ENH[illegible]ED EDITION

Microsoft® Office 2003

VOLUME I

ROBERT T. GRAUER
UNIVERSITY OF MIAMI

MARYANN BARBER
UNIVERSITY OF MIAMI

PEARSON
Prentice Hall
Upper Saddle River, New Jersey 07458

Executive Acquisitions Editor: Jodi McPherson
VP/ Publisher: Natalie E. Anderson
Senior Project Manager, Editorial: Eileen Clark
Editorial Assistants: Brian Hoehl, Alana Meyers, and Sandy Bernales
Media Project Manager: Cathleen Profitko
Marketing Manager: Emily Williams Knight
Marketing Assistant: Lisa Taylor
Project Manager, Production: Lynne Breitfeller
Production Editor: Greg Hubit
Associate Director, Manufacturing: Vincent Scelta
Manufacturing Buyer: Lynne Breitfeller
Design Manager: Maria Lange
Interior Design: Michael J. Fruhbeis
Cover Design: Michael J. Fruhbeis
Cover Printer: Phoenix Color
Composition and Project Management: The GTS Companies
Printer/ Binder: Banta Menasha

Use of the Microsoft Office Specialist Approved Courseware Logo on this product signifies that it has been independently reviewed and approved in complying with the following standards:
Acceptable coverage of all content related to the Specialist level Microsoft Office Exams entitled "Word 2003," "Excel 2003," "Access 2003," "PowerPoint 2003," and sufficient performance-based exercises that relate closely to all required content based on sampling of text.

PEARSON
Prentice Hall

10 9 8 7 6 5 4 3 2 1
ISBN 0-13-218701-9 spiral
ISBN 0-13-237038-7 adhesive

To Marion —
my wife, my lover, and my best friend

Robert Grauer

To Frank —
I love you

To Holly —
for being my friend

Maryann Barber

What does this logo mean?

It means this courseware has been approved by the Microsoft® Office Specialist Program to be among the finest available for learning **Microsoft Word 2003, Microsoft Excel 2003, Microsoft Access 2003,** and **Microsoft PowerPoint 2003.** It also means that upon completion of this courseware, you may be prepared to take an exam for Microsoft Office Specialist qualification.

What is a Microsoft Office Specialist?

A Microsoft Office Specialist is an individual who has passed exams for certifying his or her skills in one or more of the Microsoft Office desktop applications such as Microsoft Word, Microsoft Excel, Microsoft PowerPoint, Microsoft Outlook, Microsoft Access, or Microsoft Project. The Microsoft Office Specialist Program typically offers certification exams at the "Specialist" and "Expert" skill levels.* The Microsoft Office Specialist Program is the only program approved by Microsoft for testing proficiency in Microsoft Office desktop applications and Microsoft Project. This testing program can be a valuable asset in any job search or career advancement.

More Information:

To learn more about becoming a Microsoft Office Specialist, visit www.microsoft.com/officespecialist

To learn about other Microsoft Office Specialist approved courseware from Pearson Education visit www.prenhall.com

---

*The availability of Microsoft Office Specialist certification exams varies by application, application version, and language. Visit www.microsoft.com/officespecialist for exam availability.

Contents

two

Gaining Proficiency: Editing and Formatting 121

three

Enhancing a Document: The Web and Other Resources 175

four

Advanced Features: Outlines, Tables, Styles, and Sections 225

MICROSOFT® OFFICE EXCEL 2003

one

Introduction to Excel: What Is a Spreadsheet? 281

two

Gaining Proficiency: The Web and Business Applications 345

three

Graphs and Charts: Delivering a Message 389

four

Using Spreadsheets in Decision Making: What If? 439

MICROSOFT® OFFICE **ACCESS 2003**

one

Introduction to Access: What Is a Database? 497

two

Tables and Forms: Design, Properties, Views, and Wizards 545

three

Information from the Database: Reports and Queries 599

four

Proficiency: Relational Databases, Pivot Charts, and the Switchboard 657

MICROSOFT® OFFICE POWERPOINT® 2003

one

Introduction to PowerPoint: Presentations Made Easy 705

two

Gaining Proficiency: Slide Show Tools and Digital Photography 769

THE INTERNET AND THE WORLD WIDE WEB

The Internet and the World Wide Web 825

ESSENTIAL COMPUTING CONCEPTS

Getting Started 889

MICROSOFT® OFFICE OUTLOOK® 2003

Outlook 2003: A Desktop Information Manager 945

INTEGRATED CASE STUDIES

ADDITIONAL EXERCISES AND CASE STUDIES

Preface

THE EXPLORING OFFICE SERIES FOR 2003

Continuing a tradition of excellence, Prentice Hall is proud to announce the new ***Exploring Microsoft Office 2003*** series by Robert T. Grauer and Maryann Barber. The hands-on approach and conceptual framework of this comprehensive series helps students master all aspects of the Microsoft Office 2003 software, while providing the background necessary to transfer and use these skills in their personal and professional lives.

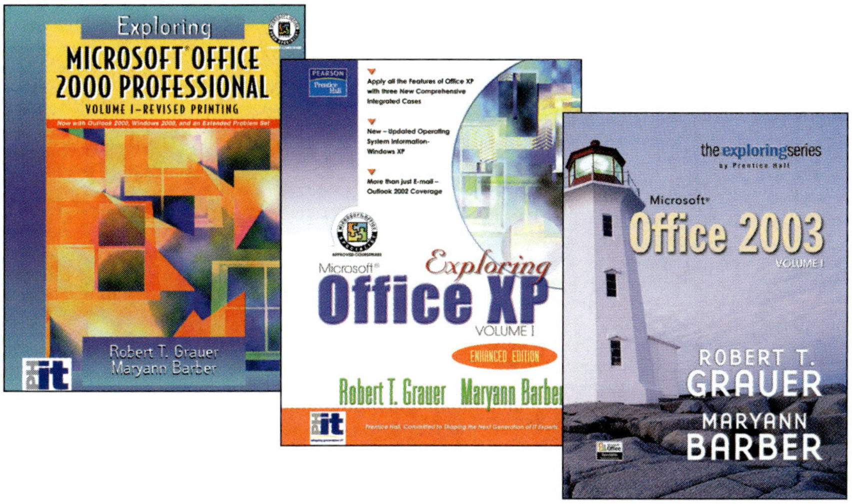

The entire series has been revised to include the new features found in the Office 2003 Suite, which contains Word 2003, Excel 2003, Access 2003, PowerPoint 2003, Publisher 2003, FrontPage 2003, and Outlook 2003.

In addition, this edition includes fully revised end-of-chapter material that provides an extensive review of concepts and techniques discussed in the chapter. Each chapter now begins with an ***introductory case study*** to provide an effective overview of what the reader will be able to accomplish, with additional ***mini cases*** at the end of each chapter for practice and review. The conceptual content within each chapter has been modified as appropriate and numerous end-of-chapter exercises have been added.

The new ***visual design*** introduces the concept of ***perfect pages***, whereby every step in every hands-on exercise, as well as every end-of-chapter exercise, begins at the top of its own page and has its own screen shot. This clean design allows for easy navigation throughout the text.

Continuing the success of the website provided for previous editions of this series, Exploring Office 2003 offers expanded resources that include online, interactive study guides, data file downloads, technology updates, additional case studies and exercises, and other helpful information. Start out at www.prenhall.com/grauer to explore these resources!

Organization of the Exploring Office 2003 Series

The new Exploring Microsoft Office 2003 series includes five combined Office 2003 texts from which to choose:

- ***Volume I*** is Microsoft Office Specialist certified in each of the core applications in the Office suite (Word, Excel, Access, and PowerPoint). Five additional modules (*Essential Computing Concepts, Getting Started with Windows XP, The Internet and the World Wide Web, Getting Started with Outlook,* and *Integrated Case Studies*) are also included. ***Volume I Enhanced Edition*** adds 18 new chapter-opening case studies, two new integrated case studies, 30 additional end-of-chapter problems, and 20 new mini cases to the existing Volume I.
- ***Volume II*** picks up where Volume I leaves off, covering the advanced topics for the individual applications. A *Getting Started with VBA* module has been added.
- The ***Plus Edition*** extends the coverage of Access and Excel to six and seven chapters, respectively (as opposed to four chapters each in Volume I). It also maintains the same level of coverage for PowerPoint and Word as in Volume I so that both applications are Microsoft Office Specialist certified. The Plus Edition includes a new module on XML but does not contain the Essential Computing Concepts or Internet modules.
- The ***Brief Microsoft Office 2003*** edition provides less coverage of the core applications than Volume I (a total of 10 chapters as opposed to 18). It also includes the *Getting Started with Windows XP* and *Getting Started with Outlook* modules.
- ***Getting Started with Office 2003*** contains the first chapter from each application (Word, Excel, Access, and PowerPoint), plus three additional modules: *Getting Started with Windows XP, The Internet and the World Wide Web,* and *Essential Computing Concepts.*

Individual texts for Word 2003, Excel 2003, Access 2003, and PowerPoint 2003 provide complete coverage of the application and are Microsoft Office Specialist certified. For shorter courses, we have created brief versions of the Exploring texts that give students a four-chapter introduction to each application. Each of these volumes is Microsoft Office Specialist certified at the Specialist level.

Microsoft® Office Specialist Approved Courseware

This series has been approved by Microsoft to be used in preparation for Microsoft Office Specialist exams.

The Microsoft Office Specialist program is globally recognized as the standard for demonstrating desktop skills with the Microsoft Office suite of business productivity applications (Microsoft Word, Microsoft Excel, Microsoft PowerPoint, Microsoft Access, and Microsoft Outlook). With a Microsoft Office Specialist certification, thousands of people have demonstrated increased productivity and have proved their ability to utilize the advanced functionality of these Microsoft applications.

By encouraging individuals to develop advanced skills with Microsoft's leading business desktop software, the Microsoft Office Specialist program helps fill the demand for qualified, knowledgeable people in the modern workplace. At the same time, Microsoft Office Specialist helps satisfy an organization's need for a qualitative assessment of employee skills.

Instructor and Student Resources

The **Instructor's CD** that accompanies the Exploring Office series contains:

- Student data files
- Solutions to all exercises and problems
- PowerPoint lectures
- Instructor's manuals in Word format that enable the instructor to annotate portions of the instructor manuals for distribution to the class
- Instructors may also use our ***test creation software,*** TestGen and QuizMaster. TestGen is a test generator program that lets you view and easily edit test-bank questions, create tests, and print in a variety of formats suitable to your teaching situation. Exams can be easily uploaded into WebCT, BlackBoard, and CourseCompass. QuizMaster allows students to take the tests created with TestGen on a local area network.

Prentice Hall's Companion Website at www.prenhall.com/grauer offers expanded IT resources and downloadable supplements. This site also includes an online study guide for students containing true/false and multiple choice questions and practice projects.

WebCT www.prenhall.com/webct
Gold level customer support available exclusively to adopters of Prentice Hall courses is provided free-of-charge upon adoption and provides you with priority assistance, training discounts, and dedicated technical support.

Blackboard www.prenhall.com/blackboard
Prentice Hall's abundant online content, combined with Blackboard's popular tools and interface, result in robust Web-based courses that are easy to implement, manage, and use—taking your courses to new heights in student interaction and learning.

CourseCompass www.coursecompass.com
CourseCompass is a dynamic, interactive online course management tool powered by Blackboard. This exciting product allows you to teach with marketing-leading Pearson Education content in an easy-to-use, customizable format.

Training and Assessment www2.phgenit.com/support

Prentice Hall offers Performance Based Training and Assessment in one product, Train&Assess IT. The Training component offers computer-based training that a student can use to preview, learn, and review Microsoft Office application skills. Web or CD-ROM delivered, Train IT offers interactive multimedia, computer-based training to augment classroom learning. Built-in prescriptive testing suggests a study path based not only on student test results but also on the specific textbook chosen for the course.

The Assessment component offers computer-based testing that shares the same user interface as Train IT and is used to evaluate a student's knowledge about specific topics in Word, Excel, Access, PowerPoint, Windows, Outlook, and the Internet. It does this in a task-oriented, performance-based environment to demonstrate proficiency as well as comprehension on the topics by the students. More extensive than the testing in Train IT, Assess IT offers more administrative features for the instructor and additional questions for the student.

Assess IT also allows professors to test students out of a course, place students in appropriate courses, and evaluate skill sets.

Opening Case Study

New! Each chapter now begins with an introductory case study to provide an effective overview of what students will accomplish by completing the chapter.

CHAPTER

1

Getting Started with Microsoft® Windows® XP

OBJECTIVES

After reading this chapter you will:

1. Describe the Windows desktop.
2. Use the Help and Support Center to obtain information.
3. Describe the My Computer and My Documents folders.
4. Differentiate between a program file and a data file.
5. Download a file from the Exploring Office Web site.
6. Copy and/or move a file from one folder to another.
7. Delete a file, and then recover it from the Recycle Bin.
8. Create and arrange shortcuts on the desktop.
9. Use the Search Companion.
10. Use the My Pictures and My Music folders.
11. Use Windows Messenger for instant messaging.

hands-on exercises

1. WELCOME TO WINDOWS XP
   Input: None
   Output: None
2. DOWNLOAD PRACTICE FILES
   Input: Data files from the Web
   Output: Welcome to Windows XP (a Word document)
3. WINDOWS EXPLORER
   Input: Data files from exercise 2
   Output: Screen Capture within a Word document
4. INCREASING PRODUCTIVITY
   Input: Data files from exercise 3
   Output: None
5. FUN WITH WINDOWS XP
   Input: None
   Output: None

CASE STUDY

UNFORESEEN CIRCUMSTANCES

Steve and his wife Shelly have poured their life savings into the dream of owning their own business, a "nanny" service agency. They have spent the last two years building their business and have created a sophisticated database with numerous entries for both families and nannies. The database is the key to their operation. Now that it is up and running, Steve and Shelly are finally at a point where they could hire someone to manage the operation on a part-time basis so that they could take some time off together.

Unfortunately, their process for selecting a person they could trust with their business was not as thorough as it should have been. Nancy, their new employee, assured them that all was well, and the couple left for an extended weekend. The place was in shambles on their return. Nancy could not handle the responsibility, and when Steve gave her two weeks' notice, neither he nor his wife thought that the unimaginable would happen. On her last day in the office Nancy "lost" all of the names in the database—the data was completely gone!

Nancy claimed that a "virus" knocked out the database, but after spending nearly $1,500 with a computer consultant, Steve was told that it had been cleverly deleted from the hard drive and could not be recovered. Of course, the consultant asked Steve and Shelly about their backup strategy, which they sheepishly admitted did not exist. They had never experienced any problems in the past, and simply assumed that their data was safe. Fortunately, they do have hard copy of the data in the form of various reports that were printed throughout the time they were in business. They have no choice but to manually reenter the data.

Your assignment is to read the chapter, paying special attention to the information on file management. Think about how Steve and Shelly could have avoided the disaster if a backup strategy had been in place, then summarize your thoughts in a brief note to your instructor. Describe the elements of a basic backup strategy. Give several other examples of unforeseen circumstances that can cause data to be lost.

1

New! A listing of the input and output files for each hands-on exercise within the chapter. Students will stay on track with what is to be accomplished.

Perfect Pages

hands-on exercise

1 Welcome to Windows XP

Each step in the hands-on exercises begins at the top of the page to ensure that students can easily navigate through the text.

Objective To log on to Windows XP and customize the desktop; to open the My Computer folder; to move and size a window; to format a floppy disk and access the Help and Support Center. Use Figure 7 as a guide.

Step 1: **Log On to Windows XP**

- Turn on the computer and all of the peripheral devices. The floppy drive should be empty prior to starting your machine.
- Windows XP will load automatically, and you should see a login screen similar to Figure 7a. (It does not matter which version of Windows XP you are using.) The number and names of the potential users and their associated icons will be different on your system.
- Click the icon for the user account you want to access. You may be prompted for a password, depending on the security options in effect.

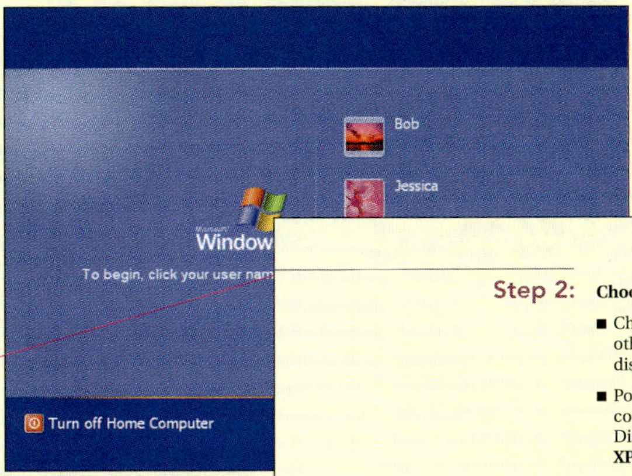

(a) Log On to Windows XP (step 1)

Figure 7 Hands-on Exercise 1

USER ACCOUNTS

The available user names are cr
Windows XP, but you can add or d
click Control Panel, switch to the Ca
the desired task, such as creating
then supply the necessary informati
user accounts in a school setting.

Step 2: **Choose the Theme and Start Menu**

- Check with your instructor to see if you are able to modify the desktop and other settings at your school or university. If your network administrator has disabled these commands, skip this step and go to step 3.
- Point to a blank area on the desktop, click the **right mouse button** to display a context-sensitive menu, then click the **Properties command** to open the Display Properties dialog box. Click the **Themes tab** and select the **Windows XP theme** if it is not already selected. Click **OK**.
- We prefer to work without any wallpaper (background picture) on the desktop. **Right click** the desktop, click **Properties**, then click the **Desktop tab** in the Display Properties dialog box. Click **None** as shown in Figure 7b, then click **OK**. The background disappears.
- The Start menu is modified independently of the theme. **Right click** a blank area of the taskbar, click the **Properties command** to display the Taskbar and Start Menu Properties dialog box, then click the **Start Menu tab**.
- Click the **Start Menu option button**. Click **OK**.

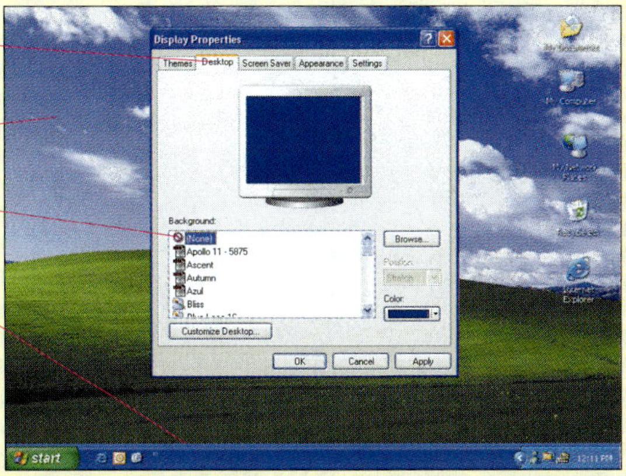

New! Larger screen shots with clear callouts.

(b) Choose the Theme and Start Menu (step 2)

Figure 7 Hands-on Exercise 1 *(continued)*

Boxed tips provide students with additional information.

IMPLEMENT A SCREEN SAVER

A screen saver is a delightful way to personalize your computer and a good way to practice with basic commands in Windows XP. Right click a blank area of the desktop, click the Properties command to open the Display Properties dialog box, then click the Screen Saver tab. Click the down arrow in the Screen Saver list box, choose the desired screen saver, then set the option to wait an appropriate amount of time before the screen saver appears. Click OK to accept the settings and close the dialog box.

Mini Cases and Practice Exercises

New!

We've added mini cases at the end of each chapter for expanded practice and review.

Mini Cases

The Financial Consultant

A friend of yours is in the process of buying a home and has asked you to compare the payments and total interest on a 15- and 30-year loan at varying interest rates. You have decided to analyze the loans in Excel, and then incorporate the results into a memo written in Microsoft Word. As of now, the principal is $150,000, but it is very likely that your friend will change his mind several times, and so you want to use the linking and embedding capability within Windows to dynamically link the worksheet to the word processing document. Your memo should include a letterhead that takes advantage of the formatting capabilities within Word; a graphic logo would be a nice touch.

Fun with the If Statement

Open the *Chapter 4 Mini Case—Fun with the If Statement* workbook in the Exploring Excel folder, then follow the directions in the worksheet to view a hidden message. The message is displayed by various If statements scattered throughout the worksheet, but the worksheet is protected so that you cannot see these formulas. (Use help to see how to protect a worksheet.) We made it easy for you, however, because you can unprotect the worksheet since a password is not required. Once the worksheet is unprotected, pull down the Format menu, click the Cells command, click the Protection tab, and clear the Hidden check box. Prove to your professor that you have done this successfully, by changing the text of our message. Print the completed worksheet to show both displayed values and cell formulas.

The Lottery

Many states raise money through lotteries that advertise prizes of several million dollars. In reality, however, the actual value of the prize is considerably less than the advertised value, although the winners almost certainly do not care. One state, for example, recently offered a twenty million dollar prize that was to be distributed in twenty annual payments of one million dollars each. How much was the prize actually worth, assuming a long-term interest rate of five percent? Use the PV (Present Value) function to determine the answer. What is the effect on the answer if payments to the recipient are made at the beginning of each year, rather than at the end of each year?

A Penny a Day

What if you had a rich un
salary each day for the n
prised at how quickly th
use the Goal Seek comm
(if any) will your uncle p
uncle pay you on the 31s

The Rule of 72

Delaying your IRA for or
on when you begin. Tha
a calculator, using the "R
long it takes money to
money earning 8% annu
money doubles again in
your IRA at age 21, rathe
initial contribution. Use
lose, assuming an 8% ra
determine the exact amo

216 CHAPTER 4: USING SPREADSHEETS IN D

New!

Each project in the end-of-chapter material begins at the top of a page—now students can easily see where their assignments begin and end.

Practice with Excel

1. **Theme Park Admissions:** A partially completed version of the worksheet in Figure 3.13 is available in the Exploring Excel folder as *Chapter 3 Practice 1*. Follow the directions in parts (a) and (b) to compute the totals and format the worksheet, then create each of the charts listed below.
   a. Use the AutoSum command to enter the formulas to compute the total number of admissions for each region and each quarter.
   b. Select the entire worksheet (cells A1 through F8), then use the AutoFormat command to format the worksheet. You do not have to accept the entire design, nor do you have to use the design we selected. You can also modify the design after it has been applied to the worksheet by changing the font size of selected cells and/or changing boldface and italics.
   c. Create a column chart showing the total number of admissions in each quarter as shown in Figure 3.13. Add the graphic shown in the figure for emphasis.
   d. Create a pie chart that shows the percentage of the total number of admissions in each region. Create this chart in its own chart sheet with an appropriate name.
   e. Create a stacked column chart that shows the total number of admissions for each region and the contribution of each quarter within each region. Create this chart in its own chart sheet with an appropriate name.
   f. Create a stacked column chart showing the total number of admissions for each quarter and the contribution of each region within each quarter. Create this chart in its own chart sheet with an appropriate name.
   g. Change the color of each of the worksheet tabs.
   h. Print the entire workbook, consisting of the worksheet in Figure 3.13 plus the three additional sheets that you create. Use portrait orientation for the Sales Data worksheet and landscape orientation for the other worksheets. Create a custom header for each worksheet that includes your name, your course, and your instructor's name. Create a custom footer for each worksheet that includes the name of the worksheet. Submit the completed assignment to your instructor.

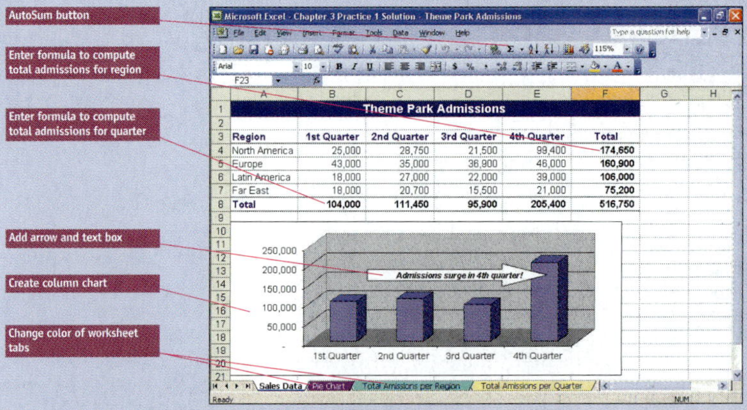

FIGURE 3.13 Theme Park Admissions (exercise 1)

150 CHAPTER 3: GRAPHS AND CHARTS

INTEGRATED CASE STUDIES

New!

Each case study contains multiple exercises that use Microsoft Office applications in conjunction with one another.

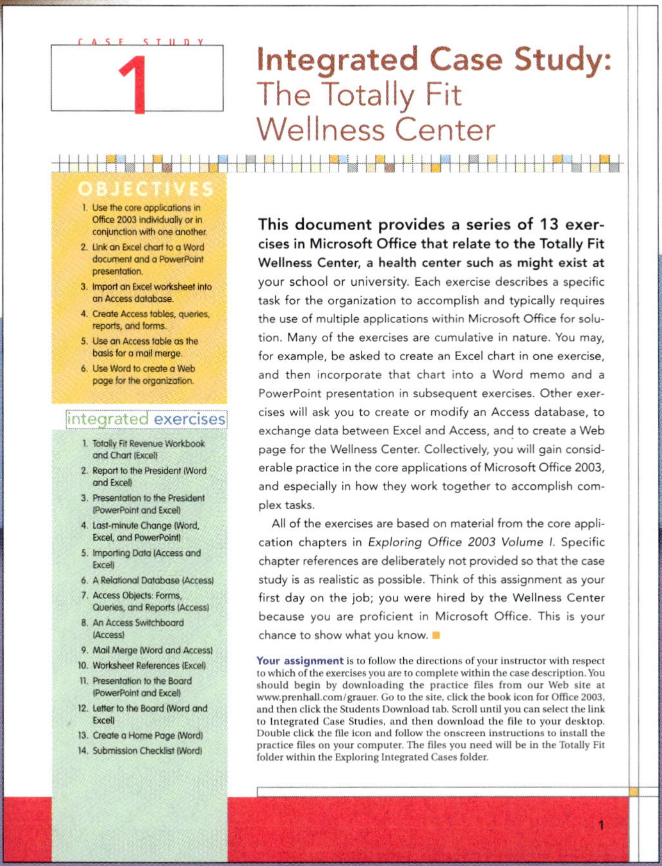

CASE STUDY 1

Integrated Case Study: The Totally Fit Wellness Center

OBJECTIVES

1. Use the core applications in Office 2003 individually or in conjunction with one another.
2. Link an Excel chart to a Word document and a PowerPoint presentation.
3. Import an Excel worksheet into an Access database.
4. Create Access tables, queries, reports, and forms.
5. Use an Access table as the basis for a mail merge.
6. Use Word to create a Web page for the organization.

integrated exercises

1. Totally Fit Revenue Workbook and Chart (Excel)
2. Report to the President (Word and Excel)
3. Presentation to the President (PowerPoint and Excel)
4. Last-minute Change (Word, Excel, and PowerPoint)
5. Importing Data (Access and Excel)
6. A Relational Database (Access)
7. Access Objects: Forms, Queries, and Reports (Access)
8. An Access Switchboard (Access)
9. Mail Merge (Word and Access)
10. Worksheet References (Excel)
11. Presentation to the Board (PowerPoint and Excel)
12. Letter to the Board (Word and Excel)
13. Create a Home Page (Word)
14. Submission Checklist (Word)

This document provides a series of 13 exercises in Microsoft Office that relate to the Totally Fit Wellness Center, a health center such as might exist at your school or university. Each exercise describes a specific task for the organization to accomplish and typically requires the use of multiple applications within Microsoft Office for solution. Many of the exercises are cumulative in nature. You may, for example, be asked to create an Excel chart in one exercise, and then incorporate that chart into a Word memo and a PowerPoint presentation in subsequent exercises. Other exercises will ask you to create or modify an Access database, to exchange data between Excel and Access, and to create a Web page for the Wellness Center. Collectively, you will gain considerable practice in the core applications of Microsoft Office 2003, and especially in how they work together to accomplish complex tasks.

All of the exercises are based on material from the core application chapters in *Exploring Office 2003 Volume I*. Specific chapter references are deliberately not provided so that the case study is as realistic as possible. Think of this assignment as your first day on the job; you were hired by the Wellness Center because you are proficient in Microsoft Office. This is your chance to show what you know.

Your assignment is to follow the directions of your instructor with respect to which of the exercises you are to complete within the case description. You should begin by downloading the practice files from our Web site at www.prenhall.com/grauer. Go to the site, click the book icon for Office 2003, and then click the Students Download tab. Scroll until you can select the link to Integrated Case Studies, and then download the file to your desktop. Double click the file icon and follow the onscreen instructions to install the practice files on your computer. The files you need will be in the Totally Fit folder within the Exploring Integrated Cases folder.

1

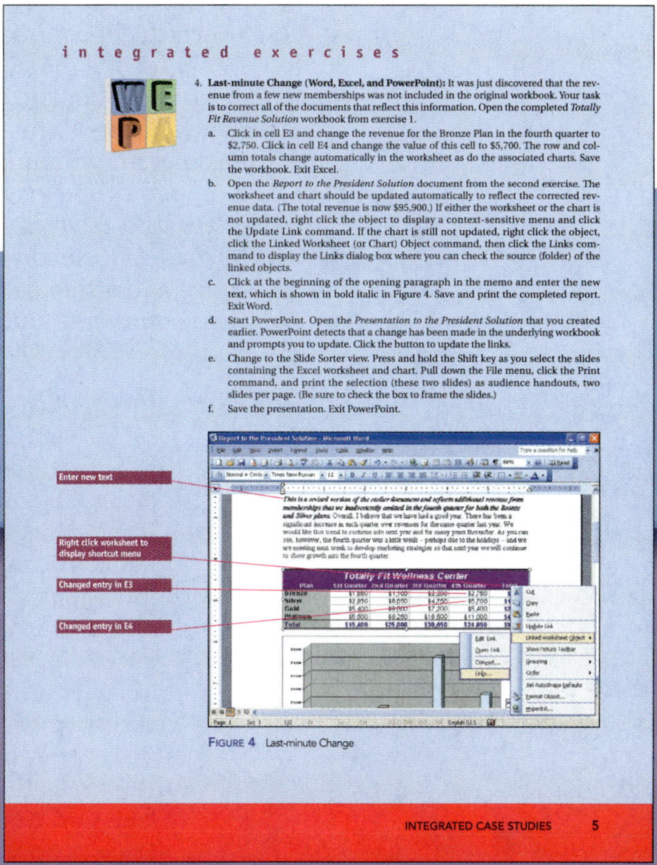

integrated exercises

4. **Last-minute Change (Word, Excel, and PowerPoint):** It was just discovered that the revenue from a few new memberships was not included in the original workbook. Your task is to correct all of the documents that reflect this information. Open the completed *Totally Fit Revenue Solution* workbook from exercise 1.
   a. Click in cell E3 and change the revenue for the Bronze Plan in the fourth quarter to $2,750. Click in cell E4 and change the value of this cell to $5,700. The row and column totals change automatically in the worksheet as do the associated charts. Save the workbook. Exit Excel.
   b. Open the *Report to the President Solution* document from the second exercise. The worksheet and chart should be updated automatically to reflect the corrected revenue data. (The total revenue is now $95,900.) If either the worksheet or the chart is not updated, right click the object to display a context-sensitive menu and click the Update Link command. If the chart is still not updated, right click the object, click the Linked Worksheet (or Chart) Object command, then click the Links command to display the Links dialog box where you can check the source (folder) of the linked objects.
   c. Click at the beginning of the opening paragraph in the memo and enter the new text, which is shown in bold italic in Figure 4. Save and print the completed report. Exit Word.
   d. Start PowerPoint. Open the *Presentation to the President Solution* that you created earlier. PowerPoint detects that a change has been made in the underlying workbook and prompts you to update. Click the button to update the links.
   e. Change to the Slide Sorter view. Press and hold the Shift key as you select the slides containing the Excel worksheet and chart. Pull down the File menu, click the Print command, and print the selection (these two slides) as audience handouts, two slides per page. (Be sure to check the box to frame the slides.)
   f. Save the presentation. Exit PowerPoint.

Enter new text

Right click worksheet to display shortcut menu

Changed entry in E3

Changed entry in E4

FIGURE 4 Last-minute Change

INTEGRATED CASE STUDIES 5

Companion Web site

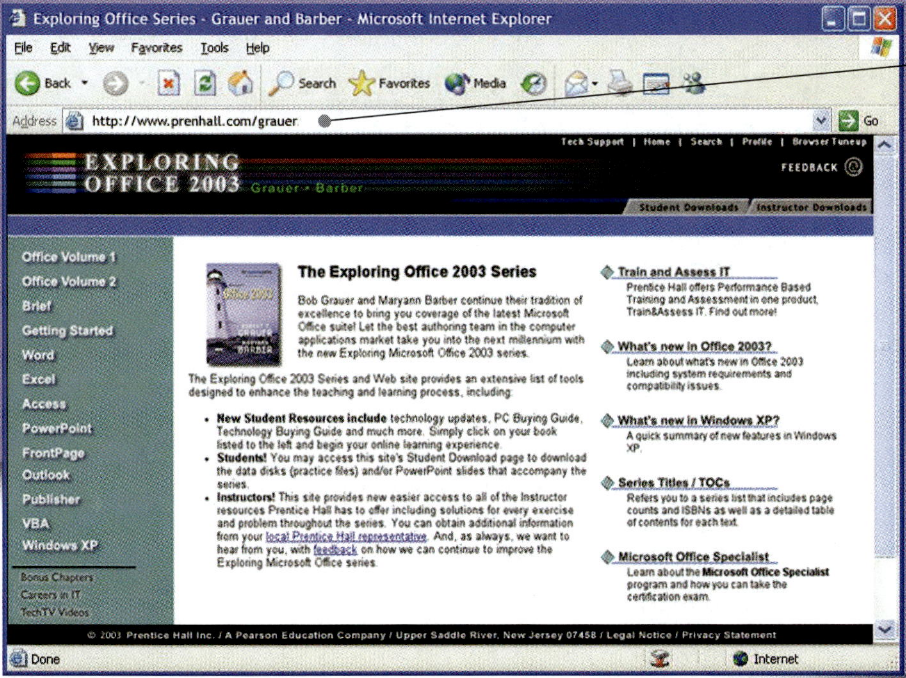

New!

Updated and enhanced Companion Web site. Find everything you need—student practice files, PowerPoint lectures, online study guides, and instructor support (solutions)!

www.prenhall.com/grauer

Acknowledgments

We want to thank the many individuals who have helped to bring this project to fruition. Jodi McPherson, executive acquisitions editor at Prentice Hall, has provided new leadership in extending the series to Office 2003. Cathi Profitko did an absolutely incredible job on our Web site. Shelly Martin was the creative force behind the chapter-opening case studies. Emily Knight coordinated the marketing and continues to inspire us with suggestions for improving the series. Greg Hubit has been masterful as the external production editor for every book in the series from its inception. Eileen Clark coordinated the myriad details of production and the certification process. Lynne Breitfeller was the project manager and manufacturing buyer. Lori Johnson was the project manager at The GTS Companies and in charge of composition. Chuck Cox did his usual fine work as copyeditor. Melissa Edwards was the supplements editor. Cindy Stevens, Tom McKenzie, and Michael Olmstead wrote the instructor manuals. Michael Fruhbeis developed the innovative and attractive design. We also want to acknowledge our reviewers who, through their comments and constructive criticism, greatly improved the series.

Gregg Asher, Minnesota State University
Lynne Band, Middlesex Community College
Don Belle, Central Piedmont Community College
Stuart P. Brian, Holy Family College
Carl M. Briggs, Indiana University School of Business
Kimberly Chambers, Scottsdale Community College
Jill Chapnick, Florida International University
Alok Charturvedi, Purdue University
Jerry Chin, Southwest Missouri State University
Charles Cole, East Stroudsburg University
Dean Combellick, Scottsdale Community College
Cody Copeland, Johnson County Community College
Larry S. Corman, Fort Lewis College
Janis Cox, Tri-County Technical College
Douglas Cross, Clackamas Community College
Martin Crossland, Southwest Missouri State University
Bill Daley, University of Oregon
Paul E. Daurelle, Western Piedmont Community College
Shawna DePlonty, Sault College of Applied Arts and Technology
Carolyn DiLeo, Westchester Community College
Judy Dolan, Palomar College
David Douglas, University of Arkansas
Carlotta Eaton, Radford University
Cheryl J. Fetterman, Cape Fear Community College
Judith M. Fitspatrick, Gulf Coast Community College
James Franck, College of St. Scholastica
Raymond Frost, Central Connecticut State University
Susan Fry, Boise State University
Midge Gerber, Southwestern Oklahoma State University
James Gips, Boston College
Vernon Griffin, Austin Community College
Ranette Halverson, Midwestern State University
Michael Hassett, Fort Hays State University
Mike Hearn, Community College of Philadelphia

Wanda D. Heller, Seminole Community College
Bonnie Homan, San Francisco State University
Ernie Ivey, Polk Community College
Walter Johnson, Community College of Philadelphia
Mike Kelly, Community College of Rhode Island
Jane King, Everett Community College
Rose M. Laird, Northern Virginia Community College
David Langley, University of Oregon
John Lesson, University of Central Florida
Maurie Lockley, University of North Carolina at Greensboro
Daniela Marghitu, Auburn University
David B. Meinert, Southwest Missouri State University
Alan Moltz, Naugatuck Valley Technical Community College
Kim Montney, Kellogg Community College
Bill Morse, DeVry Institute of Technology
Kevin Pauli, University of Nebraska
Mary McKenry Percival, University of Miami
Marguerite Nedreberg, Youngstown State University
Dr. Francisca Norales, Tennessee State University
Jim Pruitt, Central Washington University
Delores Pusins, Hillsborough Community College
Gale E. Rand, College Misericordia
Judith Rice, Santa Fe Community College
David Rinehard, Lansing Community College
Marilyn Salas, Scottsdale Community College
Herach Safarian, College of the Canyons
John Shepherd, Duquesne University
Barbara Sherman, Buffalo State College
Robert Spear, Prince George's Community College
Michael Stewardson, San Jacinto College—North
Helen Stoloff, Hudson Valley Community College
Margaret Thomas, Ohio University
Mike Thomas, Indiana University School of Business
Suzanne Tomlinson, Iowa State University
Karen Tracey, Central Connecticut State University
Antonio Vargas, El Paso Community College
Sally Visci, Lorain County Community College
David Weiner, University of San Francisco
Connie Wells, Georgia State University
Wallace John Whistance-Smith, Ryerson Polytechnic University
Jack Zeller, Kirkwood Community College

A final word of thanks to the unnamed students at the University of Miami who make it all worthwhile. Most of all, thanks to you, our readers, for choosing this book. Please feel free to contact us with any comments and suggestions.

Robert T. Grauer
rgrauer@miami.edu
www.prenhall.com/grauer

Maryann Barber
mbarber@miami.edu

CHAPTER

1

Getting Started with Microsoft® Windows® XP

OBJECTIVES

After reading this chapter you will:

1. Describe the Windows desktop.
2. Use the Help and Support Center to obtain information.
3. Describe the My Computer and My Documents folders.
4. Differentiate between a program file and a data file.
5. Download a file from the Exploring Office Web site.
6. Copy and/or move a file from one folder to another.
7. Delete a file, and then recover it from the Recycle Bin.
8. Create and arrange shortcuts on the desktop.
9. Use the Search Companion.
10. Use the My Pictures and My Music folders.
11. Use Windows Messenger for instant messaging.

hands-on exercises

1. WELCOME TO WINDOWS XP
   Input: None
   Output: None
2. DOWNLOAD PRACTICE FILES
   Input: Data files from the Web
   Output: Welcome to Windows XP (a Word document)
3. WINDOWS EXPLORER
   Input: Data files from exercise 2
   Output: Screen Capture within a Word document
4. INCREASING PRODUCTIVITY
   Input: Data files from exercise 3
   Output: None
5. FUN WITH WINDOWS XP
   Input: None
   Output: None

CASE STUDY

UNFORESEEN CIRCUMSTANCES

Steve and his wife Shelly have poured their life savings into the dream of owning their own business, a "nanny" service agency. They have spent the last two years building their business and have created a sophisticated database with numerous entries for both families and nannies. The database is the key to their operation. Now that it is up and running, Steve and Shelly are finally at a point where they could hire someone to manage the operation on a part-time basis so that they could take some time off together.

Unfortunately, their process for selecting a person they could trust with their business was not as thorough as it should have been. Nancy, their new employee, assured them that all was well, and the couple left for an extended weekend. The place was in shambles on their return. Nancy could not handle the responsibility, and when Steve gave her two weeks' notice, neither he nor his wife thought that the unimaginable would happen. On her last day in the office Nancy "lost" all of the names in the database—the data was completely gone!

Nancy claimed that a "virus" knocked out the database, but after spending nearly $1,500 with a computer consultant, Steve was told that it had been cleverly deleted from the hard drive and could not be recovered. Of course, the consultant asked Steve and Shelly about their backup strategy, which they sheepishly admitted did not exist. They had never experienced any problems in the past, and simply assumed that their data was safe. Fortunately, they do have hard copy of the data in the form of various reports that were printed throughout the time they were in business. They have no choice but to manually reenter the data. ■

Your assignment is to read the chapter, paying special attention to the information on file management. Think about how Steve and Shelly could have avoided the disaster if a backup strategy had been in place, then summarize your thoughts in a brief note to your instructor. Describe the elements of a basic backup strategy. Give several other examples of unforeseen circumstances that can cause data to be lost.

WELCOME TO WINDOWS® XP

Windows® XP is the newest and most powerful version of the Windows operating system. It has a slightly different look than earlier versions, but it maintains the conventions of its various predecessors. You have seen the Windows interface many times, but do you really understand it? Can you move and copy files with confidence? Do you know how to back up the Excel spreadsheets, Access databases, and other documents that you work so hard to create? If not, now is the time to learn.

We begin with an introduction to the desktop, the graphical user interface that lets you work in intuitive fashion by pointing at icons and clicking the mouse. We identify the basic components of a window and describe how to execute commands and supply information through different elements in a dialog box. We stress the importance of disk and file management, but begin with basic definitions of a file and a folder. We also introduce Windows Explorer and show you how to move or copy a file from one folder to another. We discuss other basic operations, such as renaming and deleting a file. We also describe how to recover a deleted file (if necessary) from the Recycle Bin.

Windows XP is available in different versions. Windows ***XP Home Edition*** is intended for entertainment and home use. It includes a media player, new support for digital photography, and an instant messenger. Windows ***XP Professional Edition*** has all of the features of the Home Edition plus additional security to encrypt files and protect data. It includes support for high-performance multiprocessor systems. It also lets you connect to your computer from a remote station.

The login screen in Figure 1 is displayed when the computer is turned on initially and/or when you are switching from one user account to another. Several individuals can share the same computer. Each user, however, retains his or her individual desktop settings, individual lists of favorite and recently visited Web sites, as well as other customized Windows settings. Multiple users can be logged on simultaneously, each with his or her programs in memory, through a feature known as ***fast user switching***.

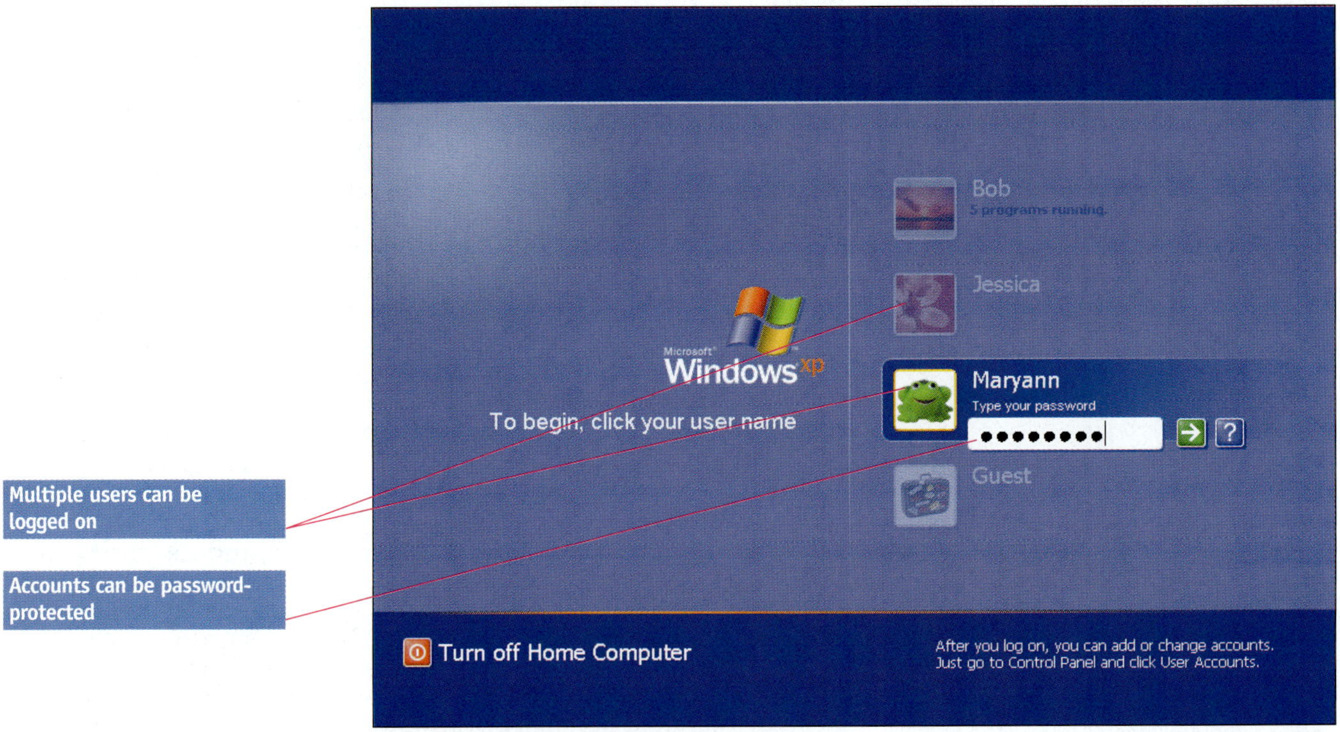

FIGURE 1 Windows XP Login

Windows XP, as well as all previous versions of Windows, creates a working environment for your computer that parallels the working environment at home or in an office. You work at a desk. Windows operations take place on the ***desktop***. There are physical objects on a desk such as folders, a dictionary, a calculator, or a phone. The computer equivalents of those objects appear as icons (pictorial symbols) on the desktop. Each object on a real desk has attributes (properties) such as size, weight, and color. In similar fashion, Windows assigns properties to every object on its desktop. And just as you can move the objects on a real desk, you can rearrange the objects on the Windows desktop.

Windows XP has a new interface, but you can retain the look and feel of earlier versions as shown in Figure 2. The desktop in Figure 2a uses the default ***Windows XP theme*** (the wallpaper has been suppressed), whereas Figure 2b displays the "same" desktop using the ***Windows Classic theme***. The icons on either desktop are used to access specific programs or other functions.

The ***Start button***, as its name suggests, is where you begin; it works identically on both desktops. Click the Start button to see a menu of programs and other functions. The Windows XP ***Start menu*** in Figure 2a is divided into two columns. The column on the left displays the most recently used programs for easy access, whereas the column on the right contains a standard set of entries. It also shows the name of the individual who is logged into the computer. The ***Classic Start menu*** in Figure 2b contains only a single column. (Note the indication of the Windows XP Professional operating system that appears at the left of the menu.)

Do not be concerned if your desktop is different from ours. Your real desk is arranged differently from those of your friends, just as your Windows desktop will also be different. Moreover, you are likely to work on different systems—at school, at work, or at home; what is important is that you recognize the common functionality that is present on all desktops.

Look now at Figure 2c, which displays an entirely different desktop, one with four open windows that is similar to a desk in the middle of a working day. Each window in Figure 2c displays a program or a folder that is currently in use. The ability to run several programs at the same time is known as ***multitasking***, and it is a major benefit of the Windows environment. Multitasking enables you to run a word processor in one window, create a spreadsheet in a second window, surf the Internet in a third window, play a game in a fourth window, and so on. You can work in a program as long as you want, then change to a different program by clicking its window.

The ***taskbar*** at the bottom of the desktop contains a button for each open window, and it enables you to switch back and forth between the open windows by clicking the appropriate button. A ***notification area*** appears at the right end of the taskbar. It displays the time and other shortcuts. It may also provide information on the status of such ongoing activities as a printer or Internet connection.

The desktop in Figure 2d is identical to the desktop in Figure 2c except that it is displayed in the Windows Classic theme. The open windows are the same, as are the contents of the taskbar and notification area. The choice between the XP theme or Windows Classic (or other) theme is one of personal preference.

Moving and Sizing a Window

A window can be sized or moved on the desktop through appropriate actions with the mouse. To ***size a window***, point to any border (the mouse pointer changes to a double arrow), then drag the border in the direction you want to go—inward to shrink the window or outward to enlarge it. You can also drag a corner (instead of a border) to change both dimensions at the same time. To ***move a window*** while retaining its current size, click and drag the title bar to a new position on the desktop.

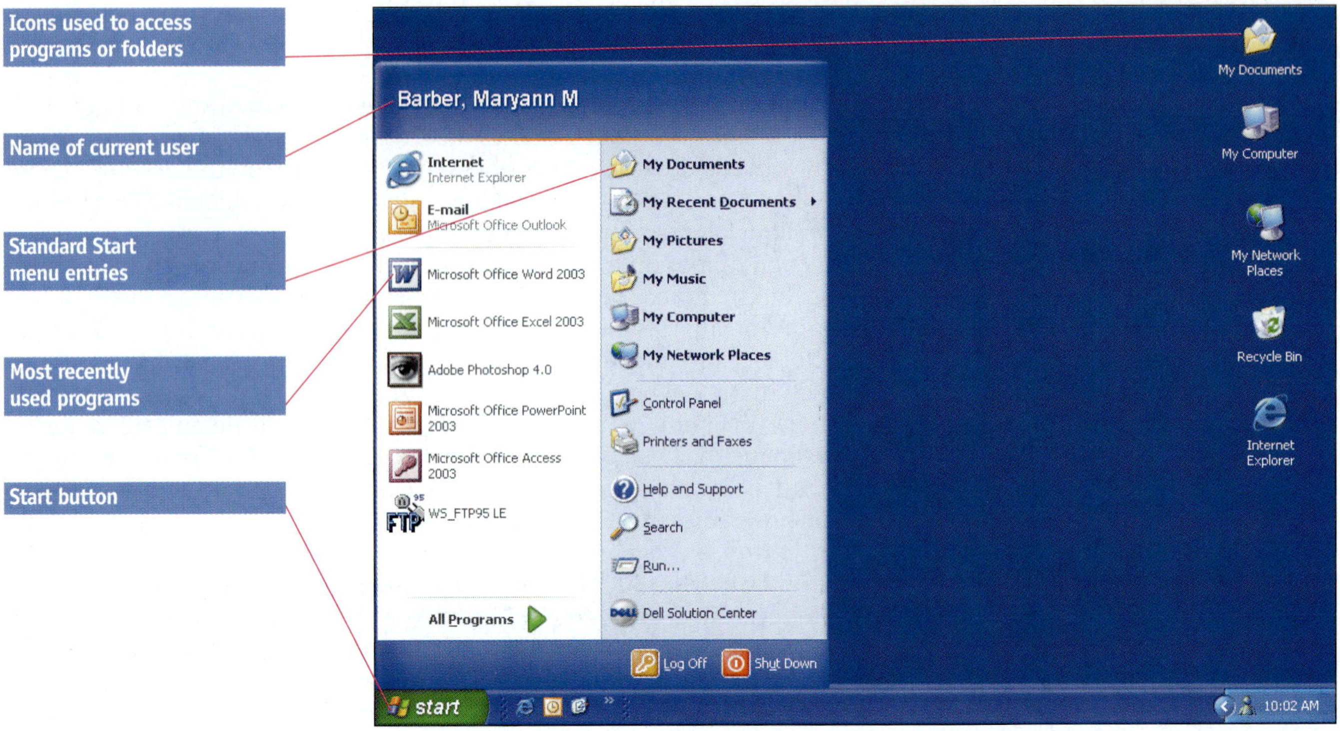

(a) Windows XP Theme and Start Menu

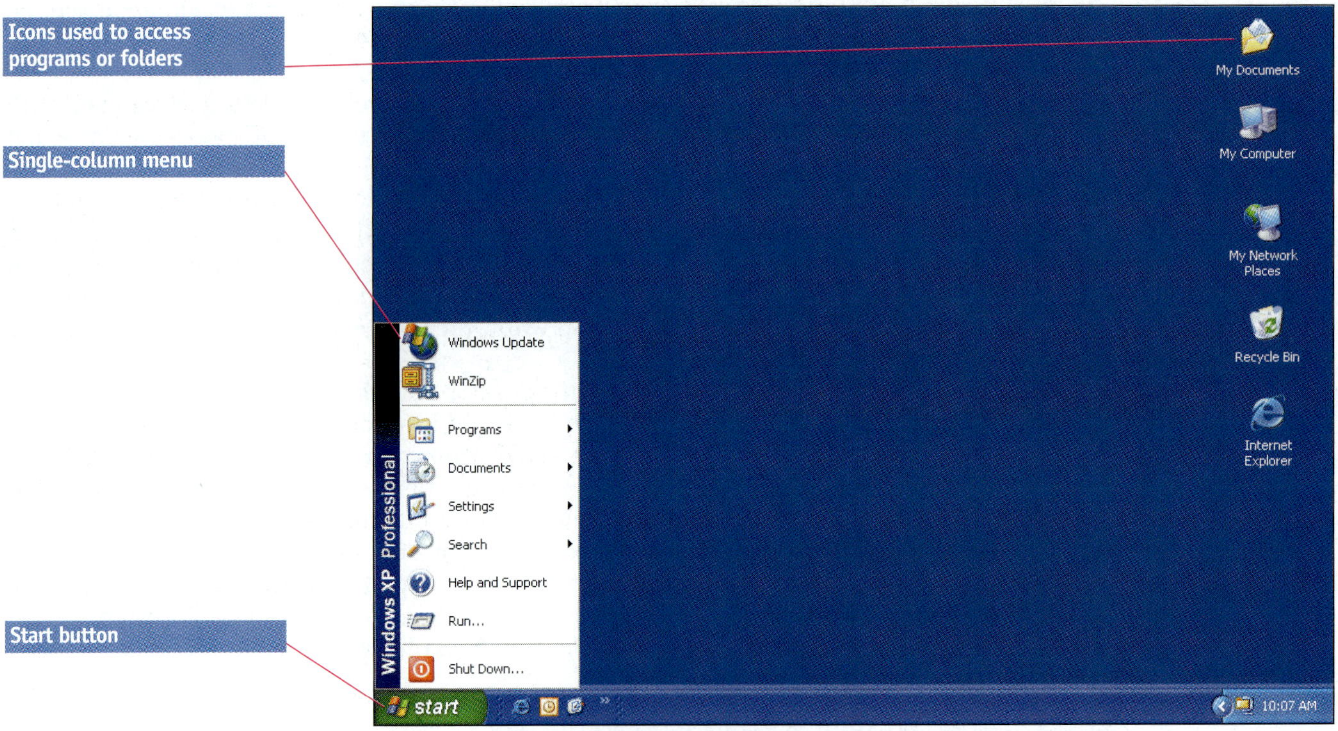

(b) Windows Classic Theme and Start Menu

FIGURE 2 The Desktop and Start Menu

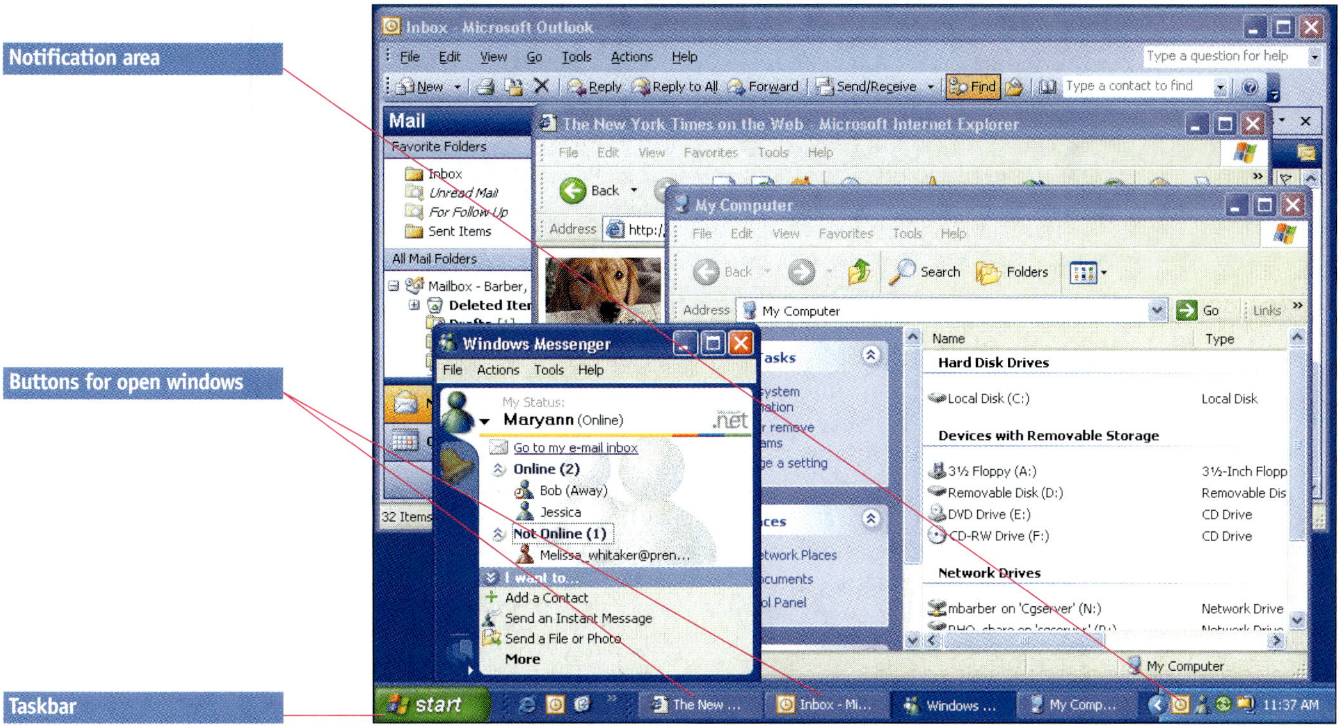

(c) Windows XP Theme

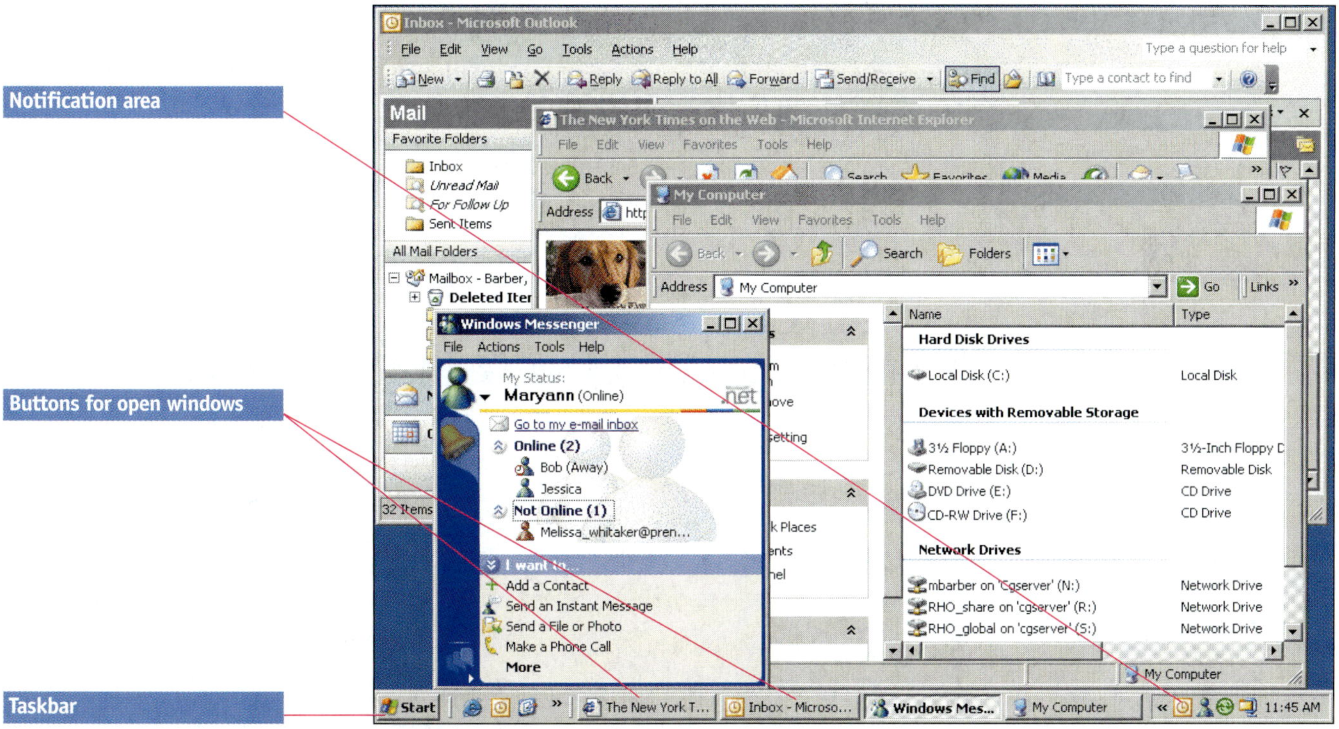

(d) Windows Classic Theme

FIGURE 2 The Desktop and Start Menu (*continued*)

ANATOMY OF A WINDOW

All Windows applications share a common user interface and possess a consistent command structure. This means that every Windows application works essentially the same way, which provides a sense of familiarity from one application to the next. In other words, once you learn the basic concepts and techniques in one application, you can apply that knowledge to every other application.

The ***My Computer folder*** in Figure 3 is used to illustrate basic technology. This folder is present on every system, and its contents depend on the hardware of the specific computer. Our system, for example, has one local disk, a floppy drive, a removable disk (an Iomega Zip® drive), a DVD drive, and a CD-RW (recordable) drive. Our intent at this time, however, is to focus on the elements that are common to every window. A ***task pane*** (also called a task panel) is displayed at the left of the window to provide easy access to various commands that you might want to access from this folder.

The ***title bar*** appears at the top of every window and displays the name of the folder or application. The icon at the extreme left of the title bar identifies the window and also provides access to a control menu with operations relevant to the window, such as moving it or sizing it. Three buttons appear at the right of the title bar. The ***Minimize button*** shrinks the window to a button on the taskbar, but leaves the window in memory. The ***Maximize button*** enlarges the window so that it takes up the entire desktop. The ***Restore button*** (not shown in Figure 3) appears instead of the Maximize button after a window has been maximized, and restores the window to its previous size. The ***Close button*** closes the window and removes it from memory and the desktop.

The ***menu bar*** appears immediately below the title bar and provides access to pull-down menus. One or more ***toolbars*** appear below the menu bar and let you execute a command by clicking a button, as opposed to pulling down a menu. The ***status bar*** at the bottom of the window displays information about the window as a whole or about a selected object within a window.

A vertical (or horizontal) ***scroll bar*** appears at the right (or bottom) border of a window when its contents are not completely visible and provides access to the unseen areas. The vertical scroll bar at the right of the task panel in Figure 3 implies that there are additional tasks available that are not currently visible. A horizontal scroll bar does not appear since all of the objects in the My Computer folder are visible at one time.

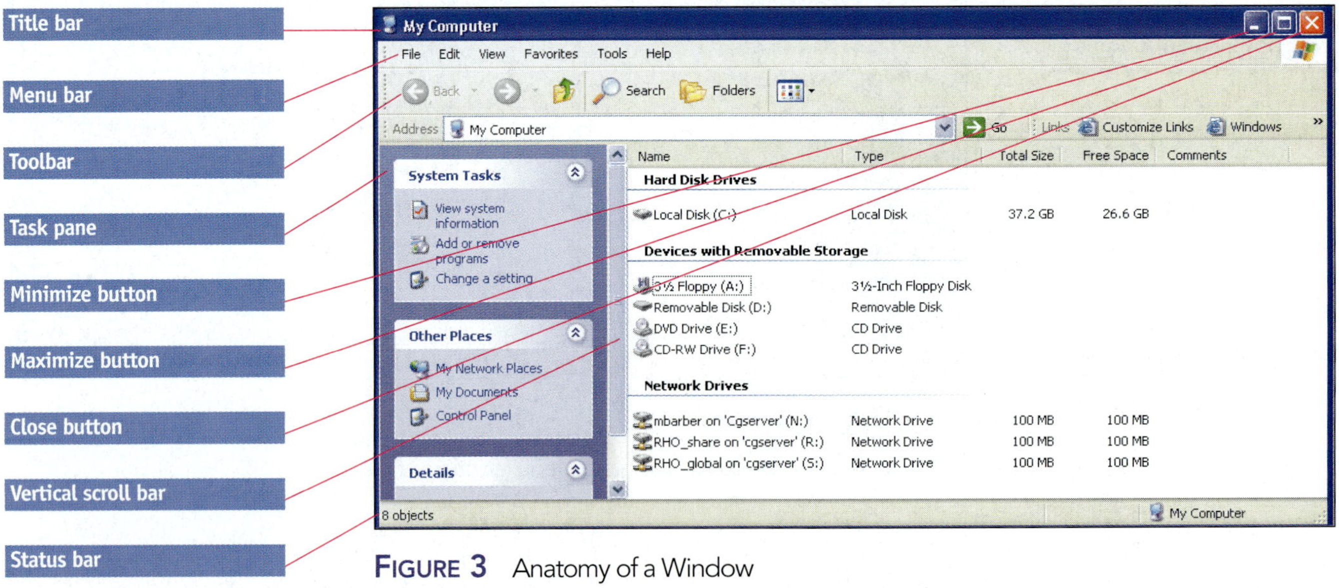

FIGURE 3 Anatomy of a Window

Pull-down Menus

The menu bar provides access to ***pull-down menus*** that enable you to execute commands within an application (program). A pull-down menu is accessed by clicking the menu name or by pressing the Alt key plus the underlined letter in the menu name; for example, press Alt+V to pull down the View menu. (You may have to press the Alt key to see the underlines.) Figure 4 displays three pull-down menus that are associated with the My Computer folder.

Commands within a menu are executed by clicking the command or by typing the underlined letter. Alternatively, you can bypass the menu entirely if you know the equivalent shortcuts shown to the right of the command in the menu (e.g., Ctrl+X, Ctrl+C, or Ctrl+V to cut, copy, or paste as shown within the Edit menu). A dimmed command (e.g., the Paste command in the Edit menu) means the command is not currently executable, and that some additional action has to be taken for the command to become available.

An ellipsis (. . .) following a command indicates that additional information is required to execute the command; for example, selection of the Format command in the File menu requires the user to specify additional information about the formatting process. This information is entered into a dialog box (discussed in the next section), which appears immediately after the command has been selected.

A check next to a command indicates a toggle switch, whereby the command is either on or off. There is a check next to the Status Bar command in the View menu of Figure 4, which means the command is in effect (and thus the status bar will be displayed). Click the Status Bar command and the check disappears, which suppresses the display of the status bar. Click the command a second time and the check reappears, as does the status bar in the associated window.

A bullet next to an item, such as Icons in the View menu, indicates a selection from a set of mutually exclusive choices. Click a different option within the group—such as Thumbnails—and the bullet will move from the previous selection (Icons) to the new selection (Thumbnails).

An arrowhead after a command (e.g., the Arrange Icons by command in the View menu) indicates that a submenu (also known as a cascaded menu) will be displayed with additional menu options.

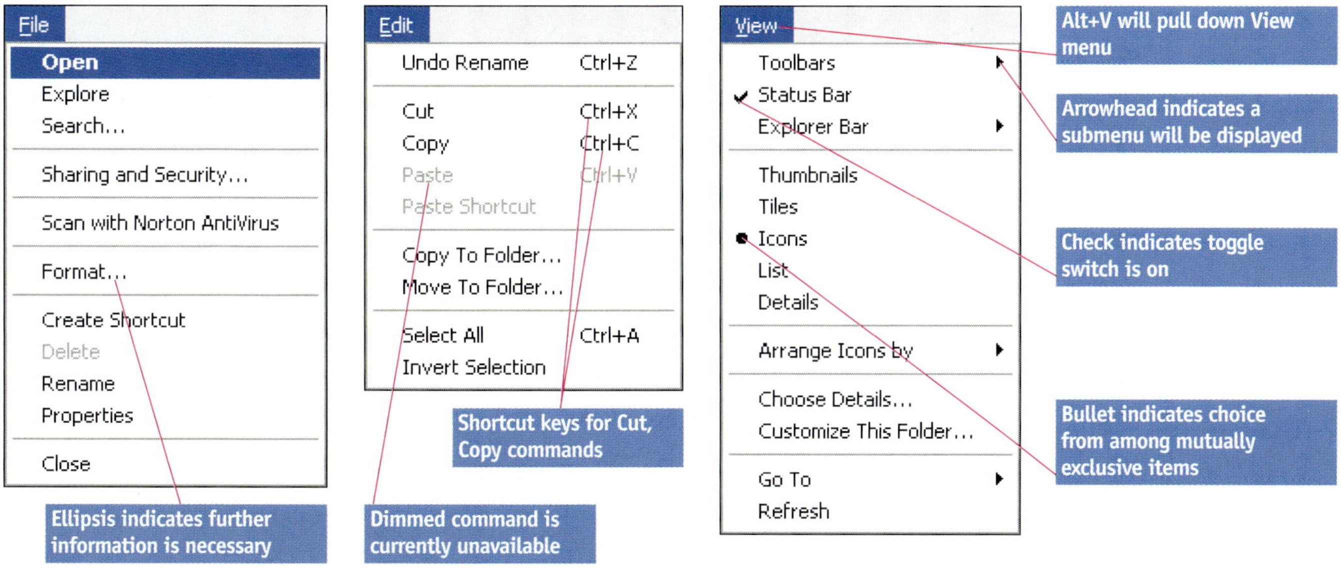

FIGURE 4 Pull-down Menus

Dialog Boxes

A ***dialog box*** appears when additional information is necessary to execute a command. Click the Print command in Internet Explorer, for example, and you are presented with the Print dialog box in Figure 5, requesting information about precisely what to print and how. The information is entered into the dialog box in different ways, depending on the type of information that is required. The tabs at the top of the dialog box provide access to different sets of options. The General tab is selected in Figure 5.

Option (radio) buttons indicate mutually exclusive choices, one of which *must* be chosen, such as the page range. In this example you can print all pages, the selection (if it is available), the current page (if there are multiple pages), or a specific set of pages (such as pages 1–4), but you can choose *one and only one* option. Any time you select (click) an option, the previous option is automatically deselected.

A ***text box*** enters specific information such as the pages that will be printed in conjunction with selecting the radio button for pages. A ***spin button*** is another way to enter specific information such as the number of copies. Click the up or down arrow to increase or decrease the number of pages, respectively. You can also enter the information explicitly by typing it into a spin box, just as you would a text box.

Check boxes are used instead of option buttons if the choices are not mutually exclusive or if an option is not required. The Collate check box is checked, whereas the Print to file box is not checked. Individual options are selected and cleared by clicking the appropriate check box, which toggles the box on and off. A ***list box*** (not shown in Figure 5) displays some or all of the available choices, any one of which is selected by clicking the desired item.

The ***Help button*** (a question mark at the right end of the title bar) provides help for any item in the dialog box. Click the button, then click the item in the dialog box for which you want additional information. The Close button (the X at the extreme right of the title bar) closes the dialog box without executing the command.

All dialog boxes also contain one or more ***command buttons***, the function of which is generally apparent from the button's name. The Print button in Figure 5, for example, initiates the printing process. The Cancel button does just the opposite and ignores (cancels) any changes made to the settings, then closes the dialog box without further action.

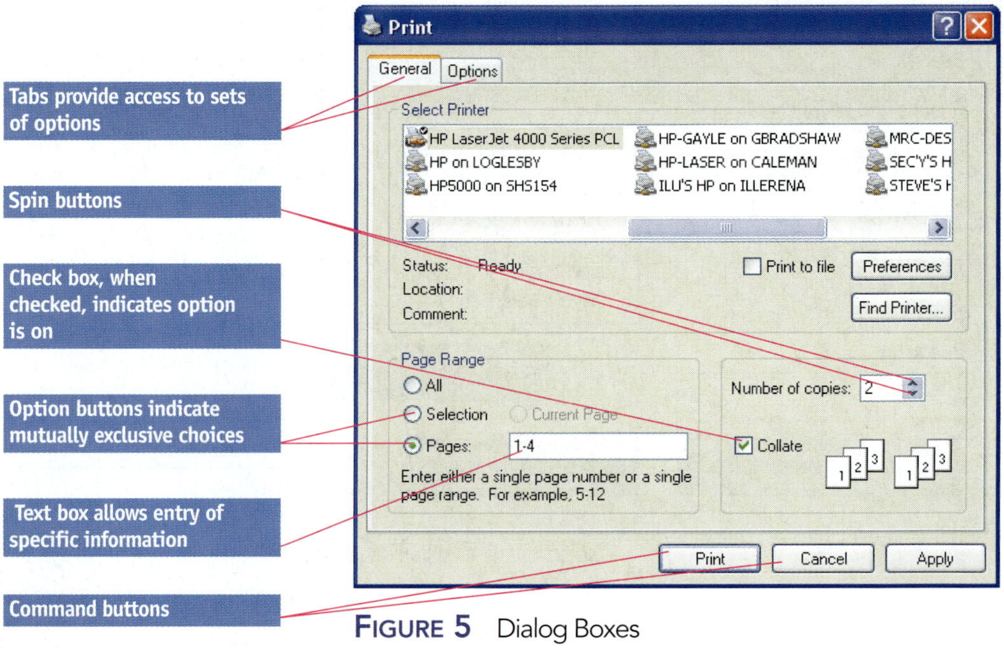

FIGURE 5 Dialog Boxes

HELP AND SUPPORT CENTER

The ***Help and Support Center*** combines such traditional features as a search function and an index of help topics. It also lets you request remote help from other Windows XP users, and/or you can access the Microsoft Knowledge base on the Microsoft Web site. Click the Index button, type the keyword you are searching for, then double click the subtopic to display the associated information in the right pane. The mouse is essential to Windows, and you are undoubtedly familiar with its basic operations such as pointing, clicking, and double clicking. Look closely, however, at the list of subtopics in Figure 6 and you might be surprised at the amount of available information. Suffice it to say, therefore, that you will find the answer to almost every conceivable question if only you will take the trouble to look.

The toolbar at the top of the window contains several buttons that are also found in ***Internet Explorer 6.0***, the Web browser that is built into Windows XP. The Back and Forward buttons enable you to navigate through the various pages that were viewed in the current session. The Favorites button displays a list of previously saved (favorite) help topics from previous sessions. The History button shows all pages that were visited in this session.

The Support button provides access to remote sources for assistance. Click the Support button, then click the link to ask a friend to help, which in turn displays a Remote Assistance screen. You will be asked to sign in to the Messenger service (Windows Messenger is discussed in more detail in a later section). Your friend has to be running Windows XP for this feature to work, but once you are connected, he or she will be able to view your computer screen. You can then chat in real time about the problem and proposed solution. And, if you give permission, your friend can use his or her mouse and keyboard to work on your computer. Be careful! It is one thing to let your friend see your screen. It is quite a leap of faith, however, to give him or her control of your machine.

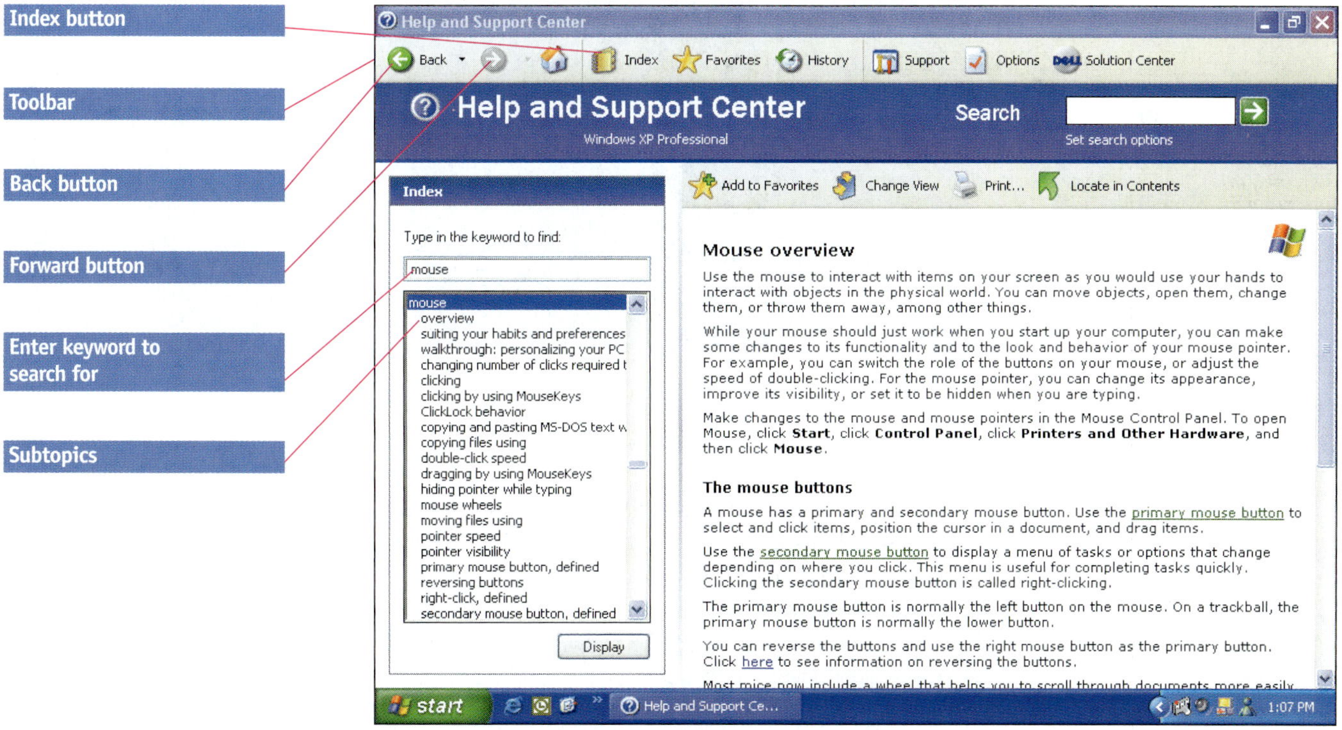

FIGURE 6 Help and Support Center

hands-on exercise

1 Welcome to Windows XP

Objective To log on to Windows XP and customize the desktop; to open the My Computer folder; to move and size a window; to format a floppy disk and access the Help and Support Center. Use Figure 7 as a guide.

Step 1: **Log On to Windows XP**

- Turn on the computer and all of the peripheral devices. The floppy drive should be empty prior to starting your machine.
- Windows XP will load automatically, and you should see a login screen similar to Figure 7a. (It does not matter which version of Windows XP you are using.) The number and names of the potential users and their associated icons will be different on your system.
- Click the icon for the user account you want to access. You may be prompted for a password, depending on the security options in effect.

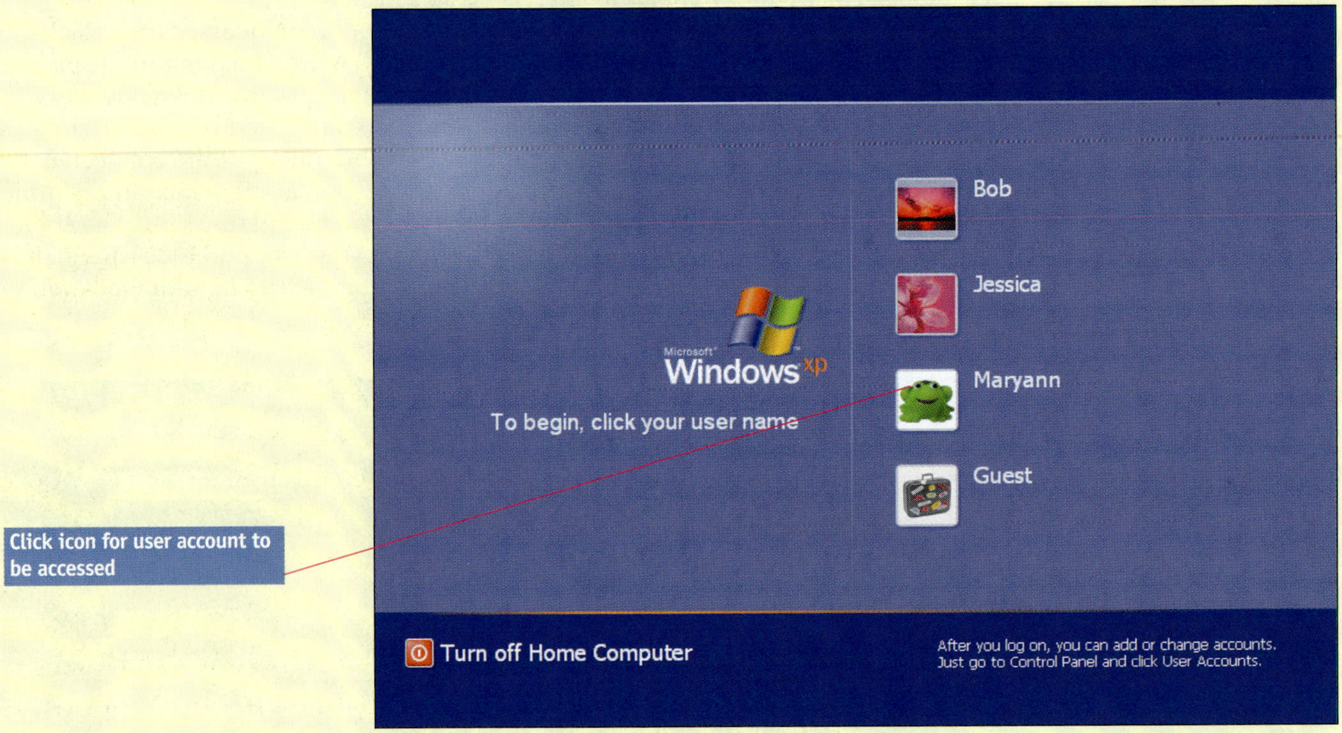

(a) Log On to Windows XP (step 1)

FIGURE 7 Hands-on Exercise 1

USER ACCOUNTS

The available user names are created automatically during the installation of Windows XP, but you can add or delete users at any time. Click the Start button, click Control Panel, switch to the Category view, and select User Accounts. Choose the desired task, such as creating a new account or changing an existing account, then supply the necessary information. Do not expect, however, to be able to modify user accounts in a school setting.

Step 2: Choose the Theme and Start Menu

- Check with your instructor to see if you are able to modify the desktop and other settings at your school or university. If your network administrator has disabled these commands, skip this step and go to step 3.
- Point to a blank area on the desktop, click the **right mouse button** to display a context-sensitive menu, then click the **Properties command** to open the Display Properties dialog box. Click the **Themes tab** and select the **Windows XP theme** if it is not already selected. Click **OK**.
- We prefer to work without any wallpaper (background picture) on the desktop. **Right click** the desktop, click **Properties**, then click the **Desktop tab** in the Display Properties dialog box. Click **None** as shown in Figure 7b, then click **OK**. The background disappears.
- The Start menu is modified independently of the theme. **Right click** a blank area of the taskbar, click the **Properties command** to display the Taskbar and Start Menu Properties dialog box, then click the **Start Menu tab**.
- Click the **Start Menu option button**. Click **OK**.

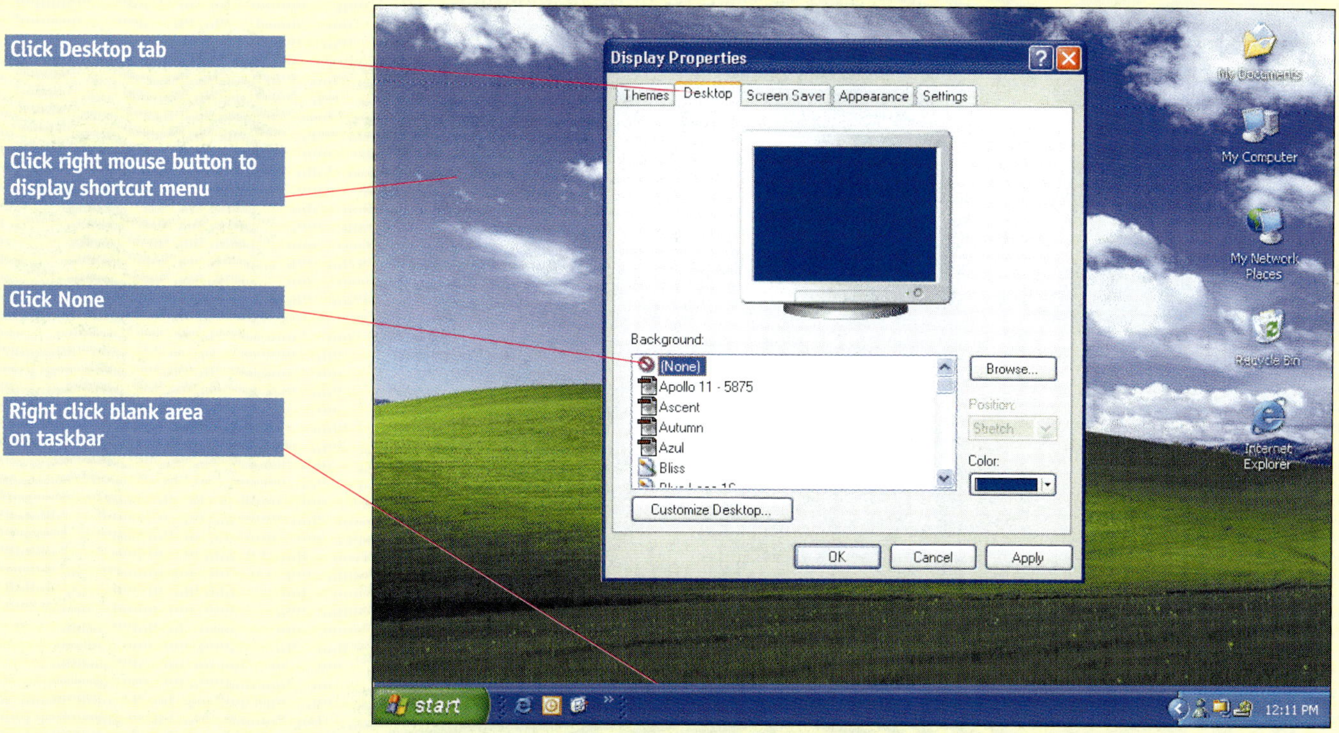

(b) Choose the Theme and Start Menu (step 2)

FIGURE 7 Hands-on Exercise 1 (*continued*)

IMPLEMENT A SCREEN SAVER

A screen saver is a delightful way to personalize your computer and a good way to practice with basic commands in Windows XP. Right click a blank area of the desktop, click the Properties command to open the Display Properties dialog box, then click the Screen Saver tab. Click the down arrow in the Screen Saver list box, choose the desired screen saver, then set the option to wait an appropriate amount of time before the screen saver appears. Click OK to accept the settings and close the dialog box.

Step 3: Open the My Computer Folder

- Click the **Start button** to display a two-column Start menu that is characteristic of Windows XP. Click **My Computer** to open the My Computer folder. The contents of your window and/or its size and position on the desktop will be different from ours.

- Pull down the **View menu** as shown in Figure 7c to make or verify the following selections. (You have to pull down the View menu each time you make an additional change.)
  - The **Status Bar command** should be checked. The Status Bar command functions as a toggle switch. Click the command and the status bar is displayed; click the command a second time and the status bar disappears.
  - Click the **Tiles command** to change to this view. Selecting the Tiles view automatically deselects the previous view.

- Pull down the **View menu**, then click (or point to) the **Toolbars command** to display a cascaded menu. If necessary, check the commands for the **Standard Buttons** and **Address Bar**, and clear the other commands.

- Click the **Folders button** on the Standard Buttons toolbar to toggle the task panel on or off. End with the task panel displayed as shown in Figure 7c.

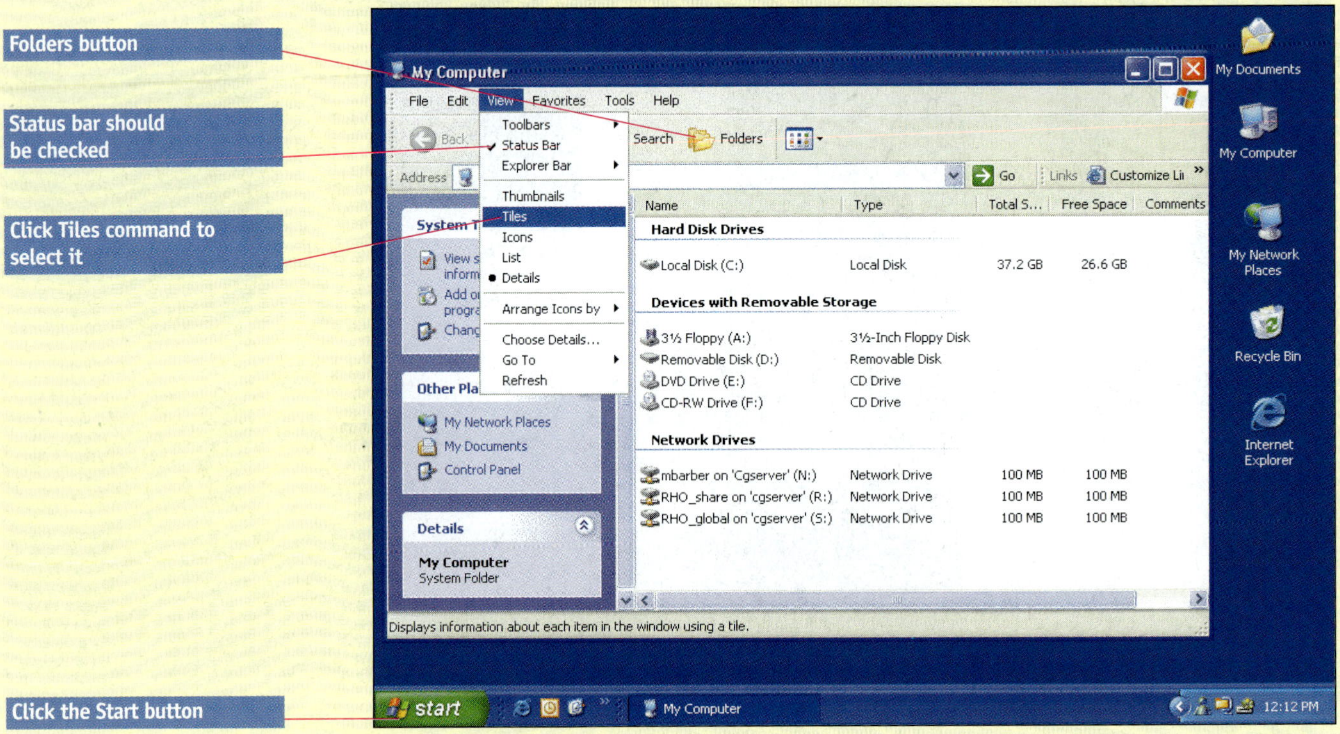

(c) Open the My Computer Folder (step 3)

FIGURE 7 Hands-on Exercise 1 (*continued*)

DESIGNATING THE DEVICES ON A SYSTEM

The first (usually only) floppy drive is always designated as drive A. (A second floppy drive, if it were present, would be drive B.) The first hard (local) disk on a system is always drive C, whether or not there are one or two floppy drives. Additional local drives, if any, such as a zip (removable storage) drive, a network drive, a CD and/or a DVD, are labeled from D on.

Step 4: Move and Size a Window

- Move and size the My Computer window on your desktop to match the display in Figure 7d.
  - To change the width or height of the window, click and drag a border (the mouse pointer changes to a double arrow) in the direction you want to go; drag the border inward to shrink the window or outward to enlarge it.
  - To change the width and height at the same time, click and drag a corner rather than a border.
  - To change the position of the window, click and drag the title bar.
- Click the **Minimize button** to shrink the My Computer window to a button on the taskbar. My Computer is still active in memory although its window is no longer visible. Click the **My Computer button** on the taskbar to reopen the window.
- Click the **Maximize button** so that the My Computer window expands to fill the entire screen. Click the **Restore button** (which replaces the Maximize button and is not shown in Figure 7d) to return the window to its previous size.
- Practice these operations until you can move and size a window with confidence.

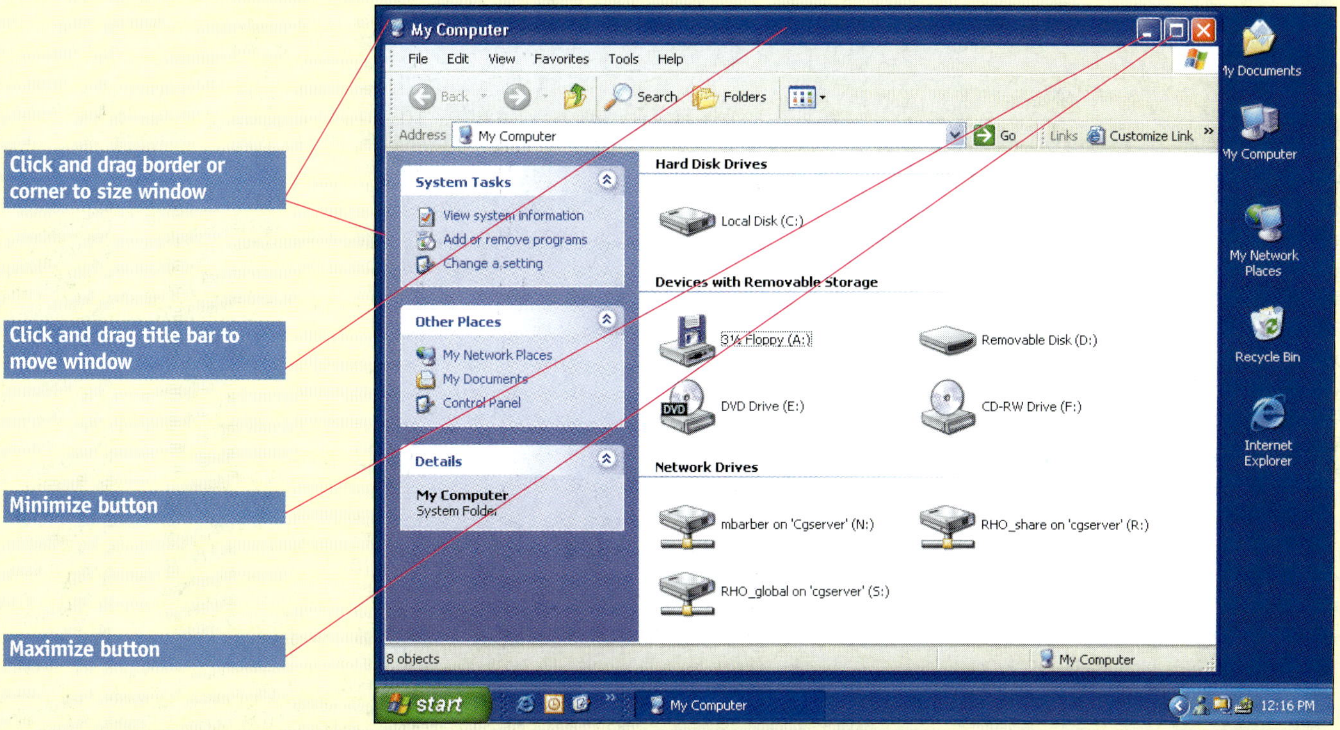

(d) Move and Size a Window (step 4)

FIGURE 7 Hands-on Exercise 1 (*continued*)

MINIMIZING VERSUS CLOSING AN APPLICATION

Minimizing a folder or an application leaves the object open in memory and available at the click of the appropriate button on the taskbar. Closing it, however, removes the object from memory, which also causes it to disappear from the taskbar. The advantage of minimizing an application or folder is that you can return to it immediately with the click of the mouse. The disadvantage is that too many open applications will eventually degrade the performance of a system.

Step 5: Capture a Screen

- Prove to your instructor that you have sized the window correctly by capturing the desktop that currently appears on your monitor. Press the **Print Screen key** to copy the current screen display to the **clipboard**, an area of memory that is available to every application.
- Nothing appears to have happened, but the screen has in fact been copied to the clipboard and can be pasted into a Word document. Click the **Start button**, click the **All Programs command**, then start **Microsoft Word** and begin a new document.
- Enter the title of your document (I Did My Homework) followed by your name as shown in Figure 7e. Press the **Enter key** two or three times to leave blank lines after your name.
- Pull down the **Edit menu** and click the **Paste command** (or click the **Paste button** on the Standard toolbar) to copy the contents of the clipboard into the Word document.
- Print this document for your instructor. There is no need to save this document. Exit Word.

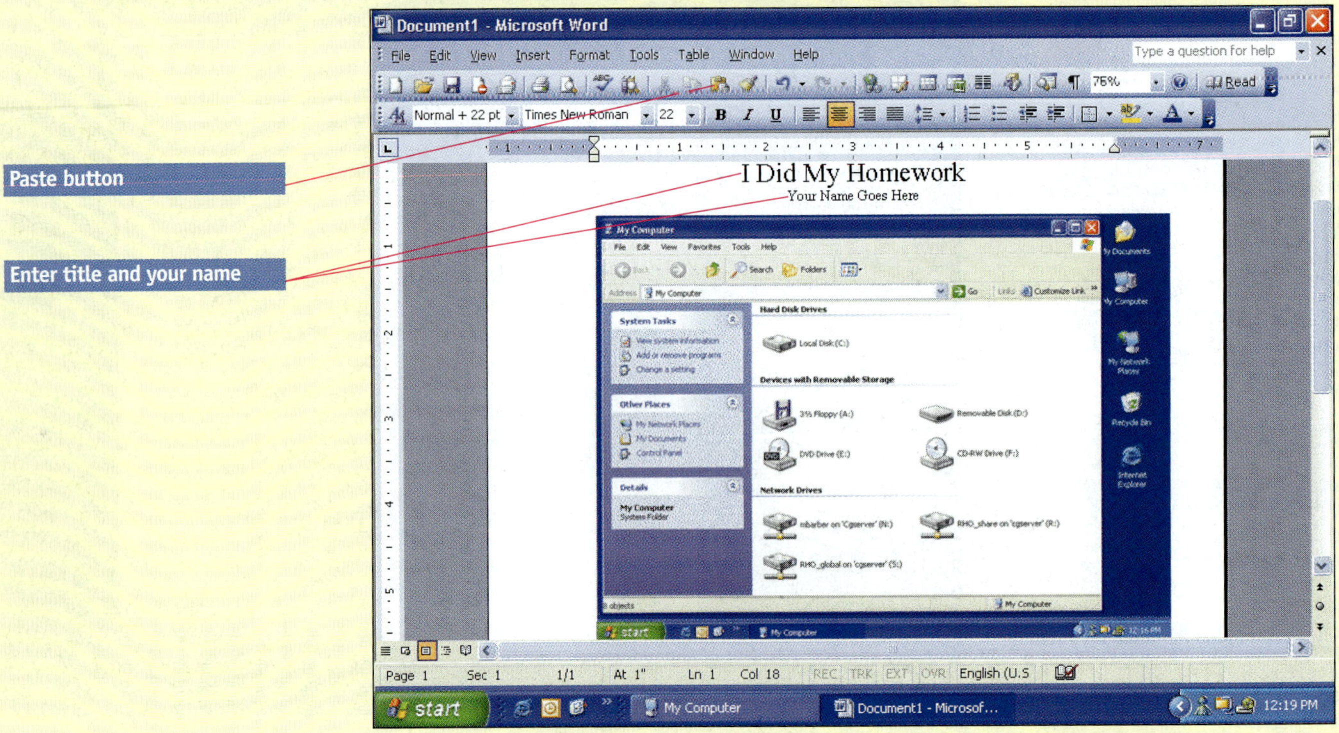

(e) Capture a Screen (step 5)

FIGURE 7 Hands-on Exercise 1 *(continued)*

THE FORMAT PICTURE COMMAND

Use the Format Picture command to facilitate moving and/or sizing an object within a Word document. Right click the picture to display a context-sensitive menu, then click the Format Picture command to display the associated dialog box. Click the Layout tab, choose any layout other than Inline with text, and click OK. You can now click and drag the picture to position it elsewhere within the document.

Step 6: Format a Floppy Disk

- Place a floppy disk into drive A. Select (click) **drive A** in the My Computer window, then pull down the **File menu** and click the **Format command** to display the Format dialog box in Figure 7f.
  - Set the **Capacity** to match the floppy disk you purchased (1.44MB for a high-density disk and 720KB for a double-density disk. The easiest way to determine the type of disk is to look for the label HD or DD, respectively.).
  - Click the **Volume label text box** if it's empty, or click and drag over the existing label if there is an entry. Enter a new label (containing up to 11 characters), such as **Bob's Disk**.
  - You can check the **Quick Format box** if the disk has been previously formatted, as a convenient way to erase the contents of the disk.
- Click the **Start button,** then click **OK**—after you have read the warning message—to begin the formatting operation. The formatting process erases anything that is on the disk, so be sure that you do not need anything on the disk.
- Click **OK** after the formatting is complete. Close the dialog box, then save the formatted disk for the next exercise. Close the My Computer window.

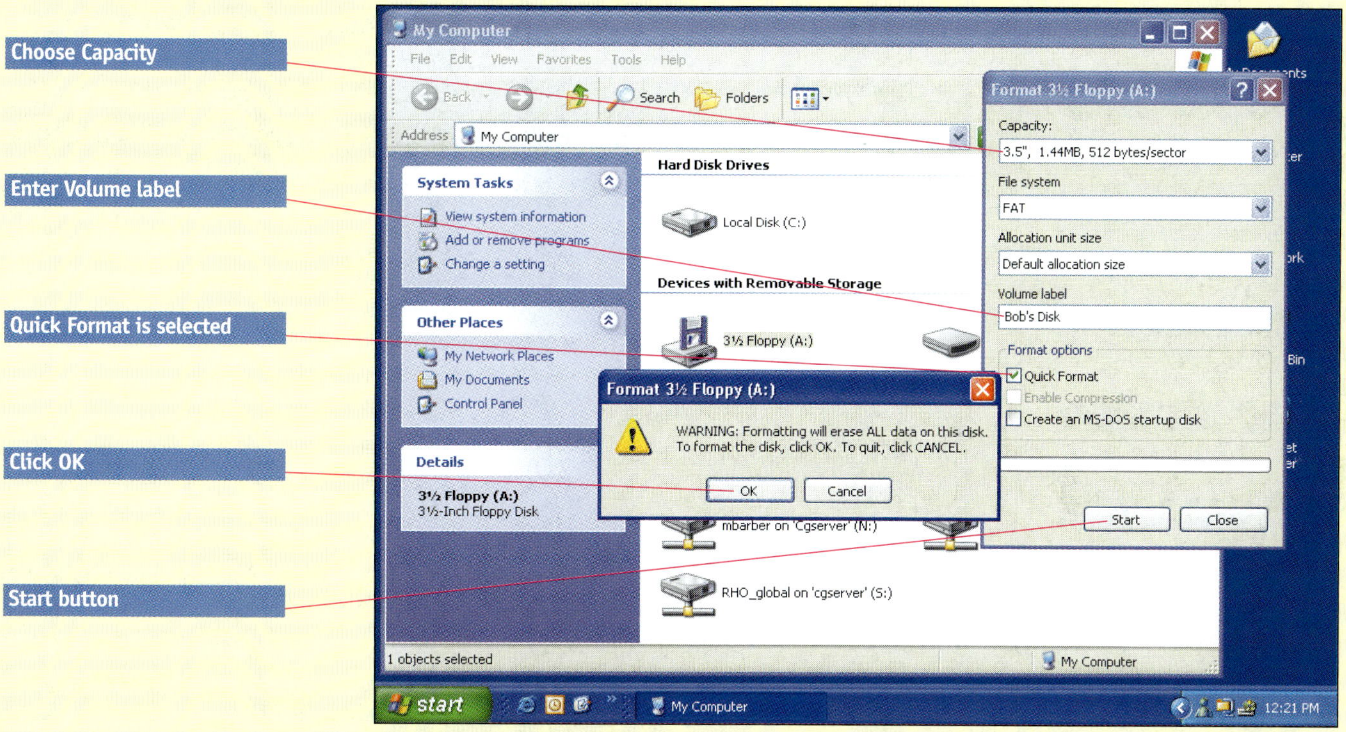

(f) Format a Floppy Disk (step 6)

FIGURE 7 Hands-on Exercise 1 (*continued*)

THE DEMISE OF THE FLOPPY DISK

You may be surprised to discover that your system no longer has a floppy disk drive, but it is only the latest victim in the march of technology. Long-playing records have come and gone. So too have 8-track tapes and the laser disk. The 3½-inch floppy disk has had a long and successful run, but it, too, is slated for obsolescence with Dell's recent announcement that it will no longer include a floppy drive as a standard component in desktop systems. Still, the floppy disk will "live forever" in the Save button that has the floppy disk as its icon.

Step 7: The Help and Support Center

- Click the **Start button**, then click the **Help and Support command** to open the Help and Support Center. Click the **Index button** to open the index pane. The insertion point moves automatically to the text box where you enter the search topic.
- Type **help**, which automatically moves you to the available topics within the index. Double click **central location for Help** to display the information in the right pane as shown in Figure 7g.
- Toggle the display of the subtopics on and off by clicking the plus and minus sign, respectively. Click the **plus sign** next to Remote Assistance, for example, and the topic opens. Click the **minus sign** next to Tours and articles, and the topic closes.
- Right click anywhere within the right pane to display the context-sensitive menu shown in Figure 7g. Click the **Print command** to print this information for your instructor.
- Close the Help and Support window.

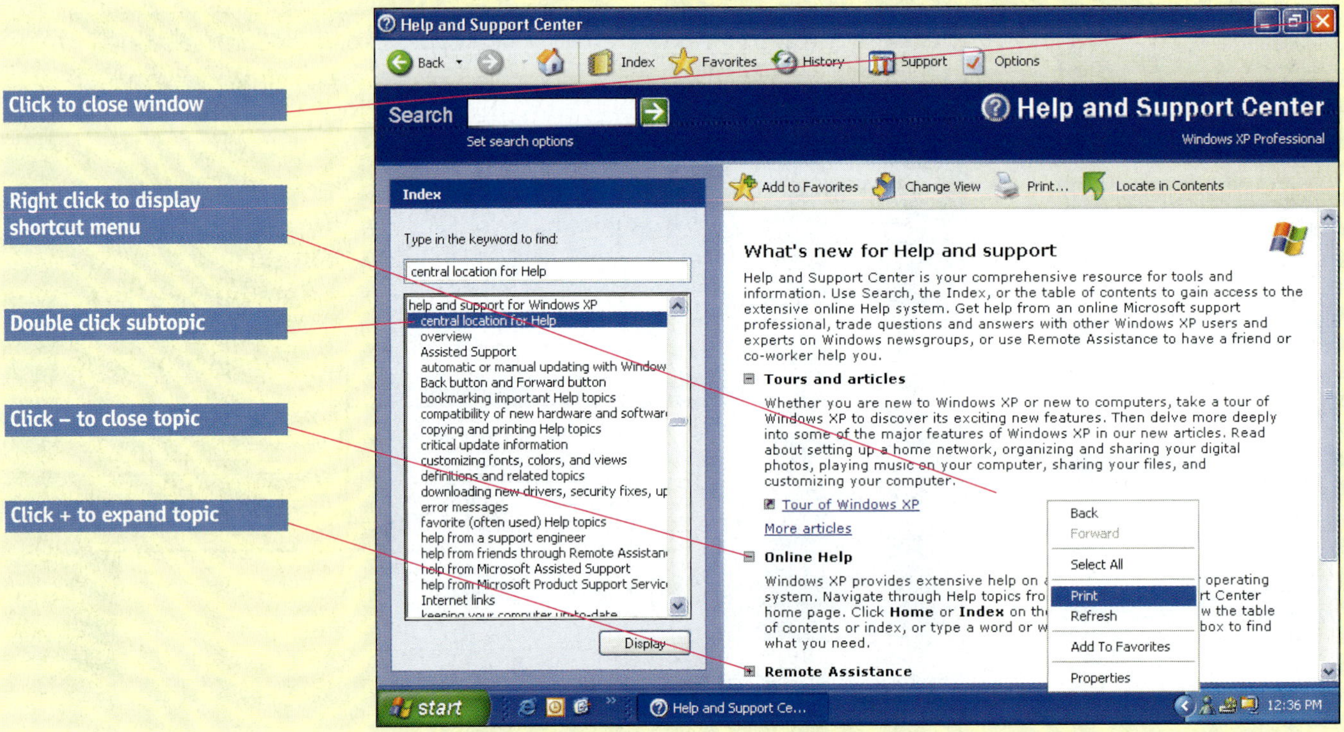

(g) The Help and Support Center (step 7)

FIGURE 7 Hands-on Exercise 1 (*continued*)

THE FAVORITES BUTTON

Do you find yourself continually searching for the same information? If so, you can make life a little easier by adding the page to a list of favorite help topics. Start the Help and Support Center, use the Index button to display the desired information in the right pane, and then click the Add to Favorites button to add the topic to your list of favorites. You can return to the topic at any time by clicking the Favorites button at the top of the Help and Support window, then double clicking the bookmark.

Step 8: Log (or Turn) Off the Computer

- It is very important that you log off properly, as opposed to just turning off the power. This enables Windows to close all of its system files and to save any changes that were made during the session.
- Click the **Start button** to display the Start menu in Figure 7h, then click the **Log Off button** at the bottom of the menu. You will see a dialog box asking whether you want to log off or switch users.
  - ❑ Switching users leaves your session active. All of your applications remain open, but control of the computer is given to another user. You can subsequently log back on (after the new user logs off) and take up exactly where you left off.
  - ❑ Logging off ends your session, but leaves the computer running at full power. This is the typical option you would select in a laboratory setting at school.
- To turn the computer off, you have to log off as just described, then select the **Turn Computer Off command** from the login screen. Welcome to Windows XP!

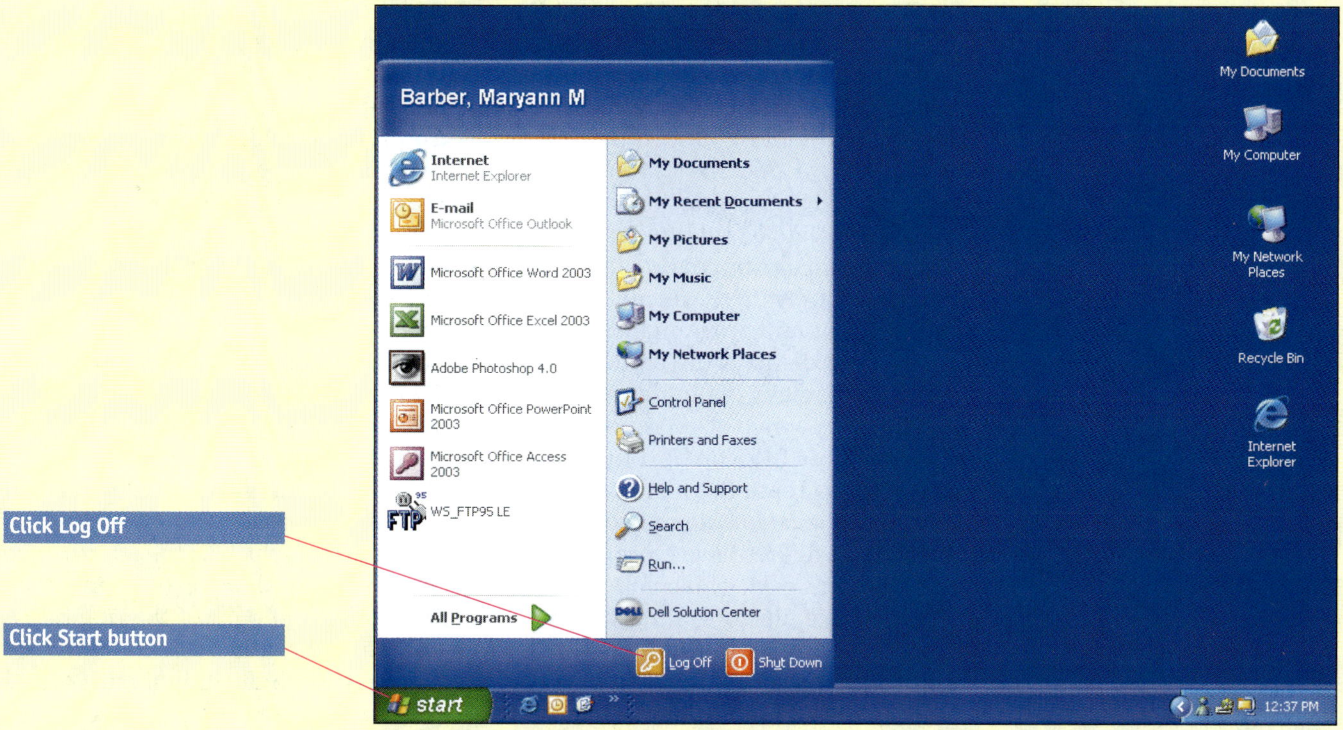

(h) Log (or Turn) Off Computer (step 8)

FIGURE 7 Hands-on Exercise 1 (*continued*)

THE TASK MANAGER

The Start button is the normal way to exit Windows. Occasionally, however, an application may "hang"—in which case you want to close the problem application but continue with your session. Press Ctrl+Alt+Del to display the Windows Task Manager dialog box, then click the Applications tab. Select the problem application (it will most likely say "not responding"), and click the End Task button. This capability is often disabled in a school setting.

FILES AND FOLDERS

A ***file*** is a set of instructions or data that has been given a name and stored on disk. There are two basic types of files, ***program files*** and ***data files***. Microsoft Word and Microsoft Excel are examples of program files. The documents and workbooks that are created by these programs are data files. A program file is executable because it contains instructions that tell the computer what to do. A data file is not executable and can be used only in conjunction with a specific program. In other words, you execute program files to create and/or edit the associated data files.

Every file has a ***filename*** that identifies it to the operating system. The filename can contain up to 255 characters and may include spaces and other punctuation. (Filenames cannot contain the following characters: \, /, :, *, ?, ", <, >, and |.) We find it easier, however, to restrict the characters in a filename to letters, numbers, and spaces, as opposed to having to remember the special characters that are not permitted.

Files are kept in ***folders*** to better organize the thousands of files on a typical system. A Windows folder is similar to an ordinary manila folder that holds one or more documents. To continue the analogy, an office worker stores his or her documents in manila folders within a filing cabinet. Windows stores its files in electronic folders that are located on a disk, CD-ROM, or other device.

Many folders are created automatically by Windows XP, such as the My Computer or My Documents folders that are present on every system. Other folders are created whenever new software is installed. Additional folders are created by the user to hold the documents he or she creates. You might, for example, create a folder for your word processing documents and a second folder for your spreadsheets. You could also create a folder to hold all of your work for a specific class, which in turn might contain a combination of word processing documents and spreadsheets. The choice is entirely up to you, and you can use any system that makes sense to you. A folder can contain program files, data files, or even other folders.

Figure 8 displays the contents of a hypothetical folder with nine documents. Figure 8a displays the folder in ***Tiles view***. Figure 8b displays the same folder in ***Details view***, which also shows the date the file was created or last modified. Both views display a file icon next to each file to indicate the ***file type*** or application that was used to create the file. *Introduction to E-mail*, for example, is a PowerPoint presentation. *Basic Financial Functions* is an Excel workbook.

The two figures have more similarities than differences, such as the name of the folder (*Homework*), which appears in the title bar next to the icon of an open folder. The Minimize, Restore, and Close buttons are found at the right of the title bar. A menu bar with six pull-down menus appears below the title bar. The Standard Buttons toolbar is below the menu, and the Address bar (indicating the drive and folder) appears below the toolbar. Both folders also contain a task pane that provides easy access to common tasks for the folder or selected object.

Look closely and you will see that the task panes are significantly different. This is because there are no documents selected in Figure 8a, whereas the *Milestones in Communications* document is selected (highlighted) in Figure 8b. Thus, the File and Folder Tasks area in Figure 8a pertains to folders in general, whereas the available tasks in Figure 8b are pertinent to the selected document. The Details areas in the two task panes are also consistent with the selected objects and display information about the Homework folder and selected document, respectively. A status bar appears at the bottom of both windows and displays the contents of the selected object.

The last difference between the task panes reflects the user's preference to open or close the Other Places area. Click the upward chevron in Figure 8a to suppress the display and gain space in the task pane, or click the downward chevron in Figure 8b to display the specific links to other places. The task pane is new to Windows XP and did not appear in previous versions of Windows.

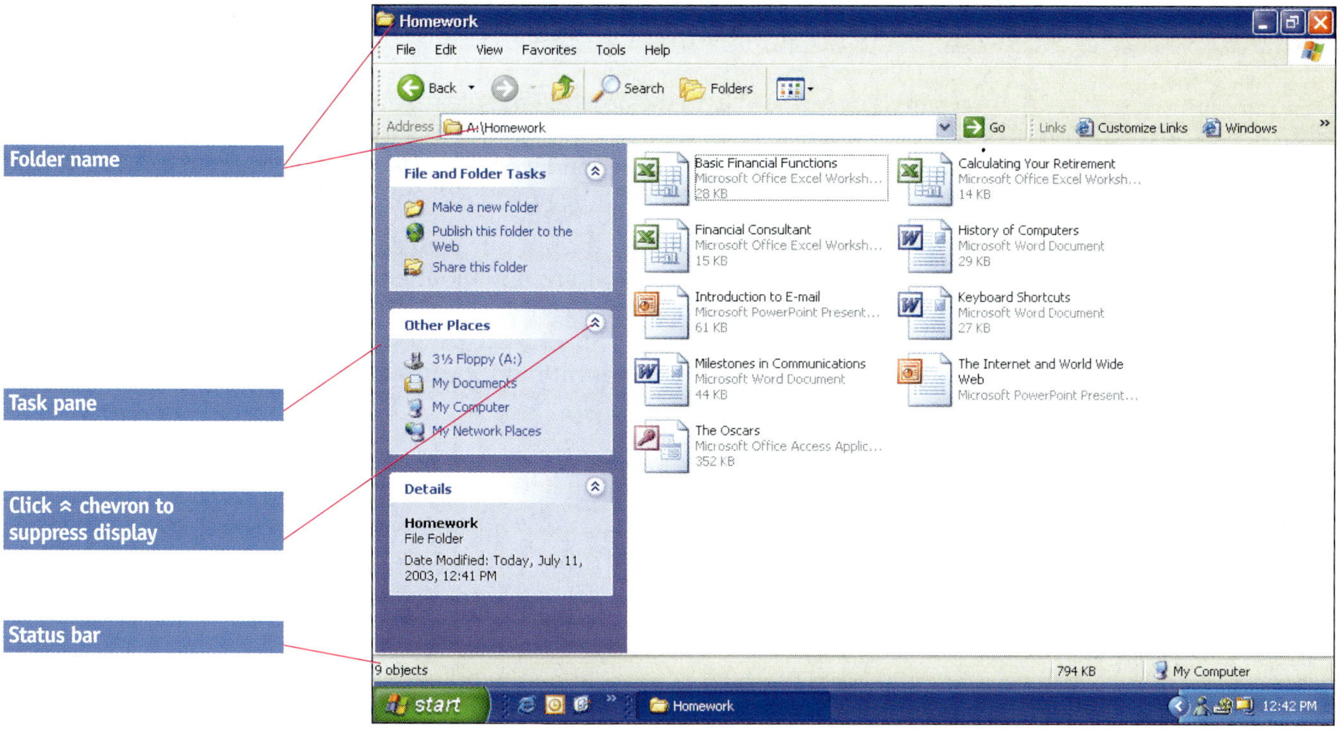

(a) Tiles View

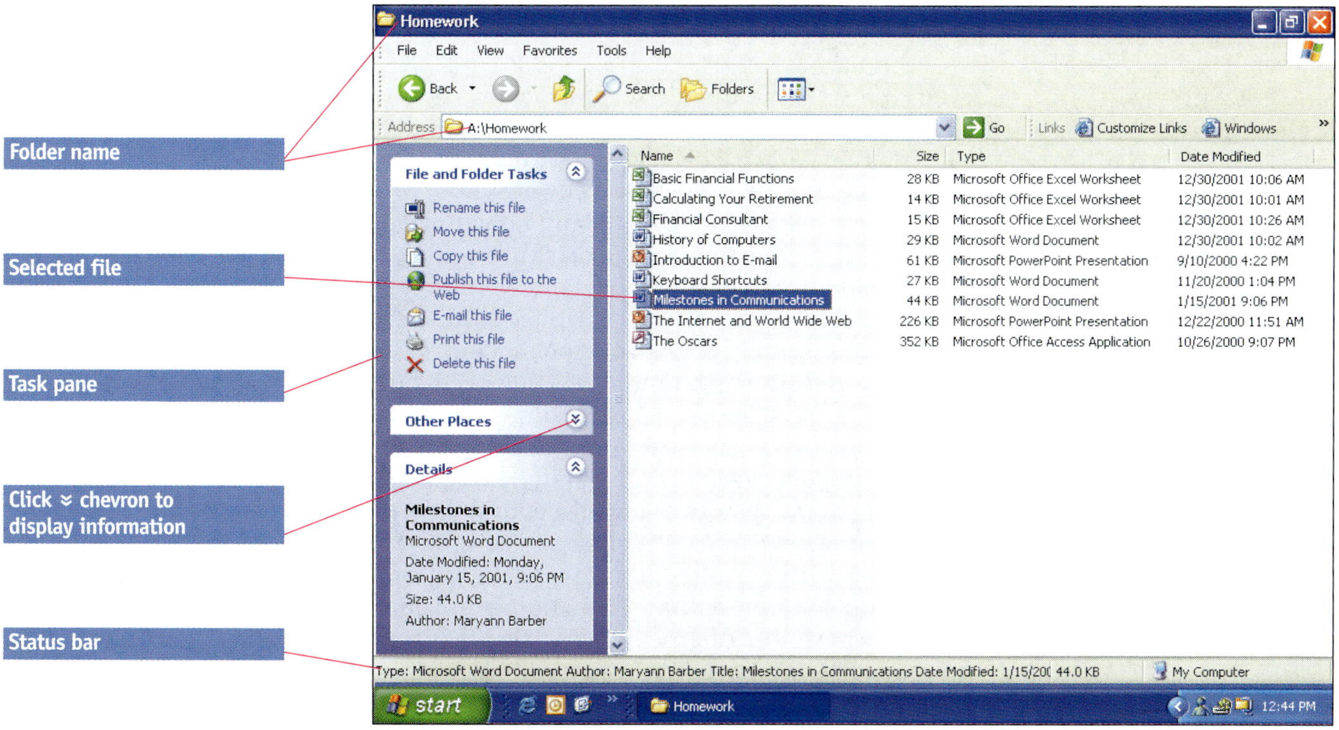

(b) Details View

FIGURE 8 Files and Folders

THE EXPLORING OFFICE PRACTICE FILES

There is only one way to master disk and file management and that is to practice at the computer. To do so requires that you have a series of files with which to work. We have created these files for you, and we use the files in the next two hands-on exercises. Your instructor will make the practice files available to you in different ways:

- The files can be downloaded from our Web site at www.prenhall.com/grauer. Software and other files that are downloaded from the Internet are typically compressed (made smaller) to reduce the amount of time it takes to transmit the file. In essence, you will download a single ***compressed file*** and then uncompress the file into multiple files onto a local drive as described in the next hands-on exercise.
- The files may be on a network drive at your school or university, in which case you can copy the files from the network drive to a floppy disk.
- There may be an actual "data disk" in the computer lab. Go to the lab with a floppy disk, then use the Copy Disk command (on the File menu of My Computer when drive A is selected) to duplicate the data disk and create a copy for yourself.

It doesn't matter how you obtain the practice files, only that you are able to do so. Indeed, you may want to try different techniques to gain additional practice with Windows XP. Note, too, that Windows XP provides a ***firewall*** to protect your computer from unauthorized access while it is connected to the Internet. (See exercise 2 at the end of the chapter.)

CONNECTING TO THE INTERNET

The easiest way to obtain the practice files is to download the files from the Web, which requires an Internet connection. There are two basic ways to connect to the Internet—from a local area network (LAN) or by dialing in. It's much easier if you connect from a LAN (typically at school or work) since the installation and setup have been done for you, and all you have to do is follow the instructions provided by your professor. If you connect from home, you will need a modem, a cable modem, or a DSL modem, and an Internet Service Provider (or ISP).

A ***modem*** is the hardware interface between your computer and the telephone system. In essence, you instruct the modem, via the appropriate software, to connect to your ISP, which in turn lets you access the Internet. A cable modem provides high-speed access (20 to 30 times that of an ordinary modem) through the same type of cable as used for cable TV. A DSL modem also provides high-speed access through a special type of phone line that lets you connect to the Internet while simultaneously carrying on a conversation.

An ***Internet Service Provider*** is a company or organization that maintains a computer with permanent access to the Internet. America Online (AOL) is the largest ISP with more than 30 million subscribers, and it provides a proprietary interface as well as Internet access. The Microsoft Network (MSN) is a direct competitor to AOL. Alternatively, you can choose from a host of other vendors who provide Internet access without the proprietary interface of AOL or MSN.

Regardless of which vendor you choose as an ISP, be sure you understand the fee structure. The monthly fee may entitle you to a set number of hours per month (after which you pay an additional fee), or it may give you unlimited access. The terms vary widely, and you should shop around for the best possible deal. Price is not the only consideration, however. Reliability of service is also important. Be sure that the equipment of your provider is adequate so that you can obtain access whenever you want.

hands-on exercise

2 Download the Practice Files

Objective To download a file from the Web and practice basic file commands. The exercise requires a formatted floppy disk and access to the Internet. Use Figure 9 as a guide.

Step 1: Start Internet Explorer

- Click the **Start button**, click the **All Programs command**, and then click **Internet Explorer** to start the program. If necessary, click the **Maximize button** so that Internet Explorer takes the entire desktop.
- Click anywhere within the **Address bar**, which automatically selects the current address (so that whatever you type replaces the current address). Enter **www.prenhall.com/grauer** (the http:// is assumed). Press **Enter**.
- You should see the Exploring Office Series home page as shown in Figure 9a. Click the book for **Office 2003**, which takes you to the Office 2003 home page.
- Click the **Student Downloads tab** (at the top of the window) to go to the Student Download page.

(a) Start Internet Explorer (step 1)

FIGURE 9 Hands-on Exercise 2

A NEW INTERNET EXPLORER

The installation of Windows XP automatically installs a new version of Internet Explorer. Pull down the Help menu and click the About Internet Explorer command to display the current release (version 6.0). Click OK to close the About Internet Explorer window.

Step 2: Download the Practice Files

- You should see the Student Download page in Figure 9b. Place the formatted floppy disk from the first exercise in drive A. Be sure there are no files on this disk.
- Scroll down the page until you see the link to the student data disk for **Windows XP**. Click the link to download the practice files.
- You will see the File Download dialog box, asking what you want to do. Click the **Save button** to display the Save As dialog box. Click the **drop-down arrow** on the Save in list box, and select (click) **drive A**.
- Click **Save** to download the file. The File Download window may reappear and show you the status of the downloading operation as it takes place.
- If necessary, click **Close** when you see the dialog box indicating that the download is complete. Minimize Internet Explorer.

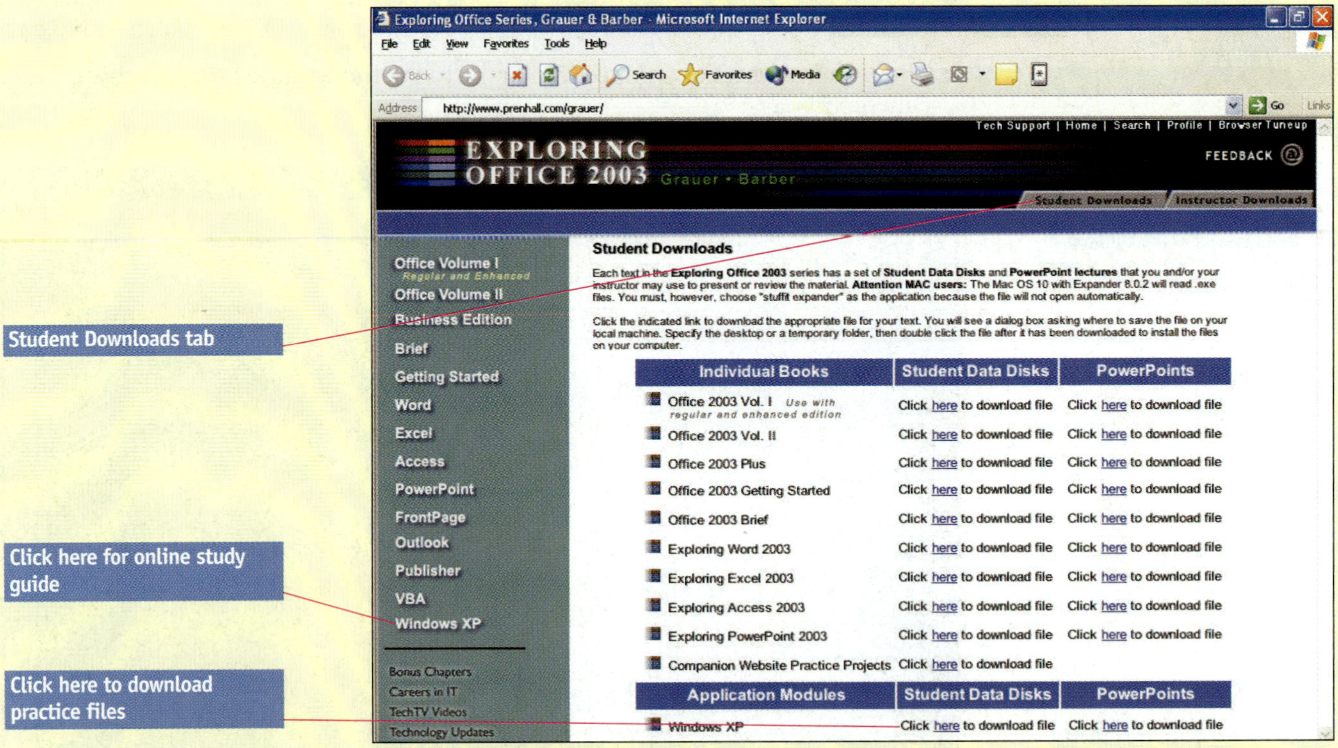

(b) Download the Practice Files (step 2)

FIGURE 9 Hands-on Exercise 2 (*continued*)

EXPLORE OUR WEB SITE

The Exploring Office Series Web site offers an online study guide (multiple-choice, true/false, and matching questions) for each individual textbook to help you review the material in each chapter. You can take practice quizzes by yourself and/or e-mail the results to your instructor. These online study guides are available via the tabs in the left navigation bar. You can return to the Student Download page at any time by clicking the tab toward the top of the window and/or you can click the link to Home to return to the home page for the Office 2003 Series. And finally, you can click the Feedback button at the top of the screen to send a message directly to Bob Grauer.

Step 3: Install the Practice Files

- Click the **Start button**, then click the **My Computer command** on the menu to open the My Computer folder. If necessary, click the Maximize button so that the My Computer window takes up the entire desktop. Change to the **Details view**.
- Click the icon for **drive A** to select it. The description of drive A appears at the left of the window. Double click the icon for **drive A** to open this drive. The contents of the My Computer window are replaced by the contents of drive A as shown in Figure 9c.
- Double click the **XPData file** to install the practice files, which displays the dialog box in Figure 9c. When you have finished reading, click **OK** to continue the installation and display the WinZip Self-Extractor dialog box.
- Check that the Unzip To Folder text box specifies **A:** to extract the files to the floppy disk. Click the **Unzip button** to extract (uncompress) the practice files and copy them onto the designated drive.
- Click **OK** after you see the message indicating that the files have been unzipped successfully. Close the WinZip dialog box.

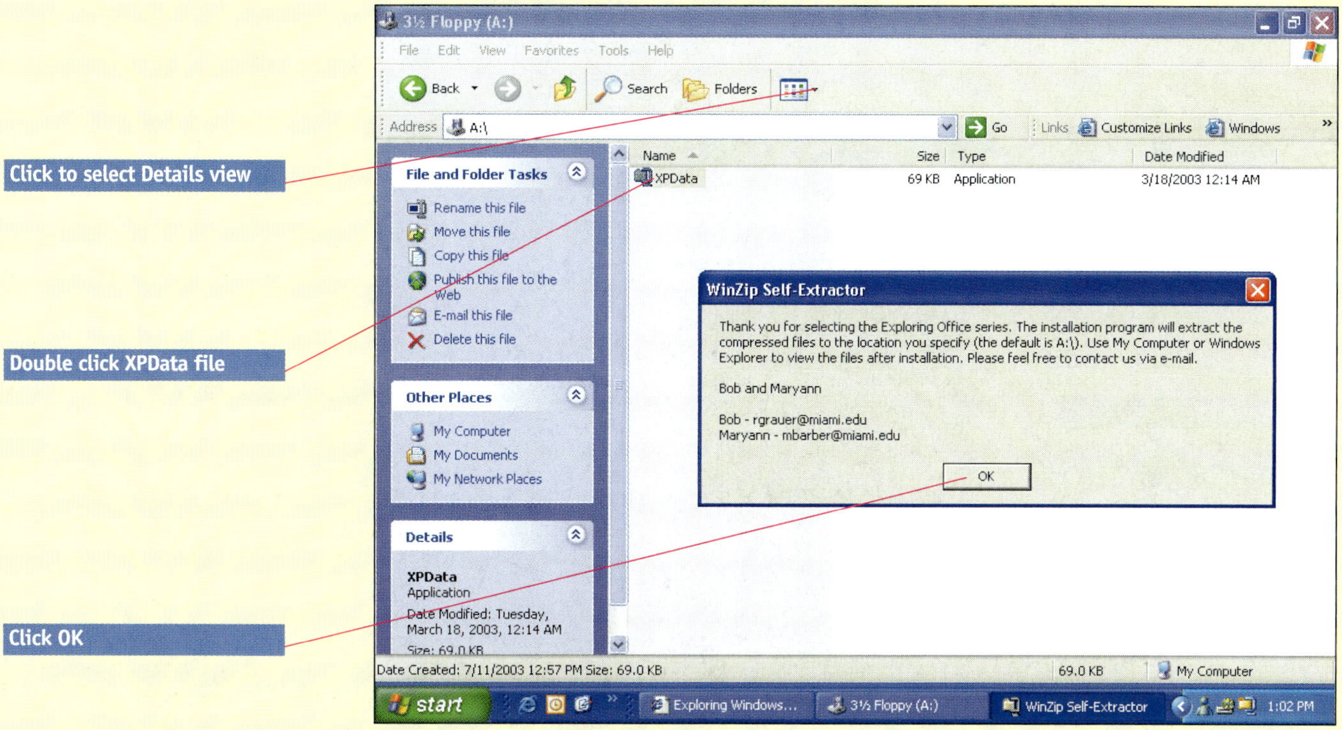

(c) Install the Practice Files (step 3)

FIGURE 9 Hands-on Exercise 2 *(continued)*

DOWNLOADING A FILE

Software and other files are typically compressed (made smaller) to reduce the amount of storage space the files require on disk and/or the time it takes to download the files. In essence, you download a compressed file (which may contain multiple individual files), then you uncompress (expand) the file on your local drive to access the individual files. After the file has been expanded, it is no longer needed and can be deleted.

Step 4: Delete the Compressed File

- The practice files have been extracted to drive A and should appear in the Drive A window. If you do not see the files, pull down the **View menu** and click the **Refresh command**.
- If necessary, pull down the **View menu** and click **Details** to change to the Details view in Figure 9e. You should see a total of eight files in the drive A window. Seven of these are the practice files on the data disk. The eighth file is the original file that you downloaded earlier. This file is no longer necessary, since it has been already been expanded.
- Select (click) the **XPData file**. Click the **Delete this file command** in the task pane (or simply press the **Del key**). Pause for a moment to be sure you want to delete this file, then click **Yes** when asked to confirm the deletion as shown in Figure 9d.
- The XPData file is permanently deleted from drive A. (Items deleted from a floppy disk or network drive are not sent to the Recycle bin, and cannot be recovered.)

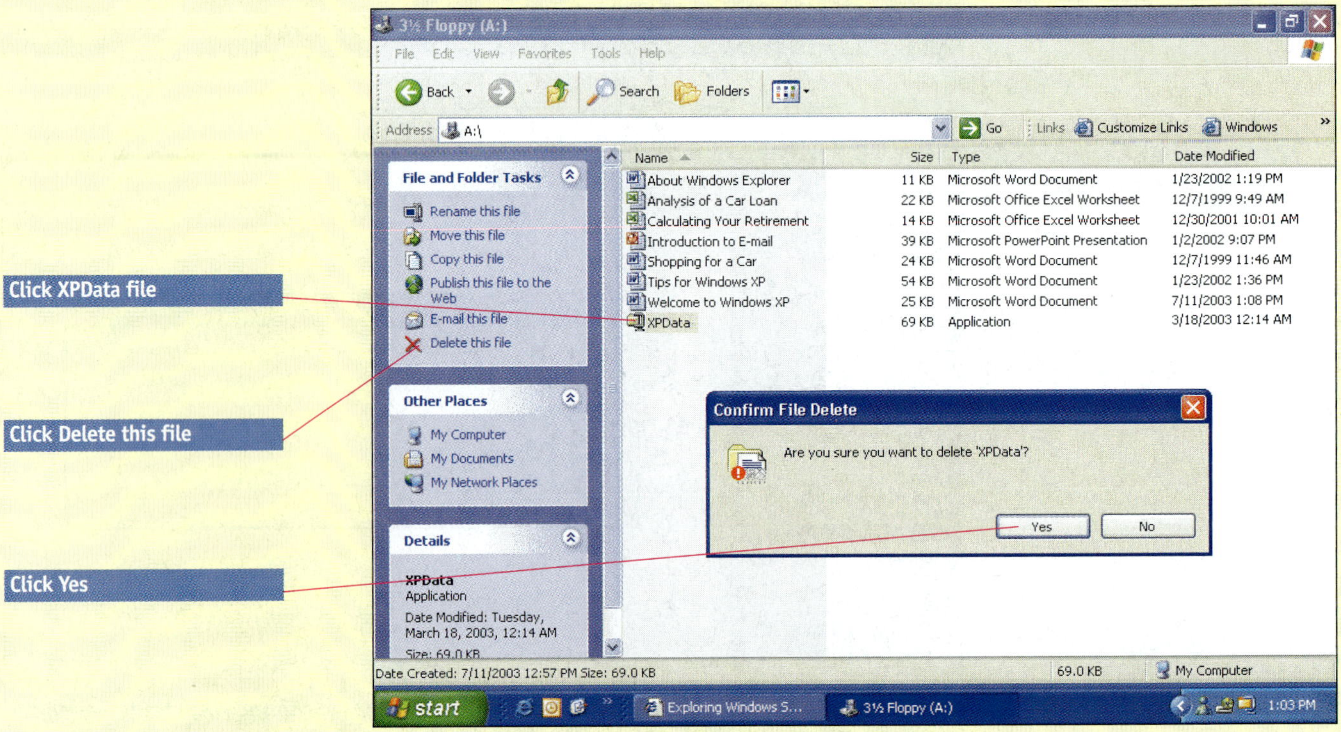

(d) Delete the Compressed File (step 4)

FIGURE 9 Hands-on Exercise 2 (*continued*)

SORT BY NAME, DATE, FILE TYPE, OR SIZE

The files in a folder can be displayed in ascending or descending sequence, by name, date modified, file type, or size, by clicking the appropriate column heading. Click Size, for example, to display files in the order of their size. Click the column heading a second time to reverse the sequence; that is, to switch from ascending to descending, and vice versa. Click a different column heading to display the files in a different sequence.

Step 5: Modify a Document

- Double click the **Welcome to Windows XP** document from within My Computer to open the document as shown in Figure 9e. (The document will open in the WordPad accessory if Microsoft Word is not installed on your machine.)
- Maximize the window for Microsoft Word. Read the document, and then press **Ctrl+End** to move to the end of the document. Do not be concerned if your screen does not match ours exactly.
- Add the sentence shown in Figure 9e, press the **Enter key** twice, then type your name. Click the **Save button** on the Standard toolbar to save the document.
- Pull down the **File menu**, click the **Print command**, and click **OK** (or click the **Print button** on the Standard toolbar) to print the document and prove to your instructor that you did the exercise.
- Pull down the **File menu** and click **Exit** to close Microsoft Word. You should be back in the My Computer folder.

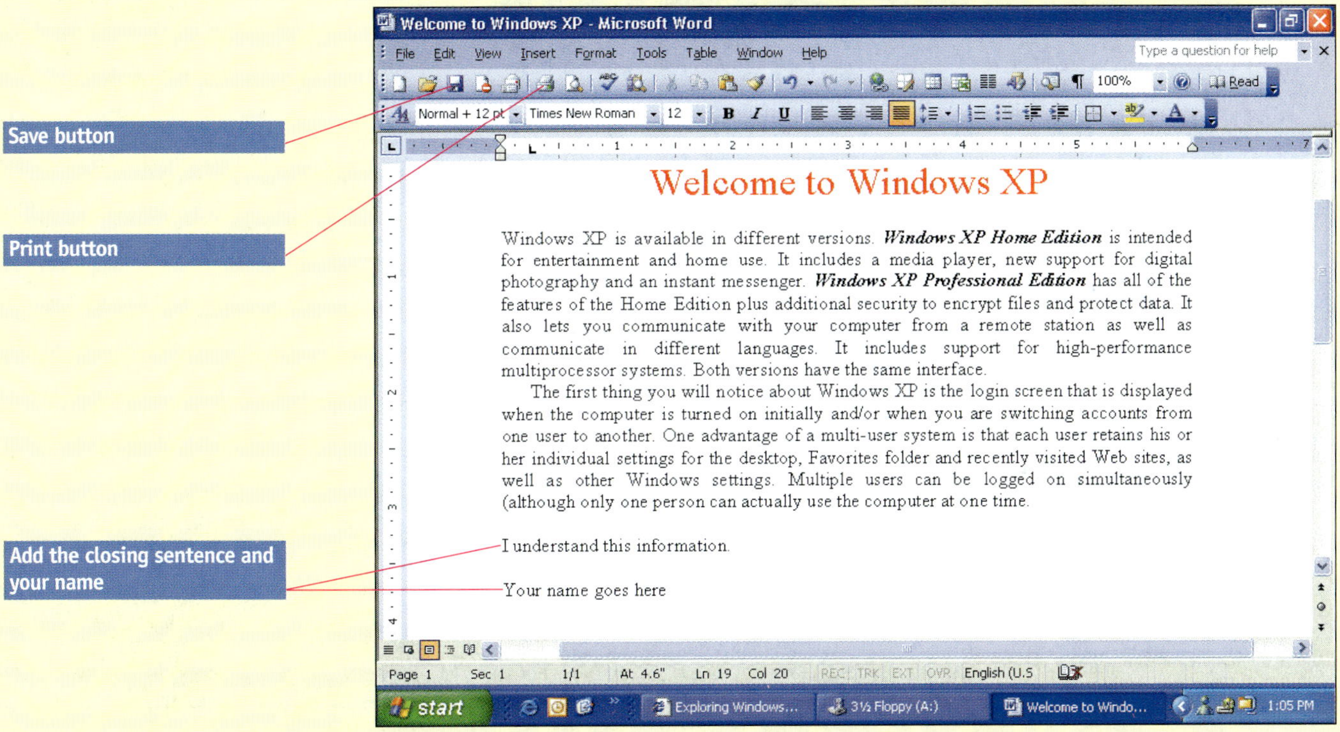

(e) Modify a Document (step 5)

FIGURE 9 Hands-on Exercise 2 (*continued*)

THE DOCUMENT, NOT THE APPLICATION

The Windows operating system is document oriented, which means that you are able to think in terms of the document rather than the application that created it. You can still open a document in traditional fashion, by starting the application that created the document, then using the File Open command in that program to retrieve the document. It's often easier, however, to open the document from within a folder by double clicking its icon. Windows will start the associated application and then open the document for you.

Step 6: Create a New Folder

- Look closely at the date and time that are displayed next to the Welcome to Windows XP document in Figure 9f. It should show today's date and the current time (give or take a minute) because that is when the document was last modified. Your date will be different from ours.
- Look closely and see that Figure 9f also contains an eighth document, called "Backup of Welcome to Windows XP." This is a backup copy of the original document that will be created automatically by Microsoft Word if the appropriate options are in effect. (See the boxed tip below.)
- Click **a blank area** in the right pane to deselect the Welcome to Windows XP document. The commands in the File and Folder Tasks area change to basic folder operations.
- Click the command to **Make a New folder**, which creates a new folder with the default name "New Folder". Enter **New Car** as the new name. You will move files into this folder in step 7.

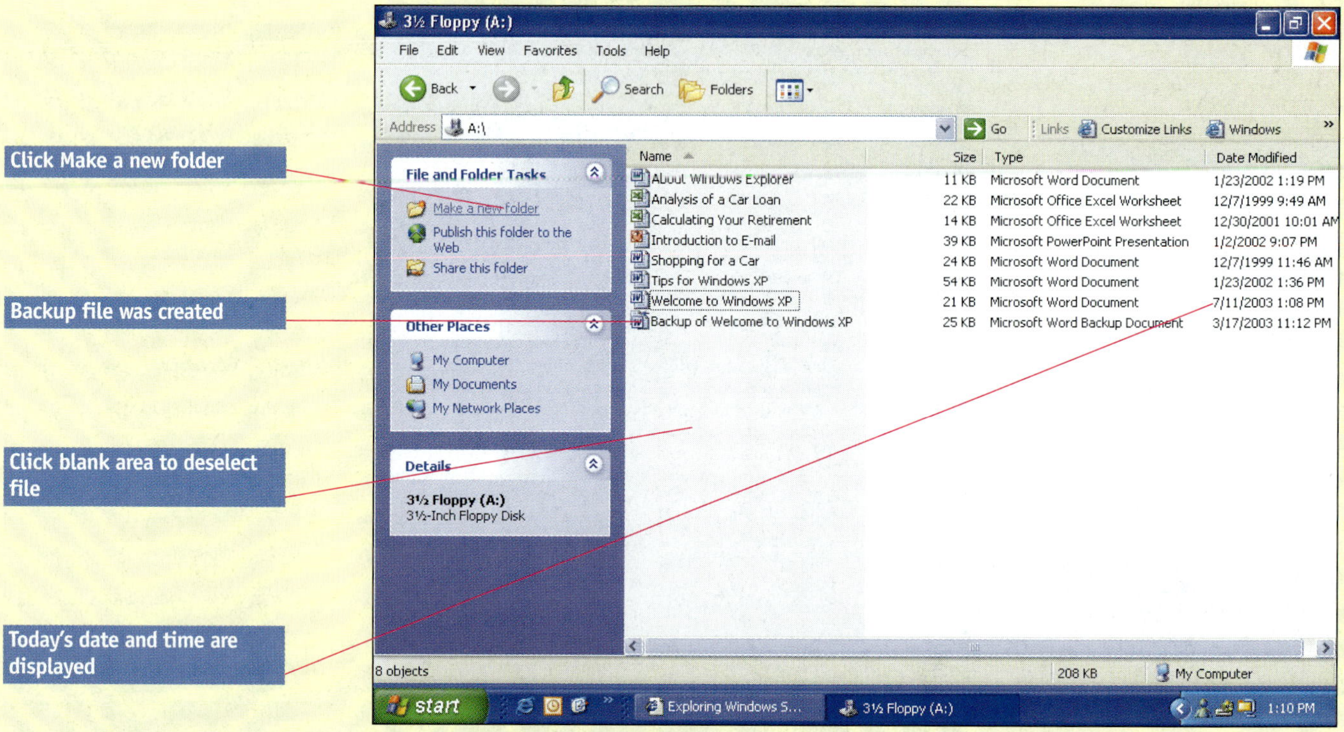

(f) Create a New Folder (step 6)

FIGURE 9 Hands-on Exercise 2 (*continued*)

USE WORD TO CREATE A BACKUP COPY

Microsoft Word enables you to automatically keep the previous version of a document as a backup copy. The next time you are in Microsoft Word, pull down the Tools menu, click the Options command, click the Save tab, then check the box to Always create backup copy. Every time you save a file from this point on, the previously saved version is renamed "Backup of document," and the document in memory is saved as the current version. The disk will contain the two most recent versions of the document, enabling you to retrieve the previous version if necessary.

Step 7: Move the Files

- There are different ways to move a file from one folder to another. The most basic technique is to
  - ❑ Select (click) the **Analysis of a Car Loan** workbook to highlight the file, then click the **Move this file command** in the task pane.
  - ❑ You will see the Move Items dialog box in Figure 9g. Click the plus sign (if it appears) next to the 3½ floppy disk to expand the disk and view its folders. Click the **New Car folder**, then click the **Move button**.
  - ❑ The selected file is moved to the New Car folder and the dialog box closes. The Analysis of a Car Loan document no longer appears in the right pane of Figure 9g because it has been moved to a new folder.
- If the source and destination folders are both on the same drive, as in this example, you can simply click and drag the file to its new destination. Thus, click and drag the **Shopping for a Car** Word document to the New Car folder. Release the mouse when the file is directly over the folder to complete the move.
- Double click the **New Car folder** to view the contents of this folder, which should contain both documents. The Address bar now says A:\New Car.

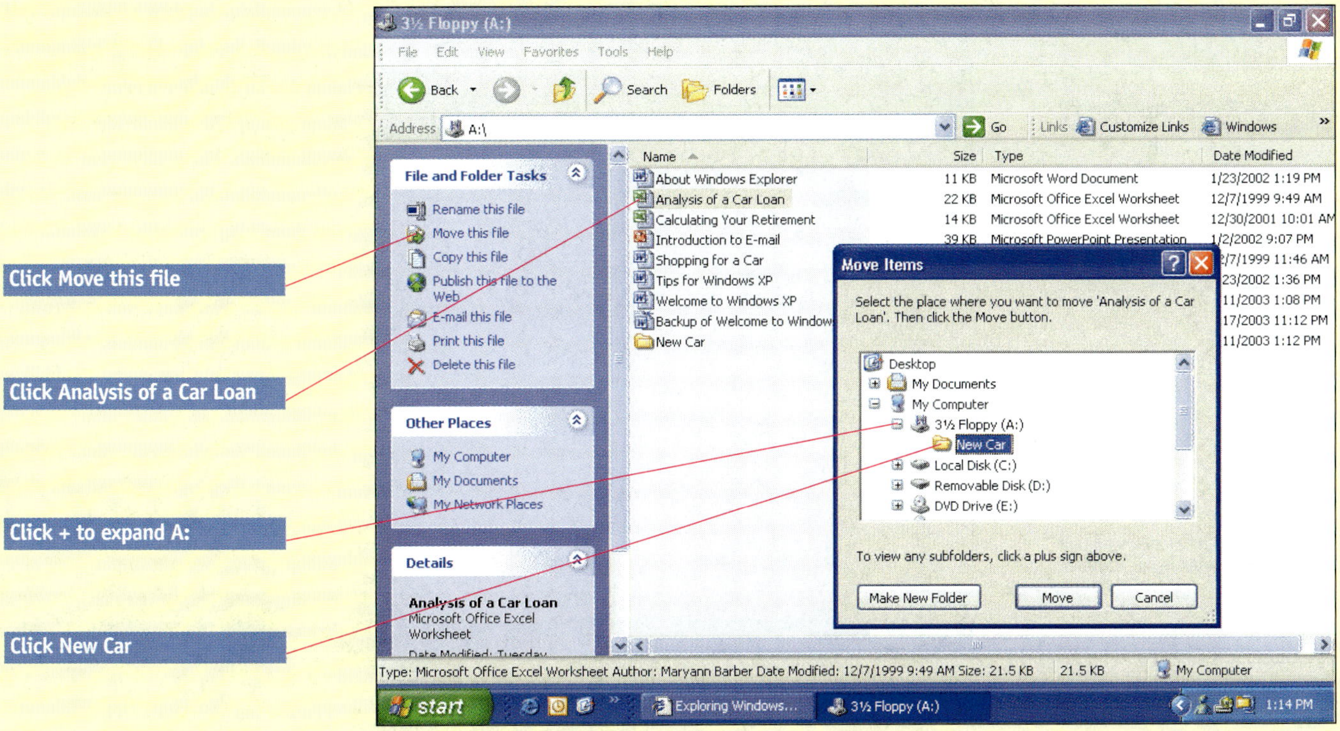

(g) Move the Files (step 7)

FIGURE 9 Hands-on Exercise 2 (*continued*)

THE PLUS AND MINUS SIGNS

Any drive, be it local or on the network, may be expanded or collapsed to display or hide its folders. A minus sign indicates that the drive has been expanded and that its folders are visible. A plus sign indicates the reverse; that is, the device is collapsed and its folders are not visible. Click either sign to toggle to the other. Clicking a plus sign, for example, expands the drive, then displays a minus sign next to the drive to indicate that the folders are visible. Clicking a minus sign has the reverse effect.

Step 8: A Look Ahead

- Click the **Folders button** to display a hierarchical view of the devices on your computer as shown in Figure 9h. This is the same screen that is displayed through Windows Explorer, a program that we will study after the exercise.
- The Folders button functions as a toggle switch; click the button a second time and the task pane (also called task panel) returns. Click the **Folders button** to return to the hierarchical view.
- The New Car folder is selected (highlighted) in the left pane because this is the folder you were working in at the previous step. The contents of this folder are displayed in the right pane.
- Click the icon for the **3½ floppy drive** to display the contents of drive A. The right pane displays the files on drive A as well as the New Car folder.
- Close the My Computer folder. Close Internet Explorer. Log off if you do not want to continue with the next exercise at this time.

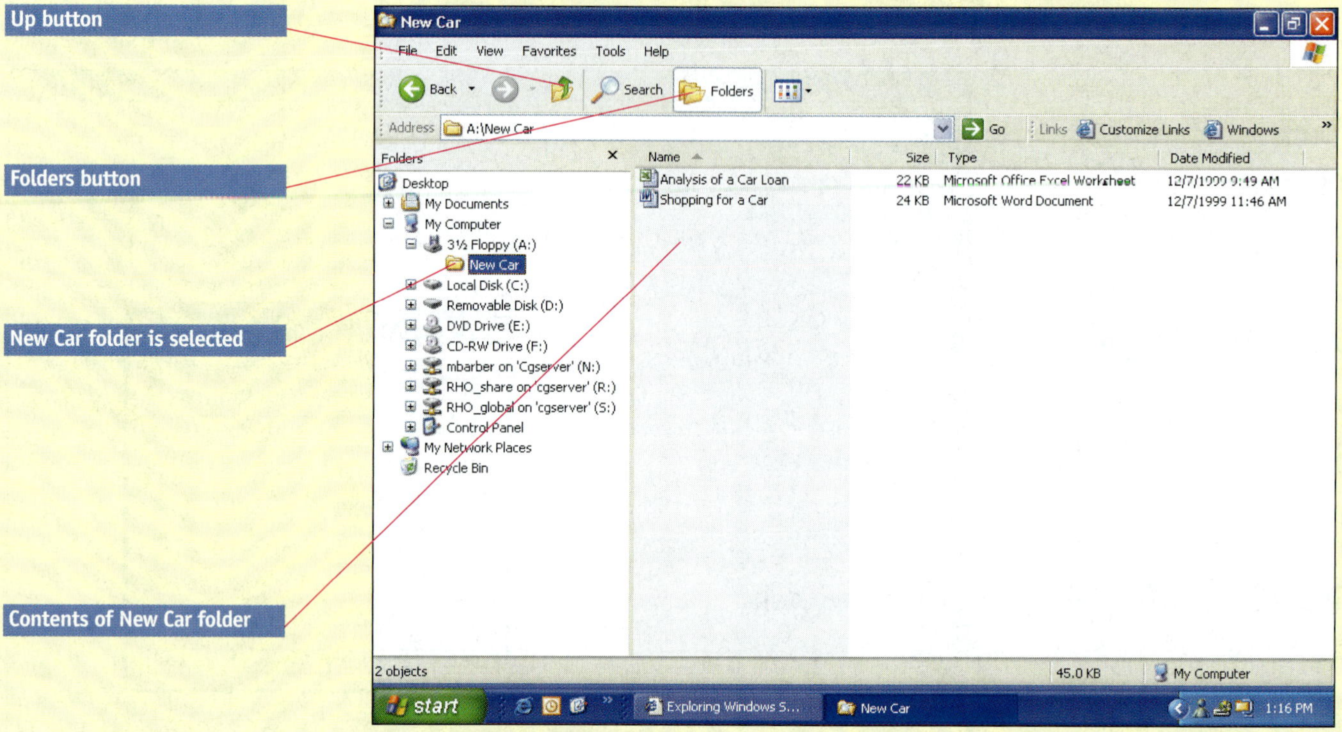

(h) A Look Ahead (step 8)

FIGURE 9 Hands-on Exercise 2 *(continued)*

NAVIGATING THE HIERARCHY

Click the Up button on the Standard Buttons toolbar to move up one level in the hierarchy in the left pane and display the associated contents in the right pane. Click the Up button when you are viewing the New Car folder, for example, and you are returned to drive A. Click the Up button a second time and you will see the contents of My Computer. Note, too, how the contents of the Address bar change each time you view a different folder in the right pane.

Windows Explorer is a program that displays a hierarchical (tree) structure of the devices on your system. Consider, for example, Figure 10a, which displays the contents of a hypothetical Homework folder as it exists on our computer. The hierarchy is displayed in the left pane, and the contents of the selected object (the Homework folder) are shown in the right pane. The advantage of viewing the folder in this way (as opposed to displaying the task pane) is that you see the location of the folder on the system; that is; the Homework folder is physically stored on drive A.

Let's explore the hierarchy in the left pane. There is a minus sign next to the icon for drive A to indicate that this drive has been expanded and thus you can see its folders. Drive C, however, has a plus sign to indicate that the drive is collapsed and that its contents are not visible. Look closely and you see that both drive A and drive C are indented under My Computer, which in turn is indented under the desktop. In other words, the desktop is at the top of the hierarchy and it contains the My Computer folder, which in turn contains drive A and drive C. The desktop also contains a My Documents folder, but the plus sign next to the My Documents folder indicates the folder is collapsed. My Computer, on the other hand, has a minus sign and you can see its contents, which consist of the drives on your system as well as other special folders (Control Panel and Shared Documents).

Look carefully at the icon next to the Homework folder in the left pane of the figure. The icon is an open folder, and it indicates that the (Homework) folder is the active folder. The folder's name is also shaded, and it appears in the title bar. Only one folder can be active at one time, and its contents are displayed in the right pane. The Milestones in Communications document is highlighted (selected) in the right pane, which means that subsequent commands will affect this document, as opposed to the entire folder. If you wanted to work with a different document in the Homework folder, you would select that document. To see the contents of a different folder, such as Financial Documents, you would select (click) the icon for that folder in the left pane (which automatically closes the Homework folder). The contents of the Financial Documents folder would then appear in the right pane.

You can create folders at any time just like the Homework and Financial Documents folders that we created on drive A. You can also create folders within folders; for example, a correspondence folder may contain two folders of its own, one for business correspondence and one for personal letters.

Personal Folders

Windows automatically creates a set of personal folders for every user. These include the ***My Documents folder*** and the ***My Pictures folder*** and ***My Music folder*** within the My Documents folder. The My Documents folder is collapsed in Figure 10a, but it is expanded in Figure 10b, and thus its contents are visible. The My Music folder is active, and its contents are visible in the right pane.

Every user has a unique set of personal folders, and thus Windows has to differentiate between the multiple "My Documents" folders that may exist. It does so by creating additional folders to hold the documents and settings for each user. Look closely at the Address bar in Figure 10b. Each back slash indicates a new folder, and you can read the complete path from right to left. Thus, the My Music folder that we are viewing is contained in My Documents folder within Maryann's folder, which in turn is stored in a Documents and Settings folder on drive C.

Fortunately, however, Windows does the housekeeping for you. All you have to do is locate the desired folder—for example, My Music or My Pictures—in the left pane, and Windows does the rest. ***Personal folders*** are just what the name implies—"personal," meaning that only one person has access to their content. Windows also provides a ***Shared Documents folder*** for files that Maryann may want to share with others.

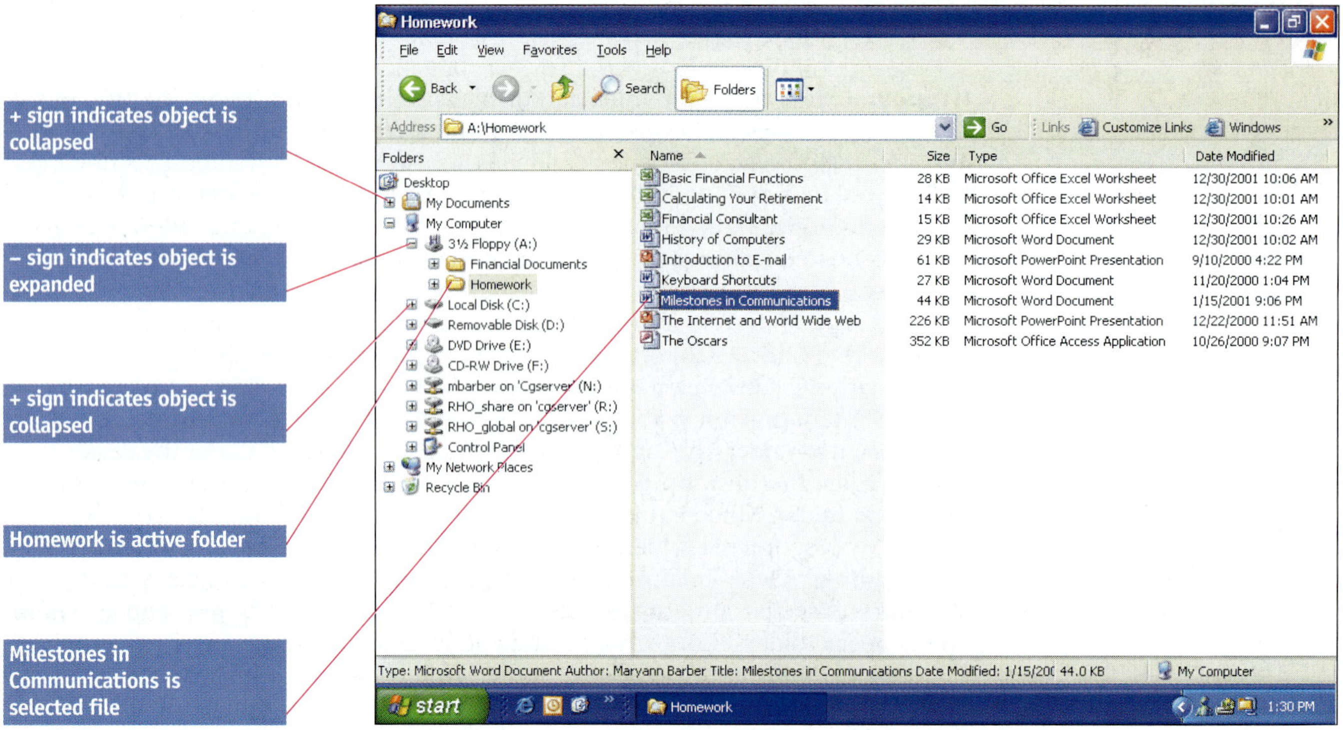

(a) Homework Folder

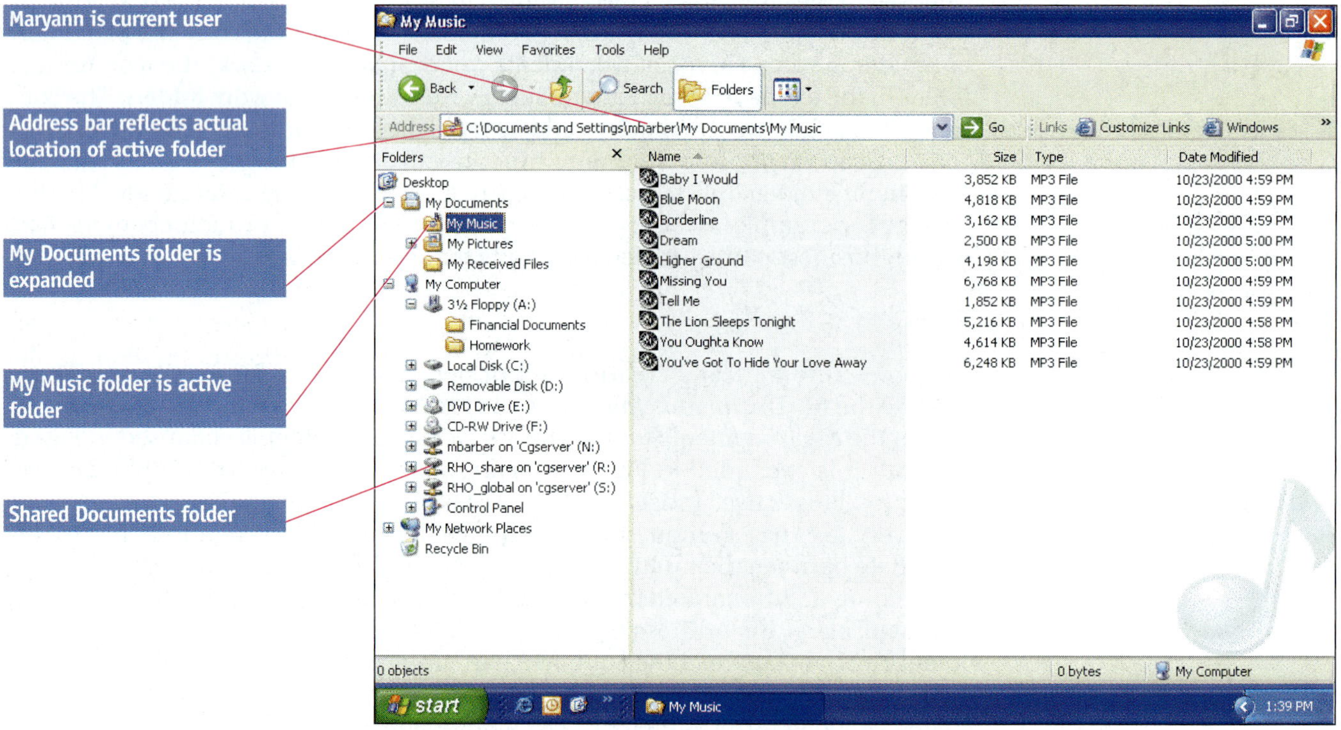

(b) My Music Folder

FIGURE 10 Windows Explorer

Moving and Copying a File

The essence of file management is to ***move*** and ***copy a file*** or folder from one location to another. This can be done in different ways. The easiest is to click and drag the file icon from the source drive or folder to the destination drive or folder, within Windows Explorer. There is one subtlety, however, in that the result of dragging a file (i.e., whether the file is moved or copied) depends on whether the source and destination are on the same or different drives. Dragging a file from one folder to another folder on the same drive moves the file. Dragging a file to a folder on a different drive copies the file. The same rules apply to dragging a folder, where the folder and every file in it are moved or copied, as per the rules for an individual file.

This process is not as arbitrary as it may seem. Windows assumes that if you drag an object (a file or folder) to a different drive (e.g., from drive C to drive A), you want the object to appear in both places. Hence, the default action when you click and drag an object to a different drive is to copy the object. You can, however, override the default and move the object by pressing and holding the Shift key as you drag.

Windows also assumes that you do not want two copies of an object on the same drive, as that would result in wasted disk space. Thus, the default action when you click and drag an object to a different folder on the same drive is to move the object. You can override the default and copy the object by pressing and holding the Ctrl key as you drag. It's not as complicated as it sounds, and you get a chance to practice in the hands-on exercise, which follows shortly.

Deleting a File

The ***Delete command*** deletes (erases) a file from a disk. The command can be executed in different ways, most easily by selecting a file, then pressing the Del key. It's also comforting to know that you can usually recover a deleted file, because the file is not (initially) removed from the disk, but moved instead to the Recycle Bin, from where it can be restored to its original location. Unfortunately, files deleted from a floppy disk are not put into the Recycle Bin and hence cannot be recovered.

The ***Recycle Bin*** is a special folder that contains all files that were previously deleted from any hard disk on your system. Think of the Recycle Bin as similar to the wastebasket in your room. You throw out (delete) a report by tossing it into a wastebasket. The report is gone (deleted) from your desk, but you can still get it back by taking it out of the wastebasket as long as the basket wasn't emptied. The Recycle Bin works the same way. Files are not deleted from the hard disk per se, but moved instead to the Recycle Bin from where they can be restored to their original location. (The protection afforded by the Recycle Bin does not extend to files deleted from a floppy disk.)

Backup

It's not a question of *if* it will happen, but *when*—hard disks die, files are lost, or viruses may infect a system. It has happened to us and it will happen to you, but you can prepare for the inevitable by creating adequate backup *before* the problem occurs. The essence of a ***backup strategy*** is to decide which files to back up, how often to do the backup, and where to keep the backup.

Our strategy is very simple—back up what you can't afford to lose, do so on a daily basis, and store the backup away from your computer. You need not copy every file, every day. Instead, copy just the files that changed during the current session. Realize, too, that it is much more important to back up your data files than your program files. You can always reinstall the application from the original disks or CD, or if necessary, go to the vendor for another copy of an application. You, however, are the only one who has a copy of the term paper that is due tomorrow. Once you decide on a strategy, follow it, and follow it faithfully!

hands-on exercise

3 Windows Explorer

Objective Use Windows Explorer to move, copy, and delete a file; recover a deleted file from the Recycle Bin. Use Figure 11 as a guide.

Step 1: Create a New Folder

- Place the floppy disk from the previous exercise into drive A. Click the **Start Button**, click the **All Programs command**, click **Accessories**, then click **Windows Explorer**. Click the **Maximize button**.
- Expand or collapse the various devices on your system so that My Computer is expanded, but all of the devices are collapsed.
- Click (select) **drive A** in the left pane to display the contents of the floppy disk. You should see the New Car folder that was created in the previous exercise.
- Point to a blank area anywhere in the **right pane**, click the **right mouse button**, click the **New command**, then click **Folder** as the type of object to create.
- The icon for a new folder will appear with the name of the folder (New Folder) highlighted. Type **Windows Information** to change the name. Press **Enter**.

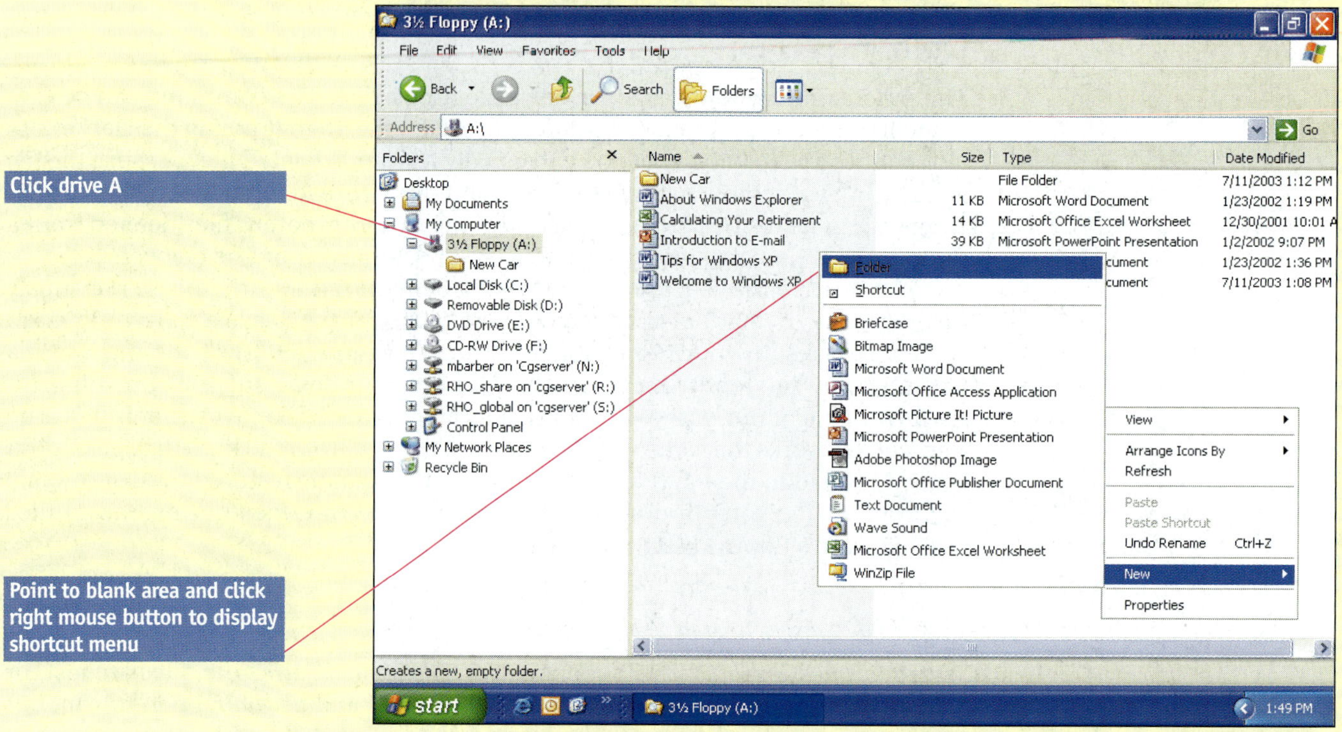

(a) Create a New Folder (step 1)

FIGURE 11 Hands-on Exercise 3 (*continued*)

THE RENAME COMMAND

Right click the file or a folder whose name you want to change to display a context-sensitive menu, and then click the Rename command. The name of the folder will be highlighted with the insertion point at the end of the name. Enter (or edit) the new (existing) name and press Enter.

Step 2: Move the Files

- If necessary, change to the **Details view** and click the **plus sign** next to drive A to expand the drive as shown in Figure 11b. Note the following:
  - The left pane shows that drive A is selected. The right pane displays the contents of drive A (the selected object in the left pane). The folders are shown first and appear in alphabetical order. If not, press the **F5 (Refresh) key** to refresh the screen.
  - There is a minus sign next to the icon for drive A in the left pane, indicating that it has been expanded and that its folders are visible. Thus, the folder names also appear under drive A in the left pane.
- Click and drag the **About Windows Explorer** document in the right pane to the **Windows Information folder** in the left pane, to move the file into that folder.
- Click and drag the **Tips for Windows XP** and the **Welcome to Windows XP** documents to move these documents to the **Windows Information folder**.
- Click the **Windows Information folder** in the left pane to select the folder and display its contents in the right pane. You should see the three files that were just moved.
- Click the **Up button** to return to drive A.

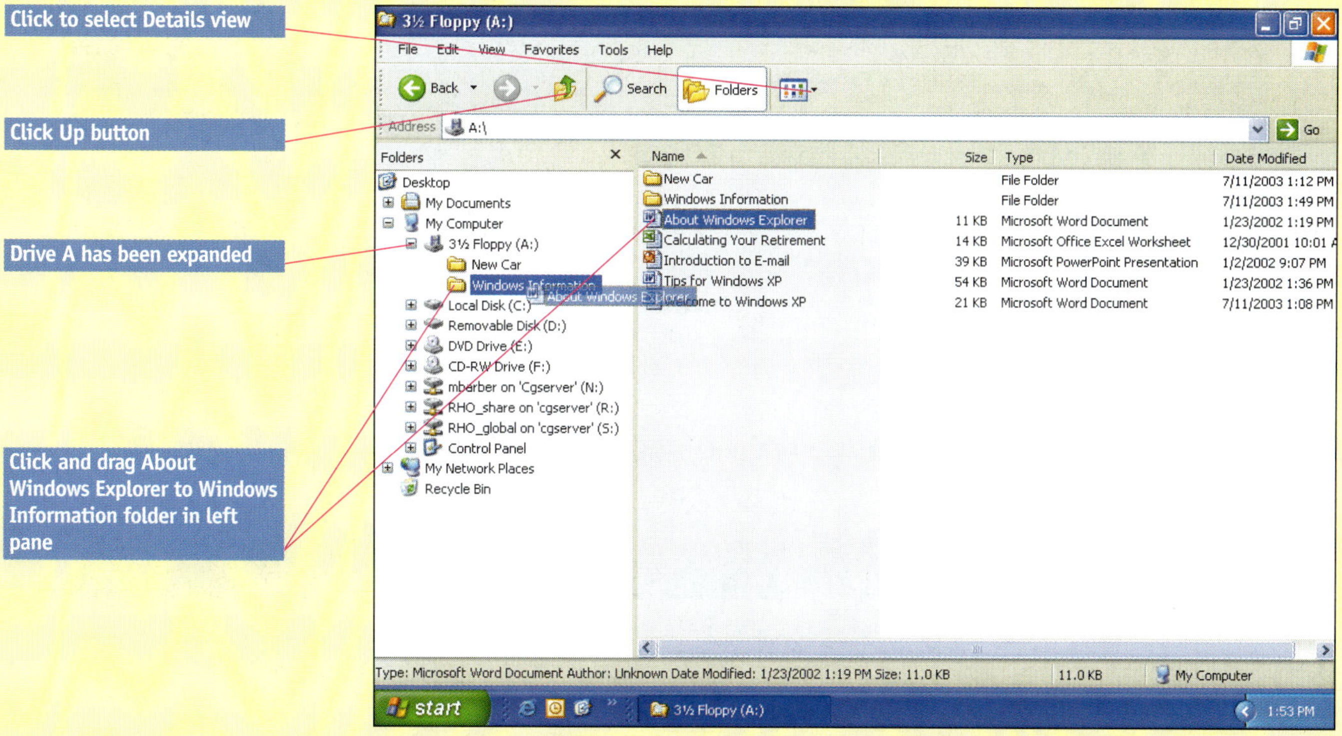

(b) Move the Files (step 2)

FIGURE 11 Hands-on Exercise 3 (*continued*)

SELECT MULTIPLE FILES

Selecting (clicking) one file automatically deselects the previously selected file. You can, however, select multiple files by clicking the first file, then pressing and holding the Ctrl key as you click each additional file. Use the Shift key to select multiple files that are adjacent to one another by clicking the icon of the first file, then pressing and holding the Shift key as you click the icon of the last file.

Step 3: Copy a Folder

- Point to the **Windows Information folder** in the right pane, then **right click and drag** this folder to the **My Documents folder** (on drive C) in the left pane. Release the mouse to display a context-sensitive menu.
- Click the **Copy Here command** as shown in Figure 11c.
  - ❑ You may see a Copy files message box as the individual files within the Windows Information folder are copied to the My Documents folder.
  - ❑ If you see the Confirm Folder Replace dialog box, it means that you (or another student) already copied these files to the My Documents folder. Click the **Yes to All button** so that your files replace the previous versions in the My Documents folder.
- Click the **My Documents folder** in the left pane. Pull down the **View menu** and click the **Refresh command** (or press the **F5 key**) so that the hierarchy shows the newly copied folder. (Please remember to delete the Windows Information folder from drive C at the end of the exercise.)

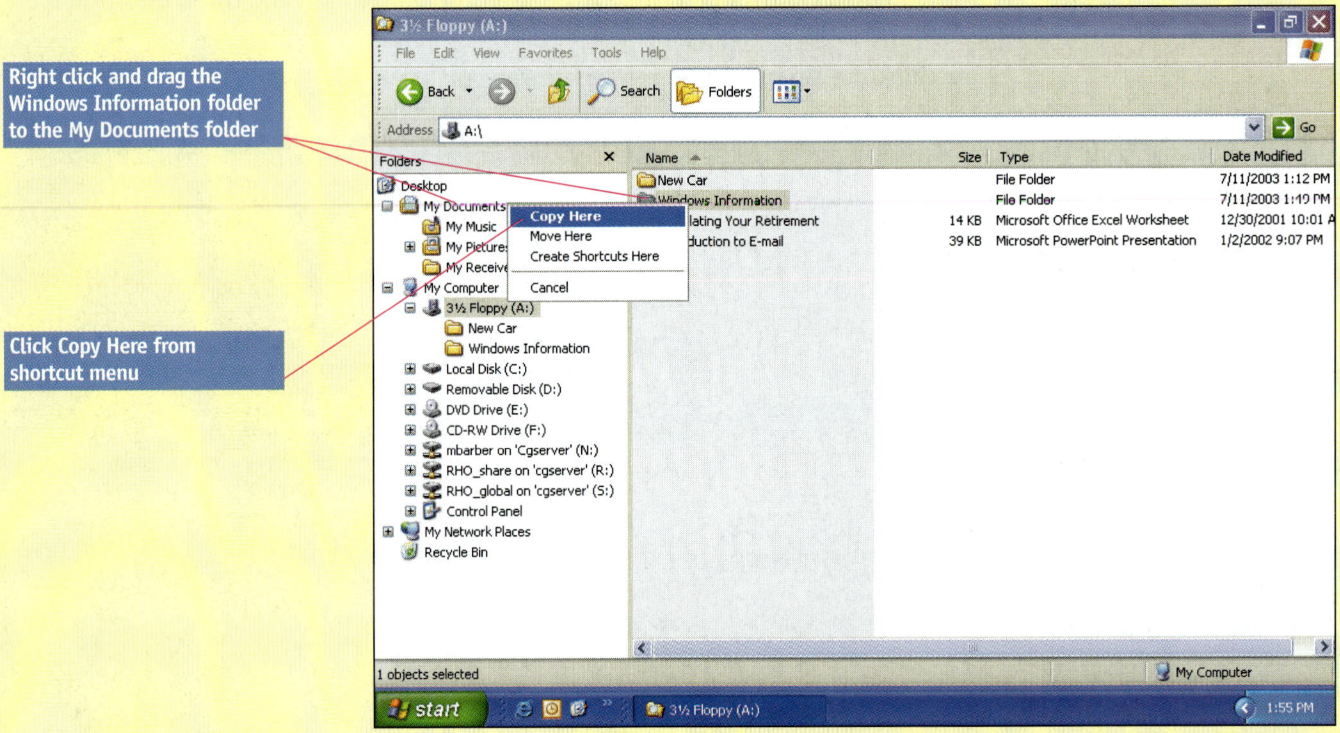

(c) Copy a Folder (step 3)

FIGURE 11 Hands-on Exercise 3 (*continued*)

RIGHT CLICK AND DRAG

The result of dragging a file with the left mouse button depends on whether the source and destination folders are on the same or different drives. Dragging a file to a folder on a different drive copies the file, whereas dragging the file to a folder on the same drive moves the file. If you find this hard to remember, and most people do, click and drag with the right mouse button to display a context-sensitive menu asking whether you want to copy or move the file. This simple tip can save you from making a careless (and potentially serious) error. Use it!

Step 4: Modify a Document

- Click the **Windows Information folder** within the My Documents folder to make it the active folder and to display its contents in the right pane. Change to the **Details view**.
- Double click the **About Windows Explorer** document to start Word and open the document. Do not be concerned if the size and/or position of the Microsoft Word window are different from ours. Read the document.
- If necessary, click inside the document window, then press **Ctrl+End** to move to the end of the document. Add the text shown in Figure 11d.
- Pull down the **File menu** and click **Save** to save the modified file (or click the **Save button** on the Standard toolbar). Pull down the **File menu** and click **Exit** to exit from Microsoft Word.
- Pull down the **View menu** and click the **Refresh command** (or press the **F5 key**) to update the contents of the right pane. The date and time associated with the About Windows Explorer document (on drive C) have been changed to indicate that the file has been modified.

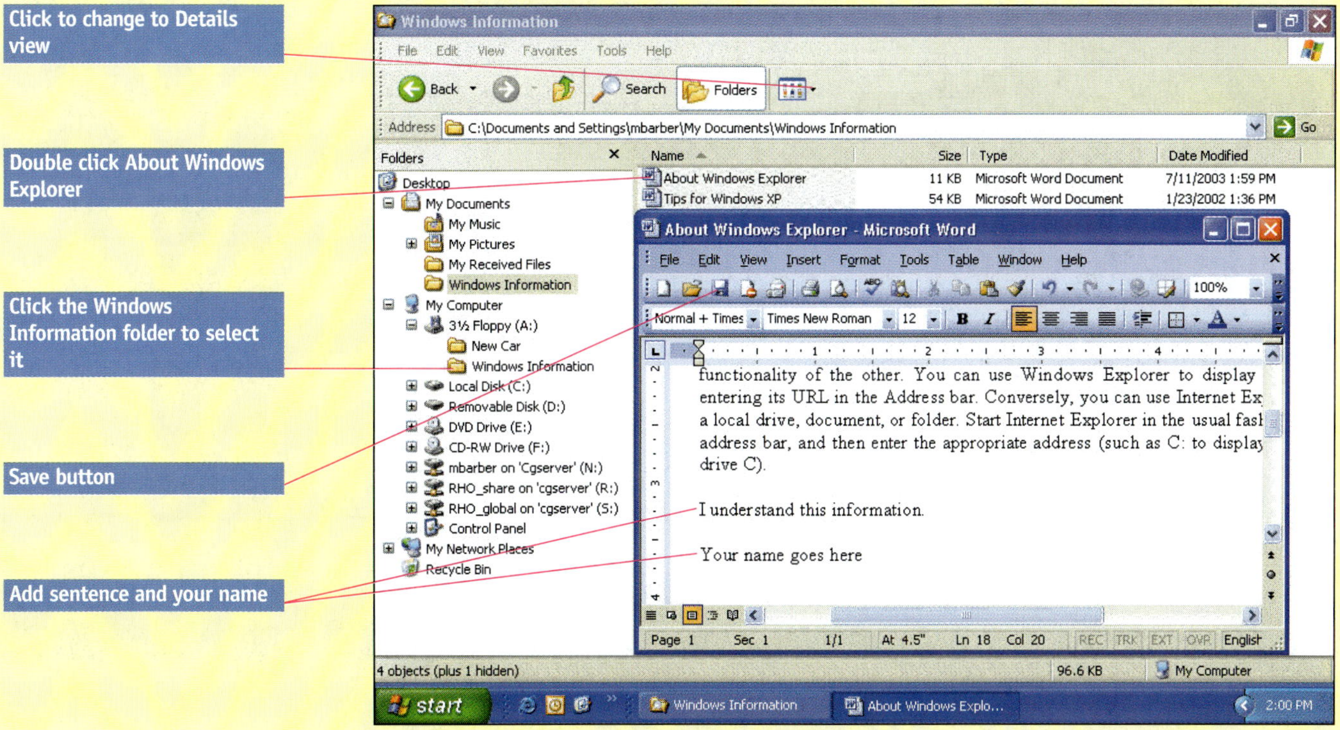

(d) Modify a Document (step 4)

FIGURE 11 Hands-on Exercise 3 (*continued*)

KEYBOARD SHORTCUTS

Most people begin with the mouse, but add keyboard shortcuts as they become more proficient. Ctrl+B, Ctrl+I, and Ctrl+U are shortcuts to boldface, italicize, and underline, respectively. Ctrl+X (the X is supposed to remind you of a pair of scissors), Ctrl+C, and Ctrl+V correspond to Cut, Copy, and Paste, respectively. Ctrl+Home and Ctrl+End move to the beginning or end of a document. These shortcuts are not unique to Microsoft Word, but are recognized in virtually every Windows application.

Step 5: Copy (Back up) a File

- Verify that the **Windows Information folder** (on drive C) is the active folder, as denoted by the open folder icon. Click and drag the icon for the **About Windows Explorer** document from the right pane to the **Windows Information folder** on **drive A** in the left pane.
- You will see the message in Figure 11e, indicating that the folder (on drive A) already contains a file called About Windows Explorer and asking whether you want to replace the existing file.
- Click **Yes** because you want to replace the previous version of the file on drive A with the updated version from the My Documents folder.
- You have just backed up a file by copying the About Windows Explorer document from a folder on drive C to the disk in drive A. In other words, you can use the floppy disk to restore the file to drive C should anything happen to it.
- Keep the floppy disk in a safe place, away from the computer.

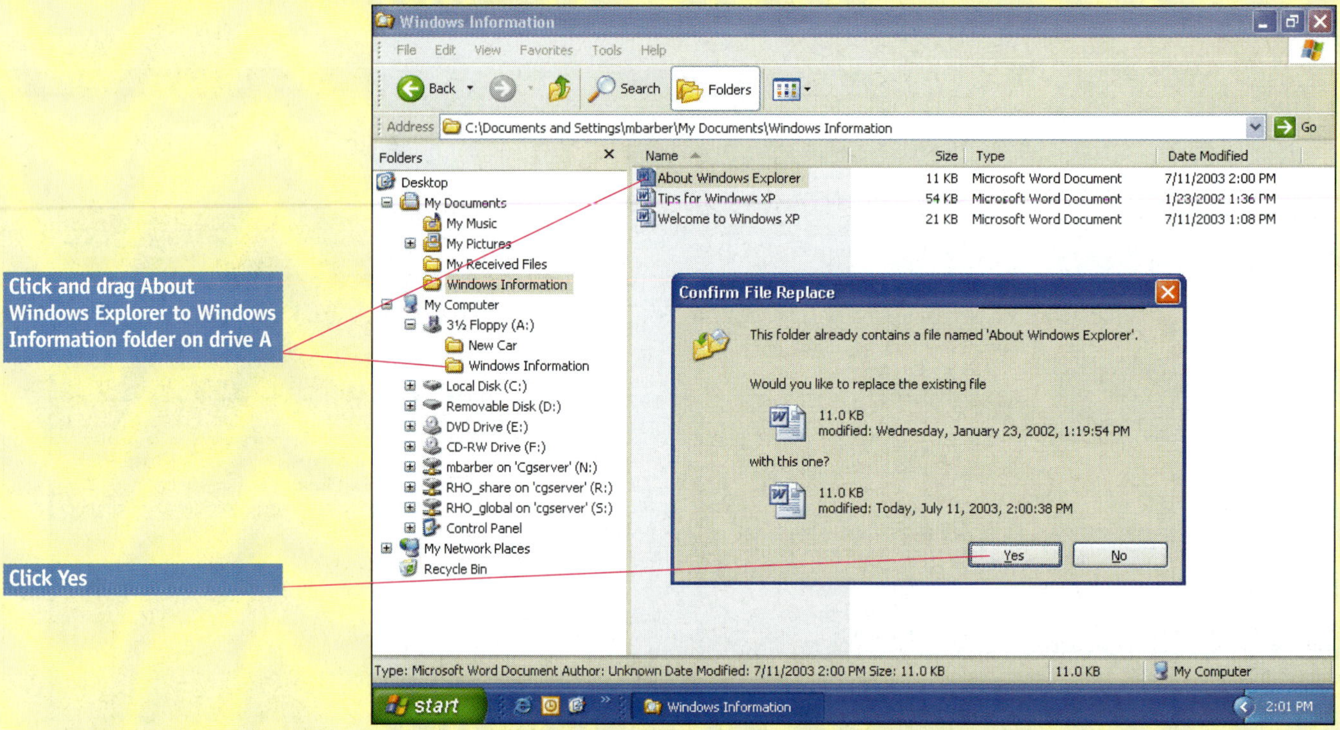

(e) Copy (Back up) a File (step 5)

FIGURE 11 Hands-on Exercise 3 (*continued*)

THE MY DOCUMENTS FOLDER

The My Documents folder is created by default with the installation of Windows XP. There is no requirement that you store your documents in this folder, but it is convenient, especially for beginners who may lack the confidence to create their own folders. The My Documents folder is also helpful in a laboratory environment where the network administrator may prevent you from modifying the desktop and/or from creating your own folders on drive C, in which case you will have to use the My Documents folder.

Step 6: Delete a Folder

- Select (click) **Windows Information folder** within the My Documents folder in the left pane. Pull down the **File menu** and click **Delete** (or press the **Del key**).
- You will see the dialog box in Figure 11f, asking whether you are sure you want to delete the folder and send its contents to the Recycle Bin, which enables you to restore the folder at a later date.
- Click **Yes** to delete the folder. The folder disappears from drive C. Note that you have deleted the folder and its contents.
- Now pretend that you do not want to delete the folder. Pull down the **Edit menu**. Click **Undo Delete**.
- The deletion is cancelled and the Windows Information folder reappears in the left pane. If you do not see the folder, pull down the **View menu** and click the **Refresh command** (or press the **F5 key**).

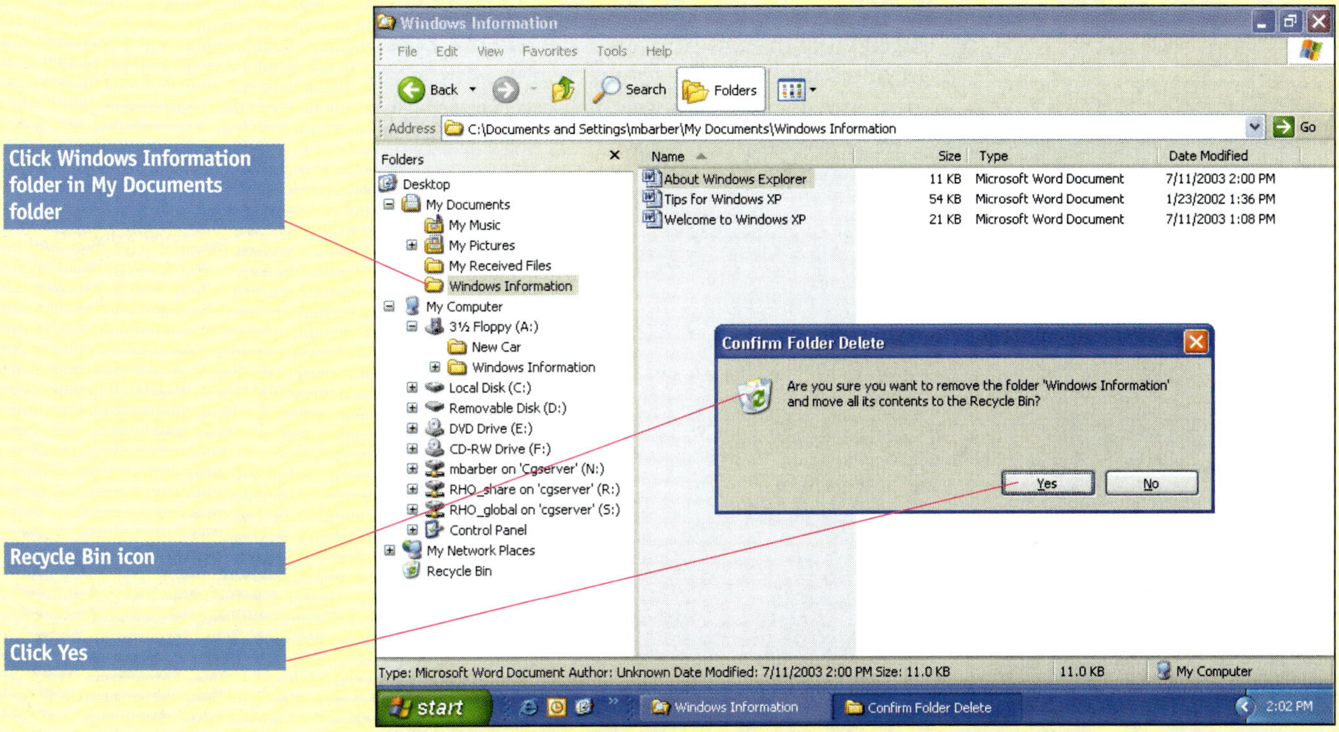

(f) Delete a Folder (step 6)

FIGURE 11 Hands-on Exercise 3 (*continued*)

CUSTOMIZE WINDOWS EXPLORER

Increase or decrease the size of the left pane within Windows Explorer by dragging the vertical line separating the left and right panes in the appropriate direction. You can also drag the right border of the various column headings (Name, Size, Type, and Modified) in the right pane to increase or decrease the width of the column and see more or less information in that column. And best of all, you can click any column heading to display the contents of the selected folder in sequence by that column. Click the heading a second time and the sequence changes from ascending to descending and vice versa.

Step 7: The Recycle Bin

- If necessary, select the **Windows Information folder** within the My Documents folder in the left pane. Select (click) the **About Windows Explorer** file in the right pane. Press the **Del key**, then click **Yes** when asked to delete the file.
- Click the **down arrow** in the vertical scroll bar in the left pane until you can click the icon for the **Recycle Bin**.
- The Recycle Bin contains all files that have been previously deleted from the local (hard) disks, and hence you will see a different number of files than those displayed in Figure 11g.
- Change to the **Details view**. Pull down the **View menu**, click (or point to) **Arrange Icons by**, then click **Date Deleted** to display the files in this sequence. Execute this command a second time (if necessary) so that the most recently deleted file appears at the top of the window.
- Right click the **About Windows Explorer** file to display the context-sensitive menu in Figure 11g, then click the **Restore command**.
- The file disappears from the Recycle bin because it has been returned to the Windows Information folder. You can open the Windows Information folder within the My Documents folder to confirm that the file has been restored.

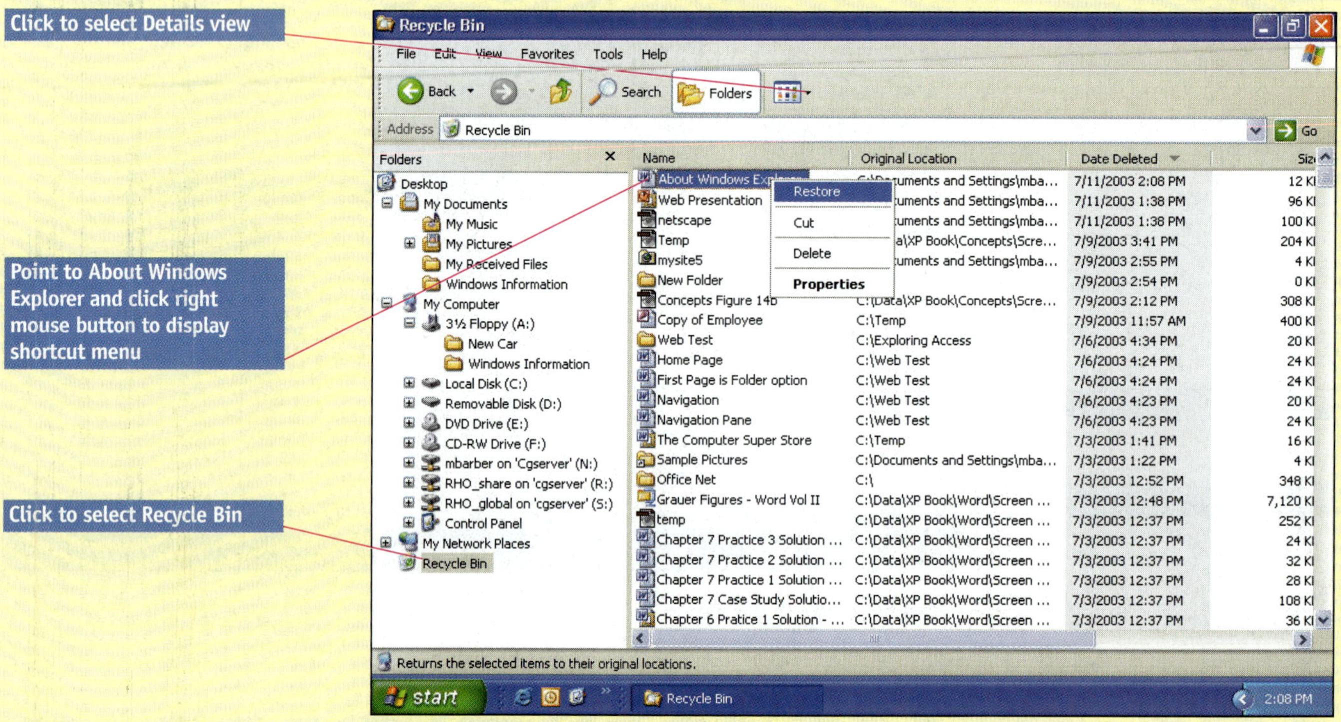

(g) The Recycle Bin (step 7)

FIGURE 11 Hands-on Exercise 3 (*continued*)

TWO WAYS TO RECOVER A FILE

The Undo command is present in Windows Explorer. Thus, you do not need to resort to the Recycle Bin to recover a deleted file provided you execute the Undo command immediately (within a few commands) after the Delete command was issued. Some operations cannot be undone (in which case the Undo command will be dimmed), but Undo is always worth a try.

Step 8: The Group By Command

- Select (click) the **Windows Information folder** on drive A. You should see the contents of this folder (three Word documents) in the right pane.
- Pull down the **View menu**, (click or) point to the **Arrange Icons by command**, then click the **Show in Groups command** from the cascaded menu.
- You see the same three files as previously, but they are displayed in groups according to the first letter in the filename. Click the **Date Modified** column, and the files are grouped according to the date they were last modified.
- The Show in Groups command functions as a toggle switch. Execute the command and the files are displayed in groups; execute the command a second time and the groups disappear.
- Select (click) the icon for **drive A** in the left pane to display the contents of drive A. You should see two folders and two files. Pull down the **View menu**, (click or) point to the **Arrange Icons by command**, and then click the **Show in Groups command** from the cascaded menu.
- Change to the **Details view**. Click the **Type column** to group the objects by folder and file type.

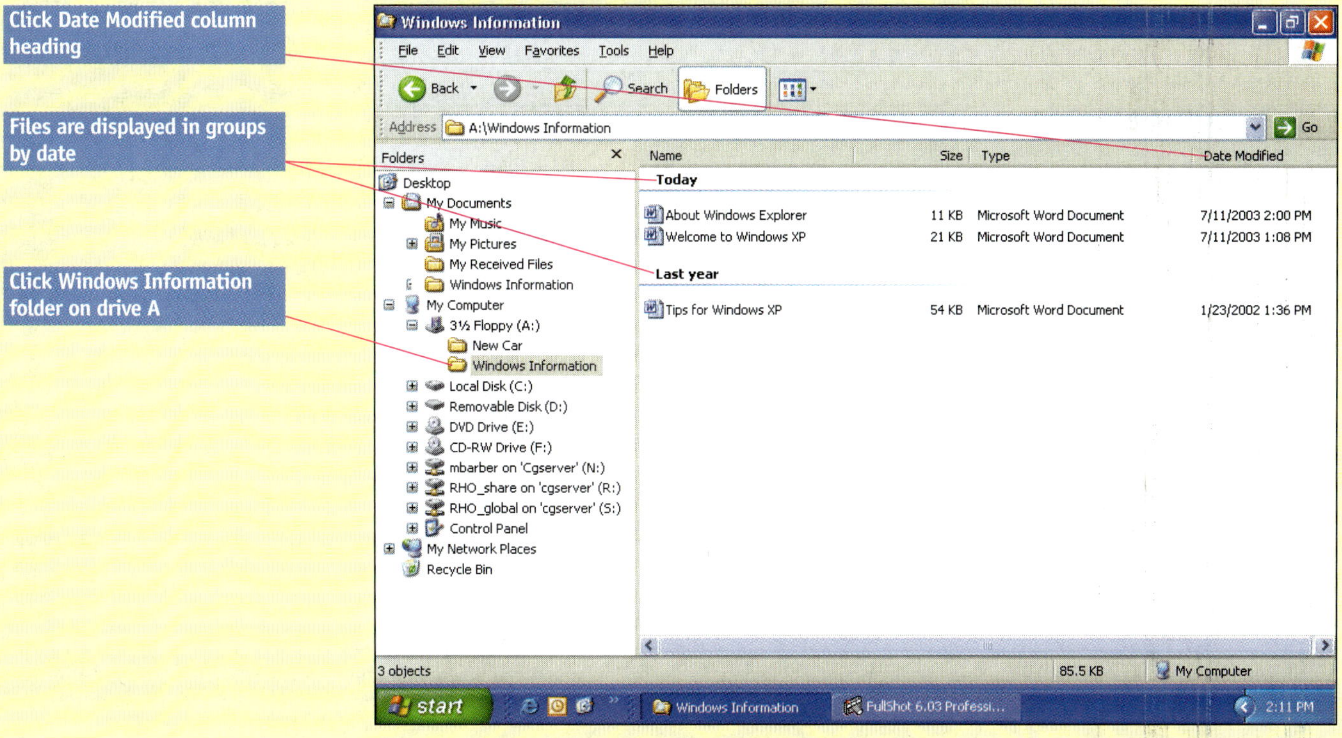

(h) The Group By Command (step 8)

FIGURE 11 Hands-on Exercise 3 (*continued*)

KEEP THE VIEW

Once you set the desired view in a folder, you may want to display every other folder according to those parameters. Pull down the Tools menu, click the Folder Options command, and click the View tab. Click the button to Apply to All folders, then click Yes when prompted to confirm. Click OK to close the Folder Options dialog box. The next time you open another folder, it will appear in the same view as the current folder.

Step 9: Complete the Exercise

- Prove to your instructor that you have completed the exercise correctly by capturing the screen on your monitor. Press the **Print Screen key**. Nothing appears to have happened, but the screen has been copied to the clipboard.
- Click the **Start button**, click the **All Programs command**, then start Microsoft Word and begin a new document. Enter the title of your document, followed by your name as shown in Figure 11i. Press the **Enter key** two or three times.
- Pull down the **Edit menu** and click the **Paste command** (or click the **Paste button** on the Standard toolbar) to copy the contents of the clipboard into the Word document.
- Print this document for your instructor. There is no need to save this document. Exit Word.
- Delete the **Windows Information folder** from the My Documents folder as a courtesy to the next student. Close Windows Explorer.
- Log off if you do not want to continue the next exercise at this time. (Click the **Start button**, click **Log Off**, then click **Log Off** a second time to end your session.)

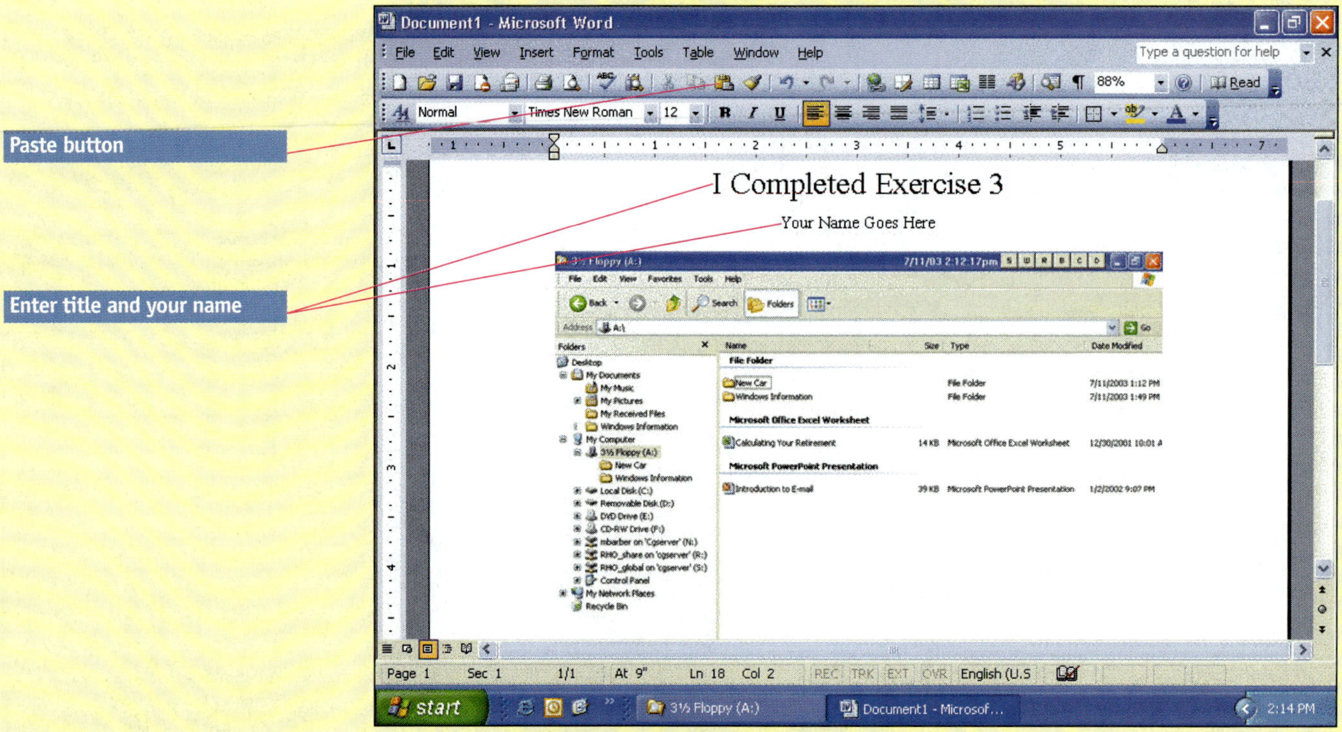

(i) Complete the Exercise (step 9)

FIGURE 11 Hands-on Exercise 3 (*continued*)

SWITCHING USERS VERSUS LOGGING OFF

Windows XP gives you the choice of switching users or logging off. Switching users leaves all of your applications open, but it relinquishes control of the computer to another user. This lets you subsequently log back on (after the new user logs off) and take up exactly where you were. Logging off, on the other hand, closes all of your applications and ends the session, but it leaves the computer running at full power and available for someone else to log on.

INCREASING PRODUCTIVITY

You have learned the basic concepts of disk and file management, but there is so much more. Windows XP has something for everyone. It is easy and intuitive for the novice, but it also contains sophisticated tools for the more knowledgeable user. This section describes three powerful features to increase your productivity. Some or all of these features may be disabled in a school environment, but the information will stand you in good stead on your own computer.

The Control Panel

The ***Control Panel*** affects every aspect of your system. It determines the appearance of your desktop, and it controls the performance of your hardware. You can, for example, change the way your mouse behaves by switching the function of the left and right mouse buttons and/or by replacing the standard mouse pointers with animated icons that move across the screen. You will not have access to the Control Panel in a lab environment, but you will need it at home whenever you install new hardware or software. You should be careful about making changes, and you should understand the nature of the new settings before you accept any of the changes.

The Control Panel in Windows XP organizes its tools by category as shown in Figure 12. Point to any category and you see a Screen Tip that describes the specific tasks within that category. The Appearance and Themes category, for example, lets you select a screen saver or customize the Start menu and taskbar. You can also switch to the Classic view that displays every tool in a single screen, which is consistent with all previous versions of Windows.

The task pane provides access to the ***Windows Update*** function, which connects you to a Web site where you can download new device drivers and other updates to Windows XP. You can also configure your system to install these updates automatically as they become available. Some updates, especially those having to do with Internet security, are absolutely critical.

Click here to switch to Classic view

Point to category and screen tip is displayed

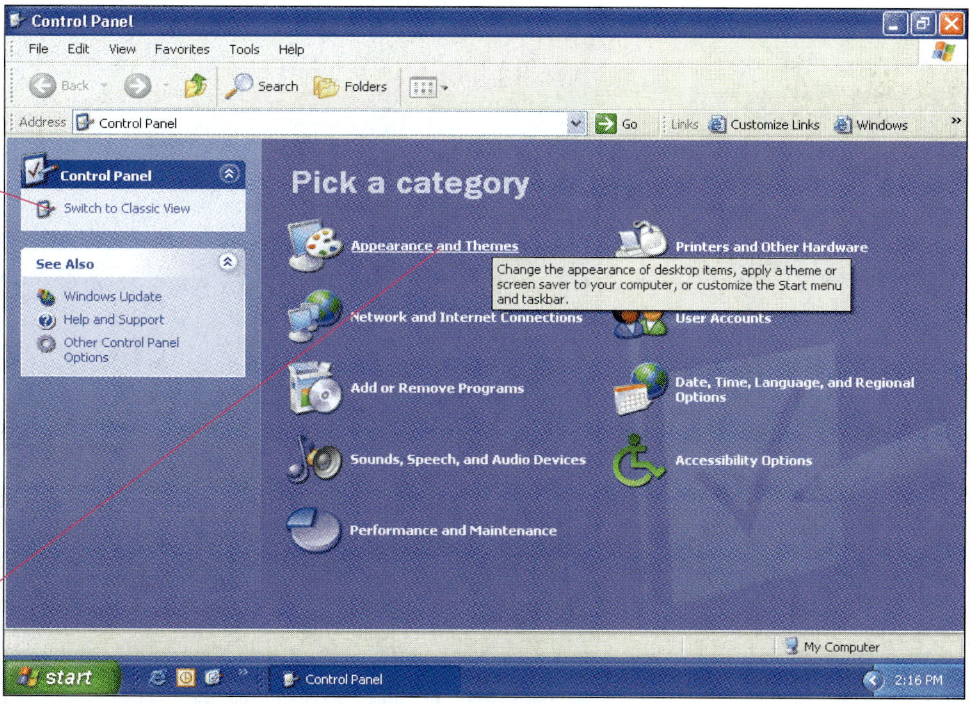

FIGURE 12 The Control Panel

Shortcuts

A ***shortcut*** is a link to any object on your computer, such as a program, file, folder, disk drive, or Web page. Shortcuts can appear anywhere, but are most often placed on the desktop or on the Start menu. The desktop in Figure 13 contains a variety of shortcuts, each of which contains a jump arrow to indicate a shortcut icon. Double click the shortcut to Election of Officers, for example, and you start Word and open this document. In similar fashion, you can double click the shortcut for a Web page (Exploring Windows Series), folder, or disk drive (drive A) to open the object and display its contents.

Creating a shortcut is a two-step process. First, you use Windows Explorer to locate the object such as a file, folder, or disk drive. Then you select the object, use the right mouse button to drag the object to the desktop, and then click the Create Shortcut command from the context-sensitive menu. A shortcut icon will appear on the desktop with the phrase "shortcut to" as part of the name. You can create as many shortcuts as you like, and you can place them anywhere on the desktop or in individual folders. You can also right click a shortcut icon after it has been created to change its name. Deleting the icon deletes the shortcut and not the object.

Windows XP also provides a set of predefined shortcuts through a series of desktop icons that are shown at the left border of the desktop in Figure 13. Double click the My Computer icon, for example, and you open the My Computer folder. These desktop icons were displayed by default in earlier versions of Windows, but not in Windows XP. They were added through the Control Panel as you will see in our next exercise.

Additional shortcuts are found in the ***Quick Launch toolbar*** that appears to the right of the Start button. Click any icon and you open the indicated program. And finally, Windows XP will automatically add to the Start menu shortcuts to your most frequently used programs. Desktop shortcuts are a powerful technique that will increase your productivity by taking you directly to a specified document or other object.

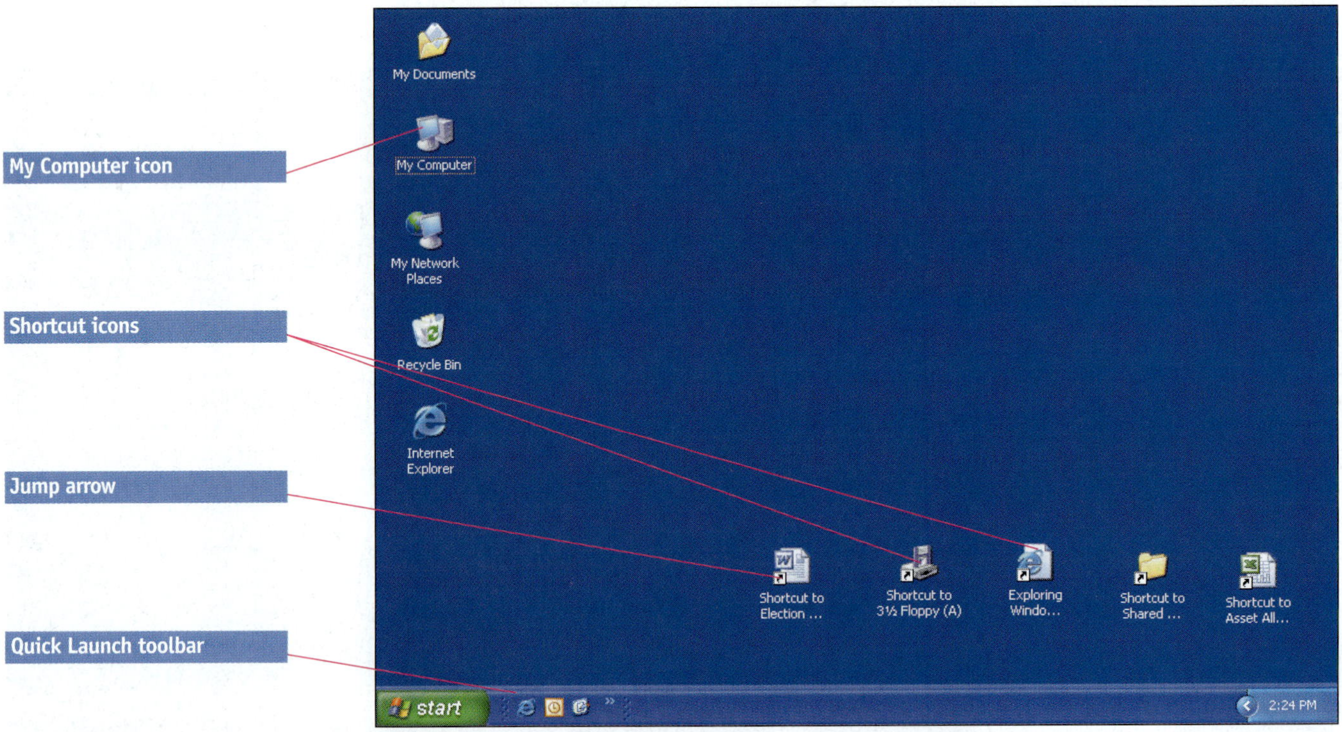

FIGURE 13 Desktop with Shortcuts

The Search Companion

Sooner or later you will create a file, and then forget where (in which folder) you saved it. Or you may create a document and forget its name, but remember a key word or phrase in the document. Or you may want to locate all files of a certain file type—for example, all of the sound files on your system. The ***Search Companion*** can help you to solve each of these problems and is illustrated in Figure 14.

The Search Companion is accessed from within any folder by clicking the Search button on the Standard Buttons toolbar to open the search pane at the left of the folder. You are presented with an initial search menu (not shown in Figure 14) that asks what you want to search for. You can search your local machine for media files (pictures, music, or video), documents (such as spreadsheets or Word documents), or any file or folder. You can also search the Help and Support Center or the Internet.

Once you choose the type of information, you are presented with a secondary search pane as shown in Figure 14. You can search according to a variety of criteria, each of which will help to narrow the search. In this example we are looking for any document on drive C that has "Windows" as part of its filename and further, contains the name "Maryann" somewhere within the document. The search is case sensitive. This example illustrates two important capabilities, namely that you can search on the document name (or part of its name) and/or its content.

Additional criteria can be entered by expanding the chevrons for date and size. You can, for example, restrict your search to all documents that were modified within the last week, the past month, or the last year. You can also restrict your search to documents of a certain size. Click the Search button after all of the criteria have been specified to initiate the search. The results of the search (the documents that satisfy the search criteria) are displayed in the right pane. You can refine the search if it is unsuccessful and/or you can open any document in which you are interested. The Search Companion also has an indexing service to make subsequent searches faster.

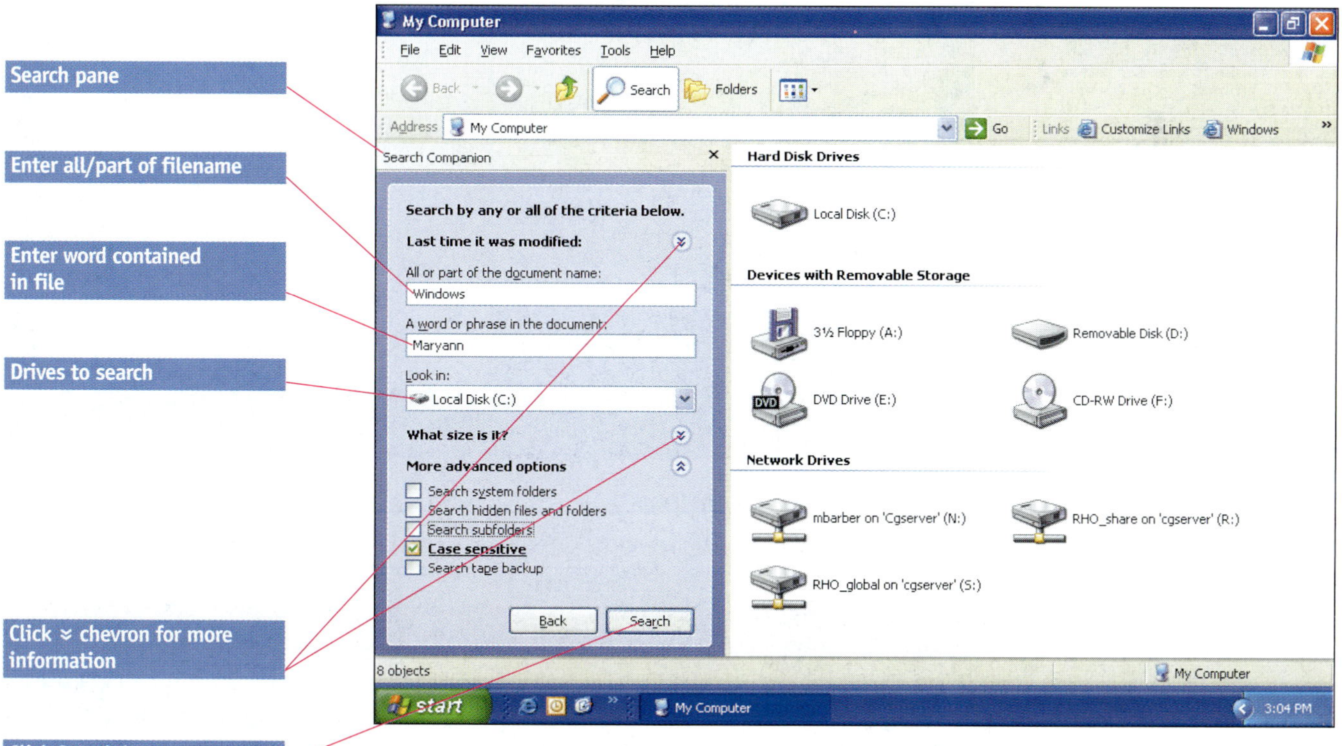

FIGURE 14 The Search Companion

hands-on exercise

4 Increasing Productivity

Objective To create and use shortcuts; to locate documents using the Search Companion; to customize your system using the Control Panel; to obtain a passport account. The exercise requires an Internet connection. Use Figure 15 as a guide.

Step 1: Display the Desktop Icons

- Log on to Windows XP. Point to a blank area on the desktop, click the **right mouse button** to display a context-sensitive menu, then click the **Properties command** to open the Display Properties dialog box in Figure 15a.
- Click the **Desktop tab** and then click the **Customize Desktop button** to display the Desktop Items dialog box.
- Check the boxes to display all four desktop icons. Click **OK** to accept these settings and close the dialog box, then click **OK** a second time to close the Display Properties dialog box.
- The desktop icons should appear on the left side of your desktop. Double click any icon to execute the indicated program or open the associated folder.

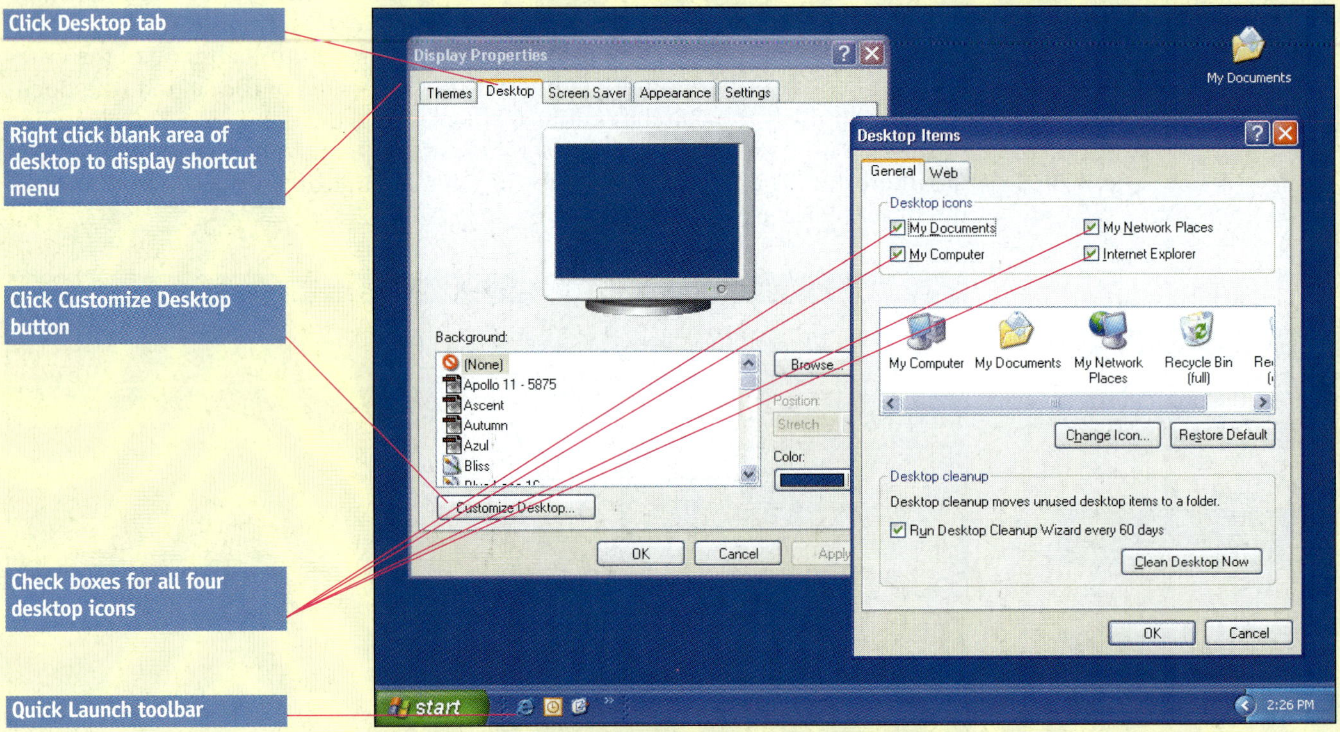

(a) Display the Desktop Icons (step 1)

FIGURE 15 Hands-on Exercise 4

THE QUICK LAUNCH TOOLBAR

The Quick Launch toolbar is a customizable toolbar that executes a program or displays the desktop with a single click. Right click a blank area of the taskbar, point to (or click) the Toolbars command, then check the Quick Launch toolbar to toggle its display on or off.

Step 2: Create a Web Shortcut

- Start Internet Explorer. You can double click the newly created icon at the left of the desktop, or you can single click its icon in the Quick Launch toolbar. Click the **Restore button** so that Internet Explorer is not maximized, that is, so that you can see a portion of the desktop.
- Click in the Address bar and enter the address **www.microsoft.com/windowsxp** to display the home page of Windows XP. Now that you see the page, you can create a shortcut to that page.
- Click the **Internet Explorer icon** in the Address bar to select the entire address, point to the Internet Explorer icon, then click and drag the icon to the desktop (you will see a jump arrow as you drag the text). Release the mouse to create the shortcut in Figure 15b.
- Prove to yourself that the shortcut works. Close Internet Explorer, and then double click the shortcut you created. Internet Explorer will open, and you should see the desired Web page. Close (or minimize) Internet Explorer since you do not need it for the remainder of the exercise.

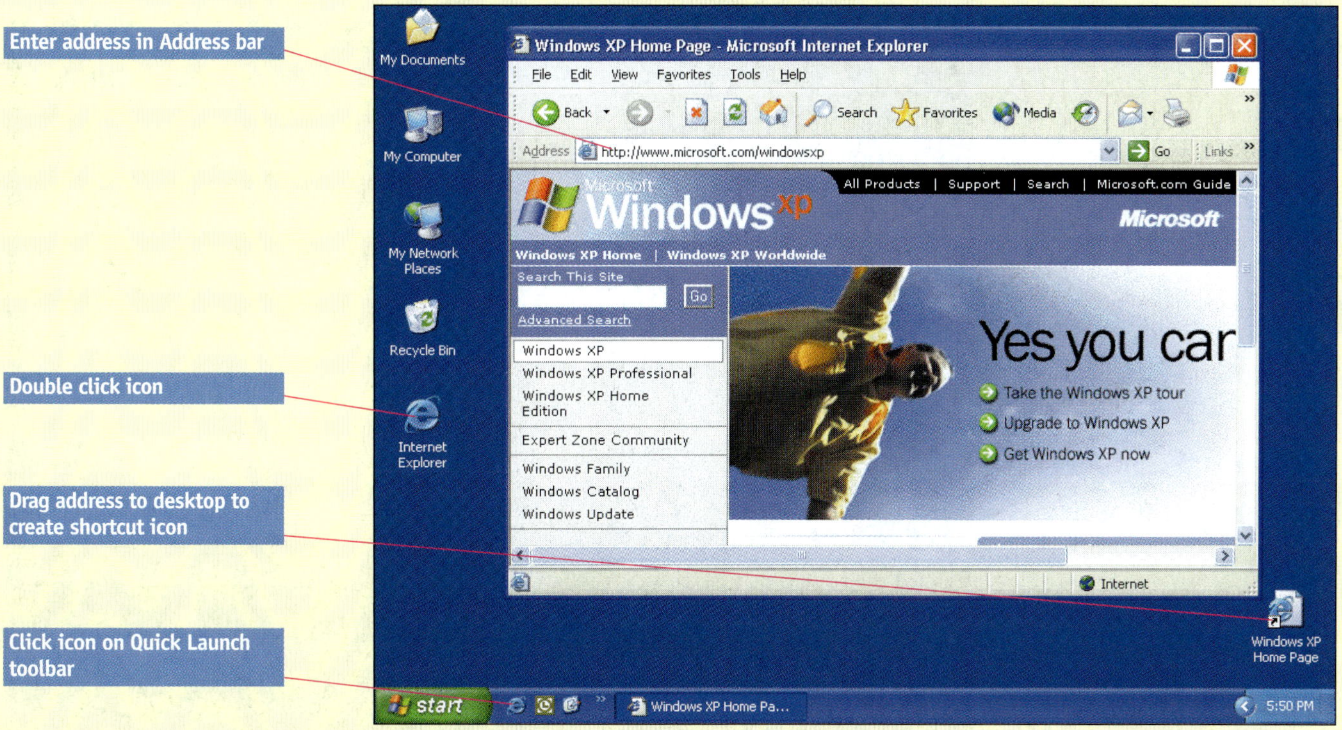

(b) Create a Web Shortcut (step 2)

FIGURE 15 Hands-on Exercise 4 (*continued*)

WORKING WITH SHORTCUTS

You can work with a shortcut icon just as you can with any other icon. To move a shortcut, drag its icon to a different location on the desktop. To rename a shortcut, right click its icon, click the Rename command, type the new name, then press the enter key. To delete a shortcut, right click its icon, click the Delete command, and click Yes in response to the confirming prompt. Deleting a shortcut deletes just the shortcut and not the object to which the shortcut refers.

Step 3: Create Additional Shortcuts

- Double click the **My Computer icon** to open this folder. Place the floppy disk from hands-on exercise 3 into the floppy drive. Double click the icon for **drive A** to display the contents of the floppy disk as shown in Figure 15c.
- The contents of the Address bar have changed to A:\ to indicate the contents of the floppy disk. You should see two folders and two files.
- Move and size the window so that you see a portion of the desktop. Right click and drag the icon for the **Windows Information folder** to the desktop, then release the mouse. Click the **Create Shortcuts Here command** to create the shortcut.
- Look for the jump arrow to be sure you have created a shortcut (as opposed to moving or copying the folder). If you made a mistake, right click a blank area of the desktop, then click the **Undo command** to reverse the unintended move or copy operation.
- Right click and drag the icon for the **PowerPoint presentation** to the desktop, release the mouse, and then click the **Create Shortcuts Here command.**

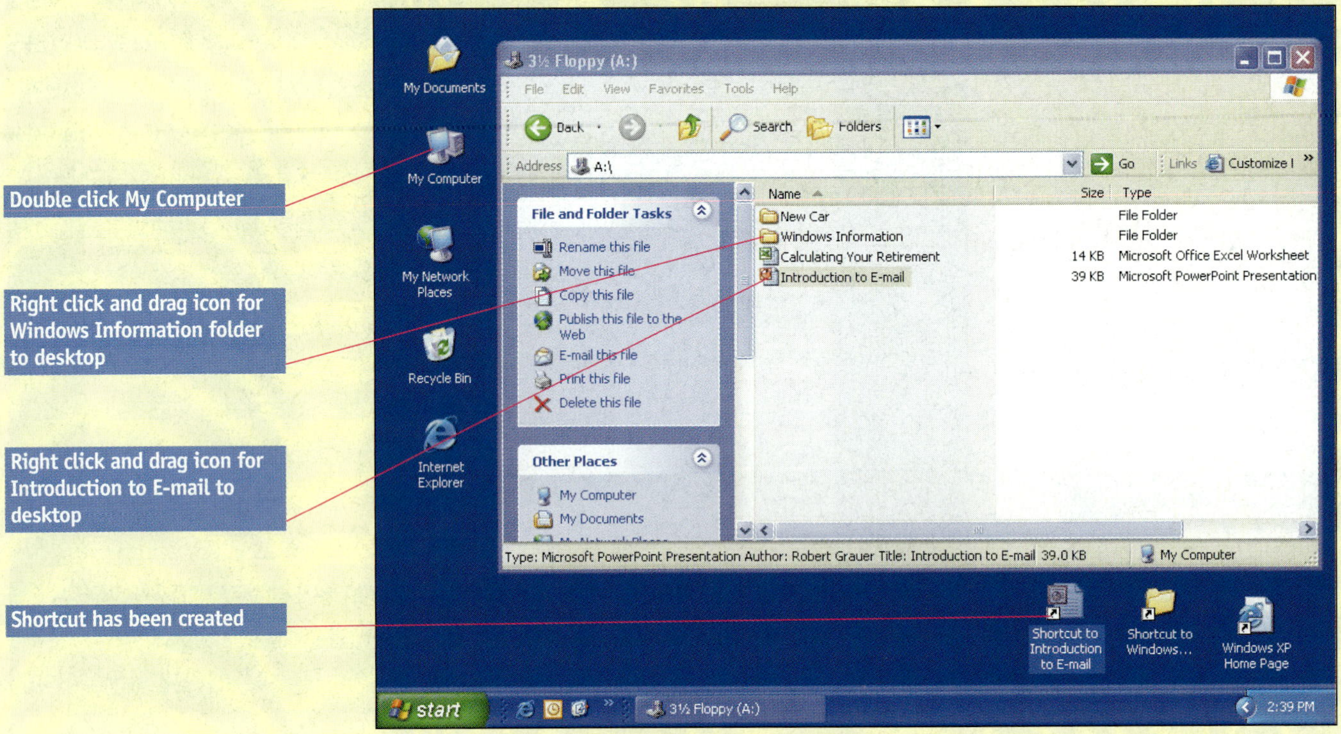

(c) Create Additional Shortcuts (step 3)

FIGURE 15 Hands-on Exercise 4 (*continued*)

THE ARRANGE ICONS COMMAND

The most basic way to arrange the icons on your desktop is to click and drag an icon from one place to another. It may be convenient, however, to have Windows arrange the icons for you. Right click a blank area of the desktop, click (or point to) the Arrange Icons by command, then click Auto Arrange. All existing shortcuts, as well as any new shortcuts, will be automatically aligned along the left edge of the desktop. Execute the Auto Arrange command a second time to cancel the command, and enable yourself to manually arrange the icons.

Step 4: Search for a Document

- Maximize the My Computer window. Click the **Search button** on the Standard Buttons toolbar to display the Search pane. The button functions as a toggle switch. Click the button and the Search pane appears. Click the button a second time and the task pane replaces the Search Companion.
- The initial screen (not shown in Figure 15d) in the Search Companion asks what you are searching for. Click **Documents (word processing, spreadsheet, etc.)**.
- You may be prompted to enter when the document was last modified. Click the option button that says **Don't Remember**, then click **Use advanced search options**. You should see the screen in Figure 15d.
- Enter the indicated search criteria. You do not know the document name and thus you leave this text box blank. The other criteria indicate that you are looking for any document that contains "interest rate" that is located on drive A, or in any subfolder on drive A.
- Click the **Search button** to initiate the search. You will see a Search dialog box to indicate the progress of the search, after which you will see the relevant documents.

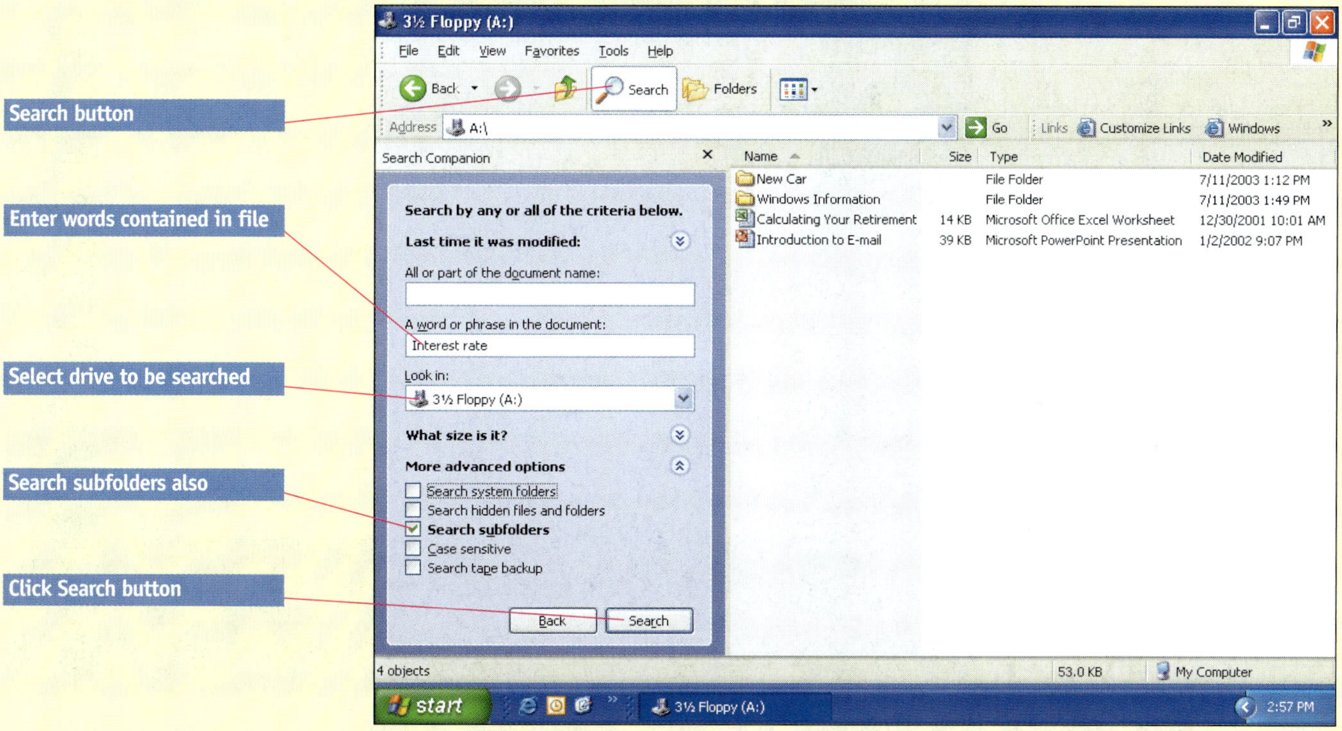

(d) Search for a Document (step 4)

FIGURE 15 Hands-on Exercise 4 (*continued*)

YOU DON'T NEED THE COMPLETE FILENAME

You can enter only a portion of the filename, and the Search Companion will still find the file(s). If, for example, you're searching for the file "Marketing Homework," you can enter the first several letters such as "Marketing" and Windows will return all files whose name begins with the letters you've entered—for example, "Marketing Homework" and "Marketing Term Paper."

Step 5: Search Results

- The search should return two files that satisfy the search criteria as shown in Figure 15e. Click the **Views button** and select **Tiles view** if you want to match our figure. If you do not see the same files, it is for one of two reasons:
  - You did not specify the correct search criteria. Click the **Back button** and reenter the search parameters as described in step 4. Repeat the search.
  - Your floppy disk is different from ours. Be sure to use the floppy disk as it existed at the end of the previous hands-on exercise.
- Click the **Restore button** so that you again see a portion of the desktop. Right click and drag the **Calculating Your Retirement** workbook to the desktop to create a shortcut on the desktop.
- Close the Search Results window, close the My Documents window, then double click the newly created shortcut to open the workbook.
- Retirement is a long way off, but you may want to experiment with our worksheet. It is never too early to start saving.
- Exit Excel when you are finished.

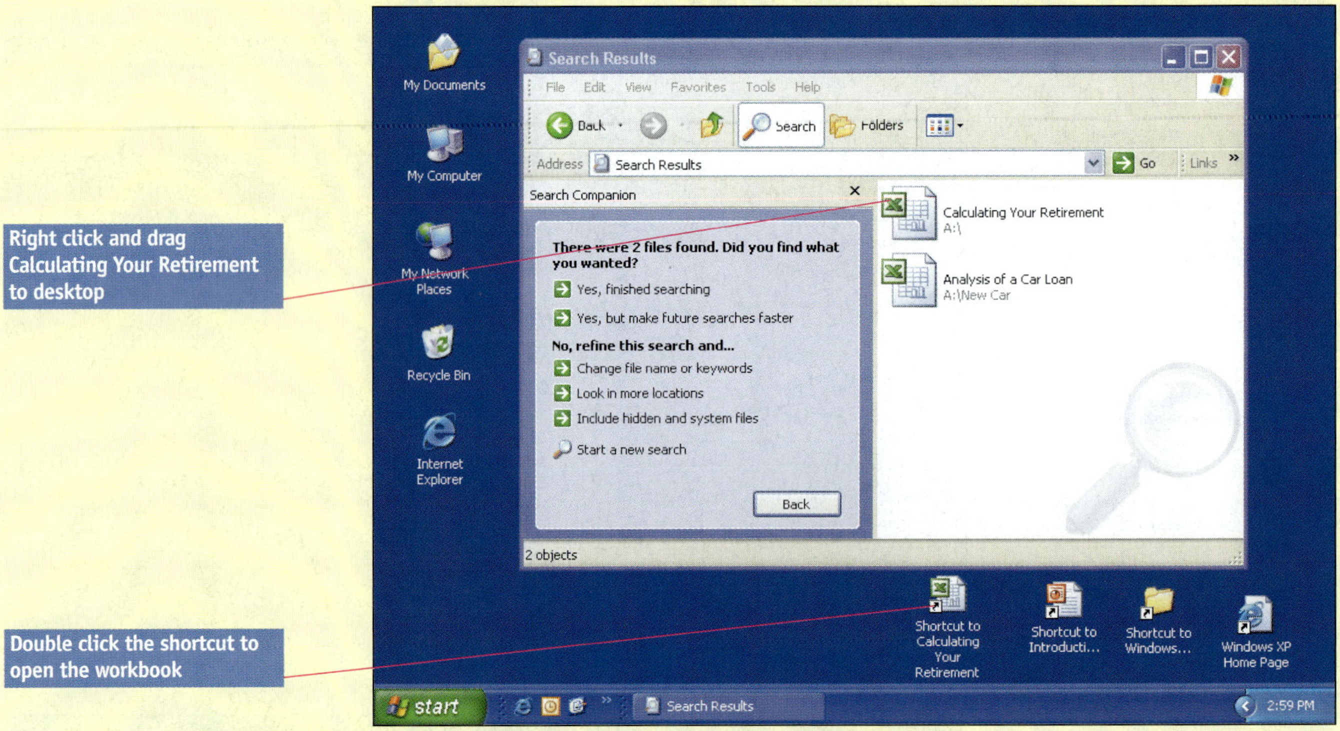

(e) Search Results (step 5)

FIGURE 15 Hands-on Exercise 4 (*continued*)

SHORTCUT WIZARD

Shortcuts can be created in many ways, including the use of a wizard. Right click a blank area of the desktop, click (or point) to the New command, then choose Shortcut to start the wizard. Enter the Web address in the indicated text box (or click the Browse button to locate a local file). Click Next, then enter the name for the shortcut as it is to appear on the desktop. Click the Finish button to exit the wizard. The new shortcut should appear on the desktop.

Step 6: Open the Control Panel Folder

- Click the **Start button**, then click **Control Panel** to open the Control Panel folder. Click the command to **Switch to Classic View** that appears in the task pane to display the individual icons as shown in Figure 15f. Maximize the window.
- Double click the **Taskbar and Start Menu icon** to display the associated dialog box. Click the **Taskbar tab**, then check the box to **Auto-hide the taskbar.** Your other settings should match those in Figure 15f. Click **OK** to accept the settings and close the dialog box.
- The taskbar (temporarily) disappears from your desktop. Now point to the bottom edge of the desktop, and the taskbar reappears. The advantage of hiding the taskbar in this way is that you have the maximum amount of room in which to work; that is, you see the taskbar only when you want to.
- Double click the **Fonts folder** to open this folder and display the fonts that are installed on your computer. Change to the **Details view**.
- Double click the icon of any font other than the standard fonts (Arial, Times New Roman, and Courier New) to open a new window that displays the font. Click the **Print button**. Close the Font window.

Click Taskbar tab

Check Auto-hide the taskbar

Double click Taskbar and Start Menu

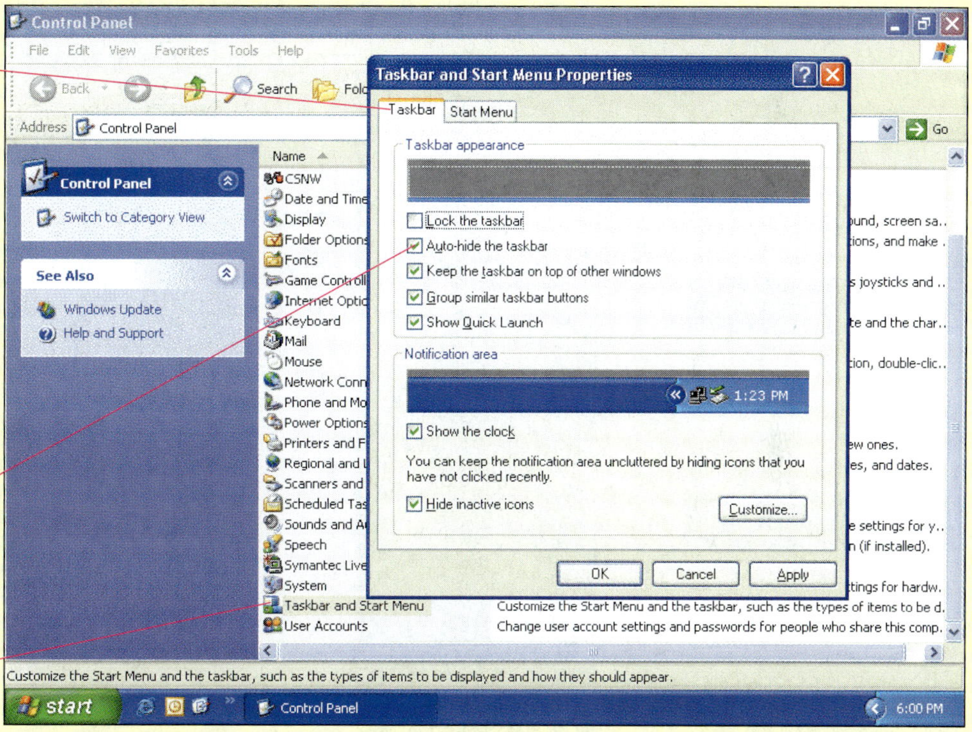

(f) Open the Control Panel Folder (step 6)

FIGURE 15 Hands-on Exercise 4 (*continued*)

MODIFY THE START MENU

Click and drag a shortcut icon to the Start button to place the shortcut on the Start menu. It does not appear that anything has happened, but the shortcut will appear at the top of the Start menu. Click the Start button to display the Start menu, then press the Esc key to exit the menu without executing a command. You can delete any item from the menu by right clicking the item and clicking the Unpin from the Start menu command.

Step 7: Obtain a .NET Passport

- Click the **Back button** to return to the Control Panel, then double click the **User Accounts icon** in the Control Panel folder. Maximize the User Accounts window so that it takes the entire desktop.
- Click the icon corresponding to the account that is currently logged to display a screen similar to Figure 15g. Click the command to **Set up my account to use a .NET passport**. You will see the first step in the Passport Wizard.
- Click the link to **View the privacy statement**. This starts Internet Explorer and goes to the .NET Passport site on the Web. Print the privacy agreement. It runs nine pages, but it contains a lot of useful information.
- Close Internet Explorer after you have printed the agreement. You are back in the Passport Wizard. Click **Next** to continue.
- Follow the instructions on the next several screens. You will be asked to enter your e-mail address and to supply a password. Click **Finish** when you have reached the last screen.
- You will receive an e-mail message after you have registered successfully. You will need your passport in our next exercise when we explore Windows Messenger and the associated instant messaging service.

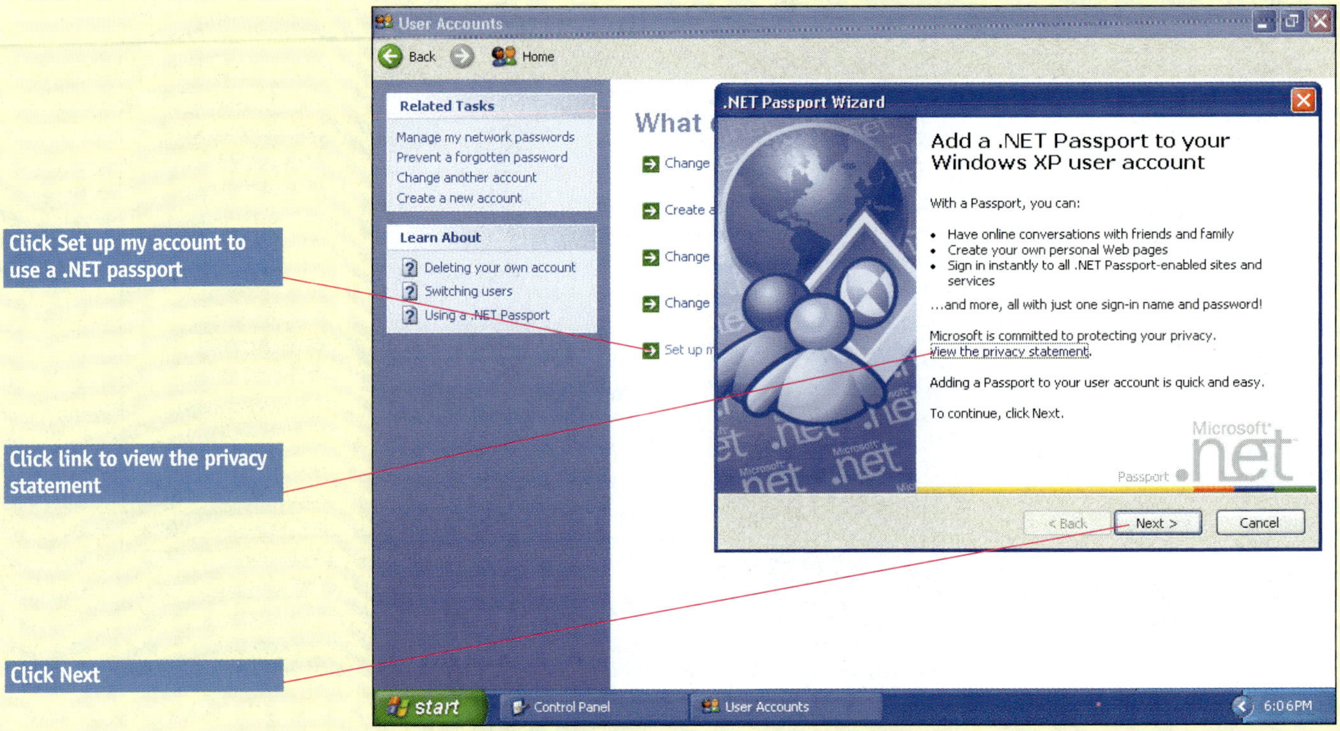

(g) Obtain a .NET Passport (step 7)

FIGURE 15 Hands-on Exercise 4 (*continued*)

UPDATING YOUR PASSPORT

You can modify the information in your passport profile at any time. Open the Control Panel, click User Accounts, select your account, then click the command to Change Your .NET passport. You can change your password, change the question that will remind you about your password should you forget it, and/or change the information that you authorize the passport service to share with others.

Step 8: Windows Update

- Close the User Accounts window to return to the Control Panel folder. Click the link to **Windows Update** to display a screen similar to Figure 15h.
- Click the command to **Scan for updates**. (This command is not visible in our figure.) This command will take several seconds as Windows determines which (if any) updates it recommends. Our system indicates that there are no critical updates but that additional updates are available.
- Click the link(s) to review the available updates. You do not have to install the vast majority of available updates. It is essential, however, that you install any updates deemed critical. One critical update appeared shortly after the release of Windows XP and closed a hole in the operating system that enabled hackers to break into some XP machines.
- Click the link to **View installation history** to see which updates were previously installed. Print this page for your instructor.
- Close the Update window. Log off the computer if you do not want to continue with the next exercise at this time.

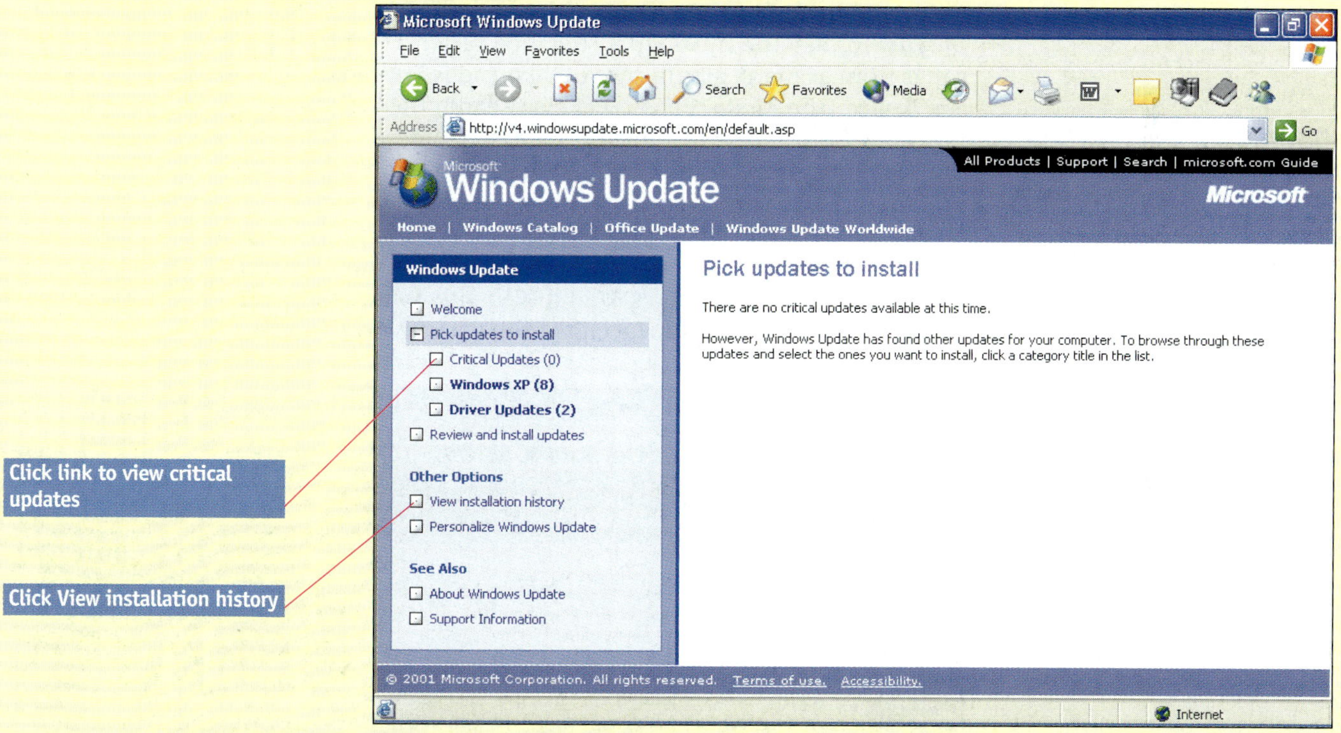

(h) Windows Update (step 8)

FIGURE 15 Hands-on Exercise 4 (*continued*)

THE SHOW DESKTOP BUTTON

The Show Desktop button or command minimizes every open window and returns you immediately to the desktop. You can get to this command in different ways, most easily by clicking the Show Desktop icon on the Quick Launch toolbar. The button functions as a toggle switch. Click it once and all windows are minimized. Click it a second time and the open windows are restored to their position on the desktop.

FUN WITH WINDOWS XP

The "XP" in Windows XP is for the experience that Microsoft promises individuals who adopt its operating system. Windows XP makes it easy to enjoy music and video, work with ***digital photographs***, and chat with your friends. This section describes these capabilities and then moves to a hands-on exercise in which you practice at the computer. All of the features are available on your own machine, but some may be disabled in a laboratory setting. It's not that your professor does not want you to have fun, but listening to music or engaging in instant messaging with your friends is not practical in a school environment. Nevertheless, the hands-on exercise that follows enables you to practice your skills in disk and file management as you work with multiple files and folders.

Windows Media Player

The ***Windows Media Player*** combines the functions of a radio, a CD, or DVD player, and an information database into a single program. It lets you listen to radio stations anywhere in the world, play a CD, or watch a DVD movie (provided you have the necessary hardware). You can copy selections from a CD to your computer, organize your music by artist and album, and then create a customized ***playlist*** to play the music in a specified order. The playlist may include as many songs from as many albums as you like and is limited only by the size of your storage device. The Media Player will also search the Web for audio or video files and play clips from a favorite movie.

The buttons at the left of the Media Player enable you to switch from one function to the next. The Radio Tuner button is active in Figure 16, and the BBC station is selected. Think of that—you are able to listen to radio stations from around the world with the click of a button. The Media Guide button connects you to the home page of the Windows Media Web site, where you can search the Web for media files and/or play movie clips from your favorite movies.

FIGURE 16 Windows Media Player

Digital Photography

Windows XP helps you to organize your pictures and share them with others. The best place to store photographs is in the My Pictures folder or in a subfolder within this folder as shown in Figure 17. The complete path to the folder appears in the Address bar and is best read from right to left. Thus, you are looking at pictures in the Romance Folder, which is in the My Pictures folder, which in turn is stored in a My Documents folder. Remember that each user has his or her unique My Documents folder, so the path must be further qualified. Hence, you are looking at the My Documents folder, within a folder for Jessica (one of several users), within the Documents and Settings folder on drive C. The latter folder maintains the settings for all of the users that are registered on this system.

The pictures in Figure 17 are shown in the ***Thumbnails view***, which displays a miniature image of each picture in the right pane. (Other views are also available and are accessed from the View menu or Views button.) The Picture Tasks area in the upper right lists the functions that are unique to photographs. You can view the pictures as a slide show, which is the equivalent of a PowerPoint presentation without having to create the presentation. You can print any picture, use it as the background on your desktop, or copy multiple pictures to a CD, provided you have the necessary hardware. You can also order prints online. You choose the company; select print sizes and quantities, supply the billing and shipping information, and your photographs are sent to you.

One photo is selected (BenWendy) in Figure 17, and the associated details are shown in the Details area of the task pane. The picture is stored as a JPG file, a common format for photographs. It was created on January 21, 2002.

The File and Folder Tasks area is collapsed in our figure, but you can expand the area to gain access to the normal file operations (move, copy, and delete). You can also e-mail the photograph from this panel. Remember, too, that you can click the Folders button on the Standard Buttons toolbar to switch to the hierarchical view of your system, which is better suited to disk and file management.

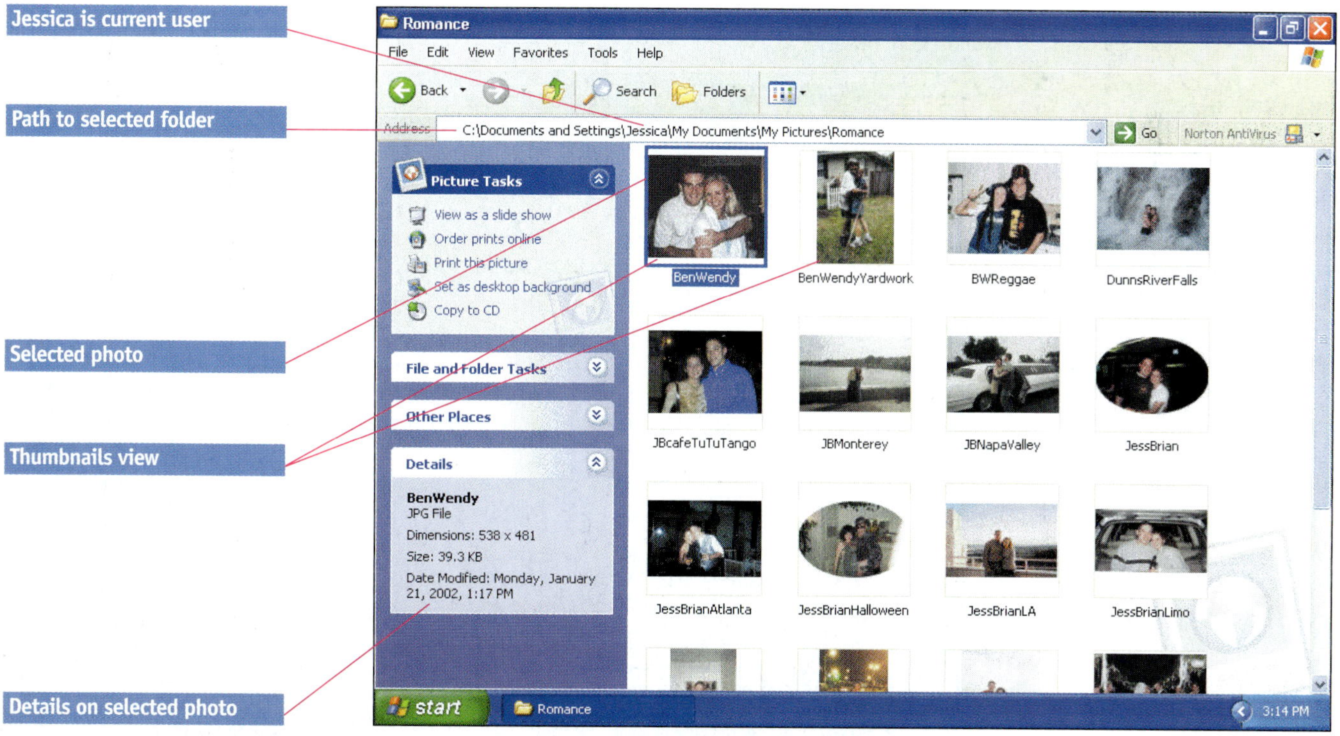

FIGURE 17 Working with Pictures

Windows Messenger

Windows Messenger is an instant messaging system in which you chat with friends and colleagues over the Internet. (It is based on the same technology as the "buddies list" that was made popular by America Online.) You need an Internet connection, a list of contacts, and a ***Microsoft passport*** that is based on your e-mail address. The passport is a free Microsoft service that enables you to access any passport-enabled Internet site with a single user name and associated password. (Step 7 in the previous hands-on exercise described how to obtain a passport.)

You can initiate a conversation at any time by monitoring the contacts list to see who is online and starting a chat session. Up to four people can participate in the same conversation. It is easy, fun, and addictive. You know the instant someone signs on, and you can begin chatting immediately. The bad news, however, is that it is all too easy to chat incessantly when you have real work to do. Hence you may want to change your status to indicate that you are busy and unable to participate in a conversation.

Figure 18 displays a conversation between Maryann and Bob. The session began when Maryann viewed her contact list, noticed that Bob was online, and started a conversation. Each person enters his or her message at the bottom of the conversation window, and then clicks the Send button. Additional messages can be sent without waiting for a response. Emoticons can be added to any message for effect. Note, too, the references to the file transfer that appear within the conversation, which are the result of Maryann clicking the command to send a file or photo, then attaching the desired file.

Windows Messenger is more than just a vehicle for chatting. If you have speakers and a microphone, you can place phone calls from your computer without paying a long distance charge. The most intriguing feature, however, is the ability to ask for remote assistance, whereby you can invite one of your contacts to view your desktop as you are working in order to ask for help. It is as if your friend were in the room looking over your shoulder. He or she will see everything that you do and can respond immediately with suggestions.

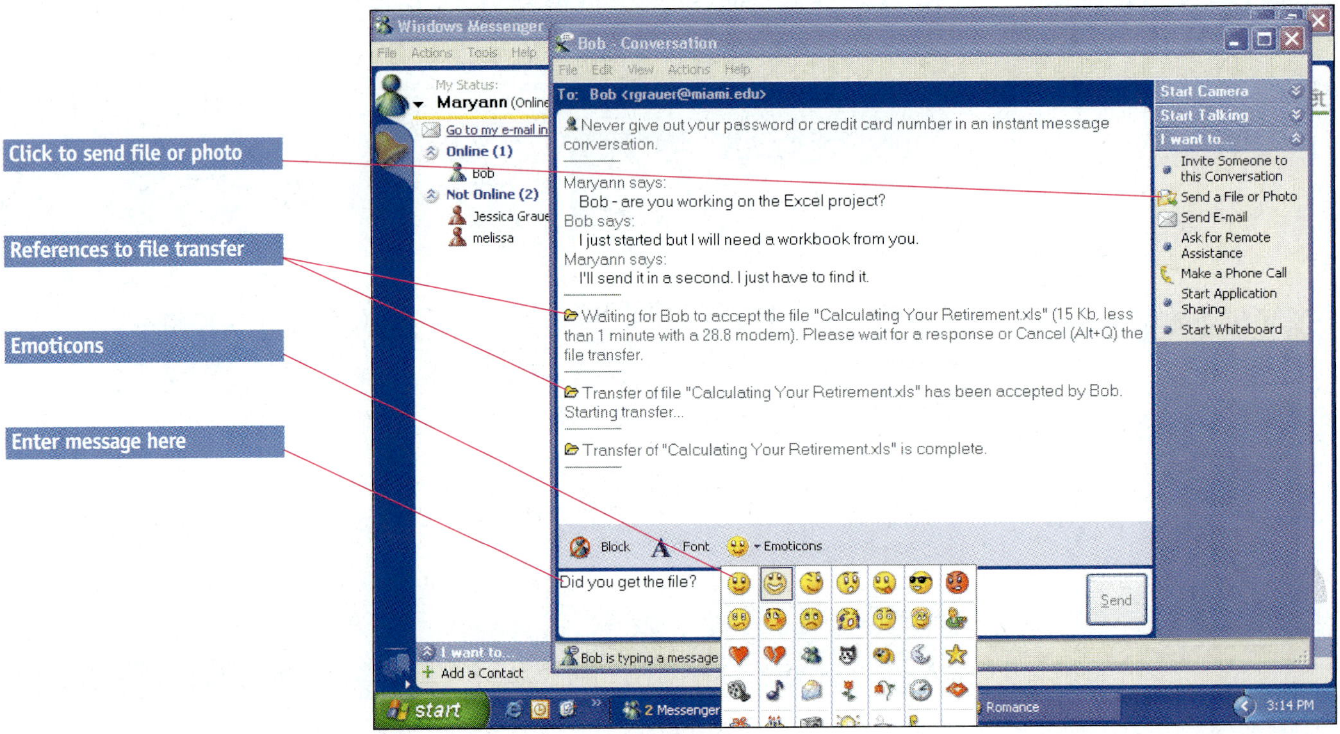

FIGURE 18 Windows Messenger

hands-on exercise

5 Fun with Windows XP

Objective To use Windows Media Player, work with photographs, and experiment with Windows Messenger. Check with your professor regarding the availability of the resources required for this exercise. Use Figure 19.

Step 1: Open the Shared Music Folder

- Start Windows Explorer. Click the **Folders button** to display the tree structure. You need to locate some music to demonstrate the Media Player.
- The typical XP installation includes some files within the Shared Documents folder. Expand the My Computer folder to show the **Shared Documents folder**, expand the **Shared Music folder**, and then open the **Sample Music folder** as shown in Figure 19a.
- Point to any file (it does not matter if you have a different selection of music) to display the ScreenTip describing the music. Double click the file to start the Media Player and play the selected music.

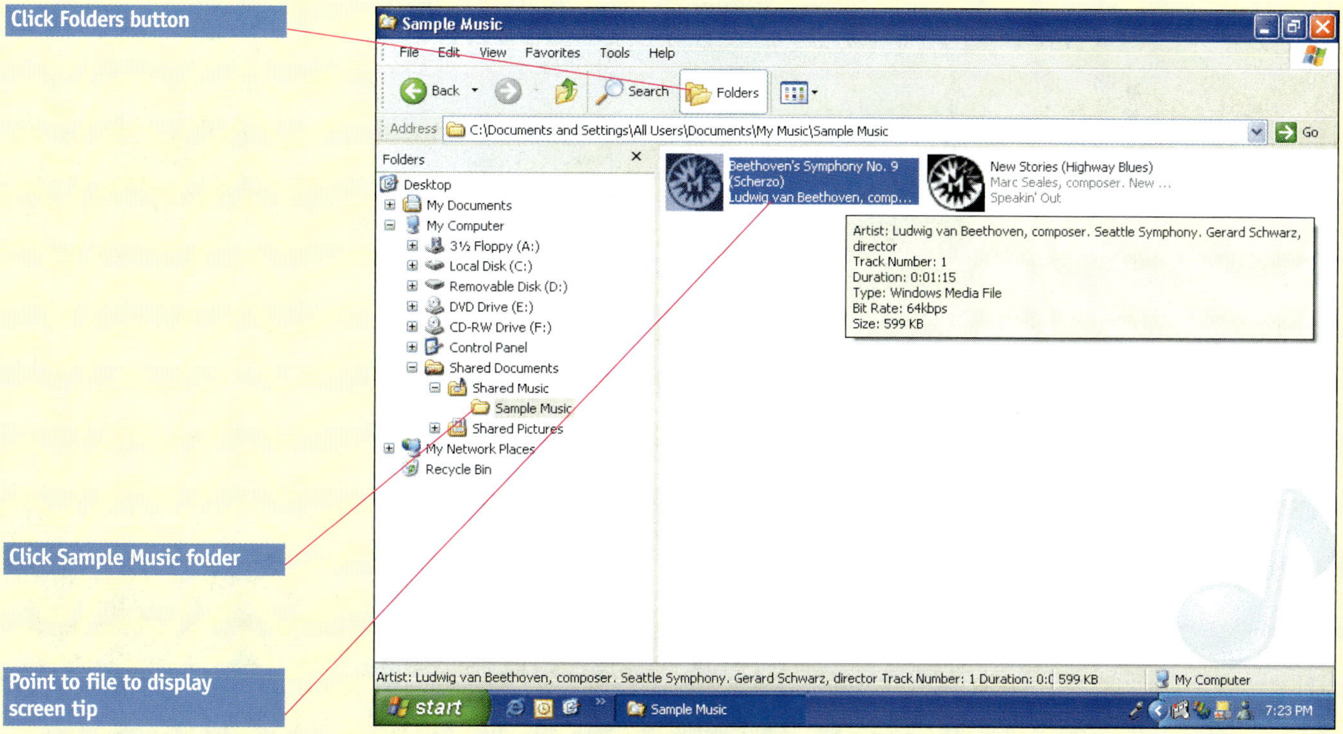

(a) Open the Shared Music Folder (step 1)

FIGURE 19 Hands-on Exercise 5

> **SHARED FOLDERS VERSUS PERSONAL FOLDERS**
>
> Windows XP automatically creates a unique My Documents folder for every user, which in turn contains a unique My Pictures folder and My Music folder within the My Documents folder. These folders are private and cannot be accessed by other users. Windows also provides a Shared Documents folder that is accessible to every user on a system.

Step 2: Listen to the Music

- You should hear the music when the Windows Media Player opens in its own window as shown in Figure 19b. The controls at the bottom of the window are similar to those on any CD player.
  - You can click the **Pause button**, then click the **Play button** to restart the music at that point.
  - You can click the **Stop button** to stop playing altogether.
  - You can also drag the slider to begin playing at a different place.
- You can also adjust the volume as shown in Figure 19b. Double click the **Volume Control icon** in the notification area at the right of the taskbar to display the Volume Control dialog box. Close this window.
- Click the **Radio Tuner button** at the side of the Media Player window. The system pauses as it tunes into the available radio stations.
- Select a radio station (e.g., **BBC World**) when you see the list of available stations, then click the **Play button** after you choose a station.
- You will see a message at the bottom of the window indicating that your computer is connecting to the media, after which you will hear the radio station.

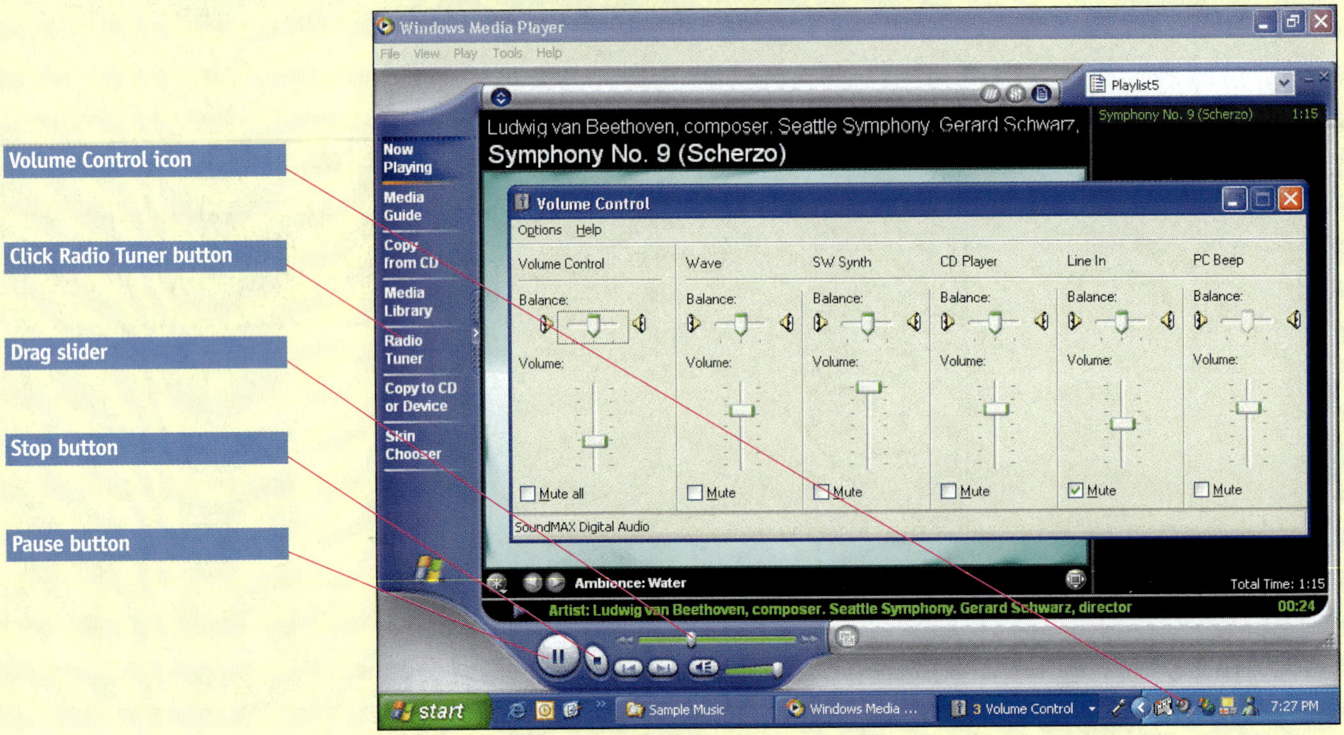

(b) Listen to the Music (step 2)

FIGURE 19 Hands-on Exercise 5 (*continued*)

OTHER MEDIA PLAYERS

If you double click a music (MP3) file, and a program other than Windows Media starts to play, it is because your system has another media player as its default program. You can still use the Windows Media Player, but you will have to start the program explicitly from the Start menu. Once the Media Player is open, pull down the File menu and click the Open command, then select the music file you want to play.

Step 3: Create a Playlist

- Click the **Media Library button** at the side of the Media player to display the media files that are currently on your computer.
  - The left pane displays a tree structure of your media library. Thus, you click the plus or minus sign to collapse or expand the indicated folder.
  - The right pane displays the contents of the selected object (the My Music playlist) in Figure 19c.
- Do not be concerned if your media library is different from ours. Click the **New playlist button**, enter **My Music** as the name of the new list, and click **OK**.
- Click the newly created playlist in the left pane to display its contents in the left pane. The playlist is currently empty.
- Start **Windows Explorer**. Open the **My Music Folder** within the My Documents folder. If necessary, click the **Restore button** to move and size Windows Explorer so that you can copy documents to the Media library.
- Click and drag one or more selections from the My Music folder to the right pane of the Media library to create the playlist. Close Windows Explorer.
- Click the **down arrow** in the list box at the upper right of the Media Gallery and select the My Music playlist to play the songs you have selected.

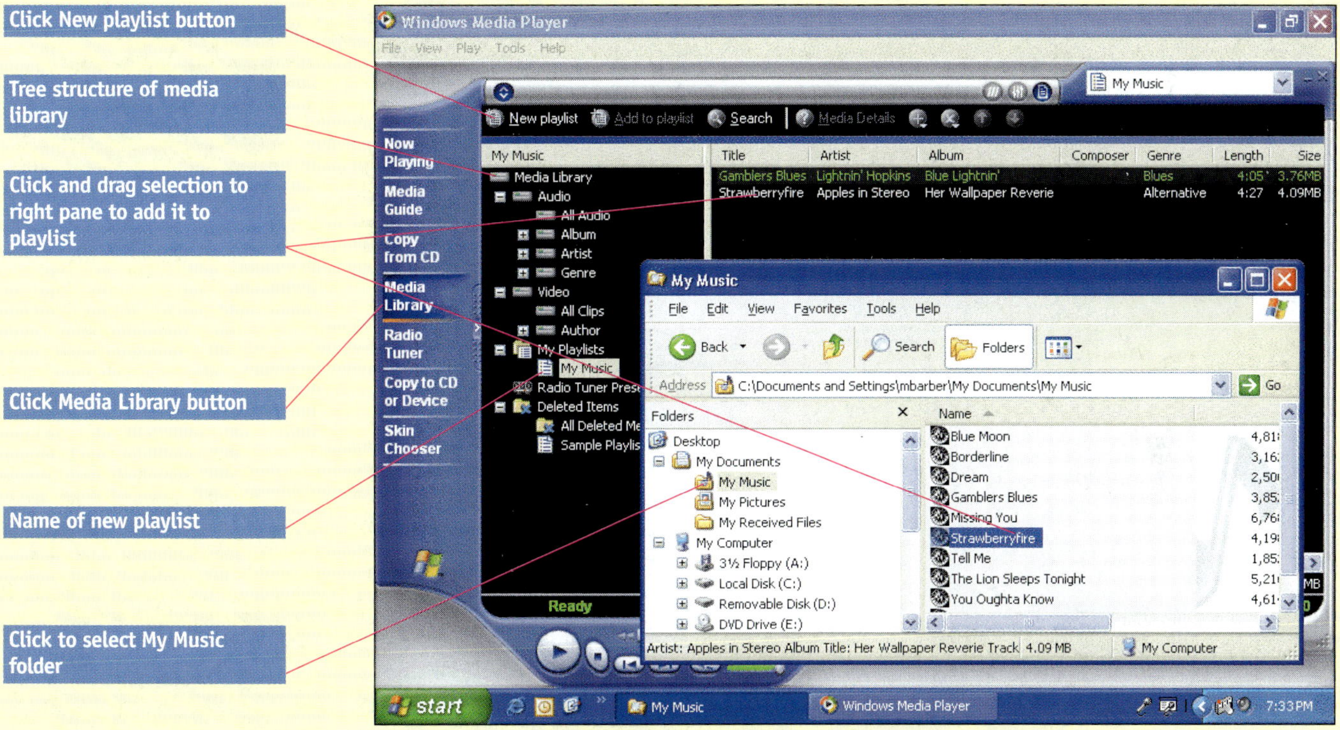

(c) Create a Playlist (step 3)

FIGURE 19 Hands-on Exercise 5 (*continued*)

THE MEDIA GUIDE

Click the Media Guide button at the left of the Media Player to display the home page of the Windows Media Site. You can also get there by starting Internet Explorer and entering windowsmedia.com in the Address bar. Either way, you will be connected to the Internet and can search the Web for media files and/or play clips from your favorite movie.

Step 4: Create a Pictures Folder

- You can use your own pictures, or if you don't have any, you can use the sample pictures provided with Windows XP. Start (or maximize) Windows Explorer. Open the **My Pictures folder** within the **My Documents folder**.
- Do not be concerned if the content of your folder is different from ours. Our folder already contains various subfolders with different types of pictures in each folder.
- Click the **Views button** and change to the **Thumbnails view**. This view is especially useful when viewing folders that contain photographs because (up to four) images are displayed on the folder icon.
- Right click anywhere in the right pane to display a context-sensitive menu as shown in Figure 19d. Click **New**, and then click **Folder** as the type of object to create.
- The icon for a new folder will appear with the name of the folder (New Folder) highlighted. Enter a more appropriate name (we chose **Romance** because our pictures are those of a happy couple), and press **Enter**.
- Copy your pictures from another folder, a CD, or floppy disk to the newly created folder.

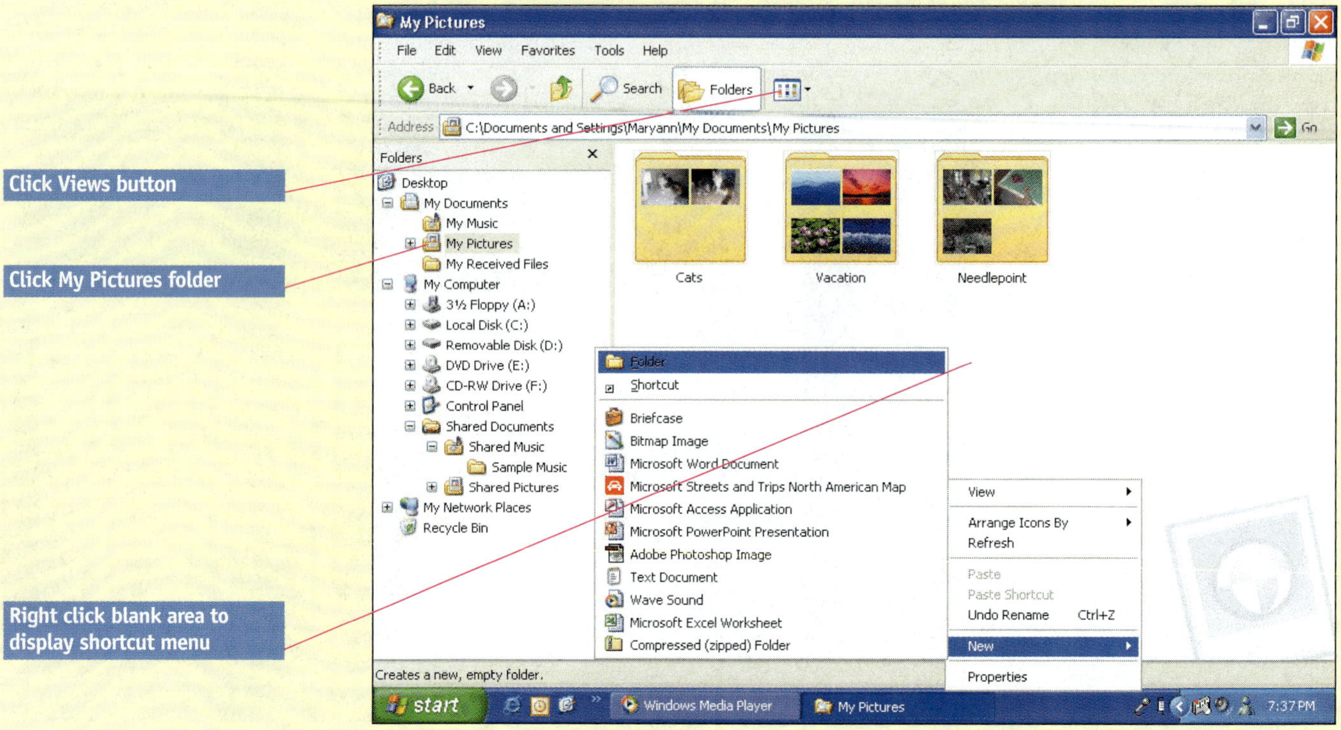

(d) Create a Pictures Folder (step 4)

FIGURE 19 Hands-on Exercise 5 *(continued)*

DESIGN GALLERY LIVE

The Microsoft Design Gallery is an excellent source of photographs and other media. Start Internet Explorer and go to the Design Gallery at dgl.microsoft.com. Enter the desired topic in the Search for text box, indicate that you want to search everywhere, and specify that the results should be photos. Download one or more of the photos that are returned by the search and use those pictures to complete this exercise.

Step 5: Display Your Pictures

- Double click the newly created folder to display its contents. Click the **Folders button** to display the Windows Explorer task pane, as opposed to the hierarchy structure. Click the **Views button** and change to the **Filmstrip view** as shown in Figure 19e.
- Click the **Next Image** or (**Previous Image**) **button** to move from one picture to the next within the folder. If necessary, click the buttons to rotate pictures clockwise or counterclockwise so that the pictures are displayed properly within the window.
- Click the command to **View as a slide show**, then display your pictures one at a time on your monitor. This is a very easy way to enjoy your photographs. Press the **Esc key** to stop.
- Choose any picture, then click the command to **Print this picture** that appears in the left pane. Submit this picture to your instructor.
- Choose a different picture and then click the command to **Set as desktop background**. Minimize Windows Explorer.

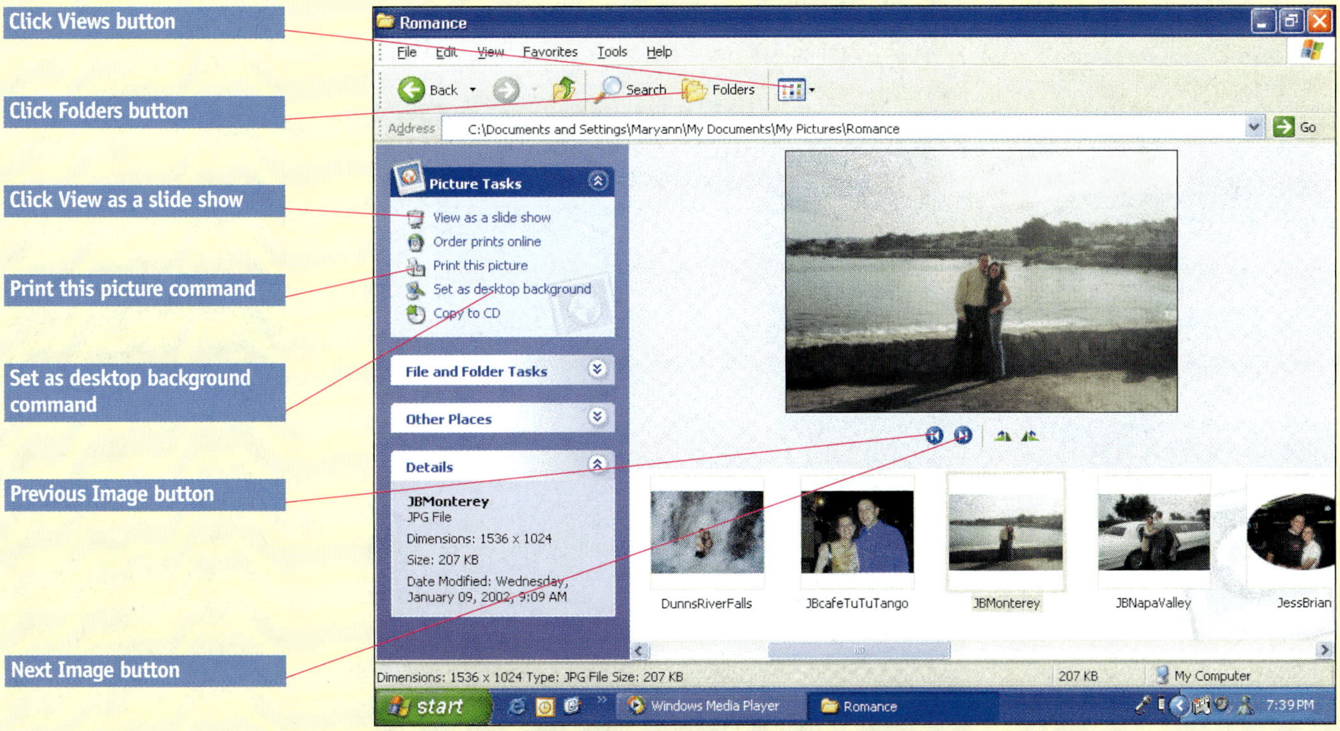

(e) Display Your Pictures (step 5)

FIGURE 19 Hands-on Exercise 5 (*continued*)

CHANGE THE VIEW

Click the down arrow next to the Views button on the Standard toolbar to change the way files are displayed within a folder. The Details view provides the most information and includes the filename, file type, file size, and the date that the file was created or last modified. (Additional attributes are also possible.) Other views are more visual. The Thumbnails view displays a miniature image of the file and is best used with clip art, photographs, or presentations. The Filmstrip view is used with photographs only.

Step 6: Customize the Desktop

- Your desktop should once again be visible, depending on which (if any) applications are open. If you do not see the desktop, right click a blank area of the taskbar, then click the **Show Desktop command**.
- You should see the picture you selected earlier as the background for your desktop. The picture is attractive (you chose it), but it may be distracting.
- To remove the picture, **right click** the background of the desktop and click the **Properties command** to display the Display Properties dialog box in Figure 19f.
- Click the **Desktop tab**, then click **None** in the Background list box. Click **OK** to accept this setting and close the dialog box. The picture disappears.
- Regardless of whether you keep the background, you can use your pictures as a screen saver. Redisplay the Display Properties dialog box. Click the **Screen Saver tab** in the Display Properties box, then choose **My Picture Slideshow** from the screen saver list box.
- Wait a few seconds and the picture within the dialog box will change, just as it will on your desktop. Click **OK** to accept the screen saver and close the Display Properties dialog box.

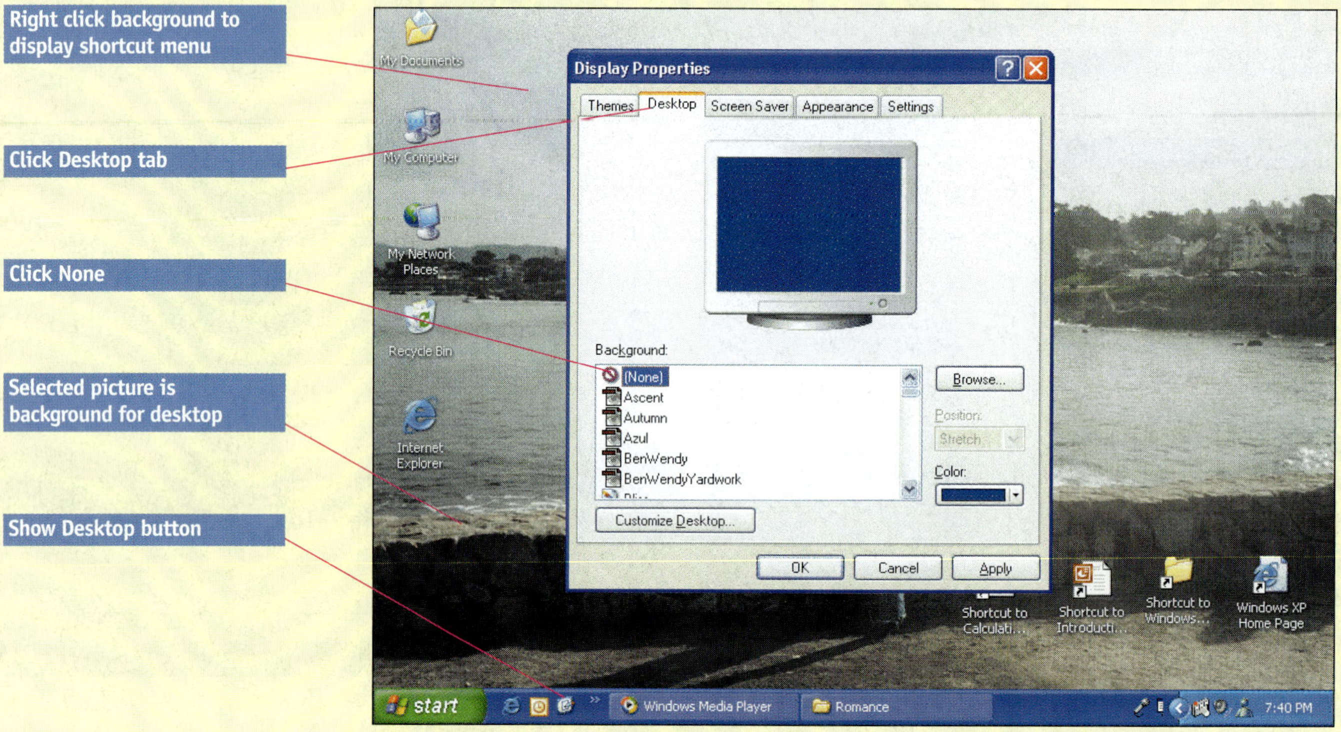

(f) Customize the Desktop (step 6)

FIGURE 19 Hands-on Exercise 5 (*continued*)

CHANGE THE RESOLUTION

The resolution of a monitor refers to the number of pixels (picture elements or dots) that are displayed at one time. The higher the resolution, the more pixels are displayed, and hence you see more of a document at one time. You can change the resolution at any time. Right click the desktop, click the Properties command to show the Display Properties dialog box, then click the Settings tab. Drag the slider bar to the new resolution, then click OK.

Step 7: Start Windows Messenger

- You need a passport to use Windows Messenger. Double click the **Windows Messenger icon** in the notification area of the taskbar to sign in.
- Maximize the Messenger window. You will see a list of your existing contacts with an indication of whether they are online.
- Add one or more contacts. Pull down the **Tools menu**, click the command to **Add a Contact**, then follow the onscreen instructions. (The contact does not have to have Windows XP to use instant messaging.)
- Double click any contact that is online to initiate a conversation and open a conversation window as shown in Figure 19g.
- Type a message at the bottom of the conversation window, then click the **Send button** to send the message. The text of your message will appear immediately on your contact's screen. Your friend's messages will appear on your screen.
- Continue the conversation by entering additional text. You can press the **Enter key** (instead of clicking the **Send button**) to send the message. You can also use **Shift + enter** to create a line break in your text.

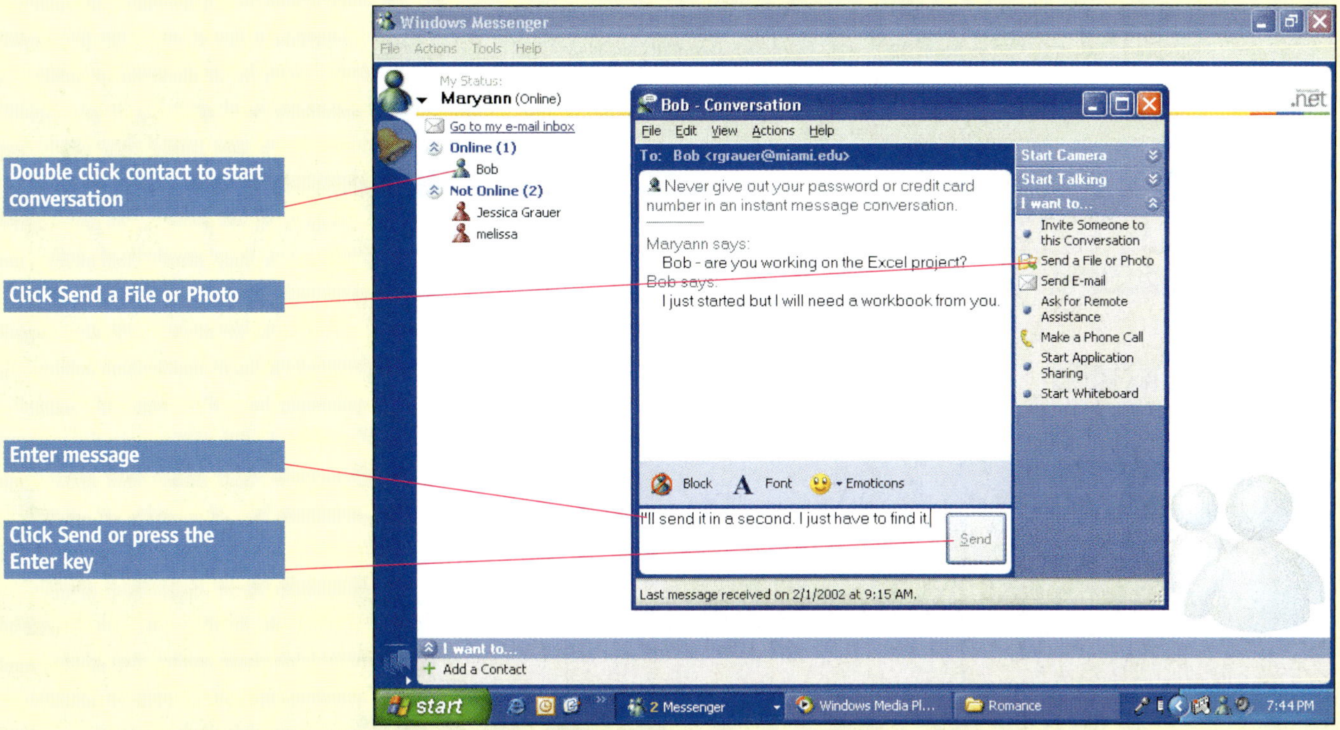

(g) Start Windows Messenger (step 7)

FIGURE 19 Hands-on Exercise 5 (*continued*)

CHANGE YOUR STATUS

Anyone on your contact list knows immediately when you log on; thus, the larger your contact list, the more likely you are to be engaged in idle chitchat when you have real work to do. You can avoid unwanted conversations without being rude by changing your status. Click the down arrow next to your name in the Messenger window and choose a different icon. You can appear offline or simply indicate that you are busy. Either way you will be more likely to get your work done.

Step 8: Attach a File

- Click the command to **Send a File or Photo**, which displays the Send a File dialog box in Figure 19h. It does not matter which file you choose, since the purpose of this step is to demonstrate the file transfer capability.
- A series of three file transfer messages will appear on your screen. Windows Messenger waits for your friend to accept the file transfer, then it indicates the transfer has begun, and finally, that the transfer was successful.
- Click the command to **Invite someone to this conversation** if you have another contact online. You will see a second dialog box in which you select the contact.
- There are now three people in the conversation. (Up to four people can participate in one conversation.) Your friends' responses will appear on your screen as soon as they are entered.
- Send your goodbye to end the conversation, then close the conversation window to end the chat session. You are still online and can participate in future conversations.
- Close Windows Messenger. You will be notified if anyone wants to contact you.

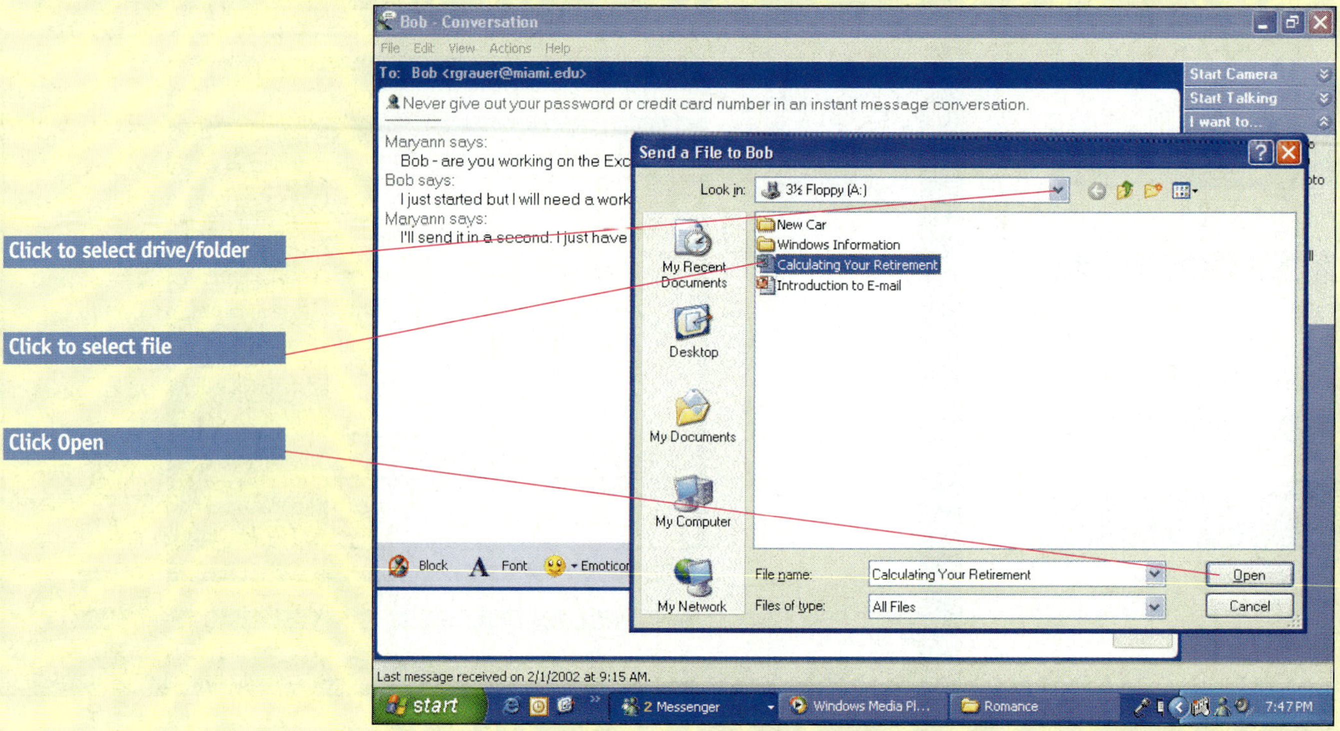

(h) Attach a File (step 8)

FIGURE 19 Hands-on Exercise 5 *(continued)*

E-MAIL VERSUS INSTANT MESSAGING

E-mail and instant messaging are both Internet communication services, but there are significant differences. E-mail does not require both participants to be online at the same time. E-mail messages are also permanent and do not disappear when you exit your e-mail program. Instant messaging, however, requires both participants to be online. Its conversations are not permanent and disappear when you end the session.

Step 9: Ask for Assistance

- Your contacts do not require Windows XP to converse with you using Windows Messenger. Windows XP is required, however, to use the remote assistance feature.
- Click the **Start button**, then click the **Help and Support command** to display the home page of the Help and Support Center. Click the **Support button**, then click the command to **Ask a friend to help**.
- A Remote Assistance screen will open in the right pane. Click the command to **Invite someone to help**, which will display your contact list as shown in Figure 19i. You can choose any contact who is online, or you can enter the e-mail address of someone else.
- You will see a dialog box indicating that an invitation has been sent. Once your friend accepts the invitation, he or she will be able to see your screen. A chat window will open up in which you can discuss the problem you are having. Close the session when you are finished.
- Pull down the **File menu** and click the command to **Sign out**. The Windows Messenger icon in the notification will indicate that you have signed out.

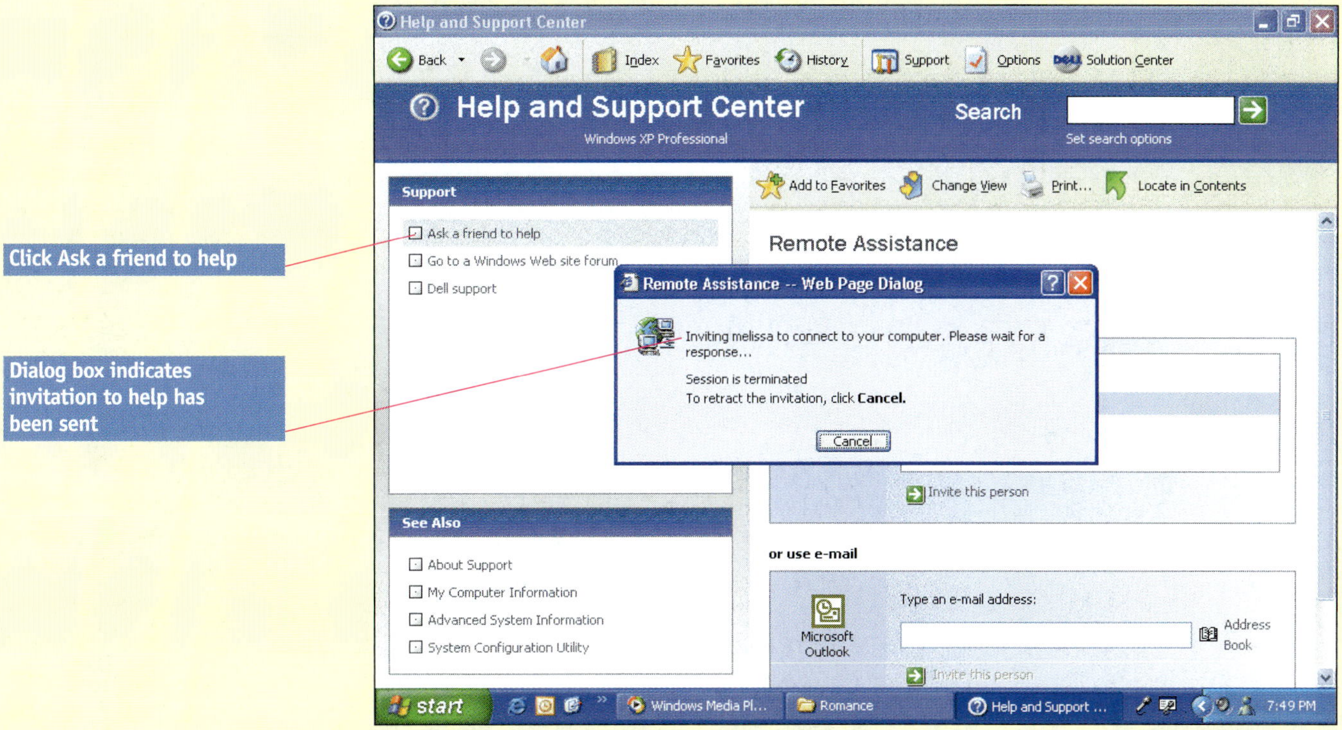

(i) Ask for Assistance (step 9)

FIGURE 19 Hands-on Exercise 5 (*continued*)

SUPPORT ONLINE

Microsoft provides extensive online support in a variety of formats. Start at the Windows XP home page (www.microsoft.com/windowsxp), then click the Support button to see what is available. You will be able to search the Microsoft Knowledge Base for detailed information on virtually any subject. You can also post questions and participate in threaded discussions in various newsgroups. Support is available for every Microsoft product.

SUMMARY

Windows XP is the newest and most powerful version of the Windows operating system. It has a slightly different look than earlier versions, but it maintains the conventions of its predecessors. All Windows operations take place on the desktop. Every window contains the same basic elements, which include a title bar, a Minimize button, a Maximize or Restore button, and a Close button. All windows may be moved and sized. The taskbar contains a button for each open program and enables you to switch back and forth between those programs by clicking the appropriate button. You can obtain information about every aspect of Windows through the Help and Support Center.

A file is a set of data or set of instructions that has been given a name and stored on disk. There are two basic types of files, program files and data files. A program file is an executable file, whereas a data file can be used only in conjunction with a specific program. Every file has a filename and a file type.

Files are stored in folders to better organize the hundreds (or thousands) of files on a disk. A folder may contain program files, data files, and/or other folders. Windows automatically creates a set of personal folders for every user. These include the My Documents folder and the My Pictures folder and My Music folder within the My Documents folder. Windows also provides a Shared Documents folder that can be accessed by every user. The My Computer folder is accessible by all users and displays the devices on a system.

Windows Explorer facilitates every aspect of disk and file management. It presents a hierarchical view of your system that displays all devices and, optionally, the folders on each device. Any device may be expanded or collapsed to display or hide its folders.

Windows XP contains several tools to help you enjoy your system. The Windows Media Player combines the functions of a radio, CD player, DVD player, and an information database into a single program. Windows Messenger is an instant messaging system in which you chat with friends and colleagues over the Internet.

The Control Panel affects every aspect of your system. It determines the appearance of your desktop and it controls the performance of your hardware. A shortcut is a link to any object on your computer, such as a program, file, folder, disk drive, or Web page. The Search Companion enables you to search for a file according to several different criteria.

KEY TERMS

MULTIPLE CHOICE

1. Which of the following is true regarding a dialog box?
   (a) Option buttons indicate mutually exclusive choices
   (b) Check boxes imply that multiple options may be selected
   (c) Both (a) and (b)
   (d) Neither (a) nor (b)

2. Which of the following is the first step in sizing a window?
   (a) Point to the title bar
   (b) Pull down the View menu to display the toolbar
   (c) Point to any corner or border
   (d) Pull down the View menu and change to large icons

3. Which of the following is the first step in moving a window?
   (a) Point to the title bar
   (b) Pull down the View menu to display the toolbar
   (c) Point to any corner or border
   (d) Pull down the View menu and change to large icons

4. Which button appears immediately after a window has been maximized?
   (a) The Close button
   (b) The Minimize button
   (c) The Maximize button
   (d) The Restore button

5. What happens to a window that has been minimized?
   (a) The window is still visible but it no longer has a Minimize button
   (b) The window shrinks to a button on the taskbar
   (c) The window is closed and the application is removed from memory
   (d) The window is still open but the application has been removed from memory

6. What is the significance of a faded (dimmed) command in a pull-down menu?
   (a) The command is not currently accessible
   (b) A dialog box appears if the command is selected
   (c) A Help window appears if the command is selected
   (d) There are no equivalent keystrokes for the particular command

7. The Recycle Bin enables you to restore a file that was deleted from
   (a) Drive A
   (b) Drive C
   (c) Both (a) and (b)
   (d) Neither (a) nor (b)

8. Which of the following was suggested as essential to a backup strategy?
   (a) Back up all program files at the end of every session
   (b) Store backup files at another location
   (c) Both (a) and (b)
   (d) Neither (a) nor (b)

9. A shortcut may be created for
   (a) An application or a document
   (b) A folder or a drive
   (c) Both (a) and (b)
   (d) Neither (a) nor (b)

10. What happens if you click the Folders button (on the Standard Buttons toolbar in the My Computer folder) twice in a row?
    (a) The left pane displays a task pane with commands for the selected object
    (b) The left pane displays a hierarchical view of the devices on your system
    (c) The left pane displays either a task pane or the hierarchical view depending on what was displayed prior to clicking the button initially
    (d) The left pane displays both the task pane and a hierarchical view

... continued

multiple choice

11. The Search Companion can

(a) Locate all files containing a specified phrase
(b) Restrict its search to a specified set of folders
(c) Both (a) and (b)
(d) Neither (a) nor (b)

12. Which views display miniature images of photographs within a folder?

(a) Tiles view and Icons view
(b) Thumbnails view and Filmstrip view
(c) Details view and List view
(d) All views display a miniature image

13. Which of the following statements is true?

(a) A plus sign next to a folder indicates that its contents are hidden
(b) A minus sign next to a folder indicates that its contents are hidden
(c) A plus sign appears next to any folder that has been expanded
(d) A minus sign appears next to any folder that has been collapsed

14. Ben and Jessica are both registered users on a Windows XP computer. Which of the following is a *false statement* regarding their personal folders?

(a) Ben and Jessica each have a My Documents folder
(b) Ben and Jessica each have a My Pictures folder that is stored within their respective My Documents folders
(c) Ben can access files in Jessica's My Documents folder
(d) Jessica cannot access files in Ben's My Documents folder

15. When is a file permanently deleted?

(a) When you delete the file from Windows Explorer
(b) When you empty the Recycle Bin
(c) When you turn the computer off
(d) All of the above

16. What happens if you (left) click and drag a file to another folder on the same drive?

(a) The file is copied
(b) The file is moved
(c) The file is deleted
(d) A shortcut menu is displayed

17. How do you shut down the computer?

(a) Click the Start button, then click the Turn Off Computer command
(b) Right click the Start button, then click the Turn Off Computer command
(c) Click the End button, then click the Turn Off Computer command
(d) Right click the End button, then click the Turn Off Computer command

18. Which of the following can be accomplished with Windows Messenger?

(a) You can chat with up to three other people in the conversation window
(b) You can place telephone calls (if you have a microphone and speaker) without paying long-distance charges
(c) You can ask for remote assistance, which enables your contact to view your screen as you are working
(d) All of the above

ANSWERS

1. c	**7.** b	**13.** a
2. c	**8.** b	**14.** c
3. a	**9.** c	**15.** b
4. d	**10.** c	**16.** b
5. b	**11.** c	**17.** a
6. a	**12.** b	**18.** d

PRACTICE WITH WINDOWS XP

1. **Two Different Views:** The document in Figure 20 is an effective way to show your instructor that you understand the My Computer folder, the various views available, the task pane, and the hierarchy structure. It also demonstrates that you can capture a screen for inclusion in a Word document. Proceed as follows:
   a. Open the My Computer folder, click the Views button, and switch to the Tiles view. Click the Folders button to display the task pane. Size the window as necessary so that you will be able to fit two folders onto a one-page document as shown in Figure 20.
   b. Press and hold the Alt key as you press the Print Screen key to copy the My Computer window to the Windows clipboard. (The Print Screen key captures the entire screen. Using the Alt key, however, copies just the current window.) Click the Start menu, click Programs, and then click Microsoft Word to start the program. Maximize the window.
   c. Enter the title of the document, press Enter, and type your name. Press the Enter key twice in a row to leave a blank line.
   d. Pull down the Edit menu. Click the Paste command to copy the contents of the clipboard to the document. Press the Enter key to add a figure caption, then press the Enter key two additional times.
   e. Click the taskbar to return to the My Computer folder. Change to the Details view. Click the Folders button to display the hierarchy structure, as opposed to the task pane. Expand My Computer in the left pane, but collapse all of the individual devices. Press Alt+Print Screen to capture the My Computer folder in this configuration.
   f. Click the taskbar to return to your Word document. Press Ctrl+V to paste the contents of the clipboard into your document. Enter an appropriate caption below the figure. Save the completed document and print it for your instructor.

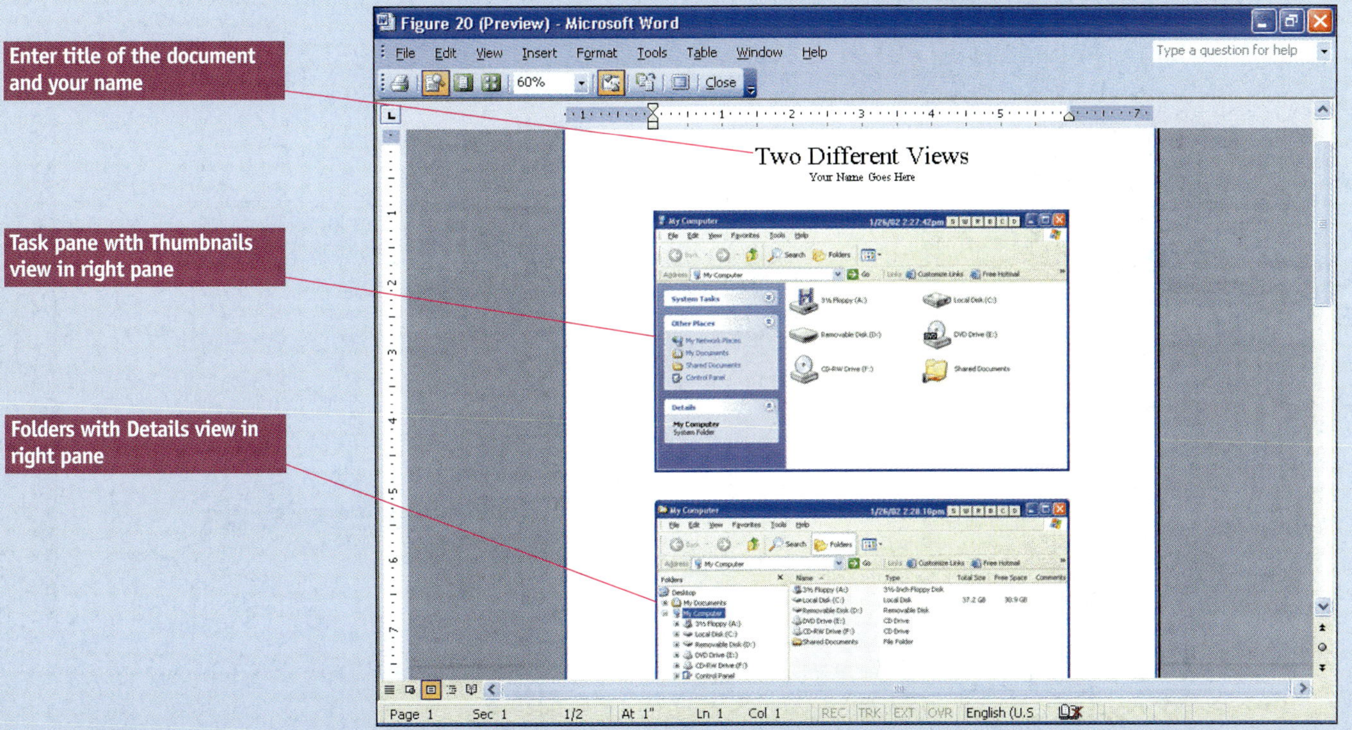

FIGURE 20 Two Different Views (exercise 1)

2. **Network Connections:** The document in Figure 21 displays the network connections on our system as well as the status of one of those connections. Your assignment is to create the equivalent document for your computer. Proceed as follows:
   a. Open the Control Panel, switch to the Classic view, then double click the Network Connections icon to display the Network Connections folder. (You can also get to this folder from My Computer, by clicking the link to My Network Places, and then clicking Network Connections from within the Network Tasks area.)
   b. Maximize the Network Connections folder so that it takes the entire desktop. Change to the Tiles view. Click the Folders button to display the task pane. Select (click) a connection, then click the link to View status of the connection, to display the associated dialog box.
   c. Press the Print Screen key to print this screen. Start Microsoft Word and open a new document. Press the Enter key several times, then click the Paste button to copy the contents of the clipboard into your document.
   d. Press Ctrl+Home to return to the beginning of the Word document, where you can enter the title of the document and your name. Compose a paragraph similar to the one in our figure that describes the network connections on your computer. Print this document for your instructor.
   e. Experiment with the first two network tasks that are displayed in the task pane. How difficult is it to set up a new connection? How do you set a firewall to protect your system from unauthorized access when connected to the Internet? How do you establish a home or small office network?
   f. Use the Help and Support Center to obtain additional information. Print one or two Help screens for your instructor.

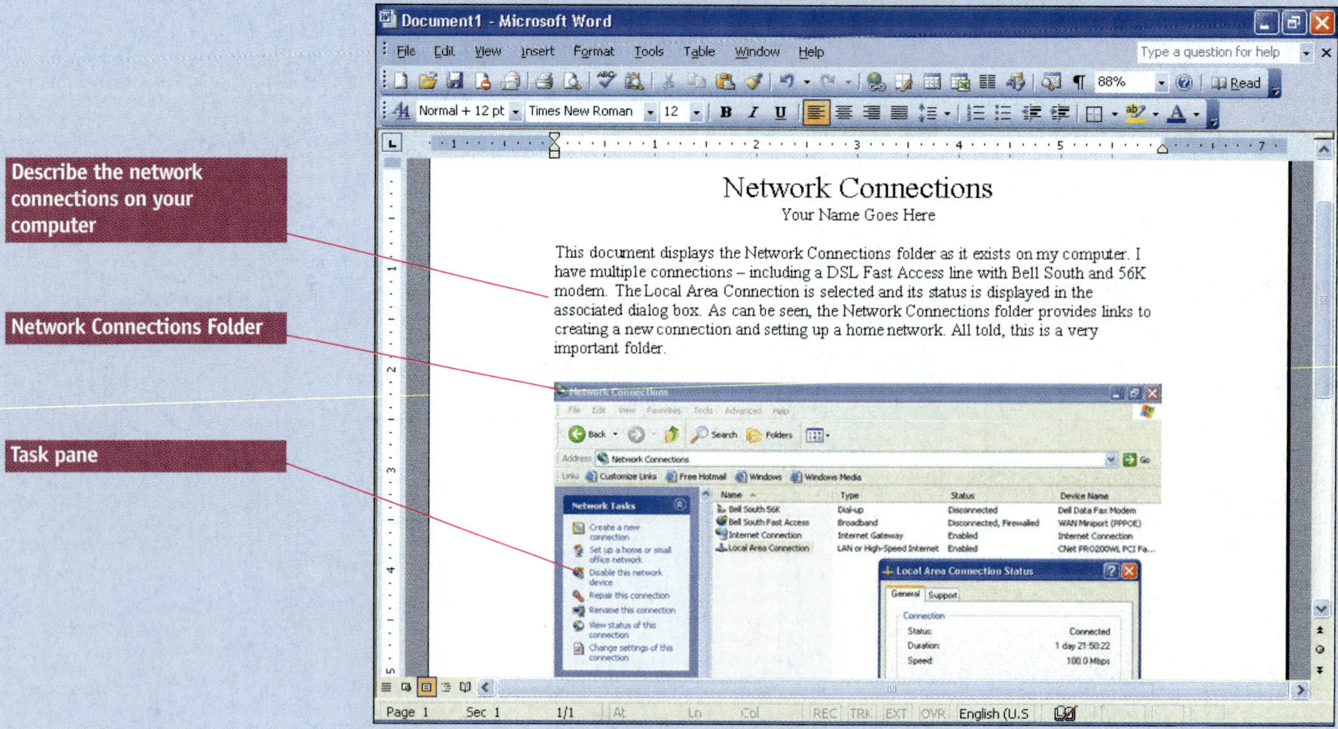

FIGURE 21 Network Connections (exercise 2)

3. **Create Your Own Folders:** Folders are the key to the Windows storage system. Folders can be created at any time and in any way that makes sense to you. The My Courses folder in Figure 22, for example, contains five folders, one folder for each class you are taking. In similar fashion, the Correspondence folder in this figure contains two additional folders according to the type of correspondence. Proceed as follows:
   a. Place the floppy disk from hands-on exercise 3 into drive A. Start Windows Explorer. Click the Folders button to display the hierarchy structure in the left pane. Change to the Details view.
   b. Create a Correspondence folder on drive A. Create a Business folder and a Personal folder within the Correspondence folder.
   c. Create a My Courses folder on drive A. Create a separate folder for each course you are taking within the My Courses folder. The names of your folders will be different from ours.
   d. Pull down the View menu, click the Arrange Icons by command, and click the command to Show in Groups. Click the Date Modified column header to group the files and folders by date. The dates you see will be different from the dates in our figure.
   e. The Show in Groups command functions as a toggle switch. Execute the command, and the files are displayed in groups; execute the command a second time, and the groups disappear. (You can change the grouping by clicking the desired column heading.)
   f. Use the technique described in problems 1 and 2 to capture the screen in Figure 22 and incorporate it into a document. Add a short paragraph that describes the folders you have created, then submit the document to your instructor.

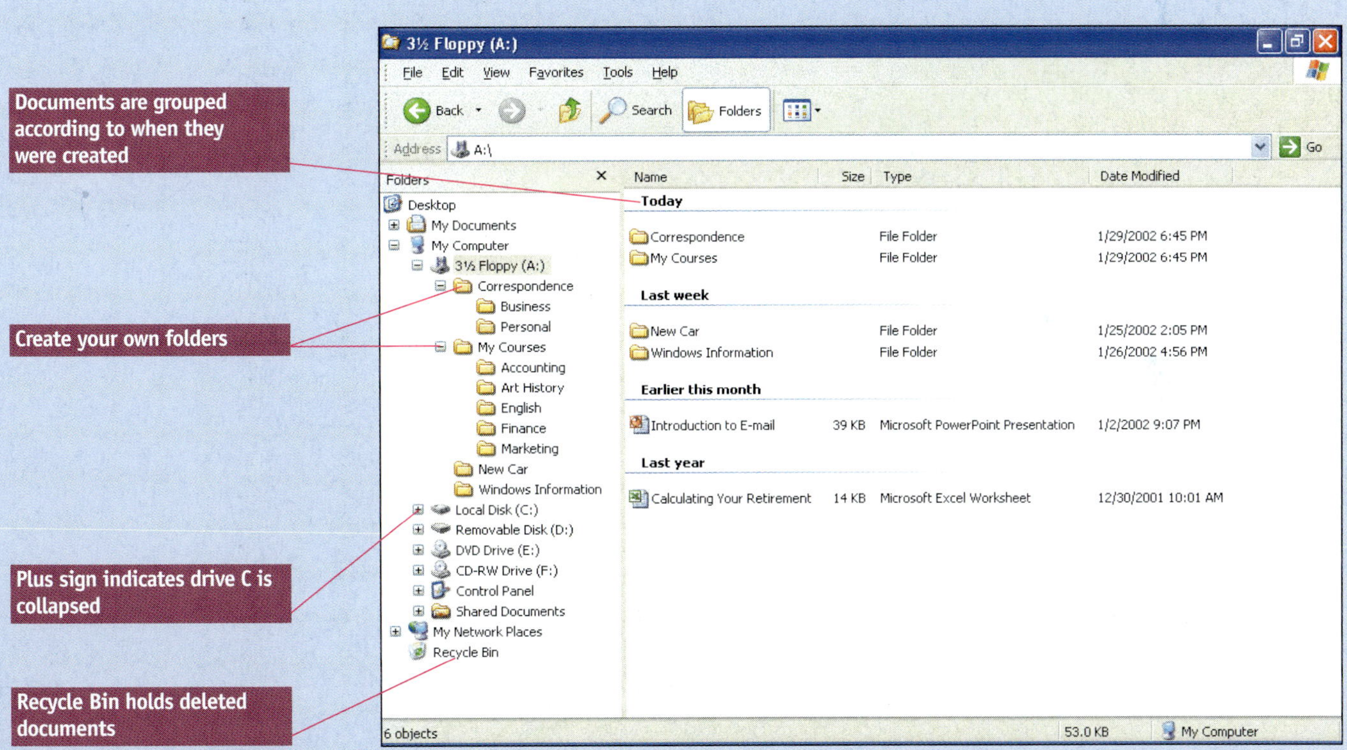

FIGURE 22 Create Your Own Folders (exercise 3)

4. **What's New in Windows XP:** Anyone, whether an experienced user or a computer novice, can benefit from a quick overview of new features in Windows XP. Click the Start button, click Help and Support, and then click the link to What's New in Windows XP. Click the second link in the task pane (taking a tour or tutorial), select the Windows XP tour, and choose the desired format. We chose the animated tour with animation, music, and voice narration.

   a. Relax and enjoy the show as shown in Figure 23. The task bar at the bottom of the figure contains three buttons to restart the show, exit, or toggle the music on and off. Exit the tutorial when you are finished. You are back in the Help and Support window, where you can take a tour of the Windows Media Player. Try it. Click the Close button at the upper right of any screen or press Escape to exit the tour. Write a short note to your instructor with comments about either tour.

   b. Return to the Help and Support Center and find the topic, "What's New in Home Networking." Print two or three subtopics that describe how to create a home network. Does the task seem less intimidating after you have read the information?

   c. Locate one or more topics on new features in digital media such as burning a CD or Windows Movie Maker. Print this information for your instructor.

   d. Return once again to the Help and Support Center to explore some of the other resources that describe new features in Windows XP. Locate the link to Windows News Groups, and then visit one of these newsgroups online. Locate a topic of interest and print several messages within a threaded discussion. Do you think newsgroups will be useful to you in the future?

   e. You can also download a PowerPoint presentation by the authors that describes new features in Windows XP. Go to www.prenhall.com/grauer, click the text for Office XP, then click the link to What's New in Windows XP, from where you can download the presentation.

Figure 23 What's New in Windows XP (exercise 4)

5. **Keyboard Shortcuts:** Almost every command in Windows can be executed in different ways, using either the mouse or the keyboard. Most people start with the mouse and add keyboard shortcuts as they become more proficient. There is no right or wrong technique, just different techniques, and the one you choose depends entirely on personal preference. If, for example, your hands are already on the keyboard, it is faster to use the keyboard equivalent if you know it.

   There is absolutely no need to memorize these shortcuts, nor should you even try. A few, however, have special appeal and everyone has favorites. You are probably familiar with general Windows shortcuts such as Ctrl+X, Ctrl+C, and Ctrl+V to cut, copy, and paste, respectively. (The X is supposed to remind you of a pair of scissors.) Ctrl+Z is less well known and corresponds to the Undo command. You can find additional shortcuts through the Help command.

   a. Use the Help and Support Center to display the information in Figure 24, which shows the available shortcuts within a dialog box. Two of these, Tab and Shift+Tab, move forward and backward, respectively, from one option to the next within the dialog box. The next time you are in a physician's office or a dentist's office, watch the assistant as he or she labors over the keyboard to enter information. That person will typically type information into a text box, then switch to the mouse to select the next entry, return to the keyboard, and so on. Tell that person about Tab and Shift+Tab; he or she will be forever grateful.

   b. The Help and Support Center organizes the shortcuts by category. Select the Natural keyboard category (not visible in Figure 24), then note what you can do with the ⊞ key. Press the ⊞ key at any time, and you display the Start menu. Press ⊞+M and you minimize all open windows. There are several other, equally good shortcuts in this category.

   c. Select your five favorite shortcuts in any category, and submit them to your instructor. Compare your selections to those of your classmates. Do you prefer the mouse or your newly discovered shortcuts?

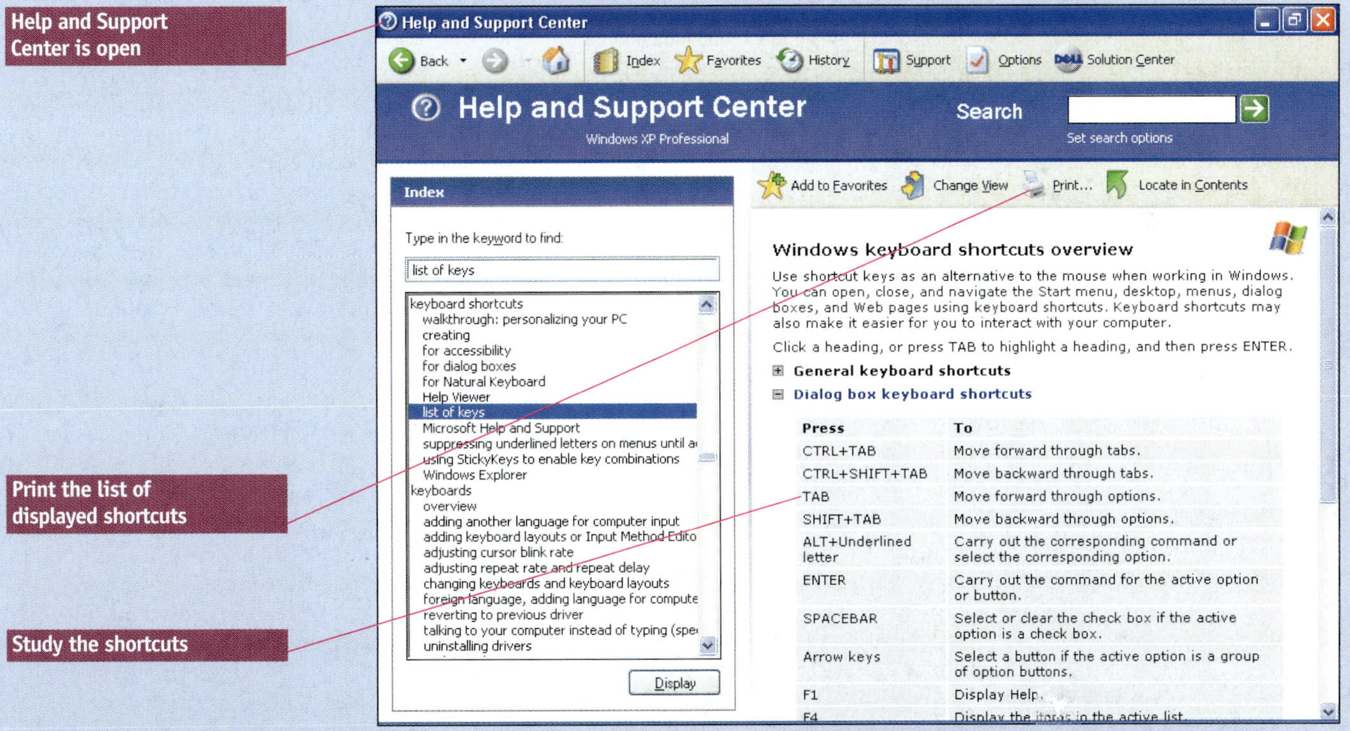

FIGURE 24 Keyboard Shortcuts (exercise 5)

MINI CASES

Planning for Disaster

Do you have a backup strategy? Do you even know what a backup strategy is? You had better learn, because sooner or later you will wish you had one. You will erase a file, be unable to read from a floppy disk, or worse yet, suffer a hardware failure in which you are unable to access the hard drive. The problem always seems to occur the night before an assignment is due. The ultimate disaster is the disappearance of your computer, by theft or natural disaster. Describe, in 250 words or less, the backup strategy you plan to implement in conjunction with your work in this class.

Tips for Windows XP

Print the *Tips for Windows XP* document that was downloaded as one of the practice files in the hands-on exercises. This document contains many of the boxed tips that appeared throughout the chapter. Read the document as a review and select five of your favorite tips. Create a new document for your instructor consisting of the five tips you selected. Add a cover page titled, "My Favorite Tips." Include your name, your professor's name, and a reference to the Grauer/Barber text from where the tips were taken.

File Compression

You've learned your lesson and have come to appreciate the importance of backing up all of your data files. The problem is that you work with large documents that exceed the 1.44MB capacity of a floppy disk. Accordingly, you might want to consider the acquisition of a file compression program to facilitate copying large documents to a floppy disk in order to transport your documents to and from school, home, or work. You can download an evaluation copy of the popular WinZip program at www.winzip.com. Investigate the subject of file compression and submit a summary of your findings to your instructor.

The Threat of Virus Infection

A computer virus is an actively infectious program that attaches itself to other programs and alters the way a computer works. Some viruses do nothing more than display an annoying message at an inopportune time. Most, however, are more harmful, and in the worst case, erase all files on the disk. Use your favorite search engine to research the subject of computer viruses to answer the following questions. When is a computer subject to infection by a virus? What precautions does your school or university take against the threat of virus infection in its computer lab? What precautions, if any, do you take at home? Can you feel confident that your machine will not be infected if you faithfully use a state-of-the-art anti-virus program that was purchased in June 2002?

Your First Consultant's Job

Go to a real installation such as a doctor's or attorney's office, the company where you work, or the computer lab at school. Determine the backup procedures that are in effect, then write a one-page report indicating whether the policy is adequate and, if necessary, offering suggestions for improvement. Your report should be addressed to the individual in charge of the business, and it should cover all aspects of the backup strategy; that is, which files are backed up and how often, and what software is used for the backup operation. Use appropriate emphasis (for example, bold italics) to identify any potential problems. This is a professional document (it is your first consultant's job), and its appearance should be perfect in every way.

CHAPTER 1

Microsoft® Word: What Will Word Processing Do for Me?

OBJECTIVES

After reading this chapter you will:

1. Define word wrap; differentiate between a hard and a soft return.
2. Distinguish between the insert and overtype modes.
3. Describe the elements on the Microsoft Word screen.
4. Create, save, edit, and print a simple document.
5. Download the practice files (data disk) for use in hands-on exercises.
6. Define select-then-do methodology; explain how it applies to formatting.
7. Check a document for spelling; explain the custom dictionary.
8. Describe the AutoCorrect and AutoText features.
9. Use the thesaurus.
10. Explain the objectives and limitations of the grammar check.
11. Differentiate between the Save and Save As commands.
12. Describe the Track Changes command and electronic editing.

hands-on exercises

1. MY FIRST DOCUMENT
   Input: None
   Output: My First Document
2. MODIFYING AN EXISTING DOCUMENT
   Input: My First Document (from exercise 1)
   Output: My First Document (additional modifications)
3. SPELL CHECK, THESAURUS, AND GRAMMAR CHECK
   Input: Language Tools
   Output: Language Tools Solution

CASE STUDY
THE STUDENT SENATOR

Jim Johnson is a well-known and well-liked freshman who is majoring in political science at your university. As one of his best friends and "political" advisors, you often engage in discussions about his political aspirations, particularly as they relate to the university. Jim has recently decided to run for student senator, and he has asked you to help him write the personal statement section of the application. The objective of the personal statement is to explain why an individual wants to become a student senator and to describe the skills and experience he or she would bring to the position.

Jim is a bright guy with great ideas and lofty goals, and has most of what it takes to succeed; he just needs a bit of help when it comes to expressing himself on paper. His request reminds you of the time in high school when you wrote several of his speeches, before and after he became student body president. It seems that ever since, Jim has expected you to polish his writing, whether it applies to politics or not. Although you know Jim well enough to write the statement for him, you think it high time that he do his own writing and thus you offer to edit his personal statement instead of simply writing it for him. Moreover, you have just discovered the Track Changes command in Microsoft Word and will do the editing electronically. ■

Your assignment is to read the chapter, paying special attention to Hands-on Exercises 2 and 3 that describe how to modify an existing document, and how to use the spell check, grammar check, and thesaurus in Microsoft Word. You will then open the document, *Chapter 1 Case Study—The Student Senator,* which is Jim's first attempt at writing his own personal statement. Pull down the Tools menu and toggle the Track Changes command on to record your changes, and then modify the document as you see fit to create the best personal statement for Jim to submit. Basic formatting is also important. Print a copy of the corrected document for your instructor to prove that you've solved the problem, and completed the case.

THE BASICS OF WORD PROCESSING

Have you ever produced what you thought was the perfect term paper only to discover that you omitted a sentence or misspelled a word, or that the paper was three pages too short or one page too long? Wouldn't it be nice to make the necessary changes, and then be able to reprint the entire paper with the touch of a key? Welcome to the world of word processing, where you are no longer stuck with having to retype anything. Instead, you retrieve your work from disk, display it on the monitor and revise it as necessary, then print it at any time, in draft or final form.

This chapter provides a broad-based introduction to word processing in general and Microsoft Word in particular. All word processors adhere to certain basic concepts that must be understood if you are to use the programs effectively. The next several pages introduce ideas that are applicable to any word processor (and which you may already know). We follow the conceptual material with a hands-on exercise that enables you to apply what you have learned.

The Insertion Point

The ***insertion point*** is a flashing vertical line that marks the place where text will be entered. The insertion point is always at the beginning of a new document, but it can be moved anywhere within an existing document. If, for example, you wanted to add text to the end of a document, you would move the insertion point to the end of the document, then begin typing.

Word Wrap

A newcomer to word processing has one major transition to make from a typewriter, and it is an absolutely critical adjustment. Whereas a typist returns the carriage at the end of every line, just the opposite is true of a word processor. One types continually *without* pressing the Enter key at the end of a line because the word processor automatically wraps text from one line to the next. This concept is known as ***word wrap*** and is illustrated in Figure 1.1.

The word *primitive* does not fit on the current line in Figure 1.1a, and is automatically shifted to the next line, *without* the user having to press the Enter key. The user continues to enter the document, with additional words being wrapped to subsequent lines as necessary. The only time you use the Enter key is at the end of a paragraph, or when you want the insertion point to move to the next line and the end of the current line doesn't reach the right margin.

Word wrap is closely associated with another concept, that of hard and soft returns. A ***hard return*** is created by the user when he or she presses the Enter key at the end of a paragraph; a ***soft return*** is created by the word processor as it wraps text from one line to the next. The locations of the soft returns change automatically as a document is edited (e.g., as text is inserted or deleted, or as margins or fonts are changed). The locations of the hard returns can be changed only by the user, who must intentionally insert or delete each hard return.

There are two hard returns in Figure 1.1b, one at the end of each paragraph. There are also six soft returns in the first paragraph (one at the end of every line except the last) and three soft returns in the second paragraph. Now suppose the margins in the document are made smaller (that is, the line is made longer) as shown in Figure 1.1c. The number of soft returns drops to four and two (in the first and second paragraphs, respectively) as more text fits on a line and fewer lines are needed. The revised document still contains the two original hard returns, one at the end of each paragraph.

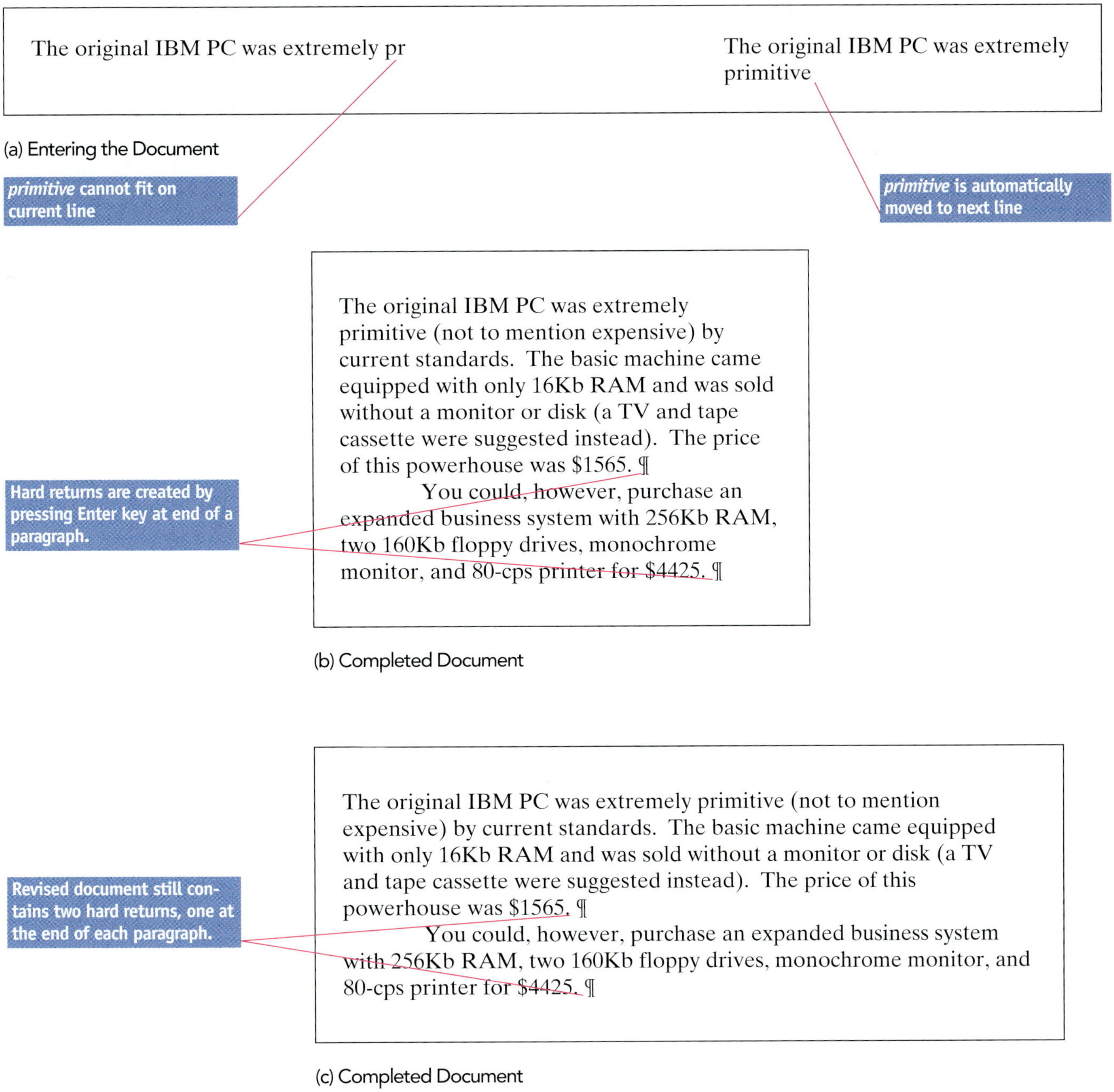

FIGURE 1.1 Word Wrap

Toggle Switches

Suppose you sat down at the keyboard and typed an entire sentence without pressing the Shift key; the sentence would be in all lowercase letters. Then you pressed the Caps Lock key and retyped the sentence, again without pressing the Shift key. This time the sentence would be in all uppercase letters. You could repeat the process as often as you like. Each time you pressed the Caps Lock key, the sentence would switch from lowercase to uppercase and vice versa.

The point of this exercise is to introduce the concept of a ***toggle switch***, a device that causes the computer to alternate between two states. The Caps Lock key is an example of a toggle switch. Each time you press it, newly typed text will change from uppercase to lowercase and back again. We will see several other examples of toggle switches as we proceed in our discussion of word processing.

Insert versus Overtype

Microsoft Word is always in one of two modes, ***insert*** or ***overtype***, and uses a toggle switch (the Ins key) to alternate between the two. Press the Ins key once and you switch from insert to overtype. Press the Ins key a second time and you go from overtype back to insert. Text that is entered into a document during the insert mode moves existing text to the right to accommodate the characters being added. Text entered from the overtype mode replaces (overtypes) existing text. Regardless of which mode you are in, text is always entered or replaced immediately to the right of the insertion point.

The insert mode is best when you enter text for the first time, but either mode can be used to make corrections. The insert mode is the better choice when the correction requires you to add new text; the overtype mode is easier when you are substituting one or more character(s) for another. The difference between the two is illustrated in Figure 1.2.

Figure 1.2a displays the text as it was originally entered, with two misspellings. The letters *se* have been omitted from the word *insert,* and an *x* has been erroneously typed instead of an *r* in the word *overtype.* The insert mode is used in Figure 1.2b to add the missing letters, which in turn moves the rest of the line to the right. The overtype mode is used in Figure 1.2c to replace the *x* with an *r.*

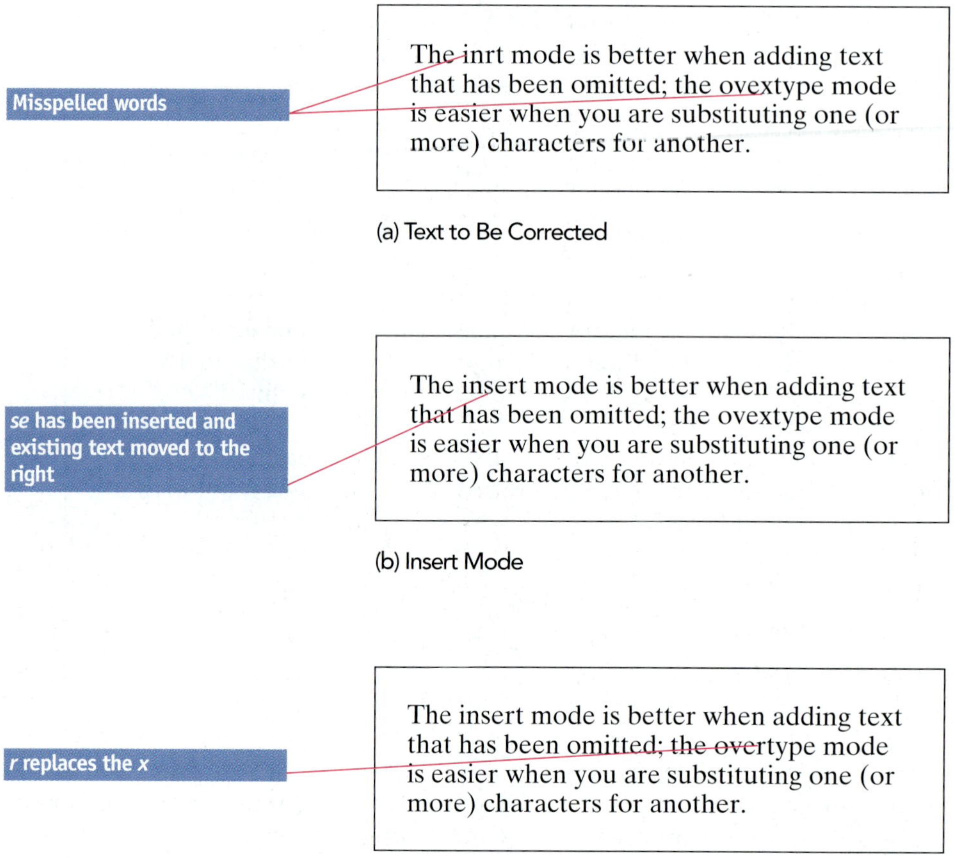

(a) Text to Be Corrected

(b) Insert Mode

(c) Overtype Mode

FIGURE 1.2 Insert and Overtype Modes

Deleting Text

The Backspace and Del keys delete one character immediately to the left or right of the insertion point, respectively. The choice between them depends on when you need to erase a character(s). The Backspace key is easier if you want to delete a character (or characters) immediately after typing. The Del key is preferable during subsequent editing.

You can delete several characters at one time by selecting (dragging the mouse over) the characters to be deleted, then pressing the Del key. And finally, you can delete and replace text in one operation by selecting the text to be replaced and then typing the new text in its place.

> **LEARN TO TYPE**
>
> The ultimate limitation of any word processor is the speed at which you enter data; hence the ability to type quickly is invaluable. Learning how to type is easy, especially with the availability of computer-based typing programs. As little as a half hour a day for a couple of weeks will have you up to speed, and if you do any significant amount of writing at all, the investment will pay off many times.

INTRODUCTION TO MICROSOFT WORD

We used Microsoft Word to write this book, as can be inferred from the screen in Figure 1.3. Your screen will be different from ours in many ways. You will not have the same document, nor is it likely that you will customize Word in exactly the same way. You should, however, be able to recognize the basic elements that are found in the Microsoft Word window that is open on the desktop.

There are actually two open windows in Figure 1.3—an application window for Microsoft Word and a document window for the specific document on which you are working. The application window has its own Minimize, Maximize (or Restore), and Close buttons. The document window has only a Close button. However, only one title bar appears at the top of the application window, and it reflects the application (Microsoft Word) as well as the document name (Word Chapter 1). A ***menu bar*** appears immediately below the title bar. Vertical and horizontal ***scroll bars*** appear at the right and bottom of the document window.

Microsoft Word is also part of the Microsoft Office suite of applications, and thus shares additional features with Excel, Access, and PowerPoint, that are also part of the Office suite. ***Toolbars*** provide immediate access to common commands and appear immediately below the menu bar. The toolbars can be displayed or hidden using the Toolbars command in the ***View menu***.

The ***Standard toolbar*** contains buttons corresponding to the most basic commands in Word—for example, opening a file or printing a document. The icon on the button is intended to be indicative of its function (e.g., a printer to indicate the Print command). You can also point to the button to display a ***ScreenTip*** showing the name of the button. The first several tools and associated keyboard shortcuts (New document, Open, Save, E-mail, and Print) are common to the other applications in Microsoft Office. Thus once you master one application in Microsoft Office, it is that much easier to learn the next.

The ***Formatting toolbar*** appears under the Standard toolbar and provides access to such common formatting operations as boldface, italics, or underlining. Other tools let you change the font or font size, highlight text, or change its color. Additional buttons enable you to change the alignment and line spacing in a paragraph, add bullets or numbering, and/or box selected text.

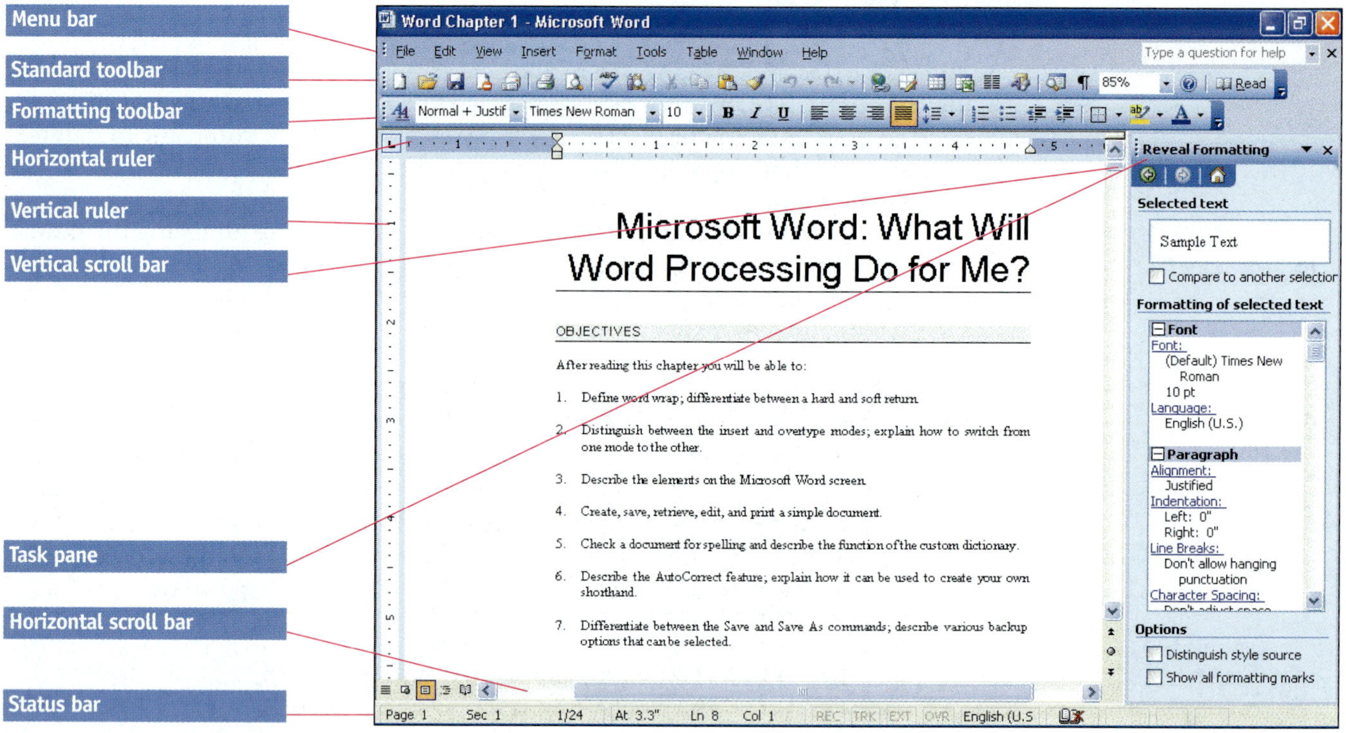

FIGURE 1.3 Microsoft Word

The toolbars may appear overwhelming at first, but there is absolutely no need to memorize what the individual buttons do. That will come with time. We suggest, however, that you will have a better appreciation for the various buttons if you consider them in groups, according to their general function, as shown in Figure 1.4a. Note, too, that many of the commands in the pull-down menus are displayed with an image that corresponds to a button on a toolbar.

The ***horizontal ruler*** is displayed underneath the toolbars and enables you to change margins, tabs, and/or indents for all or part of a document. A ***vertical ruler*** shows the vertical position of text on the page and can be used to change the top or bottom margins.

The ***status bar*** at the bottom of the document window displays the location of the insertion point (or information about the command being executed). The status bar also shows the status (settings) of various indicators—for example, OVR to show that Word is in the overtype, as opposed to the insert, mode.

The ***task pane*** at the right of the document window provides access to several basic tasks. Different task panes are displayed at different times, depending on what you want to accomplish. The Home task pane, for example, appears automatically when Word is started initially. It contains links to the last several documents that were opened to facilitate returning to an earlier document. It also provides access to a search command to obtain help on a specific topic.

The task pane can be opened explicitly at any time via the View menu by the user, who may then select a specific task pane by clicking the down arrow in the task pane itself. The Reveal Formatting task pane in Figure 1.3, for example, shows the formatting in effect at the insertion point. It describes the font (typeface) as well as the paragraph. Other task panes include Help, Clip Art, Mail Merge, and Research. You can click the Close button to close the task pane at any time. The task pane may then reopen automatically if it is required by a subsequent command, and/or the user can reopen it at any time.

Starts a new document; opens an existing document; saves the document in memory; prevents a workbook from being copied or edited; sends a document via e-mail

Prints the document; previews the document prior to printing

Checks the spelling and grammar of the document; opens Research in the task pane

Cuts or copies the selected text to the clipboard; pastes the contents of the Windows clipboard; copies the formatting of the selected text

Undoes or redoes a previously executed command

Inserts a hyperlink; displays Tables and Borders toolbar; inserts a table; inserts an Excel worksheet; creates columns; displays Drawing toolbar

Toggles the Document map on and off; toggles the display of the nonprinting characters on and off; changes the zoom percentage

Displays the Help task pane

Changes to the Reading Layout view

(a) Standard Toolbar

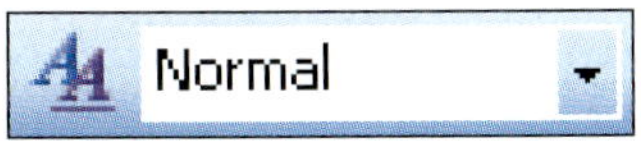

Toggles the task pane on or off to display styles and formatting; applies a specific style to the selected text

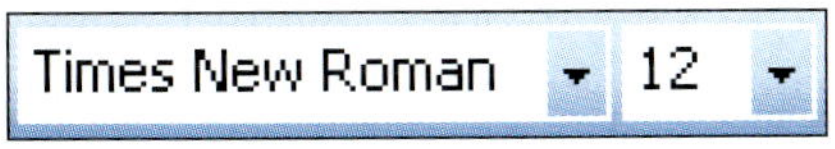

Changes the font or point size

Toggles boldface, italics, and underline on and off

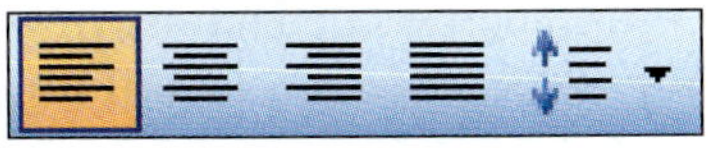

Aligns left, center, right, or full; changes the line spacing

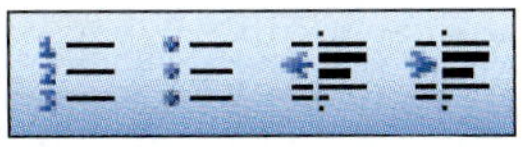

Creates a numbered or bulleted list; decreases or increases the indent

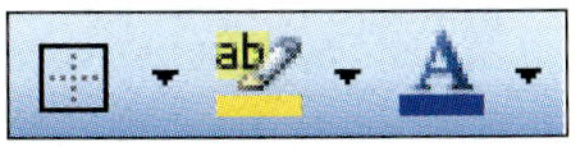

Creates a border; applies highlighting to the selected text; applies a font color to the selected text

(b) Formatting Toolbar

FIGURE 1.4 Toolbars

The File Menu

The ***File Menu*** is a critically important menu in virtually every Windows application. It contains the Save and Open commands to save a document on disk, then subsequently retrieve (open) that document at a later time. The File Menu also contains the ***Print command*** to print a document, the ***Close command*** to close the current document but continue working in the application, and the ***Exit command*** to quit the application altogether.

The ***Save command*** copies the document that you are working on (i.e., the document that is currently in memory) to disk. The command functions differently the first time it is executed for a new document, in that it displays the Save As dialog box as shown in Figure 1.5a. The dialog box requires you to specify the name of the document, the drive (and an optional folder) in which the document is stored, and its file type. All subsequent executions of the command will save the document under the assigned name, each time replacing the previously saved version with the new version.

The ***file name*** (e.g., My First Document) can contain up to 255 characters including spaces, commas, and/or periods. (Periods are discouraged, however, since they are too easily confused with DOS extensions.) The Save In list box is used to select the drive (which is not visible in Figure 1.5a) and the optional folder (e.g., Exploring Word). The ***file type*** defaults to a Word document. You can, however, choose a different format such as a Web page (HTML document), an XML document, or even a WordPerfect document.

The ***Places bar*** provides a shortcut to any of the listed folders without having to search through the Save In (or Look In) list box. The desktop icon, for example, saves a file directly to the desktop. My Recent Documents provides links to the last several documents that were opened. My Network Places takes your folders that are contained on other computers to which you have network access.

The ***Open command*** is the opposite of the Save command as it brings a copy of an existing document into memory, enabling you to work with that document. The Open command displays the Open dialog box in which you specify the file name, the drive (and optionally the folder) that contains the file, and the file type. Microsoft Word will then list all files of that type on the designated drive (and folder), enabling you to open the file you want. The Save and Open commands work in conjunction with one another. The Save As dialog box in Figure 1.5a, for example, saves the file My First Document in the Exploring Word folder. The Open dialog box in Figure 1.5b loads that file into memory so that you can work with the file, after which you can save the revised file for use at a later time.

The toolbars in the Save As and Open dialog boxes have several buttons in common that facilitate the execution of either command. The Views button lets you display the files in either dialog box in several different views. The Details view (in Figure 1.5a) shows the file size as well as the date and time a file was last modified. The Preview view (in Figure 1.5b) shows the beginning of a document, without having to open the document. The List view displays only the file names, and thus lets you see more files at one time. The Properties view shows information about the document, including the date of creation and number of revisions. The Tools button provides access to common file operations such as renaming or deleting the selected file.

Learning by Doing

Every chapter contains a series of hands-on exercises that enable you to apply what you learn at the computer. The exercises in this chapter are linked to one another in that you create a simple document in exercise 1, then open and edit that document in exercise 2. The ability to save and open a document is critical, and you do not want to spend an inordinate amount of time entering text unless you are confident in your ability to retrieve it later.

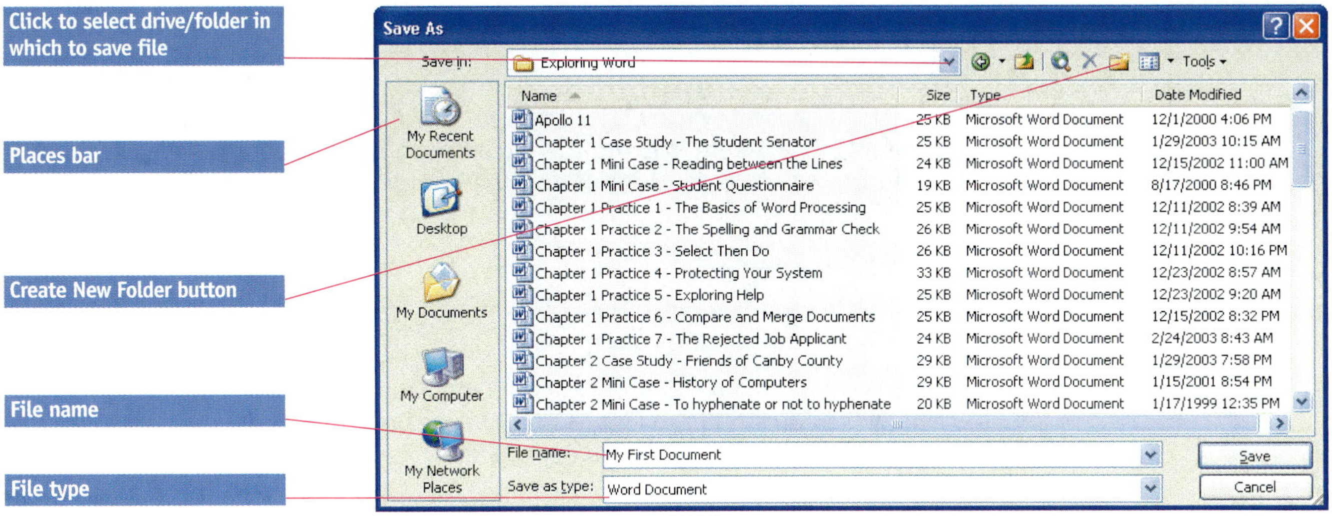

(a) Save As Dialog Box (Details view)

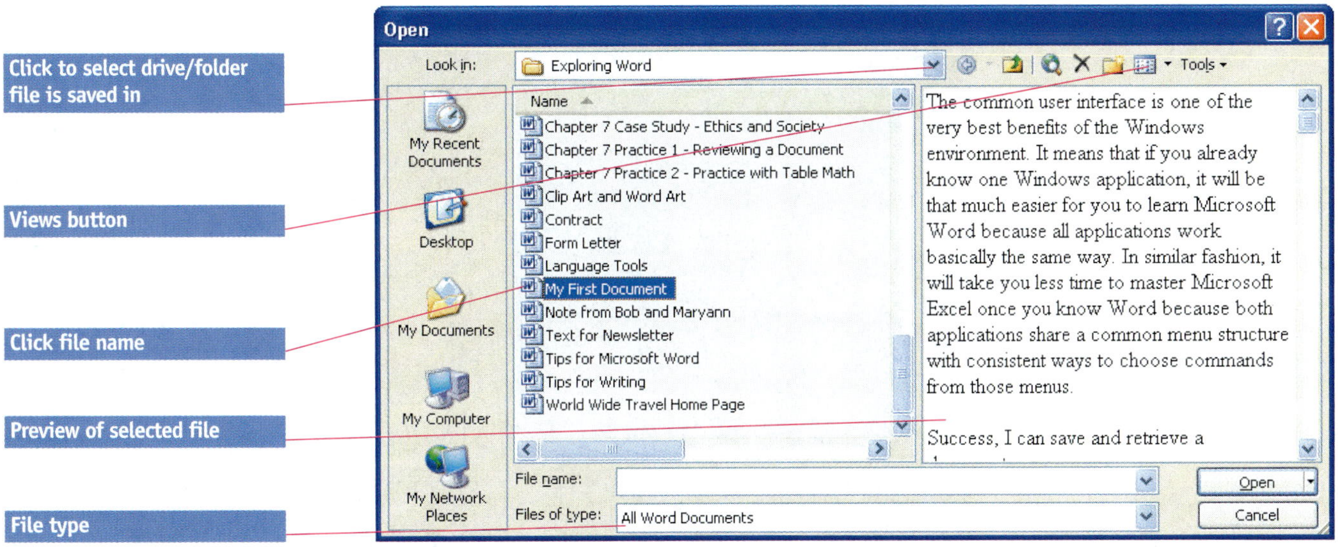

(b) Open Dialog Box (Preview view)

FIGURE 1.5 The Save and Open Commands

FILE MANAGEMENT AT YOUR FINGERTIPS

Use the toolbar in the Open and/or Save As dialog boxes to perform basic file management tasks within an Office application. You can select any existing file, then delete it or rename it. You can create a new folder, which is very useful when you begin to work with a large number of documents. Use the Views button to change the way the files are listed within the dialog box.

hands-on exercise

1 My First Document

Objective To start Microsoft Word in order to create, save, and print a simple document; to execute commands via the toolbar or from pull-down menus. Use Figure 1.6 as a guide in doing the exercise.

Step 1: Log onto Windows XP

- Turn on the computer and all of its peripherals. The floppy drive should be empty prior to starting your machine.
- Your system will take a minute or so to get started, after which you should see a logon screen similar to Figure 1.6a. Do not be concerned if the appearance of your desktop is different from ours.
- Click the icon for the user account you want to access. You may be prompted for a password, depending on the security options in effect.
- You should be familiar with basic file management and very comfortable moving and copying files from one folder to another. If not, you may want to review this material.

Click your user name

(a) Log onto Windows XP (step 1)

FIGURE 1.6 Hands-on Exercise 1

USER ACCOUNTS

The available user names are created automatically during the installation of Windows XP, but you can add or delete users at any time. Click the Start button, click Control Panel, switch to the Category view, and select User Accounts. Choose the desired task, such as creating a new account or changing an existing account. Do not expect, however, to be able to modify accounts in a school setting.

Step 2: Obtain the Practice Files

- Start Internet Explorer and go to **www.prenhall.com/grauer**. Click the book for **Office 2003**, which takes you to the Office 2003 home page. Click the **Student Downloads tab** (near the top of the window) to go to the Student Downloads page as shown in Figure 1.6b.
- Select the appropriate file to download:
  - Choose **Exploring Word** (or **Word Volume I**) if you are using a stand-alone Word text, as opposed to an Office text with multiple applications.
  - Choose **Office 2003 Volume I** (for regular or **Enhanced Edition**), **Office 2003 Plus**, or **Office 2003 Brief** if you have an Office text.
- Click the link to download the file. You will see the File Download box asking what you want to do. Click the **Save button**. The Save As dialog box appears.
- Click the **down arrow** in the Save In list box and select the drive and folder where you want to save the file. Click **Save**.
- Start Windows Explorer, select the drive and folder where you saved the file, then double click the file and follow the onscreen instructions.

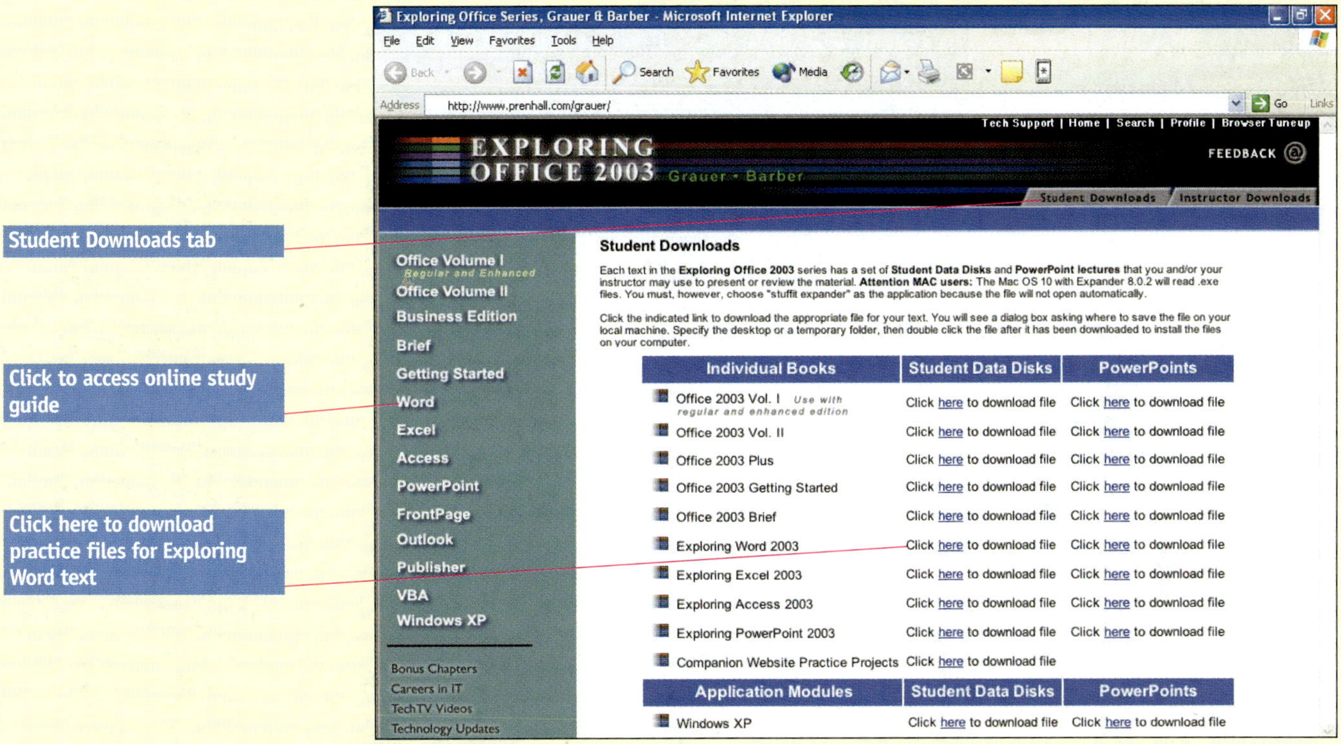

(b) Obtain the Practice Files (step 2)

FIGURE 1.6 Hands-on Exercise 1 (*continued*)

EXPLORE OUR WEB SITE

The Exploring Office Series Web site offers an online study guide (multiple-choice, true/false, and matching questions) for each individual textbook to help you review the material in each chapter. You can take practice quizzes by yourself and/or e-mail the results to your instructor. These online study guides are available via the tabs in the left navigation bar. You can return to the Student Downloads page at any time by clicking the tab toward the top of the window and/or you can click the link to Home to return to the home page for the Office 2003 Series. And finally, you can click the Feedback button at the top of the screen to send a message directly to Bob Grauer.

Step 3: Create a Document

- Click the **Start button** to display the Start menu. Click (or point to) the **All Programs button**, click **Microsoft Office**, then click **Microsoft Word 2003** to start the program.
- You should see a blank document within the Word application window. Close the task pane if it is open.
- Create the document in Figure 1.6c. Type continually from one line to the next; do *not* press the Enter key at the end of each line because Word will automatically wrap text from one line to the next.
- Press the **Enter key** at the end of the paragraph.
- You may see a red or green wavy line to indicate spelling or grammatical errors, respectively. Both features are discussed later in the chapter.
- Point to the red wavy line (if any), click the **right mouse button** to display a list of suggested corrections, then click (select) the appropriate substitution.
- Ignore the green wavy line (if any).

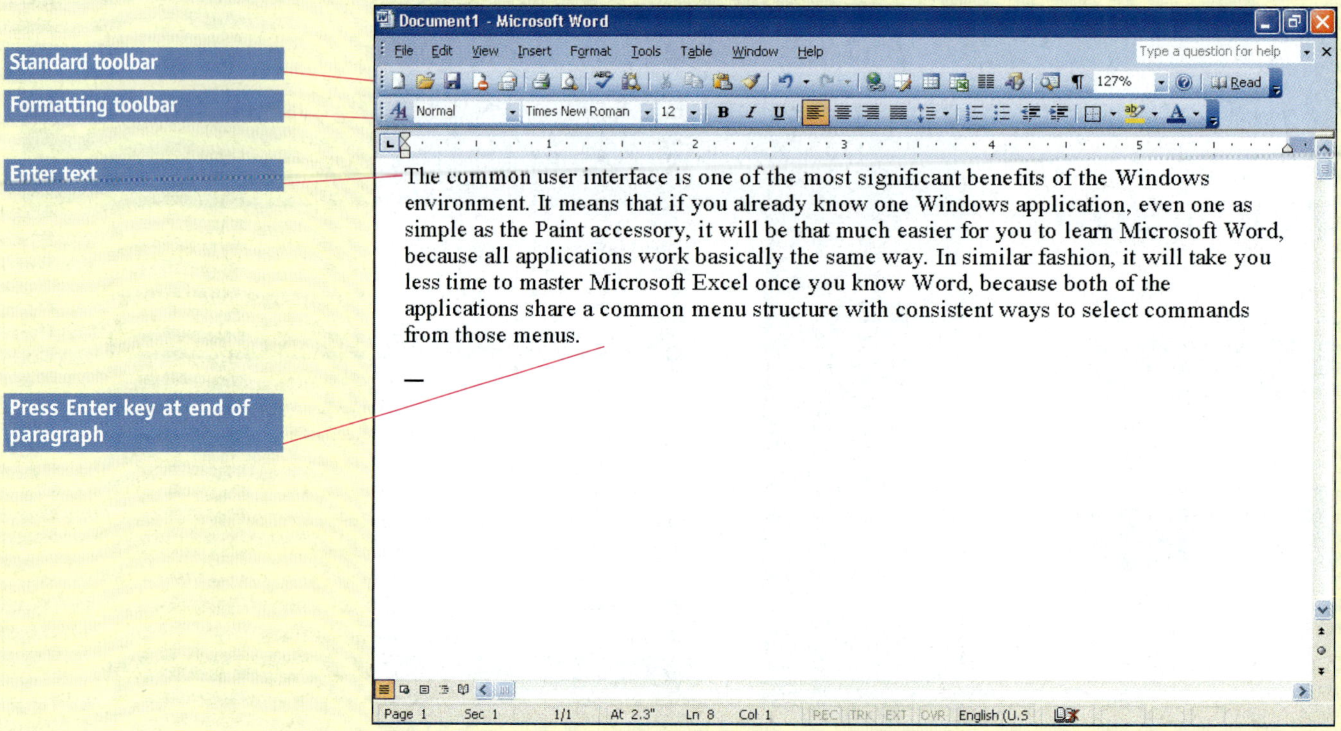

(c) Create a Document (step 3)

FIGURE 1.6 Hands-on Exercise 1 *(continued)*

SEPARATE THE TOOLBARS

You may see the Standard and Formatting toolbars displayed on one row to save space within the application window. If so, we suggest that you separate the toolbars, so that you see all of the buttons on each. Click the Toolbar Options down arrow that appears at the end of any visible toolbar to display toolbar options, then click the option to show the buttons on two rows. Click the down arrow a second time to show the buttons on one row if you want to return to the other configuration.

Step 4: Save the Document

- Pull down the **File menu** and click **Save** (or click the **Save button** on the Standard toolbar). You should see the Save As dialog box in Figure 1.6d.
- If necessary, click the **drop-down arrow** on the View button and select the **Details view**. To save the file:
  - Click the **drop-down arrow** on the Save In list box.
  - Click the appropriate drive, e.g., drive C or drive A.
  - Double click the **Exploring Word folder** to make it the active folder.
  - If necessary, click and drag over the default entry in the File name text box. Type **My First Document** as the name of your document.
  - Click **Save** or press the **Enter key**. The title bar changes to reflect the new document name (My First Document).
- Add your name at the end of the document, then click the **Save button** on the Standard toolbar to save the document with the revision.
- This time the Save As dialog box does not appear, since Word already knows the name of the document.

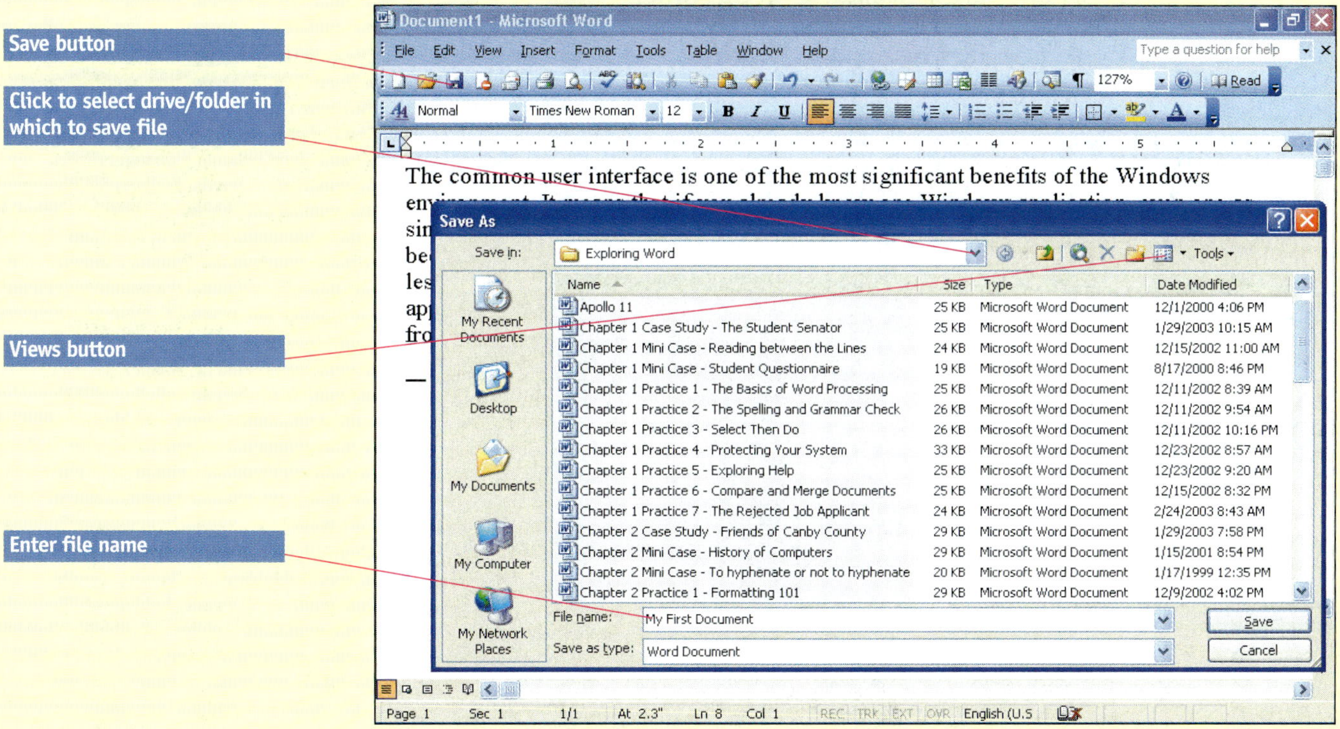

(d) Save the Document (step 4)

FIGURE 1.6 Hands-on Exercise 1 *(continued)*

THE WORD COUNT TOOLBAR

How close are you to completing the 5,000-word paper that your professor assigned? Pull down the Tools menu and click the Word Count command to display a dialog box that shows the number of pages, words, paragraphs, and characters in your document. There is also a command button to display the Word Count toolbar so that it remains on the screen throughout the session. Click the Recount button on the toolbar at any time to see the current statistics for your document.

Step 5: Help with Word

- The best time to obtain help is when you don't need it. Try either of the following:
  - ❑ Pull down the **Help menu** and click the command to **Show the Office Assistant**. Click the **Assistant**, then enter the question, **"How do I get help?"** in the Assistant's balloon and click **Search**, or
  - ❑ Type the question directly in the **Ask a Question box** in the upper right of the Word window and press **Enter**.
- Regardless of the technique you choose, Word will display a message indicating that it is searching the Office Web site for new information.
- You should see a task pane with the results of the search as shown in Figure 1.6e. Click the link that is most appropriate (e.g., About getting help while you work).
- A new window opens containing the detailed help information. Click the **Print button** in the Help window, then click the **Print command button** to print the topic for your instructor.
- Close the Help window. Close the task pane. Pull down the **Help menu** and hide the Office Assistant. Exit Word if you do not want to continue with the next exercise at this time.

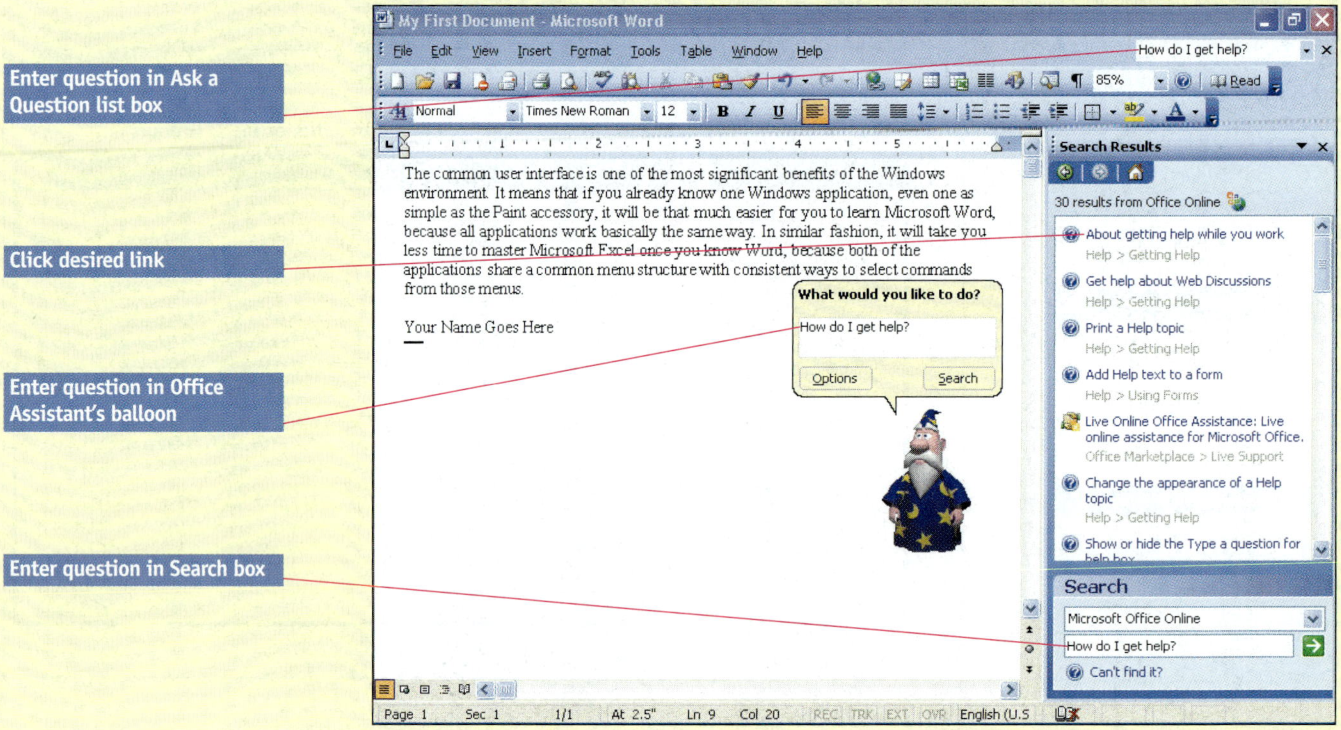

(e) Help with Word (step 5)

FIGURE 1.6 Hands-on Exercise 1 *(continued)*

TIP OF THE DAY

Pull down the Help menu, click the command to show the Office Assistant, click the Office Assistant when it appears, then click the Options button to display the Office Assistant dialog box. Click the Options tab, check the box to Show the Tip of the Day at Startup, and then click OK. The next time you start Word, you will be greeted by the Assistant, who will offer you the tip of the day.

TROUBLESHOOTING

We trust that you completed the hands-on exercise without difficulty, and that you were able to create, save, and print the document in the exercise. There is, however, considerable flexibility in the way you do the exercise in that you can display different toolbars and menus, and/or execute commands in a variety of ways. This section describes various ways in which you can customize Microsoft Word, and in so doing, will help you to troubleshoot future exercises.

Figure 1.7 displays two different views of the same document. Your screen may not match either figure, and indeed, there is no requirement that it should. You should, however, be aware of different options so that you can develop preferences of your own. Consider:

- Figure 1.7a uses short menus (note the double arrow at the bottom of the menu to display additional commands) and a shared row for the Standard and Formatting toolbars. Figure 1.7b displays the full menu and displays the toolbars on separate rows. We prefer the latter settings, which are set through the Customize command in the Tools menu.
- Figure 1.7a shows the Office Assistant (but drags it out of the way), whereas Figure 1.7b hides it. We find the Assistant distracting, and display it only when necessary by pressing the F1 key. You can also use the appropriate option in the Help menu to hide or show the Assistant, and/or you can right click the Assistant to hide it.
- Figure 1.7a shows the document with the task pane open, whereas the task pane is closed in Figure 1.7b. The task pane serves a variety of functions such as opening a document, inserting clip art, creating a mail merge, or displaying the formatting properties of selected text.
- Figure 1.7a displays the document in the ***Normal view*** whereas Figure 1.7b uses the ***Print Layout view***. The Normal view is simpler, but the Print Layout view more closely resembles the printed page as it displays top and bottom margins, headers and footers, graphic elements in their exact position, a vertical ruler, and other elements not seen in the Normal view.
- Figure 1.7a displays the ¶ and other nonprinting symbols, whereas they are hidden in Figure 1.7b. We prefer the cleaner screen without the symbols, but on occasion display the symbols if there is a problem in formatting a document. The ***Show/Hide ¶ button*** toggles the symbols on or off.
- Figure 1.7b displays an additional toolbar, the Drawing toolbar, at the bottom of the screen. Microsoft Word has more than 20 toolbars that are suppressed or displayed through the Toolbars command in the View menu. Note, too, that you can change the position of any visible toolbar by dragging its move handle (the parallel lines) at the left of the toolbar.

THE READING LAYOUT VIEW

Microsoft Word 2003 introduces the Reading Layout view, which hides the Standard and Formatting toolbars to increase the readability of a document. The pages in a document are presented to fill the screen and do not correspond to the pages as they would appear in the printed version. The Reading Layout view has its own toolbar, which includes buttons to change the font size, display the actual page layout (as it would appear on the printed page), and a Close button to return to the previous view. The Standard toolbar contains a Read button to switch to the Reading Layout. (Word documents sent as e-mail attachments are automatically opened in the Reading Layout View.)

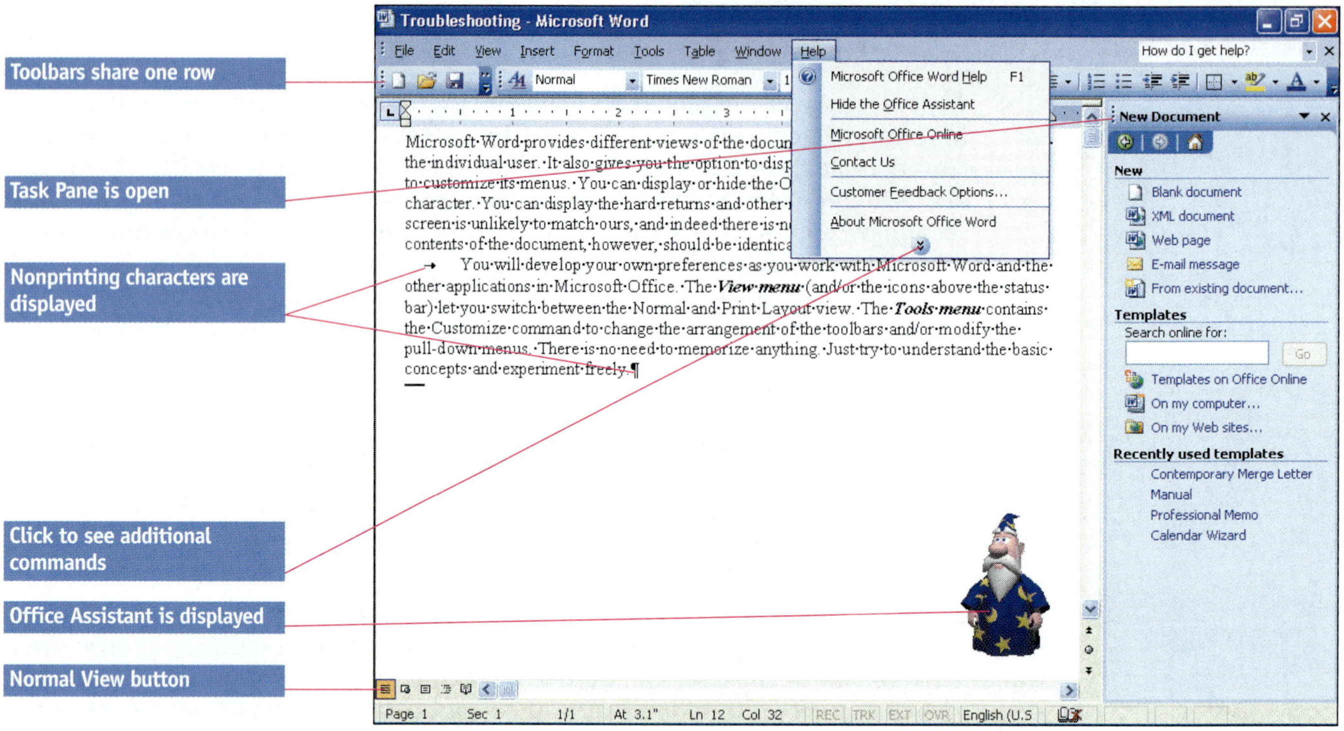

(a) Normal View

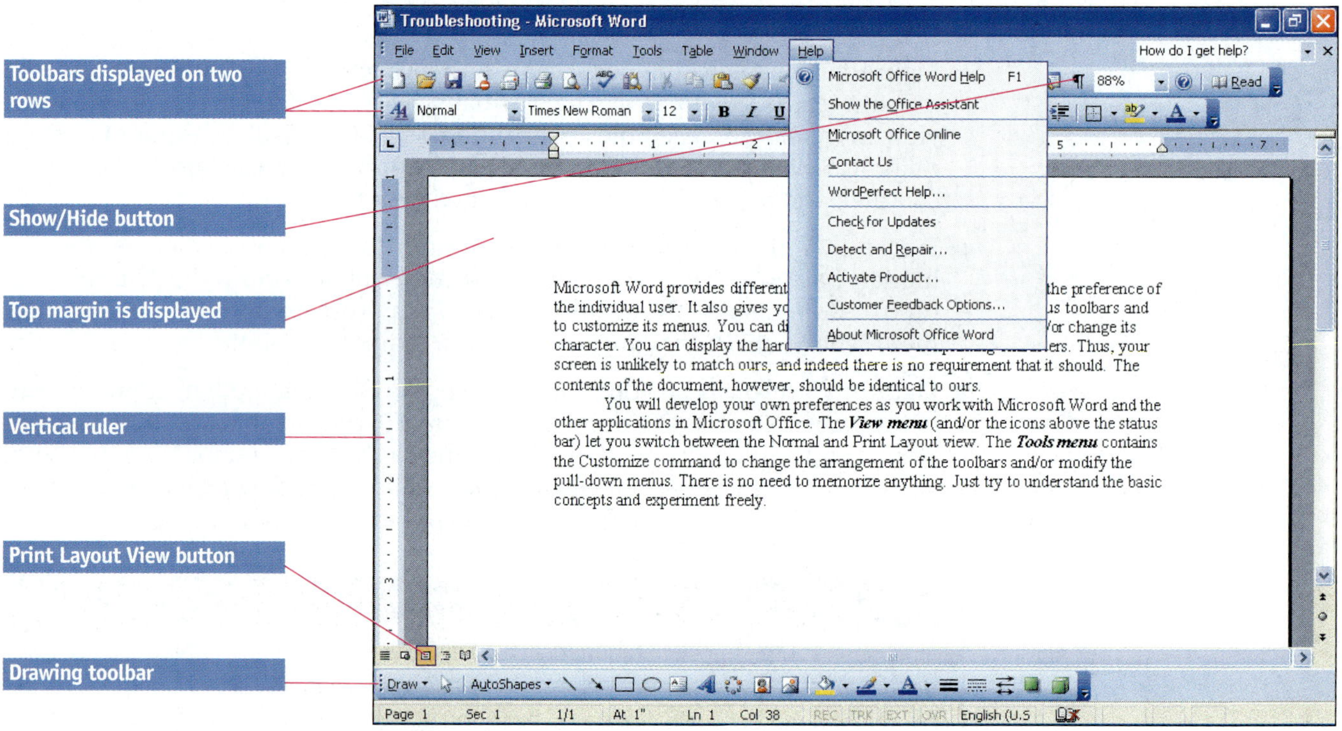

(b) Print Layout View

FIGURE 1.7 Troubleshooting

INTRODUCTION TO FORMATTING

The most important task in creating a document is to focus on its content. Once the document is written, however, you can improve its appearance through ***formatting***, which is accomplished through the concept of ***select then do***. This means that you select a block of text, and then you execute the appropriate formatting command. (The select then do concept also applies to editing commands.) Text can be selected in several ways, the most basic of which is to click and drag over the desired characters. The text continues to be selected until you click elsewhere in the document.

Formatting commands can be executed in three ways: through the Format menu, via a keyboard shortcut, or by clicking the appropriate button on the Formatting toolbar. Click the Bold or Italic buttons, for example, to change the selected text to **bold**, or *italic*, respectively. The selected text is affected by any subsequent operation. Thus you can select the text, click the Bold button, then click the Italic button to create ***bold italic***. Each command functions as a toggle switch. Click the button once to enable the effect, and then click the button a second time to cancel the effect. Each button also has a corresponding keyboard shortcut, Ctrl+B and Ctrl+I, respectively.

The Formatting toolbar also contains the Font and Font Size list boxes to change to a different font (typeface) and/or change the type size. You can also change the color of text and/or highlight text using the appropriate tool. Formatting should be done in moderation, however, or else it will lose its effectiveness.

Some formatting commands apply to the paragraph as a whole, even if the entire paragraph is not selected. You can, for example, click anywhere within a paragraph, then use the center, left-align, right-align, or justify buttons to change the alignment of the entire paragraph. The line spacing and border tools work the same way; that is, click anywhere within a paragraph, and the selected line spacing and border is applied to the entire paragraph. Figure 1.8 displays a document to illustrate different formatting options.

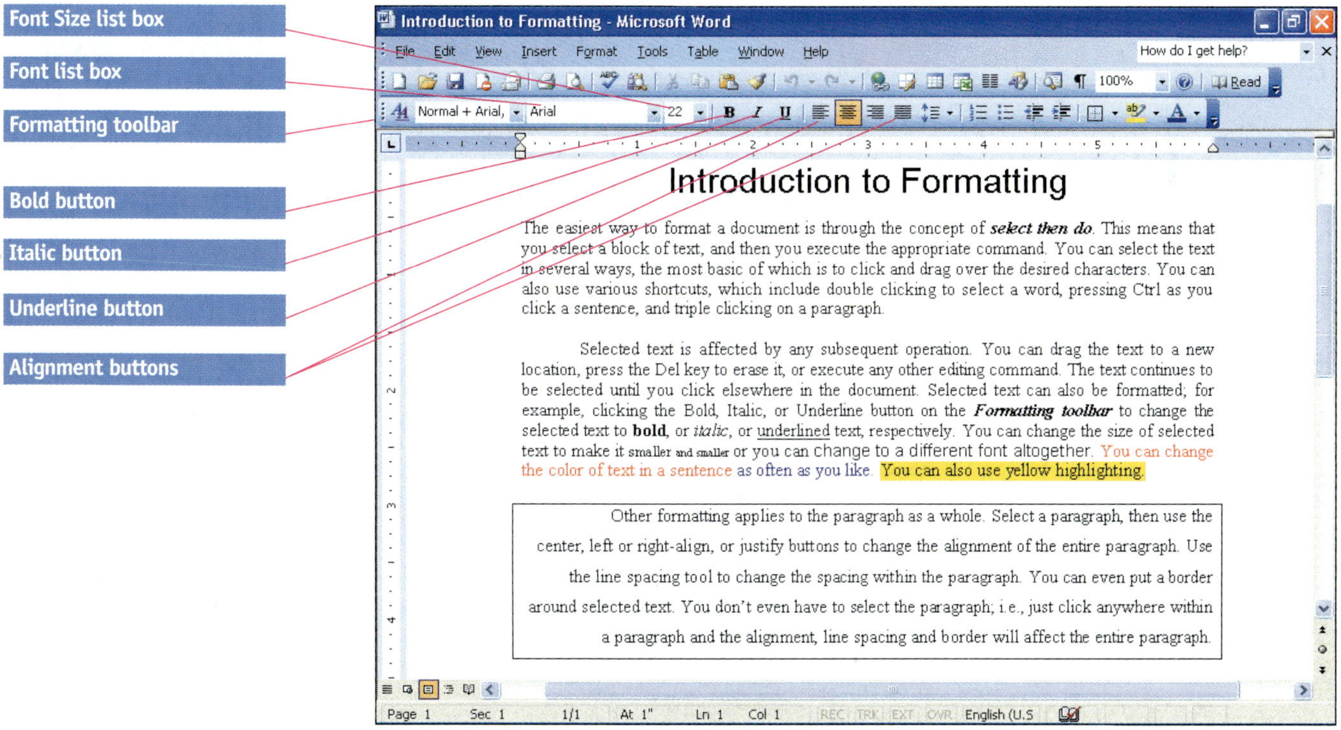

FIGURE 1.8 Introduction to Formatting

hands-on exercise

2 Modify an Existing Document

Objective To open an existing document, revise it, and save the revision; to apply basic formatting. Use Figure 1.9 as a guide in doing the exercise.

Step 1: Open an Existing Document

- Start Word. If necessary, pull down the **View menu** and click the **Task Pane command** to display the task pane.
- Click the **Home icon** in the task pane to display the most recently opened documents. Click the link to **My First Document** if it is available. (The task pane closes automatically when the document opens.)
- If you do not see the file, click the link to **More** documents to display the Open dialog box as shown in Figure 1.9a. (You can also click the **Open button** on the Standard toolbar or pull down the **File menu** and click the **Open command**.)
- If necessary, click the **drop-down arrow** on the Views button and change to the Details view. Click and drag the vertical border between columns to increase (decrease) the size of a column.
- Click the **drop-down arrow** on the Look In list box. Select (click) the drive that contains the Exploring Word folder. Double click the folder to open it.
- Click the **down arrow** on the vertical scroll bar until you can select **My First Document** from the previous exercise.
- Double click the document (or click the **Open button** within the dialog box). Your document should appear on the screen.

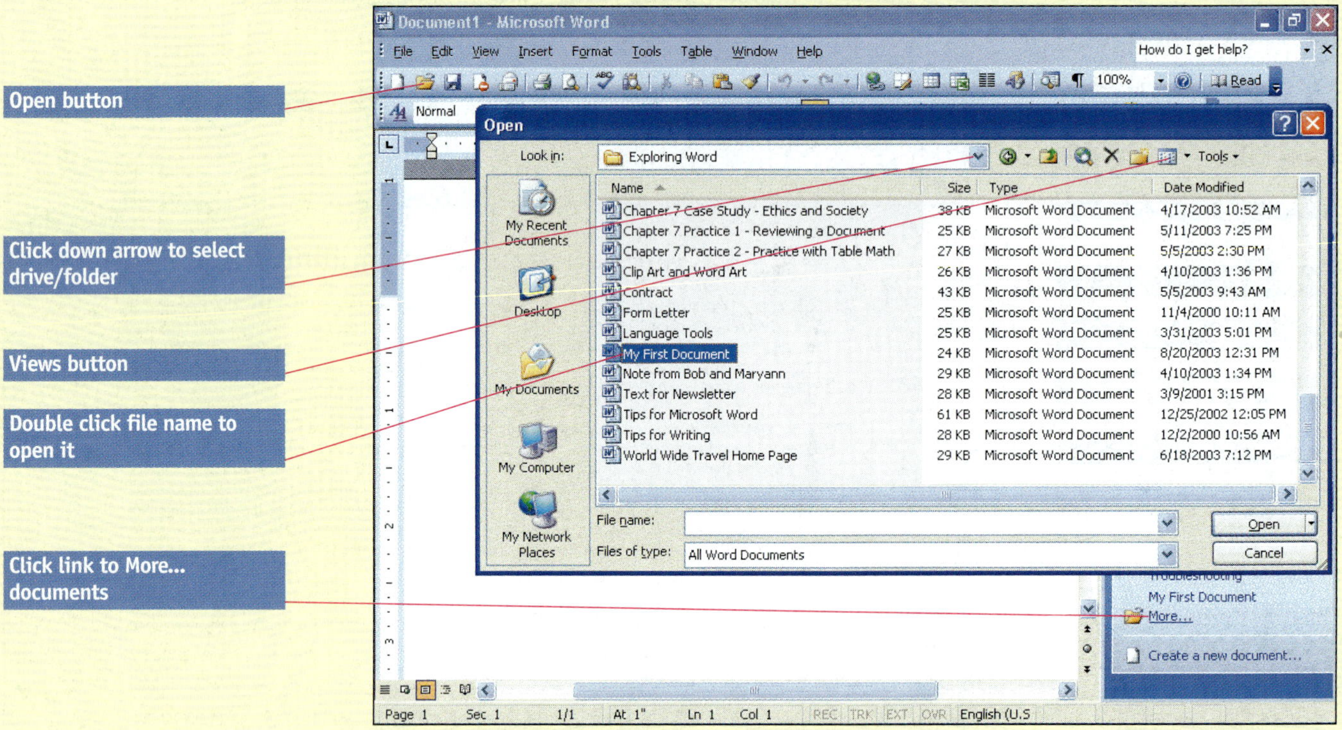

(a) Open an Existing Document (step 1)

FIGURE 1.9 Hands-on Exercise 2

Step 2: Troubleshooting

- Modify the settings within Word so that the document on your screen matches Figure 1.9b.
  - To separate the Standard and Formatting toolbars, pull down the **Tools menu**, click **Customize**, click the **Options tab**, then check the box that indicates the Standard and Formatting toolbars should be displayed on two rows. Click the **Close button**.
  - To display the complete menus, pull down the **Tools menu**, click **Customize**, click the **Options tab**, then check the box to always show full menus. Click the **Close button**.
  - To change to the Normal view, pull down the **View menu** and click **Normal** (or click the **Normal View button** at the bottom of the window).
  - To change the amount of text on the screen, click the **drop-down arrow** on the **Zoom box** on the Standard toolbar and select **Page Width**.
- Click the **Show/Hide ¶ button** to display or hide the hard returns as you see fit.
- There may still be subtle differences between your screen and ours, depending on the resolution of your monitor. These variations, if any, need not concern you as long as you are able to complete the exercise.

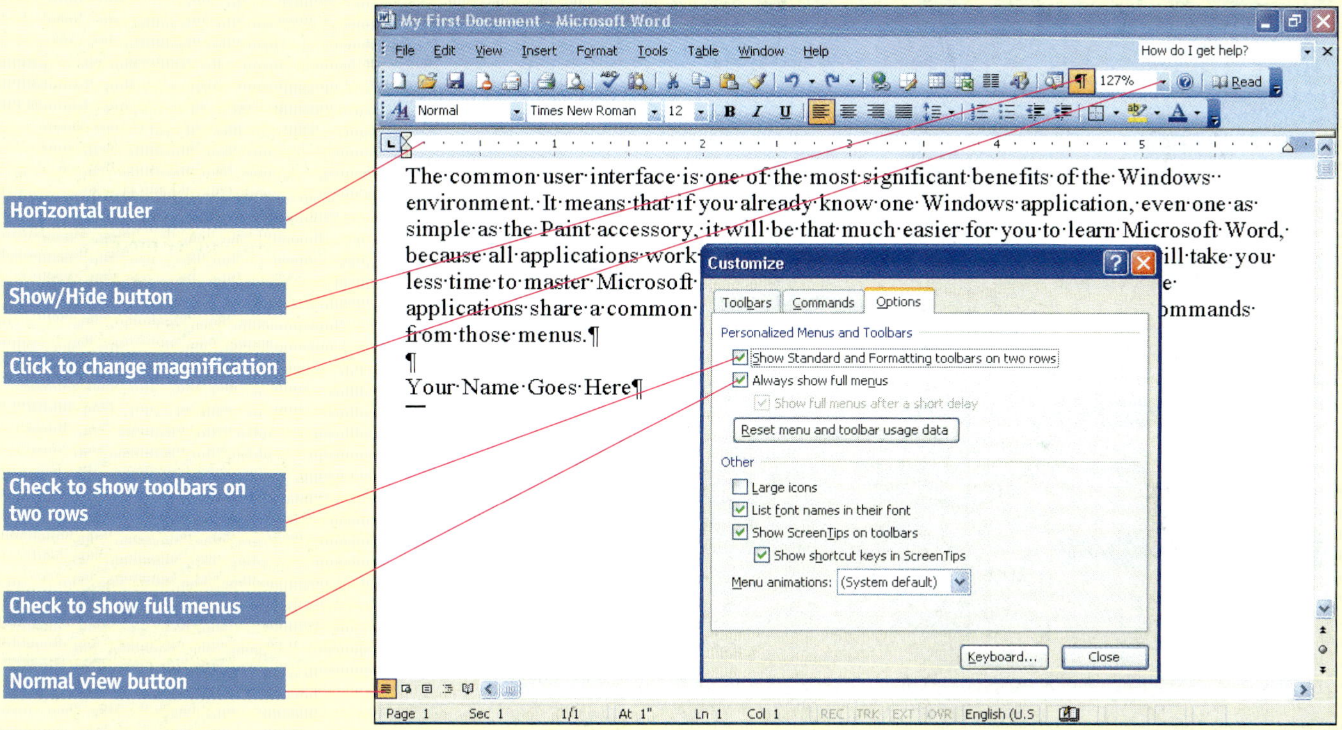

(b) Troubleshooting (step 2)

FIGURE 1.9 Hands-on Exercise 2 *(continued)*

ABOUT MICROSOFT WORD

Pull down the Help menu and click About Microsoft Word to display the specific release number and other licensing information including the Product ID. This help screen also contains two very useful command buttons, System Information and Technical support. The first button displays information about the hardware installed on your system, including the amount of memory and available space on the hard drive.

Step 3: Modify the Document

- Press **Ctrl+End** to move to the end of the document. Press the **up arrow key** once or twice until the insertion point is on a blank line above your name. If necessary, press the **Enter key** once (or twice) to add additional blank line(s).
- Add the sentence, **Success, I can save and retrieve a document!**, as shown in Figure 1.9c.
- Make the following additional modifications to practice editing:
  - ❑ Change the phrase *most significant* to **very best**.
  - ❑ Change *Paint accessory* to **game of Solitaire**.
  - ❑ Change the word *select* to **choose**.
- Use the **Ins key** to switch between insert and overtype modes as necessary. (You can also double click the **OVR indicator** on the status bar to toggle between the insert and overtype modes.)
- Pull down the **File menu** and click **Save**, or click the **Save button** to save the document. (You should do this frequently during every session.)

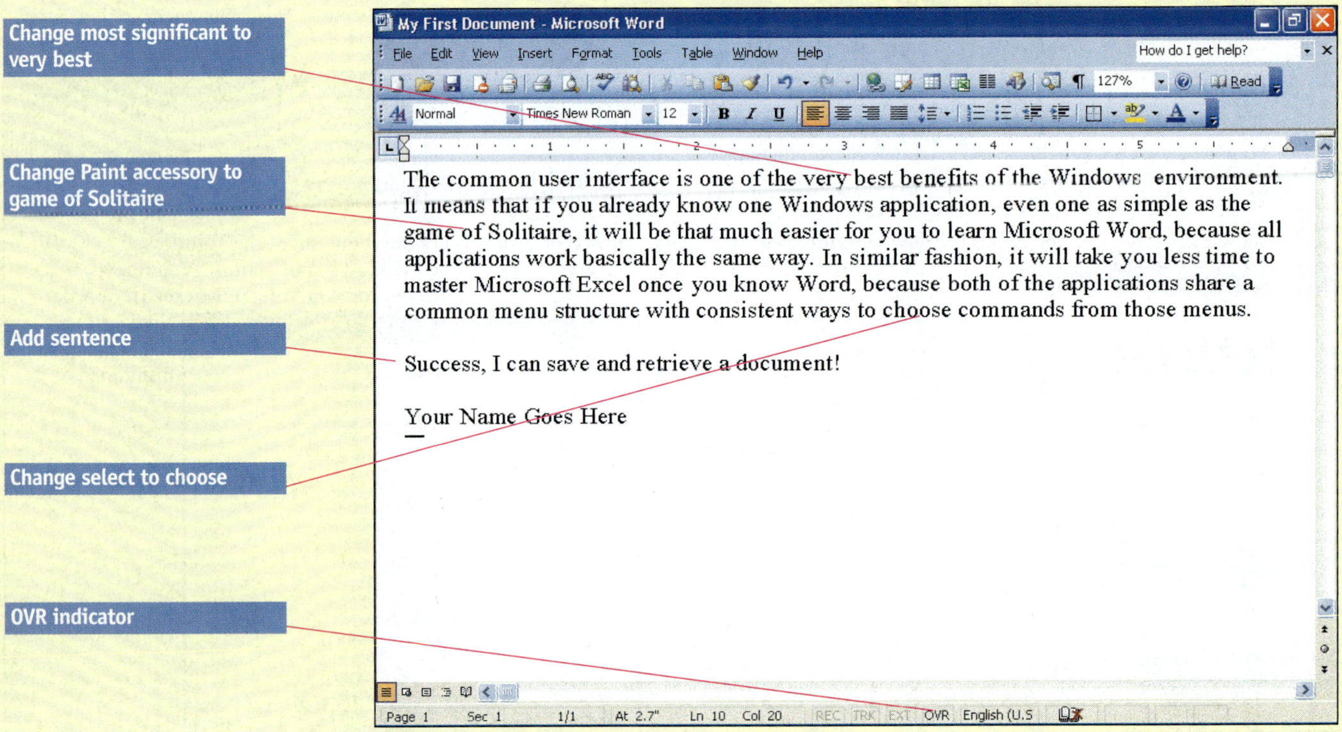

(c) Modify the Document (step 3)

FIGURE 1.9 Hands-on Exercise 2 (*continued*)

MOVING WITHIN A DOCUMENT

Press Ctrl+Home and Ctrl+End to move to the beginning and end of a document, respectively. You can also press the Home or End key to move to the beginning or end of a line. These shortcuts work not just in Word, but in any other Office application, and are worth remembering as they allow your hands to remain on the keyboard as you type.

Step 4: The Undo and Redo Commands

- Press and hold the left mouse button as you drag the mouse over the phrase, **even one as simple as the game of Solitaire**, as shown in Figure 1.9d.
- Press the **Del key** to delete the selected text from the document. Pull down the **Edit menu** and click the **Undo command** (or click the **Undo button** on the Standard toolbar) to reverse (undo) the last command. The deleted text should be returned to your document.
- Pull down the **Edit menu** a second time and click the **Redo command** (or click the **Redo button**) to repeat the Delete command.
- Try this simple experiment. Click the **Undo button** repeatedly to undo the commands one at a time, until you have effectively canceled the entire session. Now click the **Redo command** repeatedly, one command at a time, until you have put the entire document back together.
- Click the **Save button** on the Standard toolbar to save the revised document a final time.

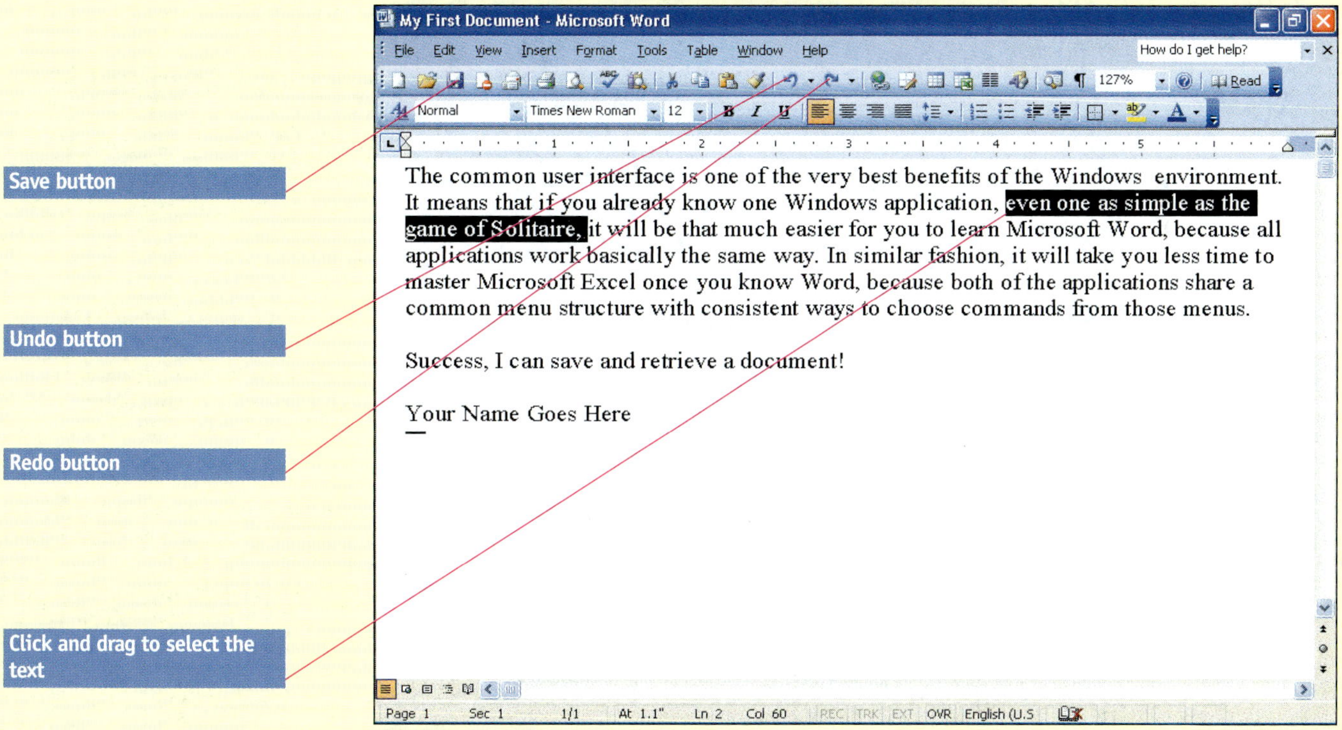

(d) The Undo and Redo Commands (step 4)

FIGURE 1.9 Hands-on Exercise 2 (*continued*)

THE UNDO AND REDO COMMANDS

Click the drop-down arrow next to the Undo button to display a list of your previous actions, then click the action you want to undo, which also undoes all of the preceding commands. Undoing the fifth command in the list, for example, will also undo the preceding four commands. The Redo command works in reverse and cancels the last Undo command.

Step 5: Format the Document

- Click and drag to select the phrase **common user interface** in the first paragraph.
- Click the **Bold button** on the Formatting toolbar (or press **Ctrl+B**) to change to bold. Click the **Italic button** (or press **Ctrl+I**) to change to italic.
- Press **Ctrl+Home** to move to the beginning of the document. Press the **Enter key** twice to add two blank lines at the top of the document. Enter **My First Document** on the first blank line as the title of the document.
- Click and drag to select the title. Click the down arrow on the **Font size box** and choose **24**. Click the **Center button** to center the title.
- Click at the end of the second paragraph to add the text shown in Figure 1.9e.
- Click and drag to select the various words and phrases in the second paragraph, and then implement the indicated formatting by clicking the appropriate button on the Formatting toolbar. (You can click the **Undo command** any time the result is not what you intended it to be.)
- Click anywhere in the second paragraph and click the **Align Right button** to change the alignment (see boxed tip below). Save the document.

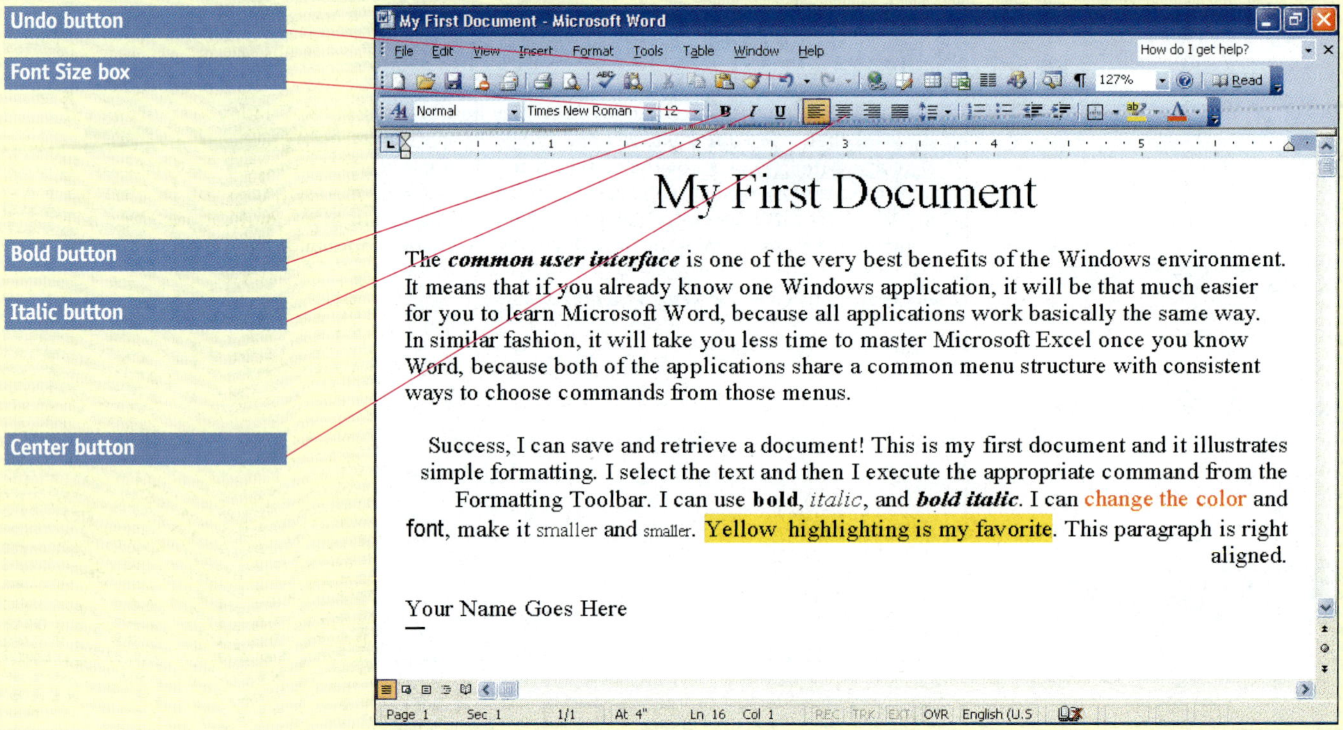

(e) Format the Document (step 5)

FIGURE 1.9 Hands-on Exercise 2 (*continued*)

FORMATTING AT THE PARAGRAPH LEVEL

Line spacing, alignment, and justification take place at the paragraph level and affect the entire paragraph even if the paragraph is not selected. In other words, you can execute these commands by clicking anywhere within the paragraph, then clicking the appropriate button on the Formatting toolbar. Formatting at the character level, however (font, type size, style or color), affects only the selected text.

Step 6: Print the Document

- Click the **Print button** on the Standard toolbar to print the completed document and submit it to your instructor. The document should print immediately, without displaying the Print dialog box.
- Pull down the **File menu** and click the **Print command** to display the Print dialog box shown in Figure 1.9f. The dialog box enables you to select additional options prior to printing:
  - The Printer Name lets you select a printer, which becomes important if you have more than one printer available to you—for example, a high-speed black-and-white network printer and an inkjet color printer.
  - The Print range gives you the option to print the entire document, the current page, or selected pages in a multipage document. Our document has only one page, so the option is not relevant here, but it becomes important as you create more complex documents.
  - The Number of copies lets you print more than one copy at a time.
- Click **OK** to print the document a second time to keep a copy for yourself.
- Pull down the **File menu** and close the document. Exit Word if you do not want to proceed with the next exercise at this time.

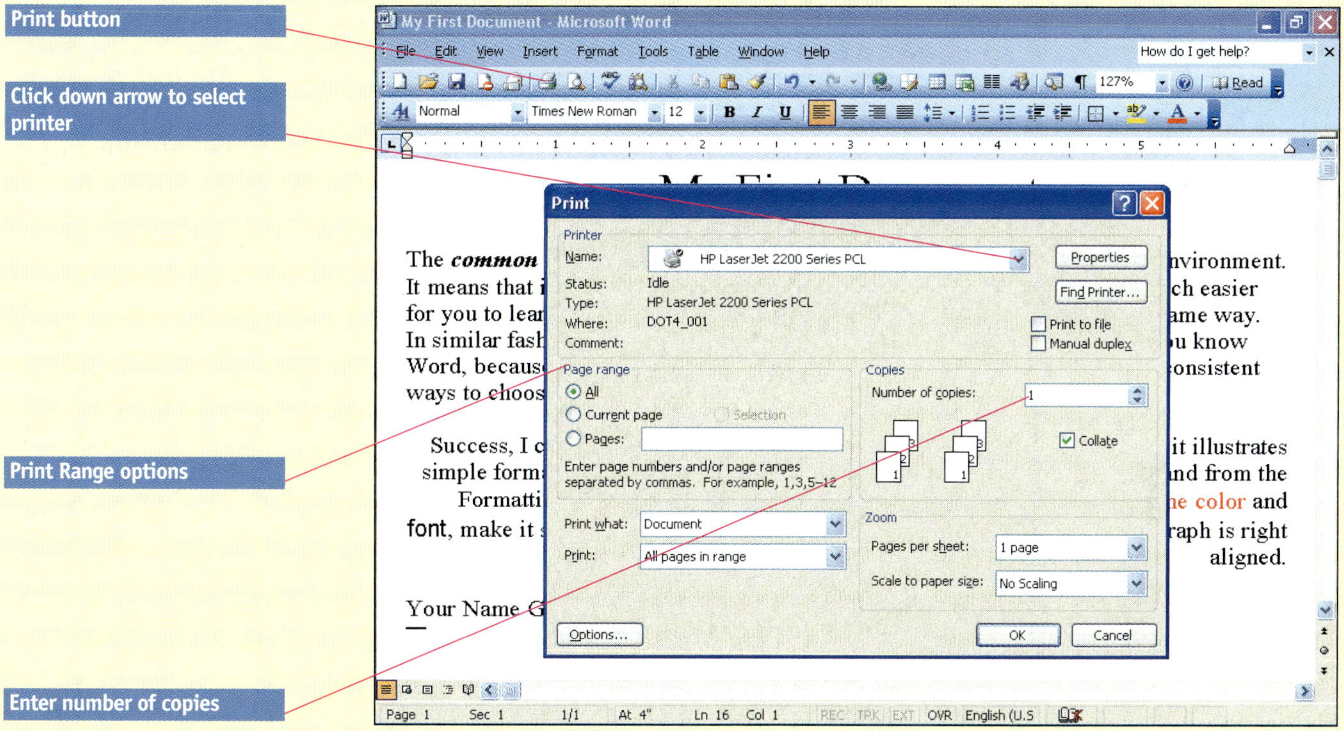

(f) Print the Document (step 6)

FIGURE 1.9 Hands-on Exercise 2 (*continued*)

DOCUMENT PROPERTIES

Prove to your instructor how hard you have worked by printing various statistics about your document, including the number of revisions and the total editing time. Pull down the File menu, click the Print command to display the Print dialog box, click the drop-down arrow in the Print What list box, select Document properties, and click OK. You can view the information (without printing) by pulling down the File menu, clicking the Properties command, and then selecting the Statistics tab.

THE SPELL CHECK

There is simply no excuse to misspell a word, since the ***spell check*** is an integral part of Microsoft Word. (The spell check is also available for every other application in the Microsoft Office.) Spelling errors make your work look sloppy and discourage the reader before he or she has read what you had to say. They can cost you a job, a grade, a lucrative contract, or an award you deserve.

The spell check can be set to automatically check a document as text is entered, or it can be called explicitly by clicking the Spelling and Grammar button on the Standard toolbar. The spell check compares each word in a document to the entries in a built-in dictionary, then flags any word that is in the document, but not in the built-in dictionary, as an error.

The dictionary included with Microsoft Office is limited to standard English and omits many proper names, acronyms, abbreviations, or specialized terms. You can, however, add such words to a ***custom dictionary*** so that they will not be flagged in the future. The spell check will inform you of repeated words and irregular capitalization. It cannot, however, flag properly spelled words that are used improperly, and thus cannot tell you that *Two be or knot to be* is not the answer.

The capabilities of the spell check are illustrated in conjunction with Figure 1.10a. Microsoft Word will indicate the errors as you type by underlining them in red. Alternatively, you can click the Spelling and Grammar button on the Standard toolbar at any time to move through the entire document. The spell check will then go through the document and return the errors one at a time, offering several options for each mistake. You can change the misspelled word to one of the alternatives suggested by Word, leave the word as is, or add the word to a custom dictionary.

The first error is the word *embarassing,* with Word's suggestion(s) for correction displayed in the list box in Figure 1.10b. To accept the highlighted suggestion, click the Change command button, and the substitution will be made automatically in the document. To accept an alternative suggestion, click the desired word, then click the Change command button. Alternatively, you can click the AutoCorrect button to correct the mistake in the current document, and, in addition, automatically correct the same mistake in any future document.

The spell check detects both irregular capitalization and duplicated words, as shown in Figures 1.10c and 1.10d, respectively. The last error, *Marder,* is not a misspelling per se, but a proper noun not found in the standard dictionary. No correction is required, and the appropriate action is to ignore the word (taking no further action)—or better yet, add it to the custom dictionary so that it will not be flagged in future sessions.

The purple dotted line under "Bernard Marder" indicates a ***smart tag***, such as a person's name. A Smart Tag Actions button will appear in the document when you point to the underlined text; click the button to see the list of actions, such as send an e-mail message using Microsoft Outlook.

A spell check will catch embarassing mistakes, iRregular capitalization, and duplicate words words. It will recognize many first names as smart tags, but last names are often flagged as a misspelling; e.g., Bernard Marder. The latter can be added to a custom dictionary so that it will not be flagged in the future. The spell check will not notice properly spelled words that are used incorrectly; for example, too bee or knot to be is not the answer.

(a) The Text

FIGURE 1.10 The Spell Check

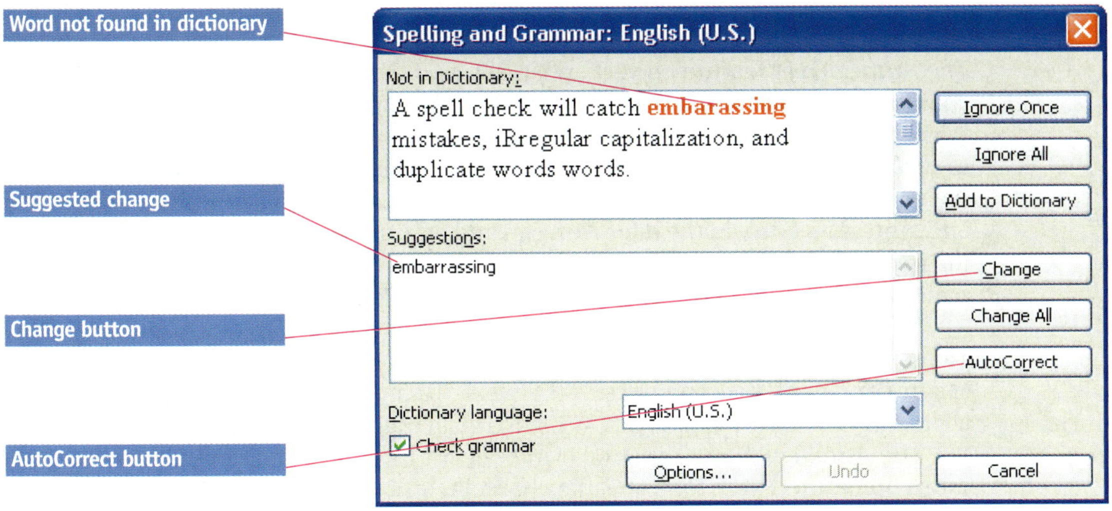

(b) Ordinary Misspelling

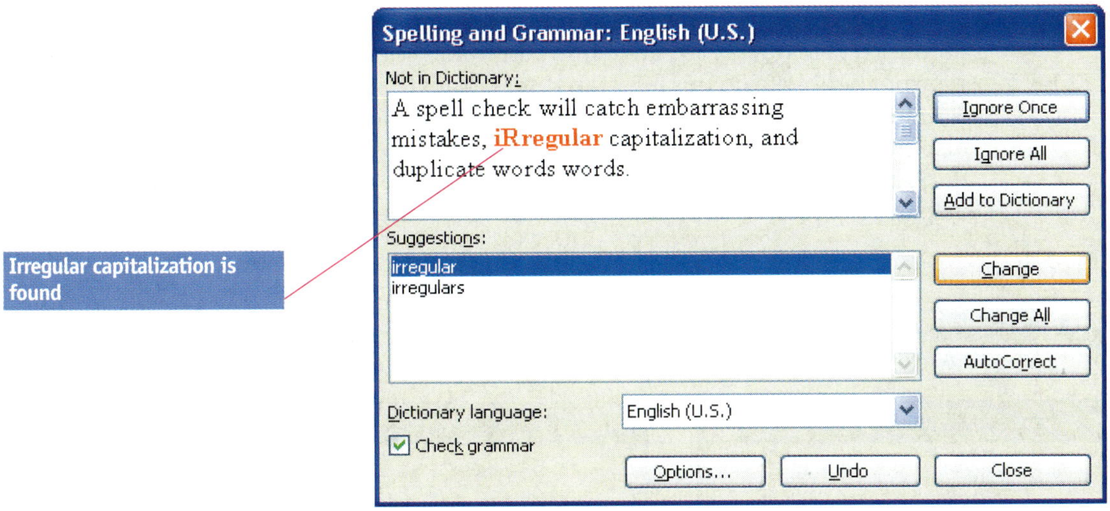

(c) Irregular Capitalization

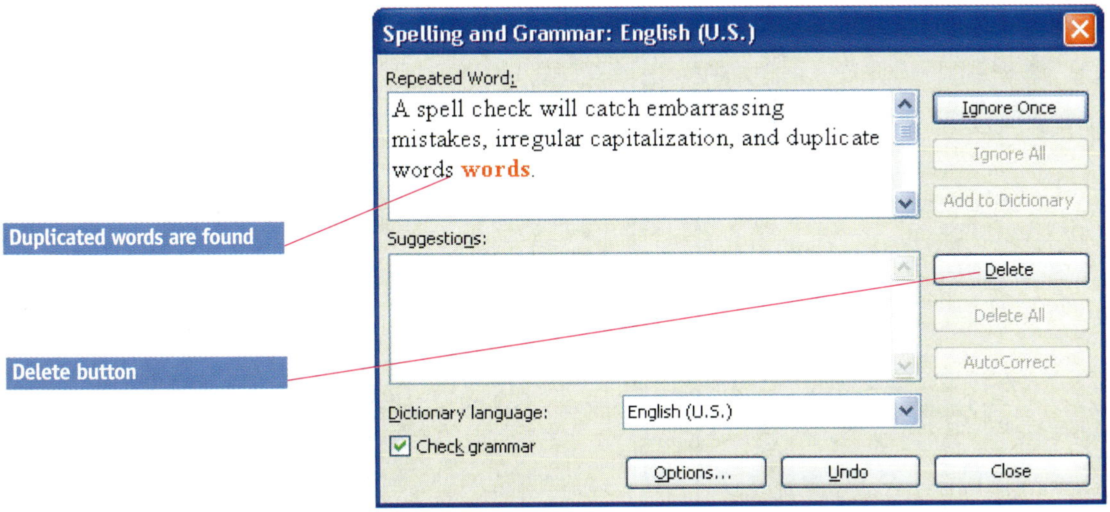

(d) Duplicated Word

FIGURE 1.10 The Spell Check (*continued*)

AutoCorrect and AutoText

The ***AutoCorrect*** feature corrects mistakes as they are made without any effort on your part. It makes you a better typist. If, for example, you typed *teh* instead of *the,* Word would change the spelling without even telling you. Word will also change *adn* to *and, i* to *I,* and occurence to occurrence. All of this is accomplished through a predefined table of common mistakes that Word uses to make substitutions whenever it encounters an entry in the table. You can add additional items to the table to include the frequent errors you make. You can also use the feature to define your own shorthand—for example, cis for Computer Information Systems as shown in Figure 1.11a.

The AutoCorrect feature will also correct mistakes in capitalization; for example, it will capitalize the first letter in a sentence, recognize that MIami should be Miami, and capitalize the days of the week. It's even smart enough to correct the accidental use of the Caps Lock key, and it will toggle the key off!

The ***AutoText*** feature is similar in concept to AutoCorrect in that both substitute a predefined item for a specific character string. The difference is that the substitution occurs automatically with the AutoCorrect entry, whereas you have to take deliberate action for the AutoText substitution to take place. AutoText entries can also include significantly more text, formatting, and even clip art.

Microsoft Word includes a host of predefined AutoText entries. And as with the AutoCorrect feature, you can define additional entries of your own. (You may, however, not be able to do this in a computer lab environment.) The entry in Figure 1.11b is named "Signature" and once created, it is available to all Word documents. To insert an AutoText entry into a new document, just type the first several letters in the AutoText name (Signature in our example), then press the Enter key when Word displays a ScreenTip containing the text of the entry.

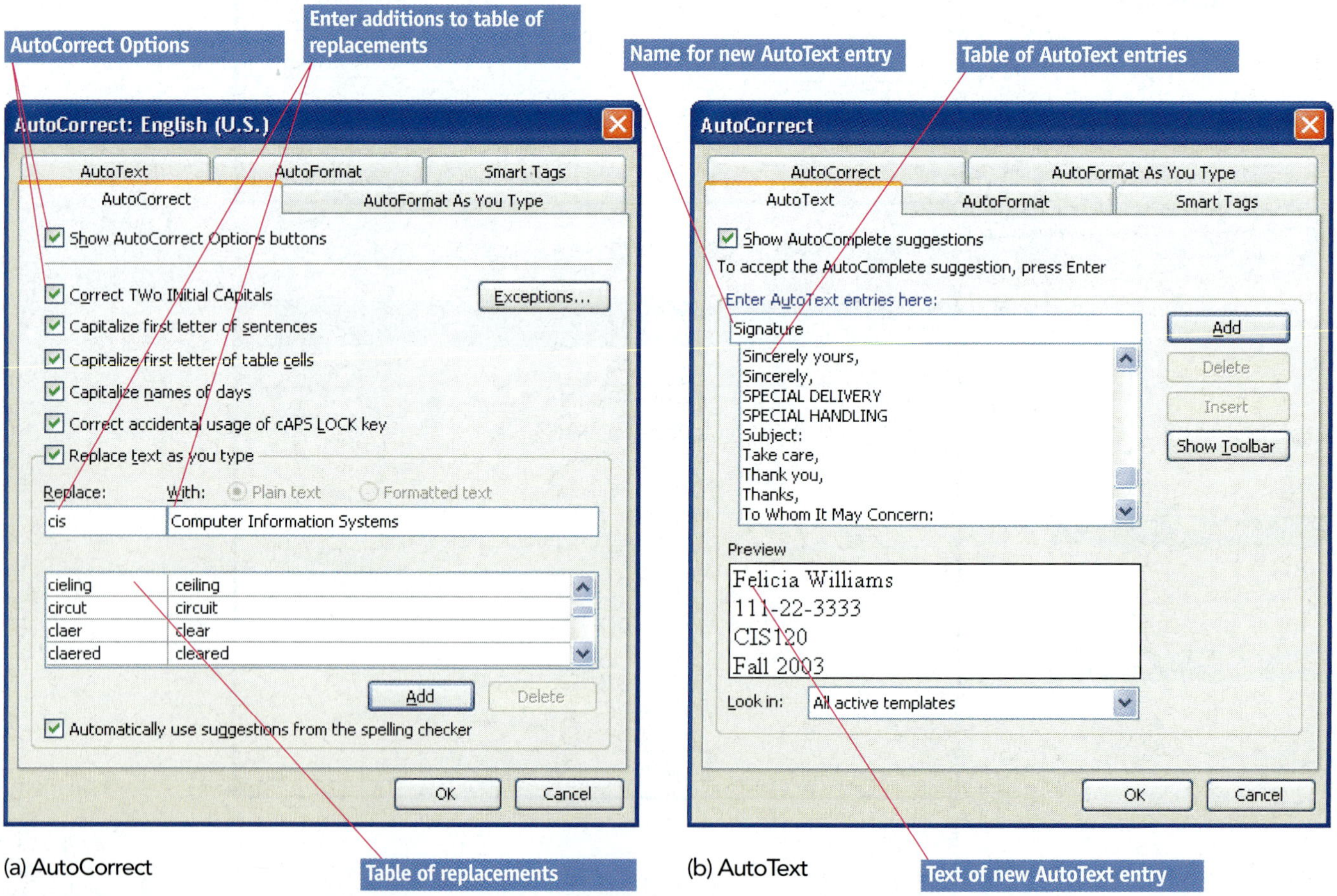

(a) AutoCorrect (b) AutoText

FIGURE 1.11 AutoCorrect and AutoText

THESAURUS

The ***thesaurus*** helps you to avoid repetition and polish your writing. The thesaurus is called from the Language command in the Tools menu and displays its results in the task pane. You position the cursor at the appropriate word within the document, then invoke the thesaurus and follow your instincts. The thesaurus recognizes multiple meanings and forms of a word (for example, adjective, noun, and verb). You can explore further alternatives by selecting a synonym and looking it up to provide additional choices.

GRAMMAR CHECK

The ***grammar check*** attempts to catch mistakes in punctuation, writing style, and word usage by comparing strings of text within a document to a series of predefined rules. As with the spell check, errors are brought to the screen, where you can accept the suggested correction and make the replacement automatically, or more often, edit the selected text and make your own changes.

You can also ask the grammar check to explain the rule it is attempting to enforce. Unlike the spell check, the grammar check is subjective, and what seems appropriate to you may be objectionable to someone else. Indeed, the grammar check is quite flexible, and can be set to check for different writing styles; that is, you can implement one set of rules to check a business letter and a different set of rules for casual writing.

Many times, however, you will find that the English language is just too complex for the grammar check to detect every error, although it will find many errors. The grammar check missed the error "no perfect" in Figure 1.12 (although it did catch "to" instead of "too"). Suffice it to say, there is no substitute for carefully proofreading every document.

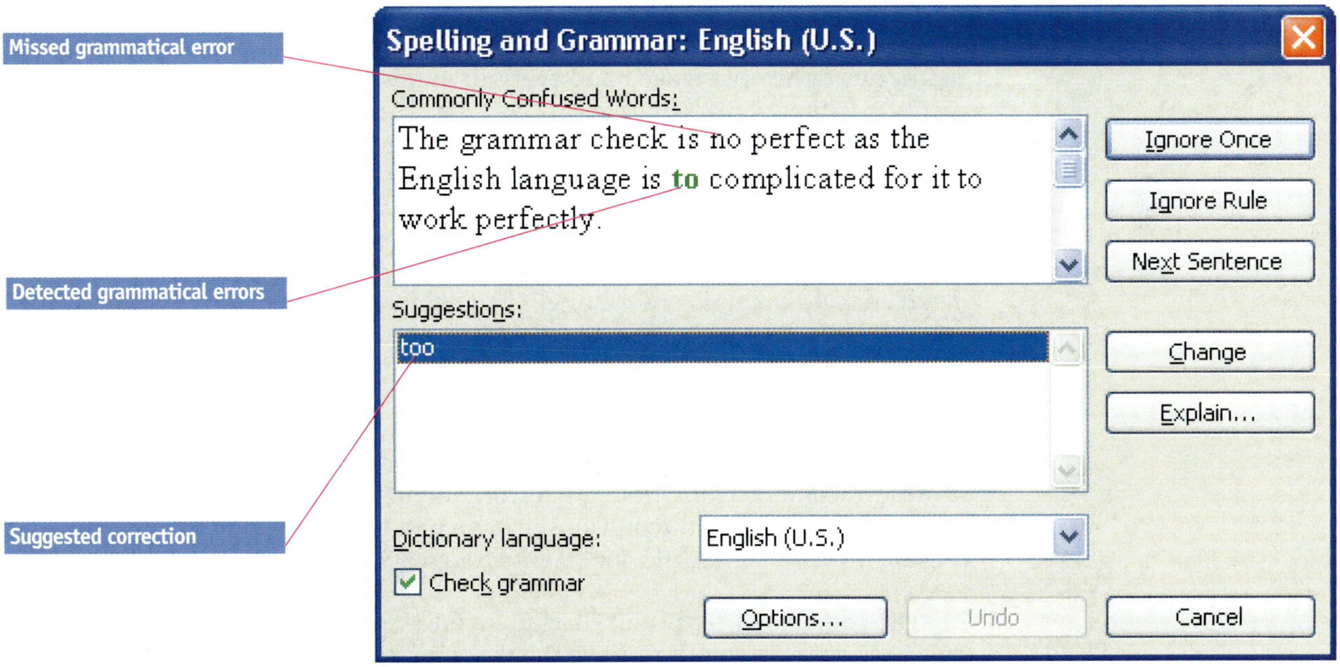

FIGURE 1.12 The Grammar Check

SAVE AS COMMAND

The Save command was used in the first two exercises. The Save As command will be introduced in the next exercise as a very useful alternative. We also introduce you to different backup options. We believe that now, when you are first starting to learn about word processing, is the time to develop good working habits.

You already know that the Save command copies the document currently being edited (the document in memory) to disk. The initial execution of the command requires you to assign a file name and to specify the drive and folder in which the file is to be stored. All subsequent executions of the Save command save the document under the original name, replacing the previously saved version with the new one.

The ***Save As command*** saves another copy of a document under a different name (and/or a different file type), and is useful when you want to retain a copy of the original document. The Save As command provides you with two copies of a document. The original document is kept on disk under its original name. A copy of the document is saved on disk under a new name and remains in memory. All subsequent editing is done on the new document.

We cannot overemphasize the importance of periodically saving a document, so that if something does go wrong, you won't lose all of your work. Nothing is more frustrating than to lose two hours of effort, due to an unexpected program crash or to a temporary loss of power. Save your work frequently, at least once every 15 minutes. Pull down the File menu and click Save, or click the Save button on the Standard toolbar. Do it!

Backup Options

Microsoft Word offers several different ***backup*** options, the most important of which is to save ***autorecovery information*** periodically. If Microsoft Word were to crash (and it will), the program will still be able to recover a previous version of your document when Word is restarted. The only work you will lose is anything you did between the time of the last autorecovery operation and the time of the crash. Set the autorecovery to take place every 10 minutes, and you will never lose more than 10 minutes of work.

You can also set Word to create a backup copy in conjunction with every Save command as shown in Figure 1.13. Assume, for example, that you have created the simple document, *The fox jumped over the fence,* and saved it under the name "Fox". Assume further that you edit the document to read, *The quick brown fox jumped over the fence,* and that you saved it a second time. The second Save command changes the name of the original document from "Fox" to "Backup of Fox", then saves the current contents of memory as "Fox". In other words, the disk now contains two versions of the document: the current version "Fox" and the most recent previous version "Backup of Fox".

The cycle goes on indefinitely, with "Fox" always containing the current version, and "Backup of Fox" the most recent previous version. Thus if you revise and save the document a third time, "Fox" will contain the latest revision while "Backup of Fox" would contain the previous version alluding to the quick brown fox. The original (first) version of the document disappears entirely since only two versions are kept.

The contents of "Fox" and "Backup of Fox" are different, but the existence of the latter enables you to retrieve the previous version if you inadvertently edit beyond repair or accidentally erase the current "Fox" version. Should this occur (and it will), you can always retrieve its predecessor and at least salvage your work prior to the last save operation.

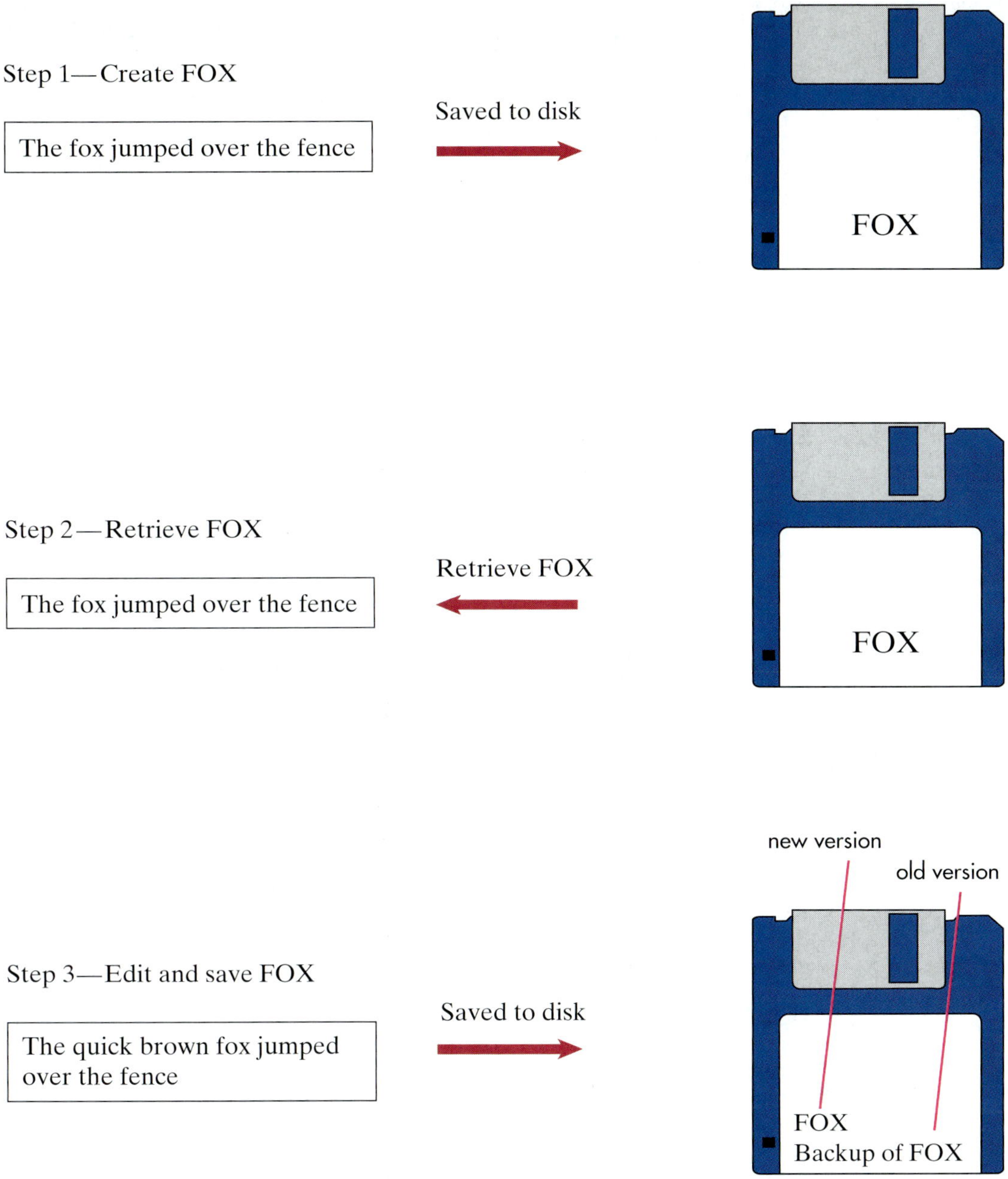

FIGURE 1.13 Backup Procedures

BACK UP YOUR WORK

It's not a question of *if* it will happen but *when*. Files are lost, systems crash, and viruses infect a system. That said, we cannot overemphasize the importance of adequate backup and urge you to back up your important files at every opportunity. Exit Word, start Windows Explorer, then copy the document from drive C to a floppy disk. If the document is too large, you can compress the file before you copy it, and/or you can burn a CD. You can also e-mail the document to yourself as an attachment. You can always get another copy of Microsoft Office, but you are the only one with a copy of the term paper due tomorrow.

hands-on exercise

3 Spell Check, Thesaurus, and Grammar Check

Objective To check a document for spelling and grammar; to use the thesaurus and practice formatting. Use Figure 1.14 as a guide in the exercise.

Step 1: The Save As Command

- Start Word. Open the **Language Tools** document in the **Exploring Word folder**. Pull down the **File menu**. Click the **Save As command** to display the dialog box in Figure 1.14a. Click the **Views button** to change to the Details view.
- Enter **Language Tools Solution** as the name of the new document. (A file name may contain up to 255 characters, and spaces are permitted.) Click the **Save button**.
- There are now two identical copies of the file on disk—**Language Tools**, which we supplied, and **Language Tools Solution** that you just created.
- The title bar displays the name of the latter document (Language Tools Solution) as it is the document currently in memory. All subsequent changes will be made to this version.

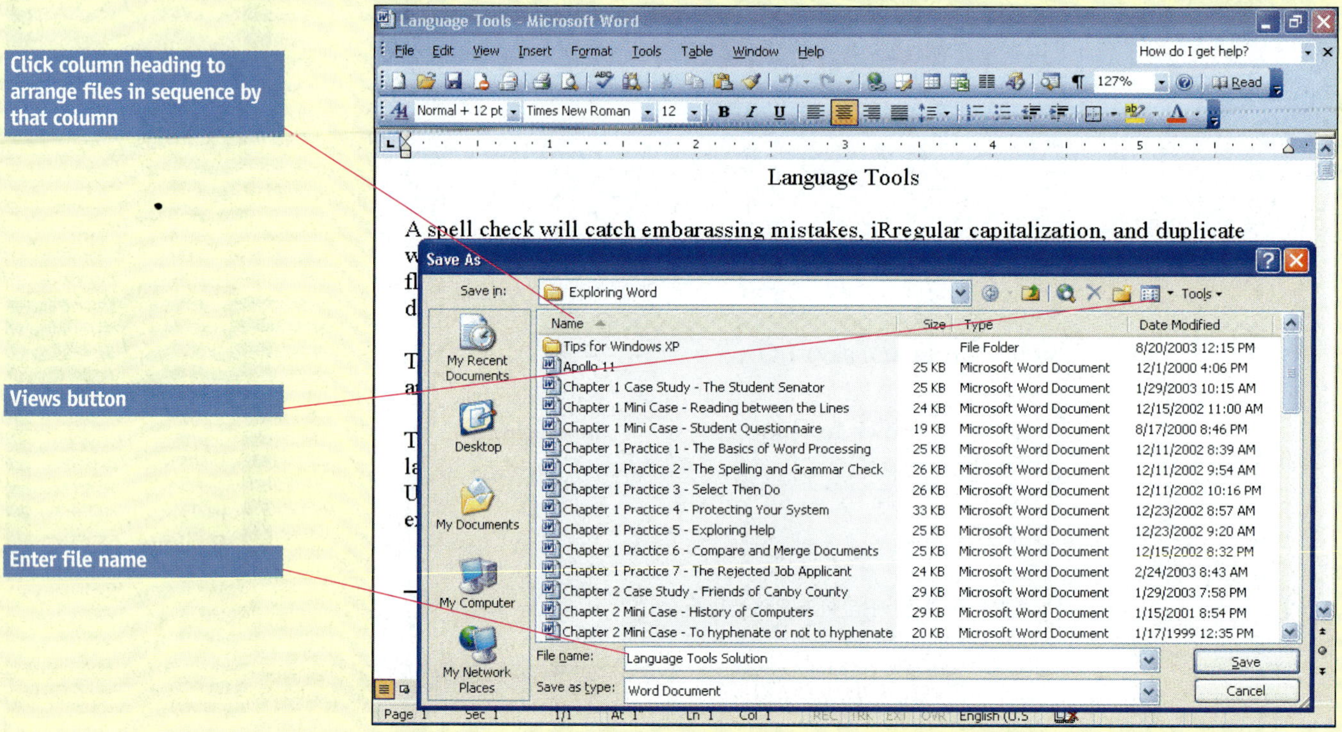

(a) The Save As Command (step 1)

FIGURE 1.14 Hands-on Exercise 3

CHANGE THE FILE TYPE

Any document created in Microsoft Word is stored in a unique file format that is not understood by other word processors. You can, however, take the document with you by changing its file type although you will lose some or all of the formatting within the document. Pull down the File menu, click the Save As command, click the down arrow in the Save as Type list box and choose a different format such as Rich Text (also known as "rtf") or Plain Text (known as "txt").

Step 2: The Spell Check

- If necessary, press **Ctrl+Home** to move to the beginning of the document. Click the **Spelling and Grammar button** on the Standard toolbar to check the document.
- "Embarassing" is flagged as the first misspelling as shown in Figure 1.14b. Click the **Change button** to accept the suggested spelling.
- "iRregular" is flagged as an example of irregular capitalization. Click the **Change button** to accept the suggested correction.
- Continue checking the document, which displays misspellings and other irregularities one at a time. Click the appropriate command button as each mistake is found.
  - Click the **Delete button** to remove the duplicated word.
  - Click the **Ignore Once button** to accept Marder (or click the **Add button** to add Marder to the custom dictionary).
- The last sentence is flagged because of a grammatical error and is discussed in the next step.

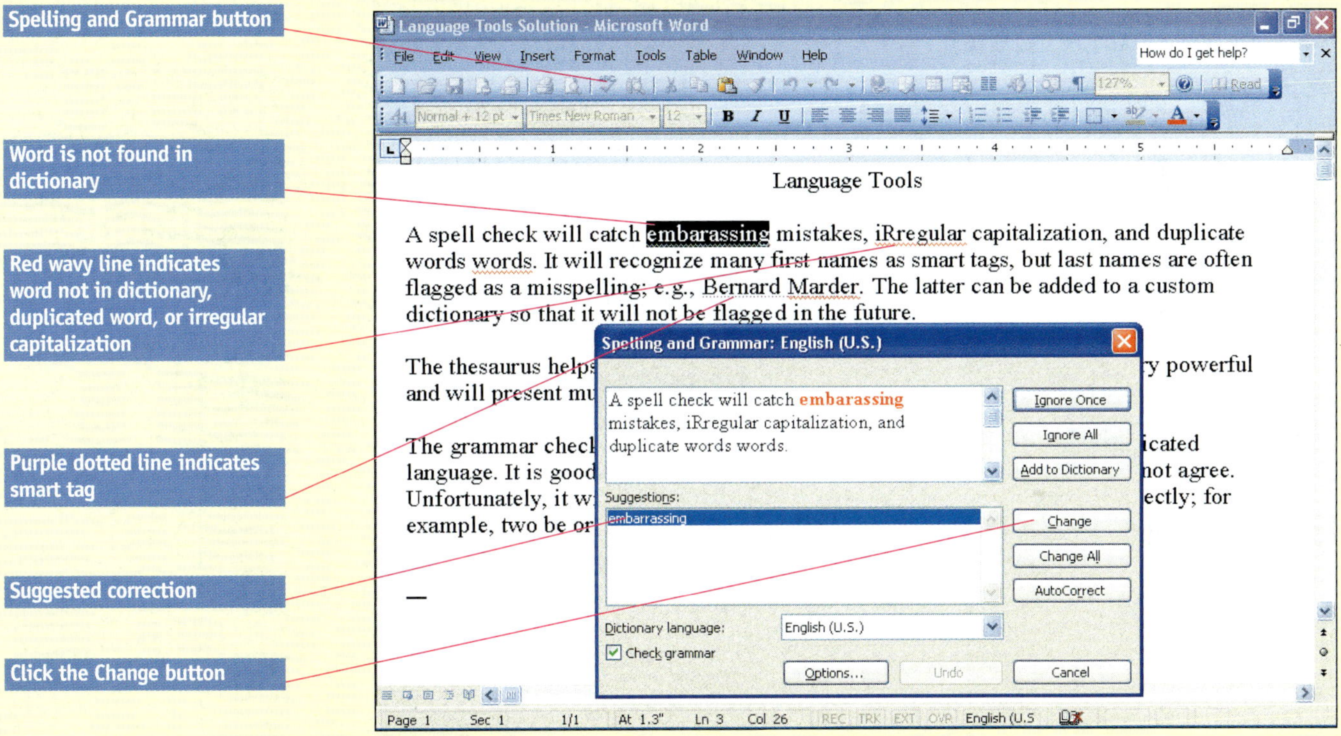

(b) The Spell Check (step 2)

FIGURE 1.14 Hands-on Exercise 3 (*continued*)

AUTOMATIC SPELLING AND GRAMMAR CHECKING

Red and green wavy lines may appear throughout a document to indicate spelling and grammatical errors, respectively. Point to any underlined word, then click the right mouse button to display a context-sensitive menu with suggested corrections. To enable (disable) these options, pull down the Tools menu, click the Options command, click the Spelling and Grammar tab, and check (clear) the options to check spelling (or grammar) as you type.

Step 3: The Grammar Check

- The phrase, "verbs and adjectives that does not agree", should be flagged as an error. If this is not the case:
  - Pull down the **Tools menu**, click **Options**, then click the **Spelling and Grammar tab**.
  - Check the box to **Check grammar** as you type, then click the button to **Recheck document**. Click **Yes** when told that the spelling and grammar check will be reset, then click **OK** to close the Options dialog box.
  - Press **Ctrl+Home** to return to the beginning of the document, then click the **Spelling and Grammar button** to recheck the document.
- Word suggests substituting "do" for "does". Click the **Change button** since this is the correct modification.
- The results are not as good in the next sentence, as can be seen in Figure 1.14c. The Grammar Check suggests substituting "are" for "be", which is not what you want. Click in the preview box and make the necessary corrections. Change "two" to "to" and "knot" to "not". Click **Change**.
- Click **OK** when you see the dialog box indicating that the spelling and grammar check is complete. Enter any additional grammatical changes manually.

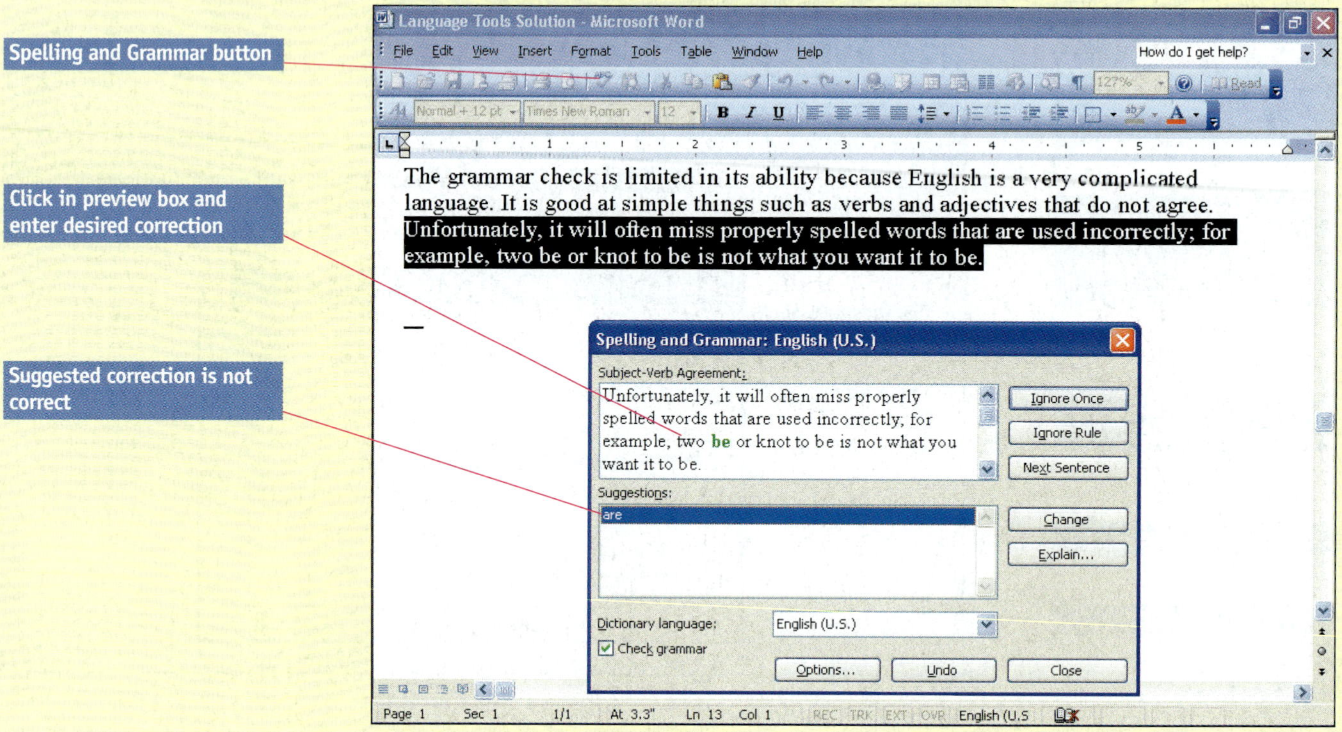

(c) The Grammar Check (step 3)

FIGURE 1.14 Hands-on Exercise 3 (*continued*)

FOREIGN LANGUAGE PROOFING TOOLS

The English version of Microsoft Word supports the spelling, grammar, and thesaurus features in more than 80 foreign languages. Support for Spanish and French is built in at no additional cost, whereas you will have to pay an additional fee for other languages. Just pull down the Tools menu and click the Select Language command to change to a different language. See practice exercise 2 at the end of the chapter.

Step 4: The Thesaurus

- Press **Ctrl+Home** to move to the beginning of the document. Select (double click) the word **"catch"** in the first sentence of the document.
- Pull down the **Tools menu**, click the **Language command** and click **Thesaurus** (or use the **Shift+F7** keyboard shortcut) to open the task pane as shown in Figure 1.14d.
- Scroll until you can click the **+ sign** next to "find (v.)", which is the same form and context for which you are seeking a synonym. The plus sign changes to a minus sign to display the list of potential changes.
- Point to the word **"spot"** and click the **down arrow** that appears to display the context-sensitive menu. Click **Insert** to replace "catch" with "spot" in the document.
- Experiment further with the thesaurus as you see fit. Close the task pane when you are finished.
- Save the document.

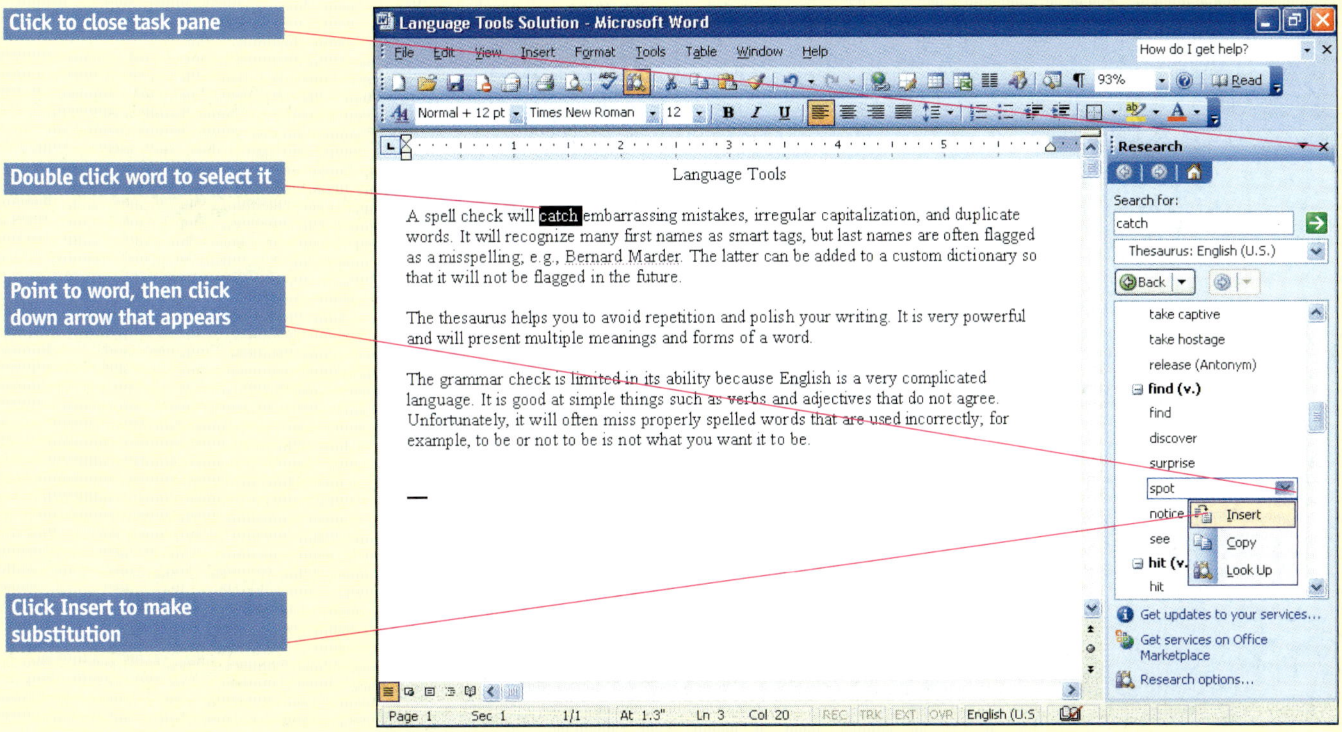

(d) The Thesaurus (step 4)

FIGURE 1.14 Hands-on Exercise 3 (*continued*)

THE RESEARCH PANE—WHAT IS TRISKAIDEKAPHOBIA?

The results of the thesaurus are displayed automatically in the Research task pane, but you can open the research pane at any time and use it to search reference materials. Pull down the Tools menu and click the Research command to display the task pane. Click in the Search for text box, type the word that you want to look up, click the down arrow to select the reference book (e.g., a dictionary, the-saurus, or encyclopedia), then click the green arrow to initiate the search. The results appear directly in the task pane. Close the task pane when you are finished. (The Research pane is a new feature in Microsoft Office Word 2003.)

Step 5: AutoCorrect

- Press **Ctrl+End** to move to the end of the document. Press the **Enter key** twice.
- Type the *misspelled* phrase, **Teh AutoCorrect feature corrects common spelling mistakes**. Word will automatically change "Teh" to "The".
- Press the **Home key** to return to the beginning of the line, where you will notice a blue line under the "T", indicating that an automatic correction has taken place. Point to the blue line, then click the **down arrow** to display the AutoCorrect options.
- Click the command to **Control AutoCorrect options**, which in turn displays the dialog box in Figure 1.14e. Click the **AutoCorrect tab**, then click the **down arrow** on the scroll bar to view the list of corrections. Close the dialog box.
- Add the sentence, **The feature also changes special symbols such as :) to ☺ to indicate I understand my work**.
- You need to restore the first :) rather than have it appear as a smiley face. Thus, point to the first ☺, point to the blue line, then click the down arrow to change the ☺ back to :).
- Save the document.

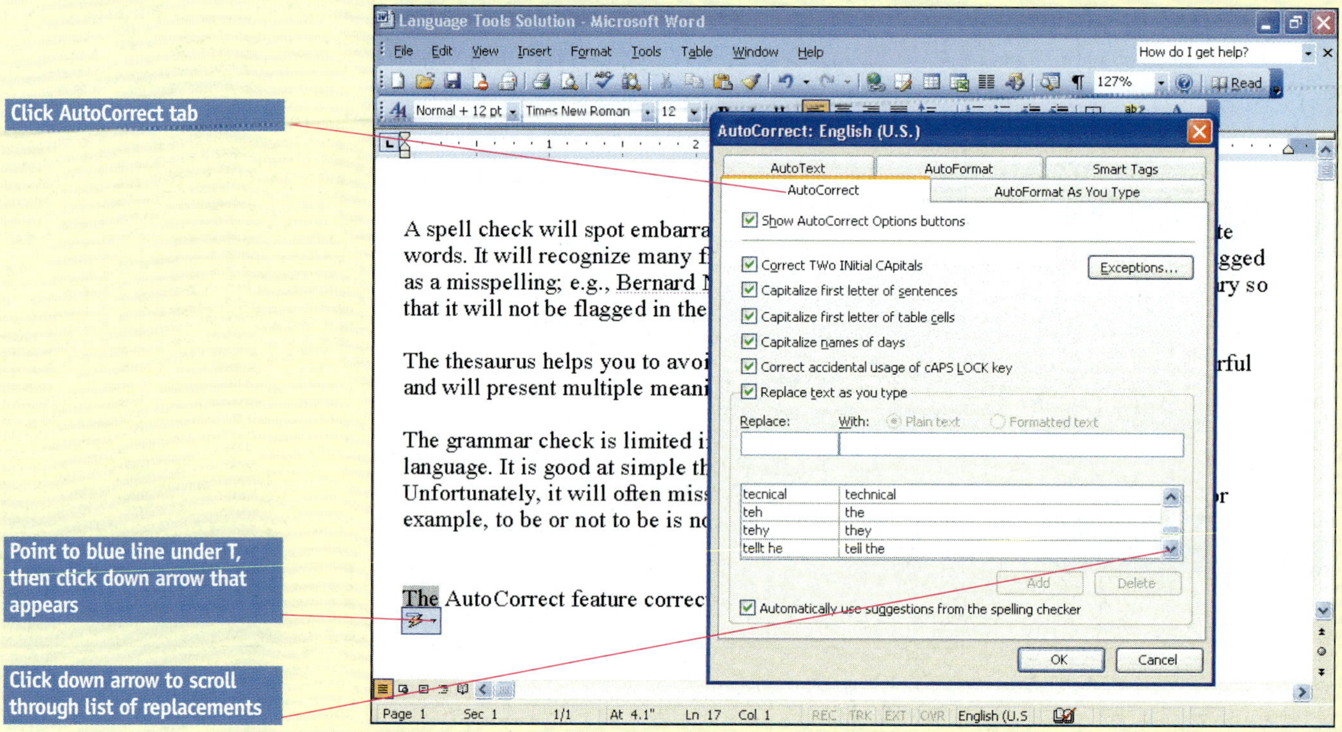

(e) AutoCorrect (step 5)

FIGURE 1.14 Hands-on Exercise 3 (*continued*)

CREATE YOUR OWN SHORTHAND

Use AutoCorrect to expand abbreviations such as "usa" for United States of America. Pull down the Tools menu, click AutoCorrect Options, type the abbreviation in the Replace text box and the expanded entry in the With text box. Click the Add command button, then click OK to exit the dialog box and return to the document. The next time you type usa in a document, it will automatically be expanded to United States of America.

Step 6: Create an AutoText Entry

- Press **Ctrl+End** to move to the end of the document. Press the **Enter key** twice. Enter your name and student number.
- Click and drag to select the information you just entered. Pull down the **Insert menu**, select the **AutoText command**, then select **AutoText** to display the AutoCorrect dialog box in Figure 1.14f.
- "Your name" is suggested automatically as the name of the AutoText entry. Click the **Add button**.
- To test the entry, you can delete your name and student number, then use the AutoText feature. Your name and other information should still be highlighted. Press the **Del key** to delete the information.
- Type the first few letters of your name and watch the screen as you do. You should see a ScreenTip containing your name and other information. Press the **Enter key** or the **F3 key** when you see the ScreenTip.
- Save the document.

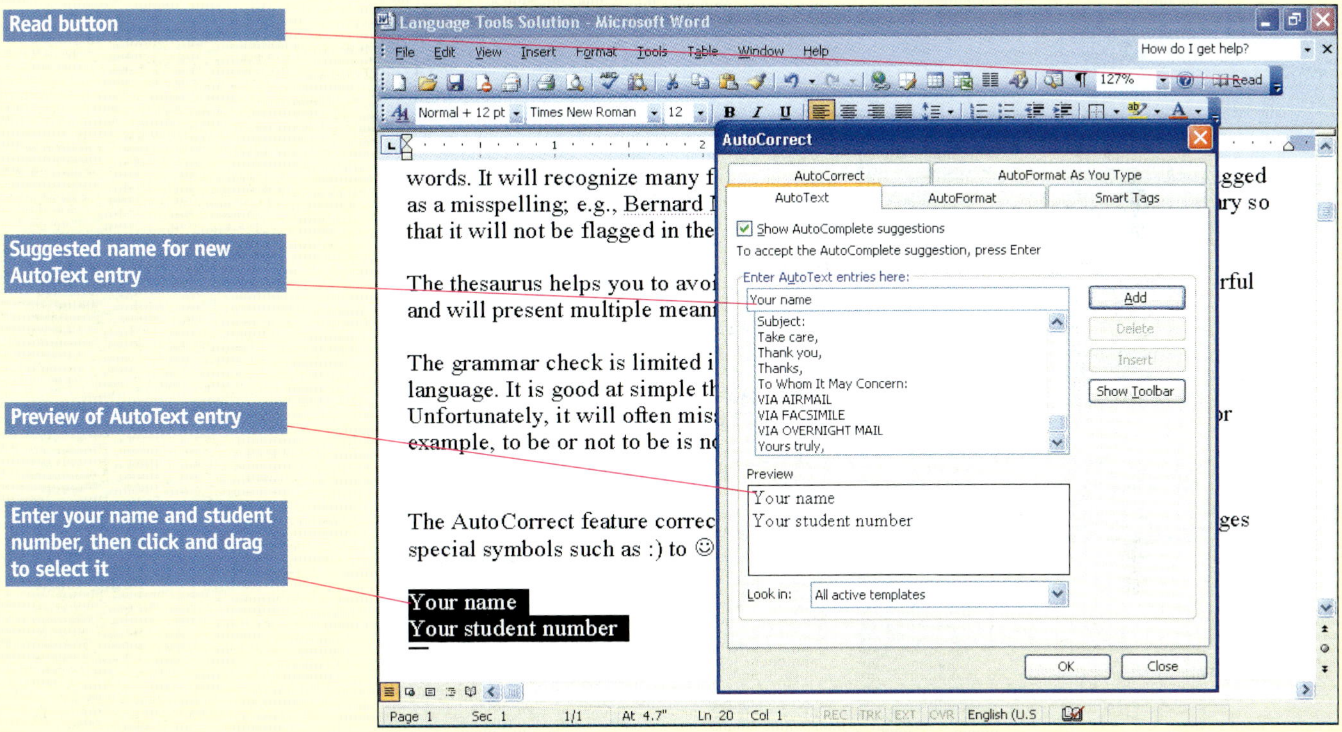

(f) Create an AutoText Entry (step 6)

FIGURE 1.14 Hands-on Exercise 3 (*continued*)

THE AUTOTEXT TOOLBAR

Point to any visible toolbar, click the right mouse button to display a context-sensitive menu, then click AutoText to display the AutoText toolbar. The AutoText toolbar groups the various AutoText entries into categories, making it easier to select the proper entry. Click the down arrow on the All Entries button to display the various categories, click a category, then select the entry you want to insert into the document.

Step 7: Start Reading

- Click the **Read button** to change to the Reading Layout view as shown in Figure 1.14g. This view is intended to proofread the final document, but you can still apply formatting through keyboard shortcuts.
- Click and drag to select "spell check", which appears in the first sentence of the document. Press **Ctrl+B**. Press **Ctrl+I**. Click elsewhere in the document to deselect the phrase, which now appears in bold italic.
- Bold face and italicize **"thesaurus", "grammar check",** and **"AutoCorrect feature"** in similar fashion.
- Click at the beginning of the document (immediately to the left of its title). Pull down the **Insert menu** and click the **Comment command**, then type the text of the comment in Figure 1.14g.
- Pull down the **File menu** and click the **Print command** to display the Print dialog box. Check that the Print What box indicates **Document showing markup**. Click **OK** to print the completed document for your instructor.
- Close the Reading Layout view. Save the document. Exit Word.

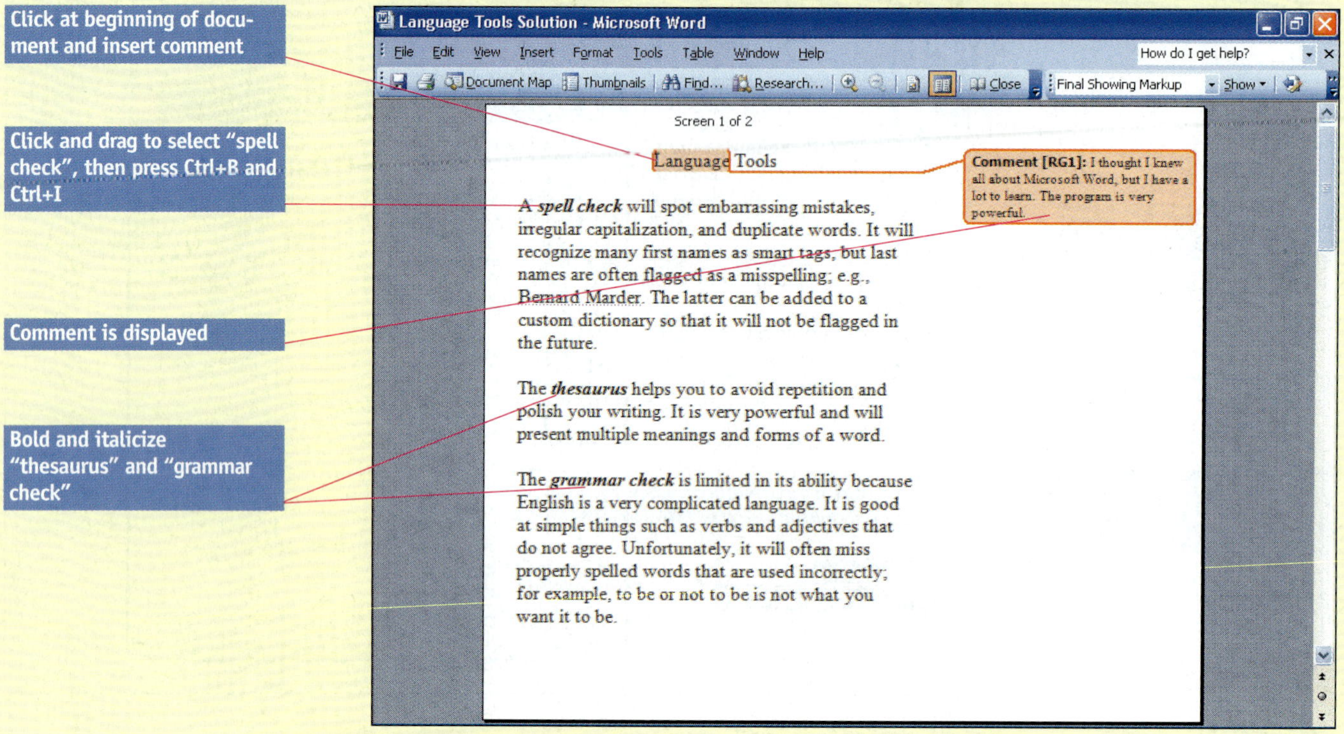

(g) Start Reading (step 7)

FIGURE 1.14 Hands-on Exercise 3 *(continued)*

THE TRACK CHANGES COMMAND

Pull down the Tools menu and click the Track Changes command to record the changes that are made in a document. (Execute the command a second time to turn the recording feature off.) Click the Read button to change the Reading Layout view, and then use the Accept or Reject Change buttons to decide if the revisions should be permanent. This technique is ideal when you are sharing a document with others. The comments of each reviewer are displayed in a different color. See problem 7 at the end of the chapter.

SUMMARY

The chapter provided a broad-based introduction to word processing in general and to Microsoft Word in particular. Help is available from many sources. You can use the Help menu or the Office Assistant as you can in any Office application. You can also go to the Microsoft Web site to obtain more recent, and often more detailed, information.

Microsoft Word is always in one of two modes, insert or overtype; the choice between the two depends on the desired editing. The insertion point marks the place within a document where text is added or replaced. Double clicking the OVR indicator on the status bar is an easy way to switch between the two modes.

The Enter key is pressed at the end of a paragraph, but not at the end of a line because Word automatically wraps text from one line to the next. A hard return is created by the user when he or she presses the Enter key; a soft return is created by Word as it wraps text and begins a new line.

The Save and Open commands work in conjunction with one another. The Save command copies the document in memory to disk under its existing name. The Open command retrieves a previously saved document. The Save As command saves the document in memory under a different name and is useful when you want to retain a copy of the current document prior to all changes.

Many operations in Microsoft Word are accomplished through the concept "select then do." This means that you select a block of text, and then you execute the appropriate editing or formatting command. Formatting commands can be executed in one of three ways: through the Format menu, via a keyboard shortcut, or by clicking the appropriate button on the Formatting toolbar. The selected text is affected by any subsequent operation, and it continues to be selected until you click elsewhere in the document.

A spell check compares the words in a document to those in a standard and/or custom dictionary and offers suggestions to correct the mistakes it finds. It will detect misspellings, duplicated phrases, and/or irregular capitalization, but will not flag properly spelled words that are used incorrectly. Foreign-language proofing tools for French and Spanish are built into the English version of Microsoft Word.

The AutoCorrect feature corrects predefined spelling errors and/or mistakes in capitalization, automatically, as the words are entered. The AutoText feature is similar in concept except that it can contain longer entries that include formatting and clip art. Either feature can be used to create a personal shorthand to expand abbreviations as they are typed.

The thesaurus suggests synonyms and/or antonyms. It can also recognize multiple forms of a word (noun, verb, and adjective) and offer suggestions for each. The grammar check searches for mistakes in punctuation, writing style, and word usage by comparing strings of text within a document to a series of predefined rules.

KEY TERMS

MULTIPLE CHOICE

1. When entering text within a document, the Enter key is normally pressed at the end of every:

(a) Line
(b) Sentence
(c) Paragraph
(d) All of the above

2. Which menu contains the commands to save the current document, or to open a previously saved document?

(a) The Tools menu
(b) The File menu
(c) The View menu
(d) The Edit menu

3. How do you execute the Print command?

(a) Click the Print button on the standard toolbar
(b) Pull down the File menu, then click the Print command
(c) Use the appropriate keyboard shortcut
(d) All of the above

4. The Open command:

(a) Brings a document from disk into memory
(b) Brings a document from disk into memory, then erases the document on disk
(c) Stores the document in memory on disk
(d) Stores the document in memory on disk, then erases the document from memory

5. What is the easiest way to change the phrase, *revenues, profits, gross margin*, to read *revenues, profits, and gross margin*?

(a) Use the insert mode, position the cursor before the *g* in *gross*, then type the word *and* followed by a space
(b) Use the insert mode, position the cursor after the *g* in *gross*, then type the word *and* followed by a space
(c) Use the overtype mode, position the cursor before the *g* in *gross*, then type the word *and* followed by a space
(d) Use the overtype mode, position the cursor after the *g* in *gross*, then type the word *and* followed by a space

6. The Save command:

(a) Brings a document from disk into memory
(b) Brings a document from disk into memory, then erases the document on disk
(c) Stores the document in memory on disk
(d) Stores the document in memory on disk, then erases the document from memory

7. A document has been entered into Word with a given set of margins, which are subsequently changed. What can you say about the number of hard and soft returns before and after the change in margins?

(a) The number of hard returns is the same, but the number and/or position of the soft returns is different
(b) The number of soft returns is the same, but the number and/or position of the hard returns is different
(c) The number and position of both hard and soft returns is unchanged
(d) The number and position of both hard and soft returns is different

8. Which of the following is detected by the spell check?

(a) Duplicate words
(b) Irregular capitalization
(c) Both (a) and (b)
(d) Neither (a) nor (b)

9. Which of the following is likely to be found in a custom dictionary?

(a) Proper names
(b) Words related to the user's particular application
(c) Acronyms created by the user for his or her application
(d) All of the above

10. Ted and Sally both use Word. Both have written a letter to Dr. Joel Stutz and have run a spell check on their respective documents. Ted's program flags *Stutz* as a misspelling, whereas Sally's accepts it as written. Why?

(a) The situation is impossible; that is, if they use identical word processing programs, they should get identical results
(b) Ted has added *Stutz* to his custom dictionary
(c) Sally has added *Stutz* to her custom dictionary
(d) All of the above reasons are equally likely as a cause of the problem

... continued

multiple choice

11. The spell check will do all of the following *except:*

(a) Flag properly spelled words used incorrectly
(b) Identify misspelled words
(c) Accept (as correctly spelled) words found in the custom dictionary
(d) Suggest alternatives to misspellings it identifies

12. The AutoCorrect feature will:

(a) Correct errors in capitalization as they occur during typing
(b) Expand user-defined abbreviations as the entries are typed
(c) Both (a) and (b)
(d) Neither (a) nor (b)

13. When does the Save As dialog box appear?

(a) The first time a file is saved using either the Save or Save As commands
(b) Every time a file is saved
(c) Both (a) and (b)
(d) Neither (a) nor (b)

14. Which of the following is true about the thesaurus?

(a) It recognizes different forms of a word; for example, a noun and a verb
(b) It provides antonyms as well as synonyms
(c) Both (a) and (b)
(d) Neither (a) nor (b)

15. The grammar check:

(a) Implements different rules for casual and business writing
(b) Will detect all subtleties in the English language
(c) Is always run in conjunction with a spell check
(d) All of the above

16. What happens if you select a word, then click the Italic button on the Formatting toolbar twice in a row?

(a) The word will be italicized
(b) The word will appear in a regular (nonitalicized) font
(c) The word will have the same appearance as before; clicking the Italic button twice in a row has no effect
(d) Impossible to determine

17. Which of the following applies to the paragraph as a whole—that is, you can apply the command anywhere within the paragraph to format the entire paragraph?

(a) Alignment
(b) Line spacing
(c) Borders
(d) All of the above

18. Which view is new to Microsoft Word 2003?

(a) Reading Layout
(b) Print Preview
(c) Normal
(d) Outline

ANSWERS

1. c	**7.** a	**13.** a
2. b	**8.** c	**14.** c
3. d	**9.** d	**15.** a
4. a	**10.** c	**16.** c
5. a	**11.** a	**17.** d
6. c	**12.** c	**18.** a

PRACTICE WITH WORD

1. **The Basics of Word Processing:** Open the *Chapter 1 Practice 1* document in the Exploring Word folder that is shown in Figure 1.15. Enter your instructor's name and your name in the To and From lines, respectively, then modify the document as described below.
   a. Change the word "worry" to "be concerned" in the first sentence of the second paragraph. Change the word "position" to "location" in the last sentence of the second paragraph.
   b. Delete the word "simply" from the second sentence in the third paragraph. Delete the word "also" in the second line of the last paragraph.
   c. Click at the end of the third paragraph, be sure you are in the insert mode, and add the sentence, "The insert mode adds characters at the insertion point while moving existing text to the right in order to make room for the new text."
   d. Click immediately to the left of the "s" in the word "test" found in the fourth line of the second paragraph. Press the Insert key to turn the OVR indicator on, and change to the overtype mode. Enter an "x", which will replace the "s". Press the Insert key a second time to return to the insert mode.
   e. Delete the two sentences in paragraph three that describe the OVR indicator.
   f. Create a new paragraph between paragraphs three and four, entering the following text: "There are two other keys that function as toggle switches of which you should be aware. The Caps Lock key toggles between upper- and lowercase letters. The Num Lock key alternates between typing numbers and using the arrow keys." As you enter the word "which" in the first sentence, type "whcih" instead. Watch what happens, as the spelling is automatically corrected. Add blank lines as needed.
   g. Select the word "present" in the second line of the first paragraph, then pull down the Tools menu and click the Language command. Click Thesaurus from the submenu. Find an appropriate meaning, click the down arrow next to the desired synonym, and check Insert. Close the task pane.
   h. Save the completed document as *Chapter 1 Practice 1 Solution*. Pull down the File menu, click the Print command, and then click the Options button in the Print dialog box. Check the box to print Document properties. Click OK to close this dialog box, and then click OK to print the document and its properties for your instructor.

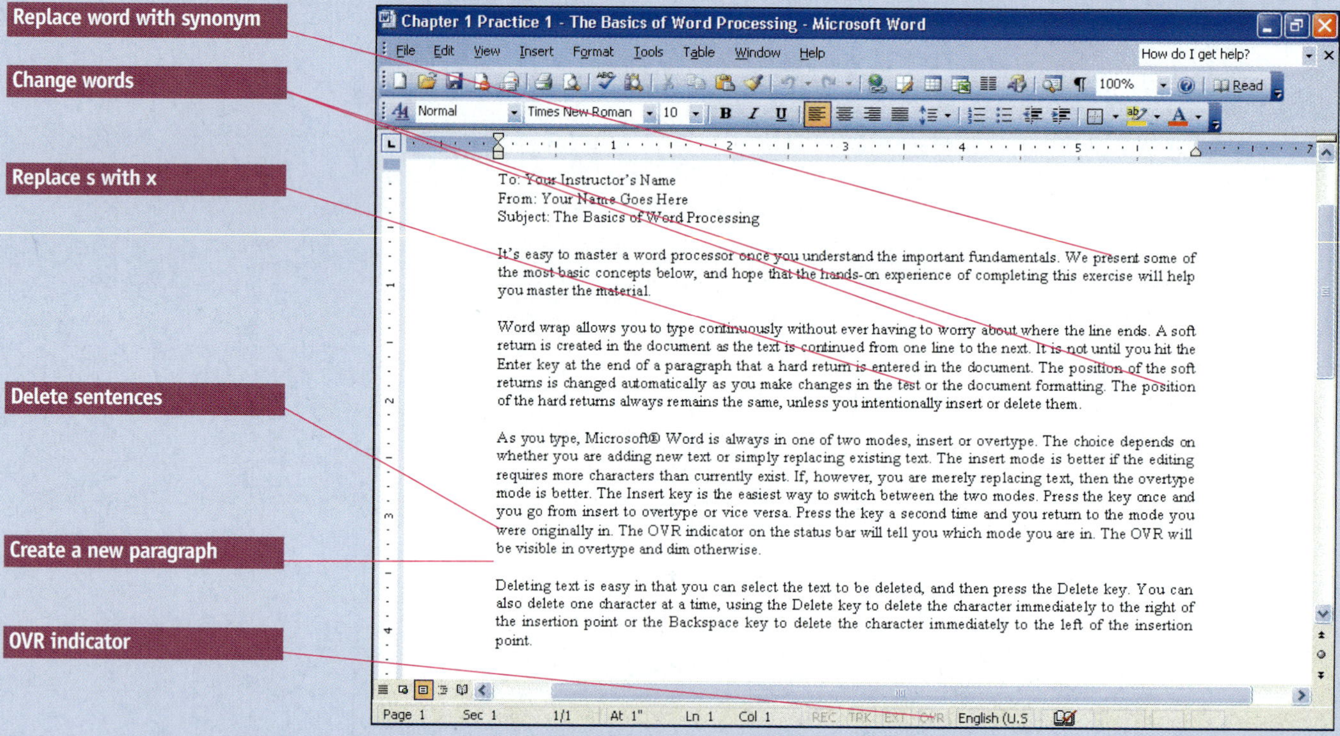

FIGURE 1.15 The Basics of Word Processing (exercise 1)

2. **The Spelling and Grammar Check:** Open the *Chapter 1 Practice 2* document in the Exploring Word folder to display the document in Figure 1.16. Word detects multiple errors in spelling and grammar as denoted by the wavy red and green lines, respectively. Your assignment is to correct the document so that it is error free. Proceed as follows:
   a. Press Ctrl+Home to move to the beginning of the document, then click the Spelling and Grammar button on the Standard toolbar to check the document for errors. Accept, reject, or make the corrections as you see fit. Do not correct the errors that are flagged at the end of the document within the French and Spanish phrases at this time. [English is the default language for spelling and grammar, but you can select other languages as you will see in parts (c) and (d).]
   b. Read the corrected document carefully and make any other necessary corrections (again, ignoring the foreign phrases). You should find several additional errors because the English language is very complicated, and it is virtually impossible to correct every error automatically.
   c. Click and drag to select the French phrases that appear near the end of the document. Pull down the Tools menu, click the Language command, click Set Language, then select French (France). Check this phrase for spelling and grammar. Do you know what the sentences mean?
   d. Click and drag to select the Spanish phrases that appear near the end of the document. Pull down the Tools menu, click the Language command, click Set Language, and then select Spanish (Spain-Modern Sort). Check this phrase for spelling and grammar. Do you know what the sentences mean?
   e. Add your name to the completed document. Save the completed document as *Chapter 1 Practice 2 Solution.*
   f. Pull down the File menu, click the Print command, and then click the Options button in the Print dialog box. Check the box to print Document properties. Click OK to close this dialog box, and then click OK to print the document and its properties for your instructor.

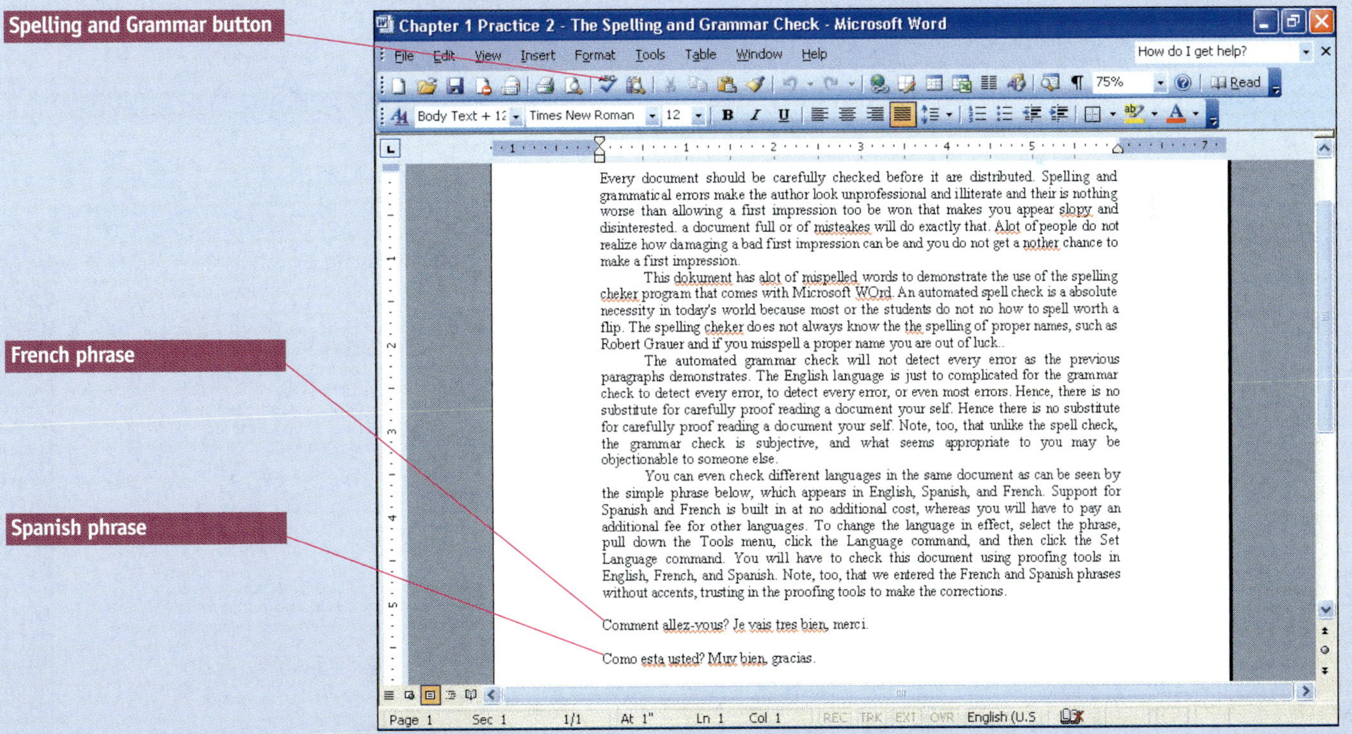

FIGURE 1.16 The Spelling and Grammar Check (exercise 2)

3. **Select Then Do:** Formatting operations are typically implemented in the context of "select then do" as described in the document of Figure 1.17. You select the text that you want to format, then you execute the appropriate formatting command, most easily by clicking the corresponding button on the Formatting toolbar. This assignment will help you to practice basic formatting. Proceed as follows:
    a. Open the *Chapter 1 Practice 3* document in the Exploring Word folder. Pull down the Edit menu and click the Select All command to select the entire document. Change the font to Times New Roman.
    b. Click and drag to select the title of the document. Change the type size to 18 points. Click the Center button on the Formatting toolbar. Select the text on the second line, type your name, and click the Center button. Change to 14 point type.
    c. Click and drag to select the term, "select-then-do" in the first paragraph. Click the Bold button. Click the Italic button. Leave the insertion point in the middle of the selected text and double click the Format Painter. Click and drag to paint the other terms in the document that use the same formatting as shown in Figure 1.17.
    d. Apply boldface, underlining, or italic as indicated in the second paragraph.
    e. Click and drag to select the word "smaller" in the second paragraph. Change the point size to 10 points. Select the words "and smaller" and change to 8 points.
    f. Click the down arrow on the Highlight tool to select yellow, and then highlight the indicated sentence in the first paragraph. Change the color of the tool to complete the highlighting for the last sentence in the second paragraph.
    g. Click anywhere in the first paragraph, then click the Justify tool. Click anywhere in the third paragraph and click the Align Right tool.
    h. Click anywhere in the last paragraph and click the Justify tool. Now click the down arrow on the line spacing tool and select 1.5. Line spacing and justification take place at the paragraph level; that is, it affects the entire paragraph that contains the insertion point even if the paragraph is not selected.
    i. Click the down arrow on the Border tool to select the Outside border. Click anywhere in the last paragraph, then click the Border tool to apply the border to the paragraph.
    j. Save the document. Print the completed document for your instructor.

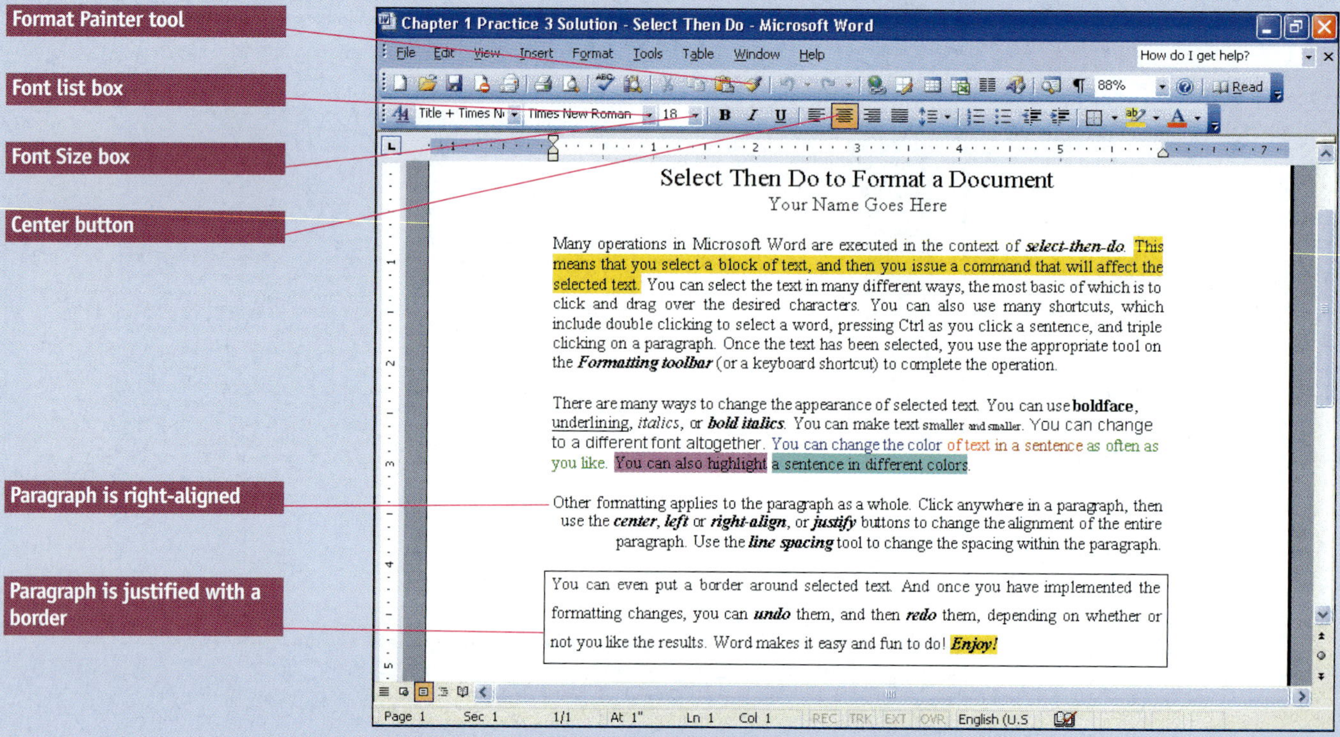

FIGURE 1.17 Select Then Do (exercise 3)

4. **Protecting Your System:** Figure 1.18 displays the first two pages in a document that discusses computer viruses and backup procedures. It's not a question of *if* it will happen, but *when*—hard disks die, files are lost, or viruses may infect a system. You can prepare for the inevitable by creating adequate backup before the problem occurs. The advice in the document is very important, and we suggest you take it to heart. Proceed as follows:
   a. Open the partially completed document in *Chapter 1 Practice 4* in the Exploring Word folder. Boldface and italicize the first occurrence of the following terms that are found on the first page: "computer virus" and "antivirus program". Read the information on this page very carefully.
   b. Start Internet Explorer and go to www.symantec.com, which is the home page of the company that supplies the Norton antivirus program. Search the Symantec Web site for the information needed to answer the questions on page 2 of the document, which asks several questions about the Norton Antivirus program. Enter your responses directly in the document.
   c. Go to www.mcafee.com to obtain information about the McAfee antivirus program. Search the Web site for the information needed to answer the questions on page 2 of the document. Enter your responses directly in the document.
   d. Go to the third page in the document, which describes a simple backup strategy. Read the information and use it to answer the indicated questions directly in the document.
   e. Press Ctrl+Home to move to the beginning of the document. Pull down the Insert menu, click the Break command, and insert a page break (or use the Ctrl+Enter keyboard shortcut).
   f. Pull down the View menu and change to the Print Layout view. Click the down arrow on the Zoom box and select Whole Page. Press Ctrl+Home a second time to move to the newly created title page. Press the Enter key several times, and then enter the title of the document, the subtitle, and your name as shown in Figure 1.18.
   g. Print the completed document for your instructor. Read the document carefully before you submit it. Don't make your definition of backup the copy you wish you had made prior to your system crashing.

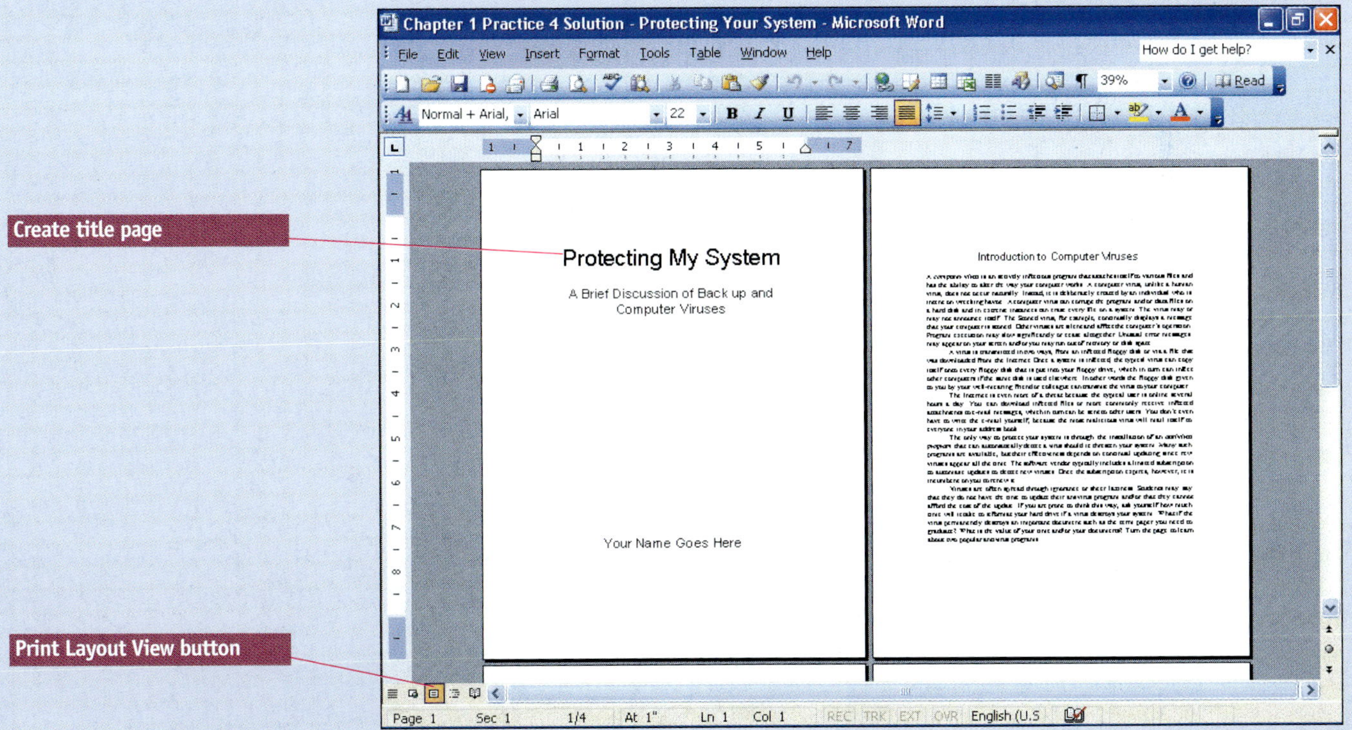

FIGURE 1.18 Protecting Your System (exercise 4)

5. **Exploring Help:** Everything you need to know about Microsoft Word is contained in its help facility. There are several types of help available, but regardless of the type you choose, the best time to look for help is when you don't need it. This exercise helps you to explore the various ways to learn more about Microsoft Word. Open the *Chapter 1 Practice 5* document in the Exploring Word folder and answer each question in the space provided.
   a. Pull down the Help menu and click the About command to see which version of Word you are currently using. Why is this information important? What other information is available from the About Microsoft Word window?
   b. How do you use the Help task pane in Figure 1.19? What other information (besides the Table of Contents) is available from this task pane?
   c. What happens if you click a closed book icon? What happens if you click an open book icon? What happens if you click a topic under an open book?
   d. How do you display (hide) the Office Assistant? When does it display a suggestion? Is it useful or just a clever annoyance? Will the same suggestion repeat itself from one session to the next? What steps are necessary to display a tip of the day each time that Microsoft Word is started?
   e. What is the Ask a Question list box? When is it available?
   f. Where would you prefer the help files to be stored, locally or on the Web? What is the advantage of storing the Help files on the Web? What is the disadvantage?
   g. How do you implement a spell check in a foreign language such as French or Spanish? Use any appropriate technique to find the answer. Print the associated help topic(s) for your instructor.
   h. Include your name at the top of the document, and then print the completed document for your instructor.

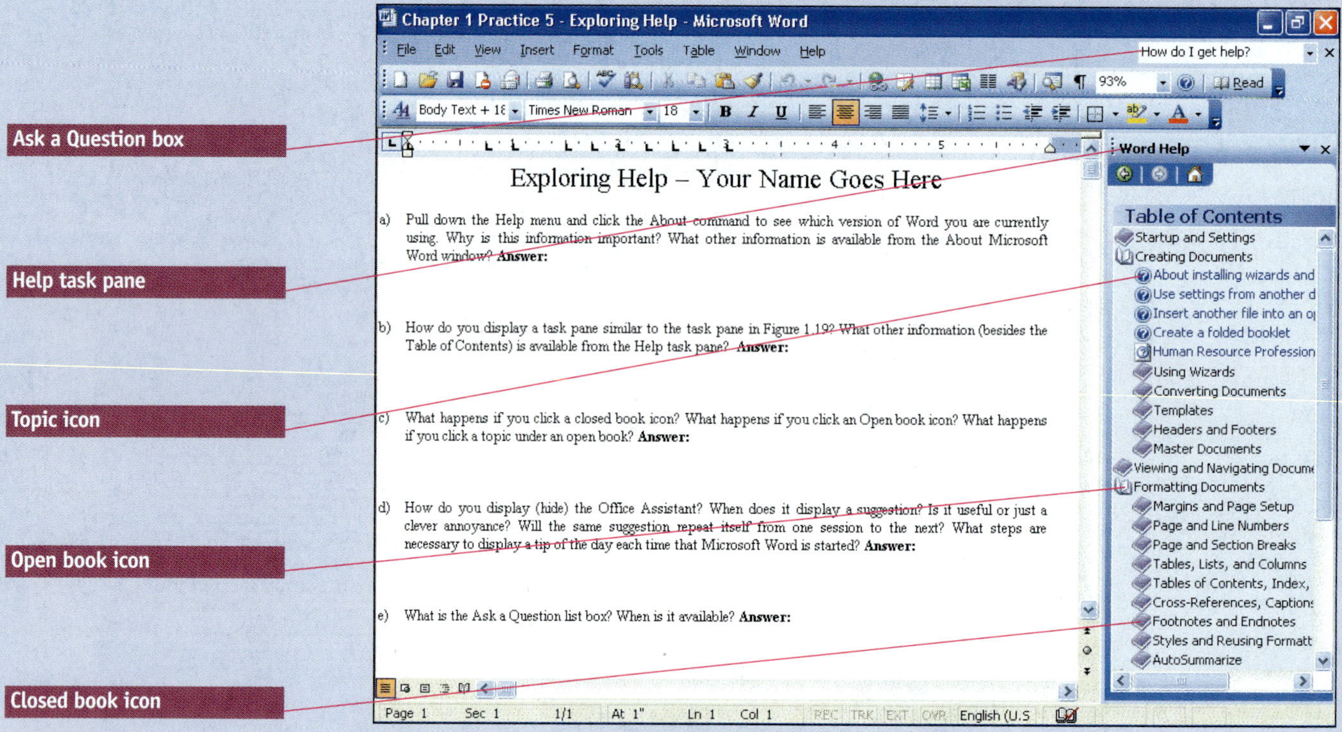

FIGURE 1.19 Exploring Help (exercise 5)

6. **Compare and Merge Documents:** The Compare and Merge Documents command lets you compare two documents in order to see the changes between those documents. You can use the command to see how well you completed the first two hands-on exercises. Proceed as follows:
   a. Open the completed *Chapter 1 Practice 6* document in the Exploring Word folder. This document contains our solution to the first two hands-on exercises followed by a paragraph that describes the Compare and Merge Documents command.
   b. Pull down the Tools menu and click the Compare and Merge Documents command to display the associated dialog box. Select *My First Document* (the document you created in the first hands-on exercise and modified in the second hands-on exercise).
   c. Check the box for Legal Blackline (to display a thin black line in the left margin showing where the changes occur), then click the Compare button. The two documents are merged together as shown in Figure 1.20. The extent of the changes in the first two paragraphs depends on how closely you followed instructions in the hands-on exercises.
   d. Click the Read button on the Standard toolbar to change to the Reading Layout view. Experiment with the Increase (Decrease) Font Size button to make the document easier to read. Accept or reject the changes as you see fit.
   e. Click the Close button to return to the Print Layout view. Pull down the File menu, click the Print command, and then click the Options button in the Print dialog box. Check the box to print Document properties. Click OK to close this dialog box, and then click OK to print the document and its properties for your instructor.
   f. Use the Help command to learn more about merging documents and tracking changes. Summarize your thoughts about these commands in a short note to your instructor.

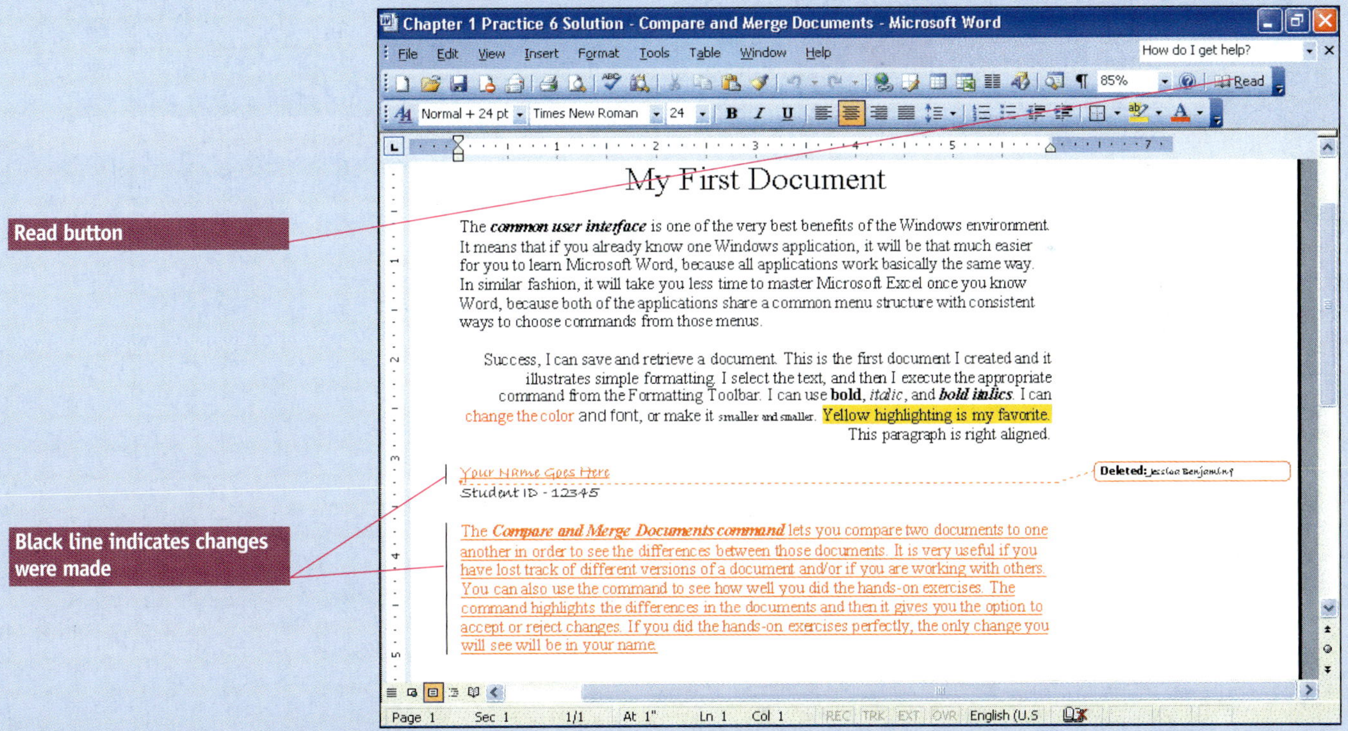

FIGURE 1.20 Compare and Merge Documents (exercise 6)

practice exercises

7. **The Rejected Job Applicant:** The Track Changes command stores the changes to a document electronically, enabling the owner of that document to accept or reject the changes as he or she sees fit. The changes may be entered in different ways; for example, the document can be sent to multiple reviewers requesting their input, in which case the changes of each reviewer are recorded in a different color. The changes may also be entered by a sole author who wants an electronic record of an editing session. Proceed as follows:
   a. Open the *Chapter 1 Practice 7* document in the Exploring Word folder. This document was written by a friend of yours who was rejected from every job for which she applied. Your assignment is to edit the letter by eliminating spelling and grammatical errors, and further by making any other changes you see fit.
   b. Pull down the Tools menu and toggle the Track Changes command on. The Reviewing toolbar should be displayed automatically. If necessary, click the down arrow in the Display for Review list box and select Final Showing Markup, to display the final version of your document with the indicated corrections as shown in Figure 1.21.
   c. Check the document for spelling and grammatical errors, making changes as appropriate. Note that each time you make a change to the document, the nature of the change is recorded in the right margin.
   d. Enter additional changes as necessary that were not detected by the tools within Word. Note, for example, that we suggested our friend apply for an entry-level rather than a senior position. We also added a letterhead to the top of the document.
   e. Click the Print button to print the document as shown—that is, the final document with the markup (editing) printed in the margin. Click the down arrow on the Display for Review list box to display the Original Showing Markup and print that version. And finally, change to the final version to print the completed document without showing the editing changes. Submit all three versions to your instructor.
   f. Save the document. Pull down the Tools menu and toggle the Track Changes command off. Pull down the View menu, click Toolbars, and toggle the display of the Reviewing Toolbar off as well.

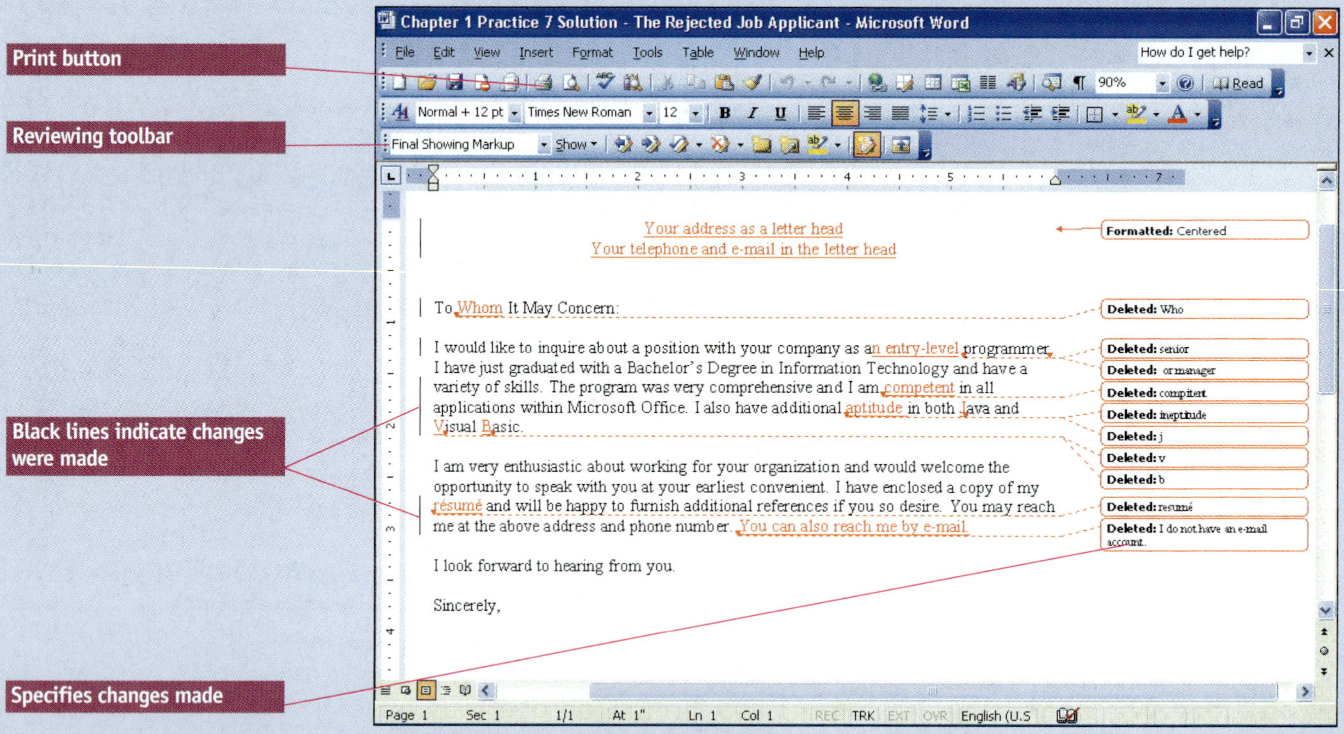

FIGURE 1.21 The Rejected Job Applicant (exercise 7)

MINI CASES

Student Questionnaire

Use the partially completed document in *Chapter 1 Mini Case—Student Questionnaire* as the basis of a document to your instructor describing your background. Click after each question and respond as indicated. If there is time in the class, your instructor can have you exchange assignments with another student, and then have you read the other student's questionnaire to the class. There are many variations on this "ice breaker," but the assignment will let you gain practice with Microsoft Word, while simultaneously learning about your classmates.

Reading Between the Lines

You were recently sent a performance appraisal by a subordinate, followed shortly by a second note with additional information. It seems that John (the individual being evaluated) was standing over your subordinate's shoulder when she wrote the evaluation, and thus her true opinion of the candidate is hidden between the lines of the original document. Open the *Chapter 1 Mini Case—Reading Between the Lines* document and delete the shaded lines within the original letter. Click the Show/Hide button to display the hidden characters, and then delete all of the hard returns (except the last one) to create a single paragraph. Change the font to 12 point Times New Roman, justify the paragraph, and set the line spacing to 2. Add your name to the revised letter and submit it to your instructor.

Acronym Finder

Do you know what the acronym PCMCIA stands for? Some might say it stands for "People Can't Memorize Computer Industry Acronyms," although the real meaning is "Personal Computer Memory Card International Association," which refers to the PC cards that are used with notebook computers. Use your favorite Internet search engine to locate a site that publishes lists of acronyms. Select five computer-related terms and create a short document with the acronym and its meaning. Select a second list of any five acronyms that appeal to you. Print the document and submit it to your instructor.

The Reference Desk

The Reference Desk, at www.refdesk.com, contains a treasure trove of information for the writer. You will find access to several online dictionaries, encyclopedias, and other references. Go to the site and select five links that you think will be of interest to you as a writer. Create a short document that contains the name of the site, its Web address, and a brief description of the information that is found at the site. Print the document and submit it to your instructor.

Planning for Disaster

Do you have a backup strategy? Do you even know what a backup strategy is? You should learn, because sooner or later you will wish you had one. You will erase a file, be unable to read from a floppy disk, or worse yet suffer a hardware failure in which you are unable to access the hard drive. The problem always seems to occur the night before an assignment is due. The ultimate disaster is the disappearance of your computer, by theft or natural disaster (e.g., Hurricane Andrew). Describe in 250 words or less the backup strategy you plan to implement in conjunction with your work in this class.

... continued

mini cases

A Letter Home

You really like this course and want very much to have your own computer, but you're strapped for cash and have decided to ask your parents for help. Write a one-page letter describing the advantages of having your own system and how it will help you in school. Tell your parents what the system will cost, and that you can save money by buying through the mail. Describe the configuration you intend to buy (don't forget to include the price of software) and then provide prices from at least three different companies. Cut out the advertisements and include them in your letter. Bring your material to class and compare your research with that of your classmates.

A Junior Year Abroad

How lucky can you get? You are spending the second half of your junior year in Paris. The problem is you will have to submit your work in French, and the English version of Microsoft Word won't do. Is there a foreign-language version available? What about the dictionary and thesaurus? How do you enter the accented characters, which occur so frequently? You are leaving in two months, so you'd better get busy. What are your options? *Bon voyage!*

Changing Menus and Toolbars

Microsoft Office enables you to display a series of short menus that contain only basic commands. The additional commands are made visible by clicking the double arrow that appears at the bottom of the menu. New commands are added to the menu as they are used, and conversely, other commands are removed if they are not used. A similar strategy is followed for the Standard and Formatting toolbars that are displayed on a single row, and thus do not show all of the buttons at one time. The intent is to simplify Office for the new user by limiting the number of commands that are visible. The consequence, however, is that the individual is not exposed to new commands, and hence may not use Office to its full potential. Which set of menus do you prefer? How do you switch from one set to the other?

CHAPTER 2

Gaining Proficiency: Editing and Formatting

OBJECTIVES

After reading this chapter you will:

1. Explain how the Undo and Redo commands are related to one another.
2. Move and copy text within a document.
3. Distinguish between the Windows clipboard and the Office clipboard.
4. Use the Find and Replace commands.
5. Define scrolling; move to the beginning and end of a document.
6. Use the Format Font command and equivalent toolbar buttons.
7. Use the Format Paragraph command and equivalent toolbar buttons.
8. Set tabs and indents using the ruler or equivalent commands.
9. Apply borders and shading.
10. Use the Page Setup command to change margins and orientation.
11. Change the column structure of a document.

hands-on exercises

1. EDITING A DOCUMENT
   Input: Note from Bob and Maryann
   Output: Note from Bob and Maryann Solution
2. CHARACTER FORMATTING
   Input: Tips for Writing
   Output: Tips for Writing Solution
3. PARAGRAPH FORMATTING
   Input: Tips for Writing Solution (from exercise 2)
   Output: Tips for Writing Solution (additional modifications)

CASE STUDY

FRIENDS OF CANBY COUNTY

It's that time of year again when auction fever is in the air! Many nonprofit businesses conduct an annual auction to raise funds to support their operation. The *Friends of Canby County* is one such organization, and it seeks to bring citizens together to effectively manage growth and reduce urban sprawl within the county. Other activities include public education and the preparation of policy statements for urban politicians.

Your first task as the new executive director is to inform citizens and local businesses of this year's auction, which is set for April 2nd in the ballroom of the Mountain View Lodge. You also have to procure the actual items that will be auctioned off at this exceedingly popular event. The goal for this year is to net $40,000 at the action, which is $4,000 more than last year.

The former director was helpful and provided copies of letters and other correspondence from last year's gala. Unfortunately, some of her files are not in their final form, and further, several changes in the content of the letter (such as the time and place of the event) have to be made. You also want to add your own touch and create a better-looking document through enhanced formatting. ■

Your assignment is to read the chapter, paying special attention to the character, paragraph, and section level formatting within the document. You are then to open last year's letter, *Chapter 2 Case Study—Friends of Canby County,* and make the necessary changes to achieve a more professional look. You have been asked to improve the letterhead and other formatting. You have also been asked to change the list of auction items to a three-column format so that the entire letter fits on one page and further, to use bullets to highlight the list of forms that are enclosed in the packet, as opposed to listing them in a paragraph. Print the completed letter for your instructor.

UNDO AND REDO COMMANDS

To err is human, but it's easy to recover from a mistake. The ***Undo command*** is executed by pulling down the Edit menu, by clicking the Undo button on the Standard toolbar, or by using the equivalent keyboard shortcut (Ctrl+Z). Each time the command is executed, it undoes a previous command; for example, executing the undo command three times in a row will undo the last three commands that were executed. You can also click the down arrow next to the Undo button on the Standard toolbar to display a reverse-order list of previous commands. Select (click) the command you want to undo, and you automatically undo all of the preceding commands. Undoing the fifth command in the list, for example, will undo the preceding four commands.

The ***Redo command*** is the opposite of Undo and reverses the last command that was undone. Clicking the down arrow next to the Redo button on the Standard toolbar will redo (re-execute) all of the previous commands prior to the one you select; for example, redoing the fifth command in the list will redo the preceding four commands. The Undo and Redo commands work in conjunction with one another; that is, every time a command is undone, it can be redone at a later time.

MOVING AND COPYING TEXT

The ability to move and/or copy text is essential in order to develop any degree of proficiency in editing. A move operation removes the text from its current location and places it elsewhere in the same (or even a different) document; a copy operation retains the text in its present location and places a duplicate elsewhere. Either operation can be accomplished using the Windows clipboard and a combination of the ***Cut***, ***Copy***, and ***Paste commands***.

The ***Windows clipboard*** is a temporary storage area available to any Windows application. Selected text is cut or copied from a document and placed onto the clipboard from where it can be pasted to a new location(s). A move requires that you select the text and execute a Cut command to remove the text from the document and place it on the clipboard. You then move the insertion point to the new location and paste the text from the clipboard into that location. A copy operation necessitates the same steps except that a Copy command is executed rather than a cut, leaving the selected text in its original location as well as placing a copy on the clipboard. (The ***Paste Special command*** can be used instead of the Paste command to paste the text without the associated formatting.)

The Cut, Copy, and Paste commands are found in the Edit menu, or alternatively, can be executed by clicking the appropriate buttons on the Standard toolbar. The contents of the Windows clipboard are replaced by each subsequent Cut or Copy command, but are unaffected by the Paste command. The contents of the clipboard can be pasted into multiple locations in the same or different documents.

Microsoft Office has its own clipboard that enables you to collect and paste multiple items. The ***Office clipboard*** differs from the Windows clipboard in that the contents of each successive Copy command are added to the clipboard. Thus, you could copy the first paragraph of a document to the Office clipboard, then copy (add) a bulleted list in the middle of the document to the Office clipboard, and finally copy (add) the last paragraph (three items in all) to the Office clipboard. You could then go to another place in the document or to a different document altogether, and paste the contents of the Office clipboard (three separate items) with a single command. The Office clipboard can hold up to 24 text or graphical elements.

Selected text is copied automatically to the Office clipboard regardless of whether you use the Copy command in the Edit menu, the Copy button on the Standard toolbar, or the Ctrl+C shortcut. The Office clipboard is accessed through the Edit menu and/or the task pane.

FIND, REPLACE, AND GO TO COMMANDS

The Find, Replace, and Go To commands share a common dialog box with different tabs for each command as shown in Figure 2.1. The ***Find command*** locates one or more occurrences of specific text (e.g., a word or phrase). The ***Replace command*** goes one step further in that it locates the text, and then enables you to optionally replace (one or more occurrences of) that text with different text. The ***Go To command*** goes directly to a specific place (e.g., a specific page) in the document.

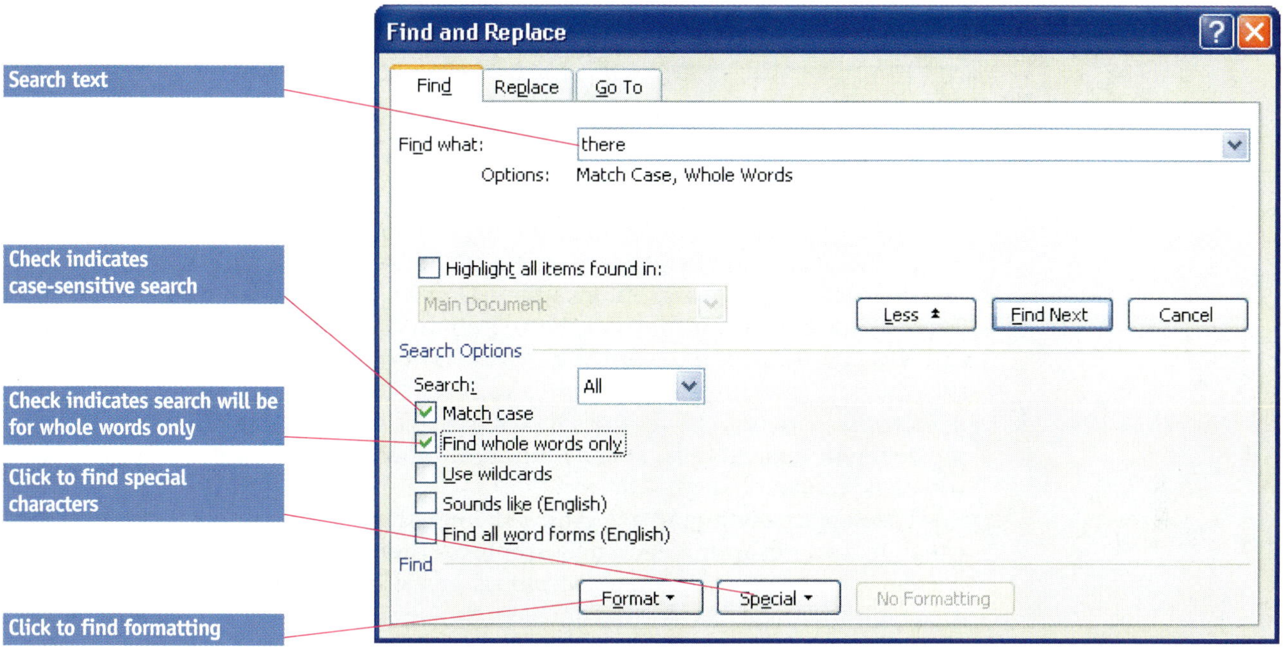

(a) Find Command

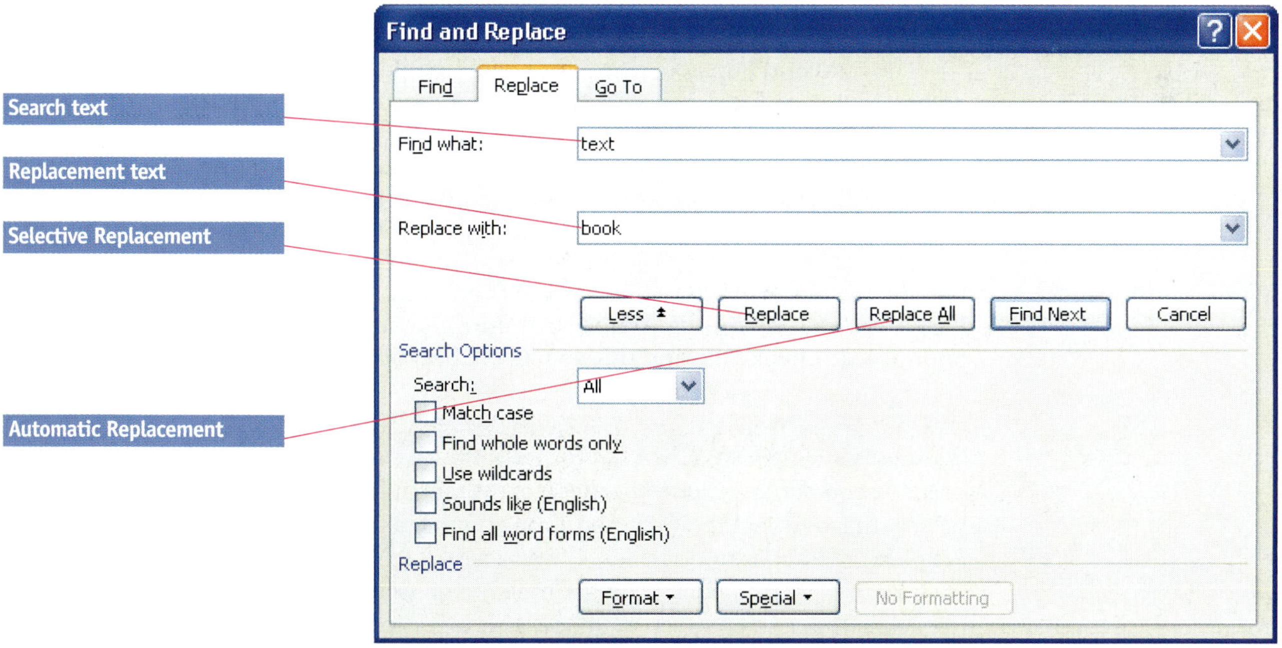

(b) Replace Command

FIGURE 2.1 The Find, Replace, and Go To Commands

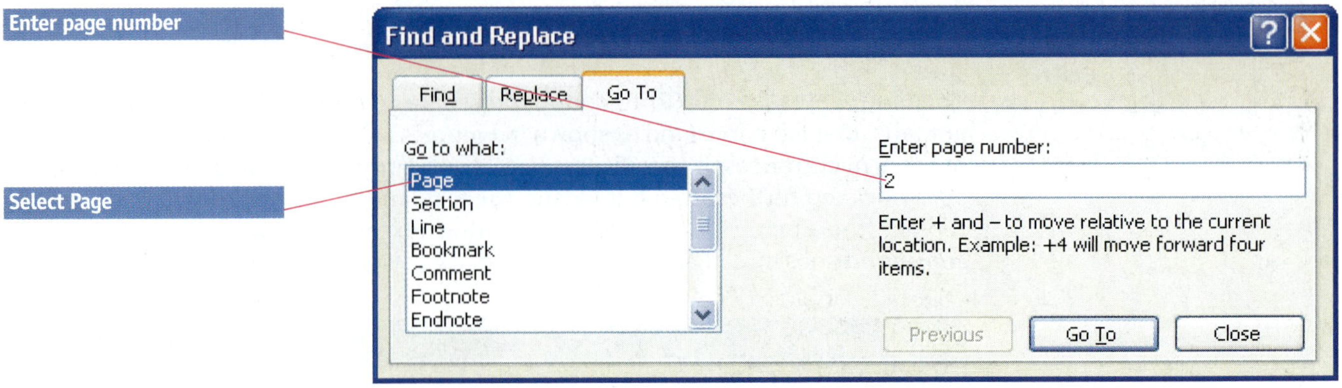

(c) Go To Command

FIGURE 2.1 The Find, Replace, and Go To Commands (*continued*)

The search in both the Find and Replace commands is case sensitive or case insensitive. A ***case-sensitive search*** (where Match Case is selected as in Figure 2.1a) matches not only the text, but also the use of upper- and lowercase letters. Thus, *There* is different from *there,* and a search on one will not identify the other. A ***case-insensitive search*** (where Match Case is *not* selected as in Figure 2.1b) is just the opposite and finds both *There* and *there.* A search may also specify ***whole words only*** to identify *there,* but not *therefore* or *thereby.* And finally, the search and replacement text can also specify different numbers of characters; for example, you could replace *16* with *sixteen.*

The Replace command in Figure 2.1b implements either ***selective replacement***, which lets you examine each occurrence of the character string in context and decide whether to replace it, or ***automatic replacement***, where the substitution is made automatically. Selective replacement is implemented by clicking the Find Next command button, then clicking (or not clicking) the Replace button to make the substitution. Automatic replacement (through the entire document) is implemented by clicking the Replace All button. This often produces unintended consequences and is not recommended; for example, if you substitute the word *text* for *book,* the word *textbook* would become *texttext,* which is not what you had in mind.

The Find and Replace commands can include formatting and/or special characters. You can, for example, change all italicized text to boldface, or you can change five consecutive spaces to a tab character. You can also use special characters in the character string such as the "any character" (consisting of ^?). For example, to find all four-letter words that begin with "f" and end with "l" (such as *fall, fill,* or *fail*), search for f^?^?l. (The question mark stands for any character, just like a ***wild card*** in a card game.) You can also search for all forms of a word; for example, if you specify *am,* it will also find *is* and *are.* You can even search for a word based on how it sounds. When searching for *Marion,* for example, check the Sounds Like check box, and the search will find both *Marion* and *Marian.*

INSERT THE DATE AND TIME

Most documents include the date and time they were created. Pull down the Insert menu, select the Date and Time command to display the Date and Time dialog box, then choose a format. Check the box to update the date automatically if you want your document to reflect the date on which it is opened, or clear the box to retain the date on which the document was created. See practice exercise 4 at the end of the chapter.

SCROLLING

Scrolling occurs when a document is too large to be seen in its entirety. Figure 2.2a displays a large printed document, only part of which is visible on the screen in Figure 2.2b. In order to see a different portion of the document, you need to scroll, whereby new lines will be brought into view as the old lines disappear.

To: Our Students
From: Bob Grauer and Maryann Barber

Welcome to the wonderful world of word processing. Over the next several chapters we will build a foundation in the basics of Microsoft Word, and then teach you to format specialized documents, create professional looking tables and charts, publish well-designed newsletters, and create Web pages. Before you know it, you will be a word processing and desktop publishing wizard!

The first chapter presented the basics of word processing and showed you how to create a simple document. You learned how to insert, replace, and/or delete text. This chapter will teach you about fonts and special effects (such as **boldfacing** and *italicizing*) and how to use them effectively — how too little is better than too much.

You will go on to experiment with margins, tab stops, line spacing, and justification, learning first to format simple documents and then going on to longer, more complex ones. It is with the latter that we explore headers and footers, page numbering, widows and orphans (yes, we really did mean widows and orphans). It is here that we bring in graphics, working with newspaper-type columns, and the elements of a good page design. And without question, we will introduce the tools that make life so much easier (and your writing so much more impressive) — the Spell Check, Grammar Check, Thesaurus, and Styles.

If you are wondering what all these things are, read on in the text and proceed with the hands-on exercises. We will show you how to create a simple newsletter, and then improve it by adding graphics, fonts, and WordArt. You will create a simple calendar using the Tables feature, and then create more intricate forms that will rival anything you have seen. You will learn how to create a résumé with your beginner's skills, and then make it look like so much more with your intermediate (even advanced) skills. You will learn how to download resources from the Internet and how to create your own Web page. Last, but not least, run a mail merge to produce the cover letters that will accompany your résumé as it is mailed to companies across the United States (and even the world).

It is up to you to practice for it is only through working at the computer, that you will learn what you need to know. Experiment and don't be afraid to make mistakes. Practice and practice some more.

Our goal is for you to learn and to enjoy what you are learning. We have great confidence in you, and in our ability to help you discover what you can do. Visit the home page for the Exploring Office series. You can also send us e-mail. You can email Bob Grauer at rgrauer@miami.edu. You can reach Maryann Barber at mbarber@miami.edu. As you read the last sentence, notice that Microsoft Word is Web-enabled and that the Internet and e-mail references appear as hyperlinks in this document. Thus, you can click the address of our home page from within this document and then you can view the page immediately, provided you have an Internet connection. You can also click the e-mail address to open your mail program, provided it has been configured correctly.

We look forward to hearing from you and hope that you will like our textbook. You are about to embark on a wonderful journey toward computer literacy. Be patient and inquisitive.

(a) Printed Document

FIGURE 2.2 Scrolling

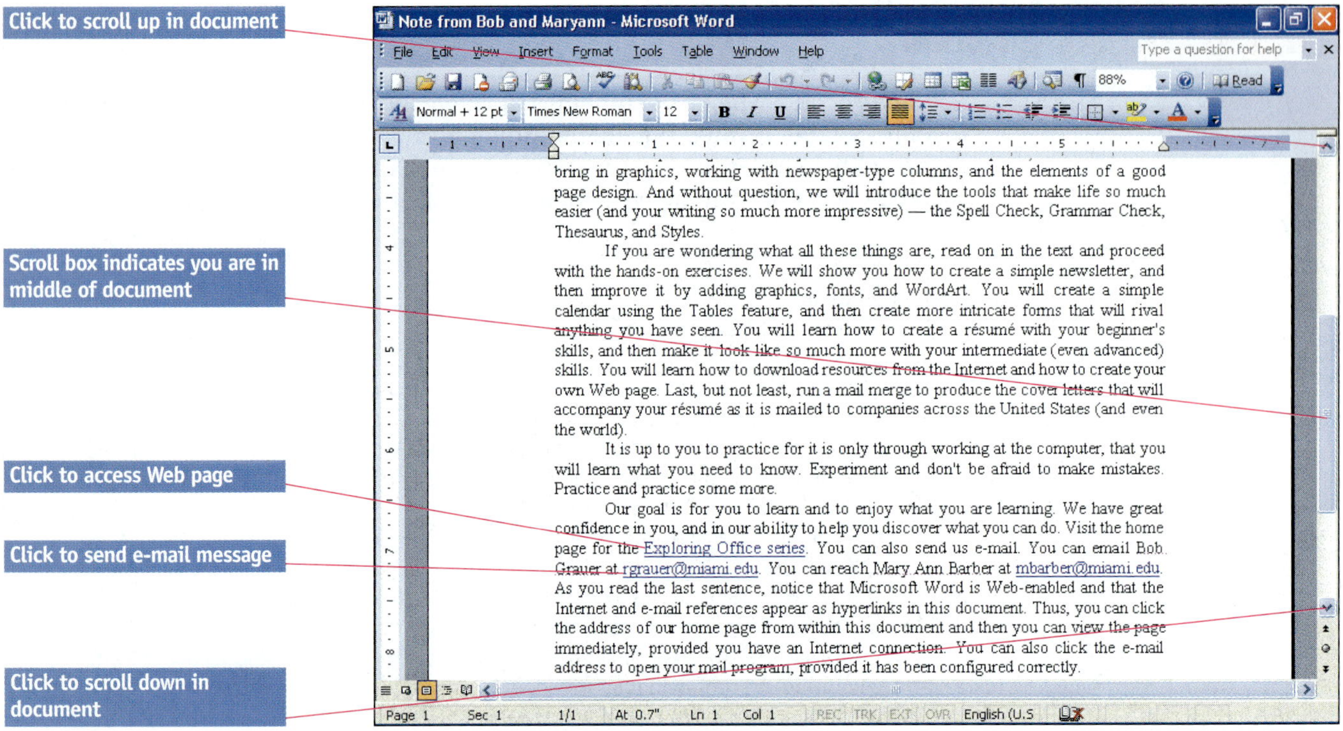

(b) Screen Display

FIGURE 2.2 Scrolling (*continued*)

Scrolling comes about automatically as you reach the bottom of the screen. Entering a new line of text, clicking on the down arrow within the scroll bar, or pressing the down arrow key brings a new line into view at the bottom of the screen and simultaneously removes a line at the top. (The process is reversed at the top of the screen.)

Scrolling can be done with either the mouse or the keyboard. Scrolling with the mouse (e.g., clicking the down arrow in the scroll bar) changes what is displayed on the screen, but does not move the insertion point, so that you must click the mouse after scrolling prior to entering the text at the new location. Scrolling with the keyboard, however (e.g., pressing Ctrl+Home or Ctrl+End to move to the beginning or end of a document, respectively), changes what is displayed on the screen as well as the location of the insertion point, and you can begin typing immediately.

Scrolling occurs most often in a vertical direction as shown in Figure 2.2. It can also occur horizontally, when the length of a line in a document exceeds the number of characters that can be displayed horizontally on the screen.

WRITE NOW, EDIT LATER

You write a sentence, then change it, and change it again, and one hour later you've produced a single paragraph. It happens to every writer—you stare at a blank screen and flashing cursor and are unable to write. The best solution is to brainstorm and write down anything that pops into your head, and to keep on writing. Don't worry about typos or spelling errors because you can fix them later. Above all, resist the temptation to continually edit the few words you've written because overediting will drain the life out of what you are writing. The important thing is to get your ideas on paper.

VIEW MENU

The ***View menu*** provides different views of a document. Each view can be displayed at different magnifications, which in turn determine the amount of scrolling necessary to see remote parts of a document.

The ***Normal view*** is the default view and it provides the fastest way to enter text. The ***Print Layout view*** more closely resembles the printed document and displays the top and bottom margins, headers and footers, page numbers, graphics, and other features that do not appear in the Normal view. The ***Reading Layout view*** eliminates unnecessary toolbars, making it easier to read your document. It also enables you to annotate a document with comments and/or highlighting of key sections.

The ***Zoom command*** displays the document on the screen at different magnifications—for example, 75%, 100%, or 200%. (The Zoom command does not affect the size of the text on the printed page.) A Zoom percentage (magnification) of 100% displays the document in the approximate size of the text on the printed page. You can increase the percentage to 200% to make the characters appear larger. You can also decrease the magnification to 75% to see more of the document at one time.

Word will automatically determine the magnification if you select one of four additional Zoom options—Page Width, Text Width, Whole Page, or Many Pages (Whole Page and Many Pages are available only in the Print Layout view). Figure 2.3, for example, displays a two-page document in Print Layout view. The 40% magnification is determined automatically once you specify the number of pages.

The View menu also provides access to two additional views—the Outline view and the Web Layout view. The Outline view does not display a conventional outline, but rather a structural view of a document that can be collapsed or expanded as necessary. The Web Layout view is used when you are creating a Web page. Both views are discussed in later chapters.

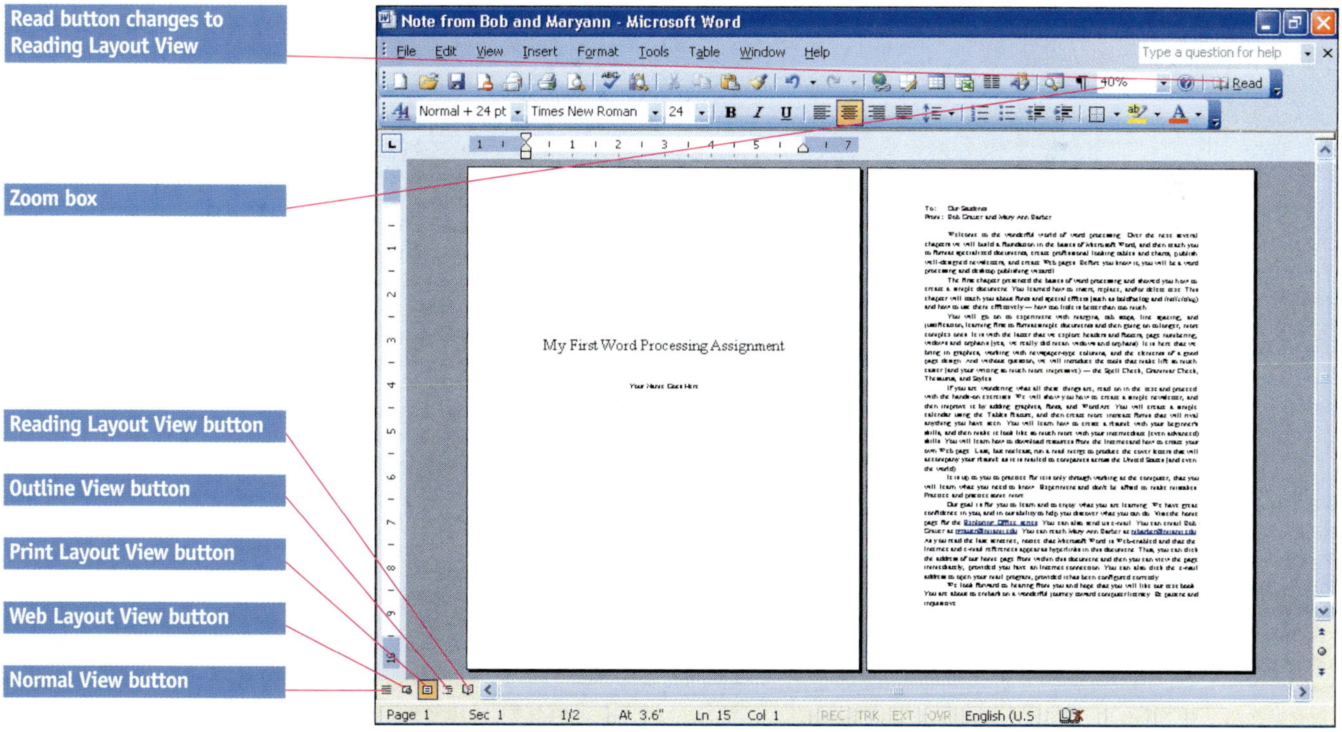

FIGURE 2.3 View Menu and Zoom Command

hands-on exercise

1 Editing a Document

Objective To edit an existing document; to use the Find and Replace commands; to move and copy text using the clipboard and the drag-and-drop facility. Use Figure 2.4 as a guide in the exercise.

Step 1: The View Menu

- Start Word as described in the hands-on exercises from Chapter 1. Pull down the **File menu** and click **Open** (or click the **Open button** on the toolbar).
  - Click the **drop-down arrow** on the Look In list box. Click the appropriate drive, drive C or drive A, depending on the location of your data.
  - Double click the **Exploring Word folder** to make it the active folder (the folder in which you will save the document).
  - Scroll in the Name list box (if necessary) until you can click the **Note from Bob and Maryann** to select this document. Double click the **document icon** or click the **Open command button** to open the file.
- The document should appear on the screen as shown in Figure 2.4a.
- Change to the Print Layout view at Page Width magnification:
  - Pull down the **View menu** and click **Print Layout** (or click the **Print Layout View button** above the status bar) as shown in Figure 2.4a.
  - Click the **down arrow** in the Zoom box to change to **Page Width**.
- Click and drag the mouse to select the phrase **Our Students**, which appears at the beginning of the document. Type your name to replace the selected text.
- Pull down the **File menu**, click the **Save As command**, then save the document as **Note from Bob and Maryann Solution**. (This creates a second copy of the document.)

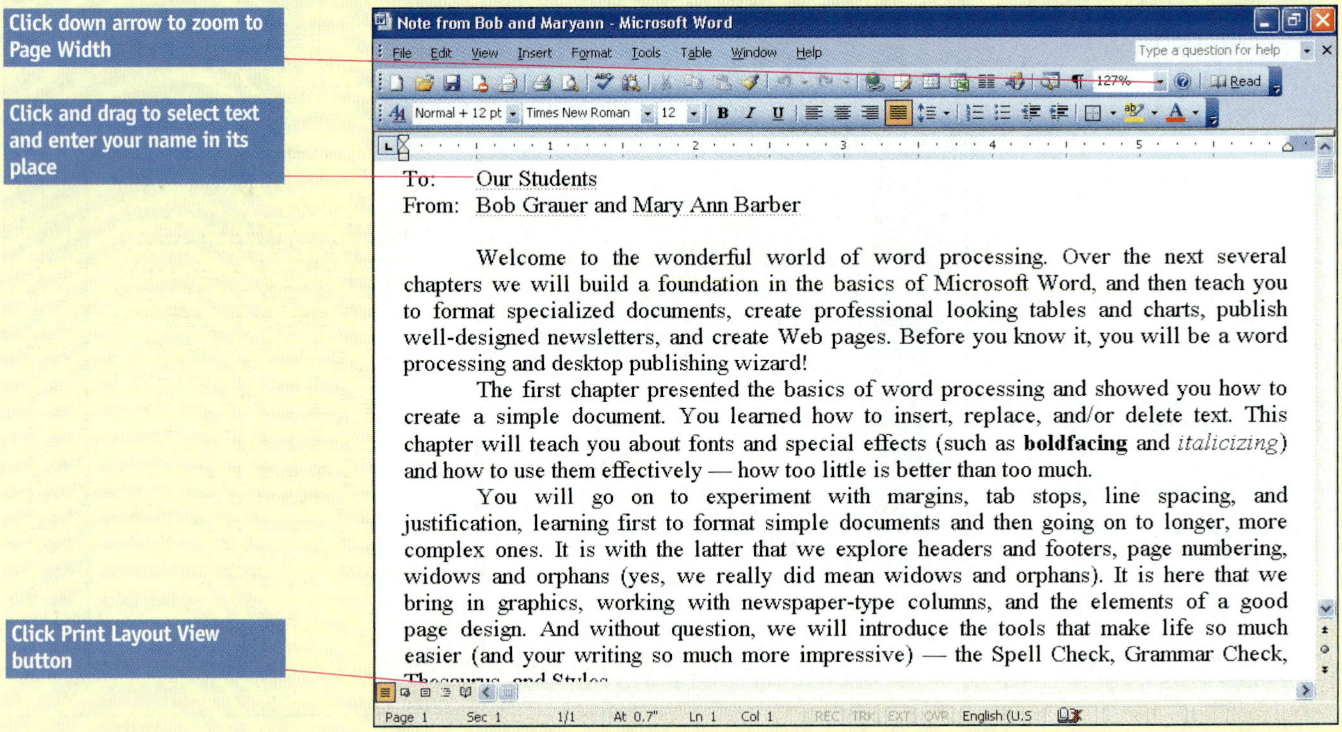

(a) The View Menu (step 1)

FIGURE 2.4 Hands-on Exercise 1

Step 2: Scrolling

- Click and drag the **scroll box** within the vertical scroll bar to scroll to the end of the document as shown in Figure 2.4b. Click immediately before the period at the end of the last sentence.
- Type a **comma** and a space, then insert the phrase **but most of all**, **enjoy**.
- Drag the **scroll box** to the top of the scroll bar to get back to the beginning of the document.
- Click immediately before the period ending the first sentence, press the **space bar**, then add the phrase **and desktop publishing**.
- Use the keyboard to practice scrolling shortcuts. Press **Ctrl+Home** and **Ctrl+End** to move to the beginning and end of a document, respectively. Press **PgUp** or **PgDn** to scroll one screen in the indicated direction.
- Save the document.

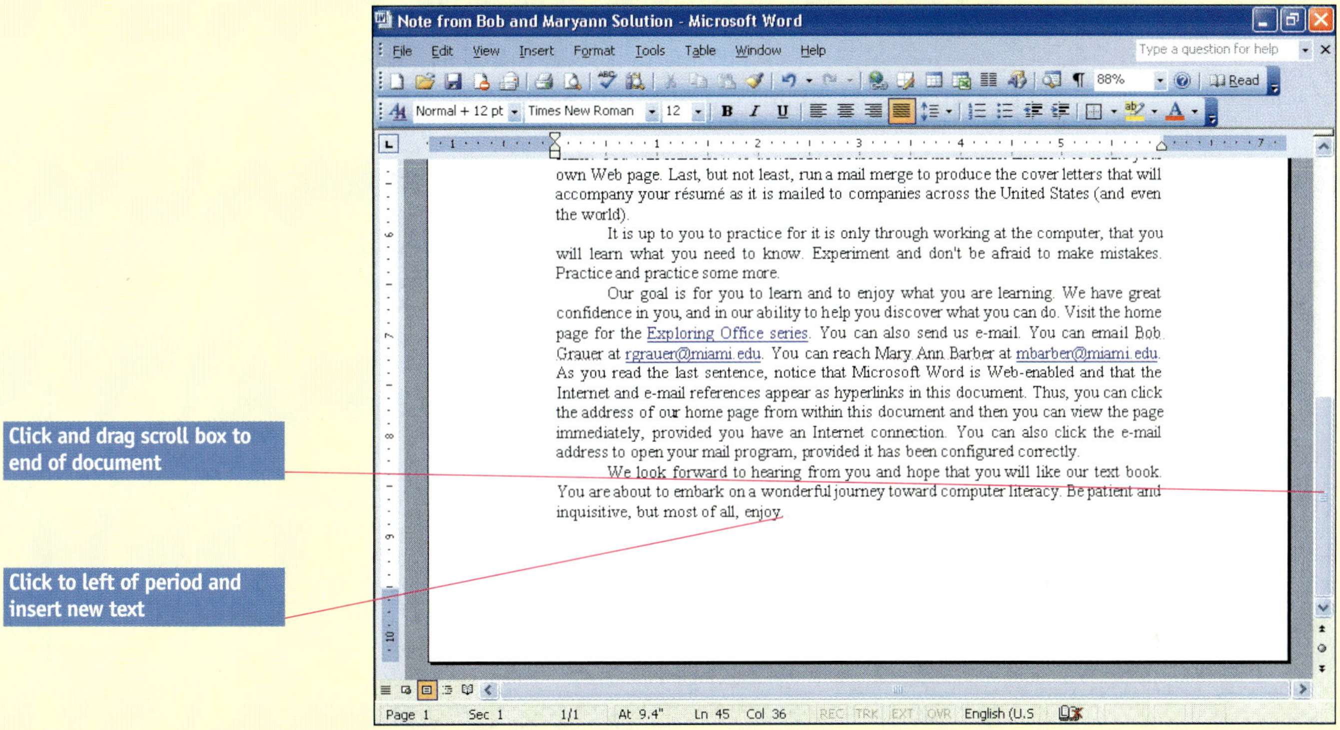

(b) Scrolling (step 2)

FIGURE 2.4 Hands-on Exercise 1 (*continued*)

THE MOUSE AND THE SCROLL BAR

Scroll quickly through a document by clicking above or below the scroll box to scroll up or down an entire screen. Move to the top, bottom, or an approximate position within a document by dragging the scroll box to the corresponding position in the scroll bar; for example, dragging the scroll box to the middle of the bar moves the mouse pointer to the middle of the document. Scrolling with the mouse does not change the location of the insertion point, however, and thus you must click the mouse at the new location prior to entering text at that location.

Step 3: The Replace Command

- Press **Ctrl+Home** to move to the beginning of the document. Pull down the **Edit menu**. Click **Replace** to produce the dialog box of Figure 2.4c. Click the **More button** to display the available options. Clear the check boxes.
- Type **text** in the Find what text box. Press the **Tab key**. Type **book** in the Replace with text box.
- Click the **Find Next button** to find the first occurrence of the word *text*. The dialog box remains on the screen, and the first occurrence of *text* is selected. This is *not* an appropriate substitution.
- Click the **Find Next button** to move to the next occurrence without making the replacement. This time the substitution is appropriate.
- Click **Replace** to make the change and automatically move to the next occurrence, where the substitution is again inappropriate. Click **Find Next** a final time. Word will indicate that it has finished searching the document. Click **OK**.
- Change the Find and Replace strings to **Mary Ann** and **Maryann**, respectively. Click the **Replace All button** to make the substitution globally without confirmation. Word will indicate that two replacements were made. Click **OK**.
- Close the dialog box. Save the document.

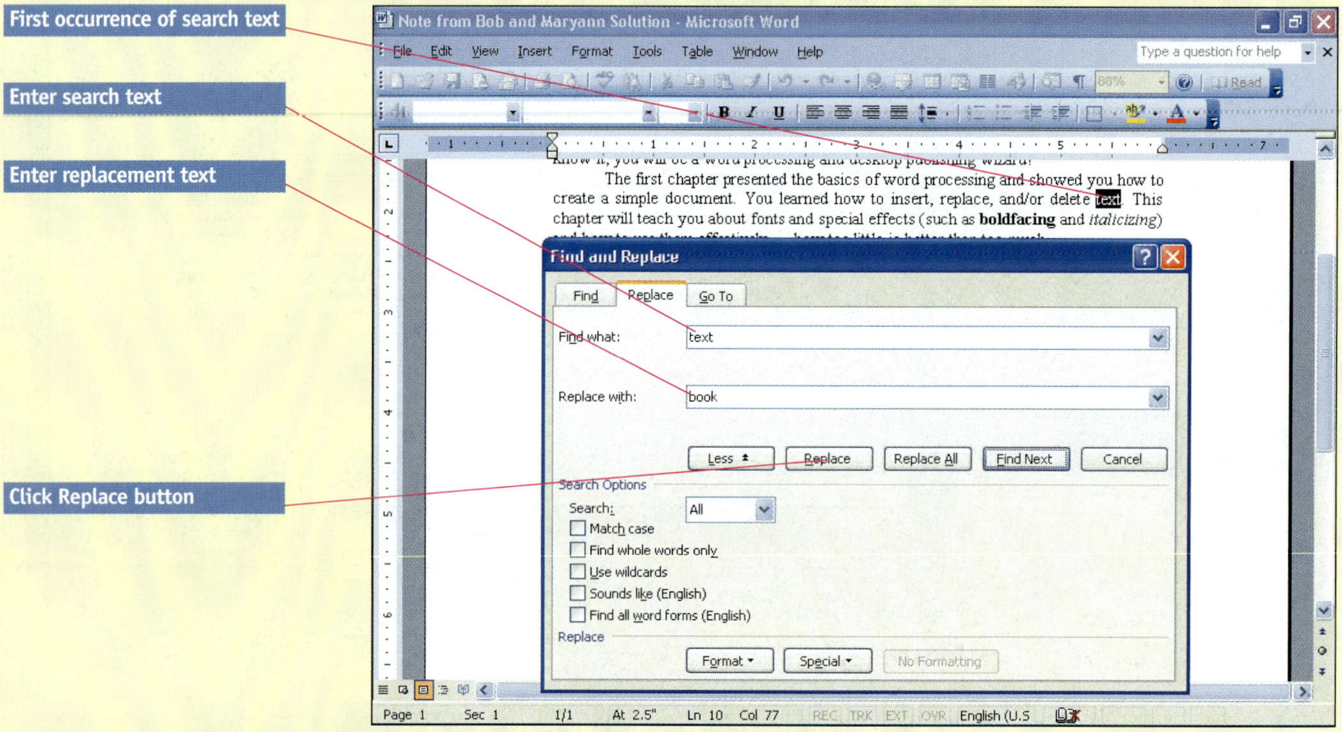

(c) The Replace Command (step 3)

FIGURE 2.4 Hands-on Exercise 1 (*continued*)

SEARCH FOR SPECIAL CHARACTERS

Use the Find and Replace commands to search for special characters such as tabs or paragraph marks. Click the More button in either dialog box, then click the Special command button that appears in the expanded dialog box to search for the additional characters. You could, for example, replace erroneous paragraph marks with a simple space, or replace five consecutive spaces with a Tab character.

Step 4: The Windows Clipboard

- Click and drag to select the sentence asking you to visit our home page, which includes a hyperlink (underlined blue text). Click the **Copy button**.
- Press **Ctrl+End** to move to the end of the document. Pull down the **Edit menu**, click the **Paste Special command** to display the Paste Special dialog box. Select **Unformatted text** and click **OK**.
- The sentence appears at the end of the document, but without the hyperlink formatting. Click the **Undo button** since we do not want the sentence. You have, however, seen the effect of the Paste Special command.
- If necessary, scroll until you see the paragraph beginning **It is up to you**. Select the sentence **Practice and practice some more** by dragging the mouse. (Be sure to include the period.)
- Pull down the **Edit menu** and click the **Copy command** or click the **Copy button**.
- Press **Ctrl+End** to scroll to the end of the document. Press the **space bar**. Pull down the **Edit menu** and click the **Paste command** (or click the **Paste button**).
- Click the **Paste Options button** if it appears as shown in Figure 2.4d to see the available options, then press **Esc** to suppress the context-sensitive menu.

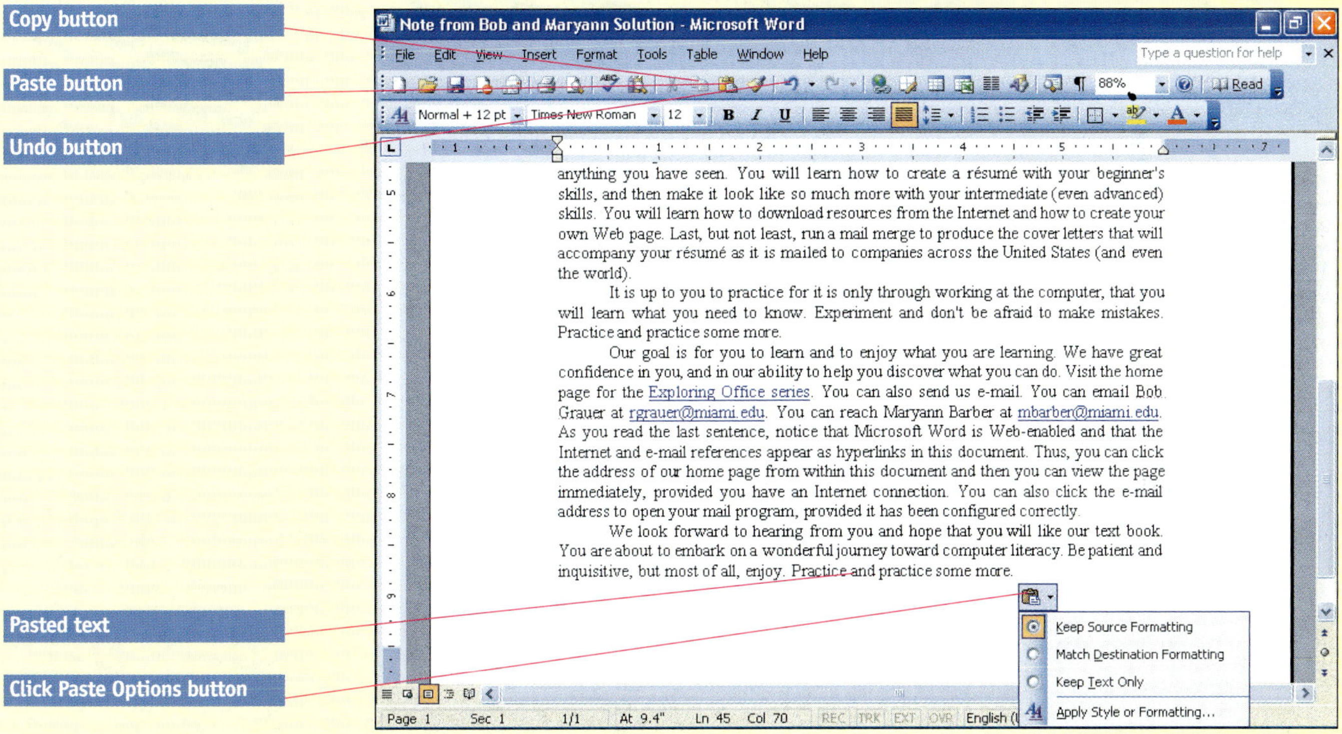

(d) The Windows Clipboard (step 4)

FIGURE 2.4 Hands-on Exercise 1 (*continued*)

PASTE OPTIONS

Text can be copied with or without the associated formatting according to the selected option in the Paste Options button. (The button appears automatically whenever the source and destination paragraphs have different formatting.) The default is to keep the source formatting (the formatting of the copied object). The button disappears as soon as you begin typing.

Step 5: The Office Clipboard

- Pull down the **Edit menu** and click the **Office Clipboard command** to open the clipboard task pane as shown in Figure 2.4e. The contents of your clipboard may differ.
- Delete any items that appear except the one urging you to practice.
- Click and drag to select the three sentences that indicate you can send us e-mail, and that contain our e-mail addresses. Click the **Copy button** to copy these sentences to the Office clipboard, which now contains two icons.
- Press **Ctrl+End** to move to the end of the document, press **Enter** to begin a new paragraph, and press the **Tab key** to indent the paragraph. Click the **Paste All button** on the Office clipboard to paste both items at the end of the document. (You may have to add a space between the two sentences.)
- Close the task pane.
- Save the document.

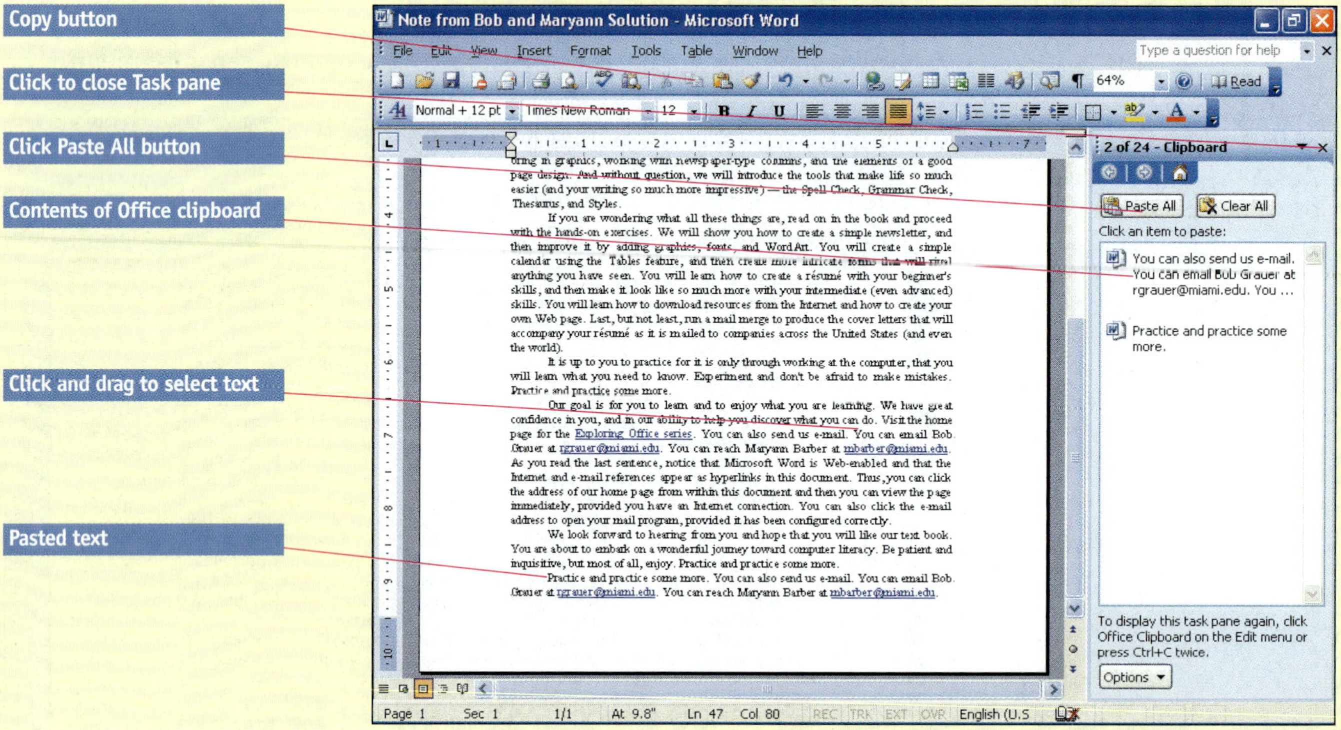

(e) The Office Clipboard (step 5)

FIGURE 2.4 Hands-on Exercise 1 (*continued*)

THE OFFICE CLIPBOARD

The Office clipboard enables you to collect up to 24 text and/or graphical elements from any Office document, and then it lets you paste those elements individually or collectively into an altogether different document. For example, you can cut or copy text from a Word document, data from an Excel worksheet, and a bulleted list from PowerPoint, then you can paste all of those elements into a new Word document. The collected items stay on the Office clipboard until you exit Office. (Press Ctrl+C twice in a row to display the Office clipboard if it is not already visible.)

Step 6: Undo and Redo Commands

- Click the **drop-down arrow** next to the Undo button to display the previously executed actions as in Figure 2.4f. The list of actions corresponds to the editing commands you have issued since the start of the exercise.
- Click **Paste** (the first command on the list) to undo the last editing command; the sentence asking you to send us e-mail disappears from the last paragraph.
- Click the **Undo button** a second time and the sentence, Practice and practice some more, disappears.
- Click the remaining steps on the undo list to retrace your steps through the exercise one command at a time. Alternatively, you can scroll to the bottom of the list and click the last command.
- Either way, when the undo list is empty, you will have the document as it existed at the start of the exercise. Click the **drop-down arrow** for the Redo command to display the list of commands you have undone.
- Click each command in sequence (or click the command at the bottom of the list), and you will restore the document.
- Save the document.

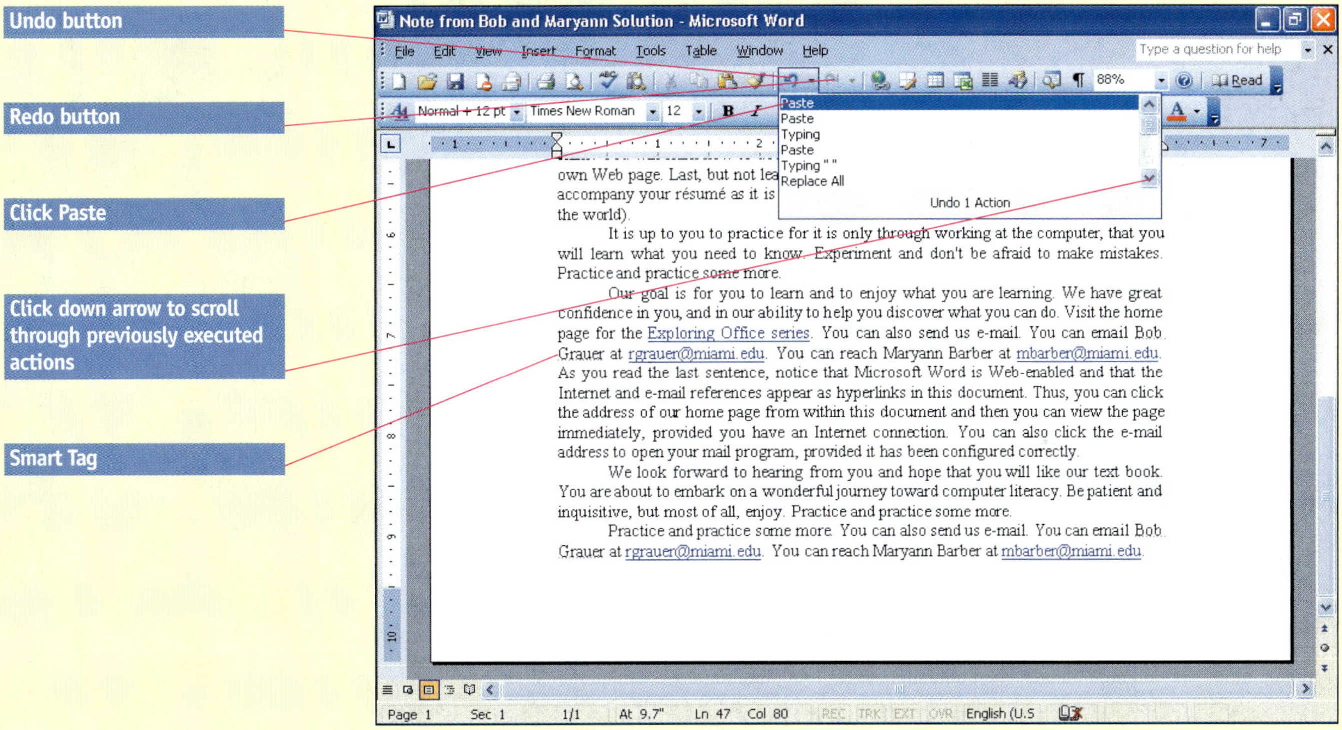

(f) Undo and Redo Commands (step 6)

FIGURE 2.4 Hands-on Exercise 1 (*continued*)

KEYBOARD SHORTCUTS—CUT, COPY AND PASTE

Ctrl+X, Ctrl+C, and Ctrl+V are keyboard shortcuts to cut, copy, and paste, respectively. The "X" is supposed to remind you of a pair of scissors. The shortcuts are easier to remember when you realize that the operative letters, X, C, and V, are next to each other on the keyboard. The shortcuts work in virtually any Windows application. See practice exercise 2 at the end of the chapter.

Step 7: Drag and Drop

- Scroll to the top of the document. Click and drag to select the phrase **format specialized documents** (including the comma and space) as shown in Figure 2.4g, then drag the phrase to its new location immediately before the word *and*. (A dotted vertical bar appears as you drag the text, to indicate its new location.)
- Release the mouse button to complete the move. Click the **drop-down arrow** for the Undo button; click **Move** to undo the move.
- To copy the selected text to the same location (instead of moving it), press and hold the **Ctrl key** as you drag the text to its new location. (A plus sign appears as you drag the text, to indicate it is being copied rather than moved.)
- Practice the drag-and-drop procedure several times until you are confident you can move and copy with precision.
- Click anywhere in the document to deselect the text. Save the document. Print the completed document for your instructor.
- Save the document.

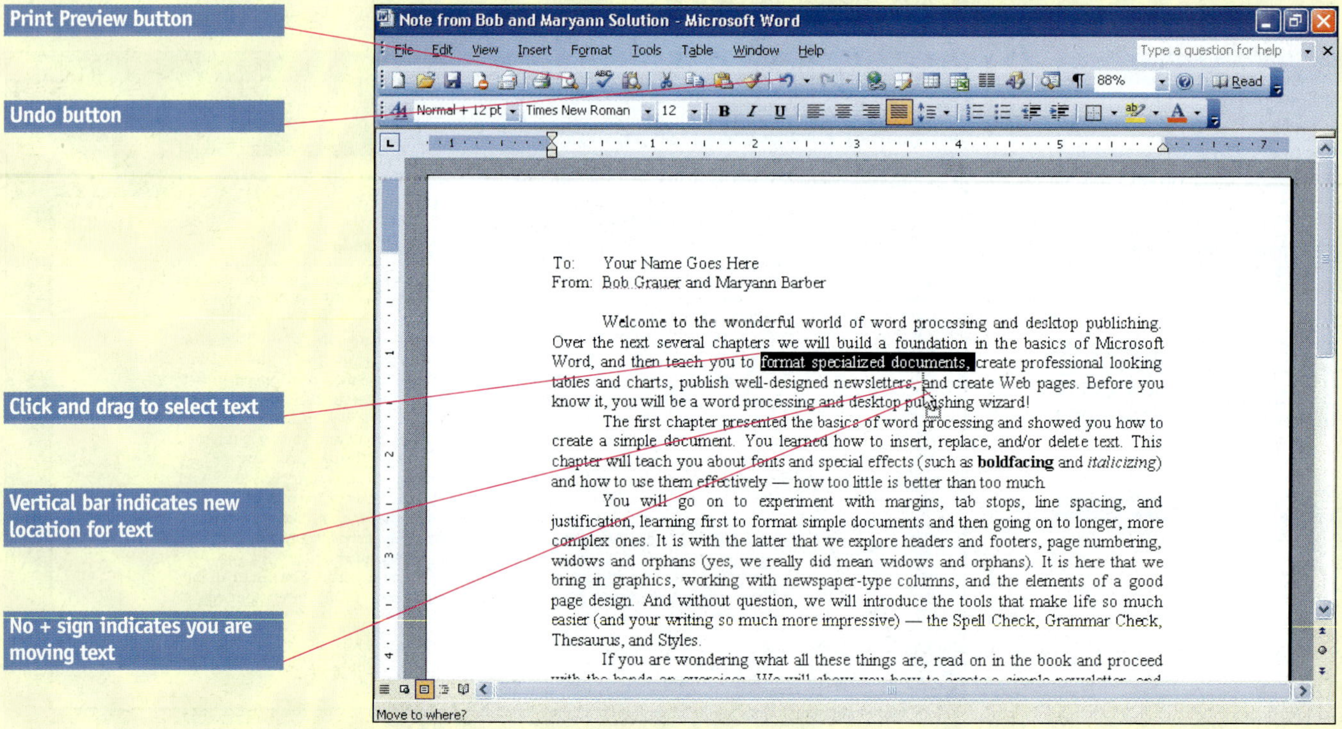

(g) Drag and Drop (step 7)

FIGURE 2.4 Hands-on Exercise 1 (*continued*)

THE PRINT PREVIEW COMMAND

Pull down the File menu and click the Print Preview command or click the Print Preview button on the Standard toolbar to see the document as it will appear when it is printed. The current document should fit on one page; if not, click the Shrink to Fit button on the Print Preview toolbar to automatically reduce the font size and force the document onto one page. Click the Print button to print the document, then close the Print Preview window.

Step 8: E-mail the Completed Document

- Check with your professor before completing this step. Pull down the **File menu**, click the **Send To command**, then choose **Mail Recipient (as Attachment)**.
- Your default e-mail program (e.g., Microsoft Outlook) is started automatically as shown in Figure 2.4h. The subject and attachment are entered automatically.
- Enter your **professor's e-mail address** in the To text box. Press the **Tab key** to move to the CC (courtesy copy) text box and enter your **e-mail address**. (It is always a good idea to send yourself a copy of important e-mail messages.)
- Press the **Tab key** three times to move to the body of the message, then enter a short note to your instructor.
- Click the **Send button** to send the message. The e-mail window closes, and you are back in Microsoft Word.
- Pull down the **File menu** and click the **Close command**. Click **Yes** if prompted to save the changes.
- Exit Word if you do not want to continue with the next exercise at this time.

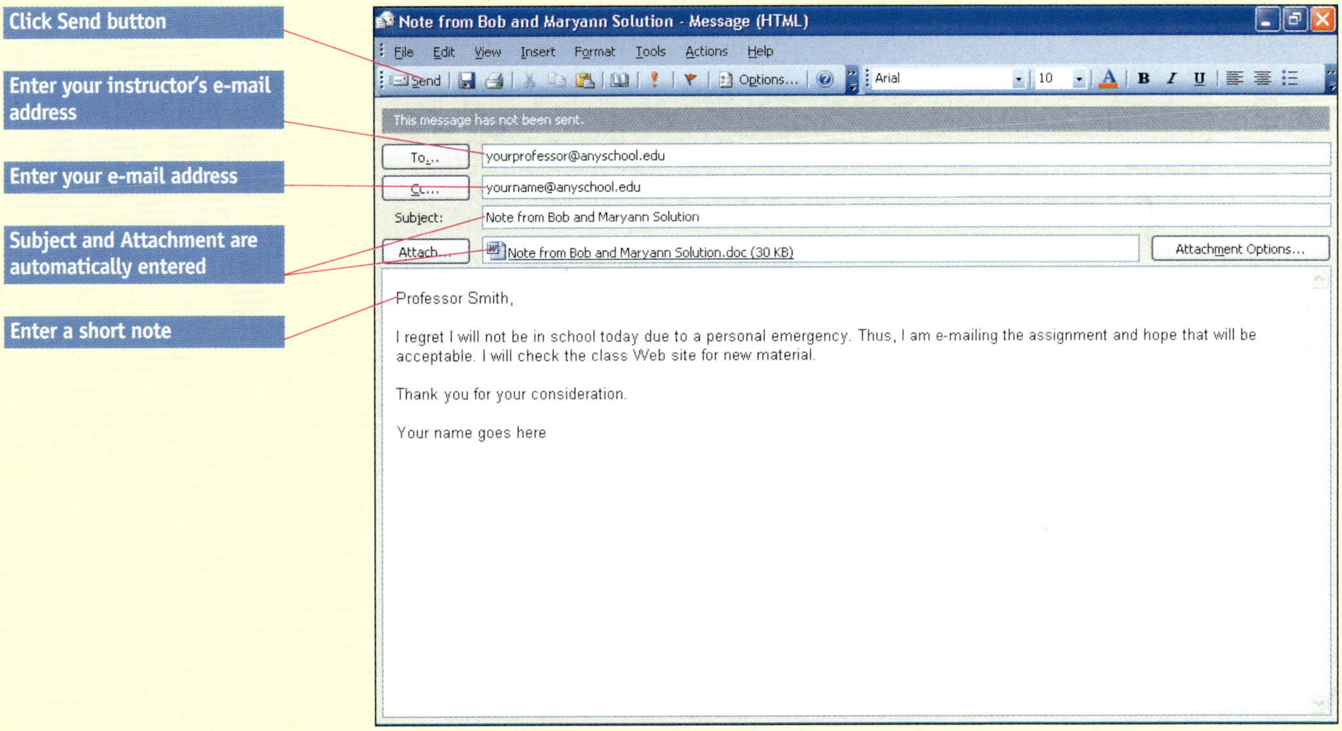

(h) E-mail the Completed Document (step 8)

FIGURE 2.4 Hands-on Exercise 1 (*continued*)

SEND A DOCUMENT FOR REVIEW

Pull down the File menu, click the Send To command, and choose Mail Recipient (for Review), as opposed to Mail Recipient (as Attachment). The result is almost the same except for a minor change in the subject line, which says "please review the attached document". The real difference between the commands occurs after the recipient reviews the document, enters his or her changes electronically, then returns the document to the sender. Word will then compare and merge the two documents (the original and the copy sent for review), giving the author the opportunity to accept or reject the reviewer's comments one at a time.

TYPOGRAPHY

Typography is the process of selecting typefaces, type styles, and type sizes. The importance of these decisions is obvious, for the ultimate success of any document depends greatly on its appearance. Type should reinforce the message without calling attention to itself and should be consistent with the information you want to convey.

A ***typeface*** or ***font*** is a complete set of characters (upper- and lowercase letters, numbers, punctuation marks, and special symbols). Figure 2.5 illustrates three typefaces—***Times New Roman***, ***Arial***, and ***Courier New***—that are accessible from any Windows application.

A definitive characteristic of any typeface is the presence or absence of tiny cross lines that end the main strokes of each letter. A ***serif typeface*** has these lines. A ***sans serif typeface*** (*sans* from the French for *without*) does not. Times New Roman and Courier New are examples of a serif typeface. Arial is a sans serif typeface.

Typography is the process of selecting typefaces, type styles, and type sizes. A serif typeface has tiny cross strokes that end the main strokes of each letter. A sans serif typeface does not have these strokes. Serif typefaces are typically used with large amounts of text. Sans serif typefaces are used for headings and limited amounts of text. A proportional typeface allocates space in accordance with the width of each character and is what you are used to seeing. A monospaced typeface uses the same amount of space for every character.

(a) Times New Roman (serif and proportional)

Typography is the process of selecting typefaces, type styles, and type sizes. A serif typeface has tiny cross strokes that end the main strokes of each letter. A sans serif typeface does not have these strokes. Serif typefaces are typically used with large amounts of text. Sans serif typefaces are used for headings and limited amounts of text. A proportional typeface allocates space in accordance with the width of each character and is what you are used to seeing. A monospaced typeface uses the same amount of space for every character.

(b) Arial (sans serif and proportional)

Typography is the process of selecting typefaces, type styles, and type sizes. A serif typeface has tiny cross strokes that end the main strokes of each letter. A sans serif typeface does not have these strokes. Serif typefaces are typically used with large amounts of text. Sans serif typefaces are used for headings and limited amounts of text. A proportional typeface allocates space in accordance with the width of each character and is what you are used to seeing. A monospaced typeface uses the same amount of space for every character.

(c) Courier New (serif and monospaced)

FIGURE 2.5 Typefaces

Serifs help the eye to connect one letter with the next and are generally used with large amounts of text. This book, for example, is set in a serif typeface. A sans serif typeface is more effective with smaller amounts of text and appears in headlines, corporate logos, airport signs, and so on.

A second characteristic of a typeface is whether it is monospaced or proportional. A ***monospaced typeface*** (such as Courier New) uses the same amount of space for every character regardless of its width. A ***proportional typeface*** (such as Times New Roman or Arial) allocates space according to the width of the character. Monospaced fonts are used in tables and financial projections where text must be precisely lined up, one character underneath the other. Proportional typefaces create a more professional appearance and are appropriate for most documents. Any typeface can be set in different ***type styles*** (such as regular, **bold**, *italic*, or ***bold italic***).

Type Size

Type size is a vertical measurement and is specified in points. One ***point*** is equal to 1/72 of an inch; that is, there are 72 points to the inch. The measurement is made from the top of the tallest letter in a character set (for example, an uppercase T) to the bottom of the lowest letter (for example, a lowercase y). Most documents are set in 10 or 12 point type. Newspaper columns may be set as small as 8 point type, but that is the smallest type size you should consider. Conversely, type sizes of 14 points or higher are ineffective for large amounts of text.

Figure 2.6 shows the same phrase set in varying type sizes. Some typefaces appear larger (smaller) than others even though they may be set in the same point size. The type in Figure 2.6a, for example, looks smaller than the corresponding type in Figure 2.6b even though both are set in the same point size. Note, too, that you can vary the type size of a specific font within a document for emphasis. The eye needs at least two points to distinguish between different type sizes.

Format Font Command

The ***Format Font command*** gives you complete control over the typeface, size, and style of the text in a document. Executing the command before entering text will set the format of the text you type from that point on. You can also use the command to change the font of existing text by selecting the text, then executing the command. Either way, you will see the dialog box in Figure 2.7, in which you specify the font (typeface), style, and point size.

You can choose any of the special effects, such as SMALL CAPS, superscripts, or subscripts. You can also change the underline options (whether or not spaces are to be underlined). You can even change the color of the text on the monitor, but you need a color printer for the printed document. (The ***Character Spacing*** and ***Text Effects*** tabs produce different sets of options in which you control the spacing and appearance of the characters.)

TYPOGRAPHY TIP—USE RESTRAINT

More is not better, especially in the case of too many typefaces and styles, which produce cluttered documents that impress no one. Try to limit yourself to a maximum of two typefaces per document, but choose multiple sizes and/or styles within those typefaces for variation. Use boldface or italic for emphasis (underlining is generally not effective). Use these styles in moderation, because if you emphasize too many elements, the effect is lost.

This is Arial 8 point type

This is Arial 10 point type

This is Arial 12 point type

This is Arial 18 point type

This is Arial 24 point type

This is Arial 30 point type

(a) Sans Serif Typeface

This is Times New Roman 8 point type

This is Times New Roman 10 point type

This is Times New Roman 12 point type

This is Times New Roman 18 point type

This is Times New Roman 24 point type

This is Times New Roman 30 point

(b) Serif Typeface

FIGURE 2.6 Type Size

The left and right indents are defined as the distance between the text and the left and right margins, respectively. Both parameters are set to zero in this paragraph and so the text aligns on both margins. Different indentation can be applied to different paragraphs in the same document.

(a) No Indents

> Positive values for the left and right indents offset a paragraph from the rest of a document and are often used for long quotations. This paragraph has left and right indents of one-half inch each. Different indentation can be applied to different paragraphs in the same document.

(b) Left and Right Indents

A first line indent affects only the first line in the paragraph and is implemented by pressing the Tab key at the beginning of the paragraph. The remainder of the paragraph is aligned at the left margin (or the left indent if it differs from the left margin) as can be seen from this example. Different indentation can be applied to different paragraphs in the same document.

(c) First Line Indent

A hanging indent sets the first line of a paragraph at the left indent and indents the remaining lines according to the amount specified. Hanging indents are often used with bulleted or numbered lists. Different indentation can be applied to different paragraphs in the same document.

(d) Hanging (Special) Indent

FIGURE 2.11 Indents

Tabs

Anyone who has used a typewriter is familiar with the function of the Tab key; that is, press Tab and the insertion point moves to the next ***tab stop*** (a measured position to align text at a specific place). The Tab key is much more powerful in Word as you can choose from four different types of tab stops (left, center, right, and decimal). You can also specify a ***leader character***, typically dots or hyphens, to draw the reader's eye across the page. Tabs are often used to create columns of text within a document.

The default tab stops are set every ½ inch and are left aligned, but you can change the alignment and/or position with the Format Tabs command. Figure 2.12 illustrates a dot leader in combination with a right tab to produce a Table of Contents. The default tab stops have been cleared in Figure 2.12a, in favor of a single right tab at 5.5 inches. The option button for a dot leader has also been checked. The resulting document is shown in Figure 2.12b.

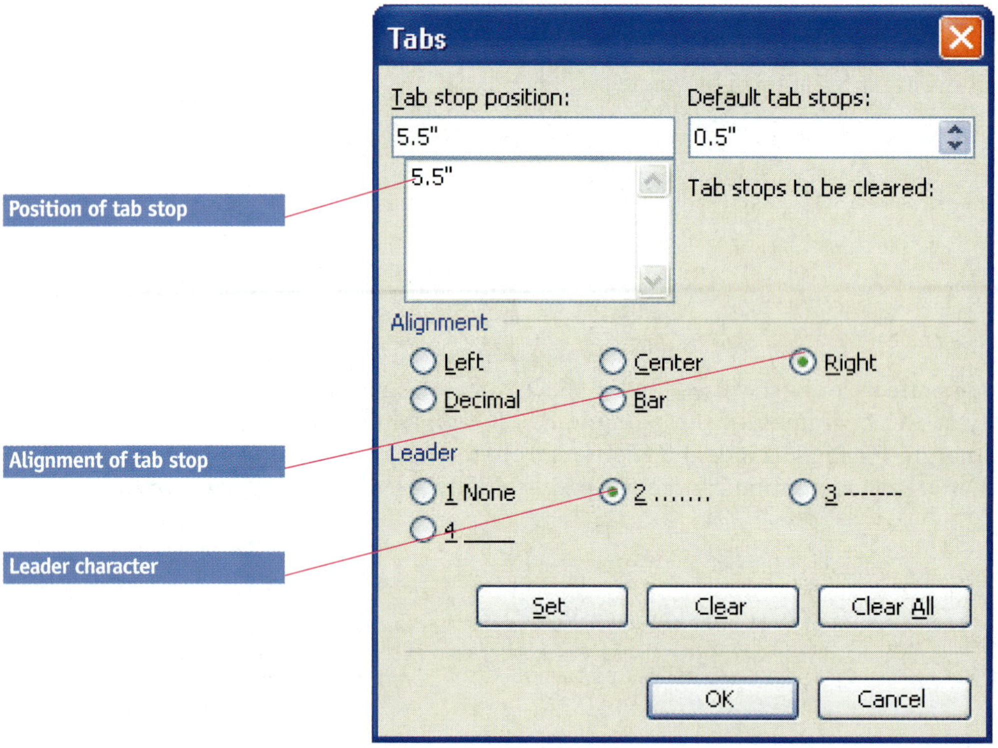

(a) Tab Stops

Right tab with dot leader

Chapter 1: Introduction 3
Chapter 2: Gaining Proficiency 32
Chapter 3: The Tools 61
Chapter 4: The Professional Document 99
Chapter 5: Desktop Publishing 124

(b) Table of Contents

FIGURE 2.12 Tabs

Hyphenation

Hyphenation gives a document a more professional look by eliminating excessive gaps of white space. It is especially useful in narrow columns and/or justified text. Hyphenation is implemented through the Language command in the Tools menu. You can choose to hyphenate a document automatically, in which case the hyphens are inserted as the document is created. (Microsoft Word will automatically rehyphenate the document to adjust for subsequent changes in editing.)

You can also hyphenate a document manually, to have Word prompt you prior to inserting each hyphen. Manual hyphenation does not, however, adjust for changes that affect the line breaks, and so it should be done only after the document is complete. And finally, you can fine-tune the use of hyphenation by preventing a hyphenated word from breaking if it falls at the end of a line. This is done by inserting a ***nonbreaking hyphen*** (press Ctrl+Shift+Hyphen) when the word is typed initially.

Line Spacing

Line spacing determines the space between the lines in a paragraph. Word provides complete flexibility and enables you to select any multiple of line spacing (single, double, line and a half, and so on). You can also specify line spacing in terms of points (there are 72 points per inch).

Line spacing is set at the paragraph level through the Format Paragraph command, which sets the spacing within a paragraph. The command also enables you to add extra spacing before the first line in a paragraph or after the last line. (Either technique is preferable to the common practice of single spacing the paragraphs within a document, then adding a blank line between paragraphs.)

FORMAT PARAGRAPH COMMAND

The ***Format Paragraph command*** is used to specify the alignment, indentation, line spacing, and pagination for the selected paragraph(s). As indicated, all of these features are implemented at the paragraph level and affect all selected paragraphs. If no paragraphs are selected, the command affects the entire current paragraph (the paragraph containing the insertion point).

The Format Paragraph command is illustrated in Figure 2.13. The Indents and Spacing tab in Figure 2.13a calls for a hanging indent, line spacing of 1.5 lines, and justified alignment. The preview area within the dialog box enables you to see how the paragraph will appear within the document.

The Line and Page Breaks tab in Figure 2.13b illustrates an entirely different set of parameters in which you control the pagination within a document. The check boxes in Figure 2.13b enable you to prevent the occurrence of awkward soft page breaks that detract from the appearance of a document.

You might, for example, want to prevent widows and orphans, terms used to describe isolated lines that seem out of place. A ***widow*** refers to the last line of a paragraph appearing by itself at the top of a page. An ***orphan*** is the first line of a paragraph appearing by itself at the bottom of a page.

You can also impose additional controls by clicking one or more check boxes. Use the Keep Lines Together option to prevent a soft page break from occurring within a paragraph and ensure that the entire paragraph appears on the same page. (The paragraph is moved to the top of the next page if it doesn't fit on the bottom of the current page.) Use the Keep with Next option to prevent a soft page break between the two paragraphs. This option is typically used to keep a heading (a one-line paragraph) with its associated text in the next paragraph.

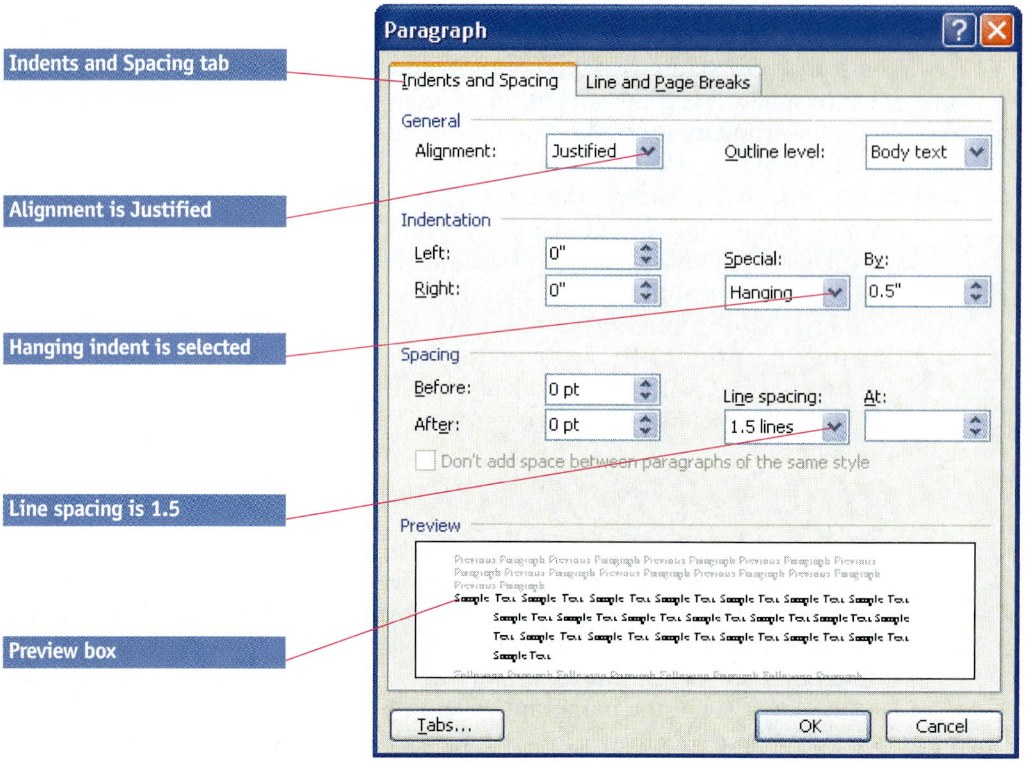

(a) Indents and Spacing

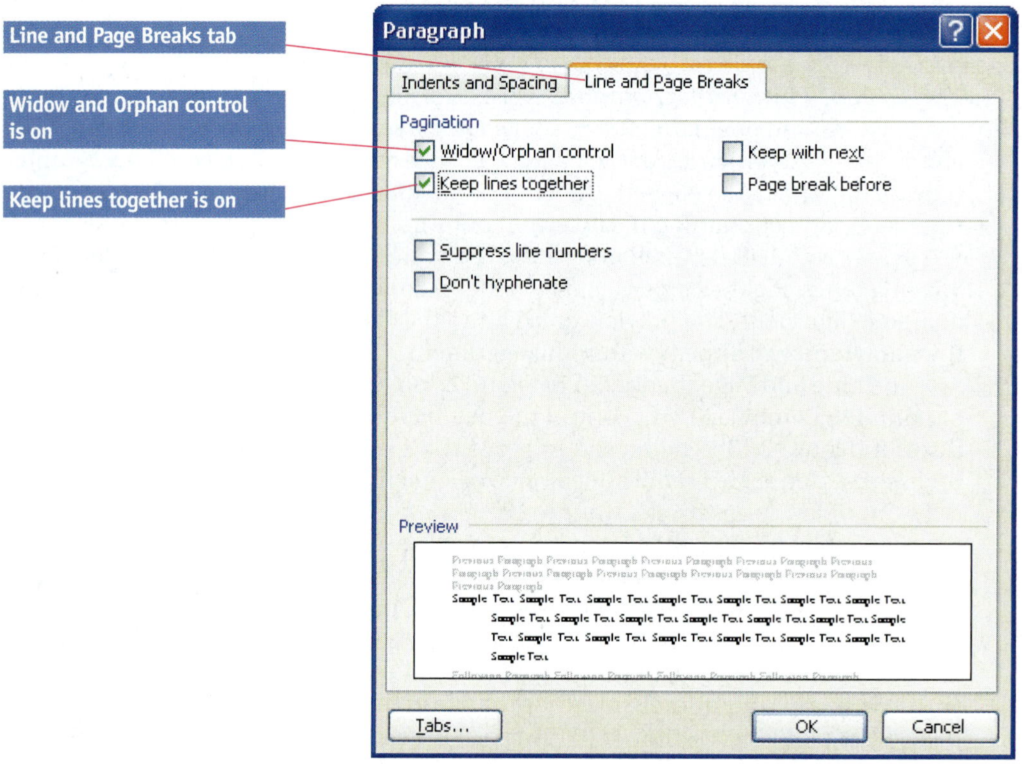

(b) Line and Page Breaks

FIGURE 2.13 Format Paragraph Command

Borders and Shading

The ***Borders and Shading command*** puts the finishing touches on a document and is illustrated in Figure 2.14. The command is applied to selected text within a paragraph, to the entire paragraph if no text is selected, or to the entire page if the Page Border tab is selected. Thus, you can create boxed and/or shaded text as well as place horizontal or vertical lines around different quantities of text.

You can choose from several different line styles in any color (assuming you have a color printer). You can place a uniform border around a paragraph (choose Box), or you can choose a shadow effect with thicker lines at the right and bottom. You can also apply lines to selected sides of a paragraph(s) by selecting a line style, then clicking the desired sides as appropriate.

The Page Border tab enables you to place a decorative border around one or more selected pages. As with a paragraph border, you can place the border around the entire page, or you can select one or more sides. The page border also provides an additional option to use preselected clip art instead of ordinary lines.

Shading is implemented independently of the border. Clear (no shading) is the default. Solid (100%) shading creates a solid box where the text is turned white so you can read it. Shading of 10 or 20 percent is generally most effective to add emphasis to the selected paragraph. The Borders and Shading command is implemented on the paragraph level and affects the entire paragraph (unless text has been selected within the paragraph)—either the current or selected paragraph(s).

The two command buttons at the bottom of the dialog box provide additional options. The Show Toolbar button displays the Tables and Borders toolbar that facilitates both borders and shading. The Horizontal Line button provides access to a variety of attractive designs.

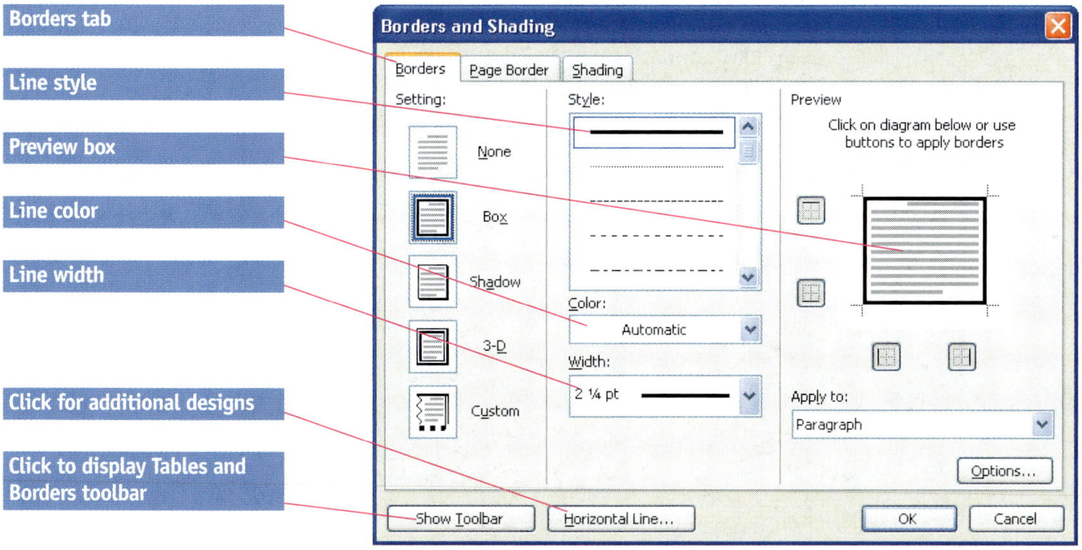

FIGURE 2.14 Paragraph Borders and Shading

FORMATTING AND THE PARAGRAPH MARK

The paragraph mark ¶ at the end of a paragraph does more than just indicate the presence of a hard return. It also stores all of the formatting in effect for the paragraph. Hence in order to preserve the formatting when you move or copy a paragraph, you must include the paragraph mark in the selected text. Click the Show/Hide ¶ button on the toolbar to display the paragraph mark and make sure it has been selected.

COLUMN FORMATTING

Columns add interest to a document and are implemented through the ***Columns command*** in the Format menu as shown in Figure 2.15. You specify the number of columns and, optionally, the space between columns. Microsoft Word does the rest, calculating the width of each column according to the left and right margins on the page and the specified (default) space between columns.

The dialog box in Figure 2.15 implements a design of three equal columns. The 2-inch width of each column is computed automatically based on left and right page margins of 1 inch each and the ¼-inch spacing between columns. The width of each column is determined by subtracting the sum of the margins and the space between the columns (a total of 2½ inches in this example) from the page width of 8½ inches. The result of the subtraction is 6 inches, which is divided by 3, resulting in a column width of 2 inches.

There is, however, one subtlety associated with column formatting, and that is the introduction of the ***section***, which controls elements such as the orientation of a page (landscape or portrait), margins, page numbers, and/or the number of columns. All of the documents in the text thus far have consisted of a single section, and therefore section formatting was not an issue. It becomes important only when you want to vary an element that is formatted at the section level. You could, for example, use section formatting to create a document that has one column on its title page and two columns on the remaining pages. This requires you to divide the document into two sections through insertion of a ***section break***. You then format each section independently and specify the number of columns in each section.

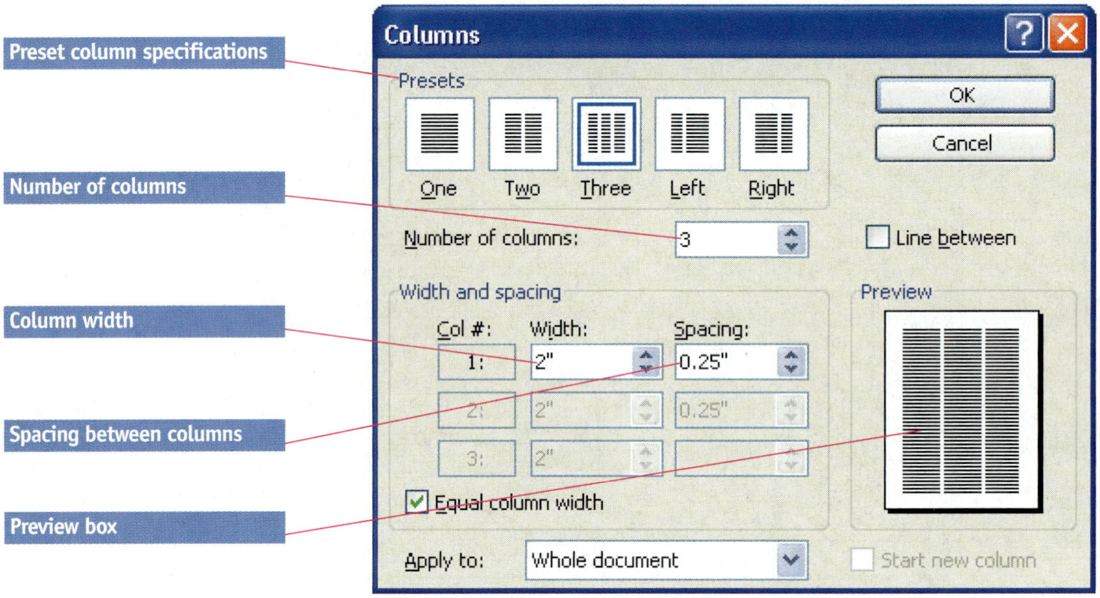

FIGURE 2.15 The Format Columns Command

THE SECTION VERSUS THE PARAGRAPH

Line spacing, alignment, tabs, and indents are implemented at the paragraph level. Change any of these parameters anywhere within the current (or selected) paragraph(s) and you change *only* those paragraph(s). Margins, page numbering, orientation, and columns are implemented at the section level. Change these parameters anywhere within a section and you change the characteristics of every page within that section.

hands-on exercise

3 Paragraph Formatting

Objective To implement line spacing, alignment, and indents; to implement widow and orphan protection; to box and shade a selected paragraph. Use Figure 2.16 as a guide in the exercise.

Step 1: Select-Then-Do

- Open the **Tips for Writing Solution** document from the previous exercise. If necessary, change to the Print Layout view.
- Click the **drop-down arrow** on the Zoom list box and click **Two Pages** to match the view in Figure 2.16a.
- Select the entire second page as shown in the figure. Point to the selected text and click the **right mouse button** to produce the shortcut menu.
- Click the **Paragraph command** to display the associated dialog box.

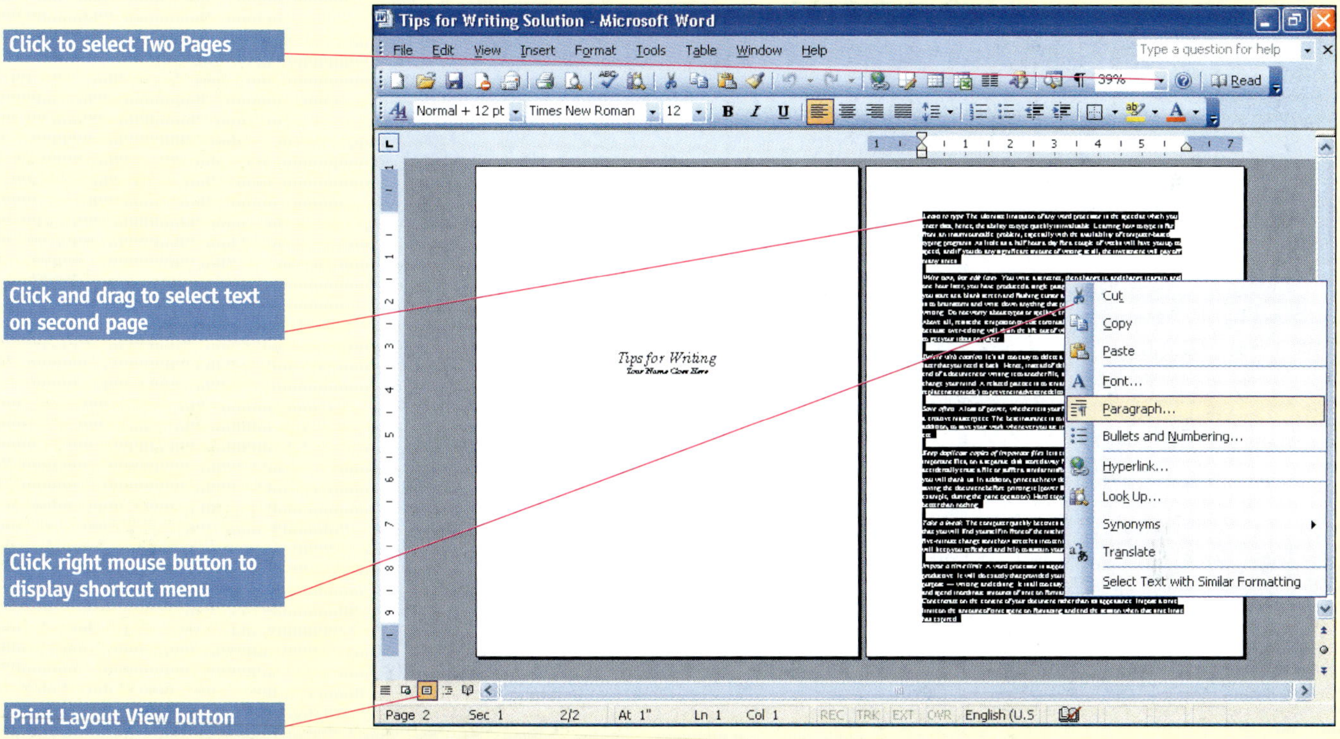

(a) Select-Then-Do (step 1)

FIGURE 2.16 Hands-on Exercise 3

SELECT TEXT WITH THE F8 (EXTEND) KEY

Move to the beginning of the text you want to select, then press the F8 (extend) key. The letters EXT will appear in the status bar. Use the arrow keys to extend the selection in the indicated direction; for example, press the down arrow key to select the line. You can also type any character—for example, a letter, space, or period—to extend the selection to the first occurrence of that character. Thus, typing a space or period is equivalent to selecting a word or sentence, respectively. Press Esc to cancel the selection mode.

Step 2: Line Spacing, Justification, and Pagination

- If necessary, click the **Indents and Spacing tab** to display the options in Figure 2.16b. Click the **down arrow** on the list box for Line Spacing and select **1.5 lines**. Click the **down arrow** on the Alignment list box and select **Justified**.
- Click the tab for **Line and Page Breaks**. Check the box for **Keep Lines Together**. If necessary, check the box for **Widow/Orphan Control**.
- Click **OK** to accept the settings and close the dialog box.
- Click anywhere in the document to deselect the text and see the effects of the formatting changes that were just specified.
- Save the document.

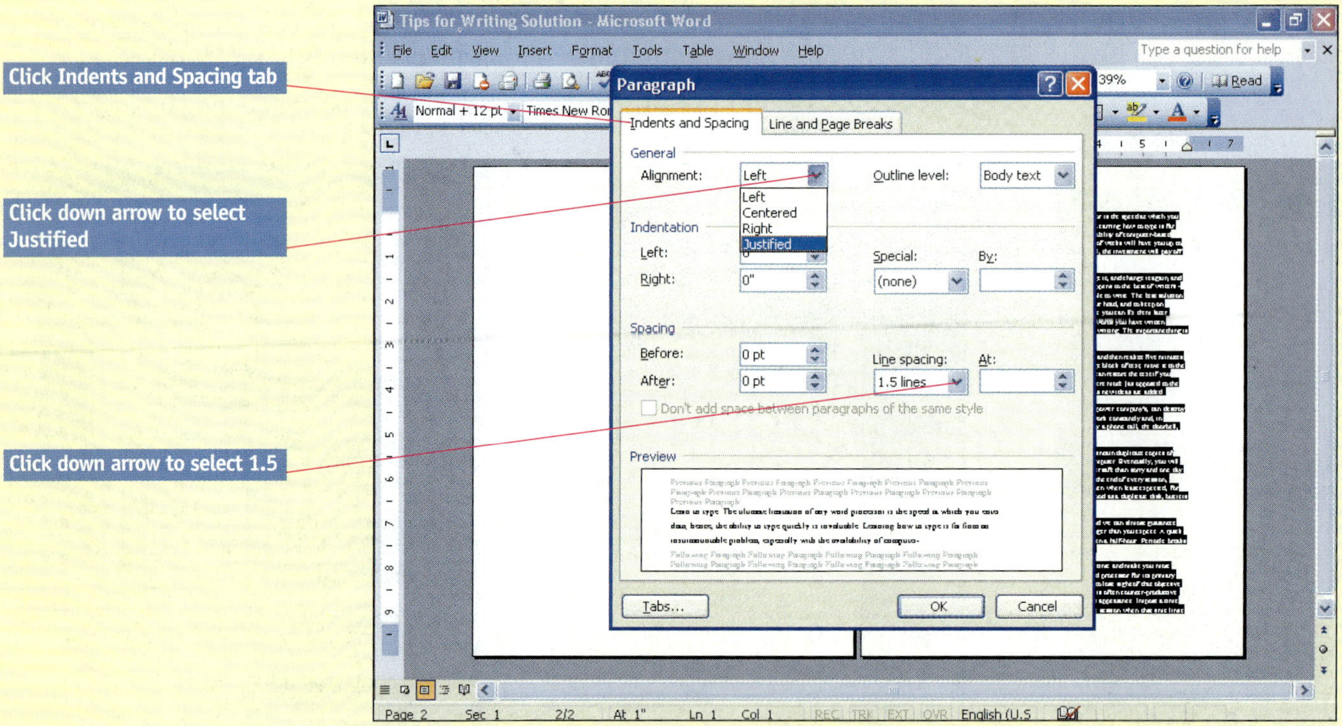

(b) Line Spacing, Justification, and Pagination (step 2)

FIGURE 2.16 Hands-on Exercise 3 (*continued*)

REVEAL THE FORMATTING

Open the task pane and click the down arrow in the title bar to select Reveal Formatting to display complete information for the selected text in the document. The properties are displayed by Font, Paragraph, and Section, enabling you to click the plus or minus sign next to each item to view or hide the underlying details. The properties in each area are links to the associated dialog boxes. Click Alignment or Justification, for example, within the Paragraph area to open the associated dialog box, where you can change the indicated property.

Step 3: Indents

- Select the second paragraph as shown in Figure 2.16c. (The second paragraph will not yet be indented.)
- Pull down the **Format menu** and click **Paragraph** (or press the **right mouse button** to produce the shortcut menu and click **Paragraph**).
- If necessary, click the **Indents and Spacing tab** in the Paragraph dialog box.
- Click the **up arrow** on the Left Indentation text box to set the **Left Indent** to **.5** inch. Set the **Right indent** to **.5** inch.
- Click **OK**. Your document should match Figure 2.16c.
- Save the document.

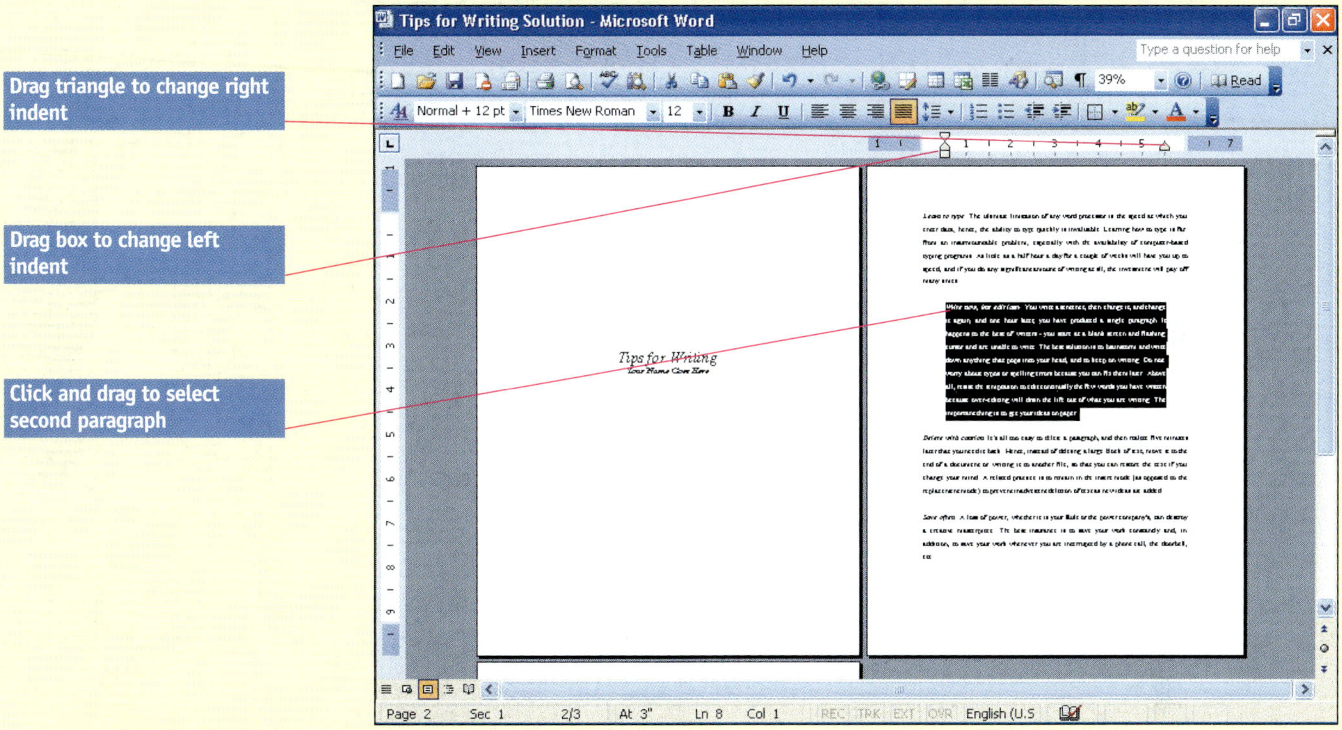

(c) Indents (step 3)

FIGURE 2.16 Hands-on Exercise 3 (*continued*)

INDENTS AND THE RULER

Use the ruler to change the special, left, and/or right indents. Select the paragraph (or paragraphs) in which you want to change indents, then drag the appropriate indent markers to the new location(s). If you get a hanging indent when you wanted to change the left indent, it means you dragged the bottom triangle instead of the box. Click the Undo button and try again. (You can always use the Format Paragraph command rather than the ruler if you continue to have difficulty.)

Step 4: Borders and Shading

- Pull down the **Format menu**. Click **Borders and Shading** to produce the dialog box in Figure 2.16d.
- If necessary, click the **Borders tab**. Select a style and width for the border. Click the rectangle labeled **Box** under Setting. You can also experiment with a partial border by clicking in the Preview area to toggle a line on or off.
- Click the **Shading Tab**. Click the **down arrow** on the Style list box. Click **10%**.
- Click **OK** to accept the settings for both Borders and Shading. Click outside the paragraph to deselect it and see the formatting in effect.
- Save the document.

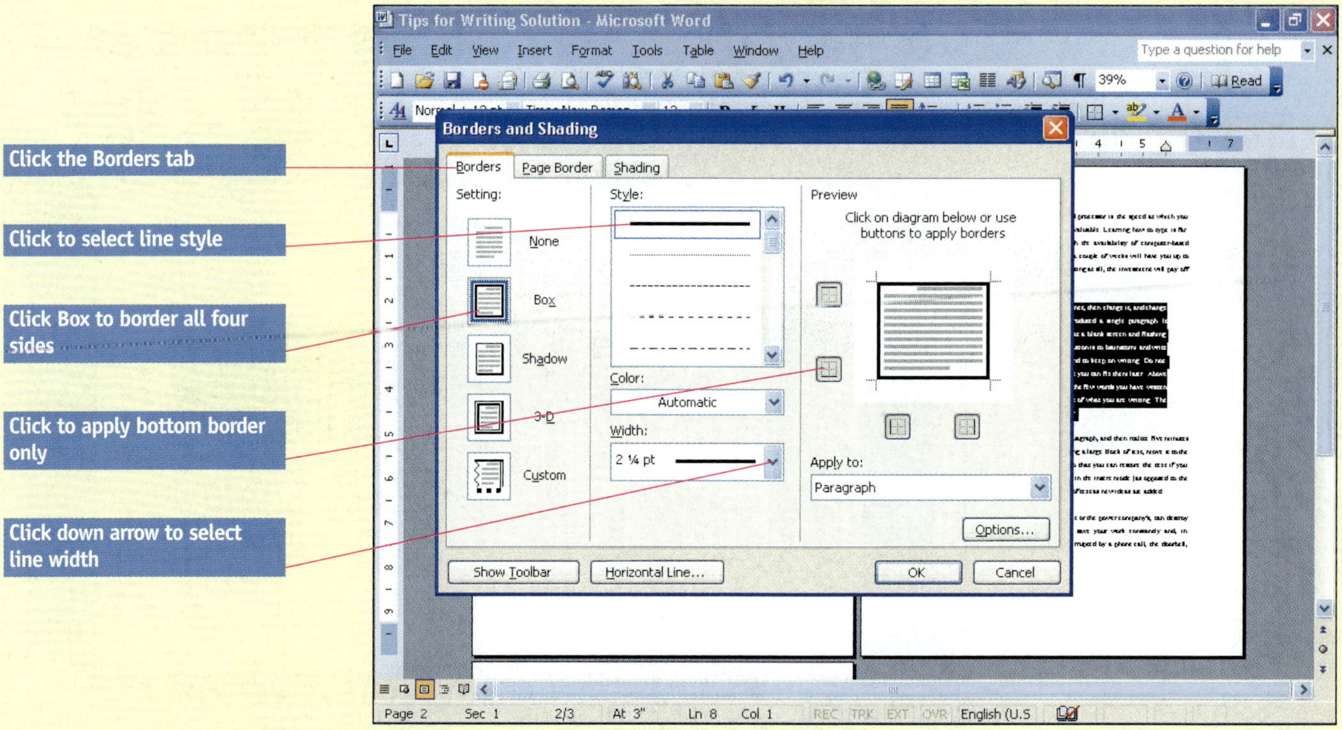

(d) Borders and Shading (step 4)

FIGURE 2.16 Hands-on Exercise 3 (*continued*)

SELECT NONCONTIGUOUS TEXT

Anyone who has used Microsoft Word prior to Office XP, will be happy to learn that you can select noncontiguous blocks of text, and then apply the same formatting to the selected text with a single command. Click and drag to select the first item, then press and hold the Ctrl key as you continue to drag the mouse over additional blocks of text. All of the selected text is highlighted within the document. Apply the desired formatting, then click anywhere in the document to deselect the text and continue working.

Step 5: View Many Pages

- Pull down the **View menu** and click **Zoom** to display the Zoom dialog box. Click the monitor icon under Many Pages, then click and drag to display three pages across. Release the mouse. Click **OK**.
- Your screen should match the one in Figure 2.16e, which displays all three pages of the document.
- The Print Layout view displays both a vertical and a horizontal ruler. The boxed and indented paragraph is clearly shown in the second page.
- The soft page break between pages two and three occurs between tips rather than within a tip; that is, the text of each tip is kept together on the same page.
- Save the document a final time. Print the document at this point in the exercise and submit it to your instructor.

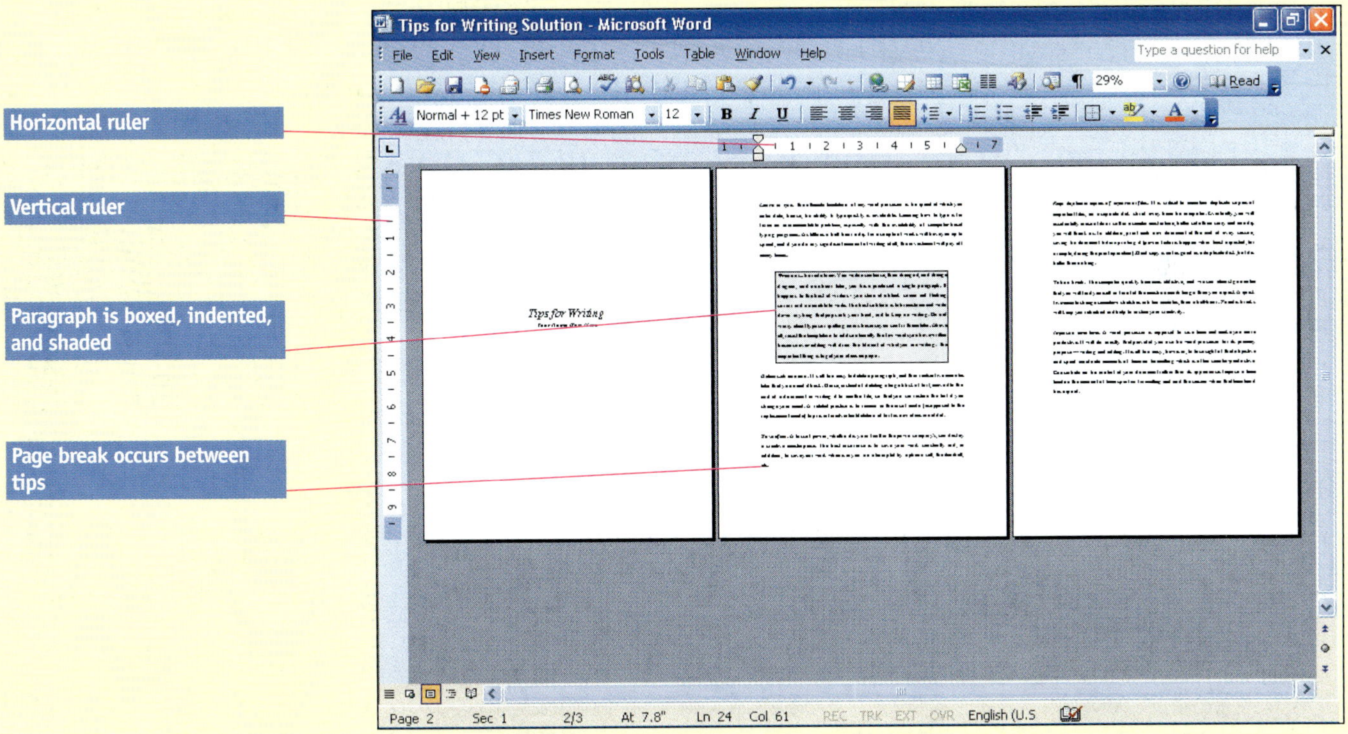

(e) View Many Pages (step 5)

FIGURE 2.16 Hands-on Exercise 3 (*continued*)

THE PAGE BORDER COMMAND

You can apply a border to the title page of your document, to every page except the title page, or to every page including the title page. Click anywhere on the page, pull down the Format menu, click Borders and Shading, and click the Page Border tab. First design the border by selecting a style, color, width, and art (if any). Then choose the page(s) to which you want to apply the border by clicking the drop-down arrow in the Apply to list box. Close the Borders and Shading dialog box.

Step 6: Change the Column Structure

- Pull down the **File menu** and click the **Page Setup command** to display the Page Setup dialog box. Click the **Margins tab**, then change the Left and Right margins to **1″** each. Click **OK** to accept the settings and close the dialog box.
- Click the **down arrow** on the Zoom list box and return to **Page Width**. Press the **PgUp** or **PgDn key** to scroll until the second page comes into view.
- Click anywhere in the paragraph, "Write Now but Edit Later". Pull down the **Format menu**, click the **Paragraph command**, click the **Indents and Spacing tab** if necessary, then change the left and right indents to **0**. Click **OK**.
- All paragraphs in the document should have the same indentation as shown in Figure 2.16f. Pull down the **Format menu** and click the **Columns command** to display the Columns dialog box.
- Click the icon for **three columns**. The default spacing between columns is .5″, which leads to a column width of 1.83″. Click in the Spacing list box and change the spacing to **.25**″, which automatically changes the column width to 2″.
- Clear the box for the **Line between** columns. Click **OK**.

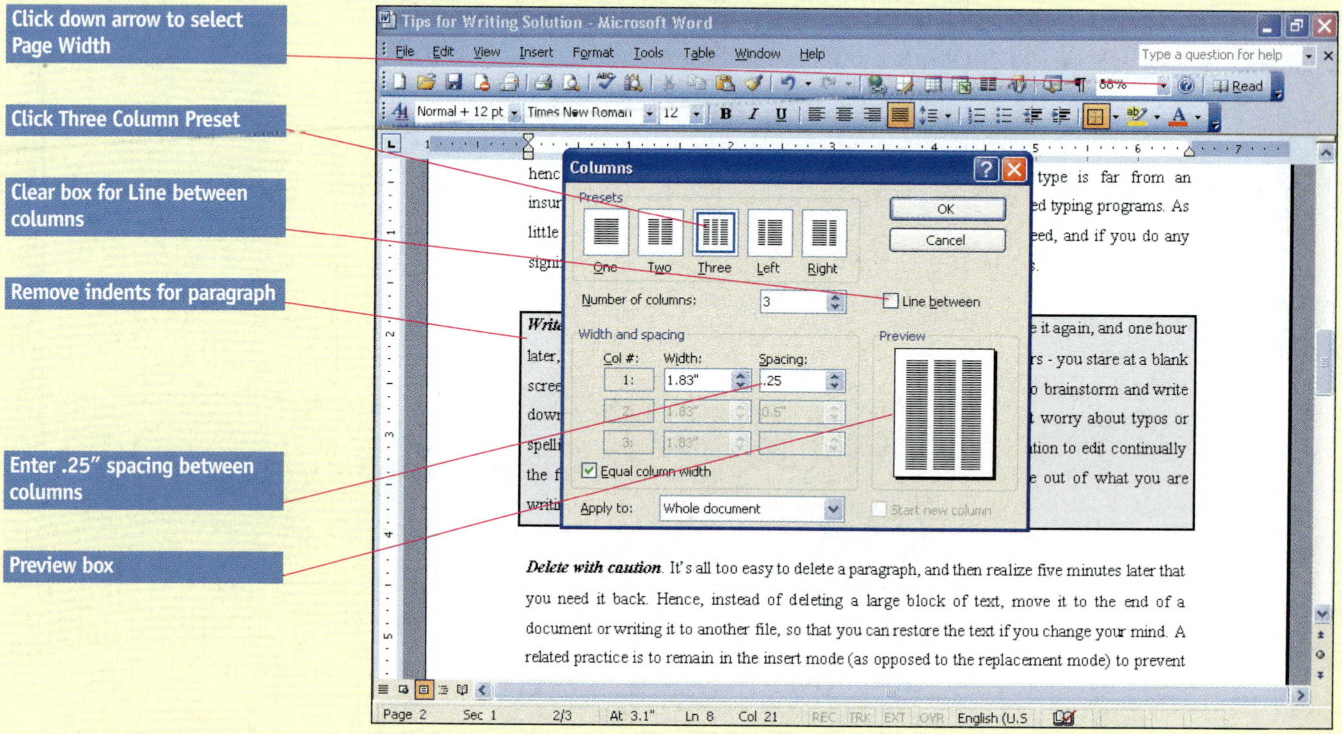

(f) Change the Column Structure (step 6)

FIGURE 2.16 Hands-on Exercise 3 (*continued*)

USE THE RULER TO CHANGE COLUMN WIDTH

Click anywhere within the column whose width you want to change, then point to the ruler and click and drag the right margin (the mouse pointer changes to a double arrow) to change the column width. Changing the width of one column in a document with equal-sized columns changes the width of all other columns so that they remain equal. Changing the width in a document with unequal columns changes only that column.

Step 7: Insert a Section Break

- Pull down the **View menu**, click the **Zoom command**, then click the monitor icon under **Many Pages**. Click and drag over 3 pages, then click **OK**. The document has switched to column formatting.
- Click at the beginning of the second page, immediately to the left of the first paragraph. Pull down the **Insert menu** and click **Break** to display the dialog box in Figure 2.16g.
- Click the **Continuous option button**, then click **OK** to accept the settings and close the dialog box.
- Click anywhere on the title page (before the section break you just inserted). Click the **Columns button**, then click the first column.
- The formatting for the first section of the document (the title page) should change to one column; the title of the document and your name are centered across the entire page.
- Print the document in this format for your instructor. Decide in which format you want to save the document—that is, as it exists now, or as it existed at the end of step 5. Exit Word.

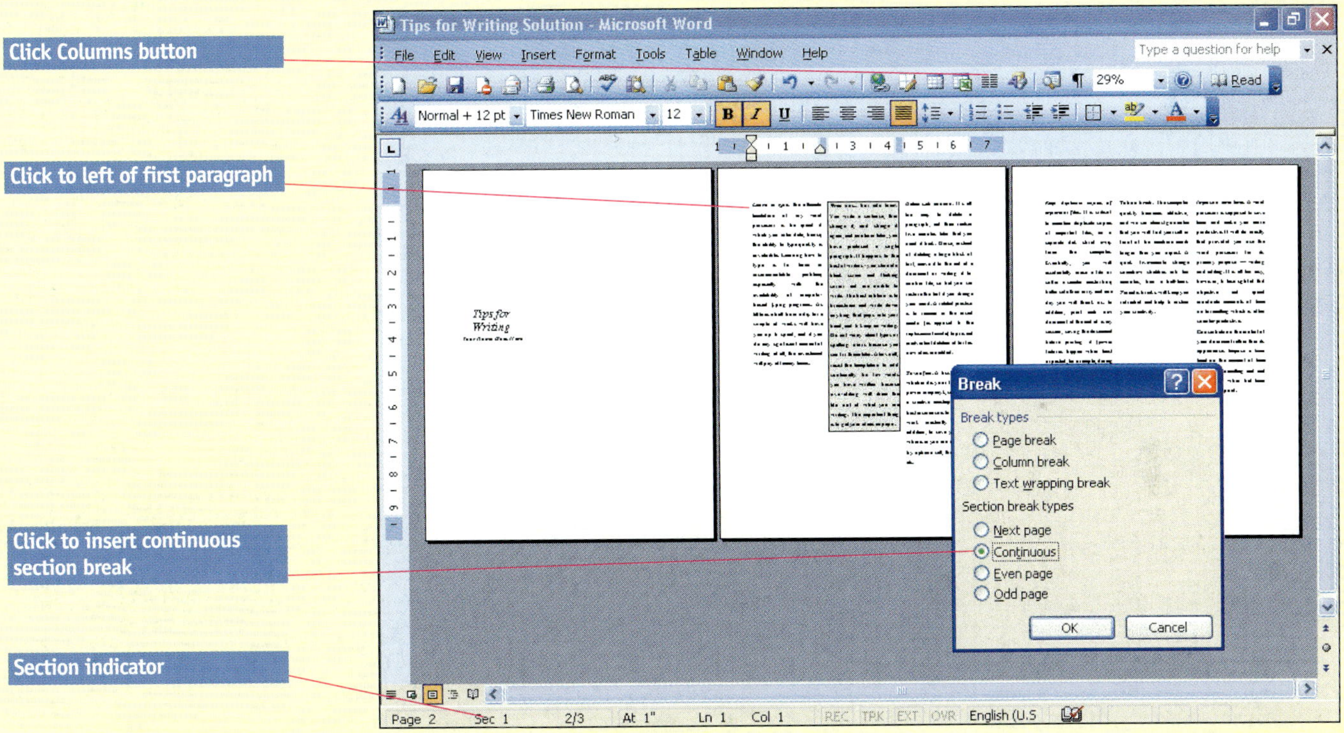

(g) Insert a Section Break (step 7)

FIGURE 2.16 Hands-on Exercise 3 (*continued*)

THE COLUMNS BUTTON

The Columns button on the Standard toolbar is the fastest way to create columns in a document. Click the button, drag the mouse to choose the number of columns, then release the mouse to create the columns. The toolbar lets you change the number of columns, but not the spacing between columns. The toolbar is also limited, in that you cannot create columns of different widths or select a line between the columns.

SUMMARY

Many operations in Word are done within the context of select-then-do; that is, select the text, then execute the necessary command. Text may be selected by dragging the mouse, by using the selection bar to the left of the document, or by using the keyboard. Text is deselected by clicking anywhere within the document.

The Undo command reverses the effect of previous commands. The Undo and Redo commands work in conjunction with one another; that is, every command that is undone can be redone at a later time.

Text is moved or copied through a combination of the Cut, Copy, and Paste commands and/or the drag-and-drop facility. The contents of the Windows clipboard are modified by any subsequent Cut or Copy command, but are unaffected by the Paste command; that is, the same text can be pasted into multiple locations. The Office clipboard retains up to 24 entries that were cut or copied.

The Find and Replace commands locate a designated character string and optionally replace one or more occurrences of that string with a different character string. The search may be case sensitive and/or restricted to whole words. The commands may also be applied to formatting and/or special characters.

Scrolling occurs when a document is too large to be seen in its entirety. Scrolling with the mouse changes what is displayed on the screen, but does not move the insertion point. Scrolling via the keyboard (for example, PgUp and PgDn) changes what is seen on the screen as well as the location of the insertion point.

The Print Layout view displays top and bottom margins, headers and footers, and other elements not seen in the Normal view. The Normal view is faster because Word spends less time formatting the display.

The Format Paragraph command determines the line spacing, alignment, indents, and text flow, all of which are set at the paragraph level. Borders and shading are set at the character or paragraph level. Margins, page size, and orientation are set in the Page Setup command at the section level.

Columns add interest to a document and are implemented through the Columns command in the Format menu and/or through the Columns button on the Standard toolbar. The number of columns is specified at the section level. The insertion of a section break enables you to create a document that contains a varying number of columns; e.g., a single column for the masthead of a newsletter and multiple columns within the body.

KEY TERMS

Arial 136
Automatic replacement 124
Borders and Shading command 155
Case-insensitive search 124
Case-sensitive search 124
Character spacing 137
Columns command 156
Copy command 122
Courier New 136
Cut command 122
Find command 123
First line indent 149
Font 136
Format Font command 137
Format Paragraph command 153
Go To command 123
Hanging indent 149
Hard page break 141
Hyphenation 153
Landscape orientation 141
Layout tab 141
Leader character 152
Left indent 149
Line spacing 153
Margins tab 141
Monospaced typeface 137
Nonbreaking hyphen 153
Normal view 127
Office clipboard 122
Orphan 153
Page break 141
Page Setup command 139
Paper tab 141
Paste command 122
Paste Special command 122
Point 137
Portrait orientation 141
Print Layout view 127
Proportional typeface 137
Reading Layout view 127
Redo command 122
Replace command 123
Right indent 149
Sans serif typeface 136
Scrolling 125
Section 156
Section break 156
Selective replacement 124
Serif typeface 136
Soft page break 141
Special indent 149
Tab stop 152
Text effects 137
Times New Roman 136
Typeface 136
Type size 137
Type style 137
Typography 136
Undo command 122
View menu 127
Whole words only 124
Widow 153
Wild card 124
Windows clipboard 122
Zoom command 127

MULTIPLE CHOICE

1. Which of the following commands does *not* place data onto the clipboard?
   (a) Cut
   (b) Copy
   (c) Paste
   (d) All of the above

2. What happens if you select a block of text, copy it, move to the beginning of the document, paste it, move to the end of the document, and paste the text again?
   (a) The selected text will appear in three places: at the original location, and at the beginning and end of the document
   (b) The selected text will appear in two places: at the beginning and end of the document
   (c) The selected text will appear in just the original location
   (d) The situation is not possible; that is, you cannot paste twice in a row without an intervening cut or copy operation

3. What happens if you select a block of text, cut it, move to the beginning of the document, paste it, move to the end of the document, and paste the text again?
   (a) The selected text will appear in three places: at the original location and at the beginning and end of the document
   (b) The selected text will appear in two places: at the beginning and end of the document
   (c) The selected text will appear in just the original location
   (d) The situation is not possible; that is, you cannot paste twice in a row without an intervening cut or copy operation

4. Which of the following are set at the paragraph level?
   (a) Alignment
   (b) Tabs and indents
   (c) Line spacing
   (d) All of the above

5. How do you change the font for *existing* text within a document?
   (a) Select the text, then choose the new font
   (b) Choose the new font, then select the text
   (c) Either (a) or (b)
   (d) Neither (a) nor (b)

6. The Page Setup command can be used to change:
   (a) The margins in a document
   (b) The orientation of a document
   (c) Both (a) and (b)
   (d) Neither (a) nor (b)

7. Which of the following is a true statement regarding indents?
   (a) Indents are measured from the edge of the page
   (b) The left, right, and first line indents must be set to the same value
   (c) The insertion point can be anywhere in the paragraph when indents are set
   (d) Indents must be set with the Format Paragraph command

8. The default tab stops are set to:
   (a) Left indents every ½ inch
   (b) Left indents every ¼ inch
   (c) Right indents every ½ inch
   (d) Right indents every ¼ inch

9. The spacing in an existing multipage document is changed from single spacing to double spacing throughout the document. What can you say about the number of hard and soft page breaks before and after the formatting change?
   (a) The number of soft page breaks is the same, but the number and/or position of the hard page breaks is different
   (b) The number of hard page breaks is the same, but the number and/or position of the soft page breaks is different
   (c) The number and position of both hard and soft page breaks is the same
   (d) The number and position of both hard and soft page breaks is different

10. Which of the following describes the Arial and Times New Roman fonts?
    (a) Arial is a sans serif font, Times New Roman is a serif font
    (b) Arial is a serif font, Times New Roman is a sans serif font
    (c) Both are serif fonts
    (d) Both are sans serif fonts

... continued

multiple choice

11. What is the effect of executing two successive Undo commands, one right after the other?

(a) The situation is not possible because the Undo command is not available

(b) The situation is not possible because the Undo command cannot be executed twice in a row

(c) The Undo commands cancel each other out; that is, the document is the same as it was prior to the first Undo command

(d) The last two commands prior to the first Undo command are reversed

12. You are in the middle of a multipage document. How do you scroll to the beginning of the document and simultaneously change the insertion point?

(a) Press Ctrl+Home

(b) Drag the scroll bar to the top of the scroll box

(c) Both (a) and (b)

(d) Neither (a) nor (b)

13. Which of the following substitutions can be accomplished by the Find and Replace command?

(a) All occurrences of the words "Times New Roman" can be replaced with the word "Arial"

(b) All text set in the Times New Roman font can be replaced by the Arial font

(c) Both (a) and (b)

(d) Neither (a) nor (b)

14. Which of the following deselects a selected block of text?

(a) Clicking anywhere outside the selected text

(b) Clicking any alignment button on the toolbar

(c) Clicking the Bold, Italic, or Underline button

(d) All of the above

15. Which point size would be most appropriate for ordinary text?

(a) 4

(b) 10

(c) 20

(d) 72

16. The find and replacement strings must be

(a) The same length

(b) The same case, either upper or lower

(c) The same length and the same case

(d) None of the above

17. Which of the following is a true statement about the Windows and Office clipboards?

(a) Both clipboards can hold only a single item

(b) Both clipboards can hold multiple items

(c) The Windows clipboard can hold only a single item, but the Office clipboard can hold multiple items

(d) The Office clipboard can hold only a single item, but the Windows clipboard can hold multiple items

18. Which of the following is set at the section level?

(a) Columns and margins

(b) Alignment and tabs

(c) Borders and shading

(d) All of the above

ANSWERS

1. c	**7.** c	**13.** c
2. a	**8.** a	**14.** a
3. b	**9.** b	**15.** b
4. d	**10.** a	**16.** d
5. a	**11.** d	**17.** c
6. c	**12.** a	**18.** a

PRACTICE WITH WORD

1. **Formatting 101:** The opening paragraph of the document in Figure 2.17 explains that formatting is implemented at three levels—the section level, the paragraph level, and the character level. The remainder of the document consists of various sentences and paragraphs that describe the formatting specifications you are to implement. The formatting commands can be executed from pull-down menus, from the Formatting toolbar, and/or through the appropriate keyboard shortcut. Open the partially completed *Chapter 2 Practice 1* document in the Exploring Word folder. Proceed as follows to create the finished document in Figure 2.17.
   a. Change the font in the title and first paragraph to Times New Roman. Center the title in 24 point Times New Roman bold. Justify the first paragraph, then boldface the indicated terms.
   b. Click at the end of the first paragraph. Press Enter. Pull down the Insert menu, click the Break command, then click the option button for a continuous section break. Click anywhere in the second section (check the status bar to confirm that you are in the second section). Pull down the Format menu, click the Columns command, and then change to two columns.
   c. Move the insertion point to the beginning of the sentence, "This paragraph is set in 10 point Times New Roman . . . ". Press Ctrl+Shift+Enter to force the paragraph to begin a new column.
   d. Follow the instructions within the document to use the appropriate font (Times New Roman or Arial), style (bold, italic, or bold italic), highlighting, and so on. Apply borders and shading as indicated.
   e. Format each of the paragraphs in the second column according to the specifications that are contained in the individual paragraphs.
   f. Add your name somewhere in the document, then print the completed document for your instructor. Do not be concerned if you do not have a color printer, but indicate this to your instructor in a note at the end of the document. Do you appreciate the difference between formatting at the character, paragraph, or section level?

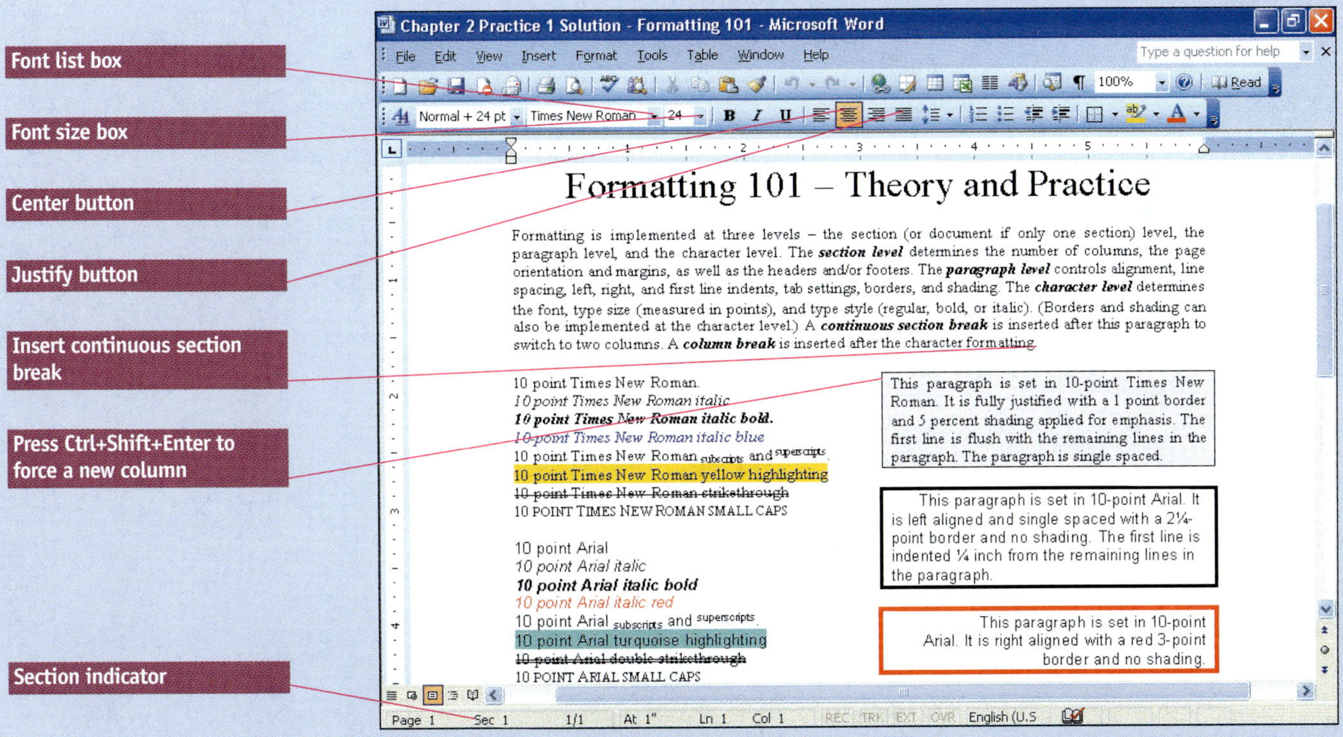

FIGURE 2.17 Formatting 101 (exercise 1)

2. **Keyboard Shortcuts:** Keyboard shortcuts are especially useful if you are a good typist because your hands can remain on the keyboard, as opposed to continually moving to and from the mouse. We never set out to memorize the shortcuts; we just learned them along the way as we continued to use Microsoft Office.

   It's much easier than you might think, because the same shortcuts apply to multiple applications. Ctrl+X, Ctrl+C, and Ctrl+V, for example, are the universal Windows shortcuts to cut, copy, and paste the selected text. The "X" is supposed to remind you of a pair of scissors, and the keys are located next to each other to link the commands to one another. Proceed as follows:

   a. Start Word. Open the *Chapter 2 Practice 2* document in the Exploring Word folder, a portion of which can be seen in Figure 2.18. Your assignment is to complete the document by entering the indicated shortcuts.

   b. Pull down the Tools menu, click the Customize command to display the Customize dialog box, click the Options tab, and then check the box to Show Shortcut Keys in ScreenTips. You can now point to any icon on any toolbar to see the associated shortcut. You can also use Help to identify the various shortcuts in Word. Click in the Ask a Question box, type "keyboard shortcuts", then click the link to keyboard shortcuts from the list of topics that are returned by the search engine.

   c. Move to the line below Ctrl+B to enter the shortcut to toggle Italic on and off. (You can point to the Italic button on the Formatting toolbar to display the ScreenTip and the associated shortcut, Ctrl+I.) Enter the remaining shortcuts in similar fashion. Use the Help menu as necessary.

   d. Enter your name in the completed document, add the appropriate formatting, and then submit the document to your instructor as proof you did this exercise. Try to learn the shortcuts in groups as they are presented in Figure 2.18. Do you think the shortcuts will help you to use Word more efficiently?

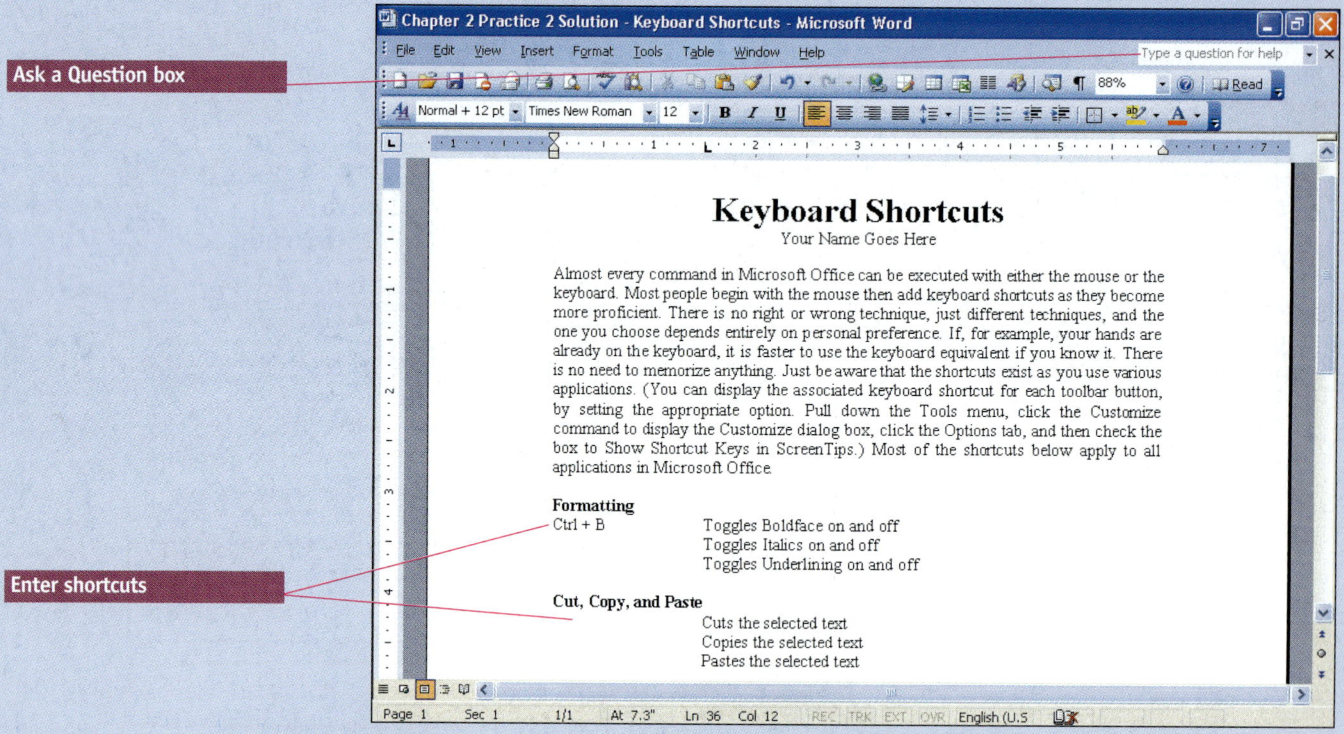

FIGURE 2.18 Keyboard Shortcuts (exercise 2)

3. **Moving Text:** There are two basic ways to move text within a document. You can use a combination of the Cut and Paste commands, or you can simply click and drag text from one location to another. The latter technique tends to be easier if you are moving text a short distance, whereas cutting and pasting is preferable if the locations are far apart within a document. This exercise will give you a chance to practice both techniques.
   a. Open the partially completed *Chapter 2 Practice 3* document, where you will find a list of the presidents of the United States together with the years that each man served.
   b. The list is out of order, and your assignment is to rearrange the names so that the presidents appear in chronological order. You don't have to be a historian to complete the exercise because you can use the years in office to determine the proper order.
   c. Center the first two lines of text. Format the title in 25 point Times New Roman. Use a smaller point size for the second line. Use the Insert Hyperlink command (or click the corresponding button on the Standard toolbar) to insert a link to the White House Web site (www.whitehouse.gov) where you can learn more about the presidents.
   d. Display the list of presidents in two columns with a line down the middle as shown in Figure 2.19. You will have to implement a section break because the first two lines (the title and the hyperlink to the White House) are in one-column format, whereas the list of presidents is in two columns. Click immediately before the first president, pull down the Insert menu, click the Break command, and then click the option button for a continuous section break.
   e. Click anywhere in the second section (check the status bar to confirm that you are in the second section.) Pull down the Format menu, click the Columns command, and then change to two columns for this section.
   f. Press Ctrl+End to move to the end of the document and insert a second continuous section break to balance the text in each column.
   g. Add your name to the completed document and submit it to your instructor.

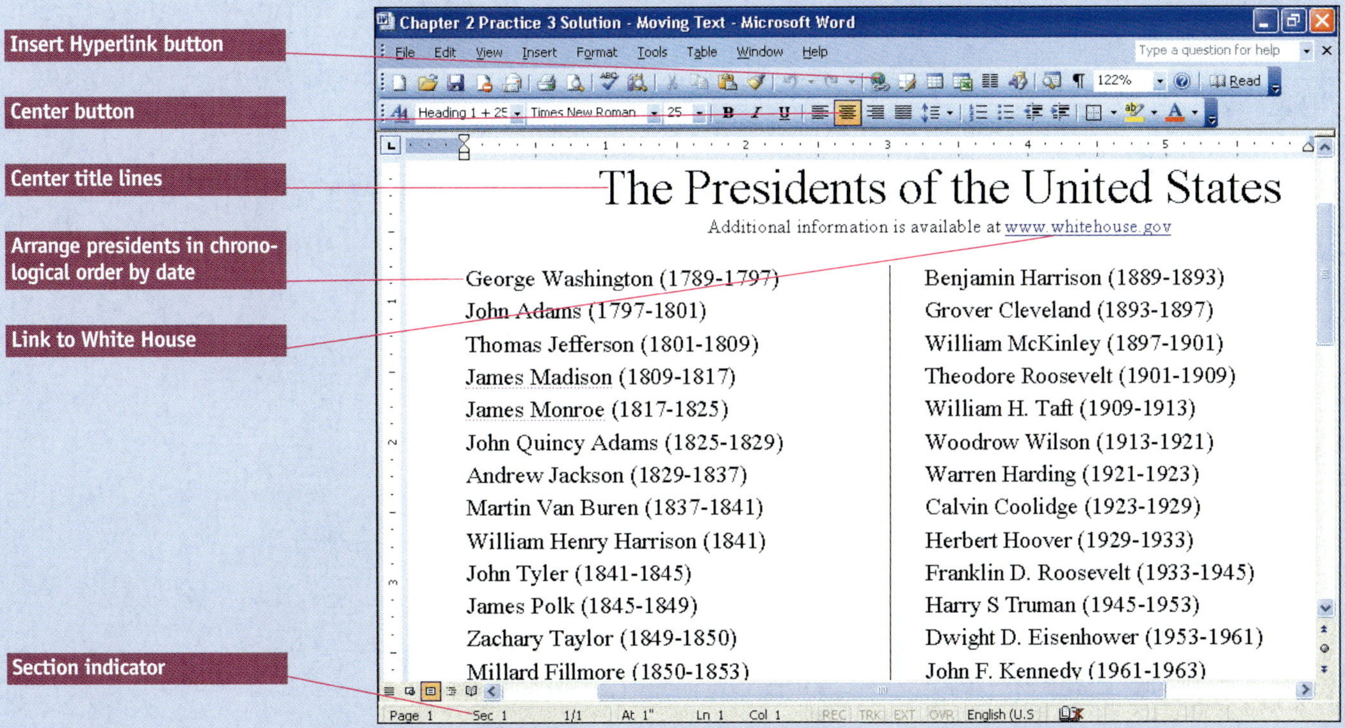

FIGURE 2.19 Moving Text (exercise 3)

4. **Inserting the Date and Time:** The document in Figure 2.20 describes the Insert Date and Time command and shows the various formats in which a date may appear. You need not duplicate our document exactly, but you are asked to insert the date multiple times, as both a fixed value and a field, in multiple formats. Divide your document into sections so that you can display the two sets of dates in adjacent columns. (Use the keyboard shortcut Ctrl+Shift+Enter to force a column break that will take you from the bottom of one column to the top of the next column.)
   a. Start Word and begin a new document. Enter the title of the document as shown in Figure 2.20. Press enter. Type the phrase, "Today's Date – ". Pull down the Insert menu, click the Date and Time command, and select the appropriate format for the date. Check the box to Update Automatically. Click OK.
   b. The date should have been entered as a code (field) because you checked the box to update automatically. Press Alt+F9 to toggle from a displayed date to a code. Press Alt+F9 a second time to show the displayed value.
   c. You can also shade all codes automatically. Pull down the Tools menu, click the Options command, select the View tab, and then click the drop-down arrow in the Field Shading list box. Select Always. Click OK.
   d. Type the first paragraph as shown in Figure 2.20. Insert a continuous section break at the end of the paragraph so that you can display text in two columns. Change to a two-column format. Pull down the Insert menu, click the Date and Time command, and enter the date in the first format shown in the figure. Do not check the box to update automatically. Enter the date four additional times using a different format each time.
   e. Press Ctrl+Shift+Enter to move to the next column, then enter the various dates as fields as shown.
   f. Insert a section break after the last date and change back to a single column. Enter the text of the last paragraph as shown in the figure. Create your document on one day, then open it a day later to be sure that the dates that were entered as fields were updated correctly.
   g. Add your name to the completed document and submit it to your instructor.

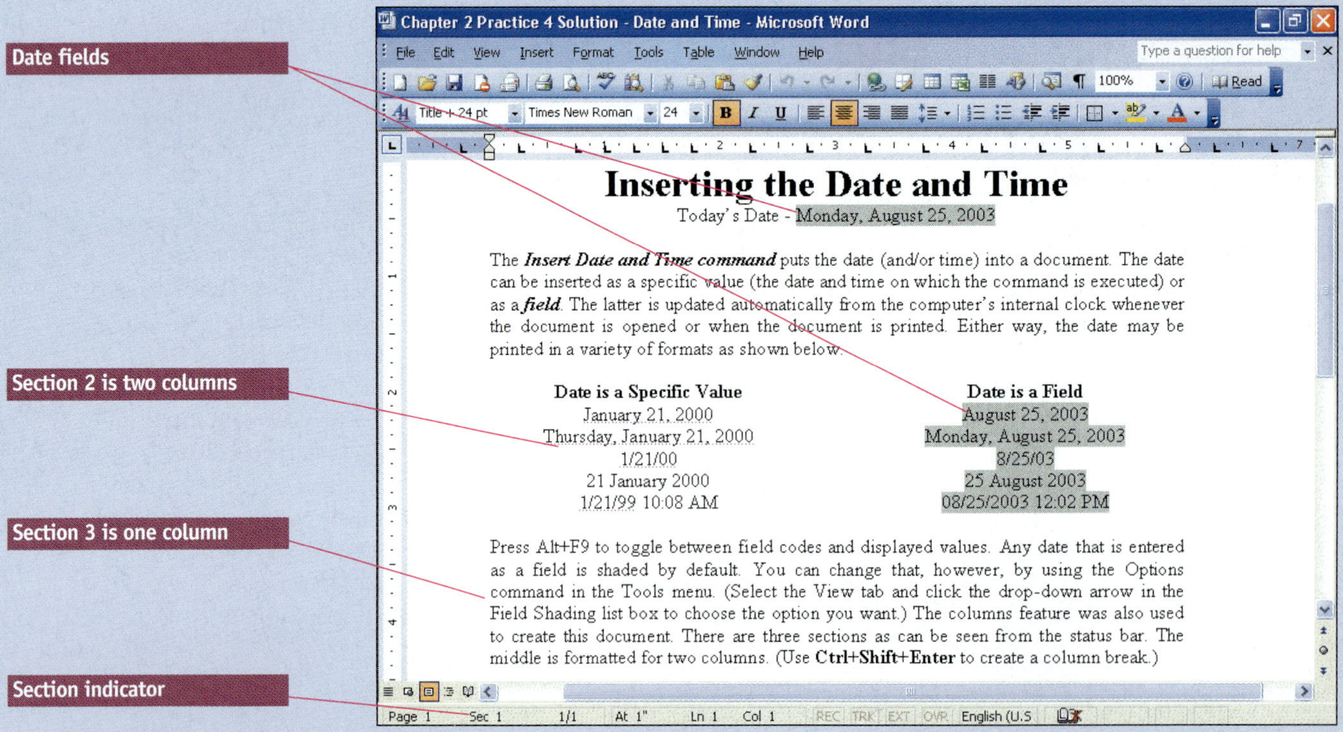

FIGURE 2.20 Inserting the Date and Time (exercise 4)

5. **Tips for Internet Explorer:** You will find a partially completed version of the document in Figure 2.21 in the file *Chapter 2 Practice 5* in the Exploring Word folder. Your assignment is to open that document, then format the various tips in an attractive fashion. You need not follow our formatting exactly, but you are to apply uniform formatting throughout the document. Proceed as follows:
   a. Pull down the View menu, open the task pane, and then click the down arrow to select Reveal Formatting as shown in Figure 2.21. This enables you to see the formatting in effect for every paragraph throughout the exercise.
   b. Format the title of the first tip, "About Internet Explorer". We used 10 point Arial in red. Look closely, however, and you will see that the paragraph formatting includes a specification to keep the heading with the next line to avoid an awkward page break. (Pull down the Format menu, click the Paragraph command to display the Paragraph dialog box, click the Line and Page Breaks tab, and check the box to Keep with next.)
   c. Check that the insertion point is anywhere within the heading. Double click the Format Painter tool on the Standard toolbar (the mouse pointer changes to a paintbrush), then paint the heading of every other tip in the document. The easiest way to do this is to click immediately to the left of each heading throughout the document. Click the Format Painter tool when you are finished to turn off the painting feature.
   d. Return to the top of the document to format the text of the first tip. We used 10 point Times New Roman and justified the paragraph. We also used the Line and Page Breaks command to keep the lines together—that is, so the paragraph does not break from one page to the next. Use the Format Painter to duplicate this formatting for the other tips in the document.
   e. Return to the beginning of the document, locate the tip entitled "Guess the URL", and use the Insert Hyperlink command to create the appropriate hyperlinks within the paragraph. Use the Edit Find (search for "www") command to locate additional instances of hyperlinks that appear in other tips.
   f. Insert a cover page that includes your name and the source of the information, and then print the entire document for your instructor. Read the completed document carefully. Did you learn anything new about Internet Explorer?

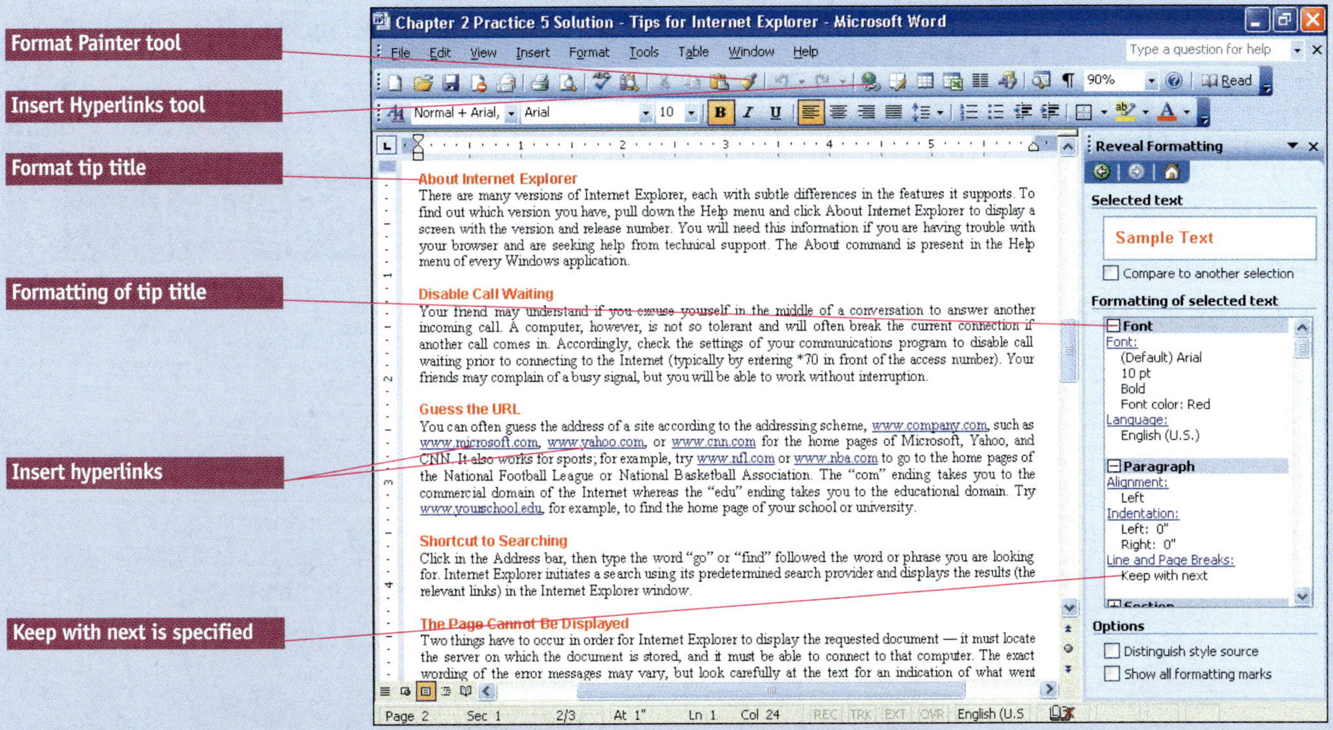

FIGURE 2.21 Tips for Internet Explorer (exercise 5)

6. **Create a Newsletter:** It's not difficult to create an effective newsletter, provided you plan effectively. Use pencil and paper to lay out the overall document before you begin. Decide how many columns you want, what clip art (if any) you will use, and what other elements you want to include. There is no requirement to write meaningful text; that is, all you have to do is write a few short sentences, then copy those sentences to fill the newsletter. You do not have to duplicate our document exactly, but you are required to include the essential elements in Figure 2.22. Proceed as follows:
   a. Choose a theme for your newsletter, and then write a short paragraph in support of that theme. Select the paragraph, copy it, and then paste it repeatedly to fill the page. Do not be concerned if you spill onto a second page. Go through the document and periodically add meaningful headings. Format the headings differently from the text.
   b. Change the default margins. We used top and bottom margins of .75 inch and left and right margins of .5 inch. Pull down the Format menu, click the Columns command, and then establish the column formatting for the body of your newsletter.
   c. Click after the first paragraph and insert clip art in support of your theme. Right click the clip art, click the Format Picture command, then use the Layout (specify square wrapping) and/or the Size tabs as necessary to move and size the clip art.
   d. Press Ctrl+Home to move to the beginning of the document. Pull down the Insert menu and select a continuous section break. Press Ctrl+Home to move to the first section, change to a single column, and then create the masthead for your newsletter. We formatted the text in 44 point Arial and used the Format Borders and Shading command (100% shading) to display light text on a solid background. Use a right tab at the right margin on the second line of the masthead, so that your name appears at the extreme right of the masthead.
   e. Create a pull quote to emphasize a specific sentence. Select the text, increase the point size, change to italic, center the text, then add a top and bottom border. Use borders and/or shading on other paragraphs as you see fit.
   f. Change to the Print Layout view, and then zoom to view the entire page. Add or delete text as necessary, so that your newsletter fills exactly one page.
   g. Print the completed newsletter for your instructor as proof you did this exercise.

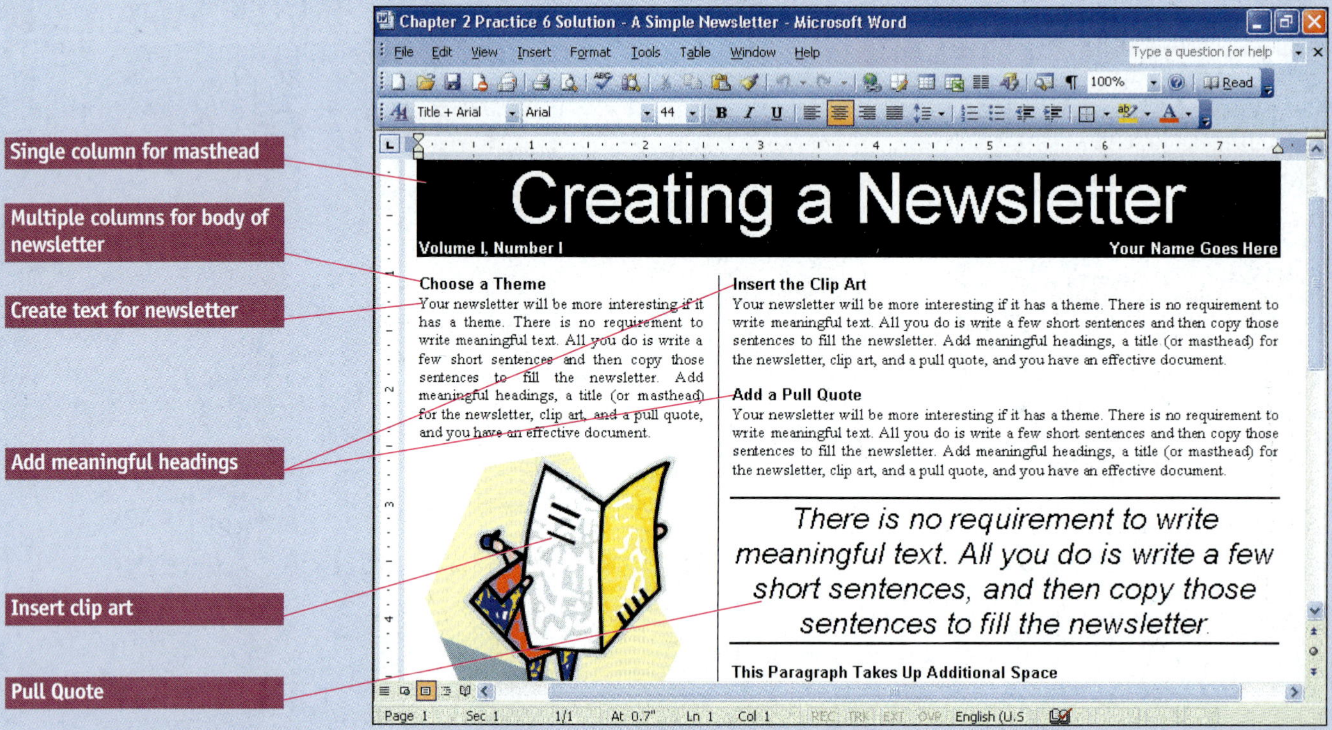

FIGURE 2.22 Create a Newsletter (exercise 6)

7. **Tracking Changes with Tab Stops:** This exercise sets different types of tabs in conjunction with tracking the editing changes during a session. Open the *Chapter 2 Practice 7* document in the Exploring Word folder, which is a partially completed version of the document in Figure 2.23. Pull down the View menu and click the Toolbars command to display the Reviewing toolbar if it is not visible. Click and drag to select the phrase "your name goes here" near the top of the document. Press the Del key, then enter your name instead. The new text will appear in a different color (magenta in our figure), and a description of the change will appear at the right of your document. If this does not occur, double click the TRK indicator on the status bar to toggle track changes on. Complete the document as follows:
   a. The tab stops for examples one and two have already been entered into the document by Bob and Maryann, and are indicated in red and green, respectively. You can point to any of the changes in the right margin to see a ScreenTip with the name of the reviewer (Bob or Maryann) and an indication of when the change was made.
   b. Click and drag to select the three lines under Example 3 to set the tabs for all three lines at the same time. Click the Tab button (at the left of the ruler) repeatedly until you see the symbol for the left tab. Now click at one inch on the ruler to set a left tab at that position. Click the Tab button until you see the symbol for a right tab, then click at 5.5 inches to set this tab. Pull down the Format menu, click the Tabs command, select the tab at 5.5 inches, and click the option button for a dotted leader. (The leader cannot be set from the ruler.) Click OK. Now press the Tab key to enter tab stops before the chapter and before the page number for all three lines.
   c. Click and drag to select the three lines of text under Example 4, then use the ruler to set decimal tabs at the indicated positions. Press the Tab key to enter a tab stop before each of the four numbers in all three lines.
   d. Click the Print button to print the document as shown—that is, the final document with the markup (editing) printed in the margin. Click the down arrow in the Display for Review list box to display the Original Showing Markup and print that version. And finally, change to the final version to print the completed document without showing the editing changes. Submit all three versions to your instructor.
   e. Click the down arrow next to the Accept Change button on the Reviewing toolbar, then click the command to Accept All Changes in Document. Pull down the Tools menu and toggle the Track Changes command off.

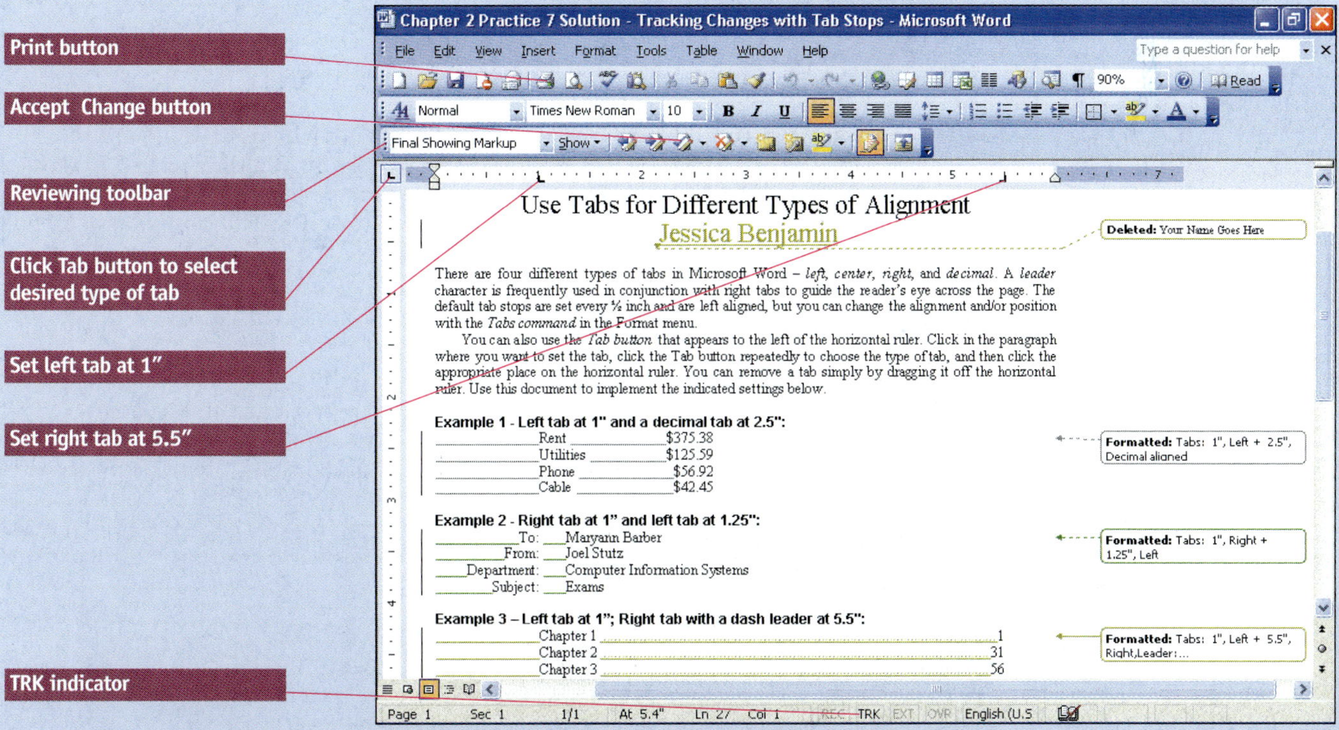

FIGURE 2.23 Tracking Changes with Tab Stops (exercise 7)

MINI CASES

Computers Past and Present

The ENIAC was the scientific marvel of its day and the world's first operational electronic computer. It could perform 5,000 additions per second, weighed 30 tons, and took 1,500 square feet of floor space. The price was a modest $486,000 in 1946 dollars. The story of the ENIAC and other influential computers of the author's choosing is found in the file *Chapter 2 Mini Case—History of Computers,* which we forgot to format, so we are asking you to do it for us.

Be sure to use appropriate emphasis for the names of the various computers. Create a title page in front of the document, then submit the completed assignment to your instructor. If you are ambitious, you can enhance this assignment by using your favorite search engine to look for computer museums on the Web. Visit one or two sites, and include this information on a separate page at the end of the document. One last task is to update the description of Today's PC (the last computer in the document).

The Preamble to the Constitution

Use your favorite search engine to locate a Web site that contains the text of the United States Constitution. Click and drag to select the text of the Preamble, use the Ctrl+C keyboard shortcut to copy the text to the Windows clipboard, start Word, and then paste the contents of the clipboard into the document. Format the Preamble in an attractive fashion, add a footnote that points to the Web page where you obtained the text, then add your name to the completed document.

To Hyphenate or Not to Hyphenate

The best way to learn about hyphenation is to experiment with an existing document. Open the *Chapter 2 Mini Case—To Hyphenate or Not to Hyphenate* document that is on the data disk. The document is currently set in 12 point type with hyphenation in effect. Experiment with various formatting changes that will change the soft line breaks to see the effect on the hyphenation within the document. You can change the point size, the number of columns, and/or the right indent. You can also suppress hyphenation altogether, as described within the document. Summarize your findings in a short note to your instructor.

The Invitation

Choose an event and produce the perfect invitation. The possibilities are endless and limited only by your imagination. You can invite people to your wedding or to a fraternity party. Your laser printer and abundance of fancy fonts enable you to do anything a professional printer can do. Special paper will add the finishing touch. Go to it—this assignment is a lot of fun.

One Space after a Period

Touch typing classes typically teach the student to place two spaces after a period. The technique worked well in the days of the typewriter and monospaced fonts, but it creates an artificially large space when used with proportional fonts and a word processor. Select any document that is at least several paragraphs in length and print the document with the current spacing. Use the Find and Replace commands to change to the alternate spacing, then print the document a second time. Which spacing looks better to you? Submit both versions of the document to your instructor with a brief note summarizing your findings.

CHAPTER 3

Enhancing a Document: The Web and Other Resources

OBJECTIVES

After reading this chapter you will:

1. Insert clip art and/or a photograph into a document.
2. Display/hide the Picture toolbar; use the crop tool as appropriate.
3. Use the Format Picture command to wrap text around clip art.
4. Use WordArt to insert decorative text into a document.
5. Use the Drawing toolbar to create simple shapes and annotations.
6. Download resources from the Web for inclusion into a Word document.
7. Insert a footnote or endnote.
8. Insert a hyperlink into a document.
9. Save a Word document as a Web page.
10. Use wizards and templates to create a document.
11. Use the Mail Merge Wizard to create a set of form letters.

hands-on exercises

1. CLIP ART AND WORDART
   Input: Clip Art and WordArt
   Output: Clip Art and WordArt Solution
2. MICROSOFT WORD AND THE WORLD WIDE WEB
   Input: Apollo 11
   Output: Apollo 11 Solution (Web page)
3. MAIL MERGE
   Input: Form Letter
   Output: Form Letter Solution (Word document); Names and Addresses (data file)

CASE STUDY

FROM DONUTS TO BAGELS

The donut shop across from campus has been receiving constant and continual feedback from students; namely, that they would like to see a healthier choice of menu options in addition to the scrumptious campus-renowned donuts for which the shop is famous. The owner, Sarah McLean, thought this was a good idea and recently added bagels to the menu to see what kind of response she would get. Sarah was optimistic that since her shop was so close to campus, students would naturally choose it over the two other bagel stores in town that were several blocks away. She hoped that the new menu would boost her business substantially.

Sarah discovered, however, that merely adding bagels to the menu was not enough to get the students through the door. She decided to take an ad in the campus paper that offered a free bagel with the purchase of a cup of tea or coffee. Sarah's fiancé is your instructor, and he in turn has assigned the ad as a design project for your class. The creator of the winning entry gets a dozen free bagels. ■

Your assignment is to read the chapter, paying special attention to the first hands-on exercise that describes how to use clip art and WordArt, and then create a colorful ad that uses both elements. The donut shop is located at 1000 Main Street, its telephone number is (111) 222-3333, and this information must appear within the ad. Size and proportion are important; the size of the ad in the campus newspaper is exactly $4\frac{1}{4} \times 5\frac{3}{4}$. Thus, you are to use the Text Box tool on the Drawing toolbar to draw a box around the completed ad that corresponds to its intended size. Somewhere in the ad include a footnote that contains your name, and then print the completed ad for your instructor for inclusion in a class contest to choose the winning entry. One more thing—the contest is purely hypothetical and there are no free bagels.

ENHANCING A DOCUMENT

This chapter describes how to enhance a document using clip art, photographs, and/or WordArt (decorative text). These objects may be stored locally or downloaded from the Web for inclusion into a document. We start with the document in Figure 3.1, which contains text, clip art, WordArt, and a scroll that was created using the Drawing toolbar. We show you the finished document, describe each of the objects within the document, and then proceed to a hands-on exercise in which you will create the document for yourself.

WordArt

Enhancing a Document

Clip art

Clip art is available from a variety of sources including the Microsoft Clip Organizer that is built into Microsoft Office. The Clip Organizer enables you to select clip art in two different ways, by searching through a predefined collection such as "transportation" or by searching on a keyword such as "automobile". The Clip Organizer also lets you specify the type of object you want—clip art, photographs, movies, or sounds. Once the object has been inserted into a document, it can be moved and sized through various options in the Format Picture command. You can wrap text around a picture, place a border around the picture, or even crop (cut out part of) the picture if necessary.

In addition to clip art, you can use WordArt to create artistic effects to enhance any document. WordArt enables you to create special effects with text. It lets you rotate and/or flip text, display it vertically on the page, shade it, slant it, arch it, or even print it upside down. Best of all, WordArt is intuitively easy to use. In essence you enter text into a dialog box, and then you choose a shape for the text from a dialog box. You can create special effects by choosing one of several different shadows. You can vary the image even further by using any TrueType font on your system. It's fun, it's easy, and you can create some truly dynamite documents.

You can insert clip art and/or WordArt into other Office documents such as PowerPoint presentations or Excel worksheets using the same commands that you will learn in this chapter. Indeed, that is one of the benefits of the Office suite because the same commands are executed from the same menus as you go from one application to another. In addition, every application in the Office suite contains a Standard toolbar and a Formatting toolbar.

The Insert Symbol command enables you to insert special symbols into a document to give it a professional look. You can, for example, use ™ rather than TM, © rather than (C), or ½ and ¼ rather than 1/2 and 1/4. It also enables you to insert accented characters as appropriate in English as in the word résumé, or in a foreign language to create properly accented words and phrases; for example, ¿Cómo está usted? And finally, you can use special symbols such as the logo for Microsoft® Windows.

AutoShape

This document was created by Your Name

FIGURE 3.1 Enhancing a Document

The Microsoft Clip Organizer

The ***Insert Picture command*** displays a task pane through which you can insert clip art, photographs, sounds, and movies (collectively called clips). The clips can come from a variety of sources. They may be installed locally in the My Collections folder, they may have been installed in conjunction with Microsoft Office in the Office Collections folder, and/or they may have been downloaded from the Web and stored in the Web Collections folder. You can insert a specific clip into a document if you know its location. You can also search for a clip that will enhance the document on which you are working.

The search is made possible by the ***Microsoft Clip Organizer***, which brings order out of potential chaos by cataloging the clips that are available to you. You enter a keyword that describes the clip you are looking for, specify the collections that are to be searched, and indicate the type of clip(s) you are looking for. The results are displayed in the task pane as shown in Figure 3.2, which returns the clips that are described by the keyword "computer". Our example restricted the search to selected collections (those stored locally, thus making it a faster search than one that searches online as well) but requested that all media types be displayed. When you see a clip that you want to use, all you have to do is point to the clip, click the down arrow that appears, and then click the Insert command from the resulting menu.

You can access the Microsoft Clip Organizer (to view the various collections) by clicking the Organize clips link at the bottom of the task pane. You can also access the Clip Organizer outside of Word by clicking the Start button on the task bar, and then clicking All Programs, Microsoft Office, Microsoft Office Tool, and Microsoft Clip Organizer. Once in the Organizer, you can search through the clips in the various collections, reorganize the existing collections, add new collections, and even add new clips (with their associated keywords) to the collections. The other links at the bottom of the task pane in Figure 3.2 provide access to additional clip art online and tips for finding more relevant clips.

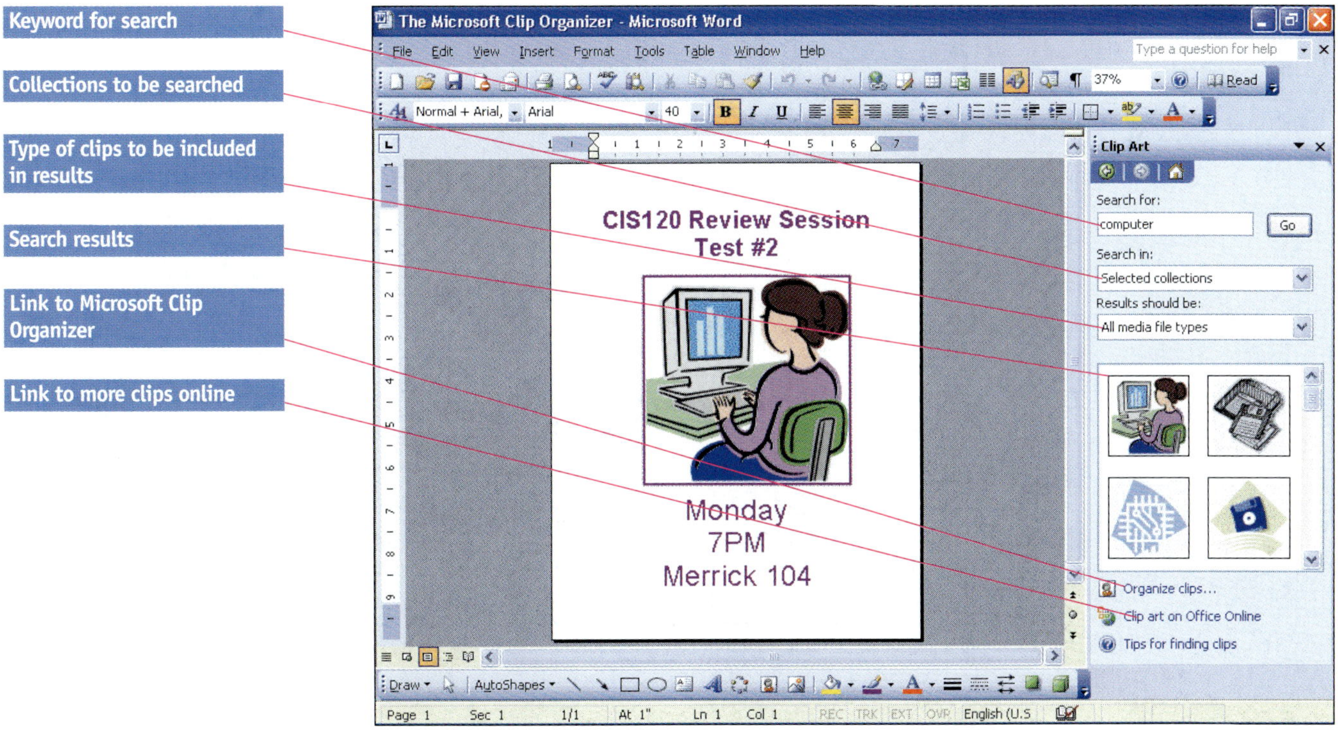

FIGURE 3.2 Insert Picture Command

The Insert Symbol Command

The ***Insert Symbol command*** enables you to enter typographic symbols and/or foreign language characters into a document in place of ordinary typing—for example, ® rather than (R), © rather than (c), ½ and ¼, rather than 1/2 and 1/4, or é rather than e (as used in the word résumé). These special characters give a document a very professional look.

You may have already discovered that some of this formatting can be done automatically through the ***AutoCorrect*** feature that is built into Word. If, for example, you type the letter "c" enclosed in parentheses, it will automatically be converted to the copyright symbol. Other symbols, such as accented letters like the é in résumé or those in a foreign language (e.g., ¿Cómo está usted?) have to be entered through the Insert Symbol command. (You could also create a macro, based on the Insert Symbol command, to simplify the process.)

The installation of Microsoft Office adds a variety of fonts onto your computer, each of which contains various symbols that can be inserted into a document. Selecting "normal text", however, as was done in Figure 3.3, provides access to the accented characters as well as other common symbols. Other fonts—especially the Wingdings, Webdings, and Symbols fonts—contain special symbols, including the Windows logo.

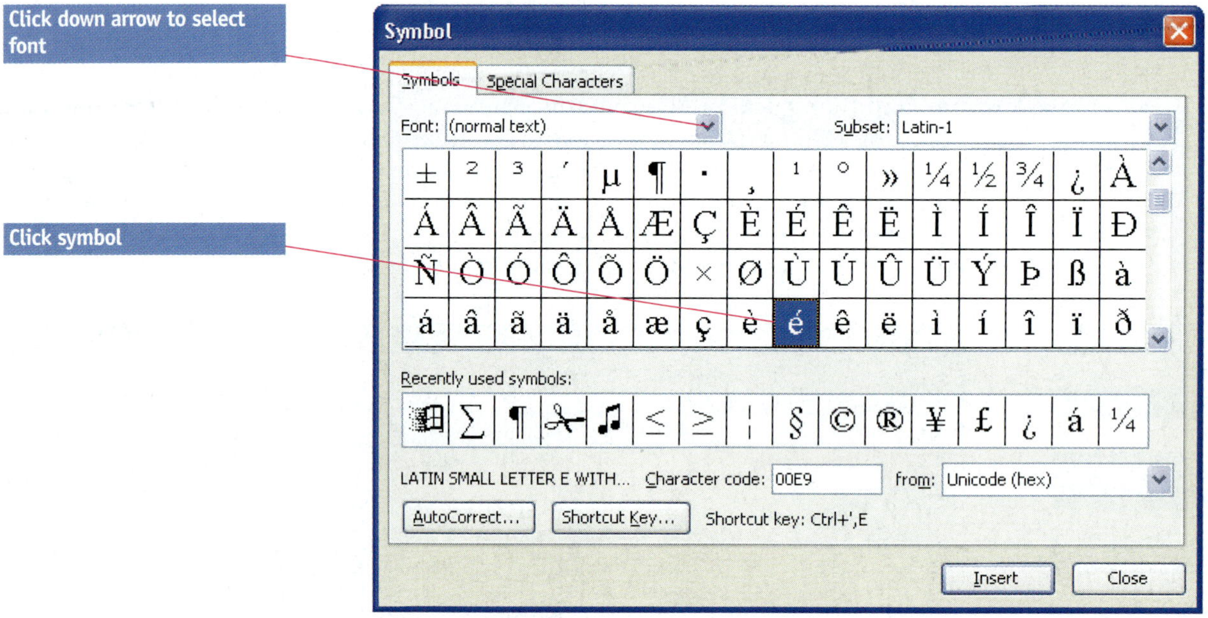

FIGURE 3.3 Insert Symbol Command

USE SYMBOLS AS CLIP ART

The Wingdings, Webdings, and Symbols fonts are among the best-kept secrets in Microsoft Office. Each font contains a variety of symbols that are actually pictures. You can insert any of these symbols into a document as text, select the character and enlarge the point size, change the color, then copy the modified character to create a truly original document. See exercise 5 at the end of the chapter.

Microsoft WordArt

Microsoft WordArt is an application within Microsoft Office that creates decorative text that can be used to add interest to a document. You can use ***WordArt*** in addition to clip art within a document, or in place of clip art if the right image is not available. You can rotate text in any direction, add three-dimensional effects, display the text vertically down the page, slant it, arch it, or even print it upside down. In short, you are limited only by your imagination.

WordArt is intuitively easy to use. In essence you choose a style for the text from among the selections in Figure 3.4a. Then you enter the specific text in a subsequent dialog box, after which the result is displayed as in Figure 3.4b. The finished WordArt is an object that can be moved and sized within a document, just like any other object. It's fun, it's easy, and you can create some truly unique documents.

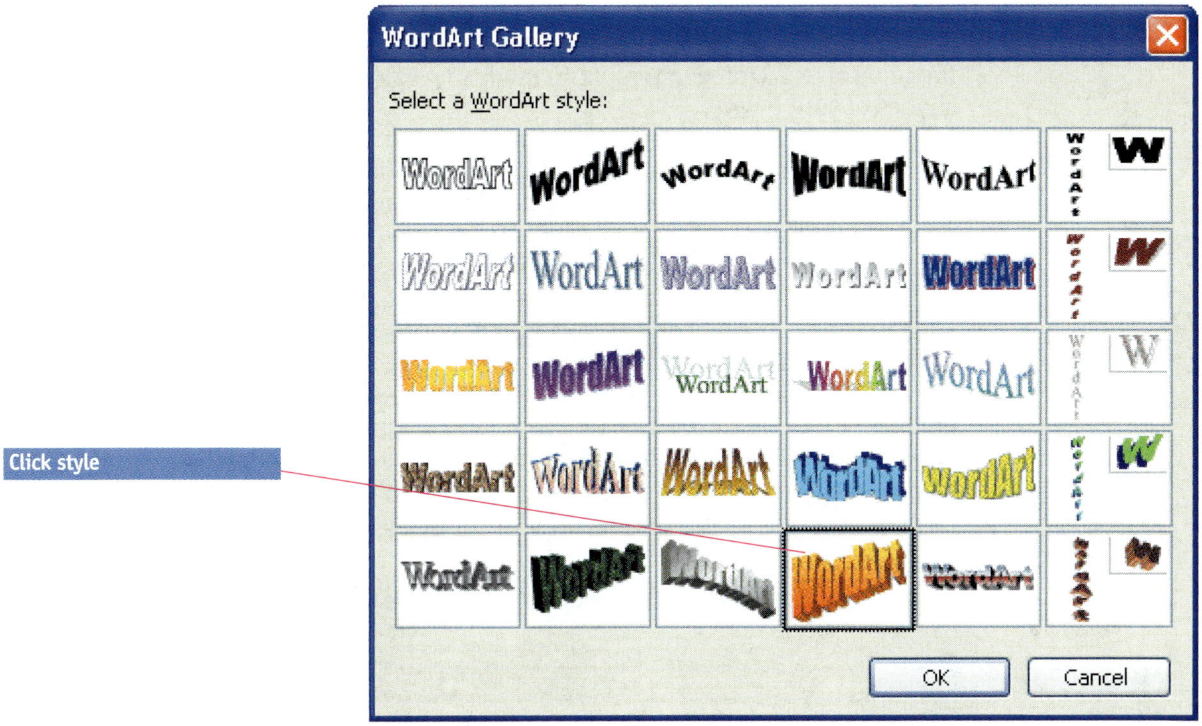

(a) Choose the Style

(b) Completed Entry

FIGURE 3.4 Microsoft WordArt

THE DRAWING TOOLBAR

All clip art is created from basic shapes, such as lines, and other basic tools that are found on the ***Drawing toolbar***. Select the Line tool, for example, then click and drag to create a line. Once the line has been created, you can select it and change its properties (such as thickness, style, or color) by using other tools on the Drawing toolbar. Draw a second line, or a curve, then depending on your ability, you have a piece of original clip art. You do not have to be an artist to use the basic tools to enhance any document.

The ***drawing canvas*** appears automatically whenever you select a tool from the Drawing toolbar and is indicated by a hashed line as shown in Figure 3.5. Each object within the canvas can be selected, at which point it displays its own ***sizing handles***. The blue rectangle is selected in Figure 3.5. You can size an object by clicking and dragging any one of the sizing handles. We don't expect you to create clip art comparable to the images provided with Microsoft Office, but you can use the tools on the Drawing toolbar to modify an existing image and/or create simple shapes of your own.

The Shift key has special significance when used in conjunction with the Line, Rectangle, and Oval tools. Press and hold the Shift key as you drag the Line tool horizontally or vertically to create a perfectly straight line in either direction. Press and hold the Shift key as you drag the Rectangle or Oval tool to create a square or circle, respectively. The AutoShapes button contains a series of selected shapes, such as a callout or banner, and is very useful to create simple drawings. And, as with any other drawing object, you can change the thickness, color, or fill by selecting the object and choosing the appropriate tool.

The Drawing toolbar also provides access to the ***Diagram Gallery***, which enables you to create a variety of charts and diagrams. Click the Insert Diagram or Organization Chart button to display the Diagram Gallery dialog box, choose the type of diagram you want, click OK, then create the diagram within the drawing canvas. (See the end-of-chapter case study on page 152.)

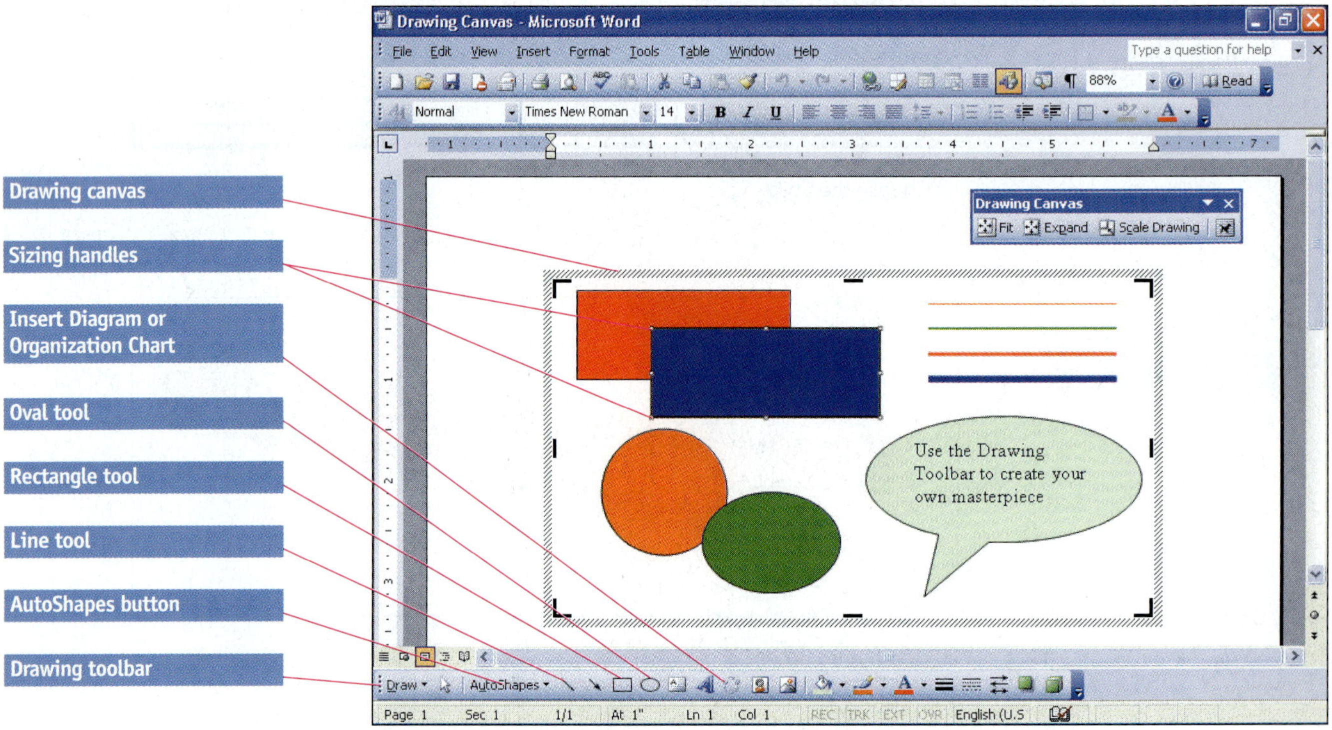

FIGURE 3.5 Drawing Canvas

hands-on exercise

1 Clip Art and WordArt

Objective To insert clip art and WordArt into a document; to use the Insert Symbol command to add typographical symbols. Use Figure 3.6 as a guide in completing the exercise.

Step 1: Insert the Clip Art

- Start Word. Open the **Clip Art and WordArt** document in the Exploring Word folder. Save the document as **Clip Art and WordArt Solution**.
- Check that the insertion point is at the beginning of the document. Pull down the **Insert menu**, click (or point to) **Picture**, then click **Clip Art**.
- The task pane opens (if it is not already open) and displays the clip art pane as shown in Figure 3.6a.
- Click in the **Search text box**. Type **computer** to search for any clip art image that is indexed with this keyword, then click the **Go button** or press **Enter**.
- The images are displayed in the task pane. Point to an image to display a drop-down arrow to its right. Click the arrow to display a context menu.
- Click **Insert** to insert the image into the document. Do not be concerned about its size or position at this time. Close the task pane.
- Save the document.

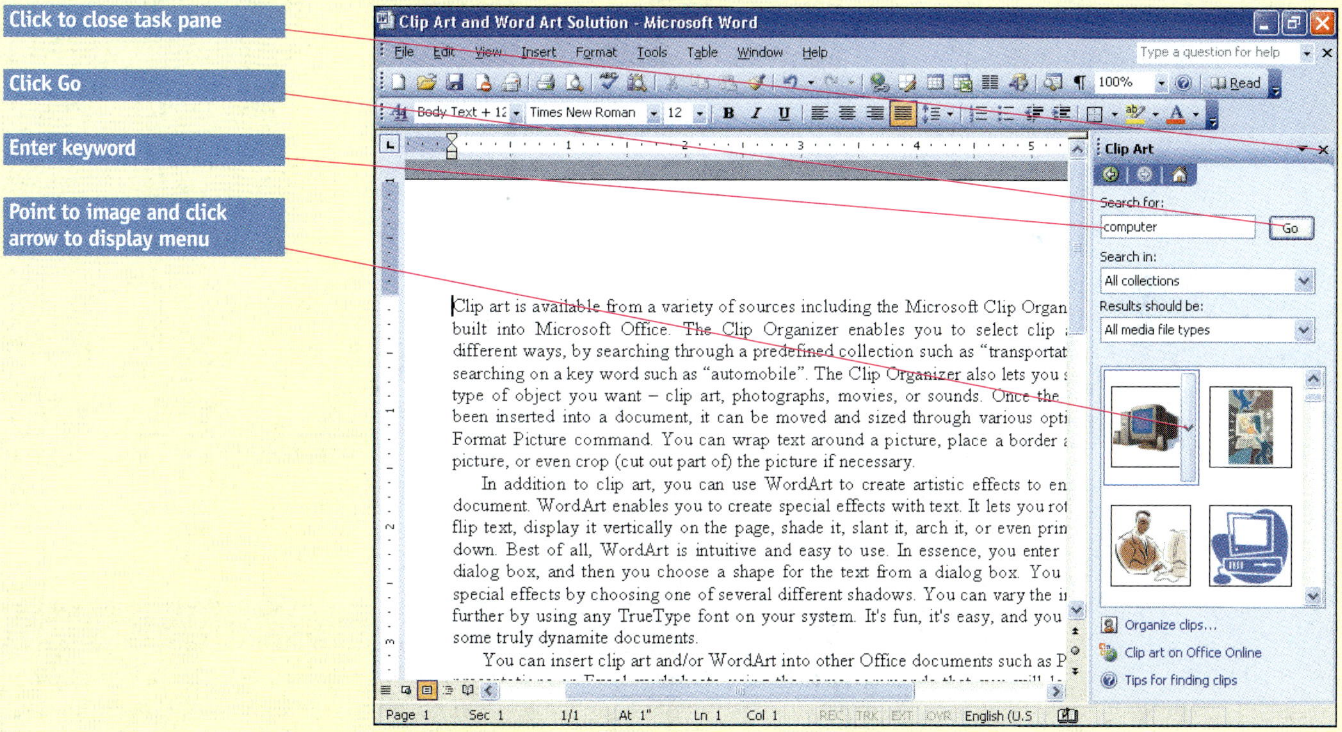

(a) Insert the Clip Art (step 1)

FIGURE 3.6 Hands-on Exercise 1

Step 2: Move and Size the Picture

- Point to the picture, click the **right mouse button** to display the context-sensitive menu, then click the **Format Picture command** to display the Format Picture dialog box in Figure 3.6b.
- You must change the layout in order to move and size the object. Click the **Layout tab**, choose the **Square layout**, then click the option button for **Left alignment**. Click **OK** to close the dialog box.
- To size the picture, click and drag a corner handle (the mouse pointer changes to a double arrow) to change the length and width simultaneously. This keeps the picture in proportion.
- To move the picture, point to any part of the image except a sizing handle (the mouse pointer changes to a four-sided arrow), then click and drag to move the image elsewhere in the document.
- Save the document.

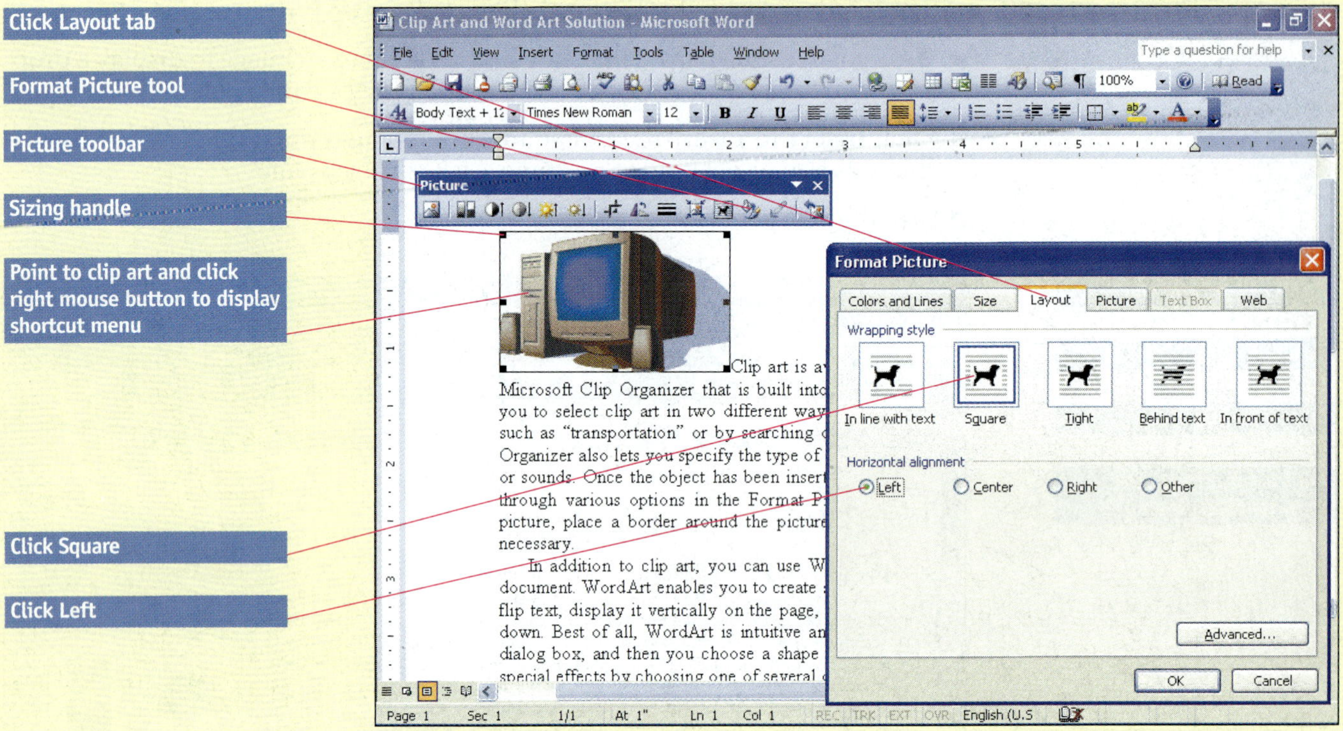

(b) Move and Size the Picture (step 2)

FIGURE 3.6 Hands-on Exercise 1 (*continued*)

THE INSERT PICTURE COMMAND

Pull down the Insert menu, click the Picture command, and click Clip Art to display the Clip Art task pane that enables you to enter the search parameters for an appropriate media object. Click the down arrow in the Search In list box and select all of the collections, including those on the Microsoft Web site. Click the down arrow in the Results list box and choose All media types, then click the Go button to initiate the search. The search may take longer than it did previously since it includes the Web, but you should have a much larger selection of potential clips from which to choose. If necessary, use the drop-down arrow on either search box to limit the search as you see fit.

Step 3: WordArt

- Press **Ctrl+End** to move to the end of the document. Pull down the **Insert menu**, click **Picture**, then click **WordArt** to display the WordArt Gallery dialog box in Figure 3.6c.
- Select the WordArt style you like (you can change it later). Click **OK**. You will see a second dialog box in which you enter the text. Enter **Enhancing a Document**. Click **OK**.
- The WordArt object appears in your document in the style you selected. Point to the WordArt object and click the **right mouse button** to display a shortcut menu. Click **Format WordArt** to display the Format WordArt dialog box.
- Click the **Layout tab**, then select **Square** as the Wrapping style. Click **OK**. It is important to select this wrapping option to facilitate placing the WordArt at the top of the document.
- Save the document.

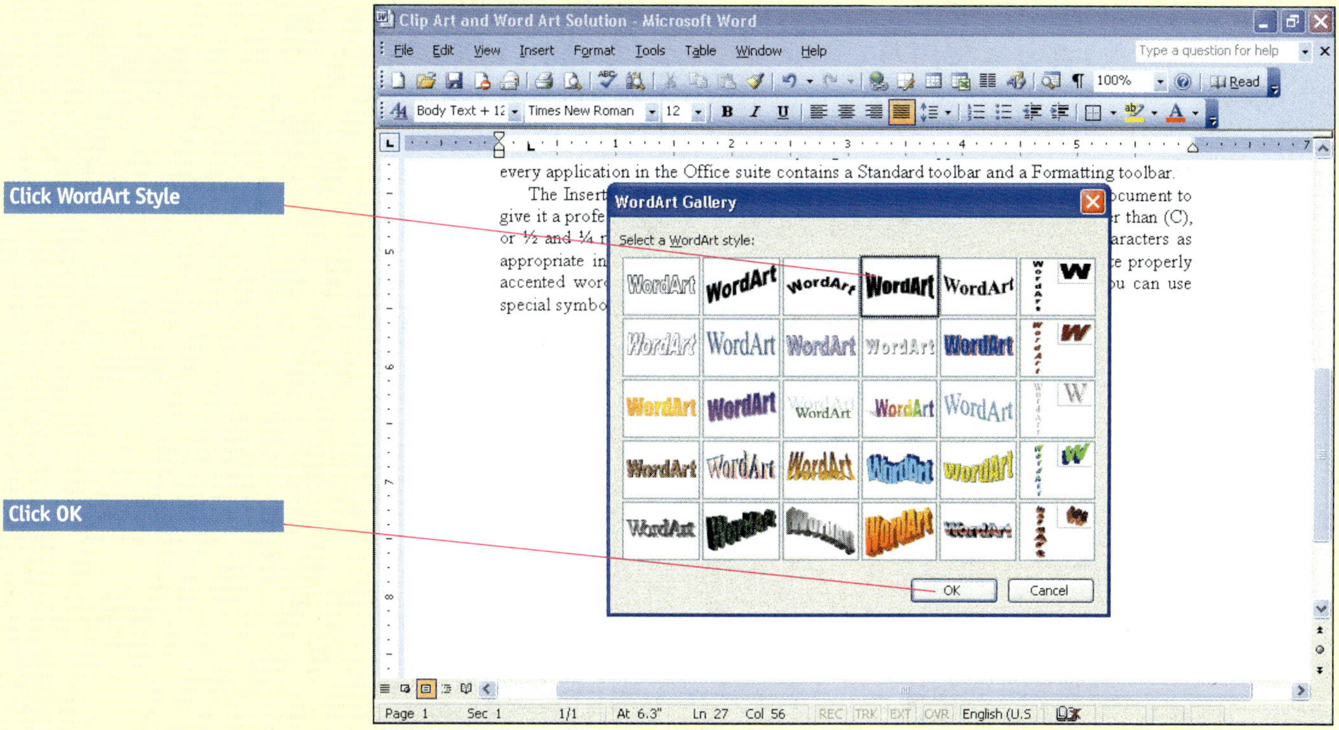

(c) WordArt (step 3)

FIGURE 3.6 Hands-on Exercise 1 (*continued*)

FORMATTING WORDART

The WordArt toolbar offers the easiest way to execute various commands associated with a WordArt object. It is displayed automatically when a WordArt object is selected and is suppressed otherwise. As with any other toolbar, you can point to a button to display a ScreenTip containing the name of the button, which is indicative of its function. The WordArt toolbar contains buttons to display the text vertically, change the style or shape, and/or edit the text.

Step 4: WordArt Continued

- Click and drag the WordArt object to move it the top of the document. (The Format WordArt dialog box is not yet visible.)
- If necessary, click to the left of the word "Clip" in the first sentence and press the **Enter key** two or three times to give yourself more room in which to work at the top of the document.
- Point to the WordArt object, click the **right mouse button** to display a shortcut menu, then click **Format WordArt** to display the Format WordArt dialog box as shown in Figure 3.6d.
- Click the **Colors and Lines tab**, then click the **Fill Color drop-down arrow** to display the available colors. Select a different color (e.g., blue). Click **OK**.
- Move and/or size the WordArt as necessary. Click the **Undo button** if necessary to cancel the action and start again.
- Save the document.

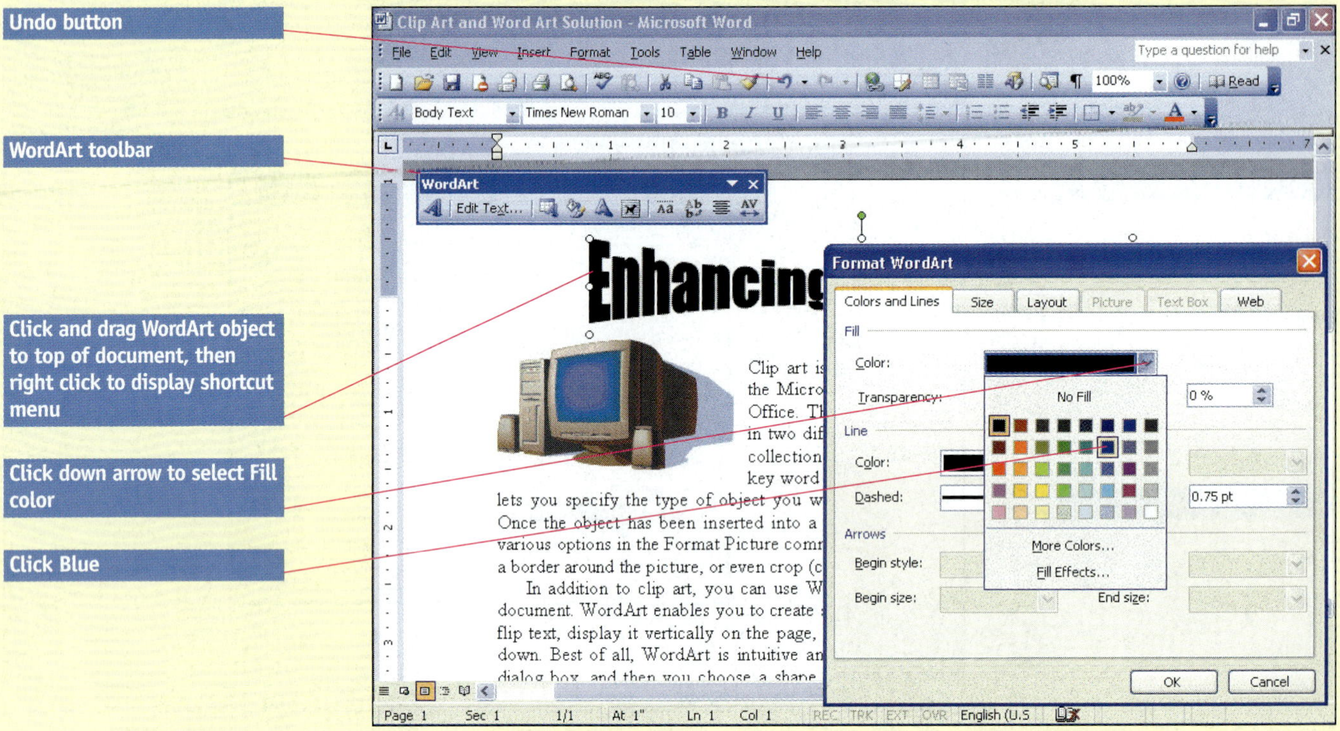

(d) WordArt Continued (step 4)

FIGURE 3.6 Hands-on Exercise 1 (*continued*)

THE THIRD DIMENSION

You can make your WordArt images even more dramatic by adding 3-D effects. You can tilt the text up or down, right or left, increase or decrease the depth, and change the shading. Pull down the View menu, click Toolbars, click Customize, then click the Toolbars tab to display the complete list of available toolbars. Check the box to display the 3-D Settings toolbar. Select the WordArt object, then experiment with various tools and special effects. The results are even better if you have a color printer.

Step 5: The Insert Symbol Command

- Press **Ctrl+End** to move to the end of the document as shown in Figure 3.6e.
- Check that you are positioned at the end of the last sentence. Press the **left arrow key** to move in front of the period.
- Pull down the **Insert menu**, click the **Symbol command**, then choose **Wingdings** from the font list box.
- Click the **Windows logo** (the last character in the last line), click **Insert**, then close the dialog box.
- Click after the word Microsoft in the same sentence, type **(r)**, and try to watch the screen as you enter the text. The (r) will be converted to the ® registered trademark symbol by the AutoCorrect feature.
- Save the document.

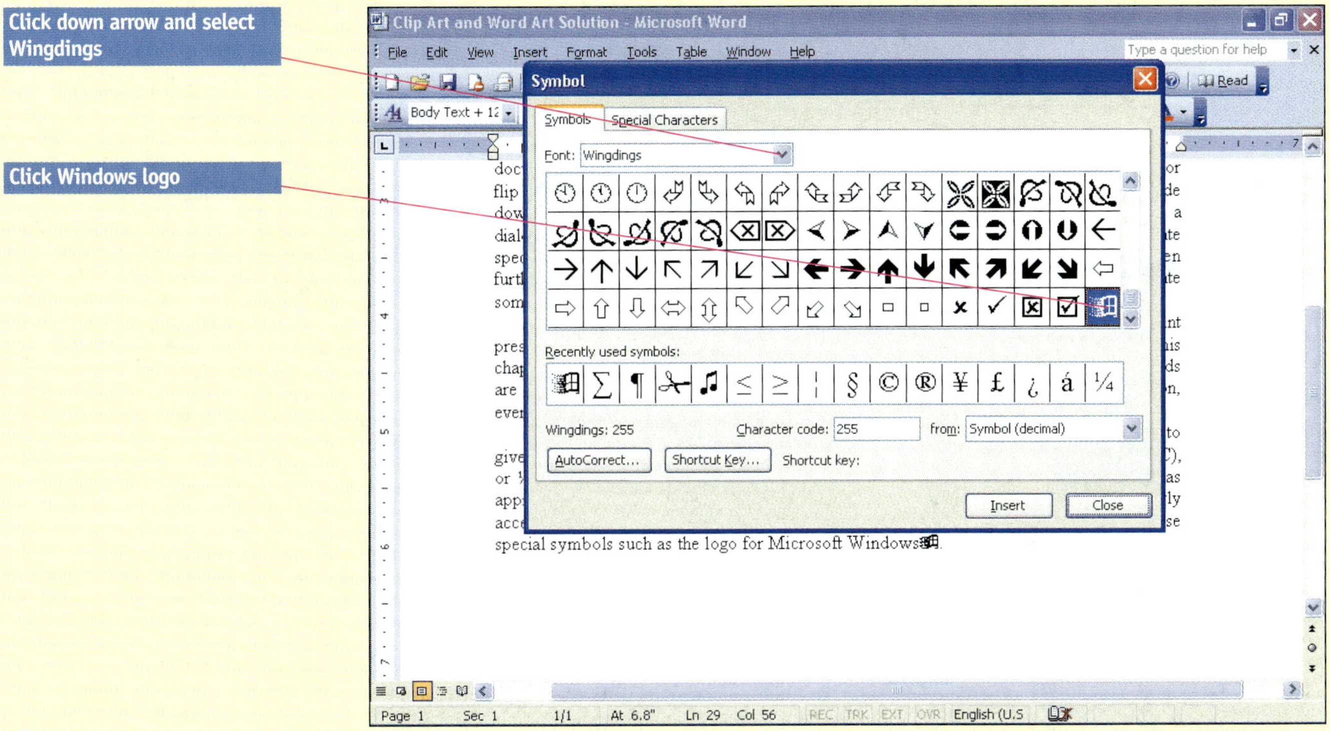

(e) The Insert Symbol Command (step 5)

FIGURE 3.6 Hands-on Exercise 1 (*continued*)

AUTOCORRECT AND AUTOFORMAT

The AutoCorrect feature not only corrects mistakes as you type by substituting one character string for another (e.g., "the" for "teh"), but it will also substitute symbols for typewritten equivalents such as © for (c), provided the entries are included in the table of substitutions. The AutoFormat feature is similar in concept and replaces common fractions such as 1/2 or 1/4 with ½ or ¼. It also converts ordinal numbers such as 1st or 2nd to 1st or 2nd.

Step 6: Create the AutoShape

- Pull down the **View menu**, click the **Toolbars command** to display the list of available toolbars, then click **Drawing toolbar**.
- Press the **End key** to move to the end of the line, then press the **Enter key** once or twice to move below the last sentence in the document.
- Click the **down arrow** on the AutoShapes tool to display the menu. Click the **Stars and Banners submenu** and select the **Horizontal Scroll**.
- The mouse pointer changes to a tiny crosshair. Press **Esc** to remove the drawing canvas (we find it easier to work without it), which in turn moves you to the bottom of the page.
- Click and drag to create a scroll, as shown in Figure 3.6f. Release the mouse. Right click in the scroll, click **Add Text**, change the font size to 18 point, then enter the text **This document was created by** (your name). Center the text.
- Click and drag the sizing handle (a circle) at the bottom of the scroll to make it narrow. Click and drag the yellow diamond at the left of the scroll to change the appearance of the scroll. The green dot at the top of the scroll allows you to rotate the scroll. Click off the scroll. Save the document.

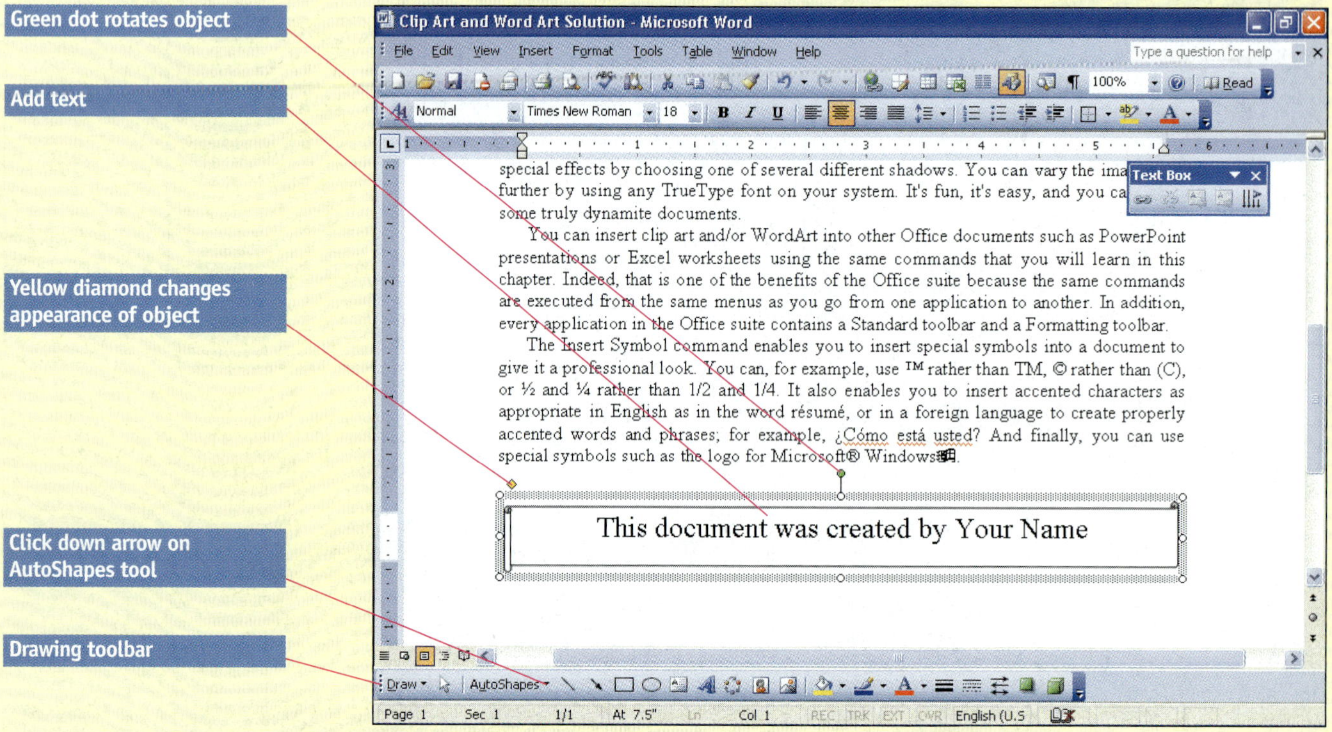

(f) Create the AutoShape (step 6)

FIGURE 3.6 Hands-on Exercise 1 (*continued*)

SUPPRESS THE DRAWING CANVAS

The drawing canvas appears by default whenever you create an AutoShape, rectangle, oval, or text box from the Drawing toolbar. You can make the canvas disappear by pressing the Esc key when the canvas appears initially. You can also prevent the canvas from appearing altogether. Pull down the Tools menu, click the Options command, click the General tab, and then clear the box to automatically create the drawing canvas when inserting AutoShapes.

Step 7: The Completed Document

- Pull down the **File menu** and click the **Page Setup command** to display the Page Setup dialog box. (You can also double click the ruler below the Formatting toolbar to display the dialog box.)
- Click the **Margins tab** and change the top margin to **1.5 inches** (to accommodate the WordArt at the top of the document). Click **OK**.
- Click the **drop-down arrow** on the Zoom box and select **Whole Page** to preview the completed document as shown in Figure 3.6g. You can change the size and position of the objects from within this view. For example:
  - Select (click) the clip art to select this object and display its sizing handles.
  - Select (click) the banner to select it (and deselect the previous selection).
  - Move and size either object as necessary.
- Print the document and submit it to your instructor as proof that you did the exercise. Save the document. Close the document.
- Exit Word if you do not want to continue with the next exercise at this time.

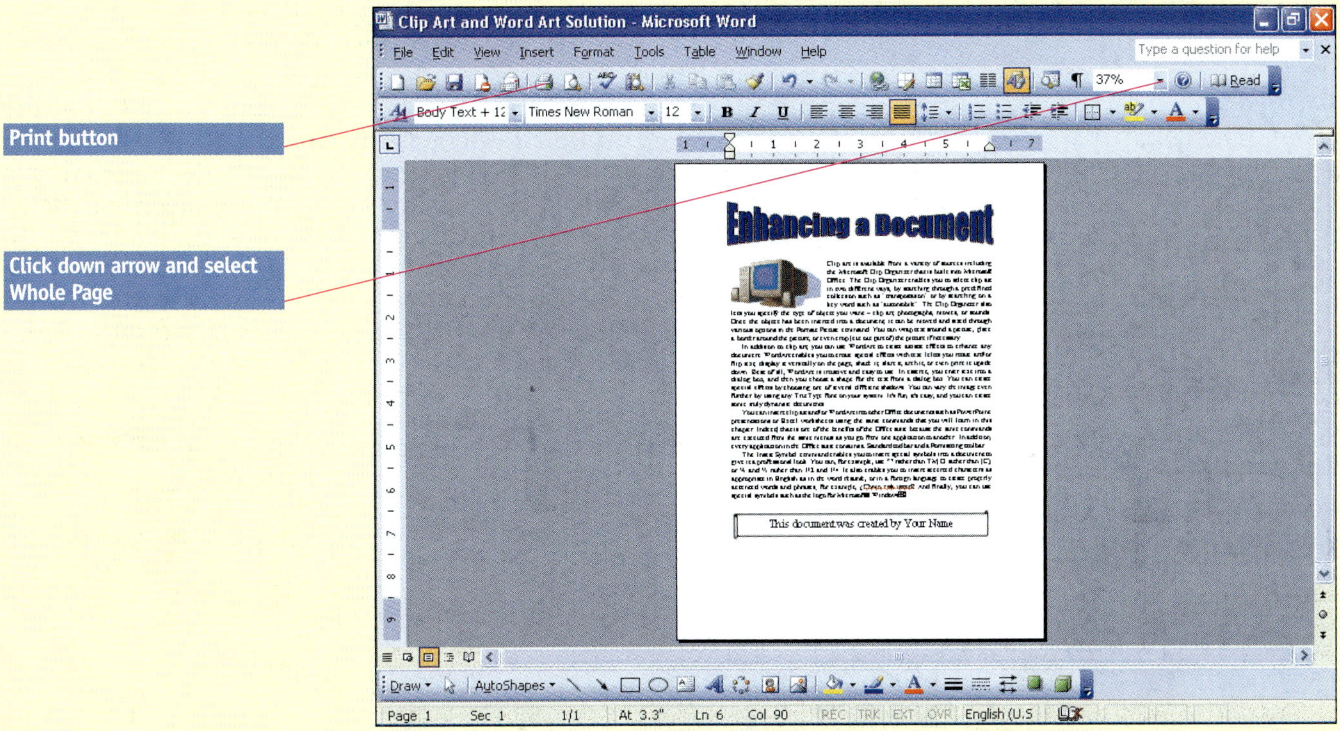

(g) The Completed Document (step 7)

FIGURE 3.6 Hands-on Exercise 1 (*continued*)

ANIMATE TEXT ON SCREEN

Select the desired text, pull down the Format menu, click the Font command to display the Font dialog box, then click the Text Effects tab. Select the desired effect such as "Blinking Background" or "Las Vegas Lights", then click OK to accept the settings and close the dialog box. The selected text should be displayed with the specified effect, which appears on the screen, but not when the document is printed. To cancel the effect, select the text, display the Font dialog box, click the Text Effects tab, select "None" as the effect, then click OK.

MICROSOFT WORD AND THE INTERNET

The ***Internet*** is a network of networks that connects computers anywhere in the world. The ***World Wide Web*** (WWW or simply, the Web) is a very large subset of the Internet, consisting of those computers that store a special type of document known as a ***Web page*** or ***HTML document***. The interesting thing about a Web page is that it contains references called ***hyperlinks*** to other Web pages, which may in turn be stored on a different computer that is located anywhere in the world. And therein lies the fascination of the Web, in that you simply click on link after link to go effortlessly from one document to the next.

Web pages are developed in a special language called ***HyperText Markup Language (HTML)***. Initially, the only way to create a Web page was to learn HTML. Microsoft Office simplifies the process because you can create the document in Word, then simply save it as a Web page. In other words, you start Word in the usual fashion, enter the text of the document with basic formatting, then use the ***Save As Web Page command*** to convert the document to a Web page. Microsoft Word does the rest and generates the HTML statements for you. (Word 2003 provides a new ***Single File Web Page*** format that makes the process even easier.) You can continue to enter text and/or change the formatting just as you can with an ordinary document.

Figure 3.7 contains the Web page you will create in the next hands-on exercise. The exercise begins by having you search the Web to locate a suitable photograph for inclusion into the document. You then download the picture to your PC and use the Insert Picture command to insert the photograph into your document. You add formatting, hyperlinks, and footnotes as appropriate, then you save the document as a Web page. The exercise is easy to do, and it will give you an appreciation for the various Web capabilities that are built into Microsoft Office.

Even if you do not place your page on the Web, you can still view it locally on your PC. This is the approach we follow in the next hands-on exercise, which shows you how to save a Word document as a Web page and then see the results of your effort in a Web browser. The Web page is stored on a local drive (e.g., on drive A or

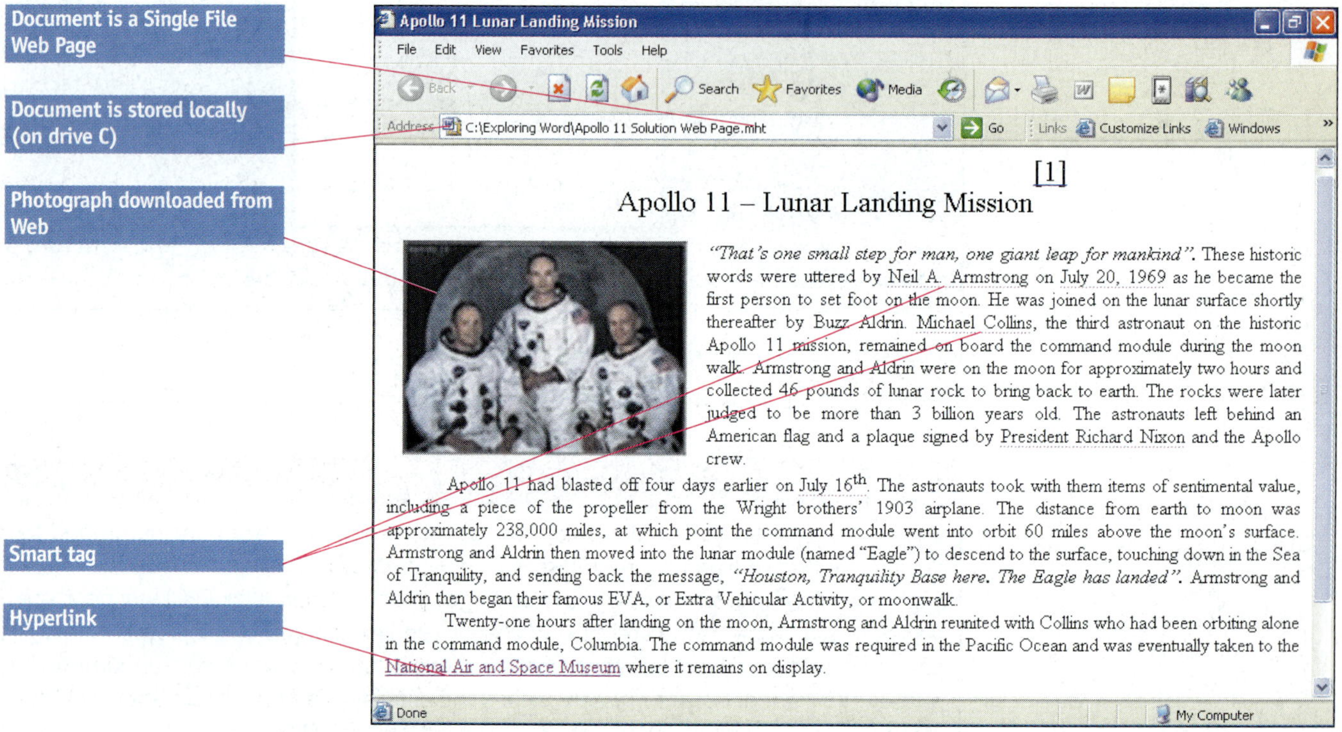

FIGURE 3.7 A Web Document

drive C) rather than on an Internet server, but it can still be viewed through Internet Explorer (or any other browser).

The ability to create links to local documents and to view those pages through a Web browser has created an entirely new way to disseminate information. Organizations of every size are taking advantage of this capability to develop an ***Intranet*** in which Web pages are placed on a local area network for use within the organizations. The documents on an intranet are available only to individuals with access to the local area network on which the documents are stored.

Copyright Protection

A ***copyright*** provides legal protection to a written or artistic work, including literary, dramatic, musical, and artistic works such as poetry, novels, movies, songs, and computer software and architecture. It gives the author of a work the exclusive right to the use and duplication of that work. A copyright does not, however, protect facts, ideas, systems, or methods of operation, although it may protect the way these things are expressed.

The owner of the copyright may sell or give up a portion of his or her rights; for example, an author may give distribution rights to a publisher and/or grant movie rights to a studio. ***Infringement of a copyright*** occurs any time a right reserved by the copyright owner is violated without permission of the owner. Anything on the Internet should be considered copyrighted unless the document specifically says it is in the ***public domain***, in which case the author is giving everyone the right to freely reproduce and distribute the material. Does copyright protection prevent you from quoting a document found on the Web in a research paper? Does copyright protection imply that you cannot download an image for inclusion in a term paper? (Facts themselves are not covered by copyright, so you can use statistical data without fear of infringement.)

The answer to what you can use from the Web depends on the amount of the information you reference, as well as the intended use of that information. It is considered ***fair use***, and thus not an infringement of copyright, to use a portion of a work for educational, nonprofit purposes, or for the purpose of critical review or commentary. In other words, you can use a quote, downloaded image, or other information from the Web, provided you cite the original work in your footnotes and/or bibliography.

A ***footnote*** provides additional information about an item, such as its source, and appears at the bottom of the page where the reference occurs. An ***endnote*** is similar in concept but appears at the end of a document. A horizontal line separates the notes from the rest of the document.

The ***Insert Reference command*** inserts either a footnote or an endnote into a document, and automatically assigns the next sequential number to that note. The command adjusts for last minute changes, either in your writing or in your professor's requirements. It will, for example, renumber all existing notes to accommodate the addition or deletion of a footnote or endnote. Existing notes are moved (or deleted) within a document by moving (deleting) the reference mark rather than the text of the footnote.

Software piracy (the unauthorized duplication or use of software products such as Microsoft Office) presents a unique problem with respect to copyright protection because of the ease with which it can be done. A program that takes years of development and costs millions of dollars can be copied in a few seconds and results in economic loss to the developer. Software piracy harms everyone in the long run, including you, the end user. It results in higher prices for legitimate licenses, reduced levels of support, and delays in the development of new software. The law imposes stiff penalties for copyright infringement. You may think that this is unduly harsh, but the intent behind the copyright law is to provide economic incentive to an artist or software developer in order that they will invest the necessary resources to create the work. You should honor and respect the copyright process.

hands-on exercise

2 Microsoft Word and the World Wide Web

Objective To download a picture from the Internet for use in a Word document; to insert a hyperlink into a Word document; to save a Word document as a Web page. Use Figure 3.8 as a reference.

Step 1: Search the Web

- Start Internet Explorer. It does not matter which page you see initially, as long as you are able to connect to the Internet and start Internet Explorer. Click the **Maximize button** so that Internet Explorer takes the entire screen.
- Click the **Search button** on the Standard Buttons toolbar to display the Search pane in the Explorer bar at the left of the Internet Explorer window.
- Enter **Apollo 11** in the text box, then click the **Go button**. The results of the search are displayed in the left pane as shown in Figure 3.8a. The results you obtain will be different from ours.
- Select (click) the link to Apollo 11 Home. (Enter the URL www.nasm.si.edu/apollo/AS11 manually if your search engine does not display this link.)
- Click the **Close button** to close the Search pane, so that your selected document takes the entire screen.

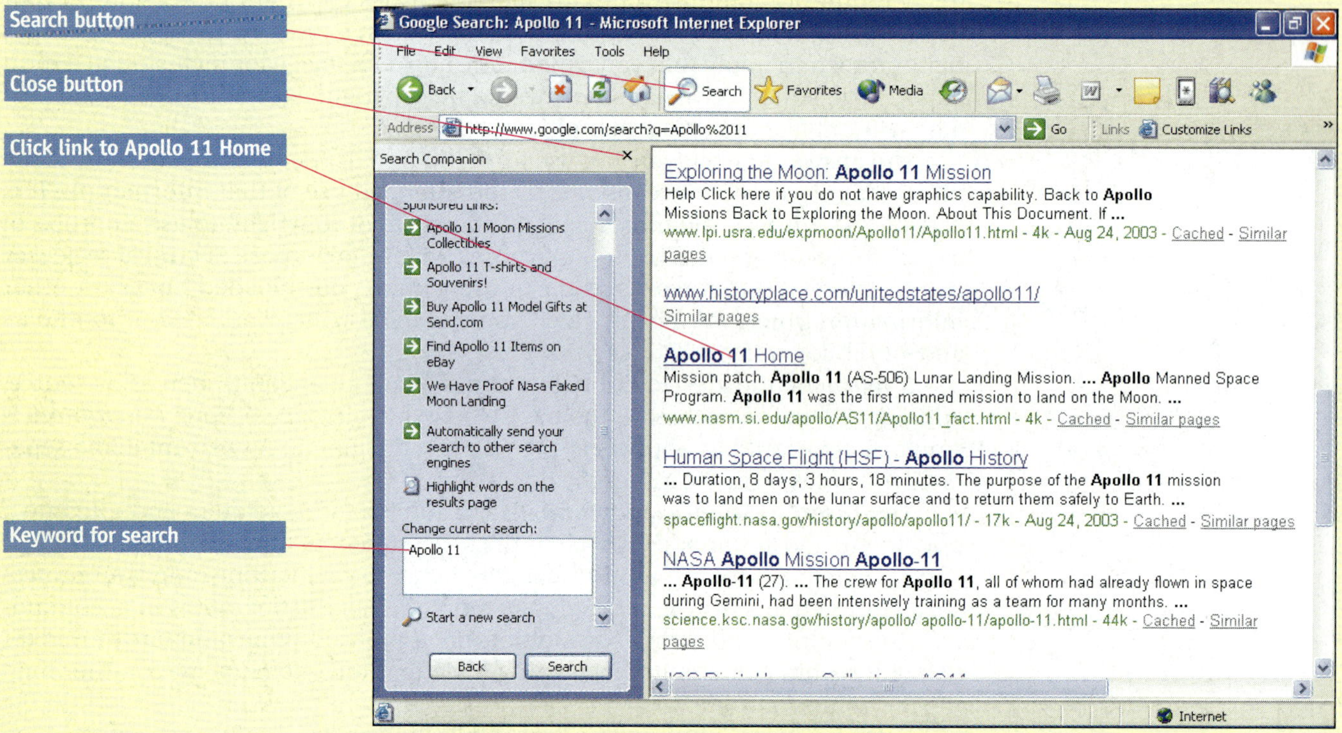

(a) Search the Web (step 1)

FIGURE 3.8 Hands-on Exercise 2

SHORTCUT TO SEARCHING

Click in the Address bar, then type the word "go" or "find" followed by the word or phrase you are looking for. Internet Explorer initiates a search using its predetermined search provider and displays the results (the relevant links) in the Internet Explorer window.

Step 2: Save the Picture

- Click the link to **Apollo 11 Crew** to display the page in Figure 3.8b. Point to the picture of the astronauts, click the **right mouse button** to display a shortcut menu, then click the **Save Picture As command** to display the Save As dialog box.
  - Click the **drop-down arrow** in the Save In list box to specify the drive and folder in which you want to save the graphic (e.g., in the **Exploring Word folder**).
  - Internet Explorer supplies the file name and file type for you. You may change the name, but you cannot change the file type.
  - Click the **Save button** to download the image. Remember the file name and location, as you will need to access the file in the next step.
- The Save As dialog box will close automatically after the picture has been downloaded to your computer.
- Click the **Minimize button** in the Internet Explorer window, since you are temporarily finished using the browser.

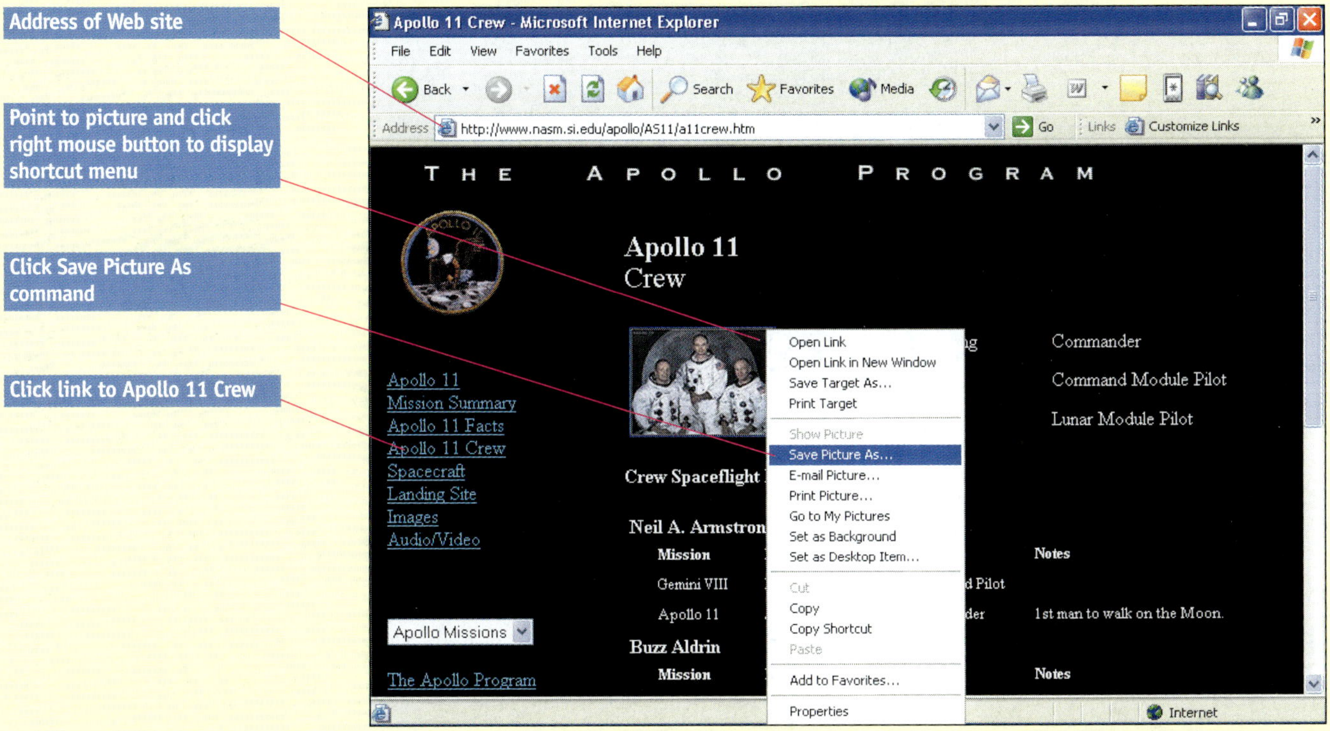

(b) Save the Picture (step 2)

FIGURE 3.8 Hands-on Exercise 2 (*continued*)

ABOUT INTERNET EXPLORER

There are multiple versions of Internet Explorer, each with subtle differences in the features it supports. To find out which version you have, pull down the Help menu and click About Internet Explorer to display a screen with the version and release number. You will need this information if you have trouble with your browser and seek help from technical support. The About command is present in the Help menu of every Windows application.

Step 3: Insert the Picture

- Start Word and open the **Apollo 11 document** in the **Exploring Word folder**. Save the document as **Apollo 11 Solution** so that you can return to the original document if necessary.
- Pull down the **View menu** to be sure that you are in the **Print Layout view** (or else you will not see the picture after it is inserted into the document). Pull down the **Insert menu**, point to (or click) **Picture command**, then click **From File** to display the Insert Picture dialog box shown in Figure 3.8c.
- Click the **down arrow** on the Look In text box to select the drive and folder where you previously saved the picture. Click the **down arrow** on the Files of type list box and specify **All files**.
- Select (click) **AS11_crew**, which is the file containing the picture that you downloaded earlier. Click the **drop-down arrow** on the **Views button**, then click **Preview** to display the picture prior to inserting. Click **Insert**.
- Save the document.

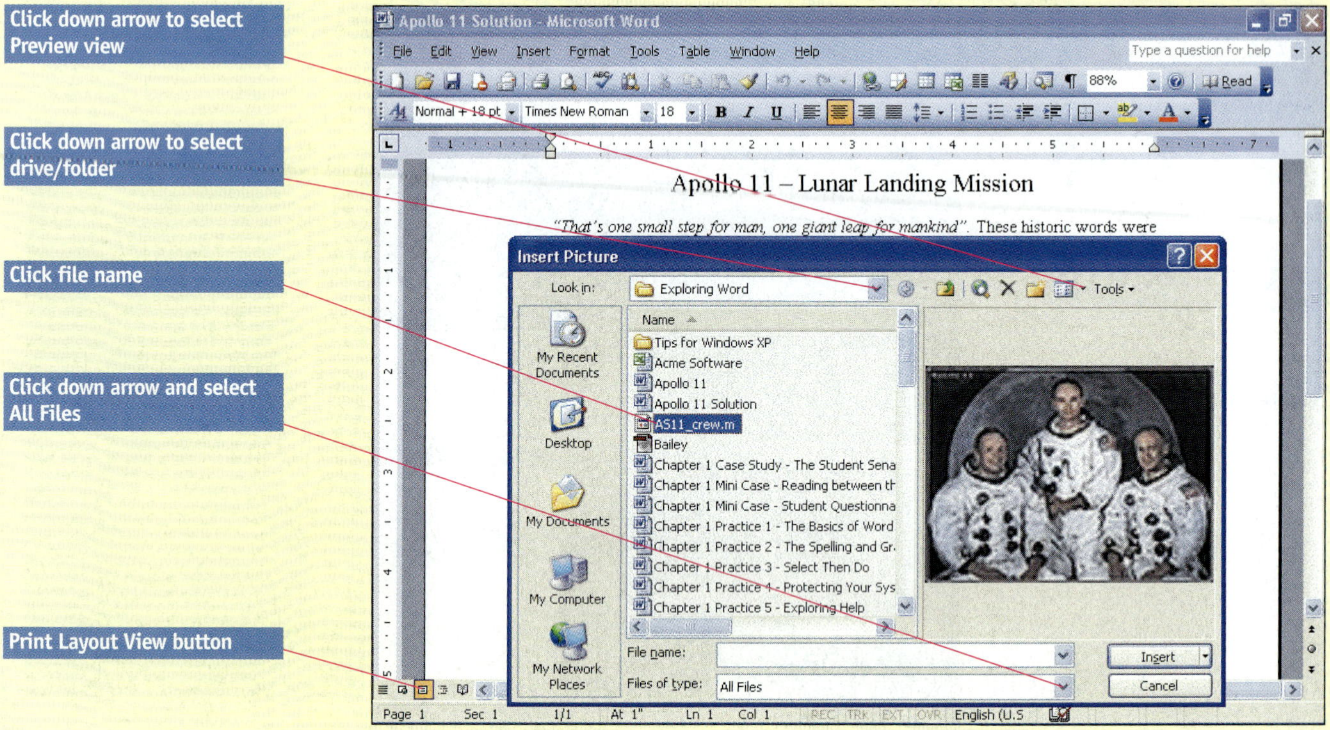

(c) Insert the Picture (step 3)

FIGURE 3.8 Hands-on Exercise 2 (*continued*)

CHANGE THE DEFAULT LOCATION

The default file location is the folder Word uses to open and save a document unless it is otherwise instructed. To change the default location, pull down the Tools menu, click Options, click the File Locations tab, click the desired File type (documents), then click the Modify command button to display the Modify Location dialog box. Click the drop-down arrow in the Look In box to select the new folder (e.g., C:\Exploring Word). Click OK to accept this selection. Click OK to close the Options dialog box. The next time you access the Open or Save commands from the File menu, the Look In text box will reflect the change.

Step 4: Move and Size the Picture

- Point to the picture after it is inserted into the document, click the **right mouse button** to display a shortcut menu, then click the **Format Picture command** to display the Format Picture dialog box.
- Click the **Layout tab** and choose **Square** in the Wrapping style area. Click **OK** to accept the settings and close the Format Picture dialog box.
- Move and/or size the picture so that it approximates the size and position in Figure 3.8d.
- Click the **Undo button** anytime that you are not satisfied with the result. (You can click Redo button to reverse the Undo command.)
- Save the document.

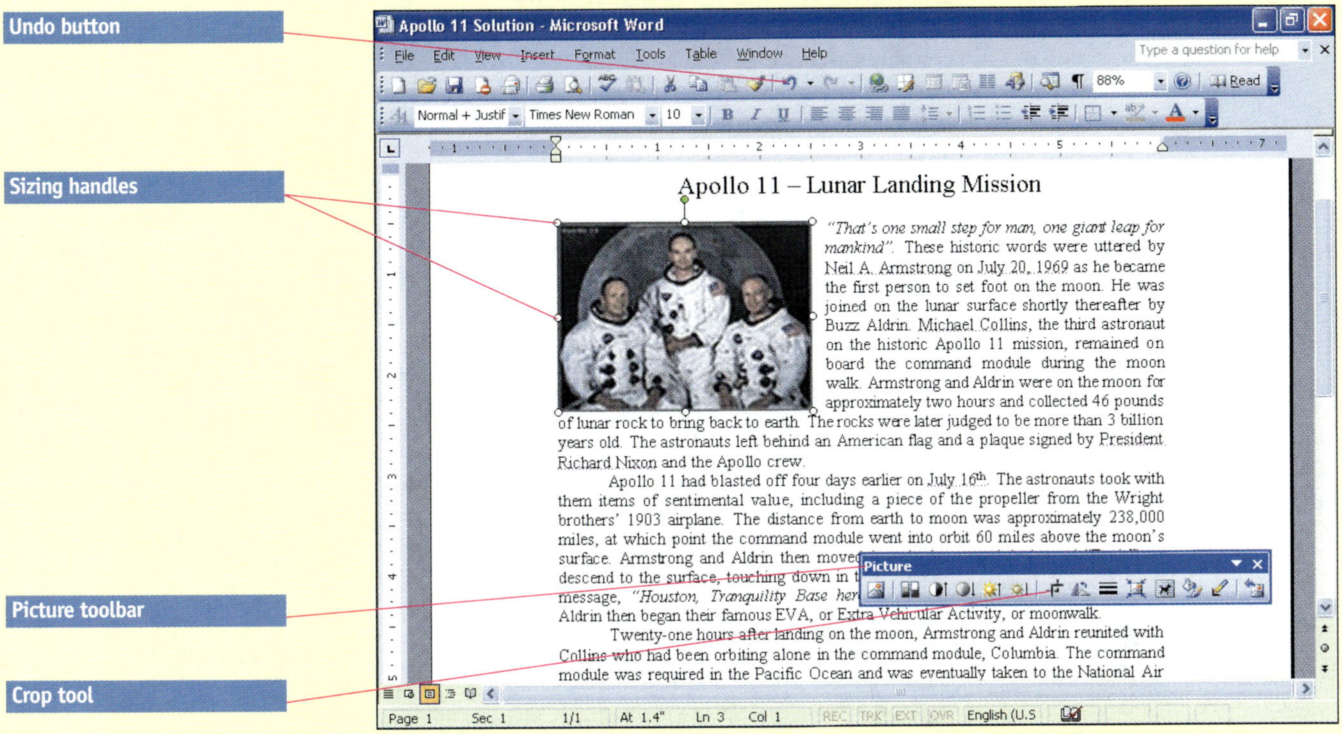

(d) Move and Size the Picture (step 4)

FIGURE 3.8 Hands-on Exercise 2 (*continued*)

CROPPING A PICTURE

The Crop tool is one of the most useful tools when dealing with a photograph as it lets you eliminate (crop) part of a picture. Select (click) the picture to display the Picture toolbar and sizing handles. (If you do not see the Picture toolbar, right click the picture and click the Show Picture Toolbar command.) Click the Crop tool (the ScreenTip will display the name of the tool), then click and drag a sizing handle to crop the part of the picture you want to eliminate. Click the Crop tool a second time to turn the feature off. To restore the picture to its original dimensions, right click the picture, click the Format Picture command, click the Picture tab, and then click the Reset button. Click OK to close the Format Picture dialog box.

Step 5: Insert a Footnote

- Press **Ctrl+Home** to move to the beginning of the document, then click after Lunar Landing Mission in the title of the document. This is where you will insert the footnote.
- Pull down the **Insert menu**. Click **Reference**, then choose **Footnote** to display the Footnote and Endnote dialog box as shown in Figure 3.8e. Check that the option button for **Footnotes** is selected and that the numbering starts at 1. Click **Insert**.
- The insertion point moves to the bottom of the page, where you type the text of the footnote, which should include the Web site from where you downloaded the picture.
- Press **Ctrl+Home** to move to the beginning of the page, where you will see a reference for the footnote you just created. If necessary, you can move (or delete) a footnote by moving (deleting) the reference mark rather than the text of the footnote.
- Save the document.

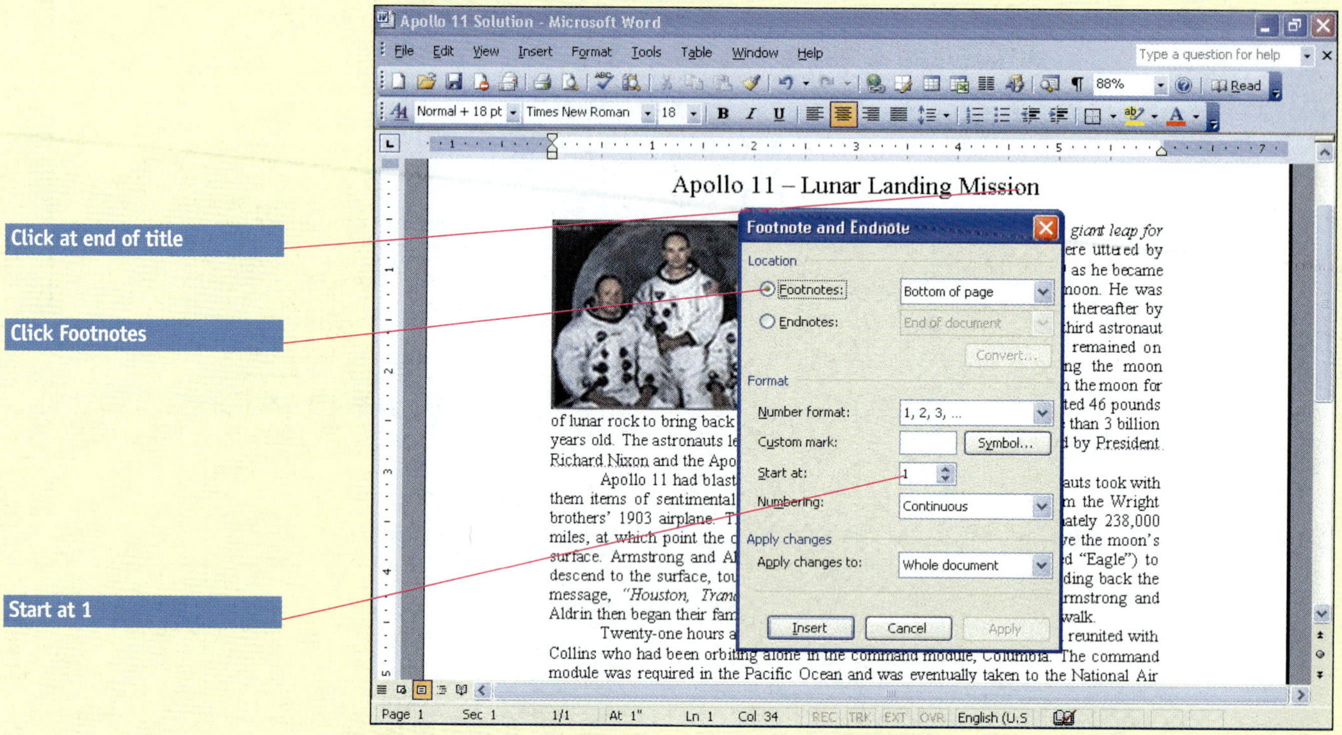

(e) Insert a Footnote (step 5)

FIGURE 3.8 Hands-on Exercise 2 (*continued*)

COPY THE WEB ADDRESS

Use the Copy command to enter a Web address from Internet Explorer into a Word document. Not only do you save time by not having to type the address yourself, but you also ensure that it is entered correctly. Click in the Address bar of Internet Explorer to select the URL, then pull down the Edit menu and click the Copy command (or use the Ctrl+C keyboard shortcut). Switch to the Word document, click at the place in the document where you want to insert the URL, pull down the Edit menu, and click the Paste command (or use the Ctrl+V keyboard shortcut).

Step 6: Insert a Hyperlink

- Scroll to the bottom of the document, then click and drag to select the text **National Air and Space Museum**.
- Pull down the **Insert menu** and click the **Hyperlink command** (or click the **Insert Hyperlink button** on the Standard toolbar) to display the Insert Hyperlink dialog box as shown in Figure 3.8f.
- National Air and Space Museum is entered automatically in the Text to display text box. Click **Existing File or Web Page**. Click **Browsed Pages**.
- Click in the **Address** text box to enter the address. Type **http://www.nasm.edu**.
- Click **OK** to accept the settings and close the dialog box. The hyperlink should appear as an underlined entry in the document.
- Save the document.

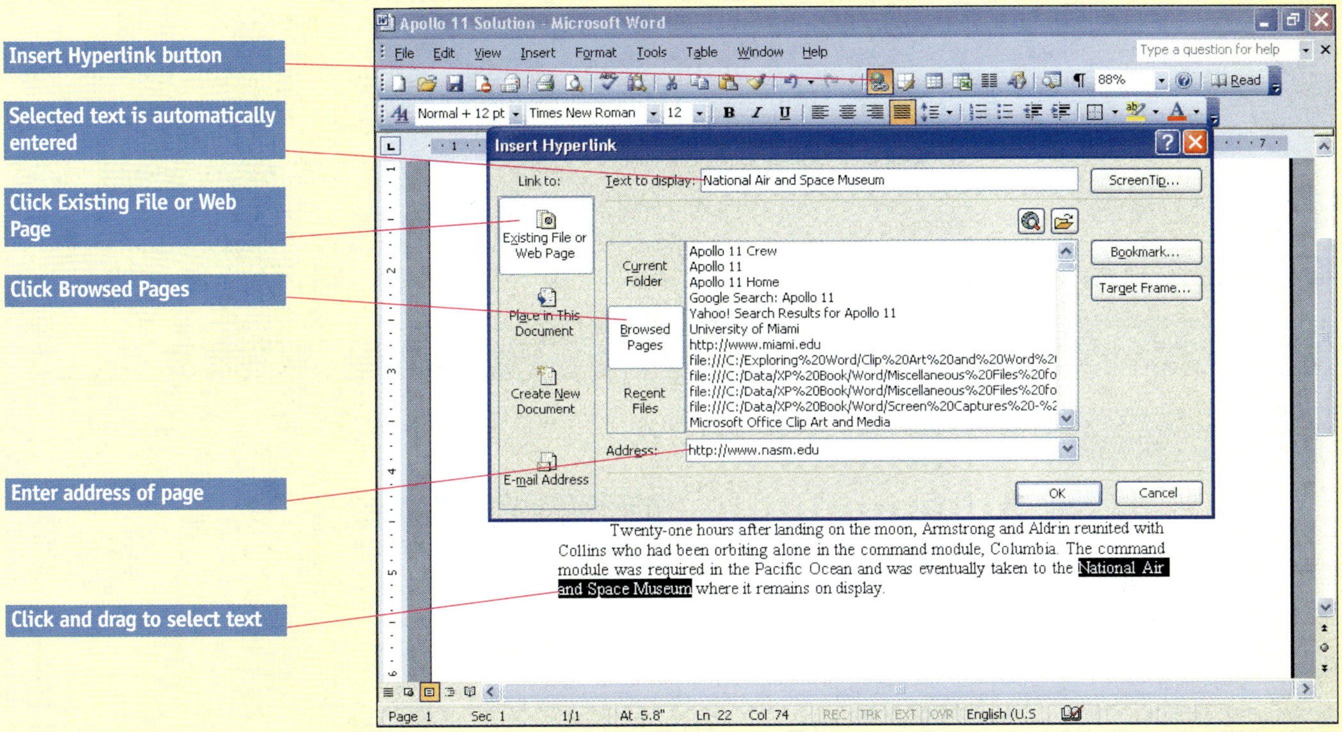

(f) Insert a Hyperlink (step 6)

FIGURE 3.8 Hands-on Exercise 2 (*continued*)

CLICK TO EDIT, CTRL+CLICK TO FOLLOW

Point to a hyperlink within a Word document and you see a ToolTip that says to press and hold the Ctrl key (Ctrl+Click) to follow the link. This is different from what you usually do, because you normally just click a link to follow it. What if, however, you wanted to edit the link? Word modifies the convention so that clicking a link enables you to edit the text of the link. Alternatively, you can right click the hyperlink to display a context-sensitive menu from where you can make the appropriate choice.

Step 7: **Create the Web Page**

- Pull down the **File menu** and click the **Save As Web Page command** to display the Save As dialog box as shown in Figure 3.8g. Be sure that **Single File Web Page** is specified as the file type.
- Click the **drop-down arrow** in the Save In list box to select the appropriate drive, then open the **Exploring Word folder**.
- Change the name of the Web page to **Apollo 11 Solution Web Page** (to differentiate it from the Word document of the same name). Click the **Change Title button** to display a dialog box in which you can change the title of the Web page to what will appear in the title bar of the Web browser, as in Figure 3.8g. Click **OK**.
- Click the **Save button**. You will see a message indicating that the pictures will be left aligned. Click **Continue**.
- The title bar changes to reflect the name of the Web page. There are now two versions of this document in the Exploring Word folder, Apollo 11 Solution and Apollo 11 Solution Web Page. The latter has been saved as a Web page.
- Click the **Print button** on the Standard toolbar to print this page for your instructor from within Microsoft Word.

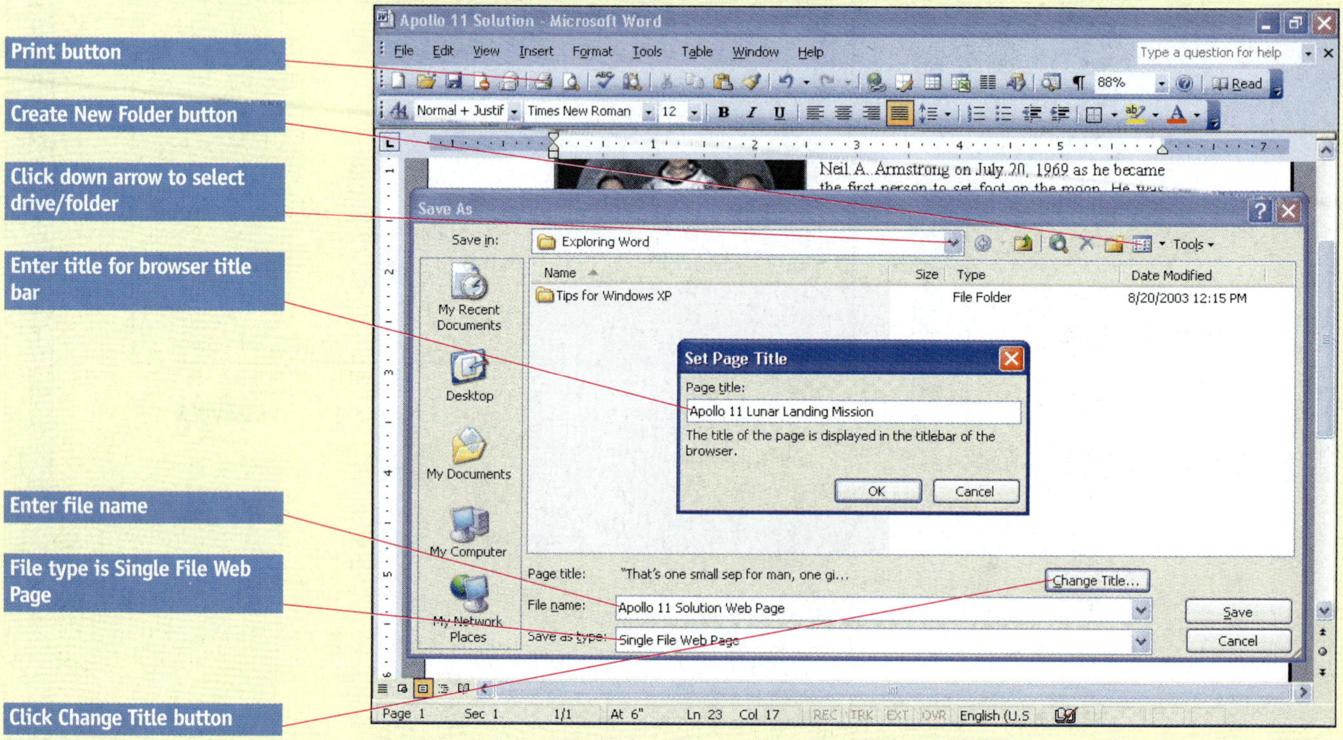

(g) Create the Web Page (step 7)

FIGURE 3.8 Hands-on Exercise 2 (*continued*)

CREATE A NEW FOLDER

Do you work with a large number of documents? If so, it may be useful to store those documents in different folders, perhaps one folder for each course you are taking. Pull down the File menu, click the Save As command to display the Save As dialog box, then click the Create New Folder button to display the associated dialog box. Enter the name of the folder, then click OK. Once the folder has been created, use the Look In box to change to that folder the next time you open that document.

Step 8: View the Web Page

- Click the taskbar button for Internet Explorer. Pull down the **File menu** and click the **Open command** to display the Open dialog box. Click the **Browse button**, then select the folder where you saved the Web page. Select the **Apollo 11 Solution Web Page** document, click **Open**, then click **OK.**
- You should see the Web page that was created earlier, as shown in Figure 3.8h. Click the **Print button** on the Internet Explorer toolbar to print this page.
- Click the hyperlink to the **National Air and Space Museum** to display the associated Web page. If you are unable to connect to the site, it is because the site is down, your Internet connection is down, and/or you entered the Web address incorrectly.
- Return to Word. Right click the hyperlink to display a context-sensitive menu, click **Edit Hyperlink**, and make the necessary correction. Save the document.
- Return to Internet Explorer. Click the **Refresh button** to load the corrected page and try the hyperlink a second time. Close Internet Explorer. Exit Word.

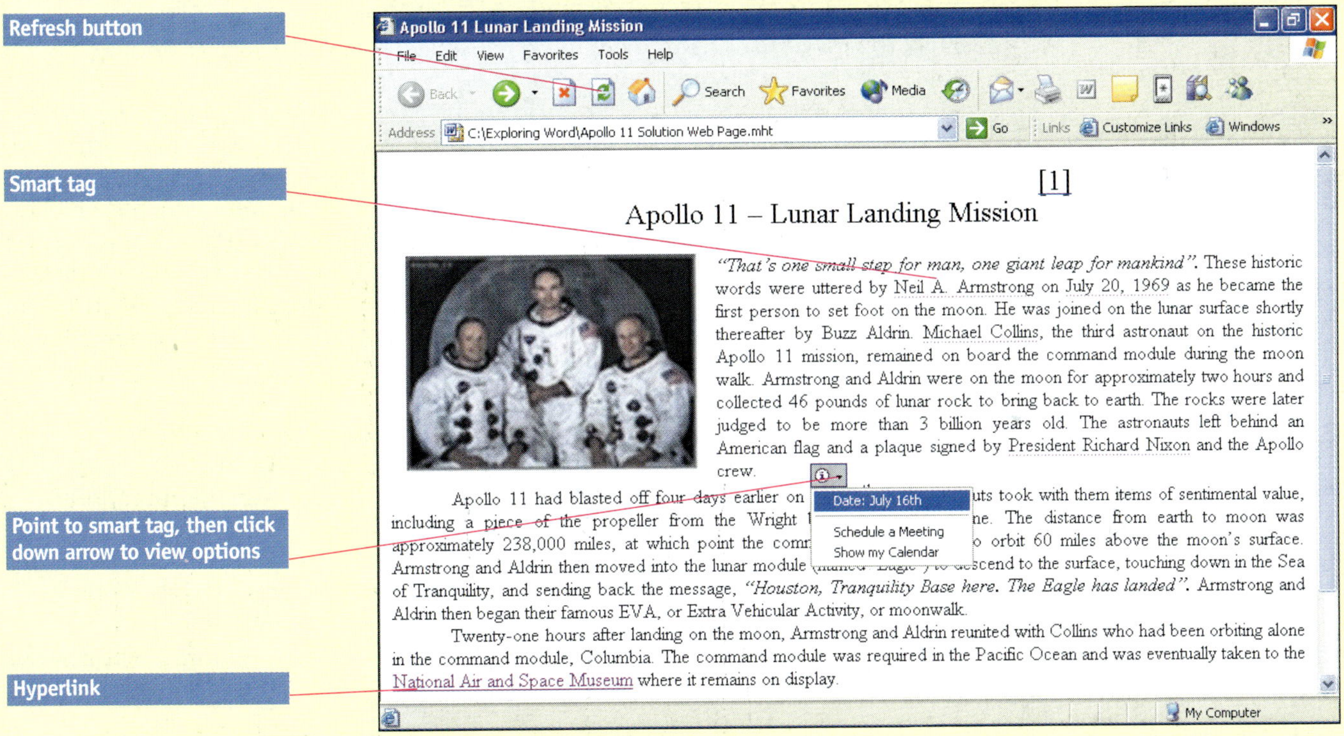

(h) View the Web Page (step 8)

FIGURE 3.8 Hands-on Exercise 2 (*continued*)

SMART TAGS

All applications in Microsoft Office identify specific data types such as a person's name or a date that may exist within a document. The data is identified by a dotted purple line and is known as a smart tag. Point to the smart tag and then click the down arrow in the Smart Tag Actions button to see the list of appropriate actions. The actions for the date in Figure 3.8h are tied to Microsoft Outlook; that is, Word is giving you the opportunity to schedule a meeting for July 16th and/or to display your calendar. The option may not exist in a lab environment.

WIZARDS AND TEMPLATES

We have created some very interesting documents throughout the text, but in every instance we have formatted the document entirely on our own. It is time now to see what is available in terms of "jump starting" the process by borrowing professional designs from others. Accordingly, we discuss the wizards and templates that are built into Microsoft Word.

A ***template*** is a partially completed document that contains formatting, text, and/or graphics. It may be as simple as a memo or as complex as a résumé or newsletter. Microsoft Word provides a variety of templates for common documents, including a résumé, agenda, and fax cover sheet. You simply open the template, then modify the existing text as necessary, while retaining the formatting in the template. A ***wizard*** makes the process even easier by asking a series of questions, then creating a customized template based on your answers. A template or wizard creates the initial document for you. It's then up to you to complete the document by entering the appropriate information.

Figure 3.9 illustrates the use of wizards and templates in conjunction with a résumé. You can choose from one of three existing styles (contemporary, elegant, and professional) to which you add personal information. Alternatively, you can select the ***Résumé Wizard*** to create a customized template, as was done in Figure 3.9a.

After the Résumé Wizard is selected, it prompts you for the information it needs to create a basic résumé. You specify the style in Figure 3.9b, enter the requested information in Figure 3.9c, and choose the categories in Figure 3.9d. The wizard asks additional questions (not shown in Figure 3.9), after which it displays the (partially) completed Résumé based on your responses. You then complete the Résumé by entering the specifics of your employment and/or additional information. As you edit the document, you can copy and paste information within the Résumé, just as you would with a regular document. You can also change the formatting. It takes a little practice, but the end result is a professionally formatted Résumé in a minimum of time.

Microsoft Word contains templates and wizards for a variety of other documents. (Look carefully at the tabs within the dialog box of Figure 3.9a and you can infer that Word will help you to create letters, faxes, memos, reports, legal pleadings, publications, and even Web pages. The Office Web site, www.microsoft.com/office, contains additional templates.) Consider, too, Figure 3.10, which displays four attractive documents that were created using the respective wizards. Realize, however, that while wizards and templates will help you to create professionally designed documents, they are only a beginning. *The content is still up to you.*

THIRTY SECONDS IS ALL YOU HAVE

Thirty seconds is the average amount of time a personnel manager spends skimming your résumé and deciding whether or not to call you for an interview. It doesn't matter how much training you have had or how good you are if your résumé and cover letter fail to project a professional image. Know your audience and use the vocabulary of your targeted field. Be positive and describe your experience from an accomplishment point of view. Maintain a separate list of references and have it available on request. Be sure all information is accurate. Be conscientious about the design of your résumé and proofread the final documents very carefully.

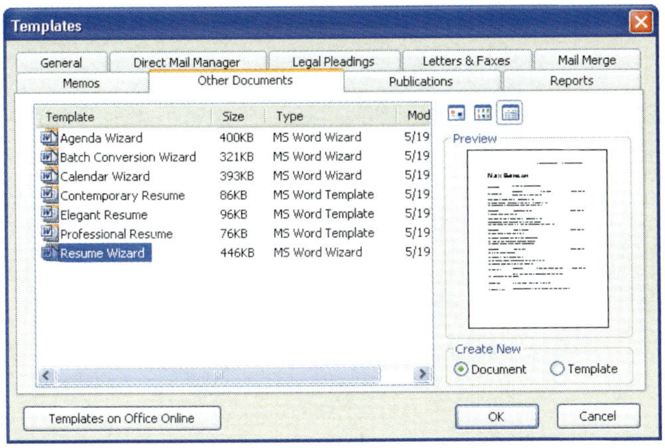

(a) Résumé Wizard

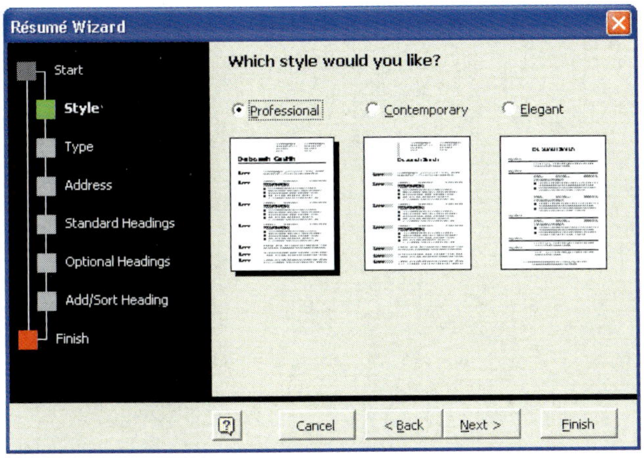

(b) Choose the Style

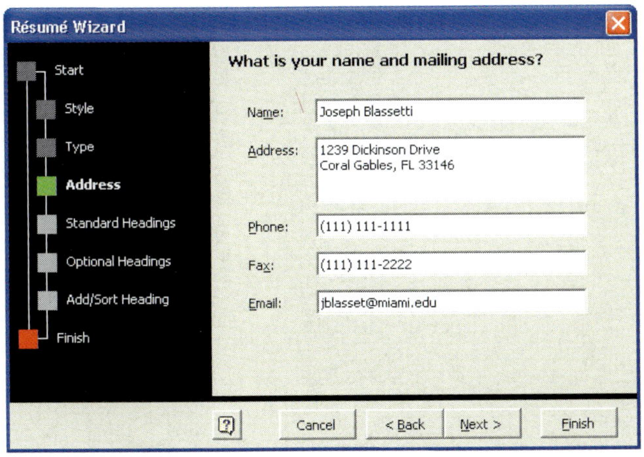

(c) Supply the Information

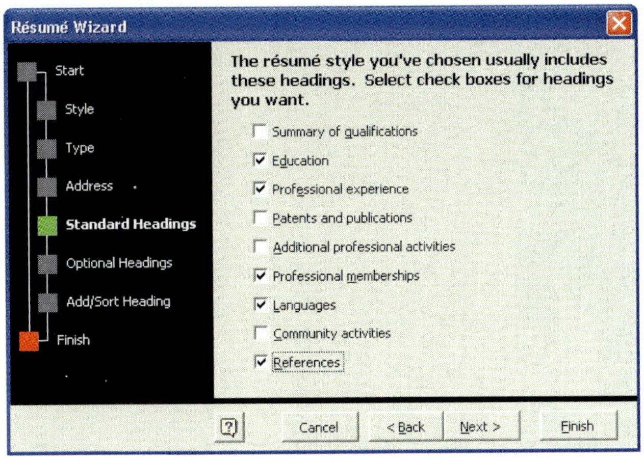

(d) Choose the Headings

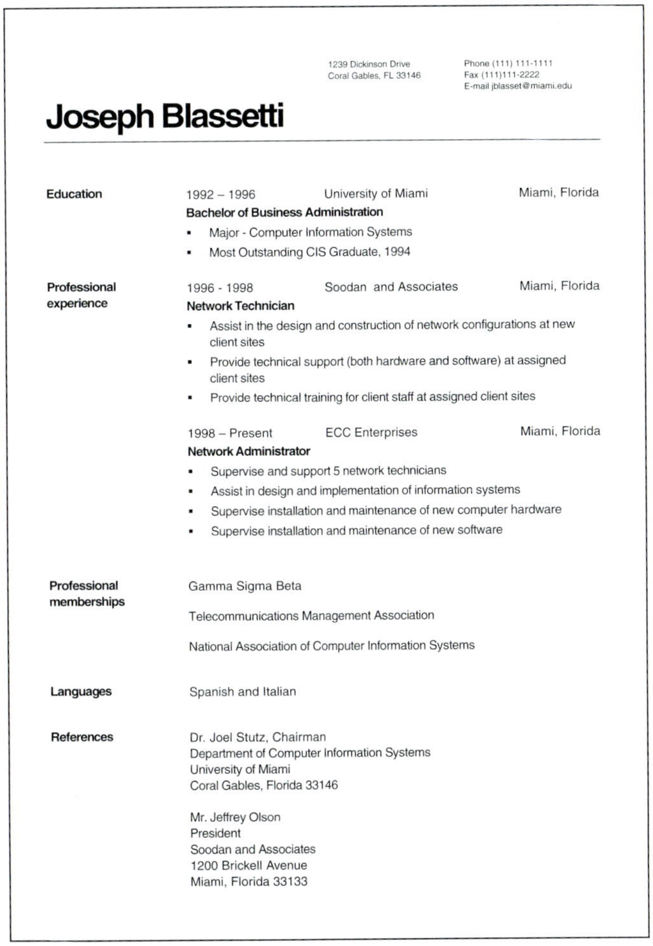
1239 Dickinson Drive
Coral Gables, FL 33146

Phone (111) 111-1111
Fax (111)111-2222
E-mail jblasset@miami.edu

Joseph Blassetti

Education

1992 – 1996 University of Miami Miami, Florida
Bachelor of Business Administration
- Major - Computer Information Systems
- Most Outstanding CIS Graduate, 1994

Professional experience

1996 - 1998 Soodan and Associates Miami, Florida
Network Technician
- Assist in the design and construction of network configurations at new client sites
- Provide technical support (both hardware and software) at assigned client sites
- Provide technical training for client staff at assigned client sites

1998 – Present ECC Enterprises Miami, Florida
Network Administrator
- Supervise and support 5 network technicians
- Assist in design and implementation of information systems
- Supervise installation and maintenance of new computer hardware
- Supervise installation and maintenance of new software

Professional memberships

Gamma Sigma Beta

Telecommunications Management Association

National Association of Computer Information Systems

Languages

Spanish and Italian

References

Dr. Joel Stutz, Chairman
Department of Computer Information Systems
University of Miami
Coral Gables, Florida 33146

Mr. Jeffrey Olson
President
Soodan and Associates
1200 Brickell Avenue
Miami, Florida 33133

(e) The Completed Résumé

FIGURE 3.9 Creating a Résumé

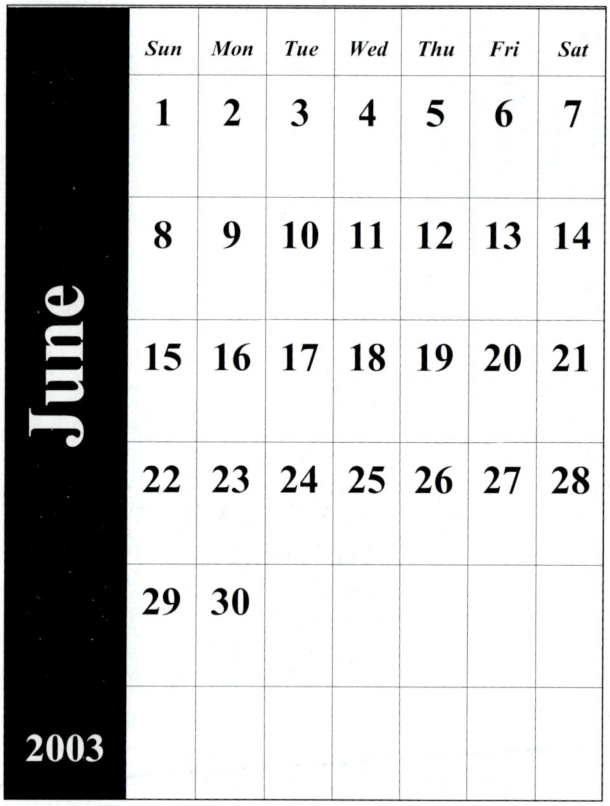

(a) Calendar

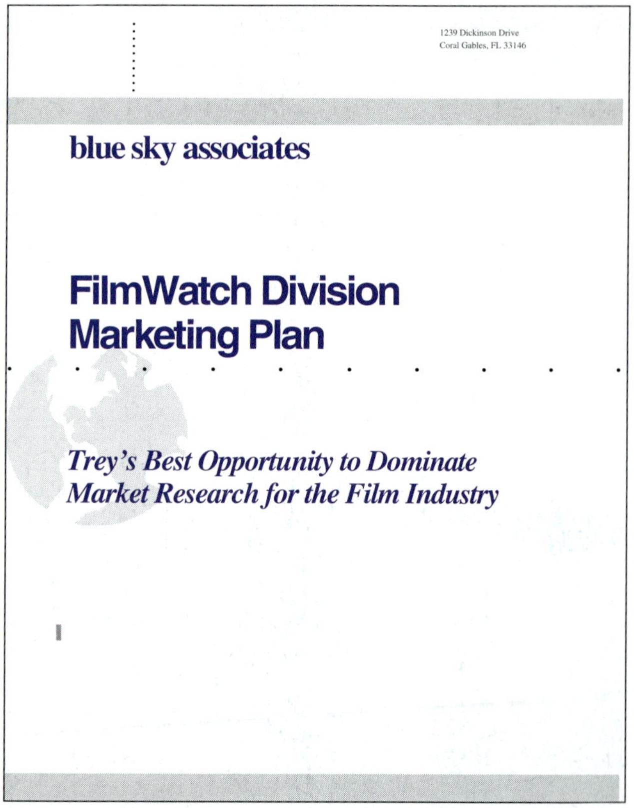

(b) Contemporary Report

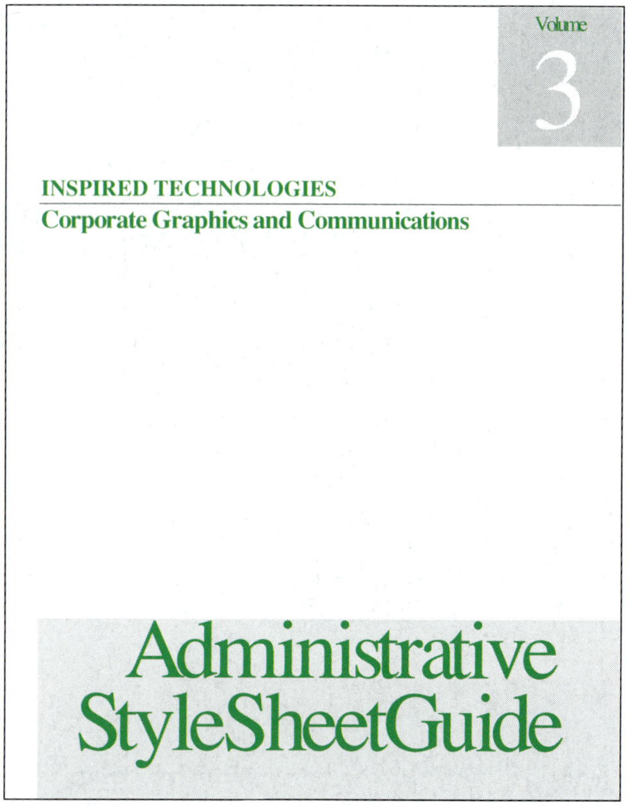

(c) Manual

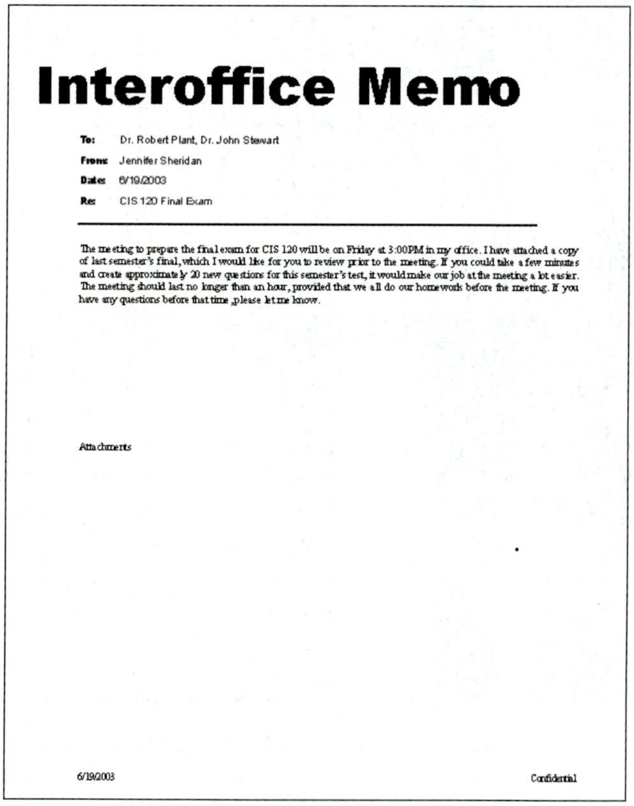

(d) Memo

FIGURE 3.10 What You Can Do with Wizards

MAIL MERGE

A ***mail merge*** can create any type of standardized document, but it is used most frequently to create a set of ***form letters***. In essence it creates the same letter many times, changing the name, address, and other information as appropriate from letter to letter. You might use a mail merge to look for a job upon graduation, when you send essentially the same cover letter to many different companies. The concept is illustrated in Figure 3.11, in which John Smith has written a letter describing his qualifications, then merges that letter with a set of names and addresses, to produce the individual letters.

The mail merge process uses two files as input, a main document and a data source (or address list). A set of form letters is created as output. The ***main document*** (e.g., the cover letter in Figure 3.11a) contains standardized text, together with one or more ***merge fields*** that serve as place holders for the variable data that will be inserted into the individual letters. The address list (the set of names and addresses in Figure 3.11b) contains the information that varies from letter to letter.

The first row in the data source is called the header row and identifies the fields in the remaining rows. Each additional row contains the data to create one letter and is called a data record. Every data record contains the same fields in the same order—for example, Title, FirstName, LastName, and so on. (The fields can also be specified collectively, but for purposes of illustration, we will show the fields individually.)

The main document and the address list work in conjunction with one another, with the merge fields in the main document referencing the corresponding fields in the data source. The first line in the address of Figure 3.11a, for example, contains three entries in angle brackets, <<Title>> <<FirstName>> <<LastName>>. (These entries are not typed explicitly but are entered through special commands, as described in the hands-on exercise that follows shortly.) The merge process examines each record in the data source and substitutes the appropriate field values for the corresponding merge fields as it creates the individual form letters. For example, the first three fields in the first record will produce Mr. Eric Simon. The same fields in the second record will produce Dr. Lauren Howard, and so on.

In similar fashion, the second line in the address of the main document contains the <<Company>> field. The third line contains the <<JobTitle>> field. The fourth line references the <<Address1>> field, and the last line contains the <<City>>, <<State>>, and <<PostalCode>> fields. The salutation repeats the <<Title>> and <<LastName>> fields. The first sentence in the letter uses the <<Company>> field a second time. The mail merge prepares the letters one at a time, with one letter created for every record in the data source until the file of names and addresses is exhausted. The individual form letters are shown in Figure 3.11c. Each letter begins automatically on a new page.

The implementation of a mail merge is accomplished through the ***Mail Merge Wizard***, which will open in the task pane and guide you through the various steps in the mail merge process. In essence there are three things you must do:

1. Create and save the main document
2. Create and save the data source
3. Merge the main document and data source to create the individual letters

The same data source can be used to create multiple sets of form letters. You could, for example, create a marketing campaign in which you send an initial letter to the entire list, and then send follow-up letters at periodic intervals to the same mailing list. Alternatively, you could filter the original mailing list to include only a subset of names, such as the individuals who responded to the initial letter. You could also use the wizard to create a different set of documents, such as envelopes and/or e-mail messages. Note, too, that you can sort the addresses to print the documents in a specified sequence, such as zip code to take advantage of bulk mail.

John Doe Computing

1239 Dickinson Drive • Coral Gables, FL 33146 • (305) 666-5555

June 22, 2003

«Title» «FirstName» «LastName»
«JobTitle»
«Company»
«Address1»
«City», «State» «PostalCode»

Dear «Title» «LastName»:

I would like to inquire about a position with «Company» as an entry-level programmer. I have graduated from the University of Miami with a Bachelor's Degree in Computer Information Systems (May 2003) and I am very interested in working for you. I am proficient in all applications in Microsoft Office and also have experience with Visual Basic, C++, and Java. I have had the opportunity to design and implement a few Web applications, both as a part of my educational program, and during my internship with Personalized Computer Designs, Inc.

I am eager to put my skills to work and would like to talk with you at your earliest convenience. I have enclosed a copy of my résumé and will be happy to furnish the names and addresses of my references. You may reach me at the above address and phone number. I look forward to hearing from you.

Sincerely,

John Doe
President

(a) The Form Letter

Title	FirstName	LastName	Company	JobTitle	Address1	City	State	PostalCode
Mr.	Eric	Simon	Arnold and Joyce Computing	President	10000 Sample Road	Coral Springs	FL	33071
Dr.	Lauren	Howard	Unique Systems	President	475 LeJeune Road	Coral Springs	FL	33071
Mr.	Peter	Gryn	Gryn Computing	Director of Human Resources	1000 Federal Highway	Miami	FL	33133
Ms.	Julie	Overby	The Overby Company	President	100 Savona Avenue	Coral Gables	FL	33146

(b) The Data Source

FIGURE 3.11 A Mail Merge

John Doe Computing
1239 Dickinson Drive • Coral Gables, FL 33146 • (305) 666-5555

June 22, 2003

Mr. Eric Simon
Arnold and Joyce Computing
President
10000 Sample Road
Coral Springs, FL 33071

Dear Mr. Simon:

I would like to inquire about a position with your company as an entry-level programmer. I have just graduated from the University of Miami with a Bachelor's Degree in Computer Information Systems (May 2003) and I am very interested in working for you. I am proficient in all applications in Microsoft Office and also have experience with Visual Basic, C++, and Java. I have had the opportunity to design and implement a few Web applications, both as a part of my educational program, and during my internship with Personalized Computer Designs, Inc.

I am eager to put my skills to work and would like to talk with you at your earliest convenience. I have enclosed a copy of my résumé and will be happy to furnish the names and addresses of my references. You may reach me at the above address and phone number. I look forward to hearing from you.

Sincerely,

John Doe
President

John Doe Computing
1239 Dickinson Drive • Coral Gables, FL 33146 • (305) 666-5555

June 22, 2003

Dr. Lauren Howard
Unique Systems
President
475 LeJeune Road
Coral Springs, FL 33071

Dear Dr. Howard:

I would like to inquire about a position with your company as an entry-level programmer. I have just graduated from the University of Miami with a Bachelor's Degree in Computer Information Systems (May 2003) and I am very interested in working for you. I am proficient in all applications in Microsoft Office and also have experience with Visual Basic, C++, and Java. I have had the opportunity to design and implement a few Web applications, both as a part of my educational program, and during my internship with Personalized Computer Designs, Inc.

I am eager to put my skills to work and would like to talk with you at your earliest convenience. I have enclosed a copy of my résumé and will be happy to furnish the names and addresses of my references. You may reach me at the above address and phone number. I look forward to hearing from you.

Sincerely,

John Doe
President

John Doe Computing
1239 Dickinson Drive • Coral Gables, FL 33146 • (305) 666-5555

June 22, 2003

Mr. Peter Gryn
Gryn Computing
Director of Human Resources
1000 Federal Highway
Miami, FL 33133

Dear Mr. Gryn:

I would like to inquire about a position with your company as an entry-level programmer. I have just graduated from the University of Miami with a Bachelor's Degree in Computer Information Systems (May 2003) and I am very interested in working for you. I am proficient in all applications in Microsoft Office and also have experience with Visual Basic, C++, and Java. I have had the opportunity to design and implement a few Web applications, both as a part of my educational program, and during my internship with Personalized Computer Designs, Inc.

I am eager to put my skills to work and would like to talk with you at your earliest convenience. I have enclosed a copy of my résumé and will be happy to furnish the names and addresses of my references. You may reach me at the above address and phone number. I look forward to hearing from you.

Sincerely,

John Doe
President

John Doe Computing
1239 Dickinson Drive • Coral Gables, FL 33146 • (305) 666-5555

June 22, 2003

Ms. Julie Overby
The Overby Company
President
100 Savona Avenue
Coral Gables, FL 33146

Dear Ms. Overby:

I would like to inquire about a position with your company as an entry-level programmer. I have just graduated from the University of Miami with a Bachelor's Degree in Computer Information Systems (May 2003) and I am very interested in working for you. I am proficient in all applications in Microsoft Office and also have experience with Visual Basic, C++, and Java. I have had the opportunity to design and implement a few Web applications, both as a part of my educational program, and during my internship with Personalized Computer Designs, Inc.

I am eager to put my skills to work and would like to talk with you at your earliest convenience. I have enclosed a copy of my résumé and will be happy to furnish the names and addresses of my references. You may reach me at the above address and phone number. I look forward to hearing from you.

Sincerely,

John Doe
President

(c) The Printed Letters

FIGURE 3.11 A Mail Merge *(continued)*

hands-on exercise

3 Mail Merge

Objective To create a main document and associated data source; to implement a mail merge and produce a set of form letters; to create a document from a template. Use Figure 3.12 as a guide.

Step 1: Open the Form Letter

- Open the **Form Letter** document in the Exploring Word folder. If necessary, change to the **Print Layout view** and zoom to **Page Width** as shown in Figure 3.12a.
- Modify the letterhead to reflect your name and address. Select **"Your Name Goes Here"**, then type a new entry to replace the selected text. Add your address information to the second line.
- Click immediately to the left of the first paragraph, then press the **Enter key** twice to insert two lines. Press the **up arrow** two times to return to the first line you inserted.
- Pull down the **Insert menu** and click the **Date and Time command** to display the dialog box in Figure 3.12a.
- Select (click) the date format you prefer and, if necessary, check the box to **Update automatically**. Click **OK** to close the dialog box.
- Save the document as **Form Letter Solution** so that you can return to the original document if necessary.

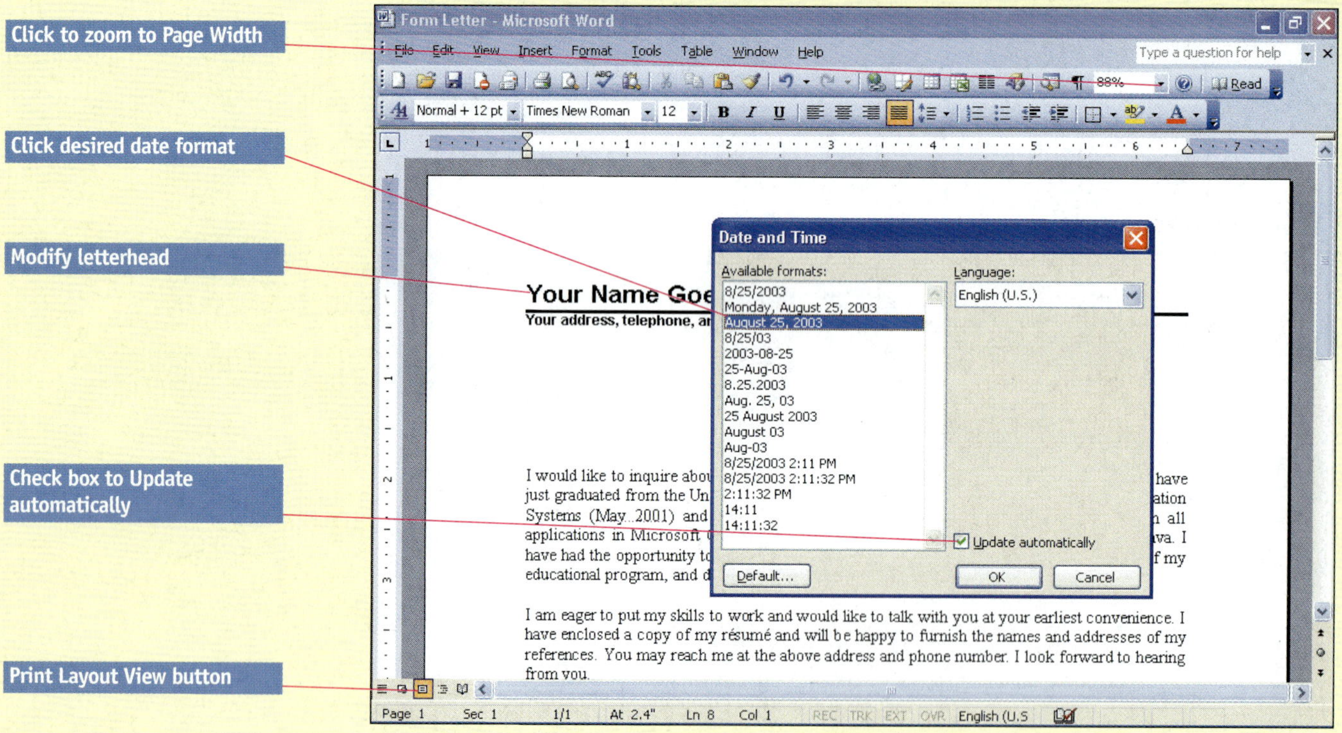

(a) Open the Form Letter (step 1)

FIGURE 3.12 Hands-on Exercise 3

Step 2: The Mail Merge Wizard

- Pull down the **Tools menu**, click **Letters and Mailings**, then click **Mail Merge...** to open the task pane.
- The option button for **Letters** is selected by default as shown in Figure 3.12b. Click **Next: Starting Document** to begin creating the document.
- The option button to **Use the current document** is selected. (We began the exercise by providing you with the text of the document, as opposed to having you create the entire form letter.)
- Click **Next: Select Recipients** to enter the list of names and addresses.
- Click the option button to **Type a New List**, then click the link to **Create** that appears within the task pane. This brings you to a new screen, where you enter the data for the recipients of your form letter.

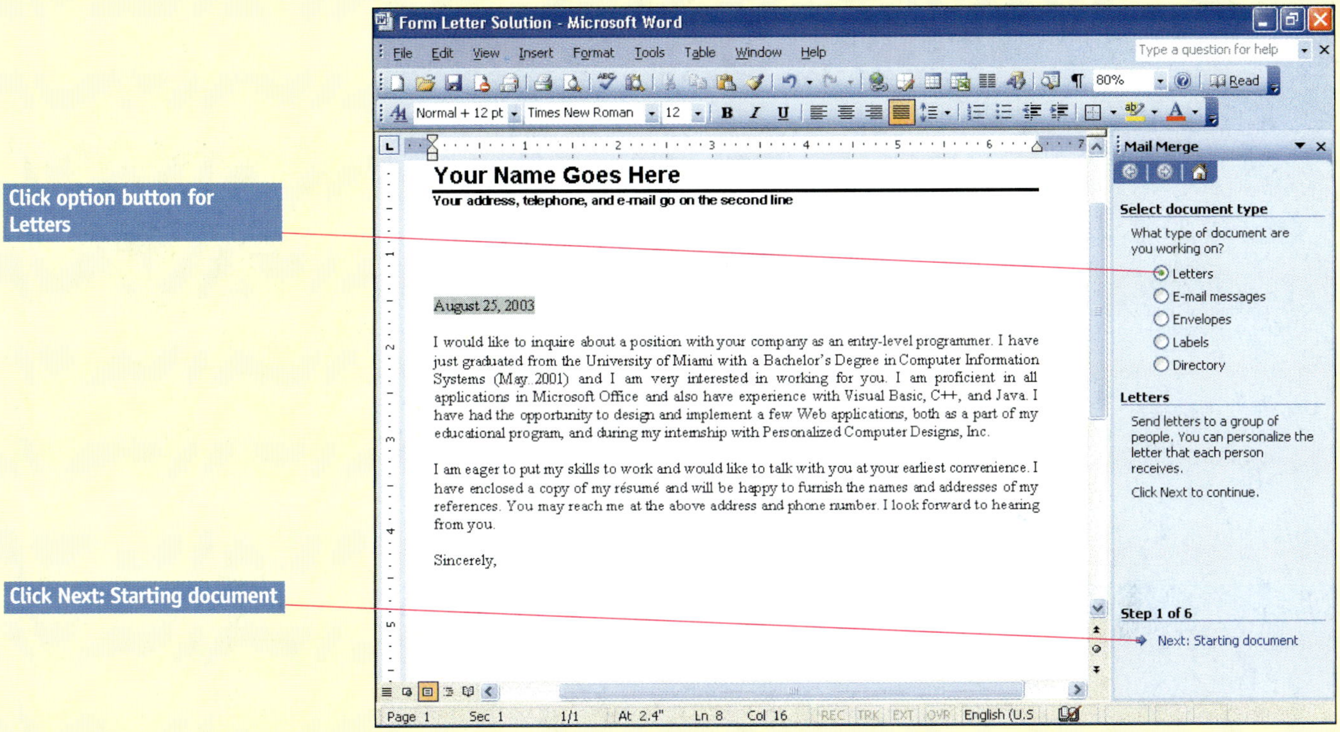

(b) The Mail Merge Wizard (step 2)

FIGURE 3.12 Hands-on Exercise 3 (*continued*)

THE MAIL MERGE WIZARD

The Mail Merge Wizard simplifies the process of creating form letters and other types of merge documents through step-by-step directions that appear automatically in the task pane. The options for the current step appear in the top portion of the task pane and are self-explanatory. Click the link to the next step at the bottom of the pane to move forward in the process, or click the link to the previous step to correct any mistakes you might have made.

Step 3: Select the Recipients

- Enter data for the first record, using your name and address as shown in Figure 3.12c. Type **Mr.** or **Ms.** in the Title field, then press **Tab** to move to the next (FirstName) field and enter your first name.
- Complete the first record by entering your address. You do not need to enter the country, phone number, or e-mail address.
- Click the **New Entry button** to enter the data for the next person. Enter your instructor's name and a hypothetical address. Enter data for one additional person, real or fictitious as you see fit. Click **Close** when you have completed the data entry.
- You will see the Save Address List dialog box, where you will be prompted to save the list of names and addresses. Save the file as **Names and Addresses** in the **Exploring Word folder**. The file type is specified as a Microsoft Office Address list.
- You will see a dialog box showing all of the records you have just entered. Click **OK** to close the dialog box. Click **Next: Write Your Letter** to continue.

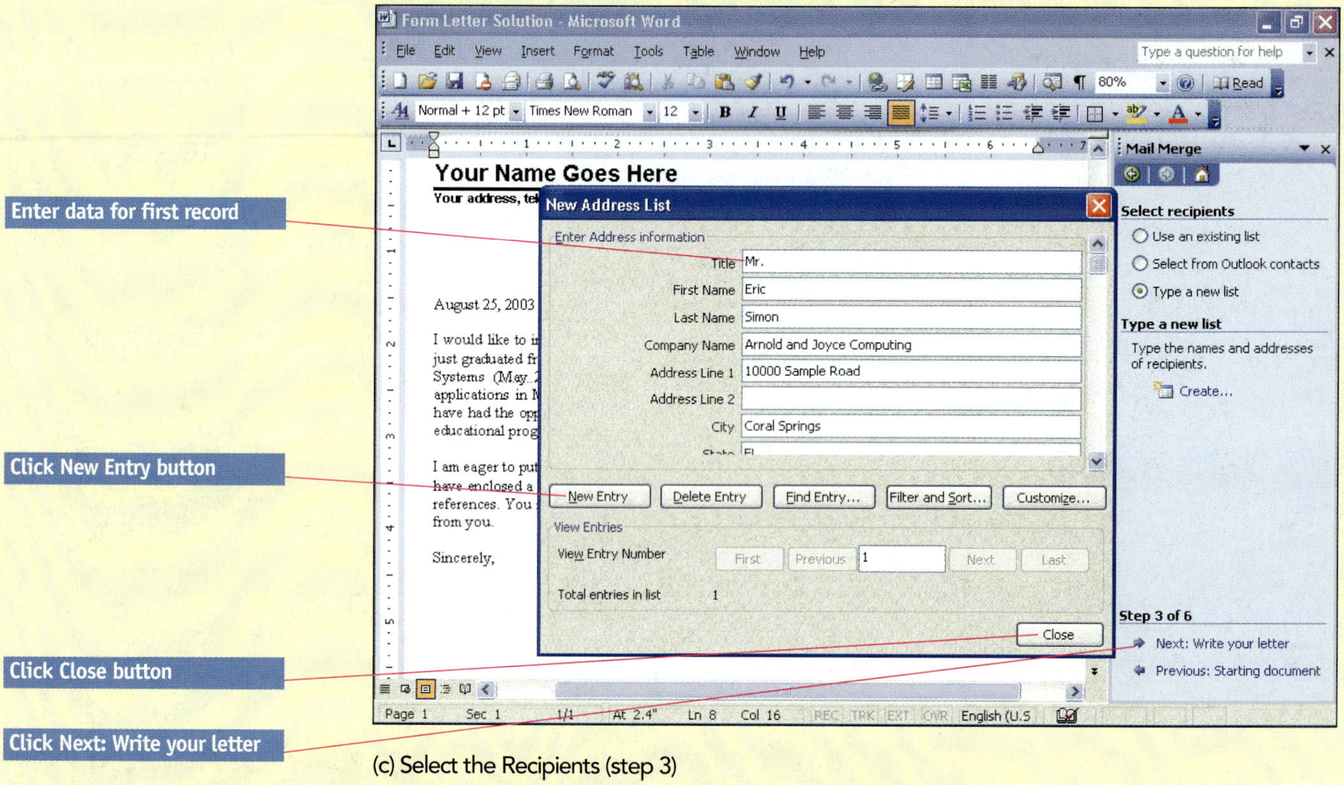

(c) Select the Recipients (step 3)

FIGURE 3.12 Hands-on Exercise 3 (*continued*)

THREE DIFFERENT FILES

A mail merge works with three different files. The main document and data source are input to the mail merge, which creates a set of merged letters as output. You can use the same data source (e.g., a set of names and addresses) with different main documents (a form letter and an envelope) and/or use the same main document with multiple data sources. You typically save, but do not print, the main document(s) and the data source(s). Conversely, you print the set of merged letters, but typically do not save them.

Step 4: Write (Complete) the Letter

- The text of the form letter is already written, but it is still necessary to insert the fields within the form letter.
- Click below the date and press the **Enter key** once or twice. Click the link to the **Address block** to select a single entry that is composed of multiple fields (Street, City, ZipCode, and so on). Click **OK**. The AddressBlock field is inserted into the document as shown in Figure 3.12d.
- Press the **Enter key** twice to leave a blank line after the address block. Click the link to the **Greeting line** to display the Greeting Line dialog box in Figure 3.12d.
- Choose the type of greeting you want. Change the comma that appears after the greeting to a colon since this is a business letter. Click **OK**. The GreetingLine field is inserted into the document and enclosed in angled brackets.
- Press **Enter** to enter a blank line. Save the document. Click **Next: Preview Your Letters** to continue.

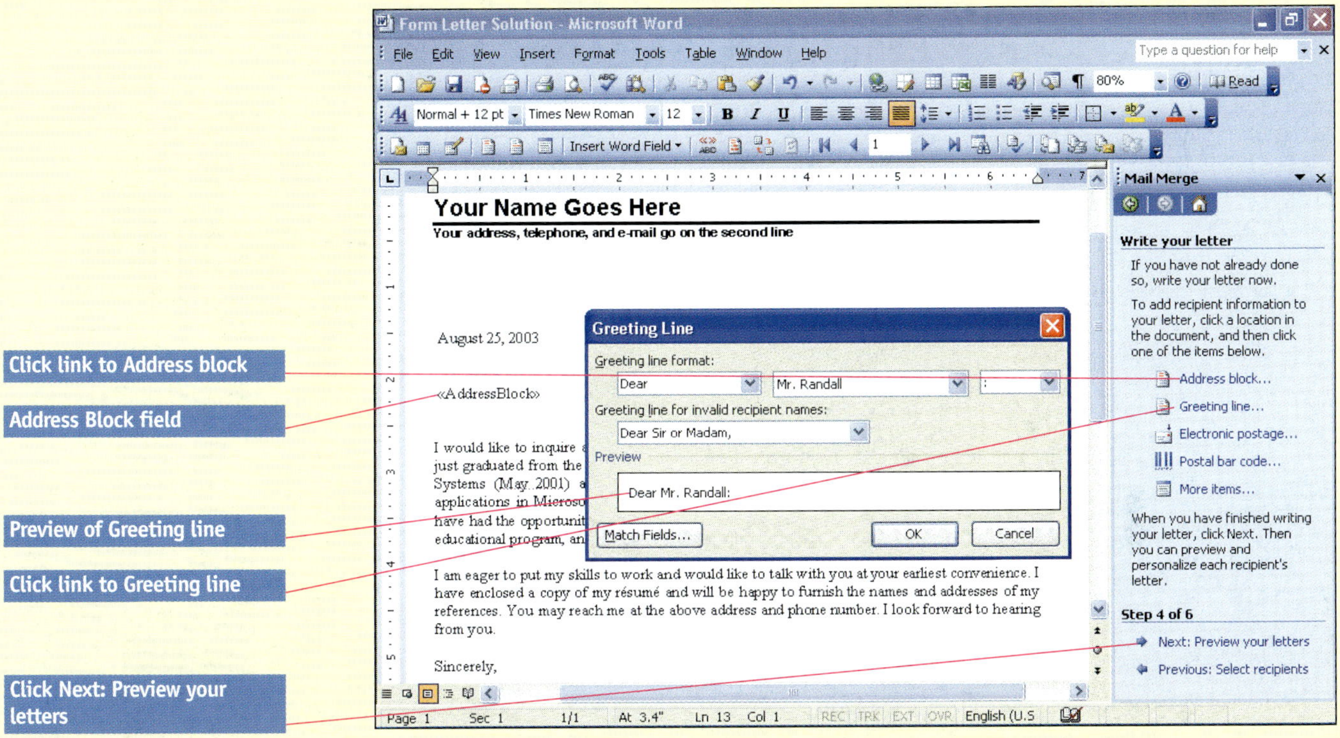

(d) Write (Complete) the Letter (step 4)

FIGURE 3.12 Hands-on Exercise 3 (*continued*)

BLOCKS VERSUS INDIVIDUAL FIELDS

The Mail Merge Wizard simplifies the process of entering field names into a form letter by supplying two predefined entries, AddressBlock and GreetingLine, which contain multiple fields that are typical of the ways in which an address and salutation appear in a conventional letter. You can still insert individual fields by clicking in the document where you want the field to go, then clicking the Insert Merge Fields button on the Mail Merge toolbar. The blocks are easier.

Step 5: View and Print the Letters

- You should see the first form letter as shown. You can click the >> or << button in the task pane (not shown in Figure 3.12e) to move to the next or previous letter, respectively. You can also use the navigation buttons that appear on the Mail Merge toolbar.
- View the records individually to be sure that the form letter is correct and that the data has been entered correctly. Make corrections if necessary.
- Click **Next: Complete the Merge**, then click **Print** to display the dialog box in Figure 3.12e. Click **OK**, then **OK** again, to print the form letters.
- Click the **<<abc>>** button to display the field codes. Pull down the **File menu** and click the **Print command** to display the Print dialog box. Check the option to print the current page. Click **OK**. Submit this page to your instructor as well.
- Pull down the **File menu** and click the **Close command** to close the Form Letter Solution and the associated set of names and addresses.
- Save the documents if you are asked about doing so.

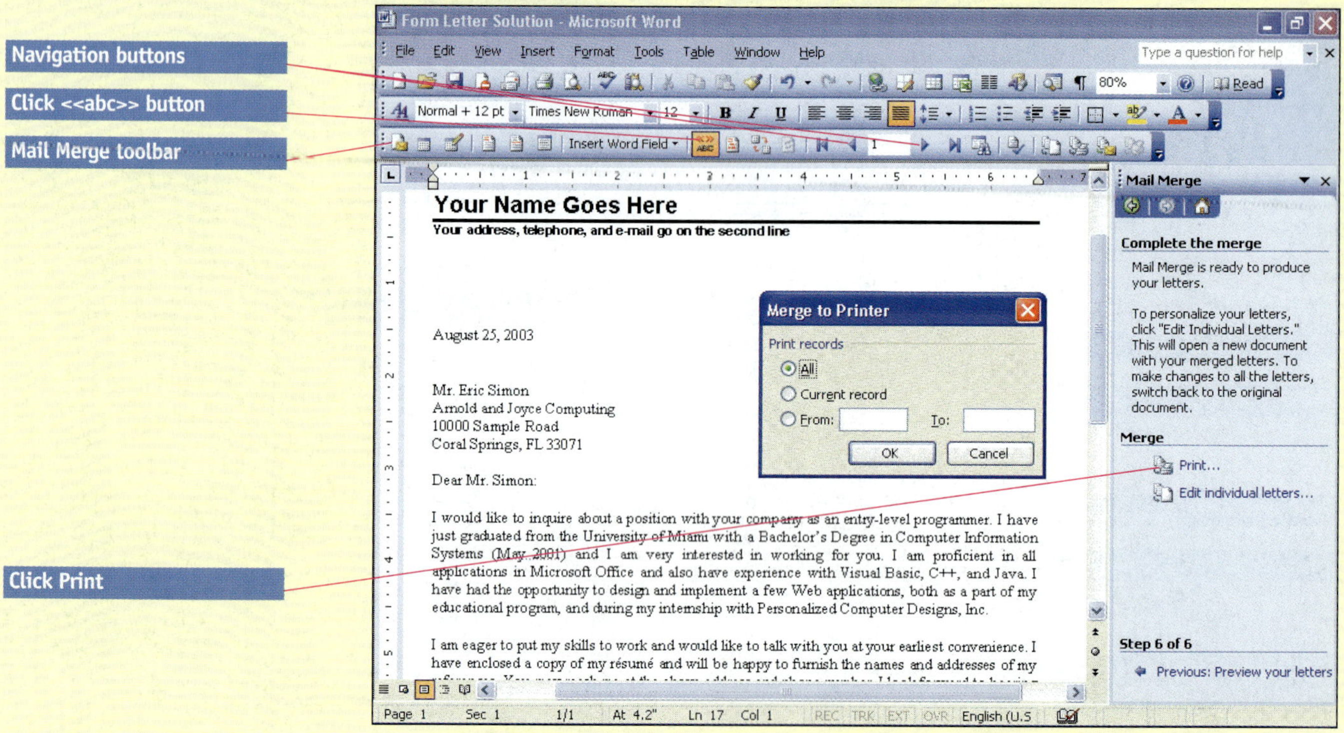

(e) View and Print the Letters (step 5)

FIGURE 3.12 Hands-on Exercise 3 (*continued*)

THE MAIL MERGE TOOLBAR

The Mail Merge toolbar appears throughout the mail merge process and contains various buttons that apply to different steps within the process. Click the <<abc>> button to display field values rather than field codes. Click the button a second time and you switch back to field codes from field values. Click the <<abc>> button to display the field values, then use the navigation buttons to view the different letters. Click the ▶ button, for example, and you move to the next letter. Click the ▶| button to display the form letter for the last record.

Step 6: Open the Contemporary Merge Letter

- Pull down the **File menu** and click the **New command**. If necessary, pull down the **View menu** and open the **task pane**.
- Click the link to **On my Computer** (under templates) in the task pane to display the Templates dialog box, then click the **Mail Merge tab** to display the Templates dialog box in Figure 3.12f.
- Select (click) the **Contemporary Merge Letter**. Be sure that the **Document option button** is selected. Click **OK** to select this document and begin the merge process.
- You will see a form letter with the AddressBlock and GreetingLine fields already entered.

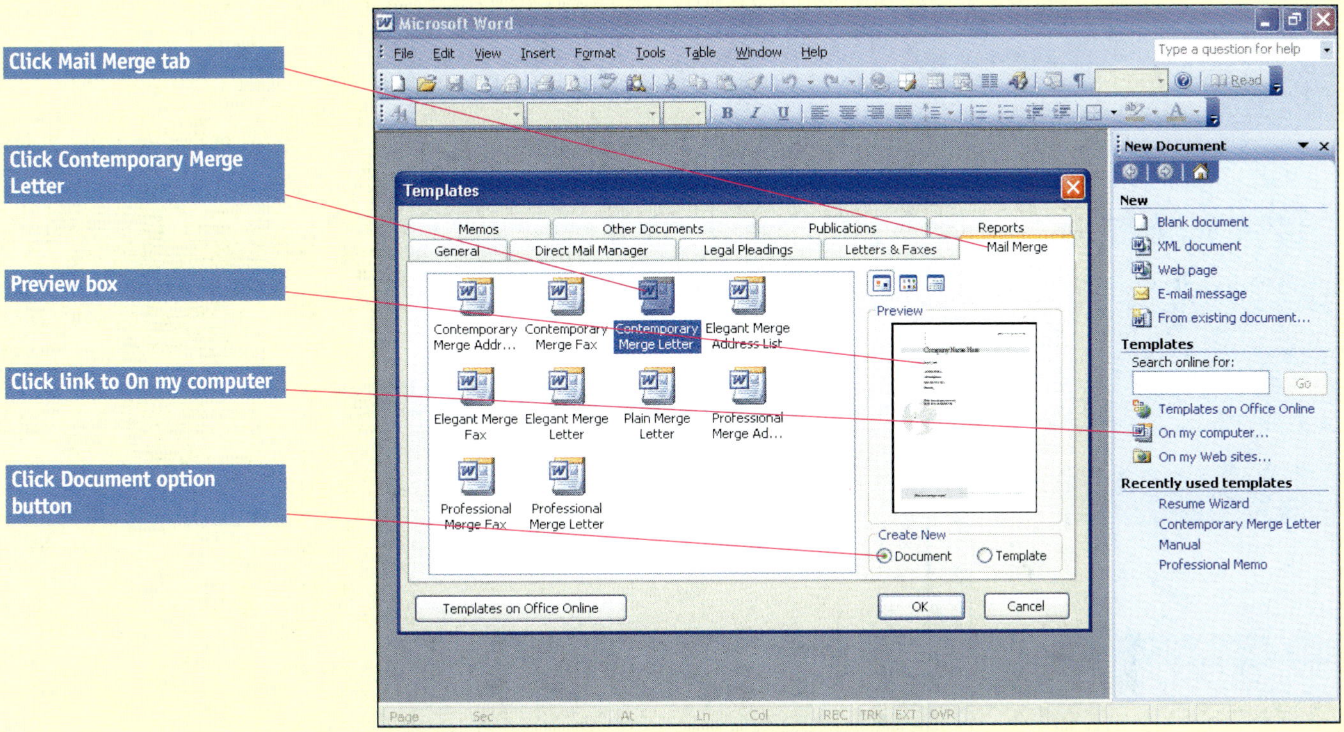

(f) Open the Contemporary Merge Letter (step 6)

FIGURE 3.12 Hands-on Exercise 3 (*continued*)

PAPER MAKES A DIFFERENCE

Most of us take paper for granted, but the right paper can make a significant difference in the effectiveness of the document, especially when you are trying to be noticed. Reports and formal correspondence are usually printed on white paper, but you would be surprised how many different shades of white there are. Other types of documents lend themselves to a specialty paper for additional impact. Consider the use of a specialty paper the next time you have an important project.

Step 7: Select the Recipients

- If necessary, display the **Mail Merge toolbar**.
- The option button to **Use an existing list** is selected. Click the link to **Browse** for the existing list to display the Select Data Source dialog box.
- We will use the same data source that you created earlier. (You could also use the list of Outlook contacts or an Access database as the source of your data.)
- Click the **down arrow** on the Look In box to select the Exploring Word folder. Click the **down arrow** on the File Type list box to select **Microsoft Office Address Lists**. Select the **Names and Addresses** file from step 3. Click **Open**.
- You should see the Mail Merge Recipients dialog box in Figure 3.12g that contains the records you entered earlier. You can use this dialog box to modify existing data, to change the order in which the form letters will appear, and/or to choose which recipients are to receive the form letter.
- Click **OK** to close the dialog box. Click **Next: Write Your Letter** to continue.

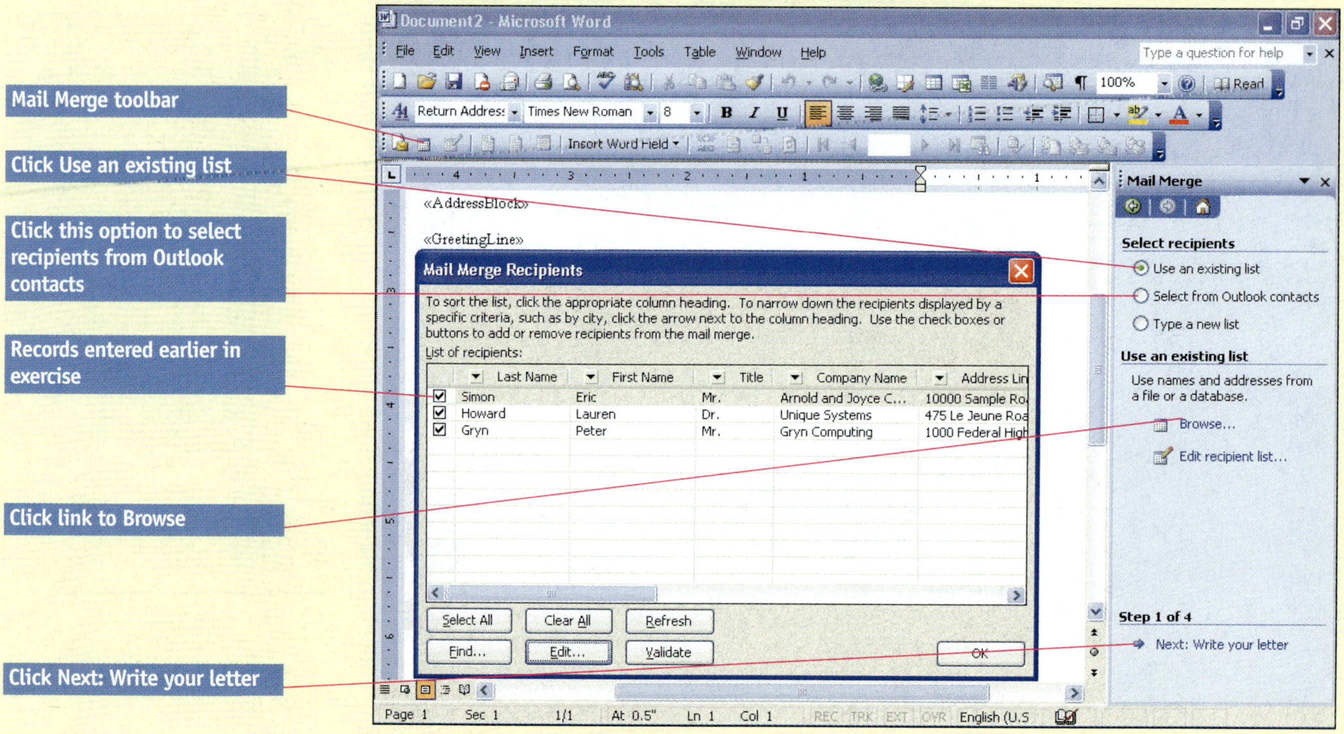

(g) Select the Recipients (step 7)

FIGURE 3.12 Hands-on Exercise 3 (*continued*)

USE OUTLOOK AS THE DATA SOURCE

Think of Microsoft Outlook as a desktop manager, or personal assistant, that keeps track of all types of information for you. You can use Outlook to maintain an address book (contact list), schedule appointments, create a task list, or send and receive e-mail. And since Outlook is an integral part of Microsoft Office, its components are easily linked to other Office applications. You could, for example, use the Outlook address book as the data source for a mail merge in Word. Just start the mail merge in the usual way, then click the option button to select recipients from the Outlook contacts.

Step 8: Write the Form Letter

- The form letter has been created as a template as shown in Figure 3.12h. The AddressBlock and GreetingLine fields have been entered for you.
- Click and drag over **Type Your Letter Here** that appears in the form letter and enter two or three sentences of your own choosing. Our letter indicates that we are seeking to acquire one or more of the consulting firms on the mailing list.
- Continue to personalize the form letter by replacing the text in the original template. Click at the upper right of the letter and enter your return address. Use your name for the company name.
- Replace the signature lines with your name and title. Select the line at the bottom of the page that reads [Click here and type a slogan] and enter a slogan of your own.
- Save the document as **Contemporary Merge Letter Solution** in the Exploring Word folder. Click the link to **Next: Preview your letters**.

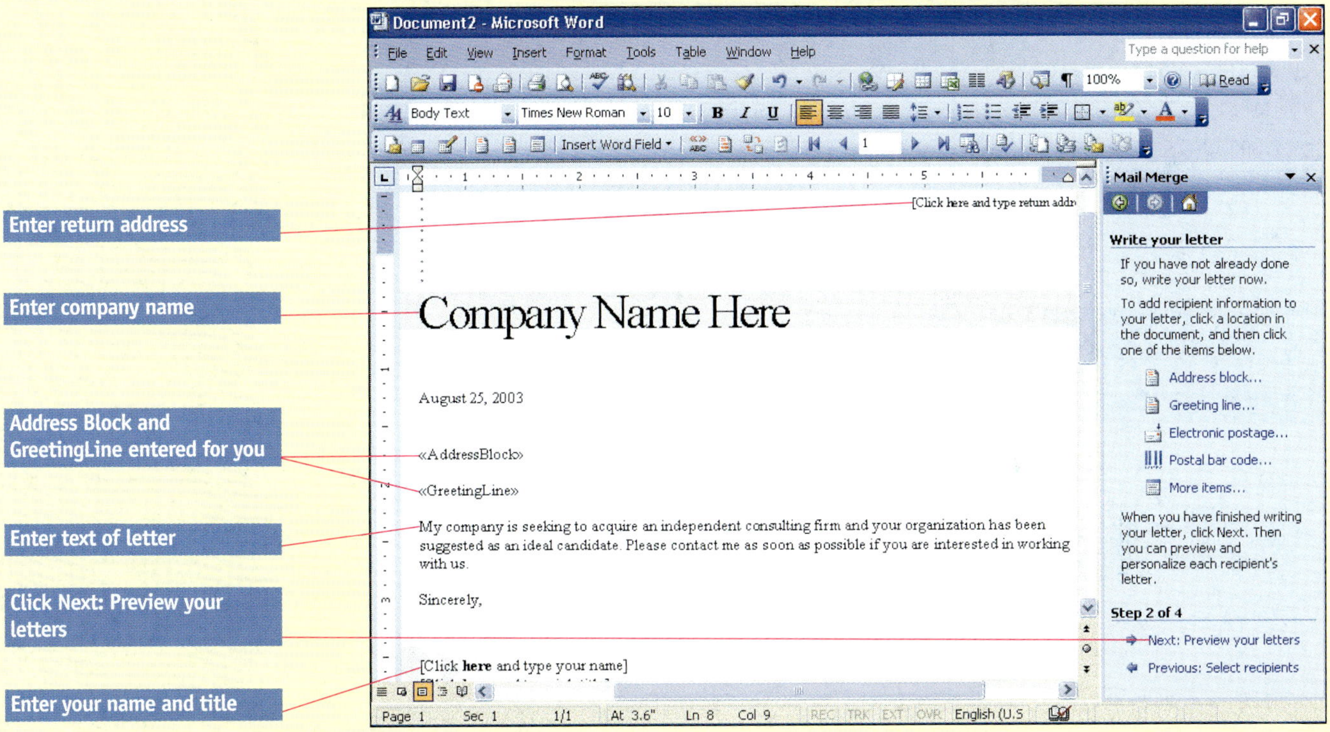

(h) Write the Form Letter (step 8)

FIGURE 3.12 Hands-on Exercise 3 (*continued*)

ENVELOPES AND MAILING LABELS

The set of form letters is only the first step in a true mail merge because you also have to create the envelopes and/or mailing labels to physically mail the letters. Start the Mail Merge Wizard as you normally do, but this time specify labels (or envelopes) instead of a form letter. Follow the instructions provided by the wizard using the same data source as for the form letters. See practice exercise 7 at the end of the chapter.

Step 9: Complete the Merge

- You should see the first form letter. The name and address of this recipient are the same as in the set of form letters created earlier. Click **Next: Complete the Merge** to display the screen in Figure 3.12i.
- Use the navigation buttons on the Mail Merge toolbar to view the three form letters. Click the link to **Print . . .** (or click the **Merge to Printer button** on the Mail Merge toolbar).
- Click the option button to print all the letters, then click **OK** to display the Print dialog box. Click **OK** to print the individual form letters.
- Exit Word. Save the form letter and/or the names and addresses document if you are asked about doing so.

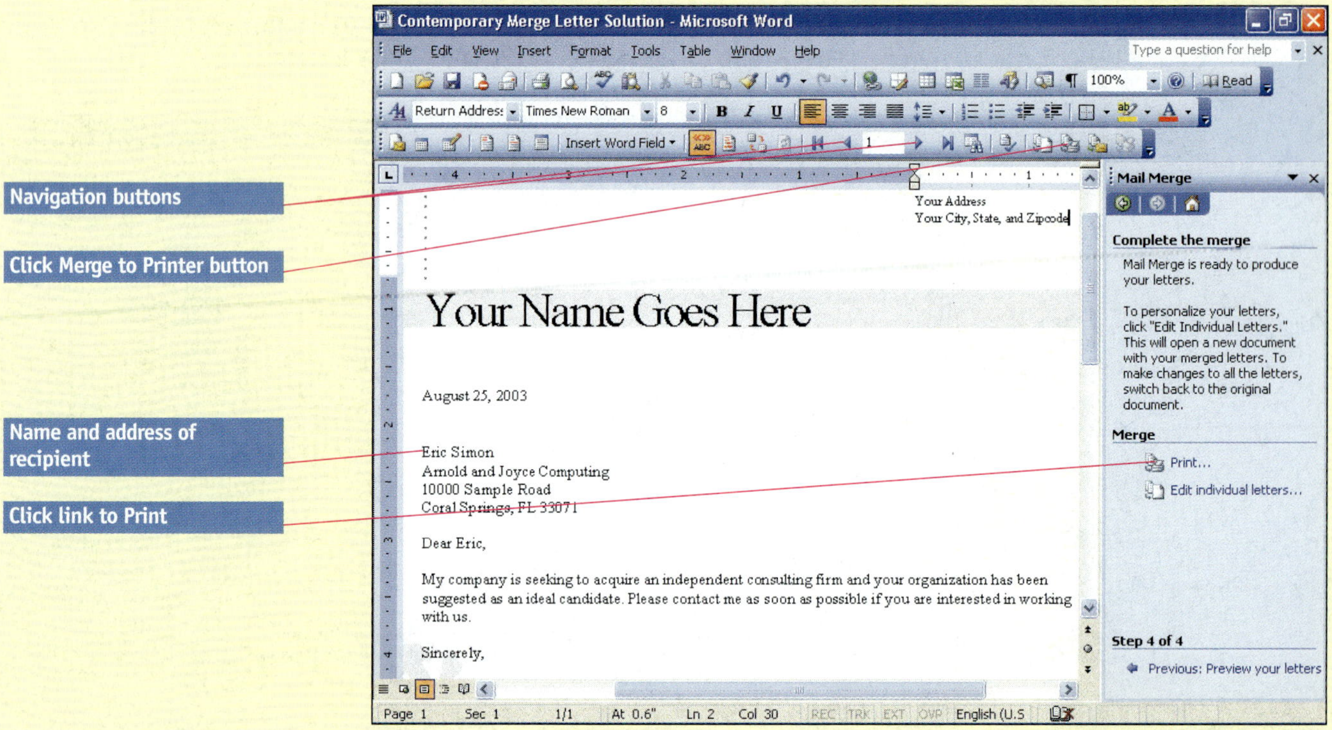

(i) Complete the Merge (step 9)

FIGURE 3.12 Hands-on Exercise 3 (*continued*)

EDIT THE INDIVIDUAL LETTERS

Click the Merge to New Document button (or click the link to Edit individual letters in the task pane) to create a third document (called Letters1 by default) consisting of the individual form letters. There are as many pages in this document as there are records in the address list. You can view and/or edit the individual letters from this document, then print the entire set of merged letters. You need not save this document, however, unless you actually made changes to the individual letters.

SUMMARY

The Insert Picture command displays a task pane in which you enter a keyword that describes the clip you are looking for. The search is made possible by the Microsoft Clip Organizer, which organizes the media files available to you into collections, then enables you to limit the search to specific media types and/or specific collections. The Drawing toolbar enables you to create your own clip art.

Microsoft WordArt is an application within Microsoft Office that creates decorative text that can be used to add interest to a document. WordArt can be used in addition to clip art or in place of clip art if the right image is not available. You can rotate text in any direction, add three-dimensional effects, display the text vertically down the page, or print it upside down.

The Insert Symbol command provides access to special characters, making it easy to place typographic characters into a document. The symbols can be taken from any font and can be displayed in any point size.

Resources (such as clip art or photographs) can be downloaded from the Web for inclusion in a Word document. Web pages are written in a language called HTML (HyperText Markup Language). The Save As Web Page command saves a Word document as a Web page. The new Single File Web Page format saves all of the elements of a Web site, including text and graphics, in a single file.

A copyright provides legal protection to a written or artistic work, giving the author exclusive rights to its use and reproduction, except as governed under the fair use exclusion. Anything on the Internet should be considered copyrighted unless the document specifically says it is in the public domain. The fair use exclusion enables you to use a portion of the work for educational, nonprofit purposes, or for the purpose of critical review or commentary. All such material should be cited through an appropriate footnote or endnote.

Wizards and templates help create professionally designed documents with a minimum of time and effort. A template is a partially completed document that contains formatting and other information. A wizard is an interactive program that creates a customized template based on the answers you supply. The resulting documentation can be modified with respect to content and/or formatting.

A mail merge creates the same letter many times, changing only the variable data, such as the addressee's name and address, from letter to letter. It is performed in conjunction with a main document and a data source, which are stored as separate documents. The mail merge can be used to create a form letter for selected records, and/or print the form letters in a sequence different from the way the records are stored in the data source. The same data source can be used to create multiple sets of form letters.

KEY TERMS

MULTIPLE CHOICE

1. How do you change the size of a selected object so that the height and width change in proportion to one another?
   (a) Click and drag any of the four corner handles in the direction you want to go
   (b) Click and drag the sizing handle on the top border, then click and drag the sizing handle on the left side
   (c) Click and drag the sizing handle on the bottom border, then click and drag the sizing handle on the right side
   (d) All of the above

2. How do you insert a hyperlink into a Word document?
   (a) Pull down the Insert menu and choose the Hyperlink command
   (b) Choose the Insert Hyperlink button on the Standard toolbar
   (c) Both (a) and (b)
   (d) Neither (a) nor (b)

3. How do you search for clip art using the Clip Organizer?
   (a) By entering a keyword that describes the image you want
   (b) By browsing through various collections
   (c) Both (a) and (b)
   (d) Neither (a) nor (b)

4. Which of the following objects can be inserted into a document?
   (a) Clip art
   (b) WordArt
   (c) Photographs
   (d) All of the above

5. Which of the following is true about a mail merge?
   (a) The same form letter can be used with different data sources
   (b) The same data source can be used with different form letters
   (c) Both (a) and (b)
   (d) Neither (a) nor (b)

6. Which of the following best describes the documents that are associated with a mail merge?
   (a) The main document is typically saved, but not necessarily printed
   (b) The names and addresses are typically saved, but not necessarily printed
   (c) The individual form letters are printed, but not necessarily saved
   (d) All of the above

7. Which of the following is true about footnotes or endnotes?
   (a) The addition of a footnote or endnote automatically renumbers the notes that follow
   (b) The deletion of a footnote or endnote automatically renumbers the notes that follow
   (c) Both (a) and (b)
   (d) Neither (a) nor (b)

8. Which of the following is true about the Insert Symbol command?
   (a) It can insert a symbol in different type sizes
   (b) It can access any font installed on the system
   (c) Both (a) and (b)
   (d) Neither (a) nor (b)

9. Which of the following is true regarding objects and the associated toolbars?
   (a) Clicking on a WordArt object displays the WordArt toolbar
   (b) Clicking on a Picture displays the Picture toolbar
   (c) Both (a) and (b)
   (d) Neither (a) nor (b)

10. Which of the following objects can be downloaded from the Web for inclusion into a Word document?
    (a) Clip art
    (b) Photographs
    (c) Sound and video files
    (d) All of the above

... continued

multiple choice

11. What is the significance of the Shift key in conjunction with various tools on the Drawing toolbar?

(a) It will draw a circle rather than an oval using the Oval tool
(b) It will draw a square rather than a rectangle using the Rectangle tool
(c) It will draw a horizontal or vertical line with the Line tool
(d) All of the above

12. What happens if you enter the text www.intel.com into a document?

(a) The entry is converted to a hyperlink, and further, the text will be underlined and displayed in a different color
(b) The associated page will be opened, provided your computer has access to the Internet
(c) Both (a) and (b)
(d) Neither (a) nor (b)

13. Which of the following is true about wizards?

(a) They are accessed from the General Templates link on the task pane
(b) They always produce a finished document with no further modification necessary
(c) Both (a) and (b)
(d) Neither (a) nor (b)

14. Which of the following is true about a Web document that was created from within Microsoft Word?

(a) It can be viewed locally
(b) It can be viewed via the Web, provided it is uploaded onto a Web server
(c) Both (a) and (b)
(d) Neither (a) nor (b)

15. Microsoft WordArt can be used to:

(a) Arch text, or print it upside down
(b) Rotate text, or add three-dimensional effects
(c) Display text vertically down a page
(d) All of these answers are correct

16. Which of the following was introduced into Word 2003 to simplify the creation of a Web page from within Microsoft Word?

(a) The Save as Web Page Command
(b) Single File Web Page format
(c) Both (a) and (b)
(d) Neither (a) nor (b)

17. What provides legal protection to the author for a written or artistic work?

(a) Public domain
(b) Copyright
(c) Fair use
(d) Footnote

18. How do you insert a date into a document so that the date is automatically updated when the document is retrieved?

(a) Type the date manually
(b) Use the Date and Time command in the Insert menu and clear the box to insert the date as a field
(c) Use the Insert Date and Time command in the Insert menu and check the box to insert the date as a field
(d) It cannot be done

ANSWERS

1. a	**7.** c	**13.** a
2. c	**8.** c	**14.** c
3. c	**9.** c	**15.** d
4. d	**10.** d	**16.** b
5. c	**11.** d	**17.** b
6. d	**12.** a	**18.** c

PRACTICE WITH WORD

1. **Runner's Paradise:** You have been asked to create a flyer to advertise an upcoming Corporate Run such as the flyer in Figure 3.13. You may create your own flyer, or you can copy our design, but you are required to use a combination of clip art, WordArt, symbols, text boxes, and lines. To create our flyer:
   a. Open a new document. Set the left and right page margins to 1″ and the top and bottom page margins to ½″.
   b. To enter the store locations at the top of the page, set a right tab at the right page margin. Enter the store locations at the left and right margins as shown in the figure.
   c. Change the font to 12 point Comic Sans (orange) and place a 3 point blue bottom border on the line. (Hint: Before you create the bottom line, press the Enter key to move to the next line in the document. Then select the line with the store locations and create the bottom border).
   d. Enter "Annual Corporate Race" in 36 point orange Comic Sans, centered between the margins. Enter the date in 24 point orange Comic Sans, also centered between the margins.
   e. Pull down the Insert menu and click the Symbol command. Select the Wingdings font, select the symbol for 8 o'clock, and then insert it into the document. Add AM, and then format the symbol to 36 point and the AM to 24 point orange Comic Sans.
   f. Insert the clip art of the running shoes. Size the clip art; change the wrapping style to Square, then move the clip art to the left of the date and time.
   g. Use WordArt to create the name of the event, and then format the WordArt. Use the WordArt toolbar to change the shape of the object and/or its color. Move, size, and rotate the object as shown in the figure.
   h. Create a text box for the entry fee information. Change the font, font size, and font color. Change the wrapping style to Square and change the line color to No Line.
   i. Enter the rest of the information at the bottom of the flyer, changing the font, font size, font color, and alignment.
   j. Print the completed flyer and submit it to your instructor.

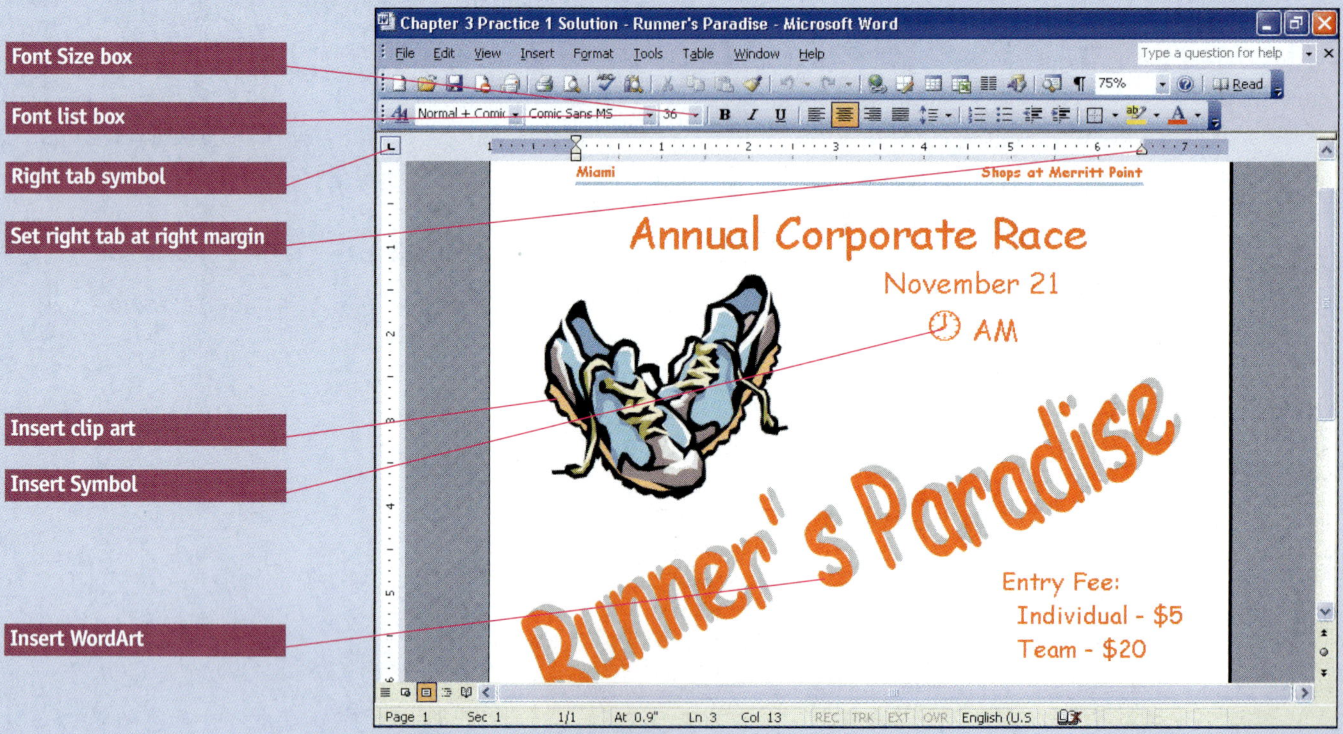

FIGURE 3.13 Runner's Paradise (exercise 1)

2. **Presidential Anecdotes:** Figure 3.14 displays the finished version of a document containing ten presidential anecdotes. The anecdotes were taken from the book *Presidential Anecdotes,* by Paul F. Boller, Jr., published by Penguin Books (New York, NY, 1981). Open the *Chapter 3 Practice 2* document and make the following changes:
    a. Add a footnote after Mr. Boller's name, which appears at the end of the second sentence in the first paragraph, citing the information about the book. This, in turn, renumbers all existing footnotes in the document.
    b. Switch the order of the paragraphs containing the anecdotes for Lincoln and Jefferson so that the presidents appear in the document in the same order in which they served. The (numbers of the) footnotes for these paragraphs are changed automatically.
    c. Click and drag to select the text of all ten anecdotes, pull down the Format menu, and click the Paragraph command to display the Format Paragraph dialog box. Click the Line and Page Breaks tab, and then check the box to keep the lines together (to avoid a page break within the paragraph.) Click the Indents and Spacing tab, and then change the spacing before each paragraph to 12 points. (This has the same visual effect as inserting a blank line before each anecdote, but it provides greater flexibility in that you can change the spacing between paragraphs with a single command.)
    d. Convert all of the footnotes to endnotes, as shown in the figure. Which style do you prefer, footnotes or endnotes?
    e. Press Ctrl+Home to move to the beginning of the document, pull down the Format menu, click the Drop Cap command, and choose the dropped letter within the paragraph as shown in Figure 3.14.
    f. Go to the White House Web site at www.whitehouse.gov and download a picture of any of the 10 presidents to use on a cover page. Press Ctrl+Home to move to the beginning of the document, then press Ctrl+Enter to create a page break. Press Ctrl+Home to return to the beginning of the document (the blank page), press the Enter key several times, and then create a title page such as the one in Figure 3.14. Be sure to cite the source of the picture with an appropriate footnote.
    g. Print the completed document for your instructor.

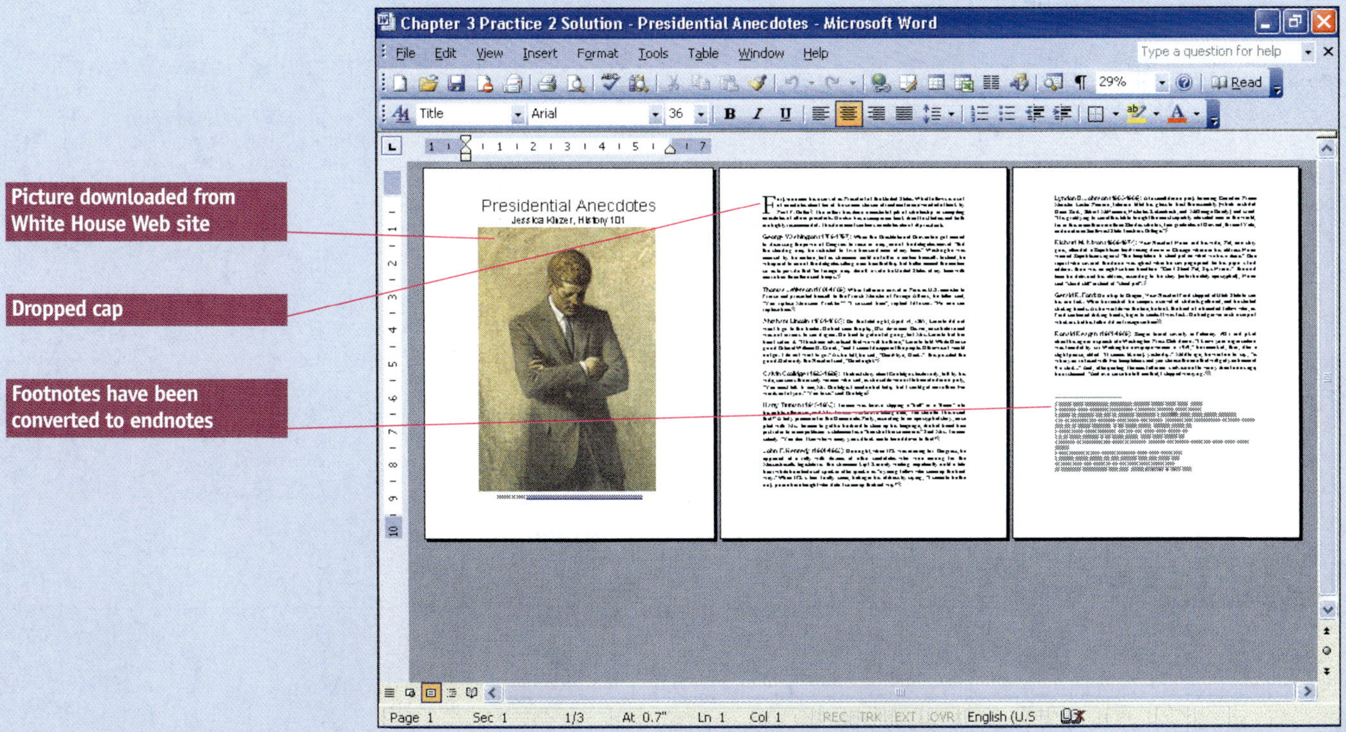

FIGURE 3.14 Presidential Anecdotes (exercise 2)

3. **Create a Home Page:** It's easy to create a home page. Start a new document and enter its text just as you would any other document. Use any and all formatting commands to create a document similar to the one in Figure 3.15. We suggest you use clip art, as opposed to a real picture. Pull down the File menu and use the Save As Web Page command to convert the Word document to a Web document. (Be sure to specify Single File Web Page as the file type.) You do not have to match our page exactly, but you are required to do the following:
   a. Use the Insert Hyperlink command to create a list of 3 to 5 hyperlinks. Be sure to enter accurate Web addresses for each of your sites.
   b. Select all of the links after they have been entered, then click the Bullets button on the Formatting toolbar to create a bulleted list.
   c. Pull down the Format menu, click the Themes command, and then select a professionally chosen design for your Web page.
   d. Save the document a final time, then exit Word. Start Windows Explorer, then go to the folder containing your home page, and double click the file you just created. Internet Explorer will start automatically (because your document was saved as a Web page).
   e. You should see the document that you just created within Internet Explorer as shown in Figure 3.15. Look carefully at the Address bar and note the local address on drive C, as opposed to a Web address. Print the document for your instructor as proof you completed the assignment.
   f. Creating the home page and viewing it locally is easy. Placing the page on the Web where it can be seen by anyone with an Internet connection is not as straightforward. You will need additional information from your instructor about how to obtain an account on a Web server (if that is available at your school), and further how to upload the Web page from your PC to the server.

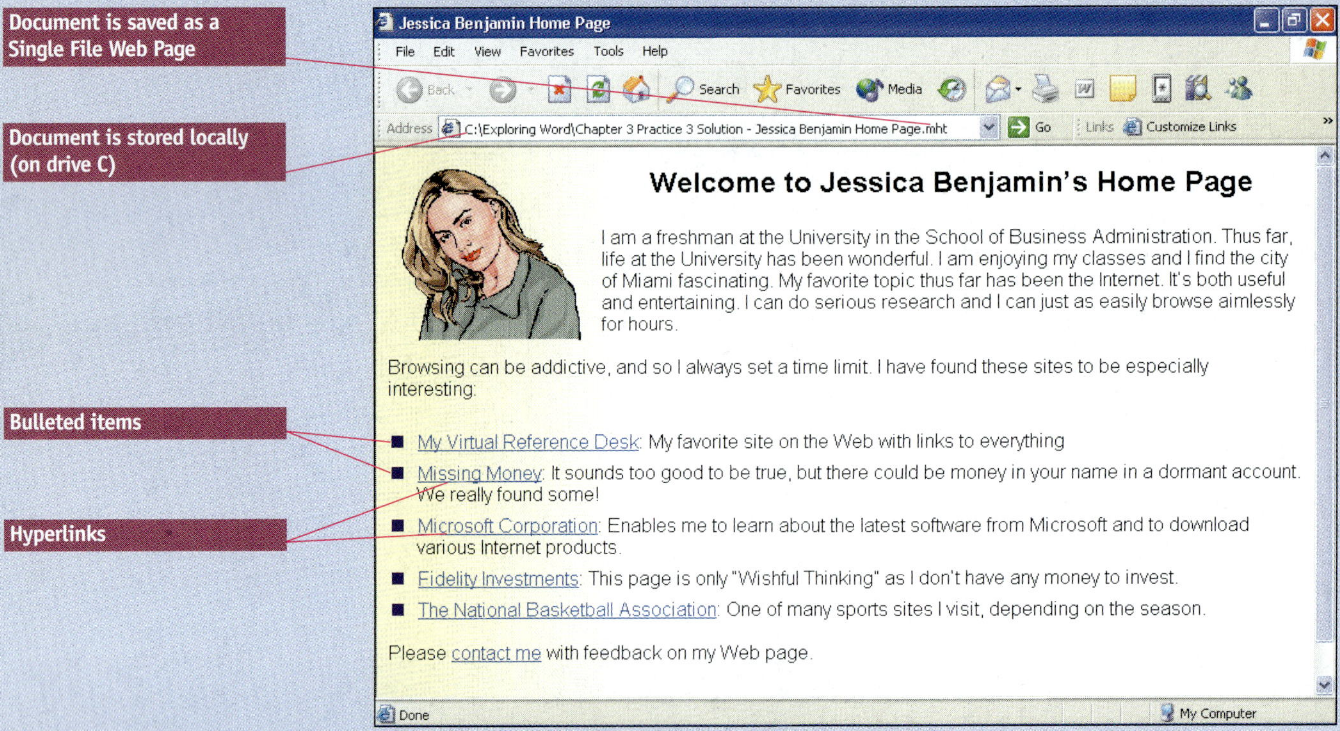

FIGURE 3.15 Create a Home Page (exercise 3)

4. **A Commercial Web Page:** Open the *Chapter 3 Practice 4* document in the Exploring Word folder. Pull down the File menu and click the Save As Web Page command to convert the Word document to a Web page. (Be sure to specify Single File Web Page as the file type.) Click Continue when a message appears that indicates pictures with text wrapping will become left or right aligned.
   a. Review the document and make the basic formatting changes you deem appropriate. Use the Themes command in the Format menu to apply an overall design to the page. Use any theme you like, but the overall document formatting should be similar to the document in Figure 3.16.
   b. Format the title if you have not already done so. Select the text, "Click here to contact us" that appears toward the top of the document. Pull down the Insert menu and click the Hyperlink command (or click the Insert Hyperlink button on the Standard toolbar), then enter your e-mail address.
   c. Go to the last paragraph and insert a hyperlink for the Boeing Company at www.boeing.com. Insert a second link for FlyteComm at www.flytecomm.com, a Web site that lets you track a flight from take-off to landing.
   d. Save the document a final time, then exit Word. Start Windows Explorer, then go to the folder containing your Web page, and double click the file you just created. Internet Explorer will start automatically (because your document was saved as a Web page). You should see your document within Internet Explorer as shown in Figure 3.16. Look carefully at the Address bar and note the local address on drive C, as opposed to a Web address. Print the document for your instructor as proof you completed the assignment.
   e. Creating the home page and viewing it locally is easy. Placing the page on the Web where it can be seen by anyone with an Internet connection is not as straightforward. You will need additional information from your instructor about how to obtain an account on a Web server (if that is available at your school), and further how to upload the Web page from your PC to the server.

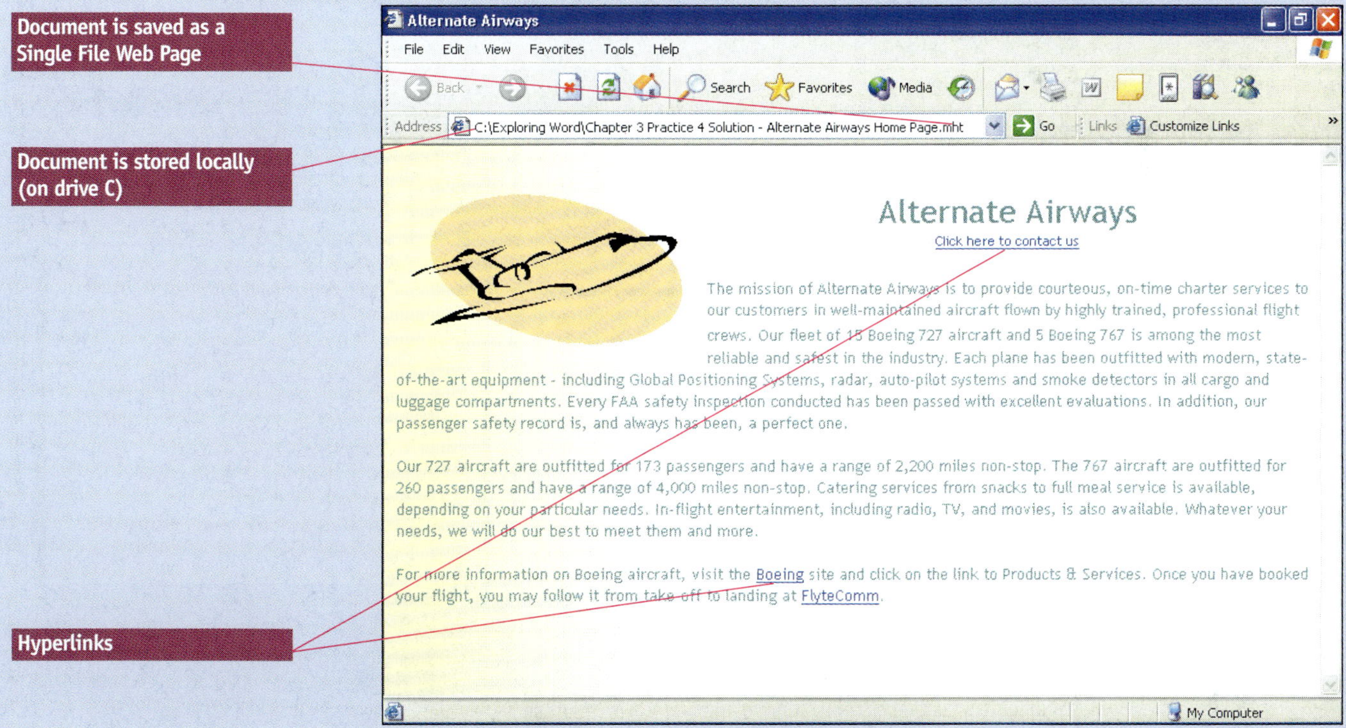

FIGURE 3.16 A Commercial Web Page (exercise 4)

5. **Symbols as Clip Art:** AutoShapes and symbols can be used to create unusual documents such as those shown in Figure 3.17. You do not have to match our documents exactly, but you are to use a combination of AutoShapes and symbols for your documents.
   a. Start a new document. Change the page orientation to landscape and set the left and right page margins to 1″. Set a Center tab at 4.5″ and a Right tab at 9″
   b. Pull down the Insert menu, click the Symbol command, then select the Webdings font. Find the fork, plate, and knife symbol, and then insert it into the document. Change the font size for the symbol to 30 points, then copy the symbol and paste it as many times as necessary to complete the line.
   c. Press the Enter key to move to the next line, and paste the symbol. Press the Tab key twice to move to the right tab, then paste the symbol again. Copy this line nine times. Create the bottom border by copying the first line.
   d. Enter the text for the invitation as shown in Figure 3.17 but use your instructor's name instead of Keith Fletcher. Increase the font size to 30 points. Change the Font color for the symbols and text to blue.
   e. Start a new document for the Music Festival flyer and change to landscape orientation. Use the AutoShapes menu on the Drawing toolbar to create the banner. Use the Insert Symbol command (Webdings font) to insert the musical note to the left of the title. Copy the symbol and paste it at the end of the title.
   f. Change the font size of the title to 50 point, then change the font color to orange. Change the fill color to tan for both the banner and the text box. Change the line color for the text box to No Line.
   g. Enter the text for the flyer, centered between the margins. Change the font size and color, as shown in the figure. Create the Explosion AutoShape, size it, and change the fill color to tan. Select the AutoShape and use the Draw menu to change its Order to send it behind the text.
   h. Use the Text Box tool on the Drawing toolbar to create a text box, and then insert the musical note inside the text box. Change the font size to 200 point and change the color as shown. Copy it. Move both text boxes as shown.
   i. Print both documents for your instructor.

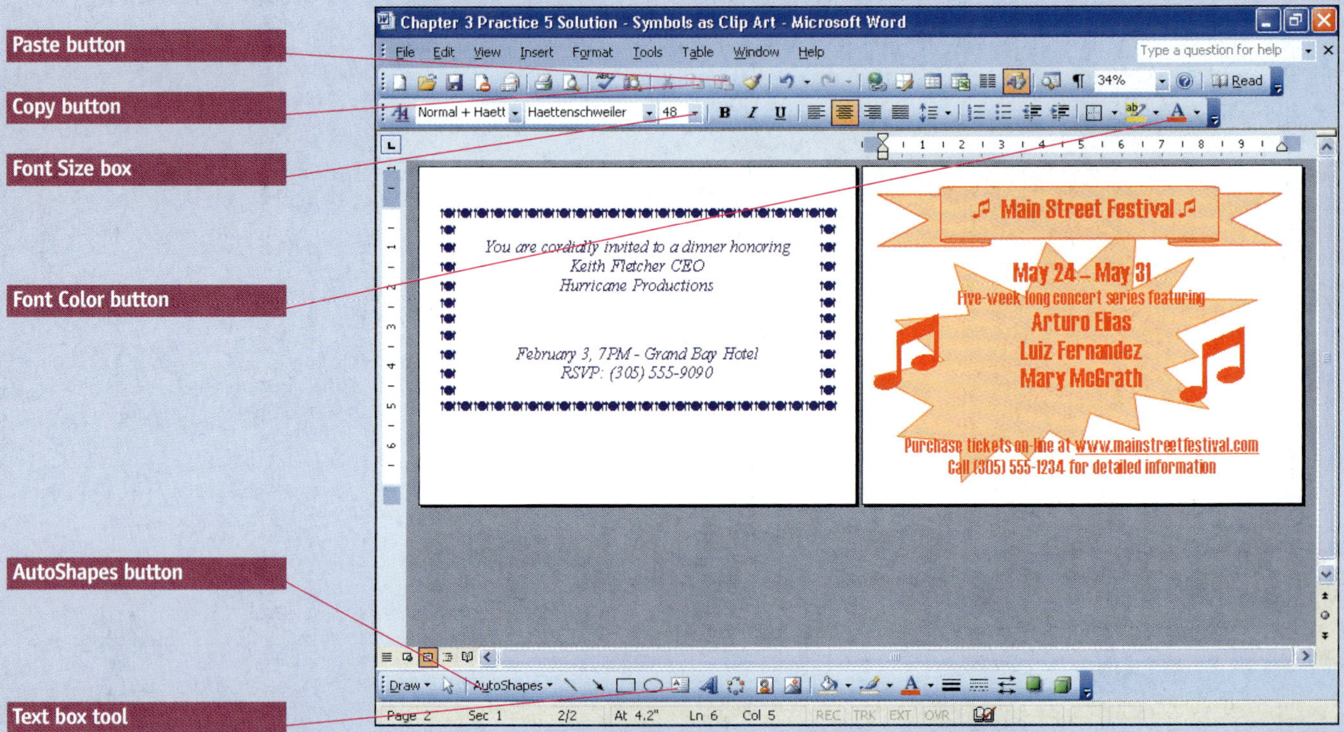

FIGURE 3.17 Symbols as Clip Art (exercise 5)

6. **Mail Merge and Templates:** This exercise combines an existing template with a mail merge to create a document similar to the one in Figure 3.18. You do not have to create the identical document, but you are required to use the indicated features. Proceed as follows:
   a. Display the task pane. Click the down arrow on the title bar of the task pane to select New Document. Click the link to the Templates home page.
   b. Choose a category (e.g., Marketing and Customer Relations), a subcategory (e.g., Letters to Customers), and a specific document (e.g., Acknowledgement of Order). Microsoft is continually changing the available templates, so you may not find the exact document. It doesn't matter. Choose any document that appeals to you. Click the link to Download now at the top of the document. Close the task pane.
   c. The template contains several bracketed entries, which are to be replaced with specific information. The template is intended for a single letter, however, whereas we are using it as the basis for a mail merge. Thus we deleted the bracketed entries to be replaced with mail merge fields in subsequent steps. We also deleted the amount and order number entries within the body of the letter, also to be replaced with mail merge fields. And finally, we specified a uniform two-week delivery time as well as a uniform phone number. Save the document.
   d. Pull down the Tools menu, click Letters and Mailings, then click Mail Merge Wizard to start the wizard. Select the Letters option. Click Next. Select the option to use the Current Document. Click Next.
   e. Select the option to select the recipients by typing a new list. Click Create to display the New Address List dialog box, then click the Customize button. Delete the Address Line 2, Country, Home Phone, Work Phone, and E-mail address. Click the Add button to add the Amount field; click the button a second time to add the OrderNumber field. Click OK to close the Customize Address List dialog box. Enter data for four recipients. Click the Close button. Save the data source as *Chapter 3 Practice 6 Solution*. Click OK.
   f. Complete the form letter by adding an address block, greeting line, amount, and order number fields as shown in Figure 3.18.
   g. Complete the remaining steps in the mail merge and then print the individual letters for your instructor. Exit Word. Save the form letter.

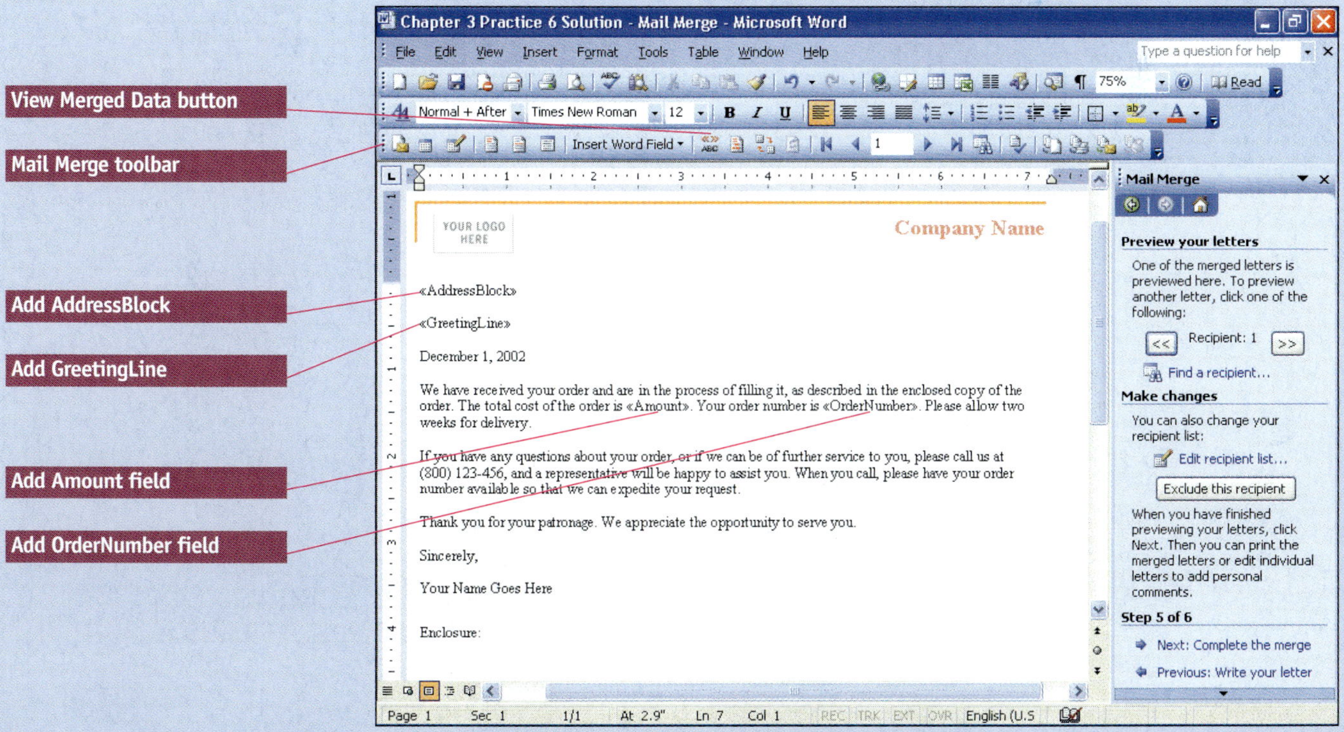

FIGURE 3.18 Mail Merge and Templates (exercise 6)

7. **Mailing Labels:** A mail merge creates the form letters for a mailing. That is only the first step, however, because you also have to create envelopes and/or mailing labels to physically mail the letters. Proceed as follows:
   a. Open a new document. Pull down the Tools menu, click Letters and Mailings, then click Mail Merge Wizard to start the Wizard. Click the Labels option and click Next. Select the option to change document layout. Click Next.
   b. You will see the Label Options dialog box. Select the type of label you want, such as 2160 Mini labels, and click OK. (The type of label you select does not matter since you are going to print the labels.) Click Next.
   c. Click Browse to locate the data source from the previous exercise (the *Chapter 3 Practice 6 Access Solution* database). Click Open. Click the Select All button, then click OK.
   d. Click Next to move to the next step, where you arrange the labels. Click Address Block, click OK, click Postal Bar Code to create the first label, and click OK. Click the button to Update All labels to copy this layout to the other labels.
   e. Click the button to Preview the labels. You should see a screen similar to Figure 3.19. The names and addresses correspond to the data we created in the previous exercise.
   f. Click Next. Do *not* attempt to print the labels unless you actually have mailing labels for the printer. Close the task pane. Save the document as *Chapter 3 Practice 7 solution.*
   g. Press the Print Screen key to capture the screen in Figure 3.19 to the Windows clipboard. Start a new Word document, then click the Paste button to paste the screen into the document. Add a sentence or two that describes the assignment. Include a cover page with your name, then print the completed document for your instructor.
   h. Repeat these steps to create a parallel set of envelopes. Pull down the View menu and click the Zoom command to view all four envelopes in one screen. Capture this screen for your instructor as well. Exit Word.

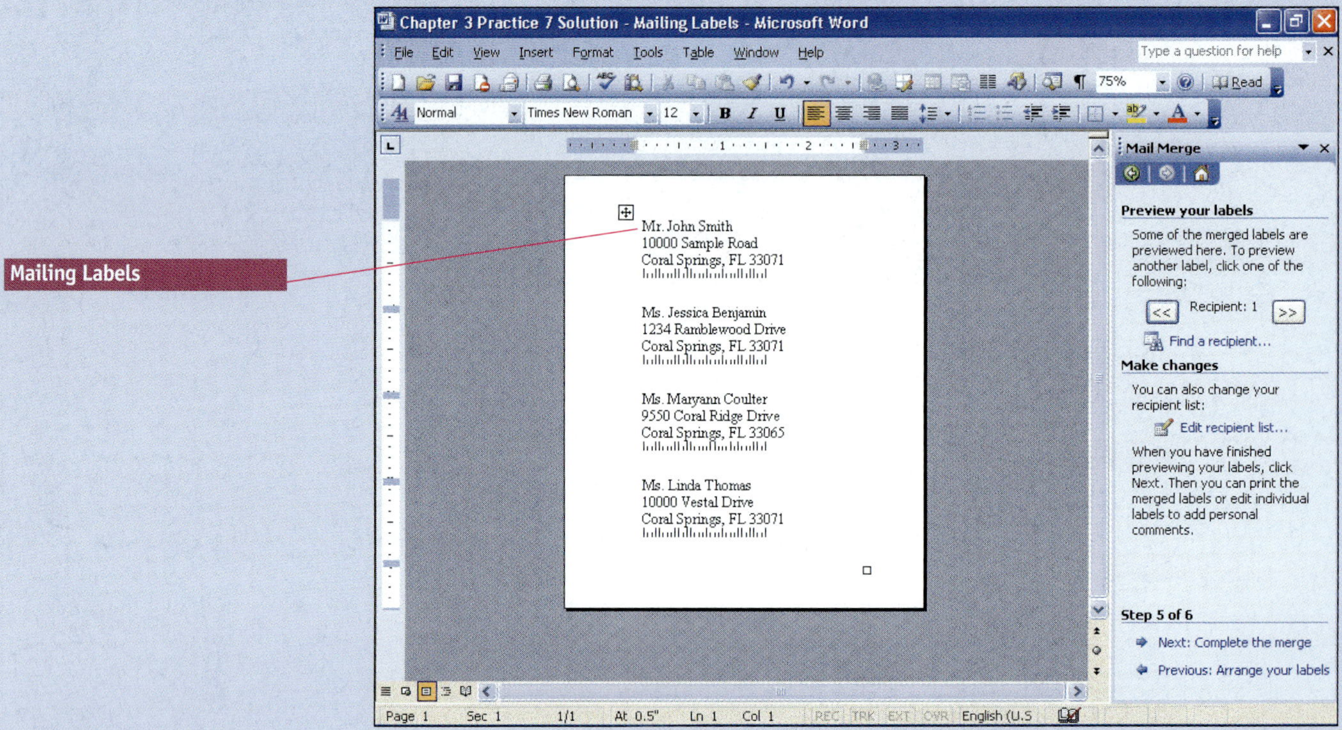

FIGURE 3.19 Mailing Labels (exercise 7)

8. **Create Your Own Stationery:** Figure 3.20 displays an envelope and matching letterhead for use as personal stationery. You do not have to match our design exactly, but you are to create both items and use the same logo for each. Proceed as follows:
   a. Begin with the stationery. Start a new document. Pull down the File menu and click the Page Setup command. Change to one-half-inch margins all around.. Enter your name, address, telephone, and e-mail information at the top of the page. Use a larger font and distinguishing color for your name, then center all of the text at the top of the page. Use the Drawing toolbar or the Borders and Shading command to add a horizontal line below the text.
   b. Pull down the Insert menu, click the Picture command, and locate an appropriate piece of clip art to use as a logo. Right click the image to display a context-sensitive menu, click the Format Picture command, click the Layout tab, and choose Square. Click OK to close the dialog box. Move and size the logo as necessary. Select the clip art, click the Copy button, click Paste, and then drag the copied image to the right side of the page.
   c. Print the completed letterhead for your instructor.
   d. Press Ctrl+Home to move to the beginning of the document. Pull down the Insert menu, click the Break command, and then click Next Page under Section breaks. (This creates a new page as well as a new section. The latter enables you to change the page orientation within a document.) Click OK.
   e. Click on the newly inserted page. Pull down the File menu, click the Page Setup command, click the Margins tab, and select the option for Landscape printing. Click the Paper tab, click the down arrow in the Paper Size list box, and choose Envelope #10 (the standard business envelope). Click OK to accept the settings and close the dialog box.
   f. Click and drag to copy the clip art from the letterhead to the envelope. Complete the envelope by adding your name and return address.
   g. Do not print the envelope in a computer lab at school unless envelopes are available for the printer. You can, however, capture the screen in Figure 3.20 to prove to your instructor that you created the envelope successfully.

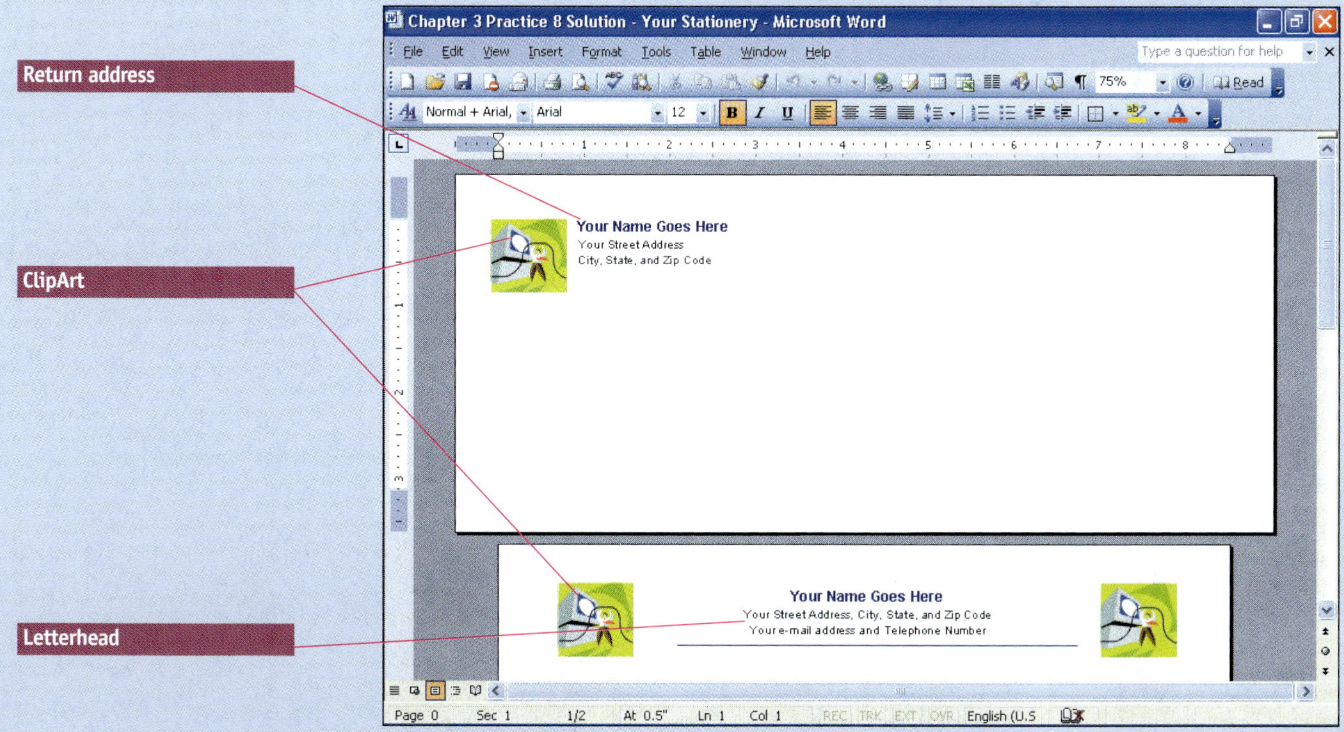

FIGURE 3.20 Create Your Own Stationery (exercise 8)

MINI CASES

Organization Charts

All applications in Microsoft Office have access to the Diagram Gallery, which helps you to create an organization chart. All you do is pull down the Insert menu and click the Diagram command to display the Diagram Gallery dialog box from where you can select the Organization chart. The default chart consists of four boxes that are displayed on two levels. The lower level has three subordinates reporting to the single box on the top level. You can modify the chart by adding (removing) boxes at various levels using the Insert Shape button on the Organization Chart toolbar. You can also click in any box to add the appropriate descriptive text. The organization chart is a single object that can be moved and sized within the document, just as any other Windows object.

Your assignment is to open the *Chapter 3 Mini Case—Organization Chart* document, which contains a basic organization chart that we have already created. Your first task is to click the various boxes in the chart to assign a specific person to each box. Copy the completed chart to a second page in the document, then experiment with the Layout and AutoFormat tools on the Organization Chart toolbar to create an alternate version of the initial chart. Print both charts for your instructor.

Travel World

You have been hired as an intern for the Travel World agency and asked to create a flyer to distribute on campus. The only requirement is to include your name and e-mail address as the travel agent. Use any combination of clip art or photographs to make the flyer as attractive as possible. Be sure to spell check the completed flyer, and then print the document for your instructor.

The Calendar Wizard

The Calendar Wizard is one of several wizards that are built into Microsoft Office. Open the Task pane, select New document from the drop-down list box, click the link to the templates on your computer to display the Templates dialog box, then click the Other Documents tab to locate the Calendar Wizard. Create a calendar for the current month using any design and orientation you like. Take advantage of the Office Assistant to add clip art and/or notes to specific dates within the selected month. Include your name somewhere within the calendar and submit it to your instructor.

MLA Guidelines

The Modern Language Association (MLA) guidelines are currently used by over 125 scholarly and literary journals, newsletters, and magazines with circulations over one thousand; by hundreds of smaller periodicals; and by many university and commercial presses. MLA style is commonly followed, not only in the United States, but in Canada and other countries as well. Use your favorite search engine to locate the MLA Web site to download the guidelines for use in a research paper. You may also go to the Microsoft Web site to see if you can locate a template that was created by Microsoft that contains this material.

Leonardo Da Vinci

Use your imagination to create a résumé for Leonardo Da Vinci. The résumé is limited to one page and will be judged for content (yes, you have to do a little research on the Web) as well as appearance. You can intersperse fact and fiction as appropriate; for example, you may want to leave space for a telephone and/or a fax number, but could indicate that these devices have not yet been invented. You can choose a format for the résumé using the Résumé Wizard, or better yet, design your own.

CHAPTER 4

Advanced Features: Outlines, Tables, Styles, and Sections

OBJECTIVES

After reading this chapter you will:

1. Create a bulleted, numbered, and/or a multilevel list (i.e., an outline).
2. Describe the tables feature.
3. Explain how styles automate the formatting process.
4. Use the AutoFormat command to apply styles to an existing document.
5. Distinguish between formatting at the character, paragraph, or section level.
6. Create a header and/or a footer; use multiple headers and/or footers within the same document.
7. Insert page numbers into a document.
8. Create an index and a table of contents.

hands-on exercises

1. BULLETS, LISTS, AND OUTLINES
   Input: None
   Output: US Constitution
2. TABLES
   Input: None
   Output: My Study Schedule
3. STYLES
   Input: Tips for Microsoft Word
   Output: Tips for Microsoft Word Solution
4. WORKING IN LONG DOCUMENTS
   Input: Tips for Microsoft Word Solution (from exercise 3)
   Output: Tips for Microsoft Word Solution (additional modifications)

CASE STUDY
THE MARTIN COMPANY

A sustainable rate of growth that can continue over time is good business. The Martin Company is committed to the concept of sustainability, be it social or economic, and it provides consulting services to businesses seeking assistance in this area. The company stresses education and offers value-added services, including environmental site audits and environmental consulting, as well as various technical support and training services.

Greg Hubit, the Director of Marketing at Martin, has asked you to review a marketing document that describes the two classes of service currently provided by the company—standard offerings and value-added services. Greg has asked that you make several changes to the document and suggested the use of styles, headers, footers, and bulleted lists where appropriate. He would like you to improve the formatting of the table on the last page, and to delete the empty rows within the table. And finally, Greg would like to see a table of contents on the first page that clearly lists each of the company's services with an appropriate page reference. You think of yourself as proficient in Microsoft Word. This is your chance to show what you can do. ■

Your assignment is to read the chapter, which focuses on several advanced features in Microsoft Word. You will then open *Chapter 4 Case Study—The Martin Company*, and insert a footer on every page that indicates the current page number and the total number of pages (e.g., page 1 of 4). A header that includes your name and the name of the case is required on every page except the title page. The Heading 1, Heading 2, and Body Text styles have been applied throughout the document, but you can modify these styles as you see fit. (The completed document will be printed in color.) Any additional formatting changes are open-ended, and we are confident that you will do a professional job. Print the completed document for your instructor.

THE REQUIREMENTS OF A TERM PAPER

This chapter presents a series of advanced features that will be especially useful the next time you have to write a term paper with very specific formatting requirements. We show you how to create a bulleted or numbered list to emphasize important items within a term paper, and how to create an outline for that paper. We introduce the tables feature, which provides an easy way to arrange text, numbers, and/or graphics. We develop the use of styles or sets of formatting instructions that provide a consistent appearance to similar elements in a document. We also discuss several items associated with longer documents, such as page numbers, headers and footers, a table of contents, and an index. We begin with lists.

Bullets and Lists

A list helps you organize information by highlighting important topics. A ***bulleted list*** emphasizes (and separates) the items. A ***numbered list*** sequences (and prioritizes) the items and is automatically updated to accommodate additions or deletions. An ***outline*** (or ***outline numbered list***) extends a numbered list to several levels, and it too is updated automatically when topics are added or deleted. Each of these lists is created through the ***Bullets and Numbering command*** in the Format menu, which displays the Bullets and Numbering dialog box in Figure 4.1.

The tabs within the Bullets and Numbering dialog box are used to choose the type of list and customize its appearance. The Bulleted tab selected in Figure 4.1a enables you to specify one of several predefined symbols for the bullet. Typically, that is all you do, although you can use the Customize button to change the default spacing (of ¼ inch) of the text from the bullet and/or to choose a different symbol for the bullet.

The Numbered tab in Figure 4.1b lets you choose Arabic or Roman numerals, or upper- or lowercase letters, for a numbered list. As with a bulleted list, the Customize button lets you change the default spacing, the numbering style, and/or the punctuation before or after the number or letter. Note, too, the option buttons to restart or continue numbering, which become important if a list appears in multiple places within a document. In other words, each occurrence of a list can start numbering anew, or it can continue from where the previous list left off.

The Outline Numbered tab in Figure 4.1c enables you to create an outline to organize your thoughts. As with the other types of lists, you can choose one of several default styles, and/or modify a style through the Customize command button. You can also specify whether each outline within a document is to restart its numbering, or whether it is to continue numbering from the previous outline.

The List Styles tab (not shown in Figure 4.1) lets you change the style (formatting specifications) associated with a list. You can change the font size, use a picture or symbol for a bullet, add color, and so on. Styles are discussed later in the chapter.

Creating an Outline

Our next exercise explores the Bullets and Numbering command in conjunction with creating an outline for a hypothetical paper on the United States Constitution. The exercise begins by having you create a bulleted list, then asking you to convert it to a numbered list, and finally to an outline. The end result is the type of outline your professor may ask you to create prior to writing a term paper.

As you do the exercise, remember that a conventional outline is created as an outline numbered list within the Bullets and Numbering command. Text for the outline is entered in the Print Layout or Normal view, *not* the Outline view. The latter provides a completely different capability—a condensed view of a document that is used in conjunction with styles and is discussed later in the chapter. We mention this to avoid confusion should you stumble into the Outline view.

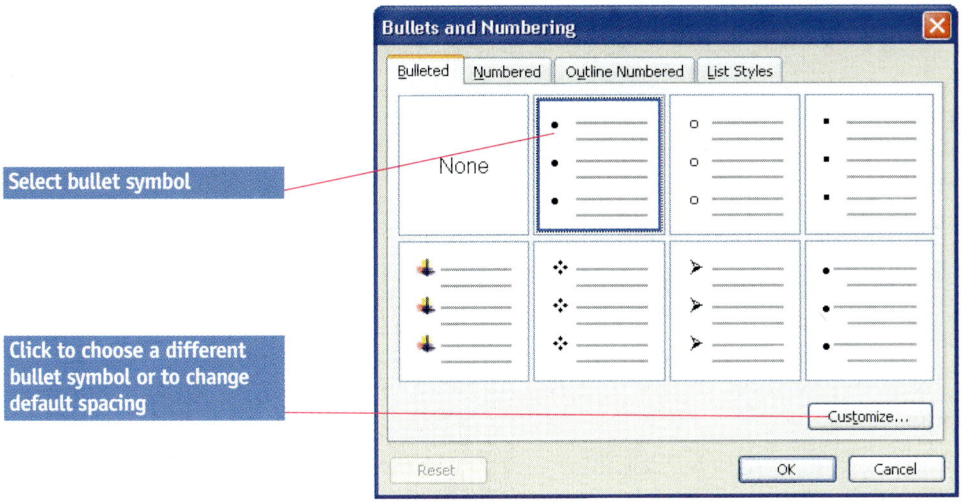

(a) Bulleted List

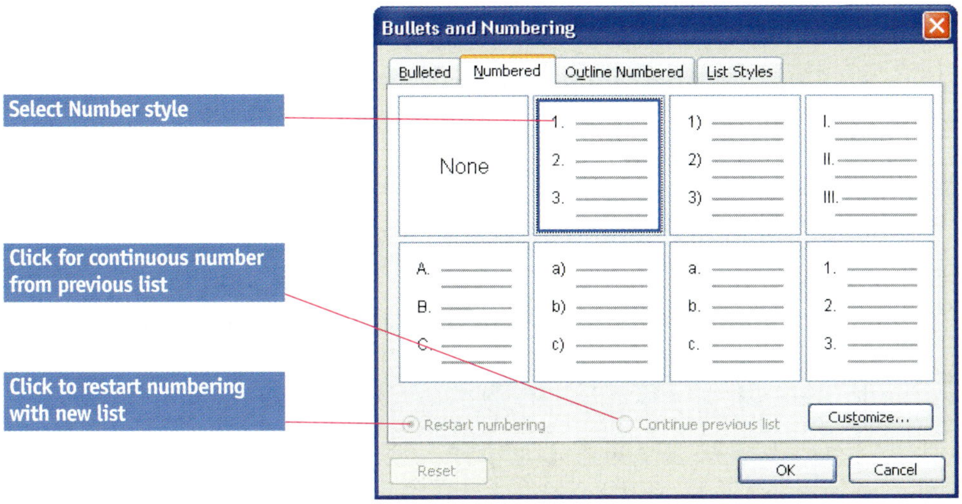

(b) Numbered List

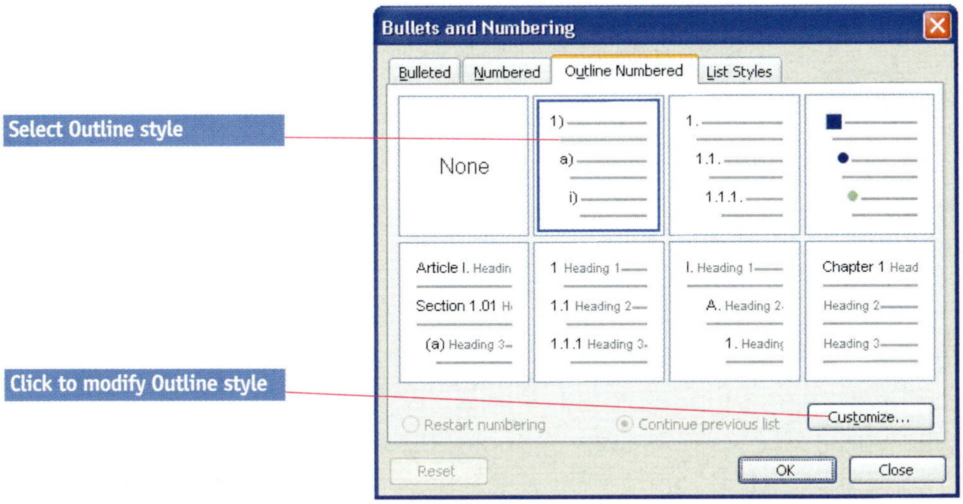

(c) Outline Numbered List

FIGURE 4.1 Bullets and Numbering

hands-on exercise

1 Bullets, Lists, and Outlines

Objective To use the Bullets and Numbering command to create a bulleted list, a numbered list, and an outline. Use Figure 4.2 as a guide.

Step 1: Create a Bulleted List

- Start Word and begin a new document. Type **Preamble**, the first topic in our list, and press **Enter**.
- Type the three remaining topics, **Article I—Legislative Branch**, **Article II—Executive Branch**, and **Article III—Judicial Branch**. Do not press Enter after the last item.
- Click and drag to select all four topics as shown in Figure 4.2a. Pull down the **Format menu** and click the **Bullets and Numbering command** to display the Bullets and Numbering dialog box.
- If necessary, click the **Bulleted tab**, select the type of bullet you want, then click **OK** to accept this setting and close the dialog box. Bullets have been added to the list.
- Click after the words **Judicial Branch** to deselect the list and also to position the insertion point at the end of the list. Press **Enter** to begin a new line. A bullet appears automatically.
- Type **Amendments**. Press **Enter** to end this line and begin the next, which already has a bullet.
- Press **Enter** a second time to terminate the bulleted list.
- Save the document as **US Constitution** in the **Exploring Word folder**.

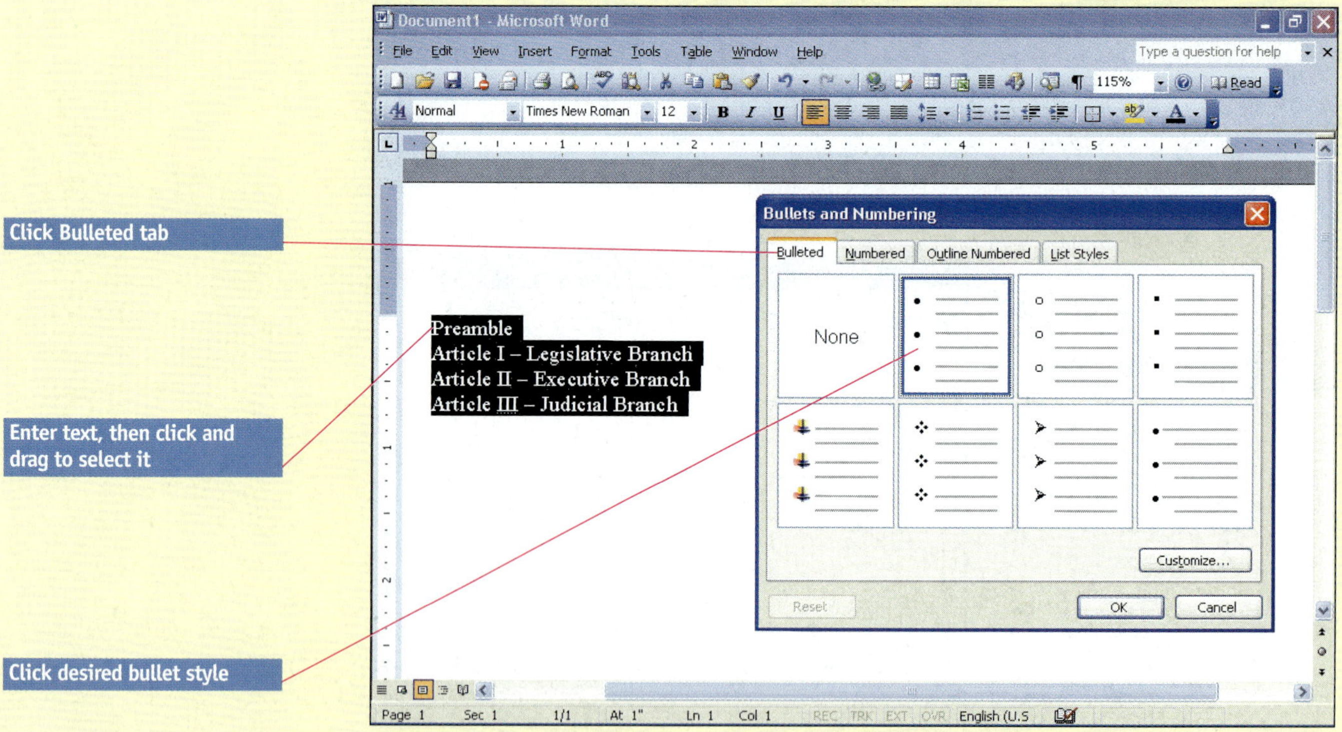

(a) Create a Bulleted List (step 1)

FIGURE 4.2 Hands-on Exercise 1

Step 2: Modify a Numbered List

- Click and drag to select the five items in the bulleted list, then click the **Numbering button** on the Standard toolbar.
- The bulleted list has been converted to a numbered list as shown in Figure 4.2b. (The last two items have not yet been added to the list.)
- Click immediately after the last item in the list and press **Enter** to begin a new line. Word automatically adds the next sequential number to the list.
- Type **History** and press **Enter**. Type **The Constitution Today** as the seventh (and last) item.
- Click in the selection area to the left of the sixth item, **History** (only the text is selected). Now drag the selected text to the beginning of the list, in front of *Preamble*. Release the mouse.
- The list is automatically renumbered. *History* is now the first item, *Preamble* is the second item, and so on.
- Save the document.

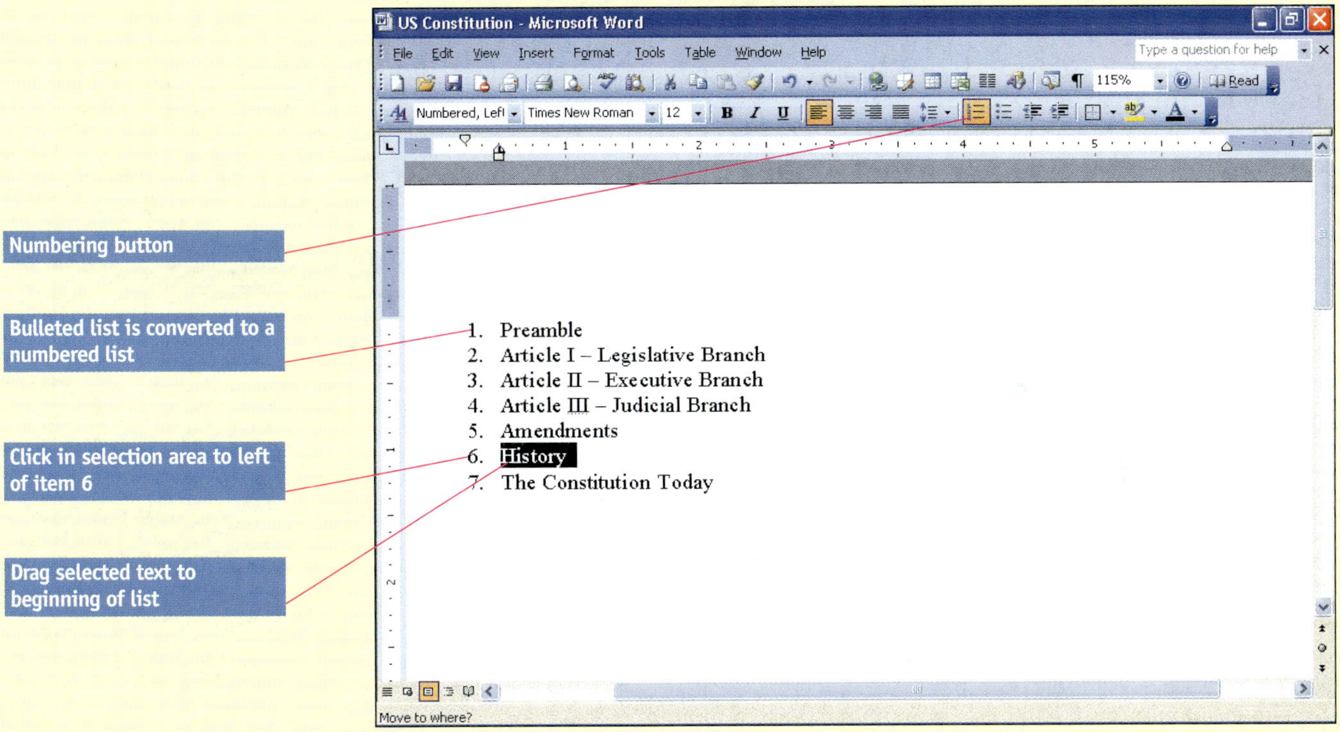

(b) Modify a Numbered List (step 2)

FIGURE 4.2 Hands-on Exercise 1 (*continued*)

THE BULLETS AND NUMBERING BUTTONS

Select the items for which you want to create a list, then click the Numbering or Bullets button on the Formatting toolbar to create a numbered or bulleted list, respectively. The buttons function as toggle switches; that is, click the button once (when the items are selected) and the list formatting is in effect. Click the button a second time and the bullets or numbers disappear. The buttons also enable you to switch from one type of list to another; that is, selecting a bulleted list and clicking the Numbering button changes the list to a numbered list, and vice versa.

Step 3: Convert to an Outline

- Click and drag to select the entire list, then click the **right mouse button** to display a context-sensitive menu.
- Click the **Bullets and Numbering command** to display the Bullets and Numbering dialog box in Figure 4.2c.
- Click the **Outline Numbered tab**, then select the type of outline you want. (Do not be concerned if the selected formatting does not display Roman numerals as we customize the outline later in the exercise.)
- Click **OK** to accept the formatting and close the dialog box. The numbered list has been converted to an outline, although that is difficult to see at this point.
- Click at the end of the third item, **Article I—Legislative Branch**. Press **Enter**. The number 4 is generated automatically for the next item in the list.
- Press the **Tab key** to indent this item and automatically move to the next level of numbering (a lowercase *a*). Type **House of Representatives**.
- Press **Enter**. The next sequential number (a lowercase *b*) is generated automatically. Type **Senate**.
- Save the document.

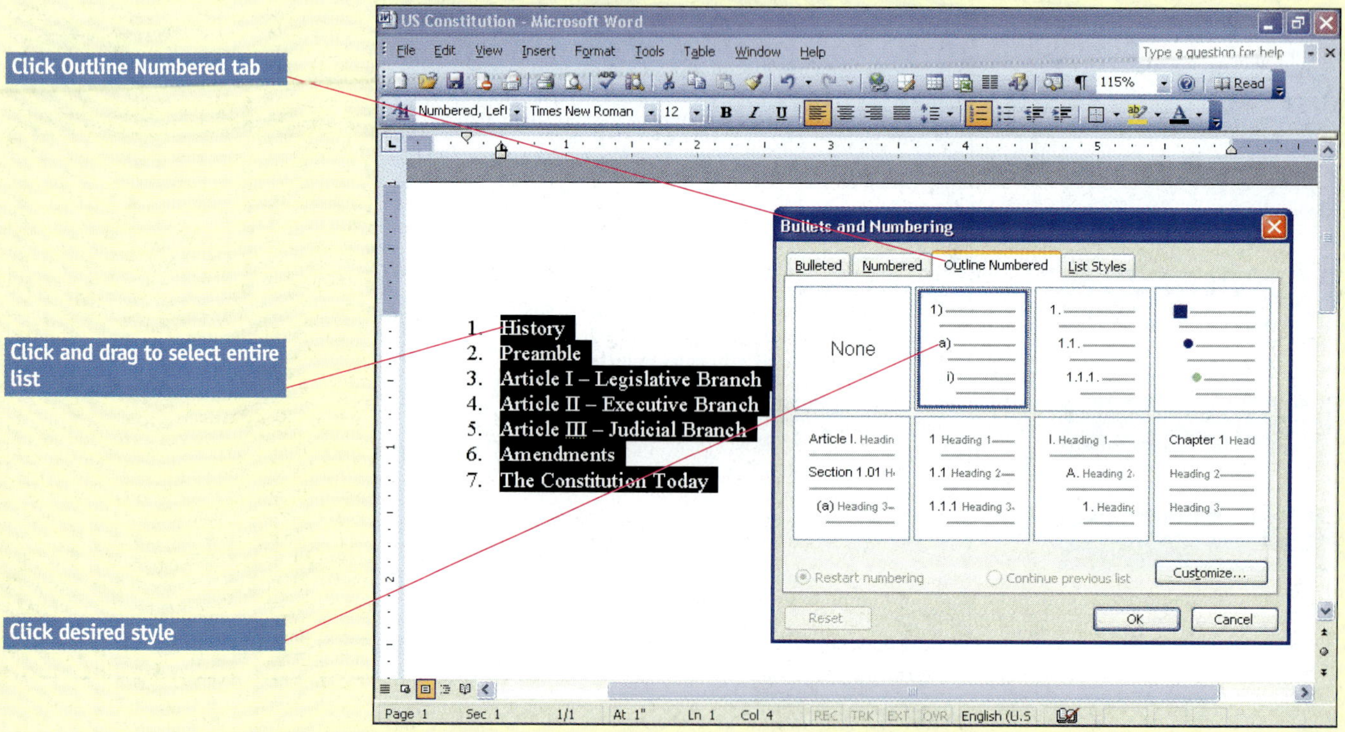

(c) Convert to an Outline (step 3)

FIGURE 4.2 Hands-on Exercise 1 (*continued*)

THE TAB AND SHIFT+TAB KEYS

The easiest way to enter text into an outline is to type continually from one line to the next, using the Tab and Shift+Tab keys as necessary. Press the Enter key after completing an item to move to the next item, which is automatically created at the same level, then continue typing if the item is to remain at this level. To change the level, press the Tab key to demote the item (move it to the next lower level), or the Shift+Tab combination to promote the item (move it to the next higher level).

Step 4: Enter Text into the Outline

- Your outline should be similar in appearance to Figure 4.2d, except that you have not yet entered most of the text. Click at the end of the line containing House of Representatives.
- Press **Enter** to start a new item (which is at level *b* in the outline). Press **Tab** to indent one level, changing the level to *i*. Type **Length of term**. Press **Enter**. Type **Requirements for office**.
- Click at the end of the line containing the word Senate. Press **Enter** to start a new line (which is at level *c*). Press **Tab** to indent one level, changing the level to an *i*. Type **Length of term**, press **Enter**, type **Requirements for office**, and press **Enter**.
- Press **Shift+Tab** to move up one level. Enter the remaining text as shown in Figure 4.2.d, using the **Tab** and **Shift+Tab** keys to demote and promote the items.
- Save the document.

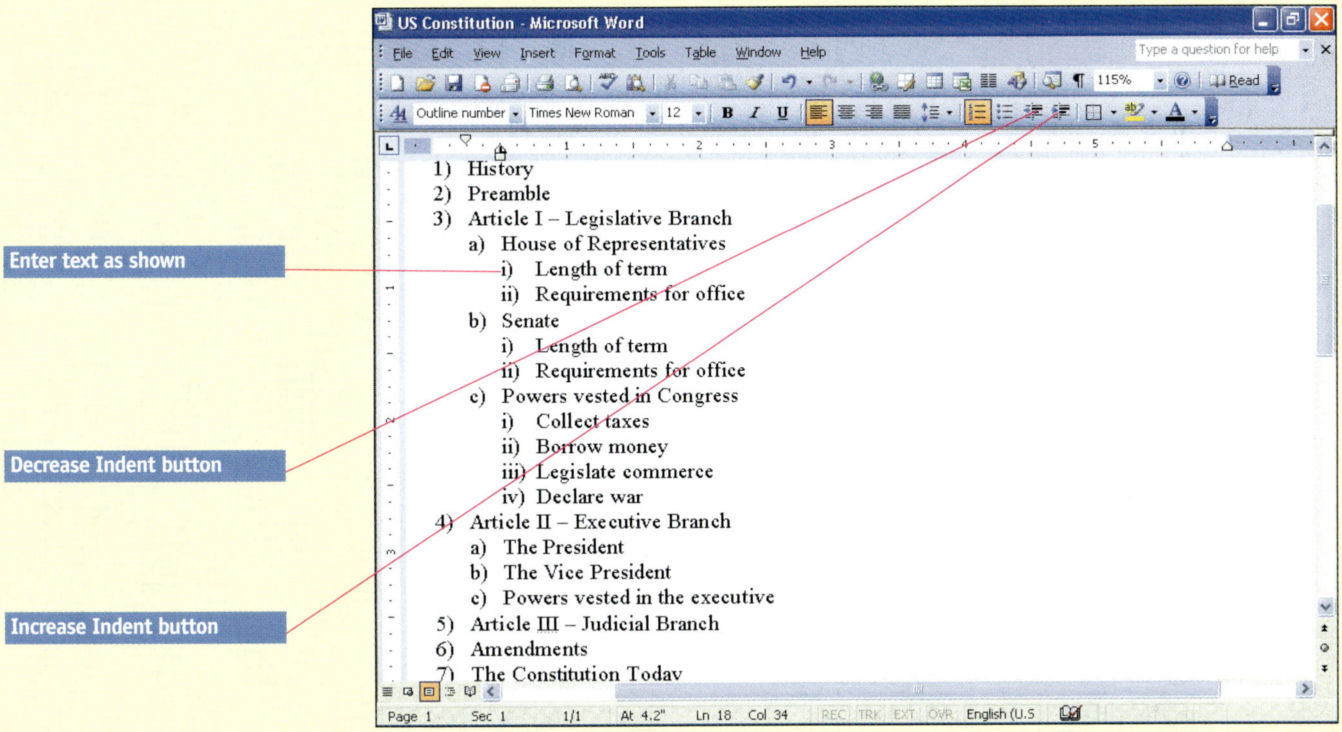

(d) Enter Text into the Outline (step 4)

FIGURE 4.2 Hands-on Exercise 1 (*continued*)

THE INCREASE AND DECREASE INDENT BUTTONS

The Increase and Decrease Indent buttons on the Standard toolbar are another way to change the level within an outline. Click anywhere within an item, then click the appropriate button to change the level within the outline. Indentation is implemented at the paragraph level, and hence you can click the button without selecting the entire item. You can also click and drag to select multiple item(s), then click the desired button.

Step 5: Customize the Outline

- Select the entire outline, pull down the **Format menu**, then click **Bullets and Numbering** to display the Bullets and Numbering dialog box.
- If necessary, click the **Outline Numbered tab** and click **Customize** to display the Customize dialog box as shown in Figure 4.2e. Level **1** should be selected.
  - Click the **drop-down arrow** in the Number style list box. Select **I, II, III**.
  - Click in the Number format text box, which now contains the Roman numeral I followed by a right parenthesis. Click and drag to select the parenthesis and replace it with a period.
  - Click the **drop-down arrow** in the Number position list box. Click **right** to right-align the Roman numerals that will appear in your outline.
- Click the number **2** in the Level list box. Select **A, B, C** as the Number style. Click in the Number format text box. Replace the right parenthesis with a period.
- Click the number **3** in the Level list box. Select **1, 2, 3** as the Number style. Click in the Number format text box. Replace the right parenthesis with a period.
- Click **OK** to accept these settings and close the dialog box. The formatting of your outline has changed to match the customization in this step.
- Save the document.

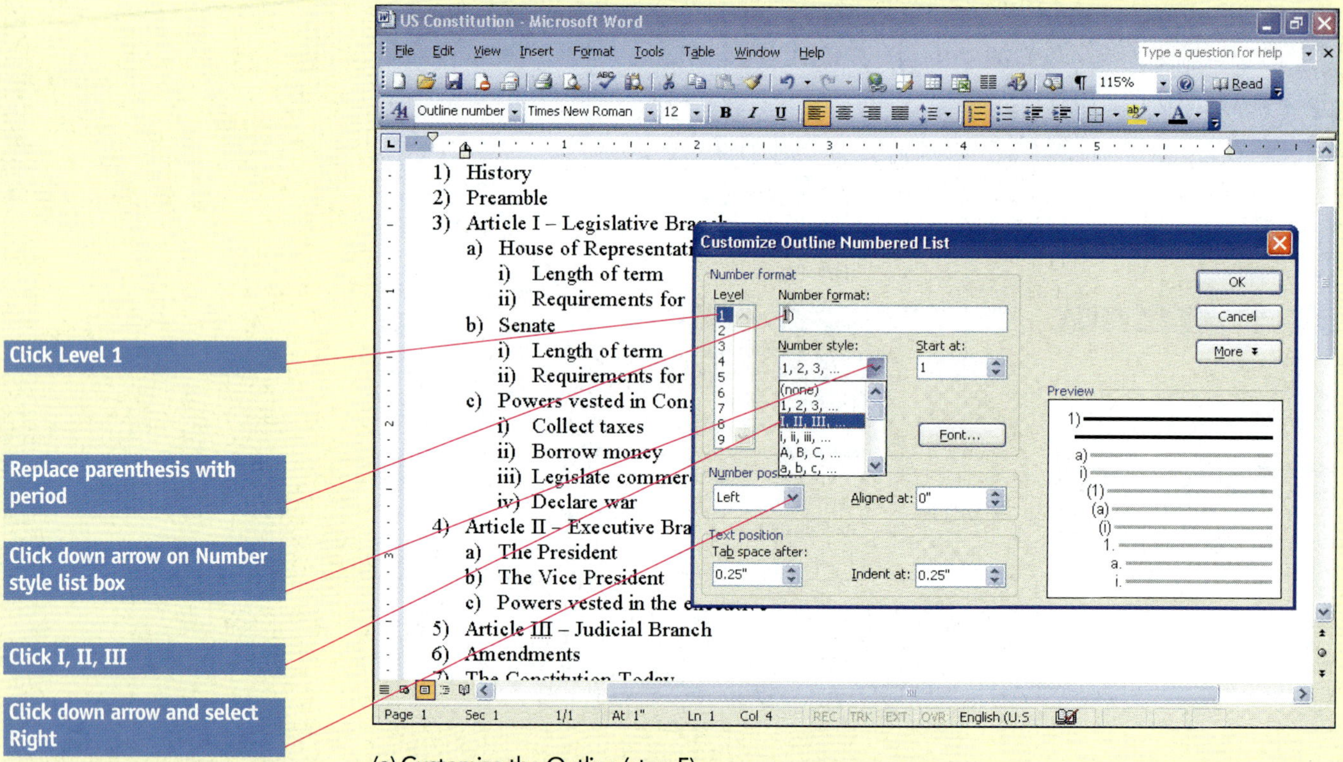

(e) Customize the Outline (step 5)

FIGURE 4.2 Hands-on Exercise 1 (*continued*)

AUTOMATIC CREATION OF A NUMBERED LIST

Word automatically creates a numbered list when you begin a paragraph with a number or letter, followed by a period, tab, or right parenthesis. Press the Enter key at the end of the line and you see the next item in the sequence. To end the list, press the Backspace key once, or press the Enter key twice.

Step 6: The Completed Outline

- Press **Ctrl+Home** to move to the beginning of the outline. The insertion point is after Roman numeral I. Type **The United States Constitution**. Press **Enter**.
- The new text appears as Roman numeral I, and all existing entries have been renumbered appropriately. The insertion point is immediately before the word History. Press **Enter** to create a blank line (for your name).
- The blank line is now Roman numeral II, and History has been moved to Roman numeral III. Move the insertion point to the blank line. Press the **Tab key** so that the blank line becomes item A. This renumbers History as Roman numeral II.
- Enter your name in the outline, then click and drag to select the first two items in the outline as shown in Figure 4.2f.
- Click the **Numbering button** to turn the outline off for the selected text. Click the **Center button** to center the text. Increase the font size to **18 points**.
- Click immediately after your name to deselect the text. Press **Enter** to add a blank line separating your name from the beginning of the outline.
- Save the document. Print the outline for your instructor. Exit Word.

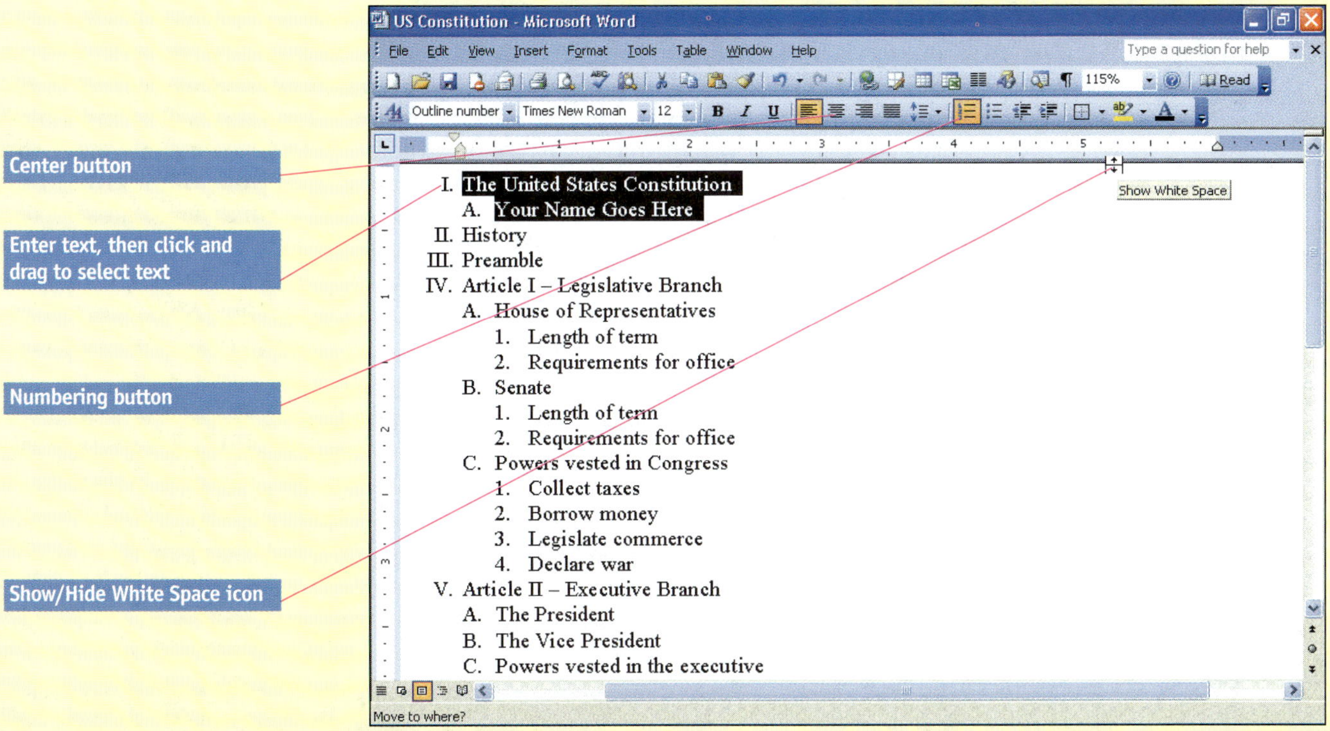

(f) The Completed Outline (step 6)

FIGURE 4.2 Hands-on Exercise 1 (*continued*)

HIDE THE WHITE SPACE

The Print Layout view displays a document as it will be printed, with margins, headers, footnotes, and/or multiple columns. You can, however, gain valuable space on the screen (and show more of your document) by hiding the white space (margins) at the top of every page and the gray space between pages. Scroll until you can see the top or bottom of the page, then click at the top of the page (you will see a Hide/Show White Space icon) to toggle the display of the white space on or off.

TABLES

The ***tables feature*** is one of the most powerful in Word and is the basis for an almost limitless variety of documents. The study schedule in Figure 4.3a, for example, is actually a 12 × 8 (12 rows and 8 columns) table as can be seen from the underlying structure in Figure 4.3b. The completed table looks quite impressive, but it is very easy to create once you understand how a table works. You can use the tables feature to create almost any type of document. (See the practice exercises at the end of the chapter for other examples.)

The rows and columns in a table intersect to form ***cells***. Each cell is formatted independently of every other cell and may contain text, numbers, and/or graphics. Commands operate on one or more cells. Individual cells can be joined together (merged) to form a larger cell as was done in the first and last rows of Figure 4.3a. Conversely, a single cell can be split into multiple cells. The rows within a table can be different heights, just as each column can be a different width. You can specify the height or width explicitly, or you can let Word determine it for you.

A cell can also contain clip art as shown in the bottom right corner of Figure 4.3a. Just click in the cell where you want the clip art to go, then use the Insert Picture command as you have throughout the text. Use the sizing handles once the clip art has been inserted to move and/or position it within the cell.

A table is created through the ***Insert Table command*** in the ***Table menu***. The command produces a dialog box in which you enter the number of rows and columns. Once the table has been defined, you enter text in individual cells. Text wraps as it is entered within a cell, so that you can add or delete text in a cell without affecting the entries in other cells. You can format the contents of an individual cell the same way you format an ordinary paragraph; that is, you can change the font, use boldface or italic, change the alignment, or apply any other formatting command. You can select multiple cells and apply the formatting to all selected cells at once.

You can also modify the structure of a table after it has been created. The ***Insert*** and ***Delete commands*** in the Table menu enable you to add new rows or columns, or delete existing rows or columns. You can invoke other commands to shade and/or border selected cells or the entire table.

You can work with a table using commands in the Table menu, or you can use the various tools on the Tables and Borders toolbar. (Just point to a button to display a ScreenTip indicative of its function.) Some of the buttons are simply shortcuts for commands within the Table menu. Other buttons offer new and intriguing possibilities, such as the button to Change Text Direction. Note, for example, how we drew an "X" to reserve Sunday morning (for sleeping).

It's easy, and as you might have guessed, it's time for another hands-on exercise in which you create the table in Figure 4.3.

LEFT	CENTER	RIGHT

Many documents call for left, centered, and/or right aligned text on the same line, an effect that is achieved through setting tabs, or more easily through a table. To achieve the effect shown in the heading of this box, create a 1 × 3 table (one row and three columns), type the text in the three cells as needed, then use the buttons on the Formatting toolbar to left align, center, and right align the respective cells. Select the table, pull down the Format menu, click Borders and Shading, then specify None as the Border setting.

Weekly Class and Study Schedule							
	Monday	Tuesday	Wednesday	Thursday	Friday	Saturday	Sunday
8:00AM							
9:00AM							
10:00AM							
11:00AM							
12:00PM							
1:00PM							
2:00PM							
3:00PM							
4:00PM							
Notes							

(a) Completed Table

(b) Underlying Structure

FIGURE 4.3 The Tables Feature

hands-on exercise

2 Tables

Objective To create a table; to change row heights and column widths; to merge cells; to apply borders and shading to selected cells. Use Figure 4.4 as a guide for the exercise.

Step 1: The Page Setup Command

- Start Word. Click the **Tables and Borders button** on the Standard toolbar to display the Tables and Borders toolbar as shown in Figure 4.4a.
- The button functions as a toggle switch—click it once and the toolbar is displayed. Click the button a second time and the toolbar is suppressed. Click and drag the title bar on the toolbar to anchor it under the Formatting toolbar.
- Pull down the **File menu** and click the **Page Setup command** to display the dialog box in Figure 4.4a.
- Click the **Margins tab** and click the **Landscape icon**. Change the top and bottom margins to **.75** inch.
- Change the left and right margins to **.5** inch each. Click **OK** to accept the settings and close the dialog box.
- Save the document as **My Study Schedule** in the **Exploring Word folder** that you have used throughout the text.
- Change to the **Print Layout view**. Zoom to **Page Width**. You are now ready to create the table.

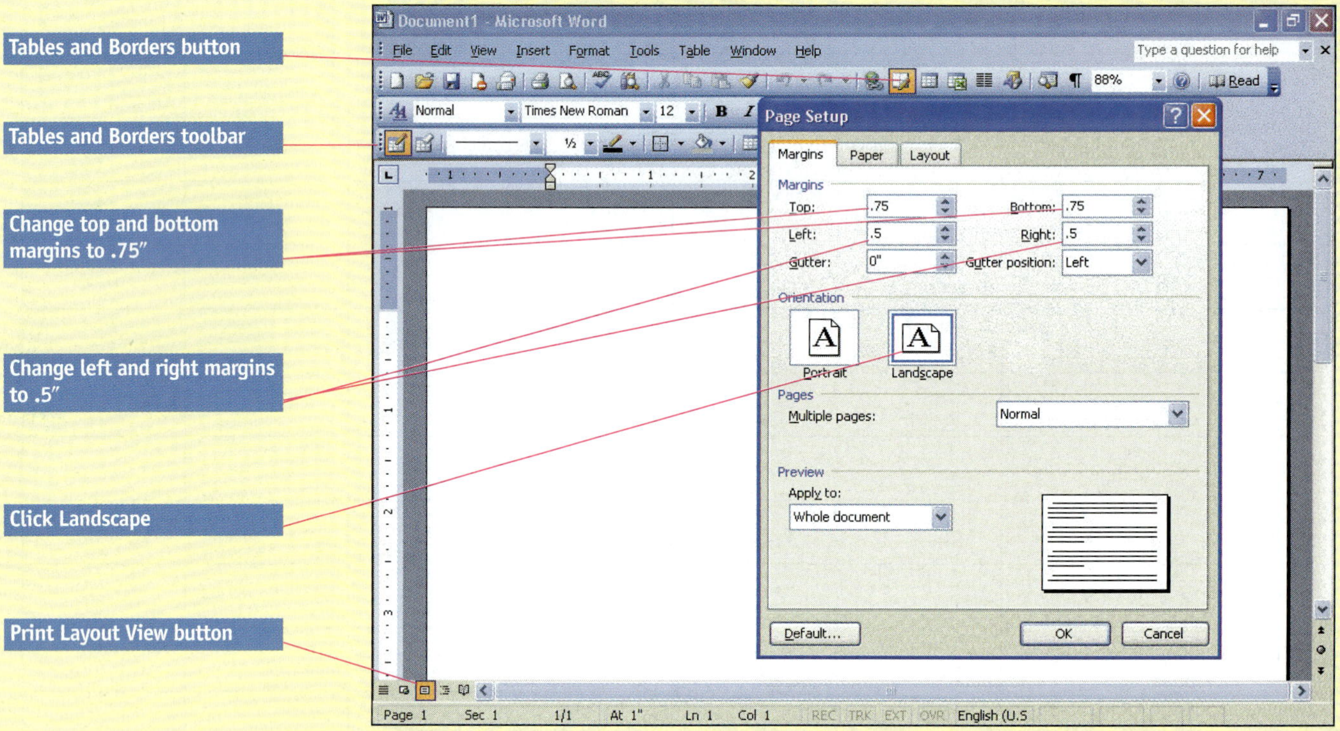

(a) The Page Setup Command (step 1)

FIGURE 4.4 Hands-on Exercise 2

Step 2: Create the Table

- Pull down the **Table menu**, click **Insert**, and click **Table** to display the dialog box in Figure 4.4b. Enter **8** and **12** as the number of columns and rows, respectively. Click **OK** and the table will be inserted into the document.
- Practice selecting various elements from the table, something that you will have to do in subsequent steps:
  - To select a single cell, click inside the left grid line (the pointer changes to an arrow when you are in the proper position).
  - To select a row, click outside the table to the left of the first cell in that row.
  - To select a column, click just above the top of the column (the pointer changes to a small black arrow).
  - To select adjacent cells, drag the mouse over the cells.
  - To select the entire table, drag the mouse over the table or click the box that appears at the upper left corner of the table.
- Click outside the table. Save the document.

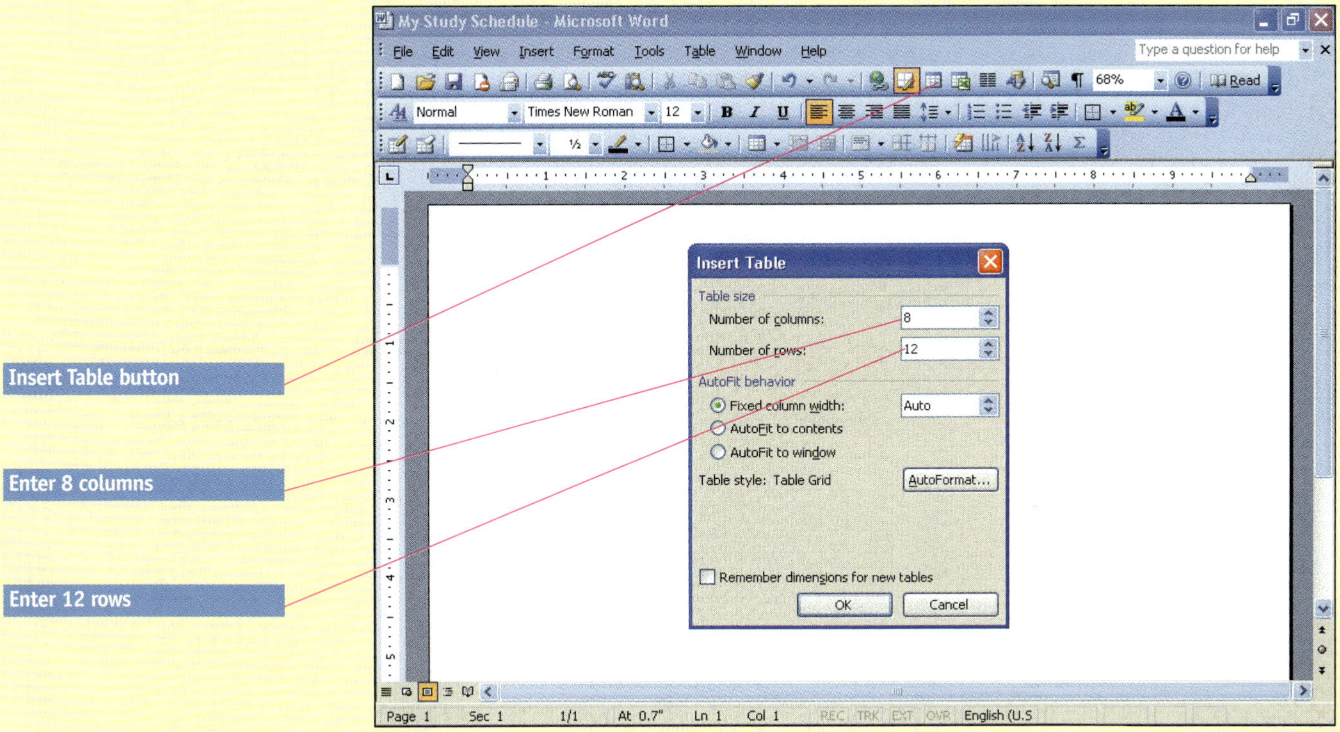

(b) Create the Table (step 2)

FIGURE 4.4 Hands-on Exercise 2 (*continued*)

TABS AND TABLES

The Tab key functions differently in a table than in a regular document. Press the Tab key to move to the next cell in the current row (or to the first cell in the next row if you are at the end of a row). Press Tab when you are in the last cell of a table to add a new blank row to the bottom of the table. Press Shift+Tab to move to the previous cell in the current row (or to the last cell in the previous row). You must press Ctrl+Tab to insert a regular tab character within a cell.

Step 3: Merge the Cells

- This step merges the cells in the first and last rows of the table. Click outside the table to the left of the first cell in the first row to select the entire first row as shown in Figure 4.4c.
- Pull down the **Table menu** and click **Merge Cells** (or click the **Merge Cells button** on the Tables and Borders toolbar). Click in the second row to deselect the first row, which now consists of a single cell.
- Click in the merged cell. Type **Weekly Class and Study Schedule** and format the text in **24 point Arial bold**. Click the **Center button** on the Formatting toolbar to center the title of the table.
- Click outside the table to the left of the first cell in the last row to select the entire row as shown in Figure 4.4c. Click the **Merge Cells button** on the Tables and Borders toolbar to merge these cells.
- Click outside the cell to deselect it, then click in the cell and type **Notes**. Press the **Enter key** five times. The height of the cell increases to accommodate the blank lines. Click and drag to select the text, then format the text in **12 point Arial bold**.
- Save the document.

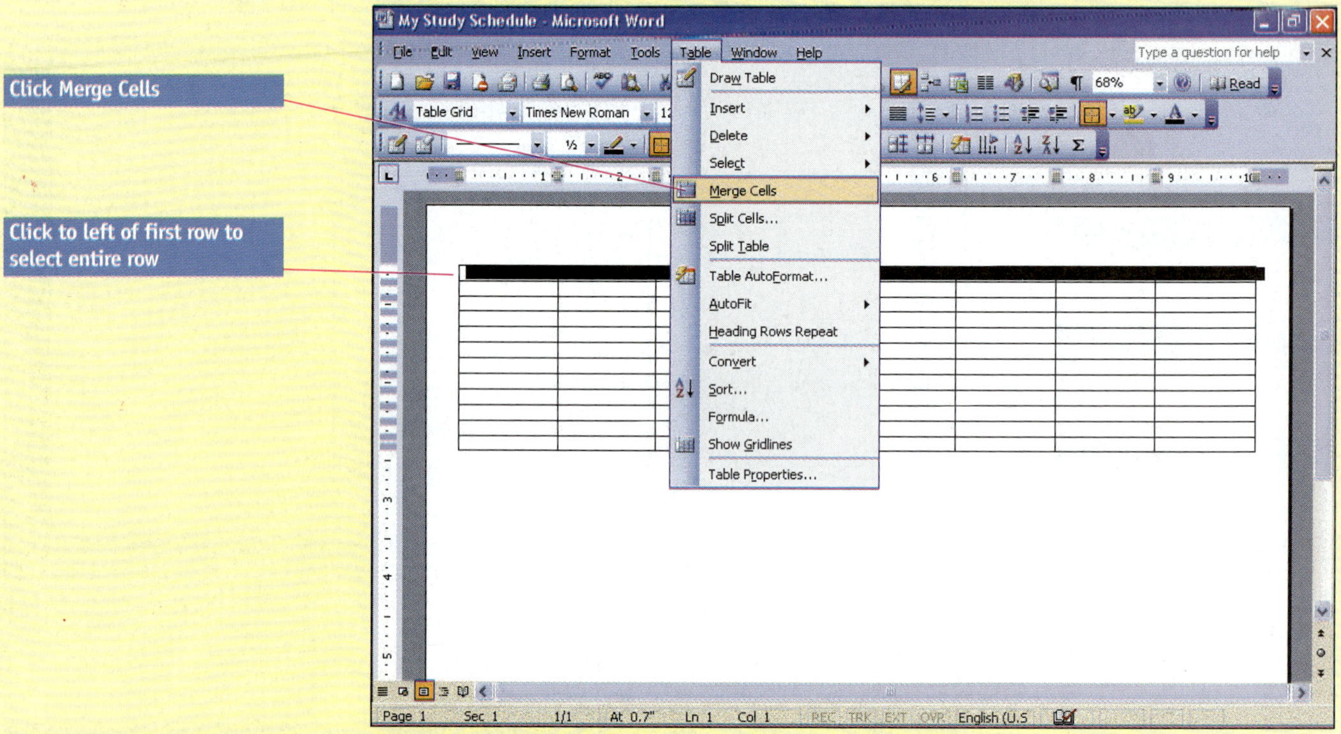

(c) Merge the Cells (step 3)

FIGURE 4.4 Hands-on Exercise 2 (*continued*)

SPLITTING A CELL

Splitting cells is the opposite of merging them. Click in any cell that you want to split, pull down the Table menu, and click the Split Cells command (or click the Split Cells button on the Tables and Borders toolbar) to display the associated dialog box. Enter the number of rows and columns that should appear after the split. Click OK to accept the settings and close the dialog box.

Step 4: Enter the Days and Hours

- Click the second cell in the second row. Type **Monday**. Press the **Tab** (or **right arrow**) **key** to move to the next cell. Type **Tuesday**. Continue until the days of the week have been entered.
- Select the entire row. Use the various tools on the Formatting toolbar to change the text to **10 point Arial Bold**. Click the **Center button** on the Formatting toolbar to center each day within the cell.
- Click the first cell in the third row. Type **8:00AM**. Press the **down arrow key** to move to the first cell in the fourth row. Type **9:00AM**. Continue to enter the hourly periods up to 4:00PM. Format as appropriate.
- Select the cells containing the hours of the day. Pull down the **Table menu**. Click **Table Properties**, then click the **Row tab** to display the Table Properties dialog box in Figure 4.4d.
- Click the **Specify height** check box. Click the **up arrow** until the height is **.5″**. Click the **drop-down arrow** on the Row height list box and select **Exactly**.
- Click the **Cell tab** in the Table Properties dialog box, then click the **Center button**. Click **OK** to accept the settings and close the dialog box. Save the document.

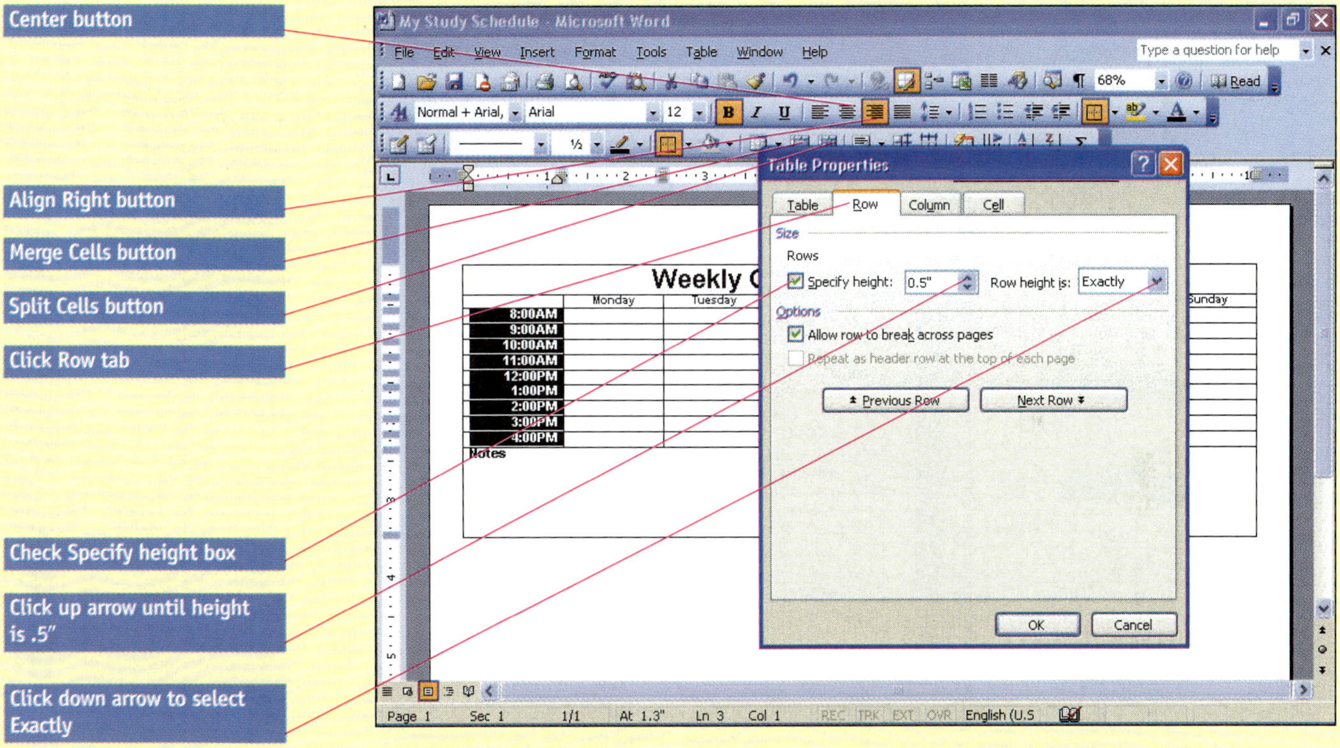

(d) Enter the Days and Hours (step 4)

FIGURE 4.4 Hands-on Exercise 2 (*continued*)

CONVERT TEXT TO A TABLE

The tables feature is outstanding. But what if you are given a lengthy list of items—for example, two items per line separated by a tab that should have been formatted as a table but weren't? All you have to do is convert the existing text to a table. Select the entire list, pull down the Table menu, click the Convert command, and click the Text to Table command. Click the Option button in the Separate text area of the dialog box, and click OK to create the table. (The command also works in reverse; i.e., you can also convert a table to text.)

Step 5: Borders and Shading

- Select (click) the cell containing the title of your table. Click the down arrow on the **Shading Color button** on the Tables and Borders toolbar to display a color palette, then choose a background color. We selected red.
- Click and drag to select the text within the cell. Click the **down arrow** on the **Font Color button** on the Formatting toolbar to display its palette, then choose **white** (that is, we want white letters on a dark background).
- Click and drag to select the first four cells under "Sunday", then click the **Merge Cells button** to merge these cells.
- Click the **down arrow** on the **Line Weight tool** and select **3** pt. Click the **down arrow** on the **Border Color tool** and select the same color you used to shade the first row.
- Click in the upper-left corner of the merged cell, then click and drag to draw a diagonal line as shown in Figure 4.4e. Click and drag to draw a second line to complete the cell.
- Save the document.

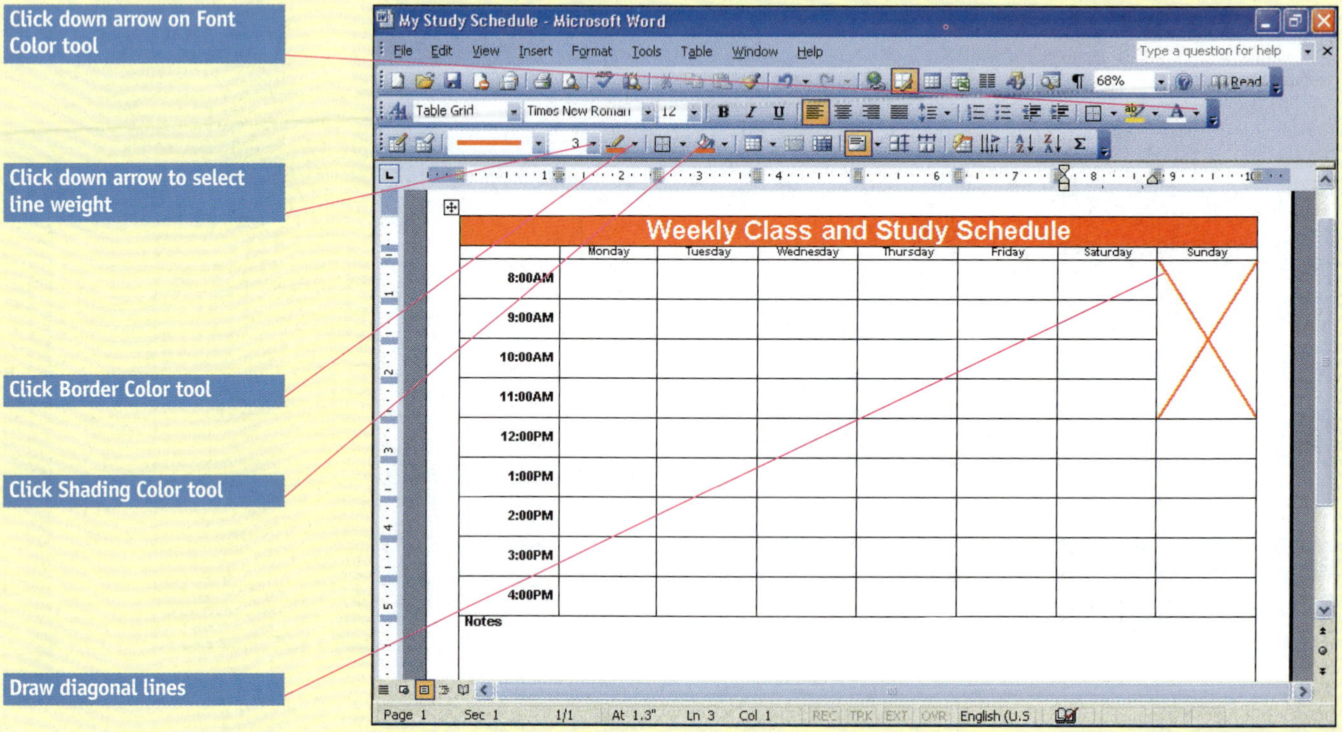

(e) Borders and Shading (step 5)

FIGURE 4.4 Hands-on Exercise 2 (*continued*)

THE AUTOFORMAT COMMAND

The AutoFormat command does not do anything that could not be done through individual formatting commands, but it does provide inspiration by suggesting attractive designs. Click anywhere in the table, pull down the Table menu, and click the Table AutoFormat command to display the associated dialog box. Choose (click) any style, click the Modify button if you want to change any aspect of the formatting, then click the Apply button to format your table in the selected style.

Step 6: Insert the Clip Art

- Click anywhere in the merged cell in the last row of the table. Pull down the **Insert menu**, click (or point to) **Picture**, then click **Clip Art**. The task pane opens and displays the Search pane as shown in Figure 4.4f.
- Click in the **Search** text box. Type **books** to search for any clip art image that is indexed with this keyword, then click the **Go button** or press **Enter**.
- The images are displayed in the task pane. Point to an image to display a drop-down arrow to its right. Click the arrow to display a context menu. Click **Insert** to insert the image into the document.
- Do not be concerned about the size or position of the image at this time as we adjust the parameters in the next step.
- Close the task pane. Save the document.

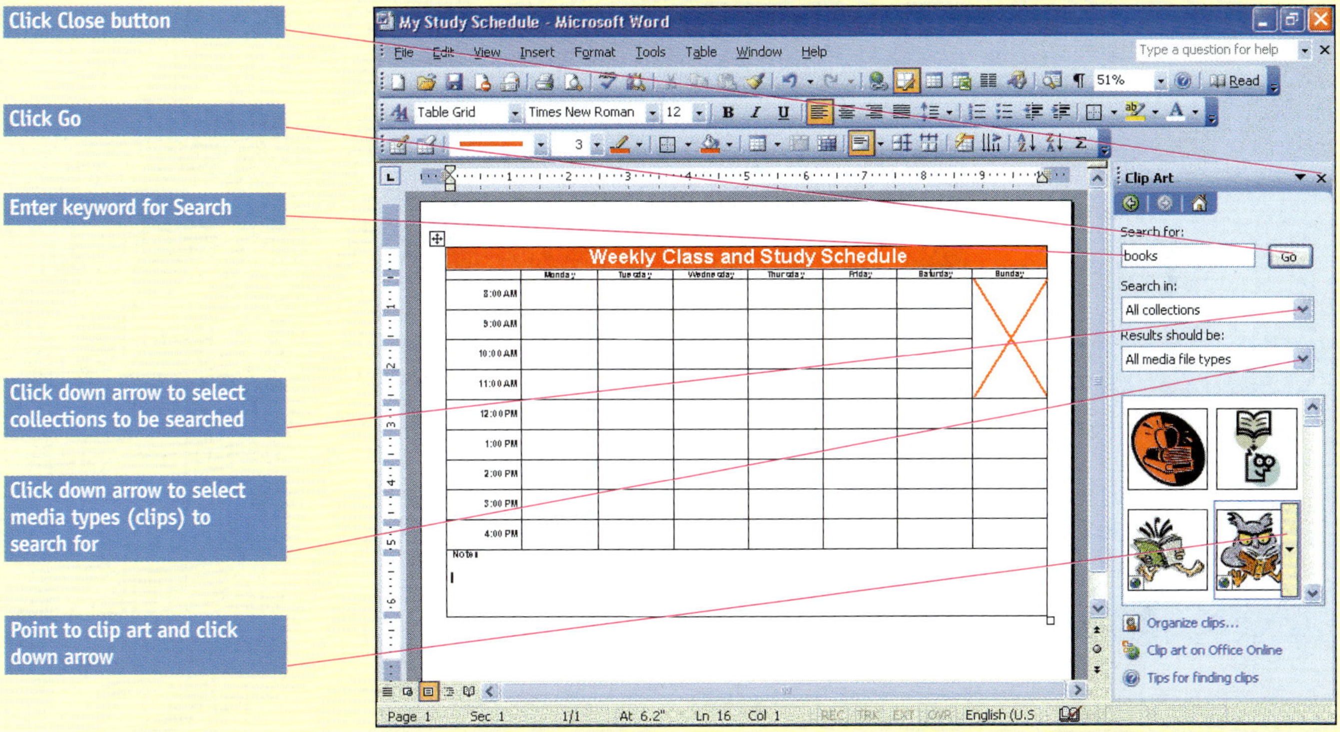

(f) Insert the Clip Art (step 6)

FIGURE 4.4 Hands-on Exercise 2 (*continued*)

SEARCHING FOR CLIP ART

The Clip Art task pane helps you to search for an appropriate media object. Click the down arrow in the Search for list box and choose all collections (including those on the Microsoft Web site). Click the down arrow in the Results should be list box and choose All media file types, then click the Go button to initiate the search. The search may take longer than previously since it includes the Web, but you should have a much larger selection of potential clips from which to choose. If necessary, use the drop-down arrow on either list box to limit the search as you see fit.

Step 7: The Finishing Touches

- Select the newly inserted clip art to display the Picture toolbar, then click the **Format Picture button** to display the Format Picture dialog box. Click the **Layout tab** and choose the **Square layout**. Click **OK** to close the dialog box.
- Select (click) the clip art to display its sizing handles as shown in Figure 4.4g. Move and size the image as necessary within its cell.
- Click anywhere in the first row of the table. Pull down the **Table menu** and click the **Table Properties command** to display the associated dialog box. Change the row height to exactly **.5 inch**. Click **OK**.
- Click the **down arrow** next to the **Align button** on the Tables and Borders toolbar and select **center alignment** to center the text vertically.
- Use the **Table Properties command** to change the row height of the second row to **.25 inch**. Center these entries vertically as well.
- Save the document, then print it for your instructor. Exit Word if you do not want to continue with the next exercise at this time.

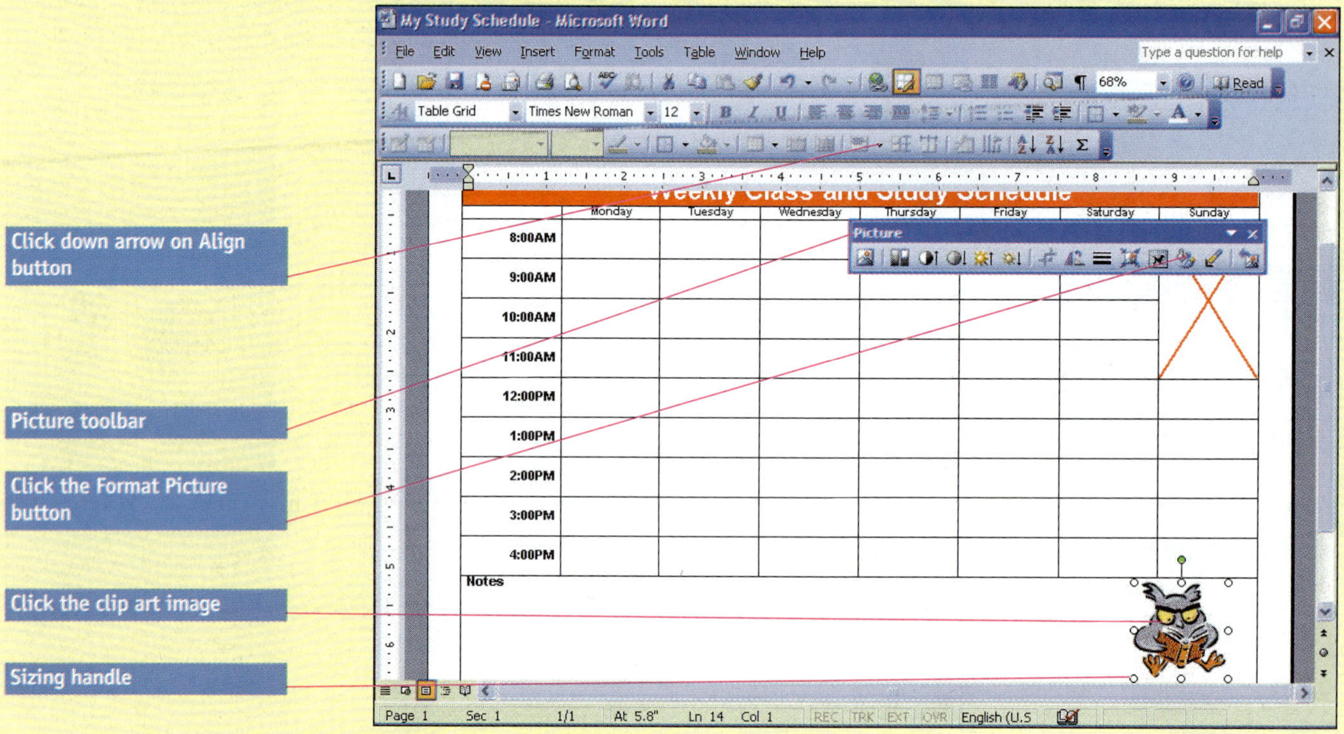

(g) The Finishing Touches (step 7)

FIGURE 4.4 Hands-on Exercise 2 (*continued*)

INSERTING OR DELETING ROWS AND COLUMNS

You can insert or delete rows and columns after a table has been created. To insert a row, click in any cell above or below where the new row should go, pull down the Table menu, click the Insert command, then choose Rows above or below as appropriate. Follow a similar procedure to insert a column, choosing whether you want the new column to go to the left or right of the selected cell.

STYLES

One characteristic of a professional document is the uniform formatting that is applied to similar elements throughout the document. Different elements have different formatting. Headings may be set in one font, color, style, and size, and the text under those headings may be set in a completely different design. The headings may be left aligned, while the text is fully justified. Lists and footnotes can be set in entirely different styles.

One way to achieve uniformity throughout the document is to use the Format Painter to copy the formatting from one occurrence of each element to the next, but this is tedious and inefficient. And if you were to change your mind after copying the formatting throughout a document, you would have to repeat the entire process all over again. A much easier way to achieve uniformity is to store the formatting information as a ***style***, then apply that style to multiple occurrences of the same element within the document. Change the style and you automatically change all text defined by that style.

Styles are created on the character or paragraph level. A ***character style*** stores character formatting (font, size, and style) and affects only the selected text. A ***paragraph style*** stores paragraph formatting (such as alignment, line spacing, indents, tabs, text flow, and borders and shading, as well as the font, size, and style of the text in the paragraph). A paragraph style affects the current paragraph or multiple paragraphs if several paragraphs are selected. Styles are created and applied through the ***Styles and Formatting command*** in the Format menu as shown in Figure 4.5.

The document in Figure 4.5a consists of multiple tips for Microsoft Word. Each tip begins with a one-line heading, followed by the associated text. The task pane in the figure displays all of the styles that are in use in the document. The ***Normal style*** contains the default paragraph settings (left aligned, single spacing, and a default font) and is automatically assigned to every paragraph unless a different style is specified. The Clear Formatting style removes all formatting from selected text. It is the ***Heading 1*** and ***Body Text styles***, however, that are of interest to us, as these styles have been applied throughout the document to the associated elements. (The style assignments are done automatically through the AutoFormat command as will be explained shortly.)

The specifications for the Heading 1 and Body Text styles are shown in Figures 4.5b and 4.5c, respectively. The current settings within the Heading 1 style call for 16 point Arial bold type in blue. The text is left justified, and the heading will always appear on the same page as the next paragraph. The Body Text style is in 10 point Times New Roman and is fully justified. The preview box in both figures shows how paragraphs formatted in the style will appear. You can change the specifications of either style using any combination of buttons or associated menu commands. (Clicking the Format button in either dialog box provides access to the various commands in the Format menu.) And as indicated earlier, any changes to the style are automatically reflected in all elements that are defined by that style.

Styles automate the formatting process and provide a consistent appearance to a document. Any type of character or paragraph formatting can be stored within a style, and once a style has been defined, it can be applied to multiple occurrences of the same element within a document to produce identical formatting.

STYLES AND PARAGRAPHS

A paragraph style affects the entire paragraph; that is, you cannot apply a paragraph style to only part of a paragraph. To apply a style to an existing paragraph, place the insertion point anywhere within the paragraph, pull down the Style list box on the Formatting toolbar, then click the name of the style you want.

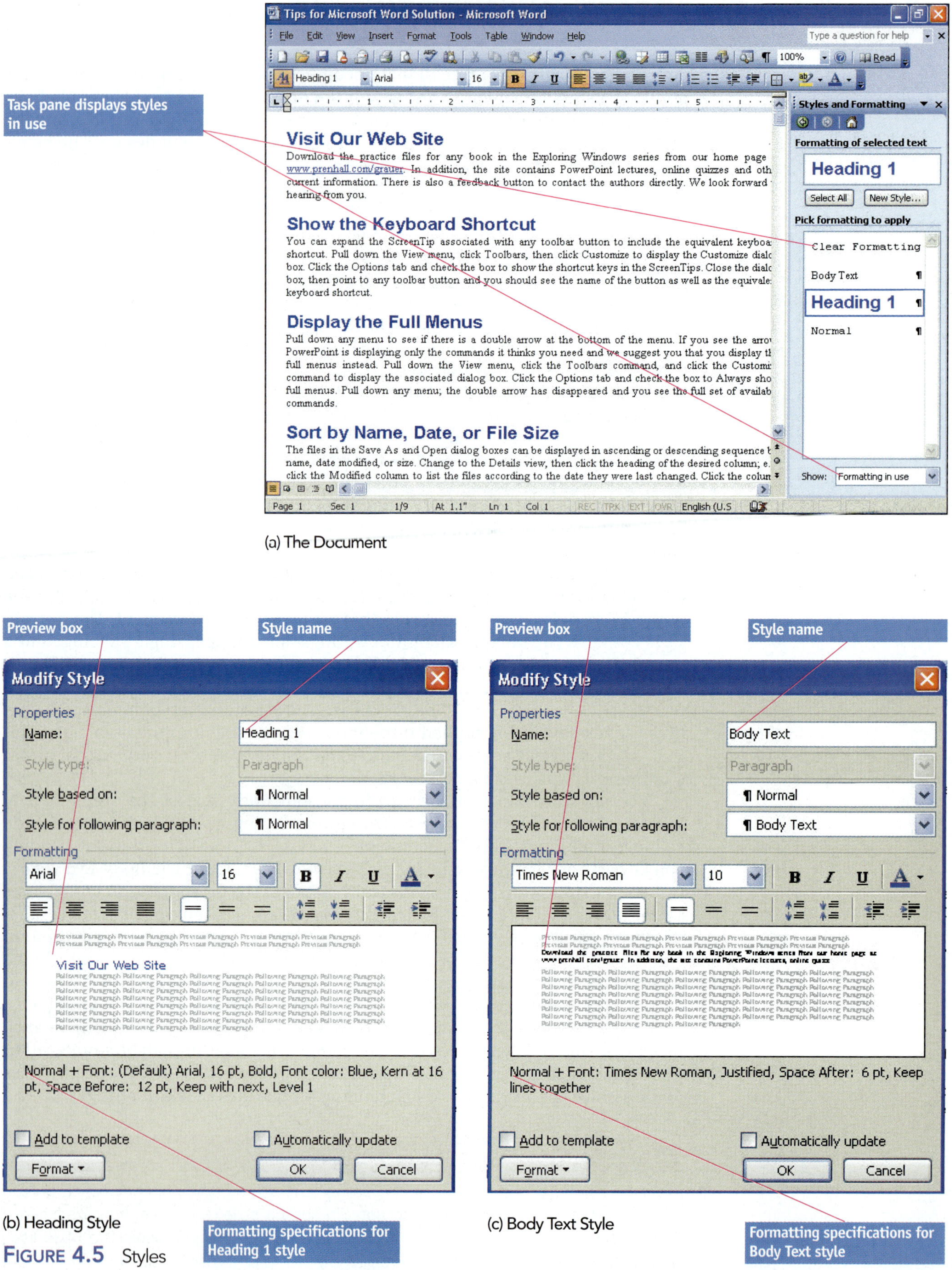

(a) The Document

(b) Heading Style

(c) Body Text Style

FIGURE 4.5 Styles

THE OUTLINE VIEW

One additional advantage of styles is that they enable you to view a document in the ***Outline view***. The Outline view does not display a conventional outline (such as the multilevel list created earlier in the chapter), but rather a structural view of a document that can be collapsed or expanded as necessary. Consider, for example, Figure 4.6, which displays the Outline view of a document that will be the basis of the next hands-on exercise. The document consists of a series of tips for Microsoft Word 2003. The heading for each tip is formatted according to the Heading 1 style. The text of each tip is formatted according to the Body Text style.

The advantage of the Outline view is that you can collapse or expand portions of a document to provide varying amounts of detail. We have, for example, collapsed almost the entire document in Figure 4.6, displaying the headings while suppressing the body text. We also expanded the text for two tips (Visit Our Web Site and Moving Within a Document) for purposes of illustration.

Now assume that you want to move the latter tip from its present position to immediately below the first tip. Without the Outline view, the text would stretch over two pages, making it difficult to see the text of both tips at the same time. Using the Outline view, however, you can collapse what you don't need to see, then simply click and drag the headings to rearrange the text within the document. The Outline view is very useful with long documents, but it requires the use of styles throughout the document.

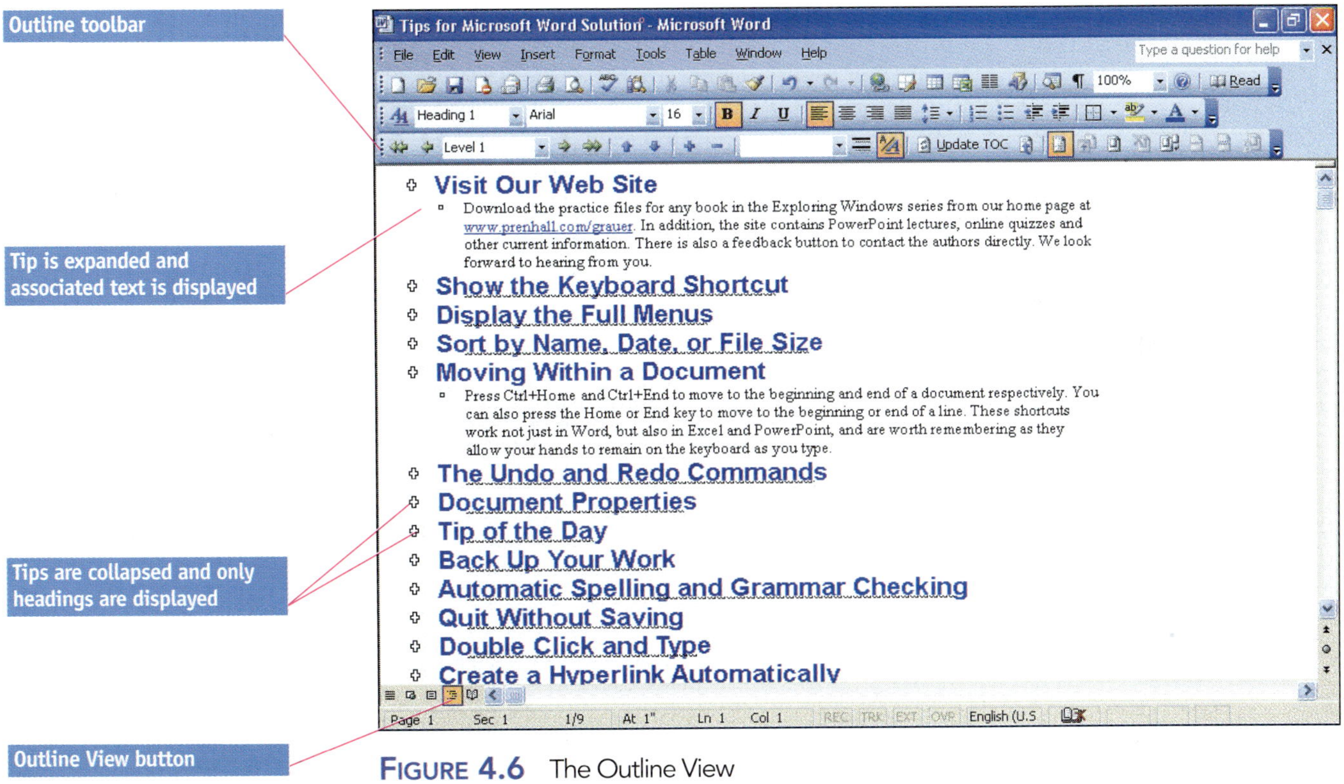

FIGURE 4.6 The Outline View

THE OUTLINE VERSUS THE OUTLINE VIEW

A conventional outline is created as a multilevel list within the Bullets and Numbering command. Text for the outline is entered in the Print Layout or Normal view, *not* the Outline view. The latter provides a condensed view of a document that is used in conjunction with styles.

The AutoFormat Command

Styles are extremely powerful. They enable you to impose uniform formatting within a document, and they let you take advantage of the Outline view. What if, however, you have an existing and/or lengthy document that does not contain any styles (other than the default Normal style, which is applied to every paragraph)? Do you have to manually go through every paragraph in order to apply the appropriate style? Fortunately the answer is no, because the AutoFormat command provides a quick solution.

The ***AutoFormat command*** enables you to format lengthy documents quickly, easily, and in a consistent fashion. In essence the command analyzes a document and formats it for you. Its most important capability is the application of styles to individual paragraphs; that is, the command goes through an entire document, determines how each paragraph is used, then applies an appropriate style to each paragraph. The formatting process assumes that one-line paragraphs are headings and applies the predefined Heading 1 style to those paragraphs. It applies the Body Text style to ordinary paragraphs and can also detect lists and apply a numbered or bulleted style to those lists.

The AutoFormat command will also add special touches to a document if you request those options. It can replace "ordinary quotation marks" with "smart quotation marks" that curl and face each other. It will replace ordinal numbers (1st, 2nd, or 3rd) with the corresponding superscripts (1st, 2nd, or 3rd), or common fractions (1/2 or 1/4) with typographical symbols (½ or ¼).

The AutoFormat command will also replace Internet references (Web addresses and e-mail addresses) with hyperlinks. It will recognize, for example, any entry beginning with http: or www. as a hyperlink and display the entry as underlined blue text (www.microsoft.com). This is not merely a change in formatting, but an actual hyperlink to a document on the Web or corporate Intranet. It also converts entries containing an @ sign, such as rgrauer@miami.edu to a hyperlink as well. (All Word documents are Web enabled. Unlike a Web document, however, you need to press and hold the Ctrl key to follow the link and display the associated page. This is different from what you usually do, because you normally just click a link to follow it. What if, however, you wanted to edit the link? Accordingly, Microsoft Word modifies the convention so that clicking a link enables you to edit the link.)

The various options for the AutoFormat command are controlled through the AutoCorrect Options command in the Tools menu. Once the options have been set, all formatting is done automatically by selecting the AutoFormat command from the Format menu. The changes are not final, however, as the command gives you the opportunity to review each formatting change individually, then accept the change or reject it as appropriate. (You can also format text automatically as it is entered according to the options specified under the AutoFormat As You Type tab.) The next exercise illustrates this powerful command.

AUTOMATIC BORDERS AND LISTS

The AutoFormat As You Type option applies sophisticated formatting as text is entered. It automatically creates a numbered list any time a number is followed by a period, tab, or right parenthesis (press Enter twice in a row to turn off the feature). It will also add a border to a paragraph any time you type three or more hyphens, equal signs, or underscores followed by the Enter key. Pull down the Tools menu, click the AutoCorrect Options command, then click the AutoFormat As You Type tab and select the desired features.

Styles

Objective To use the AutoFormat command to apply styles to an existing document; to modify existing styles; to create a new style. Use Figure 4.7 as a guide for the exercise.

Step 1: The AutoFormat Command

- Start Word. Open the document **Tips for Microsoft Word** in the **Exploring Word folder**. Save the document as **Tips for Microsoft Word Solution** so that you can return to the original if necessary.
- Press **Ctrl+Home** to move to the beginning of the document. Pull down the **Format menu**. Click **AutoFormat** to display the dialog box in Figure 4.7a.
- Click the **Options command button**. Be sure that every check box is selected to implement the maximum amount of automatic formatting. Click the **OK button** in the AutoCorrect dialog box to close the dialog box.
- If necessary, check the option to **AutoFormat now**, then click the **OK command button** to format the document.
- The status bar indicates the progress of the formatting operation, after which you will see a newly formatted document.
- Save the document.

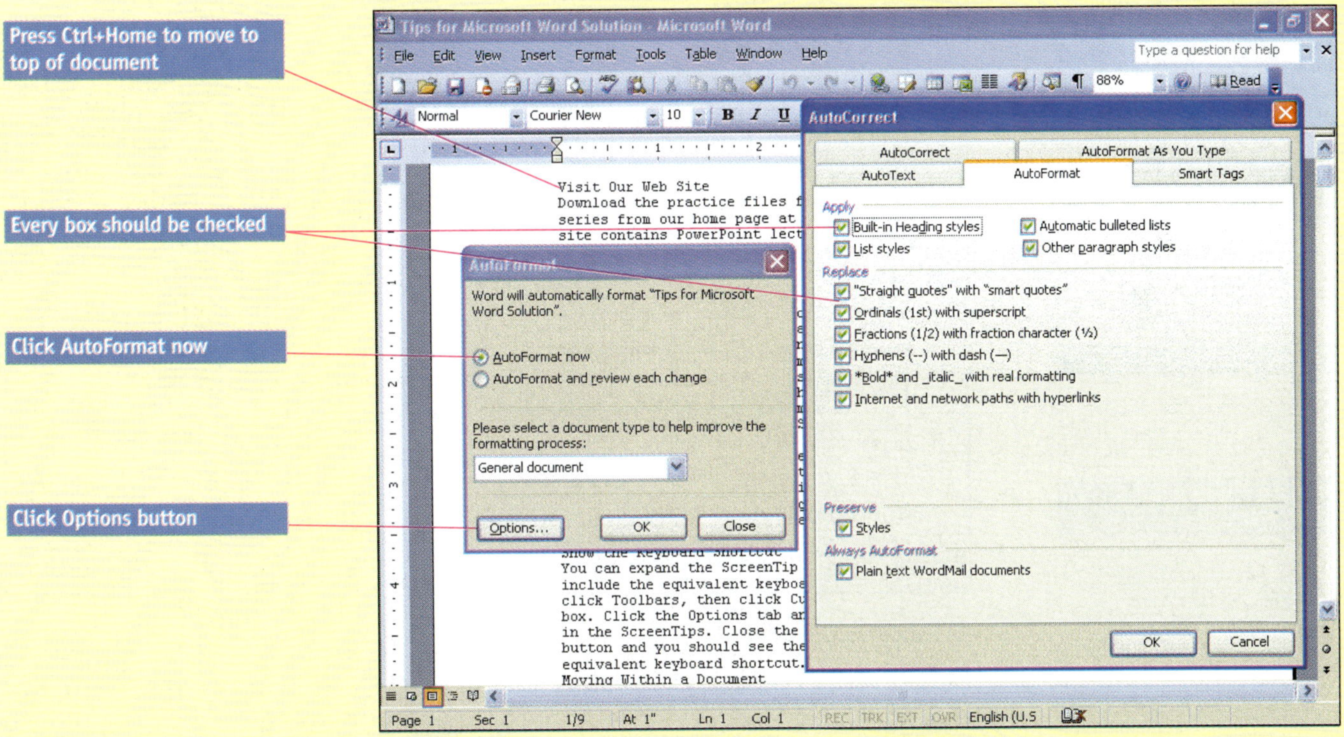

(a) The AutoFormat Command (step 1)

FIGURE 4.7 Hands-on Exercise 3

Step 2: Formatting Properties

- Pull down the **Format menu** and click the **Reveal Formatting command** to open the task pane as shown in Figure 4.7b.
- Press **Ctrl+Home** to move to the beginning of the document.
- The task pane displays the formatting properties for the first heading in your document. Heading 1 is specified as the paragraph style within the task pane. The name of the style for the selected text (Heading 1) also appears in the Style list box at the left of the Formatting toolbar.
- Click in the text of the first tip to view the associated formatting properties. This time Body Text is specified as the paragraph style in the task pane. Click the title of any tip and you will see the Heading 1 style in the Style box. Click the text of any tip and you will see the Body Text style in the Style box.
- Click the **down arrow** to the left of the Close button in the task pane and click **Styles and Formatting** to show the styles in your document. If necessary, click the **down arrow** in the Show list box to show **Formatting in use**.
- You should see the Heading 1 and Body Text styles and an option to clear formatting as the styles in your document.

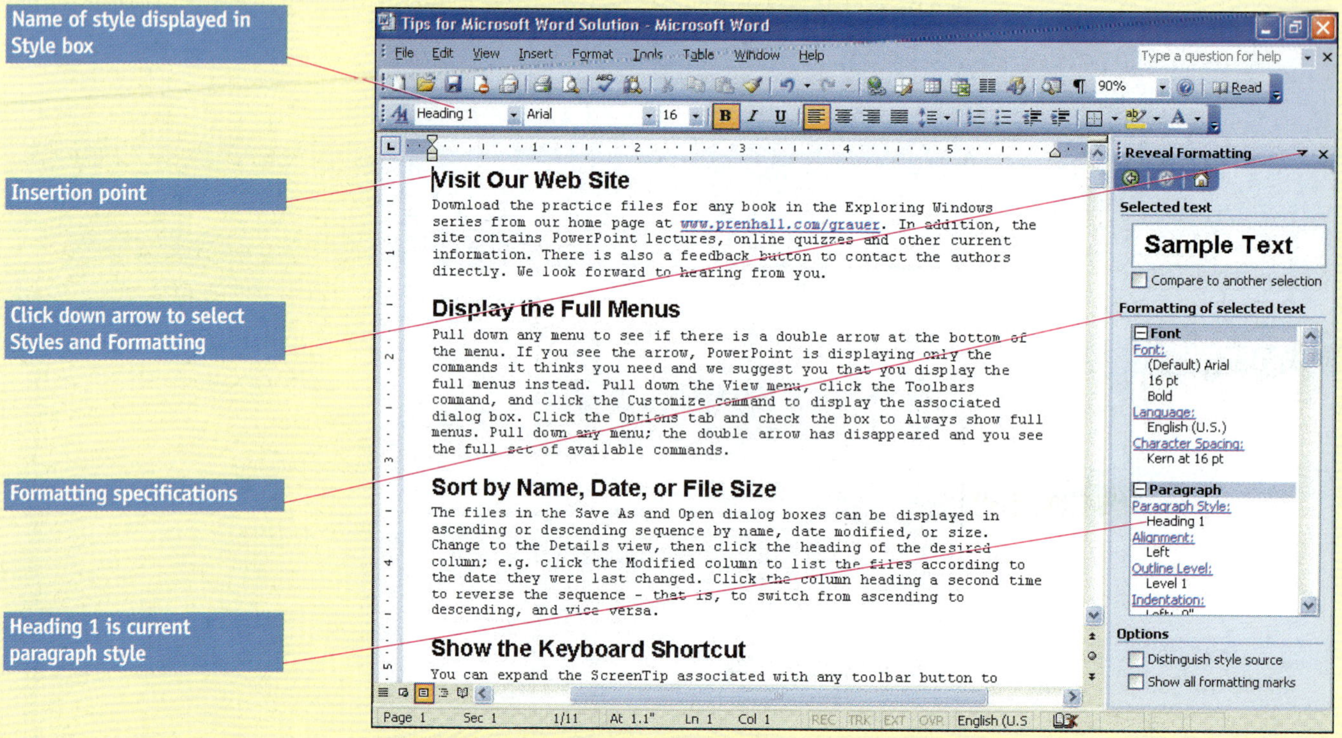

(b) Formatting Properties (step 2)

FIGURE 4.7 Hands-on Exercise 3 (*continued*)

STYLES AND THE AUTOFORMAT COMMAND

The AutoFormat command applies the Heading 1 and Body Text styles to single- and multiple-line paragraphs, respectively. Thus, all you have to do to change the appearance of the headings or paragraphs throughout the document is change the associated style. Change the Heading 1 style, for example, and you automatically change every heading throughout the document. Change the Body Text style and you change every paragraph.

Step 3: Modify the Body Text Style

- Point to the **Body Text style** in the task pane, click the **down arrow** that appears to display a context-sensitive menu, and click **Modify** to display the Modify Style dialog box.
- Click the **Justify button** to change the alignment of every Body Text paragraph in the document. Change the font to **Times New Roman**.
- Click the **down arrow** next to the **Format button**, then click **Paragraph** to display the Paragraph dialog box in Figure 4.7c. If necessary, click the **Line and Page Breaks tab**.
- The box for Widow/Orphan control is checked by default. This ensures that any paragraph defined by the Body Text style will not be split to leave a single line at the bottom or top of a page.
- Check the box to **Keep Lines Together**. This is a more stringent requirement and ensures that the entire paragraph is not split. Click **OK** to close the Paragraph dialog box. Click **OK** to close the Modify Style dialog box.
- All of the multiline paragraphs in the document change automatically to reflect the new definition of the Body Text style, which includes full justification, a new font, and ensures that the paragraph is not split across pages. Save the document.

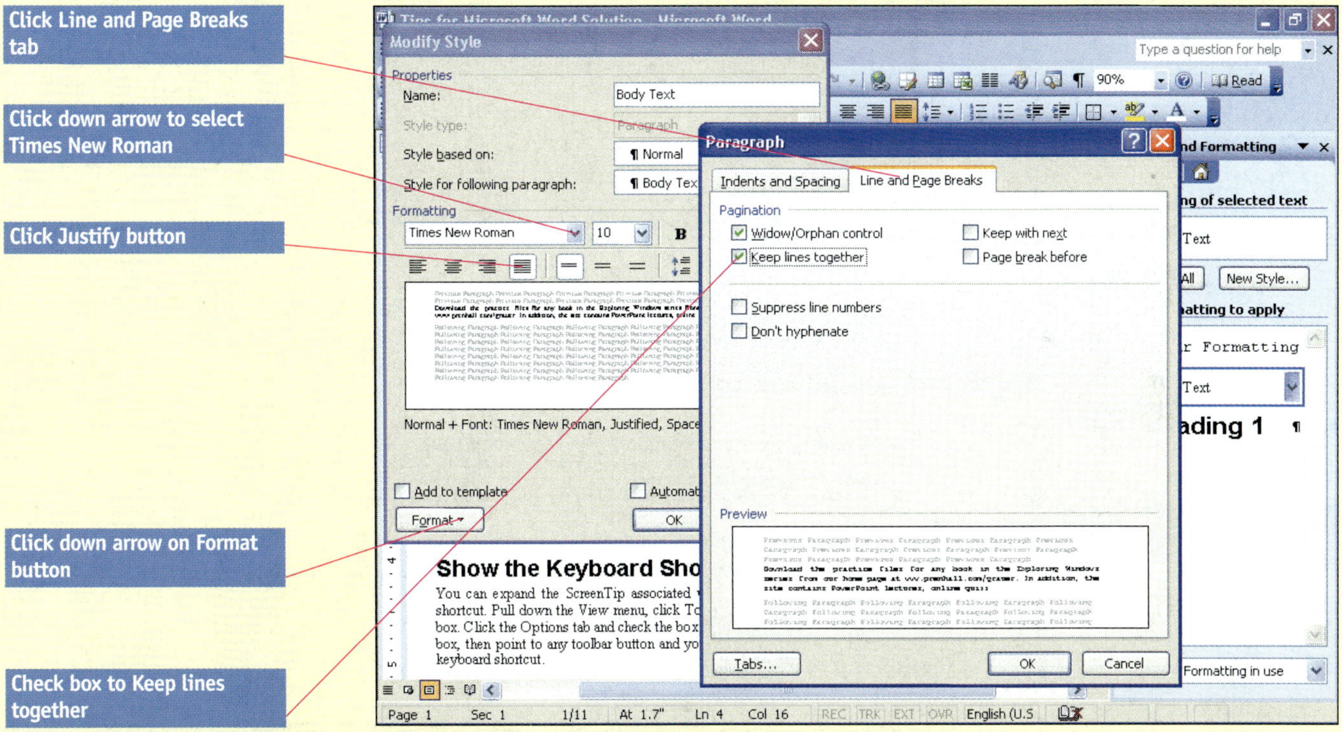

(c) Modify the Body Text Style (step 3)

FIGURE 4.7 Hands-on Exercise 3 (*continued*)

BE CAREFUL WHERE YOU CLICK

If you click the style name instead of the down arrow, you will apply the style to the selected text instead of modifying it. We know because we made this mistake. Click the Undo button to cancel the command. Click the down arrow next to the style name to display the associated menu, and click the Modify command to display the Modify Style dialog box.

Step 4: Modify the Heading 1 Style

- Point to the **Heading 1 style** in the task pane, click the **down arrow** that appears, then click **Modify** to display the Modify Style dialog box.
- Click the **Font Color drop-down arrow** to display the palette in Figure 4.7d. Click **Blue** to change the color of all of the headings in the document. The change will not take effect until you click the OK button to accept the settings and close the dialog box.
- Click the **Format button** toward the bottom of the dialog box, then click **Paragraph** to display the Paragraph dialog box. Click the **Indents and Spacing tab**. Change the **Spacing After** to **0**. Click **OK** to accept the settings and close the Paragraph dialog box.
- Click **OK** to close the Modify Style dialog box. The formatting in your document has changed to reflect the changes in the Heading 1 style.
- Save the document.

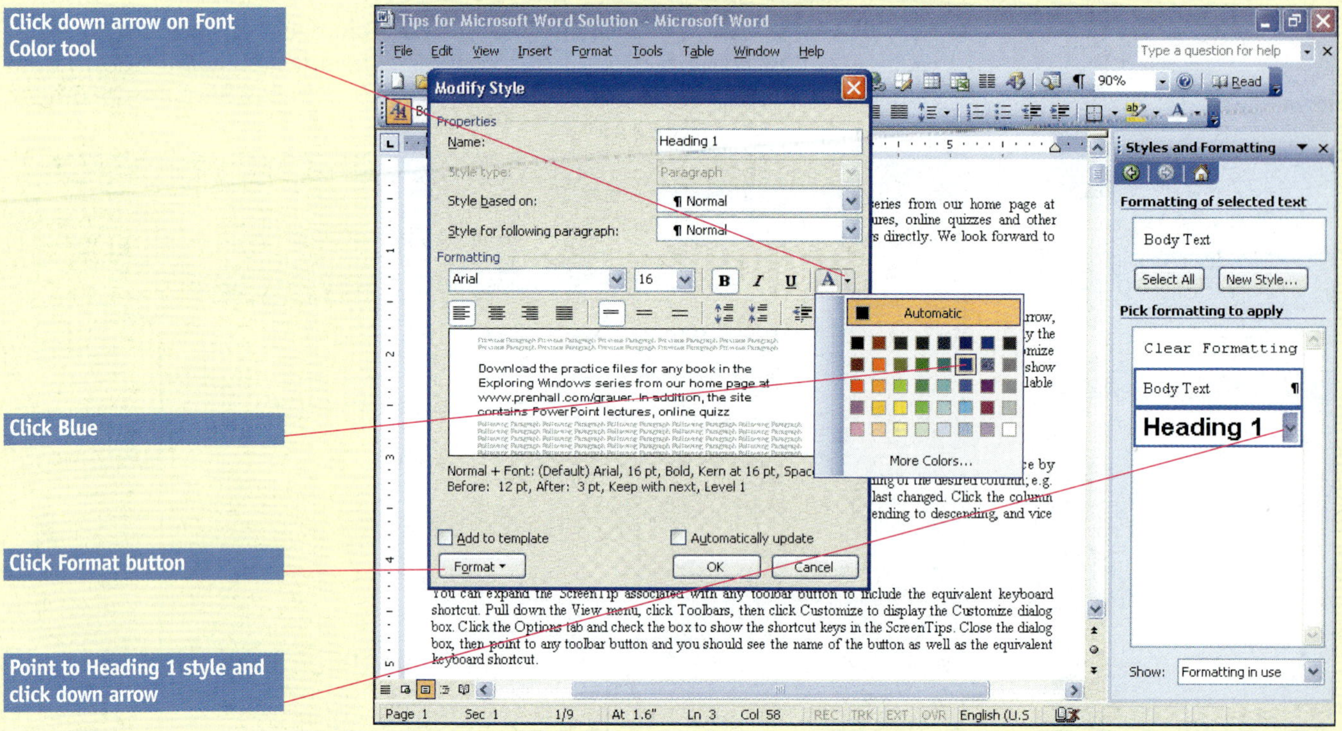

(d) Modify the Heading 1 Style (step 4)

FIGURE 4.7 Hands-on Exercise 3 (*continued*)

SPACE BEFORE AND AFTER

It's common practice to press the Enter key twice at the end of a paragraph (once to end the paragraph, and a second time to insert a blank line before the next paragraph). The same effect can be achieved by setting the spacing before or after the paragraph using the Spacing Before or After list boxes in the Format Paragraph command. The latter technique gives you greater flexibility in that you can specify any amount of spacing (e.g., 6 points) to leave only half a line before or after a paragraph. It also enables you to change the spacing between paragraphs more easily because the spacing information can be stored within the paragraph style.

Step 5: The Outline View

- Close the task pane. Pull down the **View menu** and click **Outline** (or click the **Outline View button** above the status bar) to display the document in Outline view.
- Pull down the **Edit menu** and click **Select All** (or press **Ctrl+A**) to select the entire document. Click the **Collapse button** on the Outlining toolbar to collapse the entire document so that only the headings are visible.
- If necessary, scroll down in the document until you can click in the heading of the tip entitled "Show the Keyboard Shortcut" as shown in Figure 4.7e. Click the **Expand button** on the Outlining toolbar to see the subordinate items under this heading.
- Click and drag to select the tip **Show the Keyboard Shortcut** (title and text). Point to the **plus sign** next to the selected tip (the mouse pointer changes to a double arrow), then click and drag to move the tip toward the top of the document, immediately below the first tip. Release the mouse.
- Save the document.

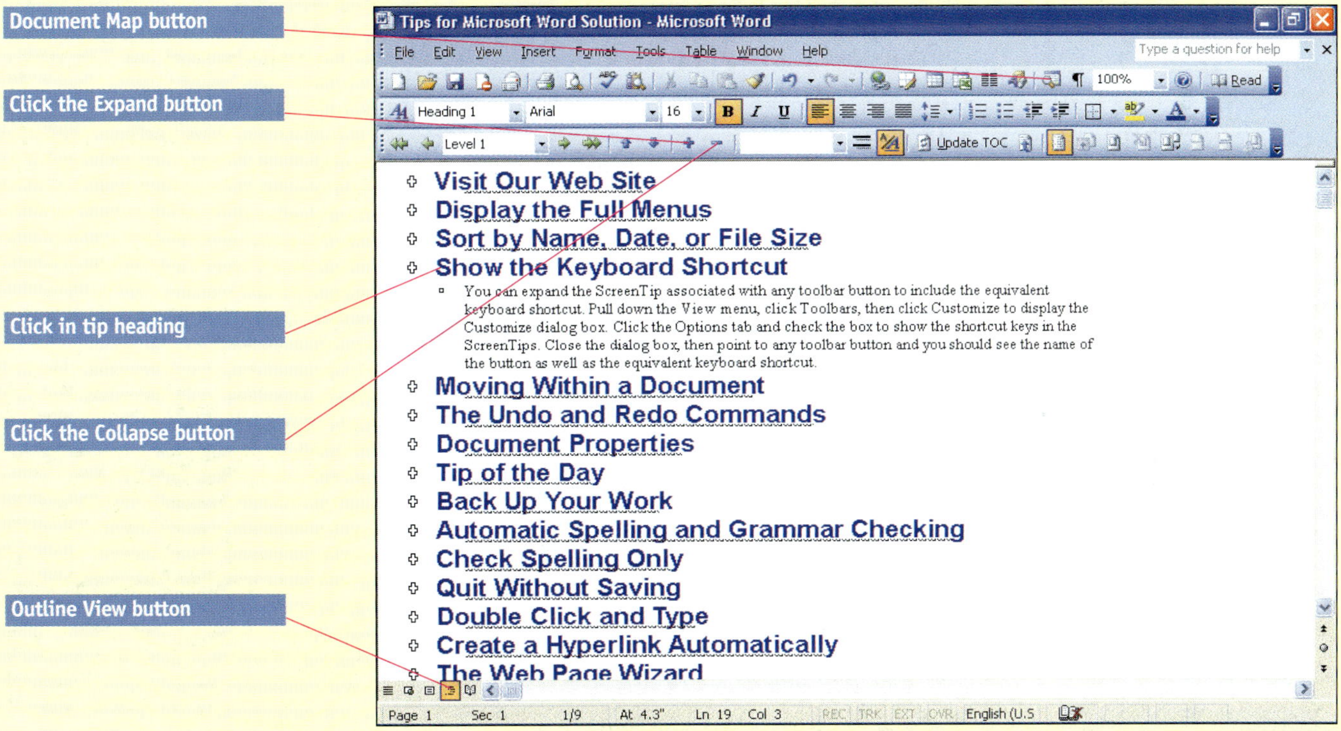

(e) The Outline View (step 5)

FIGURE 4.7 Hands-on Exercise 3 (*continued*)

THE DOCUMENT MAP

The Document Map helps you to navigate within a large document. Click the Document Map button on the Standard toolbar to divide the screen into two panes. The headings in a document are displayed in the left pane, and the text of the document is visible in the right pane. To go to a specific point in a document, click its heading in the left pane, and the insertion point is moved automatically to that point in the document, which is visible in the right pane. Click the Map button a second time to turn the feature off.

Step 6: Create a Paragraph Style

- Pull down the **View menu** and change to the **Normal view**. Pull down the **Format menu** and click **Styles and Formatting** to open the task pane as shown in Figure 4.7f.
- Press **Ctrl+Home** to move the insertion point to the beginning of the document, then press **Ctrl+Enter** to create a page break for a title page.
- Press the **up arrow** to move the insertion point to the left of the page break. Press the **Enter key** twice and press the **up arrow** to move above the page break. Select the two blank lines and click **Clear Formatting** in the task pane. Press the **up arrow**.
- Enter the title of the document, **Tips for Microsoft Word**. Change the text to **24 point Arial Bold** in **blue**. Click the **Center button** on the Formatting toolbar. Press **Enter**.
- The task pane displays the specifications for the text you just entered. You have created a new style, but the style is as yet unnamed. Point to the specification for the title (Arial, 24 pt, Centered) to display a down arrow, then click the arrow as shown in Figure 4.7f.
- Click the **Modify Style command** to display the Modify Style dialog box. Click in the **Name** text box in the Properties area and enter **Report Title** (the name of the new style). Click **OK**.
- Enter your name below the report title. Add a second line that references the authors of the textbook, Robert Grauer and Maryann Barber. Use a smaller point size. Name the associated style **Report Author**.
- Save the document.

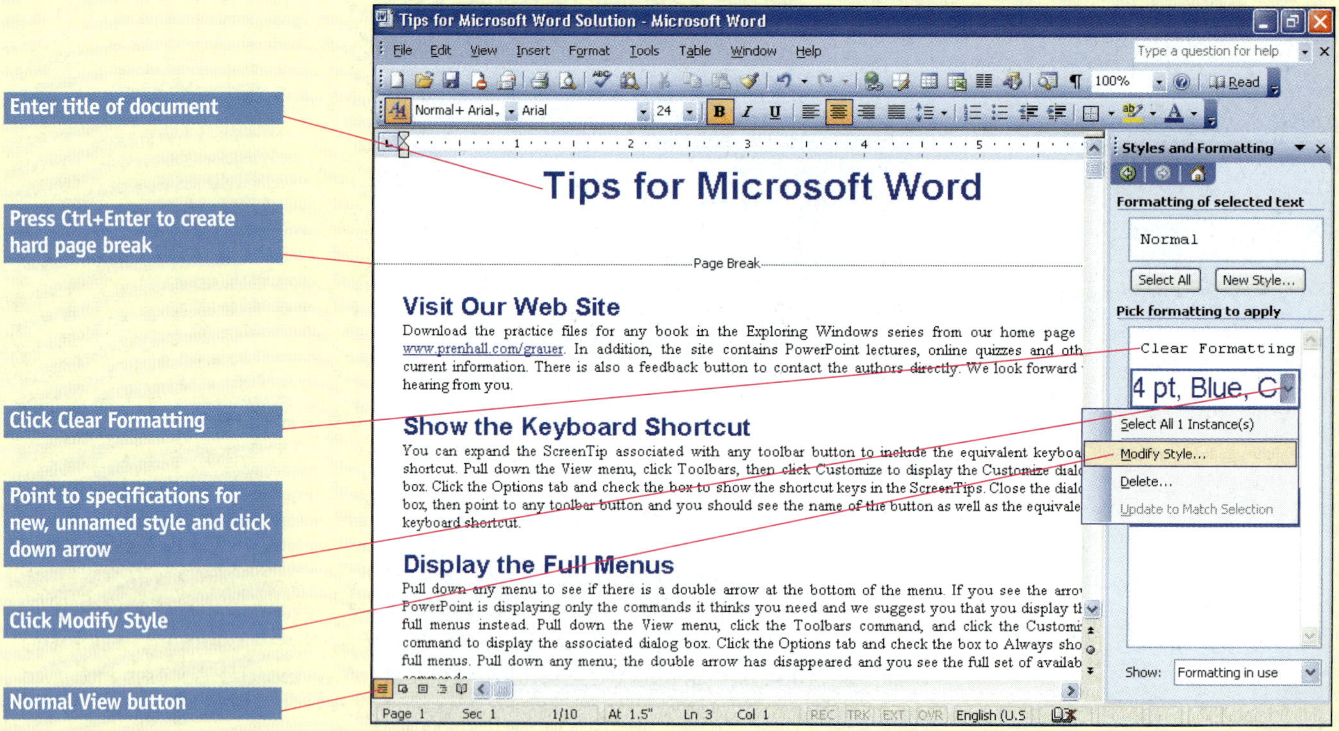

(f) Create a Paragraph Style (step 6)

FIGURE 4.7 Hands-on Exercise 3 (*continued*)

Step 7: Create a Character Style

- Click and drag to select the words **ScreenTip** (that appear within the second tip). Click the **Bold** and **Italic buttons** on the Formatting toolbar so that the selected text appears in bold and italics.
- Once again, you have created a style as can be seen in the task pane. Point to the right of the formatting specification in the task pane, click the **down arrow**, then click the **Modify Style command** to display the Modify Style dialog box in Figure 4.7g.
- Click in the **Name** text box in the Properties area and enter **Emphasize** as the name of the style. Click the **down arrow** in the Style type list box and select **Character**. Click **OK**.
- Click and drag to select the words **practice files** that appear in the first tip, click the **down arrow** in the Style list box on the Formatting toolbar, and apply the newly created Emphasize character style to the selected text.
- Save the document. Close the task pane.

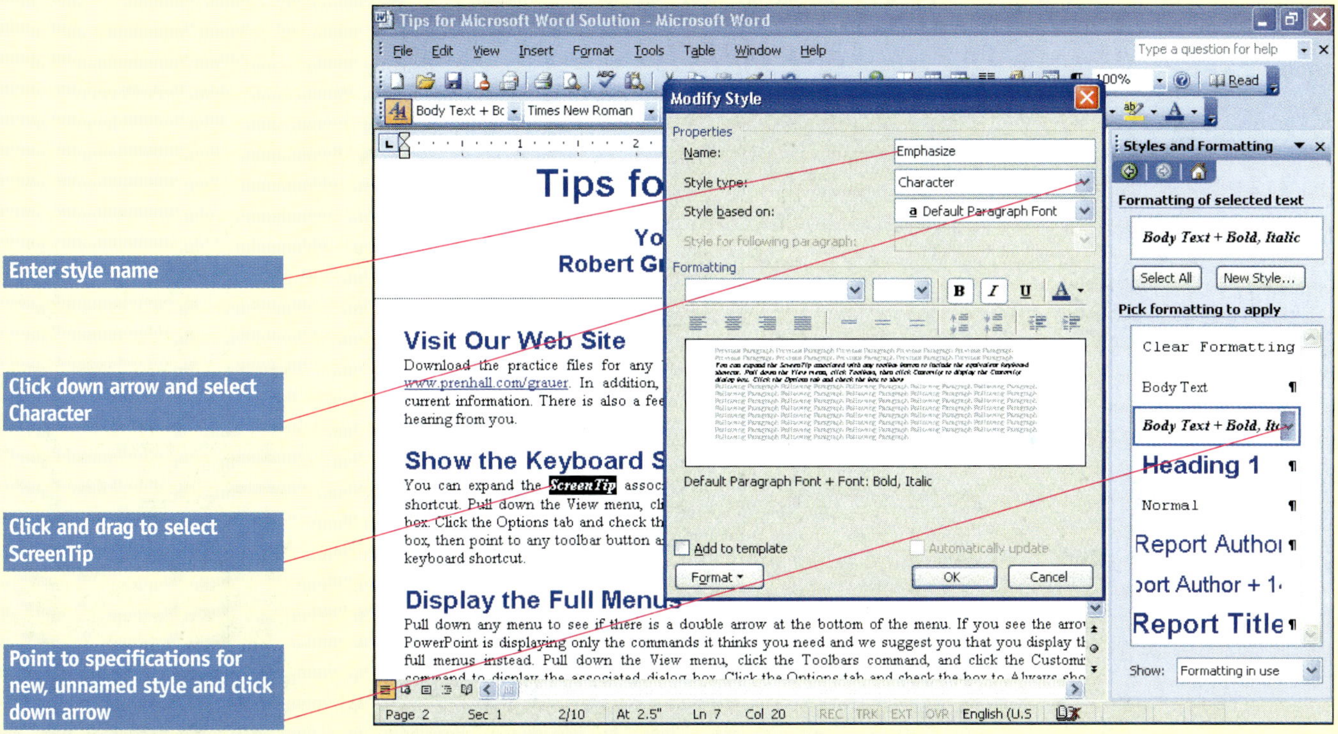

(g) Create a Character Style (step 7)

FIGURE 4.7 Hands-on Exercise 3 (*continued*)

SHOW THE KEYBOARD SHORTCUT

You can expand the ScreenTip associated with any toolbar button to include the equivalent keyboard shortcut. Pull down the View menu, click Toolbars, then click Customize to display the Customize dialog box. Click the Options tab and check the box to Show the shortcut keys in the ScreenTips. Close the dialog box, then point to any toolbar button, and you should see the name of the button as well as the equivalent keyboard shortcut. There is no need to memorize the shortcuts, but they do save time.

Step 8: The Completed Document

- Change to the **Print Layout view**. Pull down the **View menu** and click the **Zoom command** to display the Zoom dialog box. Click the option button next to **Many Pages**, then click and drag the monitor icon to display **two rows of five pages** (2 × 5) on the same screen. Click **OK**.
- You should see a multipage display similar to Figure 4.7h. The text on the individual pages is too small to read, but you can see the page breaks and overall document flow.
- The various tips should all be justified. Moreover, each tip should fit completely on one page without spilling over to the next page according to the specifications in the Body Text style.
- Click above the title on the first page and press the **Enter key** (if necessary) to position the title further down the page. Conversely, you could press the **Del key** to remove individual lines and move the title up the page.
- Save the document. Print the document only if you do not intend to do the next hands-on exercise. Exit Word if you do not want to continue with the next exercise at this time.

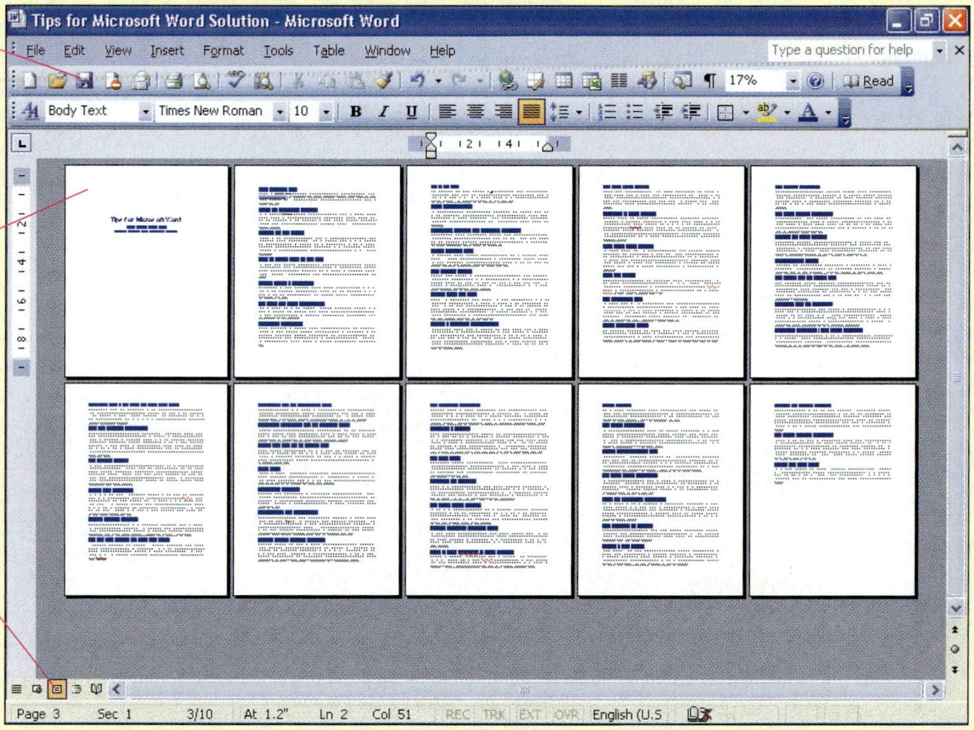

(h) The Completed Document (step 8)

FIGURE 4.7 Hands-on Exercise 3 (*continued*)

PRINT SELECTED PAGES

Why print an entire document if you want only a few pages? Pull down the File menu and click Print as you usually do, to initiate the printing process. Click the Pages option button, then enter the page numbers and/or page ranges you want; for example, 3, 6-8 will print page three and pages six through eight. You can also print multiple copies by entering the appropriate number in the Number of copies list box.

WORKING IN LONG DOCUMENTS

Long documents, such as term papers or reports, require additional formatting for better organization. These documents typically contain page numbers, headers and/or footers, a table of contents, and an index. Each of these elements is discussed in turn and will be illustrated in a hands-on exercise.

Page Numbers

The ***Insert Page Numbers command*** is the easiest way to place ***page numbers*** into a document and is illustrated in Figure 4.8. The page numbers can appear at the top or bottom of a page, and can be left, centered, or right aligned. Word provides additional flexibility in that you can use Roman rather than Arabic numerals, and you need not start at page number one.

The Insert Page Number command is limited, however, in that it does not provide for additional text next to the page number. You can overcome this restriction by creating a header or footer that contains the page number.

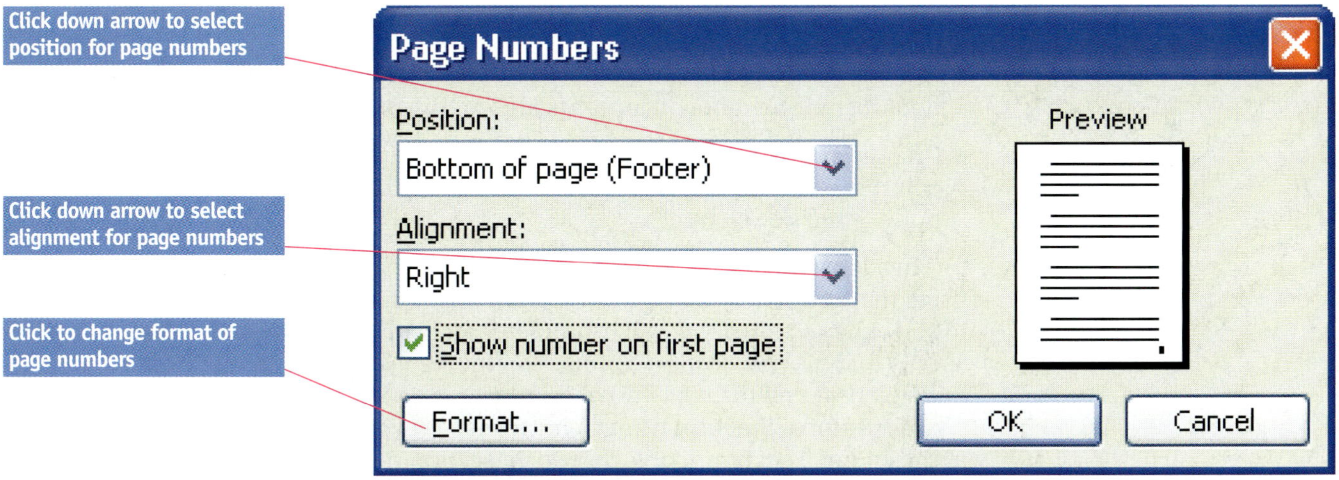

FIGURE 4.8 Page Numbers

Headers and Footers

Headers and footers give a professional appearance to a document. A ***header*** consists of one or more lines that are printed at the top of every page. A ***footer*** is printed at the bottom of the page. A document may contain headers but not footers, footers but not headers, or both headers and footers.

Headers and footers are created from the View menu. (A simple header or footer is also created automatically by the Insert Page Number command, depending on whether the page number is at the top or bottom of a page.) Headers and footers are formatted like any other paragraph and can be centered, left or right aligned. They can be formatted in any typeface or point size and can include special codes to automatically insert the page number, date, and/or time a document is printed.

The advantage of using a header or footer (over typing the text yourself at the top or bottom of every page) is that you type the text only once, after which it appears automatically according to your specifications. In addition, the placement of the headers and footers is adjusted for changes in page breaks caused by the insertion or deletion of text in the body of the document.

Headers and footers can change continually throughout a document. The Page Setup dialog box (in the File menu) enables you to specify a different header or footer for the first page, and/or different headers and footers for the odd and even pages. If, however, you wanted to change the header (or footer) midway through a document, you would need to insert a section break at the point where the new header (or footer) is to begin.

Sections

Formatting in Word occurs on three levels. You are already familiar with formatting at the character and paragraph levels that have been used throughout the text. Formatting at the section level controls headers and footers, page numbering, page size and orientation, margins, and columns. All of the documents in the text so far have consisted of a single ***section***, and thus any section formatting applied to the entire document. You can, however, divide a document into sections and format each section independently.

Formatting at the section level gives you the ability to create more sophisticated documents. You can use section formatting to do the following:

- Change the margins within a multipage letter, where the first page (the letterhead) requires a larger top margin than the other pages in the letter.
- Change the orientation from portrait to landscape to accommodate a wide table at the end of the document.
- Change the page numbering to use Roman numerals at the beginning of the document for a table of contents and Arabic numerals thereafter.
- Change the number of columns in a newsletter, which may contain a single column at the top of a page for the masthead, then two or three columns in the body of the newsletter.

In all instances, you determine where one section ends and another begins by using the ***Insert menu*** to create a ***section break***. You also have the option of deciding how the section break will be implemented on the printed page; that is, you can specify that the new section continue on the same page, that it begin on a new page, or that it begin on the next odd or even page even if a blank page has to be inserted.

Word stores the formatting characteristics of each section in the section break at the end of a section. Thus, deleting a section break also deletes the section formatting, causing the text above the break to assume the formatting characteristics of the next section.

Figure 4.9 displays a multipage view of a ten-page document. The document has been divided into two sections, and the insertion point is currently on the fourth page of the document (page four of ten), which is also the first page of the second section. Note the corresponding indications on the status bar and the position of the headers and footers throughout the document.

Figure 4.9 also displays the Header and Footer toolbar, which contains various icons associated with these elements. As indicated, a header or footer may contain text and/or special codes—for example, the word "page" followed by a code for the page number. The latter is inserted into the header by clicking the appropriate button on the Header and Footer toolbar. Remember, headers and footers are implemented at the section level. Thus, changing a header or footer within a document requires the insertion of a section break.

Table of Contents

A ***table of contents*** lists headings in the order they appear in a document and the page numbers where the entries begin. Word will create the table of contents automatically, provided you have identified each heading in the document with a built-in heading style (Heading 1 through Heading 9). Word will also update the table automatically to accommodate the addition or deletion of headings and/or changes in page numbers brought about through changes in the document.

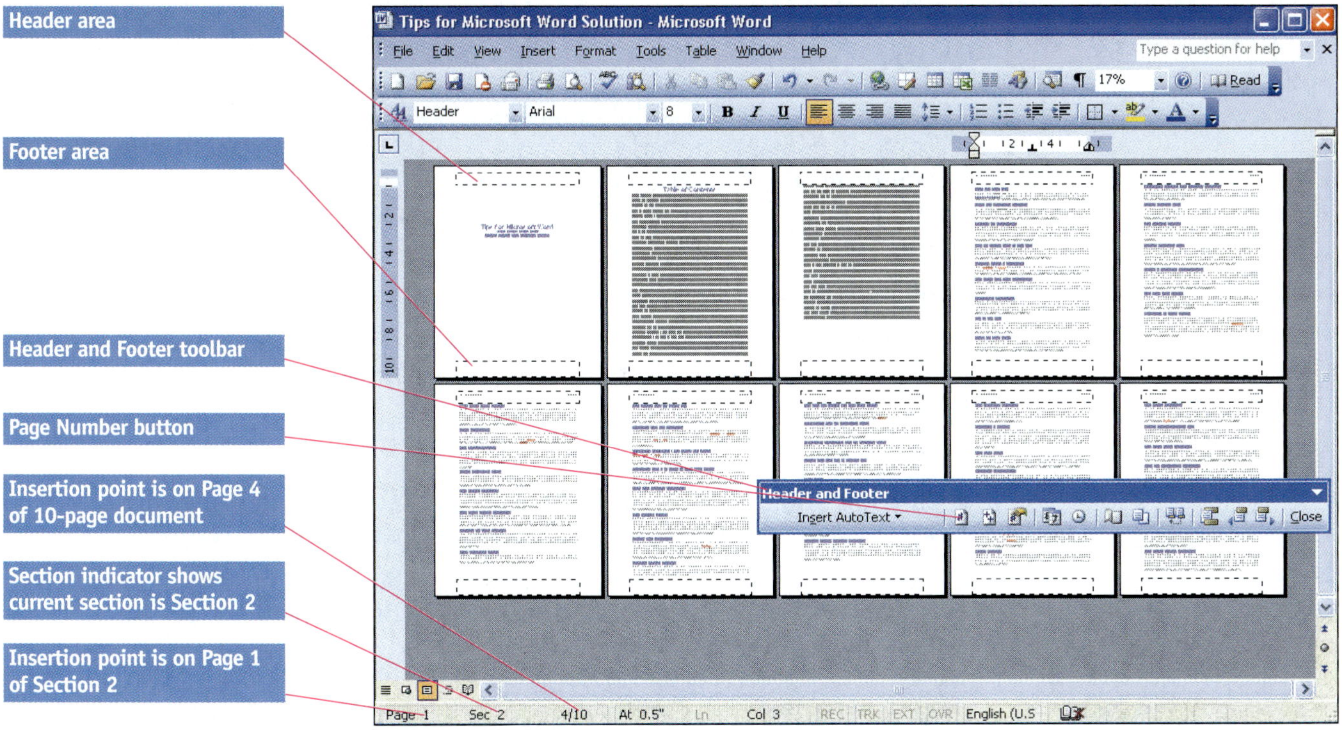

FIGURE 4.9 Headers and Footers

The table of contents is created through the ***Index and Tables command*** from the Insert menu. You have your choice of several predefined formats and the number of levels within each format; the latter correspond to the heading styles used within the document. You can also choose the ***leader character*** and whether or not to right-align the page numbers.

Creating an Index

An ***index*** is the finishing touch in a long document. Word will create an index automatically, provided that the entries for the index have been previously marked. This, in turn, requires you to go through a document, and one by one, select the terms to be included in the index and mark them accordingly. It's not as tedious as it sounds. You can, for example, select a single occurrence of an entry and tell Word to mark all occurrences of that entry for the index. You can also create cross-references, such as "see also Internet."

After the entries have been specified, you create the index by choosing the appropriate settings in the Index and Tables command. You can choose a variety of styles for the index just as you can for the table of contents. Word will put the index entries in alphabetical order and will enter the appropriate page references. You can also create additional index entries and/or move text within a document, then update the index with the click of a mouse.

The Go To Command

The ***Go To command*** moves the insertion point to the top of a designated page. The command is accessed from the Edit menu by pressing the F5 function key or by double clicking the Page number on the status bar. After the command has been executed, you are presented with a dialog box in which you enter the desired page number. You can also specify a relative page number—for example, P +2 to move forward two pages, or P –1 to move back one page.

hands-on exercise

4 Working in Long Documents

Objective To create a header (footer) that includes page numbers; to insert and update a table of contents; to add an index entry; to insert a section break and demonstrate the Go To command; to view multiple pages of a document. Use Figure 4.10 as a guide for the exercise.

Step 1: Applying a Style

- Open the **Tips for Microsoft Word Solution document** from the previous exercise. Zoom to **Page Width**. Scroll to the top of the second page.
- Click to the left of the first tip title. Type **Table of Contents**. Press the **Enter key** two times.
- Click anywhere in the phrase "Table of Contents". Click the **down arrow** on the **Styles** list box to pull down the available styles as shown in Figure 4.10a.
- Click **Report Title** (the style you created at the end of the previous exercise). "Table of Contents" is centered in 24 point blue Arial bold according to the definition of Report Title.

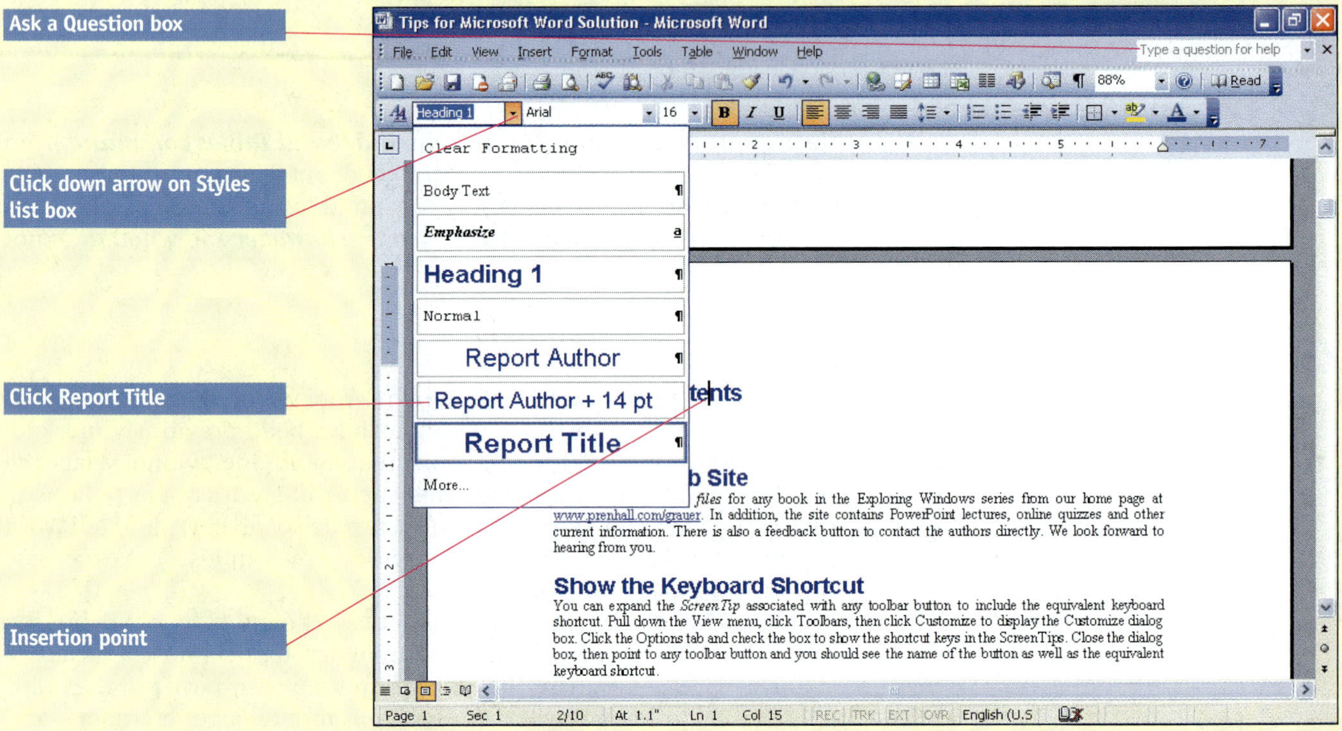

(a) Applying a Style (step 1)

FIGURE 4.10 Hands-on Exercise 4

ASK A QUESTION

Click in the Ask a Question box that appears at the right of the menu bar, enter the text of a question, press Enter, and Word returns a list of potential help topics. Click any topic that appears promising to open the Help window with detailed information. You can ask multiple questions during a session, and then click the down arrow in the list box to return to an earlier question, which will return you to the help topics.

Step 2: Table of Contents

- If necessary, change to the **Print Layout view**. Click the line immediately under the title for the table of contents. Pull down the **View menu**. Click **Zoom** to display the associated dialog box.
- Click the **monitor icon**. Click and drag the **page icons** to display two pages down by five pages across as shown in the figure. Release the mouse.
- Click **OK**. The display changes to show all ten pages in the document.
- Pull down the **Insert menu**. Click **Reference**, then click **Index and Tables**. If necessary, click the **Table of Contents tab** to display the dialog box in Figure 4.10b.
- Check the boxes to **Show Page Numbers** and to **Right Align Page Numbers**.
- Click the **down arrow** on the Formats list box, then click **Distinctive**. Click the **down arrow** in the **Tab Leader list box**. Choose a dot leader. Click **OK**. Word takes a moment to create the table of contents, which will extend to two pages.
- Save the document.

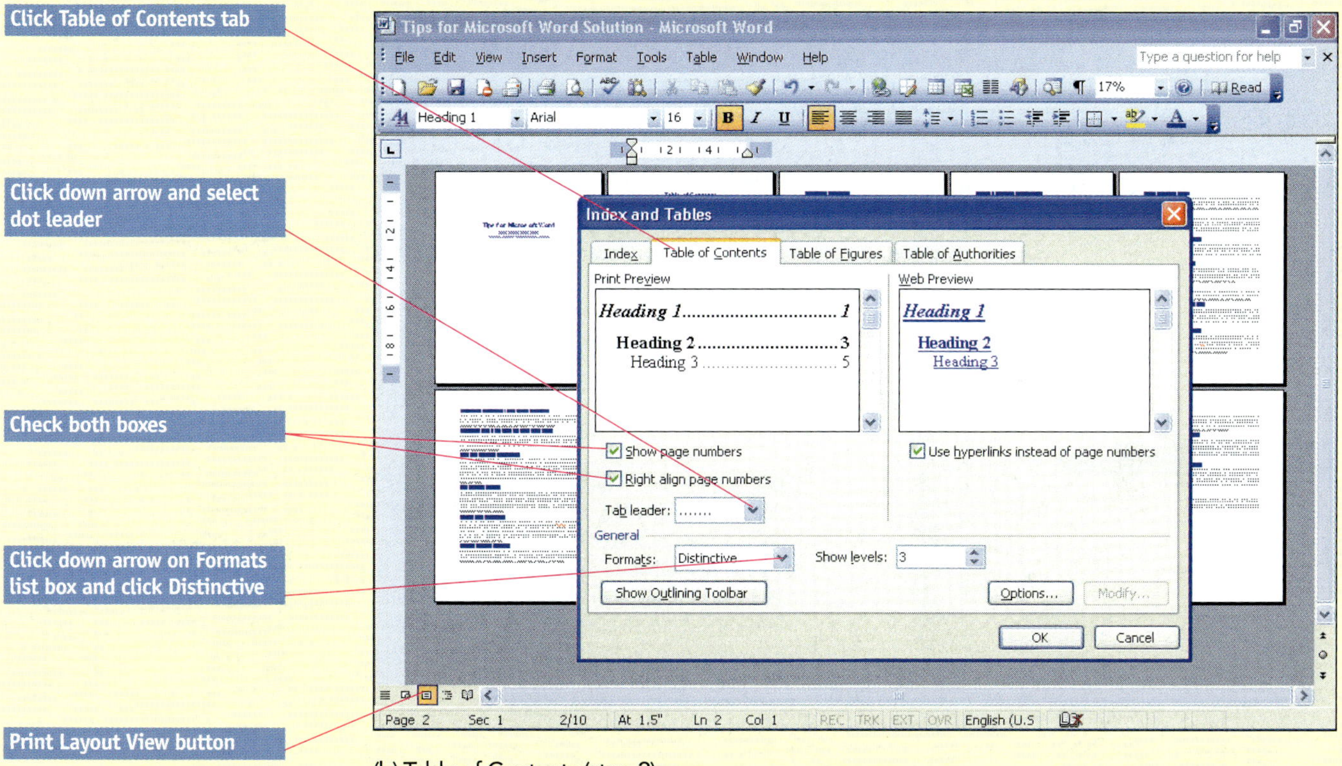

(b) Table of Contents (step 2)

FIGURE 4.10 Hands-on Exercise 4 (*continued*)

AUTOFORMAT AND THE TABLE OF CONTENTS

Word will create a table of contents automatically, provided you use the built-in heading styles to define the items for inclusion. If you have not applied the styles to the document, the AutoFormat command will do it for you. Once the heading styles are in the document, pull down the Insert command, click Reference, then click Index and Tables, then click the Table of Contents tab. Modify options as desired and click OK.

Step 3: Field Codes and Field Text

- Click the **arrow** on the **Zoom box** on the Standard toolbar. Click **Page Width** in order to read the table of contents as in Figure 4.10c.
- Use the **up arrow key** to scroll to the beginning of the table of contents. Press **Alt+F9**. The table is replaced by an entry similar to {TOC \o "1-3"\h \z \u} to indicate a field code. The exact code depends on the selections you made in step 2.
- Press **Alt+F9** a second time. The field code for the table of contents is replaced by text.
- Pull down the **Edit menu** and click the **Go To command** (or use the **Ctrl+G** keyboard shortcut) to display the dialog box in Figure 4.10c.
- Type **3** and press the **Enter key** to go to page 3, which contains the second page of the table of contents.
- Close the Find and Replace dialog box.

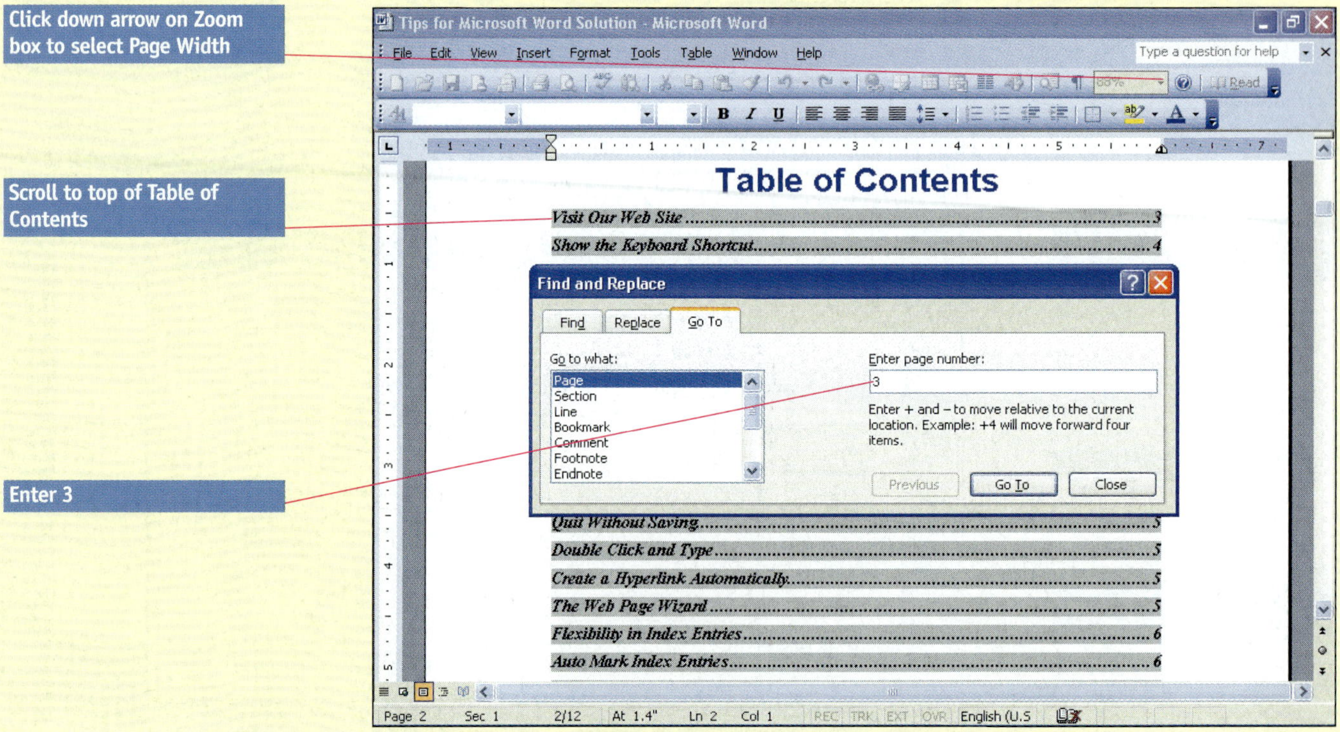

(c) Field Codes and Field Text (step 3)

FIGURE 4.10 Hands-on Exercise 4 (*continued*)

THE GO TO AND GO BACK COMMANDS

The F5 key is the shortcut equivalent of the Go To command and displays a dialog box to move to a specific location (a page or section) within a document. The Shift+F5 combination executes the Go Back command and returns to a previous location of the insertion point; press Shift+F5 repeatedly to cycle through the last three locations of the insertion point.

Step 4: Insert the Page Numbers

- Scroll down page 3 until you are at the end of the table of contents. Click to the left of the first tip heading as shown in Figure 4.10d.
- Pull down the **Insert menu.** Click **Break** to display the Break dialog box. Click the **Next Page button** under Section Break types. Click **OK** to create a section break, simultaneously forcing the first tip to begin on a new page.
- The first tip, Visit Our Web Site, moves to the top of the next page (page 4 in the document). If the status bar already displays Page 1 Section 2, a previous user has changed the default numbering to begin each section on its own page and you can go to step 5. If not, you need to change the page numbering.
- Pull down the **Insert menu** and click **Page Numbers** to display the Page Numbers dialog box. Click the **drop-down arrow** in the Position list box to position the page number at the top of page (in the header).
- Click the **Format command button** to display the Page Number Format dialog box. Click the option button to **Start at** page 1 (i.e., you want the first page in the second section to be numbered as page 1). Click **OK**.
- Click **Close** to close the Page Numbers dialog box. The status bar now displays Page 1 Sec 2. The entry 4/12 indicates that you are physically on the fourth page of a 12-page document.

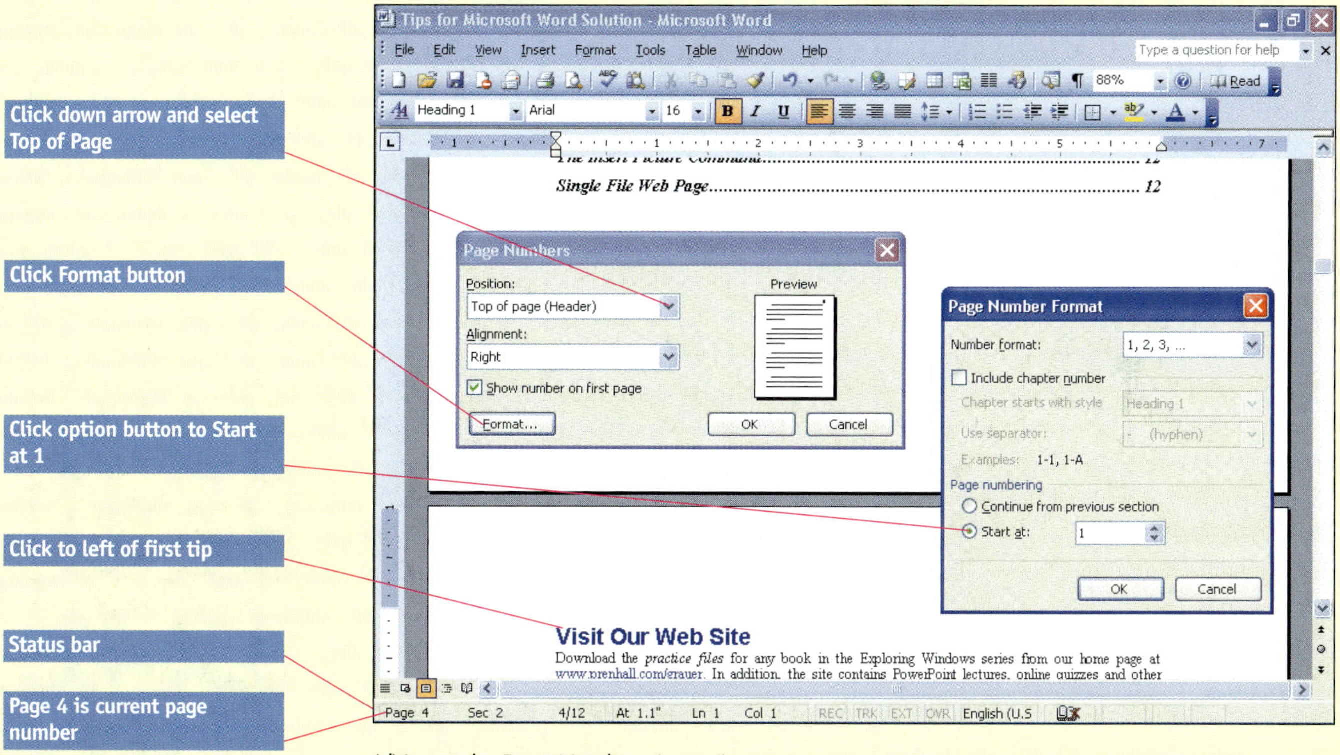

(d) Insert the Page Numbers (step 4)

FIGURE 4.10 Hands-on Exercise 4 (*continued*)

FORMATTING AT THE SECTION LEVEL

The margins, headers and footers, page numbers, orientation, and the number of columns in a document are implemented at the section level. Thus to change any of these parameters within a document, you must create a new section by inserting a section break. Look closely and you will see that the status bar indicates both the page number and the section number.

Step 5: The Page Setup Command

- Pull down the **File menu** and click the **Page Setup command** (or double click the **ruler**) to display the Page Setup dialog box.
- Click the **Layout tab** to display the options in Figure 4.10e.
- If necessary, clear the box for Different Odd and Even Pages and for Different First Page, as all pages in this section (Section 2) are to have the same header.
- Click **OK** to accept the settings and close the Page Setup dialog box.
- Save the document.

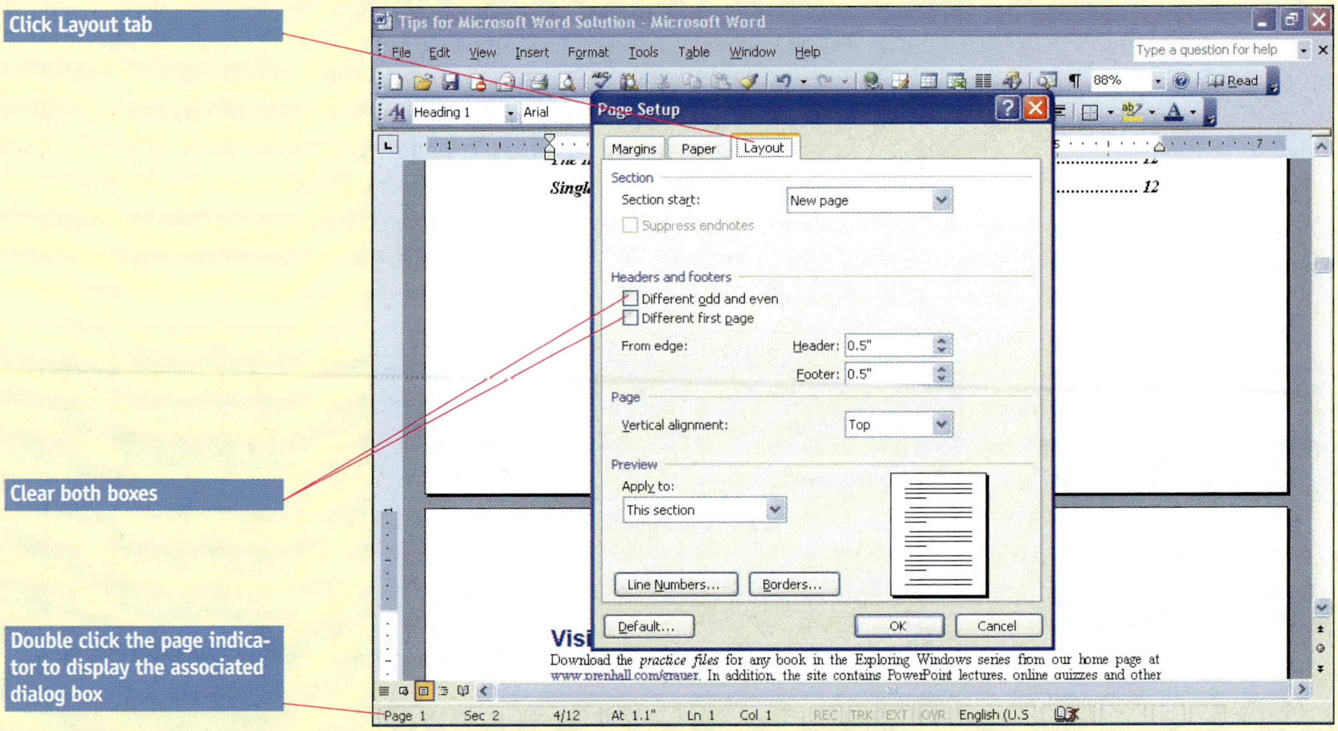

(e) The Page Setup Command (step 5)

FIGURE 4.10 Hands-on Exercise 4 (*continued*)

MOVING WITHIN LONG DOCUMENTS

Double click the page indicator on the status bar (or use the Ctrl+G keyboard shortcut) to display the dialog box for the Go To command from where you can go directly to any page within the document. You can also Ctrl+Click an entry in the table of contents to go directly to the text of that entry. And finally, you can use the Ctrl+Home and Ctrl+End keyboard shortcuts to move to the beginning or end of the document, respectively. The latter are universal shortcuts and apply to other Office documents as well.

Step 6: Create the Header

- Pull down the **View menu**. Click **Header and Footer** to produce the screen in Figure 4.10f. The text in the document is faded to indicate that you are editing the header, as opposed to the document.
- The "Link to Previous" indicator is on since Word automatically uses the header from the previous section.
- Click the **Link to Previous button** on the Header and Footer toolbar to toggle the indicator off and to create a different header for this section.
- If necessary, click in the header. Click the **arrow** on the Font list box on the Formatting toolbar. Click **Arial**. Click the **arrow** on the Font Size box. Click **8**. Type **Tips for Microsoft Word**.
- Press the **Tab key** twice. Type **PAGE**. Press the **space bar**. Click the **Insert Page Number button** on the Header and Footer toolbar.
- Click the **Show Previous button** to show the header for Section 1. Delete the page number that appears at the upper right, since we do not want to display page numbers for the table of contents.
- Click the **Close button** on the Header and Footer toolbar. The header is faded, and the document text is available for editing.

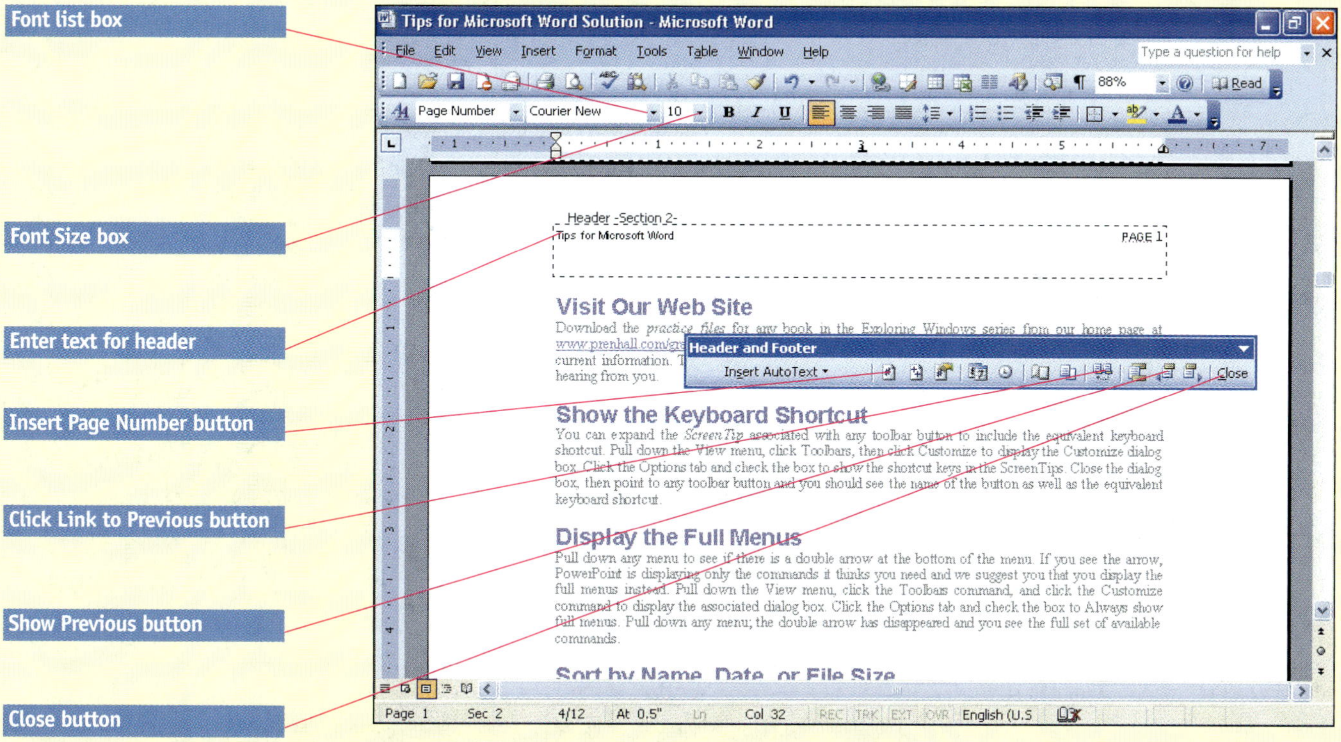

(f) Create the Header (step 6)

FIGURE 4.10 Hands-on Exercise 4 (*continued*)

HEADERS AND FOOTERS

If you do not see a header or footer, it is most likely because you are in the wrong view. Headers and footers are displayed in the Print Layout view but not in the Normal view. (Click the Print Layout button on the status bar to change the view.)

Step 7: Update the Table of Contents

- Press **Ctrl+Home** to move to the beginning of the document. The status bar indicates Page 1, Sec 1.
- Click the **Select Browse Object button** on the vertical scroll bar, then click the **Browse by Page** icon.
- If necessary, click the **Next Page button** or **Previous Page button** on the vertical scroll bar (or press **Ctrl+PgDn**) to move to the first page containing the table of contents.
- Click to the left of the first entry in the Table of Contents. Press the **F9 key** to update the table of contents. If necessary, click the **Update Entire Table button** as shown in Figure 4.10g, then click **OK**.
- The pages are renumbered to reflect the actual page numbers in the second section.
- Save the document.

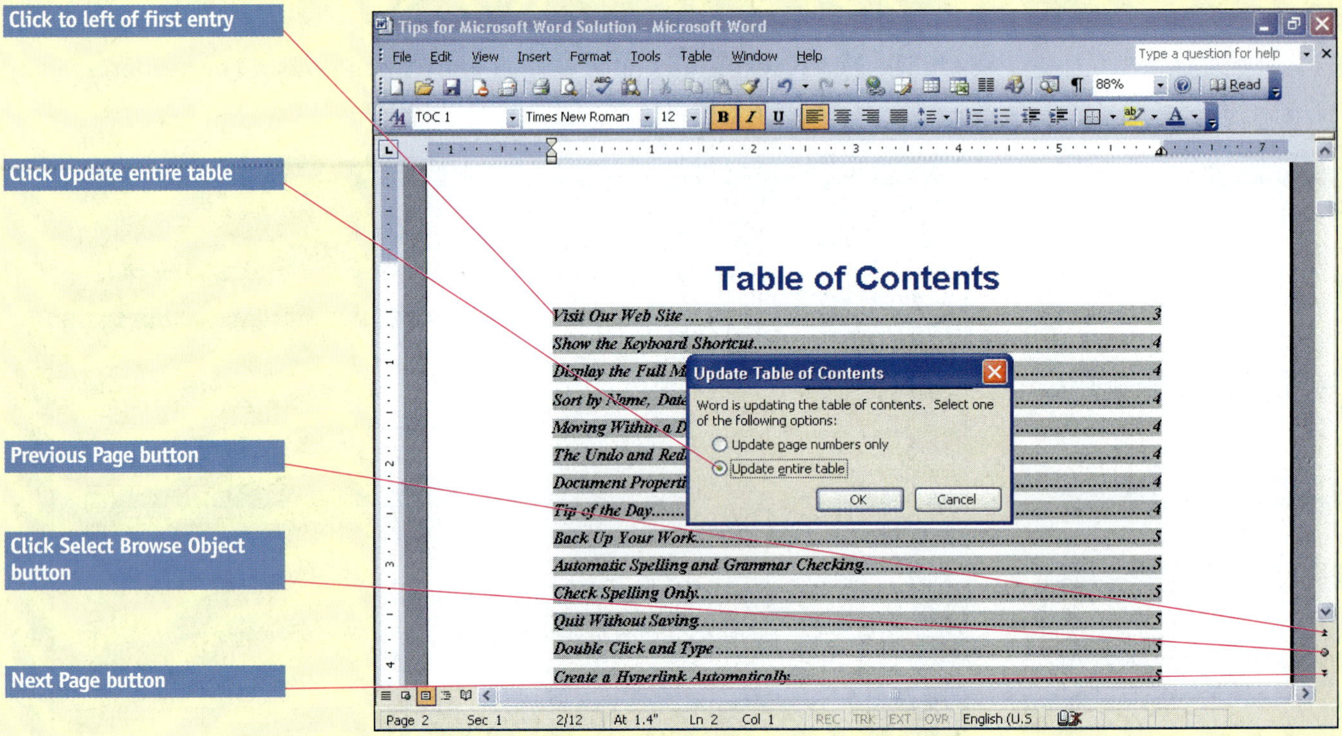

(g) Update the Table of Contents (step 7)

FIGURE 4.10 Hands-on Exercise 4 (*continued*)

SELECT BROWSE OBJECT

Click the Select Browse Object button toward the bottom of the vertical scroll bar to display a palette in which you specify how to browse through a document. Typically you browse from one page to the next, but you can browse by footnote, section, graphic, table, or any of the other objects listed. Once you select the object, click the Next or Previous buttons on the vertical scroll bar (or press Ctrl+PgDn or Ctrl+PgUp) to move to the next or previous occurrence of the selected object.

Step 8: Create an Index Entry

- Press **Ctrl+Home** to move to the beginning of the document. Pull down the **Edit menu** and click the **Find command**. Search for the first occurrence of the text "Ctrl+Home" within the document, as shown in Figure 4.10h. Close the Find and Replace dialog box.
- Click the **Show/Hide ¶ button** so you can see the nonprinting characters in the document, which include the index entries that have been previously created by the authors. (The index entries appear in curly brackets and begin with the letters XE.)
- Check that the text "Ctrl+Home" is selected within the document, then press **Alt+Shift+X** to display the Mark Index Entry dialog box. (Should you forget the shortcut, pull down the **Insert menu**, click **Reference**, click the **Index and Tables command**, click the **Index tab**, then click the **Mark command button**.)
- Click the **Mark command button** to create the index entry, after which you see the field code, {XE "Ctrl+Home"}, to indicate that the index entry has been created.
- The Mark Index Entry dialog box stays open so that you can create additional entries by selecting additional text.
- Click the option button to create a **cross-reference.** Type **keyboard shortcut** in the associated text box. Click **Mark**.
- Click in the document, click and drag to select the text "Ctrl+End," then click in the dialog box, and the Main entry changes to Ctrl+End automatically. Click the **Mark command button** to create the index entry. Close the Mark Index Entry dialog box.
- Save the document.

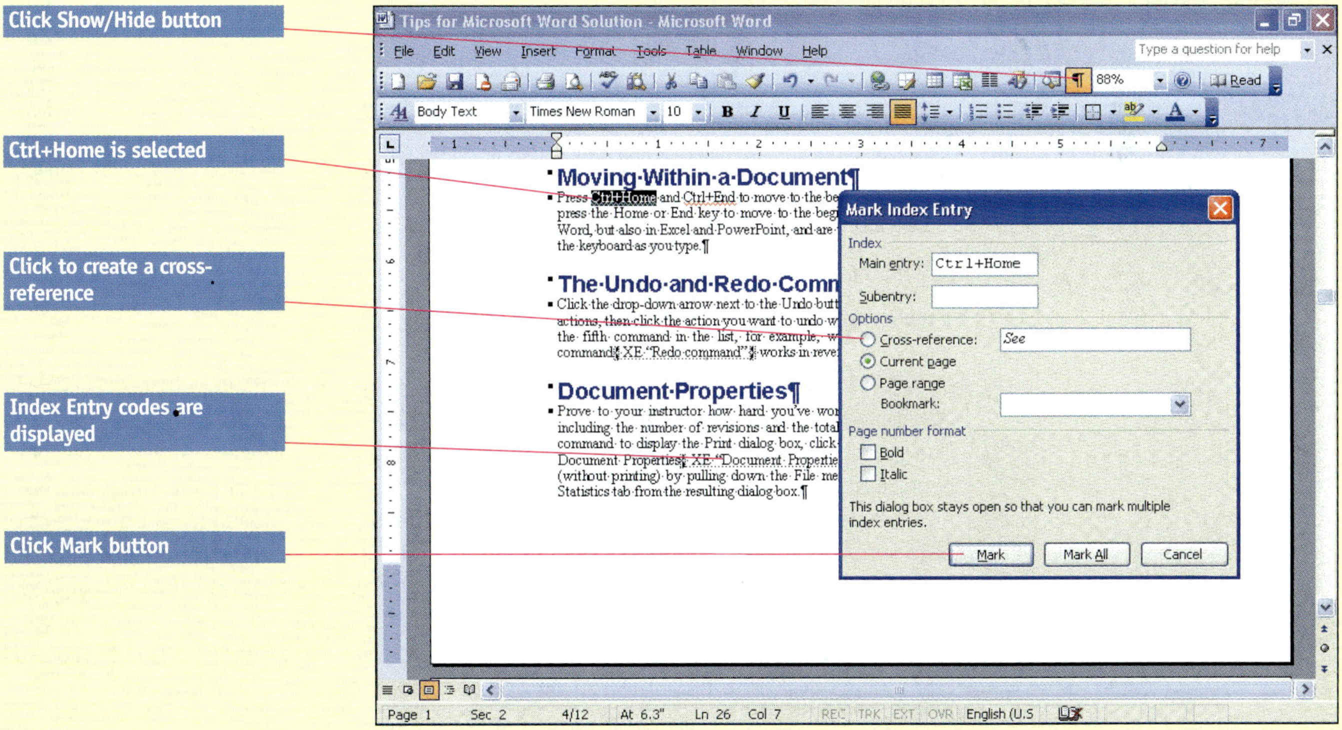

(h) Create an Index Entry (step 8)

FIGURE 4.10 Hands-on Exercise 4 (*continued*)

Step 9: Create the Index

- Press **Ctrl+End** to move to the end of the document, where you will insert the index. Press **Enter** to begin a new line.
- Pull down the **Insert menu**, click **Reference**, then click the **Index and Tables command** to display the Index and Tables dialog box in Figure 4.10i. Click the **Index tab** if necessary.
- Choose the type of index you want. We selected a **classic format** over **two columns**. Click **OK** to create the index.
- Click the **Undo button** if you are not satisfied with the appearance of the index, then repeat the process to create an index with a different style.
- Save the document.

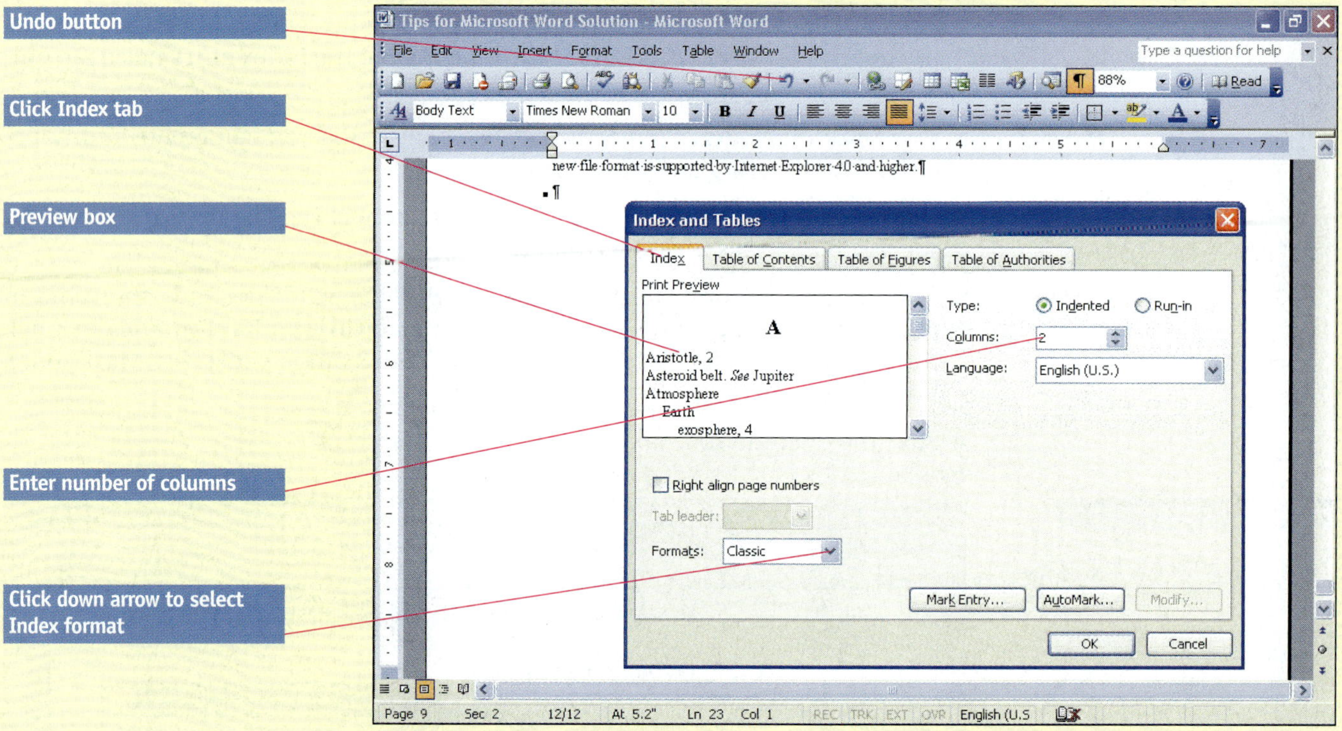

(i) Create the Index (step 9)

FIGURE 4.10 Hands-on Exercise 4 (*continued*)

AUTOMARK INDEX ENTRIES

The AutoMark command will, as the name implies, automatically mark all occurrences of all entries for inclusion in an index. To use the feature, you have to create a separate document that lists the terms you want to reference, then you execute the AutoMark command from the Index and Tables dialog box. The advantage is that it is fast. The disadvantage is that every occurrence of an entry is marked in the index so that a commonly used term may have too many page references. You can, however, delete superfluous entries by manually deleting the field codes. Click the Show/Hide button if you do not see the entries in the document.

Step 10: **Complete the Index**

- Scroll to the beginning of the index and click to the left of the letter "A." Pull down the **File menu** and click the **Page Setup command** to display the Page Setup dialog box, and click the **Layout tab**.
- Click the **down arrow** in the Section start list box and specify **New page**. Click the **down arrow** in the Apply to list box and specify **This section**. Click **OK**. The index moves to the top of a new page.
- Pull down the **Insert menu** and click the **Page numbers command** to display the Page Numbers dialog box. Click the **Format button** to display the Page Number Format dialog box. Click the option button to **Continue from previous section**. Click **OK**. Click **Close**.
- Pull down the **View menu** and click the **Header and Footer command** to display the Header and Footer toolbar as shown in Figure 4.10j. Click the **Link to Previous button** to toggle the indicator off and create a new header for this section.
- Enter **INDEX** as the text in the header. Close the Header and Footer toolbar to return to the document.
- Save the document.

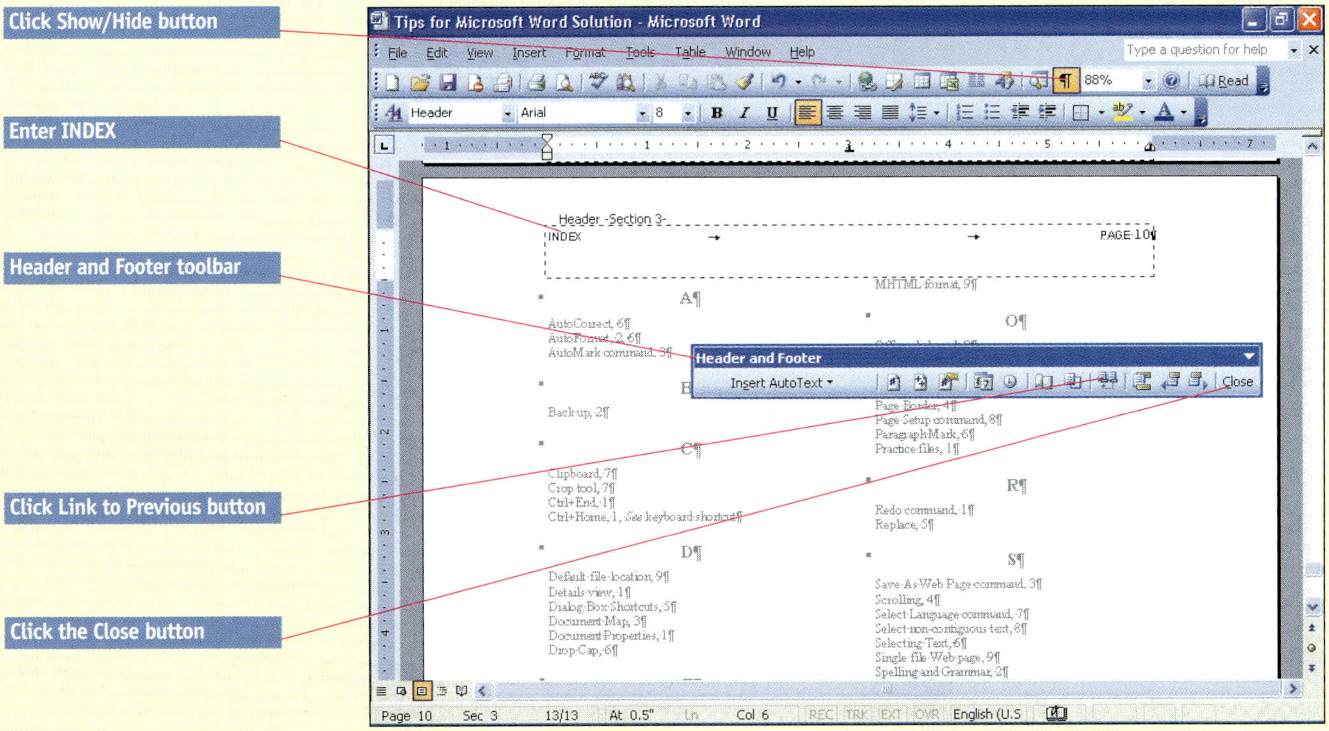

(j) Complete the Index (step 10)

FIGURE 4.10 Hands-on Exercise 4 (*continued*)

CHECK THE INDEX ENTRIES

Every entry in the index should begin with an uppercase letter. If this is not the case, it is because the origin entry within the body of the document was marked improperly. Click the Show/Hide button to display the indexed entries within the document, which appear within brackets; e.g., {XE "Practice Files"}. Change each entry to begin with an uppercase letter as necessary.

Step 11: The Completed Document

- Pull down the **View menu**. Click **Zoom**. Click **Many Pages**. Click the **monitor icon**. Click and drag the **page icon** within the monitor to display two pages down by five pages. Release the mouse. Click **OK**.
- The completed document is shown in Figure 4.10k. The index appears by itself on the last (13th) page of the document.
- Save the document, then print the completed document to prove to your instructor that you have completed the exercise.
- Congratulations on a job well done. You have created a document with page numbers, a table of contents, and an index. Exit Word.
- Read the printed document and highlight five tips you find especially useful. Try to incorporate this information in your daily work.

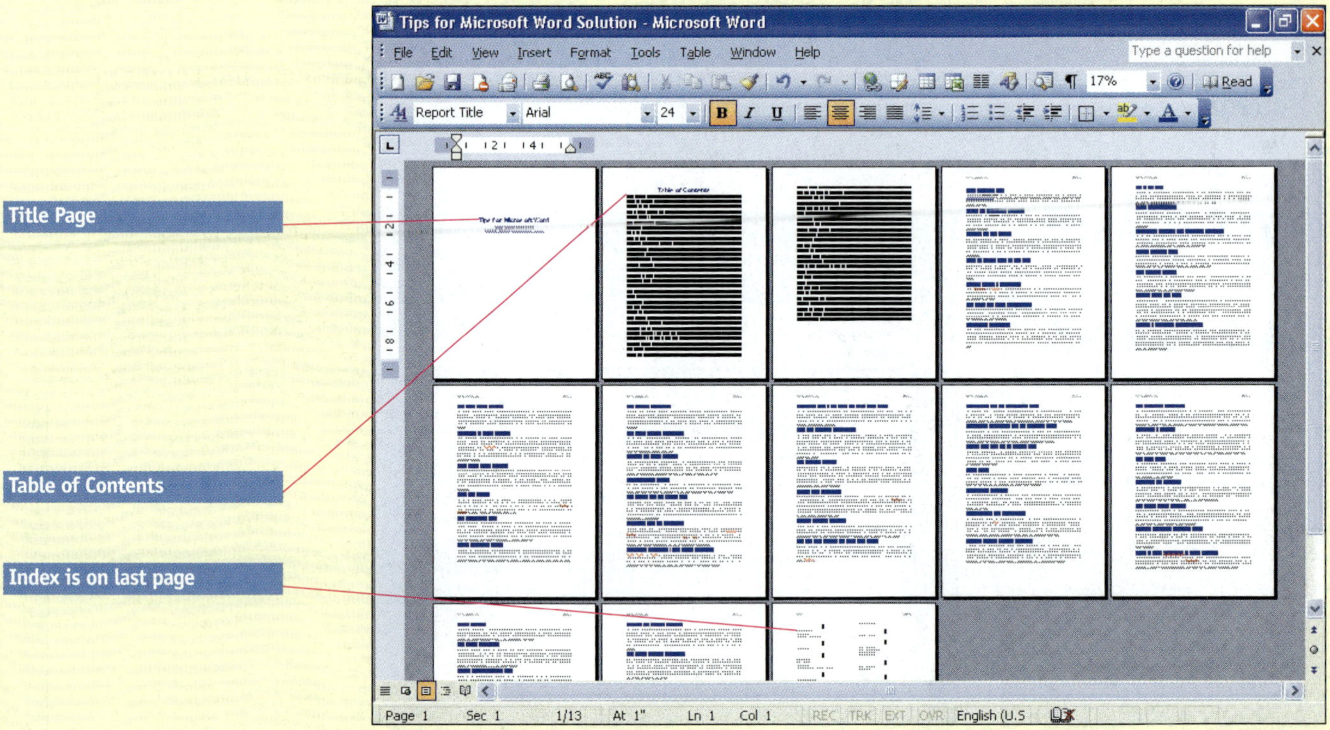

(k) The Completed Document (step 11)

FIGURE 4.10 Hands-on Exercise 4 (*continued*)

UPDATING THE TABLE OF CONTENTS

Use a shortcut menu to update the table of contents. Point to any entry in the table of contents, then press the right mouse button to display a shortcut menu. Click Update Field, click the Update Entire Table command button, and click OK. The table of contents will be adjusted automatically to reflect page number changes as well as the addition or deletion of any items defined by any built-in heading style.

SUMMARY

A list helps to organize information by emphasizing important topics. A bulleted or numbered list can be created by clicking the appropriate button on the Formatting toolbar or by executing the Bullets and Numbering command in the Format menu. An outline extends a numbered list to several levels.

Tables represent a very powerful capability within Word and are created through the Insert Table command in the Table menu or by using the Insert Table button on the Standard toolbar. Each cell in a table is formatted independently and may contain text, numbers, and/or graphics. Individual cells can be joined together to create a larger cell; e.g., the cells in the first row of a table are often merged to create a title for the table. Conversely a single cell can be split into multiple cells. The rows in a table can be different heights and/or each column can be a different width. Tables are the basis for a variety of documents.

A style is a set of formatting instructions that has been saved under a distinct name. Styles are created at the character or paragraph level and provide a consistent appearance to similar elements throughout a document. Any existing styles can be modified to change the formatting of all text defined by that style.

The Outline view displays a condensed view of a document based on styles within the document. Text may be collapsed or expanded as necessary to facilitate moving text within long documents. (The Outline view does not display a conventional outline, which is created from a multilevel list within the Bullets and Numbering command.)

The AutoFormat command analyzes a document and formats it for you. The command goes through an entire document, determines how each paragraph is used, then applies an appropriate style to each paragraph.

Formatting occurs at the character, paragraph, or section level. Section formatting controls margins, columns, page orientation and size, page numbering, and headers and footers. A header consists of one or more lines that are printed at the top of every (designated) page in a document. A footer is text that is printed at the bottom of designated pages. Page numbers may be added to either a header or footer.

A table of contents lists headings in the order they appear in a document with their respective page numbers. It can be created automatically, provided the built-in heading styles were previously applied to the items for inclusion. Word will also create an index automatically, provided that the entries for the index have been previously marked. This, in turn, requires you to go through a document, select the appropriate text, and mark the entries accordingly. The Edit Go To command enables you to move directly to a specific page, section, or bookmark within a document.

KEY TERMS

AutoFormat command 246
Body Text style 243
Bulleted list 226
Bullets and Numbering command 226
Cell 234
Character style 243
Delete command 234
Footer 255
Go To command 257
Header 255
Heading 1 style 243
Index 257
Index and Tables command 257
Insert command 234
Insert menu 256
Insert Page Numbers command 255
Insert Table command 234
Leader character 257
Normal style 243
Numbered list 226
Outline 226
Outline numbered list 226
Outline view 245
Page numbers 255
Paragraph style 243
Section 256
Section break 256
Style 243
Styles and Formatting command 243
Table menu 234
Table of contents 256
Tables feature 234

MULTIPLE CHOICE

1. Which of the following can be stored within a paragraph style?
   (a) Tabs and indents
   (b) Line spacing and alignment
   (c) Shading and borders
   (d) All of the above

2. What is the easiest way to change the alignment of five paragraphs scattered throughout a document, each of which is formatted with the same style?
   (a) Select the paragraphs individually, then click the appropriate alignment button
   (b) Select the paragraphs at the same time, then click the appropriate alignment button on the Formatting toolbar
   (c) Change the format of the existing style, which changes the paragraphs
   (d) Retype the paragraphs according to the new specifications

3. The AutoFormat command does not:
   (a) Apply styles to individual paragraphs
   (b) Apply boldface italics to terms that require additional emphasis
   (c) Replace ordinary quotes with smart quotes
   (d) Substitute typographic symbols for ordinary letters—such as © for (C)

4. Which of the following is used to create a conventional outline?
   (a) The Bullets and Numbering command
   (b) The Outline view
   (c) Both (a) and (b)
   (d) Neither (a) nor (b)

5. In which view do you see headers and/or footers?
   (a) Print Layout view
   (b) Normal view
   (c) Both (a) and (b)
   (d) Neither (a) nor (b)

6. Which of the following numbering schemes can be used with page numbers?
   (a) Roman numerals (I, II, III . . . or i, ii, iii)
   (b) Regular numbers (1, 2, 3, . . .)
   (c) Letters (A, B, C . . . or a, b, c)
   (d) All of the above

7. Which of the following is a true statement regarding headers and footers?
   (a) Every document must have at least one header
   (b) Every document must have at least one footer
   (c) Both (a) and (b)
   (d) Neither (a) nor (b)

8. Which of the following is a *false* statement regarding lists?
   (a) A bulleted list can be changed to a numbered list and vice versa
   (b) The symbol for the bulleted list can be changed to a different character
   (c) The numbers in a numbered list can be changed to letters or roman numerals
   (d) The bullets or numbers cannot be removed

9. Page numbers can be specified in:
   (a) A header but not a footer
   (b) A footer but not a header
   (c) A header or a footer
   (d) Neither a header nor a footer

10. Which of the following is true regarding the formatting within a document?
    (a) Line spacing and alignment are implemented at the section level
    (b) Margins, headers, and footers are implemented at the paragraph level
    (c) Both (a) and (b)
    (d) Neither (a) nor (b)

... continued

multiple choice

11. What happens when you press the Tab key from within a table?

(a) A Tab character is inserted just as it would be for ordinary text
(b) The insertion point moves to the next column in the same row or the first column in the next row if you are at the end of the row
(c) Both (a) and (b)
(d) Neither (a) nor (b)

12. Which of the following is true about pagination in the current document given that the status bar displays "Page 5 Section 3 7/9"?

(a) The document contains seven pages
(b) The insertion point is on the seventh page of the document, which is numbered as page 5
(c) The document cannot contain more than three sections
(d) All of the above

13. The Edit Go To command enables you to move the insertion point to:

(a) A specific page
(b) A relative page forward or backward from the current page
(c) A specific section
(d) Any of the above

14. Once a table of contents has been created and inserted into a document:

(a) Any subsequent page changes arising from the insertion or deletion of text to existing paragraphs must be entered manually
(b) Any additions to the entries in the table arising due to the insertion of new paragraphs defined by a heading style must be entered manually
(c) Both (a) and (b)
(d) Neither (a) nor (b)

15. Which of the following is a *false* statement about the Outline view?

(a) It can be collapsed to display only headings
(b) It can be expanded to show the entire document
(c) It requires the application of styles
(d) It is used to create a conventional outline

16. What is the best way to create a conventional outline in a Word document?

(a) Use the Outline view
(b) Use the Outline Numbered tab within the Bullets and Numbering command
(c) Use the Outlining toolbar
(d) All of the above are equally acceptable

17. Which of the following is a predefined Word style that is available in every document?

(a) Normal
(b) Heading 1
(c) Body Text
(d) All of these answers are correct

18. What happens if you modify the Body Text style in a Word document?

(a) Only the paragraph where the insertion point is located is changed
(b) All paragraphs in the document will be changed
(c) Only those paragraphs formatted with the Body Text style will be changed
(d) It is not possible to change a Word default style such as Body Text

ANSWERS

1. d	**7.** d	**13.** d
2. c	**8.** d	**14.** d
3. b	**9.** c	**15.** d
4. a	**10.** d	**16.** b
5. a	**11.** b	**17.** d
6. d	**12.** b	**18.** c

PRACTICE WITH WORD

1. **The Résumé:** Microsoft Word includes a Résumé Wizard, but you can achieve an equally good result through the tables feature. Follow the instructions below to create a résumé similar to the document in Figure 4.11.
   a. Start a new document. Pull down the Table menu and click the Insert command to insert a table into your document. Specify that the table should contain two columns and eight rows. Additional rows can be added as needed. Conversely, rows can be deleted at a later time if they are not needed.
   b. Select the two cells in the first row and then merge those two cells. Enter your name in the cell and then center it within the cell. Change the font and font size as shown in Figure 4.11.
   c. Enter your addresses in the next row, entering your campus address, phone, and e-mail address in the cell on the left and your permanent address and phone in the cell on the right. Left align the text in the cell on the left, right align the text in the cell on the right. Be sure to include your e-mail address with your campus address.
   d. Enter the categories in the left cell of each row, being sure to include the following categories: Objective, Education, Honors, Scholarships, Work Experience, and References. Boldface and right align the text in these cells. (Not all of these categories are visible in Figure 4.11.)
   e. Enter the associated information in the right cell of each row. Be sure to include all information that would interest a prospective employer. Left align the text in these cells, using boldface and italic as appropriate.
   f. Select the entire table and remove the borders surrounding the individual cells. (Figure 4.11 displays gridlines, which—unlike borders—do not appear in the printed document.) Print the completed résumé for your instructor.
   g. Open the task pane. Click the down arrow in the title bar of the task pane to select New document. Click the link to Templates on my computer to display the Templates dialog box and then click the Other Documents tab. Print one or more of the suggested résumé templates. How do these designs compare to the résumé based on a table? Summarize your thoughts in a short note to your instructor.

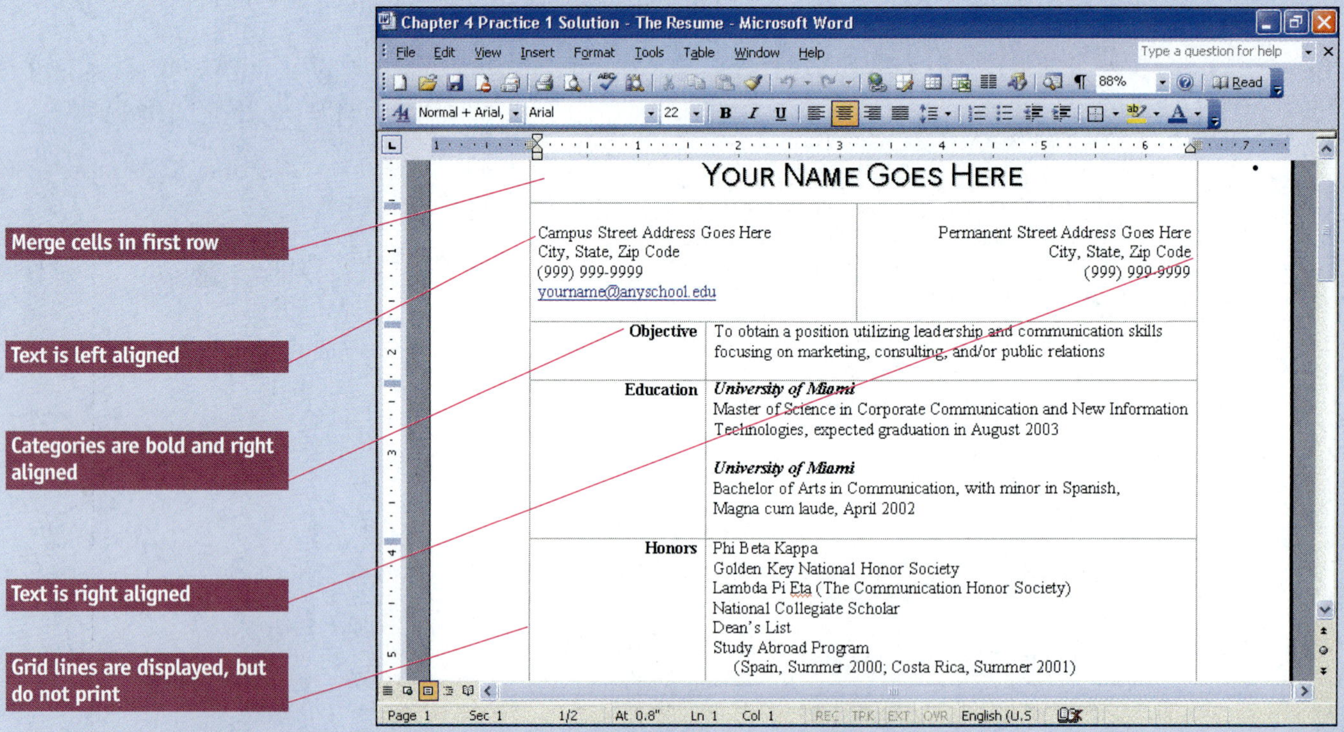

FIGURE 4.11 The Résumé (exercise 1)

2. **The Employment Application:** Use the tables feature to create a real or hypothetical employment application similar to the document in Figure 4.12. You can follow our design, or you can create your own. The Tables and Borders toolbar can be used in place of the Table menu to execute various commands during the exercise. Proceed as follows:
   a. Create an 8 × 3 (eight rows and three columns) table to match our design. Select the entire table after it is created initially. Pull down the Format menu, click the Paragraph command, and then click the Indents and Spacing tab. Click the up spin arrow in the Space Before list box to enter six points. This will drop the text in each cell half a line from the top border of the cell, and also determine the spacing between paragraphs within a cell.
   b. Merge the cells in the first row to create the title for the application. Enter the text for the first line, press Shift+Enter to create a line break instead of a paragraph break (to minimize the spacing between lines), then enter the text on the second line. Center the text. Select the first cell. Pull down the Format menu, click Borders and Shading, click the Shading tab, and choose Solid as the style. This creates white letters on a dark background.
   c. Enter the text in the next several cells as shown in Figure 4.12. Move down in the table until you can select the cell for the highest degree attained. Enter the indicated text, click and drag to select all four degrees, and then pull down the Format menu. Click the Bullets and Numbering command and select the Bulleted tab. Select any bullet style, click the Customize button, click the Character button, select the WingDings font and choose the check box for the style. Click OK.
   d. Merge the cells in row 7, then enter the text that asks the applicant to describe his or her computer skills in row 7. Merge the cells in row 8 (these cells are not visible in Figure 4.12) to create a single cell for employment references.
   e. Click the down arrow on the zoom box to view the entire document. Change the row heights as necessary so that the completed application fills the entire page.
   f. Complete the finished application as though you were applying for a job. Replace the check box next to the highest degree earned (remove the bullet) with the letter X. Submit the completed application to your instructor.

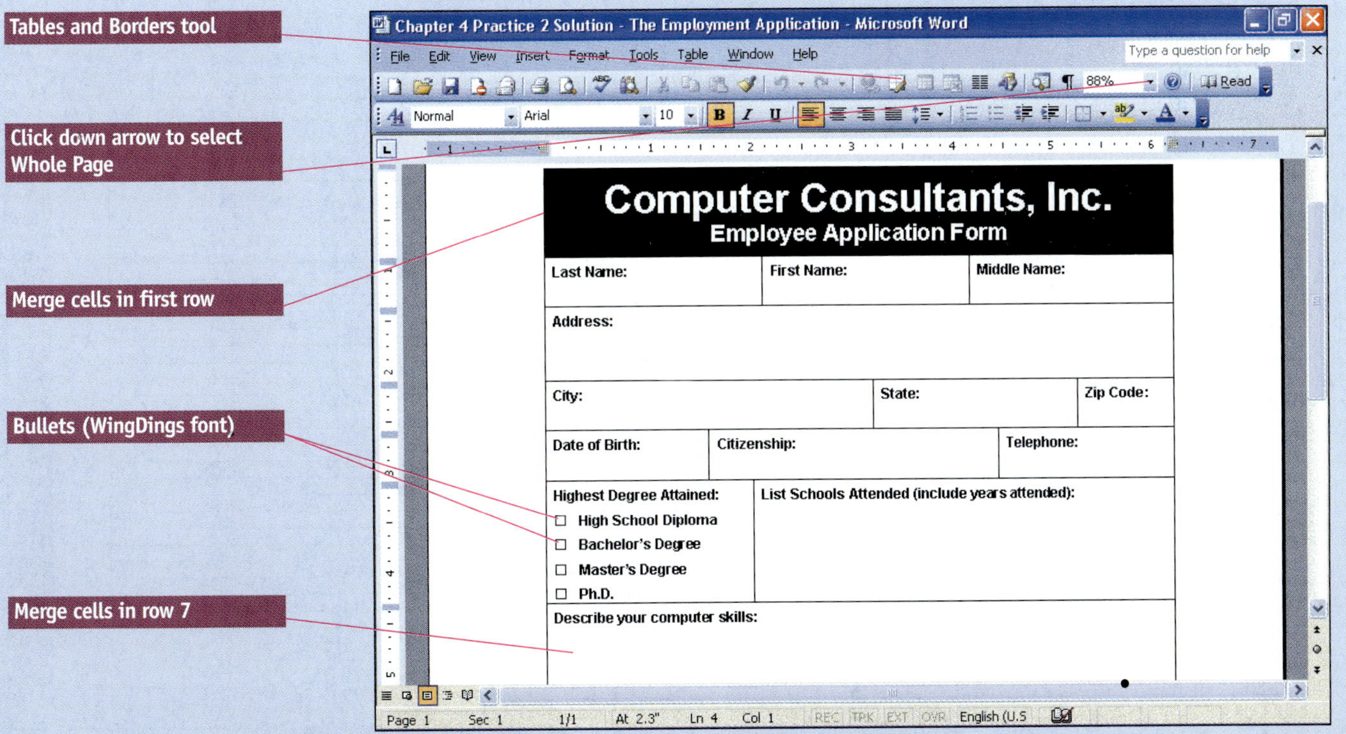

FIGURE 4.12 The Employment Application (exercise 2)

3. **The Purchase of a PC:** You can purchase a PC from any number of vendors, each of which offers multiple models and typically enable you to upgrade individual components. It is important, therefore, to compare competing systems with respect to their features and cost in a table similar to Figure 4.13. Look closely, however, and you will see that the table is the third page of a three-page document that also contains a cover page as well as a set of tips to consider when selecting a system. Proceed as follows:
   a. Open the *Chapter 4, Practice 3* document in the Exploring Word folder that contains a set of tips for purchasing a PC. Press Ctrl+Home to go to the beginning of the document, and then press Ctrl+Enter to insert a page break. Move to the beginning of the document and create a title page for this assignment that contains your name, today's date, and the same clip art image as the table in Figure 4.13.
   b. The second page of the document contains various tips that we provide, but it is up to you to complete the formatting. Insert a title at the top of this page, "Tips for Buying a PC". Create a bulleted list for the tips on this page. Use boldface or italic for the title of each tip. Change the margins and/or the font size so that all of this information fits on one page.
   c. Press Ctrl+End to move to the end of the document (the bottom of the second page). Pull down the Insert menu, click the Break command, then select Next Page under section break types. A section break is required because we are about to change the page orientation within a document.
   d. Move to the third page, pull down the File menu and click the Page Setup command to change to Landscape orientation for the third page. (Look closely at the status bar in Figure 4.13 to see that Page 3 is in Section 2 of the document. The first two pages contain the title page and list of tips, respectively, and are in Section 1.)
   e. Create the table in Figure 4.13. You need not follow our design exactly, but you are required to leave space for three competing systems. Insert the home page of each vendor as a hyperlink under the vendor's name. Insert clip art in the upper left of the table to add interest. (Use the Format Picture command to change the layout so that the clip art appears in front of the text.)
   f. Print the completed document for your instructor.

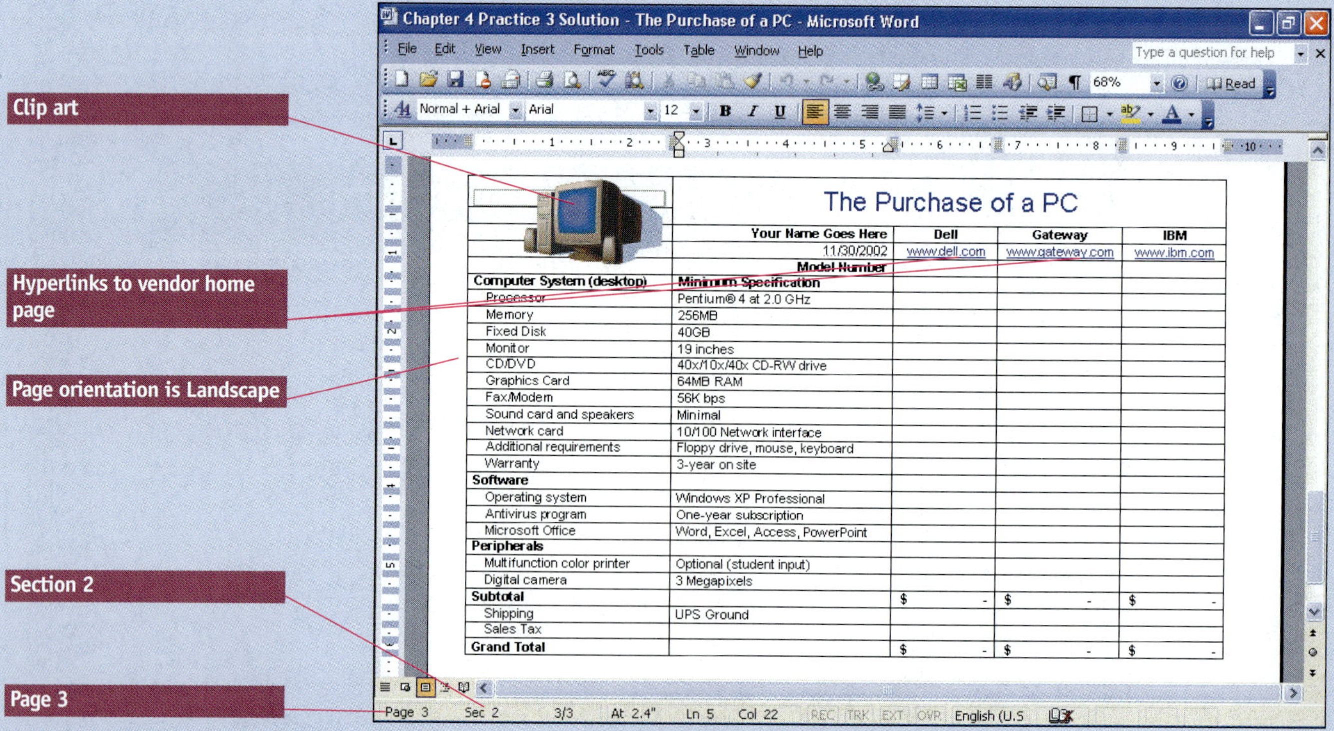

FIGURE 4.13 The Purchase of a PC (exercise 3)

4. **Bring Bailey Home:** Figure 4.14 displays a flyer that is intended to find Bailey, a combination Beagle/Jack Russell Terrier, and bring him home. You do not have to duplicate our document exactly, but you are to use a table as the basis of your document. You can create a document to search for Bailey, or you can use any pet you like. Proceed as follows:
   a. Start a new document and insert a table with four rows and ten columns. Click outside the table, immediately to the left of the first cell in the first row to select the entire row. Pull down the Table menu and click the Merge Cells command. Merge the cells in rows 2 and 3 in similar fashion.
   b. Click in the first row and enter the text of your message, e.g., "Bring Bailey Home." Select the text and increase the font size. The row height will increase automatically to accommodate the larger text. Center the text.
   c. Select (the cell in) the second row. Pull down the Format menu, click the Borders and Shading command, click the Shading tab, then select solid (100% shading) in the Style area. Click OK. This will place a black background in the cell so that the picture you insert in the next step will appear to completely fill the cell.
   d. Locate a picture of your pet. (We have provided a picture of Bailey in the Exploring Word folder.) Click in the second row, pull down the Insert menu, and insert the picture. The row height will expand automatically to accommodate the picture. Center the picture and size it appropriately.
   e. Click in the third row and enter the appropriate text to describe your pet. Increase the size of the text appropriately and center it within the cell.
   f. Enter your name and phone number in the first cell of the fourth row. Pull down the Format menu and click the Text Direction command to change the direction as shown in Figure 4.14. Align the text vertically to the top of the cell. Copy and paste the contents of this cell to the remaining cells in the row. Select the entire row and change the border style to a dashed line.
   g. Click the down arrow on the Zoom list box to view the whole page. Use the Table Properties command in the Table menu to change the row heights as necessary so that your document fills the entire page. Adjust the font sizes as necessary.
   h. Print the completed document for your instructor.

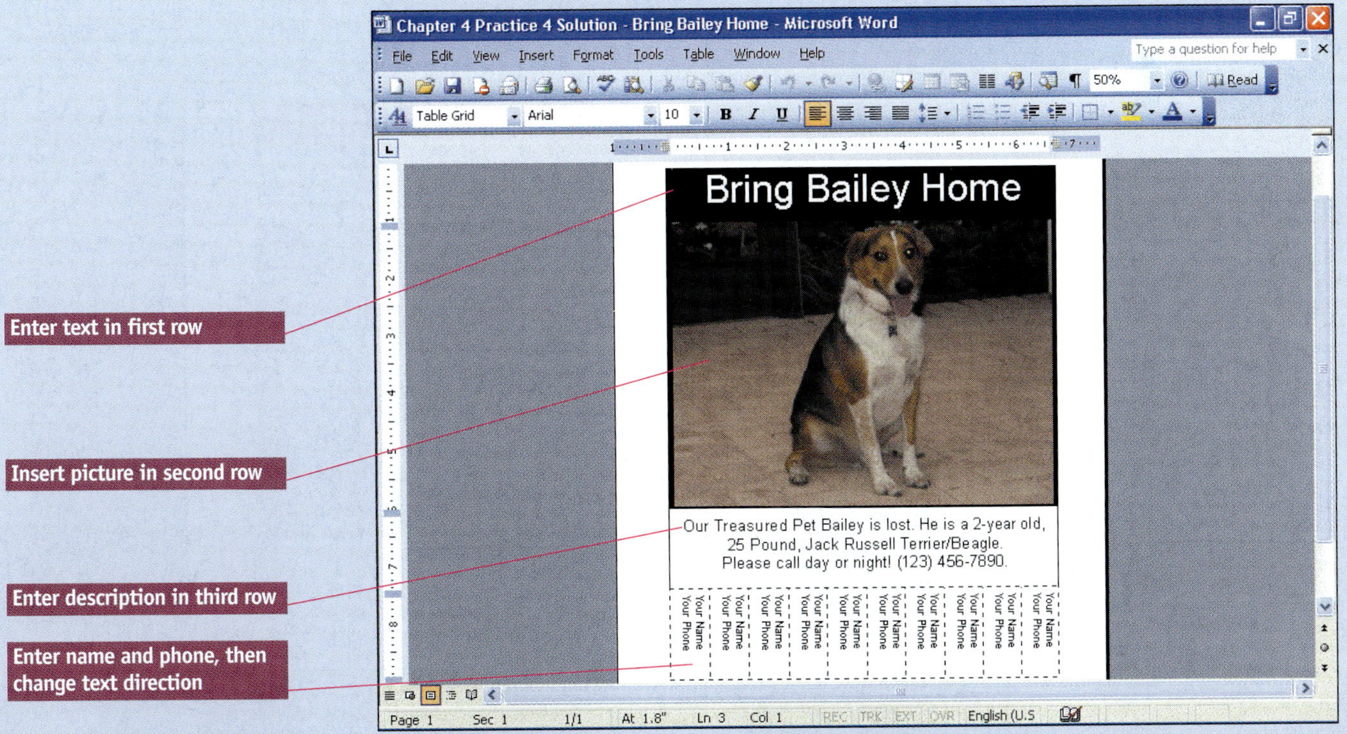

FIGURE 4.14 Bring Bailey Home (exercise 4)

5. **Classic Car for Sale:** The document in Figure 4.15 is a hypothetical flyer to advertise a classic car for sale. The document consists of text at the top of the page, three pictures, and a table with contact information. Use your imagination to create a similar document to sell any automobile. You do not have to match our design exactly, but you are required to include the table at the bottom of the document. Proceed as follows:
   a. Start a new document. Center the title of the document as shown in the figure. Use the Borders and Shading command to display the title in light text on a solid background.
   b. Write a short paragraph describing your vehicle. Include any extra equipment, a statement of condition, and the current mileage.
   c. Use your favorite search engine to locate one or more pictures of the car you wish to sell. Download those photos to your PC.
   d. Use the Insert Picture command to insert the photographs one at a time into the document. (If necessary, right click each photo after it has been inserted to display a context-sensitive menu, click the Format Picture command, and then click the Layout tab. Choose the appropriate option to help you position the picture within the text. You might also want to click the Size tab to set the dimensions of your picture more precisely.)
   e. Create a 1 × 10 table (one row and ten columns) below the pictures. Enter your name and phone number in the first cell of the table. Pull down the Format menu and click the Text Direction command to change the direction as shown in Figure 4.15. Align the text to the top of the cell.
   f. Copy and paste the contents of this cell to the remaining cells in the row. Select the entire row and change the border style to a dashed line.
   g. Click the down arrow on the Zoom list box to view the whole page. Use the Table Properties command in the Table menu to change the row heights as necessary so that your document fills the entire page. Add text and photographs as necessary.
   h. Print the completed document for your instructor.

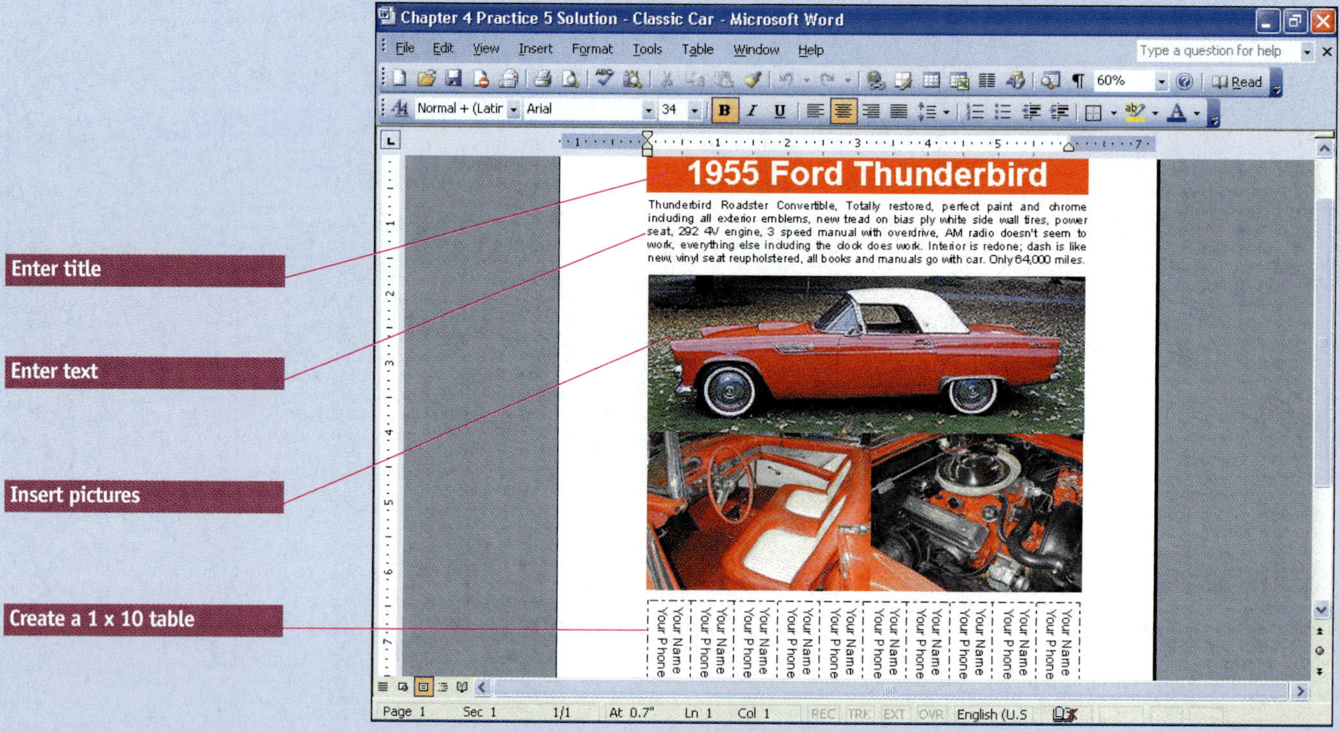

FIGURE 4.15 Classic Car for Sale (exercise 5)

6. **The Workout Schedule:** The table in Figure 4.16 is essentially an exercise in formatting, but it also tests your ability to copy efficiently within a document. You do not have to duplicate our document exactly, but you are required to have the equivalent functionality. Our schedule is for Monday through Friday (we take the weekend off), and it provides three sets for each exercise. You can create the document entirely on your own, or you can follow our suggested procedure.
   a. Start a new document. Pull down the File menu and click the Page Setup command. Change the orientation to landscape. Specify margins of one-half inch all around.
   b. Create a 5 × 17 table (5 rows and 17 columns), which includes the top portion of the table plus the first exercise. Select all but the first two cells in row two (the cells that will contain the days of the week). Pull down the Table menu, click the Table Properties command, click the Column tab, and then reduce the width of these columns to .45 inch. Change the width of the first two columns to 2.25 inches and 1 inch, respectively.
   c. Merge the cells in the first row, and then enter the indicated text. Format the text as you see fit. Insert an appropriate clip art image. (Select the clip art, pull down the Format menu, click Picture to display the Format Picture dialog box, and then click the Layout tab and change the wrapping style to position the clip art within the cell.) Copy the clip art as shown in the figure.
   d. Enter the text in rows 2 and 3 as shown. Use the Borders and Shading command in row 3 to select 100 percent (solid) shading to display white text on a dark background.
   e. Merge the first cell in rows 4 and 5. Type "Pounds" and "Reps" in the second cell in rows 4 and 5, respectively. Shade all but the first cell in row 5.
   f. Click and drag to select all of the cells in rows 4 and 5. Click the Copy button on the Standard toolbar (or use the Ctrl+C keyboard shortcut). Click the Paste button (or use the Ctrl+V keyboard shortcut) to paste the copied cells, effectively creating two additional rows for another exercise. Click the Paste button repeatedly until you have filled the page with space for additional exercises.
   g. Print the completed document for your instructor. Be sure the document fits on a single sheet of paper.

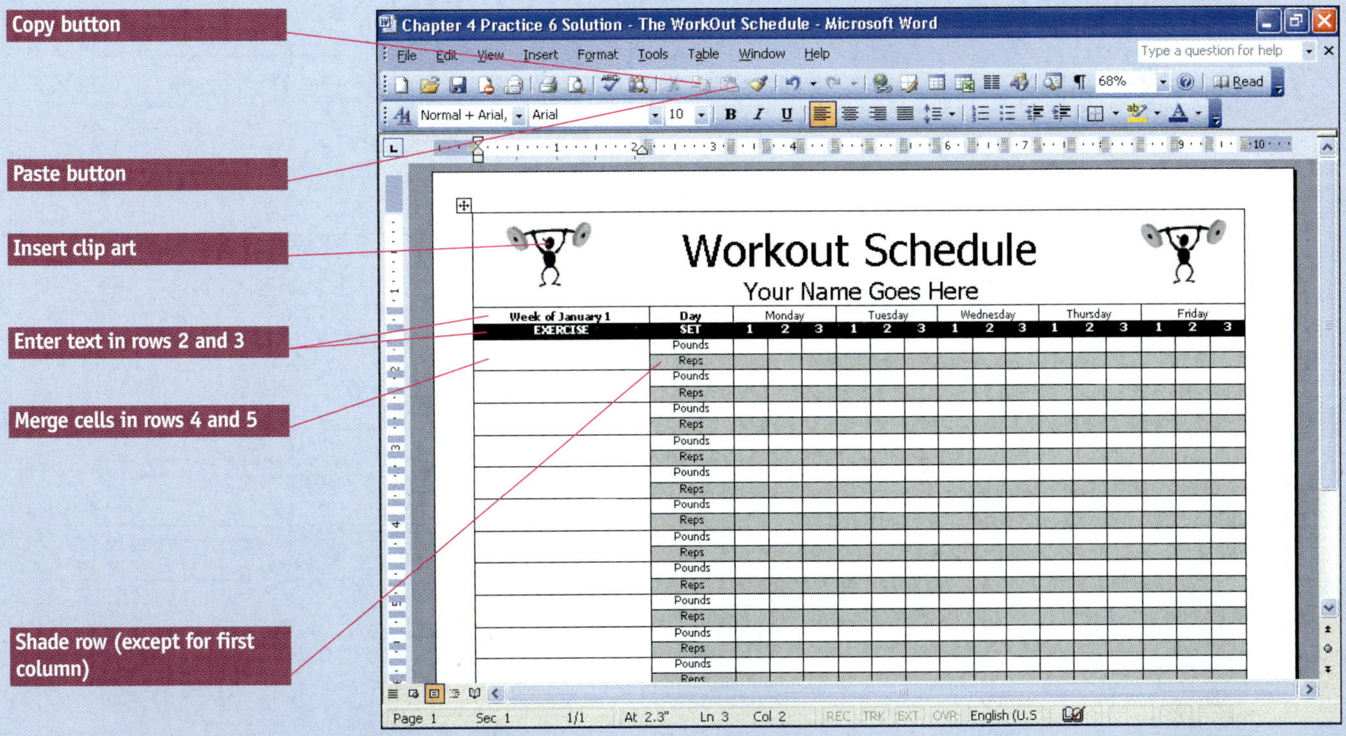

FIGURE 4.16 The Workout Schedule (exercise 6)

7. **Tips for Healthy Living:** The document in Figure 4.17 displays several tips from a document that contains tips for healthier living. The unformatted version of this document can be found in the *Chapter 4 Practice 7* document in the Exploring Word folder. Open that document, then modify it as follows:
   a. Use the AutoFormat command to apply the Heading 1 and Body Text styles throughout the document.
   b. Change the specifications for the Body Text and Heading 1 styles so that your document matches the document in the figure. The Heading 1 style calls for 12 point Arial bold with a blue top border (which requires a color printer). The Body Text style is 12 point Times New Roman, justified, with a ¼ inch left indent.
   c. Create a title page for the document consisting of the title, *Tips for Healthy Living*, the author, *Marion B. Grauer*, and an additional line, indicating that the document was prepared by you.
   d. Create a header for the document consisting of the title, *Tips for Healthy Living*, and a page number. (You can see the header in Figure 4.17.) The header is not to appear on the title page; that is, Page 1 is actually the second page of the document. Look closely at the status bar in Figure 4.17 and you will see that you are on Page 3, but that this is the fourth page of a six-page document.
   e. Click the Document Map button on the Standard toolbar to toggle the left pane on and off. The entries in the left pane correspond to all of the paragraphs in the document that are formatted in a heading style. Click any heading in the left pane and the corresponding text is displayed automatically in the right pane. (The Document Map button functions as a toggle switch.)
   f. Print the completed document for your instructor. Are you ready to follow the advice and adopt a healthier lifestyle?

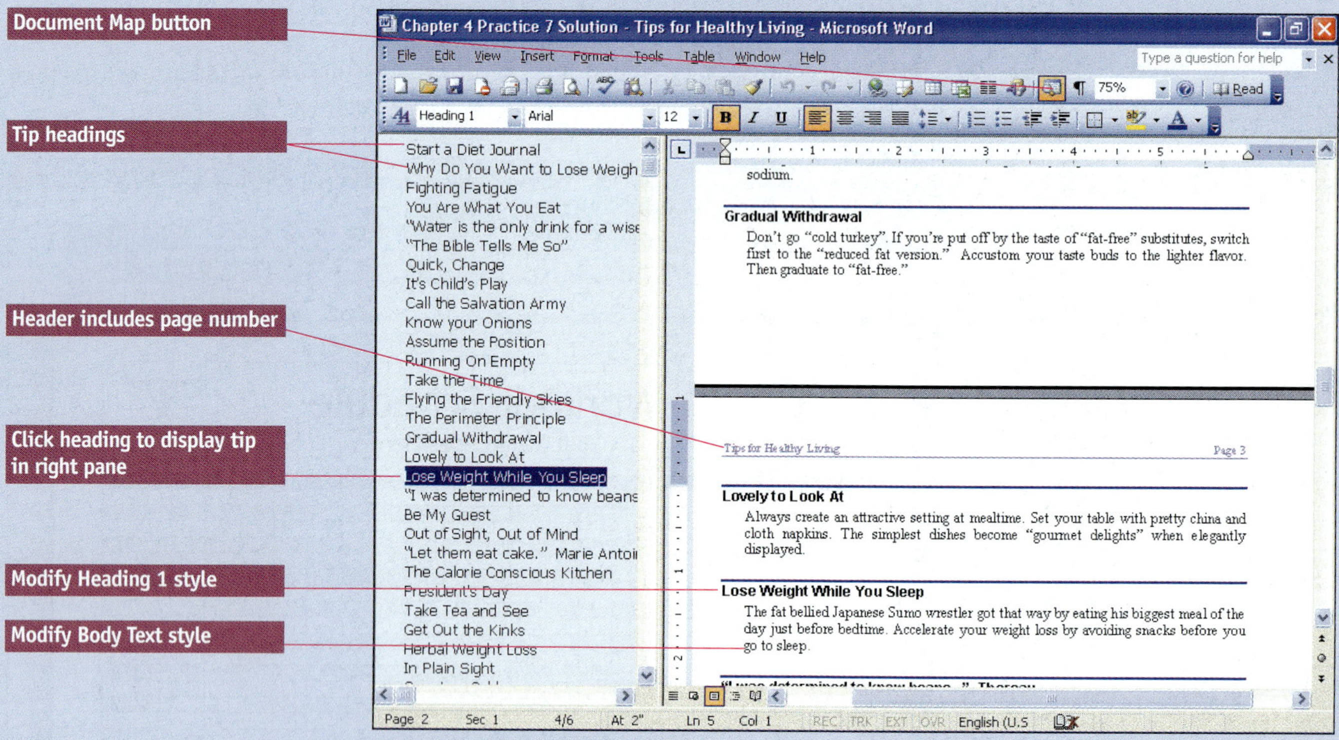

FIGURE 4.17 Tips for Healthy Living (exercise 7)

MINI CASES

Tips for Windows XP

Open the *Chapter 4 Mini Case—Tips for Windows XP* document that can be found in the Exploring Word folder. The tips are not formatted, so we would like you to use the AutoFormat command to create an attractive document. There are lots of tips, so a table of contents is also appropriate. Add a cover page with your name and date, then submit the completed document to your instructor.

Milestones in Communications

We take for granted immediate news of everything that is going on in the world, but it was not always that way. Did you know, for example, that it took five months for Queen Isabella to hear of Columbus' discovery, or that it took two weeks for Europe to learn of Lincoln's assassination? We've done some research on milestones in communications and left the file for you (*Chapter 4 Mini Case—Milestones in Communications*). It runs for two, three, or four pages, depending on the formatting, which we leave to you. We would like you to include a header, and we think you should box the quotations that appear at the end of the document (it's your call as to whether to separate the quotations or group them together). Please be sure to number the completed document and don't forget a title page.

The Term Paper

Go to your most demanding professor and obtain the formatting requirements for the submission of a term paper. Be as precise as possible; for example, ask about margins, type size, and so on. What are the requirements for a title page? Is there a table of contents? Are there footnotes or endnotes, headers or footers? What is the format for the bibliography? Summarize the requirements, then indicate the precise means of implementation within Microsoft Word.

Forms, Forms, and More Forms

Every business uses a multitude of forms. Job applicants submit an employment application, sales personnel process order forms, and customers receive invoices. Even telephone messages have a form of their own. The office manager needs forms for everything, and she has come to you for help. You remember reading something about a tables feature and suggest that as a starting point. She needs more guidance, so you sit down with her and quickly design two forms that meet with her approval. Bring the two forms to class and compare your work with that of your classmates.

Writing Style

Use your favorite search engine to locate documents that describe suggested writing style for research papers. You will find different guidelines for traditional documents versus those that are published on the Web. Can you create a sample document that implements the suggested specifications? Summarize your findings in a brief note to your professor.

CHAPTER 1

Introduction to Excel: What Is a Spreadsheet?

OBJECTIVES

After reading this chapter you will:

1. Describe several potential spreadsheet applications.
2. Distinguish among a constant, a formula, and a function.
3. Distinguish between a workbook and a worksheet.
4. Explain how the rows and columns in a worksheet are labeled.
5. Download the practice files for use in hands-on exercises.
6. Insert or delete rows and columns in a worksheet.
7. Print a worksheet to show displayed values or cell contents.
8. Distinguish between relative and absolute references.
9. Copy and/or move cell formulas within a worksheet.
10. Format a worksheet; use borders and shading; change fonts and alignment.

hands-on exercises

1. INTRODUCTION TO EXCEL
   Input: Grade Book
   Output: Grade Book Solution
2. MODIFYING A WORKSHEET
   Input: Grade Book Solution (from exercise 1)
   Output: Grade Book Solution (additional modifications)
3. CREATING A WORKBOOK
   Input: None
   Output: Better Grade Book Solution
4. FORMATTING A WORKSHEET
   Input: Better Grade Book Solution (from exercise 3)
   Output: Better Grade Book Solution (additional modifications)

CASE STUDY
THE CLARK SCHOOL

The Clark School has been severely impacted by a statewide cutback in funding for extracurricular activities. The school needs money badly and has settled on a door-to-door sale of food items by its students as the initial fund-raiser. The goal is to raise $5,000 for the purchase of new instruments for the music program. The plan is for students to present a catalog to their parents and other potential customers, who are asked to indicate their choices and provide immediate payment.

Melissa Edwards, the individual in charge of fund-raising, has settled on cookie dough as the featured product. Melissa has contracted with an organization that offers ten flavors of the dough, each in a two-pound tub that sells for $8.00 to $10.00 per tub. The school keeps a specified percentage of the selling price (50% in this instance) as profit. The students take the orders and collect the money. The organization delivers the cookie dough to the school, and the students deliver the cookie dough to their customers.

The principal has asked for a progress report midway through the fund-raiser. He wants to know whether the $5,000 goal has been met, and if not, how far the school is from meeting its goal. ■

Your assignment is to read the chapter, paying special attention to Hands-on Exercises 3 and 4, which describe how to create and format a spreadsheet. You will put yourself in Melissa's place and open the workbook, *Chapter 1 Case Study—The Clark School*, which contains the sales data through day 15 of the fund-raiser. Your task is to complete the worksheet by adding the formulas to compute the profit to date, check the profit against the intended goal, and finally, format the spreadsheet in an attractive fashion for presentation to the principal. Print the completed worksheet to show both displayed values and cell formulas.

INTRODUCTION TO SPREADSHEETS

The spreadsheet is the PC application that is used most frequently by managers and executives. This chapter provides a broad-based introduction to spreadsheets in general and to Microsoft Excel in particular. A spreadsheet (also called a worksheet) is stored within a workbook, which in turn may contain multiple worksheets.

The illustrations in this chapter are set in the context of an accountant's ledger and a professor's grade book, with the latter implemented on the computer. You will learn how students can be inserted into or removed from the worksheet and how changing a student's grade automatically recalculates the dependent values in the worksheet.

The Accountant's Ledger

A ***spreadsheet*** is the computerized equivalent of an accountant's ledger. As with the ledger, it consists of a grid of rows and columns that enables you to organize data in a readily understandable format. Figures 1.1a and 1.1b show the same information displayed in ledger and spreadsheet format, respectively.

"What is the big deal?" you might ask. The big deal is that after you change an entry (or entries), the spreadsheet will, automatically and almost instantly, recompute all of the formulas. Consider, for example, the profit projection spreadsheet shown in Figure 1.1b. As the spreadsheet is presently constructed, the unit price is \$20 and the projected sales are 1,200 units, producing gross sales of \$24,000 (\$20/unit × 1,200 units). The projected expenses are \$19,200, which yields a profit of \$4,800 (\$24,000 – \$19,200). If the unit price is increased to \$22 per unit, the spreadsheet recomputes the formulas, adjusting the values of gross sales and net profit. The modified spreadsheet of Figure 1.1c appears automatically.

With a calculator and bottle of correction fluid or a good eraser, the same changes could also be made to the ledger. But imagine a ledger with hundreds of entries and the time that would be required to make the necessary changes to the ledger by hand. The same spreadsheet will be recomputed automatically by the computer. And the computer will not make mistakes. Herein lie the advantages of a spreadsheet—the ability to make changes, and to have the computer carry out the recalculation faster and more accurately than could be accomplished manually.

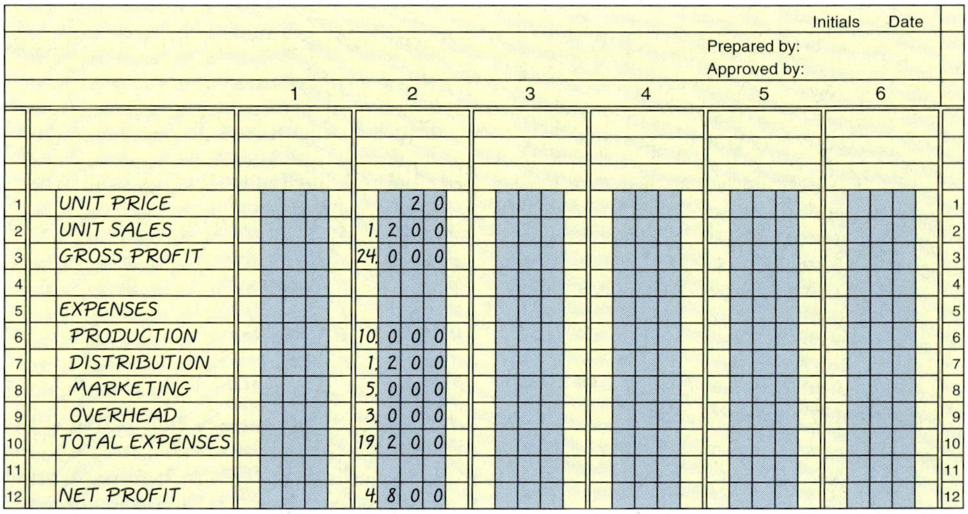

(a) The Accountant's Ledger

FIGURE 1.1 The Accountant's Ledger

Unit price is $20

Gross sales calculated automatically

	A	B
1	Profit Projection	
2		
3	Unit Price	$20
4	Unit Sales	1,200
5	Gross Sales	$24,000
6		
7	Expenses	
8	Production	$10,000
9	Distribution	$1,200
10	Marketing	$5,000
11	Overhead	$3,000
12	Total Expenses	$19,200
13		
14	Net Profit	$4,800

Net profit calculated automatically

(b) Original Spreadsheet

Gross sales are recalculated

Unit price increased to $22

	A	B
1	Profit Projection	
2		
3	Unit Price	$22
4	Unit Sales	1,200
5	Gross Sales	$26,400
6		
7	Expenses	
8	Production	$10,000
9	Distribution	$1,200
10	Marketing	$5,000
11	Overhead	$3,000
12	Total Expenses	$19,200
13		
14	Net Profit	$7,200

Net profit is recalculated

(c) Modified Spreadsheet

FIGURE 1.1 The Accountant's Ledger (*continued*)

The Professor's Grade Book

A second example of a spreadsheet, one with which you can easily identify, is that of a professor's grade book. The grades are recorded by hand in a notebook, which is nothing more than a different kind of accountant's ledger. Figure 1.2 contains both manual and spreadsheet versions of a grade book.

Figure 1.2a shows a handwritten grade book as it has been done since the days of the little red schoolhouse. For the sake of simplicity, only five students are shown, each with three grades. The professor has computed class averages for each exam, as well as a semester average for every student. The final counts *twice* as much as either test; for example, Adams's average is equal to (100+90+81+81)/4 = 88. This is the professor's grading scheme, and it is incorporated into the manual grade book and equivalent spreadsheet.

Figure 1.2b shows the grade book as it might appear in a spreadsheet, and is essentially unchanged from Figure 1.2a. Walker's grade on the final exam in Figure 1.2b is 90, giving him a semester average of 85 and producing a class average on the final of 75.2 as well. Now consider Figure 1.2c, in which the grade on Walker's final has been changed to 100, causing Walker's semester average to change from 85 to 90, and the class average on the final to go from 75.2 to 77.2. As with the profit projection, a change to any entry within the grade book automatically recalculates all other dependent formulas as well. Hence, when Walker's final exam was regraded, all dependent formulas (the class average for the final as well as Walker's semester average) were recomputed.

As simple as the idea of a spreadsheet may seem, it provided the first major reason for managers to have a personal computer on their desks. Essentially, anything that can be done with a pencil, a pad of paper, and a calculator can be done faster and far more accurately with a spreadsheet. The spreadsheet, like the personal computer, has become an integral part of every type of business. Indeed, it is hard to imagine that these calculations were ever done by hand. The spreadsheet has become an integral part of corporate culture.

Final counts twice so average is computed as (100+90+81+81)/4

	TEST 1	TEST 2	FINAL	AVERAGE
ADAMS	100	90	81	88
BAKER	90	76	87	85
GLASSMAN	90	78	78	81
MOLDOF	60	60	40	50
WALKER	80	80	90	85
CLASS AVERAGE	84.0	76.8	75.2	
NOTE: FINAL COUNTS DOUBLE				

(a) The Professor's Grade Book

Walker's original grade is 90

	A	B	C	D	E
1	Student	Test 1	Test 2	Final	Average
2					
3	Adams	100	90	81	88.0
4	Baker	90	76	87	85.0
5	Glassman	90	78	78	81.0
6	Moldof	60	60	40	50.0
7	Walker	80	80	90	85.0
8					
9	Class Average	84.0	76.8	75.2	

(b) Original Grades

Grade on Walker's final is changed to 100

Formulas recompute automatically

	A	B	C	D	E
1	Student	Test 1	Test 2	Final	Average
2					
3	Adams	100	90	81	88.0
4	Baker	90	76	87	85.0
5	Glassman	90	78	78	81.0
6	Moldof	60	60	40	50.0
7	Walker	80	80	100	90.0
8					
9	Class Average	84.0	76.8	77.2	

(c) Modified Spreadsheet

FIGURE 1.2 The Professor's Grade Book

Row and Column Headings

A spreadsheet is divided into rows and columns, with each row and column assigned a heading. Rows are given numeric headings ranging from 1 to 65,536 (the maximum number of rows allowed). Columns are assigned alphabetic headings from column A to Z, then continue from AA to AZ and then from BA to BZ and so on, until the last of 256 columns (column IV) is reached.

The intersection of a row and column forms a ***cell***, with the number of cells in a spreadsheet equal to the number of rows times the number of columns. The professor's grade book in Figure 1.2, for example, has 5 columns labeled A through E, 9 rows numbered from 1 to 9, and a total of 45 cells. Each cell has a unique ***cell reference***; for example, the cell at the intersection of column A and row 9 is known as cell A9. *The column heading always precedes the row heading in the cell reference.*

Formulas and Constants

Figure 1.3 is an alternate view of the professor's grade book that shows the cell contents rather than the computed values. Cell E3, for example, does not contain the number 88 (Adams's average for the semester), but rather the formula to compute the average from the exam grades. Indeed, it is the existence of the formula that lets you change the value of any cell containing a grade for Adams (cells B3, C3, or D3), and have the computed average in cell E3 change automatically.

To create a spreadsheet, one goes from cell to cell and enters either a constant or a formula. A ***constant*** is an entry that does not change. It may be a number, such as a student's grade on an exam, or it may be descriptive text (a label), such as a student's name. A ***formula*** is a combination of numeric constants, cell references, arithmetic operators, and/or functions (described below) that displays the result of a calculation. You can ***edit*** (change) the contents of a cell by returning to the cell and reentering the constant or formula.

A formula always begins with an equal sign. Consider, for example, the formula in cell E3, =(B3+C3+2*D3)/4, which computes Adams's semester average. The formula is built in accordance with the professor's rules for computing a student's semester average, which counts the final twice as much as the other tests. Excel uses symbols +, –, *, /, and ^ to indicate addition, subtraction, multiplication, division, and exponentiation, respectively, and follows the normal rules of arithmetic precedence. Any expression in parentheses is evaluated first, then within an expression exponentiation is performed first, followed by multiplication or division in left to right order, then finally addition or subtraction.

The formula in cell E3 takes the grade on the first exam (in cell B3), plus the grade on the second exam (in cell C3), plus two times the grade on the final (in cell D3), and divides the result by four. Thus, should any of the exam grades change, the semester average (a formula whose results depend on the individual exam grades) will also change. This, in essence, is the basic principle behind the spreadsheet and explains why, when one number changes, various other numbers throughout the spreadsheet change as well.

A formula may also include a ***function***, or predefined computational task, such as the AVERAGE function in cells B9, C9, and D9. The function in cell B9, for example, =AVERAGE(B3:B7), is interpreted to mean the average of all cells starting at cell B3 and ending at cell B7 and is equivalent to the formula =(B3+B4+B5+B6+B7)/5. You can appreciate that functions are often easier to use than the corresponding formulas, especially with larger spreadsheets (and classes with many students). Excel contains a wide variety of functions that help you to create very powerful spreadsheets. Financial functions, for example, enable you to calculate the interest payments on a car loan or home mortgage.

Constant (entry that does not change)

Function (predefined computational task)

Formula (mathematical expression)

	A	B	C	D	E
1	Student	Test 1	Test 2	Final	Average
2					
3	Adams	100	90	81	=(B3+C3+2*D3)/4
4	Baker	90	76	87	=(B4+C4+2*D4)/4
5	Glassman	90	78	78	=(B5+C5+2*D5)/4
6	Moldof	60	60	40	=(B6+C6+2*D6)/4
7	Walker	80	80	90	=(B7+C7+2*D7)/4
8					
9	Class Average	=AVERAGE(B3:B7)	=AVERAGE(C3:C7)	=AVERAGE(D3:D7)	

FIGURE 1.3 The Professor's Grade Book (cell formulas)

Figure 1.4 displays the professor's grade book as it is implemented in Microsoft Excel. Microsoft Excel is a Windows application, and thus shares the common user interface with which you are familiar. (It's even easier to learn Excel if you already know another Office application such as Microsoft Word.) You should recognize, therefore, that the desktop in Figure 1.4 has two open windows—an application window for Microsoft Excel and a document window for the workbook.

Each window has its own Minimize, Maximize (or Restore), and Close buttons. Both windows have been maximized and thus the title bars have been merged into a single title bar that appears at the top of the application window. The title bar reflects the application (Microsoft Excel) as well as the name of the workbook (Grade Book) on which you are working. A menu bar appears immediately below the title bar. Two toolbars, which are discussed in depth on page 8, appear below the menu bar. Vertical and horizontal scroll bars appear at the right and bottom of the document window.

The ***Ask a Question box*** appears to the right of the menu bar and provides instant access to the Help facility. The ***task pane*** at the right of the window provides access to several basic tasks in Excel. Different task panes are displayed at different times, depending on what you want to accomplish. The Getting Started task pane is the one you see when Excel is started initially. It lists the last several workbooks that were opened and also provides access to help. The Help task pane is shown in Figure 1.4.

The terminology is important, and we distinguish among spreadsheet, worksheet, and workbook. Excel refers to a spreadsheet as a ***worksheet***. Spreadsheet is a generic term; *workbook* and *worksheet* are unique to Excel. An Excel ***workbook*** contains one or more worksheets. The professor's grades for this class are contained in the CIS120 worksheet within the Grade Book workbook. This workbook also contains additional worksheets (CIS223 and CIS316) as indicated by the worksheet tabs at the bottom of the window. These worksheets contain the professor's grades for other courses that he or she is teaching this semester.

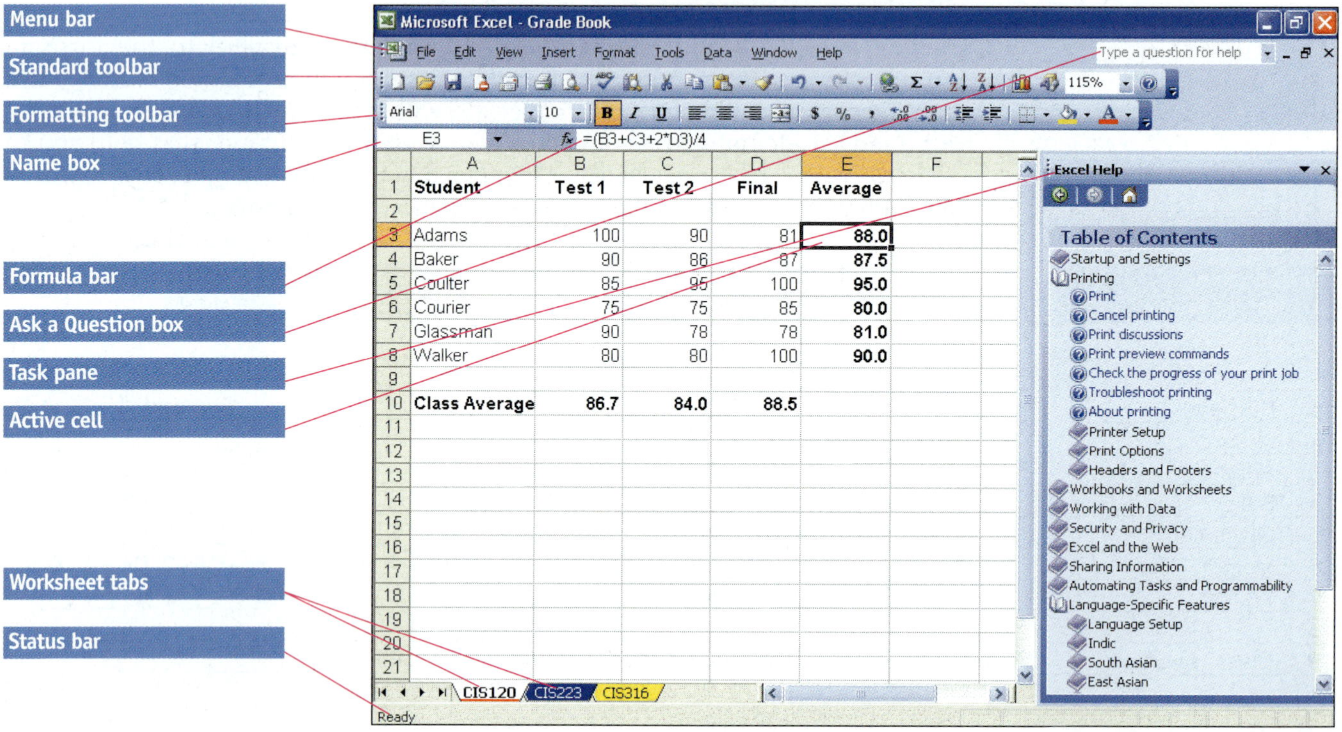

FIGURE 1.4 The Professor's Grade Book

Figure 1.4 resembles the grade book shown earlier, but it includes several other elements that enable you to create and/or edit the worksheet. The heavy border around cell E3 indicates that it (cell E3) is the ***active cell***. (The row and column headings are also highlighted to indicate the active cell.) Any entry made at this time is made into the active cell, and any commands that are executed affect the contents of the active cell. The active cell can be changed by clicking a different cell, or by using the arrow keys to move to a different cell.

The displayed value in cell E3 is 88.0, but as indicated earlier, the cell contains a formula to compute the semester average rather than the number itself. The contents of the active cell, =(B3+C3+2*D3)/4, are displayed in the ***formula bar*** near the top of the worksheet. The cell reference for the active cell, cell E3 in Figure 1.4, appears in the ***Name box*** at the left of the formula bar. The essence of Excel is the automatic recalculation of the formulas in a workbook; i.e., change a value in any cell and the entire workbook is recalculated. Change Adams's grade on the final exam, for example, and the displayed values for his semester average in cell E3, as well as the class average in cell D10, are updated automatically.

The ***status bar*** at the bottom of the worksheet keeps you informed of what is happening as you work within Excel. It displays information about a selected command or an operation in progress.

THE EXCEL WORKBOOK

An Excel workbook is the electronic equivalent of the three-ring binder. A workbook contains one or more worksheets (or chart sheets), each of which is identified by a tab at the bottom of the workbook. The worksheets in a workbook are normally related to one another; for example, each worksheet may contain the sales for a specific division within a company. The advantage of a workbook is that all of its worksheets are stored in a single file, which is accessed as a unit.

Toolbars

Excel provides several different ways to accomplish the same task. Commands may be accessed from a pull-down menu, from a shortcut menu (which is displayed by pointing to an object and clicking the right mouse button), and/or through keyboard equivalents. Commands can also be executed from one of many ***toolbars*** that appear immediately below the menu bar. The Standard and Formatting toolbars are displayed by default. The toolbars appear initially on the same line, but can be separated as described in the hands-on exercise that follows.

The ***Standard toolbar*** contains buttons corresponding to the most basic commands in Excel—for example, opening and closing a workbook, printing a workbook, and so on. The icon on the button is intended to be indicative of its function (e.g., a printer to indicate the Print command). You can also point to the button to display a ***ScreenTip*** showing the name of the button.

The ***Formatting toolbar*** appears under the Standard toolbar and provides access to common formatting operations such as boldface, italics, or underlining. It also enables you to change the alignment of entries within a cell and/or change the font or color. The easiest way to master the toolbars is to view the buttons in groups according to their general function, as shown in Figure 1.5.

The toolbars may appear overwhelming at first, but there is absolutely no need to memorize what the individual buttons do. That will come with time. Indeed, if you use another Office application such as Microsoft Word, you may already recognize many of the buttons on the Standard and Formatting toolbars. Note, too, that many of the commands in the pull-down menus are displayed with an image that corresponds to a button on a toolbar.

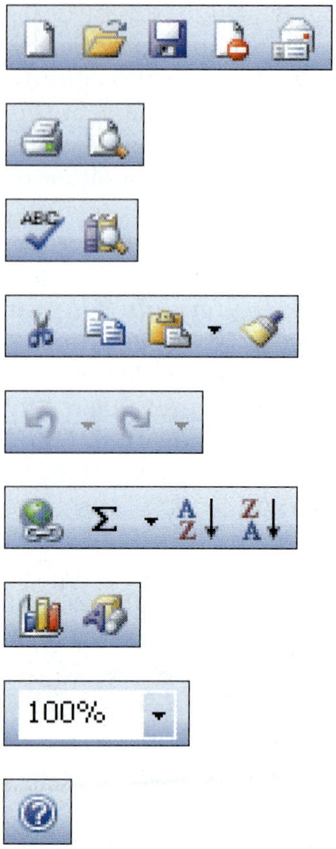

Opens a new workbook; opens an existing workbook; saves a workbook; prevents a workbook from being copied or edited; sends a workbook via e-mail

Prints the workbook; previews the workbook prior to printing

Checks the spelling; opens Research in the task pane

Cuts or copies the selecton to the clipboard; pastes the clipboard contents; copies the formatting of the selected cells

Undoes or redoes a previously executed command

Inserts a hyperlink; sums the suggested range; performs an ascending or descending sort

Starts the Chart Wizard; displays the Drawing toolbar

Changes the magnification

Opens Help in the task pane

(a) The Standard Toolbar

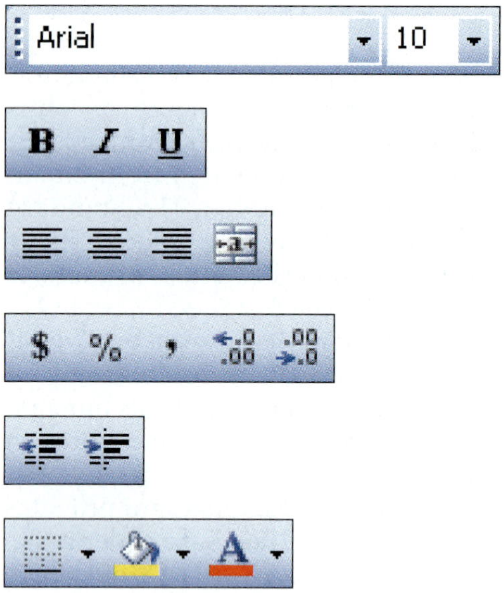

Changes the font or point size

Toggles boldface, italic, and underline on and off

Aligns left, center, right; merges cells and centers

Applies accounting, percentage, or comma formatting; increases or decreases the number of decimals

Decreases or increases the indent

Applies a border; applies a background color; applies a font color

(b) The Formatting Toolbar

FIGURE 1.5 Toolbars

THE FILE MENU

The ***File menu*** is a critically important menu in virtually every Windows application. It contains the Save and Open commands to save a workbook on disk, then subsequently retrieve (open) that workbook at a later time. The File menu also contains the ***Print command*** to print a workbook, the ***Close command*** to close the current workbook but continue working in the application, and the ***Exit command*** to quit the application altogether.

The ***Save command*** copies the workbook that you are working on (i.e., the workbook that is currently in memory) to disk. The command functions differently the first time it is executed for a new workbook, in that it displays the Save As dialog box as shown in Figure 1.6a. The dialog box requires you to specify the name of the workbook, the drive (and an optional folder) in which the workbook is to be stored, and its file type. All subsequent executions of the command save the workbook under the assigned name, replacing the previously saved version with the new version.

The ***file name*** (e.g., My First Spreadsheet) can contain up to 255 characters including spaces, commas, and/or periods. (Periods are discouraged, however, since they are too easily confused with DOS extensions.) The Save In list box is used to select the drive (which is not visible in Figure 1.6a) and the optional folder (e.g., Exploring Excel). The ***Places bar*** provides shortcuts to any of its folders without having to search through the Save In list box. Click the Desktop icon, for example, and the file is saved on the Windows desktop. You can also use the My Documents folder, which is accessible from every application in Microsoft Office.

The ***file type*** defaults to an Excel workbook. You can, however, choose a different format to maintain compatibility with earlier versions of Microsoft Excel. You can also save any Excel workbook as a Web page.

The ***Save As command*** saves a copy of an existing workbook under a different name, and/or a different file type, and is useful when you want to retain a copy of the original workbook. The command results in two copies of the workbook. The original workbook is kept on disk under the original name. A copy of the workbook is saved on disk under the new name and remains in memory. The Save As command also lets you save a workbook in a different file format such as text or CSV (comma-separated values) in order to convert the Excel data to a format required by another application.

The ***Open command*** is the opposite of the Save command as it brings a copy of an existing workbook into memory, enabling you to work with that workbook. The Open command displays the Open dialog box in which you specify the file name, the drive (and optionally the folder) that contains the file, and the file type. Microsoft Excel will then list all files of that type on the designated drive (and folder), enabling you to open the file you want.

The Save and Open commands work in conjunction with one another. The Save As dialog box in Figure 1.6a, for example, saves the file My First Spreadsheet in the Exploring Excel folder. The Open dialog box in Figure 1.6b loads that file into memory so that you can work with the file, after which you can save the revised file for use at a later time.

The toolbars in the Save As and Open dialog boxes have several buttons in common that facilitate the execution of either command. The Views button lets you display the files in many different views. The Details view shows the file size as well as the date and time a file was last modified. The Preview view shows the beginning of a workbook, without having to open the workbook. The List view displays only the file names, and thus lets you see more files at one time. The Properties view shows information about the workbook, including the date of creation and number of revisions. Other buttons provide limited file management without having to go to My Computer or Windows Explorer. You can, for example, delete a file, create a new folder, or start your Web browser from either dialog box.

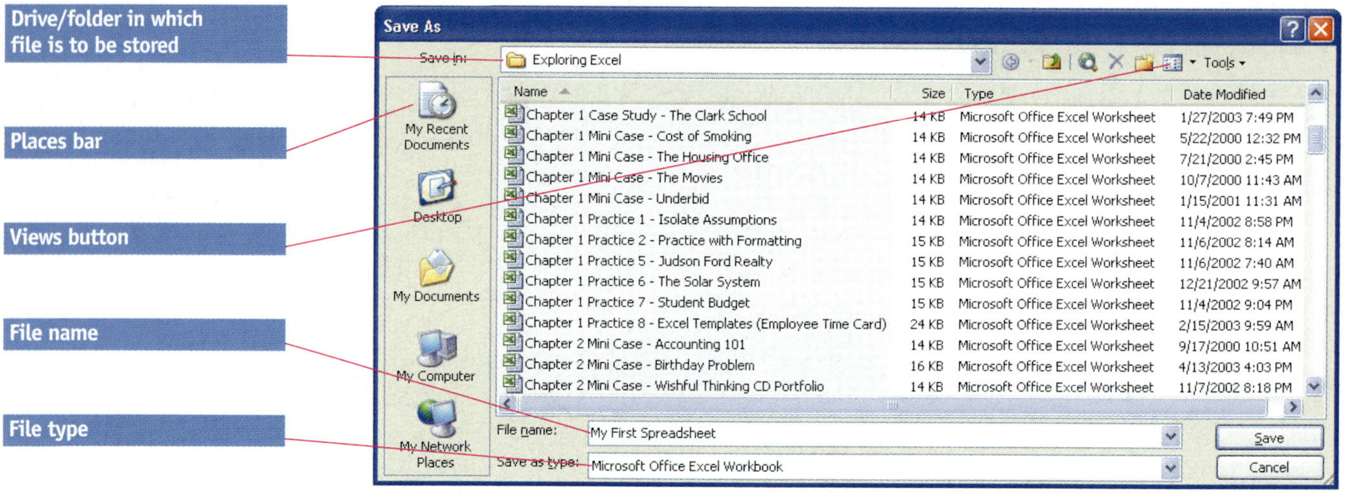

(a) Save As Dialog Box (Details View)

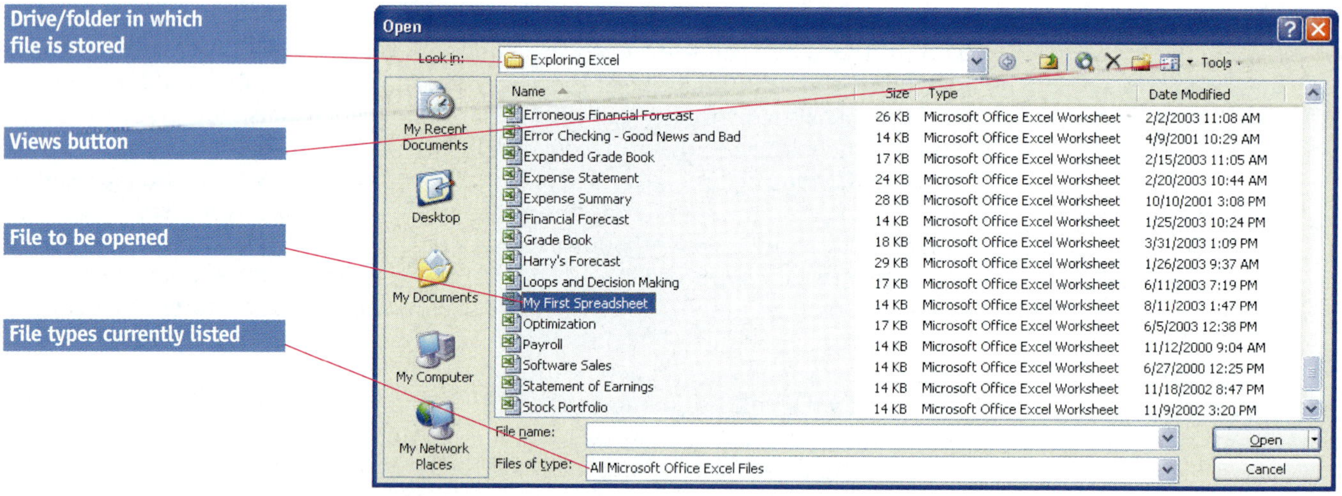

(b) Open Dialog Box (Details View)

FIGURE 1.6 The Save and Open Commands

FILE MANAGEMENT AT YOUR FINGERTIPS

Use the toolbar in the Open and/or Save As dialog box to perform basic file management within any Office application. You can select any existing file or folder, and delete it or rename it. You can also create a new folder, which is very useful when you begin to work with a large number of documents. You can also use the Views button to change the way the files are listed within the dialog box.

hands-on exercise

1 Introduction to Microsoft Excel

Objective To start Microsoft Excel; to open, modify, and print an existing workbook. Use Figure 1.7 as a guide in the exercise.

Step 1: Log On to Windows XP

- Turn on the computer and all of its peripherals. The floppy drive should be empty prior to starting your machine.
- Your system will take a minute or so to get started, after which you should see a logon screen similar to Figure 1.7a. Do not be concerned if the appearance of your desktop is different from ours.
- Click the icon for the user account you want to access. You may be prompted for a password, depending on the security options in effect.
- You should be familiar with basic file management and very comfortable moving and copying files from one folder to another. If not, you may want to review the material in the Windows XP section of this text.

Click icon for your user account

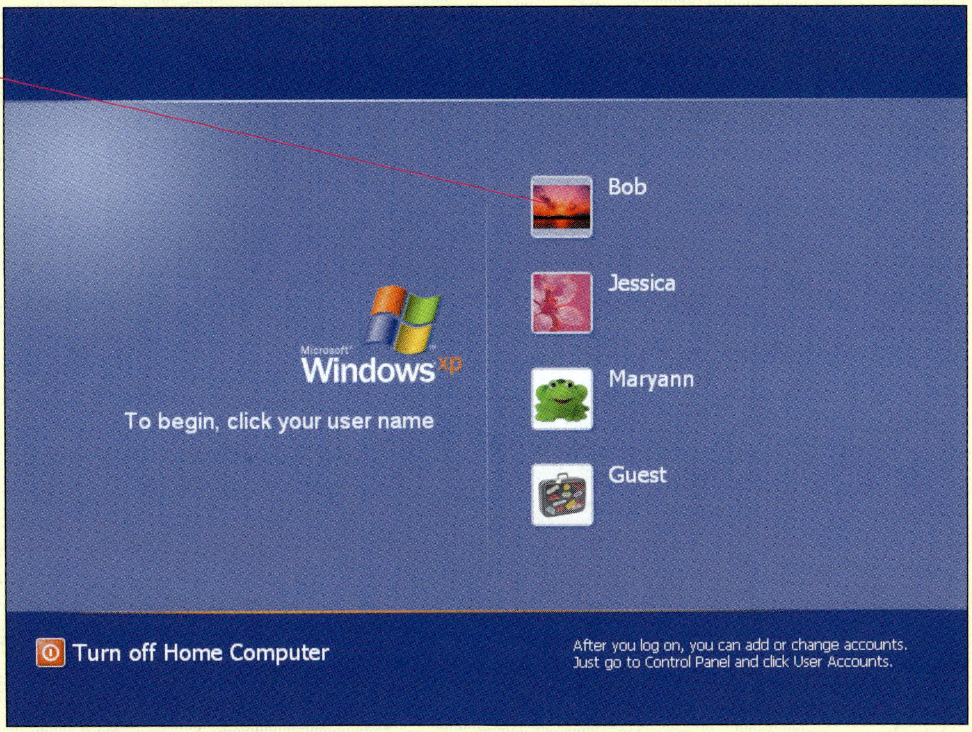

(a) Log On to Windows XP (step 1)

FIGURE 1.7 Hands-on Exercise 1

USER ACCOUNTS

The available user names are created automatically during the installation of Windows XP, but you can add or delete users at any time. Click the Start button, click Control Panel, switch to the Category view, and select User Accounts. Choose the desired task, such as creating a new account or changing an existing account, then supply the necessary information. Do not expect, however, to be able to modify accounts in a school setting.

Step 2: Download the Practice Files

- Start Internet Explorer and go to **www.prenhall.com/grauer**. Click the book for **Office 2003**, which takes you to the Office 2003 home page. Click the **Student Downloads tab** to go to the Student Download page as shown in Figure 1.7b.
- Select the appropriate file to download.
  - Choose **Exploring Excel** (or **Excel Volume I**) if you are using a stand-alone Excel text, as opposed to an Office text with multiple applications.
  - Choose **Office 2003 Volume I** (for regular or **Enhanced Edition**), **Office 2003 Plus**, or **Office 2003 Brief** with an Office text.
- Click the link to download the file. You will see the File Download box asking what you want to do. Click the **Save button**. The Save As dialog box appears.
- Click the **down arrow** in the Save In list box and select the drive and folder where you want to save the file. Click **Save**.
- Start Windows Explorer to select the drive and folder where you saved the file, then double click the file and follow the onscreen instructions.

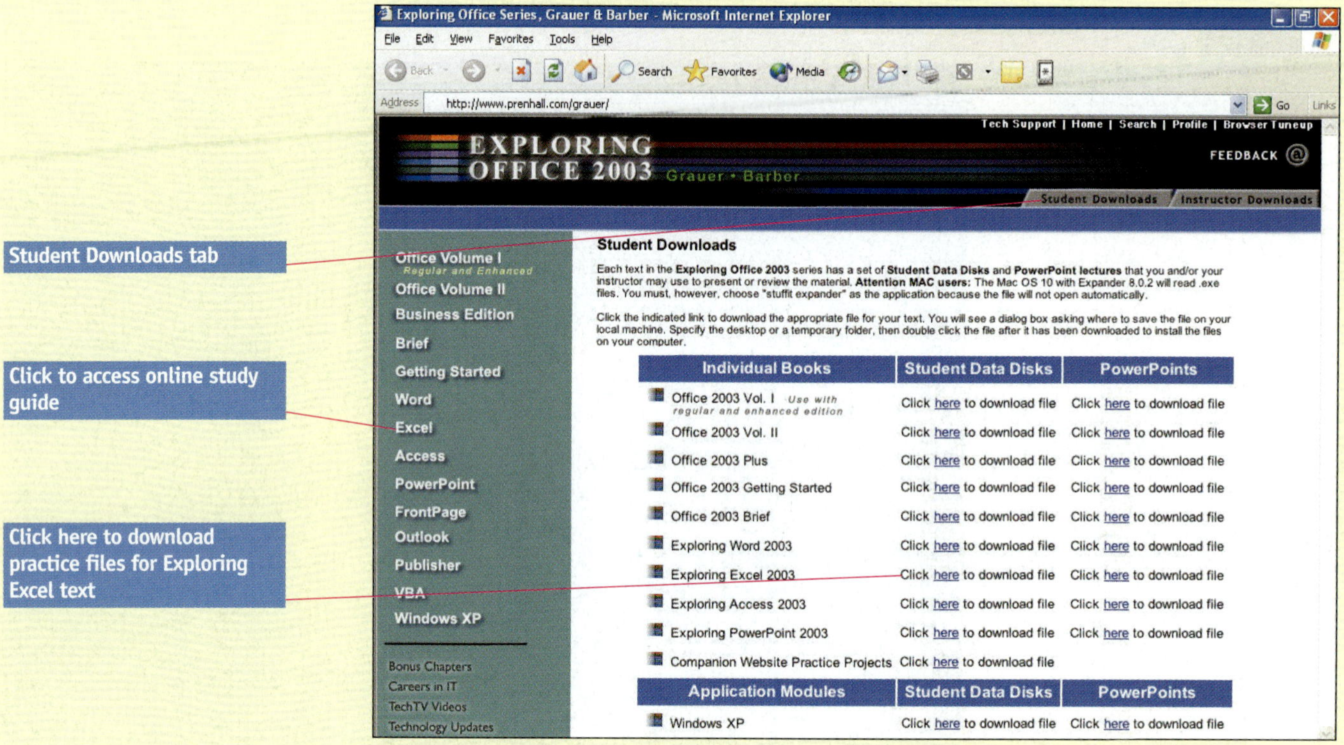

(b) Download the Practice Files (step 2)

FIGURE 1.7 Hands-on Exercise 1 (*continued*)

EXPLORE OUR WEB SITE

The Exploring Office Series Web site offers an online study guide (multiple-choice, true/false, and matching questions) for each individual textbook to help you review the material in each chapter. You can take practice quizzes by yourself and/or e-mail the results to your instructor. These online study guides are available via the tabs in the left navigation bar. You can return to the Student Download page at any time by clicking the tab toward the top of the window and/or you can click the link to Home to return to the home page for the Office 2003 Series. And finally, you can click the Feedback button at the top of the screen to send a message directly to Bob Grauer.

Step 3: Start Excel

- Click the **Start button** to display the Start menu. Click (or point to) the **All Programs button**, click **Microsoft Office**, then click **Microsoft Excel 2003** to start the program.
- Right click the Office Assistant if it appears. Click the **Hide command**.
- If necessary, click the **Maximize button** in the application window so that Excel takes the entire desktop as shown in Figure 1.7c. Click the **Maximize button** in the document window (if necessary) so that the document window is as large as possible.
- Pull down the **View menu** and click the **Task Pane command** to display (hide) the task pane. The command functions as a toggle switch; that is, execute the command and the task pane is open. Execute the command a second time and the task pane is closed.
- The Getting Started task pane appears initially. Click the down arrow in the task pane to see what other panes are available. The Help task pane is shown in Figure 1.7c. Close the task pane by clicking its **Close button**.

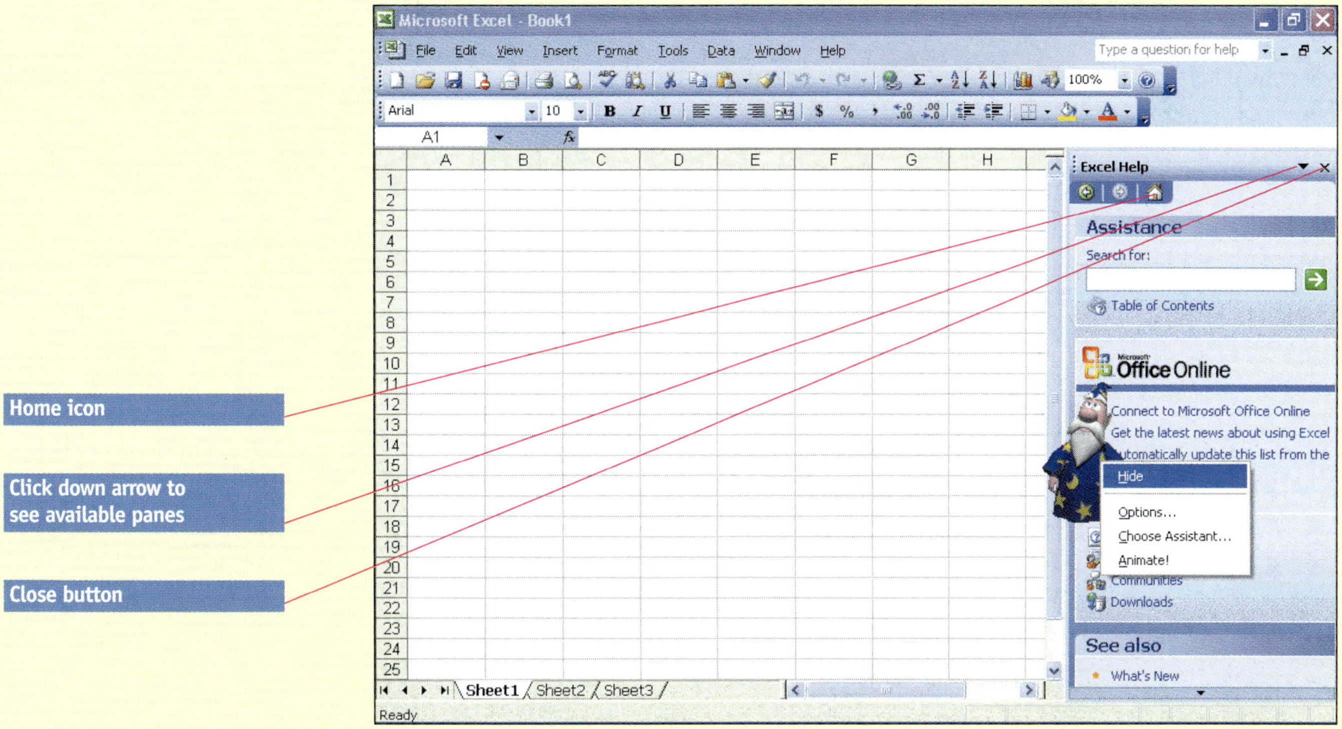

(c) Start Excel (step 3)

FIGURE 1.7 Hands-on Exercise 1 (*continued*)

SEPARATE THE TOOLBARS

You may see the Standard and Formatting toolbars displayed on one row to save space within the application window. If so, we suggest that you separate the toolbars, so that you see all of the buttons on each. Click the down arrow at the end of any visible toolbar to display toolbar options, then click the option to show the buttons on two rows. Click the down arrow a second time to show the buttons on one row if you prefer this configuration.

Step 4: Open the Workbook

- Pull down the **File menu** and click **Open** (or click the **Open button** on the Standard toolbar). You should see a dialog box similar to the one in Figure 1.7d.
- Click the **drop-down arrow** on the Views button, then click **Details** to change to the Details view. Click and drag the vertical border between two columns to increase (or decrease) the size of a column.
- Click the **drop-down arrow** on the Look In list box. Click the appropriate drive, drive C or drive A, depending on the location of your data.
- Double click the **Exploring Excel folder** to make it the active folder (the folder from which you will retrieve and into which you will save the workbook).
- Click the **down scroll arrow** if necessary in order to click **Grade Book** to select the professor's grade book. Click the **Open command button** to open the workbook and begin the exercise.

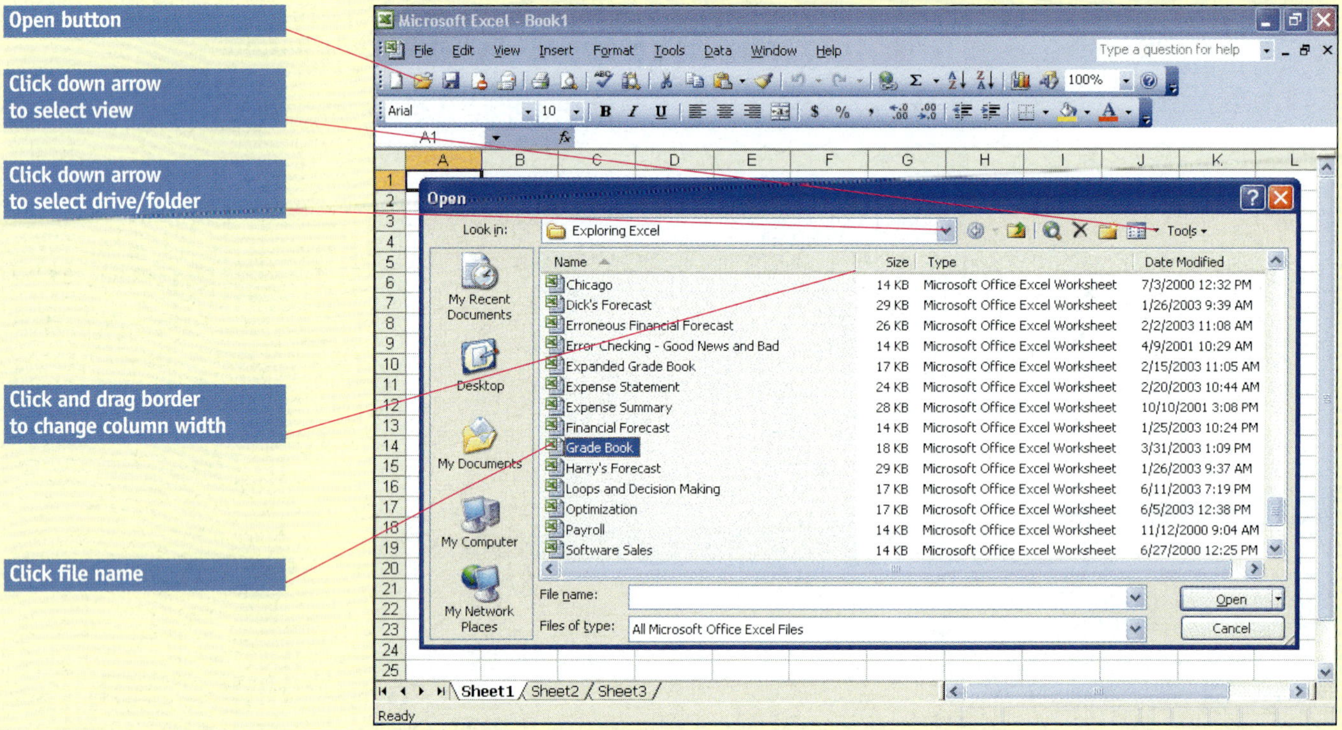

(d) Open the Workbook (step 4)

FIGURE 1.7 Hands-on Exercise 1 (*continued*)

THE MENUS MAY CHANGE

Microsoft Office gives you the option of displaying short menus (ending in a double arrow to show additional commands), as opposed to complete menus with all commands. We prefer the complete menus because that is the way you learn an application, but the settings may be different on your system. Pull down the Tools menu, click the Customize command to display the Customize dialog box, click the Options tab, and check the box to always show full menus.

Step 5: The Save As Command

- Pull down the **File menu**. Click **Save As** to display the dialog box shown in Figure 1.7e.
- Enter **Grade Book Solution** as the name of the new workbook. (A file name may contain up to 255 characters. Spaces and commas are allowed in the file name.)
- Click the **Save button**. Press the **Esc key** or click the **Close button** if you see a Properties dialog box.
- There are now two identical copies of the file on disk: "Grade Book" and "Grade Book Solution," which you just created. The title bar shows the latter name, which is the workbook currently in memory.
- You will work with "Grade Book Solution" but can always return to the original "Grade Book" if necessary.

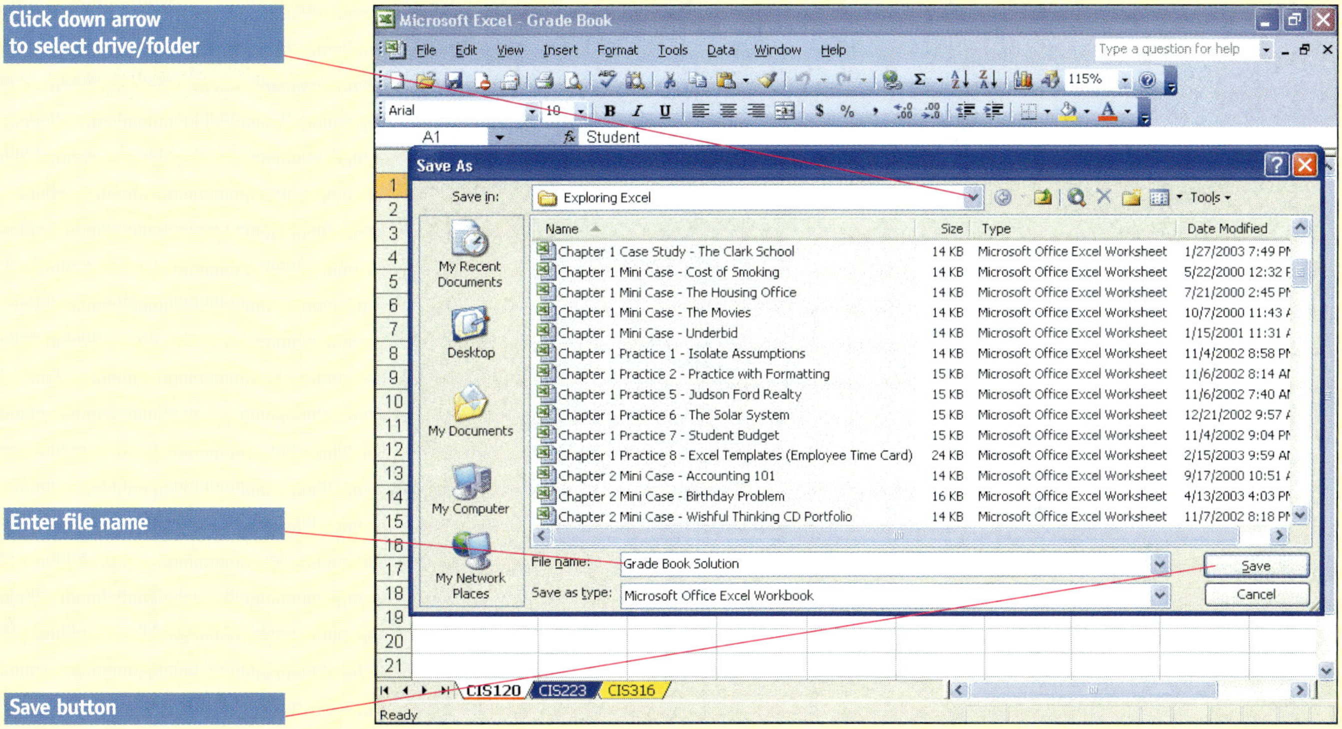

(e) The Save As Command (step 5)

FIGURE 1.7 Hands-on Exercise 1 (*continued*)

QUIT WITHOUT SAVING

There will be times when you do not want to save the changes to a workbook—for example, when you have edited it beyond recognition and wish you had never started. Pull down the File menu and click the Close command, then click No in response to the message asking whether to save the changes. Pull down the File menu, click the file's name at the bottom of the menu to reopen the file, then begin all over.

Step 6: The Active Cell, Formula Bar, and Worksheet Tabs

- You should see the workbook in Figure 1.7f. Click in **cell B3**, the cell containing Adams's grade on the first test. Cell B3 is now the active cell and is surrounded by a heavy border. The Name box indicates that cell B3 is the active cell, and its contents are displayed in the formula bar.
- Click in **cell B4** (or press the **down arrow key**) to make it the active cell. The Name box indicates cell B4 while the formula bar indicates a grade of 90.
- Click in **cell E3**, the cell containing the formula to compute Adams's semester average; the worksheet displays the computed average of 88.0, but the formula bar displays the formula, =(B3+C3+2*D3)/4, to compute that average based on the test grades.
- Click the **CIS223 tab** to view a different worksheet within the same workbook. This worksheet contains the grades for a different class.
- Click the **CIS316 tab** to view this worksheet. Click the **CIS120 tab** to return to this worksheet and continue with the exercise.

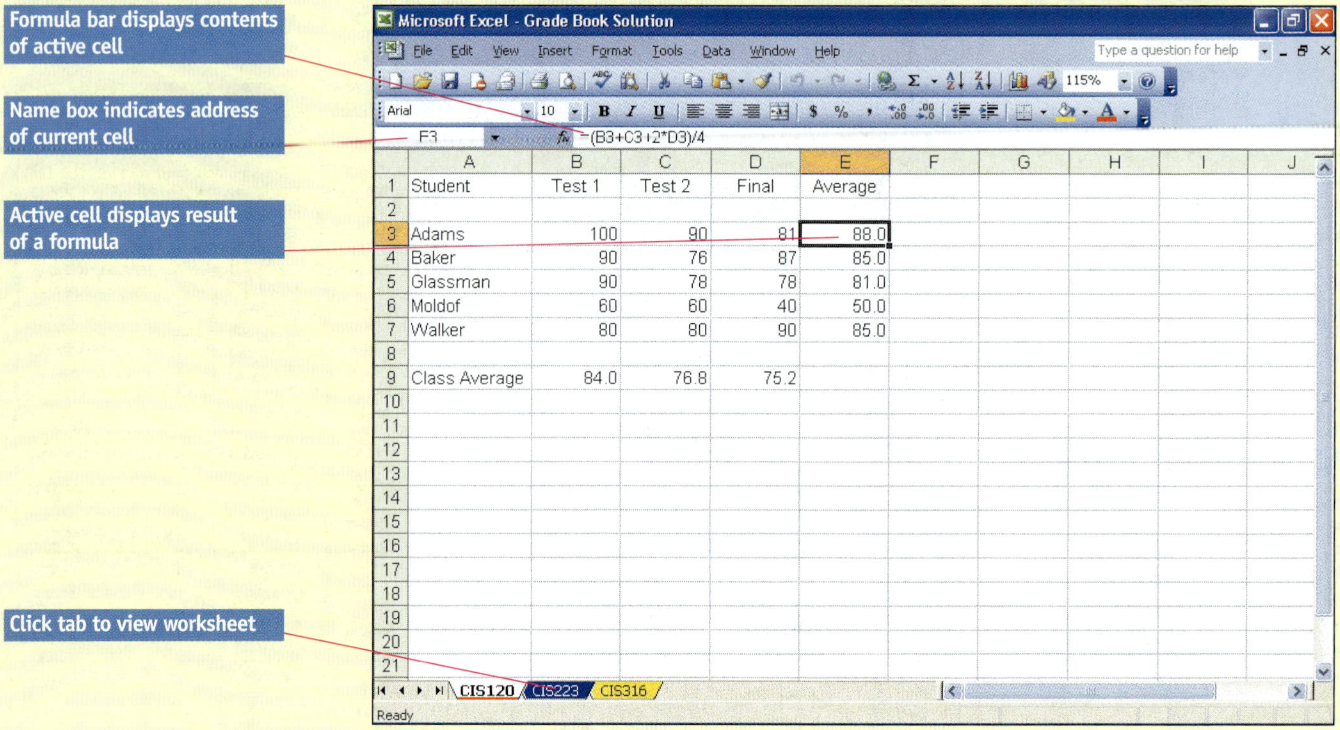

(f) The Active Cell, Formula Bar, and Worksheet Tabs (step 6)

FIGURE 1.7 Hands-on Exercise 1 (*continued*)

ADD COLOR TO THE WORKSHEET TABS

Select (click) the worksheet tab for which you want to change the tab color. (If you don't see the worksheet you want, click the tab scrolling buttons to display the tab, and then click the tab.) Pull down the Format menu, click the Sheet command, then click Tab Color to display a color palette. Click the color you want, and then click OK. You can also right click a worksheet tab to display a context-sensitive menu, and change the color from there.

Step 7: Experiment (What If?)

- Click in **cell C4**, the cell containing Baker's grade on the second test. Enter a corrected value of **86** (instead of the previous entry of 76). Press **Enter** (or click in another cell).
- The effects of this change ripple through the worksheet, automatically changing the computed value for Baker's average in cell E4 to 87.5. The class average on the second test in cell C9 changes to 78.8.
- Change Walker's grade on the final from 90 to **100**. Press **Enter** (or click in another cell). Walker's average in cell E7 changes to 90.0, while the class average in cell D9 changes to 77.2.
- Your worksheet should match Figure 1.7g. Save the workbook.

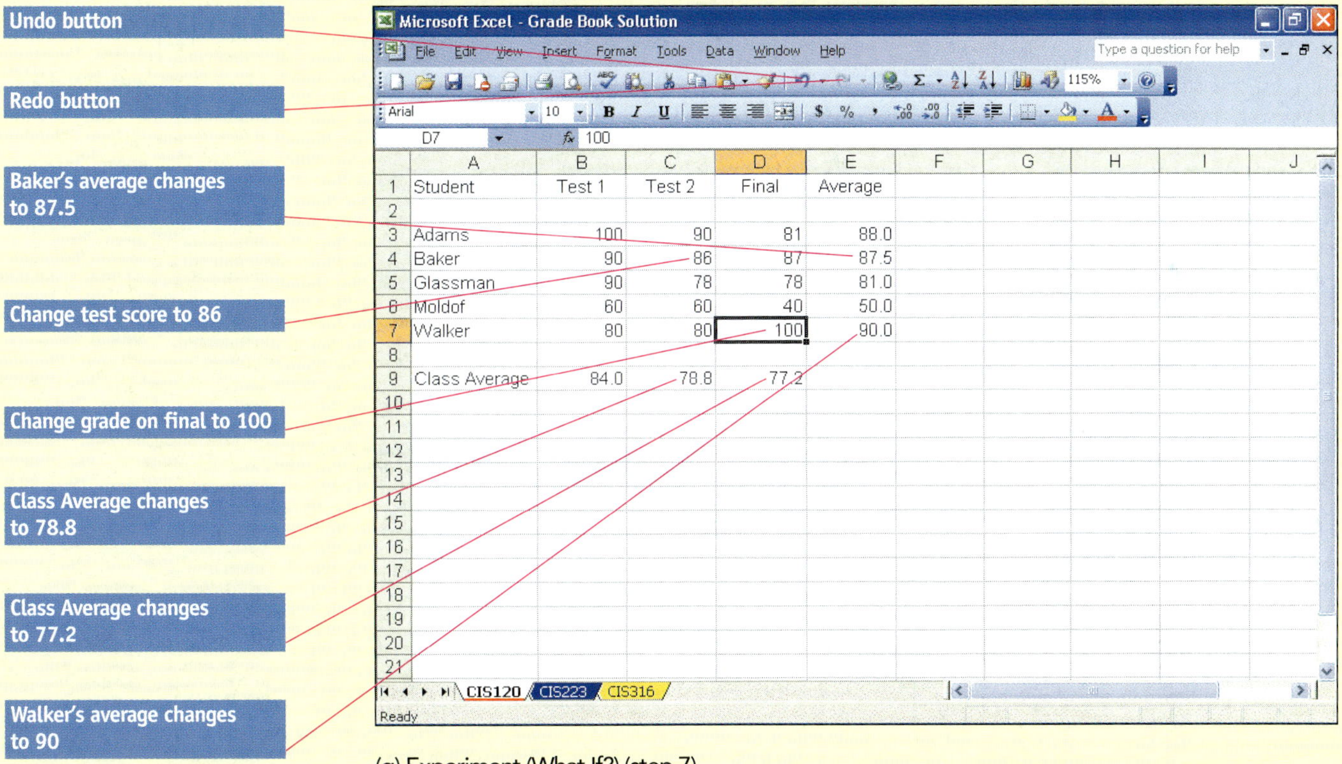

(g) Experiment (What If?) (step 7)

FIGURE 1.7 Hands-on Exercise 1 (*continued*)

THE UNDO AND REDO COMMANDS

The Undo command lets you undo the last several changes to a workbook. Click the down arrow next to the Undo button on the Standard toolbar to display a reverse-order list of your previous commands, then click the command you want to undo, which also cancels all of the preceding commands. Undoing the fifth command in the list, for example, will also undo the preceding four commands. The Redo command redoes (reverses) the last command that was undone. It, too, displays a reverse-order list of commands, so that redoing the fifth command in the list will also redo the preceding four commands.

Step 8: Help with Excel

- There are several different ways to request help, but in any event, the best time to obtain help is when you don't need any. Try either of the following:
  - Pull down the **Help menu** and click the command to **Show the Office Assistant**. Click the Assistant, then enter the question, "**How do I undo a command?**" in the Assistant's balloon and click **Search**, or
  - Type the question directly in the **Ask a Question list box** in the upper right of the Excel window and press **Enter**.
- Excel will display a message indicating that it is searching the Office Web site. You should see a task pane with the results as shown in Figure 1.7h.
- Click the link that is most appropriate, for example, **Undo or redo an action**. A new window opens containing the detailed help information. Click the **Print button** in the Help window, then click the **Print command button**.
- Close the Help window. Close the task pane. Pull down the **Help menu** and hide the Office Assistant. Exit Excel if you do not want to continue with the next exercise at this time.

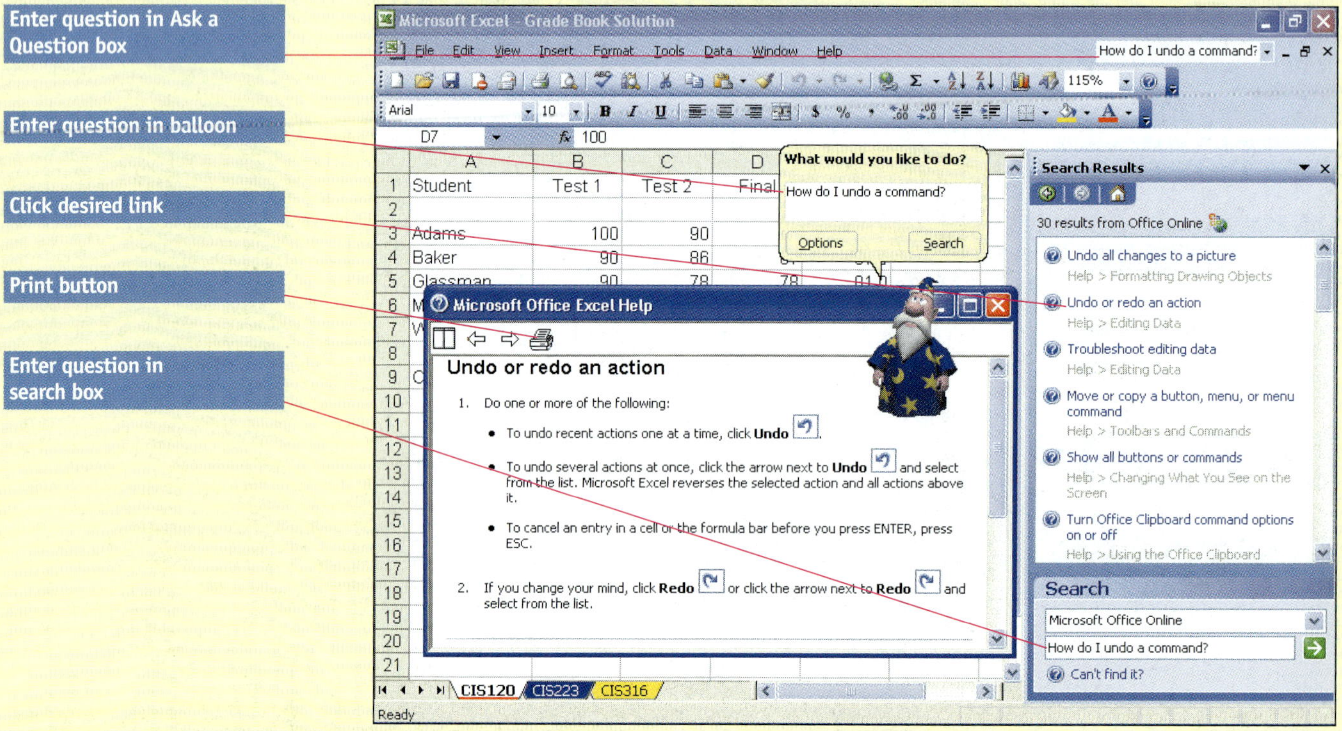

(h) Help with Excel (step 8)

FIGURE 1.7 Hands-on Exercise 1 (*continued*)

ABOUT MICROSOFT EXCEL

Pull down the Help menu and click About Microsoft Excel to display the specific release number as well as other licensing information, including the Product ID. This Help screen also contains two very useful command buttons, System Info and Technical Support. The first button displays information about the hardware installed on your system, including the amount of memory and available space on the hard drive. The Technical Support button provides information on obtaining technical assistance.

MODIFYING A WORKSHEET

We trust that you completed the hands-on exercise without difficulty and that you are more confident in your ability than when you first began. The exercise was not complicated, but it did accomplish several objectives and set the stage for a second exercise, which follows shortly.

Consider now Figure 1.8, which contains a modified version of the professor's grade book. Figure 1.8a shows the grade book at the end of the first hands-on exercise and reflects the changes made to the grades for Baker and Walker. Figure 1.8b shows the worksheet as it will appear at the end of the second exercise. Several changes bear mention:

1. One student has dropped the class and two other students have been added. Moldof appeared in the original worksheet in Figure 1.8a, but has somehow managed to withdraw; Coulter and Courier did not appear in the original grade book but have been added to the worksheet in Figure 1.8b.
2. A new column containing the students' majors has been added.

The implementation of these changes is accomplished through a combination of the ***Insert command*** (to add individual cells, rows, or columns) and/or the ***Delete command*** (to remove individual cells, rows, or columns). Execution of either command automatically adjusts the cell references in existing formulas to reflect the insertion or deletion of the various cells. The Insert and Delete commands can also be used to insert or delete a worksheet. The professor could, for example, add a new sheet to a workbook to include grades for another class and/or delete a worksheet for a class that was no longer taught. We focus initially, however, on the insertion and deletion of rows and columns within a worksheet.

Moldof will be dropped from class

	A	B	C	D	E
1	Student	Test 1	Test 2	Final	Average
2					
3	Adams	100	90	81	88.0
4	Baker	90	86	87	87.5
5	Glassman	90	78	78	81.0
6	Moldof	60	60	40	50.0
7	Walker	80	80	100	90.0
8					
9	Class Average	84.0	78.8	77.2	

(a) After Hands-on Exercise 1

A new column has been added (Major)

Two new students have been added

Moldof has been deleted

	A	B	C	D	E	F
1	Student	Major	Test 1	Test 2	Final	Average
2						
3	Adams	CIS	100	90	81	88.0
4	Baker	MKT	90	86	87	87.5
5	Coulter	ACC	85	95	100	95.0
6	Courier	FIN	75	75	85	80.0
7	Glassman	CIS	90	78	78	81.0
8	Walker	CIS	80	80	100	90.0
9						
10	Class Average		86.7	84.0	88.5	

(b) After Hands-on Exercise 2

FIGURE 1.8 The Modified Grade Book

Figure 1.9 displays the cell formulas in the professor's grade book and corresponds to the worksheets in Figure 1.8. The "before" and "after" worksheets reflect the insertion of a new column containing the students' majors, the addition of two new students, Coulter and Courier, and the deletion of an existing student, Moldof.

Let us consider the formula to compute Adams's semester average, which is contained in cell E3 of the original grade book, but in cell F3 in the modified grade book. The formula in Figure 1.9a referenced cells B3, C3, and D3 (the grades on test 1, test 2, and the final). The corresponding formula in Figure 1.9b reflects the fact that a new column has been inserted, and references cells C3, D3, and E3. The change in the formula is made automatically by Excel, without any action on the part of the user other than to insert the new column. The formulas for all other students have been adjusted in similar fashion.

Some students (all students below Baker) have had a further adjustment to reflect the addition of the new students through insertion of new rows in the worksheet. Glassman, for example, appeared in row 5 of the original worksheet, but appears in row 7 of the revised worksheet. Hence the formula to compute Glassman's semester average now references the grades in row 7, rather than in row 5 as in the original worksheet.

Finally, the formulas to compute the class averages have also been adjusted. These formulas appeared in row 9 of Figure 1.9a and averaged the grades in rows 3 through 7. The revised worksheet has a net increase of one student, which automatically moves these formulas to row 10, where the formulas are adjusted to average the grades in rows 3 through 8.

	A	B	C	D	E
1	Student	Test1	Test2	Final	Average
2					
3	Adams	100	90	81	=(B3+C3+2*D3)/4
4	Baker	90	86	87	=(B4+C4+2*D4)/4
5	Glassman	90	78	78	=(B5+C5+2*D5)/4
6	Moldof	60	60	40	=(B6+C6+2*D6)/4
7	Walker	80	80	100	=(B7+C7+2*D7)/4
8					
9	Class Average	=AVERAGE(B3:B7)	=AVERAGE(C3:C7)	=AVERAGE(D3:D7)	

Function references grades in rows 3–7

Formula references grades in B3, C3, and D3

(a) Before

	A	B	C	D	E	F
1	Student	Major	Test1	Test2	Final	Average
2						
3	Adams	CIS	100	90	81	=(C3+D3+2*E3)/4
4	Baker	MKT	90	86	87	=(C4+D4+2*E4)/4
5	Coulter	ACC	85	95	100	=(C5+D5+2*E5)/4
6	Courier	FIN	75	75	85	=(C6+D6+2*E6)/4
7	Glassman	CIS	90	78	78	=(C7+D7+2*E7)/4
8	Walker	CIS	80	80	100	=(C8+D8+2*E8)/4
9						
10	Class Average		=AVERAGE(C3:C8)	=AVERAGE(D3:D8)	=AVERAGE(E3:E8)	

Function changes to reference grades in rows 3–8 (due to addition of 2 new students and deletion of 1)

Formula changes to reference grades in C3, D3, and E3 due to addition of new column

(b) After

FIGURE 1.9 The Insert and Delete Commands

THE PAGE SETUP COMMAND

The ***Page Setup command*** gives you complete control of the printed worksheet as illustrated in Figure 1.10. Many of the options may not appear important now, but you will appreciate them as you develop larger and more complicated worksheets later in the text.

The Page tab in Figure 1.10 determines the orientation and scaling of the printed page. ***Portrait orientation*** (8½ × 11) prints vertically down the page. ***Landscape orientation*** (11 × 8½) prints horizontally across the page and is used when the worksheet is too wide to fit on a portrait page. The option buttons indicate mutually exclusive items, one of which *must* be selected; that is, a worksheet must be printed in either portrait or landscape orientation. Option buttons are also used to choose the scaling factor. You can reduce (enlarge) the output by a designated scaling factor, or you can force the output to fit on a specified number of pages. The latter option is typically used to force a worksheet to fit on a single page.

The Margins tab not only controls the margins, but will also center the worksheet horizontally and/or vertically. The Margins tab also determines the distance of the header and footer from the edge of the page.

The Header/Footer tab lets you create a header (and/or footer) that appears at the top (and/or bottom) of every page. The pull-down list boxes let you choose from several preformatted entries, or alternatively, you can click the appropriate command button to customize either entry.

The Sheet tab offers several additional options. The Gridlines option prints lines to separate the cells within the worksheet. The Row and Column Headings option displays the column letters and row numbers. Both options should be selected for most worksheets. Information about the additional entries can be obtained by clicking the Help button.

The Print Preview command button is available from all four tabs within the Page Setup dialog box. The command shows you how the worksheet will appear when printed and saves you from having to rely on trial and error.

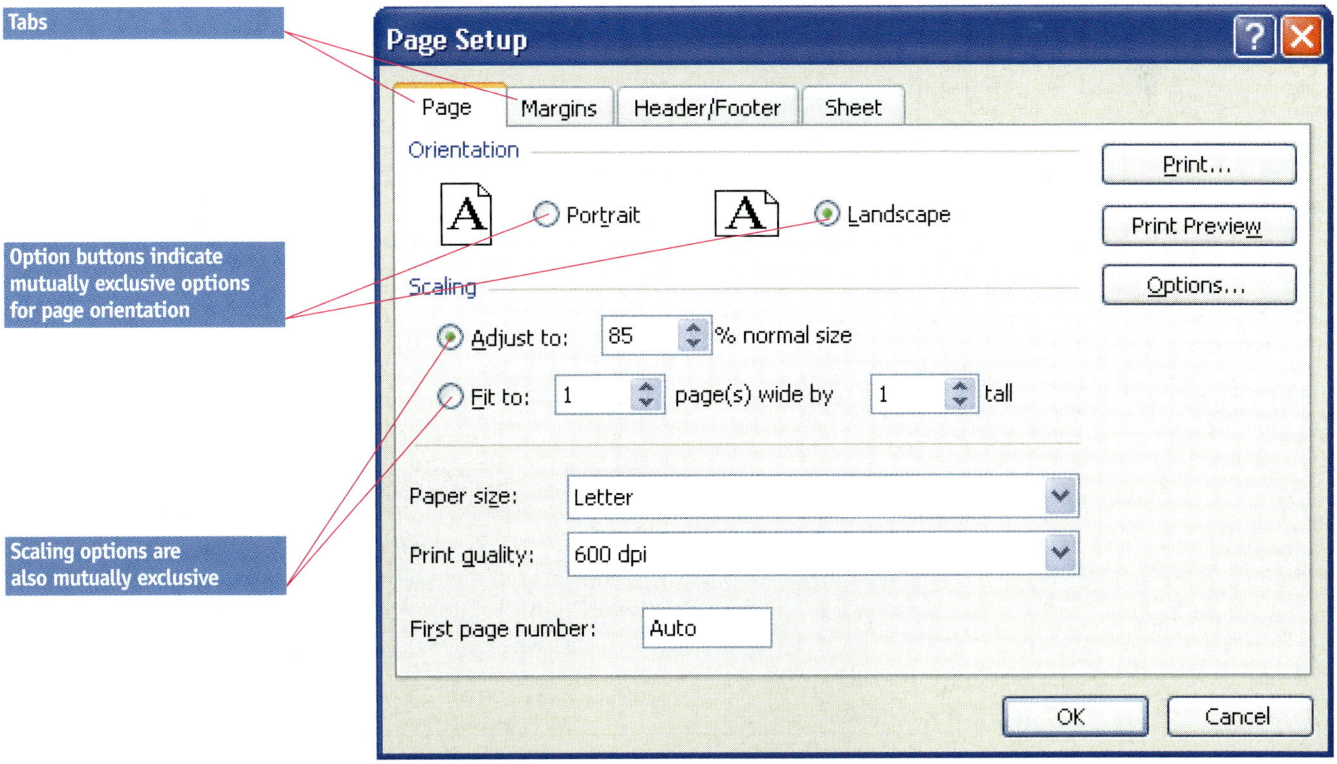

FIGURE 1.10 The Page Setup Command

hands-on exercise

2 Modifying a Worksheet

Objective To open an existing workbook; to insert and delete rows and columns of a worksheet; to print cell formulas and displayed values; to use the Page Setup command. Use Figure 1.11 as a guide.

Step 1: Open an Existing Workbook

- Start Excel. Click the **Open button** on the Standard toolbar. You should see a dialog box similar to the one in Figure 1.11a. Click the **drop-down arrow** on the Views button and click **Details** to change to the Details view.
- Click the **drop-down arrow** on the Look In list box and select drive C or drive A, depending on the location of your data. Double click the **Exploring Excel folder** to make it the active folder.
- Scroll until you can open (double click) the **Grade Book Solution** workbook from the previous exercise.

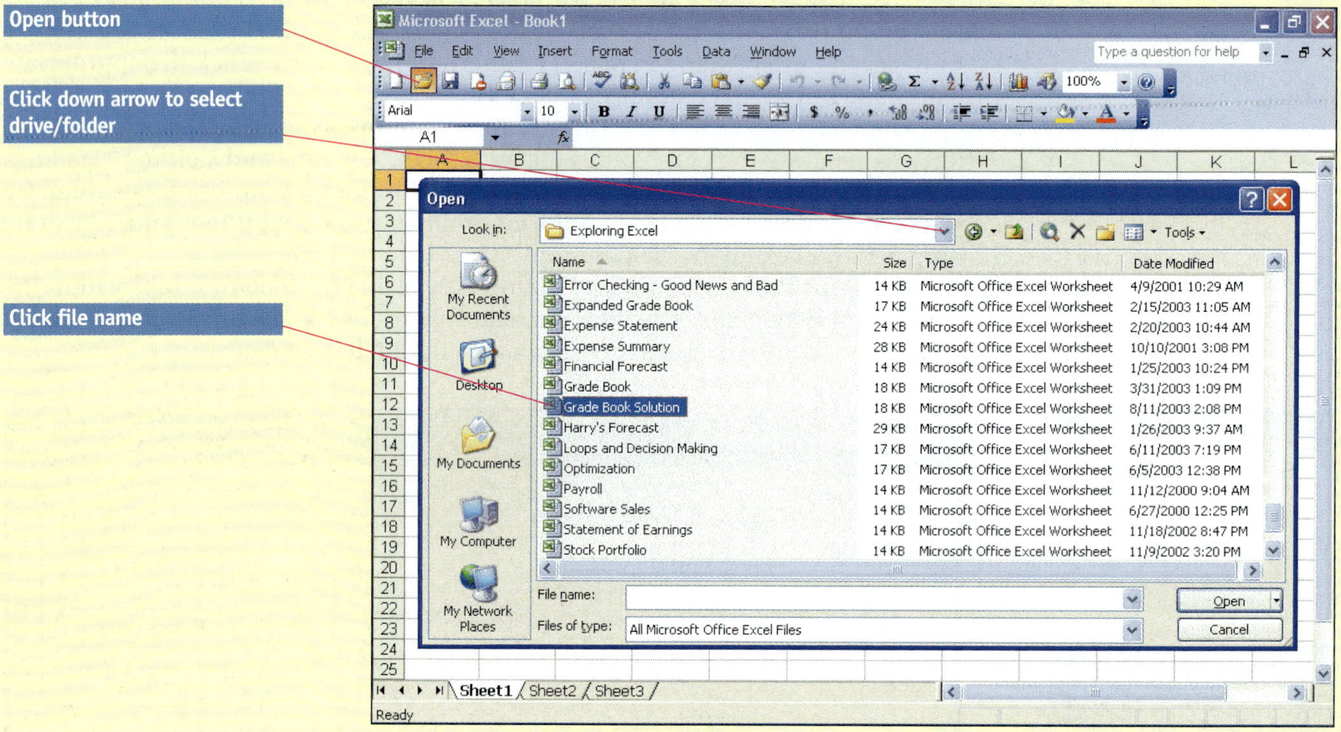

(a) Open an Existing Workbook (step 1)

FIGURE 1.11 Hands-on Exercise 2

THE GETTING STARTED TASK PANE

Pull down the View menu and click the Task Pane command to open the task pane. If necessary, click the down arrow in the task pane to select the Getting Started task pane. Look in the "Open" area of the task pane and you will see links to the last several workbooks that were opened in the application. You can also click the link to the open folder labeled "More . . . ", which will display the File Open dialog box.

Step 2: Delete a Row

- Click any cell in **row 6** (the row you will delete). Pull down the **Edit menu**. Click **Delete** to display the dialog box in Figure 1.11b. Click **Entire row**. Click **OK** to delete row 6.
- Moldof has disappeared from the grade book, and the class averages (now in row 8) have been updated automatically.
- You can restore the row you just deleted if you made a mistake. Pull down the **Edit menu** and click **Undo Delete** (or click the **Undo button** on the Standard toolbar) to reverse the last command.
- The row for Moldof has been put back into the worksheet.
- Click any cell in **row 6**, and this time delete the entire row for good.
- Save the workbook.

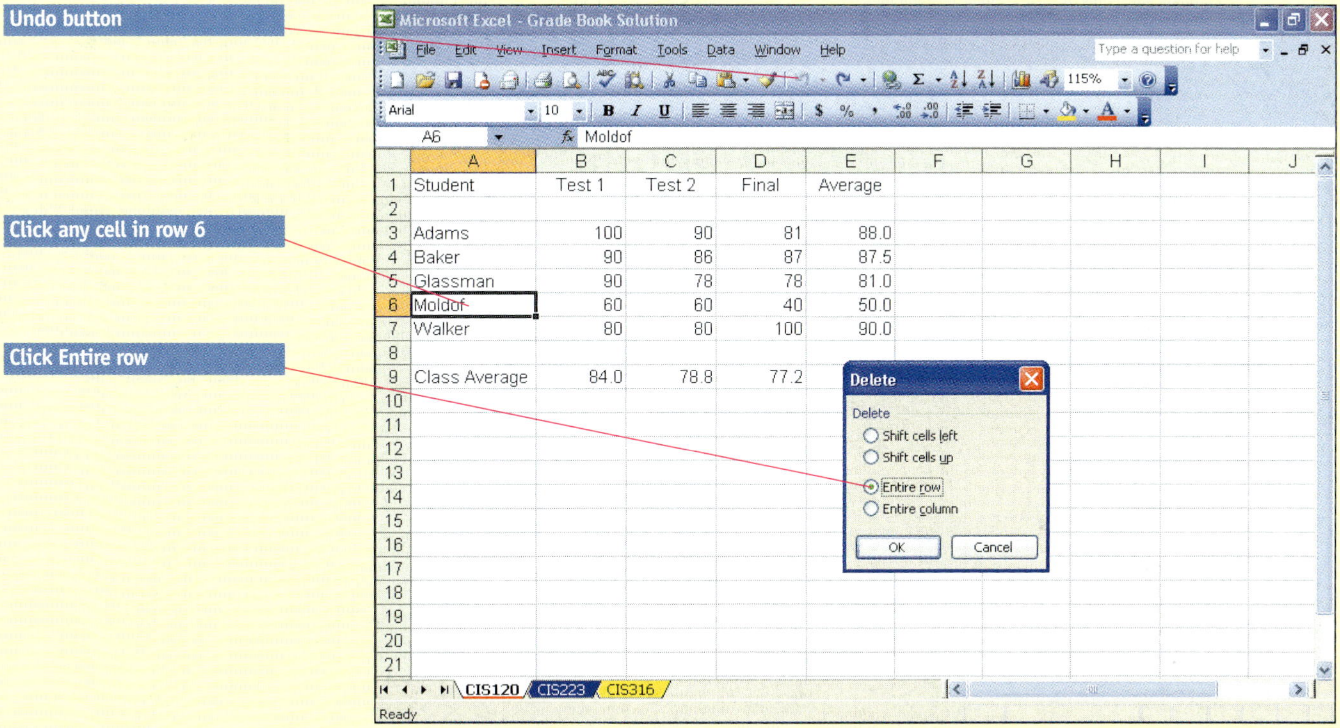

(b) Delete a Row (step 2)

FIGURE 1.11 Hands-on Exercise 2 (*continued*)

INSERT COMMENT COMMAND

You can add a comment, which displays a ScreenTip when you point to the cell, to any cell in a worksheet to explain a formula or other piece of information associated with that cell. Click in the cell that is to hold the comment, pull down the Insert menu, and click Comment to display a box in which you enter the comment. Click outside the box when you have completed the entry. Point to the cell (which should have a tiny red triangle) and you will see the comment you just created.

Step 3: Insert a Row

- Click any cell in **row 5** (the row containing Glassman's grades). Pull down the **Insert menu**. Click **Rows** to add a new row above the current row.
- A new row is inserted into the worksheet with the same formatting as in the row above. (Thus you can ignore the Format Painter button, which allows you to change the formatting.) Row 5 is now blank, and Glassman is now in row 6.
- Enter the data for the new student in row 5 as shown in Figure 1.11c. Click in **cell A5**. Type **Coulter**. Press the **right arrow key** or click in **cell B5**. Enter the test grades of 85, 95, 100 in cells B5, C5, and D5, respectively.
- Enter the formula to compute the semester average, **=(B5+C5+2*D5)/4**. Be sure to begin the formula with an equal sign. Press **Enter**.
- Click the **Save button** on the Standard toolbar, or pull down the **File menu** and click **Save** to save the changes made to this point.

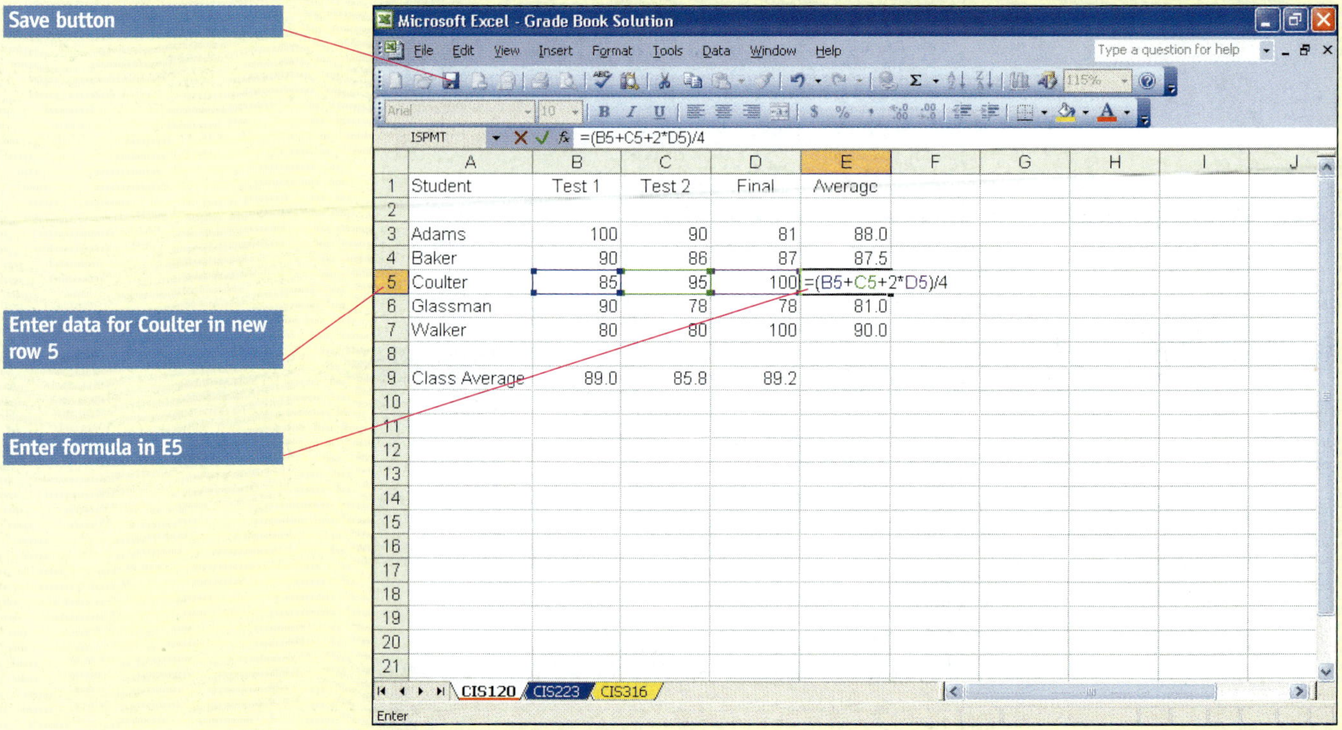

(c) Insert a Row (step 3)

FIGURE 1.11 Hands-on Exercise 2 (*continued*)

CORRECTING MISTAKES

The fastest way to change the contents of an existing cell is to double click in the cell in order to make the changes directly in the cell rather than on the formula bar. Use the mouse or arrow keys to position the insertion point at the point of correction. Press the Ins key to toggle between insert and overtype and/or use the Backspace or Del key to erase a character. Press the Home and End keys to move to the first and last characters in the cell, respectively. (If this feature does not work, pull down the Tools menu, click the Options command, select the Edit tab, and check the box to Edit directly in a cell.)

Step 4: The AutoComplete Feature

- Point to the row heading for **row 6** (which now contains Glassman's grades), then click the **right mouse button** to select the row and display a shortcut menu.
- Click **Insert** to insert a new row 6, which moves Glassman to row 7 as shown in Figure 1.11d.
- Click in **cell A6**. Type **C**, the first letter in"Courier," which also happens to be the first letter in"Coulter," a previous entry in column A. If the AutoComplete feature is on (see boxed tip), Coulter's name will be automatically inserted in cell A6 with"oulter" selected.
- Type **ourier** (the remaining letters in"Courier," which replace"oulter."
- Enter Courier's grades in the appropriate cells (75, 75, and 85 in cells B6, C6, and D6, respectively). Click in **cell E6**. Enter the formula to compute the semester average, **=(B6+C6+2*D6)/4**. Press **Enter**.
- Save the workbook.

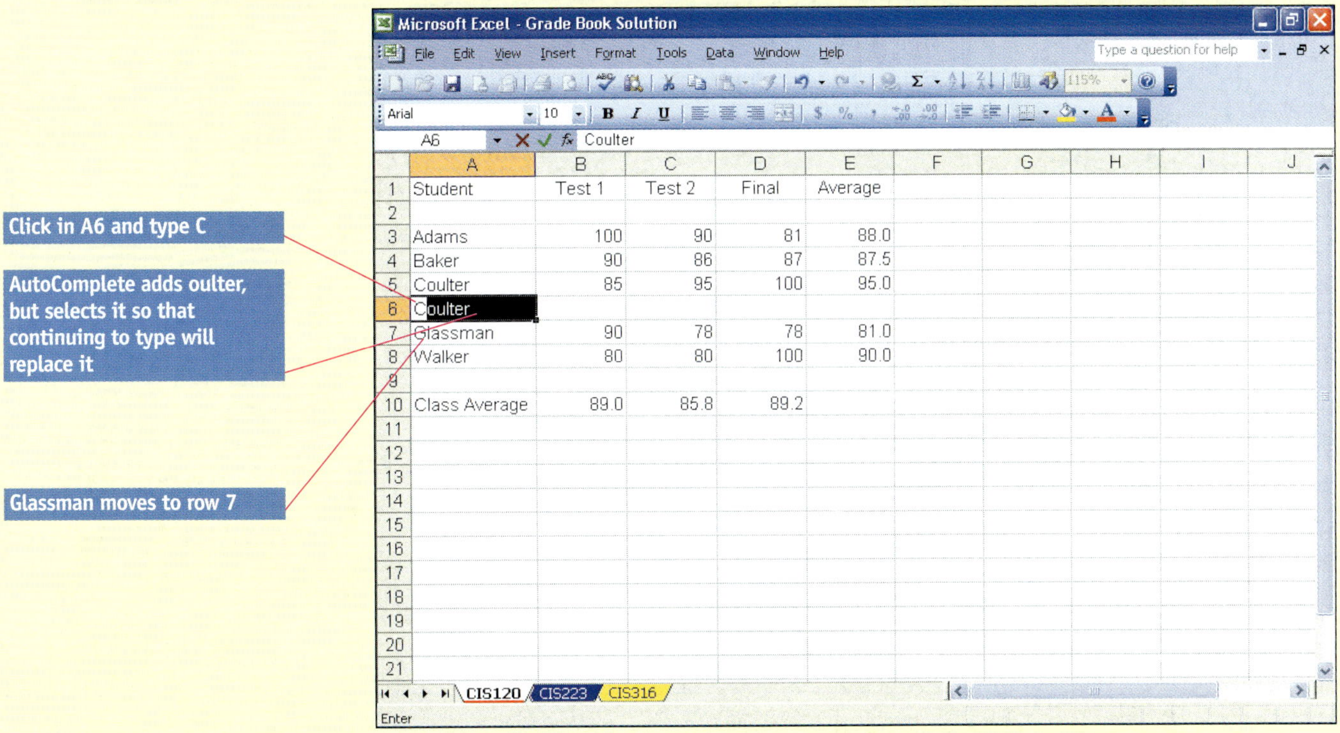

(d) The AutoComplete Feature (step 4)

FIGURE 1.11 Hands-on Exercise 2 (*continued*)

AUTOCOMPLETE

As soon as you begin typing a label into a cell, Excel searches for and (automatically) displays any other label in that column that matches the letters you typed. It's handy if you want to repeat a label, but it can be distracting if you want to enter a different label that just happens to begin with the same letter. To turn the feature on (off), pull down the Tools menu, click Options, then click the Edit tab. Check (clear) the box to enable (disable) the AutoComplete feature.

Step 5: Insert a Column

- Point to the column heading for column B, then click the **right mouse button** to display a shortcut menu as shown in Figure 1.11e.
- Click **Insert** to insert a new column, which becomes the new column B. All existing columns have been moved to the right.
- Click in **cell B1**. Type **Major**.
- Click in **cell B3**. Enter **CIS** as Adams's major. Press the **down arrow** to move automatically to the major for the next student.
- Type **MKT** in cell B4. Press the **down arrow**. Type **ACC** in cell B5. Press the **down arrow**. Type **FIN** in cell B6.
- Press the **down arrow** to move to cell B7. Type **C** (AutoComplete will automatically enter "IS" to complete the entry). Press the **down arrow** to move to cell B8. Type **C** (the AutoComplete feature again enters "IS"), then press **Enter** to complete the entry.

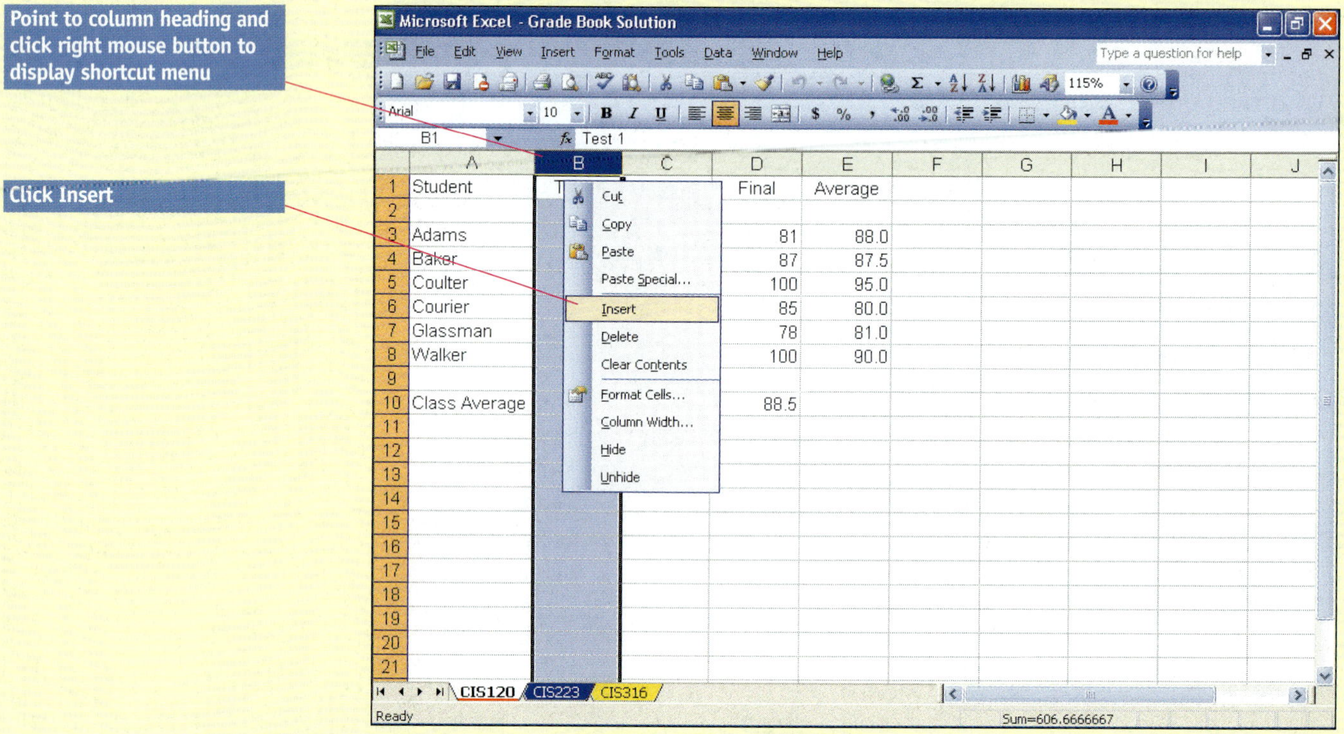

(e) Insert a Column (step 5)

FIGURE 1.11 Hands-on Exercise 2 (*continued*)

INSERTING AND DELETING INDIVIDUAL CELLS

You can insert and/or delete individual cells, as opposed to an entire row or column. To insert a cell, click in the cell where you want the new cell to go, pull down the Insert menu, then click Cells to display the Insert dialog box. Click the appropriate option button to shift cells right or down and click OK. To delete a cell or cells, select the cell(s), pull down the Edit menu, click the Delete command, then click the option button to shift cells left or up.

Step 6: Display the Cell Formulas

- Pull down the **Tools menu**. Click **Options** to display the Options dialog box. Click the **View tab**. Check the box for **Formulas**. Click **OK**. (You can also press **Ctrl+~** to toggle between cell formulas and displayed values.)
- The worksheet should display the cell formulas as shown in Figure 1.11f. The Formula Auditing toolbar is displayed automatically.
- If necessary, click the **right scroll arrow** on the horizontal scroll bar until column F, the column containing the formulas to compute the semester averages, comes into view.
- If necessary (i.e., if the formulas are not completely visible), double click the border between the column headings for columns F and G. This increases the width of column F to accommodate the widest entry in that column.

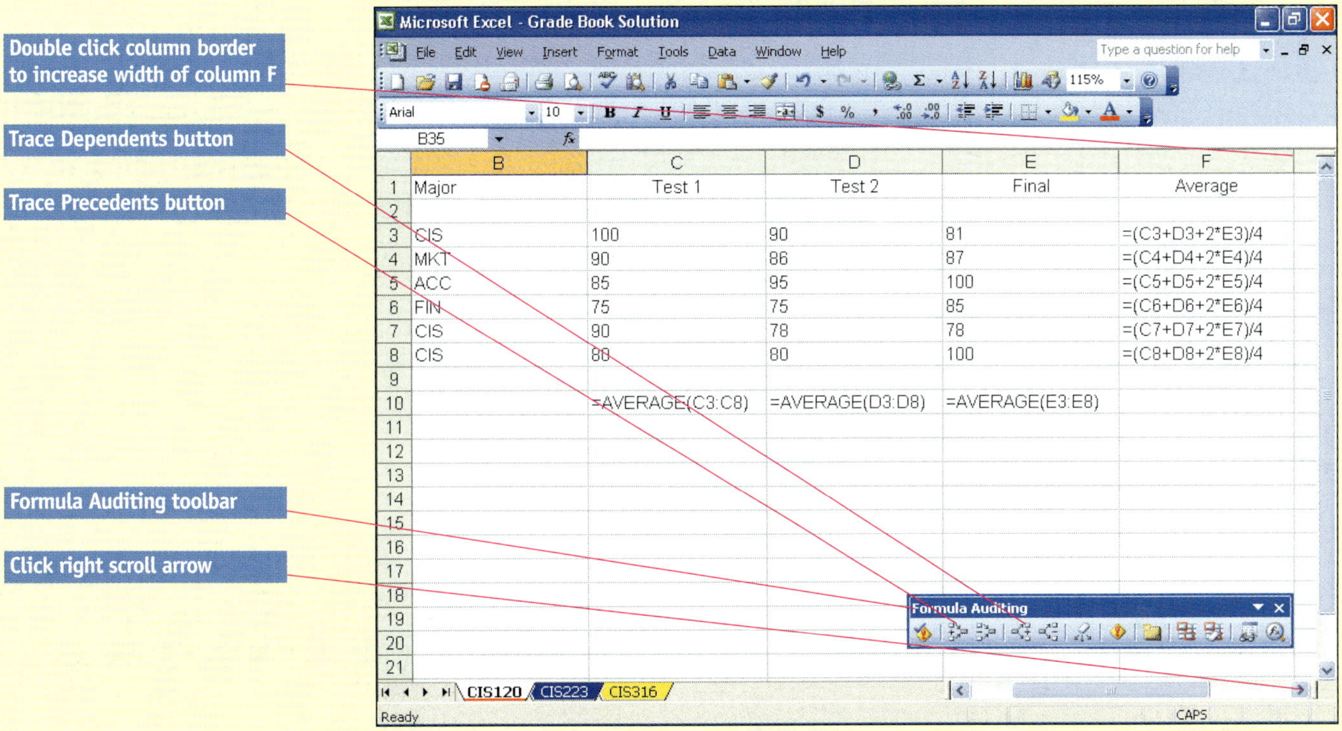

(f) Display the Cell Formulas (step 6)

FIGURE 1.11 Hands-on Exercise 2 (*continued*)

THE FORMULA AUDITING TOOLBAR

The Formula Auditing Toolbar appears automatically any time the display is changed to show cell formulas rather than displayed values. The toolbar is designed to help you detect and correct errors in cell formulas. Click in any cell containing a formula, then click the Trace Precedents button to show the cells that are used in calculating the formula in the selected cell. You can also click in any cell displaying a value and use the Trace Dependents button to show those cells whose formula references the selected cell. Click the Remove All Arrows button to erase the arrows from the display.

Step 7: The Page Setup Command

- Pull down the **File menu**. Click the **Page Setup command** to display the Page Setup dialog box as shown in Figure 1.11g.
- Click the **Page tab**. Click the **Landscape option button**. Click the option button to **Fit to 1 page**.
- Click the **Margins tab**. Check the box to center the worksheet horizontally.
- Click the **Sheet tab**. Check the boxes to print Row and Column Headings and Gridlines.
- Click the **Header/Footer tab**. Click the **drop-down arrow** on the Footer list box and select **CIS120**, which corresponds to the worksheet name.
- Click **OK** to exit the Page Setup dialog box.
- Save the workbook.

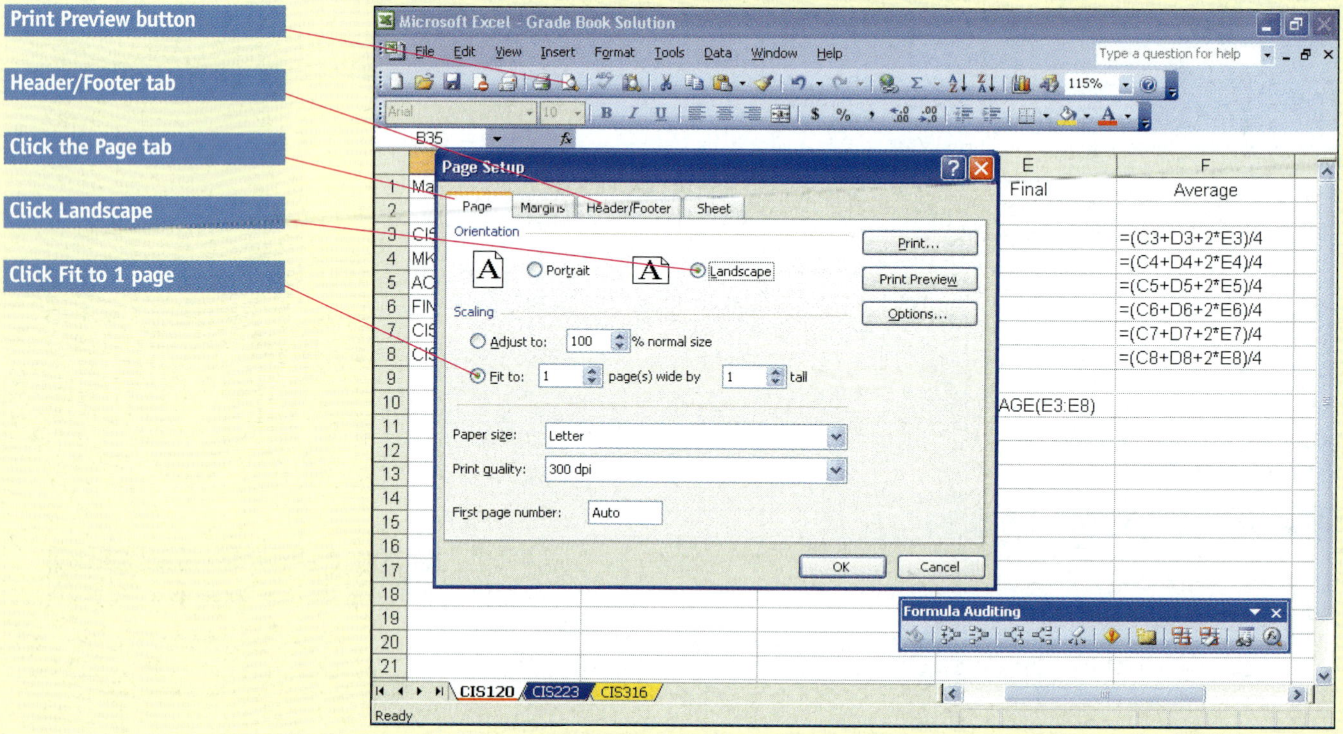

(g) The Page Setup Command (step 7)

FIGURE 1.11 Hands-on Exercise 2 (*continued*)

KEYBOARD SHORTCUTS—THE DIALOG BOX

Press Tab or Shift+Tab to move forward (backward) between fields in a dialog box, or press the Alt key plus the underlined letter to move directly to an option. Use the space bar to toggle check boxes on or off and the up (down) arrow keys to move between options in a list box. Press Enter to activate the highlighted command button and Esc to exit the dialog box without accepting the changes. These are universal shortcuts and apply to any Windows application.

Step 8: The Print Preview Command

- Pull down the **File menu** and click **Print Preview** (or click the **Print Preview button** on the Standard toolbar).
- Click the **Margins button** to toggle the margin lines on and off. (You can click and drag any margin line to change the position of the worksheet on the page and/or to change the column widths.)
- Your monitor should match the display in Figure 1.11h. (The Page Setup dialog box is also accessible from this screen.)
- Click the **Print command button** to display the Print dialog box, then click **OK** to print the worksheet.
- Press **Ctrl+~** to switch to displayed values rather than cell formulas. Click the **Print button** on the Standard toolbar to print the worksheet without displaying the Print dialog box.

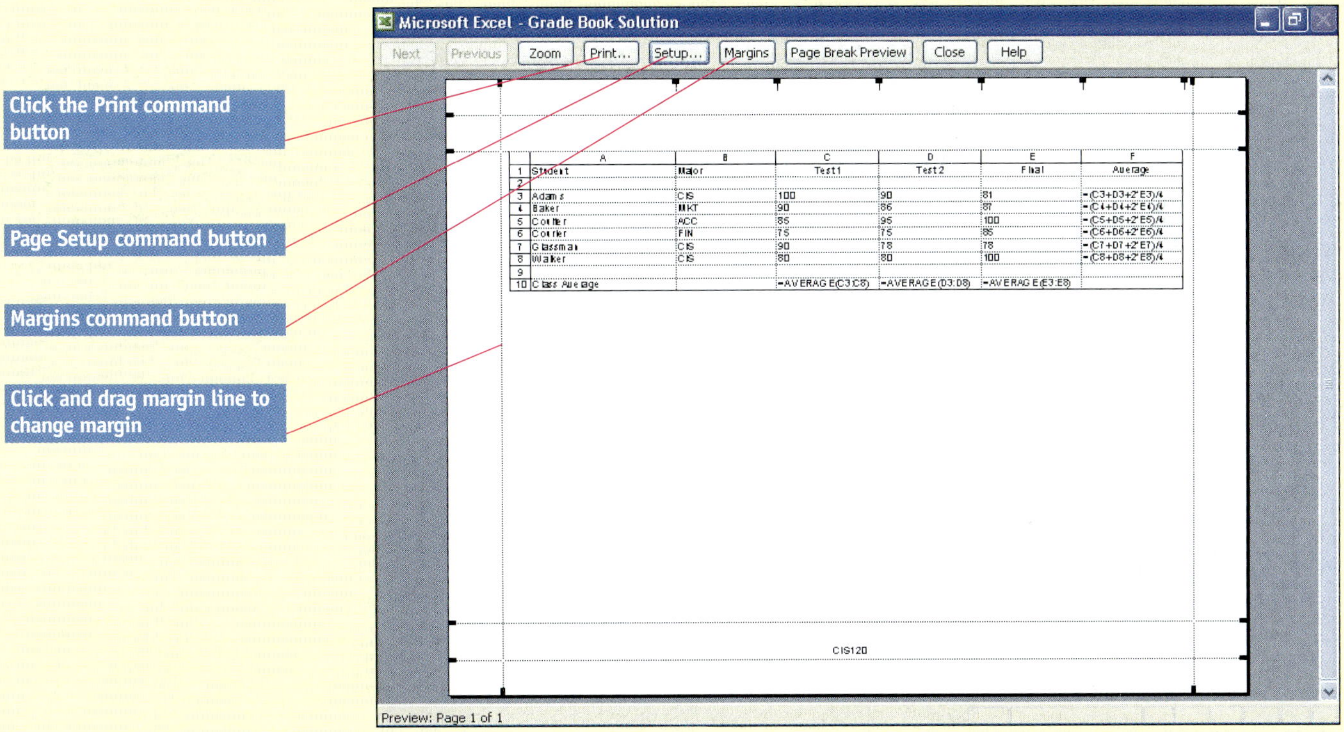

(h) The Print Preview Command (step 8)

FIGURE 1.11 Hands-on Exercise 2 (*continued*)

IDENTIFY YOUR WORKSHEETS

Use the Page Setup command to create a custom header and/or footer to identify your worksheets. Pull down the File menu, click the Page Setup command, and click the Header/Footer tab, then click the Custom Header or Custom Footer button. You can insert your own text in any desired font, as well as the date and time the worksheet was printed. You can also specify the folder, file name, and/or the worksheet name. All of the buttons are clearly marked with instructions within the dialog box.

Step 9: Insert and Delete a Worksheet

- Pull down the **Insert menu** and click the **Worksheet command** to insert a new worksheet. The worksheet is inserted as Sheet1.
- Click in **cell A1**, type **Student**, and press **Enter**. Enter the labels and student data as shown in Figure 1.11i. Enter the formulas to calculate the students' semester averages in column D. (The midterm and final count equally.)
- Enter the formulas in row 7 to compute the class averages on each exam. If necessary, click and drag the column border between the column headings for columns A and B to widen column A.
- Double click the name of the worksheet (Sheet1) to select the name. Type a new name, **CIS101**, to replace the selected text and press **Enter**. If necessary, click and drag the worksheet tab to the beginning of the workbook.
- Click the worksheet tab for **CIS223**. Pull down the **Edit menu** and click the **Delete Sheet command**. Click **Delete** when you are warned that the worksheet will be permanently deleted.
- Save the workbook. Print the new worksheet. Exit Excel if you do not want to continue with the next exercise at this time.

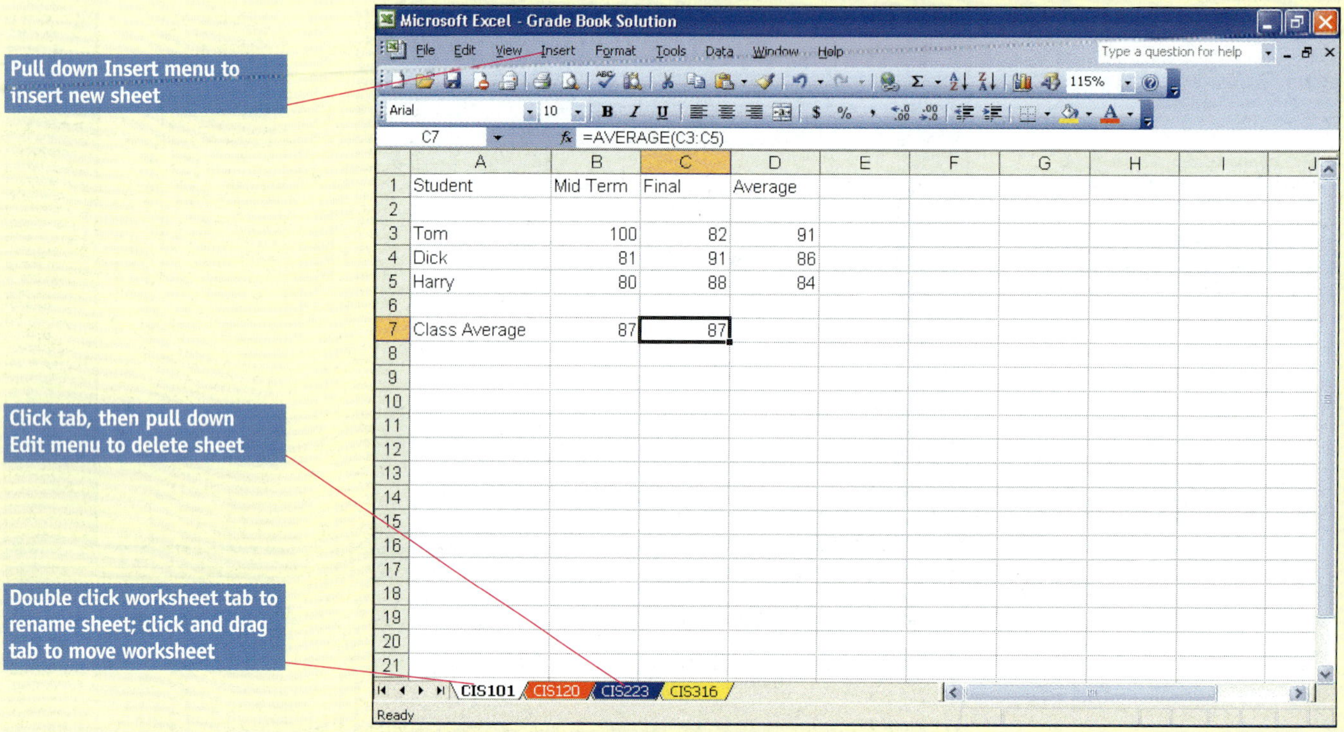

(i) Insert and Delete a Worksheet (step 9)

FIGURE 1.11 Hands-on Exercise 2 (*continued*)

MOVING, COPYING, AND RENAMING WORKSHEETS

The fastest way to move a worksheet is to click and drag the worksheet tab. You can copy a worksheet in similar fashion by pressing and holding the Ctrl key as you drag the worksheet tab. To rename a worksheet, double click its tab to select the current name, type the new name, and press the Enter key.

A BETTER GRADE BOOK

Figure 1.12 contains a much improved version of the professor's grade book. The most *obvious* difference is in the appearance of the worksheet, as a variety of formatting commands have been used to make it more attractive. The exam scores and semester averages are centered under the appropriate headings. The exam weights are formatted with percentages, and all averages are displayed with exactly one decimal point. Boldface and italics are used for emphasis. Shading and borders are used to highlight various areas of the worksheet. The title has been centered over the worksheet and is set in a larger typeface.

The most *significant* differences, however, are that the weight of each exam is indicated within the worksheet, and that the formulas to compute the students' semester averages reference these cells in their calculations. The professor can change the contents of the cells containing the exam weights and see immediately the effect on the student averages.

The isolation of cells whose values are subject to change is one of the most important concepts in the development of a spreadsheet. This technique lets the professor explore alternative grading strategies. He or she may notice, for example, that the class did significantly better on the final than on either of the first two exams. The professor may then decide to give the class a break and increase the weight of the final relative to the other tests. But before the professor says anything to the class, he or she wants to know the effect of increasing the weight of the final to 60%. What if the final should count 70%? The effect of these and other changes can be seen immediately by entering the new exam weights in the appropriate cells at the bottom of the worksheet.

Title is centered in larger font size; it is also in boldface and italics

Formatting includes boldface, shading, and borders

Exam weights are used to calculate the semester average

	A	B	C	D	E
1	***CIS120 - Spring Semester***				
2					
3	**Student**	**Test 1**	**Test 2**	**Final**	**Average**
4	Costa, Frank	70	80	90	82.5
5	Ford, Judd	70	85	80	78.8
6	Grauer, Jessica	90	80	98	91.5
7	Howard, Lauren	80	78	98	88.5
8	Krein, Darren	85	70	95	86.3
9	Moldof, Adam	75	75	80	77.5
10					
11	**Class Averages**	**78.3**	**78.0**	**90.2**	
12					
13	**Exam Weights**	**25%**	**25%**	**50%**	

FIGURE 1.12 A Better Grade Book

ISOLATE ASSUMPTIONS

The formulas in a worksheet should always be based on cell references rather than on specific values—for example, B13 or $B$13 rather than .25. The cells containing these values should be clearly labeled and set apart from the rest of the worksheet. You can then vary the inputs (or assumptions on which the worksheet is based) to see the effect within the worksheet. The chance for error is also minimized because you are changing the contents of a single cell rather than changing the multiple formulas that reference those values.

CELL RANGES

Every command in Excel operates on a rectangular group of cells known as a ***range***. A range may be as small as a single cell or as large as the entire worksheet. It may consist of a row or part of a row, a column or part of a column, or multiple rows and/or columns. The cells within a range are specified by indicating the diagonally opposite corners, typically the upper-left and lower-right corners of the rectangle. Many different ranges could be selected in conjunction with the worksheet of Figure 1.12. The exam weights, for example, are found in the range B13:D13. The students' semester averages are found in the range E4:E9. The student data is contained in the range A4:E9.

The easiest way to select a range is to click and drag—click at the beginning of the range, then press and hold the left mouse button as you drag the mouse to the end of the range where you release the mouse. Once selected, the range is highlighted and its cells will be affected by any subsequent command. The range remains selected until another range is defined or until you click another cell anywhere on the worksheet.

COPY COMMAND

The ***Copy command*** duplicates the contents of a cell, or range of cells, and saves you from having to enter the contents of every cell individually. Figure 1.13 illustrates how the command can be used to duplicate the formula to compute the class average on the different tests. The cell that you are copying from, cell B11, is called the ***source range***. The cells that you are copying to, cells C11 and D11, are the ***destination range***. The formula is not copied exactly, but is adjusted as it is copied, to compute the average for the pertinent test.

The formula to compute the average on the first test was entered in cell B11 as =AVERAGE(B4:B9). The range in the formula references the cell seven rows above the cell containing the formula (i.e., cell B4 is seven rows above cell B11) as well as the cell two rows above the formula (i.e., cell B9). When the formula in cell B11 is copied to C11, it is adjusted so that the cells referenced in the new formula are in the same relative position as those in the original formula; that is, seven and two rows above the formula. The formula in cell C11 becomes =AVERAGE(C4:C9). The formula in cell D11 becomes =AVERAGE(D4:D9).

	A	B	C	D	E
1			*CIS120 - Spring Semester*		
2					
3	**Student**	**Test 1**	**Test 2**	**Final**	**Average**
4	Costa, Frank	70	80	90	=$B$13*B4+$C$13*C4+$D$13*D4
5	Ford, Judd	70	85	80	=$B$13*B5+$C$13*C5+$D$13*D5
6	Grauer, Jessica	90	80	98	=$B$13*B6+$C$13*C6+$D$13*D6
7	Howard, Lauren	80	78	98	=$B$13*B7+$C$13*C7+$D$13*D7
8	Krein, Darren	85	70	95	=$B$13*B8+$C$13*C8+$D$13*D8
9	Moldof, Adam	75	75	80	=$B$13*B9+$C$13*C9+$D$13*D9
10					
11	**Class Averages**	**=AVERAGE(B4:B9)**	**=AVERAGE(C4:C9)**	**=AVERAGE(D4:D9)**	
12					
13	**Exam Weights**	**25%**	**25%**	**50%**	

Formula was entered in B11

Relative addresses adjust when formula is copied

Absolute addresses stay the same when formula is copied

Relative addresses adjust when formula is copied

FIGURE 1.13 The Copy Command

Figure 1.13 also illustrates how the Copy command is used to copy the formula for a student's semester average, from cell E4 (the source range) to cells E5 through E9 (the destination range). This is slightly more complicated than the previous example because the formula is based on a student's grades, which vary from one student to the next, and on the exam weights, which do not. The cells referring to the student's grades should adjust as the formula is copied, but the addresses referencing the exam weights should not.

The distinction between cell references that remain constant versus cell references that change is made by means of a dollar sign. An ***absolute reference*** remains constant throughout the copy operation and is specified with a dollar sign in front of the column and row designation, for example, $B$13. A ***relative reference***, on the other hand, adjusts during a copy operation and is specified without dollar signs, for example, B4. (A ***mixed reference*** uses a single dollar sign to make the column absolute and the row relative, for example, $A5. Alternatively, you can make the column relative and the row absolute as in A$5.)

Consider, for example, the formula to compute a student's semester average as it appears in cell E4 of Figure 1.13:

=$B$13*B4+$C$13*C4+$D$13*D4

- Final exam grade is in cell D4 and is a *relative reference*
- Weight for final exam is in cell D13 and is an *absolute reference*
- Test 2 grade is in cell C4 and is a *relative reference*
- Weight for test 2 is in cell C13 and is an *absolute reference*
- Test 1 grade is in cell B4 and is a *relative reference*
- Weight for Test 1 is in cell B13 and is an *absolute reference*

The formula in cell E4 uses a combination of relative and absolute addresses to compute the student's semester average. Relative addresses are used for the exam grades (found in cells B4, C4, and D4) and change automatically when the formula is copied to the other rows. Absolute addresses are used for the exam weights (found in cells B13, C13, and D13) and remain constant.

The copy operation is implemented by using the ***clipboard*** common to all Windows applications and a combination of the Copy and Paste commands from the Edit menu. (Office 2002 also supports the Office Clipboard that can hold 24 separate items. All references to the "clipboard" in this chapter, however, are to the Windows clipboard.) The contents of the source range are copied to the clipboard, from where they are pasted to the destination range. The contents of the clipboard are replaced with each subsequent Copy command but are unaffected by the Paste command. Thus, you can execute the Paste command several times in succession to paste the contents of the clipboard to multiple locations.

MIXED REFERENCES

Most spreadsheets can be developed using only absolute or relative references such as $A1$1 or A1 respectively. Mixed references, where only the row ($A1) or column (A$1) changes, are more subtle, and thus are typically not used by beginners. Mixed references are necessary in more sophisticated worksheets and add significantly to the power of Excel.

MOVE OPERATION

The ***move operation*** is not used in the grade book, but its presentation is essential for the sake of completeness. The move operation transfers the contents of a cell (or range of cells) from one location to another. After the move is completed, the cells where the move originated (that is, the source range) are empty. This is in contrast to the Copy command, where the entries remain in the source range and are duplicated in the destination range.

A simple move operation is depicted in Figure 1.14a, in which the contents of cell A3 are moved to cell C3, with the formula in cell C3 unchanged after the move. In other words, the move operation simply picks up the contents of cell A3 (a formula that adds the values in cells A1 and A2) and puts it down in cell C3. The source range, cell A3, is empty after the move operation has been executed.

Figure 1.14b depicts a situation where the formula itself remains in the same cell, but one of the values it references is moved to a new location; that is, the entry in A1 is moved to C1. The formula in cell A3 is adjusted to follow the moved entry to its new location; that is, the formula is now =C1+A2.

The situation is different in Figure 1.14c as the contents of all three cells—A1, A2, and A3—are moved. After the move has taken place, cells C1 and C2 contain the 5 and the 2, respectively, with the formula in cell C3 adjusted to reflect the movement of the contents of cells A1 and A2. Once again the source range (A1:A3) is empty after the move is completed.

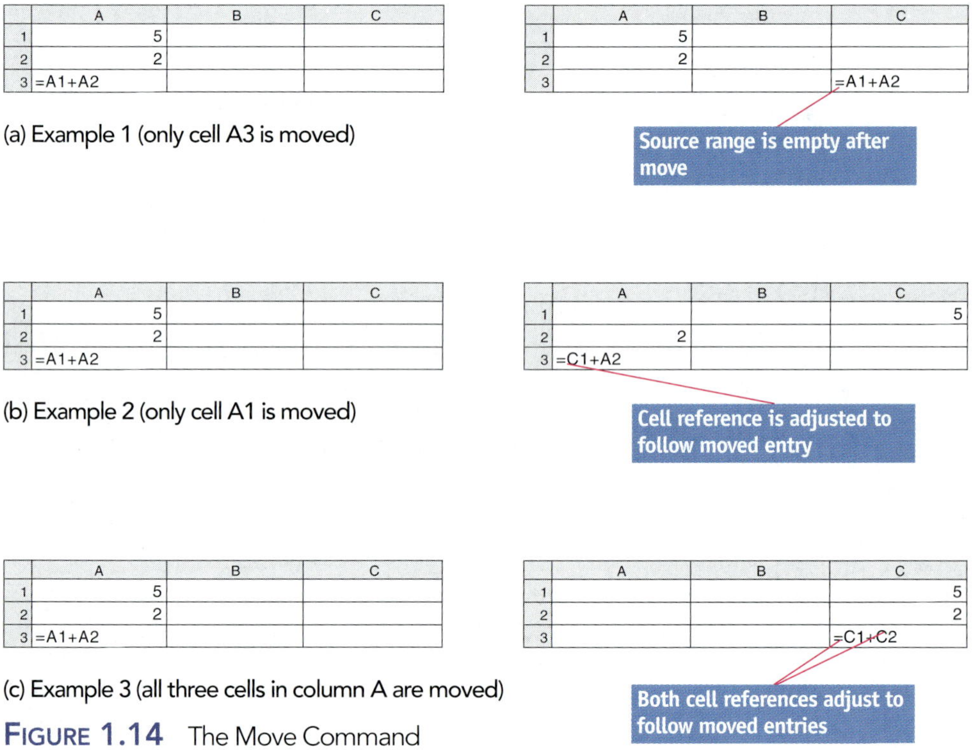

(a) Example 1 (only cell A3 is moved)

(b) Example 2 (only cell A1 is moved)

(c) Example 3 (all three cells in column A are moved)

FIGURE 1.14 The Move Command

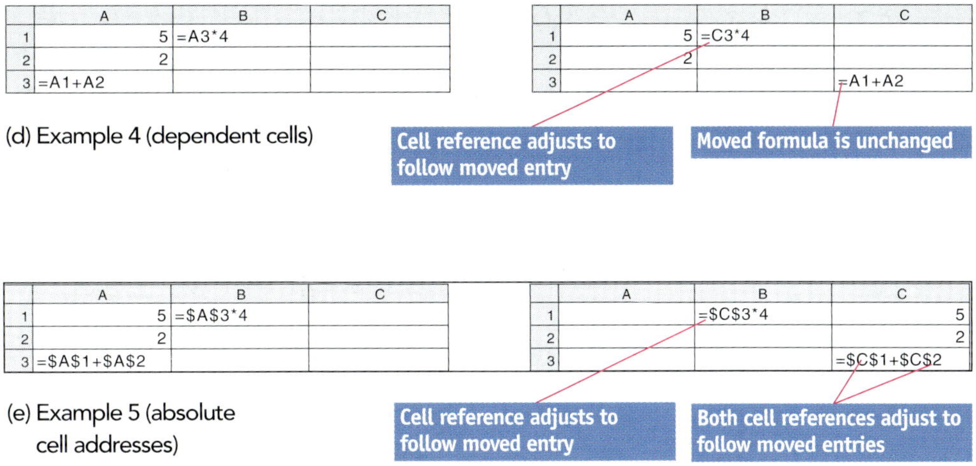

FIGURE 1.14 The Move Command (*continued*)

Figure 1.14d contains an additional formula in cell B1, which is *dependent* on cell A3, which in turn is moved to cell C3. The formula in cell C3 is unchanged after the move because *only* the formula was moved, *not* the values it referenced. The formula in cell B1 changes because cell B1 refers to an entry (cell A3) that was moved to a new location (cell C3).

Figure 1.14e shows that the specification of an absolute reference has no meaning in a move operation, because the cell addresses are adjusted as necessary to reflect the cells that have been moved. Moving a formula that contains an absolute reference does not adjust the formula. Moving a value that is specified as an absolute reference, however, adjusts the formula to follow the cell to its new location. Thus all of the absolute references in Figure 1.14e are changed to reflect the entries that were moved.

The move operation is a convenient way to improve the appearance of a worksheet after it has been developed. It is subtle in its operation, and we suggest you think twice before moving cell entries because of the complexities involved.

The move operation is implemented by using the Windows clipboard and a combination of the Cut and Paste commands from the Edit menu. The contents of the source range are transferred to the clipboard, from which they are pasted to the destination range. (Executing a Paste command after a Cut command empties the clipboard. This is different from pasting after a Copy command, which does not affect the contents of the clipboard.)

LEARNING BY DOING

As we have already indicated, there are many different ways to accomplish the same task. You can execute commands using a pull-down menu, a shortcut menu, a toolbar, or the keyboard. In the exercise that follows we emphasize pull-down menus (the most basic technique) but suggest various shortcuts as appropriate.

Realize, however, that while the shortcuts are interesting, it is far more important to focus on the underlying concepts in the exercise, rather than specific key strokes or mouse clicks. The professor's grade book was developed to emphasize the difference between relative and absolute cell references. The grade book also illustrates the importance of isolating assumptions so that alternative strategies (e.g., different exam weights) can be considered.

hands-on exercise

3 Creating a Workbook

Objective To create a new workbook; to copy formulas containing relative and absolute references. Use Figure 1.15 as a guide in doing the exercise.

Step 1: Create a New Workbook

- Start Excel. A blank workbook should appear automatically in the application window. Close the task pane.
- If necessary, separate the Standard and Formatting toolbars. Pull down the **View menu**, click **Toolbars**, click **Customize**, and click the **Options tab**. Check the box that indicates the Standard and Formatting toolbars should be displayed on two rows. Close the dialog box.
- Click in **cell A1**. Enter the title of the worksheet, **CIS120 - Spring Semester**.
- Enter the column headings in row 3 as in Figure 1.15a. Click in **cell A3** and type **Student**, then press the **right arrow key** to move to **cell B3**. Type **Test 1**.
- Press the **right arrow key** to move to **cell C3**. Type **Test 2**. Enter the words **Final** and **Average** in cells D3 and E3, respectively.

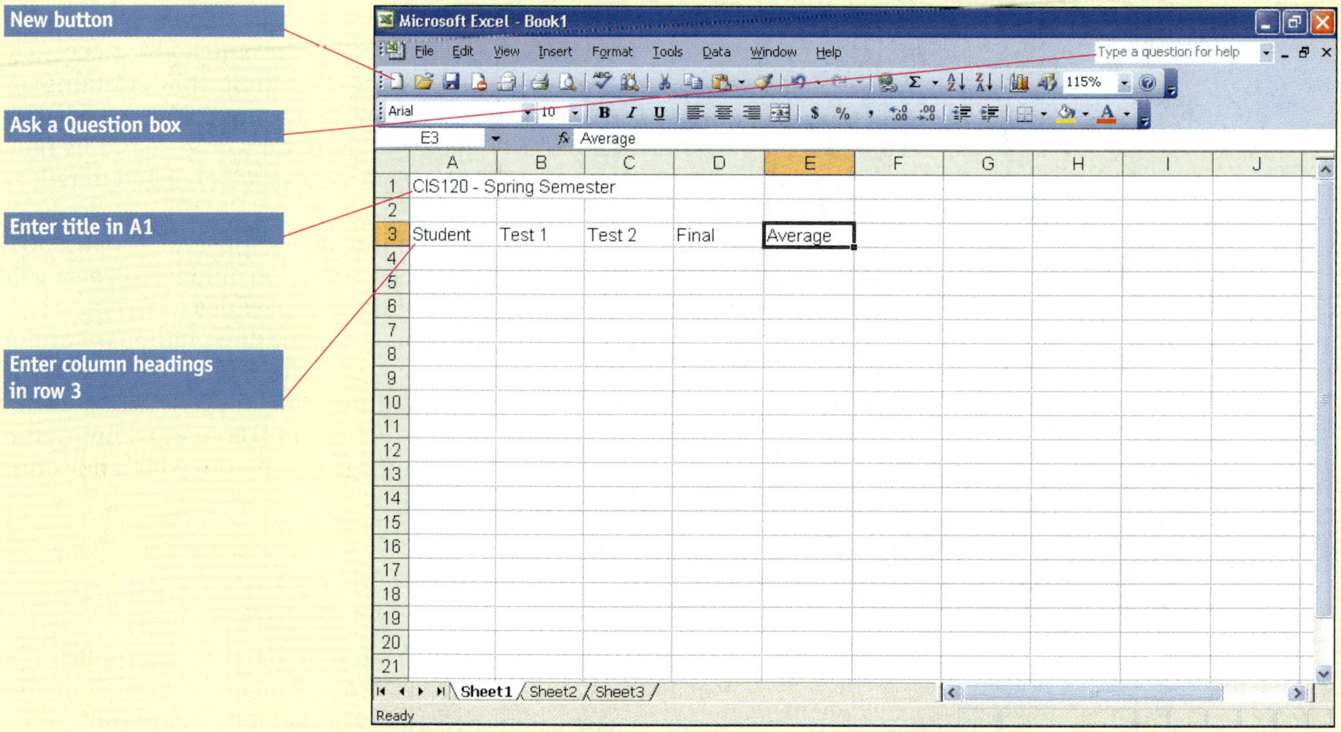

(a) Create a New Workbook (step 1)

FIGURE 1.15 Hands-on Exercise 3

ASK A QUESTION

Click in the "Ask a Question" list box to the right of the menu bar, type a question, press enter, and Excel returns a list of Help topics. Click any topic that appears to open the Help window with detailed information. You can ask multiple questions during an Excel session, then click the down arrow in the list box to return to an earlier question, which will return you to the Help topics.

Step 2: Save the Workbook

- Pull down the **File menu** and click **Save** (or click the **Save button** on the Standard toolbar) to display the Save As dialog box as shown in Figure 1.15b. (The Save As dialog box always appears the first time you save a workbook, so that you can give the workbook a name.)
- Click the **drop-down arrow** on the Save In list box. Click the appropriate drive, drive C or drive A, depending on where you are saving your Excel workbooks.
- Double click the **Exploring Excel folder** to make it the active folder (the folder in which you will save the document).
- Click and drag **Book1** (the default entry) in the File name text box to select it, then type **Better Grade Book** as the name of the workbook.
- Click the **Save button** in the Save As dialog box or press the **Enter key**. The title bar changes to reflect the name of the workbook.

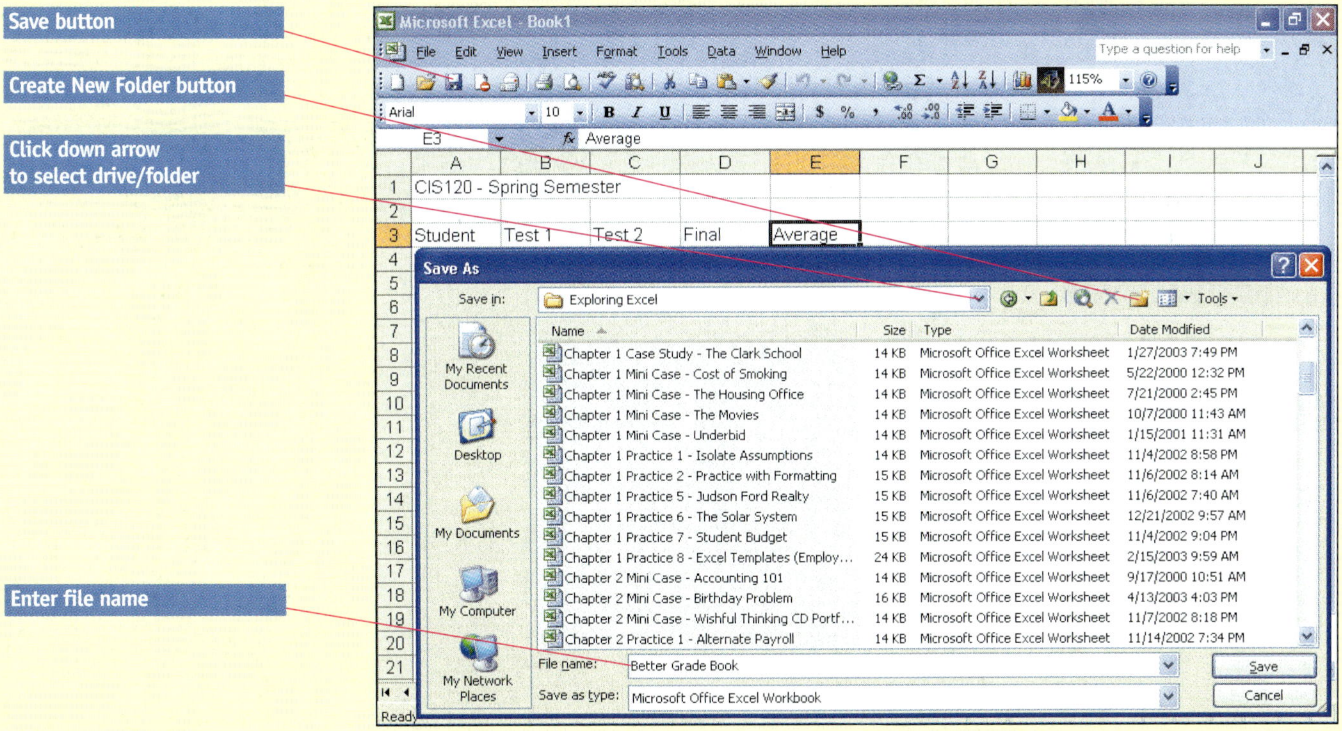

(b) Save the Workbook (step 2)

FIGURE 1.15 Hands-on Exercise 3 (*continued*)

CREATE A NEW FOLDER

Do you work with a large number of different workbooks? If so, it may be useful to store those workbooks in different folders, perhaps one folder for each subject you are taking. Pull down the File menu, click the Save As command to display the Save As dialog box, then click the Create New Folder button to display the associated dialog box. Enter the name of the folder, then click OK. Once the folder has been created, use the Look In box to change to that folder the next time you open that workbook.

Step 3: Enter Student Data and Literal Information

- Click in **cell A4** and type **Costa, Frank**, then enter Frank's grades on the two tests and the final as shown in Figure 1.15c. Do *not* enter Frank's semester average in cell E4 as that will be entered as a formula.
- If necessary, click and drag the border between columns A and B so that you can read Frank Costa's complete name. Check that you entered the data for this student correctly. If you made a mistake, return to the cell and retype the entry.
- Enter the names and grades for the other students in rows 5 through 9. Do *not* enter the student averages.
- Complete the entries in column A by typing **Class Averages** and **Exam Weights** in **cells A11** and **A13**, respectively.
- Enter the exam weights in row 13. Click in **cell B13** and enter **.25**, press the **right arrow key** to move to **cell C13** and enter **.25**, then press the **right arrow key** to move to **cell D13** and enter **.5**. Press **Enter**.
- Do *not* be concerned that the exam weights do not appear as percentages as they will be formatted in a later exercise. Save the workbook.

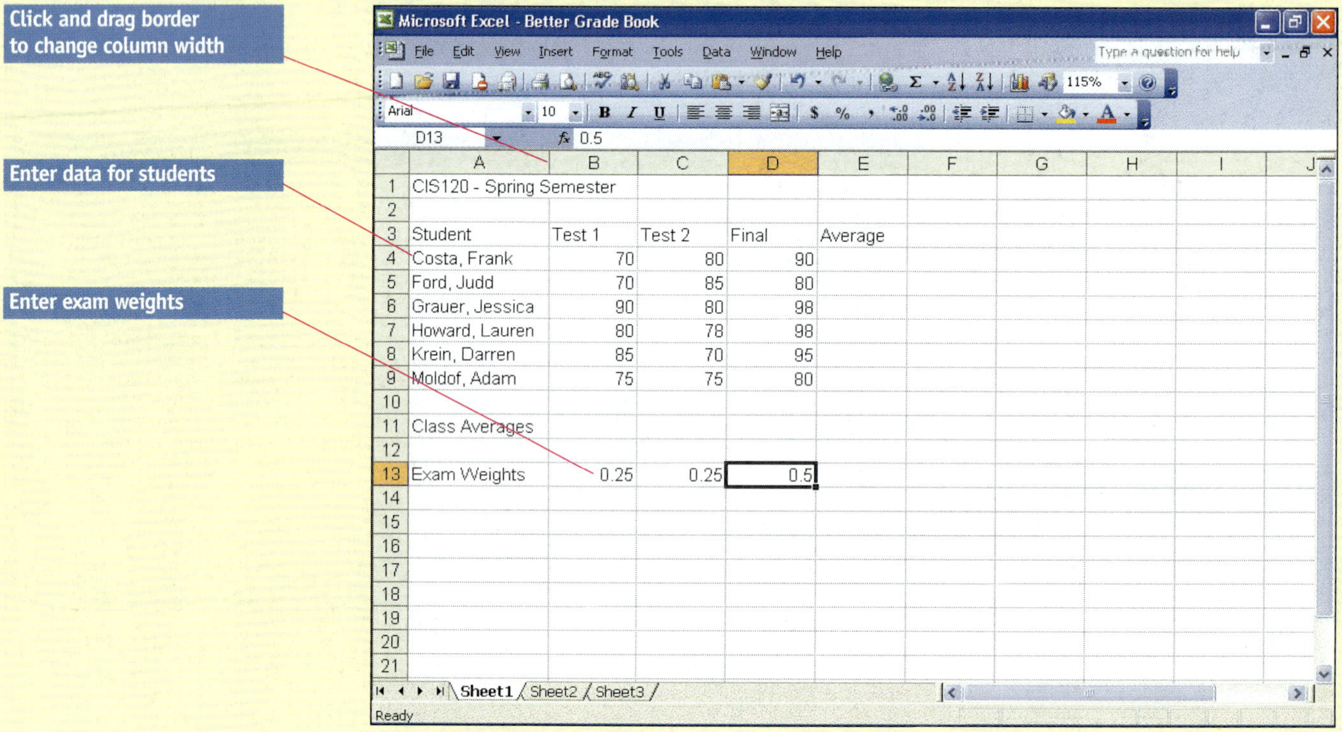

(c) Enter Student Data and Literal Information (step 3)

FIGURE 1.15 Hands-on Exercise 3 (*continued*)

COLUMN WIDTHS AND ROW HEIGHTS

Drag the border between column headings to change the column width; for example, to increase (decrease) the width of column A, drag the border between column headings A and B to the right (left). Double click the right boundary of a column heading to change the column width to accommodate the widest entry in that column. Use the same techniques to change the row heights. See practice exercise 2 at the end of the chapter.

Step 4: Compute the Student Semester Averages

- Click in **cell E4** and type the formula **=$B$13*B4+$C$13*C4+$D$13*D4** to compute the semester average for the first student. Press **Enter**. Check that the displayed value in cell E4 is 82.5 as shown in Figure 1.15d.
- Click in **cell E4** to make this the active cell, then click the **Copy button** on the Standard toolbar. A moving border will surround cell E4, indicating that its contents have been copied to the clipboard.
- Click and drag to select **cells E5** through **E9** as the destination range. Click the **Paste button** to copy the contents of the clipboard to the destination range. Ignore the Paste Options button that appears automatically any time the Paste command is executed.
- Press **Esc** to remove the moving border around cell E4. The Paste Options button also disappears.
- Click in **cell E5** and look at the formula. The cells that reference the grades have changed to B5, C5, and D5. The cells that reference the exam weights—$B$13, $C$13, and $D$13—are the same as in cell E4.
- Save the workbook.

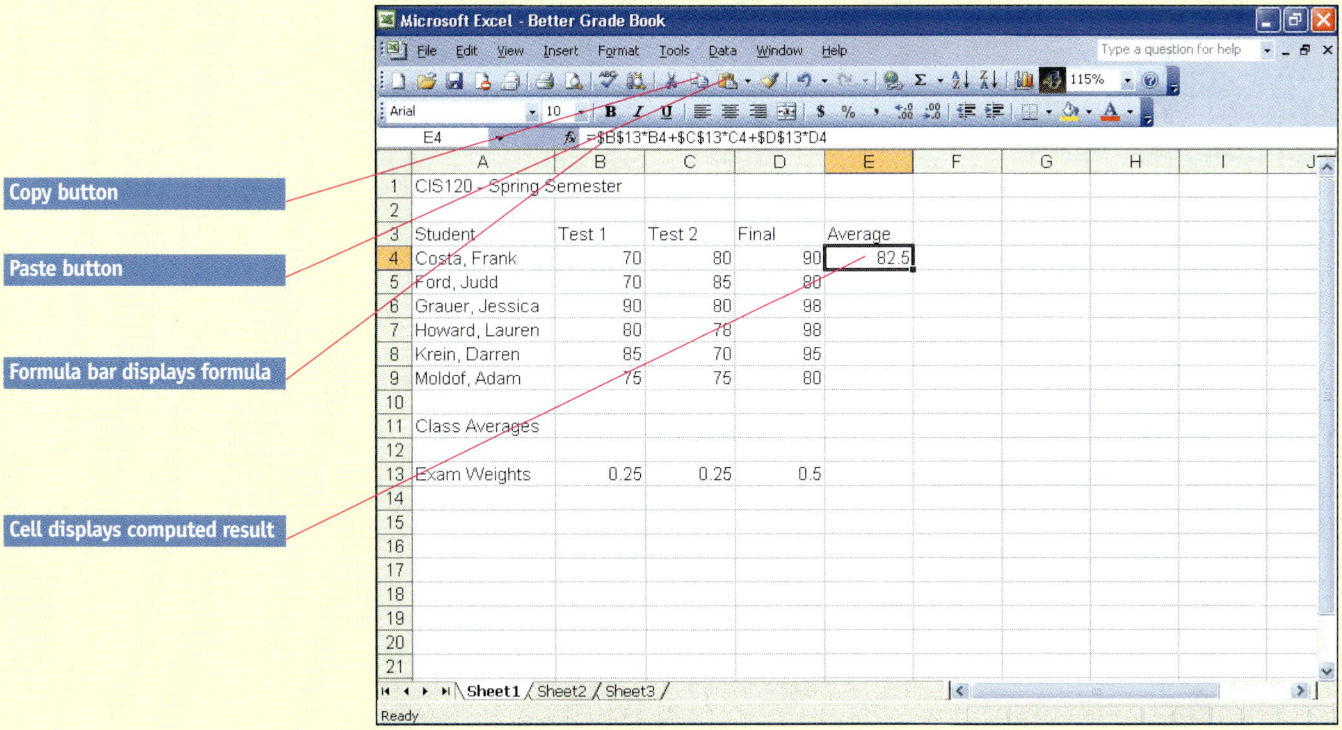

(d) Compute the student Semester Averages (step 4)

FIGURE 1.15 Hands-on Exercise 3 (*continued*)

THE PASTE OPTIONS BUTTON

The Paste Options button (includes options from the Paste Special command and) provides flexibility when you paste the contents of the clipboard into a worksheet. Press Esc to ignore the options and you automatically paste both the cell formulas and associated formatting. Alternatively, you can click the down arrow to display options to copy values rather than formulas with or without formatting, Formatting is discussed in detail later in the chapter.

Step 5: Compute the Class Averages

- Click in **cell B11** and type the formula **=AVERAGE(B4:B9)** to compute the class average on the first test. Press the **Enter key** when you have completed the formula.
- Point to cell B11, then click the **right mouse button** to display a context-sensitive menu, then click the **Copy command**. You should see a moving border around cell B11, indicating that the contents of this cell have been copied to the clipboard.
- Click and drag to select **cells C11** and **D11** as shown in Figure 1.15e. Click the **Paste button** on the standard toolbar to copy the contents of the clipboard to the destination range. Press **Esc** to remove the moving border.
- Click anywhere in the worksheet to deselect cells C11 through D11. Cells C11 and D11 should contain 78 and 90.16667, the class averages on Test 2 and the Final, respectively. Do not worry about formatting at this time.
- Save the workbook.

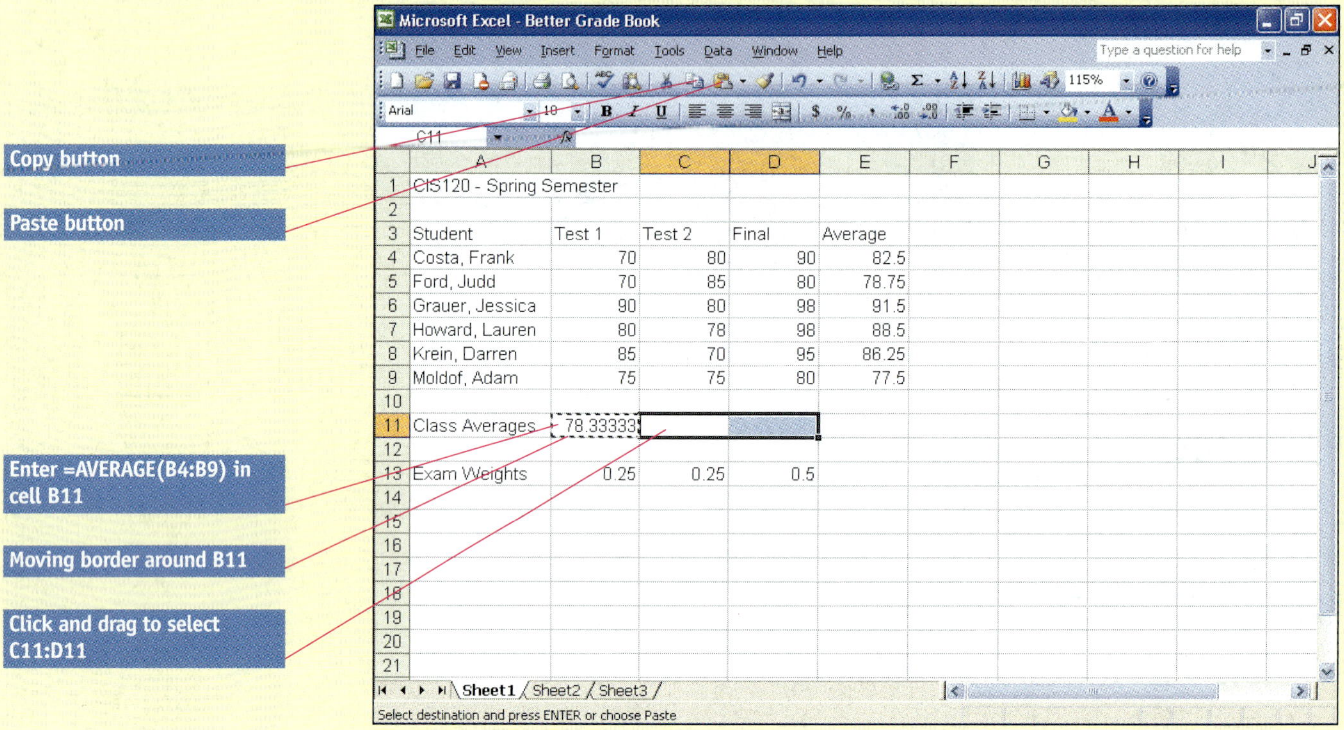

(e) Compute the Class Averages (step 5)

FIGURE 1.15 Hands-on Exercise 3 (*continued*)

TWO DIFFERENT CLIPBOARDS

The Office clipboard holds a total of up to 24 objects from multiple applications, as opposed to the Windows clipboard, which stores only the results of the last Cut or Copy command. Thus, each time you execute a Cut or Copy command, the contents of the Windows clipboard are replaced, whereas the copied object is added to the objects already in the Office clipboard. To display the Office clipboard, open the task pane, click the down arrow, and select clipboard. Leave the clipboard open as you execute multiple cut and copy operations to observe what happens.

Step 6: Change the Exam Weights

- Change the entries in **cells B13** and **C13** to **.20** and the entry in **cell D13** to **.60**. The semester average for every student changes automatically; for example, Costa and Moldof change to 84 and 78, respectively, as shown in Figure 1.15f.
- The professor decides this does not make a significant difference and wants to go back to the original weights. Click the **Undo button** three times to reverse the last three actions. You should see .25, .25, and .50 in cells B13, C13, and D13, respectively.
- Click in **cell A15** and type the label **Grading Assistant**. Press **Enter**. Type your name in **cell A16**, so that you will get credit for this assignment.
- Save the workbook. You do not need to print the workbook yet, since we will do that at the end of the next exercise, after we have formatted the workbook.
- Exit Excel if you are not ready to begin the next exercise at this time.

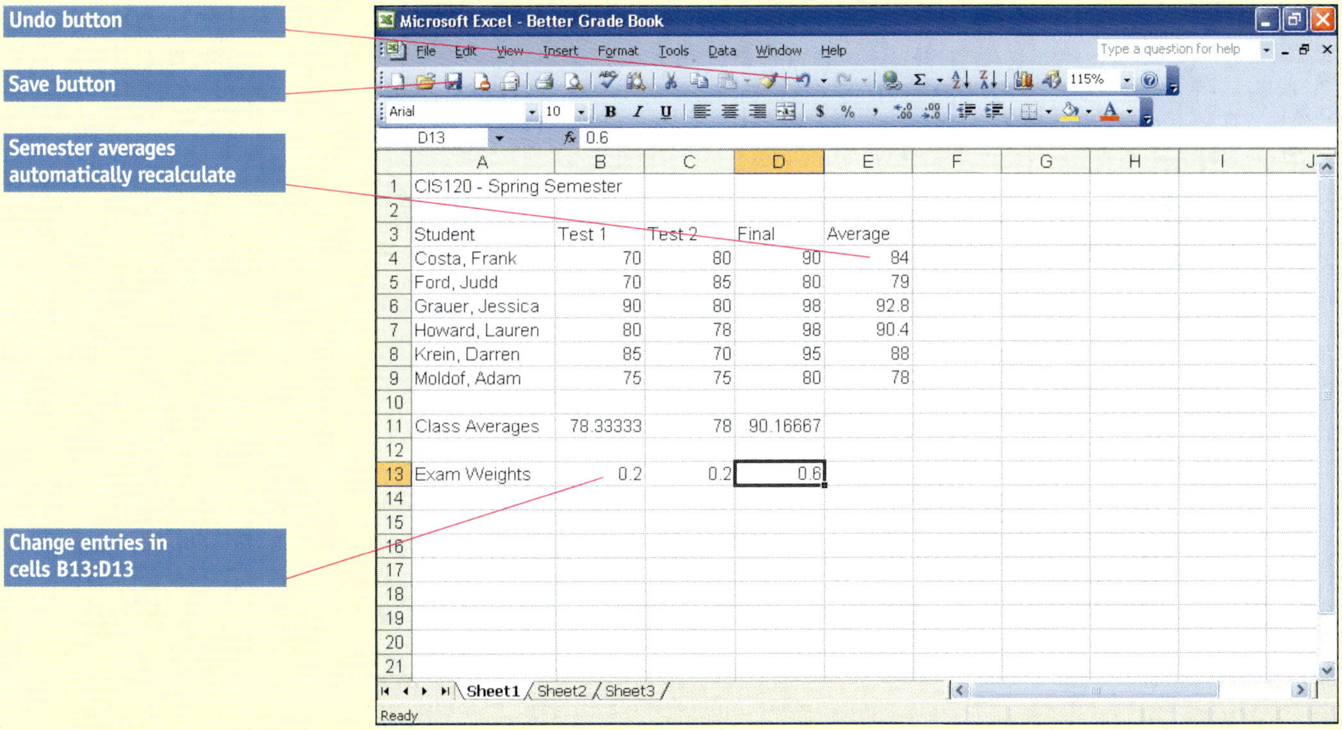

(f) Change the Exam Weights (step 6)

FIGURE 1.15 Hands-on Exercise 3 (*continued*)

CHANGE THE ZOOM PERCENTAGE

You can increase or decrease the size of a worksheet as it appears on the monitor by clicking the down arrow on the zoom box and selecting an appropriate percentage. If you are working with a large spreadsheet and cannot see it at one time on the screen, choose a number less than 100%. Conversely, if you find yourself squinting because the numbers are too small, select a percentage larger than 100%. Changing the magnification on the screen does not affect printing; that is, worksheets are always printed at 100% unless you change the scaling within the Page Setup command.

FORMATTING

Figure 1.16a shows the grade book as it exists at the end of the third hands-on exercise, without concern for its appearance. Figure 1.16b shows the grade book as it will appear at the end of the next exercise after it has been formatted. The differences between the two are due entirely to formatting. Consider:

- The exam weights are formatted as percentages in Figure 1.16b, as opposed to decimals in Figure 1.16a.
- The class and semester averages are displayed with a single decimal place in Figure 1.16b as opposed to a variable number of places in Figure 1.16a.
- Boldface and italic are used for emphasis, as are shading and borders.
- Exam grades and computed averages are centered under their respective headings, as are the exam weights.
- The worksheet title is centered across all five columns.

Class Averages are not uniformly formatted

Percentages are not formatted

	A	B	C	D	E
1	CIS120 - Spring Semester				
2					
3	Student	Test 1	Test 2	Final	Average
4	Costa, Frank	70	80	90	82.5
5	Ford, Judd	70	85	80	78.75
6	Grauer, Jessica	90	80	98	91.5
7	Howard, Lauren	80	78	98	88.5
8	Krein, Darren	85	70	95	86.25
9	Moldof, Adam	75	75	80	77.5
10					
11	Class Averages	78.33333333	78	90.16666667	
12					
13	Exam Weights	0.25	0.25	0.5	

(a) At the End of Hands-on Exercise 3

Title is centered across columns; font is larger and both bold and italic

Shading, borders, and boldface are used for emphasis

Test grades are centered in columns

Uniform number of decimal places

Percent formatting has been applied

	A	B	C	D	E
1	***CIS120 - Spring Semester***				
2					
3	**Student**	**Test 1**	**Test 2**	**Final**	**Average**
4	Costa, Frank	70	80	90	82.5
5	Ford, Judd	70	85	80	78.8
6	Grauer, Jessica	90	80	98	91.5
7	Howard, Lauren	80	78	98	88.5
8	Krein, Darren	85	70	95	86.3
9	Moldof, Adam	75	75	80	77.5
10					
11	**Class Averages**	**78.3**	**78.0**	**90.2**	
12					
13	**Exam Weights**	**25%**	**25%**	**50%**	

(b) At the End of Hands-on Exercise 4

FIGURE 1.16 Developing the Grade Book

FORMAT CELLS COMMAND

The ***Format Cells command*** controls the formatting for numbers, alignment, fonts, borders, and patterns (color). Execution of the command produces a tabbed dialog box in which you choose the particular formatting category, then enter the desired options. All formatting is done within the context of ***select-then-do***. You select the cells to which the formatting is to apply, then you execute the Format Cells command (or click the appropriate button on the Formatting toolbar).

Once a format has been assigned to a cell, the formatting remains in the cell and is applied to all subsequent values that are entered into that cell. You can, however, change the formatting by executing a new formatting command. You can also remove the formatting by using the Clear command in the Edit menu. Note, too, that changing the format of a number changes the way the number is displayed, but does not change its value. If, for example, you entered 1.2345 into a cell, but displayed the number as 1.23, the actual value (1.2345) would be used in all calculations involving that cell. The numeric formats are shown in Figure 1.17a and described below.

- ***General format*** is the default format for numeric entries and displays a number according to the way it was originally entered. Numbers are shown as integers (e.g., 123), decimal fractions (e.g., 1.23), or in scientific notation (e.g., 1.23E+10) if the number exceeds 11 digits.
- ***Number format***, which displays a number with or without the 1000 separator (e.g., a comma) and with any number of decimal places. Negative numbers can be displayed with parentheses and/or can be shown in red.
- ***Currency format***, which displays a number with the 1000 separator and an optional dollar sign (which is placed immediately to the left of the number). Negative values can be preceded by a minus sign or displayed with parentheses and/or can be shown in red.
- ***Accounting format***, which displays a number with the 1000 separator, an optional dollar sign (at the left border of the cell, vertically aligned within a column), negative values in parentheses, and zero values as hyphens.
- ***Date format***, which displays the date in different ways, such as March 14, 2001, 3/14/01, or 14-Mar-01.
- ***Time format***, which displays the time in different formats, such as 10:50 PM or the equivalent 22:50 (24-hour time).
- ***Percentage format***, whereby the number is multiplied by 100 for display purposes only, a percent sign is included, and any number of decimal places can be specified.
- ***Fraction format***, which displays a number as a fraction, and is appropriate when there is no exact decimal equivalent. A fraction is entered into a cell by preceding the fraction with an equal sign—for example, = ⅓.
- ***Scientific format***, which displays a number as a decimal fraction followed by a whole number exponent of 10; for example, the number 12345 would appear as 1.2345E+04. The exponent, +04 in the example, is the number of places the decimal point is moved to the left (or right if the exponent is negative). Very small numbers have negative exponents.
- ***Text format***, which left aligns the entry and is useful for numerical values that have leading zeros and should be treated as text, such as ZIP codes.
- ***Special format***, which displays a number with editing characters, such as hyphens in a Social Security number.
- ***Custom format***, which allows you to develop your own formats.

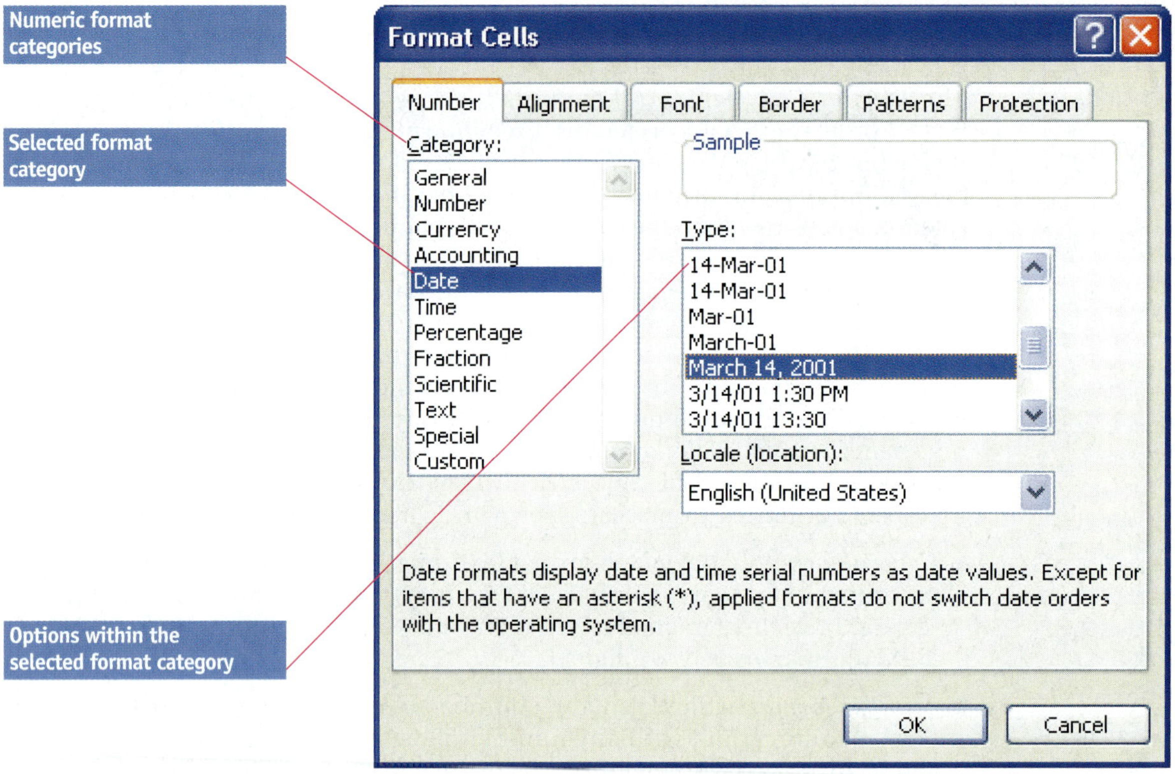

(a) The Number Tab

FIGURE 1.17 The Format Cells Command

Alignment

The contents of a cell (whether text or numeric) may be aligned horizontally and/or vertically as indicated by the dialog box of Figure 1.17b. The default horizontal ***alignment*** is general, which left-aligns text and right-aligns date and numbers. You can also center an entry across a range of selected cells (or ***merge cells***), as in the professor's grade book, which centered the title in cell A1 across columns A through E. Clear the box to merge cells if you want to ***split cells*** that have been previously merged. The Fill option under Horizontal alignment distributes the characters in the cell across the entire width of that cell.

Vertical alignment is important only if the row height is changed and the characters are smaller than the height of the row. Entries may be vertically aligned at the top, center, or bottom (the default) of a cell.

It is also possible to wrap the text within a cell to emulate the word wrap of a word processor. You select multiple cells and merge them together. And finally, you can achieve some interesting effects by rotating text up to 90° in either direction.

Fonts

You can use the same fonts in Excel as you can in any other Windows application. All fonts are WYSIWYG (What You See Is What You Get), meaning that the worksheet you see on the monitor will match the printed worksheet.

Any entry in a worksheet may be displayed in any font, style, or point size as indicated by the dialog box of Figure 1.17c. The example shows Arial, Bold Italic, and 14 points, and corresponds to the selection for the worksheet title in the improved grade book. Special effects, such as subscripts or superscripts, are also possible. You can even select a different color, but you will need a color printer to see the effect on the printed page.

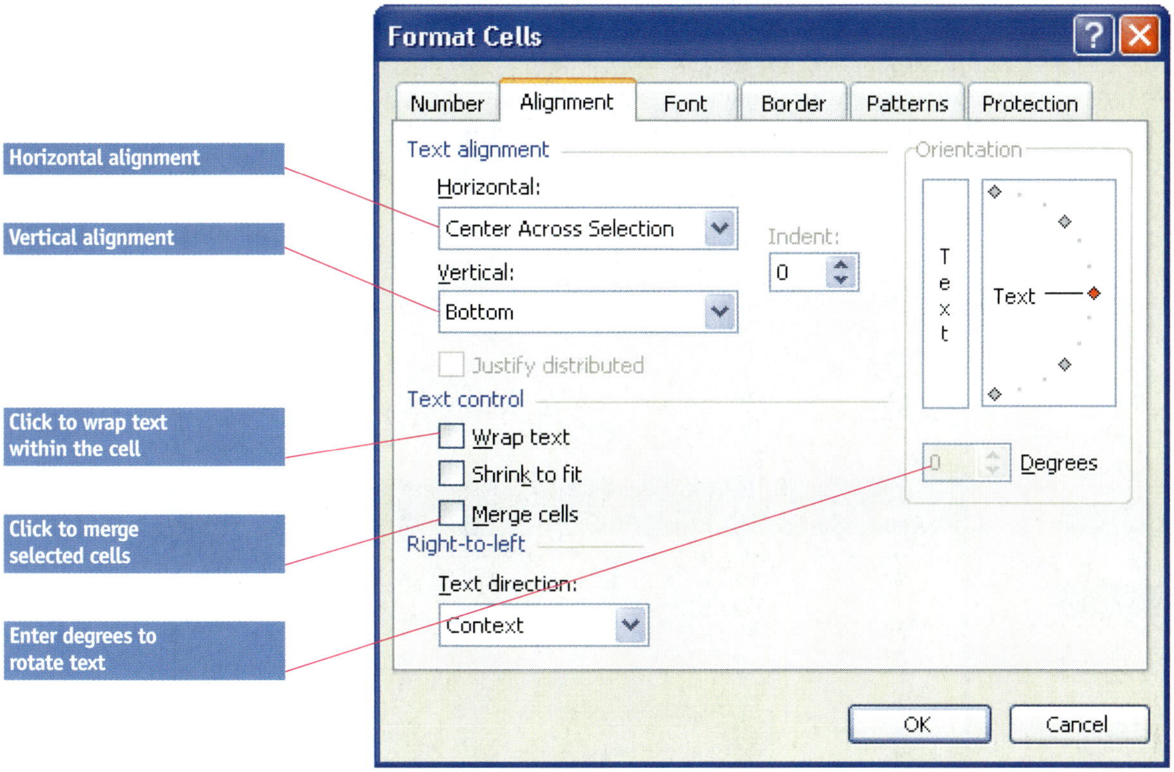

(b) The Alignment Tab

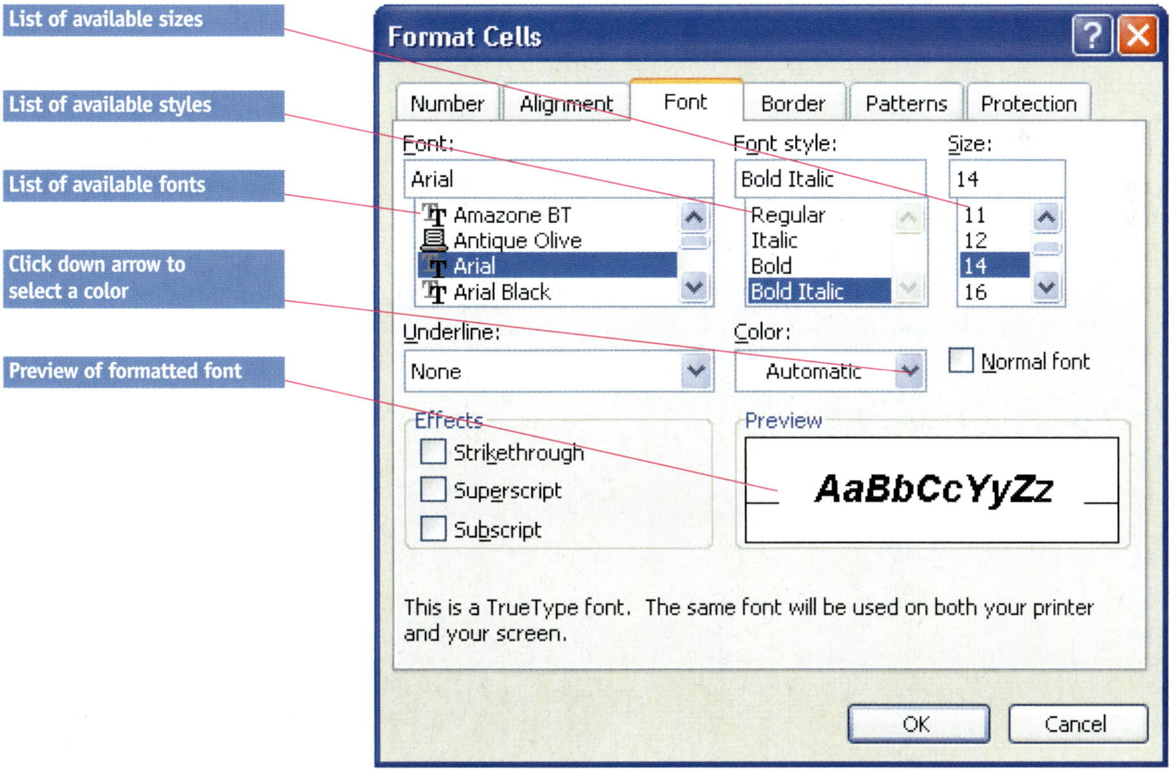

(c) The Font Tab

FIGURE 1.17 The Format Cells Command (*continued*)

Borders, Patterns, and Shading

The ***Border tab*** in Figure 1.17d enables you to create a border around a cell (or cells) for additional emphasis. You select (click) the line style at the right of the dialog box, then you click the left, right, top, and/or bottom border. You can outline the entire cell or selected cells, or you can choose the specific side or sides; for example, thicker lines on the bottom and right sides produce a drop shadow, which is very effective. You can also specify a different line style and/or a different color for the border, but you will need a color printer to see the effect on the printed output.

The ***Patterns tab*** (not shown in the figure) lets you choose a different color in which to shade the cell and further emphasize its contents. The Pattern drop-down list box lets you select an alternate pattern, such as dots or slanted lines. Click OK to accept the settings and close the dialog box.

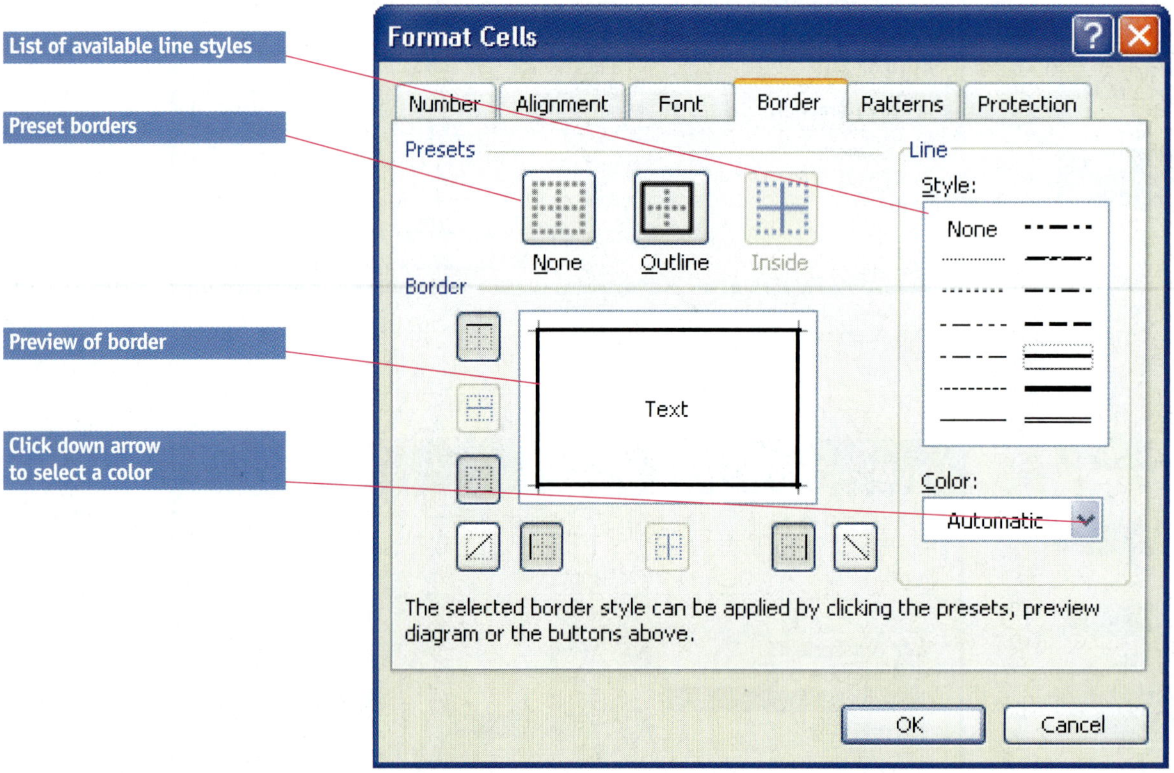

(d) The Border Tab

FIGURE 1.17 The Format Cells Command *(continued)*

USE RESTRAINT

More is not better, especially in the case of too many typefaces and styles, which produce cluttered worksheets that impress no one. Limit yourself to a maximum of two typefaces per worksheet, but choose multiple sizes and/or styles within those typefaces. Use boldface or italics for emphasis, but do so in moderation, because if you emphasize too many elements, the effect is lost.

hands-on exercise

4 Formatting a Worksheet

Objective To format a worksheet using boldface, italic, shading, and borders; to change the font and/or alignment of a selected entry. Use Figure 1.18 as a guide in the exercise.

Step 1: Center the Title

- Open **Better Grade Book** from the previous exercise. Click in **cell A1** to select the cell containing the title of the worksheet. Click the **Bold button** on the Formatting toolbar to boldface the title. Click the **Italic button** to italicize the title.
- Click in **cell A15** and click the **Bold button**. Click the **Bold button** a second time, and the boldface disappears. Click the **Bold button** again, and you are back to boldface. The same is true of the Italic button; that is, the Bold and Italic buttons function as toggle switches.
- Click in **cell A1**. Click the **down arrow** on the Font size list box and change the size to **14** to further accentuate the title.
- Click and drag to select **cells A1** through **E1**, which represents the width of the entire worksheet. Click the **Merge and Center button** on the Formatting toolbar as shown in Figure 1.18a to center the title across the width of your worksheet.
- Save the workbook.

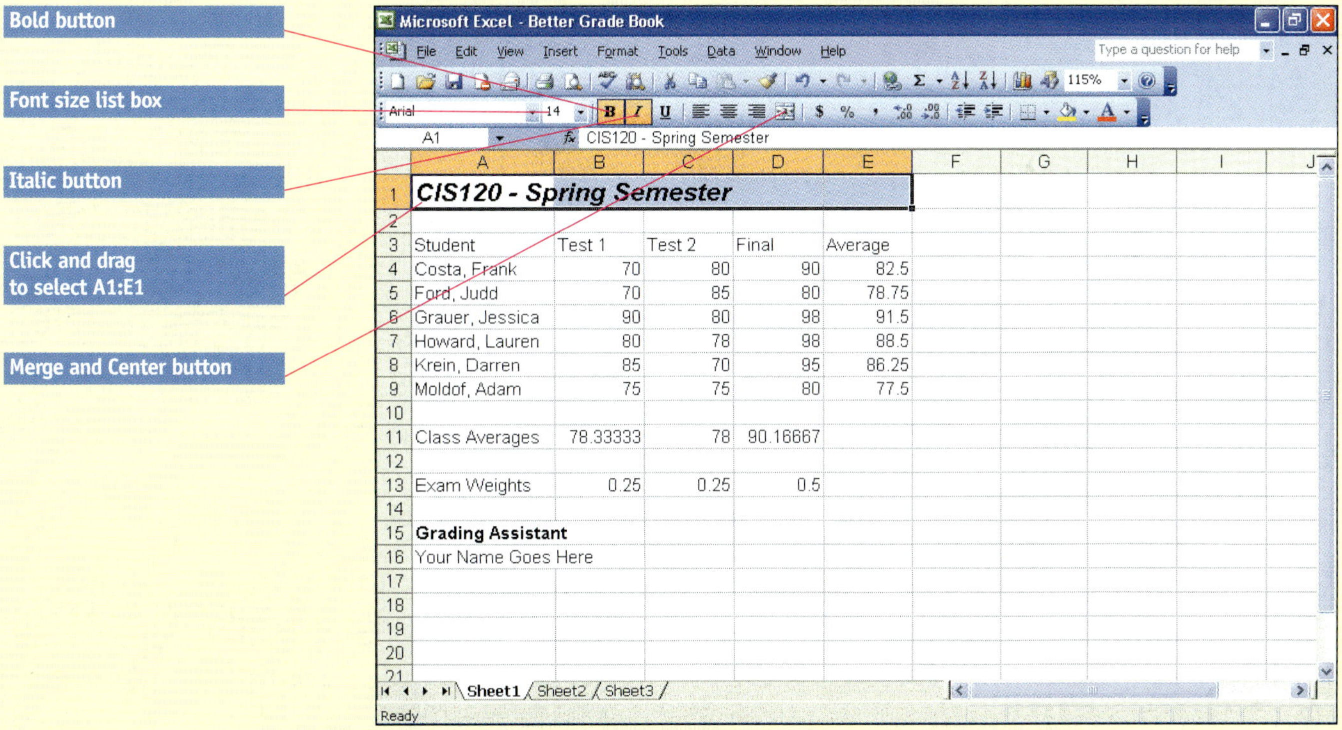

(a) Center the Title (step 1)

FIGURE 1.18 Hands-on Exercise 4

Step 2: Format the Exam Weights

- Click and drag to select **cells B13** through **D13**. Pull down the **Format menu**, then click the **Cells command** to display the dialog box in Figure 1.18b.
- If necessary, click the **Number tab**. Click **Percentage** in the Category list box. Click the **down spin arrow** in the Decimal Places box to select **zero decimals**, then click **OK**. The exam weights are displayed with percent signs and no decimal places.
- You can also use the buttons on the Formatting toolbar to accomplish the same formatting. First remove the formatting by clicking the **Undo button** on the Standard toolbar to cancel the formatting command.
- Check that cells B13 through D13 are still selected. Click the **Percent Style button** on the Formatting toolbar. (You can also pull down the **Format menu**, click the **Style command**, then choose the **Percent Style** from the Style Name list box.) Once again cells B13 through D13 are displayed in percent format.
- Save the workbook.

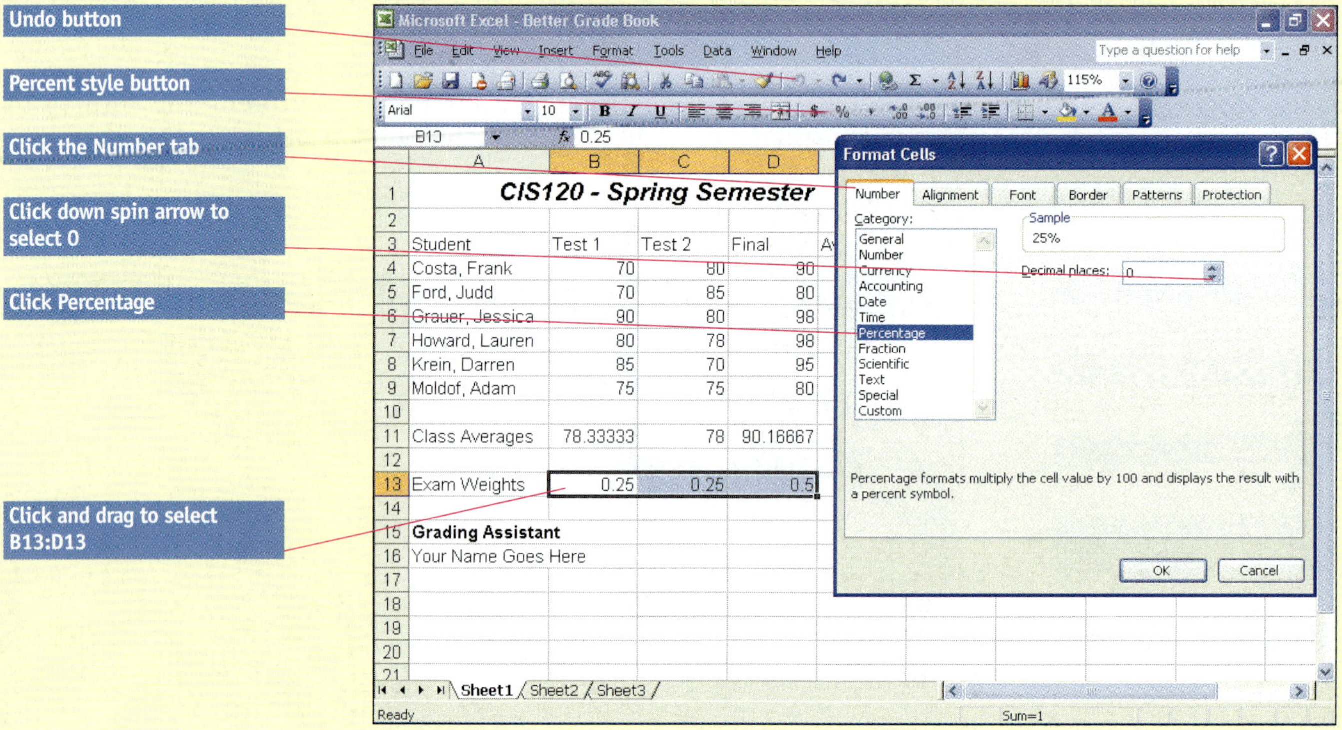

(b) Format the Exam Weights (step 2)

FIGURE 1.18 Hands-on Exercise 4 (*continued*)

THE MENU OR THE TOOLBAR

The Formatting toolbar is often the easiest way to implement a variety of formatting operations. There are buttons for boldface, italic, and underlining (each of which functions as a toggle switch). There are also buttons for alignment (including merge and center), currency, percent, and comma formats, together with buttons to increase or decrease the number of decimal places. You can find various buttons to change the font, point size, color, and borders.

Step 3: Format the Class Averages

- Click and drag to select **cells B11** through **D11**. Now press and hold the **Ctrl key** as you click and drag to select **cells E4** through **E9**. Using the Ctrl key in this way allows you to select noncontiguous (nontouching) cells as shown in Figure 1.18c.
- Format the selected cells using the Formatting toolbar or the Format menu:
  - To use the Format menu, pull down the **Format menu**, click **Cells**, click the **Number tab**, then click **Number** in the Category list box. Click the **down spin arrow** in the Decimal Places text box to reduce the decimal places to one. Click **OK**.
  - To use the Formatting toolbar, click the appropriate button repeatedly to increase or decrease the number of decimal places to one.
- Click and drag to select **cells B3** through **E13**. Click the **Center button** to center the numeric data in the worksheet under the respective column headings.
- Save the workbook.

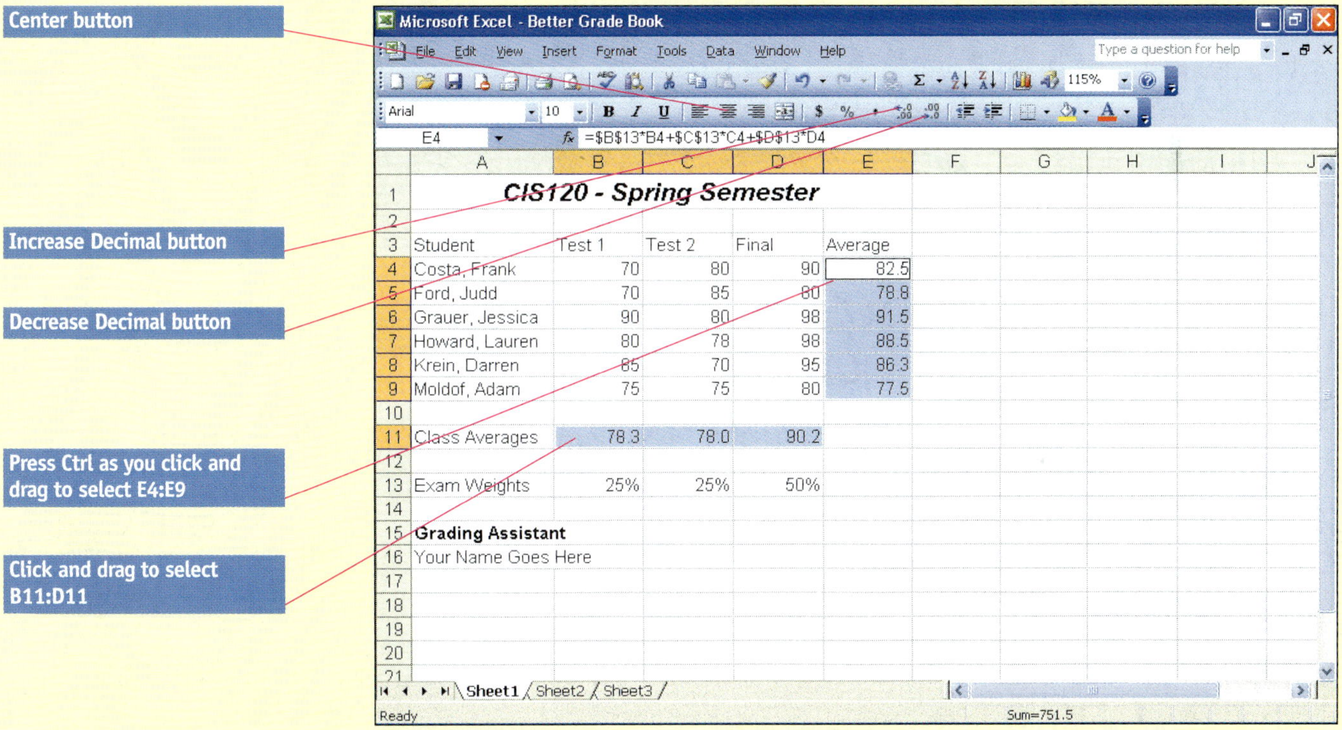

(c) Format the Class Averages (step 3)

FIGURE 1.18 Hands-on Exercise 4 (*continued*)

CLEAR THE FORMATS, BUT KEEP THE CONTENTS

You can clear the formatting in a cell and retain the contents, and/or you can clear contents but retain the formatting. Click and drag over the cell(s) for which the command is to apply, then pull down the Edit menu, click the Clear command, and choose the appropriate option—for example, the option to clear Formats. Click the tiny square immediately below the name box (to the left of the header for column A) to select the entire worksheet, then clear the formats for the worksheet. You can then repeat the steps in this exercise to practice the various formatting commands.

Step 4: Borders and Color

- Click and drag to select **cells A3** through **E3**. Press and hold the **Ctrl key** as you click and drag to select the range **A11:E11**.
- Continue to press the **Ctrl key** as you click and drag to select **cells A13:E13**. All three cell ranges should be selected, which means that any formatting command you execute will apply to all of the selected cells.
- Pull down the **Format menu** and click **Cells** (or point to any of the selected cells and click the **right mouse button** to display a shortcut menu, then click **Format Cells**). Click the **Border tab** to display the dialog box in Figure 1.18d.
- Choose a line width from the Style section. Click the **Top** and **Bottom** boxes in the Border section. Click **OK** to exit the dialog box.
- Check that all three ranges are still selected (A3:E3, A11:E11, *and* A13:E13). Click the **down arrow** on the **Fill Color button** on the Formatting toolbar. Click **yellow** (or whatever color appeals to you).
- Click the **Bold button** on the Formatting toolbar. Click outside the selected cells to see the effects of the formatting change. Save the workbook.

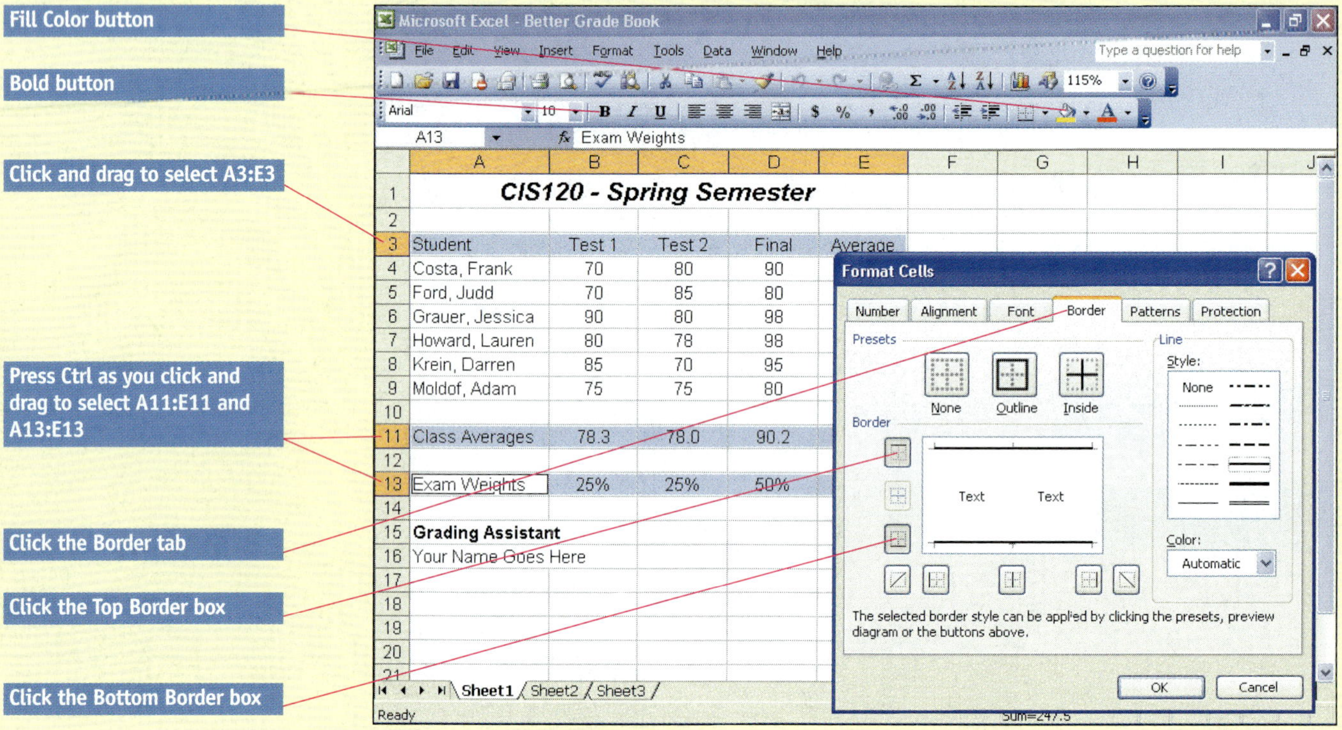

(d) Borders and Color (step 4)

FIGURE 1.18 Hands-on Exercise 4 (*continued*)

USE A PEN TO DRAW THE BORDER

You can draw borders of any thickness or color around the cells in a worksheet using a "pen," as opposed to a menu command. Click the down arrow on the Borders button on the Standard toolbar, then click the Draw Borders command to change the mouse pointer to a pen and simultaneously display the Borders toolbar. Click the Line Color or Line Style buttons to change the appearance of the border, then draw the borders directly in the worksheet. Close the Borders toolbar when you are finished.

Step 5: The Completed Worksheet

- Check that your worksheet matches ours as shown in Figure 1.18e. Pull down the **File menu**. Click **Page Setup** to display the Page Setup dialog box.
  - Click the **Margins tab**. Check the box to center the worksheet horizontally.
  - Click the **Sheet tab**. Check the boxes to print **Row and Column Headings** and **Gridlines**.
  - Click the **Header/Footer tab**. If necessary, click the **drop-down arrow** on the Header list box. Scroll to the top of the list and click **(none)** to remove the header. Click the **drop-down arrow** on the Footer list box. Scroll to the top of the list and click **(none)** to remove the footer. Click **OK**.
- Click the **Print Preview button** to preview the worksheet before printing:
  - If you are satisfied with the appearance of the worksheet, click the **Print button** within the Preview window, then click **OK** to print the worksheet.
  - If you are not satisfied with the appearance of the worksheet, click the **Setup button** within the Preview window to make the necessary changes.
- Save the workbook.

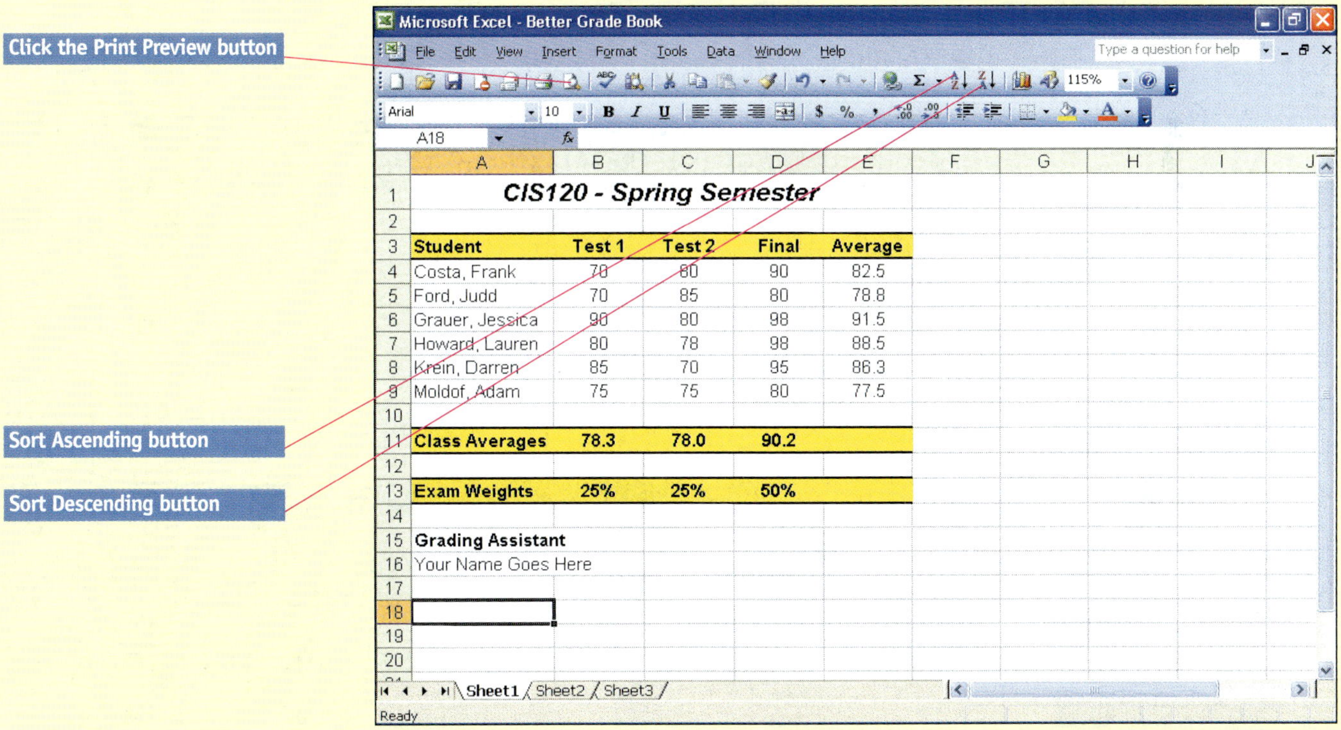

(e) The Completed Worksheet (step 5)

FIGURE 1.18 Hands-on Exercise 4 (*continued*)

SORT THE STUDENTS

The students are listed on the worksheet in alphabetical order, but you can rearrange the list according to any other field, such as the average or the result of a specific exam. Click on a single cell containing the student data in the column on which you want to sort, then click the Sort Ascending or Sort Descending button on the Standard toolbar. Click the Undo button if the result is different from what you intended.

Step 6: Print the Cell Formulas

- Pull down the **Tools menu**, click **Options**, click the **View tab**, check the box for **Formulas**, then click **OK**. You should see the cell formulas.
- Pull down the **File menu**. Click **Page Setup** to display the Page Setup dialog box. Click the **Page tab**. Click the **Landscape Orientation button**. Click the option button to **Fit to 1 Page**. Click **OK** to exit the Page Setup dialog box.
- Click the **Print Preview button** to preview the worksheet before printing.
  - Click the **Margins button** to display gridlines within the Print Preview window. Click and drag the column indicators to widen columns as necessary so that the cell formulas are completely visible.
  - Click the **Setup button** to display the Page Setup dialog box. Click the **Header/Footer tab**. Click the button to create a **Custom Header**.
  - Click in the **left section** and enter your name. Click in the **center section** and enter your course and your instructor's name.
  - Click in the **right section**. Click the **Date button**, press the **space bar**, then click the **Time button** to complete the custom header as shown in Figure 1.18f. Click **OK** to close the Header dialog box, then click **OK** to close the Page Setup dialog box. Print the worksheet.
- Pull down the **File menu**. Click **Exit**. Click **No** if prompted to save changes.

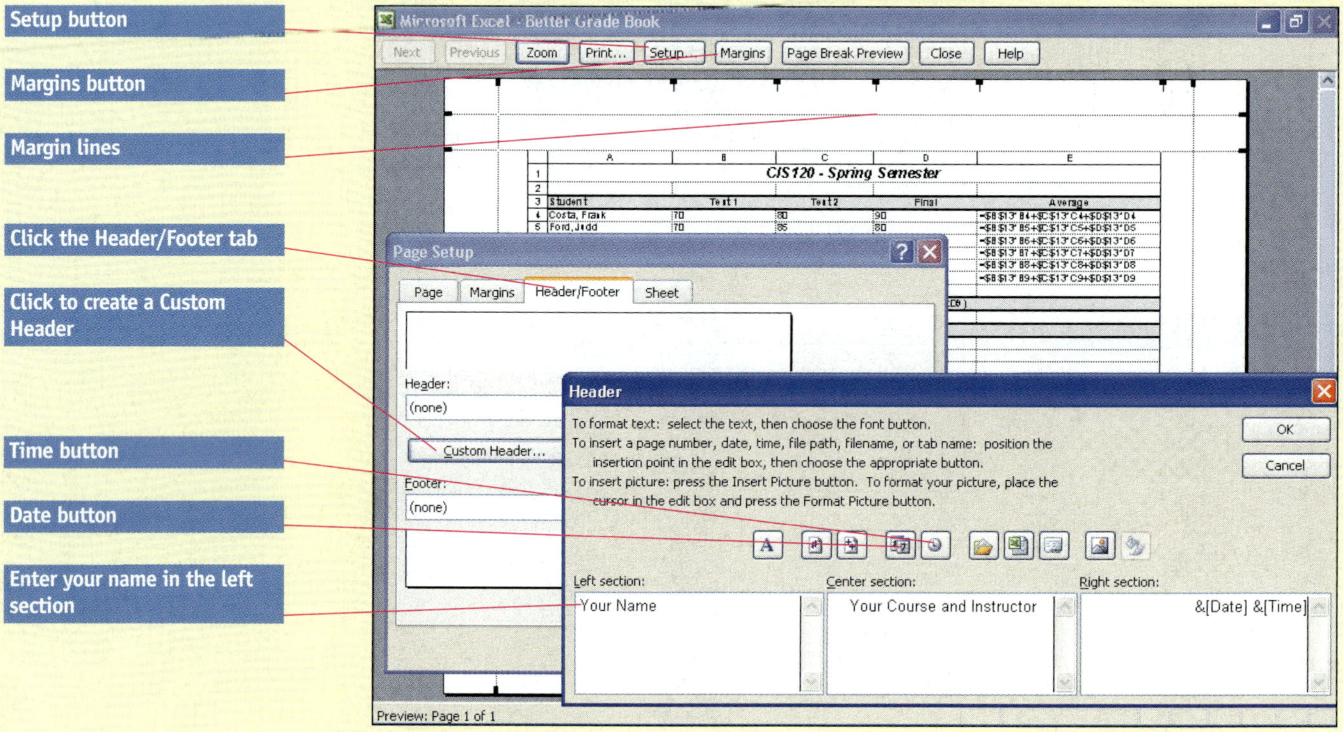

(f) Print the Cell Formulas (step 6)

FIGURE 1.18 Hands-on Exercise 4 (*continued*)

FIND AND REPLACE

Anyone familiar with a word processor takes the Find and Replace command for granted, but many people are surprised to learn that the same commands are also found in Excel. The commands are found in the Edit menu and provide the same options as in Microsoft Word. You can replace text and/or formatting throughout a worksheet. See practice exercise 5 at the end of the chapter.

SUMMARY

A spreadsheet is the computerized equivalent of an accountant's ledger. It is divided into rows and columns, with each row and column assigned a heading. The intersection of a row and column forms a cell. Spreadsheet is a generic term. Workbook and worksheet are Excel specific. An Excel workbook contains one or more worksheets.

Every cell in a worksheet (spreadsheet) contains either a formula or a constant. A formula begins with an equal sign and is a combination of numeric constants, cell references, arithmetic operators, and/or functions. A constant is an entry that does not change and may be numeric or descriptive text.

The Insert and Delete commands add or remove individual cells, rows, or columns of a worksheet. The commands are also used to insert or delete worksheets within a workbook. The Open command brings a workbook from disk into memory. The Save command copies the workbook in memory to disk.

The Page Setup command provides complete control over the printed page, enabling you to print a worksheet with or without gridlines or row and column headings. The Page Setup command also controls margins, headers and footers, centering the worksheet on a page, and orientation. The Print Preview command shows the worksheet as it will print and should be used prior to printing.

All worksheet commands operate on a cell or group of cells known as a range. A range is selected by dragging the mouse to highlight the range; the range remains selected until another range is selected or you click another cell in the worksheet. Noncontiguous (nonadjacent) ranges may be selected in conjunction with the Ctrl key.

The formulas in a cell or range of cells may be copied or moved anywhere within a worksheet. An absolute reference remains constant throughout a copy operation, whereas a relative address is adjusted for the new location. Absolute and relative references have no meaning in a move operation.

Formatting is done within the context of select-then-do; that is, select the cell or range of cells, then execute the appropriate command. The Format Cells command controls the formatting for numbers, alignment, font, borders, and patterns (colors). The Formatting toolbar simplifies the formatting process.

KEY TERMS

MULTIPLE CHOICE

1. Which of the following is true?
   (a) A worksheet contains one or more workbooks
   (b) A workbook contains one or more worksheets
   (c) A spreadsheet contains one or more worksheets
   (d) A worksheet contains one or more spreadsheets

2. The cell at the intersection of the second column and third row is cell:
   (a) B3
   (b) 3B
   (c) C2
   (d) 2C

3. What is the effect of typing F5+F6 into a cell *without* a beginning equal sign?
   (a) The entry is equivalent to the formula =F5+F6
   (b) The cell will display the contents of cell F5 plus cell F6
   (c) The entry will be treated as a text entry and display F5+F6 in the cell
   (d) The entry will be rejected by Excel, which will signal an error message

4. The Open command:
   (a) Brings a workbook from disk into memory
   (b) Brings a workbook from disk into memory, then erases the workbook on disk
   (c) Stores the workbook in memory on disk
   (d) Stores the workbook in memory on disk, then erases the workbook from memory

5. The Save command:
   (a) Brings a workbook from disk into memory
   (b) Brings a workbook from disk into memory, then erases the workbook on disk
   (c) Stores the workbook in memory on disk
   (d) Stores the workbook in memory on disk, then erases the workbook from memory

6. In the absence of parentheses, the order of operation is:
   (a) Exponentiation, addition or subtraction, multiplication or division
   (b) Addition or subtraction, multiplication or division, exponentiation
   (c) Multiplication or division, exponentiation, addition or subtraction
   (d) Exponentiation, multiplication or division, addition or subtraction

7. Cells A1, A2, and A3 contain the values 10, 20, and 40, respectively. What value will be displayed in a cell containing the cell formula =A1/A2*A3+1?
   (a) 1.125
   (b) 21
   (c) 20.125
   (d) Impossible to determine

8. The entry =AVERAGE(A4:A6):
   (a) Is invalid because the cells are not contiguous
   (b) Computes the average of cells A4 and A6
   (c) Computes the average of cells A4, A5, and A6
   (d) None of the above

9. Which of the following was suggested with respect to printing a workbook?
   (a) Print the displayed values only
   (b) Print the cell formulas only
   (c) Print both the displayed values and cell formulas
   (d) Print neither the displayed values nor the cell formulas

10. Which options are mutually exclusive in the Page Setup menu?
    (a) Portrait and landscape orientation
    (b) Cell gridlines and row and column headings
    (c) Left and right margins
    (d) All of the above

... continued

multiple choice

11. If cells A1, A2, and A3 contain the values 1, 2, and 5, respectively, what value will be displayed in a cell containing the formula =(A3-A1)/A2^2+A2?

(a) 1
(b) 3
(c) .0625
(d) .4

12. Which of the following best describes the formula used to compute a student's semester average, when the weights of each exam are isolated at the bottom of a spreadsheet?

(a) The student's individual grades are entered as absolute references and the exam weights are entered as relative references
(b) The student's individual grades are entered as relative references and the exam weights are entered as absolute references
(c) All cell references are relative
(d) All cell references are absolute

13. Cell B11 contains the formula, =SUM (B3:B9). What will the contents of cell C11 be if the formula in cell B11 is copied to cell C11?

(a) =SUM (C3:C9)
(b) =SUM (B3:B9)
(c) =SUM ($B$3:$B$9)
(d) =SUM ($C$3:$C$9)

14. Given that cell E6 contains the formula =B6*$B$12+C6*$C$12+D6*$D$12. What will be the formula in cell E7 if the contents of cell E6 are copied to that cell?

(a) =B7*$B$12+C7*$C$12+D7*$D$12
(b) =B7*$B$13+C7*$C$13+D7*$D$13
(c) =B6*$B$13+C6*$C$13+D6*$D$13
(d) None of the above

15. A formula containing the reference =D$5 is copied to a cell one column over and two rows down. How will the entry appear in its new location?

(a) =E5
(b) =E$5
(c) =E$6
(d) =$E5

16. The formula =B3+C4 is stored in cell D5. What will the formula be if row two is deleted from the worksheet?

(a) =B2+C4
(b) =B3+C3
(c) =B3+C4
(d) =B2+C3

17. You are creating a sales forecast, and have entered the sales for 2002 in cell B4. The expected rate of increase is in cell C2. What formula would you enter in cell C4 to compute the sales for 2003, given that you will copy that formula to cells D4:E4 to calculate the forecast for 2004 and 2005?

(a) =B4+B4*C2
(b) =$B$4+$B$4*C2
(c) =B4*(1+$C$2)
(d) None of the above

18. What is the end result of clicking in a cell, then clicking the Italic button on the Formatting toolbar twice in a row?

(a) The cell contents are displayed in italic
(b) The cell contents are displayed in ordinary (nonitalicized) type
(c) The cell contents are unchanged and appear exactly as they did prior to clicking the Italic button twice in a row
(d) Impossible to determine

ANSWERS

1. b	**7.** b	**13.** a
2. a	**8.** c	**14.** a
3. c	**9.** c	**15.** b
4. a	**10.** a	**16.** d
5. c	**11.** b	**17.** c
6. d	**12.** b	**18.** c

PRACTICE WITH EXCEL

1. **Isolate Assumptions:** Figure 1.19 displays a new grade book with a different grading scheme. Students take three exams worth 100 points each, submit a term paper and various homework assignments worth 50 points each, then receive a grade for the semester based on their total points. The maximum number of points (the point threshold) is 400. A student's semester average is computed by dividing his or her total points by the point threshold. Open the partially completed workbook in *Chapter 1 Practice 1* in the Exploring Excel folder and proceed as follows:
   a. Click in cell G4 and enter a formula to compute Anderson's total points. Click in cell H4 and enter a formula that will compute Anderson's semester average. Be sure this formula includes an absolute reference to cell B16.
   b. Click and drag to select the formulas in cells G4 and H4, then copy these formulas to cells G5 through H12.
   c. Click in cell B14 and enter a formula that will compute the class average on the first exam. Copy this formula to cells C14 to H14.
   d. Format the worksheet appropriately, but you need not match our formatting exactly. Note, too, that we have wrapped the text in cells B3 through H3 in order to use a narrower column width. (Select the cells, pull down the Format Cells command, click the Alignment tab, then check the box to wrap text.)
   e. Add your name as the grading assistant, then print the worksheet twice, once to show displayed values and once to show the cell formulas. Use landscape printing and be sure that the worksheet fits on one sheet of paper.
   f. The professor is concerned about the grades being too low and wants to introduce a curve. He does this by reducing the point threshold on which the students' semester averages are based. Click in cell B16 and change the threshold to 350, which automatically raises the average of every student.
   g. Print the displayed values that reflect the change in part (e). Can you see the value of isolating the assumptions within a worksheet?
   h. Add a cover page, then submit the complete assignment (four pages in all, counting the cover page) to your instructor as proof that you did this exercise.

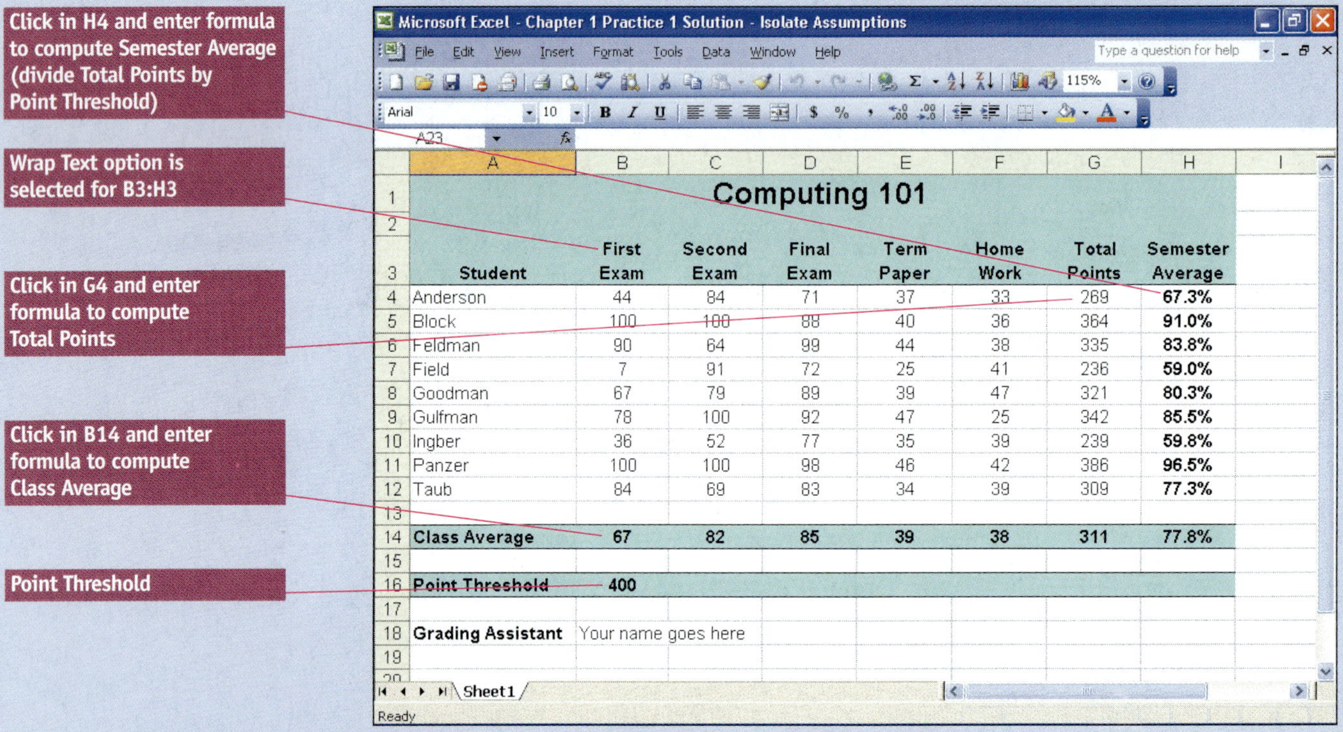

	A	B	C	D	E	F	G	H
1	Computing 101							
2								
3	Student	First Exam	Second Exam	Final Exam	Term Paper	Home Work	Total Points	Semester Average
4	Anderson	44	84	71	37	33	269	67.3%
5	Block	100	100	88	40	36	364	91.0%
6	Feldman	90	64	99	44	38	335	83.8%
7	Field	7	91	72	25	41	236	59.0%
8	Goodman	67	79	89	39	47	321	80.3%
9	Gulfman	78	100	92	47	25	342	85.5%
10	Ingber	36	52	77	35	39	239	59.8%
11	Panzer	100	100	98	46	42	386	96.5%
12	Taub	84	69	83	34	39	309	77.3%
13								
14	Class Average	67	82	85	39	38	311	77.8%
15								
16	Point Threshold	400						
17								
18	Grading Assistant	Your name goes here						
19								

FIGURE 1.19 Isolate Assumptions (exercise 1)

2. **Practice with Formatting:** The workbook in Figure 1.20 provides practice with formatting and basic cell operations. Open the partially completed workbook in *Chapter 1 Practice 2,* and then format the workbook using the instructions in each cell. The formatting is very straightforward, but inserting and deleting cells is a little trickier since it can affect cells that have been merged together. You will find it easier therefore if you start in cell A1 and work your way down the worksheet, one row at a time. Proceed as follows:
   a. Click in cell A1 and enter your name, then change the formatting to 16 point white text on a blue background as shown in the figure.
   b. Move to cell A3 and format the text as indicated. You can use the Format Cells command and/or the various tools on the Formatting toolbar as you see fit. Move to cell B3 and italicize the text in green. Format cells A4 through B7 in similar fashion. Follow the instructions in cell B5 to change the width of column B.
   c. Follow the instructions in cells A8 to A12 to format the contents of cells B8 to B12, respectively. (No additional formatting is required for cells A8 to A12 at this time.)
   d. Click in cell A13, then click the Merge and Center button to split the merged cell into two cells. (The Merge and Center button functions as a toggle switch: Click it once, the selected cells are merged; click it a second time, and the merged cell is split.) Follow the instructions in the cell to change the row height and other formatting. Cell B13 should be blank when you are finished.
   e. Click in cell A14, click the Format Painter tool, and then click and drag cells A8 through A12 to apply the formatting from cell A14.
   f. Right click the row indicator for row 15 and insert a new row, and then move the contents of cell A20 to the newly inserted cell A15.
   g. Change the width of column A to 55, merge cells A16 and B16, then complete the indicated formatting for the merged cell.
   h. Print the completed workbook for your instructor. Use the Page Setup command to display gridlines and row and column headings. Change to landscape printing and center the worksheet horizontally on the page. Create a custom header that contains your name, your school, and your instructor's name. Add a custom footer that contains the name of the workbook, and the date and time you completed the assignment.

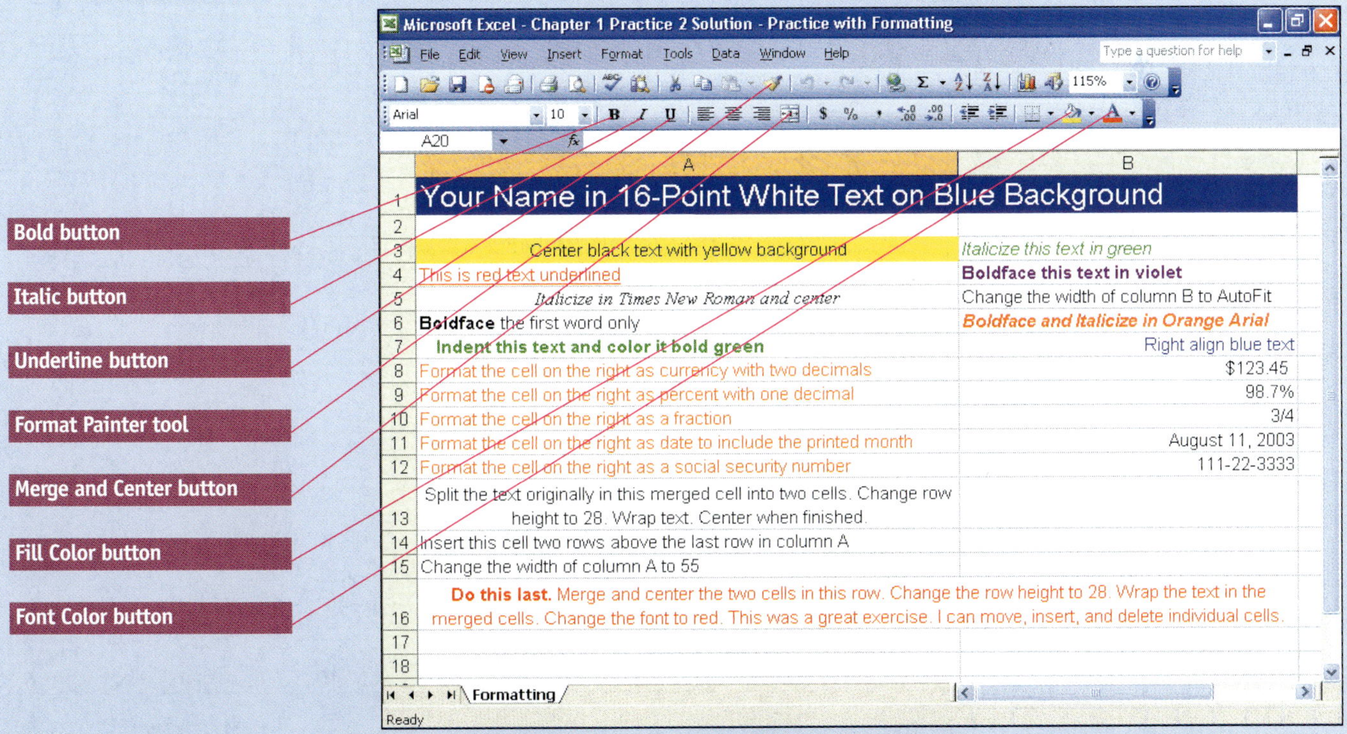

FIGURE 1.20 Practice with Formatting (exercise 2)

3. **The Calendar:** There are many way to create a calendar within Microsoft Office. The most important step, however, is to design the calendar with the computer off, then once you know the type of calendar (e.g., weekly or monthly) and the desired look, it is relatively easy to create regardless of the application.
   a. Start a new workbook. Click and drag to select cells D1 through F1, click the Merge and Center button, then change the format of the merged cells to text. Enter the month for which you will create the calendar—for example, October 2003 as shown in Figure 1.21. Click and drag to merge cells D2 through F2 in similar fashion, and enter your name. Change the row height, column width, font size, and color as appropriate.
   b. Click in cell B3 and enter "Sunday", the day on which our calendar will begin. Click and drag the fill handle to cells C3 to H3 to automatically enter the remaining days of the week (using the AutoFill capability within Excel).
   c. Click and drag to select cells B3 through H3 and click the Bold button. Pull down the Format menu, click the Cells command, click the Alignment tab, and then choose Center for the Vertical Alignment. Increase the row height to see the vertical alignment. Change the formatting of the text as desired.
   d. Click in the appropriate cell in row four (cell E4 in our figure) and enter 1 for the first day of the month. Enter the remaining days of the month in rows four through eight as appropriate, then increase the row height in rows 4 through 7 so that the calendar fills the page. (We specified a row height of 65.) Change the vertical alignment to the top of each cell and format the text as appropriate, for example, 14 point bold.
   e. Use the Insert Picture command to insert an appropriate piece of clip art. Complete the formatting by changing the fill color in cells B3 through H3, B3 through B8, and H3 through H8.
   f. Insert a second worksheet and create a weekly calendar. The calendar should show the days of the week going across the top, and the times of the day down the side. The rest of the design is up to you.
   g. Use the Page Setup command to change to landscape printing, then print both calendars for your instructor.

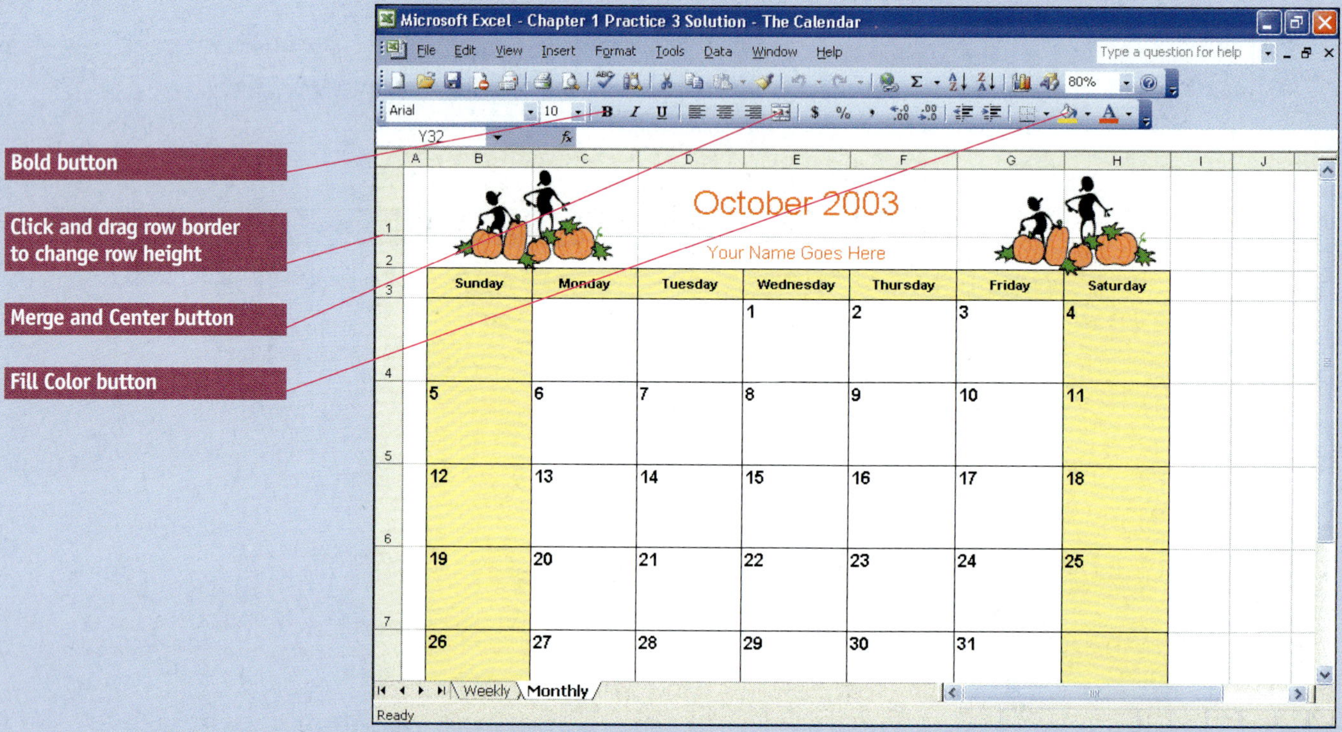

FIGURE 1.21 The Calendar (exercise 3)

4. **The Checkbook:** Figure 1.22 displays a worksheet that can be used to balance your checkbook. Your assignment is to create a similar worksheet using real or hypothetical data. Proceed as follows:
   a. Start Excel. If necessary, click the New button on the Standard toolbar to display a blank workbook. Click in cell A1 and enter the title with your name as shown. Enter the labels for cells A2 through F2. Do not worry about formatting at this time.
   b. Enter the initial balance in cell F3. Enter the data for your first check in row 4. To enter a date, just type the date without an equal sign; e.g., type 6/2 to display June 2 of the current year. Do not worry about the precise formatting at this time.
   c. Click in cell F4 and enter the formula to compute the balance. The formula should be entered in such a way that the balance is computed correctly, regardless of whether the transaction is a check (withdrawal) or deposit.
   d. Enter data for at least 6 additional transactions in cells A through E of the appropriate rows. Copy the formula to compute the balance for these transactions from cell F4.
   e. Skip one row after the last transaction, then enter the formulas to verify that the balance is correct. The formula for cell F18 (in our worksheet) is the initial balance, minus the sum of all checks and withdrawals, plus the sum of all deposits. The displayed value should equal the balance after the last transaction. Pull down the Insert menu and click the Comment command to enter a comment in that cell that explains the formula in cell F18.
   f. Format the completed worksheet as shown in Figure 1.22. You do not have to duplicate our formatting exactly, but you are to use date and currency formatting in the appropriate cells.
   g. Print the completed workbook to show both displayed values and cell formulas. Use the Page Setup command to display gridlines and row and column headings. Center the worksheet horizontally on the page. Create a custom header that contains your name, your school, and your instructor's name. Add a custom footer that contains the name of the workbook, and the date and time you completed the assignment.

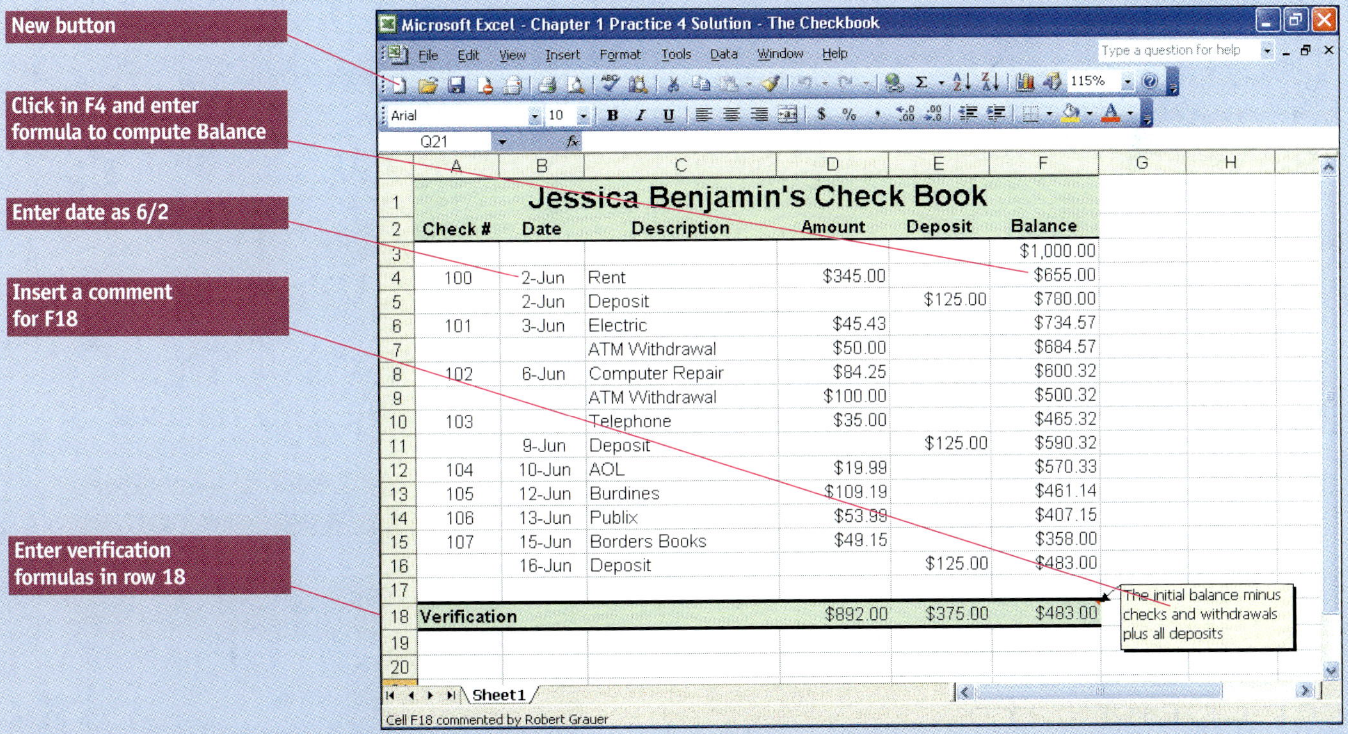

FIGURE 1.22 The Checkbook (exercise 4)

5. **Judson Ford Realty:** The worksheet in Figure 1.23 displays the sales for Judson Ford Realty for the month of October. You can open a partially completed version of this worksheet in *Chapter 1 Practice 5*, but it is up to you to complete the worksheet so that it matches Figure 1.23. The notes in the worksheet and/or the column headings should be self-explanatory with respect to entering the various formulas, but the information is repeated below.
   a. The percentage of the asking price in cell E4 is the sales price divided by the asking price. Format the result as a percent with one decimal place.
   b. The price per square foot in cell F4 is the selling price divided by the number of square feet.
   c. The realtor's commission in cell G4 is a percentage of the selling price and is based on the commission percentage in cell B14.
   d. The net to the homeowner in cell H4 is the selling price minus the commission to the realtor.
   e. Copy the formulas in row 4 to the remaining rows in the worksheet.
   f. Format the worksheet in an appropriate fashion, but you need not match our formatting exactly. Note, too, that we have wrapped the text in row 3 in order to use a narrower column width. (Select cells A3 through H3, pull down the Format Cells command, click the Alignment tab, then check the box to wrap text.)
   g. Compute the agency statistics as shown in row 12. Use the Average, Max, and Min functions in cells H17 through H19 to display these values for the properties that were sold during the month.
   h. Use the Find and Replace command to change the text in the various addresses. Change all occurrences of "Str" to "Street", "Rd" to "Road", and "Ave" to "Avenue". You also need to replace the Courier New font with Arial throughout the worksheet.
   i. Add your name in cell G14, then print the worksheet to show both displayed values and cell formulas. Change to landscape printing and add a custom header and/or a custom footer.
   j. Create a cover sheet, then submit the assignment to your instructor.

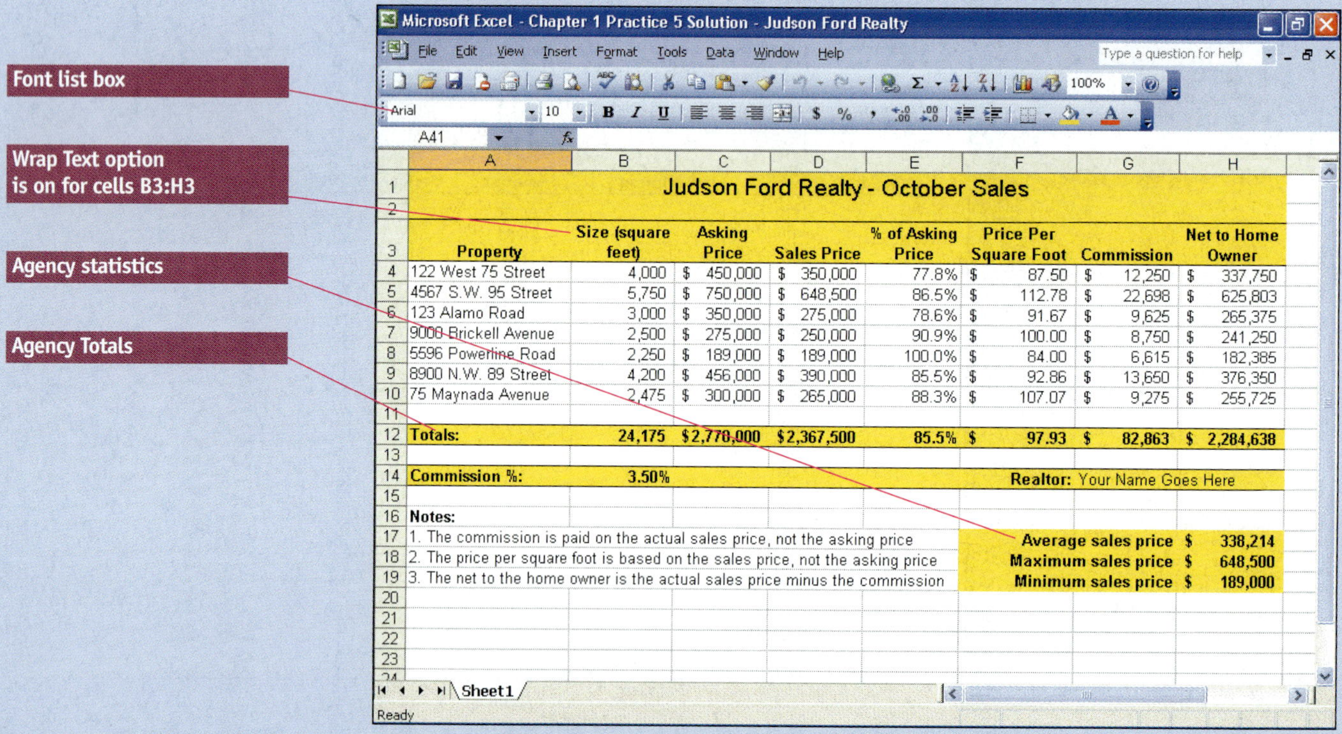

	A	B	C	D	E	F	G	H
1	Judson Ford Realty - October Sales							
2								
3	Property	Size (square feet)	Asking Price	Sales Price	% of Asking Price	Price Per Square Foot	Commission	Net to Home Owner
4	122 West 75 Street	4,000	$ 450,000	$ 350,000	77.8%	$ 87.50	$ 12,250	$ 337,750
5	4567 S.W. 95 Street	5,750	$ 750,000	$ 648,500	86.5%	$ 112.78	$ 22,698	$ 625,803
6	123 Alamo Road	3,000	$ 350,000	$ 275,000	78.6%	$ 91.67	$ 9,625	$ 265,375
7	9000 Brickell Avenue	2,500	$ 275,000	$ 250,000	90.9%	$ 100.00	$ 8,750	$ 241,250
8	5596 Powerline Road	2,250	$ 189,000	$ 189,000	100.0%	$ 84.00	$ 6,615	$ 182,385
9	8900 N.W. 89 Street	4,200	$ 456,000	$ 390,000	85.5%	$ 92.86	$ 13,650	$ 376,350
10	75 Maynada Avenue	2,475	$ 300,000	$ 265,000	88.3%	$ 107.07	$ 9,275	$ 255,725
11								
12	**Totals:**	**24,175**	**$2,770,000**	**$2,367,500**	**85.5%**	**$ 97.93**	**$ 82,863**	**$ 2,284,638**
13								
14	**Commission %:**	**3.50%**					**Realtor:** Your Name Goes Here	
15								
16	**Notes:**							
17	1. The commission is paid on the actual sales price, not the asking price						**Average sales price**	**$ 338,214**
18	2. The price per square foot is based on the sales price, not the asking price						**Maximum sales price**	**$ 648,500**
19	3. The net to the home owner is the actual sales price minus the commission						**Minimum sales price**	**$ 189,000**

FIGURE 1.23 Judson Ford Realty (exercise 5)

6. **The Solar System:** The potential uses of a spreadsheet are limited only by your imagination as can be seen by Figure 1.24, which displays a spreadsheet with information about our solar system. Open the partially completed version of the workbook in *Chapter 1 Practice 6*, then complete the worksheet by developing the formulas for the first planet, copying those formulas to the remaining rows in the worksheet, then formatting appropriately.
    a. Click in cell C15 and enter your weight on Earth. You can specify your weight in pounds rather than kilograms.
    b. Click in cell C16 and enter the function =Pi() as shown in Figure 1.23. The displayed value for the cell shows the value of Pi to several decimal places. The contents of the cell, however, contain the indicated function as can be seen in the formula bar.
    c. Click in cell D4 and enter the formula to compute the diameter of the first planet (Mercury). The diameter of a planet is equal to twice its radius.
    d. Click in cell E4 and enter the formula to compute the circumference of a planet. The circumference is equal to the diameter times the constant Pi.
    e. Click in cell F4 and enter the formula to compute the surface area, which is equal to four times Pi times the radius squared. (This is the formula to compute the surface area of a sphere, which is different from the formula to compute the area of a circle.)
    f. Click in cell G4 and enter the formula to compute your weight on Mercury, which is your weight on Earth times the relative gravity of Mercury compared to that of Earth.
    g. Copy the formulas in row 4 to the remainder of the worksheet, then format the worksheet appropriately. You need not copy our formatting exactly. Add your name in cell E15 as indicated.
    h. The worksheet contains a hyperlink to a Web site by Bill Arnett, which has additional information about the planets. If you click the hyperlink within Excel, your browser will open automatically, and you will be connected to the site, provided you have an Internet connection.
    i. Print the worksheet two ways, once with displayed values, and once to show the cell contents. Use landscape orientation and appropriate scaling so that the worksheet fits on a single page.

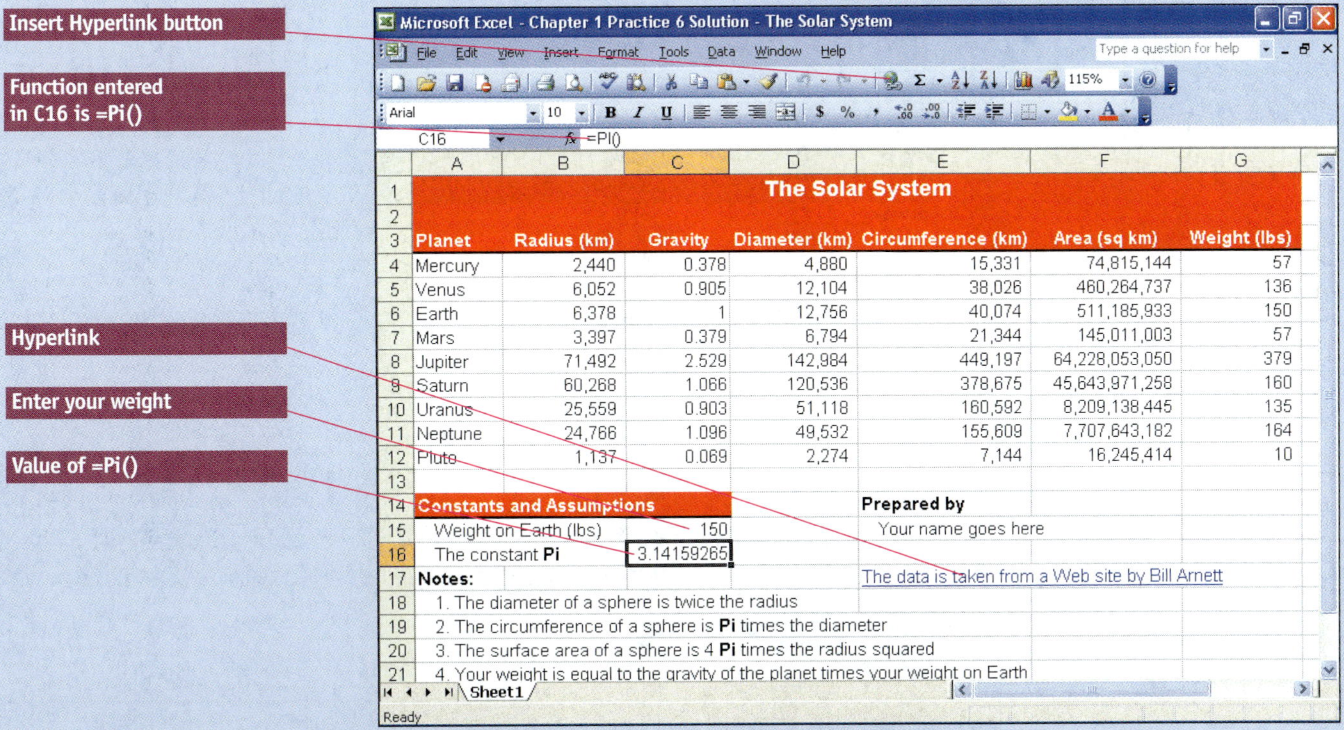

Planet	Radius (km)	Gravity	Diameter (km)	Circumference (km)	Area (sq km)	Weight (lbs)
Mercury	2,440	0.378	4,880	15,331	74,815,144	57
Venus	6,052	0.905	12,104	38,026	460,264,737	136
Earth	6,378	1	12,756	40,074	511,185,933	150
Mars	3,397	0.379	6,794	21,344	145,011,003	57
Jupiter	71,492	2.529	142,984	449,197	64,228,053,050	379
Saturn	60,268	1.066	120,536	378,675	45,643,971,258	160
Uranus	25,559	0.903	51,118	160,592	8,209,138,445	135
Neptune	24,766	1.096	49,532	155,609	7,707,643,182	164
Pluto	1,137	0.069	2,274	7,144	16,245,414	10

FIGURE 1.24 The Solar System (exercise 6)

7. **Student Budget:** Figure 1.25 displays a hypothetical budget for a nine-month academic year. You can use the partially completed version of this worksheet in the *Chapter 1 Practice 7* workbook, or you can create your own budget. If you use our file, then the totals in your worksheet should correspond exactly to those in Figure 1.25, whereas if you create your own budget, the numbers will differ. The worksheet is straightforward, but we want to call your attention to the following:
   a. Enter the data (the labels for the various income and expense categories as well as the specific amounts) in the body of the worksheet.
   b. Use the Sum function in cell K4 to compute the total for the first income source for the academic year. Copy this formula to the remaining cells in this column.
   c. Use the Sum function in cell B8 to compute the total income for September. Copy this formula to the remaining cells in this row. (The total income for the year can be obtained by summing either cells K4 through K7 or cells B8 through J8.) Use a similar approach to determine the total expenses for each month in row 18.
   d. Compute the deficit or surplus for each month in row 20. If necessary, adjust your numbers to show at least one month where you run a deficit. Negative numbers should be formatted in red and be enclosed in parentheses.
   e. Compute the minimum and maximum monthly expense in cells B22 and B23, respectively.
   f. Merge and center the cells in row 1, and enter your name to identify the worksheet as your own. Format it appropriately. Print the worksheet two ways, to show both displayed values and cell formulas, then submit both pages to your instructor. Be sure to use the Page Setup command to specify landscape printing, and appropriate scaling so that the entire worksheet fits on a single page.
   g. Extend the exercise by exploring potential sources for financial aid. Your school or university may offer scholarships or work study programs of which you are currently unaware. Outside agencies may provide similar help. Summarize your findings and bring them to class for discussion.

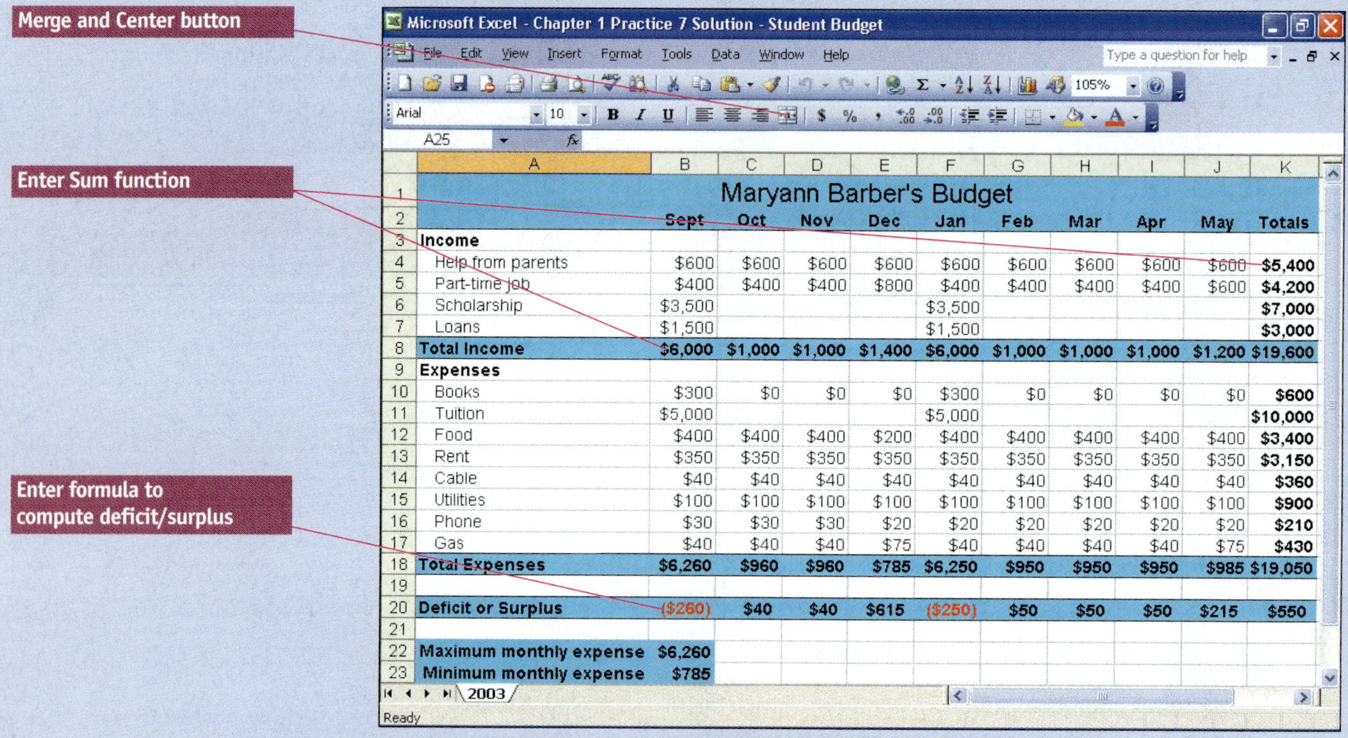

	A	B	C	D	E	F	G	H	I	J	K
1	Maryann Barber's Budget										
2		Sept	Oct	Nov	Dec	Jan	Feb	Mar	Apr	May	Totals
3	Income										
4	Help from parents	$600	$600	$600	$600	$600	$600	$600	$600	$600	$5,400
5	Part-time job	$400	$400	$400	$800	$400	$400	$400	$400	$600	$4,200
6	Scholarship	$3,500				$3,500					$7,000
7	Loans	$1,500				$1,500					$3,000
8	Total Income	$6,000	$1,000	$1,000	$1,400	$6,000	$1,000	$1,000	$1,000	$1,200	$19,600
9	Expenses										
10	Books	$300	$0	$0	$0	$300	$0	$0	$0	$0	$600
11	Tuition	$5,000				$5,000					$10,000
12	Food	$400	$400	$400	$200	$400	$400	$400	$400	$400	$3,400
13	Rent	$350	$350	$350	$350	$350	$350	$350	$350	$350	$3,150
14	Cable	$40	$40	$40	$40	$40	$40	$40	$40	$40	$360
15	Utilities	$100	$100	$100	$100	$100	$100	$100	$100	$100	$900
16	Phone	$30	$30	$30	$20	$20	$20	$20	$20	$20	$210
17	Gas	$40	$40	$40	$75	$40	$40	$40	$40	$75	$430
18	Total Expenses	$6,260	$960	$960	$785	$6,250	$950	$950	$950	$985	$19,050
19											
20	Deficit or Surplus	($260)	$40	$40	$615	($250)	$50	$50	$50	$215	$550
21											
22	Maximum monthly expense	$6,260									
23	Minimum monthly expense	$785									

FIGURE 1.25 Student Budget (exercise 7)

8. **Excel Templates:** This chapter introduced you to the basics of Excel and showed you how to create your own spreadsheets. It is often convenient, however, to use a workbook that was created by someone else that is tailored to a specific application. This type of workbook is called a template and it contains text, formulas, and formatting, but no specific data. Proceed as follows:
   a. Start Excel. Pull down the View menu to display the task pane, then click the down arrow in the task pane to display the New Workbook task pane. Look in the Other templates area and click the link to On My Computer to display the Templates dialog box. Click the Spreadsheet Solutions tab.
   b. You should see several templates that were installed locally with the installation of Microsoft Office. Select the *Timecard* template and click OK. (You can open the *Chapter 1 Practice 8* workbook in the Exploring Excel folder if this template is not available on your system.)
   c. Click in cell E10, type your name, and press the Tab key to move to cell I10. Enter your student number (do not be concerned that the worksheet asks for an employee number rather than a student number). Press the Tab key to move to cell M9 where you enter the note in Figure 1.26.
   d. Click in cell D20 and type the name of the first course you are taking. Use the Tab key to move across the row to enter your study hours for the week. You cannot, however, move to column Q because the total is calculated automatically. Click in cell D22 and start to enter the data for your second course. Enter the data for your remaining courses in similar fashion.
   e. The worksheet is currently protected, which means you cannot change the contents of the cells containing labels and formulas. Pull down the Tools menu, click Protection, and then click the Unprotect Sheet command. (A password is not required.) You can now modify the worksheet to fit your specific application, for example, logging study hours instead of an employee worksheet. Click in cell P5 and enter Study Hours. Make additional modifications as you see fit. (We changed the name of the worksheet tab to Study Schedule.) Print the completed worksheet for your instructor. Save the workbook as *Chapter 1 Practice 8 Solution—Study Schedule.*

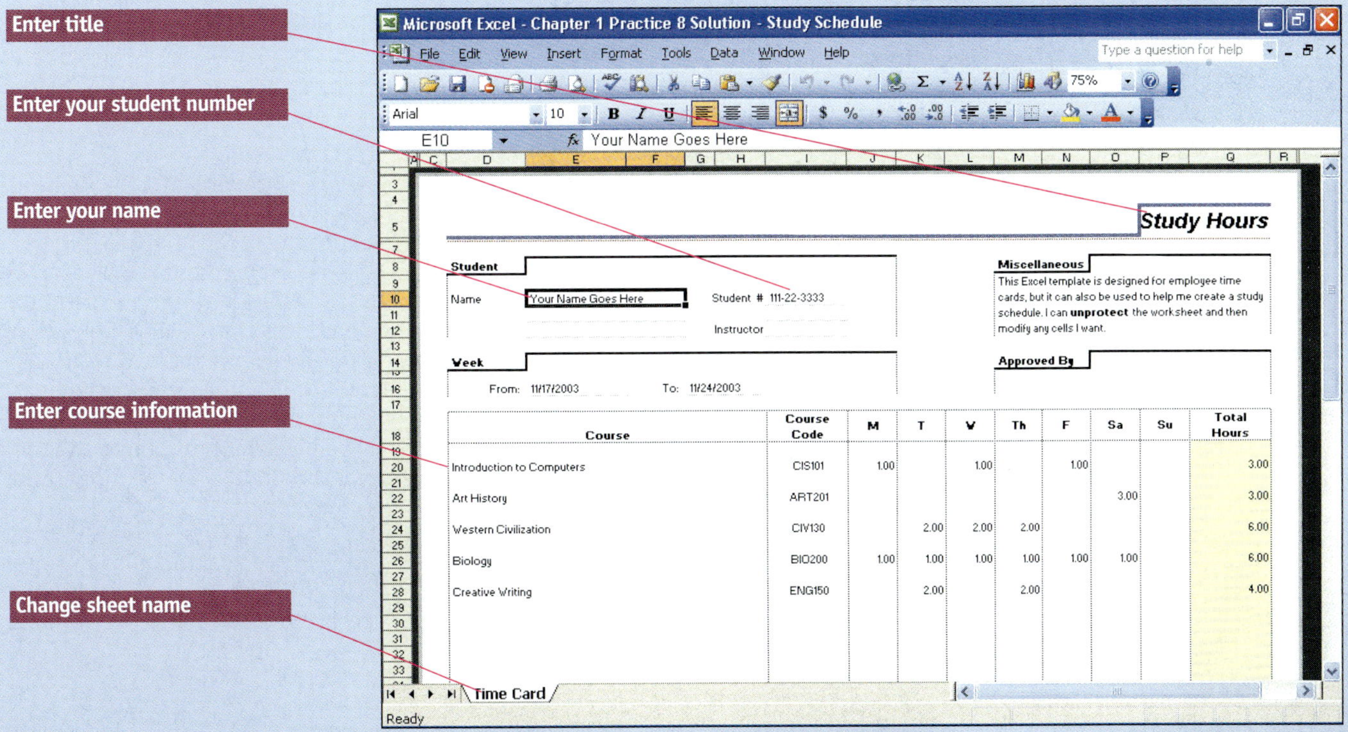

FIGURE 1.26 Excel Templates (exercise 8)

MINI CASES

The Movies

The partially completed *Chapter 1 Mini Case—The Movies* workbook in the Exploring Excel folder is intended to compute the weekly revenue for a chain of movie theatres. The revenue includes income from day and evening tickets as well as the food concession. Complete the workbook by using the appropriate combination of relative and absolute references in your cell formulas so that you can copy the formulas from the first theatre to the remaining rows in the worksheet. If you do the assignment correctly, your worksheet should display total revenue of $455,625. Format the completed worksheet as appropriate. Place your name somewhere in the worksheet, then print the worksheet two ways, to show both displayed values and cell formulas, then submit both pages to your instructor. Be sure to use the Page Setup command to specify landscape printing, and appropriate scaling so that the entire worksheet fits on a single page.

The Cost of Smoking

Smoking is hazardous to your health as well as your pocketbook. A one-pack-a-day habit, at $3/pack, will cost you more than $1000 per year. For the same money you could buy 20 concert tickets at $50 each, or more than 700 gallons of gas at $1.50 per gallon. Open the partially completed *Chapter 1 Mini Case—Cost of Smoking* workbook and compute the number of various items that you could buy over the course of a year in lieu of cigarettes. We have entered approximate prices, but you need not use our numbers and/or you can substitute additional items of your own.

Accuracy Counts

The *Chapter 1 Mini Case—Underbid* workbook in the Exploring Excel folder was the last assignment completed by your predecessor prior to his unfortunate dismissal. The worksheet contains a significant error, which caused your company to underbid a contract and assume a subsequent loss of $100,000. As you look for the error, don't be distracted by the attractive formatting. The shading, lines, and other touches are nice, but accuracy is more important than anything else. Write a memo to your instructor describing the nature of the error. Include suggestions in the memo on how to avoid mistakes of this nature in the future.

The Housing Office

The partially completed *Chapter 1 Mini Case—Housing Office* workbook in the Exploring Excel folder is intended to compute the revenue for the dorms on campus. The revenue includes the income from single rooms, double rooms, and the associated meal plans. Your assignment is to complete the workbook. If you do the assignment correctly, the total revenue for Lincoln Hall should be $4,392,500. Pay special attention to the formula for the meal plan revenue (cell G4 for the first residence hall), which uses a combination of relative and absolute addresses. Note, too, that each double room has two students, each of whom is required to pay for the meal plan. Format the completed worksheet as appropriate. Place your name somewhere in the worksheet, then print the worksheet two ways, to show both displayed values and cell formulas, then submit both pages to your instructor. Be sure to use the Page Setup command to specify landscape printing, and appropriate scaling so that the entire worksheet fits on a single page.

CHAPTER 2

Gaining Proficiency: The Web and Business Applications

OBJECTIVES

After reading this chapter you will:

1. Gain proficiency in using relative and absolute references to create a worksheet.
2. Explain the importance of isolating assumptions in a worksheet.
3. Use the fill handle to copy a formula to adjacent cells.
4. Use pointing to enter a formula.
5. Insert a hyperlink into a worksheet.
6. Save a worksheet as a Web page, and then view the page in a Web browser.
7. Import data from a Web query into a workbook; refresh the query to obtain current information.
8. Describe the Today() function and its use in date arithmetic.

hands-on exercises

1. PAYROLL
   Input: Payroll
   Output: Payroll Solution
2. CREATING A WEB PAGE
   Input: Statement of Earnings
   Output: Statement of Earnings Solution (workbook and MHT document)
3. WEB QUERIES
   Input: Stock Portfolio
   Output: Stock Portfolio Solution

CASE STUDY

THE PROPER TIP

There is no perfect answer to the question, "how much to tip." It helps to realize, however, that the word "tip" is an acronym for the phrase "to insure promptness." One should focus, therefore, on the server's ability to meet your requests: did he or she hustle and try to please you; was the server professional; did he or she try to rectify a bad situation if there was one? It is truly impolite to omit a tip even if the service was poor, but there is a range of amounts that sends a clear message to your server. This is generally accepted to be between 10% and 20% of the pretax total of the meal.

Lynne Breitfeller has decided to make the calculation easy for herself by creating a simple worksheet that will calculate the appropriate tip, based on the amount of the meal and the level of service. Lynne intends to make the worksheet completely general; she wants to be able to vary the suggested percentages and/or the amount of the bill and see the recommended tip. This is an unusual application, but it is intended to show that Excel can be applied to virtually any numeric calculation. ■

Your assignment is to read the chapter, paying special attention to Hands-on Exercises 1 and 2, which explain how to use relative and absolute references, and how to save and edit a Web page. You will then put yourself in Lynne's place and create a new workbook that calculates the suggested tip for poor, average, and excellent service on bills ranging from $10 to $200 in increments of $5. Use 10%, 15%, and 20% as the percentages for the different levels of service. Isolate all of the assumptions so that you can change the amount of the bill and/or the suggested percentages. Add a hyperlink to your favorite restaurant or dining etiquette Web site on the worksheet, then save the worksheet as a Web page. Print a copy of the completed worksheet to show both the displayed values and cell formulas. Print a second copy of the worksheet from your Internet browser.

EMPLOYEE PAYROLL

This chapter introduces several new capabilities to increase your proficiency in Excel. We begin with pointing, which is a preferred way to enter a cell formula. We present the fill handle to facilitate copying a formula to other rows or columns within a worksheet. We introduce the Today() function and the use of date arithmetic. We also discuss the various Web capabilities that are built into Excel. You will learn how to add a hyperlink to a worksheet and how to save a worksheet as a Web page for viewing in a browser such as Internet Explorer or Netscape Navigator. You will also learn how to create a Web query to download information from the Web directly into an Excel worksheet.

The spreadsheet in Figure 2.1 shows how Excel can be used to compute a simple payroll. Figure 2.1a shows the displayed values and Figure 2.1b contains the underlying formulas. The concepts necessary to develop the spreadsheet were presented in the previous chapter. The intent here is to reinforce the earlier material, with emphasis on the use of ***relative*** and ***absolute references*** in the various cell formulas.

The calculation of an individual's gross pay depends on the employment practices of the organization. The formula used in the worksheet is simply an algebraic statement of how employees are paid, in this example, straight time for regular hours, and time-and-a-half for each hour of overtime. The first employee, Adams, earns $400 for 40 regular hours (40 hours at $10/hour) plus $60 for overtime (4 overtime hours × $10/hour × 1.5 for overtime). The formula to compute Adams's gross pay is entered into cell E2 as follows:

Gross Pay = Regular Hours * Hourly Rate + Overtime Hours * Hourly Rate * 1.5

- Hourly Rate (second) — Relative reference to cell B2
- Overtime Hours — Relative reference to cell D2
- Hourly Rate (first) — Relative reference to cell B2
- Regular Hours — Relative reference to cell C2
- Gross Pay — Entered into cell E2 as =C2*B2+D2*B2*1.5

The cell references in the formula are relative references, which means that they will change when copied to another cell. Thus, you can copy the formula in cell E2 to the other rows in column E to compute the gross pay for the other employees. The formula in cell E3, for example, becomes =C3*B3+D3*B3*1.5, as can be seen from the displayed formulas in Figure 2.1b.

The withholding tax is computed by multiplying an individual's gross pay by the withholding tax rate. (This is an approximate calculation because the true withholding tax rate is implemented on a sliding scale; that is, the more an individual earns, the higher the tax rate. We use a uniform rate, however, to simplify the example.) The formula in cell F2 to compute the withholding tax uses a combination of relative and absolute references as follows:

Withholding Tax = Gross Pay * Withholding Rate

- Withholding Rate — Absolute reference to cell C11
- Gross Pay — Relative reference to cell E2
- Withholding Tax — Entered into cell F2 as =E2*$C$11

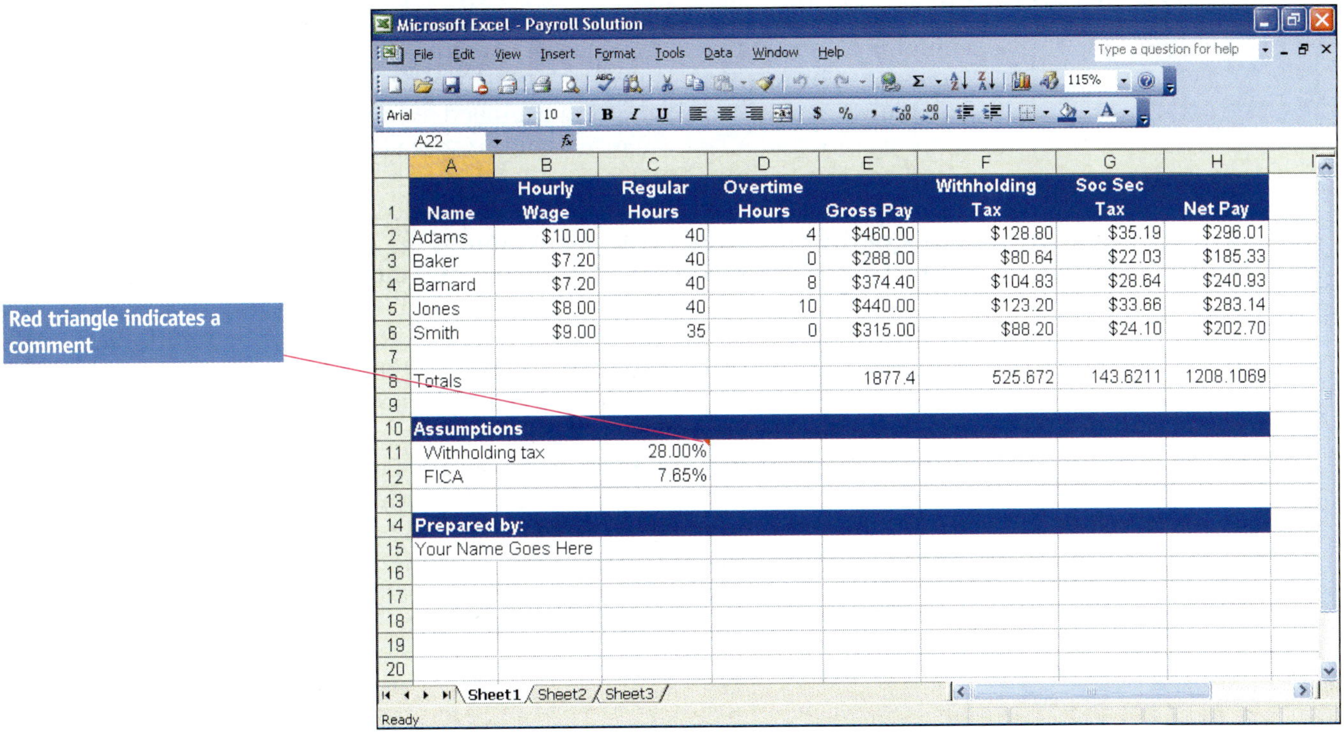

(a) Displayed Values

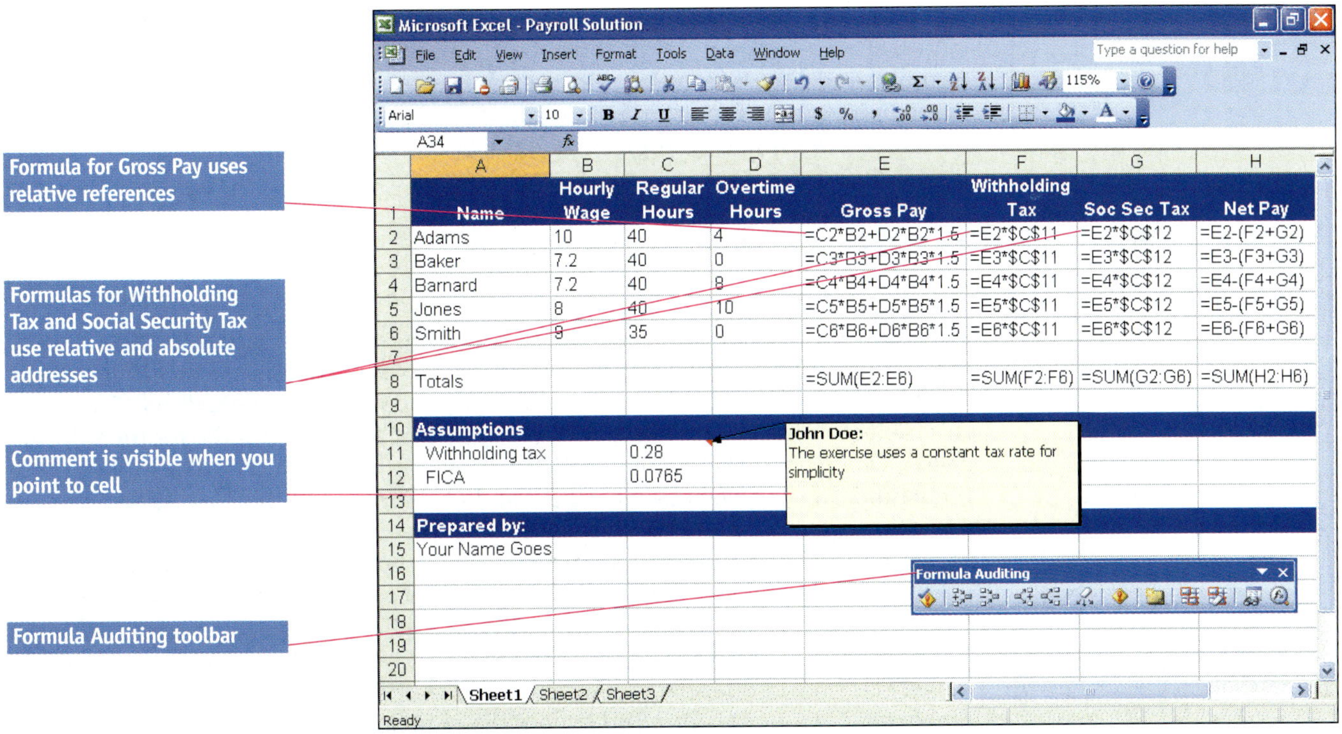

(b) Cell Formulas

FIGURE 2.1 Payroll

It is important to emphasize that the formula to compute the withholding tax contains an absolute reference to the tax rate (cell C11), as opposed to the actual constant (.28 in this example). The distinction may seem trivial, but most assuredly it is not, as two important objectives are achieved. First, the user sees those factors that affect the results of the spreadsheet in a separate assumption area (e.g., the withholding rate). Second, the user can change the value in one place, cell C11, then have the change automatically reflected in the calculations for all of the employees. The calculation of the employee's Social Security tax in cell G2 is performed in similar fashion and includes an absolute reference to cell C12.

The remaining formulas in the worksheet are also straightforward. An employee's net pay is computed by subtracting the deductions (the withholding tax and the Social Security tax) from the gross pay. Thus the net pay for the first employee is entered in cell H2 using the formula =E2–(F2+G2). The cell references are relative, which enables us to copy the formula to the remaining rows in column H, and thus calculate the net pay for the other employees.

The employee totals for gross pay, withholding tax, social security tax, and net pay are computed using the SUM function in the appropriate cells in row 8. The formula to compute the gross pay, =SUM(E2:E6), is entered into cell E8, after which it is copied to the remaining cells in row 8.

Pointing

Any cell reference can be entered into a formula by typing the address explicitly into a cell. Entering addresses in this way is not recommended, however, because it is all too easy to make a mistake, such as typing A40 when you really mean A41. ***Pointing*** to the cell is a more accurate method, since you use the mouse (or arrow keys) to select the cell directly when you build the formula. In essence you (1) Click in the cell that will contain the formula, (2) Type an equal sign to begin entering the formula, and (3) Click in the cell you want to reference. You then type any arithmetic operator, then continue pointing to additional cells using the steps we just described. And finally, you press the Enter key to complete the formula. It's easier than it sounds, and you get to practice in our next exercise.

The Fill Handle

There are several ways to copy the contents of a cell. You can use the Copy and Paste buttons on the Standard toolbar, the associated keyboard shortcuts, and/or the corresponding commands in the Edit menu. You can also use the ***fill handle,*** a tiny black square that appears in the lower-right corner of a selected cell. All you do is (1) Select the cell or cells to be copied, (2) Point to the fill handle for the selected cell(s), which changes the mouse pointer to a thin crosshair, (3) Click and drag the fill handle over the destination range, and (4) Release the mouse to complete the operation. (The fill handle can be used to copy only to adjacent cells.) Again, it's easier than it sounds, and as you may have guessed, it's time for our next hands-on exercise, in which you build the payroll worksheet in Figure 2.1.

Comments

The ***Insert Comment command*** creates the equivalent of a ScreenTip that displays information about the worksheet. Cell C11 in Figure 2.1a contains a tiny red triangle to indicate the presence of a comment, which appears as a ScreenTip when you point to the cell, as shown in Figure 2.1b. (An option can be set to display the comment permanently, but most people opt for just the triangle.) Comments may be subsequently edited, or deleted altogether if they are no longer appropriate.

hands-on exercise

1 Payroll

Objective Develop a spreadsheet for a simplified payroll to illustrate relative and absolute references. Use pointing to enter formulas and the fill handle to copy formulas. Use Figure 2.2 as a guide in the exercise.

Step 1: Compute the Gross Pay

- Start Excel. Open the **Payroll workbook** in the **Exploring Excel folder** to display the worksheet in Figure 2.2a.
- Save the workbook as **Payroll Solution** so that you may return to the original workbook if necessary.
- Click in **cell E2,** the cell that contains the gross pay for the first employee. Press the **equal sign** on the keyboard to begin pointing, click in **cell C2** (which produces a moving border around the cell), press the **Asterisk key**, then click in **cell B2**. You have entered the first part of the formula to compute an employee's gross pay.
- Press the **plus sign**, click in **cell D2**, press the **Asterisk**, click in **cell B2**, press the **Asterisk**, type **1.5**, then press **Enter**. You should see 460 as the displayed value for cell E2.
- Click in **cell E2**, then check to be sure that the formula you entered matches the formula in the formula bar in Figure 2.2a. If necessary, click in the formula bar and make the appropriate changes so that you have the correct formula in cell E2.
- Enter your name in cell A15. Save the workbook.

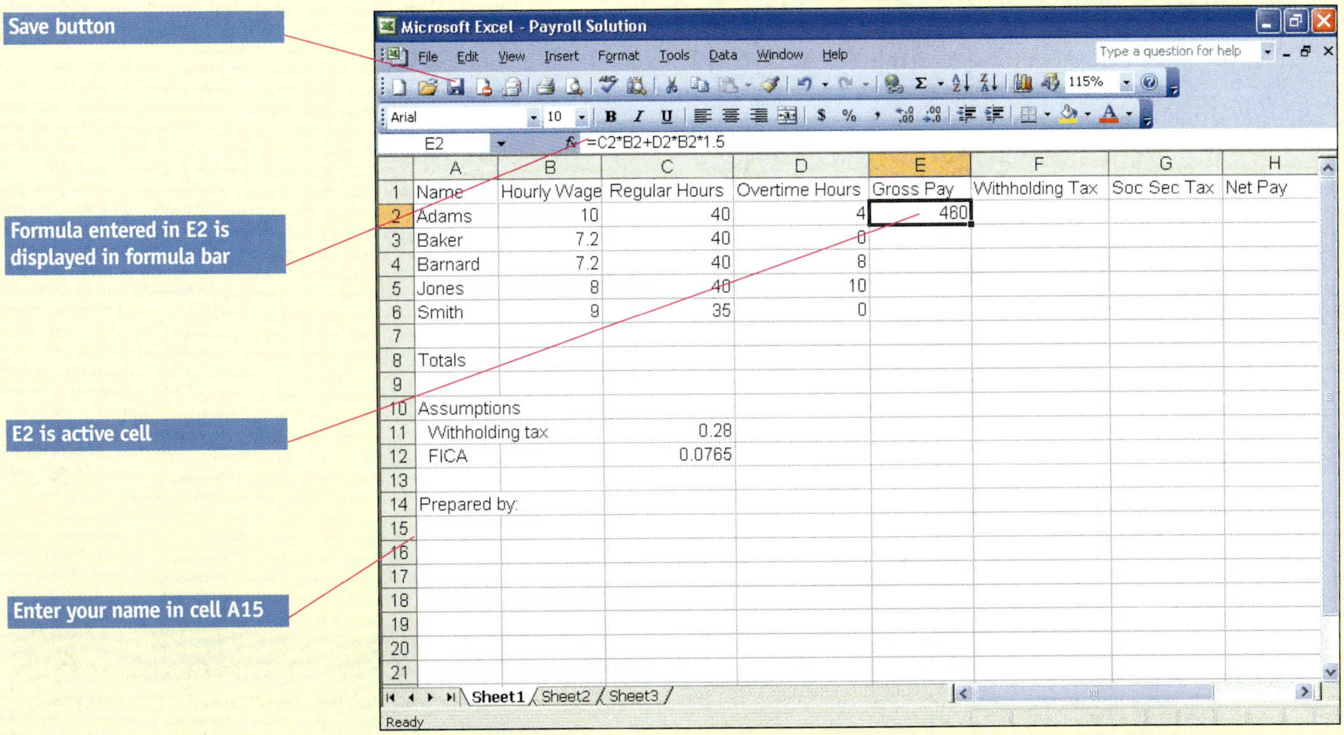

(a) Compute the Gross Pay (step 1)

FIGURE 2.2 Hands-on Exercise 1

Step 2: Complete the Calculations

- Click in **cell F2**, the cell that contains the withholding tax for the first employee. Press the **equal sign** on the keyboard to begin pointing, then click in **cell E2**, the cell that contains the employee's gross pay.
- Press the **Asterisk key**, then click in **cell C11**, the cell that contains the withholding tax. Cell F2 should now contain the formula, =E2*C11, but this is not quite correct.
- Check that the insertion point (the flashing vertical line) is within (or immediately behind) the reference to cell C11, then press the **F4 key** to change the cell reference to $C$11 as shown in Figure 2.2b.
- Press **Enter**. The displayed value in cell F2 should be 128.8, corresponding to the withholding tax for this employee.
- Use pointing to enter the remaining formulas for the first employee. Click in **cell G2**, then enter the formula **=E2*$C$12**. The displayed value is 35.19, corresponding to the Social Security Tax.
- Click in **cell H2**, and enter the formula **=E2–(F2+G2)**. The displayed value is 296.01, corresponding to the net pay for this individual.
- Save the workbook.

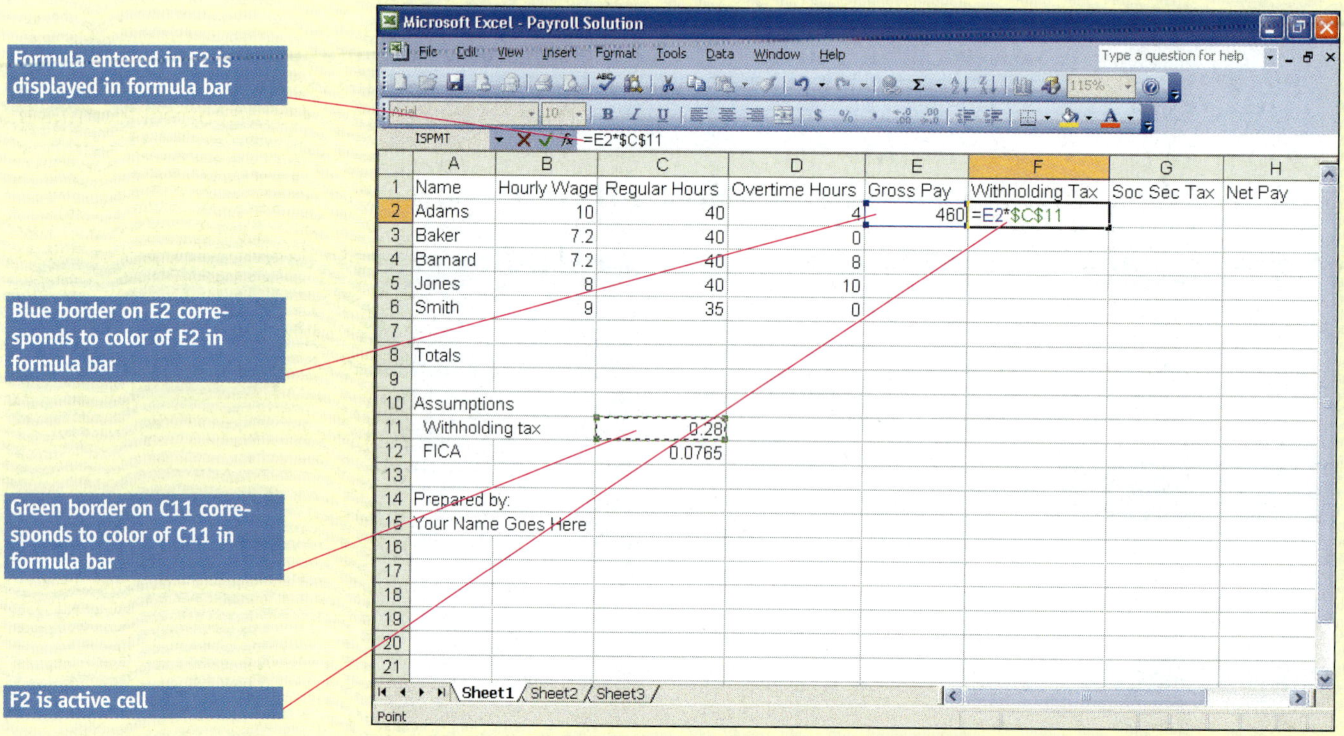

(b) Complete the Calculations (step 2)

FIGURE 2.2 Hands-on Exercise 1 (*continued*)

THE F4 KEY

The F4 key cycles through relative, absolute, and mixed references. Click on any reference within the formula bar; for example, click on A1 in the formula =A1+A2. Press the F4 key once, and it changes to an absolute reference. Press the F4 key a second time, and it becomes a mixed reference, A$1; press it again, and it is a different mixed reference, $A1. Press the F4 key a fourth time, and return to the original relative reference, A1.

Step 3: Copy the Formulas

- Click in **cell E2**, then click and drag to select **cells E2:H2**, as shown in Figure 2.2c. Point to the **fill handle** in the lower-right corner of cell H2. The mouse pointer changes to a thin crosshair.
- Drag the **fill handle** to cell H6 (the lower-right cell in the range of employee calculations). A dim border appears as you drag the fill handle as shown in Figure 2.2c.
- Release the mouse to complete the copy operation. The formulas for the first employee have been copied to the corresponding rows for the other employees.
- Click in **cell E3**, the cell containing the gross pay for the second employee. You should see the formula =C3*B3+D3*B3*1.5. Now click in **cell F3**, the cell containing the withholding tax for the second employee.
- You should see the formula =E3*$C$11, which contains a relative reference (cell E3) that is adjusted from one row to the next, and an absolute reference (cell $C$11) that remains constant from one employee to the next.
- Save the workbook.

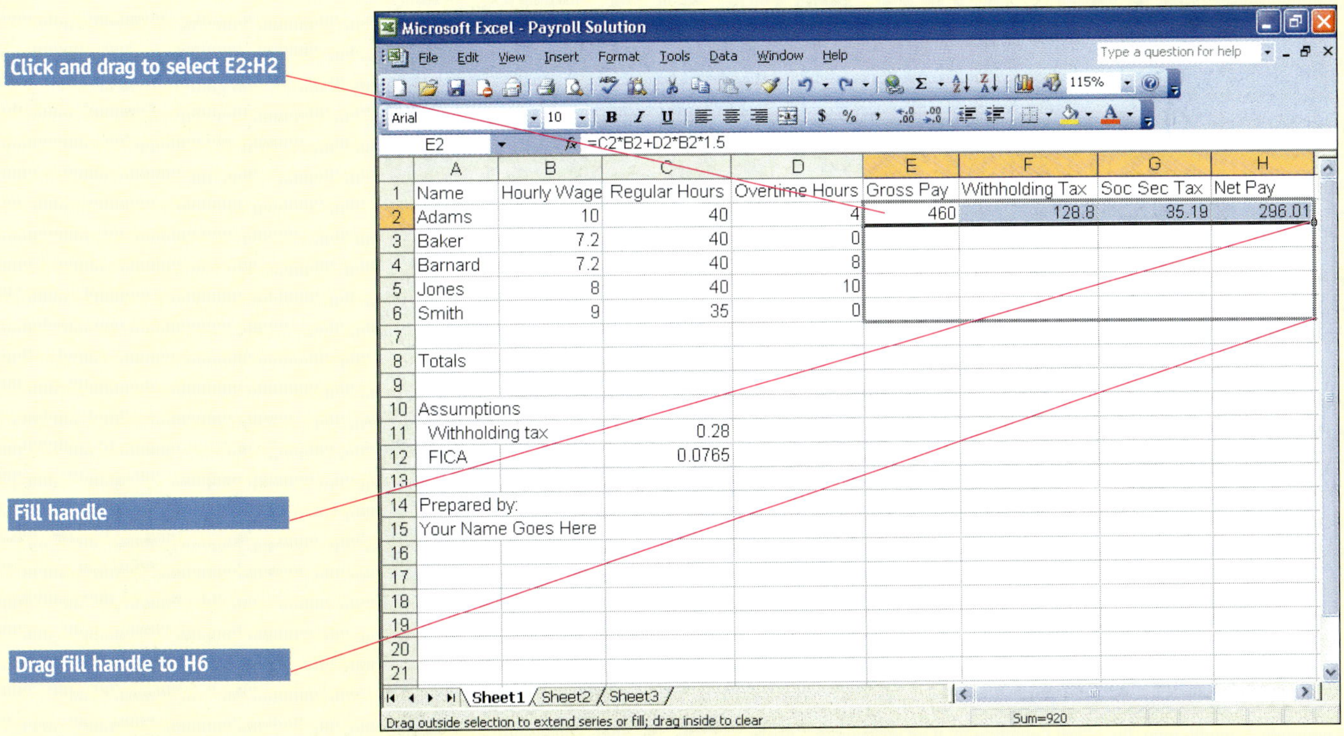

(c) Copy the Formulas (step 3)

FIGURE 2.2 Hands-on Exercise 1 (*continued*)

IT'S ONLY ALGEBRA

There are several ways to enter the formula to compute an employee's gross pay. You could, for example, factor out the hourly rate and enter the formula as =B3*(C3+D3*1.5). It doesn't matter how you enter the formula as long as the results are algebraically correct. What is important is the combination of relative and absolute references, so that the formula is copied correctly from one row to the next.

Step 4: Compute the Totals

- Click in **cell E8**, the cell that is to contain the total gross pay for all employees. Type the **=sign**, type **SUM(**, then click and drag over **cells E2** through **E6**.
- Type a **closing parenthesis**, and then press **Enter** to complete the formula. Cell E8 should display the value 1877.4. Now click in **cell E8** and you should see the function, =SUM(E2:E6).
- Click and drag the **fill handle** in cell E8 to the remaining cells in this row (cells F8 through H8). Release the mouse to complete the copy operation.
- You should see 1208.1069 in cell H8, corresponding to the total net pay for all employees. Click in **cell H8** to view the formula, =SUM(H2:H6), which results from the copy operation.
- Save the workbook.

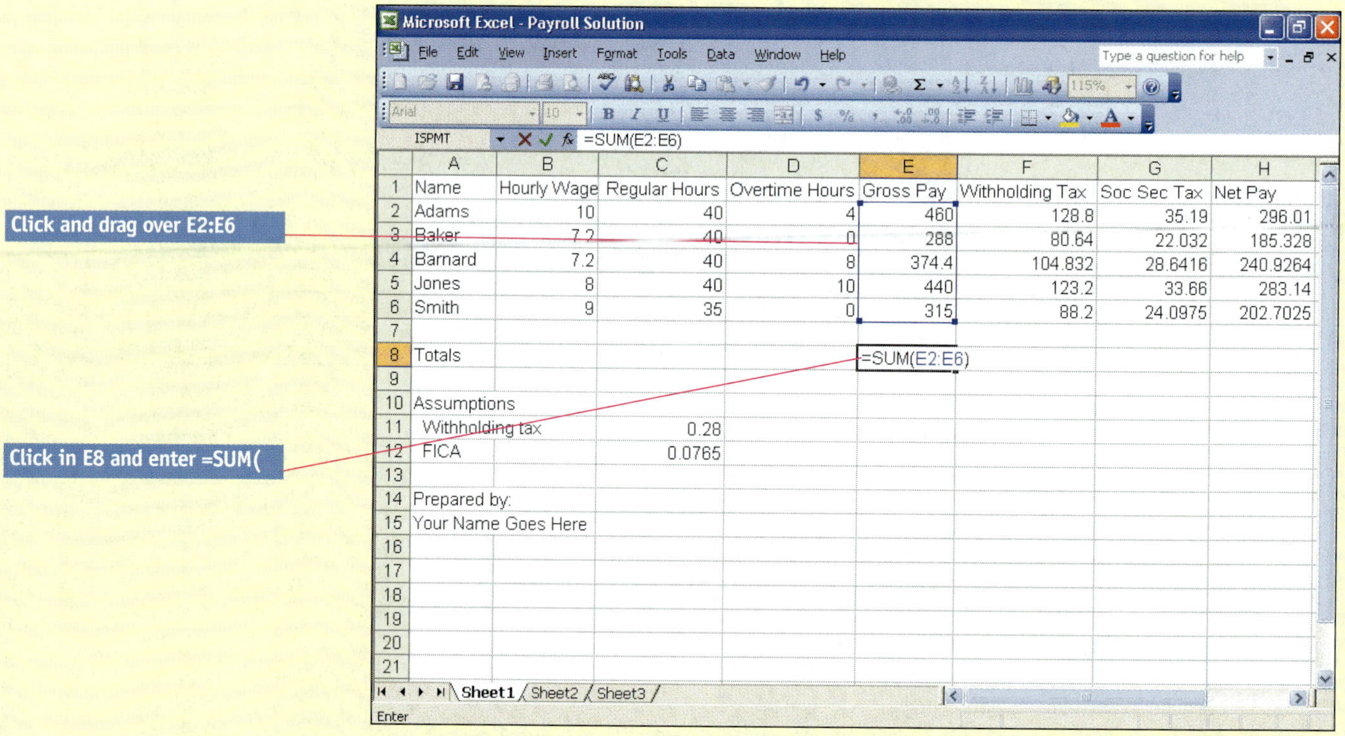

(d) Compute the Totals (step 4)

FIGURE 2.2 Hands-on Exercise 1 (*continued*)

FORMULAS VERSUS FUNCTIONS

There are in essence two ways to compute the total gross pay for all employees, using the SUM function, or the equivalent formula (e.g., =E2+E3+E4+E5+E6). The function is preferable for two reasons. First, it's easier to enter, and therefore less prone to error. Second, the function adjusts automatically to include any additional employees that will be entered within the cell range. Try inserting a new employee between the existing employees in rows 3 and 4, then observe how the values for this employee will be included automatically in the computed totals. The function also adjusts for deleted rows, whereas the formula does not.

Step 5: Format the Spreadsheet

- Click in **cell B2**, then click and drag to select **cells B2** through **B6**. Press and hold the **Ctrl key** as you click and drag to select cells **E2** through **H8** (in addition to the previously selected cells).
- Pull down the **Format menu** and click the **Cells command** to display the Format Cells dialog box in Figure 2.2e. Click the **Number tab** and choose **Currency** from the Category list box. Specify **2** as the number of decimal places.
- If necessary, choose the **$ sign** as the currency symbol. (Note, too, that you can select a variety of alternative symbols such as the British Pound or the Euro symbol for the European Community.) Click **OK** to accept the settings and close the dialog box.
- Click and drag to select **cells C11** and **C12**, then click the **Percent Style button** on the Formatting toolbar. Click the **Increase/Decrease Decimals buttons** to format each number to two decimal places.
- Save the workbook.

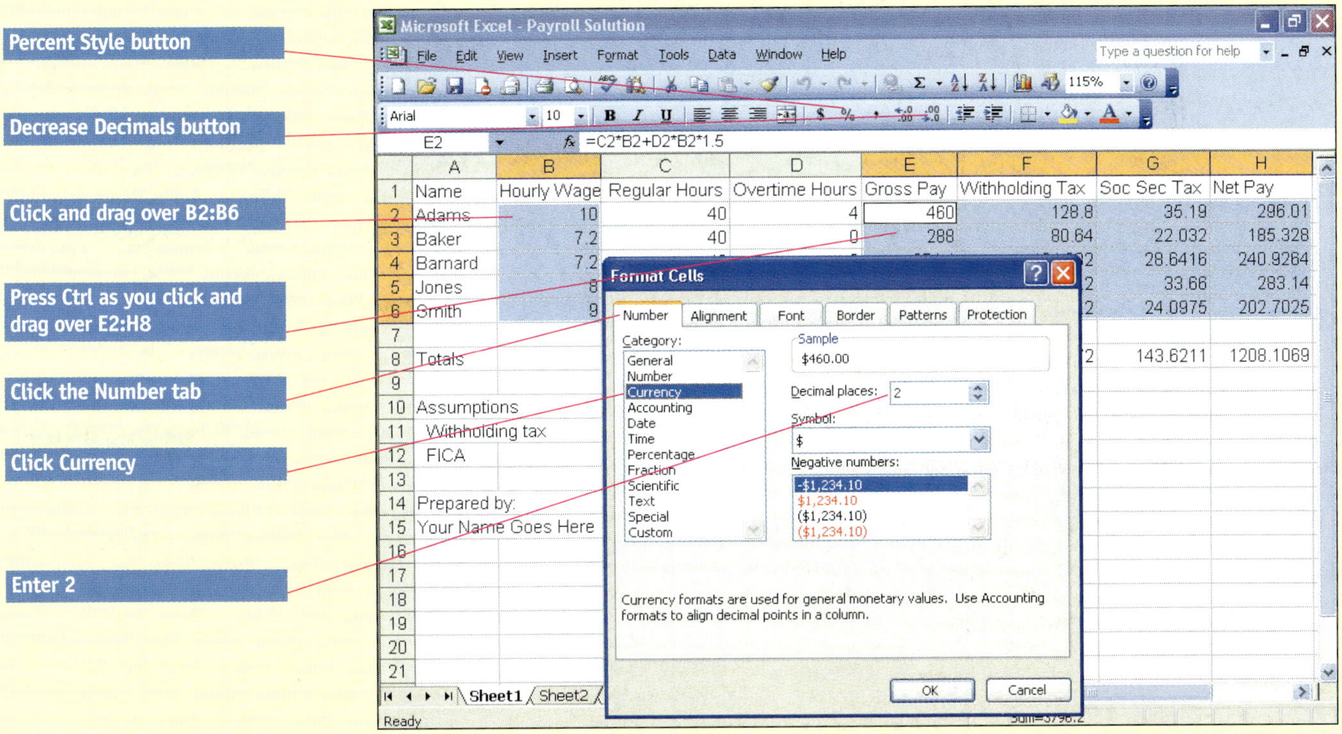

(e) Format the Spreadsheets (step 5)

FIGURE 2.2 Hands-on Exercise 1 (*continued*)

THE FORMAT STYLE COMMAND

A style is a collection of formats such as the font, alignment, and number of decimal places. Common styles, such as percent or currency, are represented by buttons on the Formatting toolbar and are most easily applied by clicking the appropriate tool. You can also apply the style by pulling down the Format menu, clicking the Style command, and selecting the style from the Style Name list box. The latter allows you to modify the definition of existing styles and/or to create a new style.

Step 6: Complete the Formatting

- Click and drag to select **cells A1** through **H1**. Press and hold the **Ctrl key**, then click and drag to select **cells A10** through **H10** in addition to the cells in row 1. Continue to press and hold the **Ctrl key**, then click and drag to select cells **A14** through **H14**.
- Click the **Fill Color arrow** on the Formatting toolbar, then select **blue** as the fill color. Click the **Font Color arrow** on the Formatting toolbar, then select **white** as the color for the text. Click the **Bold button** so that the text stands out from the fill color.
- Click and drag to select **cells A1** through **H1** (which also deselects the cells in rows 10 and 14). Click the **Right mouse button** to display a context-sensitive menu, then click the **Format Cells command** to display the dialog box in Figure 2.2f.
- Click the **Alignment tab,** then check the box to **Wrap text** in a cell. Click **OK** to accept the settings and close the dialog box.
- Click the **Center button** to center the text as well. Reduce the width of columns C and D. Save the workbook.

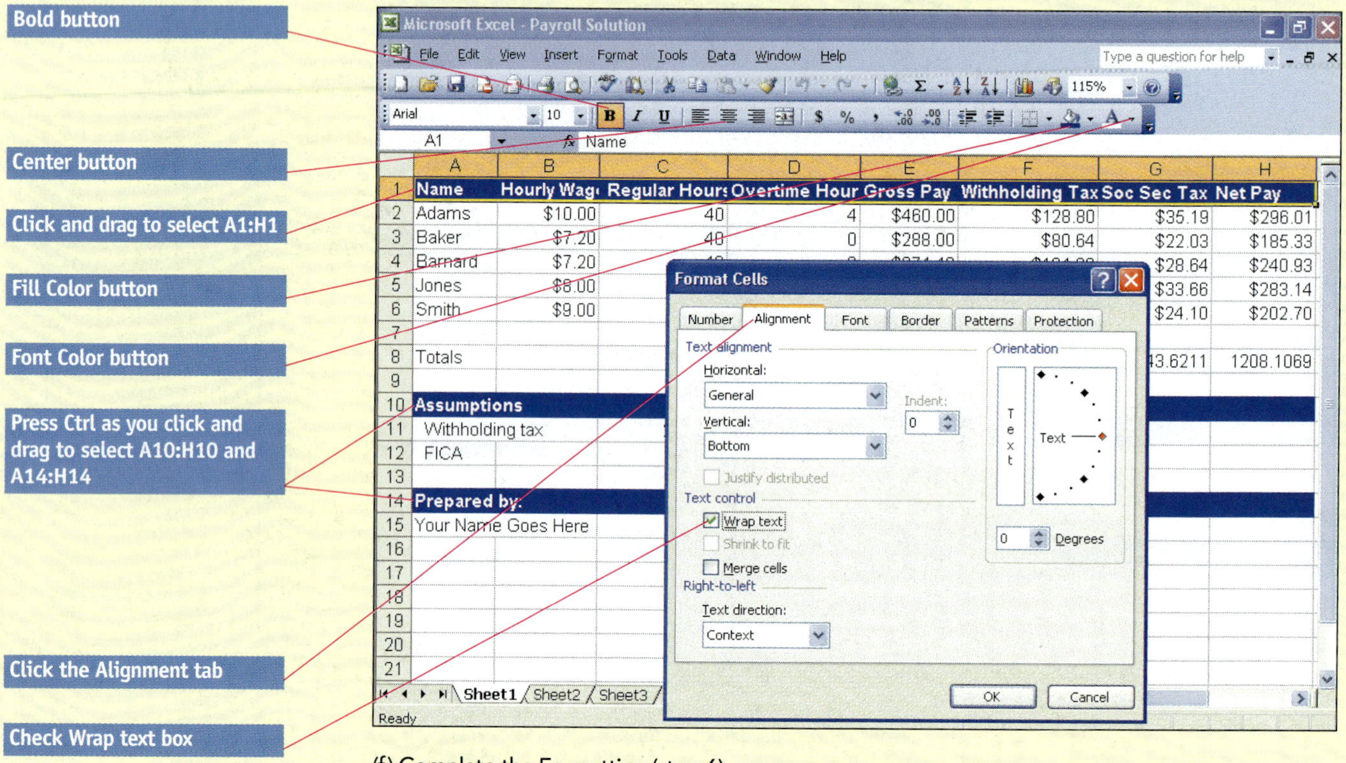

(f) Complete the Formatting (step 6)

FIGURE 2.2 Hands-on Exercise 1 (*continued*)

SORT THE EMPLOYEE LIST

The employees are listed on the worksheet in alphabetical order, but you can rearrange the list according to any other field, such as the net pay. Click a single cell containing employee data in the column on which you want to sort, then click the Sort Ascending or Sort Descending button on the Standard toolbar. Click the Undo button if the result is different from what you intended.

Step 7: The Completed Workbook

- Click in **cell C11**. Pull down the **Insert menu** and click **Comment**, then insert the text of the comment as shown in Figure 2.2g. (The name that appears in the comment box will be different on your system.)
- Click in any other cell when you have finished inserting the comment. The text of the comment is no longer visible, but you should still see the tiny triangle. Now point to cell C11 and you see the text of the comment.
- Pull down the **File menu** and click the **Page Setup command** to display the Page Setup dialog box. Click the **Page tab**. Click the **Landscape Option button**. Click the option to **Fit to 1 page**.
- Click the **Margins tab**. Check the box to center the worksheet horizontally. Click the **Sheet tab**. Check the boxes to print **Row and Column Headings** and **Gridlines.** Click **OK**. Print the worksheet.
- Save the workbook. Press **Ctrl+~** to show the cell formulas rather than the displayed values. Adjust the column widths as necessary, then print the worksheet a second time.
- Close the workbook. Exit Excel if you do not want to continue with the next exercise at this time.

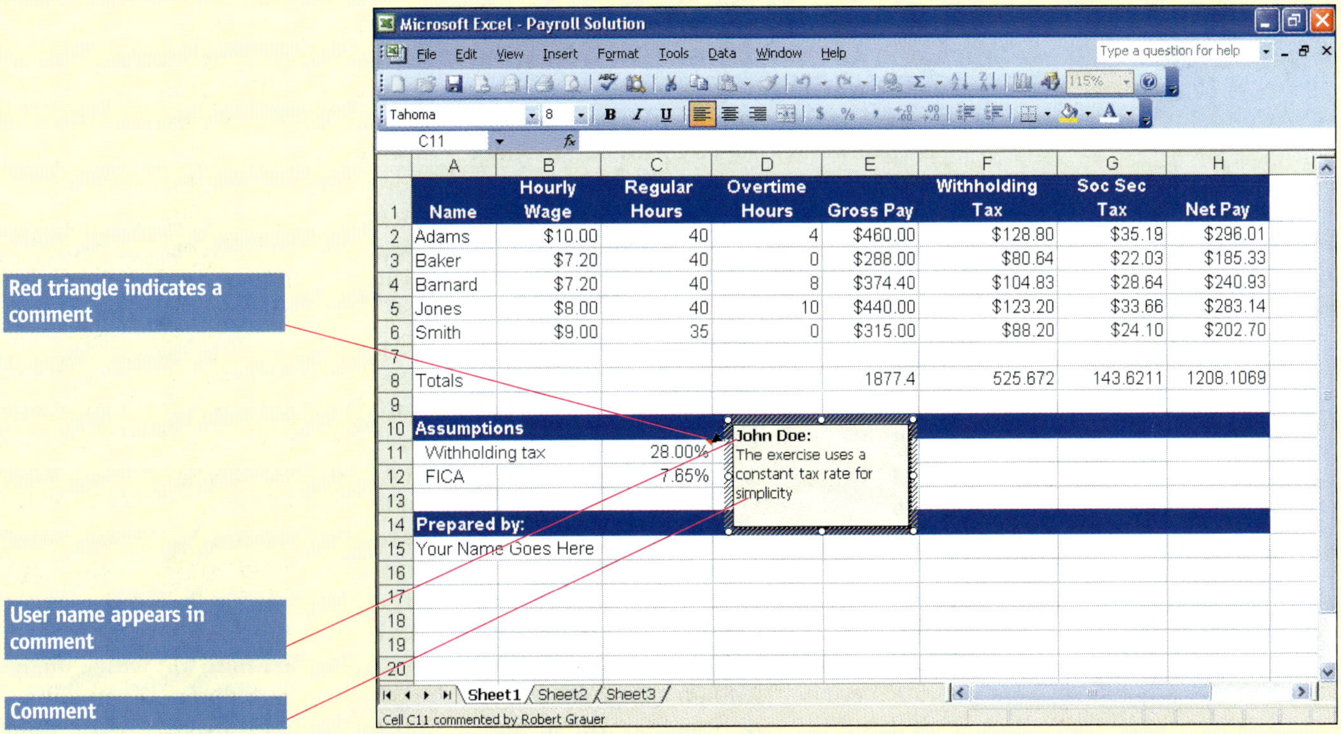

(g) The Completed Workbook (step 7)

FIGURE 2.2 Hands-on Exercise 1 (*continued*)

EDIT AND DELETE COMMENTS

Point to any cell that contains a comment, then click the right mouse button to display a context-sensitive menu with commands to edit or delete a comment. (The menu also contains the option to show or hide the comment.) The name that appears within the comment box corresponds to the user name set during installation. Pull down the Tools menu, click the Option command, click the General tab, then go to the User Name area to modify this information.

EXCEL AND THE INTERNET

The ***Internet*** is closely tied to Microsoft Excel through three basic capabilities. First, you can insert a ***hyperlink*** (a reference to another document) into any Excel worksheet, then view the associated document by clicking the link without having to start your Web browser manually. Second, you can save any Excel workbook as a ***Web page*** (or ***HTML document***), which in turn can be displayed through a Web browser. And finally, you can download information from a Web server directly into an Excel workbook through a ***Web query*** (a capability that we illustrate later in the chapter).

Consider, for example, Figure 2.3a, which contains an Excel worksheet that displays a consolidated statement of earnings for a hypothetical company. The information in this worksheet is typical of what companies publish in their annual report, a document that summarizes the financial performance of a corporation. Every public corporation is required by law to publish this type of information so that investors may evaluate the strength of the company. The annual report is mailed to the shareholders, and it is typically available online as well.

The worksheet in Figure 2.3a is easy to create, and you do not have to be a business major to understand the information. Indeed, if you have any intention of investing in the stock market, you should be able to analyze the data in the worksheet, which conveys basic information about the financial strength of a company to potential investors. In essence, the worksheet shows the sales for the company in the current year, subtracts the expenses to obtain the earnings before taxes, displays the income taxes that were paid, then arrives at the net earnings after taxes.

The worksheet also contains a calculation that divides the net earnings for the company by the number of shares to determine the earnings per share (a number that is viewed closely by investors). There is also comparable information for the previous year to show the increase or decrease for each item. And finally, the worksheet contains a hyperlink or reference to a specific Web site, such as the home page for the corporation. You can click the link from within Excel, and provided you have an Internet connection, your Web browser will display the associated page. Once you click the link, its color will change, just as it would if you were viewing the page in Netscape Navigator or Internet Explorer.

The Web page in Figure 2.3b is, for all intents and purposes, identical to the worksheet in Figure 2.3a. Look closely, however, and you will see that the Web page in Figure 2.3b is displayed in Internet Explorer, whereas the worksheet in Figure 2.3a is displayed in Microsoft Excel. The ***Save as Web Page command*** converts a worksheet to a Web page. The page can be uploaded to the Internet, but it can also be viewed from a PC or local area network, as was done in Figure 2.3b. Use the ***Web Page Preview command*** in the File menu to view the page, or open the page directly in your browser.

Our next exercise has you create the worksheet in Figure 2.3a, after which you create the Web document in Figure 2.3b. All applications in Microsoft Office incorporate a concept known as ***round trip HTML***, which means that you can subsequently edit the Web page in the application that created it originally. In other words, you start with an Excel worksheet, save it as a Web page, then you can open the Web page and return to Excel to edit the document.

SINGLE FILE WEB PAGES

Web documents are written in HTML or HyperText Markup Language. The newest version of Microsoft Office also recognizes the Single File Web Page (MHTML) format, in which all of the elements of a Web page (text and graphics) are saved as a single file. The address bar of a Web browser displays the document name and extension, which may appear as htm (or html) or mht, depending on how the Web page was created initially.

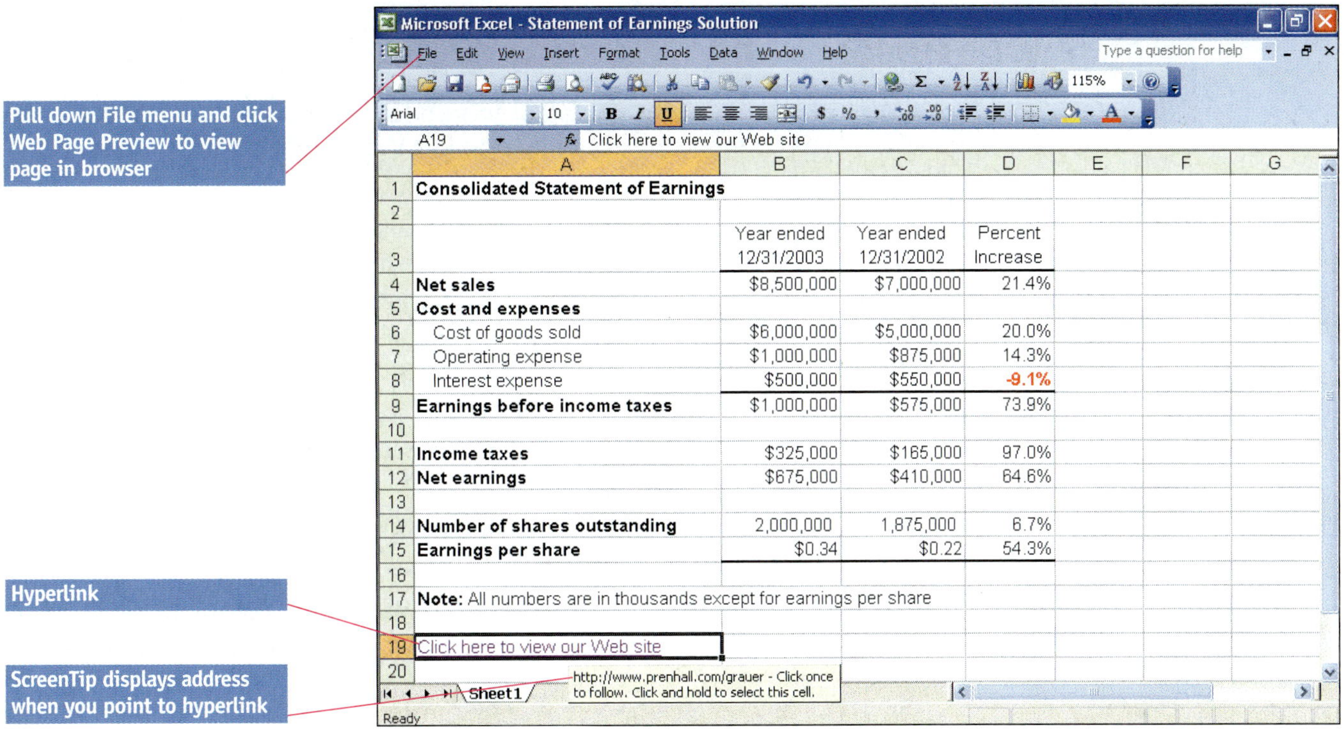

(a) Excel Worksheet

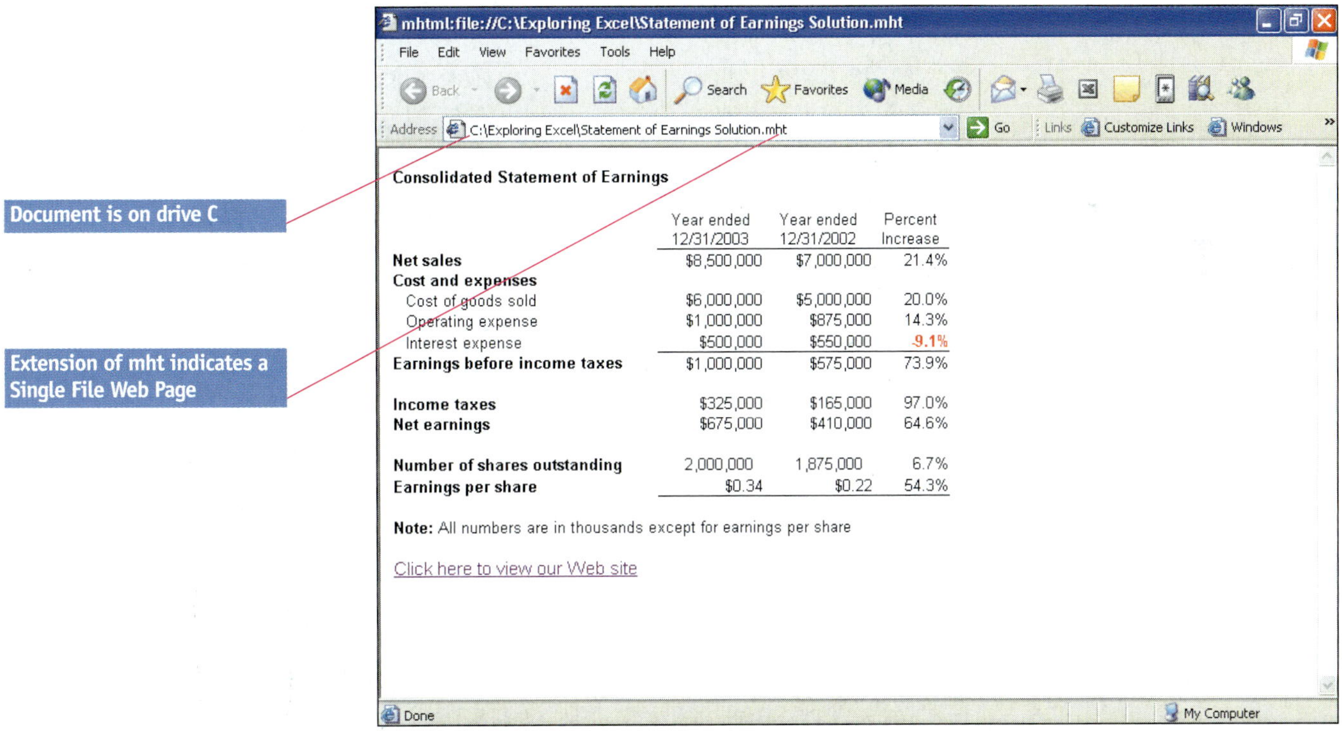

(b) Web Page

FIGURE 2.3 Consolidated Statement of Earnings

hands-on exercise

2 Creating a Web Page

Objective To insert a hyperlink into an Excel workbook; to save a workbook as an HTML document, then subsequently edit the Web page. Use Figure 2.4 as a guide in the exercise.

Step 1: Compute the Net Earnings

- Open the **Statement of Earnings workbook** in the **Exploring Excel folder**. Save the workbook as **Statement of Earnings Solution** so that you can always go back to the original workbook if necessary.
- We have entered the labels and data for you, but you have to create the formulas. Click in **cell B9**. Type an **equal sign**, then click in **cell B4** to begin the pointing operation.
- Type a **minus sign**, type **SUM(**, then click and drag to select **cells B6** through **B8** as shown in Figure 2.4a.
- Type a **closing parenthesis**, then press the **Enter key** to complete the formula. You should see 1000000 as the displayed value in cell B9.
- Click in **cell B12**, then use pointing to enter the formula for net earnings, **=B9–B11**.
- Click in **cell B15**, then use pointing to enter the formula for earnings per share, **=B12/B14**.
- Copy the formulas in cells B9, B12, and B15 to the corresponding cells in column C. You have to copy the formulas one at a time.
- Save the workbook.

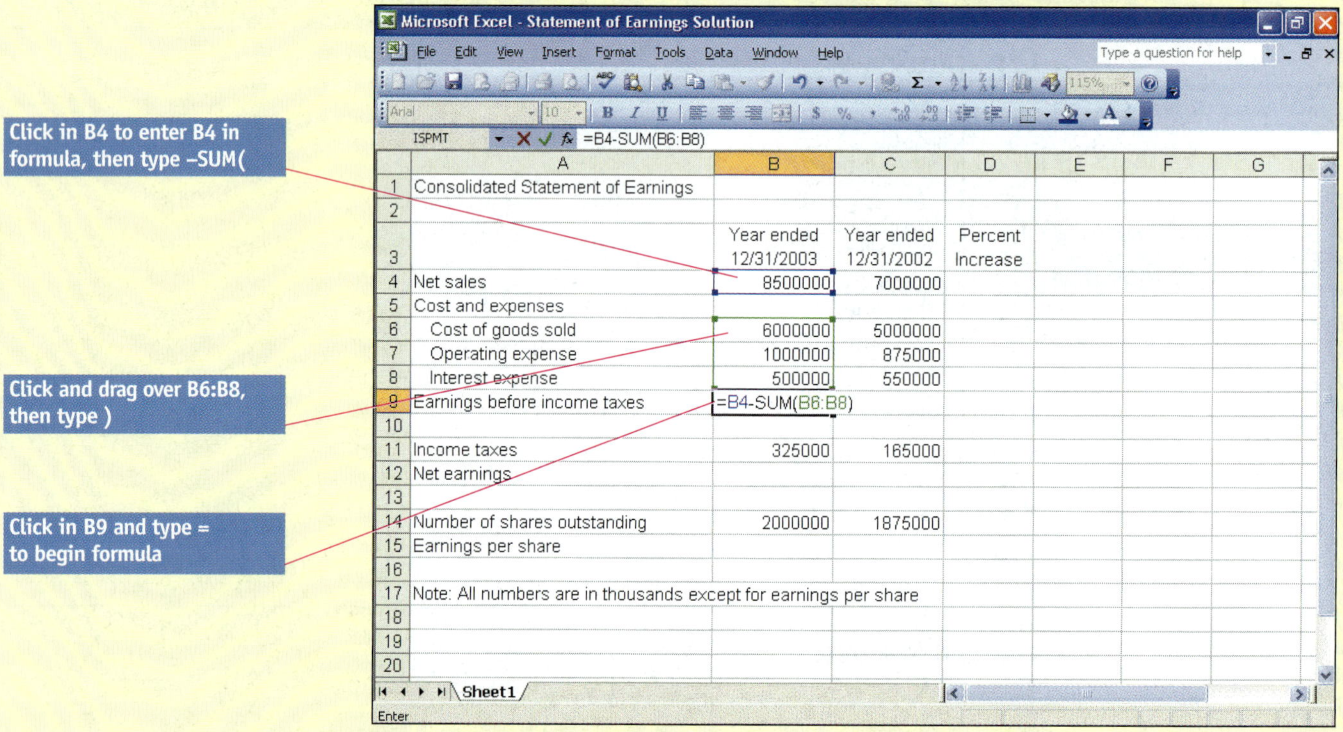

(a) Compute the Net Earnings (step 1)

FIGURE 2.4 Hands-on Exercise 2

Step 2: Compute the Percent Increase

- Click in **cell D4**, then enter the formula to compute the percent increase from the previous year. Use pointing to enter the formula, **=(B4-C4)/C4**.
- You should see .214286 as the displayed value in cell D4 as shown in Figure 2.4b. Do not worry about formatting at this time.
- Click in **cell D4**. Click the **Copy button** on the Standard toolbar (or use the **Ctrl+C** keyboard shortcut) to copy the contents of this cell to the clipboard. You should see a moving border around cell D4.
- Press and hold the **Ctrl key** to select **cells D6** through **D9**, **D11**, and **D12**, and **D14** and **D15** as shown in Figure 2.4b. (We have selected a noncontiguous range of cells, because we do not want to copy the formula to cells D10 or D13.)
- Click the **Paste button** on the Standard toolbar (or use the **Ctrl+V** keyboard shortcut) to paste the contents of cell D4 into these cells. Ignore the Paste Options button if it appears.
- Press the **Esc key** to remove the moving border around cell D4.

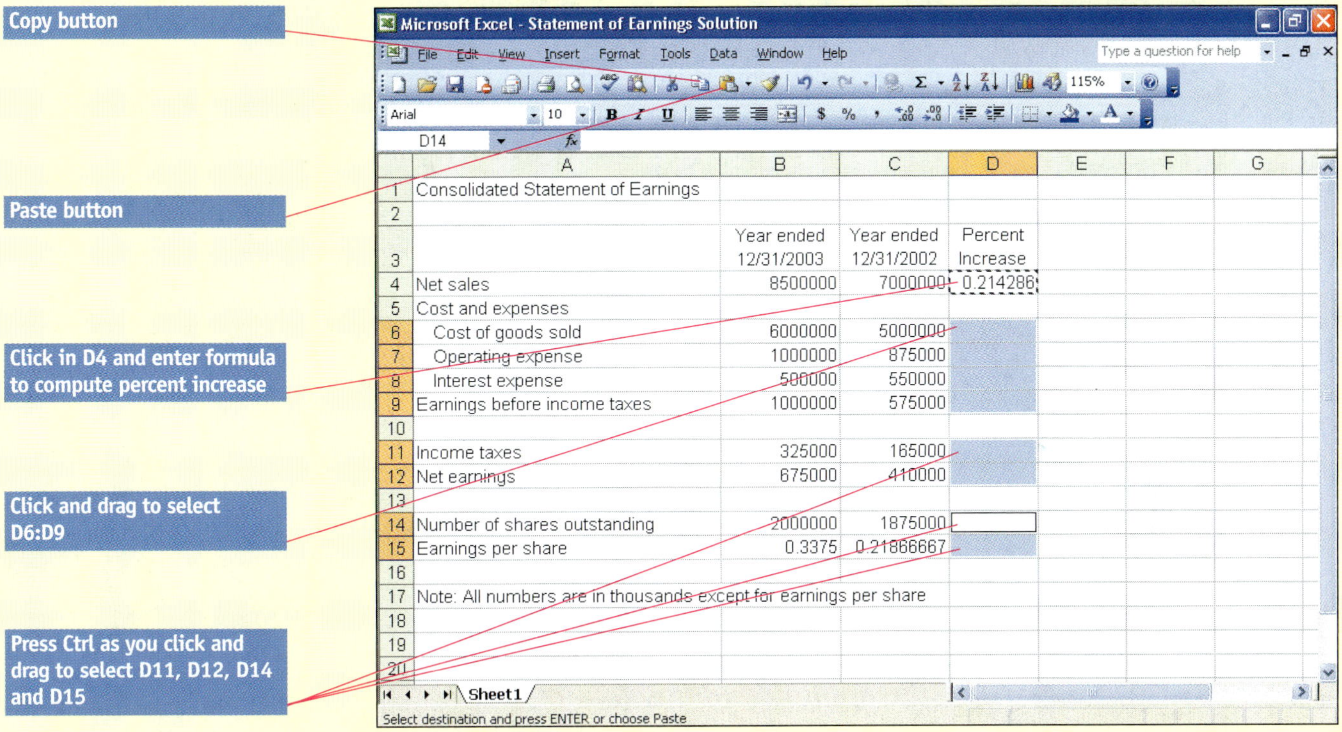

(b) Compute the Percent Increase (step 2)

FIGURE 2.4 Hands-on Exercise 2 (*continued*)

USE POINTING TO ENTER CELL FORMULAS

A cell reference can be typed directly into a formula, or it can be entered more easily through pointing. The latter is also more accurate as you use the mouse or arrow keys to reference cells directly. To use pointing, select (click) the cell to contain the formula, type an equal sign to begin entering the formula, click (or move to) the cell containing the reference, then press the F4 key as necessary to change from relative to absolute references. Type any arithmetic operator to place the cell reference in the formula, then continue pointing to additional cells. Press the Enter key to complete the formula.

Step 3: Format the Worksheet

- Format the worksheet as shown in Figure 2.4c. Click in **cell A1**, then press and hold the **Ctrl key** to select **cells A4, A5, A9, A11, A12, A14,** and **A15**. Click the **Bold button** on the Formatting toolbar (or use the **Ctrl+B** keyboard shortcut).
- Double click in **cell A17**, then click and drag over **Note**: within the cell to select this portion of the label. Press **Ctrl+B** to boldface the selected text.
- Remember that boldfacing the contents of a cell functions as a toggle switch; that is, click the Boldface button and the text is bold. Click the button a second time and the boldface is removed.
- Select **cells B3** through **D3**, **B8** through **D8**, and **B15** through **D15** as shown in Figure 2.4c. Click the **down arrow** on the Borders button on the Formatting toolbar to display the available borders. Click the bottom border icon to implement this formatting in the selected cells.
- Complete the formatting in the remainder of the worksheet by using currency, comma, and percent formats as appropriate. Save the workbook.

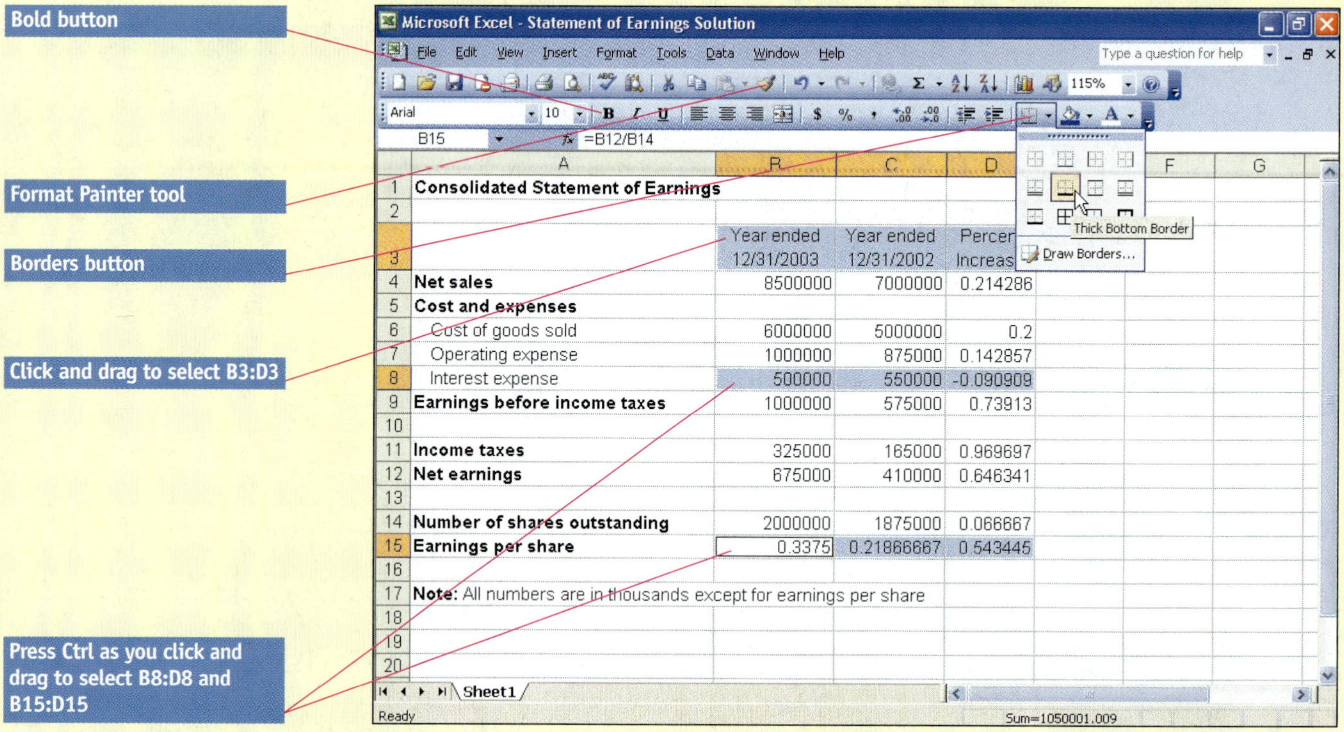

(c) Format the Worksheet (step 3)

FIGURE 2.4 Hands-on Exercise 2 (*continued*)

THE FORMAT PAINTER

The Format Painter copies the formatting of the selected cell to other cells in the worksheet. Click the cell whose formatting you want to copy, then double click the Format Painter button on the Standard toolbar. The mouse pointer changes to a paintbrush to indicate that you can copy the current formatting; just click and drag the paintbrush over the cells that you want to assume the formatting of the original cell. Repeat the painting process as often as necessary, then click the Format Painter button a second time to return to normal editing.

Step 4: Conditional Formatting

- Click and drag to select **cells D4** through **D15**, the cells that contain the percentage increase from the previous year.
- Pull down the **Format menu** and click the **Conditional Formatting command** to display the Conditional Formatting dialog box.
- Check that the Condition 1 list box displays Cell Value Is. Click the **down arrow** in the relationship list box and choose **less than**. Press **Tab** to move to the next list box and enter a **zero** as shown in Figure 2.4d.
- Click the **Format button** to display the Format Cells dialog box. Click the **Font tab**, click the **down arrow** on the Color list box and choose **Red**. Choose Bold as the Font style. Click **OK** to close the Format Cells dialog box.
- Click **OK** to close the Conditional Formatting dialog box. The decrease in the interest expense should be displayed in bold red as –9.1%.
- Save the workbook.

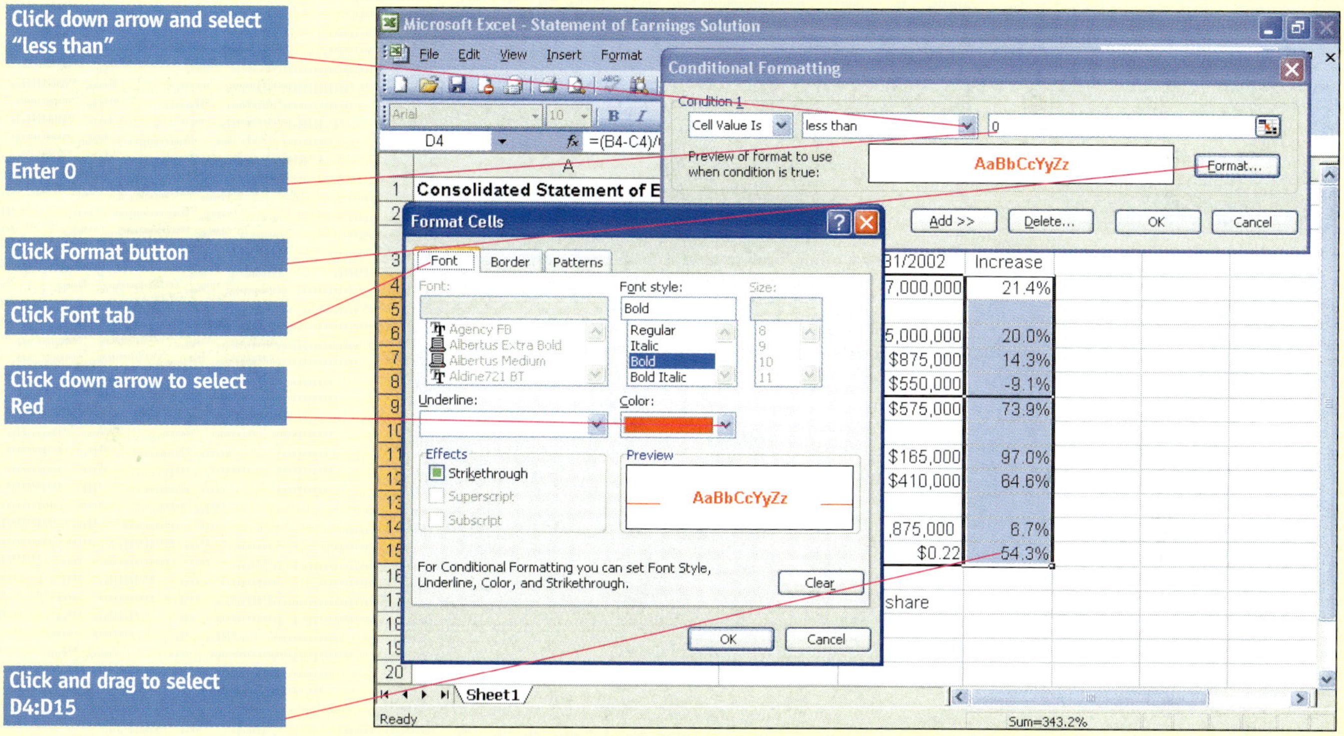

(d) Conditional Formatting (step 4)

FIGURE 2.4 Hands-on Exercise 2 (*continued*)

ADDING MULTIPLE CONDITIONS

Use the Conditional Formatting command to impose additional conditions with alternative formats depending on the value within a cell. You can, for example, display negative values in red (as was done in this example) and positive values (above a certain number) in blue. Pull down the Format menu and click the Conditional Formatting command, then click the Add button within the dialog box to add the additional conditions. Conditional formatting is a lesser-known feature that adds significantly to the appearance of a worksheet.

Step 5: Insert the Hyperlink

- Click in **cell A19**. Pull down the **Insert menu** and click the **Hyperlink command** (or click the **Insert Hyperlink button** on the Standard toolbar) to display the Insert Hyperlink dialog box in Figure 2.4e. Click in the **Text to display** text box and enter **Click here to view our Web site**.
- Click **Existing File or Web Page**, then click the button for **Browsed Pages**, then click in the Address text box (toward the bottom of the dialog box) and enter the Web address such as **www.prenhall.com/grauer** (the http:// is assumed). Click **OK** to accept the settings and close the dialog box.
- The hyperlink should appear as an underlined entry in the worksheet. Point to the hyperlink (the Web address should appear as a ScreenTip), then click the link to start your browser and view the Web page. You need an Internet connection to see the actual page.
- You are now running two applications, Excel and the Web browser, each of which has its own button on the Windows taskbar. Click the **Excel button** to continue working (and correct the hyperlink if necessary).
- Save the workbook.

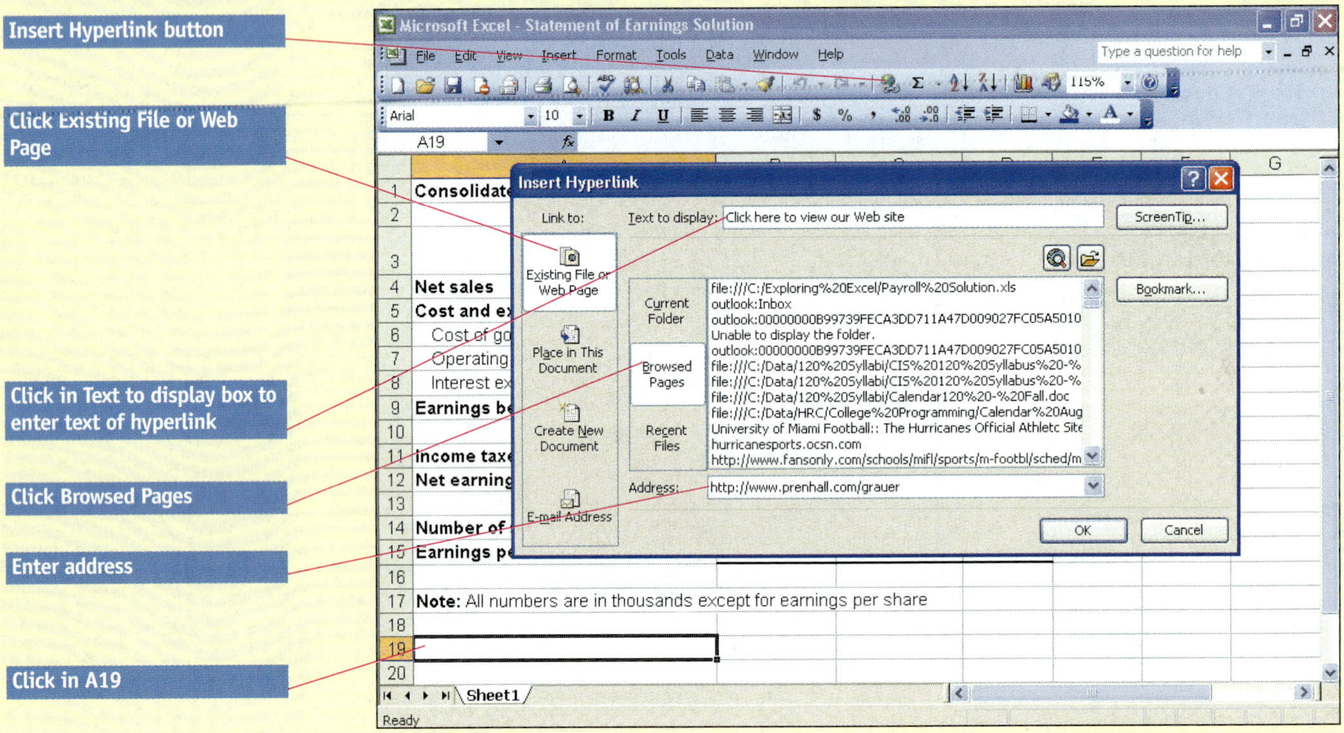

(e) Insert the Hyperlink (step 5)

FIGURE 2.4 Hands-on Exercise 2 (*continued*)

SELECTING (EDITING) A HYPERLINK

In an ideal world you will enter all the information for a hyperlink correctly on the first attempt. But what if you make a mistake and need to edit the information? You cannot select a hyperlink by clicking it, because that displays the associated Web page. You can, however, right click the cell containing the hyperlink to display a context-sensitive menu, then click the Edit Hyperlink command to display the associated dialog box in which to make the necessary changes. (The menu also enables you to remove the hyperlink.)

Step 6: Save the Web Page

- Pull down the **File menu** and click the **Save as Web Page command** to display the Save As dialog box in Figure 2.4f. Note the following:
  - The **Exploring Excel folder** is entered automatically as the default folder, since that is the location of the original workbook.
  - **Statement of Earnings Solution** is entered automatically as the name of the Web page, corresponding to the name of the workbook, Statement of Earnings Solution.
  - The default file type is **Single File Web Page**, as opposed to HTML.
  - It does not matter whether you save the entire workbook or a single sheet, since the workbook contains only a single sheet. However, you need to specify a single sheet if and when you want to add interactivity (i.e., Excel functionality) when the page is opened through a Web browser.
- Click the **Save button**. There are now two versions of the workbook on disk, both with the same name (Statement of Earnings Solution), but with different extensions, corresponding to a Web page and Excel workbook.
- Close Microsoft Excel. (We will restart the application later in the exercise.)

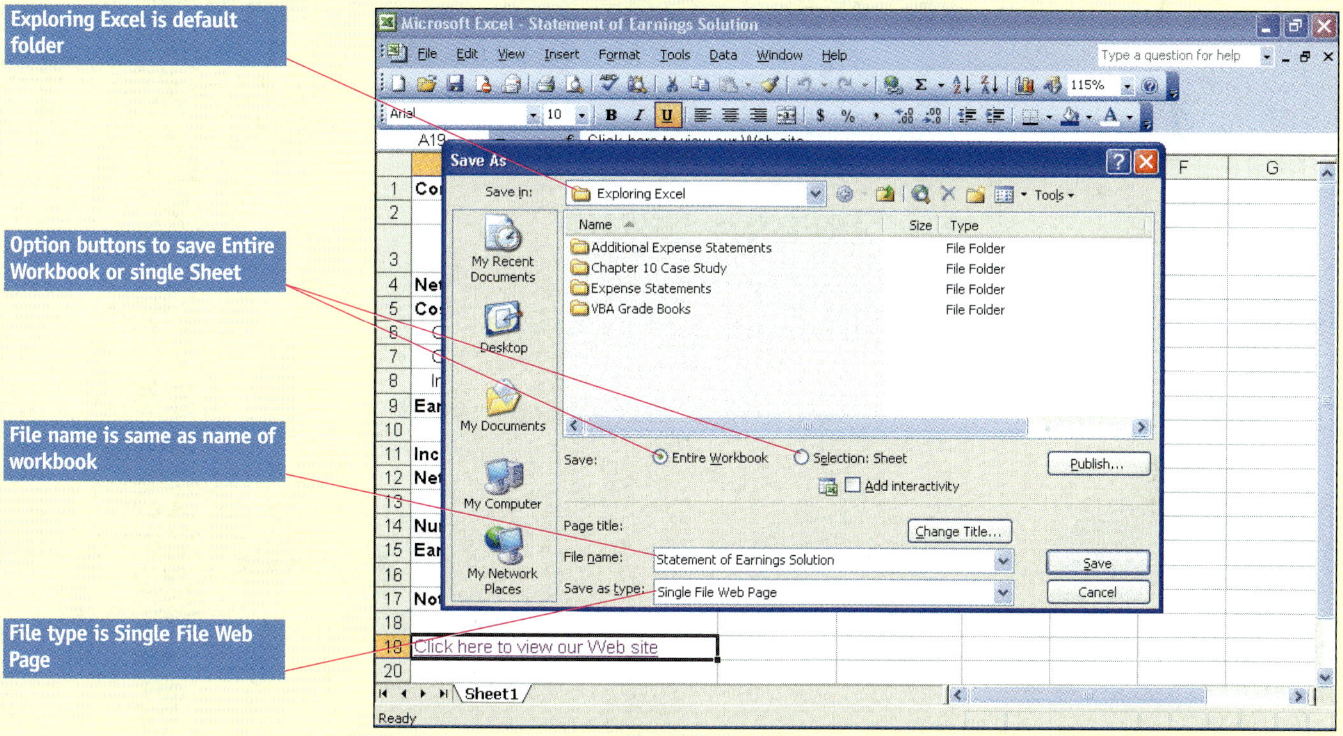

(f) Save the Web Page (step 6)

FIGURE 2.4 Hands-on Exercise 2 (*continued*)

CHANGE THE DEFAULT FILE LOCATION

The default file location is the folder Excel uses to open and save a workbook unless it is otherwise instructed. To change the default location, pull down the Tools menu, click Options, and click the General tab. Enter the name of the new folder (e.g., C:\Exploring Excel) in the Default File Location text box, then click OK. The next time you access the Open or Save command from the File menu, the Look In text box will reflect the change.

Step 7: Start Windows Explorer

- Click the **Start button,** start **Windows Explorer**, then change to the Exploring Excel folder. The location of this folder depends on whether you have your own computer.
  - If you are working from a floppy disk, select drive A in the left pane.
  - If you are working on your own computer, expand drive C in the left pane, then scroll until you can select the Exploring Excel folder.
- Either way, you should see the contents of the Exploring Excel folder in the right pane as shown in Figure 2.4g. As indicated, there are two versions of the Statement of Earnings Solution with different icons and file types.
- Right click the file with the Excel icon and file type to display a shortcut menu, then click the **Delete command** to delete this file. You do not need the Excel workbook any longer because you can edit the workbook from the Web page through the concept of round trip HTML.
- Double click the Web page version of the earnings statement to view the document in your default browser.

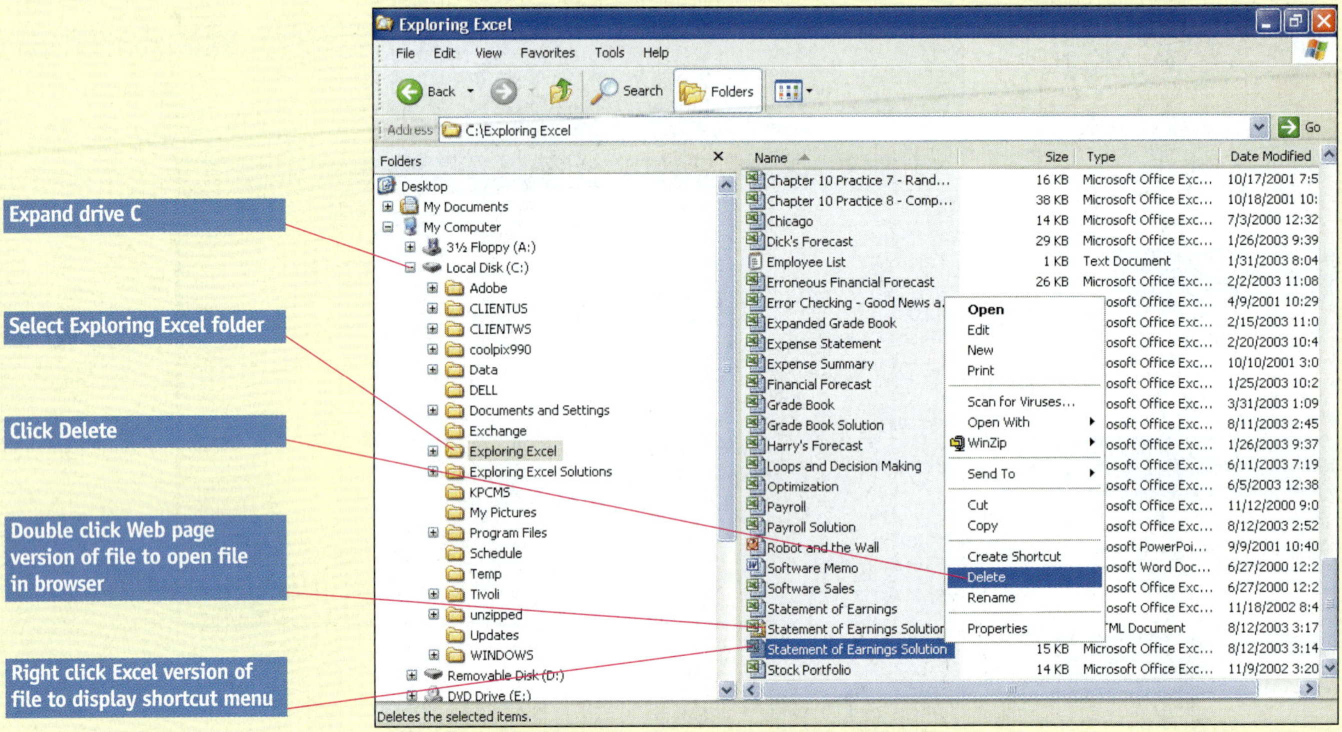

(g) Start Windows Explorer (step 7)

FIGURE 2.4 Hands-on Exercise 2 (*continued*)

ROUND TRIP HTML

Each application in Microsoft Office lets you open an HTML document in both Internet Explorer and the application that created the Web page initially. In other words, you can start with an Excel worksheet and use the Save as Web Page command to convert the document to a Web page, then view that page in a Web browser. You can then reopen the Web page in Excel (the application that created it initially) with full access to all Excel commands in order to edit the document.

Step 8: View the Web Page

- You should see the Statement of Earnings Solution displayed within Internet Explorer (or Netscape Navigator) as shown in Figure 2.4h. The Web page looks identical to the worksheet that was displayed earlier in Excel.
- Click the hyperlink that was inserted through the Insert Hyperlink command to view the Web site. You should see our Web site (**www.prenhall.com/grauer**), if that was the address you used earlier.
- Click the **Back button** on the Standard Buttons toolbar to return to the Statement of Earnings Solution Web page. Look carefully at the Address bar and note that unlike other Web documents, this page is displayed from your local system (drive C or drive A), depending on the location of the file.
- Click the **Edit with Microsoft Excel button** on the Standard Buttons toolbar to start Excel in order to modify the Web page.
- Both applications, Internet Explorer and Microsoft Excel, are open as can be seen by the taskbar, which contains buttons for both.

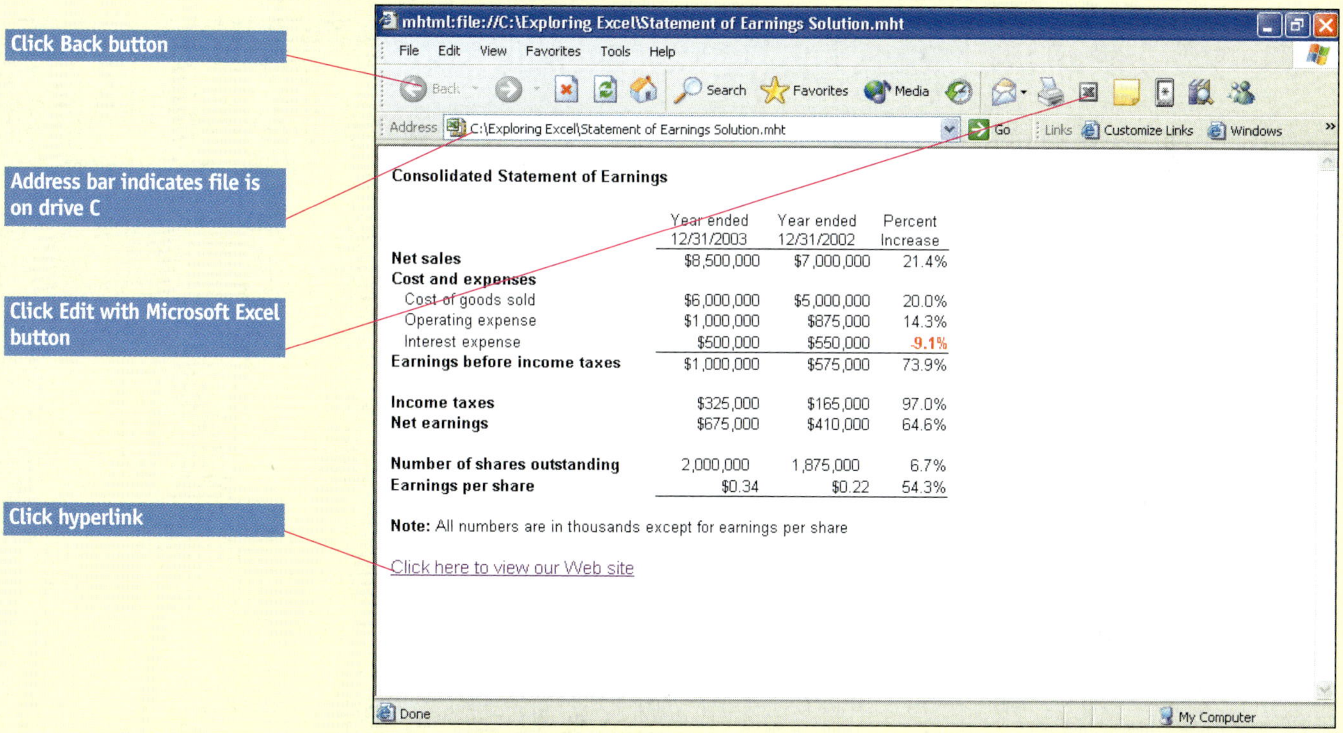

(h) View the Web Page (step 8)

FIGURE 2.4 Hands-on Exercise 2 (*continued*)

MULTITASKING

Multitasking, the ability to run multiple applications at the same time, is one of the primary advantages of the Windows environment. Minimizing an application is different from closing it, and you want to minimize, rather than close, an application to take advantage of multitasking. Closing an application removes it from memory so that you have to restart the application if you want to return to it later in the session. Minimizing, however, leaves the application open in memory, but shrinks its window to a button on the Windows taskbar.

Step 9: Edit the Web Page

- You should be back in Microsoft Excel as shown in Figure 2.4i. Click in **cell A21** and enter the label, **Prepared by**, followed by your name.
- Save the worksheet.
- Click the **Internet Explorer button** on the taskbar to return to your browser. The change you made (the addition of your name) is not yet visible because the browser displays the previous version of the page.
- Click the **Refresh button** on the Standard Buttons toolbar to bring in the most current version of the worksheet. Your changes should now be visible.(You may, however, have to close, then reopen Internet Explorer to see the change.)
- Pull down the **File menu** (within Internet Explorer) and click the **Print command,** then click the **Print command button** to print the Web page for your instructor.
- Close Internet Explorer. Exit Excel if you do not wish to continue with the next exercise at this time.

Click in A21 and enter your name

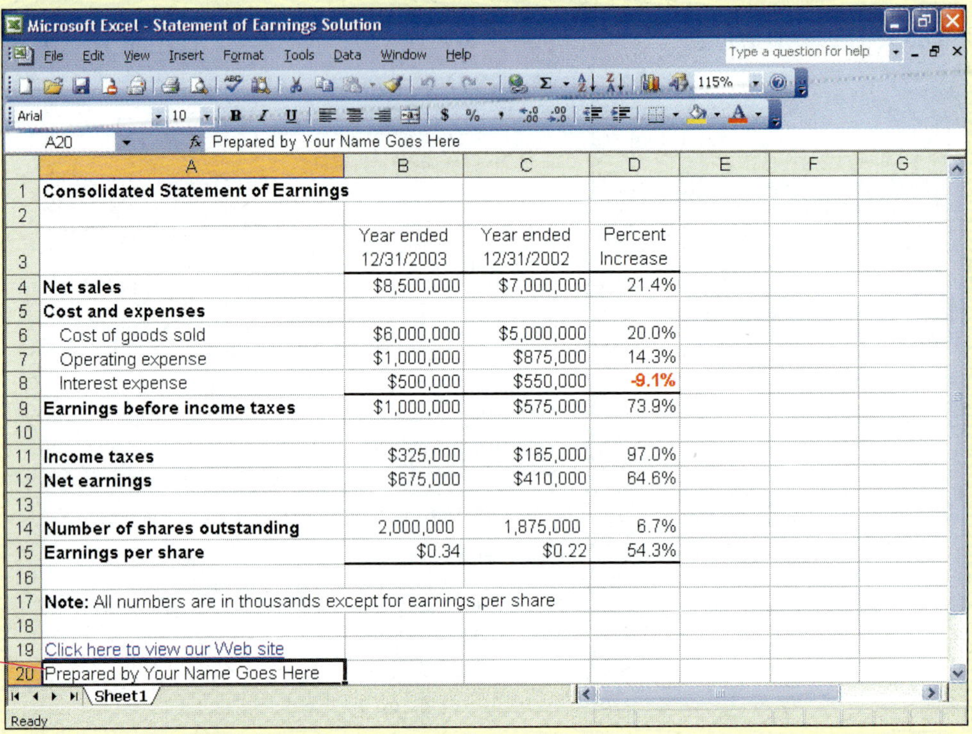

	A	B	C	D
1	**Consolidated Statement of Earnings**			
2				
3		Year ended 12/31/2003	Year ended 12/31/2002	Percent Increase
4	**Net sales**	$8,500,000	$7,000,000	21.4%
5	**Cost and expenses**			
6	Cost of goods sold	$6,000,000	$5,000,000	20.0%
7	Operating expense	$1,000,000	$875,000	14.3%
8	Interest expense	$500,000	$550,000	-9.1%
9	**Earnings before income taxes**	$1,000,000	$575,000	73.9%
10				
11	**Income taxes**	$325,000	$165,000	97.0%
12	**Net earnings**	$675,000	$410,000	64.6%
13				
14	**Number of shares outstanding**	2,000,000	1,875,000	6.7%
15	**Earnings per share**	$0.34	$0.22	54.3%
16				
17	**Note:** All numbers are in thousands except for earnings per share			
18				
19	Click here to view our Web site			
20	Prepared by Your Name Goes Here			

(i) Edit the Web Page (step 9)

FIGURE 2.4 Hands-on Exercise 2 (*continued*)

USE A TEMPLATE

A template is a partially completed workbook that is used to create other workbooks. It typically contains formulas and formatting but no specific data. Thus you open a template and enter the information that is specific to your application, then you save the template as an ordinary workbook. Excel provides several business templates.

Our next example is a worksheet to maintain a stock portfolio and compute the gain or loss associated with investment. The worksheet in Figure 2.5 lists several stocks, each with its recognized symbol, and records the purchase price, number of shares, and date of purchase of each investment. This information is "fixed" for each stock at the time of purchase. The worksheet then uses the current (today's) price to determine the gain or loss. It also uses today's date to compute the length of time the investment was held. The interesting thing about the worksheet is that the current price is obtained via a ***Web query***, a capability that enables Excel to go to a specific site on the Web to retrieve the information. The worksheet is time-sensitive and thus the values you see on your computer will be different from those in Figure 2.5.

The top half of the worksheet is typical of the worksheets we have studied thus far. The bottom portion (from row 14 down) represents the result of the Web query, which is entered into the worksheet via the ***Import External Data command***. Execution of this command prompts you for the location of the result (e.g., cell A14 in Figure 2.5) and the location of the parameters (or stock symbols), for which you want to determine the price (cells A5 through A10 in this example). Excel does the rest and places the results of the query into the worksheet. The results of the query can be continually updated through the ***Refresh command***, which is represented by the Exclamation Point button on the ***External Data toolbar***.

The worksheet in Figure 2.5 also illustrates the use of ***date arithmetic*** to determine the length of time an investment is held. (This is an important consideration for investors who can reduce their tax liability through a capital gains tax break on investments held for more than one year.) Date arithmetic is made possible through a simple concept by which Excel stores all dates as integers (serial numbers) beginning with January 1, 1900. Thus, January 1, 1900 is stored as the number 1, January 2, 1900 as the number 2, and so on.

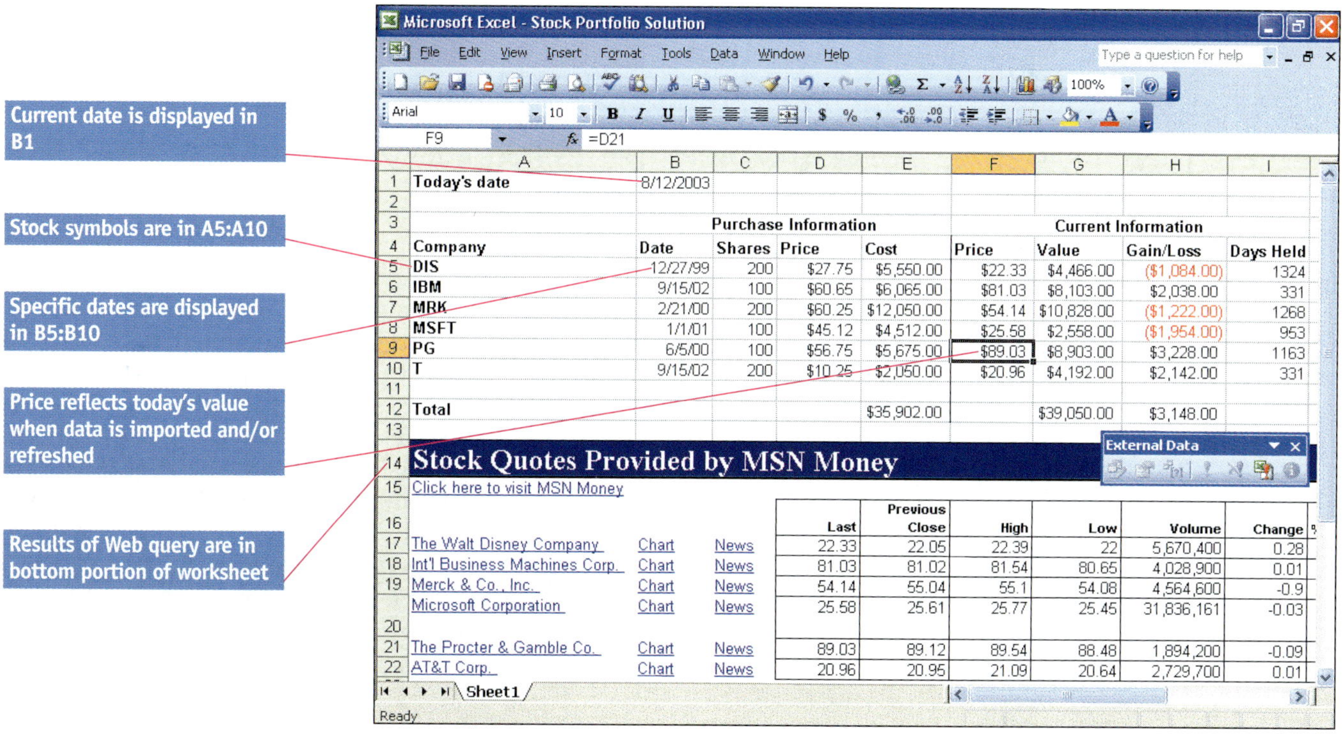

(a) The Excel Worksheet

FIGURE 2.5 Web Queries

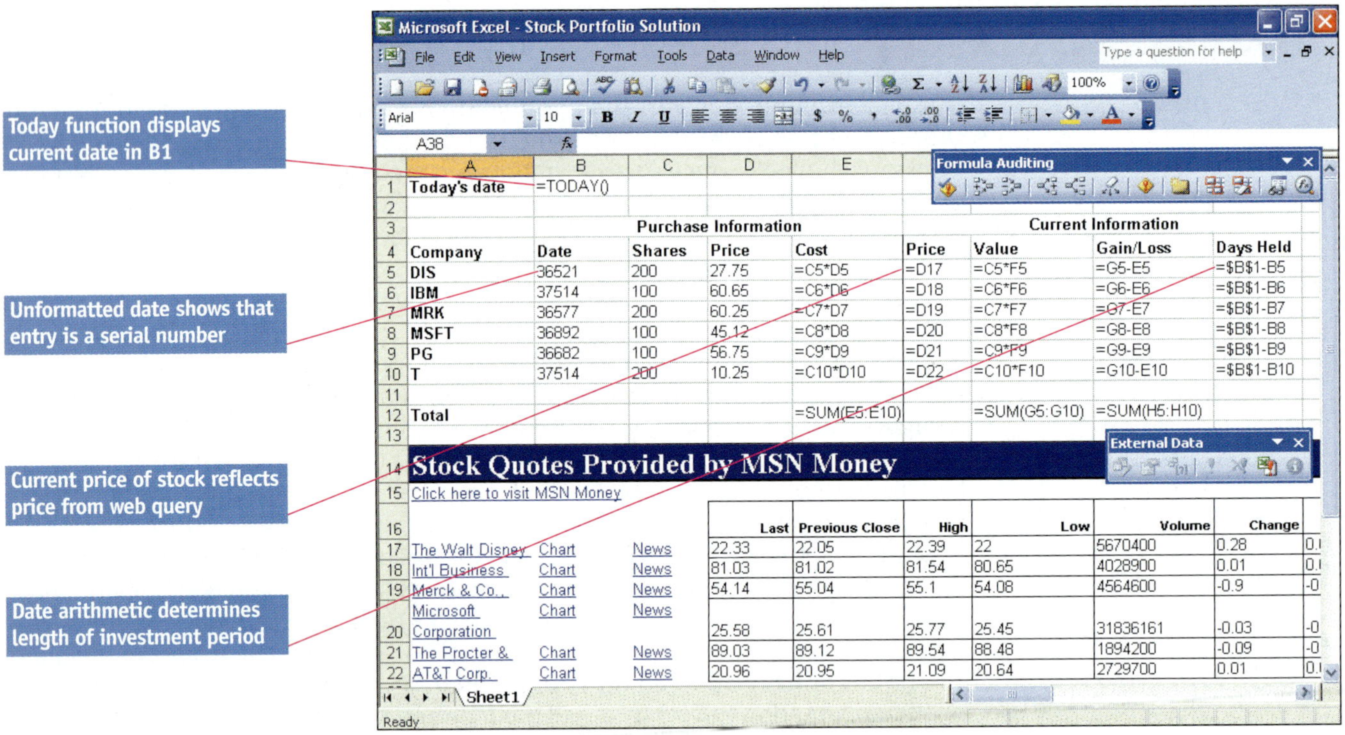

(b) Cell Formulas

FIGURE 2.5 Web Queries (*continued*)

The ***Today( ) function*** returns the current date (i.e., the date on which the spreadsheet is opened). If, for example, you entered the Today( ) function into a spreadsheet that was created on May 14, and you opened the spreadsheet a month later, the value of the function would be automatically updated to June 14. The fact that dates are stored as integers enables you to add or subtract two different dates and/or to use a date in any type of arithmetic computation. A person's age can be computed by subtracting the date of birth from today's date, and dividing the result by 365.

In similar fashion, you can subtract the purchase date of an investment from today's date to determine the number of days the investment was held. Look now at the formula in cell I5 of Figure 2.5b, which subtracts the date of purchase (cell B5) from an absolute reference to today's date (cell B1) to compute the length of the investment. The formula in cell I5 (=$B$1–B5) can then be copied to the remaining rows in column I to determine the length of each investment.

A date is entered in different ways, most easily by typing the date in conventional fashion such as 12/31/99 or 12/31/1999. If you specify a two-digit year, then any year from 00 to 29, is assumed to be in the 21st century; for example, 1/21/00, will be stored as January 21, 2000. (The number 29 is arbitrary and you will have to ask Microsoft why it was chosen.) To avoid confusion, you should enter all four digits of the year—for example, 10/31/2001 for October 31, 2001.

YOU MUST UNDERSTAND THE PROBLEM

The formulas to compute the cost of an investment, its current value, the associated gain or loss, and the number of days the investment was held have nothing to do with Excel per se. Neither did the formulas to compute the gross pay, net pay, and so on in the payroll example. In other words, Excel is a means to an end, rather than an end unto itself, and you must understand the underlying problem.

hands-on exercise

3 Web Queries

Objective

Include a Web query into a worksheet to retrieve current stock prices from the Internet. (The exercise requires an Internet connection.) Use the Today() function to illustrate the use of date arithmetic. Use Figure 2.6 as a guide in the exercise.

Step 1: Open the Stock Portfolio

- Open the **Stock Portfolio workbook** in the **Exploring Excel folder** to display the worksheet in Figure 2.6a.
- Save the workbook as **Stock Portfolio Solution** so that you can return to the original workbook if necessary.
- Cell B1 displays today's date 8/12/2003 in our figure, but a different date on your machine. If necessary, click in **cell B1**, and note that it contains the function, **=Today()**. Thus the displayed value in cell B1 will always reflect the current date.
- Click in **cell B5**, the cell containing the date on which the shares in DIS were purchased. The contents of cell B5 are 12/27/1999 (there is no equal sign). This is a "fixed" date, and its value will not change from one day to the next.
- Pull down the **Data menu**, click **the Import External Data command**, then choose **Import Data command** to display the Select Data Source dialog box in Figure 2.6a.
- Choose the **MSN MoneyCentral Investor Stock Quotes** query, then click the **Open button**.

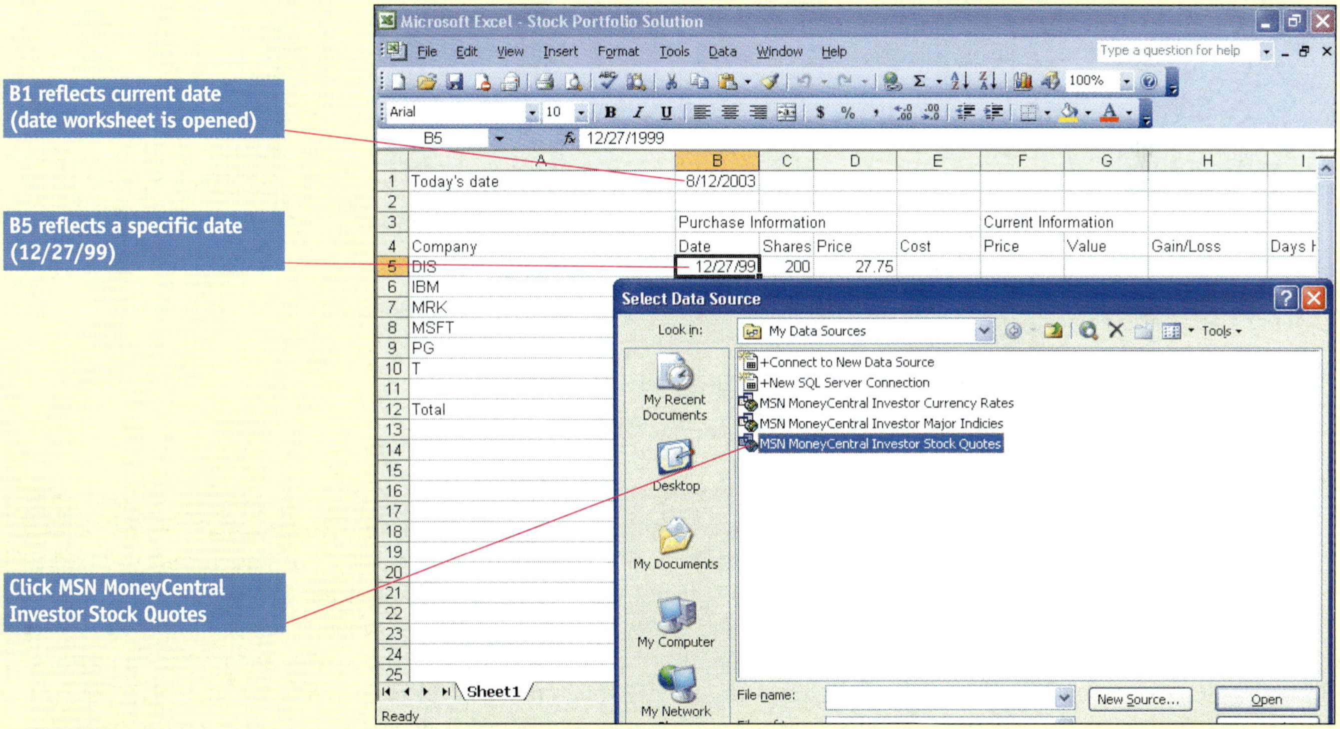

(a) Open the Stock Portfolio (step 1)

FIGURE 2.6 Hands-on Exercise 3

Step 2: Complete the Web Query

- The Import Data dialog box opens and prompts you for information about the Web query. Click the option button to put the data into the existing worksheet, then click in **cell A14** to indicate the location within the current worksheet. Click **OK**.
- Click and drag to select **cells A5** through **A10**, as the cells containing the stock symbols as shown in Figure 2.6b. Check the box to use this value reference for future refreshes. Click **OK**.
- Your system will pause as Excel goes to the Web to retrieve the information, provided you have an Internet connection. You should then see the stock quotes provided by MSN Money Central Investor.
- Do not be concerned if the column widths change as a result of the query. (You can widen them later.)
- Save the workbook.

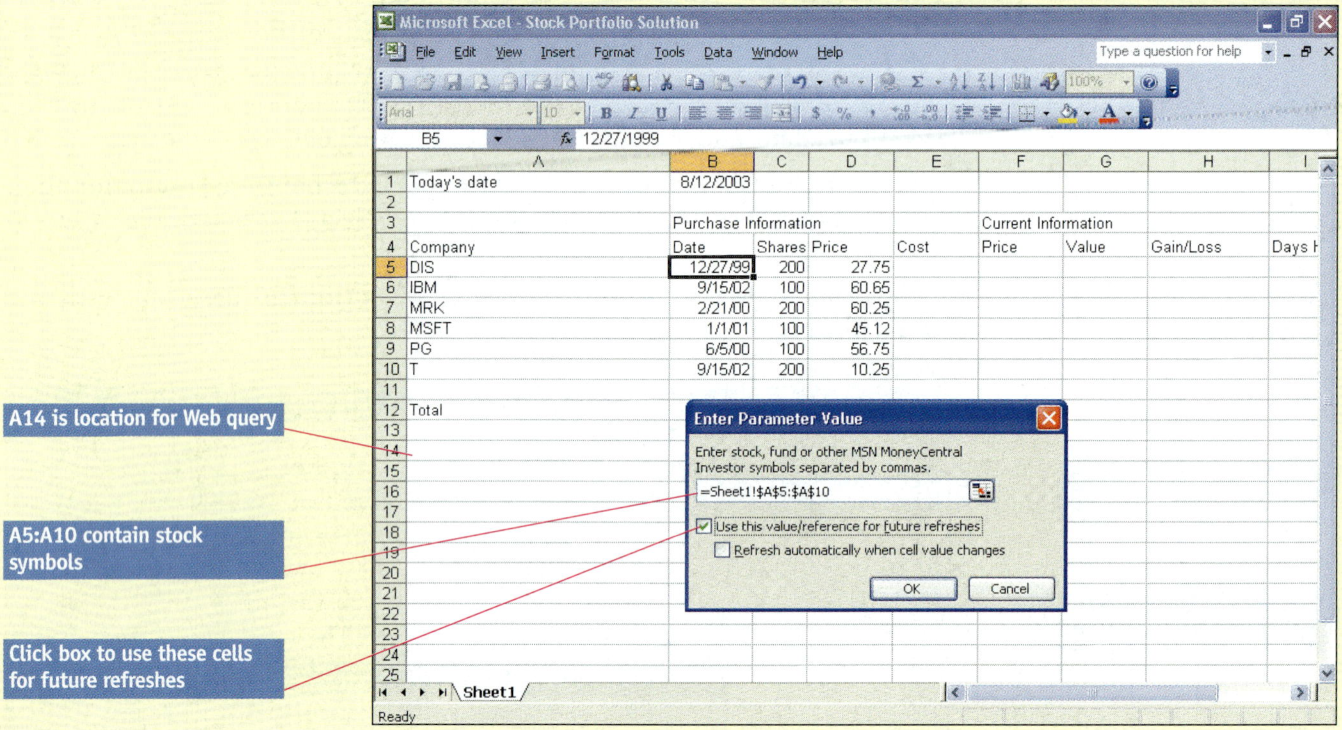

(b) Complete the Web Query (step 2)

FIGURE 2.6 Hands-on Exercise 3 (*continued*)

CREATE A NEW WEB QUERY

Web queries in earlier versions of Microsoft Office were limited in that you had to use existing queries. Office 2003, however, makes it easy to create new queries from virtually any Web page. Pull down the Data menu, click the Import External Data command, then click New Web query to display the associated dialog box. Enter the address of any Web page (try your favorite professional sport) that contains the data you want, then look for the yellow arrows that indicate the data may be imported. See problem 9 at the end of the chapter.

Step 3: Compute the Gain/Loss

- You should see the information that was obtained via the Web query as shown in Figure 2.6c. Use pointing to enter the cell references to complete the formulas for the first investment.
  - Click in **cell E5** (the cell that contains the cost of the investment) and enter the formula, **=C5*D5**.
  - Click in **cell F5** (the cell that contains today's price), and enter the formula **=D17**, which references the cell that contains the current price of **DIS**.
  - Click in **cell G5** (the cell that contains today's value of the investment) and enter the formula, **=C5*F5**.
  - Click in **cell H5** (the cell that contains the gain or loss) and enter the formula, **=G5–E5**, corresponding to today's value minus the cost.
  - Click in **cell I5** (the cell that contains the days held) and enter the formula, **=$B$1–B5**.
- If necessary, change the format in cell I5 to reflect a number, rather than a date. Click in **cell I5**, pull down the **Format menu**, click the **Cells command**, click the **Number tab**, choose **Number** as the category, and specify **zero decimal places**. Click **OK**.
- Save the workbook.

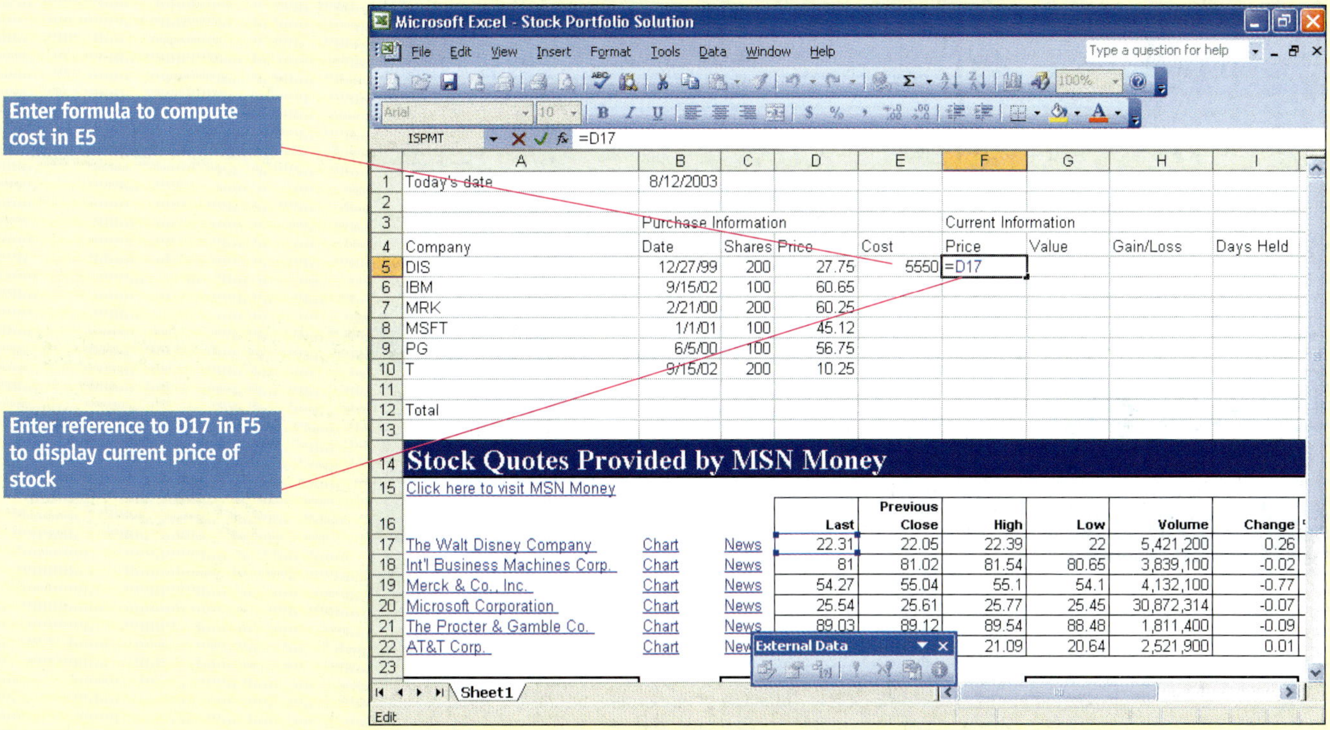

(c) Compute the Gain/Loss (step 3)

FIGURE 2.6 Hands-on Exercise 3 (*continued*)

NUMBERS, DATES, AND FORMATS

Any cell that contains a numeric value may be formatted in a variety of styles: date, number, percentage, currency, and so on. Excel does not know which format to use, and thus it is up to the user to select the cell, pull down the Format menu, click the Cells command to display the Format cells dialog box, click the Number tab, then choose the appropriate category.

Step 4: Copy the Formulas

- Click and drag to select **cells E5** through **I5**, the cells containing the formulas associated with the first investment, as shown in Figure 2.6d.
- Point to the fill handle in the lower-right corner of cell I5, then click and drag the fill handle to copy the formulas in row 5 to rows 6 through 10. Release the mouse to complete the copy operation.
- Click in **cell E12**, the cell that contains the total cost of your investments. Type **=SUM(** then click and drag to select **cells E5:E10**.
- Type a **closing parenthesis**, then press the **Enter key**. Cell E12 should contain the formula **=SUM(E5:E10)**.
- Copy the formula in cell E12 to **cells G12** and **H12**. The displayed value in cell E12 should be 35902. The displayed values in cells G12 and H12 depend on the current stock prices. The value of your portfolio will be very different from ours.
- Save the workbook.

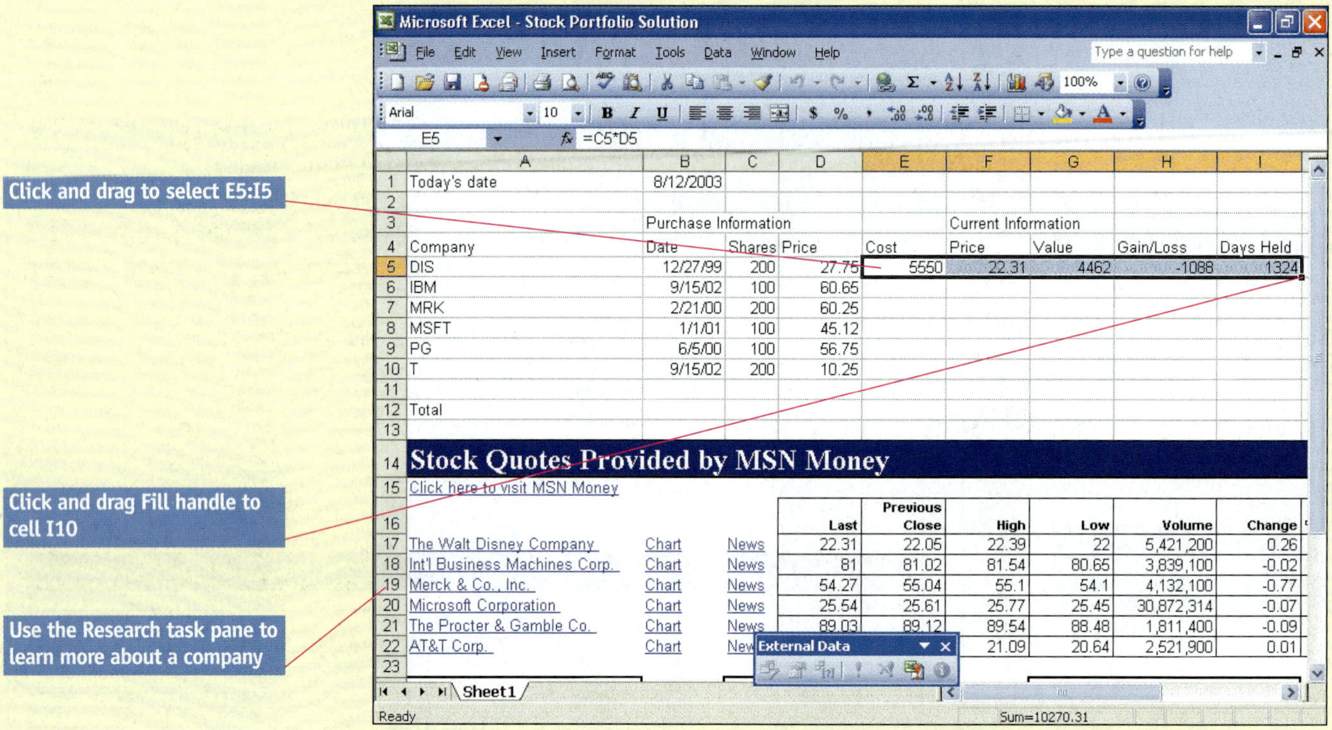

(d) Copy the Formulas (step 4)

FIGURE 2.6 Hands-on Exercise 3 (*continued*)

THE RESEARCH TASK PANE

Microsoft Office Excel 2003 introduces a research pane that connects you directly to various research tools on the Web. Pull down the Tools menu and click the Research command to display the Research task pane. Enter the name of the company for which you want information in the Search for text box, click the down arrow in the Reference Books list box, and then select Gale Company Profiles. Excel retrieves basic corporate information such as the company's address, phone, ticker symbol, and revenue, and displays the results in the task pane. Close the task pane when you are finished reading the information.

Step 5: Format the Worksheet

- Click and drag to select **cells D5** through **H12**, the cells that contain dollar amounts. Pull down the **Format menu**, click the **Cells command** to display the Format Cells dialog box, then click the **Number tab**. Format these cells in **Currency format,** with **two decimal places**. Display negative values in **red** and enclosed in **parentheses**. Click **OK**.
- Select all of the cells that contain a label (**cell A1**, **cells A3** through **I4**, **A5** through **A10**, and **cell A12**). Click the **Bold button** to boldface this information.
- Click and drag to select cells **B3** through **E3**, then click the **Merge and Center button**. Merge **cells F3** through **I3** in similar fashion.
- Click and drag to select **cells E4** through **E12.** Click the **down arrow** on the Borders button on the Formatting toolbar, then click the **right border icon** as shown in Figure 2.6e. Click **cell A1** (to deselect these cells). You should see a vertical line separating the purchase information from the current values.
- Adjust the column widths if necessary. Save the workbook.

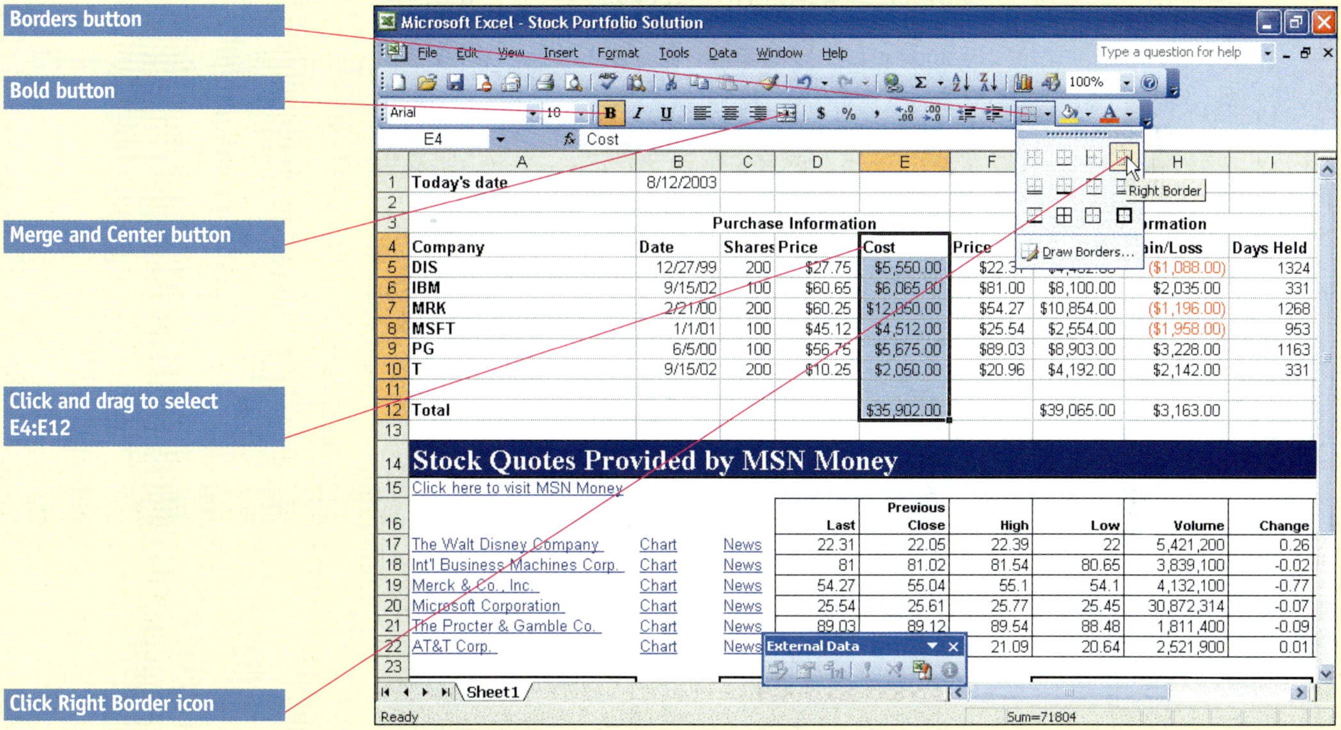

(e) Format the Worksheet (step 5)

FIGURE 2.6 Hands-on Exercise 3 (*continued*)

CAPITAL GAINS AND CONDITIONAL FORMATTING

The Internal Revenue Service offers a significant tax break on stock transactions that are considered a "long term" capital gain (more than one year under today's tax code). Click and drag to select cells I5 through I10, the cells that show how long a stock has been held. Pull down the Format menu, click the Conditional Formatting command, then enter the condition as cell value is >365. Click the Format button, click the Font tab, then choose a different color (e.g., blue) to highlight those investments that qualify for this consideration.

Step 6: Refresh the Query

- Right click anywhere within the Web query (i.e., within cells A14 to I22) to display the context-sensitive menu in Figure 2.6f. Click the **Refresh External Data command** to retrieve the current prices from the Web. Click **OK**.
- The numbers in your worksheet will change, provided you have an Internet connection and the stock market is open. The column widths may also change since the Web query automatically adjusts the width of its columns (see boxed tip).
- Adjust the column widths if necessary. (Remember, the value of your portfolio will be very different from ours.)
- Save the workbook a final time. Print the workbook twice, once to show the displayed values, and once to show the cell contents.
- Now that you have completed this exercise, you can experiment further with the various links within the Web query. Scroll to the bottom of the query, for example, then click the link for Symbol Lookup to find the symbol for your favorite stock or index.
- Good luck with your stock portfolio, and congratulations on a job well done.

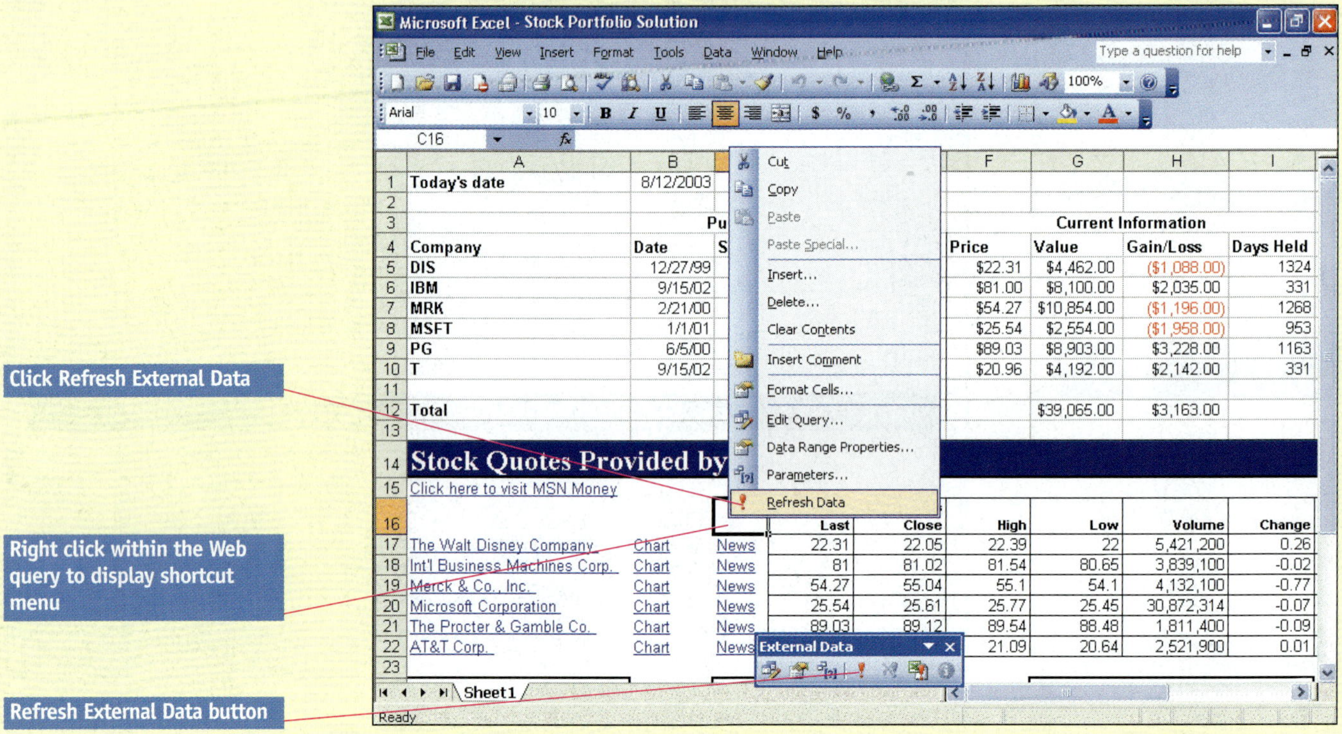

(f) Refresh the Query (step 6)

FIGURE 2.6 Hands-on Exercise 3 (*continued*)

DATA RANGE PROPERTIES

The Web query associated with MSN Stock quotes will, by default, change the column widths in the entire worksheet each time the query is refreshed. You can prevent this from happening by right clicking in the query area, then clicking the Data Range Properties command to display the associated dialog box. Clear the check box to Adjust column width, then click OK to accept the settings and close the dialog box. The next time you refresh the query, the column widths will not change.

SUMMARY

The distinction between relative, absolute, and mixed references, coupled with the importance of isolating the assumptions on which a worksheet is based, are basic concepts in spreadsheet design. A relative reference (such as A1) changes both the row and column, when the cell containing the reference is copied to other cells in the worksheet. An absolute reference (such as $A$1) remains constant throughout the copy operation. A mixed reference, either $A1 or A$1, modifies the row or column, respectively. Most spreadsheets can be built through combinations of relative and absolute addresses. Mixed references are required for more advanced spreadsheets.

The initial conditions and/or assumptions on which a spreadsheet is based should be isolated so that their values can be easily changed. The formulas in the main body of the spreadsheet typically contain absolute references to these assumptions. The placement of the assumptions and initial conditions is not a requirement of Excel per se, but is crucial to the development of accurate and flexible worksheets. The Insert Comment command creates the equivalent of a screen tip that displays information about the worksheet.

Pointing and the fill handle are two techniques that facilitate the development of a spreadsheet. Although any cell reference can be entered into a formula by typing the reference directly, it is easier and more accurate to enter the reference through pointing. In essence you click in the cell that contains the formula, type an equal sign to begin the formula, then use the mouse (or arrow keys) to enter the various cell references as you build the formula.

The fill handle, a tiny black square in the lower-right corner of the selected cell(s), is the easiest way to copy a cell formula to adjacent cells. Just select the cell or cells to be copied, point to the fill handle for the selected cell(s), click and drag the fill handle over the destination range, and release the mouse.

A hyperlink can be inserted into any Excel worksheet, then the associated page viewed by clicking the link, without having to start the Web browser manually. Any worksheet or workbook can be saved as a Web page, which in turn can be stored on a Web server and displayed through a Web browser. Microsoft Office now recognizes the Single File Web Page format, which stores all of the elements on a Web page (text and graphics) as a single file.

Information from the Web can also be downloaded and inserted directly into an Excel workbook through a Web query. Office 2003 enables you to create your own Web queries from virtually any Web page.

Dates are entered into a worksheet by typing the date in conventional fashion such as 11/24/2000 or December 24, 2000. Either way all dates are stored as integers, beginning with January 1, 1900; that is January 1, 1900 is stored as the number 1. This simple concept enables date arithmetic, whereby calculations can be made between two dates to determine the number of days that have elapsed. The Today() function always returns the current date and is used in conjunction with date arithmetic.

KEY TERMS

MULTIPLE CHOICE

1. The formula to compute the gross pay of an employee in the payroll example that was developed in this chapter uses:
   (a) Absolute references for hourly wage, regular hours, and overtime hours
   (b) Relative references for hourly wage, regular hours, and overtime hours
   (c) Mixed references for hourly wage, regular hours, and overtime hours
   (d) Impossible to determine

2. Which of the following best describes the formula to compute the withholding tax of an employee in the payroll example that was developed in this chapter?
   (a) It contains a relative reference to gross pay and an absolute reference to the withholding rate
   (b) It contains an absolute reference to gross pay and a relative reference to the withholding rate
   (c) It contains absolute references to both the gross pay and withholding tax
   (d) It contains relative references to both the gross pay and withholding tax

3. Cell D12 contains the formula, =SUM (A12:C12). What will the contents of cell D13 be, if the formula in cell D12 is copied to cell D13?
   (a) =SUM (A12:C12)
   (b) =SUM (A13:C13)
   (c) =SUM (A12:C13)
   (d) =SUM (A13:C12)

4. A formula containing the entry =$B$3 is copied to a cell one column over and two rows down. How will the entry appear in its new location?
   (a) =$C$5
   (b) =$B$3
   (c) =B3
   (d) =C5

5. How do you insert a hyperlink into a workbook?
   (a) Pull down the Insert menu and click the Hyperlink command
   (b) Click the Insert Hyperlink button on the Standard toolbar
   (c) Right click a cell and click the Hyperlink command
   (d) Any of the above

6. A Web browser such as Internet Explorer can display a page from:
   (a) A local drive such as drive A or drive C
   (b) A drive on a local area network
   (c) The World Wide Web
   (d) All of the above

7. What is the best way to enter the current price of a stock into an Excel worksheet?
   (a) Copy the price directly from today's copy of *The Wall Street Journal*
   (b) Save the worksheet as a Web page
   (c) Create a Web query, then refresh the query to obtain the current price
   (d) Use Internet Explorer to locate a Web page that contains the current price

8. The estimated sales for the first year of a financial forecast are contained in cell B3. The sales for year two are assumed to be 10% higher than the first year, with the rate of increase (10%) stored in cell C23 at the bottom of the spreadsheet. Which of the following is the best way to enter the sales for year two?
   (a) =B3+B3*.10
   (b) =B3+B3*C23
   (c) =B3+B3*$C$23
   (d) All of the above are equivalent entries

9. Which of the following requires an Internet connection?
   (a) Using Internet Explorer to view a Web page that is stored locally
   (b) Updating the values that are obtained through a Web query
   (c) Clicking a hyperlink that references a document that is stored on drive C
   (d) All of the above

10. Cell F6 contains the formula =AVERAGE(B6:D6). What will be the contents of cell F7 if the entry in cell F6 is *moved* to cell F7?
   (a) =AVERAGE(B6:D6)
   (b) =AVERAGE(B7:D7)
   (c) =AVERAGE($B$6:$D$6)
   (d) =AVERAGE($B$7:$D$7)

... continued

multiple choice

11. What will be stored in a cell if 2/5 is entered in it?

(a) 2/5
(b) .4
(c) The date value February 5 of the current year
(d) 2/5 or .4, depending on the format in effect

12. You type 11/24/00 into a cell, press the Enter key, and expect to see Nov 24, 2000. Instead you see the value 36854. Which of the following is the most likely explanation?

(a) Something is radically wrong with the date function
(b) The cell is formatted to display a numeric value rather than a date
(c) You should have used an equal sign to enter the date
(d) None of the above makes any sense at all

13. Which of the following formulas can be used to compute an individual's age, given that the individual's birth date is stored in cell A4?

(a) =(Today( )–A4)/365
(b) =(Today–A4)/365
(c) =(A4–Today)/365
(d) =(A4–Today( ))/365

14. Microsoft Excel and Internet Explorer are both open and display the "same" worksheet. You make a change in the Excel file that is not reflected in the Web page. What is the most likely explanation?

(a) The two files are not linked to one another
(b) The files are stored locally, as opposed to a Web server
(c) You did not refresh the Web page in Microsoft Excel
(d) You did not refresh the Web page in Internet Explorer

15. You notice that the values in a specific column are displayed in three different colors, red for values less than zero, blue for values greater than $100,000, and black otherwise. How is this possible?

(a) The colored formatting is automatically built into every Excel worksheet
(b) A Web query was used to implement the red and blue formatting
(c) Conditional formatting was applied to the column
(d) It is not possible; that is, the question is in error

16. A formula containing the cell reference A$4 is copied to a cell one column over and two rows down. How will the reference appear in its new location?

(a) Both the row and column will change
(b) Neither the row nor column will change
(c) The row will change but the column will remain the same
(d) The column will change but the row will remain the same

17. The formula =B3+C4 is stored in cell D5. What will the formula be if a row is inserted above the second row?

(a) =B3+C4
(b) =B4+C5
(c) =C3+D4
(d) =B2+C3

18. You want to add the contents of cells C1, C2, C3, and C4 but expect that additional values may be inserted within the column of numbers at a later time. Which formula automatically adjusts to *include* the additional entries?

(a) =C1+C2+C3+C4
(b) =SUM(C1:C4)
(c) Both entries will automatically adjust
(d) Neither entry will adjust if rows are inserted

ANSWERS

1. b	**7.** c	**13.** a
2. a	**8.** c	**14.** d
3. b	**9.** b	**15.** c
4. b	**10.** a	**16.** d
5. d	**11.** c	**17.** b
6. d	**12.** b	**18.** b

PRACTICE WITH EXCEL

1. **Alternate Payroll:** Figure 2.7 contains an alternate version of the payroll that was created in the first hands-on exercise in the chapter. The new spreadsheet includes the number of dependents for each employee and a fixed deduction per dependent, which combine to reduce an individual's taxable income. An employee with two dependents, for example, would have his or her taxable income reduced by $100 ($50 per dependent). The revised spreadsheet also isolates the overtime rate as an assumption at the bottom of the worksheet, which enables the user to change the overtime rate in a single place should that become necessary.
   a. Open the *Chapter 2 Practice 1* workbook, and then complete the spreadsheet so that the displayed values match ours. Use the appropriate combination of relative and absolute references in row 4, so that you can copy the formulas in this row to the remaining rows in the worksheet.
   b. Click in cell F12 and enter the appropriate Sum function to compute the total gross pay for all employees. Copy this formula to the remaining cells in this row.
   c. Format the worksheet in an attractive fashion. You do not have to match our formatting exactly, but you are to display all dollar amounts with the currency symbol and two decimal places.
   d. Substitute your name for the employee named "Grauer", then sort the worksheet so that the employees appear in alphabetical order. (Click anywhere within column A and click the Sort Ascending button on the Standard toolbar. Note, too, that there must be a blank row above the total row, or else it will be sorted with the other rows.) Shade the row containing your name.
   e. Print the completed worksheet twice, once with displayed values, and once to show the cell formulas. Use the Page Setup command to switch to landscape printing and force the output onto one page. Print gridlines and row and column headings. Change the column widths as appropriate.
   f. Change the overtime rate in cell E14 to 2.00; that is, an employee is paid double time for each overtime hour. Change the withholding rate in cell E16 to 25%. Print the displayed values to reflect these changes.

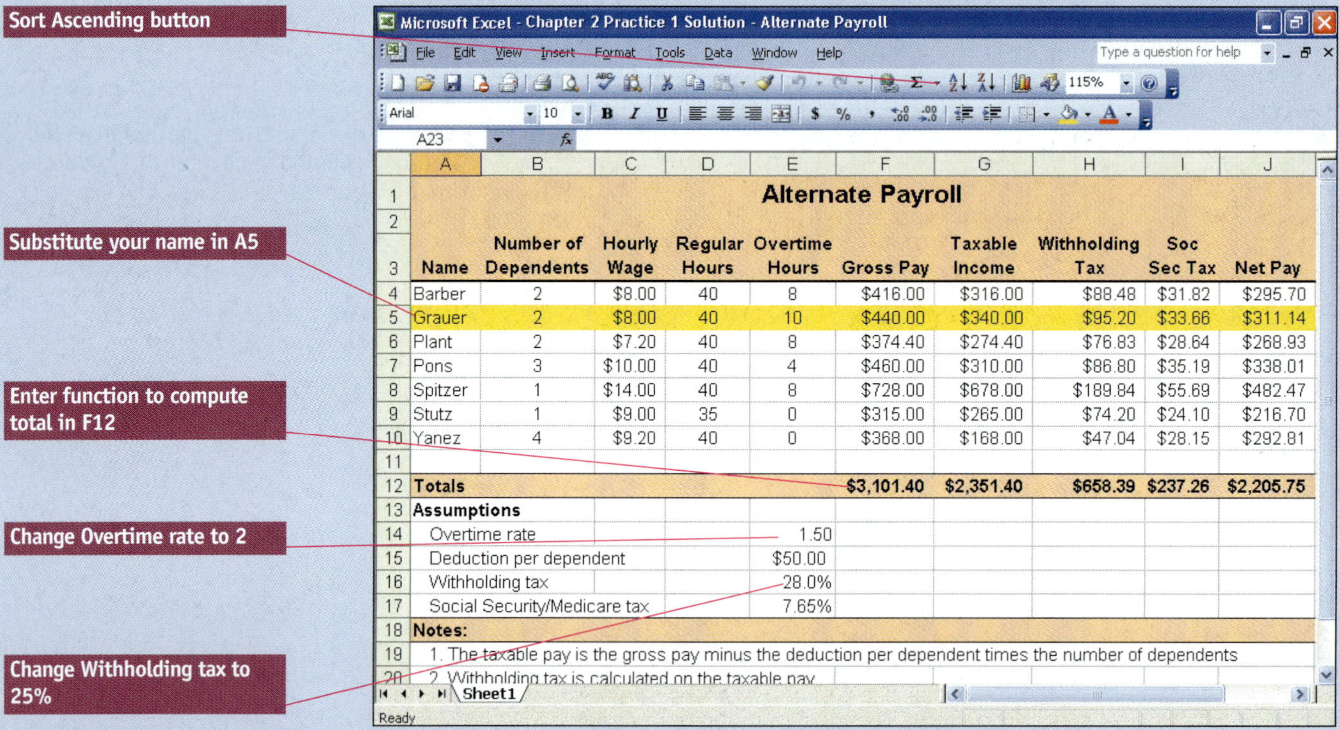

	Name	Number of Dependents	Hourly Wage	Regular Hours	Overtime Hours	Gross Pay	Taxable Income	Withholding Tax	Soc Sec Tax	Net Pay
4	Barber	2	$8.00	40	8	$416.00	$316.00	$88.48	$31.82	$295.70
5	Grauer	2	$8.00	40	10	$440.00	$340.00	$95.20	$33.66	$311.14
6	Plant	2	$7.20	40	8	$374.40	$274.40	$76.83	$28.64	$268.93
7	Pons	3	$10.00	40	4	$460.00	$310.00	$86.80	$35.19	$338.01
8	Spitzer	1	$14.00	40	8	$728.00	$678.00	$189.84	$55.69	$482.47
9	Stutz	1	$9.00	35	0	$315.00	$265.00	$74.20	$24.10	$216.70
10	Yanez	4	$9.20	40	0	$368.00	$168.00	$47.04	$28.15	$292.81
11										
12	**Totals**					$3,101.40	$2,351.40	$658.39	$237.26	$2,205.75
13	**Assumptions**									
14	Overtime rate				1.50					
15	Deduction per dependent				$50.00					
16	Withholding tax				28.0%					
17	Social Security/Medicare tax				7.65%					
18	**Notes:**									
19	1. The taxable pay is the gross pay minus the deduction per dependent times the number of dependents									
20	2. Withholding tax is calculated on the taxable pay									

FIGURE 2.7 Alternate Payroll (exercise 1)

2. **The Sports Statistician:** Figure 2.8 illustrates how Excel can be used to tabulate statistics for a hypothetical softball league. Open the partially completed worksheet in *Chapter 2 Practice 2* workbook, and proceed as follows:
   a. An individual batting average is computed by dividing the number of hits by the number of at bats (e.g., 30/80 or .375 for Maryann Barber). The batting average should be formatted to three decimal places. (Create the Custom format .000 to eliminate the 0 before the batting average to display .375, rather than the default numerical format of 0.000.)
   b. Compute the total bases for an individual by multiplying the number of singles by one, the number of doubles by two, the number of triples by three, and the number of home runs by four, then adding the results.
   c. The slugging percentage is computed by dividing the total bases by the number of at bats (e.g., 48/80 or .600 for Maryann Barber). The slugging average should be formatted to three decimal places.
   d. The team totals for all columns except batting average and slugging percentage are determined by summing the appropriate values. The team batting average and slugging percentage are computed by dividing the number of hits and total bases, respectively, by the number of at bats.
   e. Substitute your name for Jessica Grauer (our league is coed), sort the players in alphabetical order, then format the worksheet so that it matches Figure 2.8.
   f. Add an appropriate clip art image somewhere in the worksheet using the same technique as in any Office application. Pull down the Insert menu, click (or point to) Picture, then click Clip Art to open the task pane. Click in the Search text box. Enter "baseball" to search for any clip art image that is described with this keyword and click the Go button.
   g. Print the completed worksheet twice, once with displayed values, and once to show the cell formulas. Use the Page Setup command for the cell formulas to switch to landscape printing and force the output onto one page. Print gridlines and row and column headings. Add a cover sheet, then submit all three pages (cover sheet, displayed values, and cell formulas) to your instructor.

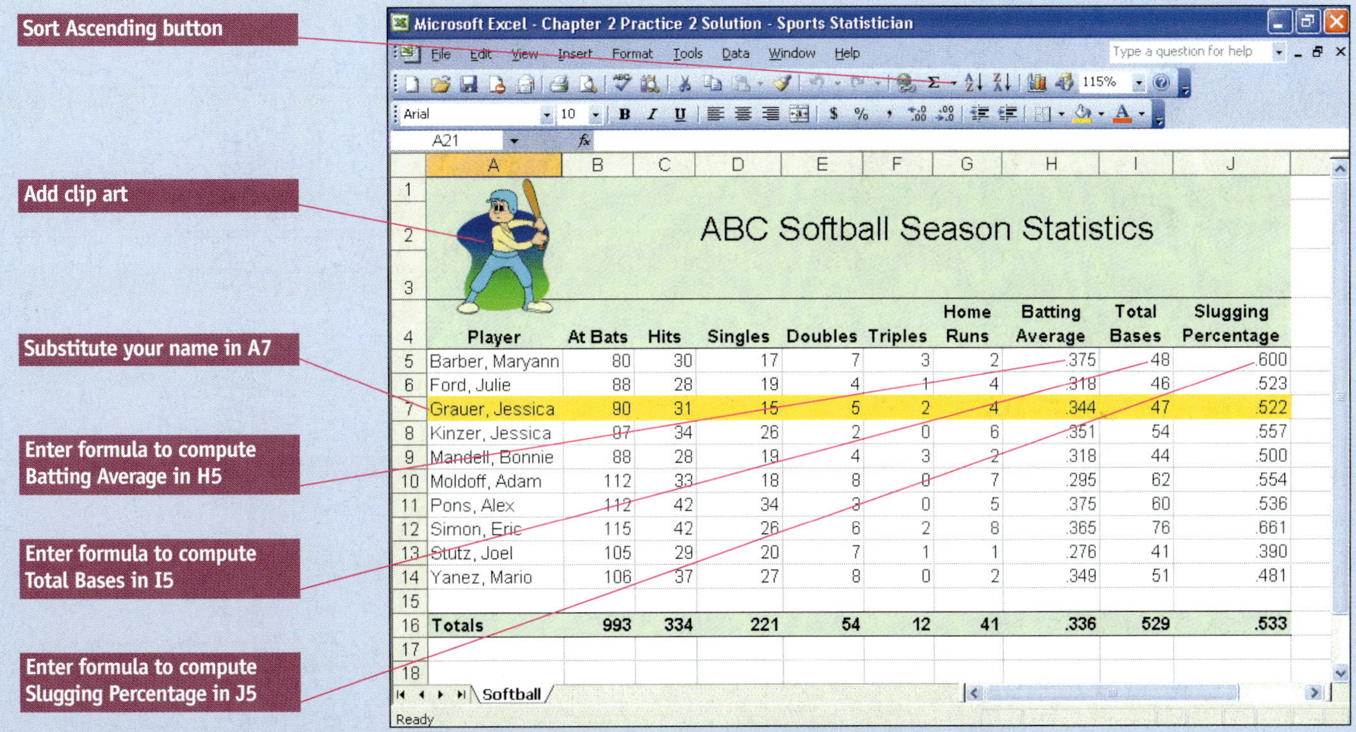

Player	At Bats	Hits	Singles	Doubles	Triples	Home Runs	Batting Average	Total Bases	Slugging Percentage
Barber, Maryann	80	30	17	7	3	2	.375	48	.600
Ford, Julie	88	28	19	4	1	4	.318	46	.523
Grauer, Jessica	90	31	15	5	2	4	.344	47	.522
Kinzer, Jessica	87	34	26	2	0	6	.351	54	.557
Mandell, Bonnie	88	28	19	4	3	2	.318	44	.500
Moldoff, Adam	112	33	18	8	0	7	.295	62	.554
Pons, Alex	112	42	34	3	0	5	.375	60	.536
Simon, Eric	115	42	26	6	2	8	.365	76	.661
Stutz, Joel	105	29	20	7	1	1	.276	41	.390
Yanez, Mario	106	37	27	8	0	2	.349	51	.481
Totals	**993**	**334**	**221**	**54**	**12**	**41**	**.336**	**529**	**.533**

FIGURE 2.8 The Sports Statistician (exercise 2)

3. **Web Pages and Hyperlinks:** The Web page in Figure 2.9 is based on the partially completed *Chapter 2 Practice 3* workbook in the Exploring Excel folder. Your assignment is to complete the workbook in Excel, then save the workbook as a Web page. (You can view the Web page locally as in Figure 2.9, without loading it onto a Web server.) Proceed as follows:
   a. Compute the total points for each player by multiplying the number of free throws, 2-point field goals, and 3-point field goals by 1, 2, and 3, respectively.
   b. Compute the points per game for each player by dividing the total points by the number of games. Display the result to one decimal point. Compute the rebounds per game in similar fashion.
   c. Add clip art as you see fit. We used the same image twice to bracket the title of the worksheet, but feel free to improve on our design. Format your page to match ours.
   d. Add your name as the statistician in the bottom of the worksheet. Instead of merely typing your name, however, add your name as a hyperlink that points to your home page if you have one. If you do not have a home page, use any Web address that is appropriate, such as www.nba.com for the National Basketball Association. In any event, the text should say, "Click here for John Doe's (substitute your name) Home Page".
   e. Print the completed workbook from Excel to show both displayed values and cell formulas. Use the Page Setup command to display gridlines and row and column headings.
   f. Save the workbook as a Web page, then open the workbook in Internet Explorer. How does the printed Web page compare to the printed workbook?
   g. This exercise demonstrates how easy it is to create a Web page from an Excel worksheet and view it locally within Internet Explorer. To place a page on the Web, you will need Internet access, and further, you will need storage space on a Web server. Check with your instructor to see if these resources are available to you, and if so, find out the steps necessary to upload your page to the server. Send a note to your instructor that contains the Web address where he or she may view your Web page.

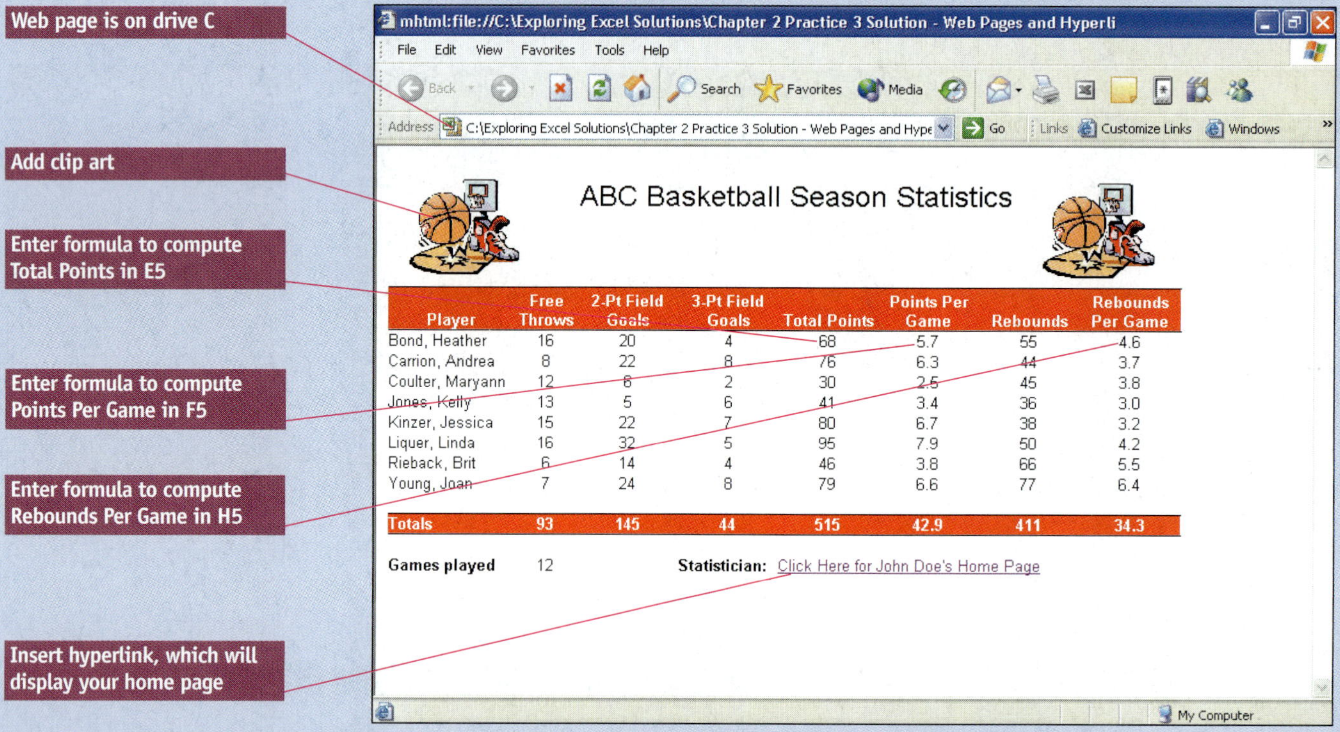

Player	Free Throws	2-Pt Field Goals	3-Pt Field Goals	Total Points	Points Per Game	Rebounds	Rebounds Per Game
Bond, Heather	16	20	4	68	5.7	55	4.6
Carrion, Andrea	8	22	8	76	6.3	44	3.7
Coulter, Maryann	12	6	2	30	2.5	45	3.8
Jones, Kelly	13	5	6	41	3.4	36	3.0
Kinzer, Jessica	15	22	7	80	6.7	38	3.2
Liquer, Linda	16	32	5	95	7.9	50	4.2
Rieback, Brit	6	14	4	46	3.8	66	5.5
Young, Joan	7	24	8	79	6.6	77	6.4
Totals	93	145	44	515	42.9	411	34.3

FIGURE 2.9 Web Pages and Hyperlinks (exercise 3)

4. **The Workout Schedule:** The worksheet in Figure 2.10 is essentially an exercise in formatting, but it also tests your ability to copy efficiently within a worksheet. You do not have to duplicate our document exactly, but you are required to have the equivalent functionality. You can create the document entirely on your own, or you can follow our suggested procedure.
    a. Open a new workbook. Click in cell B4 and enter "Day". Click in cell C4 and type "Monday". Click and drag to select cells C4 through E4, click the Merge and Center button to create a single cell, then use the Borders button to place a border around the merged cell. Drag the fill handle of this cell to enter the remaining days of the week in row 4.
    b. Enter "EXERCISE" and "SET" in cells A5 and B5, respectively. Select both cells, change the fill color to black and the text color to white. Center the text. Click the Bold button so that the text stands out.
    c. Enter 1, 2, and 3 in cells C5, D5, and E5, respectively. Click in cell B5, click the Format Painter button, and copy the formatting to cells C5 through E5. Copy these cells to the remaining cells in this row.
    d. Center "Pounds" and "Reps" in cells B6 and B7, respectively. Change the fill color in cell B7. Place a border around cells B6 and B7, then copy the formatting to the remaining cells in rows 6 and 7. (You can use the Format Painter and/or the Paste Special command, after which you choose formats.)
    e. Adjust the width of column A. Add the appropriate border around the merged cell in A6. Copy rows 6 and 7 to the remaining rows in the worksheet.
    f. Merge cells B1 through Q1 to enter the title of the worksheet. Merge cells B2 through Q2 and enter your name. Change the row height in rows 1 to 4 as appropriate, and then insert an appropriate logo in the upper-left portion of the worksheet.
    g. Print the completed worksheet in landscape mode. Be sure the worksheet fits on a single sheet of paper. Use the Page Setup command to add a footer that shows the name of the worksheet (i.e., the week of the workout).
    h. Copy the completed worksheet to two additional worksheets within the workbook. Rename all three worksheets to indicate the week of the workout.

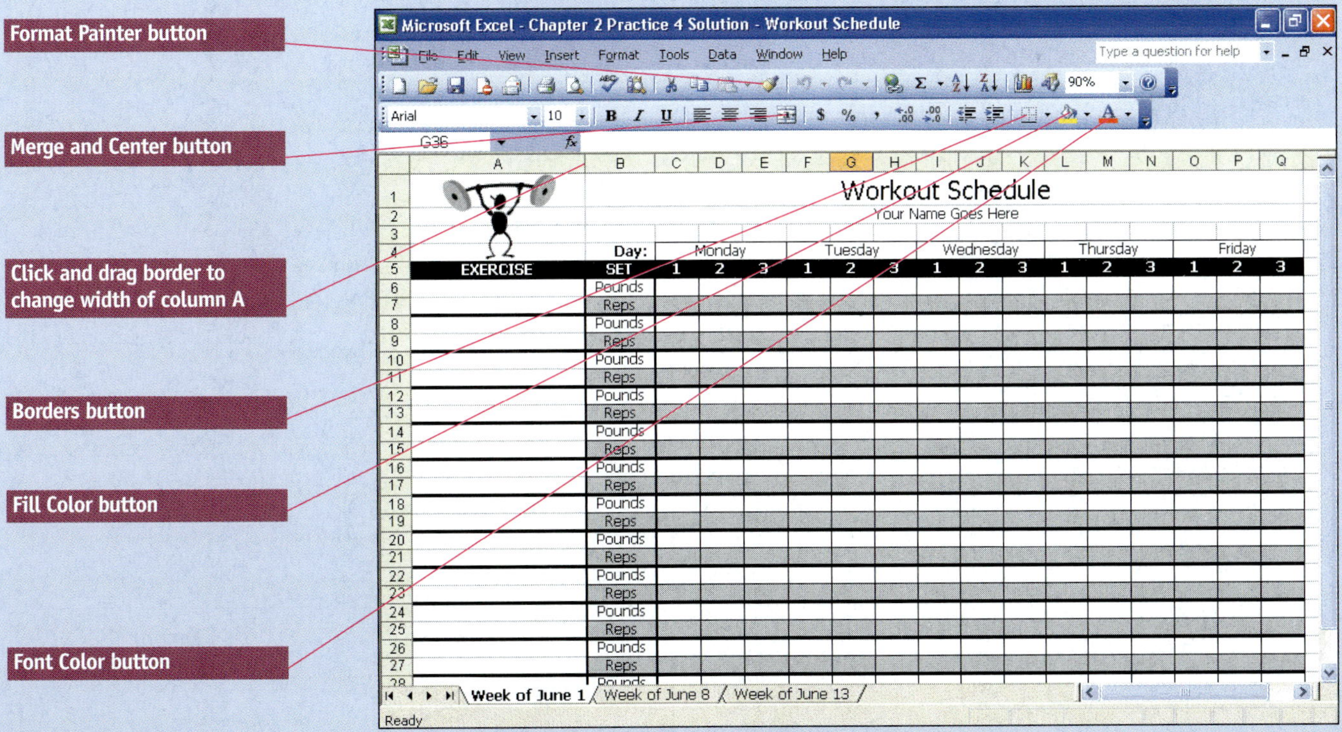

FIGURE 2.10 The Workout Schedule (exercise 4)

5. **An Exercise in Conversion:** The worksheet in Figure 2.11 displays a series of common conversion factors and the associated set of equivalent values. Open the partially completed workbook in *Chapter 2 Practice 5*, and then complete the workbook to match Figure 2.11. You do not have to match our formatting exactly, nor do you have to enter the identical values in column G.
   a. Click in cell E8 and enter the formula, =1/E7. (Cell E7 contains the value to convert inches to centimeters; the reciprocal of that value will convert centimeters to inches.) Enter the appropriate formula in cell E19 to convert kilograms to pounds.
   b. A kilobyte is mistakenly thought of as 1,000 bytes, whereas it is actually 1,024 (2^{10}) bytes. In similar fashion, a megabyte and a gigabyte are 2^{20} and 2^{30} bytes, respectively. Use this information to enter the appropriate formulas to display the conversion factors in cells E21, E22, and E23.
   c. Enter the formulas for the first conversion in row 7. Click in cell H7 and enter =C7. Click in cell J7 and enter =E7*G7. Click in cell K7 and enter =D7. Copy the formulas in row 7 to the remaining rows in the worksheet. (The use of formulas for columns H through K builds flexibility into the worksheet; that is, you can change any of the conversion factors on the left side of the worksheet, and the right side will be updated automatically.)
   d. Enter a set of values in column G for conversion; for example, enter 12 in column G7 to convert 12 inches to centimeters. The result should appear automatically in cell J7. Shade cells G7 through G23.
   e. Convert the entry in cell B3 to a hyperlink for www.onlineconversion.com.
   f. Use the Merge and Center command as necessary throughout the worksheet to approximate the formatting in Figure 2.11. Change the orientation in Column B so that the various labels are displayed as indicated.
   g. Display a border around groups of cells as shown in Figure 2.11. The easiest way to do this is to select the cells, then click the down arrow on the Borders tool on the Formatting toolbar to choose the appropriate border.
   h. Print the displayed values and the cell formulas for your instructor. Be sure to show the row and column headings as well as the gridlines. Use landscape printing to be sure the worksheet fits on a single sheet of paper.

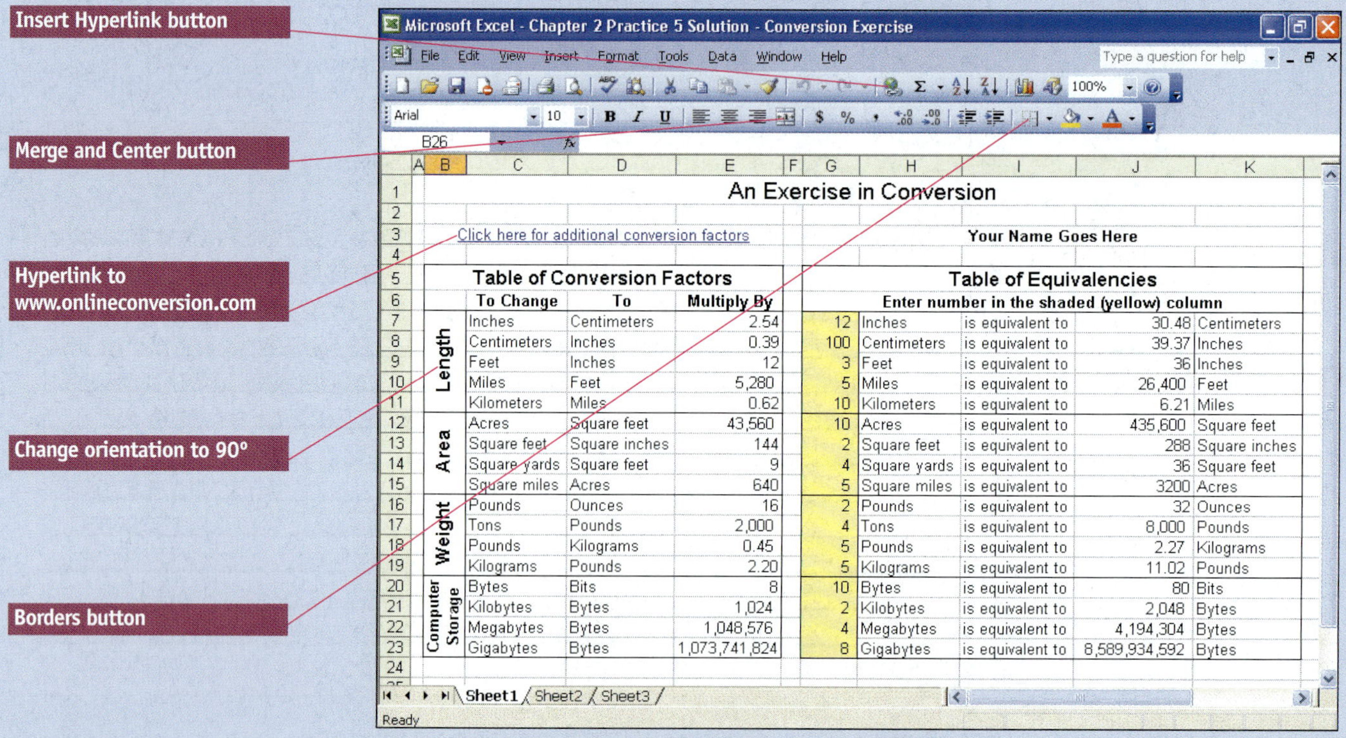

	To Change	To	Multiply By				
Length	Inches	Centimeters	2.54	12	Inches	is equivalent to	30.48 Centimeters
	Centimeters	Inches	0.39	100	Centimeters	is equivalent to	39.37 Inches
	Feet	Inches	12	3	Feet	is equivalent to	36 Inches
	Miles	Feet	5,280	5	Miles	is equivalent to	26,400 Feet
	Kilometers	Miles	0.62	10	Kilometers	is equivalent to	6.21 Miles
Area	Acres	Square feet	43,560	10	Acres	is equivalent to	435,600 Square feet
	Square feet	Square inches	144	2	Square feet	is equivalent to	288 Square inches
	Square yards	Square feet	9	4	Square yards	is equivalent to	36 Square feet
	Square miles	Acres	640	5	Square miles	is equivalent to	3200 Acres
Weight	Pounds	Ounces	16	2	Pounds	is equivalent to	32 Ounces
	Tons	Pounds	2,000	4	Tons	is equivalent to	8,000 Pounds
	Pounds	Kilograms	0.45	5	Pounds	is equivalent to	2.27 Kilograms
	Kilograms	Pounds	2.20	5	Kilograms	is equivalent to	11.02 Pounds
Computer Storage	Bytes	Bits	8	10	Bytes	is equivalent to	80 Bits
	Kilobytes	Bytes	1,024	2	Kilobytes	is equivalent to	2,048 Bytes
	Megabytes	Bytes	1,048,576	4	Megabytes	is equivalent to	4,194,304 Bytes
	Gigabytes	Bytes	1,073,741,824	8	Gigabytes	is equivalent to	8,589,934,592 Bytes

FIGURE 2.11 An Exercise in Conversion (exercise 5)

6. **Web Queries:** Microsoft Office includes a Web query to determine the exchange rates for popular currencies as can be seen in Figure 2.12. The worksheet contains formulas for two parallel sets of conversions, from British pounds to dollars, and from dollars to British pounds. Open the partially completed workbook in *Chapter 2 Practice 6,* then proceed as follows:
   a. Use the Import External Data command to enter the Web query (MS MoneyCentral Investor Currency Rates) in the worksheet, starting in cell A13. Click in cell B11 and enter the appropriate cell reference within the query (cell B24 in our example, which is not visible in Figure 2.12) to obtain the current value of the conversion factor. Use the value in cell B11 to convert the amounts in British pounds to the equivalent dollar amounts. Note that Microsoft is continually changing the content of its queries to include different currencies, so you may have to enter a different cell address.
   b. Click in cell E11 and enter the conversion factor to convert dollars to pounds. (This is the reciprocal of the value in cell B11.) Complete the entries in column E, which convert dollars to the equivalent amount in British pounds.
   c. Format the worksheet to match Figure 2.12. Be sure to use the appropriate currency symbols for dollars and pounds. Add your name and today's date as shown.
   d. Click the tab for the Euro (European Currency) worksheet and enter the formulas for the appropriate conversion from Euros to dollars and vice versa. You do not have to enter the query on this worksheet, because you can reference the values in the existing query. The entry in cell B11 of the Euro worksheet is Pounds!B34 on our worksheet (remember, the query changes continually so you may have to adjust the cell reference). Click in cell B11 of the Euro worksheet, type an equal sign to begin pointing, click the Pounds worksheet, and click in the cell containing the appropriate conversion, then click Enter to finish the formula.
   e. Format the Euro worksheet and include the European Currency Symbol as appropriate. Print both worksheets for your instructor.

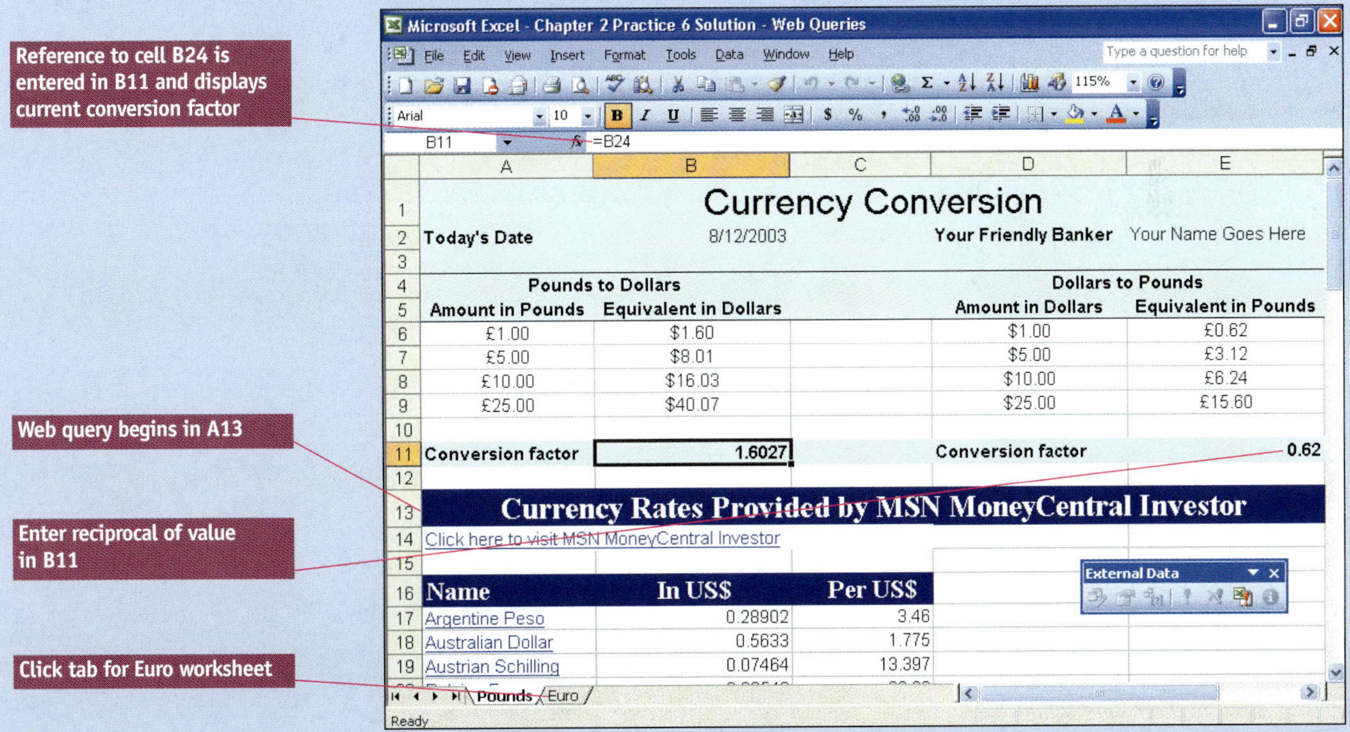

FIGURE 2.12 Web Queries (exercise 6)

7. **Buying a PC:** The worksheet in Figure 2.13 is intended to help you evaluate PC configurations from different vendors. The technical specifications for a PC are continually changing, so the minimum requirements in our worksheet may no longer be appropriate. Still, the partially completed worksheet in *Chapter 2 Practice 7* is a good starting place for your research. Open the workbook and proceed as follows:

   a. Enter the names of three vendors you would consider in cells C3, D3, and E3, respectively. Enter the associated Web sites in cells C4, D4, and E4. Visit the Web site of each vendor to determine an appropriate configuration that the vendor is currently offering. Specifications change all the time, and our minimum specifications in column B may be out of date. Thus, adjust the entries in column B as you see fit. Highlight any cell where you have modified the specification.

   b. Enter the costs associated with each system selected in part (a) in row 6. Your system will include some or all of the specifications at no additional charge. Enter the dollar amount of any item that is not included in the bundled price in the appropriate cell in the body of the worksheet.

   c. Software is probably extra. The vendor may include a basic version of the operating system; e.g., Windows XP Home edition, but there will (most likely) be a charge if you want to upgrade. The same is true for Microsoft Office; that is, you have to purchase the version of the Office suite that contains the four major applications.

   d. Enter the appropriate Sum function in cell C25. You also need to enter the shipping, sales tax, and formula for the grand total in the appropriate cells in column C. Copy the formulas for the cells in column C to the corresponding cells in columns D and E.

   e. Enter your name in cell B3 as indicated. Enter a function to determine today's date in cell B4. Insert an appropriate piece of clip art in the upper left portion of the worksheet.

   f. Format the completed worksheet. You do not have to match our formatting exactly, but you are to display dollar amounts with the currency symbol and no decimal places.

   g. Print the completed worksheet two ways, once with displayed values and once with cell formulas. Be sure the worksheet fits on one page and that you display gridlines and row and column headings.

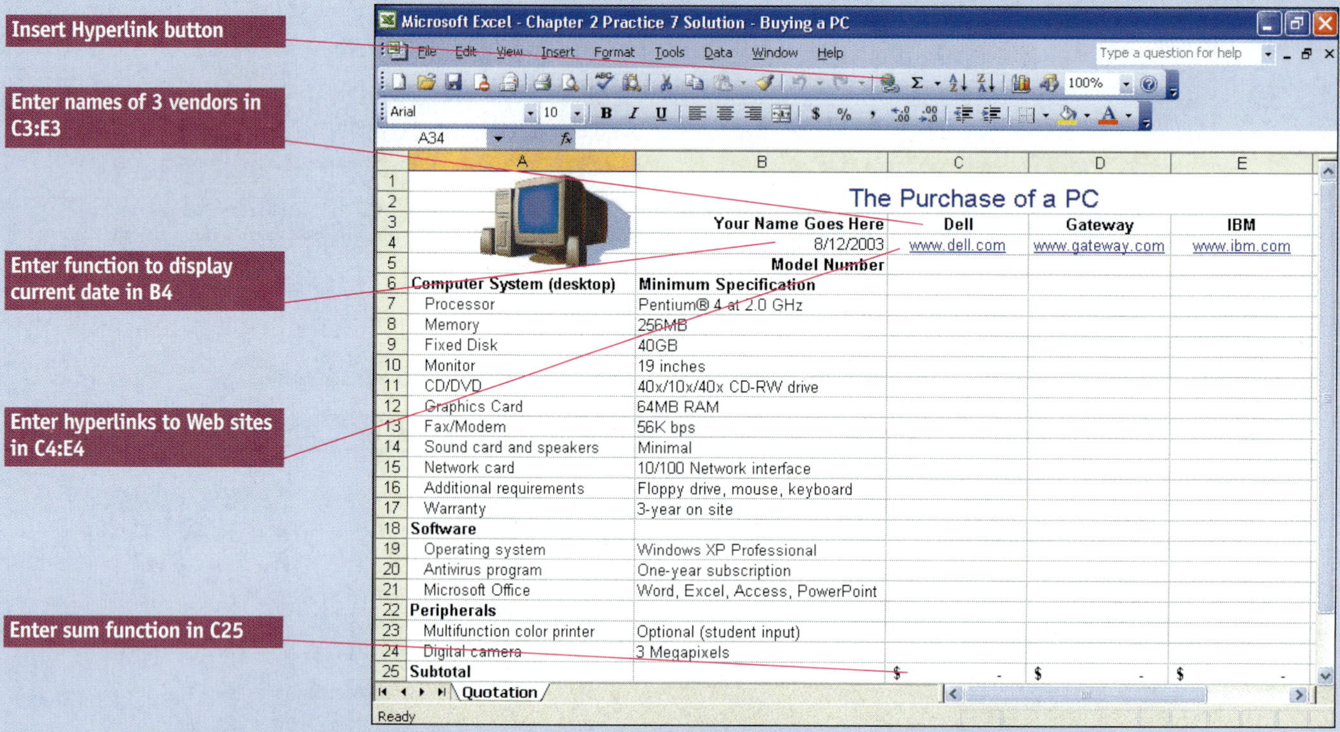

FIGURE 2.13 Buying a PC (exercise 7)

8. **Mixed References:** Most spreadsheets can be developed using a combination of relative and absolute references. Occasionally, however, you will need to incorporate mixed references as in a multiplication table. This assignment asks you to create a worksheet similar to the one in Figure 2.14. You can extend the range of the table and/or use different formatting. You are required, however, to use a formula containing mixed references in the first cell of the table (cell B4 in our figure) that can be copied to the remaining entries in this row, after which the entire row can be copied to the remaining rows in the worksheet.
    a. Enter the row and column headings in row 3 and column A, respectively. One way to create these values is through the AutoFill feature. Simply enter 1 and 2 in the first two cells for the row headings, select both of these cells, then drag the fill handle to continue the series in the remaining cells. Repeat the process to enter the column headings.
    b. The interesting part of this problem is the initial formula in the body of the worksheet (we don't want you to enter the results manually); that is, you need mixed references for the formula in cell B4. The formula is easy if you ask yourself the right questions. The product in cell B4 multiplies the value in cell A4 by the value in cell B3. Ask yourself questions to what happens to the formula when it is copied to the remaining rows and columns in the worksheet. Will the first number always come from column A? (Yes.) Will it always come from row 4? (No.) Will the second number always come from column B? (No.) Will it always come from row 3? (Yes.) The answers tell you how to create the mixed references.
    c. Copy the formula in cell B4 to the remaining columns in this row. Now copy row 4 to the remaining rows in the worksheet. Verify that the worksheet is correct by checking the displayed value at the bottom right of the table (144 in our example.)
    d. Add your name to the worksheet and submit it to your instructor. Remember, this worksheet is for a young person, so formatting is important. Print the cell formulas as well so that you can see how the mixed reference changes throughout the worksheet. Submit the complete assignment to your instructor. Using mixed references correctly is challenging, but once you arrive at the correct solution, you will have learned a lot about this very powerful spreadsheet feature.

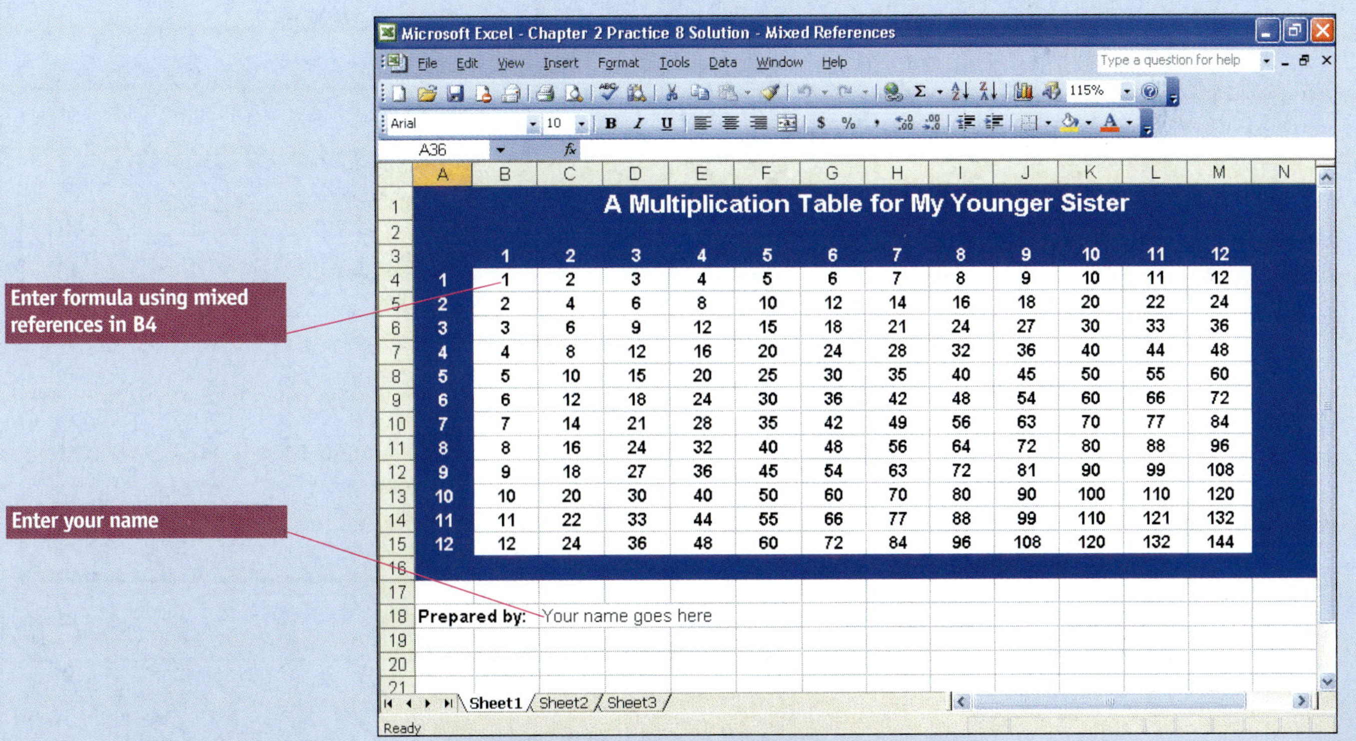

FIGURE 2.14 Mixed References (exercise 8)

9. **Create a New Web Query:** You can create a new Web query to obtain data from almost any site and then use that data as the basis of calculations within an Excel workbook. Use Internet Explorer to locate a Web site containing data you wish to import before you start Excel, then proceed as follows:
   a. Start a new workbook, pull down the Data menu, click the Import External Data command, and then click New Web query to display New Web Query dialog box as shown in Figure 2.15. Enter the address of the site containing the data. We chose the National Basketball Association at http://www. nba.com/statistics.
   b. Click the Go button to display the site that you selected. The site must contain one or more yellow arrows to indicate that data from the site can be imported via a Web query. Click the arrow next to the table you want to import; in our example this is the 2002–2003 regular season leaders in the NBA. The arrow changes to a green check to indicate the data has been selected.
   c. Click the Import button, and then click OK. The data should appear in your worksheet (in similar fashion to the stock query that was developed in the chapter). Continue to develop the worksheet using formulas that reference the data that was imported by the query.
   d. Print the worksheet containing the query for your instructor to show you completed the exercise. Save the workbook. Exit Excel.
   e. Open your workbook the next day, click anywhere within the Web query on the worksheet, then click the Refresh External Button on the External Data toolbar. The data in the query should be updated automatically. Print the worksheet containing the new values for your instructor.
   f. Add a cover sheet then submit both worksheets to your instructor. Were you successful immediately; i.e., did your initial site permit you to create a Web query, or did you have to search multiple sites? Were you able to build a useful worksheet from the query that you created?

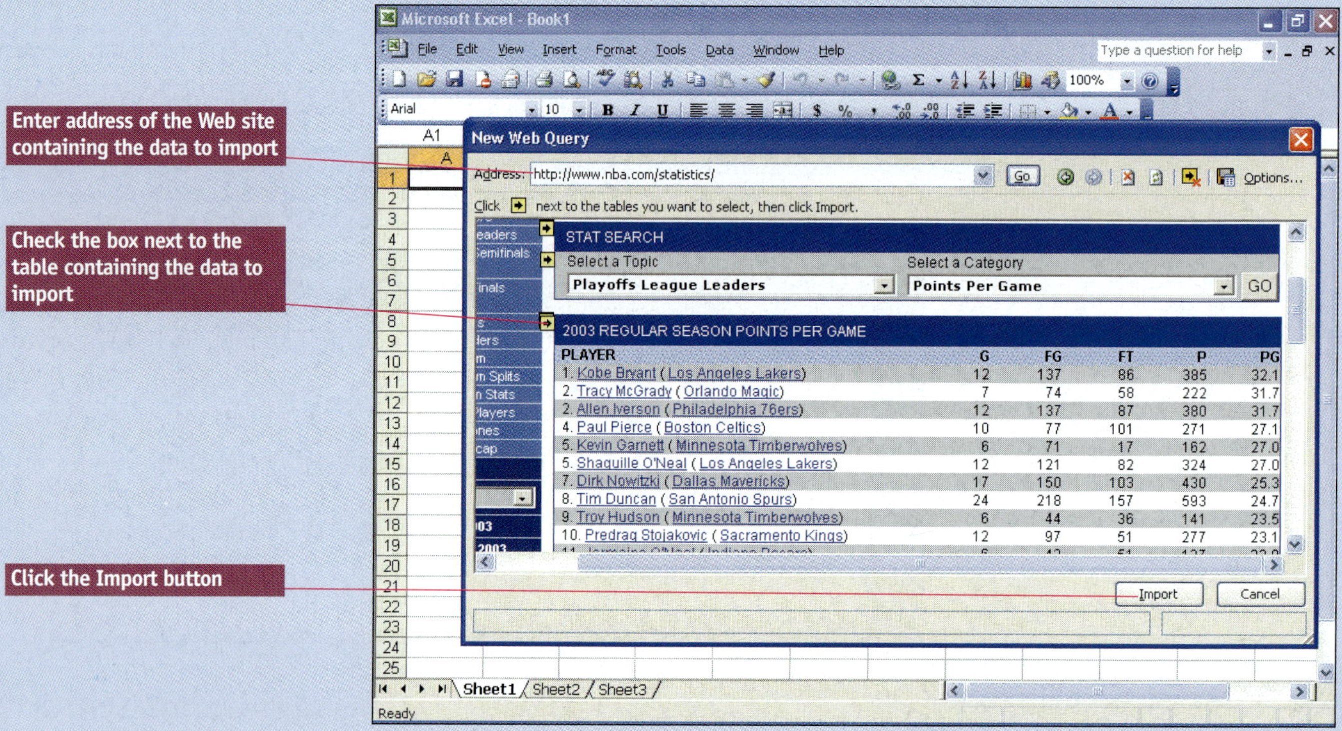

FIGURE 2.15 Create a New Web Query (exercise 9)

10. **Financial Forecast:** Financial planning and budgeting is one of the most common business applications of spreadsheets. Figure 2.16 depicts one such illustration, in which the income and expenses of Get Rich Quick Enterprises are projected over a six-year period. You don't have to be a business major to do the assignment. You do, however, need to follow a logical approach to develop the worksheet. We have entered the text in column A and the assumptions in the bottom of the partially completed workbook, *Chapter 2 Practice 10,* in the Exploring Excel folder. Open the workbook and proceed as follows.

    a. Develop the formulas for the first year of the forecast based on the initial conditions at the bottom of the spreadsheet. The projected income for the first year of the forecast (cell B7) is $225,000, based on sales of 75,000 units at a price of $3.00 per unit. The overhead (fixed costs) consists of the production facility at $50,000 and administrative expenses of $25,000. The variable costs for the same year are broken down into manufacturing of $75,000 (75,000 units at $1.00 per unit) and sales of $15,000 (75,000 units at $.20 per unit). Subtracting the total expenses from the estimated income yields a net income before taxes of $75,000. The income tax is subtracted from this amount, leaving net earnings of $38,400 in the first year.

    b. Develop the formulas for the second year, based on the values in year 1 and the assumed rates of increase at the bottom of the worksheet. Use an appropriate combination of relative and absolute references so that these formulas can be copied to the remaining columns in the worksheet. We suggest you use pointing to enter the formulas in column C.

    c. Copy the formulas for year 2 (in column C) to the remaining years of the forecast (columns D through G). Check that your worksheet is correct by comparing the displayed values to Figure 2.16.

    d. Format the completed worksheet. You do not have to match our formatting exactly, but you are to display dollar amounts with the currency symbol and appropriate decimal places.

    e. Add your name somewhere in the worksheet. Print the completed worksheet two ways, once with displayed values and once with cell formulas. Use landscape printing and force the worksheet to one page. Display gridlines and row and column headings.

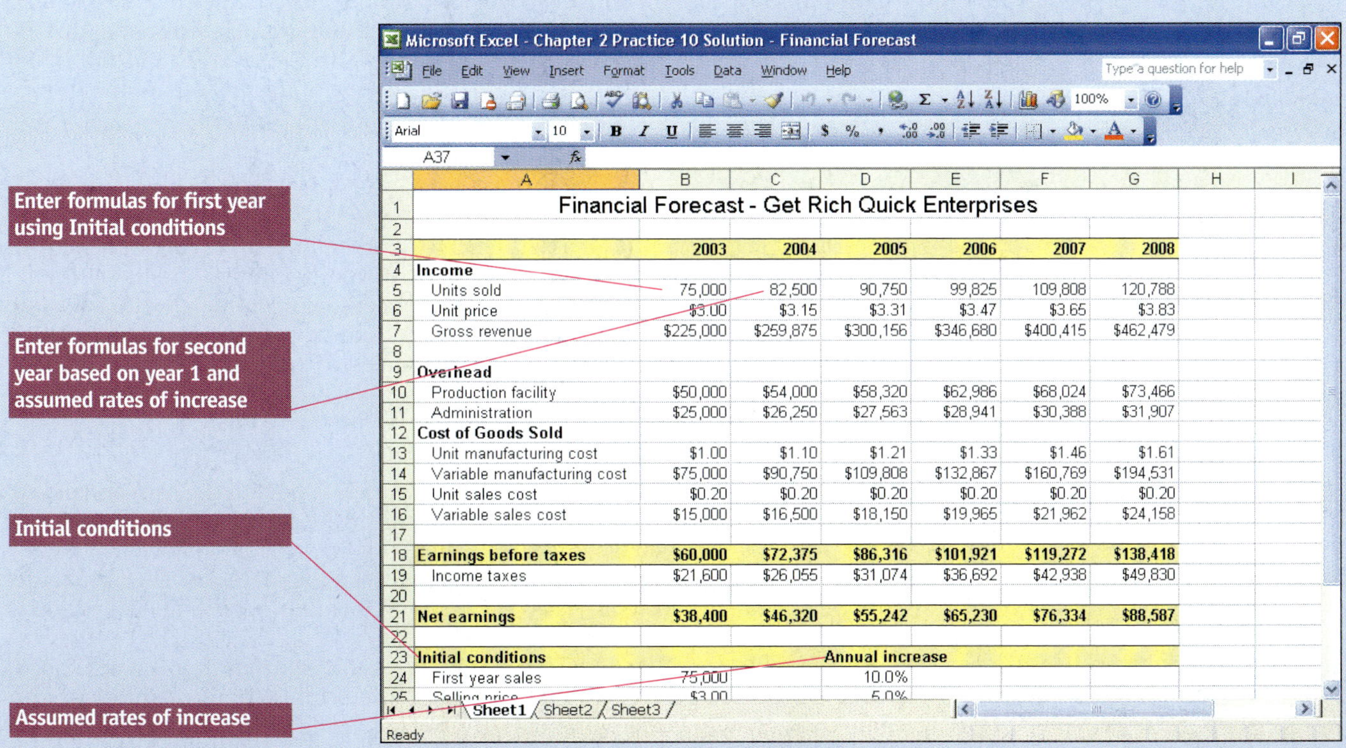

	A	B	C	D	E	F	G
1	Financial Forecast - Get Rich Quick Enterprises						
2							
3		2003	2004	2005	2006	2007	2008
4	**Income**						
5	Units sold	75,000	82,500	90,750	99,825	109,808	120,788
6	Unit price	$3.00	$3.15	$3.31	$3.47	$3.65	$3.83
7	Gross revenue	$225,000	$259,875	$300,156	$346,680	$400,415	$462,479
8							
9	**Overhead**						
10	Production facility	$50,000	$54,000	$58,320	$62,986	$68,024	$73,466
11	Administration	$25,000	$26,250	$27,563	$28,941	$30,388	$31,907
12	**Cost of Goods Sold**						
13	Unit manufacturing cost	$1.00	$1.10	$1.21	$1.33	$1.46	$1.61
14	Variable manufacturing cost	$75,000	$90,750	$109,808	$132,867	$160,769	$194,531
15	Unit sales cost	$0.20	$0.20	$0.20	$0.20	$0.20	$0.20
16	Variable sales cost	$15,000	$16,500	$18,150	$19,965	$21,962	$24,158
17							
18	**Earnings before taxes**	**$60,000**	**$72,375**	**$86,316**	**$101,921**	**$119,272**	**$138,418**
19	Income taxes	$21,600	$26,055	$31,074	$36,692	$42,938	$49,830
20							
21	**Net earnings**	**$38,400**	**$46,320**	**$55,242**	**$65,230**	**$76,334**	**$88,587**
22							
23	**Initial conditions**			**Annual increase**			
24	First year sales	75,000		10.0%			
25	Selling price	$3.00		5.0%			

FIGURE 2.16 Financial Forecast (exercise 10)

MINI CASES

Accounting 101—Straight Line Depreciation

Every asset depreciates (loses value) over time. It's similar to the value of your car, which loses value with every mile you drive. The straight line method of depreciation assumes that an asset depreciates at a uniform rate over its projected life. The amount of value that the asset loses each year is the depreciation expense for that year. To determine the depreciation amount for each year, take the cost of the asset, subtract its residual (salvage) value, and then divide the result by the number of years the asset will be used. Assume, for example, that an asset cost $25,000 new, that it will last for 8 years, at the end of which time it will have a $5,000 salvage value. The annual depreciation expense for this asset is ($25,000–$5,000)/8 or $2,500.

Your assignment is to open the *Chapter 2 Mini Case—Accounting 101* workbook in the Exploring Excel folder in order to enter the necessary formulas to compute the annual depreciation expense. You also have to determine the accumulated deprecation for each year (the sum of all depreciation taken so far, including the current year) as well as the value of the asset (its cost minus the accumulated depreciation). Add your name to the worksheet, enter today's date and the appropriate formatting, then print the worksheet twice, once with displayed values, and once to show the cell formulas.

Wishful Thinking CD Portfolio

It must be nice to have a portfolio of CDs (Certificates of Deposit) where all you do is collect the interest. Your assignment is to open the *Chapter 2 Mini Case—Wishful Thinking CD Portfolio* workbook to determine the total interest earned by the portfolio. The formulas should be straightforward. The maturity date is computed by adding the term (converted to days) to the purchase date. Determine the days until maturity by subtracting today's date from the maturity date. The annual income is determined by multiplying the amount of the CD times its interest rate. The estimated tax is found by multiplying the annual income by the tax rate. The net income is the annual income minus the estimated tax. If you do the exercise correctly, the net income should be almost $18,000.

Format the completed worksheet in an attractive fashion. Add your name in cell A19. Print the worksheet twice, once with displayed values, and once to show the cell formulas. You might also do a little research on the Web to see what the current interest rates on CDs of varying term are. What is the FDIC? Is the investment in a CD insured to its full value? Add a cover sheet, then submit all three pages, together with the answers to the discussion questions, to your instructor as proof you completed this exercise.

Your Net Worth

Your net worth is the sum of all your assets (such as cash, mutual funds, the value of your home and furniture, and so on) minus the sum of all your liabilities (credit card debt, home mortgages, taxes, etc.) Create a simple worksheet that could be used to calculate your net worth, and then complete the worksheet by adding hypothetical data. *Wishful thinking is encouraged.* Submit the completed worksheet to your instructor.

The Birthday Problem

How much would you bet *against* two people in your class having the same birthday? Don't be too hasty, for the odds of two classmates sharing the same birthday (month and day) are much higher than you would expect: There is a fifty percent chance (.5063) in a class of 23 students that two people will have been born on the same day. The probability jumps to seventy percent (.7053) in a class of thirty, and to ninety percent (.9025) in a class of forty-one.

Open the partially completed *Chapter 2 Mini Case—The Birthday Problem* workbook, which contains the basic formula you will need to determine the probabilities. Your assignment is to complete the workbook by copying the formulas we provide to the remaining rows in the worksheet. Print the completed worksheet for your instructor, and then see whether the probabilities hold in your class.

CHAPTER 3

Graphs and Charts: Delivering a Message

OBJECTIVES

After reading this chapter you will:

1. Describe how a chart can be used to deliver a message.
2. List several types of charts and describe the purpose of each.
3. Distinguish between an embedded chart versus a chart in its own chart sheet.
4. Use the Chart Wizard to create and modify a chart.
5. Use the Drawing toolbar to enhance a chart by adding lines and objects.
6. Distinguish between data series in rows versus columns.
7. Differentiate between a stacked-column chart versus a side-by-side column chart.
8. Create a Word document that is linked to a worksheet and an associated chart.

hands-on exercises

1. THE CHART WIZARD
   Input: Software Sales
   Output: Software Sales Solution
2. MULTIPLE DATA SERIES
   Input: Software Sales Solution (from first exercise)
   Output: Software Sales Solution (additional modifications)
3. OBJECT LINKING AND EMBEDDING
   Input: Software Sales Solution (from second exercise)
   Output: Software Sales Solution (additional modifications); Software Memo Solution (Word document)

CASE STUDY

TAX CUTS AND DINNER

What if people split a dinner check using the principles of the progressive income tax that is central to our tax code? Five lifelong friends of various means meet once a week for dinner and split the $100 check according to their ability to pay. Tom, Dick, and Harry are of relatively modest means and pay $1, $4, and $9, respectively. Ben and Ken are far more prosperous and pay $18 and $68, respectively.

The friends were quite satisfied with the arrangement until the owner offered a rebate. "You are excellent customers, and I will reduce the cost of your meal by $15." The question became how to divide the $15 windfall in order to give everyone his fair share? The proprietor suggested that they allocate the savings according to the amount each contributed to the original check. He made a quick calculation, and then rounded each person's share to an integer; e.g., Tom's new bill should have been 85 cents, but it was decided he would eat for free. In similar fashion, Dick now owes $3, Harry $7, Ben $15, and Ken $60. (Ken, the most prosperous individual, made up the difference with respect to the cents that were dropped.) The new total is $85 and everyone saves money.

Once outside the restaurant the friends began to compare their savings. Tom and Dick each complained that they saved only $1. Harry grumbled that he saved only $2. Ben thought it unfair that Ken saved more than the other four friends combined. Everyone continued to pick on Ken. The next week Ken felt so uncomfortable that he did not show up, so his former friends ate without him. But when the bill came they were $60 short. ■

Your assignment is to create a simple worksheet and associated set of charts that shows the amounts the friends pay before and after the rebate. The numbers in the case are not contrived; that is, they represent the proportion of income taxes that are paid by five different income groups. The 20% of families that represent the lowest income group pay approximately 1% of the total tax bill. The second 20% pays 4%, the third 20% pays 9%, the fourth 20% pays 18%, and the upper 20% pays 68%. This example was inspired by an anonymous e-mail message.

CHART TYPES

Business has always known that the graphic representation of data is an attractive, easy-to-understand way to convey information. Indeed, business graphics has become one of the most exciting Windows applications, whereby charts (graphs) are easily created from a worksheet, with just a few simple keystrokes or mouse clicks.

The chapter begins by emphasizing the importance of determining the message to be conveyed by a chart. It describes the different types of charts available within Excel and how to choose among them. It explains how to create a chart using the Chart Wizard, how to embed a chart within a worksheet, and how to create a chart in a separate chart sheet. It also describes how to use the Drawing toolbar to enhance a chart by creating lines, objects, and 3-D shapes.

The second half of the chapter explains how one chart can plot multiple sets of data, and how several charts can be based on the same worksheet. It also describes how to create a compound document, in which a chart and its associated worksheet are dynamically linked to a memo created by a word processor. All told, we think you will find this to be one of the most enjoyable chapters in the text.

A ***chart*** is a graphic representation of data in a worksheet. The chart is based on descriptive entries called ***category labels***, and on numeric values called ***data points***. The data points are grouped into one or more ***data series*** that appear in row(s) or column(s) on the worksheet. In every chart there is exactly one data point in each data series for each value of the category label.

The worksheet in Figure 3.1 will be used throughout the chapter as the basis for the charts we will create. Your manager believes that the sales data can be understood more easily from charts than from the strict numerical presentation of a worksheet. You have been given the assignment of analyzing the data in the worksheet and are developing a series of charts to convey that information.

The sales data in the worksheet can be presented several ways—for example, by city, by product, or by a combination of the two. Ask yourself which type of chart is best suited to answer the following questions:

- What percentage of the total revenue comes from each city? What percentage comes from each product?
- What is the dollar revenue produced by each city? What is the revenue produced by each product?
- What is the rank of each city with respect to sales?
- How much revenue does each product contribute in each city?

In every instance, realize that a chart exists only to deliver a message, and that *you cannot create an effective chart unless you are sure of what that message is.* The next several pages discuss various types of business charts, each of which is best suited to a particular type of message. After you understand how charts are used conceptually, we will create various charts in Excel.

	A	B	C	D	E	F
1	**Superior Software Sales**					
2						
3		**Miami**	**Denver**	**New York**	**Boston**	**Total**
4	**Word Processing**	$50,000	$67,500	$9,500	$141,000	**$268,000**
5	**Spreadsheets**	$44,000	$18,000	$11,500	$105,000	**$178,500**
6	**Database**	$12,000	$7,500	$6,000	$30,000	**$55,500**
7	**Total**	**$106,000**	**$93,000**	**$27,000**	**$276,000**	**$502,000**

FIGURE 3.1 Superior Software

Pie Charts

A ***pie chart*** is the most effective way to display proportional relationships. It is the type of chart to select whenever words like *percentage* or *market share* appear in the message to be delivered. The pie, or complete circle, denotes the total amount. Each slice of the pie corresponds to its respective percentage of the total.

The pie chart in Figure 3.2a divides the pie representing total sales into four slices, one for each city. The size of each slice is proportional to the percentage of total sales in that city. The chart depicts a single data series, which appears in cells B7 through E7 on the associated worksheet. The data series has four data points corresponding to the total sales in each city.

To create the pie chart, Excel computes the total sales ($502,000 in our example), calculates the percentage contributed by each city, and draws each slice of the pie in proportion to its computed percentage. Boston's sales of $276,000 account for 55 percent of the total, and so this slice of the pie is allotted 55 percent of the area of the circle.

An ***exploded pie chart***, as shown in Figure 3.2b, separates one or more slices of the pie for emphasis. Another way to achieve emphasis in a chart is to choose a title that reflects the message you are trying to deliver. The title in Figure 3.2a, for example, *Revenue by Geographic Area*, is neutral and leaves the reader to develop his or her own conclusion about the relative contribution of each area. By contrast, the title in Figure 3.2b, *New York Accounts for Only 5% of Revenue,* is more suggestive and emphasizes the problems in this office. Alternatively, the title could be changed to *Boston Exceeds 50% of Total Revenue* if the intent were to emphasize the contribution of Boston.

Three-dimensional pie charts may be created in exploded or nonexploded format as shown in Figures 3.2c and 3.2d, respectively. Excel also enables you to add arrows and text for emphasis.

Title is neutral

Size of slice is proportional to percentage of total sales from Boston

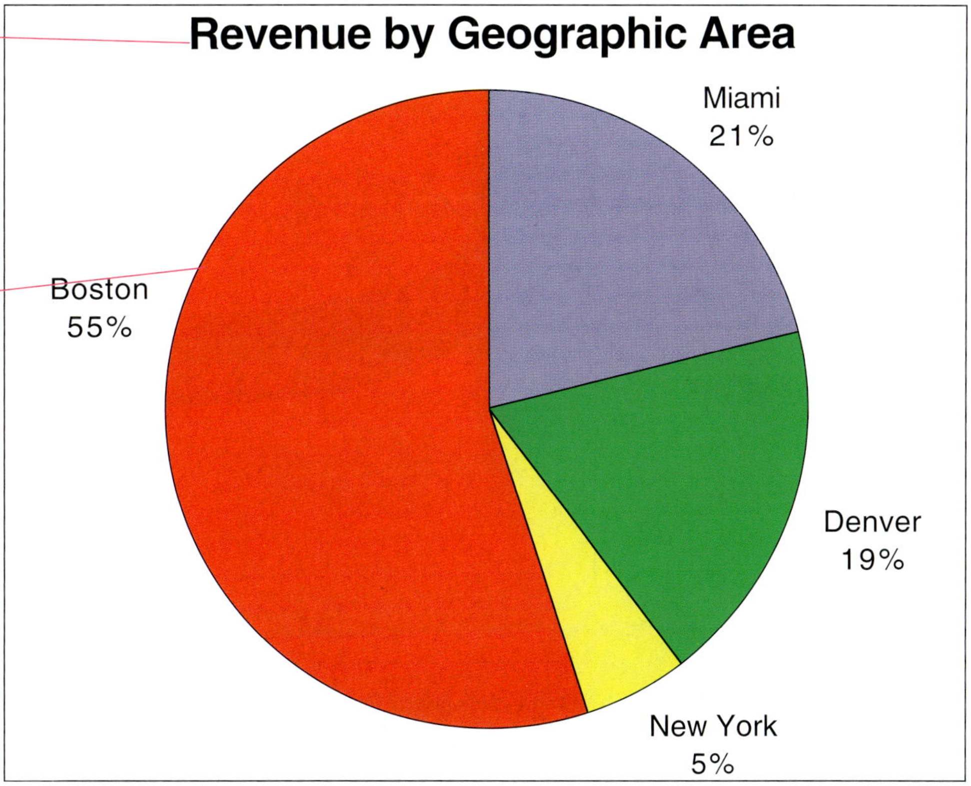

(a) Simple Pie Chart

FIGURE 3.2 Pie Charts

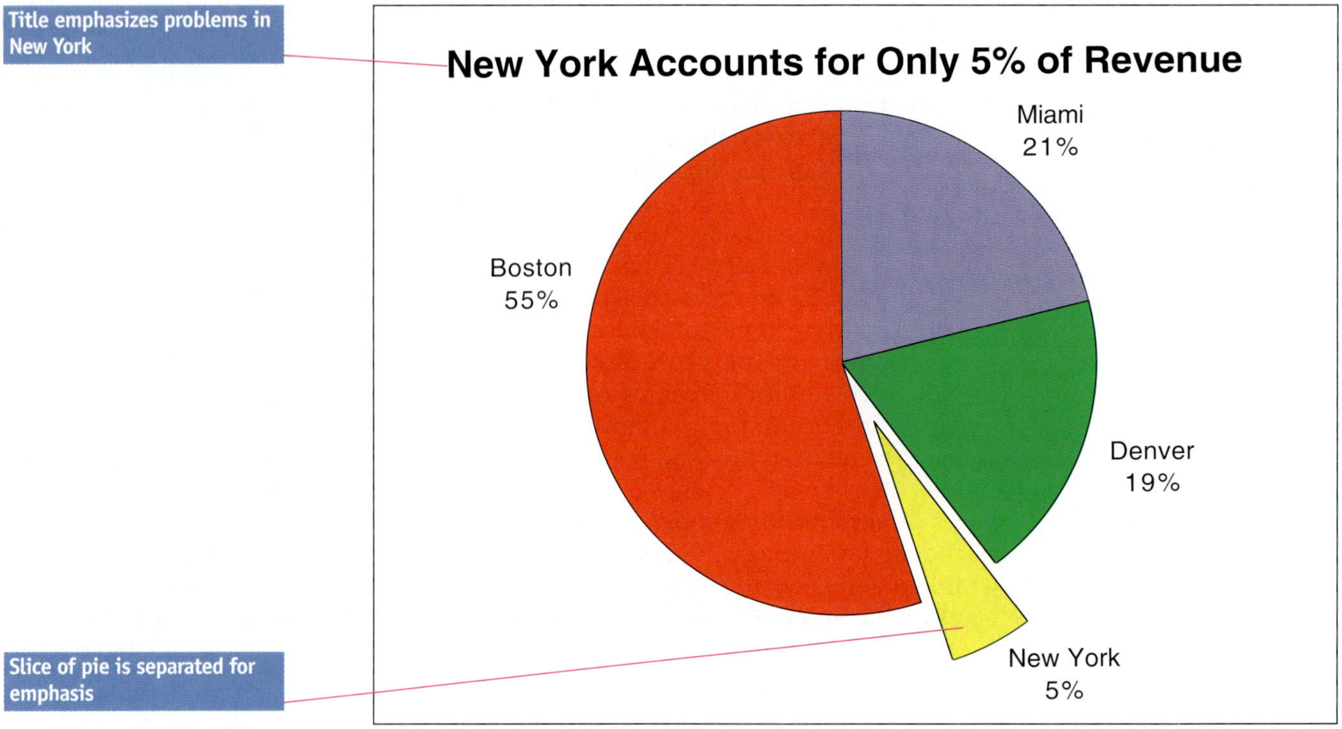

(b) Exploded Pie Chart

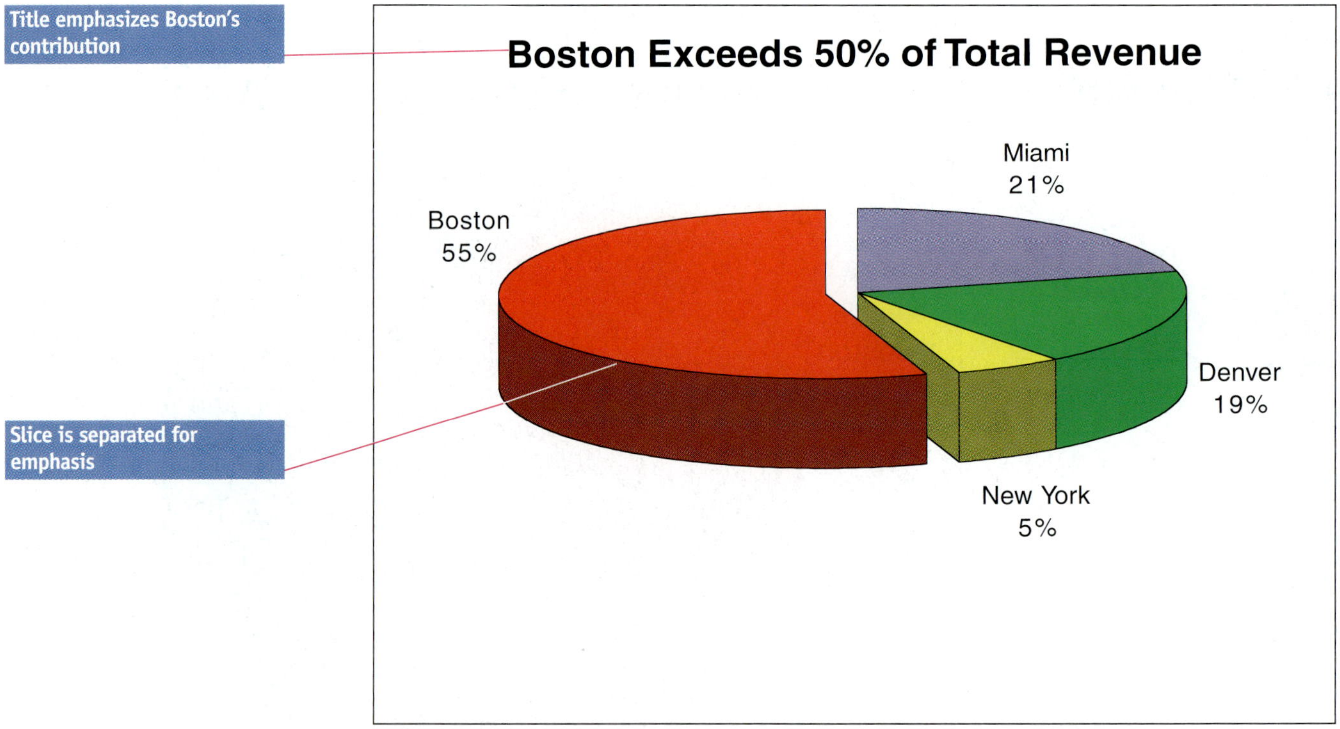

(c) Three-dimensional Pie Chart

FIGURE 3.2 Pie Charts (*continued*)

Title emphasizes Boston's contribution

Arrows and text added for emphasis

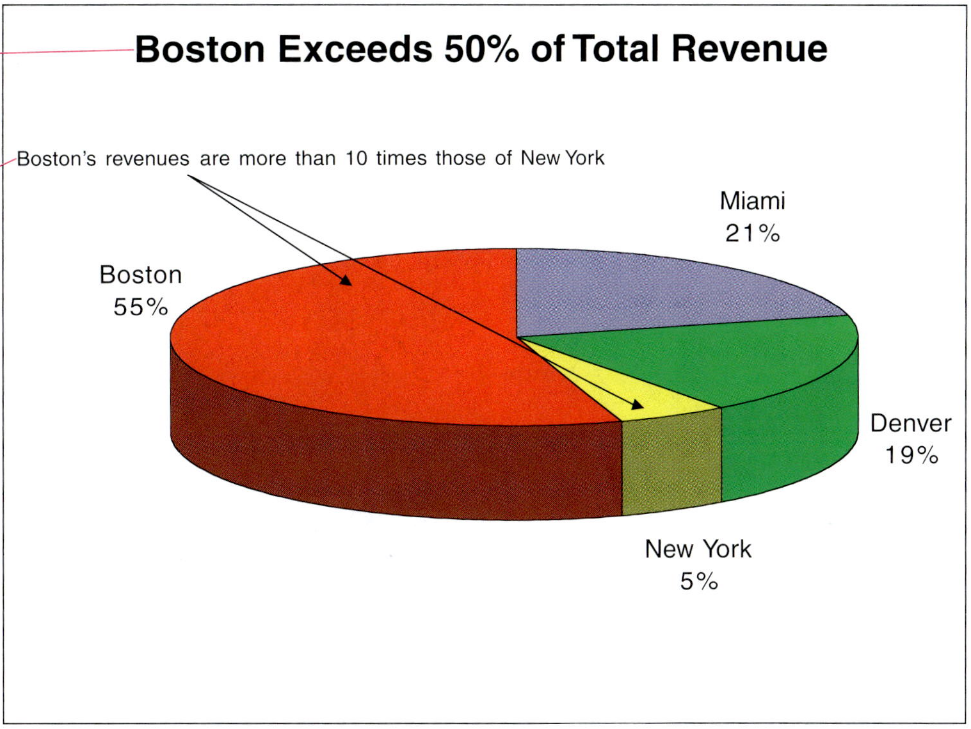

(d) Enhanced Pie Chart

FIGURE 3.2 Pie Charts (*continued*)

A pie chart is easiest to read when the number of slices is limited (i.e., not more than six or seven), and when small categories (percentages less than five) are grouped into a single category called "Other."

Column and Bar Charts

A ***column chart*** is used when there is a need to show actual numbers rather than percentages. The column chart in Figure 3.3a plots the same data series as the earlier pie chart, but displays it differently. The category labels (Miami, Denver, New York, and Boston) are shown along the ***X*** (horizontal) ***axis***. The data points (monthly sales) are plotted along the ***Y*** (vertical) ***axis***, with the height of each column reflecting the value of the data point.

A column chart can be given a horizontal orientation and converted to a ***bar chart*** as in Figure 3.3b. Some individuals prefer the bar chart over the corresponding column chart because the longer horizontal bars accentuate the difference between the items. Bar charts are also preferable when the descriptive labels are long, to eliminate the crowding that can occur along the horizontal axis of a column chart. As with the pie chart, a title can lead the reader and further emphasize the message, as with *Boston Leads All Cities* in Figure 3.3b.

KEEP IT SIMPLE

Keep it simple. This rule applies to both your message and the means of conveying that message. Excel makes it almost too easy to change fonts, styles, the shape of columns, type sizes, and colors, but such changes will often detract from, rather than enhance, a chart. More is not necessarily better, and you do not have to use a feature just because it is there. Remember that a chart must ultimately succeed on the basis of content, and content alone.

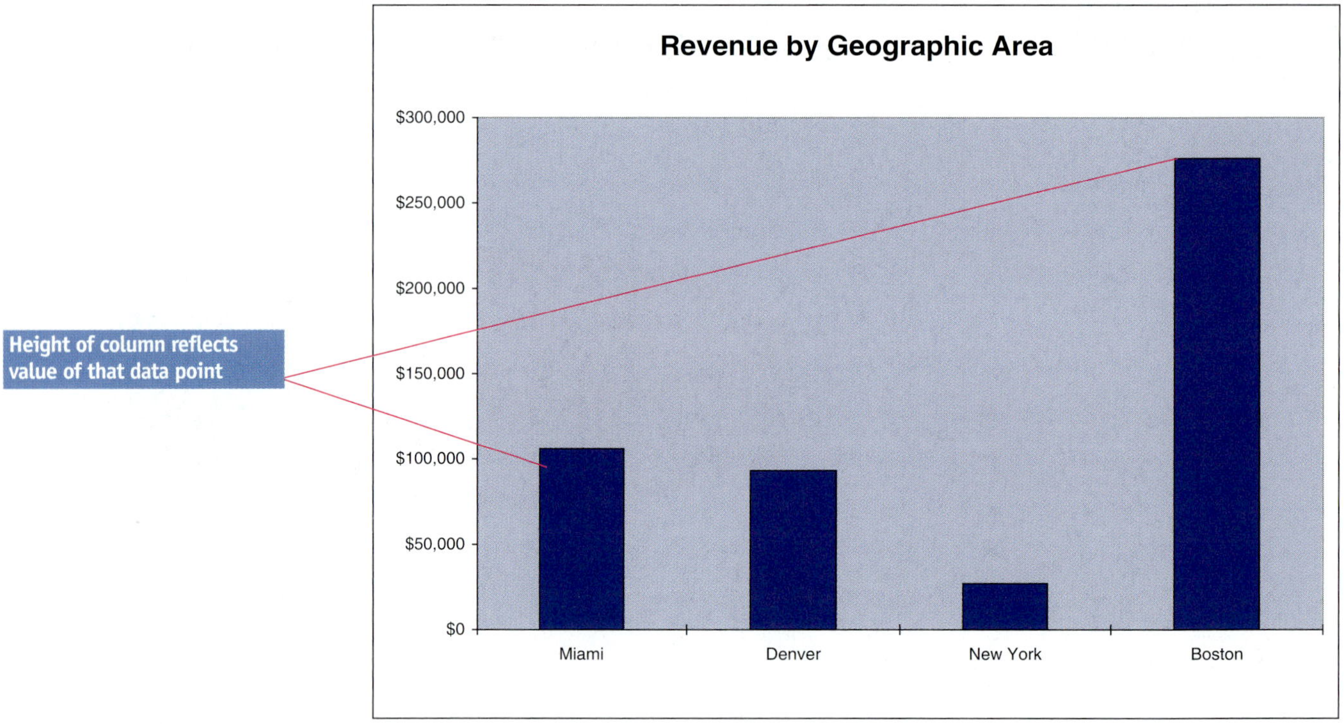

(a) Column Chart

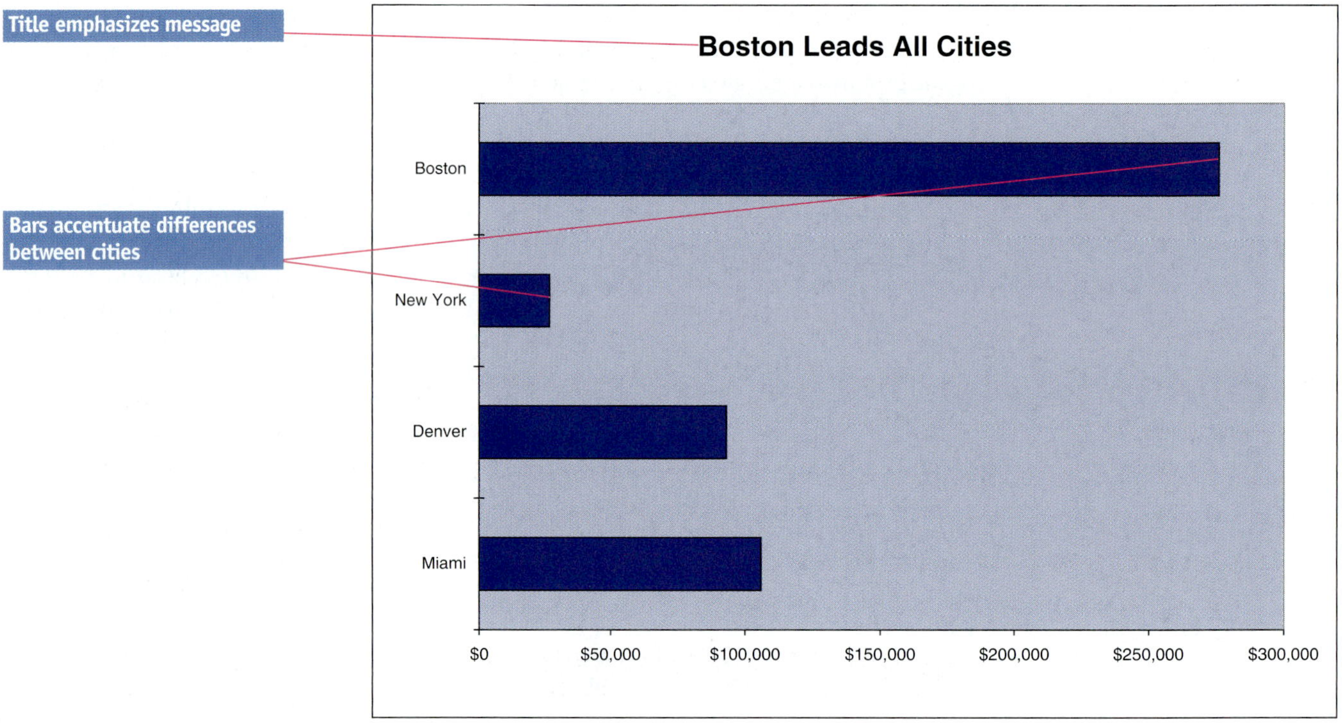

(b) Horizontal Bar Chart

FIGURE 3.3 Column/Bar Charts

3-D effect adds interest

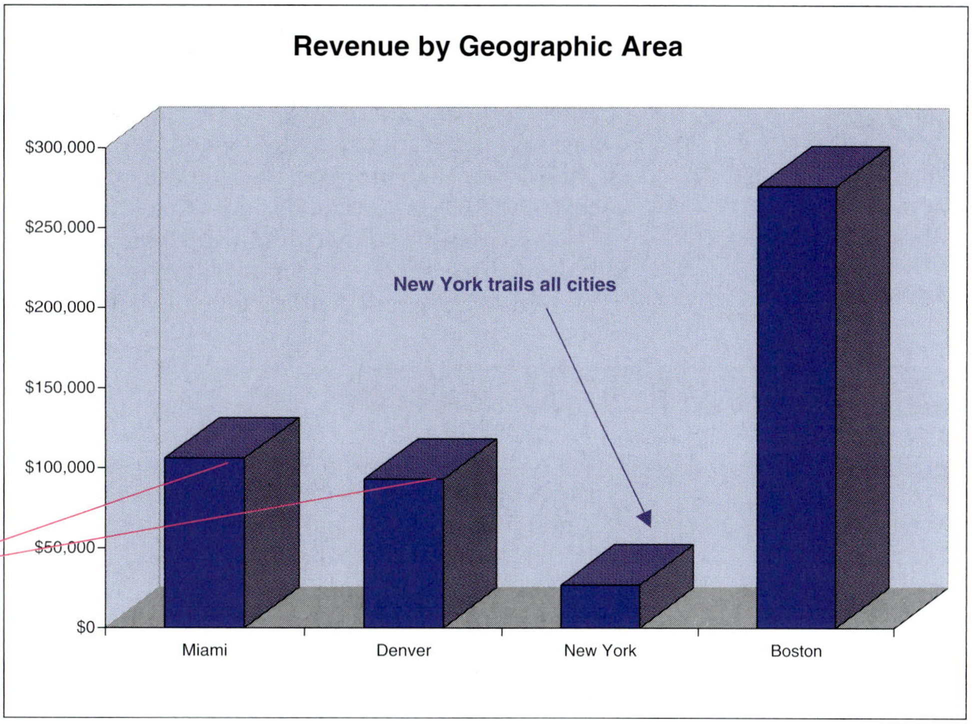

(c) Three-dimensional Column Chart

Applications are shown on *X* axis, rather than cities

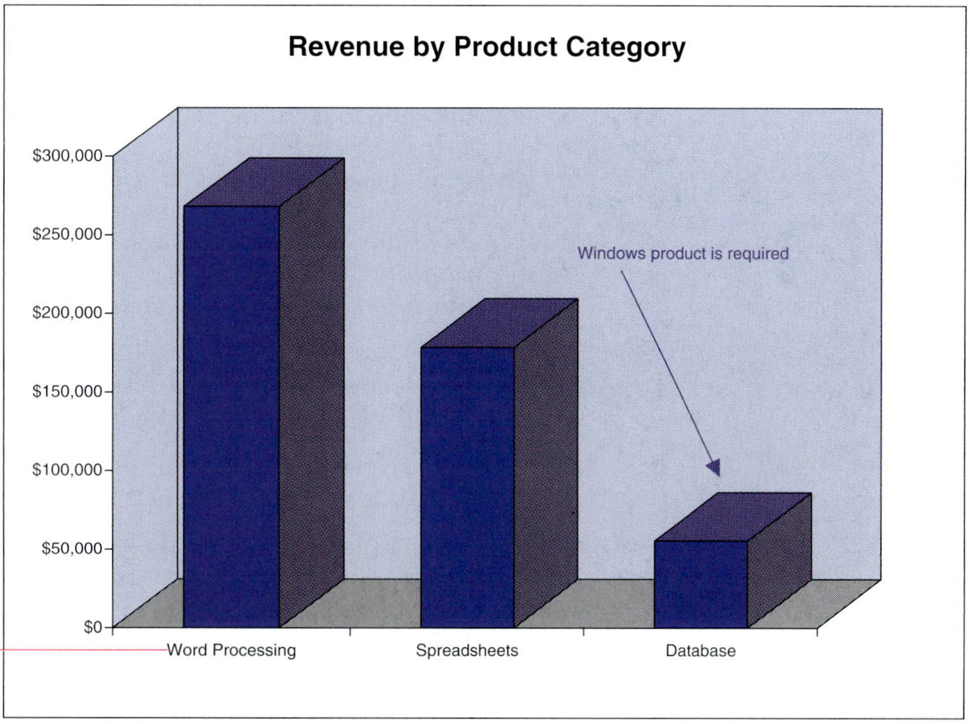

(d) Alternate Column Chart

FIGURE 3.3 Column/Bar Charts (*continued*)

The special effect of a ***three-dimensional column chart*** can produce added interest as shown in Figures 3.3c and 3.3d. Figure 3.3d plots a different set of numbers than we have seen so far (the sales for each product, rather than the sales for each city). The choice between the charts in Figures 3.3c and 3.3d depends on the message you want to convey—whether you want to emphasize the contribution of each city or each product. The title can be used to emphasize the message. Arrows, text, and 3-D shapes can be added to either chart to enhance the message.

As with a pie chart, column and bar charts are easiest to read when the number of categories is relatively small (seven or fewer). Otherwise, the columns (bars) are plotted so close together that labeling becomes impossible.

CREATING A CHART

There are two ways to create a chart in Excel. You can *embed* the chart in a worksheet, or you can create the chart in a separate ***chart sheet***. Figure 3.4a displays an embedded column chart. Figure 3.4b shows a pie chart in its own chart sheet. Both techniques are valid. The choice between the two depends on your personal preference.

Regardless of where it is kept (embedded in a worksheet or in its own chart sheet), a chart is linked to the worksheet on which it is based. The charts in Figure 3.4 plot the same data series (the total sales for each city). Change any of these data points on the worksheet, and both charts will be updated automatically to reflect the new data.

Both charts are part of the same workbook (Software Sales) as indicated in the title bar of each figure. The tabs within the workbook have been renamed to indicate the contents of the associated sheet. Additional charts may be created and embedded in the worksheet and/or placed on their own chart sheets. And, as previously stated, if you change the worksheet, the chart (or charts) based upon it will also change.

Study the column chart in Figure 3.4a to see how it corresponds to the worksheet on which it is based. The descriptive names on the *X* axis are known as category labels and match the entries in cells B3 through E3. The quantitative values (data points) are plotted on the *Y* axis and match the total sales in cells B7 through E7. Even the numeric format matches; that is, the currency format used in the worksheet appears automatically on the scale of the *Y* axis.

The ***sizing handles*** on the ***embedded chart*** indicate it is currently selected and can be sized, moved, or deleted the same way as any other Windows object:

- To size the selected chart, point to a sizing handle (the mouse pointer changes to a double arrow), then drag the handle in the desired direction.
- To move the selected chart, point to the chart (the mouse pointer is a single arrow), then drag the chart to its new location.
- To copy the selected chart, click the Copy button to copy the chart to the clipboard, click in the workbook where you want the copied chart to go, then click the Paste button to paste the chart at that location.
- To delete the selected chart, press the Del key.

The same operations apply to any of the objects within the chart (such as its title), as will be discussed in the next section on enhancing a chart. Note, too, that both figures contain the chart toolbar that enables you to modify a chart after it has been created.

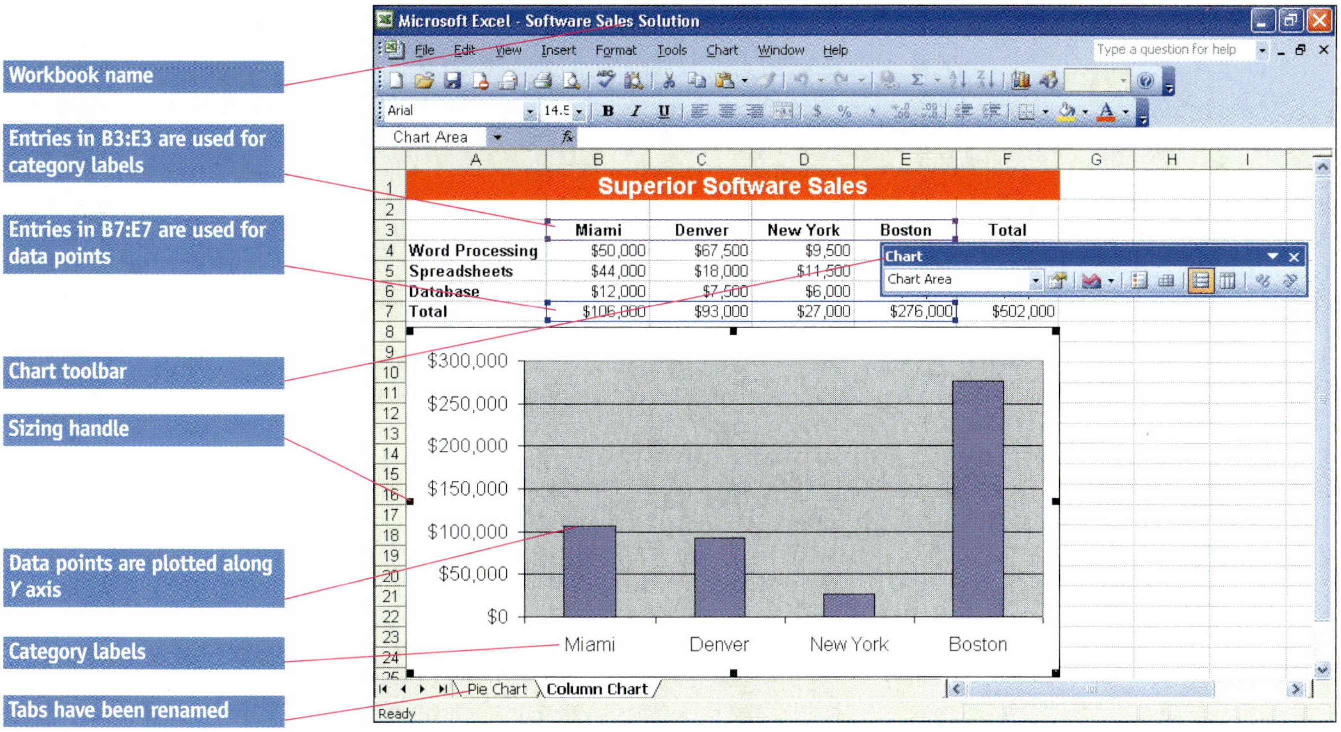

(a) Embedded Chart

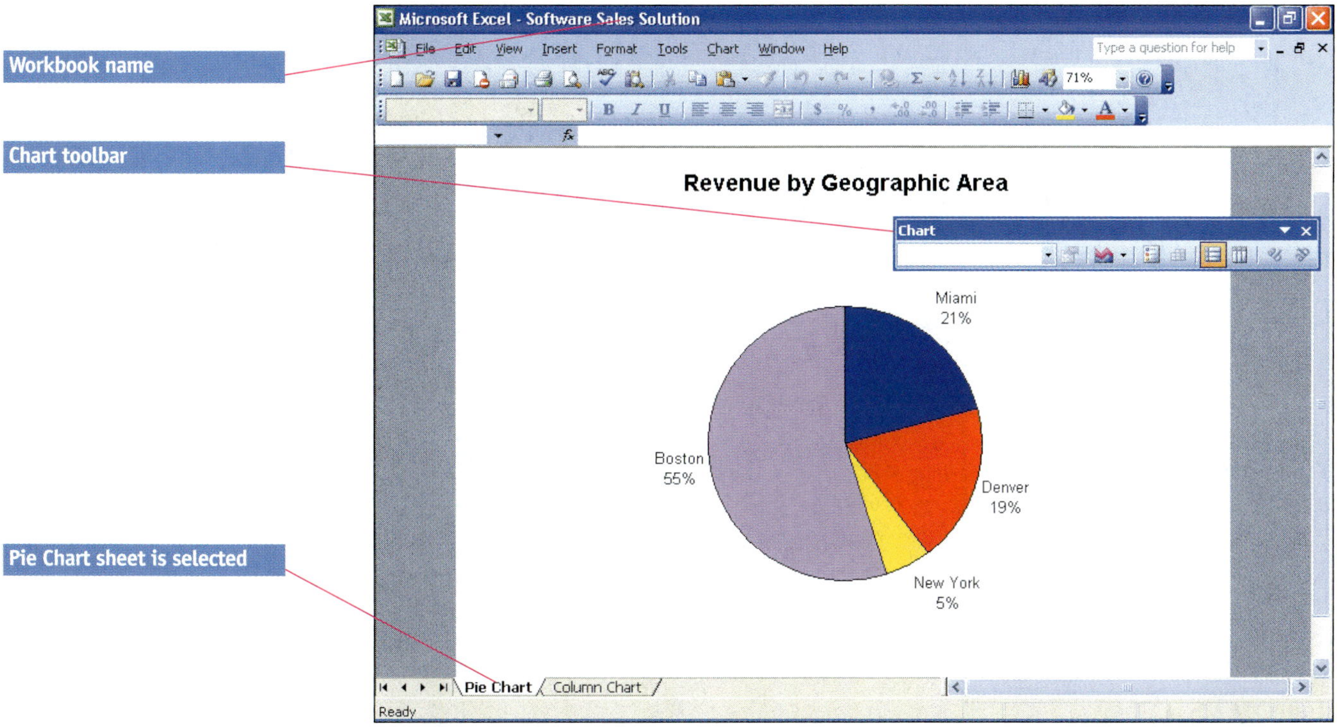

(b) Chart Sheet

FIGURE 3.4 Creating a Chart

The Chart Wizard

The ***Chart Wizard*** is the easiest way to create a chart. Just select the cells that contain the data as shown in Figure 3.5a, click the Chart Wizard button on the Standard toolbar, and let the wizard do the rest. The process is illustrated in Figure 3.5, which shows how the wizard creates a column chart to plot total sales by geographic area (city).

The steps in Figure 3.5 appear automatically as you click the Next command button to move from one step to the next. You can retrace your steps at any time by pressing the Back command button, access the Office Assistant for help with the Chart Wizard, or abort the process with the Cancel command button.

Step 1 in the Chart Wizard (Figure 3.5b) asks you to choose one of the available ***chart types***. Step 2 (Figure 3.5c) shows you a preview of the chart and enables you to confirm (and, if necessary, change) the category names and data series specified earlier. (Only one data series is plotted in this example. Multiple data series are illustrated later in the chapter.) Step 3 (Figure 3.5d) asks you to complete the chart by entering its title and specifying additional options (such as the position of a legend and gridlines). And finally, step 4 (Figure 3.5e) has you choose whether the chart is to be created as an embedded chart (an object) within a specific worksheet, or whether it is to be created in its own chart sheet. The entire process takes but a few minutes.

Selected cells (B3:E3 and B7:E7)

	A	B	C	D	E	F
1	Superior Software Sales					
2						
3		Miami	Denver	New York	Boston	Total
4	Word Processing	$50,000	$67,500	$9,500	$141,000	$268,000
5	Spreadsheets	$44,000	$18,000	$11,500	$105,000	$178,500
6	Database	$12,000	$7,500	$6,000	$30,000	$55,500
7	Total	$106,000	$93,000	$27,000	$276,000	$502,000

(a) The Worksheet

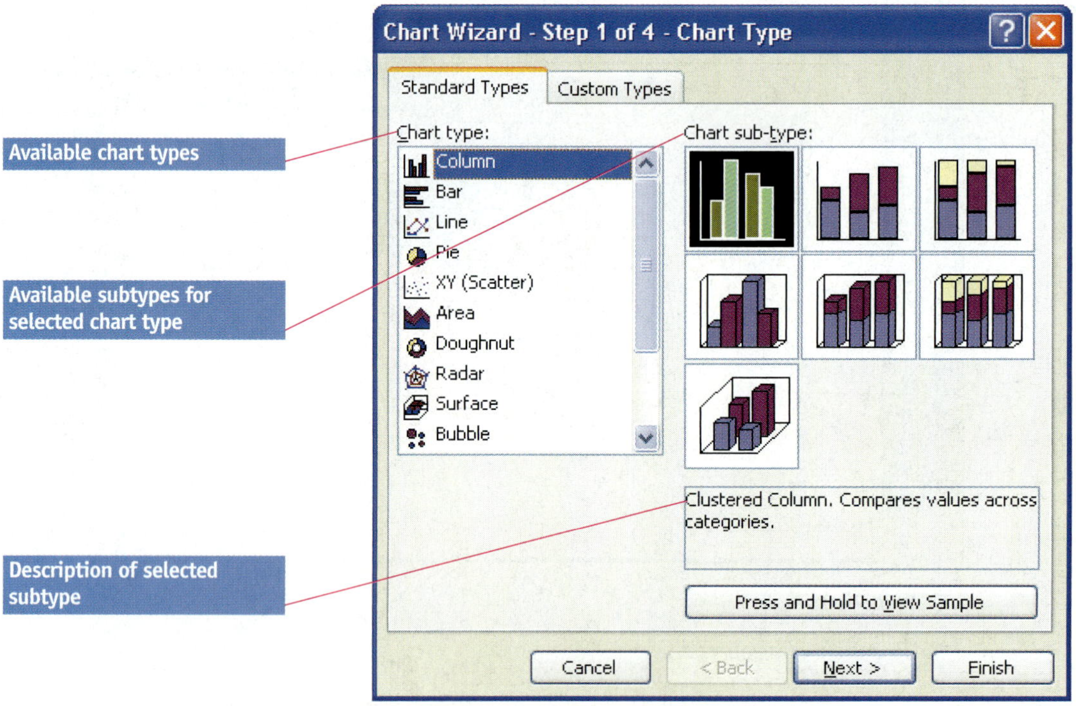

(b) Select the Chart Type (step 1)

FIGURE 3.5 The Chart Wizard

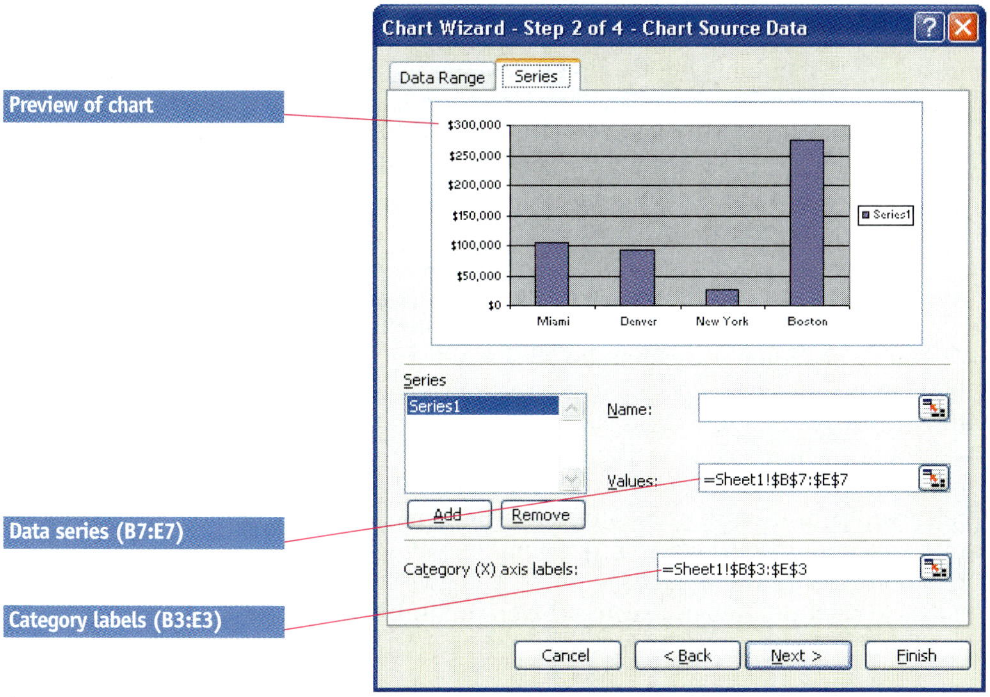

(c) Check the Data Series (step 2)

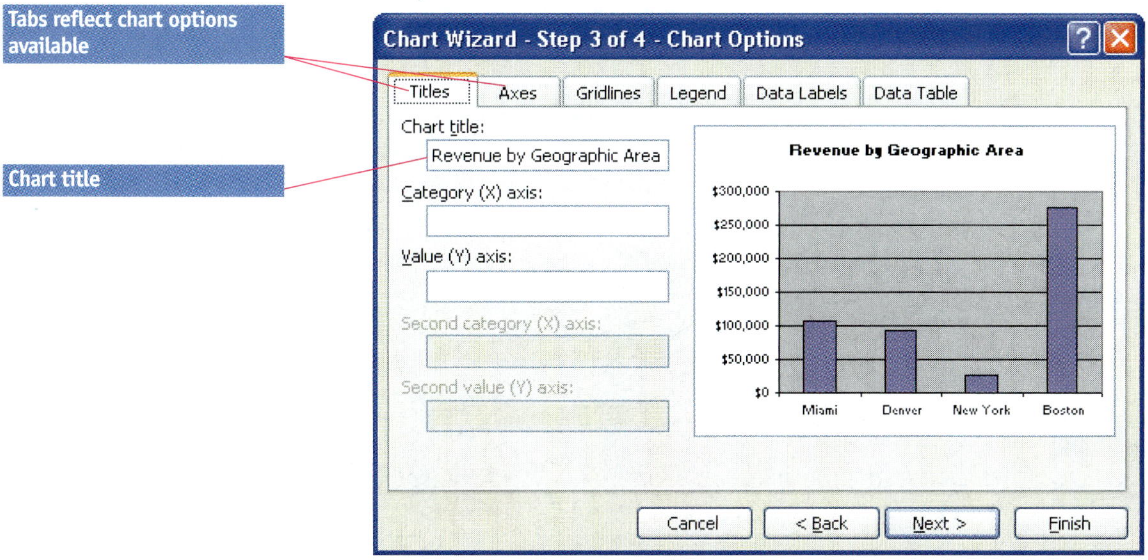

(d) Complete the Chart Options (step 3)

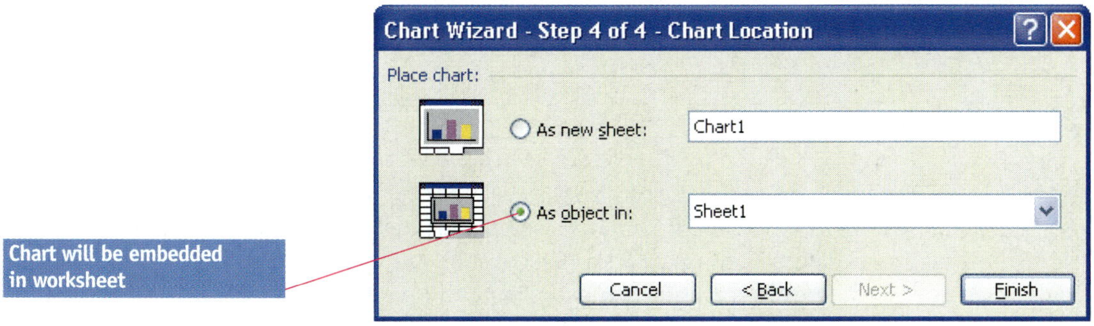

(e) Choose the Location (step 4)

FIGURE 3.5 The Chart Wizard (*continued*)

Modifying a Chart

A chart can be modified in several ways after it has been created. You can change the chart type and/or the color, shape, or pattern of the data series. You can add (or remove) gridlines and/or a legend. You can add labels to the data series. You can also change the font, size, color, and style of existing text anywhere in the chart by selecting the text, then changing its format. All of these features are implemented from the Chart menu or by using the appropriate button on the ***Chart toolbar***.

You can also use the ***Drawing toolbar*** to add text boxes, arrows, and other objects for added emphasis. Figure 3.6, for example, contains a three-dimensional arrow with a text box within the arrow to call attention to the word processing sales. It also contains a second text box with a thin arrow in reference to the database product. Each of these objects is created separately using the appropriate tool from the Drawing toolbar. It's easy, as you will see in our next exercise.

You can change the position of any toolbar by dragging the move handle of a docked toolbar or the title bar of a floating toolbar. (If you drag a floating toolbar to the edge of the program window, it becomes a docked toolbar.) To display a toolbar, pull down the View menu and click the Toolbars command, then check the toolbar. The command functions as a toggle switch; i.e., execute the command and you see the toolbar. Execute the command a second time and the toolbar is hidden.

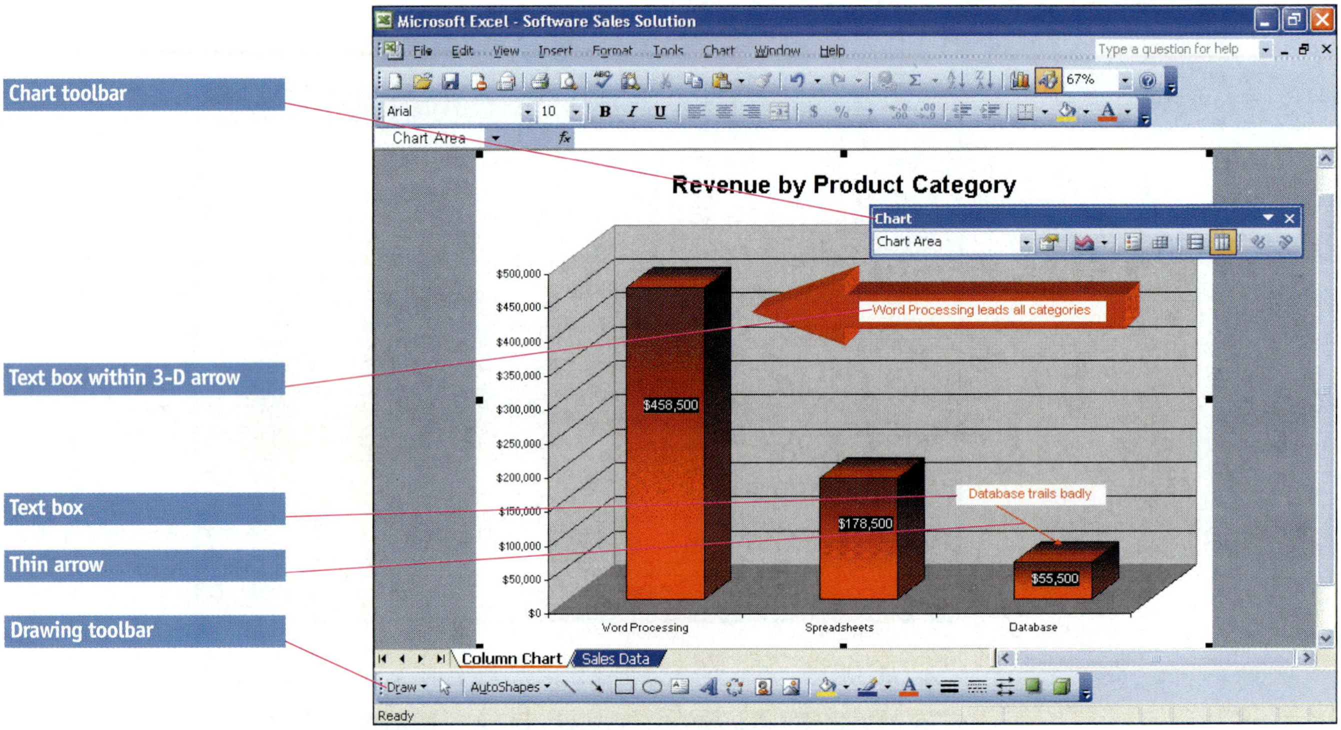

FIGURE 3.6 Enhancing a Chart

SET A TIME LIMIT

Excel enables you to customize virtually every aspect of every object within a chart. That is the good news. It's also the bad news, because you can spend inordinate amounts of time for little or no gain. It's fun to experiment, but set a time limit and stop when you reach the allocated time. The default settings are often adequate to convey your message, and further experimentation might prove counterproductive.

hands-on exercise

1 The Chart Wizard

Objective To create and modify a chart by using the Chart Wizard; to embed a chart within a worksheet; to enhance a chart to include arrows and text. Use Figure 3.7 as a guide in the exercise.

Step 1: The AutoSum Command

- Start Excel. Open the **Software Sales workbook** in the **Exploring Excel folder**. Save the workbook as **Software Sales Solution**.
- Click and drag to select **cells B7** through **E7** (the cells that will contain the total sales for each location). Click the **AutoSum button** on the Standard toolbar to compute the total for each city.
- The totals are computed automatically as shown in Figure 3.7a. The formula bar shows that Cell B7 contains the Sum function to total all of the numeric entries immediately above the cell.
- Click and drag to select **cells F4** through **F7**, then click the **AutoSum button**. The Sum function is entered automatically into these cells to total the entries to the left of the selected cells.
- Click and drag to select **cells B4** through **F7** to format these cells with the currency symbol and no decimal places.
- **Boldface** the row and column headings and the totals. Center the entries in **cells B3** through **F3**.
- Save the workbook.

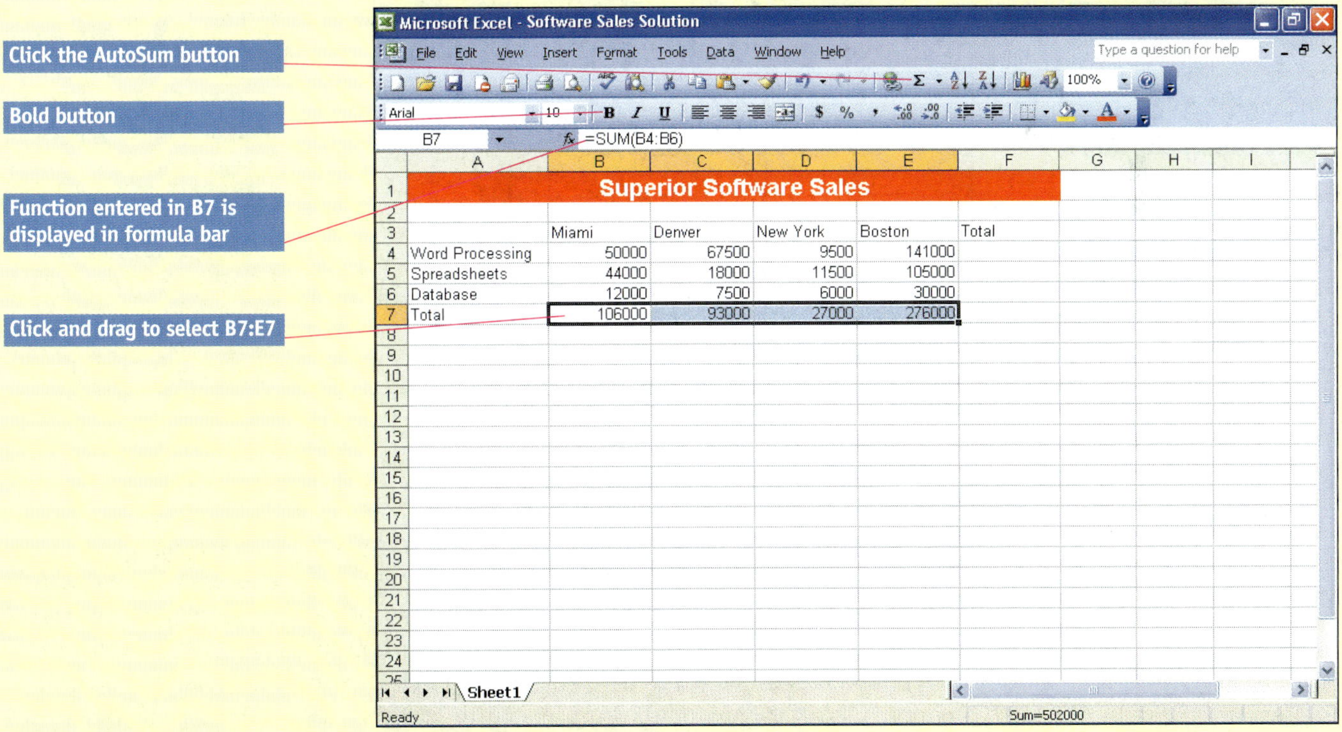

(a) The AutoSum Command (step 1)

FIGURE 3.7 Hands-on Exercise 1

Step 2: Start the Chart Wizard

- Separate the toolbars if they occupy the same row. Pull down the **Tools menu**, click the **Customize command**, click the **Options tab**, then check the box that displays the toolbars on two rows.
- Drag the mouse over **cells B3** through **E3** to select the category labels (the names of the cities). Press and hold the **Ctrl key** as you drag the mouse over **cells B7** through **E7** to select the data series (the cells containing the total sales for the individual cities).
- Check that cells B3 through E3 and B7 through E7 are selected. Click the **Chart Wizard button** on the Standard toolbar to start the wizard. If you don't see the button, pull down the **Insert menu** and click the **Chart command**.
- You should see the dialog box for step 1 of the Chart Wizard as shown in Figure 3.7b. The **Column** chart type and **Clustered column** subtype are selected.
- Click (and hold) the button to see a sample chart. Click **Next**.

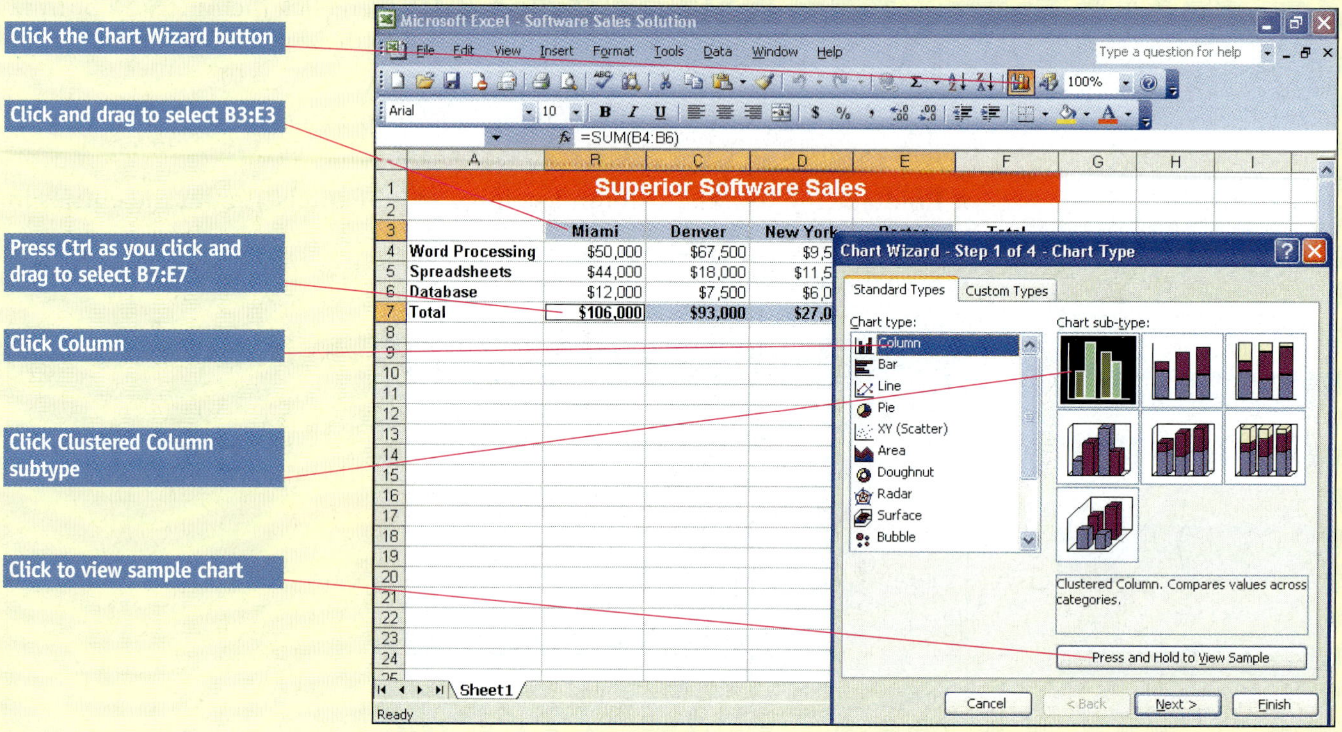

(b) Start the Chart Wizard (step 2)

FIGURE 3.7 Hands-on Exercise 1 (*continued*)

RETRACE YOUR STEPS

The Chart Wizard guides you every step of the way, but what if you make a mistake or change your mind? Click the Back command button at any time to return to a previous screen to enter different information, then continue working with the wizard. Click the Next button to proceed to the next step. Click Finish when the chart is complete.

Step 3: The Chart Wizard (continued)

- You should see step 2 of the Chart Wizard. Click the **Series tab** in the dialog box so that your screen matches Figure 3.7c.
- The values (the data being plotted) are in cells B7 through E7. The Category labels for the *X* axis are in cells B3 through E3. Click **Next** to continue.
- You should see step 3 of the Chart Wizard. If necessary, click the **Titles tab**, then click in the text box for the Chart title.
- Type **Revenue by Geographic Area**. Click the **Legend tab** and clear the box to show a legend. Click **Next**.
- You should see step 4 of the Chart Wizard. If necessary, click the option button to place the chart **As object** in Sheet1 (the name of the worksheet in which you are working).
- Click **Finish**.

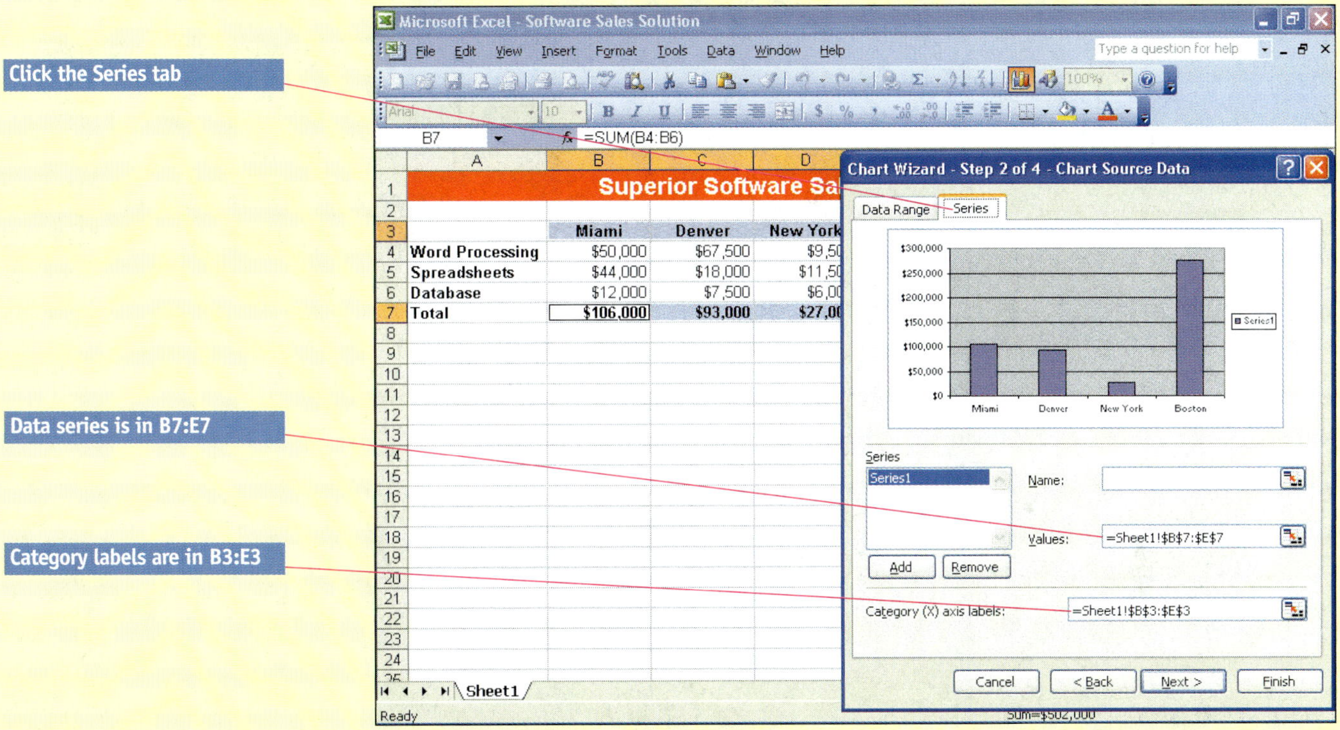

(c) The Chart Wizard (continued) (step 3)

FIGURE 3.7 Hands-on Exercise 1 (*continued*)

THE F11 KEY

The F11 key is the fastest way to create a chart in its own sheet. Select the data, including the legends and category labels, then press the F11 key to create the chart according to the default format built into the Excel column chart. After the chart has been created, you can use the menu bar, Chart toolbar, or shortcut menus to choose a different chart type and/or customize the formatting.

Step 4: Move and Size the Chart

- You should see the completed chart as shown in Figure 3.7d. The sizing handles indicate that the chart is selected and will be affected by subsequent commands. The Chart toolbar is displayed automatically whenever a chart is selected.
- Move and/or size the chart just as you would any other Windows object:
  - To move the chart, click the chart (background) area to select the chart (a ScreenTip, "Chart Area," is displayed), then click and drag (the mouse pointer changes to a four-sided arrow) to move the chart.
  - To size the chart, drag a corner handle (the mouse pointer changes to a double arrow) to change the length and width of the chart simultaneously, keeping the chart in proportion as it is resized.
- Click outside the chart to deselect it. The sizing handles disappear and the Chart toolbar is no longer visible.
- Save the workbook.

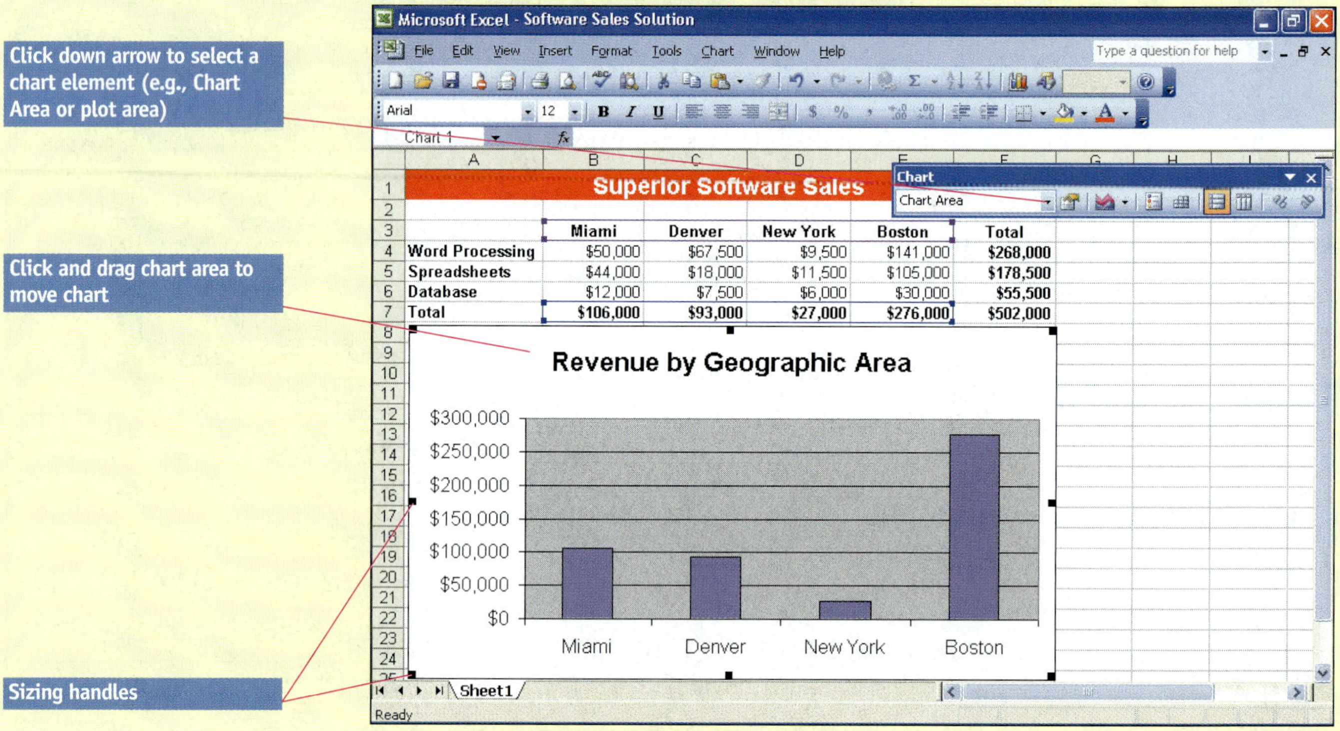

(d) Move and Size the Chart (step 4)

FIGURE 3.7 Hands-on Exercise 1 (*continued*)

EMBEDDED CHARTS

An embedded chart is treated as an object that can be moved, sized, copied, or deleted just as any other Windows object. To move an embedded chart, click the background of the chart to select the chart, then drag it to a new location in the worksheet. To size the chart, select it, then drag any of the eight sizing handles in the desired direction. To delete the chart, select it, then press the Del key. To copy the chart, select it, click the Copy button on the Standard toolbar to copy the chart to the clipboard, click elsewhere in the workbook where you want the copied chart to go, then click the Paste button.

Step 5: Change the Worksheet

- Any changes in a worksheet are automatically reflected in the associated chart. Click in **cell B4**, change the entry to **$400,000**, and press the **Enter key**.
- The total sales for Miami in cell B7 change automatically to reflect the increased sales for word processing, as shown in Figure 3.7e. The column for Miami also changes in the chart and is now larger than the column for Boston.
- Click in **cell B3**. Change the entry to **Chicago**. Press **Enter**. The category label on the *X* axis changes automatically.
- Click the **Undo button** to change the city back to Miami. Click the **Undo button** a second time to return to the initial value of $50,000. The worksheet and chart are restored to their earlier values.
- Save the workbook.

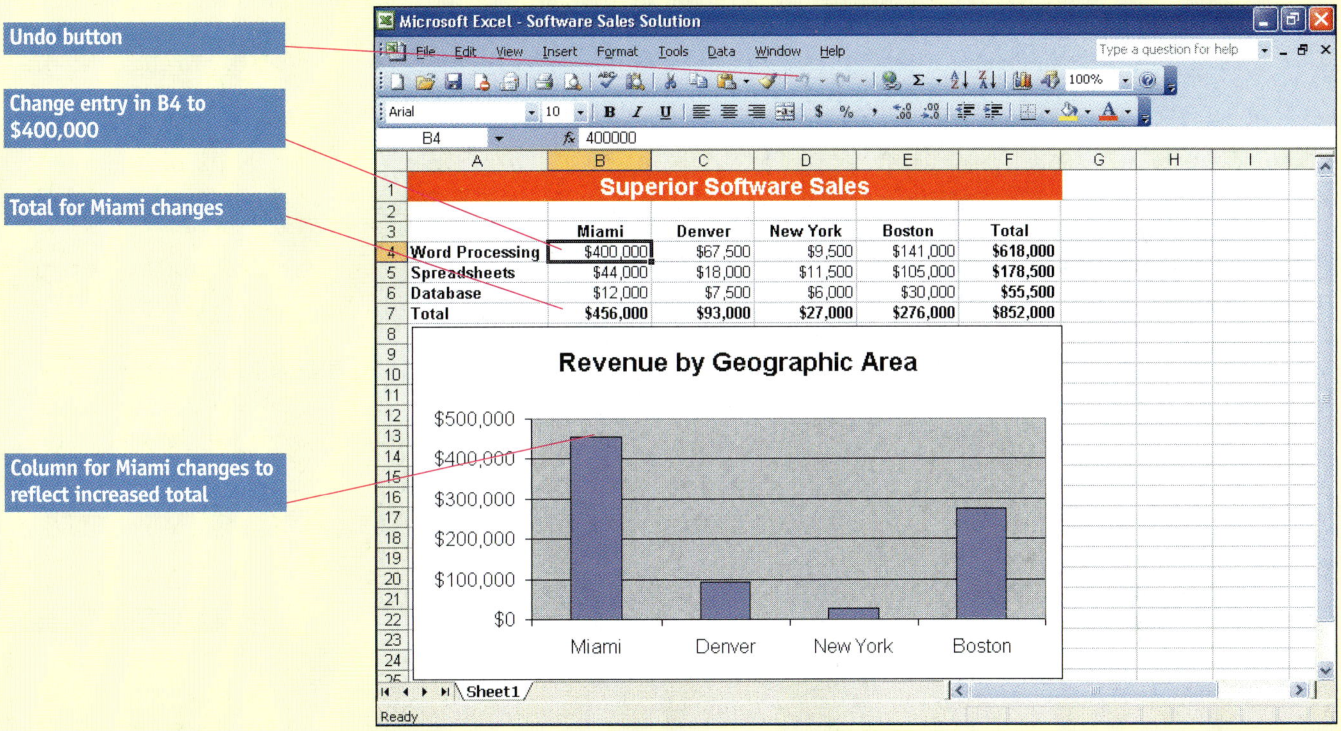

(e) Change the Worksheet (step 5)

FIGURE 3.7 Hands-on Exercise 1 (*continued*)

THE AUTOFORMAT COMMAND

The AutoFormat command does not do anything that could not be done through individual formatting commands, but it does provide inspiration by suggesting several attractive designs. Select the cells you want to format, pull down the Format menu, and click the AutoFormat command to display the AutoFormat dialog box. Select (click) a design, then click the Options button to determine the formats to apply (font, column width, patterns, and so on). Click OK to close the dialog box and apply the formatting. Click the Undo button if you do not like the result. See practice exercise 1 at the end of the chapter.

Step 6: Change the Chart Type

- Click the **chart** (background) **area** to select the chart, click the **drop-down arrow** on the Chart type button on the Chart toolbar, then click the **3-D Pie Chart icon**. The chart changes to a three-dimensional pie chart.
- Point to the chart area, click the **right mouse button** to display a shortcut menu, then click the **Chart Options command** to display the Chart Options dialog box shown in Figure 3.7f.
- Click the **Data Labels tab**, then click the check boxes for Category name and Percentage. Click **OK** to accept the settings and close the dialog box.
- The pie chart changes to reflect the options you just specified. Modify each component as necessary:
  - Select (click) the (gray) **Plot area**. Click and drag the sizing handles to increase the size of the plot area within the embedded chart.
  - Point to any of the labels, click the **right mouse button** to display a shortcut menu, and click **Format Data Labels** to display a dialog box. Click the **Font tab**, and select a smaller point size. It may also be necessary to click and drag each label away from the plot area.
- Make other changes as necessary. Save the workbook.

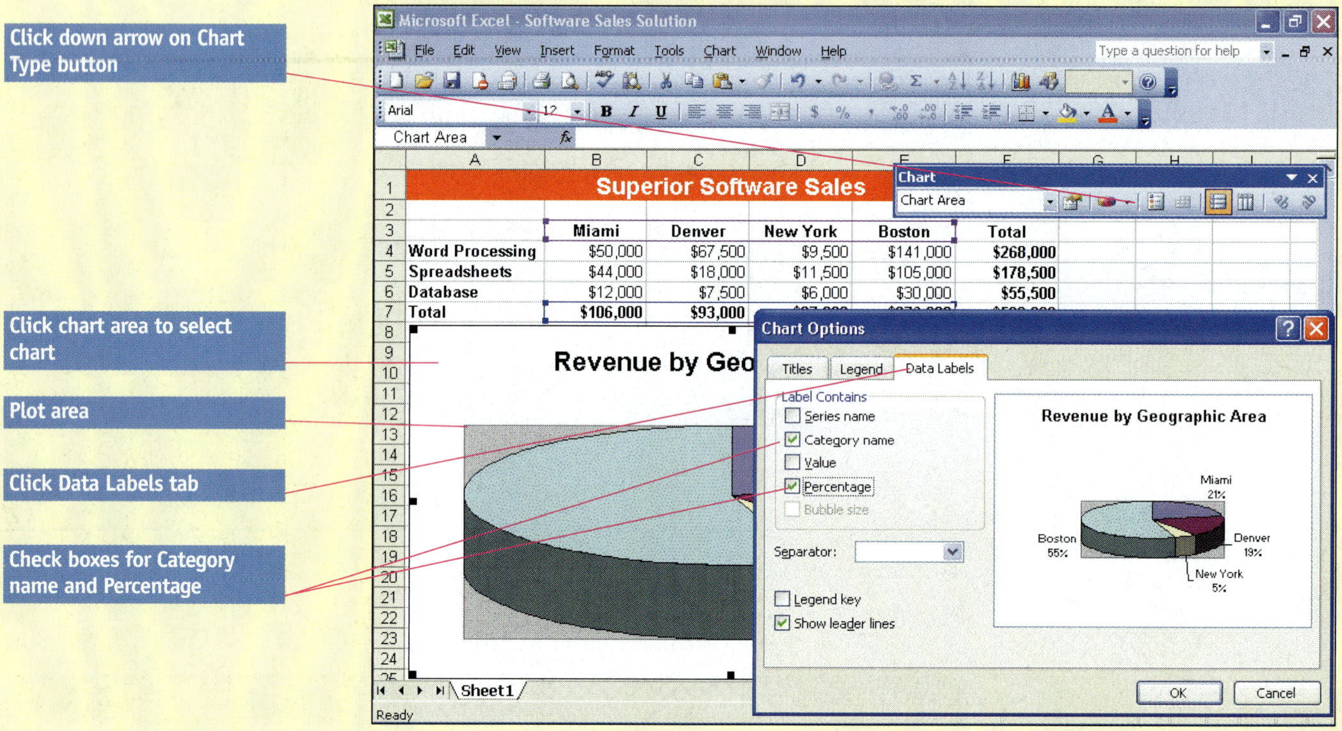

(f) Change the Chart Type (step 6)

FIGURE 3.7 Hands-on Exercise 1 (*continued*)

ADDITIONAL CHART TYPES

Excel offers multiple chart types, each with several formats. Line charts are best to display time-related information such as a five-year trend of sales or profit data. A combination chart uses two or more chart types to display different kinds of data or when different scales are required for multiple data series. See practice exercise 6 at the end of the chapter.

Step 7: Create a Second Chart

- Click and drag to select **cells A4** through **A6** in the worksheet. Press and hold the **Ctrl key** as you drag the mouse to select **cells F4** through **F6**.
- Click the **Chart Wizard button** on the Standard toolbar to start the Chart Wizard and display the dialog box for step 1 as shown in Figure 3.7g. The Column Chart type is already selected. Click the **Clustered column with a 3-D visual effect subtype**. Press and hold the indicated button to preview the chart with your data. Click **Next**.
- Click the **Series tab** in the dialog box for step 2 to confirm that you selected the correct data points. The values for Series1 should consist of cells F4 through F6. The Category labels for the *X* axis should be cells A4 through A6. Click **Next**.
- You should see step 3 of the Chart Wizard. Click the **Titles tab**, then click in the text box for the Chart title. Type **Revenue by Product Category**. Click the **Legend tab** and clear the box to show a legend. Click **Next**.
- You should see step 4 of the Chart Wizard. Select the option button to create the chart **As new sheet** (Chart1). Click **Finish**.
- The 3-D column chart has been created in the chart sheet labeled Chart1.

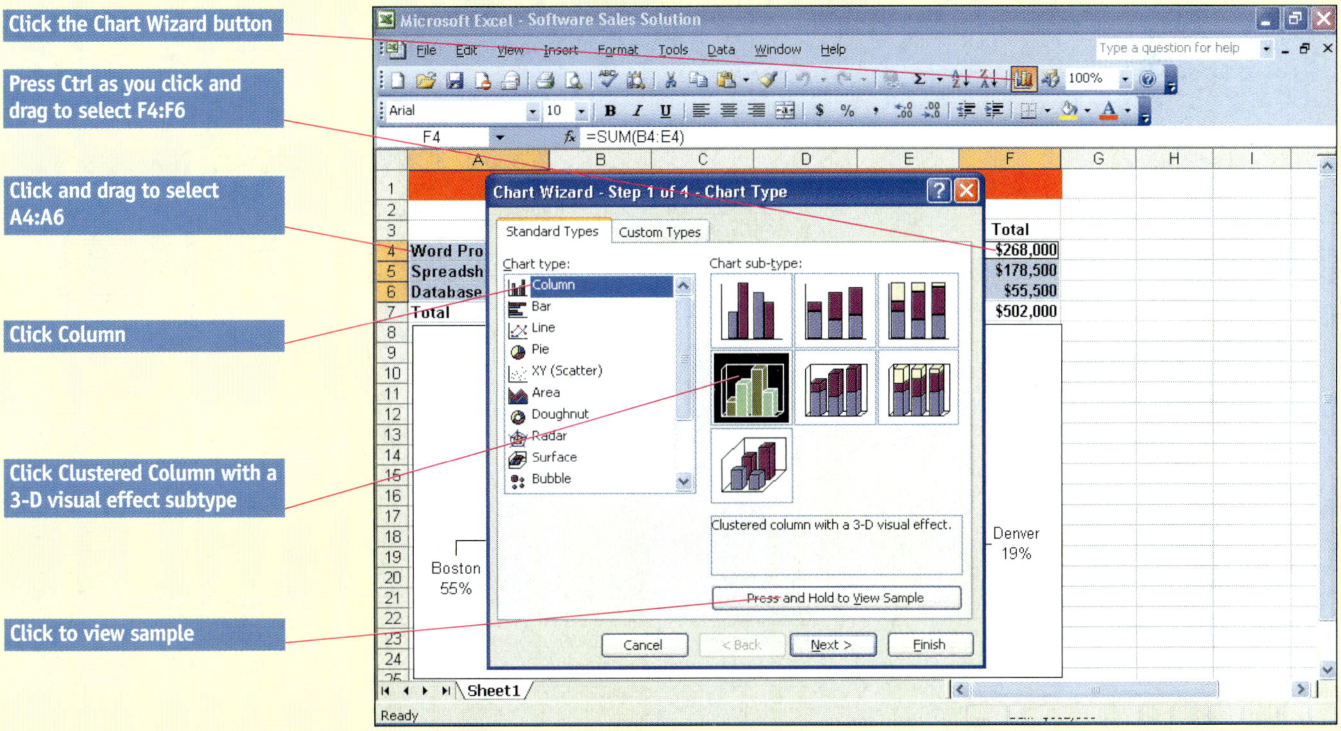

(g) Create a Second Chart (step 7)

FIGURE 3.7 Hands-on Exercise 1 (*continued*)

ANATOMY OF A CHART

A chart is composed of multiple components (objects), each of which can be selected and changed separately. Point to any part of a chart to display a ScreenTip indicating the name of the component, then click the mouse to select that component and display the sizing handles. You can then click and drag the object within the chart and/or click the right mouse button to display a shortcut menu with commands pertaining to the selected object.

Step 8: Add a Text Box

- Point to any visible toolbar, click the **right mouse button** to display a shortcut menu listing the available toolbars, then click **Drawing** to display the Drawing toolbar as shown in Figure 3.7h.
- Click the **Text Box button** on the Drawing toolbar. Click in the chart (the mouse pointer changes to a thin crosshair), then click and drag to create a text box. Release the mouse, then enter the text, **Word Processing leads all categories**.
- Point to the thatched border around the text box, then right click the border to display a context-sensitive menu. Click **Format Text Box** to display the Format Text dialog box. Click the **Font tab** and change the font to **12 point bold**. Choose **Red** as the font color.
- Click the **Colors and Lines tab** and select **white** as the fill color. Click **OK**. You should see red text on a white background. If necessary, size the text box so that the text fits on one line. Do not worry about the position of the text box.
- Click the title of the chart. You will see sizing handles around the title to indicate it has been selected. Click the **drop-down arrow** in the Font Size box on the Formatting toolbar. Click **22** to increase the size of the title. Save the workbook.

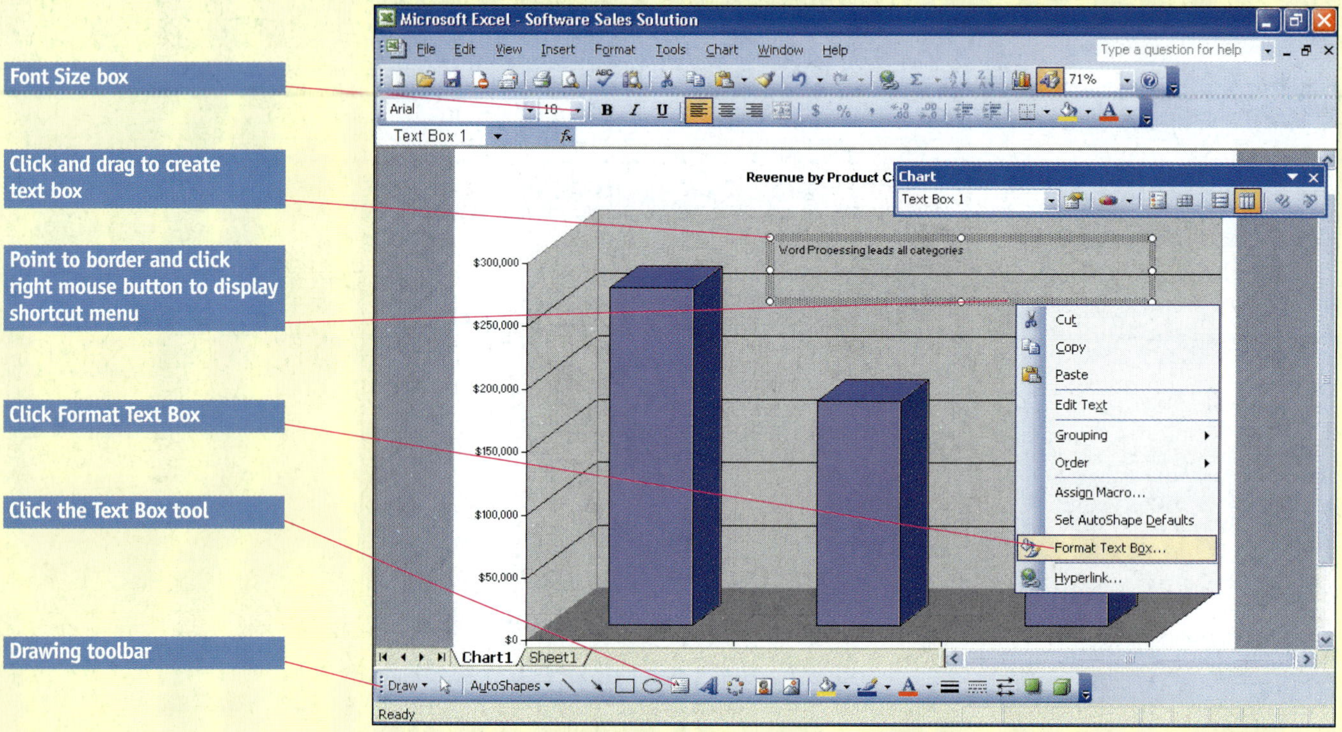

(h) Add a Text Box (step 8)

FIGURE 3.7 Hands-on Exercise 1 (*continued*)

FLOATING TOOLBARS

Any toolbar can be docked along the edge of the application window, or it can be displayed as a floating toolbar within the application window. To move a docked toolbar, drag the move handle. To move a floating toolbar, drag its title bar. To size a floating toolbar, drag any border in the direction you want to go. Double click the title bar of any floating toolbar to dock it. A floating toolbar will dim and disappear if it is not used.

Step 9: Create a 3-D Shape

- Click on the **AutoShapes button** and, if necessary, click the double arrow to display additional commands. Click **Block Arrows**. Select an arrow style.
- Click in the chart (the mouse pointer changes to a thin crosshair), then click and drag to create an arrow. Release the mouse.
- Click the **3-D button** on the drawing toolbar and click **3-D Style 1** as shown in Figure 3.7i. Right click the arrow and click the **Format AutoShape command** to display the Format AutoShape dialog box. Click the **Colors and Lines tab**. Choose **Red** as the fill color. Click **OK**, then size the arrow.
- Select (click) the text box you created in the previous step, then click and drag the text box out of the way. Select (click) the **3-D arrow** and position it next to the word processing column.
- Click and drag the text box on top of the arrow. If you do not see the text, right click the arrow, click the **Order command**, and click **Send to Back**.
- Save the workbook, but do not print it at this time. Exit Excel if you do not want to continue with the next exercise at this time.

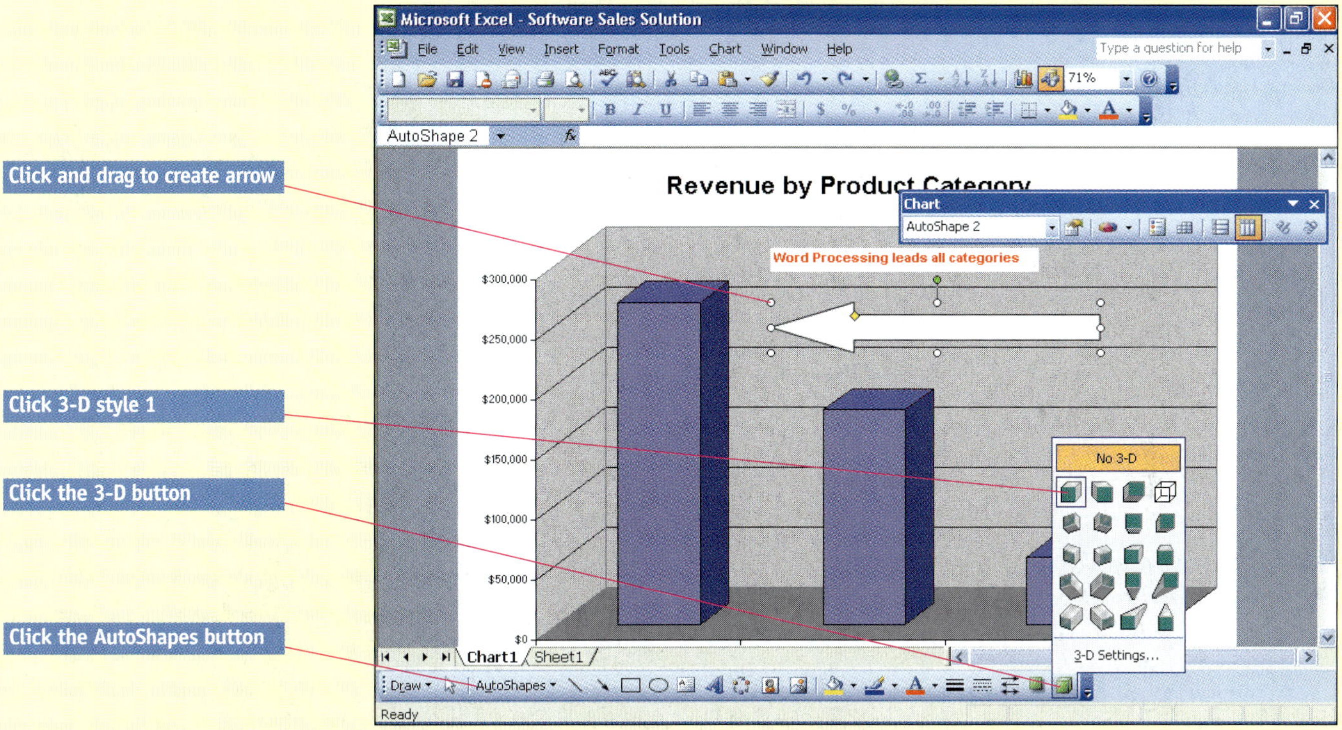

(i) Create a 3-D Shape (step 9)

FIGURE 3.7 Hands-on Exercise 1 (*continued*)

FORMAT THE DATA SERIES

Use the Format Data Series command to change the color, shape, or pattern of the columns within the chart. Right click any column to select the data series (be sure that all three columns are selected), then click Format Data Series to display the Format Data Series dialog box. Experiment with the various options, especially those on the Shape and Patterns tabs within the dialog box. Click OK when you are satisfied with the changes.

MULTIPLE DATA SERIES

The charts presented so far displayed only a single data series such as the total sales by location or the total sales by product category. Although such charts are useful, it is often more informative to view ***multiple data series*** on the same chart. Figure 3.8a displays the worksheet we have been using throughout the chapter. Figure 3.8b displays a side-by-side column chart that plots multiple data series that exist as rows (B4:E4, B5:E5, and B6:E6) within the worksheet. Figure 3.8c displays a chart based on the same data when the series are in columns (B4:B6, C4:C6, D4:D6, and E4:E6).

Both charts plot a total of twelve data points (three product categories for each of four locations), but they group the data differently. Figure 3.8b displays the data by city in which the sales of three product categories are shown for each of four cities. Figure 3.8c is the reverse and groups the data by product category. This time the sales in the four cities are shown for each of three product categories. The choice between the two charts depends on your message and whether you want to emphasize revenue by city or by product category. It sounds complicated, but it's not; Excel will create either chart for you according to your specifications.

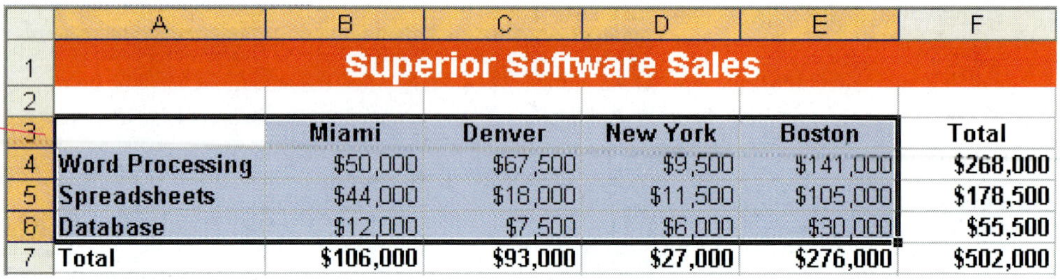

	A	B	C	D	E	F
1	Superior Software Sales					
2						
3		Miami	Denver	New York	Boston	Total
4	Word Processing	$50,000	$67,500	$9,500	$141,000	$268,000
5	Spreadsheets	$44,000	$18,000	$11,500	$105,000	$178,500
6	Database	$12,000	$7,500	$6,000	$30,000	$55,500
7	Total	$106,000	$93,000	$27,000	$276,000	$502,000

(a) Worksheet Data

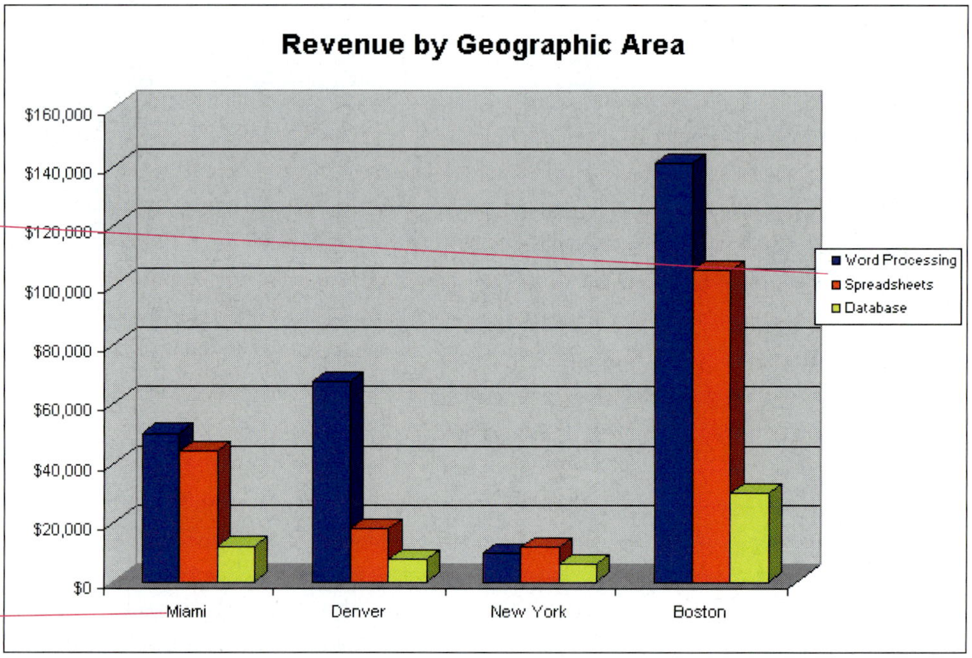

(b) Data in Rows

FIGURE 3.8 Side-by-Side Column Charts

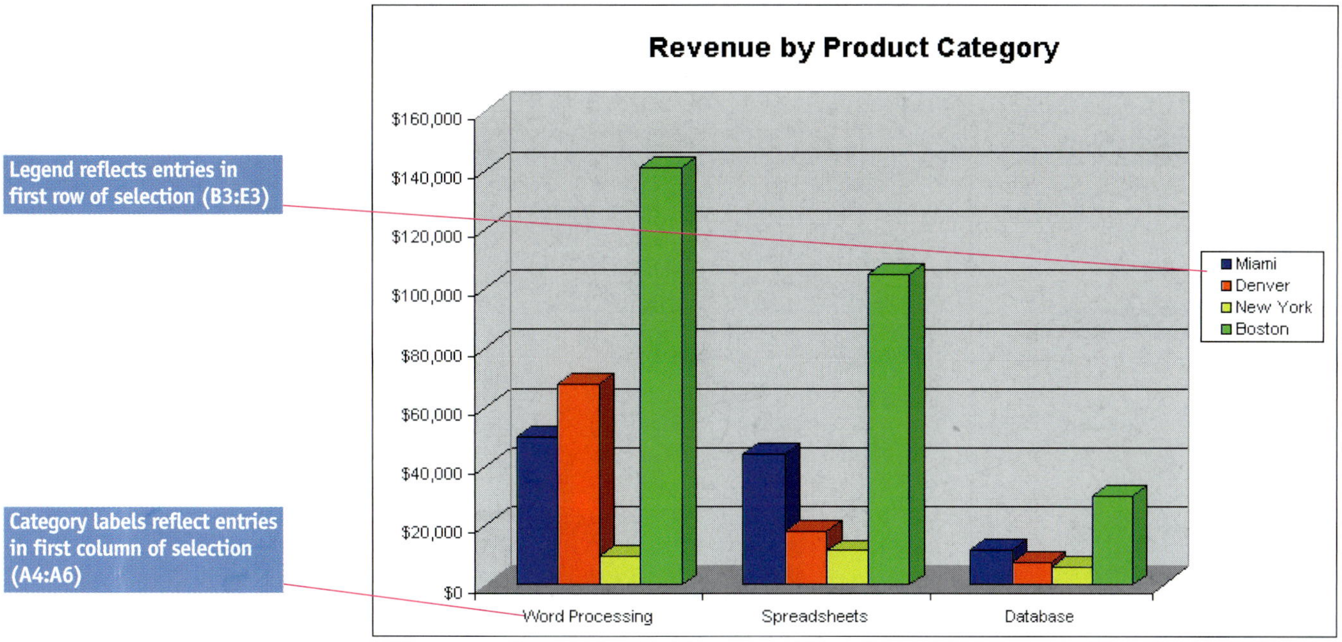

(c) Data in Columns

FIGURE 3.8 Side-by-Side Column Charts (*continued*)

- If you specify that the data series are in rows (Figure 3.8b), the wizard will:
  - Use the first row (cells B3 through E3) for the category labels
  - Use the remaining rows (rows four, five, and six) for the data series
  - Use the first column (cells A4 through A6) for the legend text
- If you specify the data series are in columns (Figure 3.8c), the wizard will:
  - Use the first column (cells A4 through A6) for the category labels
  - Use the remaining columns (columns B, C, D, and E) for the data series
  - Use the first row (cells B3 through E3) for the legend text

Stacked Column Charts

The next decision is the choice between ***side-by-side column charts*** versus ***stacked column charts*** such as those shown in Figure 3.9. Stacked column charts also group data in one of two ways, in rows or in columns. Thus Figure 3.9a is a stacked column chart with the data in rows. Figure 3.9b is also a stacked column chart, but the data is in columns.

The choice of side-by-side versus stacked column charts depends on the intended message. If you want the audience to see the individual sales in each city or product category, then the side-by-side columns in Figure 3.8 are more appropriate. If, on the other hand, you want to emphasize the total sales for each city or product category, the stacked columns are preferable. The advantage of the stacked column is that the totals are clearly shown and can be easily compared. The disadvantage is that the segments within each column do not start at the same point, making it difficult to determine the actual sales for the individual categories.

Note, too, that the scale on the *Y* axis is different for charts with side-by-side columns versus charts with stacked columns. The side-by-side columns in Figure 3.8 show the sales of each product category and so the *Y* axis goes only to $160,000. The stacked columns in Figure 3.9, however, reflect the total sales for all products in each city and thus the scale goes to $300,000. Realize, too, that for a stacked column chart to make sense, its numbers must be additive. You would not, for example, convert a column chart that plots units and dollar sales side by side to a stacked column chart, because units and dollars are not additive.

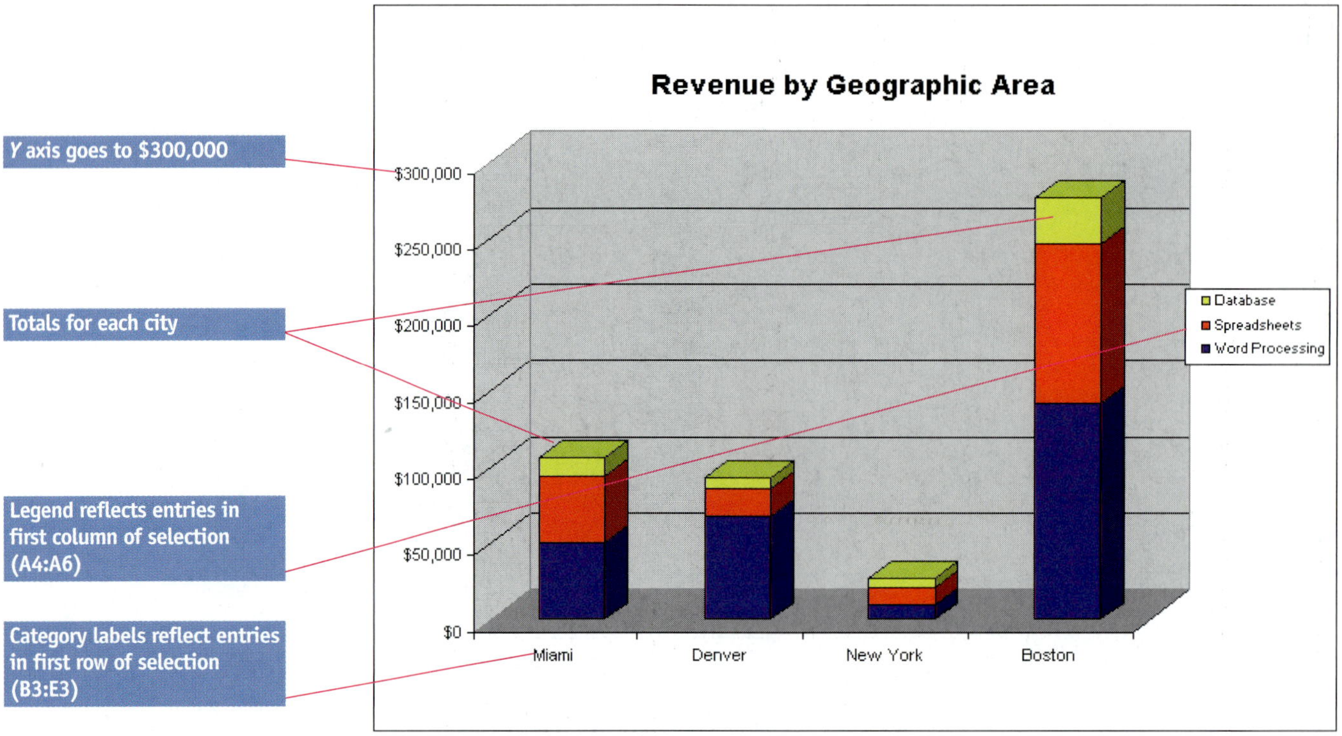

(a) Data in Rows

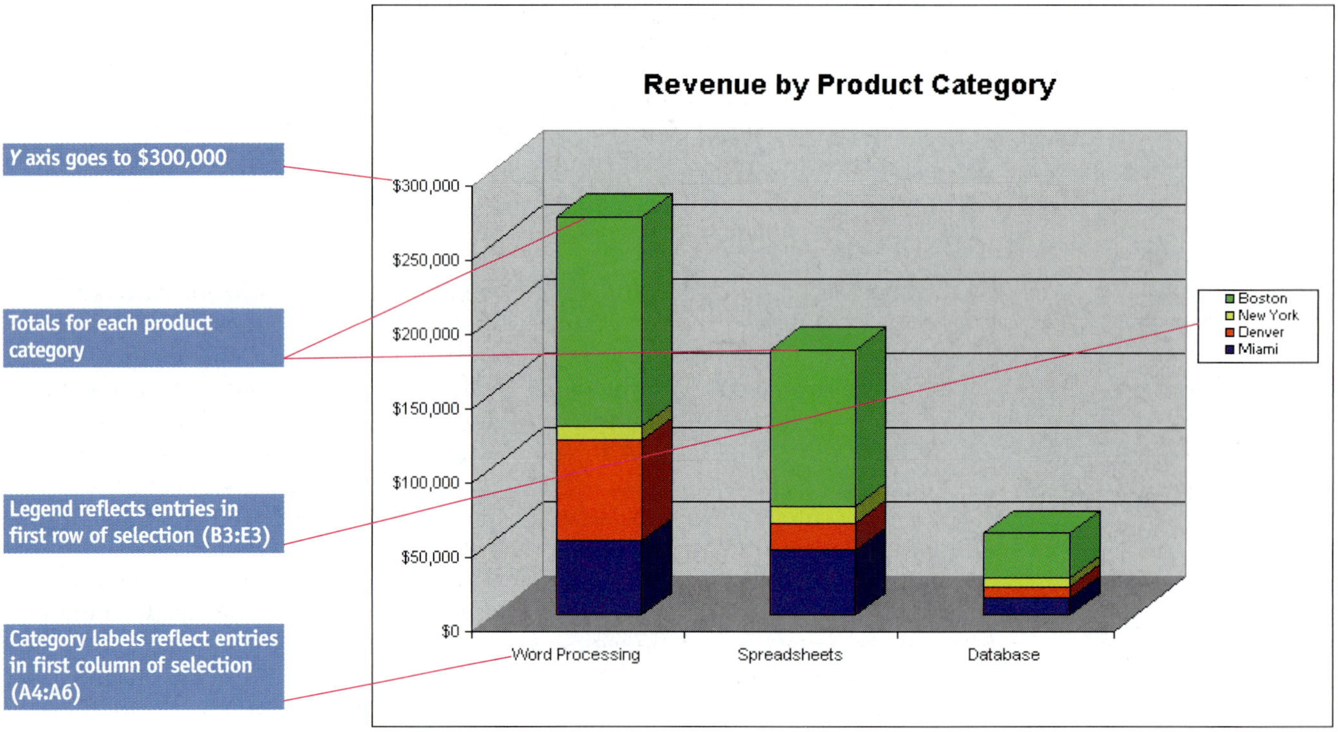

(b) Data in Columns

FIGURE 3.9 Stacked Column Charts

hands-on exercise

2 Multiple Data Series

Objective To plot multiple data series in the same chart; to differentiate between data series in rows and columns. Use Figure 3.10 as a guide.

Step 1: Rename the Worksheets

- Open the **Software Sales Solution workbook** from the previous exercise as shown in Figure 3.10a.
- Point to the workbook tab labeled **Sheet1**, click the **right mouse button** to display a shortcut menu, then click the **Rename command**. The name of the worksheet (Sheet1) is selected.
- Type **Sales Data** to change the name of the worksheet to the more descriptive name. Press the **Enter key**. Right click the worksheet tab a second time, click the **Tab Color command**, then change the color to **blue**. Click **OK**.
- Change the name of the Chart1 sheet to **Column Chart**. Change the tab color to **red**. Close the Drawing toolbar. Save the workbook.

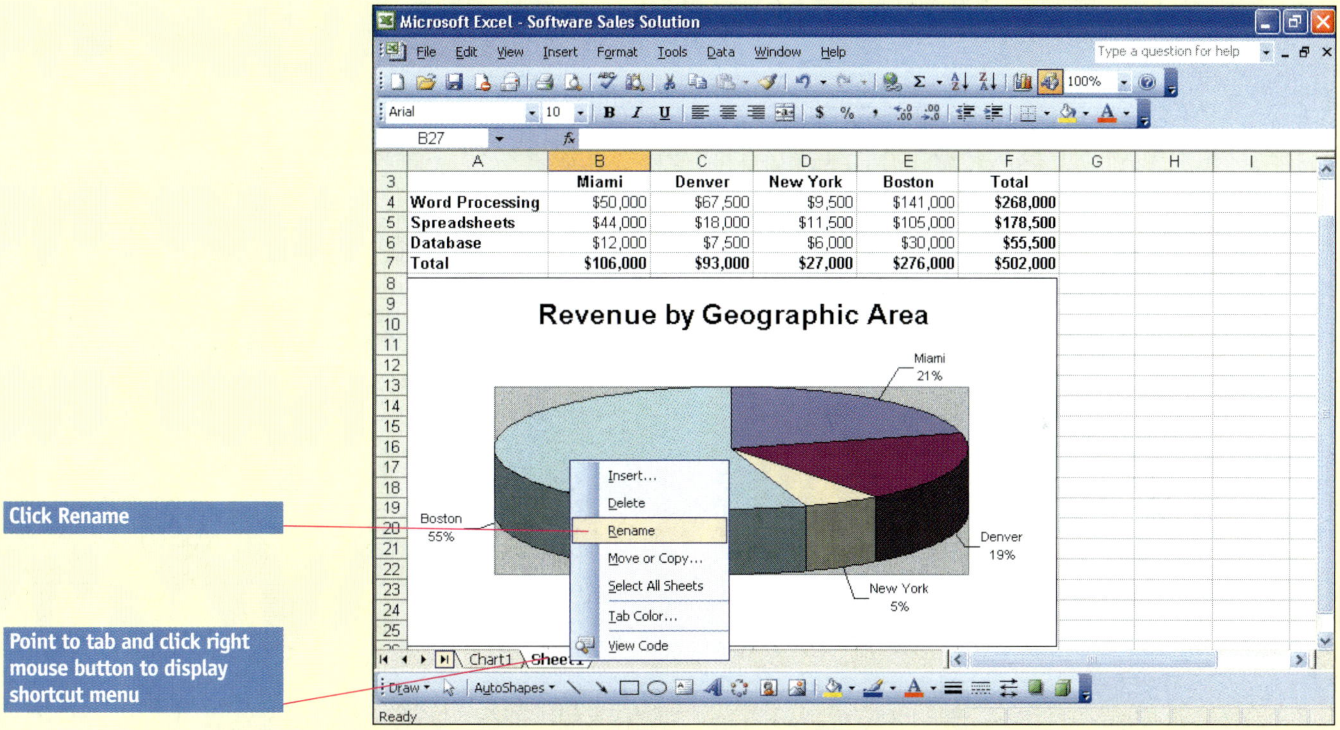

(a) Rename the Worksheets (step 1)

FIGURE 3.10 Hands-on Exercise 2

HIDING AND UNHIDING A WORKSHEET

A chart delivers a message more effectively than the corresponding numeric data, and thus it may be convenient to hide the associated worksheet on which the chart is based. Click the tab of the worksheet you want to hide, pull down the Format menu, click Sheet, and then click the Hide command. (Reverse the process to unhide the worksheet. Pull down the Format menu, click Sheet, click the Unhide command, and then click the name of the worksheet you want to see.)

Step 2: The Chart Wizard

- Click the **Sales Data tab**, then click and drag to select **cells A3** through **E6**. Click the **Chart Wizard button** on the Standard toolbar to start the wizard.
- Select **Column** as the chart type and **Clustered column with a 3-D visual effect** as the subtype. Click **Next** to continue with the Chart Wizard.
- You should see step 2 of the Chart Wizard as shown in Figure 3.10b. The data range should be specified as **Sales Data!$A$3:$E$6**. The option button for **Series in Rows** should be selected. Click **Next**.
- You should see step 3 of the Chart Wizard. Click the **Titles tab**. Click the text box for Chart title. Type **Revenue by City**. Click **Next**.
- You should see step 4 of the Chart Wizard. Click the option button for **As new sheet**. Type **Revenue by City** in the associated text box. Click **Finish**.
- Excel creates the new chart in its own sheet named Revenue by City. Change the tab color of the chart sheet to **red**. Save the workbook.

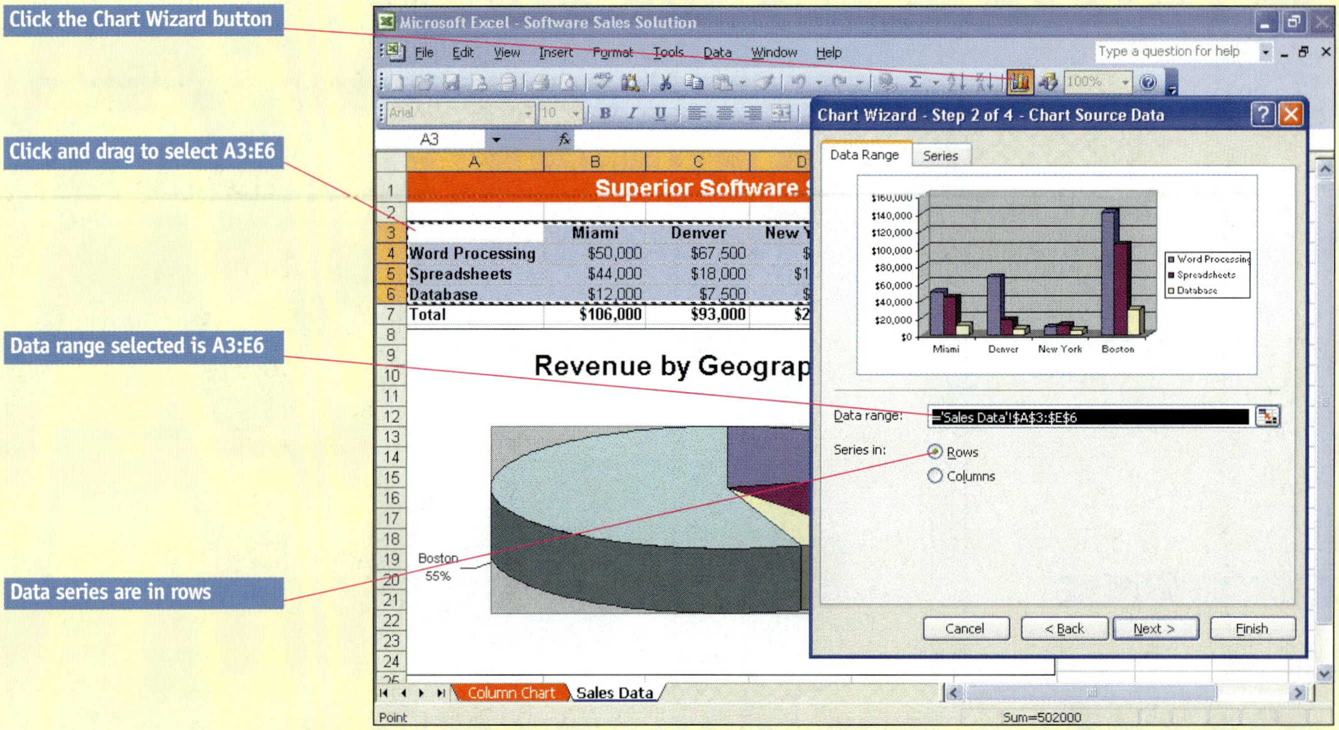

(b) The Chart Wizard (step 2)

FIGURE 3.10 Hands-on Exercise 2 (*continued*)

DATA IN ROWS VERSUS COLUMNS

The choice between data series in rows versus columns depends on the message you want to convey. If the data series are in rows (as in this example), the contribution of each city is emphasized. The first row in the selected range from the worksheet (cells A3 through E6) appears on the *X* axis, and the first column is used as the legend. To view the individual data series, pull down the Chart menu, click the Source Data command to display the associated dialog box, then click the Series tab. You will find three data series (Word processing, Spreadsheets, and Database), each with four data points.

Step 3: Copy the Chart

- Click anywhere in the chart title to select the title. Click the **Font Size list box** and change to **18 point** type to enlarge the title.
- Point to the tab named **Revenue by City**. Click the **right mouse button**. Click **Move or Copy** to display the dialog box in Figure 3.10c.
- Click **Sales Data** in the Before Sheet list box. Check the box to **Create a Copy**. Click **OK**.
- A duplicate worksheet called Revenue by City(2) is created and appears before (to the left of) the Sales Data worksheet. (You can also press and hold the Ctrl key as you drag the worksheet tab to create a copy of the worksheet.)
- Double click the newly created worksheet tab to select the name. Enter **Revenue by Product** as the new name.
- Save the workbook.

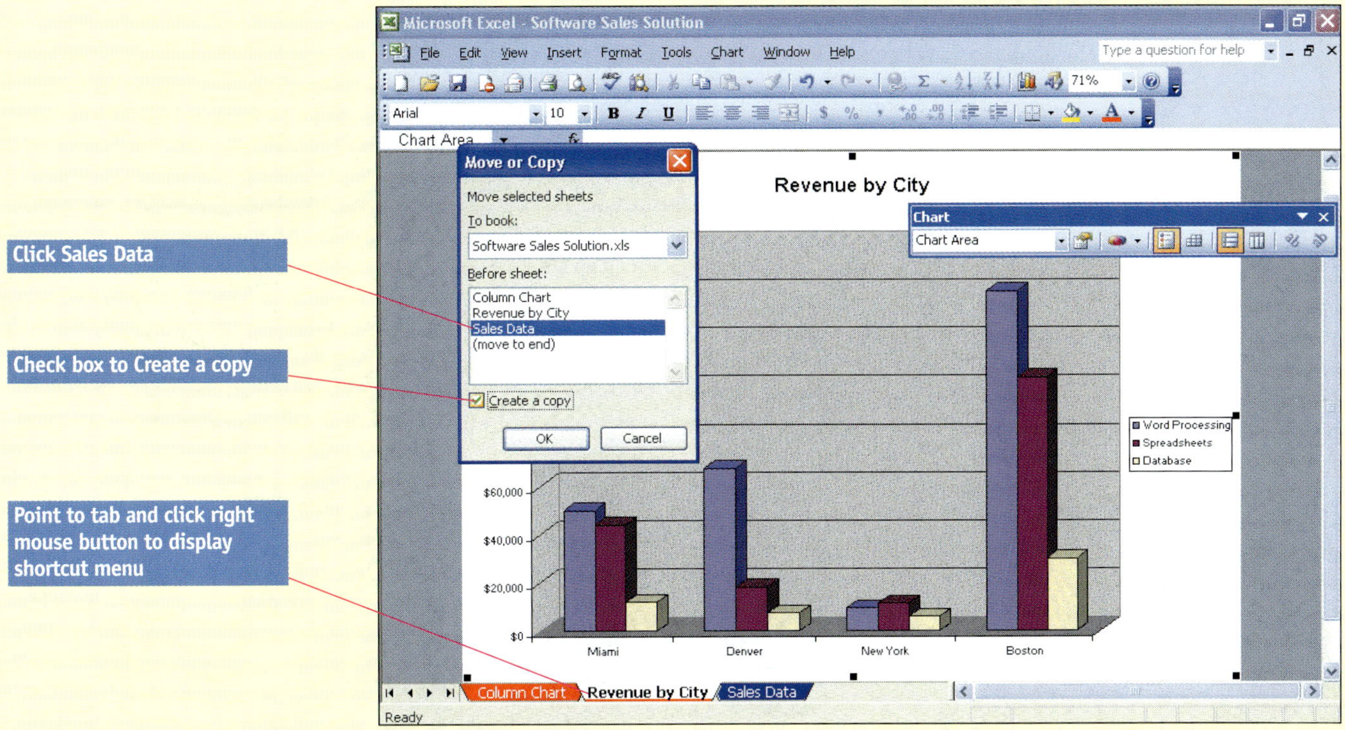

(c) Copy the Chart (step 3)

FIGURE 3.10 Hands-on Exercise 2 (*continued*)

MOVING AND COPYING A WORKSHEET

The fastest way to move or copy a chart sheet is to drag its tab. To move a sheet, point to its tab, then click and drag the tab to its new position. To copy a sheet, press and hold the Ctrl key as you drag the tab to the desired position for the second sheet. Rename the copied sheet (or any sheet for that matter) by double clicking its tab to select the existing name. Enter a new name for the worksheet, then press the Enter key. You can also right click the worksheet tab to change its color. See practice exercise 1 at the end of the chapter.

Step 4: Change the Source Data

- Click the **Revenue by Product tab** to make it the active sheet. Click anywhere in the title of the chart, drag the mouse over the word **City** to select the text, then type **Product Category** to replace the selected text. Click outside the title to deselect it.
- Pull down the **Chart menu**. If necessary, click the double arrow to see more commands, click **Source Data** and click the **Data Range tab** (you will see the Sales Data worksheet). Click the **Columns option button** so that your screen matches Figure 3.10d.
- Click the **Series tab** and note the following:
  - The original chart plotted the data in rows. There were three data series (one series for each product).
  - The new chart (shown in the dialog box) plots the data in columns. There are four data series (one for each city as indicated in the Series list box).
- Click **OK** to close the Source Data dialog box.
- Save the workbook.

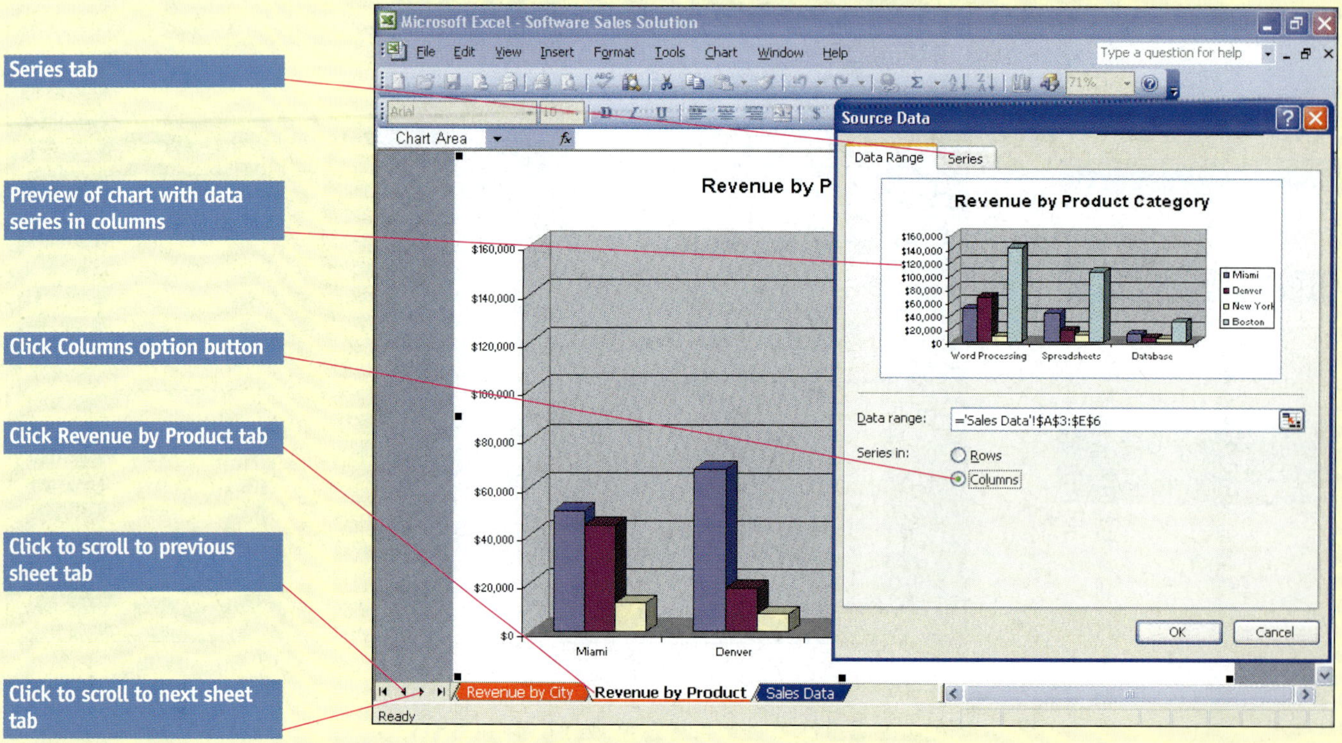

(d) Change the Source Data (step 4)

FIGURE 3.10 Hands-on Exercise 2 (*continued*)

THE HORIZONTAL SCROLL BAR

The horizontal scroll bar contains four scrolling buttons to scroll through the sheet tabs in a workbook. Click ◀ or ▶ to scroll one tab to the left or right. Click ⏮ or ⏭ to scroll to the first or last tab in the workbook. Once the desired tab is visible, click the tab to select it. Change the color of any tab by right clicking the tab and selecting Tab Color from the context-sensitive menu. See practice exercise 1 at the end of the chapter.

Step 5: Change the Chart Type

- Pull down the **Chart menu** and click the **Chart Type command** to display the associated dialog box.
- Select the **Stacked Column with a 3-D visual effect** chart (the middle entry in the second row). Click **OK**. The chart changes to a stacked column chart.
- Pull down the **Chart menu** and click the **Chart Options command** to display the associated dialog box. Click the **Legend tab** and check the option button to display the legend at the **bottom** of the chart.
- Click the **Data Labels tab**. Check the box to display the **Value** of each chart component as shown in Figure 3.10e.
- Experiment further with the various options that are available. Click the **Data Table tab**, then check the box to show the data table. We think the table is cluttered in this example, and thus we clear the box to show the table.
- Click **OK** to accept the existing settings and close the Chart Options dialog box. Save the workbook.

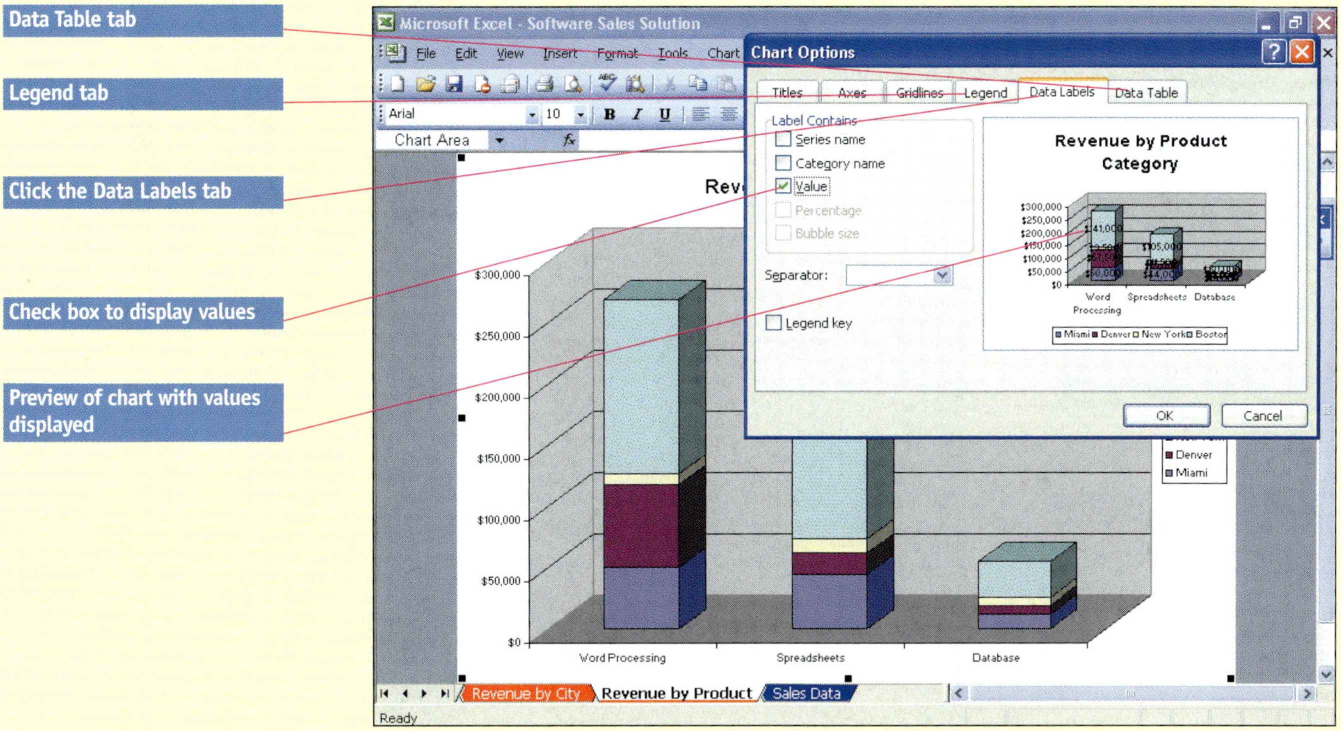

(e) Change the Chart Type (step 5)

FIGURE 3.10 Hands-on Exercise 2 (*continued*)

THE RIGHT MOUSE BUTTON

Point to a cell (or group of selected cells), a chart or worksheet tab, a toolbar, or chart (or a selected object on the chart), then click the right mouse button to display a shortcut menu. All shortcut menus are context-sensitive and display commands appropriate for the selected item. Right clicking a toolbar, for example, enables you to display (hide) additional toolbars. Right clicking a sheet tab enables you to rename, move, copy, or delete the sheet.

Step 6: Print the Workbook

- Click the **Print Preview button** on the Standard toolbar to display the Print Preview screen. Click the **Margins button** on the Print Preview toolbar to toggle the (display of the) margins on and off.
- Click the **Setup button** to display the Page Setup dialog box. Click the **Page tab** in the Page Setup dialog box. Click the option button for **landscape**.
- Click the **Header/Footer tab** in the Page Setup dialog box, then click the button to create a **Custom Footer** to display the Footer dialog box as shown in Figure 3.10f.
- Click the text box for the left section and **enter your name**. Click the text box for the center section and **enter your instructor's name**.
- Click the text box for the right section. Click the **Date button**, press the **space bar**, and then click the **Time button**. Click **OK** to accept these settings and close the Footer dialog box. Click **OK** to close the Page Setup dialog box.
- Print the completed chart for your instructor. Use the **Page Setup command** as appropriate prior to printing the other charts in the workbook.
- Save the workbook. Exit Excel if you do not want to continue with the next exercise at this time.

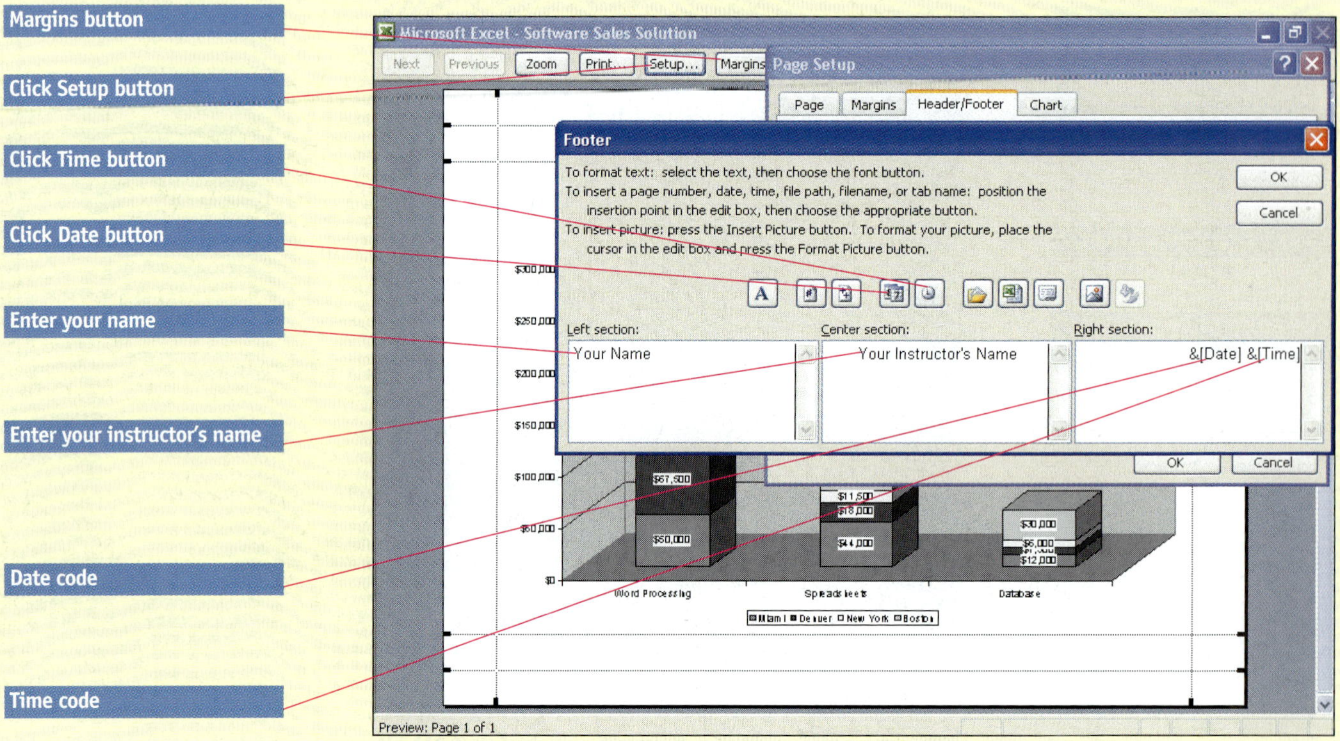

(f) Print the Workbook (step 6)

FIGURE 3.10 Hands-on Exercise 2 (*continued*)

PRINT ONLY WHAT YOU NEED

Why print an entire workbook if you need only a single worksheet? Press and hold the Ctrl key as you click the tab(s) of the worksheet(s) that you want to print. Pull down the File menu, click the Print command, click the option button for Active Sheet(s) in the Print What area, then click OK. (You can also print selected cells within a worksheet by selecting the cells, then clicking the Selection option button.)

OBJECT LINKING AND EMBEDDING

The applications within Microsoft Office enable you to create a document in one application that contains data (objects) from another application. The memo in Figure 3.11, for example, was created in Microsoft Word, and it contains ***objects*** (a worksheet and a chart) that were developed in Microsoft Excel. The Excel objects are linked to the Word document, so that any changes to the Excel workbook are automatically reflected in the Word document.

The following exercise uses ***Object Linking and Embedding (OLE)*** to create a Word document containing an Excel worksheet and chart. As you do the exercise, both applications (Word and Excel) will be open, and it will be necessary to switch back and forth between them. This in turn demonstrates the ***multitasking*** capability within Windows and the use of the ***taskbar*** to switch between the open applications.

Superior Software

To: Mr. White
Chairman, Superior Software

From: Heather Bond
Vice President, Marketing

Subject: May Sales Data

The May sales data clearly indicate that Boston is outperforming our other geographic areas. It is my feeling that Ms. Brown, the office supervisor, is directly responsible for its success and that she should be rewarded accordingly. In addition, we may want to think about transferring her to New York, as they are in desperate need of new ideas and direction. I will be awaiting your response after you have time to digest the information presented.

Superior Software Sales

	Miami	Denver	New York	Boston	Total
Word Processing	$50,000	$67,500	$200,000	$141,000	**$458,500**
Spreadsheets	$44,000	$18,000	$11,500	$105,000	**$178,500**
Database	$12,000	$7,500	$6,000	$30,000	**$55,500**
Total	**$106,000**	**$93,000**	**$217,500**	**$276,000**	**$692,500**

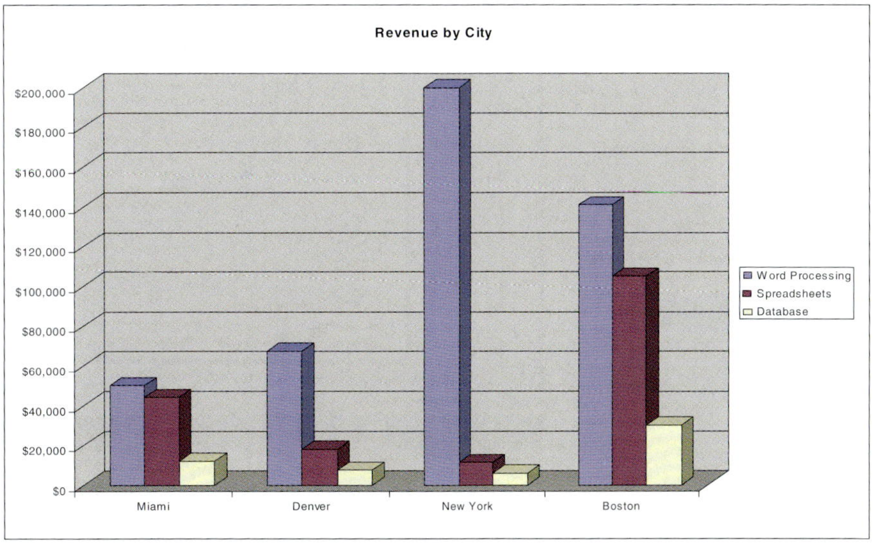

FIGURE 3.11 Object Linking and Embedding

hands-on exercise

3 Object Linking and Embedding

Objective To create a compound document consisting of a memo, worksheet, and chart. Use Figure 3.12 as a guide in the exercise.

Step 1: Open the Software Sales Document

- Click the **Start button**, click **All Programs**, click **Microsoft Office**, then click **Microsoft Office Word 2003** to start Word. Hide the Office Assistant if it appears.
- If necessary, click the **Maximize button** in the application window so that Word takes the entire desktop as shown in Figure 3.12a. (The Open dialog box is not yet visible.)
- Pull down the **File menu** and click **Open** (or click the **Open button** on the Standard toolbar).
  - Click the **drop-down arrow** in the Look In list box. Click the appropriate drive, drive C or drive A, depending on the location of your data.
  - Double click the **Exploring Excel folder** (we placed the Word memo in the Exploring Excel folder) to open the folder. Double click the **Software Memo** to open the document.
  - Save the document as **Software Memo Solution**.
- Pull down the **View menu**. Click **Print Layout** to change to the Print Layout view. Pull down the **View menu**. Click **Zoom**. Click **Page Width**. Click **Ok**.
- The software memo is open on your desktop.

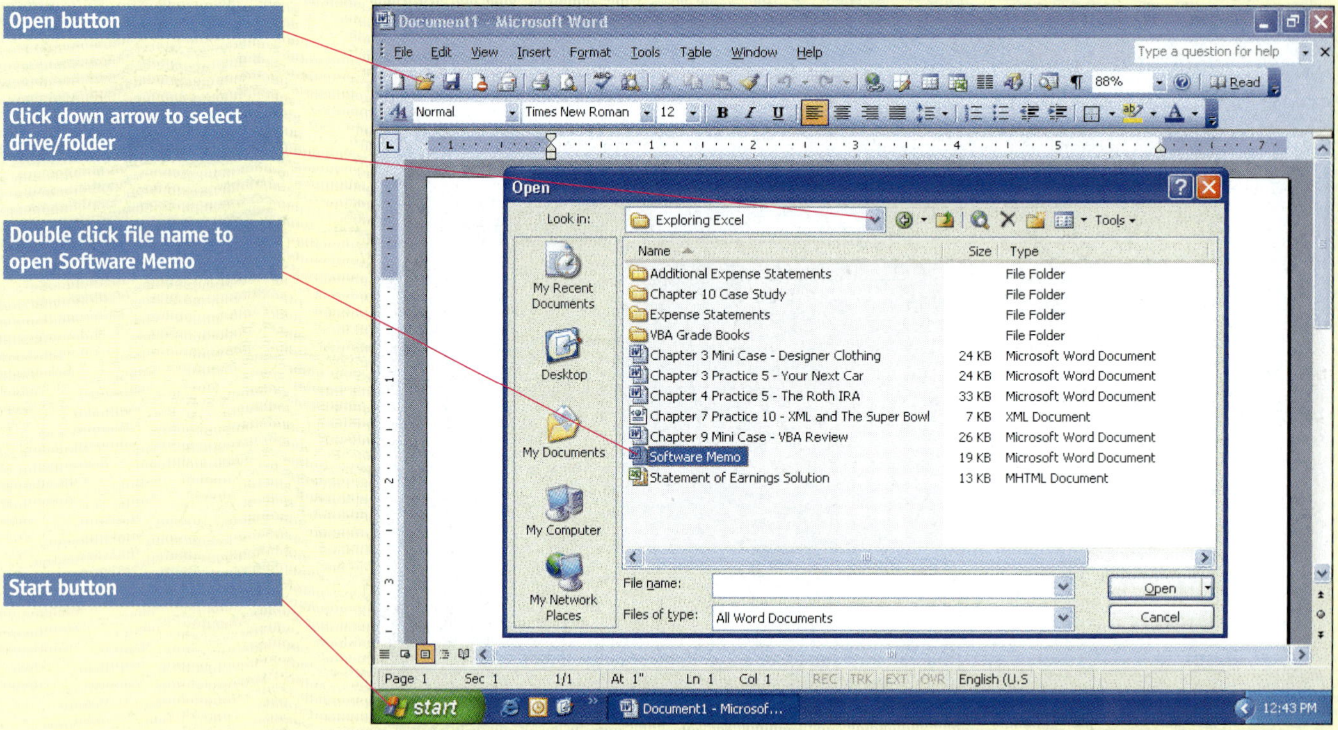

(a) Open the Software Sales Document (step 1)

FIGURE 3.12 Hands-on Exercise 3

Step 2: Copy the Worksheet

- Open the **Software Sales Solution workbook** from the previous exercise.
  - If you did not close Microsoft Excel at the end of the previous exercise, you will see its button on the taskbar. Click the **Microsoft Excel button** to return to the Software Sales Solution workbook.
  - If you closed Microsoft Excel, click the **Start button** to start Excel, then open the Software Sales Solution workbook.
- The taskbar should now contain a button for both Microsoft Word and Microsoft Excel. Click either button to move back and forth between the open applications. End by clicking the **Microsoft Excel button**.
- Click the tab for **Sales Data**. Click and drag to select **A1** through **F7** to select the entire worksheet as shown in Figure 3.12b.
- Point to the selected area and click the **right mouse button** to display the shortcut menu. Click **Copy**.
- A moving border appears around the entire worksheet, indicating that it has been copied to the clipboard.

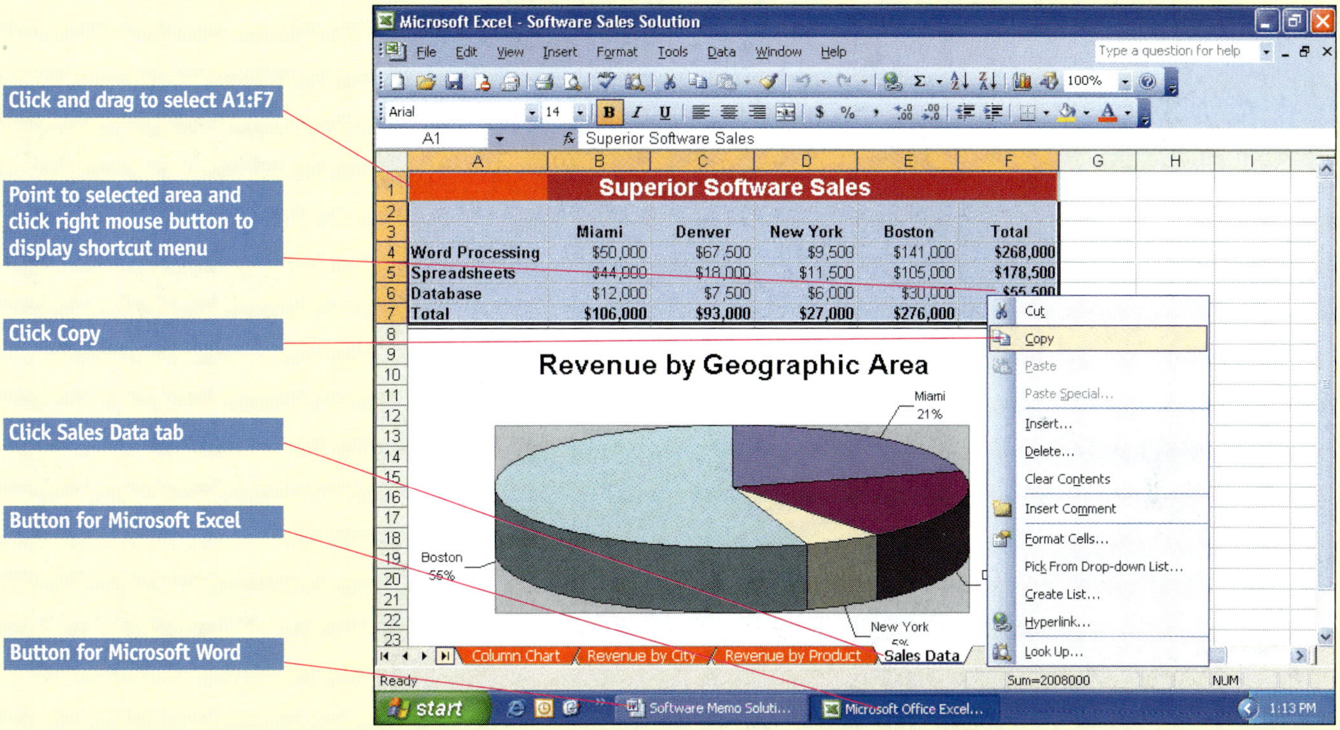

(b) Copy the Worksheet (step 2)

FIGURE 3.12 Hands-on Exercise 3 (*continued*)

THE WINDOWS TASKBAR

Multitasking, the ability to run multiple applications at the same time, is one of the primary advantages of the Windows environment. Each button on the taskbar appears automatically when its application or folder is opened, and disappears upon closing. (The buttons are resized automatically according to the number of open windows.) The taskbar can be moved to the left or right edge of the desktop, or to the top of the desktop, by dragging a blank area of the taskbar to the desired position.

Step 3: Create the Link

- Click the **Microsoft Word button** on the taskbar to return to the memo as shown in Figure 3.12c. Press **Ctrl+End** to move to the end of the memo, which is where you will insert the Excel worksheet.
- Pull down the **Edit menu**. If necessary, click the **double arrow** to see more commands, then click **Paste Special** to display the dialog box in Figure 3.12c.
- Click **Microsoft Excel Worksheet Object** in the As list. Click the **Paste link option button**. Click **OK** to insert the worksheet into the document.
- Right click the worksheet to display a context-sensitive menu, click **Format Object** to display the associated dialog box, and click the **Layout tab**.
- Choose **Square** in the Wrapping Style area, then click the option button to **Center** the object. Click **OK** to accept the settings and close the dialog box.
- Save the memo.

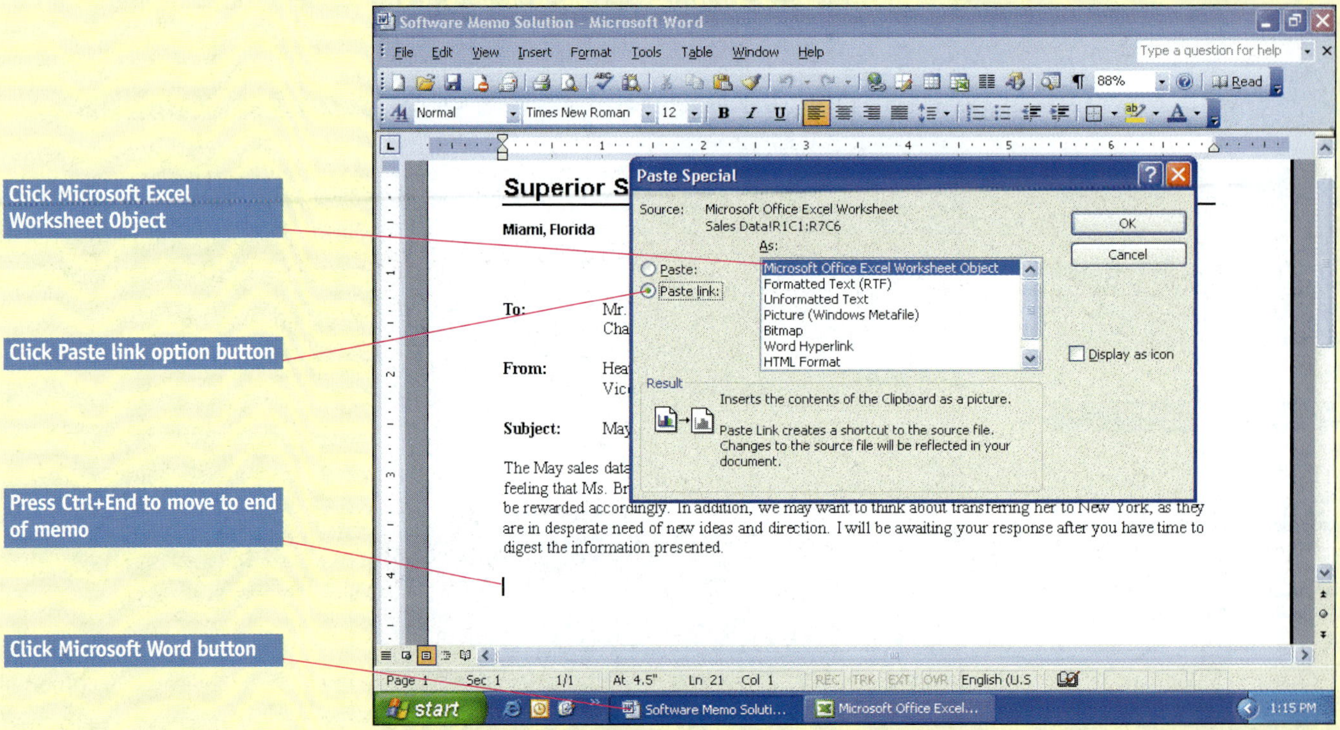

(c) Create the Link (step 3)

FIGURE 3.12 Hands-on Exercise 3 (*continued*)

THE COMMON USER INTERFACE

The common user interface provides a sense of familiarity from one Office application to the next. The applications share a common menu structure with consistent ways to execute commands from those menus. The Standard and Formatting toolbars are present in both applications. Many keyboard shortcuts are also common, such as Ctrl+Home and Ctrl+End to move to the beginning and end of a document, respectively.

Step 4: Copy the Chart

- Click the **Microsoft Excel button** on the taskbar to return to the worksheet.
- Click outside the selected area (cells A1 through F7) to deselect the cells. Press **Esc** to remove the moving border.
- Click the **Revenue by City tab** to select the chart sheet. Point to the chart area, then click the left mouse button to select the chart.
- Be sure you have selected the entire chart and that you see the same sizing handles as in Figure 3.12d.
- Pull down the **Edit menu** and click the **Copy command** (or click the **Copy button** on the Standard toolbar).
- A moving border appears around the entire chart, indicating that the chart has been copied to the clipboard. You can now link the chart to the Word document.

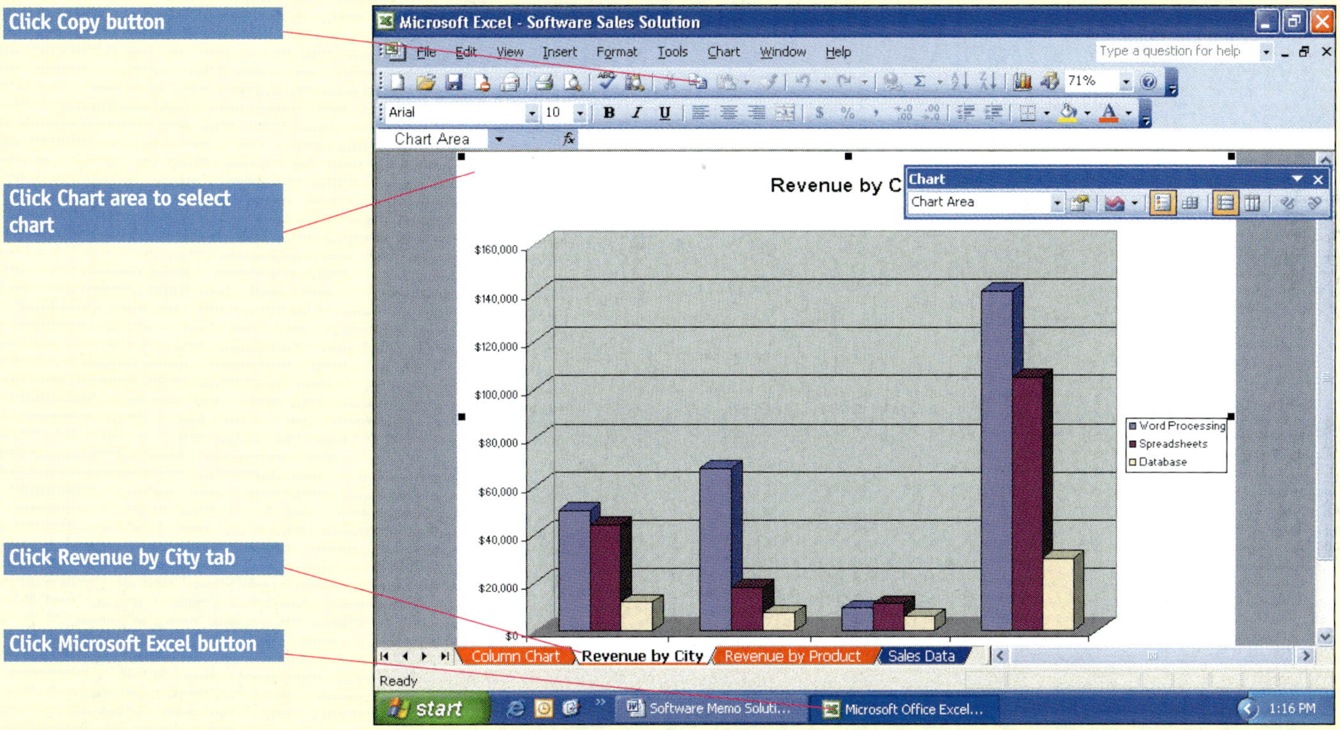

(d) Copy the Chart (step 4)

FIGURE 3.12 Hands-on Exercise 3 (*continued*)

ALT+TAB STILL WORKS

Alt+Tab was a treasured shortcut in the first version of Windows that enabled users to switch back and forth between open applications. The shortcut also works in all subsequent versions of Windows. Press and hold the Alt key while you press and release the Tab key repeatedly to cycle through the open applications, whose icons are displayed in a small rectangular window in the middle of the screen. Release the Alt key when you have selected the icon for the application you want.

Step 5: Add the Chart

- Click the **Microsoft Word button** on the taskbar to return to the memo. Double click below the worksheet to set the insertion point.
- Pull down the **Edit menu**. Click **Paste Special**. Click the **Paste link option button**. If necessary, click **Microsoft Excel Chart Object**. Click **OK** to insert the chart into the document.
- Right click the chart to display a context-sensitive menu, click **Format Object**, click the **Layout tab**, and choose **Square** in the Wrapping Style area. Click **OK**.
- Zoom to **Whole Page** to facilitate moving and sizing the chart. You need to reduce its size so that it fits on the same page as the memo. Thus scroll to the chart and click the chart to select it. This displays the sizing handles as shown in Figure 3.12e.
- Click and drag a corner sizing handle inward to make the chart smaller. Move the chart to the first page and center it on the page below the spreadsheet.
- Select the chart. Pull down the **Format menu**, and click the **Object command** to display the Format Object dialog box.
- Click the **Colors and Lines tab**. Click the **down arrow** in the Line color area, choose a color, and click **OK** to place a border around the chart.
- Zoom to **Page Width**. Look carefully at the worksheet and chart in the document. The sales for Word Processing in New York are currently $9,500, and the chart reflects this amount. Save the memo.
- Point to the **Microsoft Excel button** on the taskbar and click the **right mouse button** to display a shortcut menu. Click **Close** to close Excel. Click **Yes** if prompted to save the changes to the Software Sales Solution workbook.

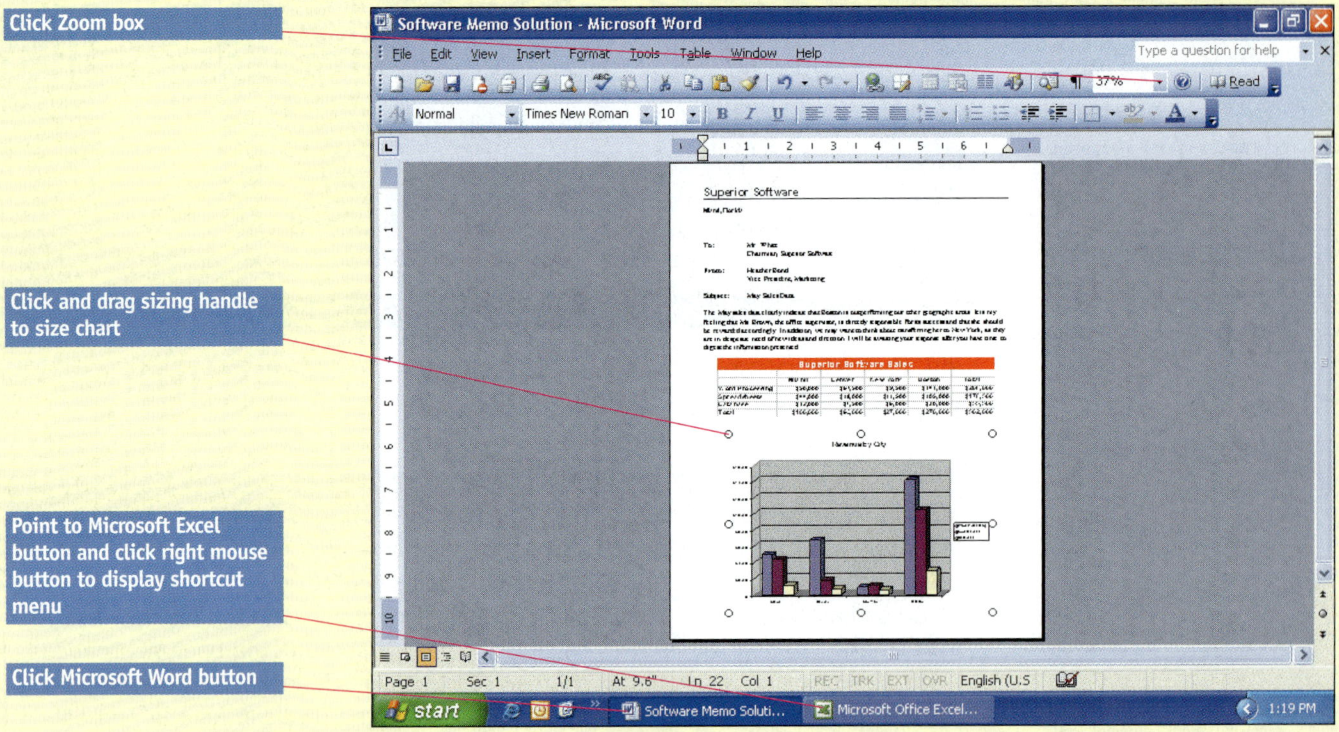

(e) Add the Chart (step 5)

FIGURE 3.12 Hands-on Exercise 3 (*continued*)

Step 6: Modify the Worksheet

- Click anywhere in the worksheet to select the worksheet and display the sizing handles as shown in Figure 3.12f.
- The status bar indicates that you can double click to edit the worksheet. Thus, double click anywhere within the worksheet to start Excel, the application that created the chart originally, in order to change the data.
- The system pauses as it loads Excel and reopens the Software Sales Solution workbook. If necessary, click the **Maximize button** to maximize the Excel window. Hide the Office Assistant if it appears.
- If necessary, click the **Sales Data tab** within the workbook. Click in **cell D4**. Type **$200,000**. Press **Enter**.
- Click the |◀ **button** to scroll to the first tab. Click the **Revenue by City tab** to select the chart sheet. The chart has been modified automatically and reflects the increased sales for New York.
- Save the workbook.

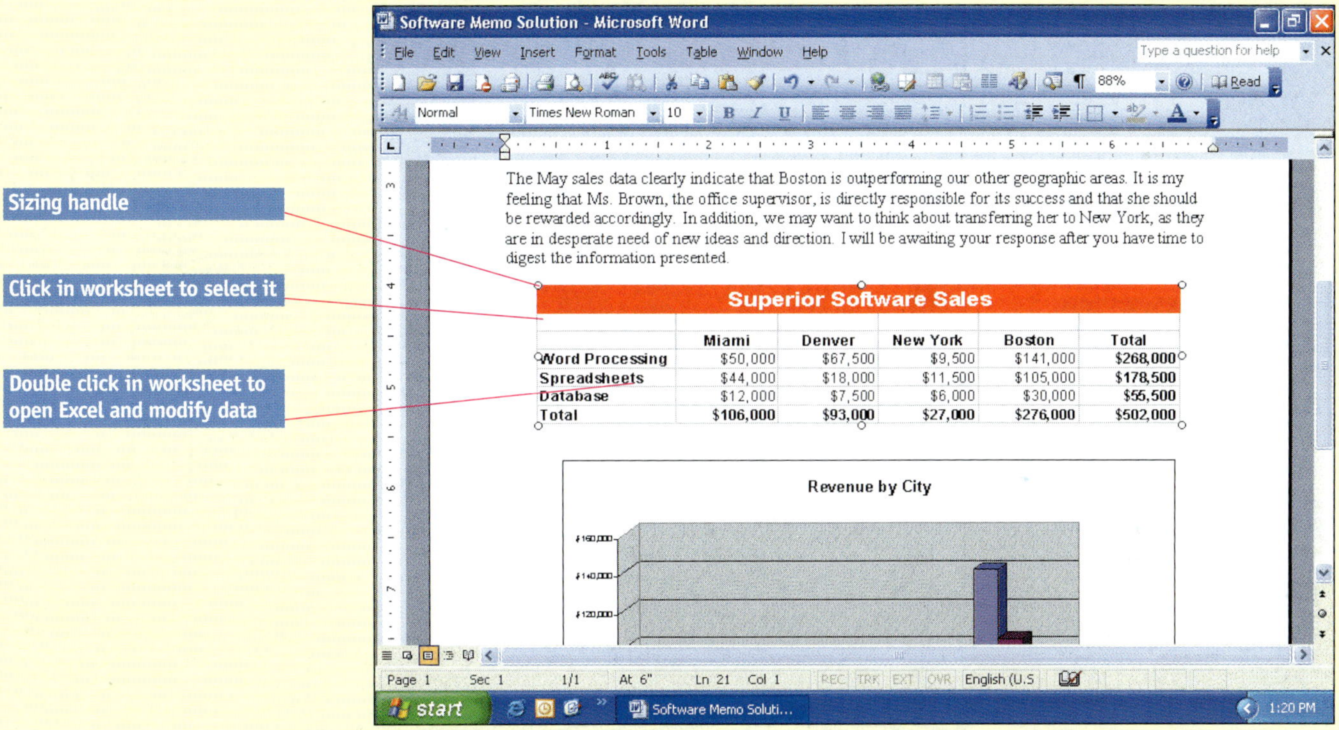

(f) Modify the Worksheet (step 6)

FIGURE 3.12 Hands-on Exercise 3 (*continued*)

LINKING VERSUS EMBEDDING

A linked object maintains its connection to the source file. An embedded object does not. Thus, a linked object can be placed in any number of destination files, each of which maintains a pointer (link) to the same source file. Any change to the object in the source file is reflected automatically in every destination file containing that object.

Step 7: Update the Links

- Click the **Microsoft Word button** on the taskbar to return to the Software Memo. The worksheet and chart should be updated automatically. If not:
  - Pull down the **Edit menu**. Click **Links** to display the Links dialog box in Figure 3.12g.
  - Select the link(s) to update. (You can press and hold the **Ctrl key** to select multiple links simultaneously.)
  - Click the **Update Now button** to update the selected links.
  - Close the Links dialog box.
- The worksheet and chart should both reflect $200,000 for word processing sales in New York.
- Zoom to the **Whole Page** to view the completed document. Click and drag the worksheet and/or the chart within the memo to make any last-minute changes. Save the memo a final time.
- Print the completed memo and submit it to your instructor. Exit Word. Exit Excel. Save the changes to the Software Sales Solution workbook if you are prompted to do so.

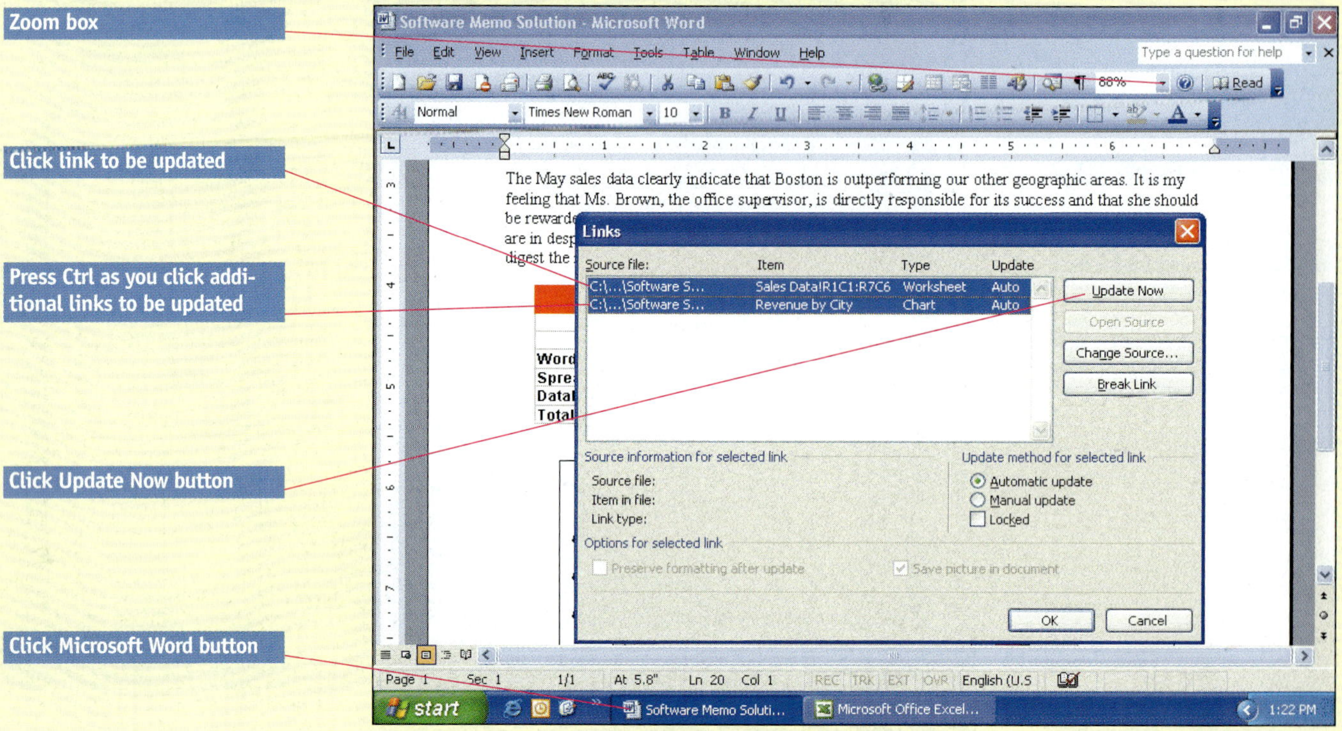

(g) Update the Links (step 7)

FIGURE 3.12 Hands-on Exercise 3 (*continued*)

LINKING WORKSHEETS

A Word document can be linked to an Excel chart and/or worksheet; that is, change the chart in Excel, and the Word document changes automatically. The chart itself is linked to the underlying worksheet; change the worksheet, and the chart changes. Worksheets can also be linked to one another; for example, a summary worksheet for the corporation as a whole can reflect data from detail worksheets for individual cities. See practice exercises 7 and 8 at the end of the chapter.

SUMMARY

A chart is a graphic representation of data in a worksheet. The type of chart chosen depends on the message to be conveyed. A pie chart is best for proportional relationships. A column or bar chart is used to show actual numbers rather than percentages. A line chart is preferable for time-related data. A combination chart uses two or more chart types when different scales are required for different data series.

The title of a chart can help to convey the message. A neutral title such as "Revenue by City" leaves the reader to draw his or her own conclusion. Using a different title such as "Boston Leads All Cities" or "New York is Trailing Badly" sends a very different message.

The Chart Wizard is an easy way to create a chart. Once created, a chart can be enhanced with arrows and text boxes found on the Drawing toolbar. These objects can be moved or sized and/or modified with respect to their color and other properties. The chart itself can also be modified using various commands from the Chart menu or tools on the Chart toolbar. A toolbar may be docked along the edge of a window or it may be floating within the window. All toolbars are displayed or hidden using the Toolbar command in the View menu.

A chart may be embedded in a worksheet or created in a separate chart sheet. An embedded chart may be moved within a worksheet by selecting it and dragging it to its new location. An embedded chart may be sized by selecting it and dragging any of the sizing handles in the desired direction.

Multiple data series may be specified in either rows or columns. If the data is in rows, the first row is assumed to contain the category labels, and the first column is assumed to contain the legend. Conversely, if the data is in columns, the first column is assumed to contain the category labels, and the first row the legend. The Chart Wizard makes it easy to switch from rows to columns and vice versa.

The choice between a side-by-side and a stacked column chart depends on the intended message. A side-by-side chart shows the contribution of each data point, but the total for each series is not as clear as with a stacked column chart. The stacked column chart, on the other hand, shows the totals clearly, but the contribution of the individual data points is obscured since the segments do not start at zero. It is important that charts are created accurately and that they do not mislead the reader. Stacked column charts should not add dissimilar quantities such as units and dollars.

Object Linking and Embedding enables the creation of a compound document containing data (objects) from multiple applications. The essential difference between linking and embedding is whether the object is stored within the compound document (embedding) or in its own file (linking). An embedded object is stored in the compound document, which in turn becomes the only user (client) of that object. A linked object is stored in its own file, and the compound document is one of many potential clients of that object. The same chart can be linked to a Word document and a PowerPoint presentation.

KEY TERMS

MULTIPLE CHOICE

1. Which type of chart is best to portray proportion or market share?
   (a) Pie chart
   (b) Line
   (c) Column chart
   (d) Combination chart

2. Which of the following is a true statement about the Chart Wizard?
   (a) It is accessed via a button on the Standard toolbar
   (b) It enables you to choose the type of chart you want as well as specify the location for that chart
   (c) It enables you to retrace your steps via the Back command button
   (d) All of the above

3. Which of the following chart types is *not* suitable to display multiple data series?
   (a) Pie chart
   (b) Horizontal bar chart
   (c) Column chart
   (d) All of the above are equally suitable

4. Which of the following is best to display additive information from multiple data series?
   (a) A column chart with the data series stacked one on top of another
   (b) A column chart with the data series side by side
   (c) Both (a) and (b) are equally appropriate
   (d) Neither (a) nor (b) is appropriate

5. A workbook must contain:
   (a) A separate chart sheet for every worksheet
   (b) A separate worksheet for every chart sheet
   (c) Both (a) and (b)
   (d) Neither (a) nor (b)

6. Which of the following is true regarding an embedded chart?
   (a) It can be moved elsewhere within the worksheet
   (b) It can be made larger or smaller
   (c) Both (a) and (b)
   (d) Neither (a) nor (b)

7. Which of the following will produce a shortcut menu?
   (a) Pointing to a workbook tab and clicking the right mouse button
   (b) Pointing to an embedded chart and clicking the right mouse button
   (c) Pointing to a selected cell range and clicking the right mouse button
   (d) All of the above

8. Which of the following is done *prior* to invoking the Chart Wizard?
   (a) The data series are selected
   (b) The location of the embedded chart within the worksheet is specified
   (c) Both (a) and (b)
   (d) Neither (a) nor (b)

9. Which of the following will display sizing handles when selected?
   (a) An embedded chart
   (b) The title of a chart
   (c) A text box or arrow
   (d) All of the above

10. How do you switch between open applications?
    (a) Click the appropriate button on the taskbar
    (b) Use Alt+Tab to cycle through the applications
    (c) Both (a) and (b)
    (d) Neither (a) nor (b)

... continued

multiple choice

11. A Word document is linked to an Excel worksheet and associated chart. Which of the following best describes the way the documents are stored on disk?

(a) A single file contains the Word document, the worksheet, and the associated chart
(b) There are two files—one for the Word document and one for the Excel workbook, which contains both the worksheet and associated chart
(c) There are three files—one for the Word document, one for the Excel worksheet, and one for the Excel chart
(d) None of the above

12. To represent multiple data series on the same chart:

(a) The data series must be in rows and the rows must be adjacent to one another on the worksheet
(b) The data series must be in columns and the columns must be adjacent to one another on the worksheet
(c) The data series may be in rows or columns so long as they are adjacent to one another
(d) The data series may be in rows or columns with no requirement to be next to one another

13. If multiple data series are selected and rows are specified:

(a) The first row will be used for the category labels
(b) The first column will be used for the legend
(c) Both (a) and (b)
(d) Neither (a) nor (b)

14. If multiple data series are selected and columns are specified:

(a) The first column will be used for the category (*X* axis) labels
(b) The first row will be used for the legend
(c) Both (a) and (b)
(d) Neither (a) nor (b)

15. Which of the following is true about the scale on the *Y* axis in a column chart that plots multiple data series side-by-side versus one that stacks the values one on top of another?

(a) The scale for the stacked columns chart contains larger values than the side-by-side chart
(b) The scale for the side-by-side columns contains larger values than the stacked columns
(c) The values on the scale will be the same for both charts
(d) The values will be different but it is not possible to tell which chart has higher values

16. A workbook includes a revenue worksheet with two embedded charts. The workbook also includes one chart in its own worksheet. How many files does it take to store this workbook?

(a) 1
(b) 2
(c) 3
(d) 4

17. Assume that cells A1 through E5 have been selected, after which the Chart Wizard is used to create a side-by-side column chart. Which of the following is true, given that the data are plotted in rows?

(a) The category names are in cells B1 through E1
(b) The legends are in cells A2 through A5
(c) Both (a) and (b)
(d) Neither (a) nor (b)

18. Which of the following creates a dynamic link between a workbook and a word processing memo?

(a) Copy, Paste Special, and Paste Link
(b) Copy and Paste
(c) Cut, Paste Special, and Paste Link
(d) Cut and Paste

ANSWERS

1. a	**7.** d	**13.** c
2. d	**8.** a	**14.** c
3. a	**9.** d	**15.** a
4. a	**10.** c	**16.** a
5. d	**11.** b	**17.** c
6. c	**12.** d	**18.** a

PRACTICE WITH EXCEL

1. **Theme Park Admissions:** A partially completed version of the worksheet in Figure 3.13 is available in the Exploring Excel folder as *Chapter 3 Practice 1*. Follow the directions in parts (a) and (b) to compute the totals and format the worksheet, then create each of the charts listed below.
   a. Use the AutoSum command to enter the formulas to compute the total number of admissions for each region and each quarter.
   b. Select the entire worksheet (cells A1 through F8), then use the AutoFormat command to format the worksheet. You do not have to accept the entire design, nor do you have to use the design we selected. You can also modify the design after it has been applied to the worksheet by changing the font size of selected cells and/or changing boldface and italics.
   c. Create a column chart showing the total number of admissions in each quarter as shown in Figure 3.13. Add the graphic shown in the figure for emphasis.
   d. Create a pie chart that shows the percentage of the total number of admissions in each region. Create this chart in its own chart sheet with an appropriate name.
   e. Create a stacked column chart that shows the total number of admissions for each region and the contribution of each quarter within each region. Create this chart in its own chart sheet with an appropriate name.
   f. Create a stacked column chart showing the total number of admissions for each quarter and the contribution of each region within each quarter. Create this chart in its own chart sheet with an appropriate name.
   g. Change the color of each of the worksheet tabs.
   h. Print the entire workbook, consisting of the worksheet in Figure 3.13 plus the three additional sheets that you create. Use portrait orientation for the Sales Data worksheet and landscape orientation for the other worksheets. Create a custom header for each worksheet that includes your name, your course, and your instructor's name. Create a custom footer for each worksheet that includes the name of the worksheet. Submit the completed assignment to your instructor.

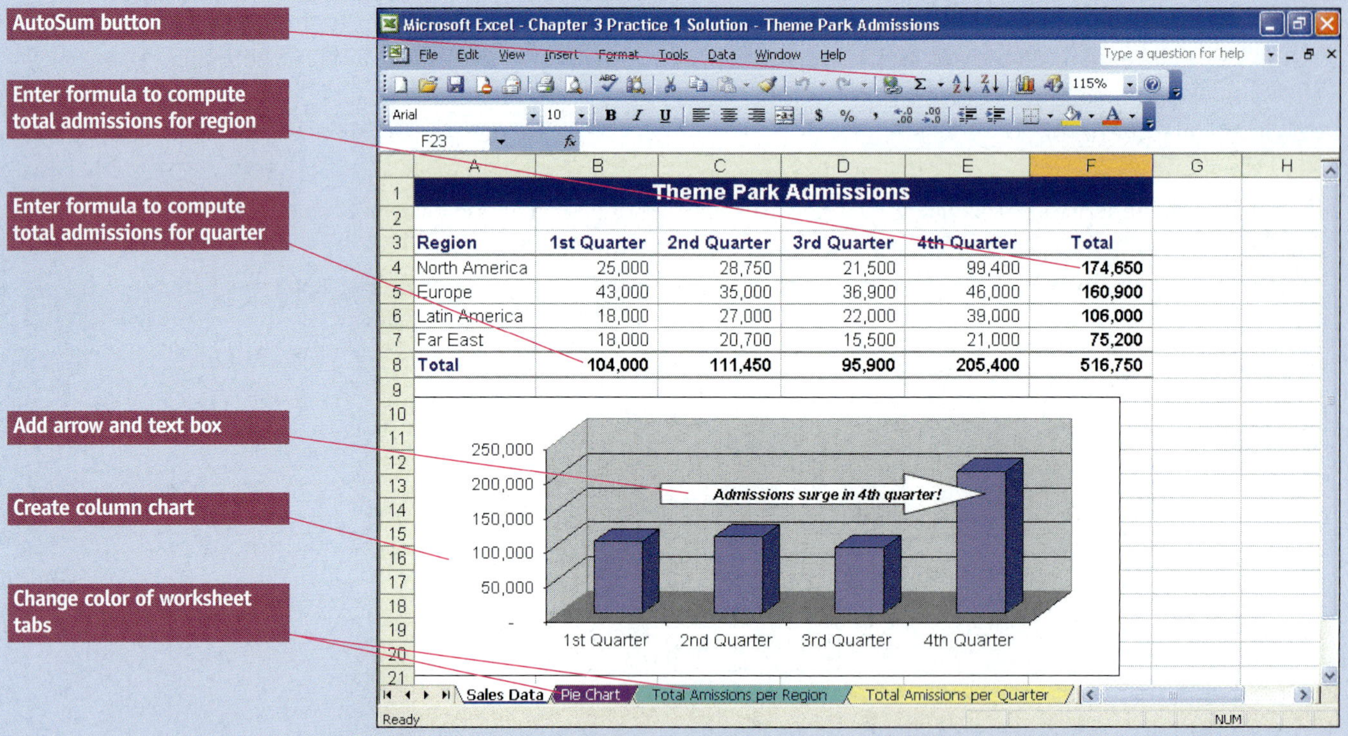

FIGURE 3.13 Theme Park Admissions (exercise 1)

2. **Rows versus Columns:** Figure 3.14 displays the Page Preview view of a worksheet with two similar charts, one that plots data by rows and the other by columns. The distinction depends on the message you want to deliver. Both charts are correct. Your assignment is to open the partially completed worksheet in the *Chapter 3 Practice 2* workbook and proceed as follows.
    a. Use the AutoSum command to compute the total number of visits for each pet category and for each quarter. Format the completed worksheet in an attractive manner. You do not have to duplicate our formatting exactly.
    b. Create each of the charts in Figure 3.14 as an embedded chart on the current worksheet. The first chart specifies that the data series are in columns. The second chart specifies the data series are in rows.
    c. Use the Page Setup command to change to landscape orientation when the chart is printed. Create a custom header that includes your name, your course, and your instructor's name. Create a custom footer with the name of the worksheet, today's date, and the current time. Specify that the worksheet will be printed at 110% to create a more attractive printed page. Be sure, however, that the worksheet and associated charts fit on a single page.
    d. Right click the Worksheet tab, click the Move or Copy command, then check the box to copy the worksheet. Double click the Worksheet tab and change the name of the duplicate worksheet to Stacked Columns.
    e. Select the first chart in the newly created Stacked Columns worksheet. Change the chart type to Stacked Columns. Check the box to use the default formatting for the chart. Change the chart type of the second chart to stacked columns as well.
    f. Print the completed workbook (both worksheets) for your instructor. Add a short note that summarizes the difference between plotting data in rows versus columns, and between side-by-side column charts and stacked column charts.

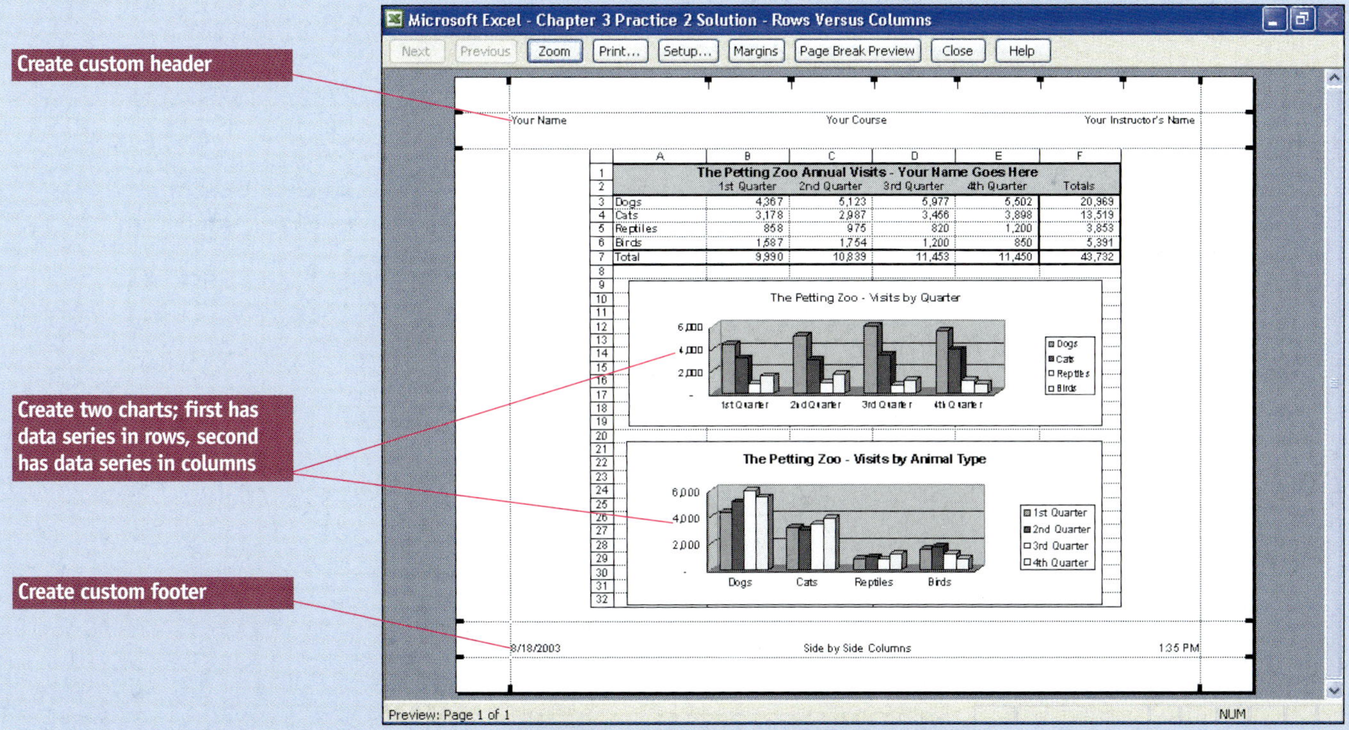

FIGURE 3.14 Rows versus Columns (exercise 2)

3. **Flexibility in Charting:** The worksheet in Figure 3.15 displays the second quarter revenues for each salesperson in TalkAway, Inc., a local cellular company. Open the partially completed workbook in *Chapter 3 Practice 3* to complete the worksheet, then create the chart in Figure 3.15. The intent of this exercise is to show you several formatting options that are available in conjunction with charts. It's fun to experiment, but set a reasonable time limit.
   a. Use the AutoSum command to enter the formulas to compute the total sales for each month and for each salesperson.
   b. Format the worksheet in attractive fashion. You do not have to duplicate our formatting exactly, but you are to highlight the data in row four. In addition, use boldface to emphasize the totals for each salesperson and each month.
   c. Use the Chart wizard to create a column chart that displays the total sales for each salesperson for the second quarter.
   d. Right click any column (data series) within the chart to display a context-sensitive menu, then click the Format Data Series command. Click the Shape tab within the dialog box to change the shape of each column. Click the Data Labels tab to display the dollar value for each salesperson.
   e. Click the second column to select just this column. Click the right mouse button, click the Format Data Point command, click the Pattern tab in the associated dialog box, then change the color of this column.
   f. Click in Cell A4 and enter your name instead of Grauer. The value on the *X* axis changes automatically to reflect the entry in cell A4.
   g. Click the AutoShapes button on the Drawing toolbar to add a callout indicating that this column represents your sales data. Right click the border of the AutoShape, click the Format AutoShape command, click the Colors and Lines tab, and add a fill color.
   h. Right click the border of the chart, click the Format Chart Area command, then change the border to include rounded corners with a shadow effect.
   i. Print the completed worksheet for your instructor.

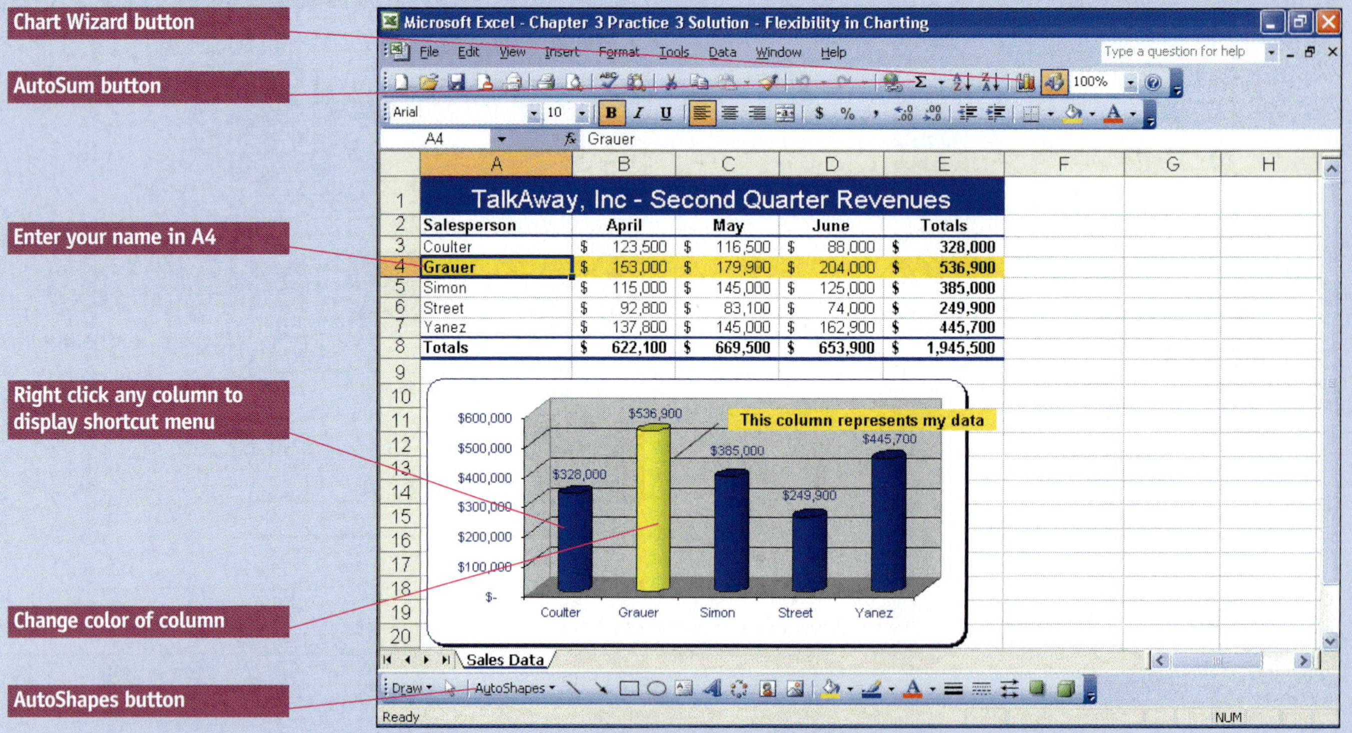

FIGURE 3.15 Flexibility in Charting (exercise 3)

4. **Page Break Preview:** Open the partially completed workbook in *Chapter 3 Practice 4* and create the four charts shown in Figure 3.16. Use the AutoSum and AutoFormat commands to complete the worksheet. Select cells A2 through E6 as the basis for each of the four charts in the figure. The charts should appear as embedded objects on the worksheet, but do not be concerned about the placement of each chart until you have completed all four charts.
   a. The first chart is a side-by-side column chart that emphasizes the sales in each city (the data is in rows).
   b. The second chart is a stacked column version of the chart in part (a).
   c. The third chart (that begins in column H of the worksheet) is a side-by-side column chart that emphasizes the sales in each product line (the data is in columns).
   d. The last chart is a stacked column version of the chart in part (c).
   e. Pull down the View command, then change to the Page Break Preview view as shown in Figure 3.16. You will see one or more dotted lines that show where the page breaks will occur. You will also see the message in Figure 3.16 indicating that you can change the location of the page breaks. Click OK after you have read the message.
   f. Remove any existing page breaks by clicking and dragging the solid blue line that indicates the break. (You can insert horizontal or vertical page breaks by clicking the appropriate cell, pulling down the Insert menu, and selecting Page Break.) Pull down the View menu and click Normal view to return to the normal view.
   g. Add your name to the completed worksheet, then print the worksheet and four embedded charts on one page. If necessary, change to landscape printing for a more attractive layout. Use the Page Setup command to create a custom header with your name, your course, and your instructor's name. Create a custom footer that contains today's date, the name of the workbook, and the current time.
   h. Write a short note to your instructor that describes the differences between the charts. Suggest a different title for one or more charts that helps to convey a specific message.

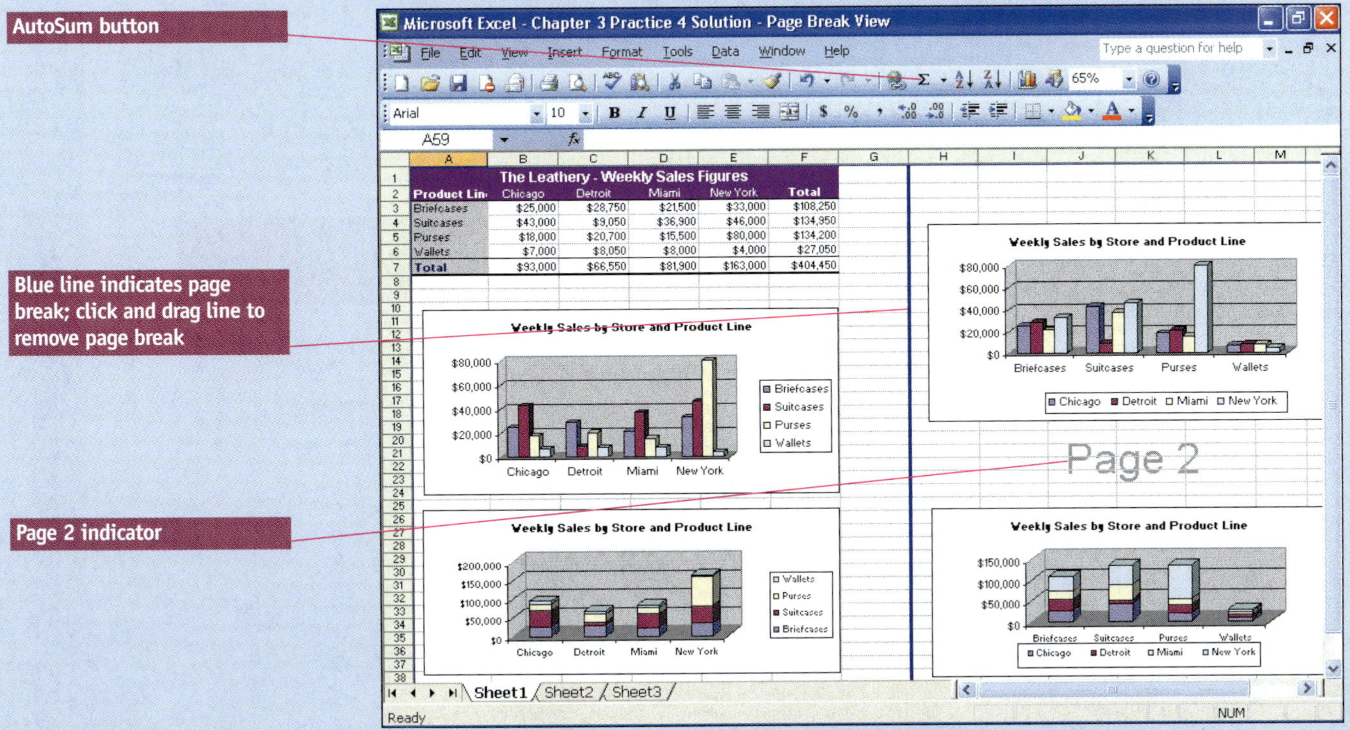

FIGURE 3.16 Page Break Preview (exercise 4)

5. **Your Next Car:** The Word document in Figure 3.17 displays descriptive information about a car you are interested in, a picture of the car, and a hyperlink to the Web site where the information was obtained. In addition, the document is linked to an Excel workbook that computes the car payment for you, based on the loan parameters that you provide. Your assignment is to create a similar document based on any car you choose. Proceed as follows:
   a. Use your favorite search engine to locate a Web site that contains information about the car you are interested in. You can go to the Web site of the manufacturer and/or you can go to a general site such as carpoint.msn.com, which contains information about all makes and models. Select the car you want and obtain the retail price of the car.
   b. Open the *Chapter 3 Practice 5* workbook in the Exploring Excel folder. Enter the price of the car, a hypothetical down payment, the interest rate of the car loan, and the term of the loan in the indicated cells. The monthly payment will be determined automatically by the PMT function that is stored in the workbook. (The PMT function is covered in detail in Chapter 4.) Save the workbook.
   c. Click and drag to select cells A3 through B9 (the cells that contain the information you want to insert into the Word document). Click the Copy button.
   d. Open the partially completed Word document, *Chapter 3 Practice 5,* that is stored in the Exploring Excel folder. Pull down the Edit menu, click the Paste Special command, and then choose the option to link the worksheet data to the Word document. Move and size the inserted worksheet to its approximate position in the document. Save the Word document.
   e. Use the taskbar to return to the Excel workbook. Change the amount of the down payment and/or the interest rate for your loan. Save the workbook. Close Excel. Return to the Word document, which should reflect the updated loan information.
   f. Return to the Web page that contains the information about your car. Right click the picture of the car that appears within the Web page, and click the Save As command to save the picture of the car to your computer. Use the Insert Picture command to insert the picture that you just obtained.
   g. Complete the Word document by inserting some descriptive information about your car. Print the completed document for your instructor.

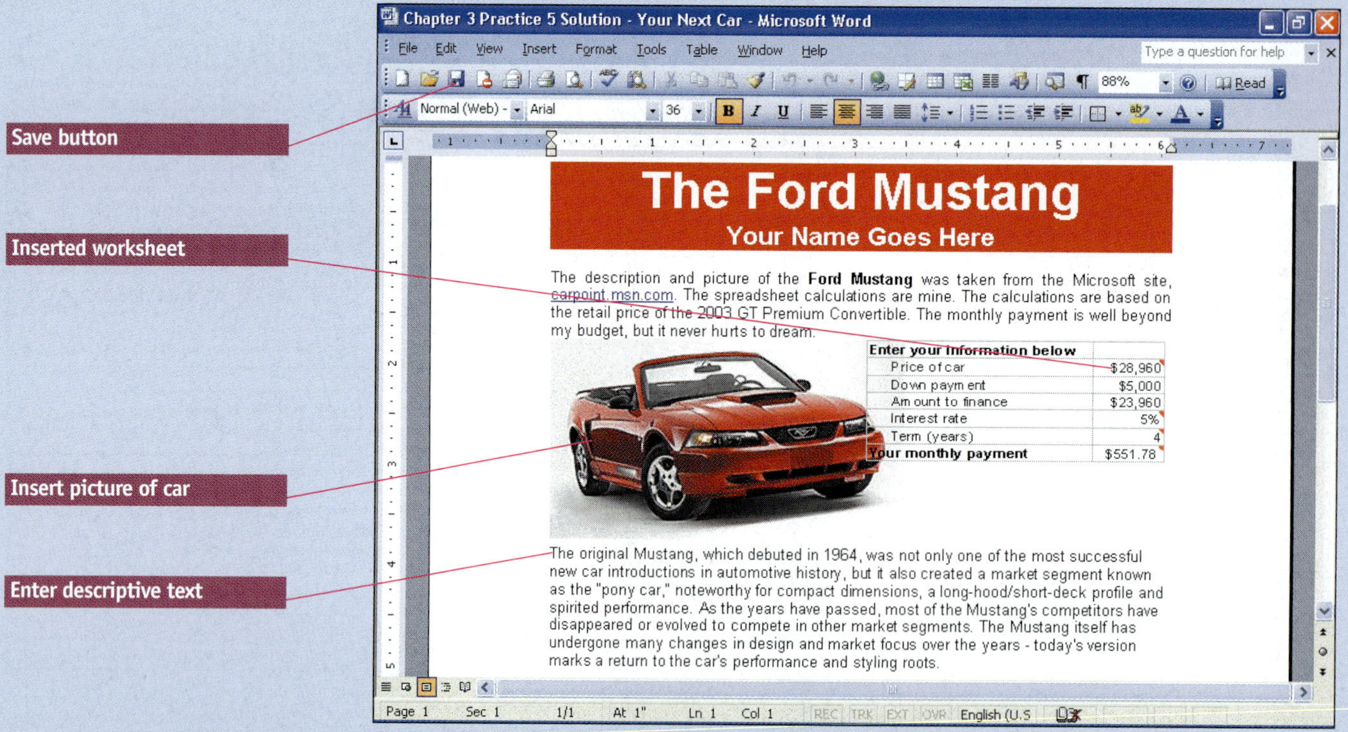

FIGURE 3.17 Your Next Car (exercise 5)

6. **Irrational Exuberance:** Figure 3.18 contains a combination chart to display different kinds of information on different scales for multiple data series. A column chart is specified for the revenue and profits, while a line chart is used for the stock price. Two different scales are necessary because the magnitudes of the numbers differ significantly.
   a. Open the partially completed workbook in *Chapter 3 Practice 6* and format the worksheet appropriately.
   b. Select the entire worksheet (cells A1 through F4), then invoke the Chart Wizard. Click the Custom Types tab in step 1 of the Chart Wizard, choose Line-Column on 2 Axes as the chart type, then in step 2 specify the data in rows. The Chart Wizard will do the rest.
   c. Modify the completed chart so that its appearance is similar to our figure. We made the chart wider and moved the legend to the bottom. (Right click the legend, click the Format Legend command, click the Placement tab, then click the Bottom option button.)
   d. Customize the border around the chart. Right click the completed chart, choose the Format Chart Area command, click the Patterns tab, then choose the style, thickness, and color of the border.
   e. Insert your name somewhere in the worksheet, then print the completed worksheet for your instructor. Use the Page Setup command to change to landscape orientation. Center the worksheet and chart horizontally on the page.
   f. Create a custom header for the worksheet that includes your name, your course, and your instructor's name. Create a custom footer that contains the name of the file in which the worksheet is contained, today's date, and the current time.
   g. What do you think should be the more important factor influencing a company's stock price, its revenue (sales) or its profit (net income)? Could the situation depicted in the worksheet occur in the real world? Summarize your thoughts in a brief note to your instructor.

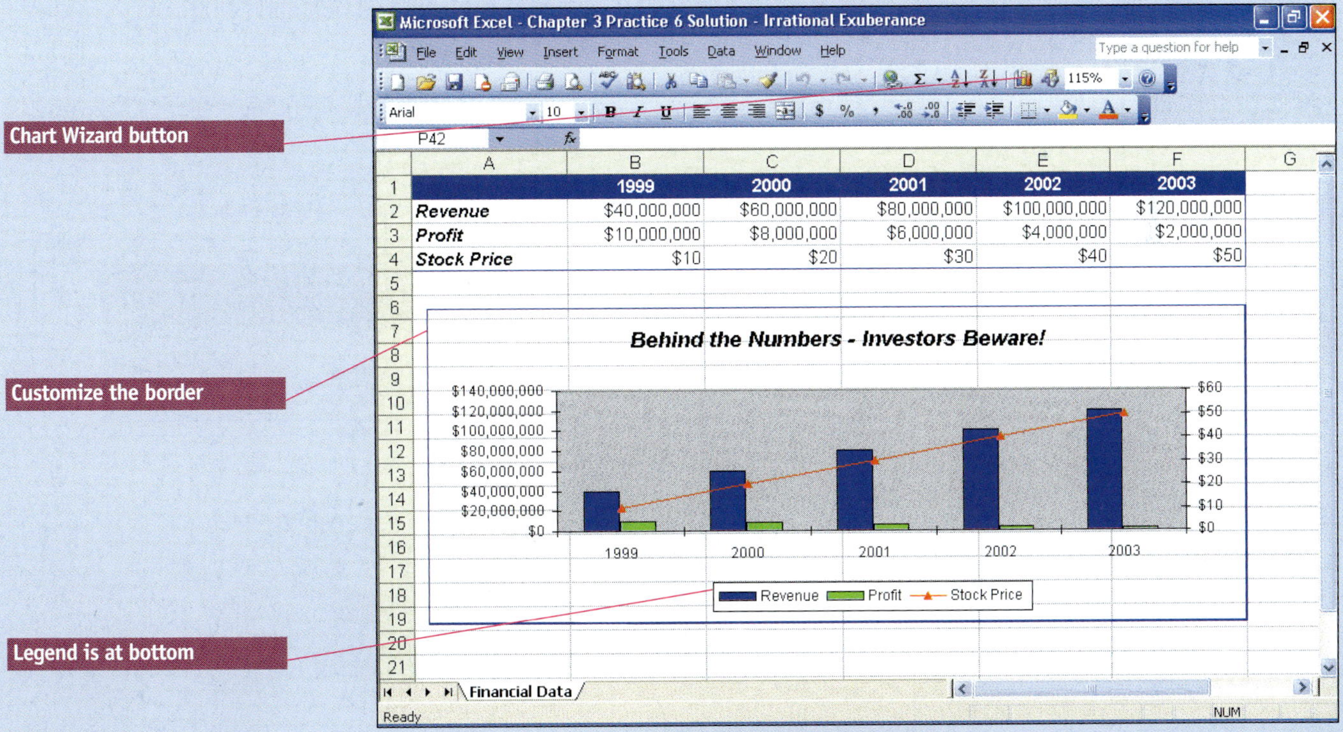

FIGURE 3.18 Irrational Exuberance (exercise 6)

7. **Worksheet References:** The worksheet in Figure 3.19 appears similar to the example that was used throughout the chapter. Look closely, however, and you will see that the workbook contains individual worksheets for each city, in addition to a worksheet for the corporation as a whole. The formulas in the corporate worksheet reference cells in the worksheets of the individual cities. For example, the entry in cell B3 of the Corporate worksheet contains the formula =Phoenix!F2 to indicate that the entry comes from cell F2 in the Phoenix worksheet. Other cells in the table reference other cells in the Phoenix worksheet as well as cells in the other worksheets.
   a. Open the *Chapter 3 Practice 7* workbook in the Exploring Excel folder. Select the Corporate worksheet by clicking the Worksheet tab. (The color of the tab for this worksheet is different from the tabs for the individual cities.) You can enter the formulas in this worksheet explicitly, but it is easier to use pointing, especially when referencing cells in other worksheets.
   b. Click (select) cell B3 in the Corporate worksheet. Type an = sign, click the Phoenix worksheet tab, click in cell F2 of this worksheet, and press the Enter key. Click in cell C3, type an = sign, click the Minneapolis tab, click in cell F2 of that worksheet, and press Enter. Repeat the process to enter the sales for San Francisco and Los Angeles.
   c. Select cells B3 through E3, then drag the fill handle to row 5 to copy the formulas for the other product lines. The copy operation works because the worksheet references are absolute, but the cell references are relative.
   d. Use the AutoSum button to compute the totals for the corporation as a whole in column F.
   e. Use the AutoFormat command to format the worksheet in an attractive fashion. (You do not have to duplicate our formatting exactly.)
   f. Use the completed worksheet as the basis for a stacked column chart with the data plotted in rows.
   g. Use the Page Setup command to display gridlines and row and column headings for each worksheet. Create a custom footer that contains your name, the name of the worksheet, and today's date. Print the entire workbook and submit the completed assignment to your instructor.

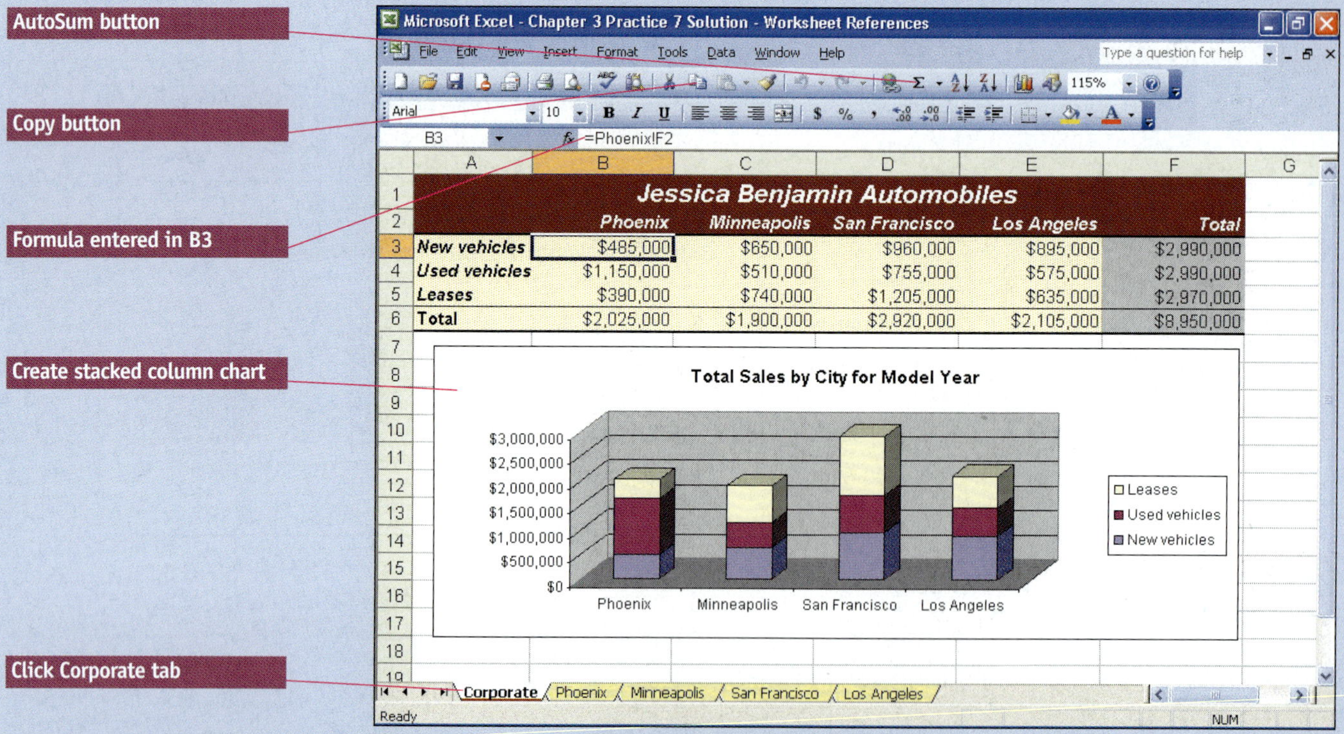

FIGURE 3.19 Worksheet References (exercise 7)

8. **Additional Practice:** The worksheet in Figure 3.20 contains a year-to-year comparison of sales data in both graphical and tabular form. Open the partially completed workbook in *Chapter 3 Practice 8* and proceed as follows:
   a. Select the Year to Year Comparison worksheet. Click in cell B3 of this worksheet, type an equal sign, click the worksheet tab labeled Previous Year, click in cell B8 of this worksheet, and press Enter. The formula for cell B3 should appear in the formula bar as ='Previous Year'!B8, indicating that the value for this cell is obtained from another worksheet in the same workbook. Copy the formula in cell B3 to cells C3 through E3.
   b. Click in cell B4 and use the same technique as in part (a) to obtain the sales for the first quarter for the current year. Copy this formula to cells C4 through E4.
   c. Use the AutoSum command to compute the total sales for the previous year (cell F3 in this worksheet). Compute the total sales for the current year in cell F4.
   d. Enter the formulas to compute the dollar increase for the first quarter in cell B5. Copy the formula in cell B5 to cells D5 through F5.
   e. Format the worksheet as shown in Figure 3.20. Try to duplicate our formatting. Use the Chart Wizard to create a side-by-side column chart that compares the sales in the current year to those in the previous year for each quarter. Display a legend at the bottom of the chart.
   f. Right click each data series individually within the chart, select the Format Data Series command, and then change the colors of the current and previous years to green and white, respectively.
   g. Use the AutoShapes button on the Drawing toolbar to create the arrow in the figure. Enter the indicated text as shown.
   h. Add your name to the title of the worksheet in cell A1. Print the completed worksheet for your instructor. Be sure to show gridlines and row and column headings.

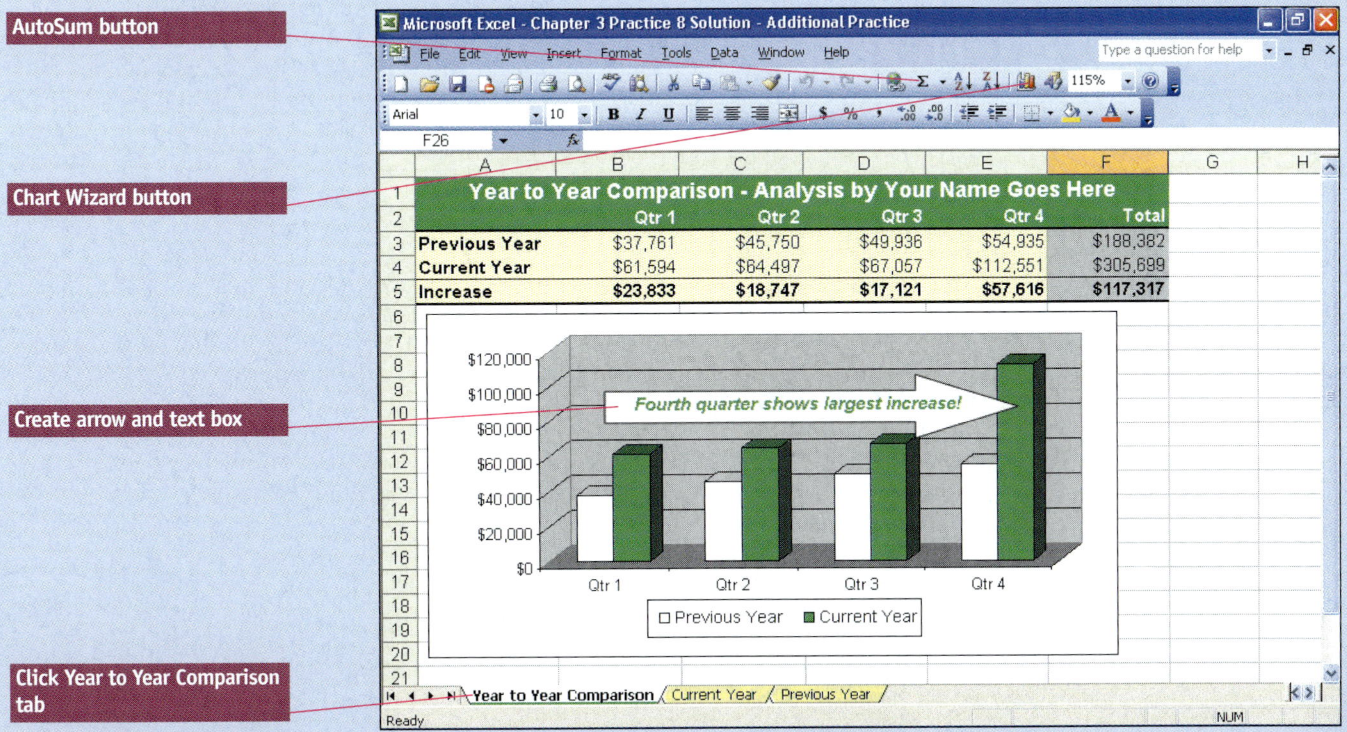

FIGURE 3.20 Additional Practice (exercise 8)

MINI CASES

The Convention Planner

Your first task as a convention planner is to evaluate the hotel capacity for the host city in order to make recommendations as to which hotels should host the convention. The data can be found in the *Chapter 3 Mini Case—Convention Planner* workbook, which contains a single worksheet showing the number of rooms in each hotel, divided into standard and deluxe categories, together with the associated room rates. Complete the worksheet by computing the total number of rooms in each category. Format the worksheet in an attractive way. Create a stacked column chart that shows the total capacity for each hotel. Create a second chart that shows the percentage of total capacity for each hotel. Store each chart in its own worksheet, and then print the entire workbook for your instructor.

Designer Clothing

This assignment asks you to complete a worksheet and associated chart for a Designer Clothing boutique, and then link these Excel objects to an appropriate memo. Open the partially completed *Chapter 3 Mini Case—Designer Clothing* workbook; compute the sales totals for each individual salesperson as well as the totals for each quarter, then format the resulting worksheet in an attractive fashion. Include your name in the title of the worksheet (cell A1). We have started the memo for you and have saved the text in the *Chapter 3 Mini Case—Designer Clothing* Word document. Open the Word document, and then link the Excel worksheet to the Word document. Repeat the process to link the Excel chart to the Word document. Print the completed document for your instructor.

PowerPoint Presentations

The chapter described how to link an Excel chart and/or worksheet to a Word document, but you can use the same technique to link these objects to a PowerPoint presentation. Open the *Chapter 3 Mini Case—Theme Park Admissions* PowerPoint presentation that is found in the Exploring Excel folder. Now open your solution to the *Chapter 3 Practice 1—Theme Park Admissions* exercise, and link the worksheet and charts in the completed workbook to the appropriate slides in the presentation. Print the completed presentation (six slides per page) for your instructor.

Exploded Pie Charts

The *Chapter 3 Mini Case—Exploded Pie Chart* workbook contains a worksheet with summary data for the Tom Laquer Men's Wear Boutique. There are four stores and three categories of sales. Your assignment is to complete the worksheet to show the summary data, using the AutoSum and AutoFormat commands as appropriate. Once this is accomplished, you can create the two required charts. The first chart is an exploded pie chart that shows the percentage of total sales that is attributed to each city. The second chart is also a pie chart that shows the percentage of sales attributed to each product line. Replace "Tom Laquer" with your name, and then print the completed workbook for your instructor.

CHAPTER

4 Using Spreadsheets in Decision Making: What If?

OBJECTIVES

After reading this chapter you will:

1. Use the PMT function to calculate the payment of a car loan or mortgage.
2. Use the FV function to determine the future value of a retirement account.
3. Explain how the Goal Seek command facilitates the decision-making process.
4. Use mixed references to vary two parameters in a table.
5. Use the AVERAGE, MAX, MIN, and COUNT functions.
6. Use the IF and VLOOKUP functions to implement decision making.
7. Freeze, unfreeze, hide, and unhide rows and columns in a worksheet.
8. Use the AutoFilter command to display selected records in a list.
9. Describe the options in the Page Setup command used with large worksheets.

hands-on exercises

1. BASIC FINANCIAL FUNCTIONS
Input: None
Output: Basic Financial Functions
2. ADVANCED FINANCIAL FUNCTIONS
Input: None
Output: Advanced Financial Functions
3. THE EXPANDED GRADE BOOK
Input: Expanded Grade Book
Output: Expanded Grade Book Solution

CASE STUDY
VACATION TIME

Emily Knight is the office manager for a regional office of a large, multinational corporation. As office manager, she handles some extremely confidential employee information, including Social Security number, salary, and bonus information. It is also her responsibility to monitor the amount of vacation time each employee has accrued, and how much of that they have used thus far this year.

The Human Resources department has asked Emily to prepare a worksheet for a selected set of employees that will show the weeks of vacation granted to each employee, the number of days already used, and the number of days remaining. The amount of vacation is based on the employee's years of service, which changes continually; that is, the worksheet must reference today's date when computing the amount of vacation time. The worksheet should also contain summary statistics for the group of employees that shows the average number of days used, as well as the maximum and minimum number of days remaining. Your predecessor began the worksheet but left unexpectedly. Emily has asked you to step in and complete the worksheet as quickly as possible. ■

Your assignment is to read the chapter, paying special attention to Hands-on Exercise 3, which describes the use of statistical and logical functions. You will then open the *Chapter 4 Case Study—Vacation Time* workbook, which contains the employee data for the regional sales office, and complete the worksheet. Use the VLOOKUP function to determine the vacation time for each employee by referencing the table at the bottom of the worksheet. You will also need the IF function to display the number of days remaining. And finally, you will have to enter the formulas for the summary statistics table at the bottom of the worksheet. Print the completed worksheet for your instructor. Print the worksheet twice to show both displayed values and cell formulas. Use the Page Setup command to create a custom footer that contains your name.

SPREADSHEETS IN DECISION MAKING

Excel is a truly fascinating program, but it is only a means to an end. A spreadsheet is first and foremost a tool for decision making, and the objective of this chapter is to show you just how valuable that tool can be. Decisions typically involve money, and so we begin by introducing two financial functions, PMT and FV, either of which is entered directly into a worksheet.

The PMT (Payment) function calculates the periodic payment on a loan, such as one you might incur with the purchase of an automobile. The FV (Future Value) function determines the future value of a series of periodic payments, such as annual contributions to a retirement account. Either function can be used in conjunction with the Goal Seek command that lets you enter the desired end result (such as the monthly payment on a car loan) and from that, determines the input (e.g., the price of the car) to produce that result.

The second half of the chapter presents an expanded version of the professor's grade book that uses several commands associated with large spreadsheets. We describe scrolling and explain how its effects are modified by freezing and/or hiding rows and columns in a worksheet. We describe various statistical functions such as MAX, MIN, COUNT, and COUNTA as well as the IF and VLOOKUP functions that provide decision making within a worksheet. We also review the important concepts of relative and absolute cell references, as well as the need to isolate the assumptions and initial conditions in a worksheet.

Analysis of a Car Loan

Figure 4.1 shows how a worksheet might be applied to the purchase of a car. In essence you need to know the monthly payment, which depends on the price of the car, the down payment, and the terms of the loan. In other words:

- Can you afford the monthly payment on the car of your choice?
- What if you settle for a less expensive car and receive a manufacturer's rebate?
- What if you work next summer to earn money for a down payment?
- What if you extend the life of the loan and receive a better interest rate?
- Have you accounted for additional items such as insurance, gas, and maintenance?

The answers to these and other questions determine whether you can afford a car, and if so, which car, and how you will pay for it. The decision is made easier by developing the worksheet in Figure 4.1, and then by changing the various parameters as indicated.

Figure 4.1a contains the ***template***, or "empty" worksheet, in which the text entries and formulas have already been entered, the formatting has already been applied, but no specific data has been input. The template requires that you enter the price of the car, the manufacturer's rebate, the down payment, the interest rate, and the length of the loan. The worksheet uses these parameters to compute the monthly payment. (Implicit in this discussion is the existence of a PMT function within the worksheet program, which is explained in the next section.)

The availability of the worksheet lets you consider several alternatives, and therein lies its true value. You quickly realize that the purchase of a $14,999 car as shown in Figure 4.1b is prohibitive because the monthly payment is almost $500. Settling for a less expensive car, coming up with a substantial down payment, and obtaining a manufacturer's rebate in Figure 4.1c help considerably, but the $317 monthly payment is still too steep. Extending the loan to a fourth year at a lower interest rate in Figure 4.1d reduces the monthly payment to (a more affordable) $244.

No specific data has been input

	A	B
1	Price of car	
2	Manufacturer's rebate	
3	Down payment	
4	Amount to finance	=B1-(B2+B3)
5	Interest rate	
6	Term (in years)	
7	Monthly payment	=PMT(B5/12,B6*12,-B4)

(a) The Template

Data entered

	A	B
1	Price of car	$14,999
2	Manufacturer's rebate	
3	Down payment	
4	Amount to finance	$14,999
5	Interest rate	9%
6	Term (in years)	3
7	Monthly payment	$476.96

(b) Initial Parameters

Less expensive car

Rebate

Down payment made

	A	B
1	Price of car	$13,999
2	Manufacturer's rebate	$1,000
3	Down payment	$3,000
4	Amount to finance	$9,999
5	Interest rate	9%
6	Term (in years)	3
7	Monthly payment	$317.97

(c) Less Expensive Car with Down Payment and Rebate

Lower interest rate

Longer term

	A	B
1	Price of car	$13,999
2	Manufacturer's rebate	$1,000
3	Down payment	$3,000
4	Amount to finance	$9,999
5	Interest rate	8%
6	Term (in years)	4
7	Monthly payment	$244.10

(d) Longer Term and Better Interest Rate

FIGURE 4.1 Spreadsheets in Decision Making

PMT Function

A ***function*** is a predefined formula that accepts one or more ***arguments*** as input, performs the indicated calculation, then returns another value as output. Excel has more than 100 different functions in various categories. Financial functions, such as the PMT function we are about to study, are especially important in business.

The ***PMT function*** requires three arguments (the interest rate per period, the number of periods, and the amount of the loan), from which it computes the associated payment on a loan. The arguments are placed in parentheses and are separated by commas. Consider the PMT function as it might apply to Figure 4.1b:

=PMT(.09/12,36,–14999)

- –14999 — Amount of loan (as a *negative* amount)
- 36 — Number of periods (3 years × 12 months/year)
- .09/12 — Interest rate per period (annual rate divided by 12)

Instead of using specific values, however, the arguments in the PMT function are supplied as cell references, so that the computed payment can be based on values supplied by the user elsewhere in the worksheet. Thus, the PMT function is entered as =PMT(B5/12,B6*12,–B4) to reflect the terms of a specific loan whose arguments are in cells B4, B5, and B6. (The principal is entered as a negative amount so that the worksheet will display a positive value.)

FV Function

The ***FV function*** returns the future value of an investment based on constant periodic payments and a constant interest rate. It can be used to determine the future value of a retirement plan such as an IRA (Individual Retirement Account) or 401K, two plans that are very popular in today's workplace. Under either plan, an individual saves for his or her retirement by making a fixed contribution each year. The money is allowed to accumulate tax-free until retirement, and it is an excellent way to save for the future.

Assume, for example, that you plan to contribute $3,000 a year to an IRA, that you expect to earn 7% annually, and that you will be contributing for 40 years (i.e., you began contributing at age 25 and will continue to contribute until age 65). The future value of that investment—the amount you will have at age 65—would be $598,905! All told, you would have contributed $120,000 ($3,000 a year for 40 years). The difference, more than $470,000, results from compound interest over the life of your investment.

The FV function is entered into a worksheet in similar fashion to the PMT function. There are three arguments—the interest rate (also called the rate of return), the number of periods, and the periodic investment. The FV function corresponding to our earlier example would be:

Amount at retirement = FV(Rate of return, Term, Periodic payment)

- Periodic payment — $3,000
- Term — 40 years
- Rate of return — 7%
- Amount at retirement — Computed value becomes $598,905

It's more practical, however, to enter the values into a worksheet, then use cell references within the FV function. If, for example, cells A1, A2, and A3 contained the rate of return, term, and annual contribution, respectively, the resulting FV function would be =FV(A1, A2, –A3). The periodic payment is preceded by a minus sign, just as the principal in the PMT function.

Inserting a Function

The ***Insert Function command*** places a function into a worksheet. You can select a function from a category as was done in Figure 4.2a, or you can enter a brief description of the function you are searching for. The Function Arguments dialog box in Figure 4.2b appears after you choose the function and is where you enter the various arguments. (Only the first three arguments are required for the Future Value function.) Excel displays the calculated value of each argument as well as the value of the function within the dialog box.

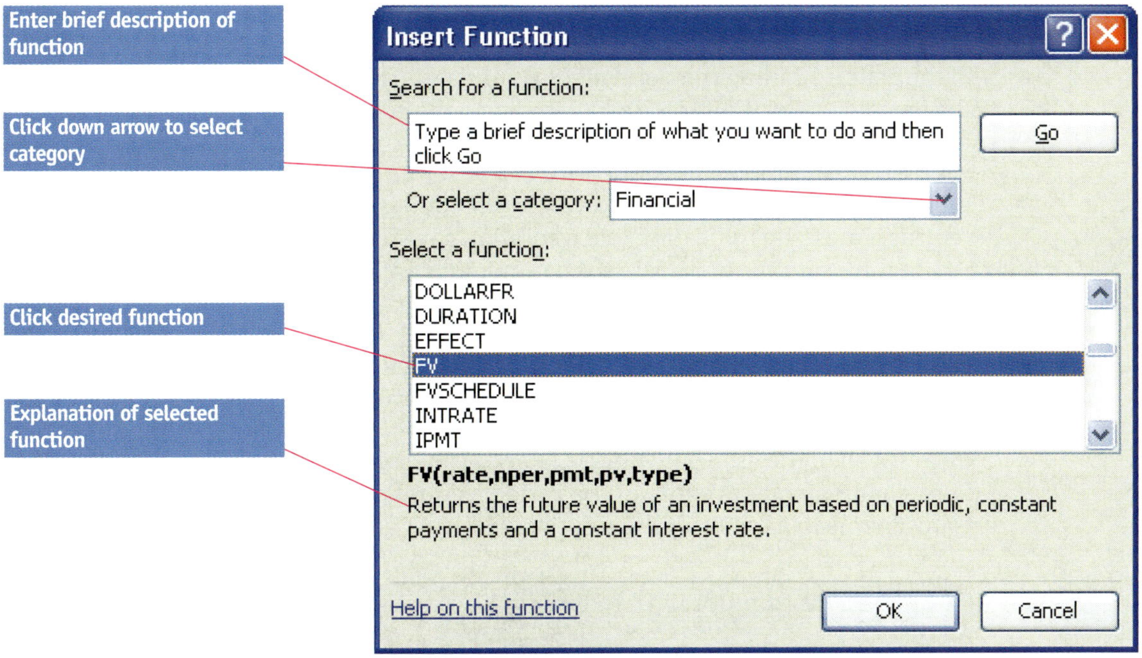

(a) Select the Function

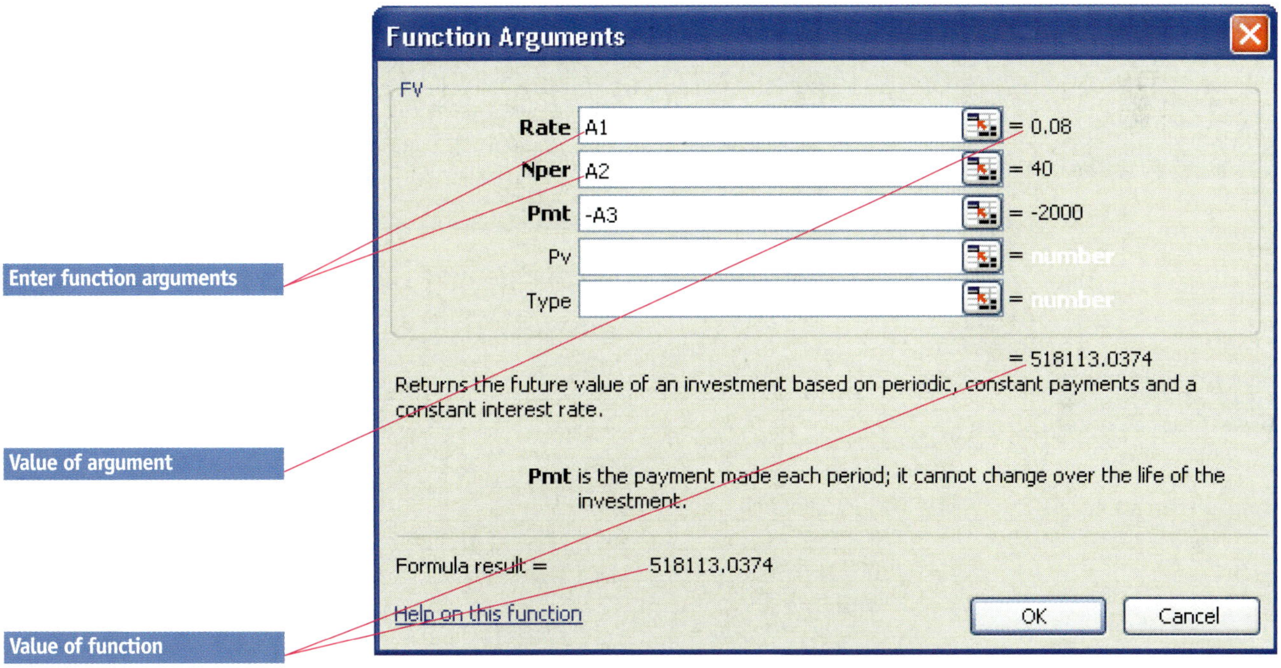

(b) Enter the Argument

FIGURE 4.2 Inserting a Function

The Goal Seek Command

The analysis in Figure 4.1 enabled us to reduce the projected monthly payment from $476 to a more affordable $244. What if, however, you can afford a payment of only $200, and you want to know the maximum you can borrow in order to keep the payment to the specified amount? The ***Goal Seek command*** is designed to solve this type of problem, as it enables you to set an end result (such as the monthly payment) in order to determine the input (the price of the car) to produce that result. Only one input (the price of the car, the interest rate, or the term) can be varied at a time.

Figure 4.3 extends our earlier analysis to illustrate the Goal Seek command. You create the spreadsheet as usual, then you pull down the Tools menu, and select the Goal Seek command to display the dialog box in Figure 4.3a. Enter the address of the cell containing the dependent formula (the monthly payment in cell B7) and the desired value of this cell ($200). Indicate the cell whose contents should be varied (the price of the car in cell B1), then click OK to execute the command. The Goal Seek command then varies the price of the car until the monthly payment returns the desired value of $200. (Not every problem has a solution, in which case Excel returns a message indicating that a solution cannot be found.)

In this example, the Goal Seek command is able to find a solution and returns a purchase price of $12,192 as shown in Figure 4.3b. You now have all the information you need. Find a car that sells for $12,192 (or less), hold the other parameters to the values shown in the figure, and your monthly payment will be (at most) $200.

The analysis in Figure 4.3 illustrates how a worksheet is used in the decision-making process. An individual defines a problem, then develops a worksheet that includes all of the associated parameters. He or she can then plug in specific numbers, changing one or more of the variables until a decision can be reached. Excel is invaluable in arriving at the solution.

Cell containing dependent formula

Desired result of formula

Cell whose contents are to be varied

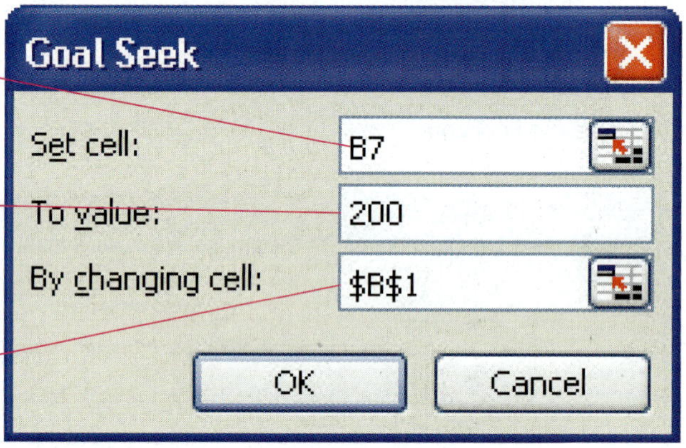

(a) Set the Maximum Payment

Required purchase price for a $200 monthly payment

	A	B
1	Price of car	$12,192
2	Manufacturer's rebate	$1,000
3	Down payment	$3,000
4	Amount to finance	$8,192
5	Interest rate	8%
6	Term (in years)	4
7	Monthly payment	$200.00

(b) Solution

FIGURE 4.3 The Goal Seek Command

hands-on exercise

1 Basic Financial Functions

Objective To illustrate the PMT and FV functions; to illustrate the Goal Seek command. Use Figure 4.4 as a guide in the exercise.

Step 1: Enter the Descriptive Labels

- Start Excel. If necessary, click the **New button** on the Standard toolbar to open a new workbook as shown in Figure 4.4a.
- Click in **cell A1**, type the label **Basic Financial Functions**, then press the **Enter key** to complete the entry. Enter the remaining labels for column A.
- Click and drag the column border between columns A and B to increase the column width of column A to accommodate the widest entry in column A (other than cell A3).
- Click in **cell B4** and type **$14,999** corresponding to the price of the automobile you hope to purchase. Be sure to include the dollar sign as you enter the data to format the cell automatically.
- Enter **$1,000** and **$3,000** in **cells B5** and **B6**, respectively, corresponding to the manufacturer's rebate and down payment, respectively.
- Click in **cell B7**. Use pointing to enter the formula **=B4–(B5+B6)**, which calculates the amount to finance (i.e., the principal of the loan).
- Enter **9%** and **3** in **cells B8** and **B9**. (If necessary, click in **cell B9**, pull down the **Edit menu**, select the **Clear command**, and choose the **Format command** to remove the dollar sign.)
- All of the loan parameters have been entered.

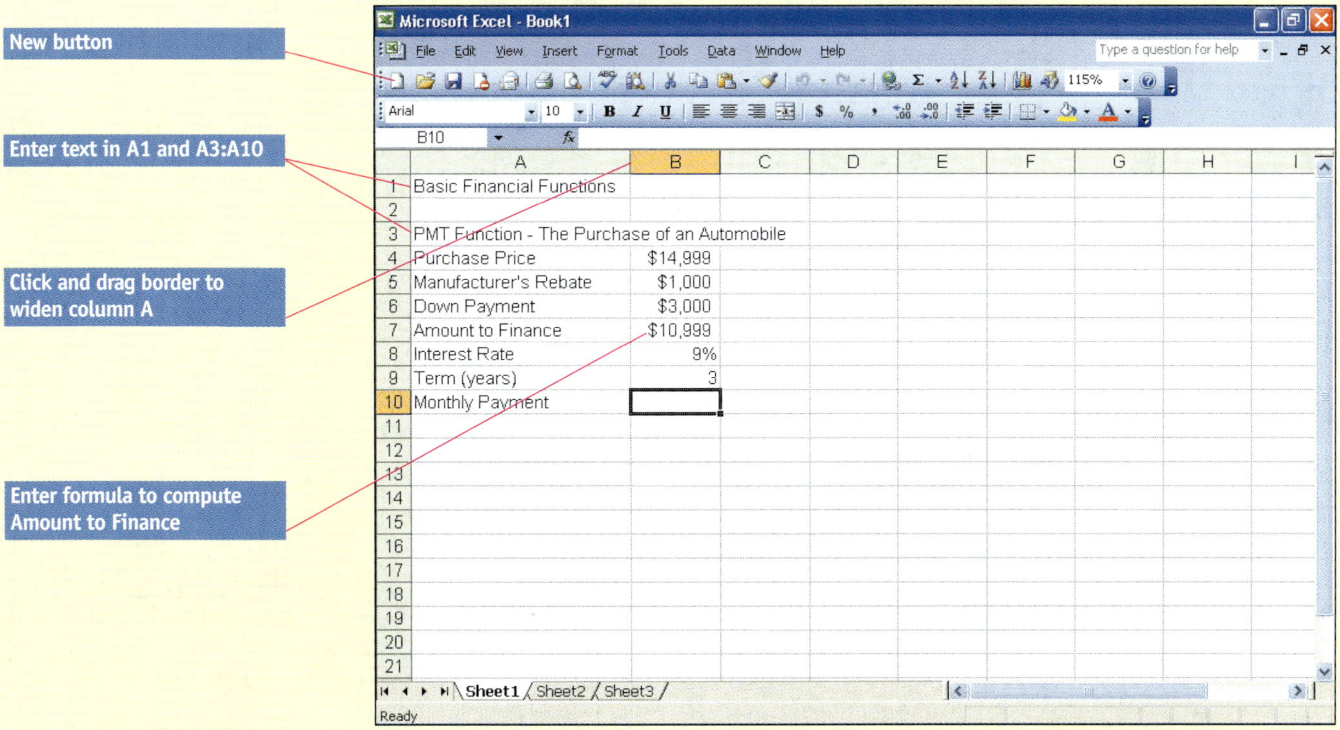

(a) Enter the Descriptive Labels (step 1)

FIGURE 4.4 Hands-on Exercise 1

Step 2: Insert a Function

- Click in **cell B10**. Pull down the **Insert menu** and click the **Function command** (or click the **Insert Function button** on the formula bar) to display the Insert Function dialog box.
- Click the **down arrow** in the Select a Category list box and select **Financial**, select the **PMT function** and click **OK** to display the Function Arguments dialog box in Figure 4.4b.
- Click the **Rate text box** and use pointing to enter the rate. Click in **cell B8** of the worksheet, then type **/12**, so that the text box contains the entry B8/12.
- Click the **Nper text box** and use pointing to enter the number of periods. Click in **cell B9**, then type ***12**, so that the formula bar contains the entry B9*12.
- Click the **Pv text box**. Type a – sign, then click in **cell B7**. You should see 349.7652595 as the value for the PMT function. Click **OK** to close the Function Arguments dialog box.
- Pull down the **File menu** and click the **Save command** (or click the **Save button** on the Standard toolbar) to display the Save As dialog box, then save the workbook as **Basic Financial Functions** in the **Exploring Excel** folder.

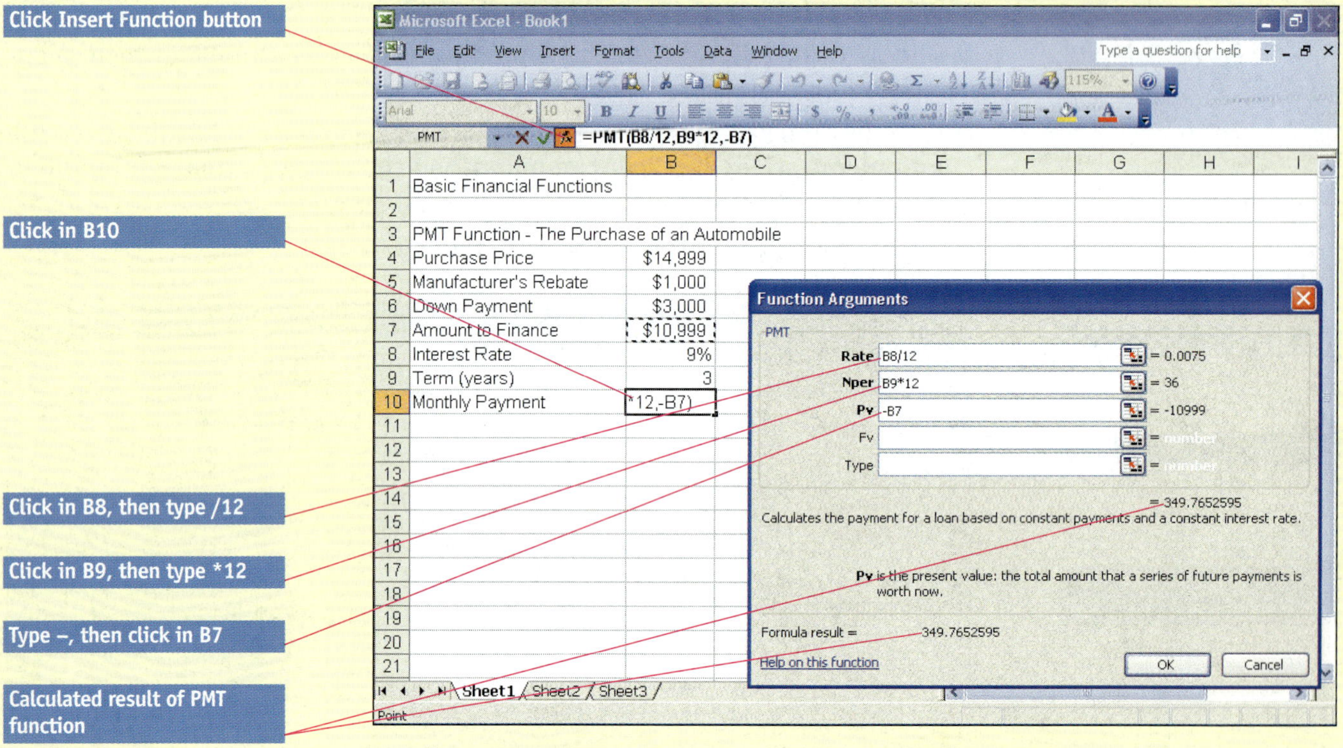

(b) Insert a Function (step 2)

FIGURE 4.4 Hands-on Exercise 1 (*continued*)

SEARCH FOR THE FUNCTION

It's easy to select a function if you know its name, but what if you are unsure of the name or don't know the category in which the function is found? Click the Insert Function button on the formula bar to display the Insert Function dialog box, type a keyword such as "payment" in the Search text box, then click the Go button. Excel returns nine functions in this example, one of which is the PMT function that you are looking for.

Step 3: The Goal Seek Command

- You can reduce the monthly payment in various ways. Click in **cell B4** and change the price of the car to **$13,999**. The monthly payment drops to $317.97.
- Change the interest rate to **8%** and the term of the loan to **4** years. The payment drops to $244.10.
- You can reduce the payment still further by using the Goal Seek command to fix the payment at a specified level. Click in **cell B10**, the cell containing the formula for the monthly payment.
- Pull down the **Tools menu**. Click **Goal Seek** to display the dialog box in Figure 4.4c. Click in the **To value** text box. Type **200** (the desired payment).
- Click in the **By changing cell** text box. Type **B4**, the cell containing the price of the car. This is the cell whose value will be determined. Click **OK**.
- The Goal Seek command returns a successful solution consisting of $12,192 and $200 in cells B4 and B10, respectively. Click **OK** to accept the solution and close the Goal Seek dialog box.
- Save the workbook.

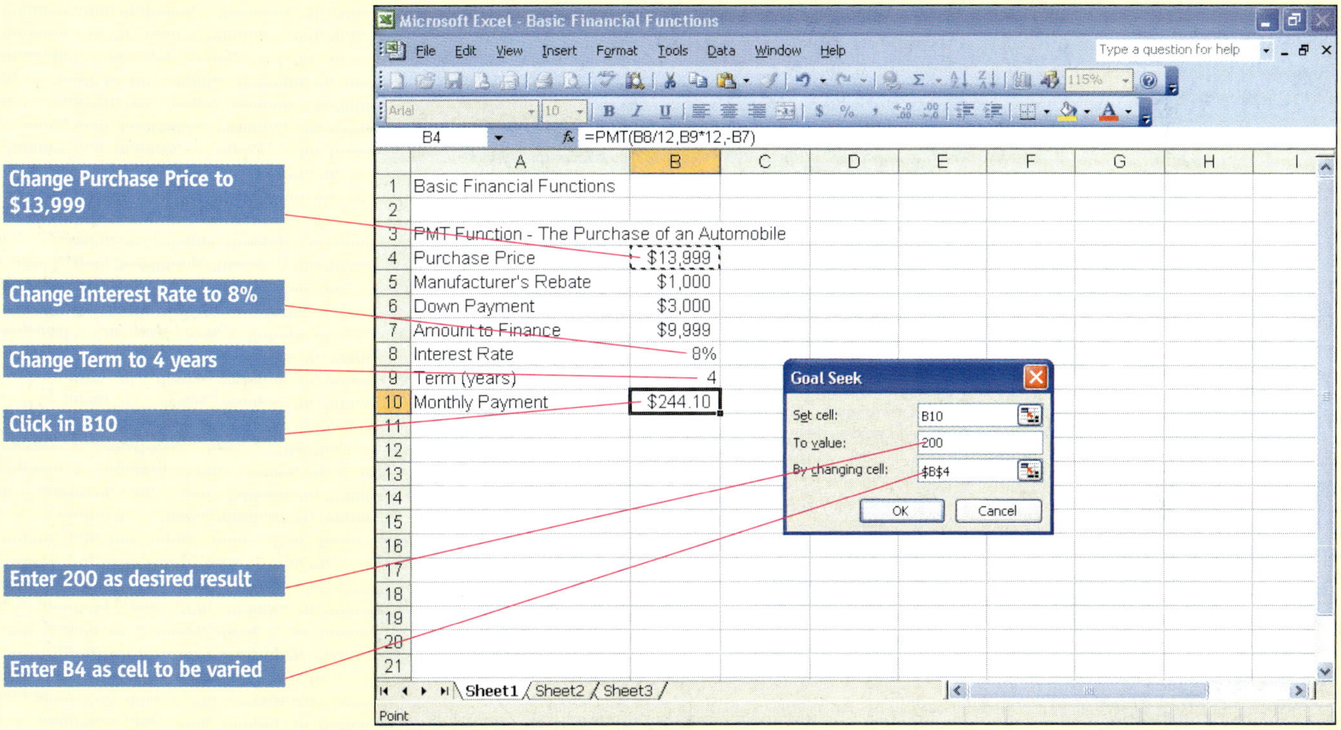

(c) The Goal Seek command (step 3)

FIGURE 4.4 Hands-on Exercise 1 (*continued*)

THE FORMATTING IS IN THE CELL

Once a number format has been assigned to a cell, either by including the format as you entered a number, or through execution of a formatting command, the formatting remains in the cell. Thus, to change the contents in a formatted cell, all you need to do is enter the new number without the formatting. Entering 5000, for example, into a cell that was previously formatted as currency will display the number as $5,000. To remove the formatting, pull down the Edit menu, select the Clear command, then choose Format.

Step 4: The Future Value Function

- Check your work carefully to be sure that your worksheet matches the top half of Figure 4.4d. Make corrections as necessary.
- Enter the labels in **cells A13** through **A17** as shown in the figure. Click in **cell B14** and type **$3,000** corresponding to the annual contribution. Be sure to include the dollar sign.
- Enter **7%** (type the percent sign) and **40** in **cells B15** and **B16**, respectively.
- Click in **cell B17**, type **=FV(**. You will see a ScreenTip that shows the arguments in the FV function. There are five arguments, but only the first three (rate, nper, and pv) are required. (The last two arguments are enclosed in square brackets to indicate they are optional.)
- Use pointing to complete the function, which is **=FV(B15,B16,–B14)**. Press **Enter** when you have finished.
- You should see $598,905.34 in cell B17. This is the amount you will have at retirement, given that you save $3,000 a year for 40 years and earn 7% interest over the life of your investment.
- Save the workbook.

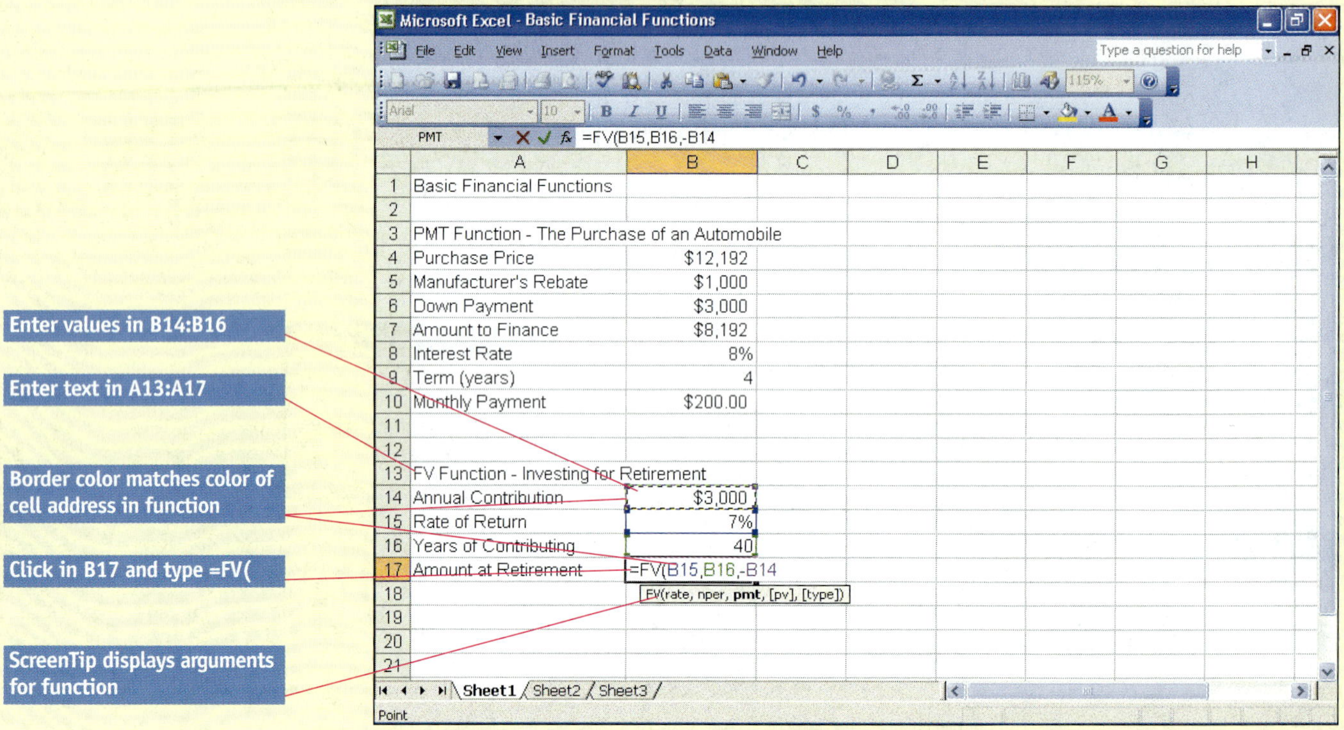

(d) The Future Value (FV) Function (step 4)

FIGURE 4.4 Hands-on Exercise 1 (*continued*)

IT'S COLOR CODED

Double click in the cell that contains the FV function, then look closely at the arguments within the function to see that each argument is a different color. Each color corresponds to the border color of the referenced cell. You can change any reference in the function (e.g., from B15 to C15) by dragging the color-coded border surrounding cell B15 (the reference you want to change) to cell C15 (the new reference).

Step 5: Format the Worksheet

- Your workbook should match Figure 4.4e except for the formatting. Click and drag **cells A1** and **B1**, then click the **Merge and Center button**.
- Click the **down arrow** on the Font Size list box to change the font size to **12**. Click the **Bold button** to boldface the title.
- Click **cell A3**. Press and hold the **Ctrl key** as you click cells **A10:B10, A13**, and **A17:B17** to select all of these cells. Click the **Bold button** to boldface the contents of these cells.
- Click and drag to select **cells A4** through **A9**. Press and hold the **Ctrl key** as you click and drag to select **cells A14** through **A16** (in addition to cells A4 through A9).
- Click the **Increase Indent button** on the Formatting toolbar to indent the labels as shown in Figure 4.4e.
- Click in **cell A19** and enter your name, then click the **Bold button** to boldface the type.
- Save the workbook.

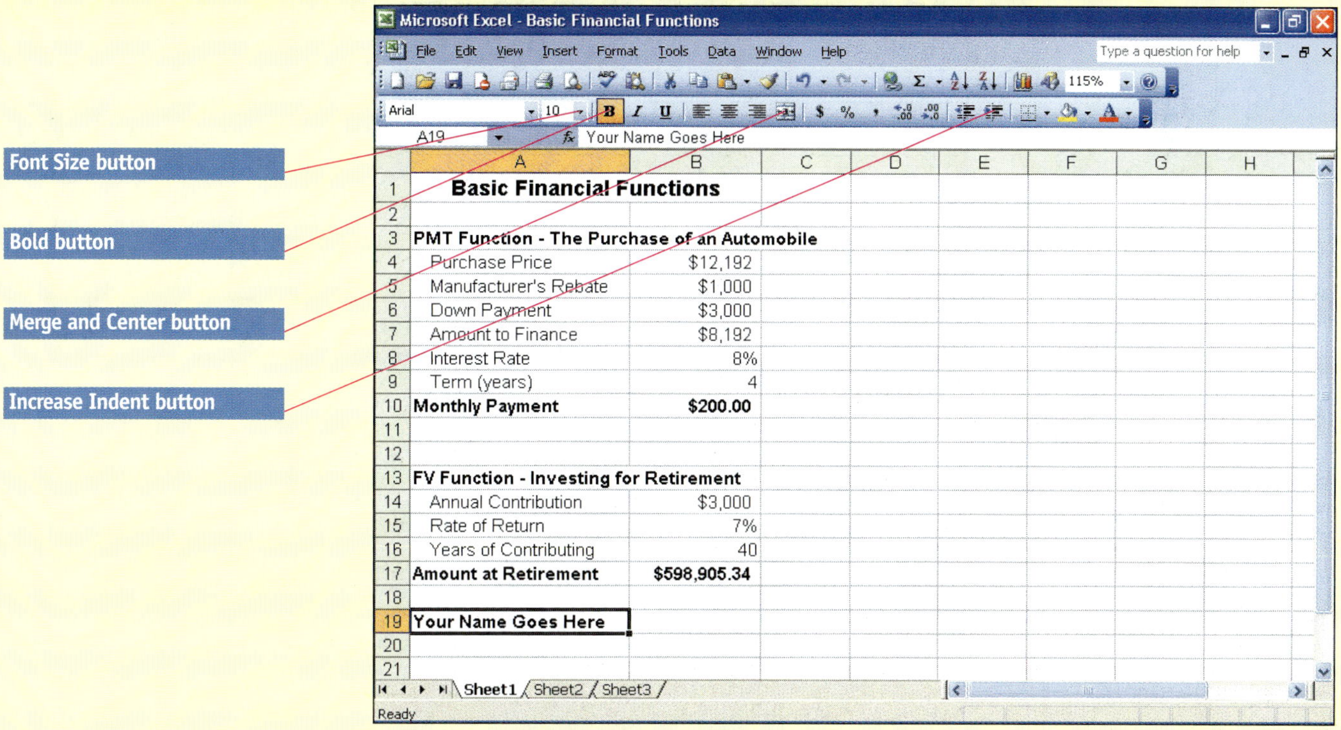

(e) Format the Worksheet (step 5)

FIGURE 4.4 Hands-on Exercise 1 (*continued*)

SELECTING NONCONTIGUOUS RANGES

You can apply the same formatting to noncontiguous (nonadjacent) cells within a worksheet by using the Ctrl key to select the cells. Click and drag to select the first cell range, then press and hold the Ctrl key as you select a second range. Continue to press the Ctrl key to select additional ranges, then format all of the selected cells with a single command. Click anywhere in the worksheet to deselect the cells.

Step 6: Print the Cell Formulas

- Pull down the **File menu** and click the **Page Setup command** to display the Page Setup dialog box. Click the **Sheet tab**, then check the boxes to print gridlines and row and column headings.
- Click the **Margins tab** and check the box to center the worksheet horizontally. Click **OK** to accept the settings and close the dialog box.
- Save the workbook. Click the **Print Preview button** on the Standard toolbar to be sure you are satisfied with the appearance of the workbook. Click the **Print button**, then click **OK** to print the worksheet.
- Press **Ctrl+`** to display the cell contents, as opposed to the displayed values. Preview the worksheet in this format, then print it when you are satisfied with its appearance. Press **Ctrl+`** to return the worksheet to displayed values.
- Submit printouts—the displayed values and the cell formulas—to your instructor as proof that you did this exercise.
- Exit Excel if you do not want to continue with the next exercise at this time.

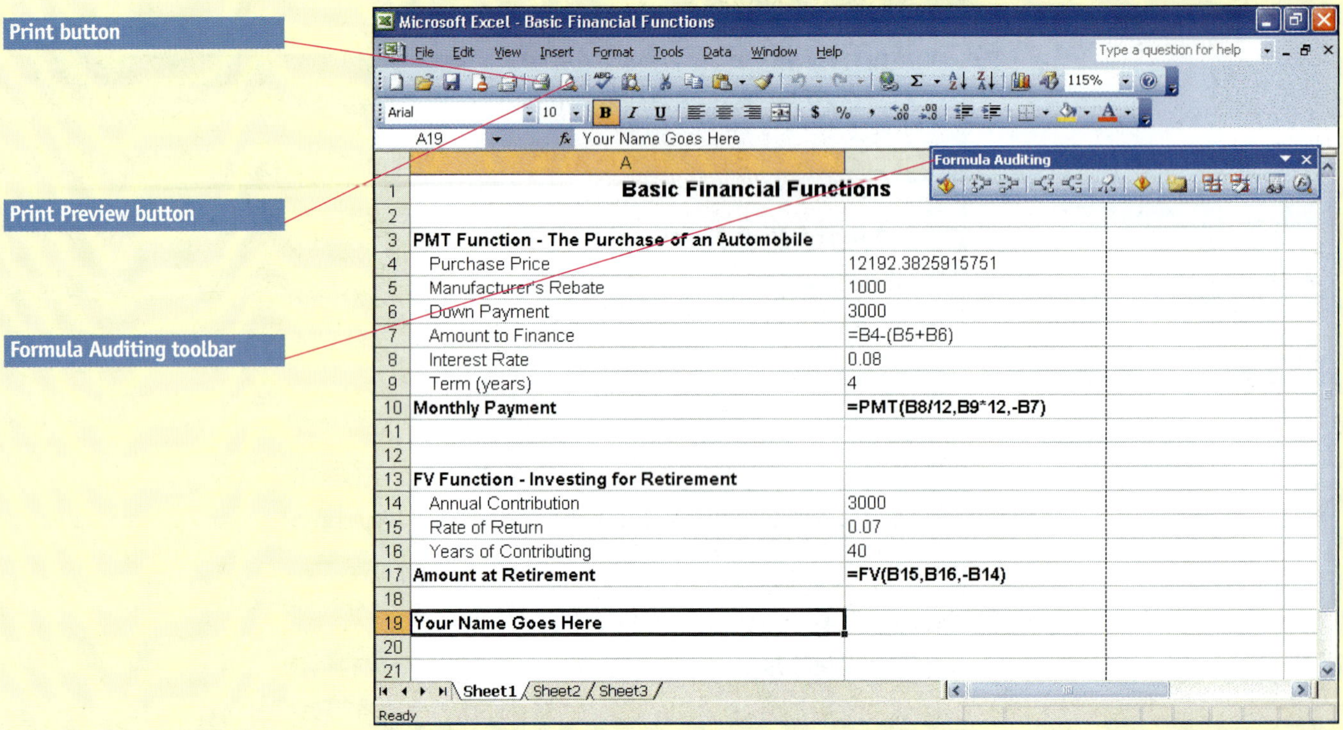

(f) Print the Cell Formulas (step 6)

FIGURE 4.4 Hands-on Exercise 1 (*continued*)

ARE THE PAYMENTS MONTHLY OR ANNUAL?

The FV function in this example computes the future value of a series of annual payments, with the term and interest rate specified as annual values, and thus there is no need to multiply or divide these values by 12. The car payment in the previous example, however, was on a monthly basis. Thus the annual interest rate was divided by 12 (to obtain the monthly rate), while the term of the loan was multiplied by 12, in order to put the numbers on a monthly basis.

HOME MORTGAGES

The PMT function is used in our next example in conjunction with the purchase of a home. The example also reviews the concept of relative and absolute addresses from Chapter 2. In addition, it introduces several other techniques to make you more proficient in Excel.

The spreadsheets in Figure 4.5 illustrate a variable rate mortgage, which will be developed over the next several pages. The user enters the amount he or she wishes to borrow and a starting interest rate, and the spreadsheet displays the associated monthly payment. The spreadsheet in Figure 4.5a enables the user to see the monthly payment at varying interest rates, and to contrast the amount of the payment for a 15- and a 30-year mortgage.

Most first-time buyers opt for the longer term, but they would do well to consider a 15-year mortgage. Note, for example, that the difference in monthly payments for a $100,000 mortgage at 7.5% is only $227.80 (the difference between $927.01 for a 15-year mortgage versus $699.21 for the 30-year mortgage). This is a significant amount of money, but when viewed as a percentage of the total cost of a home (property taxes and maintenance), it becomes less important, especially when you consider the substantial saving in interest over the life of the mortgage.

Figure 4.5b expands the spreadsheet to show the total interest over the life of the loan for both the 15- and the 30-year mortgage. The total interest on a $100,000 loan at 7.5% is $151,717 for a 30-year mortgage, but only $66,862 for a 15-year mortgage. In other words, you will pay back the $100,000 in principal plus another $151,717 in interest if you select the longer term.

Difference in monthly payment between a 30-year and a 15-year mortgage at 7.5%

	A	B	C	D
1	Amount Borrowed		$100,000	
2	Starting Interest		7.50%	
3				
4		Monthly Payment		
5	Interest	30 Years	15 Years	Difference
6	7.50%	$699.21	$927.01	$227.80
7	8.50%	$768.91	$984.74	$215.83
8	9.50%	$840.85	$1,044.22	$203.37
9	10.50%	$914.74	$1,105.40	$190.66
10	11.50%	$990.29	$1,168.19	$177.90
11	12.50%	$1,067.26	$1,232.52	$165.26

(a) Difference in Monthly Payment

Less interest is paid on a 15-year loan ($66,862 vs $151,717 on a 30-year loan)

	A	B	C	D	E
1	Amount Borrowed			$100,000	
2	Starting Interest			7.50%	
3					
4		30 Years		15 Years	
5	Interest	Monthly Payment	Total Interest	Monthly Payment	Total Interest
6	7.50%	$699.21	$151,717	$927.01	$66,862
7	8.50%	$768.91	$176,809	$984.74	$77,253
8	9.50%	$840.85	$202,708	$1,044.22	$87,960
9	10.50%	$914.74	$229,306	$1,105.40	$98,972
10	11.50%	$990.29	$256,505	$1,168.19	$110,274
11	12.50%	$1,067.26	$284,213	$1,232.52	$121,854

(b) Total Interest

FIGURE 4.5 15- versus 30-Year Mortgage

Relative versus Absolute Addresses

Figure 4.6 displays the cell formulas for the mortgage analysis. All of the formulas are based on the amount borrowed and the starting interest, in cells C1 and C2, respectively. You can vary either or both of these parameters, and the worksheet will automatically recalculate the monthly payments.

The similarity in the formulas from one row to the next implies that the copy operation will be essential to the development of the worksheet. You must, however, remember the distinction between a ***relative*** and an ***absolute reference***—that is, a cell reference that changes during a copy operation (relative) versus one that does not (absolute). Consider the PMT function as it appears in cell B6:

=PMT(A6/12,30*12,–$C$1)

- The amount of the loan, –$C$1, is an absolute reference that remains constant
- Number of periods (30 years*12 months/year)
- The interest rate, A6/12, is a relative reference that changes

The entry A6/12 (which is the first argument in the formula in cell B6) is interpreted to mean "divide the contents of the cell one column to the left by 12." Thus, when the PMT function in cell B6 is copied to cell B7, it (the copied formula) is adjusted to maintain this relationship and will contain the entry A7/12. The Copy command does not duplicate a relative address exactly, but adjusts it from row to row (or column to column) to maintain the relative relationship. The cell reference for the amount of the loan should not change when the formula is copied, and hence it is specified as an absolute address. Absolute references use a dollar sign before the row and column reference—for example, $C$1.

Relative reference (adjusts during copy operation)

Absolute reference (doesn't adjust during copy operation)

	A	B	C	D
1	Amount Borrowed		$100,000	
2	Starting Interest		7.50%	
3				
4	Monthly Payment			
5	Interest	30 Years	15 Years	Difference
6	=C2	=PMT(A6/12,30*12,-$C$1)	=PMT(A6/12,15*12,-$C$1)	=C6-B6
7	=A6+0.01	=PMT(A7/12,30*12,-$C$1)	=PMT(A7/12,15*12,-$C$1)	=C7-B7
8	=A7+0.01	=PMT(A8/12,30*12,-$C$1)	=PMT(A8/12,15*12,-$C$1)	=C8-B8
9	=A8+0.01	=PMT(A9/12,30*12,-$C$1)	=PMT(A9/12,15*12,-$C$1)	=C9-B9
10	=A9+0.01	=PMT(A10/12,30*12,-$C$1)	=PMT(A10/12,15*12,-$C$1)	=C10-B10
11	=A10+0.01	=PMT(A11/12,30*12,-$C$1)	=PMT(A11/12,15*12,-$C$1)	=C11-B11

FIGURE 4.6 Cell Formulas

ISOLATE ASSUMPTIONS

The formulas in a worksheet should be based on cell references rather than specific values—for example, C1 or $C$1 rather than $100,000. The cells containing these values should be clearly labeled and set apart from the rest of the worksheet. You can then vary the inputs (assumptions) to the worksheet and immediately see the effect. The chance for error is also minimized because you are changing the contents of a single cell, rather than changing multiple formulas.

Mixed References

Figure 4.7 displays a new worksheet that uses the FV function to calculate the value of an ***IRA (Individual Retirement Account)*** under various combinations of interest rates and years for investing. The annual contribution is $3,000 in all instances (the maximum that is allowed under current law). The interest rates appear in row 5, while the years for investing are shown in column B. The intersection of a row and column contains the future value of a series of $3,000 investments for the specific interest rate and year combination. Cell E21, for example, shows that $3,000 a year, invested over 40 years at 7%, will compound to $598,905.

The key to the worksheet is to realize that the Future Value function requires ***mixed references*** for both the interest rate and number of years. The interest rate will always come from row 5, but the column will vary. In similar fashion, the number of years will always come from column B, but the row will vary. Using this information we can enter the appropriate formula into cell C6, then copy that formula to the remaining cells in row 6, and finally copy row 6 to the remaining rows in the worksheet. The key to the worksheet is the formula in cell C6. Consider:

Future Value = FV(C$5, $B6, –$D$3)

- $D$3 — Absolute reference to cell D3, the cell containing the periodic investment
- $B6 — Mixed reference to cell $B6, the cell containing the term; the column stays constant, but the row changes
- C$5 — Mixed reference to cell C$5; the column changes, but the row stays constant.

The majority of spreadsheets can be developed using a combination of relative and absolute references. Occasionally, however, you will need to incorporate mixed references as you will see in our next exercise.

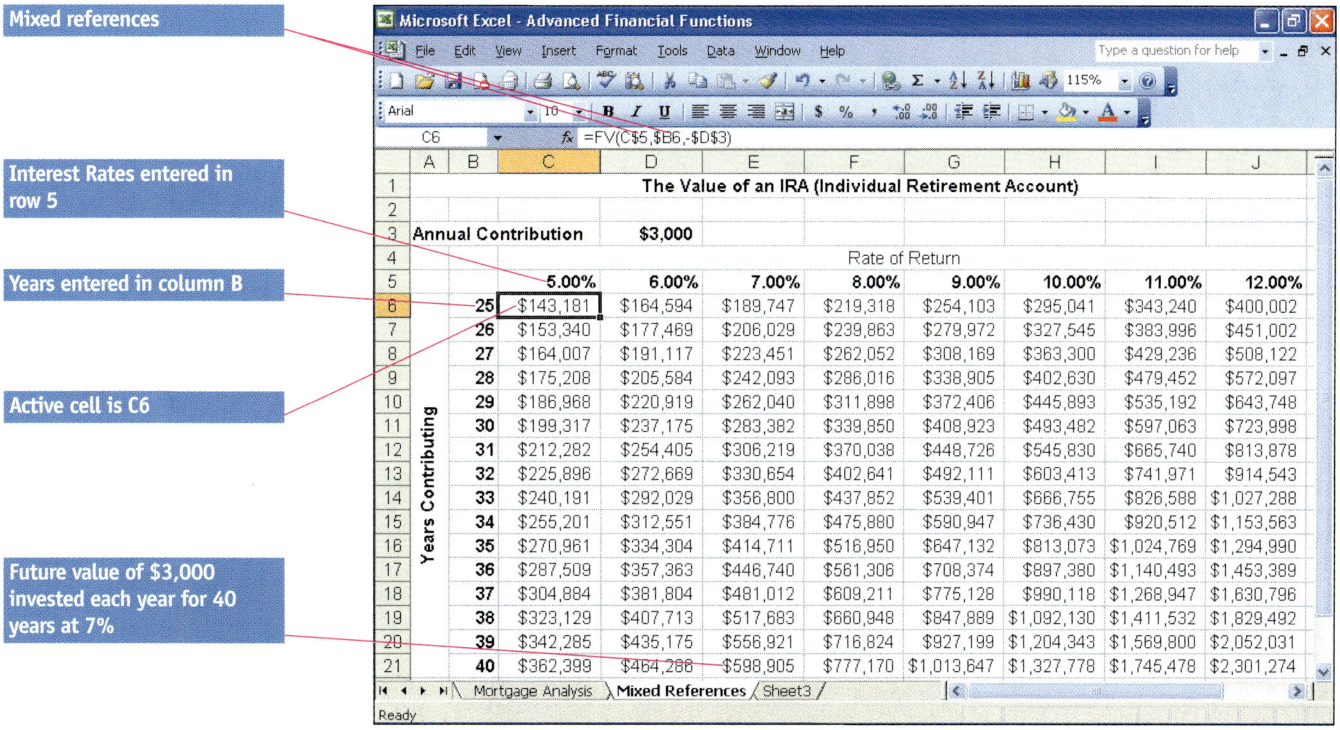

	A	B	C	D	E	F	G	H	I	J
1				The Value of an IRA (Individual Retirement Account)						
2										
3	Annual Contribution			$3,000						
4						Rate of Return				
5			5.00%	6.00%	7.00%	8.00%	9.00%	10.00%	11.00%	12.00%
6	Years Contributing	25	$143,181	$164,594	$189,747	$219,318	$254,103	$295,041	$343,240	$400,002
7		26	$153,340	$177,469	$206,029	$239,863	$279,972	$327,545	$383,996	$451,002
8		27	$164,007	$191,117	$223,451	$262,052	$308,169	$363,300	$429,236	$508,122
9		28	$175,208	$205,584	$242,093	$286,016	$338,905	$402,630	$479,452	$572,097
10		29	$186,968	$220,919	$262,040	$311,898	$372,406	$445,893	$535,192	$643,748
11		30	$199,317	$237,175	$283,382	$339,850	$408,923	$493,482	$597,063	$723,998
12		31	$212,282	$254,405	$306,219	$370,038	$448,726	$545,830	$665,740	$813,878
13		32	$225,896	$272,669	$330,654	$402,641	$492,111	$603,413	$741,971	$914,543
14		33	$240,191	$292,029	$356,800	$437,852	$539,401	$666,755	$826,588	$1,027,288
15		34	$255,201	$312,551	$384,776	$475,880	$590,947	$736,430	$920,512	$1,153,563
16		35	$270,961	$334,304	$414,711	$516,950	$647,132	$813,073	$1,024,769	$1,294,990
17		36	$287,509	$357,363	$446,740	$561,306	$708,374	$897,380	$1,140,493	$1,453,389
18		37	$304,884	$381,804	$481,012	$609,211	$775,128	$990,118	$1,268,947	$1,630,796
19		38	$323,129	$407,713	$517,683	$660,948	$847,889	$1,092,130	$1,411,532	$1,829,492
20		39	$342,285	$435,175	$556,921	$716,824	$927,199	$1,204,343	$1,569,800	$2,052,031
21		40	$362,399	$464,286	$598,905	$777,170	$1,013,647	$1,327,778	$1,745,478	$2,301,274

FIGURE 4.7 Mixed References

2 Advanced Financial Functions

Objective To use relative, absolute, and mixed references in conjunction with the PMT and FV functions; to practice various formatting commands. Use Figure 4.8 as a guide in the exercise.

Step 1: The Spell Check

- Start Excel and begin a new workbook. Click in **cell A1**. Type **Amount Borrowed**. Do not be concerned that the text is longer than the cell width, as cell B1 is empty and thus the text will be displayed in its entirety. Press the **Enter key** or **down arrow** to complete the entry.
- Type **Starting Interest** in **cell A2**. Click in **cell A4**. Type **Monthly Payment**. Enter the remaining labels in **cells A5** through **D5**, as shown in Figure 4.8a without concern for the column width.
- We suggest that you deliberately misspell one or more words in order to try the spell check. Click in **cell A1** to begin the spell check at the beginning of the worksheet.
- Click the **Spelling button** on the Standard toolbar to initiate the spell check as shown in Figure 4.8a. Make corrections, as necessary, just as you would in Microsoft Word.
- Click in **cell C1**. Type **$100,000** (include the dollar sign). Press the **Enter key** or **down arrow** to complete the entry and move to **cell C2**. Type **7.5%** (include the percent sign). Press **Enter**.
- Save the workbook as **Advanced Financial Functions** in the **Exploring Excel folder** on the appropriate drive.

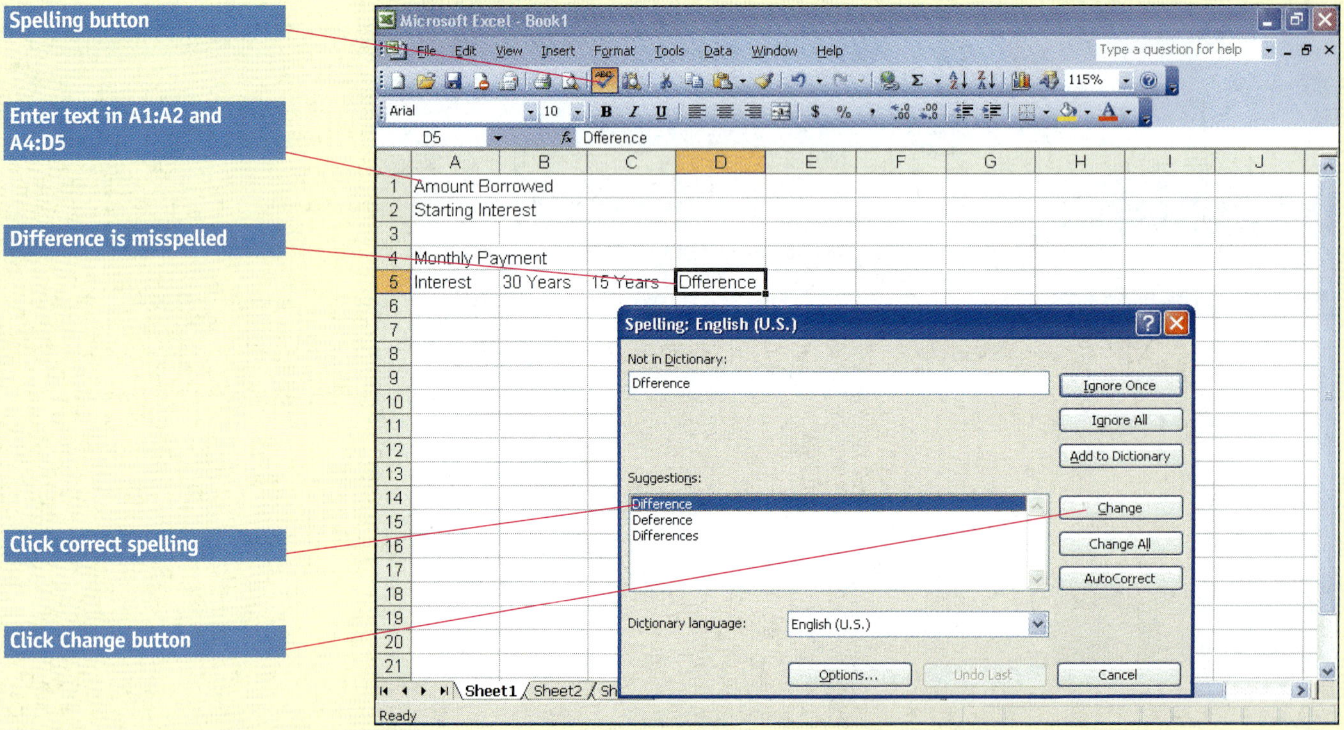

(a) The Spell Check (step 1)

FIGURE 4.8 Hands-on Exercise 2

Step 2: The Fill Handle

- Click in **cell A6**. Use pointing to enter the formula **=C2** to reference the starting interest rate in cell C2.
- Click in **cell A7**. Use pointing to enter the formula **=A6+.01** to compute the interest rate in this cell, which is one percent more than the interest rate in row 6. Press **Enter**.
- Click in **cell A7**. Point to the **fill handle** in the lower-right corner of cell A7. The mouse pointer changes to a thin crosshair.
- Drag the **fill handle** over **cells A8** through **A11**. A border appears to indicate the destination range as in Figure 4.8b. Release the mouse to complete the copy operation. The formula and associated percentage format in cell A7 have been copied to cells A8 through A11.
- Click in **cell C2**. Type **5%**. The entries in cells A6 through A11 change automatically. Click the **Undo button** on the Standard toolbar to return to the 7.5% interest rate.
- Save the workbook.

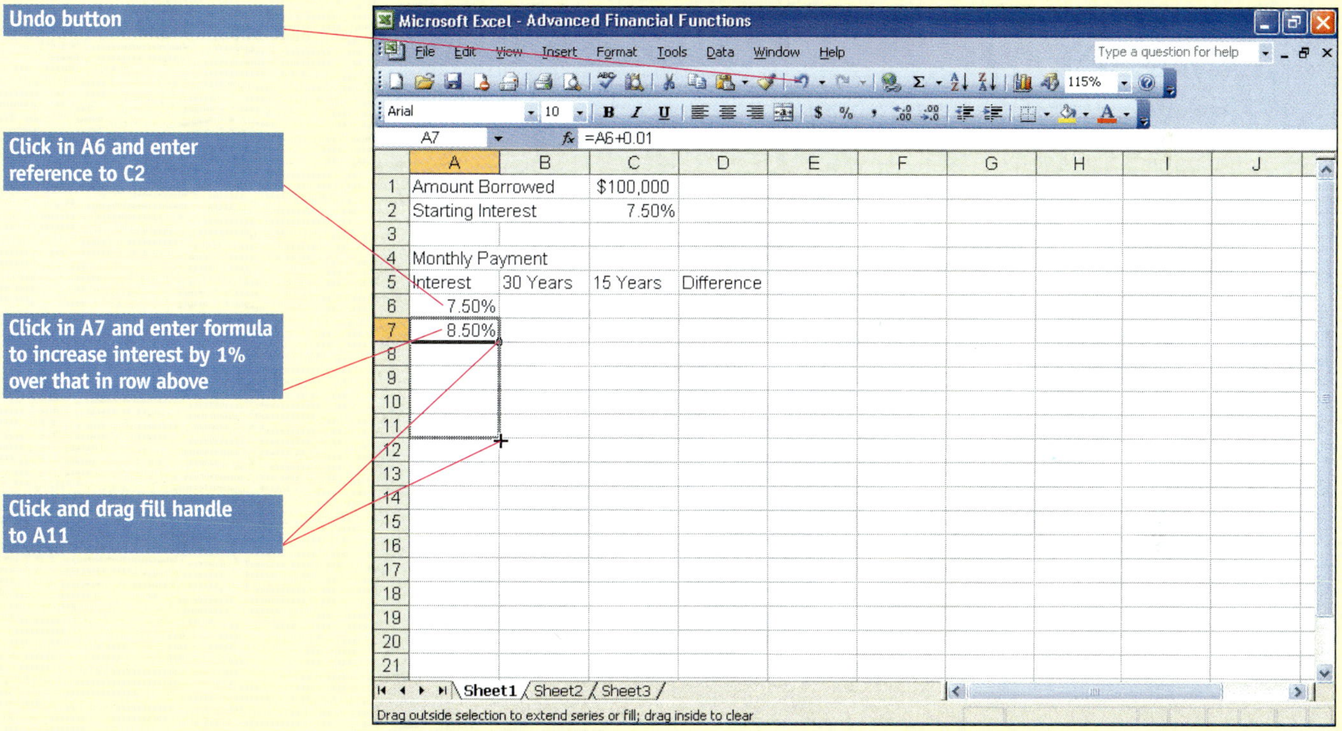

(b) The Fill Handle (step 2)

FIGURE 4.8 Hands-on Exercise 2 (*continued*)

FIND AND REPLACE

Anyone familiar with a word processor takes the Find and Replace commands for granted, but did you know the same capabilities exist in Excel? Pull down the Edit menu and choose either command. You have the same options as in the parallel command in Word, such as a case-sensitive (or insensitive) search. Use the command in the current worksheet to change "Interest" to "Interest Rate".

Step 3: Determine the 30-year Payments

- Click in **cell B6** and enter the formula **=PMT(A6/12,30*12,–$C$1)** as shown in Figure 4.8c. Note the ScreenTip that appears as you enter the function to indicate the order of the arguments. Note, too, that you can enter the references directly or you can use pointing (click the **F4 key** as necessary to change from relative to absolute addresses).
- Click in **cell B6**, which should display the value $699.21, as shown in Figure 4.8c. Click and drag the **fill handle** in the bottom-right corner of cell B6 over cells B7 through B11. Release the mouse to complete the copy operation.
- The PMT function in cell B6 has been copied to cells B7 through B11. The payment amounts are visible in cells B7 through B10, but cell B11 may display a series of number signs, meaning that the cell (column) is too narrow to display the computed results in the selected format.
- Check that cells B6:B11 are still selected. Pull down the **Format menu**, click **Column**, then click **AutoFit Selection** from the cascaded menu. Cell B11 should display $1,067.26.
- Save the workbook.

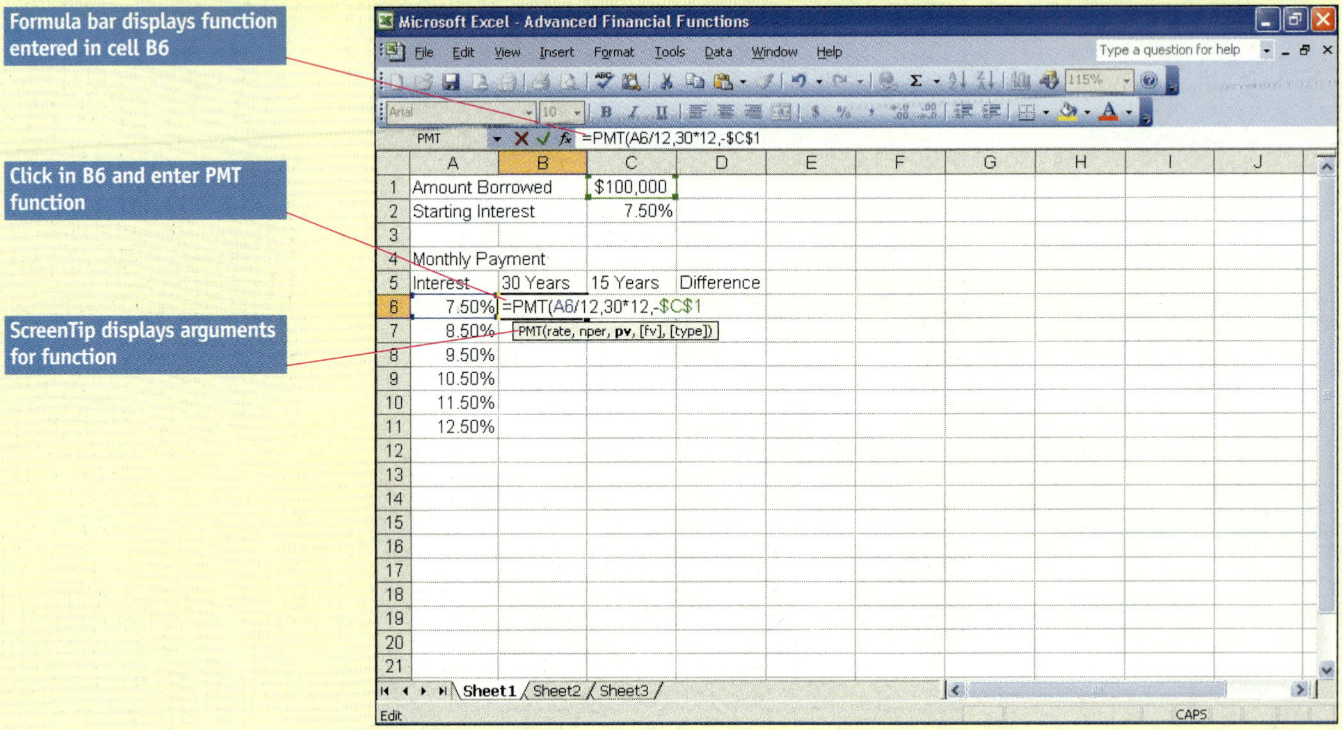

(c) Determine the 30-year Payments (step 3)

FIGURE 4.8 Hands-on Exercise 2 (*continued*)

POUND SIGNS AND COLUMN WIDTH

The appearance of pound signs within a cell indicates that the cell width (column width) is insufficient to display the computed results in the selected format. Double click the right border of the column heading to change the column width to accommodate the widest entry in that column. For example, to increase the width of column B, double click the border between the column headings for columns B and C.

Step 4: **Determine the 15-year Payments**

- Click in **cell C6** and enter the formula **=PMT(A6/12,15*12,–$C$1)** as shown in Figure 4.8d. Note the ScreenTip that appears as you enter the function to indicate the order of the arguments. You can enter the references directly, or you can use pointing (click the **F4 key** as necessary to change from relative to absolute addresses).
- Press **Enter** to complete the formula. Check that cell C6 displays the value $927.01. Make corrections as necessary.
- Use the **fill handle** to copy the contents of **cell C6** to **cells C7** through **C11**.
- If necessary, increase the width of column C. Cell C11 should display $1,232.52 if you have done this step correctly.
- Click in **cell D6** and enter the formula **=C6–B6**, then copy this formula to the remaining cells in this column. Cell D11 should display $165.26.
- Save the workbook.

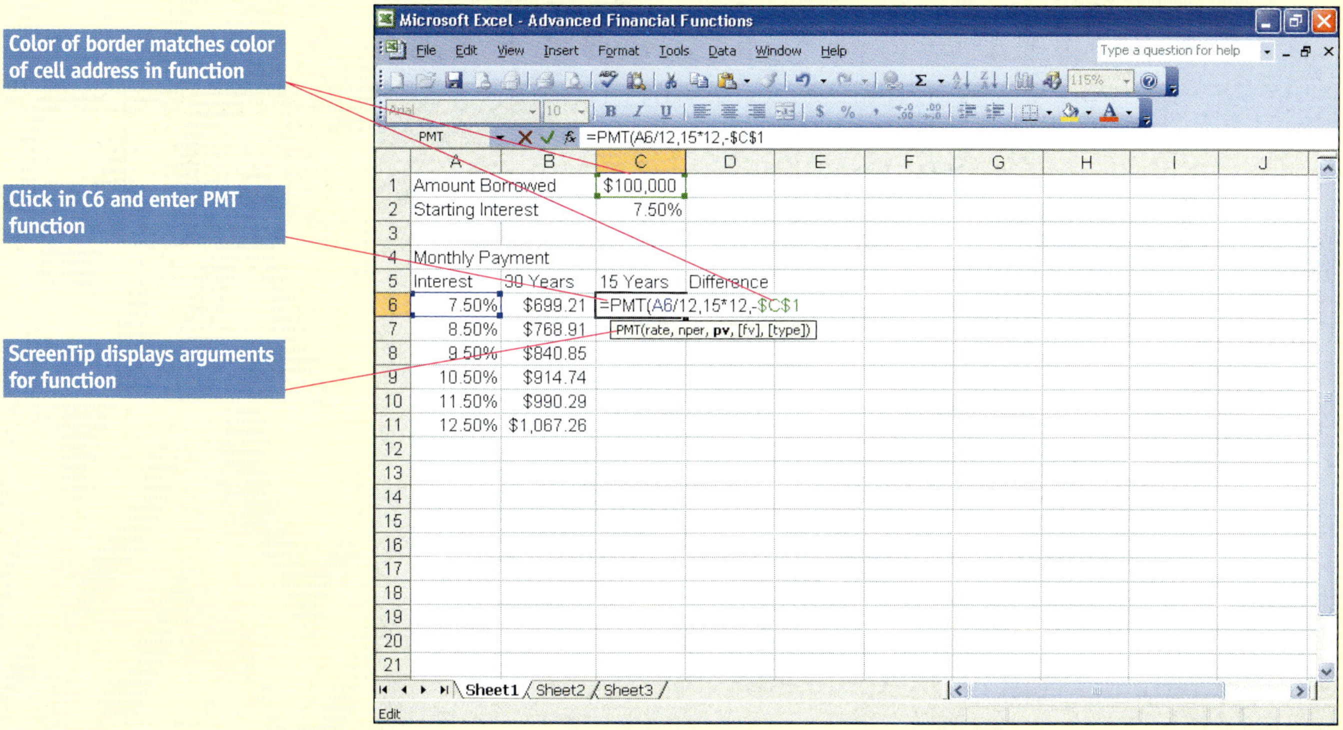

(d) Determine the 15-year Payments (step 4)

FIGURE 4.8 Hands-on Exercise 2 (*continued*)

KEYBOARD SHORTCUTS—CUT, COPY, AND PASTE

Ctrl+X (the X is supposed to remind you of a pair of scissors), Ctrl+C, and Ctrl+V are keyboard shortcuts to cut, copy, and paste, respectively, and apply to Excel as well as to Windows applications in general. The keystrokes are easier to remember when you realize that the operative letters X, C, and V are next to each other at the bottom left side of the keyboard. There is no need to memorize the keyboard shortcuts, but as you gain proficiency, they will become second nature.

Step 5: Format the Worksheet

- Click in **cell A13** and enter the label **Financial Consultant**. Enter **your name** in **cell A14**. Add formatting as necessary using Figure 4.8e as a guide.
- Click **cell A4**. Drag the mouse over cells **A4** through **D4**. Click the **Merge and Center button** on the Formatting toolbar to center the entry.
- Center the column headings in row 5. Add boldface and/or italics to the text and/or numbers as you see fit. Widen columns as necessary.
- Pull down the **File menu** and click the **Page Setup command** to display the Page Setup dialog box.
- Click the **Margins tab**. Check the box to center the worksheet horizontally. Click the **Sheet tab**. Check the boxes to include row and column headings and gridlines. Click **OK** to exit the Page Setup dialog box.
- Save the workbook. Pull down the **File menu**, click the **Print command** to display the Print dialog box, then click **OK** to print the worksheet. Press **Ctrl+~** to display the cell formulas. Widen the columns as necessary, then print.
- Press **Ctrl+~** to return to displayed values.

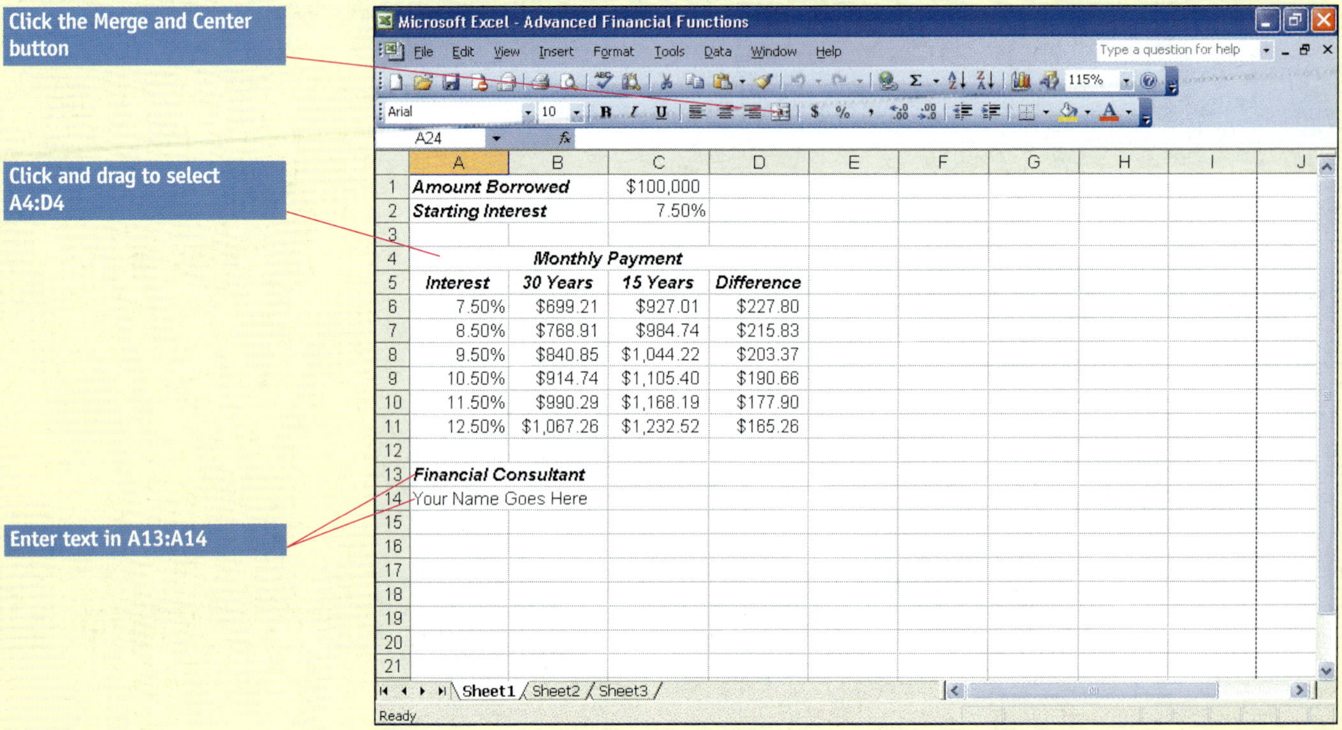

(e) Format the Worksheet (step 5)

FIGURE 4.8 Hands-on Exercise 2 (*continued*)

THE PPMT AND IPMT FUNCTIONS

The PMT function determines the periodic payment for a loan, which in turn is composed of two components, interest and principal. The amount of the payment that goes toward interest decreases each period, and conversely, the amount for the principle increases. These values can be computed through the IPMT and PPMT functions, respectively, which are used to compute the amortization (payoff) schedule for the loan.

Step 6: Merge and Center Text

- Click the **Sheet2 tab** to change to this worksheet. Click in **cell A1** and enter the title of the worksheet, **The Value of an IRA (Individual Retirement Account)**.
- Enter the indicated labels in **cells A3** and **C4** as shown in Figure 4.8f. Click in **cell A6** and type the label **Years Contributing**.
- Click and drag to select **cells A6** through **A21**, then click the **Merge and Center button** on the Standard toolbar to merge the cells. Right click within the merged cell, then click the **Format Cells command** to display the Format cells dialog box. Click the **Alignment tab**.
- Enter **90** in the Degrees list box to change to 90 degrees. Click the **down arrow** on the Vertical list box and choose **Center**. Click **OK**. Click the **Undo button** if the results are different from what you intended.
- Click and drag to select **cells A1** through **J1**, then click the **Merge and Center button** to center the title. Merge and center cells **C4** through **J4** in similar fashion.
- Click and drag the border between columns A and B to make the column narrower, as appropriate. Save the workbook.

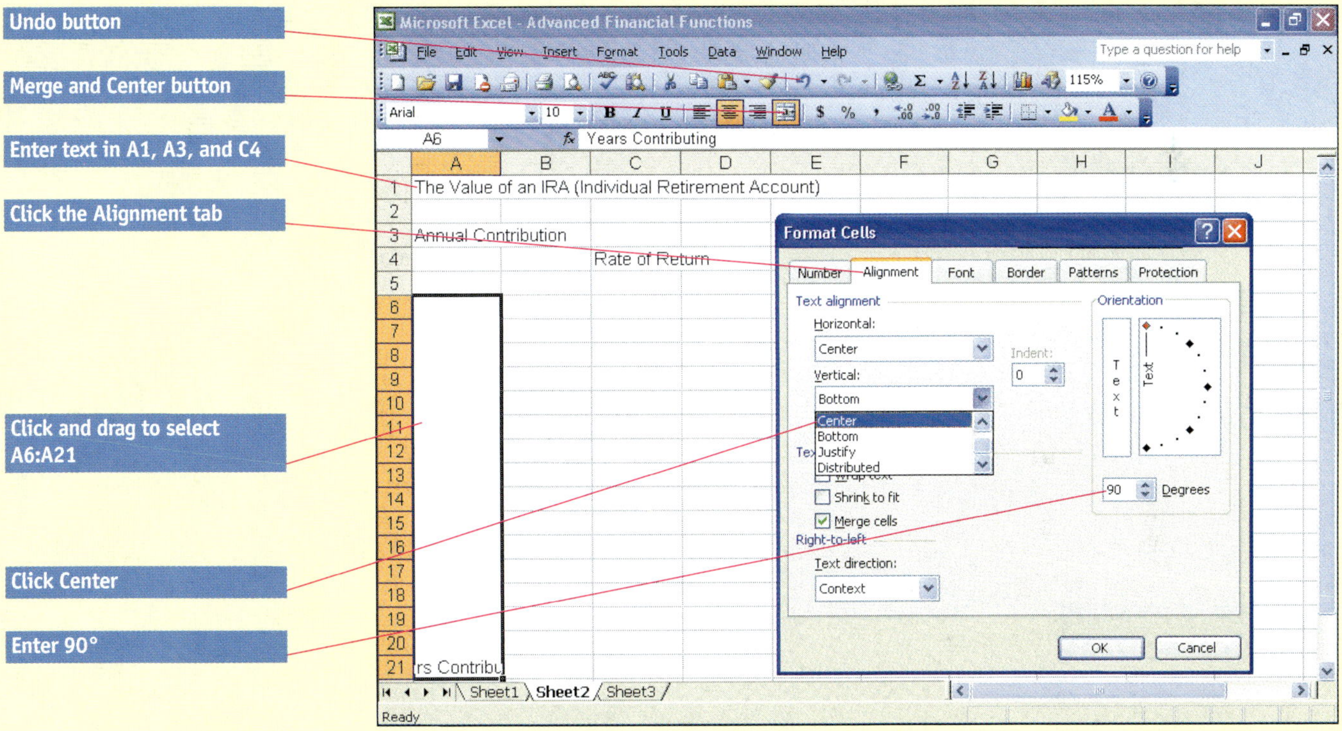

(f) Merge and Center Text (step 6)

FIGURE 4.8 Hands-on Exercise 2 (*continued*)

THE MERGE AND CENTER COMMAND

The Merge and Center command combines multiple cells into a single cell and is best used in conjunction with the headings in a worksheet. Cells can be merged horizontally or vertically, then the text in the merged cells can be aligned in a variety of styles. Text can also be rotated to provide interest in the worksheet. If necessary, you can restore the individual cells and remove the associated formatting using the Edit Clear command. Click in the merged cell, pull down the Edit menu, and click the Clear command. Click Formats to restore the individual cells to the default format.

Step 7: Enter the Row and Column Headings

- Check that the labels in your worksheet match those in Figure 4.8g. Click in **cell D3** and enter **$3,000**. Click in **cell C5** and type **5.00%**. Be sure to include the decimal point, zeros, and percent sign.
- Click in **cell D5** and enter the formula **=C5+.01**, then click and drag the **fill handle** to copy this formula to cells **E5** through **J5**.
- Click in **cell B6** and type the number **25**. Click in **cell B7** and enter the formula **=B6+1**, then click and drag the **fill handle** to copy this formula to **cells B8** through **B21**.
- Double click the **Sheet2 tab** to select the worksheet name, then type **Mixed References** as the name of this worksheet. Double click the **Sheet1 tab** to select the worksheet name, then type **Mortgage Analysis** as the name of this worksheet.
- Click the newly named **Mixed References worksheet tab** to return to this worksheet and continue working.
- Save the workbook.

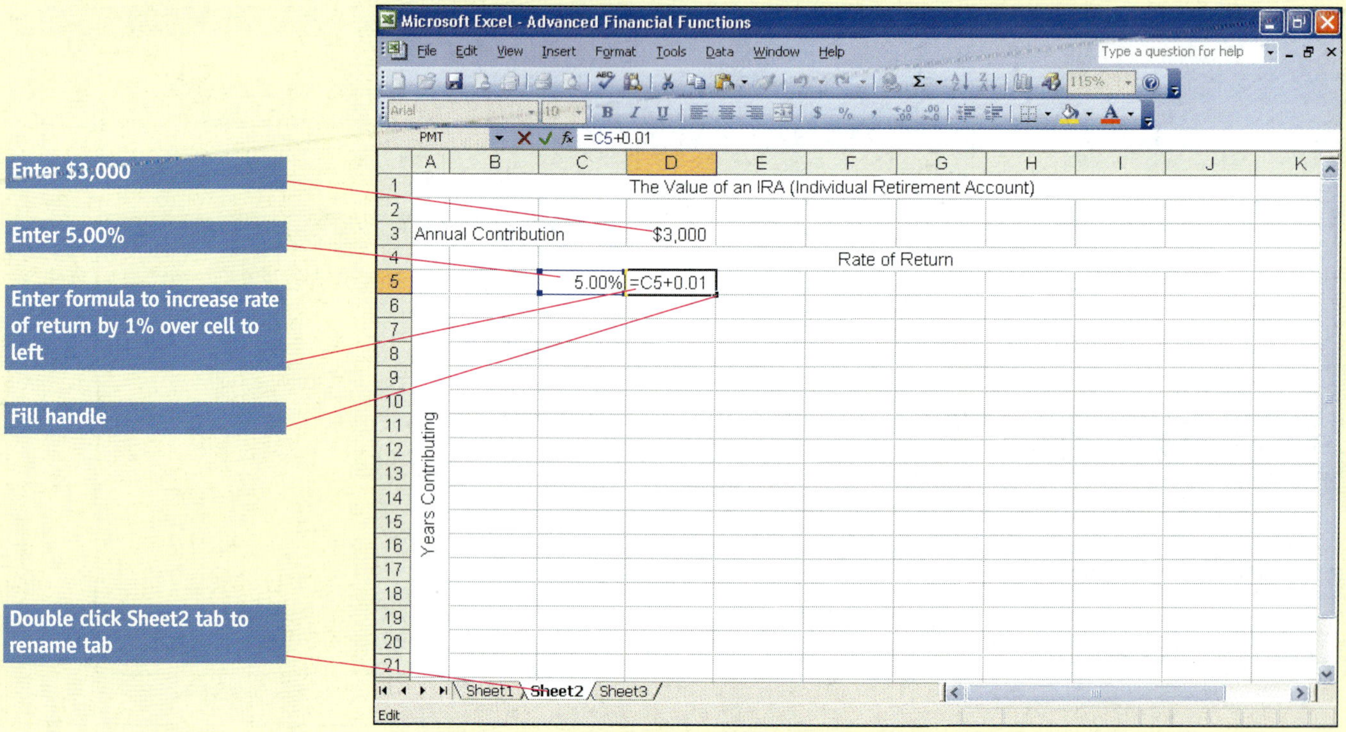

(g) Enter the Row and Column Headings (step 7)

FIGURE 4.8 Hands-on Exercise 2 (*continued*)

AUTOMATIC FORMATTING

Excel converts any number entered with a beginning dollar sign to currency format, and any number entered with an ending percent sign to percentage format. The automatic formatting enables you to save a step by typing $100,000 or 7.5% directly into a cell, rather than entering 100000 or .075 and having to format the number. The formatting is applied to the cell and affects any subsequent numbers in that cell. (Use the Clear command in the Edit menu to remove the formatting.)

Step 8: Create the Mixed References

- Click in **cell C6**. Pull down the **Insert menu** and click **Function** (or click the **Insert Function button** on the formula bar) to display the Insert Function dialog box.
- Click the **drop-down arrow**, then click **Financial** in the Select a Category list box. Click **FV** in the Select a Function list box. Click **OK**.
- Click and drag the Function Arguments dialog box so that you can see the underlying cells as shown in Figure 4.8h.
- Click the text box for rate, click in **cell C5**, then press the **F4 key** until you see **C$5** within the dialog box.
- Press **Tab** to move to (or click in) the **Nper text box**, click in **cell B6**, then press the **F4 key** until you see $B6 within the dialog box.
- Press **Tab** to move to (or click in) the **Pmt text box**, type a **minus sign**, click in **cell D3**, then press the **F4 key** until you see **–$D$3** in the dialog box.
- Check that the entries on your screen match those in Figure 4.8h, then click **OK**. Cell C6 should display the value $143,181.
- Save the workbook.

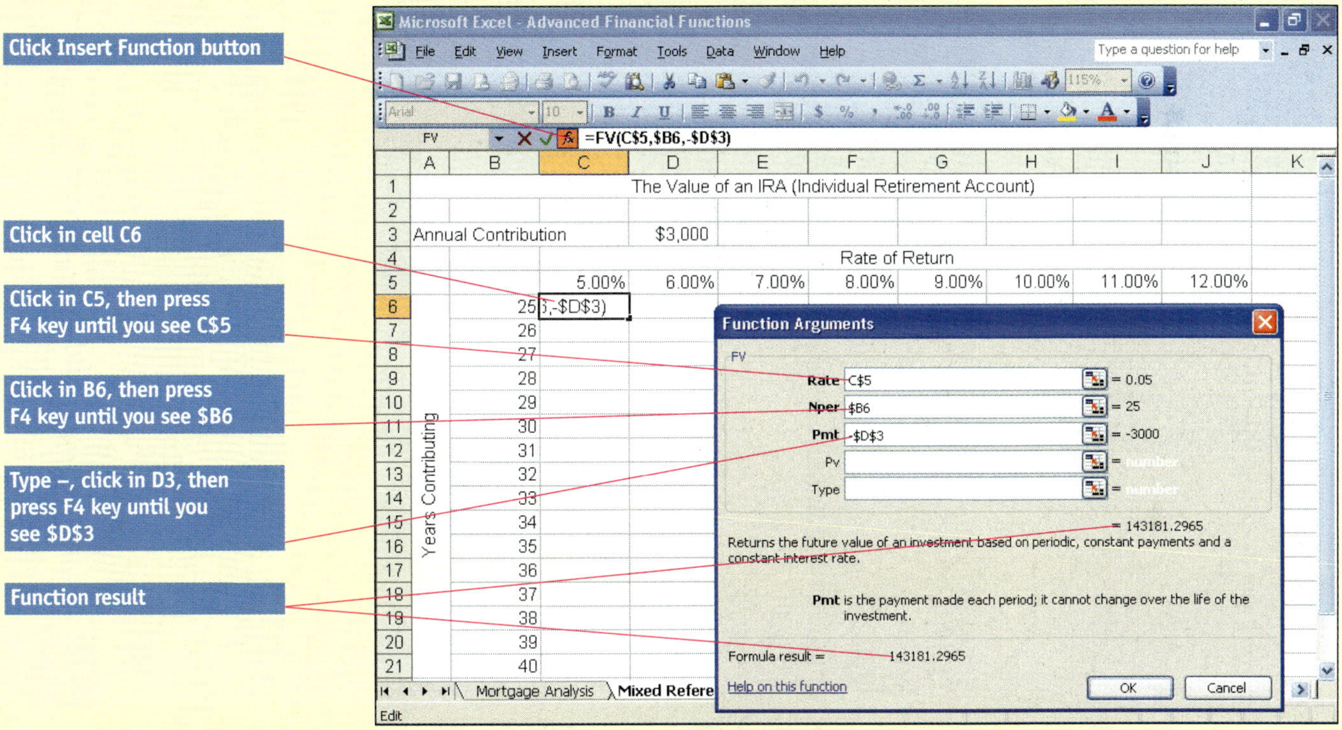

(h) Create the Mixed References (step 8)

FIGURE 4.8 Hands-on Exercise 2 (*continued*)

MIXED REFERENCES ARE NOT DIFFICULT

Mixed references are not difficult, provided you think clearly about what is required. In our example the interest rate should always come from row 5, but the column should change. Hence you enter C$5 for this parameter within the FV function. In similar fashion, the term of the investment should always come from column B, but the row should change. Thus you enter $B6 for this parameter. It's easy and it's powerful.

Step 9: Copy the Formula

- If necessary, click in **cell C6**, the cell that contains the formula you just created. Click and drag the **fill handle** in **cell C6** to **cells D6** through **J6**.
- Change the formatting to **zero decimal places**, then change column widths as necessary. Cell J6 should display the value $400,002.
- If necessary, select **cells C6** through **J6** as shown in Figure 4.8i. Click and drag the fill handle in **cell J6** to **cell J21** to copy the entire row to the remaining rows in the worksheet.
- Release the mouse. Cell J21 should display the value $2,301,274, corresponding to the future value of a $3,000 investment for 40 years at 12 percent. Change column widths as necessary.
- Click in **cell C6**, then press the **right arrow** to move from one cell to the next in this row to see how the cell formulas change to reflect the mixed references. Return to cell C6, then press the **down arrow** to view the cell formulas for the other cells in this column.
- Save the workbook.

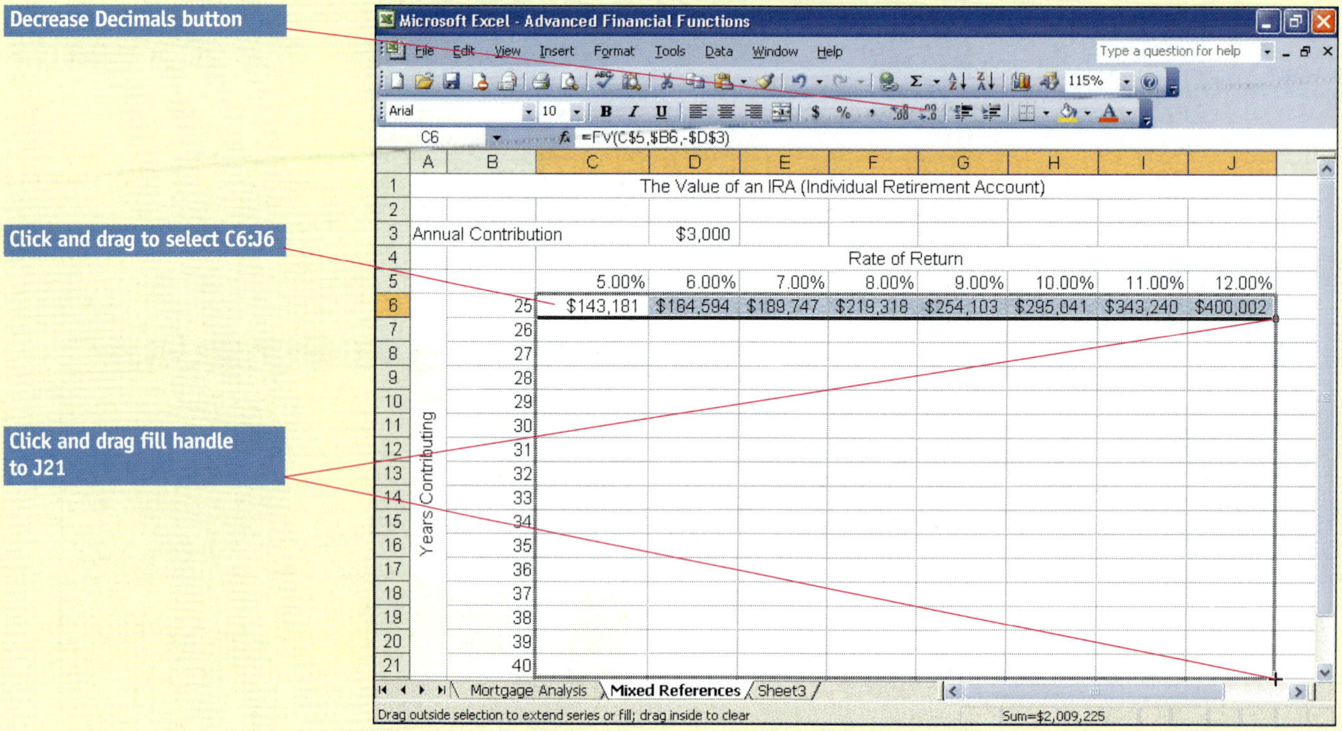

(i) Copy the Formula (step 9)

FIGURE 4.8 Hands-on Exercise 2 (*continued*)

THE ARRANGE WINDOWS COMMAND

It can be advantageous to view multiple worksheets within a workbook at the same time, with each worksheet in its own window. Pull down the Window menu and click the New Window command to open another window. Pull down the Window menu a second time, click the Arrange command, then click the option button that indicates how you want to display the windows; e.g., horizontal to display the windows one on top of another. Each window provides a different view of the workbook. Click in either window, then click the worksheet tab you want to display.

Step 10: The Finishing Touches

- Check that the numbers in your worksheet match those in Figure 4.8j. Make corrections as necessary.
- Use the **Page Setup command** to include gridlines and row and column headings. Use landscape formatting if necessary.
- Print the worksheet two ways, once with the displayed values and once with the cell contents.
- Add a cover sheet, then submit all five pages (the cover sheet, the displayed values and cell formulas for the mortgage analysis from step 5, and the displayed values and cell formulas from this step) to your instructor as proof that you completed this exercise.
- Exit Excel if you do not want to continue with the next exercise at this time.

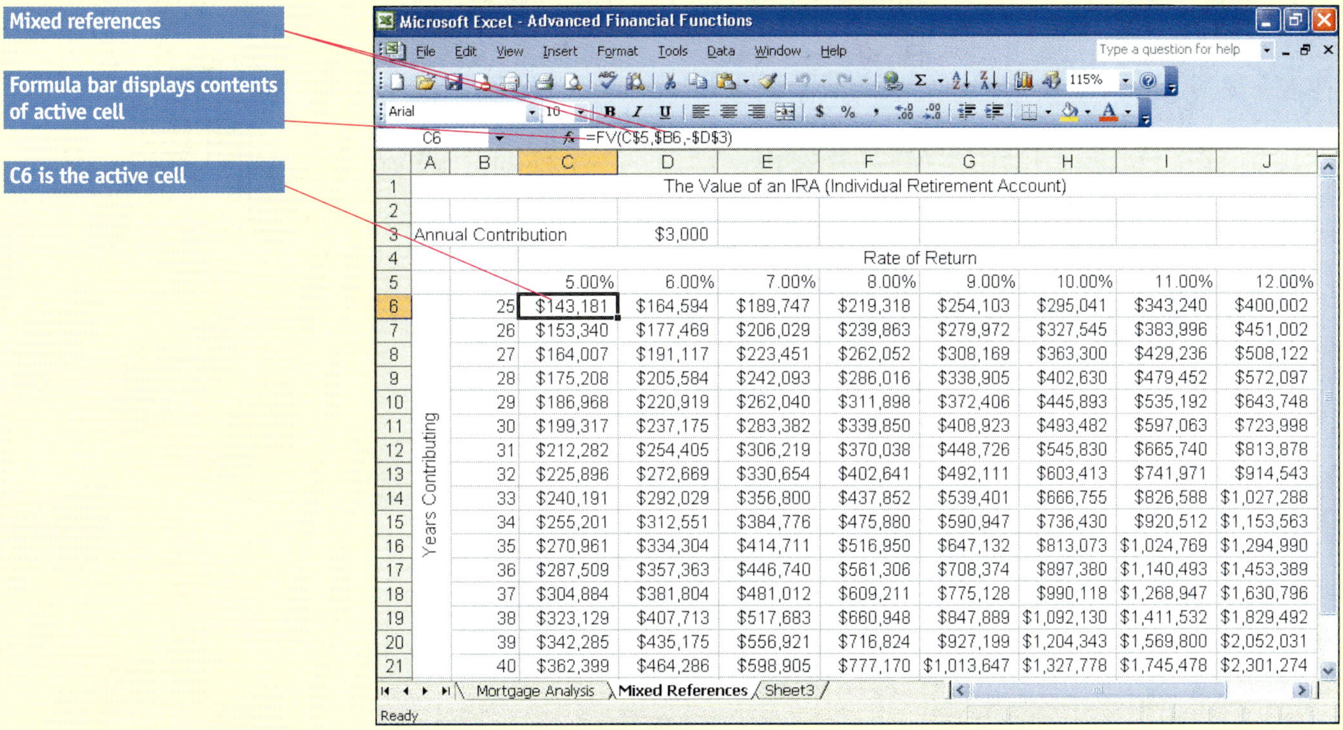

	A	B	C	D	E	F	G	H	I	J
1	The Value of an IRA (Individual Retirement Account)									
2										
3	Annual Contribution			$3,000						
4						Rate of Return				
5			5.00%	6.00%	7.00%	8.00%	9.00%	10.00%	11.00%	12.00%
6	Years Contributing	25	$143,181	$164,594	$189,747	$219,318	$254,103	$295,041	$343,240	$400,002
7		26	$153,340	$177,469	$206,029	$239,863	$279,972	$327,545	$383,996	$451,002
8		27	$164,007	$191,117	$223,451	$262,052	$308,169	$363,300	$429,236	$508,122
9		28	$175,208	$205,584	$242,093	$286,016	$338,905	$402,630	$479,452	$572,097
10		29	$186,968	$220,919	$262,040	$311,898	$372,406	$445,893	$535,192	$643,748
11		30	$199,317	$237,175	$283,382	$339,850	$408,923	$493,482	$597,063	$723,998
12		31	$212,282	$254,405	$306,219	$370,038	$448,726	$545,830	$665,740	$813,878
13		32	$225,896	$272,669	$330,654	$402,641	$492,111	$603,413	$741,971	$914,543
14		33	$240,191	$292,029	$356,800	$437,852	$539,401	$666,755	$826,588	$1,027,288
15		34	$255,201	$312,551	$384,776	$475,880	$590,947	$736,430	$920,512	$1,153,563
16		35	$270,961	$334,304	$414,711	$516,950	$647,132	$813,073	$1,024,769	$1,294,990
17		36	$287,509	$357,363	$446,740	$561,306	$708,374	$897,380	$1,140,493	$1,453,389
18		37	$304,884	$381,804	$481,012	$609,211	$775,128	$990,118	$1,268,947	$1,630,796
19		38	$323,129	$407,713	$517,683	$660,948	$847,889	$1,092,130	$1,411,532	$1,829,492
20		39	$342,285	$435,175	$556,921	$716,824	$927,199	$1,204,343	$1,569,800	$2,052,031
21		40	$362,399	$464,286	$598,905	$777,170	$1,013,647	$1,327,778	$1,745,478	$2,301,274

(j) The Finishing Touches (step 10)

FIGURE 4.8 Hands-on Exercise 2 (*continued*)

START SAVING EARLY

The longer you invest, the more time that compound interest has to work its magic. Investing $3,000 for 40 years at 7%, for example, yields a future value of $598,905. Delay for five years—that is, invest for 35 years rather than 40—and the amount goes down to $414,711. Put another way—Start your IRA at age 25, and 40 years later you will have accumulated more than half a million dollars. Wait until age 30, and you wind up with significantly less. The out-of-pocket difference is only $15,000 ($3,000 a year for five years), but the end result at retirement is more than $180,000. Too many people try to time the stock market, which is impossible. It is the time *in* the market that matters.

THE GRADE BOOK REVISITED

Financial functions are only one of several categories of functions that are included in Excel. Our next example presents an expanded version of the professor's grade book. It introduces several new functions and shows how those functions can aid in the professor's determination of a student's grade. The expanded grade book is shown in Figure 4.9. Consider:

Statistical functions: The AVERAGE, MAX, and MIN functions are used to compute the statistics on each test for the class as a whole. The range on each test is computed by subtracting the minimum value from the maximum value.

IF function: The IF function conditionally adds a homework bonus of three points to the semester average, prior to determining the letter grade. The bonus is awarded to those students whose homework is "OK." Students whose homework is not "OK" do not receive the bonus.

VLOOKUP function: The expanded grade book converts a student's semester average to a letter grade, in accordance with the table shown in the lower-right portion of the worksheet. A student with an average of 60 to 69 will receive a D, 70 to 79 a C, 80 to 89 a B, and 90 or higher an A. Any student with an average less than 60 receives an F.

The Sort command: The rows within a spreadsheet can be displayed in any sequence by clicking on the appropriate column within the list of students, then clicking the Ascending or Descending sort button on the Standard toolbar. The students in Figure 4.9 are listed alphabetically, but could just as easily have been listed by Social Security number.

	A	B	C	D	E	F	G	H	I	J
1	Professor's Grade Book - Final Semester Averages									
2										
3	**Name**	**Soc Sec Num**	**Test 1**	**Test 2**	**Test 3**	**Test 4**	**Test Average**	**Homework**	**Semester Average**	**Grade**
4	Adams, John	111-22-3333	80	71	70	84	77.8	Poor	77.8	C
5	Barber, Maryann	444-55-6666	96	98	97	90	94.2	OK	97.2	A
6	Boone, Dan	777-88-9999	78	81	70	78	77.0	OK	80.0	B
7	Borow, Jeff	123-45-6789	65	65	65	60	63.0	OK	66.0	D
8	Brown, James	999-99-9999	92	95	79	80	85.2	OK	88.2	B
9	Carson, Kit	888-88-8888	90	90	90	70	82.0	OK	85.0	B
10	Coulter, Sara	100-00-0000	60	50	40	79	61.6	OK	64.6	D
11	Fegin, Richard	222-22-2222	75	70	65	95	80.0	OK	83.0	B
12	Ford, Judd	200-00-0000	90	90	80	90	88.0	Poor	88.0	B
13	Glassman, Kris	444-44-4444	82	78	62	77	75.2	OK	78.2	C
14	Goodman, Neil	555-55-5555	92	88	65	78	80.2	OK	83.2	B
15	Milgrom, Marion	666-66-6666	94	92	86	84	88.0	OK	91.0	A
16	Moldof, Adam	300-00-0000	92	78	65	82	79.8	Poor	79.8	C
17	Smith, Adam	777-77-7777	60	50	65	80	67.0	Poor	67.0	D
18										
19	**Average**		81.9	78.3	71.4	80.5	**HW Bonus**	3	**Grading Criteria**	
20	**Highest Grade**		96.0	98.0	97.0	95.0			0	F
21	**Lowest Grade**		60.0	50.0	40.0	60.0			60	D
22	**Range**		36.0	48.0	57.0	35.0			70	C
23									80	B
24	**Exam Weights**		**20%**	**20%**	**20%**	**40%**			90	A

Statistical functions determine average, highest, and lowest grades on tests

IF function determines Semester Average

VLOOKUP Function determines Grade

FIGURE 4.9 The Expanded Grade Book

Statistical Functions

The ***MAX***, ***MIN***, and ***AVERAGE functions*** return the highest, lowest, and average values, respectively, from an argument list. The list may include individual cell references, ranges, numeric values, functions, or mathematical expressions (formulas). The ***statistical functions*** are illustrated in the worksheet of Figure 4.10.

The first example, =AVERAGE(A1:A3), computes the average for cells A1 through A3 by adding the values in the indicated range (70, 80, and 90), then dividing the result by three, to obtain an average of 80. Additional arguments in the form of values and/or cell addresses can be specified within the parentheses; for example, the function =AVERAGE(A1:A3,200), computes the average of cells A1, A2, and A3, and the number 200.

Cells that are empty or cells that contain text values are *not* included in the computation. Thus since cell A4 is empty, the function =AVERAGE(A1:A4) will also return an average value of 80 (240/3). In similar fashion, the function =AVERAGE(A1:A3,A5) includes only three values in its computation (cells A1, A2, and A3) because the text entry in cell A5 is excluded. The results of the MIN and MAX functions are obtained in a comparable way, as indicated in Figure 4.10. Empty cells and text entries are not included in the computation.

The COUNT and COUNTA functions each tally the number of entries in the argument list and are subtly different. The ***COUNT function*** returns the number of cells containing a numeric entry, including formulas that evaluate to numeric results. The ***COUNTA function*** includes cells with text as well as numeric values. The functions =COUNT(A1:A3) and =COUNTA(A1:A3) both return a value of 3 as do the two functions =COUNT(A1:A4) and =COUNTA(A1:A4). (Cell A4 is empty and is excluded from the latter computations.) The function =COUNT(A1:A3,A5) also returns a value of 3 because it does not include the text entry in cell A5. However, the function =COUNTA(A1:A3,A5) returns a value of 4 because it includes the text entry in cell A5.

Empty and/or text values are not included in the computation (AVERAGE)

Empty and/or text values are not included in the computation (COUNT)

Empty cells are not included in the computation (COUNTA)

Text values are included in the computation (COUNTA)

Function	Value
=AVERAGE(A1:A3)	80
=AVERAGE(A1:A3,200)	110
=AVERAGE(A1:A4)	80
=AVERAGE(A1:A3,A5)	80
=MAX(A1:A3)	90
=MAX(A1:A3,200)	200
=MAX(A1:A4)	90
=MAX(A1:A3,A5)	90
=MIN(A1:A3)	70
=MIN(A1:A3,200)	70
=MIN(A1:A4)	70
=MIN(A1:A3,A5)	70
=COUNT(A1:A3)	3
=COUNT(A1:A3,200)	4
=COUNT(A1:A4)	3
=COUNT(A1:A3,A5)	3
=COUNTA(A1:A3)	3
=COUNTA(A1:A3,200)	4
=COUNTA(A1:A4)	3
=COUNTA(A1:A3,A5)	4

(a) Illustrative Functions

Empty cell

Text value

	A
1	70
2	80
3	90
4	
5	Study hard

(b) The Spreadsheet

FIGURE 4.10 Statistical Functions with a Text Entry

Arithmetic Expressions versus Functions

Many worksheet calculations, such as an average or a sum, can be performed in two ways. You can enter a formula such as =(A1+A2+A3)/3, or you can use the equivalent function =AVERAGE(A1:A3). *The use of functions is generally preferable* as shown in Figure 4.11.

The two worksheets in Figure 4.11a may appear equivalent, but the ***SUM function*** is superior to the arithmetic expression. This is true despite the fact that the entries in cell A5 of both worksheets return a value of 100.

Consider what happens if a new row is inserted between existing rows 2 and 3, with the entry in the new cell equal to 25 as shown in Figure 4.11b. The SUM function adjusts automatically to include the new value (returning a sum of 125) because the SUM function was defined originally for the cell range *A1 through A4.* The new row is inserted within these cells, moving the entry in cell A4 to cell A5, and changing the range to include cell A5.

No such accommodation is made in the arithmetic expression, which was defined to include four *specific* cells rather than a range of cells. The addition of the new row modifies the cell references (since the values in cells A3 and A4 have been moved to cells A4 and A5), and does not include the new row in the adjusted expression.

Similar reasoning holds for deleting a row. Figure 4.11c deletes row 2 from the *original* worksheets, which moves the entry in cell A4 to cell A3. The SUM function adjusts automatically to =SUM(A1:A3) and returns the value 80. The formula, however, returns an error (to indicate an illegal cell reference) because it is still attempting to add the entries in four cells, one of which no longer exists. In summary, a function expands and contracts to adjust for insertions or deletions, and should be used wherever possible.

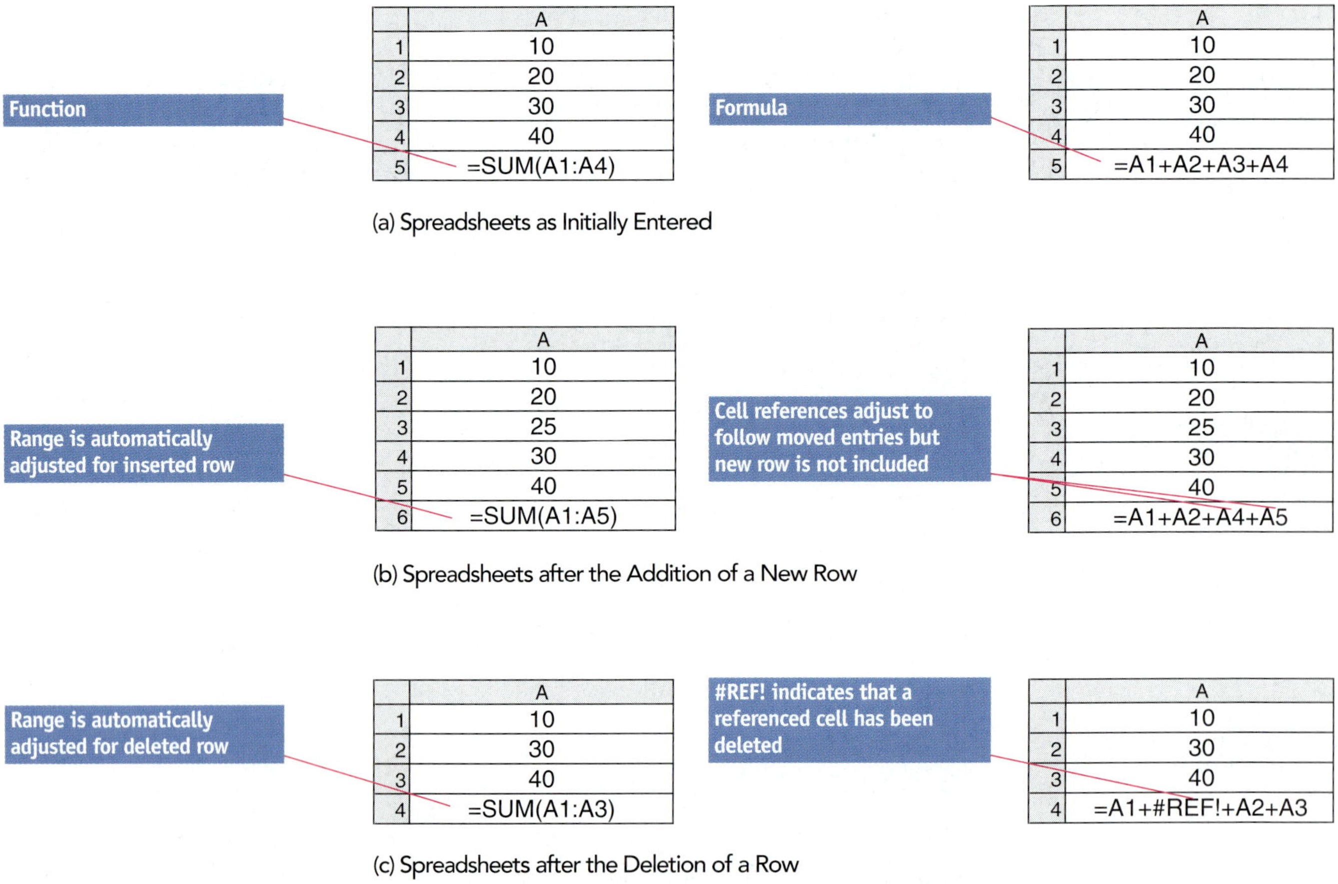

FIGURE 4.11 Arithmetic Expressions versus Functions

IF Function

The ***IF function*** enables decision making to be implemented within a worksheet. It has three arguments: a condition that is either true or false, the value if the condition is true, and the value if the condition is false. Consider:

=IF(condition,value-if-true,value-if-false)

- condition: Condition is either true or false
- value-if-true: Value returned for a true condition
- value-if-false: Value returned for a false condition

The IF function returns either the second or third argument, depending on the result of the condition; that is, if the condition is true, the function returns the second argument. If the condition is false, the function returns the third argument.

The condition includes one of the six ***relational operators*** in Figure 4.12a. The IF function is illustrated in the worksheet in Figure 4.12b, which is used to create the examples in Figure 4.12c. The arguments may be numeric (1000 or 2000), a cell reference to display the contents of the specific cell (B1 or B2), a formula (=B1+10 or =B1–10), a function (MAX(B1:B2) or MIN(B1:B2)), or a text entry enclosed in quotation marks ("Go" or "Hold").

Operator	Description
=	Equal to
<>	Not equal to
<	Less than
>	Greater than
<=	Less than or equal to
>=	Greater than or equal to

(a) Relational Operators

	A	B	C
1	10	15	April
2	10	30	May

(b) The Spreadsheet

IF Function	Evaluation	Result
=IF(A1=A2,1000,2000)	10 is equal to 10: TRUE	1000
=IF(A1<>A2,1000,2000)	10 is not equal to 10: FALSE	2000
=IF(A1<>A2,B1,B2)	10 is not equal to 10:FALSE	30
=IF(A1<B2,MAX(B1:B2),MIN(B1:B2))	10 is less than 30: TRUE	30
=IF(A1<A2,B1+10,B1-10)	10 is less than 10:FALSE	5
=IF(A1=A2,C1,C2)	10 is equal to 10: TRUE	April
=IF(SUM(A1:A2)>20,"Go","Hold")	10+10 is greater than 20:FALSE	Hold

(c) Examples

FIGURE 4.12 The IF Function

The IF function is used in the grade book of Figure 4.9 to award a bonus for homework. Students whose homework is "OK" receive the bonus, whereas other students do not. The IF function to implement this logic for the first student is:

=IF(H4="OK",G4+$H$19,G4)

- H4="OK": Condition determines if homework is "OK"
- G4+$H$19: Average is incremented by the bonus in cell H19 if homework is "OK"
- G4: Average is unchanged if homework *not* "OK"

The IF function compares the value in cell H4 (the homework grade) to the literal "OK." If the condition is true (the homework is "OK"), the bonus in cell H19 is added to the student's test average in cell G4. If, however, the condition is false (the homework is not "OK"), the average is unchanged.

VLOOKUP Function

Consider, for a moment, how the professor assigns letter grades to students at the end of the semester. He or she computes a test average for each student and conditionally awards the bonus for homework. The professor then determines a letter grade according to a predetermined scale; for example, 90 or above is an A, 80 to 89 is a B, and so on.

The ***VLOOKUP*** (vertical lookup) ***function*** duplicates this process within a worksheet by assigning an entry to a cell based on a numeric value contained in another cell. The ***HLOOKUP*** (horizontal lookup) ***function*** is similar in concept except that the table is arranged horizontally. In other words, just as the professor knows where on the grading scale a student's numerical average will fall, the VLOOKUP function determines where within a specified table (the grading criteria) a numeric value (a student's average) is found, and retrieves the corresponding entry (the letter grade).

The VLOOKUP function requires three arguments: the value to look up, the range of cells containing the table in which the value is to be looked up, and the column number within the table that contains the result. These concepts are illustrated in Figure 4.13, which was taken from the expanded grade book in Figure 4.9. The table in Figure 4.13 extends over two columns (I and J), and five rows (20 through 24); that is, the table is located in the range I20:J24. The ***breakpoints*** or matching values (the lowest numeric value for each grade) are contained in column **I** (the first column in the table) and are in ascending order. The corresponding letter grades are found in column **J**.

The VLOOKUP function in cell J4 determines the letter grade (for John Adams) based on the computed average in cell I4. Consider:

```
=VLOOKUP(I4,$I$20:$J$24,2)
    |        |         └ The column number containing the grade
    |        └ The range of the table
    └ Value to look up (the student's average)
```

The first argument is the value to look up, which in this example is Adams's computed average, found in cell I4. A relative reference is used so that the address will adjust when the formula is copied to the other rows in the worksheet.

	A	. . .	G	H	I	J
1	Professor's Grade Book - Final Semester Averages					
2						
3	Name		Test Average	Homework	Semester Average	Grade
4	Adams, John		77.8	Poor		
.	.	.	.	.	.	.
19	Average		HW Bonus	3	Grading Criteria	
20	Highest Grade				0	F
21	Lowest Grade				60	D
22	Range				70	C
23					80	B
24	Exam Weights				90	A

=VLOOKUP(14,$I$20:$J$24,2)

Breakpoints (in ascending order)

Grades are in column 2 of table

FIGURE 4.13 Table Lookup Function

A large worksheet, such as the extended grade book, can seldom be seen on the monitor in its entirety. It's necessary, therefore, to learn how to view the distant parts of a worksheet, to keep certain parts of the worksheet in constant view, and/or to hide selected rows and columns. These concepts are illustrated in Figure 4.14. Figure 4.14a displays the initial worksheet, with cell A1 selected as the active cell, so that you see the upper-left portion of the worksheet, rows 1 through 20 inclusive, and columns A through I inclusive. You cannot see the semester grades in column J, nor can you see the class averages and other statistics that begin in row 21.

Clicking the right arrow on the horizontal scroll bar (or pressing the right arrow key when the active cell is already in the rightmost column of the screen) causes the entire screen to move one column to the right. In similar fashion, clicking the down arrow in the vertical scroll bar (or pressing the down arrow key when the active cell is in the bottom row of the screen) causes the entire screen to move down one row. This is known as ***scrolling*** and it comes about automatically as the active cell is changed as you work with the worksheet.

Freezing Panes

Scrolling brings the distant portions of a worksheet into view, but it also moves the headings for existing rows and/or columns off the screen. You can, however, retain the headings by freezing panes as shown in Figure 4.14b. The letter grades and the grading criteria are visible as in the previous figure, but so too are the names at the left of the worksheet and the column headings at the top of the worksheet.

Look closely at Figure 4.14b and you will see column B (containing the Social Security numbers) is missing, as are rows 4 through 7 (the first four students). You will also notice a horizontal line under row 3 and a vertical line after column A, to indicate that these rows and columns have been frozen. This is accomplished through the ***Freeze Panes command*** that always displays the desired row or column headings (column A and rows 1, 2, and 3 in this example) regardless of the scrolling in effect. The rows and/or columns that are frozen are the ones above and to the left of the active cell when the command is issued. The ***Unfreeze Panes command*** returns to normal scrolling.

Hiding Rows and Columns

Figure 4.14c illustrates the ability to hide rows and/or columns in a worksheet. We have hidden columns C through F (inclusive) that contain the results of the individual tests, and rows 19 through 24 that contain the summary statistics. The "missing" rows and columns remain in the workbook but are hidden from view. The cells are not visible in the monitor, nor do they appear when the worksheet is printed. To hide a row or column, click the row or column heading to select the entire row or column, then execute the Hide command from within the Format menu. ***Unhiding cells*** is trickier because you need to select the adjacent rows or columns prior to executing the Unhide command.

Printing a Large Worksheet

The ***Page Break Preview command*** (in the View menu) lets you see and/or modify the page breaks that will occur when the worksheet is printed as shown in Figure 4.14d. The dashed blue line between columns H and I indicates that the worksheet will print on two pages, with columns A to H on page 1 and columns I and J on page 2. The dialog box shows that you adjust (eliminate) the page break by dragging the dashed line to the right.

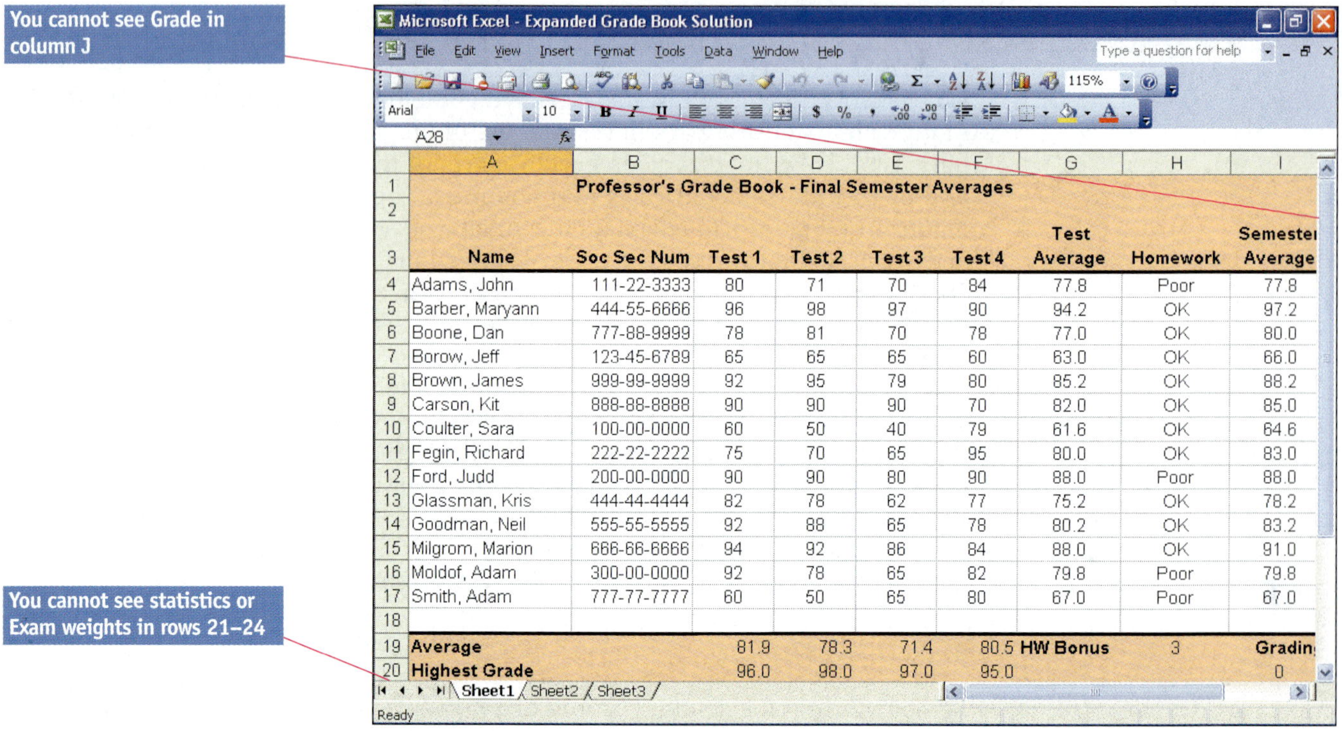

(a) The Grade Book

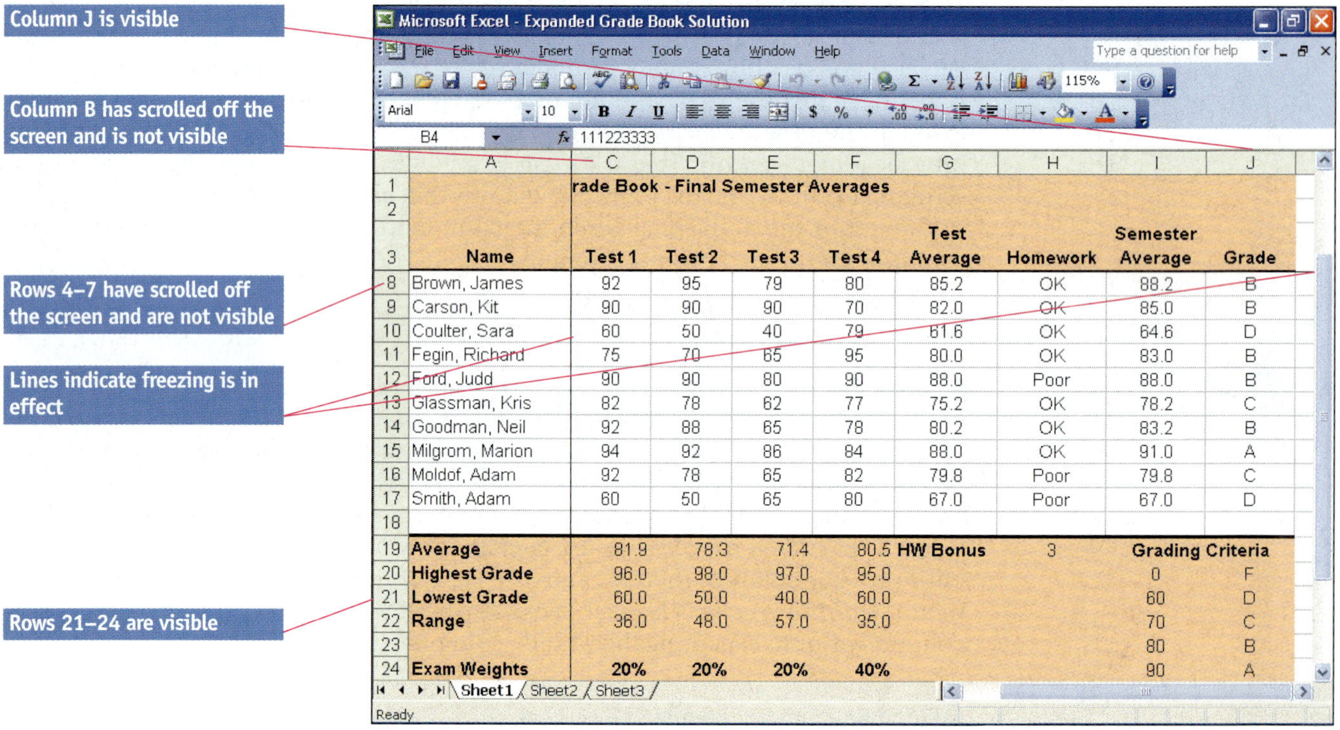

(b) Freezing Panes

FIGURE 4.14 Working with Large Spreadsheets

Columns C–F are hidden

Rows 19–24 are hidden

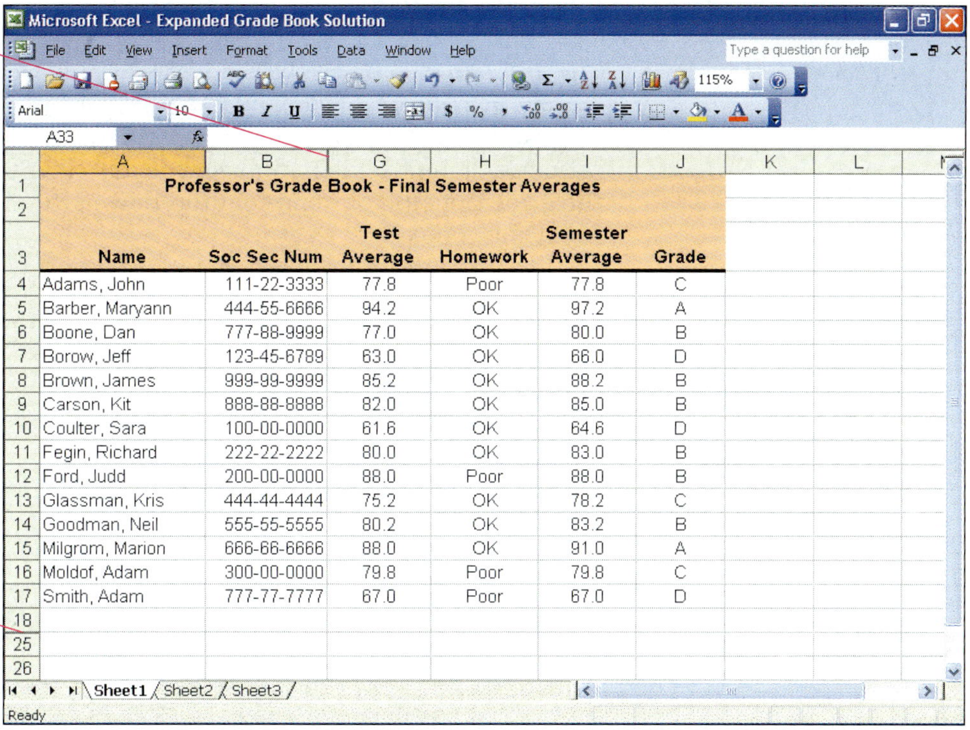

(c) Hiding Rows and Columns

Dashed blue line indicates position of page break; click and drag line to change location of page break

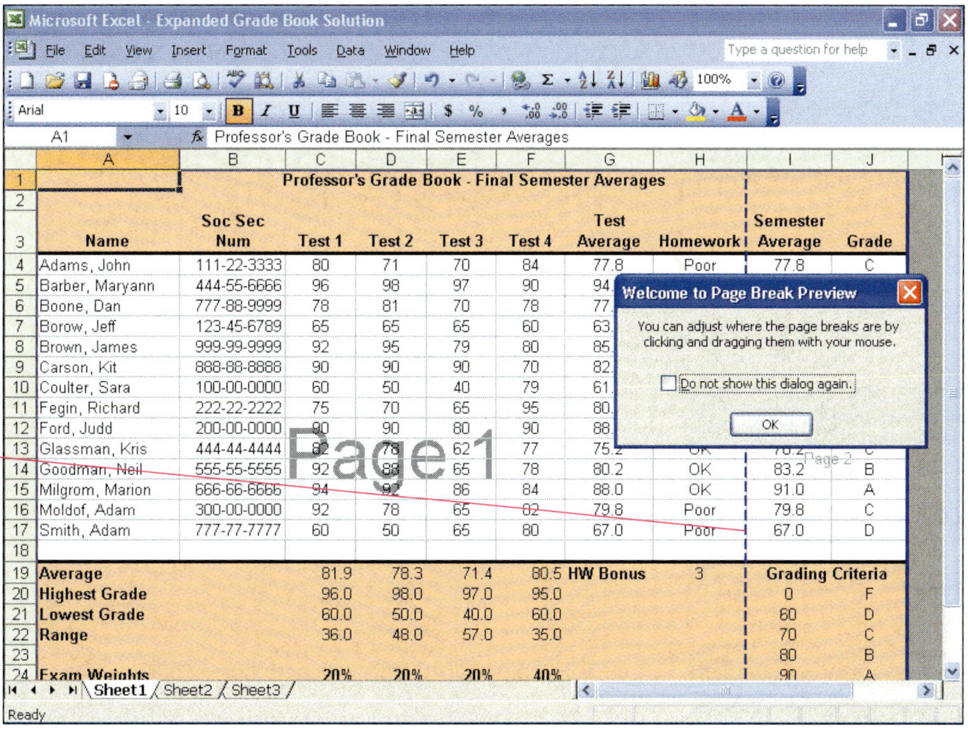

(d) Page Break Preview

FIGURE 4.14 Working with Large Spreadsheets (*continued*)

AutoFilter Command

The ***AutoFilter command*** lets you display a selected set of students (rows) within a worksheet as shown in Figure 4.15. The hidden rows are *not* deleted, but are simply not displayed. We begin with Figure 4.15a, which shows the list of all students (with selected columns hidden from view). Look closely at the column headings in row three and note the presence of drop-down arrows that appear in response to the AutoFilter command.

Clicking a drop-down arrow produces a list of the unique values for that column, enabling you to establish the criteria-selected records. To display the students with poor homework, for example, click the drop-down arrow for Homework, then click Poor from the resulting list. Figure 4.15b shows three students in rows 4, 12, and 17 that satisfy the filter. The remaining students are still in the worksheet but are not shown because of the selection criterion.

A filter condition can be imposed on multiple columns as shown in Figure 4.15c. As indicated, the worksheet in Figure 4.15b displays only the students with poor homework. Clicking the arrow next to Grade, then clicking "B", will filter the list further to display the students who received a "B" *and* who have poor homework. Only one student meets both conditions, as shown in Figure 4.15c. The drop-down arrows next to Homework and Grade are displayed in blue to indicate that a filter is in effect for these columns.

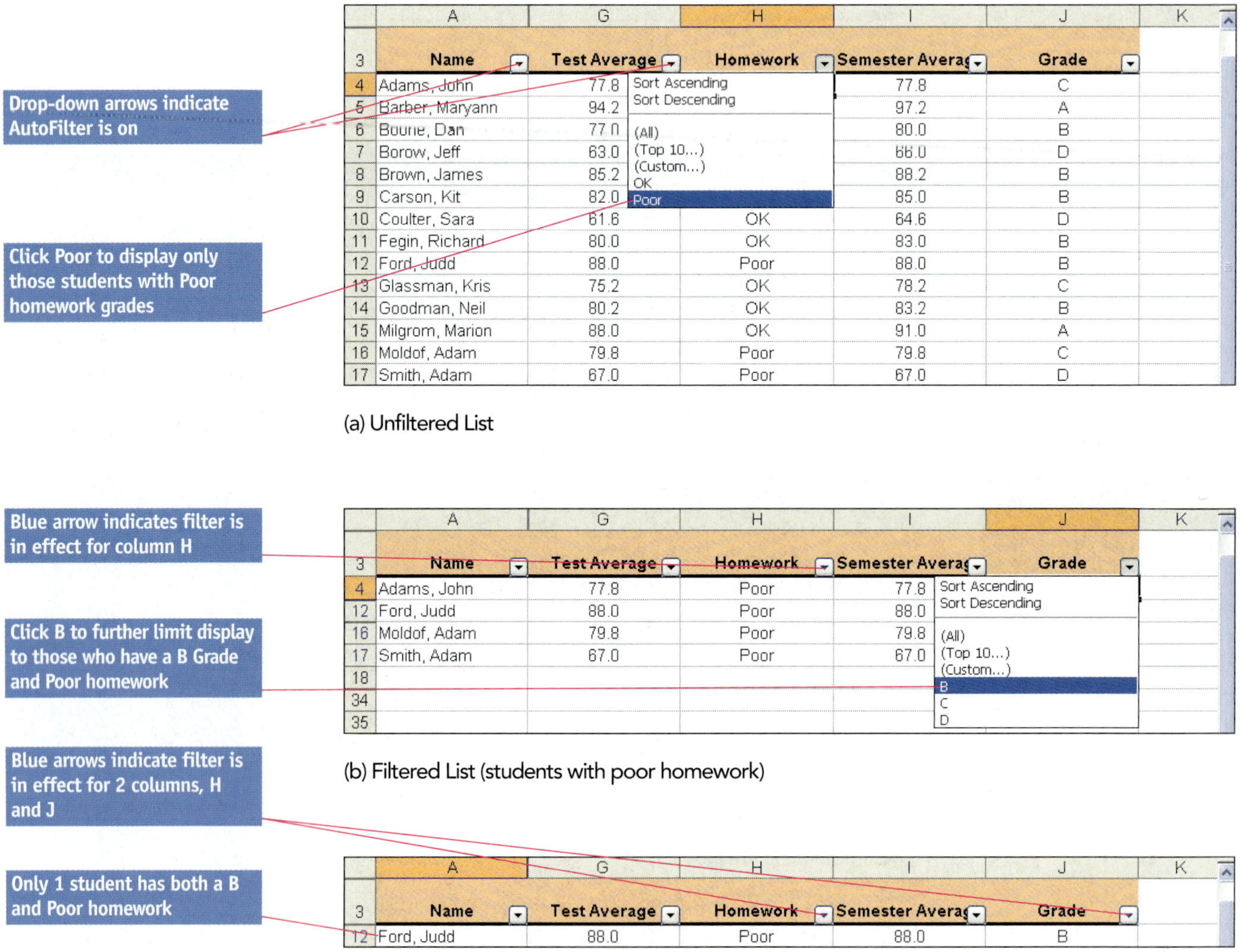

(a) Unfiltered List

(b) Filtered List (students with poor homework)

(c) Imposing a Second Condition

FIGURE 4.15 The AutoFilter Command

hands-on exercise

3 The Expanded Grade Book

Objective To develop the expanded grade book; to use statistical (AVERAGE, MAX, and MIN) and logical (IF and VLOOKUP) functions; to demonstrate scrolling and the Freeze Panes command. Use Figure 4.16 as a guide.

Step 1: The Fill Handle

- Open the **Expanded Grade Book** in the **Exploring Excel folder**. Click in **cell C3**, the cell containing the label Test 1 as shown in Figure 4.16a.
- Click and drag the **fill handle** over **cells D3**, **E3**, and **F3** (a ScreenTip shows the projected result in cell F3), then release the mouse. Cells D3, E3, and F3 contain the labels Test 2, Test 3, and Test 4, respectively.
- Save the workbook as **Expanded Grade Book Solution** so that you can always return to the original workbook if necessary.

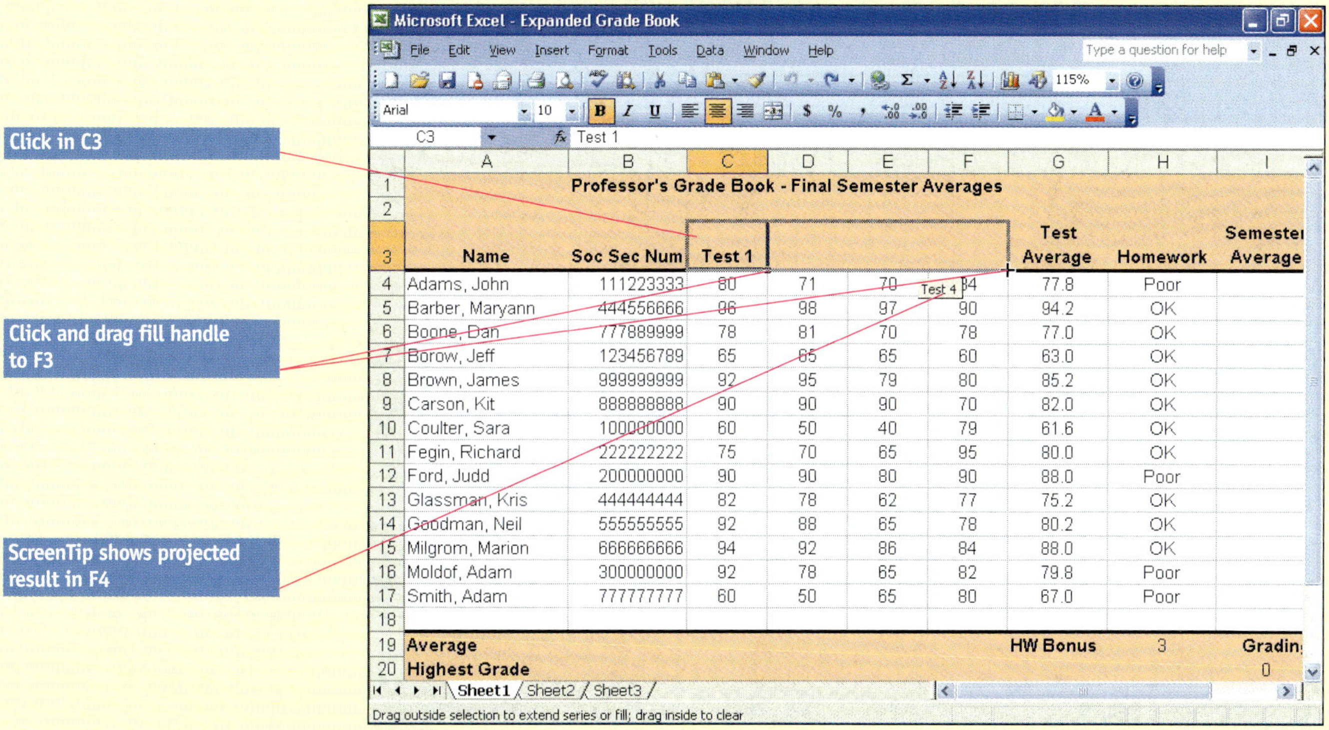

	A	B	C	D	E	F	G	H	I
1	Professor's Grade Book - Final Semester Averages								
2									
3	Name	Soc Sec Num	Test 1				Test Average	Homework	Semester Average
4	Adams, John	111223333	80	71	70	84	77.8	Poor	
5	Barber, Maryann	444556666	96	98	97	90	94.2	OK	
6	Boone, Dan	777889999	78	81	70	78	77.0	OK	
7	Borow, Jeff	123456789	65	65	65	60	63.0	OK	
8	Brown, James	999999999	92	95	79	80	85.2	OK	
9	Carson, Kit	888888888	90	90	90	70	82.0	OK	
10	Coulter, Sara	100000000	60	50	40	79	61.6	OK	
11	Fegin, Richard	222222222	75	70	65	95	80.0	OK	
12	Ford, Judd	200000000	90	90	80	90	88.0	Poor	
13	Glassman, Kris	444444444	82	78	62	77	75.2	OK	
14	Goodman, Neil	555555555	92	88	65	78	80.2	OK	
15	Milgrom, Marion	666666666	94	92	86	84	88.0	OK	
16	Moldof, Adam	300000000	92	78	65	82	79.8	Poor	
17	Smith, Adam	777777777	60	50	65	80	67.0	Poor	
18									
19	Average						HW Bonus	3	Gradin
20	Highest Grade								0

(a) The Fill Handle (step 1)

FIGURE 4.16 Hands-on Exercise 3

THE AUTOFILL CAPABILITY

The AutoFill capability is the fastest way to enter certain series into contiguous cells. Enter the starting value(s) in a series, then drag the fill handle to the adjacent cells. Excel completes the series based on the initial value. Type January (or Jan) or Monday (or Mon) then drag the fill handle in the direction you want to fill. Excel will enter the appropriate months or days of the week, respectively. You can also type text followed by a number, such as Product 1 or Quarter 1, then use the fill handle to extend the series.

Step 2: Format the Social Security Numbers

- Click and drag to select **cells B4** through **B17**, the cells containing the unformatted Social Security numbers.
- Point to the selected cells and click the **right mouse button** to display a shortcut (context-sensitive) menu.
- Click the **Format Cells command**, click the **Number tab**, then click **Special** in the Category list box as shown in Figure 4.16b.
- Click **Social Security Number** in the Type box, then click **OK** to accept the formatting and close the Format Cells dialog box. The Social Security numbers are displayed with hyphens.
- Save the workbook.

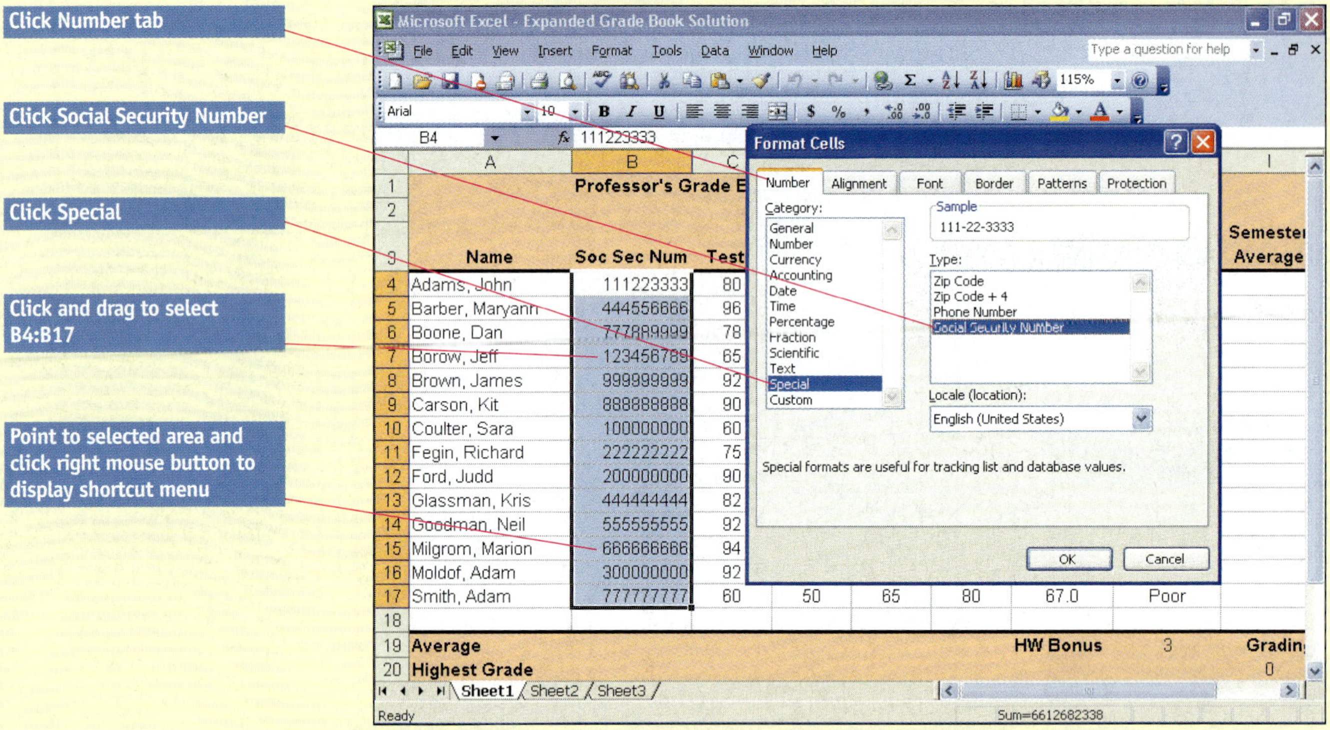

(b) Format the Social Security Numbers (step 2)

FIGURE 4.16 Hands-on Exercise 3 (*continued*)

THE LEFT AND RIGHT FUNCTIONS

A professor may want to post grades, but cannot do so by student name or Social Security number. One can, however, create an "ID number" consisting of the left- or rightmost digits in the Social Security number. Insert a new column into the worksheet, then go to the cell for the first student in this column (e.g., cell C4 if you insert a new column C). Enter the function =LEFT(B4,4) to display the first four digits from cell B4, corresponding to the first four (leftmost) digits in Adams's Social Security Number. You could also enter the function =RIGHT(B4,4) to display the last four (rightmost) digits. Hide the columns containing the names and Social Security numbers, then post the grades. See practice exercise 9 at the end of the chapter.

Step 3: The Freeze Panes Command

- Press **Ctrl+Home** to move to **cell A1**. Click the **right arrow** on the horizontal scroll bar until column A scrolls off the screen. Cell A1 is still the active cell, because scrolling with the mouse does not change the active cell.
- Press **Ctrl+Home**. Press the **right arrow key** until column A scrolls off the screen. The active cell changes as you scroll with the keyboard.
- Press **Ctrl+Home** again, then click in **cell B4**. Pull down the **Window menu**. Click **Freeze Panes** as shown in Figure 4.16c. You will see a line to the right of column A and below row 3.
- Click the **right arrow** on the horizontal scroll bar (or press the **right arrow key**) repeatedly until column J is visible. Note that column A is visible (frozen), but that one or more columns are not shown.
- Click the **down arrow** on the vertical scroll bar (or press the **down arrow key**) repeatedly until row 25 is visible. Note that rows 1 through 3 are visible (frozen), but that one or more rows are not shown.
- Press **Ctrl+Home** to go to **B4**.

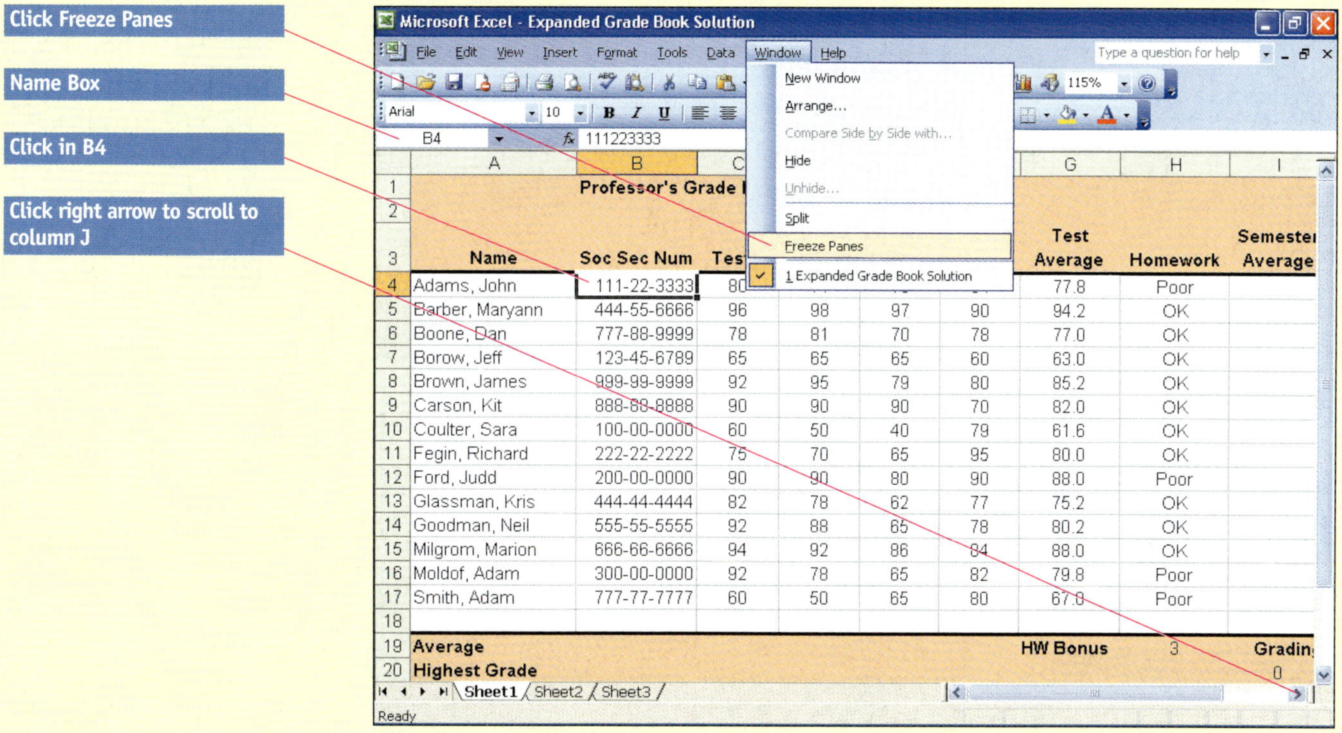

(c) The Freeze Panes Command (step 3)

FIGURE 4.16 Hands-on Exercise 3 (*continued*)

GO TO A SPECIFIC CELL

Ctrl+Home and Ctrl+End will take you to the upper-left and bottom-right cells within a worksheet, but how do you get to a specific cell? One way is to click in the Name box (to the left of the formula bar), enter the cell reference (e.g., K250), and press the Enter key. You can also pull down the Edit menu and click the Go To command (or press the F5 key) to display the Go To dialog box, enter the address of the cell in the Reference text box, then press Enter to go directly to the cell.

Step 4: The IF Function

- Scroll until Column I is visible on the screen. Click in **cell I4**.
- Click the **Insert Function button** on the formula bar. Click the **down arrow** on the Select a Category list box and click **Logical**. Click **IF** in the Select a Function list box, then click **OK** to display the Function Arguments dialog box in Figure 4.16d.
- You can enter the arguments directly, or you can use pointing as follows:
  - Click the **Logical_test** text box. Click **cell H4** in the worksheet. (You may need to click and drag the top border of the dialog box to move it out of the way.) Type **="OK"** to complete the logical test.
  - Click the **Value_if_true** text box. Click **cell G4** in the worksheet, type a **plus sign**, click **cell H19** in the worksheet (scrolling if necessary), and finally press the **F4 key** (see boxed tip) to convert the reference to cell H19 to an absolute reference ($H$19).
  - Click the **Value_if_false** text box. Click **cell G4** in the worksheet.
- Check that the dialog box on your worksheet matches the one in Figure 4.16d. Click **OK** to insert the function into your worksheet.
- Save the workbook.

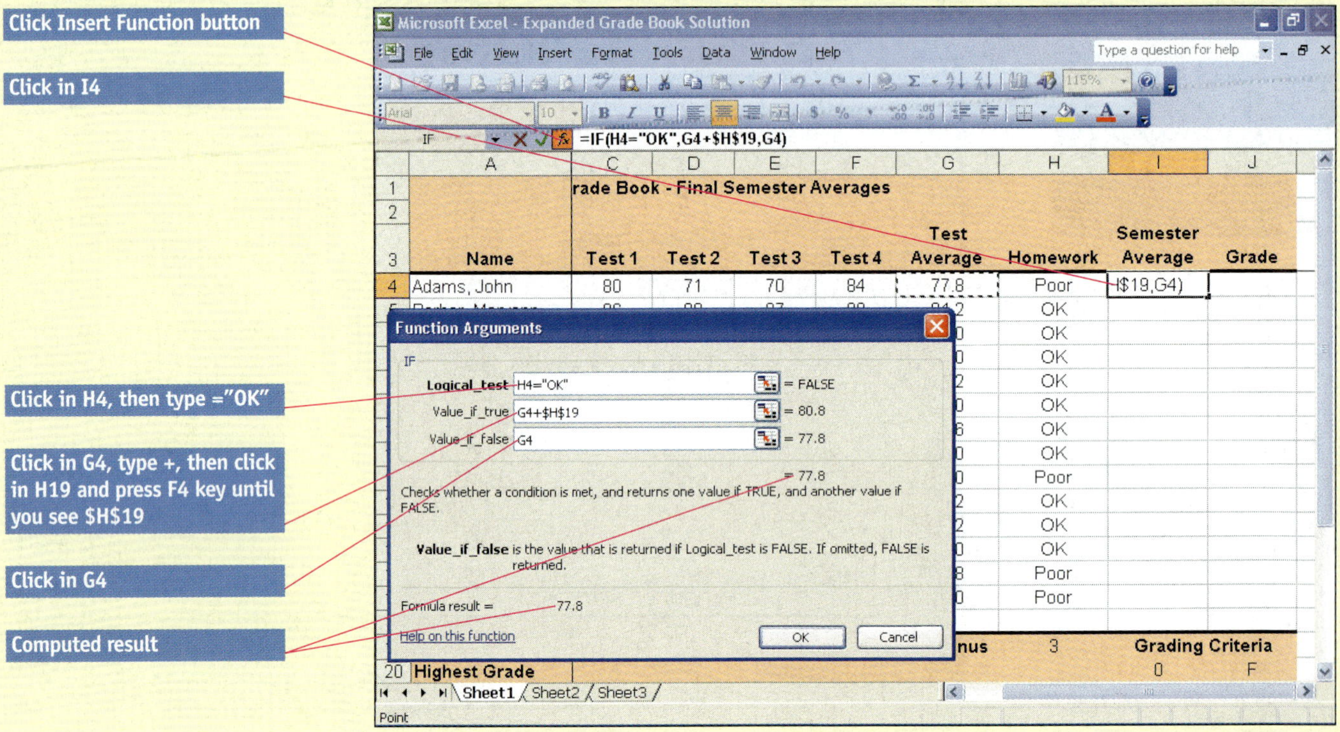

(d) The IF Function (step 4)

FIGURE 4.16 Hands-on Exercise 3 (*continued*)

THE F4 KEY

The F4 key cycles through relative, absolute, and mixed addresses. Click on any reference within the formula bar; for example, click on A1 in the formula =A1+A2. Press the F4 key once, and it changes to an absolute reference. Press the F4 key a second time, and it becomes a mixed reference, A$1; press it again, and it is a different mixed reference, $A1. Press the F4 key a fourth time, and return to the original relative address, A1.

Step 5: The VLOOKUP Function

- Click in **cell J4**. Click the **Insert Function button** on the formula bar. Click **Lookup & Reference** from the Select a Category list box. Scroll in the Function Name list box until you can select **VLOOKUP**. Click **OK** to display the Function Arguments dialog box in Figure 4.16e.
- Enter the arguments for the VLOOKUP function as shown in the figure. You can enter the arguments directly, or you can use pointing as follows:
  - Click the **Lookup_value** text box. Click **cell I4** in the worksheet.
  - Click the **Table_array** text box. Click **cell I20** and drag to **cell J24** (scrolling if necessary). Press the **F4 key** to convert to an absolute reference.
  - Click the **Col_index_num** text box. Type **2**.
- Check that the dialog box on your worksheet matches the one in Figure 4.16e. Make corrections as necessary.
- Click **OK** to insert the completed function into your worksheet.
- Save the workbook.

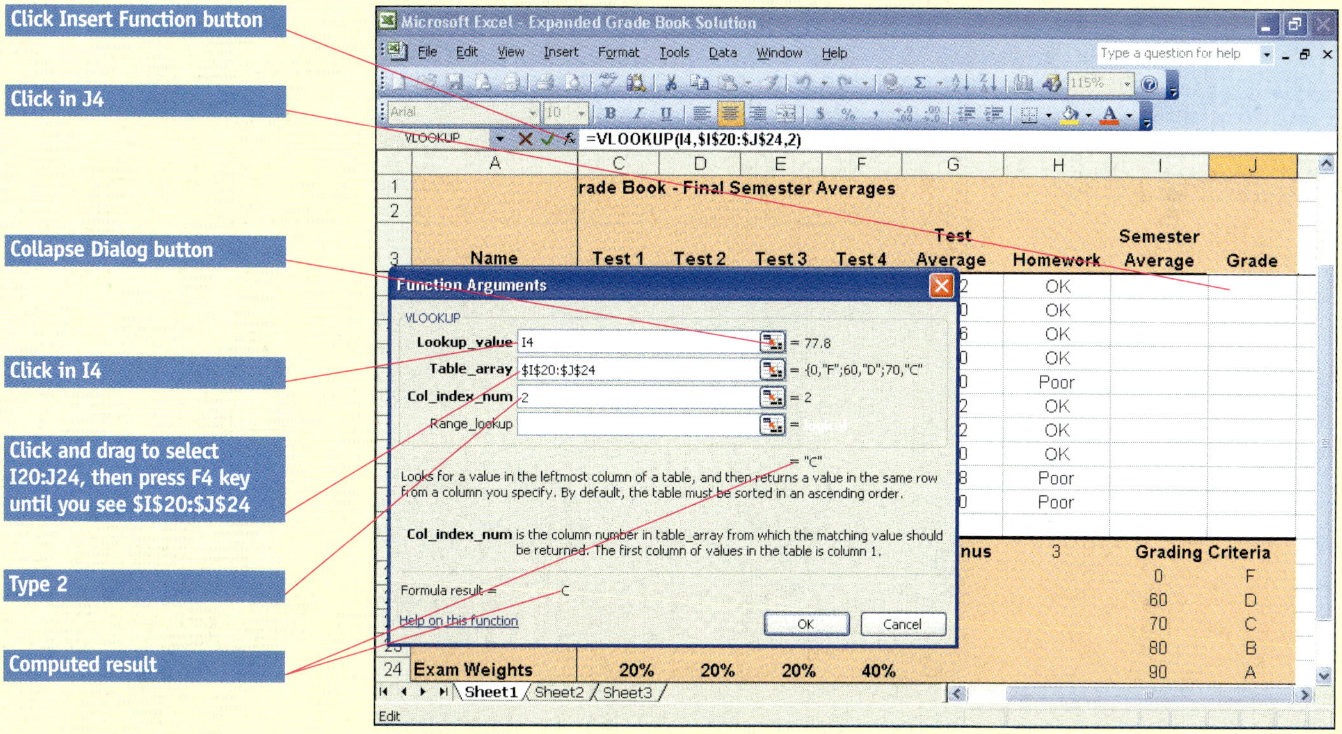

(e) The VLOOKUP Function (step 5)

FIGURE 4.16 Hands-on Exercise 3 (*continued*)

THE COLLAPSE DIALOG BUTTON

You can enter a cell reference in one of two ways: You can type it directly in the Function Arguments dialog box, or click the cell in the worksheet. The Function Arguments dialog box typically hides the necessary cell, however, in which case you can click the Collapse Dialog button (which appears to the right of any parameter within the dialog box). This collapses (hides) the Function Arguments dialog box so that you can click the underlying cell, which is now visible. Click the Collapse Dialog button a second time to display the entire dialog box.

Step 6: Copy the IF and VLOOKUP Functions

- If necessary, scroll to the top of the worksheet. Select **cells I4** and **J4** as in Figure 4.16f.
- Point to the **fill handle** in the lower-right corner of the selected range. The mouse pointer changes to a thin crosshair.
- Drag the **fill handle** over **cells I5** through **J17**. A border appears, indicating the destination range as shown in Figure 4.16f. Release the mouse to complete the copy operation.
- If you have done everything correctly, Adam Smith should have a grade of D based on a semester average of 67.
- Check that the semester averages in column I are formatted to one decimal place.
- Save the workbook.

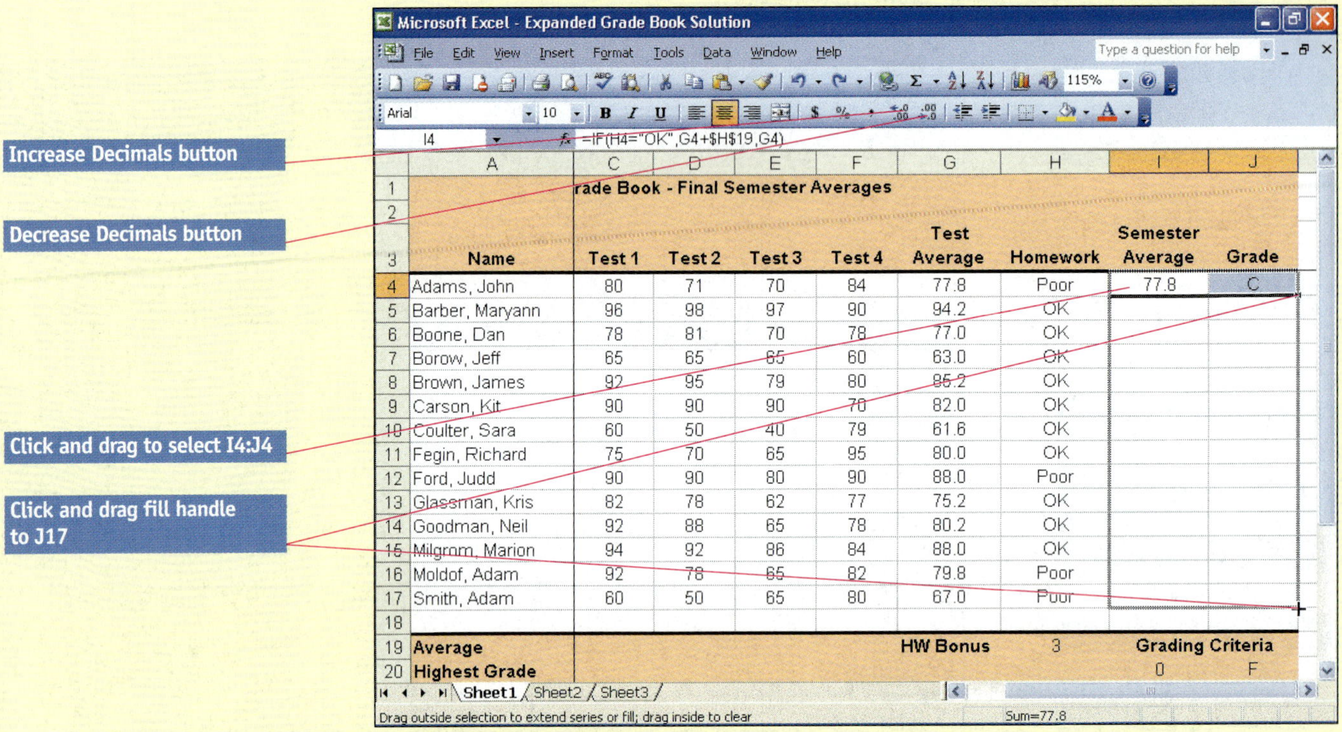

(f) Copy the IF and VLOOKUP Functions (step 6)

FIGURE 4.16 Hands-on Exercise 3 (*continued*)

THE ROUND FUNCTION

Adam Moldof has a semester average of 79.8, which returns a grade of C according to the strict interpretation of the VLOOKUP function. Your instructor might give Adam a break and round his average to 80, but the computer will not. Changing the format to display zero decimal places is not the answer, since formatting affects the display of a number, but not how the number is stored internally. The solution is to use the ROUND function in conjunction with the formula to compute the semester average. See exercise 9 at the end of the chapter.

Step 7: Create the Summary Statistics

- Scroll until you can click in **cell C19**. Type **=AVERAGE(C4:C17)**. Press **Enter**. Cell C19 should display 81.9 as shown in Figure 4.16g.
- Click in **cell C20** and enter the formula **=MAX(C4:C17)**. Click in **cell C21** and enter the formula **=MIN(C4:C17)**.
- Click in **cell C22** and enter the formula **=C20–C21**. Check that the displayed values match those in Figure 4.16g.
- Click and drag to select **cells C19** through **C22**, then click and drag the **fill handle** to **cell F22**. Release the mouse.
- Click outside the selection to deselect the cells. You will see the summary statistics for the other tests.
- Save the workbook.

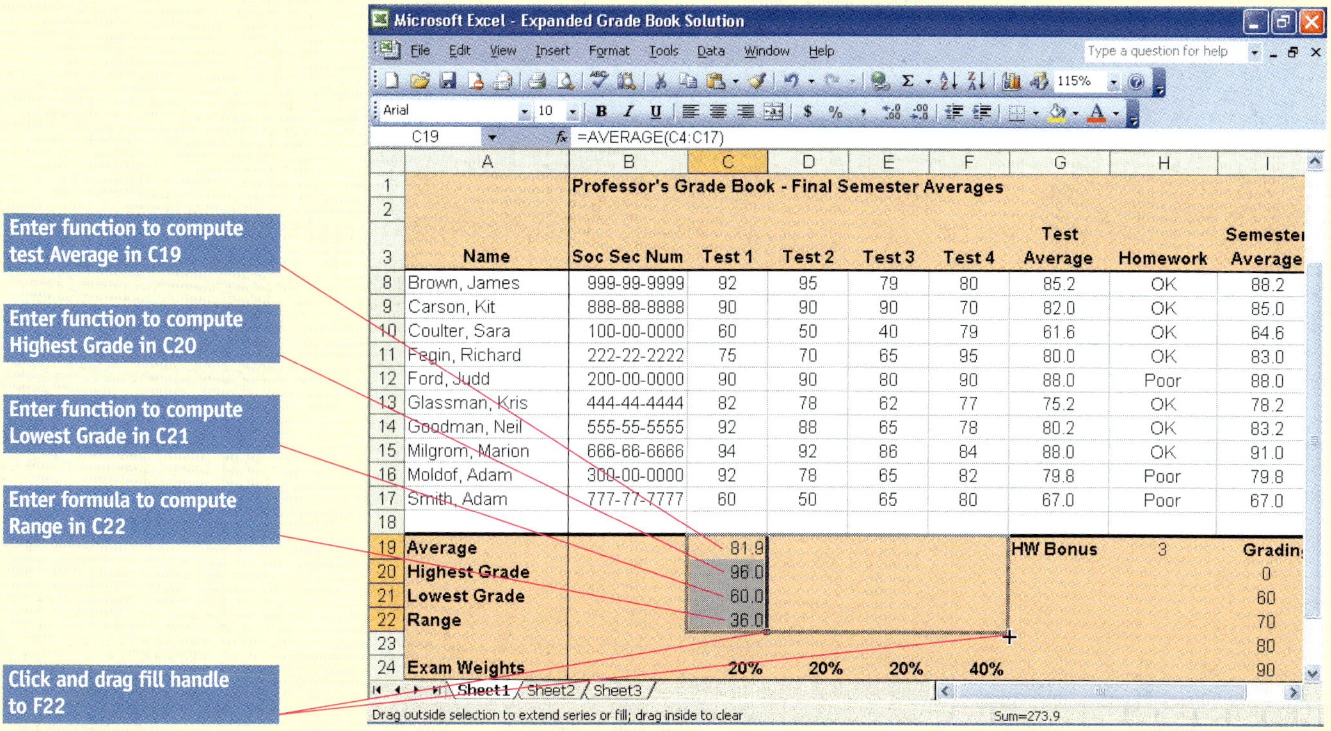

(g) Create the Summary Statistics (step 7)

FIGURE 4.16 Hands-on Exercise 3 (*continued*)

RANK IN CLASS

Use the Rank function to determine a student's rank in class. (Excel also has functions for quartiles and percentiles.) Add a new column to the worksheet, column K in this example, then click in the cell for the first student in the list (cell K4). Enter the function =RANK(I4,$I$4:$I$17), where I4 contains the value you want to look up (the individual student's semester average) and $I$4:$I$17 references the set of numbers on which to base the rank. The latter is entered as an absolute reference so that the cell formula may be copied to the remaining cells in column K. See practice exercise 9 at the end of the chapter.

Step 8: The Page Break Preview Command

- Pull down the **View menu** and click the **Page Break Preview command** to see the potential page breaks as shown in Figure 4.16h. Click **OK** if you see the welcome message.
- Click and drag the dashed blue line to the right to eliminate the page break. (You can also drag the solid blue line that appears on the right border to the left to create a page break.)
- Pull down the **View menu** and click **Normal** to return to the Normal view.
- Pull down the **File menu**. Click **Page Setup** to display the Page Setup dialog box. Click the **Margins tab**. Check the box to center the worksheet horizontally.
- Click the **Sheet tab**. Check the boxes to display the **Row and Column Headings** and the **Gridlines**.
- Click the **Print Preview button** to display the completed spreadsheet. Click the **Print button** and click **OK** to print the workbook.
- Print the worksheet with the cell formulas.

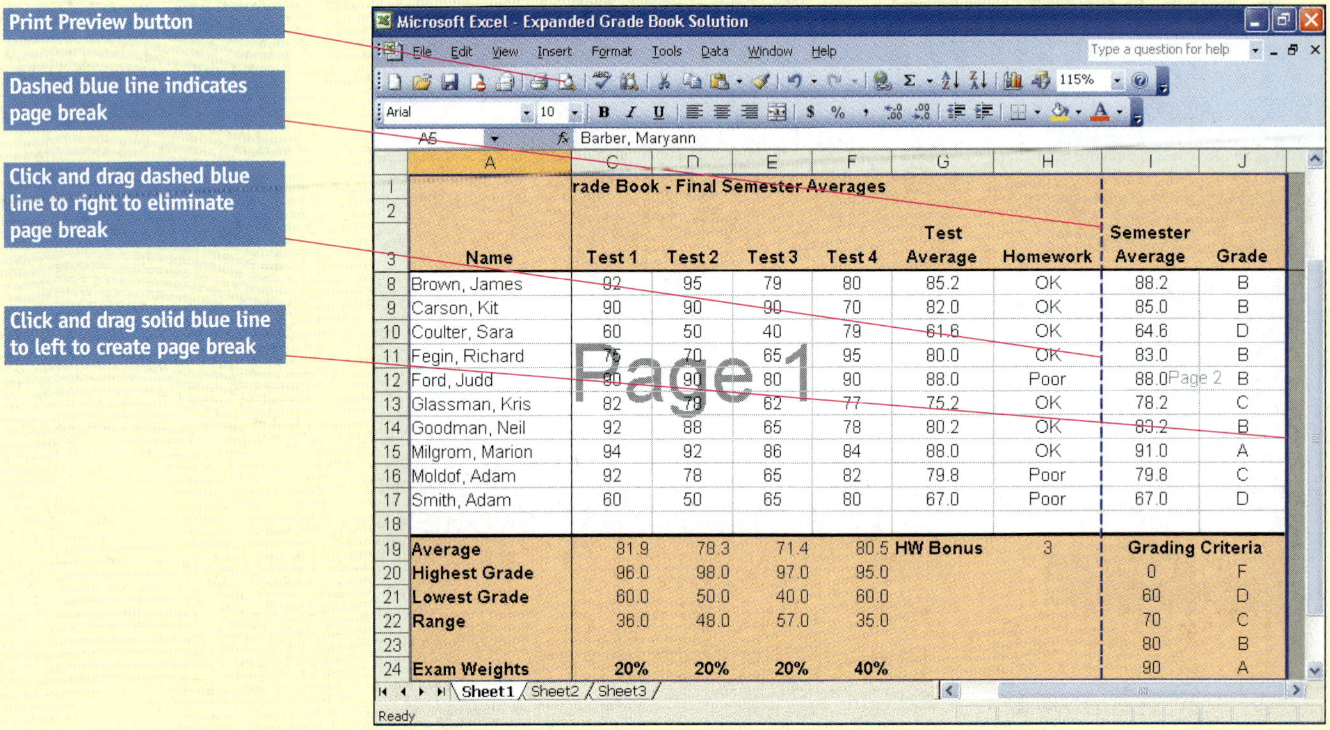

(h) The Page Break Preview Command (step 8)

FIGURE 4.16 Hands-on Exercise 3 (*continued*)

USE NESTED IFS FOR MORE COMPLEX DECISION MAKING

A "nested IF" (or "IF within an IF") is a common logic structure in every programming language. It could be used in the expanded grade book to implement more complicated logic such as a variable homework bonus (of –2, 3, and 5), depending on the grade (for poor, OK, and good, respectively). The IF function in Excel has three arguments—a condition, a value if the condition is true, and a value if the condition is false. A nested IF simply replaces the true and/or false value with another IF statement. See practice exercise 9 at the end of the chapter.

Step 9: Hide the Rows and Columns

- Click and drag the column headings for **columns C** through **F** to select these columns, point to the selected columns, then click the **right mouse button** to display the context-sensitive menu in Figure 4.16i. Click **Hide** to hide these columns.
- Click and drag the row headings for **rows 19** through **24** to select these rows, point to the selected rows, click the **right mouse button**, and click the **Hide command**. Print the worksheet.
- Now reverse the process and unhide the rows, but leave the columns hidden. Click and drag to select the row headings for **rows 18** and **25** (which are contiguous), right click to display a context-sensitive menu, then click the **Unhide command**.
- You should see all of the rows in the entire worksheet (within the limitations of scrolling). Save the workbook.

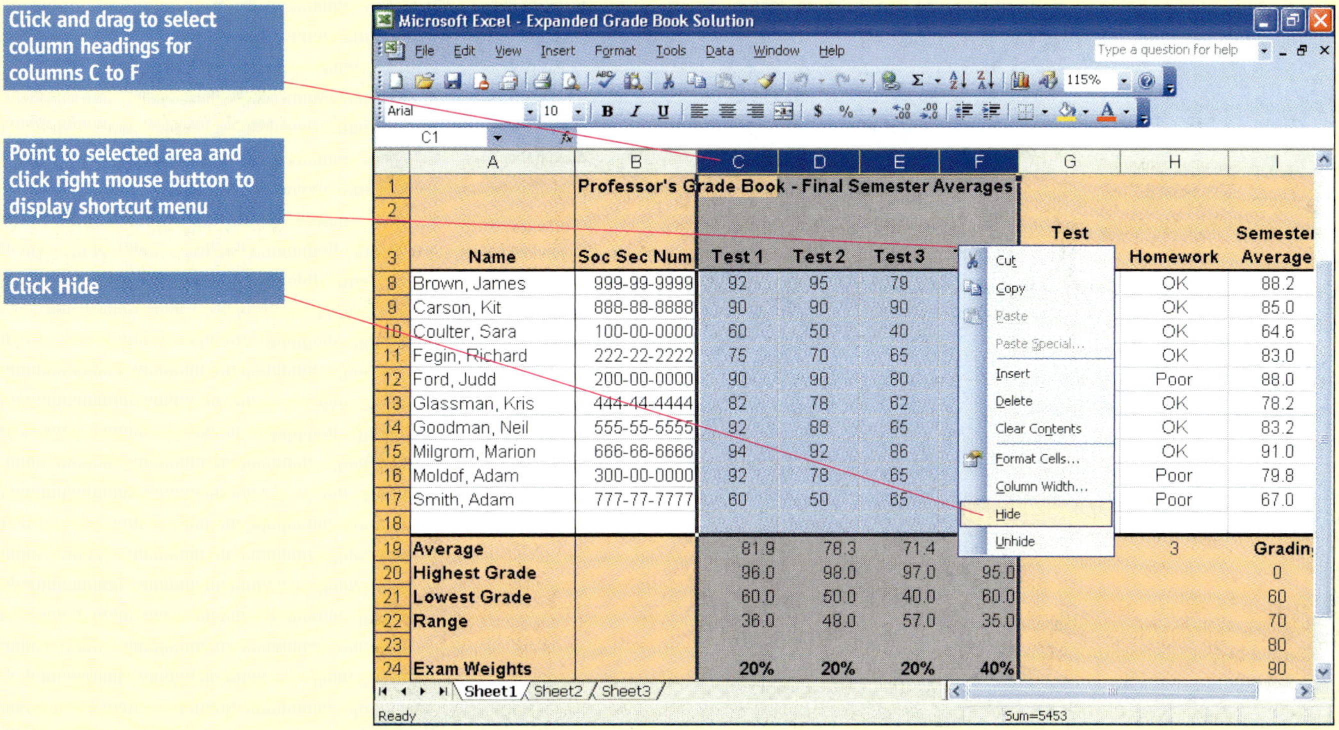

(i) Hide the Rows and Columns (step 9)

FIGURE 4.16 Hands-on Exercise 3 (*continued*)

UNHIDING ROWS AND COLUMNS

Hiding a row or column is easy: You just select the row or column(s) you want to hide, click the right mouse button, then select the Hide command from the shortcut menu. Unhiding a row or column is trickier because you cannot see the target cells. To unhide a column, for example, you need to select the columns on either side; for example, select columns A and C if you are trying to unhide column B. To unhide column A, however, click in the Name box and enter A1. Pull down the Format menu, click Column, then click the Unhide command.

Step 10: The AutoFilter Command

- Click anywhere within the list of students. Pull down the **Data menu**, click the **Filter command**, then click **AutoFilter**. The worksheet is essentially unchanged except that each column heading is followed by a drop-down arrow.
- Click the **drop-down arrow** in cell H3 (the column containing the students' homework grades). Click **Poor**. The list of students changes to show only those students who received this grade on their homework as shown in Figure 4.16j.
- Click the **drop-down arrow** in cell J3, then select **B** from the drop-down list of grade values. The list changes to show the one student who managed to receive a "B" despite having poor homework.
- Add your name and title (**Grading Assistant**) in cells G26 and G27. Save the workbook, then print it for your instructor.
- Pull down the **Data menu**, click **Filter**, and click the **AutoFilter command** to remove the filter and display all of the students.
- Exit Excel. Congratulations on a job well done.

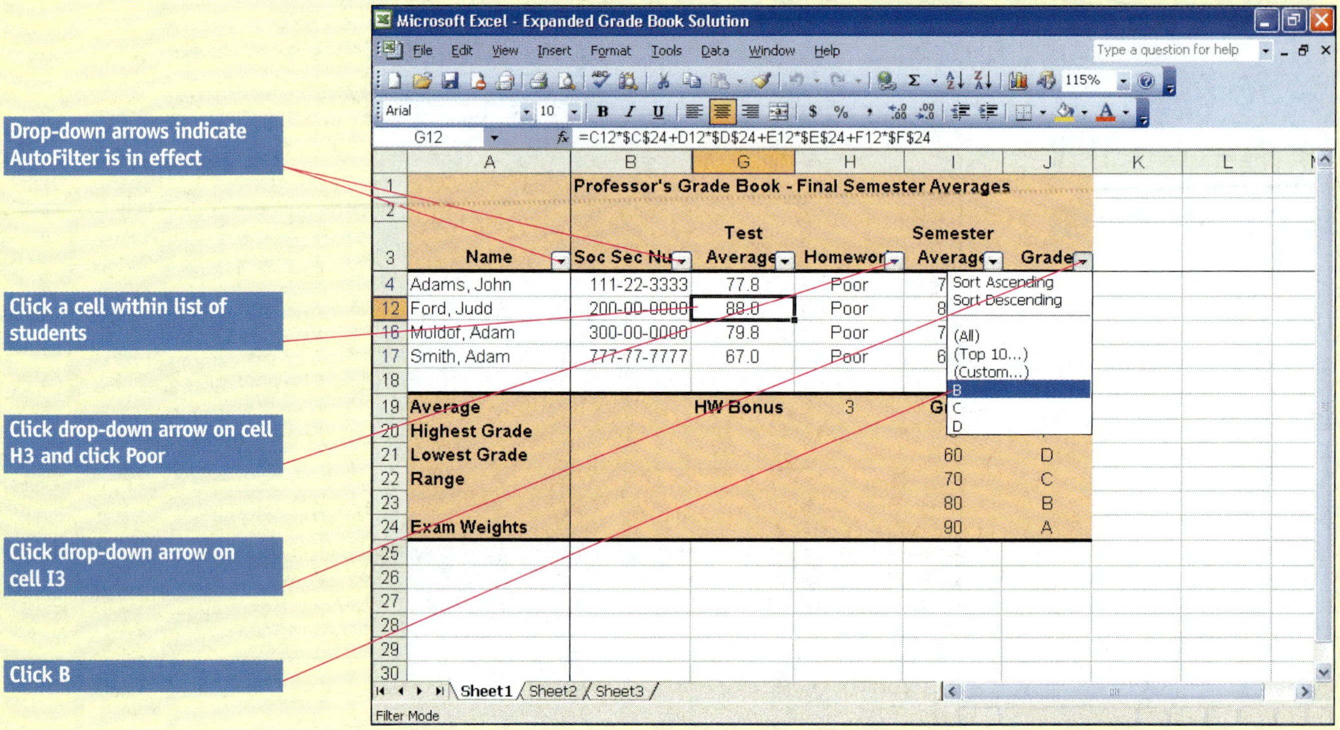

(j) The AutoFilter Command (step 10)

FIGURE 4.16 Hands-on Exercise 3 (*continued*)

SET PRINT AREAS

Press and hold the Ctrl key as you click and drag to select one or more areas in the worksheet, then pull down the File menu, select the Print Area command, and click Set Print Area. The print area is enclosed in dashed lines. The next time you execute the Print command, you will print just the print area(s), with each print area appearing on a separate page. Use the Print Area command in the File menu to clear the print area.

SUMMARY

Excel contains several categories of built-in functions. The PMT function computes the periodic payment for a loan based on three arguments (the interest rate per period, the number of periods, and the amount of the loan). The PMT function was used in worksheets to compute a car payment and a home mortgage. The IPMT and PPMT functions determine the amount of each periodic payment that goes toward interest and principal, respectively.

The FV function returns the future value of an investment based on constant periodic payments and a constant interest rate. The function is associated with Individual Retirement Accounts and 401K retirement plans. A spreadsheet was developed using mixed references to create a two-level table showing the future value of a retirement account at different interest rates and time periods.

Statistical functions were also discussed. The AVERAGE, MAX, and MIN functions return the average, highest, and lowest values in the argument list. The COUNT function returns the number of cells with numeric entries. The COUNTA function displays the number of cells with numeric and/or text entries.

The IF, VLOOKUP, and HLOOKUP functions implement decision making within a worksheet. The IF function has three arguments: a condition, which is evaluated as true or false; a value if the test is true; and a value if the test is false. The VLOOKUP and HLOOKUP functions also have three arguments: the value to look up, the range of cells containing the table, and the column or row number within the table that contains the result.

Several options were presented for working with large spreadsheets. Scrolling enables you to view any portion of a large worksheet but moves the labels for existing rows and/or columns off the screen. The Freeze Panes command keeps the row and/or column headings on the screen while scrolling within a large worksheet. The Page Break Preview command lets you see and/or modify the page breaks that will occur when a worksheet is printed. The AutoFilter command displays a selected set of rows within a worksheet according to a specified set of criteria. The hidden rows are not deleted but are simply not displayed.

A spreadsheet is first and foremost a tool for decision making, and thus Excel includes several commands to aid in that process. The Goal Seek command lets you enter the desired end result of a spreadsheet model (such as the monthly payment on a car loan) and determines the input (the price of the car) necessary to produce that result. The assumptions and initial conditions in a spreadsheet should be clearly labeled and set apart from the rest of the worksheet. This facilitates change and reduces the chance for error.

The hands-on exercises introduced several techniques to make you more proficient. The fill handle is used to copy a cell or group of cells to a range of adjacent cells. Pointing is a more accurate way to enter a cell reference into a formula as it uses the mouse or arrow keys to select the cell as you build the formula. The AutoFill capability creates a series based on the initial value(s) you supply.

KEY TERMS

MULTIPLE CHOICE

1. Which of the following options may be used to print a large worksheet?
   (a) Landscape orientation
   (b) Scaling
   (c) Reduced margins
   (d) All of the above

2. If the results of a formula contain more characters than can be displayed according to the present format and cell width,
   (a) The extra characters will be truncated under all circumstances
   (b) All of the characters will be displayed if the cell to the right is empty
   (c) A series of asterisks will be displayed
   (d) A series of pound signs will be displayed

3. Which cell—A1, A2, or A3—will contain the amount of the loan, given the function =PMT(A1,A2,A3)?
   (a) A1
   (b) A2
   (c) A3
   (d) Impossible to determine

4. Which of the following will compute the average of the values in cells D2, D3, and D4?
   (a) The function =AVERAGE(D2:D4)
   (b) The function =AVERAGE(D2,D4)
   (c) Both (a) and (b)
   (d) Neither (a) nor (b)

5. The function =IF(A1>A2,A1+A2,A1*A2) returns
   (a) The product of cells A1 and A2 if cell A1 is greater than A2
   (b) The sum of cells A1 and A2 if cell A1 is less than A2
   (c) Both (a) and (b)
   (d) Neither (a) nor (b)

6. Which of the following is the preferred way to sum the values contained in cells A1 to A4?
   (a) =SUM(A1:A4)
   (b) =A1+A2+A3+A4
   (c) Either (a) or (b) is equally good
   (d) Neither (a) nor (b) is correct

7. Which of the following will return the highest and lowest arguments from a list of arguments?
   (a) HIGH/LOW
   (b) LARGEST/SMALLEST
   (c) MAX/MIN
   (d) All of the above

8. Which of the following is a *required* technique to develop the worksheet for the mortgage analysis?
   (a) Pointing
   (b) Copying with the fill handle
   (c) Both (a) and (b)
   (d) Neither (a) nor (b)

9. Given that cells B6, C6, and D6 contain the numbers 10, 20, and 30, respectively, what value will be returned by the function =IF(B6>10,C6*2,D6*3)?
   (a) 10
   (b) 40
   (c) 60
   (d) 90

10. Which of the following is not an input parameter to the Goal Seek command?
   (a) The cell containing the end result
   (b) The desired value of the end result
   (c) The cell whose value will change to reach the end result
   (d) The value of the input cell that is required to reach the end result

... continued

multiple choice

11. What is the correct order of the arguments for the FV function?

(a) Interest Rate, Term, Principal
(b) Term, Interest Rate, Principal
(c) Interest Rate, Term, Annual Amount
(d) Term, Interest Rate, Annual Amount

12. Which function will return the number of nonempty cells in the range A2 through A6, including in the result cells that contain text as well as numeric entries?

(a) =COUNT(A2:A6)
(b) =COUNTA(A2:A6)
(c) =COUNT(A2,A6)
(d) =COUNTA(A2,A6)

13. The annual interest rate, term in years, and principal of a loan are stored in cells A1, A2, and A3, respectively. Which of the following is the correct PMT function, given monthly payments?

(a) =PMT(A1,A2,–A3)
(b) =PMT(A1/12,A2*12,–A3)
(c) =PMT(A1*12, A2/12,–A3)
(d) =PMT(A1,A2,A3)

14. The worksheet displayed in the monitor shows columns A and B, skips columns D, E, and F, then displays columns G, H, I, J, and K. What is the most likely explanation for the missing columns?

(a) The columns were previously deleted
(b) The columns are empty and thus are automatically hidden from view
(c) Either (a) or (b) is a satisfactory explanation
(d) Neither (a) nor (b) is a likely reason

15. Given the function =VLOOKUP(C6,D12:F18,3)

(a) The entries in cells D12 through D18 are in ascending order
(b) The entries in cells D12 through D18 are in descending order
(c) The entries in cells F12 through F18 are in ascending order
(d) The entries in cells F12 through F18 are in descending order

16. A formula containing the entry =$B3 is copied to a cell one column over and two rows down. How will the entry appear in its new location?

(a) =$B3
(b) =B3
(c) =$C5
(d) =$B5

17. You expect to contribute $2,000 a year for 10 years to a retirement plan and expect an annual return of 7%. Which of the following functions can you use to determine the expected future value?

(a) =FV(.07/12,10*12,–2000)
(b) =FV(.07,10,–2000)
(c) =FV(.07/12,10*12, 2000)
(d) =FV(.07,10, 2000)

18. Which of the following computes the monthly payment for a car loan of $10,000 that is amortized over 3 years at 5%?

(a) =PMT(.05/12,36,–10000)
(b) =PMT(.05,36,–10000)
(c) =PMT(.05,3,–10000)
(d) =PMT(.05,3,10000)

ANSWERS

1. d	**7.** c	**13.** b
2. d	**8.** d	**14.** d
3. c	**9.** d	**15.** a
4. a	**10.** d	**16.** d
5. d	**11.** c	**17.** b
6. a	**12.** b	**18.** a

PRACTICE WITH EXCEL

1. **Calculating Your Retirement:** Retirement is years away, but it is never too soon to start planning. The Future Value function enables you to calculate the amount of money you will have at retirement, based on a series of uniform contributions, made by you and/or your employer, during your working years. Once you reach retirement, however, you do not withdraw all of the money immediately, but withdraw it periodically as a monthly pension. Your assignment is to create a new worksheet similar to the one in Figure 4.17. Note the following:
   a. The accrual phase uses the FV value function to determine the amount of money you will accumulate. The total contribution in cell B7 is a formula based on a percentage of your annual salary, plus a matching contribution from your employer. The 6.2% in our figure corresponds to the percentages that are currently in effect for Social Security. (In actuality, the government currently deducts 7.65% from your paycheck, and allocates 6.2% for Social Security and the remaining 1.45% for Medicare.)
   b. The future value of your contributions (i.e., the amount of your "nest egg") depends on the assumptions in the left side of the worksheet. The 6% interest rate is conservative and can be achieved by investing in bonds, as opposed to equities. The 45 years of contributions corresponds to an individual entering the work force at age 22 and retiring at 67 (the age at which today's worker will begin to collect Social Security).
   c. The pension phase uses the PMT function to determine the payments you will receive in retirement. The formula in cell E4 is a simple reference to the amount accumulated in cell B10. The formula in cell E7 uses the PMT function to compute your monthly pension based on your nest egg, the interest rate, and the years in retirement. Note that accrual phase uses an *annual* contribution in its calculations, whereas the pension phase determines a *monthly* pension.
   d. Add a hyperlink to the page that goes to the Social Security Administration (www.ssa.gov), and then compare your calculation to the benefits provided by the government. Is Social Security providing a good return on your investment?
   e. Add your name to the worksheet, print the worksheet both ways to show displayed values and cell formulas, add a cover sheet, and then submit the assignment to your instructor.

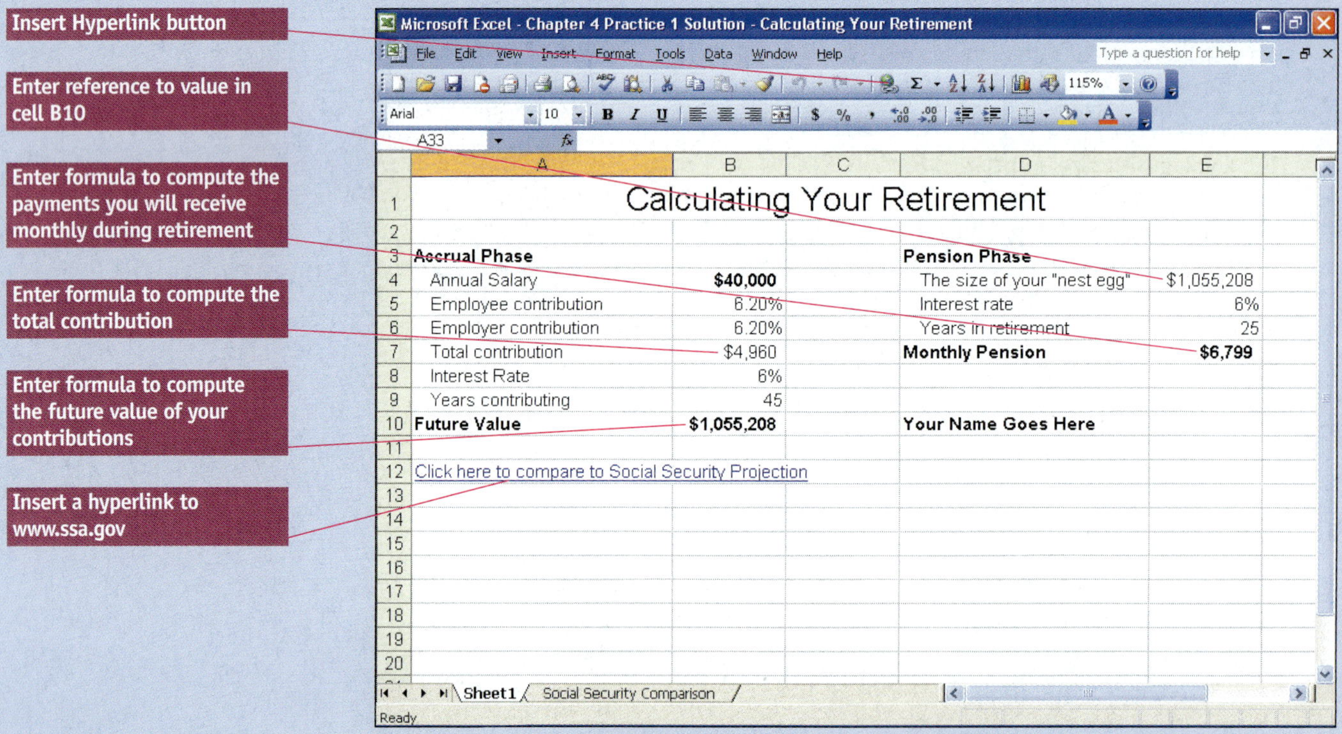

FIGURE 4.17 Calculating Your Retirement (exercise 1)

2. **Alternate Grade Book:** Figure 4.18 displays an alternate version of the grade book that was used in the third hands-on exercise. The student names have changed as has the professor's grading scheme. Open the partially completed version of this worksheet in the *Chapter 4 Practice 2* workbook in the Exploring Excel folder, then complete the workbook as follows:
   a. The test average is computed by dropping the student's lowest grade, then giving equal weight to the three remaining tests. Steve Weinstein's test average, for example, is computed by dropping the 70 on test 1, then taking the average of 80, 90, and 100, his grades for tests 2, 3, and 4. You will need to use the SUM, MIN, and COUNT functions to implement this requirement.
   b. Students are required to complete a designated number of homework assignments (12 in Figure 4.18), then receive a bonus or penalty for every additional or missing homework assignment. Andrea Carrion completed 9 homework assignments, rather than 12, and thus has a 6-point penalty (2 points per each missing assignment). The bonus or penalty is added to the test average to determine the semester average.
   c. The grade for the course is based on the semester average and table of grading criteria according to an HLOOKUP function within the worksheet.
   d. Format the worksheet in an attractive manner. You do not have to duplicate our formatting exactly, but you are to use conditional formatting to display all failing grades and homework penalties in red.
   e. Add your name to the worksheet. Print the worksheet twice, once with displayed values and once with cell formulas. Use the Page Setup command to display grid lines and row and column headings. Add a custom header with your name, the course you are taking and your instructor's name. Create a custom footer with today's date and the current time.
   f. Print the worksheet a second time to reflect Maryann's comment. Add a cover sheet, and then submit both copies of the worksheet together with the cell formulas to your instructor.

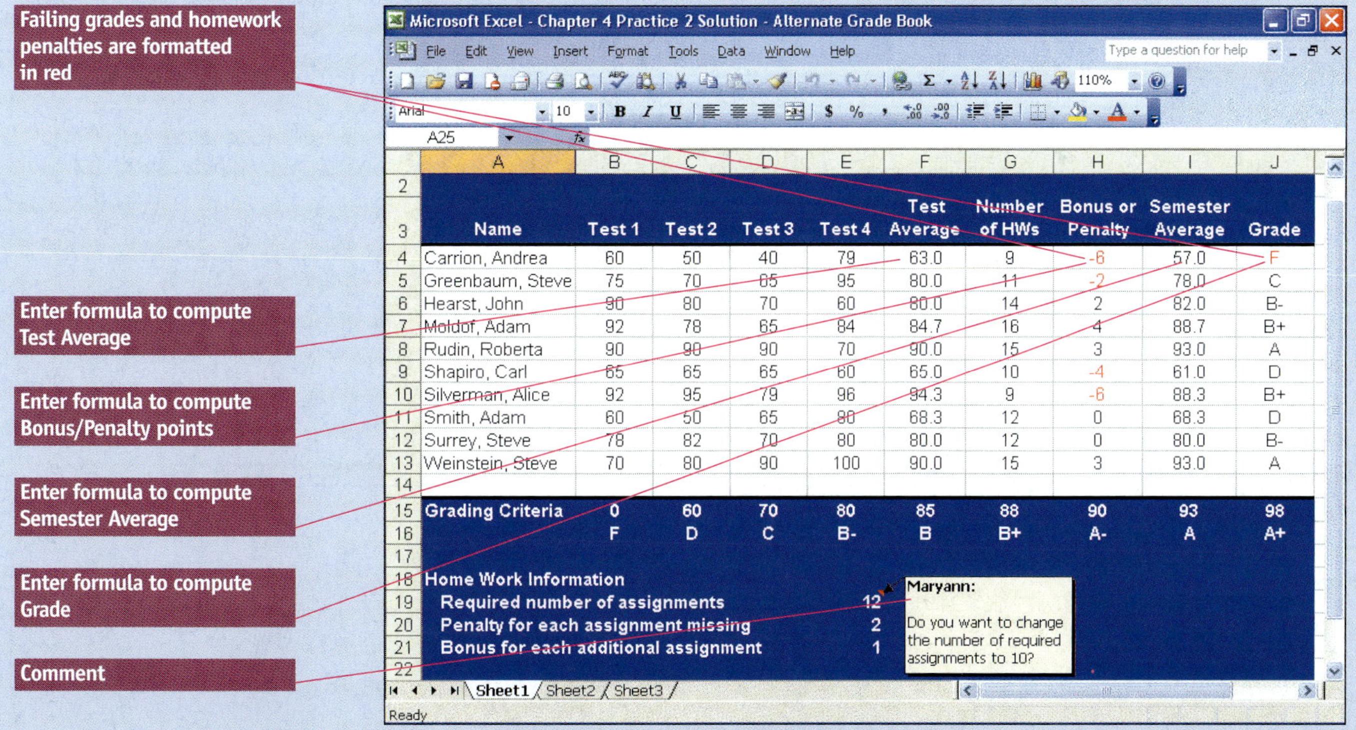

FIGURE 4.18 Alternate Grade Book (exercise 2)

3. **Expanded Payroll:** Figure 4.19 displays an expanded version of the payroll example that was used earlier in the text. The assumptions used to determine an individual's net pay are listed in the worksheet and repeated below. Open the partially completed *Chapter 4 Practice 3* workbook in the Exploring Excel folder. Be sure to use the appropriate combination of relative and absolute addresses so that the formulas in row 2 may be copied to the remaining rows in the worksheet and, further, so that you can easily modify any of the underlying assumptions.
    a. Click in cell E2 to compute the employee's regular pay (regular hours worked times the hourly wage). The number of regular hours worked does not appear explicitly in the worksheet, but is calculated from the total hours worked and the overtime threshold (which is entered in the assumption area). Barber, for example, works a total of 48 hours, 40 regular, and 8 (every hour over the threshold) of overtime.
    b. Click in cell F2 and compute the overtime pay, which is the pay for all hours above the overtime threshold (40 hours in Figure 4.19). The employee receives the overtime rate (1.5 in this worksheet) times the hourly wage for every hour over the threshold.
    c. The gross pay in cell G2 is the sum of the regular pay and the overtime pay. The taxable pay in cell H2 is computed by subtracting the deduction per dependent times the number of dependents.
    d. The withholding tax in cell I2 is based on the taxable pay and the tax table. Use a VLOOKUP function to determine the tax rate, then multiply by the taxable pay.
    e. The Social Security/Medicare tax in cell J2 is a fixed percentage of gross pay.
    f. The Net Pay in cell K2 is equal to the gross pay minus the withholding and Social Security tax.
    g. Copy the formulas in row 2 to the remaining rows in the worksheet.
    h. Add your name to the worksheet, then print the worksheet to show both displayed values and cell formulas.
    i. Change the overtime threshold in cell D13 to 35 and the overtime rate in cell D14 to 2. Print the worksheet a second time to show the resulting displayed values.
    j. Add a cover sheet and submit all of the printouts to your instructor.

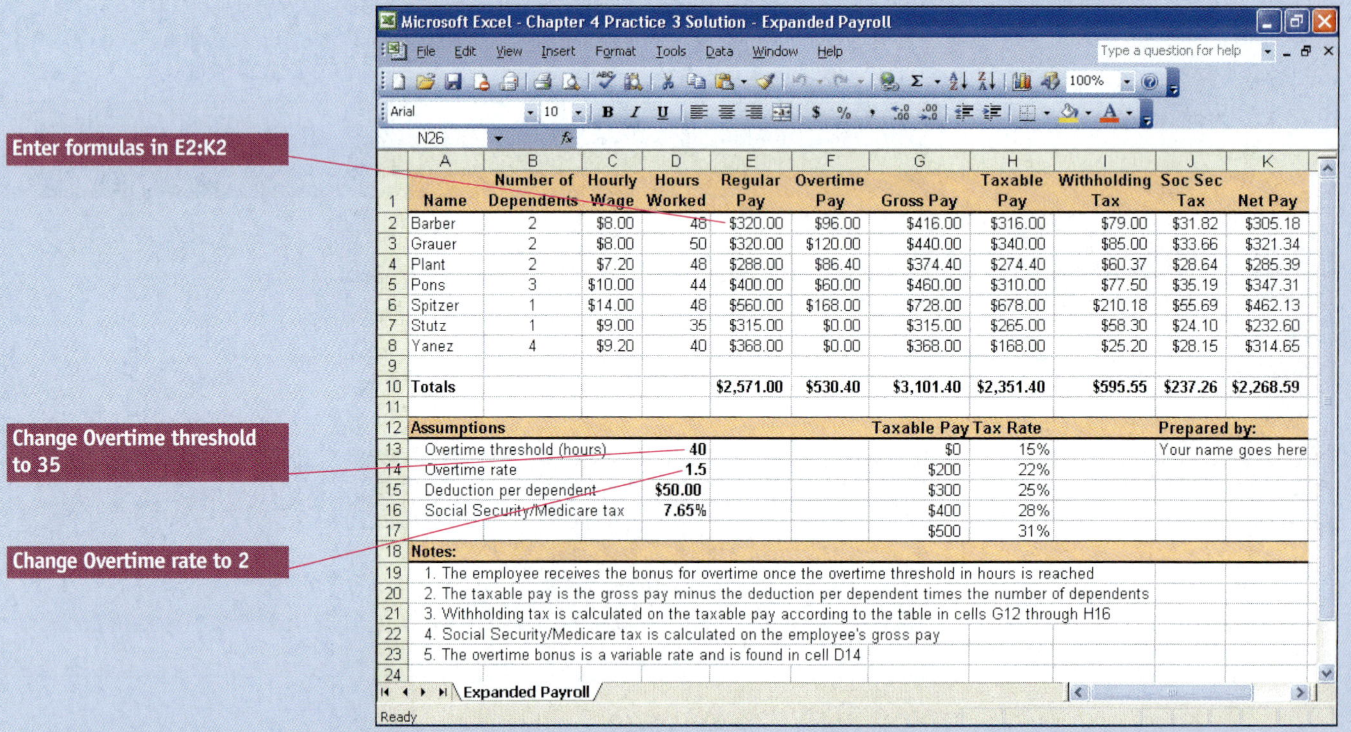

	A	B	C	D	E	F	G	H	I	J	K
1	Name	Number of Dependents	Hourly Wage	Hours Worked	Regular Pay	Overtime Pay	Gross Pay	Taxable Pay	Withholding Tax	Soc Sec Tax	Net Pay
2	Barber	2	$8.00	48	$320.00	$96.00	$416.00	$316.00	$79.00	$31.82	$305.18
3	Grauer	2	$8.00	50	$320.00	$120.00	$440.00	$340.00	$85.00	$33.66	$321.34
4	Plant	2	$7.20	48	$288.00	$86.40	$374.40	$274.40	$60.37	$28.64	$285.39
5	Pons	3	$10.00	44	$400.00	$60.00	$460.00	$310.00	$77.50	$35.19	$347.31
6	Spitzer	1	$14.00	48	$560.00	$168.00	$728.00	$678.00	$210.18	$55.69	$462.13
7	Stutz	1	$9.00	35	$315.00	$0.00	$315.00	$265.00	$58.30	$24.10	$232.60
8	Yanez	4	$9.20	40	$368.00	$0.00	$368.00	$168.00	$25.20	$28.15	$314.65
9											
10	Totals				$2,571.00	$530.40	$3,101.40	$2,351.40	$595.55	$237.26	$2,268.59
11											
12	Assumptions						Taxable Pay	Tax Rate		Prepared by:	
13	Overtime threshold (hours)			40			$0	15%		Your name goes here	
14	Overtime rate			1.5			$200	22%			
15	Deduction per dependent			$50.00			$300	25%			
16	Social Security/Medicare tax			7.65%			$400	28%			
17							$500	31%			
18	Notes:										
19	1. The employee receives the bonus for overtime once the overtime threshold in hours is reached										
20	2. The taxable pay is the gross pay minus the deduction per dependent times the number of dependents										
21	3. Withholding tax is calculated on the taxable pay according to the table in cells G12 through H16										
22	4. Social Security/Medicare tax is calculated on the employee's gross pay										
23	5. The overtime bonus is a variable rate and is found in cell D14										
24											

FIGURE 4.19 Expanded Payroll (exercise 3)

4. **Fuel Estimates:** Figure 4.20 displays a worksheet an airline uses to calculate the fuel requirements and associated cost for available flights. Open the partially completed worksheet in the *Chapter 4 Practice 4* workbook, and then complete the workbook to match our figure. Note the following:
   a. The fuel required for each flight is dependent on the type of aircraft and the number of flying hours. Use a VLOOKUP function in the formula to determine gallons per hour based on the type of plane, then multiply the result by the number of flying hours to compute the amount of fuel for each flight. (The table for the VLOOKUP function extends over three columns.)
   b. Use the fuel required from part (a) to compute the additional requirements for reserve fuel and holding fuel, which must then be added to the initial fuel requirements to get the total fuel needed for a trip. These parameters are shown at the bottom of the worksheet and are susceptible to change. Use the appropriate combination of relative and absolute references so that the formula for the first flight can be copied to the remaining rows in the worksheet.
   c. The estimated fuel cost for each flight is the number of gallons times the price per gallon. There is a price break, however, if the fuel required reaches or exceeds a threshold number of gallons. The Boeing-727 flight from Miami to Los Angeles, for example, requires 6,050 gallons, which exceeds the threshold, and therefore qualifies for the reduced price of fuel.
   d. Your worksheet should be completely flexible and amenable to change; that is, the hourly fuel requirements, price per gallon, price threshold, and holding and reserve percentages are all subject to change.
   e. Print the worksheet to show both displayed values and cell formulas. Use the Page Setup command to create a custom header and a custom footer that includes your name, your instructor's name, the name of your course, today's date, and the current time.
   f. Change the threshold for the price break to 3,500 gallons. Change the price per gallon to $1.50 and $1.75 if the threshold is met or not met, respectively. Print the spreadsheet to reflect these new values. Add a cover sheet and submit all of your printouts to your instructor.

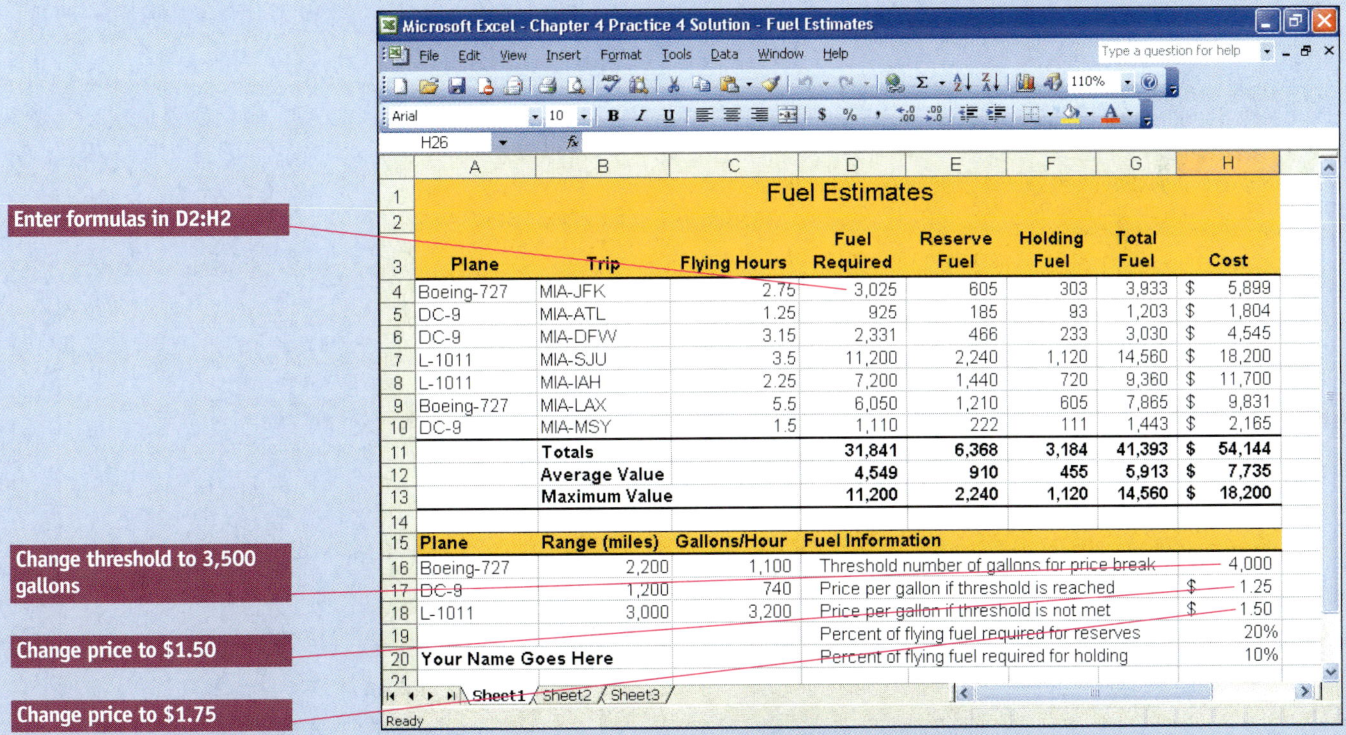

	A	B	C	D	E	F	G	H
1	Fuel Estimates							
2								
3	Plane	Trip	Flying Hours	Fuel Required	Reserve Fuel	Holding Fuel	Total Fuel	Cost
4	Boeing-727	MIA-JFK	2.75	3,025	605	303	3,933	$ 5,899
5	DC-9	MIA-ATL	1.25	925	185	93	1,203	$ 1,804
6	DC-9	MIA-DFW	3.15	2,331	466	233	3,030	$ 4,545
7	L-1011	MIA-SJU	3.5	11,200	2,240	1,120	14,560	$ 18,200
8	L-1011	MIA-IAH	2.25	7,200	1,440	720	9,360	$ 11,700
9	Boeing-727	MIA-LAX	5.5	6,050	1,210	605	7,865	$ 9,831
10	DC-9	MIA-MSY	1.5	1,110	222	111	1,443	$ 2,165
11		**Totals**		**31,841**	**6,368**	**3,184**	**41,393**	**$ 54,144**
12		**Average Value**		**4,549**	**910**	**455**	**5,913**	**$ 7,735**
13		**Maximum Value**		**11,200**	**2,240**	**1,120**	**14,560**	**$ 18,200**
14								
15	**Plane**	**Range (miles)**	**Gallons/Hour**	**Fuel Information**				
16	Boeing-727	2,200	1,100	Threshold number of gallons for price break				4,000
17	DC-9	1,200	740	Price per gallon if threshold is reached				$ 1.25
18	L-1011	3,000	3,200	Price per gallon if threshold is not met				$ 1.50
19				Percent of flying fuel required for reserves				20%
20	**Your Name Goes Here**			Percent of flying fuel required for holding				10%

FIGURE 4.20 Fuel Estimates (exercise 4)

5. **The Roth IRA:** Figure 4.21 displays a Word document with an Excel worksheet and associated chart that displays the value of an IRA for various combinations of interest rates and years invested. (The chart is not visible in Figure 4.21.) A partially completed version of that worksheet is found in the Exploring Excel folder, as is the associated Word document. Your assignment is to complete the worksheet, create the associated line chart, and then link the Excel objects to the Word document.
   a. Open the partially completed *Chapter 4 Practice 5* workbook. Click in cell C5 and enter the appropriate FV function using mixed references. Mixed references are not difficult if you ask yourself the right questions. The interest rate for the calculation in cell C5 will come from cell B5. Will the interest rate for other cells always come from column B? (Yes, so the reference to the column is absolute.) Will the interest rate always come from row 5? (No, so the reference to the column is relative.) Use similar reasoning to determine that the reference to the number of years in cell C4 should be expressed as C$4. Copy the formula in cell C5 to the remaining rows and columns in the worksheet. You should see the same dollar amounts as in Figure 4.21.
   b. The worksheet is designed so that the user can change the starting interest rate and associated increment, 4.50% and .5%, respectively in the figure, then have those values reflected in the body of the spreadsheet. The user can also change the number of years for the investment and the associated increment, as well as the annual contribution. Change the values in the assumption area of the worksheet to see how the worksheet changes.
   c. Create a line chart in its own chart sheet that shows the value of a Roth IRA at different interest rates for different time periods.
   d. Open the associated *Chapter 4 Practice 5* Word document in the Exploring Excel folder and link the portion of the worksheet shown in Figure 4.21 to the Word document. Return to Excel and link the line chart to a second page in the Word document. Save the workbook. Exit Excel.
   e. Add your name to the memo after the salutation, "To the New Graduate", then print the completed memo and submit it to your instructor. Compound interest has been called the eighth wonder of the world. Use it to your advantage!

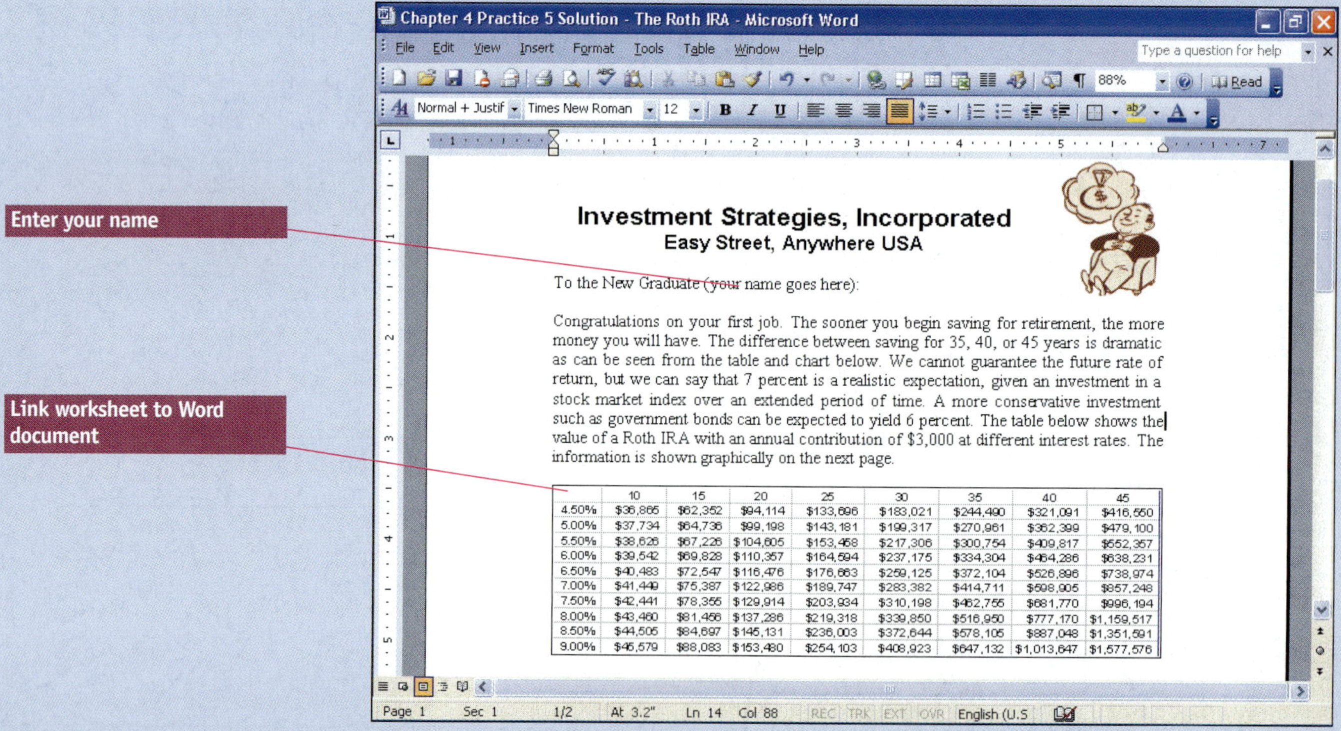

	10	15	20	25	30	35	40	45
4.50%	$36,865	$62,352	$94,114	$133,696	$183,021	$244,490	$321,091	$416,550
5.00%	$37,734	$64,736	$99,198	$143,181	$199,317	$270,961	$362,399	$479,100
5.50%	$38,626	$67,226	$104,605	$153,458	$217,306	$300,754	$409,817	$552,357
6.00%	$39,542	$69,828	$110,357	$164,594	$237,175	$334,304	$464,286	$638,231
6.50%	$40,483	$72,547	$116,476	$176,663	$259,125	$372,104	$526,896	$738,974
7.00%	$41,449	$75,387	$122,986	$189,747	$283,382	$414,711	$598,905	$857,248
7.50%	$42,441	$78,355	$129,914	$203,934	$310,198	$462,755	$681,770	$996,194
8.00%	$43,460	$81,456	$137,286	$219,318	$339,850	$516,950	$777,170	$1,159,517
8.50%	$44,505	$84,697	$145,131	$236,003	$372,644	$578,105	$887,048	$1,351,591
9.00%	$45,579	$88,083	$153,480	$254,103	$408,923	$647,132	$1,013,647	$1,577,576

FIGURE 4.21 The Roth IRA (exercise 5)

6. **Celebrity Birthdays:** The spreadsheet in Figure 4.22 compares the age of its developer to that of several celebrities. It is a sophisticated spreadsheet that uses a nested IF function, the absolute value function, and conditional formatting. Open the partially completed version of this spreadsheet in *Chapter 4 Practice 6* and proceed as follows:
   a. Enter your name and birth date in cells B4 and B5, respectively. Enter the function to display today's date in cell E4. Enter the formula to compute your age in cell E5.
   b. Click in cell C8 and enter a nested IF function to indicate whether you are older, younger, or the same age as the celebrity in this row. Start the IF function as follows: =IF($B$5<B8,"older by",IF($B$5>B8, ...)). The absolute reference is to your birth date in cell B5; that is, if your birth date is less than the celebrity's birth date, you are older. If this condition is not true, the second IF function should tell whether you are younger or you are the same age.
   c. Apply conditional formatting to the formula in cell C8 to display the result in red, blue, or green, depending on whether you are older, younger, or the same age.
   d. Click in cell D8 and enter the formula to compute the difference in age, which is to appear as a positive number, regardless of whether you are older or younger than the celebrity. The easiest way to ensure positive numbers is to use the ABS (absolute value) function. (A zero age difference should not appear in the worksheet, however. Pull down the Tools menu, click the Options command, click the View tab, and then clear the box to display zero values.)
   e. Click in cell E8 and enter the appropriate IF function to display the word "years" if you are either older or younger than the celebrity. The cell should be blank if you are the same age. Center the entry.
   f. Copy the formulas in row 8 to the remaining rows of the worksheet. Be sure to test the worksheet completely; that is, change your birth date temporarily to match the birthday of a celebrity to see if you display the same age in column D.
   g. Click the link to find celebrity birthdays and add a person who is not in the original workbook. (We added Mia Hamm.) Boldface and highlight the row you added.
   h. Print the spreadsheet to show the displayed values in alphabetical order by the celebrities' last name. Print the cell formulas.

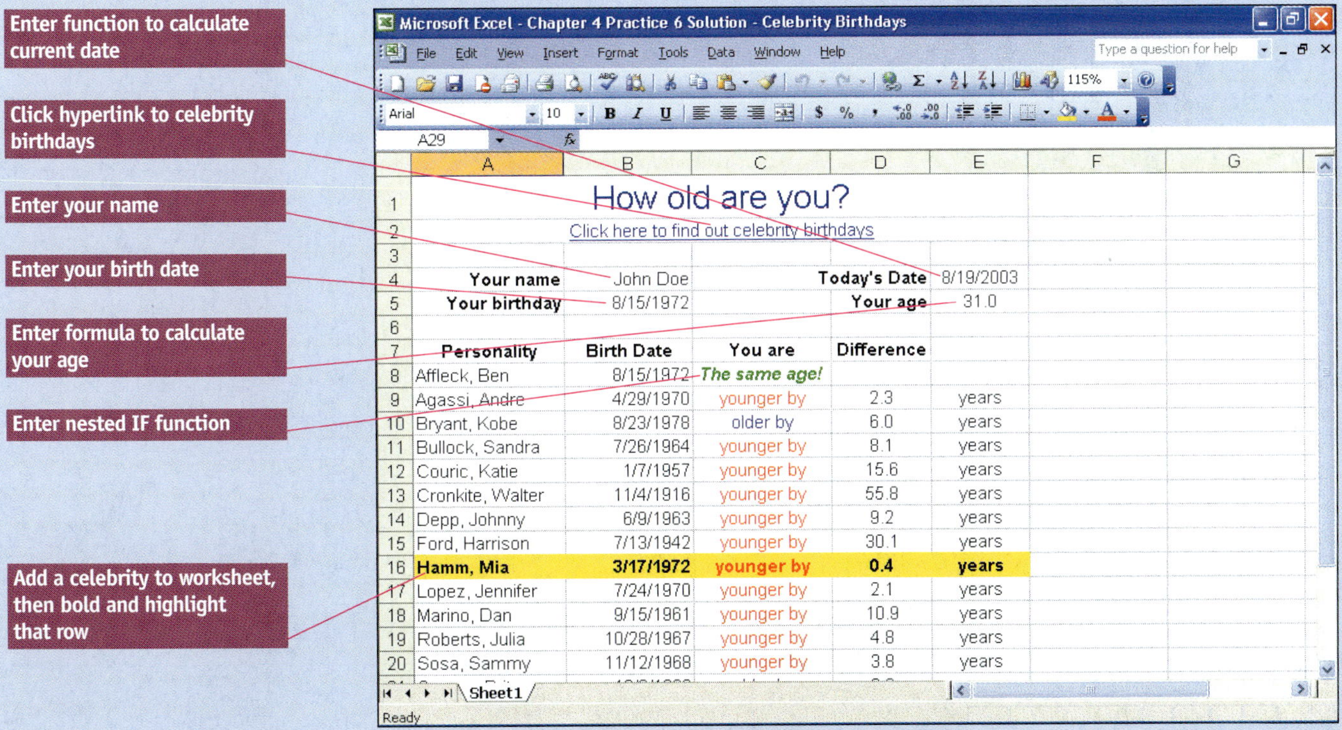

FIGURE 4.22 Celebrity Birthdays (exercise 6)

7. **The Health Club:** The worksheet in Figure 4.23 displays a list of new members in the Totally Fit Gym. Your assignment is to open the partially completed workbook in *Chapter 4 Practice 7,* in order to complete the workbook so that it matches our figure. You do not have to match our formatting exactly, but you are required to duplicate the functionality. Proceed as follows:
   a. Click in Cell C4 and enter the appropriate VLOOKUP function to determine the cost of the individual's membership. Your formula should contain an absolute reference to the table of membership costs that is contained in cells A17 through C19.
   b. Click in cell E4 and use an IF function to determine the annual total, which consists of the cost of membership plus an optional locker fee. Now click in cell G4 to compute the total amount due, which is the annual total times the number of years the individual has chosen.
   c. The down payment in cell H4 depends on the type of membership and is not dependent on the number of years. Thus Allen, George, and Grauer all have a required down payment of $250 for the deluxe membership, even though they selected a different number of years.
   d. Compute the balance (which is the total due minus the down payment) in cell I4. Use the PMT function to determine the monthly payment in cell J4.
   e. Copy the formulas in row 4 to the remaining rows in the worksheet.
   f. Enter your last name in cell A8 in place of "Grauer". Sort the client list in alphabetical order, then select the row containing your name and shade it.
   g. Enter the appropriate statistical functions in column H to determine summary statistics. Your values should match ours.
   h. Format the completed worksheet as you see fit. Insert clip art somewhere in the worksheet to serve as a logo.
   i. Print the displayed values and cell formulas for your instructor. Use landscape printing so that the worksheet fits on one page. Be sure that the grid lines and the row and column headings appear.

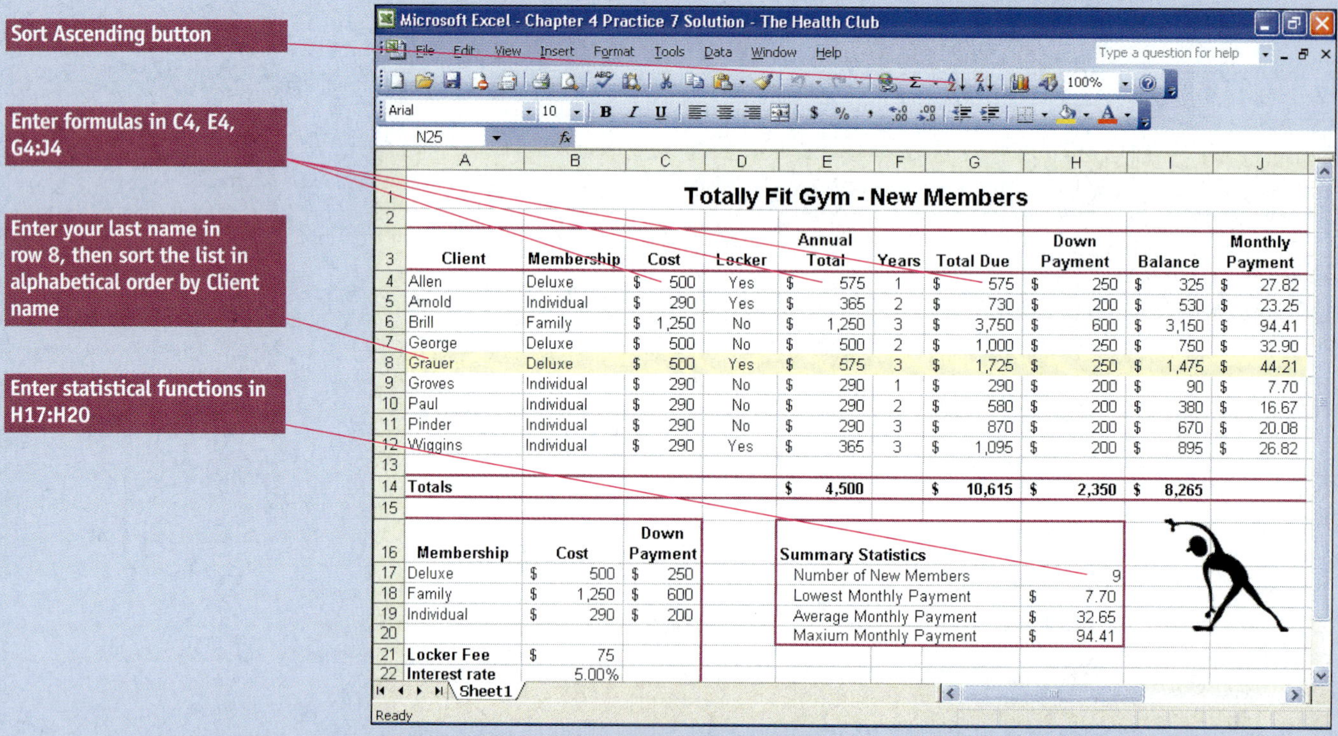

FIGURE 4.23 The Health Club (exercise 7)

8. **File Formats and Folders:** One of the most common tasks in the workplace involves the exchange of data between different applications. You might use Excel to compute student grades for the semester, and then find it necessary to export that data to a mainframe computer. Proceed as follows.
   a. Open the Expanded Grade Book Solution from Hands-on Exercise 3. Click the rectangle in the upper left corner of the worksheet to select the entire worksheet. Pull down the Format menu, click Column, then click the Unhide command.
   b. Click the Copy button. Pull down the Edit menu, click Paste Special, click the option button for Values (in the Paste area), and click OK. This converts the Excel formulas to their numeric and literal equivalents.
   c. Delete the first two rows in the worksheet (which contain the title information) and all rows below the last student. Delete every column except the student's name, Social Security number, and letter grade. Delete the Sheet2 and Sheet3 worksheets.
   d. Pull down the File menu, Click the Save As command to display the Save As dialog box. Enter Semester Grades as the file name. Click the down arrow in the Save As type list box and choose CSV (Comma delimited). Click Yes if you see a message indicating that the workbook may contain features that are incompatible with the CSV format.
   e. Pull down the File menu and click the Save As command to display the Save As dialog box. Click the Create New Folder button and enter "Original Name" as the name. Click OK.
   f. Click the up arrow on the Save As toolbar to return to the Exploring Excel folder as shown in Figure 4.24. Select the new folder, click the down arrow on the Tools button, click the Rename command, and enter Data for Export as the name of the folder. Close the dialog box. Close the workbook.
   g. Click the Open button on the Standard toolbar and change to the Exploring Excel folder. Select the Semester Grades document and drag it to the Data for Export folder. (You can also move the document using "cut and paste".)
   h. Start the Notepad accessory and open the Semester Grades document in the Data Export folder. Use Notepad to print the Semester Grades document.

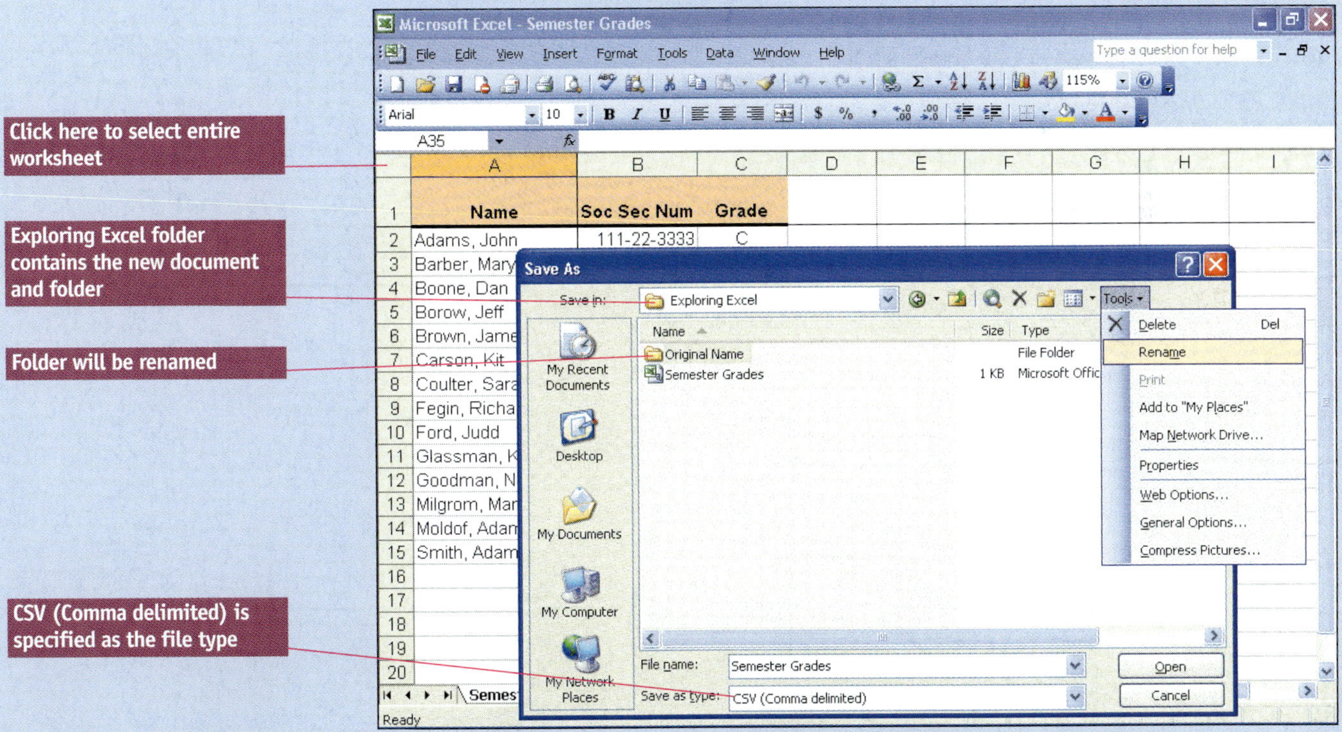

FIGURE 4.24 File Formats and Folders (exercise 8)

9. **Nested IFs and Other Functions:** Figure 4.25 displays a modified version of the expanded grade book. A Student ID has been inserted in column C, the explicit bonus or penalty for homework is displayed in column J, and the rank in class has been inserted in column M. Open the partially completed workbook in *Chapter 4 Practice 9,* then proceed as follows:
   a. Click in cell C4 and use the LEFT function to display the first four digits of the student's Social Security number in cell B4. Copy the formula to the remaining rows in the worksheet. Be sure that your results correspond to our figure. Hide columns A and B since the professor will post the worksheet by Student ID.
   b. Enter the formula to compute the student's test average in cell H4, which is based on the exam weights in row 24. Copy this formula to the remaining rows. Enter the appropriate statistical functions at the bottom of the worksheet for test 1. Copy these formulas to the appropriate cells for the other exams.
   c. Students are penalized two points for poor homework, and are rewarded two and four points, for satisfactory (OK) and good homework, respectively. Use a nested IF function in cell J4 to compute the homework bonus or penalty. Write the IF function in such a way that it will flag an invalid homework grade. Copy this formula to the remaining rows in the spreadsheet.
   d. Click in cell K4 and enter the formula for the semester average. Use a VLOOKUP function in cell L4 to determine the grade for the semester. Copy these formulas to the remaining rows in the worksheet.
   e. The VLOOKUP function does not give students a break; for example, the student with a 79.6 average (student ID is 4444) is assigned a C. (You can change the format in column K to omit decimals, but the assigned grade will not change because formatting does not change the actual value in a cell.) Thus you have to change the formula in cell K4 to round the student's grade to the nearest integer. Copy this formula to the remaining rows to be sure it works correctly.
   f. Use the Rank function to determine each student's rank in class according to the computed value of his or her semester average. (Use the Help menu if necessary.)
   g. Add your name to the worksheet as the grading assistant. Format the worksheet, then print it twice, to show both displayed values and cell formulas.

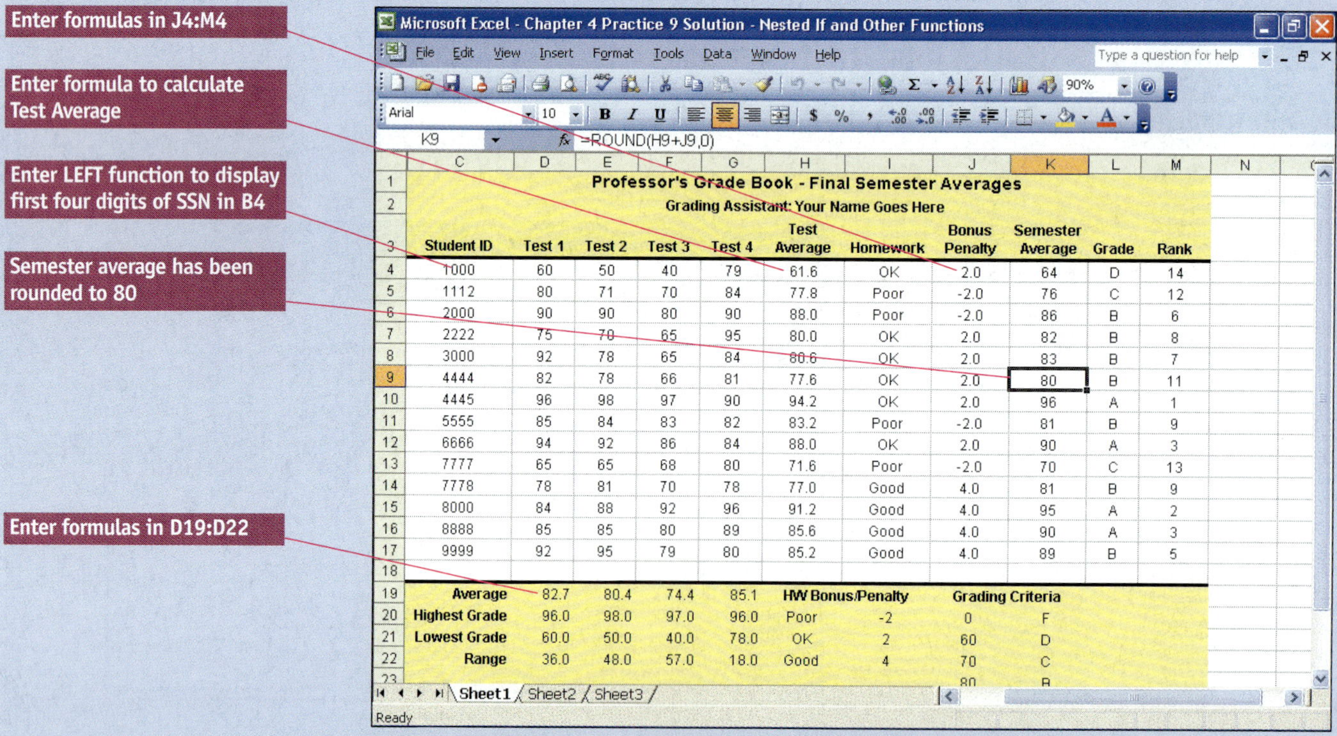

	C	D	E	F	G	H	I	J	K	L	M
1	Professor's Grade Book - Final Semester Averages										
2	Grading Assistant: Your Name Goes Here										
3	Student ID	Test 1	Test 2	Test 3	Test 4	Test Average	Homework	Bonus Penalty	Semester Average	Grade	Rank
4	1000	60	50	40	79	61.6	OK	2.0	64	D	14
5	1112	80	71	70	84	77.8	Poor	-2.0	76	C	12
6	2000	90	90	80	90	88.0	Poor	-2.0	86	B	6
7	2222	75	70	65	95	80.0	OK	2.0	82	B	8
8	3000	92	78	65	84	80.6	OK	2.0	83	B	7
9	4444	82	78	66	81	77.6	OK	2.0	80	B	11
10	4445	96	98	97	90	94.2	OK	2.0	96	A	1
11	5555	85	84	83	82	83.2	Poor	-2.0	81	B	9
12	6666	94	92	86	84	88.0	OK	2.0	90	A	3
13	7777	65	65	68	80	71.6	Poor	-2.0	70	C	13
14	7778	78	81	70	78	77.0	Good	4.0	81	B	9
15	8000	84	88	92	96	91.2	Good	4.0	95	A	2
16	8888	85	85	80	89	85.6	Good	4.0	90	A	3
17	9999	92	95	79	80	85.2	Good	4.0	89	B	5
18											
19	Average	82.7	80.4	74.4	85.1	HW Bonus/Penalty		Grading Criteria			
20	Highest Grade	96.0	98.0	97.0	96.0	Poor	-2	0	F		
21	Lowest Grade	60.0	50.0	40.0	78.0	OK	2	60	D		
22	Range	36.0	48.0	57.0	18.0	Good	4	70	C		
23								80	B		

FIGURE 4.25 Nested IFs and Other Functions (exercise 9)

10. **Election 2000:** Election 2000 has come and gone, but it will always be remembered as the closest election in our history. You will find a partially completed version of Figure 4.26 in the file, *Chapter 4 Practice 10*. Open the workbook and proceed as follows:
    a. Enter an appropriate IF function in cells D9 and F9 to determine the electoral votes for each candidate. The electoral votes are awarded on the all-or-nothing basis; that is, the candidate with the larger popular vote wins all of that states electoral votes. The other candidate gets zero votes. (Pull down the Tools menu, click the Options command, click the View tab, and then clear the box to display zero values.)
    b. Copy the entries in cells D9 and F9 to the remaining rows in the respective columns. Format these columns to display red and blue values, for Mr. Bush and Mr. Gore, respectively.
    c. Enter a formula in cell G9 to determine the difference in the popular vote between the two candidates. The result should always appear as a positive number. You can do this in one of two ways; by using either an absolute value function or an appropriate IF function. Copy this formula to the remaining rows in the column.
    d. Click in cell H9 and determine the percentage differential in the popular vote. This is the difference in the number of votes divided by the total number of votes.
    e. Enter the appropriate SUM functions in cells B4, B5, C4, and C5 to determine the electoral and popular vote totals for each candidate.
    f. Add your name and your instructor's name as indicated. Reduce the top and bottom margins to three quarters of an inch, then use the appropriate option in the Page Setup command to be sure your worksheet fits on one page. Adjust the column widths as necessary. Print the worksheet a second time to show the cell formulas.
    g. Use the Sort command to display the states in a different sequence, such as the smallest (or largest) vote differential. Print the worksheet in this sequence.
    h. Add a cover sheet. Submit all of your printouts to your instructor.

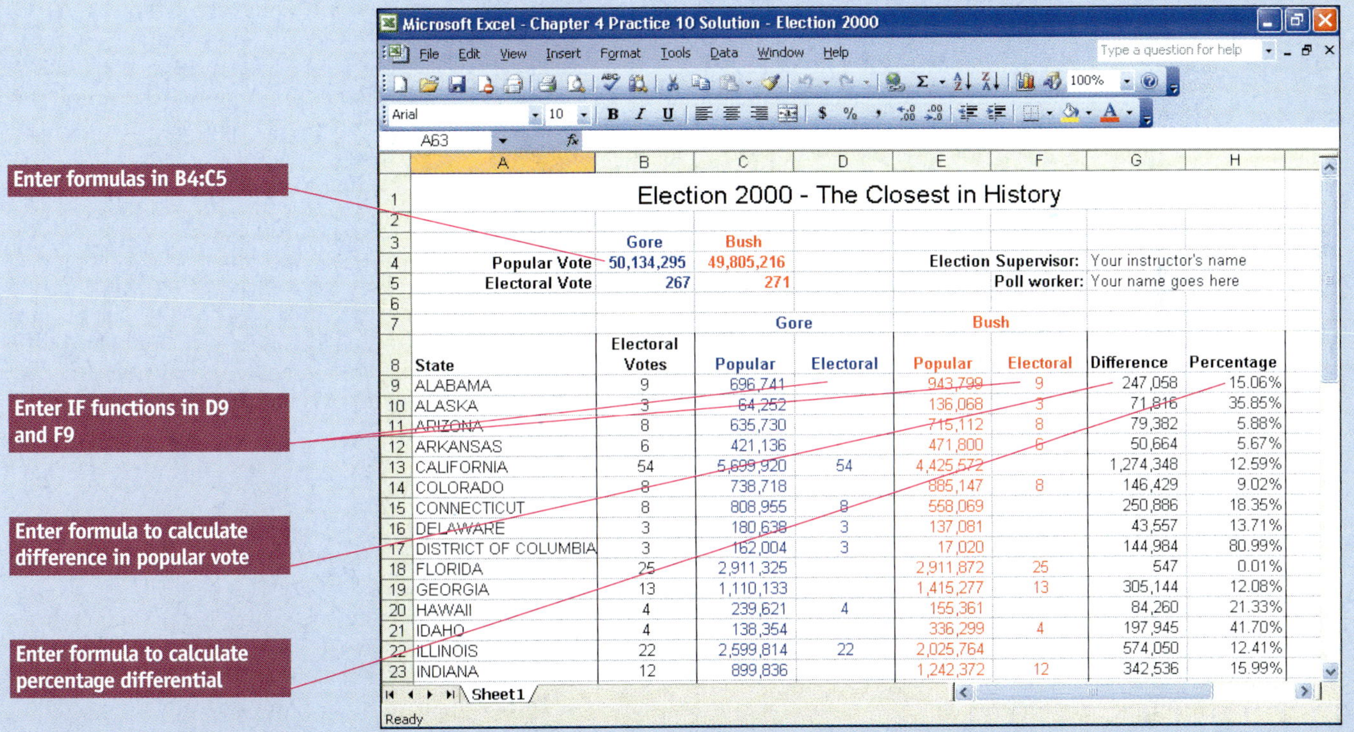

Election 2000 - The Closest in History

	Gore	Bush			
Popular Vote	50,134,295	49,805,216	Election Supervisor:	Your instructor's name	
Electoral Vote	267	271	Poll worker:	Your name goes here	

		Gore		Bush			
State	Electoral Votes	Popular	Electoral	Popular	Electoral	Difference	Percentage
ALABAMA	9	696,741		943,799	9	247,058	15.06%
ALASKA	3	64,252		136,068	3	71,816	35.85%
ARIZONA	8	635,730		715,112	8	79,382	5.88%
ARKANSAS	6	421,136		471,800	6	50,664	5.67%
CALIFORNIA	54	5,699,920	54	4,425,572		1,274,348	12.59%
COLORADO	8	738,718		885,147	8	146,429	9.02%
CONNECTICUT	8	808,955	8	558,069		250,886	18.35%
DELAWARE	3	180,638	3	137,081		43,557	13.71%
DISTRICT OF COLUMBIA	3	162,004	3	17,020		144,984	80.99%
FLORIDA	25	2,911,325		2,911,872	25	547	0.01%
GEORGIA	13	1,110,133		1,415,277	13	305,144	12.08%
HAWAII	4	239,621	4	155,361		84,260	21.33%
IDAHO	4	138,354		336,299	4	197,945	41.70%
ILLINOIS	22	2,599,814	22	2,025,764		574,050	12.41%
INDIANA	12	899,836		1,242,372	12	342,536	15.99%

FIGURE 4.26 Election 2000 (exercise 10)

MINI CASES

The Financial Consultant

A friend of yours is in the process of buying a home and has asked you to compare the payments and total interest on a 15- and 30-year loan at varying interest rates. You have decided to analyze the loans in Excel, and then incorporate the results into a memo written in Microsoft Word. As of now, the principal is $150,000, but it is very likely that your friend will change his mind several times, and so you want to use the linking and embedding capability within Windows to dynamically link the worksheet to the word processing document. Your memo should include a letterhead that takes advantage of the formatting capabilities within Word; a graphic logo would be a nice touch.

Fun with the If Statement

Open the *Chapter 4 Mini Case—Fun with the If Statement* workbook in the Exploring Excel folder, then follow the directions in the worksheet to view a hidden message. The message is displayed by various If statements scattered throughout the worksheet, but the worksheet is protected so that you cannot see these formulas. (Use help to see how to protect a worksheet.) We made it easy for you, however, because you can unprotect the worksheet since a password is not required. Once the worksheet is unprotected, pull down the Format menu, click the Cells command, click the Protection tab, and clear the Hidden check box. Prove to your professor that you have done this successfully, by changing the text of our message. Print the completed worksheet to show both displayed values and cell formulas.

The Lottery

Many states raise money through lotteries that advertise prizes of several million dollars. In reality, however, the actual value of the prize is considerably less than the advertised value, although the winners almost certainly do not care. One state, for example, recently offered a twenty million dollar prize that was to be distributed in twenty annual payments of one million dollars each. How much was the prize actually worth, assuming a long-term interest rate of five percent? Use the PV (Present Value) function to determine the answer. What is the effect on the answer if payments to the recipient are made at the beginning of each year, rather than at the end of each year?

A Penny a Day

What if you had a rich uncle who offered to pay you "a penny a day," and then double your salary each day for the next month? It does not sound very generous, but you will be surprised at how quickly the amount grows. Create a simple worksheet that enables you to use the Goal Seek command to answer the following questions. On what day of the month (if any) will your uncle pay you more than one million dollars? How much money will your uncle pay you on the 31st day?

The Rule of 72

Delaying your IRA for one year can cost you as much as $64,000 at retirement, depending on when you begin. That may be hard to believe, but you can check the numbers without a calculator, using the "Rule of 72." This financial rule of thumb states that to find out how long it takes money to double, divide the number 72 by the interest rate; for example, money earning 8% annually will double in approximately 9 years (72 divided by 8). The money doubles again in 18 years, again in 27 years, and so on. Now assume that you start your IRA at age 21, rather than 20, effectively losing 45 years of compound interest for the initial contribution. Use the rule of 72 to determine approximately how much you will lose, assuming an 8% rate of return. Check your calculation by creating a worksheet to determine the exact amount.

CHAPTER

1

Introduction to Access: What Is a Database?

OBJECTIVES

After reading this chapter you will:

1. Define the terms field, record, table, and database.
2. Describe the objects in an Access database.
3. Download the practice files (data disk) for use in hands-on exercises.
4. Add, edit, and delete records within a table.
5. Use existing forms and reports.
6. Explain the importance of data validation in maintaining a table.
7. Apply a filter by form or selection.
8. Sort a table on one or more fields.
9. Identify the one-to-many relationships in a database.
10. Explain how changes in one table of a relational database affect other the tables in the database.

hands-on exercises

1. INTRODUCTION TO ACCESS
   Input: Bookstore database
   Output: Bookstore database (modified)
2. FILTERS AND SORTING
   Input: Employee database
   Output: Employee database (modified)
3. A LOOK AHEAD
   Input: Look Ahead database
   Output: Look Ahead database (modified)

CASE STUDY

NATALIE'S CUPPA JOE

Natalie's Cuppa Joe is a locally famous coffee shop that is known for its large and very creative selection of signature espresso drinks for coffee enthusiasts. The owner, Natalie Anderson, has always believed that variety is the spice of life and that there is much more to coffee than just cream and sugar. Natalie insists on good customer relations, and her staff is expected to know regular customers by their first name. Customers are also encouraged to submit suggestions for additional signature selections.

To make it easier on her employees, Natalie has built a database with information about her customers. New customers are asked to complete a questionnaire the first time they come into the shop as they wait for their drink to be prepared. Customers provide the standard name and address information, indicate whether they want to be included on a mailing list, and whether they wish to purchase the discount "Cuppa Card." This data is then entered into the database within three to four days.

You have just been hired by Natalie's Cuppa Joe and are expected to become knowledgeable about its customers and proficient at brewing the wild coffee drinks for which they are famous. Natalie has given you time away from the front counter to become familiar with the database, to enter recent customer information, and to generate two reports that will reflect the new data. ■

Your assignment is to read the chapter, paying special attention to each of the hands-on exercises. You will then open the *Chapter 1 Case Study—Natalie's Cuppa Joe* database, and examine each of its objects (tables, forms, queries, and reports). You will use the existing Customers form to enter data about yourself as a new customer. Indicate that you want to be on the mailing list, but that you have not yet purchased the discount card. Be sure to suggest a specialty drink in the space provided. Print the completed form containing your data, and then print both of the reports within the database. (Your name should appear on both if you followed our instructions correctly.) Submit all of the printed information to your instructor.

THE COLLEGE BOOKSTORE

Imagine, if you will, that you are the manager of a college bookstore and that you maintain data for every book in the store. Accordingly, you have recorded the specifics of each book (the title, author, publisher, price, and so on) in a manila folder, and have stored the folders in one drawer of a file cabinet.

One of your major responsibilities is to order books at the beginning of each semester, which in turn requires you to contact the various publishers. You have found it convenient, therefore, to create a second set of folders with data about each publisher—such as the publisher's phone number, address, and discount policy. You also found it necessary to create a third set of folders with data about each order—such as when the order was placed, the status of the order, which books were ordered, and how many copies.

Normal business operations will require you to make repeated trips to the filing cabinet to maintain the accuracy of the data and keep it up to date. You will have to create a new folder whenever a new book is received, whenever you contract with a new publisher, or whenever you place a new order. In similar fashion, you will have to modify the data in an existing folder to reflect changes that occur, such as an increase in the price of a book, a change in a publisher's address, or an update in the status of an order. And, lastly, you will need to remove the folder of any book that is no longer carried by the bookstore, or of any publisher with whom you no longer have contact, or of any order that was canceled.

The preceding discussion describes the bookstore of 40 years ago—before the advent of computers and computerized databases. The bookstore manager of today needs the same information as his or her predecessor. Today's manager, however, has the information readily available, at the touch of a key or the click of a mouse, through the miracle of modern technology.

Information systems have their own vocabulary. A ***field*** is a basic fact (or data element)—such as the name of a book or the telephone number of a publisher. A ***record*** is a set of fields. A ***table*** is a set of records. Every record in a table contains the same fields in the same order. A ***database*** consists of one or more tables. In our example each record in the Books table will contain the identical six fields—ISBN (a unique identifying number for the book), title, author, year of publication, price, and publisher. In similar fashion, every record in the Publishers table will have the same fields for each publisher just as every record in the Orders table has the same fields for each order.

You can think of the file cabinet in the manual system as a database. Each set of folders in the file cabinet corresponds to a table within the database. Thus, the Bookstore database consists of three separate tables—of books, publishers, and orders. Each table, in turn, consists of multiple records, corresponding to the folders in the file cabinet. The Books table, for example, contains a record for every book title in the store. The Publishers table has a record for each publisher, just as the Orders table has a record for each order.

The real power of Access is derived from a database with multiple tables—such as Books, Publishers, and Orders tables within the Bookstore database. For the time being, however, we focus on a simpler database with only one table so that you can learn the basics of Access. After you are comfortable working with a single table, we will show you how to work with multiple tables and relate them to one another.

GARBAGE IN, GARBAGE OUT

The information produced by a system is only as good as the data on which the information is based. In other words, no system, be it manual or electronic, can produce valid output from invalid input. The phenomenon is described by the acronym "GIGO"—garbage in, garbage out.

INTRODUCTION TO MICROSOFT ACCESS

Microsoft Access, the fourth major application in the Microsoft Office suite, is used to create and manage a database such as the one for the college bookstore. Consider now Figure 1.1, which shows how Microsoft Access appears on the desktop. Our discussion assumes a basic familiarity with the Windows operating system and the user interface that is common to all Windows applications. You should recognize, therefore, that the desktop in Figure 1.1 has two open windows—an application window for Microsoft Access and a document (database) window for the database that is currently open. (Microsoft Office Access 2003 uses the Access 2000 file format by default, to maintain compatability with earlier versions of Access.)

Each window has its own title bar and Minimize, Maximize (or Restore), and Close buttons. The title bar in the application window contains the name of the application (Microsoft Access). The title bar in the document (database) window contains the name of the database that is currently open (Bookstore). The application window for Access has been maximized to take up the entire desktop, and hence the Restore button is visible. The database window has not been maximized.

A menu bar appears immediately below the application title bar. A toolbar (similar to those in other Office applications) appears below the menu bar and offers alternative ways to execute common commands.

The Database Window

The ***Database window*** displays the various objects in an Access database. There are seven types of objects—tables, queries, forms, reports, pages, macros, and modules. Every database must contain at least one table, and it may contain any or all (or none) of the other objects. Each object type is accessed through the appropriate button within the Database window. In this chapter we concentrate on tables, but we briefly describe the other types of objects as a preview of what you will learn as you read our book.

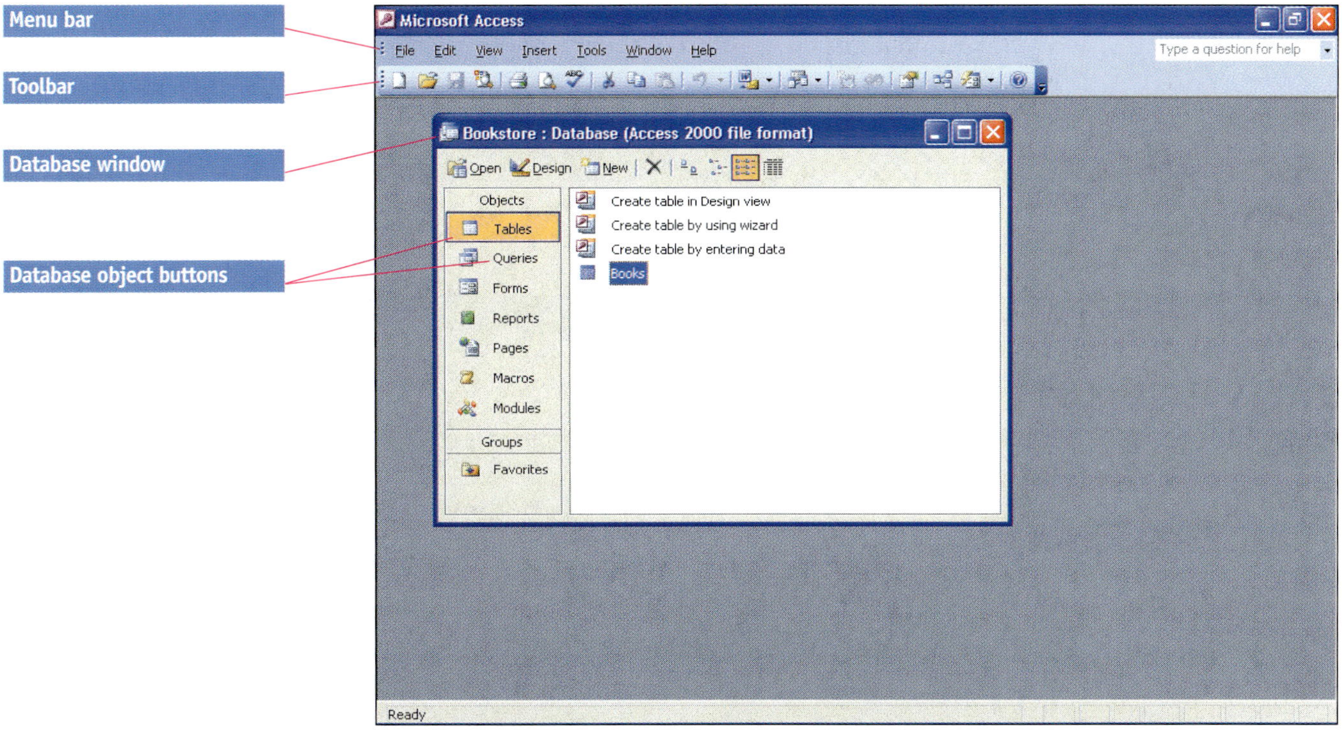

FIGURE 1.1 The Database Window

Tables

A table stores data about a physical entity such as a person, place, or thing, and it is the basic element in any database. A table is made up of records, which in turn are made up of fields. It is similar to an Excel worksheet in appearance, with each record appearing in a separate row. Each field appears in a separate column.

Access provides different ways in which to view a table. The ***Datasheet view*** is where you add, edit, and delete records of a table, and it is the view on which we concentrate throughout the chapter. The ***Design view*** is used to create (and/or modify) the table by specifying the fields it will contain and the associated properties for each field. The field type (for example, text or numeric data) and the field length are examples of field properties. (The Design view is covered in detail in Chapter 2, where we show you how to create a table.)

Access also includes two additional views that provide a convenient way to display summary information from a table. The ***PivotTable view*** is similar in concept to an Excel pivot table and provides a convenient way to summarize data about groups of records. The ***PivotChart view*** creates a chart from the associated PivotTable view. (These views are discussed further in Chapter 4 and need not concern you at this time.)

Figure 1.2 shows the Datasheet view for the Books table in our bookstore. The first row in the table displays the field names. Each additional row contains a record (the data for a specific book). Each column represents a field (one fact about a book). Every record in the table contains the same fields in the same order: ISBN number, Title, Author, Year, List Price, and Publisher.

The ***primary key*** is the field (or combination of fields) that makes each record in a table unique. The ISBN is the primary key in the Books table; it ensures that every record in a table is different from every other record, and hence it prevents the occurrence of duplicate records. A primary key is not required but is strongly recommended. (We cannot think of an example where you would not want to use a primary key.) There can be only one primary key per table.

The status bar at the bottom of Figure 1.2 indicates that there are 22 records in the table and that you are positioned on record number 13. You can work on only one record at a time. The vertical scroll bar at the right of the window indicates that there are more records in the table than can be seen at one time. The horizontal scroll bar at the bottom of the window indicates that you cannot see an entire record.

The triangle that appears to the left of the record indicates that the data in the ***current record*** has been saved. The triangle will change to a pencil as you begin to enter new data, then it will change back to a triangle after you complete the data entry and move to another record, since data is saved automatically as soon as you move from one record to the next.

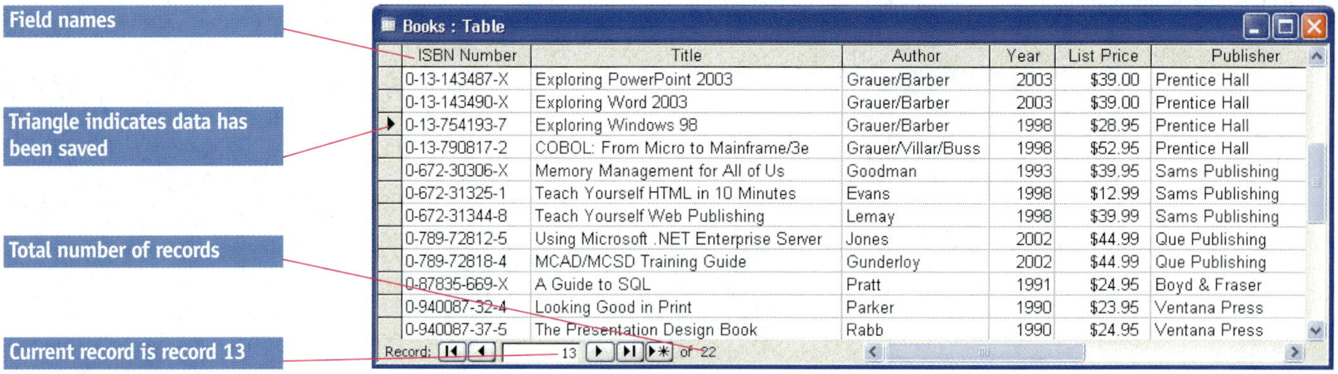

ISBN Number	Title	Author	Year	List Price	Publisher
0-13-143487-X	Exploring PowerPoint 2003	Grauer/Barber	2003	$39.00	Prentice Hall
0-13-143490-X	Exploring Word 2003	Grauer/Barber	2003	$39.00	Prentice Hall
0-13-754193-7	Exploring Windows 98	Grauer/Barber	1998	$28.95	Prentice Hall
0-13-790817-2	COBOL: From Micro to Mainframe/3e	Grauer/Villar/Buss	1998	$52.95	Prentice Hall
0-672-30306-X	Memory Management for All of Us	Goodman	1993	$39.95	Sams Publishing
0-672-31325-1	Teach Yourself HTML in 10 Minutes	Evans	1998	$12.99	Sams Publishing
0-672-31344-8	Teach Yourself Web Publishing	Lemay	1998	$39.99	Sams Publishing
0-789-72812-5	Using Microsoft .NET Enterprise Server	Jones	2002	$44.99	Que Publishing
0-789-72818-4	MCAD/MCSD Training Guide	Gunderloy	2002	$44.99	Que Publishing
0-87835-669-X	A Guide to SQL	Pratt	1991	$24.95	Boyd & Fraser
0-940087-32-4	Looking Good in Print	Parker	1990	$23.95	Ventana Press
0-940087-37-5	The Presentation Design Book	Rabb	1990	$24.95	Ventana Press

FIGURE 1.2 An Access Table

Forms, Queries, and Reports

As previously indicated, an Access database contains different types of objects. A table (or set of tables) is at the heart of any database because it contains the actual data. The other objects in a database—such as forms, queries, and reports—are based on an underlying table. Figure 1.3a displays a form based on the Books table that was shown earlier.

A ***form*** provides a friendlier interface than does a table and it is easier to use when entering or modifying data. Note, for example, the command buttons that appear in the form to add a new record, to find or delete an existing record, to print a record, and to close the form. In short, the form provides access to all of the data maintenance operations that are available through a table. The status bar and navigation buttons at the bottom of the form are similar to those that appear at the bottom of a table.

Figure 1.3b displays a query that lists the books for a particular publisher (Prentice Hall in this example). A ***query*** provides information based on the data within an underlying table. The Books table, for example, contains records for many publishers, but the query in Figure 1.3b shows only the books that were published by a specific publisher. The results of the query are similar in appearance to the underlying table, except that the query contains selected records and/or selected fields for those records. The query may also list the records in a different sequence from that of the table. (A query can also be used to add new records and/or modify existing records.)

Figure 1.3c displays a ***report*** that contains the same information as the query in Figure 1.3b. The report, however, provides the information in a more attractive format than the query. Note, too, that a report can be based on either a table or a query. Thus, you could have based the report on the Books table, rather than the query, in which case the report would list every book in the table, as opposed to a limited subset of the records within the table.

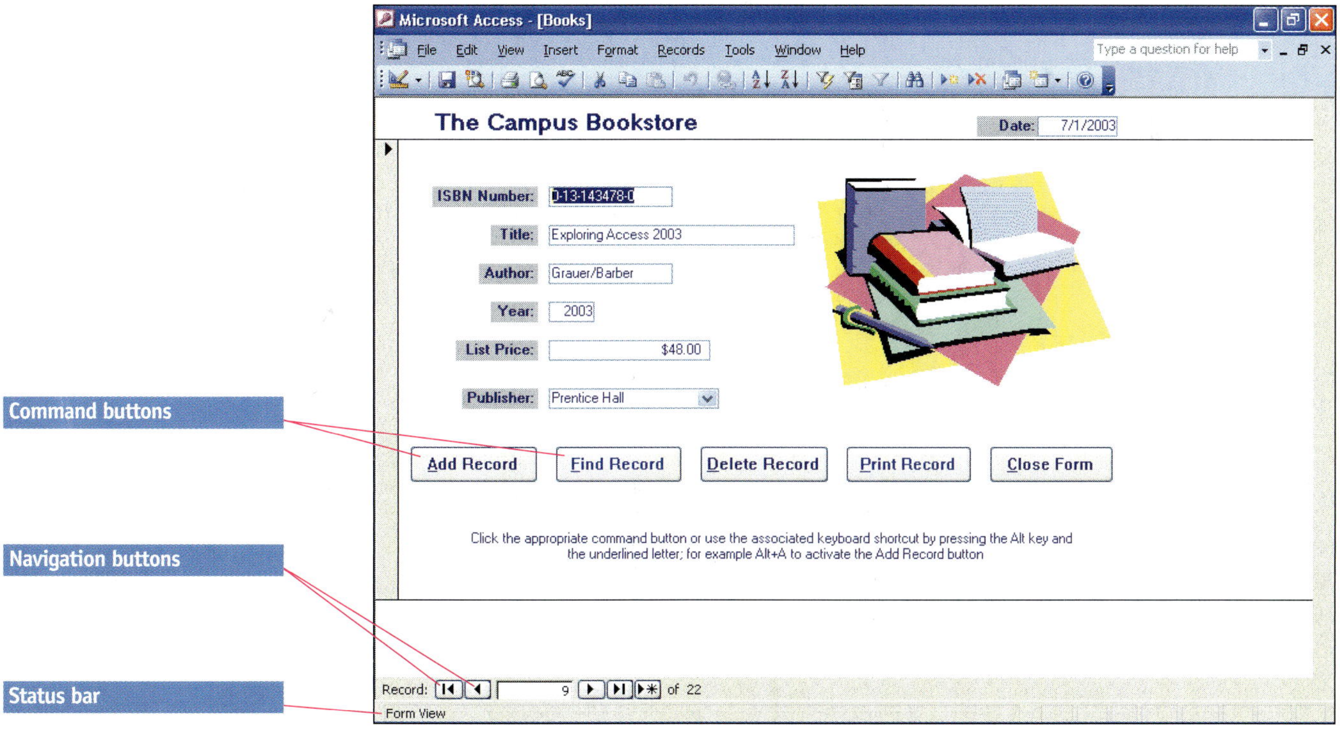

(a) Form

FIGURE 1.3 Forms, Queries, and Reports

Only books published by Prentice Hall are displayed

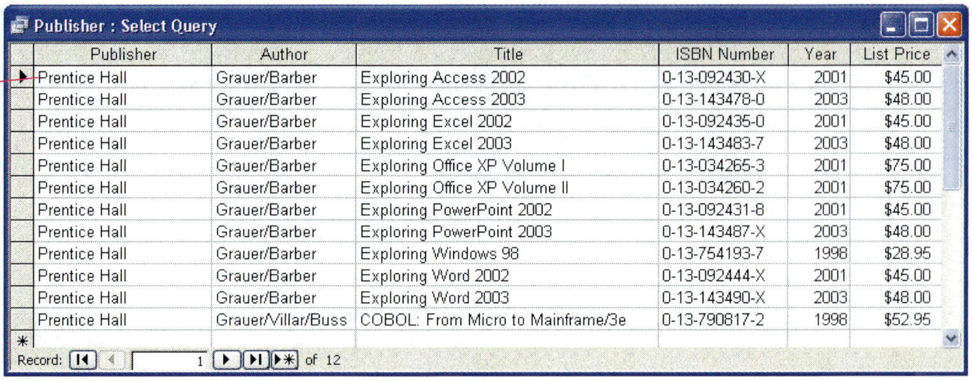

Publisher	Author	Title	ISBN Number	Year	List Price
Prentice Hall	Grauer/Barber	Exploring Access 2002	0-13-092430-X	2001	$45.00
Prentice Hall	Grauer/Barber	Exploring Access 2003	0-13-143478-0	2003	$48.00
Prentice Hall	Grauer/Barber	Exploring Excel 2002	0-13-092435-0	2001	$45.00
Prentice Hall	Grauer/Barber	Exploring Excel 2003	0-13-143483-7	2003	$48.00
Prentice Hall	Grauer/Barber	Exploring Office XP Volume I	0-13-034265-3	2001	$75.00
Prentice Hall	Grauer/Barber	Exploring Office XP Volume II	0-13-034260-2	2001	$75.00
Prentice Hall	Grauer/Barber	Exploring PowerPoint 2002	0-13-092431-8	2001	$45.00
Prentice Hall	Grauer/Barber	Exploring PowerPoint 2003	0-13-143487-X	2003	$48.00
Prentice Hall	Grauer/Barber	Exploring Windows 98	0-13-754193-7	1998	$28.95
Prentice Hall	Grauer/Barber	Exploring Word 2002	0-13-092444-X	2001	$45.00
Prentice Hall	Grauer/Barber	Exploring Word 2003	0-13-143490-X	2003	$48.00
Prentice Hall	Grauer/Villar/Buss	COBOL: From Micro to Mainframe/3e	0-13-790817-2	1998	$52.95

(b) Query

Report is based on query shown in Figure 1.3b

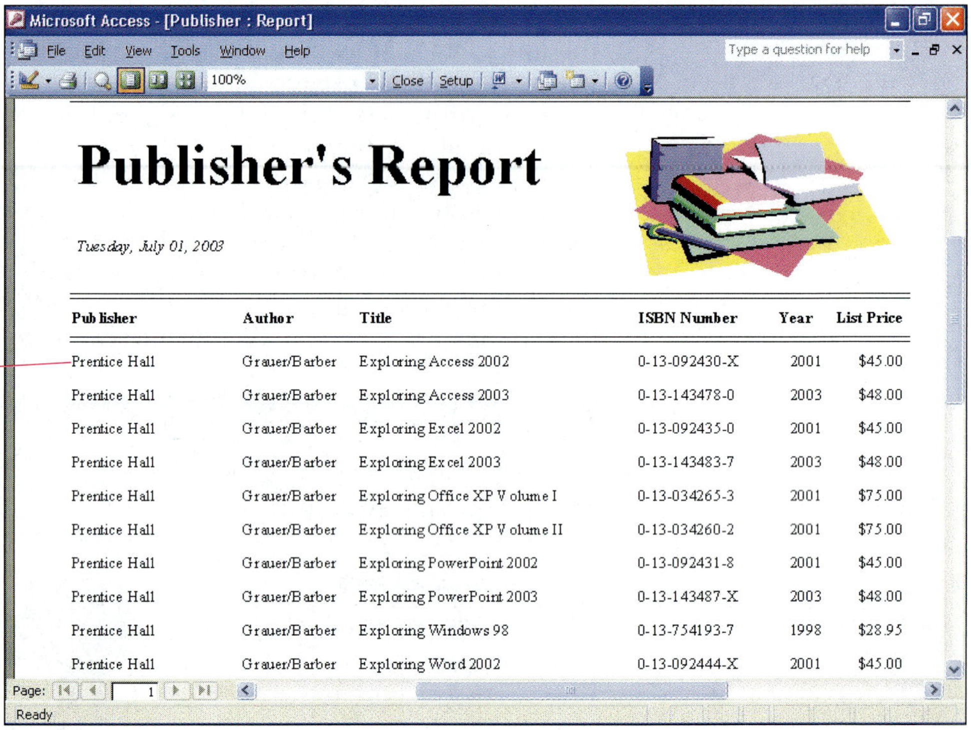

Publisher	Author	Title	ISBN Number	Year	List Price
Prentice Hall	Grauer/Barber	Exploring Access 2002	0-13-092430-X	2001	$45.00
Prentice Hall	Grauer/Barber	Exploring Access 2003	0-13-143478-0	2003	$48.00
Prentice Hall	Grauer/Barber	Exploring Excel 2002	0-13-092435-0	2001	$45.00
Prentice Hall	Grauer/Barber	Exploring Excel 2003	0-13-143483-7	2003	$48.00
Prentice Hall	Grauer/Barber	Exploring Office XP Volume I	0-13-034265-3	2001	$75.00
Prentice Hall	Grauer/Barber	Exploring Office XP Volume II	0-13-034260-2	2001	$75.00
Prentice Hall	Grauer/Barber	Exploring PowerPoint 2002	0-13-092431-8	2001	$45.00
Prentice Hall	Grauer/Barber	Exploring PowerPoint 2003	0-13-143487-X	2003	$48.00
Prentice Hall	Grauer/Barber	Exploring Windows 98	0-13-754193-7	1998	$28.95
Prentice Hall	Grauer/Barber	Exploring Word 2002	0-13-092444-X	2001	$45.00

(c) Report

FIGURE 1.3 Forms, Queries, and Reports (*continued*)

ONE FILE HOLDS EVERYTHING

All of the objects in an Access database are stored in a single file. The database can be opened from within Windows Explorer by double clicking the file name. It can also be opened from within Access through the Open command in the File menu or by clicking the Open button on the Database toolbar. The individual objects within a database are opened from the Database window.

hands-on exercise

1 Introduction to Access

Objective To open an existing Access database; to add, edit, and delete records within a table in that database; to open forms, queries, and reports within an existing database. Use Figure 1.4 as a guide in the exercise.

Step 1: Log on to Windows XP

- Turn on the computer and all of its peripherals. The floppy drive should be empty prior to starting your machine.
- Your system will take a minute or so to get started, after which you should see the desktop in Figure 1.4a. Do not be concerned if the appearance of your desktop is different from ours.
- Click the icon for the user account you want to access. You may be prompted for a password, depending on the security options in effect.
- You should be familiar with basic file management and be able to copy files from one folder to another. If not, you may want to review this material in the "Getting Started with Microsoft Windows" section in the text.

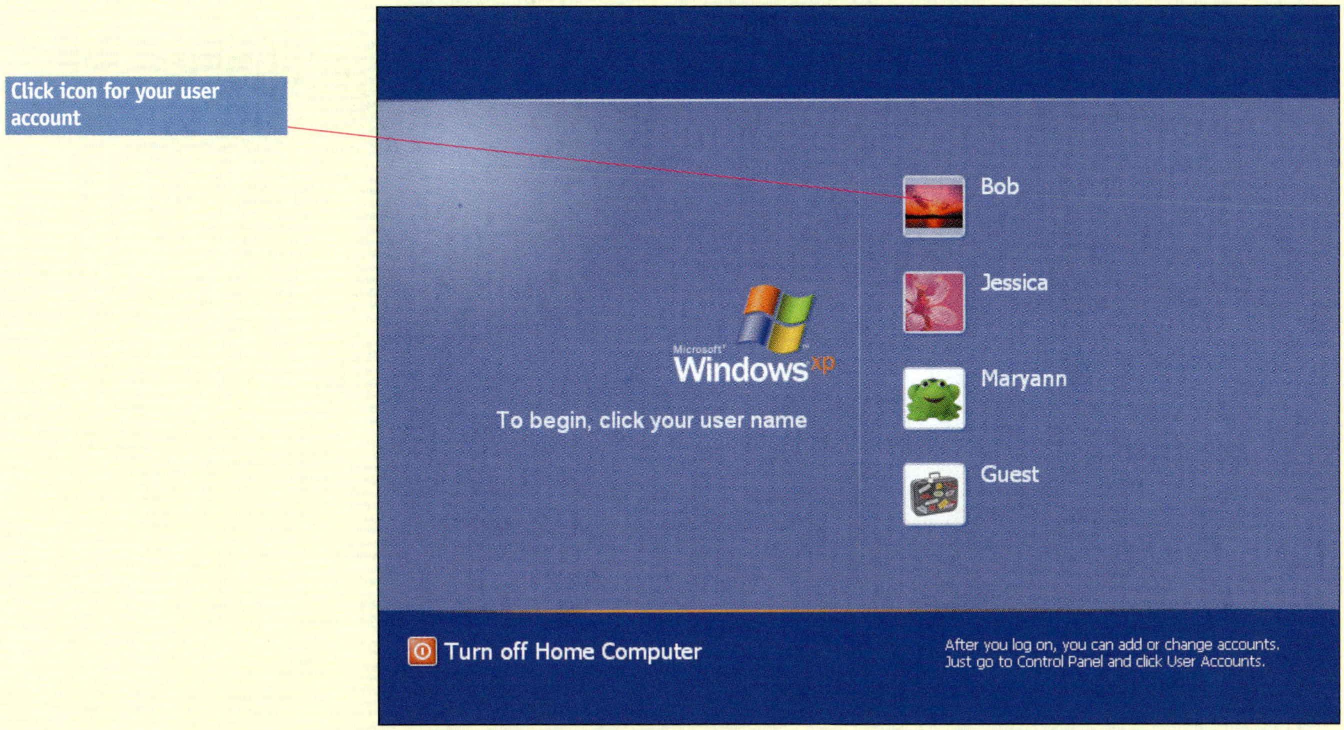

(a) Log onto Windows XP (step 1)

FIGURE 1.4 Hands-on Exercise 1

USER ACCOUNTS

The available user names are created automatically during the installation of Windows XP, but you can add or delete users at any time. Click the Start button, click Control Panel, switch to the Category view, and select User Accounts. Choose the desired task, such as creating a new account or changing an existing account. Do not expect, however, to be able to modify accounts in a school setting.

Step 2: Obtain the Practice Files

- Start Internet Explorer, and go to **www.prenhall.com/grauer**. Click the book for **Office 2003**, which takes you to the Office 2003 home page. Click the **Student Downloads tab** (near the top of the window) to go to the Student Download page as shown in Figure 1.4b.
- Select the appropriate file to download.
  - Choose **Exploring Access** (or **Access Volume I**) if you are using a stand-alone Access text, as opposed to an Office text with multiple applications.
  - Choose **Office 2003 Volume I** (for regular or **Enhanced Edition**), **Office 2003 Plus**, or **Office 2003 Brief** if you have an Office text.
- Click the link to download the file. You will see the File Download box asking what you want to do. Click the **Save button**. The Save As dialog box appears.
- Click the **down arrow** in the Save In list box and select the drive and folder where you want to save the file. Click **Save**.
- Start Windows Explorer, select the drive and folder where you saved the file, then double click the file to follow the onscreen instructions.

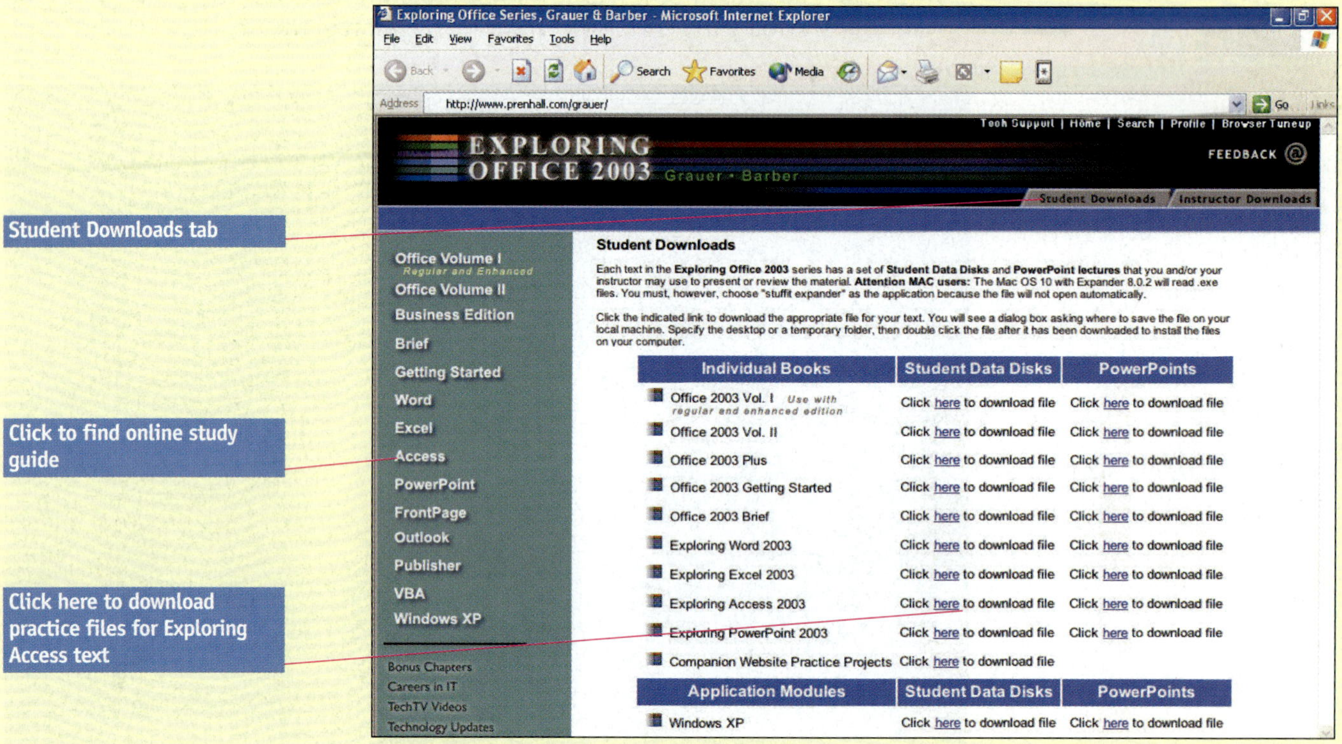

(b) Obtain the Practice Files (step 2)

FIGURE 1.4 Hands-on Exercise 1 (*continued*)

EXPLORE OUR WEB SITE

The Exploring Office Series Web site offers an online study guide (multiple-choice, true/false, and matching questions) for each individual textbook to help you review the material in each chapter. You can take practice quizzes by yourself and/or e-mail the results to your instructor. These online study guides are available via the tabs in the left navigation bar. You can return to the Student Download page at any time by clicking the tab toward the top of the window and/or you can click the link to Home to return to the home page for the Office 2003 series. And finally, you can click the Feedback button at the top of the screen to send a message directly to Bob Grauer.

Step 3: Start Microsoft Access

- Click the **Start button**, click the **All Programs button**, click **Microsoft Office**, then click **Microsoft Office Access 2003** to start the program.
- Pull down the **File menu** and click the **Open command** to display the Open dialog box in Figure 1.4c. (Do this even if the task pane is open.)
- Click the **down arrow** on the **Views button**, then click **Details** to change to the Details view.
- Click and drag the vertical border between columns to increase (or decrease) the size of a column.
- Click the **drop-down arrow** on the Look In list box. Click the appropriate drive (drive C is recommended rather than drive A) depending on the location of your data. Double click the **Exploring Access folder**.
- Click the down scroll arrow (if needed) to click the **Bookstore database**. Click the **Open command button** to open the database.
- Click the **Open button** within the Security Warning dialog box if you see a warning message saying that the database may contain code to harm your computer. (The message is caused by the programming statements that are behind the command buttons in the various forms within the database.)

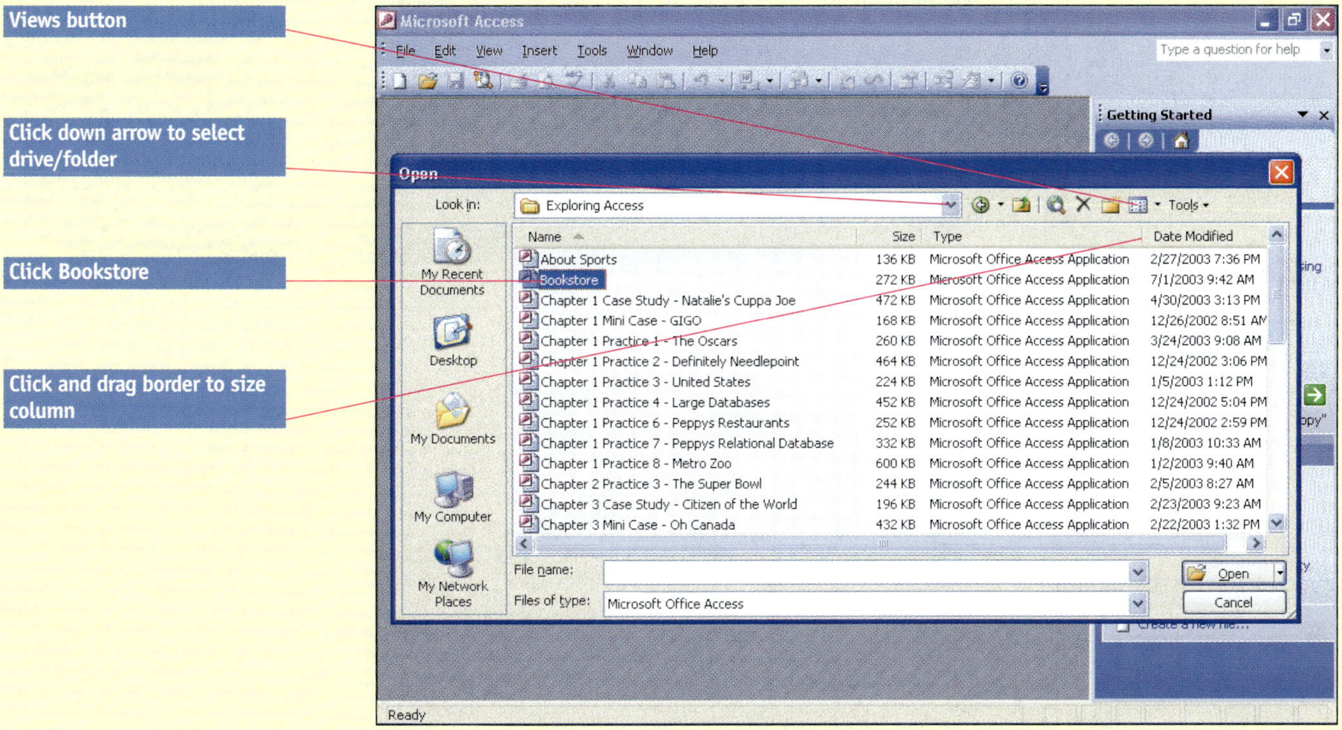

(c) Start Microsoft Access (step 3)

FIGURE 1.4 Hands-on Exercise 1 (*continued*)

FILE FORMATS

Access 2002 (Office XP) introduced a new file format that was continued in Access 2003. Access 2000, however, cannot read the new format, and thus, it is convenient to save files in the Access 2000 format to maintain compatibility with anyone using Microsoft Office 2000. Pull down the Tools menu, click Options, click the Advanced tab, and change the Default File Format to Access 2000.

Step 4: Open the Books Table

- If necessary, click the **Maximize button** in the application window so that Access takes the entire desktop.
- You should see the database window for the Bookstore database. Click the **Tables button**. Double click the icon next to Books to open the table as shown in Figure 1.4d.
- Click the **Maximize button** so that the Books table fills the Access window and reduces the clutter on the screen.
- Practice with the navigation buttons above the status bar to move from one record to the next. Click ▶ or ◀ to move forward to the next record or return to the previous record.
- Click |◀ to move to the first record in the table or ▶| to move to the last record in the table.
- Click in any field of the first record. The status indicator at the bottom of the Books table indicates record 1 of 22. The triangle symbol in the record selector column indicates that the record has not changed since it was last saved.

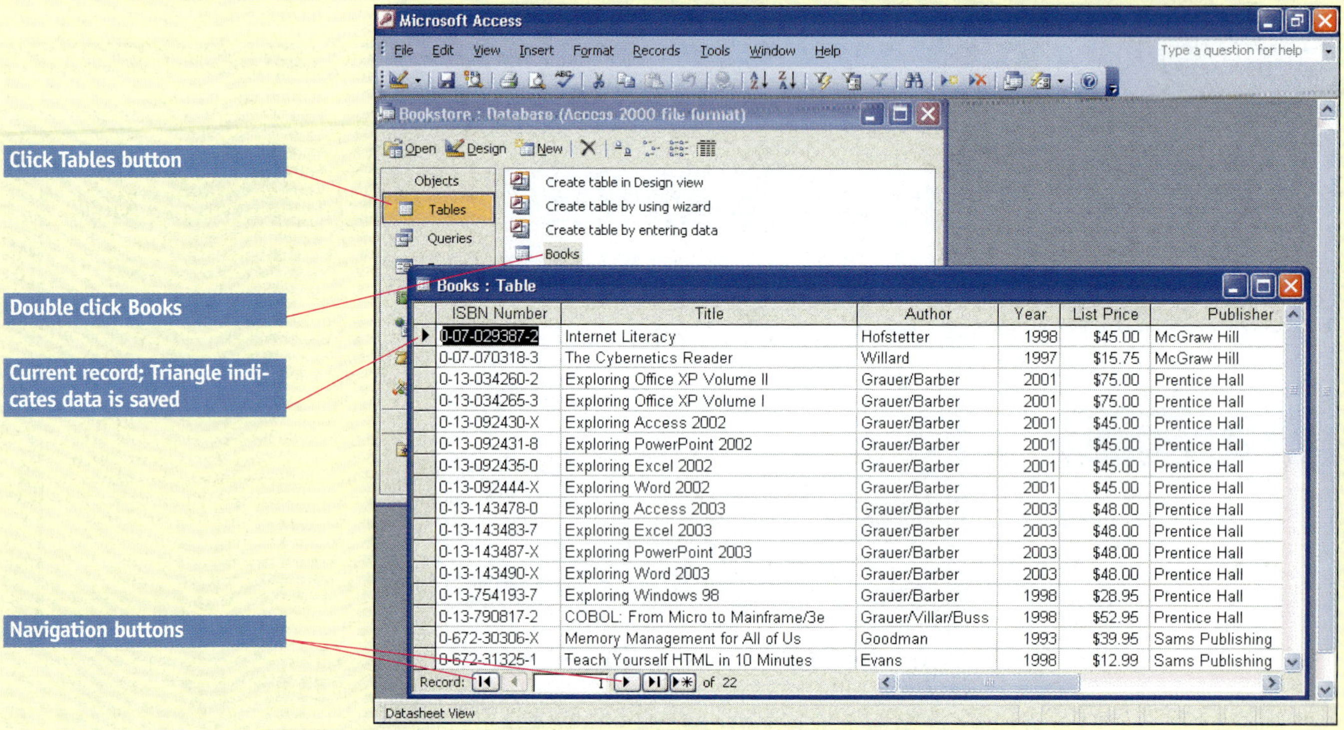

(d) Open the Books Table (step 4)

FIGURE 1.4 Hands-on Exercise 1 (*continued*)

MOVING FROM FIELD TO FIELD

Press the Tab key, the right arrow key, or the Enter key to move to the next field in the current record (or the first field in the next record if you are already in the last field of the current record). Press Shift+Tab or the left arrow key to return to the previous field in the current record (or the last field in the previous record if you are already in the first field of the current record). Press Home or End to move to the first or last field, respectively.

Step 5: Add a New Record

- Pull down the **Insert menu** and click **New Record** (or click the **New Record button** on the Table Datasheet toolbar). The record selector moves to the last record (record 23). The insertion point is positioned in the first field (ISBN Number).
- Enter data for the new book (Exploring Microsoft Office 2003 Volume I) as shown in Figure 1.4e. The record selector changes to a pencil as soon as you enter the first character in the new record.
- Press **Enter** when you have entered the last field for the record. The record has been saved to the database, and the record selector changes to a triangle.
- Add another record. Enter **0-13-143442-X** as the ISBN. The title is **Exploring Microsoft Office 2003 Volume II** by **Grauer/Barber**. The price is **$79.00**. The book was published by **Prentice Hall** in **2003**. Be sure to press **Enter** when you have completed the data entry.
- There are now 24 records in the table.

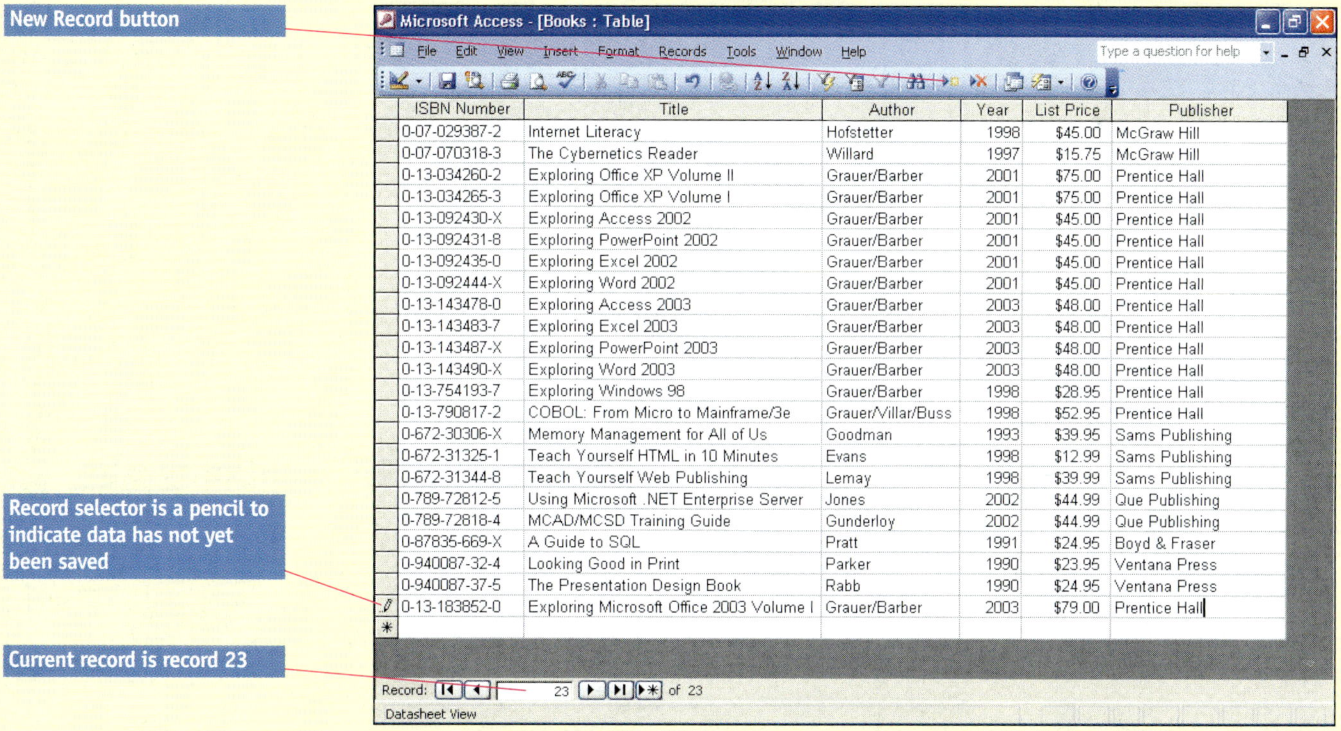

ISBN Number	Title	Author	Year	List Price	Publisher
0-07-029387-2	Internet Literacy	Hofstetter	1998	$45.00	McGraw Hill
0-07-070318-3	The Cybernetics Reader	Willard	1997	$15.75	McGraw Hill
0-13-034260-2	Exploring Office XP Volume II	Grauer/Barber	2001	$75.00	Prentice Hall
0-13-034265-3	Exploring Office XP Volume I	Grauer/Barber	2001	$75.00	Prentice Hall
0-13-092430-X	Exploring Access 2002	Grauer/Barber	2001	$45.00	Prentice Hall
0-13-092431-8	Exploring PowerPoint 2002	Grauer/Barber	2001	$45.00	Prentice Hall
0-13-092435-0	Exploring Excel 2002	Grauer/Barber	2001	$45.00	Prentice Hall
0-13-092444-X	Exploring Word 2002	Grauer/Barber	2001	$45.00	Prentice Hall
0-13-143478-0	Exploring Access 2003	Grauer/Barber	2003	$48.00	Prentice Hall
0-13-143483-7	Exploring Excel 2003	Grauer/Barber	2003	$48.00	Prentice Hall
0-13-143487-X	Exploring PowerPoint 2003	Grauer/Barber	2003	$48.00	Prentice Hall
0-13-143490-X	Exploring Word 2003	Grauer/Barber	2003	$48.00	Prentice Hall
0-13-754193-7	Exploring Windows 98	Grauer/Barber	1998	$28.95	Prentice Hall
0-13-790817-2	COBOL: From Micro to Mainframe/3e	Grauer/Villar/Buss	1998	$52.95	Prentice Hall
0-672-30306-X	Memory Management for All of Us	Goodman	1993	$39.95	Sams Publishing
0-672-31325-1	Teach Yourself HTML in 10 Minutes	Evans	1998	$12.99	Sams Publishing
0-672-31344-8	Teach Yourself Web Publishing	Lemay	1998	$39.99	Sams Publishing
0-789-72812-5	Using Microsoft .NET Enterprise Server	Jones	2002	$44.99	Que Publishing
0-789-72818-4	MCAD/MCSD Training Guide	Gunderloy	2002	$44.99	Que Publishing
0-87835-669-X	A Guide to SQL	Pratt	1991	$24.95	Boyd & Fraser
0-940087-32-4	Looking Good in Print	Parker	1990	$23.95	Ventana Press
0-940087-37-5	The Presentation Design Book	Rabb	1990	$24.95	Ventana Press
0-13-183852-0	Exploring Microsoft Office 2003 Volume I	Grauer/Barber	2003	$79.00	Prentice Hall

(e) Add a New Record (step 5)

FIGURE 1.4 Hands-on Exercise 1 (*continued*)

CREATE YOUR OWN SHORTHAND

Use the AutoCorrect feature that is common to all Office applications to expand abbreviations such as "PH" for Prentice Hall. Pull down the Tools menu, click AutoCorrect Options, type the abbreviation in the Replace text box and the expanded entry in the With text box. Click the Add command button, then click OK to exit the dialog box and return to the document. The next time you type PH (in uppercase) as you enter a record, it will be automatically expanded to Prentice Hall. (This feature may not work in a laboratory setting.)

Step 6: Edit a Record

- Click in the **Title field** for the first record, pull down the **Edit menu**, and click **Find** (or click the **Find button** on the toolbar) to display the dialog box in Figure 1.4f.
- Enter **COBOL** in the Find What text box. Check that the other parameters for the Find command match the dialog box in Figure 1.4f. Be sure that the **Title field** is selected in the Look In list box and **Any Part of Field** is selected in the Match text box.
- Click the **Find Next command button**. Access moves to record 14, the record containing the designated character string, and selects the matching word in the Title field for that record. Click **Cancel** to close the Find dialog box.
- Press the **Tab key** three times to move from the Title field to the Price field (or click directly in the price field). The current price ($52.95) is already selected.
- Type **$58.95**, then press the **down arrow** to move to the next record and save the data. (The changes are saved automatically; i.e., you do not have to click the Save button.)

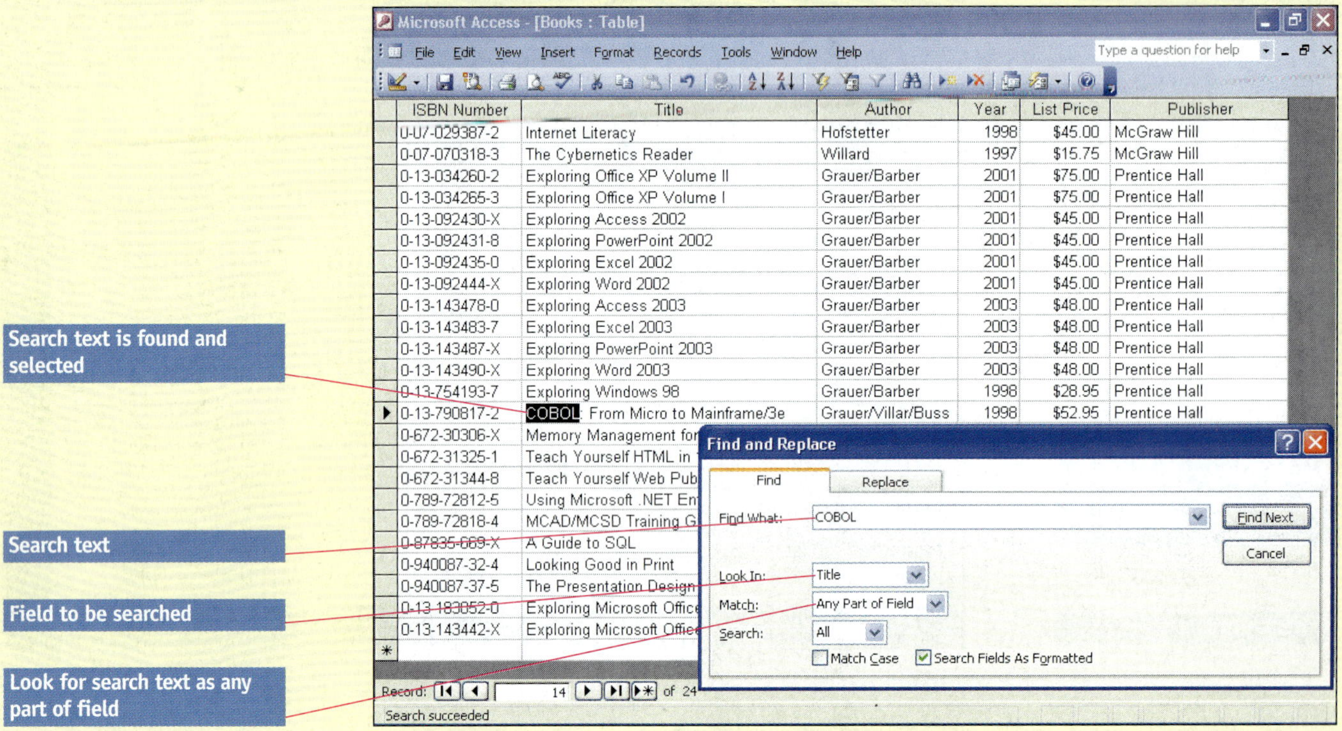

(f) Edit a Record (step 6)

FIGURE 1.4 Hands-on Exercise 1 (*continued*)

USE WHAT YOU KNOW

The Find command is contained in the Edit menu of every Office application, and it is an ideal way to search for specific records within a table. You have the option to search a single field or the entire record, to match all or part of the selected field(s), to move forward or back in a table, and to specify a case-sensitive search. The Replace command can be used to substitute one value for another. Be careful, however, about using the Replace All option for global replacement because unintended replacements are far too common.

Step 7: Delete a Record

- Use the Find command to search for the book **A Guide to SQL**. (You can click in the Title field, enter "SQL" in the Find What dialog box, then use the same search parameters as in the previous step.)
- The Find command should return the appropriate record, which is *not visible* in Figure 1.4g. (This is because we have deleted the record to display the dialog box in the figure.)
- Pull down the **Edit menu** and click the **Select Record command** to highlight the entire record. You can also click the **record selector column** (the box immediately to the left of the first field) to select the record without having to use a pull-down menu.
- Press the **Del key** (or click the **Delete Record button** on the toolbar) to delete the record. You will see the dialog box in Figure 1.4g indicating that you are about to delete a record and asking you to confirm the deletion. Click **Yes** to delete the record.
- Pull down the **Edit menu**. The Undo command is dim, indicating that you cannot undelete a record. Press **Esc** to continue working.

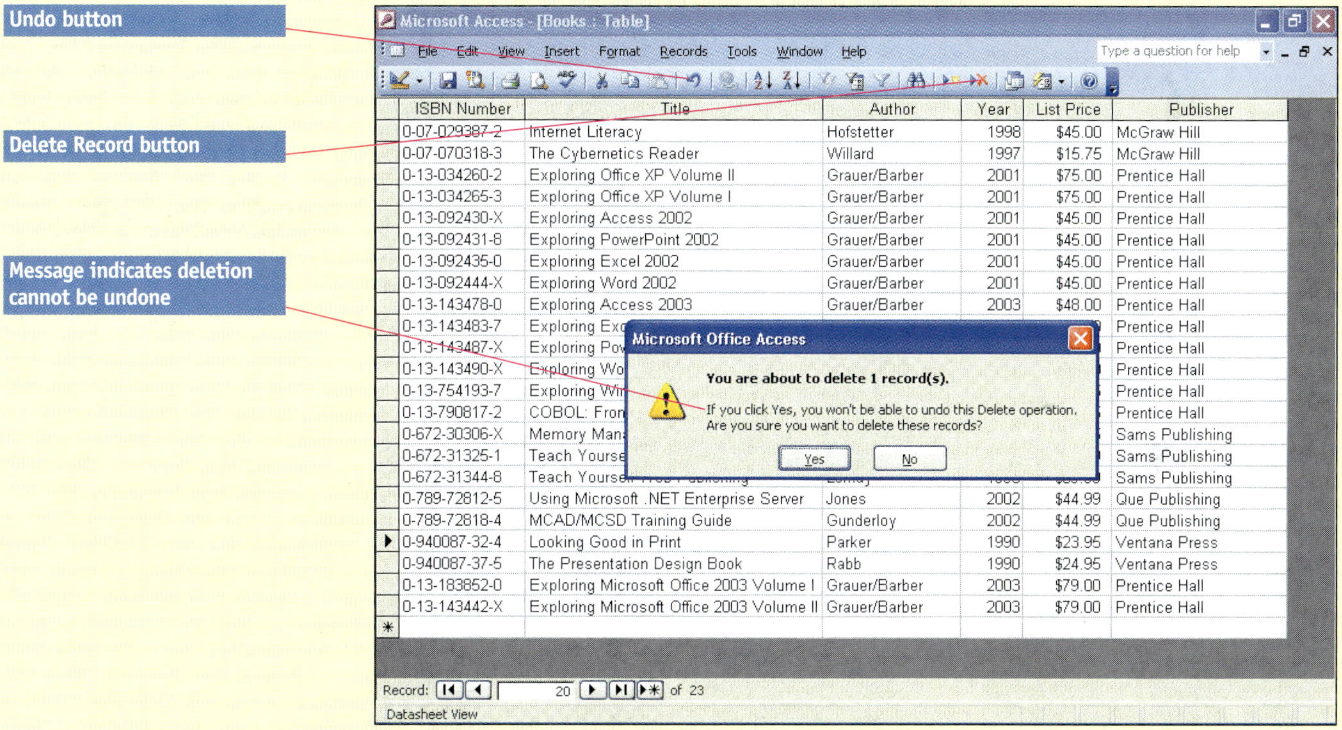

(g) Delete a Record (step 7)

FIGURE 1.4 Hands-on Exercise 1 (*continued*)

THE UNDO COMMAND

The Undo command is common to all Office applications, but it is implemented differently in Access. Word, Excel, and PowerPoint let you undo the last several operations. Access, however, because it saves changes automatically as soon as you move to the next record, lets you undo only the last command that was executed. Even this is limited, because once you delete a record, you cannot undo the deletion; that is, the record is permanently deleted.

Step 8: Print the Table

- Pull down the **File menu** and click the **Print Preview command** to see the table prior to printing. The status bar indicates that you are viewing page 1 (and further, the active scroll buttons indicate that there are additional pages).
- Click the **Setup button** on the Print Preview toolbar to display the Page Setup dialog box as shown in Figure 1.4h.
- Click the **Page tab**. Click the **Landscape option button**. Click **OK** to accept the settings and close the dialog box.
- The table should now fit on one page. (If it still does not fit on one page, click the Setup button on the Print Preview toolbar to display the Page Setup dialog box, click the **Margins tab**, and make the margins smaller.)
- Click the **Print button** to print the table. Alternatively, you can pull down the File menu, click **Print** to display the Print dialog box, click the **All options button**, then click **OK**.
- Click **Close** to close the Print Preview window. Close the table.

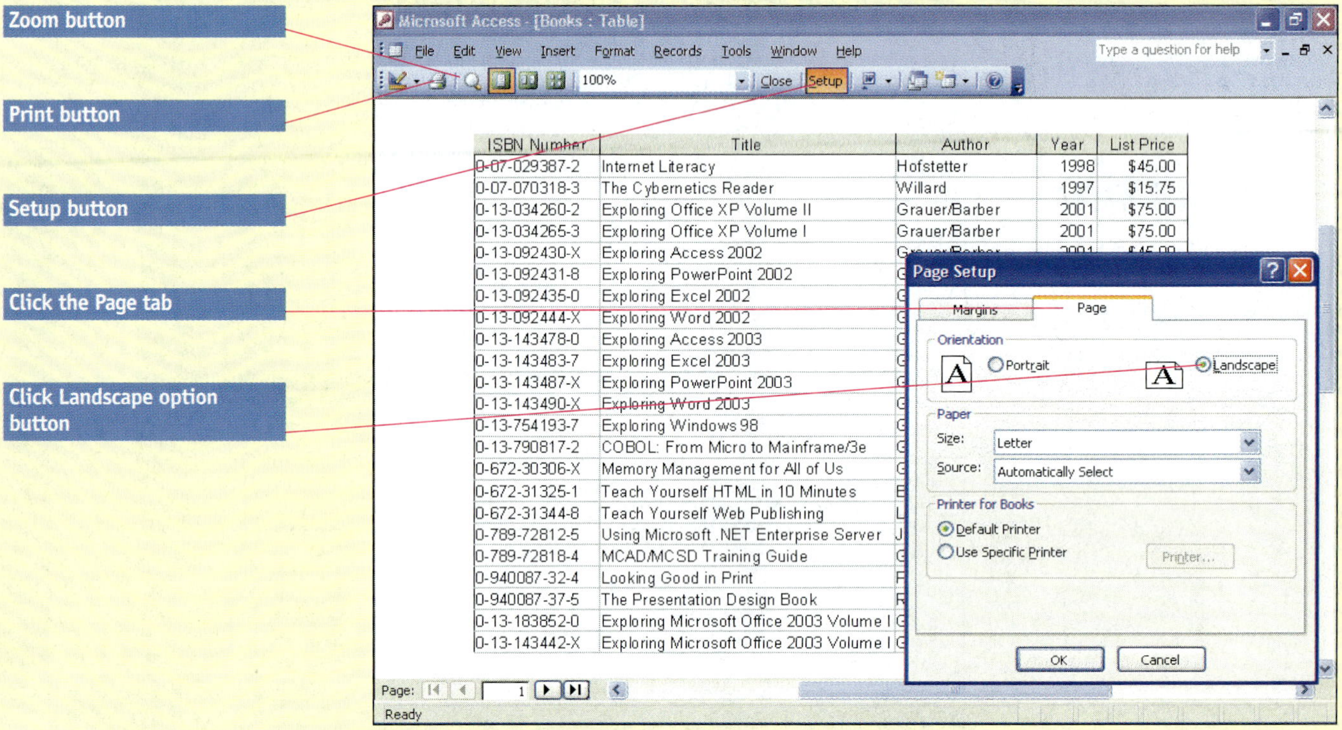

(h) Print the Table (step 8)

FIGURE 1.4 Hands-on Exercise 1 (*continued*)

THE PRINT PREVIEW TOOLBAR

The Print Preview toolbar is displayed automatically when you preview a report prior to printing. Click the Zoom button to toggle back and forth between fitting the entire page in the window and viewing the report at 100% magnification. Click the one, two, and multiple page buttons, to view different portions of the report in reports that extend over multiple pages. Use the Setup button to change the margins and/or orientation. Click the Close button to exit Print Preview.

Step 9: Open the Books Form

- Click the **Forms button** in the Database window. Double click the **Books form** to open the form, and if necessary, maximize the form so that it takes the entire window.
- Click the **Add Record command button**, or use the keyboard shortcut, **Alt+A**. (Each command button has a different underlined letter to indicate the keyboard shortcut.)
- Click in the text box for **ISBN number**, then use the **Tab key** to move from field to field as you enter data for the book as shown in Figure 1.4i.
- Enter text in the **Price field** to view the data validation that is built into Access. Click **OK** when you see the error message, then enter the indicated price. Click the **drop-down arrow** on the Publisher's list box to display the available publishers and to select the appropriate one. The use of a combo box ensures that you cannot misspell a publisher's name.
- Click the button to **Print Record** (or press **Alt+P**) to print the form for the record that you just added.
- Close the Books form to return to the Database window.

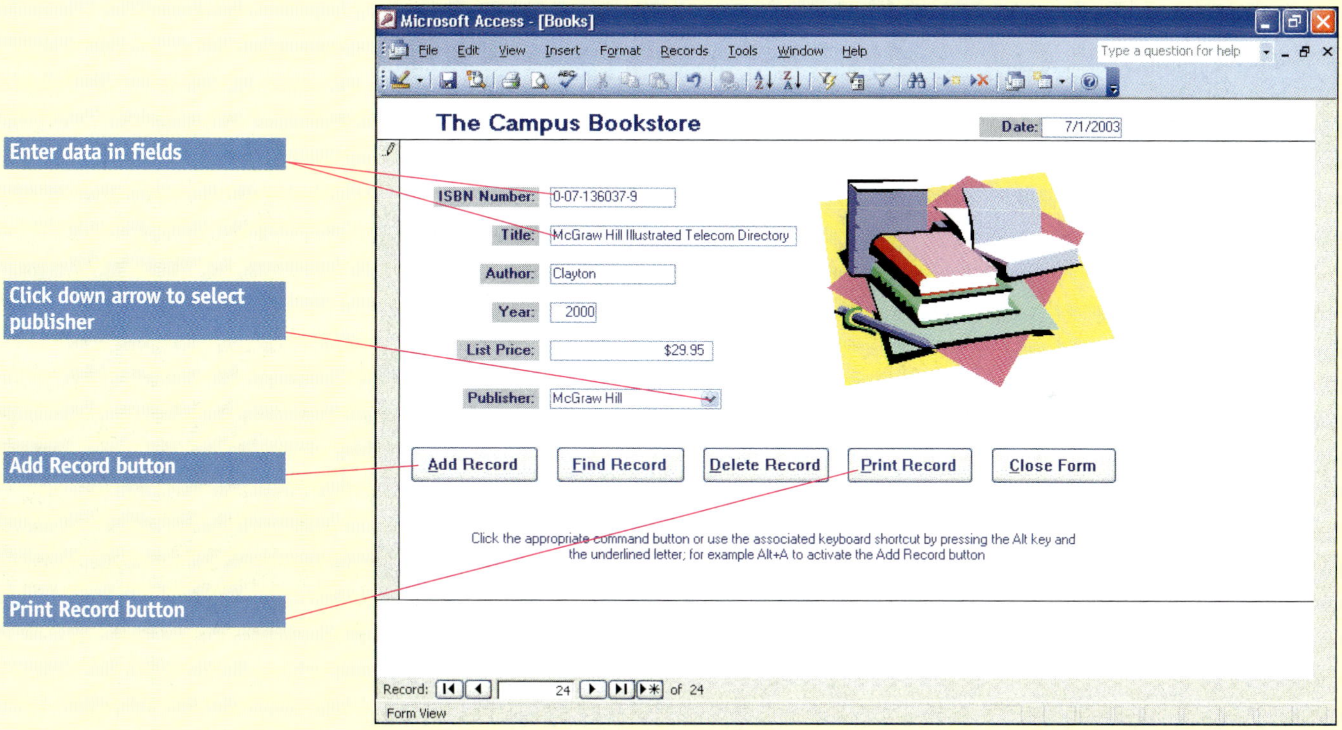

(i) Open the Books Form (step 9)

FIGURE 1.4 Hands-on Exercise 1 (*continued*)

DATA VALIDATION

No system, no matter how sophisticated, can produce valid output from invalid input. Thus, good systems are built to anticipate errors in data entry and to reject those errors prior to saving a record. Access will automatically prevent you from adding records with a duplicate primary key or entering invalid data into a numeric or date field. Other types of validation, such as requiring the author's name, are implemented by the database developer.

Step 10: Run a Query

- Click the **Queries button** in the Database window. Double click the **Publisher query** to run the query. You will see a dialog box asking you to enter the name of a publisher.
- Type **McGraw Hill** and press **Enter** to see the results of the query, which should contain three books by this publisher. (If you do not see any books, it is because you spelled the publisher incorrectly. Close the query to return to the Database window, then rerun the query.)
- You can use a query to display information, as was just done, and/or you can modify data in the underlying table. Click in the **Publisher field** for the blank record in the last row (the record selector is an asterisk). Type **McGraw Hill** to begin entering the data for a new record as shown in Figure 1.4j.
- You can enter data for any publisher within the query, but you must satisfy the requirements for data validation. See what happens if you omit the ISBN number or Author's name, or enter alphabetic data for the year or price. (The missing ISBN is **0-07-561585-1**.)
- Click the **Close button** to close the query and return to the Database window.

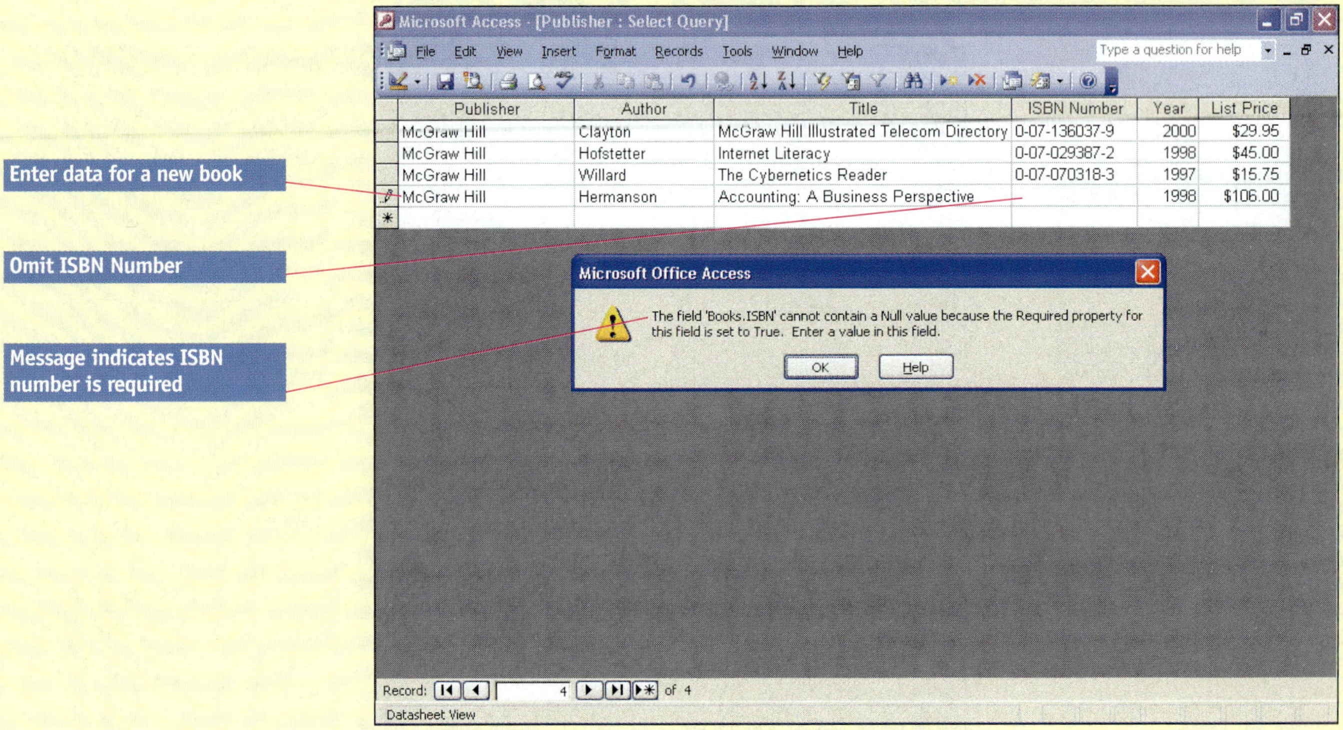

(j) Run a Query (step 10)

FIGURE 1.4 Hands-on Exercise 1 (*continued*)

FORMAT A DATASHEET

Format your tables and/or queries to make the results stand out. Click anywhere in a table or query (in Datasheet view), pull down the Format menu, and click the Datasheet command to display the Format Datasheet dialog box. You can change the style of the table to sunken or raised, change the color of the gridlines or suppress them altogether. The Format command also enables you to change the row height or column width and/or to hide columns. See practice exercise 4 at the end of the chapter.

Step 11: Open a Report

- Click the **Reports button** in the Database window to display the available reports. Double click the icon for the **Publisher report**. Type **McGraw Hill** in the Parameter dialog box. Press **Enter**.
- Click the **Maximize button** in the Report Window so that the report takes the entire screen as shown in Figure 1.4k.
- Click the **Zoom button** to toggle to 100% so that you can read the report, which should contain four records.
- Two books were in the original database. One book was entered through a form in step 9. The other book was entered through a query in step 10. All of the books in the report are published by McGraw Hill, which is consistent with the parameter you entered at the beginning of this step.
- Click the **Print button** on the Report toolbar. Click the **Close button** to close the Report window.

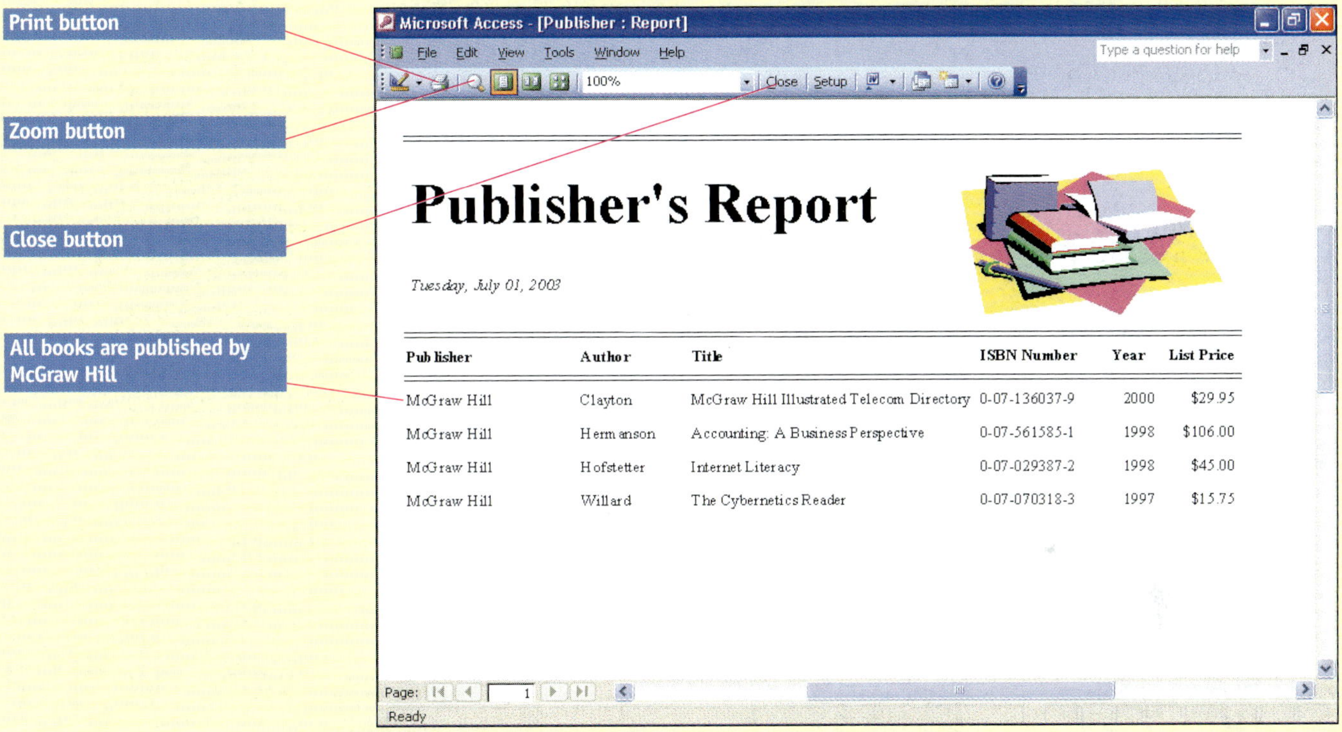

(k) Open a Report (step 11)

FIGURE 1.4 Hands-on Exercise 1 (*continued*)

TIP OF THE DAY

Pull down the Help menu, click the command to Show the Office Assistant, click the Office Assistant when it appears, then click the Options button to display the Office Assistant dialog box. Click the Options tab, check the box to Show the Tip of the Day at Startup, and then click OK. The next time you start Access, you will be greeted by the Assistant, who will offer you the tip of the day. (You can display a Tip of the Day for the other Office applications in similar fashion.)

Step 12: Help with Access

- There are several different ways to request help, but in any event, the best time to obtain help is when you don't need any. Try any of the following:
  - ❑ Pull down the **Help menu** and click the command to **Show the Office Assistant**. Click the **Assistant**, then enter the question, "**What is a table?**" in the Assistant's balloon and click **Search**, or
  - ❑ Type the question directly in the **Ask a Question list box** in the upper right of the Access window and press **Enter**, or
  - ❑ Pull down the **Help menu**, click **Microsoft Access Help** to display the task pane, enter the question in the **Search box**, and click the **Start Searching arrow**.
- Regardless of the technique you choose, Access will display a message indicating that it is searching Microsoft Office Online. (Help is not available locally, and this can be a problem with a slow Internet connection.)
- You should see a task pane with the results of the search as shown in Figure 1.4l. Click the link that is most appropriate (e.g., **About tables** in this example).
- A new window opens containing the detailed help information. Close the Help window. Close the task pane. Hide the Office Assistant.
- Exit Access if you do not want to continue with the next exercise at this time.

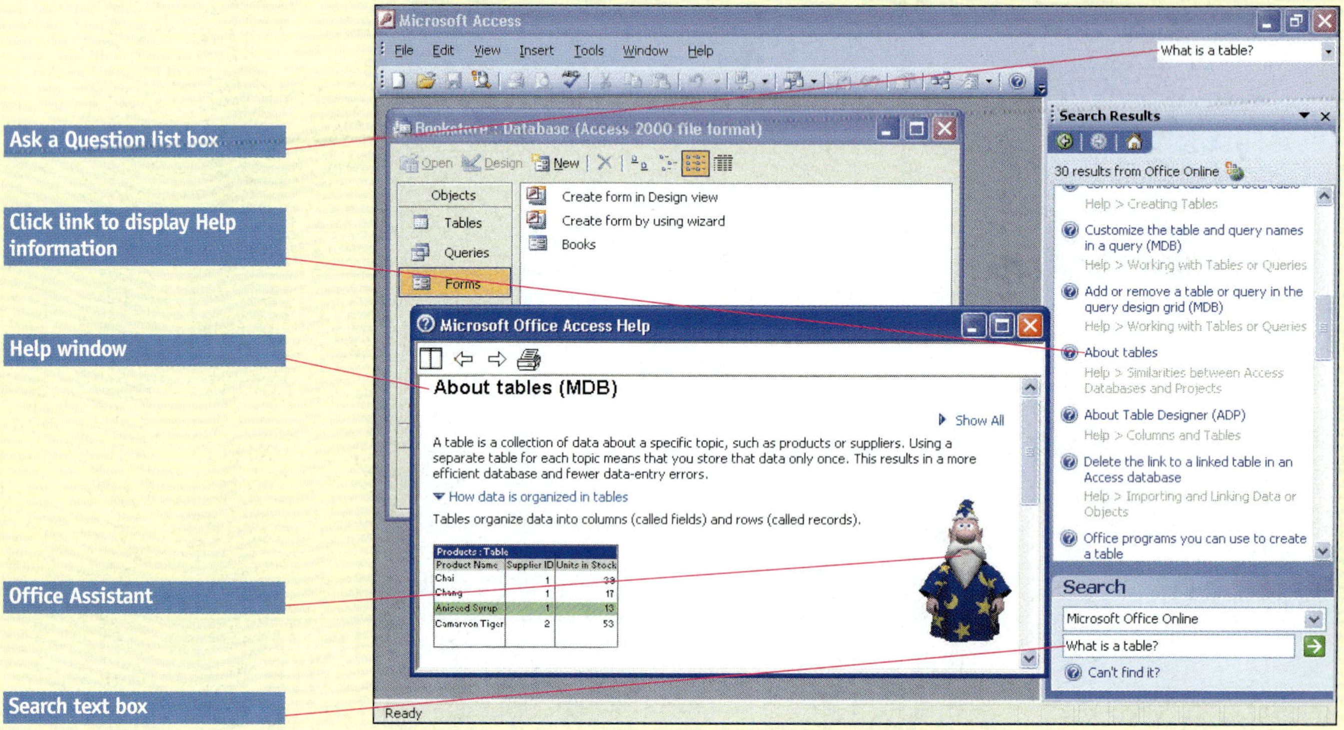

(l) Help with Access (step 12)

FIGURE 1.4 Hands-on Exercise 1 (*continued*)

CHOOSE YOUR OWN ASSISTANT

Pull down the Help menu, click the command to Show the Office Assistant, click the Office Assistant when it appears, then click the Options button to display the Office Assistant dialog box. Click the Gallery tab, then click the Next button repeatedly to cycle through the available characters. Click OK to accept the character of your choice. You're still in control, however. Pull down the Help menu and click the command to Hide the Office Assistant if it becomes annoying.

FILTERS AND SORTING

The exercise just completed described how to use an existing report to obtain information from the database. But what if you are in a hurry and don't have the time to create the report? There is a faster way. You can open the table in the Datasheet view, then apply a filter and/or a sort to the table to display selected records in any order. A ***filter*** displays a subset of records from the table according to specified criteria. A ***sort*** lists those records in a specific sequence, such as alphabetically by last name or by EmployeeID. We illustrate both of these concepts in conjunction with Figure 1.5.

Figure 1.5a displays an employee table with 14 records. Each record has 8 fields. The records in the table are displayed in sequence according to the EmployeeID, which is also the primary key (the field or combination of fields that uniquely identifies a record). The status bar indicates that there are 14 records in the table. What if, however, you wanted a partial list of those records, such as employees with a specific title?

Figure 1.5b displays a filtered view of the same table in which we see only the Account Reps. The status bar shows that this is a filtered list, and that there are 8 records that satisfy the criteria. (The employee table still contains the original 14 records, but only 8 records are visible with the filter in effect.) The table has also been sorted so that the selected employees are displayed in alphabetical order, as opposed to EmployeeID order.

Two operations are necessary to go from Figure 1.5a to Figure 1.5b—filtering and sorting, and they can be performed in either order. The easiest way to implement a filter is to click in any cell that contains the value of the desired criterion (such as any cell that contains "Account Rep" in the Title field), then click the ***Filter by Selection*** button on the Database toolbar. To sort the table, click in the field on which you want to sequence the records (the LastName field in this example), then click the ***Sort Ascending*** button on the Database toolbar. The ***Sort Descending*** button is appropriate for numeric fields such as salary, if you want to display the records with the highest value listed first.

The operations can be done in any order; that is, you can filter a table to show only selected records, then you can sort the filtered table to display the records in a different order. Conversely, you can sort a table and then apply a filter. It does not matter which operation is performed first, and indeed, you can go back and forth between the two. You can also filter the table further, by applying a second (or third) criterion; for example, click in a cell containing "Good," then click the Filter by Selection button a second time to display the Account Reps with good performance. You can also click the ***Remove Filter*** button at any time to display all of the records in the complete table.

Figure 1.5c illustrates an alternate and more powerful way to apply a filter known as ***Filter by Form***, in which you can select the criteria from a drop-down list, and/or apply multiple criteria simultaneously. However, the real advantage of the Filter by Form command extends beyond these conveniences to two additional capabilities. First, you can specify relationships within a criterion; for example, you can select employees with a salary greater than (or less than) $40,000. Filter by Selection, on the other hand, requires you to specify criteria equal to an existing value. Figure 1.5d displays the filtered table of Chicago employees earning more than $40,000.

A second advantage of the Filter by Form command is that you can specify alternative criteria (such as employees in Chicago *or* employees who are account reps) by clicking the Or tab. (The latter capability is not implemented in Figure 1.5.) Suffice it to say, however, that the availability of the various filter and sort commands enables you to obtain information from a database quickly and easily without having to create a query or report.

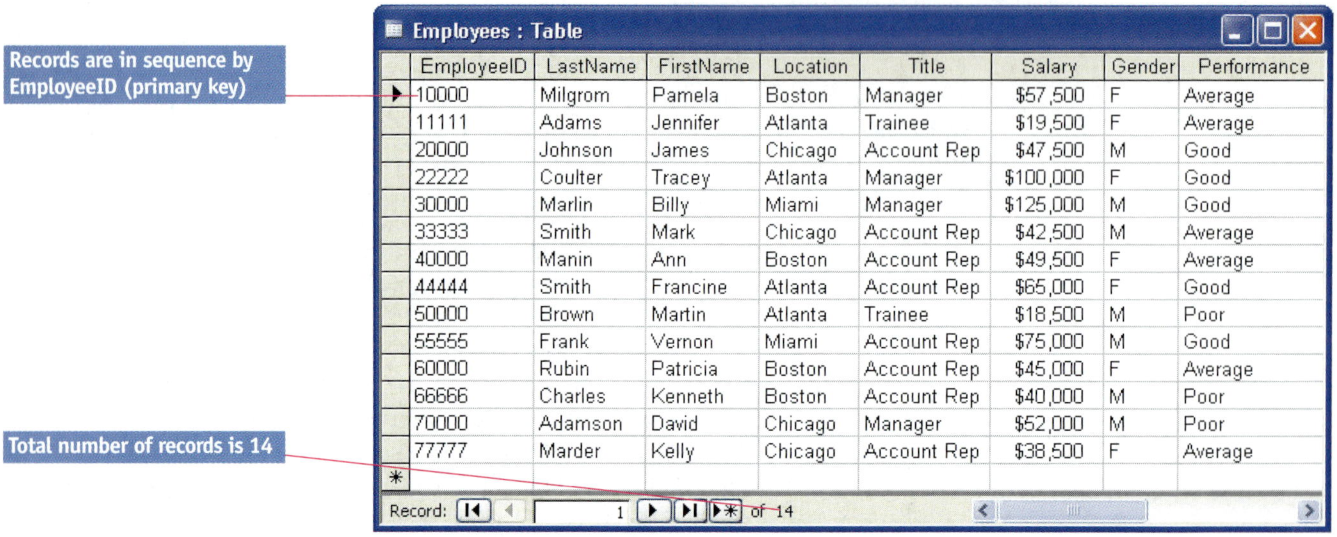

EmployeeID	LastName	FirstName	Location	Title	Salary	Gender	Performance
10000	Milgrom	Pamela	Boston	Manager	$57,500	F	Average
11111	Adams	Jennifer	Atlanta	Trainee	$19,500	F	Average
20000	Johnson	James	Chicago	Account Rep	$47,500	M	Good
22222	Coulter	Tracey	Atlanta	Manager	$100,000	F	Good
30000	Marlin	Billy	Miami	Manager	$125,000	M	Good
33333	Smith	Mark	Chicago	Account Rep	$42,500	M	Average
40000	Manin	Ann	Boston	Account Rep	$49,500	F	Average
44444	Smith	Francine	Atlanta	Account Rep	$65,000	F	Good
50000	Brown	Martin	Atlanta	Trainee	$18,500	M	Poor
55555	Frank	Vernon	Miami	Account Rep	$75,000	M	Good
60000	Rubin	Patricia	Boston	Account Rep	$45,000	F	Average
66666	Charles	Kenneth	Boston	Account Rep	$40,000	M	Poor
70000	Adamson	David	Chicago	Manager	$52,000	M	Poor
77777	Marder	Kelly	Chicago	Account Rep	$38,500	F	Average

(a) The Employees Table (by EmployeeID)

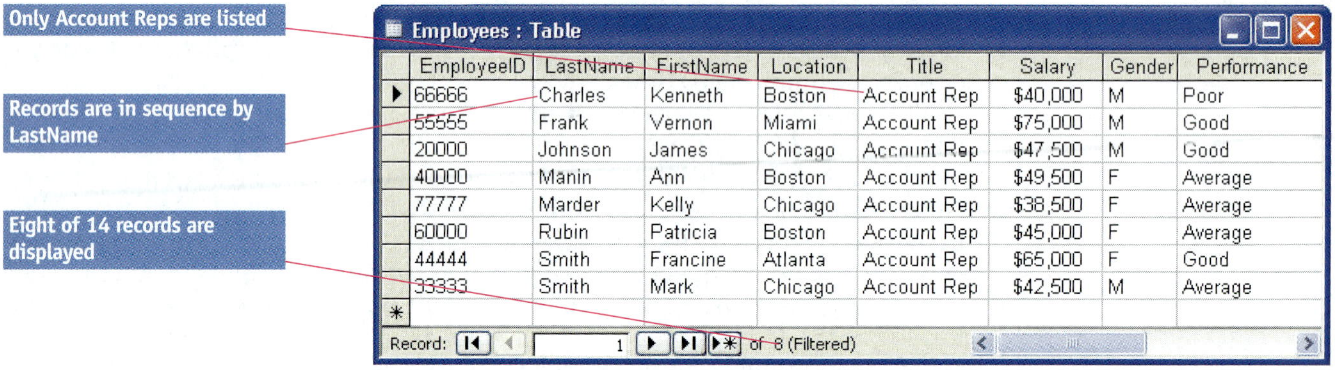

EmployeeID	LastName	FirstName	Location	Title	Salary	Gender	Performance
66666	Charles	Kenneth	Boston	Account Rep	$40,000	M	Poor
55555	Frank	Vernon	Miami	Account Rep	$75,000	M	Good
20000	Johnson	James	Chicago	Account Rep	$47,500	M	Good
40000	Manin	Ann	Boston	Account Rep	$49,500	F	Average
77777	Marder	Kelly	Chicago	Account Rep	$38,500	F	Average
60000	Rubin	Patricia	Boston	Account Rep	$45,000	F	Average
44444	Smith	Francine	Atlanta	Account Rep	$65,000	F	Good
33333	Smith	Mark	Chicago	Account Rep	$42,500	M	Average

(b) Filtered List (Account Rep by last name)

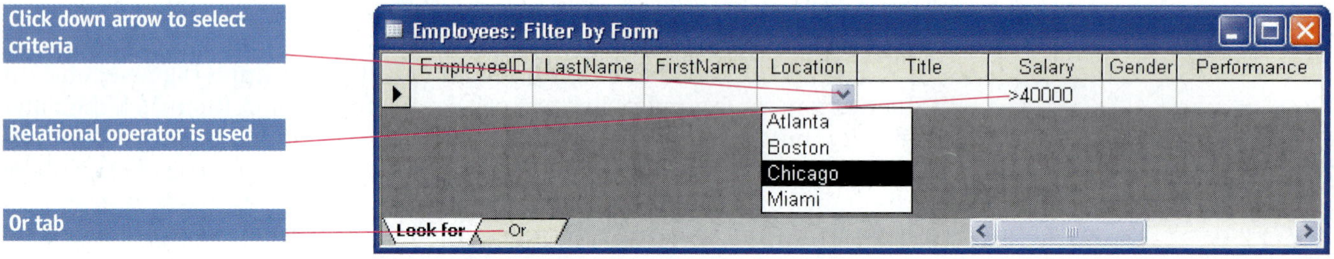

(c) Filter by Form

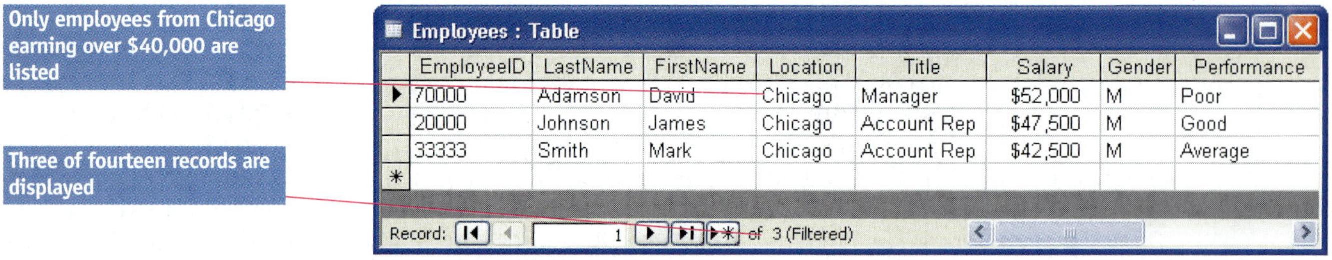

EmployeeID	LastName	FirstName	Location	Title	Salary	Gender	Performance
70000	Adamson	David	Chicago	Manager	$52,000	M	Poor
20000	Johnson	James	Chicago	Account Rep	$47,500	M	Good
33333	Smith	Mark	Chicago	Account Rep	$42,500	M	Average

(d) Filtered List (Chicago employees earning more than $40,000)

FIGURE 1.5 Filters and Sorting

hands-on exercise

2 Filters and Sorting

Objective To display selected records within a table by applying the Filter by Selection and Filter by Form criteria; to sort the records in a table. Use Figure 1.6 as a guide in the exercise.

Step 1: Open the Employees Table

- Start Access as you did in the previous exercise, but this time you will open a different database. Pull down the **File menu** and click the **Open command** to display the Open dialog box.
- Click the **down arrow** in the Look In box to select the drive (**drive C** is recommended rather than drive A) and folder (**Exploring Access**) that contains the **Employee database**.
- Click the **Open button** in the Open dialog box to open the database, then click the **Open button** within the Security Warning dialog box if you see a warning message.
- Click the **Forms button** in the Database window, then double click the **Employees form** to open the form as shown in Figure 1.6a. Click the **Maximize button** so that the Employee form fills the Access window.
- Click the **Add Record button**, then enter data for yourself, using **12345** as the EmployeeID, and your first and last name. You have been hired as an **Account Rep**. Your salary is **$40,000**, you will work in **Miami**, and your performance is **Good**.
- Click the **Print Record button** to print the record containing your data. Click the **Close Form button** to return to the Database window.

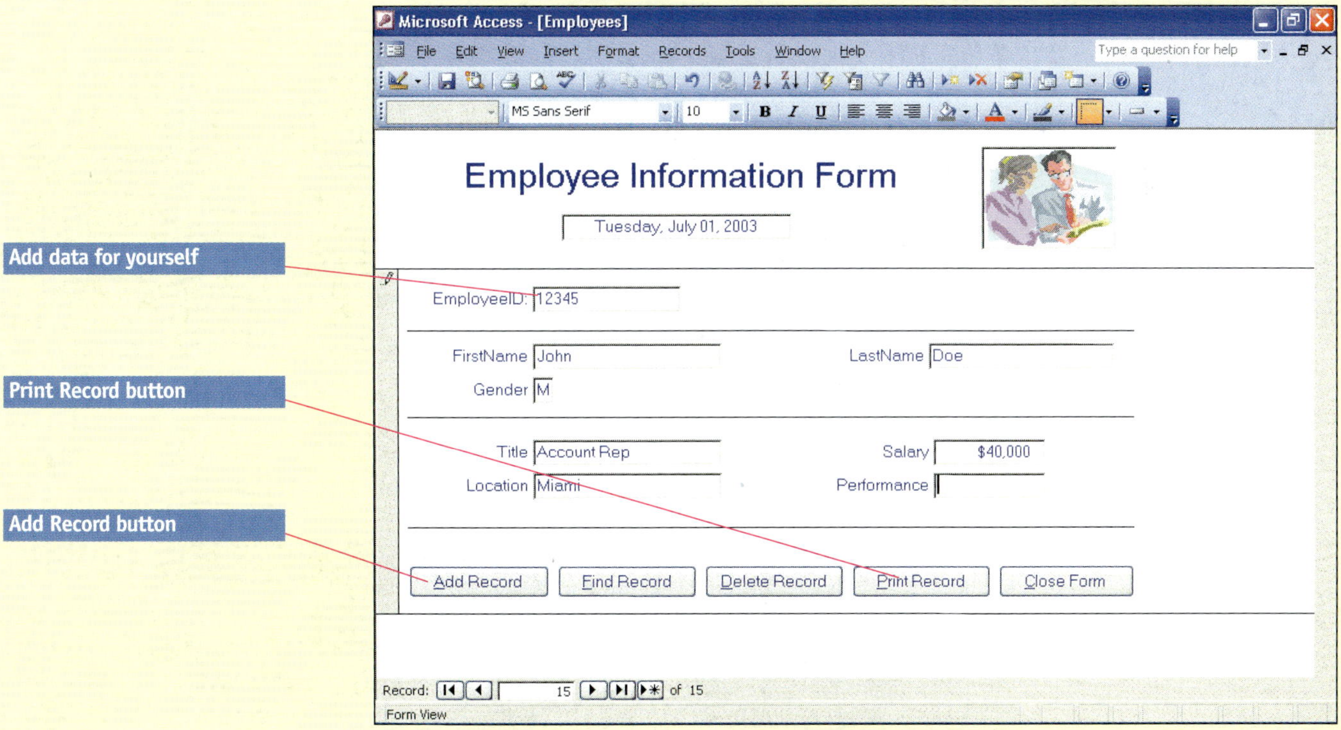

(a) Open the Employees Table (step 1)

FIGURE 1.6 Hands-on Exercise 2

Step 2: Filter by Selection

- Click the **Tables button** in the Database window. Double click the **Employees table** to open the table, which should contain 15 records, including the record you added for yourself.
- Click in the Title field of any record that contains the title **Account Rep**, then click the **Filter by Selection button**.
- You should see 9 employees, all of whom are Account Reps, as shown in Figure 1.6b. The status bar indicates that there are 9 records (as opposed to 15) and that there is a filter condition in effect.
- Click in the performance field of any employee with a Good performance (we clicked in the Performance field of the first record), then click the **Filter by Selection button** a second time.
- This time you see 4 employees, each of whom is an Account Rep with a performance evaluation of Good. The status bar indicates that 4 records satisfy this filter condition.
- Click the **Print button** to print the filtered table.

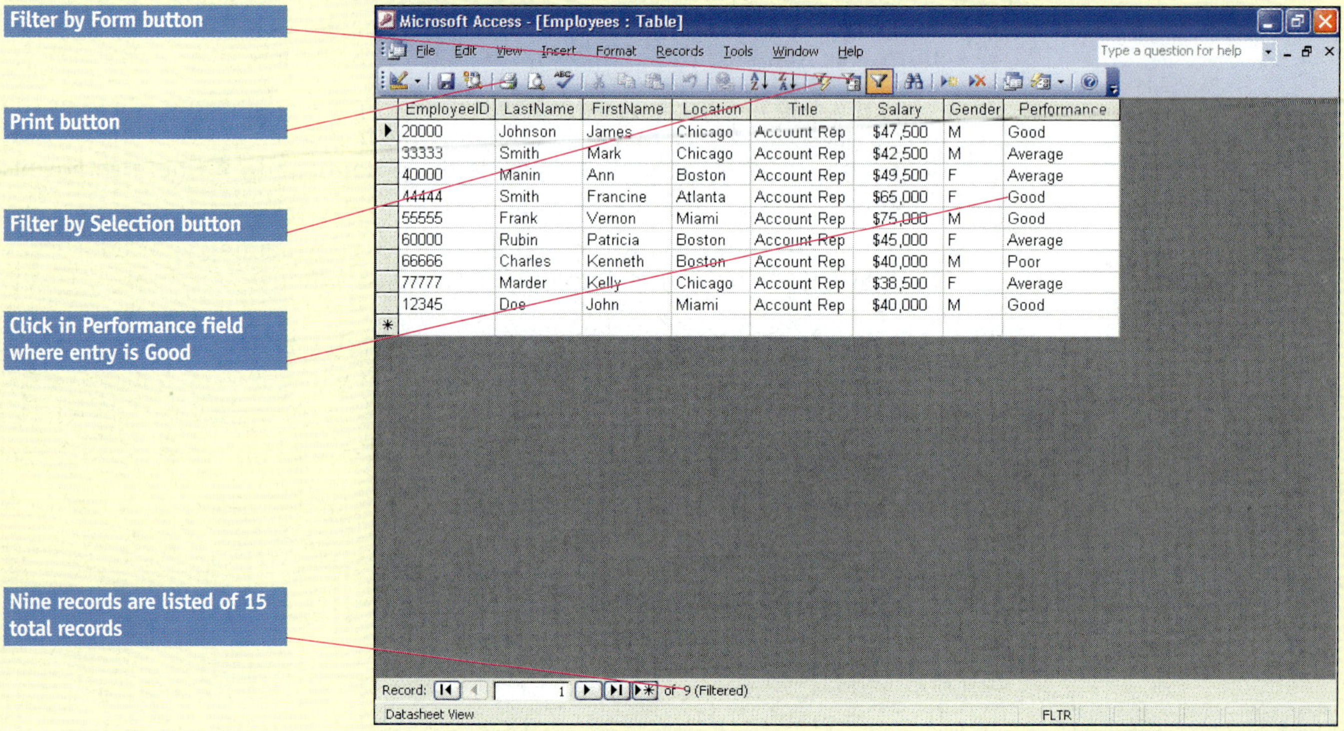

EmployeeID	LastName	FirstName	Location	Title	Salary	Gender	Performance
20000	Johnson	James	Chicago	Account Rep	$47,500	M	Good
33333	Smith	Mark	Chicago	Account Rep	$42,500	M	Average
40000	Manin	Ann	Boston	Account Rep	$49,500	F	Average
44444	Smith	Francine	Atlanta	Account Rep	$65,000	F	Good
55555	Frank	Vernon	Miami	Account Rep	$75,000	M	Good
60000	Rubin	Patricia	Boston	Account Rep	$45,000	F	Average
66666	Charles	Kenneth	Boston	Account Rep	$40,000	M	Poor
77777	Marder	Kelly	Chicago	Account Rep	$38,500	F	Average
12345	Doe	John	Miami	Account Rep	$40,000	M	Good

(b) Filter by Selection (step 2)

FIGURE 1.6 Hands-on Exercise 2 (*continued*)

FILTER EXCLUDING SELECTION

The Filter by Selection button on the Database toolbar selects all records that meet the designated criterion. The Filter Excluding Selection command does just the opposite and displays all records that do not satisfy the criterion. First, click the Remove Filter button to remove any filters that are in effect, then click in the appropriate field of any record that contains the value you want to exclude. Pull down the Records menu, click (or point to) the Filter command, then click the Filter Excluding Selection command to display the records that do not meet the criterion.

Step 3: Filter by Form

- Click the **Filter by Form button** to display the form in Figure 1.6c, where you can enter or remove criteria in any sequence. Each time you click in a field, a drop-down list appears that displays all of the values for the field that occur within the table.
- Click in the columns for **Title** and **Performance** to remove the criteria that were entered in the previous step. Select the existing entries individually and press the **Del key** as each entry is selected.
- Click in the cell underneath the **Salary field** and type **>30000** (as opposed to selecting a specific value). Click in the cell underneath the **Location Field**, click the **down arrow**, and select **Chicago**.
- Click the **Apply Filter button** to display the records that satisfy these criteria. (You should see 4 records.)
- Click the **Print button** to print the table.

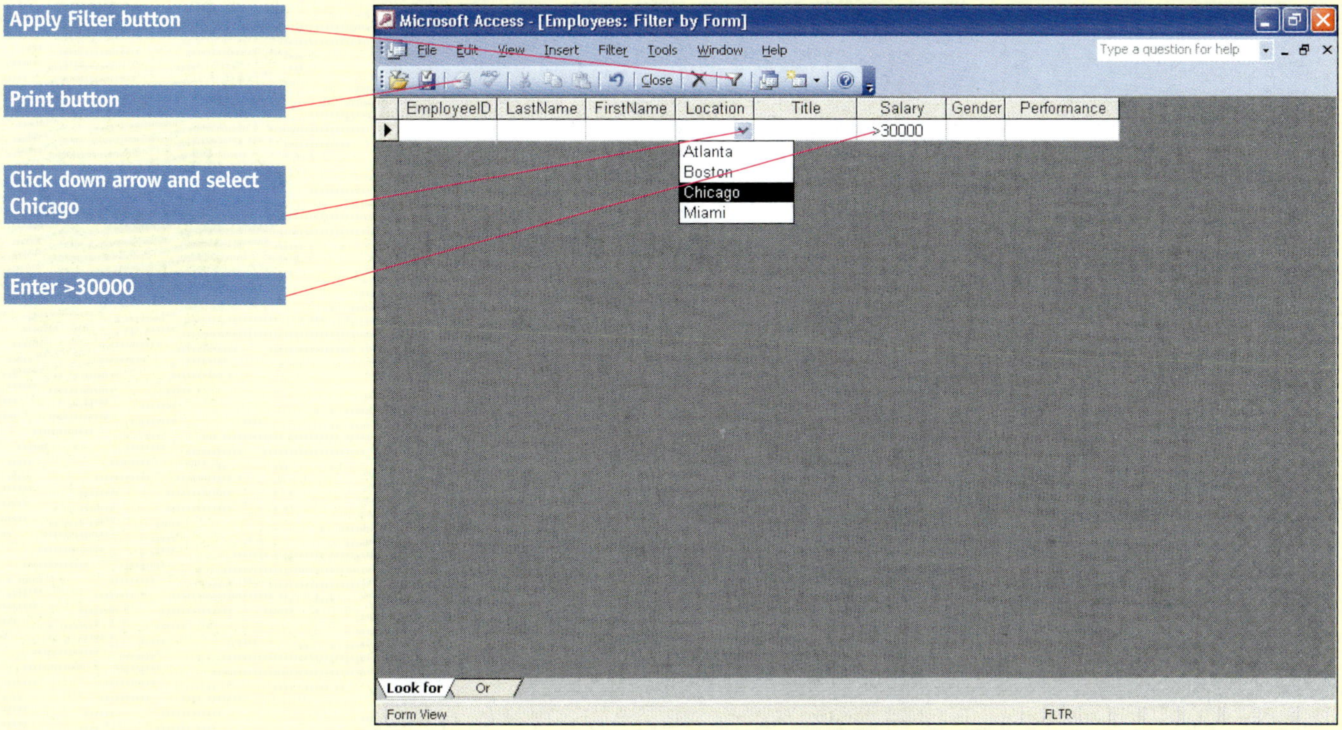

(c) Filter by Form (step 3)

FIGURE 1.6 Hands-on Exercise 2 (*continued*)

FILTER BY FORM VERSUS FILTER BY SELECTION

The Filter by Form command has all of the capabilities of the Filter by Selection command, and provides two additional capabilities. First, you can use relational operators such as >, >=, <, or <=, as opposed to searching for an exact value. Second, you can search for records that meet one of several conditions (the equivalent of an "Or" operation). Enter the first criterion as you normally would, then click the Or tab at the bottom of the window to display a second form in which you enter the alternate criteria. (To delete an alternate criterion, click the associated tab, then click the Delete button on the toolbar.)

Step 4: Sort the Table

- Click the **Remove Filter button** to display the complete table, which contains 15 employee records.
- Click in the **LastName field** of any record, then click the **Sort Ascending button**. The records are displayed in alphabetical (ascending) order by last name as shown in Figure 1.6d.
- Click in the **Salary field** of any record, then click the **Sort Descending button**. The records are in descending order of salary; that is, the employee with the highest salary is listed first.
- Click in the **Location field** of any record, then click the **Sort Ascending button** to display the records by location, although the employees within a location are not in any specific order.
- You can sort on two fields at the same time, provided the fields are next to each other, as described in the next step.

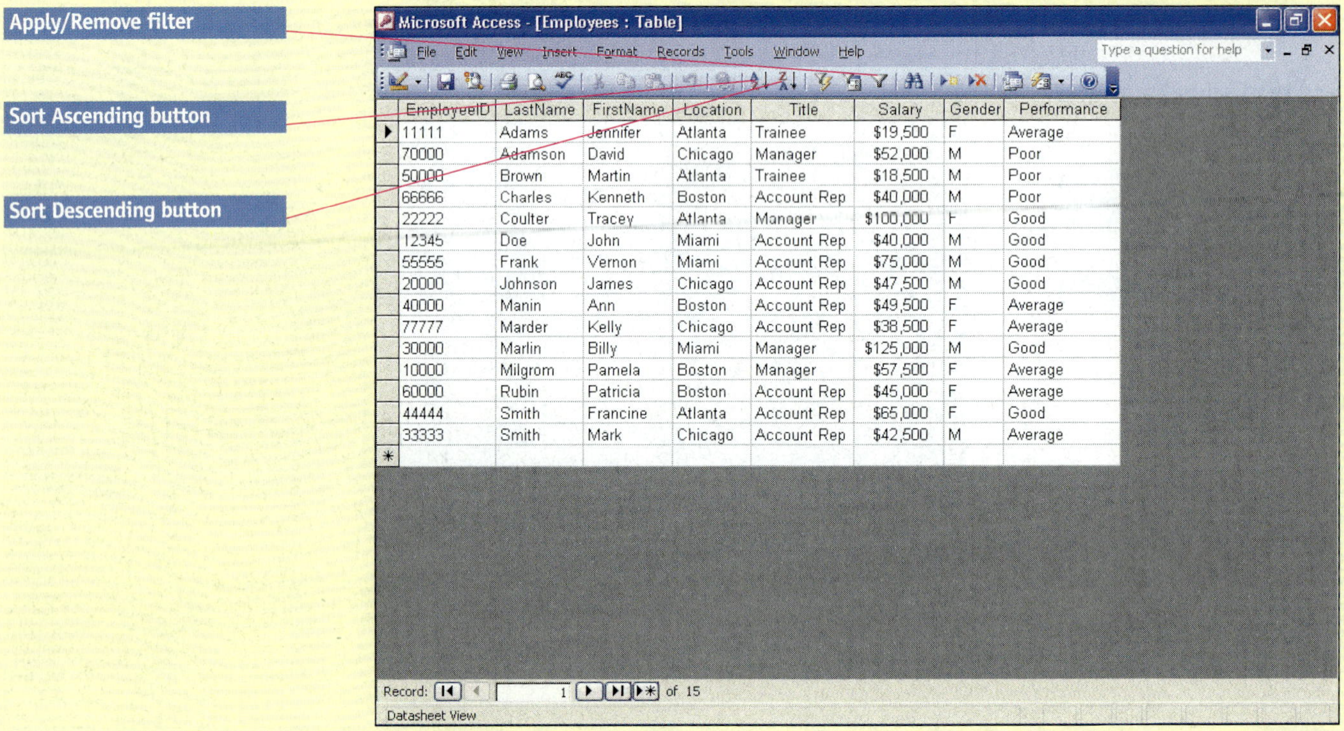

(d) Sort the Table (step 4)

FIGURE 1.6 Hands-on Exercise 2 (*continued*)

THE SORT OR FILTER—WHICH IS FIRST?

It doesn't matter whether you sort a table and then apply a filter, or filter first and then sort. The operations are cumulative. Thus, once a table has been sorted, any subsequent display of filtered records for that table will be in the specified sequence. Alternatively, you can apply a filter, then sort the filtered table by clicking in the desired field and clicking the appropriate sort button. Remember, too, that all filter commands are cumulative, and hence you must remove the filter to see the original table.

Step 5: Sort on Two Fields

- Click the header for the **Location field** to select the entire column. Click and drag the **Location header** so that the Location field is moved to the left of the LastName field.
- Click anywhere to deselect the column, then click on the **Location header** and click and drag to select both the Location header and the LastName Header as shown in Figure 1.6e.
- Click the **Sort Ascending button**. The records are sorted by location and alphabetically within location. (You could extend the sort to three fields such as Location, LastName, and FirstName by selecting all three fields prior to clicking the Sort button.)
- Print the table for your instructor. Close the table, saving the changes when prompted to do so.

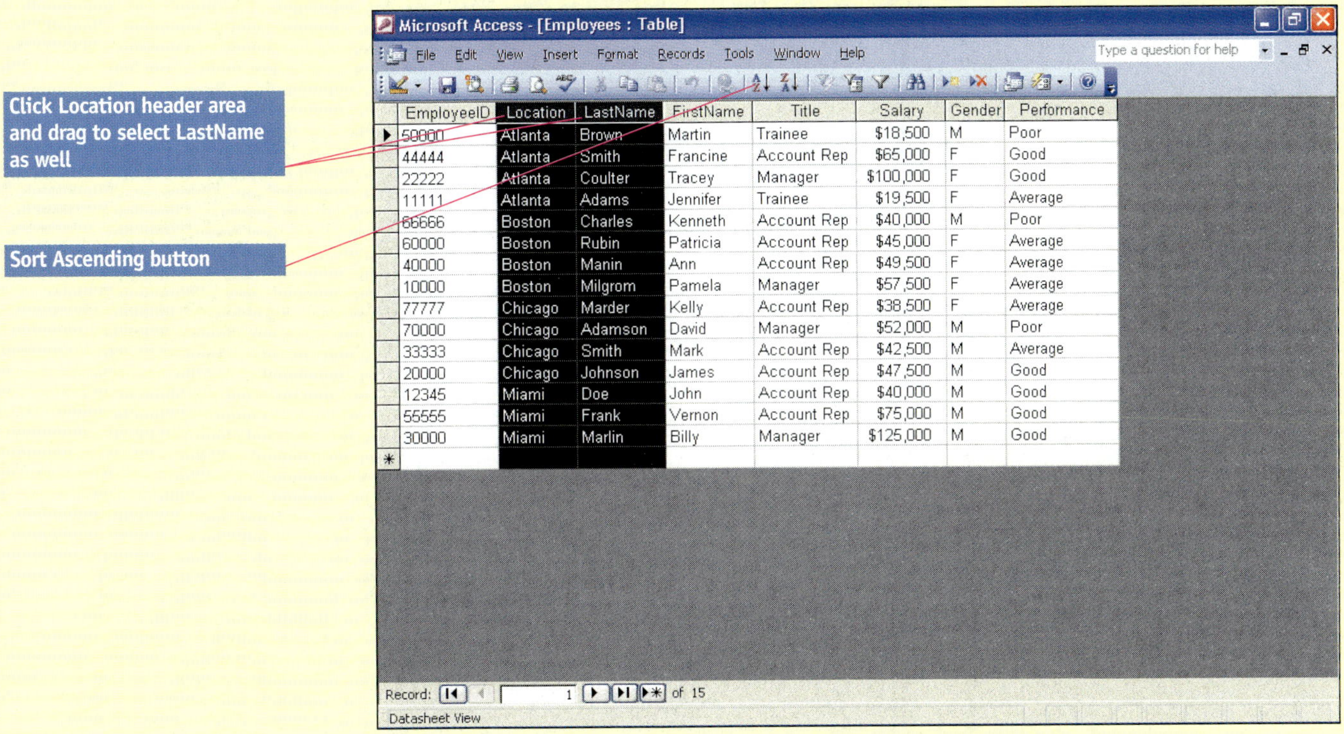

EmployeeID	Location	LastName	FirstName	Title	Salary	Gender	Performance
50000	Atlanta	Brown	Martin	Trainee	$18,500	M	Poor
44444	Atlanta	Smith	Francine	Account Rep	$65,000	F	Good
22222	Atlanta	Coulter	Tracey	Manager	$100,000	F	Good
11111	Atlanta	Adams	Jennifer	Trainee	$19,500	F	Average
66666	Boston	Charles	Kenneth	Account Rep	$40,000	M	Poor
60000	Boston	Rubin	Patricia	Account Rep	$45,000	F	Average
40000	Boston	Manin	Ann	Account Rep	$49,500	F	Average
10000	Boston	Milgrom	Pamela	Manager	$57,500	F	Average
77777	Chicago	Marder	Kelly	Account Rep	$38,500	F	Average
70000	Chicago	Adamson	David	Manager	$52,000	M	Poor
33333	Chicago	Smith	Mark	Account Rep	$42,500	M	Average
20000	Chicago	Johnson	James	Account Rep	$47,500	M	Good
12345	Miami	Doe	John	Account Rep	$40,000	M	Good
55555	Miami	Frank	Vernon	Account Rep	$75,000	M	Good
30000	Miami	Marlin	Billy	Manager	$125,000	M	Good

(e) Sort on Two Fields (step 5)

FIGURE 1.6 Hands-on Exercise 2 (*continued*)

REMOVING VERSUS DELETING A FILTER

Removing a filter displays all of the records that are in a table, but it does not delete the filter because the filter is stored permanently with the table. To delete the filter entirely is more complicated than simply removing it. Pull down the Records menu, click Filter, then click the Advanced Filter/Sort command to display a grid containing the criteria for the filter. Clear the Sort and Criteria rows by clicking in any cell containing an entry and deleting that entry, then click the Apply Filter button when all cells are clear to return to the Datasheet view. The Apply Filter button should be dim, indicating that the table does not contain a filter.

Step 6: Print a Report

- Click the **Reports button** in the Database window. Double click the icon for **Employees by Location report**.
- Click the **Maximize button** in the Report Window so that the report takes the entire screen as shown in Figure 1.6f.
- Click the **Zoom button** to toggle to 100% so that you can read the report. The report displays the employees in the same order as the sorted table from step 5. (The sequence for the report is contained in its design specification and does not depend on the sequence of the underlying table.)
- Click the **Print button** on the Report toolbar to print the report for your instructor. Submit all of the printed information to your instructor:
  - ❑ The employee form from step 1
  - ❑ The filtered table from steps 2 and 3
  - ❑ The sorted table from step 5
  - ❑ The Employees by Location report from this step
- Close the report. Exit Access if you do not want to continue with the next exercise at this time.

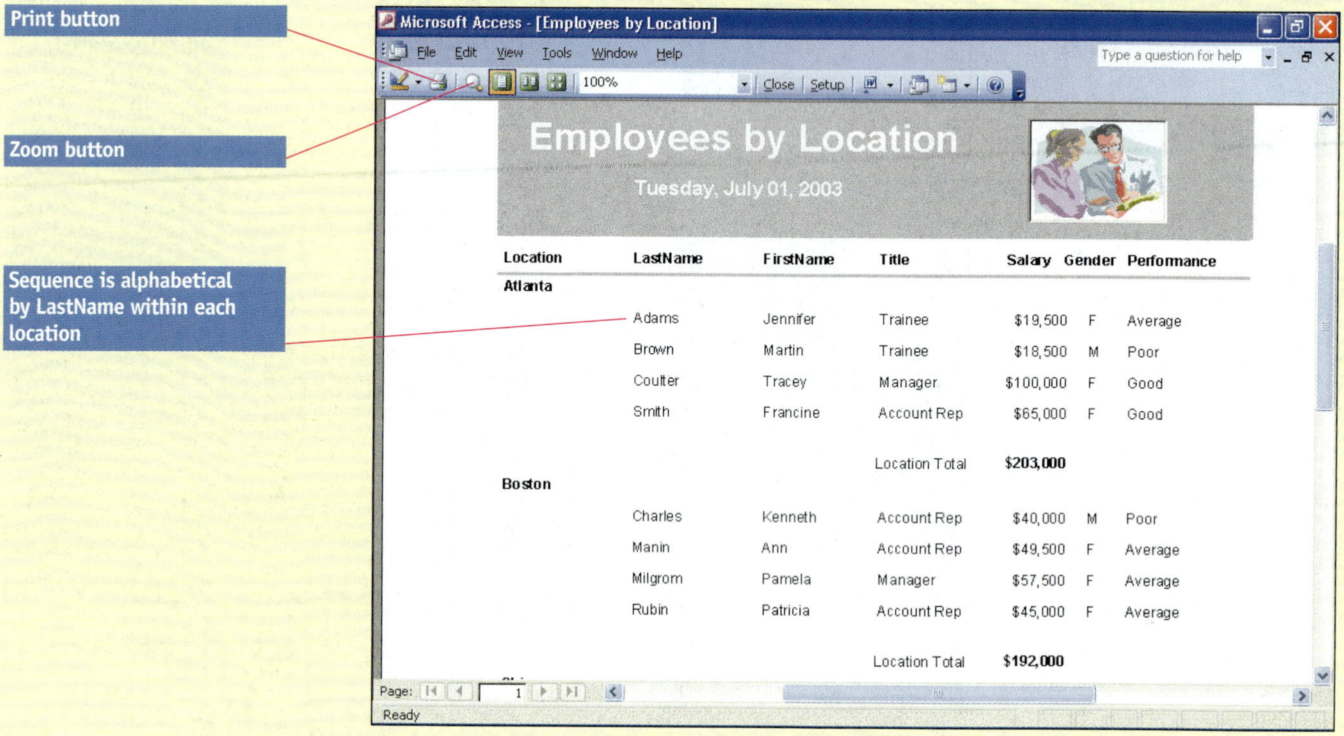

(f) Print a Report (step 6)

FIGURE 1.6 Hands-on Exercise 2 (*continued*)

DATA VERSUS INFORMATION

Data and information are not synonymous although the terms are often used interchangeably. Data is the raw material and consists of the table (or tables) that comprise a database. Information is the finished product. Data is converted to information by selecting (filtering) records, by sequencing (sorting) the selected records, and/or by summarizing data from multiple records. Decisions in an organization are based on information that is compiled from multiple records, as opposed to raw data.

LOOKING AHEAD: A RELATIONAL DATABASE

The Bookstore and Employee databases are both examples of simple databases in that they each contained only a single table. The real power of Access, however, is derived from multiple tables and the relationships between those tables. This type of database is known as a ***relational database*** and is illustrated in Figure 1.7. This figure expands the original Employee database by adding two tables, for locations and titles, respectively.

The Employees table in Figure 1.7a is the same table we used at the beginning of the previous exercise, except for the substitution of a LocationID and TitleID for the location and title, respectively. The Locations table in Figure 1.7b has all of the fields that pertain to each location: LocationID, Location, Address, State, Zipcode, and OfficePhone. One field, the LocationID, appears in both Employees and Locations tables and links the two tables to one another. In similar fashion, the Titles table in Figure 1.7c has the information for each title: the TitleID, Title, Description, EducationRequired, and Minimum and MaximumSalary. The TitleID appears in both the Employees and Titles tables to link those tables to one another.

EmployeeID	LastName	FirstName	LocationID	TitleID	Salary	Gender	Performance
10000	Milgrom	Pamela	L02	T02	$57,500	F	Average
11111	Adams	Jennifer	L01	T03	$19,500	F	Average
20000	Johnson	James	L03	T01	$47,500	M	Good
22222	Coulter	Tracey	L01	T02	$100,000	F	Good
30000	Marlin	Billy	L04	T02	$125,000	M	Good
33333	Smith	Mark	L03	T01	$42,500	M	Average
40000	Manin	Ann	L02	T01	$49,500	F	Average
44444	Smith	Francine	L01	T01	$65,000	F	Good
50000	Brown	Mark	L01	T03	$18,500	M	Poor
55555	Frank	Vernon	L04	T01	$75,000	M	Good
60000	Rubin	Patricia	L02	T01	$45,000	F	Average
66666	Charles	Kenneth	L02	T01	$40,000	M	Poor
70000	Adamson	David	L03	T02	$52,000	M	Poor
77777	Marder	Kelly	L03	T01	$38,500	F	Average

(a) The Employees Table

LocationID	Location	Address	State	Zipcode	OfficePhone
L01	Atlanta	450 Peachtree Road	GA	30316	(404) 333-5555
L02	Boston	3 Commons Blvd	MA	02190	(617) 123-4444
L03	Chicago	500 Loop Highway	IL	60620	(312) 444-6666
L04	Miami	210 Biscayne Blvd	FL	33103	(305) 787-9999

(b) The Locations Table

TitleID	Title	Description	EducationRequired	MinimumSalary	MaximumSalary
T01	Account Rep	A marketing ...	Four year degree	$25,000	$75,000
T02	Manager	A supervisory ...	Four year degree	$50,000	$150,000
T03	Trainee	An entry-level ...	Two year degree	$18,000	$25,000

(c) The Titles Table

FIGURE 1.7 A Relational Database

To obtain information about a specific employee's title or location, you go to the Employees table, then use the LocationID and TitleID to locate the appropriate records in the Locations and Titles tables, respectively. The tables are color coded to emphasize the relationships between them. It sounds complicated, but it is really quite simple and very elegant. More importantly, it enables you to obtain detailed information about any employee, location, or title. To show how it works, we will ask a series of questions that require you to look in one or more tables for the answer. Consider:

Query: At which location does Pamela Milgrom work? What is the phone number of her office?

Answer: Pamela works in the Boston office, at 3 Commons Blvd., Boston, MA, 02190. The phone number is (617) 123-4444.

Did you answer the question correctly? You had to search the Employees table for Pamela Milgrom to obtain the LocationID (L02 in this example) corresponding to her office. You then searched the Locations table for this LocationID to obtain the address and phone number for that location. The process required you to use both the Locations and Employees tables, which are linked to one another through a ***one-to-many relationship***. One location can have many employees, but a specific employee can work at only one location. Let's try another question:

Query: Which employees are managers?

Answer: There are four managers: Pamela Milgrom, Tracey Coulter, Billy Marlin, and David Adamson.

The answer to this question is based on the one-to-many relationship that exists between titles and employees. One title can have many employees, but a given employee has only one title. To answer the query, you search the Titles table for "manager" to determine its TitleID (T02). You then go to the Employees table and select those records that have this value in the TitleID field.

The design of a relational database enables us to extract information from multiple tables in a single query. Equally important, it simplifies the way data is changed in that modifications are made in only one place. Consider:

Query: Which employees work in the Boston office? What is their phone number?

Answer: There are four employees in Boston: Pamela Milgrom, Ann Manin, Patricia Rubin, and Kenneth Charles, each with the same number (617-123-4444).

Once again, we draw on the one-to-many relationship between locations and employees. Thus, we begin in the Locations table where we search for "Boston" to determine its LocationID (L02) and phone number (617 123-4444). Then we go to the Employees table to select those records with this value in the LocationID field.

Query: What change(s) are necessary to accommodate a new telephone number for the Boston office?

Answer: Only one change is necessary. One would open the Locations table, locate the record for Boston, and change the phone number.

This query illustrates the ease with which changes are made to a relational database. There are four employees in Boston, but each employee record contains the LocationID (L02), rather than the actual information for the Boston office. Thus, changing the contents of the appropriate record in the Locations table automatically changes the information for the employees in that location.

We're ready for our next hands-on exercise in which we illustrate the true power of an Access database and its ability to work with multiple tables in a relational database. (The exercise uses the same data as the tables in Figure 1.7.)

3 A Look Ahead

Objective To open a database with multiple tables; to identify the one-to-many relationships within the database; and to produce reports based on those relationships. Use Figure 1.8 as a guide in the exercise.

Step 1: Open the Relationships Window

- Start Access. Pull down the **File menu** and click the **Open command**. Open the **Look Ahead database** in the **Exploring Access folder**.
- Pull down the **Tools menu** and click the **Relationships command** to open the Relationships window as shown in Figure 1.8a. Pull down the **Relationships menu** and click the **Show Table command** to display the Show Table dialog box.
- Click (select) the **Locations table** (within the Show Table dialog box), then click the **Add button** to add this table to the Relationships window.
- Double click the **Titles** and **Employees tables** to add these tables to the Relationships window. Close the Show Table dialog box.

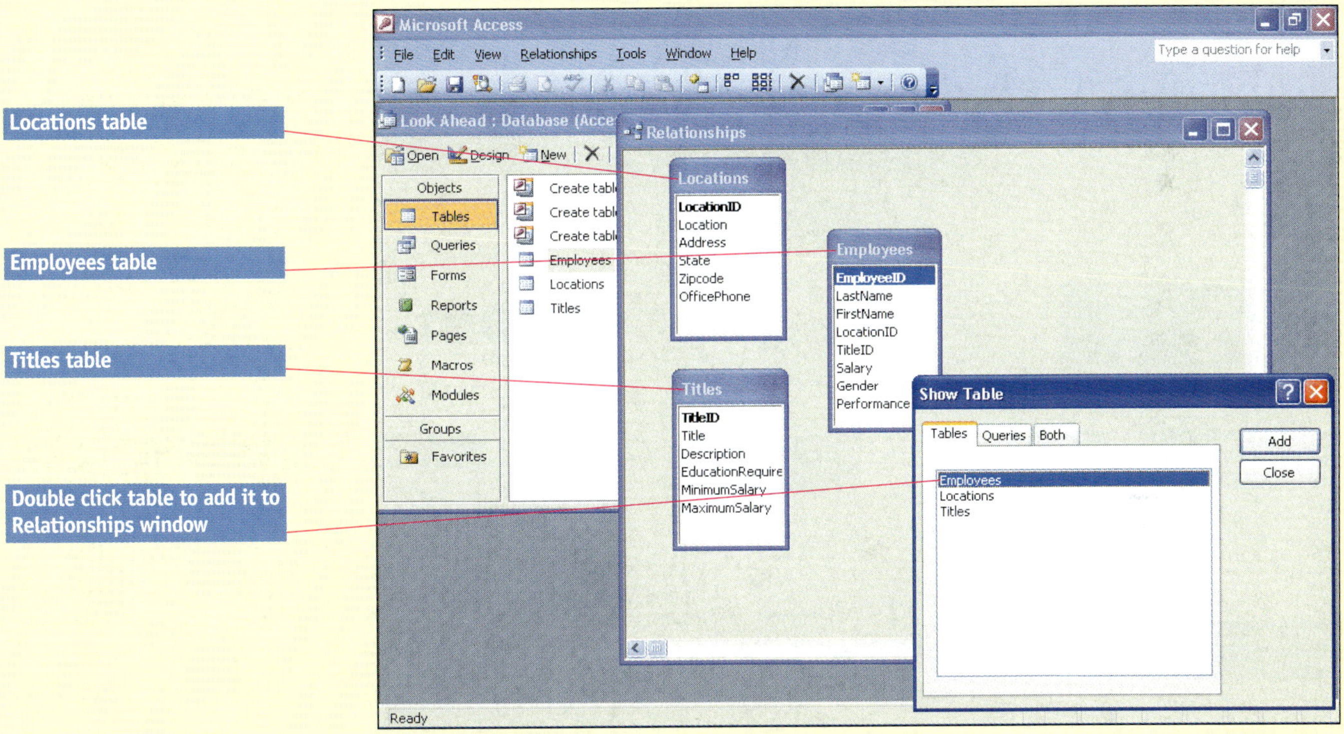

(a) Open the Relationships Window (step 1)

FIGURE 1.8 Hands-on Exercise 3

WORK ON DRIVE C

Even in a lab setting, it is preferable to work on the local hard drive, as opposed to a floppy disk. The hard drive is much faster, which is significant when working with the large files associated with Access. More importantly, the capacity of the floppy disk is limited, so that you are likely to crash as the database expands. Work on drive C throughout the exercise, then use Windows Explorer at the end of the exercise to copy the database to a floppy disk that you can take with you.

Step 2: Create the Relationships

- Maximize the Relationships windows so that you have more room in which to work. Click and drag the title bar of each table so that the positions of the tables match those in Figure 1.8b.
- Click and drag the bottom (and/or right) border of each table so that you see all of the fields in each table.
- Click and drag the **LocationID field** in the Locations table field list to the **LocationID field** in the Employees field list. Release the mouse button. You will see the Edit Relationships dialog box.
- Check the box to **Enforce Referential Integrity**. Click the **Create button** to create the relationship.
- Click and drag the **TitleID field** in the Titles table field list to the **TitleID field** in the Employees field list. Release the mouse button. You will see the Edit Relationships dialog box.
- Check the box to **Enforce Referential Integrity** as shown in Figure 1.9b. Click the **Create button** to create the relationship.
- Click the **Save button** on the Relationships toolbar to save the Relationships window, then close the Relationships window.

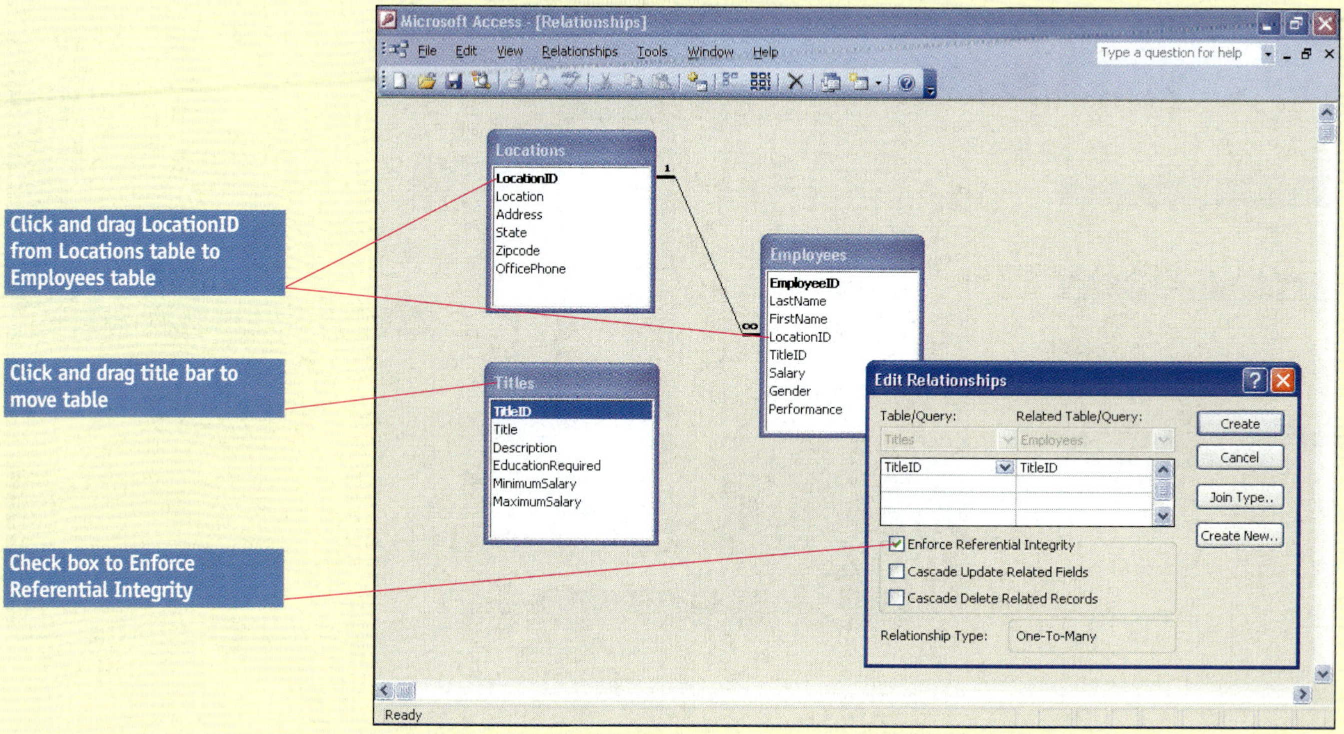

(b) Create the Relationships (step 2)

FIGURE 1.8 Hands-on Exercise 3 (*continued*)

THE RELATIONSHIPS ARE VISUAL

The tables in an Access database are created independently, then related to one another through the Relationships window. The number 1 and the infinity symbol (∞) appear at the ends of the lines to indicate the nature of the relationship—for example, a one-to-many relationship between the Locations and Employees tables.

Step 3: Referential Integrity

- Double click the **Employees table** to open the table. Maximize the window. Pull down the **Insert** menu and click the **New Record command** (or click the **New Record button** on the Table Datasheet toolbar).
- Enter data for yourself, using 12345 as the EmployeeID, and your first and last name as shown in Figure 1.8c. Enter an invalid LocationID (e.g., **L44**), then complete the record as shown in the figure.
- Press the **Enter key** when you have completed the data entry, then click **OK** when you see the error message. Access prevents you from entering a location that does not exist.
- Click in the **LocationID field** and enter **L04**, the LocationID for Miami. Press the **down arrow key** to move to the next record, which automatically saves the current record.
- Close the Employees table.

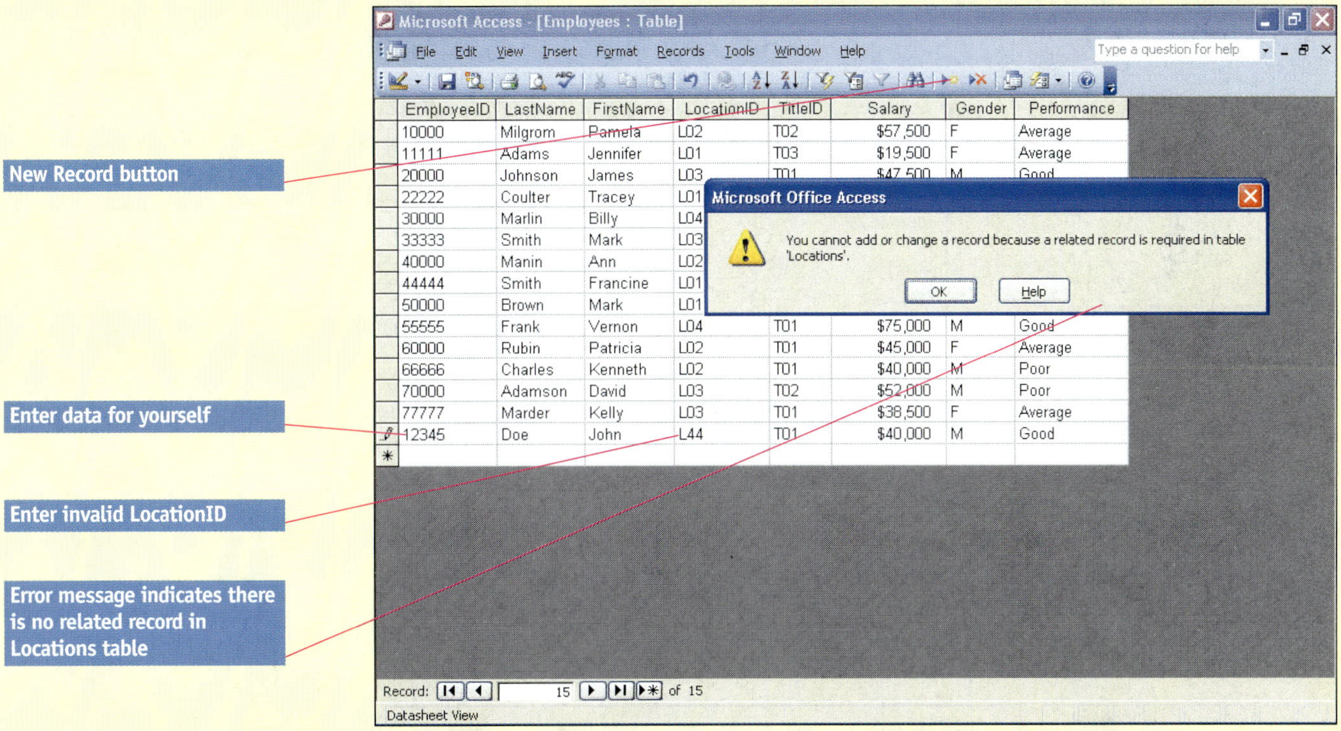

(c) Referential Integrity (step 3)

FIGURE 1.8 Hands-on Exercise 3 (*continued*)

REFERENTIAL INTEGRITY

The tables in a database must be consistent with one another, a concept known as referential integrity. Thus, Access automatically implements certain types of data validation to prevent such errors from occurring. You cannot, for example, enter a record in the Employees table that contains an invalid value for either the LocationID or the TitleID. Nor can you delete a record in the Locations or Titles table if it has related records in the Employees table. Think for a moment what the consequences would be if this type of validation was not imposed on the database.

Step 4: Simplified Data Entry

- Click the **Forms button** in the Database window, then double click the **Employees form** to open this form as shown in Figure 1.8d.
- Click the **Add Record button** (or use the **Alt+A** keyboard shortcut), then click in the text box for the EmployeeID.
- Enter the data for **Bob Grauer** one field at a time, pressing the **Tab key** to move from one field to the next. Click the **down arrow** when you come to the location field to display the available locations, then select (click) **Miami.**
- Press the **Tab key** to move to the Title field, click the **down arrow**, and choose **Account Rep**.
- Complete the data for Bob's record by entering **$150,000**, **M**, and **Excellent** in the Salary, Gender, and Performance fields, respectively.
- Click the **Close Form button** (or use the **Alt+C** keyboard shortcut) when you have finished entering the data.

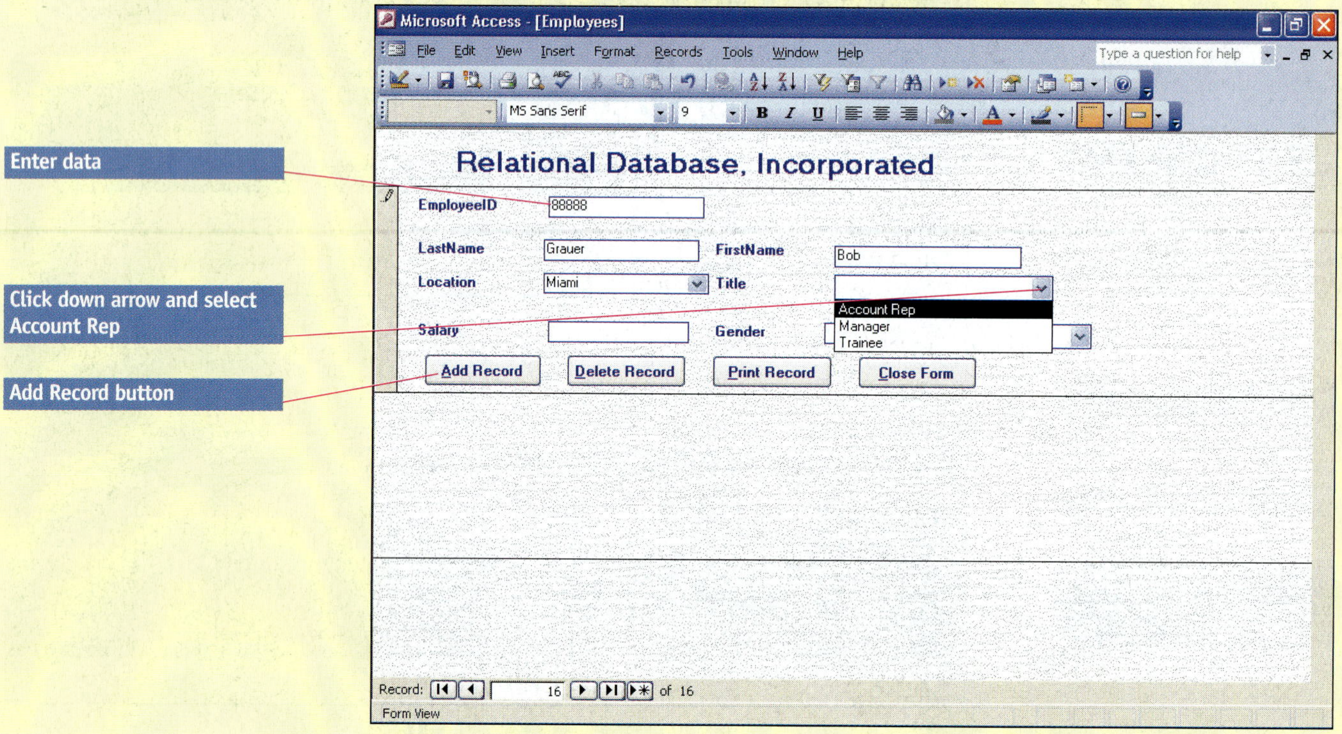

(d) Simplified Data Entry (step 4)

FIGURE 1.8 Hands-on Exercise 3 (*continued*)

SIMPLIFIED DATA ENTRY

The success of any system depends on the accuracy of its data as well as its ease of use. Both objectives are met through a well-designed form that guides the user through the process of data entry and simultaneously rejects invalid responses. The drop-down list boxes for the Location, Title, and Performance fields ensure that the user can enter only valid values in these fields. Data entry is also simplified in these fields in that you can enter just the first letter of a field, then press the Tab key to move to the next field. The command buttons at the bottom of the form provide easy access to basic commands.

Step 5: Print the Employee Master List

- Click the **Reports button** in the Database window. Double click the **Employee Master List** report to open the report as shown in Figure 1.8e.
- Click the **Maximize button** in the Report window so that the report takes the entire desktop. Click the **Zoom button** to view the report at **100%**.
- The report displays selected fields for every employee in the Employees table. The two new employees, you and Bob Grauer, appear in alphabetical order. Both employees are in the Miami office.
- The fields for each employee are taken from different tables in the database:
  - The values for last name, first name, salary, and performance are from the Employees table.
  - The name of the location and the office phone are from the Locations table, which is related to the Employees table through the LocationID field that appears in both tables.
  - The employee's title is taken from the Titles table, which is related to the Employees table through the TitleID field that appears in both tables.
- Click the **Print button** to print the report. Close the Report window.

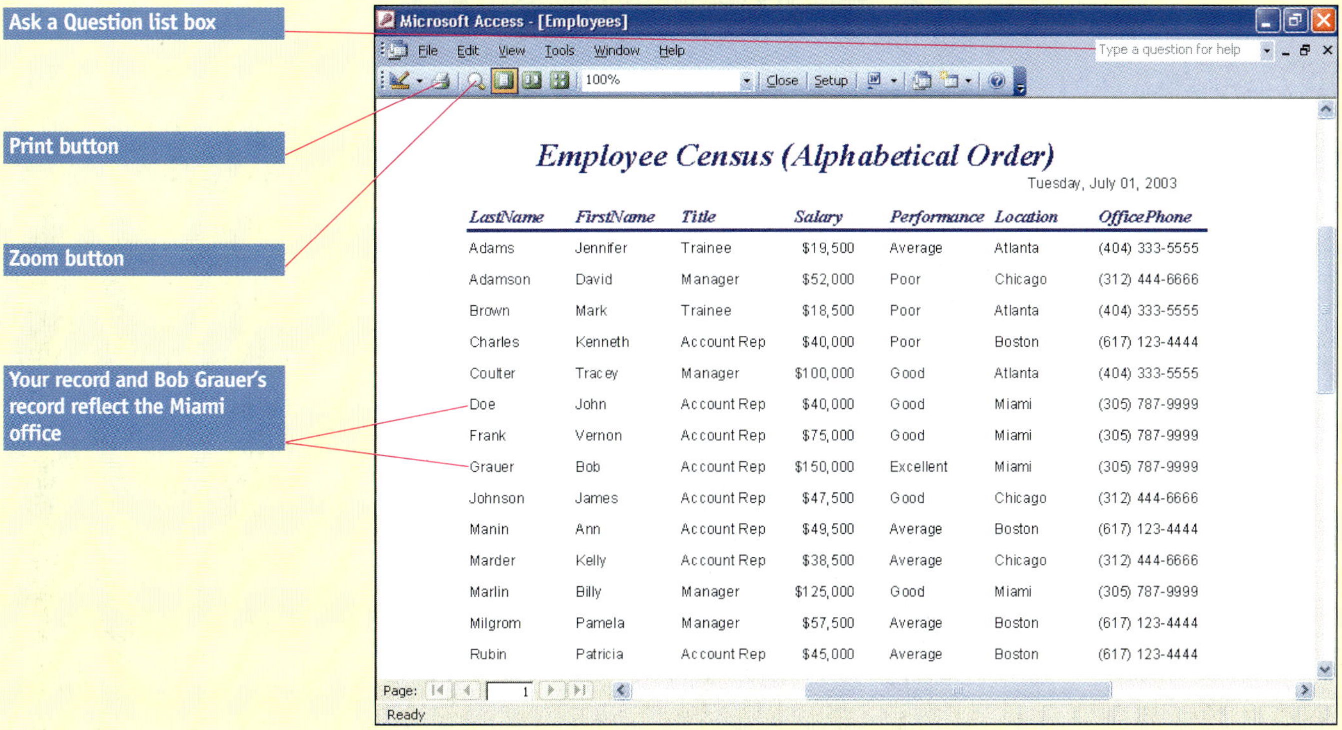

LastName	FirstName	Title	Salary	Performance	Location	OfficePhone
Adams	Jennifer	Trainee	$19,500	Average	Atlanta	(404) 333-5555
Adamson	David	Manager	$52,000	Poor	Chicago	(312) 444-6666
Brown	Mark	Trainee	$18,500	Poor	Atlanta	(404) 333-5555
Charles	Kenneth	Account Rep	$40,000	Poor	Boston	(617) 123-4444
Coulter	Tracey	Manager	$100,000	Good	Atlanta	(404) 333-5555
Doe	John	Account Rep	$40,000	Good	Miami	(305) 787-9999
Frank	Vernon	Account Rep	$75,000	Good	Miami	(305) 787-9999
Grauer	Bob	Account Rep	$150,000	Excellent	Miami	(305) 787-9999
Johnson	James	Account Rep	$47,500	Good	Chicago	(312) 444-6666
Manin	Ann	Account Rep	$49,500	Average	Boston	(617) 123-4444
Marder	Kelly	Account Rep	$38,500	Average	Chicago	(312) 444-6666
Marlin	Billy	Manager	$125,000	Good	Miami	(305) 787-9999
Milgrom	Pamela	Manager	$57,500	Average	Boston	(617) 123-4444
Rubin	Patricia	Account Rep	$45,000	Average	Boston	(617) 123-4444

(e) Print the Employee Master List (step 5)

FIGURE 1.8 Hands-on Exercise 3 (*continued*)

ASK A QUESTION

Click in the "Ask a Question" list box that appears at the right of the document window, enter the text of a question such as "How do I print a report?", press Enter, and Access returns a list of potential Help topics. Click any topic that appears promising to display the detailed information. You can ask multiple questions during an Access session, then click the down arrow in the list box to return to an earlier question, which will return you to the Help topics.

Step 6: Change the Locations Table

- Click the **Tables button** in the Database window, then double click the **Locations table** to open this table as shown in figure 1.8f. Maximize the window if necessary.
- Click the **plus sign** next to location L04 (Miami) to view the employees in this office. The plus sign changes to a minus sign as the employee records for this location are shown.
- Your name appears in this list as does Bob Grauer's. Click the **minus sign** and the list of related records disappears.
- Click and drag to select **Miami** (the current value in the Location field). Type **Orlando** and press the **Tab key**. Enter the corresponding values for the other fields: **1000 Kirkman Road, FL, 32801**, and **(407) 555-5555** for the address, state, zip code, and office phone, respectively.
- Close the **Locations table**. You have effectively moved the Miami Office to Orlando; i.e., all employees who were assigned to the Miami Office are now working out of Orlando.

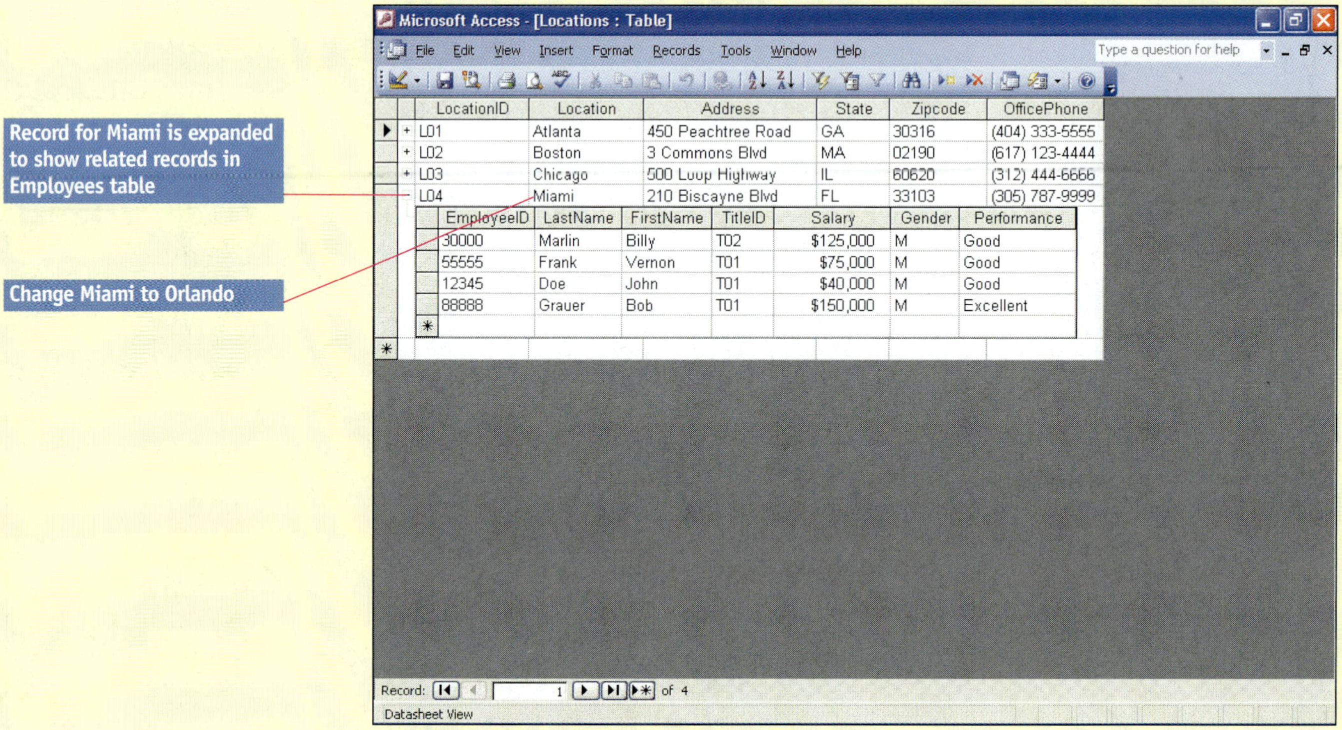

(f) Change the Locations Table (step 6)

FIGURE 1.8 Hands-on Exercise 3 (*continued*)

ADD AND DELETE RELATED RECORDS

Take advantage of the one-to-many relationship between locations and employees (or titles and employees) to add and/or delete records in the Employees table. Open the Locations table, then click the plus sign next to the location where you want to add or delete an employee record. To add a new employee, click in any employee record, click the New Record navigation button, then add the new data. To delete a record, click the record, then click the Delete Record button on the Table Datasheet toolbar. Click the minus sign to close the employee list.

Step 7: Print the Employees by Title Report

- Click the **Reports button** in the Database window, then double click the **Employees by Title report** to open the report shown in Figure 1.8g.
- Click the **Maximize button** in the Report window so that the report takes the entire desktop. Click the **Zoom button** to view the report at **100%**.
- This report lists employees by title, rather than alphabetically. Note that you and Bob Grauer are both listed as Account Reps in the Orlando office; that is, the location of the office was changed in the Locations table, and that change is automatically reflected for all employees assigned to that office.
- Pull down the **File menu** and click the **Page Setup command**. Click the **Margins tab**, then change the left and right margins to **.75 inch** each, so that the report fits on one page. Click **OK**. Print the report for your instructor to show you completed the exercise.
- Close the Report window. Close the Database window. Exit Access. Welcome to the world of relational databases.

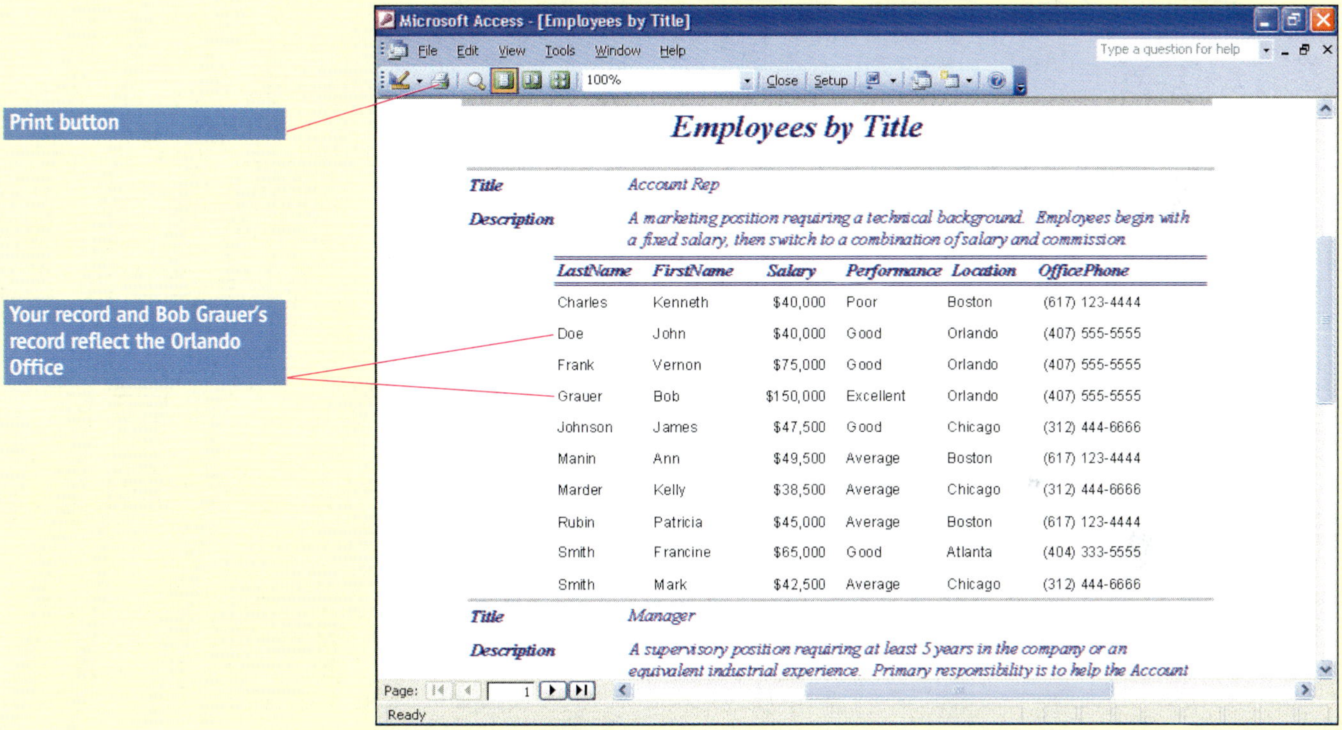

(g) Print the Employees by Title Report (step 7)

FIGURE 1.8 Hands-on Exercise 3 (*continued*)

BACK UP YOUR WORK

We cannot overemphasize the importance of adequate backup and urge you to back up your important files at every opportunity. Exit Access, start Windows Explorer, then copy the database from drive C to a floppy disk, CD, or zip drive. Remember, you can always get another copy of Microsoft Office, but your data files are irreplaceable. Make duplicate copies of any files that you cannot afford to lose, and then store those files away from your computer. Develop a backup strategy and follow it faithfully!

SUMMARY

An Access database has seven types of objects—tables, forms, queries, reports, pages, macros, and modules. The database window displays these objects and enables you to open an existing object or create a new object.

Each table in the database is composed of records, and each record is in turn composed of fields. Every record in a given table has the same fields in the same order. The primary key is the field (or combination of fields) that makes every record in a table unique. A table can have only one primary key.

A table is displayed in multiple views. The Design view is used to define the table initially and to specify the fields it will contain. The Datasheet view is the view you use to add, edit, or delete records. The PivotTable view is similar in concept to an Excel pivot table and provides a convenient way to summarize data about groups of records. The PivotChart view creates a chart from the associated PivotTable view. (The PivotTable and PivotChart views are discussed in Chapter 4.)

A record selector symbol is displayed next to the current record in Datasheet view and signifies the status of that record. A triangle indicates that the record has been saved. A pencil indicates that the record has not been saved and that you are in the process of entering (or changing) the data. An asterisk appears next to the blank record present at the end of every table, where you add a new record to the table.

Access automatically saves any changes in the current record as soon as you move to the next record or when you close the table. The Undo Current Record command cancels (undoes) the changes to the previously saved record.

A filter is a set of criteria that is applied to a table to display a subset of the records in that table. Microsoft Access lets you filter by selection or filter by form. The application of a filter does not remove the records from the table, but simply suppresses them from view. The records in a table can be displayed in ascending or descending sequence by clicking the appropriate button on the Database toolbar.

No system, no matter how sophisticated, can produce valid output from invalid input. Data validation is thus a critical part of any system. Access automatically imposes certain types of data validation during data entry. Additional checks can be implemented by the user.

A relational database contains multiple tables and enables you to extract information from those tables in a single query. The related tables must be consistent with one another, a concept known as referential integrity. Thus, Access automatically implements additional data validation to ensure the integrity of a database.

Adequate backup is essential when working with an Access database (or any other Office application). A duplicate copy of the database should be created at the end of every session and stored off site (away from the computer).

KEY TERMS

- AutoCorrect 507
- Current record 500
- Database 498
- Database window 499
- Data validation 511
- Datasheet view 500
- Design view 500
- Field 498
- Filter 515
- Filter by Form 515
- Filter by Selection 515
- Find command 508
- Form 501
- GIGO (garbage in, garbage out) . 498
- One-to-many relationship 524
- PivotChart view 500
- PivotTable view 500
- Primary key 500
- Query 501
- Record 498
- Referential Integrity 527
- Relational database 523
- Remove filter 515
- Replace command 508
- Report 501
- Sort 515
- Sort Ascending 515
- Sort Descending 515
- Table 498
- Undo command 509

MULTIPLE CHOICE

1. Which sequence represents the hierarchy of terms, from smallest to largest?
   - (a) Database, table, record, field
   - (b) Field, record, table, database
   - (c) Record, field, table, database
   - (d) Field, record, database, table

2. Which of the following is true regarding movement within a record (assuming you are not in the first or last field of that record)?
   - (a) Press Tab or the right arrow key to move to the next field
   - (b) Press Shift+Tab or the left arrow key to return to the previous field
   - (c) Both (a) and (b)
   - (d) Neither (a) nor (b)

3. You're performing routine maintenance on a table within an Access database. When should you execute the Save command?
   - (a) Immediately after you add, edit, or delete a record
   - (b) Periodically during a session—for example, after every fifth change
   - (c) Once at the end of a session
   - (d) None of the above since Access automatically saves the changes as they are made

4. Which of the following objects are contained within an Access database?
   - (a) Tables and forms
   - (b) Queries and reports
   - (c) Macros and modules
   - (d) All of the above

5. Which of the following is true about the views associated with a table?
   - (a) The Design view is used to create a table
   - (b) The Datasheet view is used to add or delete records
   - (c) Both (a) and (b)
   - (d) Neither (a) nor (b)

6. Which of the followir
   - (a) Every record in a every other reco
   - (b) Every table con as every other t
   - (c) Both (a) and (b
   - (d) Neither (a) nor

7. Which of the following is *false* about the Open Database command?
   - (a) It can be executed from the File menu
   - (b) It can be executed by clicking the Open button on the Database toolbar
   - (c) It loads a database from disk into memory
   - (d) It opens the selected table from the Database window

8. Which of the following is true regarding the record selector symbol?
   - (a) A pencil indicates that the current record has already been saved
   - (b) A triangle indicates that the current record has not changed
   - (c) An asterisk indicates the first record in the table
   - (d) All of the above

9. Which view is used to add, edit, and delete records in a table?
   - (a) The Design view
   - (b) The Datasheet view
   - (c) Either (a) or (b)
   - (d) Neither (a) nor (b)

10. What does GIGO stand for?
    - (a) Gee, I Goofed, OK
    - (b) Global Input, Global Output
    - (c) Garbage In, Garbage Out
    - (d) Gospel In, Gospel Out

... continued

ple choice

11. ...e following will be accepted as valid ...ata entry?
    - ...Adding a record with a duplicate primary key
    - ...) Entering text into a numeric field
    - (c) Entering numbers into a text field
    - (d) Omitting a required field

12. The find and replace values in a Replace command must be:
    - (a) The same length
    - (b) The same case
    - (c) Both (a) and (b)
    - (d) Neither (a) nor (b)

13. An Access table containing 10 records, and 10 fields per record, requires two pages for printing. What, if anything, can be done to print the table on one page?
    - (a) Print in Landscape rather than Portrait mode
    - (b) Decrease the left and right margins
    - (c) Both (a) and (b)
    - (d) Neither (a) nor (b)

14. Which of the following capabilities is available through Filter by Selection?
    - (a) The imposition of a relational condition
    - (b) The imposition of an alternate (OR) condition
    - (c) Both (a) and (b)
    - (d) Neither (a) nor (b)

15. Which of the following best describes the relationship between locations and employees as implemented in the Look Ahead database within the chapter?
    - (a) One to one
    - (b) One to many
    - (c) Many to many
    - (d) Impossible to determine

16. A corporate database has a one-to-many relationship between its branch offices and its employees. The Atlanta branch, which currently has 50 employees, is relocating. Where do you enter the new address and phone number?
    - (a) In the employee record of the Atlanta branch manager
    - (b) In the employee record of every employee who works in Atlanta
    - (c) In the Atlanta record in the Branch Office table
    - (d) All of the above

17. Which of the following commands can be used to replace all existing occurrences of the abbreviation CIS with Computer Information Systems?
    - (a) Find and Replace
    - (b) AutoCorrect
    - (c) Both AutoCorrect and Find and Replace
    - (d) Neither AutoCorrect nor Find and Replace

18. You are looking at an Employee table in Datasheet view. Which of the following requires an ascending sort?
    - (a) To list the employees alphabetically by their last name
    - (b) To list the employees according to their age with the youngest employee appearing first (an employee's birth date is stored in the table rather than the employee's age)
    - (c) Both (a) and (b)
    - (d) Neither (a) nor (b)

ANSWERS

1. b	**7.** d	**13.** c
2. c	**8.** b	**14.** d
3. d	**9.** b	**15.** b
4. d	**10.** c	**16.** c
5. c	**11.** c	**17.** a
6. a	**12.** d	**18.** a

PRACTICE WITH ACCESS

1. **The Oscars:** The Academy Awards®, also known as the Oscars®, are given out each year to honor the best efforts in motion pictures for the previous year. We enjoy the movies and we have created a database that contains the Oscar winners in the major categories. Your first task is to update the table in our database to include any additional awards since the publication of our text. Proceed as follows:
   a. Open the *Chapter 1 Practice 1* database in the Exploring Access folder. Click the Forms button and open the Award Winners form shown in Figure 1.9. Maximize the form. Use the navigation bar at the bottom of the form to go to the last record to determine the last year in our table.
   b. Skip this step if the database is current; otherwise, click the hyperlink in the Award Winners form to go to the Oscars site and determine the winners for the years since we published our text. Use the existing form to enter the winners for the six major awards (best picture, best actor and actress, best director, and best supporting actor and actress) into the Award Winners table.
   c. The form should display the most recent year for which data is available. Click the selection area at the left of the form to select this record. Pull down the File menu, click the Print command, then click the option button to print the selected record. Click OK. (You can also click the Print button on the form to print only the current record.) Close the form.
   d. Return to the Database window, click the Tables button and open the Award Winners table. Adjust the column widths (if necessary) so that you see all of the information for each field in each column. Pull down the File menu, click the Page Setup command, and change to landscape printing with one-half-inch margins all around. Use the Print Preview button to see how the table will appear prior to actually printing the table. Unless you change to a font that is too small to read, the data for one year will not fit on one page. Do not print the table. Close the Print Preview window, then close the table.
   e. Return to the Database window. Click the Reports button. Open the Major Winners by Year report and print the first page. (All of the data for a given year appears on the same page.) Close the report.
   f. Add a cover sheet, then submit the form and report to your instructor.

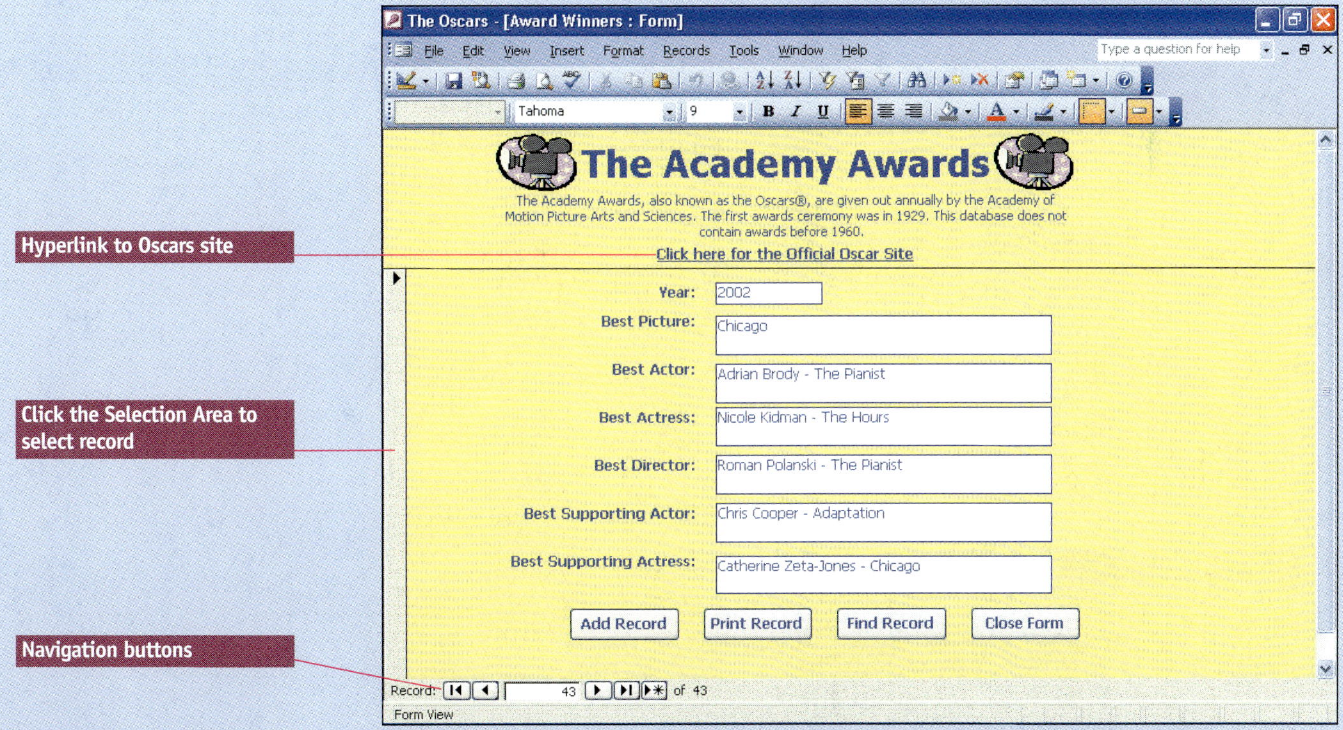

FIGURE 1.9 The Oscars (exercise 1)

2. **Definitely Needlepoint:** The Definitely Needlepoint boutique is owned and operated by four friends who wanted a friendly place to sit and stitch. They opened their store three years ago and it has grown quickly. The friends created a simple database to maintain custom records. It is your job to test the various objects in that database. Open the *Chapter 1 Practice 2* database in the Exploring Access folder and proceed as follows:
   a. Open the Customers form, maximize the form, and click the Add Record button. Enter data for yourself (even if you are not interested in needlepoint) as shown in Figure 1.10. Use customer number C1000 as shown in the figure. Indicate that you are a guild member and that you want to receive all mailings. Print the completed form for your instructor.
   b. Open the Guild Members query and uncheck the Guild Member box for Diane Battle, indicating that she is no longer a guild member. Delete the record for Anita Brockway. Close the query.
   c. Run the Guild Members report, which is based on the modified Guild Members query. Diane Battle is not listed on the report, as she is no longer a guild member. Anita Brockway is not listed either because her record has been permanently deleted from the table. Print the report for your instructor. Close the report.
   d. Open the Customers table. Filter the list by selection so that only the customers from Coral Gables are displayed. Sort the filtered list so that the customers are displayed in alphabetical order by last name. Print the filtered list. Further filter the list so that only the customers from Coral Gables who are priority 1 on the mailing list are displayed. Print this list as well. Submit both filtered lists to your instructor.
   e. Click the Filter by Form tool and delete the existing filters. Use the Filter by Form to filter the list so that only mailing list priority 1 or 2 is shown, but not priority 3. Sort the filtered list in ascending order by zip code. Print the filtered list for your instructor.
   f. Add a cover sheet to identify the assignment and submit all items to your instructor to show you completed the assignment.

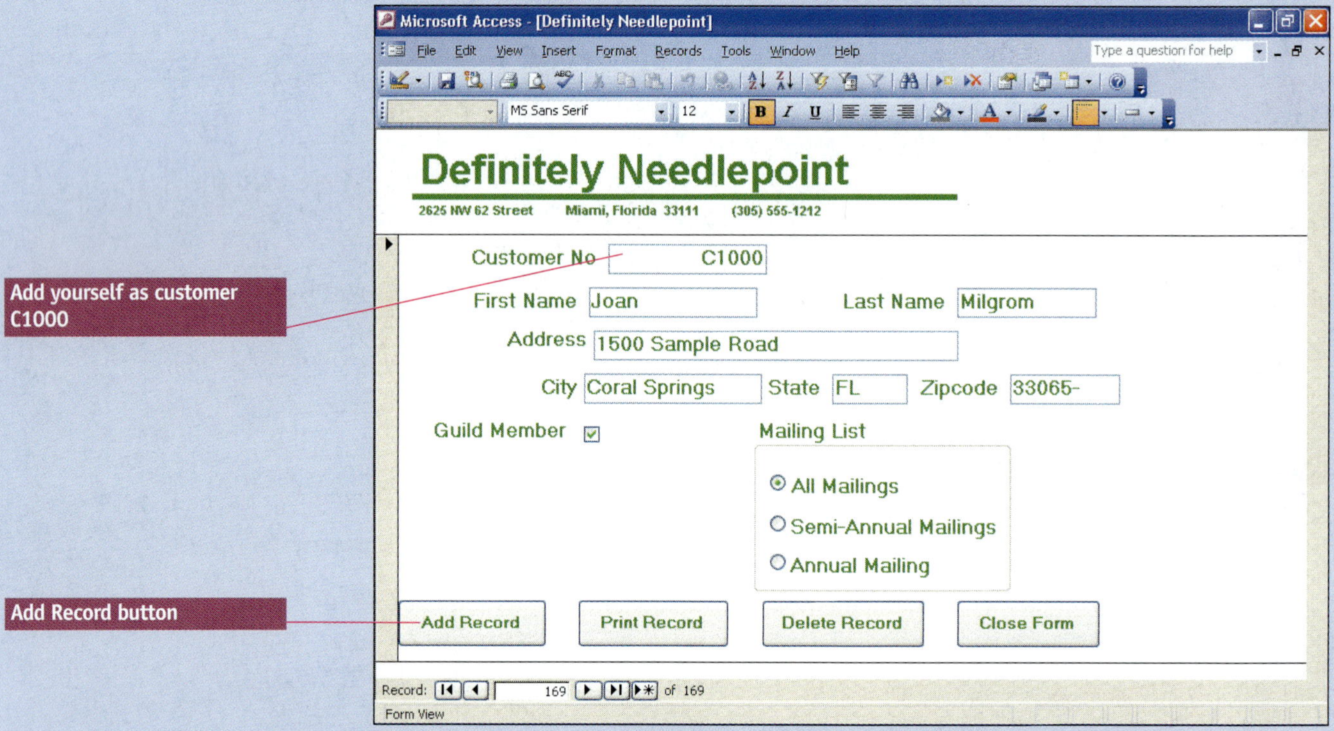

FIGURE 1.10 Definitely Needlepoint (exercise 2)

3. **The United States:** Figure 1.11 displays a table from the *Chapter 1 Practice 3* database in the Exploring Access folder. The database contains statistical data about all 50 states and enables you to create various reports such as the 10 largest states in terms of population or area.
   a. Open the *Chapter 1 Practice 3* database, and then open the States table, as shown in Figure 1.11. Pull down the File menu and click the Page Setup command to display the associated dialog box. Select landscape printing and decrease the left and right margins to half an inch. Click the Print Preview button to check that all of the fields for one record fit on one page. Print the table with all fifty records. (The table itself will take two pages because there are 50 records in the table.)
   b. Return to the Datasheet view. Click in the Population field of any state, and then click the Sort Descending button to list the states in descending order by population. Click and drag to select the first ten records so that you have selected the ten most populous states.
   c. Change to landscape printing, and then click the Print Preview button to check that all of the fields for one record fit on one page. Pull down the File menu, click the Print command, then click the option button to print the selected records (the ten states with the largest population).
   d. Return to the table and print the 10 states with the largest area. Which states (if any) appear on both listings? Close the table.
   e. Click the Queries button and open the Population Density Query. Which field is present in the query that is not present in the underlying States table? How is this field computed? How many records are displayed? What is the sequence for the displayed records? Close the query.
   f. Click the Reports button and print the Population Density Report. How does the information in this report compare to the Population Density Query? Which format do you prefer? Close the report.
   g. Print any other reports that are in the database. Are these reports based on a table or a query?
   h. Create a cover sheet. Submit the table of all 50 states, the 10 largest states by population, the 10 largest states by area, the Population Density report, as well as any additional reports that were in the database.

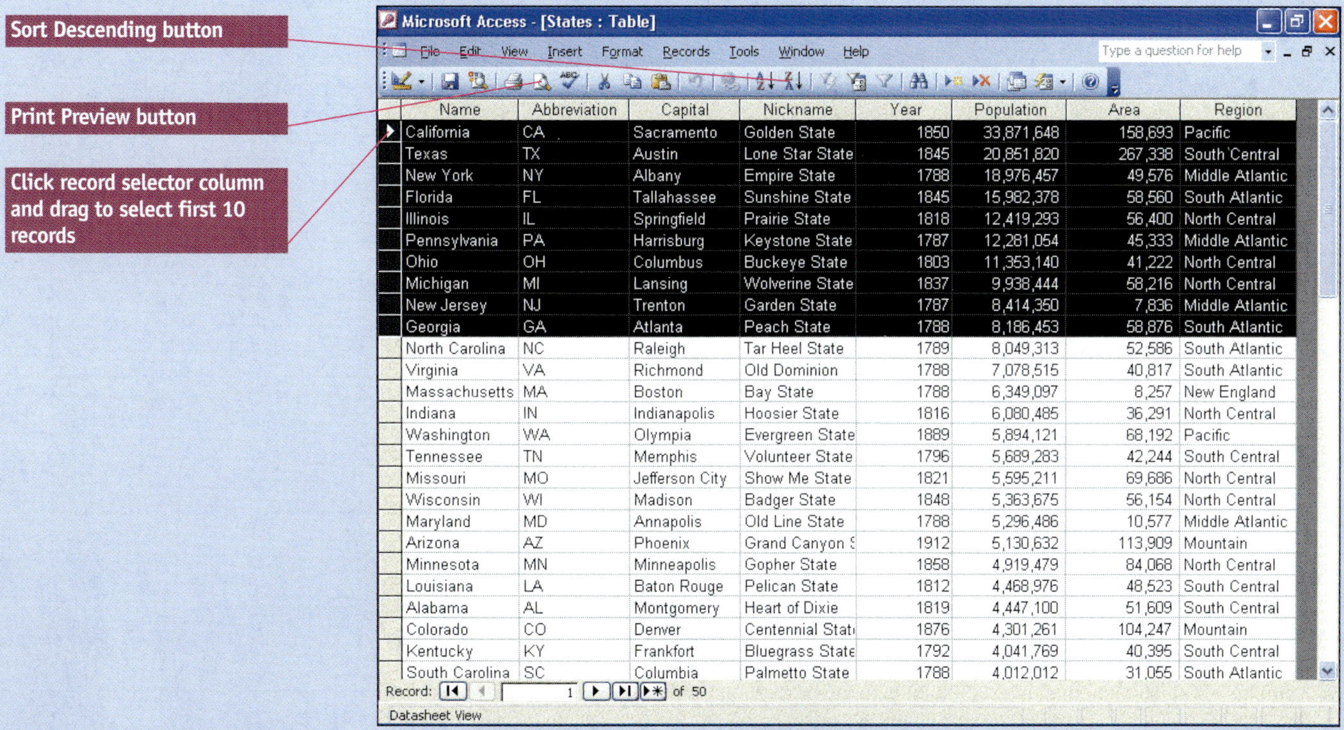

Name	Abbreviation	Capital	Nickname	Year	Population	Area	Region
California	CA	Sacramento	Golden State	1850	33,871,648	158,693	Pacific
Texas	TX	Austin	Lone Star State	1845	20,851,820	267,338	South Central
New York	NY	Albany	Empire State	1788	18,976,457	49,576	Middle Atlantic
Florida	FL	Tallahassee	Sunshine State	1845	15,982,378	58,560	South Atlantic
Illinois	IL	Springfield	Prairie State	1818	12,419,293	56,400	North Central
Pennsylvania	PA	Harrisburg	Keystone State	1787	12,281,054	45,333	Middle Atlantic
Ohio	OH	Columbus	Buckeye State	1803	11,353,140	41,222	North Central
Michigan	MI	Lansing	Wolverine State	1837	9,938,444	58,216	North Central
New Jersey	NJ	Trenton	Garden State	1787	8,414,350	7,836	Middle Atlantic
Georgia	GA	Atlanta	Peach State	1788	8,186,453	58,876	South Atlantic
North Carolina	NC	Raleigh	Tar Heel State	1789	8,049,313	52,586	South Atlantic
Virginia	VA	Richmond	Old Dominion	1788	7,078,515	40,817	South Atlantic
Massachusetts	MA	Boston	Bay State	1788	6,349,097	8,257	New England
Indiana	IN	Indianapolis	Hoosier State	1816	6,080,485	36,291	North Central
Washington	WA	Olympia	Evergreen State	1889	5,894,121	68,192	Pacific
Tennessee	TN	Memphis	Volunteer State	1796	5,689,283	42,244	South Central
Missouri	MO	Jefferson City	Show Me State	1821	5,595,211	69,686	North Central
Wisconsin	WI	Madison	Badger State	1848	5,363,675	56,154	North Central
Maryland	MD	Annapolis	Old Line State	1788	5,296,486	10,577	Middle Atlantic
Arizona	AZ	Phoenix	Grand Canyon S	1912	5,130,632	113,909	Mountain
Minnesota	MN	Minneapolis	Gopher State	1858	4,919,479	84,068	North Central
Louisiana	LA	Baton Rouge	Pelican State	1812	4,468,976	48,523	South Central
Alabama	AL	Montgomery	Heart of Dixie	1819	4,447,100	51,609	South Central
Colorado	CO	Denver	Centennial Stat	1876	4,301,261	104,247	Mountain
Kentucky	KY	Frankfort	Bluegrass State	1792	4,041,769	40,395	South Central
South Carolina	SC	Columbia	Palmetto State	1788	4,012,012	31,055	South Atlantic

FIGURE 1.11 The United States (exercise 3)

4. **Large Databases:** Figure 1.12 displays a filtered list from the *Chapter 1 Practice 4* database that is found in the Exploring Access folder. The database is similar to the Employee database that was used in the second hands-on exercise, except that it contains more than 300 records. The purpose of this exercise, however, is to provide experience working with a larger database. It also introduces the Format Datasheet command to change the default formatting for an Access table.
   a. Open the *Chapter 1 Practice 4* database and add your name as the last record in the Employees table. Assume that you are employed as an Account Rep in Boston. Your salary is $55,000, and your performance has been rated excellent. Use your own name and an EmployeeID of 99999.
   b. Filter the Employee table to display only the employees who are Account Reps in Boston as shown in Figure 1.12. Sort the filtered list by last name.
   c. Pull down the Format menu and click the Datasheet command to display the Format Datasheet dialog box in Figure 1.12. Note that the default formatting provides for both horizontal and vertical gridlines in silver. Clear the box to print vertical gridlines, and then change the color of the gridlines to dark blue. Click OK to apply the changes to the table.
   d. Pull down the File menu, click the Page Setup command, click the Page tab, and then change to landscape printing. Click the Print Preview button to be sure that the filtered table will fit on a single sheet of paper. Print the table.
   e. Remove the existing filter, then impose a new filter to display only those employees who are managers. Sort this filtered list in alphabetical order by employee number. Print the list of managers.
   f. Pull down the Format menu and explore the additional commands that are available to change the appearance of a table. How do these commands compare to similar commands in Excel? Do you think that the additional formatting enhances the appearance of a table, or are you better off to stick with the default formatting?
   g. Create a cover sheet for this assignment. Submit the printed tables together with your responses to the discussion question to your instructor.

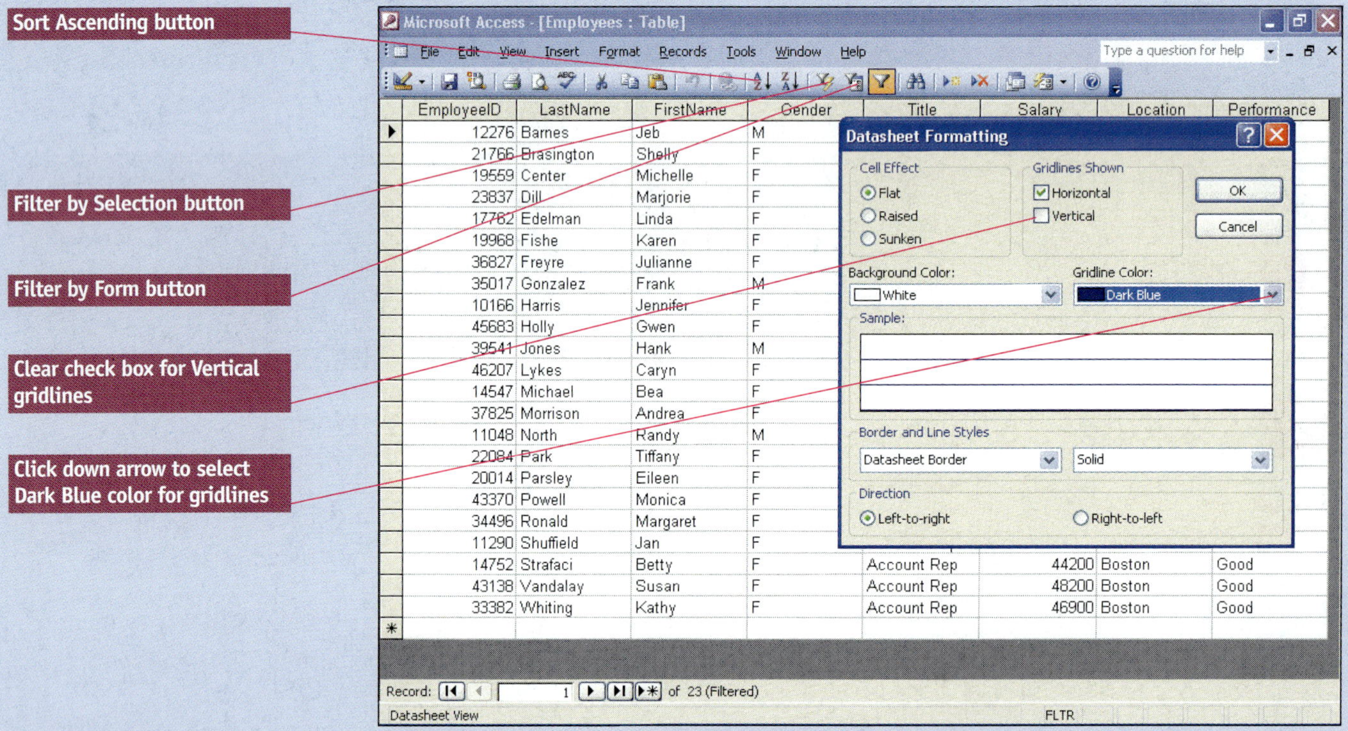

FIGURE 1.12 Large Databases (exercise 4)

5. **The Look Ahead Database:** The Look Ahead database that was introduced at the end of the chapter is a relational database that contains three tables—for employees, locations, and titles. This type of database facilitates data entry in that any change to a specific location or title is made in only one place, in the Locations or Titles tables, respectively, as opposed to having to change every employee record individually. Complete the third hands-on exercise in the chapter, and then make the following additional changes to the database.
   a. Open the *Look Ahead* database, open the Locations table, and add a new location. Use L05, Los Angeles, 1000 Rodeo Drive, CA, 90210, and (213) 666-6666 for the LocationID, Location, Address, State, ZipCode, and OfficePhone fields, respectively. Close the Locations table.
   b. Open the Titles table and change the title "Manager" to "Supervisor". Change the education requirement for a supervisor to a graduate degree. Close the Titles table.
   c. Open the Employees table. Delete the records for Kenneth Charles and David Adamson. Change the location for Bob Grauer and Francine Smith to the Los Angeles Office (location L05). Change Bob's title code to T02 so that Bob becomes the supervisor of the new office. Close the Employees table.
   d. Open the Employees form and use it to add two employees, Linda Laquer and Paul Frank, to the Los Angeles office. Both employees are Account Reps and start at $50,000. These are new employees, so no performance data is available. Assign a unique EmployeeID to each person. Is it easier to use the Employees table or the Employees form to modify data?
   e. Print all three reports in the database after the changes to the various tables have been made. (The second page of the Employees by Location report is shown in Figure 1.13 after the changes to the various tables have been made.) Submit all three reports to your instructor.
   f. Create a new report that displays the relationships within the database. Pull down the Tools menu and click Relationships to open the Relationships window, then pull down the File menu and click the Print Relationships command to display the Print Preview screen of a report that displays the contents of the Relationships window. Print this report for your instructor.

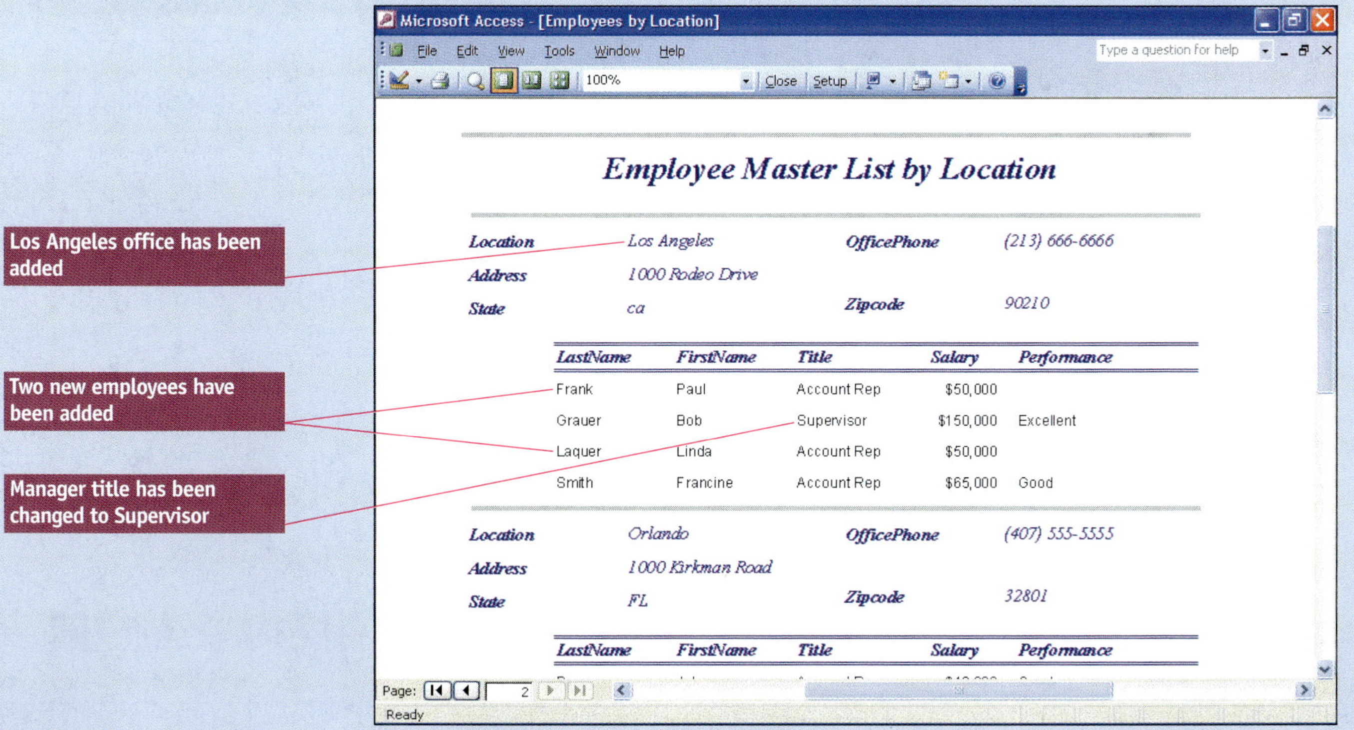

FIGURE 1.13 The Look Ahead Database (exercise 5)

6. **Peppy's Restaurants:** The Peppy's Restaurant chain is operated by individual franchisees throughout the state of Florida. Each restaurant offers the same menu, but differs in the size of the restaurant and the type of service offered. The data about all of the restaurants is maintained at corporate headquarters in an Access database. Your assignment is to open the *Chapter 1 Practice 6* database in the Exploring Access folder and test the various objects. Proceed as follows:
   a. Open the Restaurants form as shown in Figure 1.14. Add R0011 to the table, entering your name as the franchisee. Use any data that you think is appropriate. Print the record that you just added for your restaurant by clicking the Print button within the form. Close the form.
   b. Open the Restaurants table. Change the annual sales for restaurant R0003 to $1,000,000. Delete restaurant R0007.
   c. Print the Restaurants table for your instructor. Does all of the information for each restaurant fit on one page? Close the table. Return to the Database window, click the Report tab, and print the All Restaurants report. Does all of the information for each restaurant fit on one page? Do you see the restaurant that you just added in both places? Close the report.
   d. Click the Queries button in the Database window, then open both queries. Do both queries display all of the records in the Restaurants table? Does either query contain a field that is not present in the Restaurants table? Close the queries.
   e. Click the Reports button and print the two reports that correspond to the queries in part (d) for your instructor. Which is the more attractive way to display information, a query or a report?
   f. Return to the Database window. Pull down the File menu, click the Database Properties command, and then click the Contents tab. Which objects are in the database? How does this information compare to the information that is displayed in the Database Window?
   g. Submit all of the printed information to your instructor together with your answers to the discussion questions. Add a cover sheet to complete the assignment.

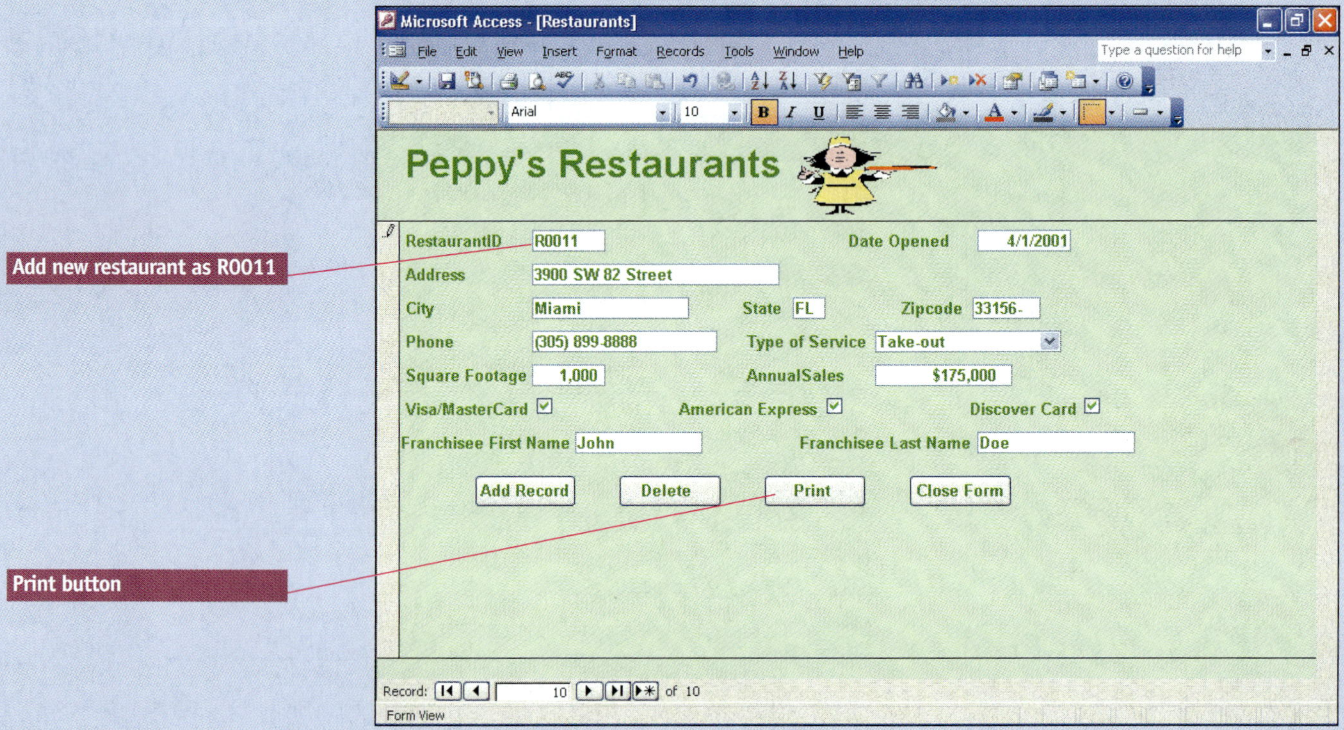

FIGURE 1.14 Peppy's Restaurants (exercise 6)

7. **Peppy's Relational Database:** The Peppy's Restaurant chain has replaced the database from the previous exercise with a relational database that contains separate tables for restaurants and franchisees. We have created a new database for you, as opposed to asking you to convert the previous database to a relational format. Nevertheless, there is still work for you to do. Accordingly, open the *Chapter 1 Practice 7* database and do the following:
   a. Create the one-to-many relationship between franchisees (i.e., owners) and restaurants as shown in Figure 1.15. The company encourages individuals to operate more than one restaurant, but a specific restaurant is run by only one franchisee.
   b. Open the Franchisees form and add yourself as Franchisee F008. Use any data that you deem appropriate. (You do not have to enter the same information as in the previous problem.)
   c. Open the Restaurants form and add restaurant R0011, using any data that you deem appropriate. You must, however, assign yourself (F008) as the franchisee.
   d. Change the FranchiseeID in restaurants 9 and 10 to F008 so that you will be associated with these restaurants as well.
   e. Print the Master Restaurant List report, which displays all restaurants in order of Restaurant ID. Print the Restaurant by Franchisee report, which lists the franchisees in order together with the restaurants they operate. Submit both reports to your instructor as proof you did the exercise.
   f. Create a new report that displays the relationships within the database. Pull down the Tools menu and click Relationships to open the Relationships window, then pull down the File menu and click the Print Relationships command to display the Print Preview screen of a report that displays the contents of the Relationships window. Print this report for your instructor.
   g. What is referential integrity and how does it pertain to Peppy's Relational Database? What happens if you assign a restaurant to a franchisee that does not exist? What happens if you attempt to delete a franchisee who owns multiple restaurants? Submit all of the printed information to your instructor together with the answers to the discussion questions.

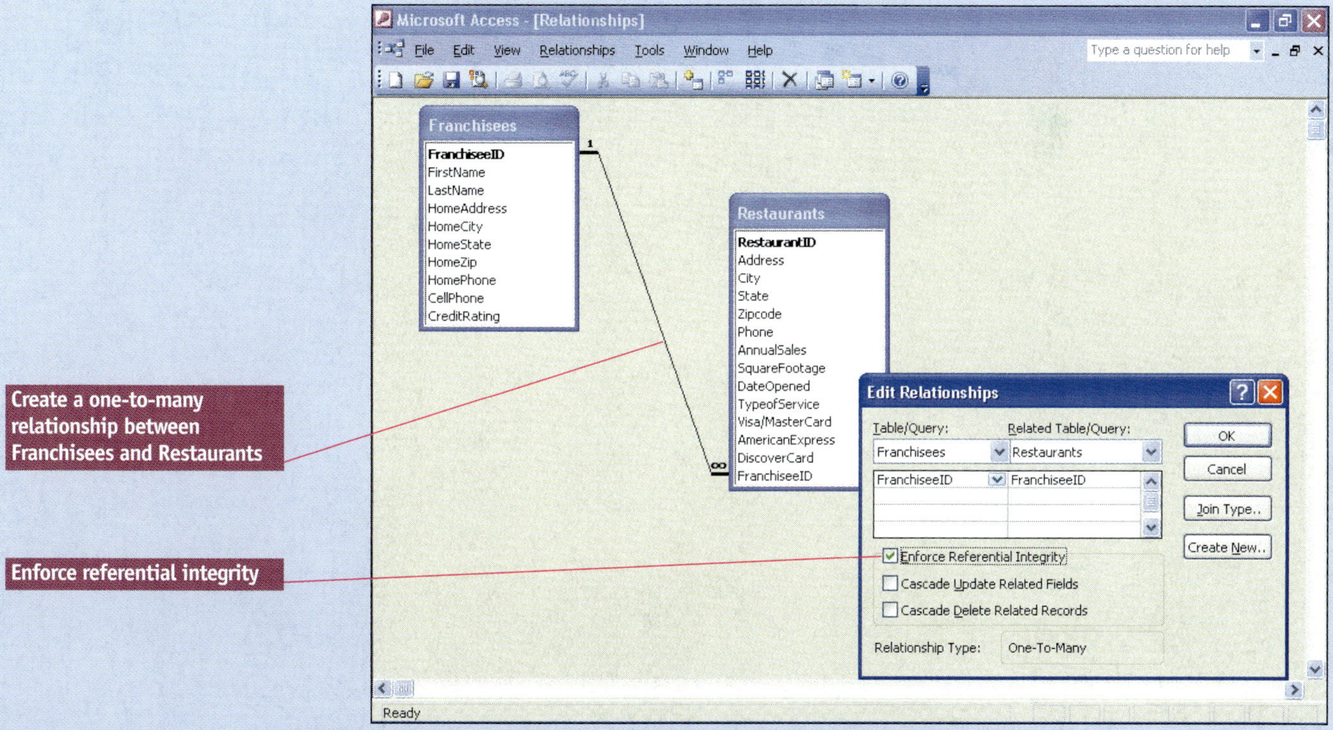

FIGURE 1.15 Peppy's Relational Database (exercise 7)

8. **Metro Zoo:** The newly opened Metro Zoo is the pride of your city. A relational database has been created with three tables: exhibits, trainers, and animals. There is a one-to-many relationship between exhibits and animals. One exhibit can have many different animals, but a specific animal is assigned to only one exhibit. A one-to-many relationship also exists between trainers and animals. One trainer can have many animals, but a specific animal has only one trainer. Open the *Chapter 1 Practice 8* database and proceed as follows:

   a. Pull down the Tools menu, click the Relationships command, and create the one-to-many relationships that exist in the system. Be sure to enforce referential integrity for both relationships.

   b. Open the Trainers form. Add yourself as a new trainer, using any information you deem appropriate. (Do not enter the TrainerID as this number is entered automatically.)

   c. Open the Animals form to add the record for the mountain tapir as shown in Figure 1.16. (Do not enter the AnimalID as this value is entered automatically.) Assign the tapir to the Americas exhibit and assign yourself as the trainer. Locate the Galapagos tortoise, black rhinoceros, and gorilla (AnimalID of 3, 11, and 12, respectively), and assign yourself as the trainer for these animals as well. Close the form.

   d. Click the Reports button in the database and print all four reports to verify that you have entered the data correctly. Which of these reports is based on data from more than one table?

   e. Create a fifth report that displays the relationships within the database. Pull down the Tools menu and click Relationships to open the Relationships window, then pull down the File menu and click the Print Relationships command to display the Print Preview screen of a report that displays the contents of the Relationships window. Print this report for your instructor.

   f. What is referential integrity, and how does it apply to the Metro Zoo database? What happens, for example, if you attempt to assign an animal to an exhibit that does not exist? What happens if you attempt to delete a trainer who has several employees? Submit all of the printed information to your instructor.

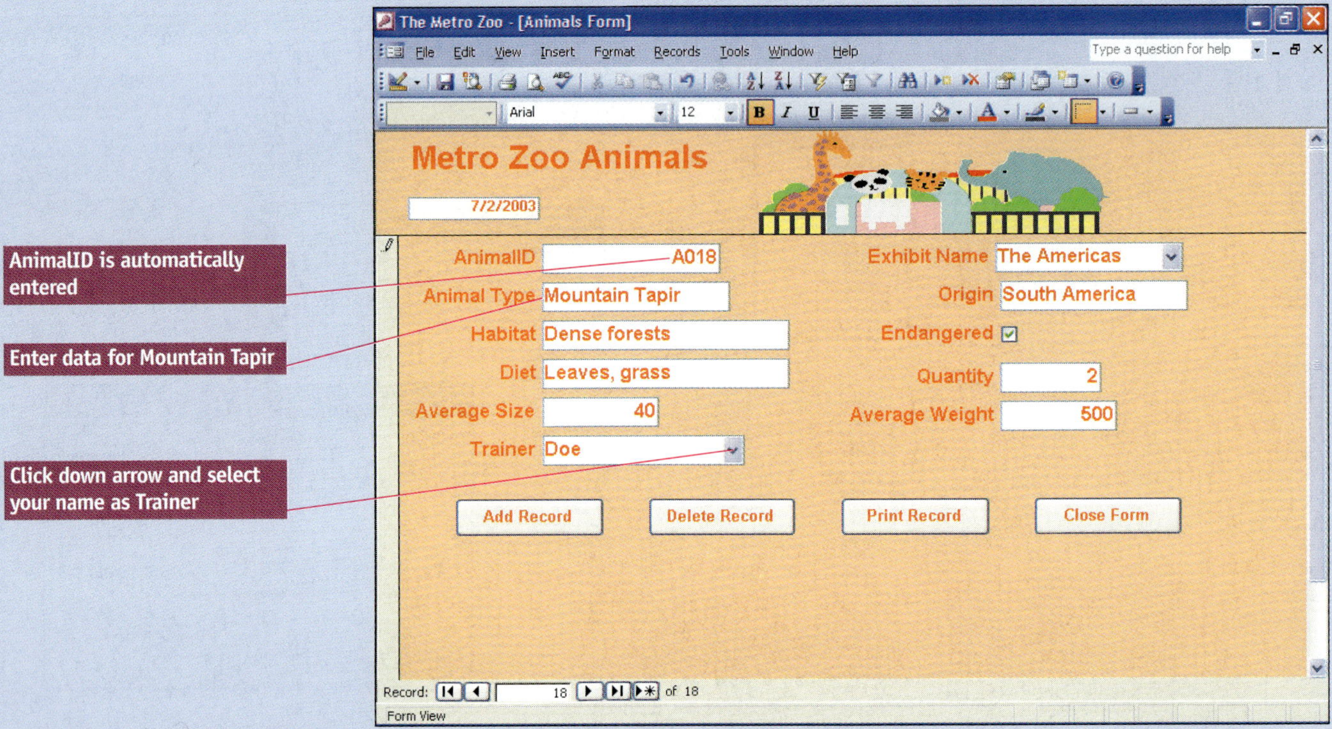

FIGURE 1.16 Metro Zoo (exercise 8)

MINI CASES

Planning for Disaster

This exercise has nothing to do with databases per se, but it is perhaps the most important assignment of all, as it deals with the question of backup. Do you have a backup strategy? Do you even know what a backup strategy is? You had better learn, because eventually you will wish you had one. You will erase a file, your system may become infected by a virus, or worse yet suffer a hardware failure in which you are unable to access the hard drive. The problem always seems to occur the night before an assignment is due. Describe in 250 words or less the backup strategy you plan to implement in conjunction with your work in this course.

Your First Consultant's Job

Go to a real installation, such as a doctor's or an attorney's office, the company where you work, or the computer lab at school. Determine the backup procedures that are in effect, then write a one-page report indicating whether the policy is adequate, and if necessary, offering suggestions for improvement. Your report should be addressed to the individual in charge of the business, and it should cover all aspects of the backup strategy—that is, which files are backed up and how often, and what software is used for the backup. Smaller organizations and professional offices (e.g., physicians and attorneys) are apt to be the installations that are most in need of assistance.

Changing Menus and Toolbars

Microsoft Office enables you to display a series of short menus that contain only basic commands. The additional commands are made visible by clicking the chevron that appears at the bottom of the menu. New commands are added to the menu as they are used, and conversely, other commands are removed if they are not used. A similar strategy is followed for the Standard and Formatting toolbars that are displayed on a single row, and thus do not show all of the buttons at one time. The intent is to simplify Office for the new user by limiting the number of visible commands. The consequence, however, is that the individual is not exposed to the new commands, and hence may not use Office to its full potential. Which set of menus do you prefer? How do you switch from one set to the other? Summarize your thoughts in a short note to your instructor.

Garbage In, Garbage Out

Your excellent work in this course has earned you an internship in the registrar's office. Your predecessor has created a student database that appears to work well, but in reality it has several problems in that the report on student grade point averages does not produce the expected information. Open the *Chapter 1 Mini Case GIGO* database in the Exploring Access folder and print the existing report. Study the results and see if you can determine the errors in the underlying data that create the erroneous output. What would you do in the future to prevent similar errors from reoccurring?

The Common User Interface

One of the most significant benefits of the Office environment is the common user interface, which provides a sense of familiarity when you go from one application to another—for example, when you go from Excel to Access. How many similarities can you find between these two applications? Which menus are common to both? Which keyboard shortcuts? Which formatting conventions? Which toolbar icons? Which shortcut menus?

CHAPTER 2

Tables and Forms: Design, Properties, Views, and Wizards

OBJECTIVES

After reading this chapter you will:

1. Discuss in general terms how to design a table.
2. Describe several data types and the associated properties.
3. Set the primary key of a table.
4. Use the Table Wizard to create a table; modify a table in Design view.
5. Describe how data validation is implemented in a table.
6. Use the Form Wizard to create a form; modify a form in Design view.
7. Distinguish between a bound control, an unbound control, and a calculated control.
8. Add a combo box and command buttons to a form.
9. Use a form to add, edit, and delete records in the underlying table.

hands-on exercises

1. CREATING A TABLE
   Input: None
   Output: My First Database
2. CREATING A FORM
   Input: My First Database (modified after exercise 1)
   Output: My First Database (modified)
3. A MORE SOPHISTICATED FORM
   Input: My First Database (modified after exercise 2)
   Output: My First Database (modified)

CASE STUDY
KAHAKAI VILLAS

Kahakai Villas, owned and operated by Kahakai Development, Inc. in Kona, Hawaii, has just broken ground on the construction of a 156-unit condominium. Kahakai Villas promises its future residents the ultimate in oceanside living, with unobstructed ocean views from every unit, in a lush tropical setting to create a true spirit of aloha. Residents choose from one, two, or three bedrooms. The base price ranges from $150,000 to $350,000, with the final price determined by the location and amenities selected. A carport is standard, whereas a garage is optional. Approximately half of the villas are adjacent to the private beach owned by the development company. The complex will also contain a spectacular swimming pool with units close to the pool paying a premium.

Joseph Murray, the project sales manager, wants to create an Access database to track the sales prospects who visit the site. He has created a simple questionnaire to capture demographic data (name, address, telephone, and so on) as well as the client's preferences in a villa. Joseph inquires about the client's price range, preferred floor, number of bedrooms, if they want a garage or carport, how soon they would be interested in moving (6 months, 9 months, 1 year, and 1 year plus), and if they would be living in the villa year-round or would be interested in offering their villa up for rental. He also leaves a space to make notes for himself. ■

Your assignment is to read the chapter and create a database for Mr. Murray. You can use the Table Wizard as the basis of your Customers (Prospects) table, but you will have to modify the table to include all of the required data as per the case description, and further to set the properties of the individual fields as appropriate. You will also need to create a form in which to enter the data. The Form Wizard is a good place to start, but you will have to modify the result to include command buttons, a suitable piece of clip art in the form header, and appropriate formatting throughout. Use the completed form to enter information about your instructor and the villa that he or she desires.

A STUDENT DATABASE

This chapter introduces a new case study, that of a student database, which we use to present the basic principles of table and form design. Tables and forms are used to input data into a system from which information can be produced. The value of that information depends entirely on the quality of the underlying data, which must be both complete and accurate. We begin, therefore, with a conceptual discussion emphasizing the importance of proper design and develop essential guidelines that are used throughout the book.

After the design has been developed, we turn our attention to implementing that design in Access. We show you how to create a table using the Table Wizard, then show you how to refine its design by changing the properties of various fields within the table. We also stress the importance of data validation during data entry.

The second half of the chapter introduces forms as a more convenient way to enter and display data. We introduce the Form Wizard to create a basic form, then show you how to modify that form to include command buttons, a list box, a check box, and an option group.

As a student you are well aware that your school maintains all types of data about you. They have your Social Security number. They have your name and address and phone number. They know whether or not you are receiving financial aid. They know your major and the number of credits you have completed. Think for a moment about the information your school requires, then write down all of the data needed to produce that information. This is the key to the design process. You must visualize the output the end user will require to determine the input to produce that output. Think of the specific fields you will need. Try to characterize each field according to the type of data it contains (such as text, numbers, or dates) as well as its size (length).

Our solution is shown in Figure 2.1, which may or may not correspond to what you have written down. The order of the fields within the table is not significant. Neither are the specific field names. What is important is that the table contain all necessary fields so that the system can perform as intended.

Field Name	Type
SSN	Text
FirstName	Text
LastName	Text
Address	Text
City	Text
State	Text
PostalCode	Text
PhoneNumber	Text
Major	Text
BirthDate	Date/Time
FinancialAid	Yes/No
Gender	Text
Credits	Number
QualityPoints	Number
DateAdmitted	Date/Time
E-mail	Text
International	Yes/No
HomePage	Hyperlink

FIGURE 2.1 The Students Table

Figure 2.1 may seem obvious upon presentation, but it does reflect the results of a careful design process based on three essential guidelines:

1. Include all of the necessary data
2. Store data in its smallest parts
3. Do not use calculated fields

Each guideline is discussed in turn. As you proceed through the text, you will be exposed to many applications that help you develop the experience necessary to design your own systems. Design is an important skill. Yes, you want to learn how to use Access, but you must first understand how to design a database and its tables if you are to use Access effectively.

Include the Necessary Data

How do you determine the necessary data? The best way is to create a rough draft of the reports you will need, then design the table so that it contains the fields necessary to create those reports. In other words, ask yourself what information will be expected from the system, then determine the data required to produce that information. Consider, for example, the type of information that can and cannot be produced from the table in Figure 2.1:

- You can contact a student by mail or by telephone. You cannot, however, contact the student's parents if the student lives on campus or has an address different from that of his or her parents.
- You can calculate a student's grade point average (GPA) by dividing the quality points by the number of credits. You cannot produce a transcript listing the courses a student has taken.
- You can calculate a student's age from his or her date of birth. You cannot determine how long the student has been at the university because the date of admission is not in the table.

Whether or not these omissions are important depends on the objectives of the system. Suffice it to say that you must design a table carefully, so that you are not disappointed when the database is implemented. *You must be absolutely certain that the data entered into a system is sufficient to provide all necessary information.* Think carefully about all of the reports you are likely to want, then be sure to capture the data to create those reports.

DESIGN FOR THE NEXT 100 YEARS

Your system will not last 100 years, but it is prudent to design as though it will. It is a fundamental law of information technology that systems evolve continually and that information requirements will change. Try to anticipate the future needs of the system, then build in the flexibility to satisfy those demands. Include the necessary data at the outset, and be sure that the field sizes are large enough to accommodate future expansion.

Store Data in Its Smallest Parts

The design in Figure 2.1 divides a student's name into two fields (first name and last name) to reference each field individually. You might think it easier to use a single field consisting of both the first and last name, but that approach is inadequate. Consider, for example, the list shown on the next page in which the student's name is stored as a single field:

List is in alphabetical order by first name

Allison Foster
Brit Reback
Carrie Graber
Danielle Ferrarro
Evelyn Adams
Frances Coulter

The first problem in this approach is one of flexibility, in that you cannot separate a student's first name from her last name. You could not, for example, create a salutation of the form "Dear Allison" or "Dear Ms. Foster" because the first and last name are not accessible individually. (In actuality you could write a procedure to divide the name field in two, but that is well beyond the capability of the Access novice.)

A second difficulty is that the list of students cannot be put into true alphabetical order because the last name begins in the middle of the field. Indeed, whether you realize it or not, the names in the list are already in alphabetical order (according to the design criteria of a single field) because sorting always begins with the leftmost position in a field. Thus the "A" in Allison comes before the "B" in Brit, and so on. The proper way to sort the data is on the last name, which can be done only if the last name is stored as a separate field. This illustrates the importance of storing data in its smallest parts.

CITY, STATE, AND ZIP CODE: ONE FIELD OR THREE?

The city, state, and zip code should always be stored as separate fields. Any type of mass mailing requires you to sort on zip code to take advantage of bulk mail. Other applications may require you to select records from a particular state or zip code, which can be done only if the data is stored as separate fields. The guideline is simple—store data in its smallest parts.

Avoid Calculated Fields

A ***calculated field*** is a field whose value is derived from a formula or function that references an existing field or combination of fields. Calculated fields should not be stored in a table because they are subject to change, waste space, and are otherwise redundant.

A student's Grade Point Average (GPA) is an example of a calculated field since it is computed by dividing the number of quality points by the number of credits. Thus it is unnecessary to store GPA in the Students table, because the table contains the fields on which the GPA is based. In other words, Access is able to calculate the GPA from these fields whenever it is needed, which is much more efficient than doing it manually. Imagine, for example, having to manually enter new values for credits and quality points and then having to recalculate the GPA for 10,000 students each semester.

BIRTH DATE VERSUS AGE

A person's age and date of birth provide equivalent information, as one is calculated from the other. It might seem easier, therefore, to store the age rather than the birth date, and thus avoid the calculation. That would be a mistake because age changes continually (and would need to be updated continually), whereas the date of birth remains constant. Similar reasoning applies to an employee's length of service versus date of hire.

CREATING A TABLE

There are two ways to create a table. The easier way is to use the ***Table Wizard***, an interactive coach that lets you choose from many predefined tables. The Table Wizard asks you questions about the fields you want to include in your table, then creates the table for you. Alternatively, you can create a table yourself by defining every field in the table. Regardless of how a table is created, you can modify it to include a new field or to delete an existing field.

Every field has a ***field name*** to identify the data that is entered into the field. The field name should be descriptive of the data and can be up to 64 characters in length, including letters, numbers, and spaces. We do not, however, use spaces in our field names, but use uppercase letters to distinguish the first letter of a new word. This is consistent with the default names provided by Access in its predefined tables.

Every field also has a ***data type*** that determines the type of data that can be entered and the operations that can be performed on that data. Access recognizes nine data types:

- A ***Number field*** contains a value that can be used in a calculation, such as the number of credits a student has earned. The contents of a number field are restricted to numbers, a decimal point, and a plus or minus sign.
- A ***Text field*** stores alphanumeric data, such as a student's name or address. It can contain alphabetic characters, numbers, and/or special characters (e.g., an apostrophe in O'Malley). Fields that contain only numbers but are not used in a calculation (e.g., Social Security Number, telephone number, or zip code) should be designated as text fields. A text field can hold up to 255 characters.
- A ***Memo field*** can be up to 65,535 characters long. Memo fields are used to hold lengthy, descriptive data (several sentences or paragraphs).
- A ***Date/Time field*** holds formatted dates or times (e.g., mm/dd/yy) and allows the values to be used in date or time arithmetic.
- A ***Currency field*** can be used in a calculation and is used for fields that contain monetary values.
- A ***Yes/No field*** (also known as a Boolean or Logical field) assumes one of two values, such as Yes or No, or True or False, or On or Off.
- An ***OLE Object field*** contains an object created by another application. OLE objects include pictures, sounds, or graphics.
- An ***AutoNumber field*** is a special data type that causes Access to assign the next consecutive number each time you add a record. The value of an AutoNumber field is unique for each record in the file, and thus AutoNumber fields are frequently used as the primary key.
- A ***Hyperlink field*** stores a Web address (URL). All Office documents are Web-enabled so that you can click a hyperlink and display the associated Web page.

Primary Key

The ***primary key*** is a field (or combination of fields) that makes each record in a table unique. The primary key is not required, but is highly recommended. There can be only one primary key per table.

A person's name is not used as the primary key because names are not unique. A Social Security Number, on the other hand, is unique and is a frequent choice for the primary key, as in the Students table in this chapter. The primary key emerges naturally in many applications, such as a part number in an inventory system, or the ISBN in the Books table of Chapter 1. If there is no apparent primary key, a new field can be created with the AutoNumber field type.

Views

A table has multiple views. The Datasheet view is the view you used in Chapter 1 to add, edit, and delete records. The Design view is the view you will use in this chapter to create (and modify) a table. The ***PivotTable view*** provides a convenient way to summarize data about groups of records. The ***PivotChart view*** displays a chart of the associated PivotTable view. (The PivotTable view and PivotChart view were introduced in Access 2002 and did not exist in previous versions. Both views are discussed in detail in Chapter 4.)

Figure 2.2a shows the Datasheet view corresponding to the table in Figure 2.1. (The horizontal scroll bar indicates that not all of the fields are visible.) The ***Datasheet view*** displays the record selector symbol for the current record (a pencil or a triangle). It also displays an asterisk in the record selector column next to the blank record at the end of the table.

Figure 2.2b shows the Design view of the same table. The ***Design view*** displays the field names in the table, the data type of each field, and the properties of the selected field. The Design view also displays a key indicator next to the field (or combination of fields) designated as the primary key.

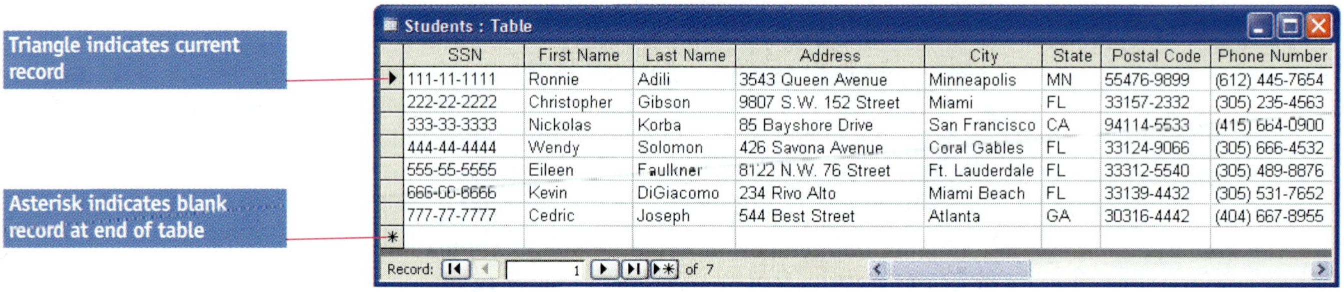

(a) Datasheet View

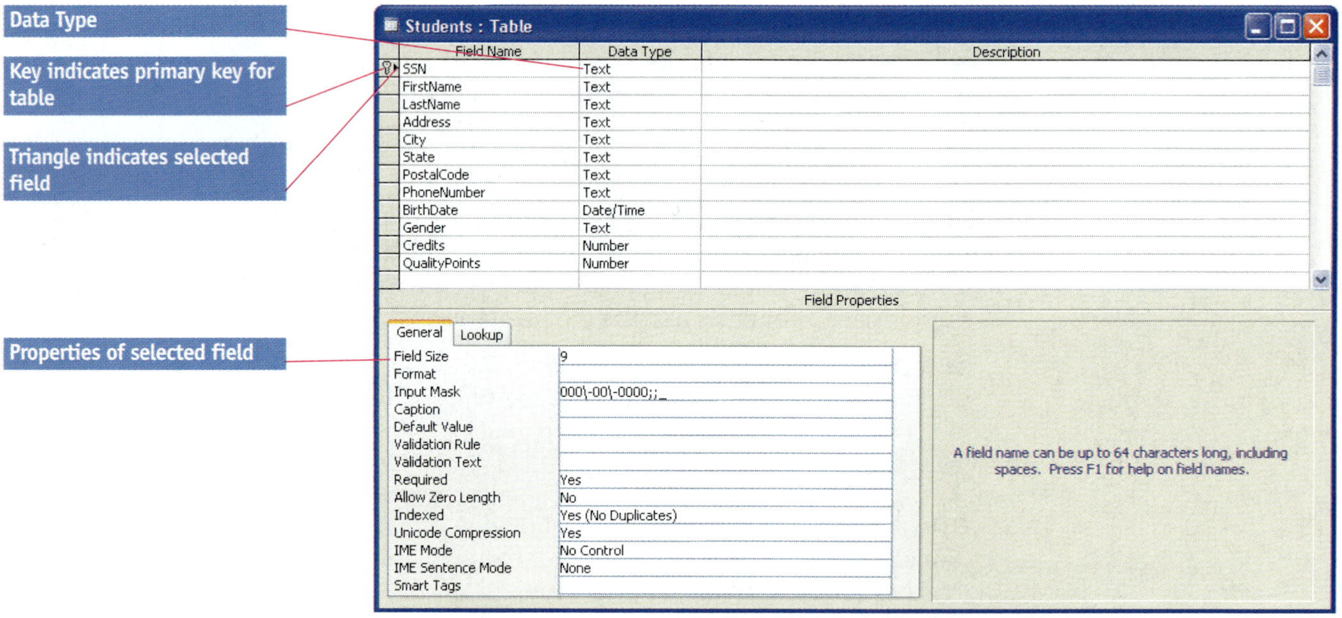

(b) Design View

FIGURE 2.2 The Views of a Table

Properties

A ***property*** is a characteristic or attribute of an object that determines how the object looks and behaves. Every Access object (tables, forms, queries, and reports) has a set of properties that determine the behavior of that object. The properties for an object are displayed and/or changed in a ***property sheet***, which is described in more detail later in the chapter.

Each field has its own set of properties that determine how the data in the field is stored and displayed. The properties are set to default values according to the data type, but can be modified as necessary. The properties are displayed in the Design view and described briefly below:

- The ***Field Size property*** adjusts the size of a text field or limits the allowable value in a number field. Microsoft Access uses only the amount of space it needs even if the field size allows a greater number.
- The ***Format property*** changes the way a field is displayed or printed, but does not affect the stored value.
- The ***Input Mask property*** facilitates data entry by displaying literal characters, that are displayed but not stored, such as hyphens in a Social Security number or slashes in a date. It also imposes data validation by ensuring that the data entered by the user fits within the mask.
- The ***Caption property*** specifies a label other than the field name for forms and reports.
- The ***Default Value property*** automatically enters a designated (default) value for the field in each record that is added to the table.
- The ***Validation Rule property*** rejects any record in which the data entered does not conform to the specified rules for data entry.
- The ***Validation Text property*** specifies the error message that is displayed when the validation rule is violated.
- The ***Required property*** rejects any record that does not have a value entered for this field.
- The ***Allow Zero Length property*** allows text or memo strings of zero length.
- The ***Indexed property*** increases the efficiency of a search on the designated field. (The primary key in a table is always indexed.)
- The ***Unicode Compression property*** is set to "Yes" by default for Text, Memo, and Hyperlink fields to store the data more efficiently.
- The ***IME Mode*** and ***IME Sentence Mode properties*** refer to the Input Method Editor for East Asian languages and are not discussed further.

There is no need to memorize the list of properties because they are readily available in the Design view of a table. And, as you may have guessed, it's time for our next hands-on exercise, in which you create a new database. We begin with the Table Wizard, then switch to the Design view to add additional fields and modify selected properties of various fields within the table.

CHANGE THE DEFAULT FOLDER

The default folder is the folder Access uses to retrieve (and save) a database unless it is otherwise instructed. To change the default folder, pull down the Tools menu, click Options, then click the General tab in the Options dialog box. Enter the name of the default database folder (e.g., C:\Exploring Access), then click OK to accept the settings and close the Options dialog box. The next time you access the File menu, the default folder will reflect the change.

hands-on exercise

1 Creating a Table

Objective To create a new database; to use the Table Wizard to create a table; to add and delete fields of an existing table. Use Figure 2.3 as a guide.

Step 1: Create a New Database

- Click the **Start button**, click the **All Programs button**, click **Microsoft Office**, then click **Microsoft Access** to start the program.
- Click **Create a new file** at the bottom of the Getting Started task pane, then click **Blank database** in the New File task pane. (If the task pane is not open, click the **New button** on the toolbar.)
- You should see the File New Database dialog box shown in Figure 2.3a.
- Click the **drop-down arrow** on the Save In list box and select the appropriate drive. Double click the **Exploring Access folder**.
- Click in the **File Name text box** and drag to select **db1**. Type **My First Database** as the name of the database you will create. Click the **Create button.**

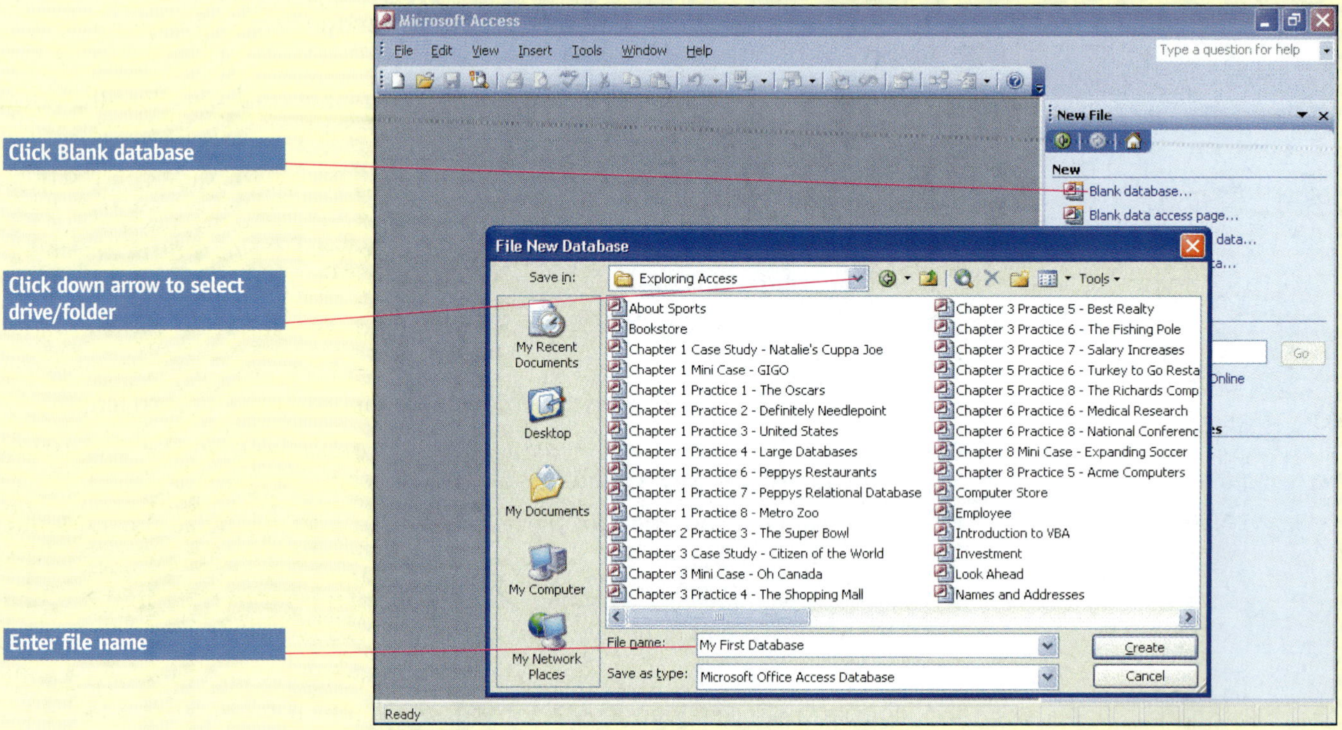

(a) Create a New Database (step 1)

FIGURE 2.3 Hands-on Exercise 1

FILE FORMATS

Access 2002 (Office XP) introduced a new file format that was continued in Access 2003. Access 2000, however, cannot read the new format; thus, it is convenient to save files in the older Access 2000 format to maintain compatibility with anyone using Microsoft Office 2000. Pull down the Tools menu, click Options, click the Advanced tab, and change the Default File Format to Access 2000. Use Help to learn about converting from one file format to another.

Step 2: The Table Wizard

- The Database window for My First Database should appear on your monitor. The Tables button is selected by default.
- Double click the icon to **Create table by using wizard** to start the Table Wizard as shown in Figure 2.3b. Click the **Business option button**.
- Click the **down arrow** on the Sample Tables list box to scroll through the available tables until you can select (click) the **Students table**. (The Students table is found near the bottom of the list.)
- The **StudentID field** is already selected in the Sample Fields list box. Click the **> button** to enter this field into the list of fields for the new table.
- Enter the additional fields for the new table by selecting the field and clicking the **> button** (or by double clicking the field). The fields to enter are **FirstName, LastName, Address, City**, and **StateOrProvince**.
- Click the **Rename Field button** after adding the StateOrProvince field to display the Rename Field dialog box. Enter **State** to shorten the name of this field. Click **OK** to accept the new name and close the dialog box.

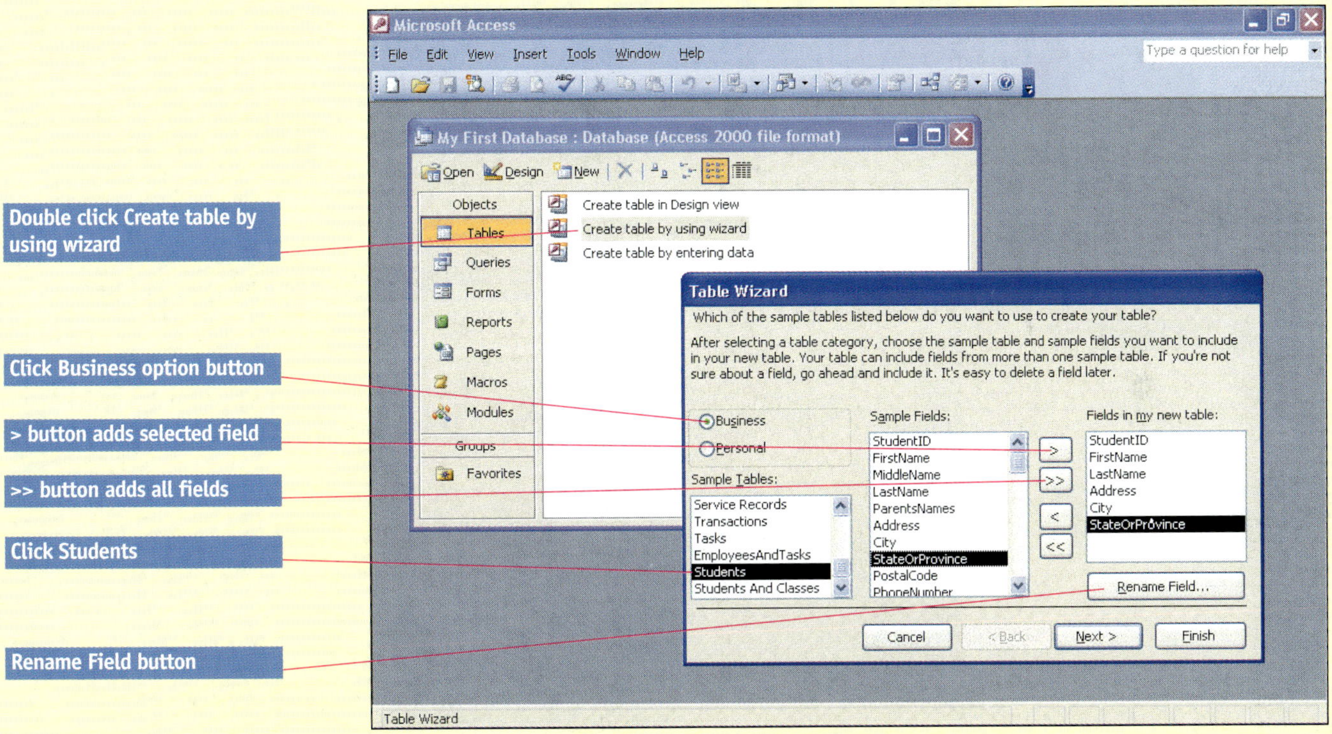

(b) The Table Wizard (step 2)

FIGURE 2.3 Hands-on Exercise 1 (*continued*)

WIZARDS AND BUTTONS

Many wizards present you with two open list boxes and expect you to copy some or all fields from the list box on the left to the list box on the right. The > and >> buttons work from left to right. The < and << buttons work in the opposite direction. The > button copies the selected field from the list box on the left to the box on the right. The >> button copies all of the fields. The < button removes the selected field from the list box on the right. The << removes all of the fields.

Step 3: The Table Wizard Continued

- Add **PostalCode** and **PhoneNumber** (you may need to click the **down arrow** to scroll). Click **Next**.
- The next screen in the Table Wizard asks you to name the table and determine the primary key.
  - ❑ Accept the Wizard's suggestion of **Students** as the name of the table.
  - ❑ Make sure that the option button **Yes, set a primary key for me** is selected as shown in Figure 2.3c.
  - ❑ Click **Next** to accept both of these options.
- The final screen in the Table Wizard asks what you want to do next.
  - ❑ Click the option button to **Modify the table design**.
  - ❑ Click the **Finish command button**.
- The Students table should appear in Design view. Pull down the **File menu** and click **Save** (or click the **Save button** on the Table Design toolbar) to save the table within the database.
- The Table Wizard provided an easy way to create the table initially. You can now modify the table in Design view as described in the next several steps.

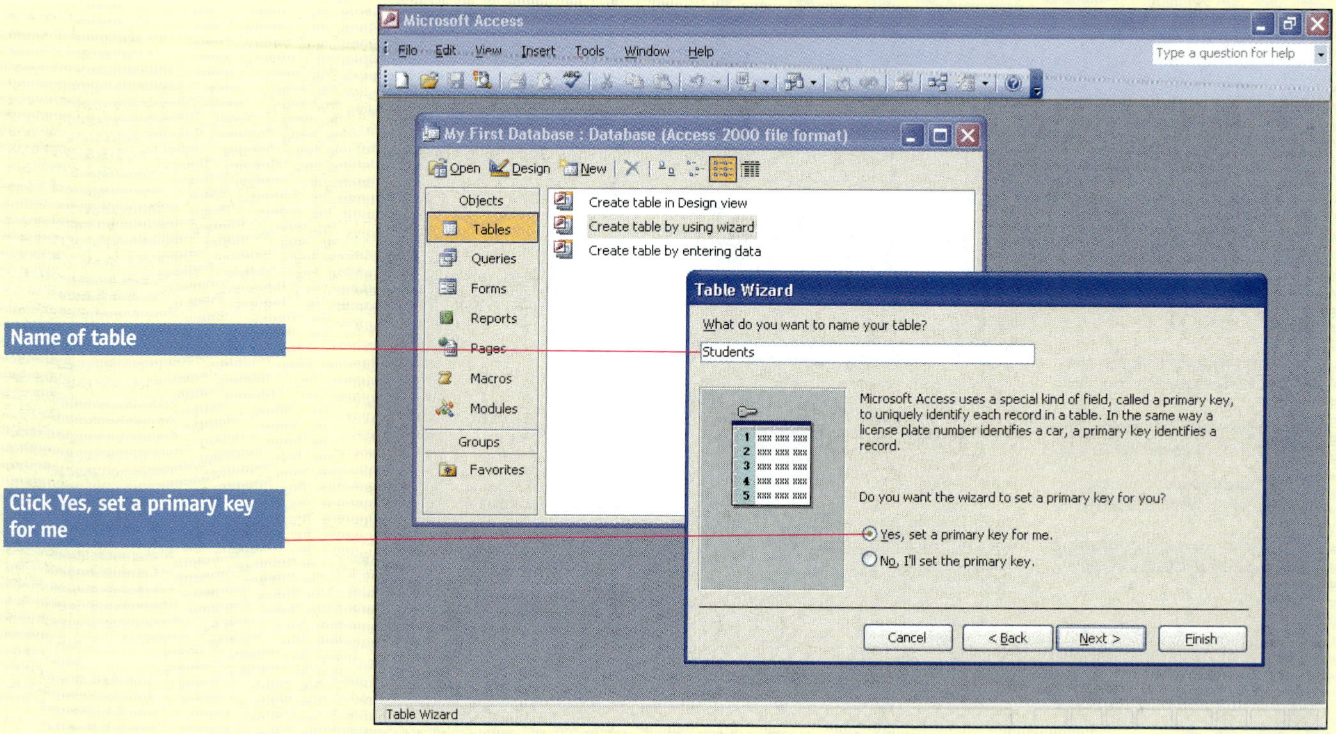

(c) The Table Wizard Continued (step 3)

FIGURE 2.3 Hands-on Exercise 1 (*continued*)

YOU DON'T HAVE TO USE THE TABLE WIZARD

There is no requirement to use the Table Wizard, especially if you are creating a table that is very different from those available through the wizard. Go to the Database window, click the Tables button, then double click the option to Create Table in Design view. Enter the field name for the first field, select the field type, then modify the field properties as necessary. Continue to work in this fashion as you enter the remaining fields into the table. See practice exercises 4, 6, and 8 at the end of the chapter.

Step 4: Add the Additional Fields

- Click the **Maximize button** to give yourself more room to work. Click the cell immediately below the last field in the table (PhoneNumber). Type **BirthDate** as shown in Figure 2.3d.
- Press the **Tab key** to move to the Data Type column. Click the **down arrow** on the drop-down list box. Click **Date/Time.** (You can also type the first letter of the field type such as **D** for Date/Time, **T** for Text, or **N** for number.)
- Add the remaining fields to the Students table.
  - ❑ Add **Gender** as a Text field.
  - ❑ Add **Credits** as a Number field.
  - ❑ Add **QualityPoints** as a Number field. (There is no space in the field name.)
- The additional fields are unique to our application and were not available in the wizard.
- Click the **Save button** to save the table.

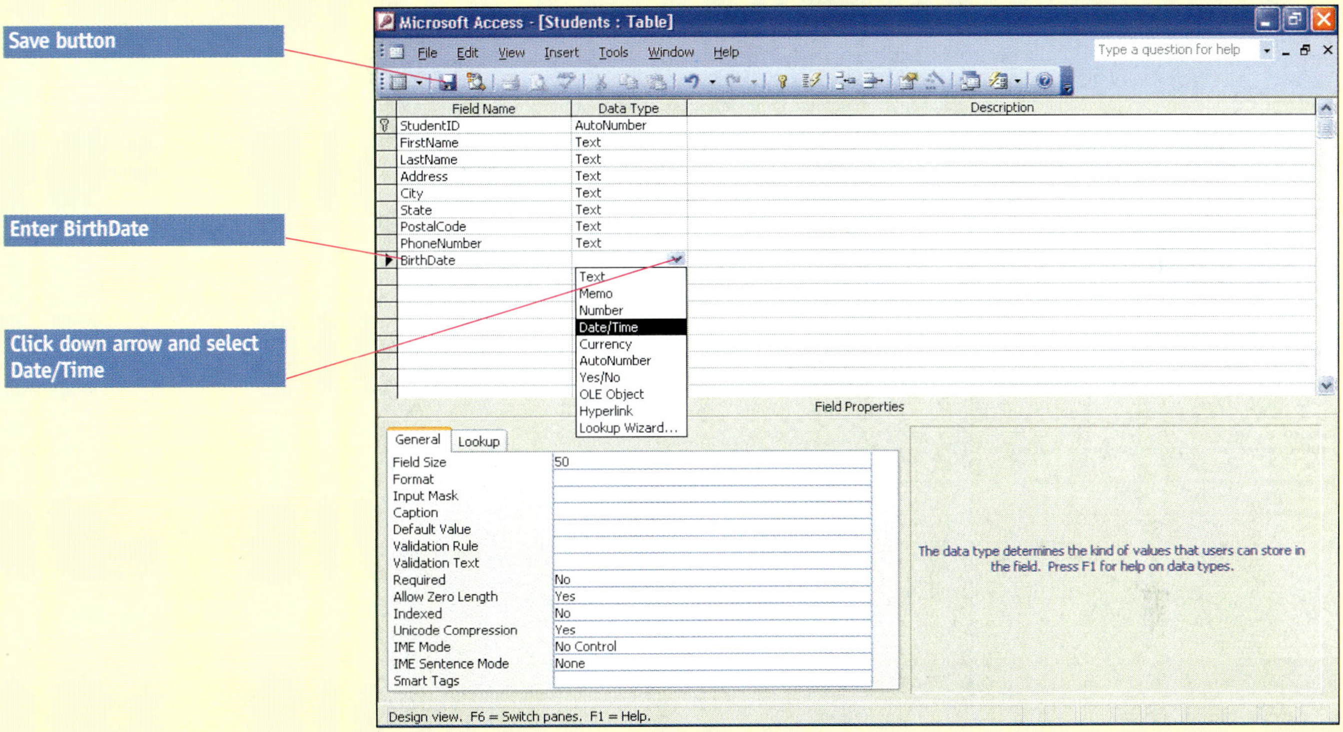

(d) Add the Additional Fields (step 4)

FIGURE 2.3 Hands-on Exercise 1 (*continued*)

NUMBERS AS TEXT FIELDS

The numeric field type should be restricted to fields on which you perform calculations, such as a student's credits or quality points. This implies that fields such as Social Security number, zip code, and telephone number are defined as text fields even though they contain numbers, as opposed to alphabetic characters. Look closely within the Students table that was created by the Table Wizard and you will see that PostalCode and PhoneNumber have been defined as text fields. (The additional characters that appear within a field, such as hyphens in a Social Security number, are entered as an input mask and are not stored within the field.)

Step 5: Change the Primary Key

- Point to the first field in the table and click the **right mouse button** to display the shortcut menu in Figure 2.3e. Click **Insert Rows**.
- Click the **Field Name column** in the newly inserted row. Type **SSN** (for Social Security Number) as the name of the new field. Press **Enter**. The data type will be set to Text by default.
- Click the **Required box** in the Properties area. Click the **drop-down arrow** and select **Yes**.
- Click in the Field Name column for **SSN**, then click the **Primary Key button** on the Table Design toolbar to change the primary key to Social Security Number. The primary key symbol has moved to SSN.
- Point to the **StudentID field** in the second row. Click the **right mouse button** to display the shortcut menu. Click **Delete Rows** to remove this field from the table definition.
- Save the table.

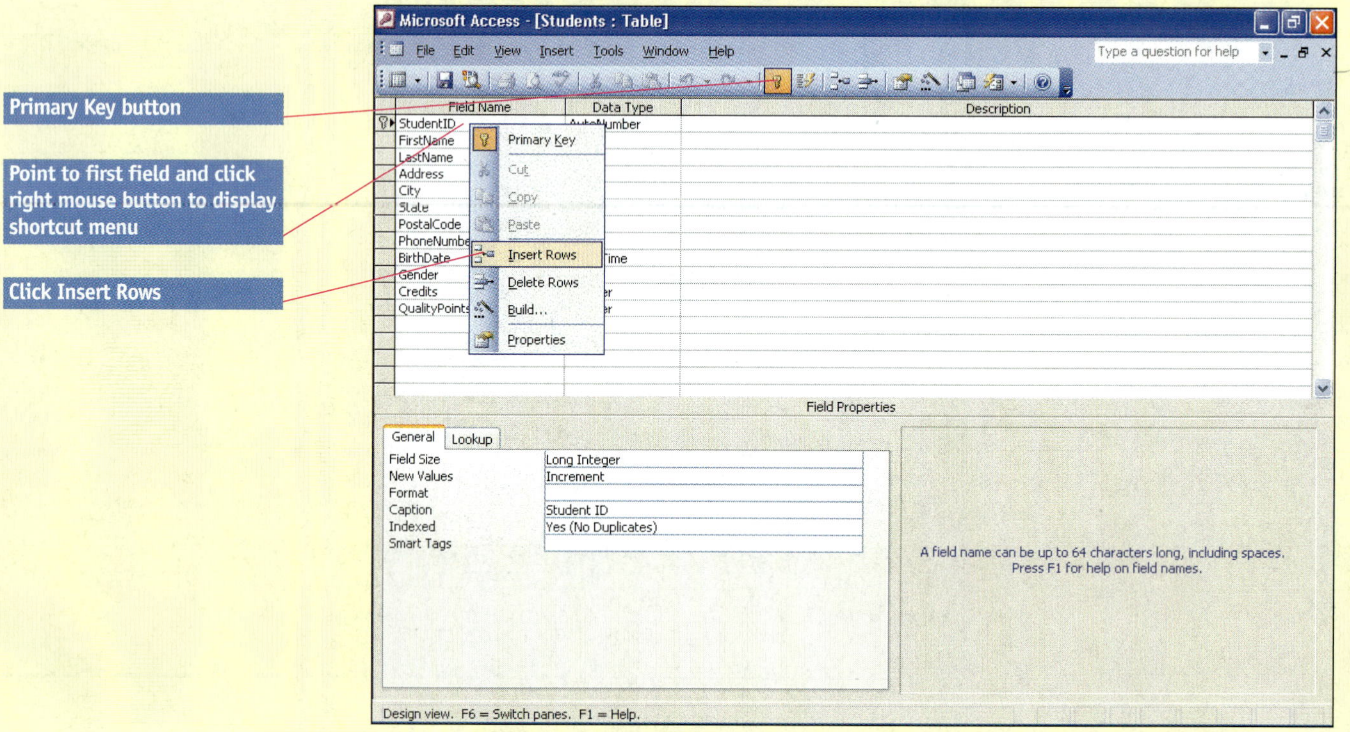

(e) Change the Primary Key (step 5)

FIGURE 2.3 Hands-on Exercise 1 (*continued*)

INSERTING OR DELETING FIELDS

To insert or delete a field, point to an existing field, then click the right mouse button to display a shortcut menu. Click Insert Rows or Delete Rows to add or remove a field as appropriate. To insert (or delete) multiple fields, point to the field selector to the left of the field name, click and drag the mouse over multiple rows to extend the selection, then click the right mouse button to display a shortcut menu.

Step 6: Create an Input Mask

- Click the field selector column for **SSN**. Click the **Input Mask box** in the Properties area. (The box is currently empty.)
- Click the **Build button** to display the Input Mask Wizard. Click **Yes** if asked to save the table. Click **Social Security Number** in the Input Mask Wizard dialog box as shown in Figure 2.3f.
- Click the **Try It** text box and enter a Social Security number to see how the mask works. If necessary, press the **left arrow key** until you are at the beginning of the text box, then enter a Social Security number (digits only). Click the **Finish command button** to accept the input mask. Click in the text box for the Field Size property and change the field size to **9**.
- Click the field selector column for **BirthDate**, then follow the steps detailed above to add an input mask. (Choose the **Short Date** format.) Click **Yes** if asked whether to save the table.
- Set an appropriate input mask for the telephone number as well. Change the field size to **10**.
- Save the table.

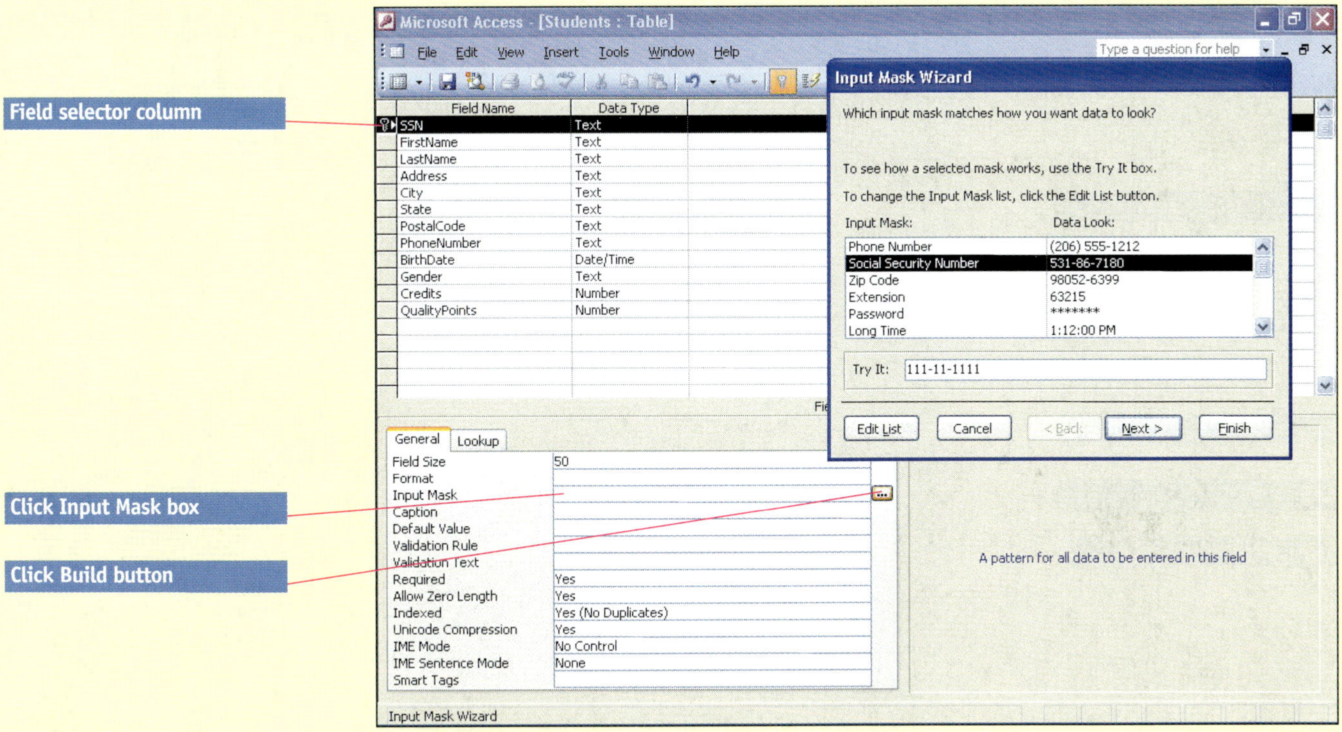

(f) Create an Input Mask (step 6)

FIGURE 2.3 Hands-on Exercise 1 (*continued*)

CREATE YOUR OWN INPUT MASK

The Input Mask imposes character-by-character data validation by requiring that data be entered in a specific way. The Social Security mask, for example, 000\-00\-0000, specifies a zero to require a numeric value from 0 to 9. The character following the slash (a hyphen in this example) is an insertion character and appears within the field during data entry but is not stored. You can create your own input masks for text fields by using the characters "L" to require a letter, or "A" to require either a letter or a digit. Use the Help command for additional information.

Step 7: Change the Field Properties

- Click the field selector column for the **FirstName field**. Click in the text box for the **Field Size property** and change the field size to **15**. Change the **Required property** to **Yes**.
- Select the **LastName field**. Set the **Field Size property** to **20** and the **Required property** to **Yes**.
- Select the **State field.** Set the **Field Size property** to two. Click the **Format box** in the Properties Area. Type a > sign to display the data in uppercase as shown in Figure 2.3g. Click in the **InputMask property** and type **LL** to require letters, as opposed to digits.
- Select the **Credits field**. Click the **Field Size box** in the Properties area, click the **down arrow** to display the available field sizes, then click **Integer**. Click in the **Default property box** and delete the default value of zero.
- Set the Field Size and Default properties for the **QualityPoints field** to match those of the Credits field.
- Save the table.

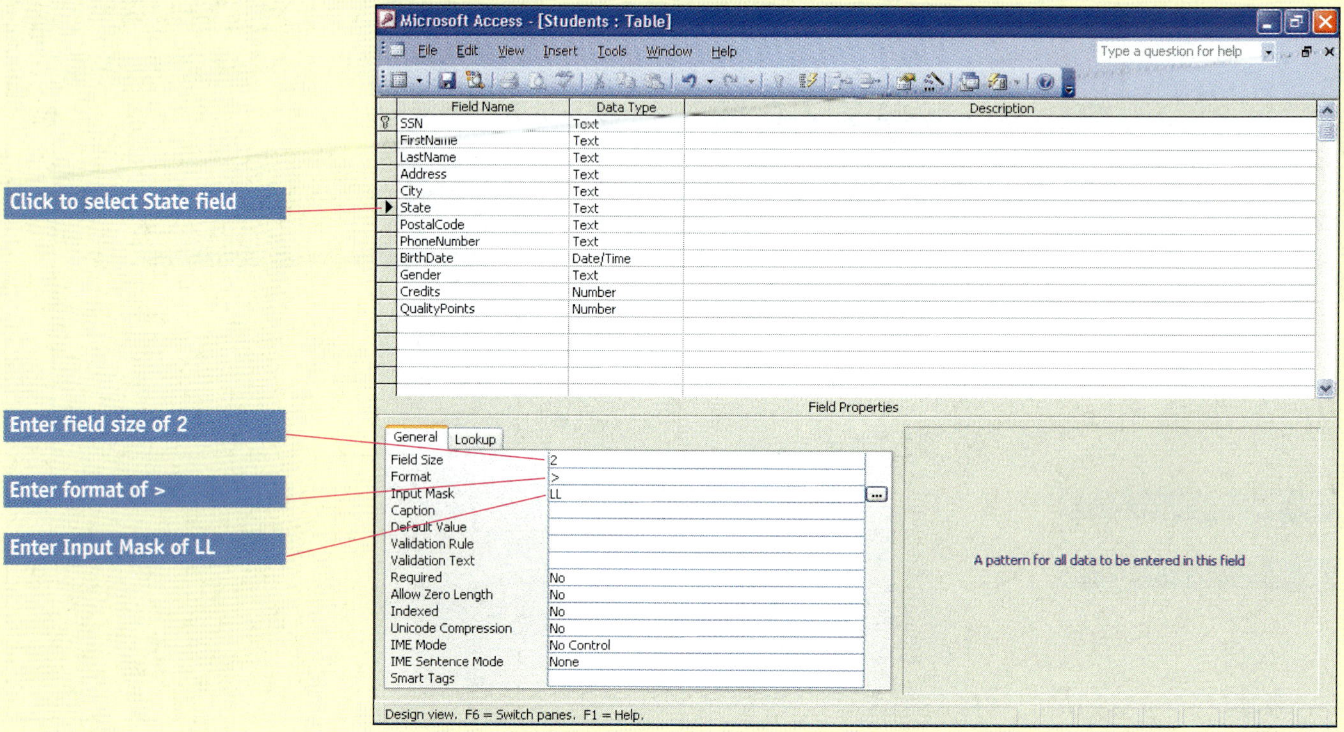

(g) Change the Field Properties (step 7)

FIGURE 2.3 Hands-on Exercise 1 (*continued*)

THE FIELD SIZE PROPERTY

The field size property should be set to the smallest possible setting because smaller data sizes are processed more efficiently. A text field can hold from 0 to 255 characters (50 is the default). Number fields which do not contain a decimal value can be set to Byte, Integer, or Long Integer field sizes, which hold values up to 255, 32,767, or 2,147,483,647, respectively. (Click in the Field Size box for a Number field and press F1 for more information.)

Step 8: Add a Validation Rule

- Data validation is implemented in several ways. You can set the Required property to Yes to ensure that a value is entered and/or you can create an input mask to accept only certain characters. You can also set the Validation Rule property.
- Select the **Gender field** as shown in Figure 2.3h. Click the **Field Size box** and change the field size to **1**.
- Click the **Format box** in the Properties area. Type a **>** sign to display the data in uppercase letters.
- Click the **Validation Rule box**. Type **="M" or "F"** to accept only these values on data entry. Click the **Validation Text box**, and type **You must specify M or F**. (This message explains the error to the user.)
- Check that the required property is set to "No" so that gender is not required. If the user enters a value, however, it must be "M" or "F".
- Save the table.

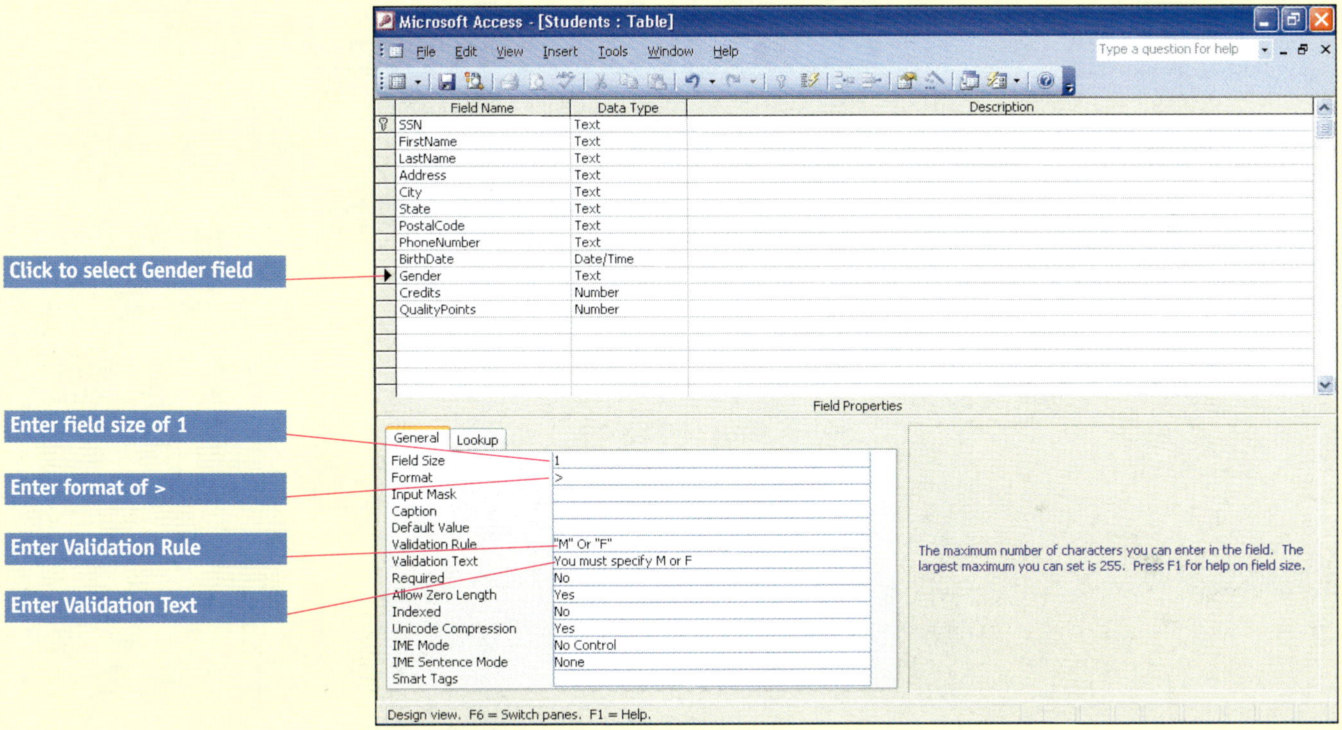

(h) Add a Validation Rule (step 8)

FIGURE 2.3 Hands-on Exercise 1 (*continued*)

VALIDATE THE INCOMING DATA

No system, no matter how sophisticated, can produce valid output from invalid input—in other words, "garbage in, garbage out." It is absolutely critical, therefore, that you take the time to validate the data as it is entered to ensure the quality of the output. Some validation is already built in by Access. You cannot, for example, enter duplicate values for a primary key, nor can you enter text into a numeric field. Other validation is built in at the initiative of the developer by setting various field properties in Design view.

Step 9: Print the Students Table

- Pull down the **View menu** and click **Datasheet View** to change to the Datasheet view as shown in Figure 2.3i. Enter data for yourself. Note the input masks that appear in conjunction with the Social Security number, phone number, and birth date.
- Pull down the **File menu** and click the **Page Setup command** to display the Page Setup dialog box. Click the **Page tab** and change to **Landscape printing**.
- Click the **Margins tab**. Change the left and right margins to **.5 inch**. Click **OK**.
- Click the **Print Preview button** to view the table to check that it fits on one page. (If not, return to the Datasheet view and reduce the column widths as necessary.)
- Pull down the **File menu**, click the **Print command**, and click **OK** to print the table. Close the Print Preview window. Close the Students table. Click **Yes** if prompted to save the changes to the table.
- Pull down the **File menu** and click the **Exit command** if you do not want to continue with the next exercise at this time.

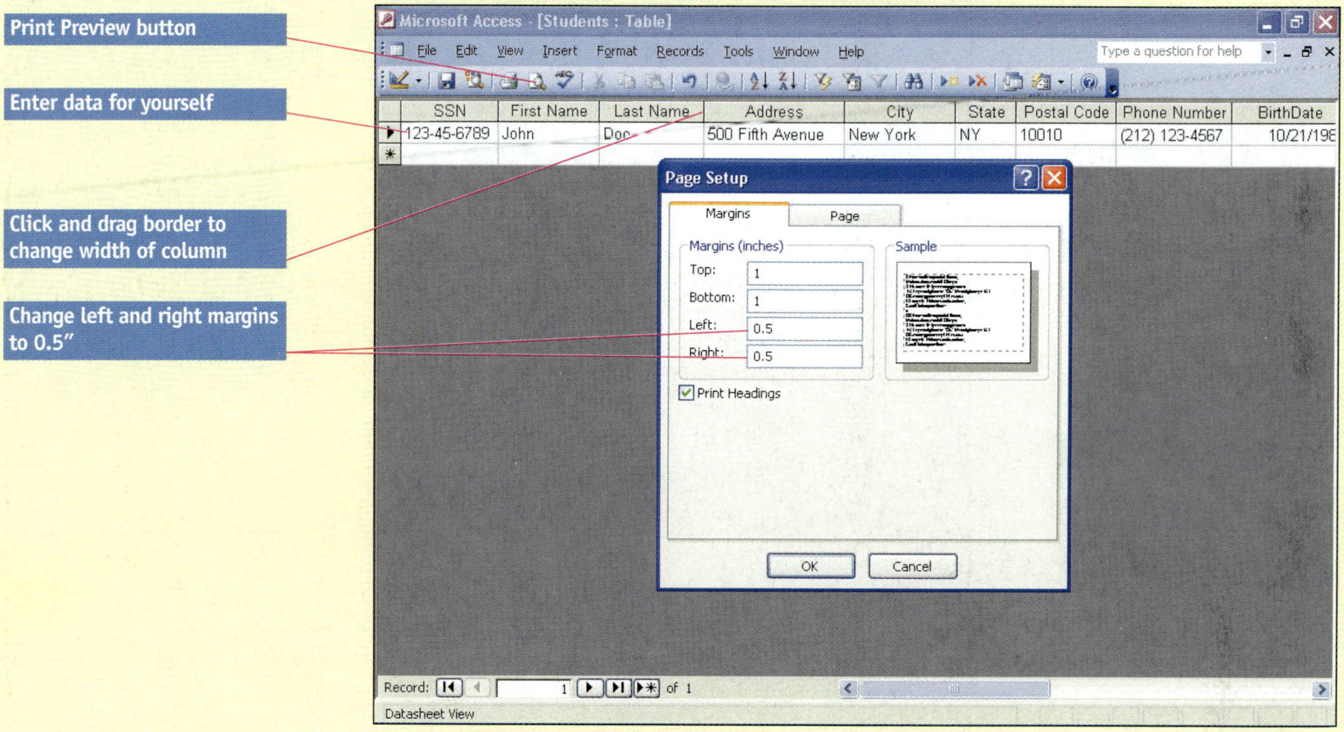

(i) Print the Students Table (step 9)

FIGURE 2.3 Hands-on Exercise 1 (*continued*)

CHANGE THE FIELD WIDTH—ACCESS AND EXCEL

Drag the border between field names to change the displayed width of a column. You can also double click the right border of a field name to change the width of the column to accommodate the widest entry in that column. This is the same convention that is followed in Microsoft Excel. Look for other similarities between the two applications. For example, you can click within a field, then click the Sort Ascending or Sort Descending buttons (in tables with multiple records) on the toolbar to display the records in the indicated sequence.

FORMS

A ***form*** provides an easy way to enter and display the data stored in a table. You type data into a form, such as the one in Figure 2.4, and Access stores the data in the corresponding (underlying) table in the database. One advantage of using a form (as opposed to entering records in the Datasheet view) is that you can see all of the fields in a single record without scrolling. A second advantage is that a form can be designed to resemble a paper form, and thus provide a sense of familiarity for the individuals who actually enter the data.

A form has different views, as does a table. The ***Form view*** in Figure 2.4a displays the completed form and is used to enter or modify the data in the underlying table. The ***Design view*** in Figure 2.4b is used to create or modify the form. A form also provides access to the PivotTable view and PivotChart view.

All forms contain ***controls*** (objects) that accept and display data, perform a specific action, decorate the form, or add descriptive information. There are three types of controls—bound, unbound, and calculated. A ***bound control*** (such as the text boxes in Figure 2.4a) has a data source (a field in the underlying table) and is used to enter or modify the data in that table.

An ***unbound control*** has no data source. Unbound controls are used to display titles, labels, lines, graphics, or pictures. Note, too, that every bound control in Figure 2.4a is associated with an unbound control (or label to identify the control). The bound control for Social Security number, for example, is preceded by a label (immediately to the left of the control) that indicates to the user the value that is to be entered. An unbound control is also used for the title of the form.

A ***calculated control*** has as its data source an expression rather than a field. An ***expression*** is a combination of operators (e.g., +, –, *, and /), field names, constants, and/or functions. A student's Grade Point Average (GPA in Figure 2.4a) is an example of a calculated control because it is computed by dividing the number of quality points by the number of credits.

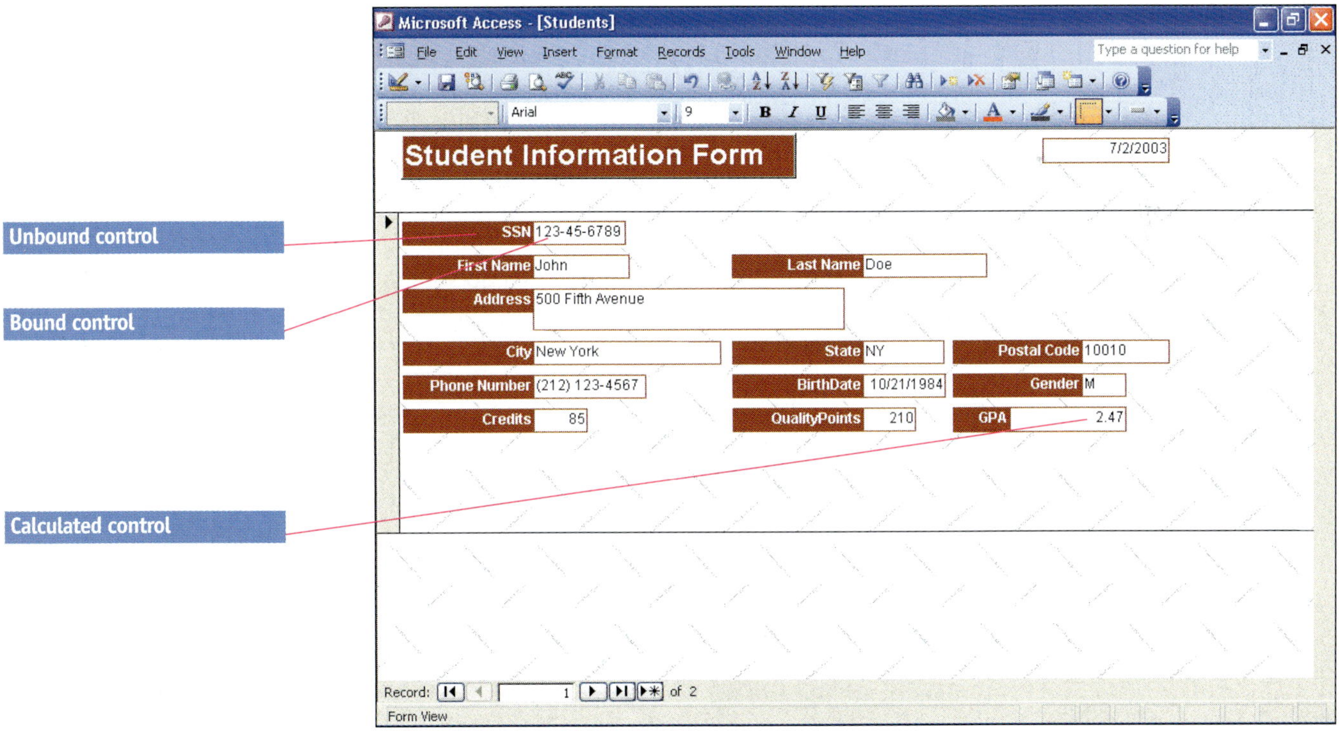

(a) Form View

FIGURE 2.4 Forms

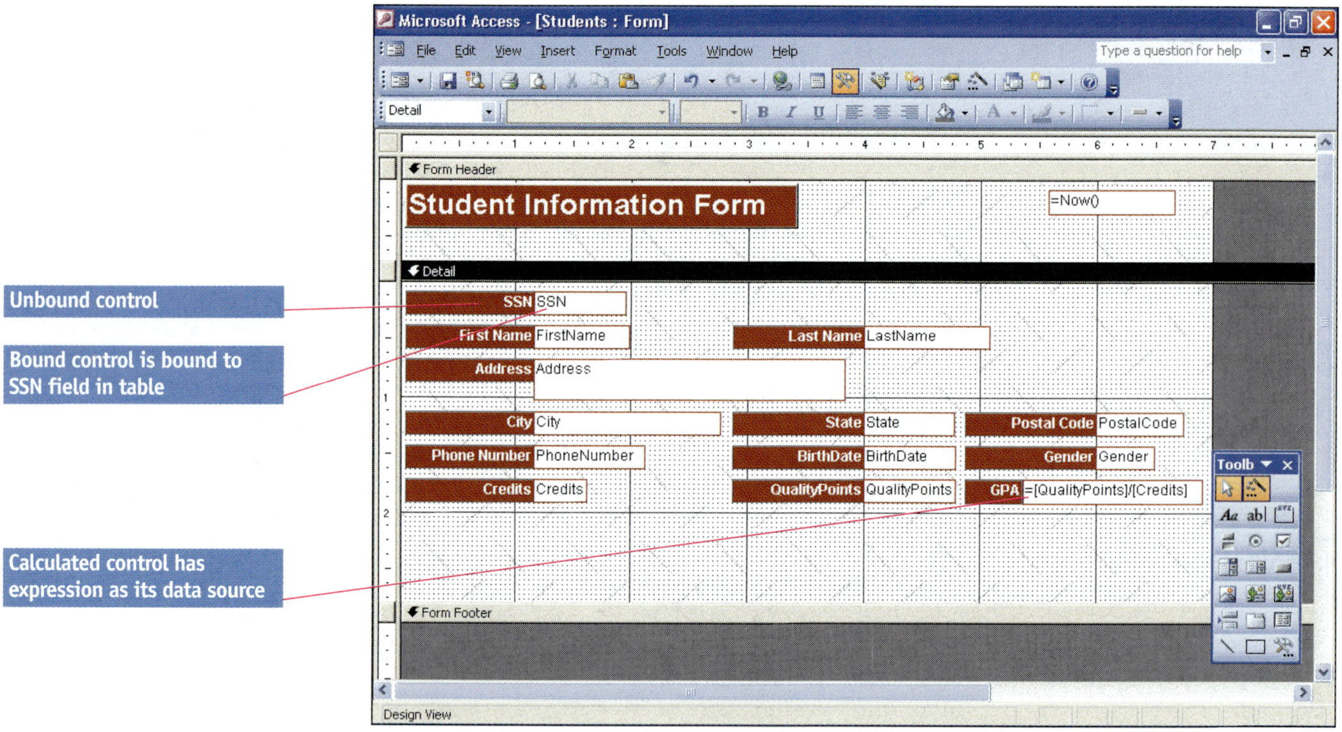

(b) Design View

FIGURE 2.4 Forms (*continued*)

Properties

As previously stated, a property is a characteristic or attribute of an object that determines how the object looks and behaves. Every control in a form has its own set of properties, just as every field in a table has its own set of properties. The properties for a control are displayed in a property sheet, as shown in Figure 2.5.

Figure 2.5a displays the property sheet for the Form Header Label. There are many different properties (note the vertical scroll bar) that control every aspect of the label's appearance. The properties are determined automatically as the object is created; that is, as you move and size the label on the form, the properties related to its size and position (Left, Top, Width, and Height in Figure 2.5a) are established for you.

Other actions, such as various formatting commands, set the properties that determine the font name and size (Arial and 18 point in Figure 2.5a). You can change the appearance of an object in two ways—by executing a command to change the object on the form, which in turn changes the property sheet, *or* by changing the property within the property sheet, which in turn changes the object's appearance on the form.

Figure 2.5b displays the property sheet for the bound SSN control. The name of the control is SSN. The source for the control is the SSN field in the Students table. Thus, various properties of the SSN control, such as the input mask, are inherited from the SSN field in the underlying table. Note, too, that the list of properties in Figure 2.5b, which reflects a bound control, is different from the list of properties in Figure 2.5a for an unbound control. Some properties, however (such as Left, Top, Width, and Height, which determine the size and position of an object), are present for every control and determine its location on the form.

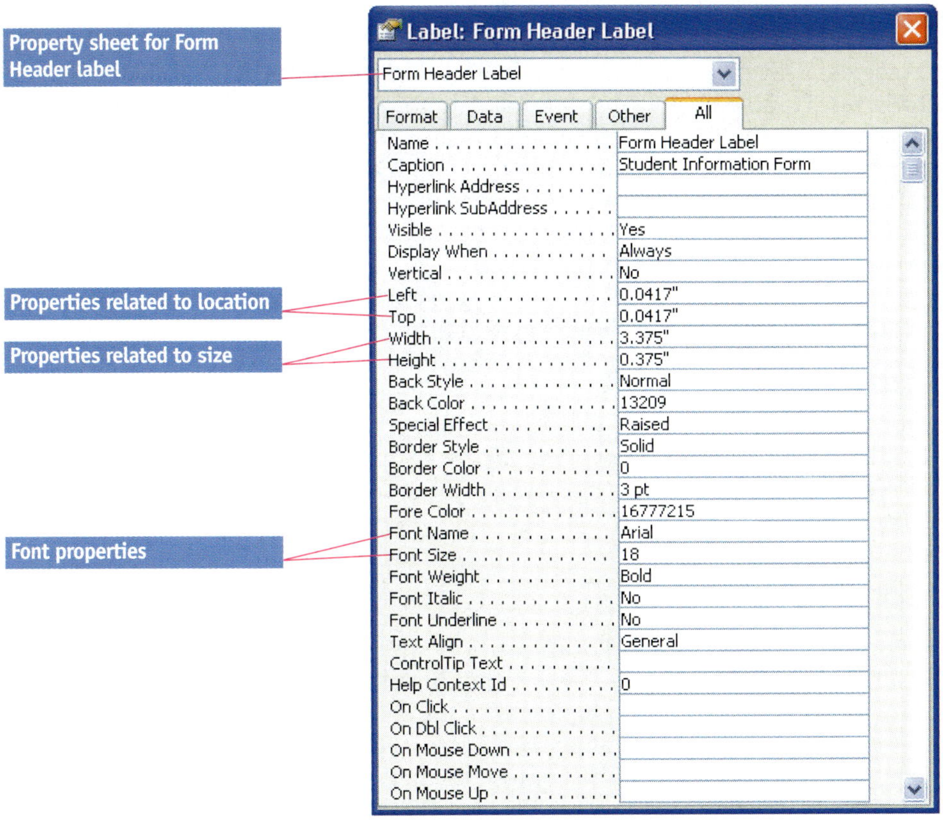

(a) From Header Label (unbound control)

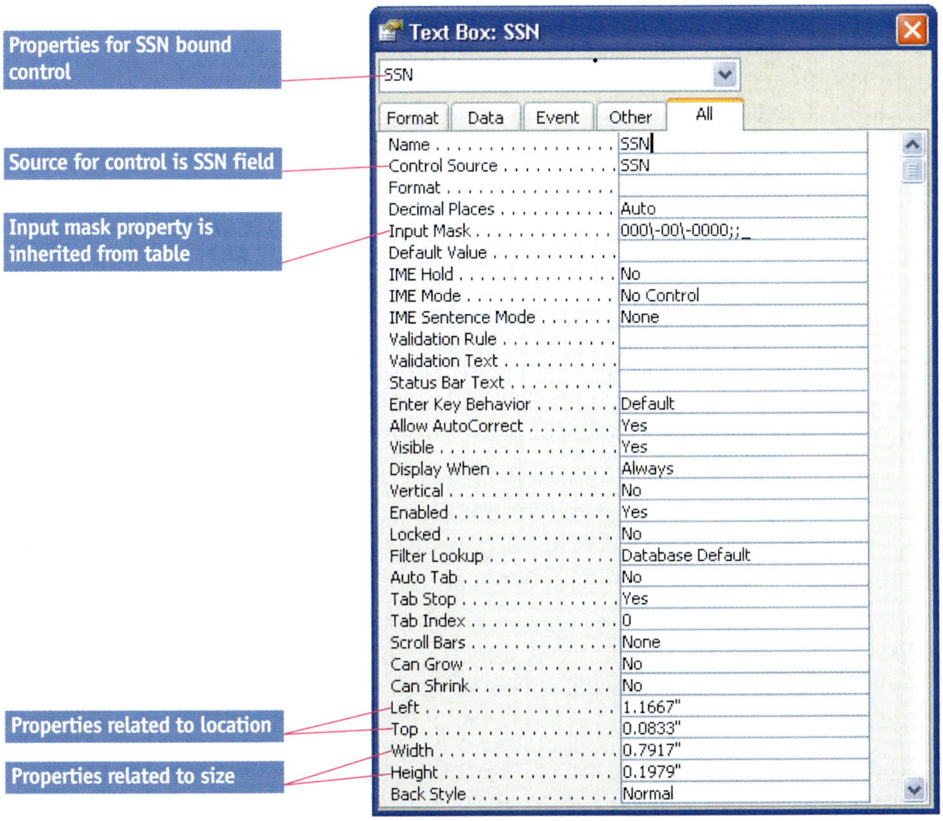

(b) SSN Text Box (bound control)

FIGURE 2.5 Property Sheets

AutoForms and the Form Wizard

The easiest way to create a form is by selecting one of several predefined ***AutoForms***. Double click the Columnar Autoform, for example, and you are presented with a form that contains all of the fields in the underlying table or query. (Queries are discussed in Chapter 3.) The ***Form Wizard*** gives you greater flexibility because you can select the fields you want and/or choose a different style from the default style provided by the AutoForm. The wizard asks you a series of questions, then builds the form according to your answers.

Figure 2.6a displays the New Form dialog box, where you choose AutoForm or select the Form Wizard, but either way you have to specify the underlying table or query. If you choose one of the AutoForm layouts, you're finished; that is, the form will be created automatically, and you can go right to the Design view to customize the form. Choosing the Form Wizard provides greater flexibility because you can select the fields you want in Figure 2.6b, the layout in Figure 2.6c, and the style in Figure 2.6d. It is at that point that you go to the Design view to further customize the form.

Modifying a Form

The Form Wizard (or an AutoForm) provides an excellent starting point, but you typically need to customize the form by adding other controls (e.g., the calculated control for GPA) and/or by modifying the controls that were created by the wizard. Each control is treated as an object, and moved or sized like any other Windows object. In essence, you select the control, then click and drag to resize the control or position it elsewhere on the form. You can also change the properties of the control through buttons on the various toolbars or by displaying the property sheet for the control and changing the appropriate property. Consider:

- *To select a bound control and its associated label (an unbound control),* click either the control or the label. If you click the control, the control has sizing handles and a move handle, but the label has only a move handle. If you click the label, the opposite occurs; that is, the label will have both sizing handles and a move handle, but the control will have only a move handle.
- *To size a control,* click the control to select the control and display the sizing handles, then drag the sizing handles in the appropriate direction. Drag the handles on the top or bottom to size the box vertically. Drag the handles on the left or right side to size the box horizontally. Drag the handles in the corner to size both horizontally and vertically.
- *To move a control and its label,* click and drag the border of either object. To move either the control or its label, click and drag the move handle (a tiny square in the upper left corner) of the appropriate object.
- *To change the properties of a control,* point to the control, click the right mouse button to display a shortcut menu, then click Properties to display the property sheet. Click the text box for the desired property, make the necessary change, then close the property sheet.
- *To select multiple controls,* press and hold the Shift key as you click each successive control. The advantage of selecting multiple controls is that you can modify the selected controls at the same time rather than working with them individually.

There is a learning curve, and it may take you a few extra minutes to create your first form. Everything you learn about forms, however, is also applicable to reports. Subsequent exercises will go much faster. And, as you may have guessed, it's time for our next hands-on exercise.

(a) Specify the Underlying Table

(b) Select the Fields

(c) Choose the Layout

(d) Choose the Style

FIGURE 2.6 The Form Wizard

TRY THE AUTOFORM FIRST

Go to the Database window, click the Forms button, then click the New button to display the New Form dialog box. Click the drop-down arrow in the Table or Query list box to select the object on which the form is based, then double click one of the AutoForm entries to create the form. If you don't like the result, don't bother to save the form. You have lost all of 30 seconds and can start again with the Form Wizard.

hands-on exercise

2 Creating a Form

Objective To use the Form Wizard to create a form; to move and size controls within a form; to use the completed form to enter data into the associated table.

Step 1: **Open the Database**

- Start Access. The **My First database** from the previous exercise should appear in the list of databases in the Open section in the task pane. Click the link to open the database.
- If the database is not listed or the task pane is not open, pull down the **File menu**, and click the **Open command** to open the database.
- Click the **Forms button** in the Database window. Click the **New command button** to display the New Form dialog box as shown in Figure 2.7a.
- Click **Form Wizard** in the list box. Click the **drop-down arrow** to display the available tables and queries in the database on which the form can be based.
- Click **Students** to select the table from the previous exercise. Click **OK**.

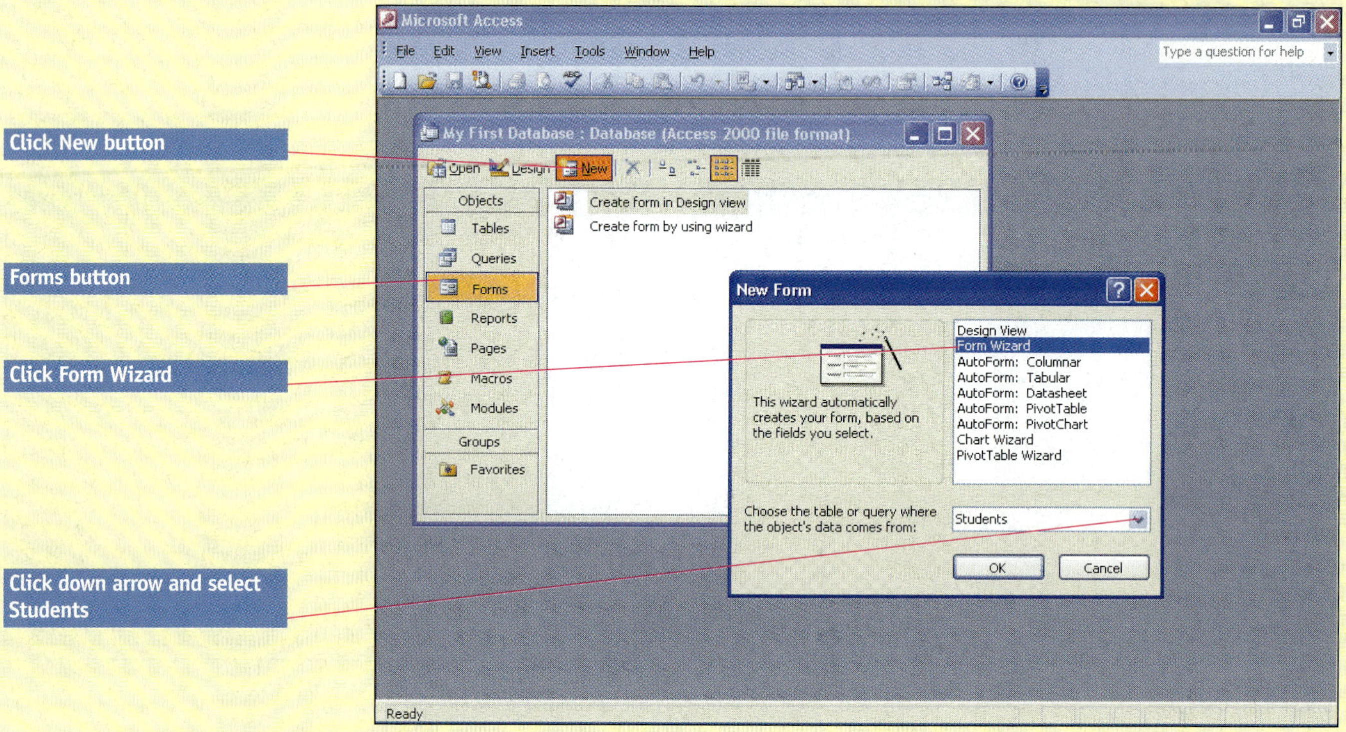

(a) Open the Database (step 1)

FIGURE 2.7 Hands-on Exercise 2

ANATOMY OF A FORM

A form is divided into one or more sections. Virtually every form has a detail section to display or enter the records in the underlying table. You can, however, increase the effectiveness or visual appeal of a form by adding a header and/or footer. Either section may contain descriptive information about the form, such as a title, instructions for using the form, or a graphic or logo.

Step 2: The Form Wizard

- You should see the dialog box in Figure 2.7b, which displays all of the fields in the Students table. Click the >> **button** to enter all of the fields in the table on the form. Click the **Next command button**.
- The **Columnar layout** is already selected. (The various layouts correspond to the different AutoForms.) Click the **Next command button**.
- Click **Industrial** as the style for your form. Click the **Next command button**.
- The Form Wizard will ask you for the title of the form and what you want to do next.
  - The Form Wizard suggests **Students** as the title of the form. Keep this entry.
  - Click the option button to **Modify the form's design**.
- Click the **Finish command button** to display the form in Design view. The wizard has created the initial form for you. You will now modify the form in Design view as described in the next several steps.

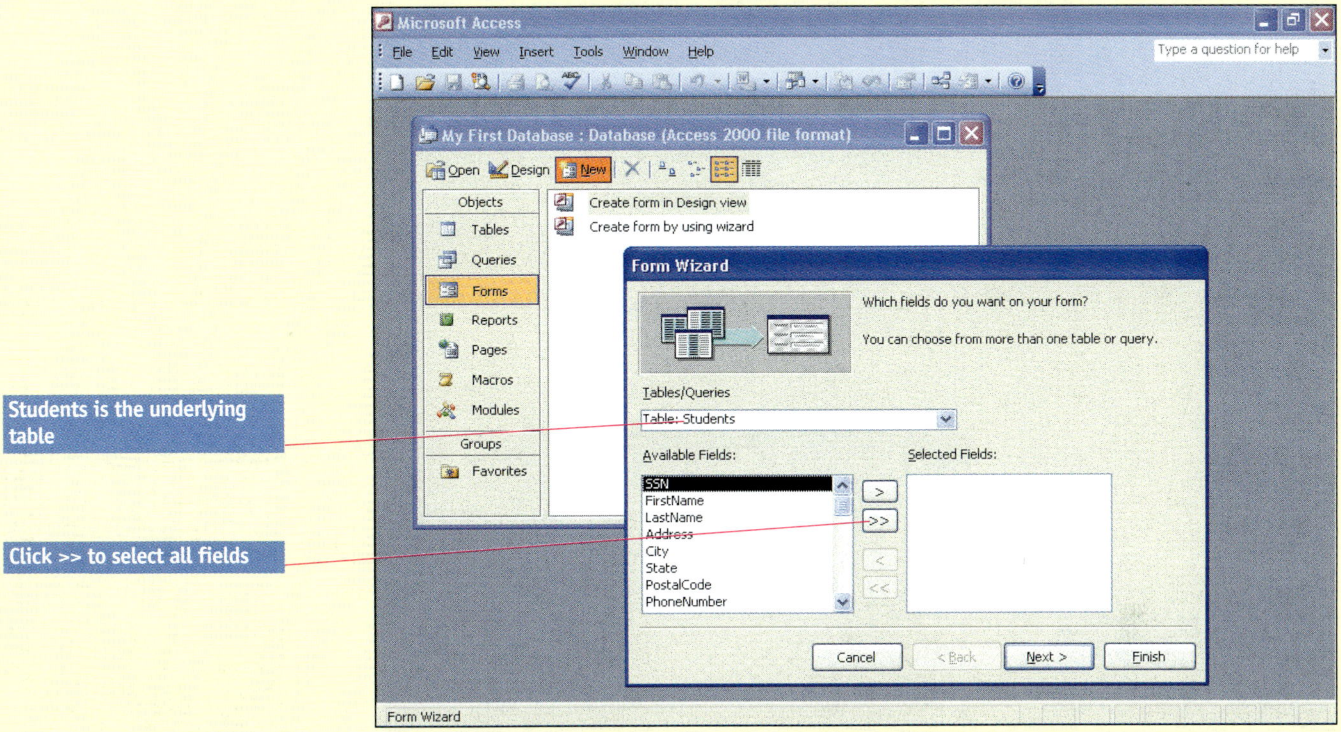

(b) The Form Wizard (step 2)

FIGURE 2.7 Hands-on Exercise 2 (*continued*)

FLOATING TOOLBARS

A toolbar is typically docked (fixed) along the edge of the application window, but it can be displayed as a floating toolbar within the application window. To move a docked toolbar, drag the toolbar background (or the toolbar's move handle). To move a floating toolbar, drag its title bar. To size a floating toolbar, drag any border in the direction you want to go. And finally, you can double click the background of any floating toolbar to dock it.

Step 3: Move the Controls

- If necessary, click the **Maximize button** so that the form takes the entire screen as shown in Figure 2.7c. Close the field list. The Form Wizard has arranged the controls in columnar format, but you need to rearrange the controls.
- Click the **Credits control** to select it. Press the **Shift key** as you click the **QualityPoints control** to select it as well. Click and drag the border of either control (the pointer changes to a hand) to move them out of the way.
- Click the **LastName control** to select the control and display the sizing handles. (Be sure to select the text box and *not* the attached label.) Click and drag the **border** of the control (the pointer changes to a hand) so that the LastName control is on the same line as the FirstName control. Use the grid to space and align the controls.
- Click and drag the **Address control** under the FirstName control (to take the space previously occupied by the last name).
- Click and drag the **right border** of the form to **7 inches** so that the City, State, and PostalCode controls will fit on the same line. (Click and drag the title bar of the Toolbox toolbar to move the toolbar out of the way.)
- Click and drag the **State control** so that it is next to the City control, then click and drag the **PostalCode control** so that it is on the same line as the other two. Press and hold the **Shift key** as you click the **City**, **State**, and **PostalCode controls** to select all three, then click and drag the selected controls under the Address control.
- Place the controls for **PhoneNumber**, **BirthDate**, and **Gender** on the same line. Move the controls under City, State, PostalCode.
- Place the controls for **Credits** and **QualityPoints** on the same line. Move the controls under PhoneNumber.
- Save the form.

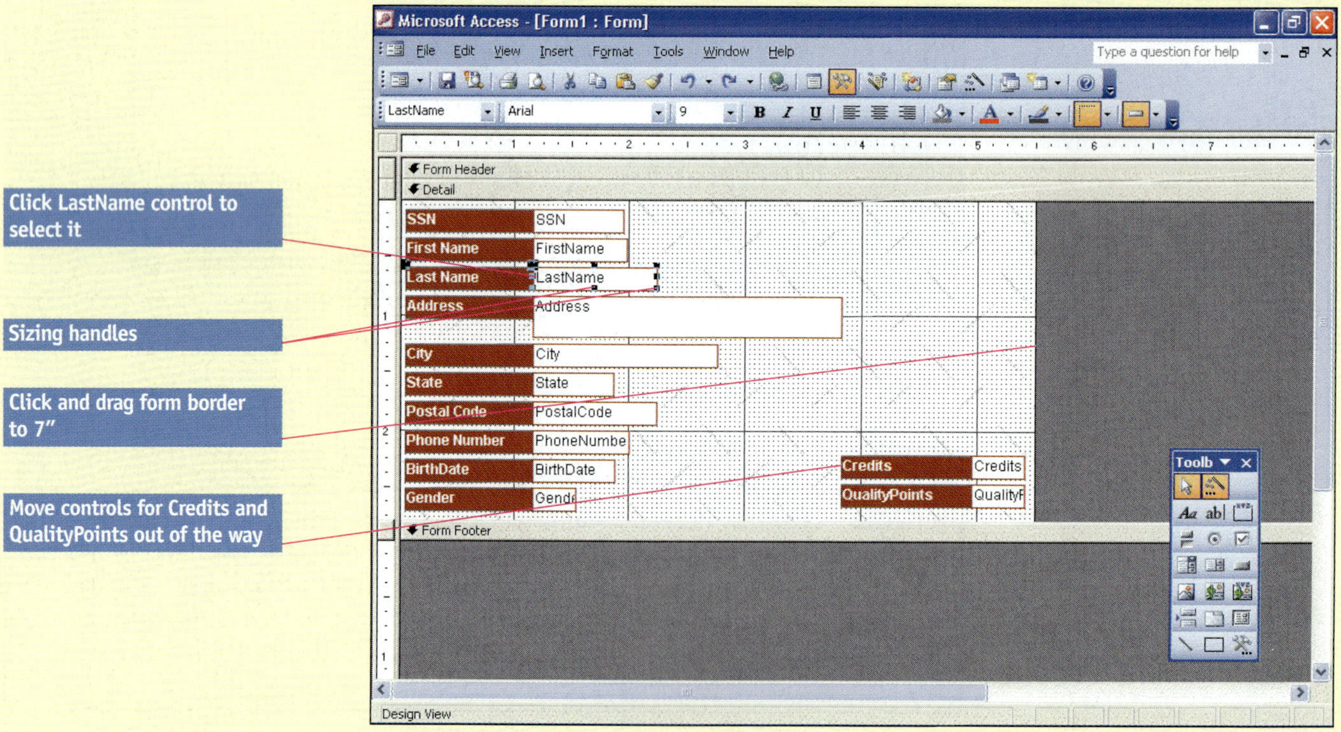

(c) Move the Controls (step 3)

FIGURE 2.7 Hands-on Exercise 2 (*continued*)

Step 4: Add a Calculated Control (GPA)

- Click the **Text Box tool** in the toolbox as shown in Figure 2.7d. The mouse pointer changes to a tiny crosshair with a text box attached.
- Click and drag in the form where you want the text box (the GPA control) to go. Release the mouse. You will see an Unbound control and an attached label containing a field number (e.g., Text24) as shown in Figure 2.7d.
- Click in the **text box** of the control. The word Unbound will disappear. Enter **=[QualityPoints]/[Credits]** to calculate a student's GPA. You must enter the field names *exactly* as they were defined in the table; that is, do *not* include a space between Quality and Points.
- Select the attached label (**Text24**), then click and drag to select the text in the attached label. Type **GPA** as the label for this control and press **Enter**.
- Size the label appropriately for GPA. Size the bound control as well. Move either control as necessary.
- Save the form.

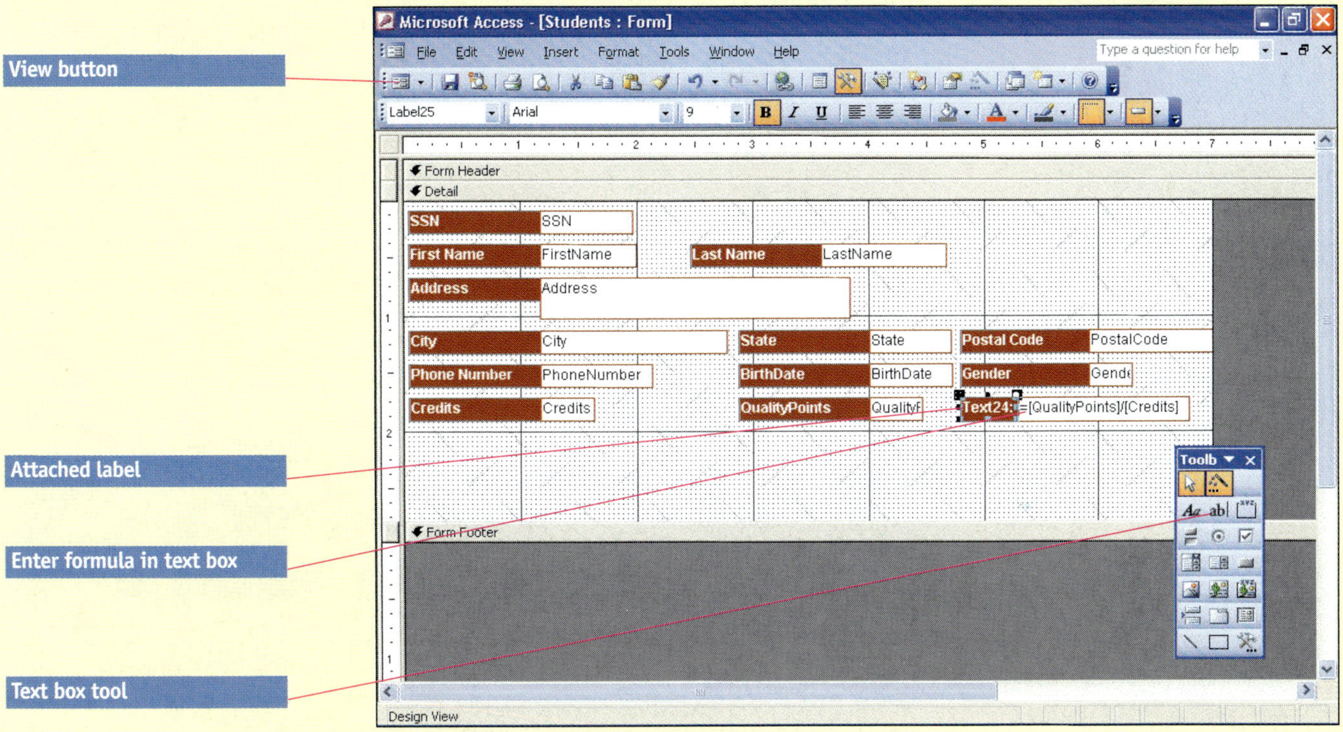

(d) Add a Calculated Control (step 4)

FIGURE 2.7 Hands-on Exercise 2 (*continued*)

SIZING OR MOVING A CONTROL AND ITS LABEL

A bound and/or an unbound control is created with an attached label. Select (click) the control, and the control has sizing handles and a move handle, but the label has only a move handle. Select the label (instead of the control), and the opposite occurs; the control has only a move handle, but the label will have both sizing handles and a move handle. To move a control and its label, click and drag the border of either object. To move either the control or its label, click and drag the move handle (a tiny square in the upper left corner) of the appropriate object.

Step 5: Modify the Property Sheet

- Point to the GPA bound control and click the **right mouse button** to display a shortcut menu. Click **Properties** to display the Properties dialog box.
- If necessary, click the **All tab** as shown in Figure 2.7e. The Control Source text box contains the entry =[QualityPoints]/[Credits] from the preceding step.
- Click the **Name text box**. Replace the original name (e.g., Text24) with **GPA**.
- Click the **Format box**. Click the **drop-down arrow**, then scroll until you can select **Fixed**.
- Click the box for the **Decimal places**. Click the **drop-down arrow** and select **2** as the number of decimal places.
- Close the Properties dialog box to accept these settings and return to the form.
- Save the form.

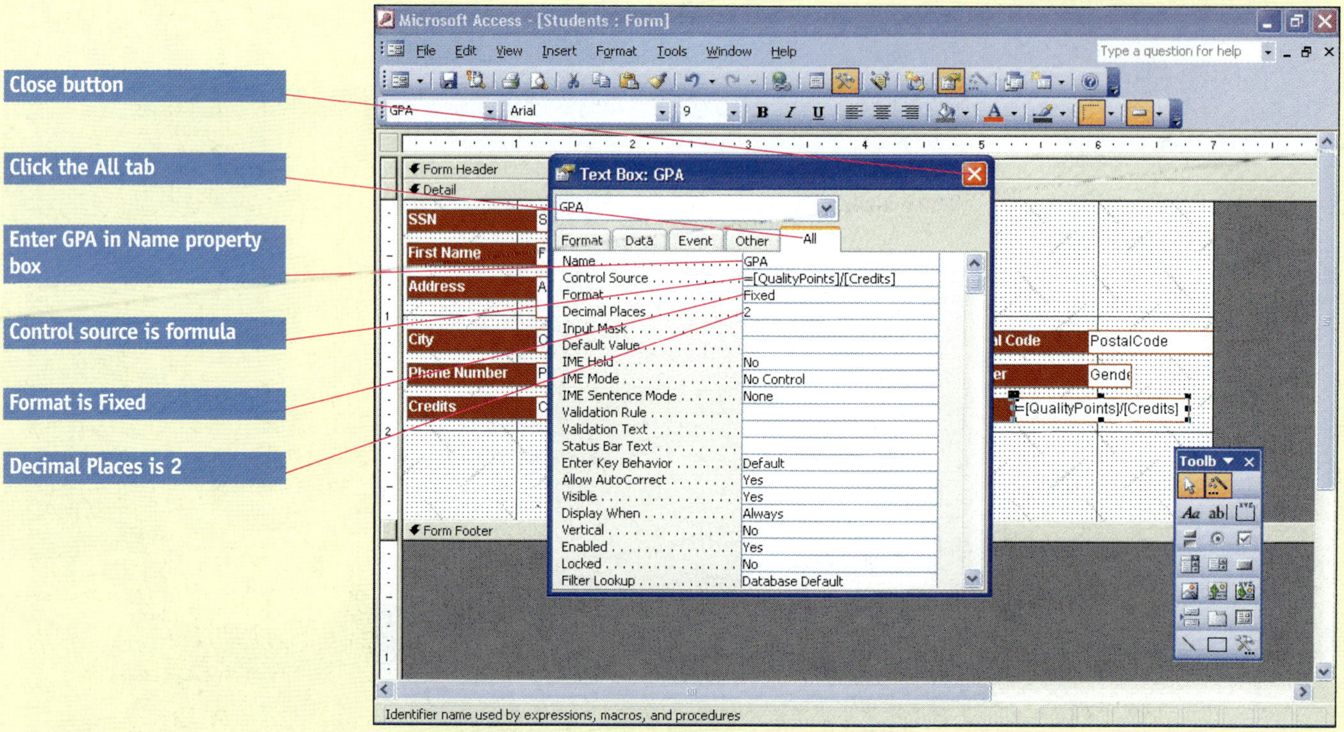

(e) Modify the Property Sheet (step 5)

FIGURE 2.7 Hands-on Exercise 2 (*continued*)

USE THE PROPERTY SHEET

You can change the appearance or behavior of a control in two ways—by changing the actual control on the form itself or by changing the underlying property sheet. Anything you do to the control automatically changes the associated property, and conversely, any change to the property sheet is reflected in the appearance or behavior of the control. In general, you can obtain greater precision through the property sheet, but we find ourselves continually switching back and forth between the two techniques. Every object in an Access database has its own property sheet.

Step 6: Align the Controls

- Click the label for SSN, then press and hold the **Shift key** as you click the labels for the other controls on the form. This enables you to select multiple controls at the same time to apply uniform formatting to the selected controls.
- All labels should be selected as shown in Figure 2.7f. Click the **Align Right button** on the Formatting toolbar to move the text to the right so that the text in each label is closer to its associated control.
- Click anywhere on the form to deselect the controls, then fine-tune the form as necessary to make it more attractive. (Use the Undo command anytime the results of a command are not what you expect.)
- Make additional changes as necessary. We moved LastName to align it with State. We also made the PostalCode and GPA controls smaller.
- Save the form.

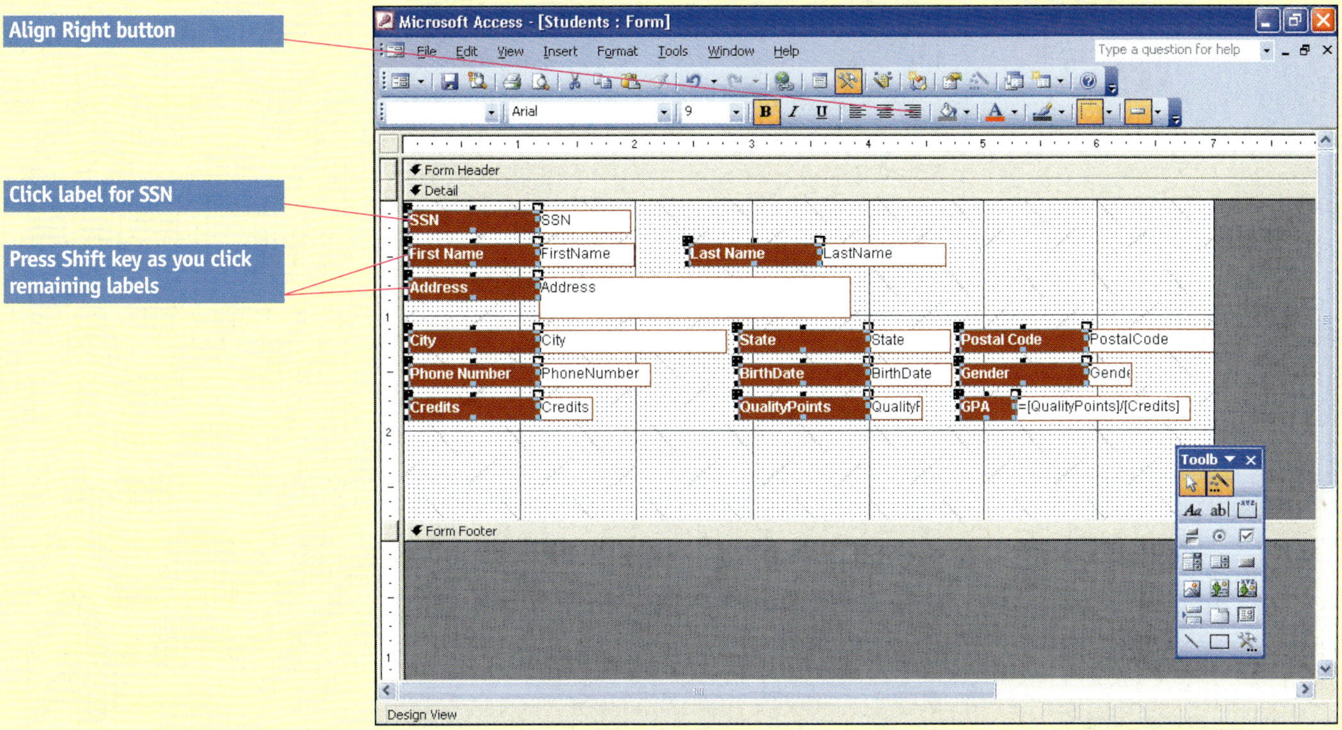

(f) Align the Controls (step 6)

FIGURE 2.7 Hands-on Exercise 2 (*continued*)

ALIGN THE CONTROLS

To align controls in a straight line (horizontally or vertically), press and hold the Shift key and click the labels of the controls to be aligned. Pull down the Format menu, click Align, then select the edge to align (Left, Right, Top, and Bottom). Click the Undo command if you are not satisfied with the result. It takes practice to master the Design view, but everything you learn about forms also applies to reports. (Reports are covered in Chapter 3.)

Step 7: Create the Form Header

- Click and drag the line separating the border of the Form Header and Detail sections to provide space for a header as shown in Figure 2.7g.
- Click the **Label tool** on the Toolbox toolbar (the mouse pointer changes to a cross hair combined with the letter A). Click and drag the mouse pointer to create a label within the header. The insertion point (a flashing vertical line) is automatically positioned within the label.
- Type **Student Information Form**. Do not be concerned about the size or alignment of the text at this time. Click outside the label when you have completed the entry, then click the control to select it.
- Click the **drop-down arrow** on the **Font Size list box** on the Formatting toolbar. Click **18**. The size of the text changes to the larger point size.
- Click the **drop-down arrow** next to the **Special Effect button** on the Formatting toolbar to display the available effects. Click the **Raised button** to highlight the label. Click outside the label to deselect it.
- Click the **Textbox tool** on the Toolbox toolbar. The mouse pointer changes to a tiny crosshair with a text box attached.
- Click and drag in the form where you want the text box for the date, then release the mouse.
- You will see an Unbound control and an attached label containing a number (e.g., Text27). Click in the text box, and the word Unbound will disappear. Type =**Now( )** to enter the current date. Click the attached label. Press the **Del key** to delete thc label.
- Right click the newly created control to display a context-sensitive menu. Click the **Properties command** and change the format to **Short Date**. Close the Properties sheet.
- Save the form.

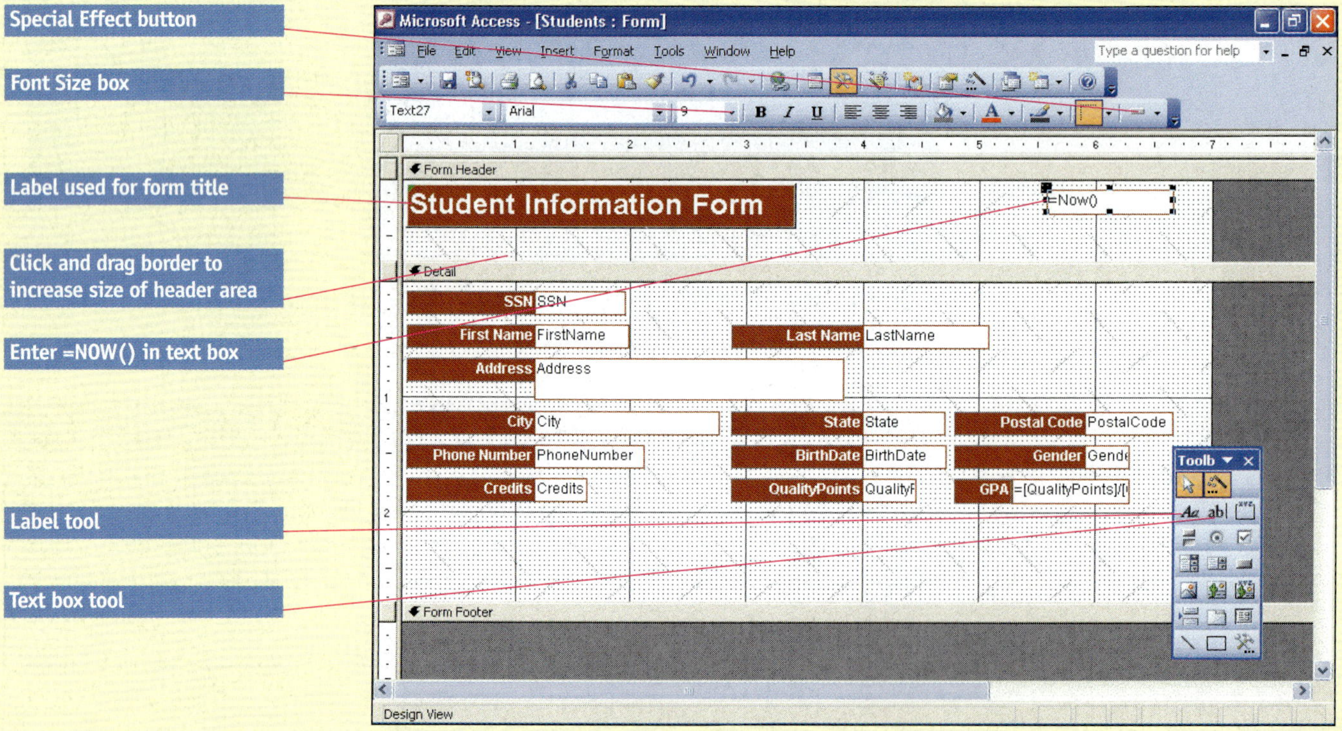

(g) Create the Form Header (step 7)

FIGURE 2.7 Hands-on Exercise 2 (*continued*)

Step 8: The Finished Form

- Click the **View button** to switch to the Form view. You will see the first record in the table that was created in the previous exercise.
- Click the **New Record button** to move to the end of the table to enter a new record as shown in Figure 2.7h. Enter data for a classmate:
  - The record selector symbol changes to a pencil as you begin to enter data as shown in Figure 2.7h.
  - Press the **Tab key** to move from one field to the next within the form. All properties (masks and data validation) have been inherited from the Students table created in the first exercise.
  - There are now two records in the table.
- Pull down the **File menu** and click **Close** to close the form. Click **Yes** if asked to save the changes to the form.
- Pull down the **File menu** and click **Close** to close the database and remain in Access. Pull down the **File menu** a second time and click **Exit** if you do not want to continue with the next exercise at this time.

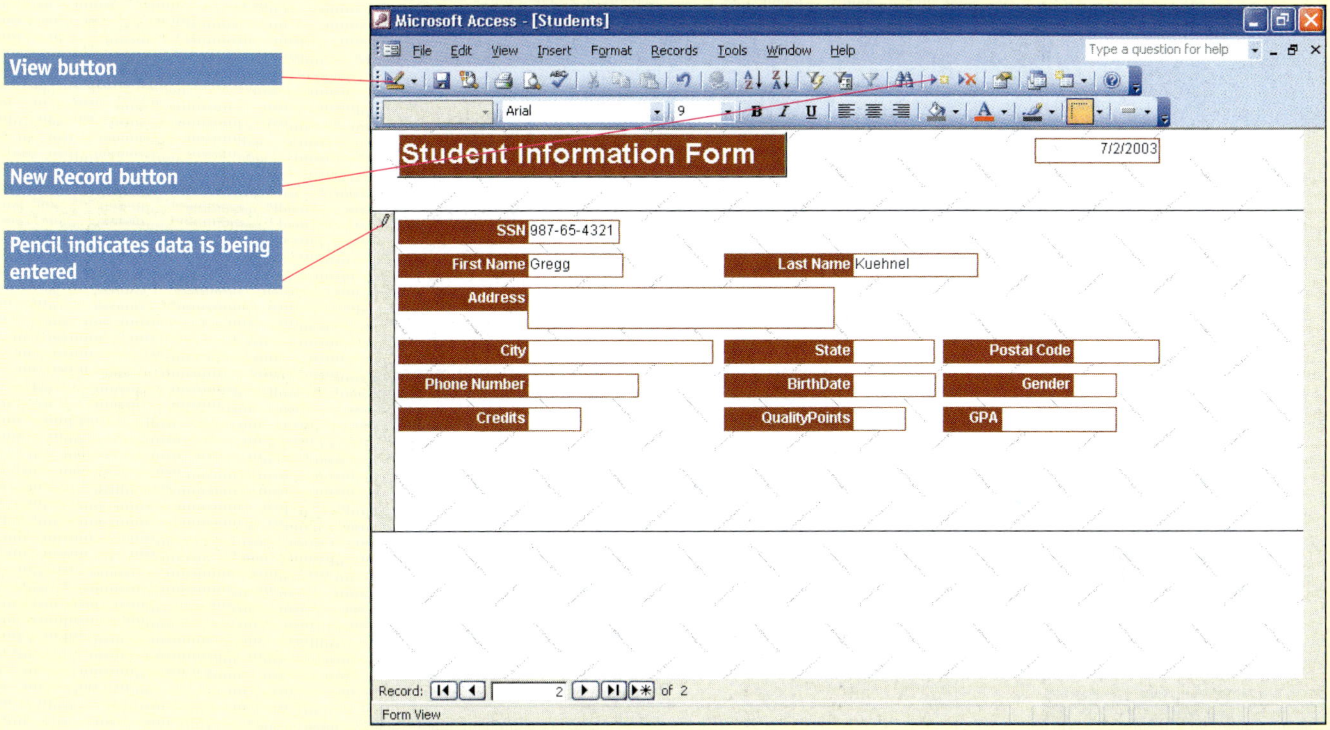

(h) The Finished Form (step 8)

FIGURE 2.7 Hands-on Exercise 2 (*continued*)

ERROR MESSAGES—#NAME? OR #ERROR?

The most common reason for either message is that the control source references a field that no longer exists, or a field whose name is misspelled. Go to the Design view, right click the control, click the Properties command, then click the All tab within the Properties dialog box. Look at the Control Source property and check the spelling of every field. Be sure there are brackets around each field in a calculated control—for example, =[QualityPoints]/[Credits].

A MORE SOPHISTICATED FORM

The Form Wizard provides an excellent starting point but stops short of creating the form you really want. The exercise just completed showed you how to add controls to a form that were not in the underlying table, such as the calculated control for the GPA. The exercise also showed how to move and size existing controls to create a more attractive and functional form.

Consider now Figure 2.8, which further improves on the form from the previous exercise. Three additional controls have been added—for major, financial aid, and campus—to illustrate other ways to enter data than through a text box. The student's major is selected from a ***drop-down list box***. The indication of financial aid (a Yes/No field) is entered through a ***check box***. The student's campus is selected from an ***option group***, in which you choose one of three mutually exclusive options.

The form in Figure 2.8 also includes clip art in the header. The way in which clip art is added to a form (or report) in Access differs from the way it is done in the other Office applications, in that the Insert Picture command does not link to the Clip Organizer as it does with Word, Excel, and PowerPoint. Execution of the command in Access is more limited and requires you to specify the file that contains the clip art image. (You can, however, start the Clip Organizer as a separate application, copy the clip art to the clipboard, then paste the contents of the clipboard into Access.)

Command buttons have also been added to the bottom of the form to facilitate the way in which the user carries out certain procedures. To add a record, for example, the user simply clicks the Add Record command button, as opposed to having to click the New Record button on the Database toolbar or having to pull down the Insert menu. Additional buttons have been added to find or delete a record and to close the form. The next exercise has you retrieve the form you created in Hands-on Exercise 2 to add these enhancements.

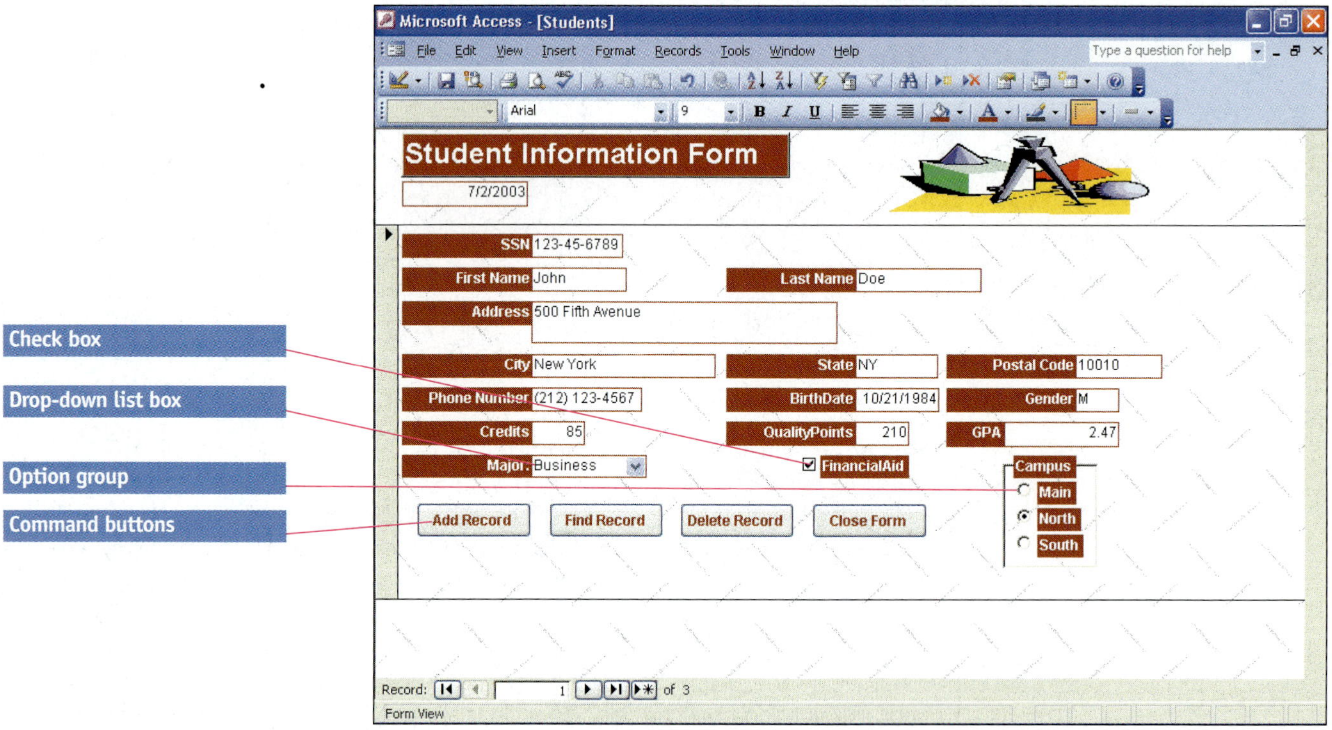

FIGURE 2.8 A More Sophisticated Form

hands-on exercise

3 A More Sophisticated Form

Objective To add fields to an existing table; to use the Lookup Wizard to create a combo box; to add controls to an existing form to demonstrate inheritance; to add command buttons to a form. Use Figure 2.9 as a guide in the exercise.

Step 1: Modify the Table

- Open **My First Database** that we have been using throughout the chapter. If necessary, click the **Tables button** in the Database window. The **Students table** is already selected since that is the only table in the database.
- Click the **Design command button** to open the table in Design view as shown in Figure 2.9a. (The FinancialAid, Campus, and Major fields have not yet been added.) Maximize the window.
- Click the **Field Name box** under QualityPoints. Enter **FinancialAid** as the name of the new field. Press the **Enter (Tab**, or **right arrow) key** to move to the Data Type column. Type **Y** (the first letter in a Yes/No field) to specify the data type.
- Click the **Field Name box** on the next row. Type **Campus**. (There is no need to specify the Data Type since Text is the default.)
- Press the **down arrow key** to move to the Field Name box on the next row. Enter **Major**. Press the **Enter (Tab**, or **right arrow) key** to move to the Data Type column. Click the **drop-down arrow** to display the list of data types as shown in Figure 2.9a. Click **Lookup Wizard**.

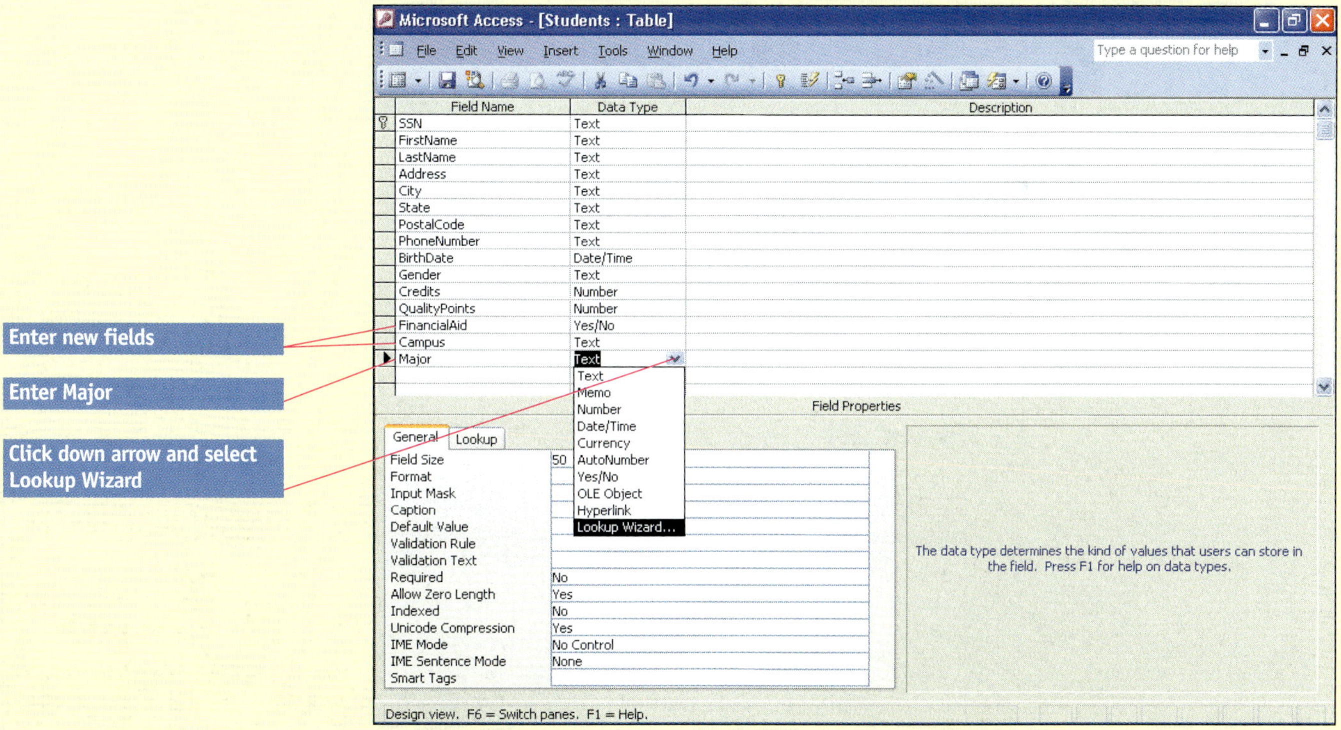

(a) Modify the Table (step 1)

FIGURE 2.9 Hands-on Exercise 3

Step 2: The Lookup Wizard

- The first screen in the Lookup Wizard asks how you want to look up the data. Click the option button that indicates **I will type in the values that I want**. Click **Next**.
- You should see the dialog box in Figure 2.9b. The number of columns is already entered as 1. Click the **text box** to enter the first major. Type **Business**. Press **Tab** or the **down arrow key** (do *not* press the Enter key) to enter the next major.
- Complete the entries shown in Figure 2.9b. Click **Next**. The wizard asks for a label to identify the column. (Major is already entered.)
- Click **Finish** to exit the wizard and return to the Design view.
- The data type has been set to Text as a result of the entries you made using the Lookup Wizard.
- Click the **Save button** to save the table. Close the table.

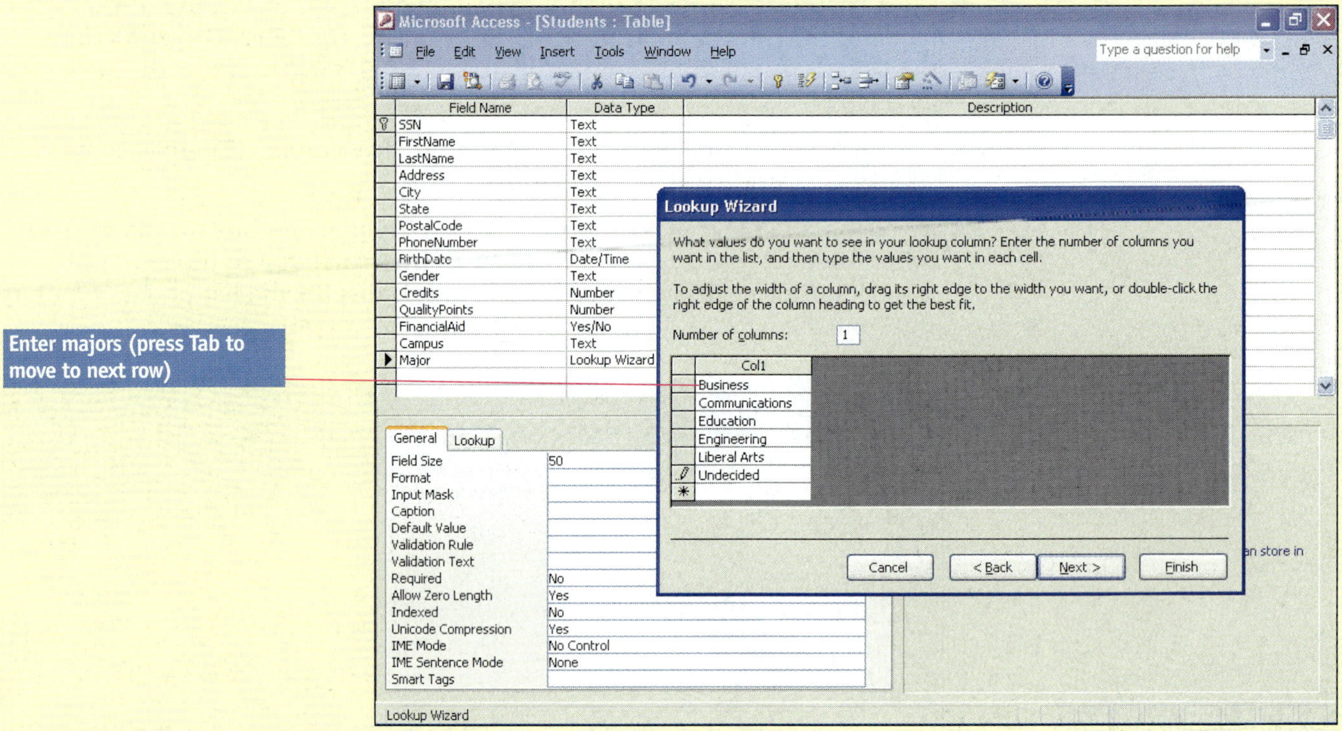

(b) The Lookup Wizard (step 2)

FIGURE 2.9 Hands-on Exercise 3 (*continued*)

RELATIONAL DATABASES—MORE SOPHISTICATED APPLICATIONS

The simplest way to use the Lookup Wizard is to type the potential values directly into the associated field. It's more powerful, however, to instruct the wizard to look up the values in a table, which in turn necessitates the creation of that table, in effect creating a relational database. Indeed, the true power of Access comes from databases with multiple tables, as was demonstrated in the Look Ahead database of Chapter 1. We develop this topic further, beginning in Chapter 4 and continue through the remaining chapters in the text.

Step 3: Add the New Controls

- Click the **Forms button** in the Database window. If necessary, click the **Students form** to select it.
- Click the **Design command button** to open the form from the previous exercise. If necessary, click the **Maximize button** so that the form takes the entire window.
- If the field list is not displayed, pull down the **View menu**. Click **Field List** to display the field list for the table on which the form is based. You can move and size the field list just like any other Windows object.
  - ❑ Click and drag the **title bar** of the field list to the position in Figure 2.9c.
  - ❑ Click and drag a **corner** or **border** of the field list so that you can see all of the fields at the same time.
- Fields can be added to the form from the field list in any order. Click and drag the **Major field** from the field list to the form. The Major control is created as a combo box because of the lookup list in the underlying table.
- Click and drag the **FinancialAid field** from the list to the form. The FinancialAid control is created as a check box because FinancialAid is a Yes/No field in the underlying table.
- Move and size the labels and bound controls as necessary. Save the form.

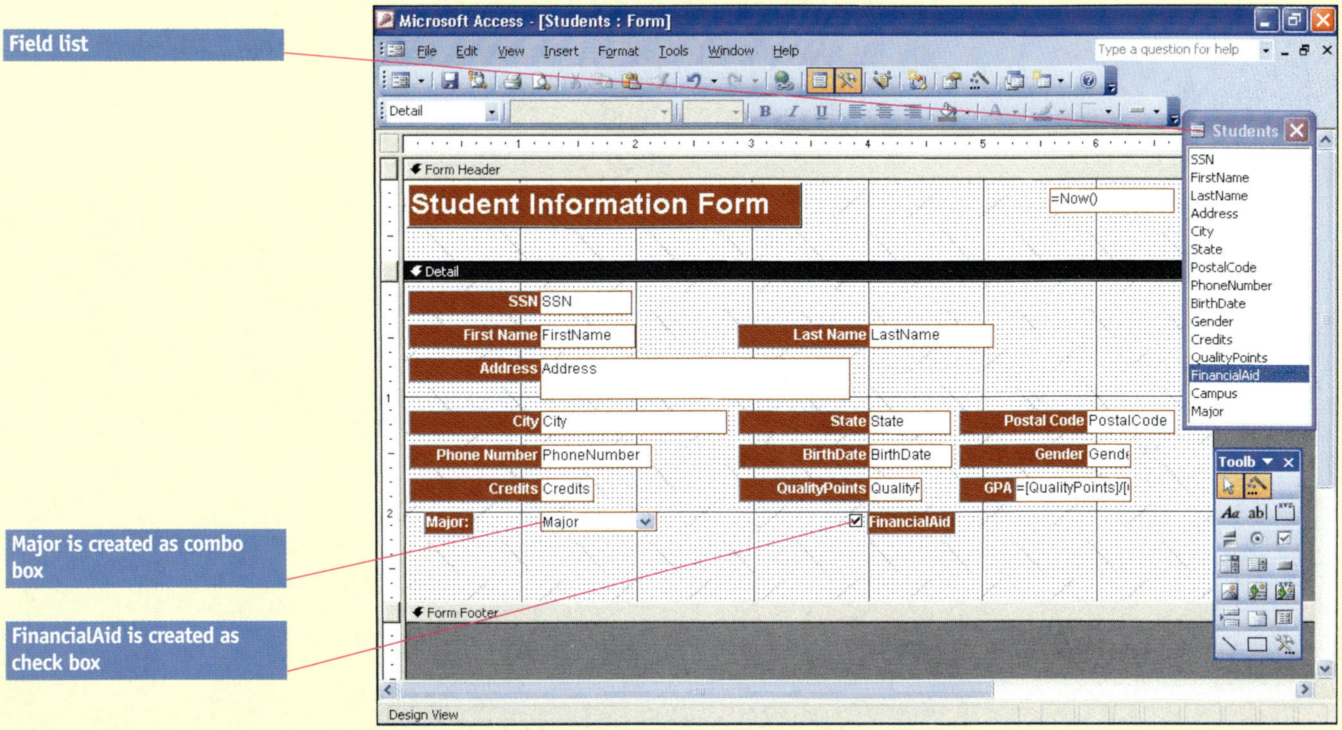

(c) Add the New Controls (step 3)

FIGURE 2.9 Hands-on Exercise 3 (*continued*)

INHERITANCE

A bound control inherits its properties from the associated field in the underlying table. A check box, for example, appears automatically for any field that was defined as a Yes/No field. In similar fashion, a drop-down list appears for any field that was defined through the Lookup Wizard. All of the other properties of the control are also inherited from the underlying table.

Step 4: Create an Option Group

- Click the **Option Group button** on the Toolbox toolbar. The mouse pointer changes to a tiny crosshair. Click and drag in the form where you want the option group to go, then release the mouse.
- You should see the Option Group Wizard as shown in Figure 2.9d. Enter **Main** as the label for the first option, then press the **Tab key** to move to the next line. Type **North** and press **Tab** to move to the next line. Enter **South** as the third and last option. Click **Next**.
- The option button to select Main (the first label that was entered) as the default is selected. Click **Next**.
- Main, North, and South will be assigned the values 1, 2, and 3, respectively. (Numeric entries are required for an option group.) Click **Next**.
- Click the **drop-down arrow** to select the field in which to store the value selected through the option group, then scroll until you can select **Campus**. Click **Next**.
- Make sure the Option button is selected as the type of control.
- Click the Option button for the **Sunken style** to match the other controls on the form. Click **Next**.
- Enter **Campus** as the caption for the group. Click the **Finish command button** to create the option group on the form. Click and drag the option group to position it on the form under the GPA control.
- Point to the border of the option group on the form, click the **right mouse button** to display a shortcut menu, and click **Properties**. Click the **All tab**. Change the name to **Campus**.
- Click the label for the **Option Group** (Campus). Click the **Fill Color button** on the Formatting toolbar to change the fill color to match that of the other labels.
- Close the dialog box. Close the field list. Save the form.

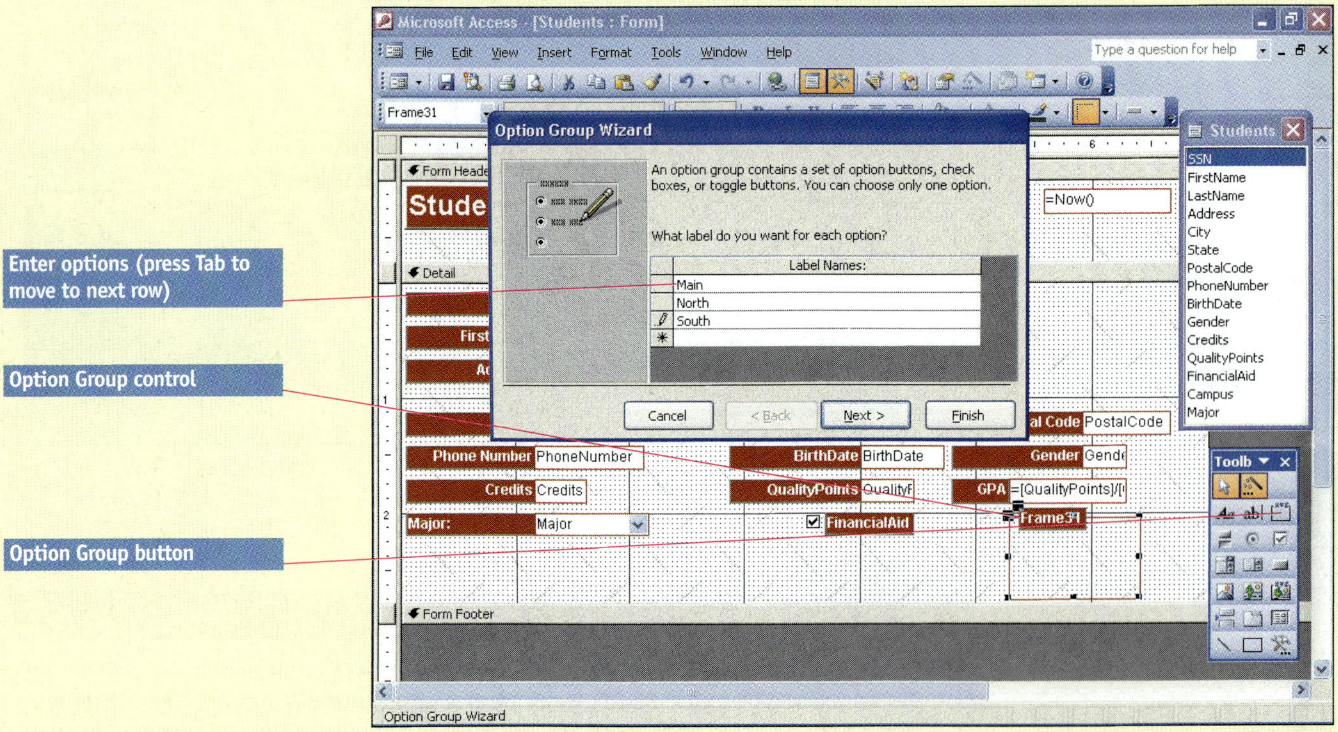

(d) Create an Option Group (step 4)

FIGURE 2.9 Hands-on Exercise 3 (*continued*)

Step 5: Add the Command Buttons

- Click the **Command Button tool**. The mouse pointer changes to a tiny crosshair that is attached to a command button when you point anywhere in the form.
- Click and drag in the form where you want the button to go, then release the mouse. This draws a button and simultaneously opens the Command Button Wizard as shown in Figure 2.9e. (The number in your button may be different from ours.)
- Click **Record Operations** in the Categories list box. Choose **Add New Record** as the operation. Click **Next**.
- Click the **Text option button** in the next screen. Click **Next**.
- Type **Add Record** as the name of the button, then click the **Finish command button**. The completed command button should appear on your form.
- Repeat these steps to add the command buttons to find a record (Record Navigation), to delete a record (Record Operations), and to close the form (Form Operations). We will adjust the size and alignment of all four buttons in the next step.

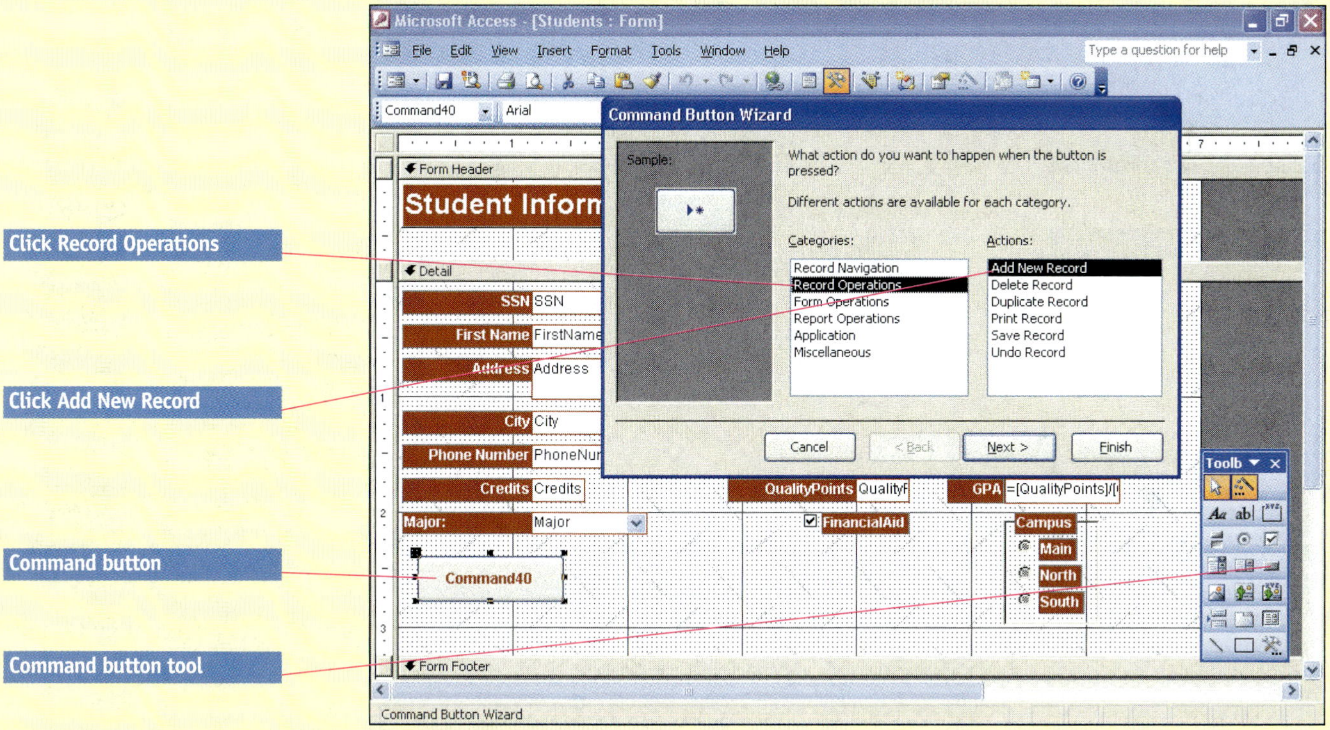

(e) Add the Command Buttons (step 5)

FIGURE 2.9 Hands-on Exercise 3 (*continued*)

WINDOWS THEMES AND ROUNDED COMMAND BUTTONS

It's a subtle difference, but we prefer the sleeker look of rounded command buttons in our forms, as opposed to the rectangular buttons that are created by default. Pull down the Tools menu, click the Options command, click the Forms/Reports tab, and check the box to use Windows Themed Controls on forms. Click the Apply button, then close the dialog box. Save the form you are working on, close the form, and then reopen it. You should see rounded buttons.

Step 6: Align the Command Buttons

- Select the four command buttons that were created in the previous step by pressing and holding the **Shift key** as you click each button. Release the Shift key when all buttons are selected.
- Pull down the **Format menu**. Click **Size** to display the cascade menu shown in Figure 2.9f. (Click the **double arrow** at the bottom of the menu if you don't see the Size command.) Click **To Widest** to set a uniform width.
- Pull down the **Format menu** a second time, click **Size**, then click **To Tallest** to set a uniform height.
- Pull down the **Format menu** again, click **Horizontal Spacing**, then click **Make Equal** so that each button is equidistant from the other buttons.
- Pull down the **Format menu** a final time, click **Align**, then click **Bottom** to complete the alignment.
- Save the form.

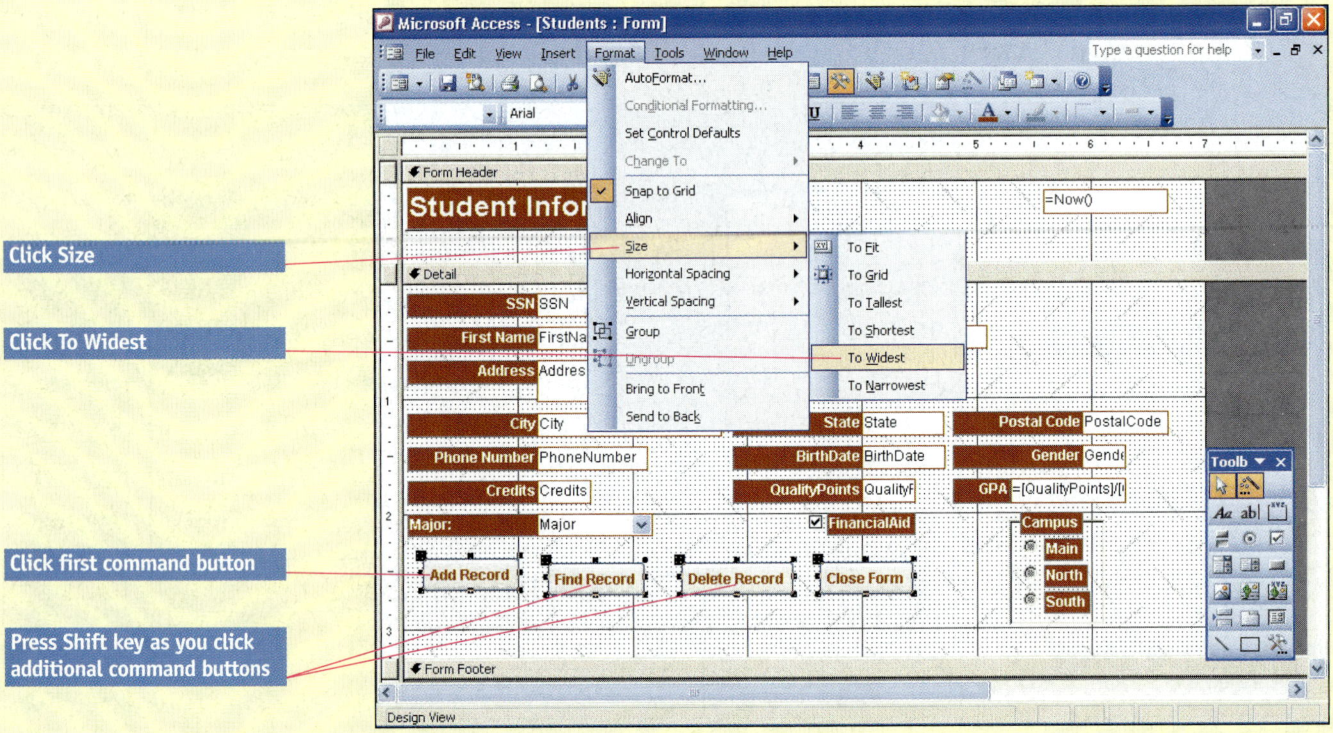

(f) Align the Command Buttons (step 6)

FIGURE 2.9 Hands-on Exercise 3 (*continued*)

MULTIPLE CONTROLS AND PROPERTIES

Press and hold the Shift key as you click one control after another to select multiple controls. To view or change the properties for the selected controls, click the right mouse button to display a shortcut menu, then click Properties to display a property sheet. If the value of a property is the same for all selected controls, that value will appear in the property sheet; otherwise the box for that property will be blank. Changing a property when multiple controls are selected changes the property for all selected controls.

Step 7: Reset the Tab Order

- Click anywhere in the Detail section. Pull down the **View menu**. Click **Tab Order** to display the Tab Order dialog box in Figure 2.9g. (Click the **double arrow** at the bottom of the menu if you don't see the Tab Order command.)
- Click the **Auto Order command button** so that the Tab key will move to fields in left-to-right, top-to-bottom order as you enter data in the form. Click **OK** to close the Tab Order dialog box.
- Right click the **GPA control**, click **Properties** to display the Properties sheet, click the **All tab**, set the **Tab Stop** property to **No**, and close the property sheet.
- Check the form one more time to make any last-minute changes. (We had to right align the label for major.)
- Save the form.

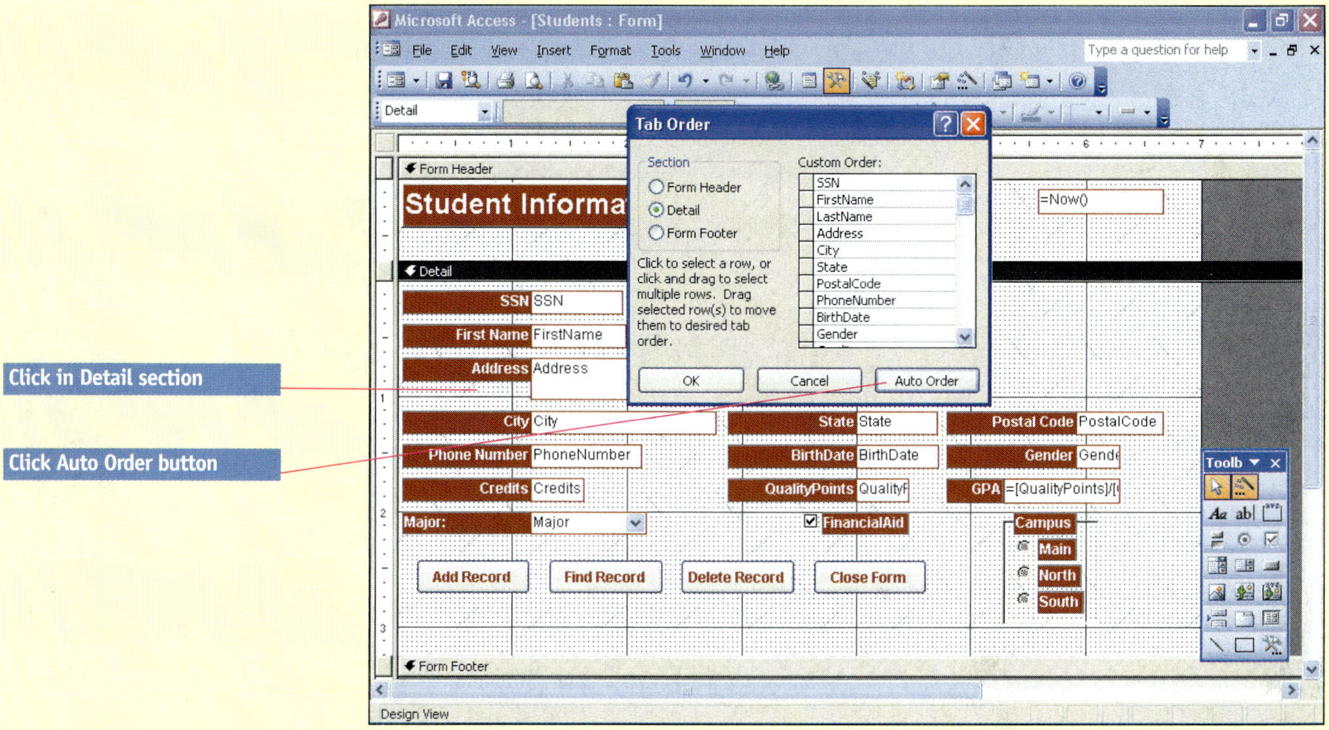

(g) Reset the Tab Order (step 7)

FIGURE 2.9 Hands-on Exercise 3 (*continued*)

THE TAB STOP PROPERTY

The Tab key provides a shortcut in the finished form to move from one field to the next. Calculated controls, such as GPA, are not entered explicitly, however, and can be bypassed by setting the Tab Stop property to no. AutoNumber fields can be bypassed in similar fashion. Note, too, that the order in which fields are selected corresponds to the sequence in which the controls were entered onto the form, and need not correspond to the physical appearance of the actual form. To restore a left-to-right, top-to-bottom sequence, pull down the View menu, click Tab Order, select AutoOrder, then click OK to close the Tab Order dialog box.

Step 8: Insert the Clip Art

- Click in the Form Header area. Pull down the **Insert menu** and click the **Picture command** to display the Insert Picture dialog box as shown in Figure 2.9h.
- Change to the **Exploring Access folder**. Click the **Views button** repeatedly until you see the **Thumbnails Views**.
- Select (click) a picture, then click **OK** to insert the picture on the form. Right click the newly inserted object to display a shortcut menu, then click **Properties** to display the Properties dialog box.
- Select the **Size Mode property** and select **Stretch** from the associated list. Close the dialog box.
- Click and drag the sizing handles on the frame to size the object appropriately for the header area. Size the form header as necessary. Move the picture and other controls in the header until you are satisfied with its appearance.
- Save the form.

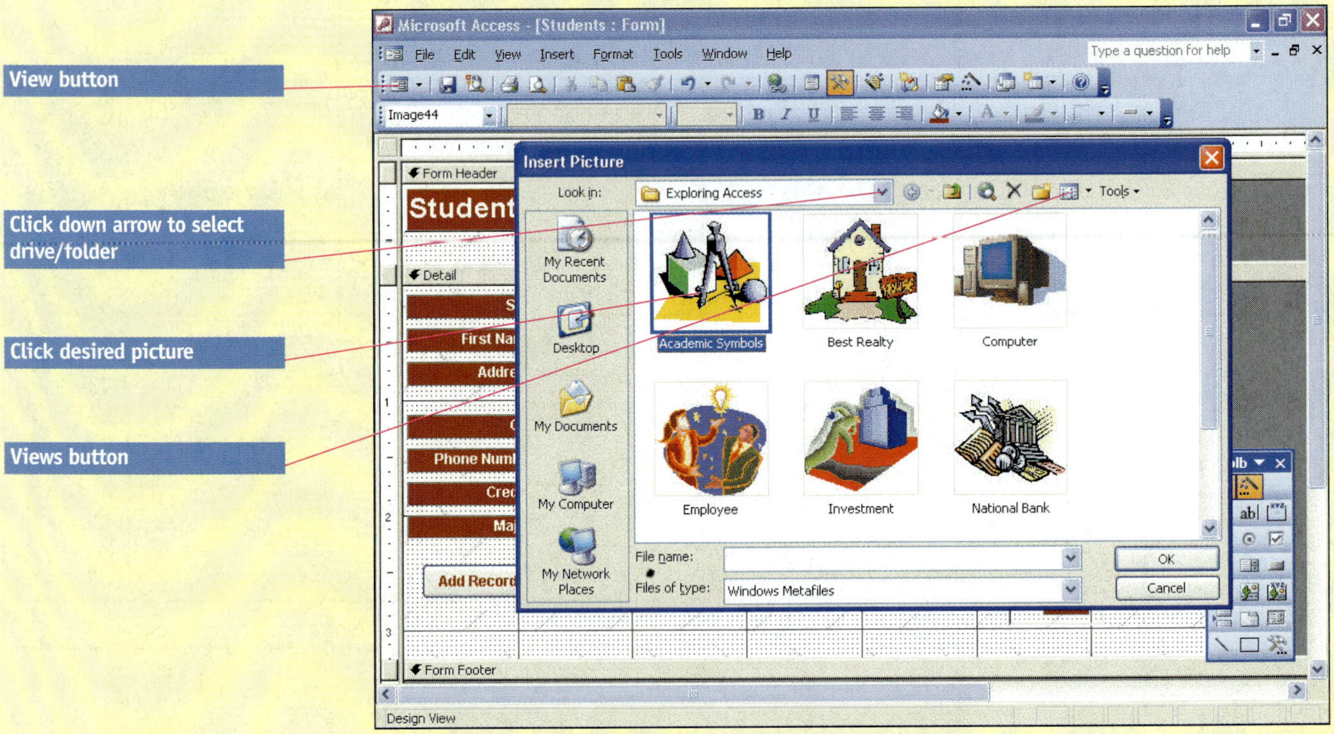

(h) Insert the Clip Art (step 8)

FIGURE 2.9 Hands-on Exercise 3 (*continued*)

MISSING TASK PANE

The Insert Picture command functions differently in Access than in the other Office applications since it does not display the Clip Art task pane. You can still search for clip art explicitly, however, by starting the Clip Organizer as a separate application. Click the Start button, click the All Programs button, click Microsoft Office Tools, then start the Clip Organizer. Select a clip art image from within the Clip Organizer, and click the Copy button. Use the Windows taskbar to return to Access, open the form in Design view, and click the Paste button.

Step 9: The Completed Form

- Click the **View button** to switch to the Form view. Click the **Add Record command button** to create a new record. Click the text box for **Social Security Number**. Add the record shown in Figure 2.9i.
- Click the **selection area** (the thin vertical column to the left of the form) to select the current record. The record selector changes to an arrow. The selection area is shaded to indicate that the record has been selected.
- Pull down the **File menu**. Click **Print** to display the Print dialog box. Click the option button to print **Selected Record**. Click **OK**.
- Examine your printed output to be sure that the form fits on a single page.
- If it doesn't, you need to adjust the margins of the form itself and/or change the margins using the Page Setup command in the File menu, then print the form a second time.
- Click the **Close Form command button** on the form after you have printed the record for your instructor.
- Click **Yes** if you see a message asking to save changes to the form design.
- Pull down the **File menu**. Click **Exit** to leave Access.

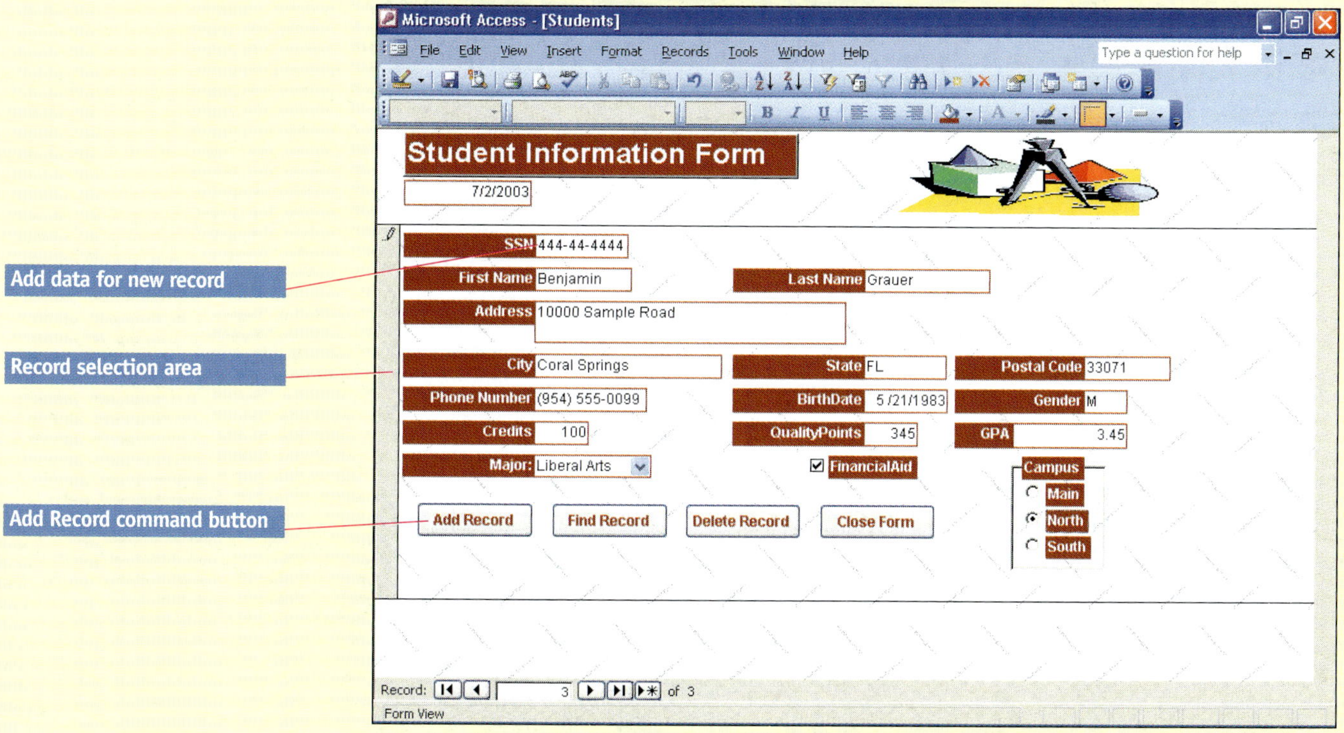

(i) The Completed Form (step 9)

FIGURE 2.9 Hands-on Exercise 3 (*continued*)

KEYBOARD SHORTCUTS

You can point and click to enter data within a form, but it's faster to use the keyboard. Use Tab (or Shift+Tab) to move forward (or backward) from field to field. Press the space bar to toggle a check box on and off. Type the first letter(s) of the desired value from a combo box to enter the value—for example "B" for "Business" within the list box for Major. These are universal shortcuts and apply to any Windows application.

SUMMARY

Access should be considered as a means to an end, rather than an end in itself. The real objective is to obtain useful information from a database, and that can be accomplished only if the database contains the necessary data to produce that information. Thus, one starts with a list of desired reports (or output), then determines the data (or input) to produce that information, after which the table can be created. The data within a table should be divided into the smallest possible units, such as separate fields for first and last name. Calculated fields should be avoided.

A table has different views—the Design view and the Datasheet view. The Design view is used to create the table and determine the fields within the table, as well as the data type and properties of each field. The Datasheet view is used after the table has been created to add, edit, and delete records. (The PivotTable view and PivotChart view display summary data and are discussed in Chapter 4.)

The Table Wizard is the easiest way to create a table. It lets you choose from a series of business or personal tables, asks you questions about the fields you want, then creates the table for you. The wizard creates the initial table for you, after which you can modify the table in Design view.

A form provides a user-friendly way to enter and display data, in that it can be made to resemble a paper form. AutoForms and the Form Wizard are easy ways to create a form. The Design view enables you to modify an existing form.

A form consists of objects called controls. A bound control has a data source such as a field in the underlying table. An unbound control has no data source. A calculated control contains an expression. Controls are selected, moved, and sized the same way as any other Windows object.

A property is a characteristic or attribute of an object that determines how the object looks and behaves. Every Access object (e.g., tables, fields, forms, and controls) has a set of properties that determine the behavior of that object. The properties for an object are displayed in a property sheet.

KEY TERMS

Allow Zero Length property 551
AutoForm 564
AutoNumber field 549
Bound control 561
Calculated control 561
Calculated field 548
Caption property 551
Check box 574
Command button 574
Control 561
Currency field 549
Data type 549
Datasheet view 550
Date/Time field 549
Default Value property 551
Design view 550
Drop-down list box 574
Expression 561
Field name 549
Field Size property 551
Form 561
Form view 561
Form Wizard 564
Format property 551
Hyperlink field 549
IME Mode property 551
IME Sentence Mode property .. 551
Indexed property 551
Input Mask property 551
Memo field 549
Number field 549
OLE Object field 549
Option group 574
PivotChart view 550
PivotTable view 550
Primary key 549
Property 551
Property sheet 551
Required property 551
Tab Order 581
Tab Stop property 581
Table Wizard 549
Text field 549
Unbound control 561
Unicode Compression property 551
Validation Rule property 551
Validation Text property 551
Yes/No field 549

MULTIPLE CHOICE

1. Which of the following is true?
   (a) The Table Wizard must be used to create a table
   (b) The Form Wizard must be used to create a form
   (c) Both (a) and (b)
   (d) Neither (a) nor (b)

2. Which of the following is implemented automatically by Access?
   (a) Rejection of a record with a duplicate value of the primary key
   (b) Rejection of numbers in a text field
   (c) Both (a) and (b)
   (d) Neither (a) nor (b)

3. Social Security number, phone number, and zip code should be designated as:
   (a) Number fields
   (b) Text fields
   (c) Yes/No fields
   (d) Any of the above depending on the application

4. Which of the following is true of the primary key?
   (a) Its values must be unique
   (b) It must be defined as a text field
   (c) It must be the first field in a table
   (d) It can never be changed

5. Social Security number rather than name is used as a primary key because:
   (a) The Social Security number is numeric, whereas the name is not
   (b) The Social Security number is unique, whereas the name is not
   (c) The Social Security number is a shorter field
   (d) All of the above

6. Which of the following is true regarding buttons within the Form Wizard?
   (a) The > button copies a selected field from a table onto a form
   (b) The < button removes a selected field from a form
   (c) Both (a) and (b)
   (d) Neither (a) nor (b)

7. Which of the following was *not* a suggested guideline for designing a table?
   (a) Include all necessary data
   (b) Store data in its smallest parts
   (c) Avoid calculated fields
   (d) Designate at least two primary keys

8. Which of the following are valid parameters for use with a form?
   (a) Portrait orientation, a width of 6 inches, left and right margins of $1\frac{1}{4}$ inch
   (b) Landscape orientation, a width of 9 inches, left and right margins of 1 inch
   (c) Both (a) and (b)
   (d) Neither (a) nor (b)

9. Which view is used to add, edit, or delete records in a table?
   (a) The Datasheet view
   (b) The Design view
   (c) The PivotTable view
   (d) The PivotChart view

10. Which of the following is true?
    (a) Any field added to a table after a form has been created is automatically added to the form as a bound control
    (b) Any calculated control that appears in a form is automatically inserted into the underlying table
    (c) Every bound and unbound control in a form has an underlying property sheet
    (d) All of the above

11. In which view will you see the record selector symbols of a pencil and a triangle?
    (a) Only the Datasheet view
    (b) Only the Form view
    (c) The Datasheet view and the Form view
    (d) The Form view, the Design view, and the Datasheet view

... continued

multiple choice

12. To move a control (in the Design view), you select the control, then:

(a) Point to a border (the pointer changes to an arrow) and click and drag the border to the new position
(b) Point to a border (the pointer changes to a hand) and click and drag the border to the new position
(c) Point to a sizing handle (the pointer changes to an arrow) and click and drag the sizing handle to the new position
(d) Point to a sizing handle (the pointer changes to a hand) and click and drag the sizing handle to the new position

13. Which fields are commonly defined with an input mask?

(a) Social Security Number and phone number
(b) First name, middle name, and last name
(c) City, state, and zip code
(d) All of the above

14. Which data type appears as a check box in a form?

(a) Text field
(b) Number field
(c) Yes/No field
(d) All of the above

15. Which properties would you use to limit a user's response to two characters, and automatically convert the response to uppercase?

(a) Field Size and Format
(b) Input Mask, Validation Rule, and Default Value
(c) Input Mask and Required
(d) Field Size, Validation Rule, Validation Text, and Required

16. Which of the following is true with respect to an individual's hire date and years of service, both of which appear on a form that is based on an employee table?

(a) Hire date should be a calculated control; years of service should be a bound control
(b) Hire date should be a bound control; years of service should be a calculated control
(c) Both should be bound controls
(d) Both should be calculated controls

17. What is the best way to store an individual's name in a table?

(a) As a single field consisting of the last name, first name, and middle initial, in that order
(b) As a single field consisting of the first name, last name, and middle initial, in that order
(c) As three separate fields for first name, last name, and middle initial
(d) All of the above are equally suitable

18. Which of the following would *not* be a good primary key?

(a) Student Number
(b) Social Security Number
(c) An e-mail address
(d) A 9-digit zip code

ANSWERS

1. d	**7.** d	**13.** a
2. a	**8.** c	**14.** c
3. b	**9.** a	**15.** a
4. a	**10.** c	**16.** b
5. b	**11.** c	**17.** c
6. c	**12.** b	**18.** d

PRACTICE WITH ACCESS

1. **A Modified Student Form:** Open the *My First Database* used in the chapter and modify the Student form created in the hands-on exercises to match the form in Figure 2.10. (The form contains three additional controls that must be added to the Students table, prior to modifying the form.)
   a. Open the Students table in Design view. Add DateAdmitted and EmailAddress as a date and a text field, respectively. Add a Yes/No field to indicate whether the student is an international student.
   b. Open the Students form in Design view. Add controls for the additional fields as shown in Figure 2.10.
   c. Modify the State field in the underlying Students table to use the Lookup Wizard, and set CA, FL, NJ, and NY as the values for the list box. (These are the most common states in the student population.) The control in the form will not, however, inherit the list box because it was added to the table after the form was created. Hence, you have to delete the existing control in the form, display the field list, then click and drag the State field from the field list to the form.)
   d. Add a hyperlink in the form header that contains the Web address of your school or university. It's easy—just click the Insert Hyperlink button on the Form Design toolbar, then enter the text and associated address in the ensuing dialog box. Click and drag the control containing the hyperlink to the appropriate place on the form.
   e. Change the Caption property in each command button to include an ampersand in front of the underlined letter (e.g., &Add Record). The resulting command button is shown with an underline under the letter (e.g., Add Record). This in turn lets you use a shortcut, Alt+A (where A is the underlined letter), to activate the command button.
   f. Resize the control in the Form Header so that *Your School or University Student Information Form* takes two lines. Press Ctrl+Enter to force a line break within the control. Resize the Form Header.
   g. Change the tab order to reflect the new fields in the form.
   h. Use the Page Setup command to change the margins and/or orientation of the page to be sure that the form fits on one page. Click the record selector column to select your record, then print the form for your instructor.

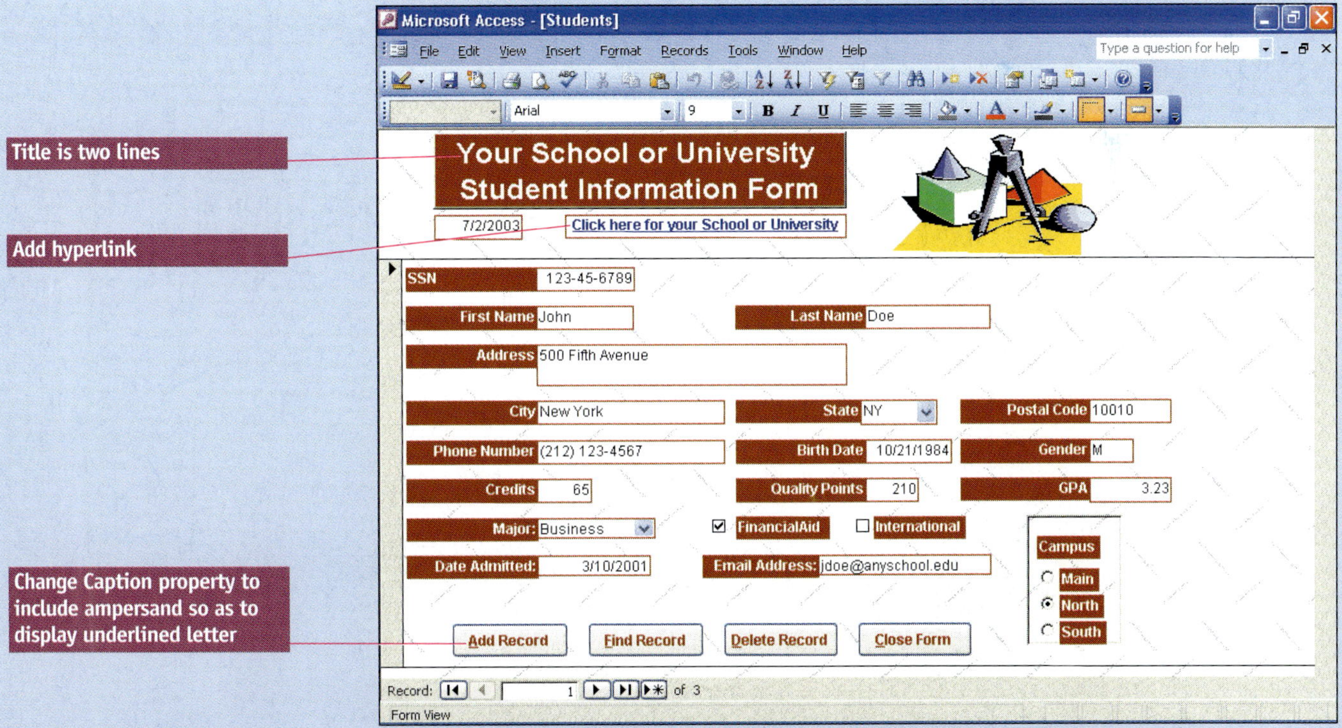

FIGURE 2.10 Modified Student Form (exercise 1)

2. **The United States Database:** This assignment builds on the United States database that was used for an earlier exercise in Chapter 1. Your assignment is to build a form similar to the one in Figure 2.11. You do not have to match our form exactly. You do, however, have to duplicate the functionality. Proceed as follows:

   a. Open the *Chapter 1 Practice 3* database in the Exploring Access folder. Click the Tables button in the Database window and open the States table in Design view. Insert a new field at the end of the table, using WebPage and hyperlink as the field name and field type, respectively.

   b. Use the Form Wizard to create the form initially, based on the States table (select all of the fields). Select a column layout and choose any style. Open the form in Design view to complete the form. Move and size the various controls as shown in Figure 2.11.

   c. Add clip art to the form header that contains an image representing the United States. (Change the Size Mode property of the clip art to Stretch.) Insert a hyperlink to the White House (www.whitehouse.gov) underneath the image. Add your name and date in the form header.

   d. Create a calculated control for the population density (population/area). Set the Tab Stop property to No.

   e. Add the indicated command buttons, using the Caption property to implement the keyboard shortcut; for example, &Find Record will underline the letter "F" and enable the Alt+F keyboard shortcut to activate the button.

   f. Pull down the View menu, click the Tab Order command to display the Tab Order dialog box, and then click the Auto Order button to set the tab order to match the physical arrangement of the controls in the form.

   g. Go to the Form view. Use the navigation buttons to locate your home state (or any state if you are an international student). Enter the address of the state's Web page, using an address of the form www.state.*abbreviation*.us (e.g., www.state.fl.us for Florida).

   h. Use the Page Setup command to change the margins and/or orientation of the page to be sure that the form fits on one page. Click the record selector column to select your state and print this record for your instructor. Click the hyperlink for your state's Web page and print that page for your instructor as well.

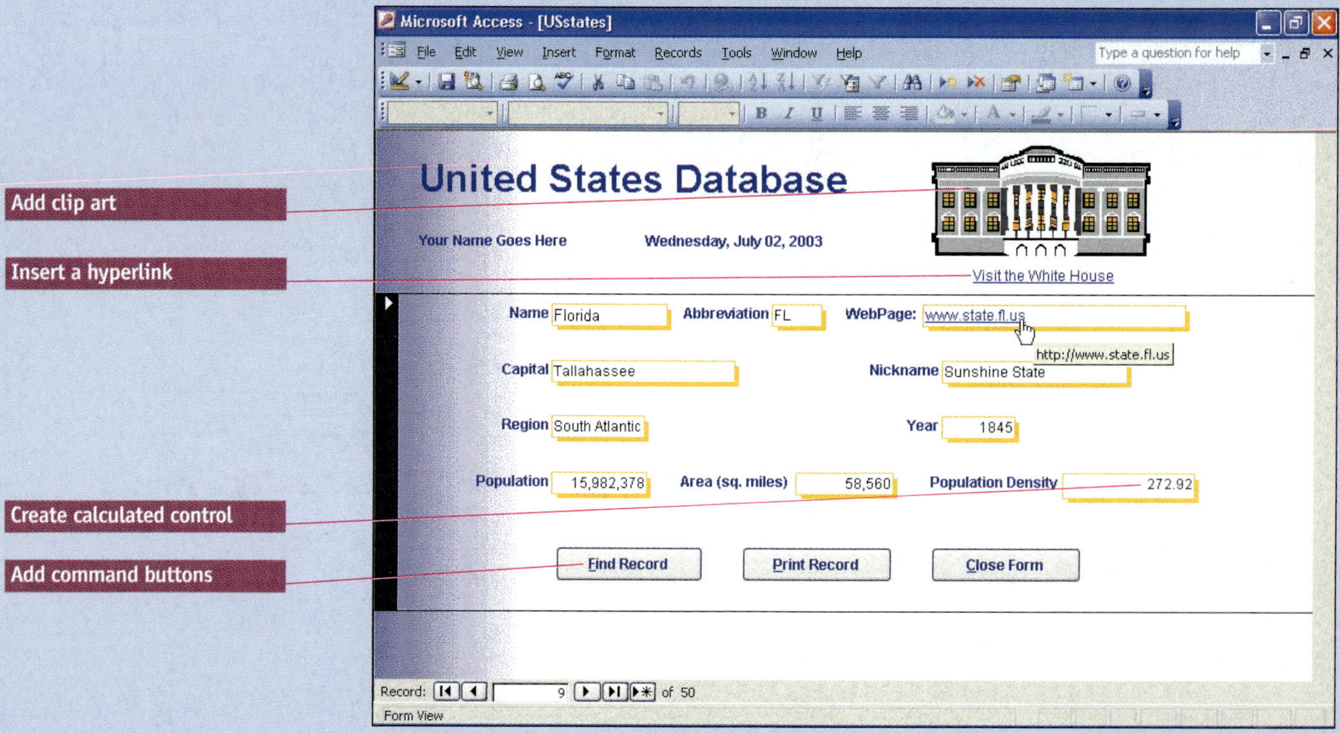

FIGURE 2.11 The United States Database (exercise 2)

3. **The Super Bowl:** Figure 2.12 displays a Web page (or Data Access page) that can be used to view and/or enter data in an underlying Access database. Look closely and you will see that the form is displayed in Internet Explorer, as opposed to Access, because the form was created as a Web page within Access. Proceed as follows:
   a. Open the *Chapter 2 Practice 3* database in the Exploring Access folder. Click the Pages tab in the Database window, and then double click the option to create the Data Access page using the wizard. The wizard will prompt you for the information it needs in a series of screens. The first screen asks you to choose the table or query (Previous Games) and the fields within that table (All). Click Next.
   b. You do not need grouping or sorting, but you should check the box to apply a theme (to make the form more attractive). End the wizard by viewing the page in Design view. Enter a title as indicated by the Click here prompt. Insert a hyperlink to the Super Bowl Web site (www.superbowl.com).
   c. Pull down the File menu, click the Save command, then save the page in the Exploring Access folder. You will be warned that you have specified an absolute path and that the network may not be able to reconnect in the future. Click OK.
   d. Close the database and exit Access. Go to the Exploring Access folder and open the Web page (HTML document) that you just created to view the records in the Super Bowl table as shown in Figure 2.12. (The HTML document exists as a separate document outside of the Access database.)
   e. Click the New button to add a record for any games that are not in our table. (You can click the link to the Super Bowl Web site to obtain the scores of the additional games.) Print the record of the most recent game from Internet Explorer. Close Internet Explorer.
   f. Start Access and reopen the *Chapter 2 Practice 3* database. Click the Tables button, open the Previous Games table, and go to the last record in the table, which should contain the data that you just entered. Now think about what you have accomplished. You were able to add a record to an Access database using a Web page as the "front end" for the database. You can continue to add, edit, or delete records using the Web page, and all changes will be reflected in the underlying Access table.

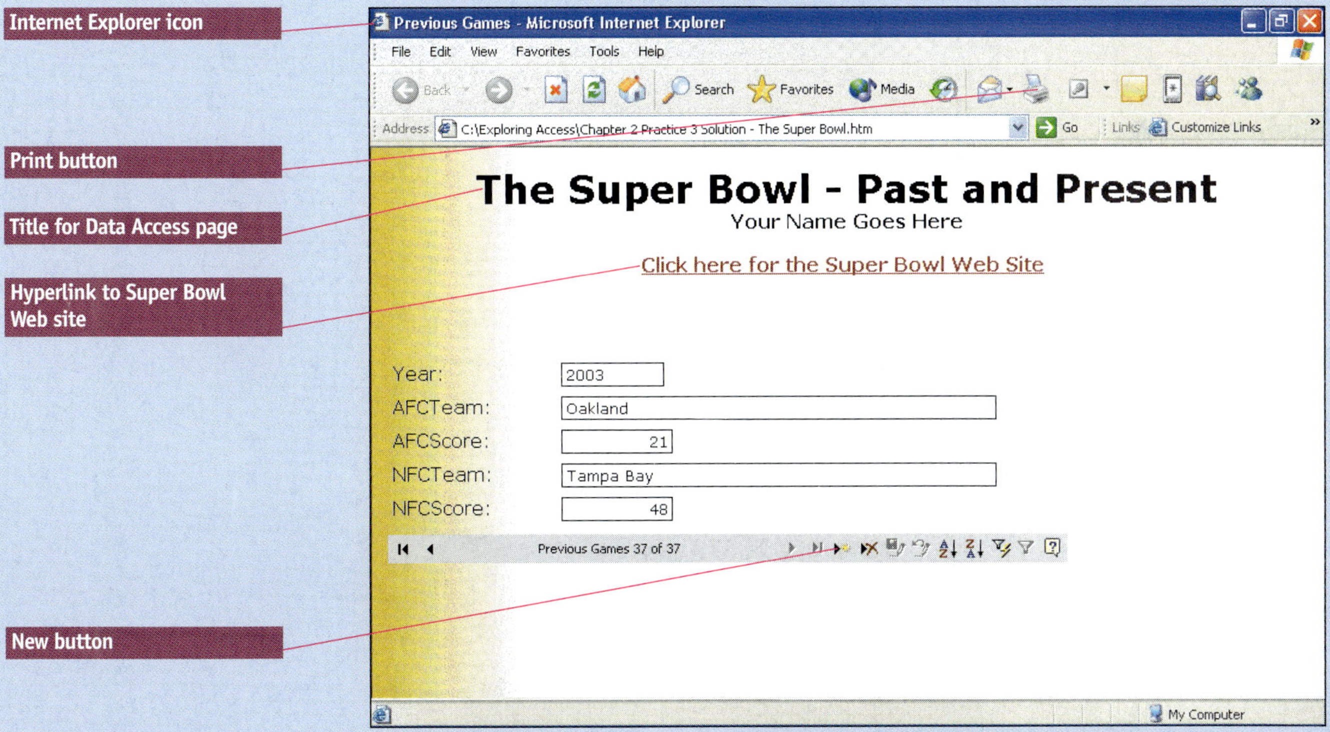

FIGURE 2.12 The Super Bowl (exercise 3)

4. **The Fishing Pole:** You have been asked by a marine hardware store to create a database that will be used to track its customers. In essence, you are to create the table in Figure 2.13 without benefit of the Table Wizard. Proceed as follows:
   a. Start Access and create a new (blank) database. Click the Tables button in the Database window and double click the option to create a new table in Design view. To enter a new field, click in the Field Name column and type the name of the field (do not use spaces in the field name). Move to the Data Type column and choose the field type.
   b. Create all of the fields in Figure 2.13. (The BoatType should be specified using the Lookup Wizard, and include Fishing, Power, and Sail as the boat types to be listed.) Save the table as Customers.
   c. The CustomerNumber is to be the primary key. It should be an AutoNumber data type, and the Format should be \C0000, which will automatically produce a Customer Number that begins with the letter C, followed by a four-digit number each time a record is added to the table.
   d. Establish input masks for the customer's zip code and phone number, as well as the initial purchase date. The initial purchase date should also have a short date format.
   e. Use the Format property so that the state is displayed in uppercase letters, regardless of how it is entered.
   f. Set appropriate field sizes for all text fields. Eliminate the default value of 0 and set a currency format with 2 decimal places for the initial purchase amount.
   g. Set the Required property for the LastName and FirstName fields to Yes.
   h. Set the Validation Rule property for the MailingList field to restrict values to 1, 2, or 3. Set the Validation Text property to display an appropriate message if the user attempts to enter invalid data.
   i. Enter one record into the completed table, entering your name as the customer name. Print the table only if you are not doing the next exercise. The table will require two pages, even if you change to landscape printing.

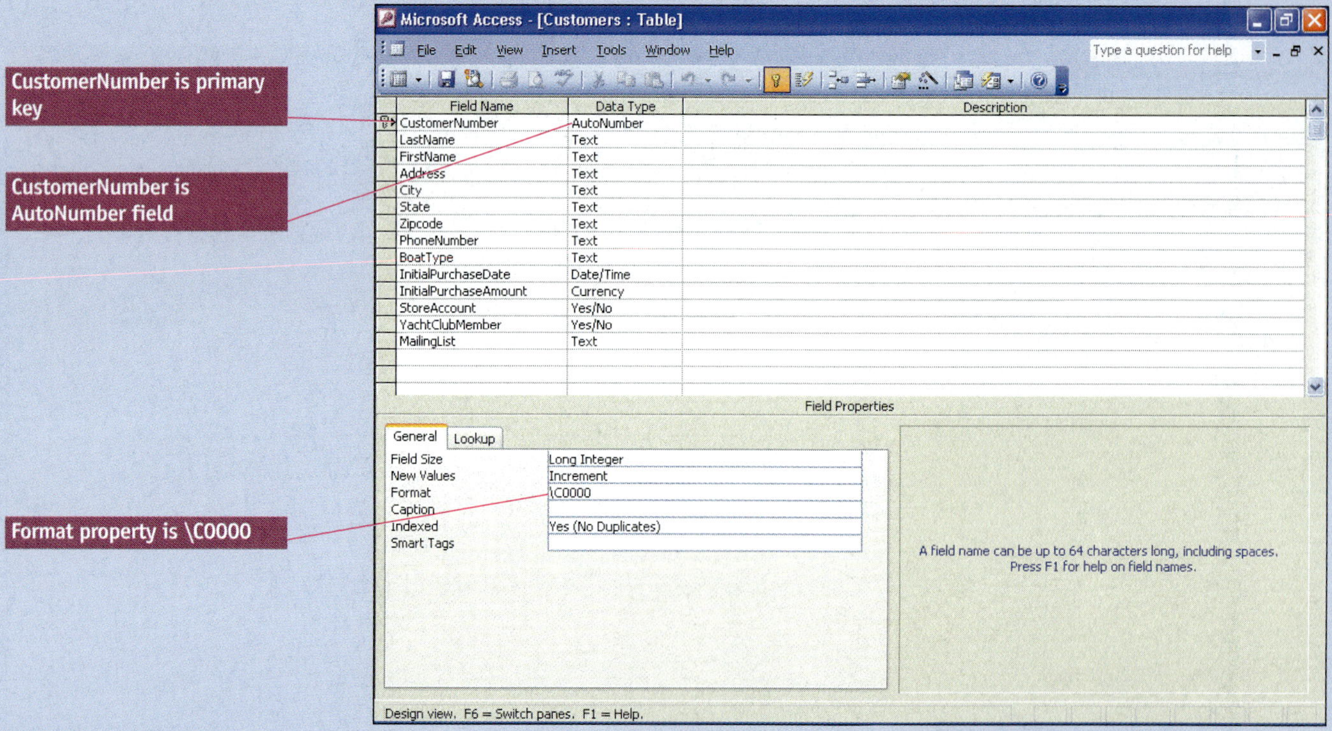

FIGURE 2.13 The Fishing Pole (exercise 4)

5. **A Form for the Fishing Pole:** Your assignment is to create a form similar to the one in Figure 2.14 that is based on the Fishing Pole database created in the previous exercise. The design of your form can be different from ours, but you must duplicate the functionality in our figure. Start with the Form Wizard, and then modify the resulting form as necessary so that your finished form accommodates all of the following:
   a. The form should contain a control for every field in the underlying table. Move, format, align, and size the controls as necessary. Change the tab order of the controls so that the user tabs through the controls from left to right, top to bottom. Set the Tab Stop property of the Customer Number to No because the user does not input this value.
   b. Use a different background color for the required fields (such as the customer's first and last name) to emphasize that these fields must be entered. Include a note at the bottom of the form to explain the color change.
   c. Insert a form header with clip art (you do not have to use the same clip art as in our figure) and an appropriate title as shown in Figure 2.14. Set the Size Mode property of the clip art to Stretch.
   d. Add command buttons as indicated. The command buttons should be a uniform size with equal spacing between them. Test each command button to be sure that it works as intended.
   e. Use the Page Setup command to be sure that the form will fit on a single page when printed. Change the margins and/or orientation of the form as necessary. The completed form should display the data that you entered for yourself when you created the table in the previous problem. Print this form for your instructor.
   f. Click the Add Record button to add a new record to the Customers table. Use your instructor's name as the customer's name, and supply other information as you see fit. Click the record selector column to select your instructor's record. Pull down the File menu, click the Print command, then select the option button to print the selected record. Submit both forms to your instructor to show that you completed this assignment.

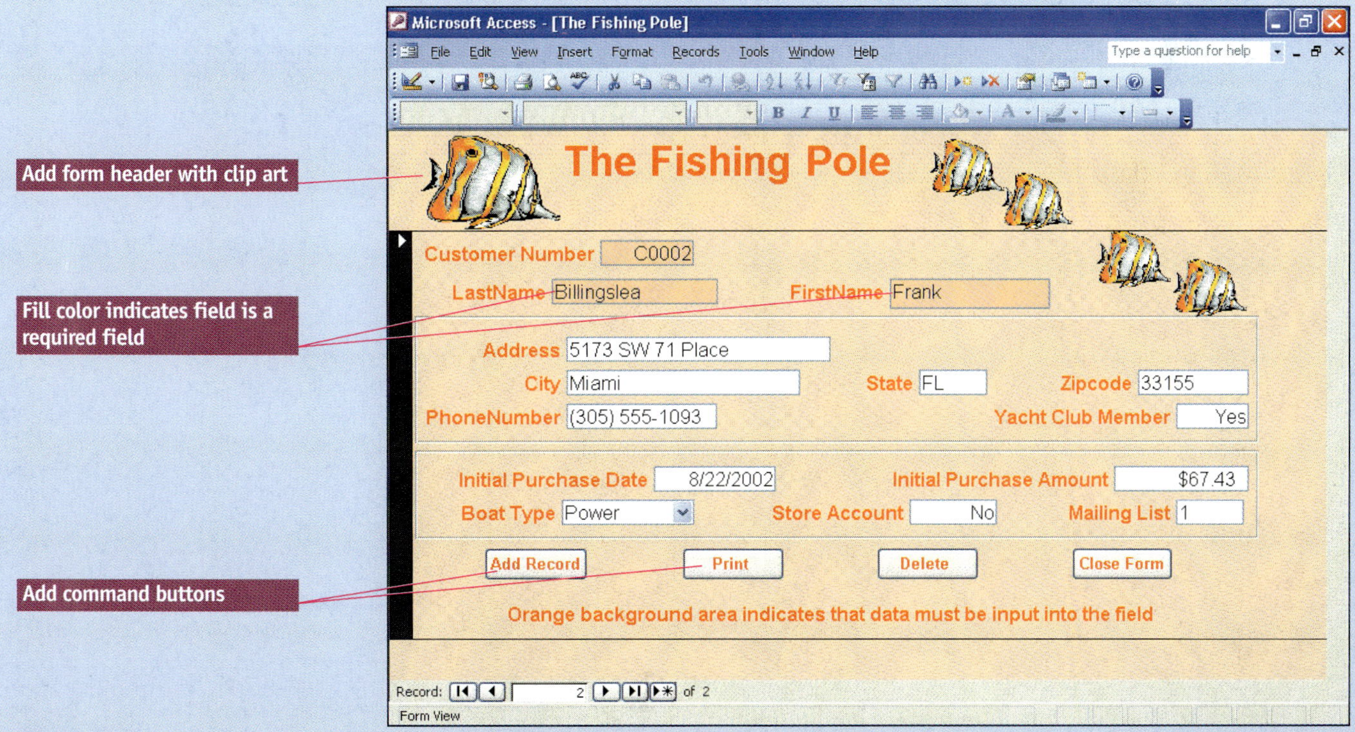

FIGURE 2.14 A Form for the Fishing Pole (exercise 5)

6. **The Shopping Mall:** You have been hired as a consultant for a shopping mall to create a database that is to track all of the stores in the mall. You have met with the mall manager several times and have decided on the various fields that need to be included in the Stores table. The results of your discussion can be summarized by the Design view of the table as shown in Figure 2.15.
   a. Create the table without benefit of the Table Wizard. Start Access and specify that you will create a new database. The database should be called Shopping Mall and it should be stored in your Exploring Access folder.
   b. Click the Tables button in the Database window and double click the option to create a new table in Design view. To enter a new field, click in the Field Name column and type the name of the field (do not use spaces in the field name). Move to the Data Type column and choose the field type. The fields in your table should match those in Figure 2.15.
   c. The StoreID is to be the primary key. Use the validation rule that is specified in the figure, which requires that the file begin with the letter S followed by four digits to indicate the store unit number.
   d. The StoreType should be specified using the Lookup Wizard, and include Clothing, Jewelry, Furniture, Home Accessories, Restaurant, and Shoes as the store types to be listed.
   e. Establish input masks for the manager's phone number, as well as the lease start date and lease end date. The latter two fields require short date formats.
   f. Set appropriate field sizes for all text fields. Eliminate the default values of 0 and set appropriate formats for the currency fields. The PricePerSquareFt is the rent per square foot and should allow two decimal places. The StoreRevenue field should be formatted without any decimal places.
   g. The StoreID, StoreName, and StoreType are required fields.
   h. Enter one record into the completed table. Use StoreID S0001 and use your name as the manager. Change to landscape printing and adjust the column width and/or the margins, so that the records fit on a single sheet of paper. Print this record for your instructor.

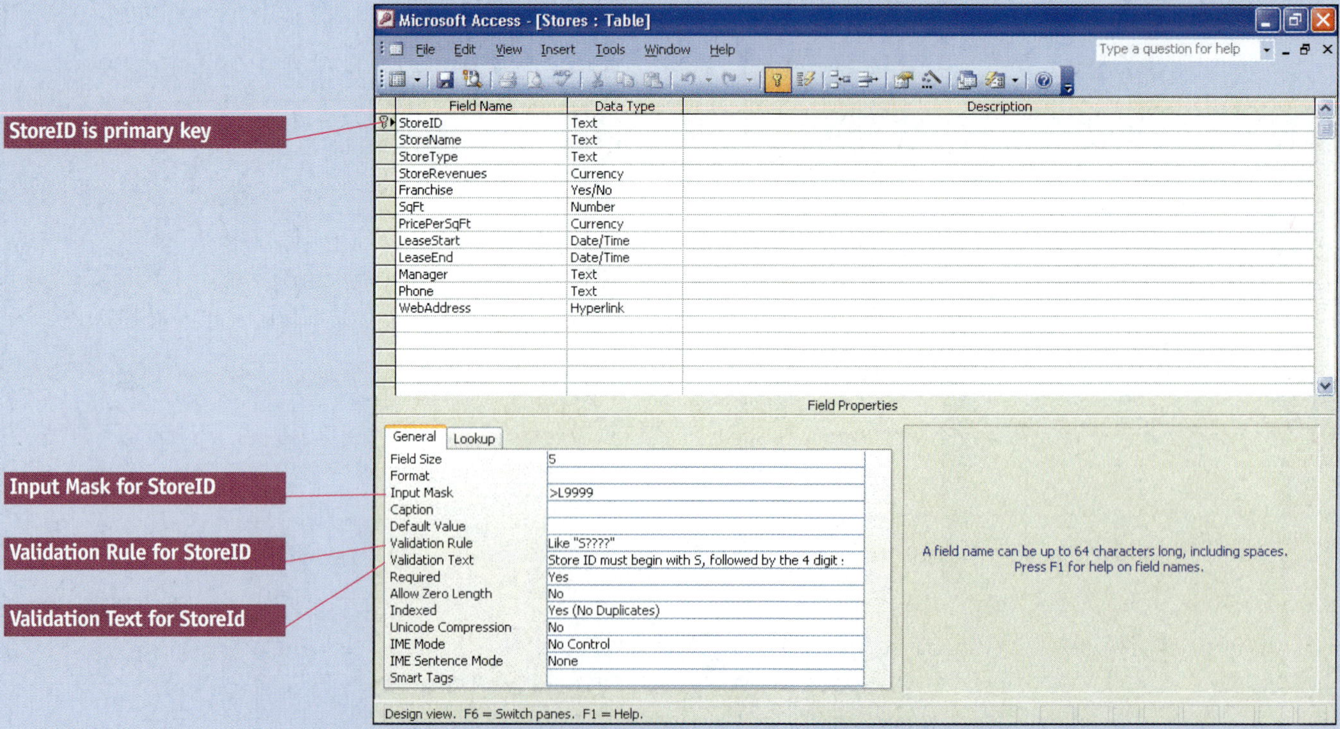

FIGURE 2.15 The Shopping Mall (exercise 6)

7. **A Form for the Shopping Mall:** Your assignment is to create a form similar to the one in Figure 2.16 that is based on the Shopping Mall database created in the previous exercise. The design of your form can be different from ours, but you must duplicate the functionality in our figure. Start with the Form Wizard, and then modify the resulting form as necessary so that your finished form accommodates all of the following:
   a. The form should contain a control for every field in the underlying table. Format, move, size, and align the controls as necessary. Change the tab order of the controls so that the user tabs through the controls from left to right, top to bottom.
   b. Include a calculated control to determine the monthly rent, which is equal to the number of square feet times the price per square foot. Change the format of this control to currency. Set the Tab Stop property to No.
   c. Use a different background for the required fields (such as the StoreID and StoreType) to emphasize that the data for these fields is required. Include a note at the bottom of the form that explains the color change.
   d. Insert a form header with clip art (you do not have to use the same clip art as in our figure) and an appropriate title. Set the Size Mode property of the clip art to Stretch.
   e. Add command buttons as indicated. The command buttons should be a uniform size with equal spacing between them. Test each command button to be sure that it works as intended.
   f. Use the Page Setup command to be sure that the form will fit on a single page when printed. The completed form should display the data that you entered for store number S0001 when you created the table in the previous problem. Print this form for your instructor.
   g. Click the Add Record button to add a new record with StoreID S0002. Use your instructor's name as the store manager, and supply other information as you see fit. Click the record selector column to select your instructor's record. Pull down the File menu, click the Print command, then select the option button to print the selected record. Submit both forms to your instructor to show that you completed this assignment.

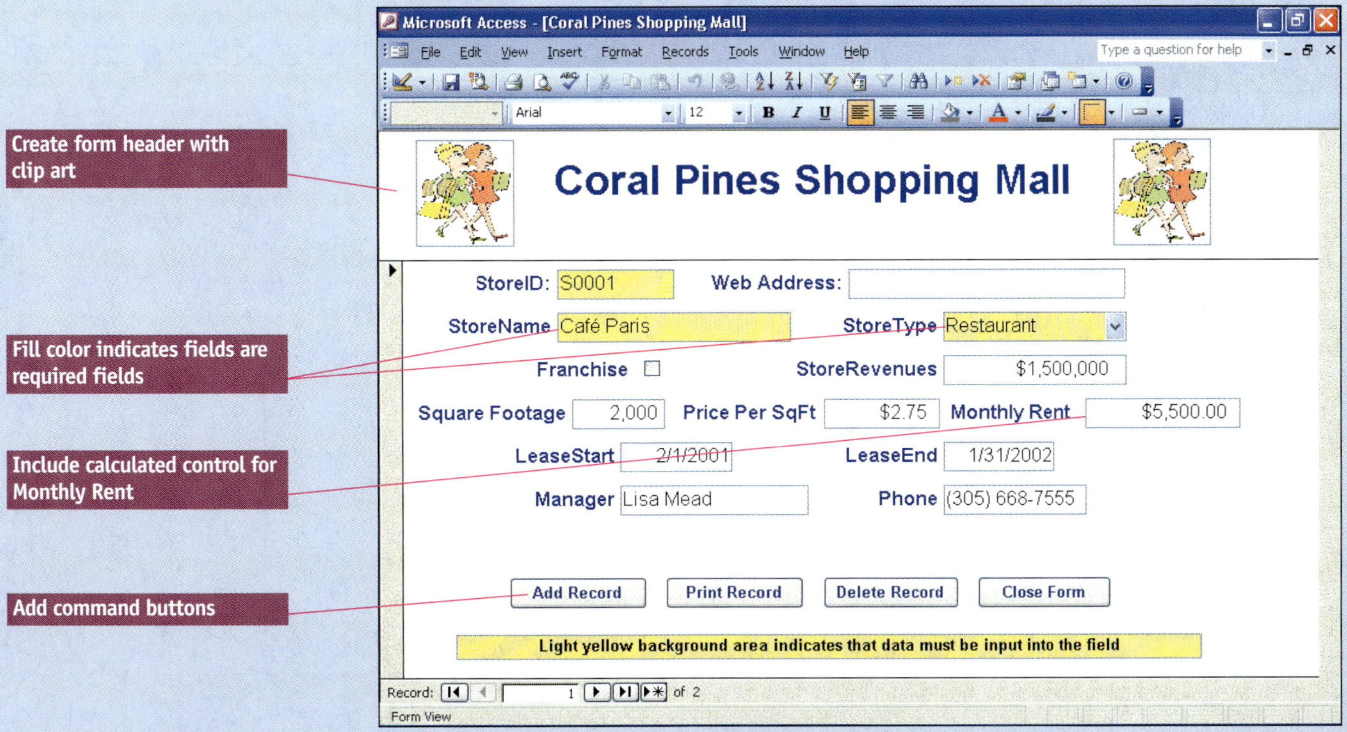

FIGURE 2.16 A Form for the Shopping Mall (exercise 7)

8. **Best Realty:** Best Realty is a real estate agency that specializes in the listing/selling of homes, including single-family dwellings as well as multiple-family dwellings. You have recently been hired by Best Realty to develop a database to track their property listings. After much thought and planning, you have decided upon the fields shown in Figure 2.17. Proceed as follows:
   a. Create the table shown *without* using the Table Wizard. After you start Access, specify that you will create a new database—then assign the name Best Realty and save it in the Exploring Access folder.
   b. Click the Tables button in the Database window and double click the option to create a new table in the Design view. To enter a new field, click in the Field Name column and type the name of the field (do not use spaces in the field name). Move to the Data Type column and choose the field type. The fields in your table should match those in Figure 2.17.
   c. The PropertyID should be designated as the primary key. Be sure to include a validation rule that specifies that the ID should be composed of the letter P followed by four digits.
   d. The PropertyType should be created using the Lookup Wizard, and include Single-Family, Townhome, Duplex, and Condominium.
   e. Set appropriate field sizes for all text fields. Eliminate the default values of 0 and set appropriate formats for the number fields.
   f. Create an input mask and format for the DateListed and DateSold fields.
   g. The PropertyID, Address, AskingPrice, and AgentLastName should be specified as required fields.
   h. Enter one record into the completed table. Use P0001 as the PropertyID and use your name as the agent. Change to landscape printing and adjust the column width and/or the margins so that the record fits on a single sheet of paper. Print this record for your instructor.

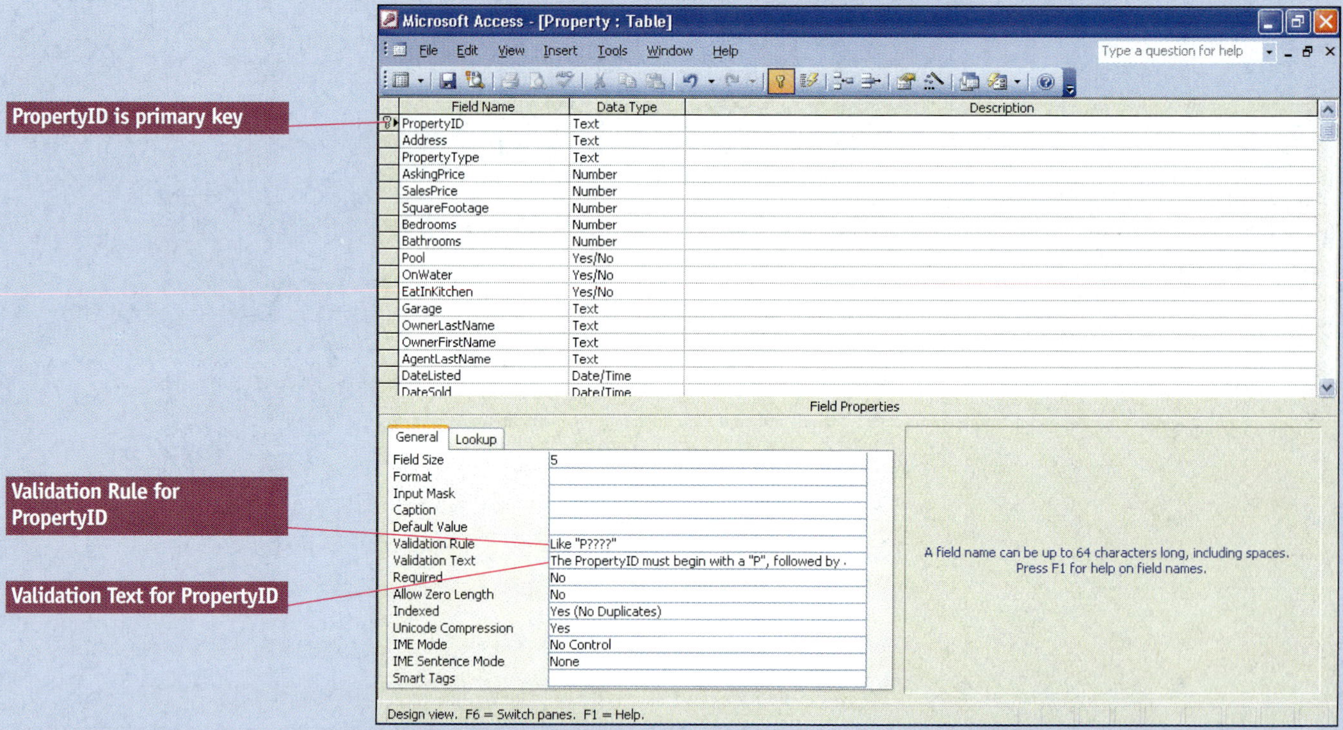

FIGURE 2.17 Best Realty (exercise 8)

9. **A Form for Best Realty:** Your assignment is to create a form similar to the one in Figure 2.18 that is based on the Best Realty database created in the previous exercise. The design of your form can be different from ours, but you must duplicate the functionality in our figure. Start with the Form Wizard, and then modify the resulting form as necessary so that your finished form accommodates all of the following:
   a. The form should contain a control for every field in the underlying table. Format, move, size, and align the controls as necessary. Change the tab order of the controls so that the user tabs through the controls from left to right, top to bottom.
   b. Add a calculated control to determine the price per square foot, which is equal to the sales price divided by the number of square feet. Change the format of this control to currency. Set the Tab Stop property to No.
   c. Use a different background for the required fields (such as the PropertyID and Address) to emphasize that the data for these fields is required. Include a note at the bottom of the form to explain the color change.
   d. Insert a form header with clip art (you do not have to use the same clip art as in our figure) and an appropriate title. Set the Size Mode property of the clip art to Stretch.
   e. Add command buttons as indicated. The command buttons should be a uniform size with equal spacing between them. Test each command button to be sure that it works as intended.
   f. Use the Page Setup command to be sure that the form will fit on a single page when printed. The completed form should display the data that you entered for the first property when you created the table in the previous problem. Print this form for your instructor.
   g. Click the Add Record button to add a new record with PropertyID P0002. Use your instructor's name as the owner, and supply other information as you see fit. Click the record selector column to select this record. Pull down the File menu, click the Print command, then select the option button to print the selected record. Submit both forms to your instructor to show that you completed this assignment.

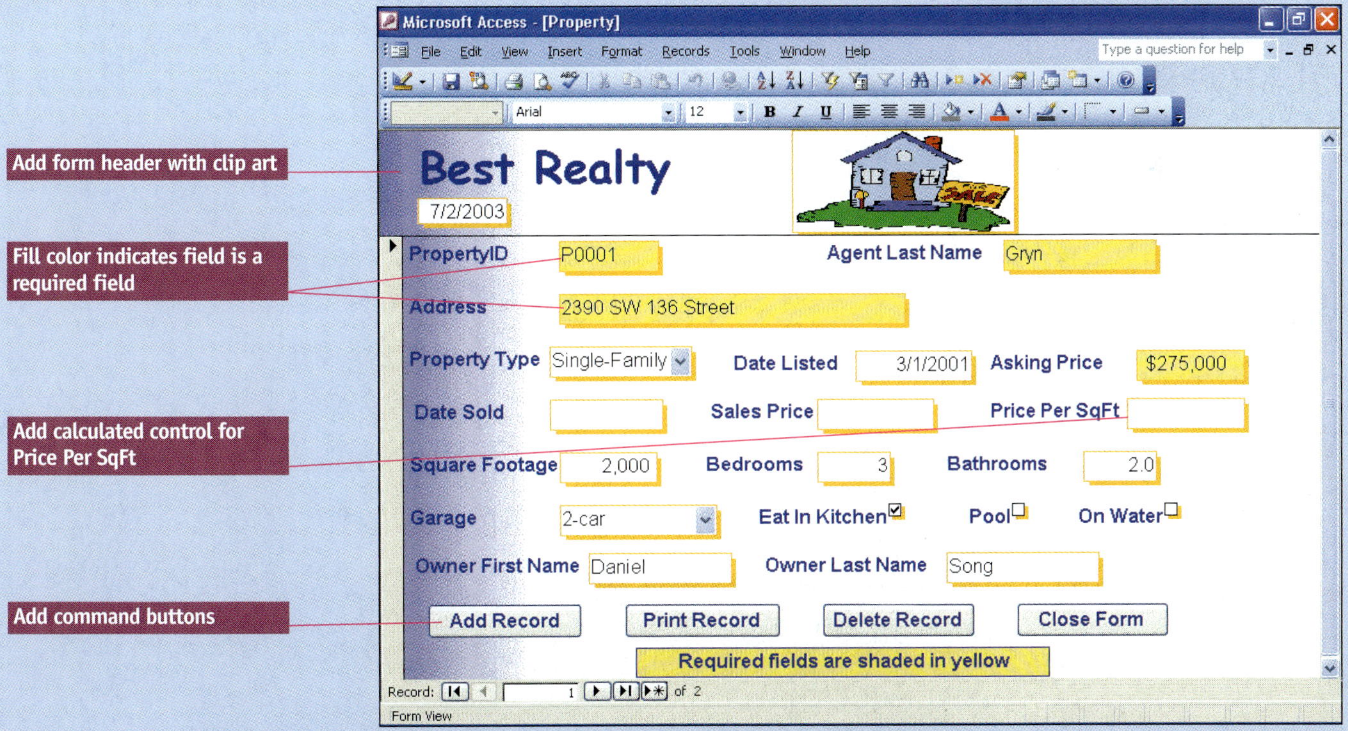

FIGURE 2.18 A Form for Best Realty (exercise 9)

10. **About Our Students:** Figure 2.19 illustrates a form that we create for all of our databases that appears automatically when the database is opened. The form is not based on a table within the database; that is, the form contains descriptive information about the database such as a version number, serial number, logo, and/or copyright notice. You can use our design and wording and/or you can modify either element as you see fit. Proceed as follows:
    a. Open the *My First Database* that you have used throughout the chapter. Click the Forms button, then double click the command to create a form in Design view. Click and drag the borders of the form so that the size of the form is approximately 3½ inches by 3½ inches.
    b. Display the Toolbox toolbar. Use the Label tool to add the various text boxes that appear on the form. We suggest an 8-point sans serif typeface (Arial, Tahoma, or MS Sans Serif).
    c. Insert the clip art logo that you used earlier for the Students form. (Set the Size Mode property to Stretch so that the clip art is not truncated.)
    d. Use the Command Button Wizard to insert a button to close the form. Change the text of the button to "OK" as shown in Figure 2.19.
    e. You have to change the properties of the form itself to suppress the scroll bars, record selector, and navigation buttons because the form is not based on an underlying table. Go to Design view, right click the Form Selector button (the tiny square in the upper-left corner) to display a context-sensitive menu, choose Properties to display the Property sheet for the form, and then look for the appropriate properties.
    f. Save the form as About Our Students. (The name of the form will appear automatically in the title bar when the form is displayed.) Go to the Form view to see the completed form. Return to Design view to make changes as necessary. Print the completed form for your instructor.
    g. The Startup property can be used to display the form automatically when the database is open. Pull down the Tools menu, click the Startup command, select About Our Students in the Display Form/Page list box, and click OK. Close the database, then reopen it to see your form.

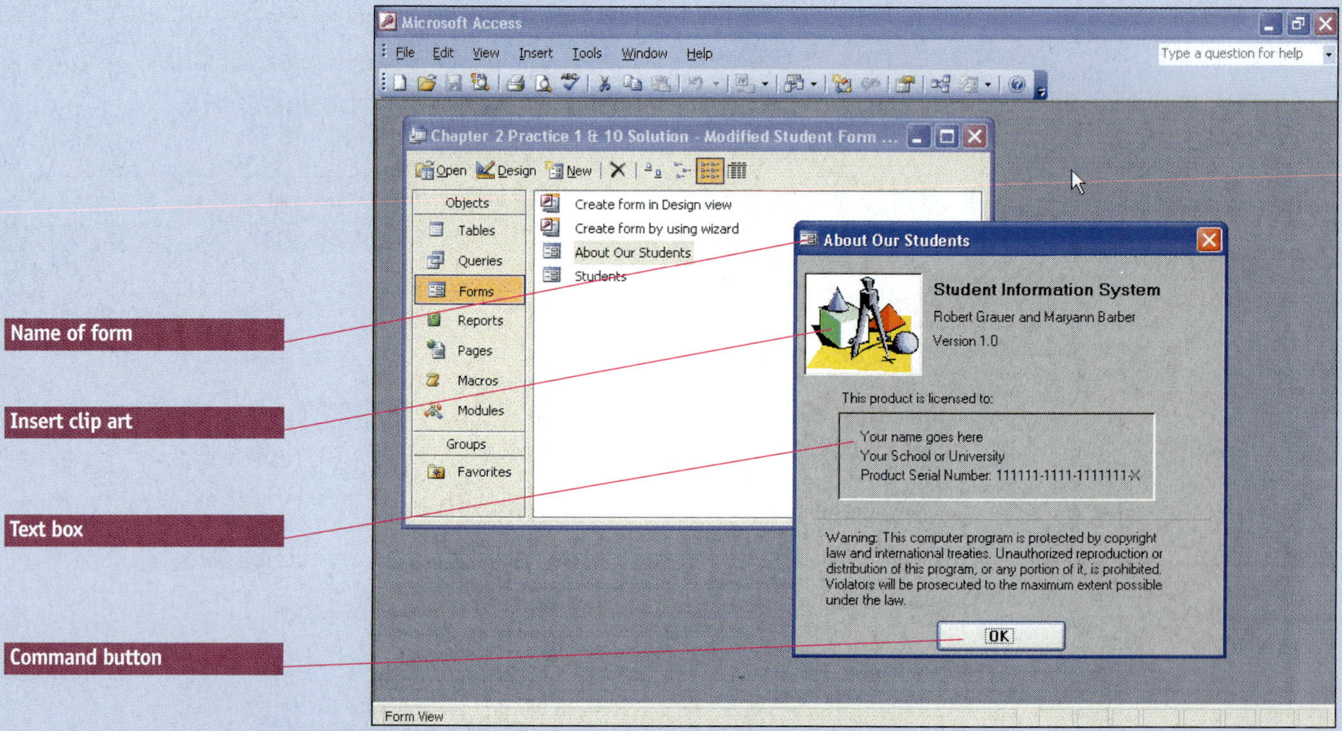

FIGURE 2.19 About Our Students (exercise 10)

MINI CASES

Employee Compensation

You have been hired as the Personnel Director for a medium-sized firm (500 employees) and are expected to implement a system to track employee compensation. You want to be able to calculate the age of every employee as well as the length of service. You want to know each employee's most recent performance evaluation. You want to be able to calculate the amount of the most recent salary increase, both in dollars and as a percentage of the previous salary. You also want to know how long the employee had to wait for that increase—that is, how much time elapsed between the present and previous salary. Design a table capable of providing this information. Create a supporting form.

The Stockbroker

A good friend has come to you for help. He is a new stockbroker whose firm provides computer support for existing clients, but does nothing in the way of data management for prospective clients. Your friend wants to use a PC to track the clients he is pursuing. He wants to know when he last contacted a person, how the contact was made (by phone or through the mail), and how interested the person was. He also wants to store the investment goals of each prospect, such as growth or income, and whether a person is interested in stocks, bonds, and/or a retirement account. And finally, he wants to record the amount of money the person has to invest. Design a table suitable for the information requirements. Create a supporting form, then use that form to enter data for two clients.

Form Design

Collect several examples of such real forms as a magazine subscription, auto registration, or employment application. Choose the form you like best and implement the design in Access. Start by creating the underlying table (with some degree of validation), then use the Form Wizard to create the form. How closely does the form you create resemble the paper form with which you began? To what extent does the data validation ensure the accuracy of the data?

File Compression

Access databases get very large very quickly. Accordingly, you might want to consider acquisition of a file compression program to facilitate copying large documents to a floppy disk in order to transport your documents to and from school, home, or work. You can download an evaluation copy of the popular WinZip program at www.winzip.com. Investigate the subject of file compression, then submit a summary of your findings to your instructor.

CHAPTER

3

Information from the Database: Reports and Queries

OBJECTIVES

After reading this chapter you will:

1. Describe the reports available through the Report Wizard.
2. Describe the similarities between forms and reports with respect to the underlying controls.
3. List the sections in a report.
4. Use conditional formatting in a report.
5. Differentiate between a query and a table; define a dynaset.
6. Use the design grid to create and modify a select query.
7. Explain the use of multiple criteria rows in a query.
8. Use concatenation to combine fields in a query or report.
9. Use an immediate If statement to create a calculated control.
10. Define an action query.
11. Create a crosstab query.

hands-on exercises

1. THE REPORT WIZARD
Input: Our Students
Output: Our Students (modified)

2. CREATING A SELECT QUERY
Input: Our Students (after Hands-on Exercise 1)
Output: Our Students (modified)

3. GROUPING RECORDS
Input: Our Students (after Hands-on Exercise 2)
Output: Our Students (modified)

4. CROSSTAB AND ACTION QUERIES
Input: Our Students (after Hands-on Exercise 3)
Output: Our Students (modified)

CASE STUDY

CITIZEN OF THE WORLD

Jodi McPherson, a student intern at the World Health Organization, was asked to conduct a study on overcrowding in countries around the world. The premise of the study is that we share one planet, that we are all "citizens of the world," and that we must work together to develop a global environmental policy. The study is to focus on population density, which is defined as the number of people per square kilometer. Jodi's supervisor has asked for a report that shows the twenty countries with the highest population density in descending order of that statistic. He has also requested two additional reports that show the twenty largest countries by area and the twenty largest countries by population. All three reports are to have a similar design with attractive formatting and a uniform logo.

Thus far, Jodi's internship has been terrific. She has a nicely equipped cubicle with a beautiful view and a state-of-the art computer with the latest version of Microsoft Access. She spent the first two weeks of her internship gathering data about each country, including its capital, area, and population. Once this was accomplished, Jodi entered the data into a table within an Access database and now needs to create various reports to analyze the data she has collected. ■

Your assignment is to put yourself in Jodi's place and develop the required reports based on the Access database, *Chapter 3 Case Study—Citizen of the World*. The database also contains an "About Citizen of the World" form that cites the source of the data. You are to read the chapter and pay special attention to Hands-on Exercises 2 and 3 that describe how to create a select query and how to create a report based on that query. Your next task will be to create a query that contains population density as a calculated field and that sorts the records in descending order of population density. You can then set the Top Values property to display the twenty countries with the highest population density. (In actuality, you will need three queries, one for each report.) Print a copy of each report for your instructor.

DATA VERSUS INFORMATION

Chapters 1 and 2 described how to enter and maintain data through the use of tables and forms. This chapter shows how to convert the data into information through queries and reports. Queries enable you to ask questions about the database. Reports provide presentation quality output and display detail as well as summary information about the records in a database.

As you read the chapter, you will see that the objects in an Access database (tables, forms, reports, and queries) have many similar characteristics. We use these similarities to build on what you have learned in previous chapters. You already know, for example, that the controls in a form inherit their properties from the corresponding fields in a table. The same concept applies to the controls in a report. You also know that there are three types of controls—bound controls, unbound controls, and calculated controls. And since you know how to move and size controls within a form, you also know how to move and size the controls in a report. As you read the chapter, look for these similarities to apply your existing knowledge to new material.

Reports

A ***report*** is a printed document that displays information from a database. Figure 3.1 shows several sample reports, each of which will be created in this chapter. The reports were created with the ***Report Wizard*** and are based on the Students table that was presented in Chapter 2. (The table has been expanded to 24 records.) As you view each report, ask yourself how the data in the table was rearranged to produce the information in the report.

The ***columnar (vertical) report*** in Figure 3.1a is the simplest type of report. It lists every field for every record in a single column (one record per page) and typically runs for many pages. The records in this report are displayed in the same sequence (by Social Security number) as the records in the table on which the report is based.

The ***tabular report*** in Figure 3.1b displays fields in a row rather than in a column. Each record in the underlying table is printed in its own row. Unlike the previous report, only selected fields are displayed, so the tabular report is more concise than the columnar report of Figure 3.1a. Note, too, that the records in the report are listed in alphabetical order rather than by Social Security number.

The report in Figure 3.1c is also a tabular report, but it is very different from the report in Figure 3.1b. The report in Figure 3.1c lists only a selected set of students (those students with a GPA of 3.50 or higher), as opposed to the earlier reports, which listed every student. The students are listed in descending order according to their GPA.

The report in Figure 3.1d displays the students in groups, according to their major, then computes the average GPA for each group. The report also contains summary information (not visible in Figure 3.1d) for the report as a whole, which computes the average GPA for all students. The individual fields within a student record are considered data. A list of students on the Dean's list, however, is information that has been produced from the data about the individual students. In similar fashion, the average GPA for each major is also information rather than data.

DATA VERSUS INFORMATION

Data and information are not synonymous although the terms are often interchanged. Data is the raw material and consists of the table (or tables) that comprise a database. Information is the finished product. Data is converted to information by selecting records, performing calculations on those records, and/or changing the sequence in which the records are displayed. Decisions in an organization are based on information rather than raw data.

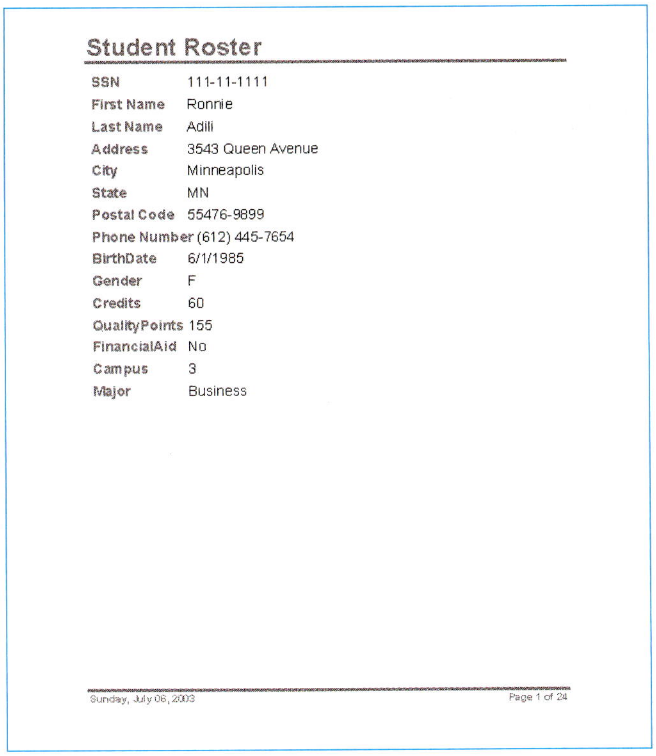

Student Roster

SSN	111-11-1111
First Name	Ronnie
Last Name	Adili
Address	3543 Queen Avenue
City	Minneapolis
State	MN
Postal Code	55476-9899
Phone Number	(612) 445-7654
BirthDate	6/1/1985
Gender	F
Credits	60
QualityPoints	155
FinancialAid	No
Campus	3
Major	Business

Sunday, July 06, 2003 Page 1 of 24

(a) Columnar Report

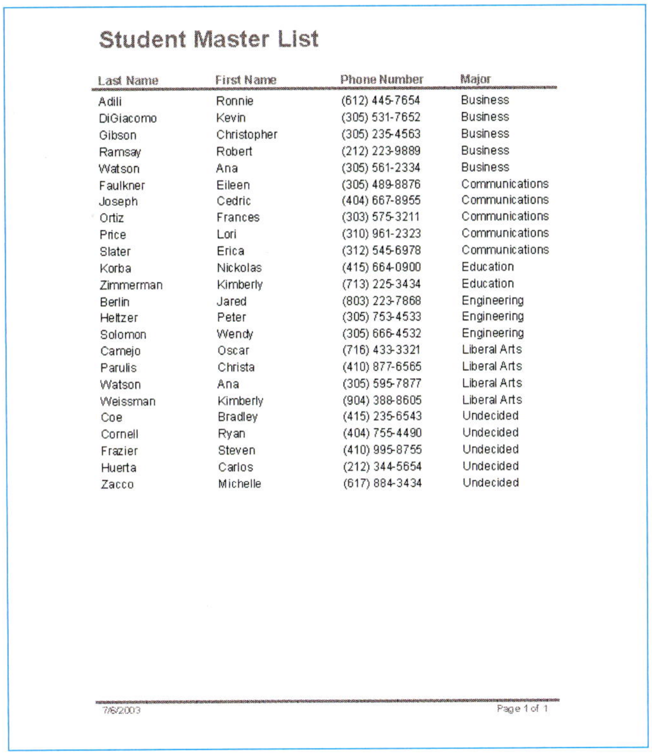

Student Master List

Last Name	First Name	Phone Number	Major
Adili	Ronnie	(612) 445-7654	Business
DiGiacomo	Kevin	(305) 531-7652	Business
Gibson	Christopher	(305) 235-4563	Business
Ramsay	Robert	(212) 223-9889	Business
Watson	Ana	(305) 561-2334	Business
Faulkner	Eileen	(305) 489-8876	Communications
Joseph	Cedric	(404) 667-8955	Communications
Ortiz	Frances	(303) 575-3211	Communications
Price	Lori	(310) 961-2323	Communications
Slater	Erica	(312) 545-6978	Communications
Korba	Nickolas	(415) 664-0900	Education
Zimmerman	Kimberly	(713) 225-3434	Education
Berlin	Jared	(803) 223-7868	Engineering
Heltzer	Peter	(305) 753-4533	Engineering
Solomon	Wendy	(305) 666-4532	Engineering
Camejo	Oscar	(716) 433-3321	Liberal Arts
Parulis	Christa	(410) 877-6565	Liberal Arts
Watson	Ana	(305) 595-7877	Liberal Arts
Weissman	Kimberly	(904) 388-8605	Liberal Arts
Coe	Bradley	(415) 235-6543	Undecided
Cornell	Ryan	(404) 755-4490	Undecided
Frazier	Steven	(410) 995-8755	Undecided
Huerta	Carlos	(212) 344-5654	Undecided
Zacco	Michelle	(617) 884-3434	Undecided

7/6/2003 Page 1 of 1

(b) Tabular Report

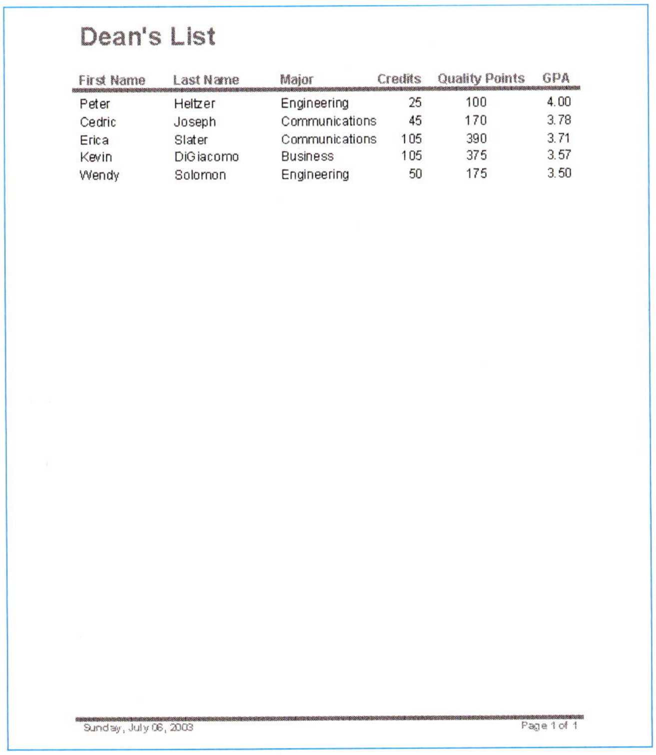

Dean's List

First Name	Last Name	Major	Credits	Quality Points	GPA
Peter	Heltzer	Engineering	25	100	4.00
Cedric	Joseph	Communications	45	170	3.78
Erica	Slater	Communications	105	390	3.71
Kevin	DiGiacomo	Business	105	375	3.57
Wendy	Solomon	Engineering	50	175	3.50

Sunday, July 06, 2003 Page 1 of 1

(c) Dean's List

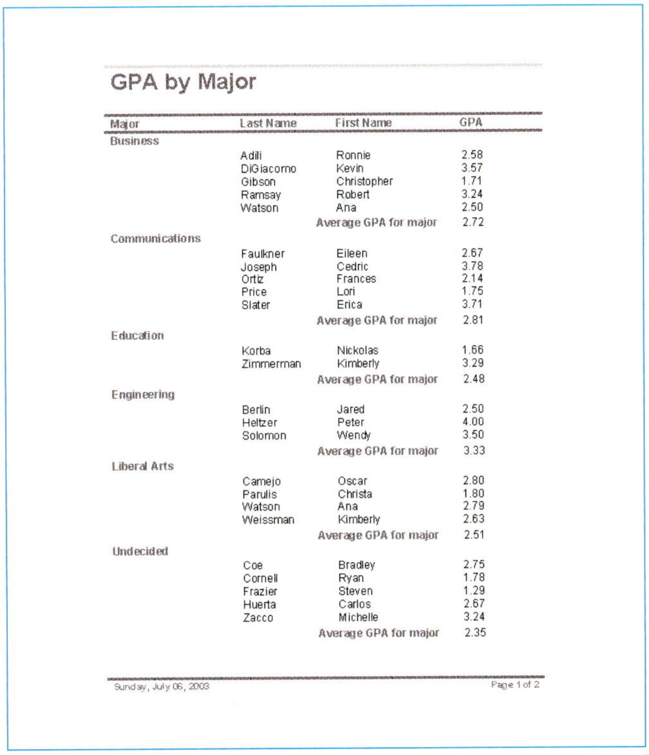

GPA by Major

Major	Last Name	First Name	GPA
Business			
	Adili	Ronnie	2.58
	DiGiacomo	Kevin	3.57
	Gibson	Christopher	1.71
	Ramsay	Robert	3.24
	Watson	Ana	2.50
		Average GPA for major	2.72
Communications			
	Faulkner	Eileen	2.67
	Joseph	Cedric	3.78
	Ortiz	Frances	2.14
	Price	Lori	1.75
	Slater	Erica	3.71
		Average GPA for major	2.81
Education			
	Korba	Nickolas	1.66
	Zimmerman	Kimberly	3.29
		Average GPA for major	2.48
Engineering			
	Berlin	Jared	2.50
	Heltzer	Peter	4.00
	Solomon	Wendy	3.50
		Average GPA for major	3.33
Liberal Arts			
	Camejo	Oscar	2.80
	Parulis	Christa	1.80
	Watson	Ana	2.79
	Weissman	Kimberly	2.63
		Average GPA for major	2.51
Undecided			
	Coe	Bradley	2.75
	Cornell	Ryan	1.78
	Frazier	Steven	1.29
	Huerta	Carlos	2.67
	Zacco	Michelle	3.24
		Average GPA for major	2.35

Sunday, July 06, 2003 Page 1 of 2

(d) Summary Report

FIGURE 3.1 Report Types

Anatomy of a Report

All reports are based on an underlying table or query within the database. (Queries are discussed later in the chapter.) A report, however, displays the data or information in a more attractive fashion because it contains various headings and/or other decorative items that are not present in either a table or a query.

The easiest way to learn about reports is to compare a printed report with its underlying design. Consider, for example, Figure 3.2a, which displays the tabular report, and Figure 3.2b, which shows the underlying design. The latter shows how a report is divided into sections, which appear at designated places when the report is printed. There are seven types of sections, but a report need not contain all seven.

The ***Report Header*** appears once, at the beginning of a report. It typically contains information describing the report, such as its title and the date the report was printed. (The report header appears above the page header on the first page of the report.) The ***Report Footer*** appears once at the end of the report, above the page footer on the last page of the report, and displays summary information for the report as a whole.

The ***Page Header*** appears at the top of every page in a report and can be used to display page numbers, column headings, and other descriptive information. The ***Page Footer*** appears at the bottom of every page and may contain page numbers (when they are not in the page header) or other descriptive information.

A ***Group Header*** appears at the beginning of a group of records to identify the group. A ***Group Footer*** appears after the last record in a group and contains summary information about the group. Group headers and footers are used only when the records in a report are sorted (grouped) according to a common value in a specific field. These sections do not appear in the report of Figure 3.2, but were shown earlier in the report of Figure 3.1d.

The ***Detail section*** appears in the main body of a report and is printed once for every record in the underlying table (or query). It displays one or more fields for each record in columnar or tabular fashion, according to the design of the report.

The Report Wizard

The Report Wizard is the easiest way to create a report, just as the Form Wizard is the easiest way to create a form. The Report Wizard asks you questions about the report you want, then builds the report for you. You can accept the report as is, or you can customize it to better suit your needs.

Figure 3.3a displays the New Report dialog box, from which you can select the Report Wizard. The Report Wizard, in turn, requires you to specify the table or query on which the report will be based. The report in this example will be based on an expanded version of the Students table that was created in Chapter 2.

After you specify the underlying table, you select one or more fields from that table, as shown in Figure 3.3b. The Report Wizard then asks you to select a layout (e.g., Tabular in Figure 3.3c.) and a style (e.g., Soft Gray in Figure 3.3d). This is all the information the Report Wizard requires, and it proceeds to create the report for you. The controls on the report correspond to the fields you selected and are displayed in accordance with the specified layout.

Apply What You Know

The Report Wizard provides an excellent starting point, but typically does not create the report exactly as you would like it to be. Accordingly, you can modify a report created by the Report Wizard, just as you can modify a form created by the Form Wizard. The techniques are the same, and you should look for similarities between forms and reports so that you can apply what you already know. Knowledge of one is helpful in understanding the other.

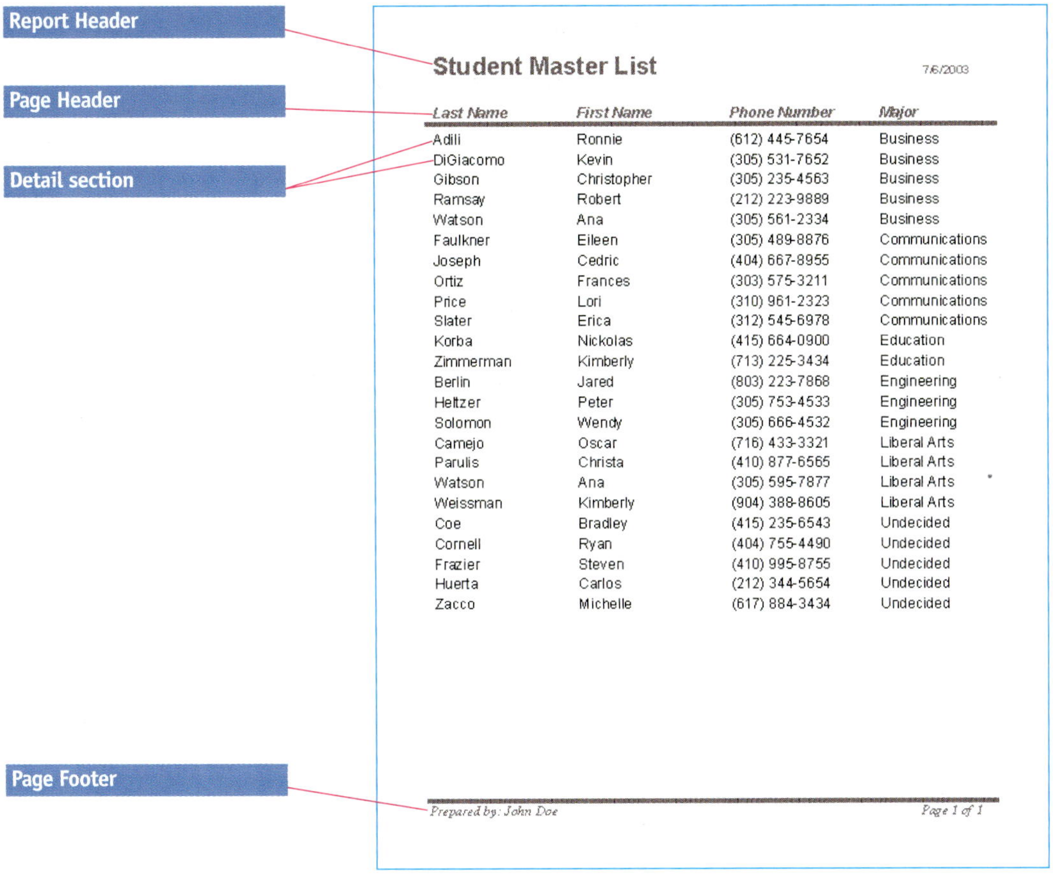

Last Name	First Name	Phone Number	Major
Adili	Ronnie	(612) 445-7654	Business
DiGiacomo	Kevin	(305) 531-7652	Business
Gibson	Christopher	(305) 235-4563	Business
Ramsay	Robert	(212) 223-9889	Business
Watson	Ana	(305) 561-2334	Business
Faulkner	Eileen	(305) 489-8876	Communications
Joseph	Cedric	(404) 667-8955	Communications
Ortiz	Frances	(303) 575-3211	Communications
Price	Lori	(310) 961-2323	Communications
Slater	Erica	(312) 545-6978	Communications
Korba	Nickolas	(415) 664-0900	Education
Zimmerman	Kimberly	(713) 225-3434	Education
Berlin	Jared	(803) 223-7868	Engineering
Heltzer	Peter	(305) 753-4533	Engineering
Solomon	Wendy	(305) 666-4532	Engineering
Camejo	Oscar	(716) 433-3321	Liberal Arts
Parulis	Christa	(410) 877-6565	Liberal Arts
Watson	Ana	(305) 595-7877	Liberal Arts
Weissman	Kimberly	(904) 388-8605	Liberal Arts
Coe	Bradley	(415) 235-6543	Undecided
Cornell	Ryan	(404) 755-4490	Undecided
Frazier	Steven	(410) 995-8755	Undecided
Huerta	Carlos	(212) 344-5654	Undecided
Zacco	Michelle	(617) 884-3434	Undecided

(a) The Printed Report

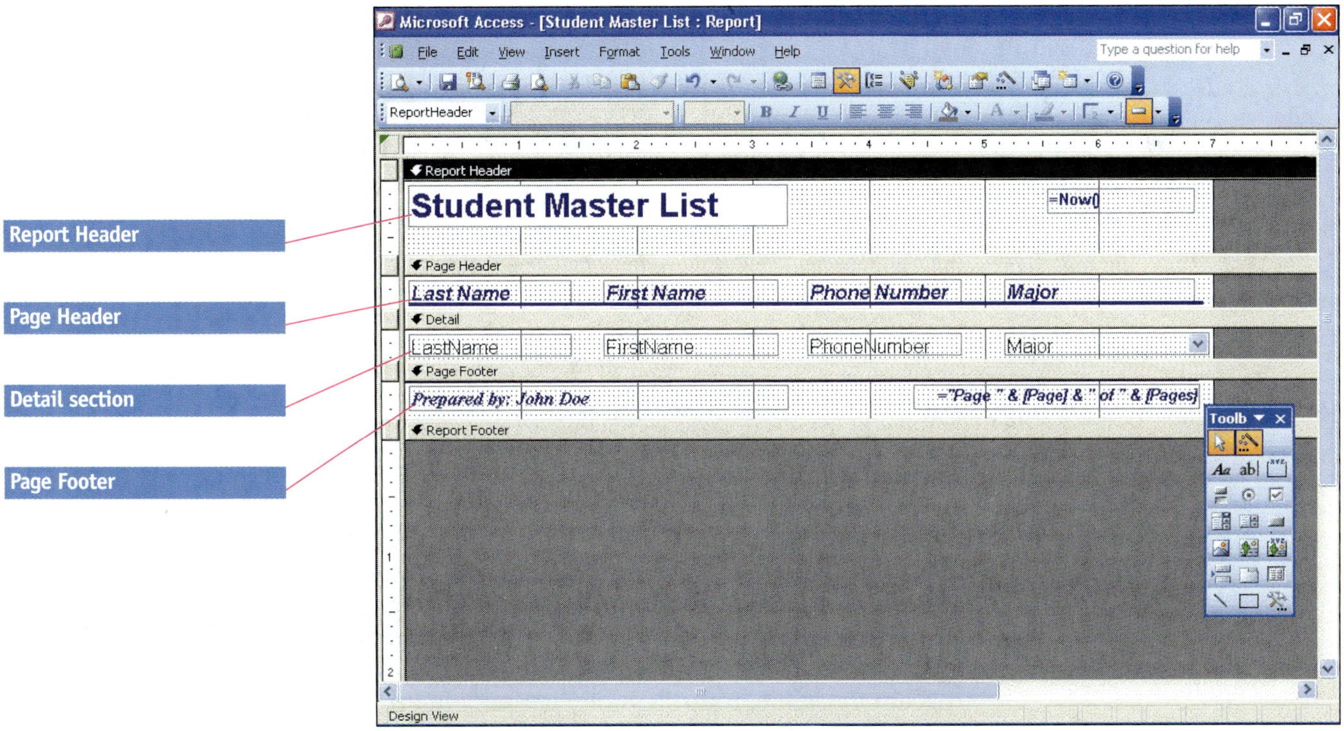

(b) Design View

FIGURE 3.2 Anatomy of a Report

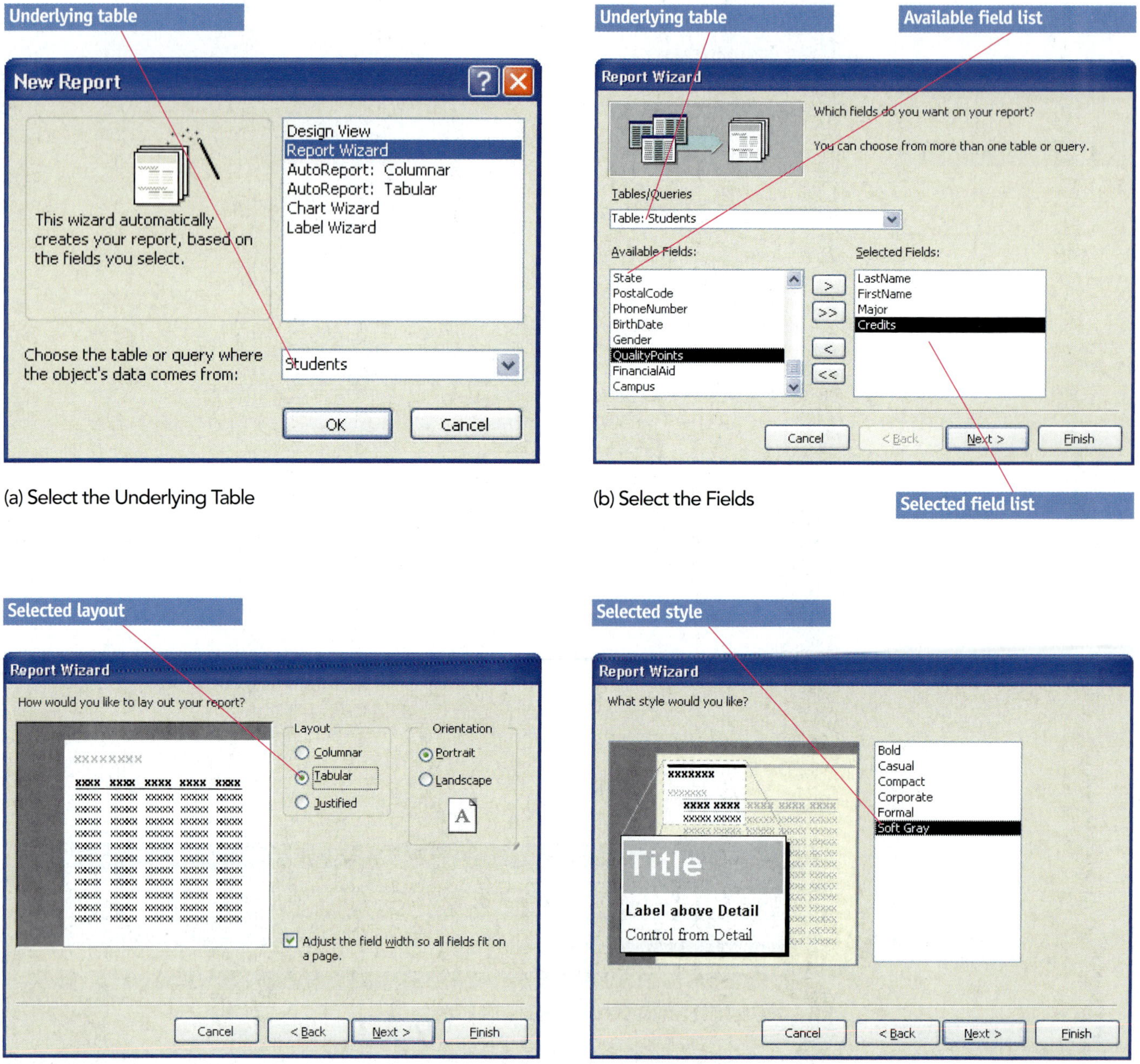

(a) Select the Underlying Table

(b) Select the Fields

(c) Choose the Layout

(d) Choose the Style

FIGURE 3.3 The Report Wizard

Bound, Unbound, and Calculated Controls

Controls appear in a report just as they do in a form, and the same definitions apply. A ***bound control*** has as its data source a field in the underlying table. An ***unbound control*** has no data source and is used to display titles, labels, lines, rectangles, and graphics. A ***calculated control*** has as its data source an expression rather than a field. A student's Grade Point Average is an example of a calculated control since it is computed by dividing the number of quality points by the number of credits. The means for selecting, sizing, moving, aligning, and deleting controls are the same, regardless of whether you are working on a form or a report. And, as you may have guessed, it is time for our next hands-on exercise.

hands-on exercise

1 The Report Wizard

Objective To use the Report Wizard to create a new report; to modify an existing report by adding, deleting, and/or modifying its controls. Use Figure 3.4 as a guide in the exercise.

Step 1: Open the Our Students Database

- Start Access. Pull down the **File menu** and click the **Open command** or click the link to **More...** if the task pane is open.
- Open the **Our Students database** in the Exploring Access folder. Click **Open** in response to the security warning.
- The Our Students database has the identical design as the database you created in Chapter 2. We have, however, expanded the Students table so that it contains 24 records to enable you to create more meaningful reports and queries from the database.
- Click the **Reports button** in the Database window, then click the **New command button** to display the New Report dialog box in Figure 3.4a. Select the **Report Wizard** as the means of creating the report.
- Click the **drop-down arrow** to display the tables and queries in the database in order to select the one on which the report will be based. (There are currently two tables and no queries.)
- Click **Students**, then click **OK** to start the Report Wizard, which prompts you for the information it needs to create a report.

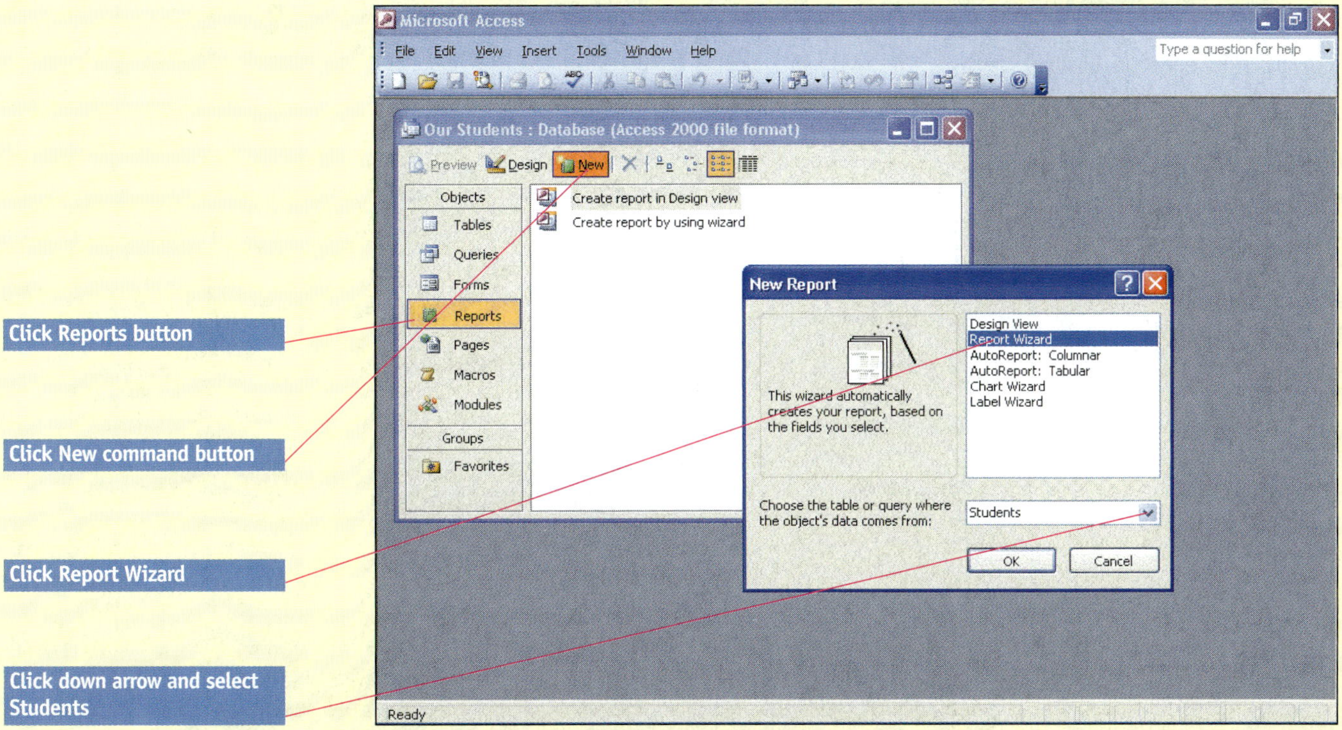

(a) Open the Our Students Database (step 1)

FIGURE 3.4 Hands-on Exercise 1

Step 2: The Report Wizard

- You should see the dialog box in Figure 3.4b, which displays all of the fields in the Students table. Double click the **LastName field** in the Available Fields list box, as shown in Figure 3.4b.
- Enter the remaining fields (**FirstName**, **PhoneNumber**, and **Major**) one at a time by double clicking the field name. Click **Next**.
- The Report Wizard displays several additional screens asking about the report you want to create. The first screen asks whether you want to choose any grouping levels. Click **Next** without specifying a grouping level.
- The next screen asks whether you want to sort the records. Click the **drop-down arrow** to display the available fields, then select **LastName**. Click **Next**.
- The **Tabular layout** is selected, as is **Portrait orientation**. Be sure the box is checked to **Adjust field width so all fields fit on a page**. Click **Next**.
- Choose **Corporate** as the style. Click **Next**.
- Enter **Student Master List** as the title for your report. The option button to **Preview the Report** is already selected.
- Click the **Finish button** to exit the Report Wizard and view the report.

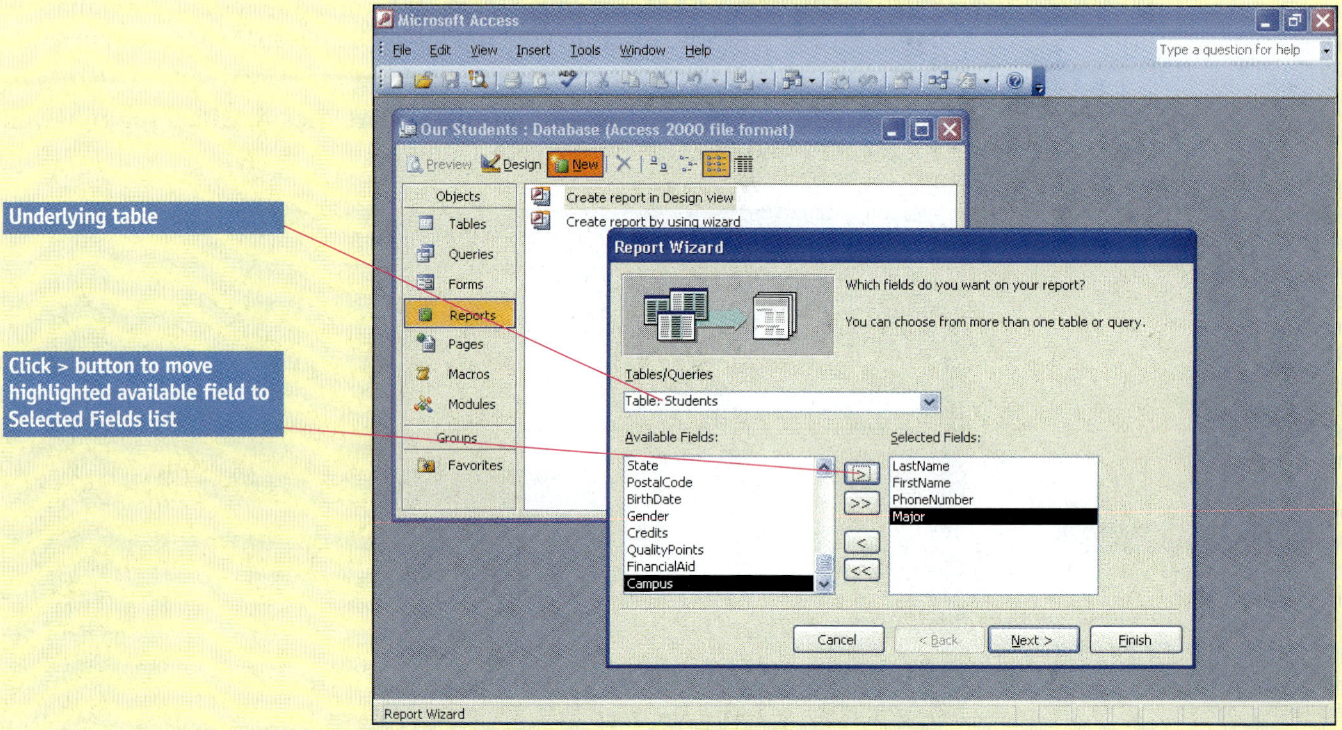

(b) The Report Wizard (step 2)

FIGURE 3.4 Hands-on Exercise 1 (*continued*)

WHAT THE REPORT WIZARD DOESN'T TELL YOU

The fastest way to select a field is by double clicking; that is, double click a field in the Available Fields list box, and it is automatically moved to the Selected Fields list for inclusion in the report. The process also works in reverse; that is, you can double click a field in the Selected Fields list to remove it from the report.

Step 3: Preview the Report

- Click the **Maximize button** so the report takes the entire window as shown in Figure 3.4c.
  - ❑ There is a Report Header (the title of the report) at the beginning of the report, a Page Header (column headings) at the top of the page, and a Page Footer at the bottom of the page.
  - ❑ There is also a detail line for every record in the underlying table.
- Click the **drop-down arrow** on the Zoom box so that you can view the report at different magnifications. We chose 75%.
- Click the **scroll arrows** on the vertical scroll bar to view the names of additional students. Click and drag the horizontal scroll bar to position the report within the window.
- Click the **Close button** to close the Print Preview window and change to the Report Design view. The next step describes how to modify the report so that the controls are spaced more attractively.

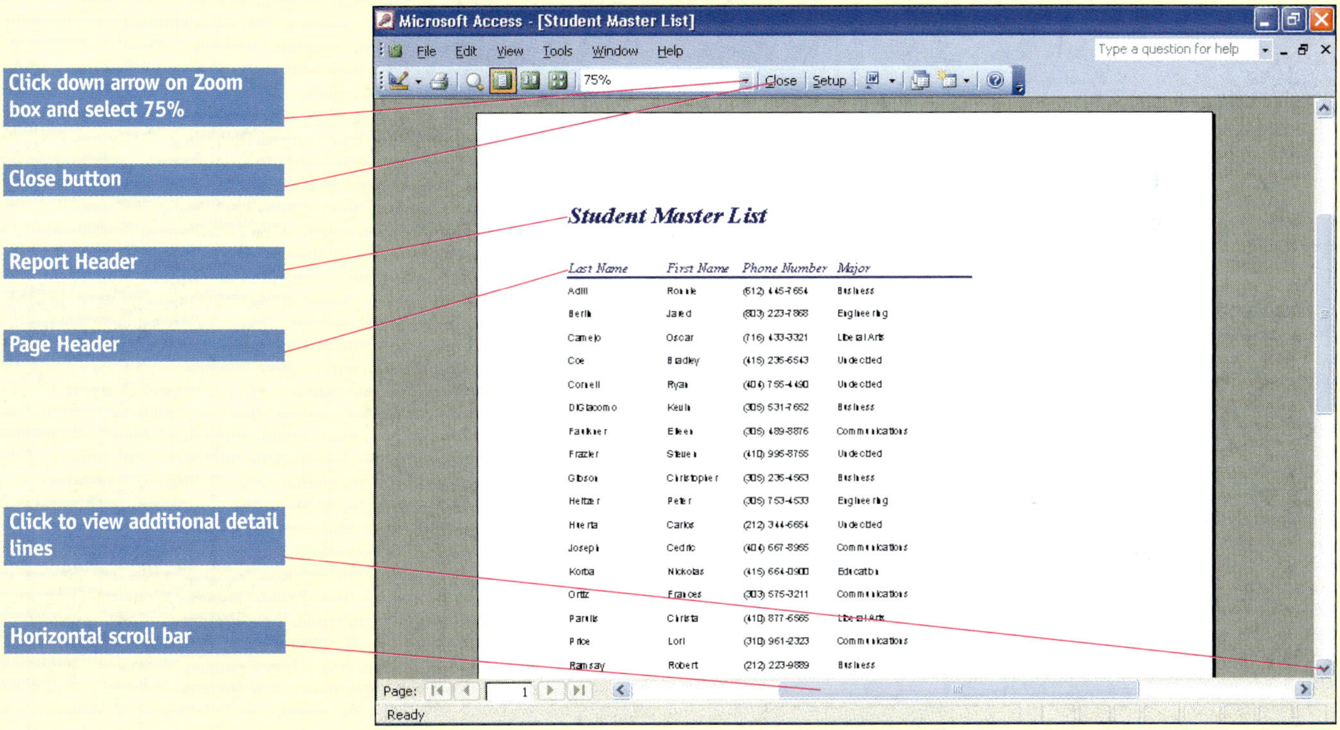

(c) Preview the Report (step 3)

FIGURE 3.4 Hands-on Exercise 1 (*continued*)

THE PRINT PREVIEW WINDOW

The Print Preview window enables you to preview a report in various ways. Click the One Page, Two Pages, or Multiple Pages buttons for different views of a report. Use the Zoom button to toggle between the full page and zoom (magnified) views, or use the Zoom box to choose a specific magnification. The Navigation buttons at the bottom of the Print Preview window enable you to preview a specific page, while the vertical scroll bar at the right side of the window lets you scroll within a page.

Step 4: Modify an Existing Control

- Click the **Major control** in the Detail section, then press the **Shift key** as you click its label in the Page Header. Point to the border of either control, then drag the controls to the right. Move the **PhoneNumber** and **FirstName** controls in similar fashion so that the fields are spaced attractively across the width of the report.
- Click the **blue line** in the Page Header to select the line. Press the **Shift key** (to retain a horizontal line) as you drag the sizing handle to the right side of the page.
- Click and drag the border of the control containing the **Now function** from the Report Footer to the Report Header as shown in Figure 3.4d.
- Size the control as necessary, then check that the control is still selected and click the **Align Right button** on the Formatting toolbar.
- Point to the control, then click the **right mouse button** to display a shortcut menu, and click **Properties** to display the Properties sheet.
- Click the **Format tab** in the Properties sheet, click the **Format property**, then click the **drop-down arrow** to display the available formats. Click **Short Date**, then close the Properties sheet.
- Pull down the **File menu** and click **Save** (or click the **Save button**) to save the modified design

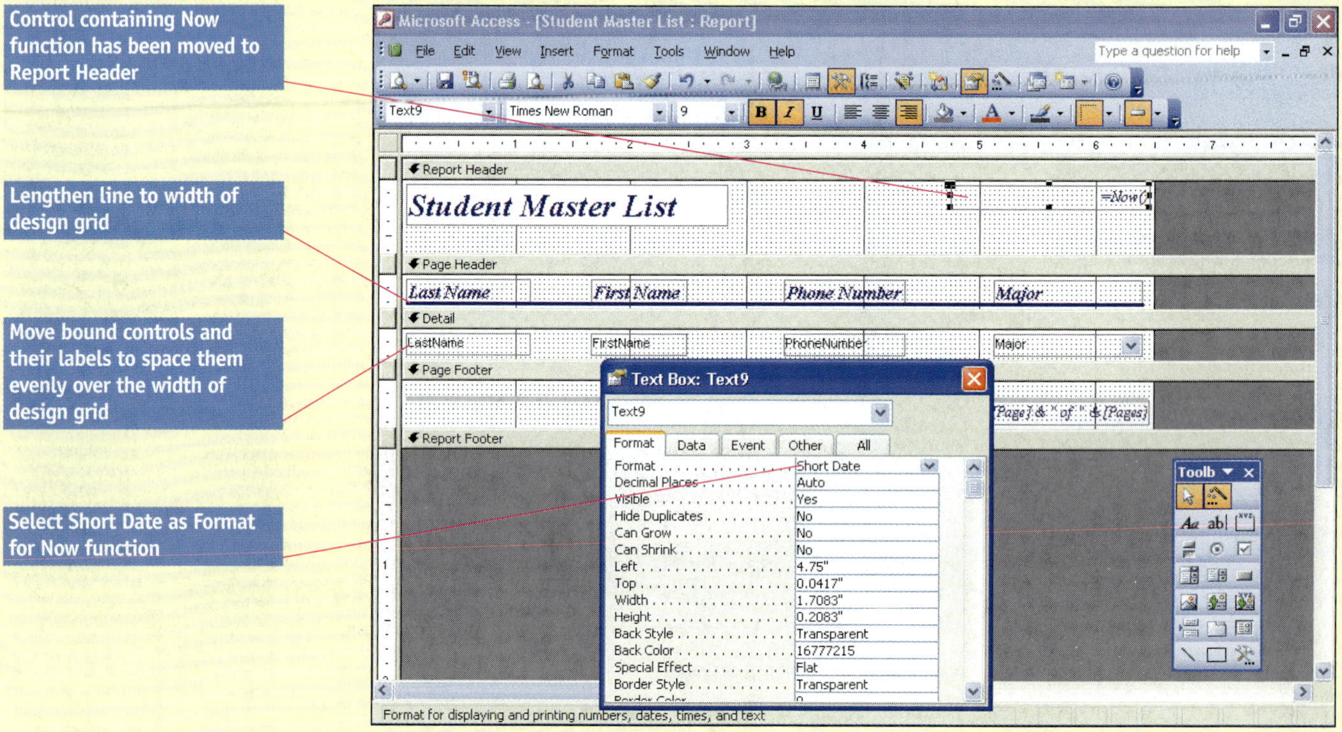

(d) Modify an Existing Control (step 4)

FIGURE 3.4 Hands-on Exercise 1 (*continued*)

THE REPORT WIZARD, FUNCTIONS, AND FIELDS

The Report Wizard automatically inserts the Now function and the Page and Pages fields to enhance the appearance of a report. The Now function returns the current date and time. The Page and Pages fields return the specific page number and the total number of pages, respectively. You can also add these controls explicitly by creating a text box, then replacing the default unbound control by an equal sign, followed by the function or field—for example, =Now() to insert the current date and time.

Step 5: Add an Unbound Control

- Click the **Label tool** on the Toolbox toolbar, then click and drag in the Report Footer where you want the label to go and release the mouse. You should see a flashing insertion point inside the label control. (If you see the word *Unbound* instead of the insertion point, it means you selected the Text Box tool rather than the Label tool; delete the text box and begin again.)
- Type **Prepared by** followed by your name as shown in Figure 3.4e. Press **Enter** to complete the entry and also select the control.
- You will see a green triangle in the upper-left corner of the control and an exclamation point icon to indicate a potential error. Point to the icon, click the **down arrow** to display the list of potential errors, then click **Ignore Error**.
- Point to the control, click the **right mouse button** to display the shortcut menu, then click **Properties** to display the Properties dialog box.
- Click the **down arrow** on the scroll bar, then scroll until you see the Font Size property. Click in the **Font Size box**, click the **drop-down arrow**, then scroll until you can change the font size to **9**. Close the Property sheet.
- Save the report.

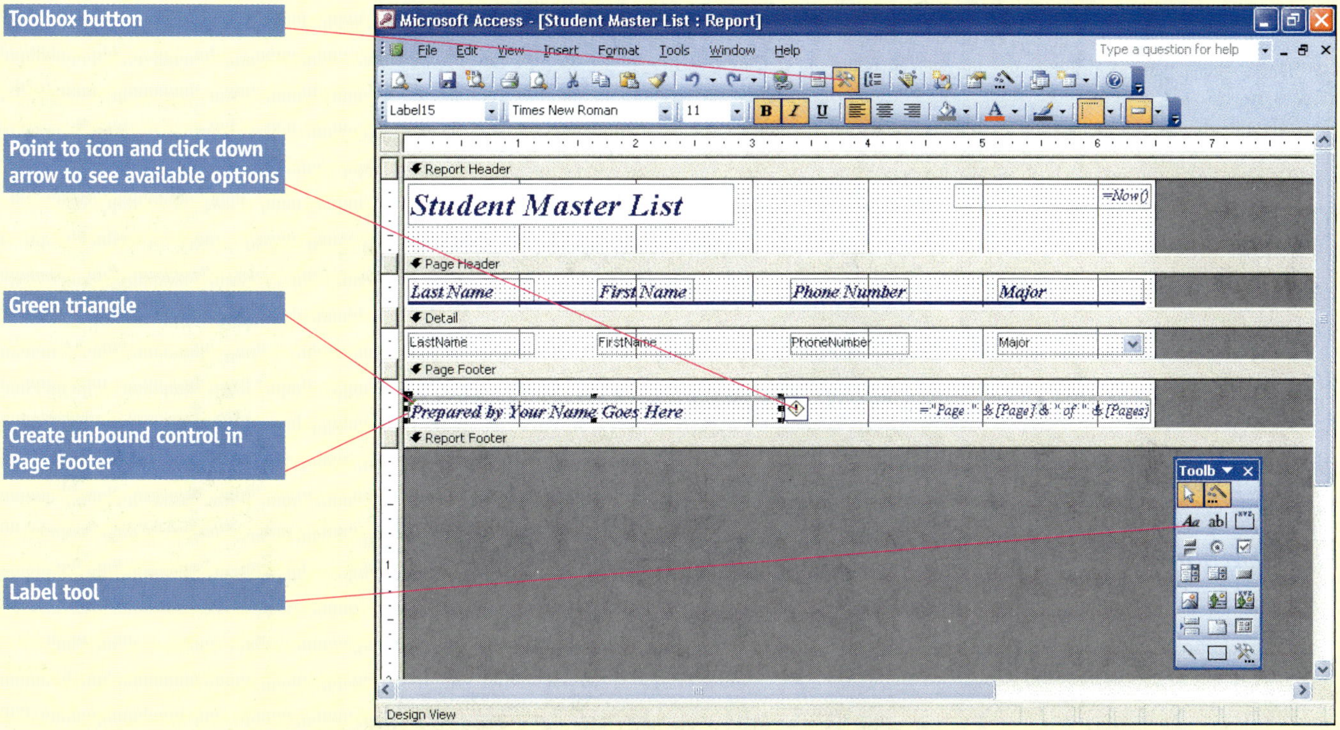

(e) Add an Unbound Control (step 5)

FIGURE 3.4 Hands-on Exercise 1 (*continued*)

MISSING TOOLBARS

The Report Design, Formatting, and Toolbox toolbars appear by default in the Report Design view, but any (or all) of these toolbars may be hidden at the discretion of the user. If any of these toolbars does not appear, point to any visible toolbar, click the right mouse button to display a shortcut menu, then click the name of the toolbar you want to display. You can also click the Toolbox button on the Report Design toolbar to display (hide) the Toolbox toolbar.

Step 6: Change the Sort Order

- Pull down the **View menu**. Click the **Sorting and Grouping command** to display the Sorting and Grouping dialog box in Figure 3.4f. The students are currently sorted by last name.
- Click the **drop-down arrow** in the Field Expression box. Click **Major**. (The ascending sequence is selected automatically.)
- Click on the next line in the Field Expression box, click the **drop-down arrow** to display the available fields, then click **LastName** to sort the students alphabetically within major.
- Close the Sorting and Grouping dialog box. The students will now be listed by major and alphabetically by last name within each major when you view the report in step 7.
- Save the report.

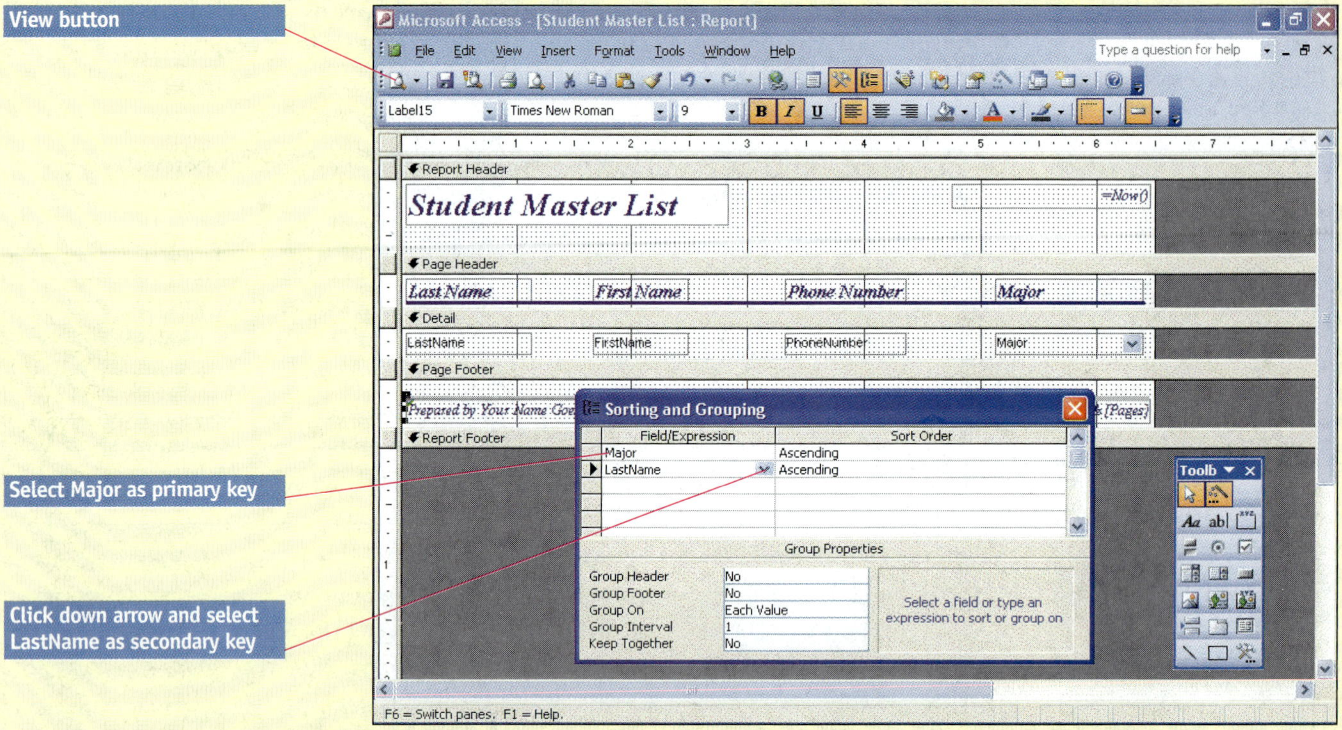

(f) Change the Sort Order (step 6)

FIGURE 3.4 Hands-on Exercise 1 (*continued*)

ADDING A GROUP HEADER OR FOOTER

You can add or remove a Group Header or Footer after a report has been created. Pull down the View menu and click the Sorting and Grouping command to display the associated dialog box. Click the line containing the field for which you want to add or remove the element, then enter Yes or No, respectively, in the Group Properties area and close the dialog box. The newly created header or footer is initially empty, and thus you will have to insert the necessary controls to complete the report.

Step 7: View the Modified Report

- Click the **View button** to preview the finished report. If necessary, click the **Zoom button** on the Print Preview toolbar so that the display on your monitor matches Figure 3.4g. The report has changed so that:
  - ❑ The date appears in the Report Header (as opposed to the Report Footer). The format of the date has changed to a numbered month, and the day of the week has been eliminated.
  - ❑ The controls are spaced attractively across the page.
  - ❑ The students are listed by major and, within each major, alphabetically according to last name.
  - ❑ Your name appears in the Report Footer. Click the **down arrow** on the vertical scroll bar to move to the bottom of the page to see your name.
- Click the **Print button** to print the report and submit it to your instructor. Click the **Close button** to exit the Print Preview window.
- Click the **Close button** in the Report Design window. Click **Yes** if asked whether to save the changes to the Student Master List report.
- Close the database. Exit Access if you do not want to continue with the next exercise at this time.

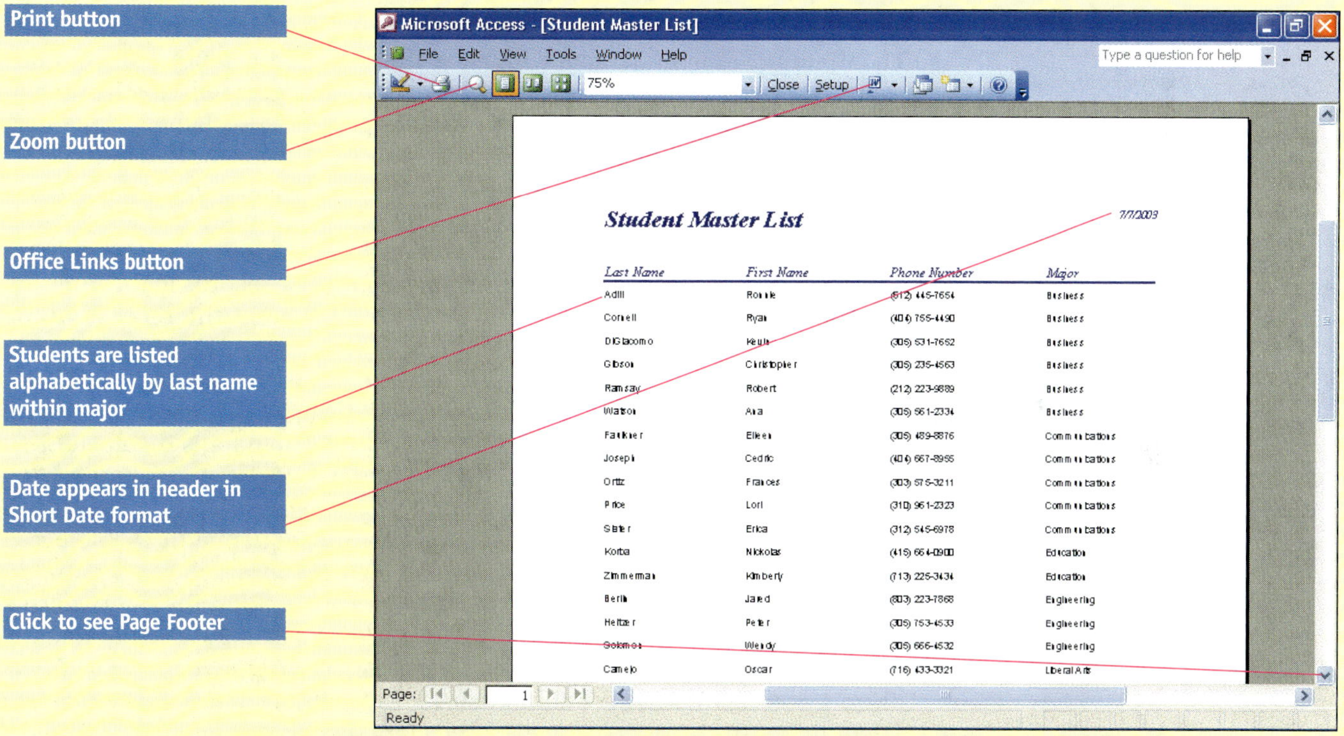

(g) View the Modified Report (step 7)

FIGURE 3.4 Hands-on Exercise 1 (*continued*)

LINK TO WORD OR EXCEL

Click the down arrow on the Office Links button to display links to Word and Excel. Click either link to start the associated application, where you can take advantage of the extended editing or analysis (including chart) capabilities in Word and Excel, respectively. You can save the report as either a Word document or Excel workbook, but any subsequent changes to the Access report are static and will not be reflected in the other applications.

INTRODUCTION TO QUERIES

The report you just created displayed every student in the underlying table. What if, however, we wanted to see just the students who are majoring in Business? Or the students who are receiving financial aid? Or the students who are majoring in Business *and* receiving financial aid? The ability to ask questions such as these, and to see the answers to those questions, is provided through a query. Queries represent the real power of a database.

A ***query*** lets you see the data you want in the sequence that you want it. It lets you select specific records from a table (or from several tables) and show some or all of the fields for the selected records. It also lets you perform calculations to display data that is not explicitly stored in the underlying table(s), such as a student's GPA.

The query is created by the ***Simple Query Wizard*** or directly in Design view. The results of the query are displayed in a ***dynaset***, which contains the records that satisfy the criteria specified in the query.

A dynaset looks and acts like a table, but it isn't a table; it is a *dyna*mic sub*set* of a table that selects and sorts records as specified in the query. A dynaset is similar to a table in appearance and, like a table, it enables you to enter a new record or modify or delete an existing record. Any changes made in the dynaset are automatically reflected in the underlying table.

Figure 3.5a displays the Students table we have been using throughout the chapter. (We omit some of the fields for ease of illustration.) Figure 3.5b contains the design grid used to select students whose major is "Undecided" and further, to list those students in alphabetical order. (The design grid is explained in the next section.) Figure 3.5c displays the answer to the query in the form of a dynaset.

The table in Figure 3.5a contains 24 records. The dynaset in Figure 3.5c has only five records, corresponding to the students who are undecided about their major. The table in Figure 3.5a has 15 fields for each record (some of the fields are hidden). The dynaset in Figure 3.5c has only four fields. The records in the table are in Social Security Number order (the primary key), whereas the records in the dynaset are in alphabetical order by last name.

The query in Figure 3.5 is an example of a ***select query***, which is the most common type of query. A select query searches the underlying table (Figure 3.5a in the example) to retrieve the data that satisfies the query. The data is displayed in a dynaset (Figure 3.5c), which can be modified to update the data in the underlying table(s). The specifications for selecting records and determining which fields will be displayed for the selected records, as well as the sequence of the selected records, are established within the design grid of Figure 3.5b.

The design grid consists of columns and rows. Each field in the query has its own column and contains multiple rows. The ***Field row*** displays the field name. The ***Sort row*** enables you to sort in ***ascending*** or ***descending sequence***. The ***Show row*** controls whether or not the field will be displayed in the dynaset. The ***Criteria row(s)*** determines the records that will be selected, such as students with an undecided major.

REPORTS, QUERIES, AND TABLES

Every report is based on either a table or a query. The design of the report may be the same with respect to the fields that are included, but the actual reports will be very different with respect to the information they provide. A report based on a table contains every record in the table. A report based on a query contains only the records that satisfy the criteria in the query.

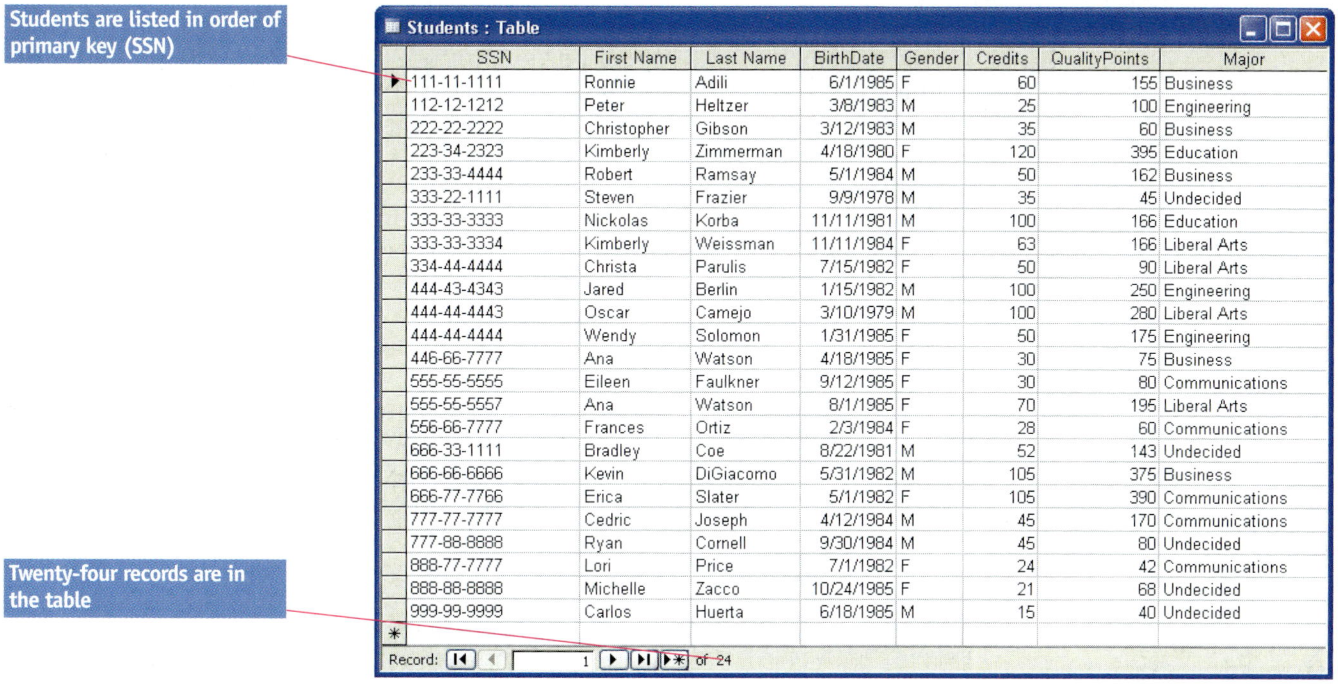

SSN	First Name	Last Name	BirthDate	Gender	Credits	QualityPoints	Major
111-11-1111	Ronnie	Adili	6/1/1985	F	60	155	Business
112-12-1212	Peter	Heltzer	3/8/1983	M	25	100	Engineering
222-22-2222	Christopher	Gibson	3/12/1983	M	35	60	Business
223-34-2323	Kimberly	Zimmerman	4/18/1980	F	120	395	Education
233-33-4444	Robert	Ramsay	5/1/1984	M	50	162	Business
333-22-1111	Steven	Frazier	9/9/1978	M	35	45	Undecided
333-33-3333	Nickolas	Korba	11/11/1981	M	100	166	Education
333-33-3334	Kimberly	Weissman	11/11/1984	F	63	166	Liberal Arts
334-44-4444	Christa	Parulis	7/15/1982	F	50	90	Liberal Arts
444-43-4343	Jared	Berlin	1/15/1982	M	100	250	Engineering
444-44-4443	Oscar	Camejo	3/10/1979	M	100	280	Liberal Arts
444-44-4444	Wendy	Solomon	1/31/1985	F	50	175	Engineering
446-66-7777	Ana	Watson	4/18/1985	F	30	75	Business
555-55-5555	Eileen	Faulkner	9/12/1985	F	30	80	Communications
555-55-5557	Ana	Watson	8/1/1985	F	70	195	Liberal Arts
556-66-7777	Frances	Ortiz	2/3/1984	F	28	60	Communications
666-33-1111	Bradley	Coe	8/22/1981	M	52	143	Undecided
666-66-6666	Kevin	DiGiacomo	5/31/1982	M	105	375	Business
666-77-7766	Erica	Slater	5/1/1982	F	105	390	Communications
777-77-7777	Cedric	Joseph	4/12/1984	M	45	170	Communications
777-88-8888	Ryan	Cornell	9/30/1984	M	45	80	Undecided
888-77-7777	Lori	Price	7/1/1982	F	24	42	Communications
888-88-8888	Michelle	Zacco	10/24/1985	F	21	68	Undecided
999-99-9999	Carlos	Huerta	6/18/1985	M	15	40	Undecided

(a) Students Table

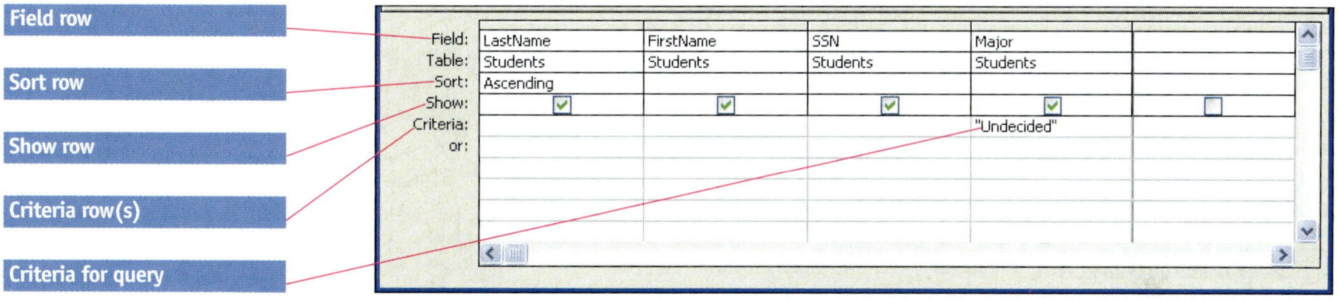

Field:	LastName	FirstName	SSN	Major	
Table:	Students	Students	Students	Students	
Sort:	Ascending				
Show:	✓	✓	✓	✓	☐
Criteria:				"Undecided"	
or:					

(b) Design Grid

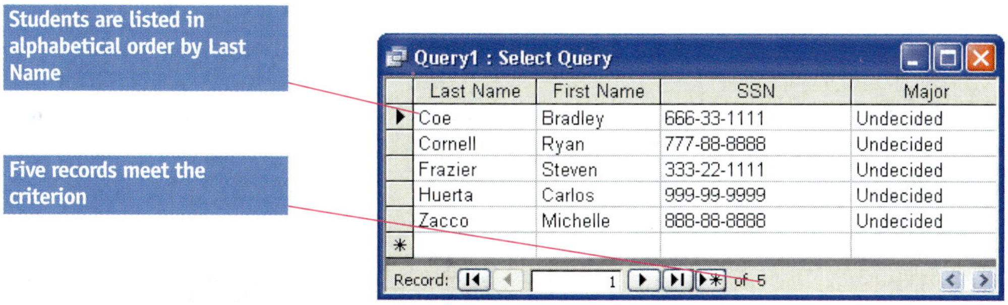

Last Name	First Name	SSN	Major
Coe	Bradley	666-33-1111	Undecided
Cornell	Ryan	777-88-8888	Undecided
Frazier	Steven	333-22-1111	Undecided
Huerta	Carlos	999-99-9999	Undecided
Zacco	Michelle	888-88-8888	Undecided

(c) Dynaset

FIGURE 3.5 Queries

Query Design View

A select query is created by the Simple Query Wizard and/or in Design view as shown in Figure 3.6. The upper portion of the Design View window contains the field list for the table(s) on which the query is based (the Students table in this example). The lower portion of the window displays the ***design grid***, which is where the specifications for the select query are entered. A field is added to the design grid by dragging it from the field list.

The data type of a field determines the way in which the criteria are specified for that field. The criterion for a text field is enclosed in quotation marks. The criteria for number, currency, and counter fields are shown as digits with or without a decimal point. (Commas and dollar signs are not allowed.) Dates are enclosed in pound signs and are entered in the mm/dd/yy format. The criterion for a Yes/No field is entered as Yes (or True) or No (or False).

Access accepts values for text and date fields in the design grid in multiple formats. The value for a text field can be entered with or without quotation marks (Undecided or "Undecided"). A date can be entered with or without pound signs (1/1/97 or #1/1/97#). Access converts your entries to standard format as soon as you move to the next cell in the design grid. Thus, text entries are always shown in quotation marks, and dates are enclosed in pound signs.

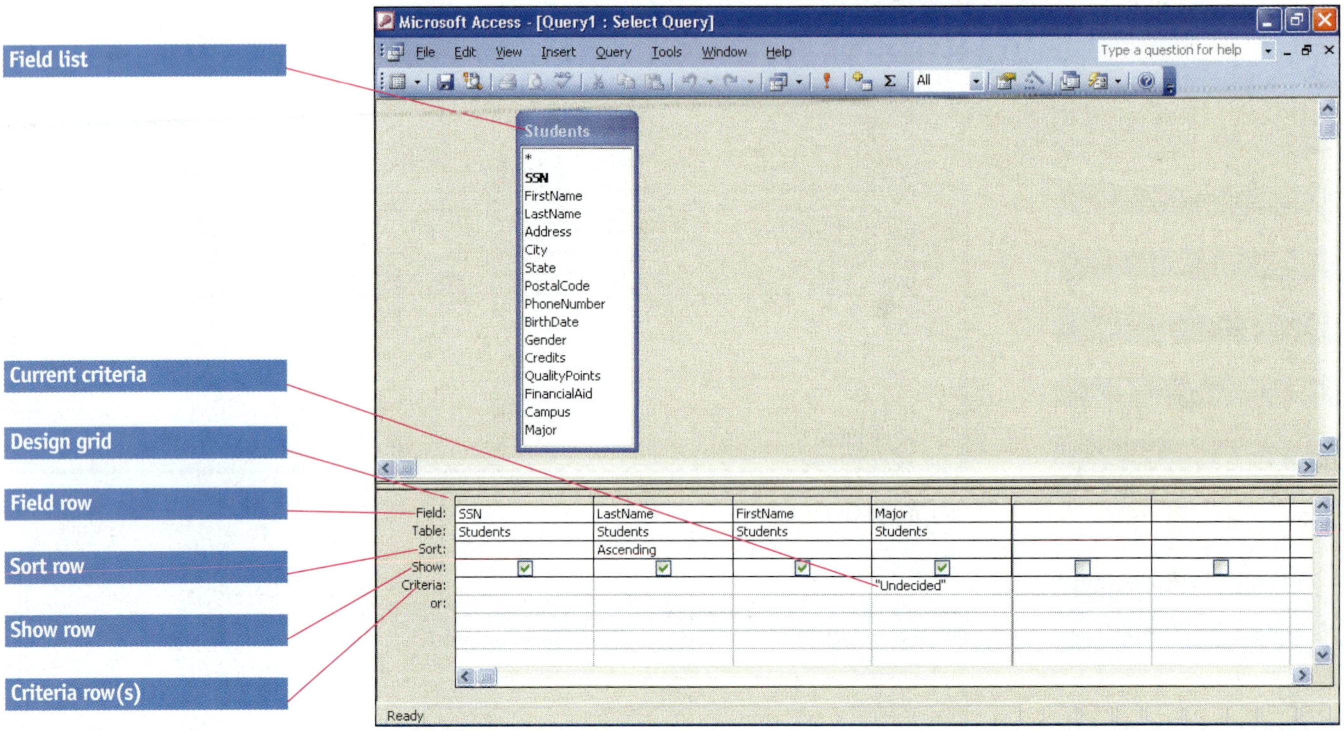

FIGURE 3.6 Query Design View

WILD CARDS

Select queries recognize the question mark and asterisk wild cards that enable you to search for a pattern within a text field. A question mark stands for a single character in the same position as the question mark; thus H?ll will return Hall, Hill, and Hull. An asterisk stands for any number of characters in the same position as the asterisk; for example, S*nd will return Sand, Stand, and Strand.

Selection Criteria

To specify selection criteria in the design grid, enter a value or expression in the Criteria row of the appropriate column. Figure 3.7 contains several examples of simple criteria and provides a basic introduction to select queries.

The criterion in Figure 3.7a selects the students majoring in Business. The criteria for text fields are case insensitive. Thus, *"Business"* is the same as *"business"* or *"BUSINESS"*.

Values entered into multiple columns of the same Criteria row implement an ***AND condition*** in which the selected records must meet *all* of the specified criteria. The criteria in Figure 3.7b select students who are majoring in Business *and* who are from the state of Florida. The criteria in Figure 3.7c select Communications majors who are receiving financial aid.

Values entered into different Criteria rows are connected by an ***OR condition*** in which the selected records may satisfy *any* of the indicated criteria. The criteria in Figure 3.7d select students who are majoring in Business *or* who are from Florida or both.

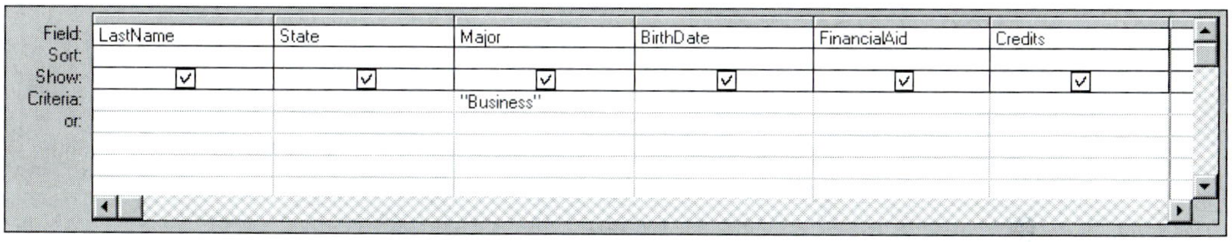

(a) Business Majors

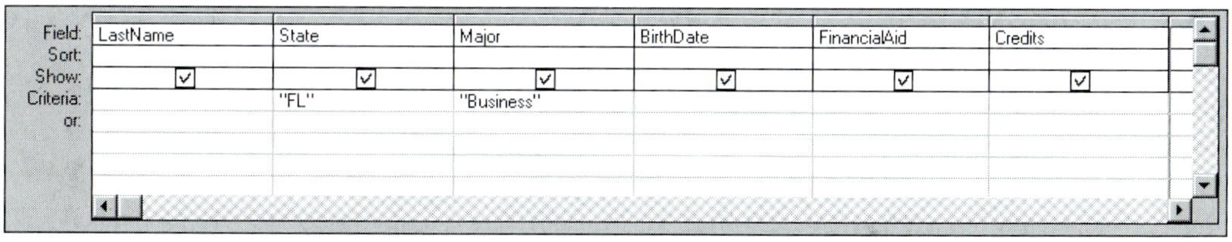

(b) Business Majors from Florida

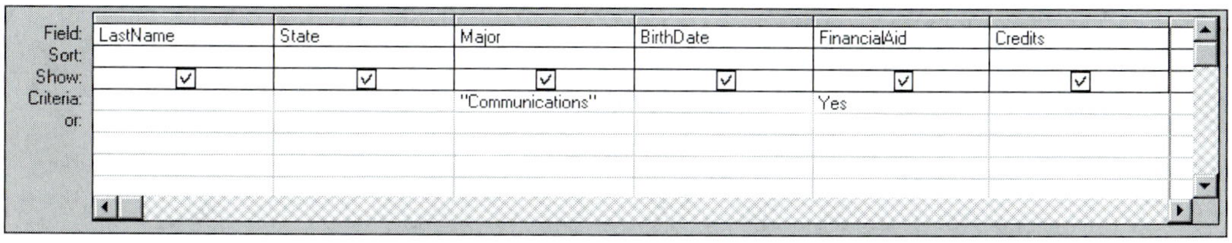

(c) Communications Majors Receiving Financial Aid

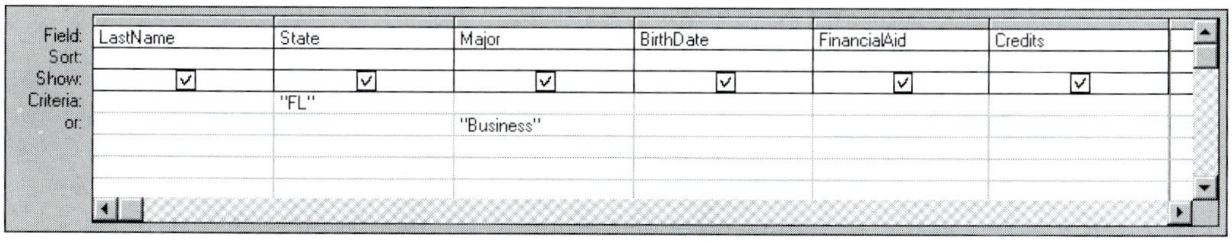

(d) Business Majors or Students from Florida

FIGURE 3.7 Selection Criteria

Relational operators (>, <, >=, <=, =, and <>) are used with date or number fields to return records within a designated range. The criteria in Figure 3.7e select Engineering majors with fewer than 60 credits.

Criteria can grow more complex by combining multiple AND and OR conditions. The criteria in Figure 3.7f select Engineering majors with fewer than 60 credits *or* Communications majors who were born on or after April 1, 1974.

Other functions enable you to impose still other criteria. The ***Between function*** selects records that fall within a range of values. The criterion in Figure 3.7g selects students who have between 60 and 90 credits. The ***NOT function*** selects records that do not contain the designated value. The criterion in Figure 3.7h selects students with majors other than Liberal Arts.

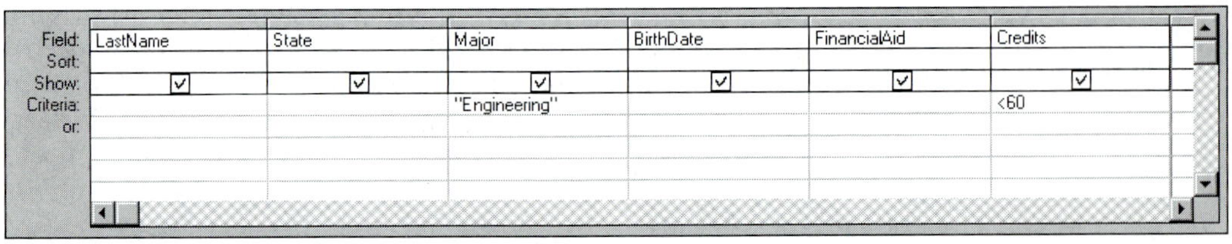

(e) Engineering Majors with Fewer than 60 Credits

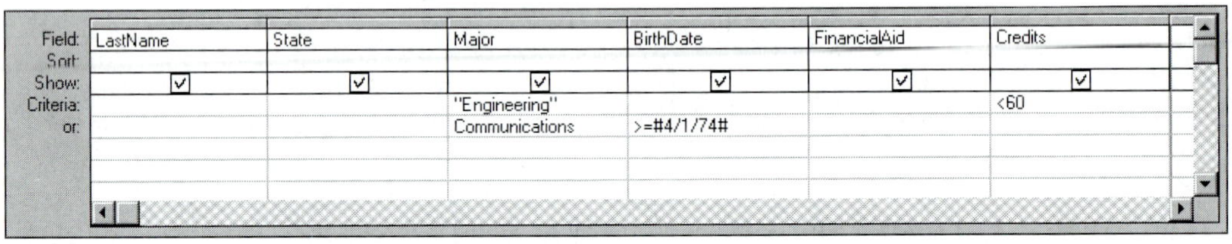

(f) Engineering Majors with Fewer than 60 Credits or Communications Majors Born on or after April 1, 1974

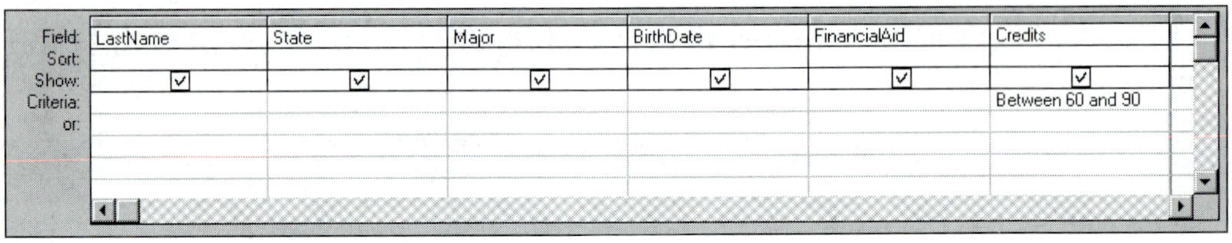

(g) Students with between 60 and 90 Credits

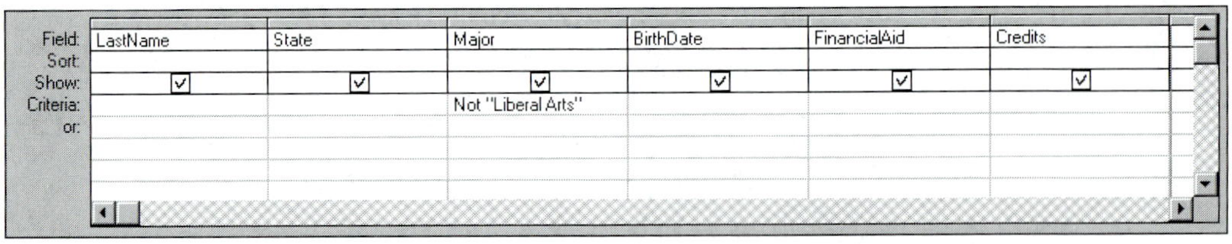

(h) Students with Majors Other than Liberal Arts

FIGURE 3.7 Selection Criteria (*continued*)

hands-on exercise

2 Creating a Select Query

Objective To create a select query using the Simple Query Wizard; to show how changing values in a dynaset changes the values in the underlying table; to create a report based on a query. Use Figure 3.8 as a guide in the exercise.

Step 1: The Simple Query Wizard

- Start Access and open the **Our Students database** from the previous exercise. Click **Open** in response to the security warning.
- Click the **Queries button** in the Database window. Double click the icon next to **Create query by using wizard** to start the Simple Query Wizard as shown in Figure 3.8a.
- The Students table should be already selected from the Tables/Queries list box. (If not, click the **drop-down arrow** in this list box and select the **Students table**.)
- Select the **LastName field** from the field list at the left, then click the > **button** to add this field to the Selected Fields list. (Use the < **button** if necessary to remove a field from the Selected Fields list.)
- Add the **FirstName**, **PhoneNumber**, **Major**, and **Credits fields** in that order to the Selected Fields list. (You can double click a field name to add it to the field list.) Click **Next**.
- The option button for a **Detail query** is selected. Click **Next**.
- Enter **Undecided Major** as the name of the query. Click the option button that says you want to **Modify the query design**. Click **Finish**.

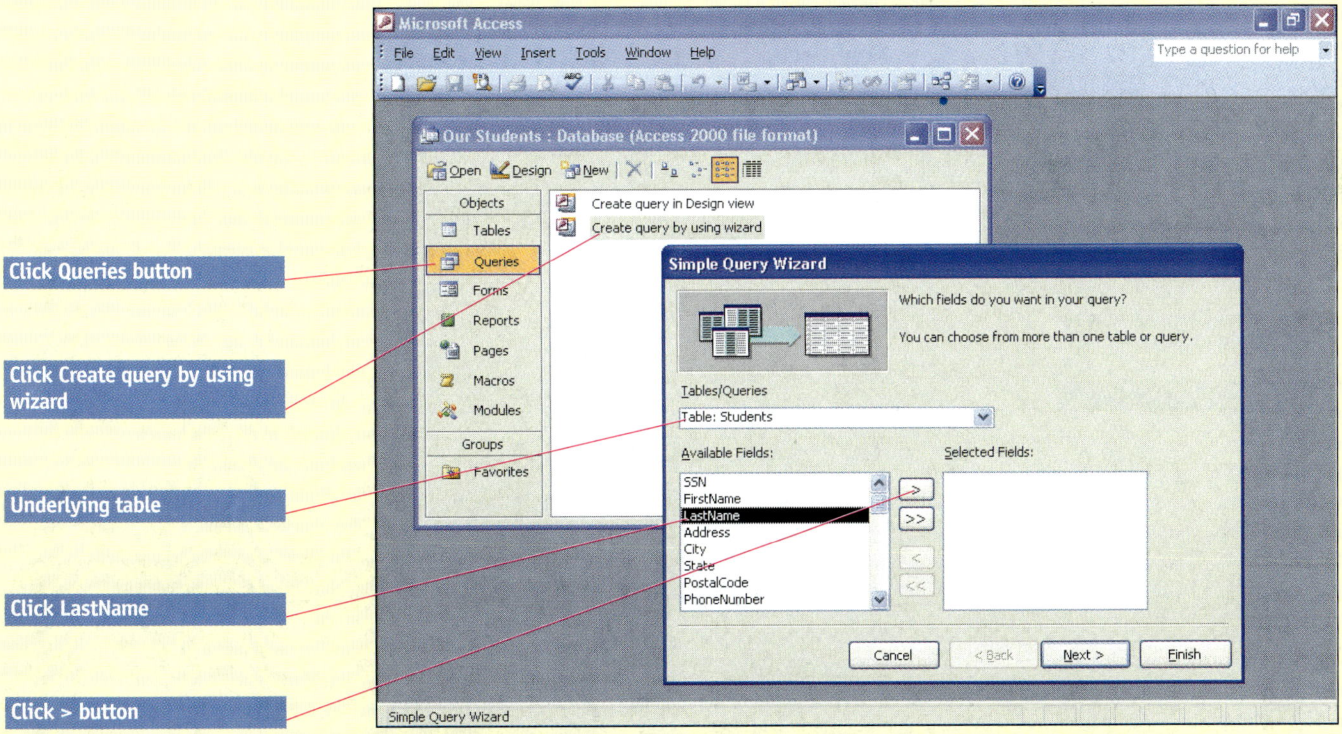

(a) The Simple Query Wizard (step 1)

FIGURE 3.8 Hands-on Exercise 2

Step 2: Complete the Query

- You should see the Query Design window as shown in Figure 3.8b. (Your query has not yet been completed, however, and so your figure does not match ours at this time.) Click the **Maximize button** so that the Design window takes the entire screen.
- Click and drag the border between the upper and lower portions of the window to give you more room in the upper half. Click and drag the bottom of the field list so that you can see all of the fields in the Students table.
- Check that you have all of the necessary fields in the lower half of the window. You can click and drag any missing field from the field list to the grid, and/or you can select a column, then drag it within the grid to rearrange the order of the fields.
- Click the **Criteria row** for **Major**. Type **Undecided**.
- Click the **Sort row** under the LastName field, click the **drop-down arrow**, then select **Ascending** as the sort sequence.
- Click the **Save button** to save the query.

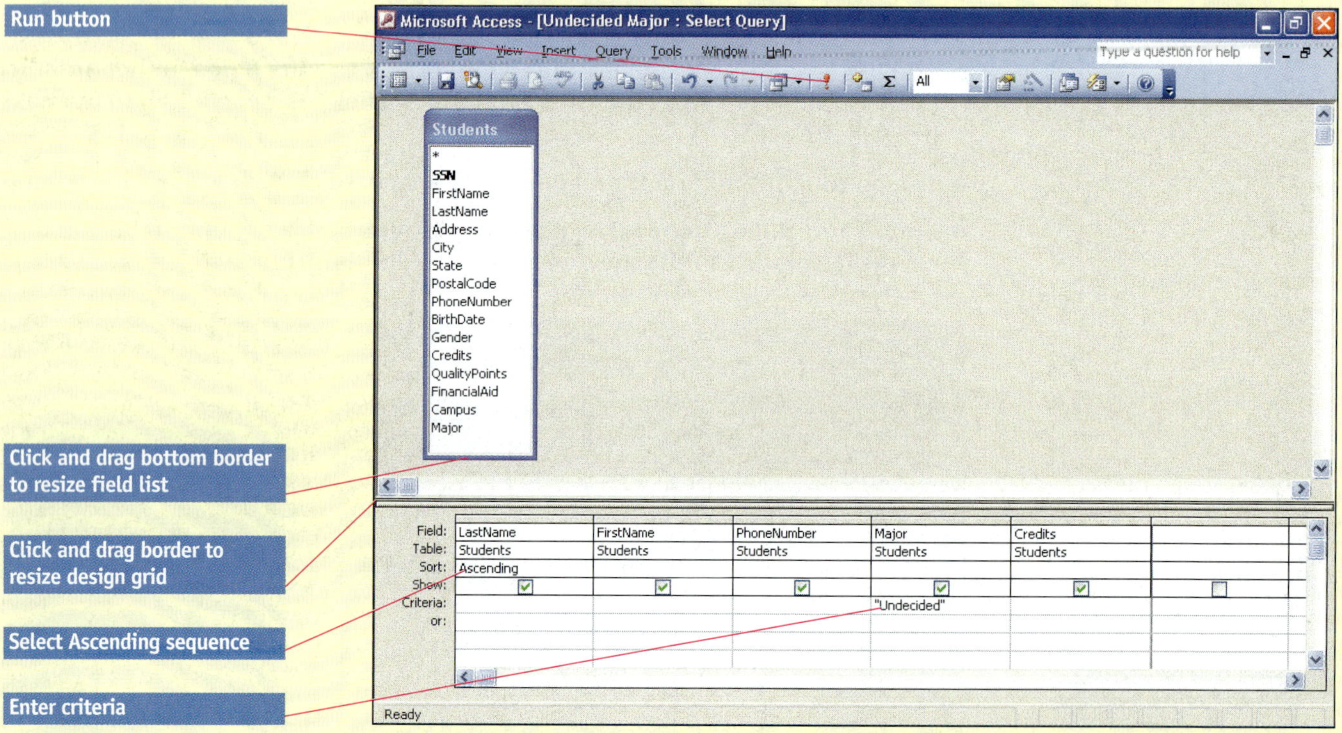

(b) Complete the Query (step 2)

FIGURE 3.8 Hands-on Exercise 2 (*continued*)

CUSTOMIZE THE QUERY WINDOW

The Query window displays the field list and design grid in its upper and lower halves, respectively. To increase (decrease) the size of either portion of the window, drag the line dividing the upper and lower sections. Drag the title bar to move a field list. You can also size a field list by dragging a border just as you would size any other window. Press the F6 key to toggle between the upper and lower halves as you work in the Design view.

Step 3: Run the Query

- Pull down the **Query menu** and click **Run** (or click the **Run button**) to run the query and change to the Datasheet view.
- You should see the five records in the dynaset of Figure 3.8c. Change Ryan Cornell's major to Business by clicking in the **Major field**, clicking the **drop-down arrow**, then choosing **Business** from the drop-down list.
- Click the **View button** to return to the Design view in order to rerun the query. Click the **Run button**.
- You should now see four students. Ryan Cornell no longer appears because he has changed his major.
- Change to the Design view.

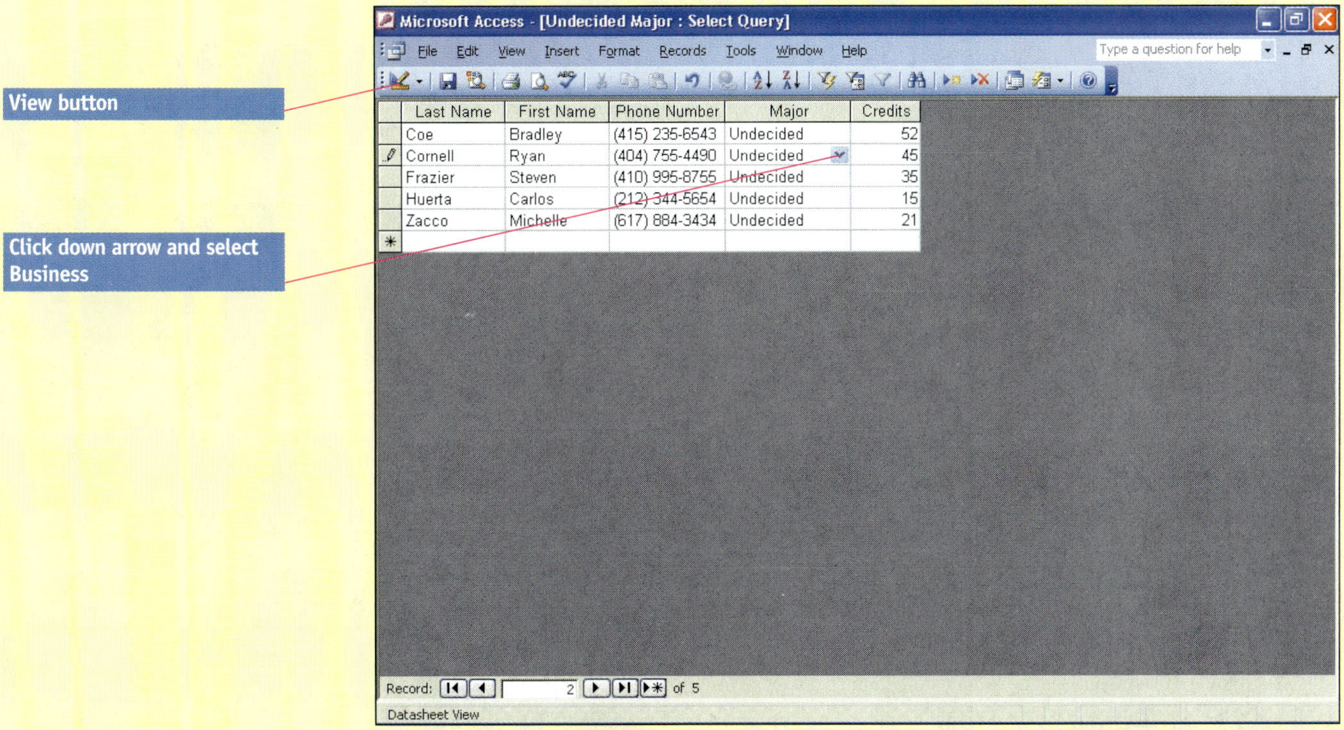

(c) Run the Query (step 3)

FIGURE 3.8 Hands-on Exercise 2 (*continued*)

THE DYNASET

A query represents a question and an answer. The question is developed by using the design grid in the Query Design view. The answer is displayed in a dynaset that contains the records that satisfy the criteria specified in the query. A dynaset looks and acts like a table, but it isn't a table; it is a dynamic subset of a table that selects and sorts records as specified in the query. A dynaset is like a table in that you can enter a new record or modify or delete an existing record. It is dynamic because the changes made to the dynaset are automatically reflected in the underlying table.

Step 4: Modify the Query

- Click the **Show check box** in the Major field to remove the check as shown in Figure 3.8d. The Major field will be used to select students, but it will not appear in the dynaset.
- Click the **Criteria row** under credits. Type **>30** to select only the Undecided majors with more than 30 credits.
- Click the **Save button** to save the revised query. Click the **Run button** to run the revised query.
- This time there are only two records (Bradley Coe and Steven Frazier) in the dynaset, and the major is no longer displayed.
- Carlos Huerta and Michelle Zacco do not appear because they do not have more than 30 credits.

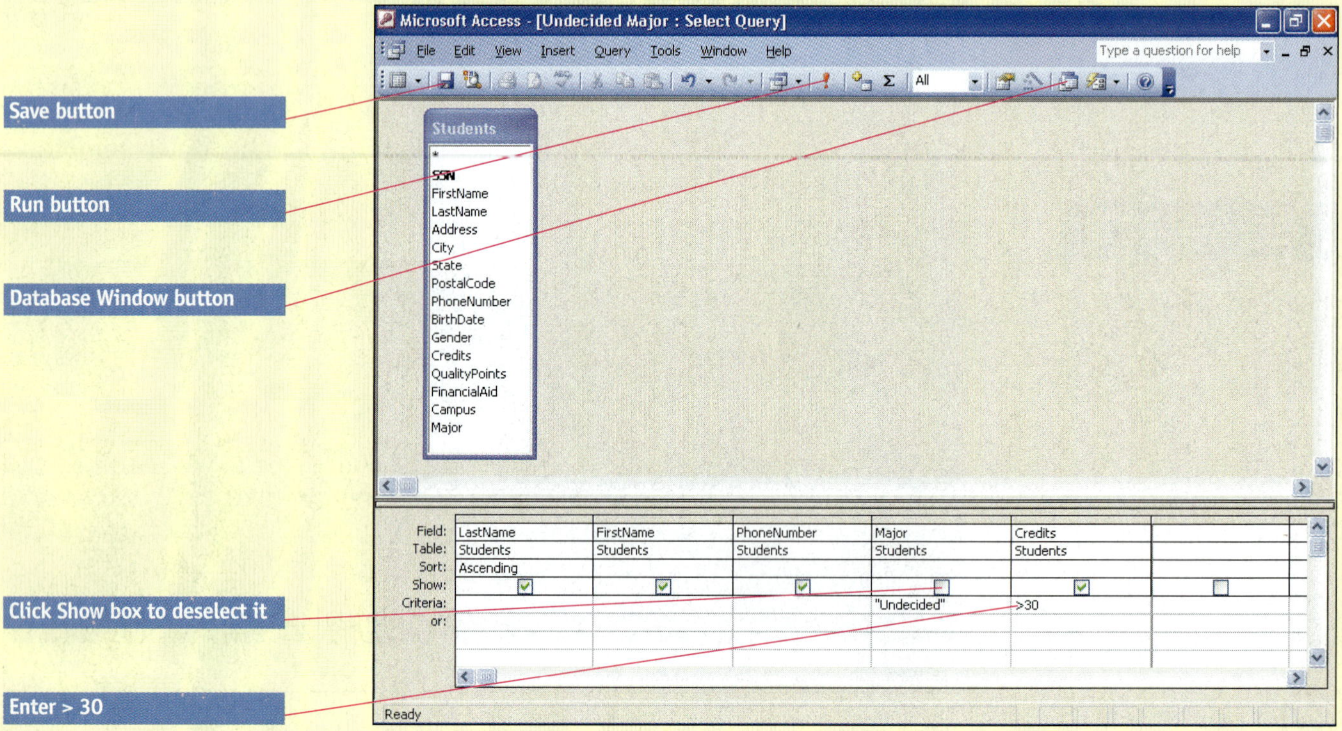

(d) Modify the Query (step 4)

FIGURE 3.8 Hands-on Exercise 2 (*continued*)

FLEXIBLE CRITERIA

Access offers a great deal of flexibility in the way you enter the criteria for a text field. Quotation marks and/or an equal sign are optional. Thus, "Undecided", Undecided, =Undecided, or ="Undecided" are all valid, and you may choose any of these formats. Access will convert your entry to standard format ("Undecided" in this example) after you have moved to the next cell. Numeric fields, however, are always entered without quotation marks.

Step 5: Create a Report

- Pull down the **Window menu** and click **1 Our Students: Database** (or click the **Database window button** on the toolbar). You will see the Database window in Figure 3.8e.
- Click the **Reports button**, then double click the icon next to **Create report by using wizard**.
- Click the **drop-down arrow** on the **Tables/Queries** list box and select **Query:Undecided Major**. All of the visible fields (major has been hidden) are displayed. Click the **>>button** to select all of the fields in the query for the report. Click **Next**.
- You do not want to choose additional grouping levels. Click **Next** to move to the next screen.
- There is no need to specify a sort sequence. Click **Next**.
- The **Tabular layout** is selected, as is **Portrait orientation**. Be sure the box is checked to **Adjust field width so all fields fit on a page**. Click **Next**.
- Choose **Soft Gray** as the style. Click **Next**.
- If necessary, enter **Undecided Major** as the title for your report. The option button to **Preview the report** is already selected. Click the **Finish command button** to exit the Report Wizard and view the report.

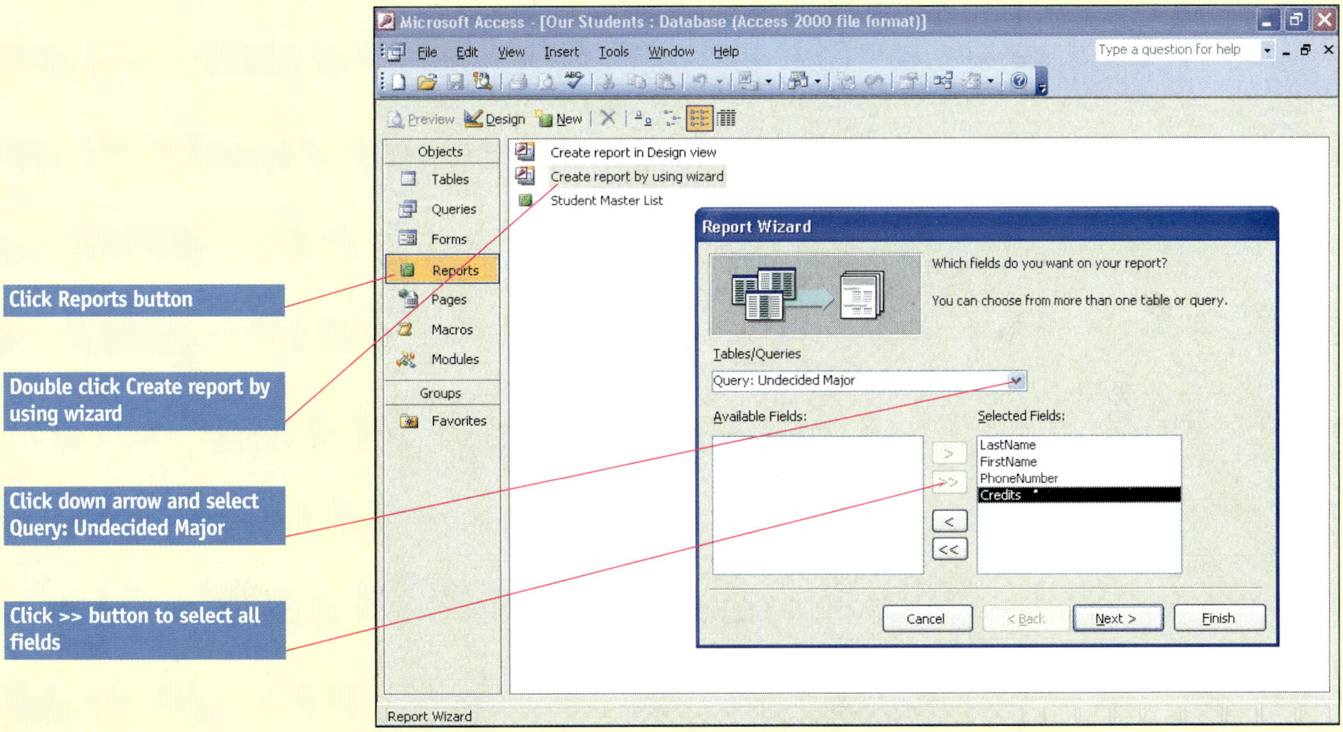

(e) Create a Report (step 5)

FIGURE 3.8 Hands-on Exercise 2 (*continued*)

THE BACK BUTTON

The Back button is present on every screen within the Report Wizard and enables you to recover from mistakes or simply to change your mind about how you want the report to look. Click the Back button at any time to return to the previous screen, then click it again if you want to return to the screen before that.

Step 6: The Completed Report

- If necessary, click the **Maximize button** to see the completed report as shown in Figure 3.8f. If necessary, return to the Design view to space the fields and their labels attractively across the page. Save the design changes.
- Click the **Print button** to print the report. Click the **Close button** to exit the Print Preview window. Close the Report design window.
- Switch to the Query window, then close the Query window.
- If necessary, click the **Database Window button** on the toolbar to return to the Database window. Click the **Maximize button**:
  - Click the **Queries button** to display the names of the queries in the Our Students database. You should see the *Undecided Major* query created in this exercise.
  - Click the **Reports button**. You should see two reports: *Student Master List* and *Undecided Major*.
- Close the **Our Students database** and exit Access if you do not wish to continue with the next exercise at this time.

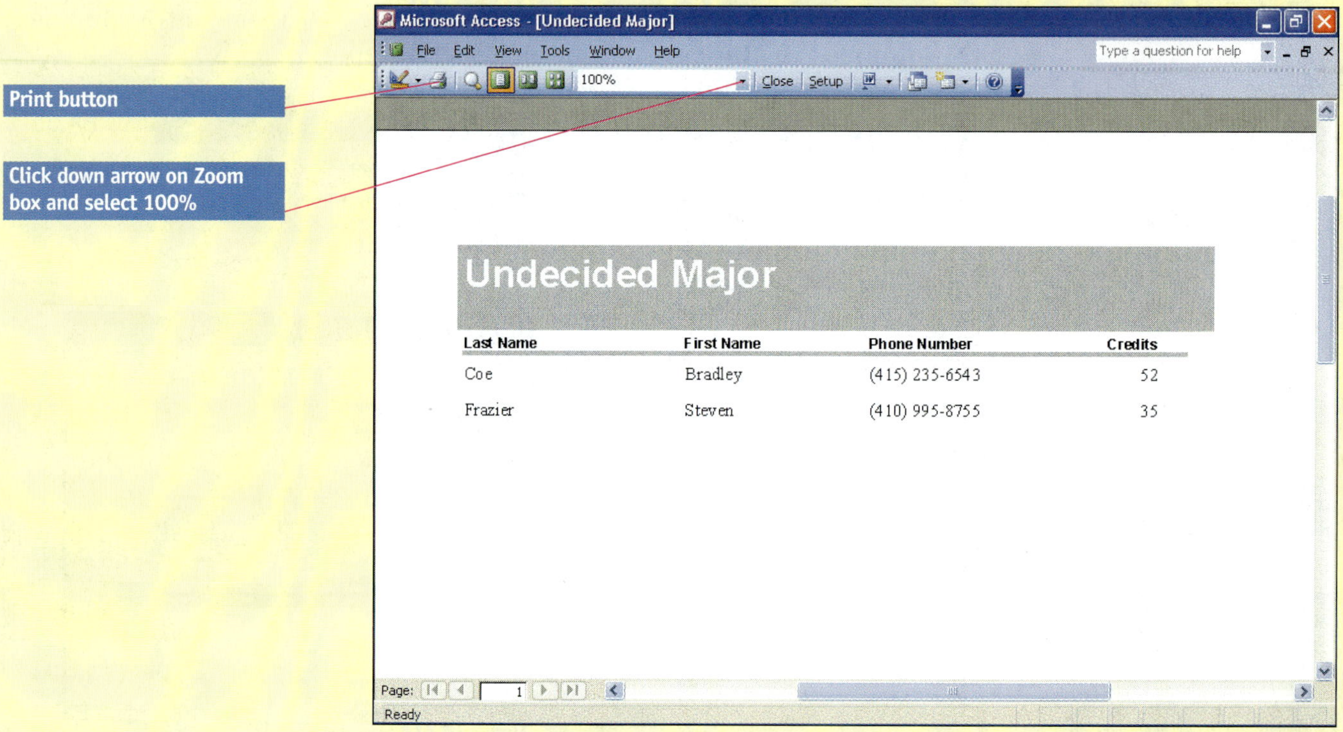

(f) The Completed Report (step 6)

FIGURE 3.8 Hands-on Exercise 2 (*continued*)

THE BORDER PROPERTY

The Border property enables you to display a border around any type of control. Point to the control (in the Design view), click the right mouse button to display a shortcut menu, then click Properties to display the Properties dialog box. Select the Format tab, click the Border Style property, then choose the type of border you want (e.g., solid to display a border or transparent to suppress a border). Use the Border Color and Border Width properties to change the appearance of the border.

A report, and/or the query on which it is based, can be enhanced through the use of Access functions to create calculated controls. Figure 3.9a displays a query in Design view, whereas Figure 3.9b shows (a portion of) the corresponding dynaset. The students appear in alphabetical order according to their major, and then alphabetically by last name within each major. Three of the controls in the query (Major, QualityPoints, and Credits) are from the underlying Students table as can be seen from the corresponding entries in the Table row. The other controls (Name, GPA, and Distinction) are calculated and thus, are not contained in an underlying table; that is, the entries in the Table row for these fields are blank.

Syntactically, the name of a calculated control is followed by a colon, a space, and then the expression. The first calculated control, Name, uses the ampersand to ***concatenate*** (join together) three components of a student's name: the last name, a comma followed by a space, and the first name. The result can be seen in the dynaset—for example, "Adili, Ronnie" for the first student in the table. Notice how the concatenated field is more visually appealing than displaying the two name fields individually.

The next calculated control, GPA, uses simple division (the quality points divided by the number of credits) to compute a student's grade point average. Jared Berlin, for example, has quality points and credits of 250 and 100, respectively, resulting in a calculated GPA of 2.50.

An ***Immediate IF (IIF) function*** is used in the last calculated control (Distinction) to determine if a student is on the Dean's list. The IIF function has three arguments—a condition that is either true or false, the result when the condition is true, and an (optional) result when the condition is false. Thus, in this example, if the GPA is greater than or equal to 3.50, the function returns the expression "Dean's List". If, however, the condition is not true, the function does not return any value; that is, the control will be left blank in the resulting data set. The query in Figure 3.9 will be the basis of the report described in the next section as well as the hands-on exercise that follows.

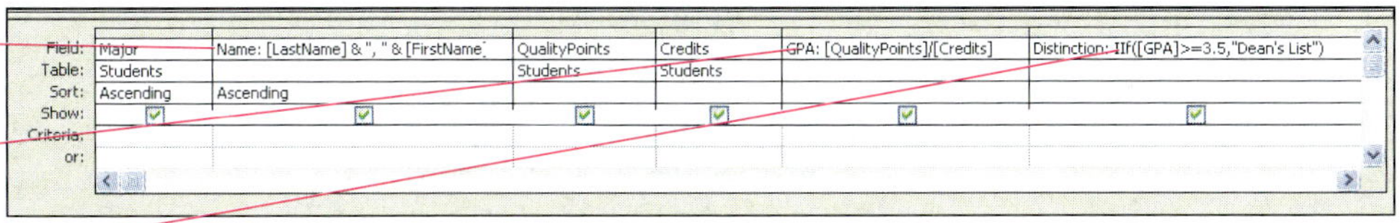

(a) Design View

Students are listed alphabetically by last name within major

Student's last name and first name have been concatenated

GPA has been calculated to 2 decimals

Dean's List is indicated only where GPA is >= 3.5

Major	Name	QualityPoints	Credits	GPA	Distinction
Business	Adili, Ronnie	155	60	2.58	
Business	Cornell, Ryan	80	45	1.78	
Business	DiGiacomo, Kevin	375	105	3.57	Dean's List
Business	Gibson, Christopher	60	35	1.71	
Business	Ramsay, Robert	162	50	3.24	
Business	Watson, Ana	75	30	2.50	
Communications	Faulkner, Eileen	80	30	2.67	
Communications	Joseph, Cedric	170	45	3.78	Dean's List
Communications	Ortiz, Frances	60	28	2.14	
Communications	Price, Lori	42	24	1.75	
Communications	Slater, Erica	390	105	3.71	Dean's List
Education	Korba, Nickolas	166	100	1.66	

(b) Dynaset

FIGURE 3.9 Access Functions

GROUPING RECORDS

The report in Figure 3.10 is based on the query just discussed; that is, look closely, and you will see that the report contains the same business majors as previously. The GPA is calculated as before, and it illustrates ***conditional formatting***; that is, the format (in this case, the font color) depends on the value of the GPA control. A GPA greater than 3.5 is printed in blue, a GPA less than 2.0 is printed in red, and all other values are printed in black.

The report in Figure 3.10a, for example, groups students according to their major, sorts them alphabetically according to last name within each major, then calculates the average GPA for all students in each major. A Group Header appears before each group of students to identify the group and display the major. A Group Footer appears at the end of each group and displays the average GPA for students in that major.

Figure 3.10b displays the Design view of the report in Figure 3.10a, which determines the appearance of the printed report. Look carefully at the design to relate each section to the corresponding portion of the printed report:

- The **Report Header** contains the title of the report and appears once, at the beginning of the printed report.
- The **Page Header** contains the column headings that appear at the top of each page. The column headings are labels (or unbound controls) and are formatted in bold.
- The **Group Header** consists of a single bound control that displays the value of the major field prior to each group of detail records.
- The **Detail section** consists of bound controls that appear directly under the corresponding heading in the Page Header. The Detail section is printed once for each record in each group.
- The **Group Footer** appears after each group of detail records. It consists of an unbound control (Average GPA for Major:) followed by a calculated control that computes the average GPA for each group of students.
- The **Page Footer** appears at the bottom of each page and contains the date, page number, and total number of pages in the report.
- The **Report Footer** appears at the end of the report. It consists of an unbound control (Average GPA for All Students:) followed by a calculated control that computes the average GPA for all students.

Grouping records within a report enables you to perform calculations on each group, as was done in the Group Footer of Figure 3.10. The calculations in our example made use of the ***Avg function***, but other types of calculations are possible:

- The ***Sum function*** computes the total for a specific field for all records in the group.
- The ***Min function*** determines the minimum value for all records in the group.
- The ***Max function*** determines the maximum value for all records in the group.
- The ***Count function*** counts the number of records in the group.

Look closely at the page footer to see the inclusion of three additional functions—Now, Page, and Pages—that display the current date, the current page, and total number of pages, respectively. The Report Wizard builds the Page Footer automatically, but you can learn from the wizard and incorporate these functions in other reports that you create.

The following exercise has you create the report in Figure 3.10. The Report Wizard is used to design the basic report, but additional modifications are necessary to create the Group Header and Group Footer.

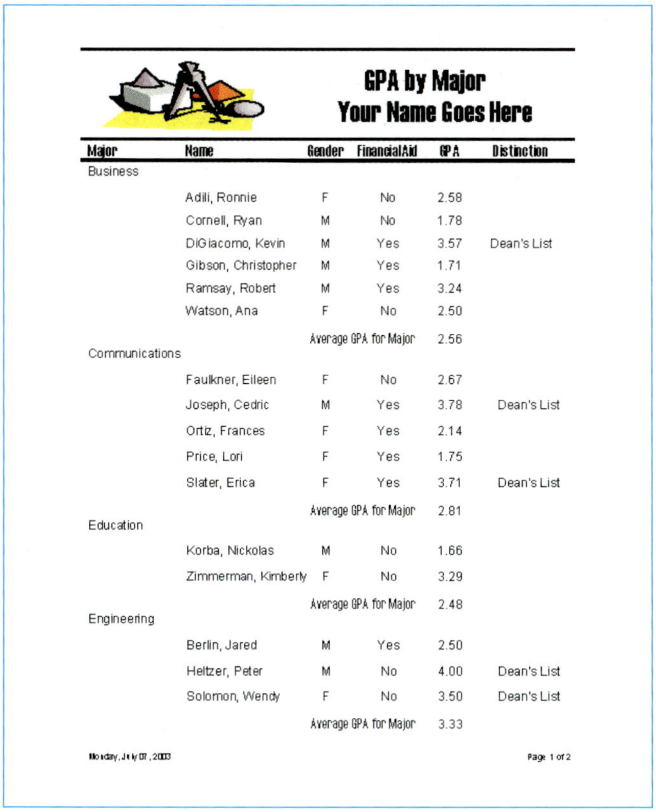

Major	Name	Gender	FinancialAid	GPA	Distinction
Business					
	Adili, Ronnie	F	No	2.58	
	Cornell, Ryan	M	No	1.78	
	DiGiacomo, Kevin	M	Yes	3.57	Dean's List
	Gibson, Christopher	M	Yes	1.71	
	Ramsay, Robert	M	Yes	3.24	
	Watson, Ana	F	No	2.50	
		Average GPA for Major		2.56	
Communications					
	Faulkner, Eileen	F	No	2.67	
	Joseph, Cedric	M	Yes	3.78	Dean's List
	Ortiz, Frances	F	Yes	2.14	
	Price, Lori	F	Yes	1.75	
	Slater, Erica	F	Yes	3.71	Dean's List
		Average GPA for Major		2.81	
Education					
	Korba, Nickolas	M	No	1.66	
	Zimmerman, Kimberly	F	No	3.29	
		Average GPA for Major		2.48	
Engineering					
	Berlin, Jared	M	Yes	2.50	
	Heltzer, Peter	M	No	4.00	Dean's List
	Solomon, Wendy	F	No	3.50	Dean's List
		Average GPA for Major		3.33	

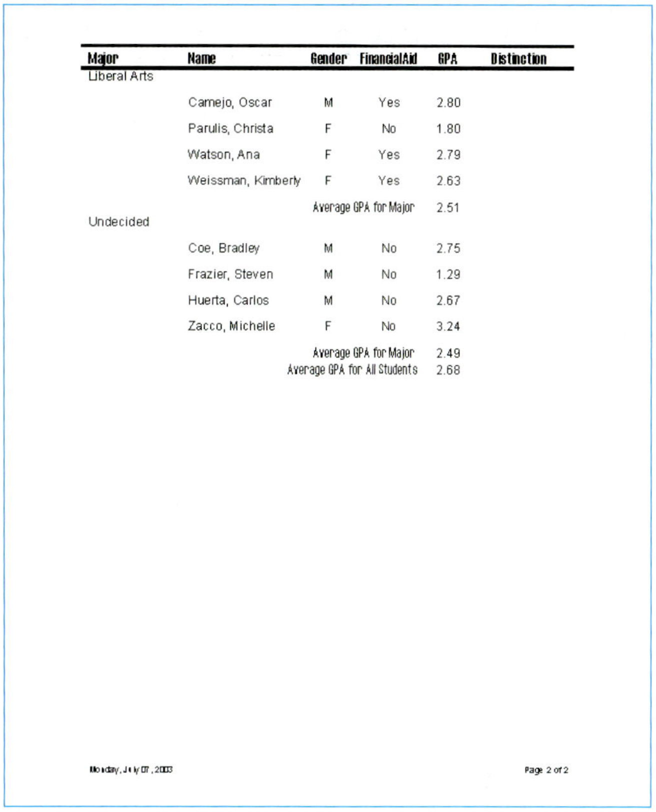

Major	Name	Gender	FinancialAid	GPA	Distinction
Liberal Arts					
	Carnejo, Oscar	M	Yes	2.80	
	Parulis, Christa	F	No	1.80	
	Watson, Ana	F	Yes	2.79	
	Weissman, Kimberly	F	Yes	2.63	
		Average GPA for Major		2.51	
Undecided					
	Coe, Bradley	M	No	2.75	
	Frazier, Steven	M	No	1.29	
	Huerta, Carlos	M	No	2.67	
	Zacco, Michelle	F	No	3.24	
		Average GPA for Major		2.49	
		Average GPA for All Students		2.68	

(a) The Printed Report

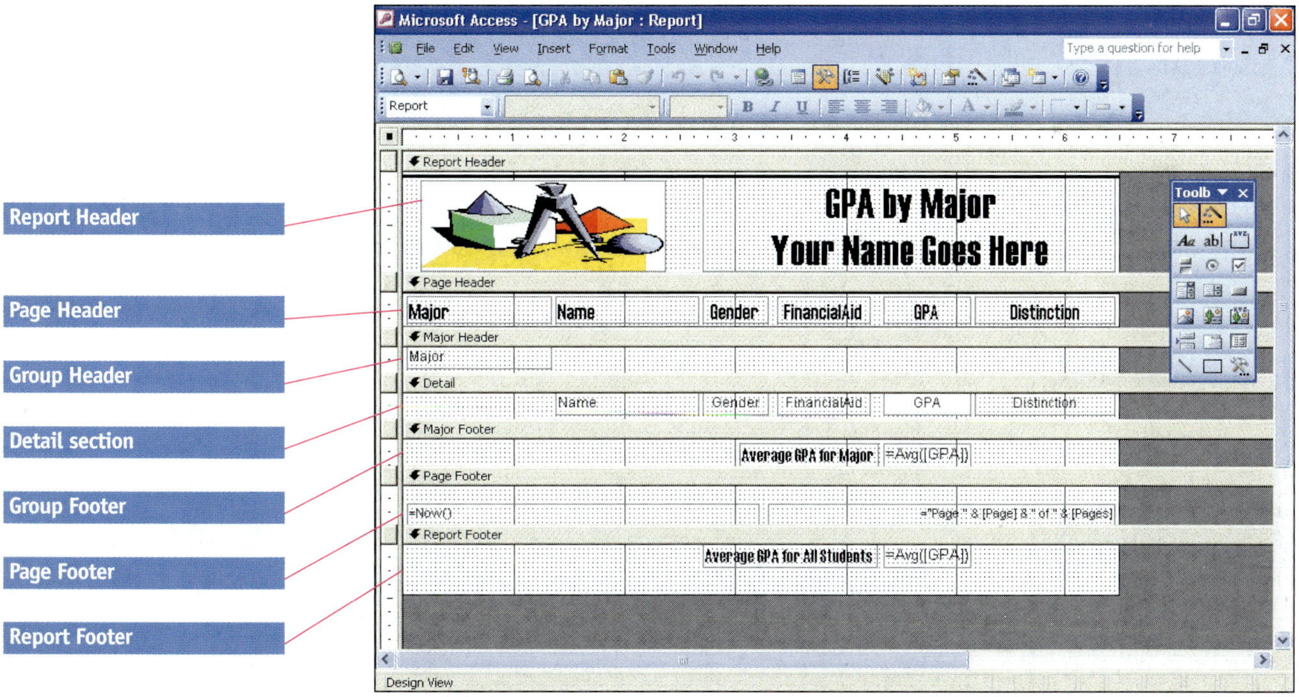

(b) Design View

FIGURE 3.10 The Summary Report

hands-on exercise

3 Grouping Records

Objective To create a query containing a calculated control, then create a report based on that query; to use the Sorting and Grouping command to add a Group Header and Group Footer to a report. Use Figure 3.11 as a guide.

Step 1: Create the Query

- Start Access and open the **Our Students database** from the previous exercise. Click **Open** in response to the security warning.
- Click the **Queries button** in the Database window. Double click **Create query in Design view** to display the Query Design window and bypass the Simple Query Wizard.
- The Show Table dialog box appears; the **Tables tab** is already selected, as is the **Students table.** Click the **Add button** to add the table to the query. Click **Close** to close the Show Table dialog box.
- Click the **Maximize button** so that the window takes up the entire screen as shown in Figure 3.11a. Drag the border between the upper and lower portions of the window to give yourself more room in the upper portion. Make the field list larger, to display more fields at one time.
- Scroll (if necessary) within the field list, then click and drag the **Major field** from the field list to the query. Click and drag the **Gender**, **FinancialAid**, **QualityPoints**, and **Credits fields** (in that order).
- Click the **Sort row** for the Major field. Click the **down arrow** to open the drop-down list box. Click **Ascending.**
- Click **Save** to display the dialog box in Figure 3.11a. Enter **GPA by Major** as the query name. Click **OK.**

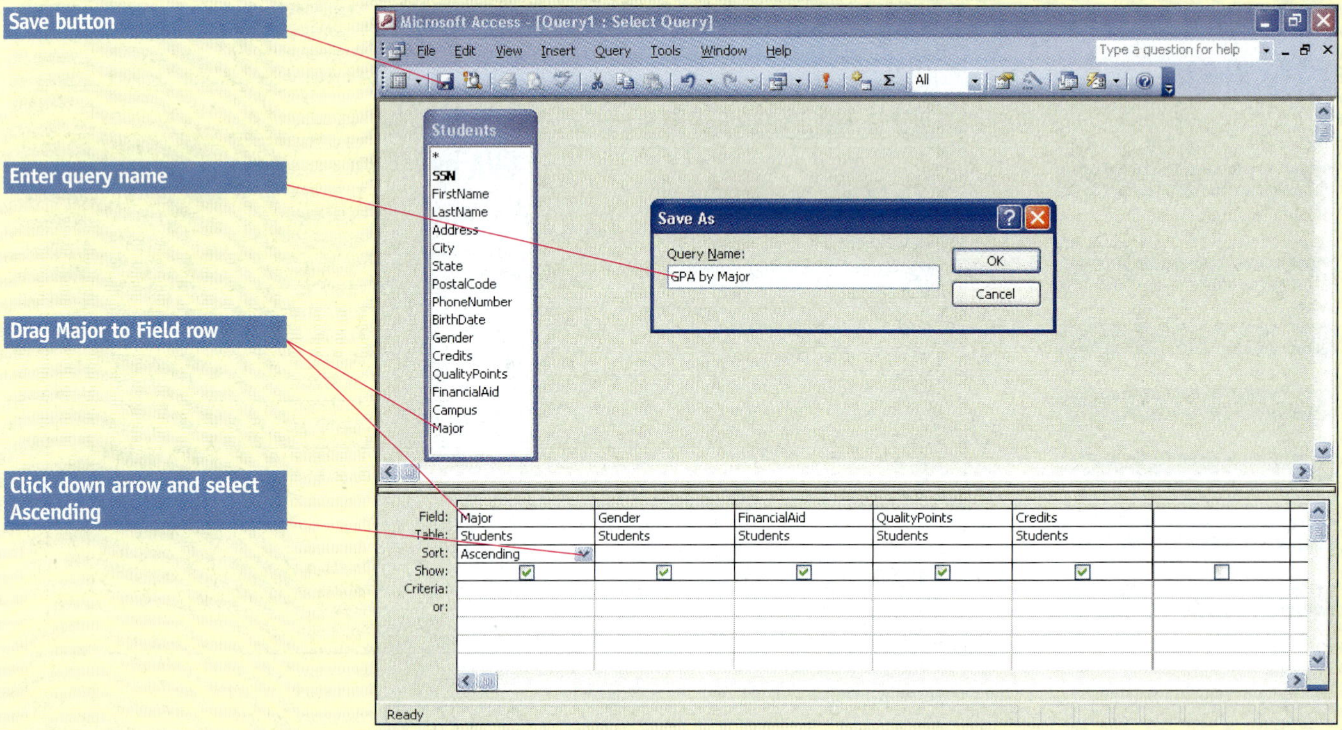

(a) Create the Query (step 1)

FIGURE 3.11 Hands-on Exercise 3

Step 2: Add the Calculated Controls

- Click anywhere in the **Gender column**. Pull down the **Insert menu** and click **Columns** to insert a blank column to the left of the Gender field.
- Click in the **Field row** of the newly inserted column to enter a calculated control. Type **Name: LastName & ", " & FirstName**, and press **Enter**. The ampersand concatenates (joins together) the various components in the name field.
- Be sure to spell the fields correctly (there are no spaces in "LastName" or "FirstName"). You are concatenating (joining together) the last name, a comma and a space, and the first name into a single field called Name.
- Click in the **Sort row** under the newly created Name control. Click the **down arrow** and choose an **Ascending** sequence as shown in Figure 3.11b.
- Click in the **Field row** of the first blank column. Type **GPA: QualityPoints/Credits**, and press **Enter**. Be sure to spell the field names correctly.
- Change the column widths as necessary to see the field contents. Save the query.

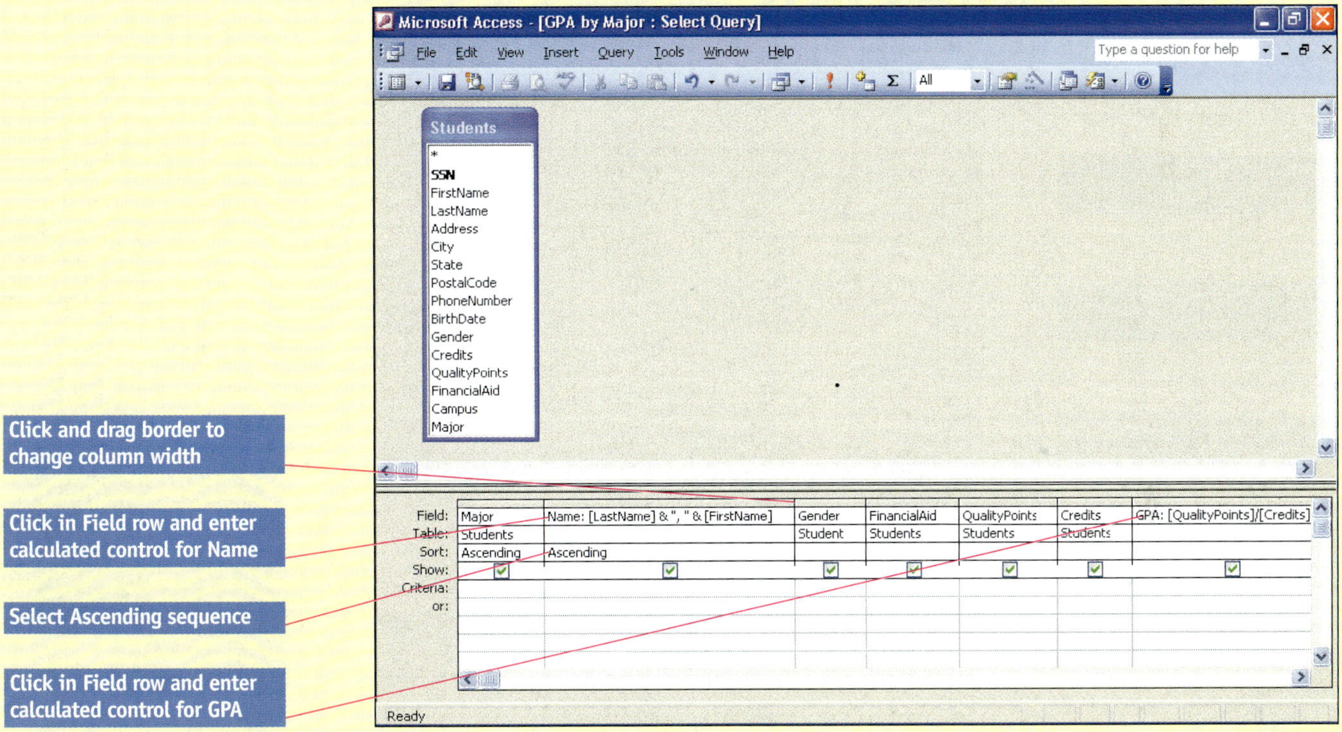

(b) Add the Calculated Controls (step 2)

FIGURE 3.11 Hands-on Exercise 3 (*continued*)

THE TOP VALUES PROPERTY

The Top Values property lets you display a specified percentage or number of the top or bottom records in a list. Remove any sort keys in the query, then sort the table according to the desired sequence, ascending or descending, to get the lowest or highest values, respectively. Click the down arrow in the Top Values list box to choose the number of records, such as 5 or 5% to show the top five or five percent, respectively. Save the query, then run it. See practice exercise 3 at the end of the chapter.

Step 3: Run the Query

- Pull down the **Query menu** and click **Run** (or click the **Run button** on the Query Design toolbar). You will see the dynaset in Figure 3.11c, which displays the records that satisfy the query.
- Students are listed by major and alphabetically by last name within major. (Access sorts from left to right according to the way in which the fields appear in the Design grid. Thus, the Major field must appear to the left of the LastName field within the Design view.)
- Change column widths as necessary by dragging the border between adjacent column headings.
- A total of seven fields appear in the dynaset, corresponding to the controls that were added to the design grid in Design view. The GPA is displayed to too many decimal places.
- Click the **View button** to modify the query.

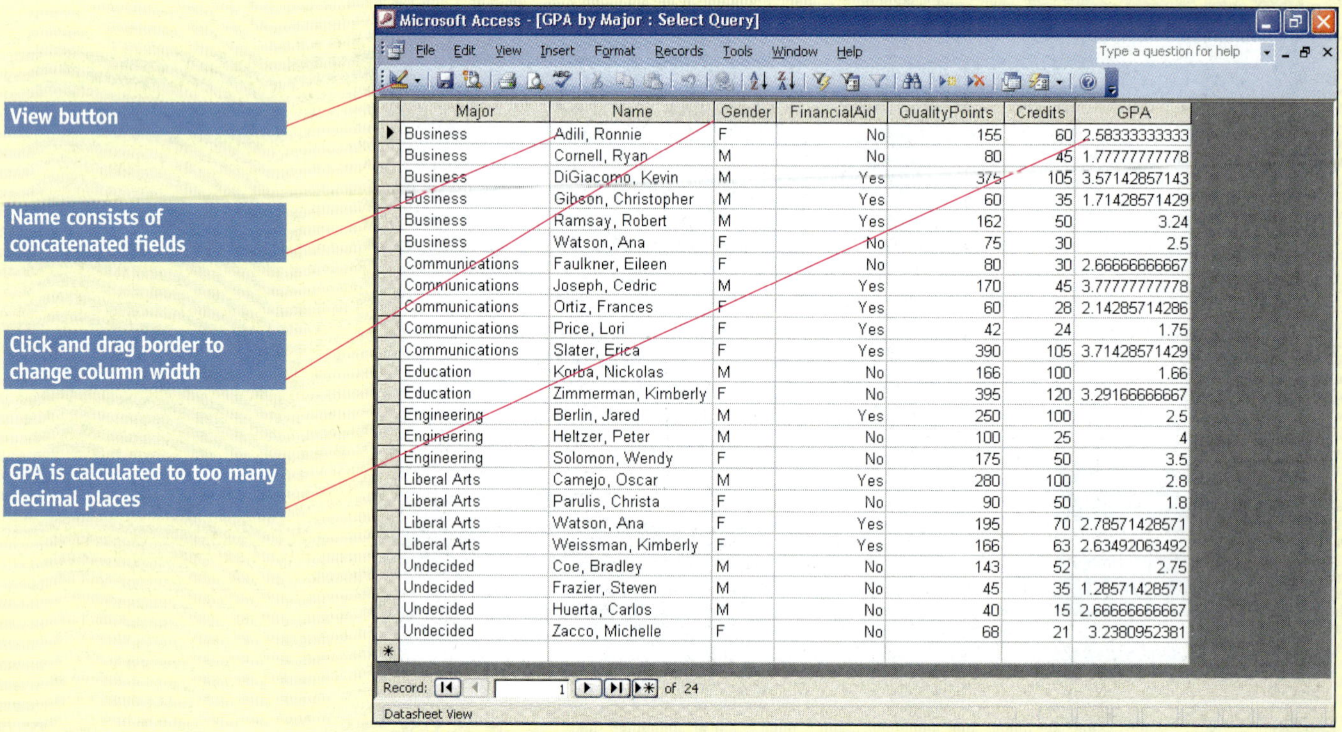

Major	Name	Gender	FinancialAid	QualityPoints	Credits	GPA
Business	Adili, Ronnie	F	No	155	60	2.58333333333
Business	Cornell, Ryan	M	No	80	45	1.77777777778
Business	DiGiacomo, Kevin	M	Yes	375	105	3.57142857143
Business	Gibson, Christopher	M	Yes	60	35	1.71428571429
Business	Ramsay, Robert	M	Yes	162	50	3.24
Business	Watson, Ana	F	No	75	30	2.5
Communications	Faulkner, Eileen	F	No	80	30	2.66666666667
Communications	Joseph, Cedric	M	Yes	170	45	3.77777777778
Communications	Ortiz, Frances	F	Yes	60	28	2.14285714286
Communications	Price, Lori	F	Yes	42	24	1.75
Communications	Slater, Erica	F	Yes	390	105	3.71428571429
Education	Korba, Nickolas	M	No	166	100	1.66
Education	Zimmerman, Kimberly	F	No	395	120	3.29166666667
Engineering	Berlin, Jared	M	Yes	250	100	2.5
Engineering	Heltzer, Peter	M	No	100	25	4
Engineering	Solomon, Wendy	F	No	175	50	3.5
Liberal Arts	Camejo, Oscar	M	Yes	280	100	2.8
Liberal Arts	Parulis, Christa	F	No	90	50	1.8
Liberal Arts	Watson, Ana	F	Yes	195	70	2.78571428571
Liberal Arts	Weissman, Kimberly	F	Yes	166	63	2.63492063492
Undecided	Coe, Bradley	M	No	143	52	2.75
Undecided	Frazier, Steven	M	No	45	35	1.28571428571
Undecided	Huerta, Carlos	M	No	40	15	2.66666666667
Undecided	Zacco, Michelle	F	No	68	21	3.2380952381

(c) Run the Query (step 3)

FIGURE 3.11 Hands-on Exercise 3 (*continued*)

ADJUST THE COLUMN WIDTH

Point to the right edge of the column you want to resize, then drag the mouse in the direction you want to go; drag to the right to make the column wider or to the left to make it narrower. Alternatively, you can double click the column selector line (right edge) to fit the longest entry in that column. Adjusting the column width in the Design view does not affect the column width in the Datasheet view, but you can use the same technique in both views.

Step 4: Modify the Query

- Point to the GPA column and click the **right mouse button** to display a shortcut menu. Click the **Properties command** to display the Field Properties dialog box in Figure 3.11d.
- Click the **General tab** if necessary. Click the **Format text box**. Click the **drop-down arrow** to display the available formats. Click **Fixed**. Close the Field Properties dialog box.
- We will add another calculated control that will display "Dean's List" if the student has earned this distinction. Click in the **Field row** in the first blank column of the design grid.
- Enter **Distinction: IIF(GPA>=3.5, "Dean's List")** for the new control as shown in Figure 3.11d. This expression will display the literal "Dean's List" if the student has a GPA greater than or equal to 3.5.
- Click the **Save button** to save the modified query.

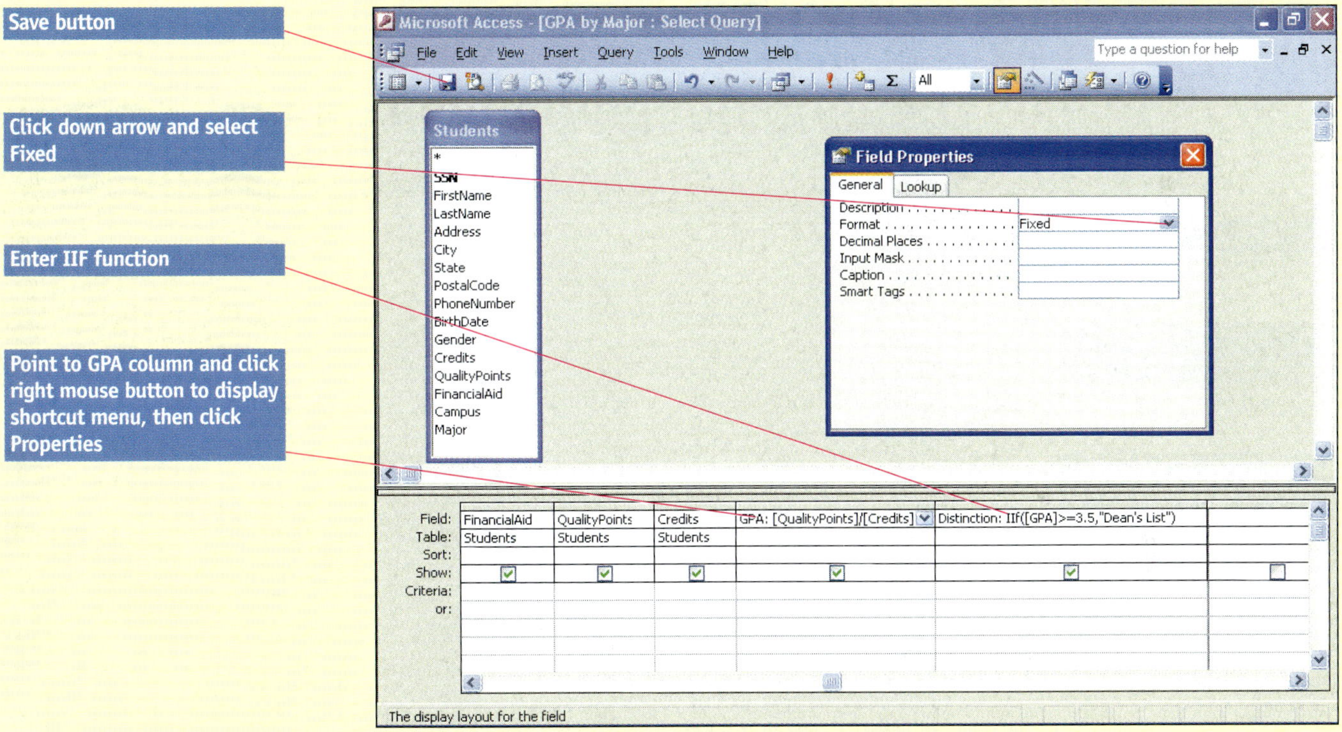

(d) Modify the Query (step 4)

FIGURE 3.11 Hands-on Exercise 3 (*continued*)

NESTED IF STATEMENTS

A "nested If" (or an If within an If) is a common logic structure in every programming language. It could be used in this example to implement more complicated logic such as displaying either "Dean's List" or "Probation", depending on the GPA. The IIF function has three arguments—a condition, the result if the condition is true, and the result if the condition is false. A nested If replaces either condition with another If. Thus, you could enter IIF(GPA>=3.5, "Dean's List", IIF(GPA<2.0, "Probation","N/A")).

Step 5: Rerun the Query

- Click the **Run button** to run the modified query. You will see a new dynaset corresponding to the modified query as shown in Figure 3.11e. Resize the column widths (as necessary) within the dynaset.
  - Students are still listed by major and alphabetically within major.
  - The GPA is calculated to two decimal places and appears under the GPA field.
  - Dean's List is indicated for those students with a GPA of 3.5 or above.
- Click the **QualityPoints field** for Christopher Gibson. Replace 60 with **70**. Press **Enter**. The GPA changes automatically to 2.
- Pull down the **Edit menu** and click **Undo Current Field/Record** (or click the **Undo button** on the Query toolbar). The GPA returns to its previous value.
- Tab to the **GPA field** for Christopher Gibson. Type **2**. Access will beep and prevent you from changing the GPA because it is a calculated field as indicated on the status bar.
- Click the **Close button** to close the query and return to the Database window. Click **Yes** if asked whether to save the changes.

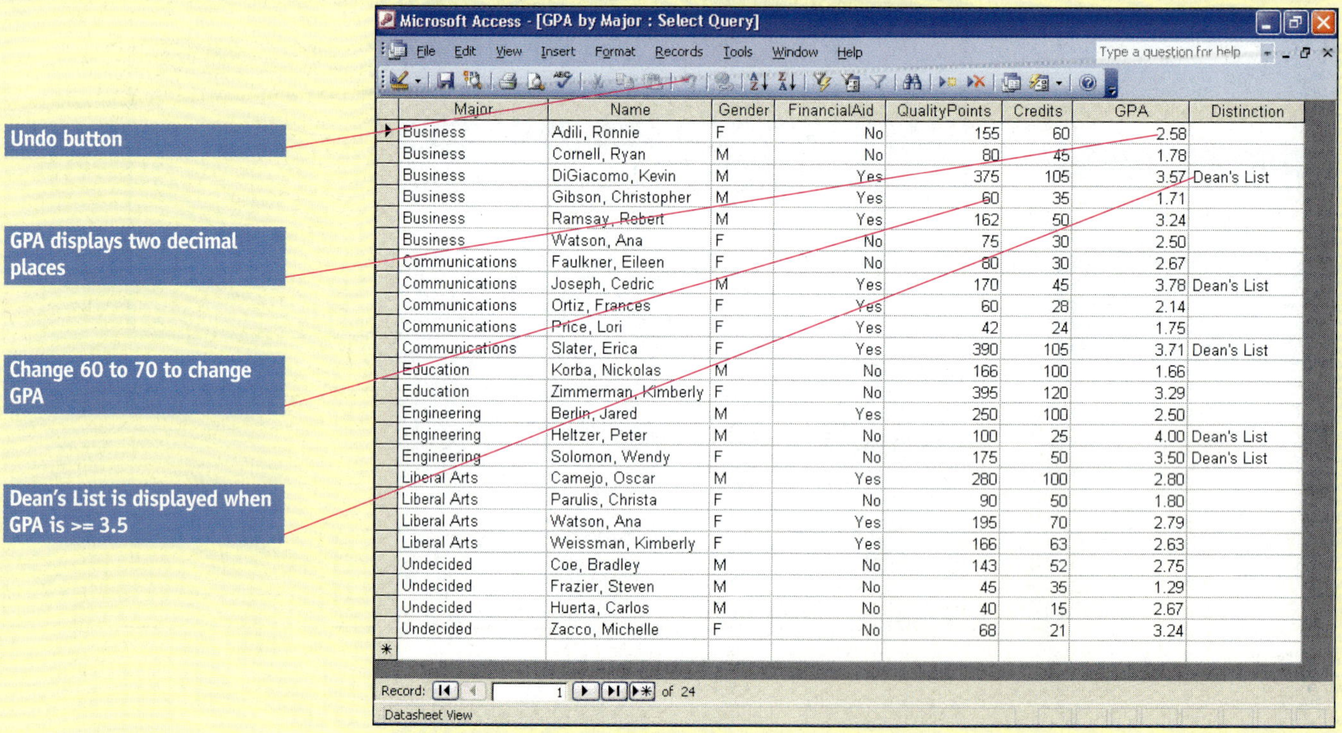

Major	Name	Gender	FinancialAid	QualityPoints	Credits	GPA	Distinction
Business	Adili, Ronnie	F	No	155	60	2.58	
Business	Cornell, Ryan	M	No	80	45	1.78	
Business	DiGiacomo, Kevin	M	Yes	375	105	3.57	Dean's List
Business	Gibson, Christopher	M	Yes	60	35	1.71	
Business	Ramsay, Robert	M	Yes	162	50	3.24	
Business	Watson, Ana	F	No	75	30	2.50	
Communications	Faulkner, Eileen	F	No	80	30	2.67	
Communications	Joseph, Cedric	M	Yes	170	45	3.78	Dean's List
Communications	Ortiz, Frances	F	Yes	60	28	2.14	
Communications	Price, Lori	F	Yes	42	24	1.75	
Communications	Slater, Erica	F	Yes	390	105	3.71	Dean's List
Education	Korba, Nickolas	M	No	166	100	1.66	
Education	Zimmerman, Kimberly	F	No	395	120	3.29	
Engineering	Berlin, Jared	M	Yes	250	100	2.50	
Engineering	Heltzer, Peter	M	No	100	25	4.00	Dean's List
Engineering	Solomon, Wendy	F	No	175	50	3.50	Dean's List
Liberal Arts	Camejo, Oscar	M	Yes	280	100	2.80	
Liberal Arts	Parulis, Christa	F	No	90	50	1.80	
Liberal Arts	Watson, Ana	F	Yes	195	70	2.79	
Liberal Arts	Weissman, Kimberly	F	Yes	166	63	2.63	
Undecided	Coe, Bradley	M	No	143	52	2.75	
Undecided	Frazier, Steven	M	No	45	35	1.29	
Undecided	Huerta, Carlos	M	No	40	15	2.67	
Undecided	Zacco, Michelle	F	No	68	21	3.24	

(e) Rerun the Query (step 5)

FIGURE 3.11 Hands-on Exercise 3 (*continued*)

USE WHAT YOU KNOW

An Access table or dynaset not only resembles an Excel worksheet in appearance, but it also accepts many of the same commands and operations. The Sort Ascending and Sort Descending buttons function identically to their Excel counterparts. You can also double click the right border of a column heading to adjust the column width. The Format menu enables you to change the row width or column height, hide or unhide columns, or freeze and unfreeze columns.

Step 6: The Report Wizard

- You should see the Database window. Click the **Reports button**, then double click **Create report by using the wizard** to start the Report Wizard.
- Select **GPA by Major** from the Tables/Queries drop-down list. The Available Fields list displays all of the fields in the GPA by Major query.
  - Click the **Major field** in the Available Fields list box. Click the **> button**.
  - Add the **Name**, **Gender**, **FinancialAid**, **GPA**, and **Distinction fields** one at a time. The easiest way to add a field is to double click the field name.
  - Do not include the QualityPoints or Credits fields. Click **Next**.
- You should see the screen asking whether you want to group the fields. Click the **Major field**, then click the **> button** to display the screen in Figure 3.11f.
- The Major field appears above the other fields to indicate that the records will be grouped according to the value of the Major field. Click **Next**.
- The next screen asks you to specify the order for the detail records. Click the **drop-down arrow** on the list box for the first field. Click **Name** to sort the records alphabetically by last name within each major. Click **Next**.
- The **Stepped Option button** is already selected for the report layout, as is **Portrait orientation**. Be sure the box is checked to **Adjust field width so all fields fit on a page**. Click **Next**.
- Choose **Compact** as the style. Click **Next**.
- **GPA by Major** (which corresponds to the name of the underlying query) is already entered as the name of the report. Click the Option button to **Modify the report's design**.
- Click **Finish** to exit the Report Wizard.

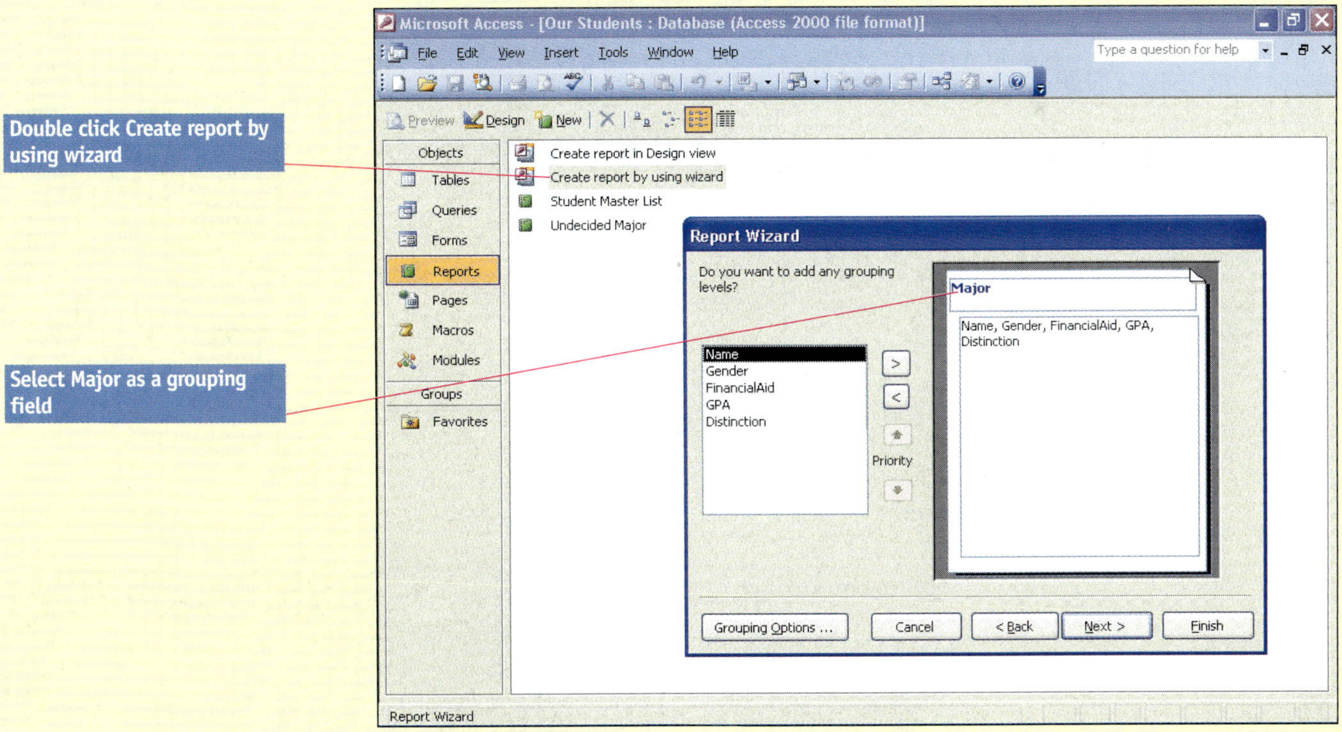

(f) The Report Wizard (step 6)

FIGURE 3.11 Hands-on Exercise 3 (*continued*)

Step 7: Sorting and Grouping

- Click and drag the right border of the label in the Report Header to the right to increase the size of the label. Press **Shift+Enter** to force a line break. Enter your name as shown in Figure 3.11g.
- Click the **Center button** to center the text within the unbound control. Click outside the label, then click and drag the label to the right.
- Move, size, and align the column headings and bound controls. You may have to go back and forth between Design view and Report Preview until you are satisfied.
- Pull down the **View menu**. Click **Sorting and Grouping** to display the Sorting and Grouping dialog box.
- The **Major field** should already be selected. Click the **Group Footer** property, click the **drop-down arrow**, then click **Yes** to create a Group Footer for the Major field. Close the dialog box.
- Click the down arrow for the **Keep Together** property. Click **Whole Group**. The Major footer has been added to the report. Close the dialog box.

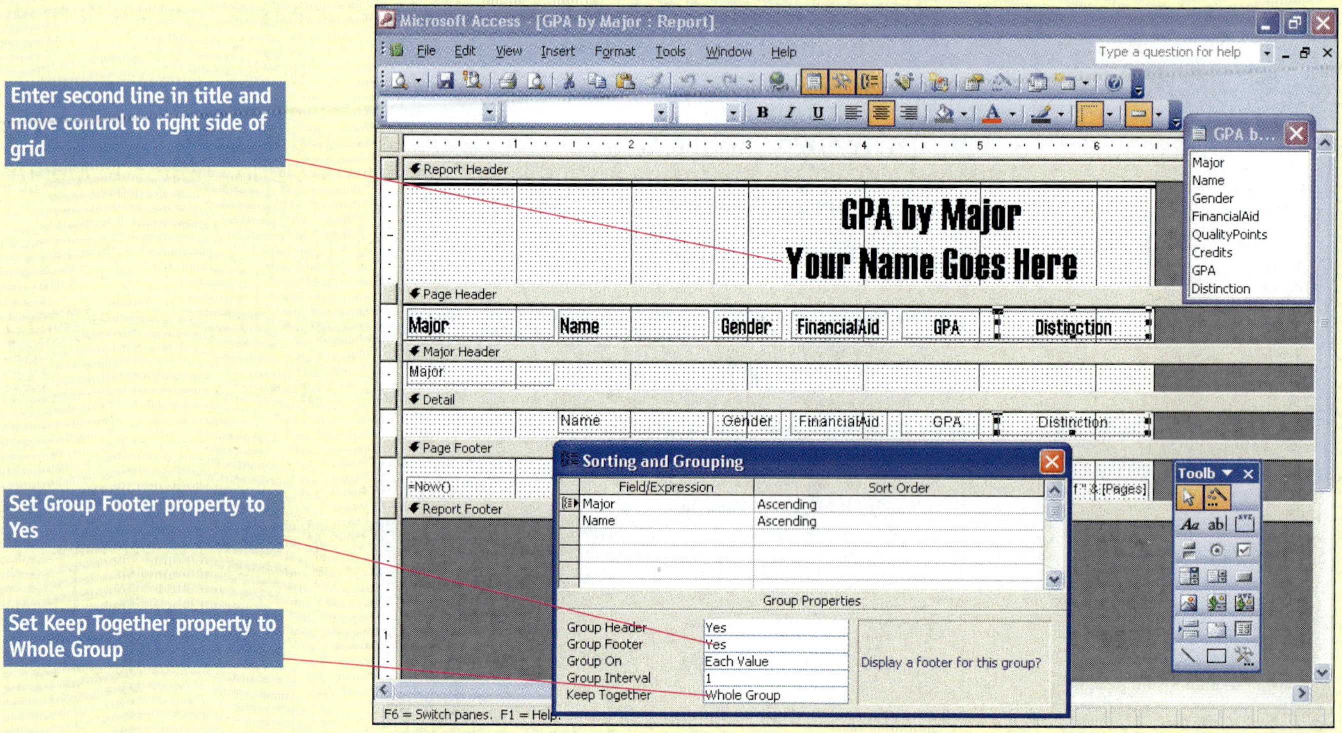

(g) Sorting and Grouping (step 7)

FIGURE 3.11 Hands-on Exercise 3 (*continued*)

SELECTING MULTIPLE CONTROLS

Select (click) a column heading in the Page Header, then press and hold the Shift key as you select the corresponding bound control in the Detail section. This selects both the column heading and the bound control and enables you to move and size the objects in conjunction with one another. Continue to work with both objects selected as you apply formatting through various buttons on the Formatting toolbar, or change properties through the property sheet. Click anywhere on the report to deselect the objects when you are finished.

Step 8: Create the Group and Report Footers

- Click the **Text Box button** on the Toolbox toolbar. The mouse pointer changes to a tiny crosshair with a text box attached.
- Click and drag in the Group Footer where you want the text box (which will contain the average GPA) to go. Release the mouse.
- You will see an Unbound control and an attached label containing a field number (e.g., Text 18).
- Click in the **text box** control (Unbound will disappear). Enter **=Avg(GPA)** to calculate the average of the GPA for all students in this group as shown in Figure 3.11h.
- Click in the attached unbound control, click and drag to select the text (Text 18), then type **Average GPA for Major** as the label for this control. Size, move, and align the label as shown in the figure.
- Point to the **Average GPA control**, click the **right mouse button** to display a shortcut menu, then click **Properties** to display the Properties dialog box.
- Click the **Format tab**. Change the format to **Fixed** and the number of decimal places to **2**. Close the Properties sheet.
- Click and drag the bottom of the Report Footer down to create space for the Report Footer. Press and hold the **Shift key** as you select the label and associated control in the Major (Group) footer. Click the **Copy Button**.
- Click in the Report Footer, then click the **Paste button** to copy the controls to the report footer. Click and drag both controls to align them under the corresponding controls in the Major footer.
- Change the text of the label in the Report Footer to reflect **all students** as shown in Figure 3.11h. Move and size the label as necessary. Save the report.

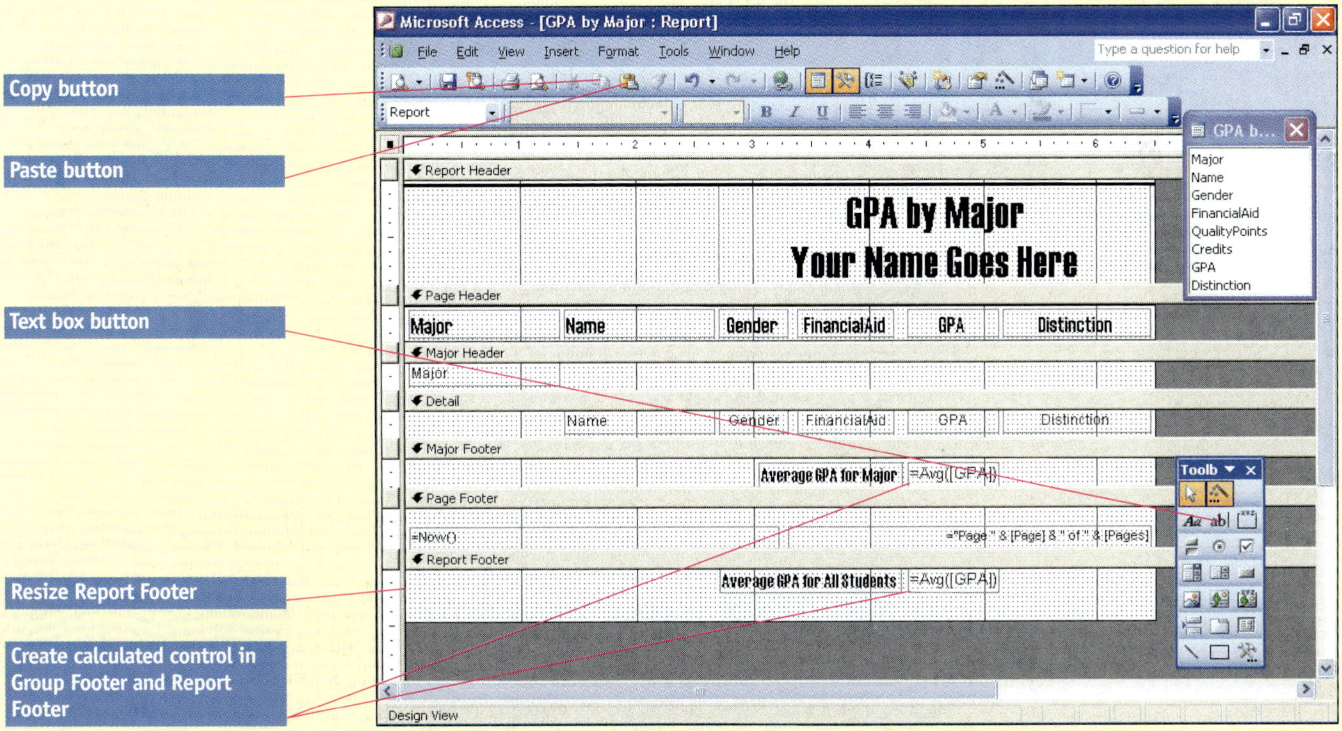

(h) Create the Group and Report Footers (step 8)

FIGURE 3.11 Hands-on Exercise 3 (*continued*)

Step 9: The Finishing Touches

- Click in the Report Header. Pull down the **Insert menu** and click the **Picture command** to display the Insert Picture dialog box. Change to the **Exploring Access folder**. Select the **Academic Symbols picture**, then click **OK**.
- **Right click** the picture to display a context-sensitive menu, then click **Properties** to display the Properties Dialog box. Click the **Size Mode property**, click the **down arrow**, and click **Stretch**. Close the Properties sheet.
- Click and drag to size the picture. Resize the Report Header as appropriate.
- Select the **GPA control** in the Detail section. Pull down the **Format menu** and click the **Conditional Formatting command** to display the associated dialog box.
- Enter the first condition as shown in Figure 3.11i. Click the **down arrow** on the font color button and click **blue**.
- Click the **Add button**, then enter the second condition, this time selecting a font color of **red**. Click **OK** to accept both conditions and close the dialog box.

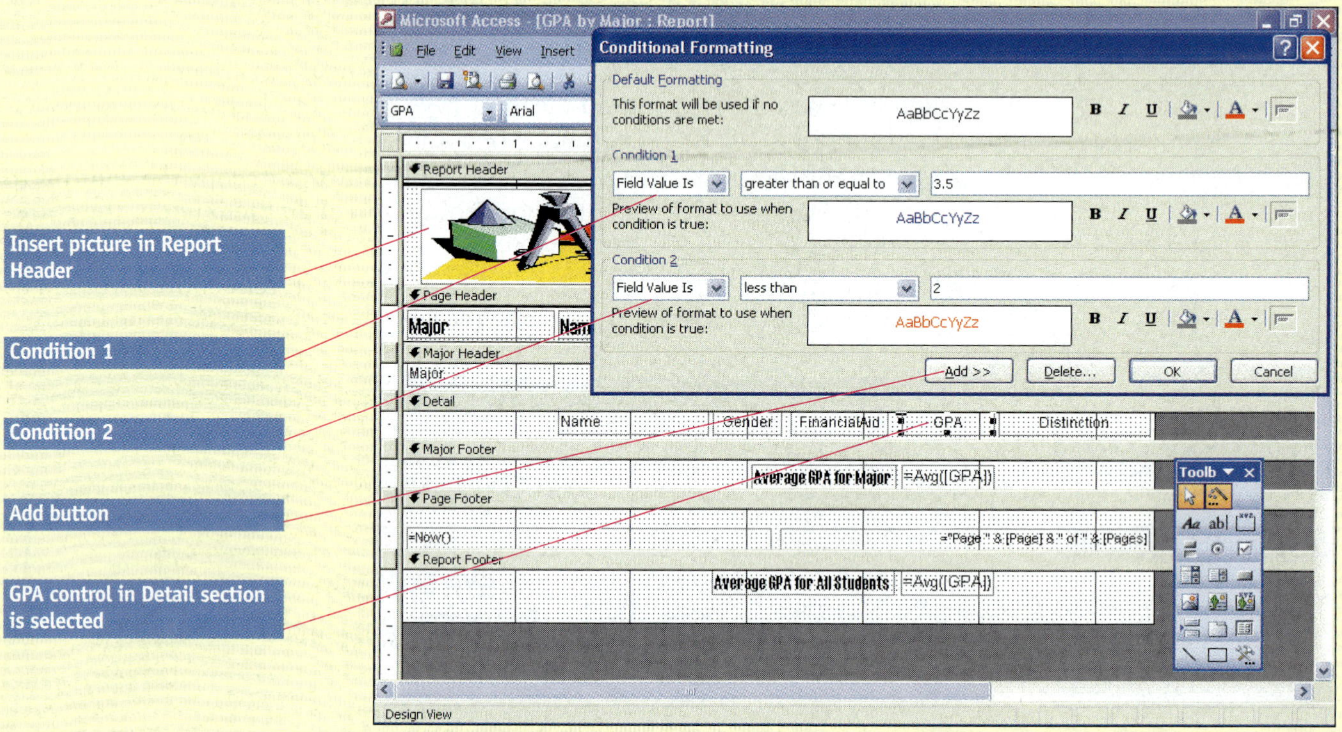

(i) The Finishing Touches (step 9)

FIGURE 3.11 Hands-on Exercise 3 (*continued*)

MISSING TASK PANE

The Insert Picture command functions differently in Access than in the other Office applications because it does not display the Clip Art task pane. You can still search for clip art explicitly, however, by starting the Clip Organizer as a separate application. Click the Start button, click the All Programs button, click Microsoft Office, click Microsoft Office Tools, then start the Microsoft Clip Organizer. Select a clip art image from within the Clip Organizer, and click the Copy button. Use the Windows taskbar to return to Access, open the form or report in Design view, and click the Paste button.

Step 10: The Completed Report

- Click the **Print Preview button** to view the completed report as shown in Figure 3.11j. The status bar shows you are on Page 1 of the report.
- Click the **Zoom button** to see the entire page. Click the **Zoom button** a second time to return to the higher magnification, which lets you read the report.
- Be sure that you are satisfied with the appearance of the report and that all controls align properly with their associated labels. If necessary, return to the Design view to modify the report.
- Pull down the **File menu** and click **Print** (or click the **Print button**) to display the Print dialog box. The **All option button** is already selected under Print Range. Click **OK** to print the report.
- Pull down the **File menu** and click **Close** to close the GPA by Major report. Click **Yes** if asked to save design changes to the report.
- Close the **Our Students database**. Exit Access if you do not want to continue with the next exercise at this time.

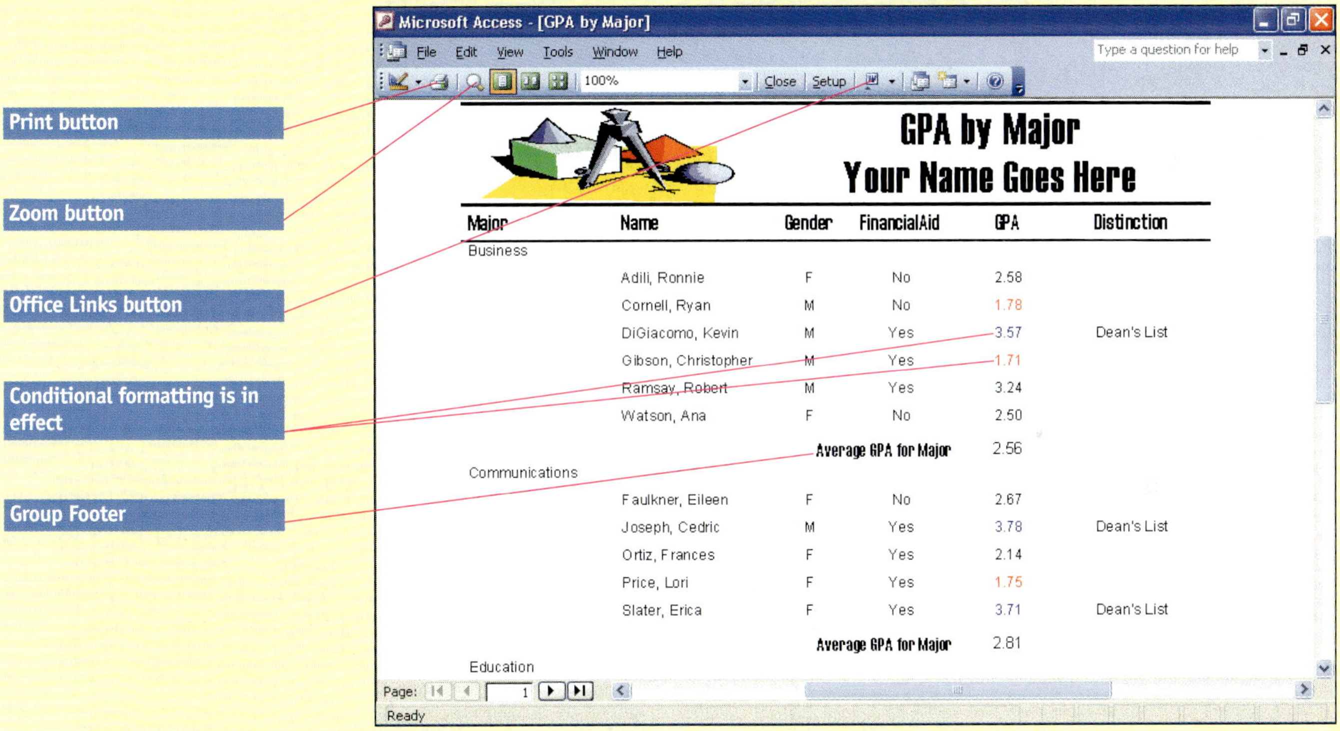

(j) The Completed Report (step 10)

FIGURE 3.11 Hands-on Exercise 3 (*continued*)

THE PRINT PREVIEW TOOLBAR

The Print Preview toolbar has several useful tools to preview a report. Click the One page, Two pages, or Multiple pages buttons, to see the indicated number of pages, and/or use the Zoom button to toggle between different magnifications. And finally, you can use the Office Links button to convert the report to a Word document or Excel workbook.

CROSSTAB QUERIES

A ***crosstab query*** consolidates data from an Access table and presents the information in a row and column format (similar to a pivot table in Excel). Figure 3.12 shows a crosstab query that displays the average GPA for all students by major and gender. A crosstab query aggregates (sums, counts, or averages) the values of one field (e.g., GPA), then groups the results according to the values of another field listed down the left side of the table (major), and a set of values listed across the top of the table (gender).

A crosstab query can be created in the Query Design view, but it is easier to use the Crosstab Query Wizard, as you will see in the next hands-on exercise. The wizard allows you to choose the table (or query) on which the crosstab query is based, then prompts you for the fields to be used for the row and column values (major and gender in our example). You then select the field that will be summarized (GPA), and choose the desired calculation (average). It's easy and you get a chance to practice in the hands-on exercise that follows shortly.

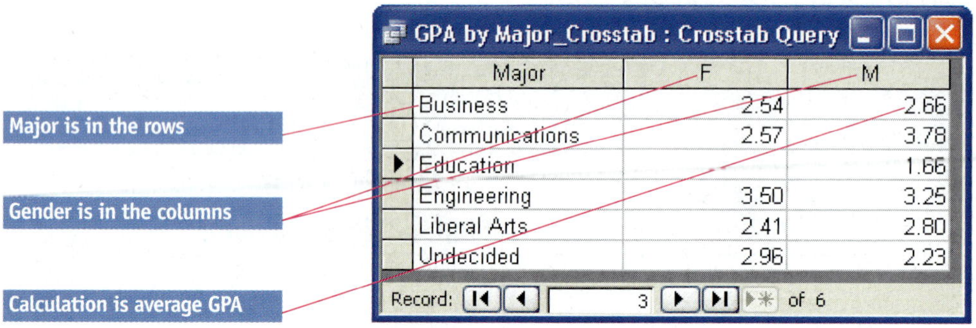

FIGURE 3.12 Crosstab Query

ACTION QUERIES

Queries are generally used to extract information from a database. A special type of query, however, known as an ***action query***, enables you to update the database by changing multiple records in a single operation. There are four types of action queries: update, append, delete, and make-table.

An ***update query*** changes multiple records within a table. You could, for example, create an update query to raise the salary of every employee by 10 percent. You can also use criteria in the update query; for example, you can increase the salaries of only those employees with a specified performance rating.

An ***append query*** adds records from one table to the end of another table. It could be used in the context of the student database to add transfer students to the Students table, given that the transfer records were stored originally in a separate table. An append query can include criteria, so that it adds only selected records from the other table, such as those students with a designated GPA.

A ***delete query*** deletes one or more records from a table according to designated criteria. You could, for example, use a delete query to remove employees who are no longer working for a company, students who have graduated, or products that are no longer kept in inventory.

A ***make-table query*** creates a new table from records in an existing table. This type of query is especially useful prior to running a delete query in that you can back up (archive) the records you are about to delete. Thus, you could use a make-table query to create a table containing those students who are about to graduate (e.g., those with 120 credits or more), then run a delete query to remove the graduates from the Students table. You're ready for another hands-on exercise.

hands-on exercise

4 Crosstab and Action Queries

Objective To use action queries to modify a database; to create a crosstab query to display summarized values from a table. Use Figure 3.13 as a guide in completing the exercise.

Step 1: Create the Make-Table Query

- Start Access and open the **Our Students database**. Click **Open** in response to the security warning. Click the **Queries button** in the Database window, then double click **Create query in Design view**.
- The Show Table dialog box appears automatically with the Tables tab already selected. If necessary, select the **Students table**, then click the **Add button** to add the table to the query as shown in Figure 3.13a. Close the Show Table dialog box. Maximize the query window, then resize the top portion of the window as well as the field list.
- Click the **SSN** (the first field) in the Students table. Press and hold the **Shift key**, then scroll (if necessary) until you can click **Major** (the last field) in the table. Click and drag the selected fields (i.e., every field in the table) from the field list to the design grid in Figure 3.13a.
- Scroll in the design grid until you can see the Credits field. Click in the **Criteria row** for the Credits field and enter **>=120**.
- Click the **drop-down arrow** next to the **Query Type button** on the toolbar and select (click) the **Make-Table query** as shown in Figure 3.13a. Enter **Graduating Seniors** as the name of the table you will create.
- Verify that the option button for Current Database is selected, then click **OK**.

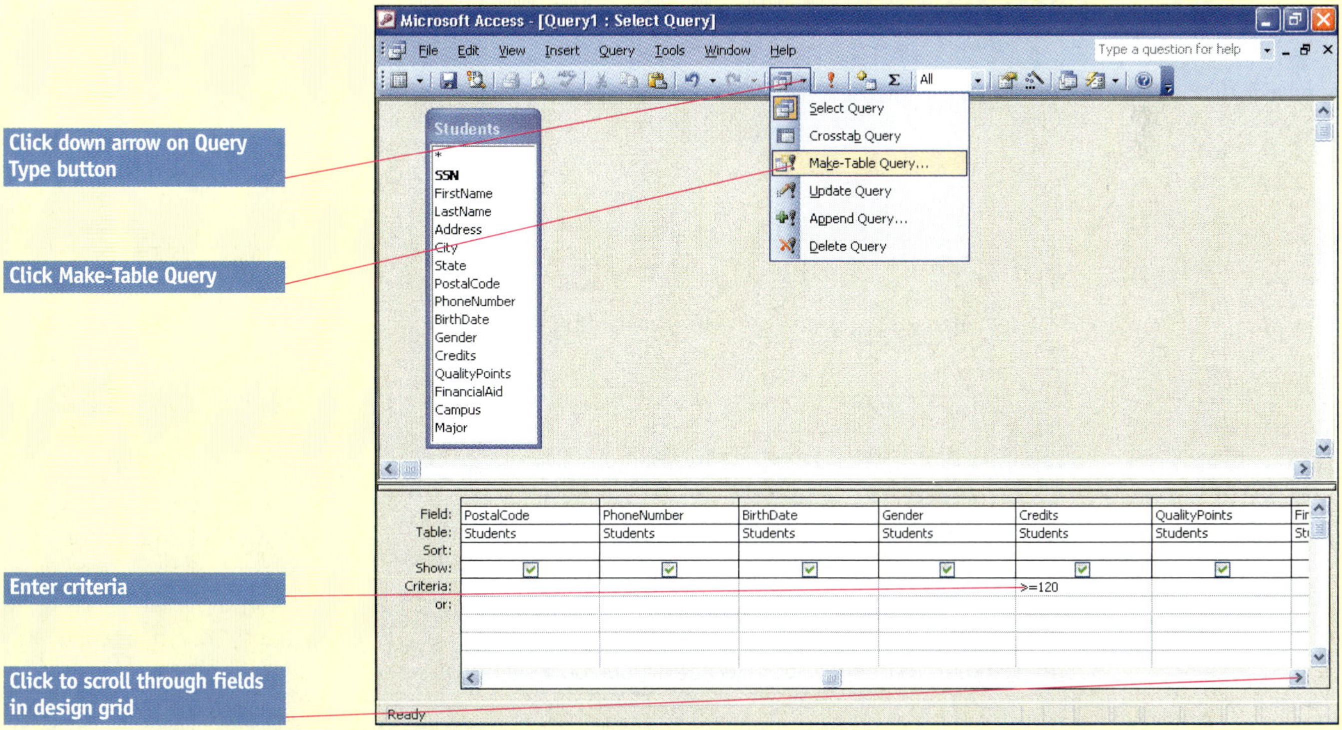

(a) Create the Make-Table Query (step 1)

FIGURE 3.13 Hands-on Exercise 4

Step 2: Run the Make-Table Query

- Click the **Run button** to run the Make-Table query. Click **Yes** in response to the message in Figure 3.13b indicating that you are about to paste one record (for the graduating seniors) into a new table.
- Do not be concerned if you do not see the Graduating Seniors table at this time; unlike a select query, you remain in the Design view after executing the Make-Table query.
- Close the Make-Table query. Save the query as **Archive Graduating Seniors**.
- Click the **Tables button** in the Database window, then open the **Graduating Seniors table** you just created. The table should contain one record (for Kim Zimmerman) with 120 or more credits.
- Close the table.

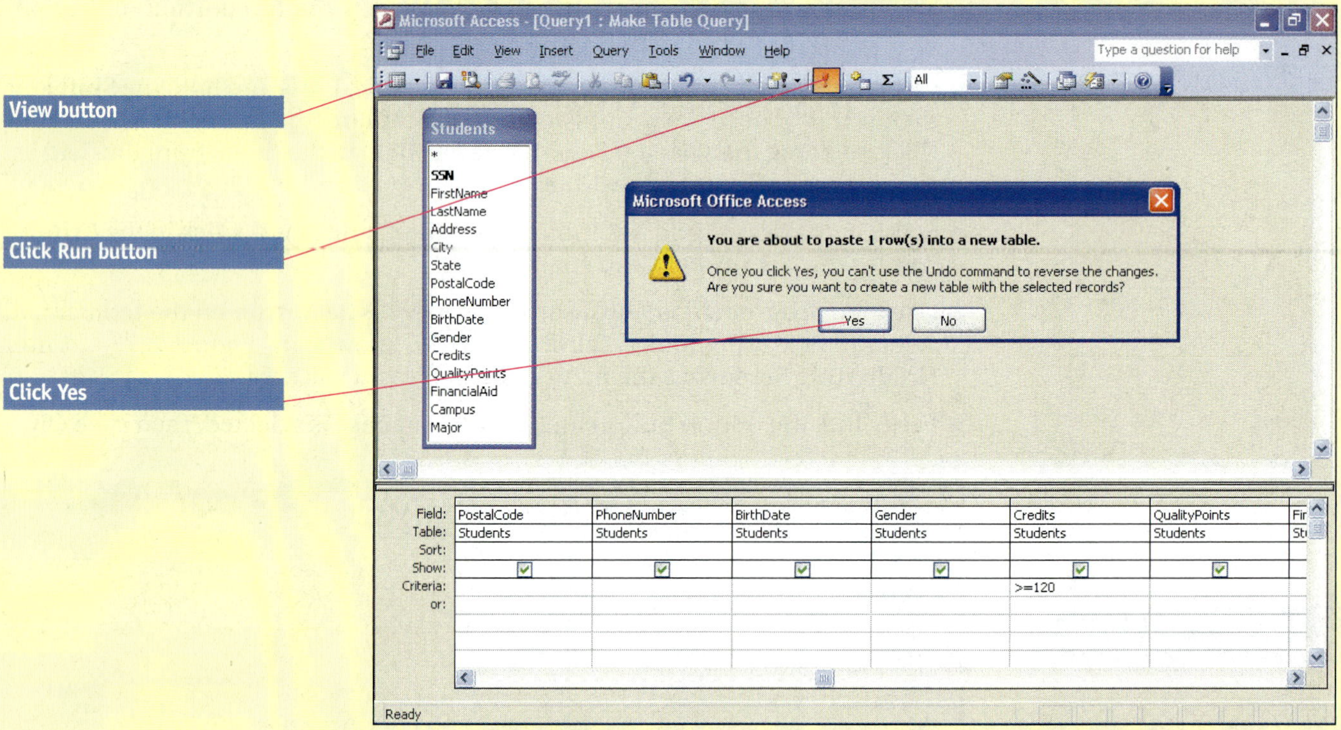

(b) Run the Make-Table Query (step 2)

FIGURE 3.13 Hands-on Exercise 4 (*continued*)

LOOK BEFORE YOU LEAP

The result of an action query is irreversible; that is, once you click Yes in the dialog box displayed by the query, you cannot undo the action. You can, however, preview the result before creating the query by clicking the View button at the left of the Query Design toolbar. Click the button and you see the results of the query displayed in a dynaset, then click the View button a second time to return to the Design view. Click the Run Query button to execute the query, but now you can click Yes with confidence since you have seen the result.

Step 3: Create the Delete Query

- Click the **Queries button** in the Database window, then click the **Archive Graduating Seniors query** to select the query.
- Pull down the **Edit menu** and click **Copy** to copy the query to the clipboard. (You can also click the Copy button on the Database toolbar.)
- Pull down the **Edit menu** a second time, then click the **Paste command** to display the Paste As dialog box in Figure 3.13c. (You can also click the Paste button on the Database toolbar.)
- Type **Purge Graduating Seniors** as the name of the query, then click **OK**.
- The Database window contains the original query (Archive Graduating Seniors) as well as the copied version (Purge Graduating Seniors) that you just created.

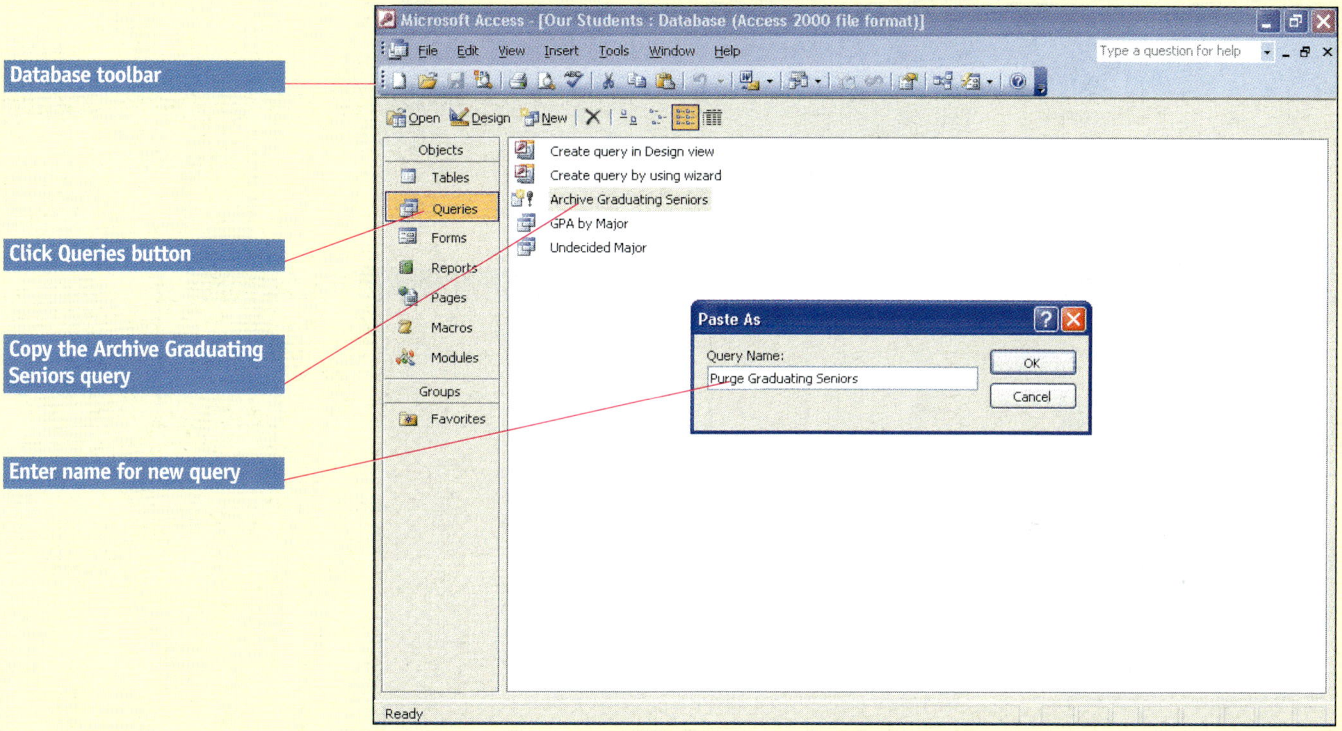

(c) Create the Delete Query (step 3)

FIGURE 3.13 Hands-on Exercise 4 (*continued*)

COPY, RENAME, OR DELETE AN ACCESS OBJECT

Use the Copy and Paste commands in the Database window to copy any object in an Access database. To copy an object, select the object, pull down the Edit menu, and click Copy (or use the Ctrl+C keyboard shortcut). Pull down the Edit menu a second time and select the Paste command (or use the Ctrl+V shortcut), then enter a name for the copied object. To delete or rename an object, point to the object, then click the right mouse button to display a shortcut menu and select the desired operation.

Step 4: Complete and Run the Delete Query

- Open the newly created query in the Design view. Maximize the window. Click the **drop-down arrow** next to the **Query Type button** on the toolbar and select (click) the **Delete Query**.
- Click and drag the box on the horizontal scroll bar until you can see the **Credits field** as shown in Figure 3.13d. The criterion, >= 120, is already entered because the Delete query was copied originally from the Make-Table query, and the criteria are identical.
- Click the **Run button** to execute the query. Click **Yes** when warned that you are about to delete one record from the specified table. Once again, you remain in the Design view after the query has been executed.
- Close the Query window. Click **Yes** if asked to save the changes.
- Open the **Students table**. The record for Kim Zimmerman is no longer there.
- Close the Students table.

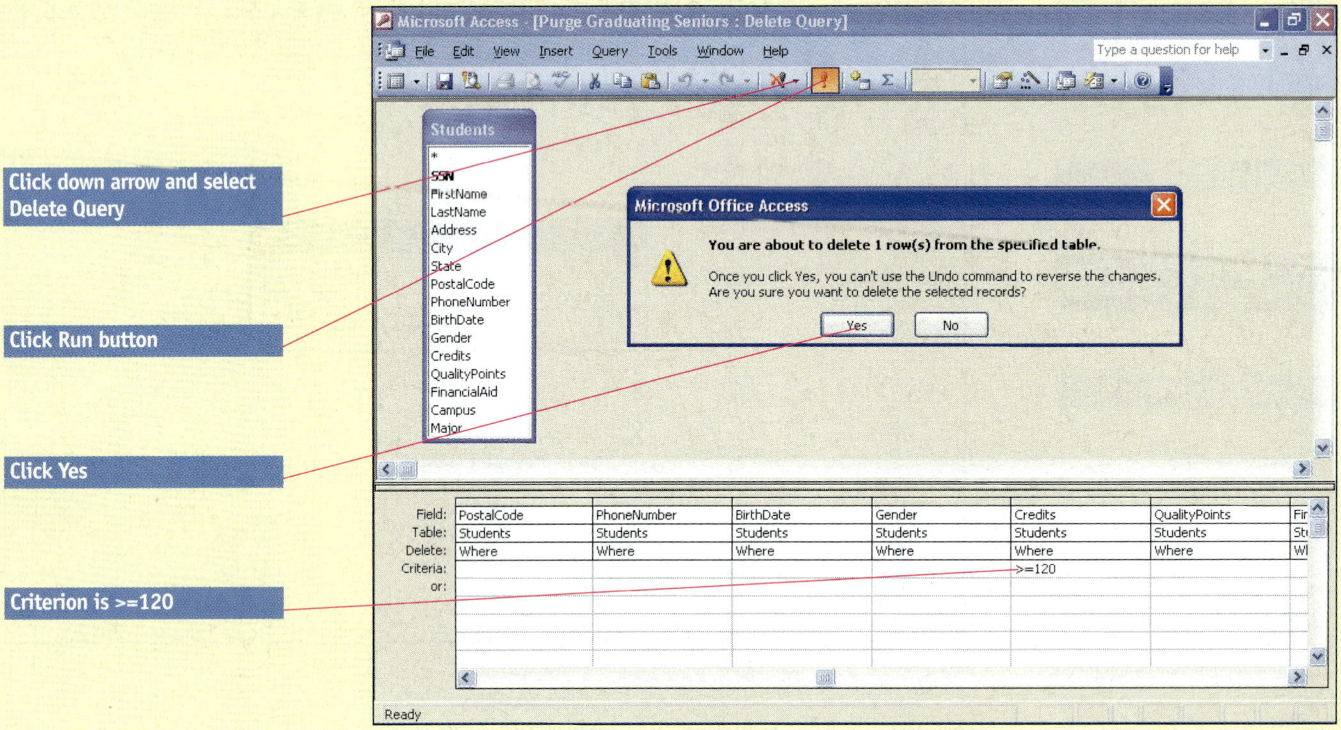

(d) Complete and Run the Delete Query (step 4)

FIGURE 3.13 Hands-on Exercise 4 (*continued*)

PLAN FOR THE UNEXPECTED

Deleting records is cause for concern in that once the records are removed from a table, they cannot be restored. This may not be a problem, but it is comforting to have some means of recovery. Accordingly, we always execute a Make-Table query, with the identical criteria as in the Delete query, prior to running the latter. The deleted records from the original table can be restored through an Append query should it be necessary.

Step 5: Create the Append Query

- Click the **Queries button**, then double click **Create query in Design view**. The Show Tables dialog box opens and contains the following tables:
  - The Students table that you have used throughout the chapter.
  - The Graduating Seniors table that you just created.
  - The Transfer Students table that will be appended to the Students table.
- Select the **Transfer Students table**, then click the **Add button** to add this table to the query. Close the Show Table dialog box. Maximize the window. Click and drag the **asterisk** from the field list to the **Field row** in the query design grid.
- Click the **drop-down arrow** next to the **Query Type button** on the toolbar and select (click) **Append Query** to display the Append dialog box. Click the **drop-down arrow** on the Append to Table Name list box and select the **Students table** as shown in Figure 3.13e. Click **OK**.
- Click the **Run button**. Click **Yes** when warned that you are about to add 4 rows (from the Transfer Students table) to the Students table.
- Save the query as **Append Transfer Students**. Close the query window.
- Open the **Students table**. Four records have been added (Liquer, Thomas, Rudolph, Milgrom). Close the table.

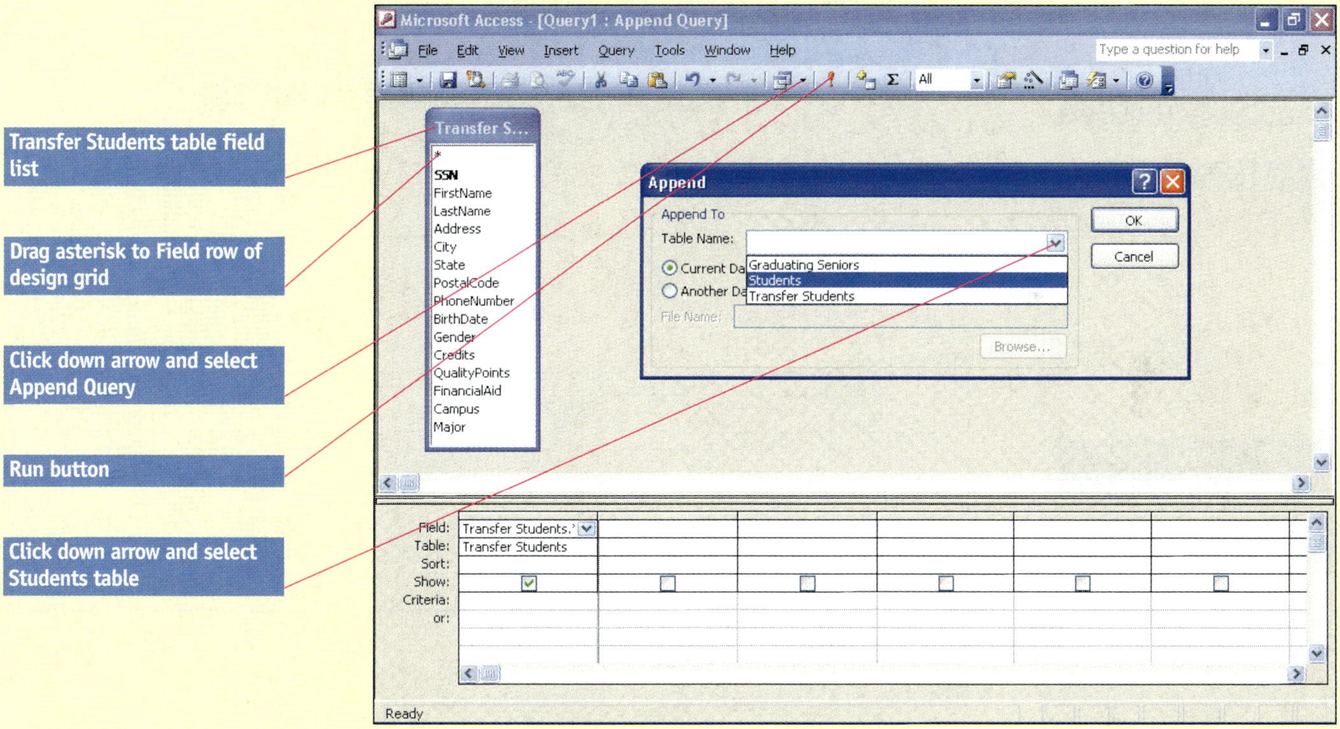

(e) Create the Append Query (step 5)

FIGURE 3.13 Hands-on Exercise 4 (*continued*)

THE ASTERISK VERSUS INDIVIDUAL FIELDS

Click and drag the asterisk in the field list to the design grid to add every field in the underlying table to the query. The advantage to this approach is that it is quicker than selecting the fields individually. The disadvantage is that you cannot sort or specify criteria for individual fields.

Step 6: Create an Update Query

- Click the **Queries button** in the Database window. Select (click) the **GPA by Major query**, press **Ctrl+C** to copy the query, then press **Ctrl+V** to display the Paste As dialog box. Enter **Update Financial Aid**. Click **OK**.
- Open the newly created query in the Design view as shown in Figure 3.13f. Click the **drop-down arrow** next to the **Query Type button** on the toolbar and select (click) **Update Query**. The design grid changes to include an Update To row, and the Sort row disappears.
- Click in the **Criteria row** for the **GPA field** and enter **>=3**. Click in the **Update To row** for the **FinancialAid field** and enter **Yes**. The combination of these entries will change the value of the Financial Aid field to "yes" for all students with a GPA of 3.00 or higher.
- Click the **Run button** to execute the query. Click **Yes** when warned that you are about to update nine records. Close the query window.
- Click **Yes** if asked whether to save the changes.

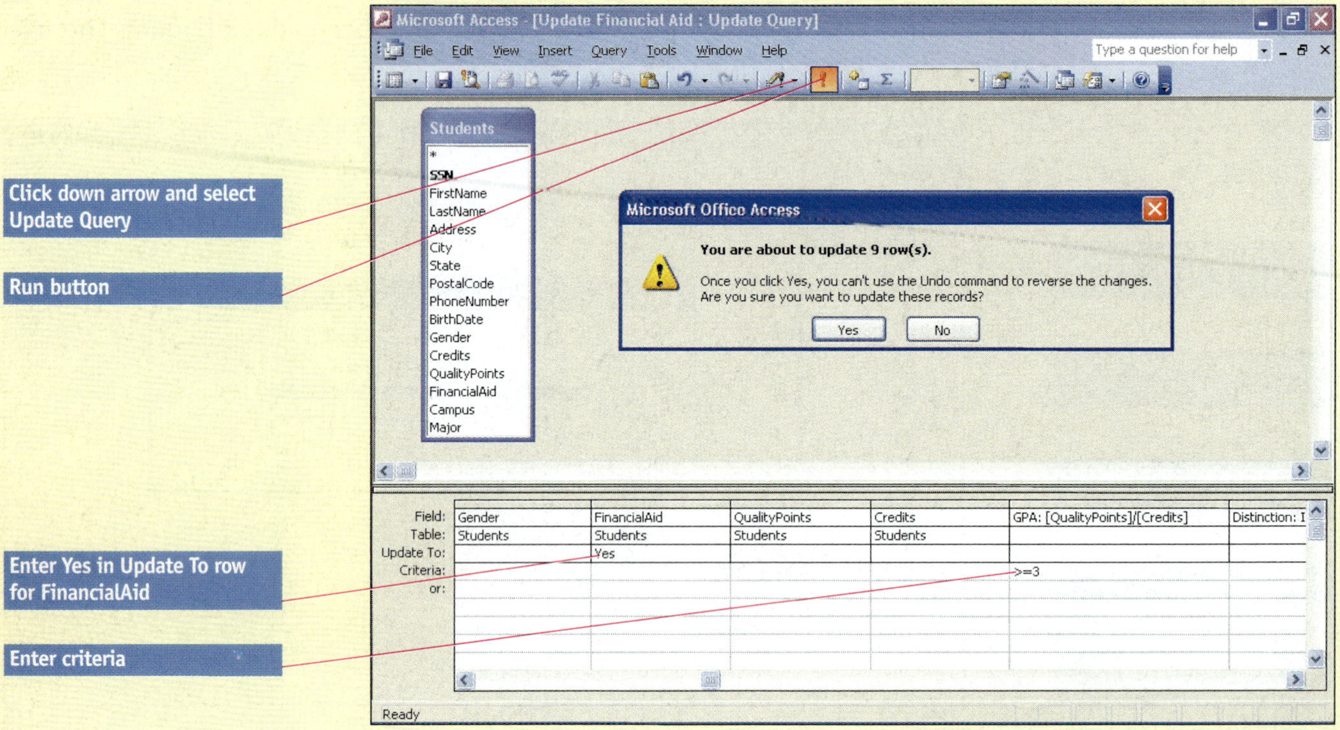

(f) Create an Update Query (step 6)

FIGURE 3.13 Hands-on Exercise 4 (*continued*)

VERIFY THE RESULTS OF THE UPDATE QUERY

You have run the Update Query, but are you sure it worked correctly? Press the F11 key to return to the Database window, click the Queries button, and rerun the GPA by Major query that was created earlier. Click in the GPA field for the first student, then click the Sort Descending button to display the students in descending order by GPA. Every student with a GPA of 3.00 or higher should be receiving financial aid.

Step 7: Check Results of the Action Queries

- Click the **Tables button** in the Database window. Open (double click) the **Students, Graduating Seniors**, and **Transfer Students tables** one after another. You have to return to the Database window each time you open a table.
- Pull down the **Window menu** and click the **Tile Vertically command** to display the tables as shown in Figure 3.13g. The arrangement of your tables may be different from ours.
- Check your progress by comparing the tables to one another:
  - Check the first record in the Transfer Students table, Lindsey Liquer, and note that it has been added to the Students table via the Append Transfer Students query.
  - Check the record in the Graduating Seniors table, Kim Zimmerman, and note that it has been removed from the Students table via the Purge Graduating Seniors query.
  - The Students table reflects the current student database. The other two tables function as backup.
- Close the Students, Transfer Students, and Graduating Seniors tables.

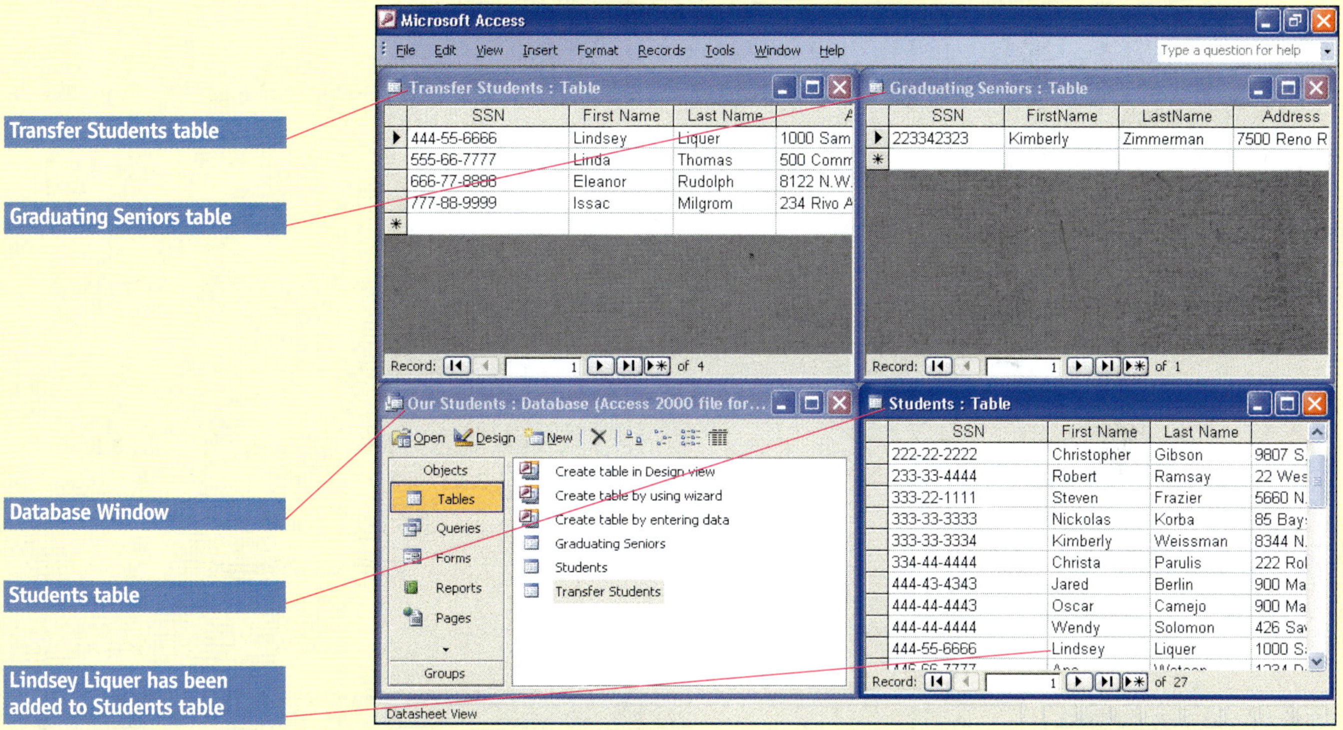

(g) Check Results of the Action Queries (step 7)

FIGURE 3.13 Hands-on Exercise 4 (*continued*)

DATABASE PROPERTIES

The buttons within the Database window display the objects within a database, but show only one type of object at a time. You can, for example, see all of the reports or all of the queries, but you cannot see the reports and queries at the same time. There is another way. Pull down the File menu, click Database Properties, then click the Contents tab to display the contents (objects) in the database.

Step 8: Create a Crosstab Query

- Click the **Queries button** in the Database window, click **New**, click the **Crosstab Query Wizard** in the New Query dialog box, and click **OK** to start the wizard.
- Click the **Queries option button** and select the **GPA by Major query**. Click **Next** to continue.
  - ❑ Click **Major** in the Available Fields list, then click > to place it in the Selected Fields list. Click **Next**.
  - ❑ Click **Gender** as the field for column headings. Click **Next**.
  - ❑ Click **GPA** as the field to calculate and select the **Avg function** as shown in Figure 3.13h. Clear the check box to include row sums. Click **Next**.
  - ❑ The name of the query is suggested for you, as is the option button to view the query. Click **Finish**.
- The results of the crosstab query are shown. The query lists the average GPA for each combination of major and gender. The display is awkward, however, in that the GPA is calculated to an unnecessary number of decimal places.
- Click the **View button** to display the Design view for this query. Right click in the **GPA column** to display a context-sensitive menu, click **Properties** to display the Field Properties dialog box, click in the **Format row**, and select **Fixed**. Set the number of decimals to **two**.
- Click the **Run button** to re-execute the query. This time the GPA is displayed to two decimal places. Save the query. Close the Query window.
- Close the Our Students database.
- Exit Access.

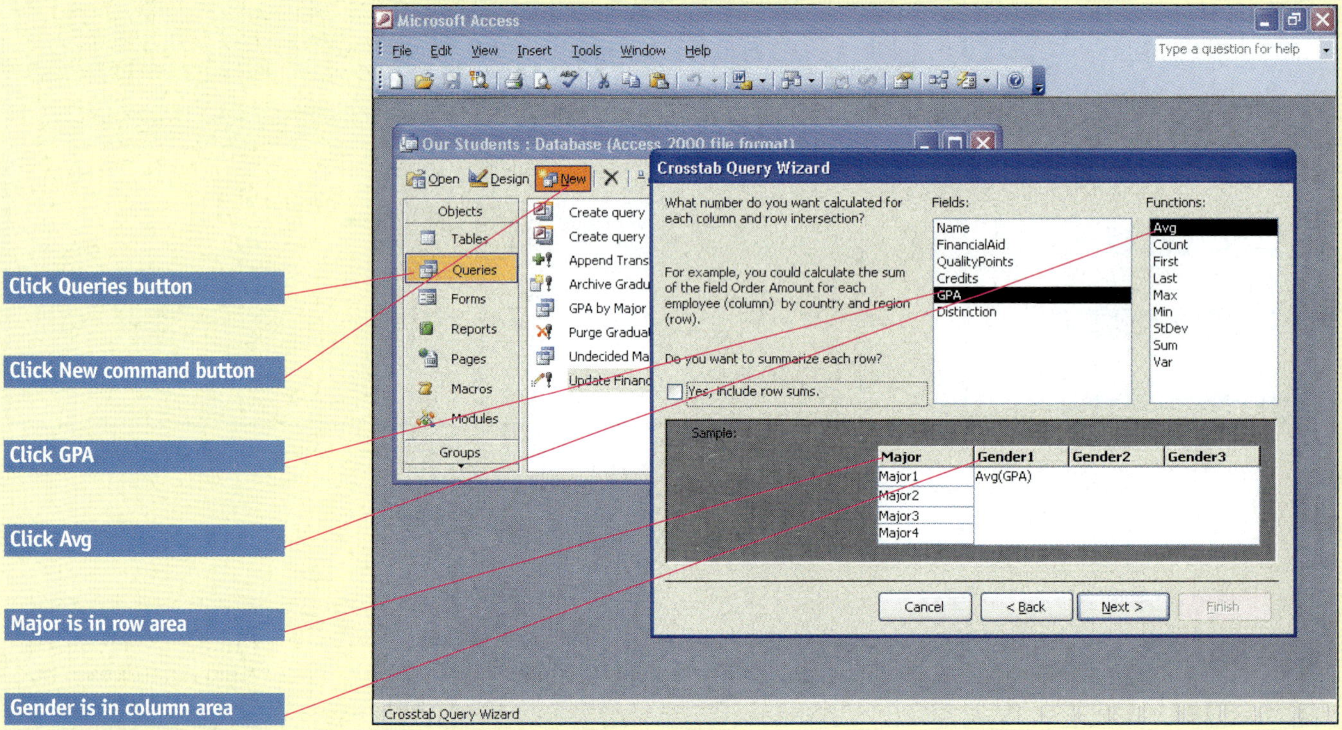

(h) Create a Crosstab Query (step 8)

FIGURE 3.13 Hands-on Exercise 4 (*continued*)

SUMMARY

Data and information are not synonymous although the terms are often interchanged. Data is the raw material and consists of the table (or tables) that comprise a database. Information is the finished product. Data is converted to information by selecting records, performing calculations on those records, and/or changing the sequence in which the records are displayed. Decisions in an organization are based on information rather than raw data.

A report is a printed document that displays information from the database. Reports are created through the Report Wizard, then modified as necessary in the Design view. A report is divided into sections. The Report Header (Footer) occurs at the beginning (end) of the report. The Page Header (Footer) appears at the top (bottom) of each page. The Detail section is found in the main body of the report and is printed once for each record in the report.

Each section is composed of objects known as controls. A bound control has a data source such as a field in the underlying table. An unbound control has no data source. A calculated control contains an expression. Controls are selected, moved, and sized the same way as any other Windows object.

Every report is based on either a table or a query. A report based on a table contains every record in that table. A report based on a query contains only the records satisfying the criteria in the query.

A query enables you to select records from a table (or from several tables), display the selected records in any order, and perform calculations on fields within the query. A select query is the most common type of query. It is created using the Simple Query Wizard and/or in Design view. A select query displays its output in a dynaset that can be used to update the data in the underlying table(s).

The records in a report are often grouped according to the value of a specific field within the record. A Group Header appears before each group to identify the group. A Group Footer appears at the end of each group and can be used to display the summary information about the group.

An action query modifies one or more records in a single operation. There are four types of action queries: update, append, delete, and make-table. An update query changes multiple records within a table. An append query adds records from one table to the end of another table. A delete query deletes one or more records from a table according to designated criteria. A make-table query creates a new table from records in an existing table.

A crosstab query displays aggregated information, as opposed to individual records. It can be created directly in the Query Design view, but is created more easily through the Crosstab Query Wizard.

KEY TERMS

Action query 636
AND condition 615
Append query 636
Ascending sequence 612
Avg function 624
Between function 616
Bound control 604
Calculated control 604
Columnar report 600
Concatenate 623
Conditional formatting 624
Count function 624
Criteria row 612
Crosstab query 636
Delete query 636
Descending sequence 612
Design grid 614
Detail section 602
Dynaset 612
Field row 612
Group Footer 602
Group Header 602
Immediate IF function 623
Make-table query 636
Max function 624
Min function 624
NOT function 616
OR condition 615
Page Footer 602
Page Header 602
Print Preview 635
Query 612
Query window 618
Relational operators 616
Report 600
Report Footer 602
Report Header 602
Report Wizard 600
Select query 612
Show row 612
Simple Query Wizard 612
Sort row 612
Sorting and Grouping 632
Sum function 624
Tabular report 600
Top Values property 627
Unbound control 604
Update query 636

MULTIPLE CHOICE

1. Why might a report be based on a query rather than a table?
   (a) To limit the report to selected records
   (b) To include a calculated field in the report
   (c) Both (a) and (b)
   (d) Neither (a) nor (b)

2. An Access database may contain:
   (a) One or more tables
   (b) One or more queries
   (c) One or more reports
   (d) All of the above

3. Which of the following is true regarding the names of objects within an Access database?
   (a) A form or report may have the same name as the underlying table
   (b) A form or report may have the same name as the underlying query
   (c) Both (a) and (b)
   (d) Neither (a) nor (b)

4. The dynaset created by a query may contain:
   (a) A subset of records from the associated table
   (b) A subset of fields from the associated table for every record
   (c) Both (a) and (b)
   (d) Neither (a) nor (b)

5. Which toolbar contains a button to display the properties of a selected object?
   (a) The Query Design toolbar
   (b) The Report Design toolbar
   (c) Both (a) and (b)
   (d) Neither (a) nor (b)

6. Which of the following does *not* have a Design view and a Datasheet view?
   (a) Tables
   (b) Forms
   (c) Queries
   (d) Reports

7. Which of the following is true regarding the wild card character?
   (a) A question mark stands for a single character in the same position as the question mark
   (b) An asterisk stands for any number of characters in the same position as the asterisk
   (c) Both (a) and (b)
   (d) Neither (a) nor (b)

8. Which of the following will print at the top of every page?
   (a) Report header
   (b) Group header
   (c) Both (a) and (b)
   (d) Neither (a) nor (b)

9. Which of the following must be present in every report?
   (a) A report header and a report footer
   (b) A page header and a page footer
   (c) Both (a) and (b)
   (d) Neither (a) nor (b)

10. A query, based on the Our Students database within the chapter, contains two fields from the Student table (QualityPoints and Credits) as well as a calculated field (GPA). Which of the following is true?
    (a) Changing the value of Credits or QualityPoints in the query's dynaset automatically changes these values in the underlying table
    (b) Changing the value of GPA automatically changes its value in the underlying table
    (c) Both (a) and (b)
    (d) Neither (a) nor (b)

... continued

multiple choice

11. Which of the following may be included in a report as well as in a form?

(a) Bound control
(b) Unbound control
(c) Calculated control
(d) All of the above

12. The navigation buttons ▶ and ◀ will:

(a) Move to the next or previous record in a table
(b) Move to the next or previous page in a report
(c) Both (a) and (b)
(d) Neither (a) nor (b)

13. Assume that you created a query based on an Employee table, and that the query contains fields for Location and Title. Assume further that there is a single criteria row and that New York and Manager have been entered under the Location and Title fields, respectively. The dynaset will contain:

(a) All employees in New York
(b) All managers
(c) Only the managers in New York
(d) All employees in New York and all managers

14. You have decided to modify the query from the previous question to include a second criteria row. The Location and Title fields are still in the query, but this time New York and Manager appear in *different* criteria rows. The dynaset will contain:

(a) All employees in New York
(b) All managers
(c) Only the managers in New York
(d) All employees in New York and all managers

15. Which of the following is true about a query that lists employees by city and alphabetically within city?

(a) The design grid should specify a descending sort on both city and employee name
(b) The City field should appear to the left of the employee name in the design grid
(c) Both (a) and (b)
(d) Neither (a) nor (b)

16. Which of the following is *not* an example of an action query?

(a) Delete query
(b) Append query
(c) Select query
(d) Make-table query

17. You want to create a query that will select all managers in New York earning less than $80,000, and all managers in San Francisco earning less than $60,000. How many criteria rows will you need in the Design grid?

(a) 1
(b) 2
(c) 3
(d) 4

18. Which of the following expressions will display a student's last name, a comma and a space, followed by the student's first name?

(a) LastName, FirstName
(b) "LastName, FirstName"
(c) LastName & ", " & FirstName
(d) LastName, ", " FirstName

ANSWERS

1. c	**7.** c	**13.** c
2. d	**8.** d	**14.** d
3. c	**9.** d	**15.** b
4. c	**10.** a	**16.** c
5. d	**11.** d	**17.** b
6. d	**12.** c	**18.** c

PRACTICE WITH ACCESS

1. **The Oscars:** Figure 3.14 displays the first of three reports that you are to create for the Oscars database, which was introduced in Chapter 1. Your first task is to update the database to include the additional awards (if any) since the publication of our text. Open the *Chapter 1 Practice 1* database, open the existing form, and go to the last record to see if the data is current. If not, go to the Oscars Web site (www.oscar.com) to obtain the winners in the six major categories—Best Picture, Best Director, Best Actor and Actress, and Best Supporting Actor and Actress—for any years that are not in the database. You can then create the required reports. Proceed as follows:
    a. Use the Report Wizard to create the report in Figure 3.14, which is based on the Awards Winners table. The wizard creates a basic report with four sections—the Report Header, Page Header, Detail, and Page Footer. It will ask whether you want to group the records (no) and whether to sort the records (select year, then click the Ascending button to change to a descending sort.) Choose any layout, style, and title when prompted.
    b. Exit the wizard and go to Design view. You do not have to duplicate our design exactly, but you are to use a clip art image in the Report Header. The width of your report should not exceed 6½ inches. Close the report.
    c. Go to the Database window and select the report that you just created. Press Ctrl+C to copy the report, then press Ctrl+V to display the Paste As dialog box. Enter *Best Actor and Actress* as the name of the new report.
    d. Open *Best Actor and Actress* report in Design view (which currently has the best picture and director information). Change the labels in the Report and Page Headers as necessary. Delete the Best Picture and Best Director controls from the Detail section. Pull down the View menu and click the Field List command to display the Award Winners table. Click and drag the BestActor control to its appropriate place in the Detail section, then delete the associated label. Click and drag the BestActress control in similar fashion. Move and size the controls as needed.
    e. Close the report. Return to the Database window. Copy the *Best Actor and Actress* report that you just created to a new *Best Supporting Actor and Actress* report, then modify that report accordingly. Print all three reports for your instructor.

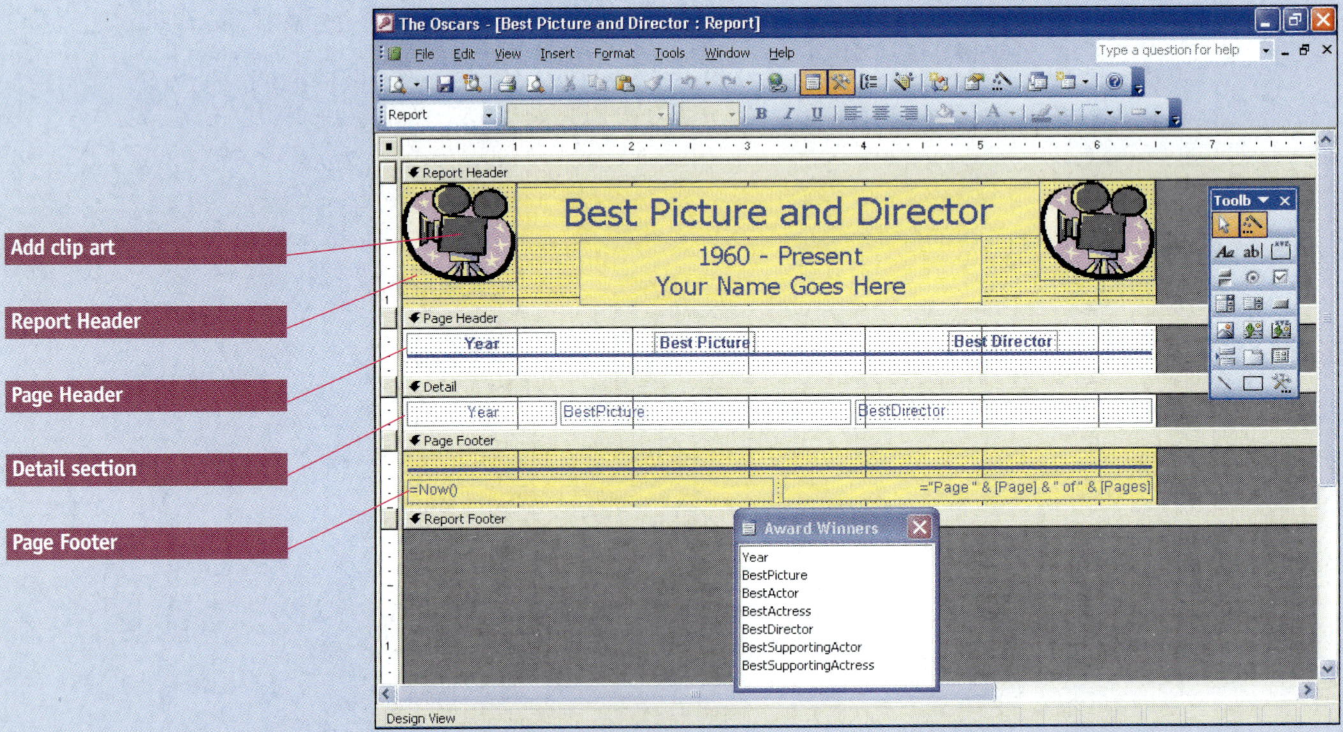

FIGURE 3.14 The Oscars (exercise 1)

2. **The United States:** The report in Figure 3.15 contains one example of every type of report section (a Report Header and Report Footer, a Page Header and Page footer, a Group header and Group footer, and a Detail section). It is based on the United States database from Chapter 1, and it computes the population and area totals for each region of the country. The report also contains a population density field that divides a state's population by its area. Open the *Chapter 1 Practice 3* database and proceed as follows:
   a. Use the Report Wizard to create the report in Figure 3.15, which is based on the Population Density query that is already in the database. The report is to be sorted by region and then sorted by the name of each state within each region. Click the Summary Options button (in the same step where you specify the sorting sequence), check the boxes to sum the Population and Area fields, and click the option button for Detail and Summary information. Check the box to adjust field width so that all fields fit on one page. Choose a stepped layout and soft gray as the style. Name the report United States by Region, click the option button to modify the report's design, then click Finish.
   b. You will see a report similar to Figure 3.15, but there is a lot of work to do. Start in the Region footer and change the contents to match Figure 3.15. You will have to delete an existing label, add new labels, increase font sizes, and move and align the various controls. You will have to further modify the footer so that it displays the average population density for each region. Click the Text Box tool, create an unbound control, then click in the control and enter the formula, =Sum([Population])/Sum([Area]). Click the button to preview the report. If you entered the formula correctly, the density for the Middle Atlantic region should be 396.54 (after you change the formatting properties of the control).
   c. Enter a similar control =Sum([Population])/Sum([Area]) in the Report Footer to compute the population density for the country as a whole.
   d. Change the formatting of the report and/or the contents of the various labels as you see fit. You do not have to match our design exactly, but be sure to add your name to the Report Header. Print the completed report for your instructor. The width of the report should not exceed 6½ inches.

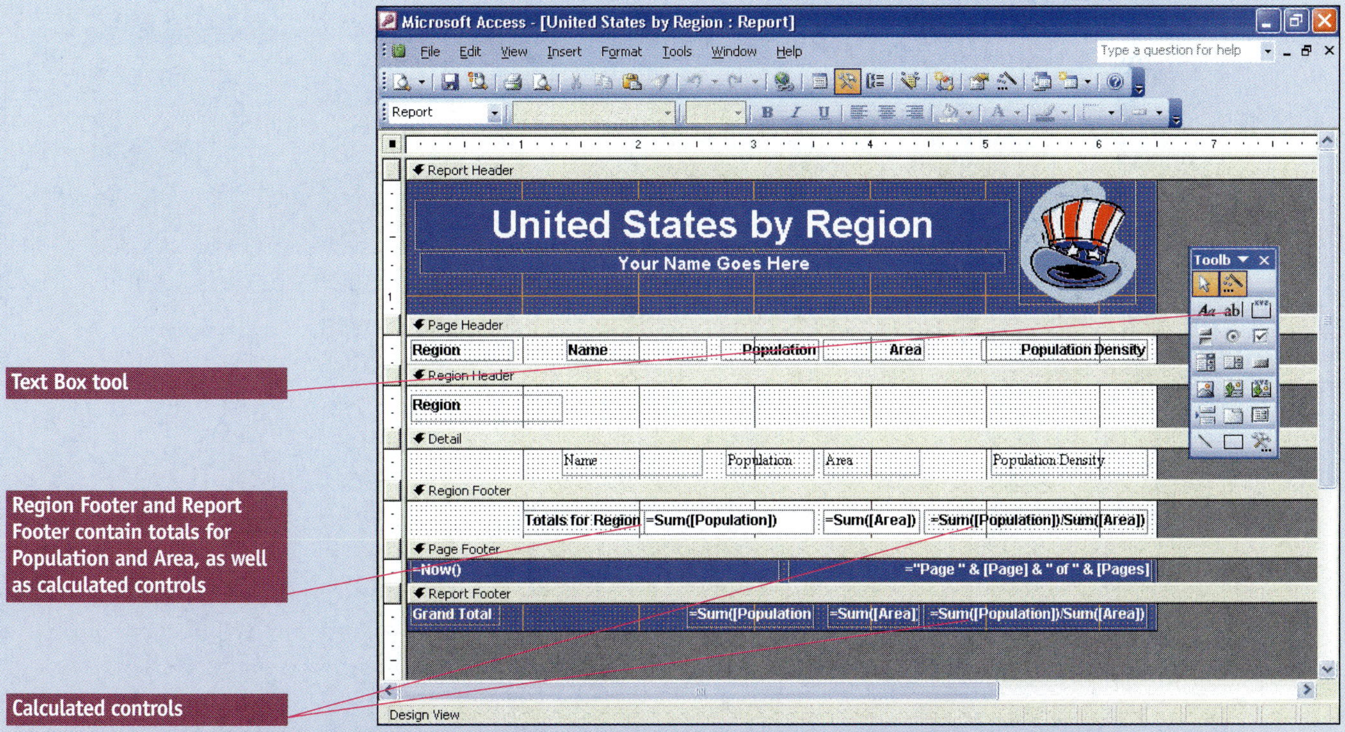

FIGURE 3.15 The United States

3. **The Super Bowl:** Figure 3.16 displays a History of the Super Bowl report that will be the basis of two subsequent reports that you will create in this exercise. Your first task is to update the database to include the additional games (if any) since the publication of our text. The database was introduced in Chapter 2 when we asked you to create a Web page for data entry. Proceed as follows:
   a. Open the *Chapter 2 Practice 3* database, open the existing table, and see if the data is current. If not, go to the Super Bowl Web site (www.superbowl.com) to obtain the results for any years that are not in the database.
   b. Go to the Database window. Click the Reports button. Modify the existing History of the Super Bowl report to include your name. Print this report.
   c. Click the Queries Button. Select the History of the Super Bowl query, press Ctrl+C to copy the query, then press Ctrl+V to display the Paste As dialog box. Enter Biggest Blowouts as the name of the query, then open the query in Design view. Change the sort sequence to display the records in descending sequence by margin of victory. Click in the Margin column, then click the down arrow on the Top Value list box and choose 5 (to list the five games with the highest margin.) Run the query to be sure it is correct.
   d. Click the Reports button. Select the History of the Super Bowl report, press Ctrl+C to copy the report, then press Ctrl+V to display the Paste As dialog box. Enter Biggest Blowouts as the name of the report. Open the report in Design view. Change the report properties so that the report is based on the Biggest Blowouts query. (Right click the Report Selector box in the upper left corner, click Properties to display the property sheet for the report as a whole, and click the All tab. Click the down arrow in the Record Source box and select the Biggest Blowouts query. Close the property sheet.) Change the report title to The Super Bowl's Biggest Blowouts. Print this report for your instructor.
   e. Repeat the process in steps (c) and (d) to create a query and associated report that shows the games in which your favorite team participated. Print this report. Add a cover sheet, then submit all three reports (History of the Super Bowl, Biggest Blowouts, and My Favorite Team) to your instructor.

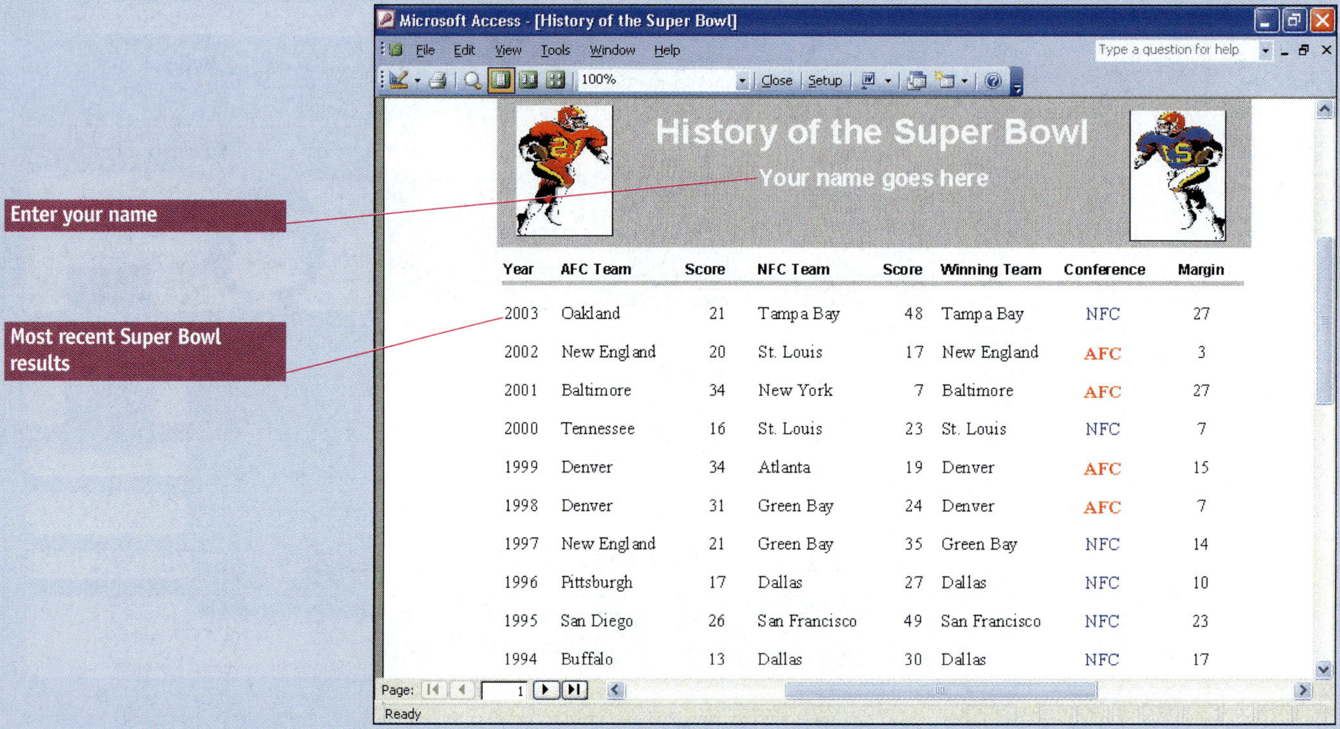

FIGURE 3.16 The Super Bowl (exercise 3)

4. **The Shopping Mall:** The partially completed *Chapter 3 Practice 4* database contains our version of the Shopping Mall database from Chapter 2. You will find a Stores table with 10 to 15 records, a form to enter data, and a form that describes the Shopping Mall database. Your assignment is to create the various reports that are described below. Each of the reports is based on an underlying query that contains a calculated control, selection criteria, and/or a sorting sequence. You should create the query first, display the associated dynaset to be sure the information is correct, then proceed to create the report. Use the Report Wizard to create the initial report, then modify the result in Design view. Proceed as follows:
   a. Create the report in Figure 3.17 that lists all stores with a monthly rental greater than $5,000. The stores are to be listed in descending order of the monthly rent. Your report should contain all of the fields that appear in our report, but you need not match the design.
   b. Create a report that shows all stores whose leases end in 2005. The stores are to be listed in chronological order by the ending date, with the earliest date shown first. Use the same design for your report as in Figure 3.17 and include all of the following fields: StoreID, StoreName, StoreType, LeaseStartDate, and LeaseEndDate.
   c. Create a report that displays all clothing stores in alphabetical order. Include the store revenue, monthly rent, manager's name, and phone number.
   d. Create a report listing those stores for which no manager has been assigned. List the stores in alphabetical order by the name of the store. The report should include the StoreID, the name of the store, whether or not it is a franchise, and the lease start and end dates.
   e. Print each of the reports and turn them in to your instructor. You may need to change the page orientation and/or margins to ensure that each report fits on one page. Add a cover sheet to complete the assignment.

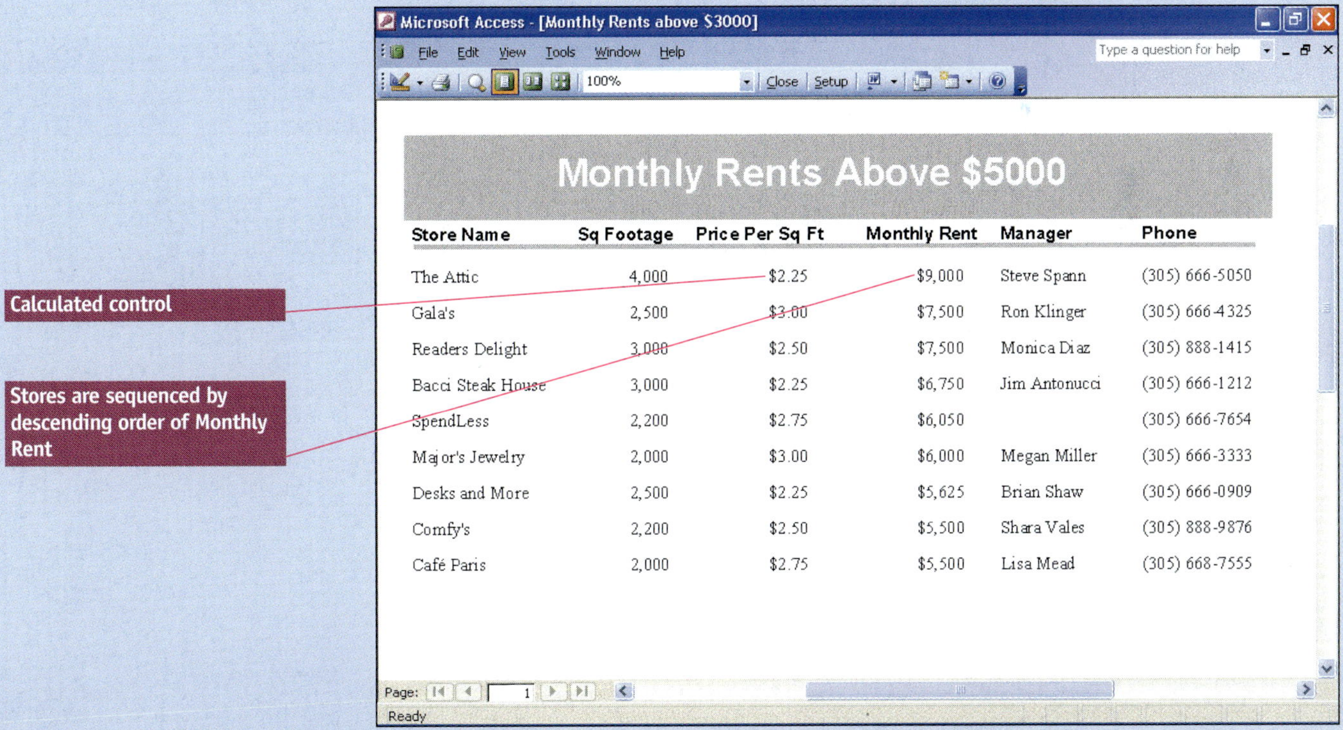

FIGURE 3.17 The Shopping Mall (exercise 4)

5. **Best Realty:** The partially completed *Chapter 3 Practice 5* database contains our version of the Best Realty database from Chapter 2. You will find a Property table with 10 to 15 records, a form to enter data, and a form that describes the Best Realty database. Your assignment is to create the various reports that are described below:
   a. The report in Figure 3.18 that shows all properties that have been sold to date. The report is based on a query that contains two calculated fields: the price per square foot (based on the selling price, as opposed to the asking price) and the number of days that the property was on the market. Your report should contain all of the fields that appear in our report, but you need not match the design.
   b. A report listing properties with an asking price of more than $250,000. The properties are to be listed from most expensive to least expensive. Include the Asking Price, PropertyID, Address, Agent's Last Name, Property Type, and Date Listed. This report should contain only properties that are available (i.e., properties that have not been sold).
   c. A report listing the available properties that are on the water. List the properties in alphabetical order by the owner's last name. Include in the report the owner's last name, the address, the asking price, the number of bedrooms and bathrooms, and whether or not the property has a pool.
   d. A report listing the available properties that have more than 3 bedrooms. List the properties in order from the one with the most to fewest bedrooms. The report should include the number of bedrooms, the agent's last name, the address, the property type, the garage information, and the date listed.
   e. Choose a different format for each report to experiment with the different designs that are available. You may need to change the page orientation and/or margins to ensure that each report fits on one page.
   f. Print each of the reports and turn them in to your instructor. Add a cover sheet to complete the assignment.

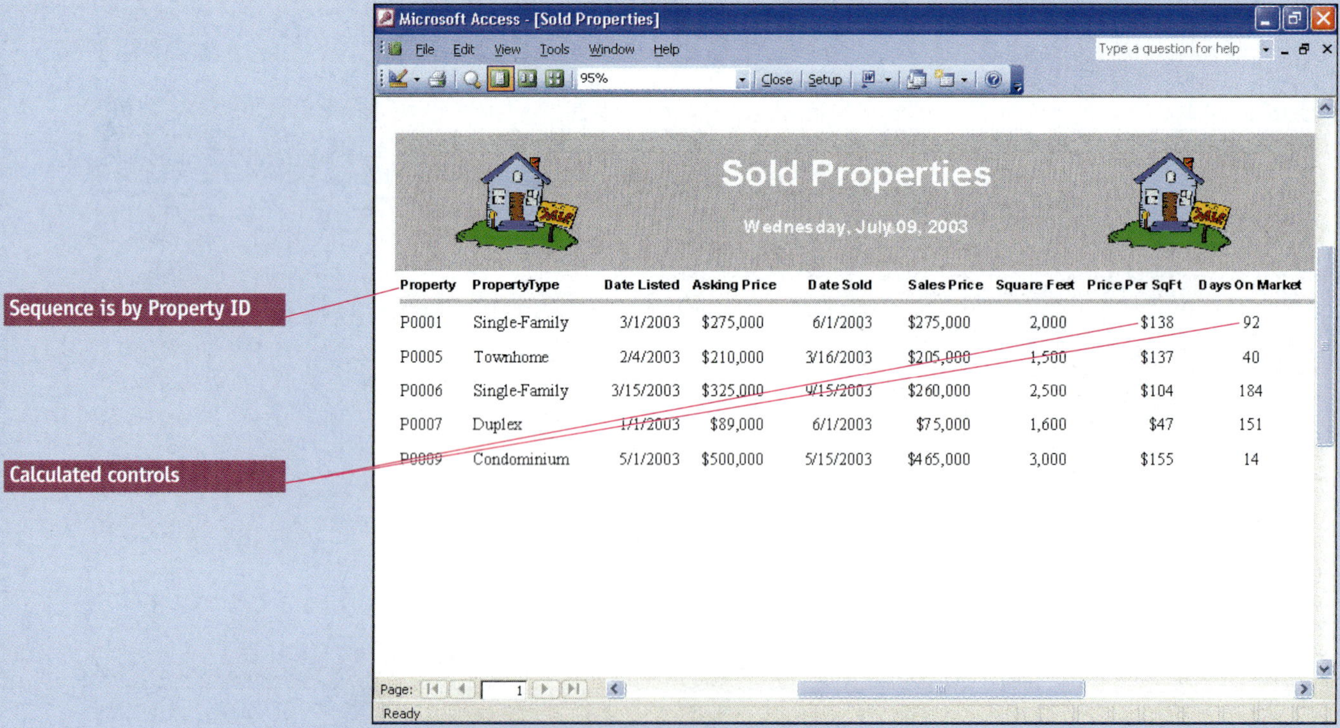

FIGURE 3.18 Best Realty (exercise 5)

6. **The Fishing Pole:** The partially completed *Chapter 3 Practice 6* database builds on an earlier example from Chapter 2. Your present assignment is to create the various reports that are described below, each of which requires its own query. We provide a Customers table with 60 records. Proceed as follows:
   a. Create a report similar to Figure 3.19 that lists all customers whose initial purchase was more than $500. The customers are to be listed in descending order of the initial purchase amount. Your report should contain all of the fields that appear in our report, but you need not match our design exactly. We suggest you start with the Report Wizard, and then modify the report in Design view.
   b. Create a report that shows all customers who own a fishing boat, listing the customers in alphabetical order by last name. Your report should include the customer's first and last name, the boat type, phone number, store account, and an indication of whether the customer is a yacht club member.
   c. Create a report that displays all the long-term customers (people who have been customers for at least two years). This report is based on an underlying query that contains a calculated field to determine the number of years since the customer's initial purchase. (You will need to use the integer function to truncate the decimal portion of the field.) The report should include the customer's name, address (on two lines), and initial purchase date, as well as the number of years since the initial purchase.
   d. Create a report that groups customers by mailing list priority. List the customers in alphabetical order by last name within each group. (The mailing list priority will appear in the group header.) The Detail section should include the customer's number, name, address, city, state, zip code, and phone number.
   e. Print each of the reports and turn them in to your instructor. Change the page orientation and/or margins if necessary to ensure that all of the fields for one record fit on one page.

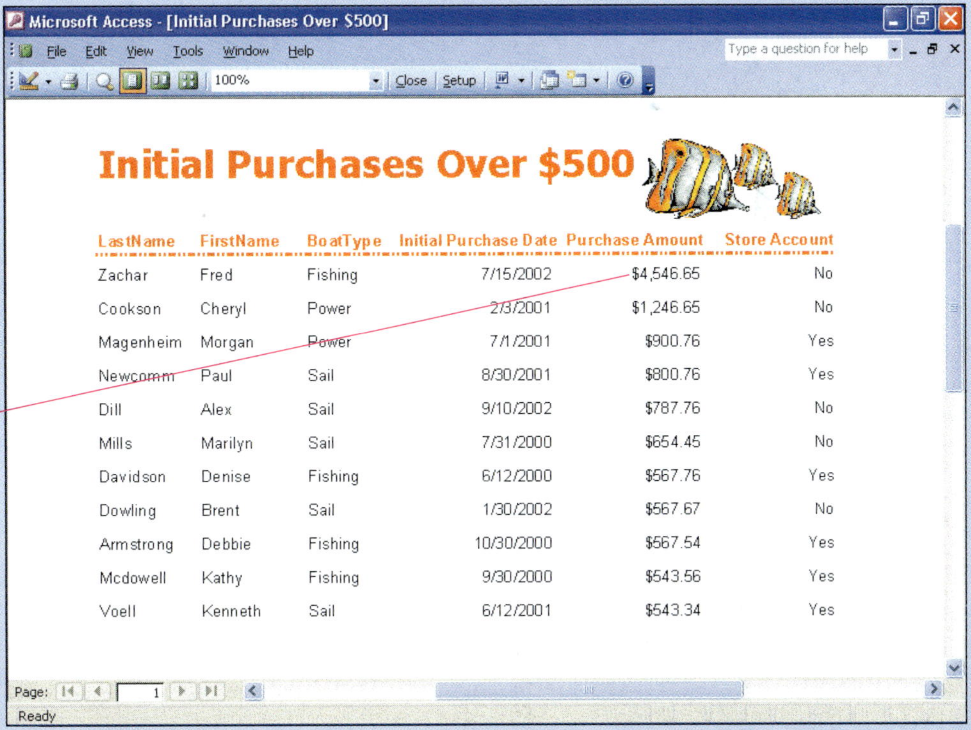

Sequence is by descending order of Purchase Amount

FIGURE 3.19 The Fishing Pole (exercise 6)

7. **Salary Increases:** The report in Figure 3.20 displays salary information for employees grouped by the location where they work. The easiest way to create this report is to use the Report Wizard, then modify the result in the Design view as necessary. You don't have to match our design exactly, but you are to include the identical information in your report. Proceed as follows:
   a. Open the *Chapter 3 Practice 7* database in the Exploring Access folder. Use the Report Wizard to create the initial version of the report in Figure 3.20. Group the data by location, and sort the records by last name. Do not specify summary options at this time. Choose a stepped layout and any style that appeals to you.
   b. Go to the Design view. Pull down the View menu, click the Sorting and Grouping command, select Location in the Field/Expression list box, then click Yes to display the Group Footer. Click in the location footer, then use the Text box to add an unbound control with the formula, =Sum(Salary). Change the label of the control to "Total Salaries for Location". Copy these controls to the Report Footer.
   c. Add clip art to the Report Header. You can copy the clip art that appears in the Report Header from either the Employees form or the Employee Census report that is included in the database. Open either object in Design view, select the clip art, and click the Copy button. Open the Employee by Location report in Design view, click in the Report Header, click the Paste button, then move and size the image as necessary. Save the report. Print the report.
   d. Create a parallel report that displays employees by title rather than location. The easiest way to create this report is to copy the location report, then modify the copied report as necessary. Go to the Database window and click the Reports button. Select the Employees by Location report. Press Ctrl+C to copy the report, then press Ctrl+V to duplicate the report as Employees by Title.
   e. Open the Employees by Title report in Design view. Pull down the View menu, click the Sorting and Grouping command, and change the grouping order from location to title. Modify the report title, column headings, and bound controls within the report as necessary. Save the report, then print it for your instructor. Add a cover sheet to complete the assignment.

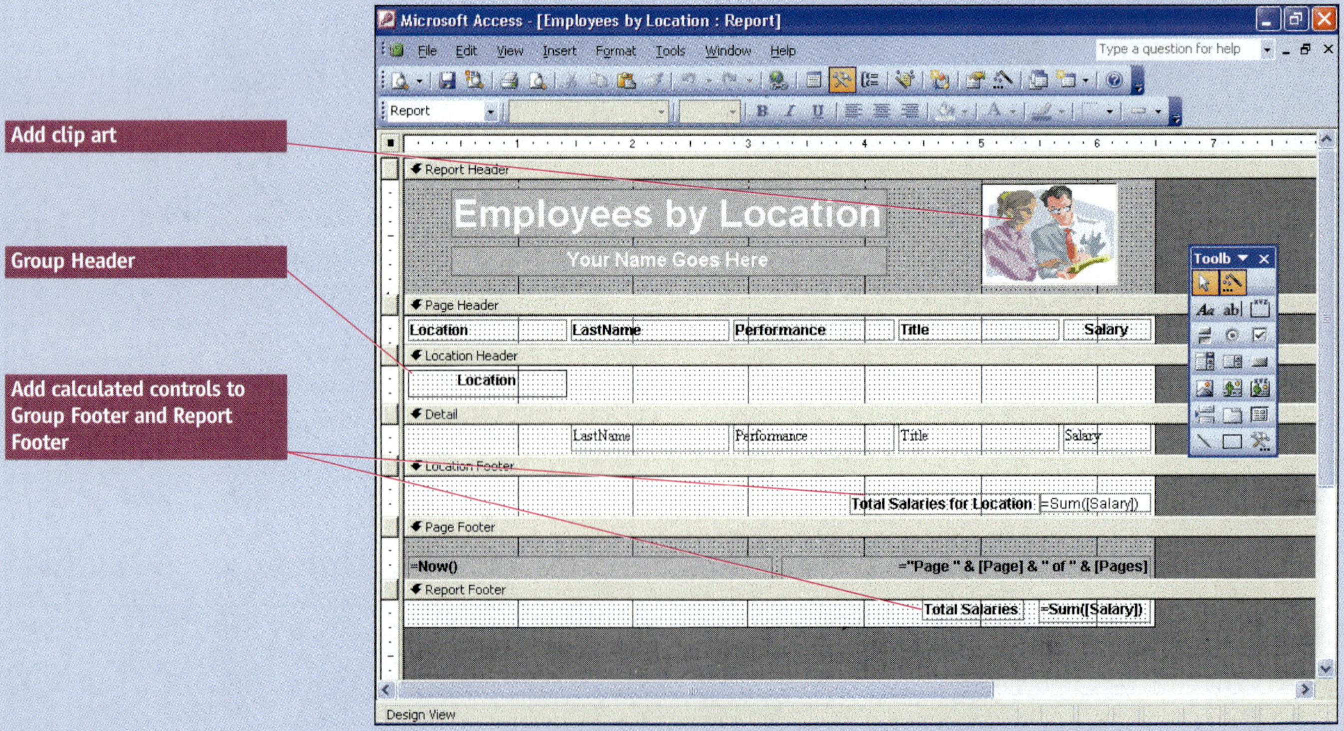

FIGURE 3.20 Salary Increases (exercise 7)

8. **Action Queries:** This problem asks you to create several action queries, after which you are to rerun a report from the previous exercise to see the effects of the action queries on the original data. Realize, however, that action queries will modify the original Employees table, and hence it is good practice to duplicate the table before you begin. Proceed as follows:
   a. Open the *Chapter 3 Practice 7* database in the Exploring Access folder. Go to the Database window, select the Employees table, pull down the Edit menu, and click the Copy command (or use the Ctrl+C keyboard shortcut). Pull down the Edit menu and click the Paste command (or use the Ctrl+V shortcut). Click the option button to copy the data and the structure. Name the copied table "Original Employees" and keep it as backup should you need to return to the original data.
   b. Create a Delete query (based on the Employees table) to delete all employees with poor performance. Run the query.
   c. Create an Update query to give all employees with Average performance a 5% raise. (The Update To row in the Salary column should contain the entry [Salary]*1.05). Be sure to run this query only once.
   d. Create two additional Update queries to give employees who had a performance of Good or Excellent, increases of 10% and 15%, respectively. Be sure to run each query only once. (If there are no employees that satisfy the criteria, the query will not update any records.)
   e. Use the Crosstab Query Wizard to create the query in Figure 3.21, which displays the total salary for each location-gender-title combination, after all of the action queries have been run. Print the query for your instructor.
   f. Rerun the Employee by Location report from the previous exercise and compare the results to the earlier version. The Atlanta manager now has a salary of $110,000, which reflects the 10% increase for Good performance. Note, too, there is only one sales coordinator in Atlanta (Bowles). Her salary is $31,500, which reflects a 5% raise ($1,500) for Average performance. Brown, the other sales coordinator in Atlanta (in the previous exercise) was terminated because of Poor performance.
   g. Add a cover sheet and submit all printouts to your instructor.

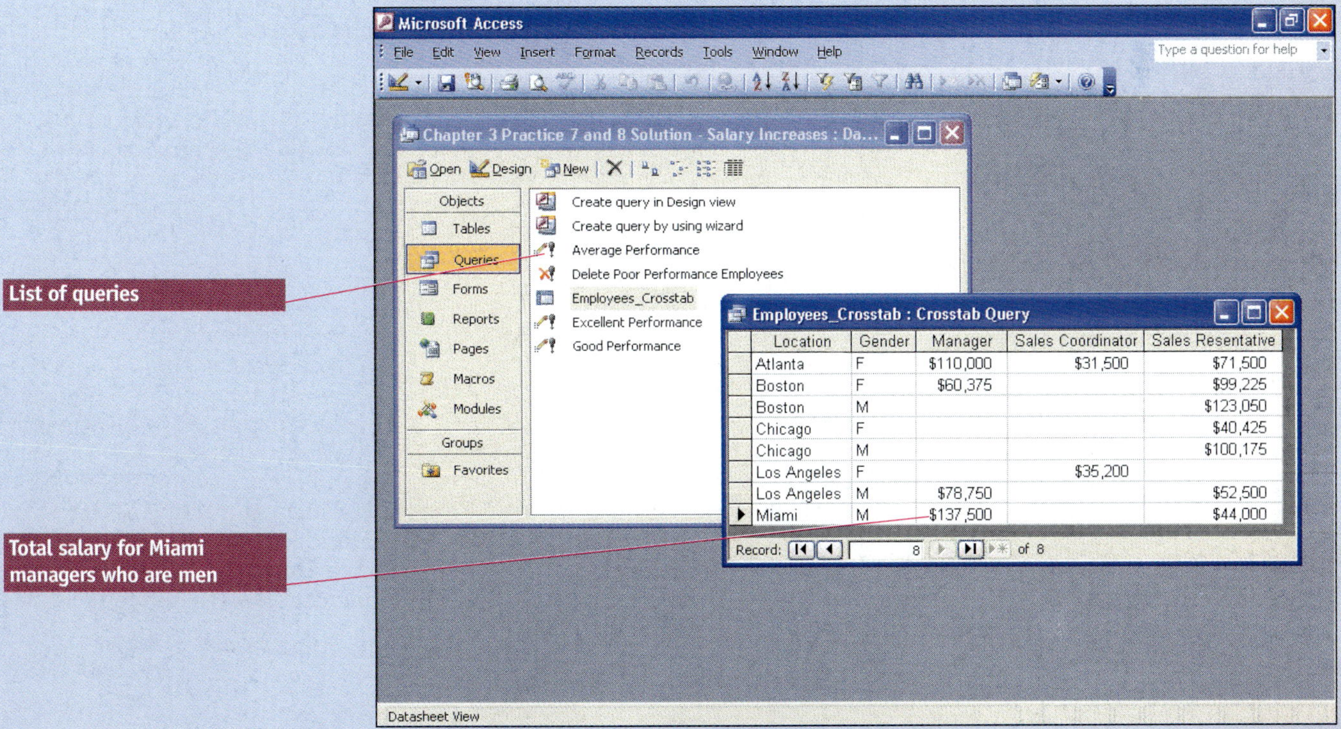

FIGURE 3.21 Action Queries (exercise 8)

MINI CASES

Mail Merge

A mail merge takes the tedium out of sending form letters, as it creates the same letter many times, changing the name, address, and other information as appropriate from letter to letter. The form letter is created in a word processor (e.g., Microsoft Word), but the data file may be taken from an Excel workbook or an Access table or query. Use the *Our Students* database that you have worked with throughout the chapter as the basis for two different form letters that are to be sent to two different groups of students. The first letter is to congratulate students on the Dean's list (GPA of 3.50 or higher). The second letter is a warning to students on academic probation (GPA of less than 2.00).

We have created the form letters for you as the Word documents *Chapter 3 Mini Case Study—Probation Letter* and *Chapter 3 Mini Case Study—Dean's List*, with both documents stored in the Exploring Access folder. Open the Access database and create the required queries, then select each query individually, pull down the Tools menu, click Office Links, and click the command to Merge it with Microsoft Word. Word provides step-by-step assistance, and you should be able to complete the mail merge without difficulty. Print the first form letter for each query to show your instructor that you have completed the assignment.

Oh Canada

If you ask the average Canadian how many states there are in the United States, you are very likely to get the correct answer. If you reverse the question and ask the average American about Canadian provinces, the response is far less accurate. This assignment enables you to learn about our neighbor to the North. Open the *Chapter 3 Mini Case Study—Oh Canada* database in the Exploring Access folder. You will find a single table with four fields—the name of the province or territory, the estimated population for 2002 (in thousands), the area in square kilometers, and an indication of whether the data pertains to a province or territory.

Your assignment is to create a report that parallels the Population Density report in the United States database that was described in practice exercise 2 on page 153. Your first task will be to create a query to compute the population density, after which you can create a report based on that query. The report should be grouped by province or territory, with population and area totals for each group, the average population density for each group, as well as statistics for Canada as a whole.

The Oh Canada database also contains an About Canada form that cites the source of the statistics that appear in the database. The form contains a map of Canada that you are asked to copy to the report you create. Last, but not least, modify the About Canada form so that it contains your name and student number. Print the completed form and report for your instructor.

Compacting versus Compressing

An Access database becomes fragmented, and thus unnecessarily large, as objects (e.g., reports and forms) are modified or deleted. It is important, therefore, to periodically compact a database to reduce its size (enabling you to back it up on a floppy disk). Choose a database with multiple objects, such as the Our Students database used in this chapter. Use the Windows Explorer to record the file size of the database as it presently exists. Start Access, open the database, pull down the Tools menu, and select Database Utilities to compact the database, then record the size of the database after compacting. You can also compress a compacted database (using a standard Windows utility such as WinZip) to further reduce the requirement for disk storage. Summarize your findings in a short report to your instructor. Try compacting and compressing at least two different databases to better appreciate these techniques.

CHAPTER 4

Proficiency: Relational Databases, Pivot Charts, and the Switchboard

OBJECTIVES

After reading this chapter you will:

1. Import data from an Excel workbook for inclusion in an Access database
2. Use the Relationships window to create a one-to-many relationship; define referential integrity.
3. Create a report that contains a relationships diagram
4. Create and modify a multiple-table select query.
5. Create a totals query.
6. Use Microsoft Graph to create a chart for inclusion in a report.
7. Create a pivot table and associated pivot chart.
8. Create and modify a switchboard.
9. Show the object dependencies that exist within a database.
10. Compact and repair a database; back up a database.

hands-on exercises

1. IMPORTING DATA FROM EXCEL
Input: Investment Data workbook; Investment database (Access)
Output: Investment Data workbook (modified); Investment database (modified)
2. TOTAL QUERIES, CHARTS, AND PIVOT TABLES
Input: Investment database (after exercise 1)
Output: Investment database (modified)
3. THE SWITCHBOARD MANAGER
Input: Investment database (after exercise 2)
Output: Investment database (modified)

CASE STUDY
ATTORNEYS FOR ATHLETES

Matt Denham was always a blue-chip athlete, and it came as no surprise when he went in the second round of the most recent NFL draft. Matt was very distrustful of professional agents and asked you to negotiate his first contract, given your recent graduation from law school at the top of your class. Matt is your best friend, and he also asked you to represent three teammates who were drafted by teams in other cities.

Your reputation for negotiating huge signing bonuses spread quickly and you now represent more than 100 athletes. As your business grew, you began to hire other attorneys, so that you have offices in several cities, each of which employs multiple attorneys. The downside is that your business has grown so quickly that it is becoming more difficult to provide the quality service of which you are so proud. A consultant has recommended that you create a relational database to store the data for your offices, attorneys, and the athletes they represent. The consultant has submitted a preliminary design in the form of a simple database that includes the required tables and the associated relationships diagram. The consultant has also chosen a logo (clip art) and color scheme, and has created a descriptive form to show the visual design. ■

Your assignment is to read the chapter and focus on the one-to-many relationships that exist within the database. Put yourself in the place of the consultant and create the initial version of the database, including the switchboard. You will need three tables to track offices, attorneys, and athletes. There is a one-to-many relationship between offices and attorneys (one office has several attorneys, but a given attorney works in only one office). There is a second one-to-many relationship between attorneys and athletes (one attorney represents many athletes, but a specific athlete is represented by only one attorney). Your switchboard should contain three menu items: to display an About Attorneys for Athletes form, to print the relationships diagram, and to exit the application. The visual design is important. Print the relationships diagram, the Switchboard form, and the Switchboard Items table for your instructor.

THE INVESTMENT DATABASE

Each application in Microsoft Office is independent of the others, but it is often necessary or advantageous to share data between the applications. Data may be collected in Excel, imported or linked to an Access database to take advantage of its relational capability, then exported back to Excel for data analysis, or to Microsoft Word for a mail merge. This chapter describes how to share data between applications in the context of a database for an investment firm.

The Investment database is a relational database with two tables, one for clients, and one for financial consultants. Data from both tables can be displayed in a single query that contains fields from each table, and therein lies the real power of Microsoft Access. The chapter also introduces the concept of a total query to produce summary information. The results of a total query are then presented in graphical form through Microsoft Graph. The last portion of the chapter describes the creation of a user interface (or switchboard) that lets a nontechnical person move easily from one object to another by clicking a menu item. The switchboard is created through the Switchboard Manager, one of several utilities in Microsoft Access.

The database in Figure 4.1 is designed for an investment firm that monitors its clients and their financial consultants. The firm requires the typical data for each client—name, birth date, telephone, assets under management, and so on. The firm also stores data about its employees who are the financial consultants that service the clients. Each entity (clients and consultants) requires its own table in the database in order to add, edit, and/or delete data for individual clients and consultants, independently of one another.

If, for example, you wanted to know (or change) the account type and assets for Bradley Adams, you would search the Clients table for Bradley's record, where you would find the account type (Retirement), and assets ($90,000). In similar

Bradley Adams' record

ConsultantID points to Andrea Carrion (ConsultantID of 1)

SSN	FirstName	LastName	ConsultantID	BirthDate	Gender	Account Type	Assets
100-00-0000	Eileen	Marder	2	9/12/1935	F	Standard	$14,000
111-11-1111	Bradley	Adams	1	8/22/1961	M	Retirement	$90,000
111-22-2333	Linda	Laquer	3	3/16/1981	F	Corporate	$25,000
200-00-0000	Kevin	Stutz	3	5/31/1972	M	Retirement	$150,000
222-22-2222	Nickolas	Gruber	2	11/11/1961	M	Corporate	$90,000
300-00-0000	Cedric	Stewart	4	4/12/1974	M	Retirement	$90,000
333-33-3333	Lori	Graber	3	7/1/1972	F	Deluxe	$120,000
400-00-0000	Ryan	Yanez	1	9/30/1974	M	Standard	$18,000
444-44-4444	Christopher	Milgrom	4	3/12/1953	M	Corporate	$100,000
444-55-5666	Jessica	Benjamin	1	10/31/1973	F	Deluxe	$125,000
500-00-0000	Erica	Milgrom	2	5/1/1972	F	Retirement	$150,000
555-55-5555	Peter	Carson	1	3/8/1953	M	Standard	$12,000
600-00-0000	Michelle	Zacco	2	10/24/1975	F	Deluxe	$90,000
666-66-6666	Kimberly	Coulter	2	11/11/1974	F	Corporate	$180,000
700-00-0000	Steven	Frazier	4	9/9/1968	M	Retirement	$150,000
777-77-7777	Ana	Johnson	3	4/18/1948	F	Standard	$12,000
800-00-0000	Christa	Parulis	1	7/15/1972	F	Corporate	$120,000
888-88-8888	David	James	4	8/1/1945	M	Deluxe	$100,000
900-00-0000	Ronnie	Jones	2	6/1/1949	F	Standard	$12,000
999-99-9999	Wendy	Simon	1	1/31/1945	F	Retirement	$10,000

(a) The Clients Table

Andrea Carrion has ConsultantID of 1

ConsultantID	FirstName	LastName	Phone	DateHired	Status
1	Andrea	Carrion	(954) 346-1980	9/1/1995	Partner
2	Ken	Grauer	(954) 346-1955	9/1/1999	Associate
3	Robert	Arnold	(954) 346-1958	10/18/2000	Associate
4	Issac	Milgrom	(954) 346-1961	3/16/2002	Partner

(b) The Consultants Table

FIGURE 4.1 The Investments Database

fashion, you could search the Consultants table for Andrea Carrion and learn that she was hired on September 1, 1995, and that she is a partner in the firm. You could also use the ConsultantID field in Bradley Adams' record to learn that Andrea Carrion is Bradley's financial consultant.

The investment firm imposes a ***one-to-many relationship*** between financial consultants and their clients. One consultant can have many clients, but a given client is assigned to only one consultant. This relationship is implemented in the database by including a common field, ConsultantID, in both tables. The ConsultantID is the ***primary key*** (the field or combination of fields that ensures each record is unique) in the Consultants table. It also appears as a ***foreign key*** (the primary key of another table) in the Clients table in order to relate the two tables to one another.

The data from both tables can be combined through this relationship to provide complete information about any client and the consultant who serves him/her, or about any consultant and the clients he or she services. For example, to determine the name, telephone number, and status of Bradley Adams' financial consultant, you would search the Clients table to determine the ConsultantID assigned to Bradley (consultant number 1). You would then search the Consultants table for that consultant number and retrieve the associated data.

Multiple-table Queries

You have just seen how to manually relate data from the Clients and Consultants tables to one another. As you might expect, it can also be done automatically through the creation of a multiple-table query as shown in Figure 4.2. Figure 4.2a shows the Design view, whereas Figure 4.2b displays the associated dynaset. Bradley Adams appears first in the dynaset since the query lists clients in alphabetical order by last name. Note, too, that Carrion appears as Bradley's financial consultant, which is the same conclusion we reached when we looked at the tables initially.

The one-to-many relationship between consultants and clients is shown graphically in the Query window. The tables are related through the ConsultantID

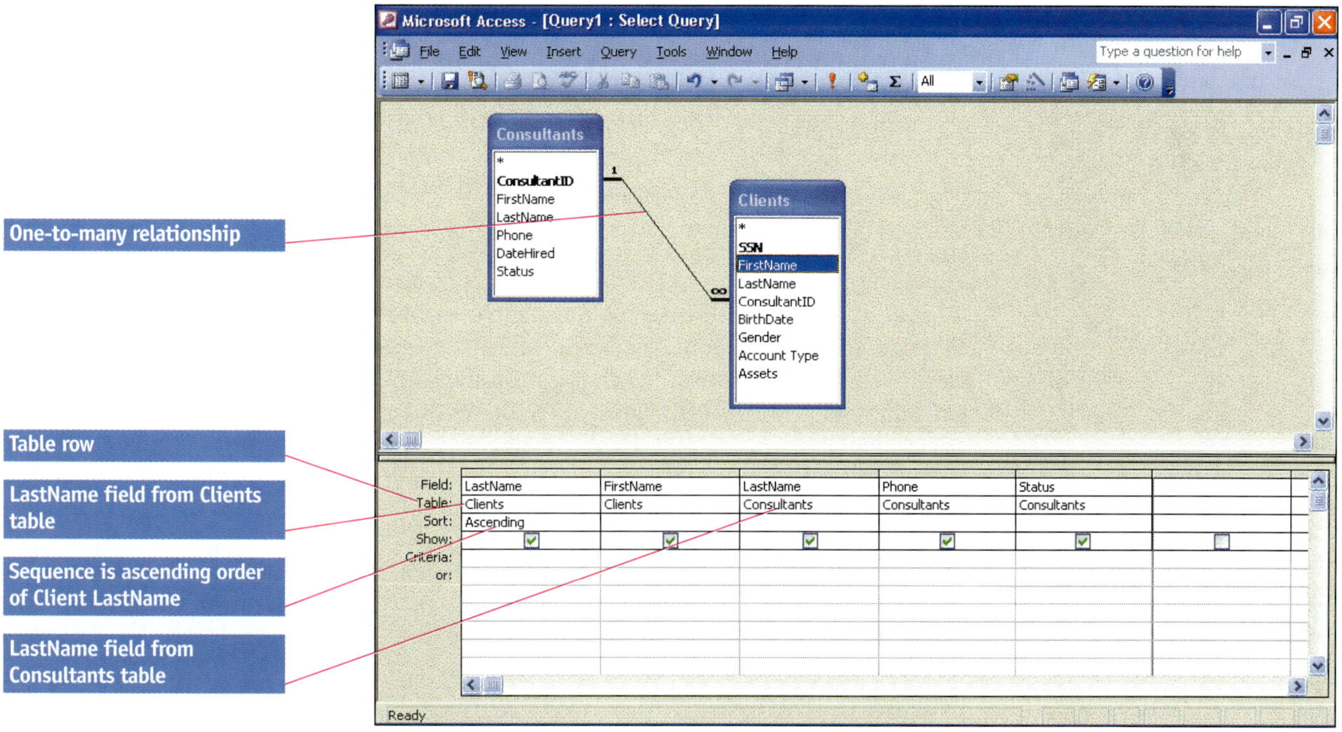

(a) Design View

FIGURE 4.2 Multiple-table Query

Sequence is alphabetical order by Client LastName

Consultant LastName

Clients.LastName	FirstName	Consultants.LastName	Phone	Status
Adams	Bradley	Carrion	(954) 346-1980	Partner
Benjamin	Jessica	Carrion	(954) 346-1980	Partner
Carson	Peter	Carrion	(954) 346-1980	Partner
Coulter	Kimberly	Grauer	(954) 346-1955	Associate
Frazier	Steven	Milgrom	(954) 346-1961	Partner
Graber	Lori	Arnold	(954) 346-1958	Associate
Gruber	Nickolas	Grauer	(954) 346-1955	Associate
James	David	Milgrom	(954) 346-1961	Partner
Johnson	Ana	Arnold	(954) 346-1958	Associate
Jones	Ronnie	Grauer	(954) 346-1955	Associate
Laquer	Linda	Arnold	(954) 346-1958	Associate
Marder	Eileen	Grauer	(954) 346-1955	Associate
Milgrom	Erica	Grauer	(954) 346-1955	Associate
Milgrom	Christopher	Milgrom	(954) 346-1961	Partner
Parulis	Christa	Carrion	(954) 346-1980	Partner
Simon	Wendy	Carrion	(954) 346-1980	Partner
Stewart	Cedric	Milgrom	(954) 346-1961	Partner
Stutz	Kevin	Arnold	(954) 346-1958	Associate
Yanez	Ryan	Carrion	(954) 346-1980	Partner
Zacco	Michelle	Grauer	(954) 346-1955	Associate

(b) Dynaset

FIGURE 4.2 Multiple-table Query (*continued*)

field that appears in both tables. ConsultantID is the primary key of the "one" table (the Consultants table in this example), but it is also a field in the "many" table (the Clients table). This in turn links the tables to one another, making it possible to join data from the two tables in a single query.

The lower half of the Query window is similar to the queries you created in Chapter 3. The difference is that the design grid contains a ***Table row*** to indicate the table from where the field was taken. The client's last name and first name are taken from the Clients table. The consultant's last name, phone, and status are taken from the Consultants table. The records appear in alphabetical order (in ascending sequence) according to the value of the client's last name.

Maintaining the Database

You have seen how easy it is to obtain information from the investment database. The design of the investment database, with separate tables for clients and consultants, makes it easy to add, edit, or delete information about a client or consultant. Thus, to add a new client or consultant, just go to the respective table and add the record. In similar fashion, to change the data for an existing client or consultant, you again go to the appropriate table, locate the record, and make the change. The advantage of the relational database, however, is that you have to change the consultant information in only one place; for example, change the phone number of a consultant, and the change will be automatically reflected for every client associated with that consultant.

Realize, too, that the tables in the database must be consistent with one another, a concept known as ***referential integrity***. For example, you can always delete a record from the Clients table (the "many" table in this example). You cannot, however, delete a record from the Consultants table (the "one" table) when there are clients assigned to that consultant, because those clients would then be assigned to a financial consultant who did not exist. Access monitors the relationships that are in effect and prevents you from making changes that do not make sense. It will enforce referential integrity automatically.

THE IMPORT SPREADSHEET WIZARD

It is important to realize that data is data regardless of where it originates. You may prefer to work in Access, but others in the organization may use Excel or vice versa. In any event, there is a need to send data back and forth between applications. The ***Get External Data command*** imports or links data from an external source into Access. The data may come from an Excel workbook (as in our next hands-on exercise), or from a text file that was created by an application outside of Microsoft Office. The ***Export command*** does the reverse and copies an Access database object to an external destination.

The ***Import Spreadsheet Wizard*** is illustrated in Figure 4.3. The Wizard asks you a series of questions, then it imports the Excel worksheet into the Access table. You select the worksheet in Figure 4.3a, designate the Excel column headings and Access field names in Figure 4.3b, and specify the primary key in Figure 4.3c. You can then view and/or modify the resulting table as shown in Figure 4.3d.

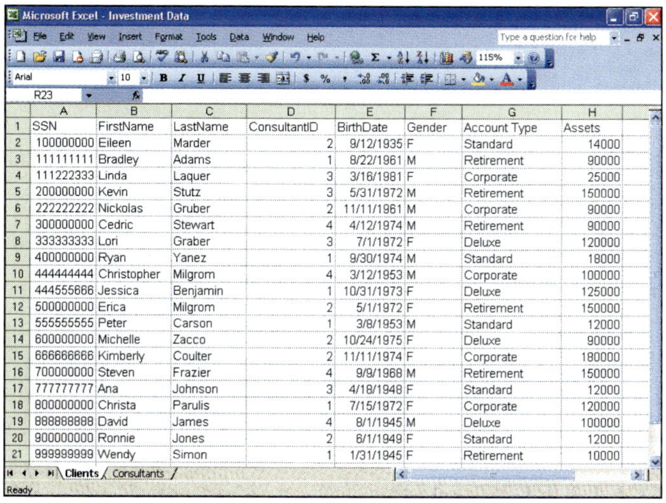

(a) The Excel Workbook

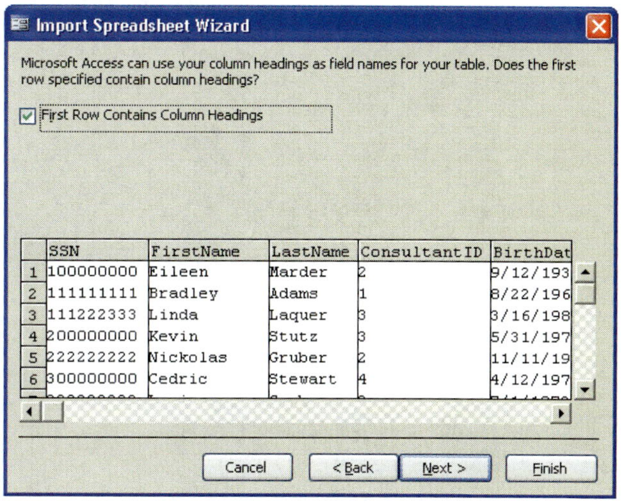

(b) Designate Column Headings (field names)

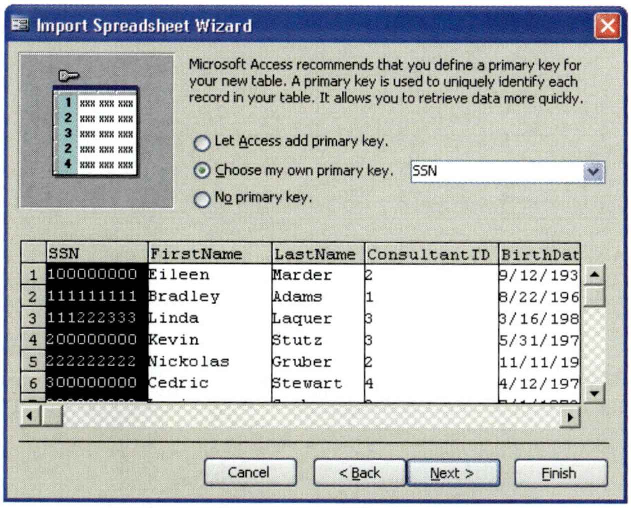

(c) Choose the Primary Key

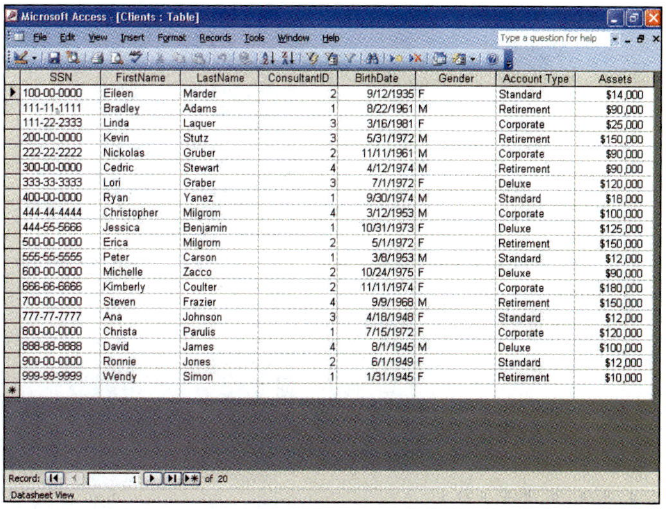

(d) The Clients Table

FIGURE 4.3 The Import Spreadsheet Wizard

hands-on exercise 1

Importing Data from Excel

Objective To import an Access table from an Excel workbook; to create a one-to-many relationship; to create a multiple-table query.

Step 1: Import the Excel Worksheet

- Start Access. Click the link to **More . . .** in the task pane, or pull down the **File menu** and click the **Open command**. Open the **Investment database** in the **Exploring Access folder**. Click **Open** in response to the security warning. If necessary, click the **Tables button**.
- Pull down the **File menu**, click (or point to) the **Get External Data command**, then click **Import** to display the Import dialog box in Figure 4.4a.
- Click the **down arrow** on the Look in list box and change to the **Exploring Access folder** (the same folder that contains the Access databases).
- Click the **down arrow** on the Files of type list box and select **Microsoft Excel**. Select the **Investment Data workbook**. Click the **Import button**.

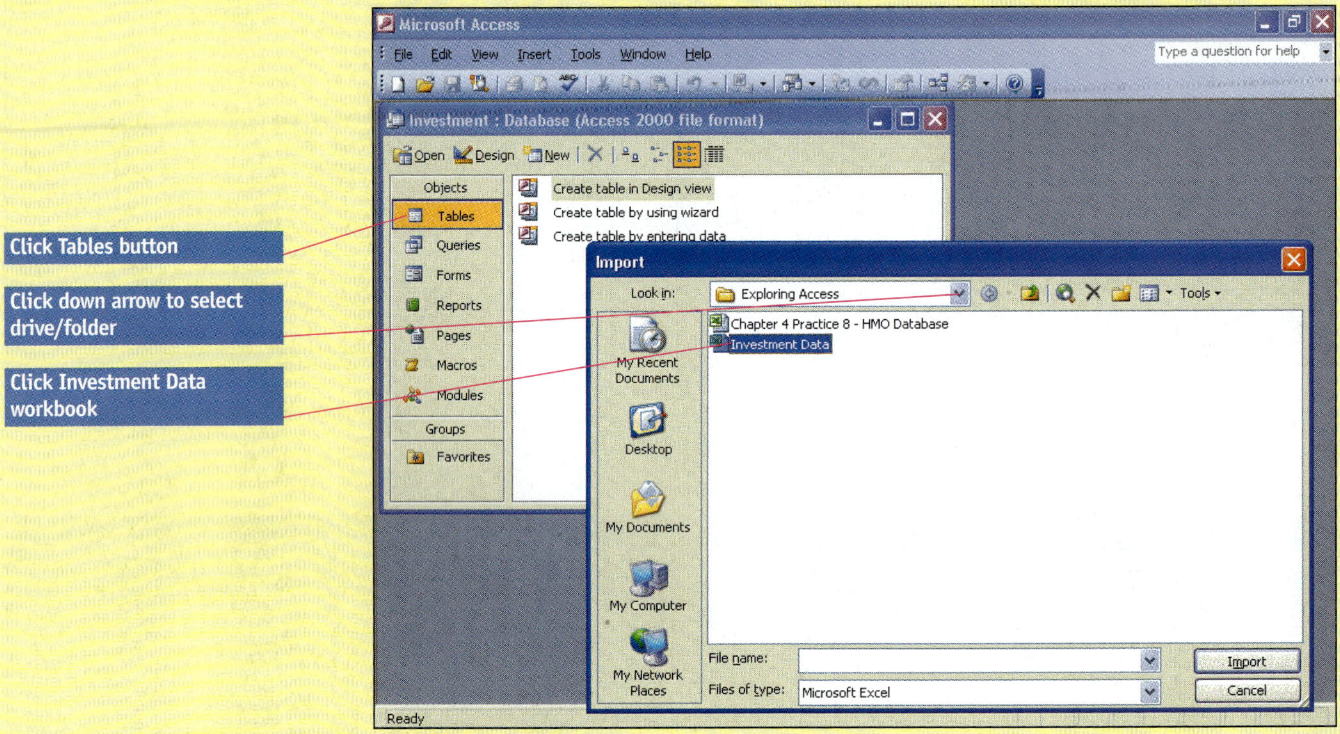

(a) Import the Excel Worksheet (step 1)

FIGURE 4.4 Hands-on Exercise 1

IMPORTING VERSUS LINKING

The Get External Data command displays a cascaded menu to import or link tables. Importing a table brings a copy of the table into the database and does not maintain a tie to the original data. Linking, on the other hand, does not bring the table into the database but only a pointer to the data source. Any changes to the data are made in the original data source and are reflected automatically in any database that is linked to that source.

Step 2: The Import Spreadsheet Wizard

- You should see the first step in the Import Spreadsheet Wizard as shown in Figure 4.4b. The option button to **Show Worksheets** is selected. The Clients worksheet is also selected. Click **Next**.
- Access will use the column headings in the Excel workbook as field names in the Access table, provided you check the box indicating that the first row contains column headings. Click **Next**.
- Select the option button to store the data in a new table. Click **Next**.
- You do not need information about the individual fields. Click **Next**.
- Select the option to choose your own primary key. Click the **drop-down arrow** on the list box, and select **SSN**. Click **Next**.
- Access indicates that it will import the data to a Clients table. Click the **Finish button**, then click **OK** when the wizard indicates it has finished importing the data. The Clients table appears within the Database window.
- Repeat the steps to import the **Consultants table** into the Investment database from the Investment Data workbook. Use the **ConsultantID field** as the primary key for this table.

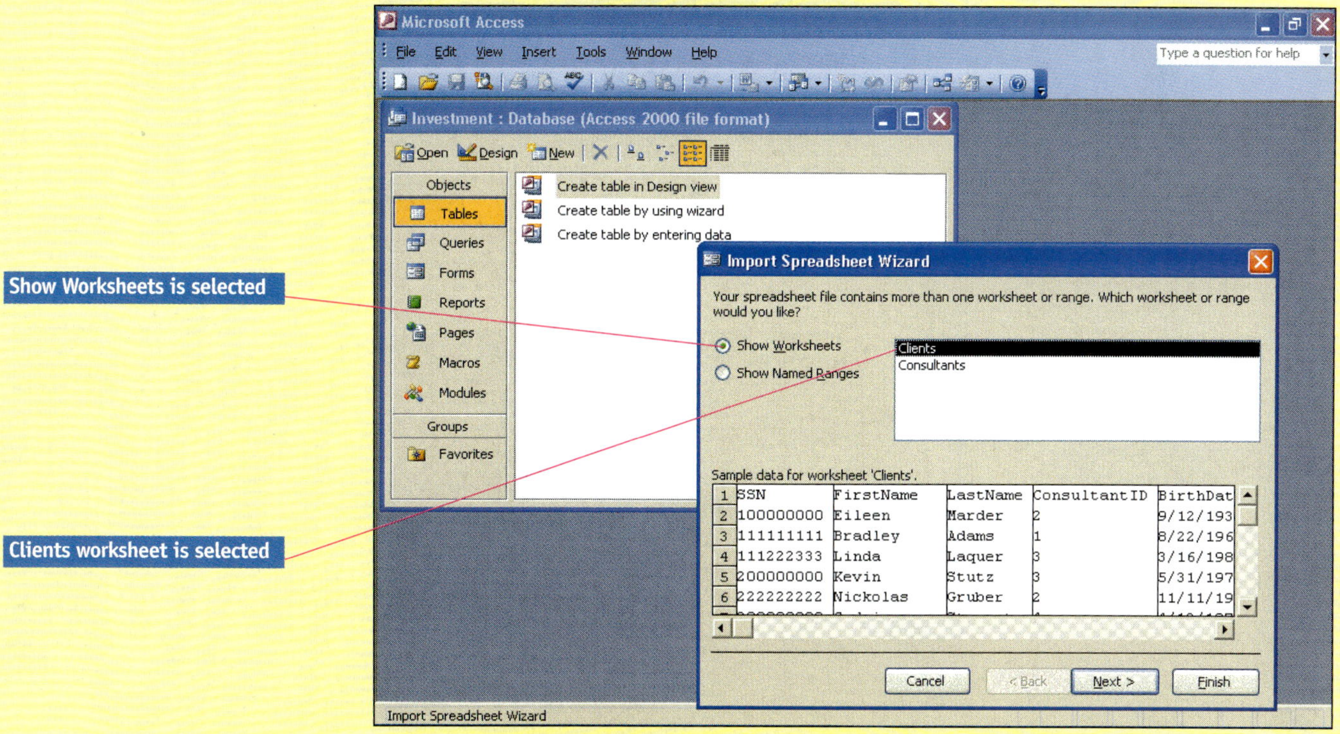

(b) The Import Spreadsheet Wizard (step 2)

FIGURE 4.4 Hands-on Exercise 1 (*continued*)

THE IMPORT TEXT WIZARD

The most common format for data originating outside of Microsoft Office is a text (or ASCII) file that stores the data without formatting of any kind. Pull down the File menu, click the Get External Data command, click Import, and specify Text Files as the file format to start the Import Text Wizard.

Step 3: Create the Relationship

- Pull down the **Tools menu** and click the **Relationships command** to open the Relationships window in Figure 4.4c. (The tables are not yet visible.)
- Pull down the **Relationships menu** and click the **Show Table command** to display the Show Table dialog box. Click (select) the **Clients table** (within the Show Table dialog box), then click the **Add button**.
- Double click the **Consultants table** to add this table to the Relationships window. Close the Show Table dialog box. Click and drag the title bar of each table so that the positions of the tables match those in Figure 4.4c.
- Click and drag the bottom (and/or right) border of each table so that you see all of the fields in each table.
- Click and drag the **ConsultantID field** in the Consultants table field list to the **ConsultantID field** in the Clients field list. You will see the Edit Relationships dialog box.
- Check the box to **Enforce Referential Integrity**. Click the **Create button** to create the relationship.
- Click the **Save button** to save the Relationships window.

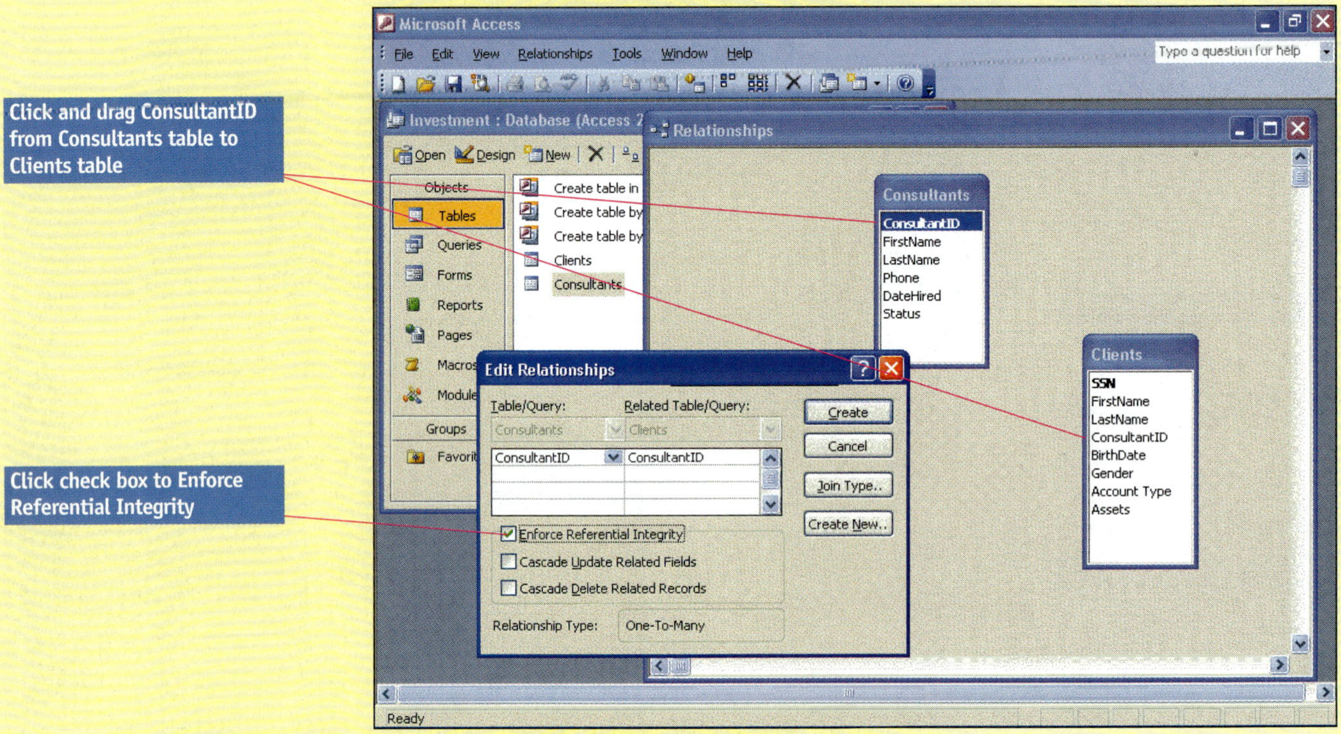

(c) Create the Relationship (step 3)

FIGURE 4.4 Hands-on Exercise 1 (*continued*)

REFERENTIAL INTEGRITY

The tables in a database must be consistent with one another, a concept known as referential integrity. Thus, Access automatically implements certain types of data validation to prevent errors of inconsistency from occurring. You cannot, for example, enter a record in the Clients table that references a Consultant who does not exist. Nor can you delete a record in the Consultants table if it has related records in the Clients table.

Step 4: Print the Relationship

- Pull down the **File menu** and click the **Print Relationships command.** You will see the Print Preview screen of a report. Maximize the window.
- Click the **View button** to change to the Design view as shown in Figure 4.4d. If necessary, click the **Toolbox button** to display the Toolbox toolbar.
- Click the **Label tool** on the Toolbox toolbar, then click and drag in the Report Header section of the report to create an unbound control.
- The insertion point is positioned automatically within the label you just created. Type **Prepared by:** followed by your name. Size the labels within the header as necessary.
- Click the **Save button** to display the Save As dialog box. Change the name of the report to **Relationships Diagram**, then click **OK**.
- Click the **View button** to change to the **Print Preview** view of the report. Click the **Print button**. Close the Print Preview window.
- Close the Report window. Close the Relationships window.

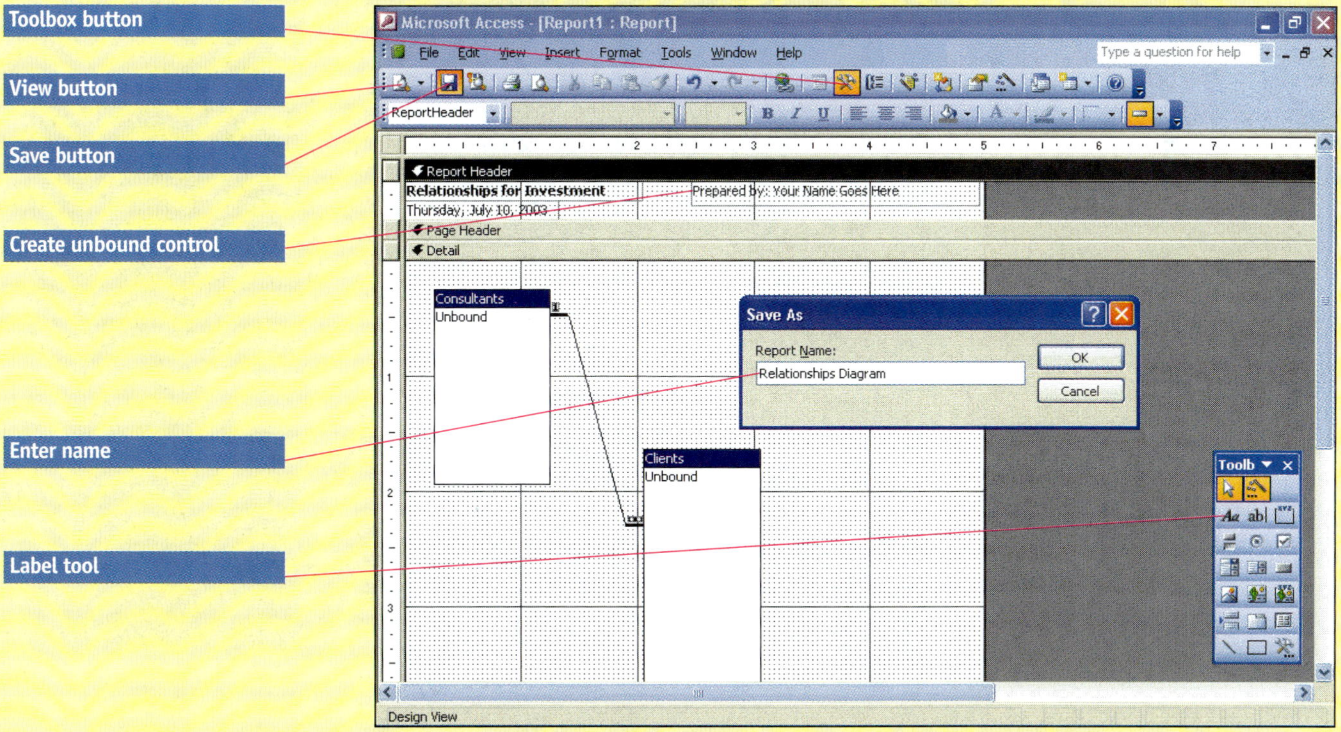

(d) Print the Relationship (step 4)

FIGURE 4.4 Hands-on Exercise 1 (*continued*)

DISPLAY THE CURRENT DATE

A report typically displays one of two dates—the date it was created, or the current date (i.e., the date on which it is printed). We prefer the latter, which is obtained through the Now() function. Click in the Report header and delete the control containing today's (fixed) date. Click the Text Box tool, click and drag where you want the date to appear, then release the mouse. Click in the text box and enter the function =Now(). Save the report. The next time you open the report, it will display the current date.

Step 5: Add Your Own Record

- Click the **Forms button** in the Database window, then double click the **Consultants form** to open the form.
- Click the **Add Record button** and enter the data for your instructor. Enter **5** as the ConsultantID, enter your **instructor's name**, and use today's date as the date of hire. Your instructor is a **partner**. Close the form.
- Double click the **Clients form** in the Database window to open the form as shown in Figure 4.4e. Click the **Add Record button**, then enter the appropriate data for yourself.
  - Click the **down arrow** on the Consultants list box, then select your instructor (Barber in our example) as your financial consultant.
  - Enter **Standard** as the Account Type.
  - Enter **$25,000** in the Assets field.
- Click the **Print Record button** to print the form.
- Click the **Close Form button.**

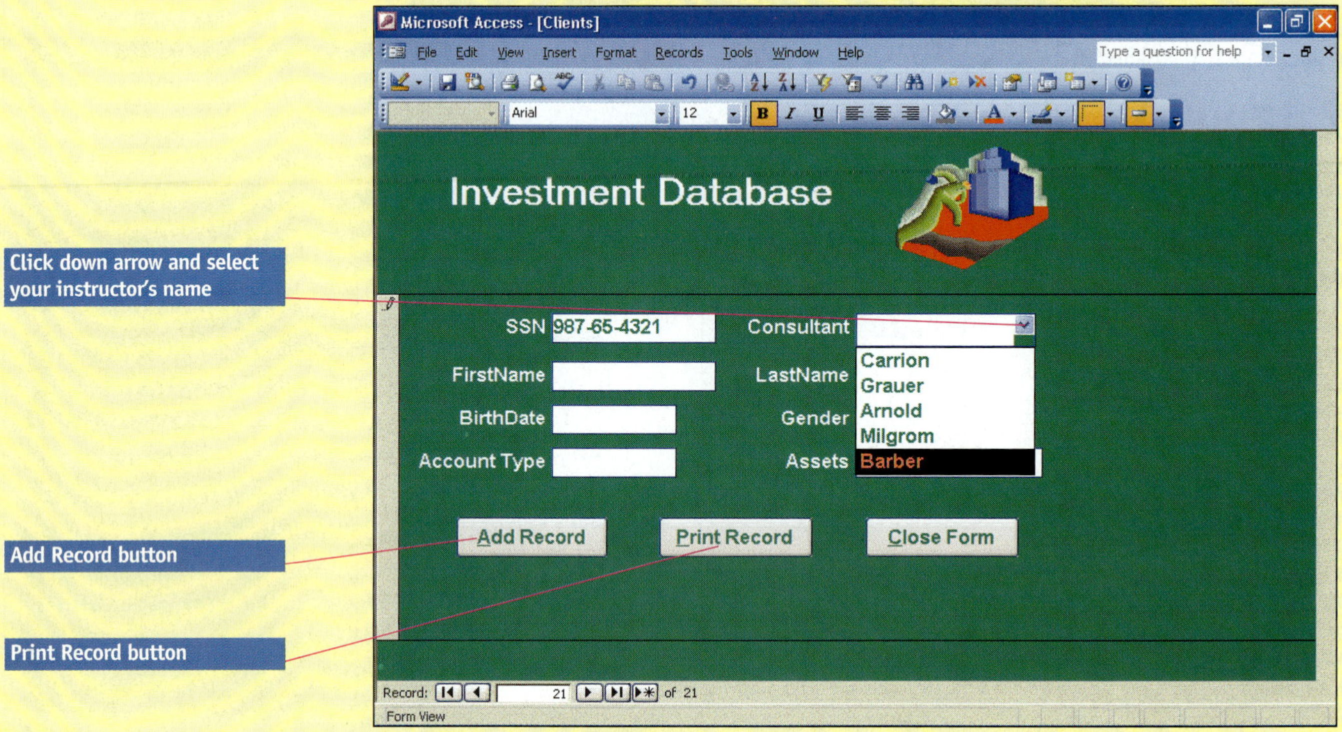

(e) Add Your Own Record (step 5)

FIGURE 4.4 Hands-on Exercise 1 (*continued*)

ADD A HYPERLINK

You can enhance the appeal of your form through inclusion of a hyperlink. Open the form in Design view, then click the Insert Hyperlink button to display the Insert Hyperlink dialog box. Enter the Web address and click OK to close the dialog box and return to the Design view. Right click the hyperlink to display a shortcut menu, click the Properties command to display the Properties dialog box, then change the caption, font, and/or point size as appropriate.

Step 6: **Create the Multiple-table Query**

- Click the **Queries button** in the Database window. Double click the icon to **Create query in design view** to open the Design window. The Show Table dialog box appears automatically.
- Press and hold the **Ctrl key** to select the Clients and Consultants tables, then click the **Add button** to add these tables to the query. Close the Show Table dialog box.
- Click the **Maximize button** so that the Query Design window takes the entire desktop. Point to the line separating the field lists from the design grid (the mouse pointer changes to a cross), then click and drag in a downward direction. This gives you more space to display the field lists.
- Click and drag the title bars of each table to arrange the tables as shown in Figure 4.4f. Click and drag the bottom of each field list until you can see all of the fields in the table.
- You are ready to complete the query, which will contain fields from both the Clients and Consultants tables.

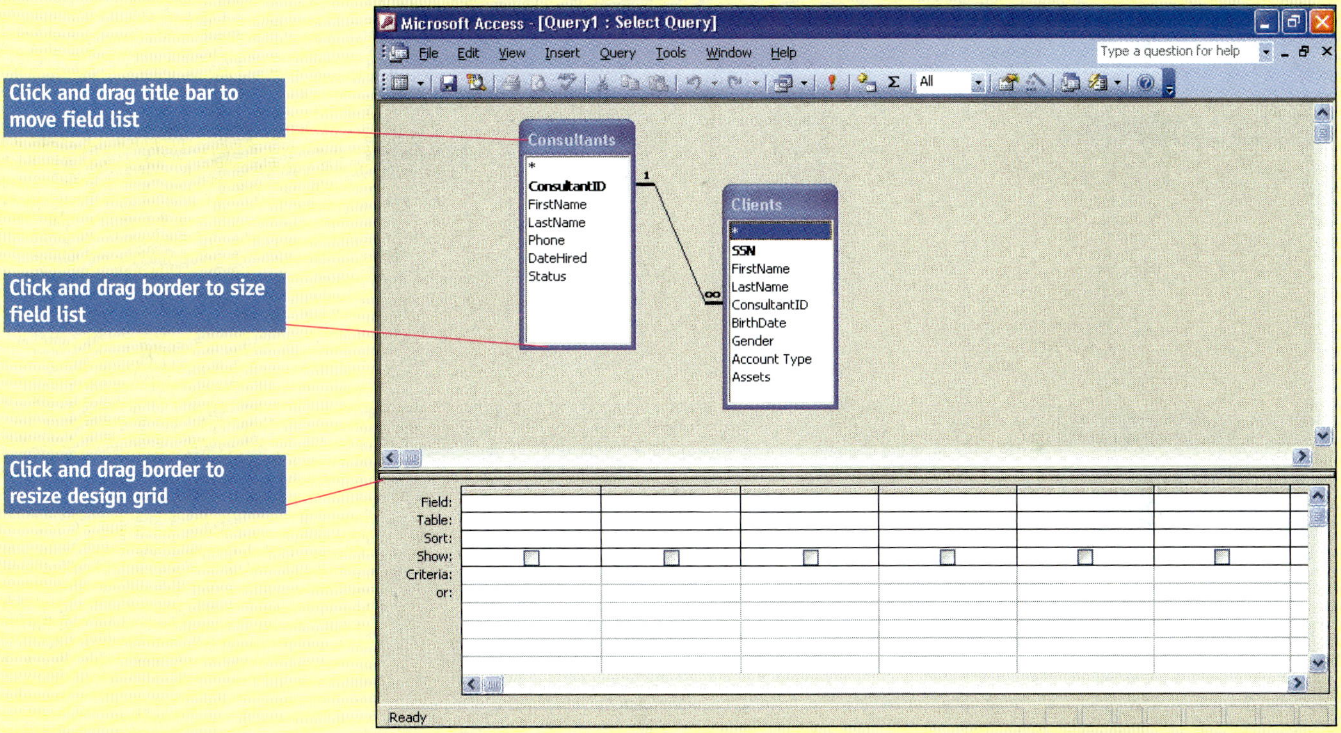

(f) Create the Multiple-table Query (step 6)

FIGURE 4.4 Hands-on Exercise 1 (*continued*)

THE JOIN LINE

Access joins the tables in a query automatically if a relationship exists between the tables within the database. Access will also join the tables (even if no relationship exists) if both tables have a field with the same name and data type, and if one of the fields is a primary key. And finally, you can create the join yourself by dragging a field from one table to the other, but this type of join applies only to the query in which it was created.

Step 7: Complete the Multiple-table Query

- The Table row should be visible within the design grid. If not, pull down the **View menu** and click **Table Names** to display the Table row in the design grid as shown in Figure 4.4g.
- Double click the **LastName** and **Status fields** from the Consultants table to add these fields to the design grid. Double click the **LastName**, **Assets**, and **Account Type fields** from the Clients table to add these fields as well.
- Click the **Sort row** under the **LastName field** from the **Consultants table**, then click the **down arrow** to open the drop-down list box. Click **Ascending**.
- Click the **Save button** on the Query Design toolbar to display the Save As dialog box. Save the query as **Assets Under Management**. Click **OK** to save the query.
- Click the **Run button** (the exclamation point) to run the query. The results are displayed on a dynaset.

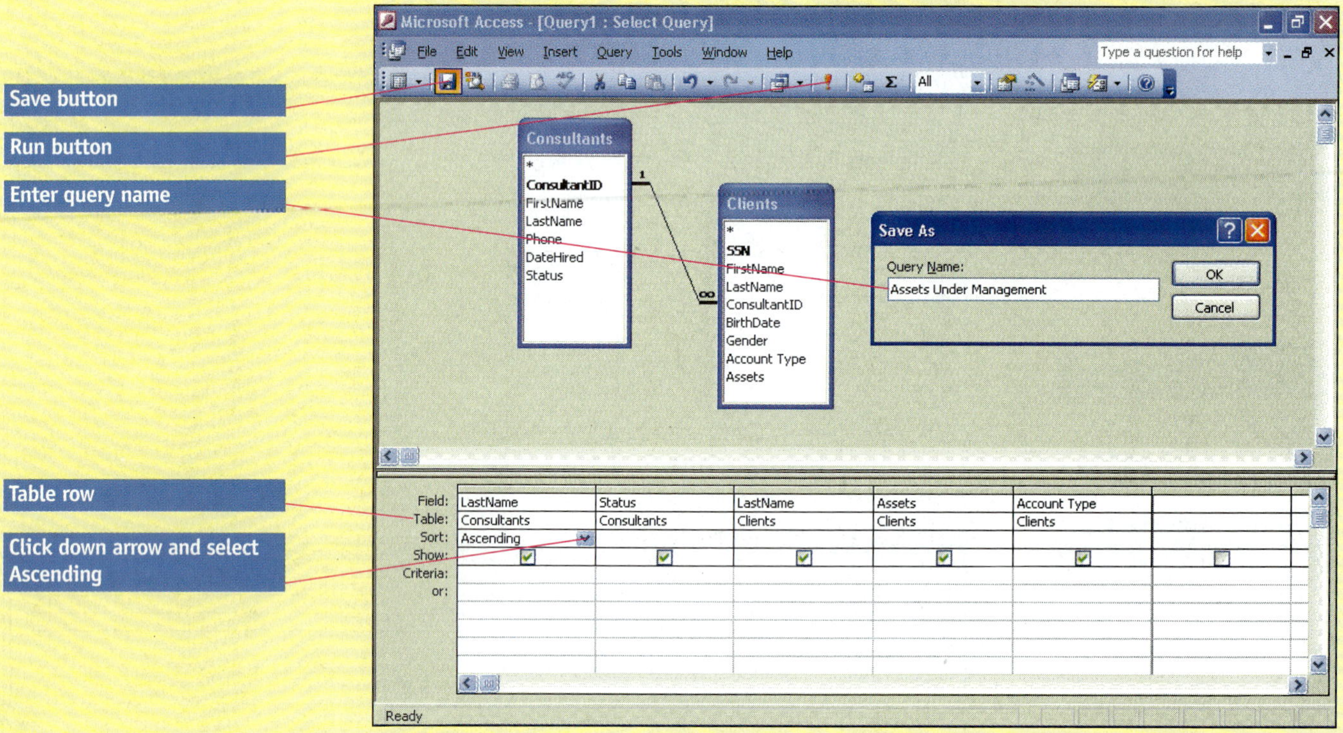

(g) Complete the Multiple-table Query (step 7)

FIGURE 4.4 Hands-on Exercise 1 (*continued*)

SORT ON MULTIPLE FIELDS

A query can be sorted on multiple fields (e.g., by consultant, and by client's last name within consultant), provided the fields are in the proper order within the design grid. Access sorts from left to right (the leftmost field is the most important field), so the consultant's last name must appear to the left of the client's last name. To move a field within the design grid, click the column selector above the field name to select the column, then drag the column to its new position. Click the Sort row for both fields and choose the ascending sequence.

PIVOT TABLES AND PIVOT CHARTS

Microsoft Graph is a simple and effective way to visualize the data in a table or query. Pivot tables and the associated pivot charts provide a more powerful way of analyzing the same data as can be seen in Figure 4.7. A ***pivot table*** computes summary statistics for the records in a table (or query) according to the parameters you supply. A ***pivot chart*** provides the same information in graphical form.

The pivot table in Figure 4.7a displays the assets under management for each combination of consultant and account type within the Investment database. Arnold, for example, has $307,000 under management that is distributed over the different account types. In similar fashion, Barber and Carrion have assets under management of $100,000 and $375,000, respectively. The combined assets for all consultants are $1,758,000. The columns show the total assets for each account type as distributed over the various consultants. The combined assets for all account types also total to $1,758,000.

A pivot table is very flexible in that the fields in the row and column areas, Consultant's LastName and Account Type in this example, can be expanded or collapsed to show detail or summary statistics. We have elected to suppress the details for all consultants except Carrion to illustrate the distinction. Carrion, for example, has two retirement accounts of $10,000 and $90,000, and the individual amounts are displayed, as opposed to the total.

There is additional flexibility in that you can display (remove) data for any consultant or account type, by clicking the down arrow in the field name and checking (or clearing) the box for the specific value of the field. Note, too, the third dimension in the pivot table (the filter area) that indicates all of the records in the database. The Status field in this example (is from the Consultant's table, and it) contains one of two values, Partner or Associate, to indicate the status of the consultant. As with the row and column fields, you can click the down arrow to filter the table to display or hide the records according to the value of the Status field.

You can also change the overall structure of the pivot table to add or remove fields by dragging the field names on or off the table. You can switch the orientation (pivot the table) by dragging a field to or from the row, column, or filter area. You can change the means of calculation by switching to the Average, Minimum, or Maximum value, as opposed to the Sum function value in the present table. And finally, you can change the data in the underlying table, then refresh the pivot table to reflect the changes in the table.

Best of all, a pivot table is very easy to create. You may recall that a table (or query) has four different views: Datasheet view, Design view, Pivot Table view, and Pivot Chart view. The pivot table is created within the Pivot Table view. In essence, all you do is click and drag a field from the ***field list*** to the indicated drop area. The Consultant's LastName, Account Type, and Status fields, for example, have been dragged to the row, column, and filter areas, respectively. The Assets field is dragged to the body of the table, and the row and column totals are specified.

The Pivot Chart view in Figure 4.7b displays the graphical equivalent of the associated pivot table. The pivot chart is created automatically when you create the associated pivot table. You can pivot the chart just as you can pivot the table, and any changes made to the pivot chart are automatically reflected in the pivot table and vice versa. You can filter the data to display (hide) selected records. You could, for example, click the down arrow next to Account Type field, then clear the check box that appears next to any of the account types to suppress these values. And finally, you can change the properties of any of the chart's components to display different fonts, formatting, styles, and so on.

Pivot tables have been available for several years in Microsoft Excel, but they are still a well-kept secret in that many otherwise knowledgeable individuals do not know of their existence. Pivot tables and charts are relatively new to Microsoft Access, however, as they were first introduced in Office XP.

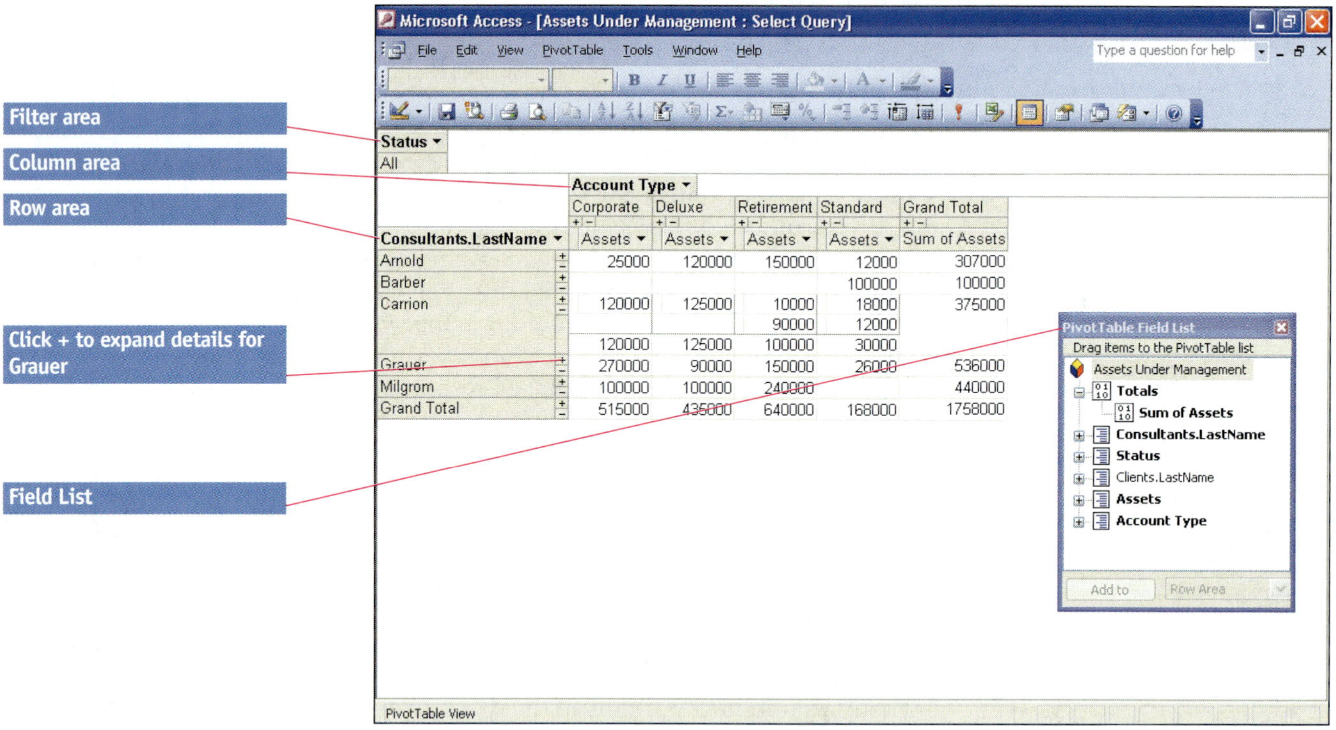

(a) Pivot Table

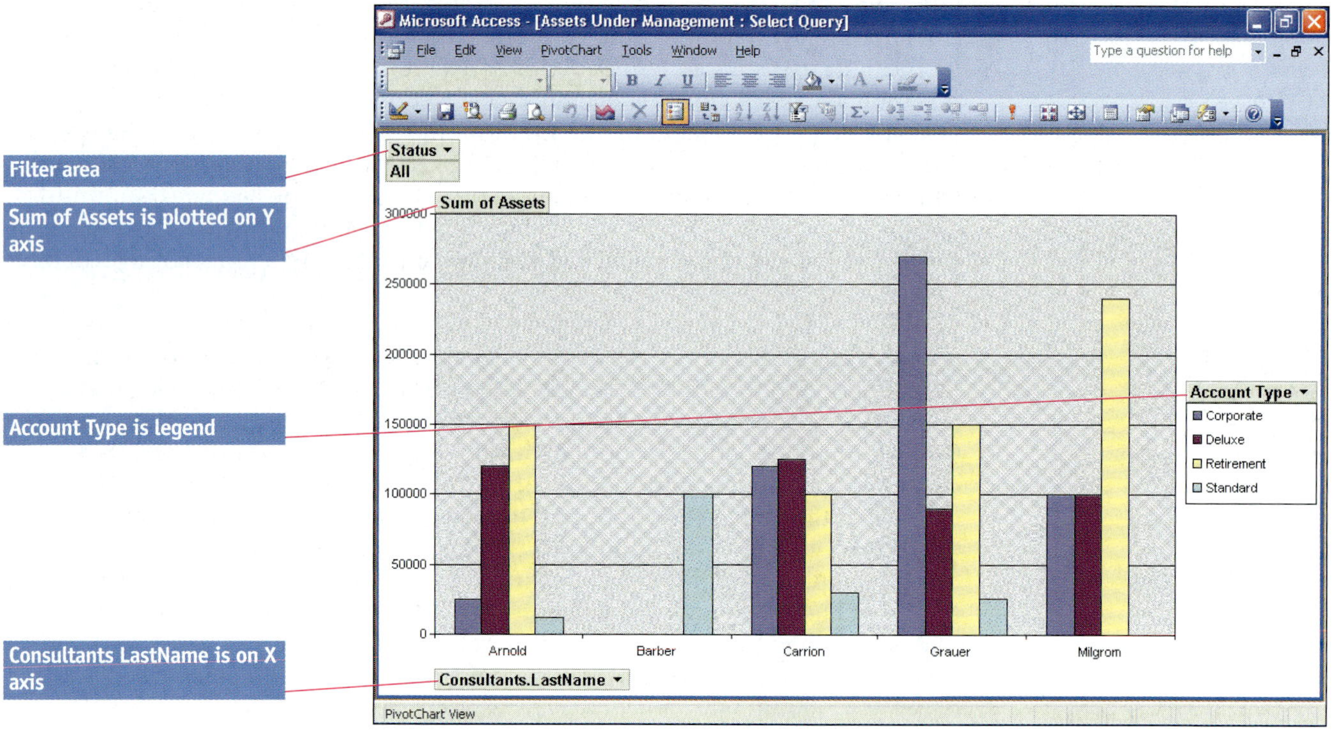

(b) Pivot Chart

FIGURE 4.7 Pivot Tables and Pivot Charts

hands-on exercise

2 Total Queries, Charts, and Pivot Tables

Objective To create a total query; to use Microsoft Graph to present data from an Access object in graphical form. Use Figure 4.8 as a guide.

Step 1: Copy the Assets Under Management Query

- Open the **Investment database**. Click the **Queries button** in the Database window and select the **Assets Under Management query** that was created earlier.
- Click the **Copy button** on the Database toolbar (or press **Ctrl+C**) to copy the query to the clipboard. Click the **Paste button** (or press **Ctrl+V**) to display the Paste As dialog box in Figure 4.8a.
- Enter **Assets Under Management Summary** as the name of the new query. Click **OK**. There are now two queries in the database window, the original query that was created in the previous exercise, as well as a copy of that query that you will modify in this exercise.
- Select (click) the **Assets Under Management Summary query** that was just created via the Copy and Paste commands. Click the **Design button** to open the query in Design view.

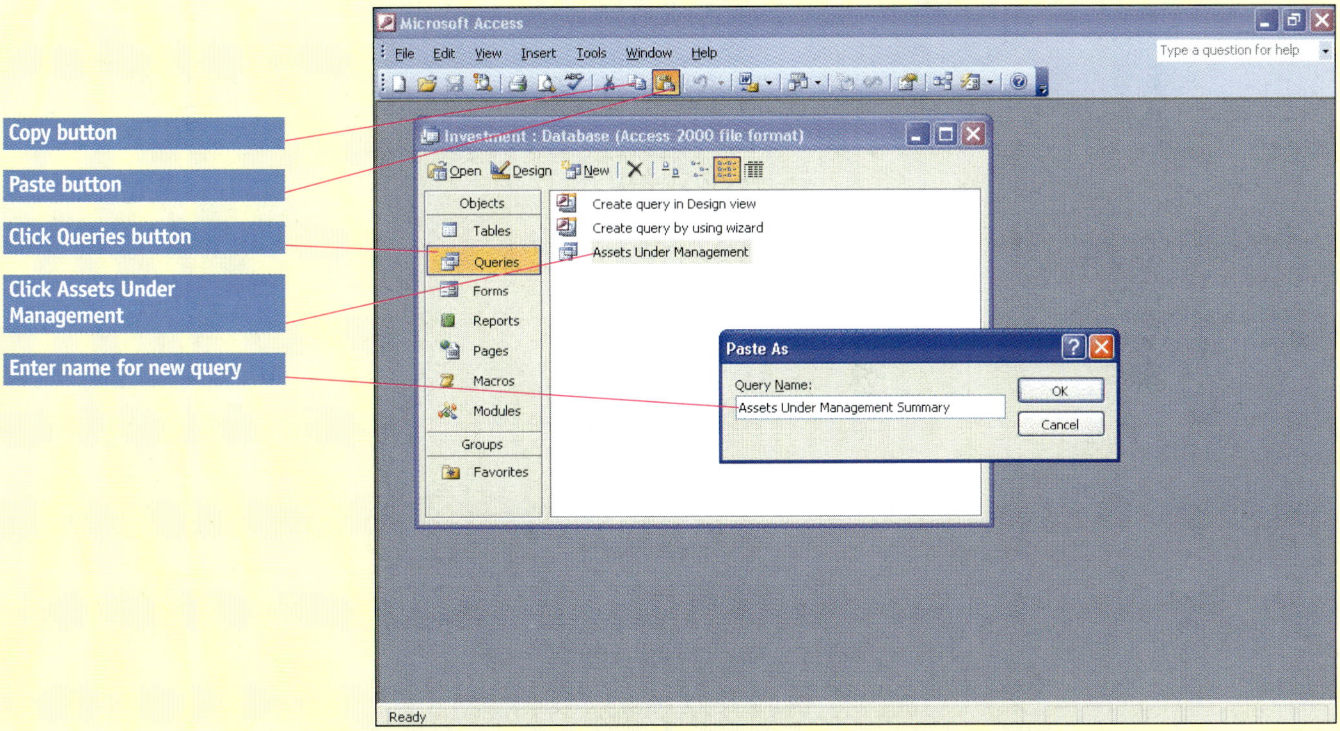

(a) Copy the Assets Under Management Query (step 1)

FIGURE 4.8 Hands-on Exercise 2

KEYBOARD SHORTCUTS—CUT, COPY, AND PASTE

Ctrl+X, Ctrl+C, and Ctrl+V are shortcuts to cut, copy, and paste, respectively, and apply to all applications in the Office suite as well as to Windows applications in general. The shortcuts are easier to remember when you realize that the operative letters X, C, and V are next to each other at the bottom left side of the keyboard.

Step 2: Create the Total Query

- You should see the Assets Under Management Summary in Design view as shown in Figure 4.8b. Maximize the window. Pull down the **View menu** and click **Totals** to display the Total row.
- Click the **Total row** under the **Client's LastName field**, click the **down arrow** to display the list of summary functions, then click the **Count function**.
- Click the **Total row** under the Assets field, click the **down arrow** to display the list of summary functions, then click the **Sum function**.
- Click the column selector for the **Consultants Status field** to select the entire column, then press the **Del key** to remove the column from the query. Delete the column containing the **Client's Account Type field** in similar fashion. Your query should now contain three fields.
- Pull down the **Query menu** and click **Run** (or click the **Run button**) to run the query. You should see a dynaset with five records, one for each financial consultant. Each record contains the total assets for one consultant.
- Save the query. Close the query.

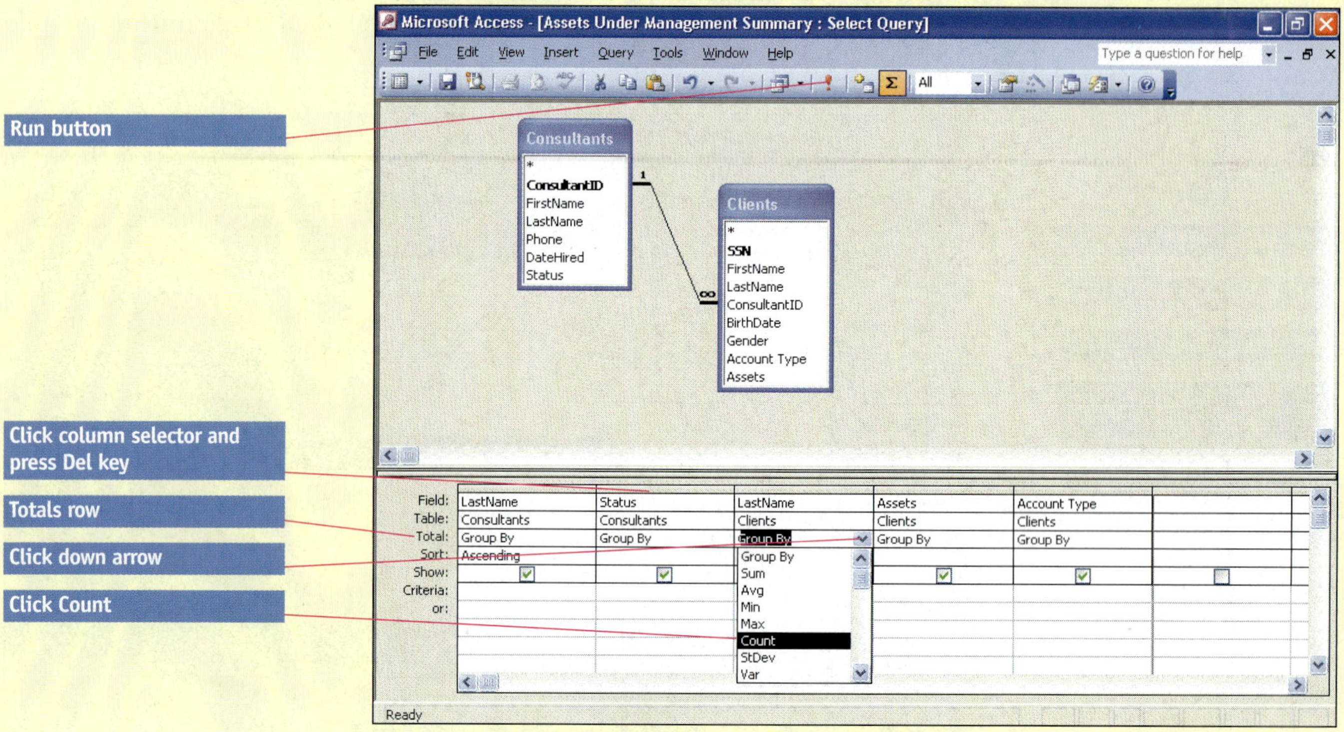

(b) Create the Total Query (step 2)

FIGURE 4.8 Hands-on Exercise 2 (*continued*)

THE UNMATCHED QUERY WIZARD

Any business wants all of its employees to be productive, and our hypothetical financial services concern is no exception. The Unmatched Query Wizard identifies records in one table (e.g., Consultants) that do not have matching records in another table (e.g., clients). In other words, it will tell you which consultants (if any) do not have any clients. Click the Queries button in the Database window, click the New button, select the Find Unmatched Query Wizard, and click OK. Answer the prompts to create the query and see the results.

Step 3: Start the Chart Wizard

- Click the **Reports button** in the Database window. Double click the **Assets Under Management report** to run the report. Click the **View button** to switch to Design view.
- You should see the Assets Under Management report in Design view as shown in Figure 4.8c. Click and drag the **Report Header** down in the report to increase the size of the Report Header.
- Click the control that is to contain the name of the person who prepared the report and enter your name. Arrange and format the controls in the Report Header as shown.
- Pull down the **Insert menu** and click the **Chart command**. The mouse pointer changes to a tiny crosshair. Click and drag in the **Report Header** to draw the outline of the chart as shown in Figure 4.8c.
- The Chart Wizard starts automatically and asks for the table or query on which to base the chart. Click the **Queries button**, click the **Assets Under Management Summary query**, and click **Next**.

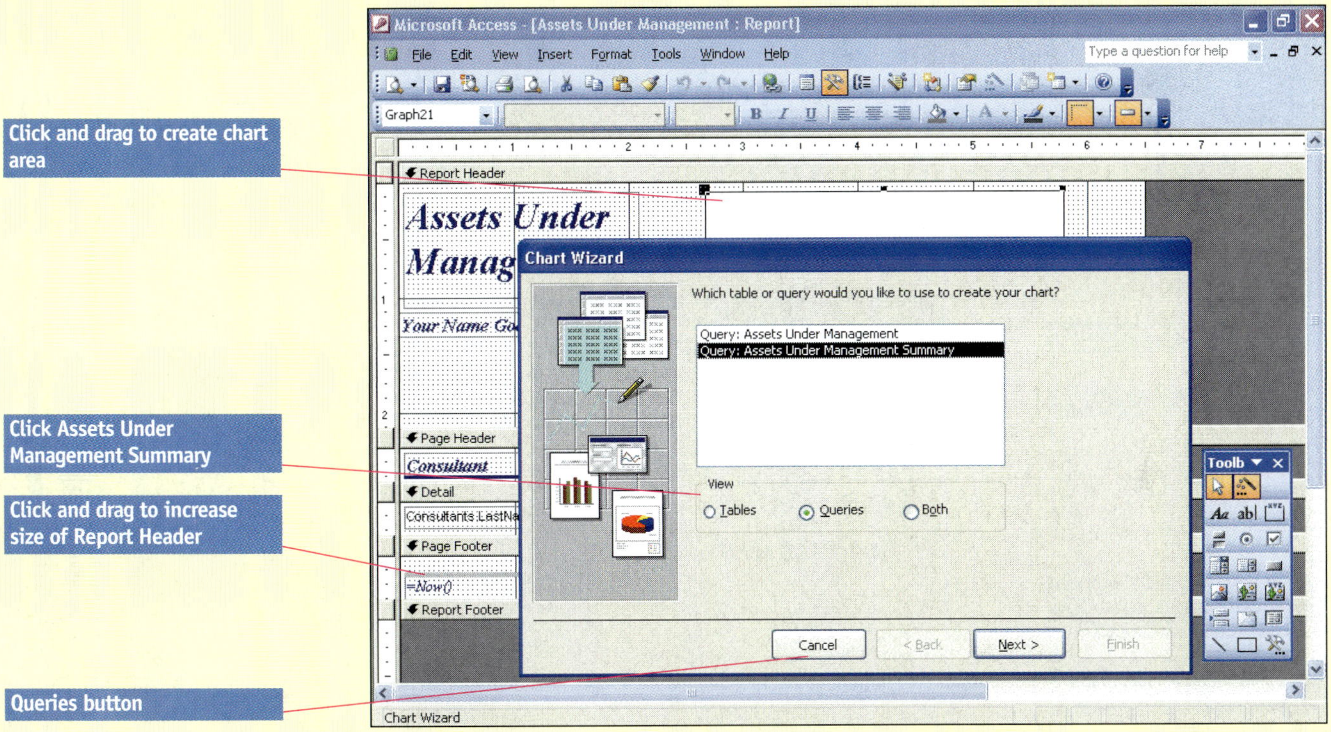

(c) Start the Chart Wizard (step 3)

FIGURE 4.8 Hands-on Exercise 2 (*continued*)

ANATOMY OF A REPORT

All reports are divided into sections that print at designated times. The Report Header and Report Footer are each printed once at the beginning and end of the report. The Page Header appears under the Report Header on the first page and at the top of every page thereafter. The Page Footer appears at the bottom of every page in the report, including the last page, where it appears after the Report Footer. The Detail section is printed once for each record in the underlying query or table.

Step 4: Complete the Chart Wizard

- Answer the questions posed by the Chart Wizard to complete the chart.
- Double click the **LastName** and **SumOfAssets fields** to move these fields from the list of Available fields to the list containing the fields for the chart. Click **Next** to continue.
- Select the **3-D Column Chart** as the chart type. Click **Next**.
- The Chart Wizard lays out the chart for you, with the SumOfAssets field on the Y axis and the LastName field on the X axis. Click **Next**.
- The chart should not change from record to record because we are plotting the total for each consultant. Thus, click the **down arrow** in both the Report Fields list and the Chart Fields list and select No Field. Click **Next**.
- Assets Under Management Summary is entered automatically as the title for the chart. Click the option button that indicates you do not want to display a legend. Click **Finish**.
- The completed chart appears in the report as shown in Figure 4.8d. Do not be concerned that the values along the Y axis do not match the Asset totals or that the labels on the X axis do not correspond to the names of the financial consultants.
- Click the **Save button** to save the report. Click anywhere in the **Report Header** to deselect the chart. Click the **View button** to view the chart within the report. The appearance of the chart more closely resembles the finished product, but the chart still needs work.
- Click the **View button** to return to the Design view.

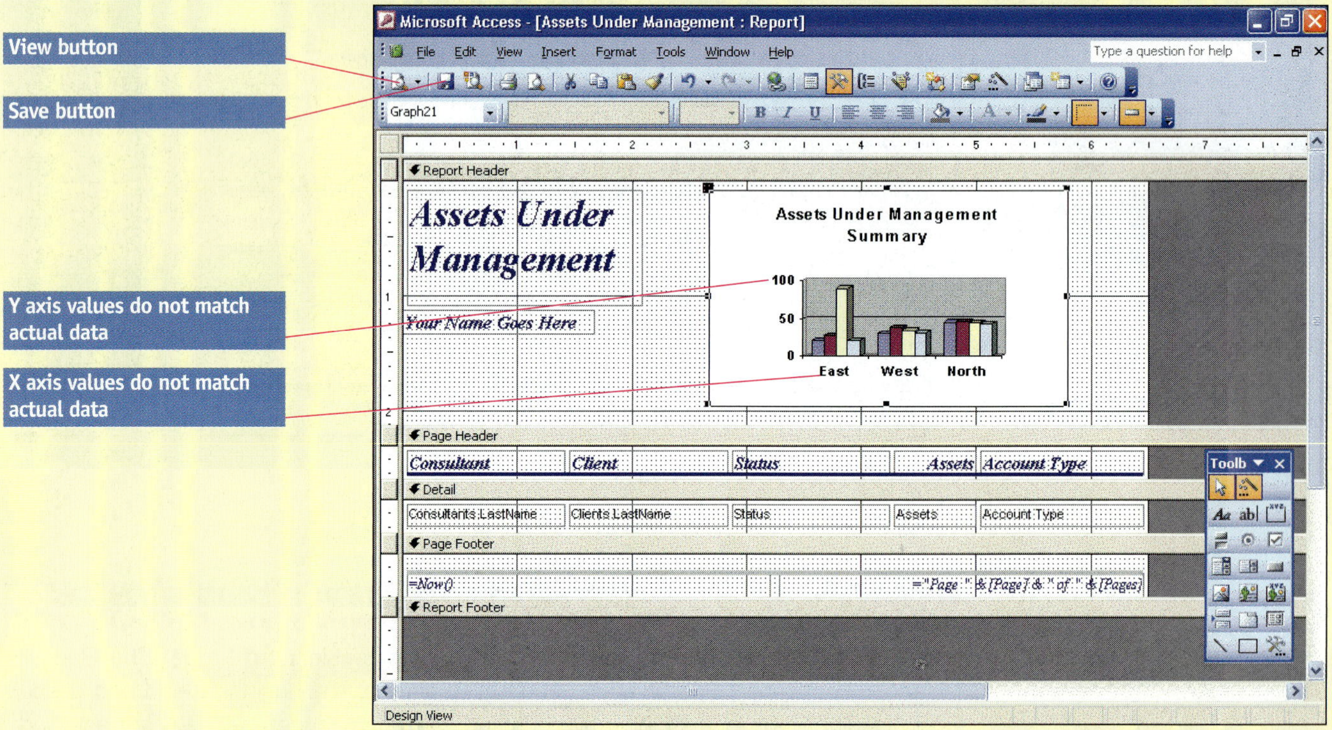

(d) Complete the Chart Wizard (step 4)

FIGURE 4.8 Hands-on Exercise 2 (*continued*)

Step 5: Increase the Plot Area

- Click anywhere in the chart to display the sizing handles, then (if necessary) drag the sizing handle on the right border to increase the width of the chart.
- You might also want to drag the Report Header down (to increase the size of the header), then click and drag the bottom border of the chart to make it deeper. The chart area should be large enough so that you will be able to see the names of all the financial consultants along the X axis.
- Click off the chart to deselect it, then double click within the chart to display the hashed border as shown in Figure 4.8e.
- Close the chart datasheet if it appears. Click (select) the title of the chart and press the **Del key**.
- Right click the **Y axis**, click **Format Axis**, click the **Number tab**, and set to **Currency format** with **zero** decimals. Click **OK**.
- Click off the chart to deselect the chart, then click the **View button**. Continue to move back and forth between the Design view and the finished report, until you can see all of the consultants' names along the X axis.
- Close the report. Click **Yes** if asked whether to save the changes to the report.

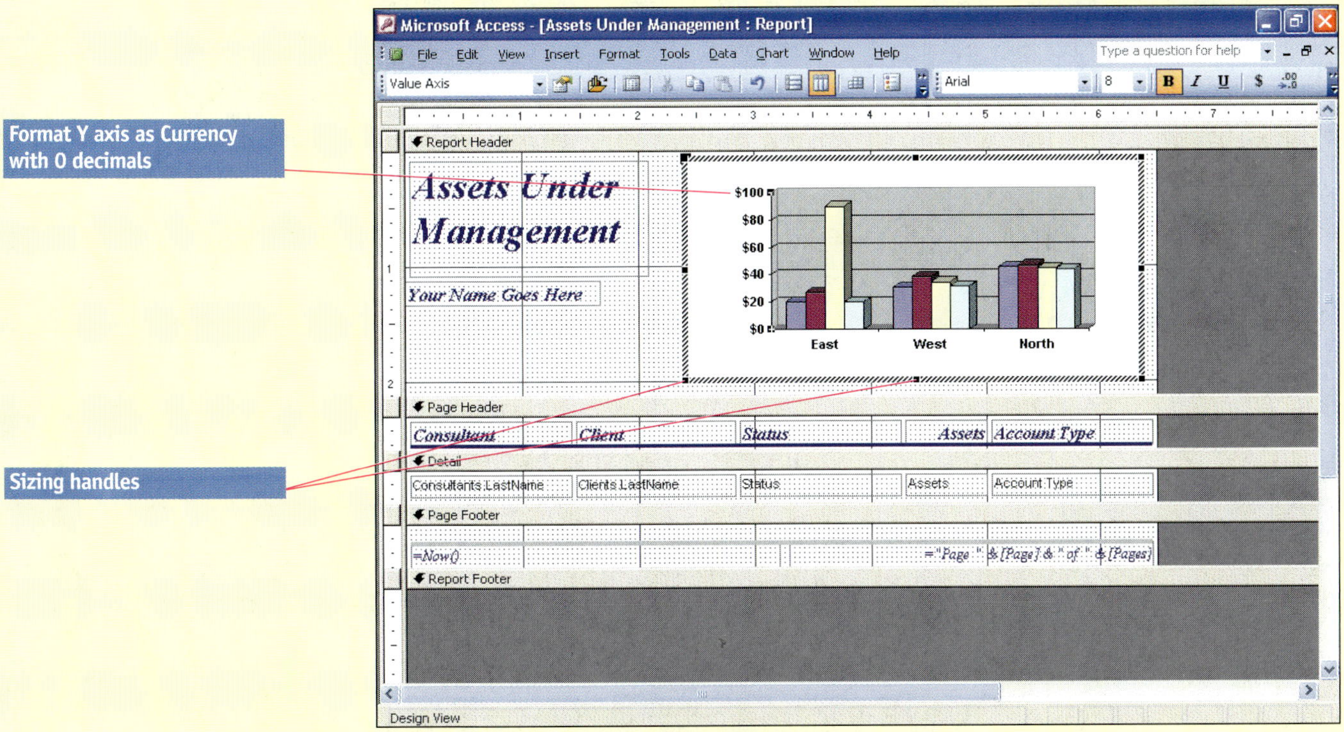

(e) Increase the Plot Area (step 5)

FIGURE 4.8 Hands-on Exercise 2 (*continued*)

TO CLICK OR NOT TO CLICK

Click anywhere on the chart to select the chart and display the sizing handles; this allows you to move and/or size the chart within the report. Click off the chart to deselect it, then double click the chart to start the Microsoft Graph in order to modify the chart itself.

Step 6: The Completed Report

- Click the **Forms button**, open the **Clients form**, locate your record, and change your assets to **$100,000**. Click the **▶ button** to record your changes and move to the next record. Close the Clients form.
- Click the **Queries button**, then double click the **Assets Under Management Summary query** to rerun the query. The increased value of your account should be reflected in the Assets Under Management of your instructor. Close the query.
- Click the **Reports button**, and double click the **Assets Under Management report** to open the report as shown in Figure 4.7f.
- The detailed information for your account (Doe in this example) appears within the detailed records in the body of the report. The value of your account ($100,000) is reflected in the total for your instructor.
- Click the **Setup button** and change all margins to **one-half an inch**. Click the **Print button** to print the report for your instructor. Close the Report window.

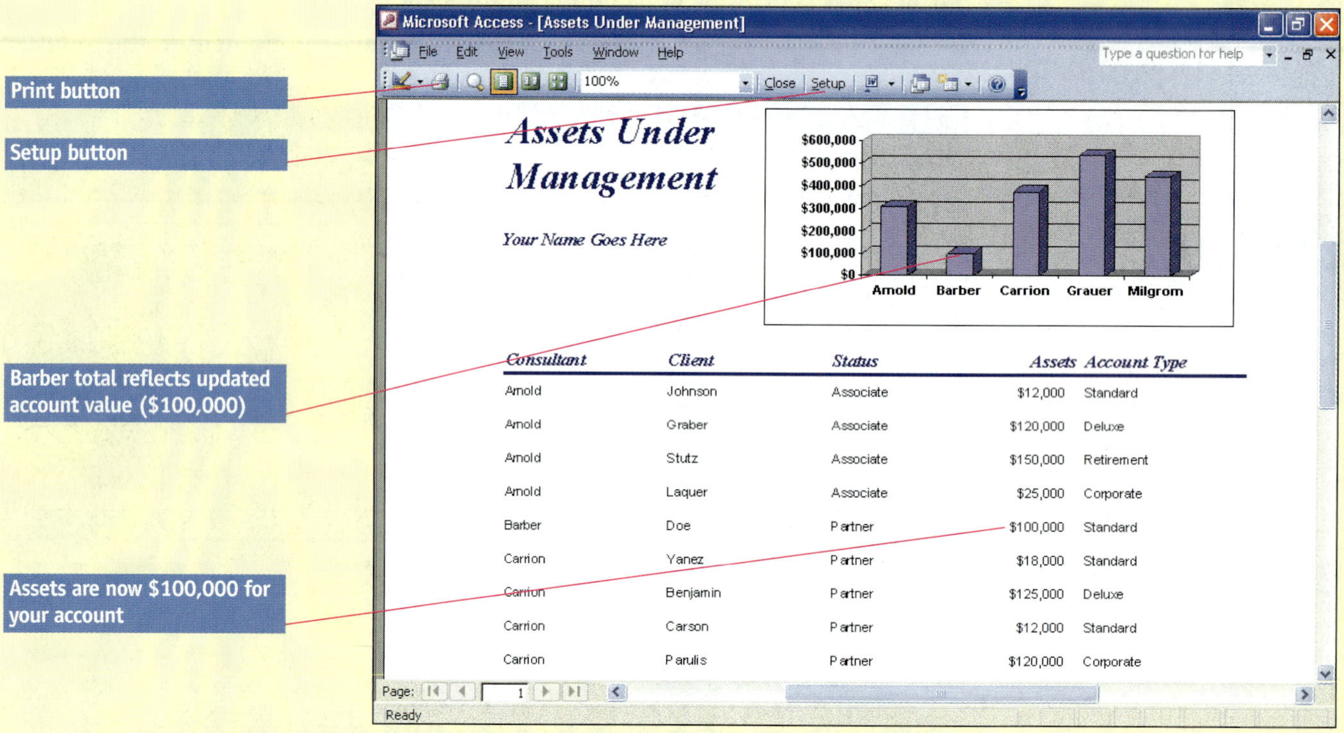

(f) The Completed Report (step 6)

FIGURE 4.8 Hands-on Exercise 2 (*continued*)

OPEN THE SUBDATASHEET

Take advantage of the one-to-many relationship that exists between consultants and clients to add and/or delete records in the Clients table while viewing the information for the associated consultant. Go to the Database window, open the Consultants table in Datasheet view, then click the plus sign next to the consultant. You now have access to all of the client records for that consultant and can add, edit, or delete a record as necessary. Click the minus sign to close the client list.

Step 7: Create the Pivot Table

- Open the **Assets Under Management query**. Pull down the **View menu** and select the **PivotTable View** to display an empty pivot table. If necessary, pull down the **View menu** a second time and click the **Field List command** (or simply click the **Field List button** on the Pivot Table toolbar) to display the field list.
- Click and drag the **Consultants.LastName field** to the row area as shown in Figure 4.8g. Click and drag the **Account Type field** to the column area and the **Status field** to the filter area.
- Click and drag the **Assets field** to the Totals or Detail Fields area as shown in Figure 4.8g. You should see the total assets for each consultant, account type, and the database as a whole. Click the **Save button**. Close the field list.
- Right click on the **25,000** Corporate Assets for Arnold. Click **AutoCalc**; click **Sum**. You will see the sum of each client's assets in the Grand Total column.
- Click the **minus sign** next to each consultant's name to show just the totals for each consultant in each Account Type category.
- Pull down the **File menu**, click the **Print command**, and click **OK** (or click the **Print button** on the PivotTable toolbar) to print the pivot table.

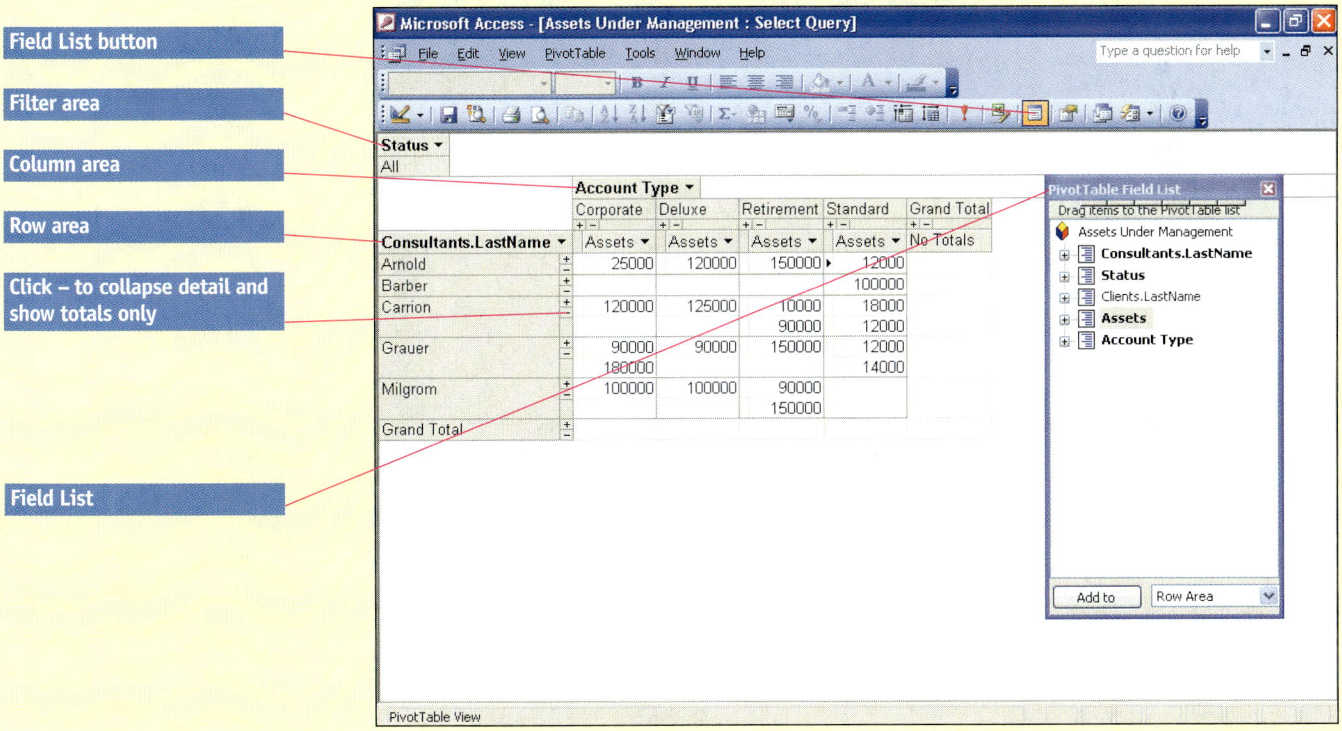

(g) Create the Pivot Table (step 7)

FIGURE 4.8 Hands-on Exercise 2 (*continued*)

CHANGE THE ORDER

Click within any row or column, then click the Ascending or Descending button on the PivotChart toolbar to display the entries in the selected sequence. Click in the Consultants.LastName column, for example, and click the Ascending button to display the rows alphabetically. Click a single cell in the Grand Total column, then click the Descending button to display the consultant with the highest assets first.

Step 8: **The Pivot Chart**

- Pull down the **View menu** and select the **PivotChart view** to display the pivot chart in Figure 4.8h. The chart corresponds to the pivot table you just created. Close the Field list.
- Pull down the **PivotChart menu** and click the **Show Legend command** (or click the **Show Legend button** on the PivotChart toolbar) to display the legend. The names of the different account types appear as a legend.
- Pull down the **PivotChart menu** and click the **By Row/By Column command** to reverse the rows and columns. The Account Types now appear as the category names, and the names of the consultants appear in the legend.
- The label "Axis Title" does not enhance either the X or Y axis. Click the label on either axis, then press the **Delete key**. Delete the other label in similar fashion.
- Pull down the **File menu**, click the **Page Setup command**, click the **Page tab**, change to **Landscape printing**, and click **OK**. Click the **Print button** on the PivotTable toolbar to print the pivot table.
- Close the query. Click **Yes** when asked whether to save the changes. Exit Access if you do not want to continue with the next exercise at this time.

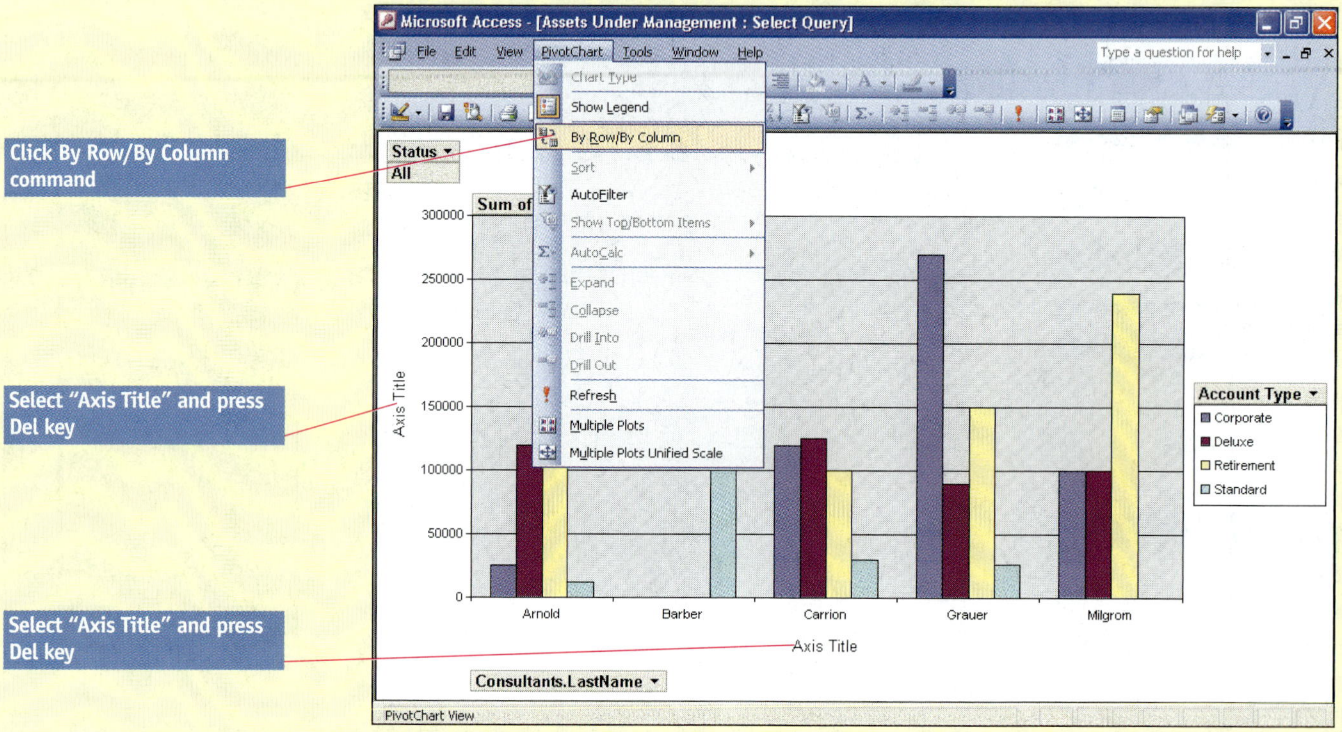

(h) The Pivot Chart (step 8)

FIGURE 4.8 Hands-on Exercise 2 (*continued*)

IMPOSE OR CLEAR A FILTER

Click the down arrow next to any field name to display all of the values for that field, then check or clear the boxes next to the field values. Click the down arrow next to the Account Type field, for example, then clear the box for the Corporate account type. Click OK and the associated column disappears from the table. There is no Undo command, but you can restore the column by reversing the process. And remember, any changes to the pivot chart are automatically reflected in the associated pivot table.

THE USER INTERFACE

The Investment database has grown in sophistication throughout the chapter. It contains two tables, for clients and consultants. There is a one-to-many relationship between consultants and clients, and referential integrity is enforced. There is a form to enter data into each table. There are also queries and reports based on these tables. You are proficient in Access and are familiar with its Database window to the extent that you can select different objects to accomplish the work you have to do. But what if the system is to be used by a nontechnical user who might not know how to open the various forms and reports within the system?

It is important, therefore, to create a user interface that ties the objects together so that the database is easy to use. The interface displays a menu (or series of menus) enabling a nontechnical person to open the various objects within the database, and to move easily from one object to another. This type of interface is called a ***switchboard***, and it is illustrated in Figure 4.9. The switchboard itself is stored as a form within the database, but it is subtly different from the forms you have developed in previous chapters. Look closely and note that the record selector and navigation buttons have been suppressed because the switchboard is not used for data entry, but rather as a menu for the user.

The switchboard is intuitive and easy to use. Click About Investments, the first button on the switchboard in Figure 4.9a, and the system displays the informational screen we like to include in all of our applications. Click any other button, and you display the indicated form or report. Close the form or report, and you will be returned to the switchboard, where you can select another item.

You should try to develop a switchboard that will appeal to your users. Speak in depth to the people who will use your application to determine what they expect from the system. Identify the tasks they consider critical, and be sure you have an easily accessible menu option for those tasks.

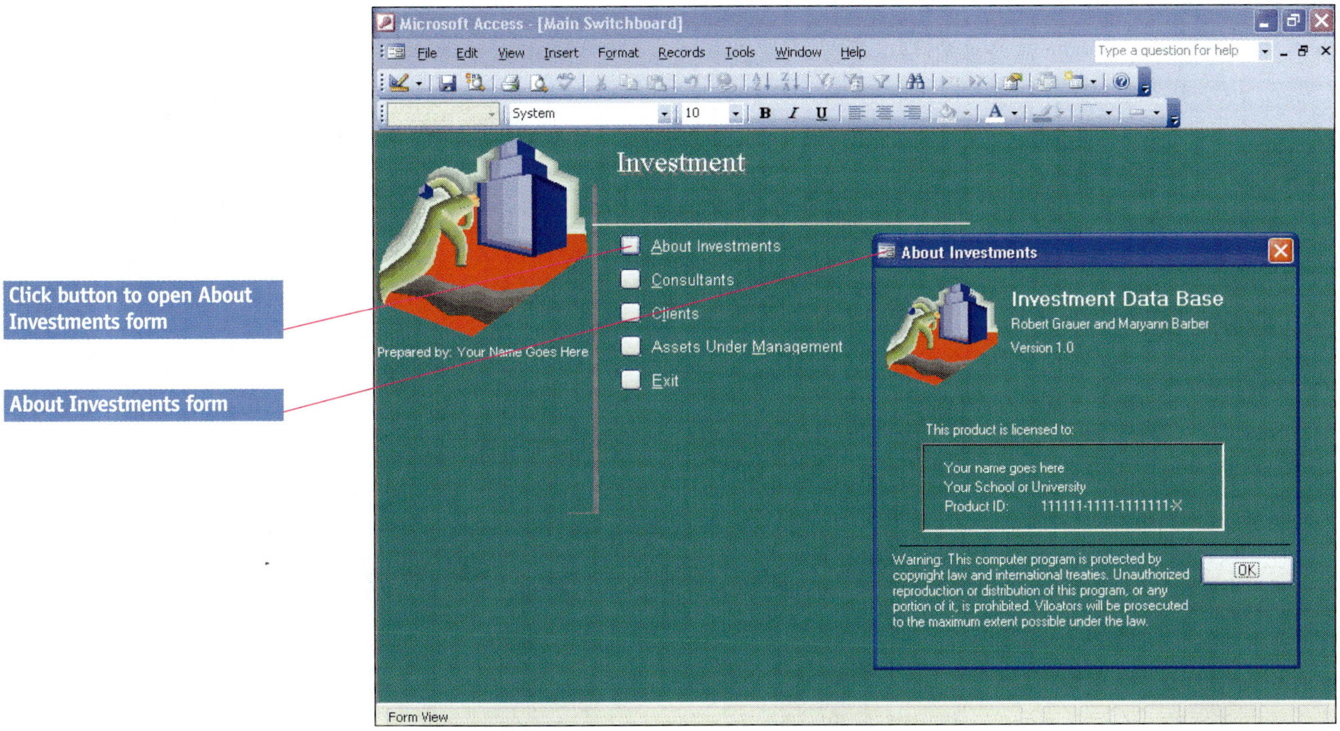

(a) The Switchboard

FIGURE 4.9 The Switchboard

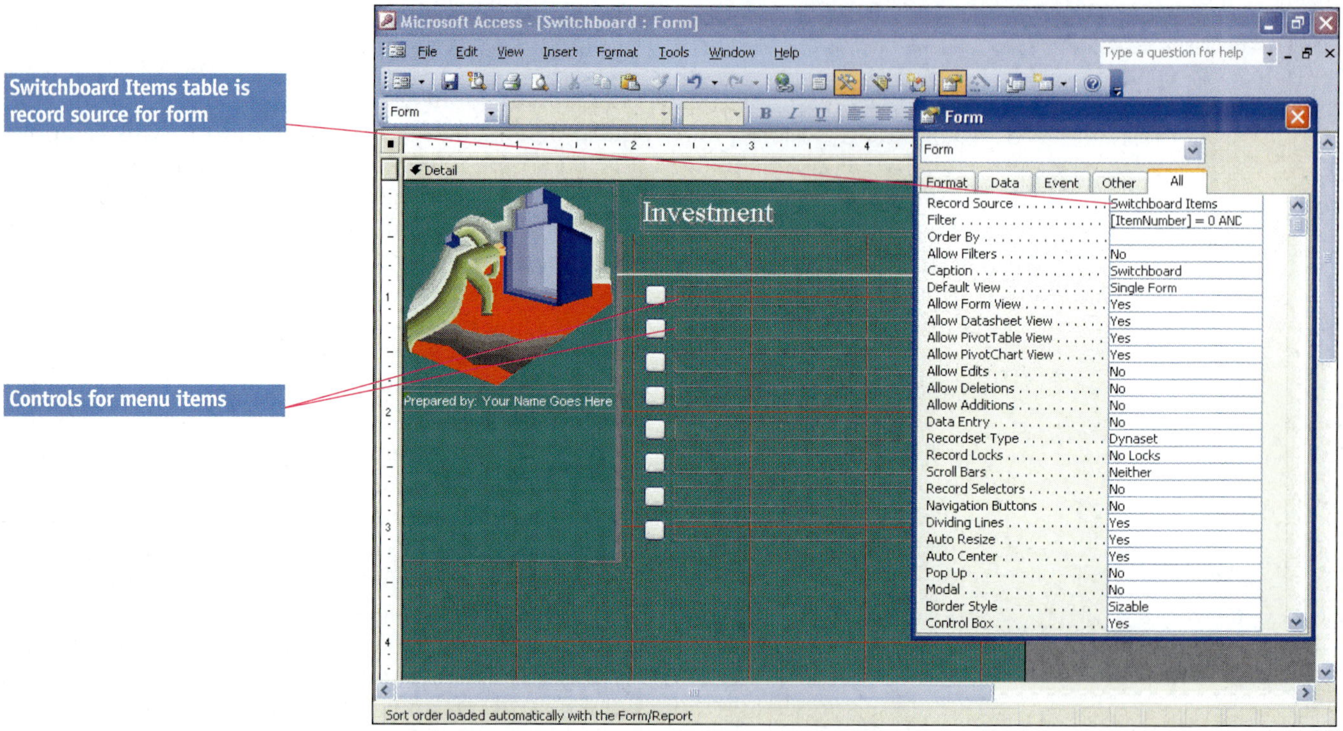

(b) Design View

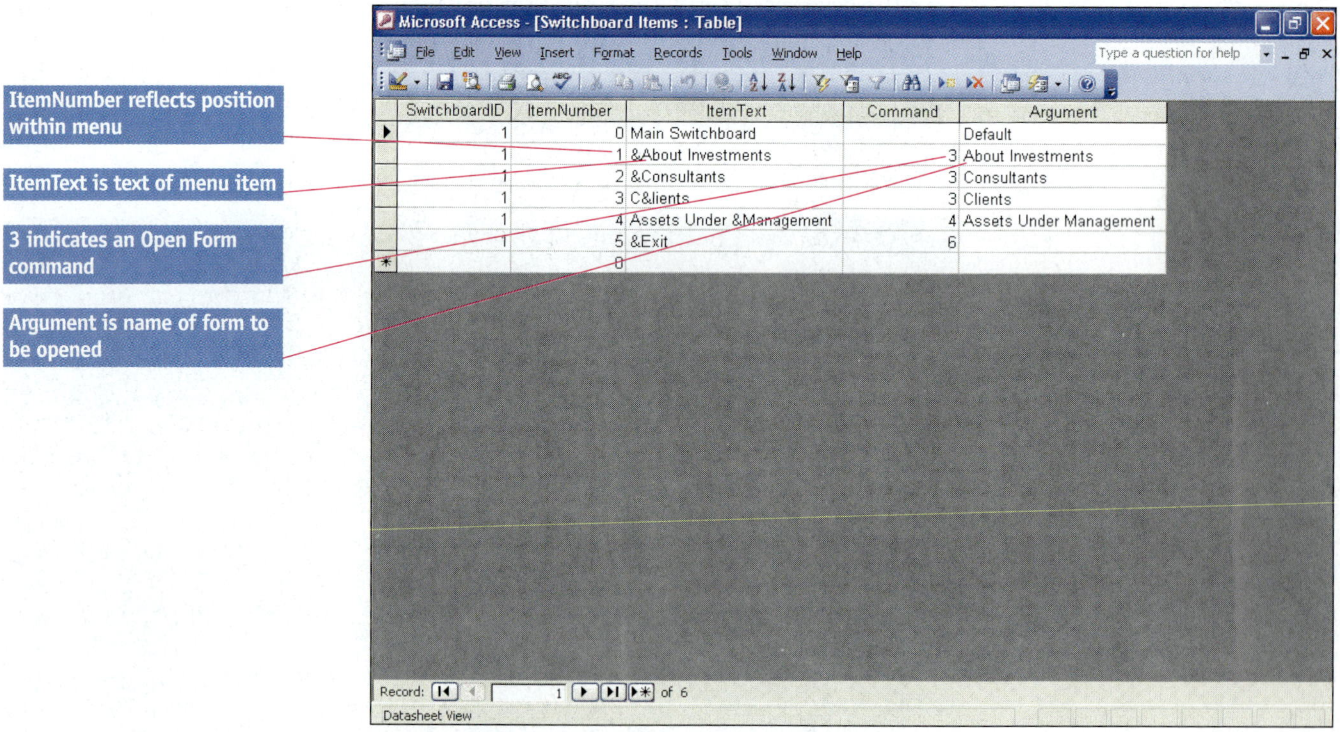

(c) The Switchboard Items Table

FIGURE 4.9 The Switchboard (*continued*)

The Switchboard Manager

The switchboard is quite powerful, but it is also very easy to create. All of the work is done by the ***Switchboard Manager***, an Access utility that prompts you for information about each menu. You supply the text of the item, as it is to appear on the switchboard (e.g., Clients), together with the underlying command (e.g., Open Clients Form). Access does the rest. It creates the switchboard form and an associated ***Switchboard Items table*** that is the basis for the switchboard. Figure 4.9b displays the Design view of the switchboard in Figure 4.9a.

At first, the two views do not appear to correspond to one another, in that text appears next to each button in the Form view, but it is absent in the Design view. This, however, is the nature of a switchboard, because the text for each button is taken from the Switchboard Items table in Figure 4.9c, which is the record source for the form, as can be inferred from the Form property sheet shown in Figure 4.9b. In other words, each record in the Switchboard Items table has a corresponding menu item in the switchboard form.

The Switchboard Items table is created automatically and need never be modified explicitly. It helps, however, to have an appreciation for each field in the table. The SwitchboardID field identifies the number of the switchboard, which becomes important in applications with more than one switchboard. Access limits each switchboard to eight items, but you can create as many switchboards as you like, each with a different value for the SwitchboardID. Every database has a main switchboard by default, which can in turn display other switchboards as necessary.

The ItemNumber and ItemText fields identify the position and text of the item, respectively, as it appears on the switchboard form. (The & that appears within the ItemText field will appear as an underlined letter on the switchboard to enable a keyboard shortcut; for example, &Consultants is displayed as Consultants and recognizes the Alt+C keyboard shortcut in lieu of clicking the button.) The Command and Argument fields determine the action that will be taken when the corresponding button is clicked. Command number 3, for example, opens a form.

Other Access Utilities

The ***Convert Database command*** changes the file format of an Access 2003 database to the format used by earlier versions. Think, for a moment, why such a command is necessary. Access 2003 is the current release of Microsoft Access, and thus it is able to read files that were created in all previous versions. The converse is not true, however. Access 2000, for example, cannot read an Access 2003 database because the latter uses a file format that was unknown when Access 2000 was developed. The Convert Database command solves the problem by translating an Access 2003 database to the earlier format. (Access 2003 also enables you to create and modify databases in the Access 2000 format, without going through the conversion process.)

The ***Compact and Repair Database command*** serves two functions, as its name suggests. The compacting process eliminates the fragmentation and wasted disk space that occur during development as you add, edit, and delete the various objects in a database. Compacting can be done when the database is open or closed. Compacting a database when it's open saves the database under the same name. Compacting a database when it is closed is safer, however, since the compacted database is stored as a new file (enabling you to return to the original file should anything go wrong). The Repair function takes place automatically if Access is unable to read a database when the database is opened initially.

The ***Back Up Database command*** compacts the open database, and then it saves the compacted database under a different name that contains the date the backup was created. Thus, if you were to back up a database named "Investment", the backup copy would be named "Investment_2003-07-16", given that the backup was created on July 16, 2003.

hands-on exercise

3 The Switchboard Manager

Objective To create a switchboard and user interface; to compact a database. Use Figure 4.10 as a guide in the exercise.

Step 1: Start the Switchboard Manager

- Open the **Investment database**. Minimize the Database window to give yourself more room in which to work.
- Pull down the **Tools menu**, click the **Options command**, click the **Forms/Report tab** to display the associated dialog box, then check the box to **Use Windows Themed Controls on Forms**.
- Pull down the **Tools menu**, click the **Database Utilities command**, and choose **Switchboard Manager**.
- Click **Yes** if you see a message indicating that there is no valid switchboard and asking if you want to create one. You should see the Switchboard Manager dialog box as shown in Figure 4.10a.
- Click the **Edit command button** to edit the Main Switchboard, which displays the Edit Switchboard Page dialog box. Click the **New command button** to add an item to this page, which in turn displays the Edit Switchboard item dialog box. Add the first switchboard item as follows.
  - Click in the **Text list box** and type **&About Investments**, which is the name of the command, as it will appear in the switchboard.
  - Click the **drop-down arrow** on the Command list box and choose the command to Open the Form in either the Add or Edit mode.
  - Click the **down arrow** in the Form list box and choose **About Investments**.
- Click **OK** to create the switchboard item. The Edit Switchboard Item dialog box closes, and the item appears in the Main Switchboard page.

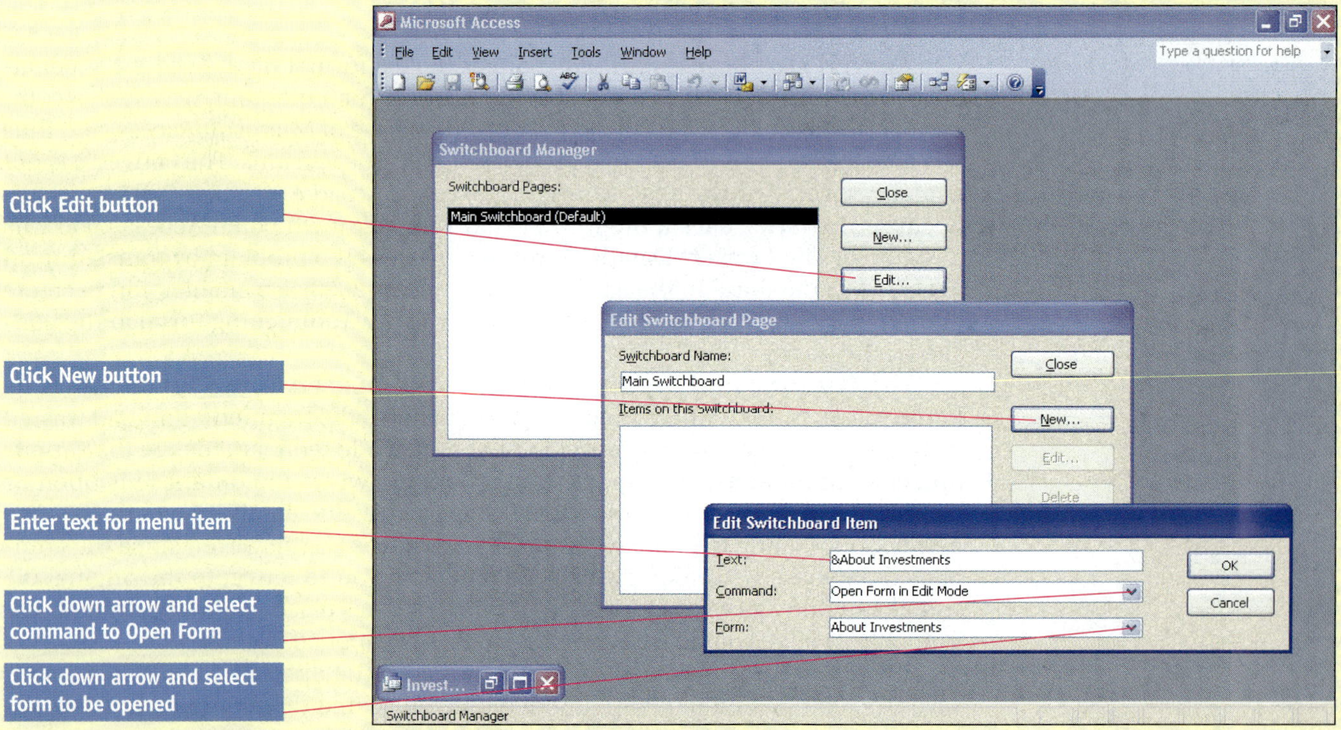

(a) Start the Switchboard Manager (step 1)

FIGURE 4.10 Hands-on Exercise 3

Step 2: Complete the Switchboard

- Click the **New command button** in the Edit Switchboard Page dialog box to add a second item to the switchboard.
- Click in the **Text list box** and type **&Consultants**. Click the **drop-down arrow** on the Command list box and choose **Open Form in Edit Mode**. Click the **drop-down arrow** in the Form list box and choose **Consultants**. Click **OK**.
- The &Consultants command appears as an item on the switchboard (The switchboard will display Consultants to indicate a keyboard shortcut—see boxed tip.)
- Add the remaining items to the switchboard as shown in Figure 4.10b. The menu items are as follows:
  - ❑ **C&lients**—Opens the Clients form in Edit mode.
  - ❑ **Assets Under &Management**—Opens the Assets report.
  - ❑ **&Exit**—Exits the application (closes the database but remains in Access).
- Click the **Close button** to close the Edit Switchboard Page dialog box after you have added the last item. Close the Switchboard Manager dialog box.

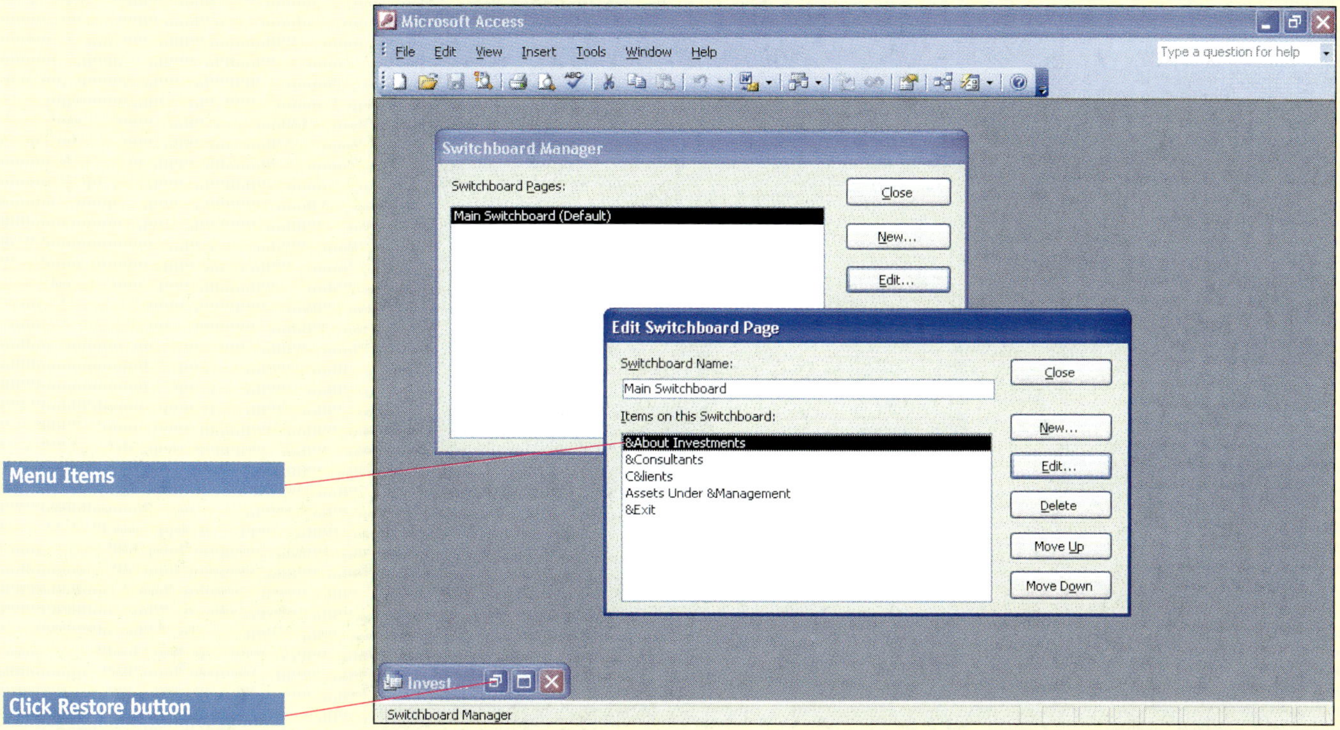

(b) Complete the Switchboard (step 2)

FIGURE 4.10 Hands-on Exercise 3 (*continued*)

CREATE A KEYBOARD SHORTCUT

The & has special significance when used within the name of an Access object because it creates a keyboard shortcut to that object. Enter "&About Investments", for example, and the letter A (the letter immediately after the ampersand) will be underlined and appear as "About Investments" on the switchboard. From there, you can execute the item by clicking its button, or you can use the Alt+A keyboard shortcut (where "A" is the underlined letter in the menu option).

Step 3: Test the Switchboard

- Click the **Restore button** in the Database window to view the objects in the database, then click the **Forms button**. The Switchboard Manager has created the Switchboard form automatically.
- Double click the **Switchboard form** to open the Main Switchboard. Do not be concerned about the design of the switchboard at this time, as your immediate objective is to make sure that the buttons work.
- Click the **About Investments button** (or use the **Alt+A** shortcut) to display the About Investments form as shown in Figure 4.10c. Click the **OK button** to close the form.
- Click the **Consultants button** (or use the **Alt+C** keyboard shortcut) to open the Consultants form. Click the **Close Form button** on the form to close this form and return to the switchboard.
- Test the remaining items on the switchboard (except the Exit button). You can click the button and/or use the keyboard shortcut as you see fit.

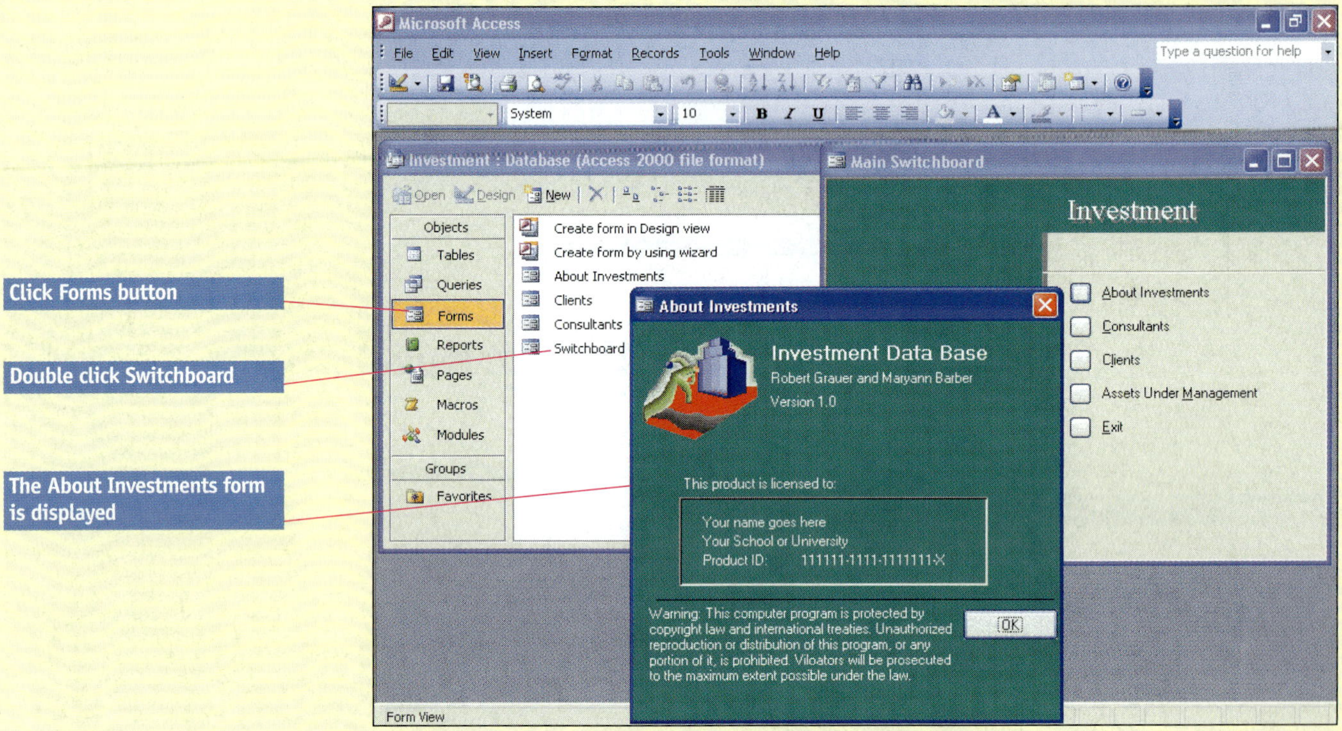

(c) Test the Switchboard (step 3)

FIGURE 4.10 Hands-on Exercise 3 (*continued*)

THE SWITCHBOARD ITEMS TABLE

You can modify an existing switchboard in one of two ways—by using the Switchboard Manager or by making changes directly in the underlying table of switchboard items. Press the F11 key to display the Database window, click the Tables button, then open the Switchboard Items table where you can make changes to the various entries on the switchboard. We encourage you to experiment, but start by changing one entry at a time. The ItemText field is a good place to begin.

Step 4: Insert the Clip Art

- Change to Design view. Maximize the window so that you have more room to work. Click in the left side of the switchboard. Pull down the **Insert menu** and click the **Picture command** to display the Insert Picture dialog box as shown in Figure 4.10d.
- Select the **Exploring Access folder**. Click the **Views button** repeatedly until you see the **Thumbnails View**. Select (click) a picture. Click **OK**.
- Move and/or size the image as necessary. Do not be concerned if you do not see the entire image as you change its size and position.
- Right click the clip art after it has been sized to display a shortcut menu, then click **Properties** to display the Properties dialog box. Select (click) the **Size Mode property**, click the **down arrow**, and select **Stretch** from the associated list. Close the dialog box.
- Click to the right of the picture in the Detail (gray) area of the form. Click the **drop-down arrow** on the **Fill/Back Color button** on the Formatting toolbar to display a color palette. Select the same shade as the rest of the form (the fifth square from the left in the second row).

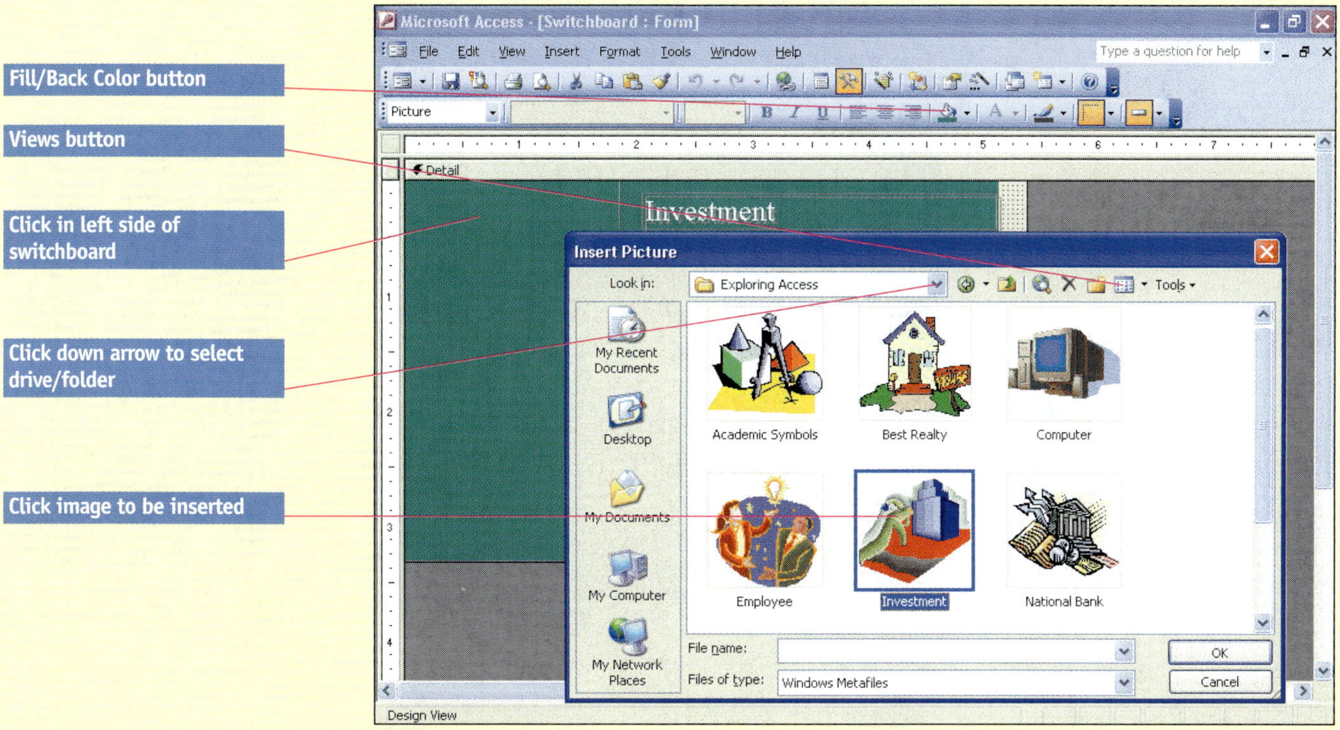

(d) Insert the Clip Art (step 4)

FIGURE 4.10 Hands-on Exercise 3 (*continued*)

SEARCHING FOR CLIP ART

The Insert Picture command functions differently in Access than in the other Office applications since it does not display the Clip Art task pane. You can still search for clip art explicitly, however, by starting the Clip Organizer as a separate application. Click the Start button, click the All Programs button, click Microsoft Office, click Microsoft Office Tools, then start the Microsoft Clip Organizer. Select a clip art image from within the Clip Organizer, and click the Copy button. Use the Windows taskbar to return to Access, open the form in Design view, and click the Paste button.

Step 5: Complete the Design

- If necessary, click the **Toolbox tool** to display the toolbox. Click the **Label tool**, then click and drag to create a text box under the picture.
- Enter your name in an appropriate font, point size, and color. Move and/or size the label containing your name as appropriate.
- Press and hold the **Shift button** as you click each text box in succession. Be sure that you select all eight, even if you do not have eight menu choices.
- Click the **drop-down arrow** on the Font/Fore color button and change the font to white as shown in Figure 4.10e. Change the font and point size to **Arial** and **10 pt**, respectively.
- Click the **Save button** to save the changes, then switch to the Form view to see the modified switchboard. Return to the Design view as necessary and make final adjustments to the switchboard. Save the form.
- Click the **View button** to see the switchboard.

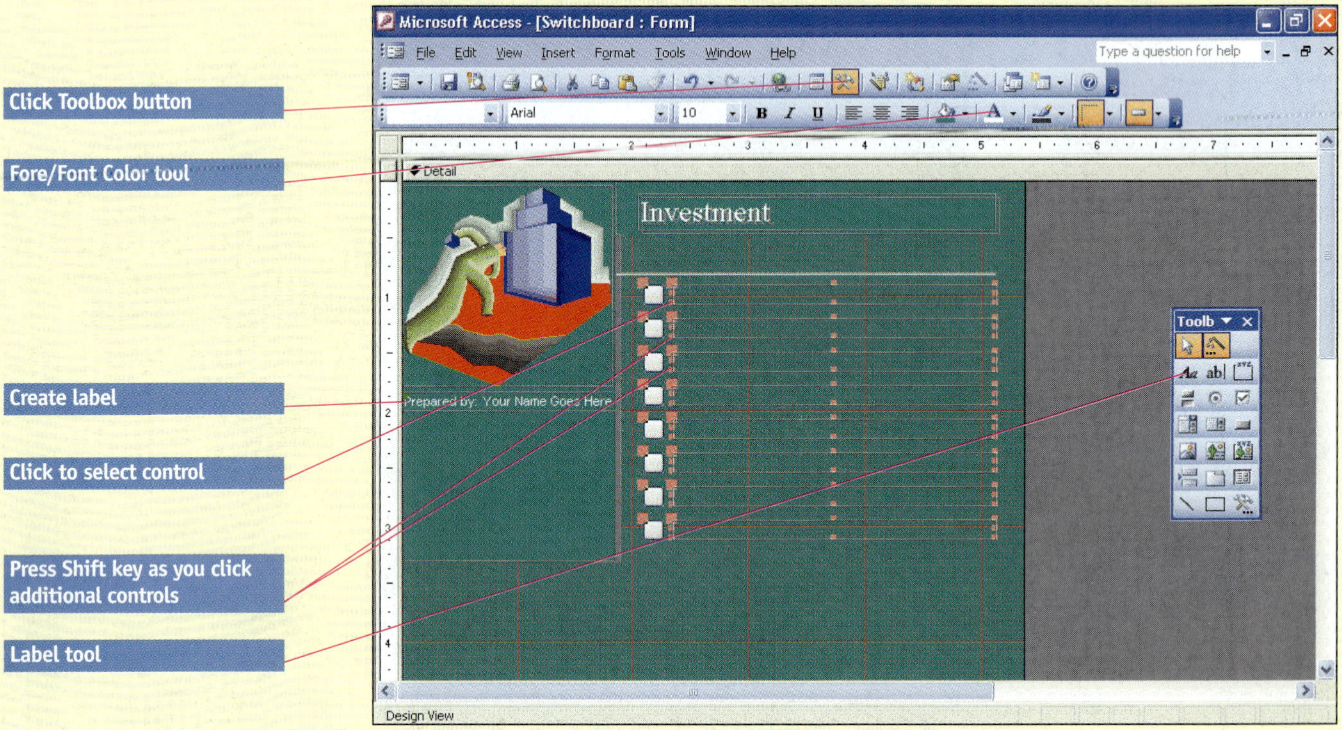

(e) Complete the Design (step 5)

FIGURE 4.10 Hands-on Exercise 3 (*continued*)

THE STARTUP PROPERTY

The ideal way to open a database is to present the user with the main switchboard, without the user having to take any special action. Pull down the Tools menu, click Startup to display the Startup dialog box, click the drop-down arrow in the Display Form/Page list box, and select the Switchboard as the form to open. Add a personal touch to the database by clicking in the Application Title text box and entering your name. Click OK to accept the settings and close the Startup dialog box. The next time the database is opened, the switchboard will be displayed automatically.

Step 6: The Completed Switchboard and Object Dependencies

- You should see the completed switchboard in Figure 4.10f. Click the **Maximize button** so that the switchboard takes the entire screen.
- Press **Alt+L** (when the switchboard is active) to open the Clients form. Locate your record. Change the Assets to $2,000,000 (wishful thinking). Close the Clients form and return to the switchboard.
- Press **Alt+M** to open the Assets Under Management report. The chart should reflect the increased value of your account. Close the report.
- Pull down the **View menu** and click the **Object Dependencies command** to open the task pane in Figure 4.10f. Click the option button that says **Objects that I depend on**.
- If necessary, click the **plus sign** that appears next to Tables within the task pane. You should see the Switchboard Items table indicating that the switchboard is dependent on an underlying table.
- Click the **Close button** at the extreme right of the menu bar to close the switchboard but leave the database open.

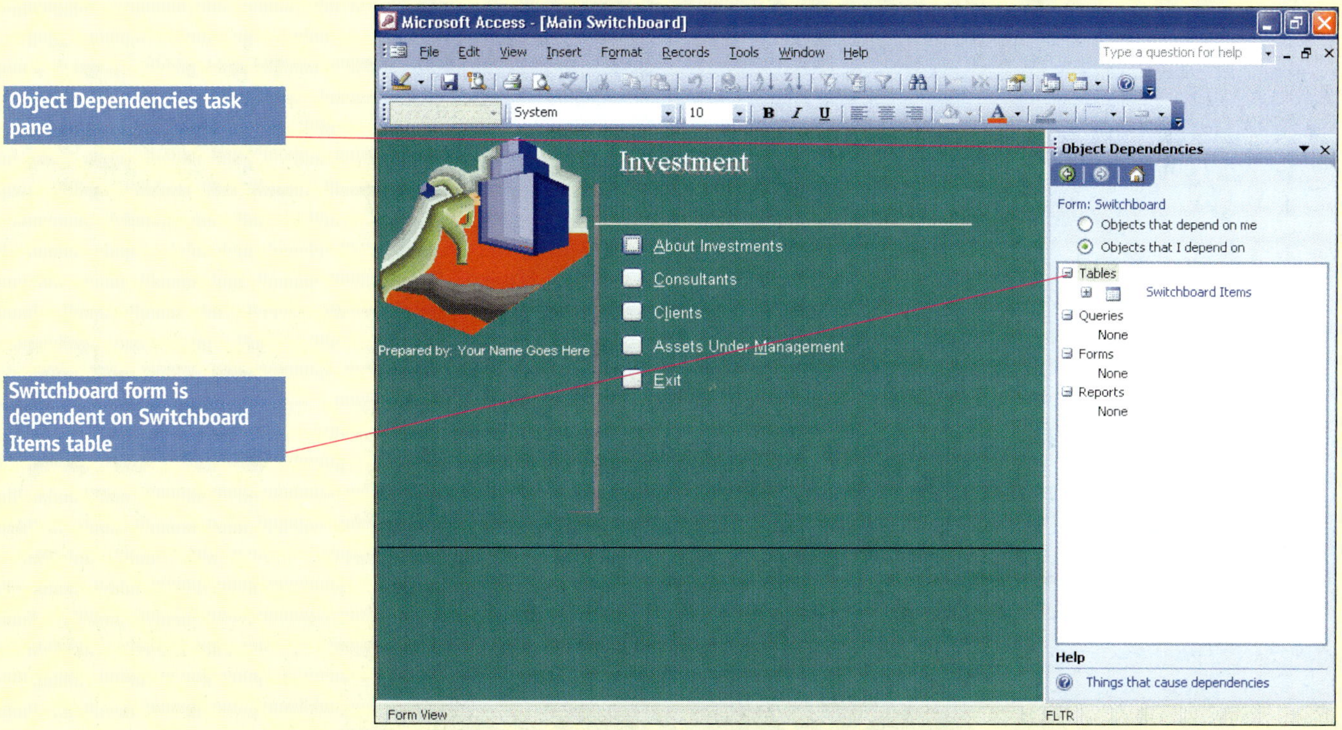

(f) The Completed Switchboard and Object Dependencies (step 6)

FIGURE 4.10 Hands-on Exercise 3 (*continued*)

OBJECT DEPENDENCIES

The objects in an Access database depend on one another; for example, a report is based on an underlying query, which in turn is based on a table. Over time, the report may become obsolete, so you delete the report and the underlying query, but if the same query were the basis of another report, the latter object would no longer function. The ability to view object dependencies can prevent this type of error from occurring. Select the object in the Database window, pull down the View menu, and click Object Dependencies to open the task pane and view the objects that depend on the selected object.

Step 7: Compact and Back Up the Database

- Pull down the **Tools menu**, click (or point to) the **Database Utilities command**, and then click the **Compact and Repair Database command**.
- The system pauses as it compacts the database, closes it, then reopens it, which in turn displays the Security Warning dialog box. Click the **Open button** to open the database. You should see the Database window for the Investment database.
- Pull down the **Tools menu**, click the **Database Utilities command**, and then click the **Back Up Database command** to display the Save Backup As dialog box as shown in Figure 4.10g.
- Access supplies a default file name consisting of the original name of the database followed by the date on which the backup was made (July 7, 2003 in our example). Click the **Save button**.
- The system pauses as it backs up the Investment database, closes the backup copy, then reopens the original Access database, which in turn displays the Security Warning dialog box.
- Click **Cancel** since we are finished working. Close Access. Congratulations on a job well done.

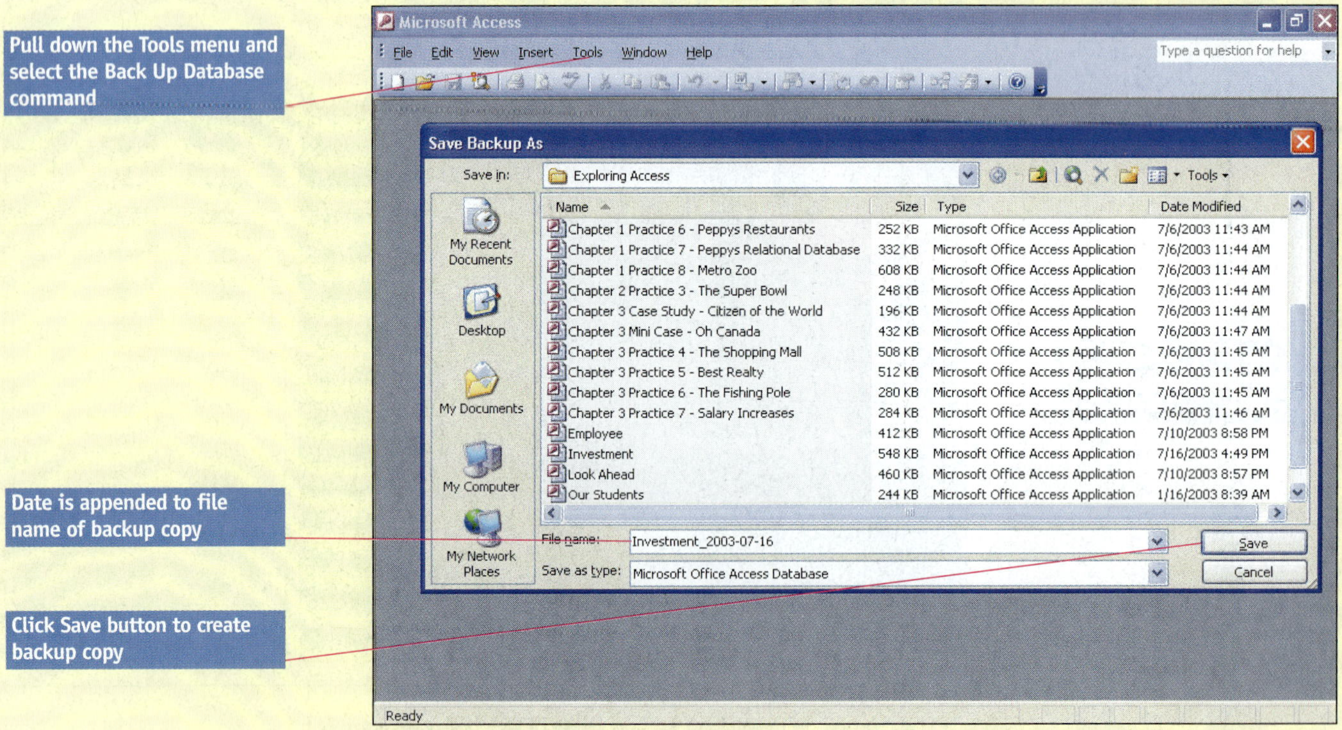

(g) Compact and Back Up the Database

FIGURE 4.10 Hands-on Exercise 3 (*continued*)

A FALSE SENSE OF SECURITY

The backup copy you just created helps to protect you against the accidental deletion or corruption of the Investment database. It does not, however, protect you against damage to your hard drive (if both copies are on the same drive). Nor does it protect you against the loss of your system due to theft or natural disaster. It is important, therefore, that you store the backup copy (or copies) offsite, away from your computer. Note, too, that any backup copy is static and that frequent backup is necessary to retain the most recent copy of your database.

SUMMARY

A relational database contains multiple tables. Each table stores data about a specific entity in the physical system, such as clients and consultants in the Investment database. The tables are related to one another through a one-to-many relationship; for example, one consultant can have many clients, as in the database from this chapter. The relationship is created in the Relationships window by dragging the join field from the one table to the related table. Referential integrity ensures that all of the data in the two tables are consistent.

A select query can contain fields from multiple tables. The relationship between those tables is shown graphically in the Query Design view. The Tables row displays the name of the table that contains each field in the query.

The Get External Data command starts a wizard that will import (or link) data from an external source—such as an Excel workbook—into an Access database. The Export command does the reverse and copies an Access object to an external destination.

A total query performs calculations on a group of records using one of several summary (aggregate) functions. Execution of the query displays a summary record for each group, and individual records do not appear. The results of a total query can be input to Microsoft Graph to display the information graphically in a form or report.

A pivot table is a very flexible way to display summary statistics for the records in a table (or query) according to the parameters you supply. A pivot chart provides the same information as the corresponding pivot table in graphical form. Any changes to the pivot table are automatically reflected in the associated pivot chart and vice versa.

A switchboard is a user interface that enables a nontechnical person to open the objects in an Access database by selecting commands from a menu. The switchboard is created through the Switchboard Manager, a tool that prompts you for the information about each menu item. The switchboard itself is stored as a form within the database that reads data from an underlying table of switchboard items.

The Convert Database command changes the file format of an Access database to the format used by earlier versions of the program. The Compact and Repair Database command serves two functions, as its name suggests. The compacting process eliminates the fragmentation and wasted disk space that occur during development as you add, edit, and delete the various objects in a database. The Repair function takes place automatically if Access is unable to read a database when the database is opened initially. The Back Up Database command compacts the open database, and then it saves the compacted database under a different name that contains the date the backup was created.

The objects in an Access database depend on one another; for example, a report is based on an underlying query, which in turn is based on a table. Over time, the report may become obsolete, and hence it is deleted along with the underlying query; but if the same query were the basis of another report, the latter object would no longer function. The ability to examine object dependencies can prevent this type of error from occurring.

KEY TERMS

Aggregate functions 670
Back Up Database command ... 685
Chart Wizard 670
Compact and Repair Database command 685
Convert Database command ... 685
Count function 670
Export command 661
Field list 673
Foreign key 659
Get External Data command 661
Group By 670
Import Spreadsheet Wizard 661
Microsoft Graph 670
Object Dependencies 691
One-to-many relationship 659
Pivot chart 673
Pivot table 673
Primary key 659
Referential integrity 660
Startup property 690
Sum function 670
Switchboard 683
Switchboard Items table 685
Switchboard Manager 685
Table row 660
Total query 670
Total row 670

MULTIPLE CHOICE

1. A database has a one-to-many relationship between physicians and patients (one physician can have many patients). Which of the following is true?
   (a) The PhysicianID will appear in the Patients table
   (b) The PatientID will appear in the Physicians table
   (c) Both (a) and (b)
   (d) Neither (a) nor (b)

2. You are creating a database for an intramural league that has a one-to-many relationship between teams and players. Which of the following describes the correct database design?
   (a) Each record in the Teams table should contain the PlayerID field
   (b) Each record in the Players table should contain the TeamID field
   (c) Both (a) and (b)
   (d) Neither (a) nor (b)

3. Which of the following will create a problem of referential integrity in the Investments database that was developed in the chapter?
   (a) The deletion of a consultant record with a corresponding client record
   (b) The deletion of a consultant record that does not have any client records
   (c) The deletion of a client record who is assigned to a consultant
   (d) All of the above

4. Which of the following is true about a select query?
   (a) It may reference fields from more than one table
   (b) It may have one or more criteria rows
   (c) It may sort on one or more fields
   (d) All of the above

5. Which of the following is a true statement about Access tables?
   (a) An Access query can be exported to an Excel workbook
   (b) An Excel worksheet can be imported as an Access table
   (c) Both (a) and (b)
   (d) Neither (a) nor (b)

6. The Get External Data command will:
   (a) Import a worksheet from an Excel workbook as a new Access table
   (b) Import a text file as a new Access table
   (c) Both (a) and (b)
   (d) Neither (a) nor (b)

7. An Excel worksheet has been imported into an Access database as a new table, after which the data has been modified. Which of the following is *false*?
   (a) The Excel worksheet will be updated to reflect the modified table
   (b) A query run after the table has been modified will reflect the new data
   (c) A report run after the table has been modified will reflect the new data
   (d) All of the above

8. Which of the following is true about the rows in the Query Design grid?
   (a) The Total row can contain different functions for different fields
   (b) The Table row can reflect different tables
   (c) The Sort row can include entries for multiple fields
   (d) All of the above

9. Which of the following is available as an aggregate function within a query?
   (a) Sum and Avg
   (b) Min and Max
   (c) Both (a) and (b)
   (d) Neither (a) nor (b)

10. Which of the following is true about clicking and double clicking a chart within a report?
    (a) Clicking the chart selects the chart, enabling you to change the size of the chart, click and drag it to a new position, or delete it altogether
    (b) Double clicking the chart opens the underlying application (Microsoft Graph), enabling you to change the appearance of the chart
    (c) Both (a) and (b)
    (d) Neither (a) nor (b)

... continued

multiple choice

11. Which of the following is created by the Switchboard Manager?

(a) A switchboard form
(b) A Switchboard Items table
(c) Both (a) and (b)
(d) Neither (a) nor (b)

12. How do you insert clip art into a switchboard?

(a) Start the Switchboard Manager, then use the Insert Clip Art command
(b) Open the switchboard form in Design view, then add the clip art using the same techniques as for any other form
(c) Both (a) and (b)
(d) Neither (a) nor (b)

13. Which of the following is true about compacting a database?

(a) Compacting a database when the database is open saves the compacted database under the original file name
(b) Compacting a closed database saves the compacted database under a different file name
(c) Both (a) and (b)
(d Neither (a) nor (b)

14. Which of the following best describes how to create a pivot chart?

(a) Use the Get External Data command to import an Excel worksheet into an Access database
(b) Use Microsoft Graph to create a multicolumn chart, then convert that chart to a pivot chart
(c) Use the Import Spreadsheet Wizard command to convert a worksheet to a pivot chart
(d) None of the above

15. The database of a commercial bank has a one-to-many relationship between Customers and Loans; that is, one customer can have many loans, but a specific loan is associated with only one customer. Which table(s) should contain the LoanID?

(a) Only the Loans table
(b) Only the Customers table
(c) Both the Loans table and the Customers table
(d) None of the above; the LoanID is not relevant to the database

16. The database of a commercial bank has a one-to-many relationship between Customers and Loans; that is, one customer can have many loans, but a specific loan is associated with only one customer. Which table(s) should contain the CustomerID?

(a) Only the Loans table
(b) Only the Customers table
(c) Both the Loans table and the Customers table
(d) None of the above; the CustomerID is not relevant to the database

17. Which of the following was suggested as essential to a backup strategy?

(a) Backing up data files at the end of every session
(b) Storing the backup file(s) at another location
(c) Both (a) and (b)
(d) Neither (a) nor (b)

18. Which of the following is an advantage of a pivot table?

(a) You can add or remove fields by dragging the field names on or off the table.
(b) You can switch the orientation by dragging a field to or from the row, column, or filter area.
(c) You can change the means of calculation by changing the average value to sum, minimum, or maximum value.
(d) All of the above

ANSWERS

1. a	**7.** a	**13.** c
2. b	**8.** d	**14.** d
3. a	**9.** c	**15.** a
4. d	**10.** c	**16.** c
5. c	**11.** c	**17.** c
6. c	**12.** b	**18.** d

PRACTICE WITH ACCESS

1. **The Oscars:** The switchboard in Figure 4.11 contains seven commands, three of which reference reports that were created in an end-of-chapter exercise in Chapter 3. You can do this exercise even if you did not create the reports, since the other objects are already in the database. You do, however, have to create the About the Oscars form, which is best accomplished by importing (and modifying) the similar form from the Investment database.
   a. Open the *Chapter 1 Practice 1* database in the Exploring Access folder. Click the Forms button in the Database window, pull down the File menu, click the Get External Data command, click Import, and then import the About Investments form from the Investment database. Return to the Database window. Right click the newly imported form, and change the name of the form to About the Oscars, then open that form in Design view. Change the clip art, labels, and colors as necessary. And finally, right click the form selector button, click Properties, select the Caption property and change the text to reflect the Oscars.
   b. Use the Switchboard Manager to create the switchboard in Figure 4.11. The Award Winners form, which is used to enter Oscar data, is already in the database (open the form in Edit mode). The report to list the major winners by year is also in the database, but the availability of the additional reports depends on whether you completed the end-of-chapter exercise in Chapter 3. Format the switchboard so that its appearance is consistent with Figure 4.11.
   c. Test each button on the switchboard to be sure that the commands work properly. Click the button to enter Oscar data, and then view the last record in the table to see the most recent awards. If necessary, click the link on the form to go to the Oscars Web site to obtain the additional awards (if any) since the publication of our book. Enter that data into the database.
   d. Click the appropriate button to view, and then print each report in the database.
   e. Pull down the Tools menu, and click the Startup command. Select the switchboard as the form to display when the database is opened. Click OK to close the Startup dialog box. Pull down the Tools menu, click Database Utilities, and then click the Compact and Repair Database command. The database should compact itself and reopen with the switchboard displayed automatically.
   f. Print the Switchboard form and Switchboard Items table for your instructor.

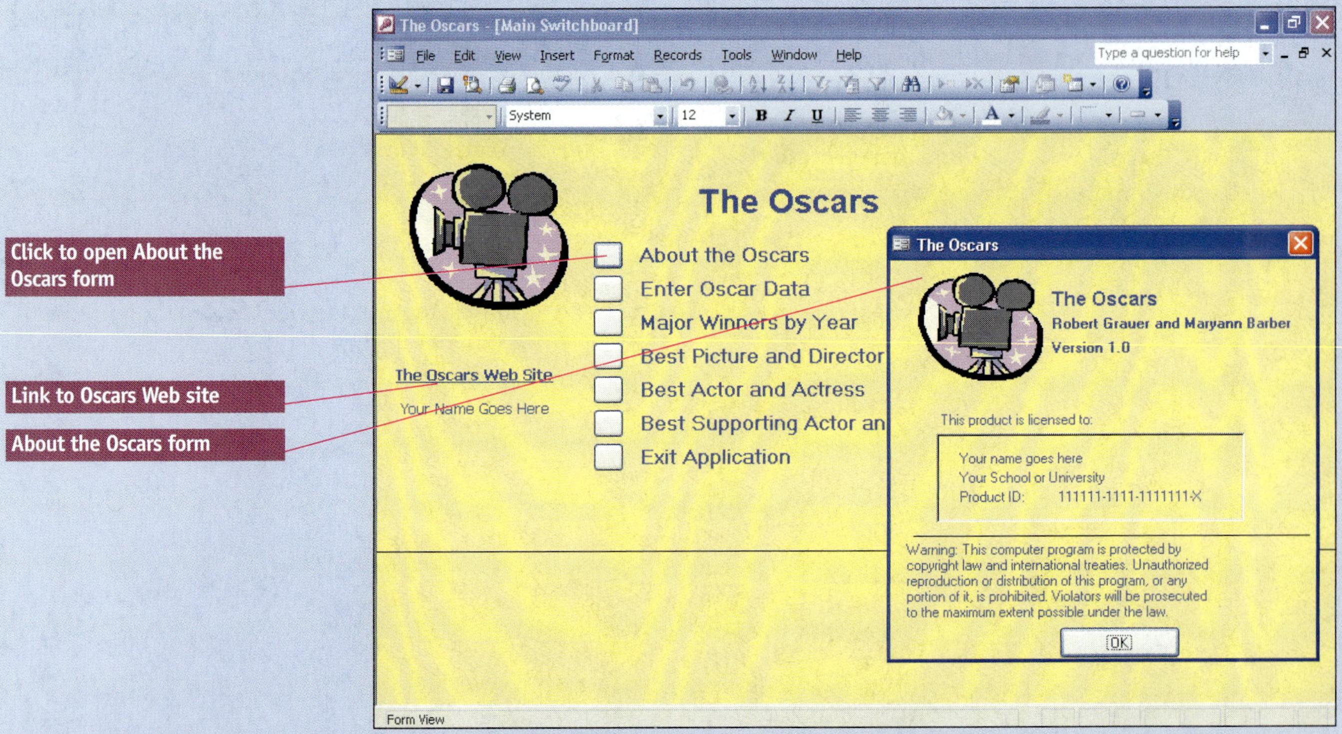

FIGURE 4.11 The Oscars (exercise 1)

2. **Employee Health Plans:** Figure 4.12 displays the relationships diagram of a database that tracks employees, the cities in which they work, and the health plans to which they subscribe. The database contains the typical data for every employee (name, birth date, salary, and so on) and for every office location (address, telephone, and so on). The database also stores data about the available health plans such as the name and description of the plan, the monthly contribution, the deductible each employee is required to pay, and the percent of expenses that an employee will be reimbursed. Your task is to create the tables (you do not have to enter any data), implement the relationships, and create a simple switchboard. Note the following:
   a. Each employee is assigned to one city, but a given city has multiple employees. In similar fashion, each employee chooses one health plan, but a given health plan has multiple employees. An employee cannot be hired without being assigned to a city. New employees have 30 days, however, to decide on a health plan.
   b. The report in Figure 4.12 is created from the Relationships window after the relationships have been specified. Pull down the Tools menu and click Relationships to open the Relationships window, then pull down the File menu and click the Print Relationships command to display the Print Preview screen of a report that displays the contents of the Relationships window. Change to the Design view to modify the report to include your name and an appropriate clip art image.
   c. Create a simple About the Employee Health Plans form similar to the other forms in this chapter.
   d. Create a switchboard with three menu options—a button to display the About Employee Health Plans form, a button to print the relationships diagram, and a button to exit the application. The switchboard should contain the same clip art as the relationships diagram. Use the Startup property to display the switchboard automatically when the database is opened.
   e. Test the switchboard thoroughly to be sure it works correctly. Use the Startup property in the Tools menu to display the switchboard automatically when the database is opened initially. Print the relationships diagram, the Switchboard form, and the Switchboard Items table for your instructor.

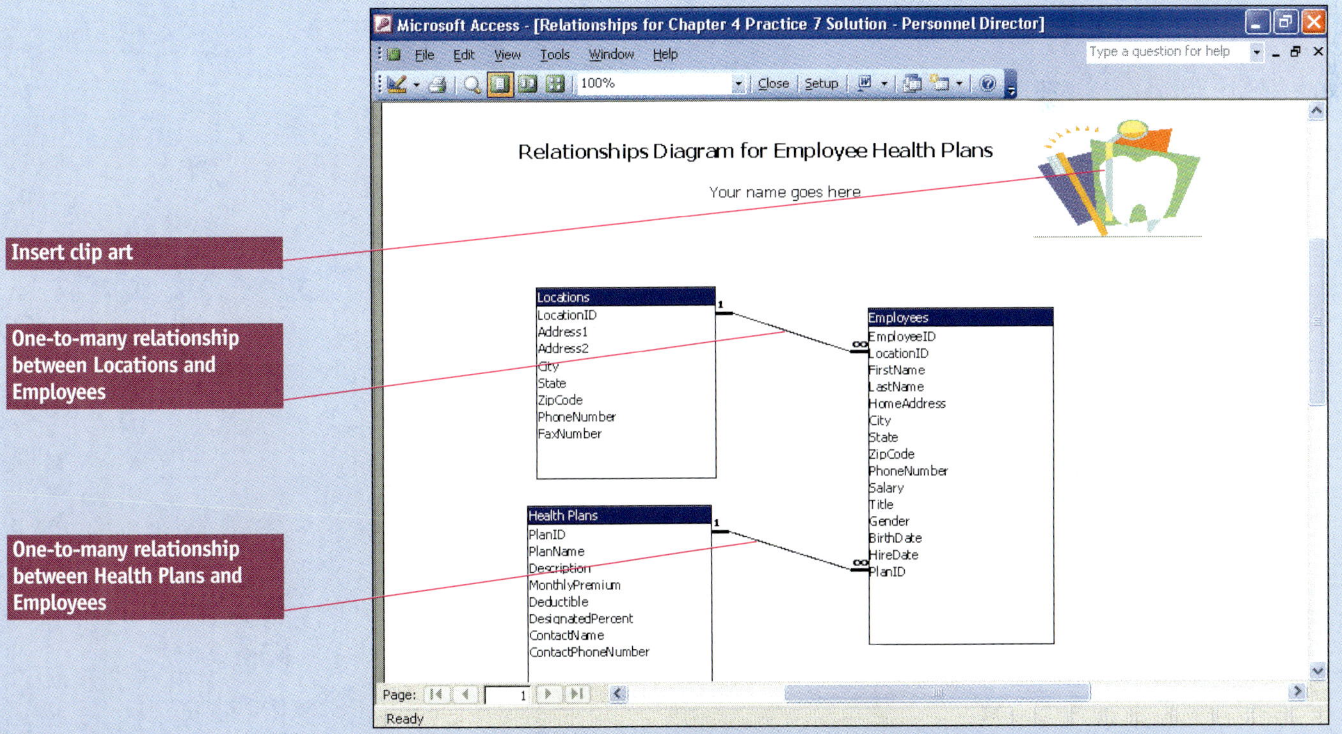

FIGURE 4.12 Employee Health Plans (exercise 2)

3. **The Metro Zoo:** The switchboard in Figure 4.13 is based on the Metro Zoo database that was introduced in Chapter 1. You do not have to match our design exactly, but you are required to duplicate the functionality. All of the objects (i.e., the forms and reports) have been created for you and are found in the database. Proceed as follows:
   a. Open the *Chapter 1 Practice 8* database and complete that exercise if you have not already done so. Pull down the Tools menu, click the Relationships command, and create the one-to-many relationships that exist in the system. Enforce referential integrity for every relationship.
   b. Start the Switchboard Manager, which will display the Switchboard Manager dialog box. Click New to create a new switchboard (in addition to the main switchboard that is created by default). Enter Report Menu as the name of the new switchboard page, then click OK.
   c. You will return to the Switchboard Manager dialog box. Select the Main Switchboard, click Edit, and build the items for the main switchboard as shown in Figure 4.13. Be sure to open all of the forms in the Edit mode. After you have built the main switchboard, click Close on the Edit Switchboard Page dialog box to return to the Switchboard Manager dialog box.
   d. Select the Report Menu switchboard, and click Edit. Build the items for the Report Menu, which consist of a separate command for each report plus a command to return to main menu. (The latter is a Go To Switchboard command that opens the Main switchboard.) Close the switchboard page. Close the Switchboard Manager.
   e. Open the Switchboard form in Design view to format the switchboard as shown in Figure 4.13. You do not have to match our design exactly.
   f. Test both switchboards to be sure that they work correctly. Verify that the data entry operations for the Trainer and Animal tables have been implemented correctly as described in Chapter 1. Use the report menu to print each report in the database.
   g. Which report is based on a query rather than a table? How many tables are referenced in that query? Go to the Database window and print the dynaset for the underlying query for the report in question. Print the Switchboard form and Switchboard Items table and then submit all items to your instructor.

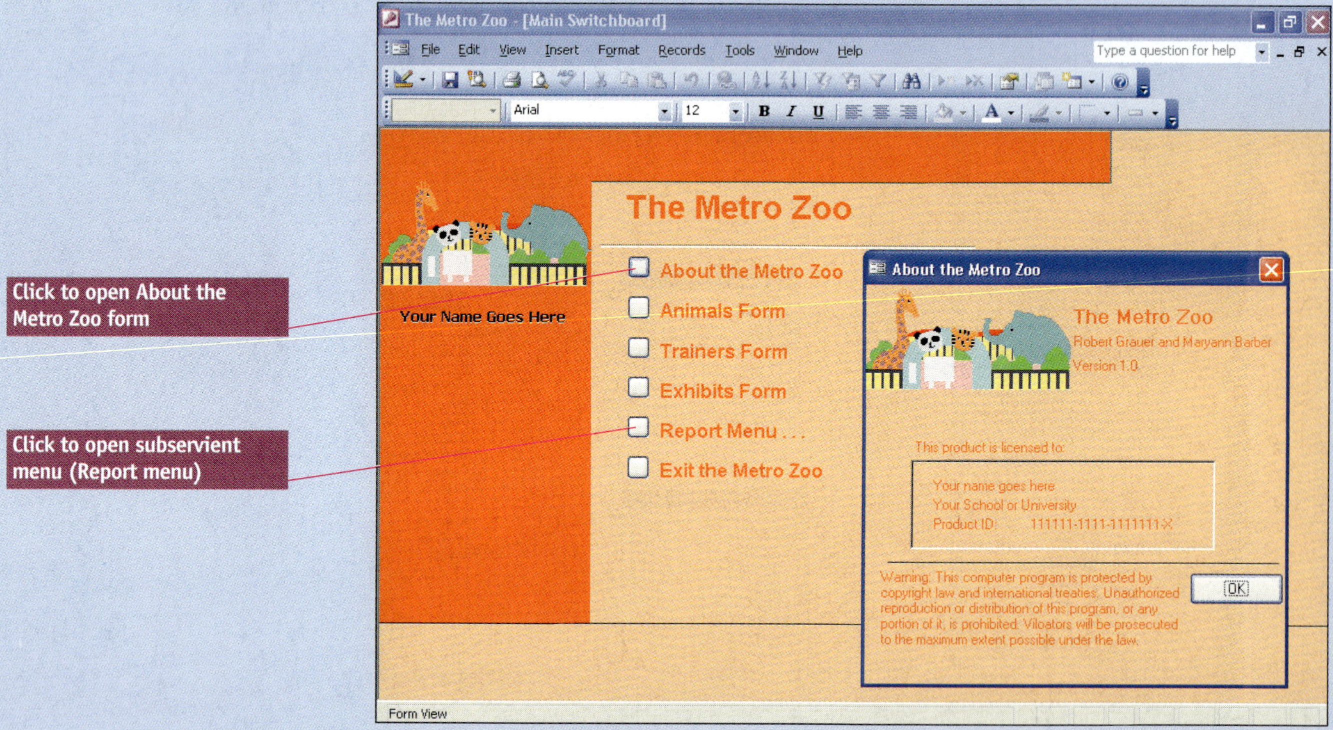

FIGURE 4.13 The Metro Zoo (exercise 3)

4. **The Shopping Mall (secondary switchboard):** Figure 4.14 displays a switchboard for the Shopping Mall database that has been developed in previous chapters, most recently in Chapter 3. Your present assignment is to create the switchboard in Figure 4.14, which includes an option to display a report menu. The latter is a second (subsidiary) switchboard that includes commands to print all of the reports that were created in Chapter 3, as well as an option to return to the Main Menu. Proceed as follows:
   a. Start the Switchboard Manager. At the Switchboard Manager dialog box, click New to create a new switchboard. In the Create New dialog box, enter a name for the new switchboard, such as Report Menu, then click OK.
   b. You will return to the Switchboard Manager dialog box. Select the Main Switchboard, click Edit, and build the items for the Main Switchboard (open the "About the Mall" form, open the Coral Pines Shopping Mall form to enter/edit data, go to the Report Menu switchboard, and Exit). After you have built the main switchboard, click Close on the Edit Switchboard Page dialog box to return to the Switchboard Manager.
   c. Select the Report Menu switchboard, and click Edit. Build the items for the Report Menu (one each to open the individual reports and one to return to the Main Menu—which is actually a Go To Switchboard command that opens the Main Switchboard).
   d. Open the Switchboard form in Design view to format the switchboard in an attractive fashion. You do not have to match our design exactly, but your switchboard should enhance the default design.
   e. Use the Startup property in the Tools menu to display the switchboard automatically when the database is opened initially. Pull down the Tools menu, click the Database Utilities command, then click the command to Compact and Repair the Database. Access will close, and then reopen, the database; the switchboard should be displayed automatically.
   f. Be sure you test both switchboards completely to be sure that they work correctly. Print the Switchboard form and the Switchboard Items table for your instructor.
   g. Take a minute to reflect on what you have accomplished over the last several chapters. You created the database and designed a table and associated form in Chapter 2, you created various reports in Chapter 3, and you put everything together via the switchboard in this exercise. Well done!

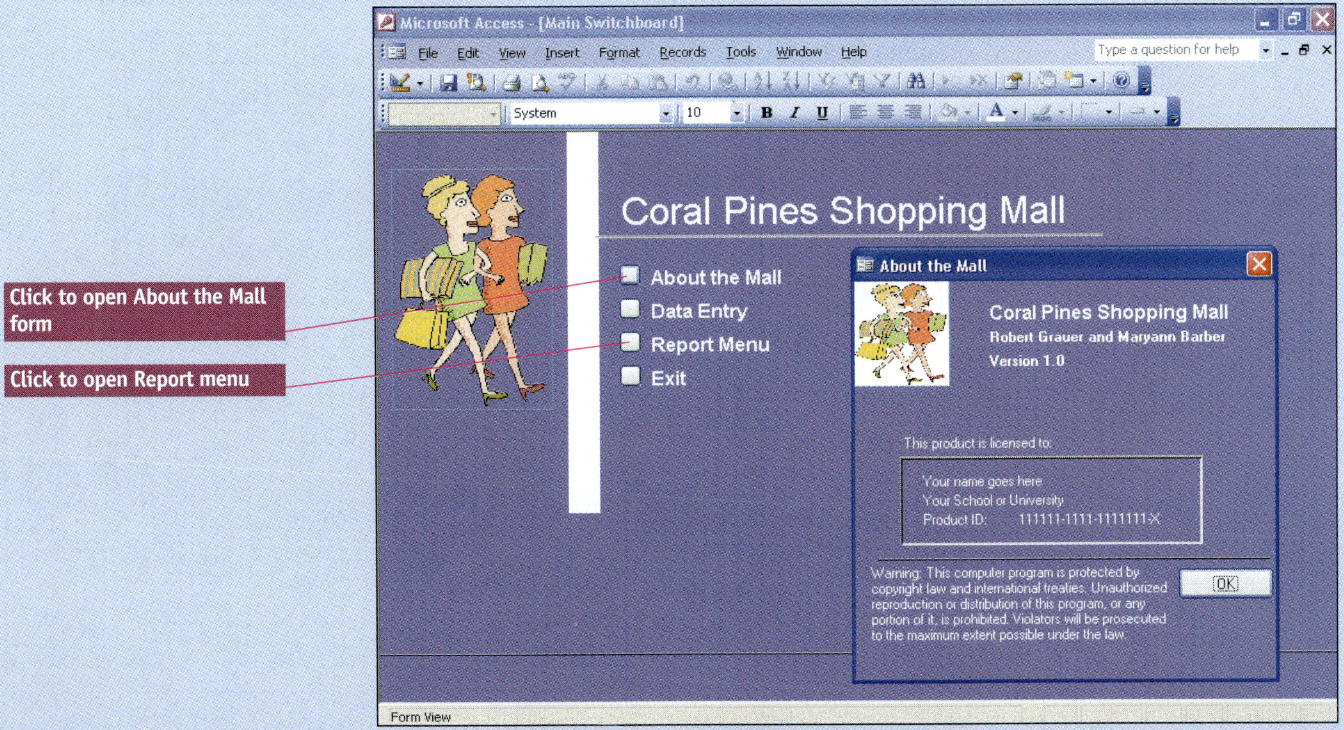

FIGURE 4.14 The Shopping Mall (exercise 4)

5. **Best Realty (secondary switchboard):** Figure 4.15 displays a switchboard for the *Best Realty* database that has been developed in previous chapters, most recently in Chapter 3. Your present assignment is to create the switchboard shown in Figure 4.15, which includes an option to display a report menu. The latter is a second (subsidiary) switchboard that includes commands to print all of the reports that were created in Chapter 3, as well as an option to return to the Main Menu. The technique for creating the subsidiary menu was described in the previous problem.
   a. Create the switchboards as indicated in Figure 4.15. You do not have to copy our design exactly, but you are to incorporate all of the indicated functionality. Format the switchboard in an attractive way and include clip art. The report menu is to provide access to all of the reports that were created in Chapter 3.
   b. Go to the main menu, and open the form to modify the property data. Use the form to indicate that property P0008 has sold for $140,000. Use today's date as the date the property was sold.
   c. Go to the Report menu, and open the report that shows the properties that have been sold. This report should include the property from part (b). Print this report for your instructor.
   d. Use the Startup property in the Tools menu to display the switchboard automatically when the database is opened initially. Pull down the Tools menu, click the Database Utilities command, then click the command to Compact and Repair the Database. Access will close, and then reopen, the database; the switchboard should be displayed automatically.
   e. Be sure that you test both switchboards completely to be sure that they work correctly. Print the switchboard form and table of Switchboard Items. Use landscape printing if necessary to be sure that each item fits on one page. Add a cover sheet and submit everything to your instructor.
   f. Take a minute to reflect on what you have accomplished over the last several chapters. You created the database and designed a table and associated form in Chapter 2, you created various reports in Chapter 3, and you put everything together via the switchboard in this exercise. Well done!

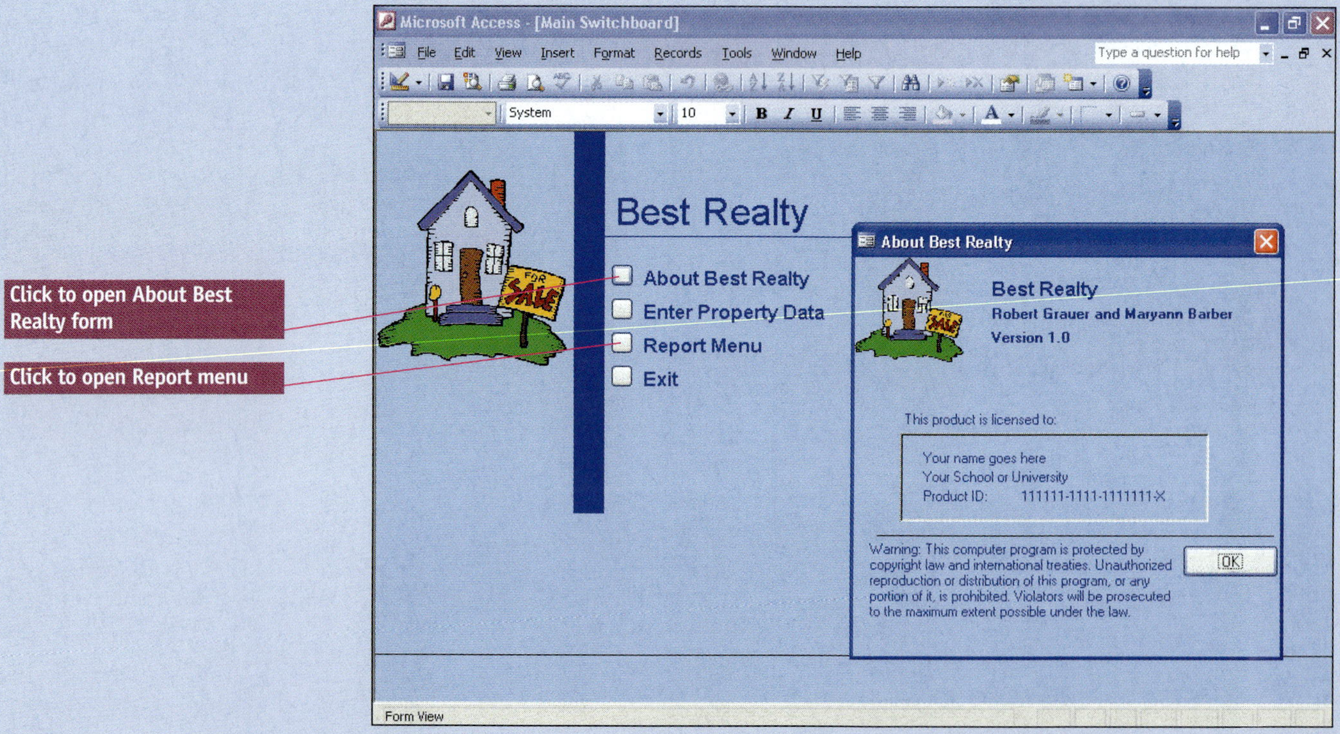

FIGURE 4.15 Best Realty (exercise 5)

6. **The Fishing Pole:** Figure 4.16 displays a switchboard for the Fishing Pole database that has been developed in previous chapters. Your assignment is to create a comparable switchboard that includes an option to display a report menu. The latter is a second (subsidiary) switchboard that includes commands to print all of the reports in the database, as well as an option to return to the Main Menu. Open the *Chapter 3 Practice 6* database in the Exploring Access folder and proceed as follows:
   a. Start the Switchboard Manager, which will display the Switchboard Manager dialog box. Click New to create a new switchboard (in addition to the main switchboard that is created by default). Enter Report Menu as the name of the new switchboard page, then click OK.
   b. You will return to the Switchboard Manager dialog box. Select the Main Switchboard, click Edit, and build the items for the main switchboard (open the About the Fishing Pole form, which is included in the database, open the Customers form in edit mode, open the Report Menu switchboard, and exit the application). After you have built the main switchboard, close the Switchboard Page dialog box to return to the Switchboard Manager dialog box.
   c. Select the Report Menu switchboard, and click Edit. Build the items for the Report Menu, which consist of a separate command for each report in the database, plus a command to return to main menu. (The latter is a Go To Switchboard command that opens the Main switchboard.) Close the switchboard page. Close the Switchboard Manager.
   d. Open the Switchboard form in Design view to format the switchboard as shown in Figure 4.16. You do not have to match our design exactly, but your switchboard should enhance the default design.
   e. Use the Startup property in the Tools menu to display the switchboard automatically when the database is opened initially. Pull down the Tools menu, click the Database Utilities command, then click the command to Compact and Repair the Database. Access will close, and then reopen; the database and the switchboard should be displayed automatically. Test both switchboards completely.
   f. Print the Switchboard form and Switchboard Items table for your instructor.

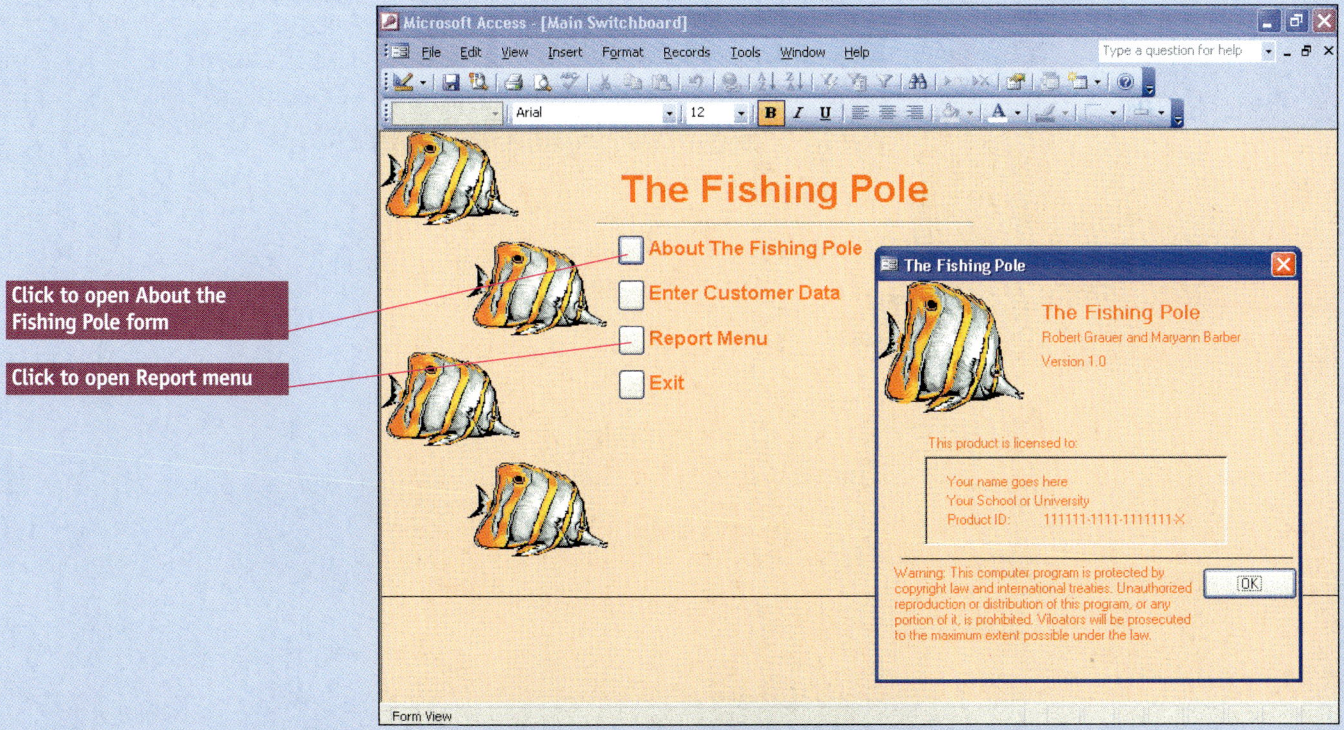

FIGURE 4.16 The Fishing Pole (exercise 6)

7. **The Database Wizard:** The switchboard in Figure 4.17 is for a contact management database that maintains information about the individuals contacted and the associated telephone calls. There is nothing remarkable in the switchboard per se, except that it and the underlying database (the tables, forms, queries, and reports) were created in a matter of minutes using one of several Database Wizards that are built into Microsoft Access. Proceed as follows:
   a. Start Access. Pull down the File menu and select the New command to open the task pane. Click the link to Other templates on My Computer to display the Templates dialog box. Click the Databases tab, then double click the Contact Management database to start the Database Wizard. You should see the File New Database dialog box in which you specify the name of the database (use Contact Management) and the folder where to store the database (use the Exploring Access folder). Click Create.
   b. You will see several screens that prompt you for information about the database that you want to create. The first screen tells you that the database stores contact and call information. Click Next.
   c. The next screen displays the tables in the database. You have to accept all of the tables, but you have the option of adding or removing fields within each table. Accept all fields for all of the tables. Click Next.
   d. The third and fourth screens let you choose the style for your forms and reports, respectively. These choices parallel those for the Form and Report Wizards. Select any style and click Next at each screen.
   e. The next two screens ask you for the title of your database (as it is to appear in the switchboard) and also give you the option of including a picture on the forms and reports. Check the option to start the database after it is built, and click the Finish button to display a switchboard similar to Figure 4.17.
   f. Explore the functionality of the database that was just created. Write a paragraph or two to your instructor describing whether the database is useful and what additional information you would like to see included. Are you able to modify the database to include the additional features you suggested?

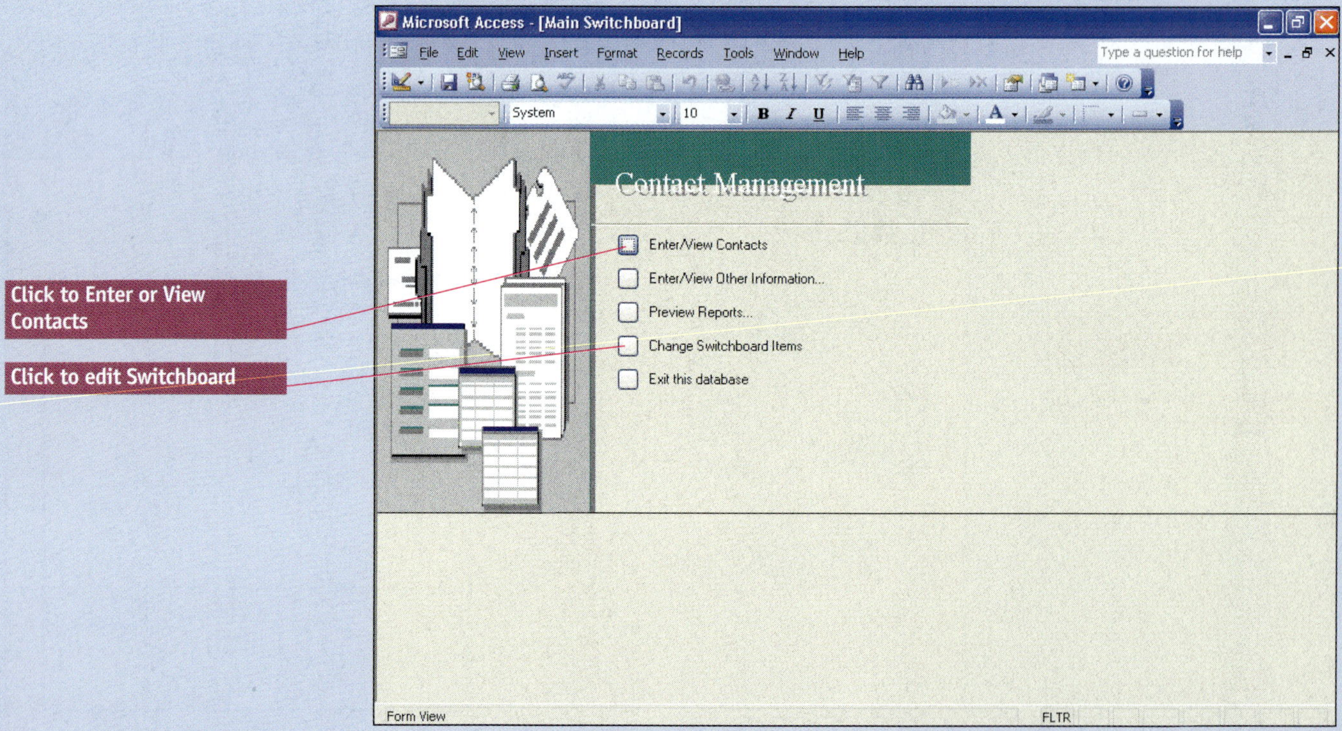

FIGURE 4.17 The Database Wizard (exercise 7)

8. **The HMO Database:** This comprehensive exercise asks you to create an Access database from the Excel workbook in Figure 4.18. There is a one-to-many relationship between physicians and patients; that is, one physician can have many patients, but a specific patient sees only one physician. Proceed as follows:
   a. Start Access and create a new database. Use the Get External Data command to import the worksheets from the *Chapter 4 Practice 8* Excel workbook into the new Access database. Specify that Social Security Number and PhysicianID are the primary keys in the Patients and Physicians tables, respectively.
   b. Use the Relationships window to create a one-to-many relationship between Physicians and Patients. Check the box to enforce referential integrity. Create a report that displays the relationships diagram.
   c. Create a query that lists all patients in alphabetical order by last name. The query should include the patient's first and last name, birth date, and gender, as well as the last name of the patient's physician and the physician's phone number. Create a report based on this query, grouping patients by physician. Format the report and add appropriate clip art.
   d. Create two simple forms for data entry, one for patients, and one for physicians. The patients form should include a list box that enables you to select a physician by name, as opposed to entering the physician's ID.
   e. Create an "About the HMO" form similar to the examples in the other exercises. You can create this form from scratch in the Design view, and/or you can import a similar form from another database, then modify the form for the HMO database.
   f. Create a simple (one-level) switchboard that provides access to six commands: About the HMO, the Patient's form, the Physician's form, the relationships diagram, the report to list patients by physician, and a command to exit the database. Format the switchboard to include your name and an appropriate clip art image.
   g. Test the switchboard completely. Use the Physician's form to enter a record for your instructor, then use the Patient's form to enter data for yourself, with your instructor as your physician. Print both of these forms, print both reports, and finally, print the Switchboard form and the Switchboard Items table.

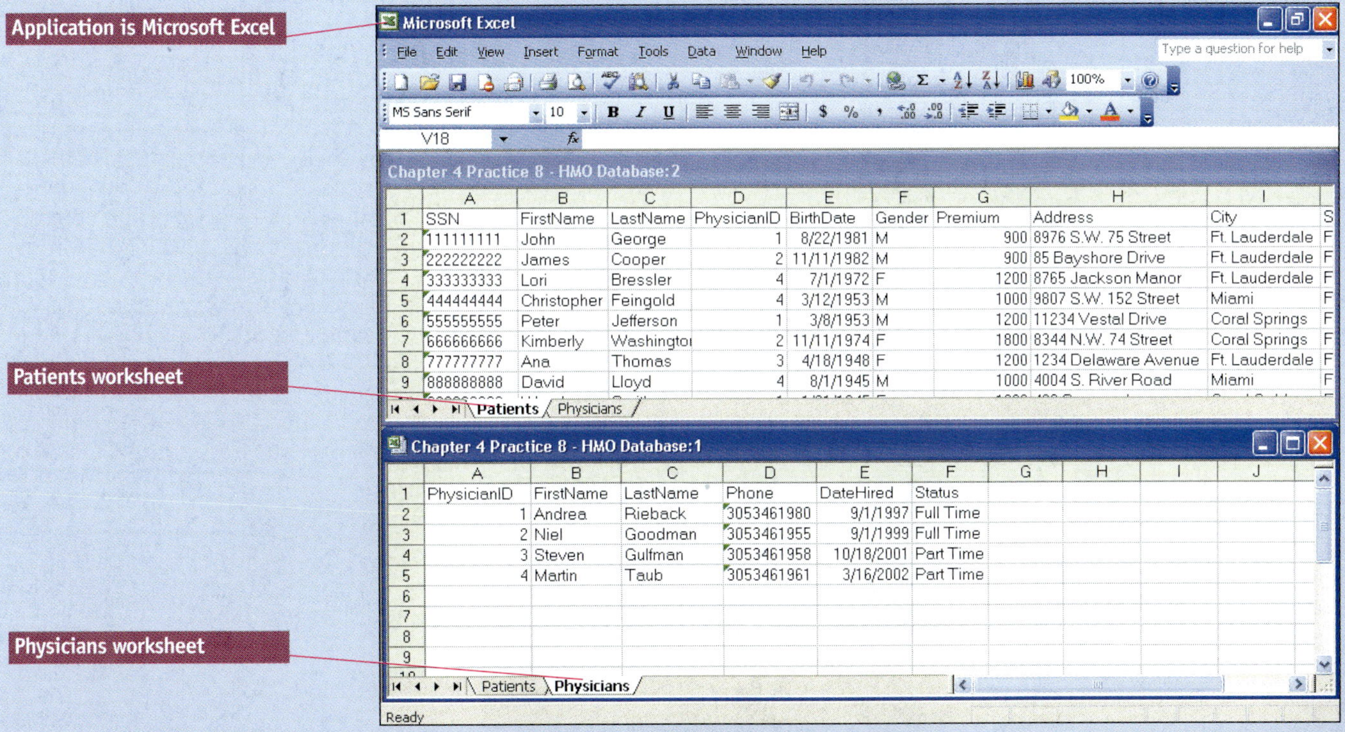

FIGURE 4.18 The HMO Database (exercise 8)

MINI CASES

Recreational Sports League

Design a database for a recreational sports league to maintain data on the league's teams, players, coaches, and sponsors. There can be any number of teams in the league. Each team has multiple players, but a specific player is associated with only one team. A team may have multiple coaches, but a given coach is associated with only one team. The league also depends on local businesses to sponsor various teams to offset the cost of uniforms and referees. One business can sponsor many teams, but a team cannot have more than one sponsor.

Design a database with four tables, for teams, players, coaches, and sponsors. You do not have to enter data into any of the tables, but you do need to design the tables in order to create a relationships diagram. Print the report containing the relationships diagram for your instructor as proof that you completed this exercise.

The Franchise

The management of a national restaurant chain is automating its procedure for monitoring its restaurants, restaurant-owners (franchisees), and the contracts that govern the two. Each restaurant has one owner (franchisee), but a given individual can own multiple restaurants.

The payment from the franchisee to the company varies according to the contract in effect for the particular restaurant. The company offers a choice of contracts, which vary according to the length of the contract, the franchise fee, and the percentage of the restaurant's sales paid to the company for marketing and royalty fees. Each restaurant has one contract, but a given contract may pertain to many restaurants.

The company needs a database capable of retrieving all data for a given restaurant, such as its annual sales, location, phone number, owner, and type of contract in effect. It would also like to know all restaurants owned by one person as well as all restaurants governed by a specific contract type.

Design a database with the necessary tables. You do not have to enter data into any of the tables, but you do need to design the tables in order to create a relationships diagram. Print the report containing the relationships diagram for your instructor as proof that you completed this exercise.

The Loan Officer

You are working in the IT department of a commercial bank and have been asked to design a database for customer loans. The bank needs to track its customers, the loans for each customer, the loan officer who approved the individual loan, and the payments received for each loan. One customer can have multiple loans, but a specific loan is associated with only one customer. A loan officer (who is an employee of the bank) must approve each loan before it is made.

One critical report is the list of all loans for each loan officer. Another important report is the list of all payments for each loan, which contains the amount of the payment and the date the payment was received. You do not have to enter data into any of the tables, but you do need to create the tables in order to create a relationships diagram and associated report. Be sure to set the required property properly for the various fields in different tables. You should not, for example, be able to create a new record in the Loans table unless that loan has been assigned to a customer and was approved by a loan officer. Print the report containing the relationships diagram for your instructor as proof that you completed this exercise.

CHAPTER 1

Introduction to PowerPoint: Presentations Made Easy

OBJECTIVES

After reading this chapter you will:

1. Start PowerPoint; edit and view an existing presentation.
2. Describe the different PowerPoint views and the features in each view.
3. Use the outline to create and edit the text of a presentation.
4. Insert a new slide; change the layout of an existing slide.
5. Use the Clip Organizer to add or change the clip art on a slide.
6. Apply a design template to a presentation.
7. Add animation and transition effects to a presentation.
8. Insert comments into a presentation.
9. Insert WordArt into a presentation.
10. Insert a Word table and an Excel chart into a presentation.

hands-on exercises

1. INTRODUCTION TO POWERPOINT
   Input: Introduction to PowerPoint
   Output: Introduction to PowerPoint Solution
2. CREATING A PRESENTATION
   Input: None
   Output: My First Presentation
3. ANIMATING A PRESENTATION
   Input: My First Presentation (from exercise 2)
   Output: My First Presentation (additional modifications)
4. ENHANCING A PRESENTATION
   Input: Enhancing a Presentation; My Study Schedule (Word document); Software Sales (Excel workbook)
   Output: Enhancing a Presentation Solution

CASE STUDY
GAME WORLD

Dave Moles and Cathi Profitko started Game World five years ago. Their vision was, and still is, to create a chain of stores that offers its customers a complete collection of video games for sale, trade, or rent. The two friends struggled initially until they realized that they should focus on the three top players in the market: PlayStation, Xbox, and Nintendo. Sales and profits have climbed steadily ever since. Last year, they broke through the one million dollar barrier as they recorded a 50% increase in sales over the previous year.

Dave and Cathi have already rejected several offers to sell their growing business and are looking to expand. They have demonstrated that their concept is successful and are seeking to franchise their operation, but realize they will need a substantial amount of cash to do so. Thus, they have decided to seek venture capital from outside. One potential source has asked that they create a PowerPoint presentation for their initial meeting that provides a comparison of quarterly revenues between this year and last year. The budding entrepreneurs have asked you to create the presentation and have provided some content in the form of an Excel workbook with financial data, as well as a partially completed presentation. This is an excellent opportunity—you love video games and you have the chance to get in on the ground floor. ■

Your assignment is to read the chapter and then complete the presentation for Dave and Cathi. The Exploring PowerPoint folder contains the two files you will need: the *Chapter 1 Case Study – Game World* presentation and an Excel workbook by the same name. The workbook contains several worksheets, so be sure to link the correct worksheet to the appropriate slide in the presentation. You have also been asked to insert at least one clip art image on slide two and/or slide six for interest. Add transition or animation effects as you see fit. Print the completed presentation as audience handouts.

INTRODUCTION TO POWERPOINT

This chapter introduces you to PowerPoint, one of the four major applications in Microsoft Office (Microsoft Word, Microsoft Excel, and Microsoft Access are the other three). PowerPoint enables you to create a professional presentation without relying on others, then it lets you deliver that presentation in a variety of ways. You can show the presentation on the computer, on the World Wide Web, or even on overhead transparencies.

PowerPoint is easy to learn because it is a Windows application and follows the conventions associated with the common user interface. Thus, if you already know one Windows application, it is that much easier to learn PowerPoint because you can apply what you know. It's even easier if you use Word, Excel, or Access since there are over 100 commands that are common to Microsoft Office.

The chapter begins by showing you an existing PowerPoint presentation so that you can better appreciate what PowerPoint is all about. We discuss the various views within PowerPoint and the advantages of each. We describe how to modify an existing presentation and how to view a presentation on the computer. You are then ready to create your own presentation, a process that requires you to focus on the content and the message you want to deliver. We show you how to enter the text of the presentation, how to add and/or change the format of a slide, and how to apply a design template. We also explain how to animate the presentation to create additional interest. The last portion of the chapter describes how to enhance a presentation through the inclusion of other objects such as a Word table or an Excel chart.

A PowerPoint presentation consists of a series of slides such as those in Figure 1.1. The various slides contain different elements (such as text, photographs, and WordArt), yet the presentation has a consistent look with respect to its overall design and color scheme. You might think that creating this type of presentation is difficult, but it isn't. It is remarkably easy, and that is the beauty of PowerPoint. In essence, PowerPoint allows you to concentrate on the content of a presentation without worrying about its appearance. You supply the text and supporting elements and leave the formatting to PowerPoint.

In addition to helping you create the presentation, PowerPoint provides a variety of ways to deliver it. You can show the presentation on a computer using animated transition effects as you move from one slide to the next. You can include sound and/or video in the presentation, provided your system has a sound card and speakers. You can also automate the presentation and distribute it on a disk for display at a convention booth or kiosk. If you cannot show the presentation on a computer, you can easily convert it to overhead transparencies.

PowerPoint also gives you the ability to print the presentation in various ways to distribute to your audience. You can print one slide per page, or you can print miniature versions of each slide and choose among two, three, four, six, or even nine slides per page. You can prepare notes for yourself consisting of a picture of each slide together with notes about the slide. You can also print the text of the presentation in outline form. Giving the audience a copy of the presentation (in any format) enables them to follow it more closely, and to take it home when the session is over.

POLISH YOUR DELIVERY

The speaker is still the most important part of any presentation, and a poor delivery will kill even the best presentation. Look at the audience as you speak to open communication and gain credibility. Don't read from a prepared script. Speak slowly and clearly and try to vary your delivery. Pause to emphasize key points, and be sure the person in the last row can hear you.

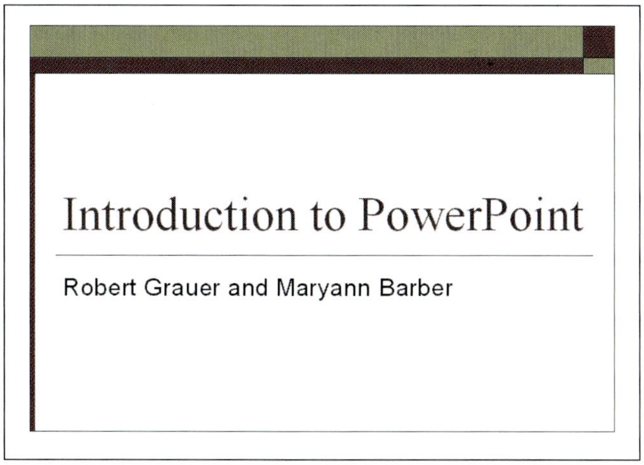

(a) Title Slide

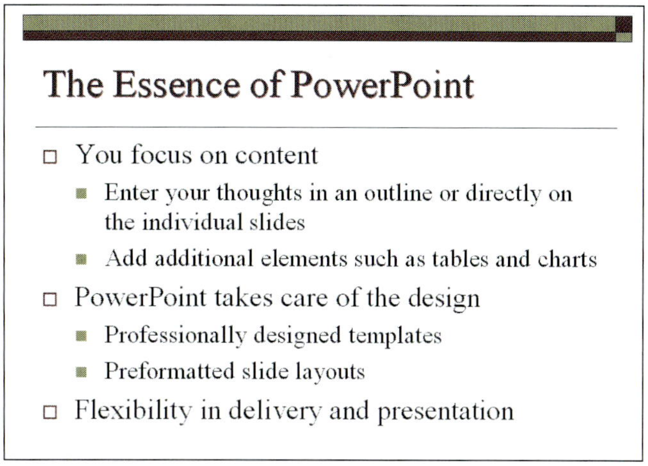

(b) Bullet Slide

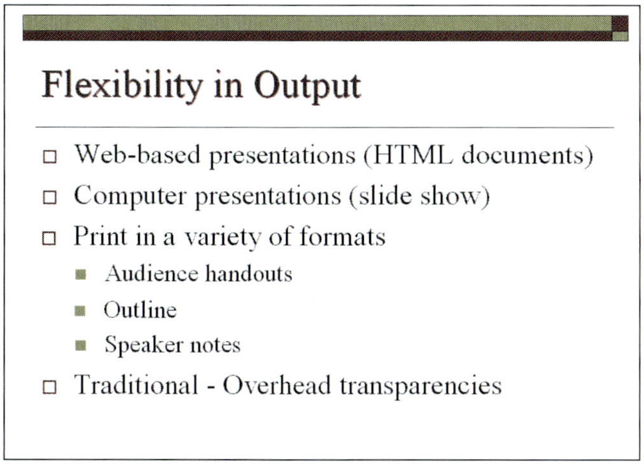

(c) Bullet Slide

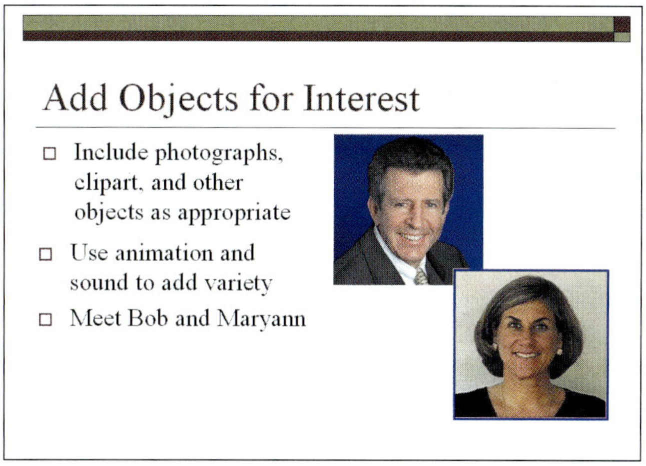

(d) Photographs

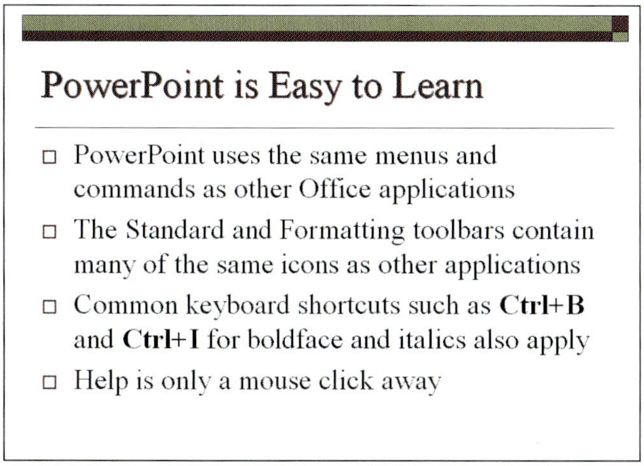

(e) Bullet Slide with Animation

(f) WordArt

FIGURE 1.1 A PowerPoint Presentation

The Common User Interface

The desktop in Figure 1.2 should look somewhat familiar even if you have never used PowerPoint, because PowerPoint shares the common user interface of every Windows application. You should recognize, therefore, the two open windows in Figure 1.2—the application window for PowerPoint and the document window for the current presentation.

The PowerPoint window contains the Minimize, Maximize (or Restore), and Close buttons. The document window, however, contains only a Close button for the current presentation, allowing you to close the presentation, but keep PowerPoint open. The title bar indicates the application (Microsoft PowerPoint) as well as the name of the presentation on which you are working (Introduction to PowerPoint). The ***menu bar*** appears immediately below the title bar and provides access to the pull-down menus within the application. The presentation appears within the document window and shows the outline of the entire presentation, a graphical image of one slide (the title slide in this example), and speaker notes for the selected slide.

The Standard and Formatting toolbars are displayed below the menu bar and are similar to those in Word and Excel. Hence, you may recognize several buttons from those applications. The ***Standard toolbar*** contains buttons for the most basic commands in PowerPoint such as opening, saving, and printing a presentation. The ***Formatting toolbar***, under the Standard toolbar, provides access to formatting operations such as boldface, italic, and underlining.

The vertical ***scroll bar*** is seen at the right of the document window and indicates that the presentation contains additional slides that are not visible. This is consistent with the ***status bar*** at the bottom of the window that indicates you are working on slide 1 of 6. The ***Drawing toolbar*** appears above the status bar and contains additional tools for working on the slide. The view buttons above the Drawing toolbar are used to switch between the different views of a presentation. PowerPoint views are discussed in the next section.

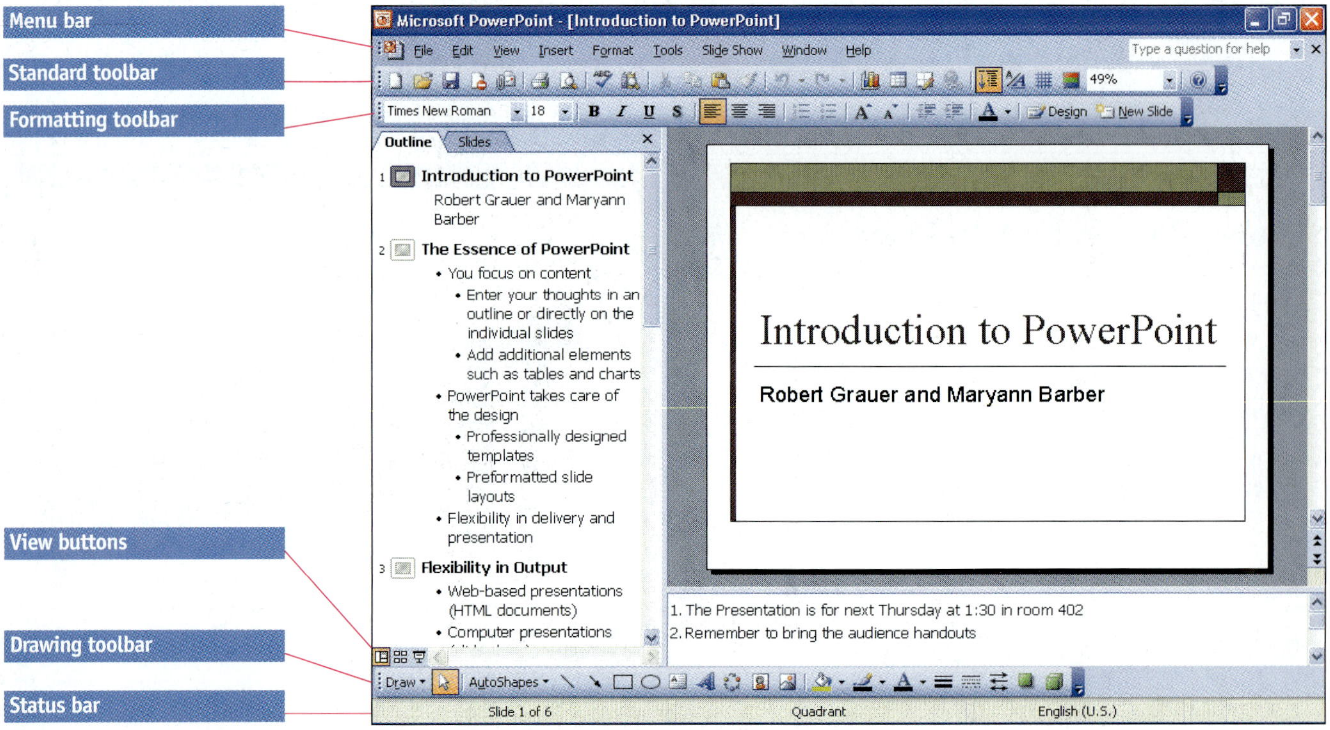

FIGURE 1.2 Introduction to PowerPoint

PowerPoint Views

PowerPoint offers multiple views in which to create, modify, and/or deliver a presentation. Each view represents a different way of looking at the presentation, and each view has unique capabilities. (There is some redundancy among the views in that certain tasks can be accomplished from multiple views.) The View menu and/or the View buttons at the bottom of the presentation enable you to switch from one view to another.

The ***Normal view*** in Figure 1.3a divides the screen into three panes containing an outline of the presentation, an enlarged view of one slide, and the associated speaker notes (if any) for the selected slide. The ***outline*** provides the fastest way to enter or edit text for the presentation. You type directly into the outline and can move easily from one slide to the next. The outline can also be used to move and copy text from one slide to another and/or to rearrange the order of the slides within a presentation. The outline is limited, however, in that it does not show graphic elements that may be present on individual slides. Thus, you may want to switch to the Normal view in Figure 1.3b that contains ***thumbnail images*** (slide miniatures) rather than the outline. This view also lets you change the order of the slides by clicking and dragging a slide to a new position. The Outline and Slides tabs in the left pane let you switch between the two variations of the Normal view.

The Normal view also provides access to the individual slides and/or speaker notes, each of which appears in its own pane. The size of the individual panes in the Normal view can be changed by dragging the border that separates one pane from another. The Normal view is all that you will ever need, but many individuals like to close the left pane completely to see just an individual slide as shown in Figure 1.3c. The individual slide, whether it is in the Normal view or displayed in a window by itself, is where you change text or formatting, add graphical elements, or apply various animation effects.

You can also elect to work in the Notes Page and/or Slide Sorter view. The ***Notes Page view*** in Figure 1.3d is redundant in that speaker notes can be entered from the Normal view. It is convenient, however, to print audience handouts of this view, since each page will contain a picture of the slide plus the associated speaker notes. The notes do not appear when the presentation is shown, but are intended for use by the speaker to help him or her remember the key points about each slide.

The ***Slide Sorter view*** in Figure 1.3e offers yet another view in which to reorder the slides within a presentation. It also provides a convenient way to delete one or more slides and/or to set transition effects for multiple slides simultaneously. Anything that you do in one view is automatically reflected in the other view. If, for example, you change the order of the slides in the Slide Sorter view, the changes will be automatically reflected in the outline or thumbnail images within the Normal view.

The ***Slide Show view*** in Figure 1.3f is used to deliver the completed presentation to an audience, one slide at a time, as an electronic presentation on the computer. The show may be presented manually where the speaker clicks the mouse to move from one slide to the next. The presentation can also be shown automatically, where each slide stays on the screen for a predetermined amount of time, after which the next slide appears automatically. Either way, the slide show may contain various transition effects from one slide to the next.

THE TASK PANE

All views in PowerPoint provide access to a task pane, which facilitates the execution of subsequent commands. The task pane serves many functions. It can be used to open an existing presentation, apply clip art to a slide, change the layout of the elements on a slide, apply transition and animation effects, or change the template of the entire presentation.

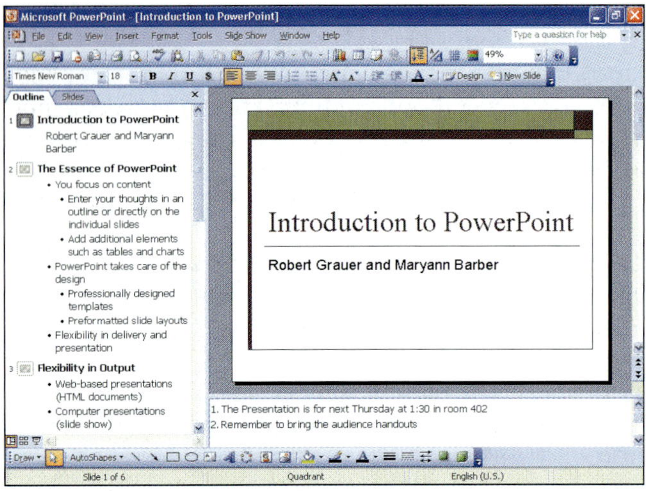

(a) Normal View with Outline

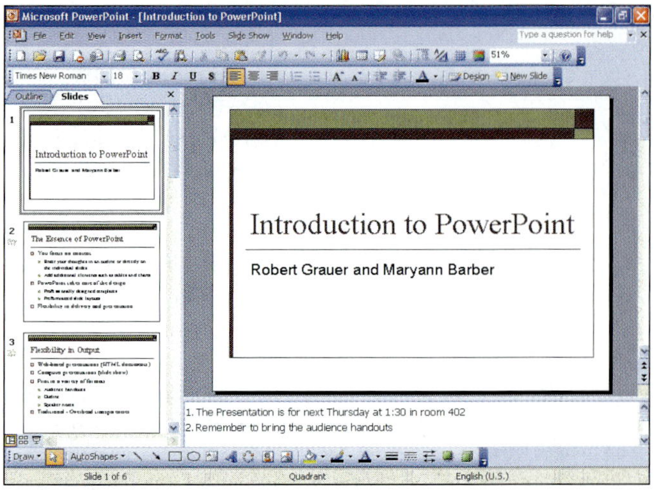

(b) Normal View with Thumbnail Images

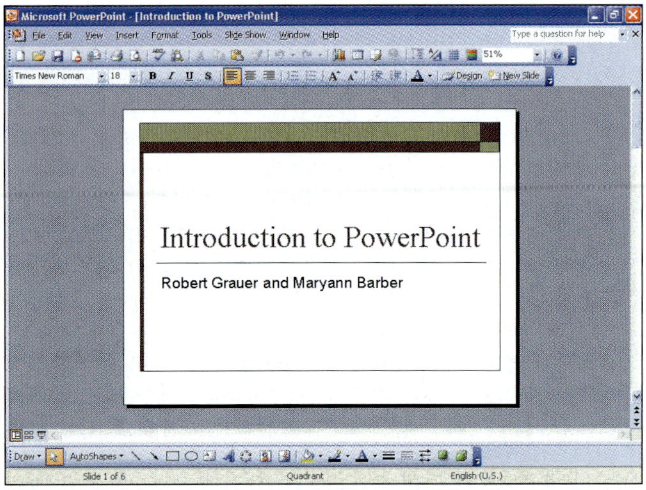

(c) Individual Slide

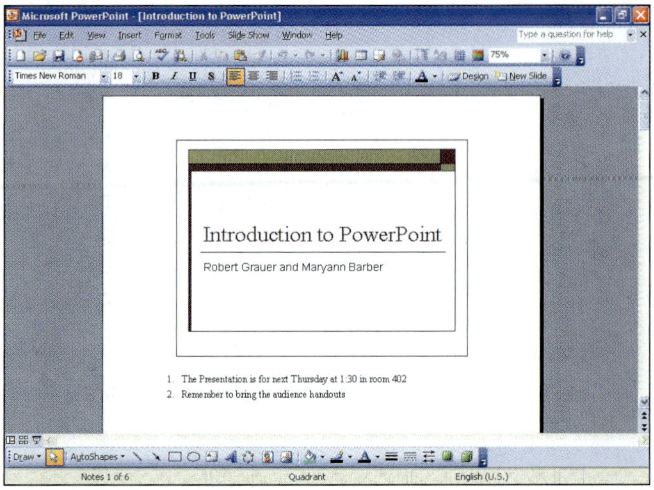

(d) Notes Page View

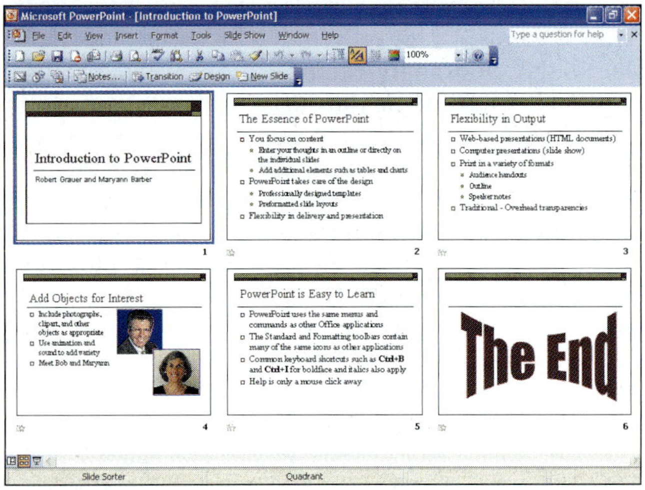

(e) Slide Sorter View

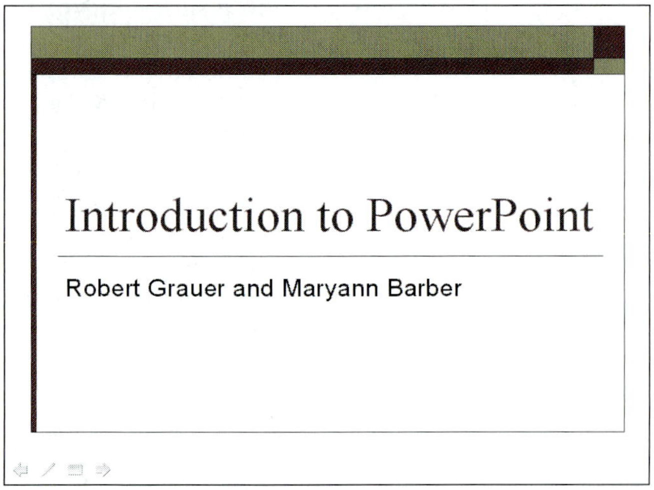

(f) Slide Show View

FIGURE 1.3 Multiple Views

The File Menu

The ***File menu*** is a critically important menu in virtually every Windows application. It contains the Save and Open commands to save a presentation on disk, then retrieve (open) that presentation at a later time. The File menu also contains the ***Print command*** to print a presentation, the ***Close command*** to close the current presentation but continue working in the application, and the ***Exit command*** to quit the application altogether.

The ***Save command*** copies the presentation that you are working on (i.e., the presentation that is currently in memory) to disk. The command functions differently the first time it is executed for a new presentation, in that it displays the Save As dialog box as shown in Figure 1.4a. The dialog box requires you to specify the name of the presentation, the drive (and an optional folder) in which the presentation is to be stored, and its file type. All subsequent executions of the command save the presentation under the assigned name, replacing the previously saved version with the new version.

The ***file name*** (e.g., My First Presentation) can contain up to 255 characters including spaces, commas, and/or periods. (Periods are discouraged, however, since they are too easily confused with DOS extensions.) The Save In list box is used to select the drive (which is not visible in Figure 1.4a) and the folder (e.g., Exploring PowerPoint) in which the file will be saved. The ***Places bar*** provides shortcuts to frequently used folders without having to search through the Save In list box. Click the Desktop icon, for example, and the file is saved on the Windows desktop. The ***file type*** defaults to a PowerPoint presentation. You can, however, choose a different format, such as an RTF (Rich Text Format) outline that can be imported into Microsoft Word. You can also save any PowerPoint presentation as a Web page (or HTML document).

The ***Open command*** is the opposite of the Save command as it brings a copy of an existing presentation into memory, enabling you to work with that presentation. The Open command displays the Open dialog box in which you specify the file name, the drive (and optionally the folder) that contains the file, and the file type. PowerPoint will then list all files of that type on the designated drive (and folder), enabling you to open the file you want.

The Save and Open commands work in conjunction with one another. The Save As dialog box in Figure 1.4a, for example, saves the file My First Presentation in the Exploring PowerPoint folder. The Open dialog box in Figure 1.4b loads that file into memory so that you can work with the file, after which you can save the revised file for use at a later time.

The toolbars in the Save As and Open dialog boxes have several buttons in common that facilitate the execution of either command. The Views button lets you display the files in different views. The Details view (in Figure 1.4a) shows the file size as well as the date and time that the file was last modified. The Preview view (in Figure 1.4b) shows the first slide in a presentation, without having to open the presentation. The List view displays only the file names, and thus lets you see more files at one time. The Properties view shows information about the presentation, including the date of creation and number of revisions.

FILE MANAGEMENT AT YOUR FINGERTIPS

Use the toolbar in the Open and/or Save As dialog boxes to perform basic file management within an Office application. You can select any existing file, and delete it or rename it. You can create a new folder, which is very useful when you begin to work with a large number of documents. You can also use the Views button to change the way the files are listed within the dialog box. Point to any tool to display a ScreenTip indicative of its function.

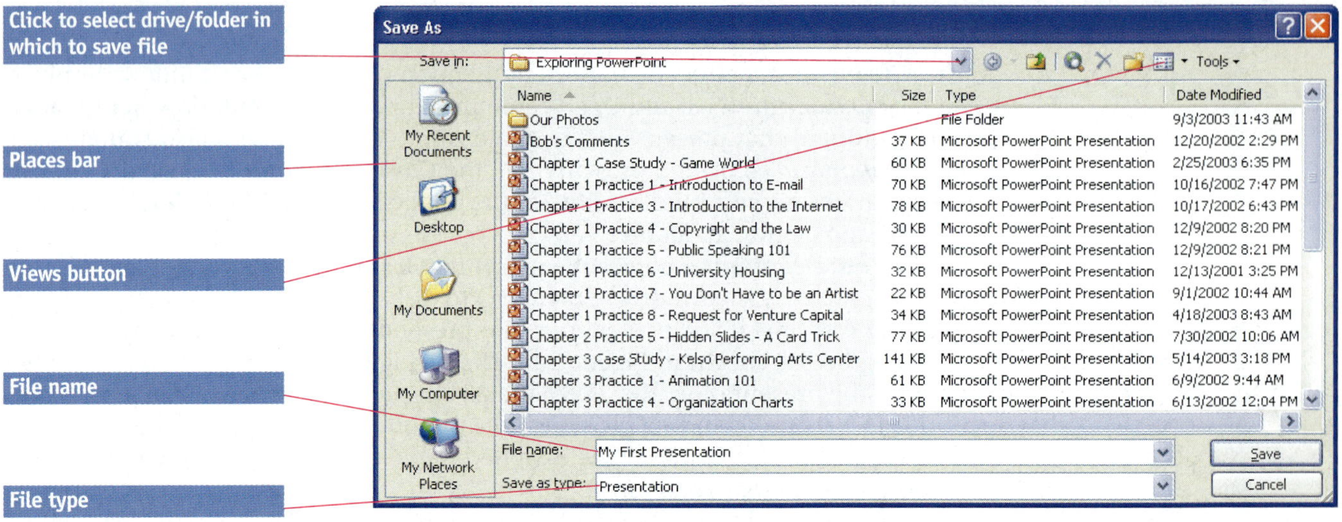

(a) Save As Dialog Box (Details view)

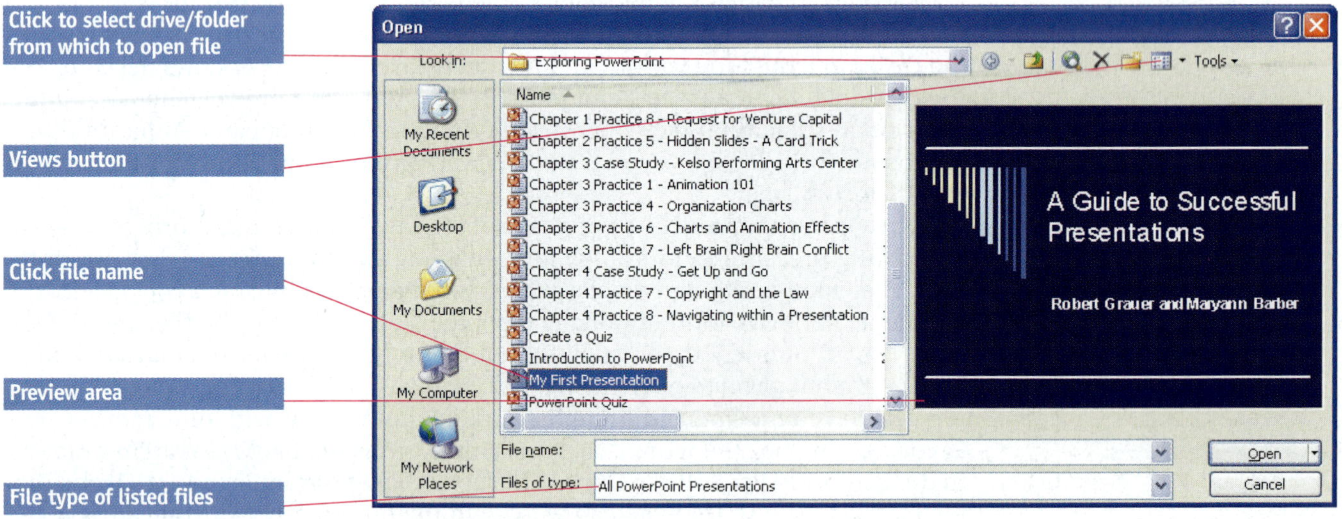

(b) Open Dialog Box (Preview view)

FIGURE 1.4 The Save and Open Commands

SORT BY NAME, DATE, OR FILE SIZE

The files in the Save As and Open dialog boxes can be displayed in ascending or descending sequence by name, date modified, or size. Change to the Details view, then click the heading of the desired column; for example, click the Modified column to list the files according to the date they were last changed. Click the column heading a second time to reverse the sequence—that is, to switch from ascending to descending, and vice versa.

hands-on exercise

1 Introduction to PowerPoint

Objective To start PowerPoint, open an existing presentation, and modify the text on an existing slide; to show an existing presentation and print handouts of its slides. Use Figure 1.5 as a guide in the exercise.

Step 1: Log on to Windows XP

- Turn on the computer and all of its peripherals. The floppy drive should be empty prior to starting your machine.
- Your system will take a minute or so to get started, after which you should see a logon screen similar to Figure 1.5a. Do not be concerned if the appearance of your desktop is different from ours.
- Click the icon for the user account you want to access. You may be prompted for a password, depending on the security options in effect.
- You should be familiar with basic file management and very comfortable moving and copying files from one folder to another. If not, you may want to review the material in the Windows XP section of this text.

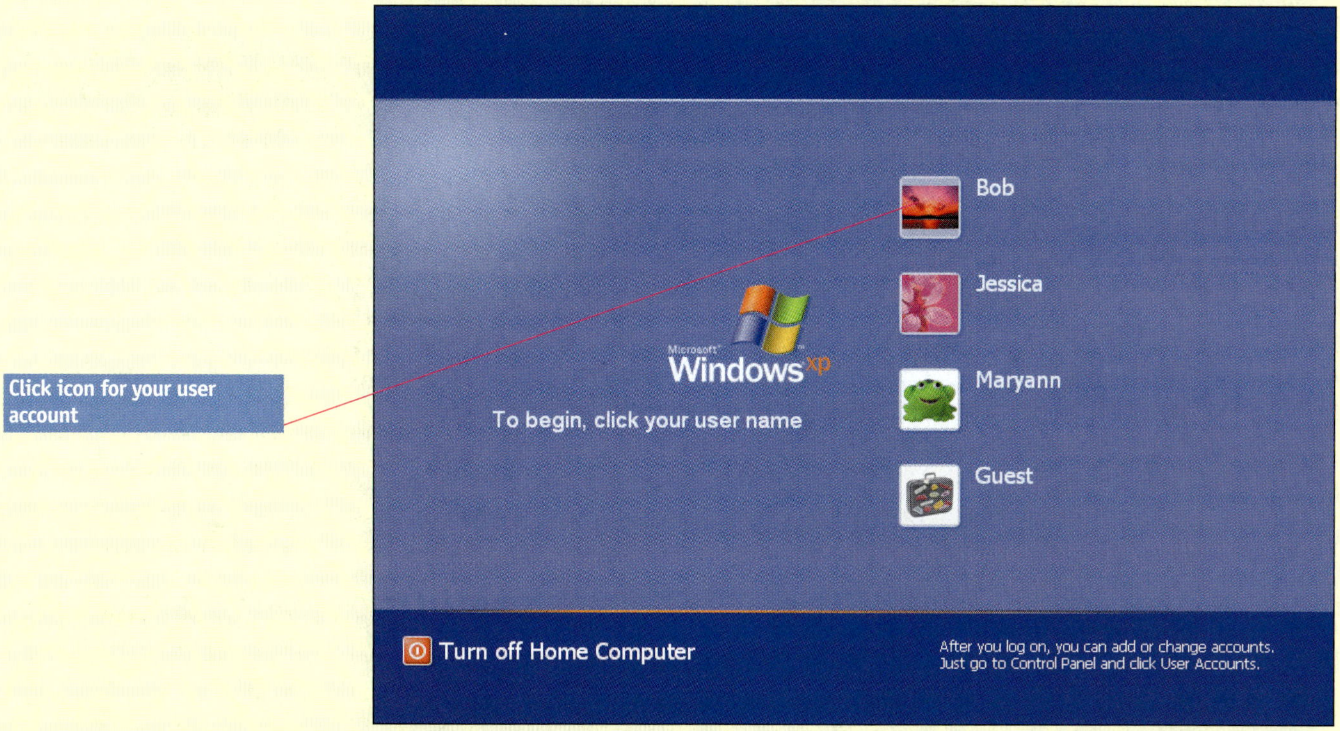

(a) Log on to Windows XP (step 1)

FIGURE 1.5 Hands-on Exercise 1

USER ACCOUNTS

The available user names are created automatically during the installation of Windows XP, but you can add or delete users at any time. Click the Start button, click Control Panel, switch to the Category view, and select User Accounts. Choose the desired task, such as creating a new account or changing an existing account. Do not expect, however, to be able to modify accounts in a school setting.

Step 2: Obtain the Practice Files

- Start Internet Explorer and go to **www.prenhall.com/grauer**. Click the book for **Office 2003**, which takes you to the Office 2003 home page. Click the **Student Downloads tab** (near the top of the window) to go to the Student Downloads page as shown in Figure 1.5b.
- Select the appropriate file to download.
  - Choose **Exploring PowerPoint** (or **PowerPoint Volume I**) if you are using a stand-alone PowerPoint text.
  - Choose **Office 2003 Volume I** (for regular or **Enhanced Edition**), **Office 2003 Plus**, or **Office 2003 Brief** if you have an Office text.
- Click the link to download the file. You will see the File Download box asking what you want to do. Click the **Save button**. The Save As dialog box appears.
- Click the **down arrow** in the Save In list box and select the drive and folder where you want to save the file. Click **Save**.
- Start Windows Explorer, select the drive and folder where you saved the file, then double click the file and follow the onscreen instructions.

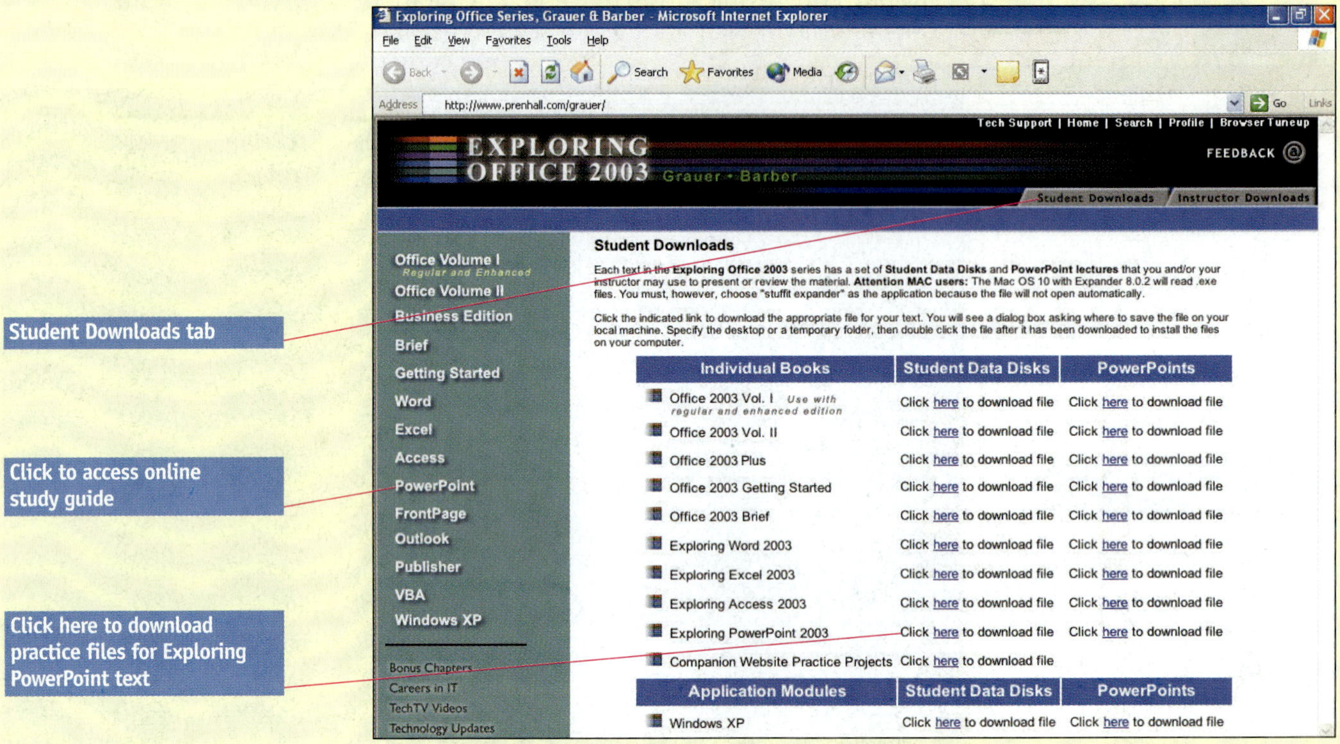

(b) Obtain the Practice Files (step 2)

FIGURE 1.5 Hands-on Exercise 1 (*continued*)

> **EXPLORE OUR WEB SITE**
>
> The Exploring Office Series Web site offers an online study guide (multiple-choice, true/false, and matching questions) for each individual textbook to help you review the material in each chapter. You can take practice quizzes by yourself and/or e-mail the results to your instructor. These online study guides are available via the tabs in the left navigation bar. You can return to the Student Downloads page at any time by clicking the tab toward the top of the window and/or you can click the link to Home to return to the home page for the Office 2003 Series. And finally, you can click the Feedback button at the top of the screen to send a message directly to Bob Grauer.

Step 3: Open a Presentation

- Click the **Start button** to display the Start menu. Click (or point to) the **All Programs button**, click **Microsoft Office**, then click **Microsoft Office PowerPoint 2003** to start the program. Close the task pane.
- Pull down the **File menu** and click the **Open command** (or click the **Open button** on the Standard toolbar).
- You should see an Open dialog box similar to the one in Figure 1.5c. Click the **drop-down arrow** on the Look In list box. Click the appropriate drive, drive C or drive A, depending on the location of your data.
- Double click the **Exploring PowerPoint folder** within the Look In box to make it the active folder. This is the folder from which you will retrieve and into which you will save the presentation.
- Click the **Views button** repeatedly to cycle through the different views. We selected the Preview view in Figure 1.5c.
- Double click **Introduction to PowerPoint** to open the presentation and begin the exercise.

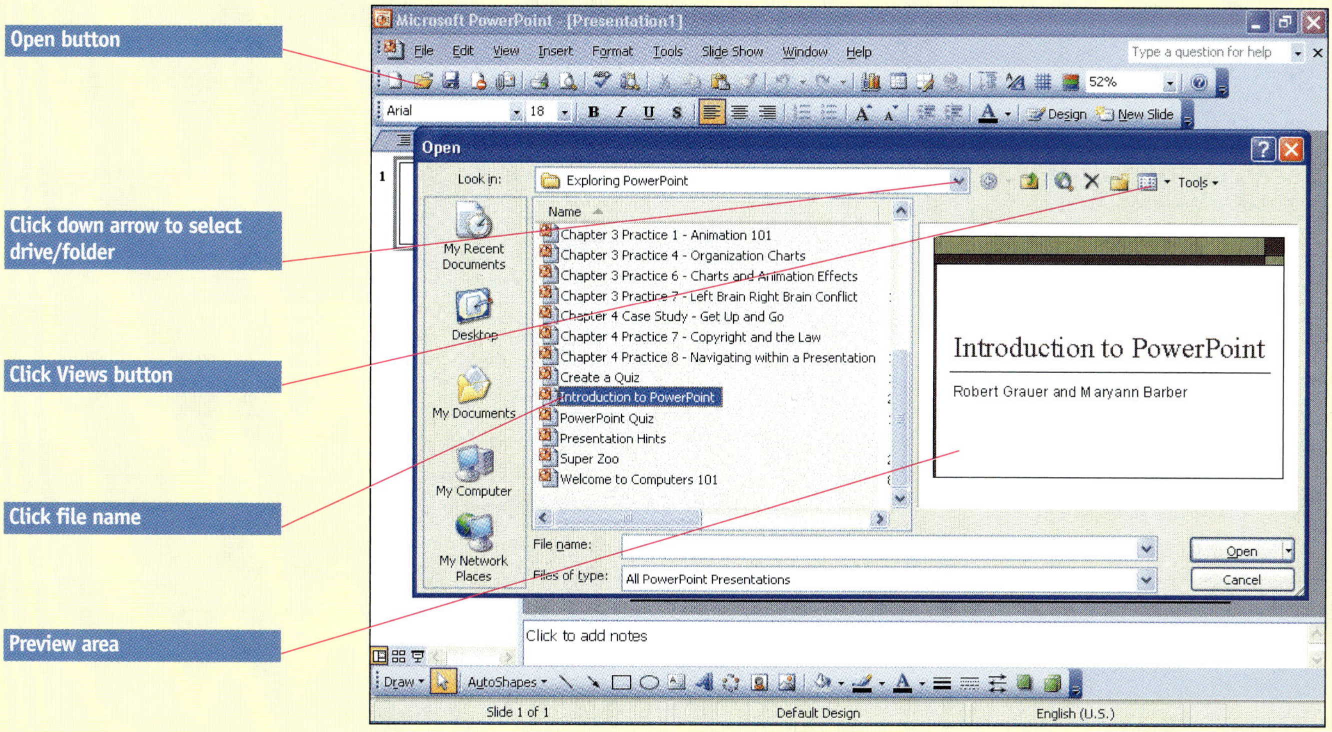

(c) Open a Presentation (step 3)

FIGURE 1.5 Hands-on Exercise 1 (*continued*)

SEPARATE THE TOOLBARS

You may see the Standard and Formatting toolbars displayed on one row to save space within the application window. If so, we suggest you separate the toolbars, so that you see all of the buttons on each. The easiest way to do this is to click the down arrow at the end of any toolbar, then click the option to show the buttons on two rows. You can click the down arrow a second time to show the buttons on one row if you want to return to the other configuration.

Step 4: The Save As Command

- If necessary, click the **Maximize button** in the application window so that PowerPoint takes the entire desktop.
- Pull down the **File menu**. Click the **Save As command** to display the dialog box shown in Figure 1.5d.
- Enter **Introduction to PowerPoint Solution** as the name of the new presentation. Click the **Save button**.
- There are now two identical copies of the file on disk, "Introduction to PowerPoint", which is the original presentation that we supplied, and "Introduction to PowerPoint Solution", which you just created.
- The title bar shows the latter name, as it is the presentation currently in memory. All subsequent changes will be made to this version. (You can always return to the original presentation if necessary.)

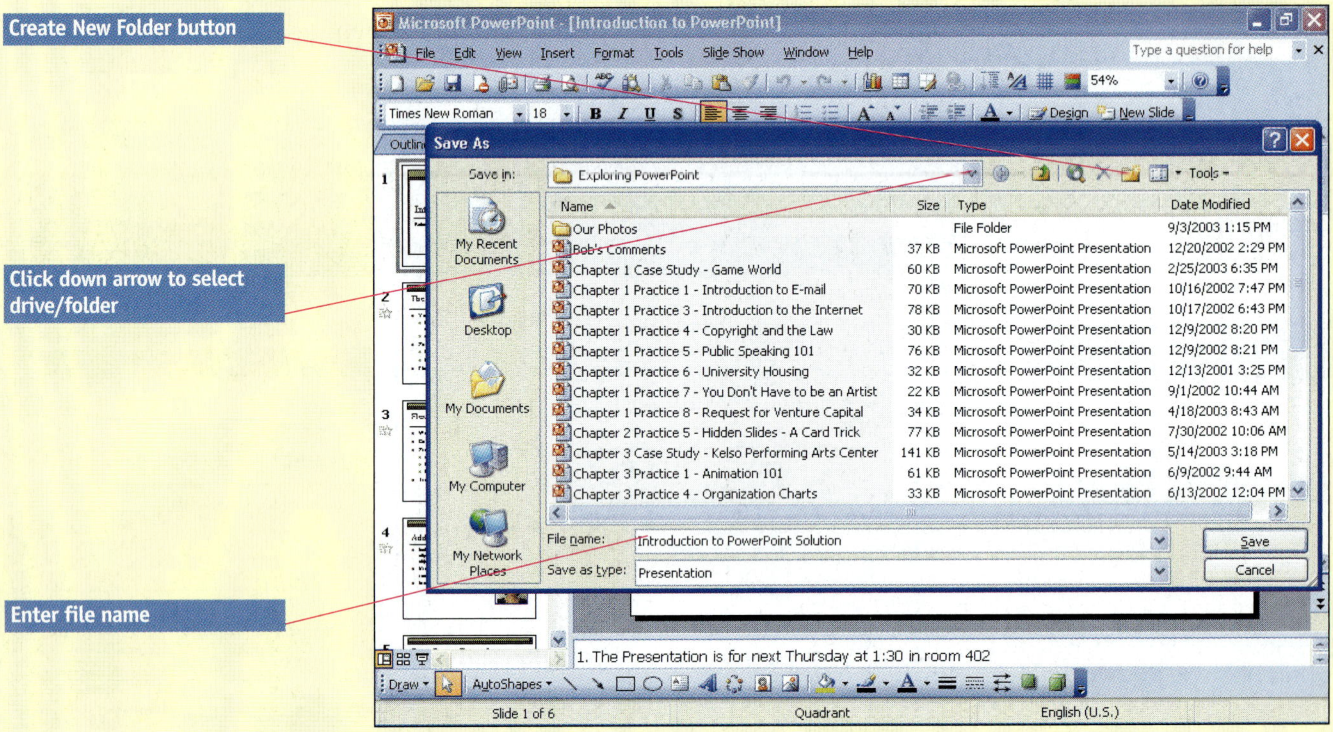

(d) The Save As Command (step 4)

FIGURE 1.5 Hands-on Exercise 1 (*continued*)

CREATE A NEW FOLDER

All Office documents are stored in the My Documents folder by default. It's helpful, however, to create additional folders, especially if you work with a large number of different documents. You can create one folder for school and another for work, and/or you can create different folders for different applications. To create a folder, pull down the File menu, click the Save As command, then click the Create New Folder button to display the New Folder dialog box. Enter the name of the folder, then click OK to create the folder. Once the folder has been created, use the Look In box to change to that folder the next time you open or save a presentation.

Step 5: Modify a Slide

- Click the *Outline tab* in the left pane. Click and drag the border separating the outline from the slide to give yourself more room to work.
- Press and hold the left mouse button as you drag the mouse over the presenters' names, **Robert Grauer and Maryann Barber**. You can select the text in either the outline or the slide pane.
- Release the mouse. The names should be highlighted (selected) as shown in Figure 1.5e. The selected text is affected by the next command.
- Type your name, which automatically replaces the selected text in both the outline and the slide pane. Press **Enter**.
- Type your class on the next line and note that the entry is made in both the slide and the outline panes.
- Pull down the **File menu** and click the **Save command** (or click the **Save button** on the Standard toolbar).

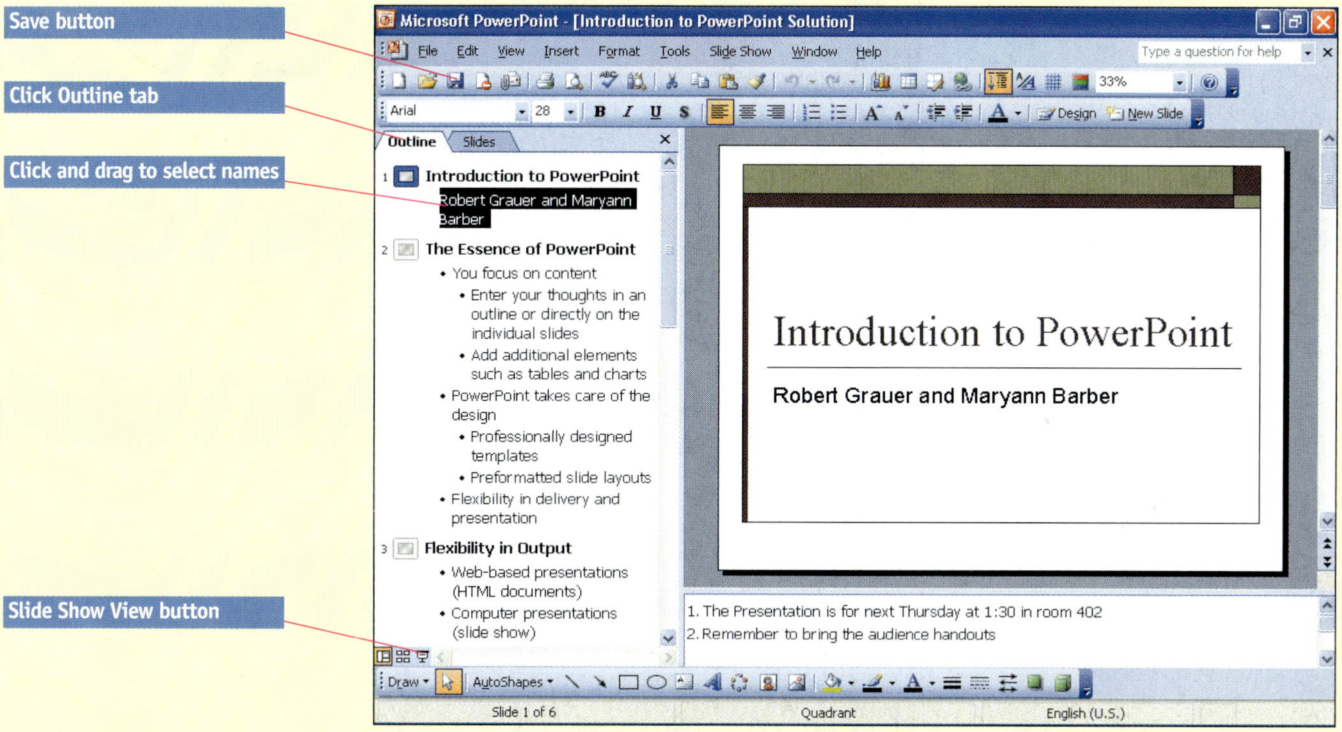

(e) Modify a Slide (step 5)

FIGURE 1.5 Hands-on Exercise 1 (*continued*)

THE AUTOMATIC SPELL CHECK

A red wavy line under a word indicates that the word is misspelled, or in the case of a proper name, that the word may be spelled correctly, but that it is not in the dictionary. In either event, point to the underlined word and click the right mouse button to display a shortcut menu. Select the appropriate spelling from the list of suggestions or add the word to the supplementary dictionary. To enable (disable) the automatic spell check, pull down the Tools menu, click the Options command, click the Spelling and Style tab, then check (clear) the option to check spelling as you type.

Step 6: Show the Presentation

- Press **Ctrl+Home** to return to the first slide. Click the **Slide Show button** above the status bar, or pull down the **View menu** and click **Slide Show**.
- The presentation will begin with the first slide as shown in Figure 1.5f.
- Click the mouse to move to the second slide. The first slide exits to the left, which is one of several transition effects used to add interest to a presentation.
- Click the mouse to go to the next (third) slide, which illustrates an animation effect. This requires you to click the mouse to display each succeeding bullet.
- Continue to view the show until you come to the end of the presentation. You can press the **Esc key** at any time to cancel the show and return to the PowerPoint window. Note the transition effects and the use of sound (provided you have speakers on your system) to enhance the presentation.
- Do you see how PowerPoint will help you to become a better public speaker?

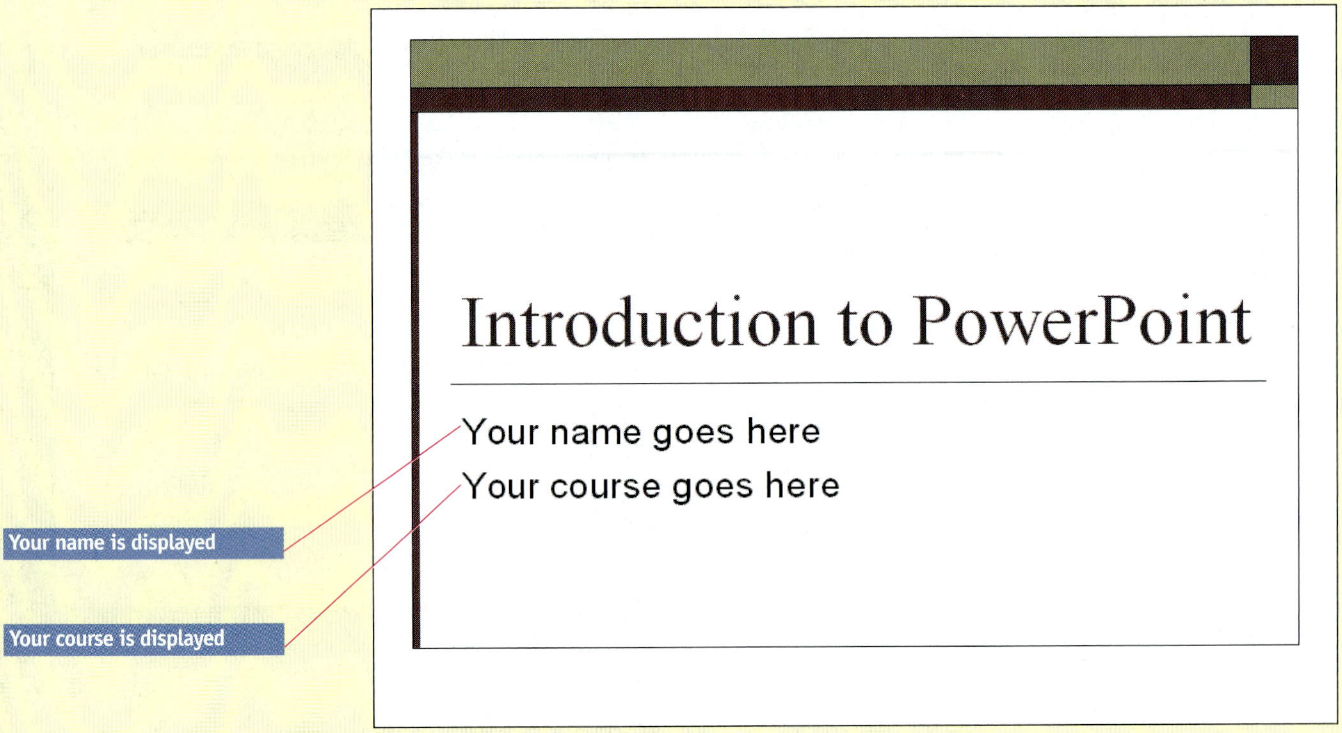

(f) Show the Presentation (step 6)

FIGURE 1.5 Hands-on Exercise 1 (*continued*)

ANNOTATE A SLIDE

Press Ctrl+P to change the mouse pointer to a point, then click and drag on the slide during the presentation to annotate the slide in much the same way your favorite football announcer diagrams a play. Use the PgDn and PgUp keys to move forward and back in the presentation while the annotation is in effect. The annotations will disappear when you exit the slide show unless you elect to keep them permanently when prompted at the end of the show. You can also type the letter E at any time to erase the annotations from a specific slide. Press Ctrl+A to change the mouse pointer back to an arrow.

Step 7: Print the Presentation

- Pull down the **File menu**. Click **Print** to display the Print dialog box in Figure 1.5g. (Clicking the Print button on the Standard toolbar does not display the Print dialog box.)
- Click the **down arrow** in the **Print what** drop-down list box, click **Handouts**, and specify **6** slides per page as shown in Figure 1.5g.
- Check the box to **Frame Slides**. Check that the **All option button** is selected under Print range. Click the **OK command button** to print the handouts for the presentation.
- Pull down the **File menu** a second time and click the **Print command**. Click the **down arrow** in the Print what list box and select **Outline View** to print the presentation in outline form. Click **OK**.
- Execute the **File Print command** a third and final time. Click the **Slides option button**, then type **1** in the associated text box to print only the first slide. Click the **down arrow** in the Print what list box and select **Slides** to print the first slide as a cover sheet. Click **OK**.

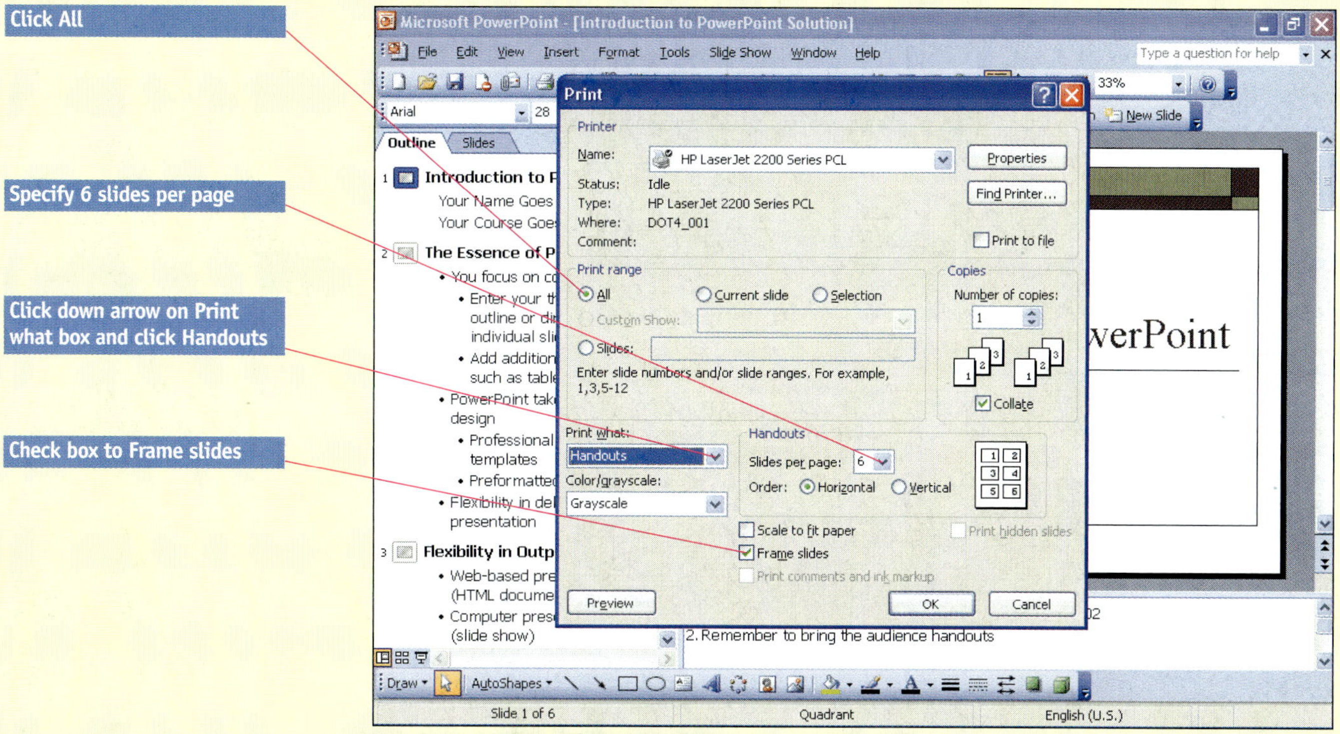

(g) Print the Presentation (step 7)

FIGURE 1.5 Hands-on Exercise 1 (*continued*)

SHOW THE KEYBOARD SHORTCUT IN A SCREENTIP

You can expand the ScreenTip associated with any toolbar button to include the equivalent keyboard shortcut. Pull down the View menu, click Toolbars, then click Customize to display the Customize dialog box. Click the Options tab and check the box to show the shortcut keys in the ScreenTips. Close the dialog box, then point to any toolbar button, and you should see the name of the button as well as the equivalent keyboard shortcut. There is no need to memorize the shortcuts, but they are useful.

Step 8: Help With PowerPoint

- The best time to obtain help is when you don't need any. Try either of the following:
  - Pull down the **Help menu** and click the command to **Show the Office Assistant**. Click the **Assistant**, then enter the question, **"How do I get help?"** in the Assistant's balloon and click **Search**, or
  - Type the question directly in the **Ask a Question box** in the upper right of the PowerPoint window and press **Enter**.
- Regardless of the technique you choose, PowerPoint will display a message indicating that it is searching the Office Web site. (Help is not available locally, and this can be a problem with a slow Internet connection.)
- You should see a task pane with the results of the search as shown in Figure 1.5h. Click the link that is most appropriate (e.g., About getting help while you work in this example).
- A new window opens containing the detailed help information. Click the **Print button** in the Help window to print the help topic for your instructor.
- Close the Help window. Close the task pane. Hide the Office Assistant. Exit PowerPoint if you do not want to continue with the next exercise at this time.

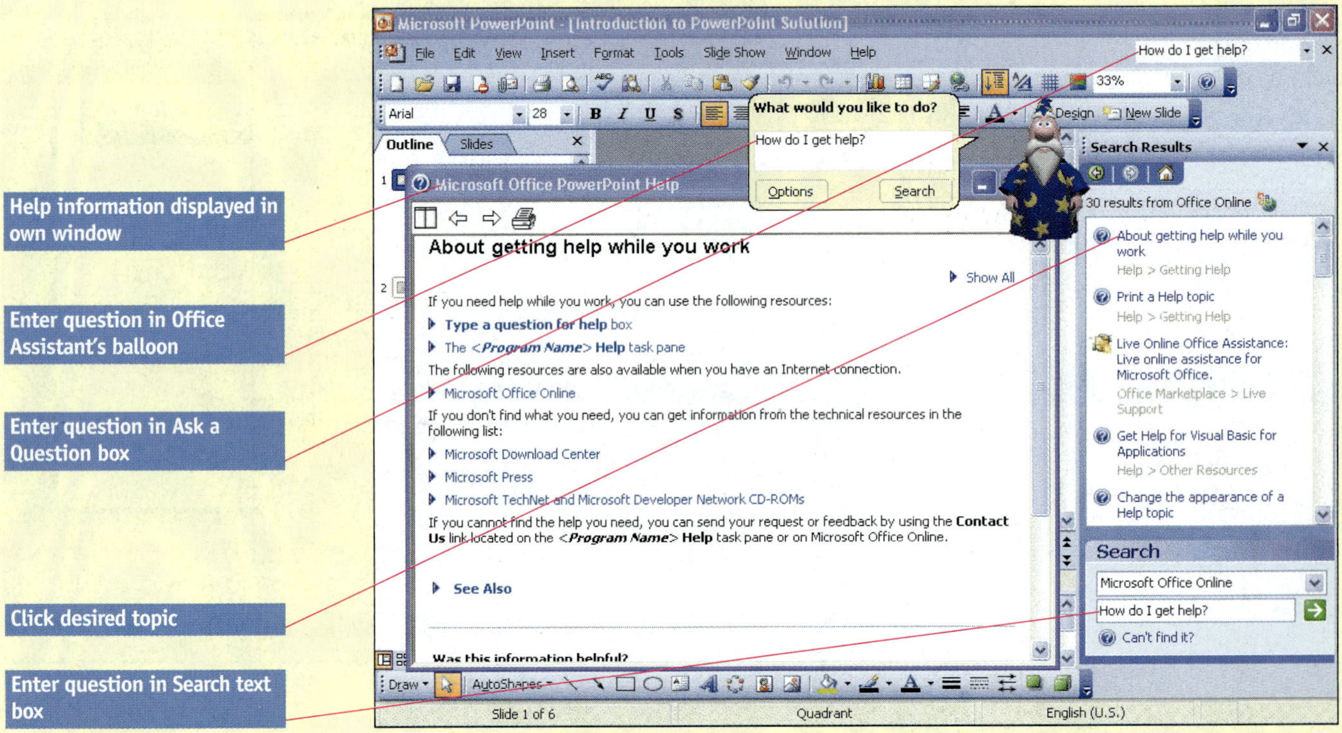

(h) Help with PowerPoint (step 8)

FIGURE 1.5 Hands-on Exercise 1 (*continued*)

TIP OF THE DAY

Pull down the Help menu, click the command to show the Office Assistant, click the Office Assistant when it appears, then click the Options button to display the Office Assistant dialog box. Click the Options tab, check the box to Show the Tip of the Day at Startup, then click OK. The next time you start PowerPoint, you will be greeted by the Assistant, who will offer you the tip of the day.

CREATING A PRESENTATION

You are ready to create your own presentation, a process that requires you to develop its content and apply the formatting through the use of a template or design specification. You can do the steps in either order, but we suggest you start with the content. Both steps are iterative in nature, and you are likely to go back and forth many times before you are finished.

You will also find yourself switching from one view to another as you develop the presentation. It doesn't matter which view you use, as long as you can accomplish what you set out to do. You can, for example, enter text one slide at a time in the Slide Normal view. You can also use the outline as shown in Figure 1.6, to view the text of many slides at the same time and thus gain a better sense of the overall presentation.

Each slide in the outline contains a title, followed by bulleted items, which are indented one to five levels, corresponding to the importance of the item. The main points appear on level one. Subsidiary items are indented below the main point to which they apply. Any item can be ***promoted*** to a higher level or ***demoted*** to a lower level, either before or after the text is entered. Each slide in the outline is numbered, and the numbers adjust automatically for the insertion or deletion of slides as you edit the presentation.

Consider, for example, slide 4 in Figure 1.6a. The title of the slide, *Develop the Content*, appears immediately after the slide number and icon. The first bullet, *Use the outline*, is indented one level under the title, and it in turn has two subsidiary bullets. The next main bullet, *Review the flow of ideas*, is moved back to level one, and it, too, has two subsidiary bullets.

The outline is (to us) the ideal way to create and edit the presentation. The ***insertion point*** marks the place where new text is entered and is established by clicking anywhere in the outline. (The insertion point is automatically placed at the title of the first slide in a new presentation.) Press Enter after typing the title or after entering the text of a bulleted item, which starts a new slide or bullet, respectively. The new item may then be promoted or demoted as necessary.

Editing is accomplished through the same techniques used in other Windows applications. For example, you can use the Cut, Copy, and Paste commands in the Edit menu (or the corresponding buttons on the Standard toolbar) to move and copy selected text, or you can simply drag and drop text from one place to another. You can also use the Find and Replace commands that are found in every Office application.

Note, too, that you can format text in the outline by using the ***select-then-do*** approach common to all Office applications; that is, you select the text, then you execute the appropriate command or click the appropriate button. The selected text remains highlighted and is affected by all subsequent commands until you click elsewhere in the outline.

Figure 1.6b displays a collapsed view of the outline, which displays only the title of each slide. The advantage to this view is that you see more slides on the screen at the same time, making it easier to move slides within the presentation. The slides are expanded or collapsed using tools on the ***Outlining toolbar***.

CRYSTALLIZE YOUR MESSAGE

Every presentation exists to deliver a message, whether it's to sell a product, present an idea, or provide instruction. Decide on the message you want to deliver, then write the text for the presentation. Edit the text to be sure it is consistent with your objective. Then, and only then, should you think about formatting, but you should always keep the message foremost in your mind. The success of any presentation will ultimately depend on its content.

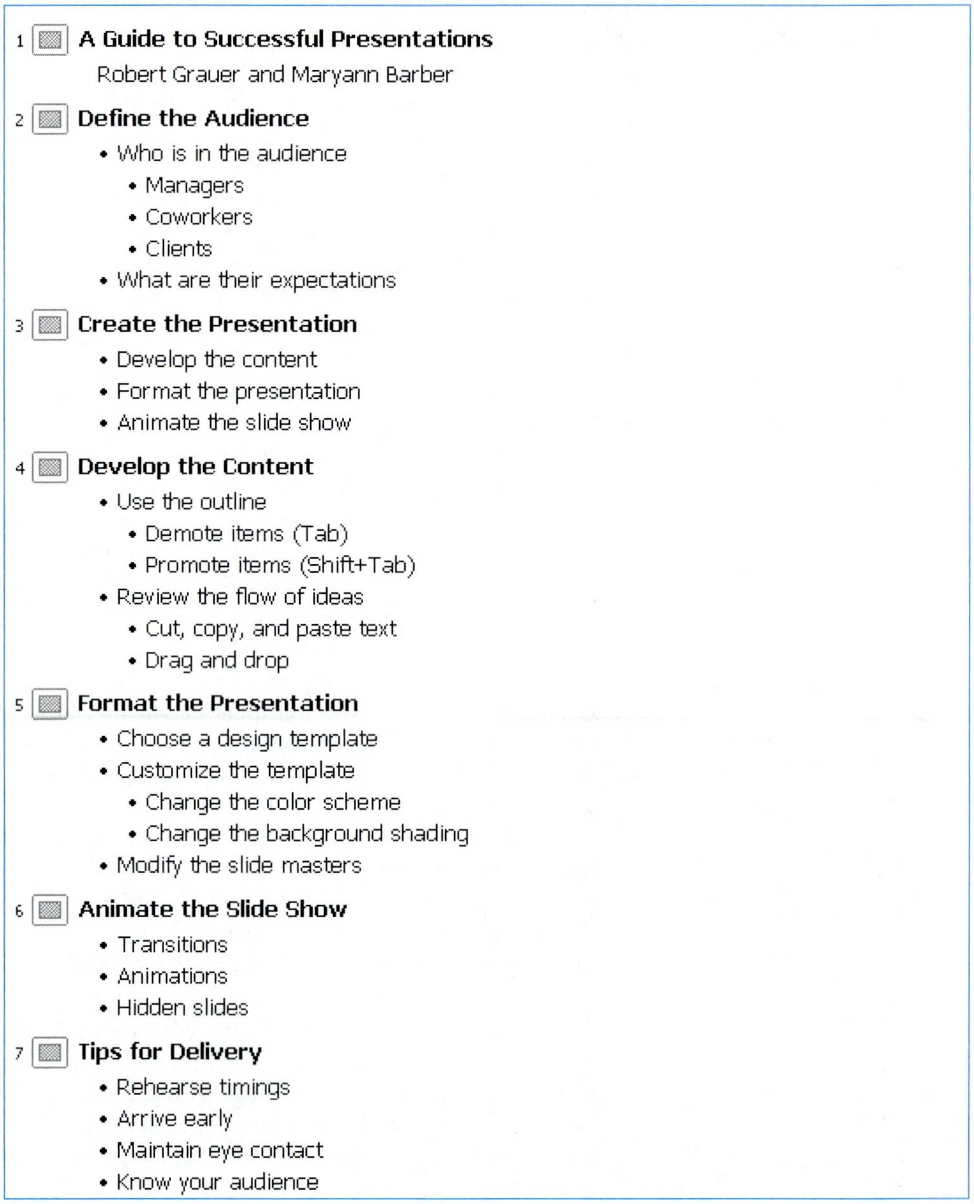

(a) The Expanded Outline

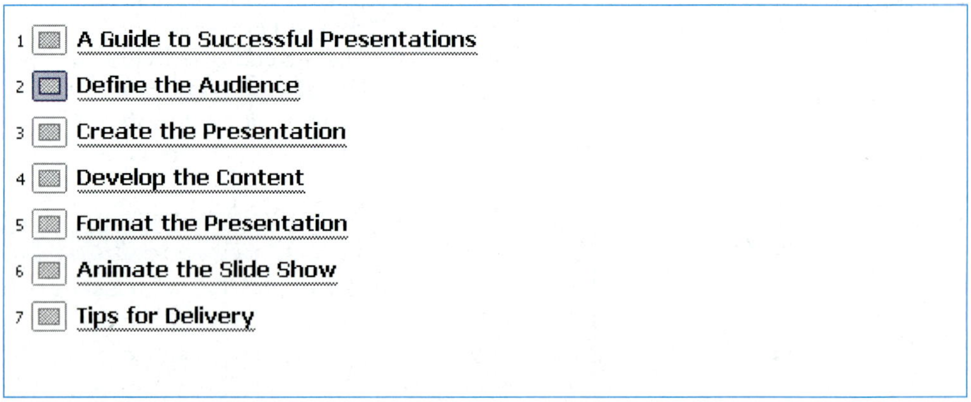

(b) The Collapsed Outline

FIGURE 1.6 The Presentation Outline

Slide Layouts

New slides are typically created as text slides, consisting of a slide title and a single column of bullets. The layout of a text (or any other) slide can be changed, however, to include clip art or other objects, and/or to display a double column of bullets. The new elements can be added manually by using the various tools on the Drawing toolbar or by letting PowerPoint change the layout for you.

PowerPoint provides a set of predefined ***slide layouts*** that determine the nature and position of the objects on a slide. The layouts are displayed by default within the task pane whenever the Insert menu is used to add a slide. Just insert the slide, then select the desired layout from the task pane. You can also change the layout of an existing slide by selecting the slide and choosing a different layout from the task pane. (Use the View menu to toggle the task pane open, then click the down arrow within the task pane to display the slide layouts.)

Figure 1.7 illustrates the creation of a two-column text slide, which in turn has three ***placeholders*** that determine the position of each object. Once the layout has been selected, you simply click the appropriate placeholder to add the title or text. Thus, you would click on the placeholder for the title and enter the text of the title as indicated. In similar fashion, you click the placeholder for either column of bullets and enter the associated text.

Other layouts include clip art, organization charts, and other objects. There are additional content layouts for a table, picture, diagram, or media clip. (You can change the size and/or position of the placeholders by moving and sizing the placeholders just as you would any other object.) It's easy, as you will see in the hands-on exercise, which follows shortly.

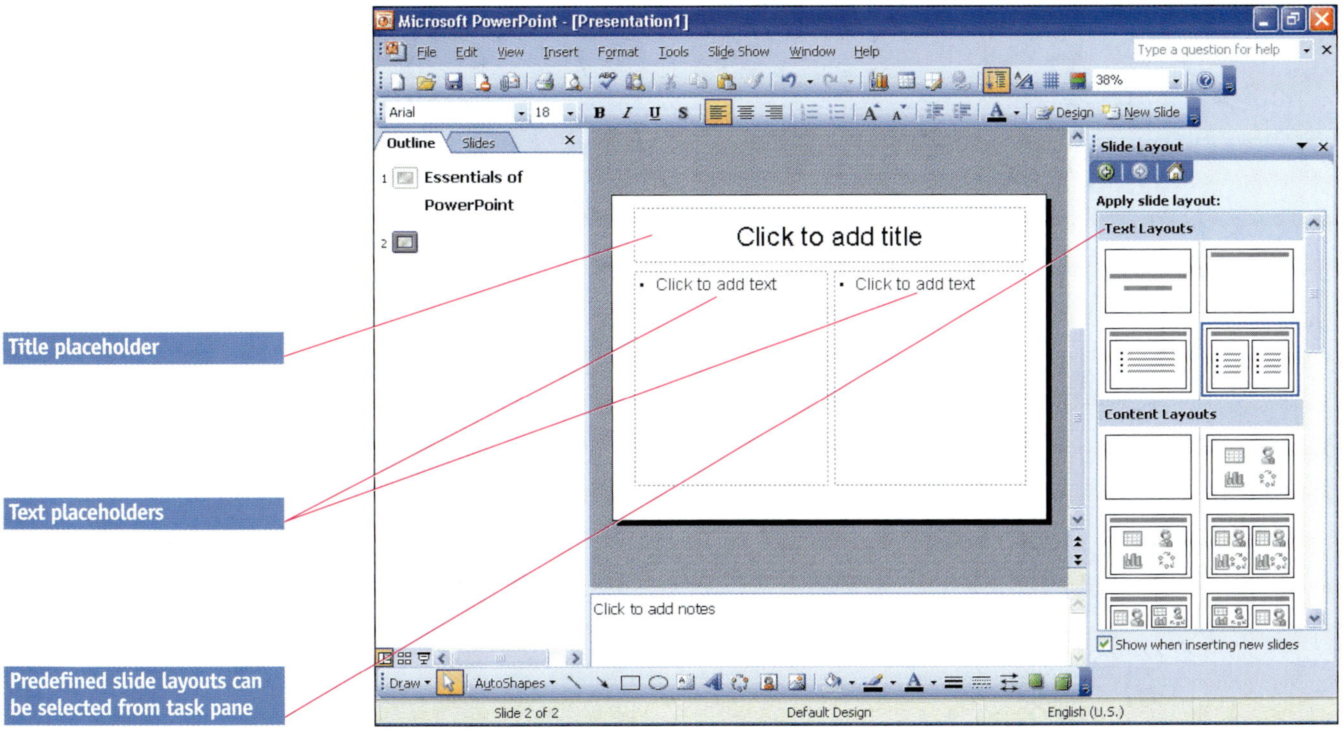

FIGURE 1.7 Slide Layouts

TEMPLATES

PowerPoint enables you to concentrate on the content of a presentation without concern for its appearance. You focus on what you are going to say, and trust in PowerPoint to format the presentation attractively. The formatting is implemented automatically by selecting one of the many templates that are supplied with PowerPoint.

A ***template*** is a design specification that controls every element in a presentation. It specifies the color scheme for the slides and the arrangement of the different elements (placeholders) on each slide. It determines the formatting of the text, the fonts that are used, and the size and placement of the bulleted text.

Figure 1.8 displays the title slide of a presentation in four different templates. Just choose the template you like, and PowerPoint formats the entire presentation according to that template. And don't be afraid to change your mind. You can use the Slide Design command at any time to select a different template and change the look of your presentation.

(a) Glass Layers

(b) Fireworks

(c) Maple

(d) Ocean

FIGURE 1.8 Templates

hands-on exercise

2 Creating a Presentation

Objective To create a new presentation; to apply a design template to a presentation. Use Figure 1.9 as a guide.

Step 1: Create a New Presentation

- Click the **Start button**, click the **All Programs button**, click **Microsoft Office**, then click **Microsoft PowerPoint** to start PowerPoint. PowerPoint opens with a new blank presentation.
- If necessary, pull down the **View menu** and switch to the **Normal view** and click the **Outline tab** as shown in Figure 1.9a.
- Hide the Office Assistant if it appears. You can get help without the Assistant by using the Ask a Question box.
- Close the task pane.

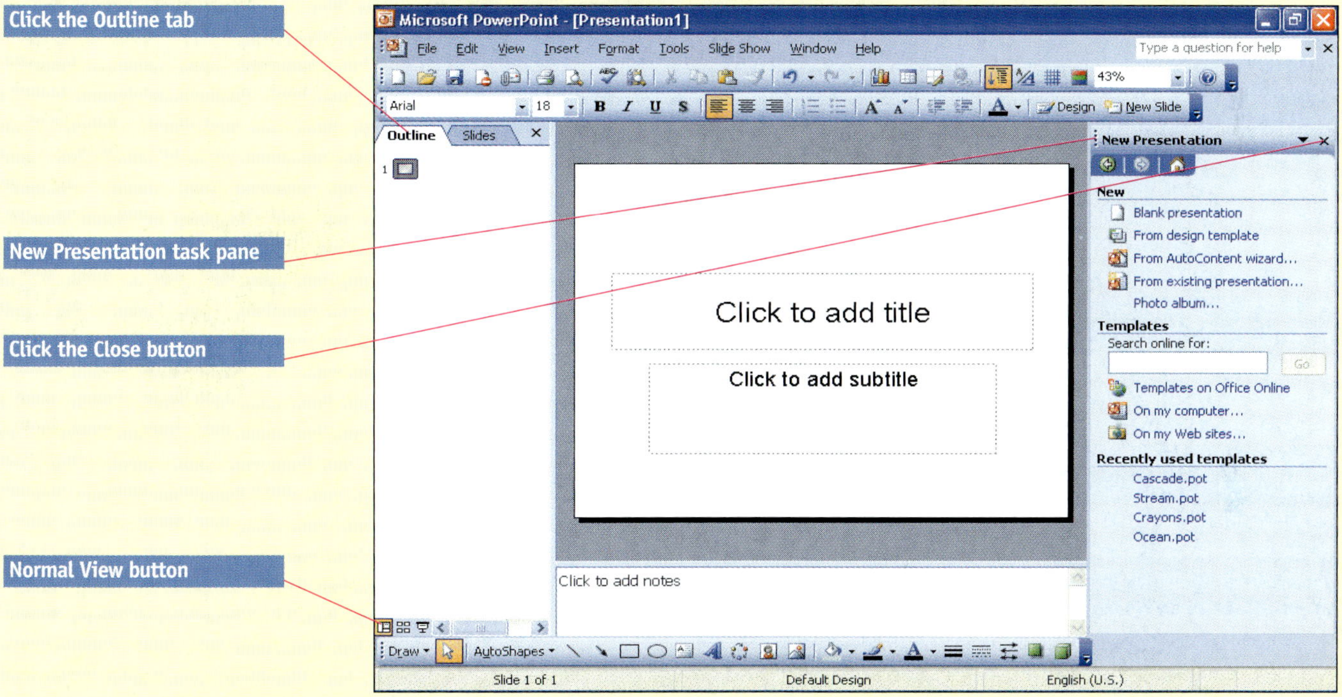

(a) Create a New Presentation (step 1)

FIGURE 1.9 Hands-on Exercise 2

EXPLORE THE TASK PANE

Different task panes are displayed at different times, depending on what you want to accomplish. The Getting Started task pane is displayed when PowerPoint is started initially, and it contains links to the last several presentations that were opened. The New Presentation task pane suggests different ways to create a presentation; e.g., by using the AutoContent Wizard, which is discussed in Chapter 2. Other task panes are displayed automatically according to the selected command. You can also use the Ctrl+F1 keyboard shortcut to open (close) the task pane at any time.

Step 2: **Create the Title Slide**

- Click anywhere in the box containing **Click to add title**, then type the title, **A Guide to Successful Presentations**, as shown in Figure 1.9b. The title will automatically wrap to a second line.
- Click anywhere in the box containing **Click to add subtitle** and enter your name. Click outside the subtitle placeholder when you have entered your name on the slide.
- The outline now contains the title of the presentation as well as your name. You can use the outline to change either element.
- Click in the Notes pane and enter a note that pertains to the title slide—for example, the date and time that the presentation is scheduled. The notes are primarily for the speaker, but can also be distributed to the audience.

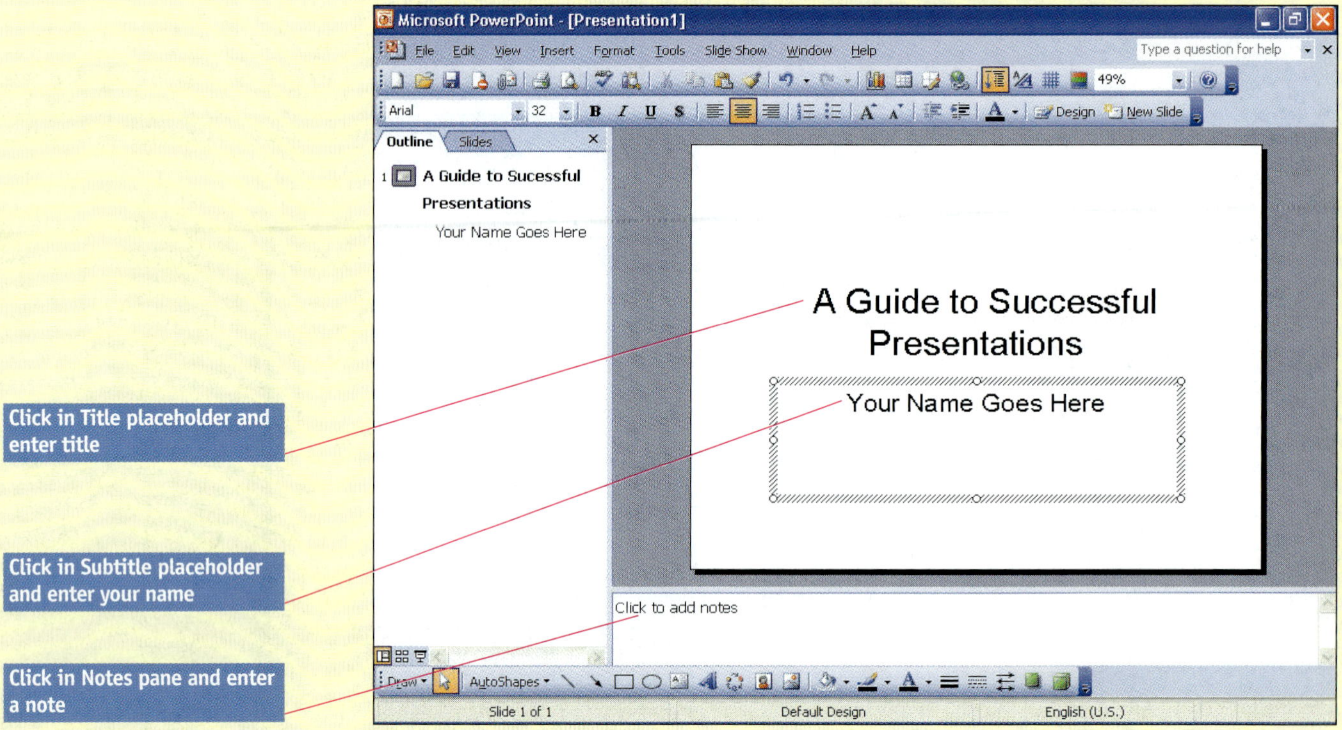

(b) Create the Title Slide (step 2)

FIGURE 1.9 Hands-on Exercise 2 (*continued*)

THE UNDO AND REDO COMMANDS

Click the drop-down arrow next to the Undo button to display a list of your previous actions, then click the action you want to undo, which also undoes all of the preceding commands. Undoing the fifth command in the list, for example, will also undo the preceding four commands. The Redo command works in reverse and cancels the last Undo command.

Step 3: Save the Presentation

- Pull down the **File menu** and click **Save** (or click the **Save button** on the Standard toolbar). You should see the Save As dialog box in Figure 1.9c. If necessary, click the **down arrow** on the **Views button** and click **Details**.
- To save the file:
  - ❑ Click the **drop-down arrow** on the Save In list box.
  - ❑ Click the appropriate drive, drive C or drive A, depending on whether or not you installed the data disk on your hard drive.
  - ❑ Double click the **Exploring PowerPoint folder** to make it the active folder (the folder in which you will save the document).
  - ❑ Enter **My First Presentation** as the name of the presentation.
- Click **Save** or press the **Enter key**. The title bar changes to reflect the name of the presentation.

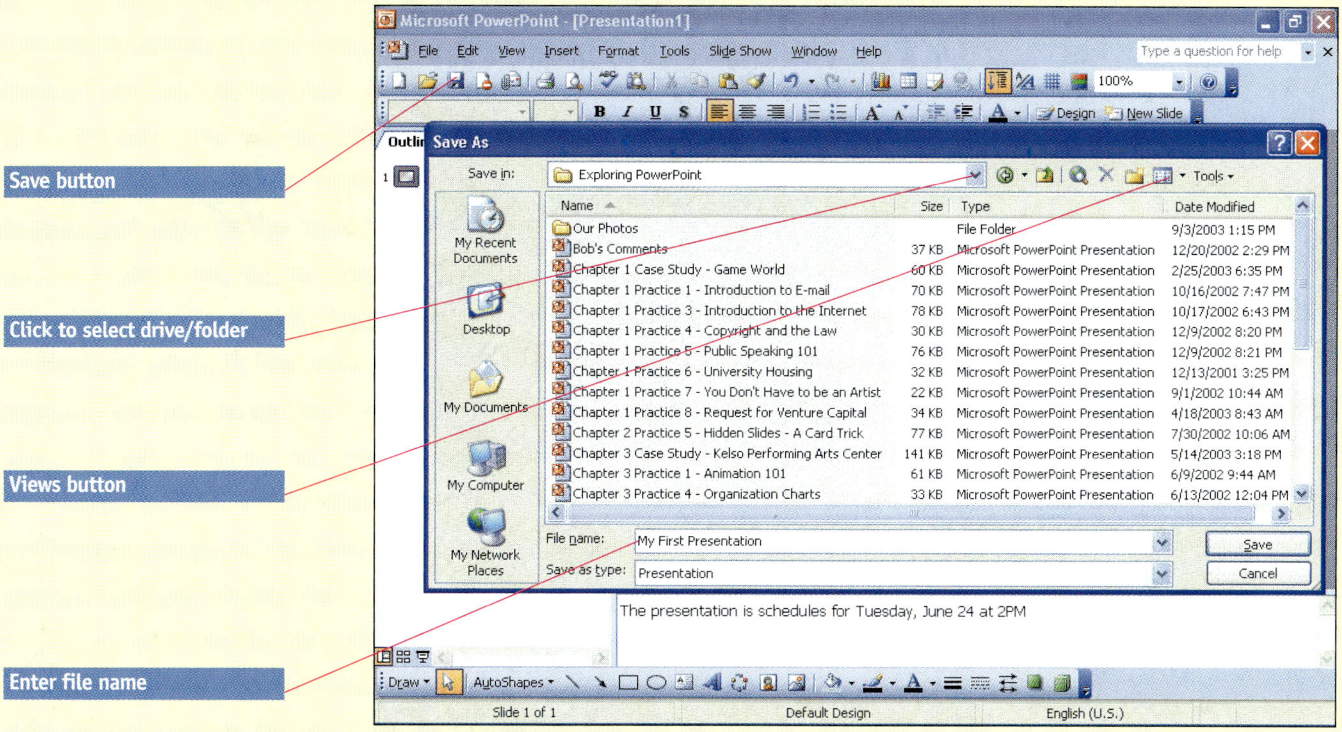

(c) Save the Presentation (step 3)

FIGURE 1.9 Hands-on Exercise 2 (*continued*)

CHANGE THE DEFAULT FOLDER

The default folder is where PowerPoint goes initially to open an existing presentation or to save a new presentation. If you have your own machine, however, you may find it useful to change the default folder. Pull down the Tools menu, click the Options command, then click the Save tab within the Options dialog box. Click in the text box that contains the default file location, enter a new folder, and click OK. The next time you open or save a file, PowerPoint will go automatically to that location.

Step 4: Enter the Text

- Check that the Outlining toolbar is displayed. If not, pull down the **View menu**, click the **Toolbars command**, then click **Outlining** to show the toolbar.
- Click and drag the border between the outline pane and the slide pane to enlarge the outline pane.
- Click after your name in the outline pane. Press **Enter** to begin a new item, then press **Shift+Tab** to promote the item and create slide 2. Type **Define the Audience**. Press **Enter**.
- Press the **Tab key** (or click the **Demote button** on the Outlining toolbar) to enter the first bullet. Type **Who is in the audience** and press **Enter**.
- Press the **Tab key** to enter the second-level bullets. Type **Managers**. Press **Enter**. Type **Coworkers**. Press **Enter**. Type **Clients**. Press **enter**.
- Press **Shift+Tab** (or click the **Promote button** on the Outlining toolbar) to return to the first-level bullets. Type **What are their expectations**. Press **Enter**.
- Press **Shift+Tab** to enter the title of the third slide. Type **Tips for Delivery**. Press **Enter**, then press the **Tab key** to create the first bullet.
- Add the remaining text for this slide and for slide 4 as shown in Figure 1.9d.

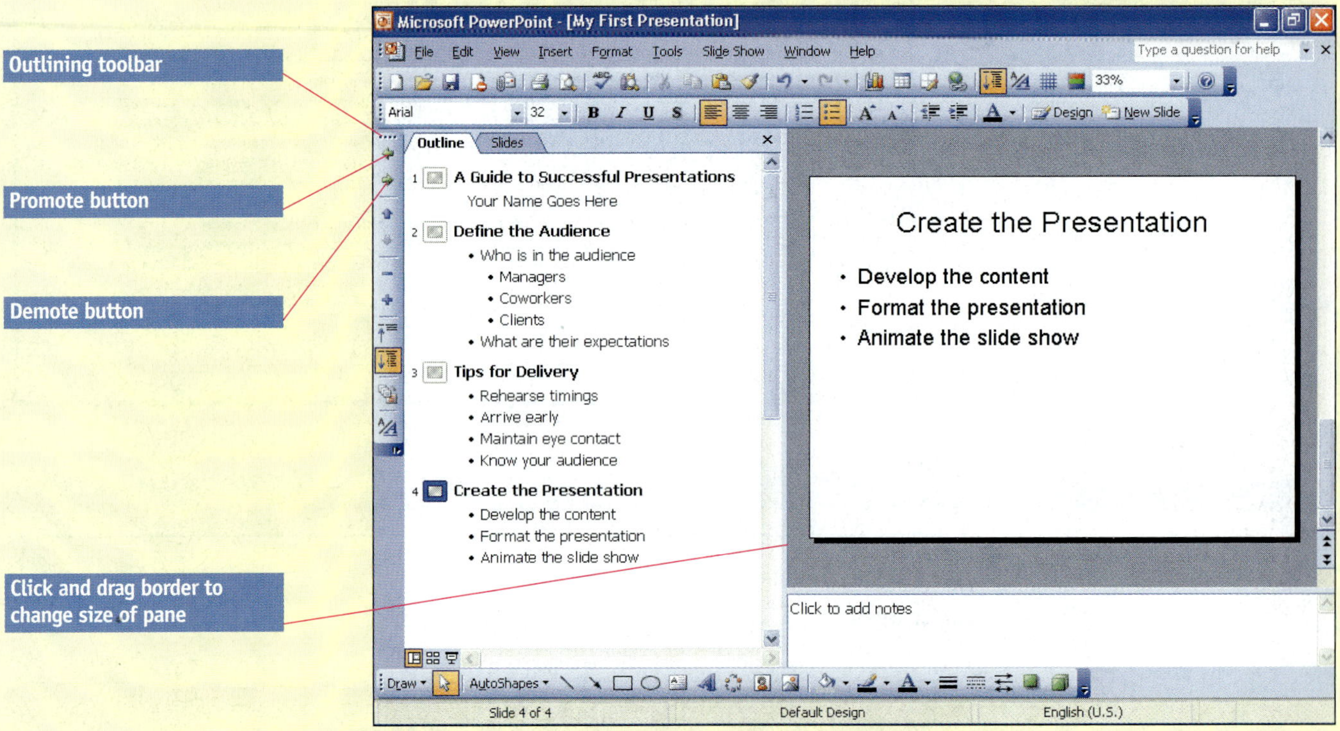

(d) Enter the Text (step 4)

FIGURE 1.9 Hands-on Exercise 2 (*continued*)

JUST KEEP TYPING

The easiest way to enter the text for a presentation is to type continually in the outline. Just type an item, then press Enter to move to the next item. You will be automatically positioned at the next item on the same level, where you can type the next entry. Continue to enter text in this manner. Press the Tab key as necessary to demote an item (move it to the next lower level). Press Shift+Tab to promote an item (move it to the next higher level).

Step 5: The Thesaurus and Spell Check

- Enter the text of the remaining slides as shown in Figure 1.9e. Do *not* press Enter after entering the last bullet on the last slide or else you will get a blank bullet.
- Click anywhere within the word "**Hidden**" that appears on the last slide. Pull down the **Tools menu** and click the **Thesaurus command** to open the research task pane, which automatically displays synonyms for the selected word.
- Point to the desired replacement (e.g., concealed), click the **drop-down arrow** to display a menu, and click **Insert** to replace "hidden" with "concealed". Click the **Undo button** to return to the original text if you prefer the original word.
- Click the **Spelling button** on the Standard toolbar to check for spelling. The result of the spell check depends on how accurately you entered the text of the presentation. We deliberately misspelled the word *Transitions.*
- Continue to check the document for spelling errors. Click **OK** when PowerPoint indicates it has checked the entire presentation.
- Click the **Save button** on the Standard toolbar to save the presentation.

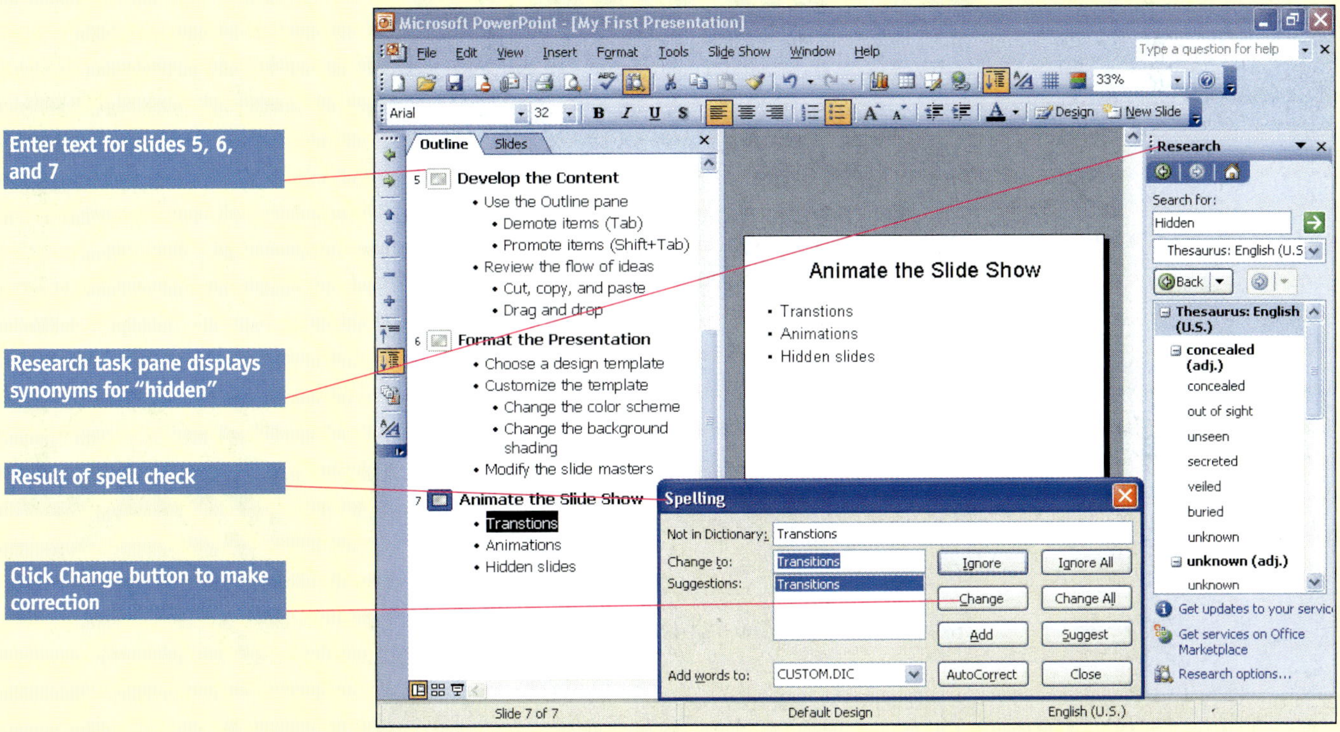

(e) The Thesaurus and Spell Check (step 5)

FIGURE 1.9 Hands-on Exercise 2 (*continued*)

THE RESEARCH TASK PANE

Microsoft Office 2003 brings the resources of the Web directly into the application. Pull down the Tools menu and click the Research command to open the Research task pane. Type the entry you are searching for, click the down arrow to choose a reference book, then click the green arrow to initiate the search. You have access to a dictionary, thesaurus, and encyclopedia. You even have an online bilingual dictionary. Research has never been easier.

Step 6: Drag and Drop

- Press **Ctrl+Home** to move to the beginning of the presentation. (If you don't see the Outlining toolbar, pull down the **View menu**, click the **Toolbars command**, and check **Outlining** to display the toolbar.)
- Click the **Collapse All button** on the Outlining toolbar to collapse the outline as shown in Figure 1.9f.
- Click the **icon** for **slide 3** (Tips for Delivery) to select the slide. Point to the **Slide icon** (the mouse pointer changes to a four-headed arrow), then click and drag to move the slide to the end of the presentation.
- All of the slides have been renumbered. The slide titled Tips for Delivery has been moved to the end of the presentation and appears as slide 7. Click the **Expand All button** to display the contents of each slide.
- Click anywhere in the presentation to deselect the last slide.
- Save the presentation.

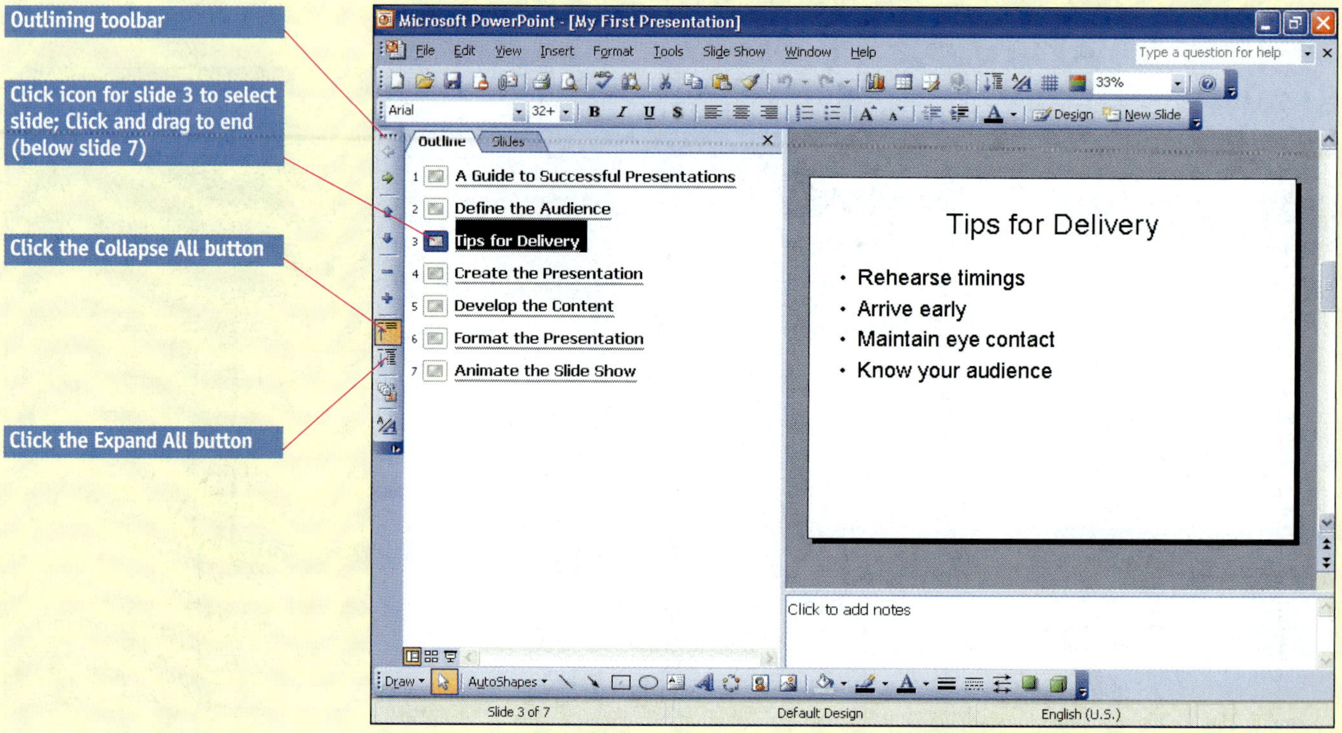

(f) Drag and Drop (step 6)

FIGURE 1.9 Hands-on Exercise 2 (*continued*)

SELECTING SLIDES IN THE OUTLINE

Click the slide icon or the slide number next to the slide title to select the slide. PowerPoint will select the entire slide (including its title, text, and any other objects that are not visible in the outline). Click the first slide, then press and hold the Shift key as you click the ending slide to select a group of sequential slides. Press Ctrl+A to select the entire outline. You can use these techniques to select multiple slides regardless of whether the outline is collapsed or expanded. The selected slides can be copied, moved, expanded, collapsed, or deleted as a unit.

Step 7: Choose a Design Template

- Pull down the **Format menu** and click the **Slide Design command** to open the task pane as shown in Figure 1.9g. (This command will change the contents of the task pane if the task pane is already open.)
- Click the **down arrow** on the scroll bar within the task pane to scroll through the available designs until you find one that you like. (We chose the Ocean design.) Click the selected design in the task pane to apply this template to your presentation.
- Select a different design to see how your presentation looks when set in another template.
- Click the **Undo button** to cancel the last command and return to the previous design. Click the **Redo button** to reverse the undo operation.
- Spend a few minutes (and *limit* yourself to a few minutes) until you have the design you like.
- Save the presentation.

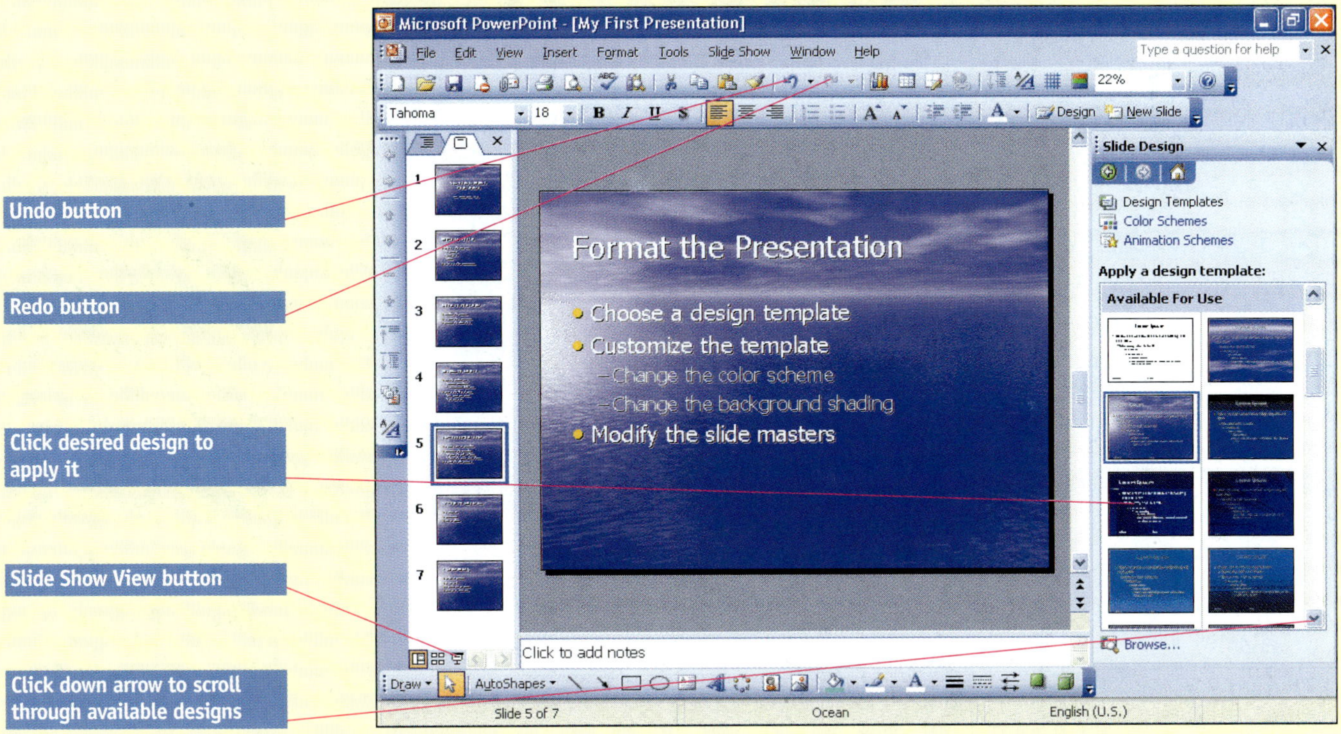

(g) Choose a Design Template (step 7)

FIGURE 1.9 Hands-on Exercise 2 (*continued*)

CUSTOMIZE THE SELECTED TEMPLATE

PowerPoint offers a wide variety of professional templates that are suitable for virtually every presentation. Even so, you will find yourself wanting to customize a template, perhaps by adding a unifying corporate logo, modifying a placeholder, changing a font style or size, or moving a placeholder. You could change every slide individually, but it is much easier to modify the underlying slide master, which controls the formatting and other elements that appear on the individual slides. Any change to the slide master is automatically reflected in every slide except the title slide. See practice exercise 9 at the end of the chapter.

Step 8: View the Presentation

- Press **Ctrl+Home** to move to the beginning of the presentation. Click the **Slide Show button** on the status bar to view the presentation as shown in Figure 1.9h.
  - To move to the next slide: Click the **left mouse button**, type the letter **N**, or press the **PgDn key**.
  - To move to the previous slide: Type the letter **P** or press the **PgUp key**.
- Continue to move from one slide to the next until you come to the end of the presentation and are returned to the Normal view.
- Save the presentation. Exit PowerPoint if you do not want to continue with the next exercise at this time.

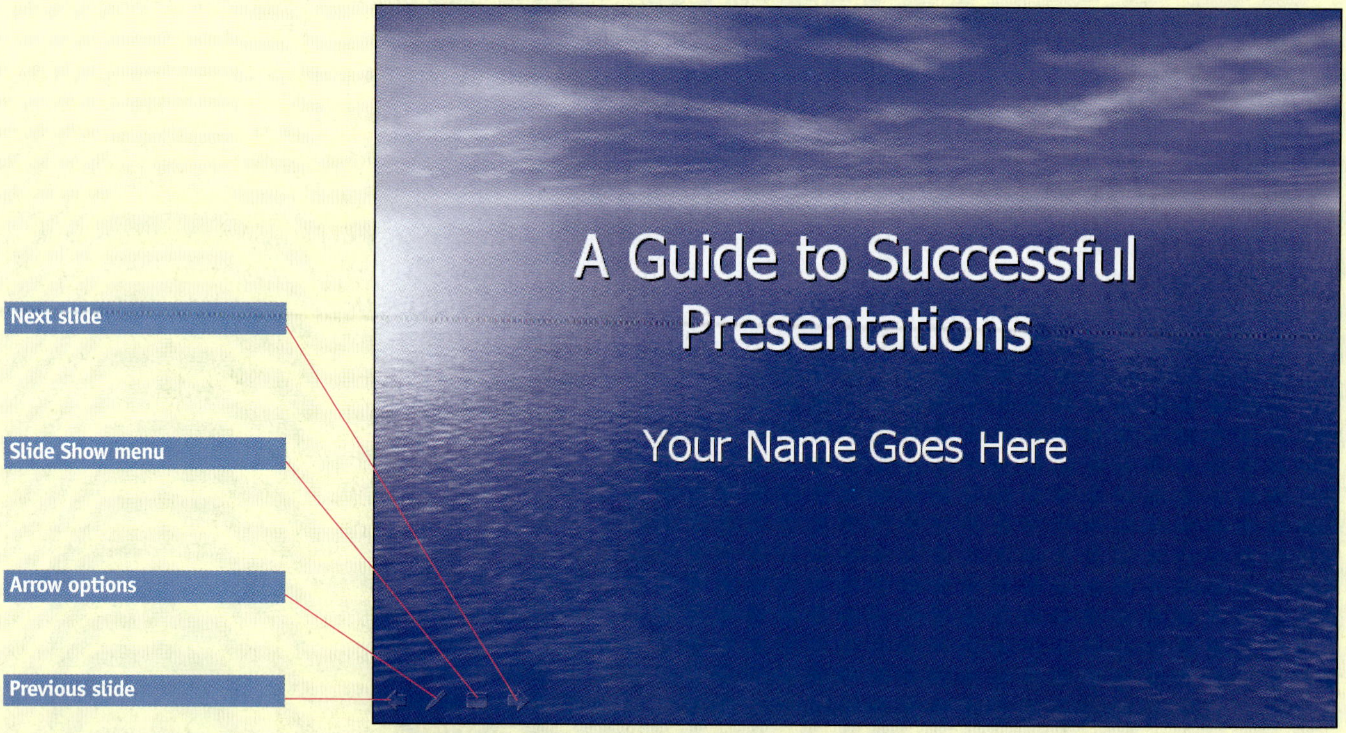

(h) View the Presentation (step 8)

FIGURE 1.9 Hands-on Exercise 2 (*continued*)

BACK UP YOUR WORK

We cannot overemphasize the importance of adequate backup and urge you to back up your important files at every opportunity. Exit PowerPoint, start Windows Explorer, then copy the presentation from drive C to a floppy disk. If the presentation is too large, you can compress the file before you copy it, and/or you can burn a CD. You can also e-mail the presentation to yourself as an attachment. Remember, you can always get another copy of Microsoft Office, but your data files are irreplaceable. Make duplicate copies of any files that you cannot afford to lose, and then store those files away from your computer.

You have successfully created a PowerPoint presentation, but the most important step is yet to come—the delivery of the presentation to an audience. This is best accomplished through a computerized slide show (as opposed to using overhead transparencies or 35mm slides). The computer becomes the equivalent of a slide projector, and the presentation is called a slide show.

PowerPoint can help you add interest to the slide show in two ways, transitions and animations. ***Transitions*** apply to the slide as a whole and control the way a slide moves on and off the screen. ***Animations*** control the entrance and/or exit of individual elements on a single slide. Transitions and animations are applied from the task pane within the Normal view as shown in Figure 1.10. (Pull down the Slide Show menu and select the Slide Transition or Custom Animation command to open the task pane with the appropriate options.)

The task pane in Figure 1.10a contains a list box with the available ***transition effects***. Slides may move on to the screen from the left or right, be uncovered by horizontal or vertical blinds, fade, dissolve, and so on. You select a slide, choose the effect, select a speed and sound, then indicate when you want to advance the slide (either on a mouse click or after a specified number of seconds). Click the Play button at the bottom of the pane to preview the transition, or click the Slide Show button to move directly to a complete show. (Transition effects can also be applied from the Slide Sorter view, where you can apply the same transition to multiple slides by selecting the slides prior to applying the effect.)

Figure 1.10b shows the application of animation effects to a specific slide. You can select a predefined animation scheme for the slide as a whole, or you can animate each object individually. The animation schemes are divided into subtle, moderate, and exciting, and it is fun to experiment with the various effects. ***Custom animation*** requires you to select an animation effect for each object on the slide, then specify the order in which the objects are to appear. The slide in Figure 1.10b, for example, displays the title, the four bullets in succession, and the clip art in that order. Look closely at the icons in the task pane and you will see that different effects are chosen for the various objects.

Delivering the Presentation

PowerPoint can help you to create attractive presentations, but the content and delivery are still up to you. You have worked hard to gain the opportunity to present your ideas and you want to be well prepared for the session. Practice aloud several times, preferably under the same conditions as the actual presentation. Time your delivery to be sure that you do not exceed your allotted time. Everyone is nervous, but the more you practice, the more confident you will be.

Arrive early. You need time to gather your thoughts as well as to set up the presentation. Start PowerPoint and open your presentation prior to addressing the audience. Be sure that your notes are with you and check that water is available for you during the presentation. Look at the audience to open communication and gain credibility. Speak clearly and vary your delivery. Try to relax. You'll be great!

QUESTIONS AND ANSWERS (Q & A)

Indicate at the beginning of your talk whether you will take questions during the presentation or collectively at the end. Announce the length of time that will be allocated to questions. Rephrase all questions so the audience can hear. If you do receive a hostile question, rephrase it in a neutral way and try to disarm the challenger by paying a compliment. If you don't know the answer, say so.

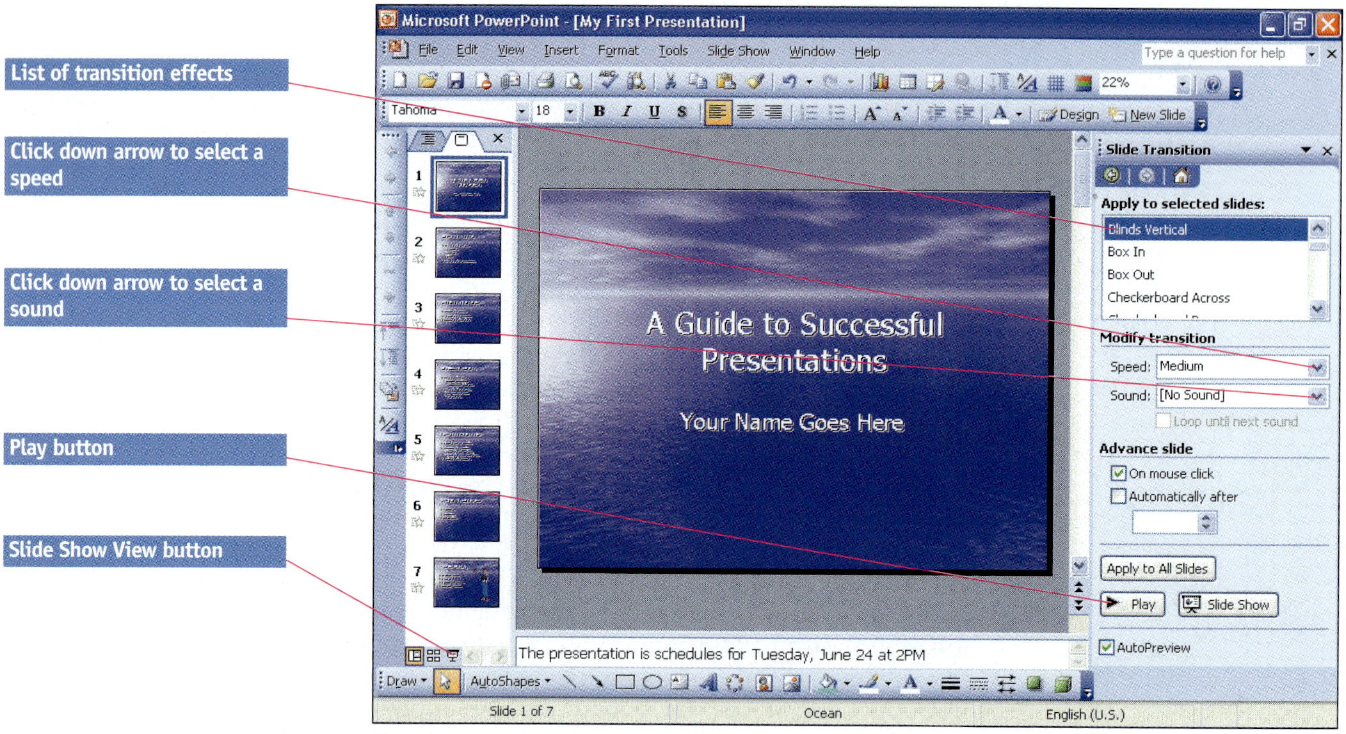

(a) Slide Transition

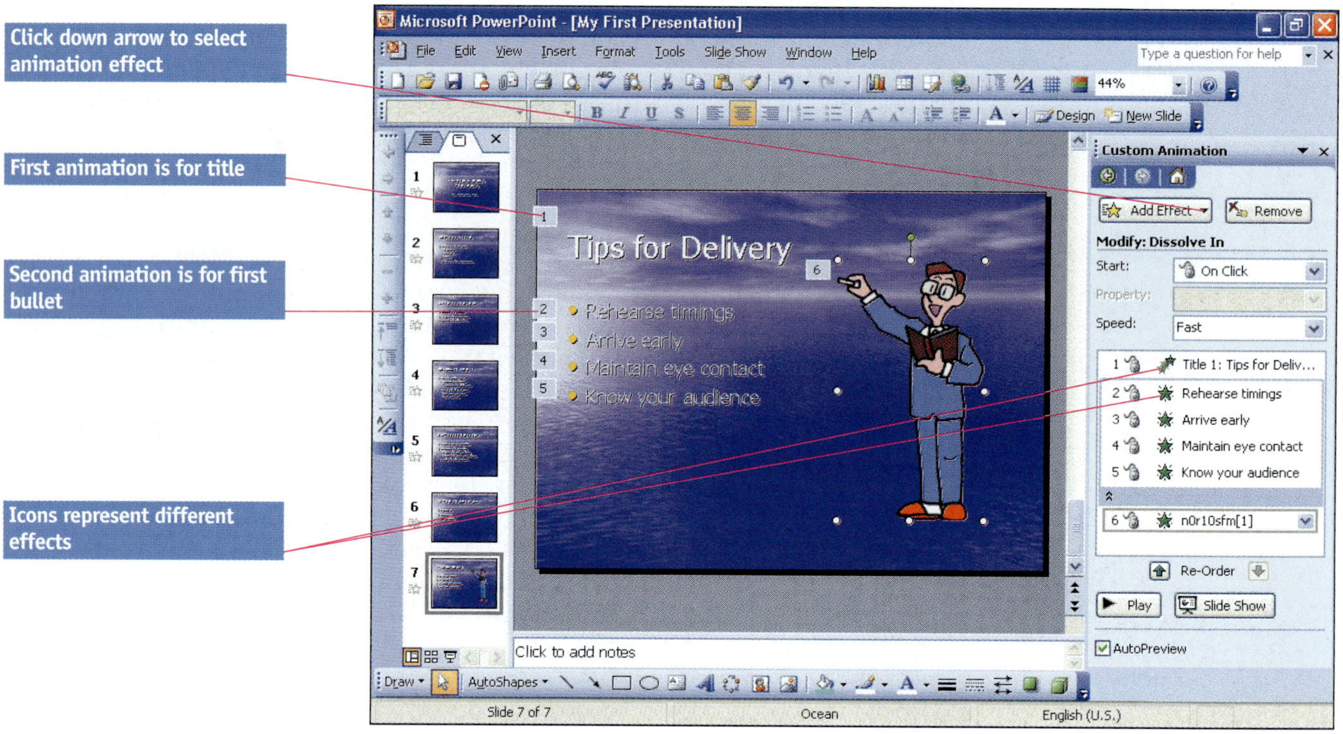

(b) Custom Animation

FIGURE 1.10 Transition and Animation Effects

hands-on exercise

3 Animating a Presentation

Objective To change the layout of an existing slide; to establish transition and animation effects. Use Figure 1.11 as a guide in the exercise.

Step 1: Change the Slide Layout

- Start PowerPoint. There are two basic ways to open an existing presentation. You can use the Open command in the File menu, or you can open the presentation from the task pane.
- Pull down the **View menu** and click the **Task pane command** to display the task pane, then (if necessary) click the **down arrow** in the task pane to select **Getting Started**.
- You should see My First Presentation from the previous exercise since the most recently used presentations are listed automatically.
- Click **My First Presentation**. (Click the link to **More** if the presentation is not listed, to display the Open dialog box, where you can select the drive and folder to locate your presentation.)
- Click the **Outline tab**, then scroll in the left pane until you can select the **Tips for Delivery slide**.
- Open the task pane. Click the **down arrow** on the task pane to select **Slide Layout** as shown in Figure 1.11a. Now scroll in the task pane until you can select the **Title, Text & Clip Art layout** as shown in Figure 1.11a. Click the layout to apply it to the current slide.

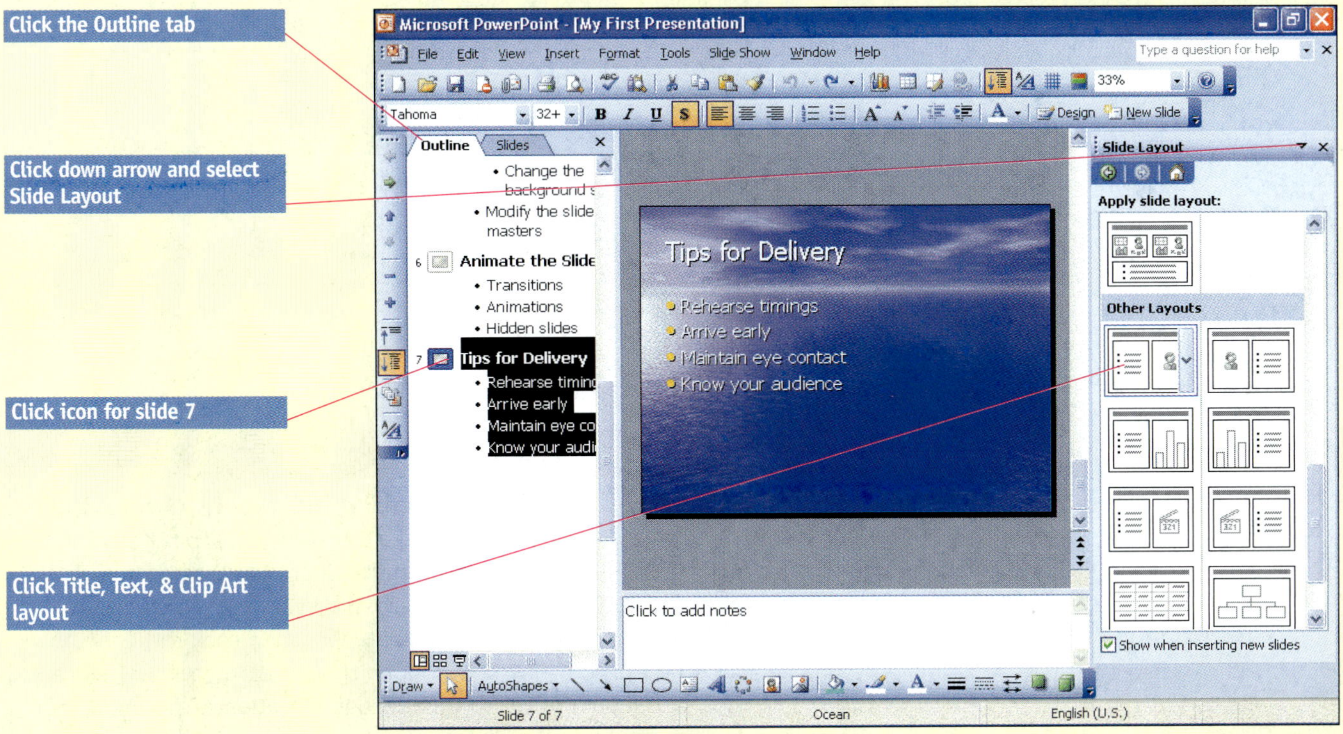

(a) Change the Slide Layout (step 1)

FIGURE 1.11 Hands-on Exercise 3

Step 2: Add the Clip Art

- Double click the **placeholder** on the slide to add the clip art. You will see the Select Picture dialog box as shown in Figure 1.11b, although the size, position, and content will be different on your screen.
- Click in the **Search** text box and enter the keyword **education**, then click the **Go button** to look for clip art that is described by this term.
- Select (click) the clip art you want and click **OK**. The clip art should appear on the slide.
- The clip art is sized automatically. You can, however, move and size the clip art just like any other Windows object.
- Save the presentation.

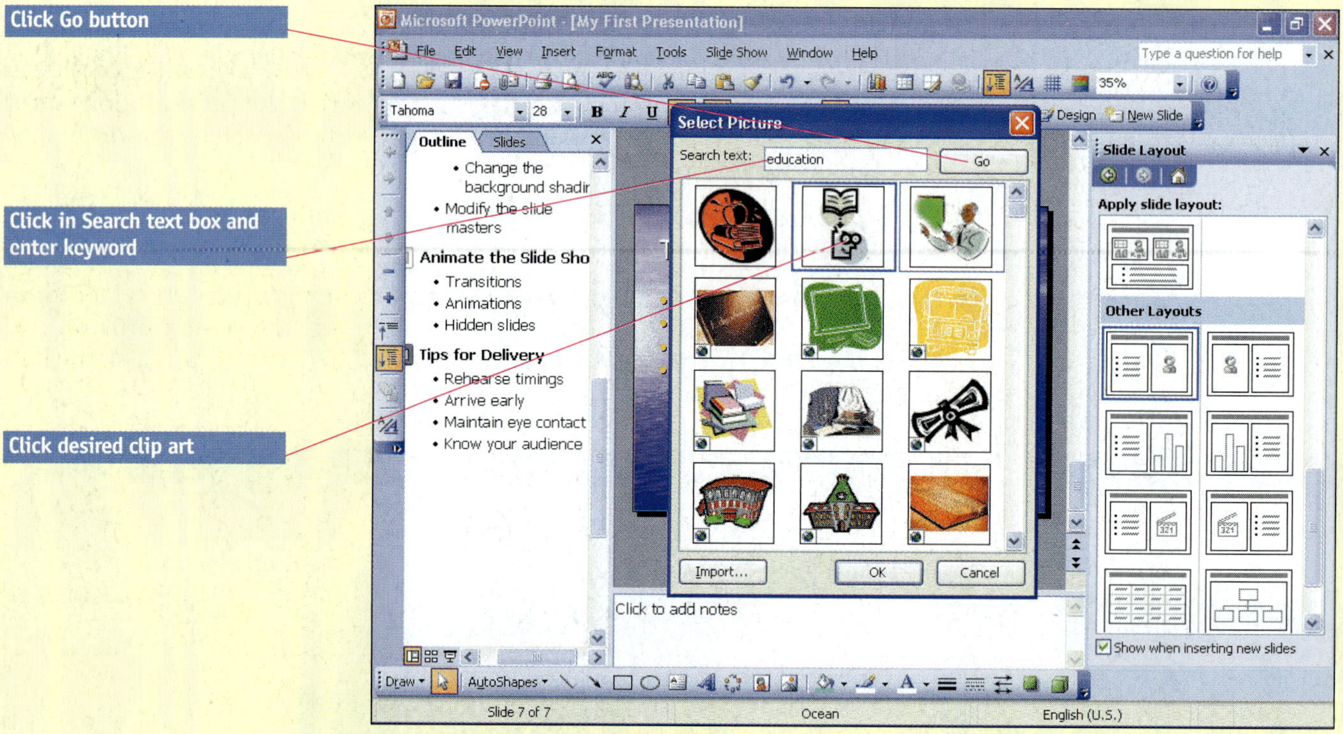

(b) Add the Clip Art (step 2)

FIGURE 1.11 Hands-on Exercise 3 (*continued*)

THE INSERT PICTURE COMMAND

Pull down the Insert menu, click the Picture command, and click Clip Art to display the Clip Art task pane that enables you to extend the search parameters for an appropriate media object. Click the down arrow in the Search in list box and select all of the collections including those on the Microsoft Web site. Click the down arrow in the Results list box and choose All media types, then click the Go button to initiate the search. The search may take longer than it did previously since it includes the Web, but you should have a much larger selection of potential clips from which to choose. If necessary, use the drop-down arrow on either search box to limit the search as you see fit.

Step 3: Add Transition Effects

- You can apply transitions either in the Normal view (with the thumbnail images) or in the Slide Sorter view. We chose the latter. Thus, click the **Slide Sorter View button** above the status bar to change to this view.
- Select (click) the first slide. Click the **Transition button** on the Slide Sorter toolbar to display the transition effects in the task pane.
- Click in the list box to select the **Blinds Vertical** transition effect (a preview plays automatically) as shown in Figure 1.11c.
- A Transition icon appears under the slide after the effect has been applied. Change the speed to **Medium**.
- Select (click) slide 2 and apply the **Checkerboard Across** transition effect to this slide. Change the speed to **Medium**.
- Apply different transition effects to the other slides in the presentation.
- Save the presentation.

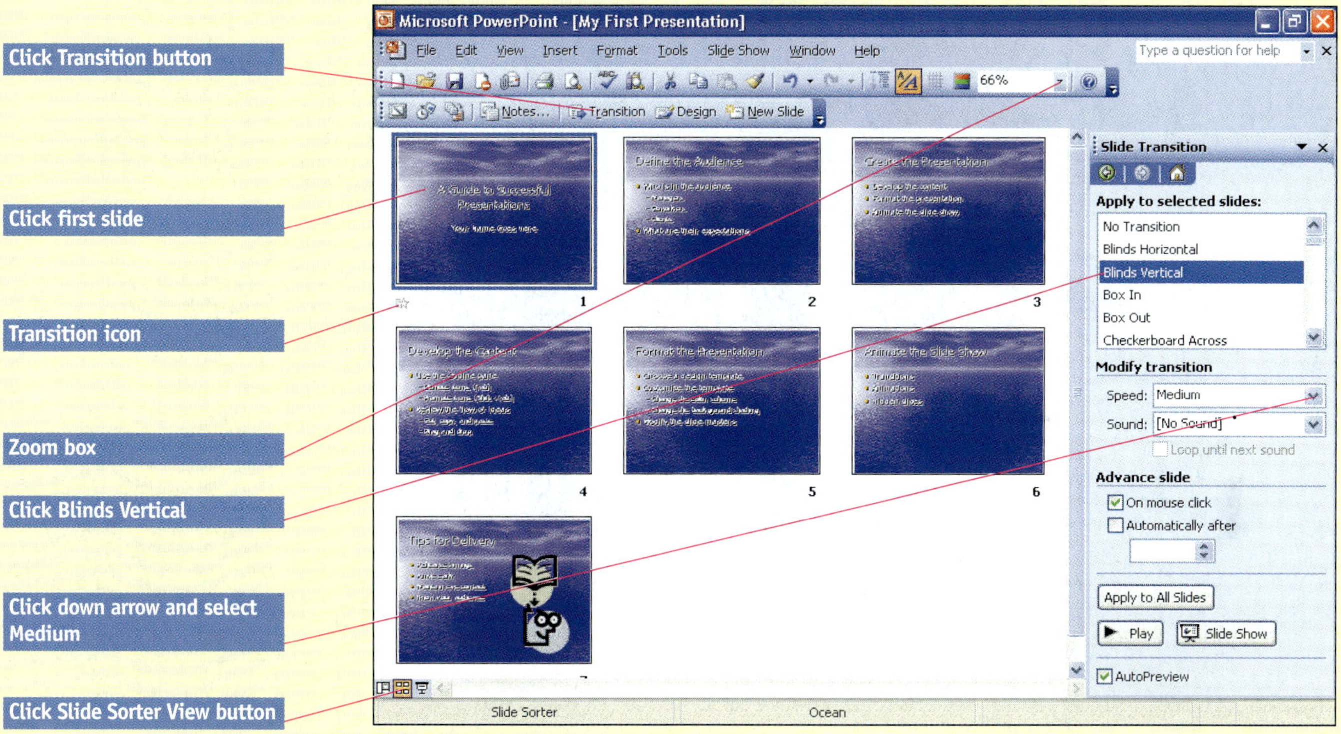

(c) Add Transition Effects (step 3)

FIGURE 1.11 Hands-on Exercise 3 (*continued*)

CHANGE THE MAGNIFICATION

Click the down arrow on the Zoom box to change the display magnification, which in turn controls the size of individual slides. The higher the magnification, the easier it is to read the text of an individual slide, but the fewer slides you see at one time. Conversely, changing to a smaller magnification decreases the size of the individual slides, but enables you to see more of the presentation.

Step 4: Create a Summary Slide

- Pull down the **Edit menu** and press **Select All** to select every slide in the presentation. (You can also press **Ctrl+A** or press and hold the **Ctrl key** as you click each slide in succession.)
- Click the **Summary Slide button** on the Slide Sorter toolbar to create a summary slide containing a bullet with the title of each selected slide. The new slide appears at the beginning of the presentation as shown in Figure 1.11d.
- Click and drag the **Summary Slide** to the end of the presentation. (As you drag the slide, the mouse pointer changes to include the outline of a miniature slide, and a vertical line appears to indicate the new position of the slide.)
- Release the mouse. The Summary Slide has been moved to the end of the presentation, and the slides are renumbered automatically.
- Save the presentation.

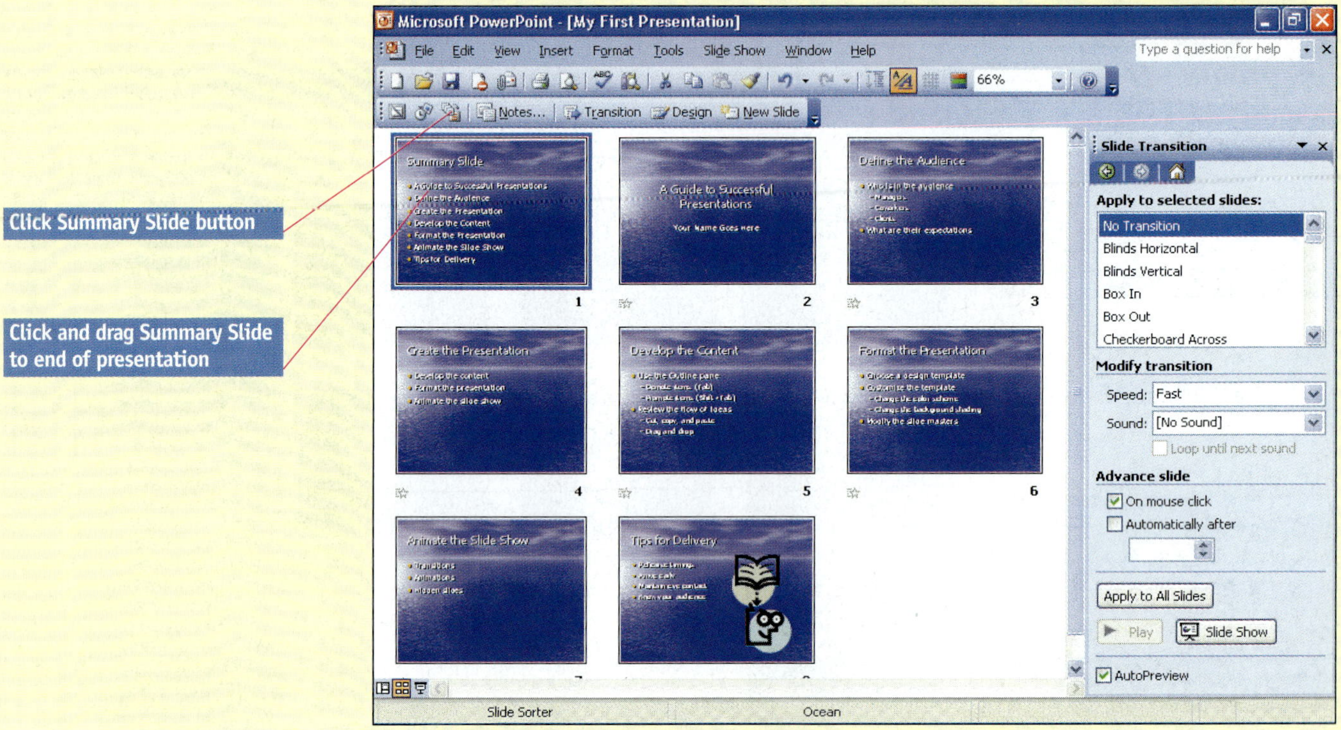

(d) Create a Summary Slide (step 4)

FIGURE 1.11 Hands-on Exercise 3 (*continued*)

SELECTING MULTIPLE SLIDES

You can apply the same transition or animation effect to multiple slides with a single command. Change to the Slide Sorter view, then select the slides by pressing and holding the Ctrl key as you click the slides. Use the task pane to choose the desired transition when all the slides have been selected. Click anywhere in the Slide Sorter view to deselect the slides and continue working.

Step 5: Create Animation Effects

- Double click the **Summary Slide** to change to the Normal view. The task pane should still be open. Click the **down arrow** on the task pane to choose **Slide Design—Animation Schemes**.
- Scroll in the Open list box to the **Moderate category**, and choose **Spin** as shown in Figure 1.11e. You will automatically see a preview of the effect.
- Scroll in the Open list box to the **Exciting category** and choose a different effect. (We're not sure who rates the effects and why one is deemed to be exciting, while the other is only moderate.)
- Click the **Undo button** if you prefer the original animation scheme.
- Save the presentation.

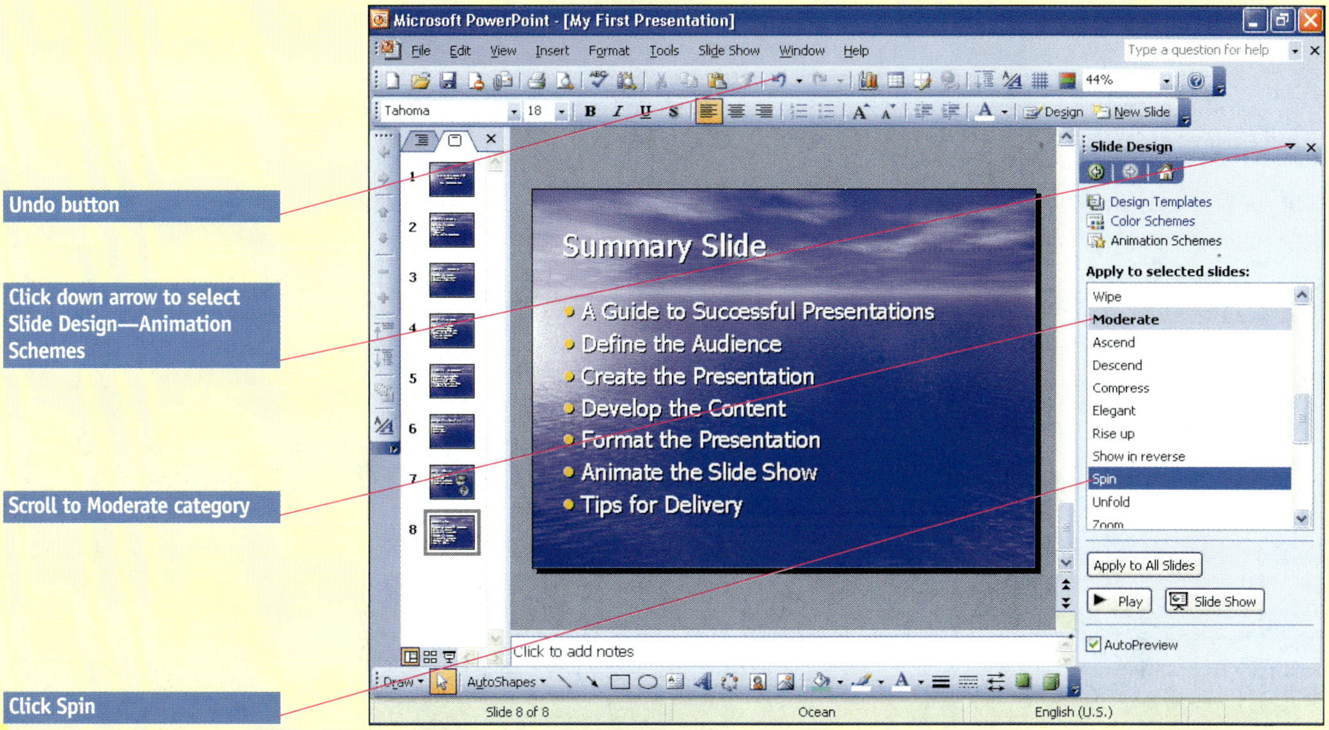

(e) Create Animation Effects (step 5)

FIGURE 1.11 Hands-on Exercise 3 (*continued*)

CUSTOMIZE THE ANIMATION

You can modify the effects of a predefined animation scheme for selected slides and/or objects on those slides. Click the down arrow in the task pane and choose Custom Animation. Select the slide, select the object on the slide that is to receive special treatment, click the Add Effect button to display a menu, choose the category (Entrance, Emphasis, etc.), and choose the effect, which will preview automatically. (Click the Remove button if you do not like the result.) Set a time limit because PowerPoint gives you virtually unlimited flexibility.

Step 6: Show the Presentation

- Press **Ctrl+Home** to return to the first slide, then click the **Slide Show button** above the status bar to view the presentation. You should see the opening slide in Figure 1.11f.
- Click the **left mouse button** to move to the next slide (or to the next bullet on the current slide when animation is in effect).
- Click the **right mouse button** to display the Shortcut menu and return to the previous slide (or to the previous bullet on the current slide when an animation is in effect).
- Continue to view the presentation until you come to the end. Click the **left mouse button** a final time to return to the regular PowerPoint window.
- Close the presentation. Exit PowerPoint if you do not want to continue with the next exercise at this time.

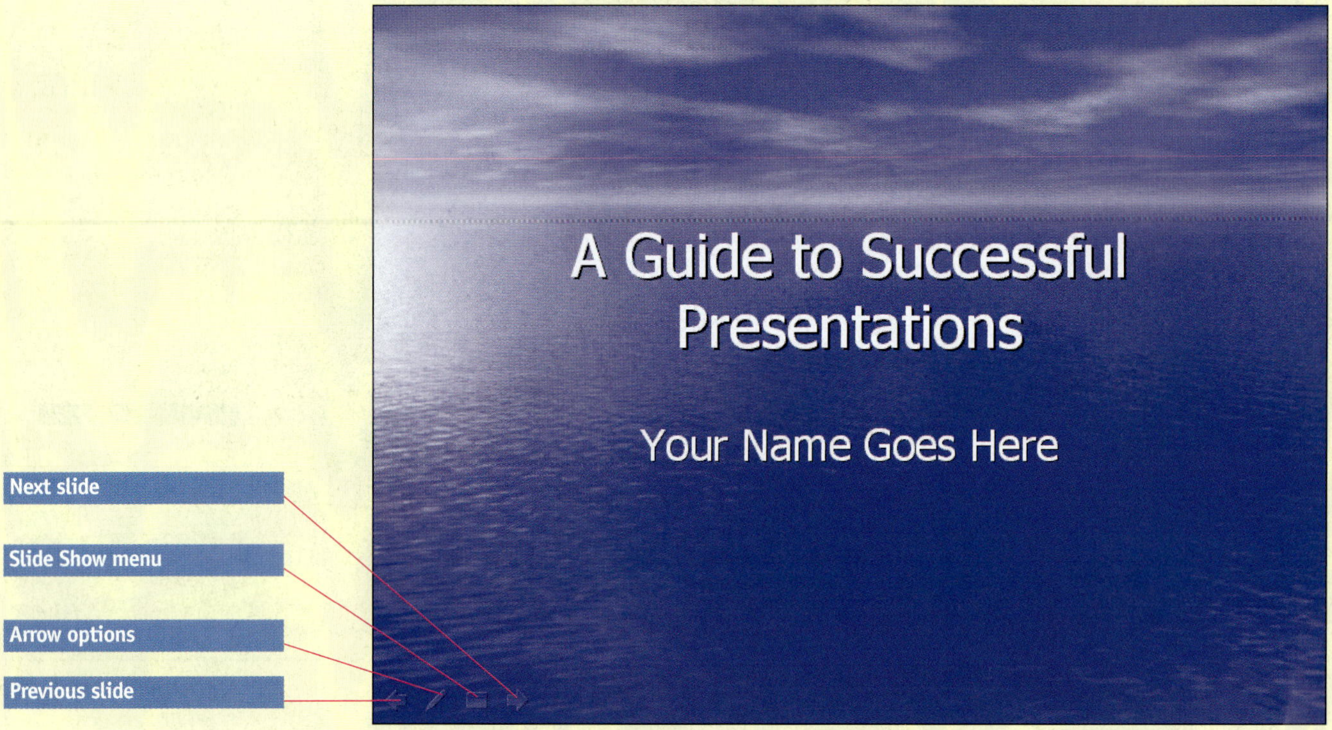

(f) Show the Presentation (step 6)

FIGURE 1.11 Hands-on Exercise 3 (*continued*)

CREATE A CUSTOM SHOW

Many presenters have to create nearly identical shows for different audiences. You could create multiple presentations and store each presentation in its own file, but it is much more efficient to create custom shows within a single presentation. Pull down the Slide Show menu, click the Custom Shows command, and click the New button to select the slides for the first custom show. Repeat the process to create additional custom shows, then select the show you want to view from the Custom Show dialog box.

ENHANCING A PRESENTATION

Thus far we have focused on presentations that consisted largely of text. PowerPoint also enables you to include a variety of visual elements that add impact to a presentation as can be seen in Figure 1.12. (This is the presentation that we will create in the next hands-on exercise.) You can add clip art, sound, or animated clips that are stored on your computer and/or you can download additional objects from the Microsoft Web site. You can also use the supplement applications that are included with Microsoft Office to add organization charts and WordArt. You can insert objects that were created in other applications, such as a chart from Microsoft Excel or a table from Microsoft Word.

A chart or table is inserted into a presentation through linking or embedding. The essential difference between the two techniques is that embedding places the object into the presentation, whereas linking does not. In other words, an ***embedded object*** is stored within the presentation. A ***linked object***, on the other hand, is stored in its own file, and the presentation is one of many potential documents that are linked to that object. The advantage of linking over embedding is that the presentation is updated automatically if the original object is changed.

Linking is also preferable if the same object is referenced in many documents, so that any change to the object has to be made in only one place (the source document). An Excel chart, for example, may be linked to a Word document and a PowerPoint presentation. You can subsequently change the chart, and both the document and presentation are updated automatically.

You can also add ***comments*** to any presentation to explain your thoughts to colleagues who may review the presentation prior to delivery. The comments appear on a slide during editing, but not during delivery as you will see in the hands-on exercise that follows shortly.

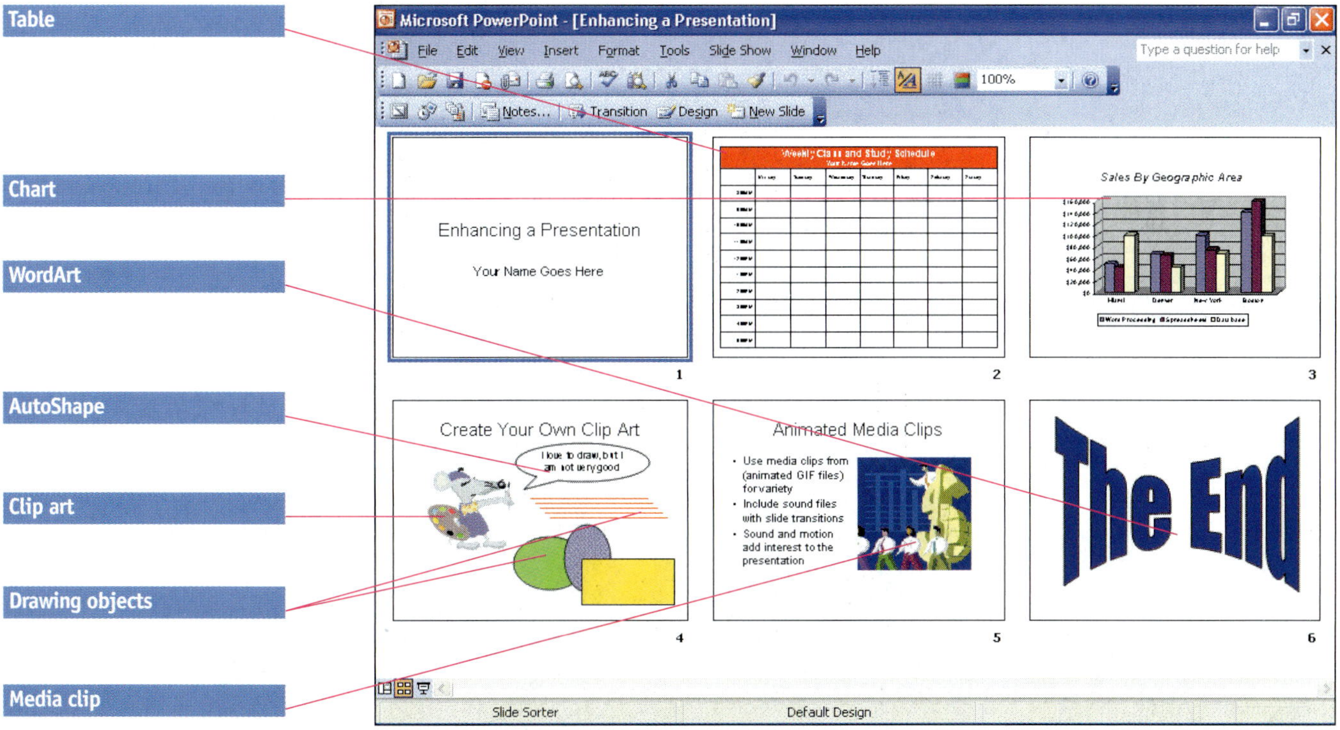

FIGURE 1.12 Enhancing a Presentation

The Microsoft Clip Organizer

The ***Insert Picture command*** displays a task pane through which you can insert clip art, photographs, sounds, and movies (collectively called clips). The clips can come from a variety of sources. They may be installed locally in the My Collections folder, they may have been installed in conjunction with Microsoft Office in the Office Collections folder, and/or they may have been downloaded from the Web and stored in the Web Collections folder. You can insert a specific clip into a document if you know its location. You can also search for a clip that will enhance the document on which you are working.

The search is made possible by the ***Microsoft Clip Organizer***, which brings order out of potential chaos by cataloging the clips that are available to you. You enter a keyword that describes the clip you are looking for, specify the ***collections*** that are to be searched, and indicate the type of clip(s) you are looking for. The results are displayed in the task pane as shown in Figure 1.13, which returns the clips that are described by the keyword "artist". Our example is searching all collections for all media types in order to return the greatest number of potential clips. When you see a clip that you want to use, all you have to do is point to the clip, click the down arrow that appears, and then click the Insert command from the resulting menu.

You can access the Microsoft Clip Organizer (to view the various collections) by clicking the Organize clips link at the bottom of the task pane. You can also access the Clip Organizer outside of PowerPoint by clicking the Start button on the task bar, and then clicking All Programs, Microsoft Office, Microsoft Office Tool, and Microsoft Clip Organizer. Once in the Organizer, you can search through the clips in the various collections, reorganize the existing collections, add new collections, and even add new clips (with their associated keywords) to the collections. The other links at the bottom of the task pane in Figure 1.13 provide access to additional clip art online and tips for finding more relevant clips.

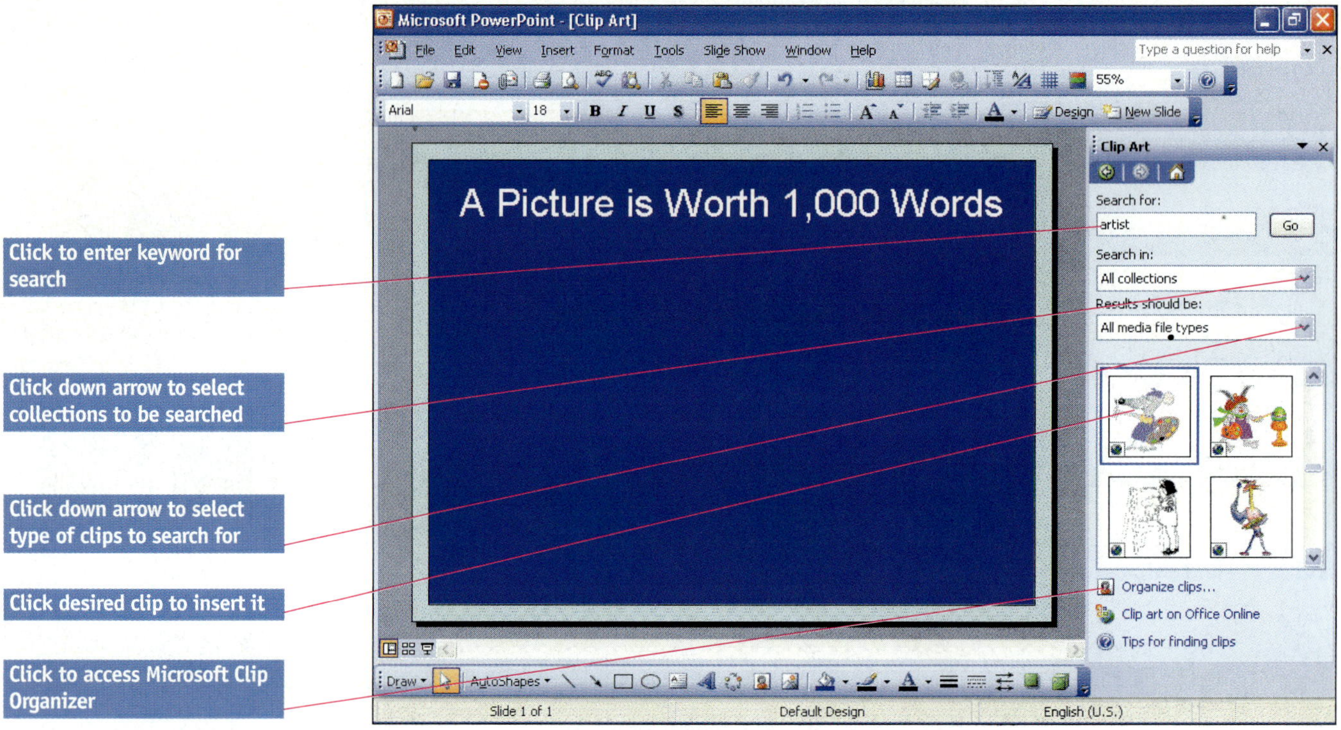

FIGURE 1.13 The Insert Picture Command

Office Art

Everyone likes ***clip art***, but relatively few individuals think in terms of enhancing it. It takes a lot of talent to create original clip art, but it takes only a little imagination to create a drawing from existing clip art as shown in Figure 1.14. There is no way that we could have drawn the artist, but it was very easy to copy the artist and create the slide, given the original clip art.

Any piece of clip art is an object that can be copied, moved, and sized like any other Windows object. Thus, we clicked on the original clip art (the artist in the upper right of the slide) to display the sizing handles, clicked the copy and paste buttons to duplicate the object, then moved and sized the copied image to the bottom of the slide. We then copied the smaller artist across the bottom of the slide.

Next we used various tools on the Drawing toolbar to complete the slide. Select the Line tool, for example, then click and drag to create a line. Once the line has been created, you can select it and change its properties (such as thickness, style, or color) by using other tools on the Drawing toolbar. The oval and rectangle tools work the same way. The AutoShapes button on the Drawing toolbar provides access to the balloon and other callouts in which you enter the text.

There are other techniques you can use as well. You can, for example, select multiple objects simultaneously and group them together to move and/or size those objects with a single mouse click. Press and hold the Shift key to select multiple objects (e.g., the large artist, the balloon, and the three circles), click the Draw button, then click the Group command. The five objects have been combined into one larger object with a single set of sizing handles.

All it takes is a little imagination and a sense of what you can do. Use different clip art images on the same slide and you get something entirely different. It is fun and it is easy. Just be flexible and willing to experiment. We think you will be pleased with the results.

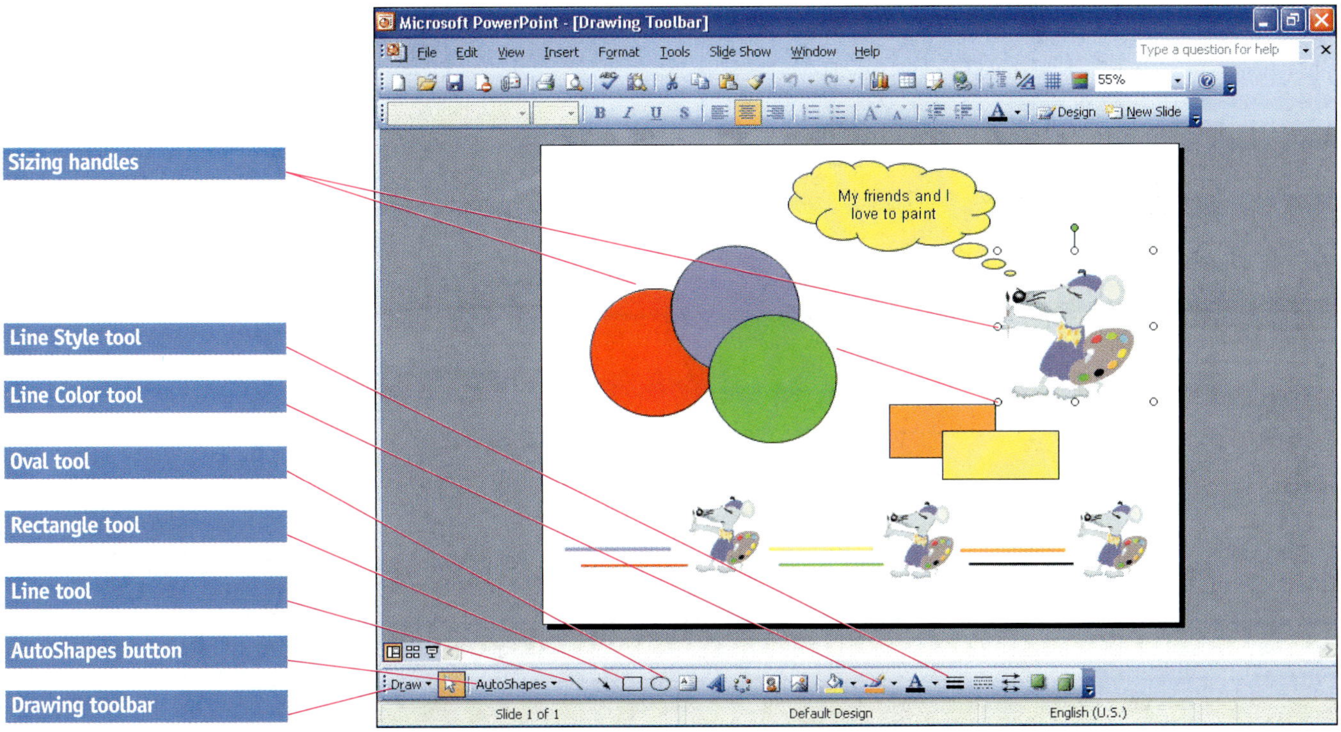

FIGURE 1.14 Office Art

Microsoft WordArt

Microsoft WordArt is an application within Microsoft Office that creates decorative text that can be used to add interest to a document. You can use WordArt in addition to clip art within a document, or in place of clip art if the right image is not available. You can rotate text in any direction, add three-dimensional effects, display the text vertically down the page, slant it, arch it, or even print it upside down. In short, you are limited only by your imagination.

WordArt is intuitive and easy to use. In essence, you choose a style for the text from among the selections in Figure 1.15a. Then you enter the specific text in a subsequent dialog box, after which the result is displayed in Figure 1.15b. The finished WordArt is an object that can be moved and sized within a presentation.

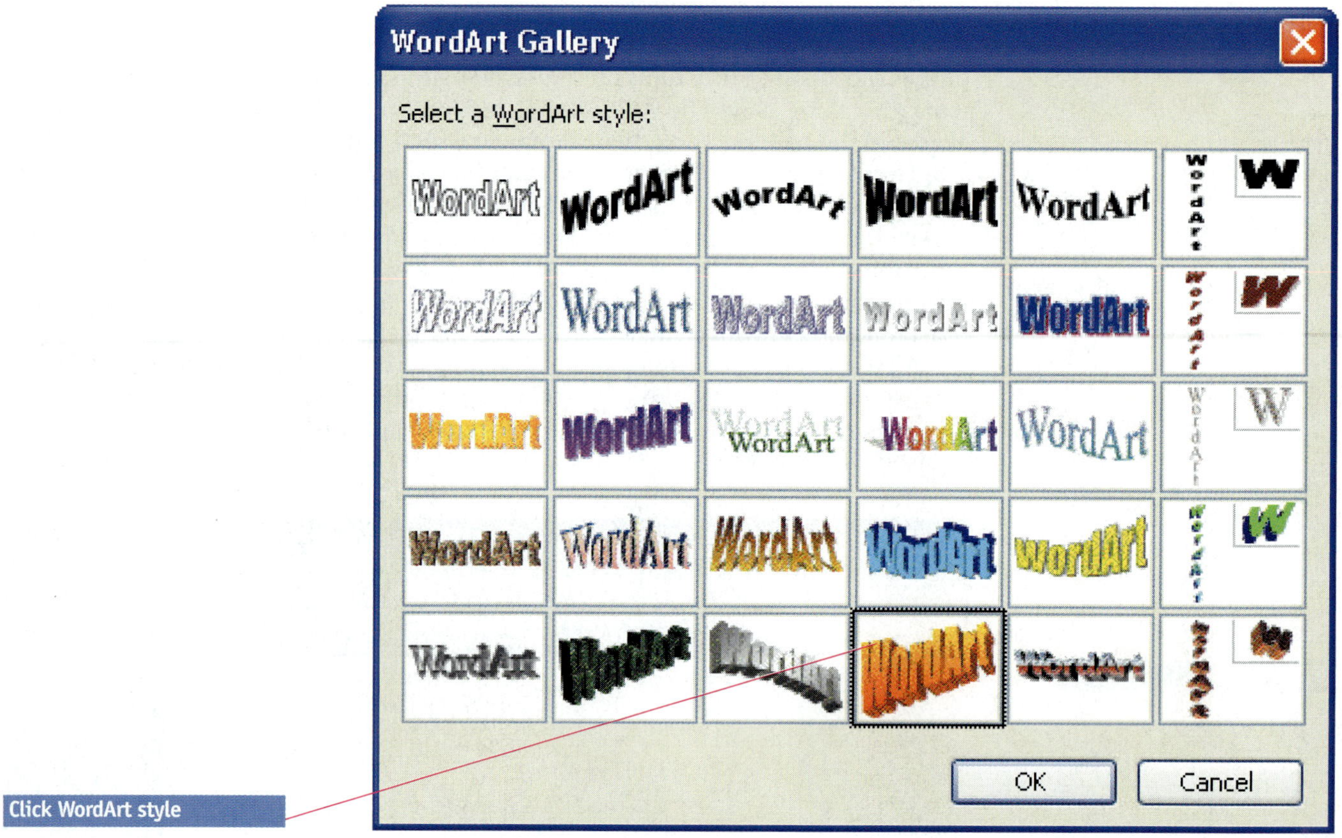

(a) Choose the Style

(b) Completed Entry

FIGURE 1.15 Microsoft WordArt

hands-on exercise

4 Enhancing a Presentation

Objective To include a Word table and an Excel chart in a presentation; to modify existing clip art and create a WordArt object. Use Figure 1.16 as a guide.

Step 1: Insert a Comment

- Start PowerPoint. Click the **New button** on the Standard toolbar to begin a new presentation. Close the task pane. Enter the title of the presentation and your name on the title slide. Save the presentation as **Enhancing a Presentation** in the **Exploring PowerPoint folder**.
- Click the **Normal View button** above the status bar if you are not in the Normal view. Click the **Slides tab** to display the slides in the left pane.
- Pull down the **Insert menu** and click the **Comment command** to insert a comment onto the slide as shown in Figure 1.16a.
- You will see an empty balloon that contains the name of the person who has registered this copy of Office, together with today's date. Enter any text at all as a comment.
- Click anywhere outside the comment. The balloon closes, and you see a comment marker. Click the marker, and the comment reappears.
- The Reviewing toolbar appears automatically whenever you are working with comments. The Markup button at the extreme left of the toolbar toggles the comment markers on and off.
- Click the **New Slide button** on the Formatting toolbar. (This will open the task pane if it is not already open.) Scroll down in the task pane until you can select a **blank layout**.

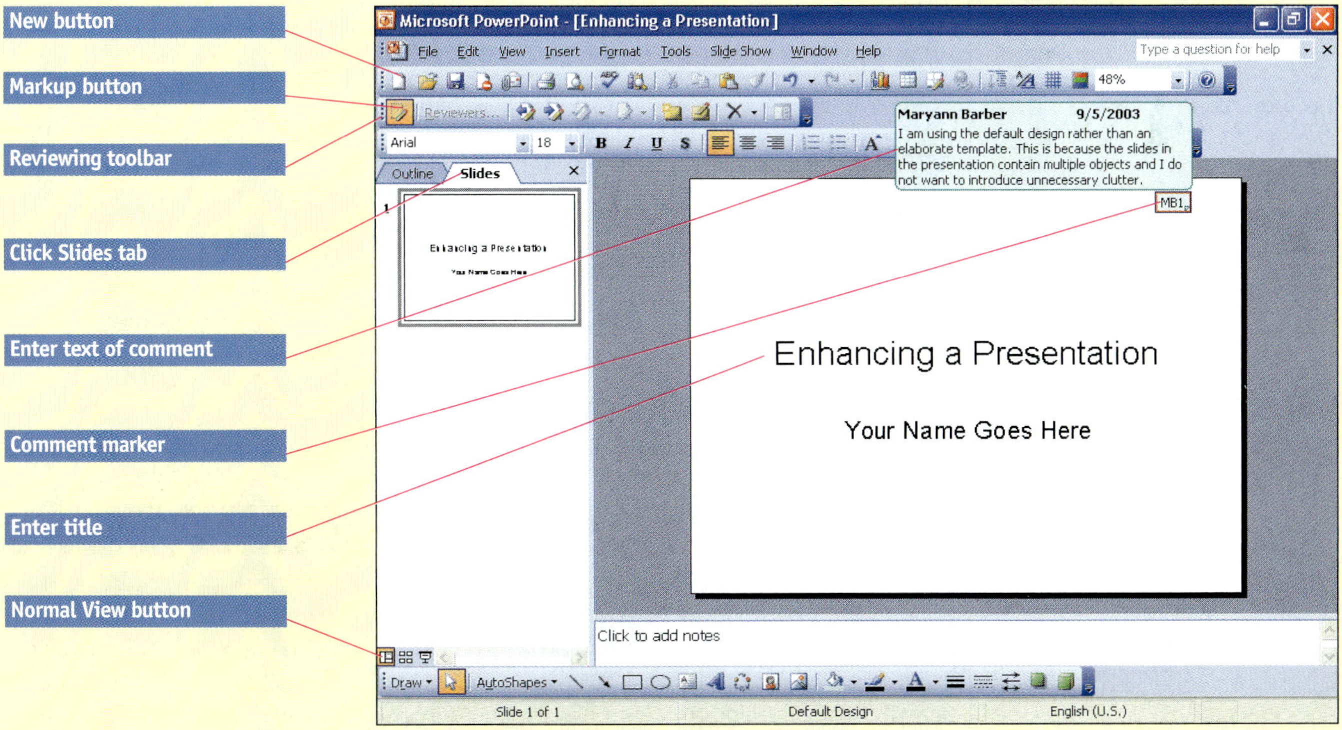

(a) Insert a Comment (step 1)

FIGURE 1.16 Hands-on Exercise 4

Step 2: Copy the Word Table

- Start Word. Open the **My Study Schedule** Word document in the **Exploring PowerPoint folder** as shown in Figure 1.16b. The document consists entirely of a Word table.
- Click and drag to select the text **Your Name Goes Here** that appears at the top of the table. Type your first and last name, which automatically replaces the selected text.
- You can click in any cell and enter an activity. The text will automatically flow from one line to the next within the cell. Limit the entry to two lines, however, or else the table may not fit on one page (or one slide). Save the document.
- Point to the table. Click the tiny square at the upper left of the table to select the entire table. Be sure that every cell is highlighted, or else the table will not be copied successfully. Click the **Copy button** to copy the table to the clipboard.
- Exit Word. The copied text remains in the clipboard even though Microsoft Word is no longer open.

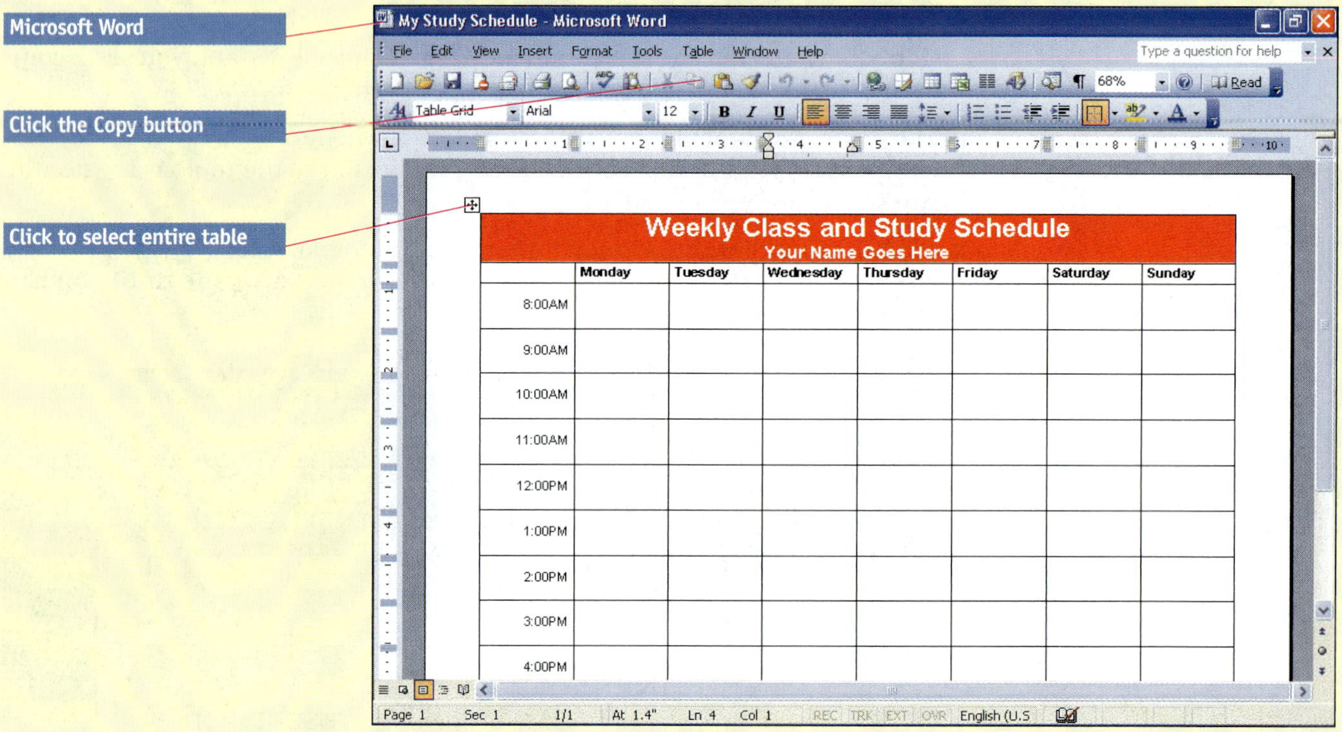

(b) Copy the Word Table (step 2)

FIGURE 1.16 Hands-on Exercise 4 (*continued*)

THE WINDOWS CLIPBOARD

The Windows clipboard is an area of memory that is available to every Windows application. Execution of the Copy command in one application places the copied text (or other object) on the clipboard from where it can be accessed by any other application. Microsoft Office has its own clipboard (in addition to the Windows clipboard) that can hold up to 24 objects. You can open the Office clipboard from any Office application by pulling down the Edit menu and selecting the Office Clipboard command.

Step 3: Insert the Table

- You should be back in PowerPoint as shown in Figure 1.16c. (If not, click the **PowerPoint button** on the Windows taskbar.)
- Click anywhere on the second slide to select this slide. Click the **Paste button** on the Standard toolbar to paste (embed) the Word table onto this slide.
- Pull down the **Insert menu** and click the **Comment command**. Enter the text of the comment shown in the figure, which indicates that the table has been embedded (rather than linked) into the presentation.
- Click anywhere outside the comment after you have finished.
- Click the **Previous Item button** on the Reviewing toolbar to move to the previous comment. Click the **Next Item button** to return to this comment.
- Save the presentation.

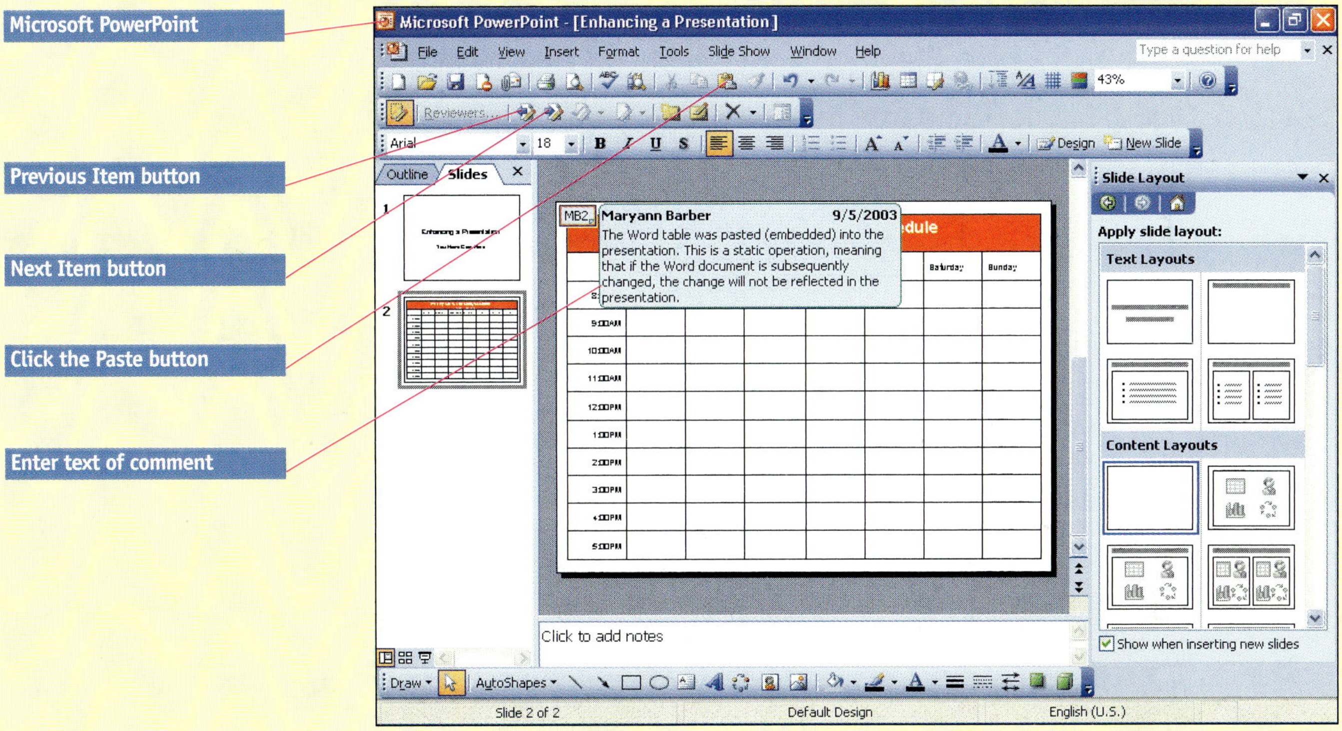

(c) Insert the Table (step 3)

FIGURE 1.16 Hands-on Exercise 4 (*continued*)

SEND SLIDES TO A WORD DOCUMENT

You can embed and/or link Word documents and PowerPoint presentations in either direction; that is, you can insert a Word document into a PowerPoint presentation as was done here, and/or you can send PowerPoint slides to a Word document. Pull down the File menu and click the Send To command, then choose Microsoft Word to display the associated dialog box. You will be given the choice of how to arrange the PowerPoint slides in the resulting Word document.

Step 4: Insert the Excel Chart

- Start Excel. Open the **Software Sales** workbook in the **Exploring PowerPoint folder**. The workbook consists of a single sheet that contains data and a chart.
- Click anywhere in the chart background to select the entire chart. You should see sizing handles around the white border of the chart. Click the **Copy button** on the Standard toolbar to copy the chart to the clipboard. Do not close the workbook as we will return to it momentarily.
- Click the **PowerPoint button** on the Windows taskbar to return to the PowerPoint presentation. Click the **New slide button** and use the Slide Layout task pane to insert a blank slide into the presentation. Close the task pane.
- Pull down the **Edit menu** and click the **Paste Special command** to display the Paste Special dialog box in Figure 1.16d. Click the **Paste link option button**. Click **OK** to insert the chart onto the slide. Do not be concerned about the size or position of the chart at this time.
- Save the presentation.

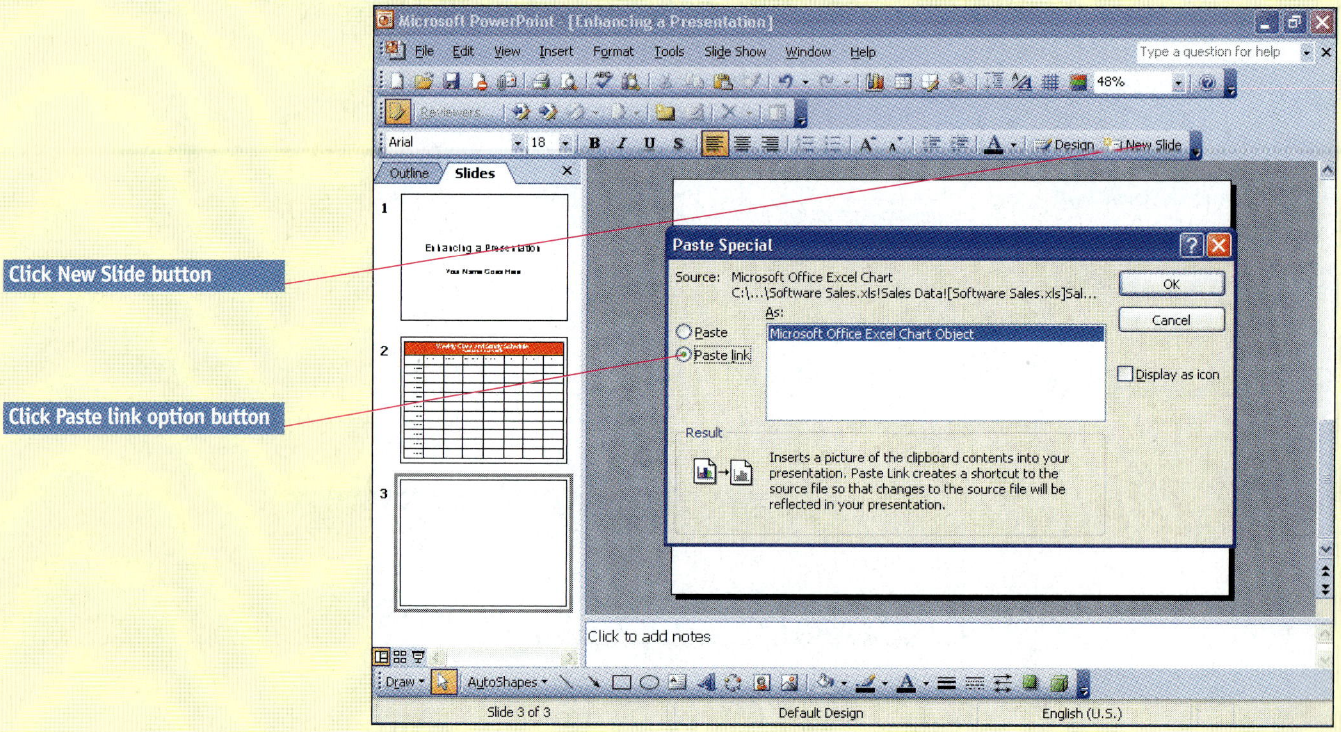

(d) Insert the Excel Chart (step 4)

FIGURE 1.16 Hands-on Exercise 4 (*continued*)

LINKING VERSUS EMBEDDING

Linking is very different from embedding as it provides a dynamic connection to the source document. A linked object, such as an Excel chart, is tied to its source, so that any changes to the source file are reflected in the PowerPoint presentation. Linking is especially useful when the same object is inserted into multiple documents, as changes to the object are made in only one place (in the source file). A linked object must always be saved in its file.

Step 5: Update the Chart

- You should see the chart as shown in Figure 1.16e. The sizing handles indicate that the chart is currently selected and can be moved and sized like any other Windows object.
- Click and drag a corner handle (the pointer changes to a two-headed arrow) to proportionally increase (decrease) the size of the chart. Point to any border (the pointer changes to a four-headed arrow) to move the chart on the slide.
- Note that the database sales for Miami are very low ($12,000). Double click the chart to return to Excel (or click the **Excel button** on the Windows taskbar). Click in **cell B4** and change the database sales for Miami to **$100,000**. Save the workbook. Exit Excel.
- Return to PowerPoint. The chart may automatically reflect the change in database sales. If not, right click the chart and select the **Update Link command**.
- Pull down the **Insert menu** and click the **Comment command** to insert an appropriate comment indicating that the chart in the presentation is linked to an Excel workbook. Close the Reviewing toolbar. Save the presentation.

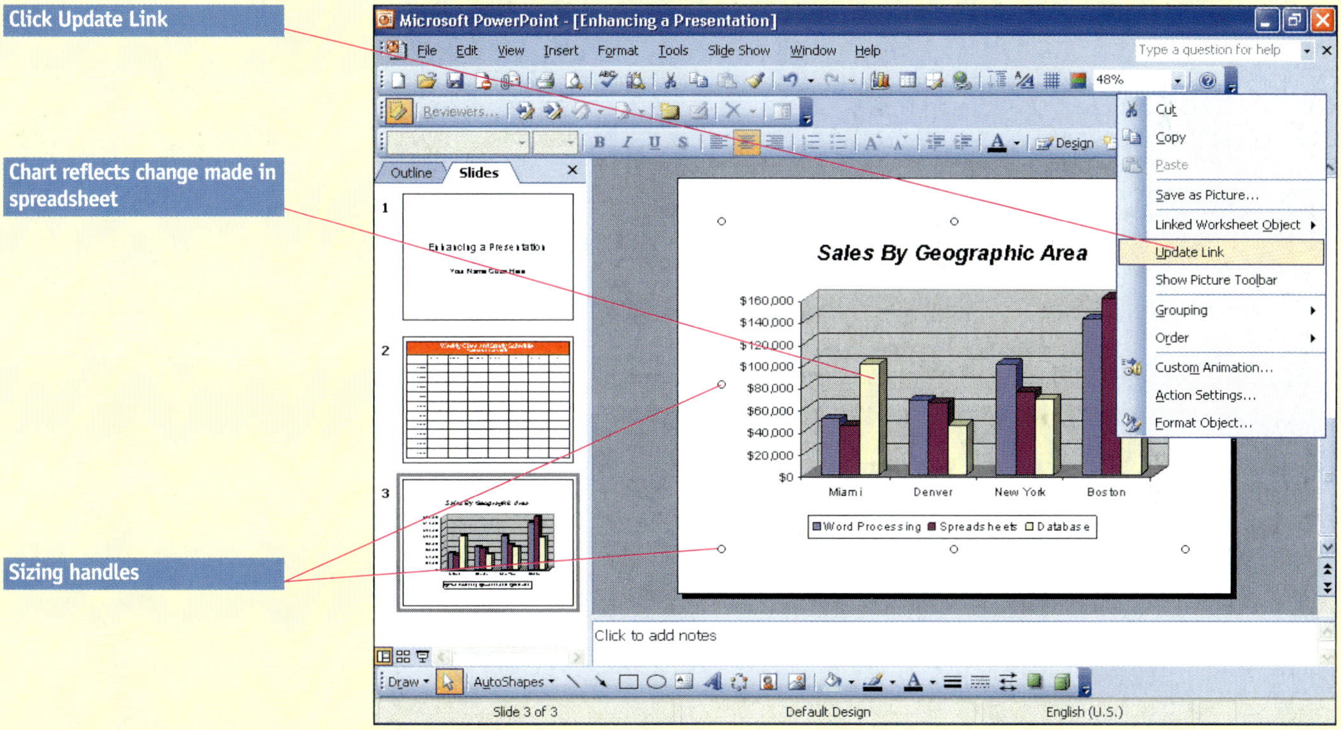

(e) Update the Chart (step 5)

FIGURE 1.16 Hands-on Exercise 4 (*continued*)

UPDATING LINKS

The next time you open this presentation you will see a message indicating that links are present and further, that the links can be updated. You should respond by clicking the Update Links command button, which in turn will bring in the most current version of the chart to the presentation. This assumes that the Excel workbook is still in the same folder where it was created initially. If there is a problem, perhaps because the workbook has been moved or renamed, pull down the Edit menu and click the Links command to modify the link.

Step 6: Insert the Clip Art

- Click the **New Slide button** and select the **Title Only** layout. Click in the title placeholder and type **Create Your Own Clip Art**.
- Pull down the **Insert menu**, click **Picture**, and then click **Clip Art** (or click the **Insert Clip Art button** on the Drawing toolbar). The contents of the task pane change automatically.
- Type **Artist** in the Search text box. Be sure the list boxes show you are searching all collections and are looking for all media types. Click the **Go button** to initiate the search.
- The system pauses, then starts to return all objects that satisfy the search criteria.
- Click the **down arrow** in the task pane to scroll through the images until you find the one that you want. Point to the right side of the image, then click the **down arrow** that appears to display a menu. Click **Insert**.
- Click the mouse to select our artist. Click the **Draw button**, click **Rotate or Flip**, then click the **Flip Horizontal command** to turn the artist around.
- Move and size the clip art so that it is positioned as shown in Figure 1.16f. Close the task pane. Save the presentation.

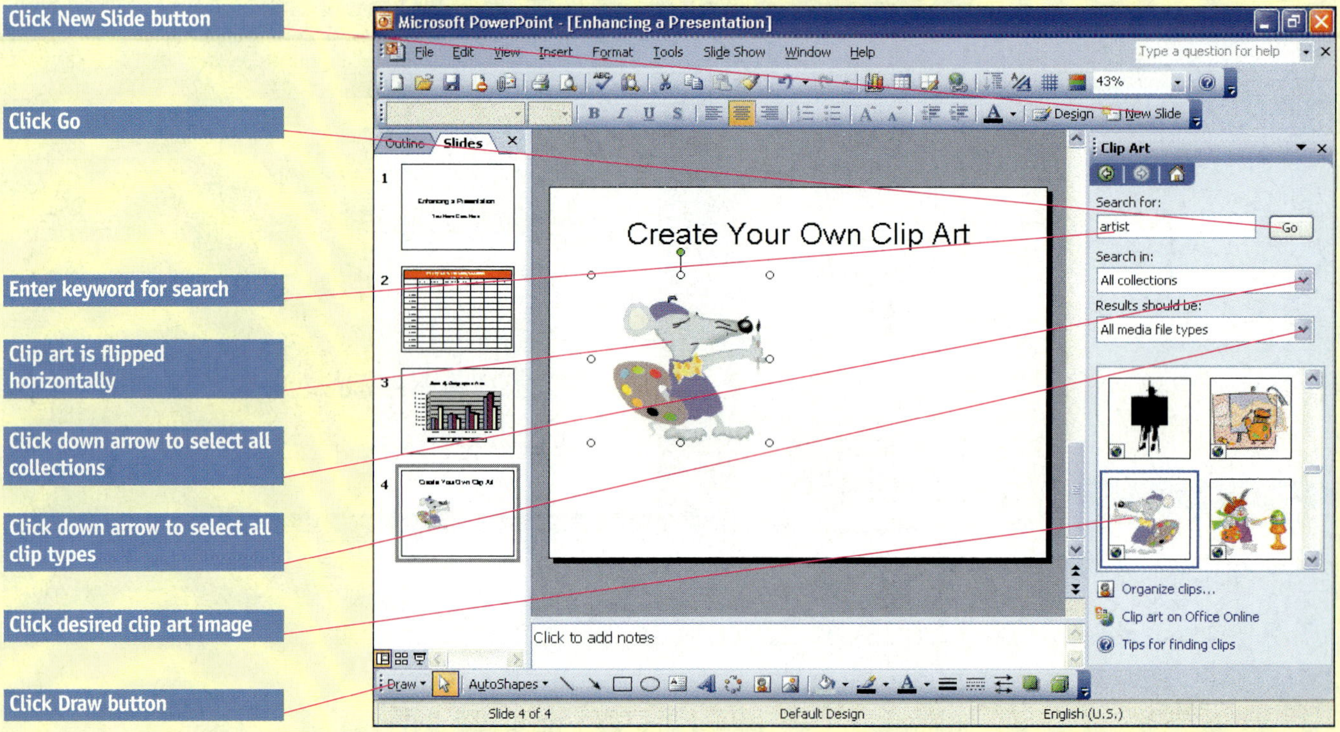

(f) Insert the Clip Art (step 6)

FIGURE 1.16 Hands-on Exercise 4 (*continued*)

THE SHIFT KEY

The Shift key has special significance when used in conjunction with the Line, Rectangle, and Oval tools. Press and hold the Shift key as you drag the line tool horizontally or vertically to create a perfectly straight line in either direction. Press and hold the Shift key as you drag the Rectangle and Oval tool to create a square and circle, respectively.

Step 7: Use the Drawing Toolbar

- Click the **AutoShapes button** on the Drawing toolbar, click **Callouts**, then click the desired balloon. The mouse pointer changes to a tiny crosshair.
- Click and drag on the slide where you want the balloon to go. Release the mouse. The balloon is selected automatically, and the sizing handles are displayed. If necessary, click and drag the balloon to adjust its size or position.
- Type the phrase shown in the figure. You can select the text, then change its font, size, or alignment. Click elsewhere on the slide to deselect the balloon.
- Click the **Line tool** on the Drawing toolbar, then click and drag to draw a line on the slide. To change the color or thickness, select the line (the sizing handles appear), click the appropriate tool on the Drawing toolbar, then select a new color or thickness.
- Select the completed line, click the **Copy button**, then click the **Paste button** several times to copy the line. Use the **Oval** or **Rectangle tools** to draw additional shapes, then use the **Fill Color tool** to change their color.
- Move and size the objects as necessary. Save the presentation.

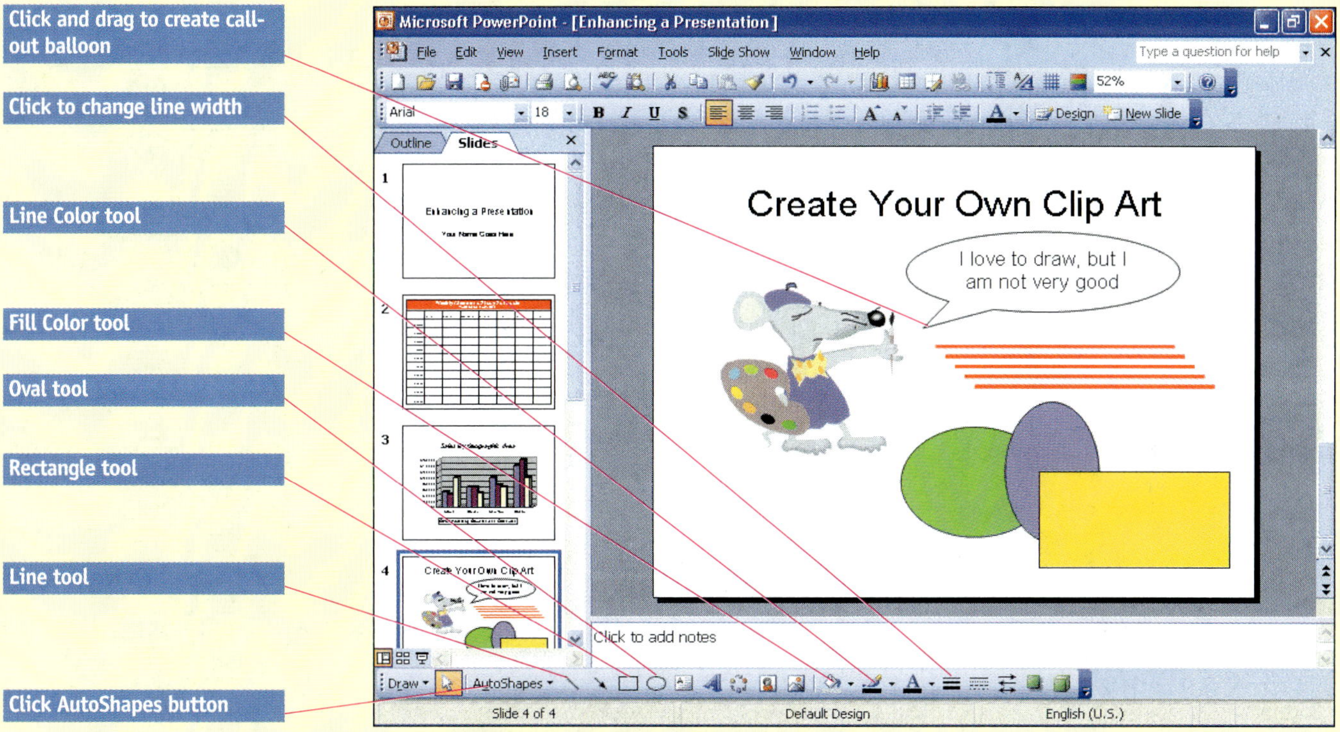

(g) Use the Drawing Toolbar (step 7)

FIGURE 1.16 Hands-on Exercise 4 (*continued*)

AUTOSHAPES

An AutoShape is a predefined shape that is drawn automatically when you select its icon from the AutoShapes toolbar, then click and drag in the slide. (To display the AutoShapes menu, click the AutoShape button on the Drawing toolbar.) To place text inside an AutoShape, select the shape and start typing. You can also change the fill color or line thickness by selecting the shape, then clicking the appropriate button on the Drawing toolbar.

Step 8: Add a Media Clip

- Click the **New Slide button** and select the **Title, Text & Media Clip** layout. Enter **Animated Media Clips** as the title of the slide. Enter the bulleted text as shown in Figure 1.16h.
- Double click the Media placeholder to add the media clip, which in turn displays the Media Clip dialog box.
- Select any clip that appeals to you. (The clip in the figure is available in the Exploring PowerPoint folder as **CashRegister**.)
- Click **OK** to insert the clip onto the slide. Size the media clip art after it appears on the slide.
- Pull down the **Slide Show menu** and click **Slide Transition** to display these options in the task pane. Click the **down arrow** in the Sound list box and select **Cash Register**. Check the box to **Loop until next sound**.
- Click the **Play button** to preview the effect. You should see the men passing an object to the sound of a cash register. (You need a sound card and speakers to hear the sound.)
- Save the presentation.

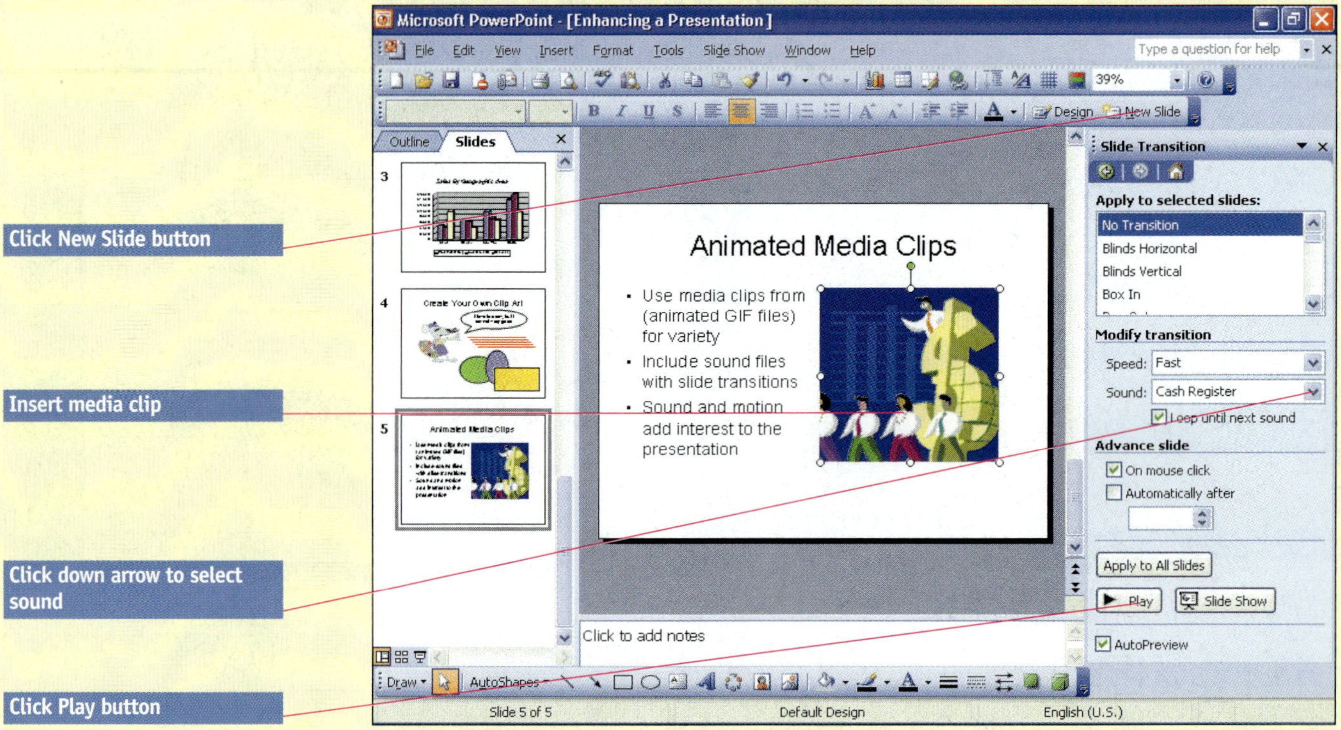

(h) Add a Media Clip (step 8)

FIGURE 1.16 Hands-on Exercise 4 (*continued*)

INSERT SLIDES FROM OTHER PRESENTATIONS

You work hard to develop individual slides and thus you may find it useful to reuse a slide from one presentation to the next. Pull down the Insert menu, click the Slides from Files command to display the Slide Finder dialog box, and click the Browse button to locate the presentation that contains the slides you want. Press and hold the Ctrl key to select multiple slides from this presentation, then click the Insert button to bring the selected slides into the current presentation.

Step 9: Add the WordArt

- We're ready to add the sixth and final slide. Click the **New Slide button** and select the **blank slide layout**. Close the task pane.
- Click the **Insert WordArt button** on the Drawing toolbar to display the WordArt Gallery dialog box as shown in Figure 1.16i. Choose any style you like (we took the fourth style from the left in the first row). Click **OK.**
- You should see the Edit WordArt text box. Enter **The End** as the text for your WordArt object. Click **OK** to close the Edit WordArt text box and insert the WordArt into your presentation.
- Move and size the WordArt object just as you would any other Windows object. Click and drag a corner sizing handle to increase the size of the WordArt until it takes the entire slide.
- Point to the middle of the WordArt object (the mouse pointer changes to a four-headed arrow), then click and drag to position the WordArt in the middle of the slide.
- Save the presentation.

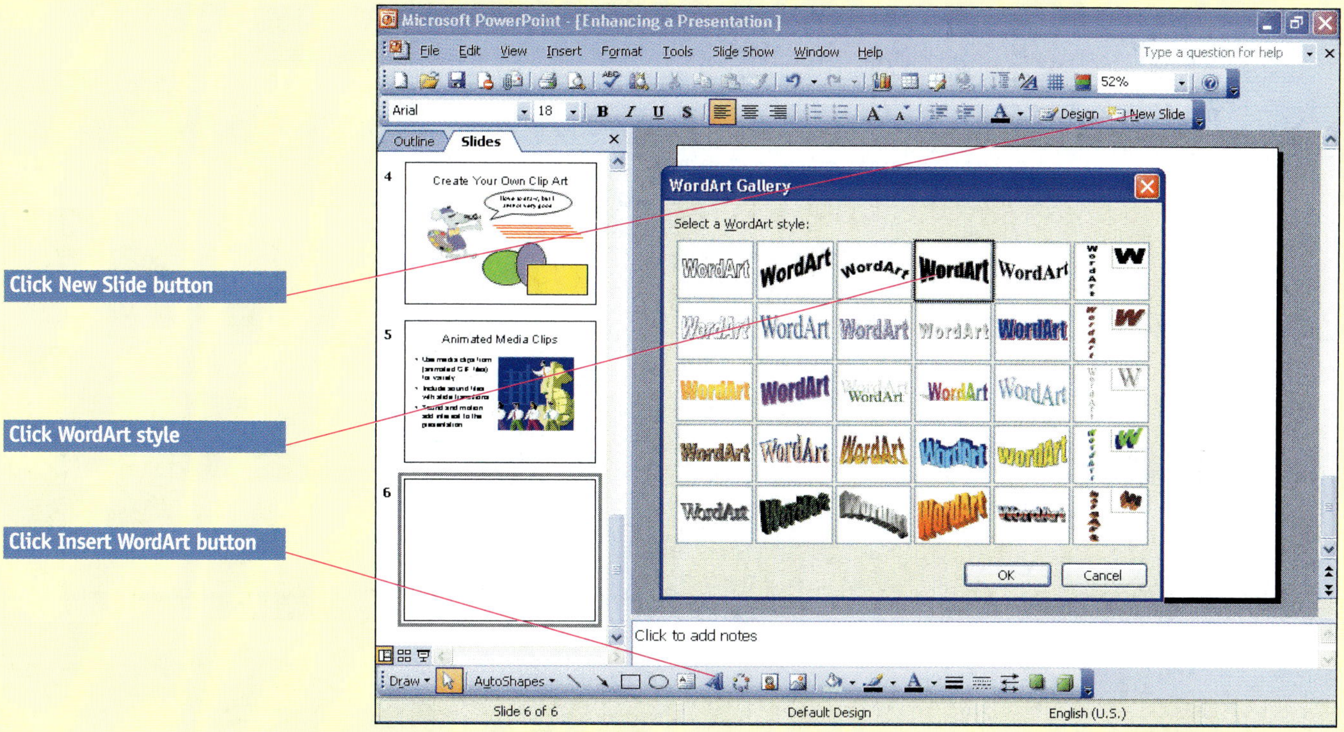

(i) Add the WordArt (step 9)

FIGURE 1.16 Hands-on Exercise 4 (*continued*)

THE WORDART TOOLBAR

The WordArt toolbar is the easiest way to change an existing WordArt object. It is displayed automatically when a WordArt object is selected and is suppressed otherwise. As with any other toolbar, you can point to a button to display a ScreenTip containing the name of the button, which is indicative of its function. You will find buttons to display the text vertically, change the style or shape, and/or edit the text.

Step 10: Complete the WordArt

- You should see the WordArt as shown in Figure 1.16j. You can click and drag the yellow diamond to change the slope of the text and/or you can click and drag the green circle to rotate the text.
- Click the WordArt object. Click the **down arrow** for the **Fill Color tool** on the Drawing toolbar to display the available fill colors. Select (click) **blue** to change the color of the WordArt object.
- Experiment with other tools on the Drawing and/or WordArt toolbars to enhance the WordArt image. Set a time limit. (Use the Undo command if the results are not what you intended.)
- Pull down the **Slide Show menu** and click **Slide Transition** to display these options in the task pane. Click the **down arrow** in the Sound list box and select **Applause**.
- Click the **Play button** to preview the effect. (You will need a sound card and speakers to hear the sound.)
- Close the task pane. Save the presentation.

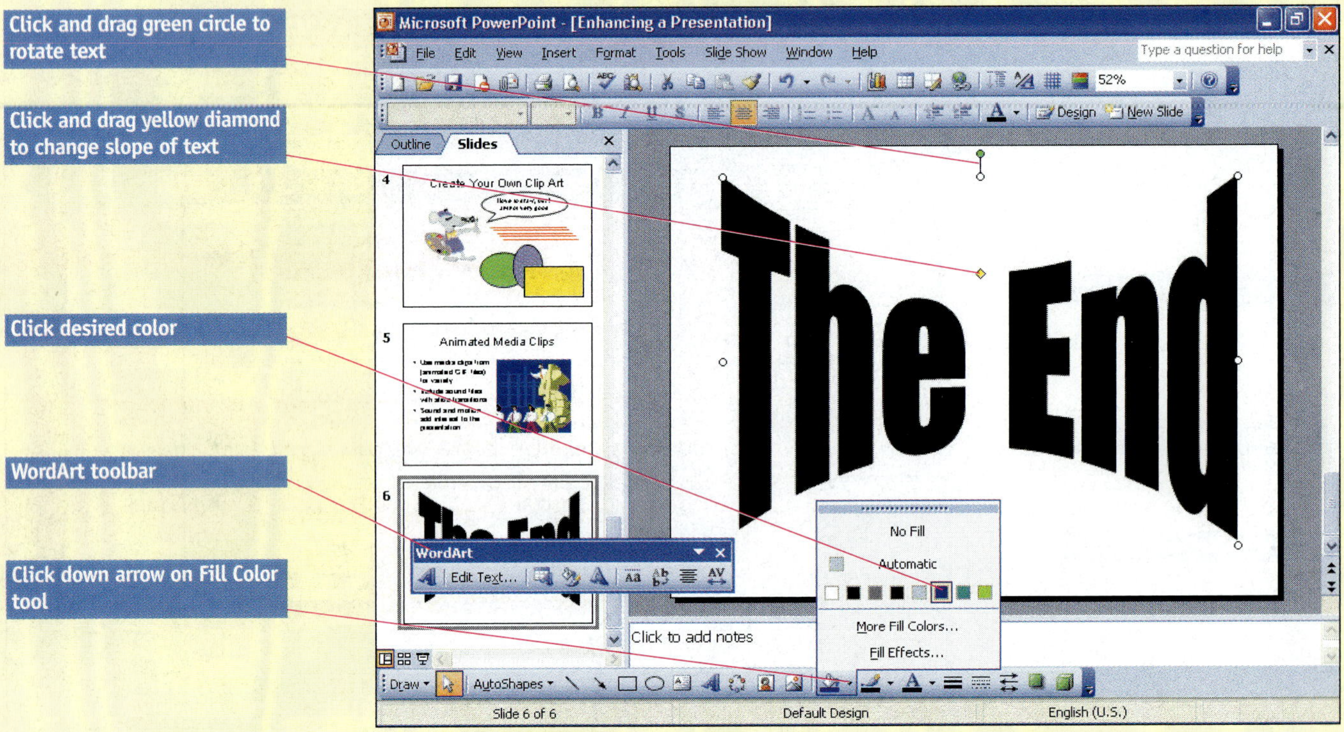

(j) Complete the WordArt (step 10)

FIGURE 1.16 Hands-on Exercise 4 (*continued*)

THE THIRD DIMENSION

You can make your WordArt images even more dramatic by adding 3-D effects. You can tilt the text up or down, right or left, increase or decrease the depth, and change the shading. Pull down the View menu, click Toolbars, click Customize to display the complete list of available toolbars, then check the box to display the 3-D Settings toolbar. Select the WordArt object, then experiment with various tools and special effects. The results are even better if you have a color printer.

Step 11: Print the Comments Pages

- Click the **Print Preview button** to preview the presentation. Click the **down arrow** on the Print What list box to select **Handouts (6 per page)**.
- Click the **down arrow** on the Options list box and toggle **Print Comments and Ink Markup** on, as shown in Figure 1.16k.
- The status bar indicates that you are on the first of two pages. Page 1 contains the six handouts. Page 2 contains the comments you entered earlier. Press the **PgDn key** to move to the second page, then scroll to the top of the page to see the comments.
- Click the **Print button** to display the Print dialog box, which contains the same information as the Print Preview screen; that is, you are printing audience handouts and will include comments. Click **OK** to print the presentation. Close the Print Preview window.
- Press **Ctrl+Home** to move to the first slide in the presentation, then click the **Slide Show button** to view the presentation.
- Save the presentation a final time. Exit PowerPoint. Well done!

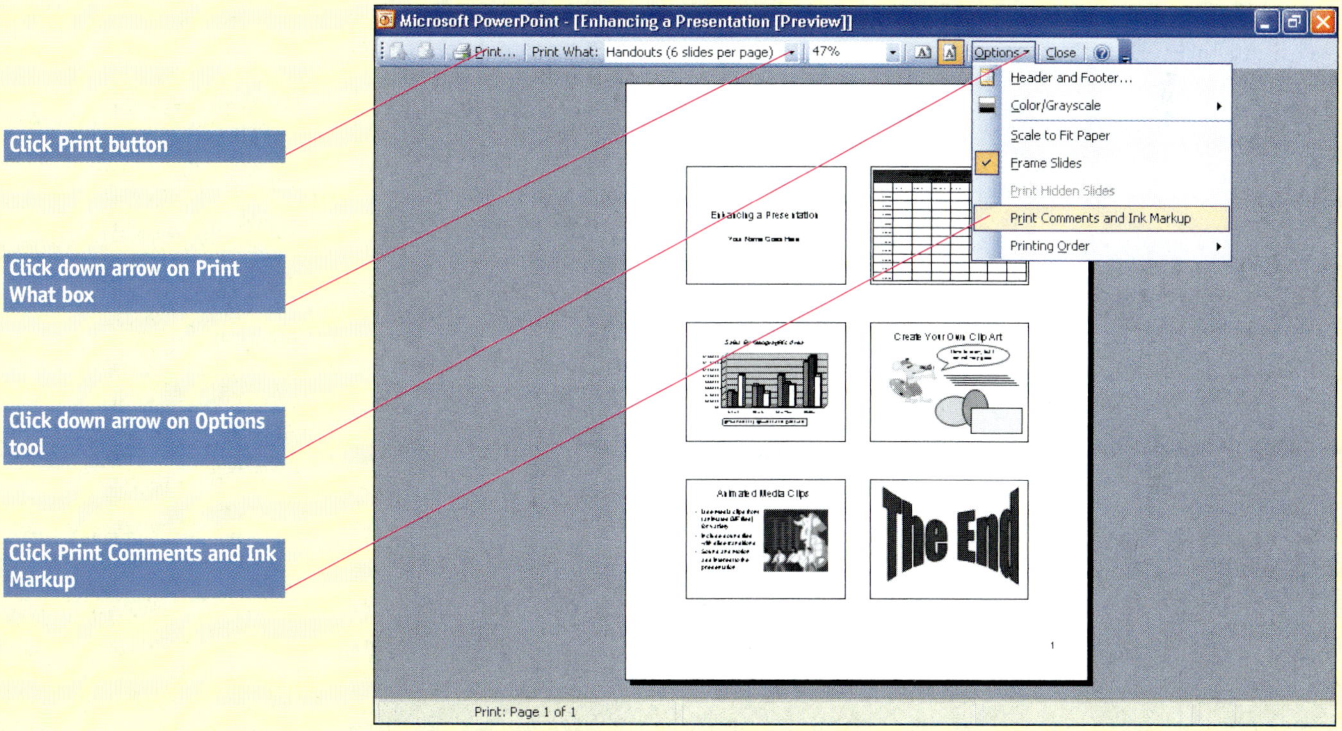

(k) Print the Comments Pages (step 11)

FIGURE 1.16 Hands-on Exercise 4 (*continued*)

THE PAGE SETUP COMMAND

The Print command determines what you will print—e.g., slides, an outline or note pages—but it does not control how the information appears on the printed page. This is controlled by the Page Setup command, which is present in virtually every Windows application. Pull down the File menu and click the Page Setup command to display the associated dialog box. This enables you to change the orientation (portrait or landscape) and/or the paper size.

SUMMARY

Microsoft PowerPoint enables you to focus on the content of a presentation without worrying about its appearance. You supply the text and supporting elements and leave the formatting to PowerPoint. The resulting presentation consists of a series of slides with a consistent design and color scheme. The presentation can be delivered in a variety of ways, such as a computer slide show, via the Web, or using overhead transparencies. It can also be printed in a variety of formats.

PowerPoint has different views, each with unique capabilities. The Normal view displays the Slide, Outline or Thumbnail images, and Notes Page views in a single window. The Slide Sorter view displays multiple slides on one screen (each slide is in miniature) and lets you see the overall flow of the presentation. The Notes Page view is best suited to printing audience handouts that display the slide and the associated speaker notes. The Slide Show view displays one slide at a time with transition and animation effects.

The outline is the easiest way to enter the text of a presentation. Text is entered continually in the outline, then promoted or demoted so that it appears on the proper level in the slide. The outline can be collapsed to show multiple slides on one screen, thus enabling you to change the order of the slides and/or move text from one slide to another.

The Insert Picture command displays a task pane in which you enter a keyword that describes the clip you are looking for. The search is made possible by the Microsoft Clip Organizer, which organizes the media files available to you into collections, then enables you to limit a search to specific media types and/or specific collections.

PowerPoint provides a set of predefined slide layouts that determine the nature and position of the objects on a slide. Each layout contains one or more placeholders to determine the position of the associated object. A template is a design specification that controls every aspect of a presentation. It specifies the formatting of the text, the fonts and colors that are used, and the design, size, and placement of the bullets.

Transitions and animations can be added to a presentation for additional interest. Transitions control the way in which one slide moves off the screen and the next slide appears. Animations control the appearance of individual elements on a single slide.

Clip art may be copied, moved, and/or sized to create modified drawings known as Office Art. The Drawing toolbar contains various tools to further enhance the clip art. WordArt is an application within Microsoft Office that creates decorative text.

Objects from other applications such as Excel charts or Word tables may be linked or embedded into a PowerPoint presentation. Linking is a dynamic technique, which means that if the underlying object changes, that change is automatically reflected in the presentation. Embedding, however, is static, and subsequent changes are not reflected in the presentation.

KEY TERMS

MULTIPLE CHOICE

1. How do you save changes to a PowerPoint presentation?
   (a) Pull down the File menu and click the Save command
   (b) Click the Save button on the Standard toolbar
   (c) Either (a) and (b)
   (d) Neither (a) nor (b)

2. Which of the following can be printed in support of a PowerPoint presentation?
   (a) Audience handouts
   (b) Notes
   (c) An outline
   (d) All of the above

3. Which toolbars are typically displayed in the Normal view?
   (a) The Standard toolbar
   (b) The Formatting toolbar
   (c) The Drawing toolbar
   (d) All of the above

4. Ctrl+Home and Ctrl+End are keyboard shortcuts that move to the beginning or end of the presentation in the:
   (a) Outline view
   (b) Slide Sorter view
   (c) Either (a) or (b)
   (d) Neither (a) nor (b)

5. The predefined slide formats in PowerPoint are known as:
   (a) View
   (b) Slide layouts
   (c) Audience handouts
   (d) Speaker notes

6. Which menu contains the commands to save the current presentation, or to open a previously saved presentation?
   (a) The Tools menu
   (b) The File menu
   (c) The View menu
   (d) The Edit menu

7. The Open command:
   (a) Brings a presentation from disk into memory
   (b) Brings a presentation from disk into memory, then erases the presentation on disk
   (c) Stores the presentation in memory on disk
   (d) Stores the presentation in memory on disk, then erases the presentation from memory

8. The Save command:
   (a) Brings a presentation from disk into memory
   (b) Brings a presentation from disk into memory, then erases the presentation on disk
   (c) Stores the presentation in memory on disk
   (d) Stores the presentation in memory on disk, then erases the presentation from memory

9. Which of the following can be displayed in the task pane?
   (a) Animation and transition effects
   (b) Design templates and slide layouts
   (c) Both (a) and (b)
   (d) Neither (a) nor (b)

10. Where will the insertion point be after you complete the text for a bullet in the outline and press the Enter key?
    (a) On the next bullet at the same level of indentation
    (b) On the next bullet at a higher level of indentation
    (c) On the next bullet at a lower level of indentation
    (d) It is impossible to determine

11. Which of the following is true about an Excel chart that is linked to both a Word document and a PowerPoint presentation?
    (a) The chart cannot be linked to any other presentations or Word documents
    (b) The chart cannot be modified since it is already linked to two documents
    (c) The chart can be modified, but any changes have to be made in two places, once in the Word document and once in the PowerPoint presentation
    (d) Any changes to the chart will be reflected automatically in both the Word document and the PowerPoint presentation.

. . . continued

multiple choice

12. What advantage, if any, is there to collapsing the outline so that only the slide titles are visible?

(a) More slides are displayed at one time, making it easier to rearrange the slides in the presentation

(b) Transition and build effects can be added

(c) Graphic objects become visible

(d) All of the above

13. Which of the following is a true statement regarding transition and build effects?

(a) Every slide must have the same transition effect

(b) Every bullet must have the same build effect

(c) Both (a) and (b)

(d) Neither (a) nor (b)

14. Which of the following is true?

(a) Slides can be added to a presentation after a template has been chosen

(b) The template can be changed after all of the slides have been created

(c) Both (a) and (b)

(d) Neither (a) nor (b)

15. Which of the following is a true statement regarding the Microsoft Clip Organizer?

(a) The search may be limited to a specific media type

(b) The search may be limited to specific collections

(c) Both (a) and (b)

(d) Neither (a) nor (b)

16. You are working on a PowerPoint presentation called First Presentation. You pull down the File menu, click the Save As command, and save the file with a new name, First Presentation Solution. Which of the following statements is true?

(a) The title bar at the top of the PowerPoint window shows First Presentation Solution

(b) There are two files on disk, First Presentation and First Presentation Solution

(c) Both (a) and (b)

(d) Neither (a) nor (b)

17. What is the effect of executing two successive Undo commands, one right after the other?

(a) The situation is not possible because the Undo command is not available

(b) The situation is not possible because the Undo command cannot be executed twice in a row

(c) The Undo commands cancel each other out; that is, the document is the same as it was prior to the first Undo command

(d) The last two commands prior to the first Undo command are reversed

18. Which of the following is a true statement about the Windows and Office clipboards?

(a) Both clipboards can hold only a single item

(b) Both clipboards can hold multiple items

(c) The Windows clipboard holds only a single item; the Office clipboard can hold multiple items

(d) The Office clipboard can hold only a single item; the Windows clipboard can hold multiple items

ANSWERS

1. c	**7.** a	**13.** d
2. d	**8.** c	**14.** c
3. d	**9.** c	**15.** c
4. d	**10.** a	**16.** c
5. b	**11.** d	**17.** d
6. b	**12.** a	**18.** c

PRACTICE WITH POWERPOINT

1. **Introduction to E-Mail:** The presentation in Figure 1.17 reviews the basics of e-mail and simultaneously provides practice with modifying an existing PowerPoint presentation. The presentation also contains two slides on computer viruses and reminds you that your computer is at risk whenever you receive an e-mail message with an attachment. Open the partially completed presentation in *Chapter 1 Practice 1* within the Exploring PowerPoint folder and do the following:
   a. Modify the title slide to include your name and your e-mail address. Replace the sample e-mail address with your address on slide 4.
   b. Boldface and italicize the four basic capabilities in any e-mail program (Send, Compose, Reply, and Forward) on slide 2. Boldface and italicize the name of each e-mail folder on slide 3.
   c. Move the last two slides (Be Aware of Computer Viruses and Protect Yourself) to the indicated positions in Figure 1.17. Read the content of these two slides very carefully. Which antivirus program do you use?
   d. Set a limit of five minutes to experiment with different design templates, and then choose a template for the completed presentation.
   e. Add transition effects throughout the presentation as you see fit.
   f. Print the presentation in multiple ways. Print the title slide as a slide (full page) to serve as a cover page. Print the outline of the presentation, then print audience handouts for the entire presentation (six per page). Be sure to frame the individual slides.
   g. View the completed presentation, paying special attention to slide 6, which contains hyperlinks to the Norton and McAfee Web sites. Visit both sites. What is the cost of each program and the associated cost of an annual update? How do the sites provide protection against new viruses? When was the last time you updated your antivirus program?
   h. Be prepared to present your findings in a class discussion.

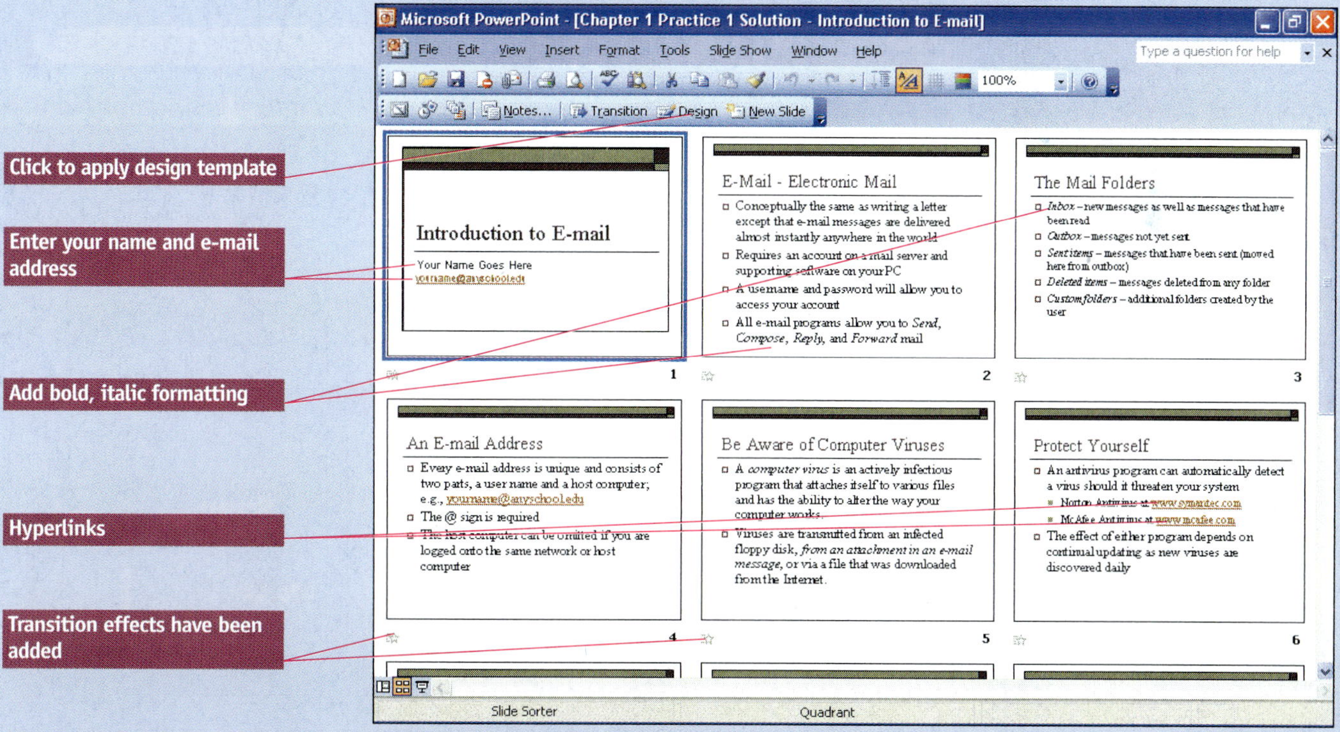

FIGURE 1.17 Introduction to E-mail (exercise 1)

2. **What's New in Windows® XP?:** Windows XP is the newest and most powerful version of the Windows operating system. It has a slightly different look than earlier versions, but it maintains the conventions of its various predecessors. The Windows XP Home Edition is intended for entertainment and home use. It includes a media player, support for digital photography, and an instant messenger. The Windows XP Professional Edition has all of the features of the Home Edition plus additional security to encrypt files and protect data.
   a. Go to the Exploring Office Web site at www.prenhall.com/grauer; click the link to Office 2003, then click the link to "What's New in Windows XP?"
   b. Read the summary description of Windows XP, then click the link to download the PowerPoint presentation. Save the file to your desktop, then go to your desktop, double click the file that you just downloaded, and follow the onscreen instructions to unzip the presentation in Figure 1.18.
   c. Start PowerPoint. Pull down the File menu, click the Open command, and change to the drive and folder where you just unzipped the "What's New in Windows XP?" presentation. Open the presentation.
   d. Pull down the Slide Show menu and click the View Show command to view the presentation. There are 25 slides in all, and it should take you no more than 10 or 15 minutes to go through the entire presentation. We think you will learn something, even if you have been using Windows XP for several months.
   e. Go to the title slide, add your name after Bob's, and replace Bob's e-mail address with your own.
   f. Create a new slide immediately after the title slide. Choose the Title and Text layout, title the slide "My Favorite New Features", then list at least three new features in Windows XP.
   g. Print the presentation in multiple ways. Print the title slide as a slide (full page) to serve as a cover page for the assignment. Print the audience handouts for the entire presentation (six per page). Be sure to frame the individual slides.

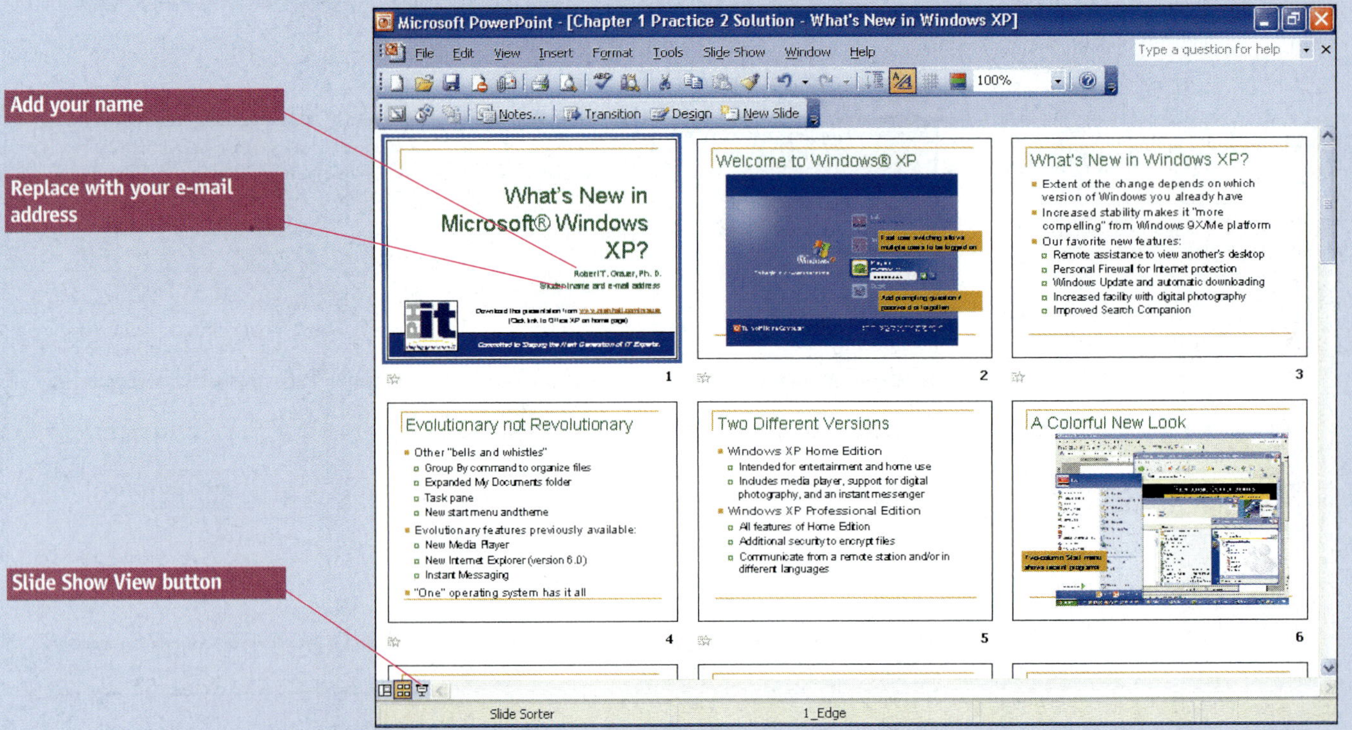

FIGURE 1.18 What's New in Windows XP? (exercise 2)

3. **Introduction to the Internet:** The presentation in Figure 1.19 is intended to review the basics of the Internet and provide practice with modifying an existing PowerPoint presentation. Open the partially completed presentation in *Chapter 1 Practice 3* within the Exploring PowerPoint folder and do the following:
   a. Add your name to the title slide as indicated. Add a note to this slide to identify your class and your professor.
   b. Search the presentation to find the slide containing the acronyms HTTP, HTTPS, HTML, and ISP (all of the terms are on the same slide). Boldface and italicize these acronyms.
   c. Delete the clip art on the "Connecting to the Internet" slide. Change the layout of this slide to a two-column bulleted slide, and then describe your Internet connection(s) in the second column.
   d. Add a bulleted slide after slide 6 (The Uniform Resource Locator). The new slide should list five specific Web sites. The first bullet should reference your school or professor. The second bullet should reference the Exploring Office Web site. Each bullet should name the site followed by its URL, e.g., The Exploring Office Web site at www.prenhall.com/grauer.
   e. Set a limit of five minutes to experiment with different design templates, and then choose a template for the completed presentation.
   f. Add transition effects throughout the presentation as you see fit.
   g. Print the presentation in multiple ways. Print the title slide as a slide (full page) to serve as a cover page. Print the notes for the first slide. Print the audience handouts for the entire presentation (six per page). Be sure to frame the individual slides. And finally, print the presentation in outline form.
   h. Go through the presentation one slide at a time to learn and/or review the material. Did you learn anything new? Are you surprised at the age of the Internet? What additional material (if any) would you include in the presentation? Summarize your thoughts in a brief note to your instructor.

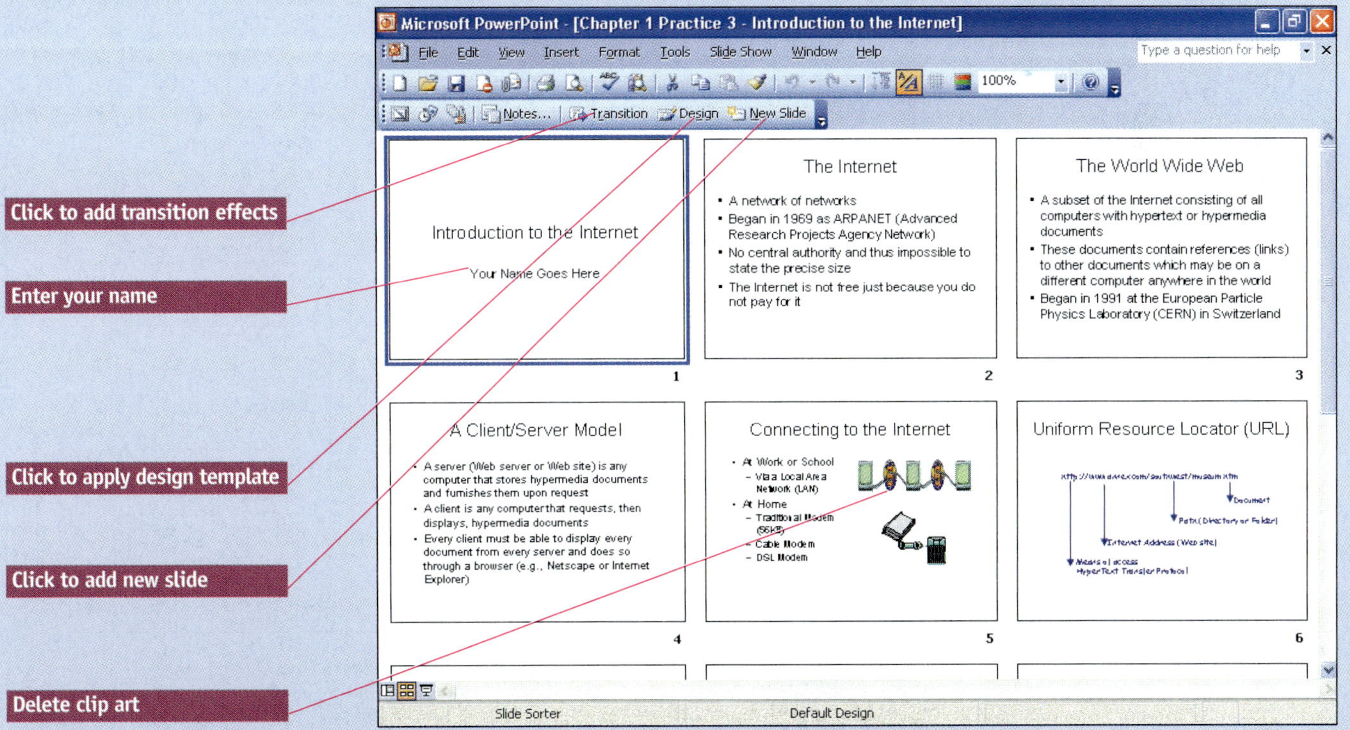

FIGURE 1.19 Introduction to the Internet (exercise 3)

4. **Copyright and the Law:** The presentation in Figure 1.20 is intended to review basic copyright law and software licensing and also to provide practice with modifying an existing PowerPoint presentation. Open the partially completed presentation in *Chapter 1 Practice 4* within the Exploring PowerPoint folder and do the following:

   a. Add a copyright logo to the title slide. Our logo is actually a piece of clip art, which has a built-in animation effect. Pull down the Insert menu, click Picture, click Clip Art to display the Insert Clip Art task pane, and then search on the keyword, copyright. (We have included the clip art image as a GIF file in the Exploring PowerPoint folder if your search is unsuccessful.) Add your name to the title slide as indicated.

   b. Boldface and italicize the terms "copyright" on slide 2 (first bullet only), "End User License Agreement" and "Site License" on slide 4, and "public domain" and "fair use exclusion" on slide 7.

   c. Set a limit of five minutes to experiment with different design templates, and then choose a template for the completed presentation.

   d. Add transition effects throughout the presentation as you see fit.

   e. Insert a new slide immediately before the last slide that contains the following text. *Individuals who violate copyright law and/or software licensing agreements may be subject to criminal or civil action by the copyright or license owners. This means you!* Choose a font size and style so that the text fills the entire slide.

   f. Visit one or more of the Web sites that are indicated on the last slide to obtain additional information. How do you feel about the copyright law with respect to downloading music from the Web? Be prepared to discuss the content of these sites in class.

   g. Print the presentation in multiple ways. Print the title slide as a slide (full page) to serve as a cover page for the assignment. Print audience handouts for the entire presentation (six per page). Be sure to frame the individual slides. And finally, print the presentation in outline form.

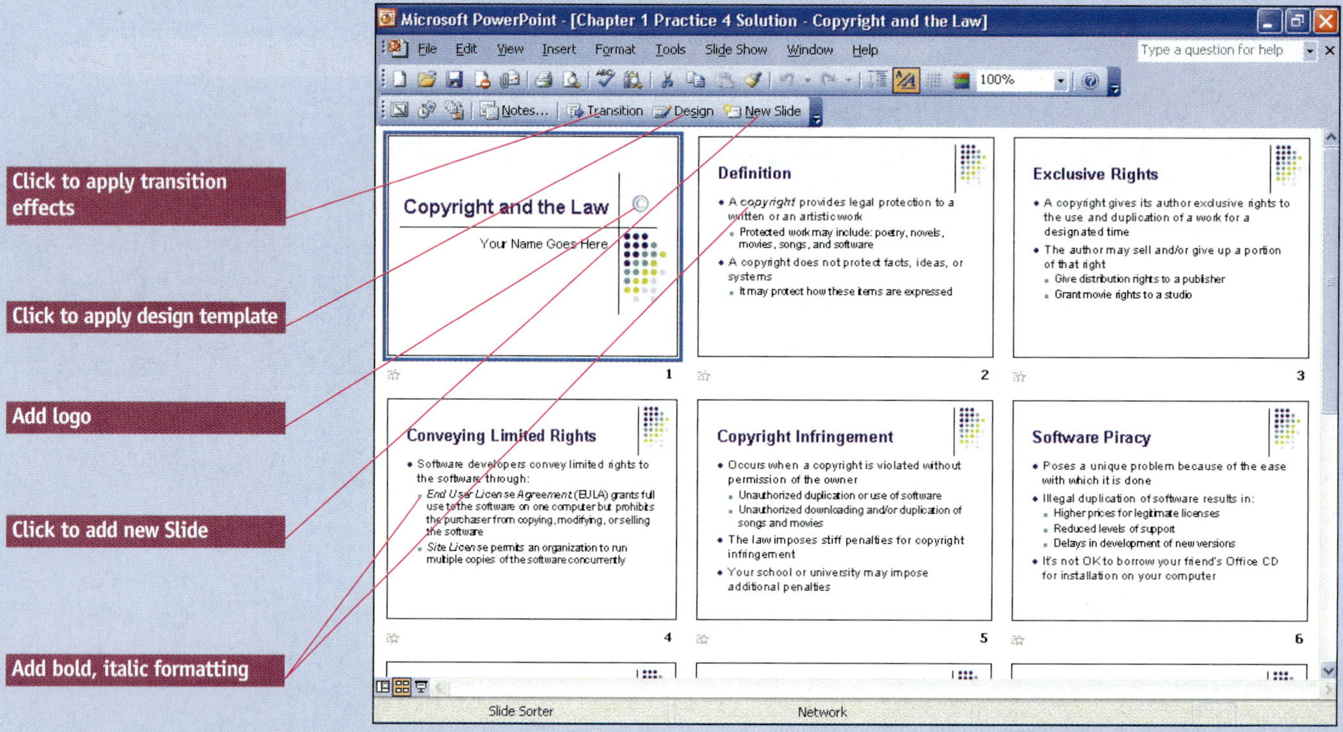

FIGURE 1.20 Copyright and the Law (exercise 4)

5. **Public Speaking 101:** PowerPoint will help you to create an attractive presentation, but the delivery is still up to you. It's easier than you think, and you should not be intimidated at the prospect of facing an audience. You can become an effective speaker by following the basic tenets of good public speaking as described in the presentation of Figure 1.21.
    a. Open the *Chapter 1 Practice 5* presentation that describes the basics of good public speaking. Add your name to the title slide.
    b. Print the notes for the presentation, then view the slide show, looking at the appropriate notes for each slide.
    c. Which slides have notes attached? Are the notes redundant, or do they add something extra? Do you see how the notes help a speaker to deliver an effective presentation?
    d. What different delivery styles were referenced in the learning activity slide? Was the class able to see the problem inherent with the ineffective delivery of each topic?
    e. Which slide contains the phrase, "Common sense is not common practice"? In what context is the phrase used within the presentation?
    f. Which personality said, "You can observe a lot by watching"? In what context is the phrase used during the presentation?
    g. Public speaking is like any other skill; the more you practice, the better you become. All you need is a friendly audience. Ask your instructor to create groups of four or five students, and then practice delivering the presentation to your classmates. Were you able to follow the tenets of good public speaking?
    h. What suggestions were made in the presentation to create a positive learning environment? Do you have any additional suggestions?
    i. Summarize your thoughts about this presentation in a short note to your instructor.

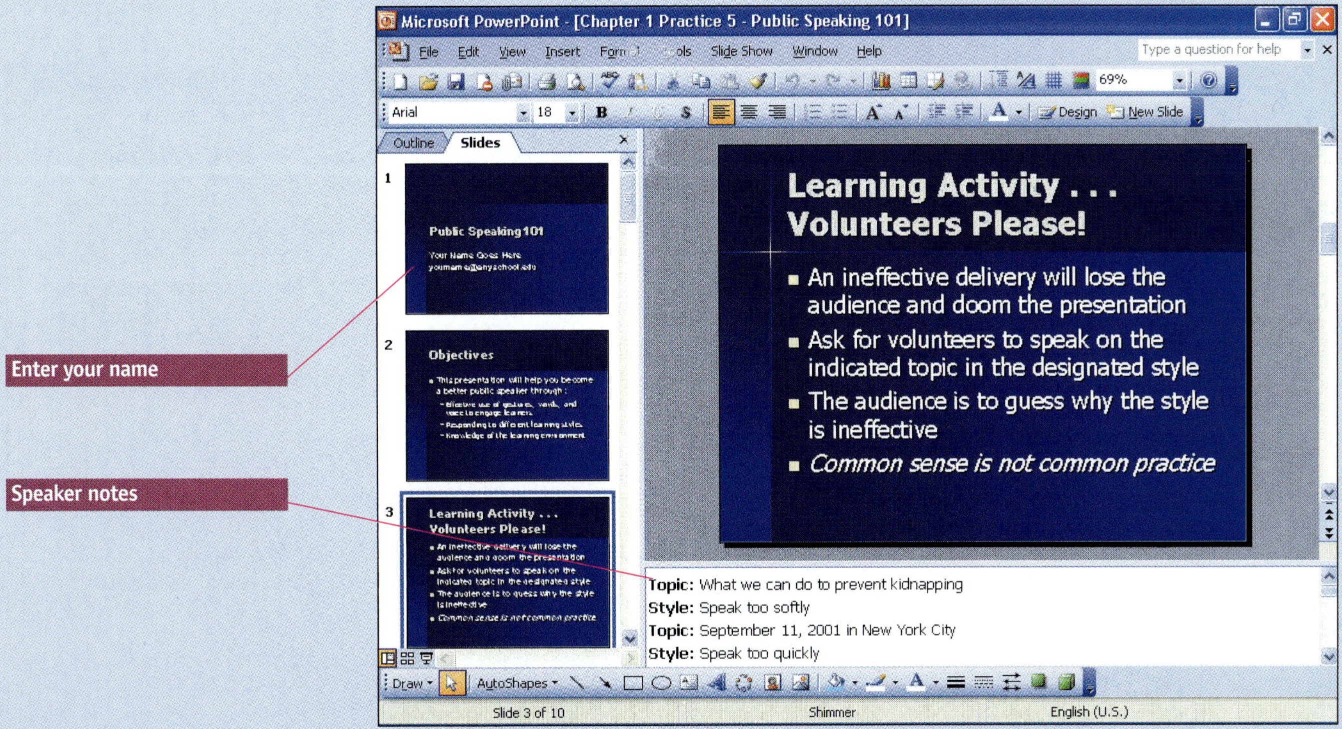

FIGURE 1.21 Public Speaking 101 (exercise 5)

6. **University Housing:** A partially completed version of the presentation in Figure 1.22 has been saved as the *Chapter 1 Practice 6* presentation in the Exploring PowerPoint folder. Open this presentation and save it as *Chapter 1 Practice 6 Solution* so that you can return to the original presentation if necessary.
   a. Insert a new slide that contains a mission statement as the fifth slide in the presentation. The mission statement should read as follows: *The mission of the* ***University Housing Office*** *is to provide a total environment that will enrich the educational experience of its residents. It seeks to promote increased interaction between faculty and students through resident masters, special programs, and intramural activities.*
   b. Open the *Chapter 1 Practice 6* workbook that is in the Exploring PowerPoint folder. Click the worksheet tab containing the side-by-side column chart. If necessary, click the Zoom button and change the magnification so that you can select the entire chart. Click the Copy button. Return to PowerPoint and go to the fourth slide. Pull down the Edit menu, click Paste Special, select Microsoft Excel Chart Object, click Paste Link, and click OK.
   c. The chart should appear in the presentation. The only tricky part (if any) is to display the entire chart (it may be cropped initially). Select the chart, then click and drag a corner sizing handle to make the chart smaller. Right click the chart and click the command to display the Picture toolbar. Select the Crop tool, then click and drag the side handle at the right of the chart to show the portion of the chart that may have been cropped initially. Move and size the chart as necessary.
   d. Use the same technique as in steps b and c to link the worksheet for room and meal revenues to the appropriate slide in the presentation. Move and/or size these objects after they have been added to the presentation.
   e. Add your name to the title slide. Print the audience handouts of the completed presentation (six per page) for your instructor. Be sure to frame the slides. Exit PowerPoint. Close the Excel workbook and exit Excel.

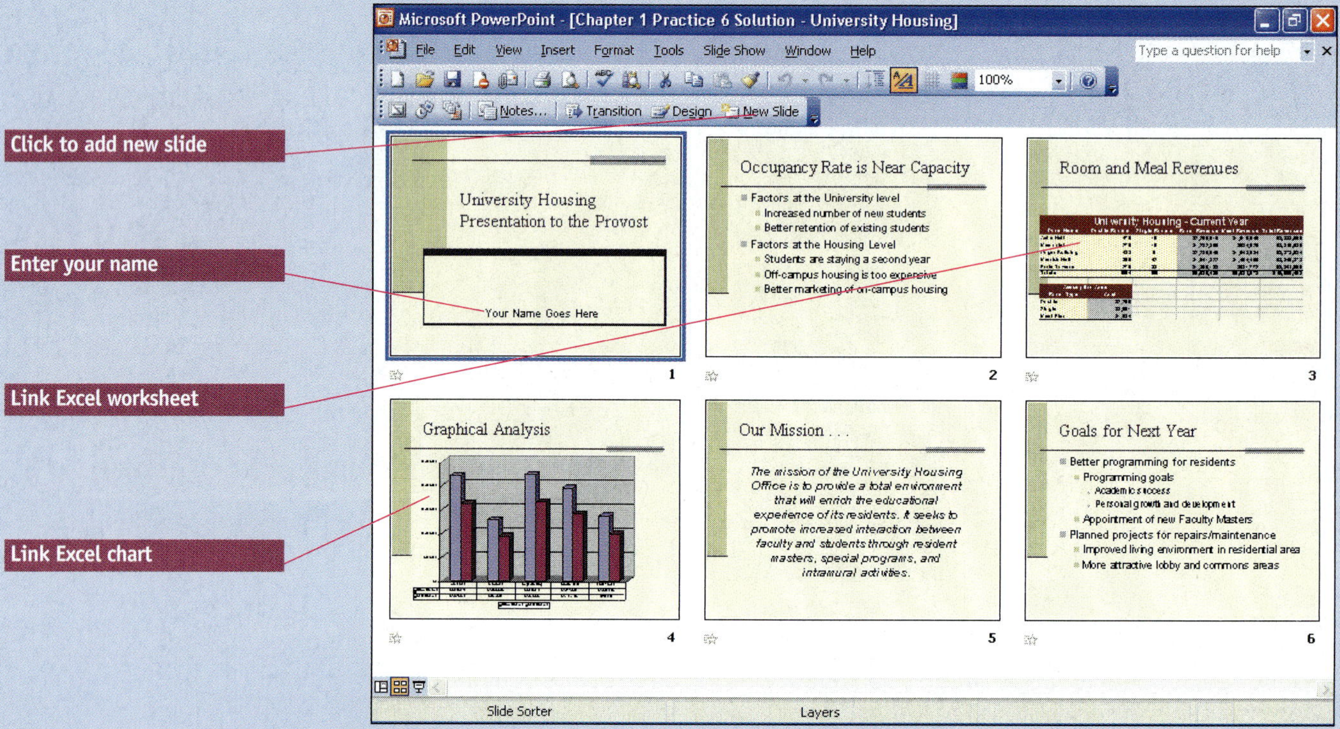

FIGURE 1.22 University Housing (exercise 6)

7. **You Don't Have to Be an Artist:** Figure 1.23 illustrates how you can modify existing clip art to create entirely different images. Open the presentation in *Chapter 1 Practice 7*. Add your name to the title slide. Change to the Slide Sorter view. Select the second slide (The Original Clip Art), click the Copy button, then click the Paste button to duplicate the original slide.
   a. Double click the copied slide (slide 3) to return to the Normal view. Select The Original Clip Art. Click the down arrow on the Draw button, and then click the Ungroup command. Click Yes to convert the picture to a Microsoft Office Drawing Object. Click on the clip art, and then ungroup it a second time. You should see two sets of sizing handles, one around the duck, and one around the computer and table.
   b. Click in the background area of the slide to deselect both objects. Now click on the duck and experiment with the various tools on the Drawing toolbar to flip the image horizontally or vertically. Change the title of the slide to describe the modification.
   c. Click in the outline pane, click on slide 2 (the slide that contains The Original Clip Art), click the Copy button, then click on slide 3 and click the paste button three times. Select (click) slide 4 and use the appropriate tools on the Drawing toolbar to create this slide. Change the title of slide 4 to reflect the modification. Create slides 5 and 6 in similar fashion, changing the title each time.
   d. Add a seventh slide of your own design, then copy the clip art from that slide to the title slide. You will have to group the objects on the seventh slide in order to move the clip art as a unit. Pull down the Edit menu, click Select All to select all of the objects, then press and hold the Ctrl key as you click the title to deselect the title. Now, right click the selected clip art, click Grouping from the context-sensitive menu, then click the Group command. You can now select the image (consisting of multiple ducks) as a single object and copy it to the title slide.
   e. Print the completed presentation for your instructor. Print the title slide as a full page, then print audience handouts of slides 2 through 7.

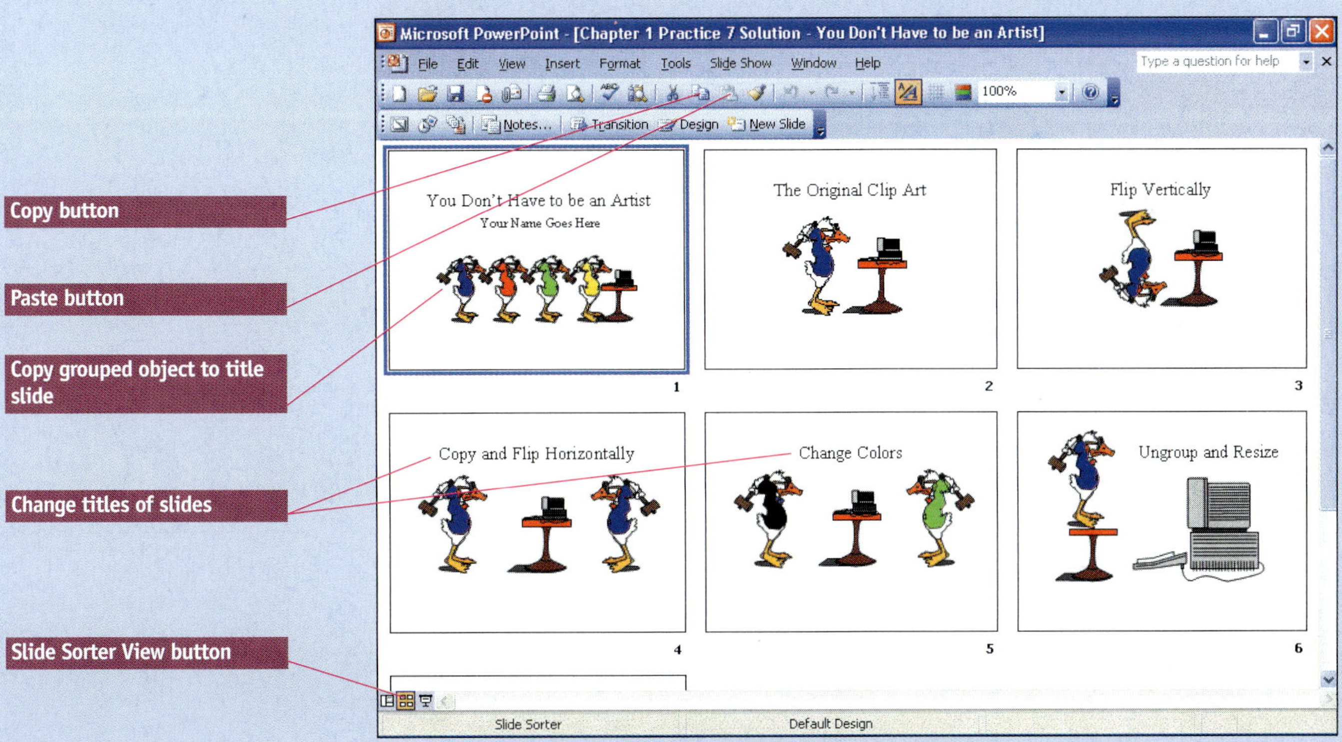

FIGURE 1.23 You Don't Have to Be an Artist (exercise 7)

8. **Request for Venture Capital:** Definitely Needlepoint is a successful retail store owned by four close friends who enjoy needlepoint. The store has been in operation for three years and has increased its revenue and profit for each year. The partners are looking to expand their operation by requesting venture capital. They have an important meeting scheduled for next week and have decided to use PowerPoint to present their case. Your assignment is to open the partially completed version of the *Chapter 1 Practice 8* presentation that is displayed in Figure 1.24 and proceed as follows:
   a. Insert a new slide containing the mission statement as the second slide in the presentation. The mission statement should read as follows: *Definitely Needlepoint provides an intimate setting in which to stitch. Our customers are our friends and participate in a variety of social and educational activities that encourage and develop the art of needlepoint.*
   b. Open the *Chapter 1 Practice 8* workbook in the Exploring PowerPoint folder. Select the worksheet that contains sales data for last year, and link that data to the slide containing the year-to-year comparison (slide 4). Now select the worksheet with sales data for the current year and link this data to the same slide. Move and/or size the worksheets after they have been added to the presentation.
   c. Locate the worksheet containing the chart that shows the sales increase by category. Link this chart to slide 5.
   d. Locate the chart that shows the sales increase by quarter and link the chart to slide 6.
   e. Add your name to the title slide in the indicated position. Print the audience handouts of the completed presentation (six per page) for your instructor. Print the outline. Print the title slide as a full slide to use as a cover page for the assignment.
   f. Save the completed presentation. Exit PowerPoint. Close the Excel workbook. Exit Excel.

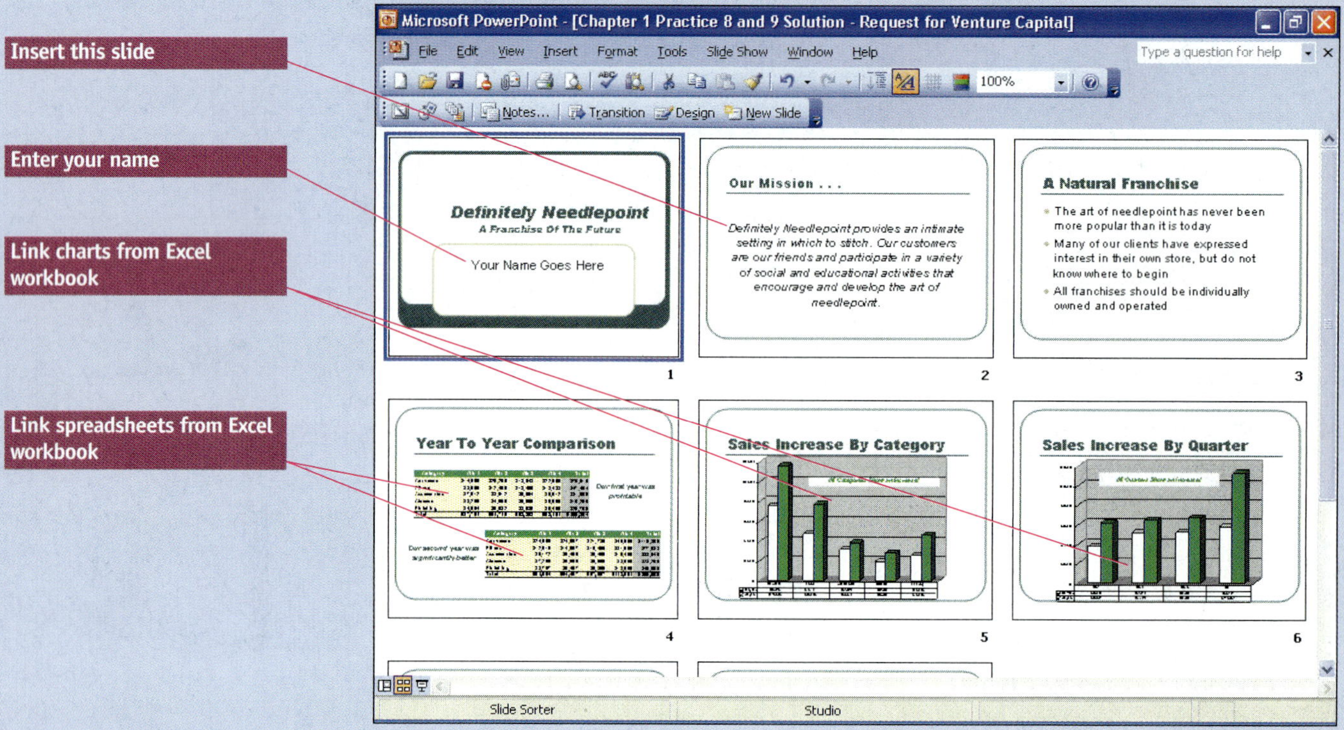

FIGURE 1.24 Request for Venture Capital (exercise 8)

9. **A Look Ahead—Action Buttons and Slide Masters:** The presentation in Figure 1.25 appears to be identical to the presentation in the previous exercise. Look closely, however, and you will see a set of four action buttons at the bottom of the second and third slides in the presentation. (The buttons are used during the slide show to provide easy navigation to the first, previous, next, and last slides in the presentation.) The buttons are on every slide except for the title slide, but the additional slides are not visible in Figure 1.25. The buttons are added to the slide master, which in turn displays them on every slide. Proceed as follows:
   a. Open the completed presentation from the previous exercise. Pull down the View menu, click the Master command, then select the Slide Master. (Be sure the bulleted slide is selected, as opposed to the title slide.) Pull down the Slide Show menu, click the Action Buttons command, and select (click) the beginning |◀ button that indicates the first slide.
   b. The mouse pointer changes to a tiny crosshair. Click in the footer area at the bottom of the slide, then drag the mouse to create an action button. Release the mouse. The Action Settings dialog box is displayed automatically. The Hyperlink to Option button is selected and First Slide is specified in the associated list box. Click OK to accept the default settings and close the Action Settings dialog box. Repeat this process three additional times to create action buttons for the previous, next, and ending slides in that sequence.
   c. Click and drag the individual action buttons so that there is sufficient space between the buttons to increase their size to ½ inch each. Press and hold the Shift key as you click each action button to select all four buttons. Point to any button, click the right mouse button to display a context-sensitive menu, then click Format AutoShape to display the Format AutoShape dialog box. Click the Size tab, then enter .35 and .5 as the height and width of each button. Click OK to accept the settings and close the dialog box.
   d. Change to the Slide Sorter view. The action buttons should appear on every slide.
   e. Save the presentation. Press Ctrl+Home to move to the first slide. Pull down the Slide Show menu and click the View Show command. Test the action buttons to be sure that they work as intended.

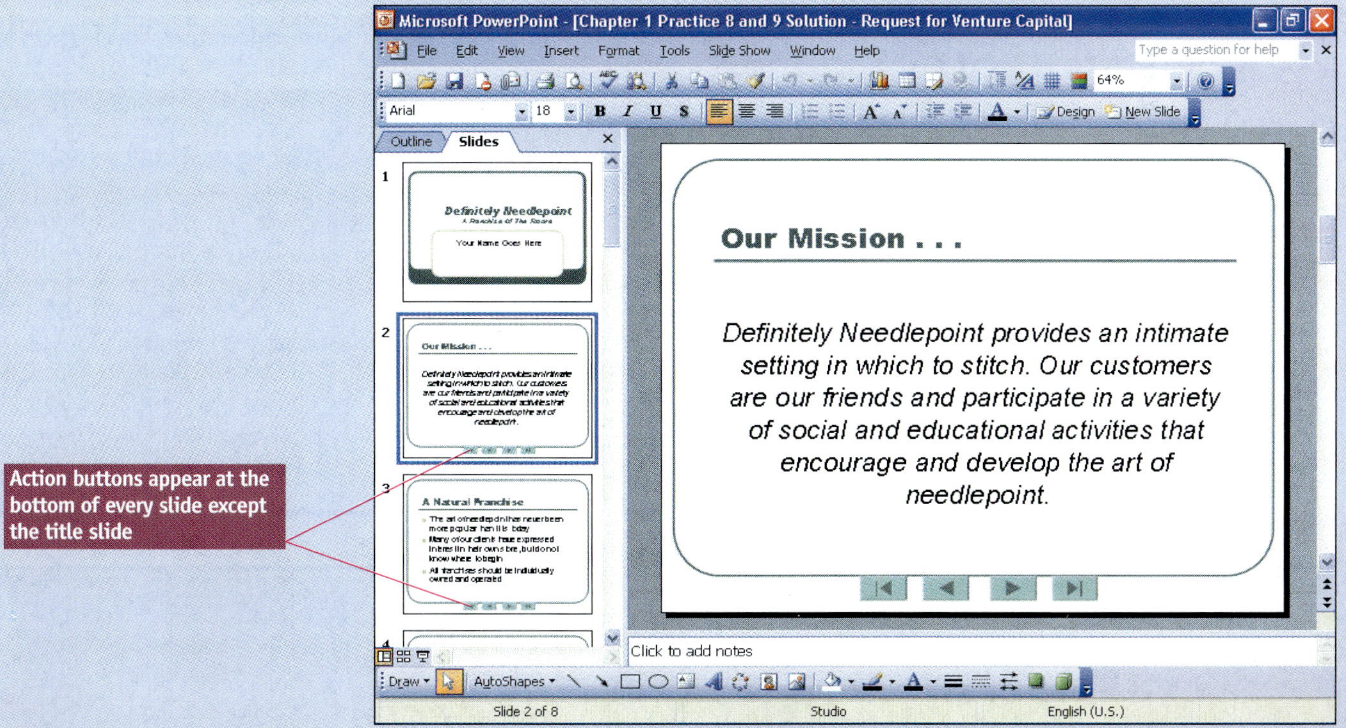

FIGURE 1.25 A Look Ahead—Action Buttons and Slide Masters (exercise 9)

MINI CASES

Planning for Disaster

This case has nothing to do with presentations per se, but it is perhaps the most important case of all, as it deals with the question of backup. Do you have a backup strategy? Do you even know what a backup strategy is? This is a good time to learn, because sooner or later you will need to recover a file. The problem always seems to occur the night before an assignment is due. You accidentally erased a file, are unable to read from a floppy disk, or worse yet, suffer a hardware failure in which you are unable to access the hard drive. The ultimate disaster is the disappearance of your computer, by theft or natural disaster. Describe in 250 words or fewer the backup strategy you plan to implement in conjunction with your work in this class.

Changing Menus and Toolbars

Office 2003 lets you switch to a series of short menus that contain only basic commands. The additional commands are made visible by clicking the double arrow that appears at the bottom of the menu. New commands are added to the menu as they are used, and conversely, other commands are removed if they are not used. A similar strategy is followed for the Standard and Formatting toolbars, which are displayed on a single row, and thus do not show all of the buttons at one time. The intent is to simplify Office 2003 for the new user by limiting the number of commands that are visible. The consequence, however, is that the individual is not exposed to new commands, and hence may not use Office to its full potential. Which set of menus do you prefer? How do you switch from one set to the other?

Be Creative

One interesting way of exploring the potential of presentation graphics is to imagine it might have been used by historical figures had it been available. Choose any historical figure or current personality and create at least a six-slide presentation. You could, for example, show how Columbus might have used PowerPoint to request funding from Queen Isabella, or how Elvis Presley might have pleaded for his first recording contract. The content of your presentation should be reasonable, but you don't have to spend an inordinate amount of time on research. Just be creative and use your imagination. Use clip art as appropriate, but don't overdo it. Place your name on the title slide as technical adviser.

The National Debt

The national debt is staggering—more than $6 trillion, or approximately $20,000 for every man, woman, and child in the United States. The annual budget is approximately $2 trillion. Use the Internet to obtain exact figures for the current year, then use this information to create a presentation on income and expenditures. Do some additional research and obtain data on the budget, the deficit, and the national debt for the years 1945, 1967, and 1980. The numbers may surprise you. For example, how does the interest expense for the current year compare to the total budget in 1967 (at the height of the Vietnam War)? To the total budget in 1945 (at the end of World War II)?

CHAPTER 2

Gaining Proficiency: Slide Show Tools and Digital Photography

OBJECTIVES

After reading this chapter you will:

1. Insert a table onto a PowerPoint slide.
2. Add headers and footers to slides and/or the audience handouts.
3. Use the Rehearse Timings feature.
4. Create a hidden slide.
5. Send a presentation for review; accept and reject reviewer edits.
6. Import a Word outline as the basis for a presentation.
7. Download a photograph from the Web for inclusion in a presentation.
8. Insert a hyperlink into a presentation.
9. Insert a photo album into a presentation.
10. Use the AutoContent Wizard as the basis for a presentation.

hands-on exercises

1. SLIDE SHOW TOOLS
   Input: Presentation Hints; Bob's Comments
   Output: Presentation Hints Solution
2. THE INTERNET AS A RESOURCE
   Input: Extinction of the Dinosaurs (Word document)
   Output: Extinction of the Dinosaurs
3. FUN WITH PHOTOGRAPHS
   Input: None
   Output: My Photo Album
4. THE AUTOCONTENT WIZARD
   Input: None
   Output: Our First Exam

CASE STUDY

FEATURE FILMS, INC.

Shelly Daniels has a bright, creative, and energetic personality. She is currently a senior majoring in Motion Pictures within the Communication Department and studying for her bachelor's degree. She hopes to become a producer or director for a major film company, following the footsteps of her grandfather, Norman A. Daniels.

This term she is taking COM400: Administration of Studio Operations. The capstone project requires every student to create their own feature film company and present an overview of their company to the class. The presentation is to be in the form of an employee orientation; it should include a description of the company's history, organizational structure, past and present projects, corporate policies, and employee benefits. The assignment was given at the beginning of the semester with the understanding that it would be developed as the topics were presented. It is now the end of the semester, and Shelly, a procrastinator by nature, is in a real bind. She has 24 hours to complete the entire assignment before presenting it to the class. In a flash of inspiration, she turns to the AutoContent Wizard for help and finds the *Employee Orientation* template, which is the perfect place to start her presentation. ■

Your assignment is to read the chapter, paying special attention to Hands-on Exercise 4, which describes the AutoContent Wizard. Put yourself in Shelly's shoes and create a presentation based on the Employee Orientation template. You will, however, have to add your own content to comply with the requirements of the assignment. You will also be graded on how well you present to the class. Thus, you should practice several times to rehearse your timing and delivery. Use animation and/or transition effects to add interest. Add notes throughout the presentation and then print the completed presentation in multiple ways. Print audience handouts (six per page). Print an outline of the presentation. Print at least one slide to show the notes that you have added. Print the title slide as a slide (full page) to serve as a cover page.

SLIDE SHOW TOOLS

PowerPoint provides a series of slide show tools to help you deliver a presentation effectively. The tools are discussed briefly in conjunction with the presentation in Figure 2.1, and then described in detail in a hands-on exercise. The text on the second slide is worthy of special mention as it was entered into a table, as an alternative to the standard bulleted text slide. The table was created through the ***Insert Table command*** to provide variety within a presentation.

Each slide in the presentation (except for the title slide) contains the identical text that was entered through the ***Header and Footer command***. The inclusion of a header or footer personalizes a presentation by adding items such as the date, place of the presentation, and/or the slide number. You can also include a clip art or logo to create additional interest.

Look carefully under each slide and you will see a number that represents the amount of time the presenter intends to devote to the slide. The timings were entered through the ***Rehearse Timings*** feature that lets you time a presentation as you practice your delivery. The Rehearse Timings feature can also be used with the ***Set Up Show command*** to automate a presentation so that each slide will be shown for the set time period.

The icon under slide number 5 indicates that it is a ***hidden slide***, which prevents the slide from appearing during a regular slide show. This is a common practice among experienced speakers who anticipate probing questions that may arise during the presentation. The presenter prefers not to address the topic initially, but creates a slide to hold in reserve should the topic arise. The hidden slide can be displayed during a slide show by right clicking the slide and choosing the Go To Slide command.

The ability to annotate slides by drawing on the slide (just like your favorite football announcer) is not visible in Figure 2.1, since the annotation takes place during the actual slide show. This is a favorite technique and one we will illustrate in the next hands-on exercise.

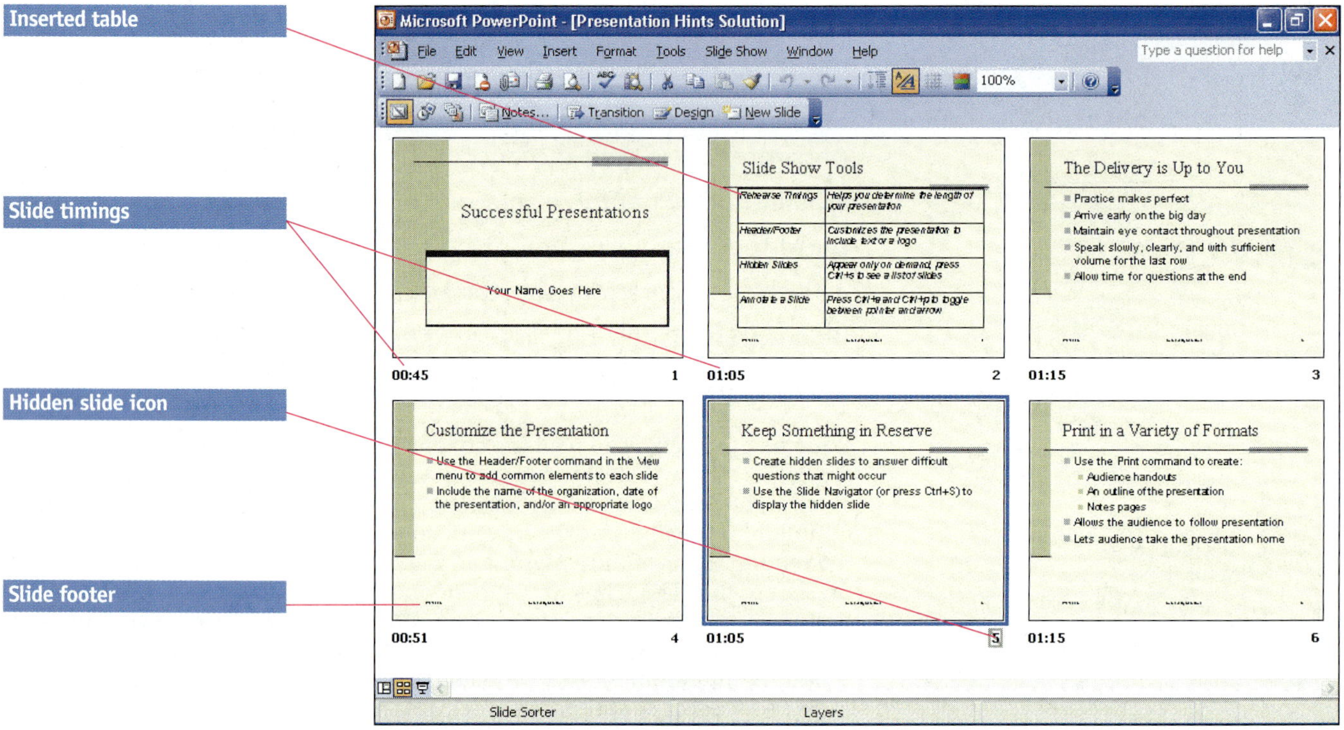

FIGURE 2.1 Presentation Tools

REVIEWING A PRESENTATION

The American workplace is team oriented, with many people typically collaborating on the same document. Microsoft Office XP facilitates this process by enabling the revisions to be stored and accepted (or rejected) electronically. In PowerPoint the process works as follows. You create the initial presentation, then use the ***Send To command*** to send the presentation to one or more people for review. PowerPoint automatically links to your e-mail program and sends the presentation as an attachment.

Each reviewer receives a copy of the presentation, enters his or her changes, then returns the revised presentation as an attachment in an e-mail message. You save each reviewer's attachment as its own file (such as Bob's Comments), then you use the ***Compare and Merge Presentations command*** to open all of the reviewers' presentations and optionally merge the comments with the original presentation. You can merge the comments from multiple reviewers in a single session.

Figure 2.2 shows the suggested changes to the first slide in the selected presentation. The ***revisions pane*** at the right shows how the title slide would look according to the changes for each reviewer. Robert Grauer changes the title to "Successful Presentations", but retains the current template. Maryann Barber, on the other hand, retains the title, but modifies the template. You can accept either or both changes by checking the box next to each reviewer's name in the revisions pane. You can expand any proposed changes in text (such as Bob's change in title) and accept or reject the suggestions individually. You can also use the Undo command to cancel your changes.

The developer of the presentation goes from one slide to the next, accepting or rejecting the changes, as he or she sees fit. The ***Reviewing toolbar*** contains several buttons to aid in this process, such as the Next and Previous Item buttons to move from one revision to the next. The toolbar also provides buttons to insert, edit, or delete comments. The reviewer ends the review, which in turn closes the revisions pane and removes the reviewers' presentations from memory. You can then send the revised presentation as an e-mail attachment.

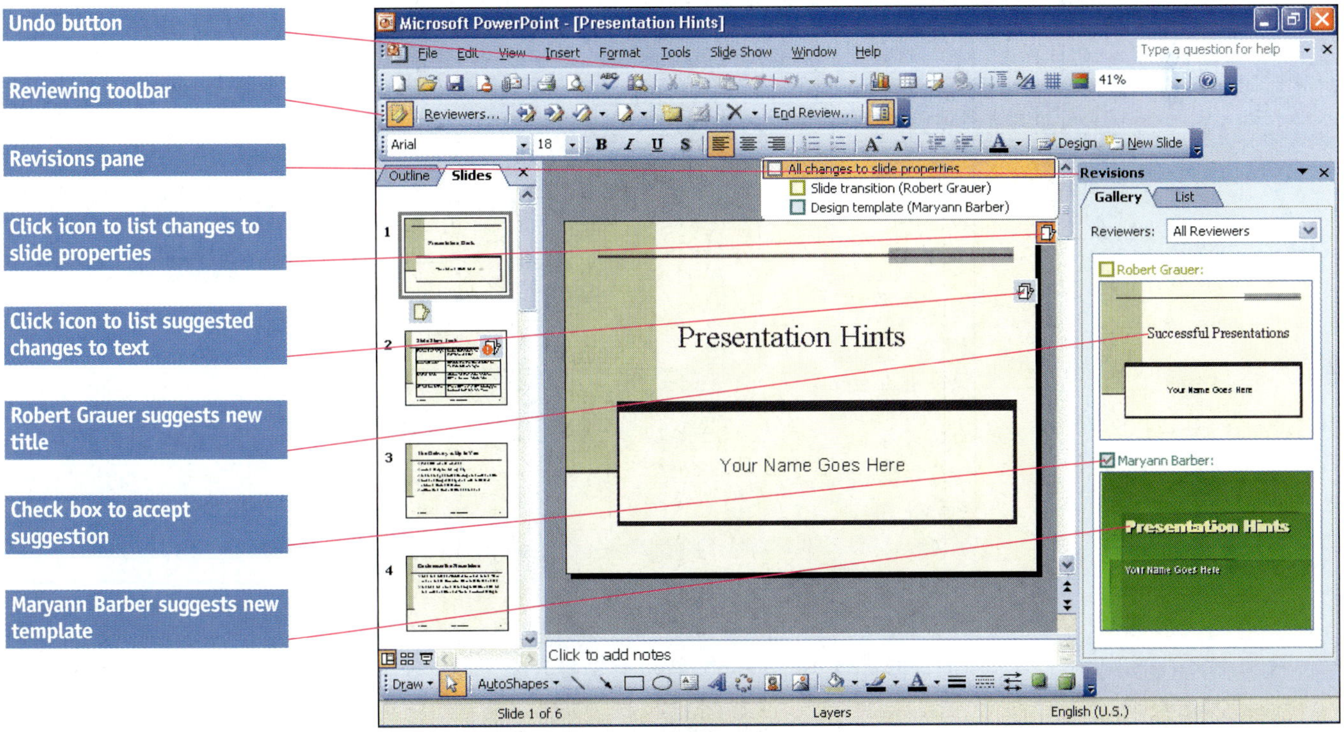

FIGURE 2.2 Reviewing Changes

hands-on exercise

1 Slide Show Tools

Objective To use the Rehearse Timings feature to practice your delivery; to use the Slide Navigator and pen during a presentation; to send a presentation for review; to compare and merge documents. Use Figure 2.3 as a guide in the exercise.

Step 1: Create the Table

- Start PowerPoint. Open **Presentation Hints** in the **Exploring PowerPoint folder**. Click on the placeholder for the subtitle and add your name to the title slide.
- Pull down the **File menu**, click the **Save As command** to display the File Save dialog box, then save the presentation as **Presentation Hints Solution**.
- Pull down the **Insert menu** and click the **New Slide command** (or click the **New Slide button** on the Formatting toolbar). The task pane opens as shown in Figure 2.3a with a text slide selected by default.
- Click the **Title Only layout** to change the layout of the new slide. Click in the Title placeholder and enter the title **Slide Show Tools** as shown in the figure.
- Click outside the title placeholder. Pull down the **Insert menu** and click the **Table command** to display the Insert Table dialog box in Figure 2.3a.
- Enter **2** as the number of columns and **4** as the number of rows. Click **OK**. The table will be inserted into the document.
- Close the task pane. Save the presentation.

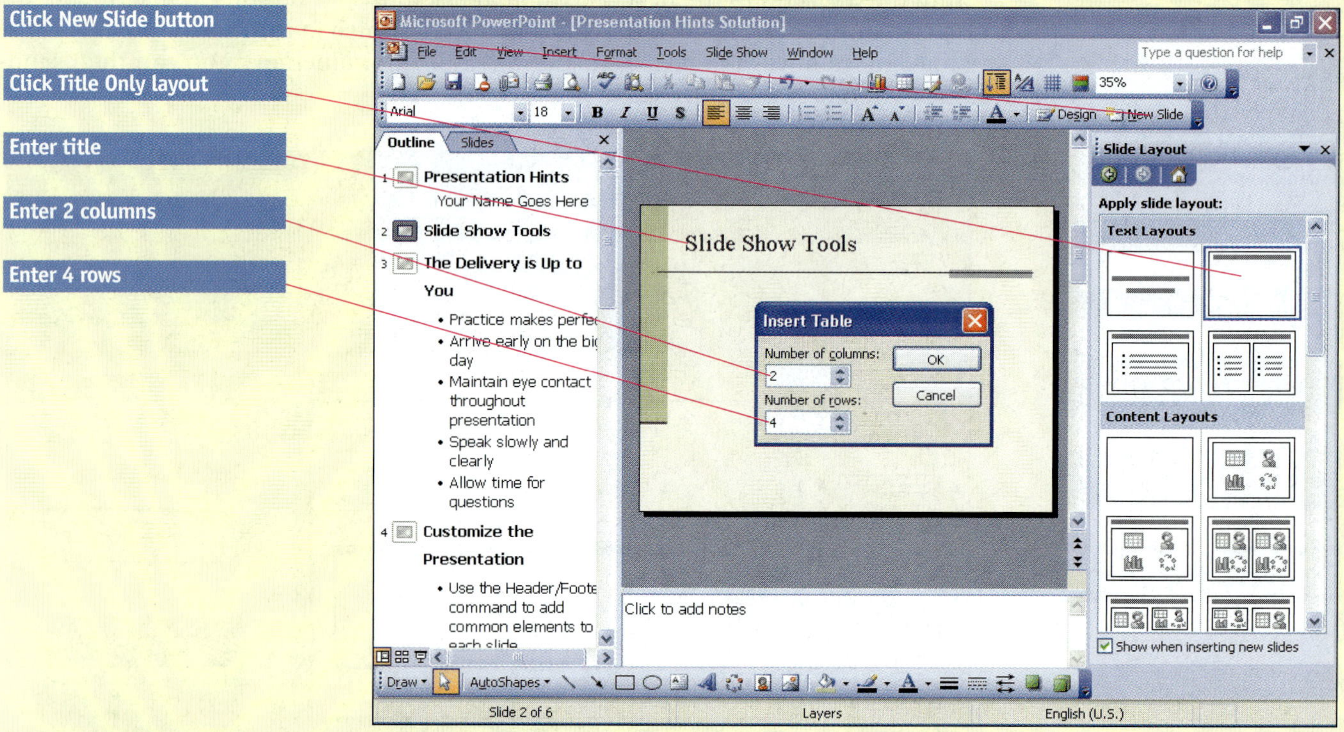

(a) Create the Table (step 1)

FIGURE 2.3 Hands-on Exercise 1

Step 2: Complete the Table

- Click anywhere in the table to select the table and display a hashed border.
- Click and drag the vertical line dividing the two columns to the left so that the first column is narrower and the second column is wider. Drag the left and/or right border to make the table larger or smaller as necessary.
- Enter the text into the table as shown in Figure 2.3b. Text is entered into each cell independently of the other cells.
- Click in a cell, type the appropriate text, then press the **Tab key** to move to the next cell. Complete the table as shown in the figure.
- Click and drag to select multiple cells simultaneously, then use the various buttons on the Formatting toolbar to format the text in these cells as you see fit. Click outside the table to deselect it.
- Save the presentation.

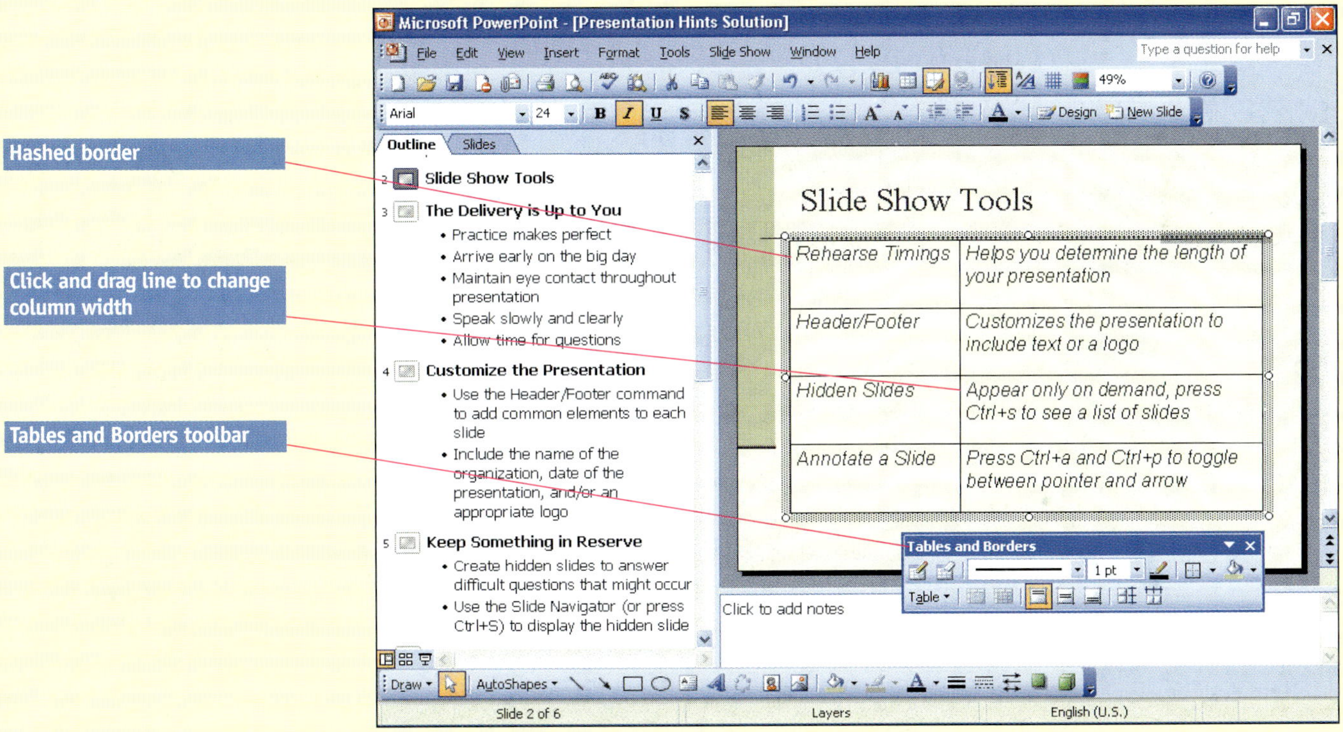

(b) Complete the Table (step 2)

FIGURE 2.3 Hands-on Exercise 1 (*continued*)

THE TABLES AND BORDERS TOOLBAR

The Tables and Borders toolbar contains a variety of tools for use in creating and/or modifying a table. Click the Border Color button (to change the color) or click the Border Width down arrow (to change the thickness), then use the mouse (the pointer changes to a pencil) to paint the table borders according to the new settings. Click the down arrow on the Table button to see the commands that are available. If you do not see the toolbar, pull down the View menu, click (or point to) the Toolbars command, then click the Tables and Borders toolbar.

Step 3: Add the Slide Footer

- Pull down the **View menu** and click the **Header and Footer command** to display the Header and Footer dialog box in Figure 2.3c.
- Click the **Slide tab**. Click the check box for the Date and time, then click the **Option button** to Update the date automatically. The presentation will always show the current date when this option is in effect. (Alternatively, you can choose the option to enter a fixed date.)
- Check the Slide number and Footer check boxes as shown. Click in the text box associated with the footer and enter the appropriate text to reflect your school or university.
- Check the box, **Don't show on title slide**, to suppress the footer on the first slide. Click the **Apply to All button** to accept these settings and close the Header and Footer dialog box.
- Save the presentation.

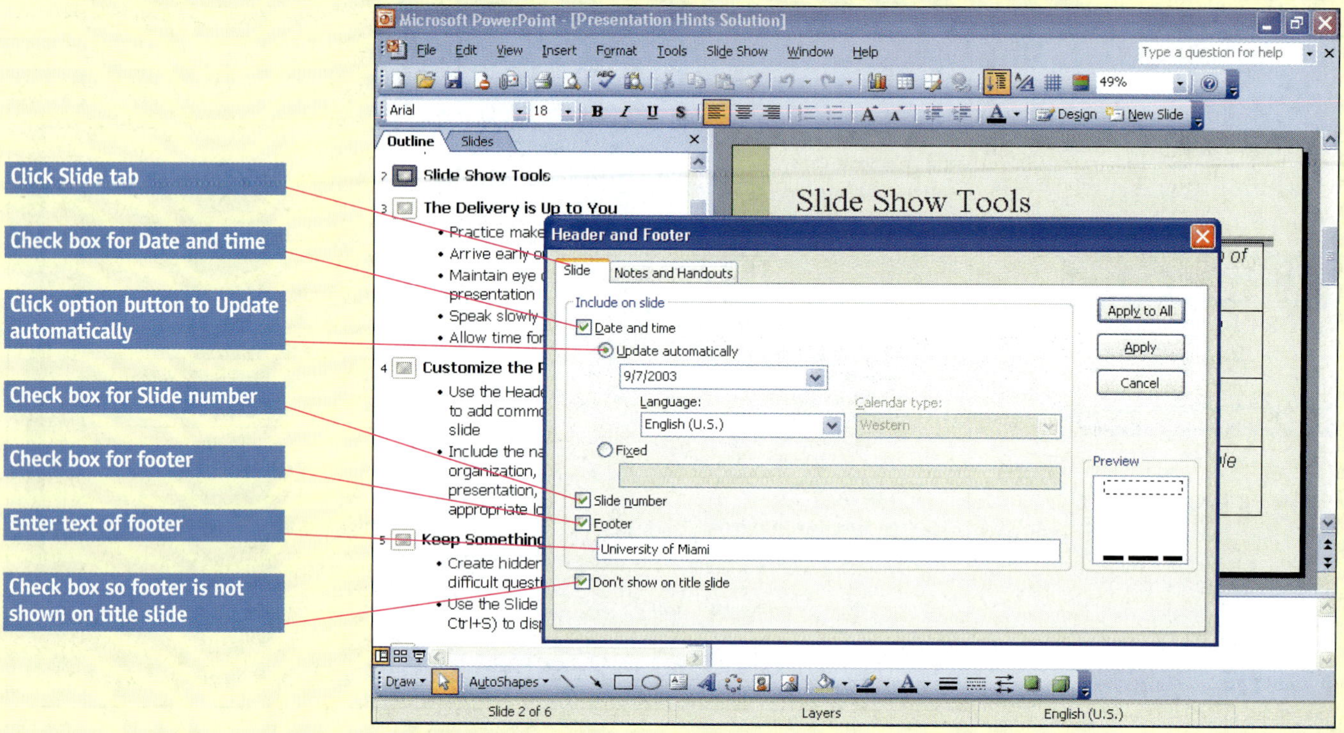

(c) Add the Slide Footer (step 3)

FIGURE 2.3 Hands-on Exercise 1 (*continued*)

CUSTOMIZE THE TABLE LAYOUT

Click and drag to select one or more cells within a table, then pull down the Format menu and click the Tables command to display the Format Table dialog box. You can change the border, fill, or text alignment by clicking the appropriate tab within the dialog box, then executing the appropriate command. Click the Undo command if the result is different from what you intended. You might also want to set a time limit, because there are almost too many options from which to choose.

Step 4: Send for Review

- Pull down the **File menu**, click (or point to) the **Send To command**, then choose **Mail Recipient (for Review)**. Your e-mail program will open automatically and display a new message as shown in Figure 2.3d. (Skip this step if your e-mail program does not appear, as might happen in a computer lab.)
- The subject, attachment, and text of the note are entered automatically for you. The name of the current presentation, "Presentation Hints Solution" appears in both the subject line and the attachment.
- Enter the e-mail address of a recipient (e.g., a fellow student). You can enter the addresses of multiple individuals if you want more than one person to review the presentation. Sign your name in the message area and click the **Send button**.
- Normally, you would need the reviewer to return the presentation to you with his or her comments.
- We have, however, supplied a presentation for you with comments from our reviewer, so that you do not have to wait for a response.

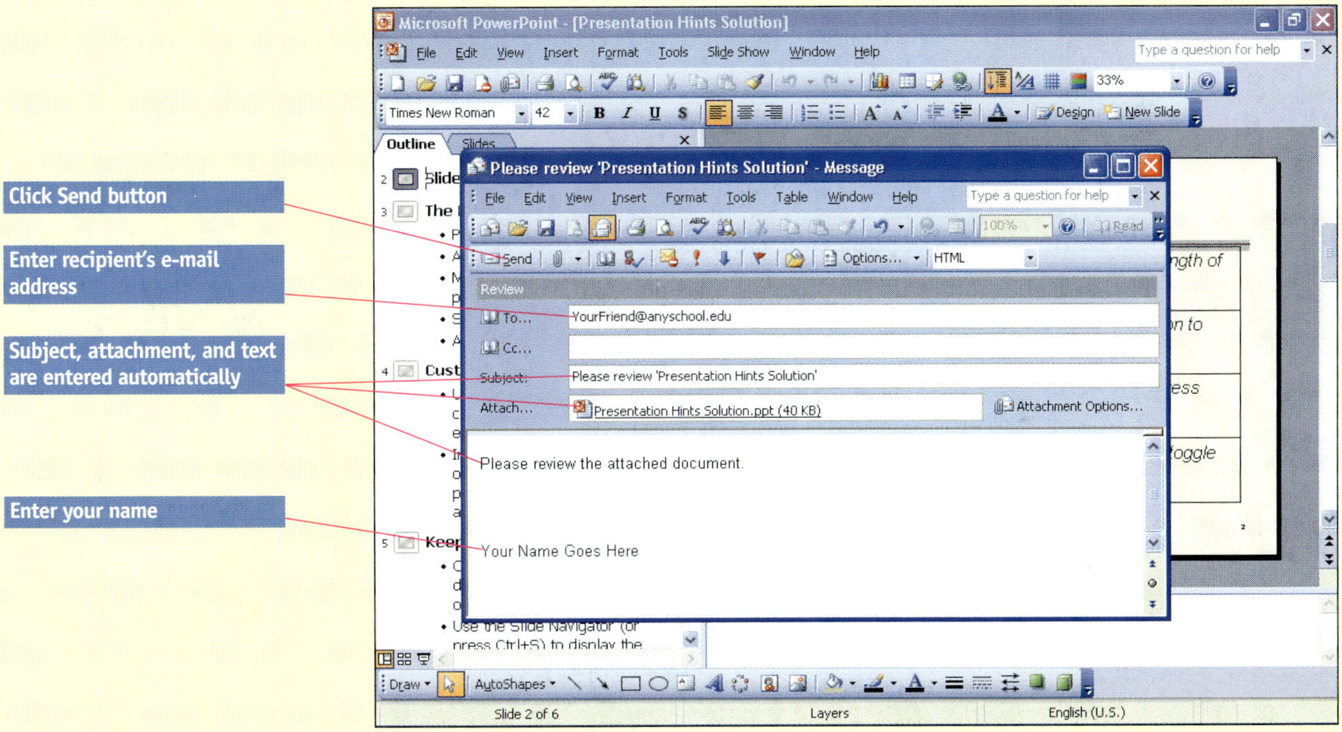

(d) Send for Review (step 4)

FIGURE 2.3 Hands-on Exercise 1 (*continued*)

SEND THE PRESENTATION AS AN ATTACHMENT

Send the completed presentation as an attachment, as opposed to sending it for review. Pull down the File menu, click the Send To command, then choose the second option to send the open presentation as an attachment to an e-mail message. This is an option with which you are probably familiar and is similar in concept to mailing a Word document or Excel workbook. (PowerPoint presentations are generally large files, and thus you may want to compress the file before sending it.)

Step 5: Compare and Merge Presentations

- Pull down the **Tools menu** and click the **Compare and Merge Presentations command**. Select the **Bob's Comments** presentation (which represents a review of your presentation) in the Exploring PowerPoint folder. Click the **Merge button**.
- Click **Continue** if you see a message indicating that one presentation was not sent for review. The Revisions Pane opens as shown in Figure 2.3e. Click the **Outline** and **Gallery tabs** in the left and right panes, respectively.
- Select the title slide. Click the icon to the right of the title slide to see suggestions from the reviewer (Robert Grauer in this example). Check the box to accept all changes to the title slide.
- Click the **Next Item button** on the Reviewing toolbar to move to the next revision. This takes you to the third slide, titled "The Delivery is Up to You". Check the box to accept all changes on this slide.
- Continue to click the **Next Item button** and accept all suggested changes until you reach the last slide. PowerPoint indicates that you have reached the end of the presentation and asks if you want to continue. Click **Cancel** since you have reviewed all of the changes.
- Click the **End Review button** on the Reviewing toolbar. Click **Yes** when asked whether to end the review. Save the presentation.

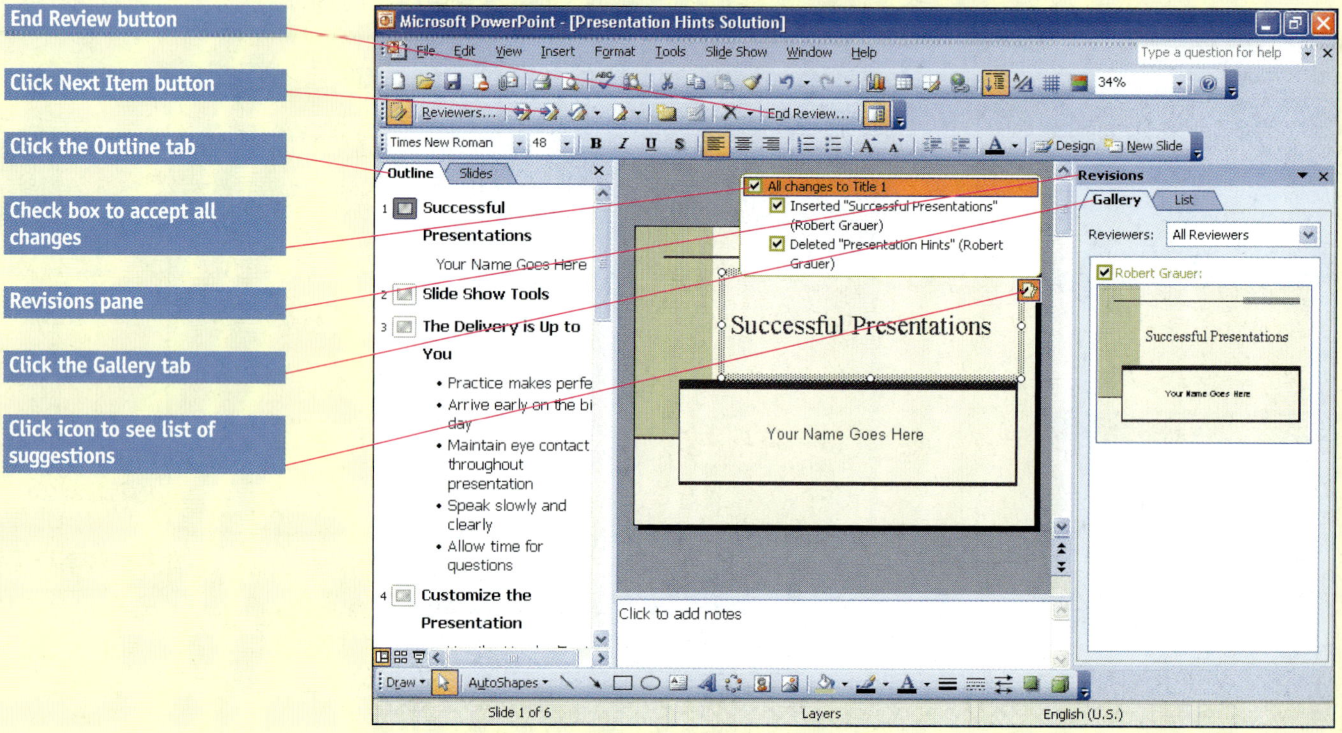

(e) Compare and Merge Presentations (step 5)

FIGURE 2.3 Hands-on Exercise 1 (*continued*)

INSERT COMMENTS INTO THE PRESENTATION

Pull down the Insert menu and click the Comment command (or click the Insert Comment button on the Reviewing toolbar) to insert a comment. The comments are for information only and do not change the actual presentation. Click the Markup button on the Reviewing toolbar to toggle the comment (and reviewer remarks) on and off.

Step 6: Rehearse the Presentation

- Press **Ctrl+Home** to return to the first slide. Pull down the **Slide Show menu** and click the **Rehearse Timings command**.
- The first slide appears in the Slide Show view. The Rehearsal toolbar is displayed in the upper-left corner of the screen. Speak as though you were presenting the slide, then click the mouse to register the elapsed time for that slide and move to the next slide.
- The second slide in the presentation should appear as shown in Figure 2.3f. Speak as though you were presenting the slide and, as you do, watch the Rehearsal toolbar:
  - The time for the specific slide (1 minute and 5 seconds) is displayed in the Slide Time box. The cumulative time for the presentation (1 minute and 50 seconds) is also shown.
  - Click the **Repeat button** to redo the timing for the slide.
  - Click the **Pause button** to (temporarily) stop the clock. Click the **Pause button** a second time to resume the clock.
  - Click the **Next button** to record the timing and move to the next slide.
- Continue rehearsing the show until you reach the end of the presentation. You should see a dialog box at the end of the presentation that indicates the total time of the slide show.
- Click **Yes** when asked whether you want to record the new timings. PowerPoint returns to the Slide Sorter view and records the timings under each slide.
- Pull down the **Slide Show menu** and click the **Set Up Show command** to display the Set Up Show dialog box.
- Check the option button to advance slides **Manually** (otherwise the slides will be automatically advanced according to the times you just recorded). Click **OK** to accept the settings and close the dialog box.

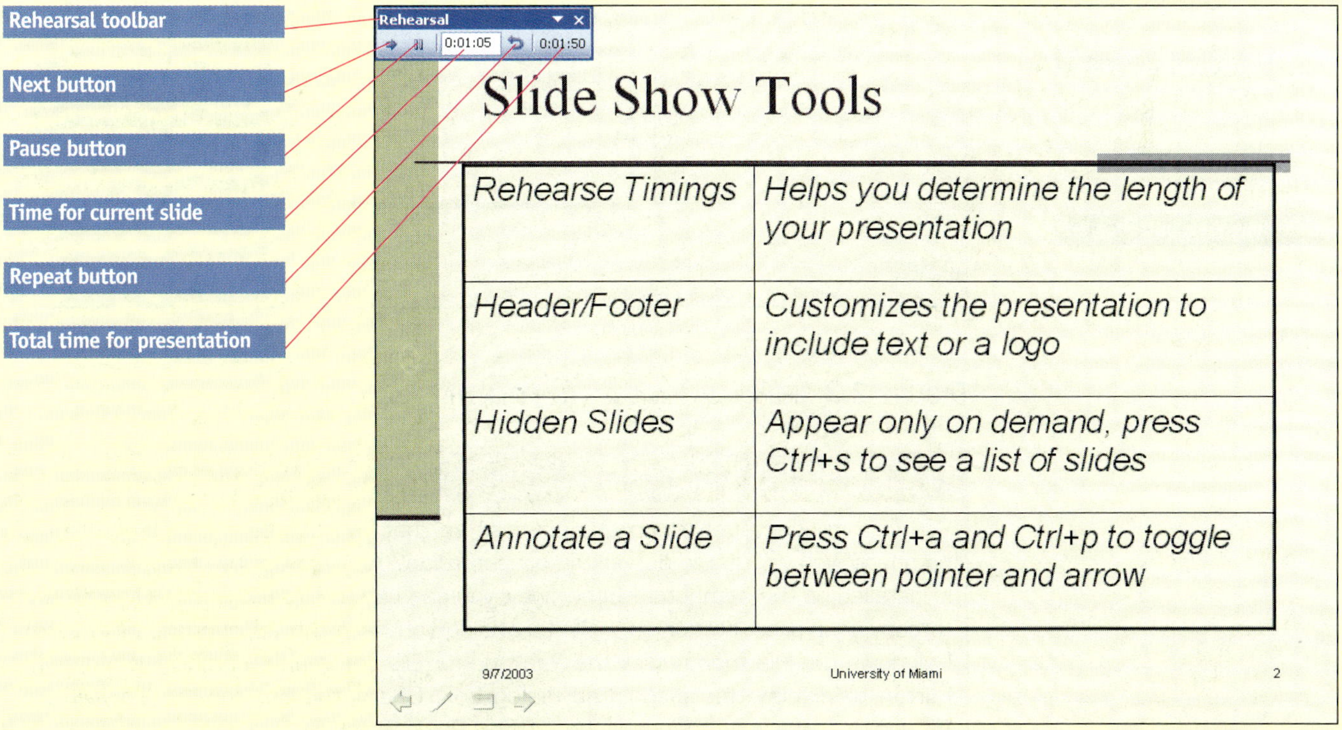

(f) Rehearse the Presentation (step 6)

FIGURE 2.3 Hands-on Exercise 1 (*continued*)

Step 7: **Hide a Slide**

- If necessary, click the **down arrow** on the Zoom box to zoom to 100%. The slides are larger and easier to read.
- Select (click) the fifth slide (Keep Something in Reserve) then click the **Hide Slide button** as shown in Figure 2.3g. The slide remains in the presentation, but it will *not* be displayed during the slide show.
- The Hide Slide button functions as a toggle switch. Click it once and the slide is hidden. Click the command a second time and the slide is no longer hidden. Leave the slide hidden.
- Click Slide 1, then click the **Slide Show View button** and move quickly through the presentation. You will not see the slide titled Keep Something in Reserve because it has been hidden. (You can still access this slide during the presentation as described in the next step.)
- Save the presentation.

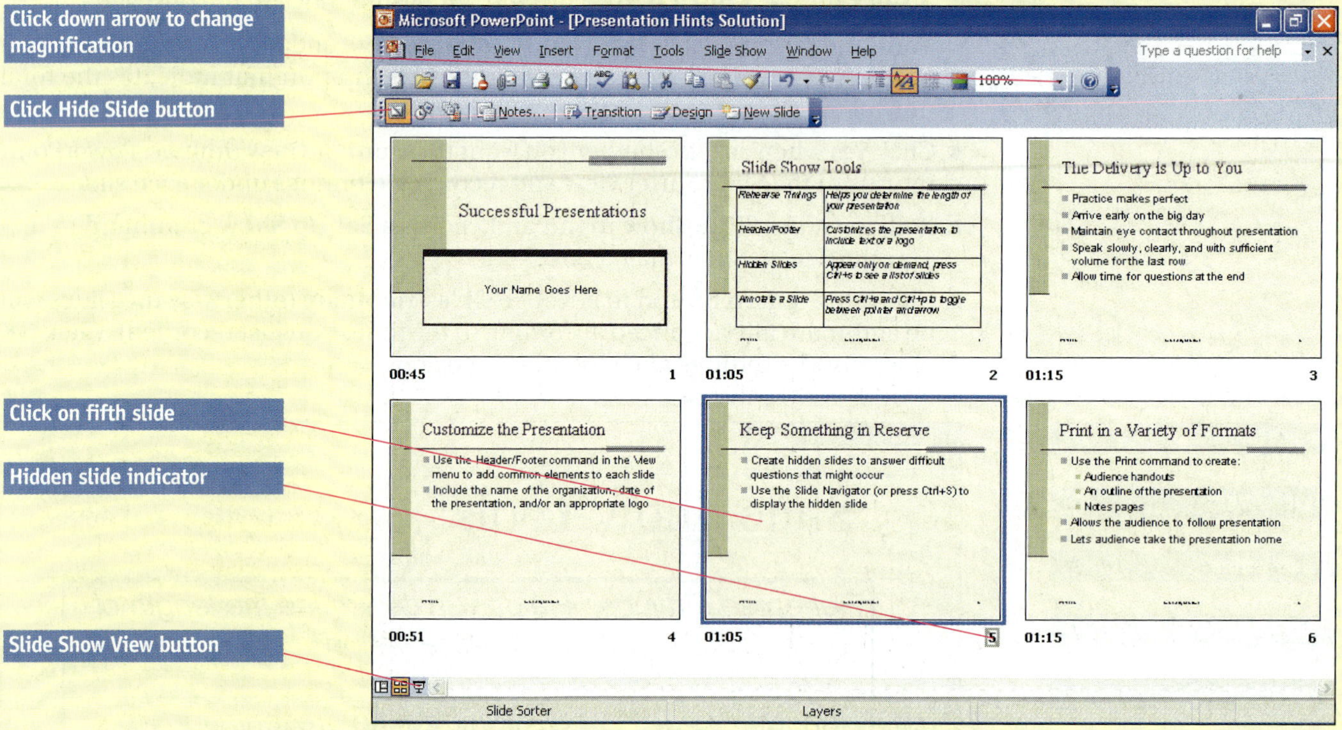

(g) Hide a Slide (step 7)

FIGURE 2.3 Hands-on Exercise 1 *(continued)*

PACKAGE FOR CD

Will your presentation fit on a floppy disk so that you can take it with you to the computer you will use to deliver the presentation? Are you positive that PowerPoint is installed on the computer? Either way, you can use the Package for CD command to copy your presentation to a CD (providing you have the appropriate hardware). Pull down the File menu, click the Package for CD command, and click the options button to display the associated dialog box. Check the box for the PowerPoint Viewer to play presentations without using PowerPoint.

Step 8: Display the Hidden Slide

- Press **Ctrl+Home** to move to the first slide in the presentation. Click the **Slide Show View button** above the status bar to show the presentation. You should see the title slide.
- Click the **left mouse button** or press the **PgDn key** to move from one slide to the next. Look at the slide number in the lower-right corner of each slide as the show progresses. You will see slides, 1, 2, 3, 4, and 6; i.e., you will skip slide 5 because it is hidden.
- Right click anywhere on the slide to display a context-sensitive menu as shown in Figure 2.3h. (You can also click the **up arrow** in the lower-left portion of the screen).
- Click the **Go to Slide command** to display a list of the slides in your presentation. Click the **fifth slide** to display the hidden slide. (Note the parentheses around the number 5 to indicate the slide is hidden.)

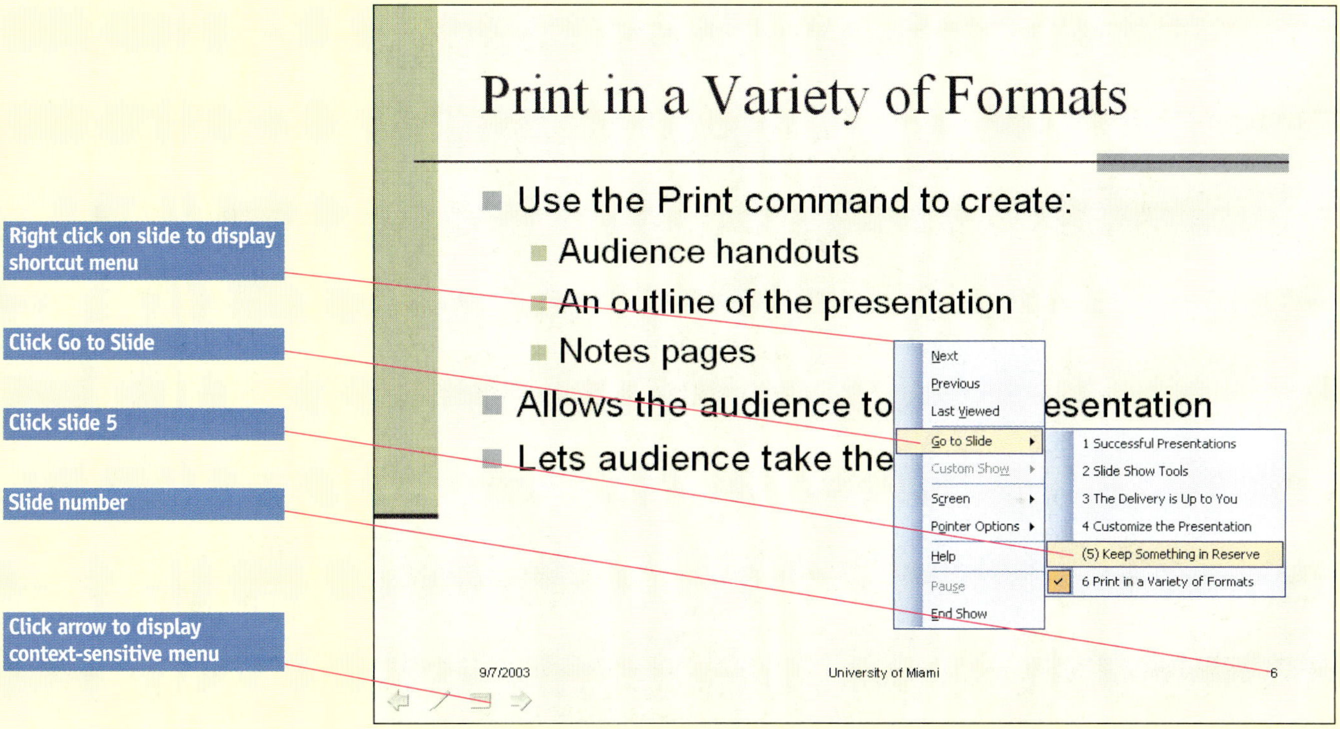

(h) Display the Hidden Slide (step 8)

FIGURE 2.3 Hands-on Exercise 1 (*continued*)

SETTING UP A SLIDE SHOW

You can start a slide show on any slide, advance the slides automatically according to preset timings (established through the Rehearse Timings command), and/or loop through the slide show continually until the user presses the Esc key. Pull down the Slide Show menu, click the Set Up Show command to display the associated dialog box, then experiment with the various options. Click OK to accept the settings and close the dialog box.

Step 9: Annotate a Slide

- You should see slide 5. Press **Ctrl+P** to change the mouse arrow to a point, then click and drag to annotate the slide as shown in Figure 2.3i. Type the letter **E.** The annotation disappears.
- Click the **pen icon** (at the lower left of the slide) to display the pointer options, and then click any of the available options. You can change the pointer thickness and/or change the annotation color.
- Draw a new annotation on the slide, then use the **PgDn key** to move to the last slide in the presentation. (Clicking with either the left or right mouse button has no effect when the mouse is set for annotation.)
- Press **Ctrl+A** to return the mouse to an arrow. Click the left mouse button repeatedly to finish the show, then click **Discard** when asked whether to keep the annotations.
- Exit PowerPoint if you do not want to continue with the next hands-on exercise at this time.

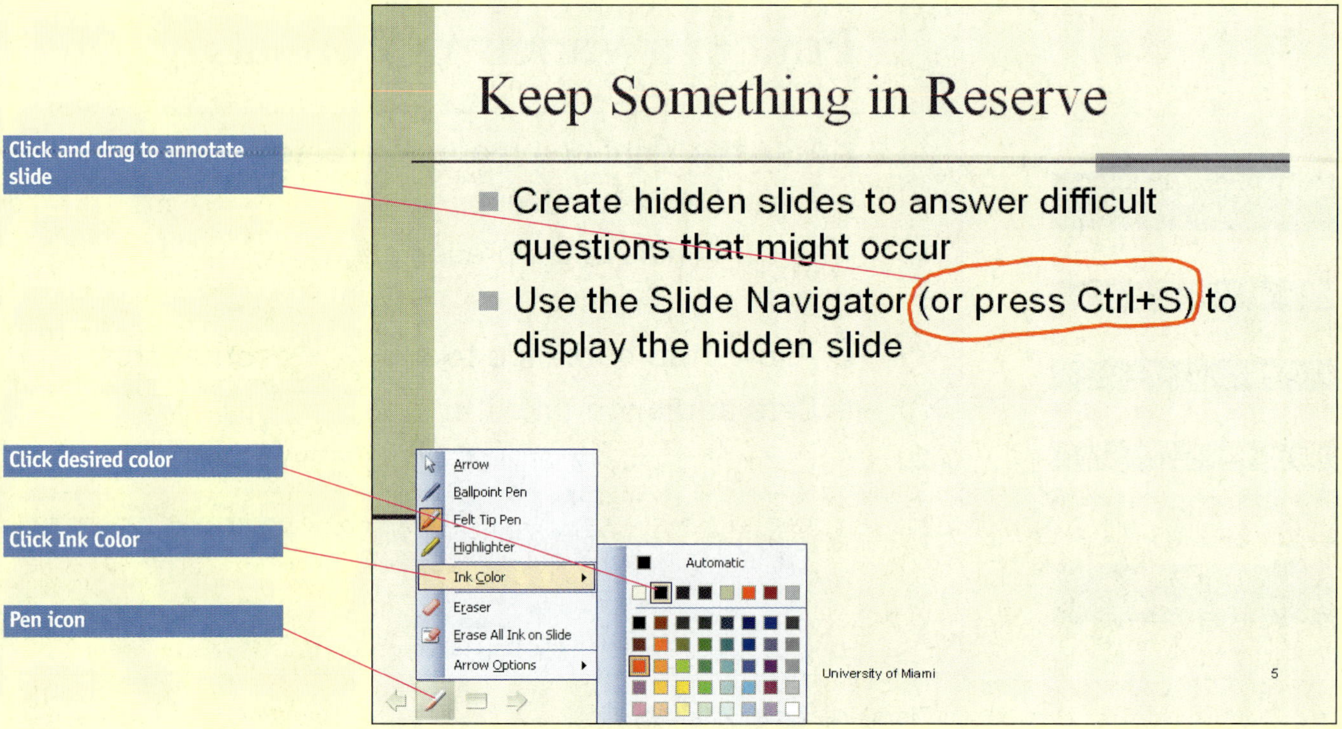

(i) Annotate a Slide (step 9)

FIGURE 2.3 Hands-on Exercise 1 (*continued*)

USE KEYBOARD SHORTCUTS DURING THE SLIDE SHOW

Press Ctrl+S to display a list of the slides in a presentation, including the hidden slides, then double click the slide you want to view. You can also type a number plus the Enter key to go to a specific slide, or press the letter H plus the Enter key to display the next hidden slide. Use Ctrl+P to change the mouse pointer to a point to annotate the slide, then press E to erase the annotations. Press Ctrl+A to change the mouse pointer back to an arrow. If you can't remember these shortcuts, press the F1 key to see the entire list.

POWERPOINT AND THE INTERNET

The ***Internet*** and ***World Wide Web*** are thoroughly integrated into all applications in Microsoft Office in three important ways. First, you can download resources from any Web page for inclusion in a PowerPoint presentation, as you will see in our next hands-on exercise. Second, you can insert hyperlinks into any Office document, then click those links to display the associated Web page in your Web browser. And finally, you can convert any Office document into a Web page for display on your Web server or local area network.

Figure 2.4 illustrates how resources from the Internet can be used to enhance a PowerPoint presentation. The title slide in Figure 2.4a displays a photograph that was downloaded from the Smithsonian Institution's collection of online photographs. The photograph is displayed as an object on a slide and is typical of how most people use a photograph within a presentation. The slide in Figure 2.4b is much more dramatic, and indeed does not even look like a PowerPoint slide. It too displays a photograph, but as background, rather than an object. The text has been entered into a ***text box*** using the appropriate tool on the Drawing toolbar. (You can right click the text box after it has been created, so that the box will expand and wrap text automatically if additional text is entered.)

Regardless of how you choose to use a photograph, your first task is to access the Web and locate the resource. Thus, you start your Web browser, then you use a search engine to locate the required information (e.g., a photograph of a dinosaur). Once this is done, right click on the photograph to display the context-sensitive menu in the figure, then click the Save Picture As command to download the file to your hard drive. Next, you start PowerPoint where you use the ***Insert Picture command*** to insert the picture that was just downloaded into a presentation. You can also use the ***Insert Hyperlink command*** to insert a ***hyperlink*** onto a slide, which you can click during the slide show, and provided you have an Internet connection, your Web browser will display the associated page.

Copyright Protection

A ***copyright*** provides legal protection to a written or artistic work, including literary, dramatic, musical, and artistic works such as poetry, novels, movies, songs, and computer software and architecture. It gives the author of a work the exclusive right to the use and duplication of that work. A copyright does not, however, protect facts, ideas, systems, or methods of operation, although it may protect the way these things are expressed.

The owner of the copyright may sell or give up a portion of his or her rights; for example, an author may give distribution rights to a publisher and/or grant movie rights to a studio. ***Infringement of a copyright*** occurs any time a right reserved by the copyright owner is violated without permission of the owner. Anything on the Internet should be considered copyrighted unless the document specifically says it is in the ***public domain***, in which case the author is giving everyone the right to freely reproduce and distribute the material. Does copyright protection prevent you from quoting a document found on the Web in a research paper? Does copyright protection imply that you cannot download an image for inclusion in a term paper? (Facts themselves are not covered by copyright, so you can use statistical data without fear of infringement.)

The answer to what you can use from the Web depends on the amount of the information you reference, as well as the intended use of that information. It is considered ***fair use***, and thus not an infringement of copyright, to use a portion of a work for educational, nonprofit purposes, or for the purpose of critical review or commentary. In other words, you can use a quote, downloaded image, or other information from the Web, provided you cite the original work in your footnotes and/or bibliography.

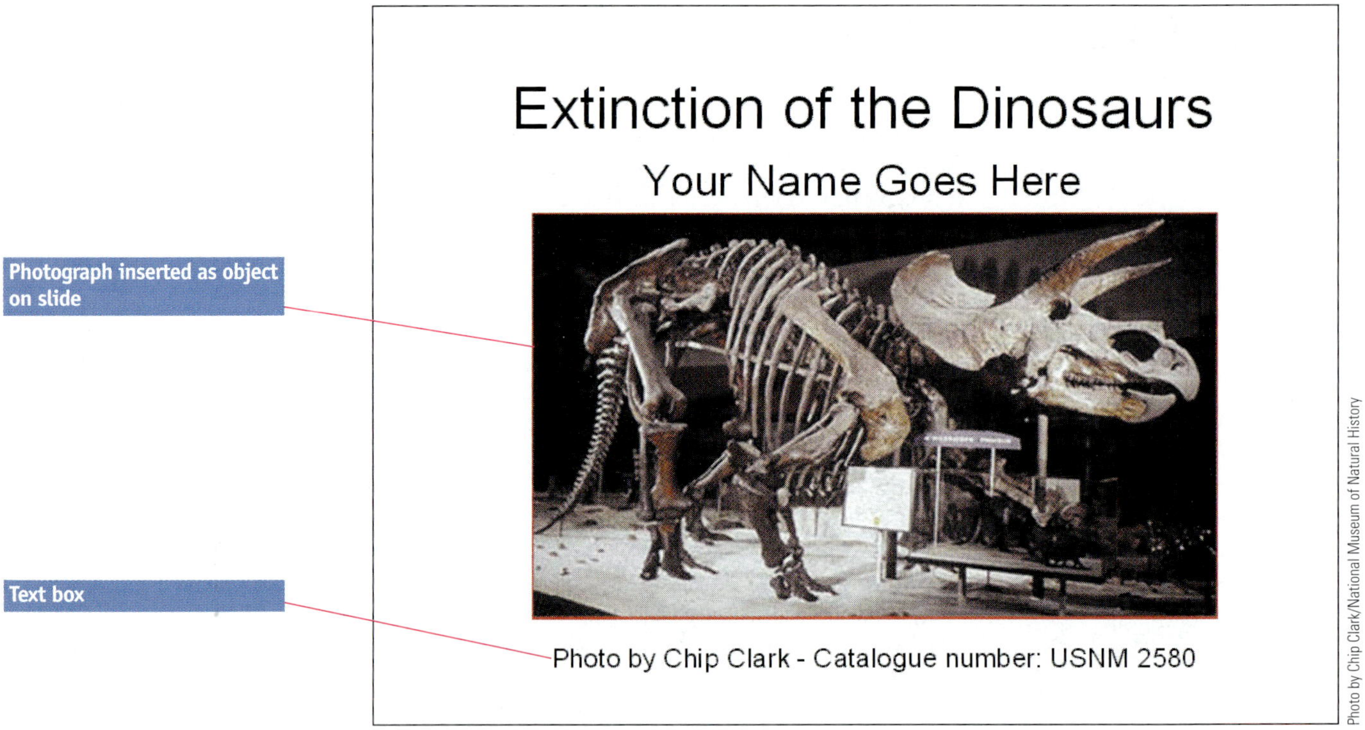

(a) Title Slide

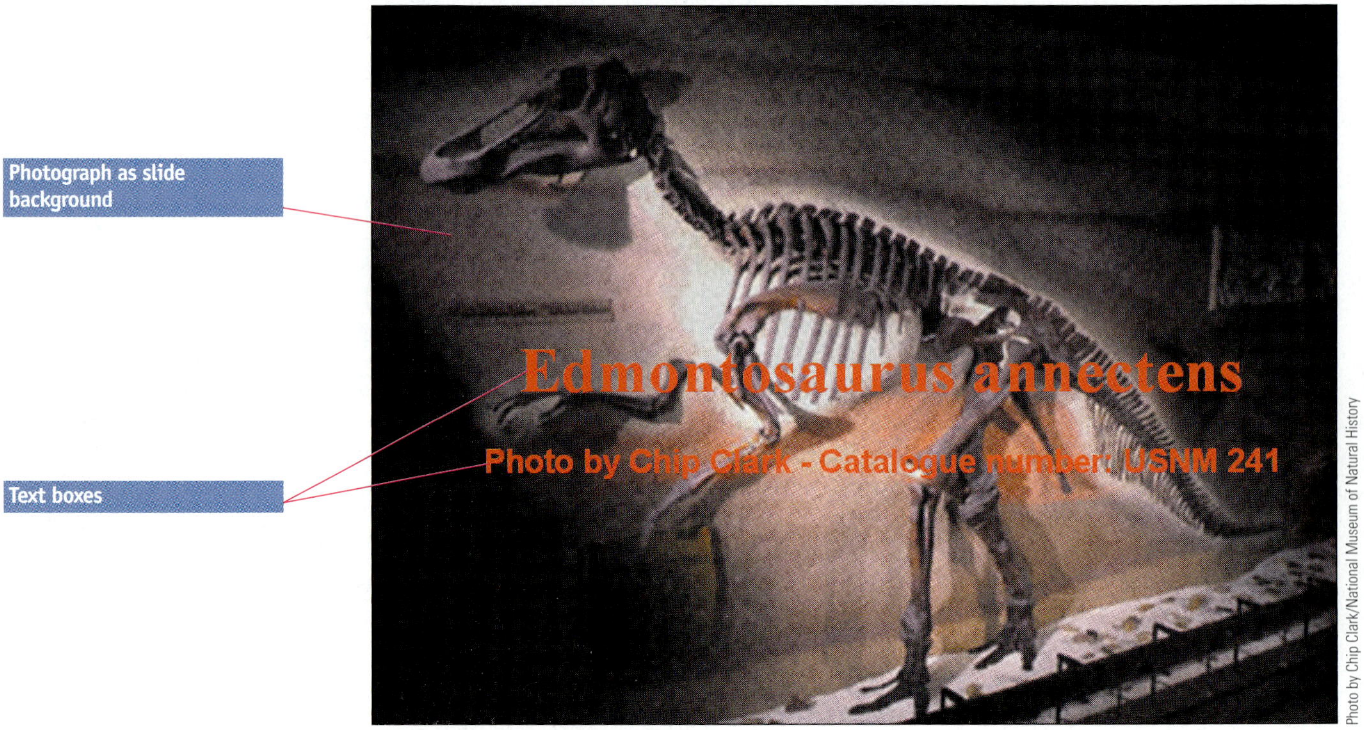

(b) Photograph as Background

FIGURE 2.4 The Web as a Resource

hands-on exercise

2 The Internet as a Resource

Objective To import slides from an outline; to download a picture from the Internet and use it in a PowerPoint presentation. Use Figure 2.5 as a guide.

Step 1: Insert the Word Outline

- Start PowerPoint, which in turn opens a new blank presentation with the title slide already selected. Close the task pane. Click the **Outline tab** in the left pane.
- Enter **Extinction of the Dinosaurs** as the title of the presentation and your name as the author. Save the presentation as **Extinction of the Dinosaurs**.
- Pull down the **Insert menu** and click the **Slides from Outline command** to display the Insert Outline dialog box in Figure 2.5a.
- Click the **drop-down arrow** on the Look in list box to select the Exploring PowerPoint folder. Select the **Extinction of the Dinosaurs** Word document.
- Click the **Insert button**. The Word document is imported into the presentation and converted to individual slides.

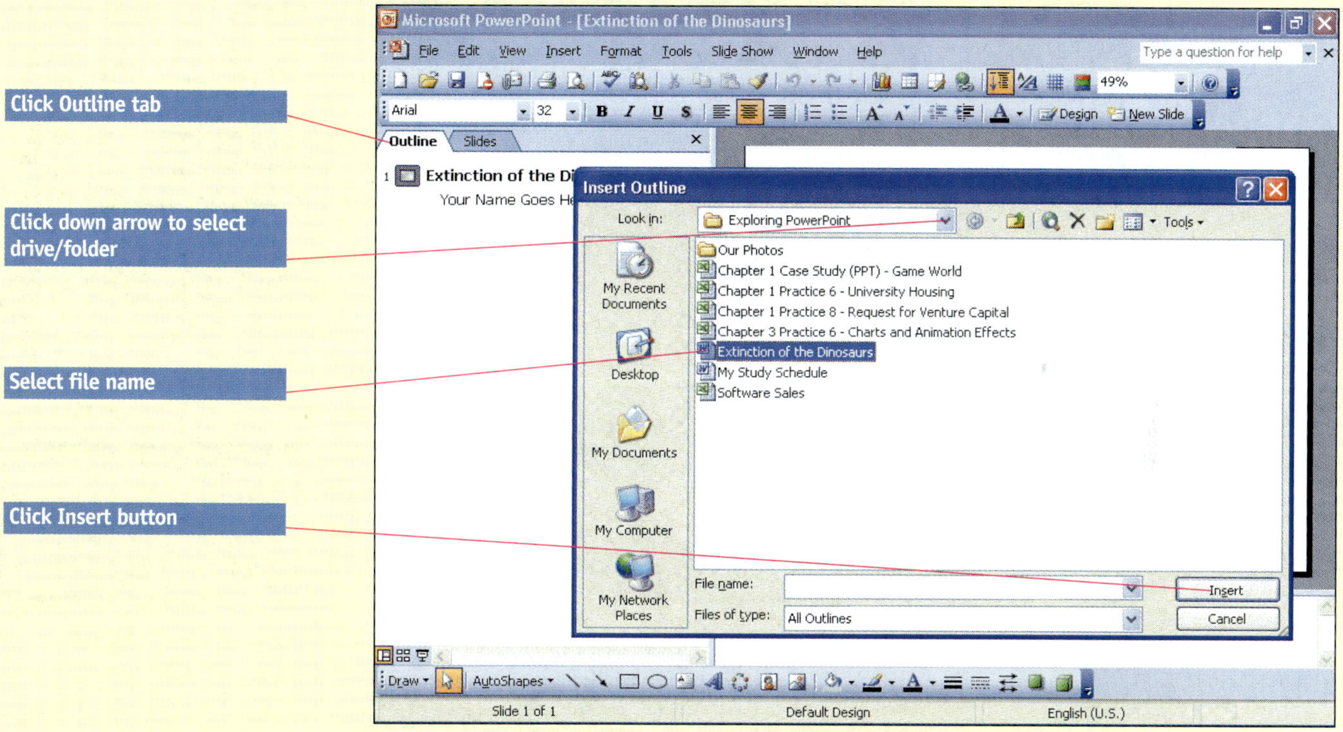

(a) Insert the Word Outline (step 1)

FIGURE 2.5 Hands-on Exercise 2

DISPLAY THE FULL MENUS

Pull down any menu to see if there is a double arrow at the bottom of the menu. If you see the arrow, PowerPoint is displaying only the commands it thinks you need, and we suggest that you display the full menus instead. Pull down the View menu, click the Toolbars command, and click the Customize command. Click the Options tab and check the box to Always show full menus. Pull down any menu; the double arrow has disappeared, and you see the full set of available commands.

Step 2: Complete the Outline

- You should see the text of the presentation as shown in Figure 2.5b. Click on the fourth slide that describes the origin of the word *dinosaur*.
- Right click the word "deinos" that is flagged as a misspelling because it is not in the English dictionary. Click **Ignore All** to accept the term without flagging it as a misspelling. Accept the spelling of "sauros" in similar fashion.
- Select (double click) **deinos**, then click the **Bold** and **Italic buttons** on the Formatting toolbar. (You can also use the Ctrl+B and Ctrl+I keyboard shortcuts that apply to all Office applications.)
- Use the **Format Painter** (see boxed tip) to copy this formatting to "sauros" and to "Sir Richard Owen".
- Click outside the placeholder to continue working.
- Save the presentation.

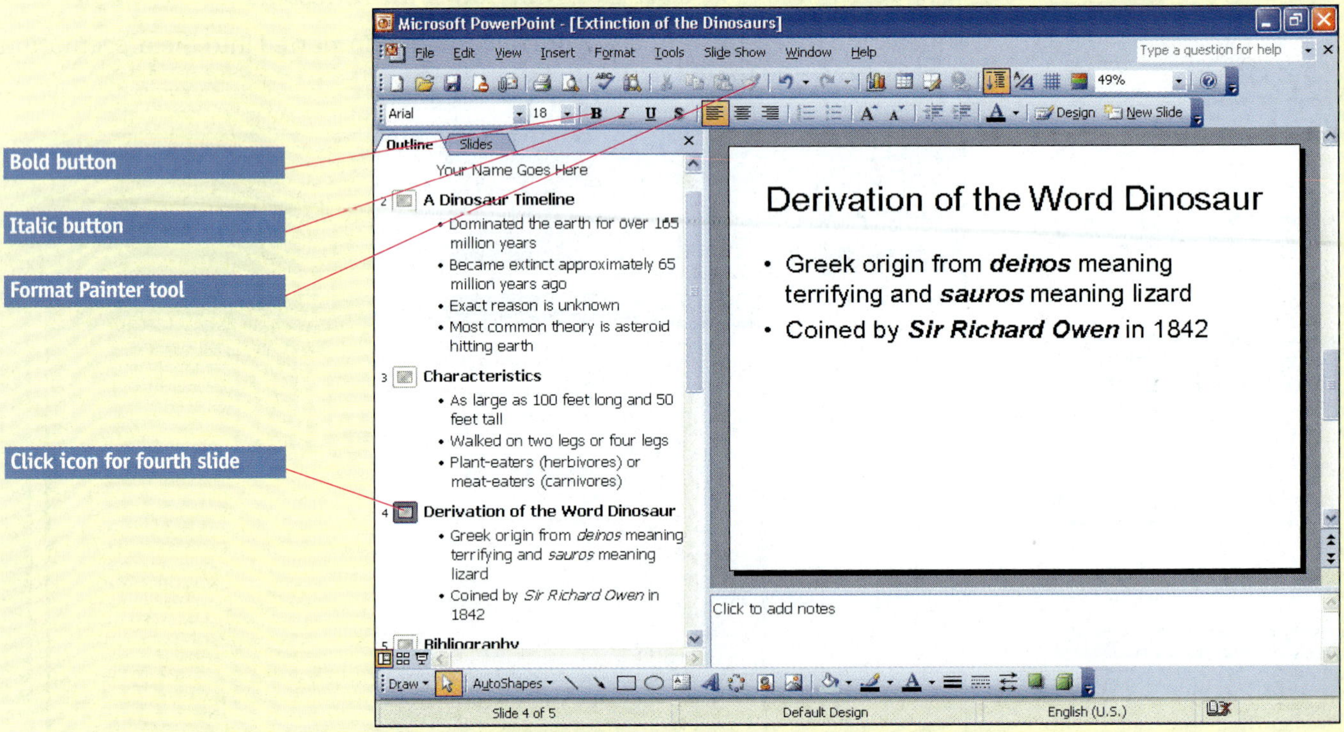

(b) Complete the Outline (step 2)

FIGURE 2.5 Hands-on Exercise 2 (*continued*)

THE FORMAT PAINTER

The Format Painter copies the formatting of the selected text to other places in a presentation. Select the text with the formatting you want to copy, then click or double click the Format Painter button on the Standard toolbar. Clicking the button will paint only one selection. Double clicking the button will paint multiple selections until the feature is turned off by again clicking the Format Painter button. Either way, the mouse pointer changes to a paintbrush, which you can drag over text to give it the identical formatting characteristics as the original selection.

Step 3: Search the Web

- Start Internet Explorer. Click the **Search button** on the Internet Explorer toolbar to open the Search pane as shown in Figure 2.5c. Enter **Smithsonian+ dinosaur** then click the **Search button**.
- The results of our search are displayed, but you will undoubtedly see a different set of links.
- Click the link to the **National Museum of Natural History** if it appears. Alternatively, you can click any link that seems promising.
- Try to find a page that contains one or more photographs. You can also enter the address (**www.nmnh.si.edu/paleo/dino**) directly to duplicate the remainder of the exercise.
- Click the **Close button** for the Search pane.

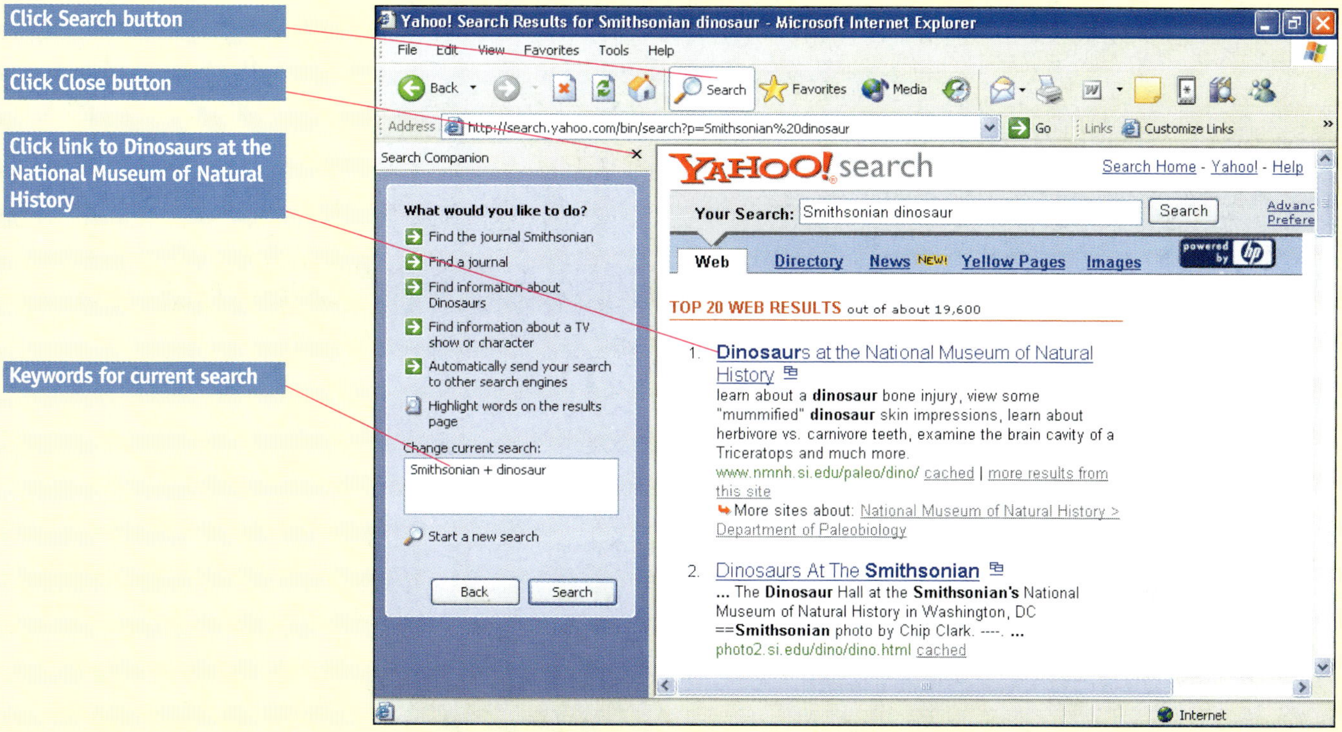

(c) Search the Web (step 3)

FIGURE 2.5 Hands-on Exercise 2 (*continued*)

ABOUT INTERNET EXPLORER

Which version of Internet Explorer are you using? It probably doesn't matter since all recent versions have essentially the same commands, except for slight variations in the toolbar and associated buttons. If your screen does not match ours, it is most likely because you are using a different version of the program. Pull down the Help menu and click the Help Internet Explorer command to see the version of Internet Explorer that is currently installed on your computer. The Help About command works for all Windows applications.

Step 4: Download the Photograph

- Select any picture on the site, click the **right mouse button** to display a shortcut menu, then click the **Save Picture As command** to display the Save As dialog box in Figure 2.5d.
- Click the **drop-down arrow** in the Save in list box to specify the drive and folder in which you want to save the graphic (e.g., the Exploring PowerPoint folder on drive C).
- The file name and file type are entered automatically. You can change the name, but do not change the file type.
- Click the **Save button** to download the image. Remember the file name and location, as you will need to access the file later in the exercise. The Save As dialog box closes automatically as soon as the picture has been downloaded.
- You need to download at least two pictures for your presentation; thus, repeat the process to download a second picture.

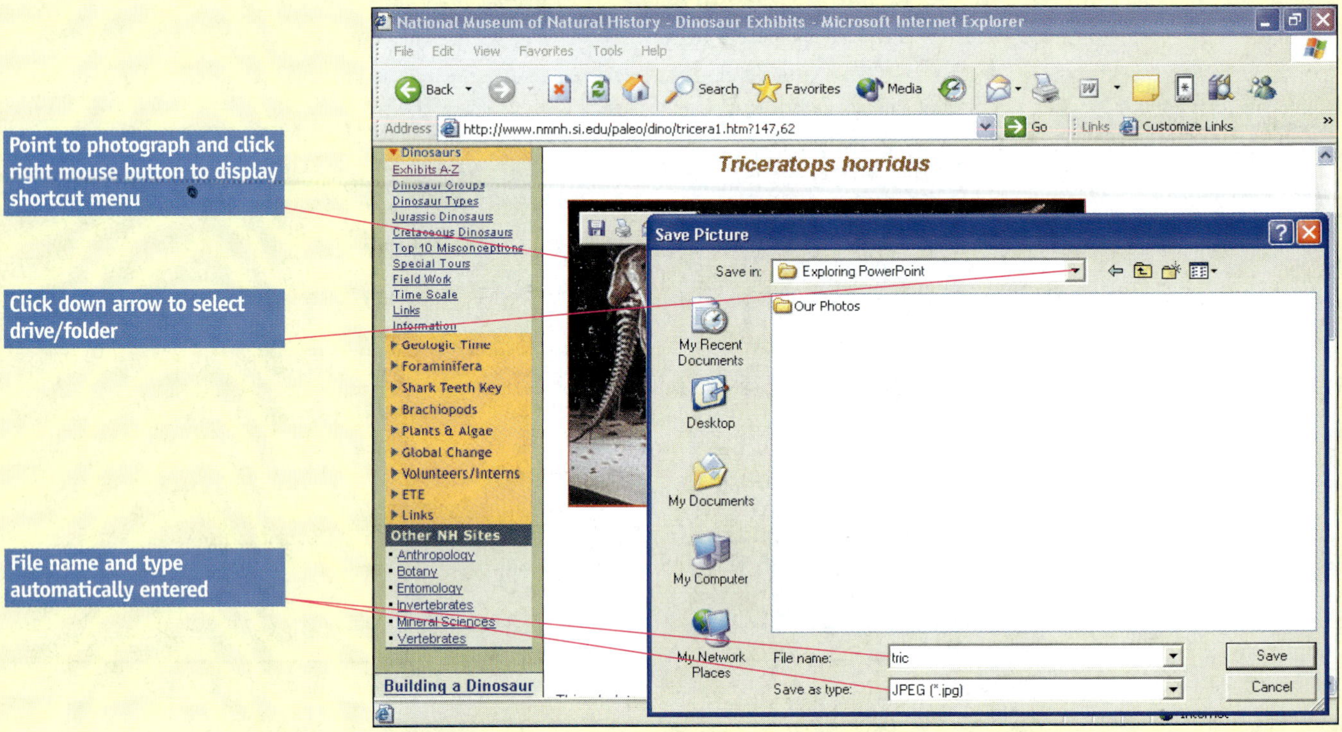

(d) Download the Photograph (step 4)

FIGURE 2.5 Hands-on Exercise 2 (*continued*)

MULTITASKING

Multitasking, the ability to run multiple applications at the same time, is one of the primary advantages of the Windows environment. Switching from one application to another is easy—just click the appropriate button on the Windows taskbar. (If the taskbar is not visible on your screen, it is because the Auto Hide feature is in effect—just point to the bottom edge of the window, and the taskbar will come into view.) You can also use the classic Alt+Tab shortcut. Press and hold the Alt key as you click the Tab key repeatedly to display icons for the open applications, then release the Tab key when the desired application is selected.

Step 5: Insert the Photograph

- Click the **PowerPoint button** on the taskbar, then press **Ctrl+Home** to display the first slide. Click below the placeholder for your name in the title slide.
- Pull down the **Insert menu**, point to (or click) **Picture**, then click **From File** to display the Insert Picture dialog box shown in Figure 2.5e.
- Click the **down arrow** on the Views button to select the **Preview view**. Click the **down arrow** on the Look in text box to select the drive and folder where you previously saved the pictures (for example, the Exploring PowerPoint folder on drive C).
- Select (click) one of the photographs you downloaded and a preview should appear within the Insert Picture dialog box. Click the **Insert button**.
- Click and drag the photograph to the bottom-right side of the slide. Click the slide title and drag the placeholder to the top of the slide.
- Click the placeholder for your name and drag it underneath the title. Click and drag the picture underneath your name. Size the picture as necessary.
- Save the presentation.

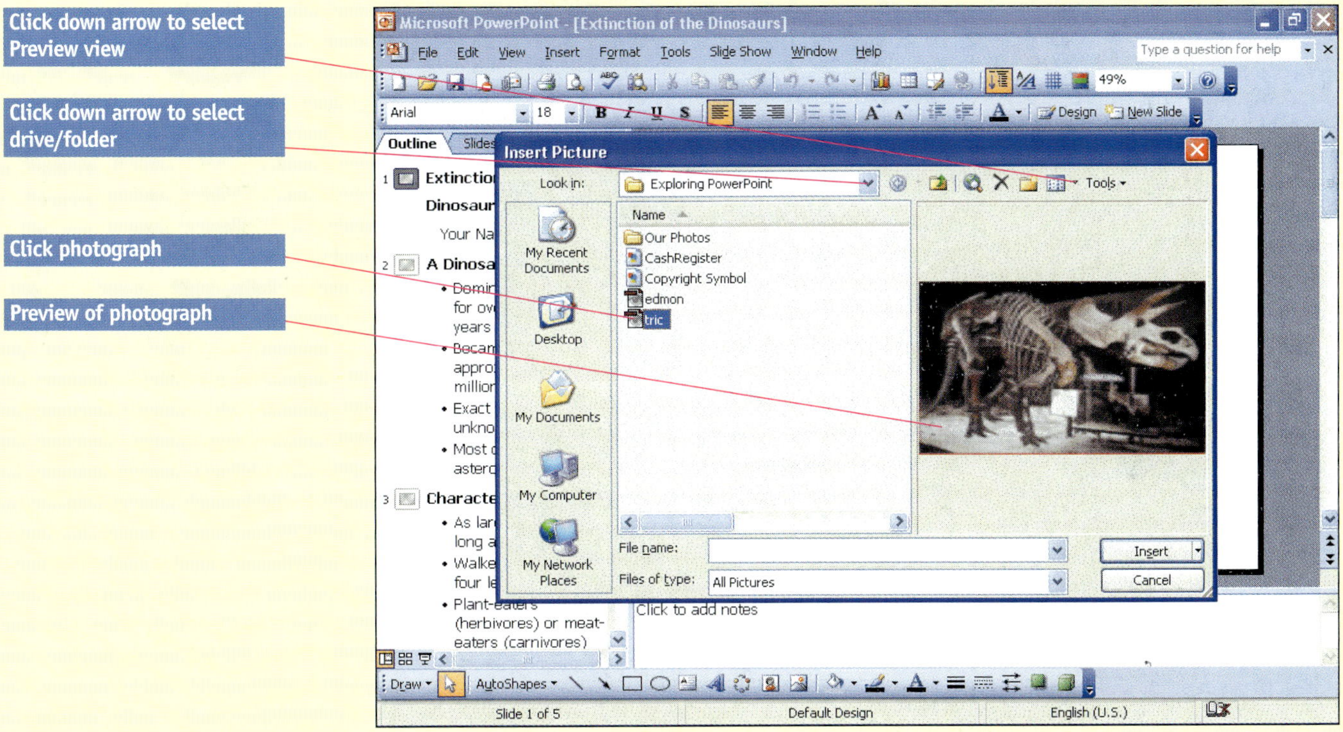

(e) Insert the Photograph (step 5)

FIGURE 2.5 Hands-on Exercise 2 (*continued*)

CROPPING A PICTURE

The Crop tool lets you eliminate (crop) part of a picture. Select (click) the picture to display the Picture toolbar and sizing handles. (If you do not see the Picture toolbar, pull down the View menu, click the Toolbars command, then click the Picture toolbar.) Click the Crop tool (the ScreenTip will display the name of the tool), then click and drag a sizing handle to crop the part of the picture you want to eliminate.

Step 6: Move and Size the Objects

- Your title slide should be similar to Figure 2.5f. Click the **Text Box tool**, then click and drag below the picture to create a text box. Enter text to cite the source for your picture as shown in Figure 2.5f. If necessary, change to an appropriate font and point size.
- Move and size the objects on the slide as necessary. To size an object:
  - ❑ Click the object to display the sizing handles.
  - ❑ Drag a corner handle (the mouse pointer changes to a double arrow) to change the length and width of the object simultaneously.
  - ❑ Drag a handle on the horizontal or vertical border to change one dimension.
- To move an object:
  - ❑ Click the object to display the sizing handles.
  - ❑ Point to any part of the border except a sizing handle (the mouse pointer changes to a four-sided arrow), then click and drag to move the object.
- Save the presentation.

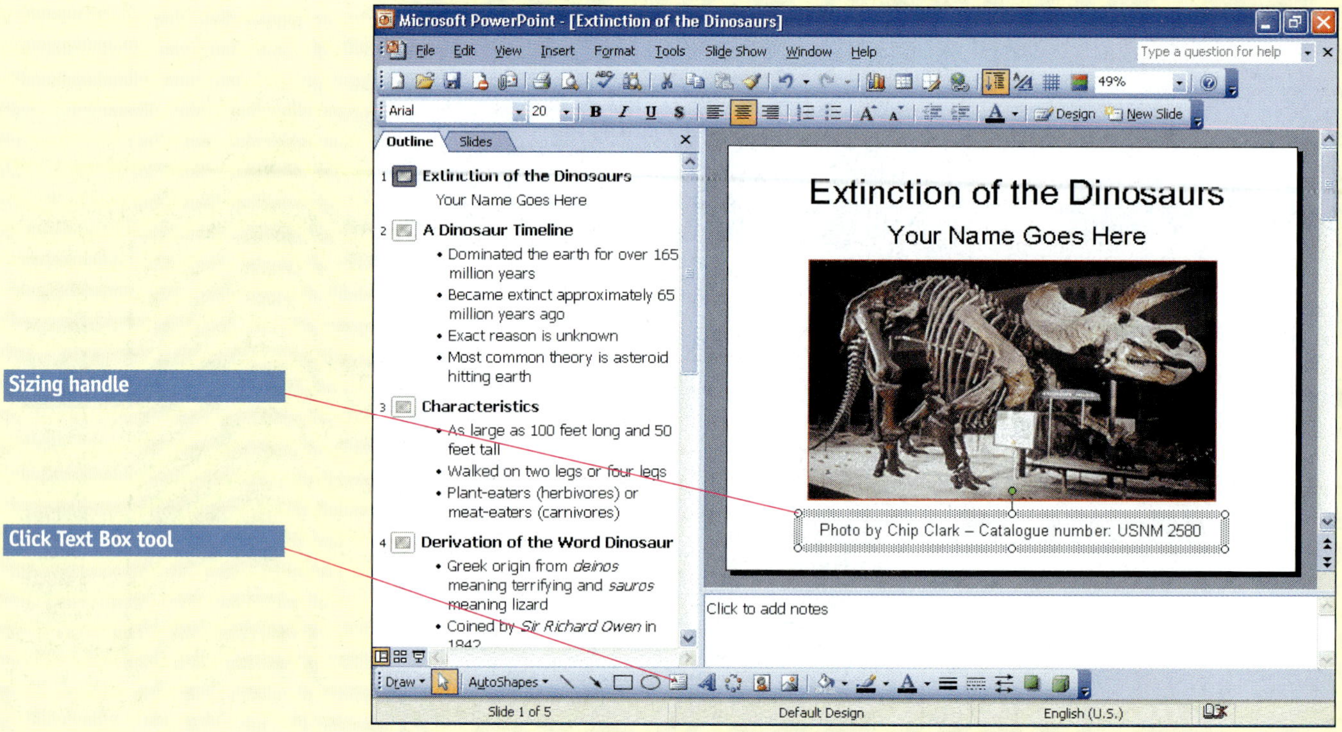

(f) Move and Size the Objects (step 6)

FIGURE 2.5 Hands-on Exercise 2 (*continued*)

ENTER THE URL AUTOMATICALLY

Use the Copy command to enter the URL into a presentation and ensure that it is entered correctly. Click in the Address bar of Internet Explorer to select the URL, then pull down the Edit menu and click the Copy command (or use the Ctrl+C shortcut). Switch to the PowerPoint presentation, click on the slide where you want to insert the URL, then pull down the Edit menu and click Paste (or press Ctrl+V). (The Cut command does not apply here, but it can be executed by the Ctrl+X keyboard shortcut. The "X" is supposed to remind you of a pair of scissors.)

Step 7: The Picture as Background

- Click the **New Slide button** to display slide layouts in the task pane. Click the blank slide layout.
- Pull down the **Format menu** and click the **Background command** to display the Background dialog box in Figure 2.5g.
- Click the **down arrow** in the Background fill list box, click **Fill Effects** to display the Fill Effects dialog box, click the **Picture tab**, then click the **Select Picture button** to display the Select Picture dialog box.
- Click the **down arrow** on the Look in text box to select the drive and folder where you saved the picture, select the photograph, then click the **Insert button** so that the photograph appears in the Fill Effects dialog box.
- Click **OK** to accept the picture and close the Fill Effects dialog box. Click the **Apply button** on the Background dialog box. The photograph should now appear as the background for your slide.
- Save the presentation.

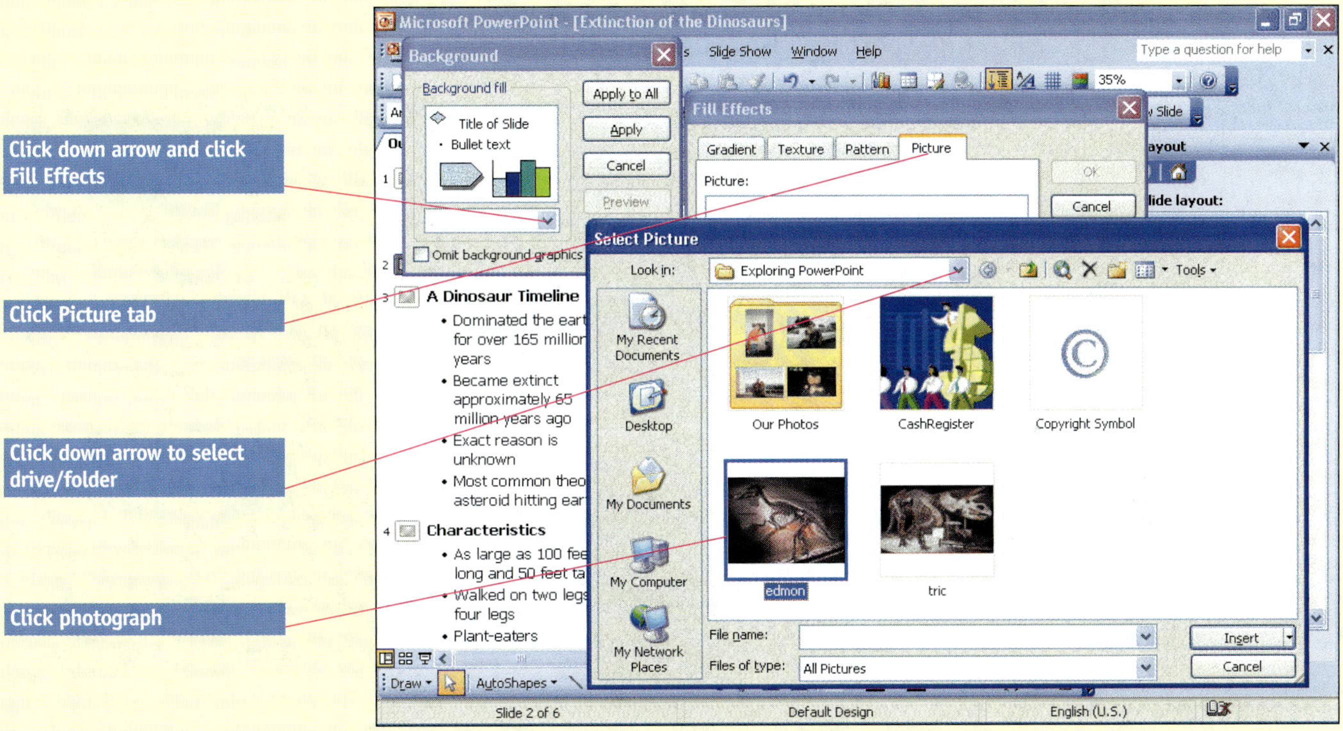

(g) The Picture as Background (step 7)

FIGURE 2.5 Hands-on Exercise 2 *(continued)*

IT'S A DIFFERENT LOOK

The slide you just created does not look like a PowerPoint slide, but it is, and it will make a tremendous impact during your next presentation. Use your imagination to expand the technique to an entire presentation. You could, for example, do a report on Impressionist paintings and show one painting per slide. You can also add a second (and smaller) photograph (perhaps of the artist) on the slide that will show both artist and painting. See practice exercise 2 at the end of the chapter.

Step 8: Add a Text Box

- Click the **Text Box tool** on the Drawing toolbar, then click and drag on the slide to create a text box. Enter the dinosaur name as shown in Figure 2.5h. If necessary, change to an appropriate font, color, and point size, such as **48 point red Times New Roman bold**. Size the text box as necessary.
- Click the **Text Box tool** a second time, then click and drag to create a second text box. Enter text to cite the source as shown in the figure. We used the same font as in the previous text box (Times New Roman), but chose a smaller size (**24 point**).
- You may need to change the font color and/or move the text box to read the text more easily. Save the presentation.
- Pull down the **File menu** and click the **Print command** to display the Print dialog box. Select **Handouts** in the Print What dialog box and choose **6 slides per page**. Click **OK**.
- Pull down the **File menu** a second time and click the **Print command**. Print an outline of the presentation.
- Close Internet Explorer. Exit PowerPoint if you do not want to continue with the next exercise at this time.

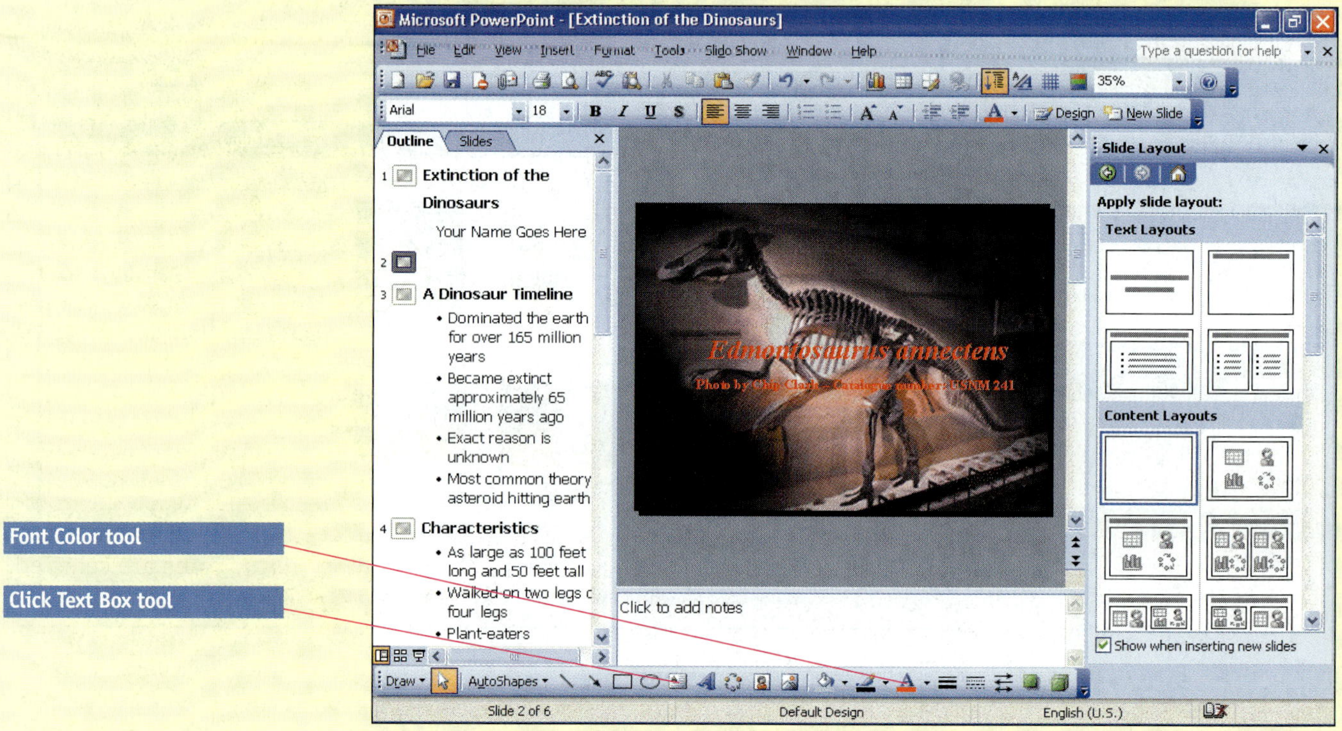

(h) Add a Text Box (step 8)

FIGURE 2.5 Hands-on Exercise 2 (*continued*)

CHANGE THE ALIGNMENT

Use the Left, Center, or Right-Align buttons to change the alignment of any bullet, slide title, or text box. Just click anywhere in the item, then click the appropriate button on the Formatting toolbar. You can also use the corresponding keyboard shortcuts (Ctrl+L, Ctrl+E, Ctrl+R), for left, center, or right alignment. The shortcuts also work in Microsoft Word.

Figure 2.6 displays multiple slides from our first presentation, which illustrates how to work with photographs. The presentation is created from a series of pictures that are stored in their own folder from where they are inserted into the presentation. Each slide in Figure 2.6 illustrates a different capability.

The ***photo album*** in Figure 2.6a imports multiple photographs into a presentation, without having to format each picture individually. The photos may be taken from your hard disk, a scanner, or a digital camera. Regardless of the origin or file format of the photographs, you can specify how many pictures you want per slide (one, two, or four), choose from a variety of picture frames (rounded corners are used in our figure), and/or insert a caption below each picture.

Figure 2.6b displays cropped versions of two pictures in the original album. Compare these photographs to their counterparts in Figure 2.6a to see how we eliminated part of the background in order to focus on the happy couple. This was accomplished through the ***Crop tool*** on the ***Picture toolbar***, which also contains additional tools to rotate a photograph and/or change the color or brightness. You can also compress a photograph (generally without a loss in quality) within a presentation to reduce the file size.

Figure 2.6c illustrates one of our favorite techniques, which is to use a photograph as a fill effect for the background of the slide. The slide itself is "empty"; it does not contain a photograph or even a title (although a title could be added to describe the photograph). Instead, the ***Format Background command*** was used to select the photograph as a background for the slide, in effect, creating a presentation that bears no resemblance to a typical PowerPoint presentation.

Figure 2.6d applies a custom animation effect to dissolve a black-and-white photograph into its color counterpart. The original color photograph is duplicated and saved as a black-and-white photograph, with the latter placed directly on top. An exit effect (dissolve out) is applied to the black-and-white picture, thus creating the transition. It's a simple and effective technique that adds variety to a presentation.

Figure 2.6e combines WordArt with a picture background. WordArt was used to create the initial object (the word "love"), after which the ***Format WordArt command*** was used to apply the photograph as fill. The only tricky part (if any) is to choose the photograph and text in such a way as to not obscure an essential portion of the underlying picture. The crop tool may be useful, therefore, to alter a picture prior to selecting it as fill.

Figure 2.6f uses animation in conjunction with a sound file to create a musical ending in which the photographs scroll continuously on the slide while the music plays in the background. The four original photographs are arranged one on top of another, extending above and below the slide. All four photographs are selected, and the custom animation command is applied. The sound (music) file is inserted independently and timed to play simultaneously with the scrolling of the pictures.

Photographs, File Formats, and File Folders

A photograph may be stored anywhere on a hard disk, although beginners typically store all photographs in the ***My Pictures folder*** within their My Documents folder. You may create additional folders (within the My Pictures folder and/or anywhere on your system) to hold groups of pictures. You can move and copy photographs from one folder to another, or from one device to another, such as from a hard disk to a zip drive, floppy disk, or CD (provided you have the software to write to the CD).

A photograph has the same attributes as any other file, which include the file name, type, file size, and date the file was created or last modified. There are many different file types for graphic work. The ***Joint Photographic Experts Group*** (***JPEG***, pronounced "jpeg") ***format*** is the most common for photographs. The ***Graphics Interchange Format*** (***GIF***, pronounced "jif") is used for clip art and similar images.

(a) Photo Album

(b) Revised (cropped) Photos

(c) Photo as Background

(d) Black-and-white Transition

(e) WordArt

(f) Credits and Sound

FIGURE 2.6 Fun with Photographs

Transitions and Animations

Transitions and animations are similar in that both add interest to a presentation through movement and (optionally) sound. A ***transition*** applies to the slide as a whole and controls the way the entire slide moves on and off the screen. An ***animation*** controls the appearance of individual elements on a single slide. PowerPoint includes a selection of animation schemes that can be applied to selected slides and/or to the presentation as a whole. PowerPoint also gives you the ability to create a ***custom animation***, which requires that you determine when (in what sequence) the objects appear and how the objects make their entrance (e.g., whether they fly in from the top or bottom). You can also control how long the objects are to remain on the screen and if (how) they are to exit. The objects on a slide may include text boxes, clip art, photographs, and so on.

Each slide in Figure 2.7 has its own entrance and exit effect, denoted by a green and red icon, respectively. (The effects from which you can choose are divided into subtle, moderate, and exciting, and it is fun to experiment.) The sequence and duration of the individual animations are seen in the associated timeline. The entrance of the Los Angeles photo is triggered by clicking the mouse during the slide show. This is followed automatically by the exit of this object, followed by the entrance of the next photo, followed by the exit of the photo. Each effect takes two seconds (medium speed) as indicated on the timeline. Most animation options include an optional sound effect; for example, you can specify the sound of a clicking camera as each photograph makes its appearance.

Any animated slide can be thought of as a theatrical production unto itself. The objects on a PowerPoint slide, just like the actors in a Broadway show, must be thoroughly scripted so that the performance is as effective as possible. You can select multiple objects at the same time in order to apply the same effects in a single command. You can resequence an animation by clicking the reorder arrows up or down within the custom animation task pane. You can change and/or remove effects as necessary. It's fun, it's easy, and as you may have guessed, it's time for our next hands-on exercise.

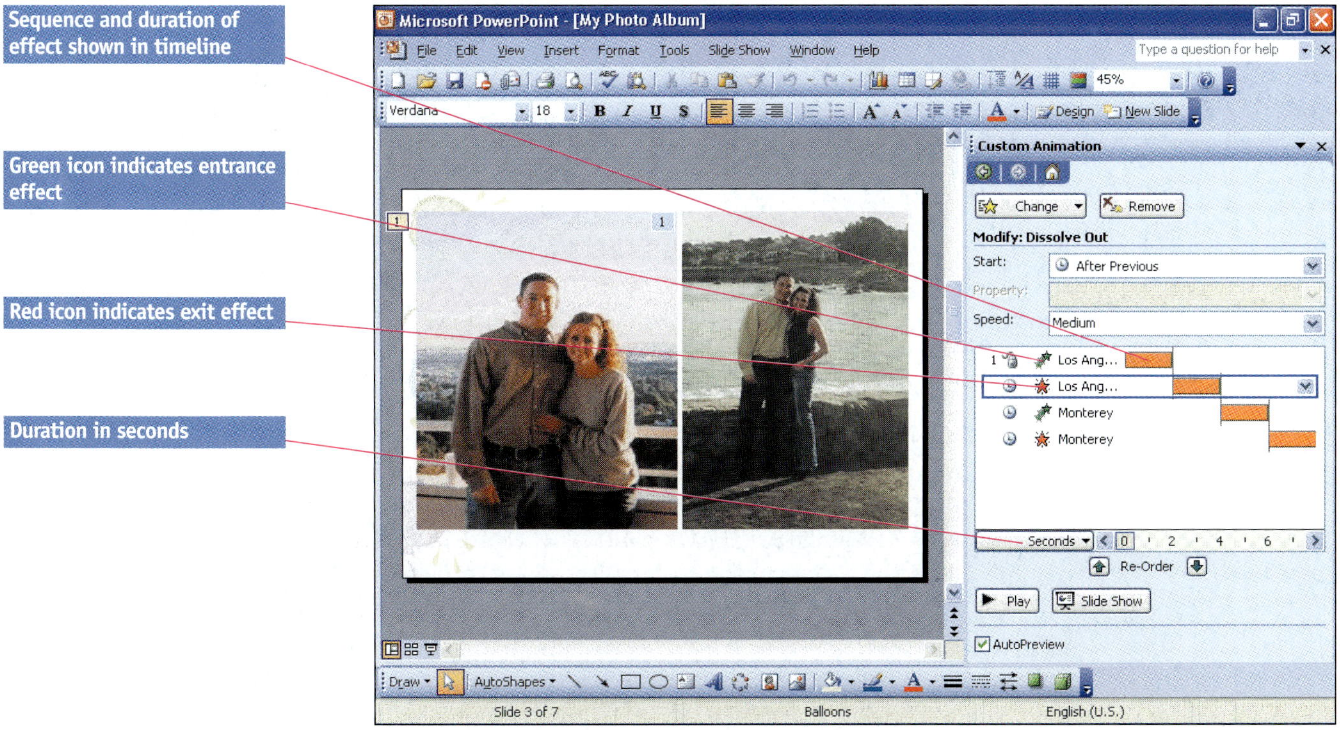

FIGURE 2.7 The Basics of Custom Animation

hands-on exercise

3 Fun with Photographs

Objective Create a photo album; use cropping and other techniques to enhance individual photographs; apply custom animation to various slides. Use Figure 2.8 as a guide.

Step 1: Create a Photo Album

- Start PowerPoint. Close the task pane and any open presentations. Pull down the **Insert menu**, click **Picture**, then click **New Photo Album** to display the Photo Album dialog box.
- Click the **File/Disk command button** to select from existing photos on your computer. You can use your own photos or you can use our pictures, which are in the **Our Photos folder** within the **Exploring PowerPoint folder**.
- Press and hold the **Ctrl key** as you select the four pictures in Figure 2.8a. (Be sure to include **Los Angeles** and **Monterey** as we will crop these photos in a later step.) Click the **Insert button**.

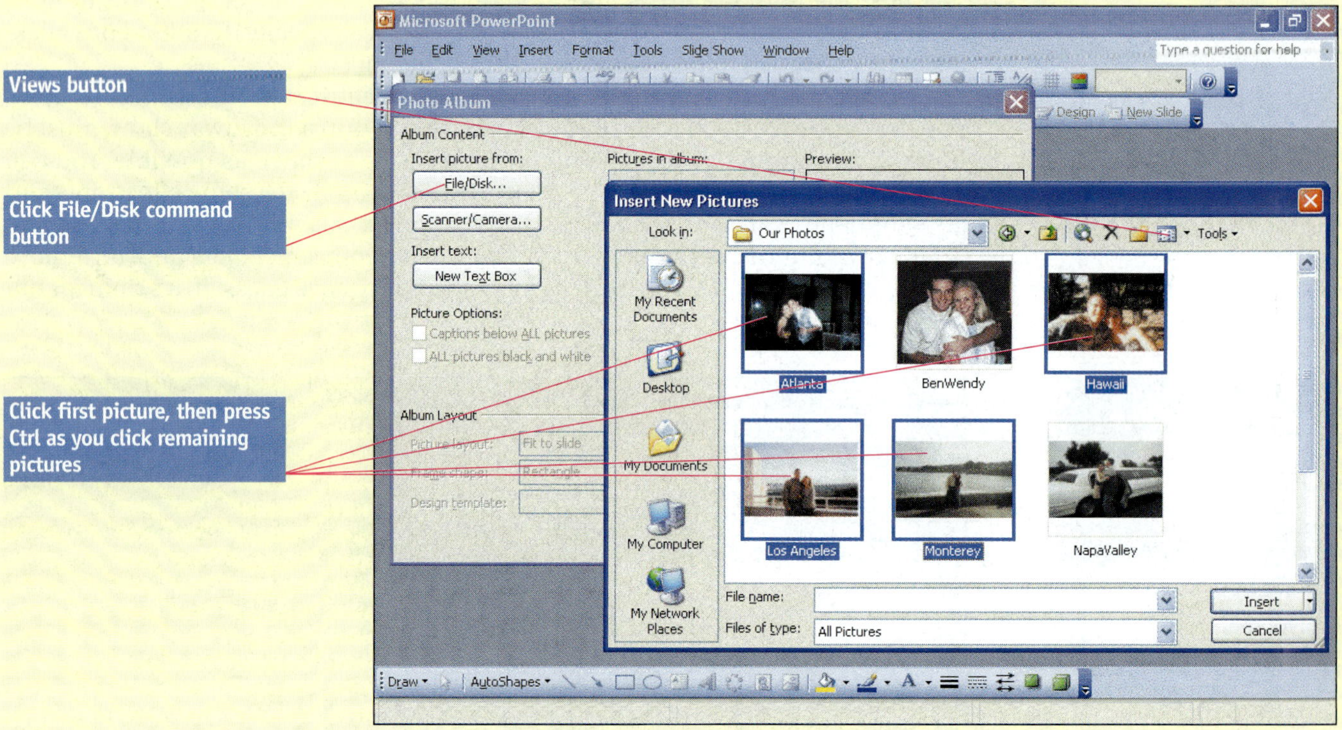

(a) Create a Photo Album (step 1)

FIGURE 2.8 Hands-on Exercise 3

CHANGE THE VIEW

Use the Views button to cycle through the different views that are available with photographs. The Thumbnails view is ideal for selecting a picture as it displays a miniature version of the photograph. The Details view provides the most information, and further, it enables you to sequence your files according to any attribute. Click the Size column, for example, and you arrange the pictures according to file size. Click the column a second time to switch from ascending to descending sequence and vice versa.

Step 2: Choose the Album Layout

- You should see the Photo Album dialog box as shown in Figure 2.8b. You can change the order of the photos within the album by selecting a photo, then pressing the **up** or **down arrow** as necessary.
- Look toward the bottom of the dialog box (in the Album Layout area) and make the indicated selections. We chose **4 pictures** for the layout and **Rounded Rectangle** for the Frame shape.
- Click the **Browse button**, double click the **Presentation Designs folder**, select a design template (we chose **Balloons**), then click **Select** to close the dialog box. Click the **Create button** to create the album.
- You should see a presentation consisting of two slides. The first slide is the title slide. The second slide contains the four pictures you selected.
- If your layout is different from ours, pull down the **Format menu**, click the **Photo Album command** to display the associated dialog box, and enter the correct parameters. Click the **Update button**.
- If necessary, change the title slide to include your name. Save the presentation as **My Photo Album**.

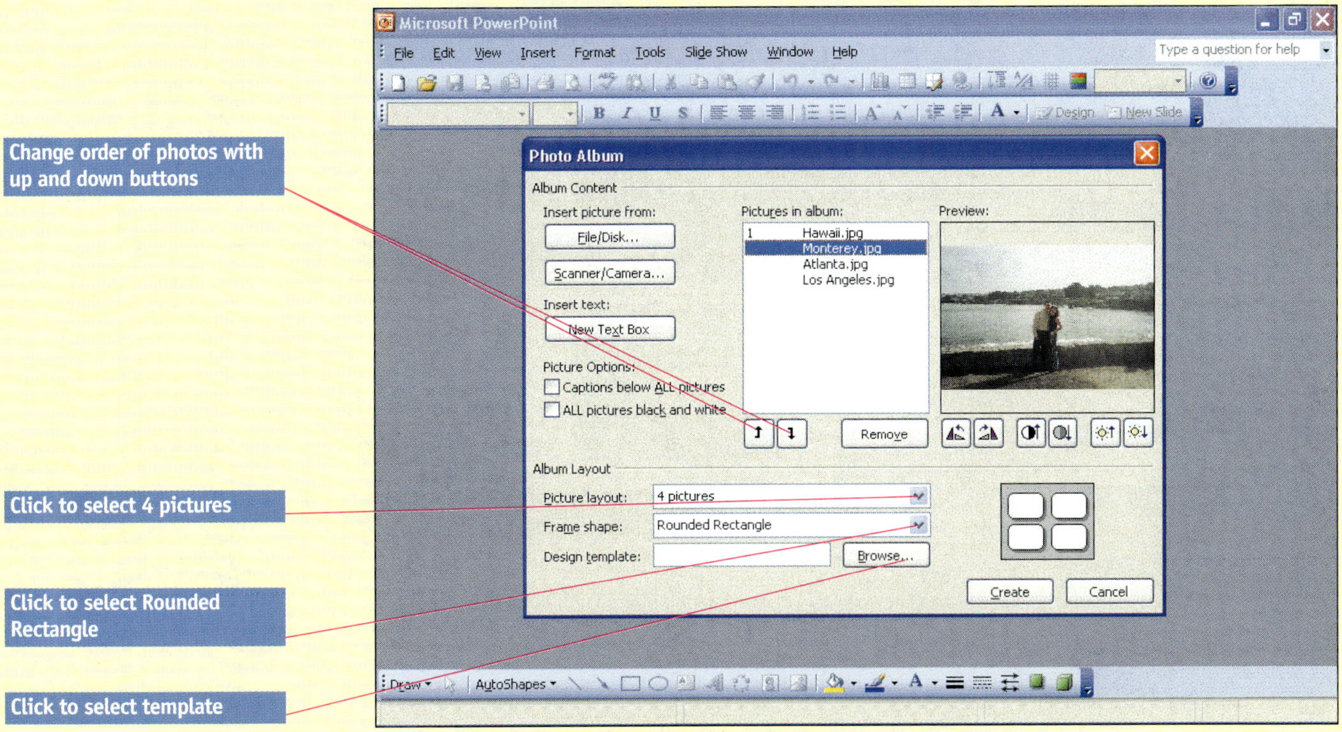

(b) Choose the Album Layout (step 2)

FIGURE 2.8 Hands-on Exercise 3 (*continued*)

TOUCH UP YOUR PHOTOS

It's not PhotoShop, but the Format Photo Album command provides limited capability to modify a photograph. Select the appropriate picture within the Format Photo Album dialog box, then use the appropriate tool within the dialog box. You can rotate a picture left or right, increase or decrease the contrast, and/or increase or decrease the brightness. You can also point to any tool to display a ScreenTip that is indicative of its function.

Step 3: Add Custom Animation

- Change to the **Normal view** if necessary. Click the **Slides tab** in the left pane. Pull down the **Slide Show menu** and click **Custom Animation** to open the task pane as shown in Figure 2.8c.
- Select the second slide. Press and hold the **Ctrl key** as you select all four photos. Click the **Add Effect button**, click **Entrance**, then select **Dissolve In** for the effect. (Click the **More Effects subcommand** if you do not see the Dissolve In effect.) Click the **down arrow** in the **Speed list box** and select **Slow**.
- Click a **down arrow** next to any effect and click **Start After Previous** so that the pictures are displayed one after another, without having to click the mouse.
- Be sure that all four animation effects are still selected, then click a **down arrow** next to any effect, and click **Effect Options** to display the Dissolve In dialog box. Click the **Effect tab**, click the **down arrow** for the **Sound list box** and (scroll if necessary to) choose **Camera**.
- Click **OK** to accept the sound and close the dialog box. Save the presentation.

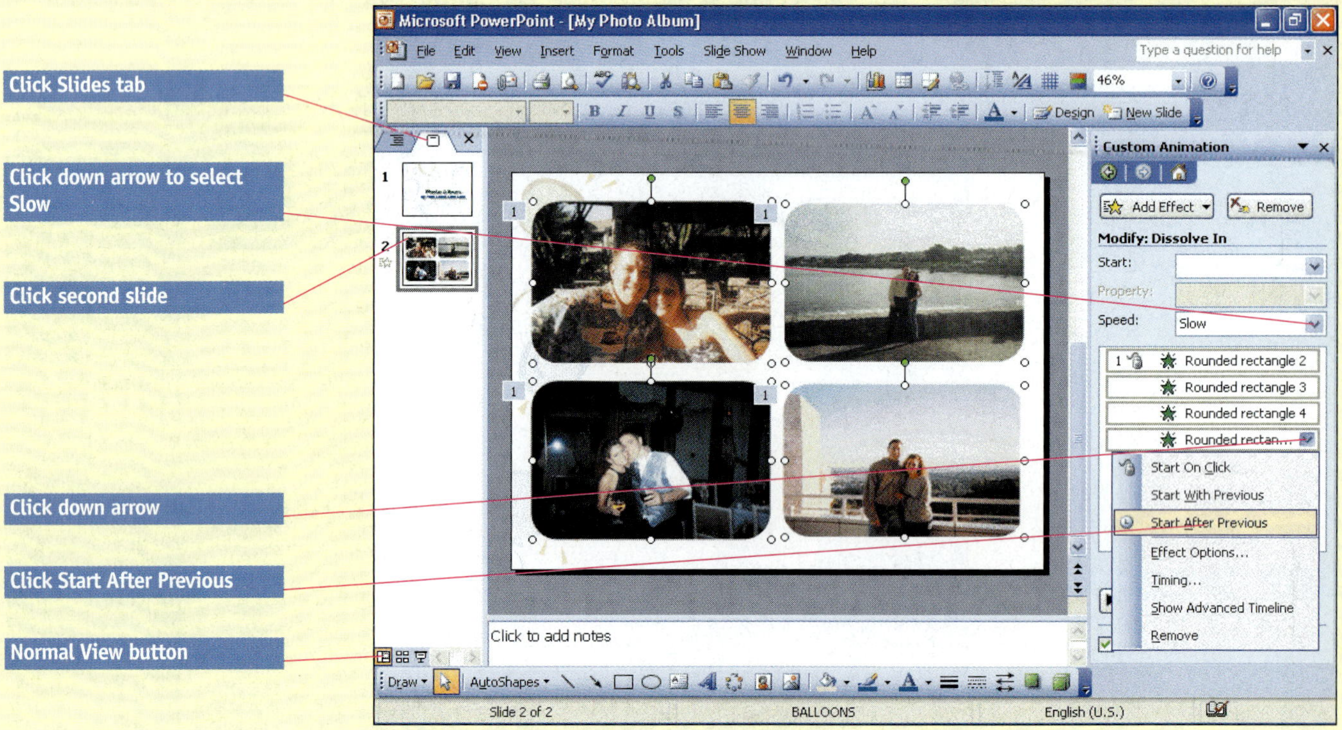

(c) Add Custom Animation (step 3)

FIGURE 2.8 Hands-on Exercise 3 (*continued*)

COMPRESS YOUR PICTURES

Use the Compress Pictures command to (attempt to) reduce the size of a presentation. Save the presentation before you begin because the command cannot be undone. Select any picture, then click the Compress Pictures tool on the Picture toolbar to display the associated dialog box. Check the options to compress pictures and to delete the cropped areas of pictures. Click OK, then click the Apply button when warned that you might reduce the quality of the photographs. Review the presentation. If the quality is significantly less (it rarely is), exit the presentation without saving to return to the original.

Step 4: Crop a Picture

- Click the **New Slide button** to insert a new slide. Change the slide layout to a blank slide. Close the task pane.
- Pull down the **Insert menu**, click **Picture**, click **From File**, then select the **Monterey picture** from the **Our Photos folder** in the **Exploring PowerPoint folder**. Click **Insert** and move it to the right side of the slide.
- Insert the **LA picture** in similar fashion and move it to the left of the slide. (You must insert the original pictures; you cannot copy the photographs from slide 2 because the Photo Album command disables cropping.)
- Select the LA photo as shown in the figure. The Picture toolbar should be visible, but if not, pull down the **View menu**, click **Toolbars**, then click the **Picture toolbar**. Use the **cropping tool** to crop the picture as shown in Figure 2.8d.
- Once you are satisfied with the result, click off the picture, then click and drag a corner to resize (enlarge) the cropped image. Crop the Monterey photo in similar fashion. Add animation as you see fit.
- Try to size the resulting photos identically for symmetry on this slide. Save the presentation.

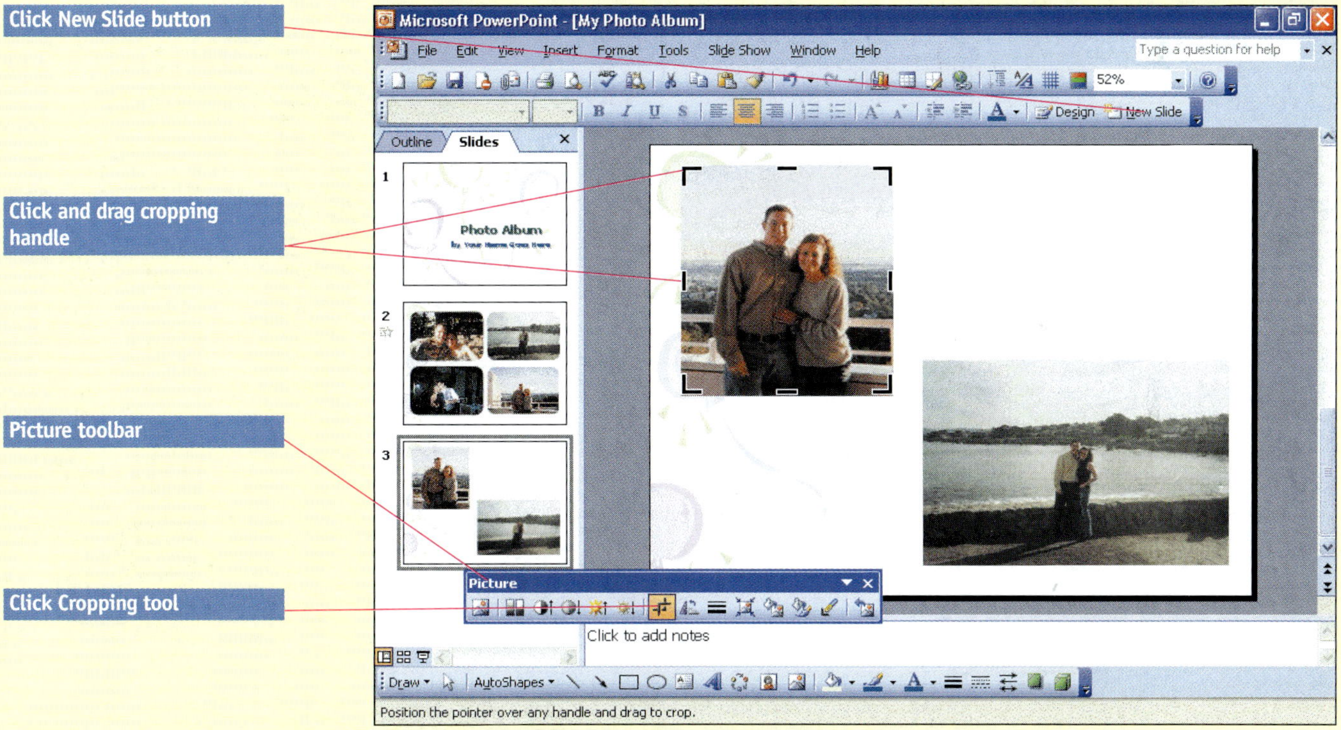

(d) Crop a Picture (step 4)

FIGURE 2.8 Hands-on Exercise 3 (*continued*)

SAVE THE NEW PICTURE

Once you have modified a picture, by cropping, shading, or any other technique, you can save the new picture as a replacement for the original. Right click the photo to display a context-sensitive menu. Choose the Save as Picture command, specify JPEG or GIF as the file format, then choose the folder where you want to save the photo. Click the Save button. You can now use the modified picture in all subsequent photo albums.

Step 5: Set a Picture as the Background

- Our favorite technique is to create presentations that do not look as though they were created in PowerPoint. One way to accomplish this is to create a blank slide that contains nothing other than a single photograph as the slide background.
- Insert a blank slide at the end of the presentation. Close the task pane. Pull down the **Format command** and click the **Background command** to display the Background dialog box in Figure 2.8e.
- Click the **down arrow** in the **Background Fill** area, click **Fill Effects** to display the associated dialog box, then click the **Picture tab**.
- Click the **Select Picture command button**, then select the desired photo (e.g., **BenWendy** in the **Our Photos folder**).
- Click **Insert** to select the picture, click **OK**, then click the **Apply button** to set the photograph as the background for this slide.
- It's easy and effective. The only "trick" is to choose a photo that has the approximate proportions of the slide.
- Save the presentation.

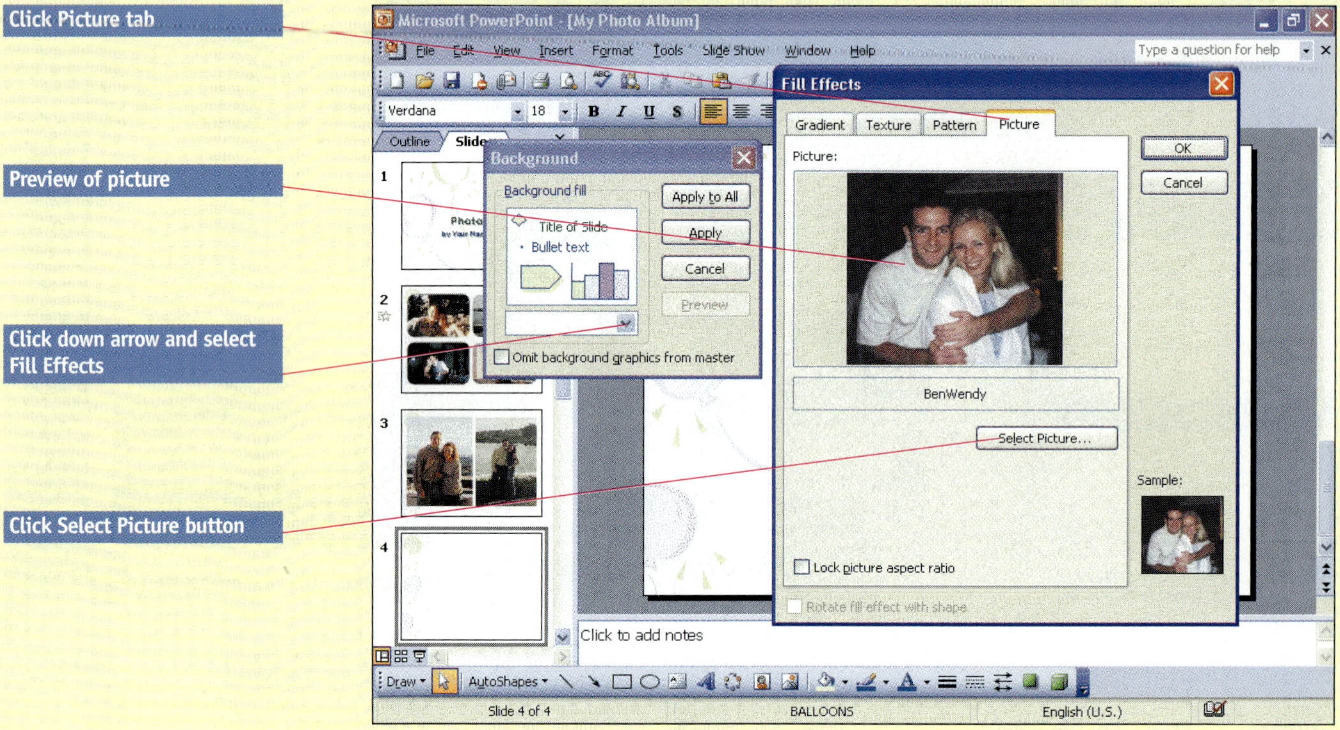

(e) Set a Picture as the Background (step 5)

FIGURE 2.8 Hands-on Exercise 3 (*continued*)

PRINTING THE PRESENTATION

We're not sure why, but the slide background may not print on a black-and-white printer. If this is true on your configuration (click the Print Preview button to find out), pull down the File menu, click the Print command, then choose Color in the Color/Grayscale list box even if you have a black-and-white printer.

Step 6: From Black and White to Color

- Insert a blank slide at the end of the presentation. Pull down the **Insert menu**, click **Picture**, click **From File**, then select the **BenWendy picture** from the **Our Photos folder**. Click **Insert**.
- Ben and Wendy should appear on a blank slide, with the picture selected. Size the picture, press **Ctrl+C** to copy it, then press **Ctrl+V** to duplicate it.
- Right click the top picture, then click the **Format Picture command** to display the associated dialog box. Click the **Picture tab**, then click the **down arrow** on the **Color list box** in the Image control area. Select **Black and White** and click **OK**.
- Check that the top picture is still selected, pull down the **Slide Show menu**, and click **Custom Animation** to open the task pane as shown in Figure 2.8f. Click the **Add Effect button**, click **Exit**, then click **Dissolve Out**. Change the speed to **Very slow**. Close the task pane.
- Click and drag the black-and-white photo so that it is directly on top of the color photo (see the boxed tip for additional hints). Click the **Slide Show button** to see the finished slide, then click the black-and-white photograph to dissolve to color. Press **Esc**.

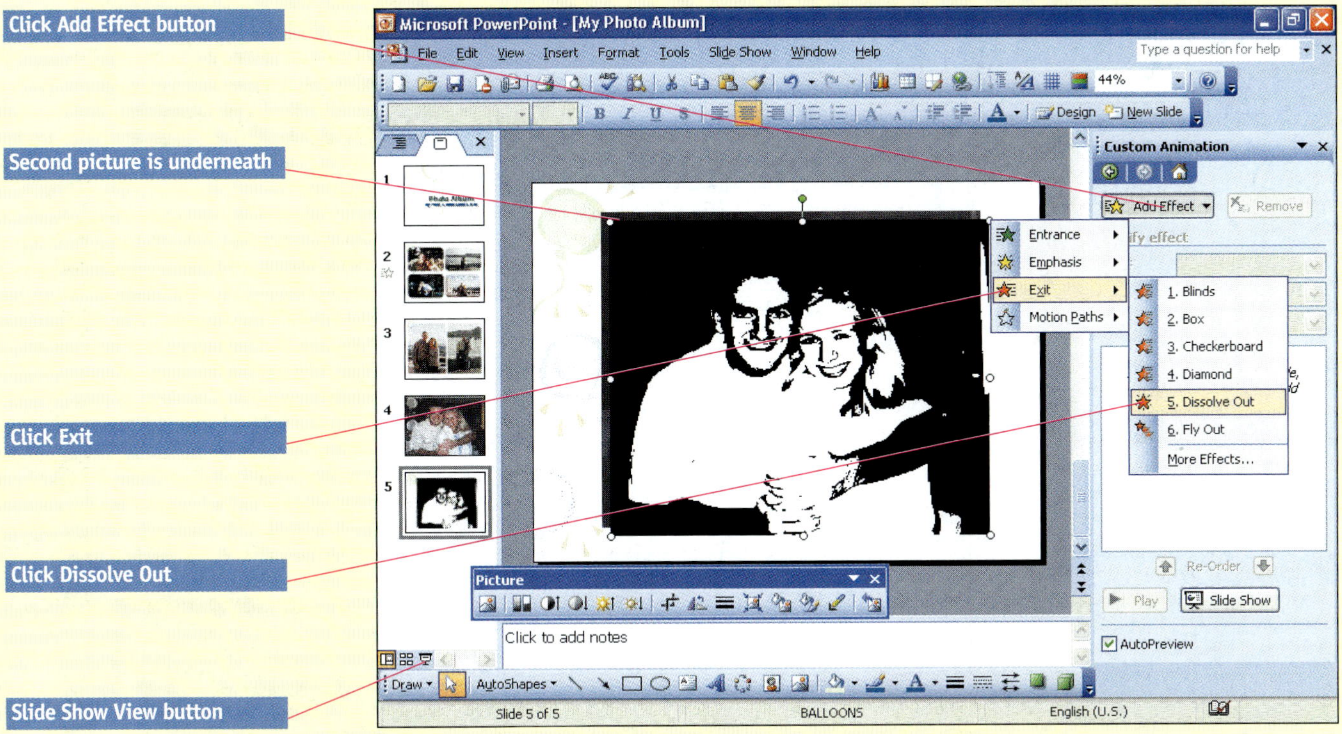

(f) From Black and White to Color (step 6)

FIGURE 2.8 Hands-on Exercise 3 (*continued*)

PLACE ONE PHOTO ON TOP OF ANOTHER

Press and hold the Ctrl key to select both pictures, pull down the Format menu, and click Picture to display the Format Picture dialog box. Click the Size tab, then enter the appropriate dimensions (e.g., a width of 7 inches for Ben and Wendy). Check the box to lock the aspect ratio so as not to distort the picture. Click the Position tab and enter horizontal and vertical distances from the left corner. Click OK. Both photos are still selected, and you can click and drag to "fine tune" the size and position.

Step 7: Create the WordArt

- Insert a blank slide at the end of the presentation, then close the task pane. Click the **Insert WordArt button** on the Drawing toolbar to display the WordArt Gallery dialog box. Choose any style you like (we took the first style in the first row). Click **OK**.
- You should see the Edit Text box. Enter **LOVE** (in uppercase) as the text for your WordArt object. Click **OK** to insert the WordArt into your presentation. Move and size the WordArt object so that it takes the entire slide as shown in Figure 2.8g.
- Pull down the **Format menu** and click **WordArt** to display the Format WordArt dialog box. Click the **Colors and Lines tab**, click the **down arrow** in the **Color list box** (in the Fill section), and select **Fill Effects** to display the dialog box.
- Click the **Picture tab**. Click the **Select Picture button**. Select the **BenWendy photo** and click **Insert**. Click **OK** to close the Fill Effects dialog box. Click **OK** a second time to close the Format WordArt dialog box.
- You should see the completed WordArt object with the photo as the fill for the letters. (You may have to resize the WordArt and/or use a cropped photo to better position the photo inside the text.) Save the presentation.

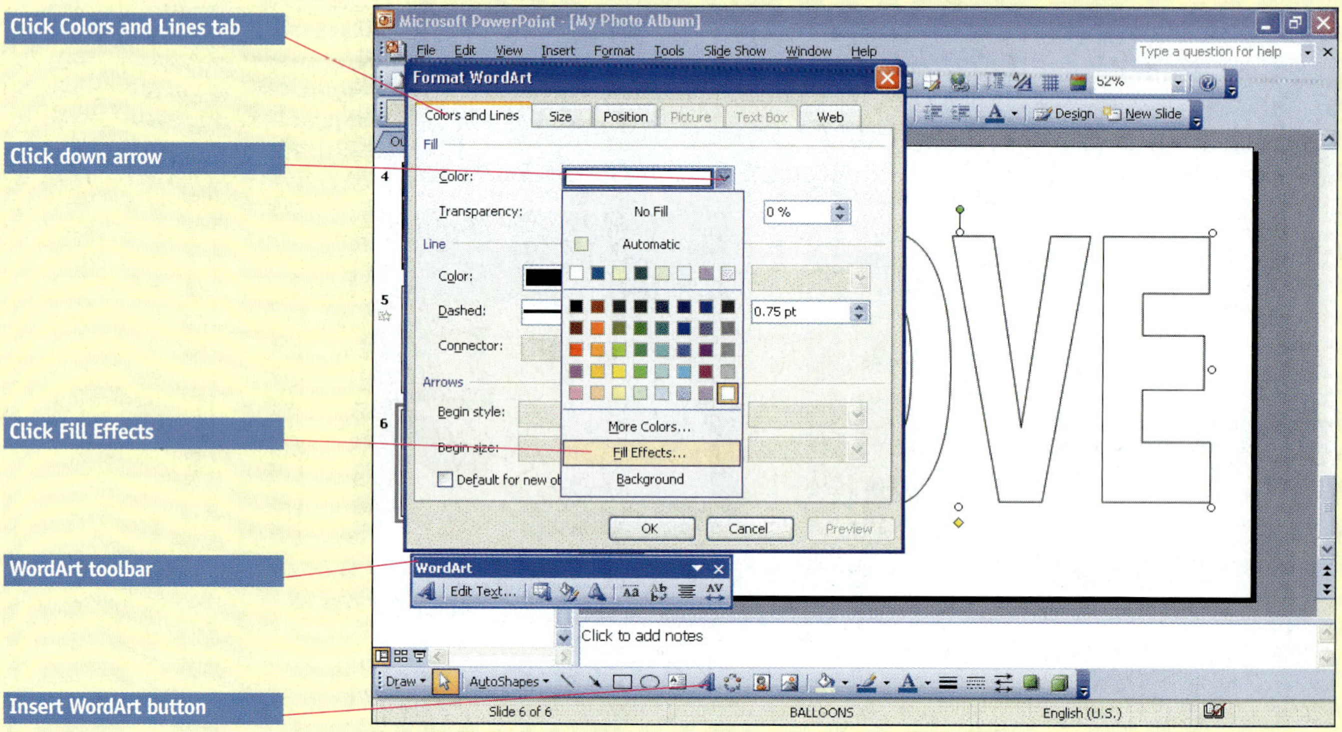

(g) Create the WordArt (step 7)

FIGURE 2.8 Hands-on Exercise 3 (*continued*)

THE WORDART TOOLBAR

The WordArt toolbar provides the easiest way to change an existing WordArt object. It is displayed automatically when a WordArt object is selected (and suppressed otherwise). As with any toolbar, you can point to a button to display a ScreenTip containing the name of the button, which is indicative of its function. You will find buttons to display the text vertically, change the style or shape, and/or edit the text.

Step 8: Create the Credits Slide

- Press **Ctrl+Home** to move to the beginning of the presentation. Select (click) the second slide, which is the original "photo album" that contains the four photographs. Press **Ctrl+C** to copy the slide.
- Press **Ctrl+End** to move to the end of the presentation. Press **Ctrl+V** to paste the slide at the end of the presentation.
- Arrange the photographs in a filmstrip. The end result will have a picture above and below the actual slide as shown in Figure 2.8h. Give yourself additional room in which to work by changing the zoom percentage and/or making the notes pane smaller.
- Pull down the **Slide Show menu** and click **Custom Animation**. Delete all of the existing animation effects. (The existing effects are the transition to the sound of a camera that we added at the beginning of the presentation.)
- Press and hold the **Ctrl key** to select all four pictures. Click the **Add Effect button**, click **Entrance**, click **More Effects**, scroll to the **Exciting category**, then choose **Credits**.
- You should see a preview of the effect in which the pictures scroll onto the screen just as in a list of movie credits. Click **OK**. Save the presentation.

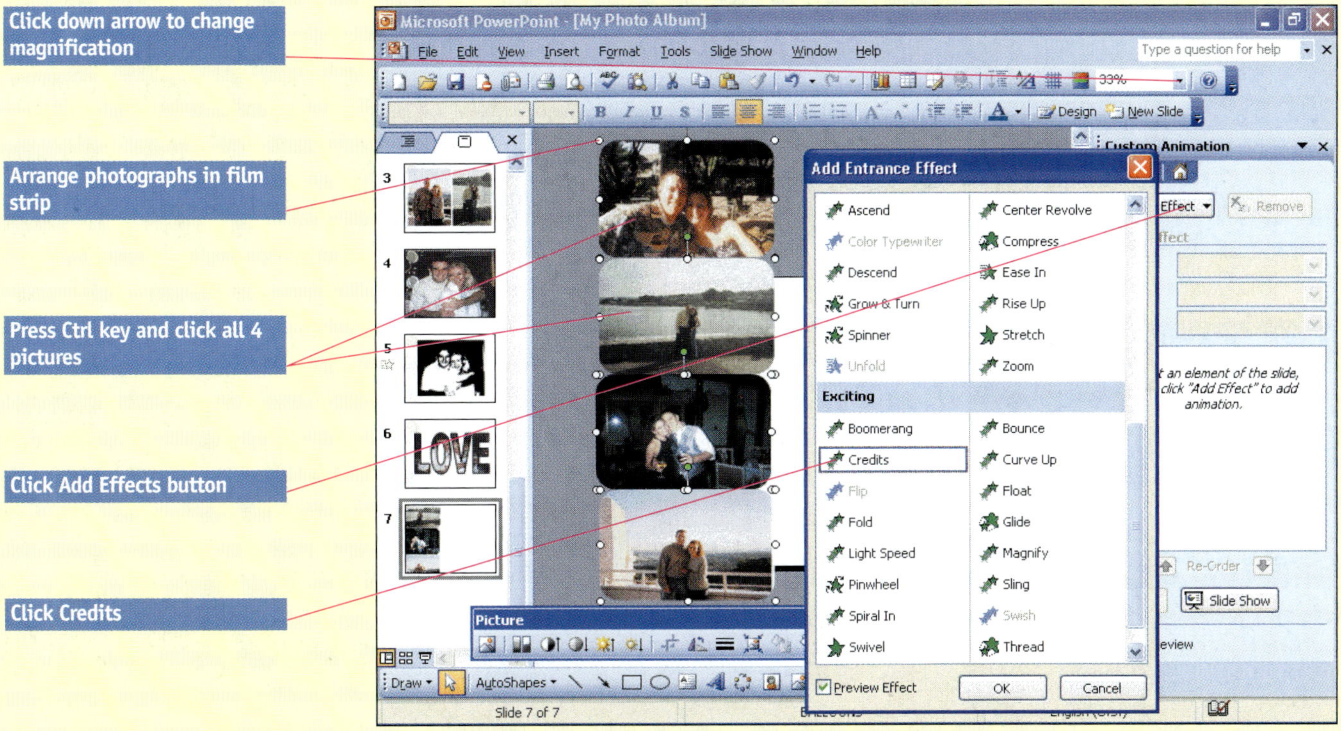

(h) Create the Credits Slide (step 8)

FIGURE 2.8 Hands-on Exercise 3 (*continued*)

USE THE GRID FOR EASY ALIGNMENT

Pull down the View menu, click the Grid and Guides command to display the associated dialog box, then check the boxes to snap objects to the grid and to display the grid on screen. The grid is visible when you work in PowerPoint, but it does not appear during a slide show or on the printed version of a presentation. Use the grid to align objects more precisely on a slide, especially in relation to one another.

Step 9: Add the Sound and Animation

- Pull down the **Insert menu**, click **Movies and Sounds**, then choose **Sound from File** to display the Insert Sound dialog box. Change to the **Our Photos folder**, specify **All Files** as the file type, then insert **Beethoven's Symphony 9**. Click **OK**.
- Click **Automatically** when asked how you want the sound to start during the show. Click and drag the animation for Beethoven's symphony to the top of the Custom animation list as shown in Figure 2.8i. (The zero next to the effect indicates that the sound will play automatically.)
- Click the animation for the first rounded rectangle (photograph), then press and hold the **Ctrl key** as you select the transition effects for the other photographs. Click the **down arrow** next to the last rectangle, then click **Start With Previous**.
- Click the **down arrow** next to the last effect, click **Timing** to display the Credits list box, then set the Repeat list box **Until Next Click** so that the pictures scroll continually. Click **OK**. Move the pictures to the middle of the slide.
- Turn up the sound on your computer, then click the **Play button**. Close the task pane. Click and drag the **Sound icon** to the lower-right portion of the slide.
- Save the presentation.

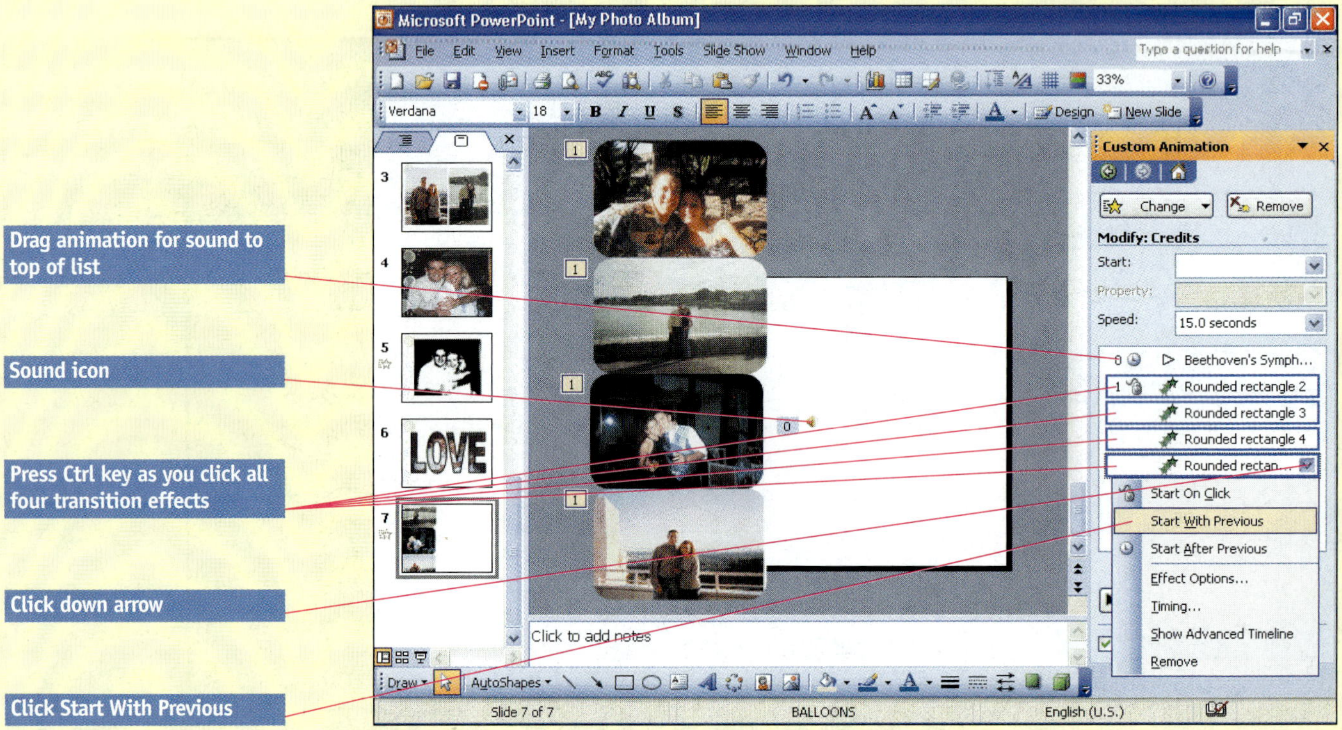

(i) Add the Sound and Animation (step 9)

FIGURE 2.8 Hands-on Exercise 3 (*continued*)

PRESENTATION PROPERTIES

How long did it take you to create this presentation? What was the total editing time? How many words does the presentation contain? How many slides have speaker notes? The answers to these and other questions are found in the presentation properties. Pull down the File menu, click the Properties command, and click the Statistics tab to see this information. Explore the other tabs to see what other information is (can be) stored to describe your presentation.

Step 10: Show Time

- Press **Ctrl+Home** to move to the first slide. Print the presentation in the form of audience handouts for your instructor. Save the presentation a final time.
- Click the **Slide Show button** (at the bottom of the window) to show the presentation as shown in Figure 2.8j. Think about the various techniques that were used to create the slides:
  - Slide 2 (the four photographs) was created initially as a photo album. The animation effects (the click of the camera) were added manually.
  - Slide 3 contains two photos that were cropped for better composition.
  - Slide 4 displays a photo as the background for a slide.
  - Slide 5 uses a transition effect to colorize a black-and-white photograph.
  - Slide 6 uses a photograph as the background for a WordArt object.
  - Slide 7 uses sound and the credits animation effect.
- Press **Esc** to end the presentation. Exit PowerPoint if you do not want to continue with the next exercise at this time.

(j) Show Time (step 10)

FIGURE 2.8 Hands-on Exercise 3 (*continued*)

USE YOUR PICTURES AS A SCREEN SAVER

Right click the desktop to display a context-sensitive menu, click Properties to display the Properties dialog box, click the Screen Saver tab, and choose My Picture Slide Slideshow. Click the Settings tab, click the Browse button, and select the folder containing your photographs. We suggest that you change the picture every seven seconds, that the pictures take the entire screen, and that you use transition effects between pictures. Click OK to accept the settings you have chosen, then click the Preview button to view the screen saver. (This tip works in Windows XP and may not work in previous versions.)

THE AUTOCONTENT WIZARD

One of the hardest things about creating a presentation is getting started. You have a general idea of what you want to say, but the words do not come easily to you. The ***AutoContent Wizard*** offers a potential solution. It eliminates writer's block and moves you immediately into a presentation. The wizard asks you a series of questions, then it uses your answers to suggest a presentation. The presentation is not complete, but it does provide an excellent beginning.

The AutoContent Wizard is accessed through the New Presentation view in the task pane and is illustrated in Figure 2.9. The wizard prompts you for the type of presentation in Figure 2.9a, for the style of the presentation in Figure 2.9b, and for additional information in Figure 2.9c. The wizard then has all the information it needs and proceeds to create a presentation for you. It even chooses a design template as illustrated by the title slide in Figure 2.9d. The template contains a color scheme and custom formatting to give your presentation a certain "look." You can change the design at any time to give your presentation a completely different look while retaining its content.

The real benefit of the wizard, however, is the outline shown in Figure 2.9e, which corresponds to the topic you selected earlier (Marketing Plan). The outline is very general, as it must be, but it provides the essential topics to include in your presentation. You work with the outline provided by the AutoContent Wizard just as you would with any other outline. You can type over existing text, add or delete slides, move slides around, promote or demote items, and so on. In short, you don't use the AutoContent outline exactly as it is presented; instead you use the outline as a starting point, then modify it to fit the needs of your presentation. The wizard has accomplished its goal, however, by giving you a solid beginning.

The presentation created by the AutoContent Wizard is based on one of several presentations that are provided with PowerPoint. You can use the wizard as just described, or you can bypass the wizard entirely and select the outline directly from the presentation templates on your computer in the New Presentation task pane. Either way, you wind up with a professional presentation with respect to design and content. Naturally, you have to modify the content to fit your needs, but you have jump-started the creative process. You simply open the presentation, then you modify the existing text as necessary, while retaining the formatting in the selected template.

Figure 2.10 displays the title slides of several sample presentations that are included with PowerPoint. The presentations vary considerably in content and design. There is a presentation for recommending a strategy in Figure 2.10a, a business plan in Figure 2.10b, and even a presentation to communicate bad news in Figure 2.10c. The presentation in Figure 2.10d contains an award certificate that is also suitable for printing. The presentations in Figure 2.10e and 2.10f are for an employee orientation and a project overview, respectively. Animation and branching are also built into several of the presentations. The AutoContent Wizard is an excellent way to start a presentation, as you shall see in our next exercise.

CHOOSE AN APPROPRIATE DESIGN

A design should enhance a presentation without calling attention to itself. It should be consistent with your message, and as authoritative or informal as the situation demands. Choosing the right template requires common sense and good taste. What works in one instance will not necessarily work in another. You would not, for example, use the same template to proclaim a year-end bonus as you would to announce a fourth-quarter loss and impending layoffs. Set a time limit, or else you will spend too much time on the formatting and lose sight of the content.

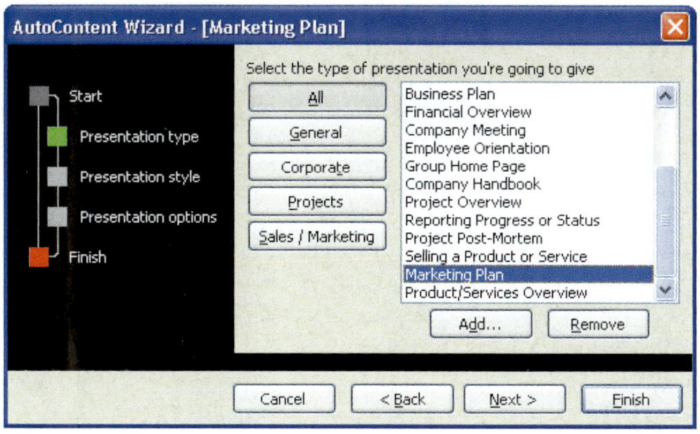

(a) Presentation Type

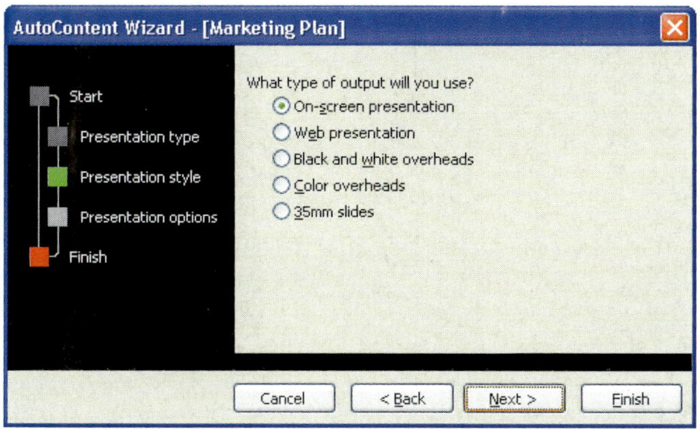

(b) Presentation Style

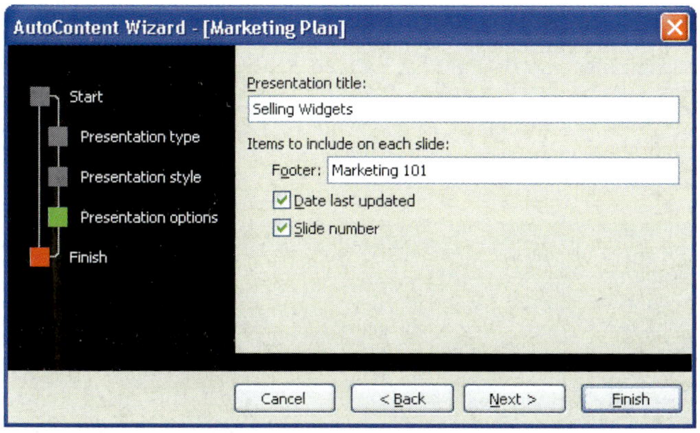

(c) Presentation Options

FIGURE 2.9 The AutoContent Wizard

(d) Title Slide and Selected Template

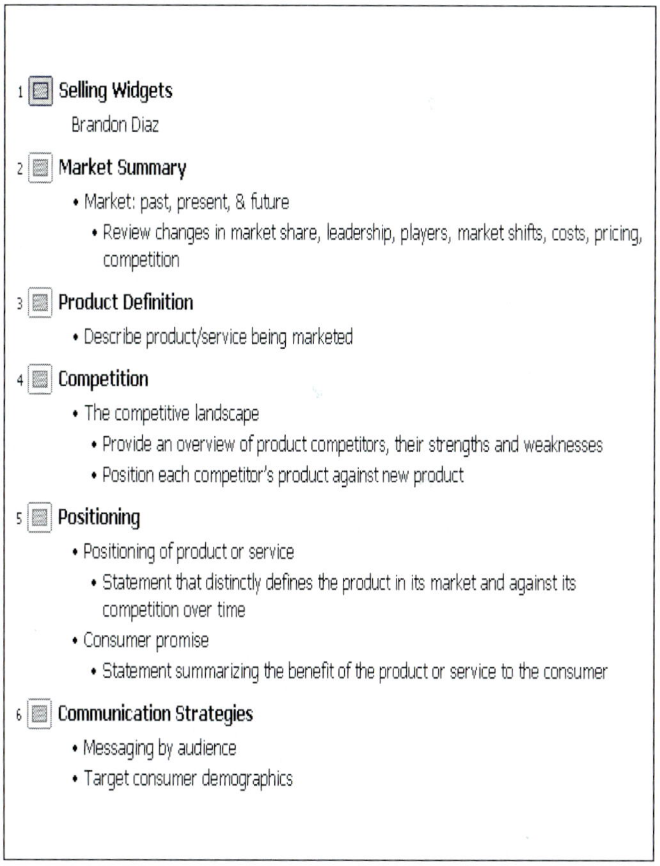

(e) Suggested Outline (additional slides not shown)

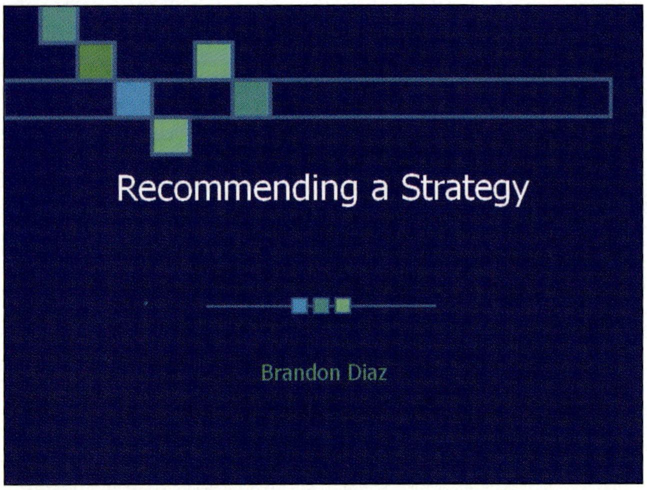

(a) Recommending a Strategy

(b) Business Plan

(c) Communicating Bad News

(d) Award Certificate

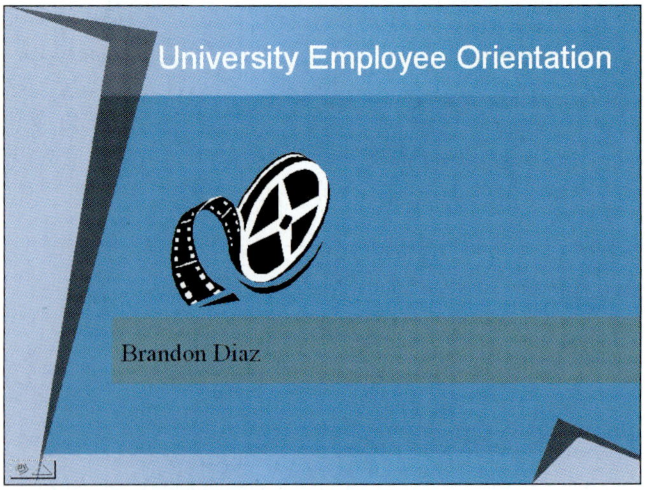

(e) Employee Orientation

(f) Project Overview

FIGURE 2.10 Suggested Presentations

hands-on exercise

4 The AutoContent Wizard

Objective Use the AutoContent Wizard to create a generic presentation for subsequent modification; insert a hyperlink on a presentation slide. Use Figure 2.11.

Step 1: The AutoContent Wizard

- Start PowerPoint and if necessary open the task pane. Click the **down arrow** in the task pane and select **New Presentation.** Click the **From AutoContent Wizard** link in the New Presentation area. You should see the first screen in the AutoContent Wizard.
- Click the **Next button** (within the wizard's dialog box) to select the presentation type. Click the **General button** as shown in Figure 2.11a.
- Select the **Communicating Bad News presentation**. Click **Next**. The option button for Onscreen presentation is selected by default. Click **Next**.
- Click in the Presentation title text box and enter **Our First Exam** as the name of the presentation. Check the boxes for **Date last updated** and **Slide Number**. Click **Next**.
- The wizard indicates it has all the answers. Click **Finish**.

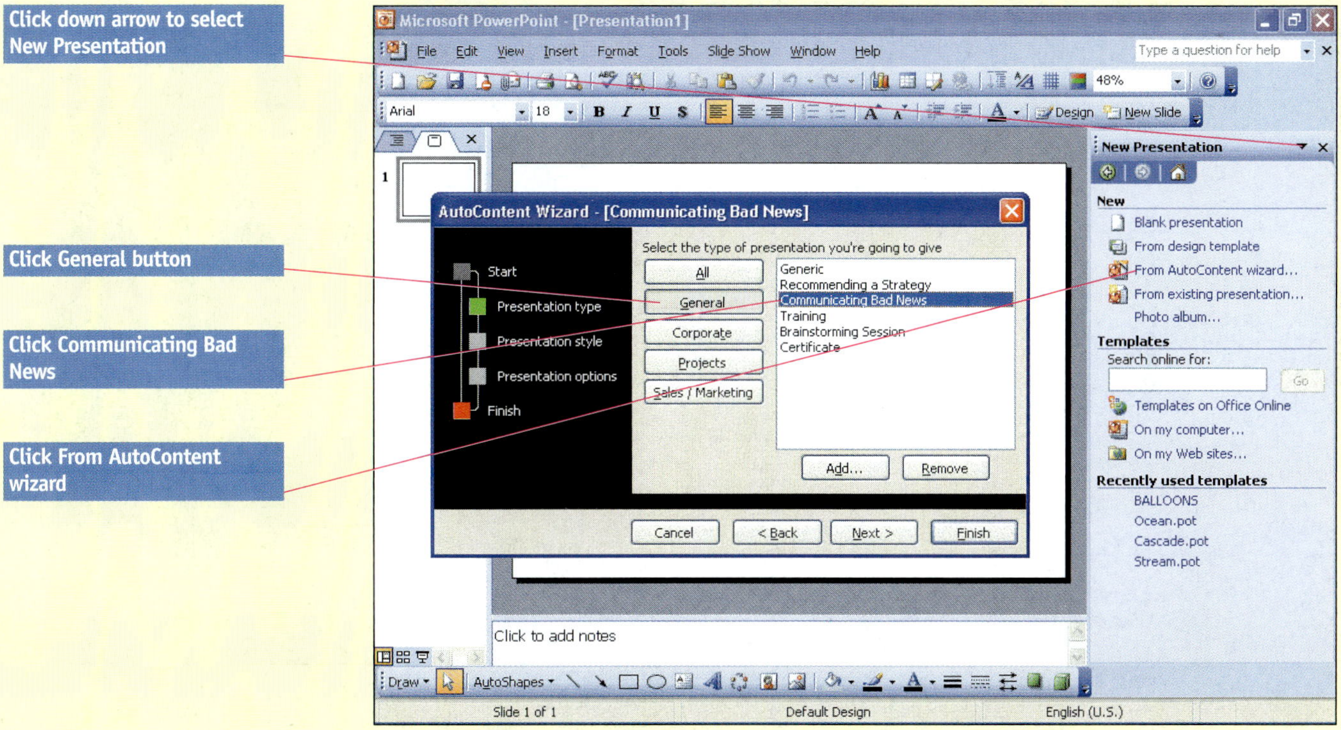

(a) The AutoContent Wizard (step 1)

FIGURE 2.11 Hands-on Exercise 4

THE HEADER AND FOOTER COMMAND

The Header and Footer command provides an easy way to display the same information on every slide. Pull down the View menu, click the Header and Footer command, then enter the date of the presentation, a descriptive footer, and/or the slide number. Click the Apply to All button to display these fields on every slide (or check the box to suppress the information on the title slide).

Step 2: Modify the Presentation

- Your presentation should be displayed in the Normal view. Note that each slide contains a footer, with the date and slide number, according to the settings you entered within the AutoContent Wizard when you created the presentation.
- Modify the title slide to include **your name**, **your e-mail address**, and **your instructor's name**.
- The AutoContent Wizard creates a generic presentation for communicating bad news. It is up to you, however, to change the text to make it relevant to the specific presentation as shown in Figure 2.11b.
  - ❑ Change the second slide (Our Situation) to describe the need for an exam.
  - ❑ Click the icon next to the third slide to select the entire slide. Press the **Del key** to delete the slide.
  - ❑ Change the fourth slide (Alternatives Considered) as shown in Figure 2.11b.
- Change the last slide (Summary) to a single item that says **Study for the Exam**. Click the **Bullets button** on the Formatting toolbar to remove the bullet from this item. Click the **Center button** to center the text.
- Save the presentation as **Our First Exam** in the **Exploring PowerPoint folder**.

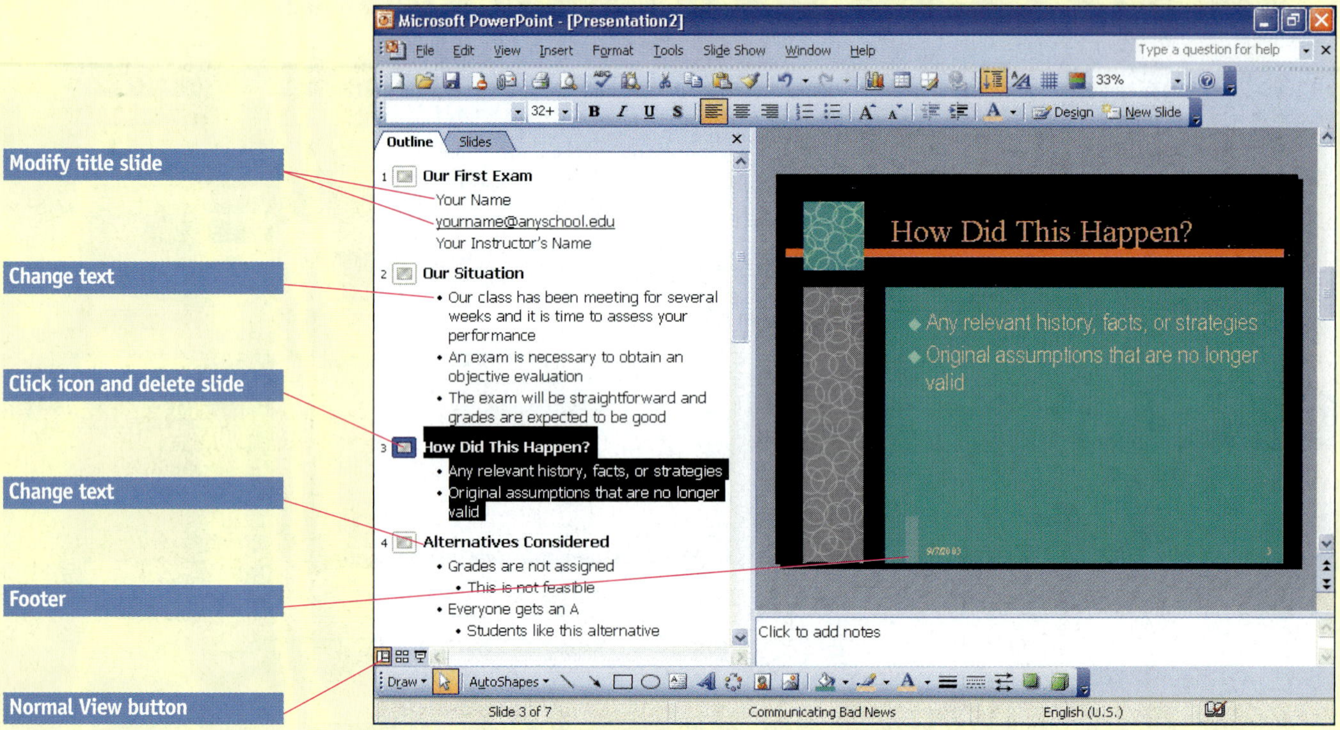

(b) Modify the Presentation (step 2)

FIGURE 2.11 Hands-on Exercise 4 (*continued*)

DELETING SLIDES

Slides may be deleted in either the Normal (tri-pane) view or the Slide Sorter view. Select (click) the Slide icon in the Outline pane of the Normal view to select one slide (or press and hold the Shift key as you click to select multiple slides), then press the Del key. You can also click the Slides tab in the Normal view, then press and hold the Ctrl key to select multiple slides prior to pressing the Delete key. Use the same technique in the Slide Sorter view.

Step 3: Insert a Hyperlink

- Change the text on slides 4 and 5 as shown in Figure 2.11c. Click and drag to select **Class Web Site** (the displayed text for the hyperlink you will add).
- Click the **Insert Hyperlink button** on the Standard toolbar (the button is not visible in Figure 2.11c) or pull down the **Insert menu** and click the **Hyperlink command**. Either way, you will see the Insert Hyperlink dialog box.
- The link to **Existing File or Web Page** is selected. Click the **Browsed Pages Button** at the left of the dialog box, then click in the **Address list box** and enter **www.prenhall.com/grauer**. (The http:// is entered automatically for you.)
- Click **OK** to create the link and close the Insert Hyperlink dialog box. Click outside the placeholder.
- Save the presentation.

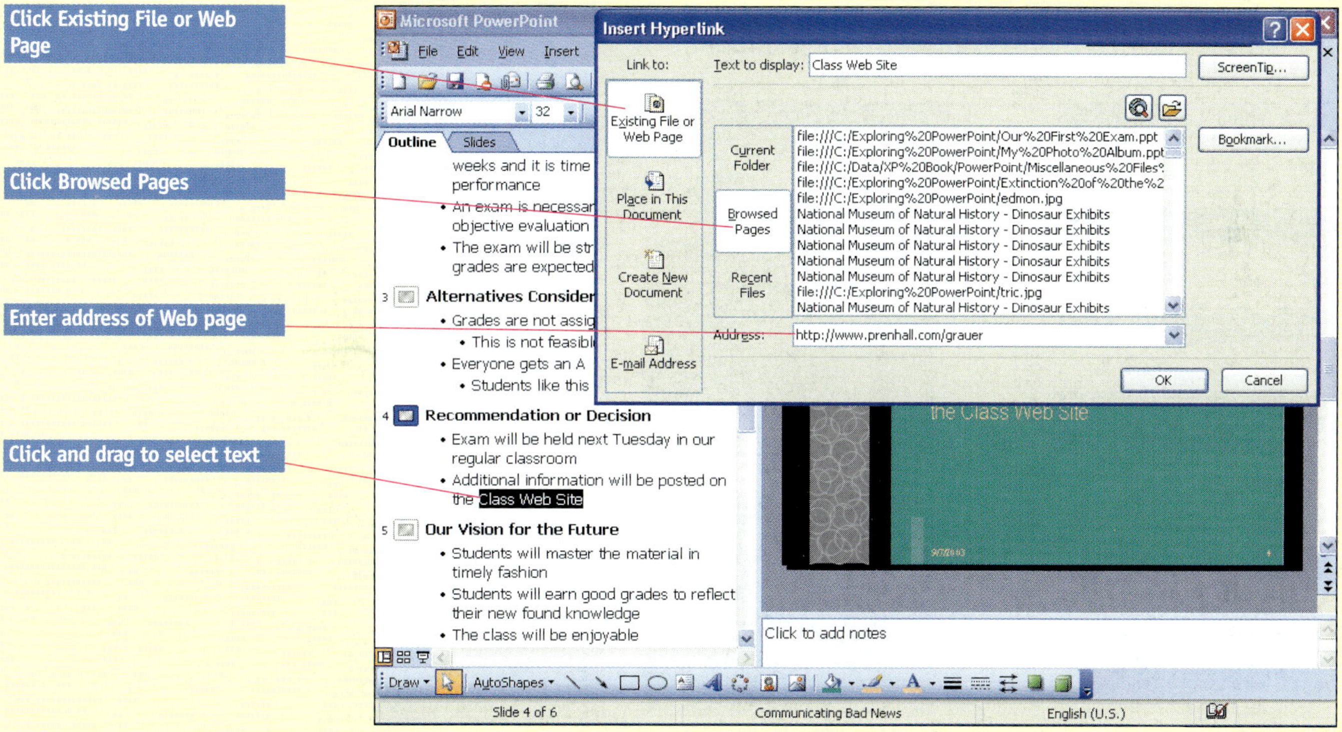

(c) Insert a Hyperlink (step 3)

FIGURE 2.11 Hands-on Exercise 4 (*continued*)

AUTOFORMAT AS YOU TYPE

Type any Web or e-mail address, then press the Enter key and the address is automatically converted to a hyperlink. (The Web address must begin with www or http:). Both conversions are performed through the AutoFormat as you Type command within Microsoft Office. If this does not work for you, pull down the Tools menu, click AutoCorrect Options, then click the AutoFormat as You Type tab. Check the box for Internet and network paths with hyperlinks, then click OK to accept the settings and close the dialog box.

Step 4: Customize the Presentation

- Change to the **Slide Sorter view** to view your presentation as shown in Figure 2.11d. (The task pane is not yet open.) Look closely at slides 1 and 4 to note that the hyperlinks have been added.
- Click the **Transition button** on the Slide Sorter toolbar to open the task pane. Click the **down arrow** on the Speed list box and change the speed to **Medium**. Click the **Apply to All Slides button** to change the speed on every slide.
- Click the **Design button** on the Slide Sorter toolbar to display the Design templates in the task pane. (You can also double click the name of the template, "Communicating Bad News", that appears in the middle of the status bar at the bottom of the window.)
- Choose a different design template (we chose the **Slit design**, which has a red background). Choose yet another design if you are still not satisfied. Close the task pane.
- Save the presentation.

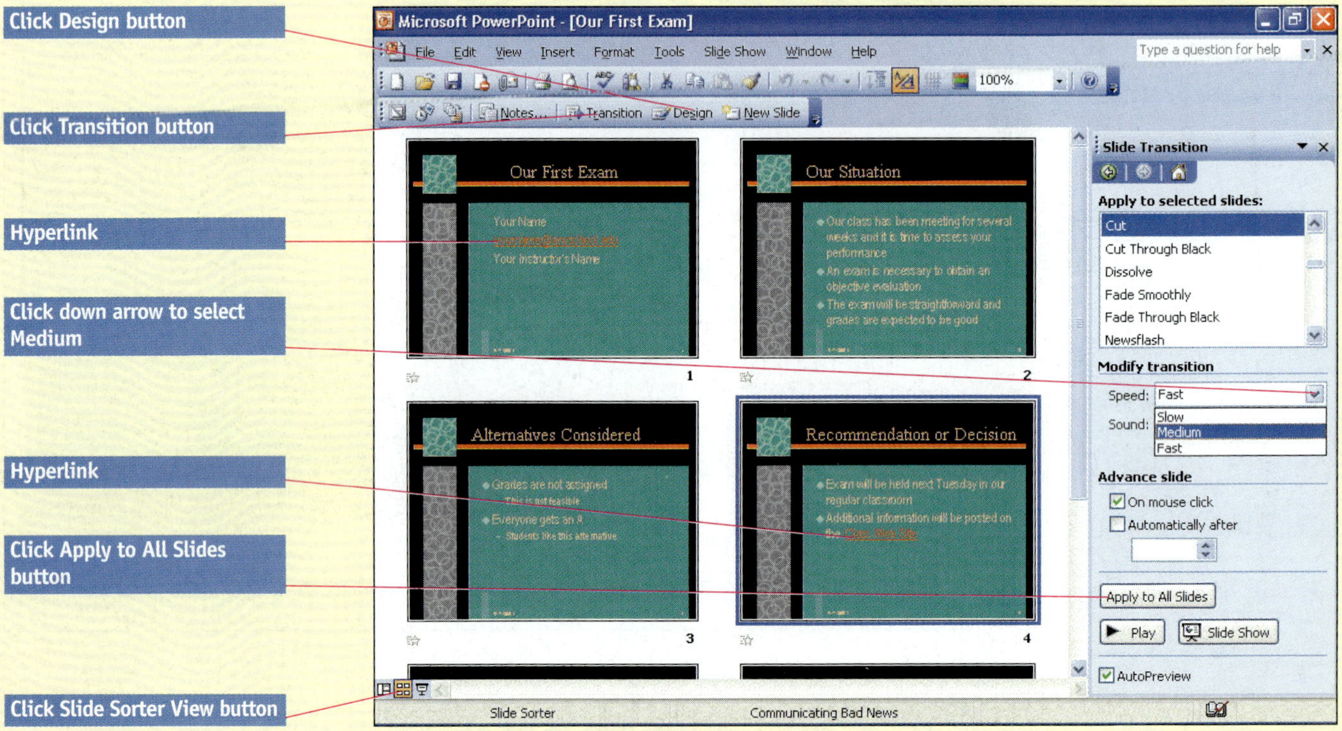

(d) Customize the Presentation (step 4)

FIGURE 2.11 Hands-on Exercise 4 (*continued*)

SET A TIME LIMIT

It's addictive, but it's not always productive, and while it's fun to experiment with different templates and animation effects, it is all too easy to spend too much time fine-tuning your presentation. It's much more important to focus on the content of your presentation rather than subtle changes in its appearance. Impose a time limit on the amount of time you will spend on this activity, and end the session when the limit is reached.

Step 5: Add Speaker Notes

- Return to the **Normal view**. Click the **Slides tab** in the left pane. The template of the presentation has changed to the Slit design as shown in Figure 2.11e.
- If necessary, press **Ctrl+Home** to go to the first slide. Click in the speaker notes area and enter an appropriate note. You can use our text, or make up your own. Save the presentation a final time.
- Print the presentation in multiple ways.
  - ❑ Print the **Notes Page** for the title slide to serve as a cover page.
  - ❑ Print the **outline** of the presentation.
  - ❑ Print **audience handouts** for the entire presentation (six per page).
  - ❑ Be sure to frame the individual slides.
  - ❑ Submit the various printouts to your instructor.
- Press **Ctrl+Home** to return to the first slide, then click the **Slide Show button** to view the presentation. Press **Esc** at the end of the show. Close the presentation. Exit PowerPoint.

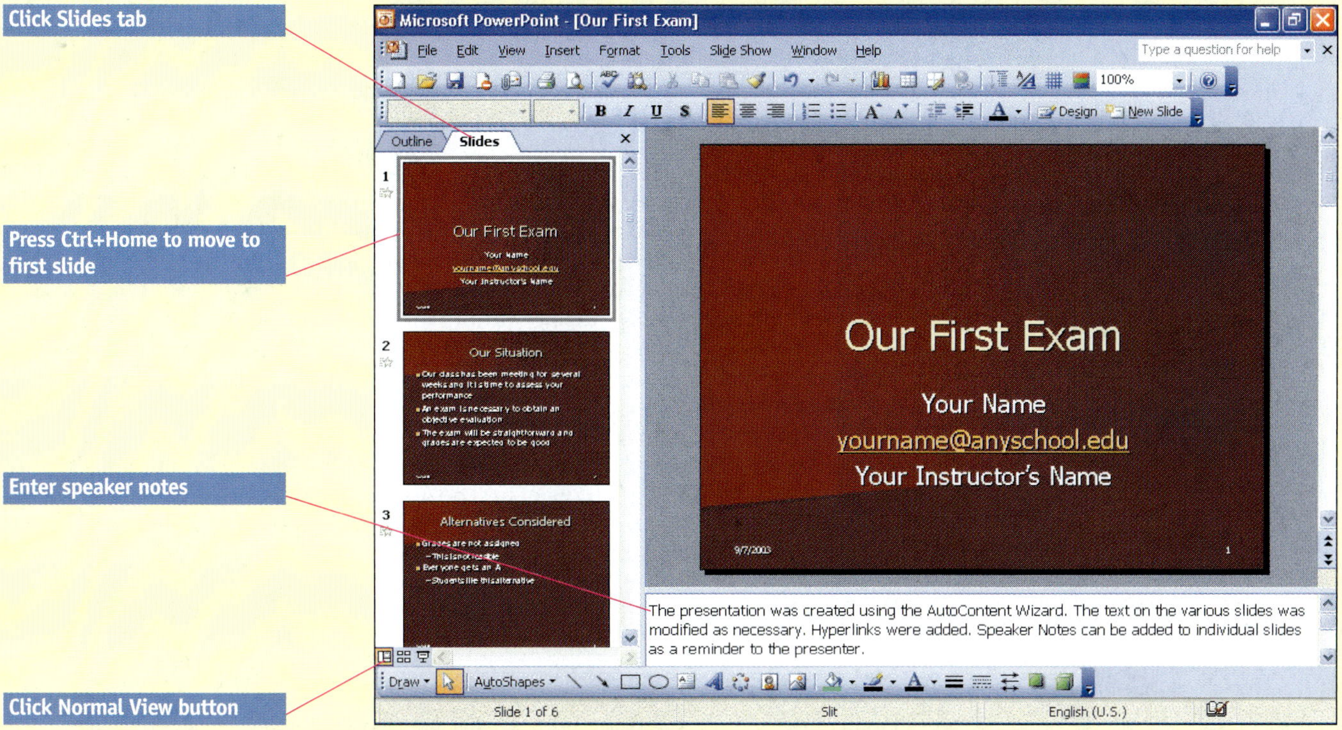

(e) Add Speaker Notes (step 5)

FIGURE 2.11 Hands-on Exercise 4 (*continued*)

ADD NUMBERED OR GRAPHICAL BULLETS

Why settle for simple bullets when you can have numbers or pictures? Click and drag to select the bulleted text on a slide, then click the Numbering button on the formatting toolbar to change to numbered bullets. You can also right click the selected text to display a context-sensitive menu, then click the Bullets and Numbering command to display the associated dialog box, where you can customize the bullets by selecting symbols, pictures, and/or special characters.

SUMMARY

A presentation can be sent electronically to multiple individuals for review. Each reviewer receives a copy of the presentation, enters his or her changes, and then returns the revised presentation as an attachment in an e-mail message. Comments from multiple reviewers can be merged in a single session.

The Header and Footer command is used to personalize a presentation by inserting a common element on every slide, such as the date, time, and/or place of the presentation. The Rehearse Timings feature times each slide as you practice your delivery so that you can estimate the duration of your presentation. Other tools are provided for use during the actual presentation. Slides can be hidden (prior to the presentation) then displayed by right clicking any slide during a slide show, clicking the Go To command, then choosing the hidden slide from a list of slides.

The new Package for CD command copies your presentation to a CD (providing you have the appropriate hardware). The command also gives you the option to save the presentation with the PowerPoint Viewer, so that the presentation may be viewed on computers that do not have PowerPoint installed.

Photographs and other resources can be downloaded from the Web for inclusion in a PowerPoint presentation. Information on the Web is protected by copyright, but you are permitted to use a portion of the work for educational or nonprofit uses under the fair use exclusion. Be sure to cite the work appropriately. The Insert Hyperlink command adds a hyperlink to a slide, which can be accessed during a presentation, provided you have an Internet connection.

A photo album imports multiple photographs into a presentation, without having to format each picture individually. The photos may be taken from a hard disk, a scanner, or a digital camera. The Joint Photographic Experts Group (JPEG, pronounced "jpeg") format is the most common file type for photographs. The Graphics Interchange Format (GIF, pronounced "jif") is used for clip art and similar images.

Photographs may be cropped using the appropriate tool on the Picture toolbar and/or special effects can be applied to enhance a presentation. The Format Background command uses a photograph as the background for a slide, creating a very different type of Powerpoint presentation. A photograph may also be used as the background for a WordArt object.

The AutoContent Wizard facilitates the creation of a new presentation. The wizard asks a series of questions, then it uses the answers to suggest a presentation based on one of several general presentations included within PowerPoint. The end result of the wizard is an outline based on the topic you selected. The outline is very general, as it must be, but it provides the essential topics to include in your presentation. The AutoContent Wizard is the best way to jump-start the creative process.

KEY TERMS

- Animation 793
- AutoContent Wizard 804
- Compare and Merge Presentations command 771
- Copyright 781
- Crop tool 791
- Custom animation 793
- Fair use 781
- Format Background command . 791
- Format WordArt command 791
- GIF format 791
- Header and Footer command ... 770
- Hidden Slide 770
- Hyperlink 781
- Insert Hyperlink command 781
- Insert Picture command 781
- Insert Table command 770
- Infringement of a copyright 781
- Internet 781
- JPEG format 791
- My Pictures Folder 791
- Package for CD command 778
- Photo album 791
- Picture toolbar 791
- Public domain 781
- Rehearse Timings 770
- Reviewing toolbar 771
- Revisions pane 771
- Set Up Show command 770
- Send To command 771
- Text box 781
- Transition 793
- World Wide Web 781

MULTIPLE CHOICE

1. How do you insert a hyperlink into a PowerPoint presentation?
   (a) Pull down the Insert menu and click the Hyperlink command
   (b) Click the Insert Hyperlink button on the Standard toolbar
   (c) Both (a) and (b)
   (d) Neither (a) nor (b)

2. Which of the following is true about hidden slides?
   (a) Hidden slides are invisible in every view
   (b) Hidden slides cannot be accessed during a slide show
   (c) Both (a) and (b)
   (d) Neither (a) nor (b)

3. Which view displays the timings for individual slides after the timings have been established by rehearsing the presentation?
   (a) Slide view
   (b) Outline view
   (c) Slide Sorter view
   (d) All of the above

4. Which of the following is true about annotating a slide?
   (a) The annotations are permanent; that is, once entered on a slide, they cannot be erased
   (b) The annotations are entered using the pen during the slide show
   (c) Both (a) and (b)
   (d) Neither (a) nor (b)

5. Which of the following can be printed for a presentation?
   (a) Audience handouts
   (b) An outline
   (c) Notes
   (d) All of the above

6. Which of the following is a true statement regarding the review of a presentation?
   (a) A presentation must have multiple reviewers
   (b) The review process is initiated outside of PowerPoint by sending a presentation as an ordinary e-mail attachment
   (c) Each reviewer's comments must be examined in a separate session
   (d) The comments of multiple reviewers can be merged in a single session

7. Which of the following *cannot* be accomplished directly by using the Format Photo Album command?
   (a) Changing the number of photographs on a slide
   (b) Changing the shape of the photographs
   (c) Inserting captions below the photographs
   (d) Adding custom animation to the individual photos

8. How do you crop a picture and then enlarge the result?
   (a) Select the crop tool, click and drag any border away from the center, click off the picture, then click and drag any corner inward
   (b) Select the crop tool, click and drag any border toward the center, click off the picture, then click and drag any corner inward
   (c) Select the crop tool, click and drag any border toward the center, click off the picture, then click and drag any corner outward
   (d) It cannot be done

9. Which of the following is *not required* to dissolve a black-and-white photograph into a color photograph?
   (a) Copy the original color photograph, then change the copied photograph to black and white
   (b) Place the black-and-white photograph on top of the color photograph
   (c) Apply the "dissolve out" exit effect to the black-and-white photograph
   (d) Apply the "dissolve in" entrance effect to the color photograph

... continued

multiple choice

10. Which of the following can be applied to a given object on a specific slide?

(a) An entrance effect, but not an exit effect
(b) An exit effect, but not an entrance effect
(c) Both an entrance and an exit effect
(d) Neither an entrance nor an exit effect

11. Which entrance effect(s) should be applied to multiple objects on a slide so that the objects appear one after another without having to click the mouse?

(a) Any entrance effect starting after the previous object
(b) Any entrance effect starting with the previous object
(c) Any entrance effect starting with a mouse click
(d) It cannot be done

12. Which of the following parameters can be set for the "fly in" entrance effect?

(a) The direction (left, right, top, or bottom)
(b) The speed (e.g., fast, medium, or slow)
(c) The starting time (e.g., automatically after the previous object appears)
(d) All of the above

13. Where can you store photographs for use in a subsequent presentation?

(a) In the My Pictures folder
(b) In a folder within the My Pictures folder
(c) In any folder on drive C
(d) All of the above

14. The AutoContent Wizard:

(a) Creates a generic presentation that can be customized as necessary
(b) Inserts a clip art image on every slide according to its content
(c) Inserts the author's name on every slide
(d) All of the above

15. Which of the following can be done to customize a presentation created by the AutoContent Wizard?

(a) Insert or delete a slide
(b) Change the template
(c) Change the transition effect
(d) All of the above

16. Which of the following provides legal protection to the author for a written or artistic work?

(a) Public domain
(b) Copyright
(c) Fair use exclusion
(d) Footnote

17. Which of the following keyboard shortcuts is correct with respect to animating a presentation?

(a) Press Ctrl+P to change the mouse pointer to a pen to animate the slide
(b) Press Ctrl+A to change the mouse pointer back to an arrow
(c) Both (a) and (b)
(d) Neither (a) nor (b)

18. Which format is most commonly associated with photographs?

(a) Joint Photograph Experts Group (JPEG), which is pronounced "jpeg"
(b) Graphics Interchange Format (GIF), which is pronounced "gif"
(c) Both (a) and (b)
(d) Neither (a) nor (b)

ANSWERS

1. c	**7.** d	**13.** d
2. d	**8.** c	**14.** a
3. c	**9.** d	**15.** d
4. b	**10.** c	**16.** b
5. d	**11.** a	**17.** c
6. d	**12.** d	**18.** a

PRACTICE WITH POWERPOINT

1. **Composite Photographs:** The presentation in Figure 2.12 builds on the first hands-on exercise to create two additional slides, each of which contains multiple photographs. You can add these slides to the original presentation and/or you can create a new presentation as shown. As with the original presentation, you can use our photographs or substitute your own.
   a. Start a new presentation. Change the slide layout to a blank slide, and then insert the photographs of Brian and Jessica (in the Our Photos folder) onto a single slide. Arrange the photographs in an attractive overlapping fashion. You can use your own pictures instead of ours.
   b. Select all of the photographs, then use the Format Picture command to apply a black 4 point border around every picture.
   c. Check that all of the photographs are still selected. Click the Compress tool on the Picture toolbar to compress the pictures and reduce their file size.
   d. Click outside the slide to deselect all of the pictures. Now select the pictures individually, pull down the Slide Show menu, click Custom Animation, and apply an entrance effect to each photograph. Set the timing for each entrance effect so that it begins automatically after the previous animation.
   e. You can create a composite picture from the individual photographs for use in any Office document. Click anywhere on the slide and press Ctrl+A to select all of the photographs. Right click the slide to display a context-sensitive menu, click the Grouping command, and then click Group. The sizing handles appear on the border of the slide to indicate a single object. Right click the slide once again; click the Save as Picture command, then save the slide as a JPEG image.
   f. Insert a new slide for the wordArt. Create four separate WordArt objects, each of which is a single letter, (L, O, V, and E), and each of which has a fill based on a different photograph.
   g. Use custom animation so that the objects appear in sequence, one after the other. Include the sound of applause in conjunction with the letter E.
   h. Print the presentation as an audience handout (two slides per page) for your instructor. Be sure to frame the individual slides.

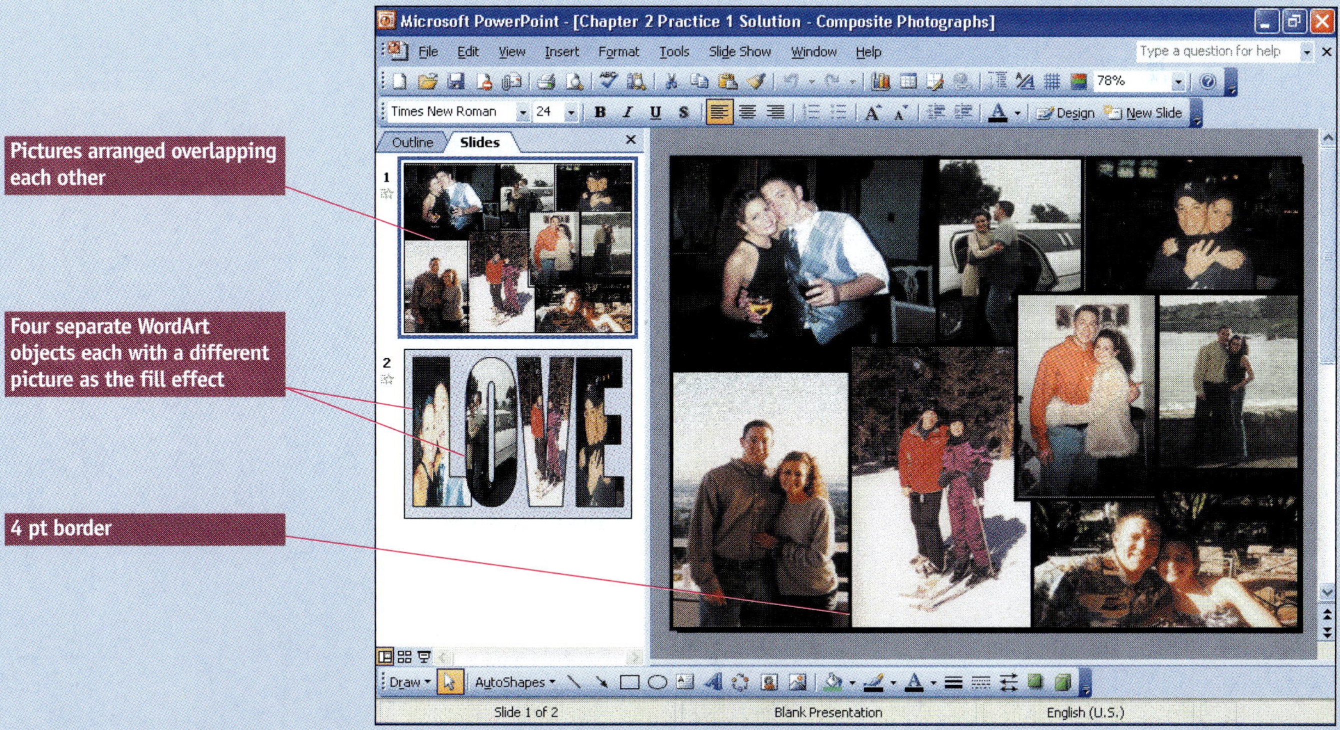

FIGURE 2.12 Composite Photographs (exercise 1)

2. **Impressionist Paintings:** The paintings in Figure 2.13 may be viewed at the Web Museum (www.ibiblio.org/wm), which currently welcomes over 200,000 visitors per week from all over the world. The museum is maintained by Nicolas Pioch and is one of our favorite sites on the Web. Start Internet Explorer to go to the museum, click the link to Famous Artworks (or search for Impressionist paintings), and then to the main page for impressionist paintings. Use that page as the basis for this assignment.
   a. Choose any artist and any painting by that artist. Click the thumbnail image of the painting you select to enlarge the painting, then right click the painting and save the image in a new folder called Impressionist Paintings. If necessary, change the name of the file to include the artist and the name of the painting. Repeat this process to download five to ten paintings.
   b. Start PowerPoint. Use the Insert Picture command to create a new photo album. Insert the paintings into the presentation, so that the paintings are displayed one painting per slide. Display a caption under each painting as shown in Figure 2.12.
   c. Change the title of the presentation to Impressionist Paintings and include your name on the title slide. Add a hyperlink on the title slide that points to the Web Museum. (Pull down the Insert menu, click the Hyperlink command, specify "The Web Museum" as the text to display, and enter the corresponding Web address.)
   d. View the completed presentation and enjoy a private showing of priceless art. Print the completed presentation as audience handouts (six per page) for your instructor.
   e. Create your own screen saver based on the impressionist paintings that you saved earlier. (This technique works in Windows XP and has to be modified for earlier versions of Windows.) Right click the desktop to display a context-sensitive menu, click Properties, then click the Screen Saver tab and choose the My Picture Slideshow from the Screen Saver list box. Click the Settings button, click the Browse button, and select the folder containing the impressionist paintings. Check the boxes to use transition effects and to include file names (to see the name of the artist with the painting).

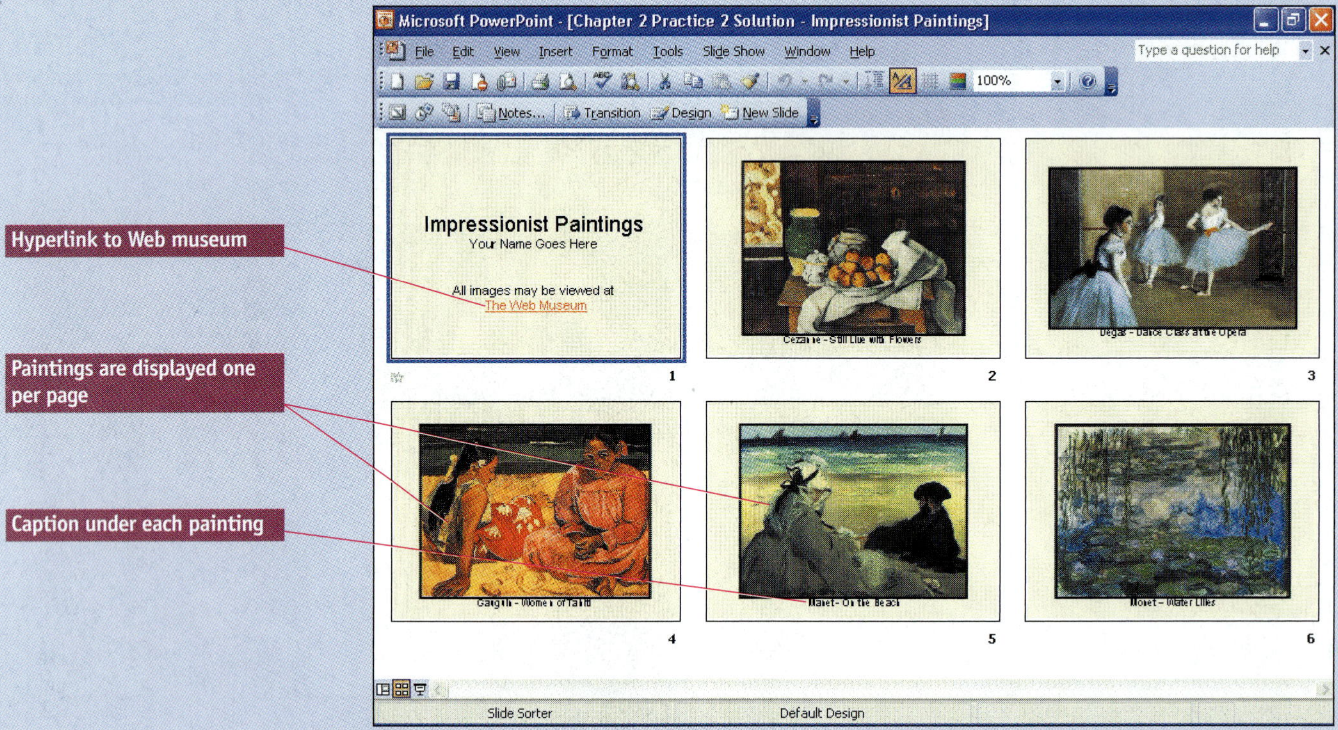

FIGURE 2.13 Impressionist Paintings (exercise 2)

Credits: Cezanne, Giraudon/Art Resource, NY; Degas: Scala/Art Resource, NY; Gaugin, Erich Lessing/Art Resource, NY; Manet, Réunion des Musées Nationaux/Art Resource, NY; Monet, Erich Lessing/Art Resource, NY.

3. **My Favorite Presidents:** Create a presentation similar to the one in Figure 2.14. The presentation contains six slides. The title slide contains your name and provides a hyperlink to the White House Web site (www.whitehouse.gov), which is the source of our photographs. Each additional slide contains a photograph and quote from one of our favorite presidents. Start a new presentation and create the title slide.
   a. Start Internet Explorer, go to the White House Web site, and locate the list of past presidents. Select any president, point to his picture, click the right mouse button to display a shortcut menu, and save the picture on your PC. Be sure you remember the location of the file when you save it on your local machine.
   b. Use the Windows taskbar to switch to PowerPoint. Insert a new slide and select the Title, Text, and Content layout. Click in the title area of this slide and add the president's name and years in office. Click in the text area, press the backspace key to delete the bullet that appears automatically, and then enter a quotation or short sentence pertaining to this president.
   c. Click the Insert Picture icon in the Content placeholder (the first icon in the second row) to display the Insert Picture dialog box. Select the folder where you saved the file in part (a). Select the picture, then click the Insert button to insert the picture onto the slide. Move and size the picture as appropriate. Save the presentation.
   d. Repeat these steps for the additional presidents. Print the title slide as a full slide to serve as a cover sheet for your assignment, then print the completed presentation as audience handouts (six per page). Be sure to frame the slides.
   e. Create your own screen saver based on the pictures of the presidents that you saved earlier. (This technique works in Windows XP and has to be modified for earlier versions of Windows.) Right click the desktop to display a context-sensitive menu, click Properties, then click the Screen Saver tab and choose the My Picture Slideshow from the Screen Saver list box. Click the Settings button, click the Browse button, and select the folder containing the presidents. Check the boxes to use transition effects and to include file names.

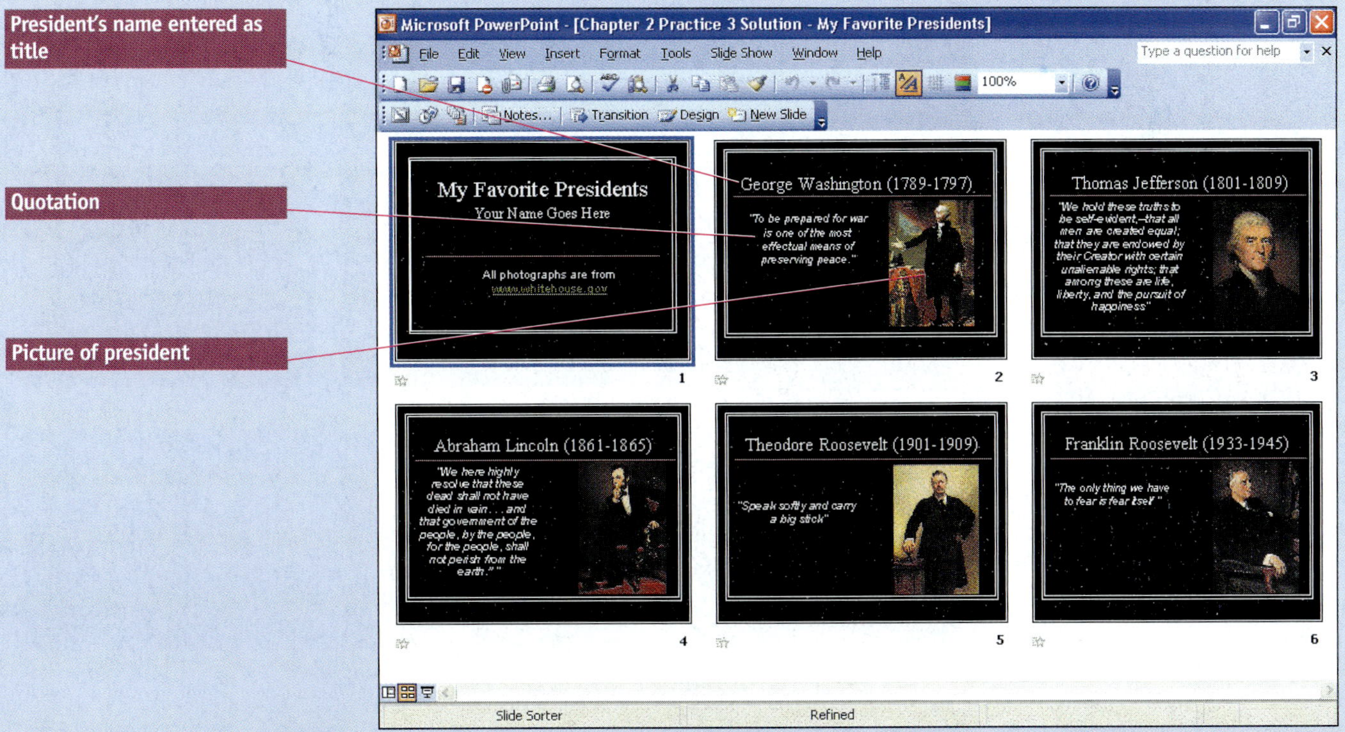

FIGURE 2.14 My Favorite Presidents (exercise 3)

4. **My State or Country:** Create (at least) a six-slide presentation that describes your home state or country of origin, similar to the presentation in Figure 2.15. You do not have to duplicate our presentation exactly, but you are required to include the equivalent information. Proceed as follows:
   a. Start a new presentation. Enter the name of your state or country on the title slide. Add your name to the title slide as well.
   b. Add notes to the title slide that contain the name of the course you are taking, your instructor's name, and the days and times your class meets. Boldface the name of your course as well as the name of your instructor.
   c. Add four additional slides that describe the history, government (include the name of the current governor, president, or prime minister), fun facts (include the population and area), and various symbols pertaining to your state or country.
   d. Add a fifth slide on major attractions that contains hyperlinks to each listed attraction. Visit at least two of the associated Web sites and print a page from each site for your instructor.
   e. Add clip art and/or photographs to the various slides as you see fit.
   f. Apply an appropriate design template to the presentation.
   g. Apply transition effects to all slides.
   h. Print the presentation in multiple ways. Print the title slide as a slide (full page) to serve as a cover page for the assignment. Print the title slide a second time, this time with speaker notes. Print audience handouts for the entire presentation (six per page). Be sure to frame the individual slides. And finally, print the presentation in outline form.
   i. Exchange your assignment with another classmate to learn more about that person. Your instructor may also use the assignment to learn more about the class as a whole; e.g., how many states are represented in your class? How many countries are represented? Which classmates are bilingual? Do any of your classmates speak more than two languages?

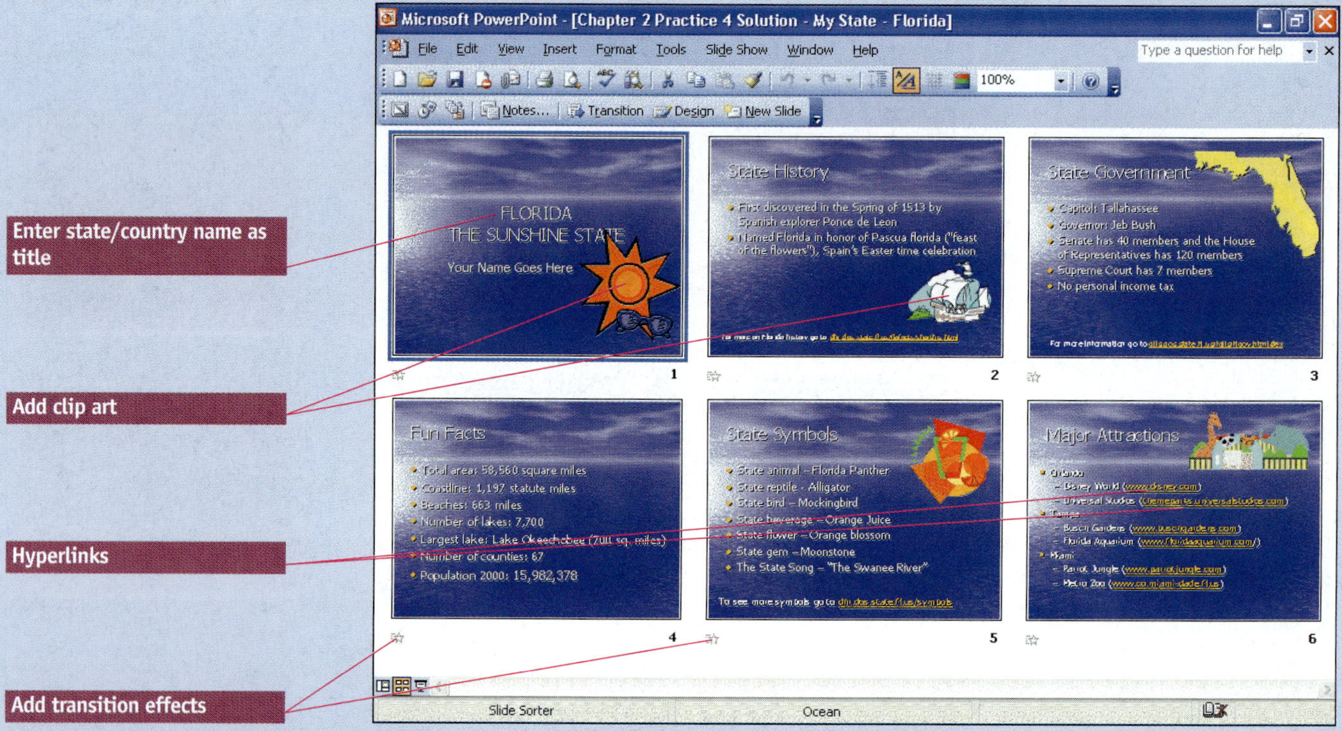

FIGURE 2.15 My State or Country (exercise 4)

5. **Hidden Slides (a card trick):** You didn't expect a card trick in a book on PowerPoint, but we think you will enjoy this exercise. Open the presentation in *Chapter 2 Practice 5*, pull down the Slide Show menu and click the View Show command (or simply press the F5 key to start the show).
   a. You will see the title slide, followed by the slide in Figure 2.16. Choose a card and then click the mouse as instructed.
   b. Concentrate as directed and then click the mouse to move to the next slide. The card you chose originally will be removed from the stack and only five cards will remain. Try it as often as you like, choosing a different card each time. We will continue to "read your mind" and will always remove your card from the pile.
   c. The solution is contained within the original presentation as a hidden slide. Change to the Slide Sorter view, locate the hidden slide, and then double click the slide to return to the Normal view so that you can read the solution. Run through the slide show once again. You can see how easy it is to perform the card trick once you know the answer.
   d. Insert a hyperlink on the title slide that will display the slide containing the solution. (You need to specify that the hyperlink is to a place in this document—that is, to an existing slide, as opposed to an external Web page.) Clicking the newly inserted hyperlink during the slide show will display the slide even if it is a hidden slide.
   e. Insert a hyperlink on the solution slide that takes you to the second slide in the presentation that describes the card trick. (Once again, specify that the hyperlink is to a place in this document, as opposed to a Web page.)
   f. View the presentation a final time to be sure it works as intended.
   g. Print the title slide as a full slide to serve as a cover sheet for your assignment. Print the completed presentation as audience handouts (six per page). Be sure to frame the individual slides.

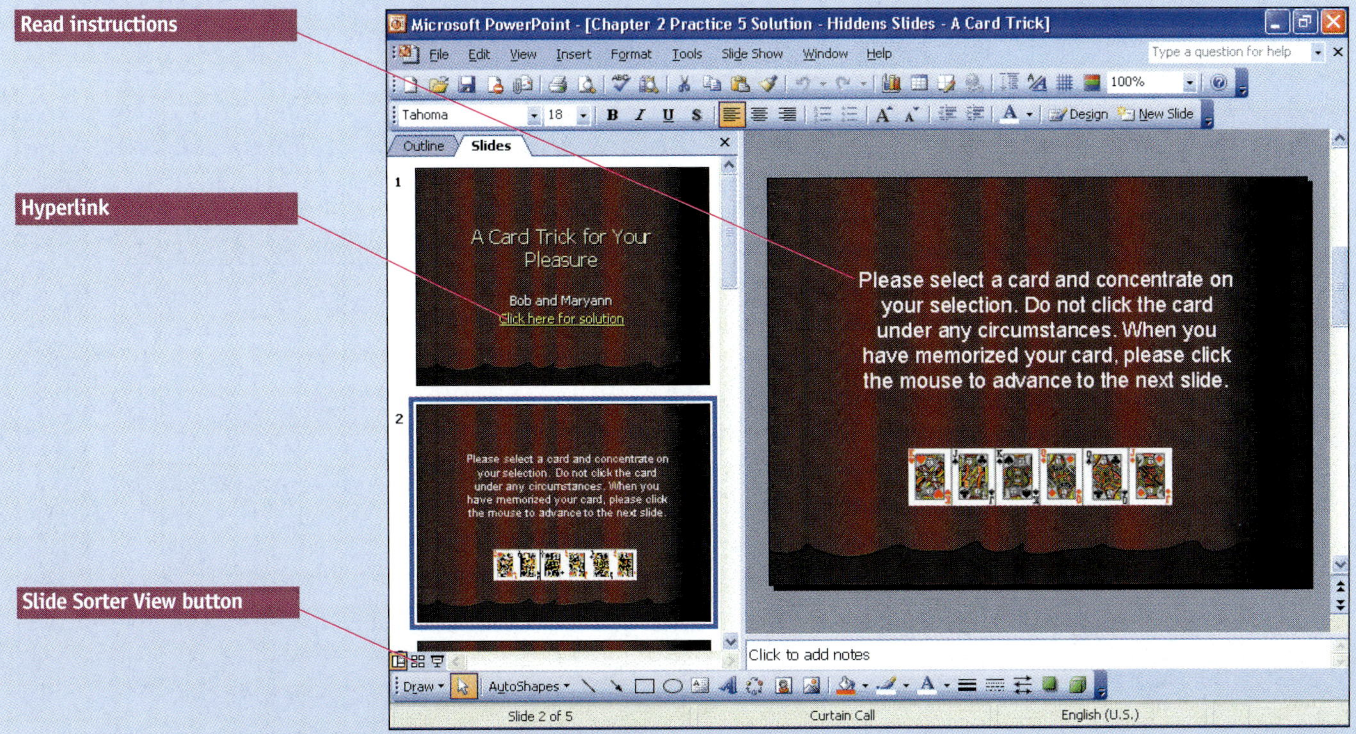

FIGURE 2.16 Hidden Slides (exercise 5)

6. **Creating a Timeline:** The presentation in Figure 2.17 displays a timeline that contains milestones for a hypothetical event. The slide looks quite impressive and is very easy to create. Choose a real or hypothetical event, then create a timeline with at least four milestones. Proceed as follows:
   a. Start PowerPoint and create a new presentation. Enter your name and an appropriate title on the title slide.
   b. Insert a second slide in the Title and Content layout. Click the icon to insert a table. Enter 12 and 2, for the number of columns and rows, respectively. Click OK to create the table.
   c. Click and drag the line separating the two rows, so that the first row is much narrower than the second. Drag the bottom border of the table down to increase the depth of the second row.
   d. Select all of the cells in the first row. Change the font size to 17 or 18 points, and then enter the months of the year. Center and boldface the text, then select an appropriate fill color.
   e. Click the AutoShapes tool and then create a block arrow for the first milestone. Enter appropriate text to describe the milestone.
   f. Use the same fill color as for the months in the first row. Copy the block arrow for the additional milestones, changing the text as necessary for each milestone.
   g. You can add a header and/or a footer to the audience handouts by modifying the handout master. Pull down the View menu, click the Master command, and then click Audience Handout. Insert your instructor's name at the upper left of the handout master and today's date at the upper right. Put your name at the lower left of the handout master, and put the page (slide) number on the lower right.
   h. Print the completed presentation as audience handouts, two slides per page. Be sure to frame the slides.

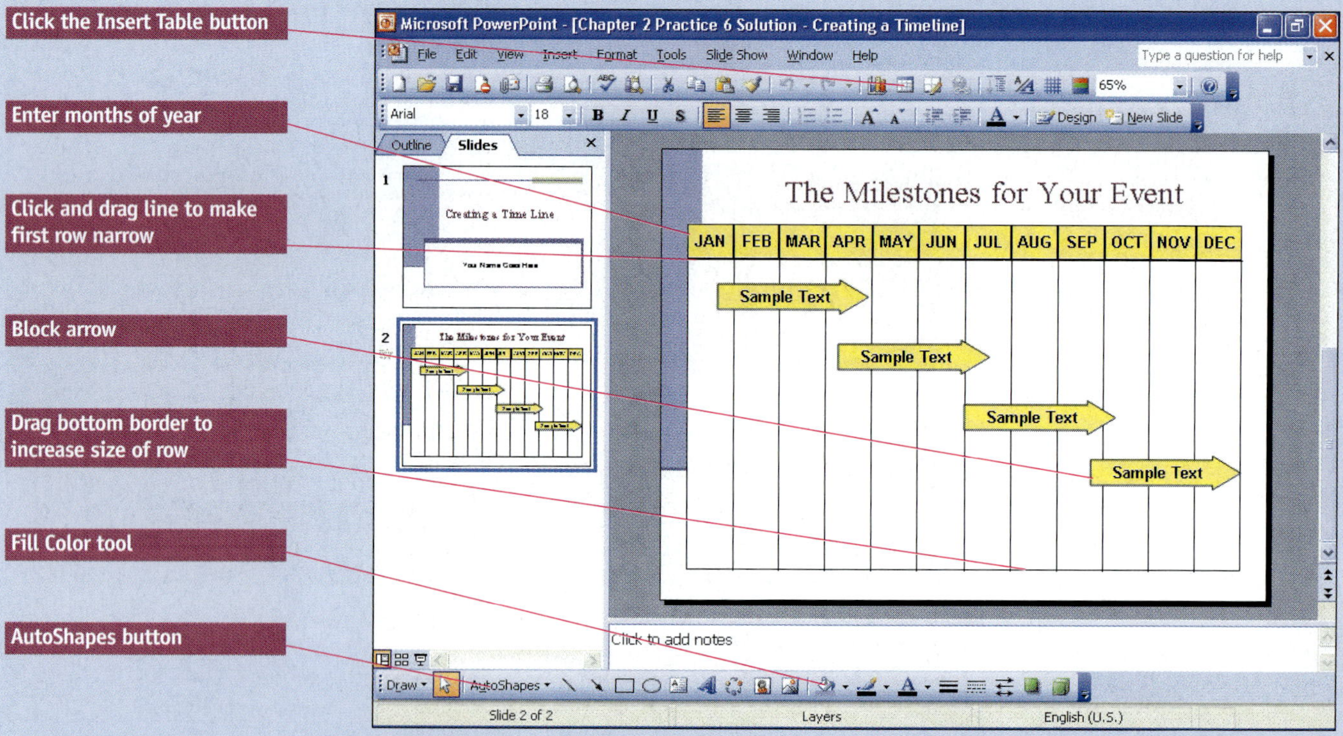

FIGURE 2.17 Creating a Timeline (exercise 6)

7. **Look Ahead—Creating a Web Page:** A PowerPoint presentation can be converted to a Web page so that it can be viewed within an Internet browser. In the early days of the Internet, the only way to create a Web page was to learn HTML. Today, however, it's much easier. You can create a presentation (Word document or Excel workbook), then use the Save as Web Page command to convert the document to a Web page.
   a. Open the *Our First Exam* presentation that was created in the fourth hands-on exercise. Pull down the File menu and click the Save As Web Page command to display the Save As dialog box. The file name (Our First Exam) is specified by default. Check that the file type is Single File Web Page (as opposed to Web Page) so that all of the HTML elements are stored in a single document. (The Single File Web Page format was introduced in PowerPoint 2003 and was not available in previous versions of Microsoft Office.)
   b. Select the Exploring PowerPoint folder, then click the Save button. The presentation does not change in any noticeable way. Close PowerPoint.
   c. Start Windows Explorer and switch to the Exploring PowerPoint folder. Look closely and you will see two files with the same name (Our First Exam). The file types are different, however. You have the original PowerPoint presentation as well as a new MHTML document.
   d. Double click the MHTML document to view the presentation as a Web page as shown in Figure 2.18. Experiment with the various controls at the bottom of the Internet Explorer window to view the presentation. How do you go to a specific slide? What happens if you click the Outline button? What happens if you click the Slide Show button in Internet Explorer?
   e. Print the title slide from Internet Explorer to prove to your instructor that you have created the Web page.
   f. The address bar in Figure 2.18 indicates that you are viewing the Web page locally (from your C drive). What additional steps are necessary if you want to place your presentation on the Web so that it can be viewed by others?

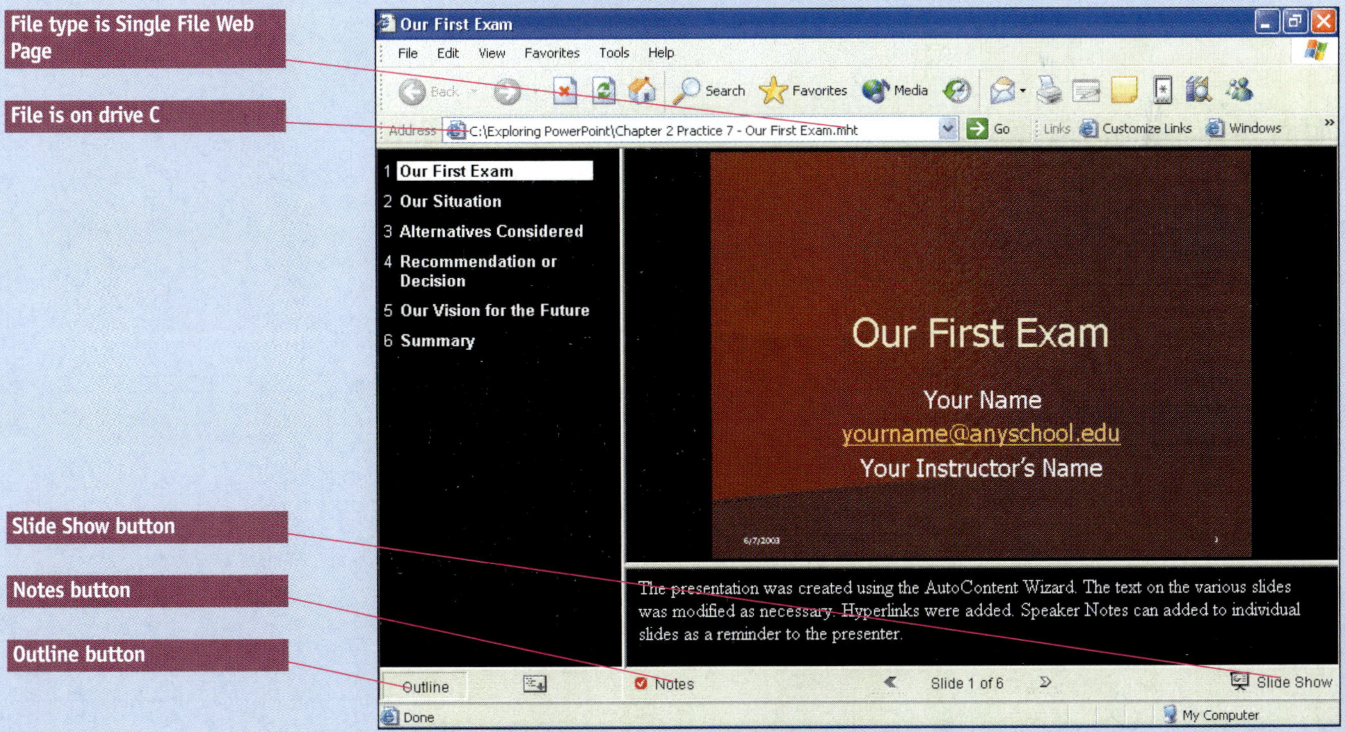

FIGURE 2.18 Look Ahead—Creating a Web Page (exercise 7)

8. **A Look Ahead—Templates and Color Schemes:** The ability to include multiple design templates in a single presentation was first introduced in Office XP. Start a new presentation and enter "Templates and Color" as the title of the presentation. Add your name to the title slide in the indicated placeholder. Choose a design template (we selected the Layers design) and add that information to the title slide. Proceed as follows to create the remainder of the presentation.
   a. Go to the Slide Sorter view as shown in Figure 2.19, copy the title slide, and then change the color scheme in the second slide. Try to use contrasting color schemes—that is, light text on a dark background, versus dark text on a light background. Which color scheme do you prefer? What does PowerPoint suggest? (See the tip for new users that appears on the Standard tab within the Edit Color Scheme dialog box.)
   b. Copy the original title slide, change to the Blends design, and modify the information in the appropriate placeholder. Duplicate this slide and change the color scheme. Repeat this process at least one additional time, so that your complete presentation has a minimum of six slides.
   c. Print the completed presentation as audience handouts (six per page) for your instructor. Use a color printer if possible to appreciate the different color schemes within the presentation.
   d. How many colors comprise a color scheme? How do you change a specific color within a particular color scheme? Be prepared to answer these questions in a class discussion.
   e. Search the Web for additional templates that are not provided in the default installation of Microsoft Office. How much do these templates cost? Are they superior to those provided with Office?
   f. Print the title slide as a full slide to use as a cover sheet for this assignment. Include written answers to the various discussion questions and submit the entire assignment to your instructor.

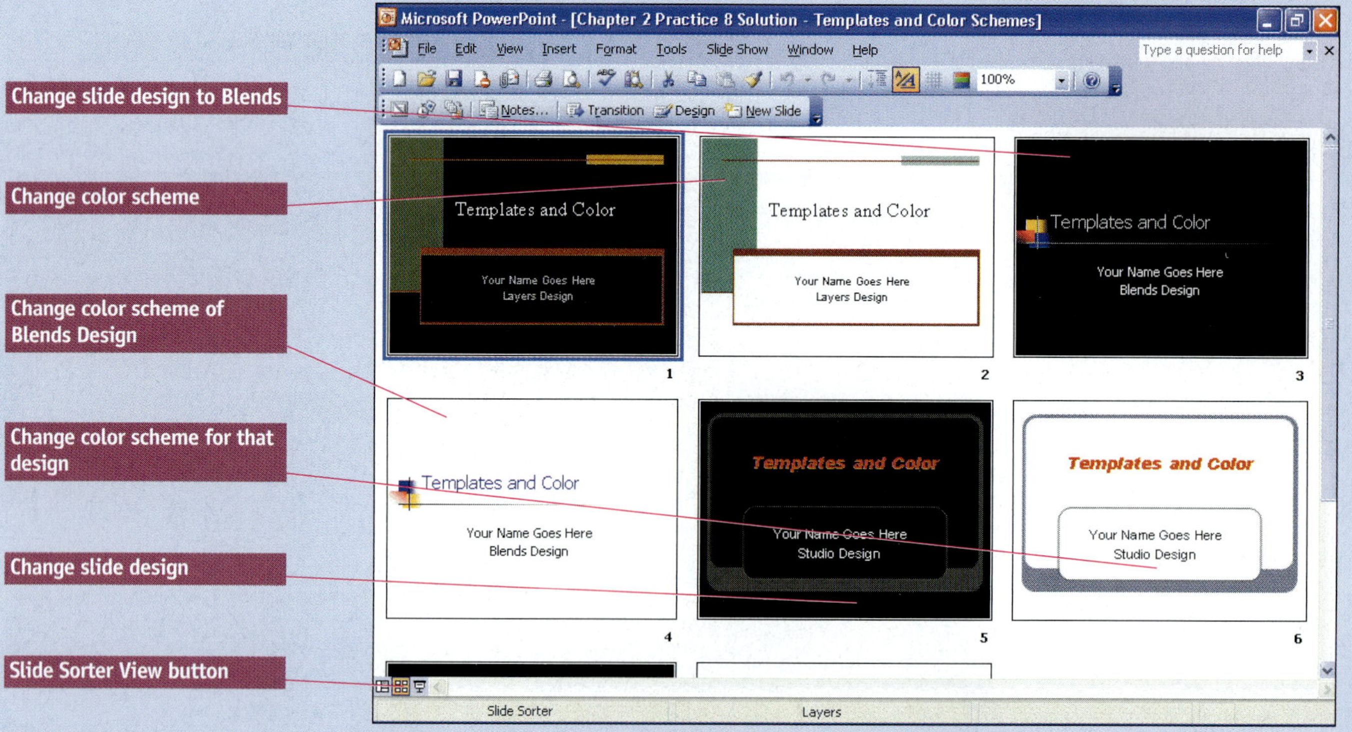

FIGURE 2.19 A Look Ahead—Templates and Color Schemes (exercise 8)

9. **A Look Ahead—Scheduling an Online Broadcast:** Any presentation, even one including video and audio, can be delivered as a Web broadcast. The broadcast can be live or recorded. A live broadcast is scheduled at a precise time, and invitations are sent to a designated list of attendees. A recorded broadcast is uploaded to a Web server and configured for on-demand viewing. Either type of broadcast is ideal for reaching large and/or geographically dispersed audiences. PowerPoint alone is sufficient to broadcast to groups of ten or fewer. Additional software, such as Microsoft Windows Media Server, is required to reach larger audiences. Check with your instructor about the facilities available to you, then proceed as follows:
   a. Choose any presentation for your broadcast. It need not be long and it need not include video or audio files, as your objective at this time is to schedule the broadcast and establish basic settings.
   b. Pull down the Slide Show menu, click the Online Broadcast command, then click Schedule a Live Broadcast to display the associated dialog box in Figure 2.20. Enter the requested information, which will appear on the lobby page (opening screen) of your broadcast.
   c. Click the Tips for Broadcast button to display a help window with detailed information about scheduling a broadcast. Print this information for your instructor. Close the Help window.
   d. Click the Settings button in the Schedule Presentation Broadcast dialog box to display the Broadcast Settings dialog box. Click the Presenter tab and then test your video and/or audio devices as necessary.
   e. Click the Advanced tab to establish additional settings; e.g., the URL of a chat room, or whether you will use the Windows Media server. Click the Help button in the Broadcast Settings dialog box to learn more. Print the associated information for your instructor. Close the Help window. Close the dialog box.
   f. Click the Schedule button to display the associated dialog box and schedule the actual broadcast (if possible). Notify your instructor when your broadcast is to take place in order to get credit for the assignment.
   g. Summarize your thoughts about scheduling a broadcast in a short note to your instructor. Add a cover sheet to complete the assignment.

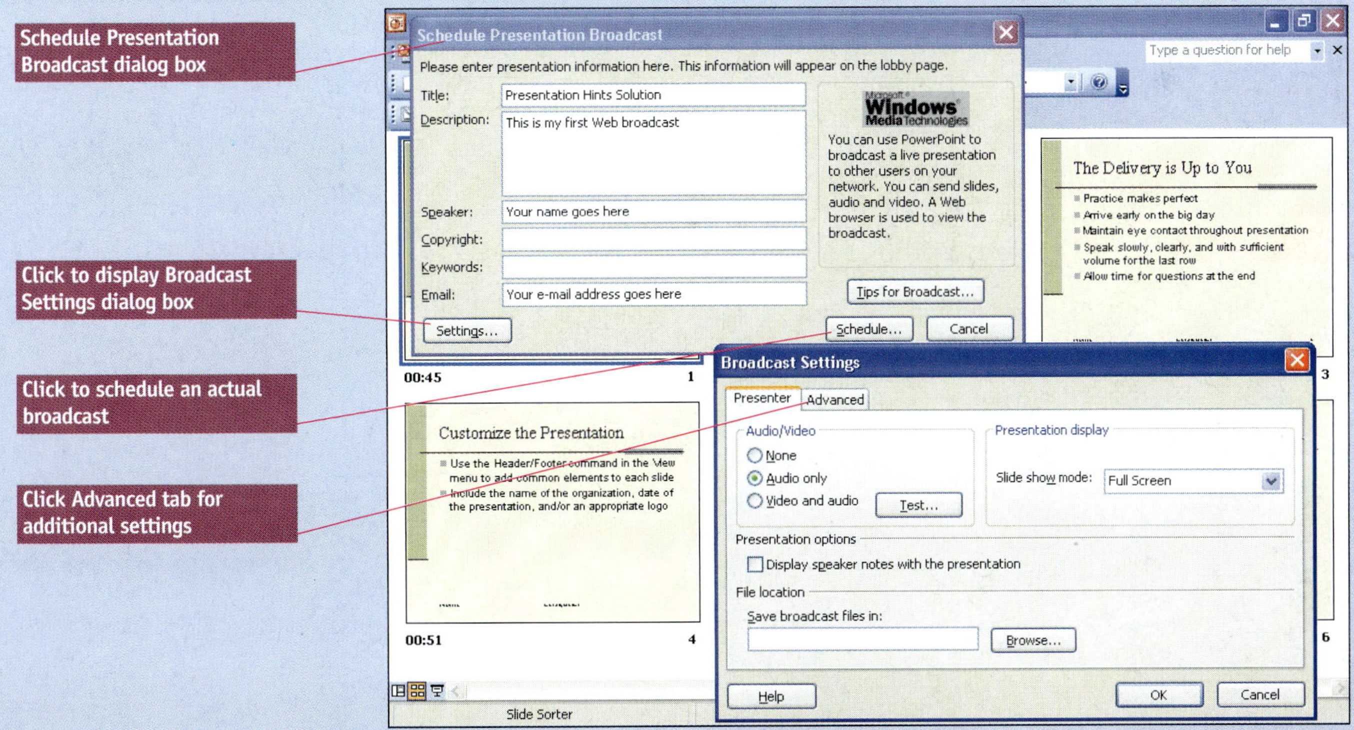

FIGURE 2.20 A Look Ahead—Scheduling an Online Broadcast (exercise 9)

MINI CASES

Digital Cameras

As with all technology, the price of a digital camera has come down significantly while performance has gone up dramatically. What are the most significant capabilities in a digital camera? What is the least amount of money you have to spend to purchase (what you consider) a worthwhile camera? What are the parameters and cost of your ideal camera? Be sure to consider the size and weight of the camera—the more functionality, the larger the camera. The worst picture is the one you do not take because the camera is too big to take with you.

The Annual Report

Corporate America spends a small fortune to produce its annual reports, which are readily available to the public. Choose any company and obtain a copy of its most recent annual report. Use your imagination on how best to obtain the data. You might try a stockbroker, the 800 directory, or even the Internet. Use the information in the annual report as the basis for a PowerPoint presentation. PowerPoint is one step ahead of you and offers a suggested financial report through the AutoContent Wizard.

Two Different Clipboards

The Office clipboard is different from the Windows clipboard, but both clipboards share some functionality. Thus, whenever you copy an object to the Office clipboard, it is also copied to the Windows clipboard. However, each successive copy operation *adds* an object to the Office clipboard (up to a maximum of 24 objects), whereas it *replaces* the contents of the Windows clipboard. The Office clipboard also has its own task pane. Experiment with the Office clipboard from different applications, then summarize your findings in a brief note to your instructor.

Director of Marketing

Congratulations on your appointment as Director of Marketing. The company into which you have been hired has 50 sales representatives across the United States. Laptop computers have just been ordered for the entire sales staff and will be delivered at next week's annual sales meeting. Your job is to prepare a PowerPoint presentation that can be used by the sales staff in future sales calls. It's short notice, but it is a critical assignment. Use the Selling a Product template provided by the AutoContent Wizard as the basis for your presentation.

CHAPTER 1

The Internet and the World Wide Web: Welcome to Cyberspace

OBJECTIVES

After reading this chapter you will:

1. Define the Internet and give a brief overview of its history.
2. Explain how the World Wide Web differs from the Internet.
3. Describe the structure of a Web address.
4. Describe the various buttons on the Internet Explorer toolbar.
5. Explain how to return to a Web site; distinguish between the History and Favorites lists.
6. Name three different search engines; explain the advantage of using multiple engines with the same query.
7. Distinguish between the AND, OR, and NOT operations with respect to a Web search.
8. Download a picture from the Web.
9. Discuss similarities and differences between e-commerce and traditional commerce.
10. Distinguish between the http and https protocols.
11. Create a Web page.

hands-on exercises

1. INTRODUCTION TO THE WORLD WIDE WEB
   Input: None
   Output: None
2. SEARCHING THE WEB
   Input: None
   Output: Apollo 11 (Word document)
3. SHOPPING IN CYBERSPACE
   Input: None
   Output: None
4. INTRODUCTION TO HTML
   Input: None
   Output: The Computer Super Store (Single File Web Page)

CASE STUDY

CREATING A HOME PAGE

Shawna Deplonty, a freshman at the University of Miami, is enrolled in CIS120, Introduction to Computer Information Systems. It is the first week of the semester, and her current assignment is to create a personal Web page. Shawna is from Canada; she and many of her classmates are international students. The professor thought it would be interesting, therefore, to require information about the student's country of origin, or if a U.S. citizen, information about the state in which the student resides. The completed page must include at least four links to appropriate Web sites plus one or two graphic images in the form of clip art, a map, and/or a photograph.

Shawna is excited about the assignment and eager to tell her classmates about her native country. She knows that she has to create a Word document and save it as a Web page, but she must first obtain the required information about Canada. Shawna is familiar with the Internet in general and currently uses e-mail and Instant Messenger to keep in touch with friends and family, but is less confident about searching for specific topics. A friend suggested that she start with the Google search engine, but she knows there are many others. The professor insists that she use at least two different search engines, because different engines will turn up different results to the same query. ■

Your assignment is to read the chapter, paying special attention to Hands-on Exercises 2 and 4 that describe how to search the Web and how to create a Web page. Search the Web to locate various sites about Canada (or your home state or country), after which you can write the text for your page. Include at least three hyperlinks on your page to the sites that you have found. Use the Themes command to enhance the formatting of the finished page, and then print the completed page from your Internet browser. If possible, upload the completed page to your school or university's Web server to share it with your classmates.

THE INTERNET

The Internet has transformed the world and is arguably the most important invention of the twentieth century. You can download music or software, view movie clips, do research, and shop for virtually anything. You can post your résumé, bank electronically, get the score of any sporting event as it happens, or check the price of a stock. You may start or end your day with e-mail.

If you are doing these things, you already know how to use the Internet, but do you really understand it? Do you know how to search for information efficiently, as opposed to casually browsing? Do you know the difference between an Internet Service Provider and a browser or between a modem and a cable modem? Are you truly comfortable with privacy and security issues that permeate the news? Do you know how to create a Web page? This introduction will answer these and other questions as you begin your journey through ***cyberspace***, the term used to describe the invisible realm of the Internet.

We begin with a brief history of the Internet and World Wide Web, describe how Web documents are accessed on a server, and define basic terms such as HTTP (HyperText Transfer Protocol). We show you how to organize your favorite sites into folders. We also describe the History folder, which provides an easy way to return to sites that you viewed previously. We define a search engine and present several tips to search efficiently. We describe the lure of e-commerce and discuss issues of privacy and security. We also show you how to create a Web page.

The ***Internet*** is a network of networks that connects computers across the country and around the world. It grew out of a U.S. Department of Defense (DOD) experimental project begun in 1969 to test the feasibility of a wide area (long distance) computer network over which scientists and military personnel could share messages and data. The country was in the midst of the Cold War, and the military imposed the additional requirement that the network be able to function with partial outages in times of national emergency (e.g., a nuclear disaster), when one or more computers in the network might be down.

The proposed solution was to create a network with no central authority. Each ***node*** (computer attached to the network) would be equal to every other node, with the ability to originate, pass, and receive messages. The path that a particular message took in getting to its destination would be insignificant. Only the final result was important, as the message would be passed from node to node until it arrived at its destination.

The experiment was (to say the least) enormously successful. Known originally as the ARPANet (Advanced Research Projects Agency Network), the original network of four computers has grown exponentially to include tens of millions of computers. To say that the Internet is large is a gross understatement, but by its very nature, it's impossible to determine just how large it really is. How many networks there are, and how many users are connected to those networks, is of no importance as long as you yourself have access.

The Internet is a network of networks, but if that were all it was, there would hardly be so much commotion. It's what you can do on the Internet, coupled with the ease of access, that makes the Internet so exciting. In essence, the Internet provides two basic capabilities: information retrieval and worldwide communication, functions that are already provided by libraries and print media, the postal system and the telephone, television, and other types of long distance media. The difference, however, is that the Internet is interactive in nature, and more importantly, it is both global and immediate.

The Internet enables you to request a document from virtually anywhere in the world, and to begin to receive that document almost instantly. No other medium lets you do that. Television, for example, has the capability to send information globally and in real time (while events are unfolding), but it is not interactive in that you cannot request a specific program. Federal Express promises overnight delivery, but that is hardly immediate. The stacks in your university library provide access to the information that is physically in that library, but that is not global access. Indeed, the Internet, and in particular the World Wide Web, is truly unique.

The World Wide Web

The original language of the Internet was uninviting and difficult to use. The potential was exciting, but you had to use a variety of esoteric programs (such as Archie and Gopher) to locate and download data. The programs were based on the Unix operating system, and you had to know the precise syntax of the commands within each program. There was no common user interface to speed learning. And, even if you were able to find what you wanted, everything was communicated in plain text, as graphics and sound were not available. All of this changed in 1991 with the introduction of the World Wide Web.

The ***World Wide Web*** (***WWW***, or simply the Web) is a very large subset of the Internet, consisting of documents with links to one another. Each document contains a ***hyperlink*** (reference) to another document, which may be on the same computer, or even on a different computer, with the latter located anywhere in the world. Hyperlinks may reference graphic, sound, and video files in addition to text files.

Hyperlinks enable you to move effortlessly from one document (or computer) to another. And therein lies the fascination of the Web, in that you simply click on link after link to go effortlessly from one document to the next. You can start your journey at your professor's home page in New York, for example, which may link to a document in the Library of Congress, which in turn may take you to a different document, and so on. So, off you go to Washington, DC, and from there to a reference across the country or perhaps around the world.

Any computer that stores a document anywhere on the Web, and makes that document available to other computers, is known as a ***server*** (or ***Web server***). Any computer that is connected to the Web, and requests a document from a server, is known as a ***client***. In other words, you work on a client computer (e.g., a node on a local area network or your PC at home) and by clicking a link in a hypermedia document, you are requesting a document from a Web server.

In order for the Web to work, every client (be it a PC or a Mac) must be able to display every document from every server. This is accomplished by imposing a set of standards known as a protocol to govern the way data is transmitted across the Web. Thus, data travels from client to server, and back, through a protocol known as the ***HyperText Transfer Protocol (http)***. In addition, to access the documents that are transmitted through this protocol, you need a special type of program known as a ***browser***. Indeed, a browser is aptly named because it enables you to visit the Web in a leisurely and casual way (the dictionary definition of the word "browse"). ***Internet Explorer*** is the browser we use throughout the text, but the concepts apply equally well to ***Netscape Navigator***, the other browser that is popular in today's environment.

Internet Explorer is easy to use because it shares the common user interface and consistent command structure that are present in every Windows application. Every screen contains several familiar elements that include the title bar, and the Minimize, Maximize (or Restore), and Close buttons. Commands are executed from pull-down menus or from command buttons that appear on a toolbar under the menu bar. A vertical and/or horizontal scroll bar appears if the entire document is not visible at one time. The title bar displays the name of the document you are currently viewing.

Figure 1 depicts the use of Internet Explorer during a typical session in which we "surf the Web" to visit various Web sites. Our journey begins through a ***portal***, or gateway into the Internet. A portal is a very general site that contains a series of links to a variety of topics. We have chosen to start with usatoday.com, but there are many such sites on the Web (Yahoo.com and Excite.com are other examples). The developers of these sites make them as interesting and as comprehensive as possible to entice visitors to the sites.

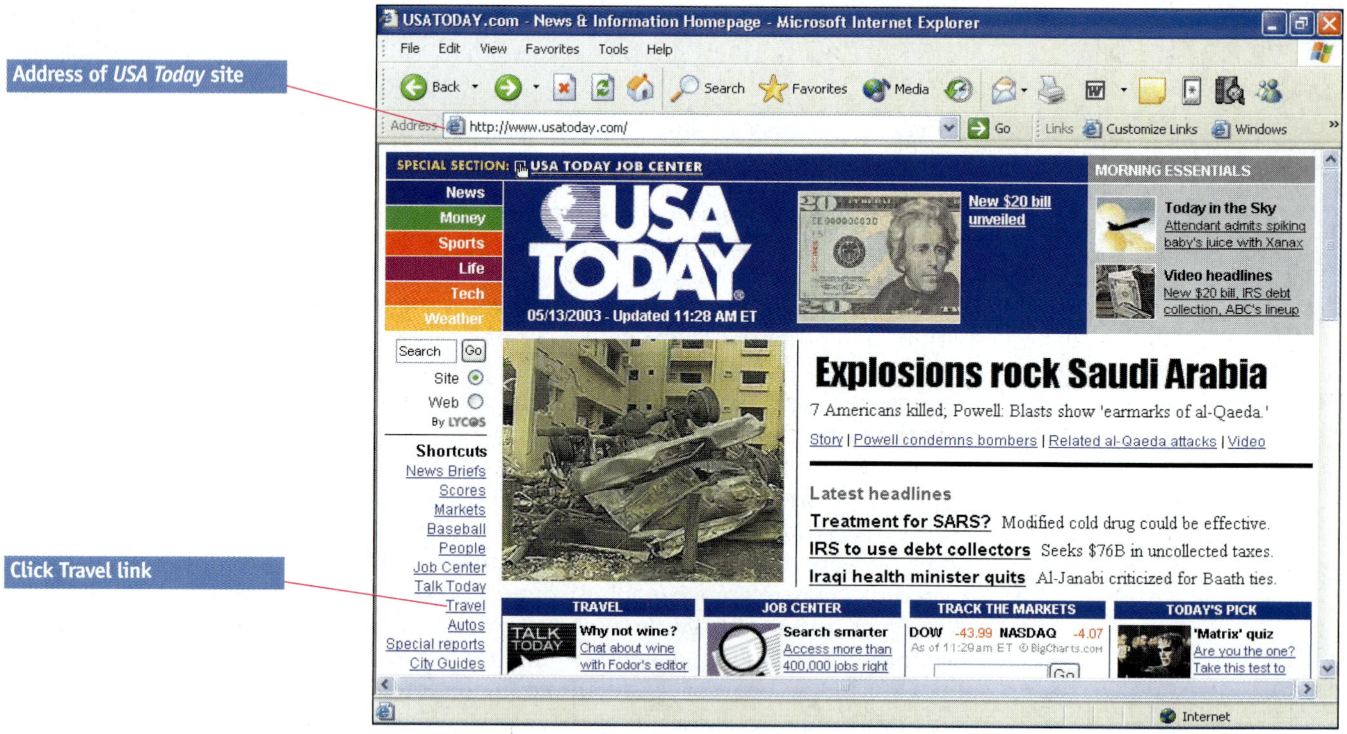

(a) *USA Today* Home Page (portal)

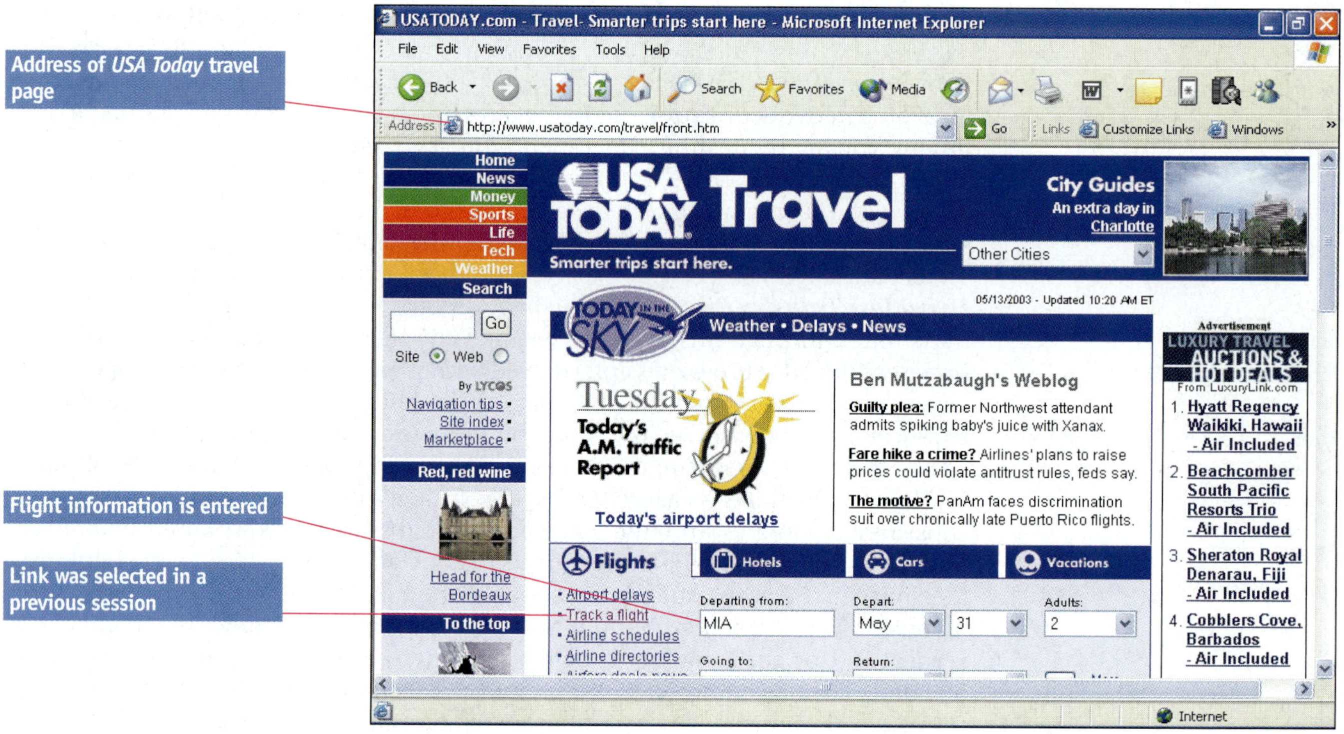

(b) *USA Today* Travel Page

FIGURE 1 The World Wide Web

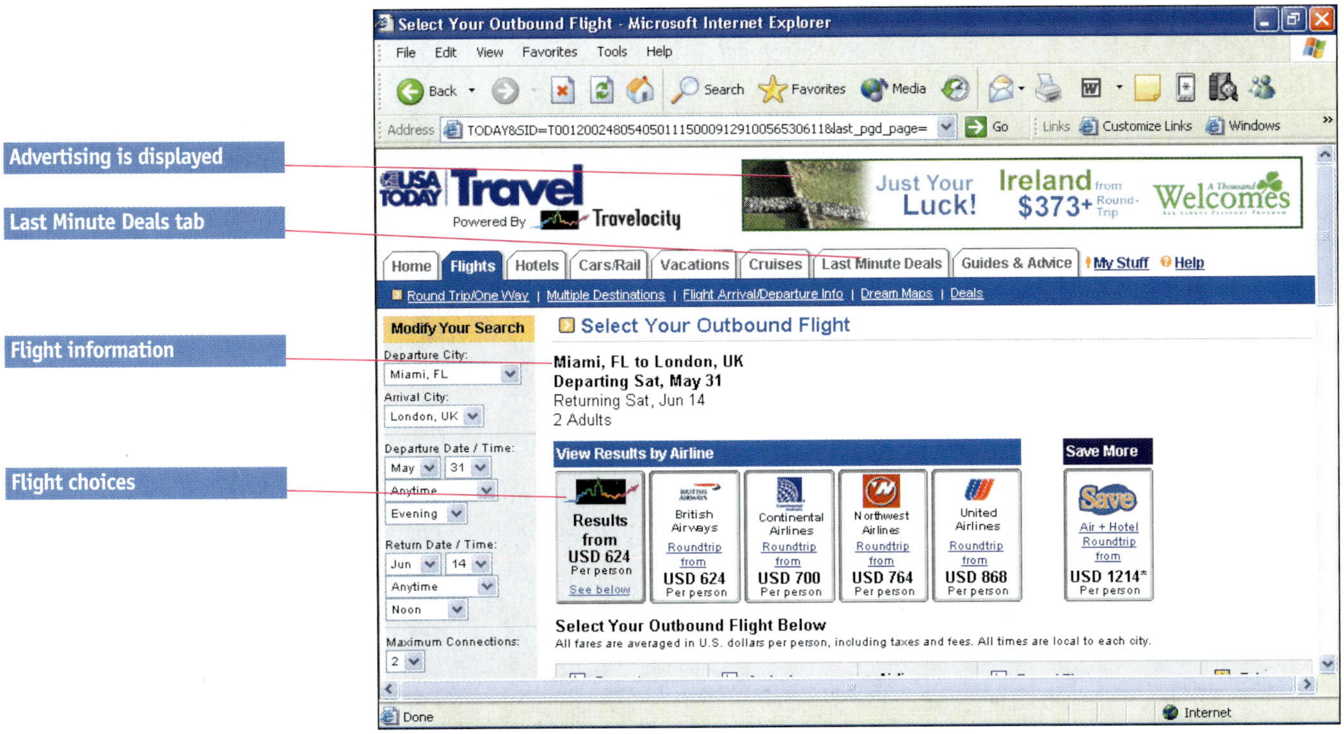

(c) Air Fares to London

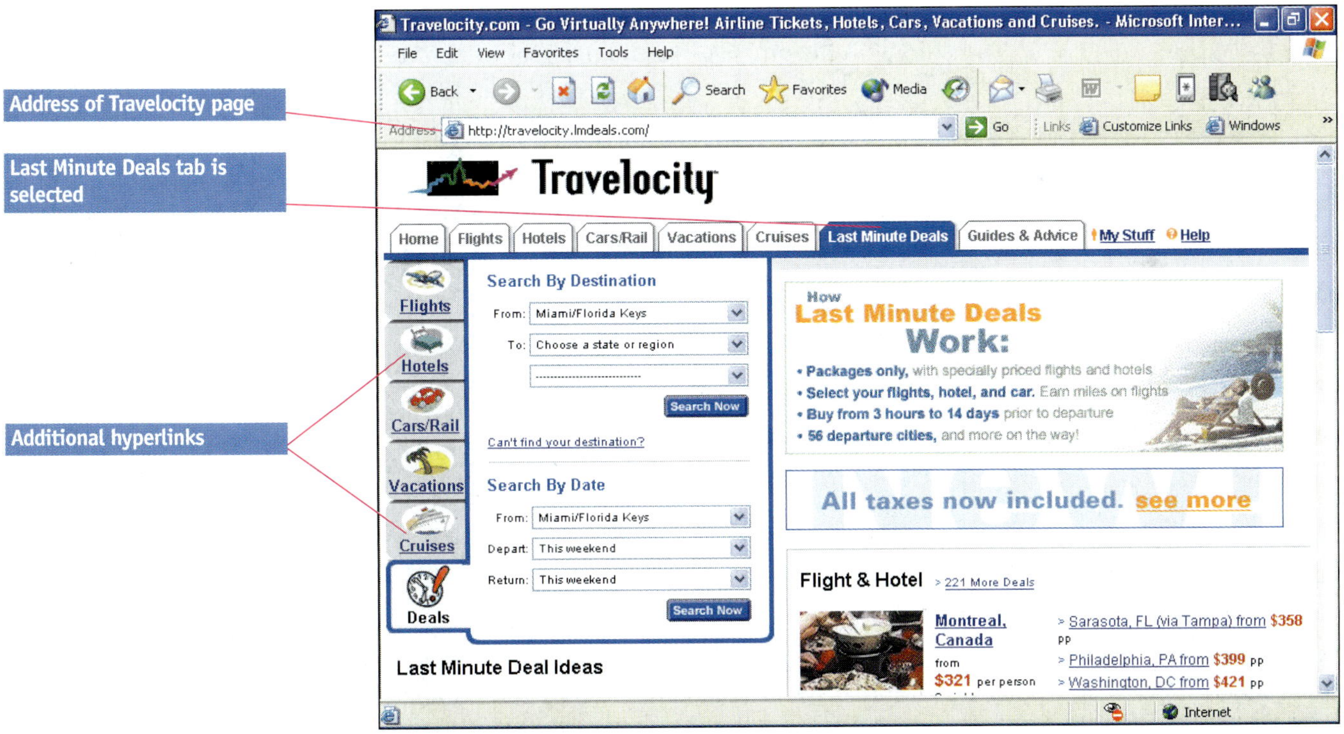

(d) Last Minute Deals

FIGURE 1 The World Wide Web (*continued*)

There is no charge to you to visit a portal, but the developers have an ulterior motive. Most sites contain one or more advertisements, as can be seen in Figure 1a. The developer sells advertising just as commercial billboards on a highway sell advertising. The more visitors to the site, the more the developer can charge for advertising on the site. Nevertheless, portals perform an invaluable service and enable you to browse the Web in leisurely fashion. Once you arrive at the portal (by entering its address into your browser), you can click any link that interests you. A newspaper site such as *USA Today*, the *New York Times*, or the major paper in your hometown is a perfect portal as it lets you begin by reading the day's events, then going wherever your inclination takes you.

Let's assume, for example, that after you have read the news, you are interested in the travel section. You click the appropriate link in Figure 1a, which in turn takes you to the travel section in Figure 1b. You see the flight information area and that reminds you to make reservations for your vacation. You enter the requested information and click Go, which in turn takes you to the Travelocity Web site in Figure 1c, where you are presented with a series of choices until you eventually make a reservation. Once there, you decide to explore the last-minute deals that may be available, which takes you to Figure 1d. The address bar changes automatically as you go from one document to the next. The documents may be stored on the same computer as with multiple pages from the *USA* Web site or on an entirely different computer, but either way, it is entirely transparent to the user.

Think for a moment of what we have just accomplished. We started with the front page of today's newspaper and shortly thereafter you were booking a flight to London. There is no beginning (other than the starting point or Web portal) and no end. You simply read the various Web documents in any way that makes sense to you, jumping to explore whatever topic you want to see next. All of this is accomplished with a graphical browser such as Internet Explorer and a connection between your computer and the Internet. The process of "surfing the net" in this fashion has become an integral part of our culture.

The underlined links that appear in Figure 1 are displayed in one of two colors, magenta or blue, depending on whether or not the link has been previously selected. Any link in blue (the majority of links) indicates the document has not yet been viewed. Links in magenta, however (such as Track a Flight in Figure 1b), imply the associated document has been retrieved earlier in that session or in a previous session. Note, too, the presence of advertising in Figure 1, such as the Ireland trip in Figure 1c. The vendor pays the owner of the site for the advertising, which helps to underwrite the investment in developing and maintaining the site.

Realize that the pages displayed in Figure 1 were available on the day that we wrote this particular chapter. They are not available today, and there is no way that you will be able to duplicate our figure. You can, however, still go to the *USA Today* Web site (www.usatoday.com), and click the link to its travel section, provided that the layout of the online newspaper is unchanged. In other words, the address of the Web site does not change, only the content.

AP/Wide World Photo

Tim Berners-Lee

Tim Berners-Lee, Creator of the Web

Tim Berners-Lee was a software engineer working in Switzerland, where he developed a hypertext program to keep track of random notes. His goal was to create an open-ended system with no boundaries, so that scientists everywhere could share their work. He single-handedly developed the URL addressing scheme for giving each document a unique address. He also created HTML to display the hypertext documents and the HTTP protocol to transmit the documents across the Web. Most incredibly, perhaps, he made his ideas freely available to the public, as opposed to profiting by his invention.

The Uniform Resource Locator (URL)

The address (or location) of a document appears in the ***Address bar*** and is known as a ***Uniform Resource Locator*** (URL), or more simply as a Web address. The URL is the primary means of navigating the Web, and indicates the Web server (computer) from which you have requested a document. Change the URL (e.g., by clicking a link or by entering a new address in the Address bar) and you jump to a different document, and possibly a different server.

A URL consists of several parts: the method of access, the domain name, a path in the directory (folder) structure within the domain, and finally the document name. Each time you click a link within a browser, you are effectively entering the URL of a new document. The general format of a Web address is as follows:

```
http://www.prenhall.com/grauer/index.html
|          |              |      |
|          |              |      └ Document
|          |              └ Path (directories or folders)
|          └ Domain name
└ Method of access (HyperText Transfer Protocol)
```

The components in the address are read from right to left. Thus our URL references the *index.html* document, in the *Grauer* folder, in the *www.prenhall.com* Internet domain, and is accessed according to the *http* protocol.

The document name is sometimes omitted, in which case the browser displays a default document called index.html. The folder (path) may not exist and thus it would not be specified. The method of access is often omitted and defaults to http. Thus, the URL *www.prenhall.com* will take you to the home page of the Prentice Hall Web site. In similar fashion, www.prenhall.com/grauer, will take you to the default page for the Grauer folder within the Prentice Hall site.

The ***domain name***, www.prenhall.com in our example, always ends with a two- or three-letter prefix called a top-level domain to help identify the site. The Internet originally provided six top-level domains as follows: **.edu** (education), **.com** (commercial), **.gov** (government), **.mil** (military), **.net** (network administration), and **.org** (nonprofit). Additional top-level domain names have been subsequently created such as **.biz** (business), **.pro** (licensed professionals), and **.info** (information services). Each country is also assigned a code that functions as a top-level domain; e.g., **.uk** (United Kingdom), **.ca** (Canada), or **.au** (Australia).

You can often guess the Internet domain of an organization by using the general format, www.organization.domain, such as www.ibm.com, www.miami.edu, and www.irs.gov, for IBM, the University of Miami, and the Internal Revenue Service, respectively. Anyone can register their own Internet domain for approximately $20 a year, provided the domain name was not registered previously.

The Domain Name Server

A mnemonic name such as www.prenhall.com/grauer may be easy for individuals to remember, but it is of no use to the computers that comprise the Internet. Every computer connected to the Web has a unique IP address that consists of four groups of numbers; e.g. 201.102.85.123. The ***domain name servers*** are a vital, but hidden part of the Internet, which translate the mnemonic domain name specified in a URL to a numeric IP address. It may sound like a simple task, but consider that there are billions of IP addresses currently in use, that IP addresses change, and that new domain names are added daily.

CONNECTING TO THE INTERNET

There are two basic ways to connect to the Internet—from a ***local area network (LAN)*** or by dialing in. It's much easier if you connect from a LAN (typically at school or work) because the installation and setup have been done for you, and all you have to do is follow the instructions provided by your professor. If you connect from home, you will need an analog modem, a cable modem, or a DSL modem, and an ***Internet Service Provider*** (or ***ISP***).

A ***modem*** is the hardware interface between your computer and the telephone system. In essence, you instruct the modem, via the appropriate software, to connect to your ISP, which in turn lets you access the Internet. A ***cable modem*** provides high-speed access (20 to 30 times that of an ordinary modem) through the same cable as used for cable TV. A ***DSL modem*** also provides high-speed access through a special type of phone line.

An Internet Service Provider is a company or organization that maintains a computer with permanent access to the Internet. Typically, you have to pay for this service, but you may be able to dial into your school or university at no charge. If not, you need to sign up with a commercial vendor such as America Online (AOL). Not only does AOL provide access to the Internet, but it also offers a proprietary interface and other services such as local chat rooms. The Microsoft Network (MSN) is a direct competitor to AOL, and it, too, offers Internet access as well as a proprietary interface and extra services. Alternatively, you can choose from a host of other vendors who provide Internet access without the proprietary interface of AOL or MSN.

Regardless of whom you choose as an ISP, be sure you understand the fee structure. The monthly fee may entitle you to a set number of hours per month (after which you pay an additional fee), or it may give you unlimited access. The terms vary widely, and we suggest you shop around for the best possible deal. If you are using a dial-up service, be sure you are given a local access number (i.e., that you are not making a long-distance call), or else your telephone bill will be outrageous. Check that the equipment of your provider is adequate and that you can obtain access whenever you want. Few things are more frustrating than to receive continual busy signals when you are trying to log on.

DISABLE CALL WAITING

Your friend may understand if you excuse yourself in the middle of a conversation to answer another incoming call. A computer, however, is not so tolerant and will often break the current connection if another call comes in. Accordingly, check the settings of your communications program to disable call waiting prior to connecting to the Internet (typically by entering *70 in front of the access number). Your friends may complain of a busy signal, but you will be able to work without interruption.

LEARNING BY DOING

The Web cannot be appreciated until you experience it for yourself, and so we come to our first hands-on exercise. We suggest a specific starting point, a portal known as the Reference Desk (at refdesk.com), then browse leisurely through a series of documents. The exercise will illustrate the concept of browsing as well as basic commands in Internet Explorer. Remember, too, that the World Wide Web is a "living document" that changes continually, so don't be surprised if you cannot duplicate the hands-on exercise exactly. It doesn't matter, because you want current information, not "yesterday's headlines."

hands-on exercise

1 Introduction to the World Wide Web

Objective To access the Internet and World Wide Web and to practice basic commands in Internet Explorer. Use Figure 2 as a guide in the exercise.

Step 1: Start Internet Explorer

- Click the **Start button**, click (or point to) **All Programs**, and then click **Internet Explorer**. (You can also double click the **Internet Explorer icon** on the desktop if it is present.)
- It does not matter which page you see initially as long as you are able to start Internet Explorer and connect to the Internet. If necessary, click the **Maximize button** so that Internet Explorer takes the entire desktop.
- Enter the address of the Reference Desk, which is the portal we shall use throughout this exercise:
  - ❑ Pull down the **File menu** and click the **Open command** to display the Open dialog box in Figure 2a. Enter the address of the Web site you want to explore—in this case, **www.refdesk.com** (you don't have to enter http:// as it is assumed). Click **OK**.
  - ❑ *Or,* click in the **Address bar**, which automatically selects the current address. Enter **www.refdesk.com** (the http:// is assumed). Press **Enter**.
- Be sure that you enter the Web address correctly, or else you will not be able to get to the site.
- If necessary, pull down the **View menu**, click the **Toolbars command**, and check the **Standard Buttons**, **Address Bar**, and **Links commands** so that your toolbars match ours.

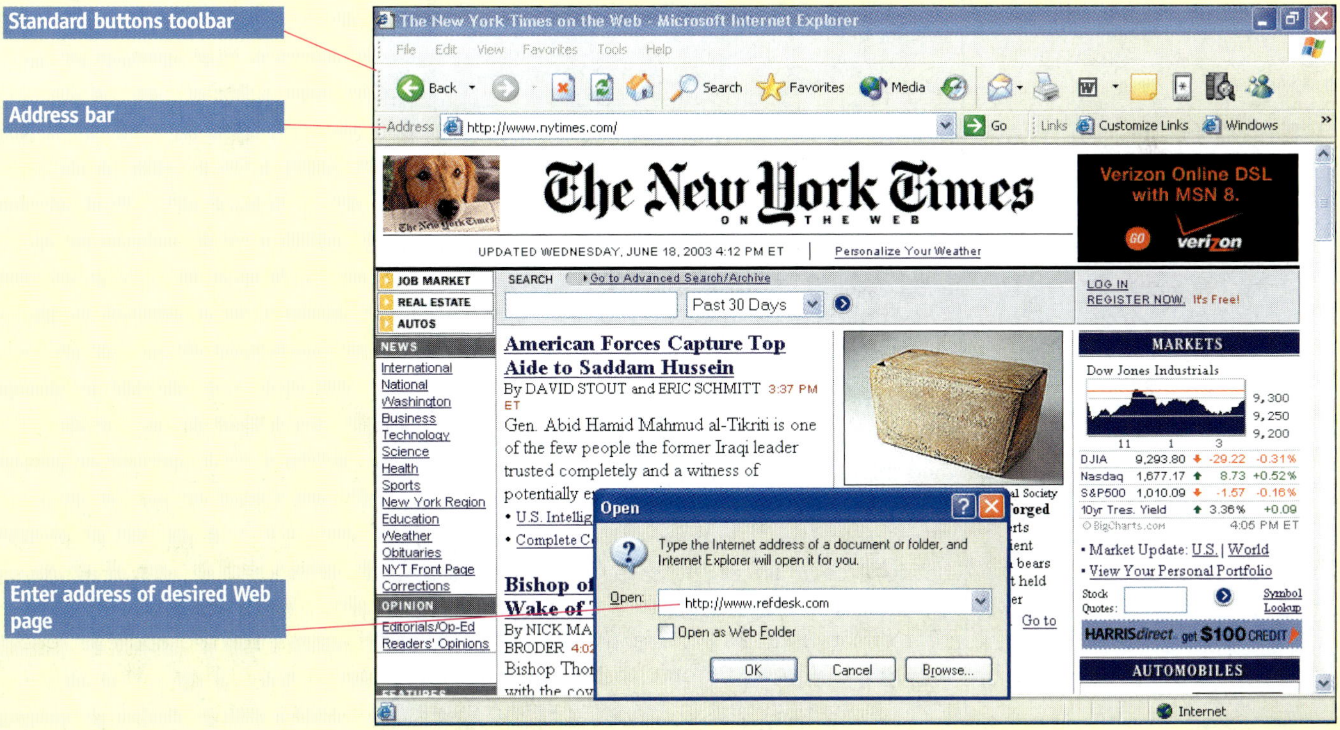

(a) Start Internet Explorer (step 1)

FIGURE 2 Hands-on Exercise 1

Step 2: The Reference Desk

- You should see the home page of the Reference Desk, as shown in Figure 2b, although the content will surely be different.
- Scroll down the page until you can select one of the three associated links in the Word of the Day area. We chose **MW** for the *Merriam Webster Dictionary*. Click the link.
- If you are unable to get to the Reference Desk, pull down the **File menu**, click the **Open command**, and reenter the address shown in the Address bar in Figure 2b. Press **Enter**.
- If you are still unable to get to the site, enter the address of any other site you wish to explore. You will not be able to duplicate the exercise exactly, but you will be able to practice with commands in Internet Explorer.

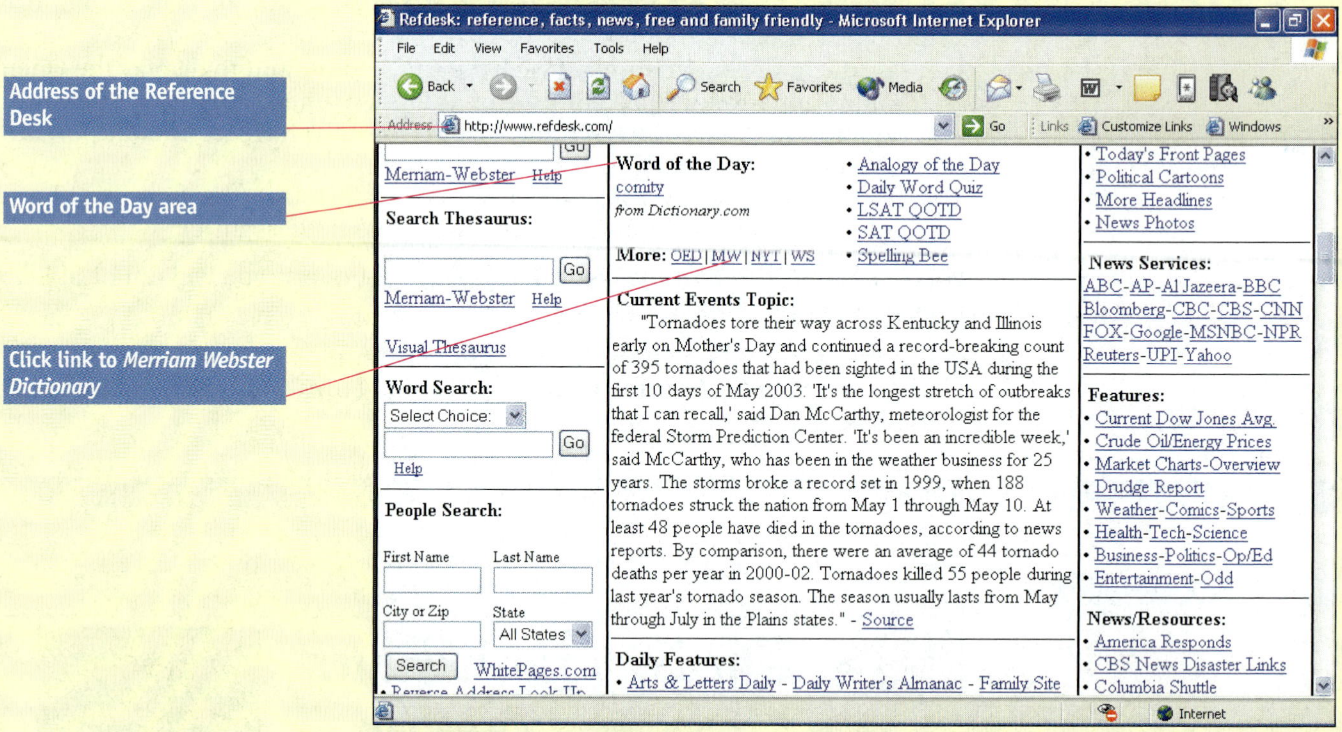

(b) The Reference Desk (step 2)

FIGURE 2 Hands-on Exercise 1 (*continued*)

THE PAGE CANNOT BE DISPLAYED

Two things have to occur for Internet Explorer to display the requested document—it must locate the server on which the document is stored, and it must be able to connect to that computer. The exact wording of the error messages may vary, but look carefully at the text for an indication of what went wrong. A message such as "The Page Cannot Be Displayed" generally means that you entered some part of the address incorrectly. Click the Address bar, reenter the address, and try again. If you still cannot display the page, the site may be down or your Internet connection may not be working. Enter the address of a different site and try to connect. If you fail to display the second site, your connection is down.

Step 3: The Word of the Day

- You should see the Word of the Day as shown in Figure 2c, but the word you see will be different from ours.
- Click the **Sound icon** to hear the pronunciation of the word.
- Click the **Print button** on the Standard Buttons toolbar to print this page for your instructor.
- Click the **Back button** on the Standard Buttons toolbar to return to the main page for the Reference Desk. Note that the link to the *Merriam Webster Dictionary* has changed color (from blue to magenta on our page) to indicate that you have viewed the associated page.
- Click the **Forward button** from the Reference Desk home page to return to the *Merriam Webster Dictionary*. The left pane on the Merriam Webster page provides several additional links that are related to building your vocabulary.
- Click the link to **Word Games** and then play today's game. Were you able to win? Did you learn anything? Print this page for your instructor as well.

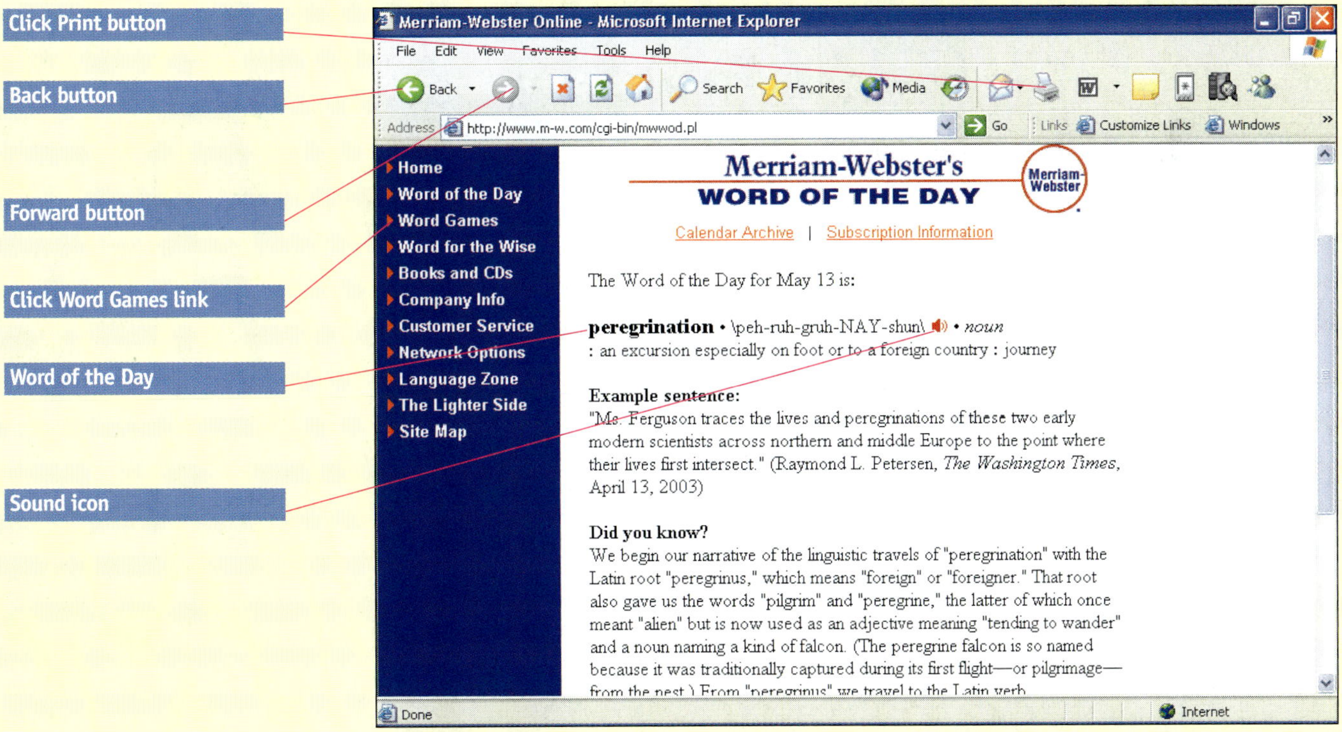

(c) The Word of the Day (step 3)

FIGURE 2 Hands-on Exercise 1 (*continued*)

THE FAVORITES LIST

The easiest way to return to a page is to add it to the Favorites list. Once you arrive at a page that you consider special, pull down the Favorites menu and click the Add to Favorites command to display the Add Favorites dialog box. Internet Explorer provides a default name for the page, but you can enter a more descriptive name if you prefer. Click OK to add the site and close the dialog box. To return to the page in the future, pull down the Favorites menu and click the indicated link from your list of favorite sites.

Step 4: The Page Setup Command

- Click the **down arrow** next to the Back button to display a list of the sites you have visited, then click the link to the **Reference Desk** to return to that page.
- Pull down the **Edit menu** and click the **Find command** to search for **Today in History**, which in turn will provide you with multiple links. Choose any link to display a page similar to Figure 2d.
- Pull down the **File menu** and click the **Page Setup command** to display the Page Setup dialog box. You do not have to change any of these options at this time, just be aware that they exist (see the boxed tip below). Click **OK** to close the dialog box.
- Click the **Print button** on the Standard Buttons toolbar to print this page for your instructor.

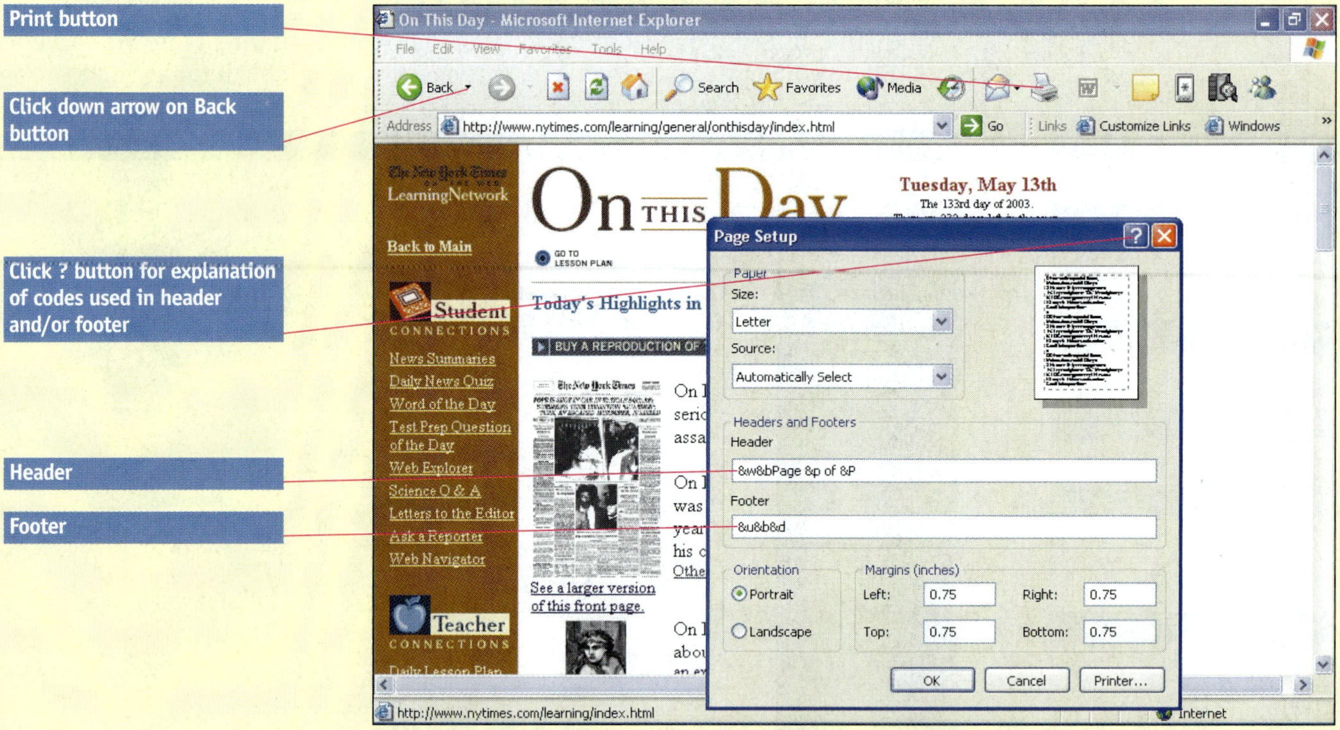

(d) The Page Setup Command (step 4)

FIGURE 2 Hands-on Exercise 1 (*continued*)

THE PAGE SETUP COMMAND

The header and/or footer in Web pages printed by Internet Explorer typically contain the address of the page and the date it was printed. Pull down the File menu and click the Page Setup command to display the Page Setup dialog box. Click the question mark in the title bar of the Page Setup dialog box, then click the Header or Footer text box to see the meaning of the various codes. (&U, for example, displays the URL or Web page address.) Right click within the list of codes and click the Print Topic command to obtain hard copy, then modify the Header and/or Footer text boxes to display the information you want.

Step 5: The Help Command

- Pull down the **Help menu** and click the **Contents and Index command** to display the Help window. If necessary, click the **Contents tab** to see a list of major help topics, each of which is represented by a book. Maximize the window.
- Click the **book icon** next to **Finding the Web Pages You Want**, then click the topic **Changing your home page** to display this information in the right pane as shown in Figure 2e.
- Right click anywhere in the left pane, then click **Print** to display the Print Topics dialog box. Click the option button to print the selected topic, click **OK**, then click **Print** to print this topic.
- The best time to learn about help is when you don't need it. Click the **Index tab** to search for information on a different topic. Click the **Search tab** and look for information from that page. Can you appreciate the different ways to obtain information?
- Click the **Close button** to exit Help.

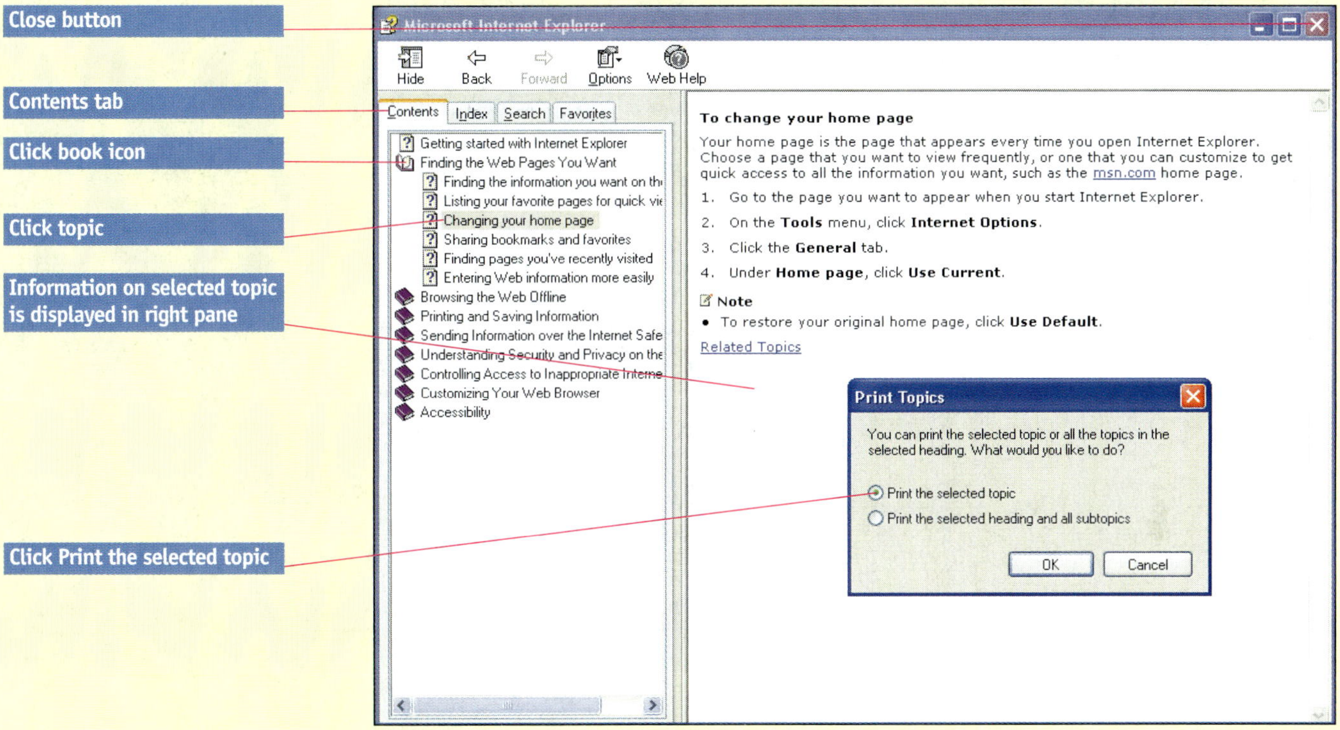

(e) The Help Command (step 5)

FIGURE 2 Hands-on Exercise 1 (*continued*)

ABOUT INTERNET EXPLORER

There are many versions of Internet Explorer, each with subtle differences in the features it supports. To find out which version you have, pull down the Help menu and click About Internet Explorer to display a screen with the version and release number. You will need this information if you are having trouble with your browser and are seeking help from technical support. The About command is present in the Help menu of every Windows application.

Step 6: Change the Start Page

- Do this step only if you are working on your own machine and you want to change your start (home) page. Click the **Back button** repeatedly until you return to the home page for the Reference Desk.
- Pull down the **Tools menu** and click the **Internet Options command** to display the Internet Options dialog box as shown in Figure 2f.
- Click the **General tab**, then click the **Use Current command button** in the Home Page area. Click the **Apply button** to change the home page. Examine the other options in this dialog box; e.g., how long are pages kept in history?
- Click the **Programs tab**. Which program is used for e-mail? Which program is used with newsgroups? Close the dialog box.
- Close Internet Explorer and then open it. The Reference Desk should be displayed as the new home page because of the changes you made in this step.

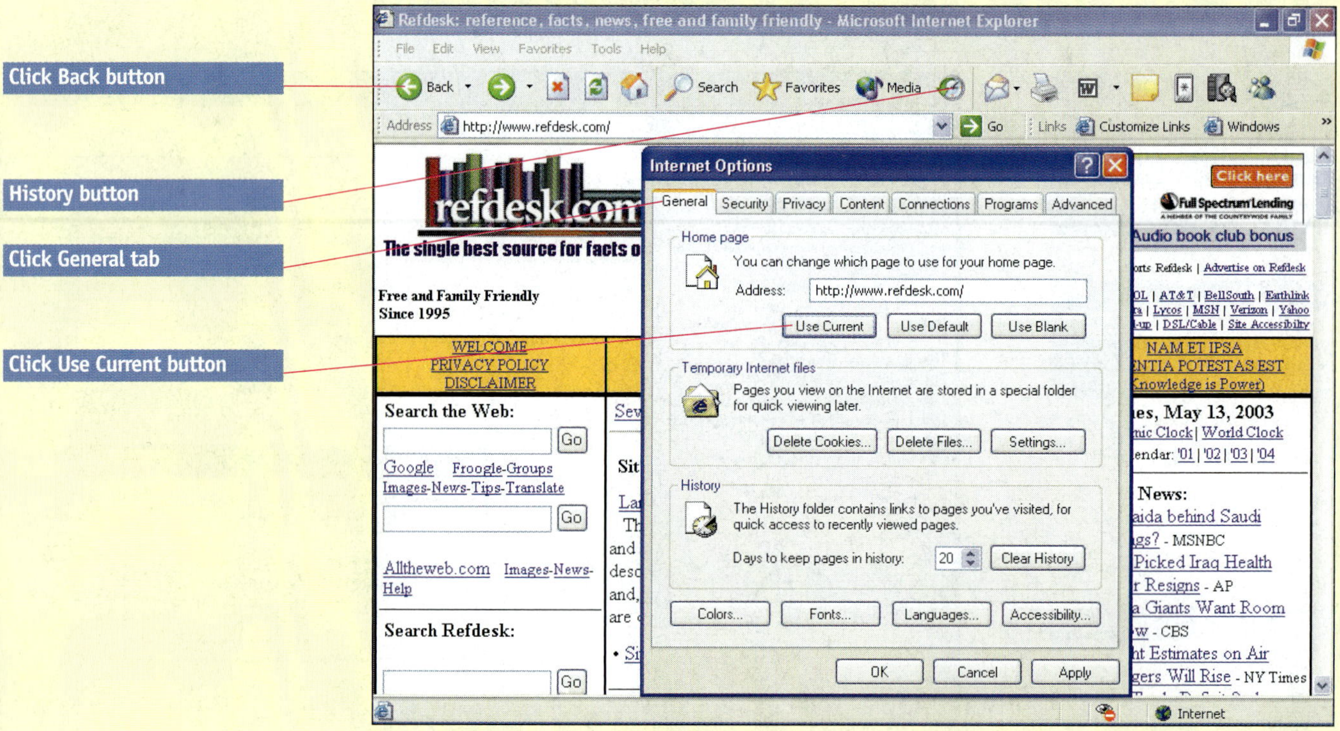

(f) Change the Start Page (step 6)

FIGURE 2 Hands-on Exercise 1 (*continued*)

THE HISTORY LIST

The History list contains links to all pages that you have recently visited for easy access to those sites. It also makes it possible for anyone looking at your computer (e.g., your instructor or employer) to see all of the sites that you have visited. Click the History button on the Standard Buttons toolbar to display the list of sites, click the down arrow next to the View button under the History title bar to sort by date, then click any week or day to view the sites you visited. Use the Internet Options command in the Tools menu to clear the History list if you want to delete this information.

Step 7: Surf the Web

- You've done what we have asked and have gotten a taste of the World Wide Web. Now it's time to explore on your own by going to new and different sites.
- Return to the Reference Desk and try any of the myriad links that are on this page. Click any link that interests you, and off you go. Use the **Print button** to print an additional page from a second site to prove to your instructor that you did the exercise.
- You can also guess at the address of a site you might want to visit according to the boxed tip below. Type **www.nba.com**, for example, and you will go to the home page of the National Basketball Association as shown in Figure 2g.
- Set a time limit for yourself, as the Web is addicting and you have other work to do. Close Internet Explorer when you are finished exploring. Shut down your computer if you do not wish to do the next exercise at this time.

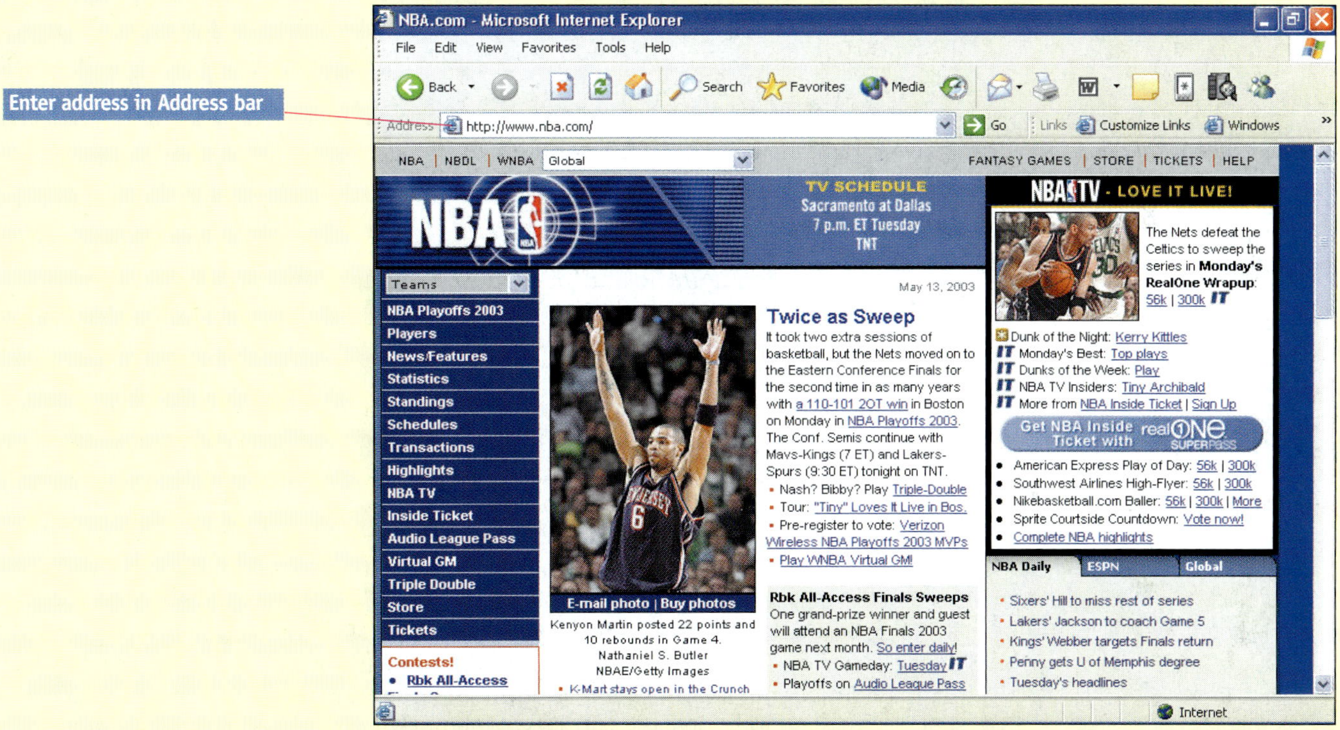

(g) Surf the Web (step 7)

FIGURE 2 Hands-on Exercise 1 (*continued*)

GUESS THE URL

You can often guess the address of a site according to the addressing scheme, www.company.com; e.g., www.microsoft.com, www.yahoo.com, or www.cnn.com for the home page of Microsoft, Yahoo!, and CNN, respectively. It also works for sports; for example, try www.nfl.com or www.nba.com to go to the home pages of the National Football League or National Basketball Association. The "com" ending takes you to the commercial domain of the Internet, whereas the "edu" ending takes you to the educational domain. Try www.yourschool.edu, for example, to find the home page of your school or university.

SEARCH ENGINES

The Internet contains a wealth of information. That is the good news. The bad news is that the Internet contains so much information that it is often difficult to find what you are looking for. A leisurely stroll from site to site may be interesting, but it is not efficient. There is a better way.

A ***search engine*** is a program that systematically searches the Web for documents in response to a specific request ***(query)*** for information. All search engines work essentially the same way. You enter a keyword or phrase and then the engine looks for documents that are related to the keywords you entered. The engine returns the titles and/or abstracts of the documents it finds (if any), together with a link to each document.

There are many search engines available, each of which may return different results to the same query. Figures 3a and 3b, for example, display the results of a query on Albert Einstein as returned by the Ask Jeeves and AltaVista search engines, respectively. The results are very different. The links in Figure 3a appear more promising, and certainly less commercial, than those in Figure 3b. The latter displays a series of ***sponsored matches***, which generate search results by allowing advertisers to bid for placement on specific keywords. Thus "Albert Einstein on eBay" or "Albert Einstein Imagination T-Shirt", while relevant to the query, are most likely not what the researcher intended.

AltaVista also provides links to more academic sources via the column of underlined links in Figure 3b, each of which will take you to a specific category related to Albert Einstein. You can also refine your search by adding additional keywords as shown in Figure 3c and/or requesting images in Figure 3d.

Other search engines will return different sets of documents because every engine maintains its own database through a program known as a ***spider***, which continually searches the Web for new pages. Each time the spider finds a new document it extracts information about that document, such as the URL (Web address) and keywords that describe the document. Some search engines store only the document's title, others contain the first few lines of text, and still others contain every word in the document. This, too, affects the results of a search. And finally, search engines differ with respect to the algorithm (or process) used to go through the database, as well as the way in which the documents are ranked with respect to their relevancy or likelihood that the document matches the query.

What, then, is the Internet Researcher to do? Is there a single search engine that is better than all the others? The answer is no, although everyone has a favorite engine. Suffice it to say, however, that the most important guideline for a successful Internet search is to use multiple search engines, because as we have seen, the same query will return different results with different search engines. Table 1 lists several popular search engines in alphabetical order. Dogpile and Metacrawler are known as ***meta search engines*** and return results from multiple search engines. The hits provided for each engine are less than if the engines were accessed directly, but the advantage of the meta search is that it uses multiple databases.

◆ AltaVista (www.altavista.com)	◆ Infoseek (www.infoseek.com)
◆ Ask Jeeves (www.askjeeves.com)	◆ Metacrawler (www.metacrawler.com)
◆ Dogpile (www.dogpile.com)	◆ MSN Internet Search (search.msn.com)
◆ Excite (www.excite.com)	◆ Northern Light (www.northernlight.com)
◆ Google (www.google.com)	◆ Snap (www.snap.com)
◆ HotBot (www.hotbot.com)	◆ Yahoo! (www.yahoo.com)

TABLE 1 Internet Search Engines

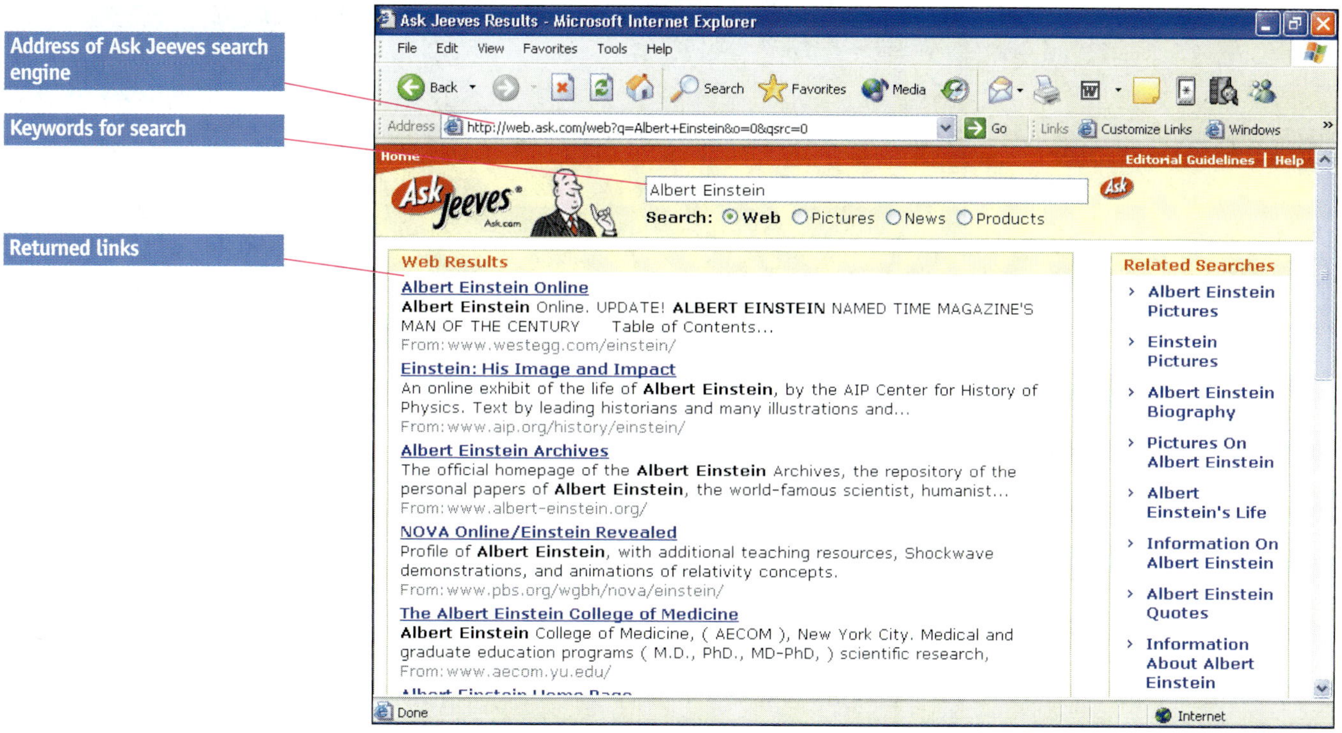

(a) Ask Jeeves Search Engine

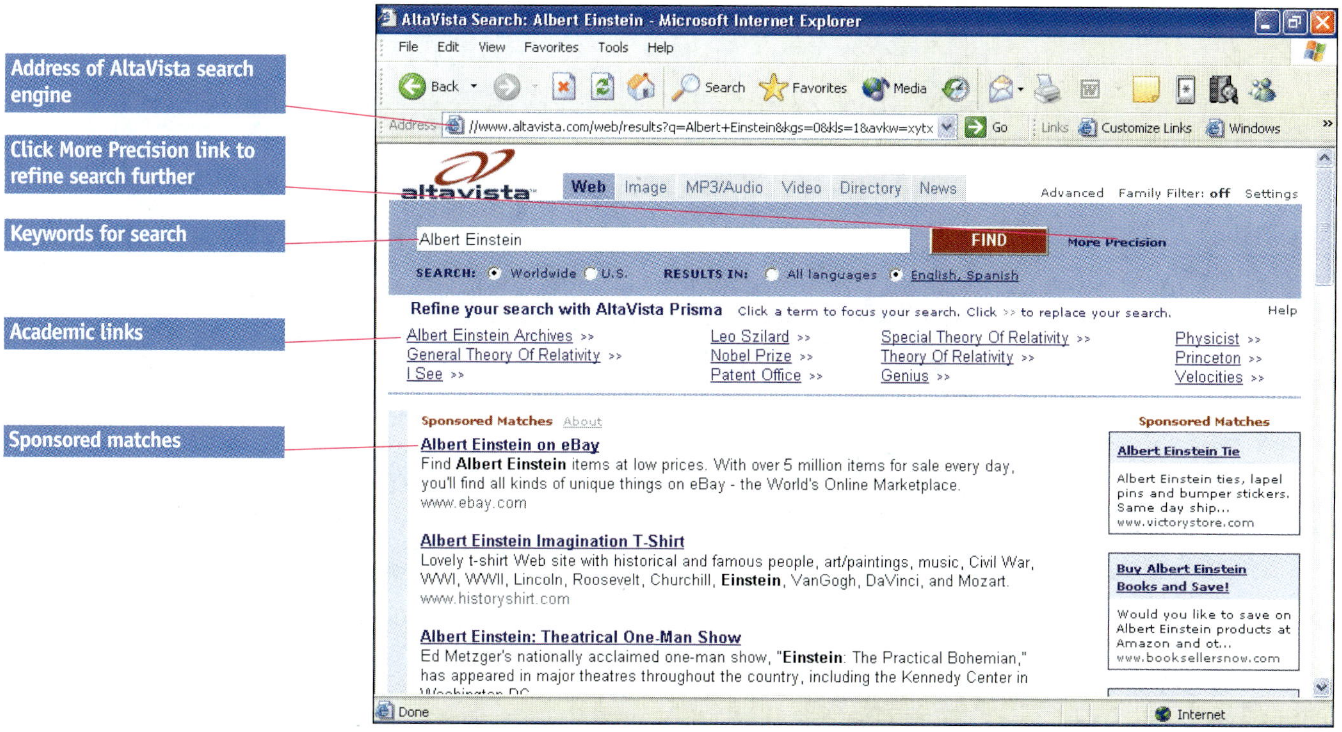

(b) AltaVista Search Engine

FIGURE 3 Search Engines

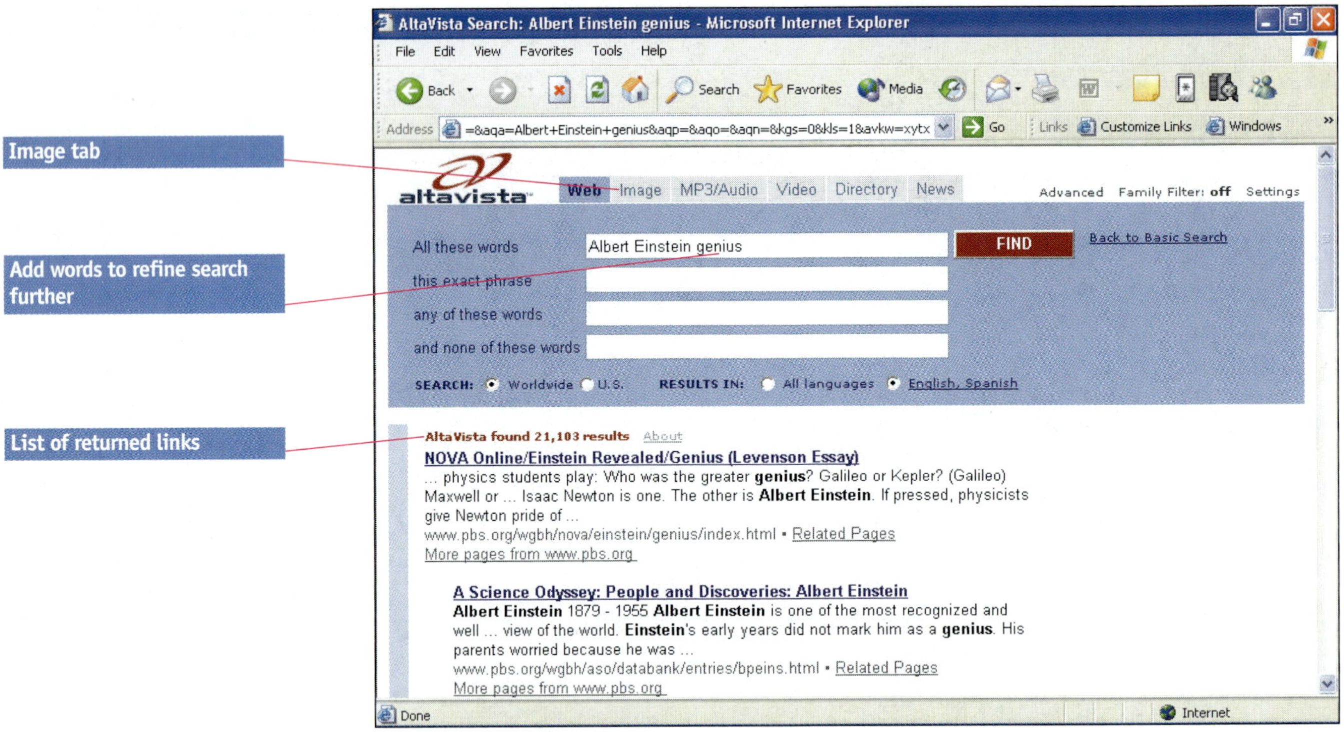

(c) Expanding the Search

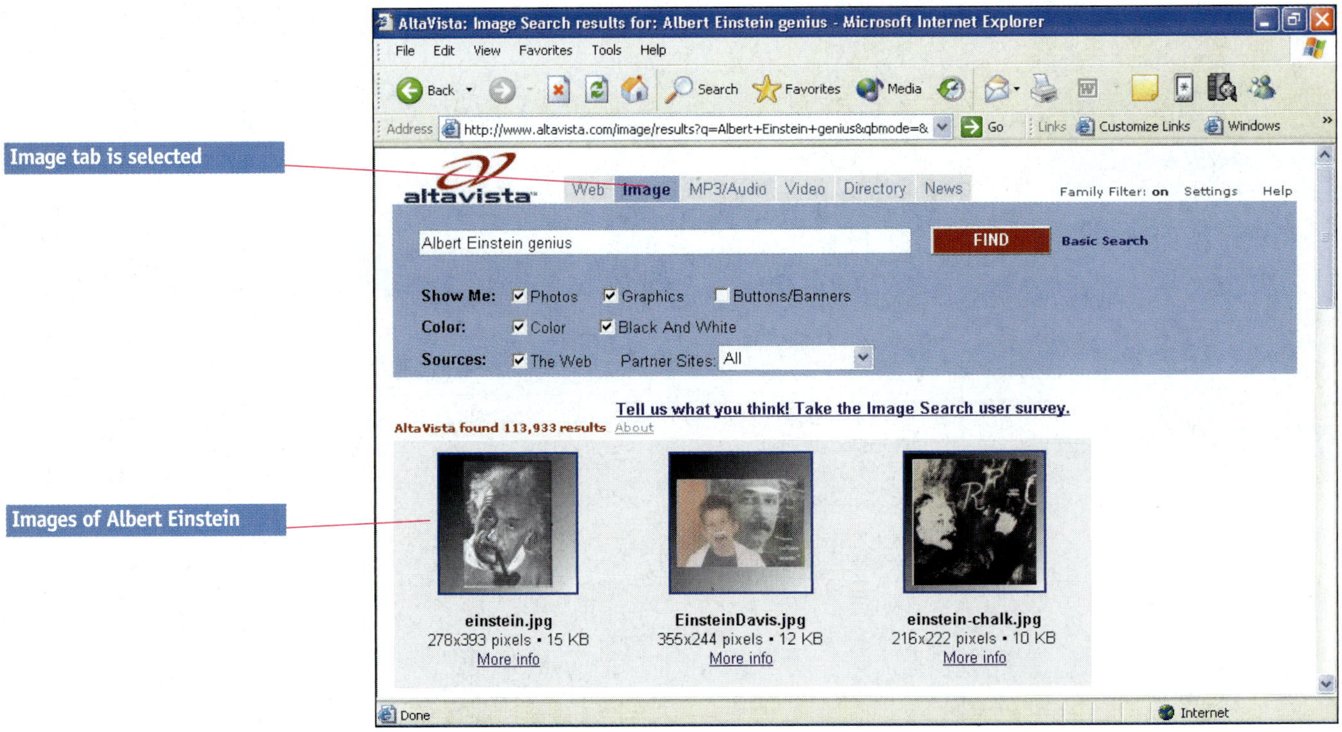

(d) Including Images

FIGURE 3 Search Engines (*continued*)

Logical (Boolean) Operators

The Web continues to grow exponentially, and as it does, the number of ***hits*** (documents matching your query) that will be returned by a search also increases. A large number of hits does not necessarily guarantee a successful search, however, because you also need to be concerned with the relevancy of those hits. The AltaVista search in Figure 3c returned more than 20,000 potential documents, far too many to review individually. All of those documents contained the keywords "Albert Einstein" but many of the documents referred to various hospitals named for the scientist. If you are looking for information about Einstein's life, you are not interested in these documents.

You can limit the documents that are returned by a search through a combination of the logical ***(Boolean) operators AND***, ***OR***, and ***NOT***. The AND operator requires that every keyword must be present. Searching for "American" AND "Airlines", for example, will return documents that contain both words such as documents that deal with American Airlines (the airline). The OR operator, however, requires that only one of the terms be present, so that searching for "American" OR "Airlines" will return documents containing "American" (anything with American) OR "Airlines" (any airline). Some search engines also enable you to use the NOT operator. Searching for "American Airlines" and NOT "Arena" will return documents about "American Airlines", but not the American Airlines Arena (in Miami). The way in which you specify the Boolean operators depends on the search engine and is described in its online help.

Figure 4 displays a ***search form*** to conduct an advanced search using the Yahoo! engine. The required document is to contain the words "Albert Einstein", the exact phrase "atomic bomb", and must not contain the word "hospital". The AND operator is implied because the document must contain both "Einstein" and "atomic bomb". The NOT operator prevents returning any documents with the word hospital and thus precludes hospitals named for Albert Einstein. The form also enables you to restrict the documents you receive to a specific language, to limit your search to specific Internet domains, and/or to filter out "mature" content.

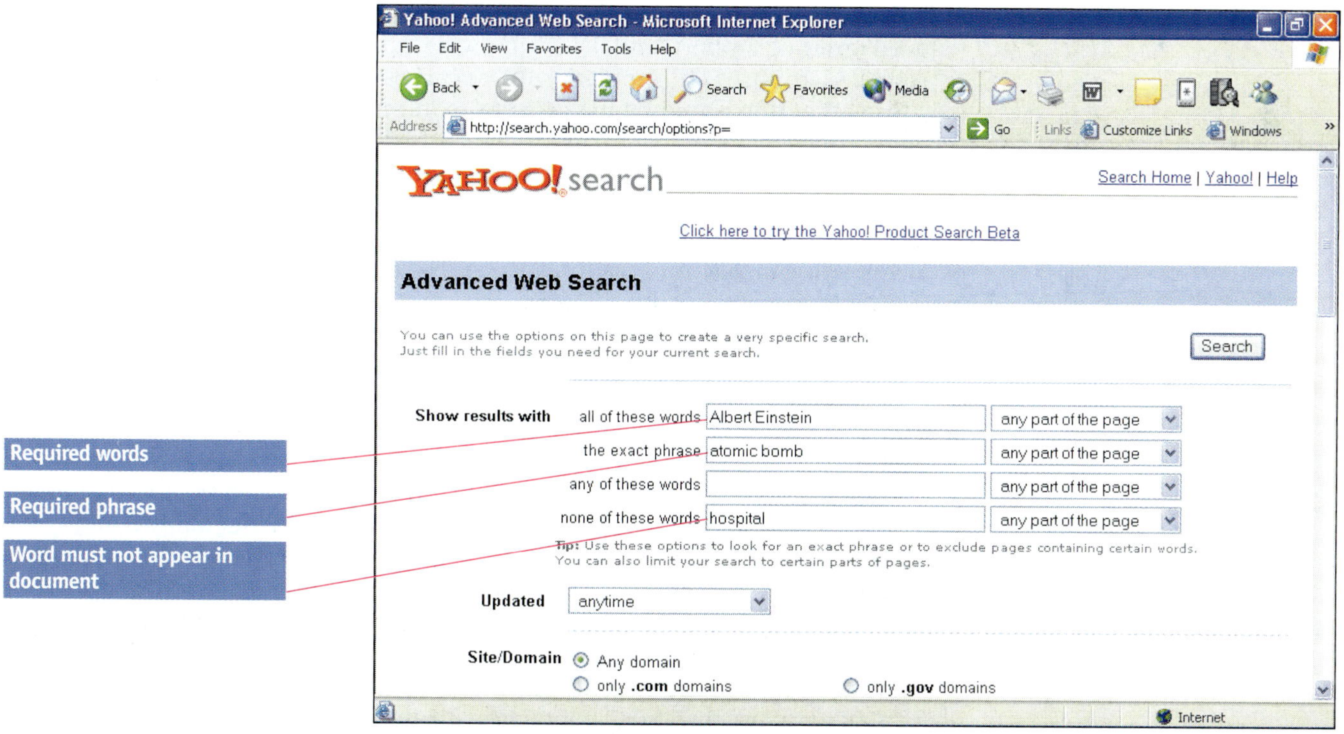

FIGURE 4 Advanced Search

Copyright Protection

A ***copyright*** provides legal protection to a written or artistic work, including literary, dramatic, musical, and artistic works such as poetry, novels, movies, songs, computer software, and architecture. It is granted by the US Copyright Office (www.loc.gov/copyright) and it gives the author the exclusive right to the use and duplication of the work. A copyright does not, however, protect facts, ideas, systems, or methods of operation, although it may protect the way these things are expressed.

The owner of the copyright may sell or give up a portion of his or her rights; for example, an author may give distribution rights to a publisher and/or grant movie rights to a studio. ***Infringement of a copyright*** occurs any time a right reserved by the copyright owner is violated without permission of the owner. Anything on the Internet should be considered copyrighted unless the document specifically says it is in the ***public domain***, in which case the author is giving everyone the right to freely reproduce and distribute the material.

Does copyright protection prevent you from quoting a document found on the Web in a research paper? Does copyright protection imply that you cannot download an image for inclusion in a term paper? (Facts themselves are not covered by copyright, so you can use statistical data without fear of infringement.) The answer to what you can use from the Web depends on the amount of the information you reference, as well as the intended use of that information. It is considered ***fair use***, and thus not an infringement of copyright, to use a portion of a work for educational or nonprofit purposes, or for the purpose of critical review or commentary. In other words, you can use a quote, downloaded image, or other information from the Web in a term paper—provided you cite the original work in your bibliography. (The Insert Reference Footnote command is used in Microsoft Word to insert footnotes or endnotes into a document.)

Software piracy (the unauthorized duplication or use of software products such as Microsoft Office) presents a unique problem with respect to copyright protection because of the ease with which it can be done. A program that takes millions of dollars and years to develop can be copied in a few seconds and results in economic loss to the developer. Software piracy harms everyone in the end, including you, the end user. It results in higher prices for legitimate licenses, reduced levels of support, and delays in the development of new software.

The law imposes stiff penalties for copyright infringement of any kind. You may think that this is unduly harsh, but the intent behind the copyright law is to provide economic incentive to an artist or software developer so that they invest the necessary resources to create the work. You would not think of walking into a music store, picking up a CD by your favorite artist, putting it under your coat, then walking out of the store without paying for the CD. Yet most people think nothing of downloading music from the Internet, and indeed are proud of the fact that they have not purchased a record, CD, cassette tape, or any other form of music since the invention of MP3. This may be great for you as a consumer, but imagine that you actually wrote and produced a particular song, and that your livelihood depends on the funds generated from the sale of that song. Do you still think it is appropriate to obtain copies of songs for free? You should honor and respect the copyright process.

The best-known example is the Napster Web site that created a virtual music store where every song was free. The Napster Web site did not actually contain illegal copies of the music. Instead it created a central directory with links to anyone signing on to the site, and then it used peer-to-peer technology to make the music files on individual PCs available to everyone else. Napster was found guilty of violating federal copyright law and forced to suspend business. But the genie was out of the bottle and other sites found ways to get around the court ruling, by avoiding the central directory but still enabling ***peer-to-peer file sharing***. What if music fans everywhere decided to stop buying music and simply wait for it to be uploaded to the Web? What effect would this have on the music industry?

Explore the URL

The document in Figure 5 is the result of a search on the Sistine Chapel and the works of Michelangelo. The address looks complicated, but it is easily broken down, which in turn can lead to other relevant documents. The URL in Figure 5 is divided as follows:

http://www.ibiblio.org/wm/paint/auth/michelangelo/michelangelo.creation.jpg

- Document: michelangelo.creation.jpg
- Path (folders): wm/paint/auth/michelangelo
- Server (computer): www.ibiblio.org
- Means of access (HyperText Transfer Protocol): http

In other words, we found a specific server (whose address is www.ibiblio.org) that contained a picture of a fragment from the ceiling of the Sistine Chapel by Michelangelo. It's logical to think that the same computer may contain other pictures or information in which we would be interested. You can get to that information by backing up one level at a time in the address, starting from the right and moving to the left. Thus you can click in the Address bar and delete the last portion of the address, up to and including the forward slash so that the URL ends simply in "Michelangelo". This will take you to a folder containing information and other works about the artist.

Go back one or two levels so that you end on "paint", which takes you to a folder with all painters on the site. Continue to backtrack in this way until you get to the Web site itself. Aside from being a wonderful way to browse, it may also be a boon to your research, because you are often searching for a concept rather than a specific term. You might, for example, be interested in Renaissance artists in general, rather than just Michelangelo. If so, you have just discovered an invaluable resource.

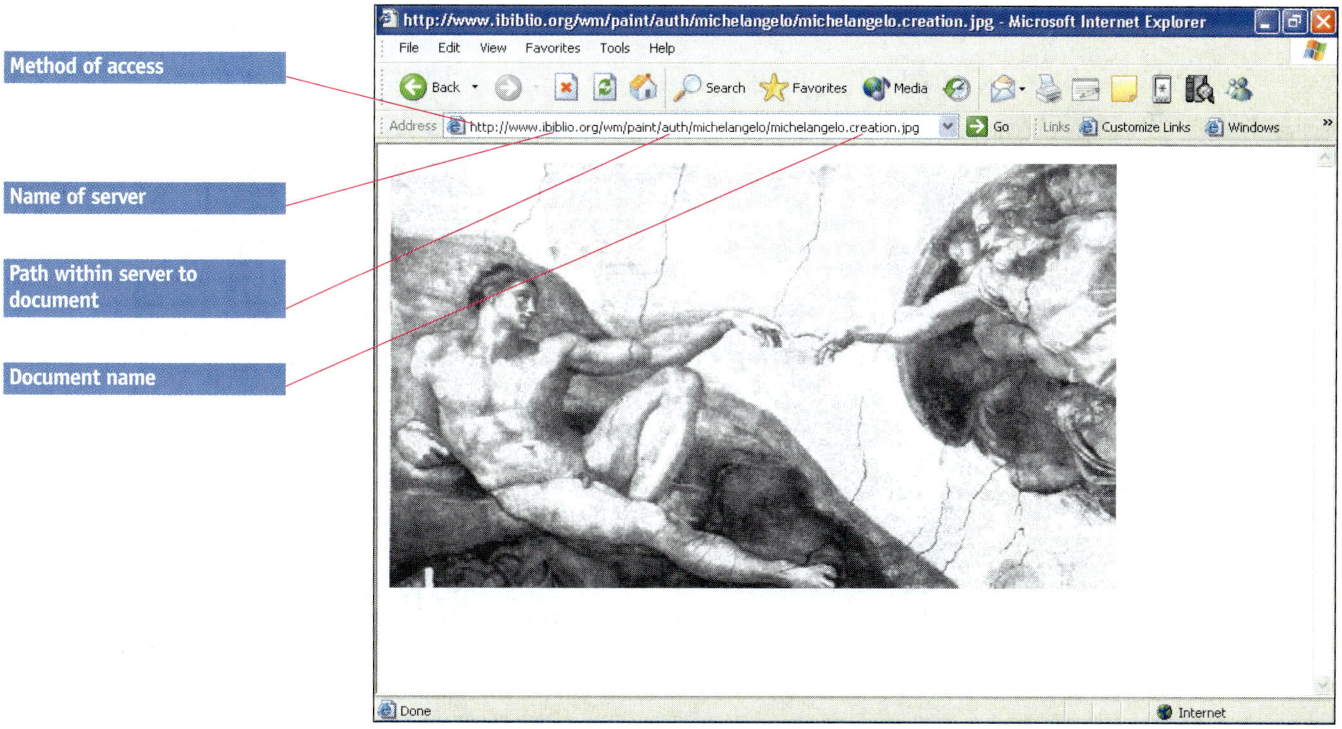

FIGURE 5 Explore the URL

hands-on exercise

2 Searching the Web

Objective To search the Web for specific information; to download a photograph and include it in a Word document; to locate an audio file. Use Figure 6 as a guide in the exercise.

Step 1: Search the Web

- Start Internet Explorer. It does not matter which page you see initially, as long as you are able to connect to the Internet and start Internet Explorer. Click the **Maximize button** so that Internet Explorer takes the entire screen.
- The objective of this exercise is to search for information from the Apollo 11 mission to the moon. There are several ways to initiate a search. You can:
  - Click the **Search button** on the Standard Buttons toolbar in Internet Explorer and enter **Apollo 11** as the text you are searching for.
  - Go directly to the Web site of an Internet search engine—for example, **www.google.com**—and enter the text of your search.
  - Click in the **Address bar**, type the keyword **Go**, followed by the topic you are searching for, such as **Go Apollo 11**.
- It does not matter if the results of your search are different from ours. Your system may use a different search engine, the Windows XP search companion may not be active, and/or the available documents on the Web may have changed since the publication of our text.
- Close the search pane. Click the link to **Apollo 11 Image Gallery** if it is present; if not, you can enter the Web site directly as described in step 2.

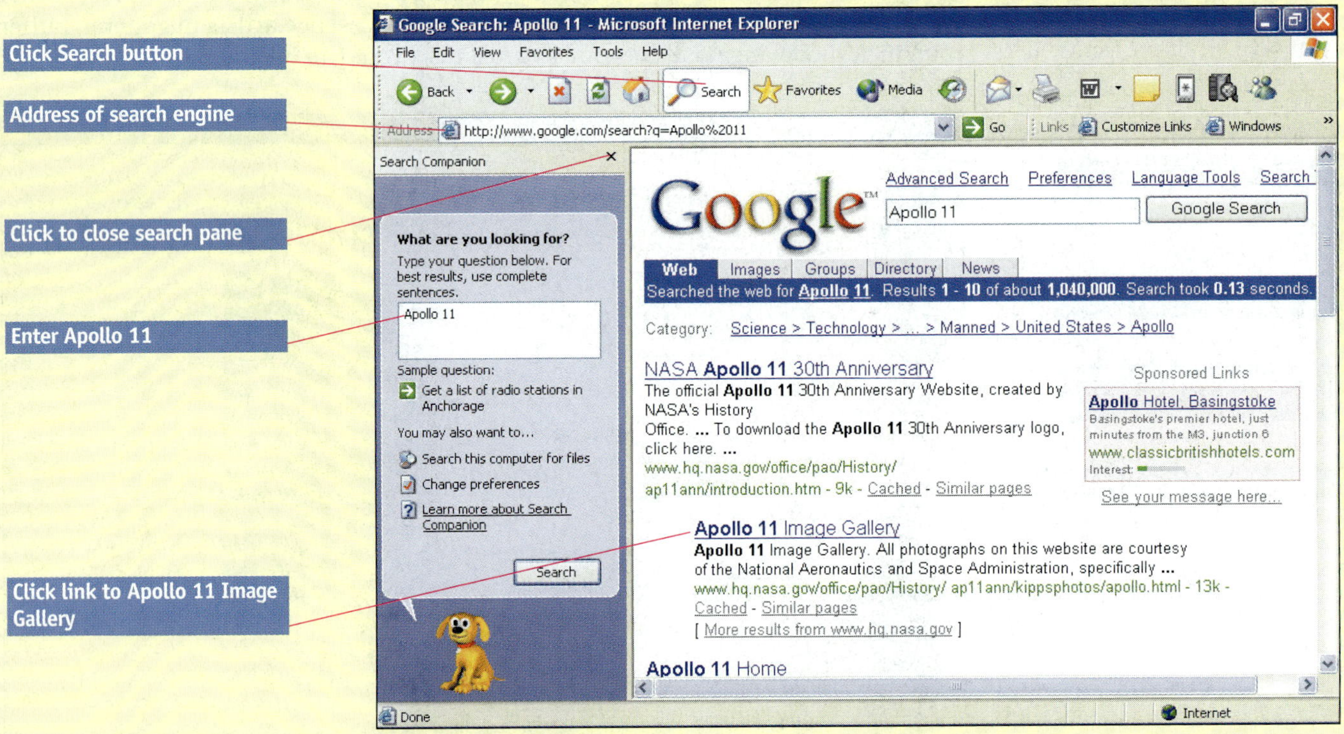

(a) Search the Web (step 1)

FIGURE 6 Hands-on Exercise 2

Step 2: Choose a Picture

- If necessary, click in the **Address bar** and enter the URL in Figure 6b to display the photographs from the Apollo 11 mission.
- Scroll down the page to select the photograph you wish to download. Click the photograph so that it expands in its own window, then right click the photo to display a context-sensitive menu.
- Click the **Save Picture As command** to display the Save As dialog box.
  - Click the **drop-down arrow** in the Save In list box to specify the drive and folder in which to save the graphic (e.g., in the **My Pictures folder**).
  - Internet Explorer supplies the file name and file type for you. You may change the name, but you cannot change the file type.
  - Click the **Save button** to download the image. Remember the file name and location, as you will need to access the file in the next step.
- The Save As dialog box will close automatically after the picture has been downloaded. Close the window containing the picture you just saved. Click the **Minimize button** in the Internet Explorer window. The window shrinks to a button on the Windows taskbar.

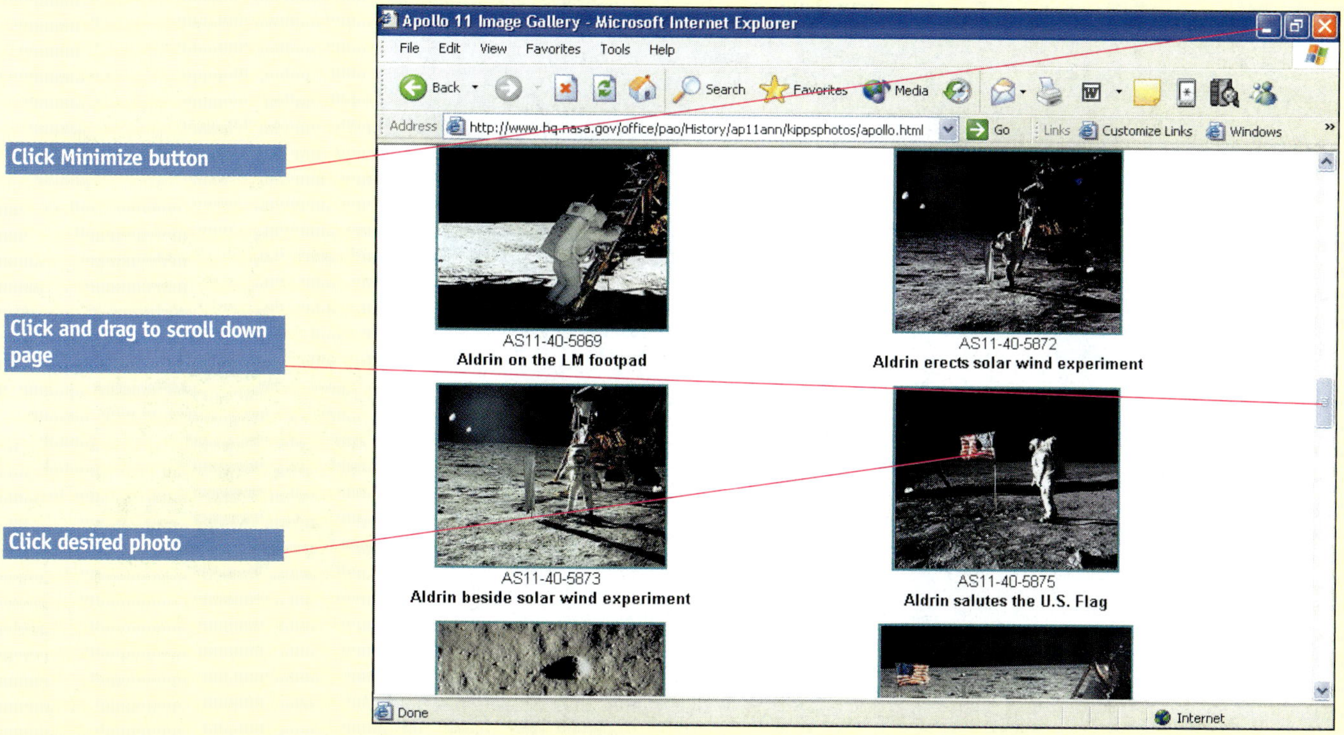

(b) Choose a Picture (step 2)

FIGURE 6 Hands-on Exercise 2 (*continued*)

THE AUTOSEARCH FEATURE

The fastest way to initiate a search is to click in the Address box, enter the keyword "Go" followed by the topic (e.g., Go University of Miami), then press the Enter key. Internet Explorer automatically invokes the default search engine and returns the relevant documents. Remember, too, that you can guess a Web address by typing www.organization.domain—for example, www.nasa.gov to display the home page for NASA.

Step 3: Insert the Picture

- Start Word, and if necessary, maximize the application window. Close the task pane. Pull down the **View menu** to be sure that you are in the **Print Layout view**.
- Enter the title and quotation in an appropriate font and point size as shown in Figure 6c. (The Insert Picture dialog box is not yet visible.) Type your name under the quotation. Press **Enter**.
- Enter any additional information required by your instructor. Center all of the text. Press **Enter** to begin a new line.
- Pull down the **Insert menu**, click **Picture**, then click **From File** to display the Insert Picture dialog box. Select the drive and folder in which you saved the picture (e.g., My Pictures on drive C).
- Select (click) the picture (e.g., **Apollo 11-5875**), then click **Insert**, and the picture is inserted into the Word document. Do not worry about its size or position at this time.
- Save the document as **Apollo 11**.

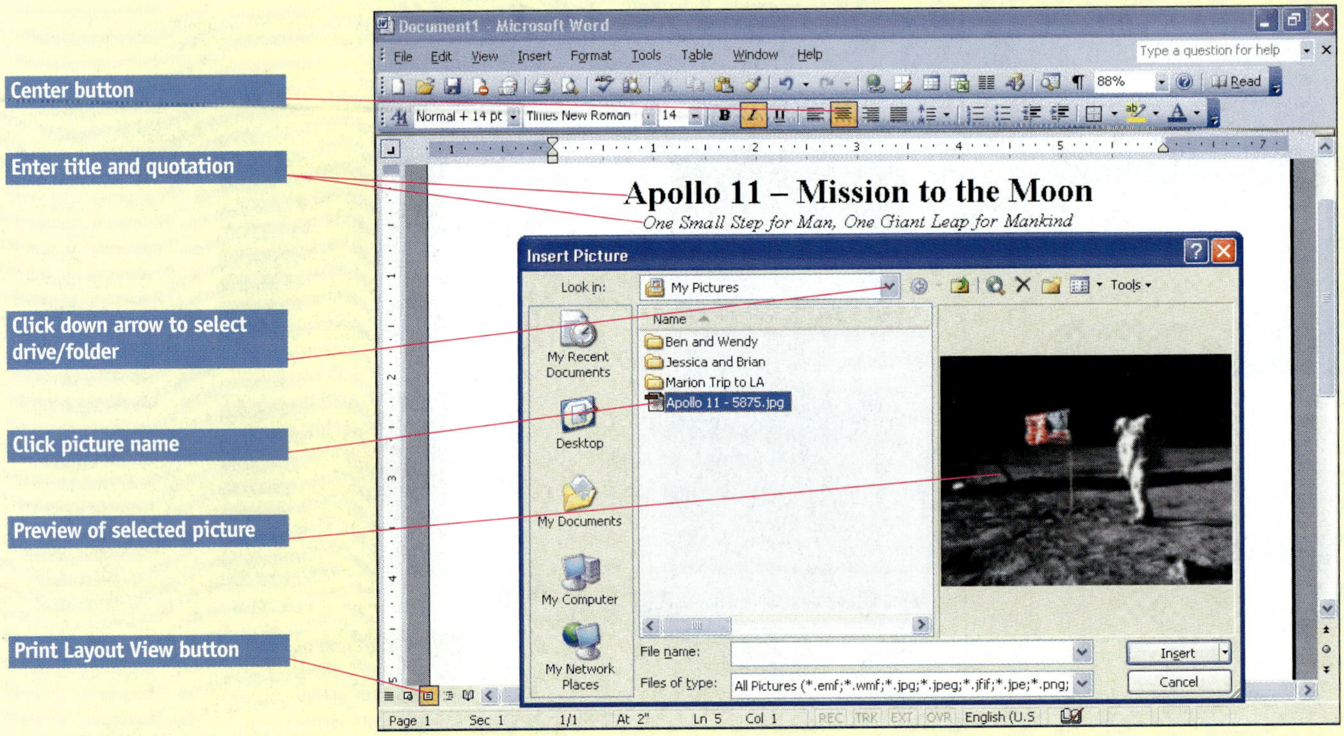

(c) Insert the Picture (step 3)

FIGURE 6 Hands-on Exercise 2 (*continued*)

MULTITASKING

Multitasking, the ability to run multiple applications at the same time, is one of the primary advantages of the Windows environment. Switching from one application to another is easy—just click the appropriate button on the Windows taskbar. You can also use the classic Alt+Tab shortcut. Press and hold the Alt key as you click the Tab key repeatedly to display and select icons for the open applications, then release the Tab key when the desired application icon is selected.

Step 4: Move and Size the Picture

- Pull down the **View menu**, click **Zoom**, then click the option button to zoom to **Whole Page**. Click **OK**. Right click the picture to display a context-sensitive menu, then click the **Format Picture command** to display the Format Picture dialog box.
- Click the **Layout tab**, then choose any wrapping style other than In line with text. Click **OK** to close the dialog box. You will now be able to move and size the picture as shown in Figure 6d.
  - To size the picture, drag a corner handle (the mouse pointer changes to a double arrow) to keep the object in proportion.
  - To move the picture, point to any part of the picture except a sizing handle (the mouse pointer changes to a four-sided arrow) and click and drag the picture elsewhere in the document.
- Click the **Undo button** on the Standard toolbar if the result is not what you expected. Save the document.

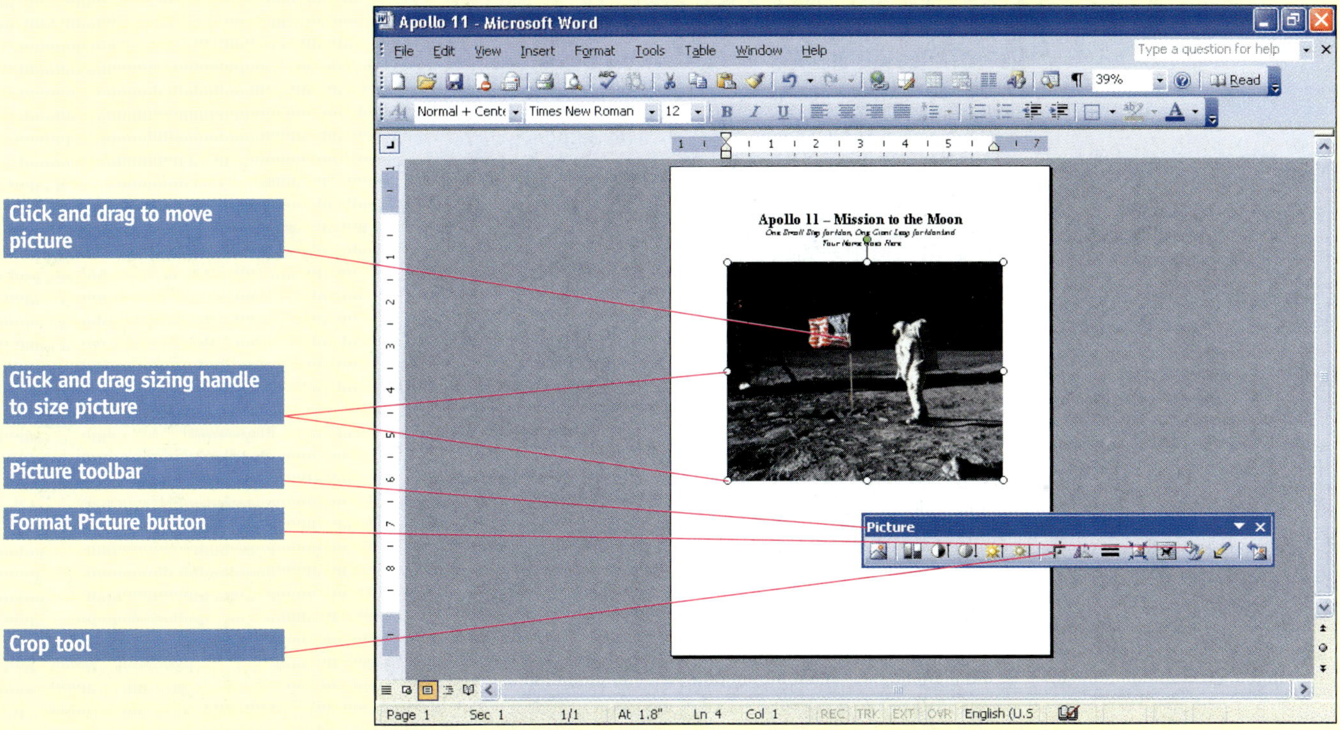

(d) Move and Size the Picture (step 4)

FIGURE 6 Hands-on Exercise 2 (*continued*)

CROPPING A PICTURE

The Crop tool is one of the most useful tools when dealing with a photograph as it lets you eliminate (crop) part of a picture. Select (click) the picture to display the Picture toolbar and sizing handles. (If you do not see the Picture toolbar, right click the picture to display a context-sensitive menu, then click the Show Picture Toolbar command. Click the Crop tool (the ScreenTip will display the name of the tool), then click and drag a sizing handle to crop the part of the picture you want to eliminate. Click the Crop button a second time to turn the feature off.

Step 5: Insert a Footnote

- Click after the words Apollo 11 (the point at which you will insert the footnote) in the title of the document. Pull down the **Insert menu**. Click **Reference**, then click **Footnote** to display the Footnote and Endnote dialog box in Figure 6e.
- Check that the option button for Footnotes is selected and that the Numbering drop-down list is set to Continuous. Click **Insert**.
- Word inserts a new footnote and simultaneously moves the insertion point to the bottom of the page to add the actual note. Zoom to **Page Width**.
- Enter the address of the Web page from where you took the picture, together with an appropriate reference.
- Click at the end of the quotation, and insert a second footnote indicating that these are the words of Neil Armstrong as he became the first person to set foot on the moon.
- Save the document. Print the cover page for your instructor as proof you did this exercise. Close Word.

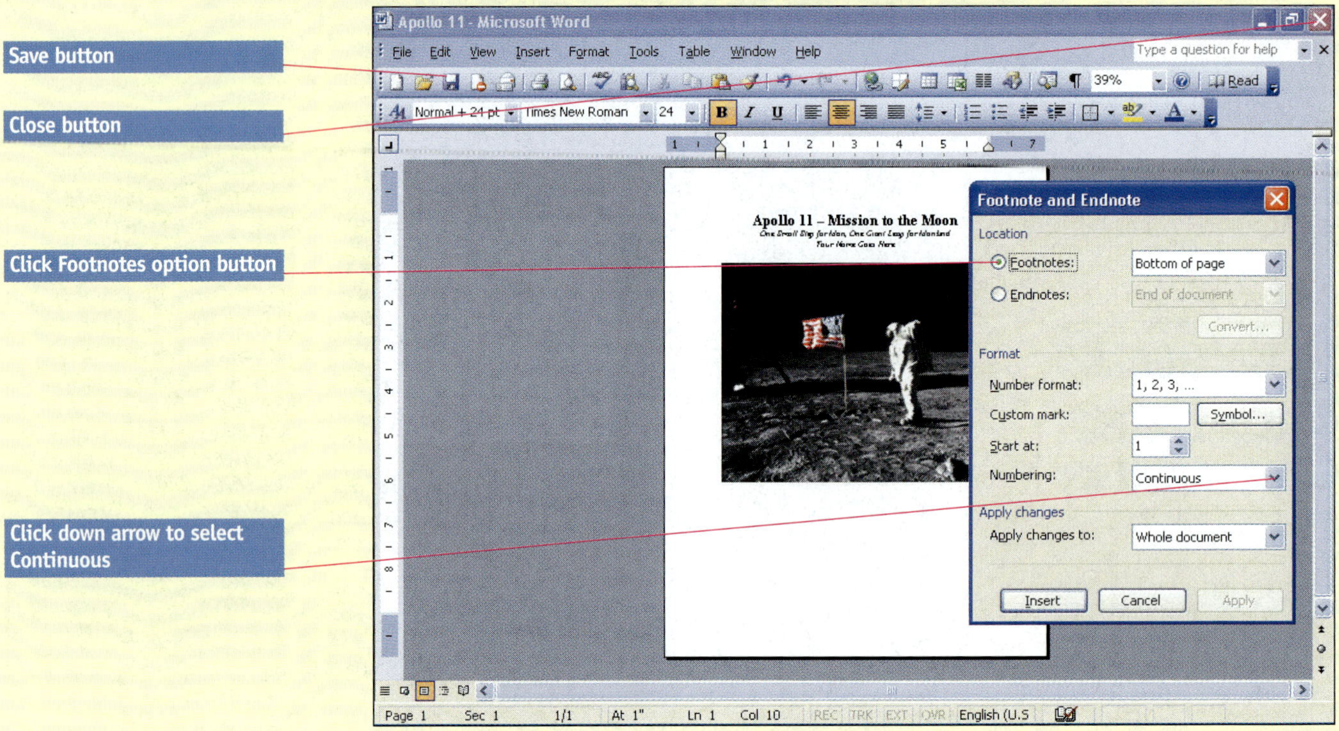

(e) Insert a Footnote (step 5)

FIGURE 6 Hands-on Exercise 2 (*continued*)

ENTER THE URL AUTOMATICALLY

Use the Copy command to enter the URL into a footnote. Not only do you save time by not having to type the address yourself, but you also ensure that it is entered correctly. Click in the Address bar of Internet Explorer to select the URL, then pull down the Edit menu and click the Copy command (or use the Ctrl+C Windows shortcut). Switch to the Word document, click at the place in the document where you want to insert the URL, then pull down the Edit menu and click Paste (or press Ctrl+V).

Step 6: Use Multiple Search Engines

- If necessary, point to the bottom of the screen to display the taskbar, then click the button for **Internet Explorer**.
- Click in the **Address bar** and enter the address of a different search engine—for example, www.askjeeves.com (or simply **www.ask.com**), to go to the home page of the Ask Jeeves search engine.
- Enter **Apollo 11 audio** as the text you are searching for, then click the **Ask button** to the right of the text box. The results of our search are displayed in Figure 6f.
- Do not be concerned if you see a different set of links and do not be dismayed by the presence of sponsored (paid) results as the advertising pays for the site.
- Click the link to **Apollo 11 Audio and Video**. If you do not see this link, click in the Address bar, type **www.nasm.si.edu/apollo/AS11/a11av.htm**, and press **Enter**. Be sure to enter the address correctly. (It is case sensitive.)

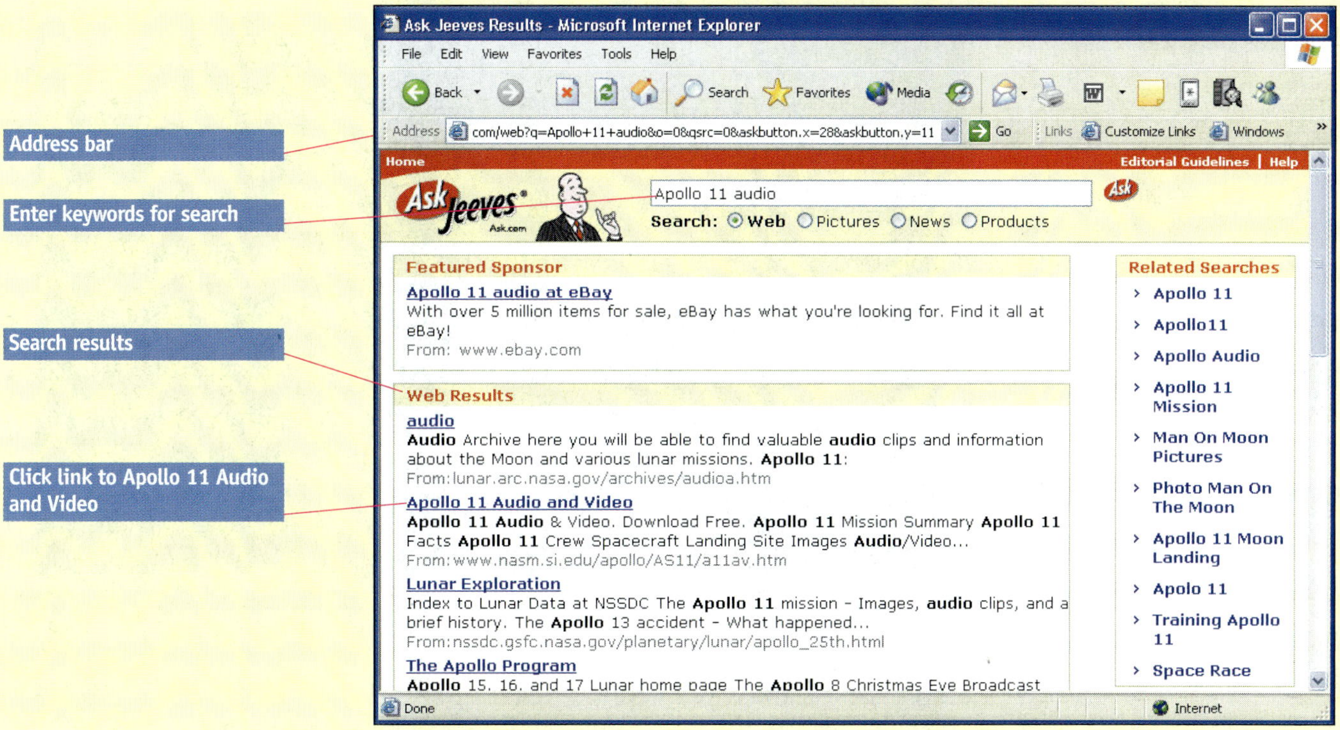

(f) Use Multiple Search Engines (step 6)

FIGURE 6 Hands-on Exercise 2 (*continued*)

CHANGE THE SEARCH BEHAVIOR

Do you have a favorite search engine? If so, you may want to change the Internet preferences on your system to use that engine by default. In Windows XP click the Start button, click the Search command, click the link to Change Preferences, and then click the link to Change Internet Search behavior. Click the Option button for Classic Internet Search, select your favorite engine, and click OK. (This command may not be available to you in a laboratory setting.)

Step 7: Windows Media Player

- You should see the Web page in Figure 6g. Scroll down the page until you find the audio clip that you want to hear, such as **First Step**.
- Click the link underneath the photo to hear the audio clip. (The text of the link, **1845K avi**, indicates the file size and the file type. An "avi" file is a standard Windows format with audio and/or video content.)
- The Windows media player should open automatically in the left pane as the clip begins to play. You should hear Neil Armstrong's voice as he first set foot on the moon, "That's one small step for man, one giant leap for mankind."
- Close Internet Explorer if you do not want to continue with the next exercise at this time. Welcome to the world of online research.

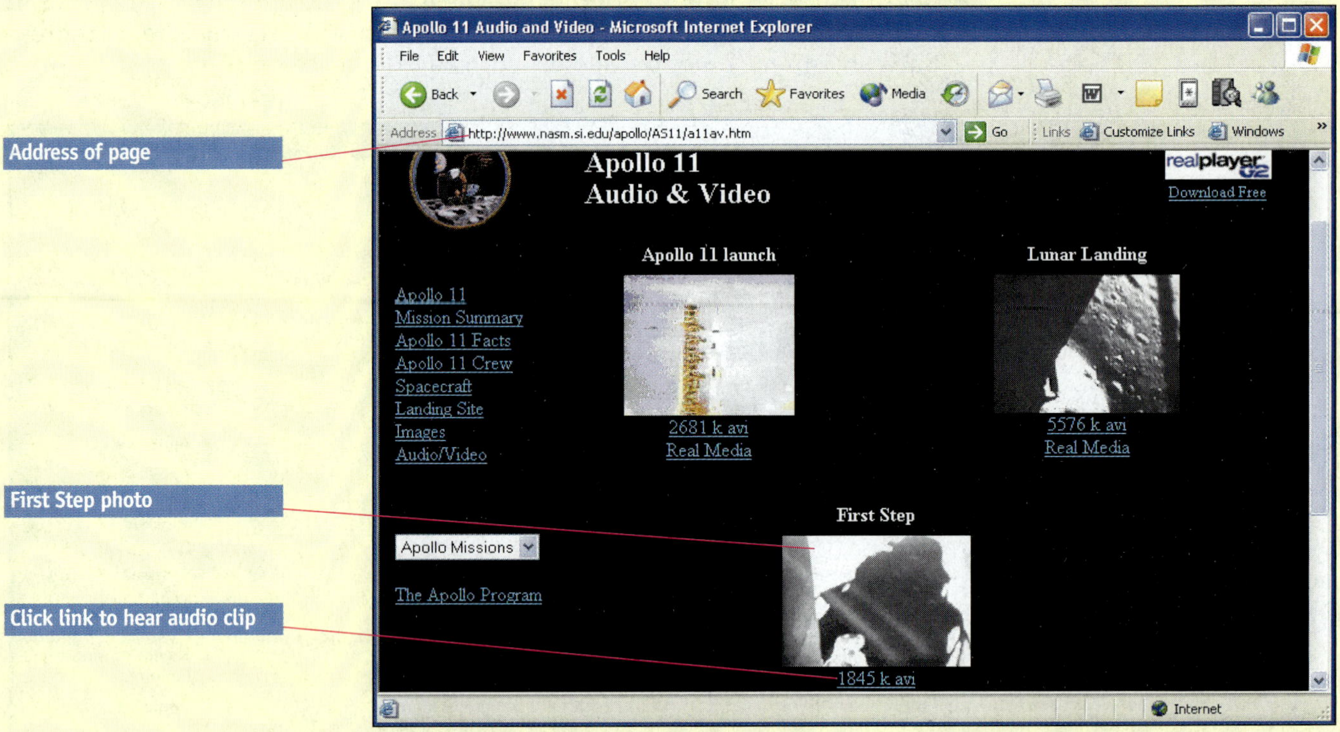

(g) Windows Media Player (step 7)

FIGURE 6 Hands-on Exercise 2 (*continued*)

INTERNET PLUG-INS

It's a simple matter for a browser to display text or graphics files, but audio and video files are more complex and cannot be played directly. A plug-in is a special-purpose program that is supplied by a company to support an innovation by that company. RealPlayer and ShockWave are two of the more common plug-ins and support streaming audio and animation, respectively. Such plug-ins are generally available for free.

THE COMMERCIALIZATION OF CYBERSPACE

It's difficult to think of the Internet as existing without any type of commercial enterprise. The Internet began, however, as a project of the United States government with a strict prohibition against commercial activity. It was not until 1991, some twenty years after its inception, that the National Science Foundation lifted the prohibition on commercial use. The subsequent growth has been both unprecedented and exponential, as companies of every size, from multinational corporations to "mom and pop" shops, maintain sites and conduct business on the Web.

The world has truly changed, and you cannot escape (nor do you want to) the excitement and potential of the new economy. The best way to appreciate the impact of ***e-commerce*** is to step back and think of commerce in the traditional sense, which is nothing more than the exchange of goods and services. The same elements are present, regardless of whether you go to a mall or shop on the Web. Commerce of either type involves buyers and sellers, products and services, and suppliers or producers of the products and services. The buyer and seller need a place to meet for the transaction to take place. The seller employs various marketing strategies to attract the buyer to the place of business, where it can accept an order, deliver the goods or services, then accept payment.

What, then, is so special about e-commerce? The answer is that it enables both the buyer and seller to do things that are not possible with the traditional model. The buyer can shop 24 hours a day, 7 days a week, without ever leaving home. There is no need to walk up and down the aisles, because you can search the entire product line with the click of a mouse. You can shop as long as you like, even taking several days to build an order as you add items to a virtual shopping cart. You can also assure yourself of the best price because it is so easy to obtain prices of a given item from multiple vendors.

The seller enjoys similar advantages because it is much less expensive to implement and maintain a Web site than it is to build a store with "bricks and mortar." The customers can come from all over the world, as opposed to having to live in the neighborhood. The seller can stock more items because there is no need to physically display products or even to print a catalog. The cost per transaction is significantly lower because the personnel costs are reduced. There need not be a salesperson although many Web sites do provide telephone support. And, best of all, the business remains open around the clock.

We tend to think of e-commerce in terms of the traditional business-to-consumer or retail model, where the consumer purchases directly from the business. Money does not even have to change hands, however, for both business and consumer to reap benefits through e-commerce or more generally, through e-business. For example, a business can provide information electronically over the Web and save the cost of printing and distribution. Consumers benefit as well by having instant access to their accounts 24 hours a day, as opposed to having to wait for a monthly statement. The Web also makes it possible to build consumer-to-consumer sites such as eBay.com (the online auction site). And all of this activity pales before the potential of the ***business-to-business (B2B)*** model in which businesses interact electronically to exchange goods and services.

THE MALL WILL NOT GO AWAY

It's convenient to shop on the Web, especially if you know exactly what you want and/or you are pressed for time. It's not as much fun, however, as going to the mall, meeting your friends, trying on clothes, seeing and touching a real product, or having a snack at the "Food Court." In short, shopping is a social experience, and the mall is not going to disappear.

Security

The advent of commercial activity brought about a fundamental rethinking of the way data is transmitted across the Internet. ***Security*** was suddenly essential, but this contradicted the original vision of the Internet as an open network that allowed all users open access to resources on remote computers. The Internet was built on data traveling freely from one computer to another, as it is routed through multiple networks to reach its destination. Each computer along the way has access to that data, which is a potential problem if the information is confidential (e.g., a credit card number).

E-commerce, however, depends entirely on the availability of secure transactions. The buyer and seller must both be assured that data is safe and cannot be compromised. This is accomplished through ***encryption***, the process of encoding data so that it is no longer in its original form when it is sent across the Internet. The precise way in which data is encrypted prior to being sent, then decrypted on the receiving end, is beyond the scope of our description. Just realize that encryption is built into Internet Explorer and that it takes place automatically when you communicate with a secure site.

Figures 7a and 7b illustrate a nonsecure and a secure connection, respectively. Any information that is transmitted in connection with Figure 7a (e.g., clicking on any of the links on the page) is of a nonconfidential nature and need not be encrypted. You can tell that the transmission is not secure in two ways—the transmission protocol is http, and the status bar does not contain a padlock icon. The form in Figure 7b, however, contains confidential data (a Login ID and password) and thus it needs to be encrypted before it is sent. You can tell that the connection is secure because a different protocol, ***https*** rather than http, is in effect, and further because the status bar in Internet Explorer displays a padlock icon.

If you intend to participate in e-commerce in any way, you should be aware of the different ways to transmit data (encrypted versus unencrypted) and the implications of each. You can feel comfortable, for example, transmitting data of a nonpersonal nature via the http (nonsecure) protocol. Anything of a confidential nature, however, such as a credit card or account number, should be sent only if the site provides a secure protocol.

A SIMPLE ENCRYPTION ALGORITHM

Julius Caesar is given credit for developing one of the oldest encryption schemes. Caesar used a simple substitution algorithm in which each letter in the original text was replaced by the letter three positions further in the alphabet. The letter "a" was replaced by the letter "d", the letter "b" by the letter "e", and so on. The word "cat", for example, would be encrypted as "fdw". It was simple, but it worked as long as the recipient knew the key, which was the number of letters to jump in the alphabet.

Privacy

You can't have it both ways. The convenience of returning to a site and having the site know your likes and dislikes to steer you to the goods or information you are most likely to request, is offset by the thought that the site knows all about you. How much it knows, and what it will do with that information, are growing concerns. It is all a function of ***cookies***—the small files that are written to your hard drive each time you visit a site. There is nothing harmful about a cookie per se. It is not a virus, and it will not erase or alter the programs on your computer. It is simply a text file that contains information about your visit to a site.

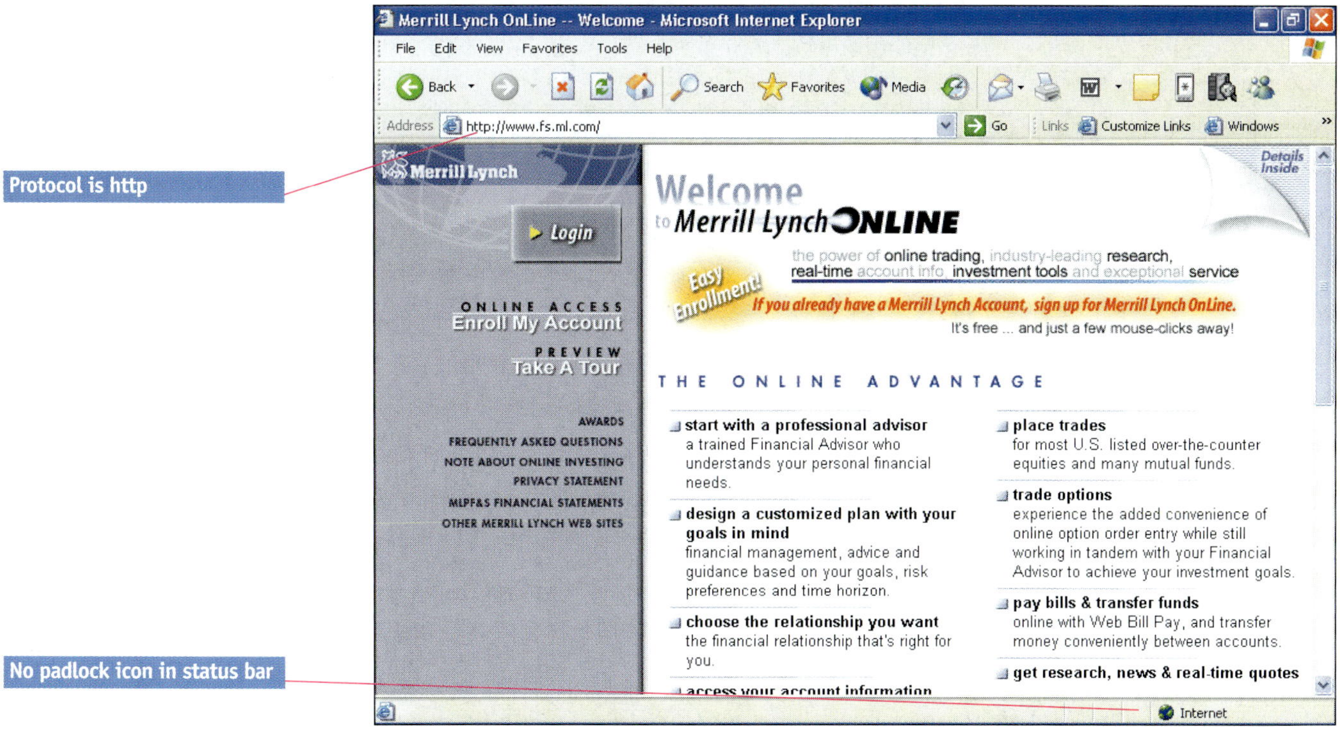

(a) Nonsecure Connection (http protocol)

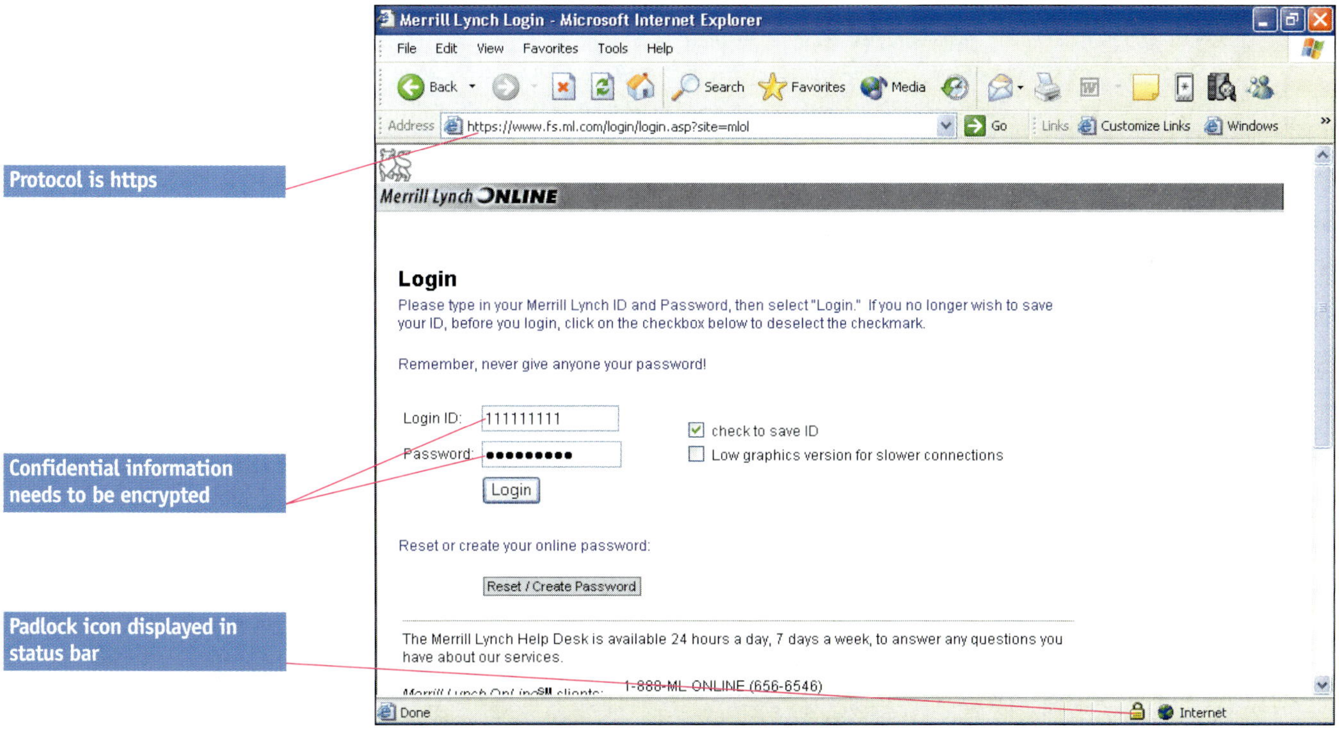

(b) Secure Connection (https protocol)

FIGURE 7 Security on the Web

In essence, cookies enable you to personalize your interaction with a Web site and thus offer a tremendous convenience while simultaneously raising a threat to your privacy. If, for example, you are interrupted in the middle of downloading a large file, a cookie makes it possible for you to reconnect to the site and begin downloading at the point where you were disconnected. Most people would agree that's good, but it is possible only because the site wrote a cookie to your computer with information about your progress. Cookies also make it possible for a retail site to send you information about the types of products you are likely to buy. Many people would think that's good, but it also means that the site knows your shopping habits, which it learned by recording the types of links you selected and the purchases you made. Cookies also let you customize various sites so that you see immediately the news or stock prices of interest to you. That can be good, but it means that the site can make inferences about stocks you own.

Cookies have always been present, but it is only recently that they have raised a furor. Most people would agree that individual cookies are not harmful. If, for example, you purchase CDs online, it is convenient for the site to know the type of music and/or artists that you like in order to notify you of new releases. One cookie from one site is not likely to invade your ***privacy***.

But what if one site could read the cookies from several sites? That is precisely what a company called DoubleClick.com has accomplished. DoubleClick is in the business of placing ads on multiple Web sites, enabling it to write cookies to a machine from multiple places, and thereby track the movements of that machine across many sites. It can tell not only what was purchased, but also which sites were visited along the way, and even the identity of the person on the machine. Some people are indifferent, whereas others are incensed at the invasion of privacy. Our objective is simply to make you aware of what is technically possible.

Returning to a Previous Site

Internet Explorer enables you to move effortlessly from one Web document to another. As you browse through the Web, it's all too easy to forget how you arrived at a particular site, making it difficult to return to that site. You could click the ***Back button*** repeatedly, but that is somewhat tedious, and further, it works only for the particular session. What if you wanted to return to a site you visited last Monday? Internet Explorer anticipates the problem and provides two different sets of links, the Favorites list and the History list.

The ***Favorites list*** in Figure 8a consists of sites that you save with the expectation of returning to those sites at a future time. (Favorites are not restricted to Web sites and can include folders and/or documents on your machine.) Once you arrive at a site that you consider special, just pull down the Favorites menu and click the Add to Favorites command. Internet Explorer then creates a link to that site within the Favorites list. The links can be stored individually, or they can be stored with related links in a folder. The typical user starts by creating individual links, then eventually opts for folders to organize the links more efficiently.

The ***History list*** in Figure 8b is even easier to use in that the links are created automatically and consist of all sites that were visited during a specified time span. (The default is 20 days.) The links in the History list are organized automatically into subfolders, one for each day of the current week, then a separate folder for previous weeks. The links are further divided to show the site, then the various pages at that site.

Either list can be displayed by clicking the appropriate button on the Internet Explorer toolbar. The buttons function as toggle switches; that is, click the Favorites button, and the Favorites list is displayed in a separate pane. Click the Favorites button a second time and the pane is closed.

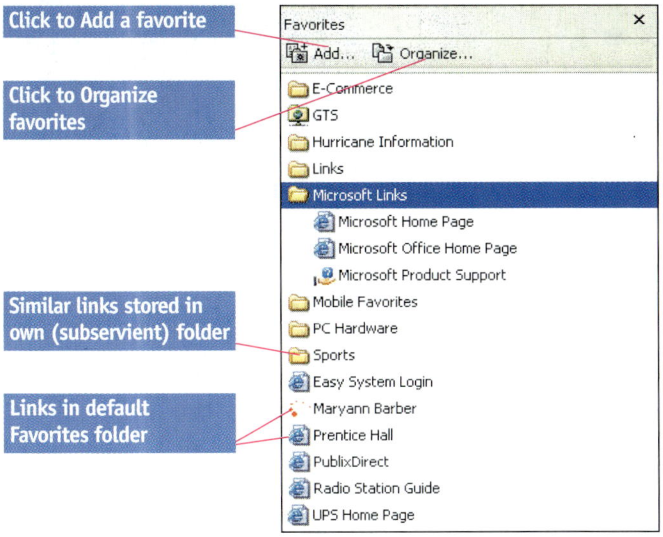

(a) Favorites Folder

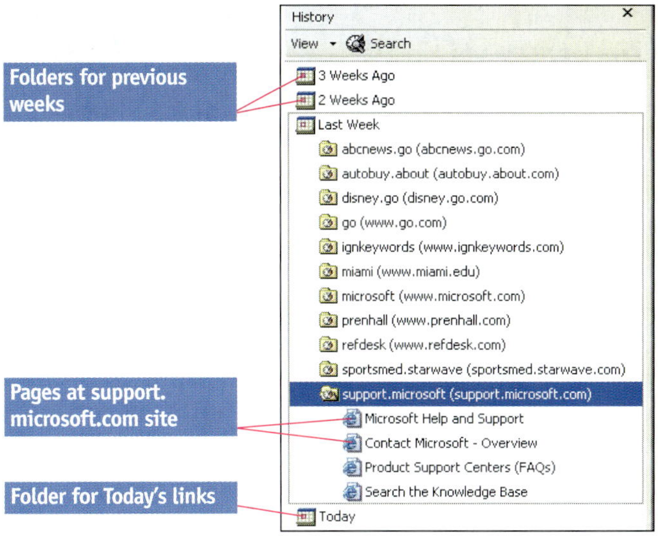

(b) History Folder

FIGURE 8 Returning to a Previous Site

OUR NEXT EXERCISE

Our next exercise takes you on a virtual shopping spree in which you visit several well-known commercial sites. Window shopping is perfectly acceptable, and there is no requirement to buy anything. Our objective is to show you the potential of shopping on the Web, to illustrate the security protocols we have been discussing, and to demonstrate the creation of a cookie. We also illustrate the Favorites list and the History list.

Our exercise focuses on the Barnes & Noble Web site, which is "traditional" in the sense that you browse through a well-defined inventory and purchase items at a specified price. We deliberately limited our shopping spree, but you might want to include additional stops. Start with eBay (www.ebay.com), where buyers and sellers are brought together in an online auction. As exciting as the concept of an auction may be, there is another class of buyers that wants a bargain, knows exactly what they want, but simply does not have the patience to wait for bidding to be completed. If that describes your shopping preference, visit www.half.com, where you can obtain previously owned items at no more than one half of their original price. The price is posted and there is no waiting for the auction to be complete. And finally, you can visit www.priceline.com, where you name your price for airline tickets, hotel rooms, and rental cars.

SET A TIME LIMIT

The exercise you are about to do has you browse continually, looking for interesting sites on which to hone your skills. We warn you that the Web is addictive, and that once you start surfing, it is difficult to stop. We suggest, therefore, that you set a time limit before you begin, and that you stick to it when the time has expired. Tomorrow is another day, with new places to explore.

hands-on exercise

3 Shopping in Cyberspace

Objective To explore shopping on the Web and to illustrate the use of the https protocol; to organize favorites more efficiently through creation of a folder. Use Figure 9 as a guide in the exercise.

Step 1: Visit Barnes & Noble

- Start Internet Explorer as you did in the previous exercises. Click in the **Address bar** and type **www.barnesandnoble.com.** Press **Enter**.
- You should see the home page of Barnes & Noble. Pull down the **Favorites menu** and click the **Add to Favorites command** to display the Add Favorite dialog box in Figure 9a. Click **OK** to add this site to the list of favorites.
- Click the **Favorites button** on the Standard Buttons toolbar to display the Favorites list in the left pane, which should now contain the Barnes & Noble Web site. (The link is added to the end of the favorites list, so you may have to scroll to see the new link.
- The Favorites button functions as a toggle switch; that is, click the button, and the Favorites list is displayed. Click the button a second time, and the list is closed.

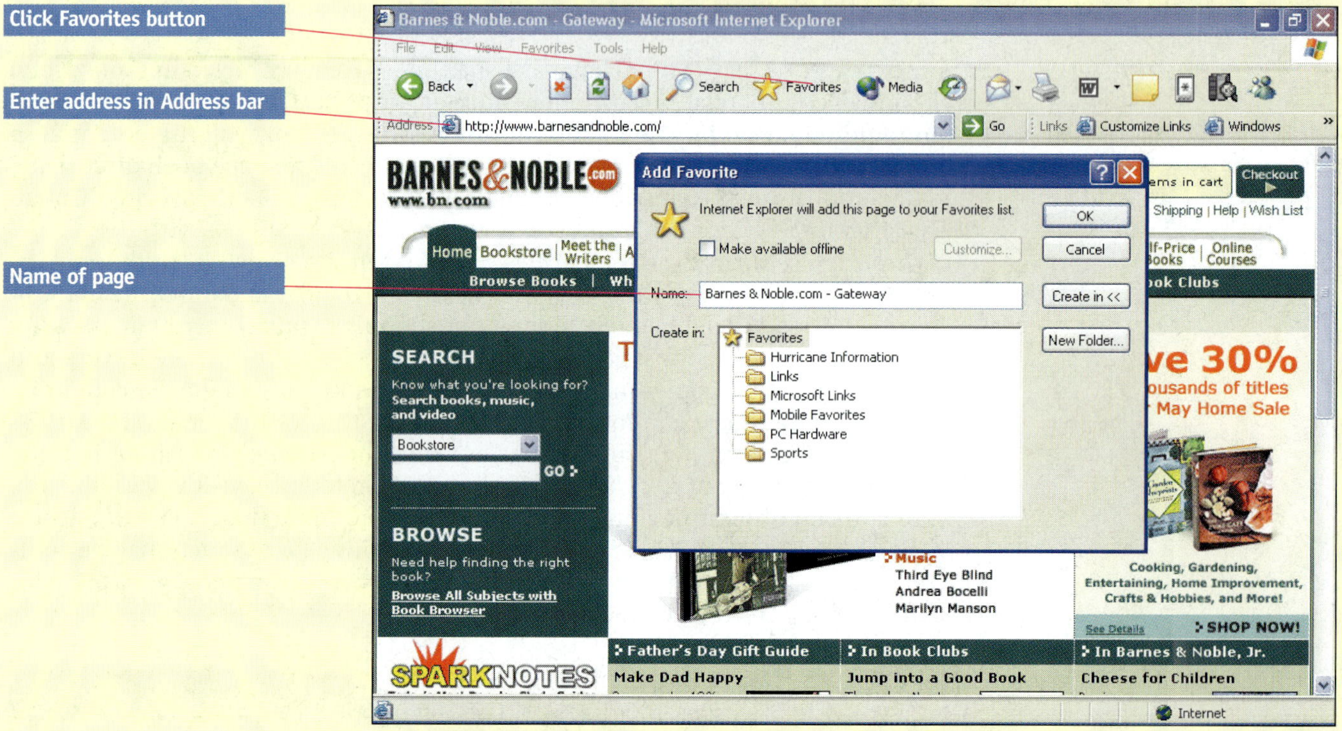

(a) Visit Barnes & Noble (step 1)

FIGURE 9 Hands-on Exercise 3

REARRANGE YOUR FAVORITES

The links within the Favorites list appear according to the sequence in which they were added to the list; the most recent link appears at the bottom of the list. Unfortunately, we have yet to discover an easy way to alphabetize the list. You can, however, click and drag any link in the list to change its place within the list. We suggest you do this each time you add a new link to maintain an alphabetic list.

Step 2: Create the E-Commerce Folder

- It's more efficient to store related links in a folder, as opposed to a single list of favorites. Pull down the **Favorites menu** and click the **Organize Favorites command** to display the Organize Favorites dialog box.
- Click the **Create Folder button**. A new folder appears within the dialog box, with the default name of the folder (New Folder). Type **E-Commerce** as the name of the folder and press **Enter**.
- Select (click) the link to Barnes & Noble that you added in the previous step. Click the **Move to Folder button** within the Organize Favorites dialog box as shown in Figure 9b. Select the newly created E-Commerce folder and click **OK**.
- The Barnes & Noble link disappears from within the Organize Favorites dialog box because it has been moved to the E-commerce folder. Click the folder to open it, and you will see the Barnes & Noble link within the folder. Close the Organize Favorites dialog box.
- Click the **Favorites button** on the Standard Buttons toolbar to open the Favorites pane, which now contains the E-commerce folder. Click the **Favorites button** a second time to close the Favorites pane.

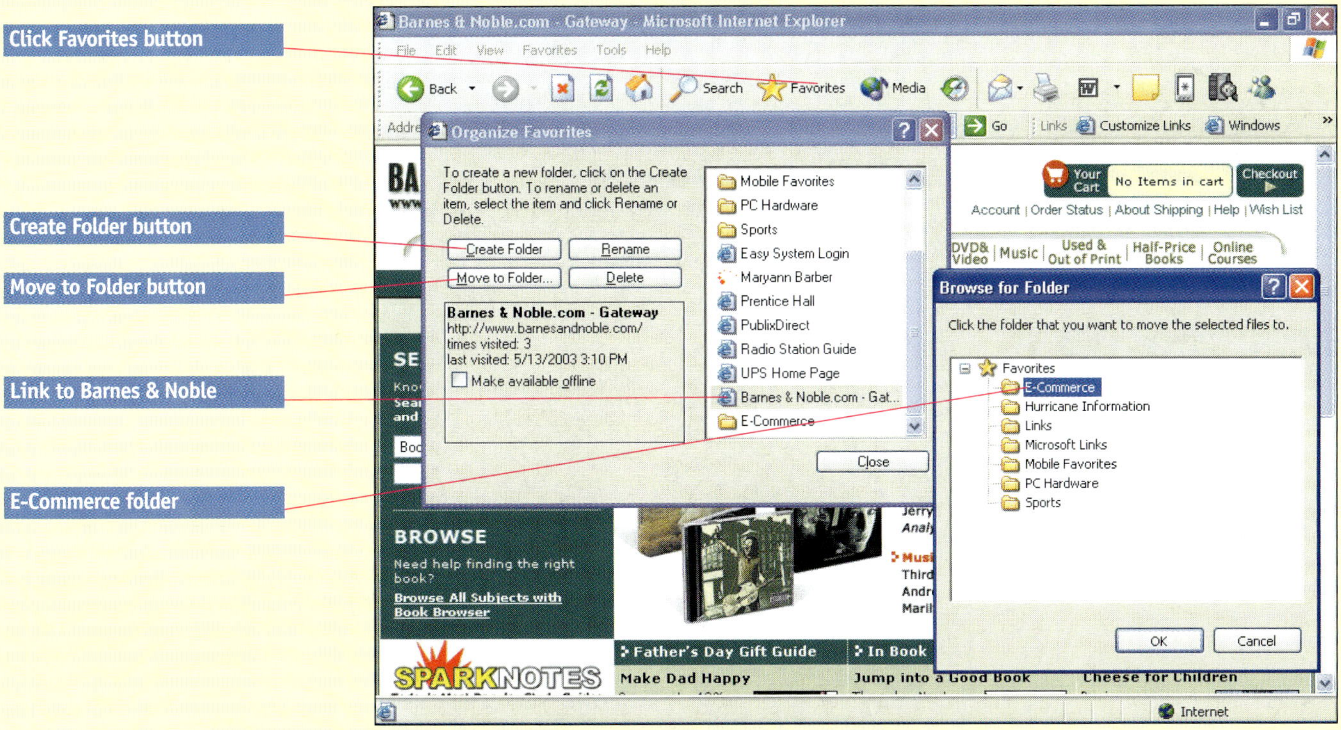

(b) Create the E-Commerce Folder (step 2)

FIGURE 9 Hands-on Exercise 3 (*continued*)

EXPORT YOUR FAVORITES LIST

Over time the average user accumulates a lengthy list of favorites that he or she will want to take to another computer. Pull down the File menu, click the Import/Export command, then follow the steps in the Import/Export Wizard to export your Favorites list. The result is a single HTML document that contains all of your links in the current set of favorite folders. You can copy that file to a floppy disk, then take it with you to another machine, where you can import the file to reestablish your complete Favorites list.

Step 3: Search for a Book

- Click the **Bookstore tab** at the top of the Barnes & Noble site. Click the **down arrow** in the Keyword list box (near the top of the screen) and select **Title**.
- Type **Harry Potter** in the Search text box, then click the **Go button** at the top of the page. You should see a list of all titles that contain Harry Potter as shown in Figure 9c. (The large number of titles is attributed to the many different editions that exist for each book in the series.)
- You can add any title to your shopping cart immediately by clicking the **Add to Cart button**. Alternatively, you can select the link to any title to read more about a selection, then decide if you want to purchase the book.
- Add at least one item to your shopping cart, then click the link to **Proceed to Checkout** to view your shopping cart. Click the **Proceed to Checkout button** to initiate the actual purchase.
- We will *not* ask you to purchase a book, but we want you to see the beginning of the checkout process.
- Click **OK** if you see a security alert indicating that you are about to view a secure page.

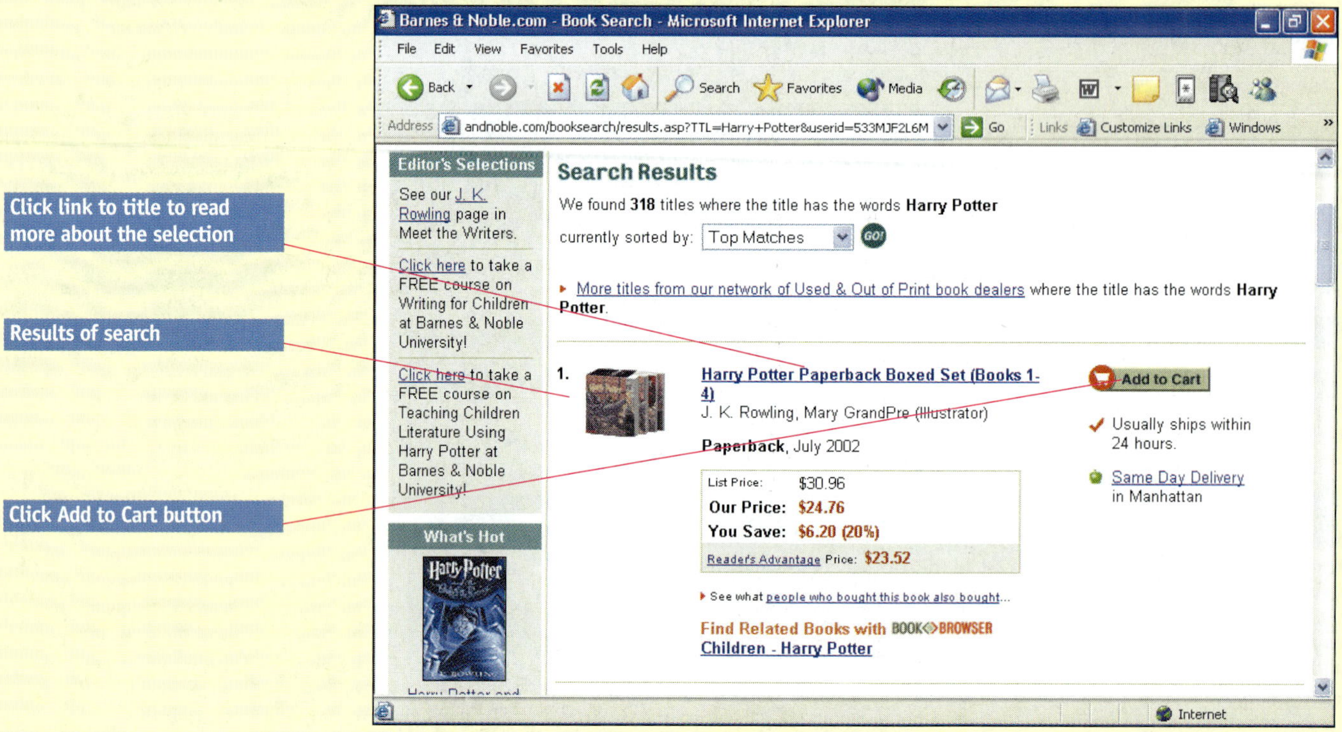

(c) Search for a Book (step 3)

FIGURE 9 Hands-on Exercise 3 (*continued*)

CHANGE THE FONT

The Web designer selects the font size he or she deems most appropriate. You can, however, change the font size of the displayed page to display more or less information as you see fit. Pull down the View menu and click the Text Size command to display a menu with five different sizes. The sizes are relative (from smallest to largest), as opposed to a specific point size. Click the size you prefer, and the display changes automatically. This command affects only the monitor and not the printed output.

Step 4: Check Out Now

- Enter your e-mail address and a password when prompted to do so. You should see a screen similar to the screen in Figure 9d. This is a secure screen as can be seen by the https protocol in the Address bar and padlock icon in the status bar.
- There is no need for you to complete the form at this time, since you will not be making an actual purchase. Note, however, some fields are asterisked (e.g., last name), whereas others (company name) are not, indicating required and optional fields, respectively.
- Click the **Back button** to return to the previous screen and cancel the checkout process. You may see the Security Alert in Figure 9d, indicating that you are leaving a secure site.
- Click **Yes** to confirm that you want to leave.

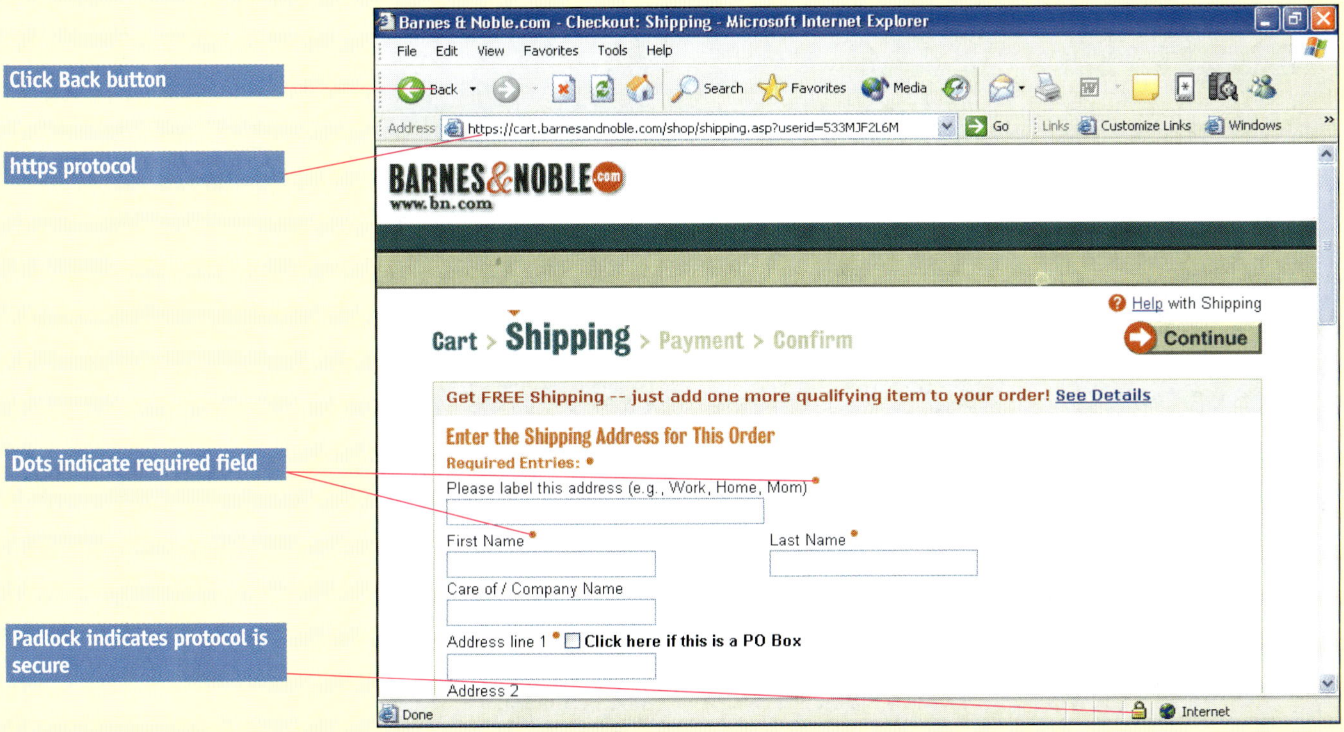

(d) Check Out Now (step 4)

FIGURE 9 Hands-on Exercise 3 (*continued*)

COMMON SENSE IS THE BEST SECURITY

You can complete your purchase over the Web and transmit confidential information, including your credit card number, in safety, provided you have a secure connection as indicated by the lock on the IE status bar. Even so, the best security protocol is common sense. Do not submit your credit card number over a computer that is not your own as the information may be stored permanently on that computer. Nor should you release confidential information to a company or Web site that you do not know. Forewarned is forearmed. And never give a password to anyone, no matter how innocent the request.

Step 5: Add Sites to the E-Commerce Folder

- Click in the **Address bar**, type **autos.msn.com**, and press **Enter** to go to the Web site.
- Pull down the **Favorites menu** and click the **Add to Favorites command** to display the Add Favorites dialog box in Figure 9e.
- Click the **Create in command button** if you do not see the set of Favorites folders, then click the **E-Commerce folder** to open the folder and save the current site within this folder. Click **OK**.
- Add at least two additional sites to the E-commerce folder. We added Dell Computer **(www.dell.com)** and the E-bay auction site **(www.ebay.com)**, but you are free to choose any sites you like.

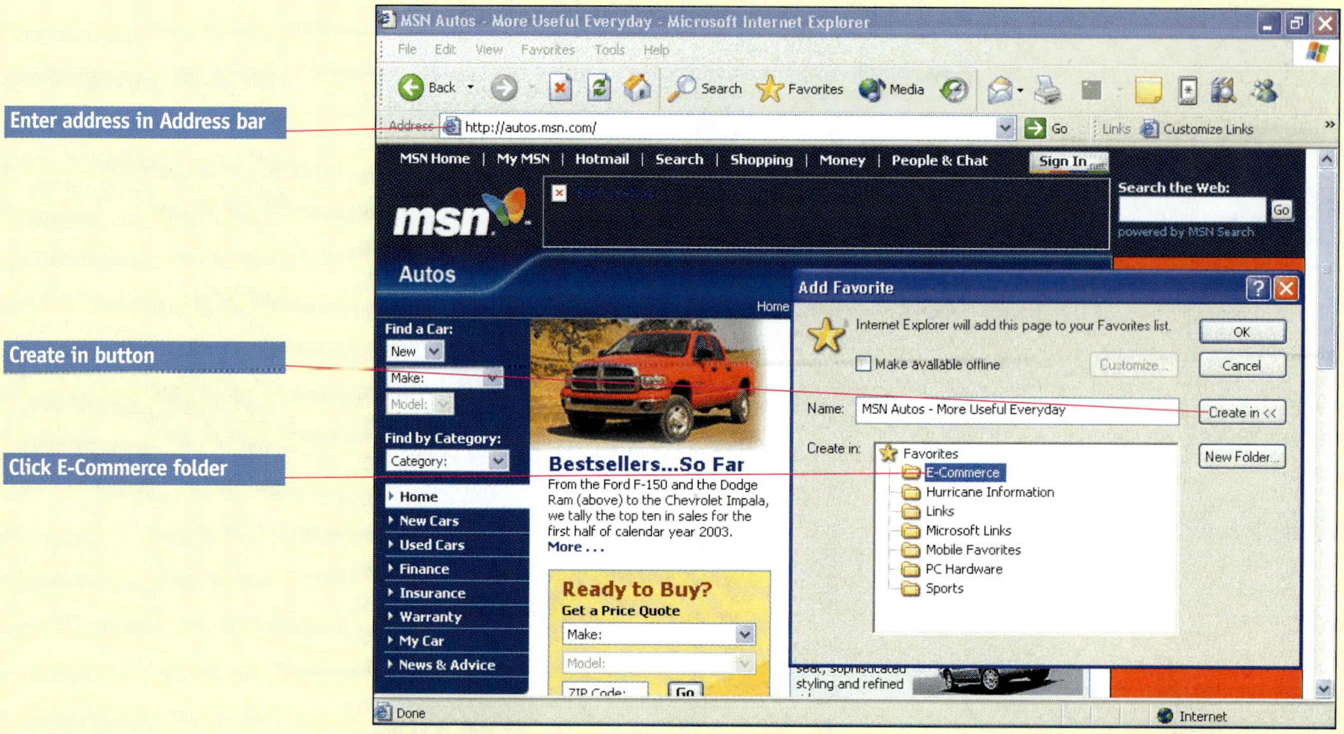

(e) Add Sites to the E-Commerce Folder (step 5)

FIGURE 9 Hands-on Exercise 3 (*continued*)

INSIST ON 30-DAY PRICE PROTECTION

Computer prices are always falling, but that doesn't mean you should wait for a better price to buy a computer. Any reputable vendor will provide a 30-day price-protection policy, which credits your account with any price reductions during the first 30 days you own your system. It is incumbent on you, however, to contact the vendor within the allotted time frame to request a refund. Don't forget to do so (and send us an e-mail message if we save you some money).

Step 6: Return to a Favorite

- Click the **Favorites button** on the Standard Buttons toolbar to display the Favorites list, then if necessary, click the **E-Commerce folder** to open the folder and display its contents as shown in Figure 9f.
- You should see the various sites that were added to this folder in the previous step. Click any link within the E-commerce folder to return to a previous site.
- You can also click and drag a link from one folder to another (or you can click the **Organize button** to move the links from one folder to another).
- Click the **E-Commerce folder** a second time to close the folder. (Each time you click a folder, you toggle the folder open or closed.)
- Close the Favorites pane.

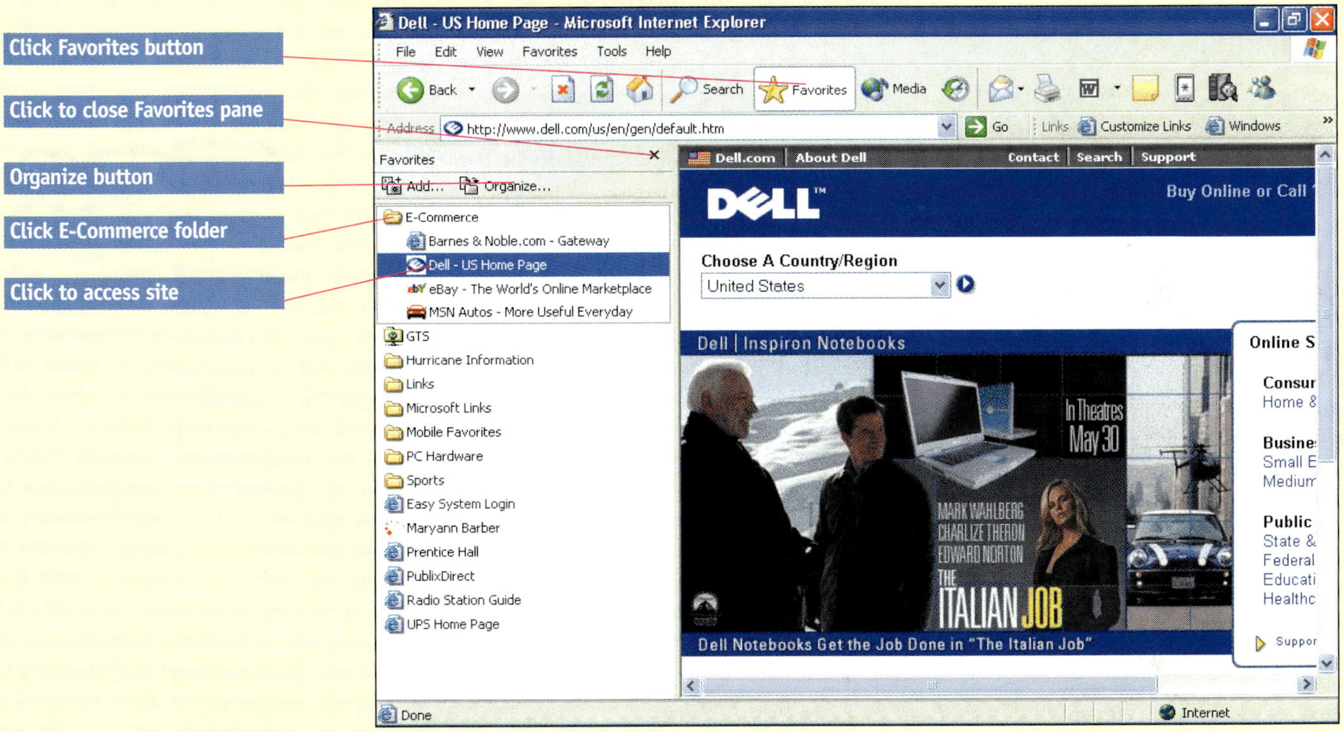

(f) Return to a Favorite (step 6)

FIGURE 9 Hands-on Exercise 3 (*continued*)

DOUBLE THE WARRANTY

You can double the warranty of any purchase (up to one additional year) by using a major credit card that offers a "buyer's protection" policy. Check with your credit card company to see whether it has this feature, and if it doesn't, consider getting a different credit card. The extended warranty is free, and it goes into effect automatically when you charge the purchase. It is applicable to any item except an automobile.

Step 7: The History List

- Click the **History button** on the Standard Buttons toolbar to open the History list as shown in Figure 9g. The History button functions as a toggle switch; click the button, and the History list is displayed. Click the button a second time, and the pane is closed.
- Click the **down arrow** next to the View button to see the different ways in which the contents of the folder can be displayed. If necessary, click **By Date**, so that the contents of the folder are displayed in chronological order.
- Click the **Today folder** to toggle this folder open or closed. Leave the folder open as shown in Figure 9g, so that you can see the sites that you visited in this exercise. Click any link within the Today folder to return to that link.
- The History list provides a complete log of your session. It is very useful in the context of shopping and/or searching the Web for information you accessed recently.
- Close Internet Explorer.

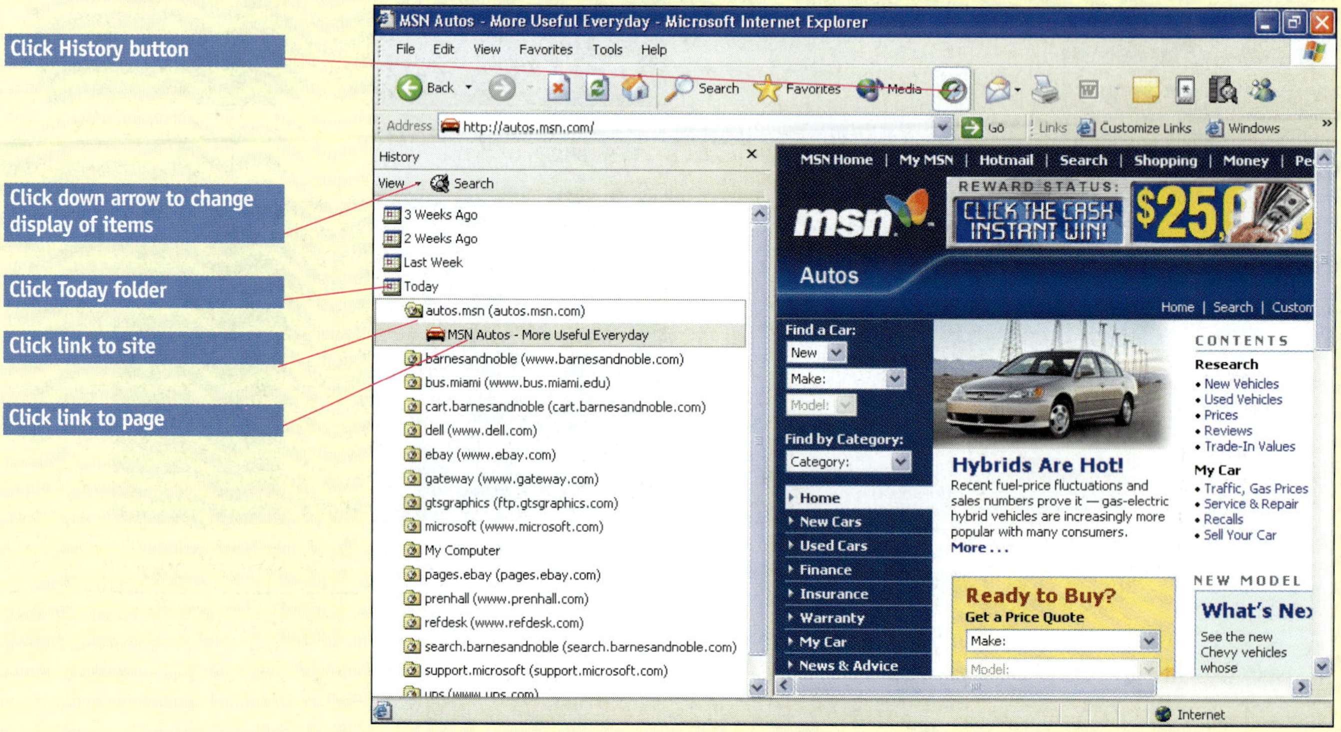

(g) The History List (step 7)

FIGURE 9 Hands-on Exercise 3 (*continued*)

WHAT IS CACHE?

Cache stores the Web pages you have accessed on your PC in an attempt to improve performance. The pages are stored in two places—in RAM and on the hard drive. The first time you request a page, it is downloaded from a Web server, which, depending on the size of the page and the traffic on the Internet, can take considerable time. The next time you request the page, Internet Explorer checks to see if it is already in cache (first memory, then disk), and if so, displays it from there. This explains why it takes several seconds (or longer) to display a page initially, and why the same page appears almost instantly if you return to it later in the session.

INTRODUCTION TO HTML

It's only a matter of time before you will want to create a home page and/or a Web site of your own. That, in turn, requires an appreciation for ***Hypertext Markup Language (HTML)***, the language in which all Web pages are written. A Web page (HTML document) consists of text and graphics, together with a set of codes (or ***tags***) that describe how the document is to appear when viewed in a Web browser such as Internet Explorer.

Initially, anyone who wanted to create a Web document had to learn each of these codes and enter them explicitly. Today, it's much easier as you can create a Web document directly in any application in Microsoft Office. In essence, you enter the text of a document, apply basic formatting—such as boldface or italic—then simply save the file as a Web document. There are, of course, other commands that you will need to learn, but all commands are executed from within the Office application, through pull-down menus, toolbars, or keyboard shortcuts. You can create a single document (called a ***home page***), or you can create multiple documents to build a simple Web site. Either way, the document(s) can be viewed locally within a Web browser—such as Internet Explorer—and/or they can be placed on a Web server, where they can be accessed by anyone with an Internet connection.

The procedure to place a document on the Web is straightforward, but it requires you to have an account on a Web server, a username, and a password. You can obtain the account from your professor and/or your ISP. You then upload the document from your machine to the server using a program known as FTP (File Transfer Protocol). Once the page has been loaded onto the Web server, it is part of the Web and can be viewed by anyone with Internet access, provided they know the address of your page.

Figure 10 displays a simple Web page that includes different types of formatting, a bulleted list, underlined links, and a heading displayed in a larger font. All of these elements are associated with specific HTML codes that identify the appearance and characteristics of the item. Figure 10a displays the document as it would appear when viewed in Internet Explorer. Figure 10b shows the underlying HTML codes (tags) that are necessary to format the page.

Fortunately, however, it is not necessary to memorize the HTML tags since you can usually determine their meaning from the codes themselves. Nor is it even necessary for you to enter the tags, as Word will create the HTML tags for you based on the formatting in the document. Nevertheless, we think it worthwhile for you to gain an appreciation for HTML by comparing the two views of the document.

HTML codes become less intimidating when you realize that they are enclosed in angle brackets and are used consistently from document to document. Most tags occur in pairs, at the beginning and end of the text to be formatted, with the ending code preceded by a slash, such as <p> and </p> to indicate the beginning and end of a paragraph. Links to other pages (which are known as hyperlinks) are enclosed within a pair of anchor tags <A> and </A> in which you specify the URL address of the document through the HREF parameter.

WHAT IS XML?

Extensible Markup Language, or XML, is an industry standard for structuring data. It is very different from HTML and serves an entirely different function. HTML describes how a document should look; for example, <B>John Doe</B> indicates that John Doe should appear in boldface, but it does not tell us anything more. You don't know that "John" is the first name or that "Doe" is the last name. XML, on the other hand, is data about data, and it lets you define your own tags, such as <name><first>John</first><last>Doe</last></name>. The XML codes can be read by any XML-compliant application and processed accordingly.

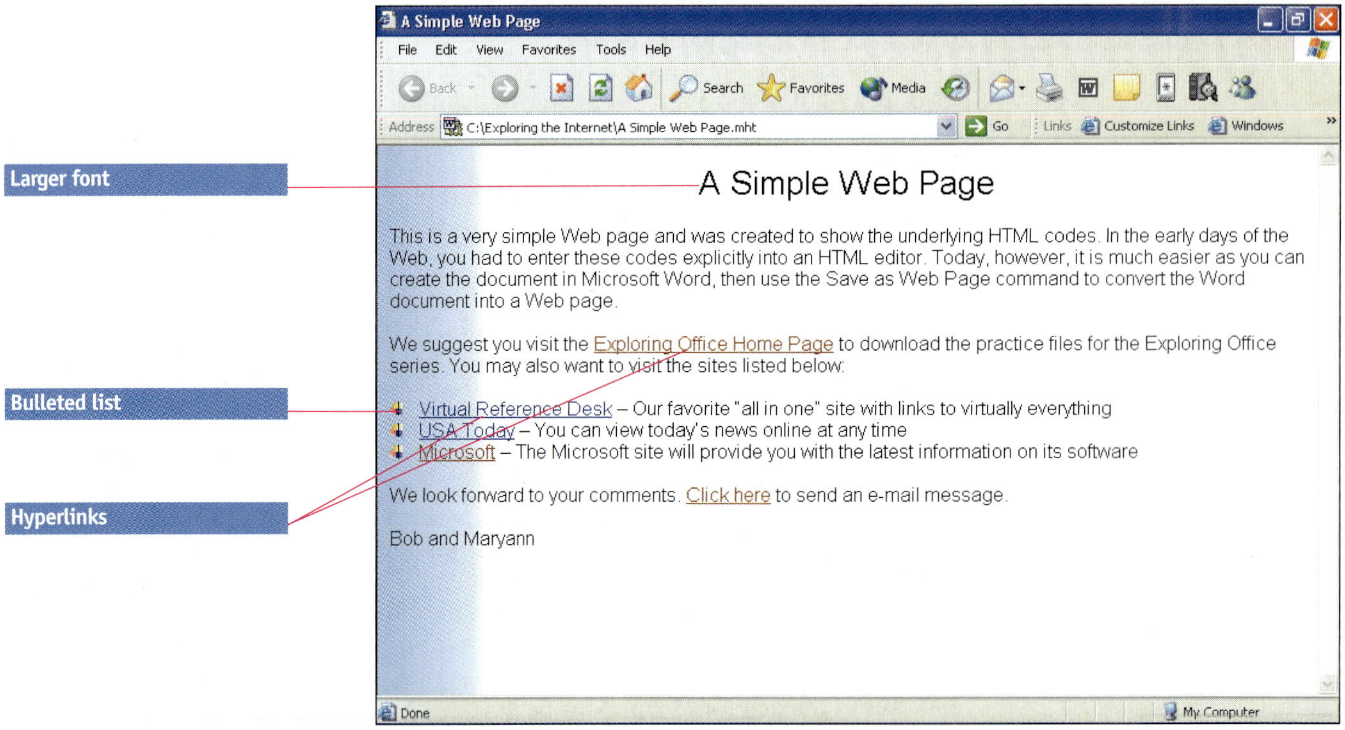

(a) Internet Explorer

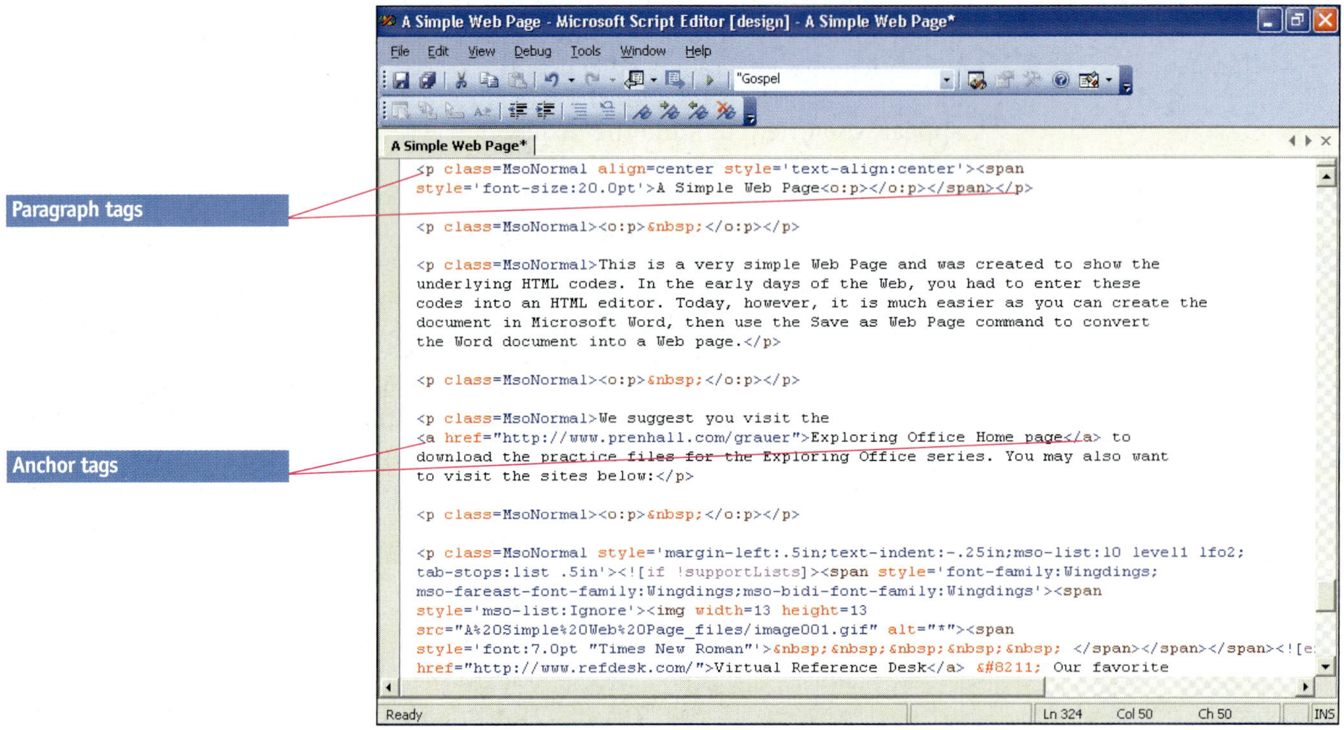

(b) HTML Source Code

FIGURE 10 Introduction to HTML

Microsoft Word

As indicated, there are different ways to create an HTML document. The original (and more difficult) method was to enter the codes explicitly in a text editor, such as the Notepad accessory that is built into Windows. An easier way (and the only method you need to consider) is to use Microsoft Word (or a specialized Web editor) to create the document for you, without having to enter the HTML codes at all.

Figure 11 displays the home page of a hypothetical computer super store as it might be created in Microsoft Word. You can create a similar page using Word by entering and formatting the text just as you would enter the text of an ordinary document. The only difference is that instead of saving the document in the default format (as a Word document), you use the ***Save As Web Page command*** to convert the document to a Web page. (Word 2003 provides a new ***Single File Web Page*** format that makes the process even easier.)

You can enter text and/or change the formatting of existing text just as you would with an ordinary Word document. Hyperlinks are entered through the Insert Hyperlink button on the Standard toolbar or through the corresponding command in the Insert menu. You can format the elements of the document (the heading, bullets, text, and so on) individually, or you can select a ***theme*** from those provided by Microsoft Word. A theme (or template) is a set of unified design elements and color schemes that will save you time while making your document more attractive.

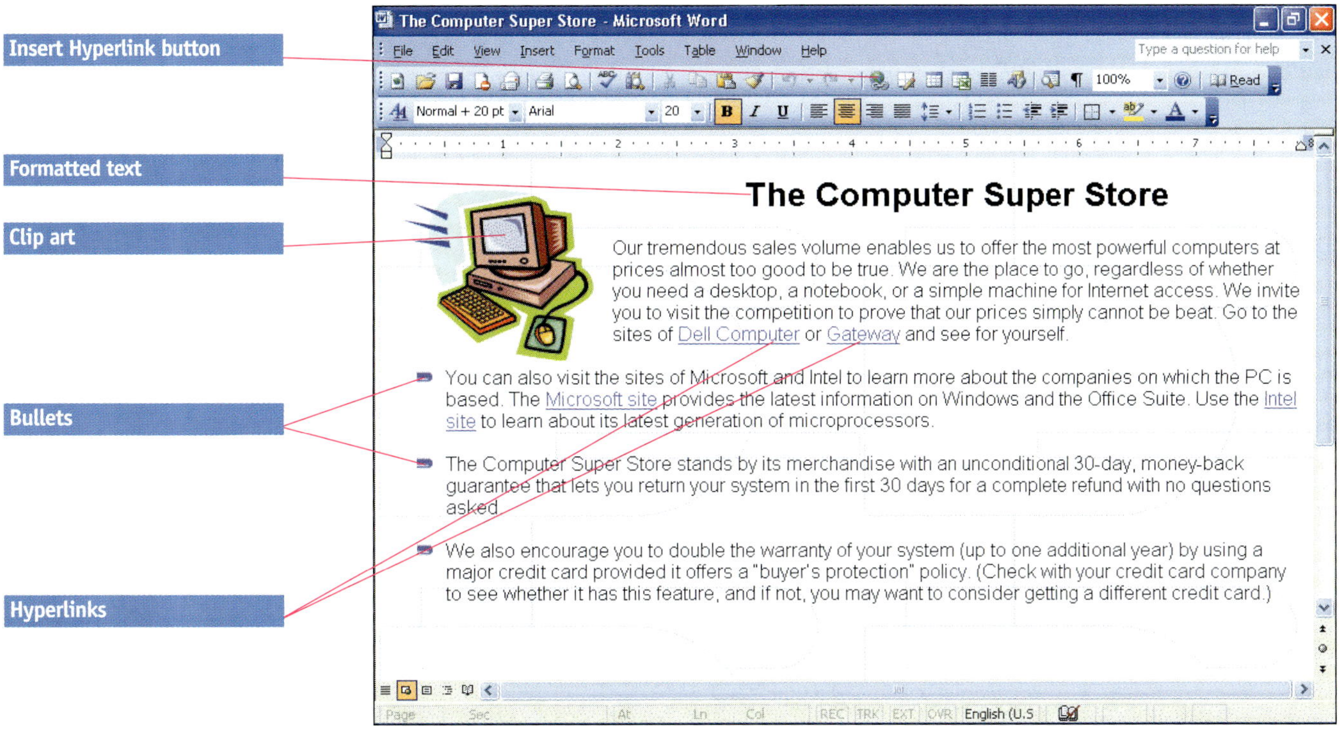

FIGURE 11 A Web Page in Microsoft Word

REGISTER YOUR SITE

You can apply for a domain name (Web address) through any of a number of independent companies. The company will verify that the name has not been previously taken, then register that name with InterNIC, the government agency that actually assigns the name. The cost is approximately $20 a year for the domain name. See practice exercise 6 at the end of the chapter.

hands-on exercise

4 Introduction to HTML

Objective To use Microsoft Word to create a simple Web page with clip art and multiple hyperlinks. Use Figure 12 as a guide in the exercise.

Step 1: Enter the Text

- Click the **Start button** on the Windows taskbar to start Microsoft Word. Close the task pane. Pull down the **View menu** and click the **Web Layout command.** Enter the text of the document as shown in Figure 12a.
- Click and drag to select the second, third, and fourth paragraphs, then click the **Bullets button** to precede each paragraph with a bullet. If necessary, click the **Decrease Indent button** to move the bullets to the left margin.
- Click the **Spelling and Grammar button** to check the document for spelling. Correct the errors (if any) as they are detected.

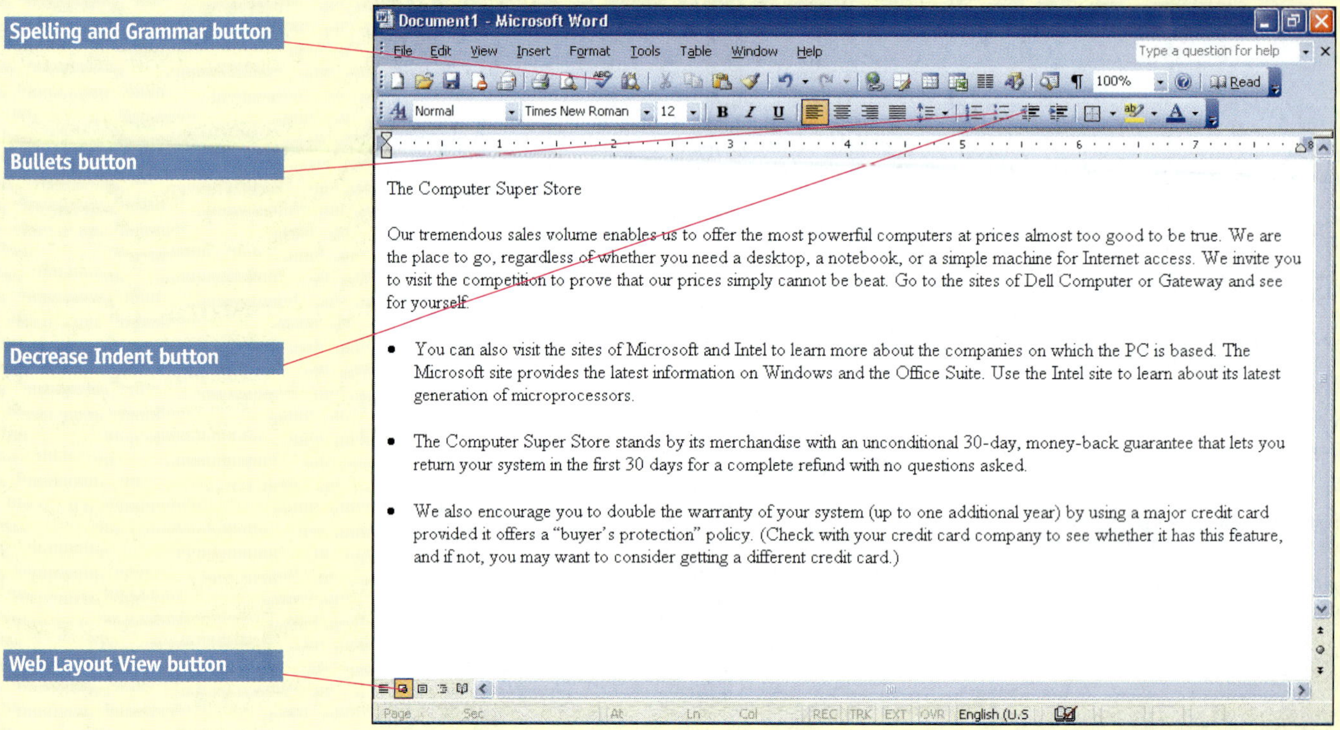

(a) Enter the Text (step 1)

FIGURE 12 Hands-on Exercise 4

MICROSOFT FRONTPAGE 2003

Microsoft Word is an excellent way to begin creating Web documents. It is only a beginning, however, and there are many specialty programs that have significantly more capability. One such product is FrontPage, a product aimed at creating a Web site, as opposed to isolated documents. Search the Microsoft Web site for information on FrontPage, and then summarize your findings in a short note to your instructor. Be sure to include information on capabilities that are included in FrontPage that are not found in Word.

Step 2: **Save the Document**

- Pull down the **File menu** and click the **Save As Web Page command** to display the Save As dialog box in Figure 12. Be sure that **Single File Web Page** is specified as the file format.
- Click the **drop-down arrow** in the Save In list box to select the appropriate drive, drive C or drive A. If necessary, click the **Up One Level button** on the Save As toolbar continually until you come to the drive itself, then click the **Create New Folder button** and create the **Exploring the Internet folder**.
- Check that the name of the document is **The Computer Super Store**. Click the **Change Title button** if you want to change the title of the Web page as it will appear in the title bar of the Web browser.
- Click the **Save button**. The title bar reflects the name of the Web page (The Computer Super Store), but the screen does not change in any other way. In other words, you can continue to work in Microsoft Word, and enhance your page through ordinary Word commands.

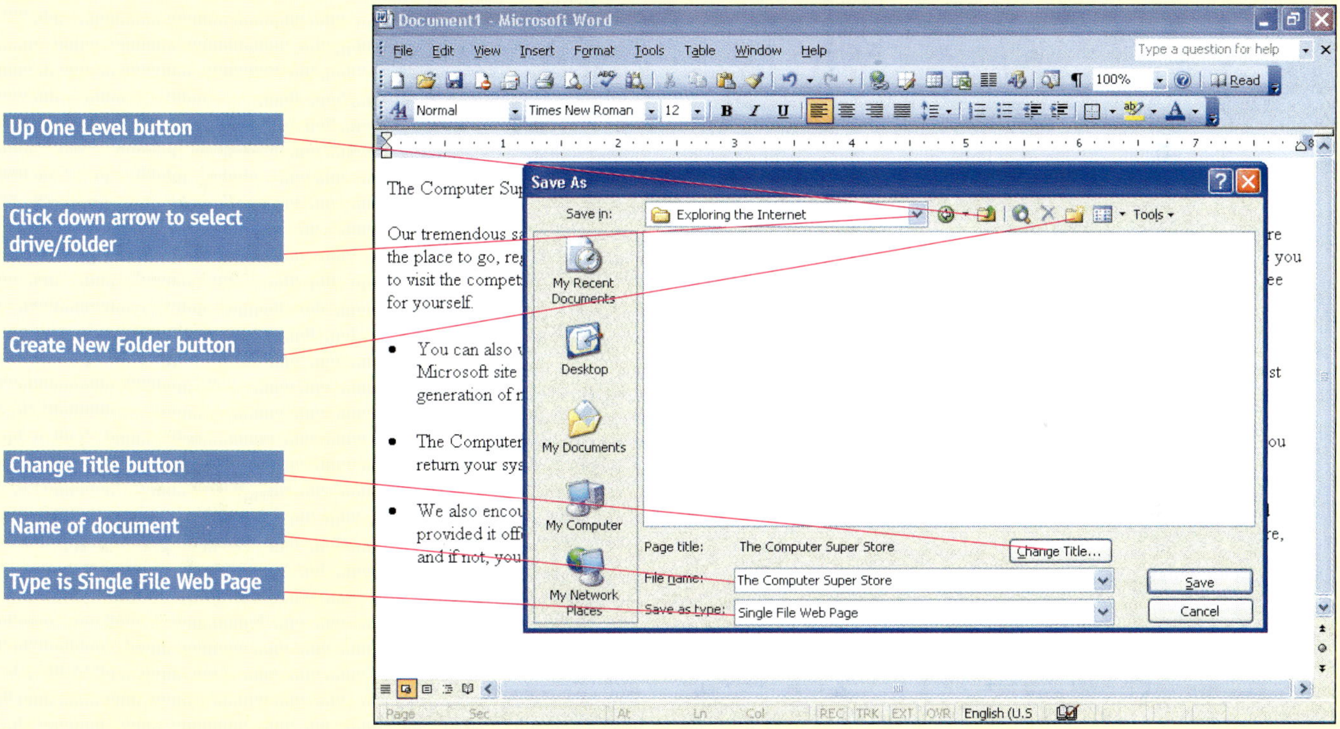

(b) Save the Document (step 2)

FIGURE 12 Hands-on Exercise 4 (*continued*)

THE FILE TYPES ARE DIFFERENT

Click the Start button, click (or point to) the All Programs command, click Accessories, then start Windows Explorer. Select the drive and folder where you saved the Web document. If necessary, pull down the View menu and change to the Details view. Look for the Web document you just created, and note that it is displayed with the icon of a Web browser (Internet Explorer or Netscape Navigator) to indicate that it is an MHTML or HTML document, rather than a Word document.

Step 3: Insert the Clip Art

- Pull down the **Insert menu**, click (or point to) **Picture**, then click **Clip Art**. The task pane opens (if it is not already open) and displays the Clip Art search pane as shown in Figure 12c.
- Click in the **Search for text box**. Type **computer** to search for any clip art image that is indexed with this keyword, then click the **Go button** or press **Enter**.
- The images are displayed in the Results box. Point to an image to display a drop-down arrow to its right. Click the arrow to display a context menu. Click **Insert** to insert the image into the document. Close the task pane.
- Point to the picture, click the **right mouse button** to display the context-sensitive menu, then click the **Format Picture command** to display the Format Picture dialog box.
- Click the **Layout tab**, choose the **Square layout**, then click the option button for **Left alignment**. Click **OK** to close the dialog box. Click and drag the sizing handles on the picture as appropriate, then drag the picture to the left of the first paragraph. Save the document.

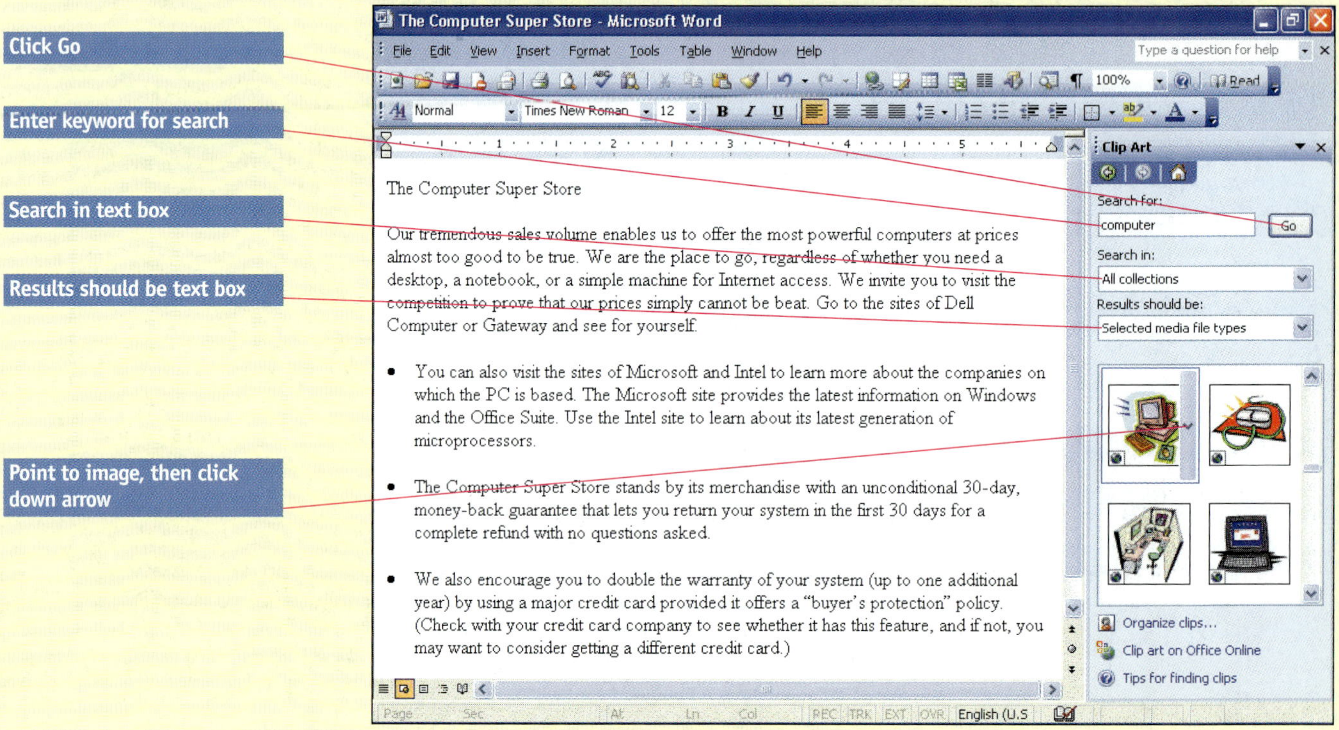

(c) Insert the Clip Art (step 3)

FIGURE 12 Hands-on Exercise 4 (*continued*)

THE INSERT PICTURE COMMAND

Pull down the Insert menu, click the Picture command, and click Clip Art to display the Clip Art task pane that enables you to enter search parameters for an appropriate media object. Click the down arrow in the Search in list box and select All collections. Click the down arrow in the Results list box, choose All media file types, then click the Go button to initiate the search. The search may take a little while as it includes the Web, but you should have a much larger selection of potential clips from which to choose. If necessary, use the drop-down arrow on either search box to limit the search as you see fit.

Step 4: **Add the Hyperlinks**

- Select **Dell Computer** (the text for the first hyperlink). Pull down the **Insert menu** and click **Hyperlink** (or click the **Insert Hyperlink button** on the Standard toolbar) to display the Insert Hyperlink dialog box in Figure 12d.
- The text to display (Dell Computer) is already entered because the text was selected prior to executing the Insert Hyperlink command. If necessary, click the icon for **Existing File or Web Page**. Click the **Browsed Pages button**.
- Click in the **Address text box** and enter the desired Web address **www.dell.com** (the http is assumed).
- Click **OK** to accept the settings and close the dialog box. The hyperlink should appear as an underlined entry in the document.
- Add the additional links in similar fashion. The addresses in our document are **www.gateway.com**, **www.microsoft.com**, and **www.intel.com**.
- Save the document.

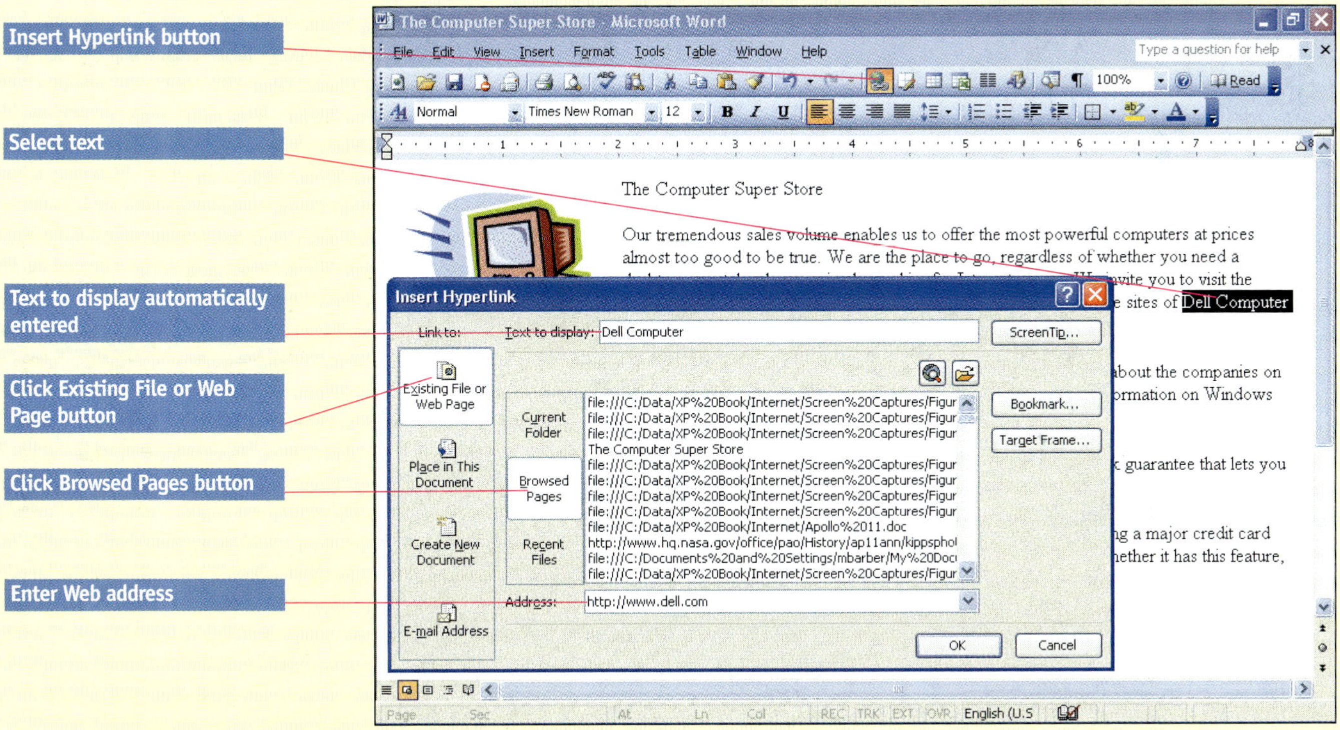

(d) Add the Hyperlinks (step 4)

FIGURE 12 Hands-on Exercise 4 (*continued*)

CLICK TO SELECT, CTRL+CLICK TO VIEW THE PAGE

Point to a hyperlink within a Word document, and you see a ScreenTip indicating that you have to press and hold the Ctrl key (Ctrl+Click) to follow the link. This is a different convention from what you are used to, because you typically just click a link to follow it. In Word, however, clicking the hyperlink simply selects the link. It's easier, therefore, to right click the link to display a context-sensitive menu from where you can make the appropriate choice to edit or remove the link.

Step 5: Apply a Theme

- You should see underlined hyperlinks in your document. Pull down the **Format menu** and click the **Theme command** to display the Theme dialog box as shown in Figure 12e.
- Select (click) a theme (we chose the Radial theme) from the list box on the left, and a sample of the design appears in the right. Click **OK**. (Only a limited number of the listed themes are installed by default, however, and thus you may be prompted for the Microsoft Office CD, depending on your selection.)
- You can go from one theme to the next by clicking the new theme. There are approximately 65 themes to choose from, and they are all visually appealing. Every theme offers a professionally designed set of formatting specifications for the various headings, horizontal lines, bullets, and links.
- Save the document.

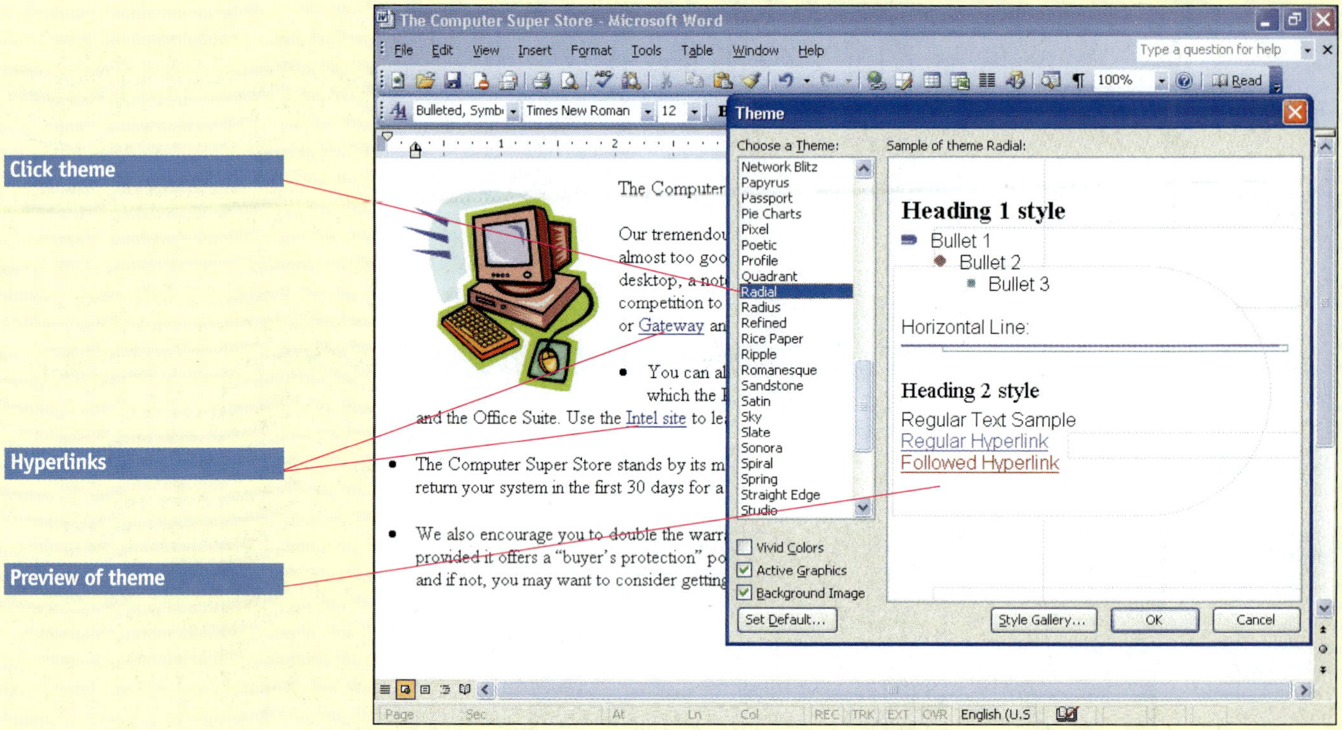

(e) Apply a Theme (step 5)

FIGURE 12 Hands-on Exercise 4 (*continued*)

KEEP IT SIMPLE

Too many would-be designers clutter a page unnecessarily by importing a complex background, which tends to obscure the text. The best design is a simple design—either no background or a very simple pattern. We also prefer light backgrounds with dark text (e.g., black or dark blue text on a white background), as opposed to the other way around. Design, however, is subjective, and there is no consensus as to what makes an attractive page. Variety is indeed the spice of life.

Step 6: The Finishing Touches

- Your document should be similar to the one in Figure 12f. It should contain clip art, a theme, and three bulleted paragraphs.
- Make any final adjustments to the size and position of the clip art. The Picture toolbar appears automatically when the clip art is selected.
- You can position the image at the left or right of the paragraph, but not in the middle (because Word is limited as an HTML editor).
- Increase the size of the title, then bold and center the title as shown. Make any additional adjustments that you see fit. The final appearance of the document is left to you.
- Save the document a final time.

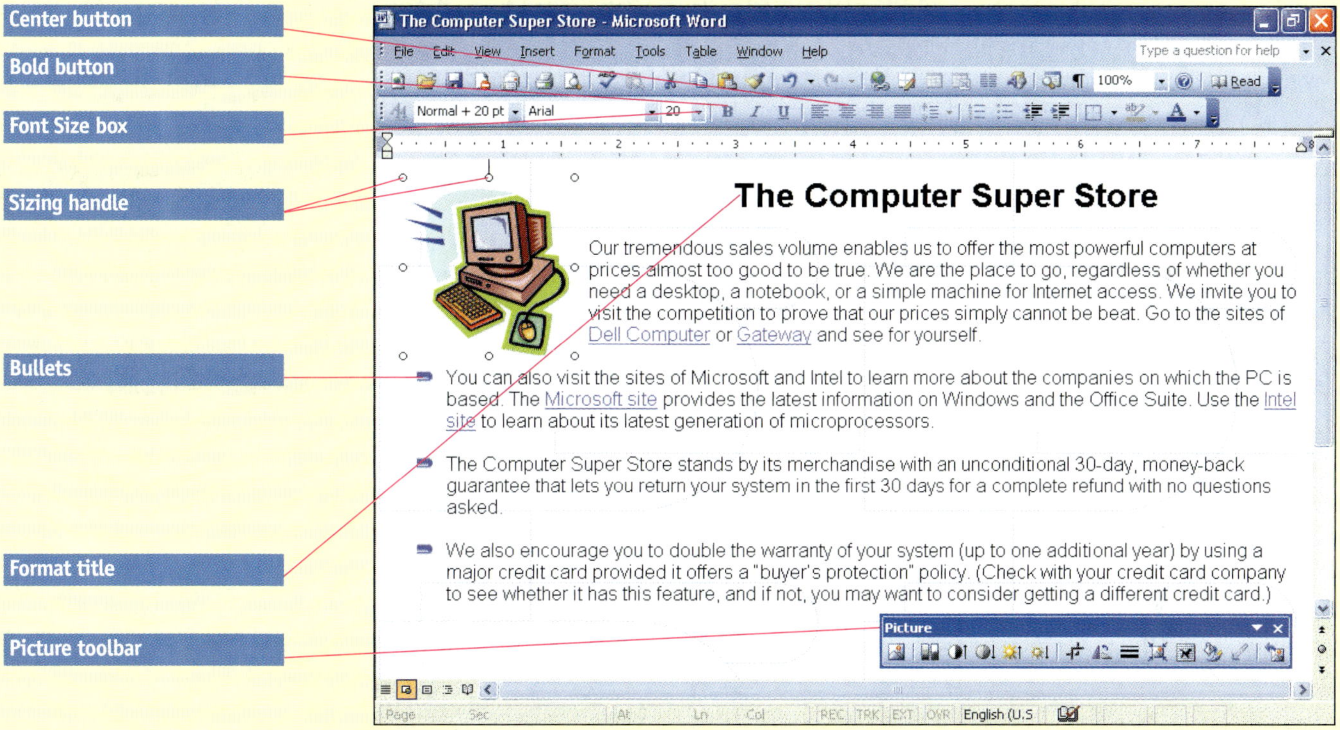

(f) The Finishing Touches (step 6)

FIGURE 12 Hands-on Exercise 4 (*continued*)

ROUND TRIP HTML

The concept of "round trip HTML" enables you to open a Web document in both Internet Explorer and Microsoft Word. You start with a Word document and use the Save As Web Page command to convert the document to a Web page. You then use Internet Explorer to view the page, but you can return to Word to edit the document by clicking the Edit button on the Standard Buttons toolbar. You can also right click the mhtml or html document in Windows Explorer, then choose Open or Edit to view or edit the document in Internet Explorer or Word, respectively.

Step 7: Open the Web Page

- Start your Web browser. Pull down the **File menu** and click the **Open command** to display the Open dialog box in Figure 12g.
- Click the **Browse button**, click the **drop-down arrow** in the Look In box, and select the drive and folder (e.g., Exploring the Internet on drive C) where you saved the Web page.
- Select (click) **The Computer Super Store** document, click **Open**, then click **OK** to open the document. You should see the Web page that was just created except that you are viewing it in a browser rather than in Microsoft Word.
- The Address bar shows the local address (C:\Exploring the Internet\The Computer Super Store.mht) of the document. (You can also open the document from the Address bar, by clicking in the **Address bar**, then typing the address of the document; for example, C:\Exploring the Internet\The Computer Super Store.mht)
- Click the **Print button** on the Internet Explorer toolbar to print this page for your instructor.

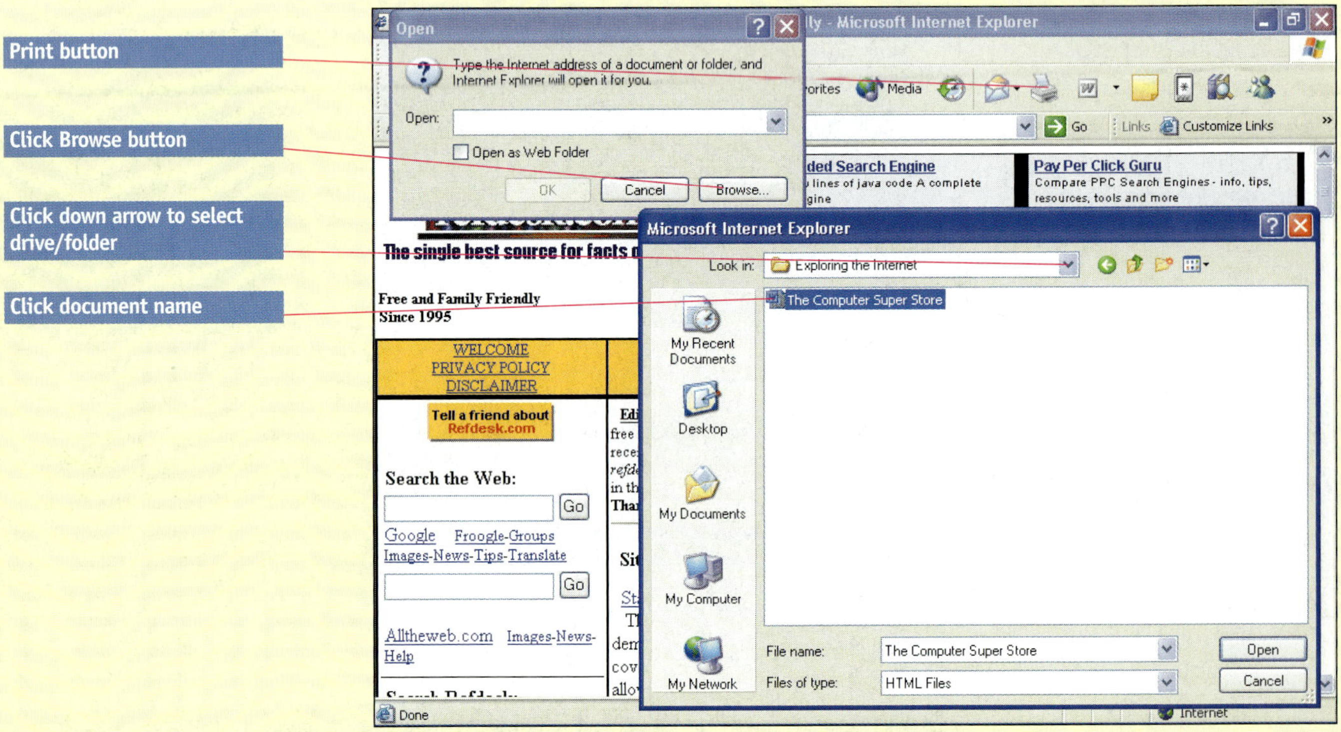

(g) Open the Web Page (step 7)

FIGURE 12 Hands-on Exercise 4 (*continued*)

SINGLE FILE WEB PAGE

Microsoft Office 2003 introduces a Single File Web Page format that saves all of the elements of a Web page, including text and graphics, in a single file. The new MHTML format lets you upload your page to a Web server as a single file, as opposed to sending multiple files and folders. It also lets you send the entire page as a single e-mail attachment. The new file format is supported by Internet Explorer 4.0 and higher.

Step 8: Test the Web Page

- This step requires an Internet connection because you will be verifying the addresses you entered earlier.
- Click the hyperlink to the **Microsoft** site to display the Web page in Figure 12h. You can explore this site, or you can click the **Back button** to return to your Web page and test another link.
- If you are unable to connect to the Microsoft site, click the **Back button** to return to your Web page, then click a second hyperlink to see if you can connect to that site. If you connect to one site, but not the other, you should return to your original document to correct the URL.
  - ❑ Click the **Word button** on the taskbar to return to the Web page, **right click** the hyperlink to display a context-sensitive menu, click **Edit Hyperlink**, and make the necessary correction. Save the corrected document.
  - ❑ Click the **Browser button** on the Windows taskbar to return to the browser, click the **Refresh button** to load the corrected page, then try the hyperlink a second time.
- Exit Word and Internet Explorer.

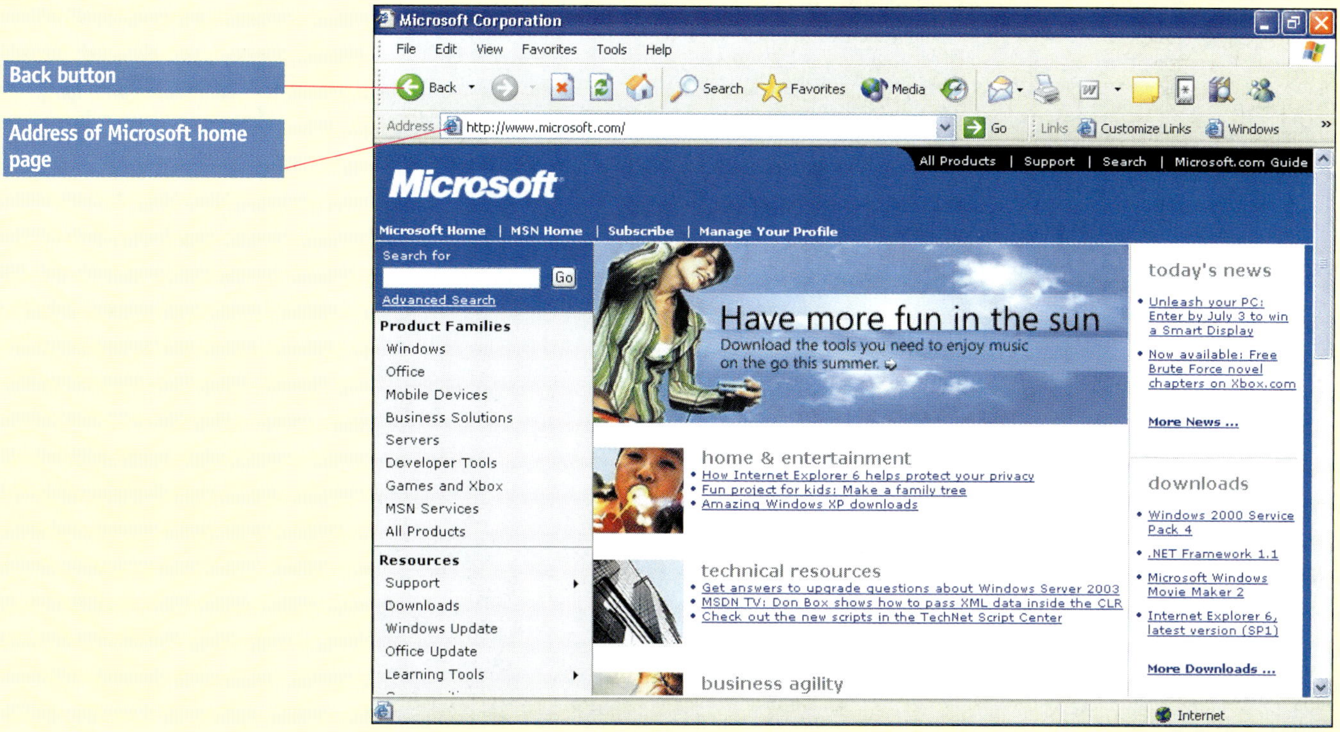

(h) Test the Web Page (step 8)

FIGURE 12 Hands-on Exercise 4 (*continued*)

VIEW THE HTML SOURCE CODE

Pull down the View menu in Internet Explorer and click the Source command to view the HTML statements that comprise the Web page. The statements are displayed in their own window, which is typically the Notepad accessory. Pull down the File menu in Notepad and click the Print command to print the HTML code. Do you see any relationship between the HTML statements and the Web page?

SUMMARY

The Internet is a network of networks. The World Wide Web (or simply the Web) is a very large subset of the Internet, consisting of hypertext and/or hypermedia documents. A program known as a browser is required to view documents that are stored on the Web. Internet Explorer and Netscape Navigator are competing browsers. The location (or address) of the Web page appears in the Address bar and is known as a Uniform Resource Locator (URL).

Search engines provide an efficient way to look for information. You enter a query consisting of the keywords you are searching for, and the search engine responds with a number of "hits," or Web documents that meet the search criteria.

Many different search engines are available, each of which uses a different database and different search algorithm. Each database stores information about its set of Web documents (running into the millions) and consists of the document's URL (i.e., its Web address) and information (keywords) about what is contained in each document. It is important, therefore, to try different engines with the same query, and further, to continually refine a query during the course of a search.

A copyright provides legal protection to a written or artistic work, giving the author exclusive rights to its use and reproduction. Anything on the Internet or World Wide Web should be considered copyrighted unless the document specifically says it is in the public domain. The fair use exclusion, however, lets you use a portion of the work for educational, nonprofit purposes, provided you cite the original work in your footnotes and/or bibliography.

Commerce, whether it is electronic or traditional, is the exchange of goods and services. Commerce of either type involves buyers and sellers, products and services, and suppliers or producers of the products and services. The advantage of e-commerce is that it enables the buyer and seller to come together in ways that are not possible with a traditional storefront. A cookie is a small file that is written to the user's hard drive by a specific site, which makes it possible to personalize the user's interaction with that site, but may also compromise the privacy of the individual.

Web documents are written in HyperText Markup Language (HTML), a language that consists of codes (or tags) that format a document for display on the World Wide Web. HTML describes how a document should look; for example, it might specify that "John Doe" is to appear in bold when viewed in a browser. Extensible Markup Language (XML) is very different as it describes the structure of the data. It might specify that "John" and "Doe" represent an individual's first and last name, respectively, and it makes that information known to virtually any application.

KEY TERMS

MULTIPLE CHOICE

1. Which of the following statements about the Internet is true?
   - (a) The Internet is less than 10 years old
   - (b) The Internet is accessed by millions of people, the exact number of which is impossible to determine
   - (c) The Internet is maintained and administered by the federal government
   - (d) All of the above

2. Web documents are created in
   - (a) HyperText Transfer Protocol (HTTP)
   - (b) HyperText Markup Language (HTML)
   - (c) Transmission Control Protocol (TCP)
   - (d) Internet Protocol (IP)

3. Which of the following is true about the hyperlinks that appear as text within a Web document?
   - (a) They are shown in different colors, depending on whether or not the links have been previously accessed
   - (b) They appear as underlined text to indicate that they are hyperlinks
   - (c) They may access documents on different computers
   - (d) All of the above

4. What is the likely address of IBM's home page?
   - (a) ibm@internet.com
   - (b) www.ibm.com
   - (c) www.ibm.edu
   - (d) internet.ibm.com

5. The Favorites list is currently displayed in the left pane of the Internet Explorer window. What will happen if you click the Favorites button on the Standard Buttons toolbar?
   - (a) An error message is displayed to indicate that the list is already open
   - (b) The Favorites list remains open and all folders within the Favorites list are open as well
   - (c) There is no visible change in the display because the list is already open
   - (d) The Favorites list disappears and the left pane is closed

6. Which of the following is a true statement regarding search engines?
   - (a) Different search engines can return different results for the same query
   - (b) The same search engine can return different results for the same query at different times (e.g., a month apart)
   - (c) Both (a) and (b)
   - (d) Neither (a) nor (b)

7. Which of the following is considered the best search engine, and thus the only engine you need to use?
   - (a) Yahoo!
   - (b) Lycos
   - (c) Excite
   - (d) There is no agreement on the best search engine

8. Which of the following will return the largest number of documents regardless of the search engine in use?
   - (a) "Tiger" or "Woods"
   - (b) "Tiger" and "Woods"
   - (c) "Tiger" not "Woods"
   - (d) Impossible to determine

9. A spider is a program that:
   - (a) Prevents cookies from being stored on a PC
   - (b) Automatically crawls through the Web searching for new pages to add to the database of a search engine
   - (c) Searches the Web for documents in response to a specific query
   - (d) Protects a computer against infection from viruses

10. Which of the following appear together within Internet Explorer to indicate that the transmission of information will be secure?
    - (a) The https protocol with a padlock icon on the status bar
    - (b) The http protocol with a padlock icon on the status bar
    - (c) The https protocol with the word "secure" on the status bar
    - (d) The http protocol with the word "secure" on the status bar

... continued

multiple choice

11. Which part of the URL http://www.prenhall.com/grauer/winXP/index.html identifies the Internet domain?

(a) http://
(b) www.prenhall.com
(c) winXP
(d) index.html

12. What is the general rule regarding the use of information that was downloaded from the Internet?

(a) It should be assumed that the material is under copyright protection unless the author states that the document is in the public domain
(b) Factual material may be cited even if the material has been copyrighted
(c) A limited portion of copyrighted material may be used for noncommercial purposes under the fair use exclusion, provided the source is cited
(d) All of the above

13. What is the easiest way to switch back and forth between Word and Internet Explorer, given that both are open?

(a) Click the appropriate button on the Windows taskbar
(b) Click the Start button, click Programs, then choose the appropriate program
(c) Minimize all applications to display the Windows desktop, then double click the icon for the appropriate application
(d) All of the above are equally convenient

14. How do you save a Word document as a Web page?

(a) Pull down the Tools menu and click the Convert to Web Page command
(b) Pull down the File menu and click the Save As Web Page command
(c) Both (a) and (b)
(d) Neither (a) nor (b)

15. Internet Explorer can display an HTML page that is stored on:

(a) A local area network
(b) A Web server
(c) Drive A or drive C of a stand-alone PC
(d) All of the above

16. Which of the following is an *invalid* URL (assume that the domain name www.company.com exists)

(a) http://www.company.com
(b) https://www.company.com
(c) html://www.company.com
(d) All of the above are valid

17. Internet Explorer and Netscape Navigator are best described as:

(a) Internet servers
(b) Web browsers
(c) Search engines
(d) Web pages

18. You are currently viewing a Web page at http://www.house.gov/house/Visitor.html. What would be the likely effect of changing the URL to http://www.house.gov?

(a) A "Page Not Found" message would be displayed
(b) A "Server down or not responding" message would be displayed
(c) You would see the home page of the server at www.house.gov
(d) Impossible to determine

ANSWERS

1. b	**7.** d	**13.** a
2. b	**8.** a	**14.** b
3. d	**9.** b	**15.** d
4. b	**10.** a	**16.** c
5. d	**11.** b	**17.** b
6. c	**12.** d	**18.** c

EXPLORING THE INTERNET

1. **Your School or University:** The questions below are intended to help you explore the Web site of your school or university. Although every site is different, there is a common goal to disseminate information to students, prospective students, faculty, and alumni. Answer the following:
   a. On average over the semester, how many times a week do you visit the site? Answer with respect to the main site for your school, as opposed to visiting the Web site for a specific course.
   b. Is there an e-mail and/or a telephone directory? If so, print the entry containing your telephone number and the one with the e-mail address for your instructor.
   c. Is there an academic calendar? If so, print the calendar for this semester.
   d. Is there a link to the athletics office? If so, print one article (page) to submit to your instructor. How often do you think the information changes?
   e. Is there a link to the admissions office? If so, do you think your school's representation on the Web is appealing to prospective students?
   f. Are you able to access your grades online? Are you able to register online?
   g. Does your current course have its own Web site? How many of your other courses have their own sites? How frequently is the content changed?
   h. Which parts of the site are secure and require a userid and password?
   i. Is the navigation on the site intuitive? If not, how would you improve it? Is there a site map? If so, does it help you to navigate the site more easily?
   j. What do you think of the visual design? How would you change it?
   k. Visit the Web site of at least one other school that is comparable in size to your school. How does its Web site compare?
   l. Summarize your answers in a short note to your instructor. Download an image from the site to use on a cover page that also contains your name, your course, and today's date, and then submit the completed assignment to your instructor.

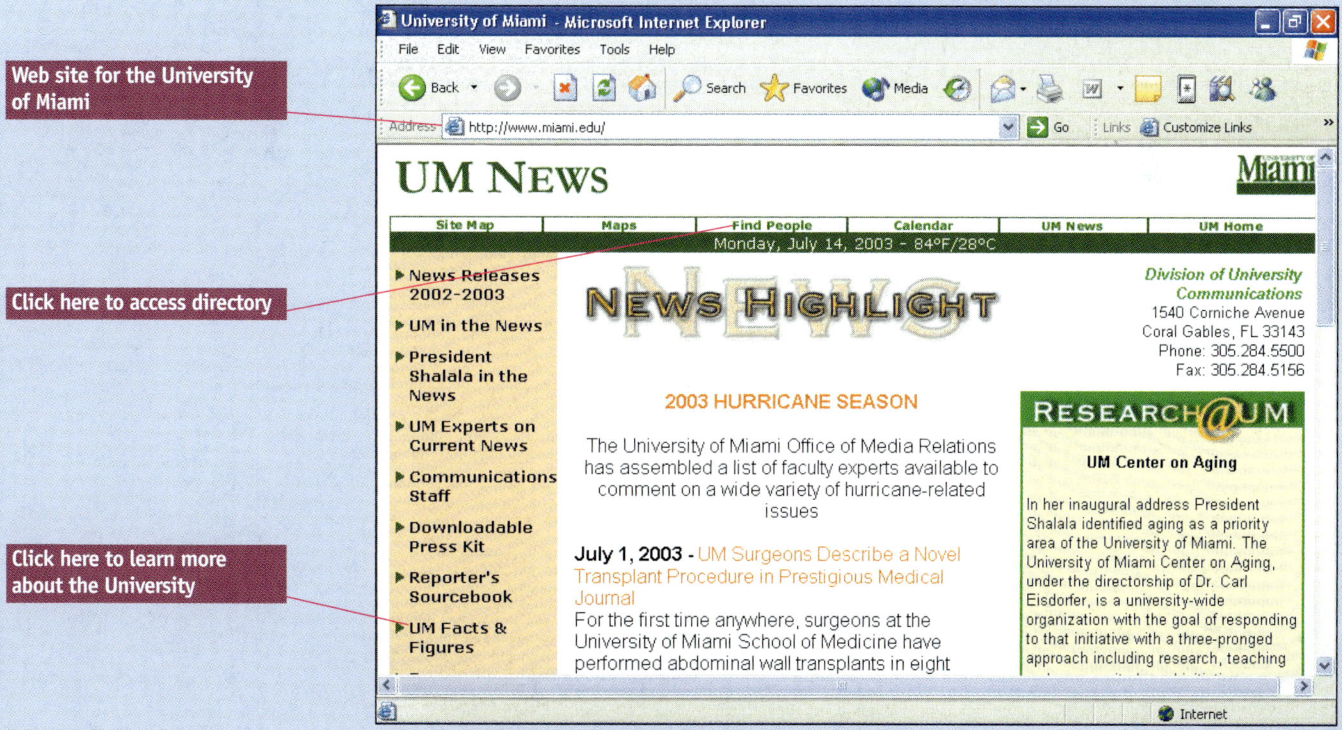

FIGURE 13 Your School or University (Exercise 1)

2. **Look it Up:** The Reference Desk in Figure 14 is an excellent source for a variety of information as it provides direct links to many specialized search engines. Give yourself one half hour and see how many of the following questions you are able to answer. You can use any site or any search engine; you are not obligated to use the Reference Desk. Print the Web page that supplies the requested information for your instructor.
   a. Use a population clock to obtain the estimated population of the world. Annotate the page to show the date and time of your answer.
   b. What was the score of the most recent Super Bowl?
   c. What is triskaidekaphobia?
   d. What does PCMCIA stand for? (People Can't Memorize Computer Industry Acronyms is not the answer we are looking for.)
   e. Find the cheapest nonstop flight from Miami to Los Angeles, leaving exactly 30 days from today and returning to Miami one week later.
   f. What is the zip code for the address, 42-15 81 Street, Apartment 3B, Elmhurst NY? What is the telephone area code for this address?
   g. Name one celebrity who was born on today's date.
   h. What is today's conversion rate of the U.S. dollar to the Japanese yen?
   i. What is the current price of one share of Microsoft stock?
   j. How many pounds are there in a kilogram?
   k. Where is the Ukraine? What is its capital?
   l. How many amendments are there to the United States Constitution?
   m. Who was Susan B. Anthony?
   n. What is the cheapest price for one dozen roses sent to your Mom today? Support your answer with a printed quote from the Web site.
   o. Use the same population clock as in part (a) to once again obtain the estimated population of the world. How much time has elapsed between the two readings? How many more people are there?

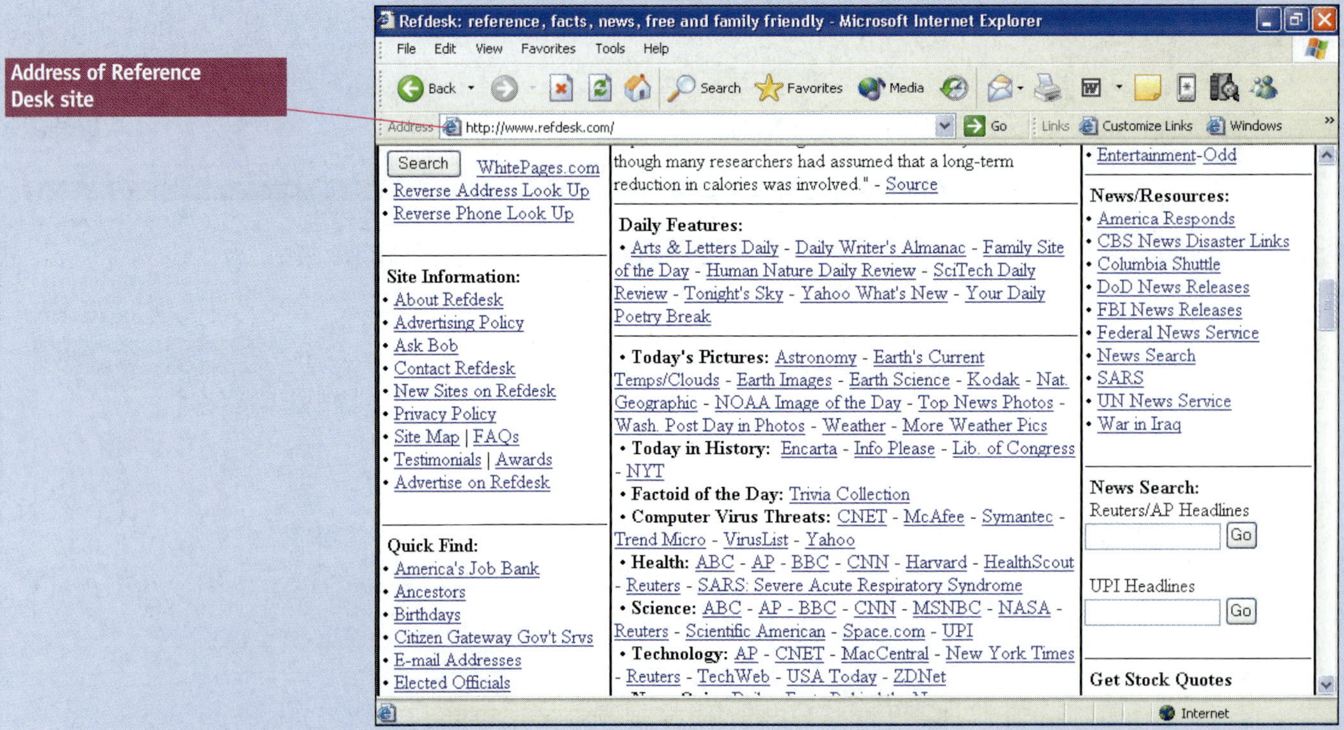

FIGURE 14 Look It Up (Exercise 2)

3. **Explore the URL:** The Web Museum (at www.ibiblio.org/wm) welcomes more than 200,000 visitors a week from all over the world. The museum is maintained by Nicolas Pioch and is one of our favorite sites on the Web. Start Internet Explorer, go to the museum, click the link to Famous Artworks (or search for impressionist paintings), and then go to the main page for impressionist paintings. Use that page to locate the painting in Figure 15, *Fishing Boats Leaving the Harbor at Le Havre* by Claude Monet. Print the picture for your instructor.

    a. Once you have found the picture, you can learn a lot more about the museum by exploring the URL that is displayed in the address bar of Figure 15. The address may look complicated, but it is really quite simple. Every URL is comprised of several components in the following sequence from left to right: the means of access (typically http), the Internet domain (or address of the server on which the document is located), the path (or folders) within the domain (if any) to get to the document, and finally the document itself.

    b. Click in the Address bar and press the End key to move to the end of the URL. Now back up one level within the URL by deleting the file name (le-havre.jpg) at the end of the address. Press Enter. What do you find?

    c. Back up another level by deleting the next part of the address (the folder). What do you find now? Continue to back up one level at a time, making a note of what you find each step along the way.

    d. Which folder provides access to other early works by Monet? Which folder contains all works by Monet? Which folder provides access to an index of all the artists at the museum? Which folder contains links to various themes (periods)?

    e. Download the painting in Figure 15 to use as a cover sheet for your assignment, then submit the completed assignment to your instructor. Include the URL of the painting in a footnote to cite your source.

    f. Do you see how backing up a level at a time within the URL can lead to interesting related documents?

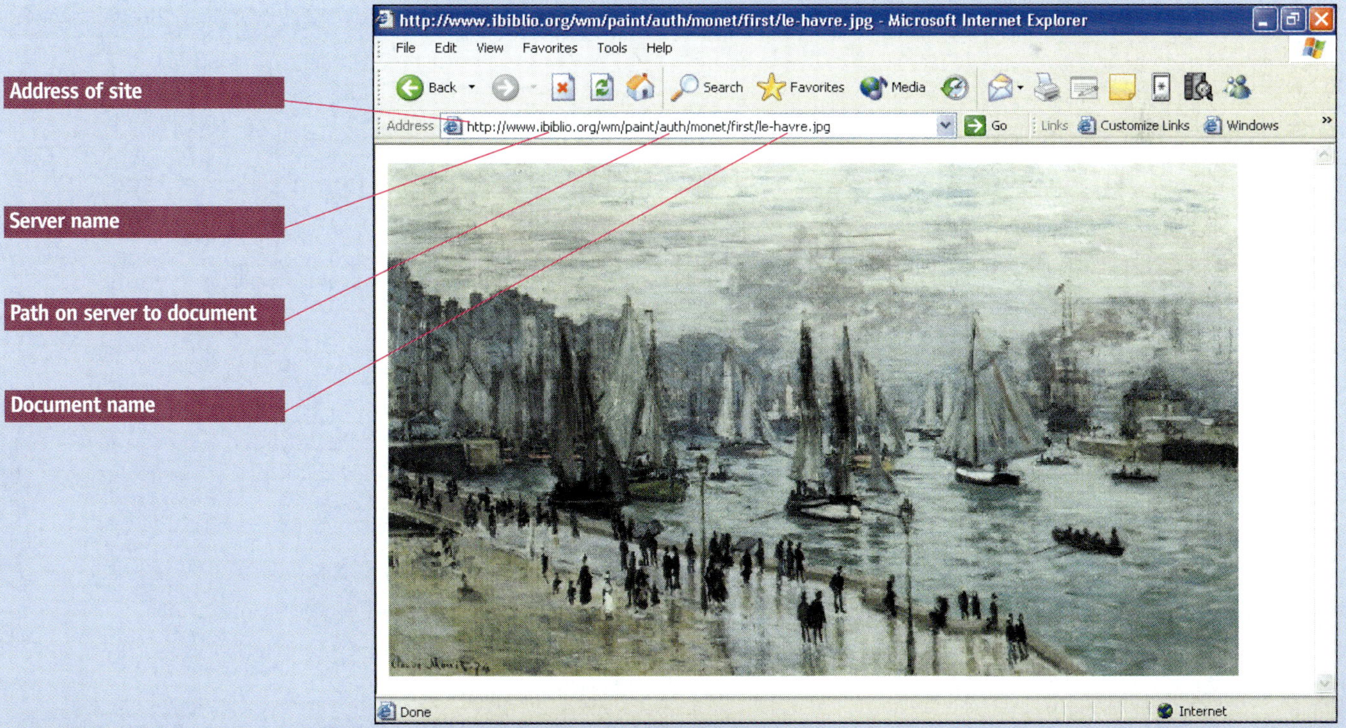

FIGURE 15 Explore the URL (Exercise 3)

4. **Create a Home Page:** It's easy to create a home page. Start a new document and enter its text just as you would any other document. Use any and all formatting commands to create a document similar to the one in Figure 16. We suggest you use clip art, as opposed to a real picture. Pull down the File menu and use the Save as Web Page command to convert the Word document to a Web document. (Be sure to specify the Single File Web Page format introduced in Office 2003 as the file type.) You do not have to match our page exactly, but you are required to do the following:
   a. Use the Insert Hyperlink command to create a list of three to five hyperlinks. Be sure to enter accurate Web addresses for each of your sites.
   b. Use the spell check to find and correct any errors that might exist.
   c. Select all of the links after they have been entered, then click the Bullets button on the Formatting toolbar to create a bulleted list.
   d. Add an additional link after the bulleted list of hyperlinks that contains your e-mail address, enabling visitors to your page to send you an e-mail message.
   e. Pull down the Format menu, click the Theme command, and then select a professionally chosen design for your Web page.
   f. Save the document a final time, then exit Word. Start Windows Explorer, then go to the folder containing your home page, and double click the file you just created. Internet Explorer will start automatically (because your document was saved as a Web page). You should see your document within Internet Explorer as shown in Figure 16. Look carefully at the Address bar and note the local address on drive C, as opposed to a Web address. Print the document for your instructor as proof you completed the assignment.
   g. Creating the home page and viewing it locally is easy. Placing the page on the Web where it can be seen by anyone with an Internet connection is not as straightforward. You will need additional information from your instructor about how to obtain an account on a Web server (if that is available at your school), and further how to upload the Web page from your PC to the server.

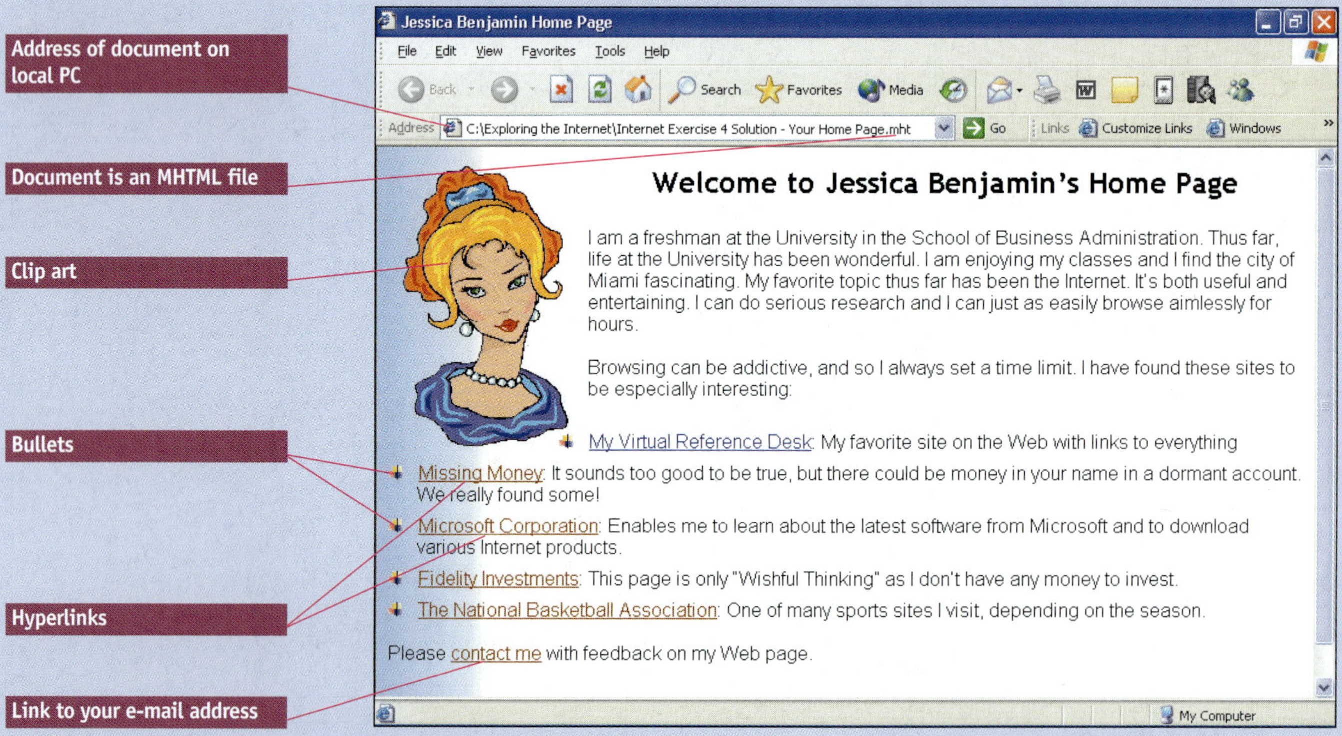

FIGURE 16 Create a Home Page (Exercise 4)

5. **A Commercial Web Page:** Create a simple Web page for the hypothetical World Wide Travel agency as shown in Figure 17. You can use our text, or you can write your own. The completed page is to include clip art or a photograph. Proceed as follows:
   a. Start Word and create the basic document. We suggest that you insert a table toward the top of the document to hold the clip art or photograph to facilitate the placement of the object within the Web page.
   b. Pull down the File menu and click the Save as Web Page command to convert the Word document to a Web page. (Be sure to specify the Single File Web Page format introduced in Office 2003 as the file type.) Click Continue if you see a message indicating that certain formatting may be lost.
   c. Review the document and make the basic formatting changes you deem appropriate. Use the spell check to be sure that your document is free from error. Use the Theme command in the Format menu to apply an overall design to the page.
   d. Insert at least one hyperlink in the document to an external Web site; for example, we included a link that will display the weather anywhere in the world.
   e. Include a second hyperlink to send an e-mail message to the agency.
   f. Save the document a final time, then exit Word. Start Windows Explorer, then go to the folder containing your Web page, and double click the file you just created. Internet Explorer will start automatically (because your document was saved as a Web page). You should see your document within Internet Explorer as shown in Figure 17. Look carefully at the Address bar and note the local address on drive C, as opposed to a Web address. Print the document for your instructor as proof you completed the assignment.
   g. Creating the home page and viewing it locally is easy. Placing the page on the Web where it can be seen by anyone with an Internet connection is not as straightforward. You will need additional information from your instructor about how to obtain an account on a Web server (if that is available at your school), and further how to upload the Web page from your PC to the server.

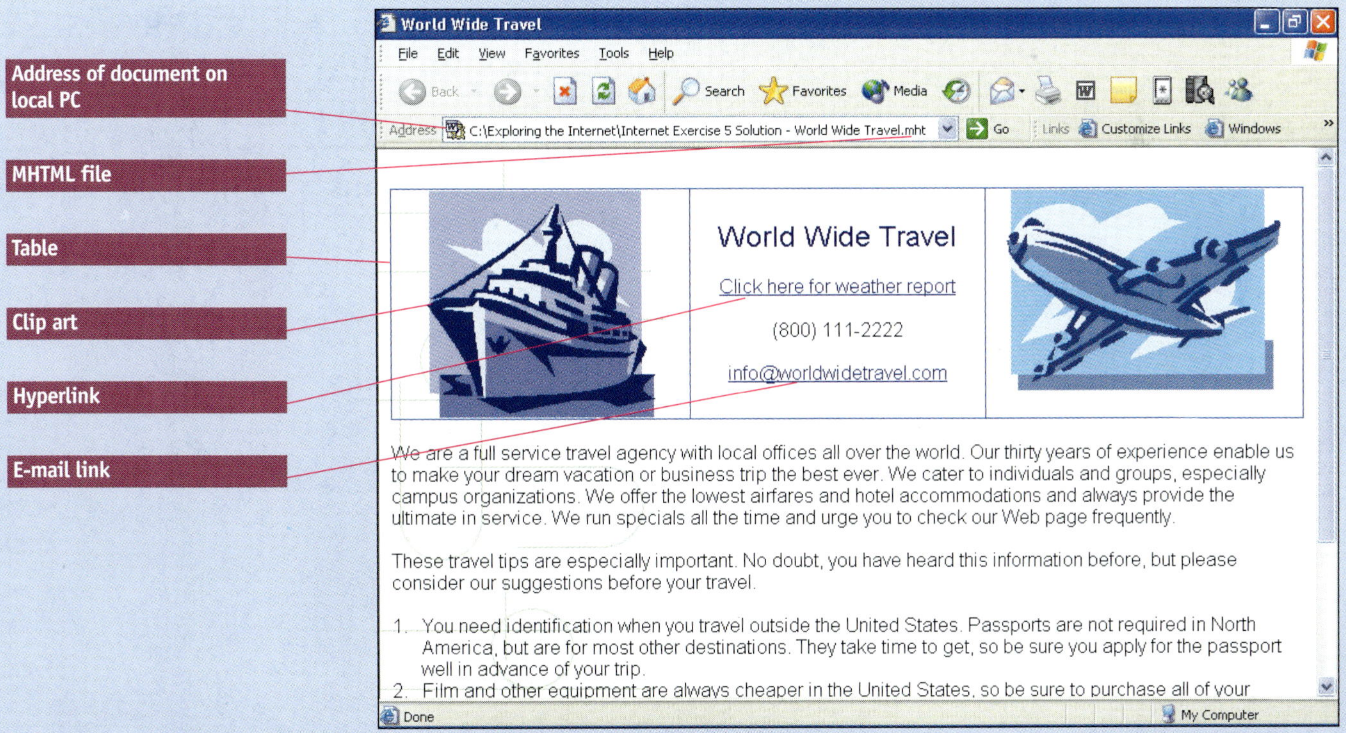

FIGURE 17 A Commercial Web Page (Exercise 5)

6. **Create a Web Site:** Figure 18 expands the previous problem to display a Web site, as opposed to a Web page. The home page is comprised of two frames; the frame at the left provides the overall navigation though the site; the frame on the right displays the Web page associated with the selected link. We do not necessarily expect you to create the actual site. We are asking you to think about the content and navigation and to investigate how to register an Internet domain name. Proceed as follows:
   a. Use any search engine to locate an accredited registrar who can register a domain name. Is www.worldwidetravel.com available? If not, who owns the domain? When does their registration expire? How much does it cost to register a domain name?
   b. Assume that you have registered a domain name and that you want to create the actual Web site. Use any search engine to locate a Web developer, and then obtain approximate costs for developing a simple site such as Figure 18.
   c. Use any search engine to locate at least one company to host your site. What is the approximate cost to host the site for one year?
   d. You do not have to create the site, but it is easier than you might think. The first step is to create individual Web pages corresponding to the links in the left frame. (The pages can be partially completed and "under construction" initially.)
   e. Open the home page (in Microsoft Word) from exercise 5, display the Frames toolbar, and insert a new frame to the left of the existing page.
   f. You now have a Web page with two frames. The left frame is currently empty, but it will contain the navigation for the site. Click in the frame, and then add descriptive text and hyperlinks to the other pages. Right click the first hyperlink to display a context-sensitive menu, click Edit Hyperlink to display the associated dialog box, and click the Target Frame button to display the Set Target Frame dialog box. Click the right frame within the box, then click OK. Check the box to set as default for all hyperlinks. Click OK to close the Edit Hyperlink dialog box.
   g. Save the completed page. Exit Word, then open the site in Internet Explorer. Click any link in the left frame and you should see the corresponding page in the right frame.

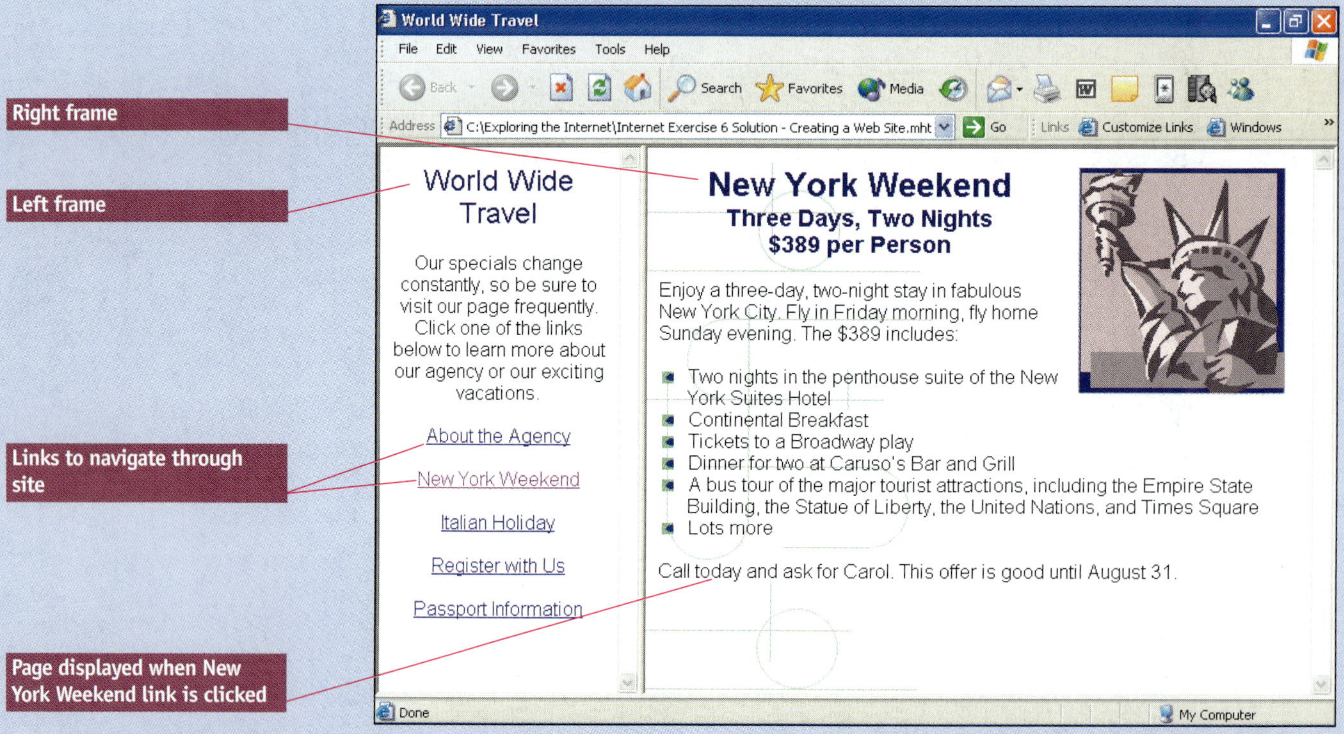

FIGURE 18 Create a Web Site (Exercise 6)

7. **Photography on the Web:** The Ofoto Web site in Figure 19 is typical of many sites that enable you to share pictures with friends and family. (The photograph was one of the author's first efforts with an entry-level digital camera, and he was very pleased with the result. The picture was taken at night with no lighting other than the built-in flash.) Do you have a digital camera? If not, find a friend or colleague who has a digital camera or use an ordinary camera and request a CD when you develop your next roll of film. Now that you have a digital photograph, proceed as follows:
   a. Use any search engine to locate a site where you can post photographs and register at the site. There should not be any charge to register or to post photographs.
   b. Create a photo album at the site and then upload two or three photographs to the album. The photo album will have a name ("Vacation to the British Isles" in Figure 19), and each photo will have its own caption (Military Tattoo—Edinburgh, Scotland).
   c. Follow the procedures at the site to share your album with a family member and/or at least one other student in your class. Are you notified by the site when your classmate looks at your pictures?
   d. Think about what has just transpired. You were able to post pictures to the Web and share those pictures with as many people as you like, and further it did not cost you a penny. How does the site stay in business?
   e. What is the posted cost for a 4 × 6 inch print? How does this compare to the cost at the corner drugstore? What other services or products are available at the site?
   f. Which large company owns the Ofoto Web site? When was that company founded? What are its most recent annual sales? (Use a search engine as appropriate to obtain the answers to these questions.) How has the advent of the digital camera affected its primary business? Do you see how the advent of the Web has enabled the company to reinvent itself?
   g. What is the Edinburgh Military Tattoo? Use any search engine to locate the home page for this event, and then print that page for your instructor.

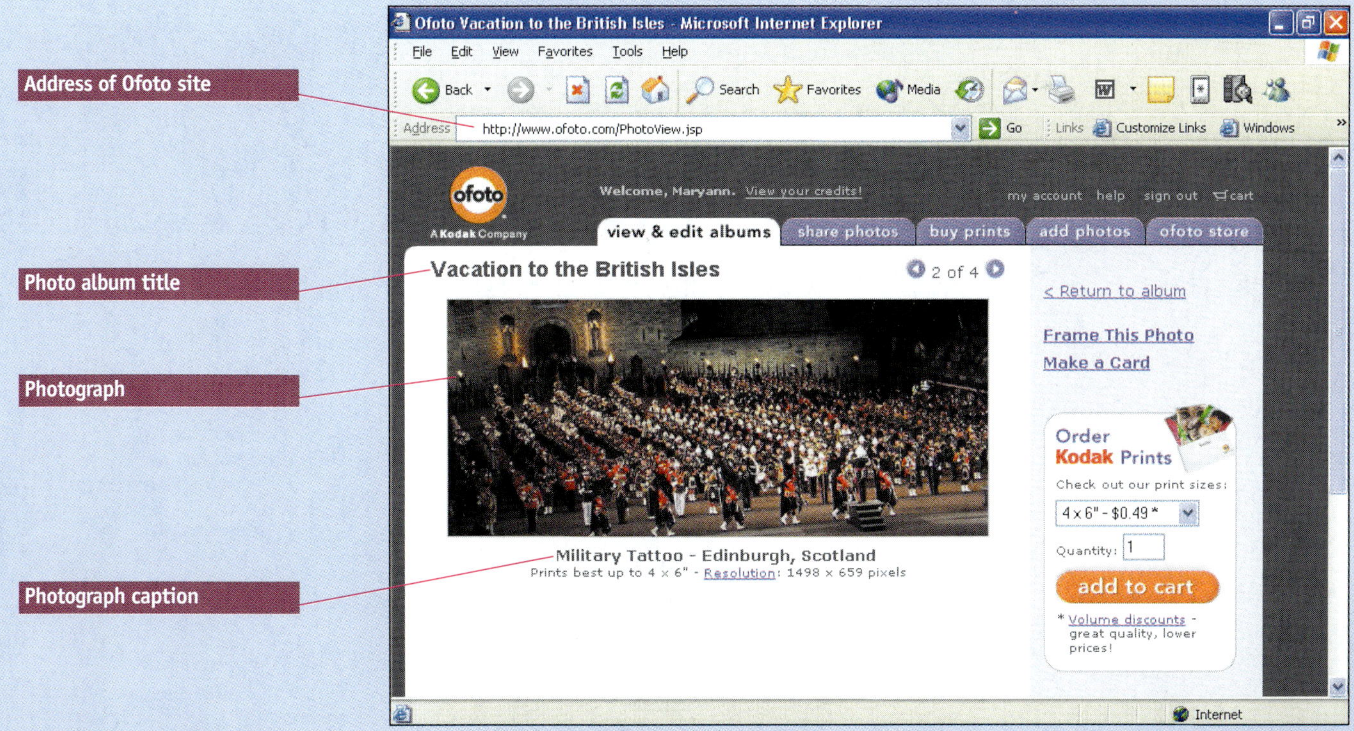

FIGURE 19 Photography on the Web (Exercise 7)

8. **Social Security Online:** You are too young to think about retirement. Even so, you should be concerned about the Social Security system (if you live in the United States) as the financial viability of the system is continually in the news. You can still do this exercise if you are enrolled in a school or university outside of the US and/or you can investigate the comparable program in your country. Proceed as follows:
   a. Use any search engine to locate the Social Security Online Web site as shown in Figure 20. Search the site to locate the financial calculators that enable you to estimate the amount of your retirement benefits.
   b. Select the "Simple Rough Estimate" calculator and enter the required parameters, which include your age at the end of this year and your earnings for this year. To make the calculation more realistic, enter your earnings as though you were working full time. Select the option to display your retirement in "today's dollars." Are you surprised at the amount? Is it more or less than you thought it would be?
   c. Under current law you contribute 6.2% of your salary (up to a maximum of $84,000) towards Social Security. Multiply this percentage by the annual earnings you entered in part (b) to determine your contribution to Social Security for the current year. This amount is in addition to your federal income tax. Note, too, that your employer matches that amount and also contributes 6.2% of your salary.
   d. Is Social Security a "good deal" for you? What if the system were changed so that your contributions and those of your employer went directly into a private pension fund that grew at 4% a year? Would the monthly pension from such a system be more or less than the amount you can expect to receive when you reach retirement age? What parameters will affect your answer?
   e. Search the site to learn more about the future of Social Security. Why is the system in financial jeopardy? What solutions have been proposed? When was Social Security started? How have the assumptions on which the system is based changed from the time of inception to today? Does this help to explain why the viability of the system is in doubt?

FIGURE 20 Social Security Online (Exercise 8)

MINI CASES

Downloading Music from the Web

The Internet has been a great friend to your pocketbook; you haven't purchased a record, CD, cassette tape, or any other form of music since the invention of MP3. This may be great for you as a consumer, but imagine that you actually wrote and produced a particular song, and that your livelihood depends on the funds generated from the sale of that song. Do you still think it is appropriate to obtain copies of songs for free? What if music fans everywhere decided to stop buying music and simply wait for it to be uploaded to the Web? What effect would this have on the music industry? Summarize your thoughts in a brief note to your instructor.

Campus Access to the Internet

The easiest way to access the Internet is from a local area network on campus. But which students are given access, and what—if anything—do you have to do to open an account? Does the university provide an e-mail account? If so, what is your username and password? What is your e-mail address? Does your e-mail account expire at the end of the semester, or does it continue throughout your stay at the university? You don't have to put your answers in writing, but you will need to know this information if you are to be successful in this class.

The Internet Service Provider

You can use at least three different technologies to connect to the Internet from home: a regular modem, a cable modem, or a DSL line. What is the rated speed of each technology? How reliable is the technology? What are the installation cost (if any) and the monthly service charge? Contact at least two different Internet Service Providers in your area to compare prices. Summarize the results in a short note to your instructor.

It's the URL, Not the Browser

Our text focuses on Internet Explorer, but the concepts apply equally well to any other browser. Choose a different browser (Netscape Navigator) and use it to display several pages that were referenced in this chapter. What difference (if any) do you see in a given page when it is viewed in Netscape rather than Internet Explorer? Which browser is better from a developer's point of view? Which is better from a user's point of view?

Employment on the Web

Graduation is fast approaching and you need a job. How can the Web help you in your search for full-time employment? Is it also useful to secure an internship or part-time job? Use your favorite search engine to locate at least two sites where you can post a résumé and/or search through a job bank. Do you think you have a realistic expectation for success by using the Web?

On Your Own

This loosely structured exercise asks you to experiment with different search engines and search parameters. Select any topic in which you are interested, then choose a search engine, construct an initial query, then record the number of hits the engine returns. Choose a different engine, enter the identical query, and record the number of hits you get with that engine. Select the more promising result, then submit a new query that limits your search through inclusion of additional keywords or other logical operators. Summarize the results in a one- or two-page Word document that you will submit to the instructor. The document should contain all the information you recorded manually in the preceding steps.

... continued

Going Abroad

Congratulations! You have just won a scholarship to spend your junior year abroad. You need a passport, and you need it quickly. Search the Web to learn how to apply for a passport. You should be able to find a site that enables you to download an actual passport application with specific instructions on where to apply; that is, an address in the city in which you live or attend school. What additional software, if any, do you need to print the application?

Tax Time

April 15 is just around the corner and you have yet to file your income tax. Search the Web to download the necessary tax forms to file your federal income tax. What other information regarding your income taxes is available from this site? What additional software, if any, do you need to print the form on your PC? Extend your search to the necessary forms for state income taxes if you live in a state that has an income tax.

The Contest

Almost everyone enjoys some form of competition. Ask your instructor to choose a theme for a Web site such as a school club, and to declare a contest in the class to produce the "best" document. Submit your entry, but write your name on the back of the document so that it can be judged anonymously. Your instructor may want to select a set of semifinalists, then distribute copies of those documents so that the class can vote on the winner.

Missing Money

The Missing Money Web site (www.missingmoney.com) is not a gag, and you really do have a chance at finding money in your name, or the name of a relative. In essence, the site stores public records of abandoned money—bank accounts, utility deposits, tax refunds, and so on. There is no charge to search the database to see whether there is an account in your name; there is, however, a charge for detailed information on any hits that you receive if you elect to pursue that information. Try it, and let us know if you find any money.

CHAPTER 1

Getting Started: Essential Computing Concepts

OBJECTIVES

After reading this chapter you will:

1. Describe components of a computer system.
2. Describe the contribution of IBM, Microsoft, and Intel in the evolution of the PC.
3. Discuss several considerations in the purchase of a computer.
4. Define the terms used to measure the capacity of memory and auxiliary storage.
5. List several auxiliary storage devices; distinguish between CD and DVD technology.
6. Describe the similarities and differences of a digital camera versus a traditional camera.
7. Describe the evolution of Microsoft Windows.
8. Describe how to safeguard a system through an antivirus program and periodic backup.
9. Define FTP; describe several ways in which it may be used.
10. Distinguish between a compressed file and a self-extracting file.
11. Describe the four major (core) applications in Microsoft Office; list at least two additional applications in the Office suite.
12. Distinguish between HTML and XML; explain how XML enables data sharing.
13. Describe InfoPath and OneNote, two new applications in Microsoft Office 2003.
14. Define a local area network.
15. Define the Internet and the World Wide Web.
16. Describe the functions in every e-mail system.
17. Describe Microsoft .Net and XML Web services.

CASE STUDY

THE SMITH FAMILY NETWORK

Mike Smith is the "Michael Brady" of the Smith family with six adopted children, ranging in age from six to sixteen. The family makes extensive use of four computers in their home. There are two machines in Mike's office, one in the family room, and one in the kitchen. The two oldest children have suggested a home network, but Mike has shown little interest. He thinks that each computer should serve a specific purpose. He is a renowned architect and uses the Macintosh in his office for architectural drawings. Mrs. Smith uses the other machine in the office to run the business. The computer in the family room is dedicated to games while the machine in the kitchen is used for e-mail and instant messaging. There are two Internet connections: a dial-up line in Mike's office and a DSL connection in the kitchen.

Mike thinks a network will be difficult and expensive to implement, and does not believe the end result will be worth the trouble. In addition, he doesn't think that his Mac and the PCs can be connected due to compatibility issues. His children disagree, stating that a network enables the connected computers to share resources such as the graphics printer in Mike's office and the DSL line in the kitchen. Mike asks the children to prove their case—stating that he will consider the idea, given that they present him with written reasons why this is a good idea.

Your assignment is to read the chapter, paying special attention to the section on local area networks (LANs) and home networks. Pretend you are one of Mike's children and write a short document describing the advantages of a home network. Include a brief discussion of what additional equipment is needed to set up a LAN. You may want to include a conceptual view of how their home network would look by inserting Clip Art into your document. Once you have finished, print a copy of the document and submit it to your instructor.

WHAT IS A COMPUTER?

Computer literacy is the absolute requirement of the new millennium. Corporations require their employees to be computer literate, parents expect their children to be computer literate, and you are probably taking this course in order to fulfill the computer literacy requirement at your school or university. We hope, therefore, that when you finish reading this section, you will feel comfortable with the computer and be able to use it effectively in a world of rapidly changing technology. This module introduces you to the essential computing concepts you will need.

A ***computer*** is an electronic device that accepts data (input), then manipulates or processes that data to produce information (output). It operates under the control of a ***program*** (or set of instructions) that is stored internally within the computer's memory. A computer system consists of the computer and its memory, peripheral devices such as a keyboard, disk drives, monitor, and printer, and the various programs that enable it to perform its intended function.

The idea of a general-purpose machine to solve mathematical problems was first proposed over 150 years ago by an Englishman named Charles Babbage. Babbage's machine would have been the world's first computer, but the technology of his day was incapable of producing the mechanical components to the required precision. Babbage died alone and penniless, having lost a personal fortune in a vain attempt to build his computer.

As happens so often with geniuses who are ahead of their time, Babbage's theory was validated a century after his death, since all modern computers are designed along the lines he proposed. Thus, every computer system, from Babbage's dream (called the Analytical Engine) to today's PC, includes the following components:

Stock Montage, Inc.

Charles Babbage

- The ***central processing unit (CPU)*** is the "brain" of the computer and performs the actual calculations.
- ***Memory*** (which is also known as ***r***andom ***a***ccess ***m***emory or ***RAM***) temporarily stores any program being executed by the computer, as well as the data on which the program operates.
- ***Auxiliary storage*** (also called secondary storage or external storage) provides a place where data can be permanently stored, and then transferred to and from main memory. A floppy disk, hard disk, CD, DVD, high-capacity removable media (such as a zip disk), and tape are the primary types of auxiliary storage used with a PC.
- ***Input devices*** accept data from an external source and convert it to electric signals, which are sent to the CPU. Virtually every PC is configured with a keyboard and mouse as its input devices. A joystick, scanner, and microphone are other common input devices.
- ***Output devices*** accept electric signals from the CPU and convert them to a form suitable for output. The monitor and printer are common output devices. Speakers are also considered an output device and are necessary to hear sound from a PC. Auxiliary storage is also considered an output device.

The relationship between the components in a computer system is shown graphically in Figure 1. In essence, the CPU accepts data from an input device or auxiliary storage, stores it temporarily in memory while it computes an answer, then sends the results to an output device or auxiliary storage. All of this happens under the control of the ***operating system***, a computer program (actually many programs) that links the various hardware components to one another. The operating system is stored on the hard disk, and it is loaded into memory when the computer is turned on. Once in memory, the operating system takes over, and it manages the system throughout the session.

AHEAD OF THEIR TIME

Charles Babbage (1792–1871) went broke trying to build a general-purpose computing device he called the Analytical Engine. Babbage worked closely with Ada Lovelace (Lord Byron's daughter), who realized the potential of the machine and formulated basic programming principles. She is credited with being history's first programmer.

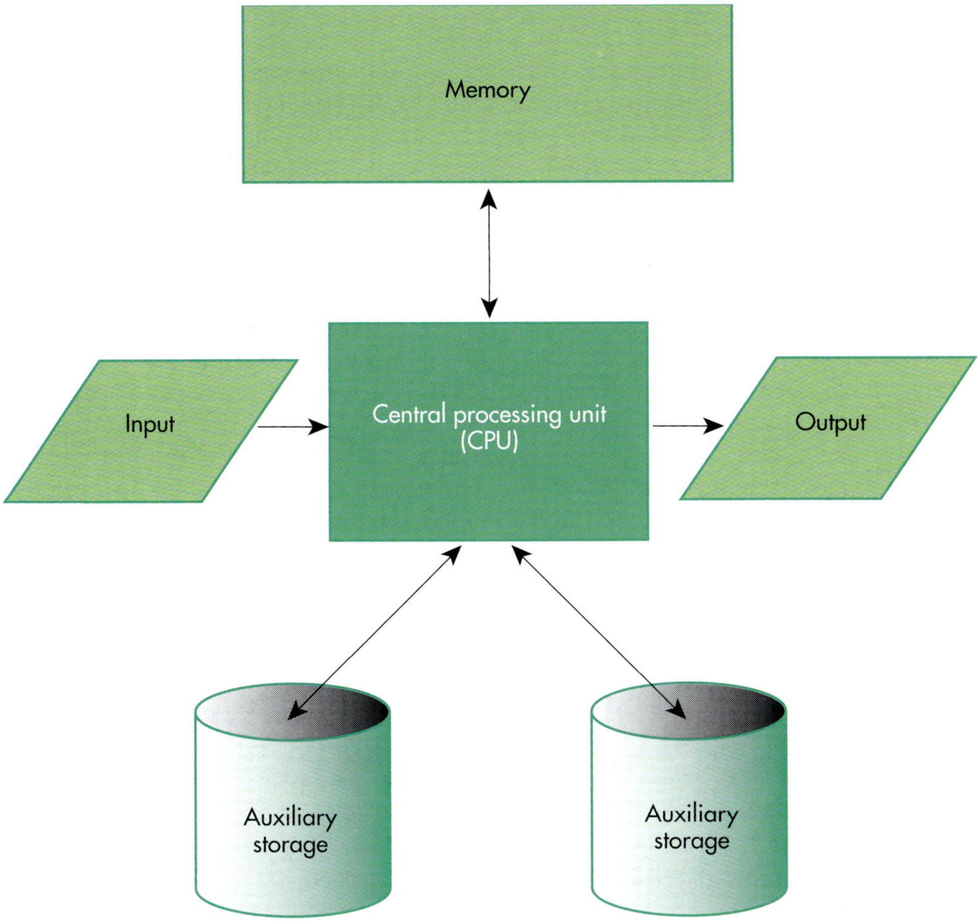

FIGURE 1 Components of a Computer System

WHAT IS AN OPERATING SYSTEM?

Every computer functions the same way. The CPU accepts data from an input device or auxiliary storage, stores it temporarily in memory while it computes an answer, then sends the result to an output device or auxiliary storage. All of this happens under the control of an operating system, a computer program (actually many programs) that links the various components of a computer to one another.

Think for a moment about what happens when you sit down at the PC. You turn on the computer, which automatically loads the operating system from auxiliary storage (e.g., a hard disk) into memory (RAM), from where the instructions are processed by the CPU. The initial commands in the operating system direct the monitor (an output device) to display the Windows desktop. You react to the output displayed on the screen by using the mouse (an input device) to click an icon such as the Start button, and then follow with subsequent clicks to start a program. The operating system processes your commands, then determines it needs to load an application program (such as Microsoft Word or Microsoft Excel) from auxiliary storage (the hard disk) into memory.

Now you are ready to go to work. You type at the keyboard (an input device) and enter the text of your document, which is stored in the computer's memory and simultaneously displayed on the monitor (an output device). When you're finished with the document, you execute a Print command to transfer the contents of memory to the printer (an alternate output device). And, of course, you will save the document, which copies the contents of memory to a disk (auxiliary storage). The next time you want to access the document, you execute the Open command, which copies the document from disk into memory, at which point you can further edit the document. You make the necessary changes, save the corrected document to disk, then print the revised document. The cycle continues indefinitely.

As you gain proficiency, you will take these operations for granted. It helps, however, if you reflect on the components of a computer system and how they interact with one another. And remember these principles apply to every computer system, from a PC to a massive mainframe.

From Micro to Mainframe

Computers can be divided into two basic groups: ***mainframes*** and ***microcomputers***. The classification is primarily one of scale. Mainframes support hundreds (or even thousands) of users simultaneously and are at the core of national and global networks. They are much larger, faster, cost significantly more money, and have much greater memory and auxiliary storage capacities than microcomputers. The distinction is becoming increasingly difficult, however, as mainframes continue to become smaller while PCs grow more powerful. Indeed, the machine on your desk has more processing power and storage capability than the mainframe of a decade ago.

A microcomputer can be defined as any computer smaller than a mainframe. It may be a server, desktop, notebook, tablet, or a handheld device. A server is a high-end desktop computer that is intended to support a local area network. A desktop, as its name implies, sits on (or under) a desk and has a monitor, mouse, and keyboard as separate components. The notebook (or laptop computer) also sits on a desk, but it is easily portable, and has the keyboard, mouse, and monitor built into the unit for easy storage. A Tablet PC extends the functionality of a notebook computer to include "pencil and paper"; that is, you can write directly on the screen using a pen and save the notes in your own handwriting. A handheld computer (also called a Personal Digital Assistant or PDA) fits into a jacket pocket and values mobility over a full-sized keyboard and screen.

WHICH COMPANY IS LARGER?

Which company is larger, IBM or Microsoft? The answer depends of course on the numbers you use to evaluate the relative size of the two computer giants. IBM's annual sales of $82 billion are almost three times those of Microsoft ($33 billion), yet the net income of both companies is approximately the same ($7 billion). The market capitalization (the total value of all outstanding shares of stock) of Microsoft, however, is nearly double that of IBM, $300 billion to $150 billion at the time we went to press.

(a) **The Universal Automatic Computer** (Univac I), the first commercially viable electronic computer, received national exposure when CBS news used the computer to predict Dwight Eisenhower's victory in the 1952 presidential election. The system cost $1 million and weighed 30 tons.

(b) **Cray Supercomputers:** Fish-eye lens view of some Cray T3E supercomputers at the National Energy Research Scientific Computing Center (NERSC) in Berkeley, California. The computers are used for complex and large-scale computation on scientific and engineering projects and research.

FIGURE 2 Computers Then and Now

Bits and Bytes

A computer is first and foremost a numerical machine. It is designed to perform mathematical calculations, and it does so very efficiently. It also works with text, graphics, and multimedia files such as sound and video, all of which are converted to numeric equivalents. You need not be concerned with precisely how this is accomplished. What is important is that you realize that computers work exclusively with numerical data.

In addition, computers use binary numbers (zeros and ones) rather than decimal numbers. Why binary, and not decimal? The answer is that a binary machine is easy to build, as only two values are required. A current may be on or off, or a switch may be up or down. A decimal computer would be far more difficult.

The binary system is described in terms of bits and bytes. A ***bit*** (binary digit) has two values, zero and one. Individual bits do not, however, convey meaningful information, and so computer storage is divided into bytes, where one ***byte*** consists of eight bits. In other words, a byte is the smallest addressable unit of memory, and any reference to the size of a computer's memory or to the capacity of its disk drive is in terms of bytes.

As indicated, a byte consists of eight bits, each of which can be either a zero or a one. Thus, there are 2^8 (or 256) possible combinations of zeros and ones that can be stored in a byte. We need, however, a way to make sense of the bits and bytes that are processed by the computer. Accordingly, a code was developed in which each combination of eight bits (one byte) represents a different character. It is known as the American Standard Code for Information Interchange (***ASCII*** for short and pronounced "as key").

The ASCII code provides for 256 different characters, which is more than enough to represent the 26 letters of the alphabet (both upper- and lowercase), the digits, 0 through 9, the punctuation marks, and various special keys you find on the typical keyboard. The ASCII codes for the uppercase letters are shown in Figure 3a. Can you see how those representations are used to create the message in Figure 3b, which represents the contents of five contiguous (adjacent) bytes in memory?

ASCII CODES

Character	ASCII Code
A	01000001
B	01000010
C	01000011
D	01000100
E	01000101
F	01000110
G	01000111
H	01001000
I	01001001
J	01001010
K	01001011
L	01001100
M	01001101
N	01001110
O	01001111
P	01010000
Q	01010001
R	01010010
S	01010011
T	01010100
U	01010101
V	01010110
W	01010111
X	01011000
Y	01011001
Z	01011010
space	00000000

(a) ASCII Codes

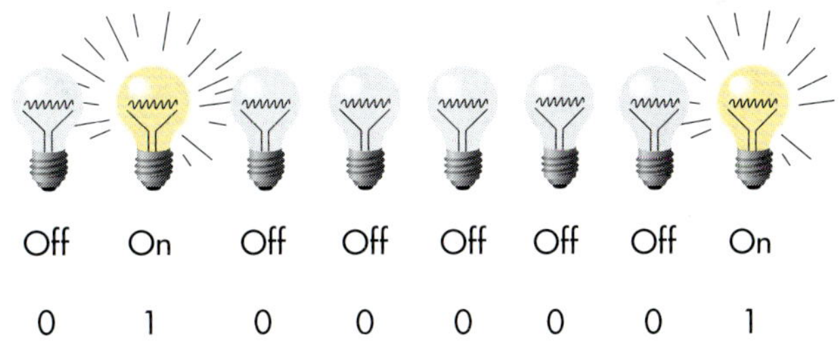

This Pattern of Electrical Circuits Represents the Capital Letter A

01001000	01000101	01001100	01001100	01001111
H	**E**	**L**	**L**	**O**

(b) "Hello" in ASCII

FIGURE 3 ASCII

INSIDE THE PC

IBM Corporation announced its version of the personal computer (PC) in 1981 and broke a long-standing corporate tradition by going to external sources for supporting hardware and software. ***Intel Corporation*** designed the microprocessor. ***Microsoft Corporation*** developed the operating system. Both companies retained the right to sell their products to other vendors.

The decision to go outside the corporation was motivated in part because IBM was playing "catch up." The Apple II and the Radio Shack TRS-80 had each been available for three years. More to the point, IBM was a mainframe company and simply did not believe in the future of the PC, a decision that the company would later regret.

The IBM PC was an instant success, in large part because of its open design that let independent vendors offer supporting products to enhance the functionality of the machine. This was accomplished by creating ***expansion slots*** on the ***motherboard*** (the main system board inside the PC) that could accommodate ***adapter cards*** from sources outside IBM. The motherboard contains the circuitry that connects the components of the PC to one another, and thus plugging in an adapter card is the equivalent of adding another device to the machine. IBM made public the necessary technical information to create the adapter cards, enabling other companies to build peripheral devices for the PC and enhance its overall capability.

The open design of the PC was a mixed blessing for IBM, in that ***PC compatibles*** based on the same microprocessor and able to run the same software began to appear as early as 1982 and offered superior performance for less money. Companies and individuals that were once willing to pay a premium for the IBM name began ordering the "same" machine from other vendors. IBM today has less than ten percent of the market it was so instrumental in creating, as the personal computer has become a commodity. "PC" is a generic term for any computer based on Intel-compatible microprocessors that are capable of running Microsoft Windows.

Apple by contrast built a closed system; that is, the only place to purchase an Apple II or Mac computer was from Apple itself. The company retained 100% of its market, but it was a much smaller market. The eventual winner was neither IBM nor Apple, but the general public, as computers have continued to come down in price while increasing exponentially in capability.

Figure 4 illustrates a typical Windows workstation, as it exists today. We view the system from the front (Figure 4a), the rear (Figure 4b), and from inside the system unit (Figure 4c). Your system will be different from ours, but you should be able to recognize the various components regardless of whether you use a desktop, tower, or notebook computer. We continue with a discussion of each component.

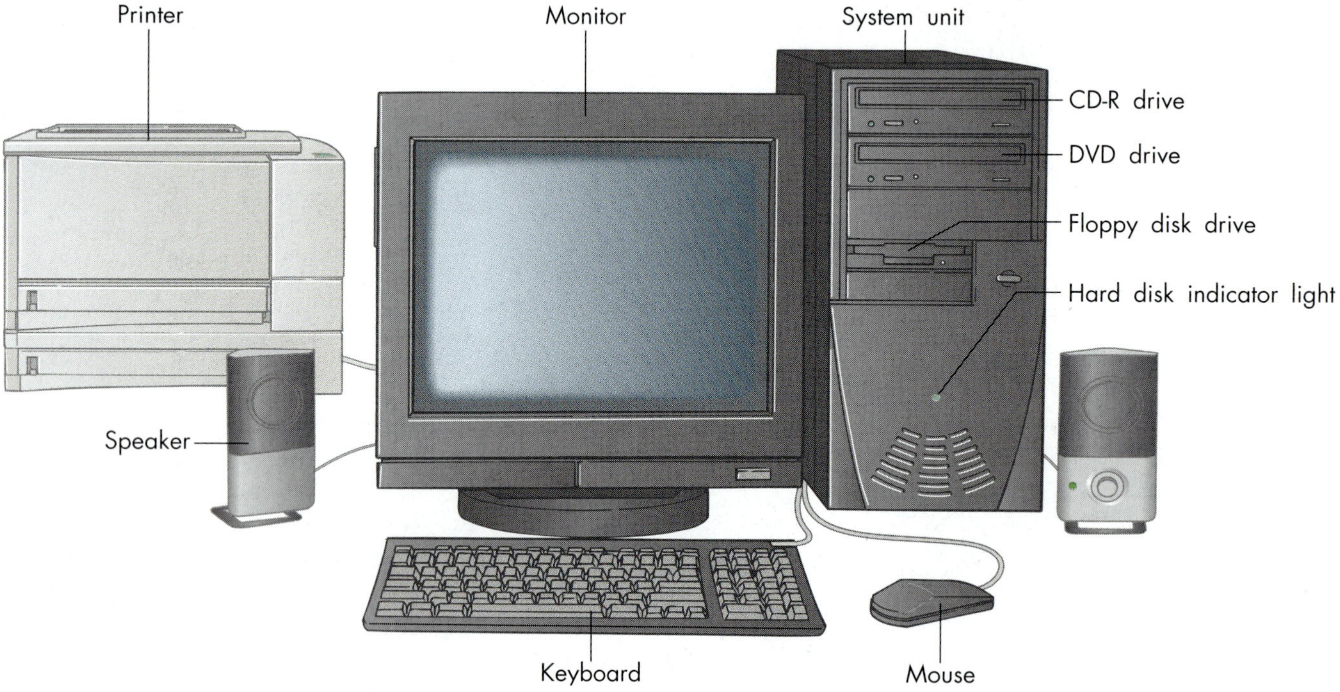

(a) Front View

FIGURE 4 A Windows Workstation

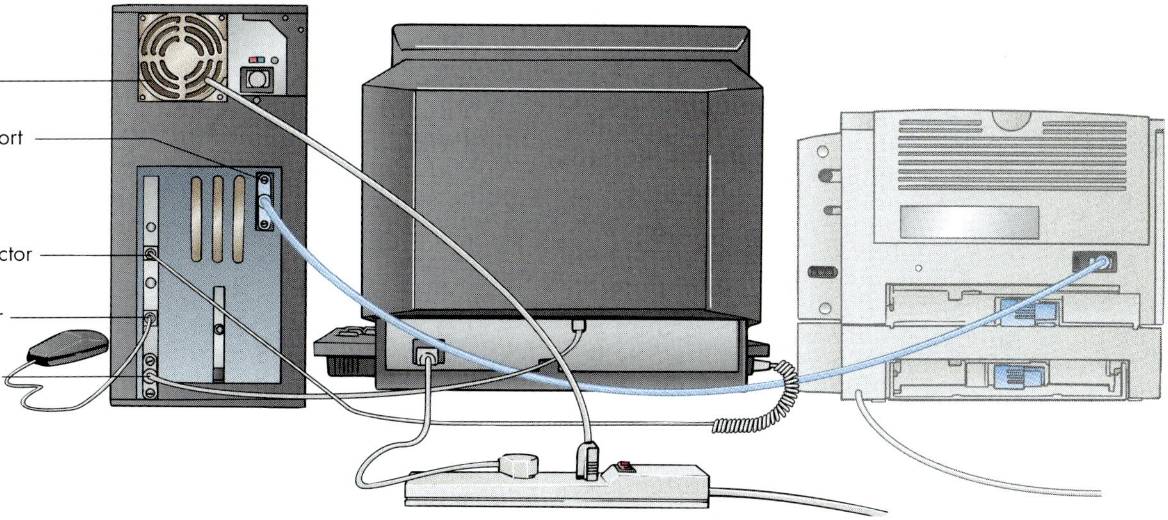

(b) Rear View

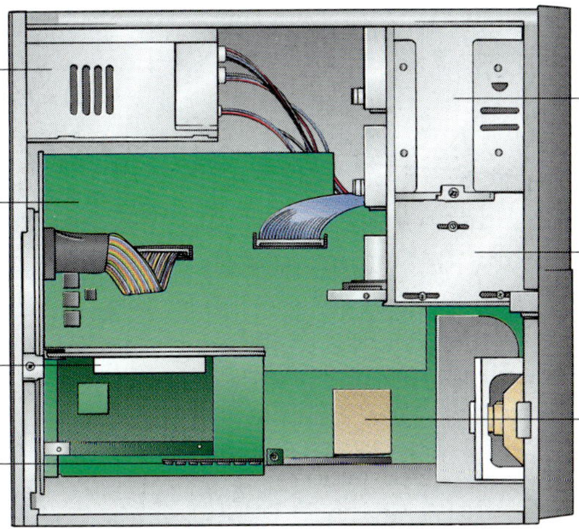

(c) Inside the Computer

FIGURE 4 A Windows Workstation (*continued*)

PLUG AND PLAY

The Universal Serial Bus (USB) simplifies the way that peripheral devices are connected to a computer. It supports plug and play, which is the ability of a computer system to automatically configure itself to detect peripheral devices such as a mouse, keyboard, printer, or digital camera. A USB port also supports hot plugging, which means that you can add or remove a device while the computer is running, and the operating system will detect the change automatically.

The Microprocessor

The CPU of the PC (or any microcomputer) is contained on a single silicon chip called a ***microprocessor***. The original Intel microprocessors were known by a number, but other vendors such as AMD and Cyrix produced functionally equivalent chips using the same numbering scheme. Then, in a stroke of marketing genius, Intel trademarked the ***Pentium*** name to differentiate its chips from the competition, and followed up with the Pentium II, Pentium III, and Pentium 4 (ordinal rather than Roman number). You can still purchase Intel-compatible chips from other vendors, but only Intel has the Pentium, a highly recognized brand name. The "Intel Inside" logo and its distinctive sound in TV commercials have earned the company tremendous customer loyalty.

The microprocessors within a given generation are also differentiated by ***clock speed***, which is measured in ***megahertz*** (MHz or millions of cycles) and/or ***gigahertz*** (GHz or billions of cycles). The higher the clock speed, the more instructions can be executed each second, and the faster the microprocessor; for example, a 3.0 GHz Pentium 4 is faster than a 2.0 MHz Pentium 4, and you can expect to pay more for the first machine.

Are the faster chips worth the extra money? Not necessarily, since virtually any new machine will be more than adequate to run Microsoft Office (provided the amount of memory is also sufficient). The numbers tend to be overwhelming, and you need not be unduly concerned with the precise characteristics of the microprocessor inside your computer. Indeed, the most cost-effective system typically uses a microprocessor that is two or three levels from the top. Today's speed demon will soon be replaced by something better; you have only to look at Figure 5 to see how far we have come. Note too that there are other ways to increase the speed of a system—by adding memory and by selecting the appropriate graphics adapter (or video card).

MOORE'S LAW

The fundamental unit of the microprocessor is the transistor—the on/off, zero/one switch that is at the heart of the digital computer. The key to improving the performance of a microprocessor is to increase the number of transistors; the more transistors, the more powerful the microprocessor. In 1965 Gordon Moore, the founder of Intel, predicted that transistor densities would continue to double every 18 months, a prediction that has held, and that accounts for the incredible increase in computer power.

Courtesy of Intel® Corporation/© 2001

Year	Chip	Clock Speed	Transistors
1979	8088	4.7 MHz	29,000
1982	80286	12 MHz	134,000
1985	80386	33 MHz	275,000
1989	80486	Up to 100 MHz	1.6 million
1993	Pentium	Up to 200 MHz	3.3 million
1998	Pentium II	233 MHz and higher	7.5 million
1999	Pentium III	450 MHz and higher	28.1 million
2000	Pentium 4	1.4 GHz and higher	34 million

FIGURE 5 The Evolution of the Intel Microprocessor

Memory

The microprocessor is the brain of the PC, but it needs instructions that tell it what to do, data on which to work, and a place to temporarily store the result of its calculations. All of this takes place in memory, a temporary storage area that holds data, instructions, and results, and passes everything back and forth to the CPU. The amount of memory a system has is important because the larger the memory, the more sophisticated the programs are that the computer is capable of executing, and further, the more programs and data that can remain in memory at the same time. Increasing the memory of a computer also increases the speed at which those programs are executed.

As depicted in Figure 6, the memory of a computer is divided into individual storage locations, each of which holds one byte. In the early days of the PC, memory was measured in ***kilobytes (KB)***. Today RAM is measured in ***megabytes (MB)***. One KB and MB are equal to approximately one thousand and one million characters, respectively. In actuality 1KB equals 1,024 (or 2^{10}) bytes, whereas 1MB is 1,048,576 (or 2^{20}) bytes. A Windows workstation has 256MB or 512MB of memory in today's environment. This is truly a fantastic amount, especially when you consider that mainframes that once cost millions of dollars had memories of 128KB and less.

The microprocessor also reads data from a second type of memory known as ***read-only memory (ROM)***. Read-only memory is accessed only when the computer is first turned on, as it contains the instructions telling the computer to check itself, and then to load the essential portion of the operating system into memory. The contents of ROM are established at the factory and cannot be altered by application programs, hence the name "read only."

The size of a computer's memory refers only to the amount of RAM available. The contents of RAM are volatile and change constantly as different programs are executed, or every time the same program is executed with different data. RAM is also transient, which means that shutting off (or losing) the power to the system erases the contents of memory. Auxiliary storage media, however, retain their contents even when there is no power.

HOW LARGE IS 256MB?

Imagine that you have been assigned the task of checking the contents of each byte of a computer with 256MB of RAM, and that it takes you one second per byte. At that rate, it would take approximately eight years to view the contents of every location.

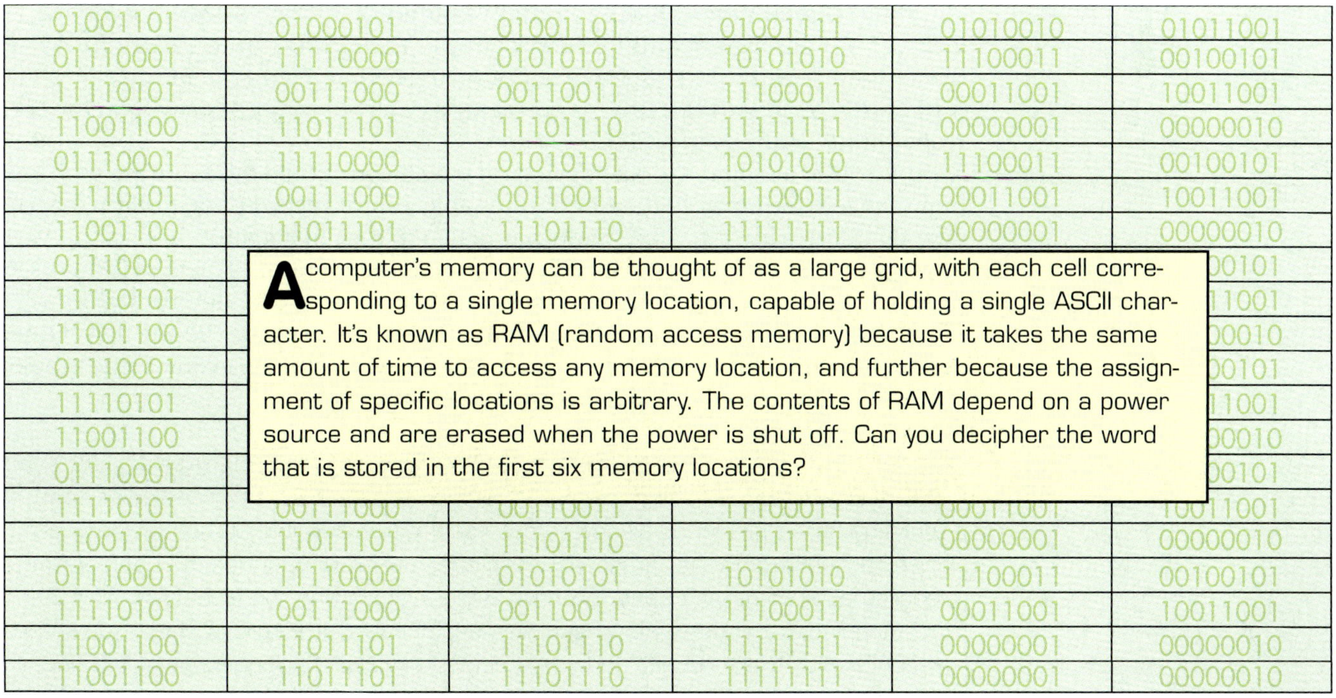

FIGURE 6 Memory

Auxiliary Storage

A disk drive is the most common type of auxiliary storage. The ***floppy disk*** gets its name because it is made of a flexible plastic (although it is enclosed in a hard plastic case). A ***hard disk*** (also called a ***fixed disk*** because it is permanently inside the system unit) uses rigid metal platters. A hard disk holds significantly more data than a floppy disk, and it accesses that data much faster.

All disks have to be formatted to store data, although that is typically done at the factory for you. The formatting process divides the surface of a disk into sectors (pie-slice wedges) and tracks (concentric circles) to enable a disk to store data. The number of sectors and tracks determines the storage capacity.

The PC uses a 3½-inch floppy disk with a capacity of 1.44MB. (The floppy disk is passing into obsolescence and is no longer standard on new computer systems.) The capacity of a hard disk is much greater than that of a floppy disk, and is measured in ***gigabytes*** (GB), where 1GB is approximately one billion (2^{30}) bytes. There is no such item as a standard hard disk, but disks with 30 to 60 GB or more are typical. Disk drives for mainframe computers have capacities that are measured in ***terabytes*** (TB), where one TB is approximately one trillion (2^{40}) bytes.

The ***CD-ROM***, once a high-priced optional device, is standard on today's PC. CD-ROM stands for Compact Disk, Read Only Memory, meaning that you can read from the CD but you cannot write to the CD. The standard CD has a storage capacity of 650 to 700 MB (compared to 1.44MB on a floppy disk). The large capacity of a CD, coupled with the modest cost of duplication (less than one dollar in quantity) makes it the ideal way to distribute software, as opposed to multiple floppy disks of years past. Computer games and reference material, such as an encyclopedia, are also distributed via a CD.

The CD-ROM has evolved from "read only" to "read and write", enabling the end user to create (burn) a CD. The ***CD-R*** (**C**ompact **D**isk–**R**ecordable) is rapidly becoming the new standard, but it is limited by the fact that the CD can be used only once. Even so, the cost of a blank CD is so modest (fifty cents or less) that the single use is not an issue. Nevertheless, the ***CD-RW*** (**C**ompact **D**isk–**ReW**ritable) goes one step further and allows the user to rewrite to the CD multiple times just as one does with a floppy disk.

DVD (Digital Video Disk or Digital Versatile Disk) technology is evolving as well. A DVD has significantly greater capacity than a CD (up to 17GB). A ***DVD-R*** device is analogous to CD-R, but it supports the higher recording density of a DVD. A ***DVD-RW*** (or DVD-RAM) drive is emerging as well but is more costly than the corresponding capability in a CD.

Two other auxiliary storage devices of which you should be aware are tape and high-capacity removable media. Both enable you to record data, and further, to take that data with you. Tape backup units enable an installation to back up very large quantities of data with virtually no human intervention. The tape is not used to access the data per se, only as insurance against hard disk failure. The Iomega Zip disk has a capacity of 250MB, and functions as a very large floppy disk. Other vendors manufacture other types of removable media. In any event, some type of removable media is essential to back up your data.

THE DEMISE OF THE FLOPPY DISK

You may be surprised to discover that your system no longer has a floppy disk drive, but it is only the latest victim in the march of technology. Long-playing records have come and gone. So have 8-track tapes and the laser disk. The 3½-inch floppy disk has had a long and successful run, but it too, is slated for obsolescence with Dell's recent announcement that it will no longer include a floppy drive as a standard component in desktop systems. Still, the floppy disk will "live forever" in the Save button that has the floppy disk as its icon.

Courtesy of IBM Corporation

(a) Floppy Disks

Courtesy of Seagate Technology/C&I Photography

(b) Hard Disk

© Michael Newman/Photo Edit

(c) CD-ROMs and DVDs

Courtesy of Iomega Corporation

(d) Zip Disk

FIGURE 7 Auxiliary Storage

WHAT IS DRIVE C?

The CPU needs to differentiate one auxiliary storage device from another and does so by designating each device with a letter. The floppy drive is always drive A. (A second floppy drive, if it were present, would be drive B.) The hard disk is always drive C with other auxiliary devices assigned letters from D on. Thus, a system with one floppy drive, a hard disk, and a CD-ROM would have devices as A, C, and D, corresponding to the floppy disk, hard disk, and CD-ROM, respectively.

Input Devices

The ***keyboard*** and the ***mouse*** are the primary input devices for the PC. The keys on the keyboard are arranged much like those of a typewriter, in the standard QWERTY pattern (named for the first six characters in the third row). In addition, there are several special keys that are unique to the PC as shown in Figure 8.

The Caps Lock key eliminates the need to continually press the Shift key to enter uppercase letters. The Caps Lock key functions as a toggle switch; that is, pressing it once causes all uppercase letters to be entered, pressing it a second time returns to lowercase, pressing it again returns to uppercase, and so on. The Num Lock key is similar in concept and activates the numeric keypad at the right side of the keyboard.

Function keys (F1 through F12) are special-purpose keys, used by various application programs to execute specific commands and/or save keystrokes. The exact purpose of a particular function key varies from program to program. The Ctrl and Alt keys work in similar fashion and are used with other keys to execute a specific command.

Cursor keys [the four arrow keys, up (↑), down (↓), right (→), and left (←)] control movement of the cursor (the blinking line or box), which shows where on the monitor the data will be entered. The Home, End, PgUp, and PgDn keys also serve to move the cursor.

The Enter (Return) key signals the completion of an entry and correspondingly causes the characters typed on the keyboard to be transmitted to the CPU. Other special keys include the Insert (Ins) and Delete (Del) keys that insert and/or delete characters, respectively. The Escape (Esc) key is used by many programs to cancel (or escape from) current actions. The Print Screen key copies the image on the monitor into memory, from where it can be inserted into a document. The Windows key (found only on newer keyboards) is equivalent to clicking the Start button in Microsoft Windows.

The standard mouse has two buttons and recognizes four basic operations with which you must become familiar:

- To point to an object, move the mouse pointer onto the object.
- To click an object, point to it, then press and release the left mouse button; to right click an object, point to the object, then press and release the right mouse button.
- To double click an object, point to it, then quickly click the left button twice in succession.
- To drag an object, move the pointer to the object, then press and hold the left button while you move the mouse to place the object in a new position.

The keyboard and mouse are the primary input devices for the PC, but there are others. A ***microphone*** is required to record your own sound files, which can then be played through the soundboard and speakers. A ***scanner*** enables you to convert a graphic image on paper into its digital equivalent for subsequent inclusion in a document. A scanner also enables you to convert the text in a paper document to a digital file that can be edited with a word processor. And don't forget a ***joystick***, which is an essential component on many computer games.

THE WINDOWS ⊞ KEY

Use the Windows ⊞ key in conjunction with various other letters as valuable keyboard shortcuts. Press and hold the Windows key with the letter "D", for example, to minimize or restore all open applications. ⊞ + E will open My Computer, and ⊞ + F opens the Search window to look for a file or folder. ⊞ by itself displays the Start menu.

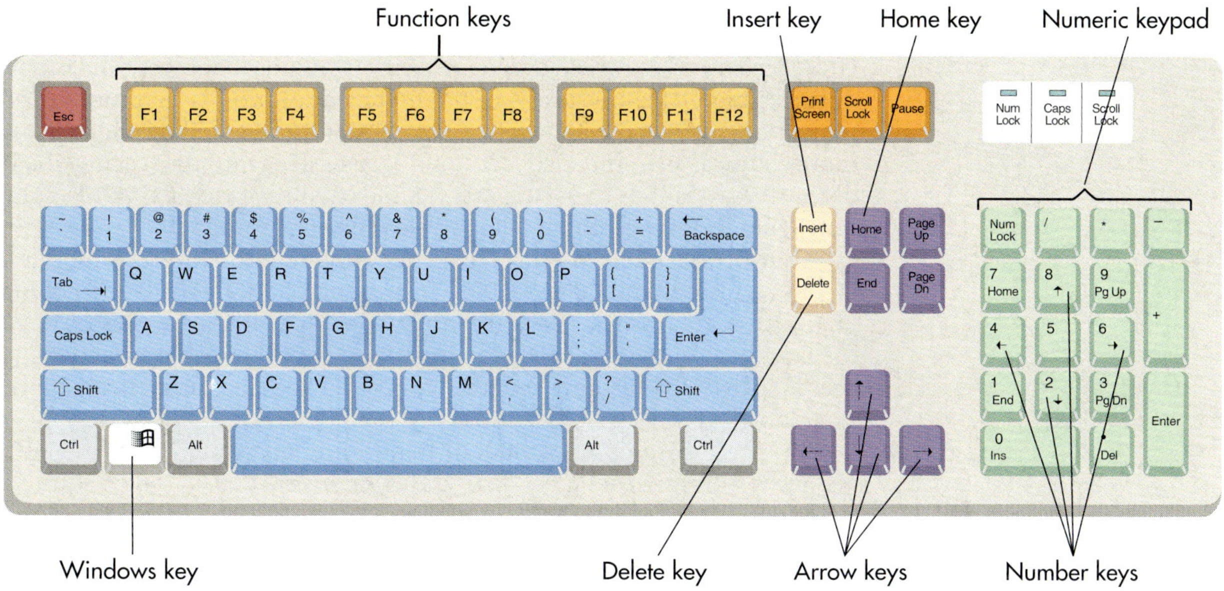

Keyboard

Courtesy of Microsoft Corporation

Mouse

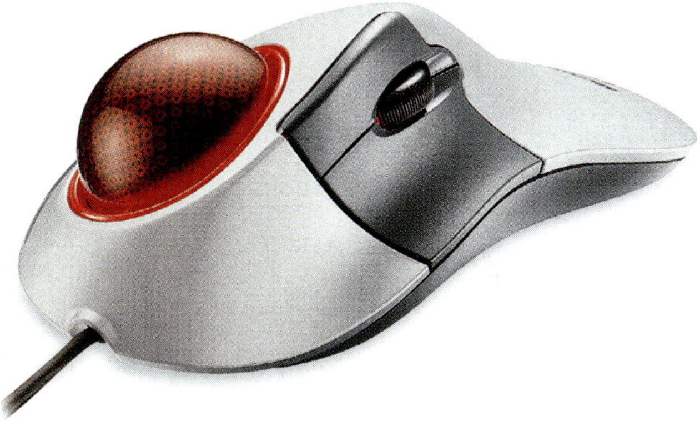

Courtesy of Microsoft Corporation

Trackball

Courtesy of Microsoft Corporation

Joystick

FIGURE 8 Input Devices

THE MOUSE OR THE KEYBOARD

Almost every command in Windows can be executed in different ways, using either the mouse or the keyboard. Most people start with the mouse and add keyboard shortcuts as they become more proficient. There is no right or wrong technique, just different techniques, and the one you choose depends entirely on personal preference in a specific situation. If, for example, your hands are already on the keyboard, it is faster to use the keyboard shortcut. Other times, your hand will be on the mouse and that will be the fastest way.

The Monitor

The ***resolution*** of a monitor is the number of ***pixels*** (tiny dots or *pic*ture *el*ements) that are displayed at one time. Several resolutions are possible, but you are most likely to see either *800 × 600* (800 pixels across by 600 pixels down) or *1024 × 768* (1024 pixels across by 768 down). An earlier standard of 640 × 480 has passed into obsolescence. The advantage of the higher resolution is that more pixels are displayed on the screen and hence you see more of the document—for example, more columns in a spreadsheet or more pages in a word processing document. The disadvantage is that the size of the text is smaller at the higher resolutions. Thus, the higher the resolution, the larger the monitor should be.

Figure 9 illustrates the effect of higher resolutions on the same monitor. Figure 9a is set to a resolution of 800 × 600, which displays rows 1 to 20 and columns A to H. Figure 9b increases the resolution to 1024 × 768, which enables us to view rows 1 to 28 and columns A to K. We see more data, but the text is smaller. Figure 9c further increases the resolution with similar effects. You choose the resolution in conjunction with the size of the monitor. A 17-inch monitor, for example, works well with a resolution of 800 × 600, or depending on your vision, even 1024 × 768. Higher resolutions, such as 1280 × 1024 or even 1600 × 1200, require larger and (considerably) more expensive monitors.

The processing requirements imposed on the system at higher resolutions are enormous. At 800 × 600, for example, the CPU has to send 480,000 bytes to display a single screen (given that each pixel requires only one byte), and that is only the beginning. The screen has to be refreshed approximately 70 times a second, and each pixel typically takes two or three bytes, rather than one. The requirements become even more demanding at higher resolutions. To speed processing, a PC is equipped with a video (display) adapter (or graphics card). You can think of the video adapter as an assistant to the CPU in that the task of displaying and refreshing a screen is shifted from the microprocessor to the graphics card. A graphics card also has its own memory, which is known as video memory.

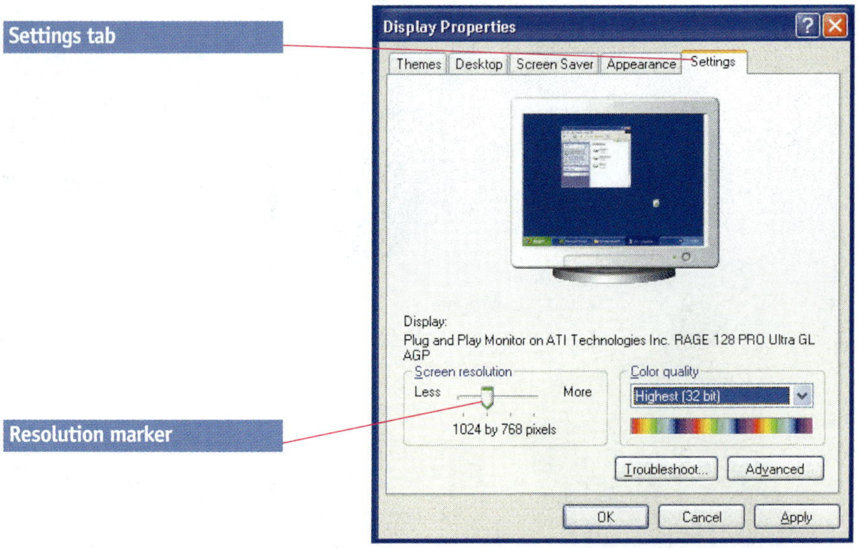

CHANGE THE RESOLUTION

Windows enables you to change the resolution of your system as you work. Right click a blank area of the desktop to display a context-sensitive menu, click the Properties command, then click the Settings tab to display the associated dialog box. Drag the screen resolution marker to the indicated setting, then click OK to accept the new setting and close the dialog box.

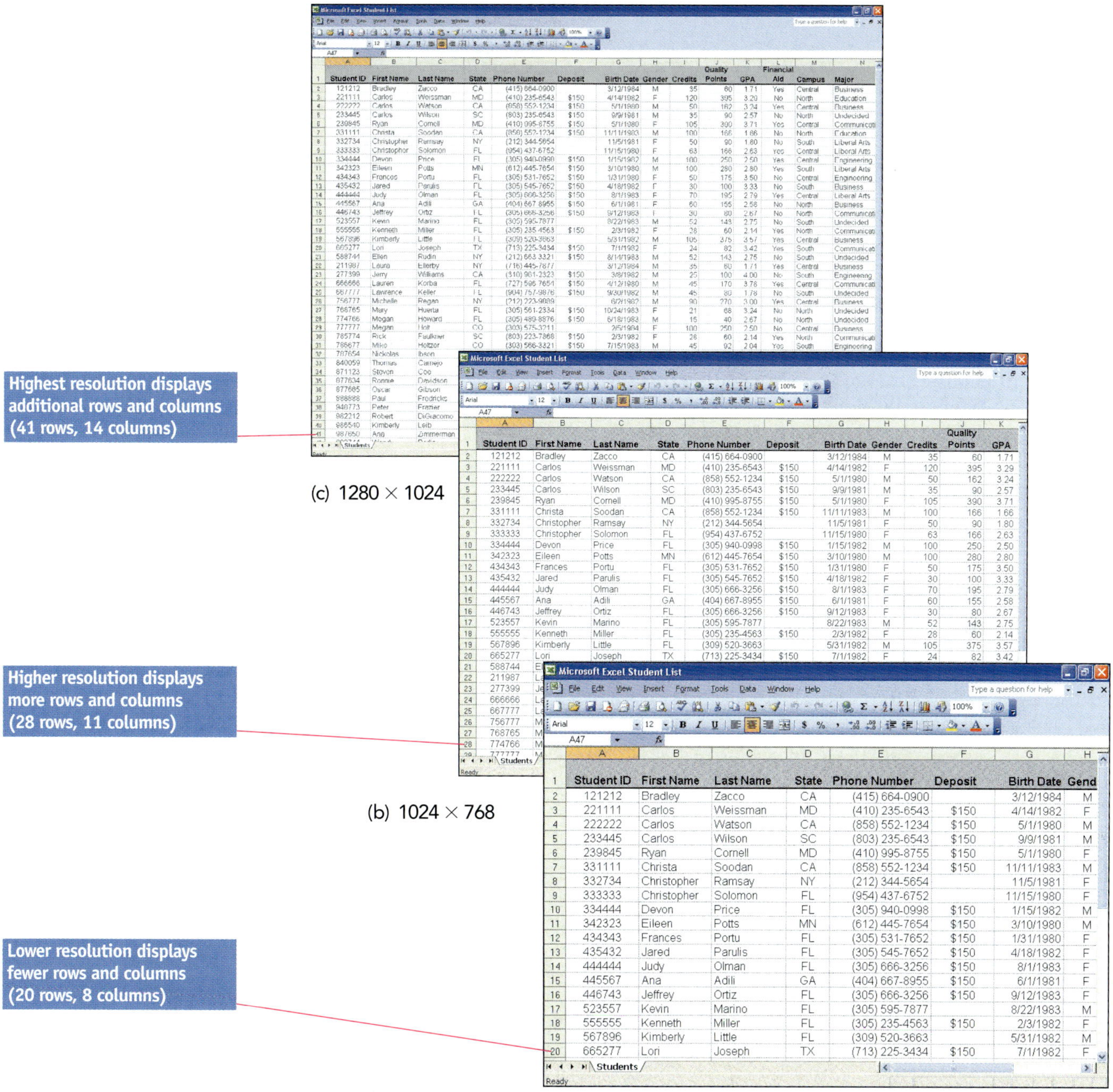

(c) 1280 × 1024

(b) 1024 × 768

(a) 800 × 600

FIGURE 9 Monitor Size and Resolution

CHOOSING A MONITOR

The difference between monitors is often due to information that is may be buried in the fine print. The dot pitch is the distance between adjacent pixels. The smaller the dot pitch, the crisper the image—or conversely, the larger the dot pitch, the grainier the picture. Choose a monitor with a dot pitch of .28 or less.

The vertical refresh rate determines how frequently the screen is repainted from top to bottom. A rate that is too slow causes the screen to flicker because it is not being redrawn fast enough to fool the eye into seeing a constant pattern. A rate of 70 Hz (70 cycles per second) is the minimum you should accept.

The Printer

A printer produces output on paper or acetate transparencies. The output is referred to as ***hard copy*** because it is more tangible than the files written to a disk or other electronic devices. Printers vary greatly in terms of design, price, and capability as can be seen in Figure 10.

The dot matrix printer was the entry-level printer of choice for many years. It was inexpensive and versatile, but suffered from two major drawbacks—it was noisy and it had a less-than-perfect print quality because each character was created with a pattern of dots. The dot matrix printer has become virtually obsolete, due to the emergence of the ink-jet printer. It is still used occasionally, however, for multipart forms.

The ***ink-jet printer*** is today's entry-level printer. It is quieter than a dot matrix printer, its print quality is much better, and it prints in color. The downside is that supplies (replacement cartridges for the colored ink) are expensive when compared to the cost of the printer.

The ***laser printer*** is the top-of-the-line device, and it offers speed and quality superior to that of an ink-jet. A personal laser printer is only slightly more expensive than an ink-jet, and it prints considerably faster, albeit in black and white. The resolution (quality) of a laser printer is measured in dots per inch (e.g., 1,200 dpi), and its speed is measured in pages per minute (e.g., 8 ppm).

You will also need to learn about ***typography***, which is the process of selecting typefaces, type styles, and type sizes. It is a critical, often subtle element in the success of a document. Good typography goes almost unnoticed, whereas poor typography calls attention to itself and detracts from a document.

A typeface (or ***font***) is a complete set of characters (upper- and lowercase letters, numbers, punctuation marks, and special symbols). Typefaces are divided into two general categories, serif and sans serif. A serif typeface (e.g., Times New Roman) has tiny cross lines at the ends of the characters to help the eye connect one letter with the next. A sans serif typeface (e.g., Arial) does not have these lines. A commonly accepted practice is to use serif typefaces with larger amounts of text and sans serif typefaces for smaller amounts such as headings or titles.

Typefaces are also characterized as monospaced or proportional. A monospaced typeface uses the same amount of space for every character, whereas a proportional typeface allocates space according to the width of the character.

Type size is a vertical measurement and is specified in points. One point is equal to $1/72$ of an inch. The text in most documents is set in 10 or 12 point type. (The text you are reading is set in a 10 point serif typeface.) Different elements in the same document are often set in different type sizes to provide emphasis.

This is Times New Roman 10 point

This is Times New Roman 12 point

This is Times New Roman 18 point

This is Times New Roman 24 point

This is Times New Roman 30 point

This is Arial 10 point

This is Arial 12 point

This is Arial 18 point

This is Arial 24 point

This is Arial 30 point

Basics of Typography—Typefaces and Point Sizes

Courtesy of IBM Corporation

(a) Network Printer

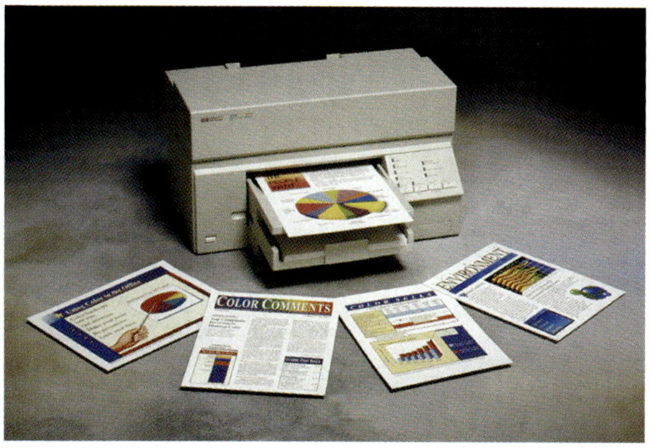

Courtesy of Hewlett-Packard Company

(b) Ink-Jet Printer

Courtesy of Hewlett-Packard Company

(c) Laser Printer

Courtesy of Hewlett-Packard Company

(d) Multifunction Printer, Copier, Scanner, Fax

FIGURE 10 Printers

CHOOSING A PRINTER

A company or organization is going to select a high-speed network printer with multiple trays and the ability to print on oversized paper (11 × 17). Individuals will choose from an entry-level ink-jet printer, a personal laser printer, or a four-in-one combination device. The latter includes the ability to print, scan, fax, or copy a document. Some machines (such as the HP officejet 145) include a fifth function to upload photographs from a flash memory card.

The Digital Camera

How many times have you shot a roll of film, waited two days for it to be developed, only to be disappointed when the pictures were out of focus? Those days are over with the advent of the ***digital camera***. You can see the picture immediately after you take it, erase the picture if you don't like it, and then later you can download multiple pictures at one time to your computer. You can edit a photograph, crop it, or rotate it, then print the result or send it as an e-mail attachment. You can even upload your pictures to various Web sites where friends and family can view your handiwork for free.

A digital camera has a lens, shutter, and optical viewfinder just like a traditional camera. Its inner workings are very different, however, as the image is stored on a photosensitive computer chip that converts the image to a series of pixels (picture elements or dots). The more pixels in the camera, the sharper the picture. Entry-level cameras provide two ***megapixels*** and produce quality prints at sizes up to 5×7 inches. A three-megapixel camera is necessary for a quality 8×10 image.

A digital camera stores its pictures on a flash memory card, as opposed to film. (Two technologies, CompactFlash and SmartMedia, are commonly used.) The more memory you have, the more pictures your camera can store. Most cameras come with a 16MB card, but we suggest you upgrade to 64MB or 128MB. If you still need more "film," you can carry additional cards and swap them in and out of the camera.

Once the pictures are taken, you will need to transfer them to your computer, which can be done in different ways. The camera may connect directly to the computer with its own cable, you may purchase a stand-alone reader to read the flash memory card that stores the images, and/or your printer may have the memory reader built in. After the pictures are transferred to your computer, you can erase the images from the memory card and reuse it as though you had purchased a new roll of film.

Courtesy of Canon USA, Inc.

(a) The Camera

(b) Bob and Marion on Vacation

(c) Stonehenge

(d) White Cliffs of Dover

FIGURE 11 The Digital Camera

THE RISE OF THE PERSONAL COMPUTER

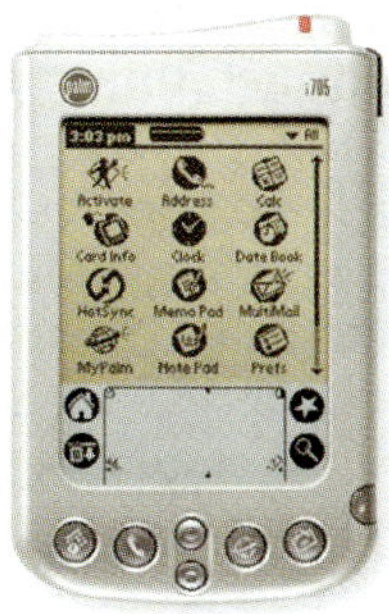

(a) Handheld "Organizer"

(b) Apple iMac

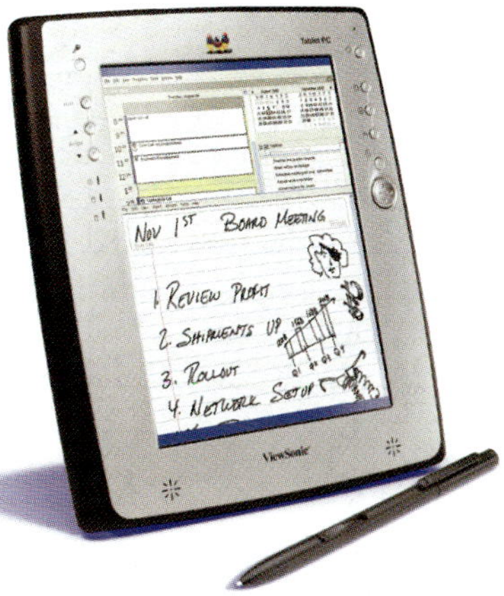

(c) Tablet PC

(d) Notebook PC

The **IBM PC** was introduced in 1981, literally a lifetime ago, because it predates today's college generation. IBM was neither first (the Apple II, TRS-80, and Commodore 64 all preceded the PC) nor technologically innovative, but its announcement put the personal computer on the desks of American business, just as Apple had put the computer in the home. By 1985 IBM had manufactured its three millionth PC, and had spawned an entire industry in the process. To appreciate how far we've come, consider this subjective list of innovative computers.

Altair 8800 (1975): The January 1975 issue of *Popular Electronics* featured the Altair 8800 on its cover: The world's first PC had to be built from a kit that cost $439. It had no keyboard or monitor, no software, and was programmed by switches on the front panel.

Apple II (1977): The Apple II was a fully assembled home computer in an attractive case, complete with keyboard, connection to a TV screen, color, memory to 64KB, and the BASIC programming language. The machine was to launch the personal computer revolution and vault its founders, Steve Wozniak and Steve Jobs, from garage to glory.

Apple Macintosh (1984): The Macintosh was far from an instant success, but once Apple got the bugs out and added an internal hard disk, laser printer, and expanded memory, the machine took off. Its ease of use and graphical interface offered an entirely different perspective on computing.

Palm Pilot 1000 (1996): The Palm Pilot 1000 began as a handheld "organizer" intended to make people's lives easier. The original applications of a date book, address book, and "to do" list have evolved into an Internet connectivity device that provides instant access to all types of information, from e-mail to stock quotes, medical data, and corporate-level database information.

Apple iMac (1998): The "i" in iMac is to remind the public of the easy-to-use Internet features that are built into this colorful and innovative computer that restored profitability to Apple. It supports wireless communication and is quieter than a PC because it is built without an internal fan. It's also a powerful computer that intrigues its users with the ability to create movies on the desktop.

The Portable PC: The first portable PC was introduced by Compaq Computer in 1983, but at 35 pounds it was more "luggable" than portable. A notebook computer today weighs in at less than 5 pounds and is equipped with 256MB of RAM and a 30GB hard disk, capabilities that exceed mainframe computers from the 1980s. (These parameters may well increase by the time you read our text.) A Tablet PC lets you write directly on the screen and take notes in your own handwriting, whereas a PDA will fit in your shirt pocket.

A PC BUYING GUIDE

Are you confused about all the ads for personal computers? You can buy from hundreds of companies, retail or through the mail, with no such thing as a standard configuration. The PC has, in effect, become a commodity where the consumer is able to select each component. We suggest you approach the purchase of a PC just as you would the purchase of any big-ticket item, with research and planning. Be sure you know your hardware requirements before you walk into a computer store, or else you will spend too much money or buy the wrong system. Stick to your requirements and don't be swayed to a different item if the vendor is out of stock. You've waited this long to buy a computer, and another week or two won't matter.

Mail order will almost always offer better prices than a retail establishment, but price should not be the sole consideration. Local service and support are also important, especially if you are a nontechnical new user. A little research, however, and you can purchase through the mail with confidence, and save yourself money in the process. If you do purchase by mail, confirm the order in writing, stating exactly what you are expecting to receive and when. Include the specific brands and/or model numbers and the agreed-upon price, including shipping and handling, to have documentation in the event of a dispute.

The vast majority of dealers, both retail and mail order, are reputable, but as with any purchase, *caveat emptor*. Good luck, good shopping, and keep the following in mind.

	**THE PURCHASE OF A PC**		
		Vendor 1	**Vendor 2**
Computer System (desktop)	Minimum Specification		
Processor	Pentium®4 at 2.0 GHz		
Memory	512MB		
Floppy Disk	No longer standard		
Fixed Disk	40GB		
Monitor	19 inches		
CD	CD-R or CD-RW		
DVD	DVD-R is optional		
Graphics Card	64MB RAM		
Fax/Modem	56K bps		
Sound card and speakers	Minimal		
Network card	10/100 Network interface		
Additional requirements	Mouse and keyboard		
Warranty	3-year on site		
Software			
Operating system	Windows XP Professional		
Antivirus program	One-year subscription		
Microsoft Office Professional			
Peripherals			
Multifunction color printer			
Digital camera	3 Megapixels		
Subtotal		$	$
Shipping	UPS Ground		
Sales Tax			
Grand Total		$	$

FIGURE 12 The Purchase of a PC

EVALUATE COMPETING SYSTEMS

Determine the requirements before you buy, or else you are apt to choose the wrong system, forget something, and/or pay too much money. Spend your money on extra memory, as opposed to a faster CPU. Your system will run just as quickly, and you will wind up paying less. Build a simple spreadsheet or Word document and compare the cost of at least two alternative systems.

Tips for Buying a PC

Don't forget the software. Any machine you buy will come with some version of the Windows operating system, but that is only the beginning since you must also purchase the application software you intend to run. Many first-time buyers are surprised that they have to pay extra for software, but you had better allow for software in your budget. Ideally, Microsoft Office will be bundled with your machine, but if not, the university bookstore is generally your best bet as it offers a substantial educational discount. Buy the edition of Office that you need; not every edition includes Access and PowerPoint. You will also need to acquire an antivirus program.

Don't skimp on memory. The more memory a system has, the better its overall performance. The Office suite is very powerful, but it requires adequate resources to run efficiently. 256MB of RAM is recommended as the absolute minimum you should consider, but 512MB is increasingly common. Either way, be sure your system can accommodate additional memory easily and inexpensively.

Buy more disk space than you think you need. We purchased our first hard disk as an upgrade to the original PC in 1984. It was a "whopping" 10MB, and our biggest concern was that we would never fill it all. The storage requirements of application programs and graphical files have increased significantly. Today's version of Microsoft Office requires several hundred megabytes for a complete installation. A 30GB drive is the minimum you should consider, but for a few dollars more, you can add significantly more storage. It is money well spent.

Let your fingers do the walking. A single issue of a computer magazine contains advertisements from many vendors, making it possible to comparison shop from multiple mail-order vendors from the convenience of home. You can also shop online and can visit a vendor's Web site to obtain the latest information. Be sure to check the price of at least two computing systems. Go to the Exploring Office home page, www.prenhall.com/grauer, click the link to additional resources, then click the link to a PC Buying Guide to visit some suggested sites.

Look for 30-day price protection. An unconditional 30-day money-back guarantee is an industry standard. Insist on this guarantee and be sure you have it in writing. A reputable vendor will also refund the amount of any price reduction that occurs during the first 30 days after delivery, but it is incumbent on you to contact the vendor and request a refund. Don't forget to do so.

Use a credit card. You can double the warranty of any system (up to one additional year) by using a major credit card, provided it offers a "buyer's protection" policy. (Check with your credit card company to see whether it has this feature, and if not, you may want to consider getting a different credit card.) The extended warranty is free, and it goes into effect automatically when you charge your computer. The use of a credit card also gives you additional leverage if you are dissatisfied with an item. Try, however, to pay off your system immediately to avoid going into debt.

Don't forget the extras. The standard PC does not include a network card or removable mass storage device. You need a network card if you plan to connect to the Internet via a cable modem, DSL, or through a local area network in your dorm. A mass storage device such as a CD-R or an Iomega Zip drive is essential for backup. Speakers may also be extra. An Uninterrupted Power Supply is also a worthwhile addition. Any vendor will gladly sell you these components. Just remember to ask.

Don't be frustrated when prices drop. The system you buy today will invariably cost less tomorrow, and further, tomorrow's machine will run circles around today's most powerful system. The IBM/XT, for example, sold for approximately $5,000 and was configured with an 8088 microprocessor, a 10MB hard disk, 128KB of RAM, and monochrome monitor, but it was the best system you could buy in 1983. The point of this example is that you enjoy the machine you buy today without concern for future technology. Indeed, if you wait until prices come down, you will never buy anything, because there will always be something better and less expensive.

BE KIND TO YOURSELF

Are you the type of person who will spend thousands on a new computer, only to set it up on your regular desk and sit on a $10 bridge chair? Don't. A conventional desk (or the dining room table) is 30 inches high, but the recommended typing height is 27 inches. The difference accounts for the stiff neck, tight shoulders, and aching backs reported by many people who sit at a computer over an extended period of time. Be kind to yourself and include a computer table with lots of room as well as a comfortable chair in your budget.

SOFTWARE

The most powerful computer system is useless without appropriate ***software***. Indeed, it is the availability of the software that justifies the purchase of the ***hardware*** and dictates how the computer will be used. Without software, the computer is just an expensive paperweight. Software is divided broadly into two classes, ***system software*** (consisting of the operating system and supporting programs) and ***application software***. The wonderful thing about application software is that replacing one application with another completely changes the personality of the computer. The same computer that is used for word processing can also be used to surf the Internet, prepare long-range financial forecasts, compose music, or play a computer game, merely by changing the application program.

The application programs depend, however, on the operating system, a program (actually many programs) that links the application to the hardware and links hardware components to one another. Thus, it is the operating system that lets you enter text at a keyboard, have that text displayed on a monitor, stored permanently on disk, then appear as hard copy on the printer. An application program (such as Microsoft Word) simply forwards your commands to the operating system, which does its work unobtrusively behind the scenes. A portion of the operating system is loaded into memory at the time the computer is turned on and it remains there throughout the session, enabling you to do the work that you want to do.

The Evolution of the Desktop

The operating system for the PC has improved continually over time. As new hardware became available, new versions of the operating system were written to take advantage of the increased performance. Each improvement in hardware brought with it a new and better operating system, which in turn demanded faster hardware with more storage capability. Figure 12 displays a screen from three different versions of Windows—Windows 3.1, Windows 95 (the first of the so-called "modern" Windows), and Windows XP—and provides an appreciation of the achievements of the last several years. Before Windows, however, there was ***MS-DOS***.

MS-DOS 1.0 was announced with the PC in 1981. The hardware was primitive by today's standards, as a fully loaded PC came with 64KB of RAM, two 5¼ floppy drives (a hard disk was not yet available), and a monochrome monitor that displayed only text (not graphics). The operating system was equally basic and required only 20KB of disk storage, but it was perfectly matched to the available hardware.

MS-DOS improved significantly over the years, but it was always a text-based system. The flashing cursor and cryptic A:\> or C:\> prompt that was displayed on the screen was intimidating to the new user, who had to know which commands to enter. The applications were also limited in that they were text-based and totally unrelated to one another. WordPerfect, Lotus, and dBase, for example, were the dominant applications of their day, but each had a completely different interface, so that knowledge of one did not help you to learn the other. And even if you knew all three applications, you could run only one application at a time.

All of this changed with the introduction of *Windows 3.1* in 1991, which introduced the ***graphical user interface*** (***GUI*** and pronounced "gooey") that let you use a mouse to point and click icons instead of having to enter text-based commands. Windows 3.1 also provided a ***WYSIWYG*** (pronounced "wizzywig" and standing for What You See Is What You Get) interface in which text and graphic elements appeared on the screen exactly as they appeared on the printer. Boldface and italics were displayed in different point sizes and different typefaces. The Windows 3.1 interface looks primitive today, but it was a very big deal at the time. It was slow to catch on initially, but it signaled the beginning of the end for MS-DOS.

WINDOWS 3.1

Windows 3.1 (1991) introduced the graphical user interface as well as a common user interface and consistent command structure for all applications. It also provided multitasking and Object Linking and Embedding.

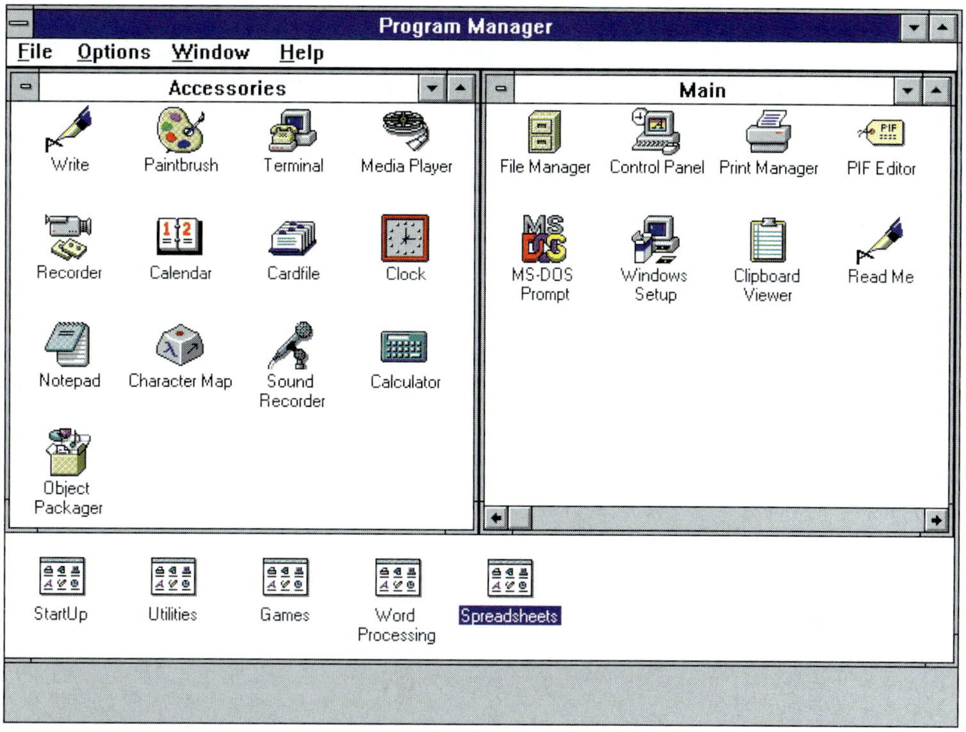

WINDOWS 95

Windows 95 (1995) simplified the desktop by providing a Start button to simplify program execution, as well as a taskbar to facilitate multitasking. File management was made easier through My Computer.

FIGURE 13 Evolution of the Desktop

WINDOWS XP

Windows XP is the successor to all current breeds of Windows—Windows 95, 98, Me, NT, and 2000. This desktop is typical of what might appear on a home computer, in which individual accounts are established for everyone who uses the computer.

THE WORKING DESKTOP

The Working Desktop is common to all versions of Windows and shows multiple open windows, each with a different application open. The taskbar is one way to switch from one application to another.

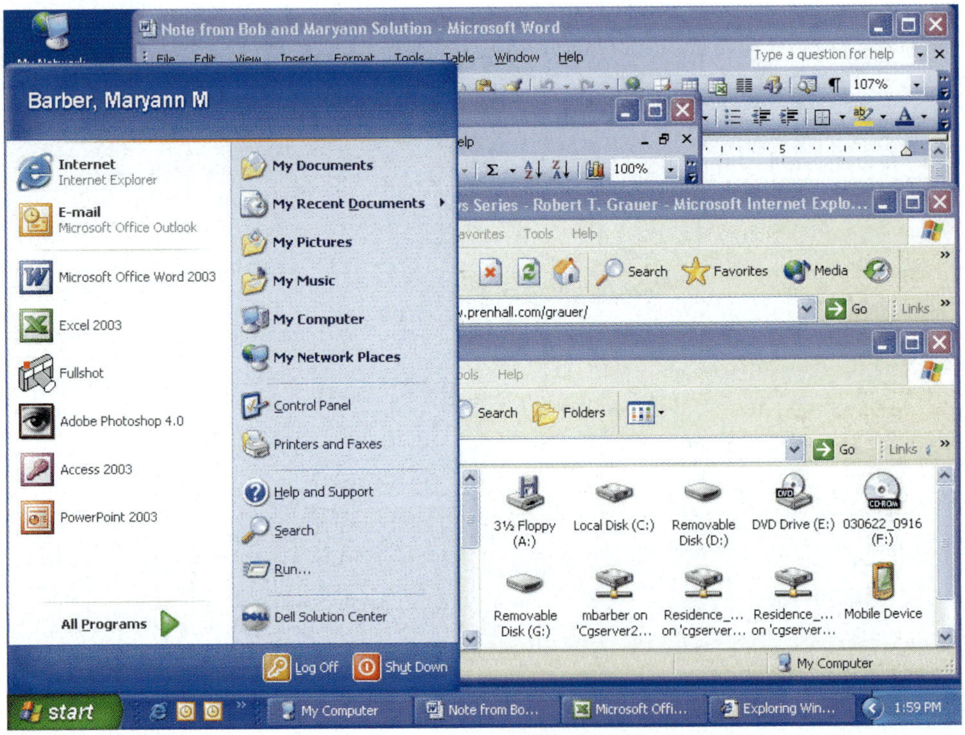

FIGURE 13 Evolution of the Desktop (*continued*)

Windows 3.1 was much more than just a pretty facelift because it also introduced three significant innovations. First and foremost is the ***common user interface***, whereby all applications adhere to the same conventions and work basically the same way. This means that once you learn one Windows application, it is that much easier to learn the next because all applications follow a consistent command structure. Think about the significance of this capability. Anyone can sit down at a computer, start an entirely new application with which they are unfamiliar, yet know how to proceed intuitively.

Windows 3.1 also introduced ***multitasking***, which lets you run more than one program at a time. This enables you to go back and forth between tasks, putting down a word processing document, for example, to read an e-mail message. This, too, is tremendously important because you previously had to close one application in order to start another.

The third innovation, ***Object Linking and Embedding*** (abbreviated ***OLE*** and pronounced "olay"), enables you to share data between applications. Using OLE you can create a document with data (objects) from multiple applications—for example, a Word document that contains an Excel spreadsheet and chart.

Windows 95 was announced in 1995 and sought to make the PC even easier to use. The simpler desktop in Windows 95 lets the user click the Start button to begin. Multitasking is implemented by clicking a button on the Windows 95 taskbar (as opposed to having to use the Alt+Tab shortcut in Windows 3.1). File management was made more intuitive through introduction of the My Computer icon on the desktop. Windows 95 also introduced long file names (up to 255 characters), as opposed to the eight-character file names that existed under MS-DOS.

Windows 95 was the first of the so-called "modern Windows" and was followed by Windows NT, Windows 98, Windows 2000, and Windows Me (the Millennium edition). It's difficult to keep track of the different versions and the subtle variations in each, especially since the biggest differences are "behind the scenes." Windows 98 and Windows Me were geared for the home user and provided extensive support for games and peripheral devices. Windows NT and Windows 2000 were aimed at the business user and provided increased security and reliability.

Windows XP replaces all previous versions of the operating system. Windows XP Home Edition is intended for entertainment and home use. It includes a media player, new support for digital photography, and an instant messenger. Windows XP Professional Edition has all of the features of the Home Edition plus additional security to encrypt files, and it includes support for high-performance multiprocessor systems. It also lets you connect to your computer from a remote station and/or communicate in different languages.

The desktop in Figure 12d is appliable to *every* version of Windows. It has four open windows, each of which displays a program that is currently in use. Multitasking enables you to do word processing in one window, create a spreadsheet in a second window, surf the Internet in a third window, play a game in a fourth window, and so on. You can work in a program as long as you want, then change to a different program by clicking its window or by using the taskbar at the bottom of the desktop. The taskbar contains a button for each open program, and it enables you to switch back and forth between those programs by clicking the appropriate button.

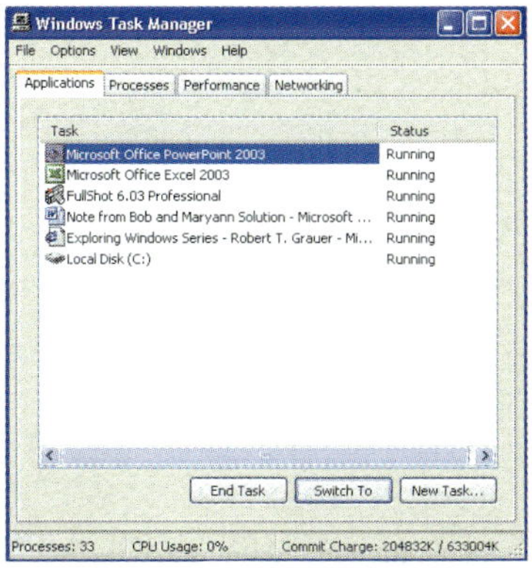

FIGURE 14 The Task Manager

THE TASK MANAGER

Does your system ever "hang" or display the message, "program not responding"? If so, you can use the Task Manager to end the problem program without shutting your system down. Press Ctrl+Alt+Del to display the Task Manager as shown in Figure 14, click the Applications tab to locate the nonresponsive program, and then click the End Task button to terminate the program. The Task Manager can also be used to navigate between programs and/or to report on the performance of your system. It may be disabled in a laboratory environment.

Disk and File Management

The hard disk on your system holds 30GB or more of data. Every CD-ROM has a capacity of 650 to 700 MB, while the capacity of DVD is considerably greater. All of this space is used to hold the various documents on your system that you worked so hard to create. But where exactly is your term paper located? Do you know how to create a ***backup*** copy that you can retrieve in the event that something happens to the original? Can you locate the group presentation that was sent to you as an e-mail attachment? Can you find the photograph that you downloaded from a Web site? In short, can you move and copy files with confidence? Suffice it to say that proficiency in disk and file management is one of the most important skills that you will acquire in this course.

A ***file*** is a set of instructions or data that has been given a name and stored on disk. There are two basic types of files, ***program files*** and ***data files***. Microsoft Word and Microsoft Excel are examples of program files. The documents and workbooks that are created by these programs are data files. Every file has a ***file name*** that identifies it to the operating system. The file name can contain up to 255 characters and may include spaces and other punctuation. Look closely at the right side of Figure 15 and you will see several data files, each with an icon to identify the associated program file. Note, too, the additional information that is displayed for each file—the file size, the type of file, and the date and time the file was created or last modified.

Files are kept in ***folders*** to better organize the thousands of files on a typical system. Many folders are created automatically by Windows such as the My Computer or My Documents folders that are present on every system. Other folders are created whenever new software is installed. Additional folders are created by the user to hold the documents he or she creates. You might, for example, create a folder for your word processing documents and a second folder for your spreadsheets. You could also create a folder to hold all of your work for a specific class, which in turn might contain a combination of word processing documents and spreadsheets. A folder can contain program files, data files, or even other folders.

Windows Explorer is the program used to move and copy files. The left pane of Windows Explorer displays a hierarchical (tree) structure of the devices on your

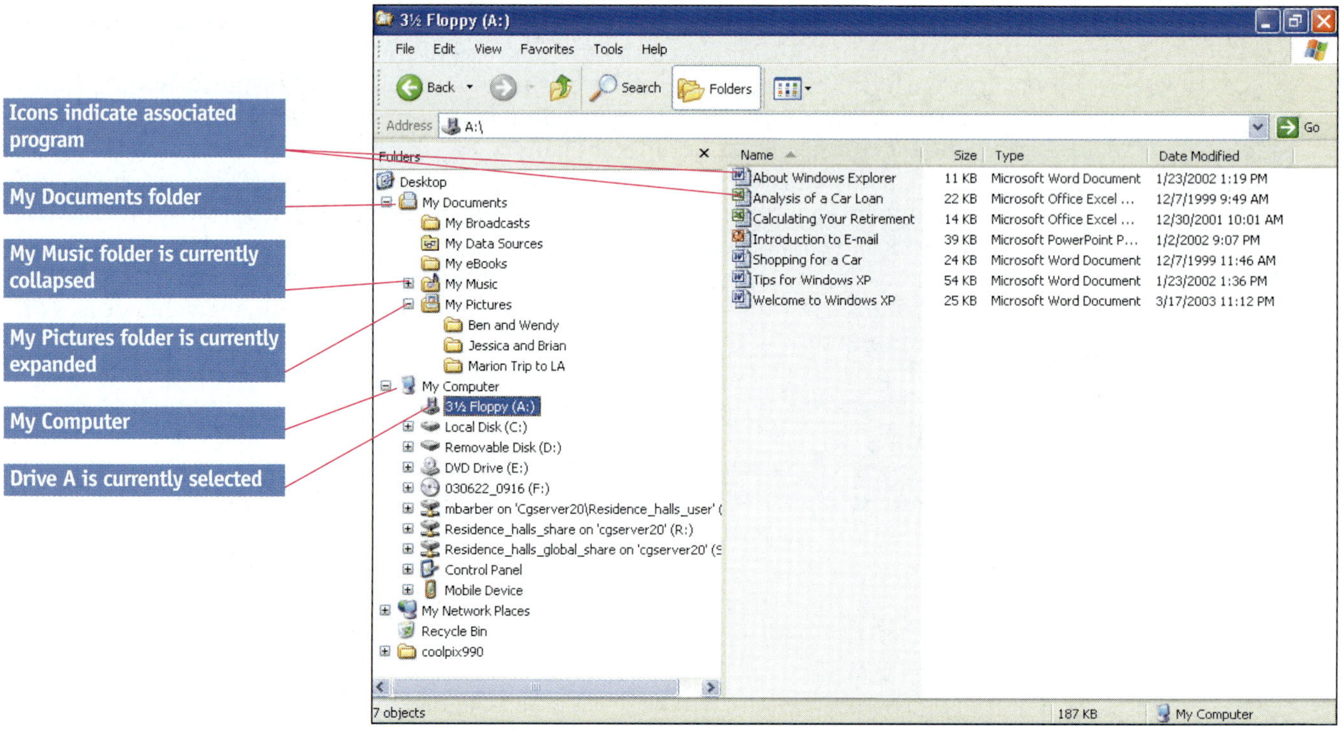

FIGURE 15 Disk and File Management

system. The desktop sits at the top of the hierarchy. The My Documents folder is found within the desktop, and it in turn contains several additional folders. The folders may be expanded (e.g., My Pictures) or collapsed (My Music). New folders can be created within My Documents or anywhere else on your hard drive(s).

The My Computer folder is also found within the desktop, and it provides access to the various devices on the system. Drive A (the floppy disk) is shaded to indicate that it is currently selected, and that its contents (data files created using programs in the Microsoft Office suite) are displayed in the right pane. Your instructor will most likely assign the various hands-on exercises in the Windows module (elsewhere in this text) so that you learn how to move and copy files efficiently. In the interim Figure 15 is intended as a brief introduction to the all-important topic of disk and file management.

Maintaining Your System

Students in a laboratory environment are almost invariably prevented from making changes to the system. If you have your own computer, however, you will need to become your own network administrator. You may have to add or remove hardware or software, and/or you may want to add another user (e.g., a younger sibling) with limited privileges. You may want to change the appearance of your desktop, modify the appearance of the taskbar or Start menu, or change the behavior of your mouse or keyboard. All of these functions are accomplished through the Control Panel as shown in Figure 16.

The ***Control Panel*** affects every aspect of your system as can be seen by the tools that are displayed in Figure 16. To make a change to your system, just double click the indicated tool and follow the onscreen prompts. Be very careful, however, and get help from a knowledgeable individual if you have any questions whatsoever. The Control Panel also provides access to the ***Windows Update*** function, which connects you to a Web site where you can download new device drivers and other updates to Windows XP. You can also configure your system to install these updates automatically as they become available. Some updates, especially those having to do with Internet security, are absolutely critical.

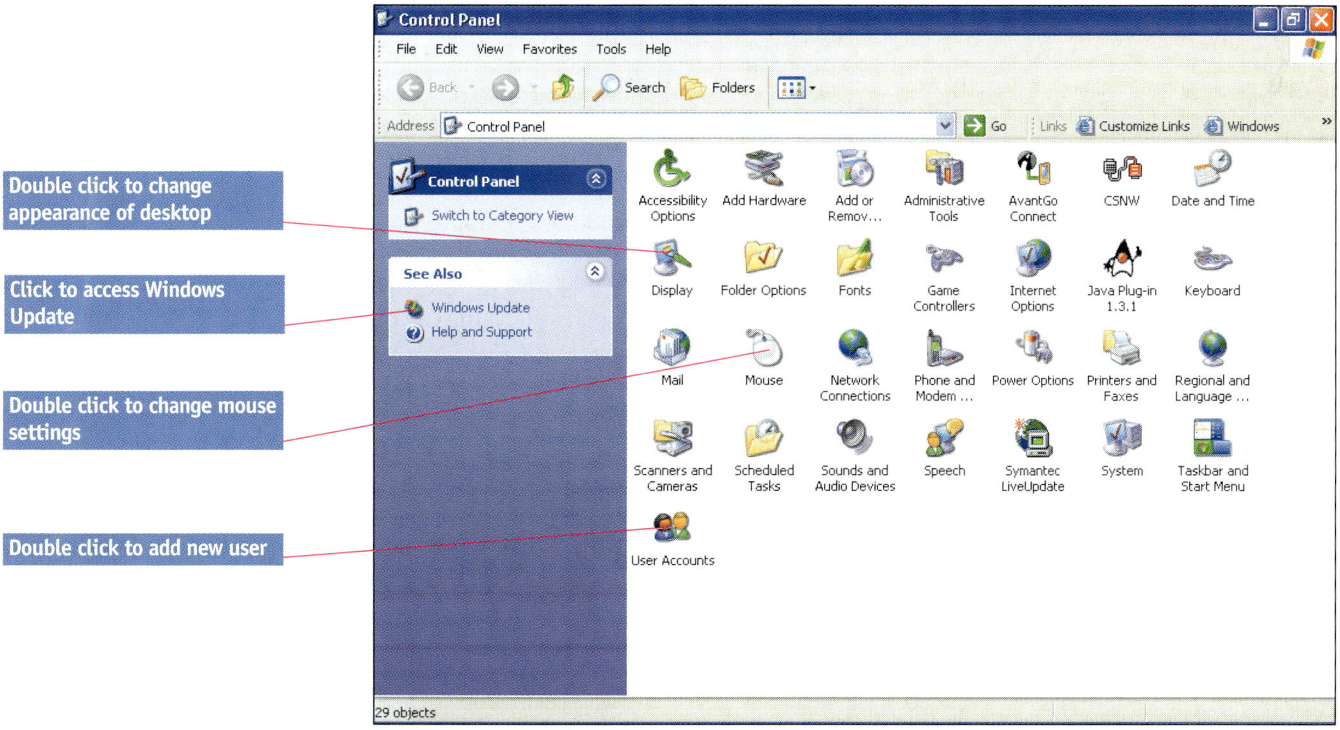

FIGURE 16 The Control Panel

WHAT WINDOWS DOESN'T HAVE

Microsoft® Windows consumes vast amounts of disk storage, yet it is missing three essential functions—antivirus protection, a graphical FTP (file transfer protocol) program, and an intuitive, easy-to-use file compression program. It would have been a simple matter for Microsoft to have included these functions (Microsoft DOS once included an antivirus program), but in the opinion of the authors the omission is deliberate and was done to avoid antitrust legislation.

Antivirus Software

A ***computer virus*** is an actively infectious program that attaches itself to various files and has the ability to alter the way your computer works. Worms and Trojan horses are different types of infectious programs, but for the purposes of this discussion we will classify all three as computer viruses; they are all bad and you want to avoid them. A computer virus, unlike a human virus, does not occur naturally. Instead, it is deliberately created by an individual who is intent on wrecking havoc.

A computer virus can corrupt the program and/or data files on a hard disk and in extreme instances erase every file on a system. The virus may or may not announce itself. The Stoned virus, for example, continually displays a message that your computer is stoned. Other viruses are silent and affect the computer's operation. Program execution may slow significantly or cease altogether. Unusual error messages may appear on your screen and/or you may run out of memory or disk space.

A virus is transmitted in two ways, from an infected floppy disk or via a file that was downloaded from the Internet. Once a system is infected, the typical virus can copy itself onto every floppy disk that is put into your floppy drive, which in turn can infect other computers if the same disk is used elsewhere.

The Internet is even more of a threat because the typical user is online several hours a day. You can download infected files or more commonly receive infected attachments to e-mail messages. You don't even have to write the e-mail yourself, because the most malicious virus will mail itself to everyone in your address book.

The best way to protect your system is through the installation of an ***antivirus program*** that can automatically detect a virus should it threaten your system. Many such programs are available, but their effectiveness depends on continual updating since new viruses appear all the time. The software vendor typically includes a limited subscription to automatic updates to detect new viruses. Once the subscription expires, however, it is incumbent on you to renew it.

Viruses are often spread through ignorance or sheer laziness. Students may say that they do not have the time to update their antivirus program and/or that they cannot afford the cost of the update. If you are prone to think this way, ask yourself how much time it will take to reformat your hard drive if a virus destroys your system. What if the virus permanently destroys an important document such as the term paper you need to graduate? What is the value of your time and/or your documents?

IS YOUR PROTECTION UP TO DATE?

Try this simple classroom test. Take a show of hands to see how many students have an antivirus program installed on their home computer. Our guess is that the vast majority will respond in the affirmative. Now ask your classmates how many have updated their protection in the last week or two. Our guess is that the number of positive responses will be much less. In other words, most of your classmates are operating under a false sense of security, thinking that their systems are protected, when in fact they are susceptible to the most recent (and often the most virulent) computer virus.

File Transfer Protocol (FTP)

File Transfer Protocol (FTP) specifies the rules by which files are sent and received across the Internet. In essence, it lets you log onto a remote computer, browse through one or more folders (directories) on that computer until you find the file you are looking for, then download that file to your computer. You use FTP every time you click on a link in your Internet browser to download a file from the Web to your PC. Uploading a file requires a little more effort, and you will want to acquire a graphical FTP program as shown in Figure 17. The left pane of the screen shows the files and folders on your computer. The right pane displays the files and folders on the FTP server. You select a file (or folder) in either pane, then you click the appropriate arrow to upload or download the file as necessary.

You may upload a file for several reasons—for example, to share photographs with friends and family, to store a backup copy of important files at a remote site, and/or to upload Web pages to an Internet server, where they can be viewed through a browser such as Internet Explorer or Netscape Navigator. Most sites require a username and password to gain access to the FTP server. Some FTP servers, however, make files freely available to the general public and provide access through anonymous FTP. It's anonymous because you log on by typing "anonymous" instead of a user name, and you supply your e-mail address as the password.

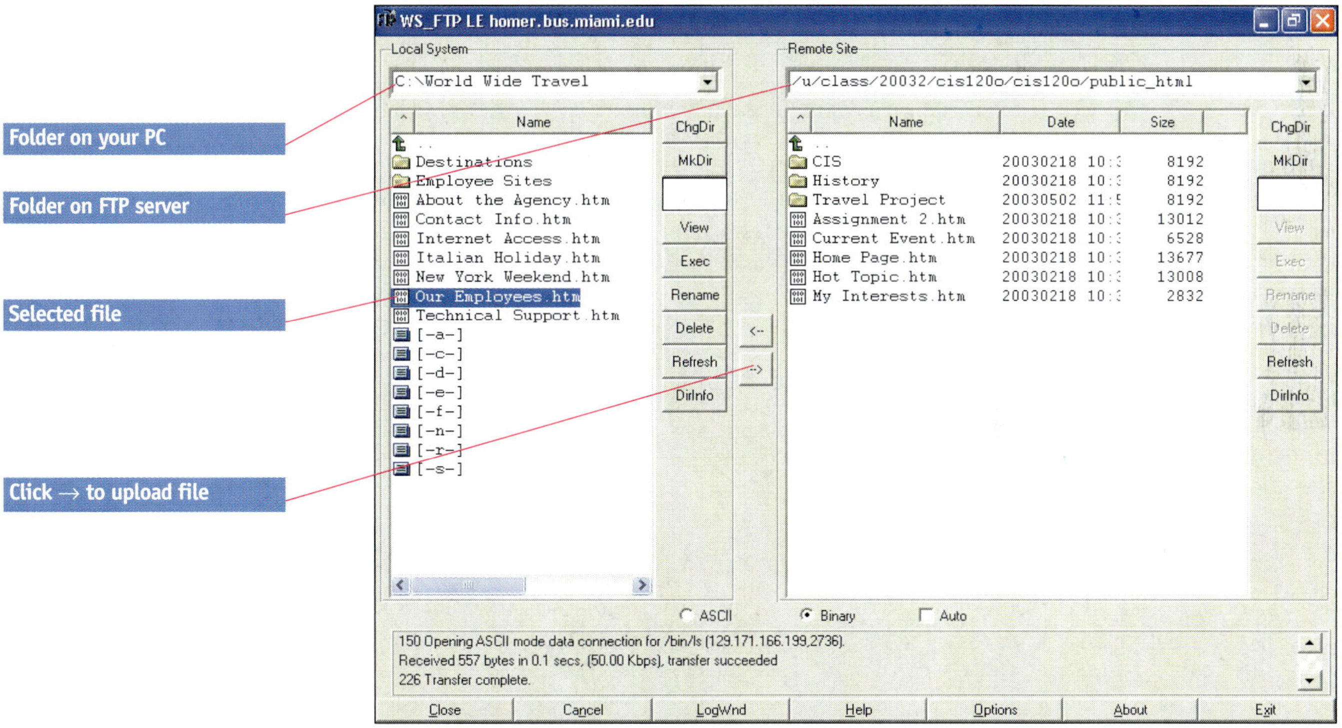

FIGURE 17 FTP (File Transfer Protocol)

BACK UP YOUR DATA

How much would you pay for another copy of your term paper or company project that just disappeared from your hard drive? It's not a question of *if* it will happen, but *when*—hard disks die, files are lost, or viruses may infect a system. We urge you, therefore, to back up your data to prepare for the inevitable. Our strategy is very simple—back up what you can't afford to lose at the end of every session, and store the backup away from your computer. FTP is an ideal way to send the files offsite for safekeeping.

File Compression

Files are often compressed (zipped) to reduce their size, especially when sending a file via e-mail or FTP. ***File compression*** also lets you place multiple documents into a single ***compressed file*** (called an ***archive***), enabling you to send or receive a single file, after which the compressed files can be extracted and accessed individually. It's a lot easier than having to **send** and receive multiple files one at a time.

Compression algorithms are very sophisticated, and the details of how they work are beyond this discussion. What is important is that you understand the concept of file compression and the advantage of creating a ***self-extracting file***, as opposed to a simple archive. Figure 18a illustrates a two-stage compression process (the second step is optional). Step 1 uses a file compression program to place three individual files (that total 500KB in size) into a single compressed file of 100KB. Step 2 takes the compressed file (archive) that was just created and runs it through the compression program a second time to create a self-extracting file of 125KB. The latter is slightly larger than the original compressed file, but it is still significantly smaller than the combined size of the individual files.

Figures 18b and 18c illustrate two different ways in which the individual files within the compressed file are extracted. Figure 18b extracts the individual files from the archive, but it requires a file compression program to do so. (This is a potential problem because a compression program is *not* built into all versions of Windows. Windows XP does include file compression, but it is not as easy or intuitive to use as the well-known WinZip or equivalent program.) Figure 18c shows that the files can be extracted automatically without the need for the compression program if the user was given a self-extracting file.

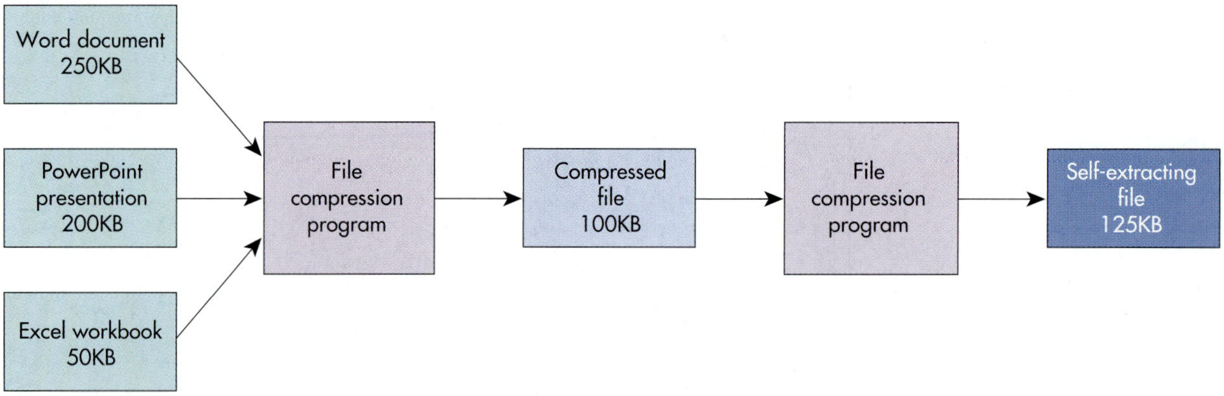

(a) File Compression

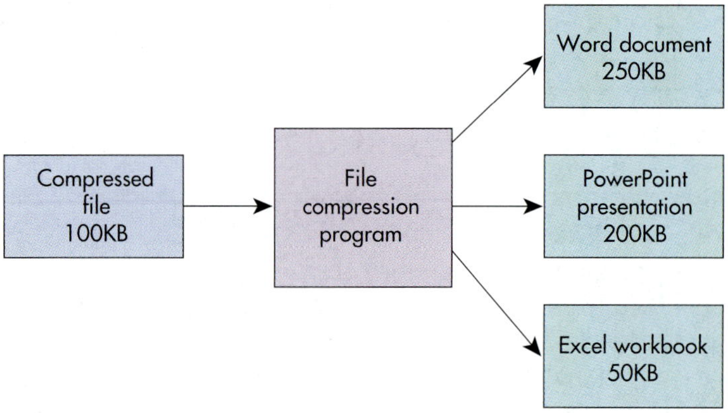

(b) Uncompressing a File

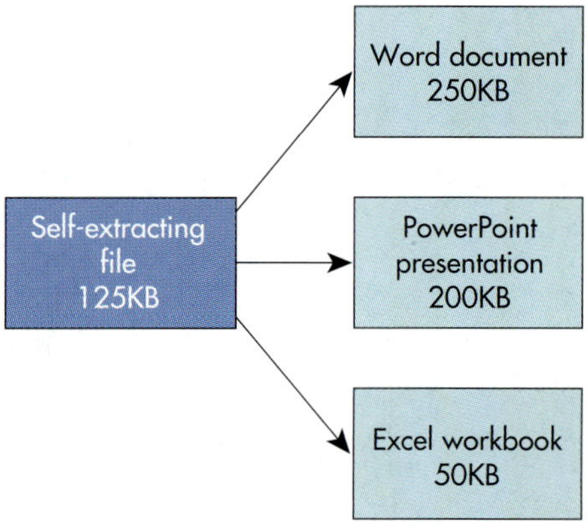

(c) Self-extracting File

FIGURE 18 File Compression

Microsoft Office 2003 contains the same four core applications as each of its predecessors—***Word, Excel, Access,*** and ***PowerPoint.*** The suite is published in multiple editions, which can lead to unpleasant surprises. Not every edition, for example, contains PowerPoint or Access, and most editions contain additional programs such as Outlook, FrontPage, Publisher, InfoPath, or OneNote (the latter two applications are new in Office 2003). Microsoft has also added the word "Office" to the official name of each application—for example, "Microsoft Office Word 2003" to emphasize that the application belongs to the Office family of products.

This section describes the similarities between the core applications in Microsoft Office, where you will find the same commands in the same menus, you will see the same toolbar buttons from one application to the next, and you will be able to take advantage of the same keyboard shortcuts. Figure 19 displays a screen from each core application in Office—Word, Excel, PowerPoint, and Access, in Figures 19a, 19b, 19c, and 19d, respectively. Look closely at Figure 19, and realize that each screen contains both an application window and a document window, and that each document window has been maximized within the application window. The title bars of the application and document windows have been merged into a single title bar that appears at the top of the application window. The title bar displays the application (e.g., Microsoft Office Word 2003 in Figure 19a) as well as the name of the document on which you are working.

All four screens in Figure 19 are similar in appearance even though the applications accomplish very different tasks. Each application window has an identifying icon, a menu bar, a title bar, and a Minimize, a Maximize or Restore, and a Close button. Each document window has its own Close button. The status bar displays information relevant to the window or selected object.

The applications in Microsoft Office have a consistent command structure in which the same basic menus (the File, Edit, View, Format, Insert, Tools, Window, and Help menus) are present in each application. In addition, the same commands are found in the same menus. The Save, Open, Print, and Exit commands, for example, are contained in the File menu. The Cut, Copy, Paste, and Undo commands are found in the Edit menu.

The means for accessing the pull-down menus are consistent from one application to the next. Click the menu name on the menu bar, or press the Alt key plus the underlined letter of the menu name; for example, press Alt+F to pull down the File menu. If you already know some keyboard shortcuts in one application, there is a good chance that the shortcuts will work in another application. Ctrl+Home and Ctrl+End, for example, move to the beginning and end of a document, respectively. Ctrl+B and Ctrl+I denote boldface and italics, respectively.

All four applications use consistent (and often identical) dialog boxes. The dialog boxes to open and close a file, for example, are identical in every application. All four applications also share a common dictionary that is accessed whenever a spell check is executed.

There are, of course, differences between the applications. Each application has its own unique menus and associated toolbars. Nevertheless, the Standard and Formatting toolbars contain many of the same tools (especially the first several tools on the left of each toolbar). The ***Standard toolbar*** contains buttons for basic commands such as Open, Save, and Print. It also contains buttons to cut, copy, and paste, and all of these buttons are identical in all four applications. The ***Formatting toolbar*** provides access to common formatting operations such as boldface, italic, or underlining, or changing the font or point size, and again, these buttons are identical in all four applications. ScreenTips that identify the purpose of a tool are present in all applications. Suffice it to say, therefore, that once you know one Office application, you have a tremendous head start in learning another. You can also use help at any time in any application.

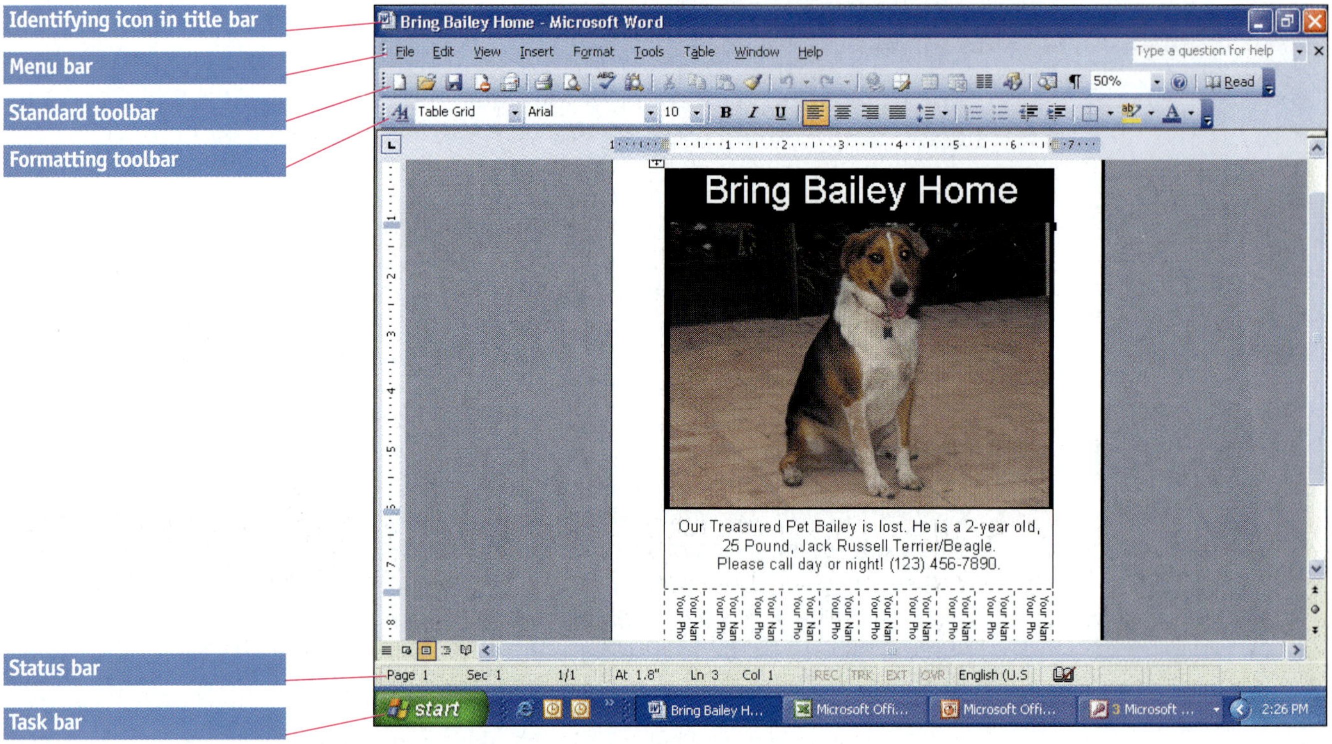

(a) Microsoft Office Word 2003

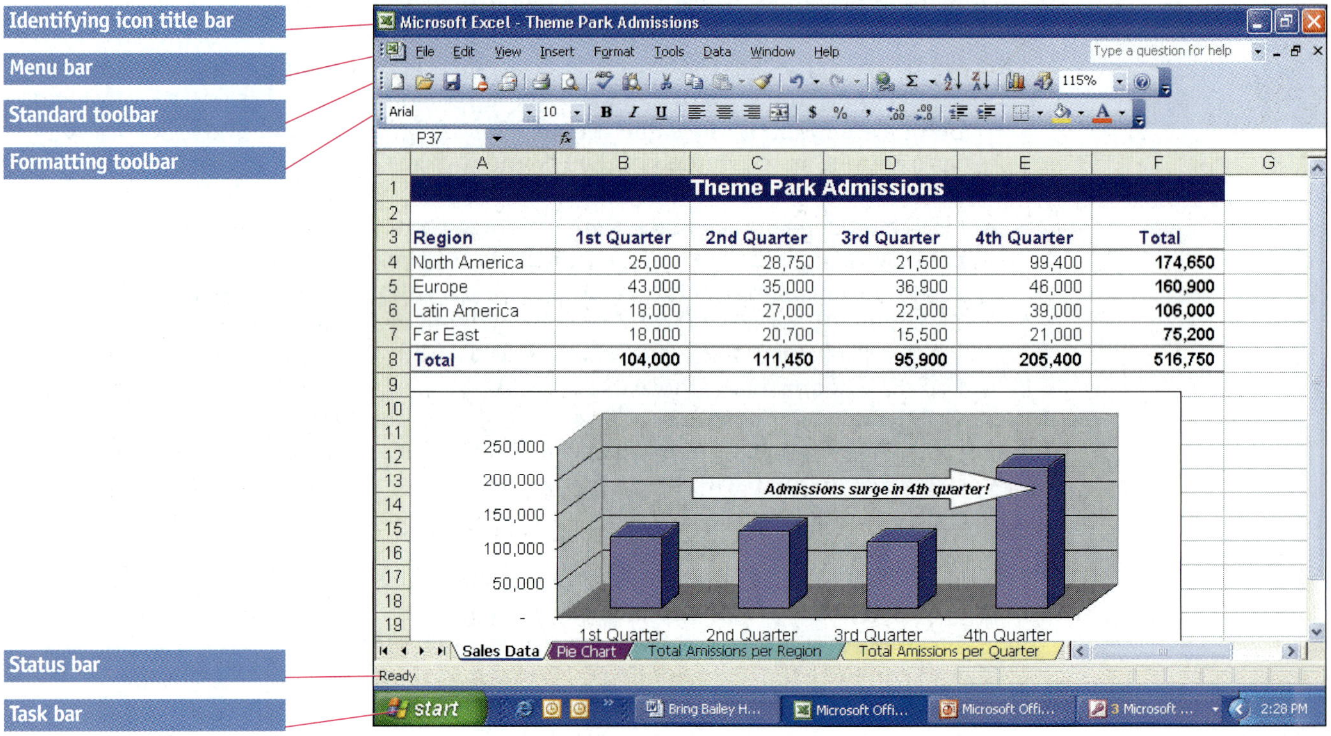

(b) Microsoft Office Excel 2003

FIGURE 19 Microsoft Office 2003 Core Applications

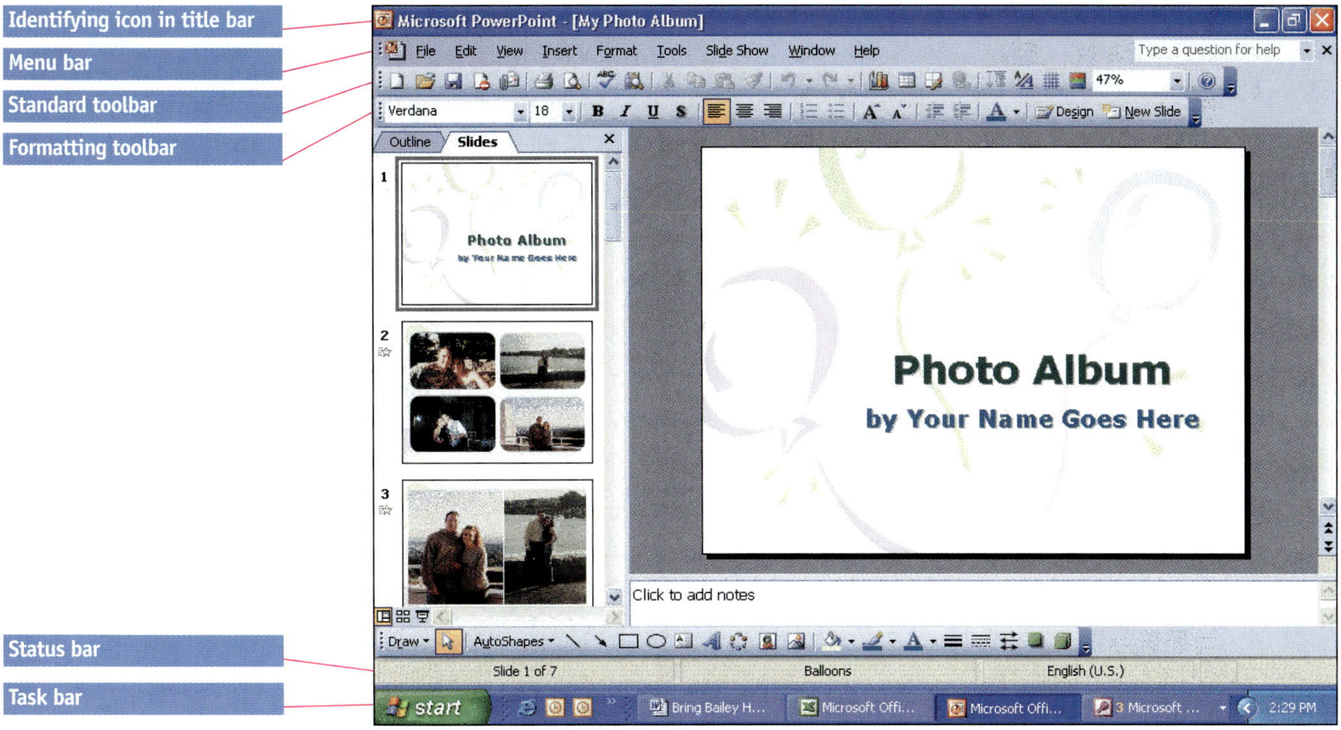

(c) Microsoft Office PowerPoint 2003

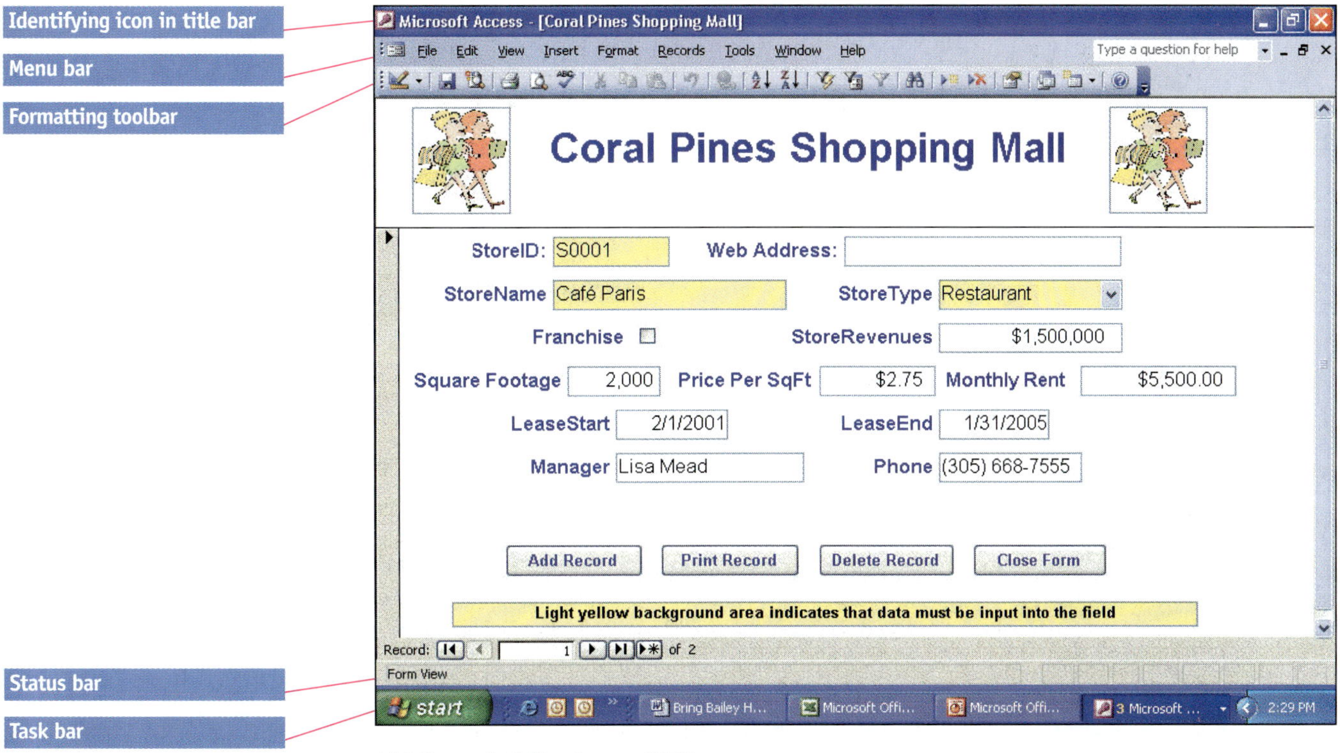

(d) Microsoft Office Access 2003

FIGURE 19 Microsoft Office 2003 Core Applications (*continued*)

Microsoft Office Outlook 2003

Microsoft Outlook is an integral part of Microsoft Office, although it is not considered one of the core applications. You can think of Outlook as a personal assistant whose job it is to keep track of all types of information for you. You can use Outlook to maintain an address book, schedule appointments, write notes to yourself, or send and receive e-mail. (The e-mail functions of Outlook are described in more detail on pages 48–50.)

We like to begin each session by reviewing the Outlook Today screen as shown in Figure 20. This screen provides an overview of our activity for the week by displaying a calendar, a "to do" list that consists of various tasks we have entered, and the status of our mail folders. The mail folders themselves are listed in the left pane. The left pane also contains links to various other functions that include a calendar, contacts, tasks, notes, and a journal.

The Calendar function enables you to create a detailed appointment book and to display those appointments in different views (daily, weekly, or monthly). You can create recurring appointments (e.g., the same class or weekly appointment), and you can instruct Outlook to remind you a few minutes before each appointment. You can also print your appointment book and take it with you.

The Contacts function maintains a detailed address book, which in turn is linked to other functions in Microsoft Office. You store an individual's name, title, one or more addresses (e.g., business and home), and one or more phone numbers (home, business, fax, and cell). There is also room for multiple e-mail addresses, a Web address, a person's birthday and anniversary, even those of the spouse.

The Journal can be set to record all of the activity on your system by generating an entry every time you access an Office document. The Notes function enables you to create the electronic equivalent of the ubiquitous yellow "post-it-note" that can be left open on the screen as you work. The task list is an effective way to organize the work you have to do. A task is simpler than an appointment (in the calendar) in that it is not associated with a specific date or time; the Tasks folder is nothing more than a simple "to do" list.

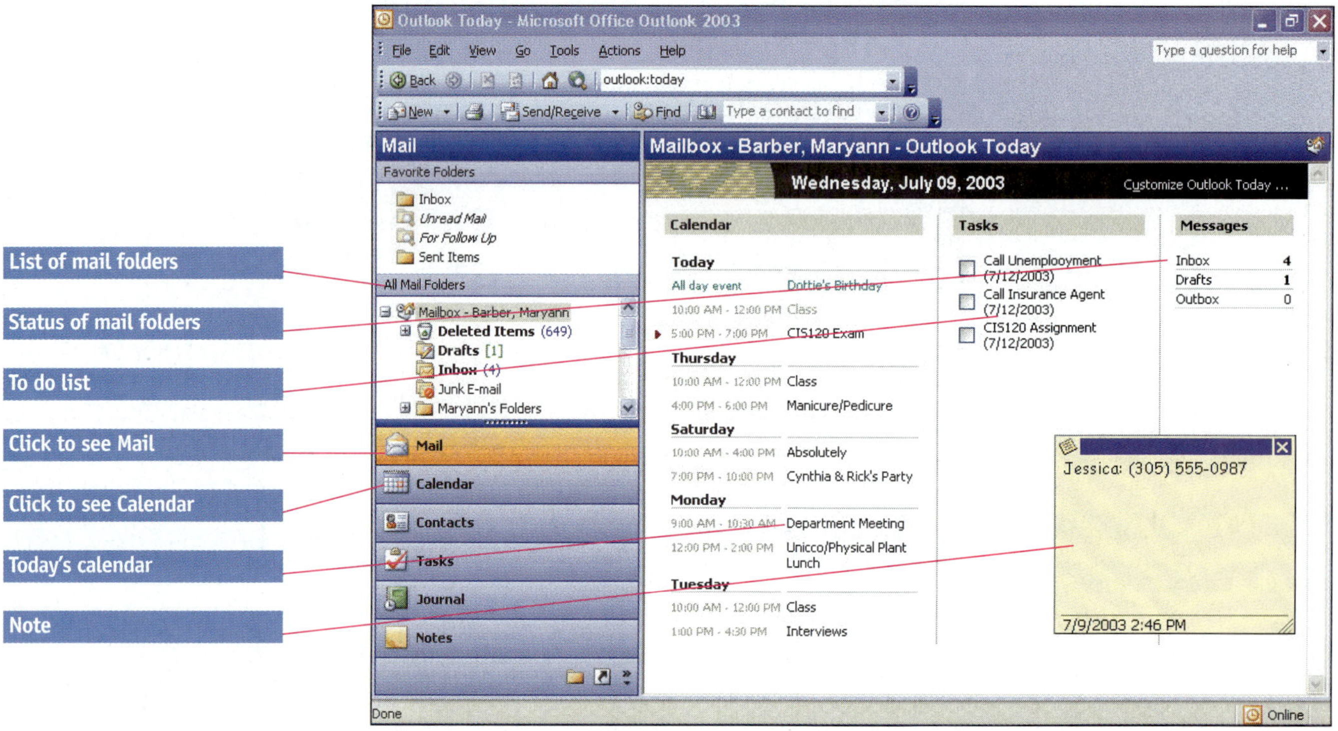

FIGURE 20 Microsoft Office Outlook 2003

Microsoft Office FrontPage® 2003

The Save as Web Page command enables you to create a Web page in Word, Excel, or PowerPoint. Why, then, would you use ***Microsoft FrontPage***, an entirely separate application in Microsoft Office? The answer can be seen by looking at Figure 21, which shows how FrontPage is designed to create a Web site, as opposed to a single Web page.

The navigation pane at the left shows the organization of the site, which currently contains a total of 16 pages, all of which are the same visual design. The Home page is at the top of the hierarchy. The News, Products, and Services pages are subservient to the Home page, whereas the Feedback, Contents, and Search pages are on the same level as the Home page.

The Home page (index.htm) for the site is shown in Design view in the right pane. The content has not yet been entered (note the under construction logo), but the navigation is complete. The navigation bar at the top of the page contains hyperlinks to the Feedback, Contents, and Search pages, and it will appear at the top of every page of the site. A second navigation bar provides hyperlinks to the News, Products, and Services pages, each of which has a navigation bar of its own. Note how these navigation bars are consistent with the layout of the entire site as shown in the left pane.

It took approximately five minutes to create the site that you see in Figure 21 using a wizard provided by FrontPage. The hard part (the navigation and site design) is done for you. You can keep the navigation, but change the look by using the Format Theme command to apply a different visual design. You can also start over and use a different wizard to create an entirely different Web site. You can also add new pages or delete existing pages at any time.

Once you settle on the overall design of the site, it is now a relatively simple matter to complete the individual pages by adding text and other elements as necessary. Look closely and you will see that the menus and toolbars in FrontPage are consistent with the other applications in Microsoft Office. FrontPage is not one of the core applications in Microsoft Office, but it should be given strong consideration any time you need to design a Web site.

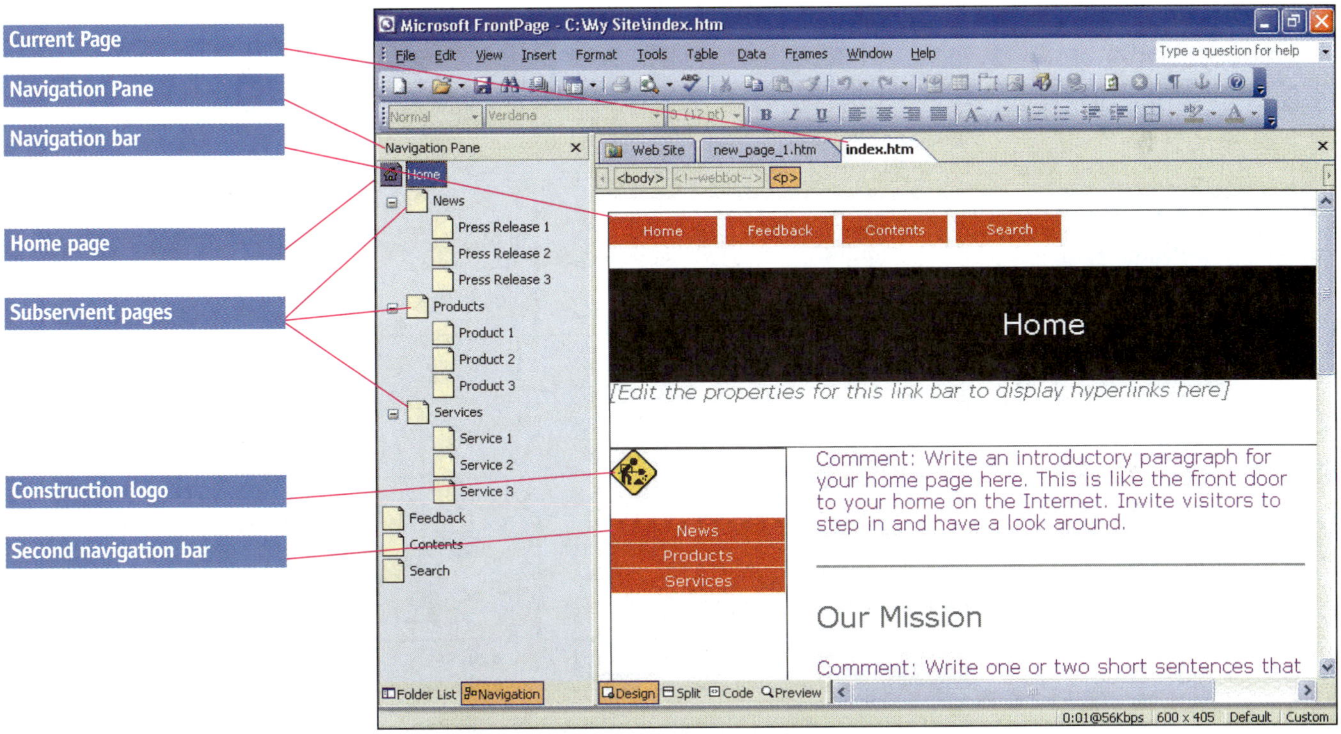

FIGURE 21 Microsoft Office FrontPage 2003

Microsoft Office Publisher 2003

Microsoft Word enables you to create virtually any type of document, with full formatting, clip art, and photographs. ***Microsoft Publisher*** takes desktop publishing one step further by providing a wide selection of documents and templates from which to choose. It enables you to create a variety of professional-looking publications without reliance on graphic designers or other services.

Publisher is ideal for any type of business communication, as it facilitates a uniform look across multiple publications through a series of templates or Master Design Sets. Each set contains the same design (logo and color scheme) for common publications such as newsletters, flyers, postcards, CD/DVD labels, and other publications. You will also find new Web site wizards, such as the Easy Web Site Builder or the E-mail Wizard to create an electronic newsletter. Additional templates are provided for stationery, greeting cards, and invitations. Publisher also includes multiple easy-builder or quick-start template guides to help create new publications quickly and easily.

Publisher is also easier to use than Microsoft Word because its templates guide you as to where to place text, pictures, and/or other objects on the page. You can customize the color scheme or font selection and/or change the layout according to your preference or organization's requirements. You can publish a completed document in multiple ways—for example, to your printer, on the Web, or as an e-mail attachment. You can also take the file to a commercial printer to publish in quantity. Publisher enables rich color and photo reproduction and advanced printing options such as a full-page bleed (running color to the edge of a page). It also provides full support for the four-color commercial printing process.

Publisher is not one of the core Office applications, but it does have the same "look and feel" of the other applications. Figure 22 shows two variations (Banner Bar and Compass Point) for the We've Moved Design Set. Each design contains three documents. Select a design, and then a document within the design, and then add your custom text to complete the document. It's fun, it's easy, and your documents will never look better.

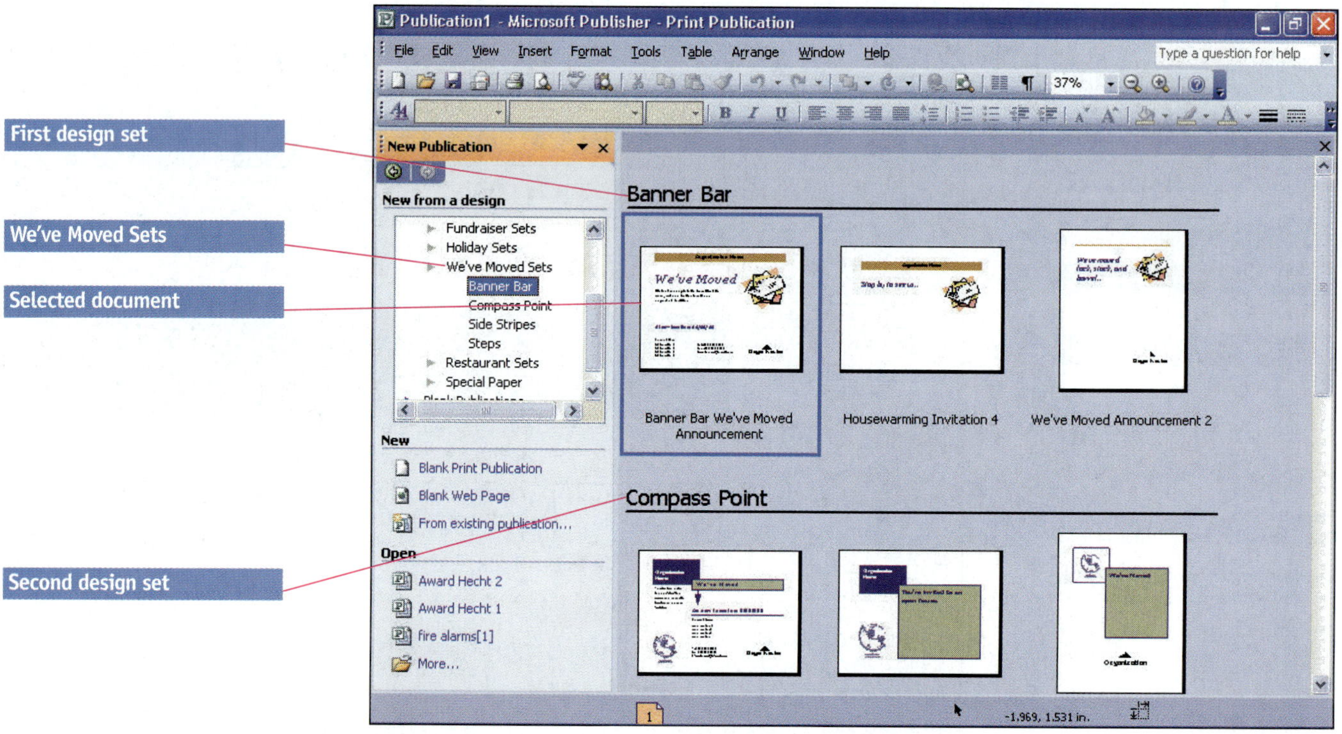

FIGURE 22 Microsoft Office Publisher 2003

Microsoft Office OneNote™ 2003

Everyone takes notes, whether it is in school, at a meeting, or simply doodling on a napkin in a restaurant. ***Microsoft Office OneNote 2003*** is a new application in the Microsoft Office suite that helps you to take notes, and then organize and reuse that information as necessary. It can be used with a Tablet PC to capture handwritten information, but it is just as effective with a notebook or desktop PC. OneNote can be installed with Office 2003, or it can be installed as a stand-alone application. It is different from the other Office applications in that it is used to create a "work product," which is designed to help a user gather information, as opposed to creating a finished document.

Figure 23 displays the OneNote notebook. You see the title bar and menu bar, followed by the Standard and Formatting toolbars, just as in other Office applications. The rest of the screen is divided into the title pane and the input area. The title pane contains the name of the notebook (My Notebook is the default) followed by the sections (tabs) within the notebook. You can have as many sections as you want, and each section can contain multiple pages. We are looking at page 2 in the Meetings section. The title of this page (Residence Hall Opening Meeting) appears on the title bar of the application. The date and time are entered for you automatically when the page is created. The rest of the page contains a variety of notes.

Taking notes is easy; just click anywhere on the page and start to type. You can apply basic formatting as you do in Word or PowerPoint—for example, bold, italic, or underlining; numbered or bulleted lists; different fonts and point sizes; font colors; highlighting; and so on. You can check spelling, move and copy text, or search for a specific character string.

OneNote also provides alternate ways to enter information on the page; for example, you can use the pen tool to draw on the page. You can also use the microphone to record external audio in conjunction with your notes. The audio is linked to and synchronized with your notes, so that you can re-create what was being said in a room at the time you were taking notes. In other words, you can take notes in the traditional way by entering text using the keyboard, but you can play back the audio at a later time to fill in the details of anything you may have missed.

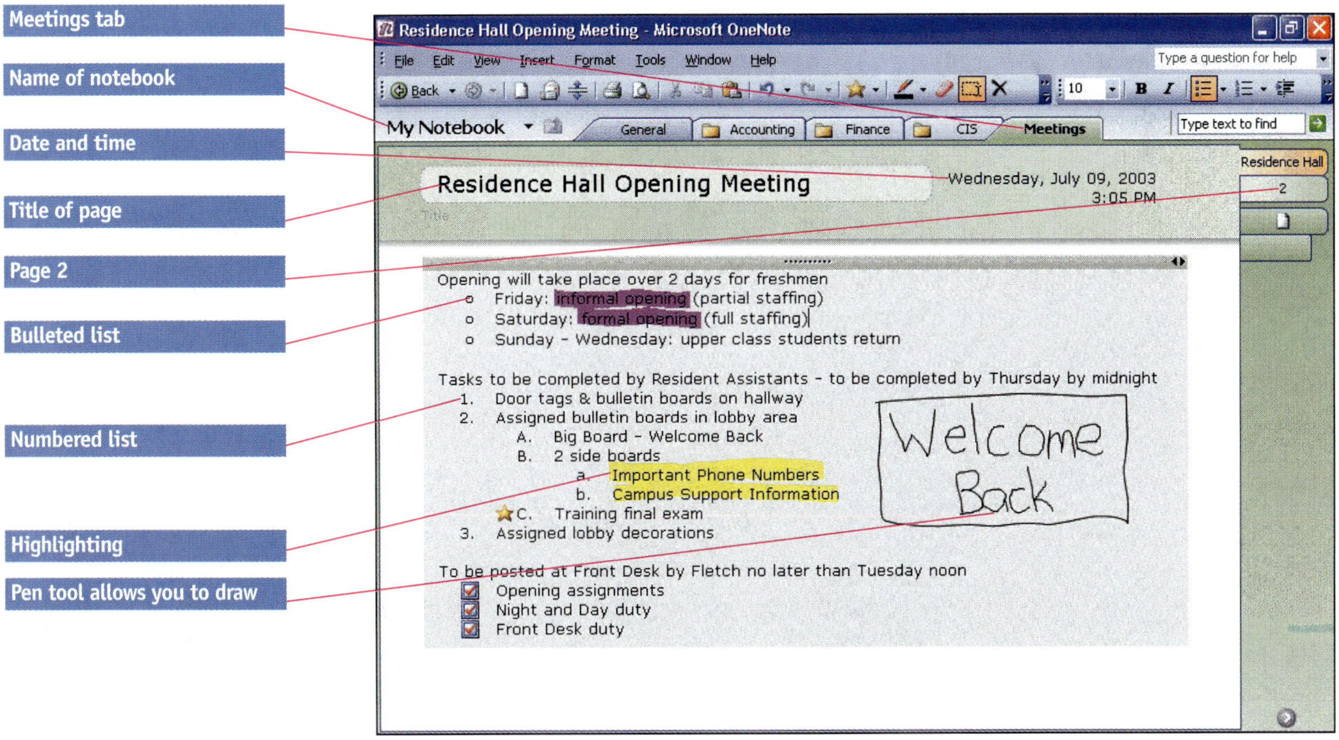

FIGURE 23 Microsoft Office OneNote 2003

Microsoft Office InfoPath 2003

Data is a valuable resource to an organization and is used over and over within an organization. ***Microsoft Office InfoPath 2003*** is a new application within Microsoft Office that simplifies the way data is captured. It enables a developer to develop a form that uses Microsoft Office as a "front end" to capture the data, and then it stores that data in XML format for use throughout the organization. You can think of XML as a "universal data format" that enables data to be captured once, and then used in any application. Thus, you cannot appreciate what InfoPath is trying to accomplish unless you have a basic understanding of ***XML (Extensible Markup Language)***.

XML is not to be confused with ***HTML (Hypertext Markup Language)***, which has only one purpose: to display a document within a browser. HTML describes how a document should look, and it has only a finite set of tags—for example, <B> and <UL>, for bold and underlining, respectively. XML is much more general. It describes the data, rather than the appearance of the data, and it has an infinite number of tags as defined by different developers for different applications. Consider:

HTML:	**XML:**
<B>John Doe</B>	<name>
	<first>John</first>
	<last>Doe</last>
	</name>

The HTML code tells us that "John Doe" will appear in boldface, but it does not tell us anything more. We don't know that "John" is the first name or that "Doe" is the last name. XML (Extensible Markup Language), on the other hand, is "data about data." You can see at a glance that it is conveying information about a name, and that there is a first name and a last name, within the name. The real advantage of XML, however, is that it is easily expanded (extensible) to include additional information about a person's name, such as "Mr. John Doe", "John J. Doe", or "Mr. John J. Doe Junior". We just extend the definition of the elements within the name to include the additional data, and then we mark up the data accordingly. Each application has access to the entire definition (schema), but it can include only those fields that are needed by the specific application. Thus:

Mr. John J. Doe Junior	**Jessica Elana Benjamin**
<name>	<name>
<prefix>Mr.</prefix>	<prefix></prefix>
<first>John</first>	<first>Jessica</first>
<middle>J.</middle>	<middle>Elana</middle>
<last>Doe</last>	<last>Benjamin</last>
<suffix>Junior</suffix>	<suffix></suffix>
<entirename></entirename>	<entirename></entirename>
</name>	</name>

Figure 24a displays the Design view of an Expense Account form as it is developed in InfoPath. The application has the same look and feel as the other applications in Microsoft Office. One sees the Standard and Formatting toolbars toward the top of the window and the task pane open at the right of the window. The latter displays the data source and shows the various fields that are available within the expenseReport definition. The employee field contains a name and an address field, each of which has multiple fields available. The developer has chosen to include the singleName field, as opposed to separating the first and last name.

Figure 24b displays the completed form as seen by the user. Jessica Benjamin completes her expense report and saves the completed form. The latter generates an XML document that contains data independent of the way it is presented in a form.

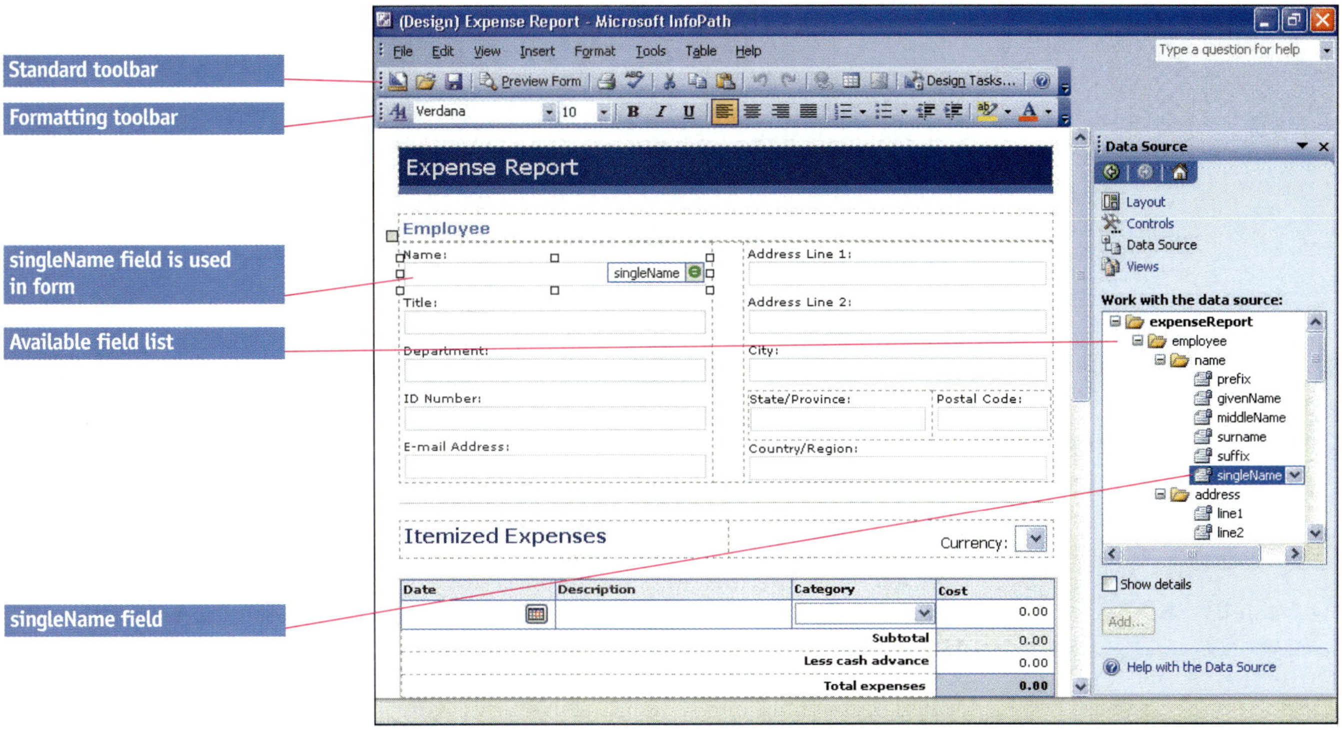

(a) Design View

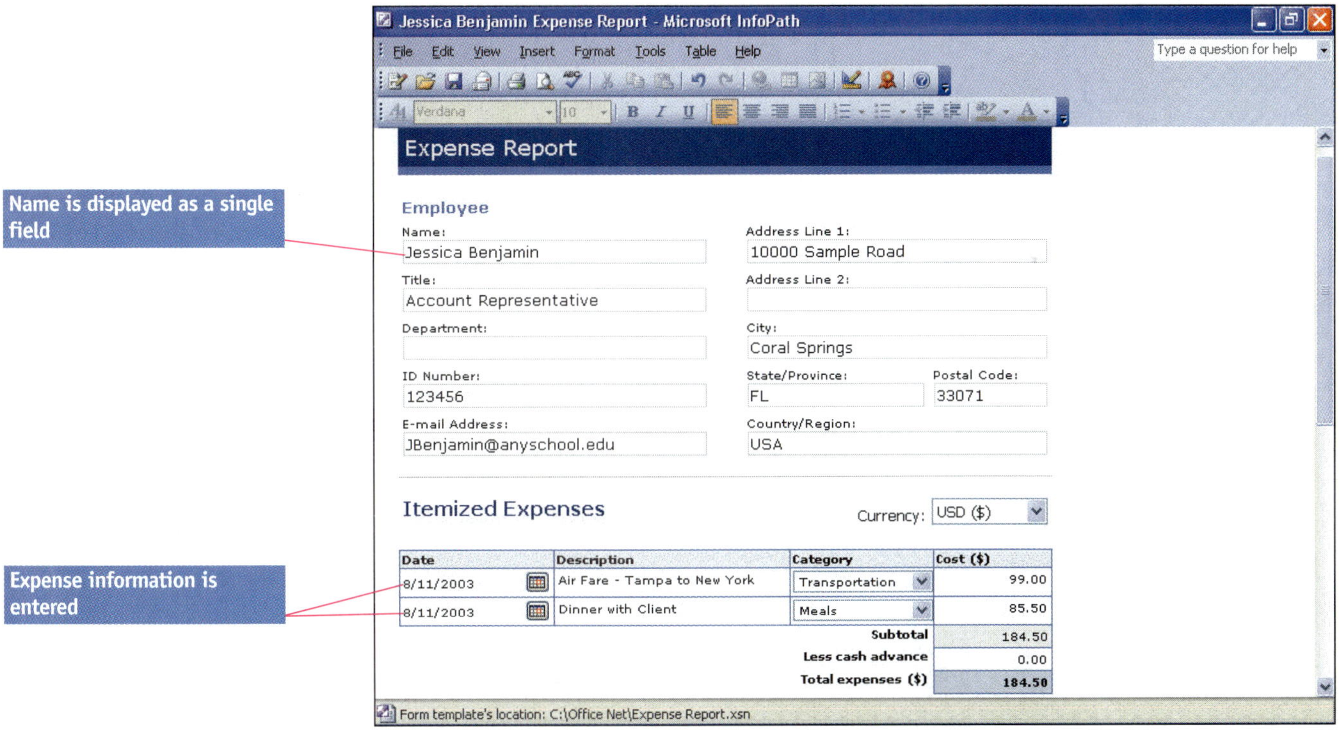

(b) User's View

FIGURE 24 Microsoft Office InfoPath 2003

INTRODUCTION TO NETWORKS

A ***network*** is a combination of hardware and software that enables the connected computers to share resources and communicate with one another. A ***local area network*** (or ***LAN***) connects its computers, typically (PCs), over short distances of a mile or two. A LAN may be created within a home or office, a building or adjacent buildings, or across a college campus. A ***wide area network*** (or ***WAN***) is similar in concept except that its computers are separated by significantly longer distances. A WAN may span an entire country or cross several continents.

The idea behind any network is very simple: to enable the connected computers, called workstations or nodes, to share resources. The home network in Figure 25a consists of two computers that share one printer and a common Internet connection. The computers may be connected to one another through the telephone wiring that is already in your home, through twisted pair wiring or coaxial cable, and/or the connection may be wireless. It doesn't matter—what is important is that the computers can communicate directly with one another to share resources, that both computers have access to the common printer, and that both computers have access to the Internet. The latter is accomplished through a ***router***, a device that sends data from the LAN to the Internet, and which directs (routes) the data received from the Internet to the appropriate computer on the network.

The local area network in Figure 25b is typical of what you might find in a computer lab at school or in a corporate office. There are many more workstations than the home network, and while it is possible to wire all of the computers to one another, it is much easier to connect each computer to a central hub, which has several ports or network connections. The hub is connected to a ***gateway*** that enables the LAN to communicate with other networks. The gateway may also include a ***firewall*** that enables computers on the LAN outside access, but prevents computers outside the LAN from gaining access to the network.

The local area network in Figure 25b also has two dedicated computers (servers) that perform tasks for the network as a whole. The printer server manages the printing for the entire network and enables every workstation to use either of the two network printers—a high-speed laser printer or an ink-jet color printer. The file server controls access to data and/or application software; to use a network application on your workstation, you click the icon to load the program, which issues a request to the server. The ***file server*** in turn verifies that you are permitted access to the program, then it loads the application into your PC's memory, and the application appears on your screen.

The wide area network in Figure 25c is composed of multiple local area networks and/or mainframe computers. The disparate networks are connected by different physical media such as microwave or radio signals, fiber optic cable, or satellites. Microwave and radio signals travel only in a straight line and thus have to be relayed several times by repeater stations (think of the radio towers that you have seen at the tops of tall buildings or mountains) before reaching their destination. Satellites eliminate this "line of site" limitation because microwaves can be bounced off satellites and avoid the obstructions on the surface of the earth.

CHOOSE YOUR PASSWORD CAREFULLY

A good password should be easy to remember but difficult to break. One way of creating such a password is to think of a sentence and use the first letter in each word to create the password; for example, "My wife's birthday is March 23", yields MwbiM23 as a password. The password may look like a series of random characters, but it should be easy for you to remember since you created the sentence in the first place. This technique yields passwords with upper- and lowercase letters as well as numbers, making it even more difficult to guess.

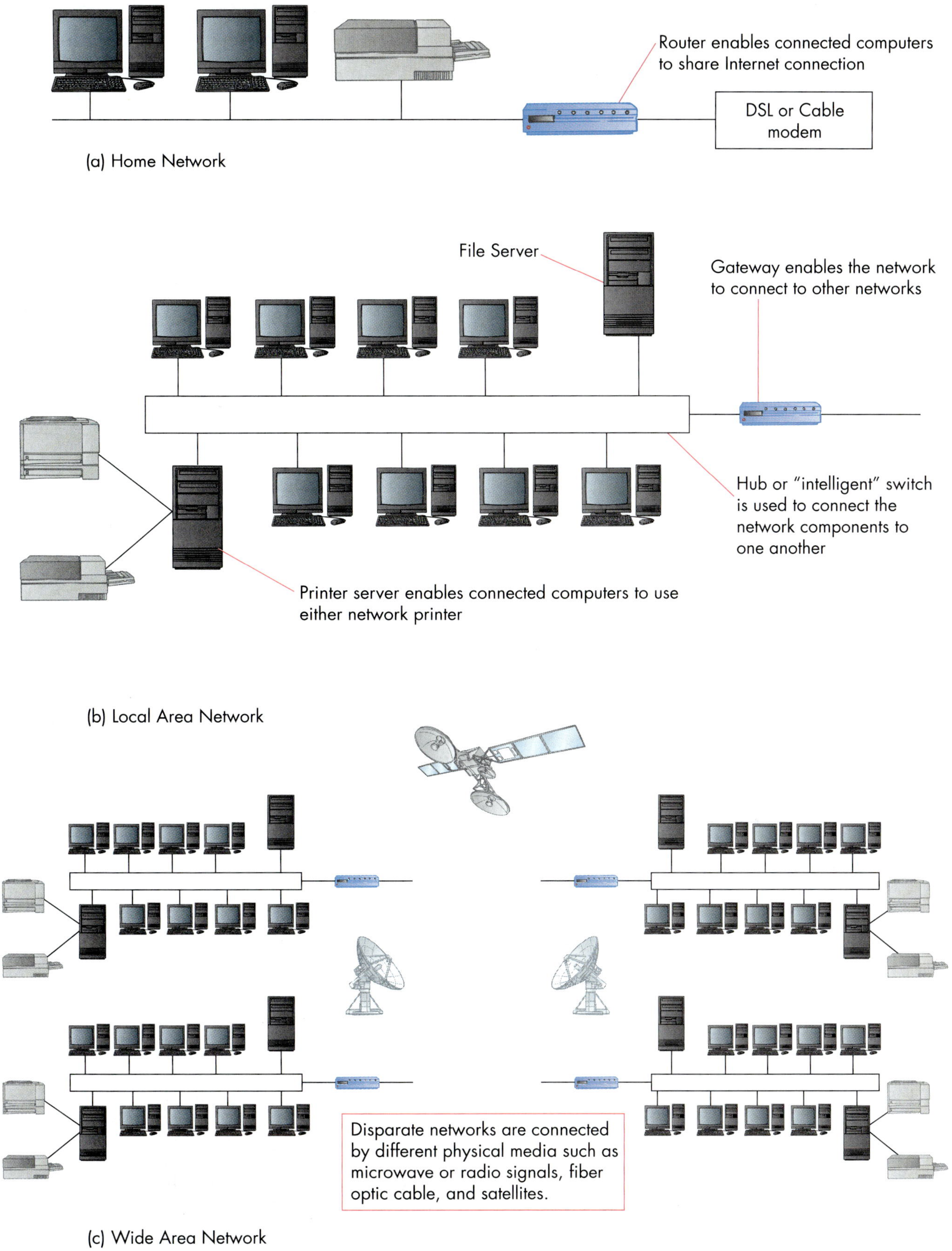

FIGURE 25 From LAN to WAN

THE INTERNET AND WORLD WIDE WEB

The ***Internet*** is a network of networks that spans the globe. It grew out of a government project that began in 1969 to test the feasibility of a network where scientists and military personnel could share messages and data no matter where they were. The original network consisted of only four computers. Today, there are literally millions of computers with an Internet connection (the exact number is impossible to determine) and tens of millions of people with Internet access.

Yes, the Internet is a collection of networks, but if that were all it was, there would hardly be so much commotion. It's what you can do on the Internet, coupled with the ease of access that makes the Internet so exciting. In essence, the Internet provides two basic capabilities, information retrieval and worldwide communication, functions that are already provided by libraries and print media, the postal system and the telephone, television, and other types of long-distance media. The difference is that the Internet is interactive in nature, and more importantly, it is both global and immediate. The Internet enables you to request a document from virtually anywhere in the world, and to begin to receive that document almost instantly. No other medium lets you do that.

The potential of the Internet was exciting from its inception, but you had to use a variety of esoteric programs (such as Archie and Gopher) to locate and download data. The programs were based on the Unix operating system, and you had to know the precise syntax of the commands within each program. There was no common user interface to speed learning. And, even if you were able to find what you wanted, everything was communicated in plain text, as graphics and sound were not available. All of this changed in 1991 with the introduction of the World Wide Web.

The ***World Wide Web (WWW)*** (or simply the Web) can be thought of as a very large subset of the Internet, consisting of hypertext and/or hypermedia documents. These documents contain links to other documents that may be stored on the same computer, or even on a different computer, with the latter located anywhere in the world. And therein lies the fascination of the Web, in that you simply click on link after link to go effortlessly from one document to the next. You can start your journey at your professor's home page in New York, which may link to a document in the Library of Congress, which in turn may take you to a different document, and so on. So, off you go to Washington DC and from there to a reference across the country or perhaps around the world.

Any computer that stores hypertext documents and makes those documents available to other computers, is known as a ***server*** (or Web server), whereas a computer that requests a document from a server is known as a ***client***. In order for the Web to work, every client (be it a PC or a Mac) must be able to display every document from every server. This is accomplished by imposing a set of standards or protocols to govern the way data is transmitted across the Web. Data travels from client to server and back, through a protocol known as the ***HyperText Transfer Protocol (http)***.

In addition, to access the documents that are transmitted through this protocol, you need a special type of program known as a ***browser***. Indeed, a browser is aptly named because it enables you inspect the Web in a leisurely and casual way (the dictionary definition of the word "browse"). ***Internet Explorer*** is the browser provided by Microsoft. ***Netscape Navigator*** is a competing product. Microsoft and Netscape are constantly trying to outdo one another, but both programs are incredibly good. Figures 26a and 26b display the Exploring Windows home page (www.prenhall.com/grauer) in Netscape Navigator and Internet Explorer, respectively. The toolbars and menu bars are different, but both programs have similar capabilities and share the common user interface common to all Windows applications. Either program will suffice. Your main concern is gaining access to the Internet.

IT'S THE URL, NOT THE BROWSER

Microsoft and Netscape argue vehemently about which is the superior browser. In actuality, however, both products are so feature-rich that it doesn't really matter which one you choose. To see for yourself, try viewing the same Web page in both browsers. What difference (if any) do you see when a page is viewed in Netscape rather than Internet Explorer? Do you agree with our statement that it is the URL (Web address) that is important, rather than the actual browser?

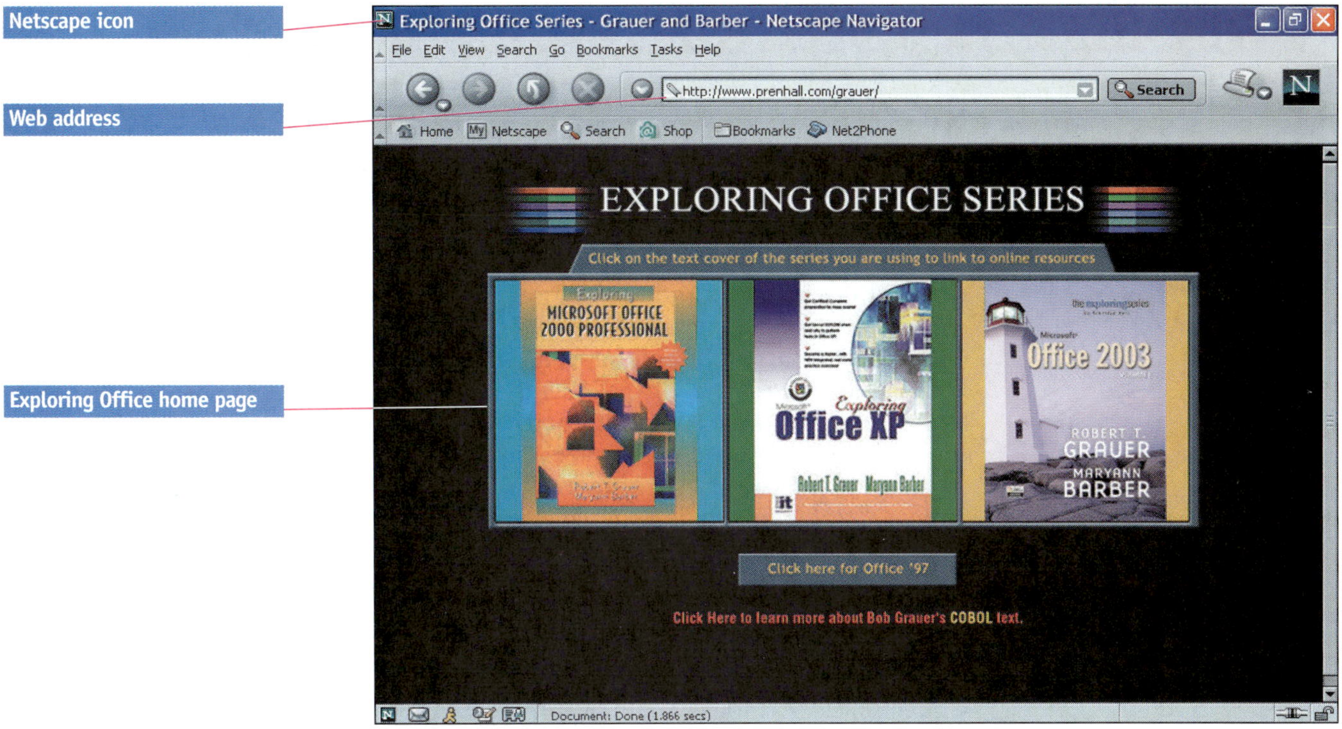

(a) Netscape Navigator

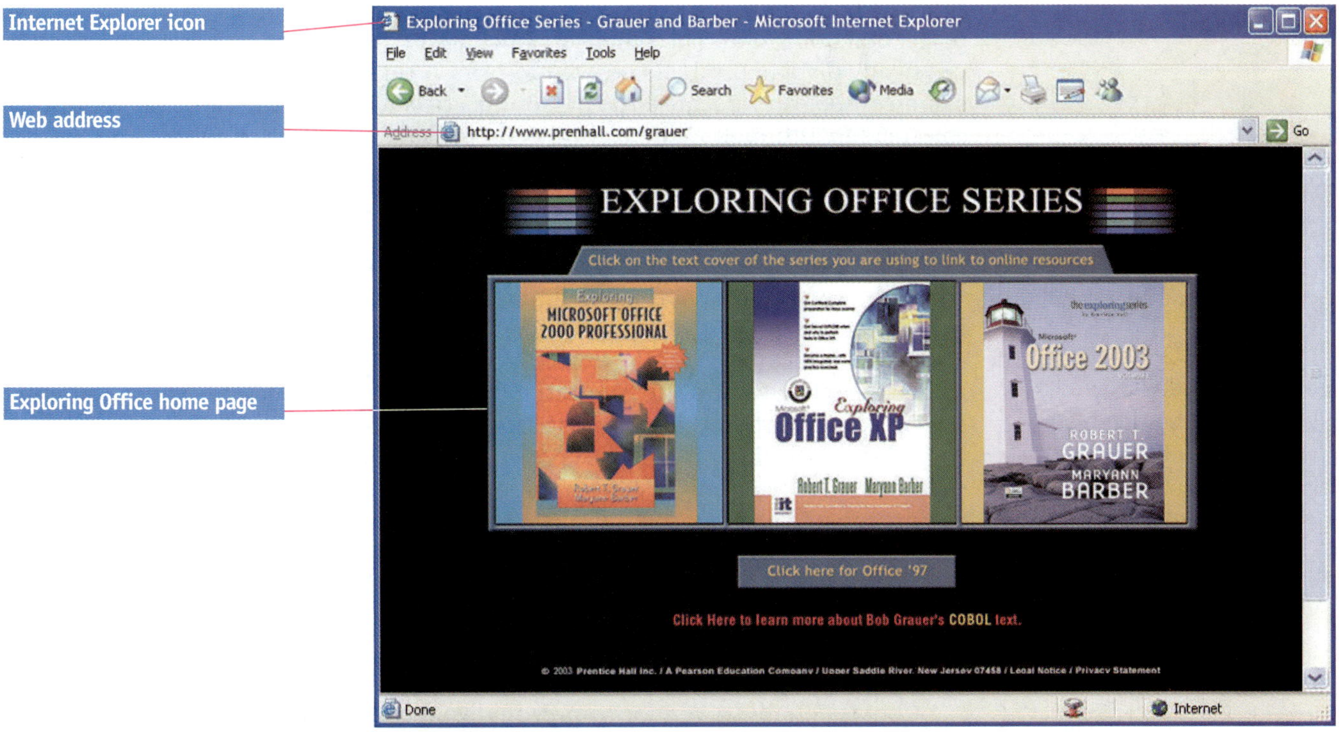

(b) Internet Explorer

FIGURE 26 Internet Browsers

THE COMMERCIALIZATION OF CYBERSPACE

It's difficult to think of the Internet as existing without any type of commercial enterprise. The Internet began, however, as a project of the United States government with a strict prohibition against commercial activity. It was not until 1991, some twenty years after its inception, that the National Science Foundation lifted the prohibition on commercial use. The subsequent growth has been both unprecedented and exponential, as companies of every size, from multinational corporations to "mom and pop" shops, conduct business on the Web.

The best way to appreciate the impact of ***e-commerce*** is to step back and think of commerce in the traditional sense, which is nothing more than the exchange of goods and services. The same elements are present, regardless of whether you go to a mall or shop on the Web. Commerce of either type involves buyers and sellers, products and services, and suppliers or producers of the products and services. The buyer and seller need a place to meet for the transaction to take place. The seller employs various marketing strategies to attract the buyer to the place of business, where it can accept an order, deliver the goods or services, and then accept payment.

What then is so special about e-commerce? The answer is that it enables both the buyer and seller to do things that are not possible with the traditional model. The buyer can shop 24 hours a day, 7 days a week, without ever leaving home. There is no need to walk up and down the aisles, because you can search the entire product line with the click of a mouse. You can shop as long as you like, even taking several days to build an order in a virtual shopping cart. You can also assure yourself the best price because it is so easy to obtain prices of a given item from multiple vendors.

The seller enjoys similar advantages because it is much less expensive to implement and maintain a Web site than it is to build a store with "bricks and mortar." The customers can come from all over the world, as opposed to having to live in the neighborhood. The seller can stock more items because there is no need to physically display products or even to print a catalog. The cost per transaction is significantly lower because the personnel costs are reduced. There need not be a salesperson although many Web sites do provide telephone support. And, best of all, the business remains open around the clock.

E-commerce depends entirely on the availability of secure transactions, which is accomplished through ***encryption***, the process of encoding data so that it is no longer in its original form when it is sent across the Internet. The precise way in which data is encrypted prior to being sent, then decrypted on the receiving end, is beyond the scope of our description. Encryption is built into both Netscape Navigator and Internet Explorer, and it takes place automatically when you communicate with a secure site. You can tell a transmission is secure when a different protocol, https rather than http, appears in the Address bar of the browser.

Privacy is another issue. The convenience of returning to a site and having the site know your likes and dislikes in order to steer you to the goods or information you are most likely to request, is offset by the thought that the site knows all about you. How much it knows, and what it will do with that information, is a growing concern. It is all a function of ***cookies***—the small files that are written to your hard drive each time you visit a site. There is nothing harmful about a cookie per se. It is not a virus and it will not erase or alter the programs on your computer. It is simply a text file that contains information about your visit to a site.

Cookies enable a vendor to personalize a customer's interaction with a Web site by sending only selected information about the types of products a customer is likely to buy. It's good for the vendor because it increases the chance of a sale. The consumer also likes the concept because he or she is not inundated with information that is of no interest. The process is possible only because the site knows your shopping habits, which it learned by recording the types of links you selected and the purchases you made. Is that good, or is it an invasion of privacy? Opinion is divided, to say the least.

A SIMPLE ENCRYPTION ALGORITHM

Julius Caesar is given credit for developing one of the oldest encryption schemes. Caesar used a simple substitution algorithm in which each letter in the original text was replaced by the letter three positions further in the alphabet. The letter "a" was replaced by the letter "d," the letter "b" by the letter "e," and so on. The word "cat," for example, would be encrypted as "fdw." It was simple, but it worked as long as the recipient knew the key—the number of letters to jump in the alphabet.

Connecting to the Internet

Your connection to the Internet begins with the selection of an ***Internet Service Provider (ISP)***, a company or organization that maintains a computer with permanent access to the Internet. You may already have free Internet access through your school or university, but if not, you will have to sign up with a commercial vendor. America Online (AOL) is perhaps the best known because of its proprietary interface, but there are many other choices.

The next decision is the means of access, whether it is a regular modem, a cable modem, or a DSL modem. A ***modem*** is the interface between a computer and the telephone. It converts the digital signal from your computer to an analog signal that traverses the phone system, then back again to a digital signal on the other end, as shown conceptually in Figure 27. In essence, you instruct the modem to dial the phone number of your ISP, which in turn lets you access the Internet. You should purchase the fastest modem available, which is 56Kbps (Kilobits per second). This speed is adequate to transmit text and limited graphics, but it pales when compared to the new technologies.

A ***cable modem*** attaches a PC to a local TV cable and receives data at about 1.5 Mbps. This is approximately 30 times faster than an ordinary modem, but the service is also more expensive. Whether or not it is worth the extra money depends on your budget and the amount of time you spend online. A cable modem requires a network card in your computer.

DSL (Digital Subscriber Line) is a newer technology that lets you transmit voice and digital data simultaneously over a telephone line. In other words, you can be speaking on the phone at the same time you are connected to the Internet. (This is in contrast to an ordinary modem that ties up your phone line.) DSL has a theoretical transmission rate of up to 8.4Mbps, but the typical connection is at 1.5Mbps, which competes directly with a cable modem.

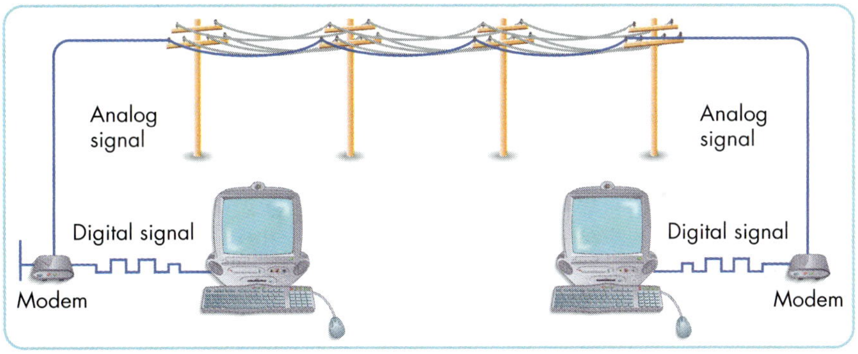

FIGURE 27 How a Modem Works

WHEN YOU USE A MODEM

1. The communication software in your computer sends a command to your modem to dial the phone number of the remote computer. The modem dials the number.
2. The remote computer answers the phone and returns a whistling sound. Your modem answers with a sound of its own.
3. The modems exchange information, a process called handshaking, to enable the communication to take place.
4. The sending computer transmits the data to its modem, which converts the data to a sound wave and sends it over the phone line.
5. The receiving modem converts the sound wave to a digital signal for the receiving computer, which processes the data and sends a reply.
6. Communications continue back and forth until eventually one of the computers instructs its modem to end the session.

TCP/IP—How the Internet Works

The Internet works and we take it for granted. Spend a few minutes, however, to learn how it works. Our explanation is not overly technical, and it will give you a better appreciation for the incredible technology at your fingertips.

Data is transmitted across the Internet through a series of protocols known collectively as ***TCP/IP*** (Transmission Control Protocol/Internet Protocol). A protocol is a set of conventions that define the rules of communication. You follow a protocol in class; for example, you raise your hand and wait to be acknowledged by your professor. In similar fashion, the sending and receiving computers on the Internet follow the TCP/IP protocol to ensure that data is transmitted correctly.

The postal system provides a good analogy of how (but certainly not how fast) TCP/IP is implemented. (The post office analogy was suggested by Ed Krol in his excellent book, *The Whole Internet*, published by O'Reilly and Associates, Inc., Sebastopol, CA, 1992.) When you mail a regular letter, you drop it into a mailbox, where it is picked up along with a lot of other letters and delivered to the local post office. The letters are sorted and sent on their way to a larger post office, where the letters are sorted again, until eventually each letter reaches the post office closest to its destination, where it is delivered to the addressee by the local mail carrier. If, for example, you sent a letter from Coral Springs, Florida, to Upper Saddle River, New Jersey, the letter would not travel directly. Instead, the Postal Service would forward the letter from one substation to the next, making a new decision at each substation as to the best (most efficient) route—for example, from Coral Springs, to Miami, to Newark, and finally, to Upper Saddle River.

Each postal substation considers all of the routes it has available to the next substation and makes the best possible decision according to the prevailing conditions. This means that the next time you mail a letter from Coral Springs to Upper Saddle River, the letter may travel a completely different path. If the mail truck from Coral Springs to Miami had already left or was full to capacity, the letter could be routed through Fort Lauderdale to New York City, and then to Upper Saddle River. The actual route taken by the letter is not important. All that matters is that the letter arrives at its destination.

The Internet works the same way, as data travels across the Internet through several levels of networks until it gets to its destination. E-mail messages arrive at the local post office (the mail server) from a remote PC connected by modem, or from a node on a local area network. The messages then leave the local post office and pass through a special-purpose computer known as a router that ensures each message is sent to its correct destination.

A message may pass through several networks to get to its destination. Each network has its own router that determines how best to move the message closer to its destination, taking into account the traffic on the network. A message passes from one network to the next, until it arrives at the destination network, from where it can be sent to the recipient, who has a mailbox on that network. The process is depicted graphically in Figure 28.

In actuality, the TCP/IP protocol is slightly more complicated than what we have been portraying, and it applies to all types of data, not just e-mail. To continue with the post office analogy, let's assume that you are sending a book, rather

ONLY THE DESTINATION MATTERS

Data is sent across the Internet in "packets," with each packet passing through several networks to get to its destination. The only thing that matters is a packet's eventual destination. Each network has its own router that determines how best to move the message forward, taking into account the traffic on the network. This means that the next time a message is sent from "point A to point B," it could travel an entirely different path. The entire process is governed by the TCP/IP protocol that sends data across the globe in seconds.

than a letter, and that the post office (for whatever reason) does not accept large packages. One alternative would be to rip the pages out of the book, mail each page individually by placing it into its own envelope, then trust that all of the envelopes arrive at the destination, and finally, that the person on the other end would be able to reassemble the individual pages. That may sound awkward, but it is a truer picture of how the Internet works.

Data (whether it is an e-mail message or a Web page) is sent across the Internet in ***packets***, with each packet limited in size. The rules for creating, addressing, and sending the packets are specified by TCP/IP, which is actually two separate protocols. The TCP portion divides the file that you want to send into packets, then numbers each packet so that the message can be reconstructed at the other end. The IP portion sends each packet on its way by specifying the addresses of the sending and receiving computers so that the routers will be able to do their job.

The TCP/IP protocol may seem unnecessarily complicated, but it is actually very clever. Dividing large files into smaller pieces ensures that no single file monopolizes the network. A second advantage ensures that the data arrives correctly. Static or noise on a telephone line is merely annoying to people having a conversation, but devastating when a file (especially a computer program) is transmitted and a byte or two is lost or corrupted. The larger the file being sent, the greater the chance that noise will be introduced and that the file will be corrupted. Sending the data in smaller pieces (packets), and verifying that the packets were received correctly, helps ensure the integrity of the data. If one packet is received incorrectly, the entire file does not have to be sent again, only the corrupted packet.

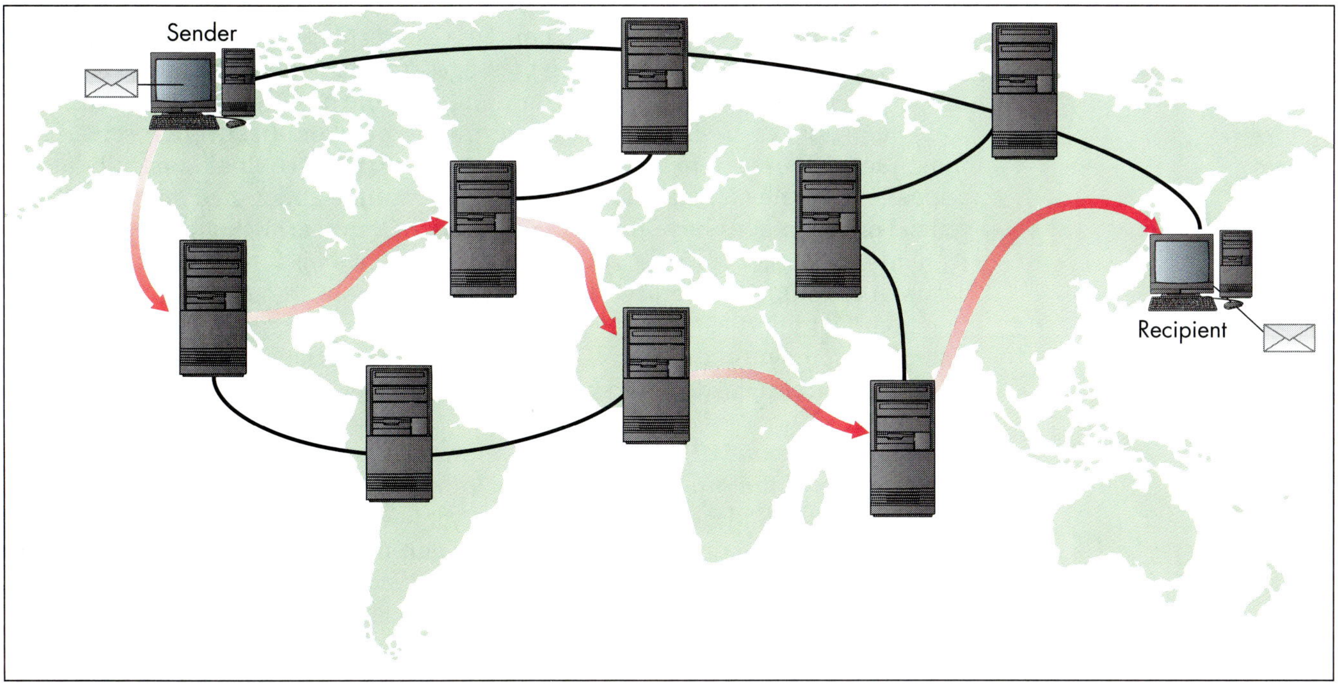

FIGURE 28 A Message Travels the Internet

WHAT SHOULD BE DONE ABOUT SPAM?

Spam is a popular meat product. It is also the name for unsolicited e-mail, the Internet equivalent of junk mail, which is proliferating at an alarming rate. Technology has progressed to the point that a mass marketer can send a million spam messages for approximately $500. Programs such as Microsoft Outlook include a junk-mail filter that is only partially effective. Relief may come in the form of new legislation, so write your representative, but please, one letter per person.

Introduction to E-mail

Electronic mail, or ***e-mail***, is conceptually the same as writing a letter and sending it through the US Postal Service with one very significant advantage—e-mail messages are delivered almost instantly, as opposed to regular (snail) mail, which requires several days. E-mail was unknown to the general public only a few years ago, but it has become an integral part of American culture.

All Windows-based e-mail systems work basically the same way. You need access to a ***mail server*** (a computer with a network connection) to receive your incoming messages and to deliver the messages you send. You also need an e-mail program such as Microsoft Outlook in order to read and compose e-mail messages, and to transfer mail back and forth to the server. You send a message when it is convenient for you. The recipient reads the message when it is convenient to do so.

The mail server functions as a central post office and provides private mailboxes to persons authorized to use its services. It receives mail around the clock and holds it until you sign on to retrieve it. You gain access to your mailbox via a ***username*** and a ***password***. The username identifies you to the server. The password protects your account from unauthorized use by others. Once you log on successfully, you can read your mail. It can be downloaded (sent from the server and stored locally), or it can be left on the server, in which case you can access it from another computer at another time. Outgoing mail is uploaded (sent from your PC) to the server, where it is sent on its way across a local area network to another person within your organization or across the Internet to the world at large.

Figure 29 displays a typical screen in Outlook. The various mail folders are shown in the left pane. Only one folder can be selected at a time, for example, the *Inbox folder* in Figure 29a, and its contents are displayed in the right pane. The inbox displays a list of all incoming messages, the person who sent the message, the subject of the message, and the date and time the message was received.

The messages are listed in order according to when they were received (the most recent message is listed at the bottom of the list). Look carefully at the appearance of the messages in the inbox to learn more about their status and contents. Four messages have not yet been read and appear with a sealed envelope icon and the subject in bold. All other messages have been read and appear with an open envelope icon and in regular type. Several of the messages also have a paper clip icon indicating that they contain an attached file. A red exclamation point (!) next to one of the messages indicates the sender labeled it as a high-priority message. Double click the message to open it, after which you can reply, forward it, or delete it.

The inbox is one of several folders within Outlook for use with Internet mail. The purpose of the other folders can be inferred from their names. The *Outbox folder* contains all messages that have not yet been sent (uploaded) to the server. Once a message is sent, however, it is moved automatically to the *Sent Items folder*. Messages remain indefinitely in the Inbox and Sent Items folders unless they are moved to another folder or deleted, in which case they are moved to the *Deleted Items folder*. Messages that you close before completing and sending them are stored in the *Drafts folder*.

An E-mail Address

All e-mail addresses follow the general format, username@mailserver. The combination of the username and mail server is unique. Bob Grauer, for example, is the only individual in the world with the e-mail address rgrauer@miami.edu. There can be many individuals who go by the username "rgrauer", and there are many more individuals who use the miami.edu mail server. But Bob is the only person who has the e-mail address rgrauer@miami.edu.

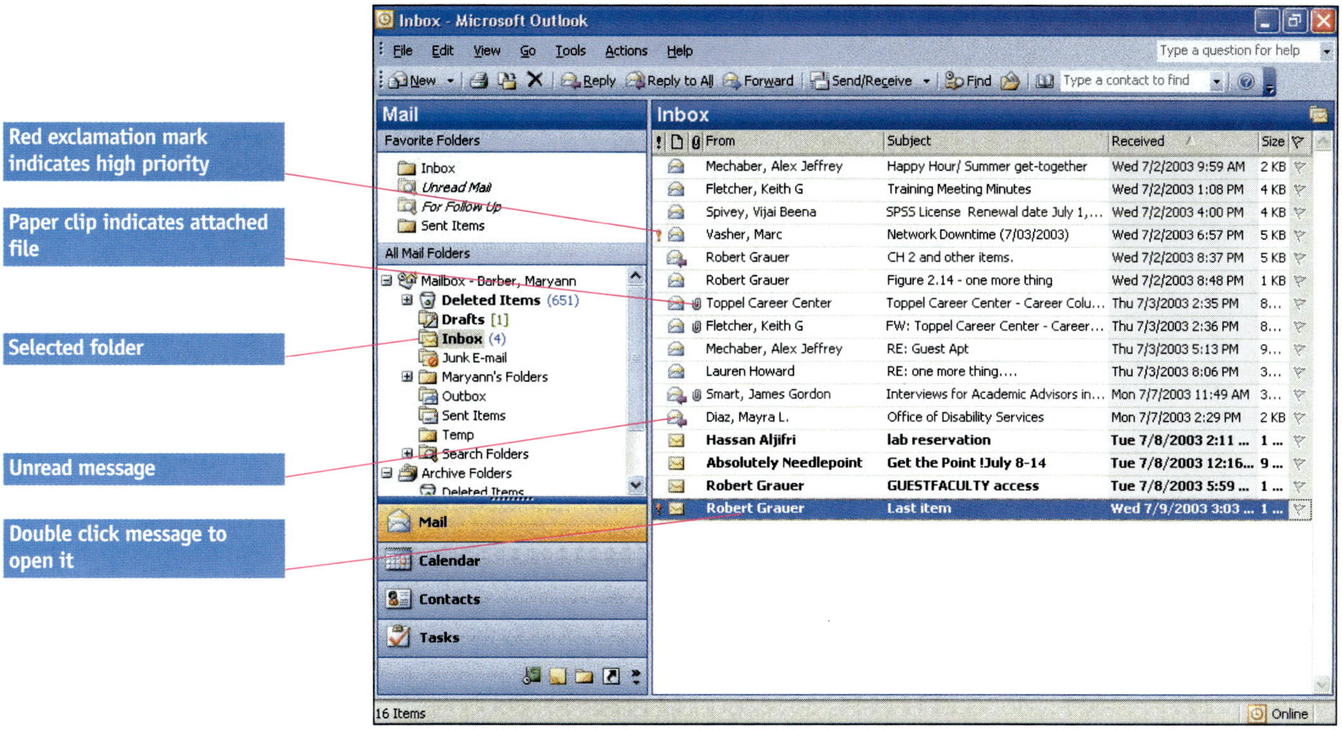

(a) The Inbox

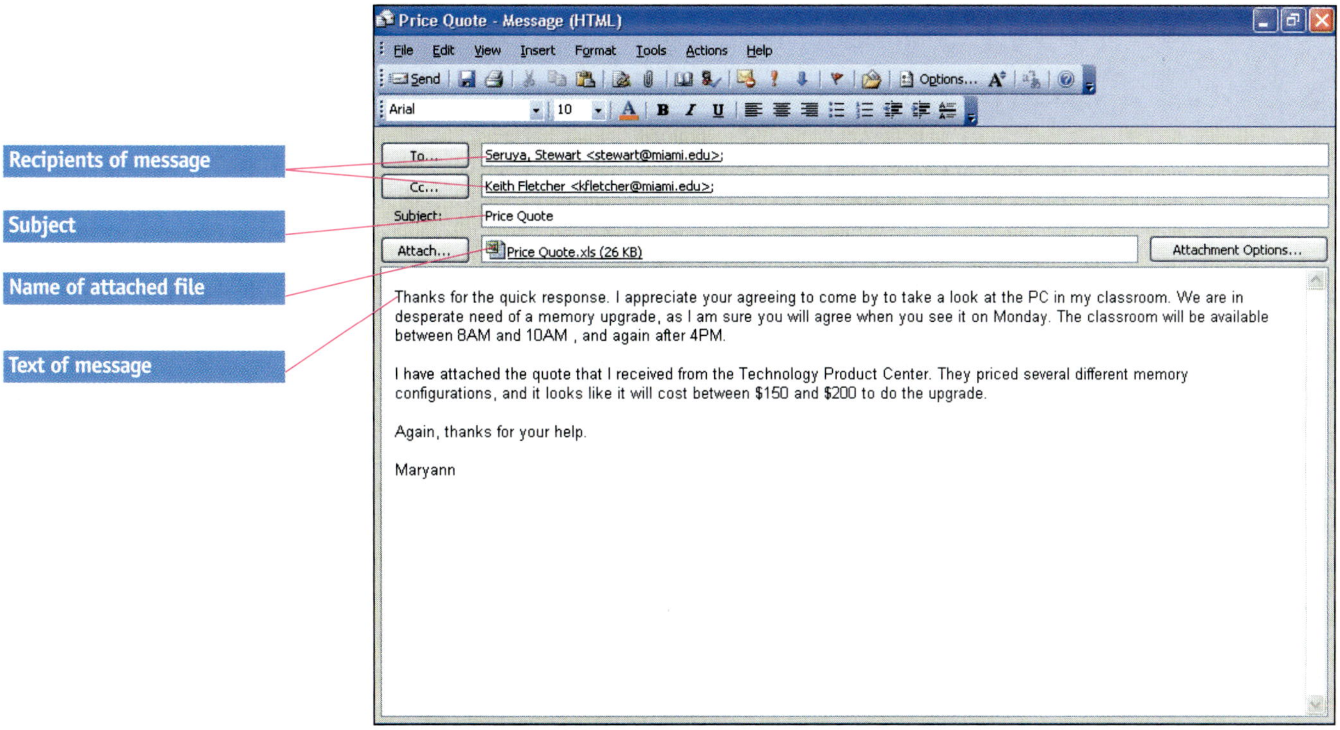

(b) Composing a Message

FIGURE 29 Introduction to E-mail

Anatomy of an E-mail Message

All e-mail systems provide the same basic commands to compose, send, reply, and forward e-mail. You start by composing (or creating) a new message on your PC, then you execute the Send command to upload the message from your PC to the mail server, where it goes out to the Internet. You reply to messages that appear in your inbox, and/or you can forward messages you receive to others. Figure 29b displays the Outlook window in which you compose a new message.

The function of the text boxes at the top of the message is apparent from their names. The To text box contains the address of the recipient(s). The Cc (courtesy or carbon copy) text box indicates the names of other people who are to receive copies of the message. The text of the message appears in the message area below the subject line. You can also attach one or more files to the e-mail message such as a Word document or an Excel workbook. The recipient reads the message as usual, and then has the ability to view and/or edit the attached file (provided that the associated application is installed on his or her machine). To mail the message, click the Send button when you have finished. That's all there is to it.

Replying to an existing message is similar in concept to creating a new message, except that Outlook automatically enters the addressee for you. You open a message from the inbox to read it, click the Reply button to open a window similar to Figure 29b, then enter the text of your message. You can enter additional recipients to your reply and/or forward the original message to someone else.

The ability to forward an e-mail message to a third party is quite useful. Select the message in any folder, click the Forward Message button on the Outlook toolbar to open the editing window, then enter the recipient's e-mail address in the To box. The subject is entered automatically and begins with the letters FW to indicate the message has been forwarded. The text of the original message and any attached files appear in the editing window. You can edit the message and/or add additional comments of your own. Click the Send button to send the message.

The Address Book

Most of us use some type of personal address book to look up the telephone numbers or addresses of friends, family, and colleagues. The ***address book*** (or contacts list) in an e-mail program works conceptually the same way, except the e-mail program looks up the information for you. You enter the addressee's name in the To field, and Outlook will look up and insert the address for you. It's a lot easier than having to remember the complete address.

A ***distribution list*** is a set of Internet addresses that is stored under a single group name. Your professor, for example, might create a distribution list for this class, consisting of the addresses of everyone in the class. To send a message to the entire class, the professor enters the name of the distribution list (e.g., CIS120) in the To field (or selects the group from the address book). The mail program then locates the list and automatically retrieves the e-mail addresses of all recipients in the list.

PRIVACY ISSUES

One of the most significant differences between e-mail and regular mail is privacy or the lack thereof. The network administrator has the ability to read the messages in your inbox, and indeed, many employers maintain they have the legal right to read their employees' e-mail—and the courts have agreed. Sending private e-mail on company time is potential grounds for dismissal. Send e-mail on your own time, and think twice about putting anything of a personal nature in an e-mail message, regardless of whether the message is personal or professional.

Microsoft® .NET is a combination of technologies that collectively build complex applications over the Internet. It is based on the concept of ***interoperability***, whereby a user can access data in any application, on any platform, on any device. In theory, you can start a transaction on a PC at your office, check on the status of that transaction on your way home using a cell phone or PDA, then check further on your PC when you arrive home.

To say that .NET is ambitious is an understatement. Bill Gates has described his company's initiative as "one of the toughest software problems ever tackled, easily greater than getting to the moon or designing the 747." Indeed, there is no shortage of hyperbole as Microsoft has, in effect; "bet the company" to fulfill the vision of its founder. So what, exactly, is .NET? Is it a product or suite of products? Is it for the end user or the developer? Is it hardware? Is it software? The answer is all of the above, but simply stated, .NET connects people and technology through XML Web services. (Extensible Markup Language, or XML for short, is an industry standard for structuring data. It is not a Microsoft product.)

Figure 30 depicts the .NET view of the world. The icon for developer tools represents the ***Visual Studio®*** suite of software that was created for developers to enable them to build and deploy XML services. The various devices are "smart devices" in the sense that they allow your information to be accessed from anywhere at any time. A smart device will verify your .NET identity, and then collect and present information in the form appropriate for that device. It may convert text to speech to speak to you on your cell phone, and/or it may recognize your handwriting as you input data on a tablet PC.

The part of .NET that you see is impressive, but the part that you don't see is even more impressive. Think of .NET as an iceberg in that only a small portion of the whole is visible. The user sees the application and the hardware. He or she does not see what lies below the surface, which is the .NET framework that makes the interconnectivity possible. Unlike a real iceberg, however, the .NET iceberg can be connected to any other .NET iceberg within the (Internet) ocean.

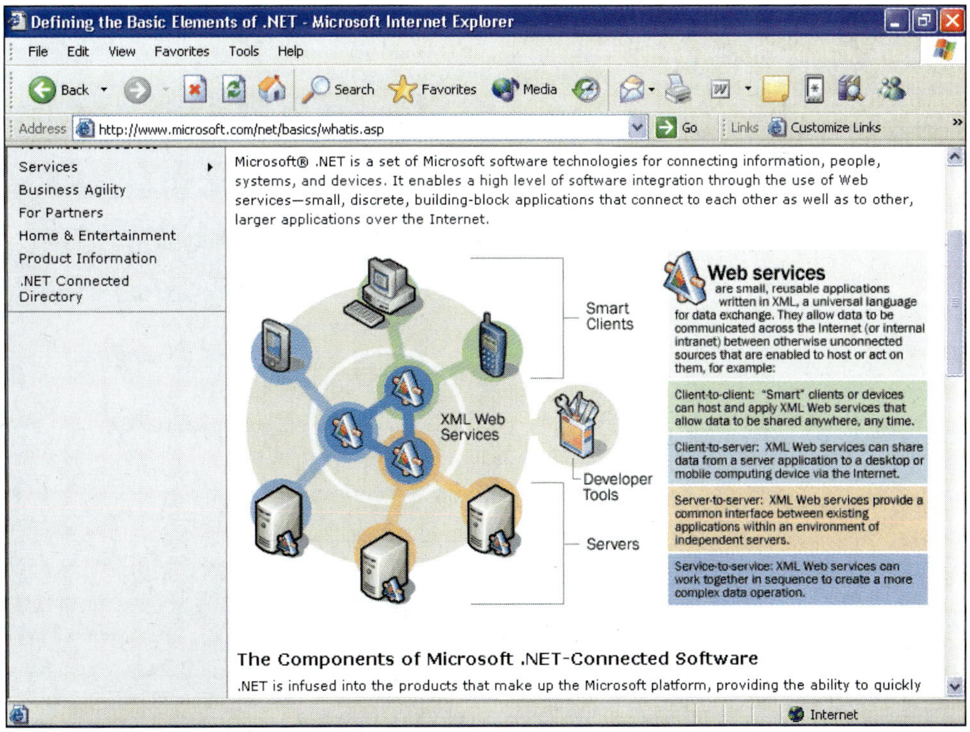

FIGURE 30 Microsoft® .NET (www.microsoft.com/net/basics/whatis.asp)

An ***XML Web service*** is a basic building block that is incorporated into a .NET application. The service is developed once, and then it can be exported to different applications running on different platforms. Companies can develop their own services and/or can use services developed by Microsoft. For example, have you logged on to a Web site to check on the arrival time of an incoming flight, and then left your cell phone number to be notified when the flight arrived? If so, the site is using the .NET Alert Web service, which sends time-sensitive information to a customer at the customer's request. Think of the connections that are made possible by the .NET framework—you log on to the Web site using a PC, and then you receive information via your cell phone.

The best known Web service is ***Microsoft® Passport***, which enables participating sites to authenticate a user with a single username and password. A passport is also used in conjunction with Windows Messenger. Figure 31a depicts the login procedure outside of .NET, whereby the user has to log in separately to every Web site, typically with a different username and password. Figure 31b illustrates the procedure after a .NET passport has been obtained. The user logs into any participating site, and then the information is shared with all other participating sites. Figure 31c depicts the home page of the .NET Passport service. The service is free.

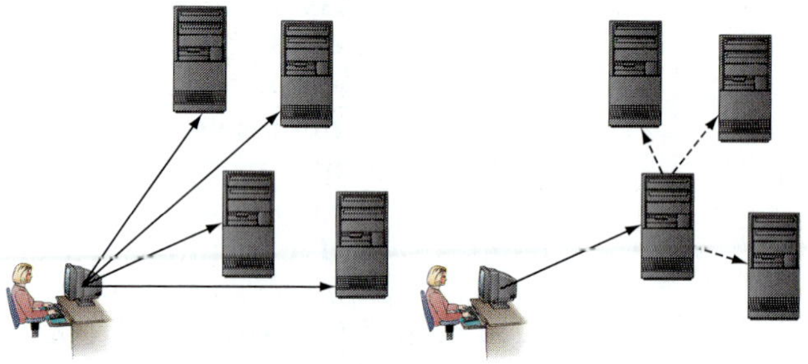

(a) Before .Net (multiple logon) (b) After .Net (single logon)

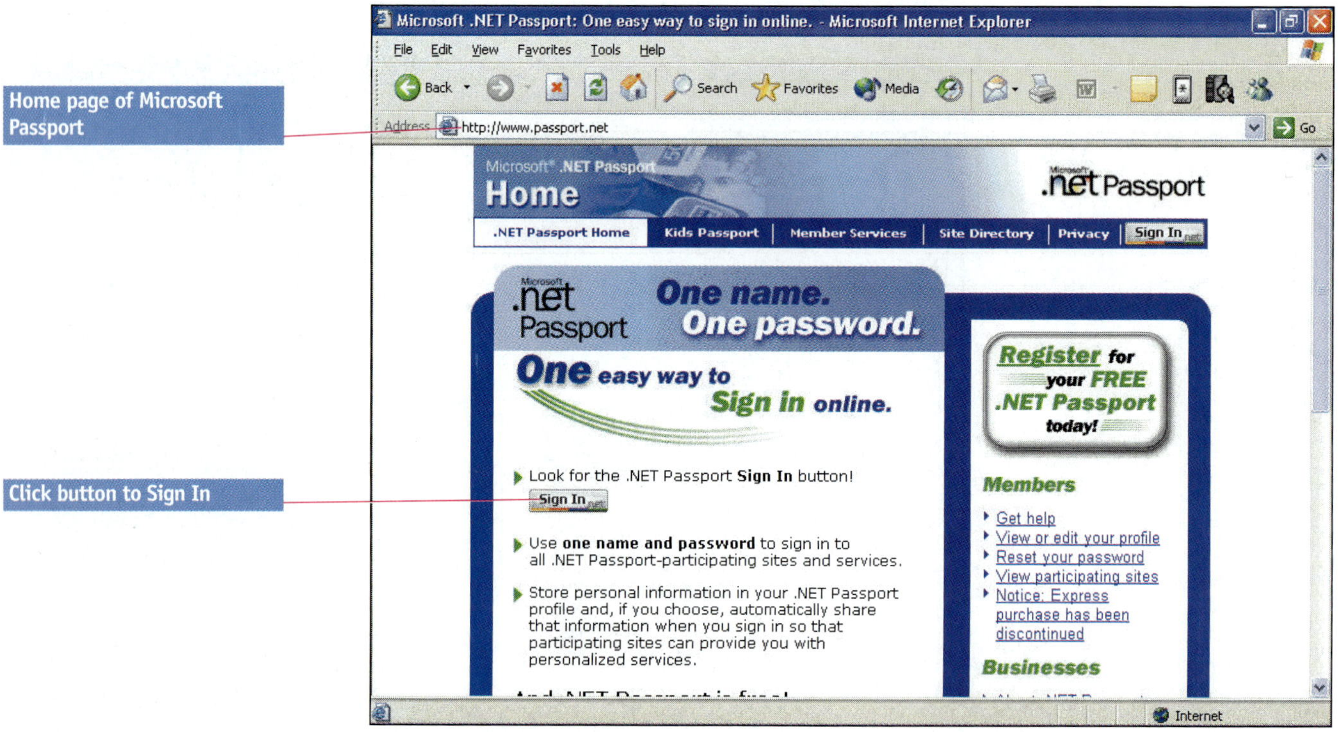

(c) Microsoft Passport Web Site

FIGURE 31 Net Passport (XML Web Services)

SUMMARY

A computer is an electronic device that accepts data (input), then manipulates or processes that data to produce information (output). A computer system consists of the computer and its memory; peripheral devices such as a keyboard, disk, monitor, and printer; and the various programs that enable it to perform its intended function.

IBM announced its version of the personal computer (PC) in 1981 and broke a long-standing corporate tradition by going to external sources for supporting hardware and software. Intel designed the microprocessor. Microsoft developed the operating system. Today, PC is a generic term for any computer that is based on Intel-compatible hardware and that runs Microsoft software.

Computer memory and storage capacity are measured in bytes. Each byte holds 8 bits (binary digits) or one ASCII character. A kilobyte, megabyte, gigabyte, and terabyte are approximately one thousand, one million, one billion, and one trillion bytes, respectively.

A hard disk holds significantly more data than a floppy disk, and it accesses that data much faster. The floppy disk is passing into obsolescence and is no longer standard on new computer systems.

A CD-ROM (Compact Disk, Read Only Memory) is standard on every system, but the technology is evolving from "read only" to "read and write," enabling the end user to create (burn) a CD. A CD-R (Compact Disk–Recordable) is now commonplace, but it is limited by the fact that the CD can be used only once. The CD-RW (Compact Disk ReWritable) goes one step further and allows the user to rewrite to the CD multiple times. A DVD (Digital Video Disk or Digital Versatile Disk) has significantly greater capacity than a CD (up to 17GB, as opposed to 700MB for a CD). A DVD-R device is analogous to CD-R, but it supports the higher recording density of a DVD. A DVD-RW (or DVD-RAM) drive is emerging as well but is more costly than the corresponding capability in a CD.

The keyboard and the mouse are the primary input devices for the PC. The standard mouse has two buttons and recognizes four basic operations: point, click (with either button), double click, and drag.

The resolution of a monitor is defined as the number of pixels (picture elements) that are displayed at one time; for example, 800×600 or 1024×768. Higher resolutions require larger monitors. The quality of a monitor is measured by its dot pitch; the smaller the dot pitch, the crisper the image.

A printer produces output on paper or acetate transparencies. The output is referred to as hard copy because it is more tangible than the files written to a disk or other electronic device. Printers vary greatly in terms of design, price, and capability. Ink-jet and laser printers are today's common technologies.

A digital camera has a lens, shutter, and optical viewfinder just like a traditional camera. Its inner workings are very different, however, as the image is stored on a photosensitive computer chip that converts the image to a series of pixels (picture elements or dots). Entry-level cameras provide two megapixels and produce quality prints at sizes up to 5×7 inches.

Software is divided broadly into two classes—system software (referred to as the operating system) and application software. Windows XP replaces all previous versions of the Windows operating system. Windows XP Home Edition is intended for entertainment and home use. It includes a media player, support for digital photography, and an instant messenger. Windows XP Professional Edition has all of the features of the Home Edition plus additional security to encrypt files and protect data.

A file is a set of instructions or data that has been given a name and stored on disk. There are two basic types of files, program files and data files. Microsoft Word and Microsoft Excel are examples of program files. The documents and workbooks that are created by these programs are data files. Files are kept in folders to better organize the thousands of files on a typical system. Windows Explorer is the program used to move and copy files and folders within a system. Adequate backup should also be created for all essential documents on a regular basis and stored offsite.

Microsoft Windows does not include three essential functions—antivirus protection, a graphical FTP (file transfer protocol) program, and an easy-to-use intuitive file compression program. An antivirus program is absolutely critical and should be installed when you buy your computer. Its effectiveness depends on continual updating since new viruses appear all the time.

File Transfer Protocol (FTP) specifies the rules by which files are sent and received across the Internet. It enables you to upload files from your machine to a remote computer and/or to download files from the FTP server to your computer.

Files are often compressed (zipped) to reduce their size, especially when sending files from one location to another. Multiple documents can be placed inside a single compressed file (called an archive), enabling you to send or receive a single file, from which the compressed files can be extracted and accessed individually.

Microsoft Office 2003 contains the same four core applications as all of its predecessors—Word, Excel, Access, and PowerPoint. The suite is published in multiple editions, each of which contains a different set of programs. Other applications in the Office family include Microsoft Outlook, FrontPage, Publisher, InfoPath, and OneNote (the latter two applications are new in Office 2003).

A network is a combination of hardware and software that enables the connected computers to share resources and communicate with one another. A local area network (or LAN) connects its computers, typically PCs, over short distances of a mile or two. A LAN may be created within a home or office, a building or adjacent buildings, or across a college campus. A wide area network (or WAN) is similar in concept except that its computers are separated by significantly longer distances. A WAN may span an entire country or cross several continents.

The Internet is a network of networks. The World Wide Web (or simply the Web) is a very large subset of the Internet, consisting of those computers that store hypertext and hypermedia documents. A browser such as Internet Explorer or Netscape Navigator is required to view documents from the Web. A connection to the Internet is established through a local area network (LAN) or by connecting to an Internet Service Provider (ISP) via a modem, cable modem, or DSL line.

E-commerce involves many of the same concepts as traditional commerce, namely the exchange of goods and services between buyers and sellers. E-commerce also enables both buyer and seller to conduct business in ways that are not possible with traditional bricks and mortar. A cookie is a small file that a Web site writes to a PC each time the site is visited, enabling a vendor to customize a user's interaction with a Web site.

Electronic mail, or e-mail, is the most widely used Internet service. An e-mail address follows the general format username@mailserver. All e-mail systems provide the same basic commands to compose, send, reply, and forward e-mail.

Microsoft® .NET is a combination of technologies that enable a user to access data in any application, on any platform, on any device. It is made possible through XML Web services, which are the basic building blocks within the .NET framework. The best known Web service is Microsoft® Passport, which enables participating sites to authenticate a user with a single username and password.

KEY WORDS AND CONCEPTS

Adapter cards ... 894
Address book ... 938
Antivirus program ... 916
Application software ... 910
Archive ... 918
ASCII ... 893
Auxiliary storage ... 890
Backup ... 914
Bit ... 893
Browser ... 930
Byte ... 893
Cable modem ... 933
CD-R ... 898
CD-ROM ... 898
CD-RW ... 898
Central processing unit (CPU) ... 890
Client ... 930
Clock speed ... 896
Common user interface ... 913
Compressed file ... 918
Computer ... 890
Computer virus ... 916
Control Panel ... 915
Cookies ... 932
Data files ... 914
Digital camera ... 906
Distribution list ... 938
DSL ... 933
DVD ... 898
DVD-R ... 898
DVD-RW ... 898
E-commerce ... 932
E-mail ... 936
Encryption ... 932
Expansion slots ... 894
Extensible Markup Language (XML) ... 926
File ... 914
File compression ... 918
File name ... 914
File server ... 928
File Transfer Protocol (FTP) ... 917
Firewall ... 928
Fixed disk ... 898
Floppy disk ... 898
Folders ... 914
Font ... 904
Formatting toolbar ... 919
Gateway ... 928
Gigabyte (GB) ... 898
Gigahertz ... 896
Graphical user interface (GUI) ... 910
Hard copy ... 904
Hard disk ... 898
Hardware ... 910
Hypertext Markup Language (HTML) ... 926
Hypertext Transfer Protocol (http) ... 930
IBM Corporation ... 894
Ink-jet printer ... 904
Input devices ... 890
Intel Corporation ... 894
Internet ... 930
Internet Explorer ... 930
Internet Service Provider (ISP) ... 933
Interoperability ... 939
Joystick ... 900
Keyboard ... 900
Kilobyte (KB) ... 897
Laser printer ... 904
Local area network (LAN) ... 928
Mail server ... 936
Mainframe computer ... 892
Megabyte (MB) ... 897
Megahertz (MHz) ... 896
Megapixel ... 906
Memory ... 890
Microcomputer ... 892
Microphone ... 900
Microprocessor ... 896
Microsoft .NET ... 939
Microsoft Access ... 919
Microsoft Corporation ... 894
Microsoft Excel ... 919
Microsoft FrontPage ... 923
Microsoft InfoPath ... 926
Microsoft Office 2003 ... 919
Microsoft OneNote ... 925
Microsoft Outlook ... 922
Microsoft Passport ... 940
Microsoft PowerPoint ... 919
Microsoft Publisher ... 924
Microsoft Word ... 919
Modem ... 933
Monitor ... 902
Motherboard ... 894
Mouse ... 900
MS-DOS ... 910
Multitasking ... 913
Netscape Navigator ... 930
Network ... 928
Object Linking and Embedding ... 913
Operating system ... 890
Output devices ... 890
Packets ... 934
Password ... 936
PC compatible ... 894
Pentium ... 896
Pixel ... 902
Program ... 890
Program files ... 914
Protocol ... 934
Random-access memory (RAM) 890
Read-only memory (ROM) ... 897
Removable mass storage ... 909
Resolution ... 902
Router ... 928
Scanner ... 900
Self-extracting file ... 918
Server ... 930
Software ... 910
Standard toolbar ... 919
System software ... 910
Task manager ... 913
TCP/IP ... 934
Terabyte ... 898
Typography ... 904
User name ... 936
Visual Studio ... 939
Wide area network ... 928
Windows Explorer ... 914
Windows Update ... 915
Windows XP ... 913
World Wide Web (WWW) ... 930
WYSIWYG ... 910
XML ... 926
XML Web service ... 940

MULTIPLE CHOICE

1. The idea for a general purpose computer was first proposed by:
   (a) Charles Babbage
   (b) Thomas J. Watson (the founder of IBM)
   (c) Watson and Crick
   (d) Bill Gates

2. Approximately how many bytes are in 1KB?
   (a) One thousand
   (b) One million
   (c) One billion
   (d) One trillion

3. The size of a computer's memory refers to:
   (a) The capacity of its hard disk
   (b) The capacity of its floppy disk
   (c) The amount of ROM available
   (d) The amount of RAM available

4. Hard copy refers to:
   (a) The difficulty of duplicating disk
   (b) Information stored on a hard drive
   (c) Written material that is difficult to read
   (d) None of the above

5. Which of the following would never be valid as a drive designation?
   (a) Drives A and C for a floppy and fixed disk, respectively
   (b) Drives 1 and 2 for a floppy and fixed disk, respectively
   (c) Drives D and E for a CD-RW and DVD, respectively
   (d) All of the above are valid designations

6. Which of the following devices is best suited to back up data from a PC?
   (a) Hard (fixed) disk
   (b) Multiple floppy disks
   (c) CD-ROM
   (d) CD-R or CD-RW

7. Which of the following displays capacities from smallest to largest?
   (a) KB, GB, MB, TB
   (b) KB, MB, GB, TB
   (c) KB, MB, TB, GB
   (d) GB, KB, MB, TB (alphabetical order)

8. Which of the following is true regarding the resolution of a monitor?
   (a) The higher the resolution, the less you see of a document at one time
   (b) The resolution cannot be changed unless the computer is restarted
   (c) Three megapixels is the most common resolution in today's environment.
   (d) Larger monitors enable you to work with higher resolutions

9. Which of the following allows a user to record multiple times to the same CD?
   (a) CD-ROM
   (b) CD-R
   (c) CR-RW
   (d) All of the above

10. Which of the following best describes the memory and fixed disk in an entry-level PC that you would buy today?
    (a) The capacity of RAM is measured in megabytes, the capacity of a fixed disk is measured in gigabytes
    (b) The capacity of RAM is measured in gigabytes, the capacity of a fixed disk is measured in megabytes
    (c) The capacities of RAM and a fixed disk are both measured in gigabytes
    (d) The capacities of RAM and a fixed disk are both measured in megabytes

11. Which applications are new to Microsoft Office 2003?
    (a) Word, Excel, Access, and PowerPoint
    (b) Outlook, Publisher, and FrontPage
    (c) OneNote and InfoPath
    (d) All of the above

... continued

multiple choice

12. What is the best and cheapest way to double the warranty of a new computer up to an additional year?

(a) Pay for the warranty at the time you purchase the computer
(b) Pay for the warranty at the end of the 30-day money-back guarantee period
(c) Use a major credit card that doubles the warranty for free
(d) You do not need to double the warranty since most computers come with a lifetime guarantee

13. When is a file compression program *not* necessary?

(a) To compress individual files into a compressed (zip) file
(b) To create a self-extracting file from a compressed file
(c) To extract files from a compressed (zip) file
(d) To extract files from a self-extracting file

14. Which of the following capabilities is built into the Microsoft Windows?

(a) A graphical FTP program
(b) Antivirus software
(c) Both (a) and (b)
(d) Neither (a) nor (b)

15. Which of the following is true about Microsoft Office?

(a) It is bundled with Microsoft Windows at no additional cost
(b) All versions of Office include the same applications
(c) Both (a) and (b)
(d) Neither (a) nor (b)

16. Which of the following means of Internet access will tie up your telephone line and prevent you from speaking when the Internet connection is in effect?

(a) An analog modem
(b) A cable modem
(c) A DSL line from your local telephone company
(d) All of the above

17. What is a cookie?

(a) A computer virus
(b) A small file that is written to a PC by a Web site
(c) A self-extracting file
(d) A file compression program

18. A local area network is intended to:

(a) Share data among connected computers
(b) Share peripheral devices among computers
(c) Share programs among connected computers
(d) All of the above

19. A virus can be transmitted when you:

(a) Download files from the Internet
(b) Copy files from a floppy disk to your hard drive
(c) Both (a) and (b)
(d) Neither (a) nor (b)

20. Which of the following is an example of an XML Web service?

(a) Microsoft Passport
(b) The Windows Control Panel
(c) FTP
(d) OneNote

ANSWERS

1. a	**8.** d	**15.** d
2. a	**9.** c	**16.** a
3. d	**10.** a	**17.** b
4. d	**11.** c	**18.** d
5. b	**12.** c	**19.** c
6. d	**13.** d	**20.** a
7. b	**14.** d	

CHAPTER 1

Outlook 2003: A Desktop Information Manager

OBJECTIVES

After reading this chapter you will:

1. Describe the components of the Outlook window.
2. Distinguish between a mail server and a mail client; explain the use of a username and password in conjunction with e-mail.
3. Send and receive e-mail; display and print messages.
4. Attach a file to an e-mail message.
5. List the mail folders that are created by default for Outlook mail; create a new mail folder and move a message to it.
6. Create a contact and add it to a category; view contacts by category.
7. Add a distribution list in Outlook; send a message using the distribution list.
8. Schedule a meeting or appointment; create a task list, note, or journal entry; print the calendar and contact list.

hands-on exercises

1. INTRODUCTION TO E-MAIL
   Input: None
   Output: E-mail messages
2. OUTLOOK CONTACTS
   Input: None
   Output: Contact list
3. THE OUTLOOK CALENDAR
   Input: None
   Output: Appointments

CASE STUDY

T-SHIRTS TO GO

Janet Olson and Beth Reilly are college roommates with big plans. They have designed a logo for their business school entrepreneurship team and want to make and sell silk-screened T-shirts to raise money to send the team to the national championships in June.

They are very busy running their fledgling operation, and have scheduling and communication needs that Outlook can help them with. They need to send messages to teammates on campus and to their suppliers. They must be able to attach drawings, worksheets, and documents to the messages.

Janet and Beth also want to set up meetings with the rest of their teammates. Given their busy schedules, they should be able to print their calendars to take with them, and they would like the computer to remind them when it's time to go to an appointment.

Janet and Beth will need the names of all suppliers that they use, such as T-shirt distributors, fabric paint suppliers, ground shipping companies, and student workers. They plan to store the e-mail address, phone number, cell phone number, mailing address, and other pertinent information on each of their contacts. They need an efficient way to keep the contact information organized. They would also like to note whether a contact is a supplier, a student, an alumna, or belongs to some other category.

Lastly, Janet and Beth have, on occasion, forgotten what files they used or in what folder they saved them. They would like to be able to easily locate recently used files. ■

Your assignment is to read the chapter and complete the hands-on exercises. You should then add several fictional entries to the Outlook contacts list, assigning each to a category (supplier, alumna, student, shipper). After you have completed the entries, print the first page of the contacts list by category to hand in. Open a blank Word document and write a fictional memo describing the T-shirt business. Save the memo, then attach it to an e-mail message to your instructor to show that you have completed the case. Open the Journal to view the Word document that you just created.

INTRODUCTION TO OUTLOOK

This supplement introduces you to the basic functions in Microsoft Outlook. Outlook is an integral part of Microsoft Office 2003. It can be used on a stand-alone PC to manage your own work, or on a network to facilitate communication with others in your organization. Think of Outlook as a personal assistant or desktop manager that keeps track of all types of information for you. Intuitively, you already know how Outlook works. Do you carry an address book or an appointment book? Do you write yourself a list of things to do? Outlook simply automates the process and in so doing adds considerable flexibility to the way you enter and reference your data.

We begin with a brief overview of each component, then move immediately to e-mail, perhaps the most widely used function in Outlook. Our discussion introduces (or reviews) the basic commands present in any e-mail system to compose, send, read, and reply to e-mail messages. We show you how to attach files to an e-mail message and how to create different folders so that you can organize the messages you send and receive. As always, the hands-on exercises are essential to the learn-by-doing philosophy we follow throughout the text.

Next you will learn to use your contact list (address book). You will find that keeping track of all of the people you have dealings with can be pretty helpful. In the third exercise we introduce the calendar portion of Outlook. You will learn how to set up meetings and appointments, and keep track of your work using the Outlook Journal. The Journal is, in essence, a log that tracks every document you access. You can then reference the Journal to find out when you last worked on a document and to find lost documents on your system.

THE OUTLOOK WINDOW

The Outlook window has similar menus and toolbars to that of the other applications in Microsoft Office, which we will describe in the various exercises that follow. A significant difference in Outlook is the ***Navigation Pane*** at the left of the window. The appearance of the Navigation Pane changes depending on what Outlook feature you are using. When you are using e-mail as in Figure 1a, the Navigation Pane displays all of your mail folders as well as ***Favorite Folders*** that contain folders you use most frequently. These folders are created by default when Outlook is installed. The buttons at the bottom of the Navigation Pane are shortcuts to the other Outlook features such as the calendar and address book.

The ***Inbox***, one of several e-mail folders in Figure 1a, displays all incoming messages (including faxes), the person who sent the message, the subject of the message, and the date and time the message was received. (You may have to expand the Inbox frame to see all of this information.) In this view the messages have been sorted and grouped by date received, with the folder showing those messages received today expanded. The ***Reading Pane*** to the right of the Inbox shows the text of the selected message. We will discuss the Inbox in more detail shortly.

The ***Contacts folder*** is shown in Figure 1b. As with the calendar, contacts can be displayed in different views (the Address Cards view is selected in Figure 1b). You can enter as much (or as little) information for each contact as you like. Once it is updated with the addresses of friends and associates, the Contacts folder becomes the basis for other Office functions. For example, the address an e-mail message is to be sent to can be selected from the Contacts folder. Postal addresses can also be selected from the Contacts folder, a feature we use all the time from Microsoft Word when we are addressing a letter. As with all Outlook features, you can print the contents of the Contacts folder; for instance, you can create a hard copy of your telephone directory.

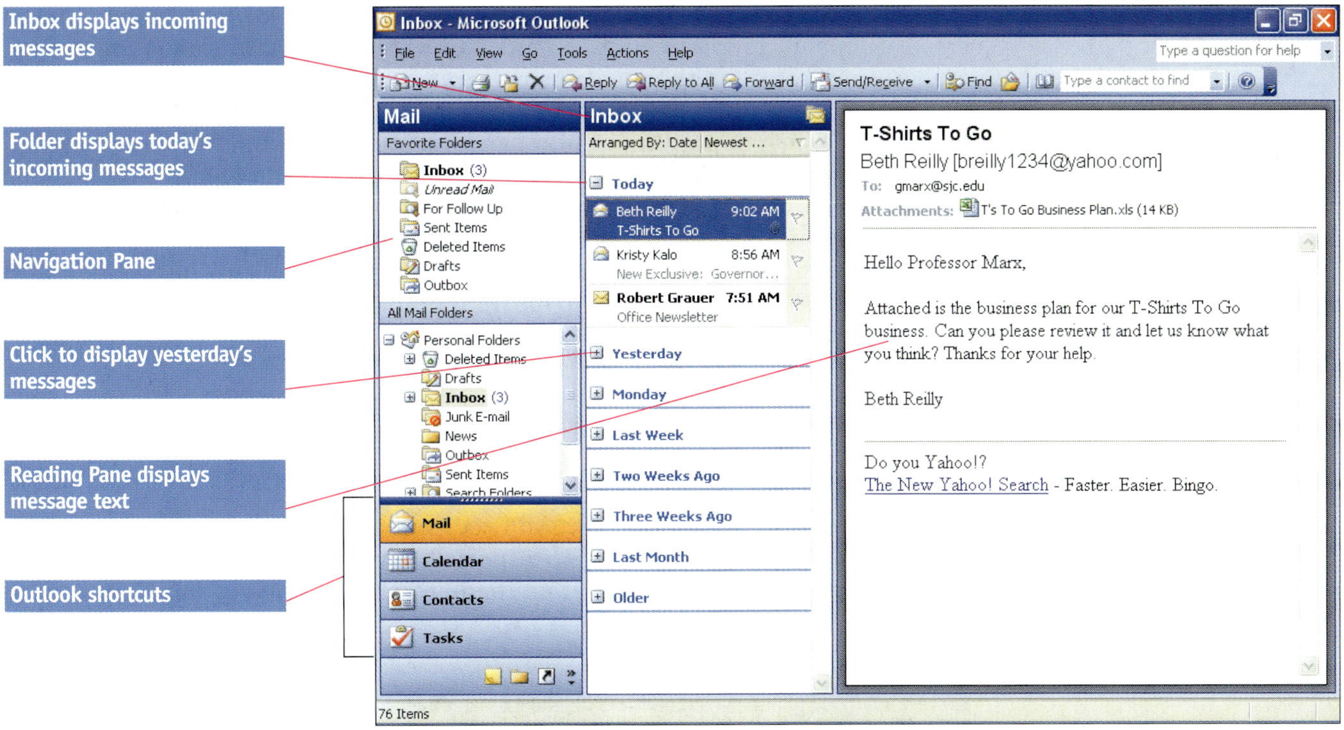

(a) The E-mail Window

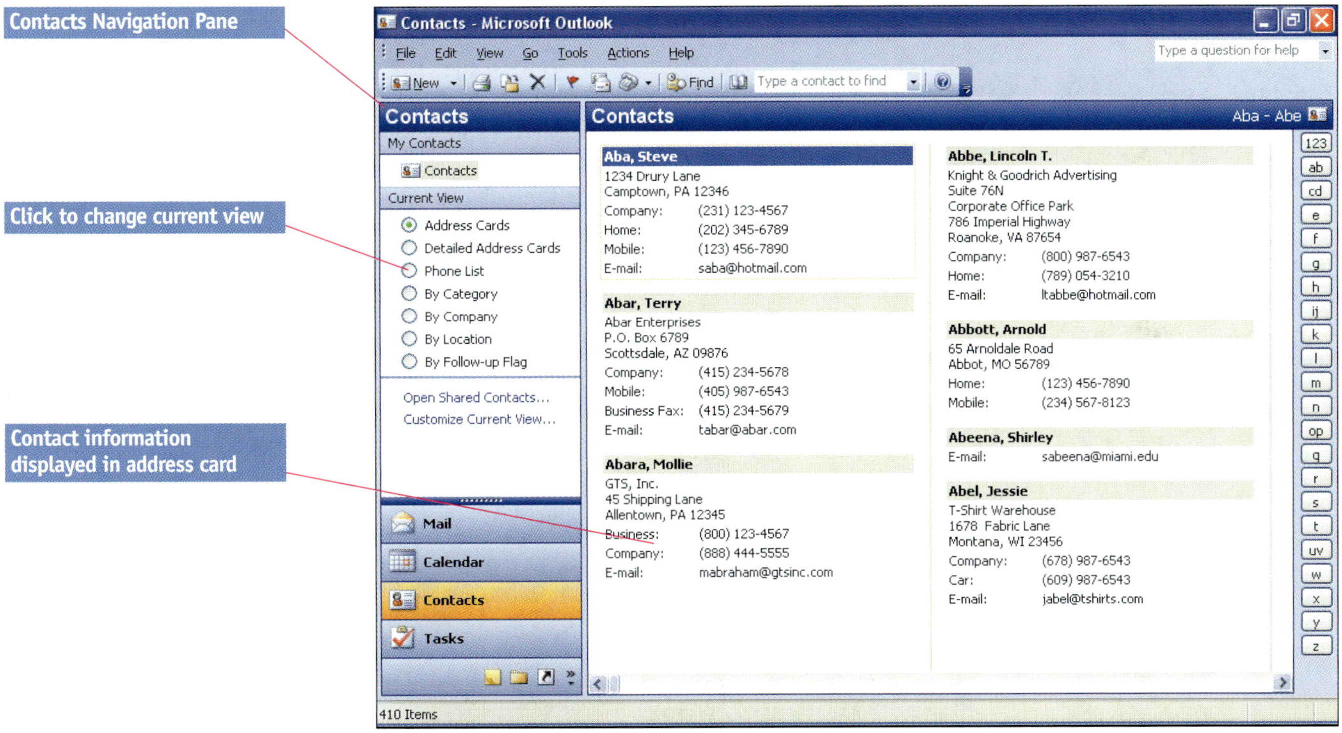

(b) The Contacts Folder

FIGURE 1 Outlook

The ***Calendar*** is selected in Figure 1c. The Outlook Calendar enables you to create a detailed appointment book and to display appointments in different views (daily, weekly, or monthly). You can create recurring appointments (e.g., the same appointment repeating on different days), and you can instruct Outlook to remind you prior to each appointment. You can also print your appointment book and take it with you. The ***Task list*** below the monthly calendar in Figure 1c is a simple but effective "to do" list that will help you organize your work. A ***task*** is simpler than an appointment and is not necessarily associated with a specific date or time. You can check off a task just as you can with pencil and paper. Unlike a paper "to do" list, overdue tasks are shown in red, reminding you to get busy.

The ***Journal*** in Figure 1d (opened from an icon on the Navigation Pane) is a log of the activity on your computer. If you have turned the Journal on, Outlook automatically generates a journal entry every time you access an Office document. As with the other features, the Journal can be displayed in different views (for example, weekly in Figure 1d). You can collapse or expand the entries for different activities. Excel, Word, and phone entries, for example, are tracked in Figure 1d, which shows that the user accessed several Excel spreadsheets on Wednesday, July 2, 2003. This is very useful information, especially if you need to retrace the steps you took on a specific day. Note, too, that the Journal also provides shortcut icons to reopen the documents it displays.

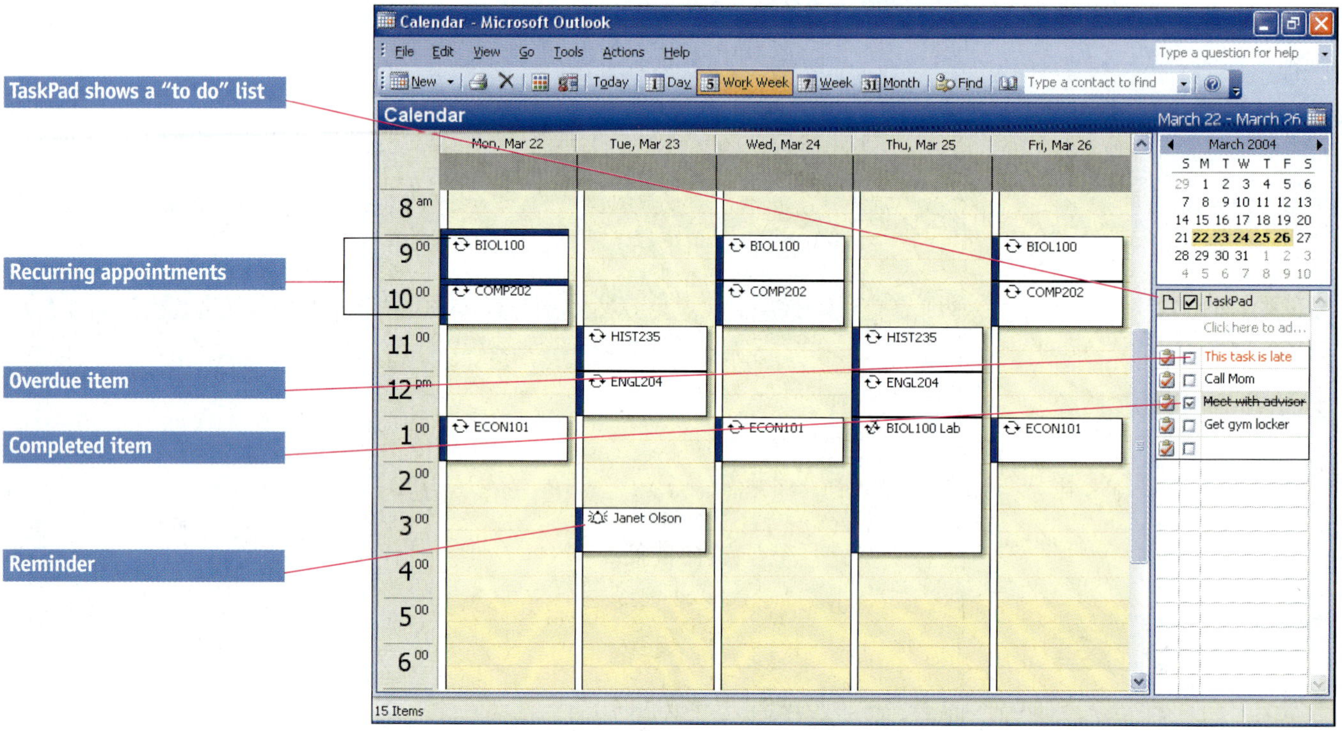

(c) The Calendar

FIGURE 1 Outlook (*continued*)

IT'S SYNERGISTIC

The functions in Outlook are thoroughly integrated with one another, making each function more valuable as a part of the whole. E-mail, for example, can be generated automatically from appointments on the calendar (perhaps to remind attendees of a scheduled meeting) using entries in the address book. You can also go in the other direction and create entries in your address book or events on your calendar directly from an e-mail message.

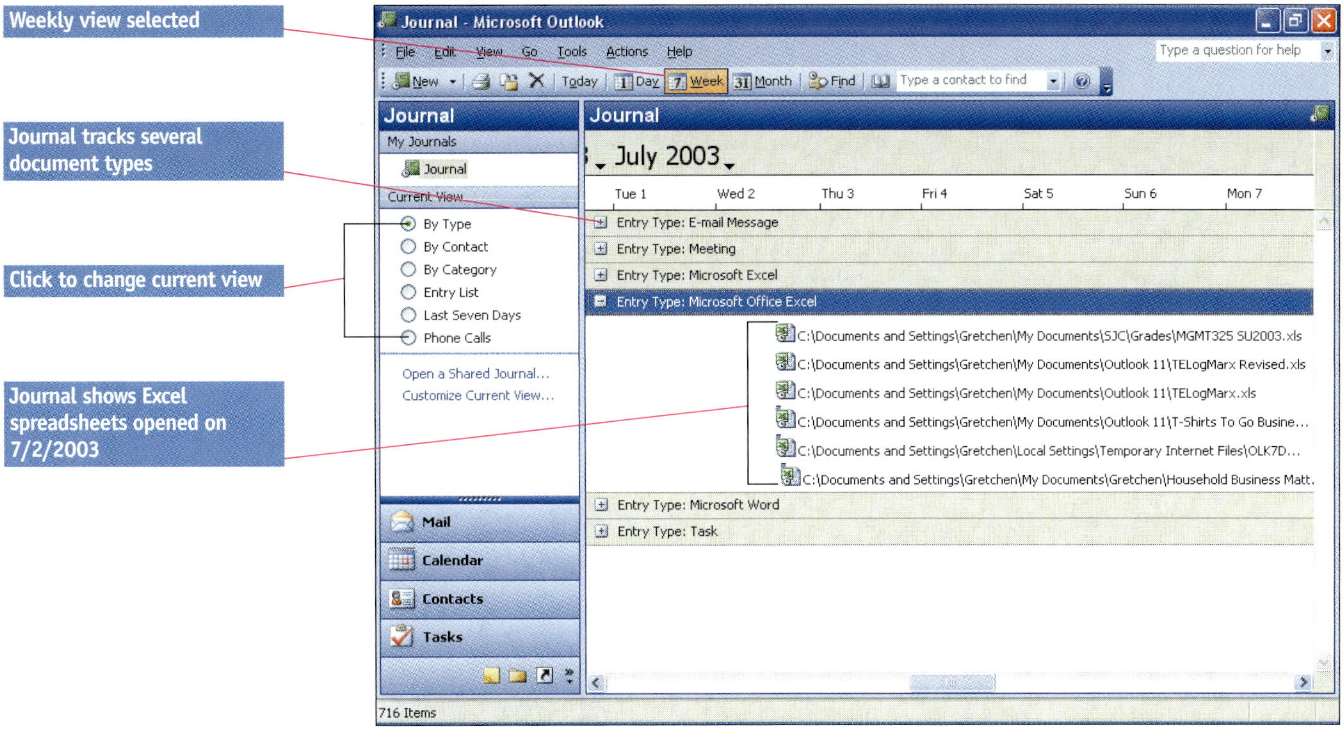

(d) The Journal

FIGURE 1 Outlook (*continued*)

INTRODUCTION TO E-MAIL

Electronic mail, or ***e-mail***, while conceptually the same as writing a letter and sending it through the U.S. Postal Service, has one very significant advantage—e-mail messages are delivered almost instantly anywhere in the world via the Internet. All Windows-based e-mail systems work essentially the same way. A ***mail client***, a program on your PC such as Microsoft Outlook, allows you to compose, send, and receive e-mail messages. Outlook, your mail client, sets up the connection with the mail server to receive your incoming messages and to deliver the messages you send.

A ***mail server*** is a special-purpose computer with an Internet connection such as you might have in your campus computer network, or it is a computer at your Internet service provider such as AOL, MSN, or your cable company. The mail server functions as a central post office and provides private ***mailboxes*** to persons authorized to use its services. The mail server receives messages around the clock from the Internet and any local networks that are attached to it, and will hold your messages for you until you log in to retrieve them.

When you open Outlook, it connects you to the server, where you gain access to your mailbox via a ***username*** and a ***password***. Your username identifies you to the server; your password protects your account from unauthorized use by others.

Once you log in to the server, outgoing mail is ***uploaded*** from your PC to the server, where it is sent on its way across a local area network to another person within your organization or across the Internet to recipients wherever they are located. New mail is ***downloaded*** from the server and stored in the Inbox in Outlook.

In order to use Outlook to connect to a mail server, you must have already established an e-mail account. The many methods for doing so are beyond the scope of this text. You should check with your instructor or campus help desk for information on how to connect to your campus mail server, or your ISP help desk if you have an e-mail account through another Internet provider.

Figure 2 displays another view of the Inbox as it appears in Microsoft Outlook. The Navigation Pane still displays the folder list, but this time the Reading Pane is at the bottom of the window. The fields at the top of the message list show all incoming messages, the name of the sender, the subject, the date and time the message was received, and the size of the message. In this view the most recent messages appear at the top of the list. Look carefully at the messages in the Inbox to learn more about their status and contents.

Messages that have been read appear in regular type; messages that have not been read appear in boldface. The number in parentheses next to the Inbox icon in the Favorite Folders list in the Navigation Pane shows a count of unread messages. One message was marked by the sender as urgent as shown by the exclamation point. The message from Beth Reilly needs further attention so the recipient has flagged it for follow-up. The icon with a magenta arrow denotes a message that has been read and replied to. The message icon with a blue arrow indicates that the message has been forwarded to another recipient. Messages with attachments show a paper clip icon.

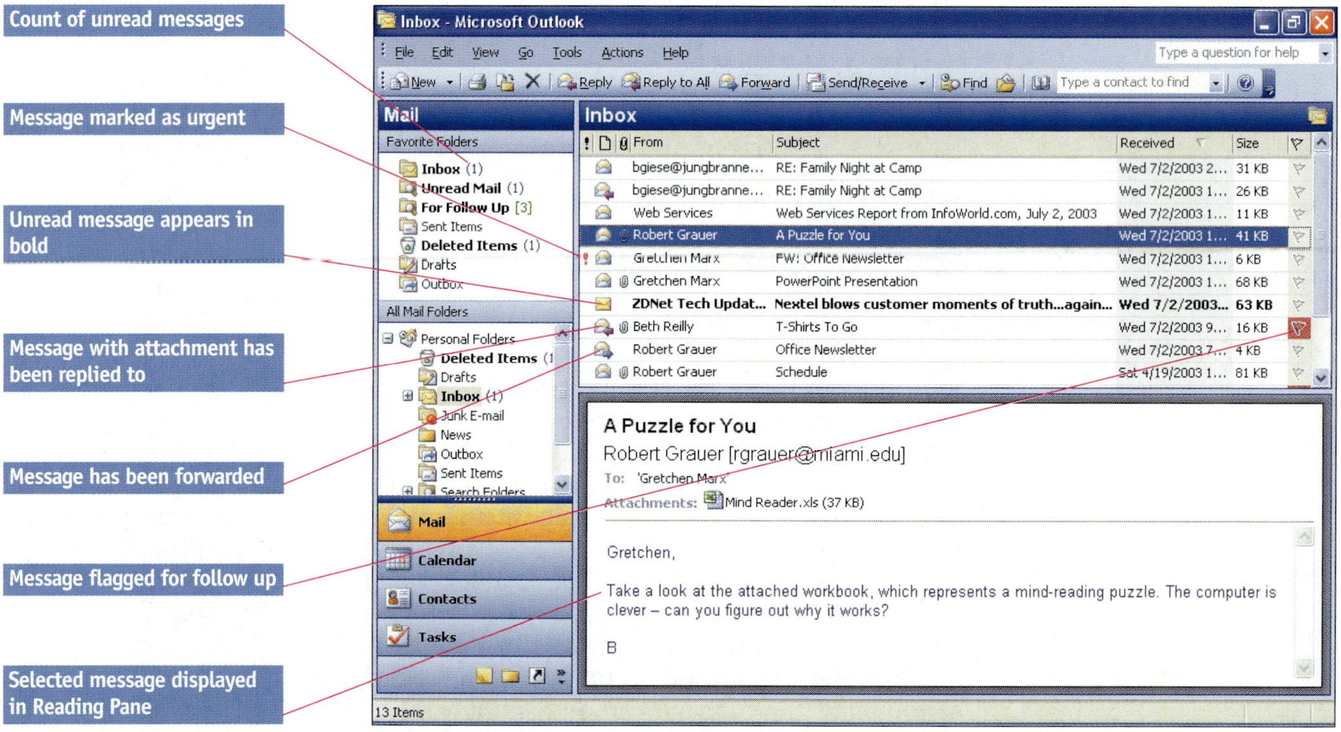

FIGURE 2 The Inbox

IT'S NOT AS PRIVATE AS YOU THINK

One of the most significant differences between e-mail and regular mail is privacy—or the lack thereof. When you receive a sealed letter through the mail, you can assume that no one else has read the letter. Not so with e-mail. The network administrator can read the messages in your inbox, and indeed, many employers maintain they have the legal right to read their employees' e-mail. Don't assume that deleting a message protects your privacy, since most organizations maintain extensive backup systems and can recover a deleted message. In other words, never put anything in an e-mail message that you would be uncomfortable seeing in tomorrow's newspaper.

Mail Folders

The purpose of Outlook's mail folders, shown in Figure 3, can be inferred from their names. The ***Outbox*** folder contains all of the messages you have written that have not yet been sent (uploaded) to the server. Once Outlook sends a message, it is automatically moved from the Outbox to the ***Sent Items folder***. Messages will remain indefinitely in both the Inbox and Sent Items folders unless you delete them, in which case they are moved to the ***Deleted Items folder***. If you close Outlook while you are in the midst of creating an e-mail, Outlook saves the unfinished message in the ***Drafts folder***.

Think, for a moment, about how you process your regular mail. You bring it into your house from the mailbox and read it at your leisure. Some mail is junk mail, which you immediately throw away. Other mail is important and you file it away with other important papers. And some mail you want to share with others in your household; you leave it on the kitchen table to reread at a later time.

E-mail is very similar. Once you begin using it, you will receive many unsolicited messages, just as you receive junk mail through the U.S. post office. You will eventually delete most of the messages you receive. Even if you save only the most important ones, after you have been receiving e-mail for some time, you will discover that there is too much mail to keep in your Inbox—it simply gets too full. You can alleviate the mess by creating folders with which to organize the various types of mail you receive. Messages can be moved or copied from one mail folder to another. Follow the same conventions as you do in Windows Explorer; that is, click and drag to move a message from one folder to another.

Only one e-mail folder can be selected at a time (for example, the Unread Mail folder in Figure 3), and its contents are displayed in the Reading Pane of the Outlook window. Click a different icon in either folder list in the Navigation Pane to display its contents in the Reading Pane. The ***Unread Mail*** and ***For Follow Up folders*** in the Favorite Folders list act as search folders. When you click them, they will display all messages in your mail folders that are either unread or require follow-up, respectively.

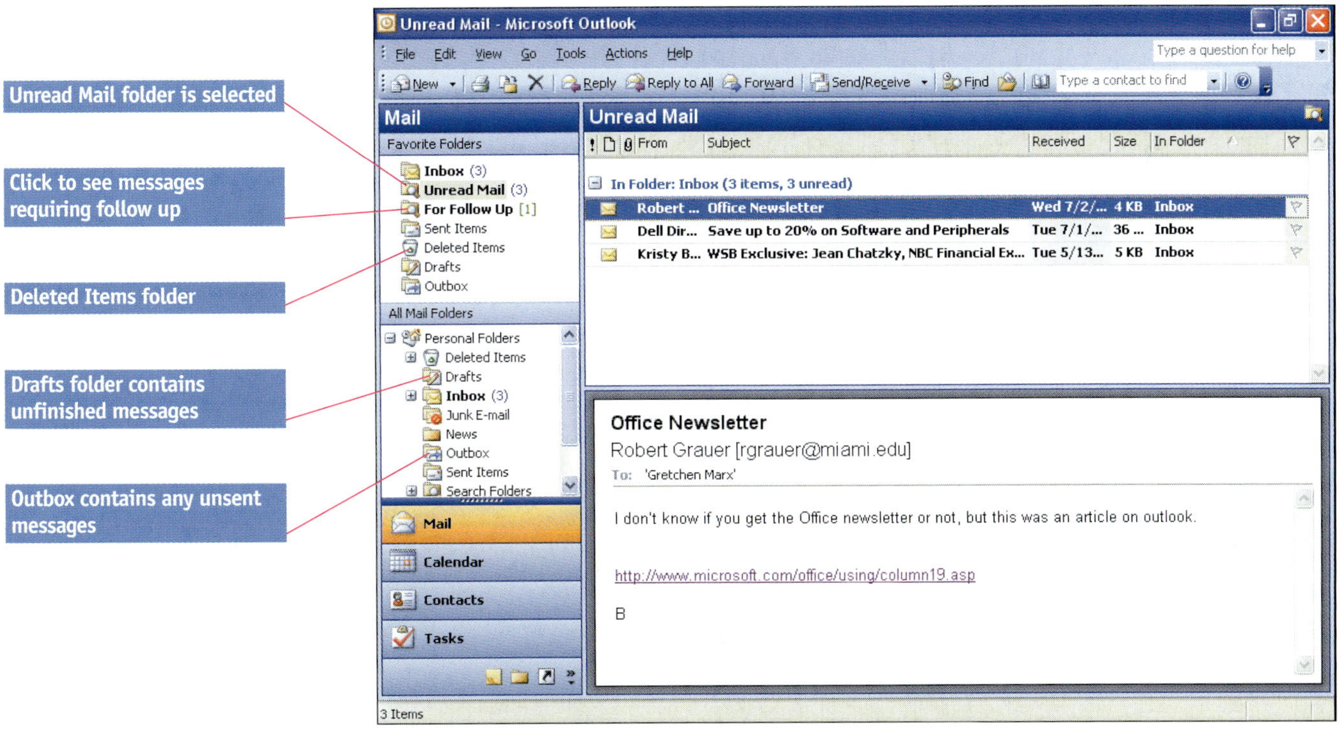

FIGURE 3 Mail Folders

Anatomy of an E-mail Message

Creating an e-mail message is easy. Just click the New Mail Message button on the Standard toolbar to display a window similar to Figure 4. The function of the various text boxes at the top of the message window is apparent from their names. The To text box, for example, contains the ***e-mail address*** of the recipient(s). The Cc text box (courtesy or carbon copy) indicates the names of other people who are to receive copies of the message. The Subject text box is filled in with an appropriate indicator of the message contents so that the recipient can determine at a glance what the message is about.

The message text appears in the message area below the subject line. Enter the text of the message, then click the Send button to mail it. That's it. The message itself can be simple or more sophisticated, such as our example in Figure 4. For example, Outlook documents are Web-enabled, meaning that you (or the recipient) can click a hyperlink within an e-mail message, and provided you have an Internet connection, be automatically connected to the Web page. The message in Figure 4 also shows Outlook stationery that you can select as a background for your messages.

The message in Figure 4 also contains three ***attached files***—an Excel workbook, a Word document, and a PowerPoint presentation. The recipient reads the message as usual, then has the ability to view, save, and/or edit the attached file on his or her PC in its original format. Both capabilities are illustrated in the first hands-on exercise.

Replying to an existing message is similar in concept to creating a new message except that Outlook automatically enters the addressee for you. You open a message from the Inbox to read it, click the ***Reply button***, then enter the text of your message. You can enter additional recipients and/or forward the original message to someone else.

As with any other Office application, Outlook commands are executed in a variety of ways. You can execute a command by pulling down a menu, by clicking a button on a toolbar, or by a keyboard shortcut. It is the underlying capabilities that are important, however, rather than the specific means of execution.

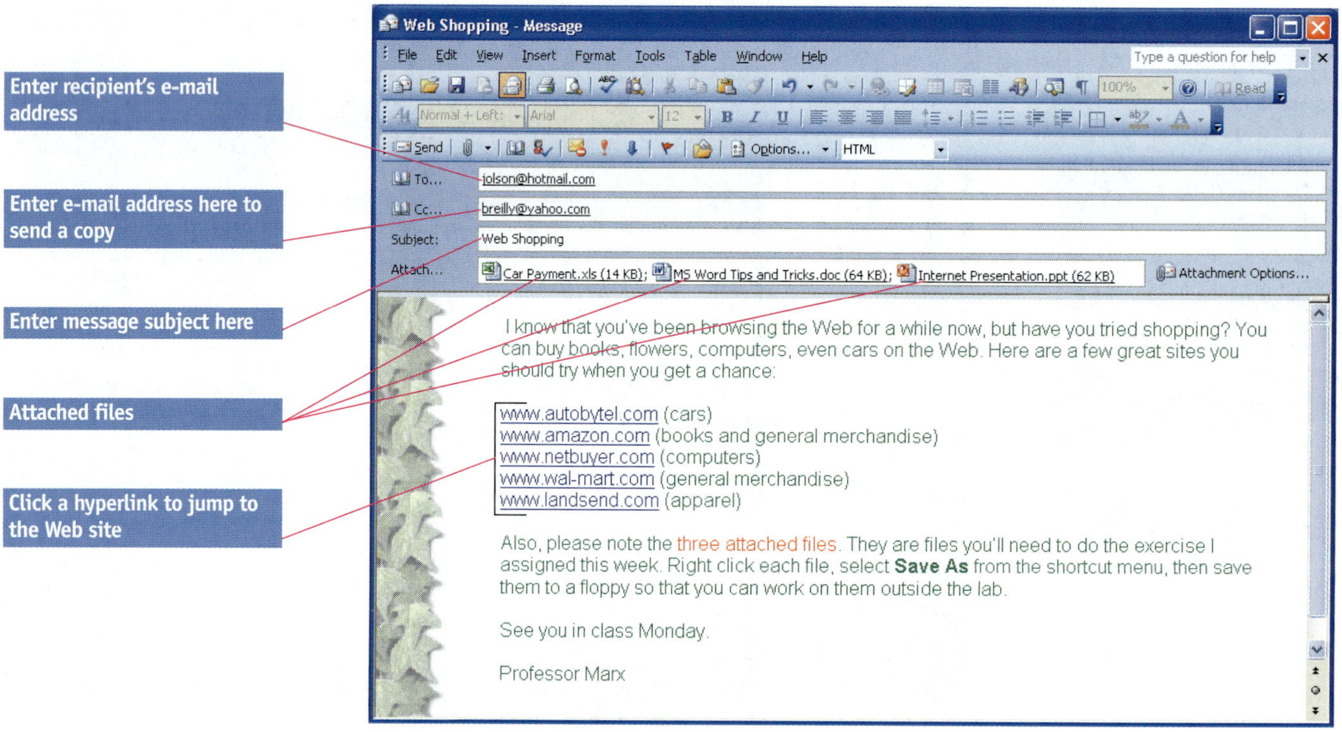

FIGURE 4 An Outlook Mail Message

hands-on exercise

1 Introduction to E-mail

Objective To send and receive an e-mail message. To complete this exercise, you must have a network connection and an e-mail account. Use Figure 5 as a guide in the exercise.

Step 1: Open Outlook

- You need to initiate a network connection in order to send and receive e-mail. The precise directions depend on where you are doing the exercise.
  - If you are using your campus network, your network center, help desk, or instructor will provide you with a username and password to log into your network.
  - If you are doing the exercise at home, you will need to connect to your Internet service provider (ISP) by modem.
- Click the **Start button** on the Windows taskbar, click **Programs** or **All Programs** depending on your version of Windows, then click **Outlook**.
- Close the Office Assistant if it appears. If necessary, maximize the Outlook window so that it takes the entire desktop.
- If you do not see the Navigation Pane shown in Figure 5a, pull down the **View menu** and click **Navigation Pane**.
- Pull down the **Tools menu**, click **Options**, click the **Mail Format tab**, then click **Use Microsoft Word to edit e-mail messages**. (This will display the Standard and Formatting toolbars when you create a message.)
- If necessary, click the **down arrow** in the **Message Format box** and select **HTML**. Click **OK** to close the dialog box.

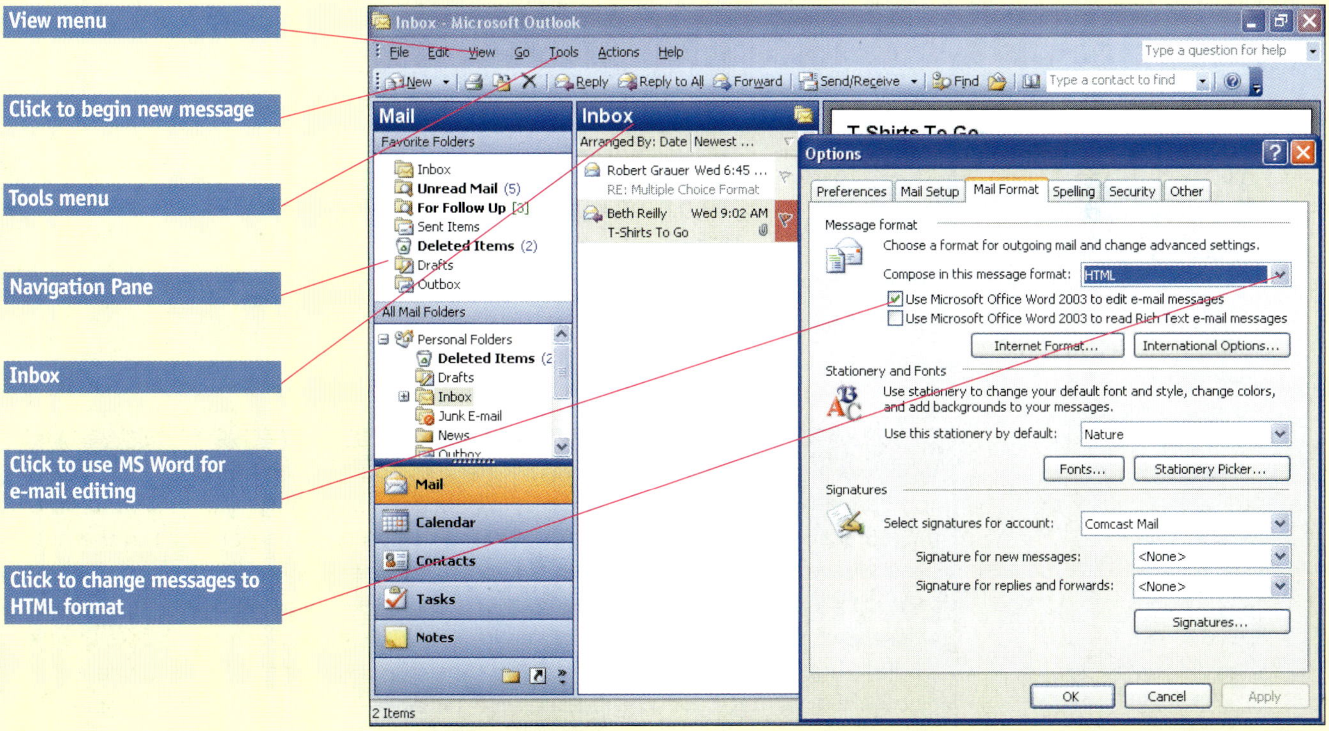

(a) Open Outlook (step 1)

FIGURE 5 Hands-on Exercise 1

Step 2: Send a Message

- Click the **New Mail Message button** on the Standard toolbar to display the editing window in Figure 5b. Maximize the window.
- Enter the Internet address of the recipient in the **To text box**. (Enter your own address or your professor's if you don't know any others.)
- Press the **Tab key** to move the insertion point to the **Cc text box** (Courtesy or Carbon copy). Enter your e-mail address so you will get a copy of the message.
- Press the **Tab key** to move the insertion point to (or click in) the **Subject text box**. Type the subject, then press the **Tab key** again to move to the message area.
- Enter the text of your message, pressing the **Enter key** only at the end of a paragraph. Correct any mistakes, then click the **Send button**. The editing window closes automatically, and you are returned to the Inbox folder.

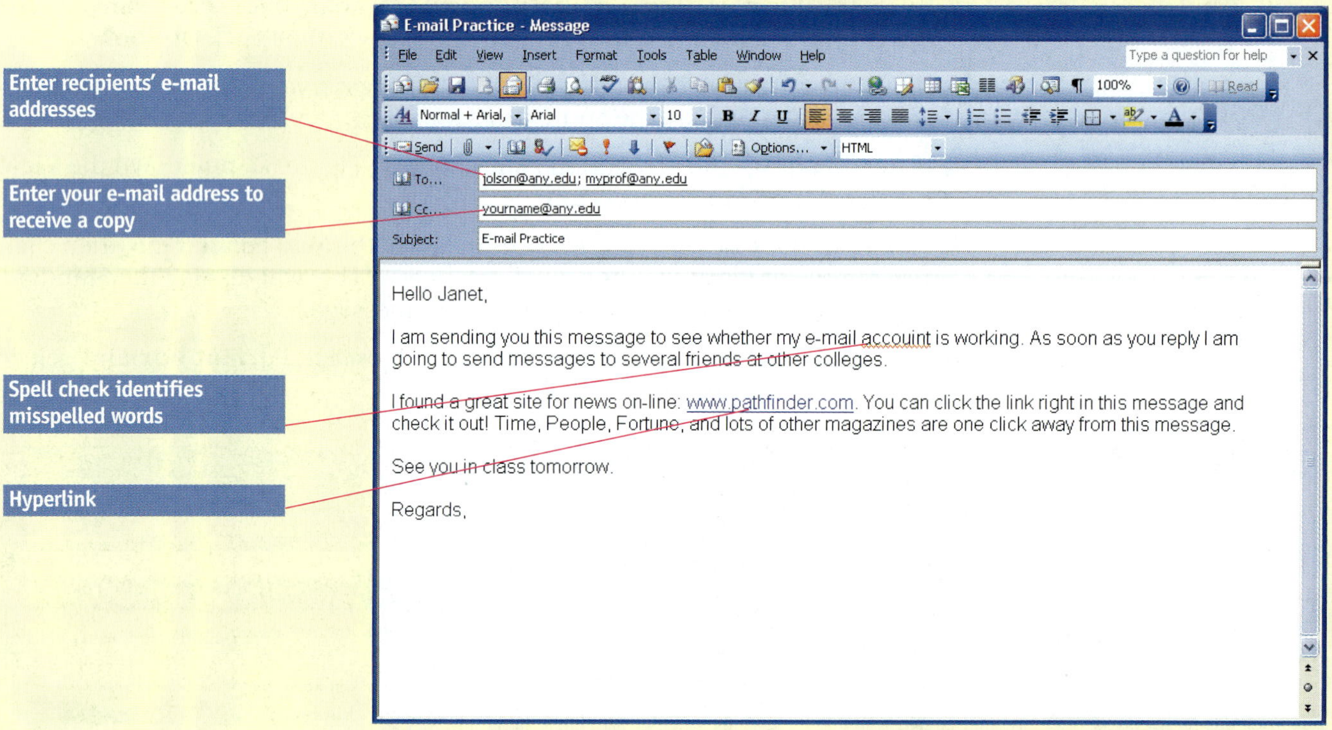

(b) Send a Message (step 2)

FIGURE 5 Hands-on Exercise 1 (*continued*)

INSERTING A PICTURE INTO YOUR MESSAGE

You can insert a picture into an e-mail message—we suggest that you send home a picture of you hard at work at your desk. Position the insertion point in the message where you want the picture. Pull down the Insert menu and select Picture, then click From File to display the Insert Picture dialog box. Navigate to the folder where your picture is saved, select the image(s), then click Insert to insert the picture(s). The picture is inserted into the message in its original size. Since not all picture file formats are compatible with all e-mail clients, you should generally include only .gif and .jpg files. And you have to be careful that your e-mail message does not get so large that your ISP refuses to send it. If the picture is too large, try changing its size using a photo editor such as Microsoft PhotoDraw.

Step 3: **Read Your Mail**

- Wait a minute or two, then click the **Send/Receive button** on the Standard toolbar to retrieve your mail from the mailer server.
- Pull down the **View menu**, select **Reading Pane**, then click **Bottom** to display the selected message in the lower half of the window as shown in Figure 5c.
- Pull down the **View menu** once again, this time selecting **AutoPreview**. The message list in the Inbox includes the first few lines of the message text. Repeat this procedure to close the AutoPreview feature.
- Click the **message** in the Inbox that you just sent yourself to display it in the Reading Pane in the lower half of the window. If necessary, drag the scroll bar down in the Reading Pane to see the rest of the message text.
- Click and drag the top edge of the Reading Pane upward to enlarge its size so that you can see more of the message. (You will, by default, see fewer of your messages listed in the Inbox.) Click and drag the top edge downward to return the Reading Pane to its original size. Click and drag the left edge of the Reading Pane to the left to widen it.
- Pull down the **View menu**, then select **Navigation Pane** to remove the Navigation Pane so that you can see more of the message.
- Press **Alt+F1** to display the Navigation Pane again. (Alt+F1 works as a toggle switch to open and close the Navigation Pane.)
- Click the **Print button** on the Standard toolbar to print the message.

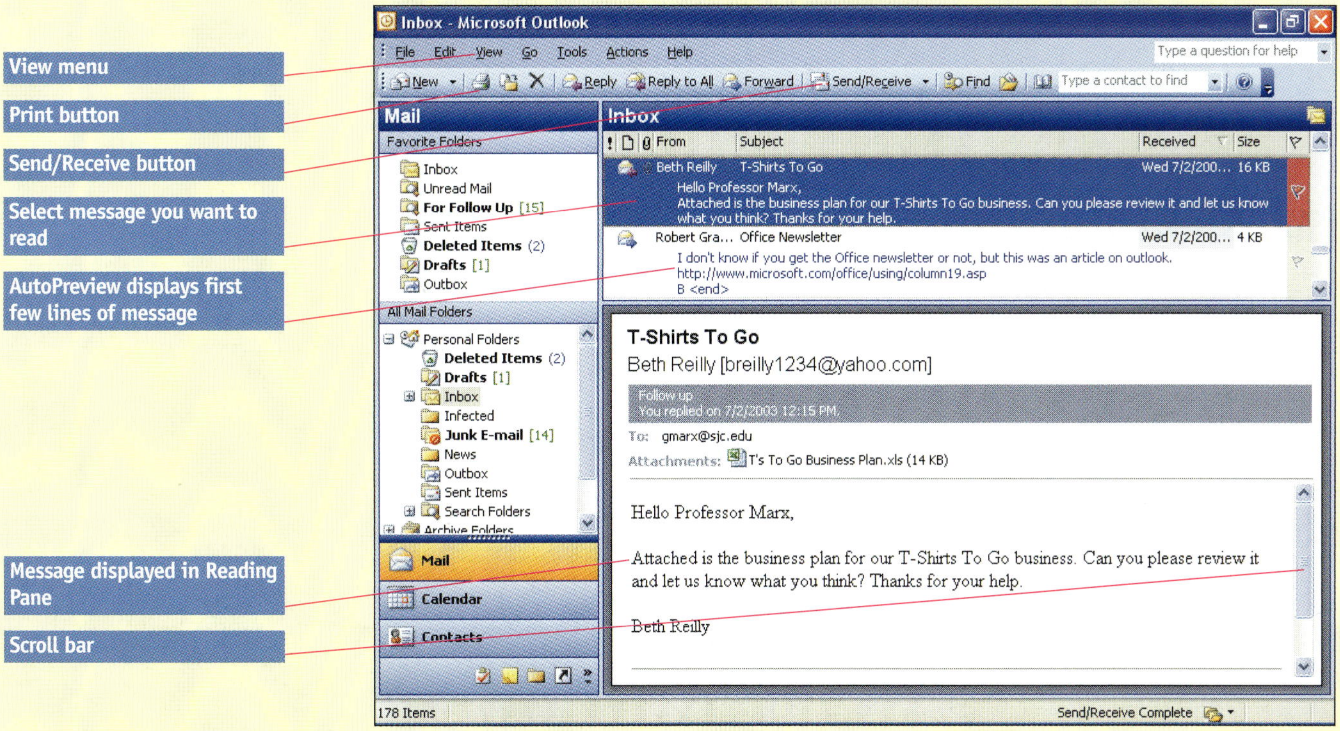

(c) Read Your Mail (step 3)

FIGURE 5 Hands-on Exercise 1 (*continued*)

Step 4: Reply to a Message

- Pull down the **Tools menu** and click **Options** to display the Options dialog box. If necessary, click the **Preferences tab**, then click the **E-mail Options button** to display the E-mail Options dialog box.
- Click the down arrow in the **When replying to a message list box** and choose the option to **Include original message text**. Select the same option in the **When forwarding a message list box**.
- Click **OK** to close the dialog box, then click **OK** again to close the Options dialog box.
- Select a message to which you want to reply, then click the **Reply button** to display a screen similar to Figure 5d. The recipient's e-mail address and the subject are entered automatically. The original e-mail message appears below a blank area where you can enter your reply.
- Enter the text of your reply using the same editing commands as when you created the original message in step 2. Right click any spelling mistakes and pick the corrected word from the list.
- Click the **Importance: High** or **Importance: Low button** (as you deem appropriate) to flag your reply when it appears in the recipient's Inbox.
- Click the **Send button** when you have completed your reply. If necessary, close the window containing the original message to return to your Inbox.

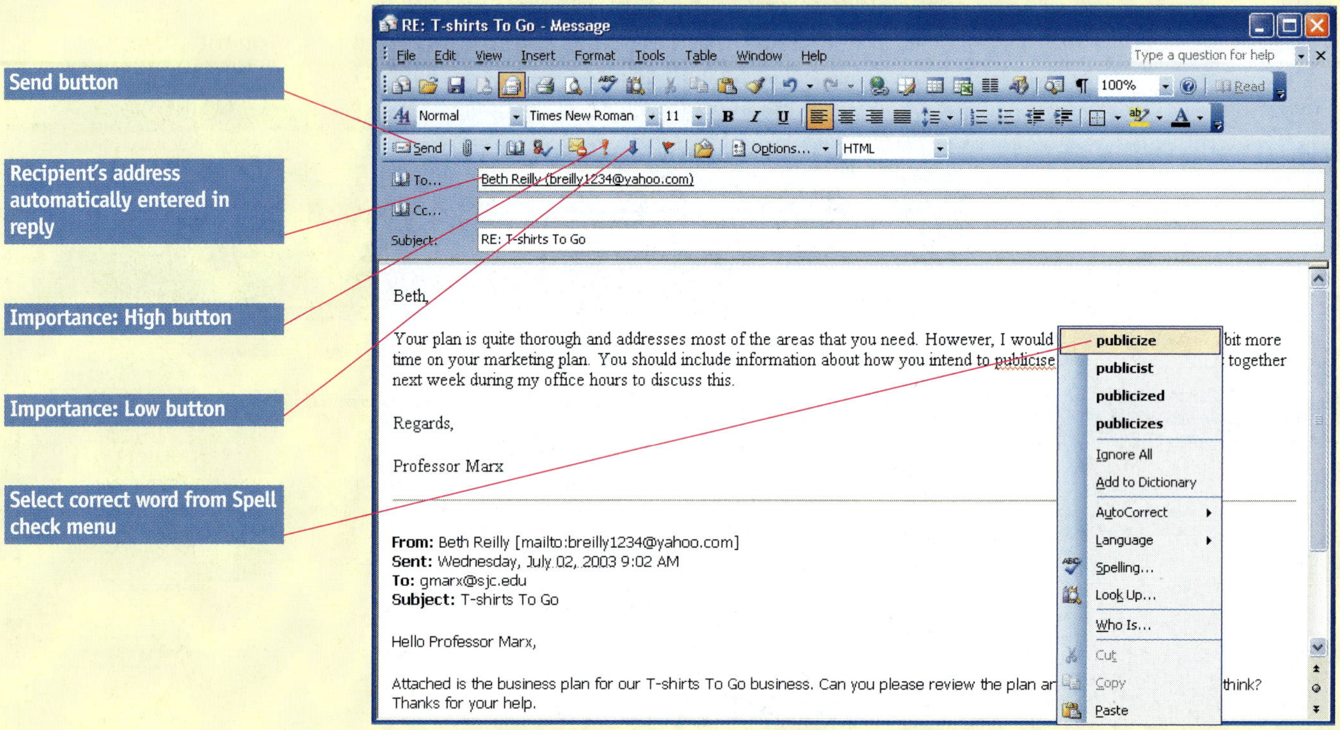

(d) Reply to a Message (step 4)

FIGURE 5 Hands-on Exercise 1 (*continued*)

CUSTOMIZING THE READING PANE

You can change the settings for the Reading Pane by right clicking the top edge of the pane. This will display a shortcut menu that allows you to remove the message header, change the font in which the messages in the Reading Pane are displayed, and so on.

Step 5: Attach a File; Enter Hyperlinks

- Enter the text of a new message as shown in Figure 5e, being sure to enter the Web addresses exactly as they appear (**www.foundmoney.com** and **www.ebay.com**). Send the message to yourself and anyone else you wish.
- Pull down the **Insert menu** and click **File** (or click the **Insert File button** on the Standard toolbar) to display the Insert File dialog box.
- Click the **down arrow** on the Look in text box and select any folder in My Documents, then select a small file within that folder. Click **Insert** to attach the selected file to your message. You will see an attachment icon at the top of your message.
- Click the **Send button** to send the message. The editing window closes automatically, and you are once again returned to the Inbox folder.

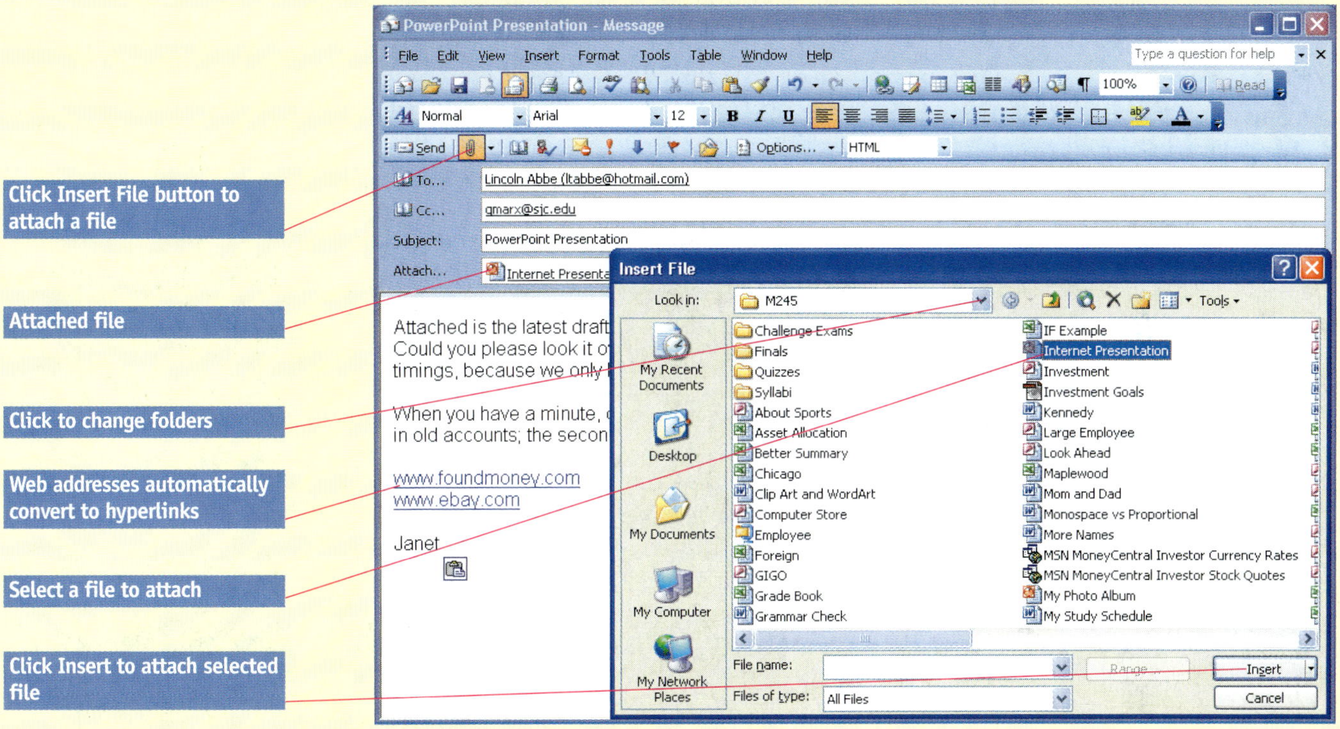

(e) Attach a File; Enter Hyperlinks (step 5)

FIGURE 5 Hands-on Exercise 1 (*continued*)

CREATE A SIGNATURE FILE

You can set up Outlook to automatically end your e-mail messages with a consistent closing (called a signature), consisting of your name, title, address, telephone, and other information. To create a signature, first be sure that you have your Inbox open on your desktop. Pull down the Tools menu, select Options, click the Mail Format tab, then click the Signatures button to display the Create Signature dialog box. Click New and follow the prompts to enter a signature. Click OK to close the Create Signature dialog box, then click the down arrow next to the Signature for new messages text box. Select the signature you just created, then click OK to close the Options dialog box. To test the signature, click the Inbox folder, then click New to create a new message. Your signature should automatically appear in the message area. You can use the same procedure to set a signature for replies and forwards.

Step 6: Open an Attachment; Test the Hyperlinks

- When the message you created and sent in step 5 appears in your Inbox, double click it to open the message as in Figure 5f.
- The Web addresses you entered in step 5 appear as hyperlinks (they appear in magenta or blue, depending on whether you have already visited them or not).
  - At www.foundmoney.com you can search for funds that you have unknowingly abandoned, such as a closed bank account or an unrefunded security deposit.
  - www.ebay.com is a popular Web auction site. We suggest you click the link to find out what people are selling over the Internet.
- Double click the file in the Attachments line. If the Opening Mail Attachment dialog box shown in the figure displays a warning message, click **Open**. The attached document opens in its own window. (Note that Windows opens the application appropriate for the attached file. That is, if the file is a worksheet, Windows opens Excel to display the file. If it is a letter, memo, or report, Windows opens Word, and if it is a presentation, Windows opens PowerPoint to display the attachment.)
- Close the document, then close the message window to return to the Inbox.

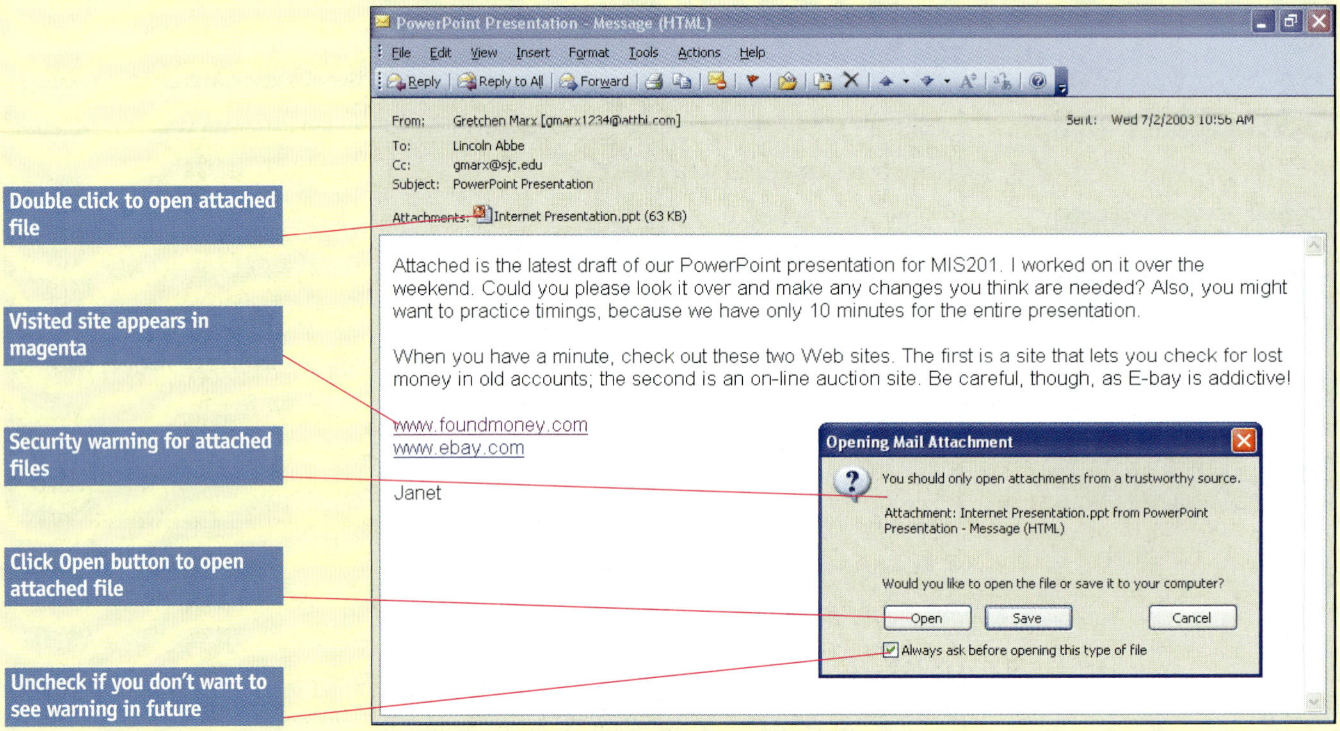

(f) Open an Attachment; Test the Hyperlinks (step 6)

FIGURE 5 Hands-on Exercise 1 (*continued*)

FORWARD A MESSAGE

To forward a message to someone else, select the message, click the Forward button on the Standard toolbar to open the editing window, then enter the recipient's e-mail address in the To text box. The subject, preceded by the letters FW to indicate the message has been forwarded, is entered automatically. You can add to or edit the text of the original message if it appears in the editing window. Click the Send button when you are finished.

Step 7: Customize the View

- Pull down the **View menu**, select **Arrange by**, click the **Expand button** at the bottom of the submenu, then click **Custom** to display the Customize View: Messages dialog box shown in the background of Figure 5g.
- Click **Fields** to view the Show Fields dialog box. Click **Flag Status** in the field list at the right of the dialog box, then click **Move Up** until flag status is immediately after icon as shown.
- Click **Cancel** to return to the Custom View dialog box without adding any fields. Click **Cancel** to return to the Inbox.
- Click the **From field** at the top of the Inbox to sort your messages by the sender's name. Pull down the **View menu**, select **Arrange By**, then click **Show in Groups** to display the messages grouped by sender. Click the **plus sign (+)** next to the sender's name to display the messages from that person.
- Pull down the **View menu,** select **Current View**, then click the other buttons in the Current View menu to explore other views in Outlook.
- Pull down the **View menu**, click **Arrange by**, then click **Show in Groups** to remove the message grouping.

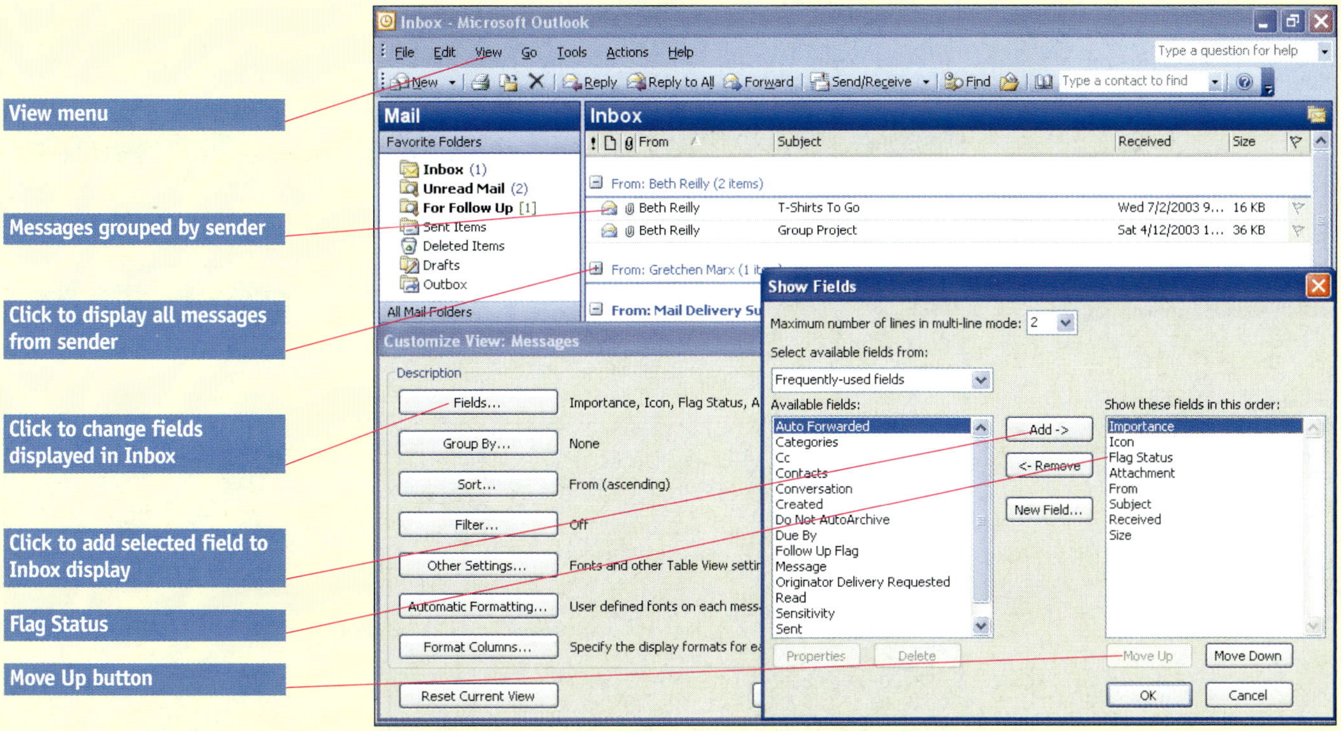

(g) Customize the View (step 7)

FIGURE 5 Hands-on Exercise 1 (*continued*)

SORT YOUR MESSAGES

Click a field name at the top of the Inbox folder to sort the messages in that order. For example, click From to display messages in ascending alphabetical order by the sender's name, click it again to display messages in descending alphabetical order. Click Received once to display in ascending date sequence, click again to display in descending date order (most recent messages at the top of the folder list).

Step 8: Create a New Folder

- If necessary, press **Alt+F1** to display the Navigation Pane. With the Inbox open, pull down the **File menu**, click **New**, then select **Folder** to display the Create New Folder dialog box shown in Figure 5h.
- Enter **COMP100** as the name of the new folder as shown in Figure 5h. If necessary, click the **down arrow** in the **Folder contains list box** and select **Mail and Post Items**.
- Click **Inbox** to place the new folder in the Outlook Inbox. Click **OK** to create the new folder.
- If necessary, click the + (plus sign) next to the Inbox to display COMP100 and any other folders within the Inbox.
- Click **Inbox** on the Navigation Pane, select one or more files in the Inbox and drag it (them) to the COMP100 folder in the Folder list. (Press and hold the **Ctrl key** while clicking messages to select more than one.)
- Click the **COMP100 folder icon** in the Navigation Pane to open the folder. The messages that you dragged to the COMP100 folder are displayed in the message list, while the name at the top of the list changes to COMP100.
- Click **Inbox** in the folder list in the Navigation Pane to return to your Inbox.

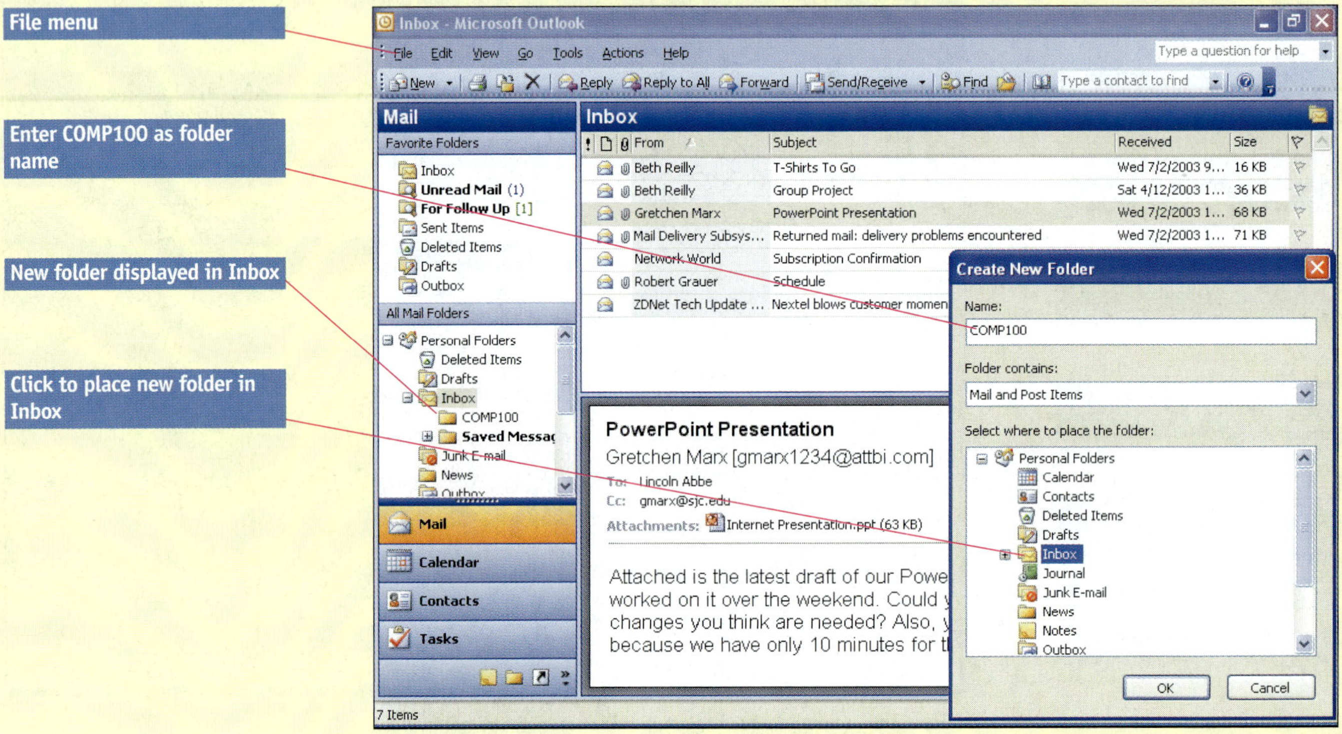

(h) Create a New Folder (step 8)

FIGURE 5 Hands-on Exercise 1 (*continued*)

CLEAN UP YOUR INBOX

Don't let too much mail accumulate in your Inbox. Delete messages that you don't need, and move messages that you want to keep to a new folder. Depending on the amount of mail you receive, you may want to set up rules so that mail from certain sources is automatically moved to specific folders (see practice exercise 1 at the end of the chapter).

Step 9: Add Stationery to a Mail Message

- Pull down the **Tools menu**, click **Options**, then select the **Mail Format tab** to display the Options dialog box in Figure 5i.
- If necessary, click the **down arrow** next to the **Compose in this message format** list box and select **HTML**.
- Click the **Stationery Picker button** to display the Stationery Picker dialog box in Figure 5i. Try several stationery formats until you find one that you like (we chose Nature), then click **OK** to select it.
- Click the **Fonts button** to display the Fonts dialog box. (Note that you can choose a different font for replies and forwarded messages so the recipient can readily see the text you have added to the message.)
- Click the **Choose Font button** for replying and forwarding and change the font color to **red**.
- Click **OK** to close the Font dialog box, click **OK** again to close the Fonts dialog box, then click **OK** once again to close the Options dialog box.
- Click the **New Mail Message button** to open a new message window. It is formatted with the stationery you selected. Compose and send a message to yourself for use in the next step.

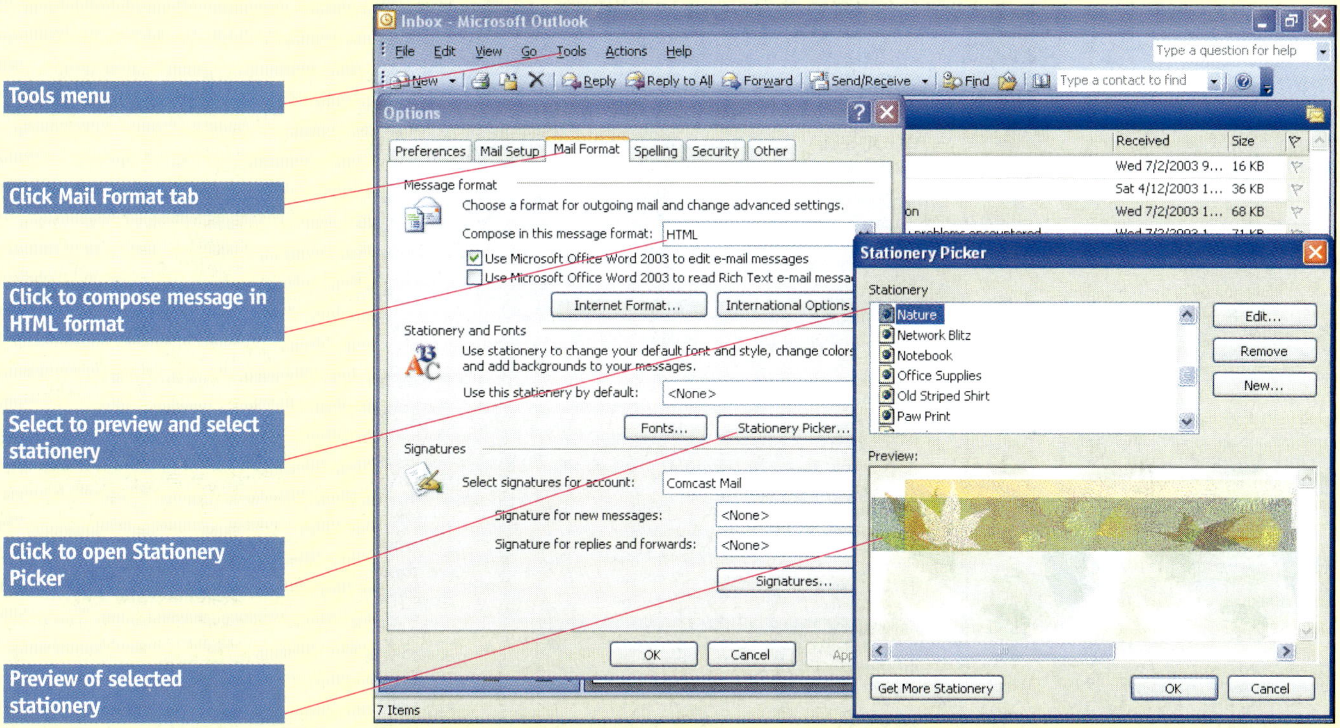

(i) Add Stationery to a Mail Message (step 9)

FIGURE 5 Hands-on Exercise 1 (*continued*)

INCOMPATIBLE MAIL CLIENTS

Some mail clients will not accept messages in HTML or rich text (word processing) format. If a recipient of a message cannot open it, change the format to plain text and send it again. Messages in plain text format are smaller in size and take less time and fewer resources to send and receive. However, you will not be able to apply stationery to the messages. You also cannot format the text or insert graphics into a message sent in plain text.

Step 10: Flag a Message for Follow Up

- Click the **Send/Receive button** on the Standard toolbar to download from the mail server the message you sent in step 9. Select the message to see the stationery.
- Right click the message, click **Follow Up** on the context-sensitive menu, then click **Add Reminder** to display the Flag for Follow Up dialog box in Figure 5j.
- Click the drop-down arrow next to the **Due by text box**, then click the **Today button** to create a due date.
- Click the drop-down arrow next to the text box that displays **None** and select a time earlier than the current time. (This will cause Outlook to display the flagged message as overdue for follow up.)
- Click **OK** to close the dialog box. Flag a second message without entering a due date.
- Click **For Follow Up** in the **Favorite Folders list** to display the For Follow Up folder in the preview pane. The message you flagged as due today is past due and is displayed in red. (If necessary, click a different message so that you can see the red highlight in the first.)
- A reminder window pops up to indicate that you have a past-due flagged item in one of your mail folders. Click **Dismiss** to close the reminder dialog box.
- Right click one of the messages and select **Delete**. The For Follow Up folder on the Navigation Pane shows only one message remaining for follow up. Close Outlook if you do not plan to go on at this point.

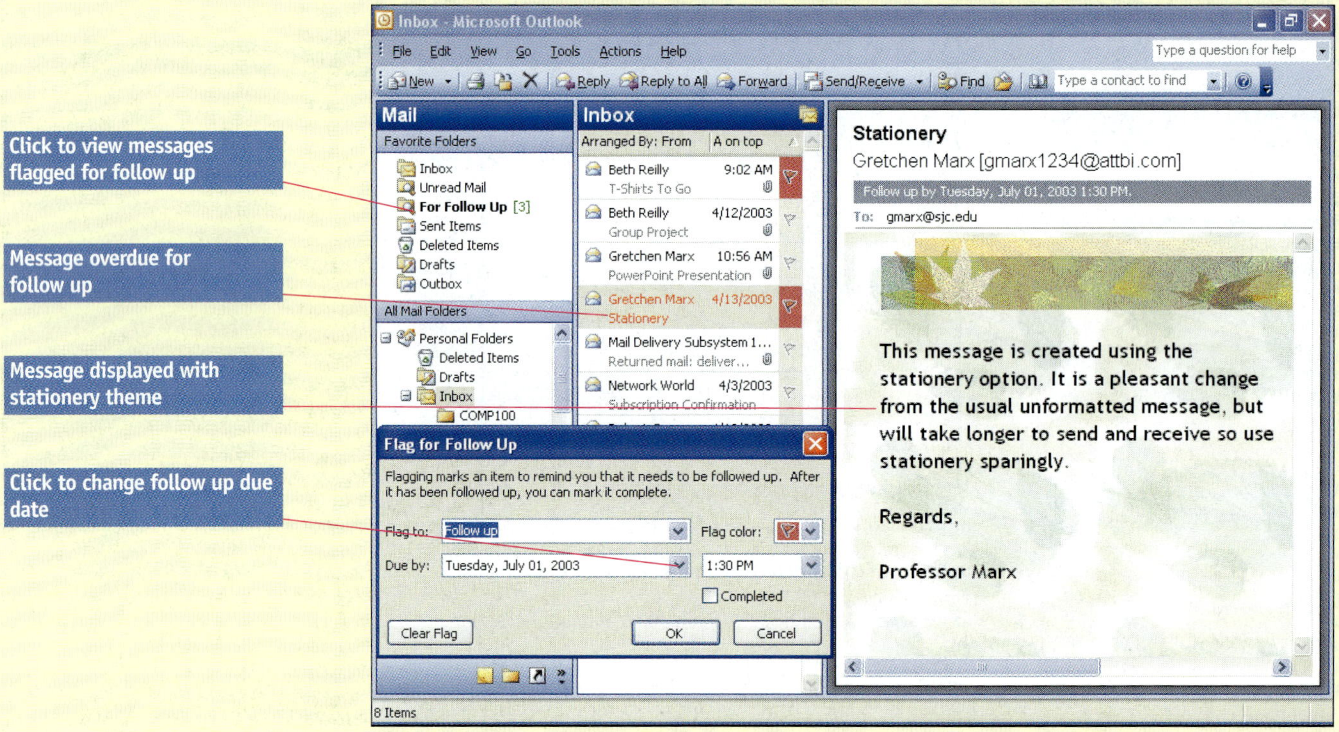

(j) Flag a Message for Follow Up (step 10)

FIGURE 5 Hands-on Exercise 1 (*continued*)

OUTLOOK CONTACTS

Just about everyone you know has an e-mail address. You could write each friend's or classmate's address in a paper address book, and then type the address into a message each time you send one. However, it is much easier to use the Contacts folder in Outlook to keep track of the addresses. When it is time to send a new message, you select the recipient from the Contacts folder without having to type his or her entire e-mail address.

As with other Outlook features, the Contacts folder can be customized to your needs. In Figure 1b you saw the Address Cards view of the folder. Default ***categories*** in Outlook allow you to assign your contacts to categories and then view contacts by categories, as shown in Figure 6a. Note that a person can be assigned to more than one category, holiday cards and personal for instance.

Note also that you can sort the contacts within categories by clicking the field at the top of the Contacts list. For instance, should you want to see all of your contacts within a particular organization, you could click the Company field. Clicking the + (plus sign) next to a category expands all of the entries within it.

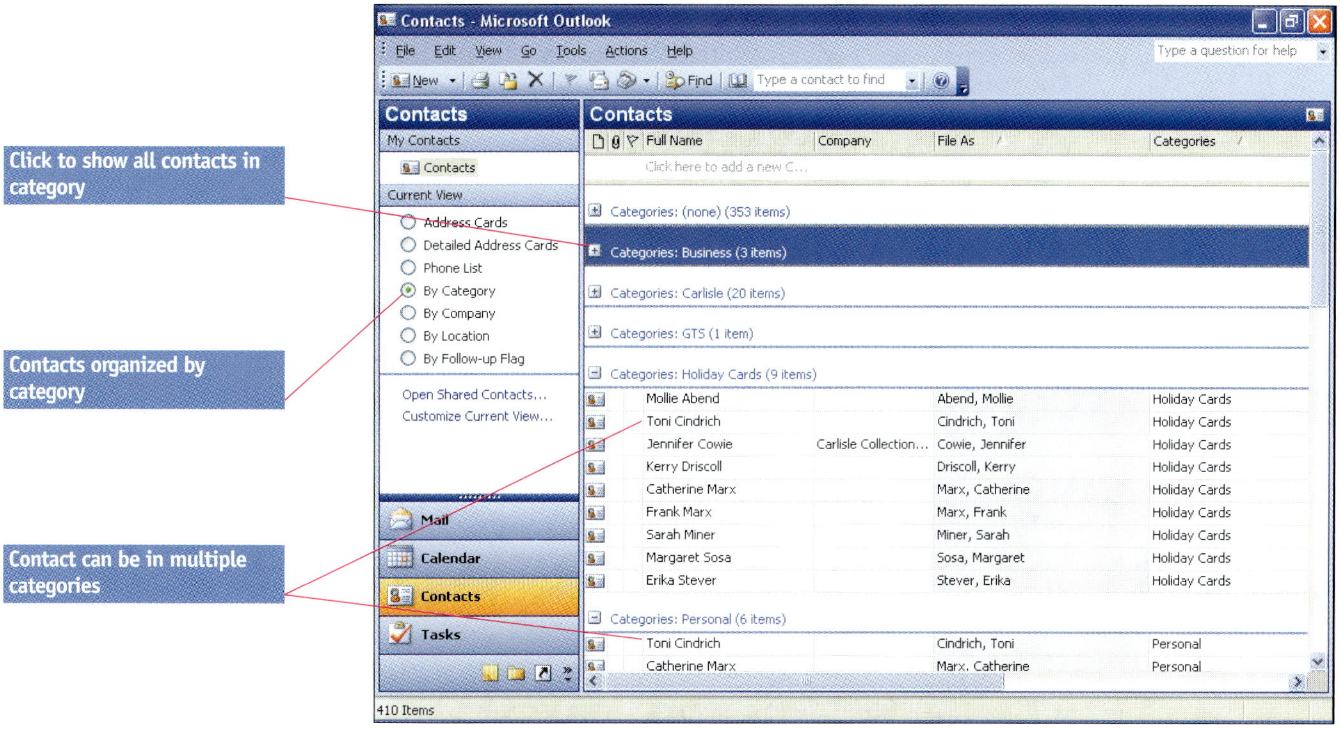

(a) Contacts Organized by Categories

FIGURE 6 Outlook Contacts

FINDING AN E-MAIL ADDRESS

What happens if you want to send an e-mail message to a friend or colleague, but you don't know the e-mail address? One solution is to consult an e-mail directory (or Internet white pages). Start Internet Explorer, then enter the Web address of a white pages search engine. We use www.whowhere.lycos.com and/or people.yahoo.com, both of which also provide telephone numbers. Be aware, however, that the information may be inaccurate. People change their e-mail addresses for a variety of reasons. Your best bet may be the old-fashioned way—simply call the person and ask for his/her address!

You can also organize your contacts as a phone list, as shown in Figure 6b. You can customize the view to show whatever fields you wish—we show last and first names, the company the person works for, and both company and car phone numbers. Note that you can change the Contacts view by using the Current View buttons in the Navigation Pane.

The information about each person in your Contacts folder is entered into an address card as shown in Figure 6c. You can enter as much or little information as you want, but generally you will at least enter a name and e-mail address. It is in this window that you select the categories, if any, you want to assign a contact to.

As the figure shows, you can add notes in the text box at the right of the dialog box. The address card is very flexible in that it allows you to enter more than one e-mail and/or address for each person. It also has fields for multiple phone numbers, a necessity in this world where everyone is connected 24/7.

The Contacts folder allows you to organize your contacts another way that we find very useful. You can set up a distribution list as shown in Figure 6d. Once the list is set up, you can send e-mail to the entire list at once by entering the list name in the address box in a new message. You can also notify the entire distribution list at one time of a meeting you are trying to arrange, or assign everyone on the list to a task. Outlook has made keeping in touch with teammates on group projects much easier. Once established, your distribution list will display in your Contacts folder in alphabetical order with the rest of the names.

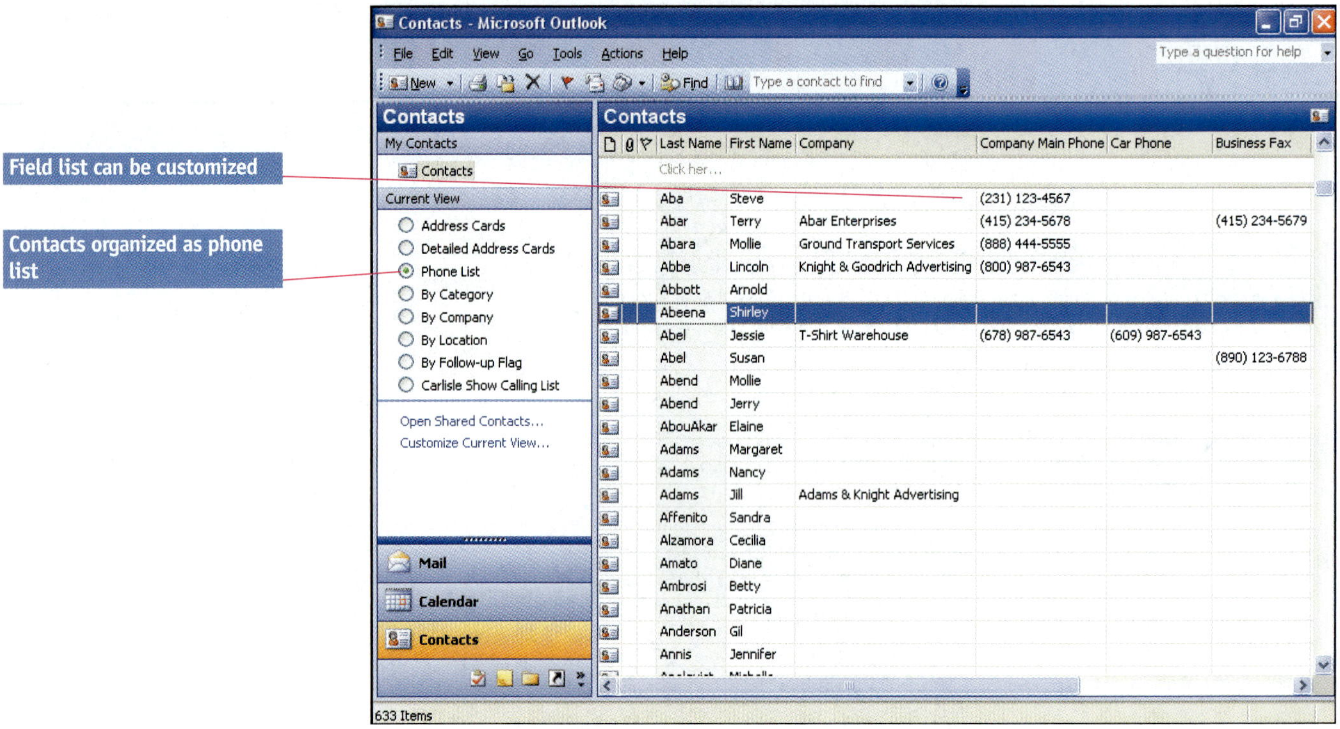

(b) Contacts Organized as a Phone List

FIGURE 6 Outlook Contacts (*continued*)

MORE ABOUT ADDRESS CARDS

The Address Cards window contains multiple tabs that allow you to add additional information about a contact. In the Details tab, for instance, you can enter the department in which the contact works, the names of his/her manager and assistant, the person's nickname, spouse's name, birthday and anniversary dates. The only problem: Now you'll have no excuse for forgetting to send a card!

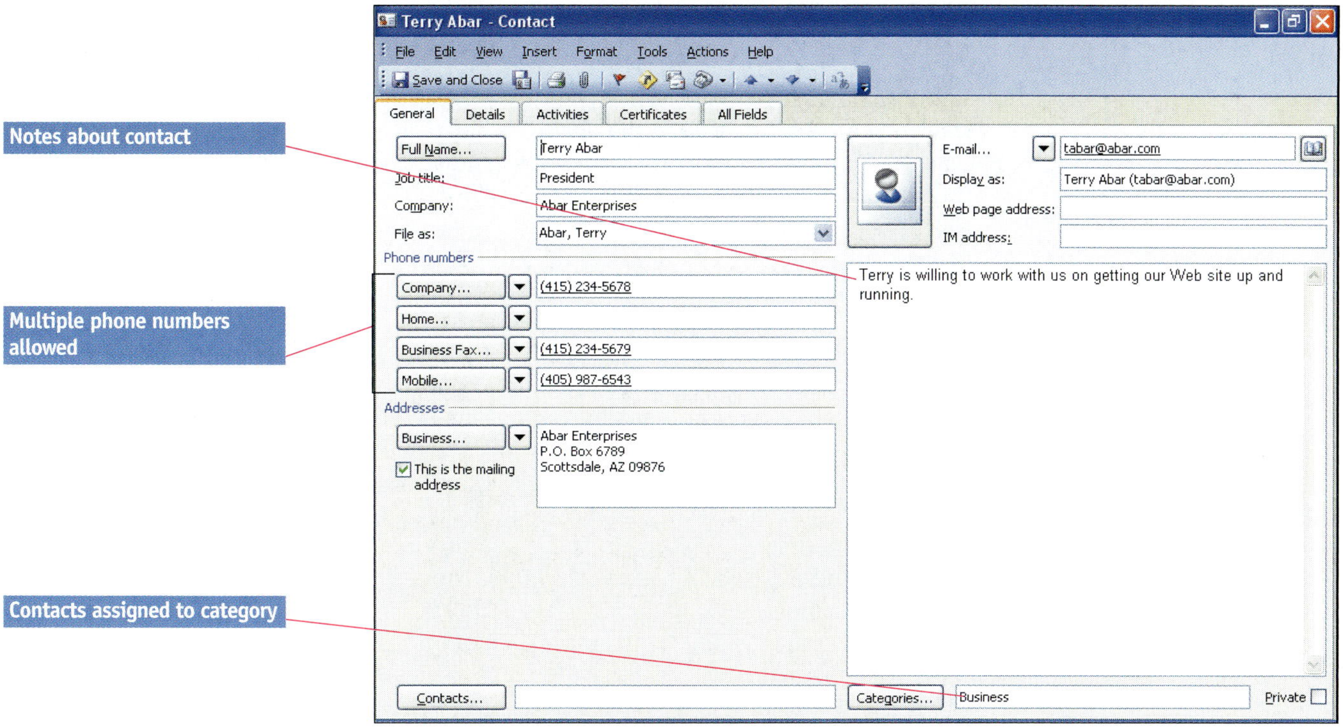

(c) Contacts Address Cards

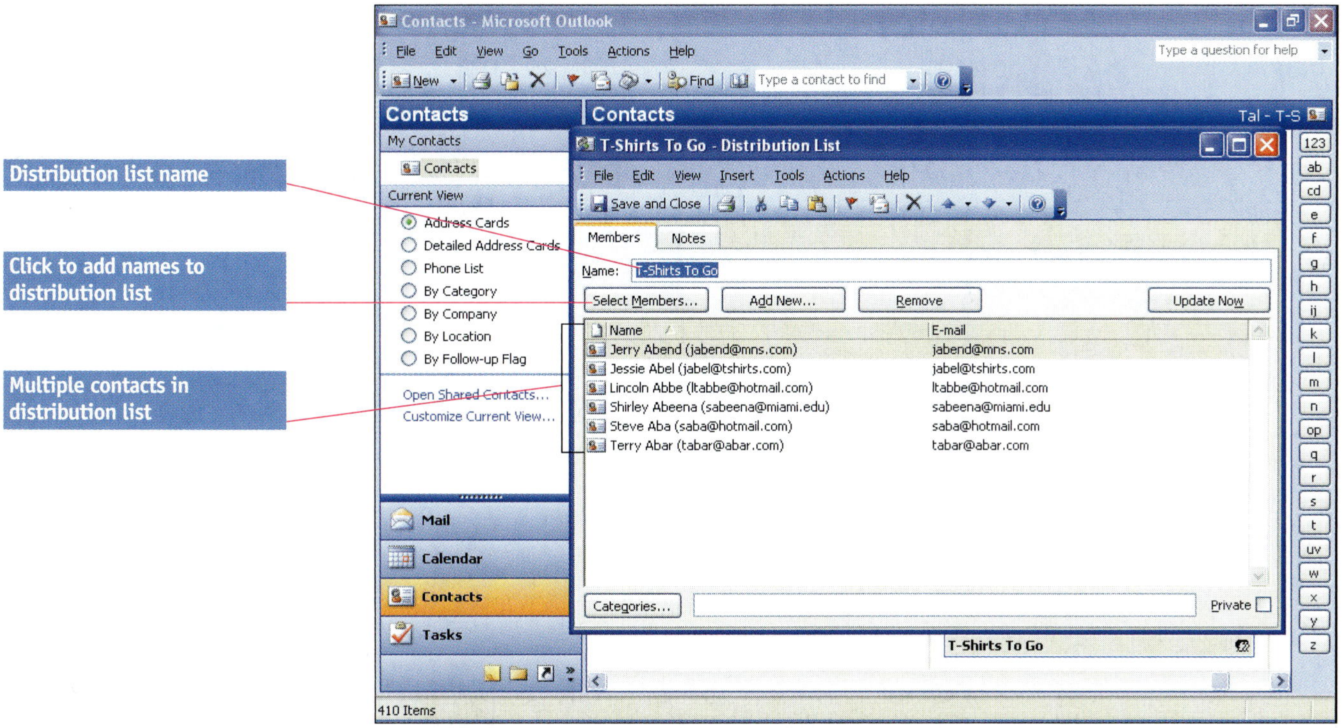

(d) A Distribution List

FIGURE 6 Outlook Contacts (*continued*)

THE OUTLOOK JOURNAL

The Journal tracks documents you have worked on; if you so choose, it can also track e-mail. Like a paper journal, you can also add your own entries in the Journal, using it much like you would a diary, as shown in Figure 7. If at some point in the future you have forgotten what projects you worked on, you can view the Journal for that day, and it will show the documents you accessed. The Journal can also be used to track meeting requests, cancellations, and task assignments.

In the figure we organize the Journal by type of entry so that all e-mail messages are shown first, then meetings, then Excel documents, Word documents, and so on. Clicking the + (plus sign) next to the entry type will display all of the documents of that type. We have expanded the meetings in the figure. You can also organize the Journal by contact, to show all of the items associated with a contact.

Clicking the Phone Calls option button on the Navigation Pane will show all of the phone calls you made on a particular day, a very useful feature if you are using Outlook to track sales calls. Clicking the Last Seven Days option button displays the Journal in list form, showing every document, e-mail message, and so on, that you are tracking. If you group the list, Outlook displays today's items, then last week's items. This view also indicates how long you were working on the document, which would be particularly useful if you are billing time worked on a project.

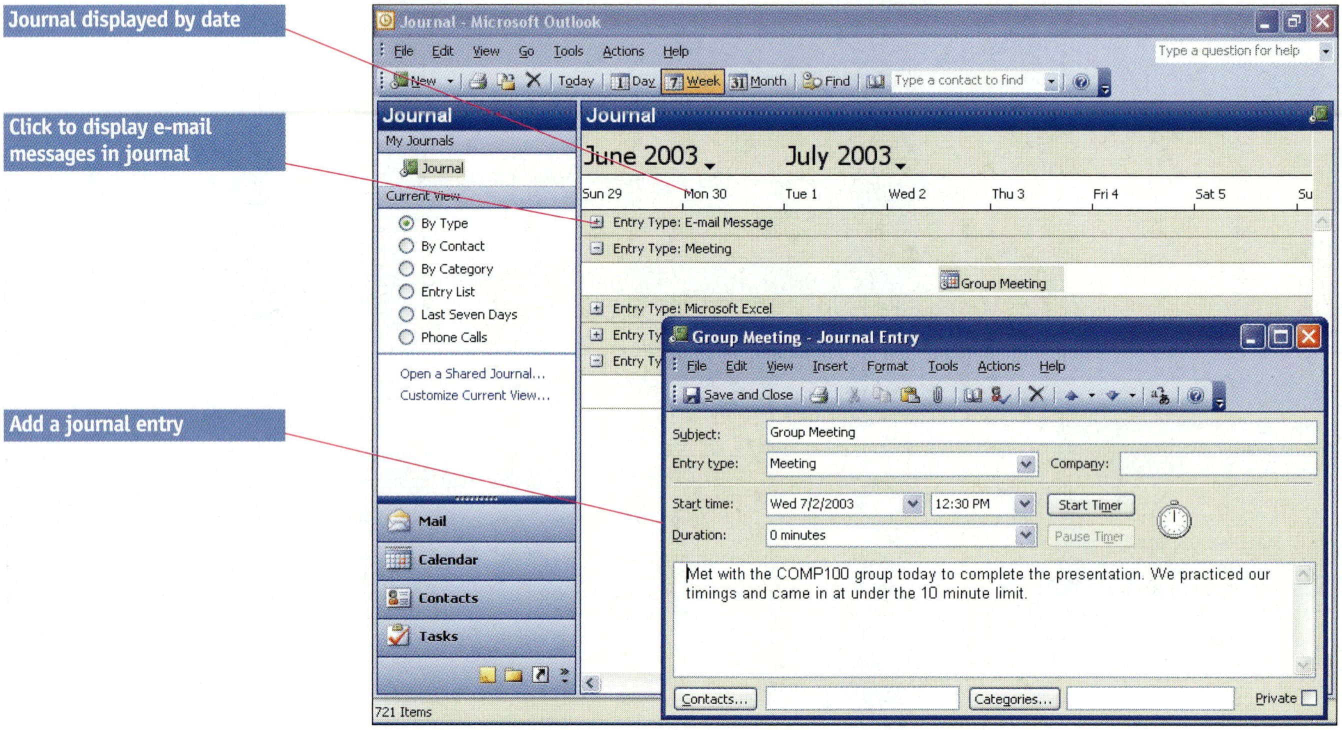

FIGURE 7 The Outlook Journal

USE THE CONTACTS LIST TO TRACK E-MAIL

When you start the Journal for the first time, you may see a message indicating that the Contacts folder is a better way to track e-mail. This is because people generally get so much e-mail that the Journal file would quickly become overloaded. To track e-mail in the Contacts folder, open Contacts, open the address card of the person for whom you want to track all correspondence, then click the Activities tab. All messages, whether in the Sent Items file, the Inbox, the Deleted Items file, and so on, are displayed.

hands-on exercise

2 Outlook Contacts

Objective To create and print a contact list. Use Figure 8 as a guide in the exercise. This exercise does not require an Internet connection.

Step 1: Create a Contact

- Click the **Start button** to display the Start menu. Click (or point to) the **All Programs**, then click **Microsoft Outlook** to start the program.
- If necessary, click the **Maximize button** so that Outlook takes the entire desktop. The Navigation Pane should be displayed by default. If not, pull down the **View menu** and click **Navigation Pane**.
- Click the **Contacts icon** on the Navigation Pane. Click the **New Contact button** on the Standard toolbar to open the Contact window in Figure 8a.
- Enter your friend's full name, e-mail address, and home phone number.
- Click the down arrow next to the **Business button** in the address section and select **Home**.
- Click in the address text box and enter your friend's home address (or a fictitious address if you don't know it).
- Click the **drop-down arrow** in the **File as list box**, then choose how you want to file the contact in the Contacts folder. (You can file by first or last name.)

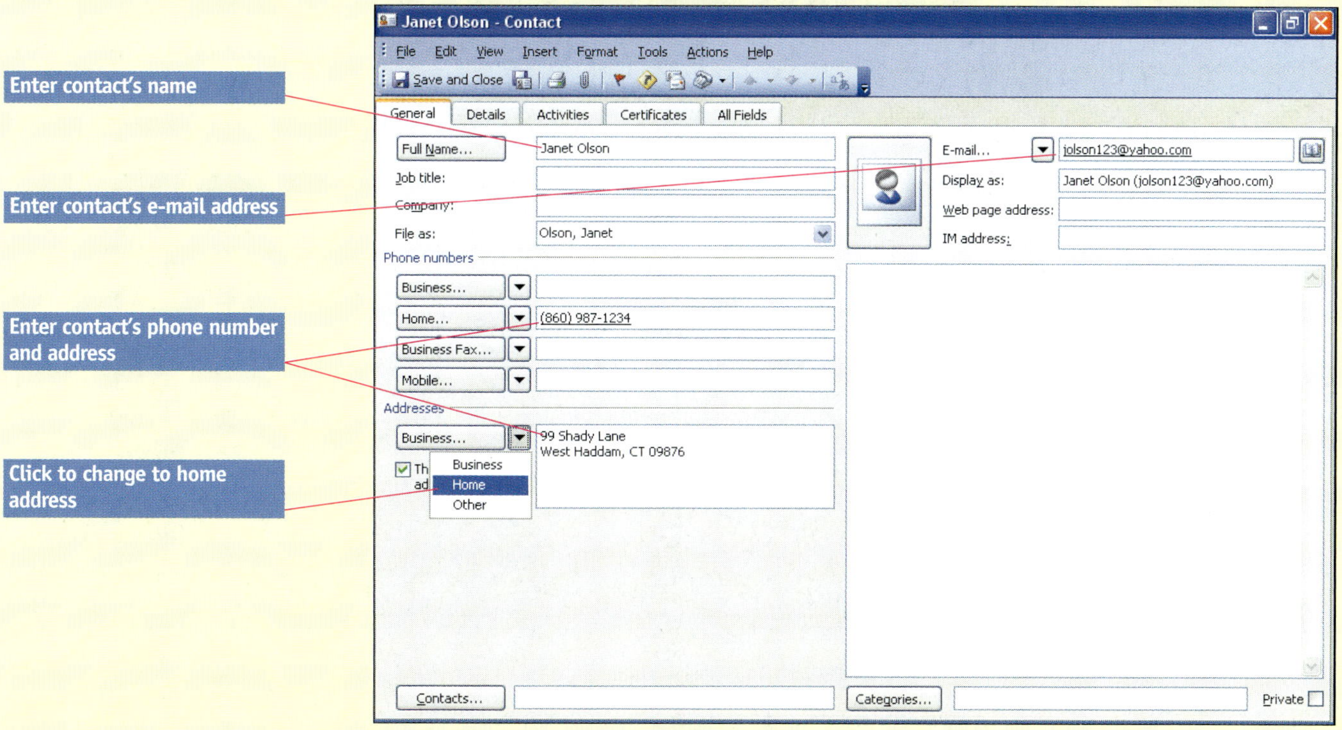

(a) Create a Contact (step 1)

FIGURE 8 Hands-on Exercise 2

Step 2: Add a Contact Category

- Click the **Categories button** to display the Categories dialog box shown in Figure 8b. Click any categories you want the contact to belong to, such as Holiday and Personal as shown.
- Click the **Master Category List button** at the bottom of the Categories dialog box to display the Master Category List and add your own category (we added **School** in the New Category box), click **Add**, then click **OK**.
- Click **School** in the Available categories list in the Categories dialog box to add the contact to the School category. Click **OK** to close the Categories dialog box.
- Click the **Details tab** and enter your friend's birth date into the **Birthday list box**. When you open the Calendar in Hands-on Exercise 3, your friend's birthday will be listed as an event on the appropriate date.
- Click the **Save and New button** to save the information for your friend and simultaneously open a new Contact window.
- Create a new contact entry for another friend, then enter your own e-mail address and other information on a third address card. Be sure to select categories for both contacts.
- Click the **Save and Close button** to save the information and return to the Contacts folder.

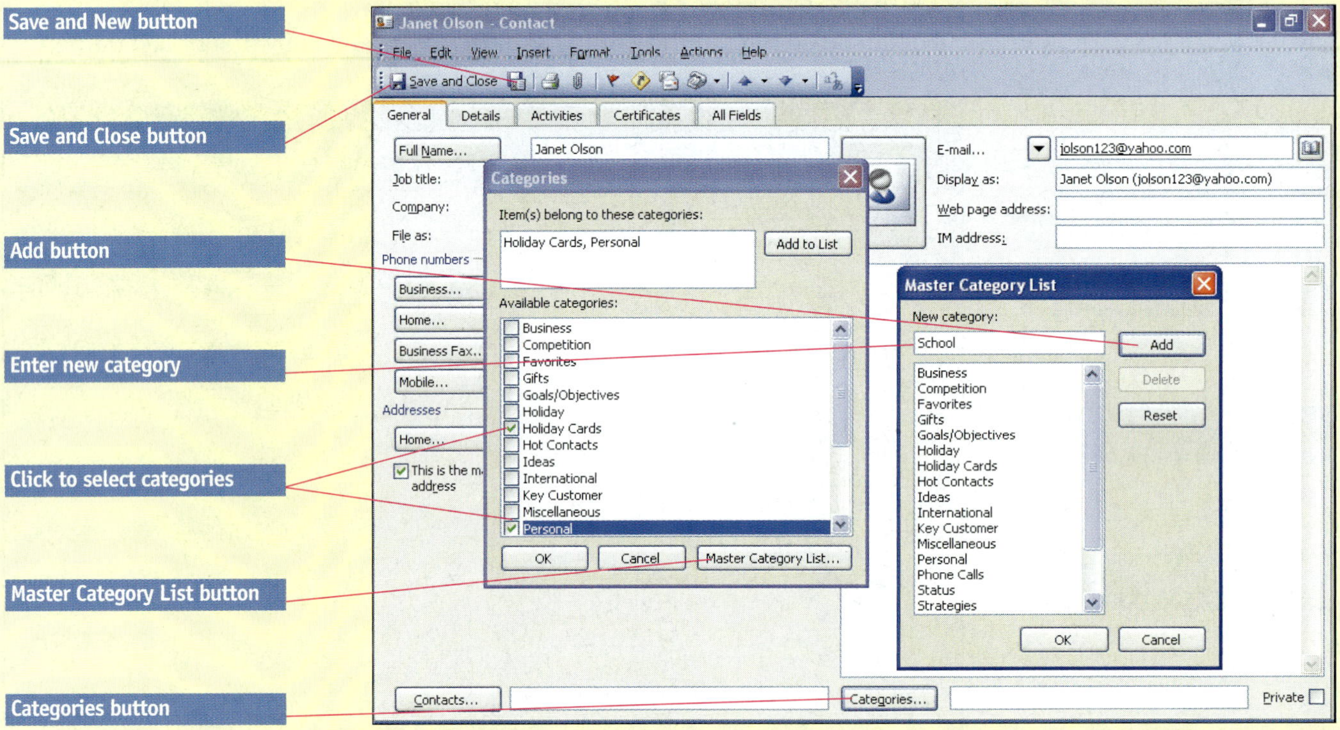

(b) Add a Contact Category (step 2)

FIGURE 8 Hands-on Exercise 2 (*continued*)

CONTACT CATEGORIES

Categories allow you to organize your Contacts list by holiday cards or gifts, for example. If you are as bad at remembering birthdays and anniversaries as we are, you may want to create those categories, then print your Contacts list sorted accordingly. If only Outlook would go to the store and buy the cards for you!

Step 3: Change the Contacts View

- Click the **Detailed Address Cards option button** in the Navigation Pane to match the view in Figure 8c.
- Click the button at the right of the window that displays the first letter of your friend's last name (e.g., "M" for Gretchen Marx), corresponding to the contact you entered in the previous step. Address cards of contacts whose last names begin with "M" are displayed.
- If necessary, scroll to the right until you see your friend's address card and check the information. If changes are necessary, click the line(s) containing the invalid data to make the correction directly in this view.
- Click the **Find button** on the Standard toolbar to display the Find dialog box at the top of the Contacts list as shown in Figure 8c. Enter the name of the contact you want to find in the **Look for text box**, then click **Find Now**. Any contacts with the name anywhere in the address card are displayed. Click the **Find button** on the Standard toolbar again to close the dialog box.
- Click the **Phone list option button** in the Navigation Pane to display the Contacts list in Phone list order.
- Click the **Print button** on the Standard toolbar to display the Print dialog box, then click **OK** again to print your Phone list.

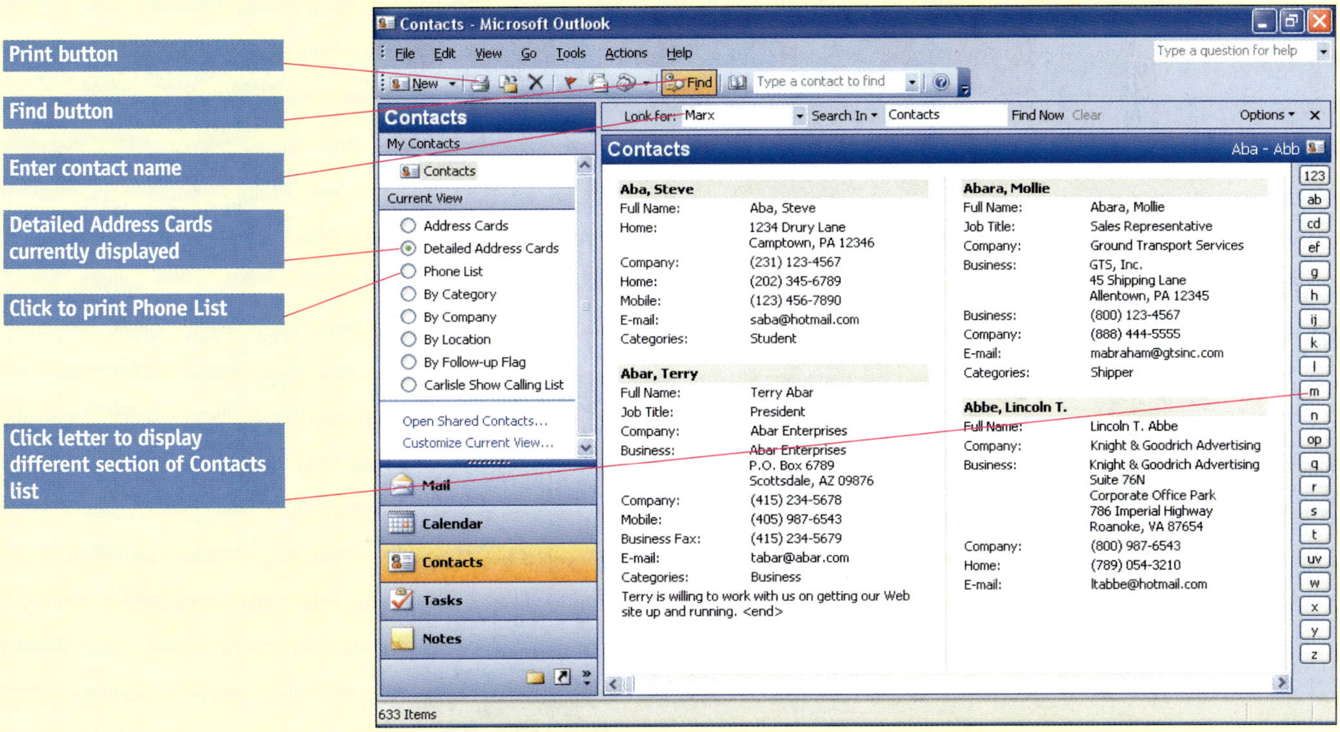

(c) Change the Contacts View (step 3)

FIGURE 8 Hands-on Exercise 2 (*continued*)

THE PAGE SETUP COMMAND

Outlook is very flexible in the way it displays and prints information. Click the Print button on the Standard toolbar, then click the Page Setup command to display the Page Setup dialog box. You can change the font of both column headers and rows, print headers or footers, change margins, and/or print your Phone list in landscape mode.

Step 4: Organize Your Contacts

- Click the **By Category option button** on the Navigation Pane. The entire Contacts list is displayed, showing first those contacts that are not in a category.
- Pull down the **View menu** and select **Expand/Collapse Groups**, then select **Collapse All Groups** so you can see the categories that you created in step 2.
- Click the **plus sign** (+) next to the categories you selected in step 2 to display the contacts within each category as shown in Figure 8d.
- Click the **Customize Current View link** on the Navigation Pane to display the Customize View: By Category dialog box. Click the **Fields button** to display the Show Fields dialog box in the figure.
- Click a field in the **Available fields list box**, then click **Add** to send it to the bottom of the field list at the right of the dialog box. Click **Move Up** to move the field to the position where you want it to appear. Add and position additional fields as you wish. Click **OK** to close the Show Fields dialog box.
- Click the **Filter button** in the Customize View dialog box to display the Filter dialog box. Click the **More Choices tab**, click the **Categories button**, then select the category that you added in step 2. We selected School.
- Click **OK** to close the Categories dialog box, click **OK** to close the Filter dialog box, then click **OK** once again to close the Customize View dialog box. One category is displayed with the fields you added.

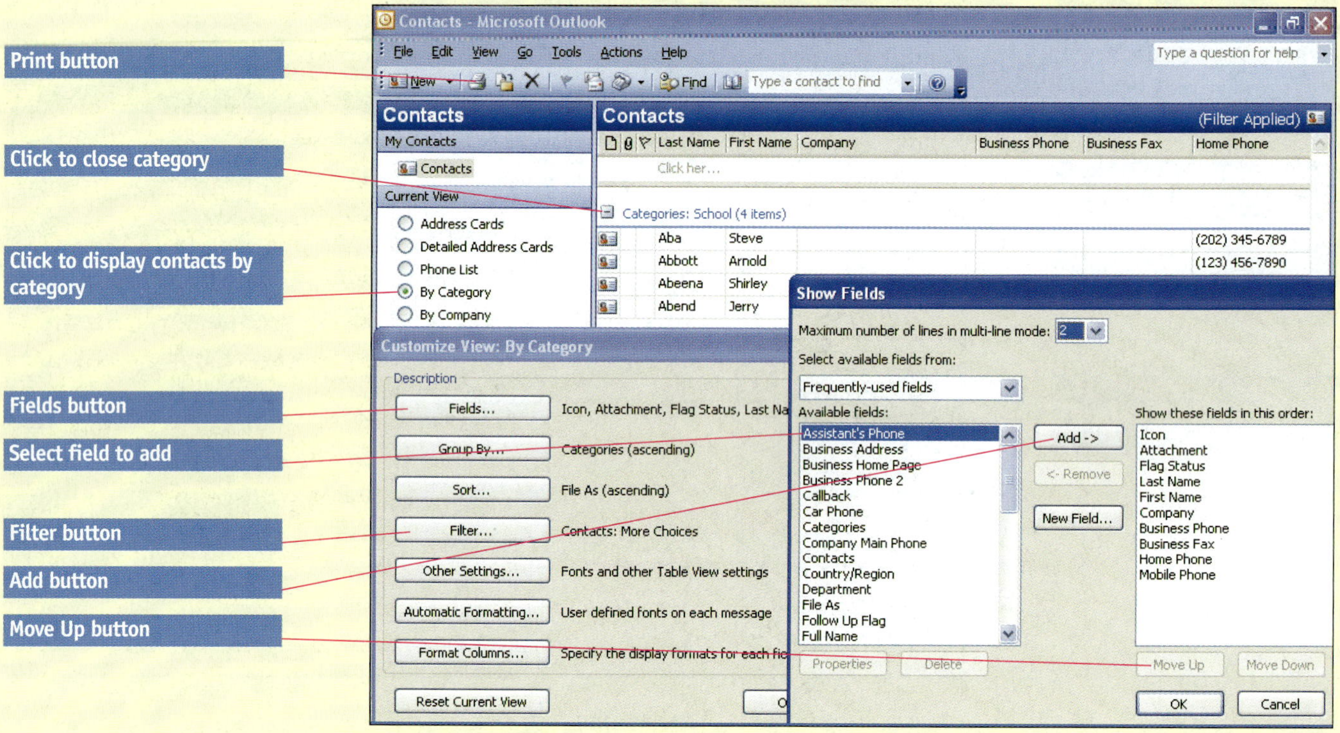

(d) Organize Your Contacts (step 4)

FIGURE 8 Hands-on Exercise 2 (*continued*)

SORTING YOUR CONTACTS

Click at the top of any column in your Contacts list to sort in ascending alphabetical or numeric order. Click again to sort in descending order. You could sort by company, for instance, so that all your contacts at that site are listed together.

Step 5: Start the Journal

- Pull down the **Go menu** and click **Journal**. Click **Yes** if a dialog box appears asking whether you want to start the Journal.
- Pull down the **Tools menu**, click **Options** to display the Options dialog box in Figure 8e, then click the **Journal Options button** to display the Journal Options dialog box.
- In the **Automatically record these items list box** at the top left of the dialog box check off **E-mail Message**, **Meeting cancellation**, **Meeting request**, and **Task request** as shown in Figure 8e.
- Scroll down in the **For these contacts list box** until you see the contacts you entered in step 1 and select them.
- In the **Also record files from list box** check **Microsoft Office Excel** and **Microsoft Word**, then click **OK** to close the Journal Options dialog box. Click **OK** again to close the Options dialog box.
- All subsequent events will be recorded in the Journal. You will not see any events in the Journal as you just turned it on. We will return to the Journal in Hands-on Exercise 3 to see the events recorded in it.

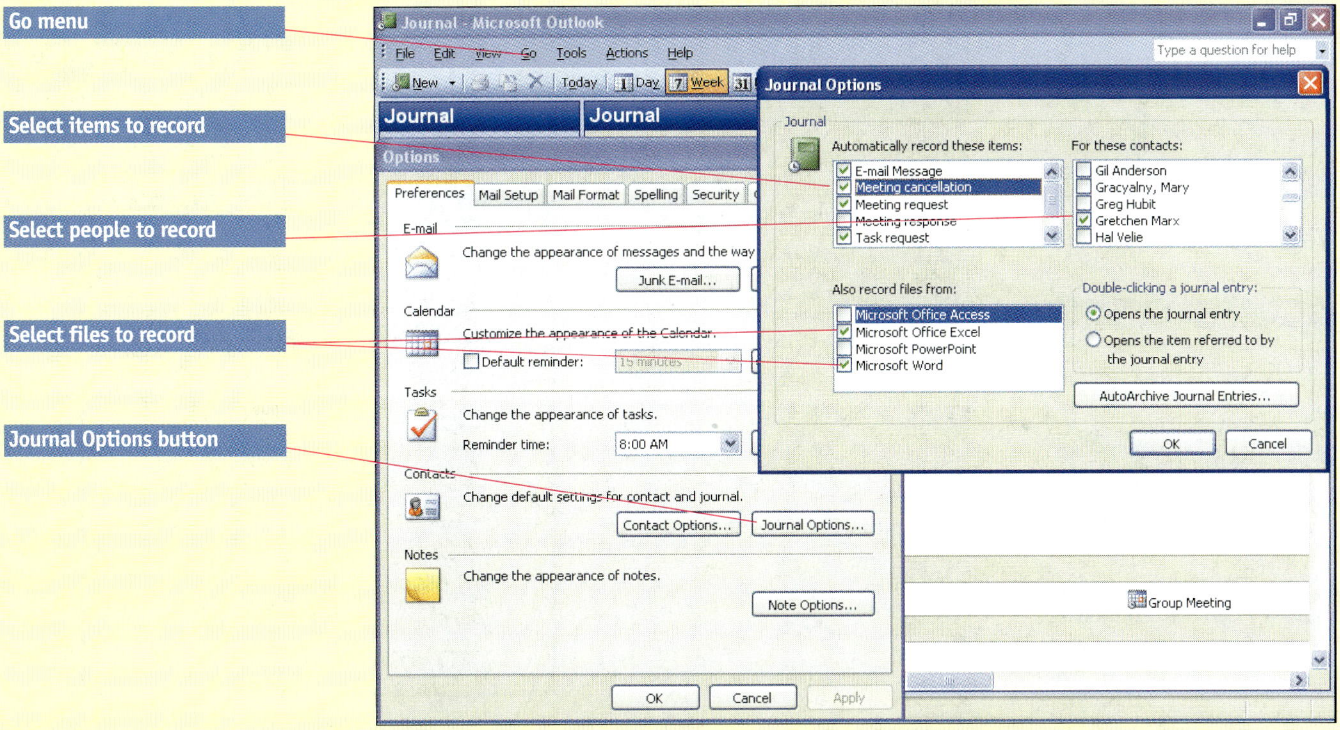

(e) Start the Journal (step 5)

FIGURE 8 Hands-on Exercise 2 (*continued*)

FIND THAT MISSING DOCUMENT

You know a file is on your computer, you can't remember its name or the folder where it's saved, but you know you worked on it last Monday. The Outlook Journal will help. Open the Journal, change to the Week or Month view, then go to the day when you last worked on the document. Double click the shortcut in the Journal to open the document and retrieve your work.

Step 6: Create a Distribution List

- Click the down arrow next to the **New button** on the Standard toolbar and click **Distribution List** to display the Distribution List dialog box in Figure 8f. Enter a name for your list—we entered **COMP100 Project Group**.
- Click **Select Members** to display the Select Members dialog box shown in Figure 8f.
- Begin typing the first few letters of the first name of one of your contacts. The selection bar jumps to the first occurrence that contains those characters. Double click the name of the contact you want to add to the Distribution list (or select the name, then click the **Members button** below the Address list).
- Click in the name box above the Contact list once more to enter another contact's name. Repeat the steps to add two or three more names to your Distribution list.
- Click **OK** to close the Select Members dialog box. The Distribution List dialog box shows all of the members you have added to the list.
- Click the **Save and Close button** on the Standard toolbar to close the dialog box. The Distribution list is stored in alphabetical order as an address card in your Contacts list.

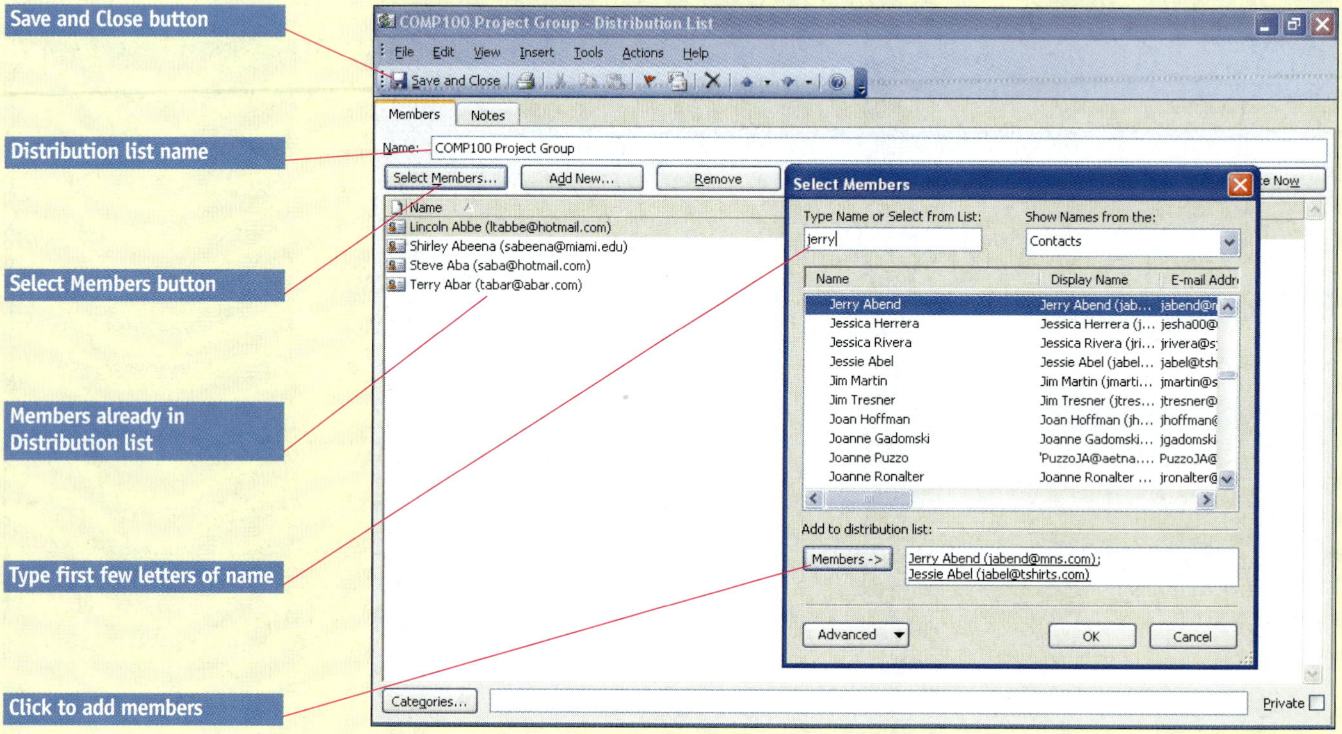

(f) Create a Distribution List (step 6)

FIGURE 8 Hands-on Exercise 2 (*continued*)

MODIFY A DISTRIBUTION LIST

You can add members to or delete them from a Distribution list at any time. Open the Contacts window, navigate to the address card containing the name of the Distribution list, and double click it to open the list. Click the Add New or Delete buttons as appropriate to update your list.

Step 7: Use the Distribution List

- Click the **Mail button** on the Standard toolbar to display the Inbox.
- Click **New Mail Message button** on the Standard toolbar, then click the **To button** to display the Select Names dialog box in Figure 8g.
- Type the first few letters of the Distribution list name you entered in Step 6. The Contact list will jump to the first entry that contains that letter combination.
- Select the Distribution list, then click the **To button** to add the list to those who will receive the message.
- Select your name within the list of contacts, then click the **Cc button** to add your name to the list of recipients. Click **OK** to close the Select Names dialog box when you are finished.
- Press the **Tab key** to move to the Subject dialog box. Enter **Advanced Features** as the subject of your message, then press the **Tab key** once again to move to the message area.
- Type a greeting to your teammates, then click the **Send button** on the E-mail toolbar to send the message to everyone on the list.

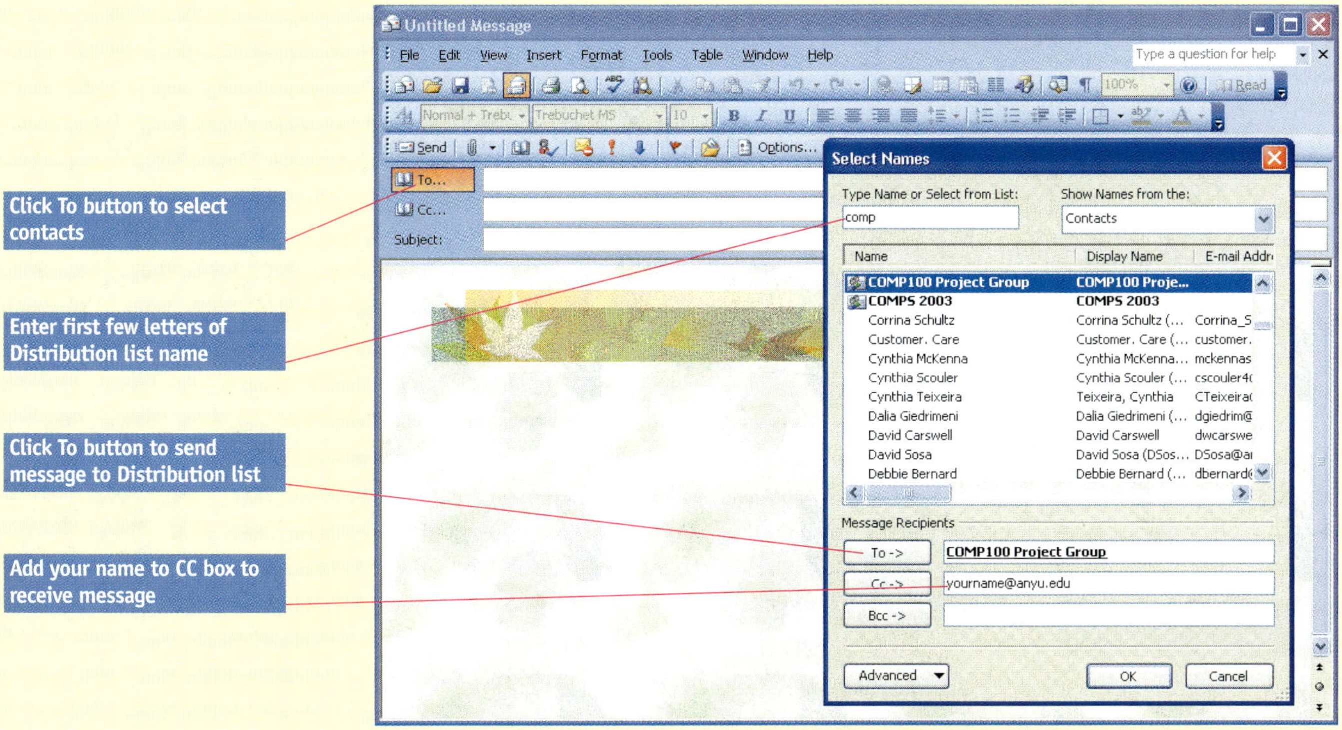

(g) Use the Distribution List (step 7)

FIGURE 8 Hands-on Exercise 2 (*continued*)

INSTANT ADDRESS BOOK

Use Outlook to automatically create entries in your Contacts list. Right click the From field in the preview pane to display a context-sensitive menu, then click the Add to Contacts command. Outlook will display the new Contact window, where you can edit the information as appropriate. Click the Save and Close button to save the contact.

Step 8: Create a Note

- Click the **Notes button** on the Navigation Pane, click the **Large Icons button** on the Standard toolbar, then click the **New button** on the Standard toolbar to display a blank sticky note. (The dialog boxes shown in Figure 8h are not yet displayed.)
- Type a reminder to yourself on the note, then click the **Close button** in the upper-right corner of the note. The note is minimized to line up with any other notes in the Reading Pane.
- Pull down the **Tools menu**, select **Options**, then click the **Note Options button** near the bottom of the **Preferences tab**.
- Select the Color and Size that you want for your notes, then click **OK** to close the Note Options dialog box and apply your selections. (New notes will have the new color and size; old notes will stay the same size and color as before.)
- Follow the procedure above to create another note. It should be the new color and size. Your notes will stay in the Notes folder until you delete them and will display on the desktop until you close them. Close Outlook if you do not want to continue to the next exercise.

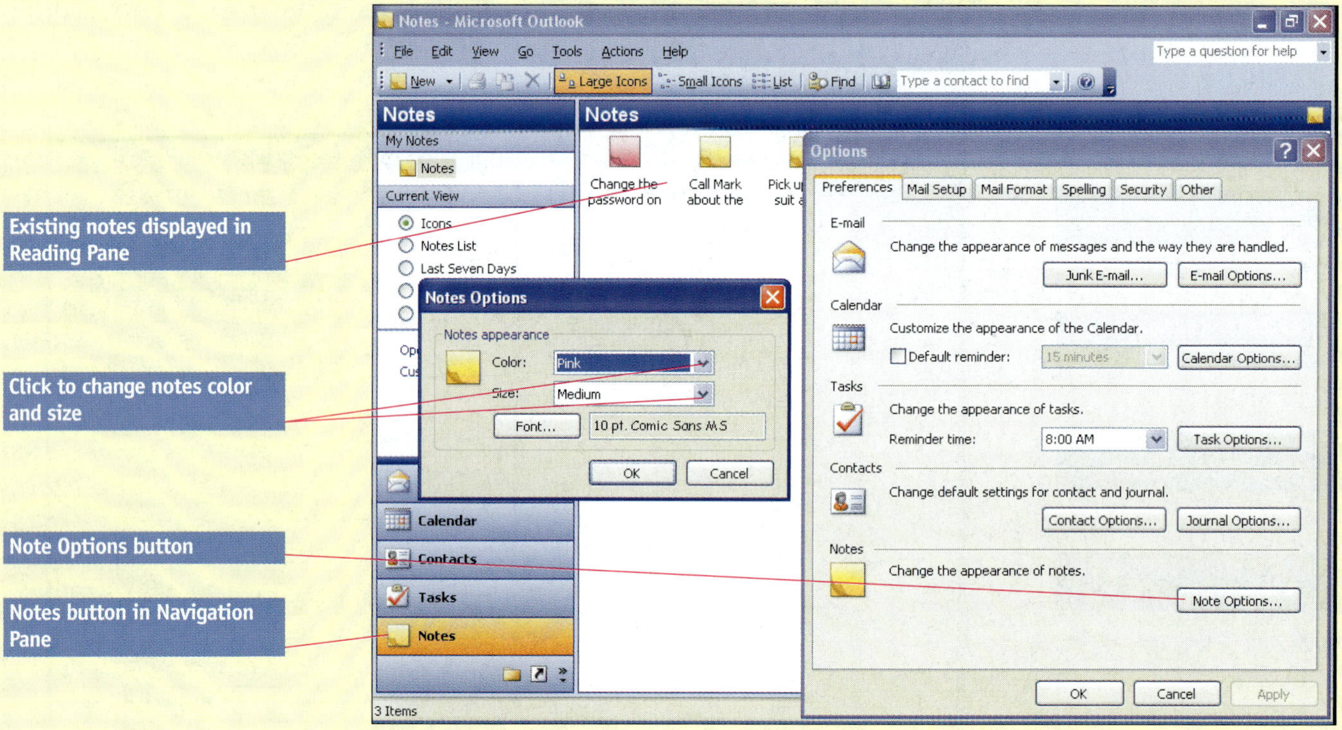

(h) Create a Note (step 8)

FIGURE 8 Hands-on Exercise 2 (*continued*)

WORKING WITH NOTES

Double click a note in the Notes folder to open it and modify the text. Right click a sticky note in the Notes folder to display a drop-down menu. Select Forward to send the note as an e-mail attachment, or try the other options to change the note color, to print, or to delete the note. Click the Current View option buttons on the Navigation Pane to organize and display your notes a different way.

THE OUTLOOK CALENDAR

Any busy manager will tell you that the majority of his/her time is spent in meetings, making and returning phone calls, and managing his/her schedule. Outlook provides several useful calendar management functions. Figure 9a shows several of these calendaring features in the daily view.

The left side of the calendar window displays the schedule for the day that is selected in the ***Date Navigator***, the monthly calendar at the upper right of the Calendar frame. Today's date is outlined in red on the monthly calendar.

Days with appointments, meetings, or recurring items on the schedule are shown in bold in the Date Navigator. Clicking a different day of the month will show the schedule for that day. Clicking the right (left) arrow next to the month will advance (step back) the calendar one month at a time.

An ***appointment*** is defined in Outlook as an assignment of time for which you do not have to schedule other people or resources such as rooms. ***Meetings*** are scheduled with one or more attendees for whom Outlook will automatically create and send e-mail notifications.

Overlapping meetings are shown adjacent to one another in the same time period in the figure. Outlook allows you to set up ***recurring events*** and to select the number of times the meeting or appointment recurs. It then reserves the time for all future occurrences in the series.

The schedule in Figure 9a shows half-hour time blocks by default. You can change the default time settings to 5, 6, 10, 15, 30, or 60-minute increments. You can also change the workweek to start on any day, for someone who works Tuesday through Saturday, for instance. The default start time can be changed to any hour of the day to accommodate someone with a different shift. If the ***Reminder option*** is turned on, as in the first appointment in Figure 9a, Outlook will notify you 15 minutes prior to the meeting.

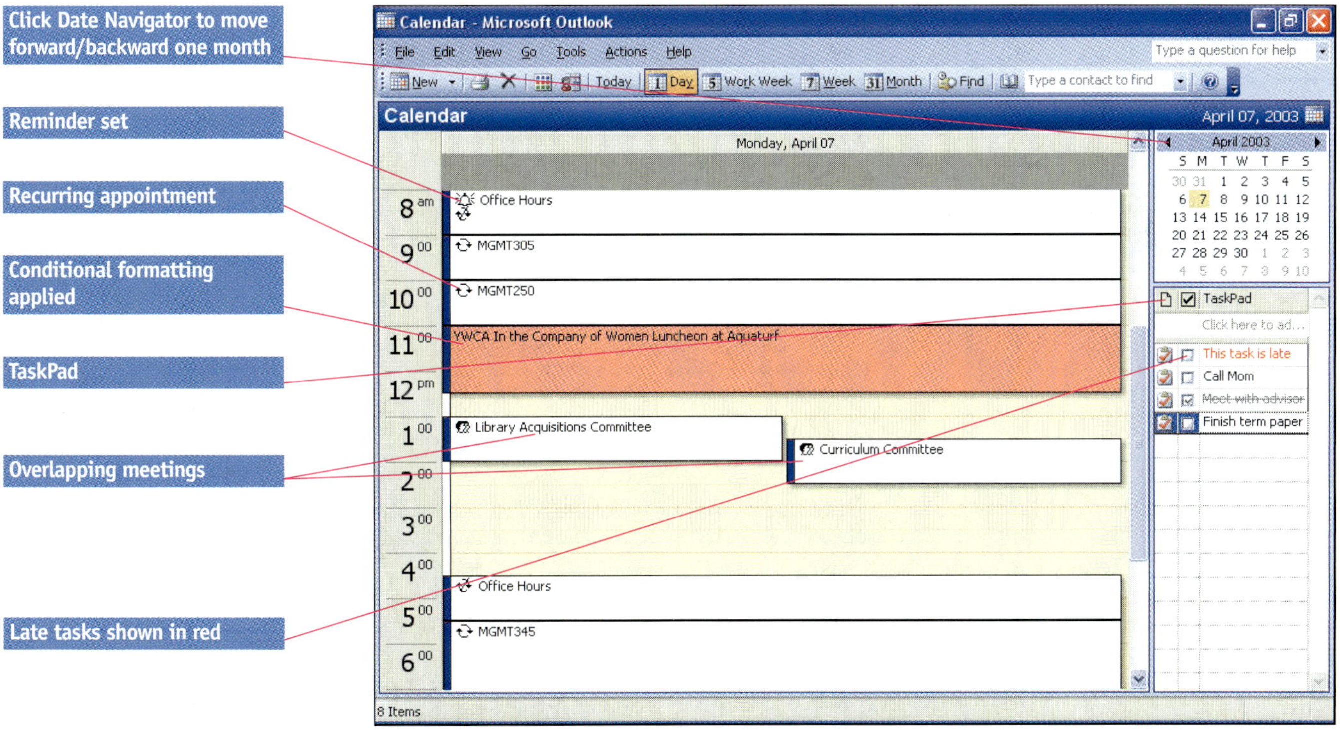

(a) The Daily View

FIGURE 9 The Outlook Calendar

You can apply conditional formatting, such as blue or green shading, to appointments on your calendar to remind yourself that a meeting is important, requires preparation or a phone call beforehand, and so on. ***Conditional formatting*** requires that you enter a rule that Outlook uses to apply the formatting. If you enter the name of the project as the rule, for example, any other appointments or meetings that you set up later that contain that project name will be displayed with the conditional format you selected. You'll do this in the following hands-on exercise.

Below the Date Navigator in Figure 9a is the ***TaskPad*** that shows each task you have entered with an indication of its status. Completed tasks are lined out, and overdue tasks are shown in a contrasting color (in this case, red). New tasks can be added simply by typing the task description in the box at the top of the TaskPad. Time can be reserved for tasks by dragging and dropping any task onto the calendar. The TaskPad and Date Navigator can be widened to show two months by clicking and dragging the left edge of the TaskPad to the left. We show the calendar without the Navigation Pane to display more of the daily events.

Figure 9b shows the calendar in monthly view. (The Navigation Pane, Date Navigator, and TaskPad were removed to show more of the calendar.) Days in the previous or next month are shaded. If there are too many meetings and appointments in one day to display in the monthly view, you can access a specific day's appointments and meetings by clicking the drop-down button within that day. Double clicking an item on the schedule will bring up details about that appointment or meeting. All-day ***events*** such as the College Symposium Day on April 10 are boxed.

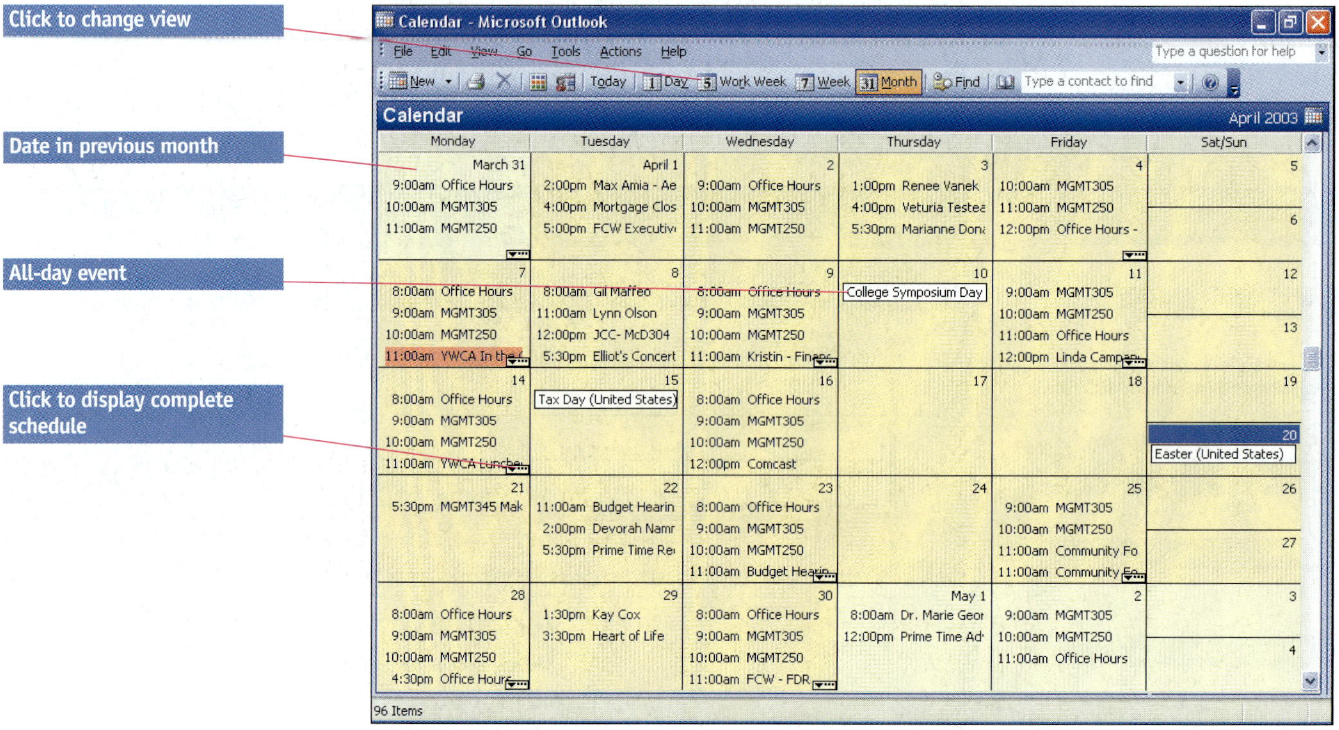

(b) The Monthly View

FIGURE 9 The Outlook Calendar (*continued*)

ORGANIZE TASKS FOR YOUR CLASSES

You can create a category for each class you are taking, then assign each task to a category. Then in Tasks view you can view your tasks by category to display all of the tasks for each class.

hands-on exercise

3 The Outlook Calendar

Objective To add appointments and schedule meetings using the Outlook calendar; to manage tasks. Use Figure 10 as a guide in the exercise.

Step 1: Enter an Appointment

- Click the **Start button** on the Windows taskbar, click **Programs** or **All Programs**, then click **Outlook**.
- Click the **Calendar button** on the Navigation Pane to display the Calendar window. The Date Navigator and TaskPad may not be visible.
- If necessary, click the **Today button** on the Standard toolbar, then click the **1 Day button** on the Standard toolbar. You should see your schedule for today.
- Click the **New Appointment button** on the Standard toolbar to open the Appointment dialog box shown in Figure 10a.
- Enter the subject, **COMP100 Group Meeting**, and location of the appointment, **Computer lab**. Enter the starting time of the appointment as 30 minutes from now. Enter the ending time one hour after that.
- Check the **Reminder box** to be notified 15 minutes before the appointment is to begin. (When the message box pops up to remind you of this hypothetical appointment, click the **Dismiss button** to close the Reminder dialog box and continue working.)
- Click the **Save and Close button** to save the appointment. Your appointment will appear in the daily schedule at the time you entered.

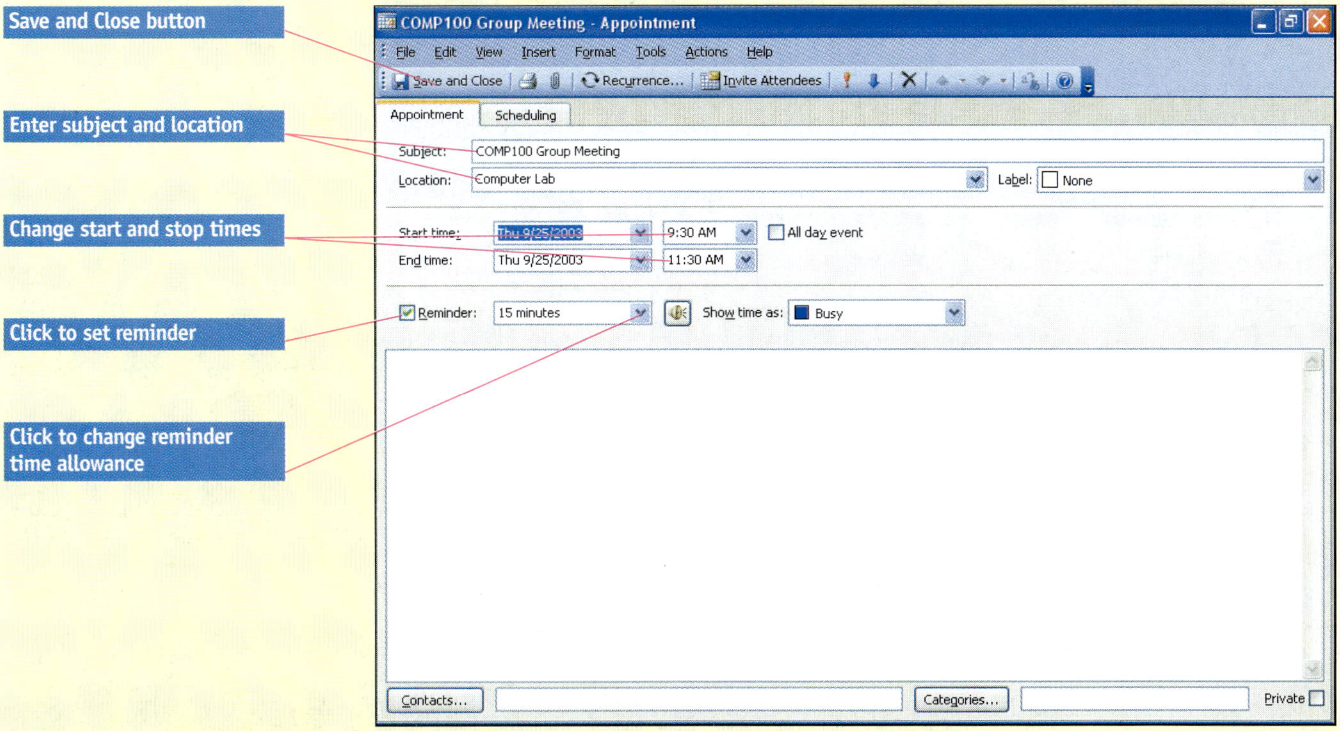

(a) Enter an Appointment (step 1)

FIGURE 10 Hands-on Exercise 3

Step 2: Add Conditional Formatting

- Click the **Calendar Coloring button** on the Standard toolbar, then select **Automatic Formatting** to display the dialog box in Figure 10b. Click the **Add button**, then type a name for this format rule in the **Name text box**—we used the name of our group meeting, **COMP100**.
- Click the **Condition button** to display the Filter dialog box. Enter **COMP100** in the **Search for the word(s) text box**. If necessary, change the **In text box** to show **subject field only**, then click **OK** to close the dialog box.
- Click the **down arrow** next to the **Label text box** to display the possible formats you can apply to this meeting. We chose **Important**. Click **OK** to close the Automatic Formatting dialog box.
- Create a new appointment with the keyword COMP100 in the subject line. The appointment will display in the conditional format you chose.
- Pull down the **Go menu** and select **Go To Date**. Enter your friend's birth date that you used in step 2 of Hands-on Exercise 2 in the dialog box, then click **OK** to close the dialog box and display the day.
- Click the **all-day birthday event** to select it, then click the **Calendar Coloring button** on the Standard toolbar and select **Birthday** from the menu of colors. The birthday and all subsequent birthdays are colored lilac.

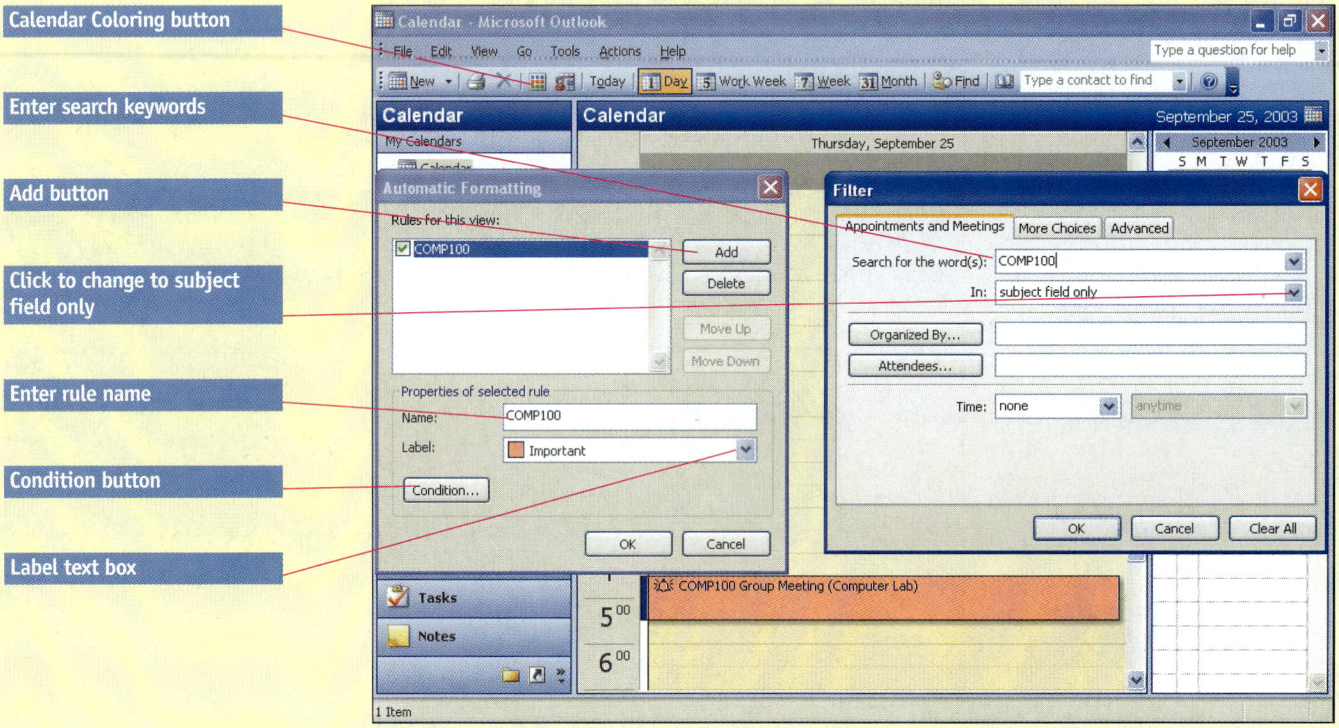

(b) Add Conditional Formatting (step 2)

FIGURE 10 Hands-on Exercise 3 (*continued*)

REMOVING A CONDITIONAL FORMAT

You can remove a conditional format that you have created by right clicking the appointment, then selecting Automatic Formatting. Click the format you do not want to display in this view to remove the check mark. When you return to the schedule, the conditional format is no longer displayed.

Step 3: **Create a Task**

- Pull down the **View menu** and select **Navigation Pane** to close it.
- If the Date Navigator and TaskPad are not visible on your screen, pull down the **View menu**, then select **TaskPad**.
- Drag the left side of the TaskPad to the left to widen the pane to show two months in the Date Navigator.
- Click in the **TaskPad text box**. Type **Finish history paper** and Press **Enter** to create the first task. Add the additional tasks shown in Figure 10c.
- Click tomorrow's date in the Date Navigator to display the next day's schedule. The task list displays the same tasks, but no appointments are scheduled.
- Click and drag any task from the task list to any time period on the schedule. The Appointment dialog box is displayed.
- Change any details if you wish, then click the **Save and Close button** to close the Appointment dialog box. The task displays as both a task in the TaskPad and as an appointment.

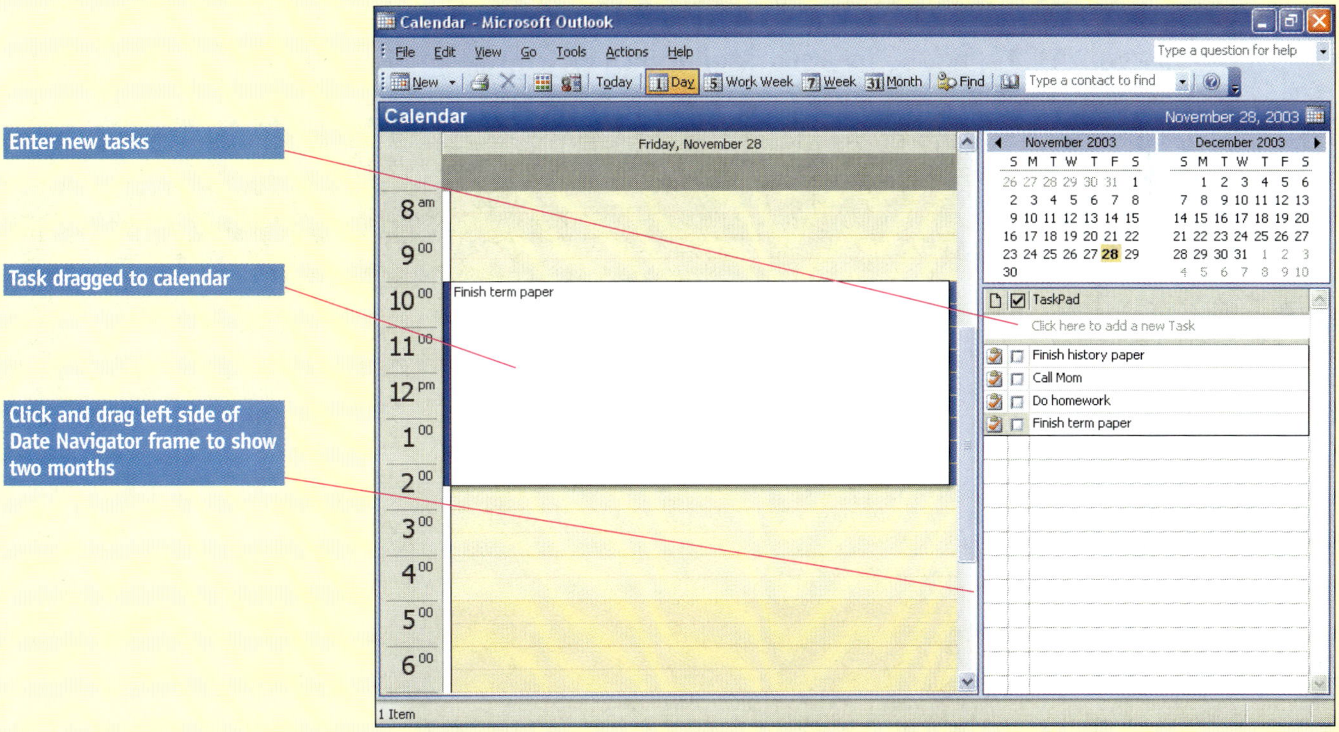

(c) Create a Task (step 3)

FIGURE 10 Hands-on Exercise 3 (*continued*)

CHANGING AN ITEM IN OUTLOOK

You can change any item in Outlook to another type of item simply by dragging it into the folder on the Navigation Pane that contains the type of item you want to create. For instance, if you want a task to become an e-mail message to someone in your Address Book, drag the task to the Inbox icon. The details entered in the Appointment window for the task will be transferred to the text portion of the e-mail message.

Step 4: Modify the Task List

- Pull down the **View menu** and select **Navigation Pane**. Click the **Tasks button** on the Navigation Pane to display the Tasks folder shown in Figure 10d.
- Click the **check box** next to Call Mom (or any of the tasks in your list). A line appears through the item to indicate that the task has been completed.
- Click in the text box to add a new task. Enter **This task is late**. Click in the **Due Date text box**, click the **drop-down arrow** that appears when you click this box, then click yesterday's date. Press **Enter**.
- Click any other task in the list to deselect the current task. The task that you just created appears in red to remind you it is overdue.
- Click the **Overdue Tasks option button** in the Current View list in the Navigation Pane. Any overdue tasks in your task list are displayed.
- Click the **Detailed List option button** in the Navigation Pane to show the Status, Due Date, % Complete, and so on.
- Press and hold the **Ctrl key** as you select any tasks that you want to delete from the list (they can be completed or not). Press the **Delete button** on the Standard toolbar to remove these tasks from the list.
- Click the **Calendar button** on the Navigation Pane to return to your schedule.

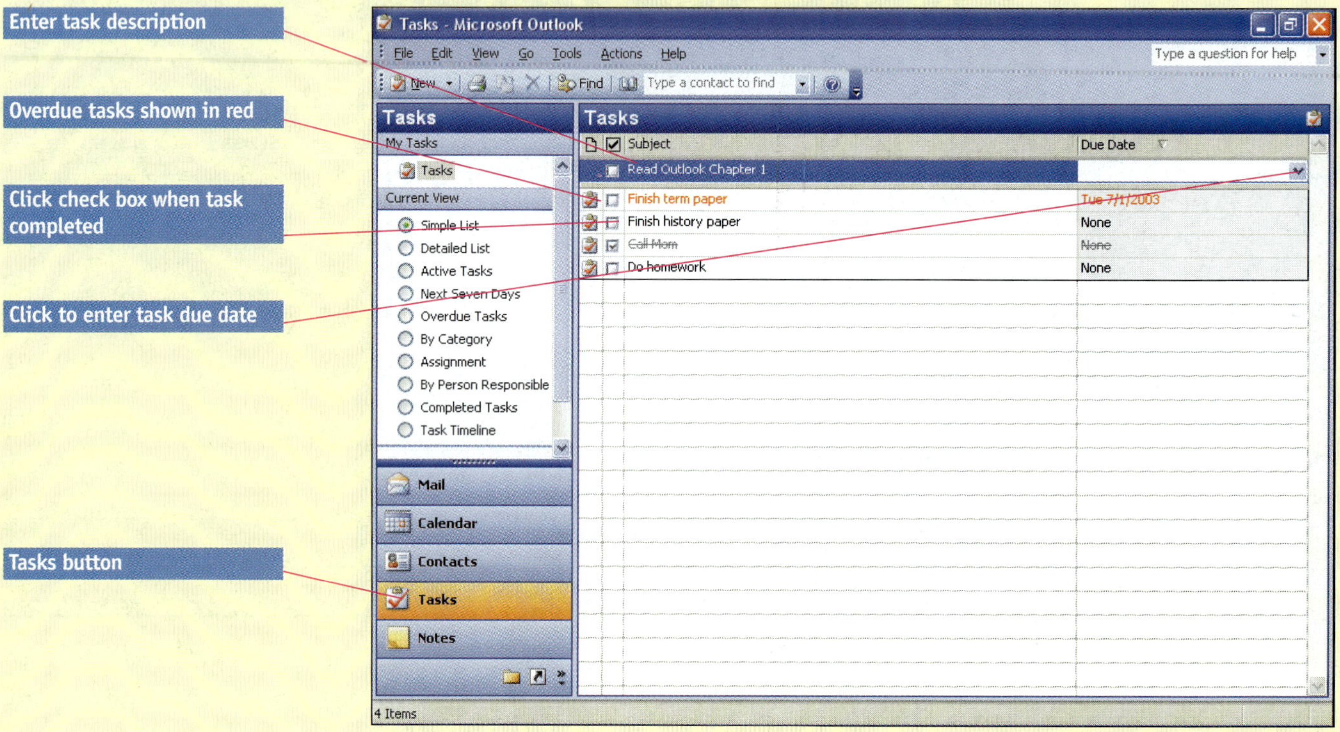

(d) Modify the Task List (step 4)

FIGURE 10 Hands-on Exercise 3 (*continued*)

ASSIGN A TASK TO SOMEONE ELSE

A task can contain more information such as a due date, whether or not the task has been started and, if so, the percentage of the task that has been completed. Best of all, you can assign a task to someone else, which you will do in practice exercise 3 at the end of the chapter.

Step 5: The Print Preview Command

- Pull down the **View menu** and click the **Work Week view** (or click the **Work Week button** on the Standard toolbar). Your schedule for the week is displayed, including the task and the appointments added in previous steps.
- Pull down the **File menu**, click **Print** to display the Print dialog box, then click **Weekly style** in the Print Style list box.
- Click **Print preview** to see a preview of your calendar with one page per week.
- Click the **Print button** on the toolbar and select **Tri-fold Style** in the Print Style selection box.
- Click the **Preview button** to preview your schedule as shown in Figure 10e. The current day is shown in the left fold, the task list in the center, and the weekly calendar in the right fold. Click the **Print button** to close the preview window.
- Click the down arrow next to **Start date** and select today's date from the calendar. Change the end date to today's date also to print only one day of your calendar. Click **OK** to print your schedule for the day.

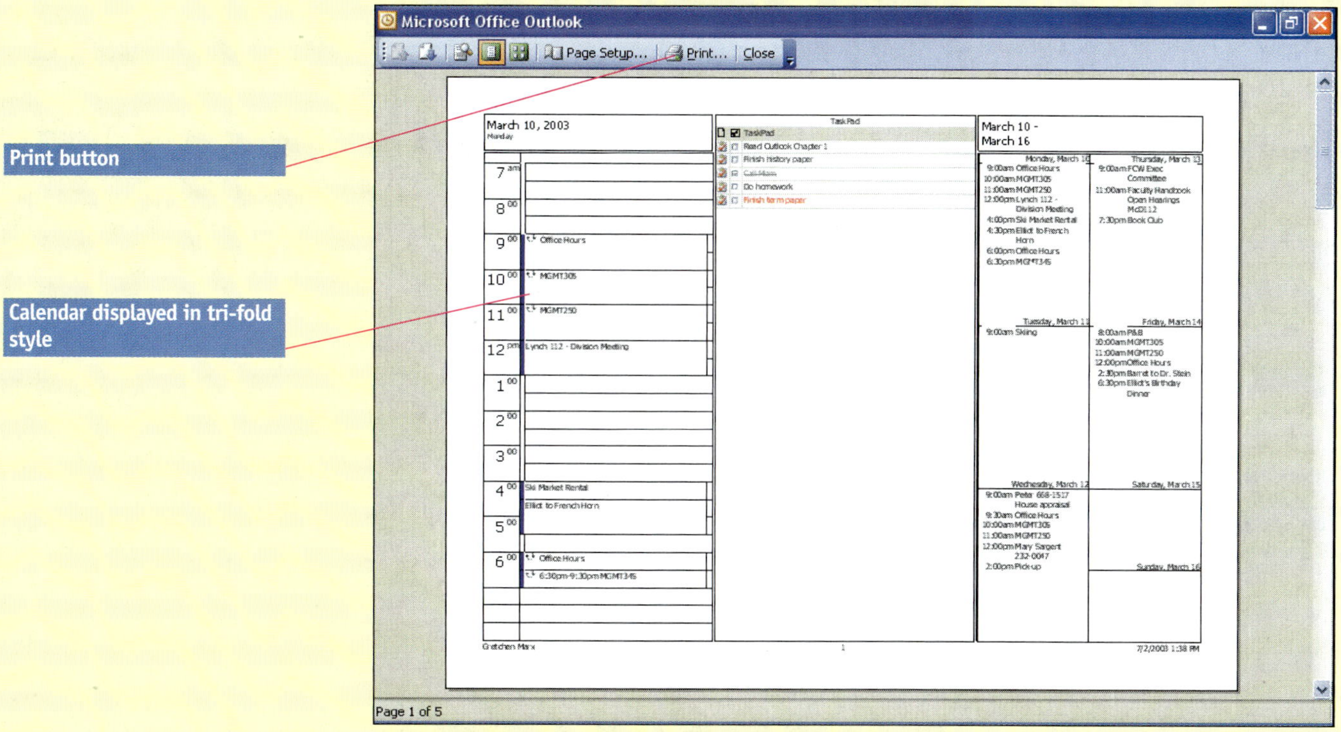

(e) The Print Preview Command (step 5)

FIGURE 10 Hands-on Exercise 3 (*continued*)

THE RECURRING APPOINTMENT

You can schedule all occurrences of a recurring appointment (such as a class or weekly office meeting) when you enter the first appointment. When you create the appointment, click the Recurrence button on the toolbar to display the Appointment Recurrence dialog box. Enter the pattern (e.g., daily or weekly) and the number of occurrences or the starting and ending date, then click OK to close the dialog box. Save the appointment, then change to a weekly or monthly view in the Schedule folder to see how the multiple appointments were entered.

Step 6: View the Journal

- Click the **Windows Start button**, select **Programs** or **All Programs**, then select **Microsoft Word** and open any Word document you have stored on your system. Make a minor modification to the document, then save and close it.
- Pull down the **Go menu**, then select **Journal** to display it.
- Click the **Day button** on the Standard toolbar to change to the Daily view, then click the **Today button** to see the Journal timeline in Figure 10f.
- Click the **plus sign** (+) next to the Microsoft Word entry type. **Double click** the Journal entry for the Word document that you just modified to display details about the entry.
- Click the **Contacts button** in the Journal Entry window to display your contact list. Select a name from the list, then click **OK** to close the Select Contacts dialog box. Click **Save and Close** to close the Journal Entry window.
- Click the **By Contact option button** in the Navigation Pane to show Journal entries listed by contact. Click the **plus sign** (+) next to the contact's name to see the Journal entries associated with that contact.

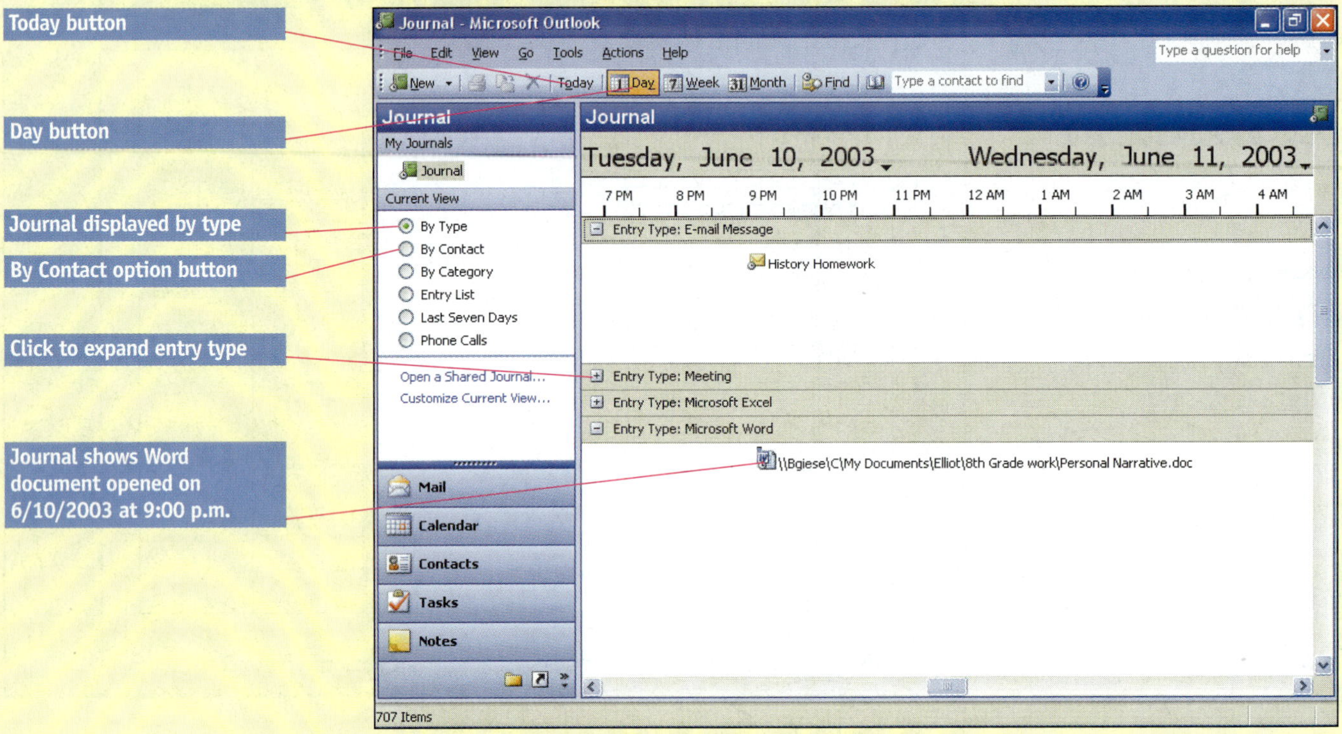

(f) View the Journal (step 6)

FIGURE 10 Hands-on Exercise 3 (*continued*)

LINKING CONTACTS TO OUTLOOK OBJECTS

You can link contacts to any Outlook appointment, event, e-mail message, or task. Click the Contacts button at the bottom of the Appointment window to display the Select Contacts dialog box and select the contact. Open a task in its own window and click the Contacts button. Click the icon in the upper-left corner of a sticky note to display the Contacts option. Right click an e-mail message in the Inbox and select Options to display a dialog box with a Contacts button.

Step 7: Outlook Today

- Pull down the **Go menu** and select **Folder** to display the Go to Folder dialog box shown in Figure 10g.
- Select **Personal Folders**, then click **OK**. The Outlook Today window shows the appointments you scheduled as well as a list of tasks you entered but have not yet completed.
- Click the text at the top of the window that says **Customize Outlook Today**. Check (clear) the Startup box that determines what you want to see when you start Outlook. (Clearing the Startup box will display the Inbox.)
- Click the **down arrow** in the Calendar area to change the number of days for which calendar events are displayed.
- Click the **down arrow** in the Styles area to change the appearance of the Outlook Today window.
- Click **Save Changes** (near the top of the window) to accept these changes and return to Outlook Today.
- Pull down the **File menu** and click the **Print command** (or click the **Print button** on the toolbar) to display the Print dialog box.
- Click **OK** to print Outlook Today. Close Outlook.

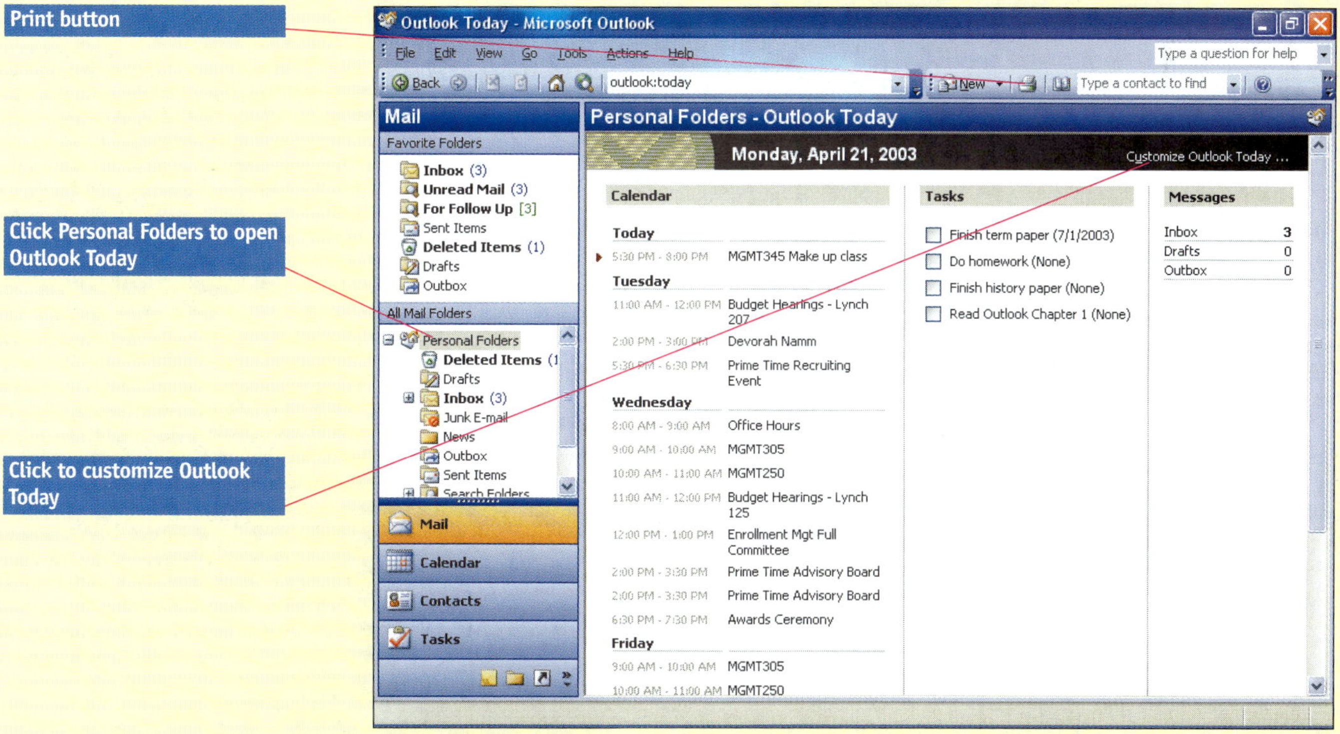

(g) Outlook Today (step 7)

FIGURE 10 Hands-on Exercise 3 (*continued*)

TURN OFF THE DEFAULT REMINDER

If you don't want a reminder for every appointment, pull down the Tools menu, click Options, then select the Preferences tab. Clear the Default reminder check box so new messages will not automatically have the reminder set.

SUMMARY

Microsoft Outlook is a desktop information manager that you can use to send and receive e-mail, maintain a Contact list (address book), schedule appointments, create and track tasks, write notes to yourself, and activate a Journal that monitors the activity on your PC.

The Navigation Pane at the left of the Outlook window provides the easiest way to switch from one feature to another. The Navigation Pane contains icons for each major Outlook feature (Inbox, Calendar, Contacts, Tasks, Journal, Notes, and Sent and Deleted Items). The Favorite Folders list is also displayed in the Navigation Pane. It contains the Unread Mail and For Follow Up search folders that allow you to instantly find messages that may be of particular interest. The Navigation Pane also displays variable information related to the feature being used, such as the Current View buttons in Calendar.

The Reading Pane shows you the content of your mail messages, and can be displayed at the right of the Inbox or below it. The appearance of message icons in the Inbox indicates whether a message has attachments; is high priority; has been read, replied to, or forwarded; or whether it needs to be followed up. You can create personal mail folders to organize your messages. E-mail messages can be sent in HTML format, which allows you to apply stationery elements to your messages. You can also attach files to messages, allowing you to send (and receive) files to (and from) anyone on the Internet.

The Outlook calendar and TaskPad allow you to organize your time and daily activities. The calendar, which can be displayed in daily, weekly, or monthly view, shows your meetings and appointments with a reminder if desired. You can add and delete tasks from the TaskPad, which also shows overdue and completed items.

The Options command in the Tools menu lets you customize virtually every aspect of Outlook. You can also customize various views, to show daily, weekly, and monthly calendars, for instance, or to organize your e-mail by contacts. You can further organize your work by applying conditional formatting, which allows you to specify the way appointments are displayed. You can also customize each of the windows within Outlook. For instance, you can show different fields in your Inbox or in your contact list when displayed as a phone list.

The features in Outlook are thoroughly integrated with one another, making each more valuable as a part of the whole. An e-mail message, for example, can be generated automatically from appointments on the calendar (perhaps to remind attendees of a scheduled meeting) using entries in the contact list. You can create entries in your Contact list or events on your calendar directly from an e-mail message. Objects within Outlook can be e-mailed, printed, and added to the Journal.

KEY TERMS

- Appointment 975
- Attached file 952
- Calendar 946
- Category 963
- Conditional formatting 976
- Contacts folder 946
- Date Navigator 975
- Deleted Items folder 951
- Download 949
- Drafts folder 951
- E-mail 949
- E-mail address 952
- Event 976
- Favorite Folders 946
- For Follow Up folder 951
- Inbox 946
- Journal 948
- Mailbox 949
- Mail client 949
- Mail server 949
- Meeting 975
- Navigation Pane 946
- Outbox 951
- Password 949
- Reading Pane 946
- Recurring events 975
- Reminder option 975
- Reply button 952
- Sent Items folder 951
- Task 948
- Task list 948
- TaskPad 976
- Unread mail folder 951
- Upload 949
- Username 949

MULTIPLE CHOICE

1. Which of the following is not a default category within the Outlook categories list?
   (a) Holiday cards
   (b) Business
   (c) Personal
   (d) School

2. Which of the following capabilities is available in Outlook e-mail?
   (a) Send a message to multiple recipients
   (b) Forward a message
   (c) Reply to a message
   (d) All of the above

3. What is the easiest way to sort your mail by the name of the sender?
   (a) Pull down the View menu, select Current View, then click By Sender
   (b) Click the From selection at the top of the column in the Inbox
   (c) Right click a message in the Inbox, then click Sort by Sender
   (d) It is possible to sort messages in the Inbox only by Date Received

4. Which of the following statements regarding Outlook is false?
   (a) You can move a message from one folder to another
   (b) You can create a Contact list of people you correspond with frequently
   (c) You can send meeting reminders to people in your Contact list
   (d) You can assign a task only to yourself

5. How are completed tasks displayed in Outlook?
   (a) They are shown in green
   (b) They are shown in red
   (c) They are lined through
   (d) Completed tasks are not displayed in the task list

6. Which of the following is a *false* statement about Outlook folders?
   (a) Mail is moved automatically from the Outbox to the Sent Items folder as the mail is picked up and delivered by the mail server
   (b) Messages deleted from the Inbox folder are automatically moved to the Deleted Items folder
   (c) Messages are moved automatically from the Inbox to the Outbox when you exit Outlook
   (d) Only one folder can be open at a time

7. Which of the following is not displayed in the Outlook calendar?
   (a) A summary count of the messages in your Inbox
   (b) The Date Navigator
   (c) Your schedule
   (d) The TaskPad

8. E-mail allows you to send messages to:
   (a) Another user on your local network
   (b) Another person on the Internet
   (c) Both (a) and (b)
   (d) Neither (a) nor (b)

9. What does the paper clip icon next to a message in the Outlook e-mail window indicate?
   (a) The sender has given the message high priority
   (b) The recipient has flagged the message for further review
   (c) The message has attachments
   (d) The message has been forwarded to one or more people

10. Which of the following can be e-mailed to a person in your contact list?
    (a) A meeting reminder
    (b) A task assignment
    (c) Both (a) and (b)
    (d) Neither (a) nor (b)

... continued

multiple choice

11. Which of the following is true about Outlook meetings?

(a) An appointment can be turned into a meeting
(b) A meeting can be assigned to a category
(c) A meeting can appear multiple times on the calendar
(d) All of the above

12. Which of the following is true about the Outlook Contacts folder?

(a) It can be printed as a telephone list
(b) It can be printed as detailed cards
(c) Both (a) and (b)
(d) Neither (a) nor (b)

13. Which of the following does not appear as an option in the Outlook Journal?

(a) Phone calls
(b) Notes
(c) Microsoft Word documents
(d) Microsoft Excel workbooks

14. Which of the following is not displayed in Outlook Today?

(a) Journal entries
(b) Tasks
(c) Meetings
(d) Message summary

15. All of the following are icons on the Navigation Pane except:

(a) Tasks
(b) Inbox
(c) Calendar
(d) Journal

16. Which of the following is *not* a view in Calendar?

(a) Daily
(b) Weekly
(c) Monthly
(d) Holiday

17. A message in your Inbox that appears in red indicates that:

(a) The message is overdue for follow up
(b) You have forwarded the message
(c) You have marked the message for follow up
(d) You have read and responded to the message

18. The Outlook Journal can track:

(a) E-mail messages
(b) Word documents
(c) Excel spreadsheets
(d) All of the above

ANSWERS

1. d	**7.** a	**13.** b
2. d	**8.** c	**14.** a
3. b	**9.** c	**15.** d
4. d	**10.** c	**16.** d
5. c	**11.** d	**17.** a
6. c	**12.** c	**18.** d

PRACTICE WITH OUTLOOK

1. **Create a Rule:** If you need to refer to a specific message in your Inbox or Sent Items folder, you may end up scrolling through hundreds if not thousands of messages. In this practice exercise you will organize incoming and outgoing messages by creating a rule to move messages containing a certain subject to a folder you set up for this purpose.
   a. Send yourself an e-mail with COMP100 as the subject. Right click the message when it appears in your Inbox, then select Create Rule from the context-sensitive menu to display the Create Rule dialog box shown in Figure 11. (If you receive a message indicating that rules do not work on HTTP e-mail accounts, click OK to close the message.)
   b. Click the check box next to Subject contains. Click the check the box next to Move e-mail to folder, then click Select Folder to display the Rules and Alerts dialog box.
   c. Select the COMP100 folder that you created in the first hands-on exercise, then click OK twice to close both dialog boxes.
   d. In the message box telling you that you have successfully created a rule, check the box to run this rule now on messages already in the current folder, then click OK. Another message box indicates that Outlook is running the rule, and the message you sent yourself is moved to the COMP100 folder.
   e. Send yourself a test message with COMP100 in the subject line. In a few minutes check the COMP100 folder. It should contain the new message.
   f. Pull down the Tools menu, select Rules and Alerts, then click New Rule to start the Rules Wizard. Click the option button to Start from a blank rule, select Check messages after sending, then click Next.
   g. Continue with the wizard to indicate that messages sent to your COMP100 distribution list should be copied to a new COMP100 folder within the Sent Items folder.
   h. Send yourself a message with the COMP100 in the subject line to test the rule. Scroll down in the All Mail Folders list to see the new folder.

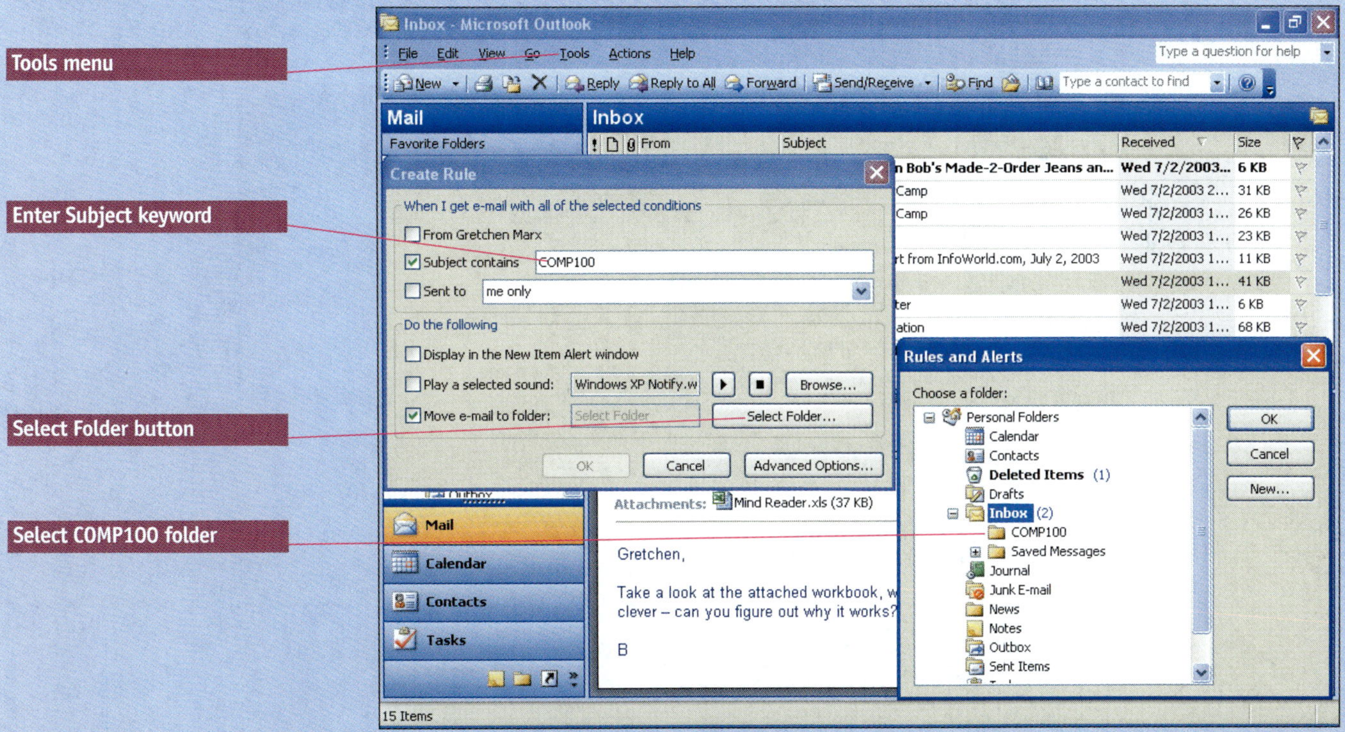

FIGURE 11 Create a Rule (exercise 1)

2. **Manage Your Mail:** Eventually your mailboxes will be very full, and take more disk space than you want. In some cases you will simply delete old messages. On the other hand, there are messages that you sent or received that you want to keep. You can do this by using Outlook's archiving capabilities. By default, Outlook is set to automatically archive messages that are more than six months old. In this exercise you will learn to manage your e-mail.
   a. Open your Inbox and delete a message that you no longer want. The message is moved to the Deleted Items folder.
   b. To delete the contents of the Deleted Items folder, right click it in the Folder list, then select Empty "Deleted Items" Folder.
   c. To archive a single folder according to your own schedule, first select the folder, then pull down the File menu and select Archive to display the Archive dialog box in Figure 12.
   d. Select the folder that you want to archive, change the archive date if you wish, then click OK.
   e. A new icon, Archive Folders, will appear in your Folder list as shown in the figure. It will contain all the folders you archive.
   f. Press the Print Screen key on your keyboard, then open Word and paste the screen image into a blank Word document. Print the document as proof for your instructor that you have archived your files.
   g. To customize AutoArchive options, pull down the Tools menu, select Options, click the Other tab, then click AutoArchive. Change settings as you wish.

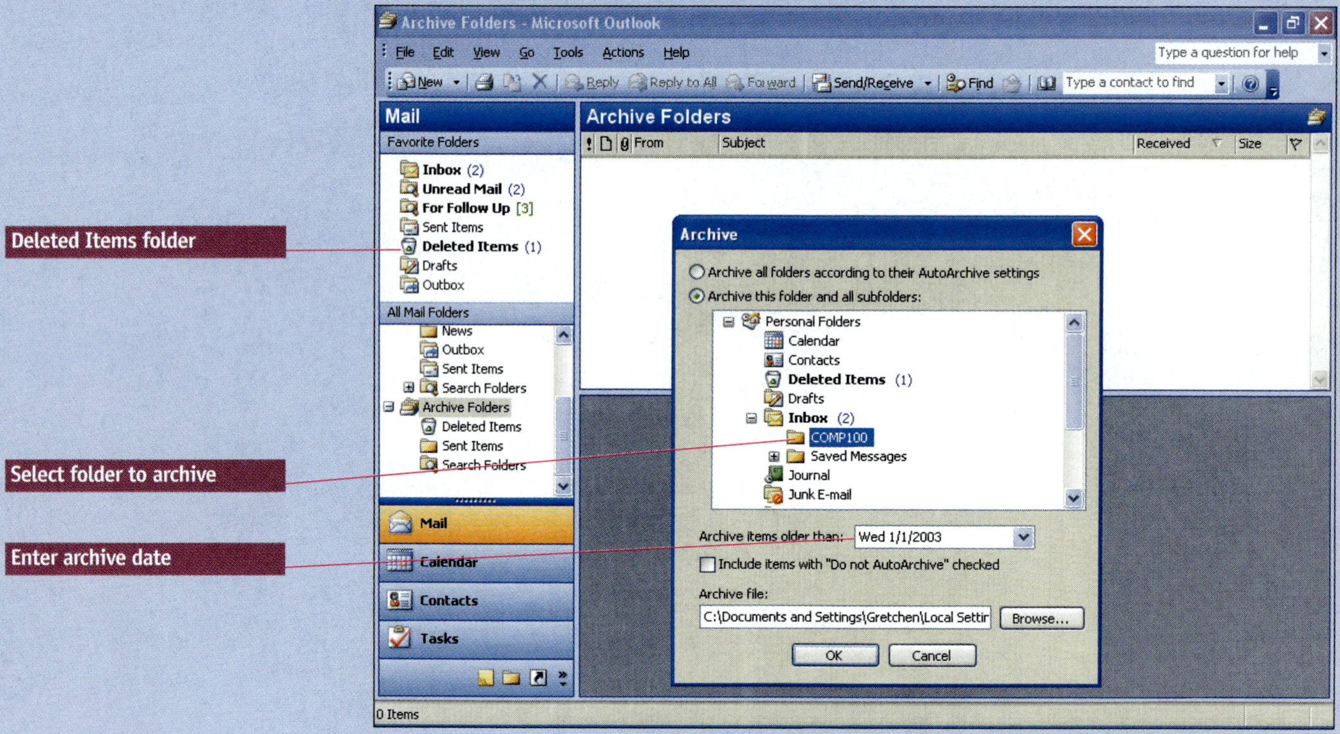

FIGURE 12 Manage Your Mail (exercise 2)

3. **Accept a Task:** Outlook is designed not only for the individual user, but also to simplify the management of many people working together on tasks, meetings, and or projects. Find a partner in your class with whom to work on this exercise.
   a. Click the Calendar icon on the Navigation Pane, then if necessary pull down the View menu and select TaskPad.
   b. Right click a task in the TaskPad. Select Assign Task from the shortcut menu to display the task as an e-mail message as shown in Figure 13.
   c. Click the To button to open your Contact list, then select your partner's name to assign him(her) to this task.
   d. Click the drop-down arrow next to the Due date text box and select a date from the calendar. Change the priority to High. Click Send.
   e. Have your partner follow the same procedure to assign you a task.
   f. When the task your partner assigns you arrives in your Inbox, double click the task message to open it.
   g. Click the Accept button on the Standard toolbar to accept the assignment. A new mail message to your partner is displayed.
   h. Enter a short message in the Notes section of the task to let your partner know that you received the task assignment, then click Send to send the acceptance message.
   i. Click the Tasks icon on the Navigation Pane. The task you accepted should be displayed in the task list. Double click the task. You are listed as the task owner.
   j. Click the Detailed List option button in the Navigation Pane, then click Customize Current View in the Navigation Pane to display the Customize View: Detailed List dialog box.
   k. Click the Fields button, then select the additional fields that you want to display in the Task window. Click OK twice to close the dialog boxes.
   l. Click the button at the top of the % Complete column to list the tasks that you have not yet started first. Click it again to show completed tasks first.

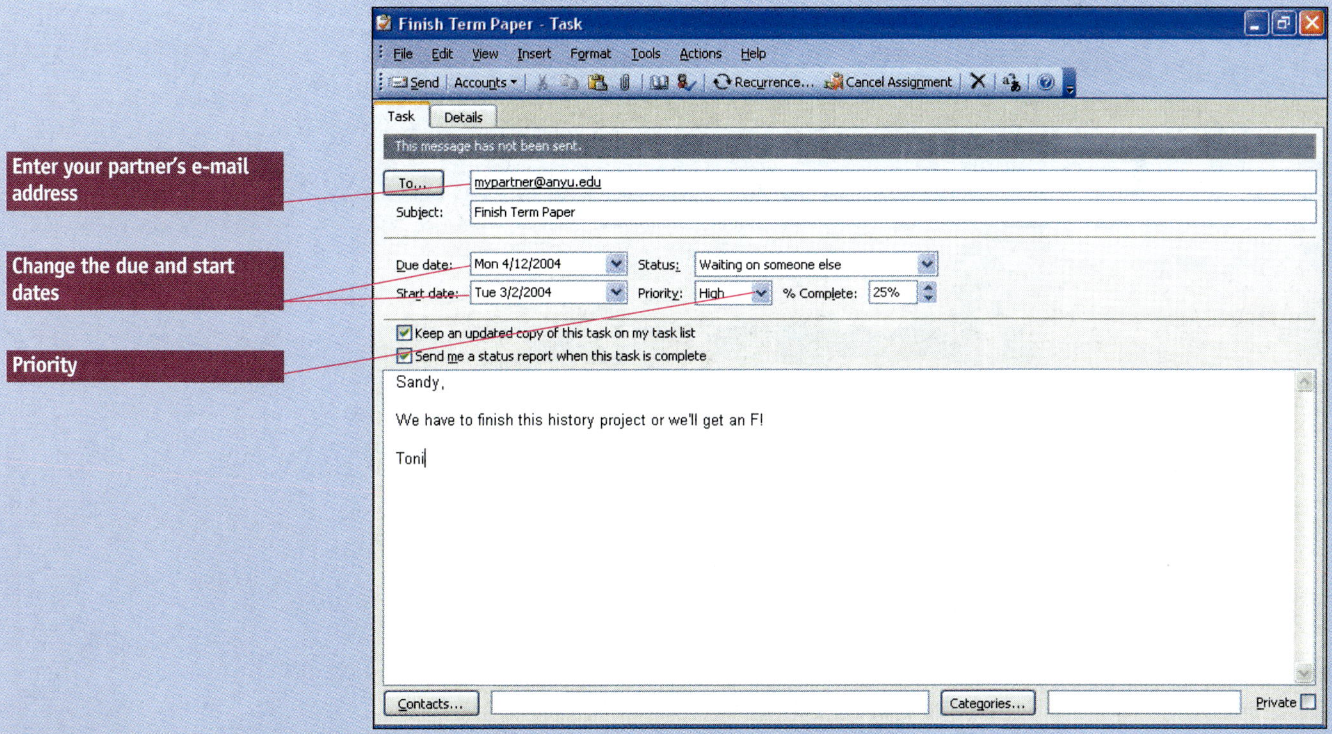

FIGURE 13 Accept a Task (exercise 3)

4. **Customize Toolbars:** Microsoft makes it easy to add functions to Outlook toolbars using the Customize command. Before doing that we will explore the Advanced toolbar in the Inbox.
   a. Open the Outlook Inbox, then right click the Standard toolbar and select Advanced. The Advanced toolbar in Figure 14 is displayed.
   b. Click the Outlook Today button to show that view, then click the Back button to return to the Inbox. Click the Reading Pane button to turn the reading pane off; click it again to restore it.
   c. Click the down arrow next to the Current View drop-down list (it says Messages when you first display the toolbar). Explore the various view options. We show Last Seven Days in the figure. Click AutoPreview to view the first three lines of each message. Click AutoPreview again to remove the three-line display.
   d. Right click either toolbar and select Customize from the shortcut menu to display the Customize dialog box at the left side of Figure 14. Click the Options tab, then click the option to Always show full menus, then click the option to Show shortcut keys in ScreenTips.
   e. Click Close to return to the Inbox. Pull down the Tools menu. Instead of a double arrow at the bottom of the menu indicating that there are more choices, the entire menu is displayed. Press Escape to close the menu. Hover over the Reply button on the Standard toolbar to see the shortcut key (Ctrl+R) displayed.
   f. Pull down the Tools menu and select Customize. This time click the Commands tab to display the Customize dialog box at the right of the screen in the figure. (We show the dialog box twice in the figure, which you will not see on your screen.)
   g. Click on File in the categories list, then scroll down in the Commands list until you see Task. Drag and drop the Task icon at the right end of the Advanced Toolbar just after the AutoPreview icon. Close the Customize dialog box and return to the Inbox.
   h. Click the Task icon on the Advanced toolbar to display a new task. Close the task. You can remove the Task button from the toolbar by opening the Commands tab in the Customize dialog box and dragging the icon off the toolbar to the Commands list.

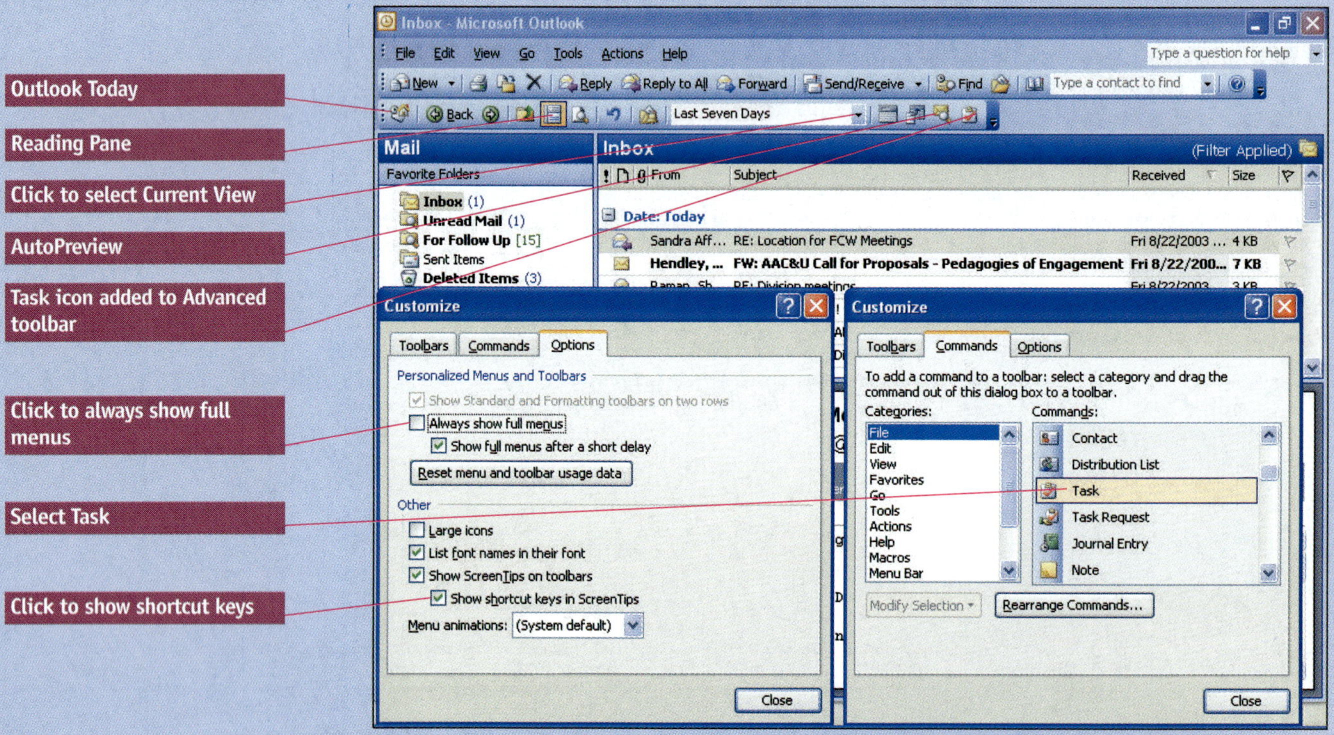

FIGURE 14 Customize Toolbars (exercise 4)

5. **Outlook Help:** Like other Microsoft Office applications, Outlook has an extensive Help function, which you should explore at your leisure to learn more about Outlook's features. In addition to basic help information, online tutorial training is also available.
   a. Open Outlook as you usually do and maximize the window. Pull down the Help menu, then select Microsoft Outlook Help to open the Help Task Pane at the right of the Outlook window.
   b. Click Table of Contents, then click on a subject of interest to you—we chose Contacts, then Pictures in Contacts, then Add a picture to a contact as shown in Figure 15. Outlook contracts, and the information pertaining to the topic you selected is displayed in a Help window at the right of the screen.
   c. Follow the instructions to add a picture to a contact, then press Print Screen. Open a new blank document in Word and paste the screen image into it. Print the document for your instructor to indicate that you know how to add a picture to the address book. Close Word and return to Outlook.
   d. Click the Close button at the upper right of the Help window that contains the detailed instructions, in this case how to add a picture to a contact. The Help window closes, Outlook expands, and the Outlook Help Table of Contents is displayed within the Task Pane.
   e. Click the Back button at the top of the Table of Contents to display the opening help screen. Type the keyword signature in the search text box, then click the Start Searching button. Outlook connects to Microsoft.com and displays a list of topics from Office Online that are related to the keyword signature.
   f. Click on one of the topics. The Help window opens once again to display instructions for that particular topic.
   g. Close the Help window, then click the Back button at the top of the Help Task Pane until you reach the main Help screen. Click the Training icon two-thirds of the way down the screen. Internet Explorer opens the Microsoft Online training site.
   h. Select Outlook in the Browse Training Courses section of the page, then select a training course to preview. Write and send a brief e-mail note to your instructor about what you learned.

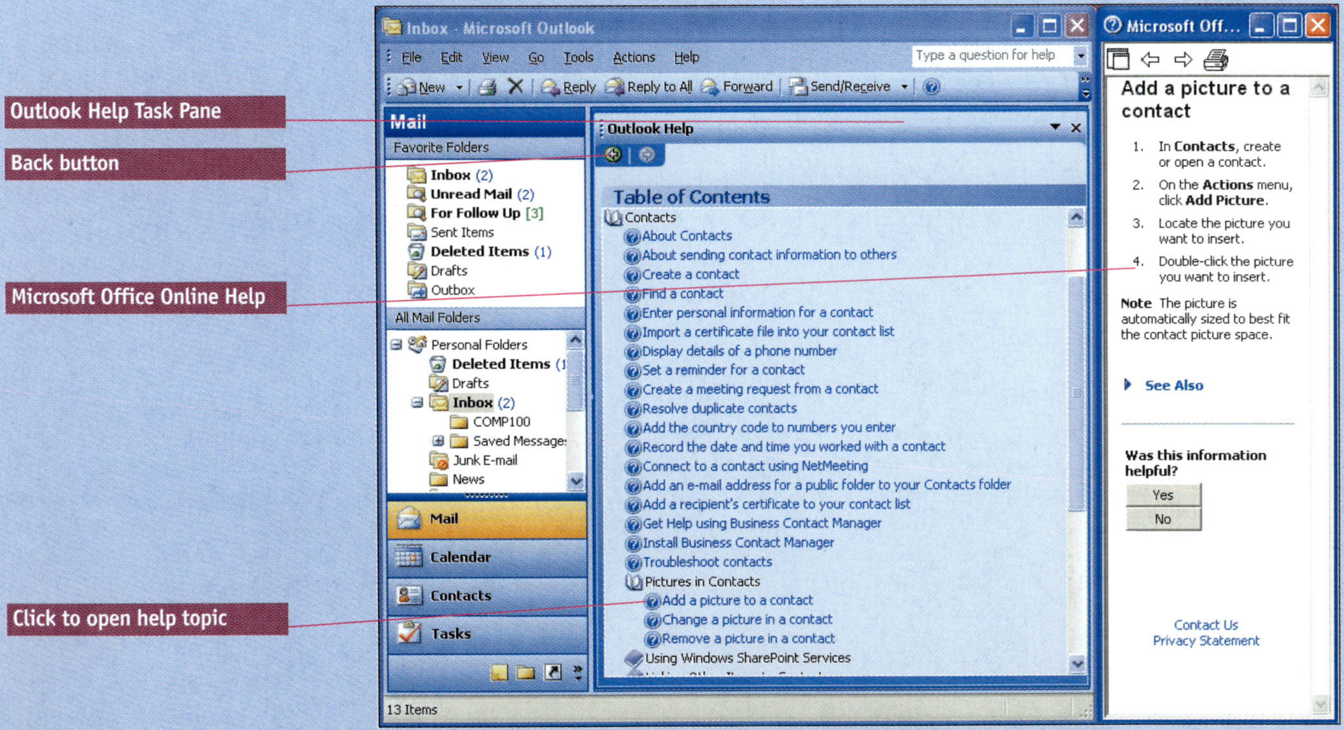

FIGURE 15 Outlook Help (exercise 5)

MINI CASES

Sign Up for a Mailing List

You can sign up on the Web to receive e-mail messages from many different sources. These mailing lists are available on every conceivable subject, which you can find at www.list-universe.com. You can sign up for a particularly good source of information about computers and the Internet at www.topica.com. Go to the site, then select the lists you want to join and begin getting great tips on how to increase your proficiency with Word, Excel, Outlook, or whatever you select. Be warned, however, that you will get lots of mail! Forward a tip you receive to your instructor to indicate that you have completed this case.

Find a Friend

You can find the e-mail address of a friend using several Web services. Try BigFoot at www.bigfoot.com, or WhoWhere at www.whowhere.lycos.com. Both services allow you to enter the person's name and other information to narrow the search, such as the city and state where they live. If the individual has an address with an Internet service provider such as AOL or MSN, chances are good that you will find it. If you need someone's corporate e-mail address, you will probably have more luck searching the organization's Web site. The availability of all of this information raises interesting questions about privacy. Is it a good idea that anyone can find anyone else so easily? What does this imply about your privacy (there is none!), and about what you put up on your own Web page? Write a short essay on the subject of Internet privacy and hand it in to your instructor.

Microsoft Outlook Home Page

Microsoft provides extensive support for its products on the Web. The home page of Microsoft Outlook can be found at www.microsoft.com/office/outlook. Go to the home page and click Tips and Tricks to learn more about how to get the most out of Outlook. Write a brief description of what you learned at the Microsoft Web site.

Outlook Handles Junk Mail

One of the enduring problems on the Internet is the explosion of junk mail, a multibillion dollar problem for organizations and a major annoyance for individuals. Microsoft Research has developed sophisticated sampling techniques that check the content of a message to determine whether or not it is junk mail and automatically move the message out of your Inbox and into the Junk E-mail folder if it is. Read more about the junk mail filter and how to customize it in Outlook Help. Print the Help screen and write a short essay for your instructor on the costs and problems associated with junk mail.

Keeping Multiple Calendars

Do you have multiple lives—that is, things you do in school, or at work, and then appointments, meetings, and so on, that you keep track of with friends and family? Outlook allows you to set up multiple calendars and display them side-by-side on the screen. On the left side of your screen you can show your meetings at work, for instance, and on the right the dentist appointments, meetings with the school principal, family birthdays, anniversaries, and so on. Open Outlook Help, click the Training link, then click the link to browse Outlook training. Click the training course to see and share multiple calendars. Create a second calendar, enter a few appointments in it, display it with your other calendar, then print the pages for your instructor as proof of completing this case.

CASE STUDY

1

Integrated Case Study: The Totally Fit Wellness Center

OBJECTIVES

1. Use the core applications in Office 2003 individually or in conjunction with one another.
2. Link an Excel chart to a Word document and a PowerPoint presentation.
3. Import an Excel worksheet into an Access database.
4. Create Access tables, queries, reports, and forms.
5. Use an Access table as the basis for a mail merge.
6. Use Word to create a Web page for the organization.

integrated exercises

1. Totally Fit Revenue Workbook and Chart (Excel)
2. Report to the President (Word and Excel)
3. Presentation to the President (PowerPoint and Excel)
4. Last-minute Change (Word, Excel, and PowerPoint)
5. Importing Data (Access and Excel)
6. A Relational Database (Access)
7. Access Objects: Forms, Queries, and Reports (Access)
8. An Access Switchboard (Access)
9. Mail Merge (Word and Access)
10. Worksheet References (Excel)
11. Presentation to the Board (PowerPoint and Excel)
12. Letter to the Board (Word and Excel)
13. Create a Home Page (Word)
14. Submission Checklist (Word)

This document provides a series of 13 exercises in Microsoft Office that relate to the Totally Fit Wellness Center, a health center such as might exist at your school or university. Each exercise describes a specific task for the organization to accomplish and typically requires the use of multiple applications within Microsoft Office for solution. Many of the exercises are cumulative in nature. You may, for example, be asked to create an Excel chart in one exercise, and then incorporate that chart into a Word memo and a PowerPoint presentation in subsequent exercises. Other exercises will ask you to create or modify an Access database, to exchange data between Excel and Access, and to create a Web page for the Wellness Center. Collectively, you will gain considerable practice in the core applications of Microsoft Office 2003, and especially in how they work together to accomplish complex tasks.

All of the exercises are based on material from the core application chapters in *Exploring Office 2003 Volume I.* Specific chapter references are deliberately not provided so that the case study is as realistic as possible. Think of this assignment as your first day on the job; you were hired by the Totally Fit Wellness Center because you are proficient in Microsoft Office. This is your chance to show what you know.

Your assignment is to follow the directions of your instructor with respect to which of the exercises you are to complete within the case description. You should begin by downloading the practice files from our Web site at www.prenhall.com/grauer. Go to the site, click the book icon for Office 2003, and then click the Student Downloads tab. Scroll until you can select the link to Integrated Case Studies, and then download the file to your desktop. Double click the file icon and follow the onscreen instructions to install the practice files on your computer. The files you need will be in the Totally Fit folder within the Exploring Integrated Cases folder.

INTEGRATED EXERCISES

1. **Totally Fit Revenue Workbook and Chart (Excel):** You will find a partially completed version of the spreadsheet in Figure 1 in the *Totally Fit Revenue* workbook in the *Totally Fit Folder*. (You can download the practice files for this case study from our Web site at www.prenhall.com/grauer.) Open the workbook and save it as *Totally Fit Revenue Solution* so that you can return to the original workbook if necessary. Proceed as follows:
   a. Click in cell F3 and enter the formula to compute the total revenue for the first fitness plan, the Bronze Plan. Copy this formula to the remaining cells in column F.
   b. Click in cell B7 and compute the total revenue for the first quarter. Copy this formula to the remaining cells in this row.
   c. Use the AutoFormat command as the basis for formatting your worksheet in an attractive fashion. You can match our formatting, or you can use your own design.
   d. Select the data in cells A2 through E6 to create a side-by-side column chart. Specify that the data series are in columns so that the different plans appear on the X axis. Save this chart in its own sheet called Revenues by Plan. Print the completed chart for your instructor.
   e. Create a second side-by-side column chart using the same data as in part (d). This time, however, specify that the data are in rows so that the quarters appear on the X axis. Save this chart in its own sheet called Revenues by Quarter. You do not have to print this chart at this time.
   f. Enter your name in the worksheet as shown.
   g. Print the completed worksheet twice, once to show displayed values and once to show the cell formulas.
   h. Save the completed workbook for use in subsequent exercises. Exit Excel.

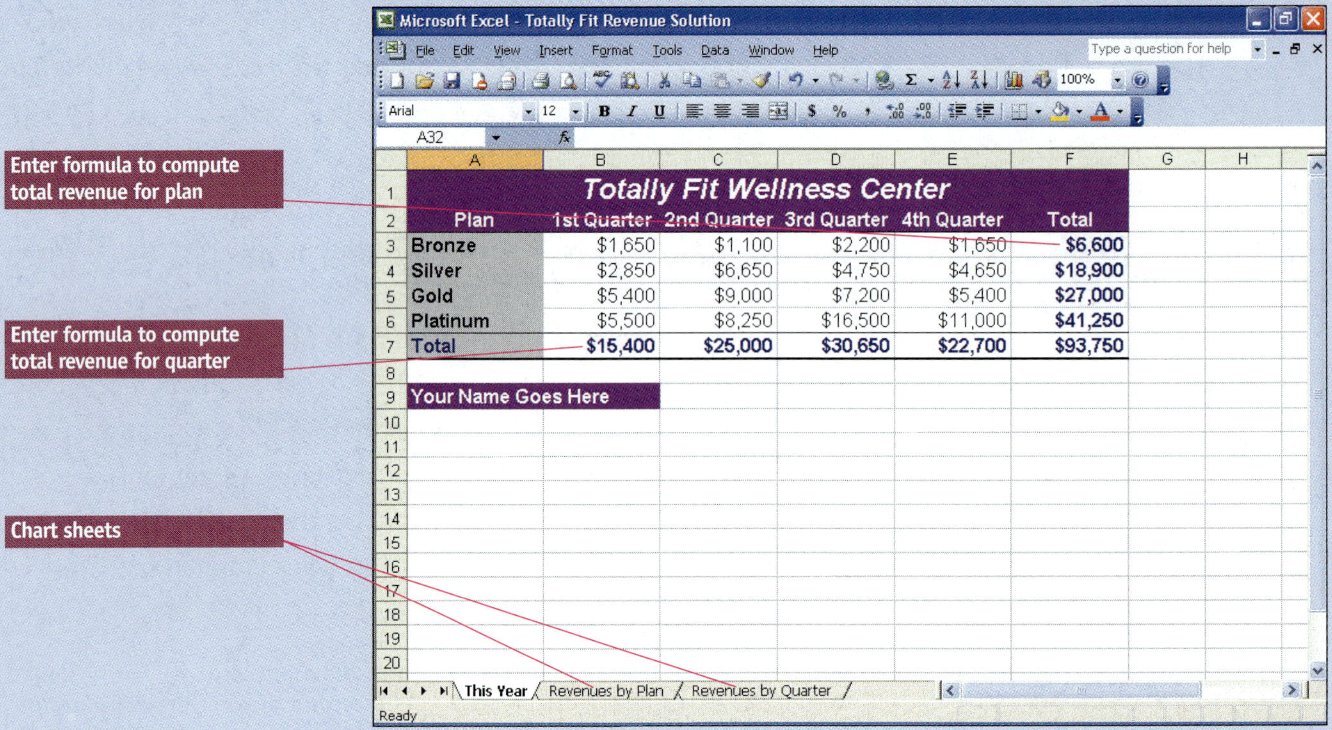

Totally Fit Wellness Center					
Plan	1st Quarter	2nd Quarter	3rd Quarter	4th Quarter	Total
Bronze	$1,650	$1,100	$2,200	$1,650	$6,600
Silver	$2,850	$6,650	$4,750	$4,650	$18,900
Gold	$5,400	$9,000	$7,200	$5,400	$27,000
Platinum	$5,500	$8,250	$16,500	$11,000	$41,250
Total	$15,400	$25,000	$30,650	$22,700	$93,750
Your Name Goes Here					

FIGURE 1 Totally Fit Revenue Workbook and Chart

2. **Report to the President (Word and Excel):** This exercise builds on the previous exercise by creating a Word document that contains the Excel worksheet and a chart. The latter is to be dynamically linked to the Word document, so that any changes in the workbook are automatically reflected in the memo.
   a. You will find a partially completed version of the document in Figure 2 in the *Report to the President* document in the *Totally Fit Folder*. Open this document, and then save it as *Report to the President Solution*. Change the To and From lines in the memo to contain your instructor's name and your name, respectively.
   b. Open the completed workbook from the previous exercise if it is not already open. Click and drag to select the completed worksheet, then click the Copy button on the Standard toolbar.
   c. Click the Microsoft Word button on the Windows taskbar to return to the Word document. Click below the first paragraph. Pull down the Edit menu and click the Paste Special command to display the Paste Special dialog box. Select Microsoft Excel Worksheet Object in the displayed list, click the Paste Link button, and then click OK to insert the worksheet. Do not worry about the size or position at this time.
   d. Move the cursor so that it is below the worksheet. Press Enter. Use the same technique as in parts (b) and (c) to link the side-by-side column chart (that displays quarters on the X axis) to the Word document. The Excel chart should appear. The only tricky part (if any) is to display the entire chart (it may be cropped initially). Select the chart, then click and drag a corner sizing handle to make the chart smaller. Right click the chart and click the command to display the Picture toolbar. Select the Crop tool, then click and drag the side handle at the right of the chart to show the portion of the chart that may have been cropped initially.
   e. Move and size the chart within the memo as necessary. You may find it convenient to change the zoom specification to "Whole Page" so that you can position the chart more easily.
   f. Save the completed document. Print the completed document for your instructor. Exit Word.

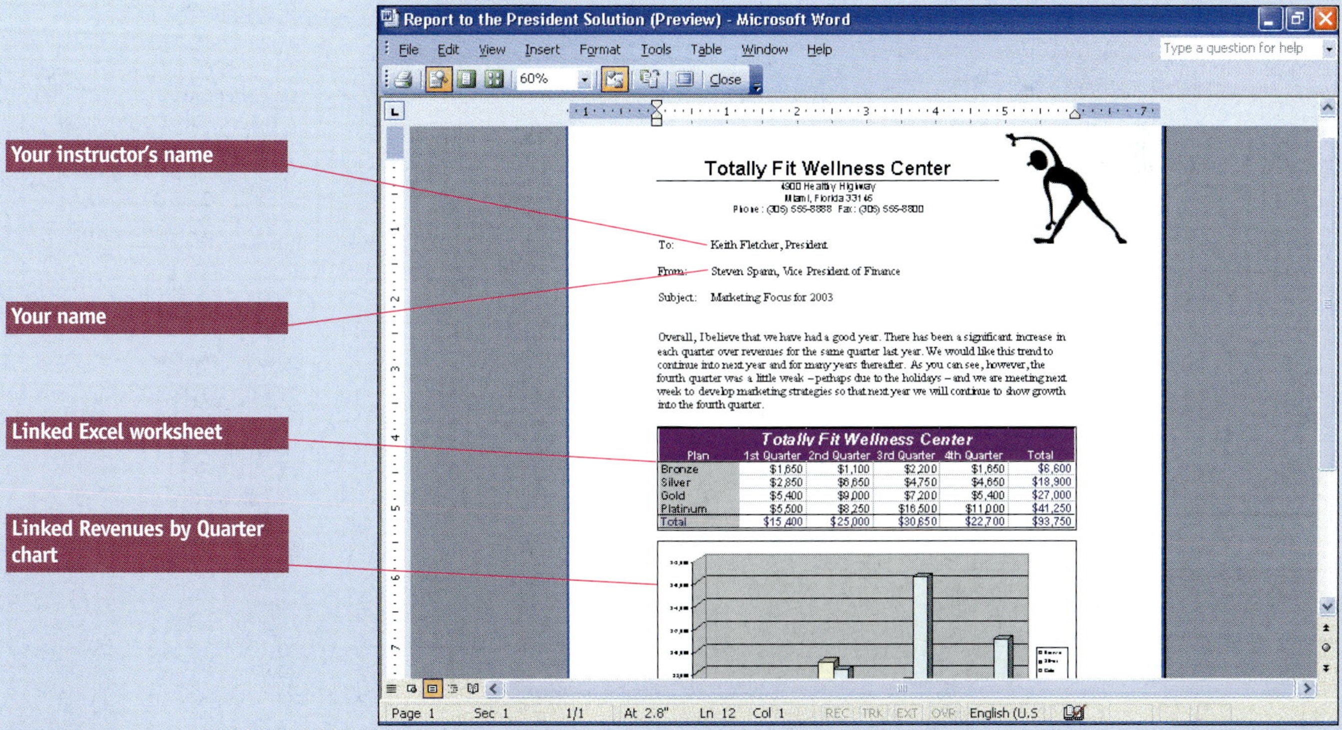

FIGURE 2 Report to the President

3. **Presentation to the President (PowerPoint and Excel):** A partially completed version of the presentation in Figure 3 has been saved as the *Presentation to the President* in the *Totally Fit Folder*. Open this presentation and save it as *Presentation to the President Solution* so that you can return to the original presentation if necessary.
   a. Insert a new slide that contains a mission statement as the second slide in the presentation. The mission statement should read as follows: *The mission of the Totally Fit Wellness Center is to provide modern, well-maintained fitness equipment and a knowledgeable, highly trained staff in order to give our members an effective and personalized exercise and wellness experience.*
   b. Open the completed workbook from exercise 1. Use the same technique as described in the previous problem to link the worksheet and the side-by-side column chart (with the data in rows) to the appropriate slides in the presentation, as shown in Figure 3.
   c. Move and/or size the worksheet and chart after they have been added to the presentation. Save the presentation.
   d. Add to the slide containing the worksheet a text box that points to the total revenue in the worksheet. The text box should indicate that the total revenue is over $90,000.
   e. Include animation effects as you see fit within a slide and add transition effects from one slide to the next.
   f. Experiment with a different design template, but limit yourself to five minutes. Choose the template you like best. Save the presentation.
   g. Add your name to the title slide. Print the audience handouts of the completed presentation (six per page) for your instructor. (Be sure to check the box to frame the slides.)
   h. Save the completed presentation. Exit PowerPoint. Close the Excel workbook and exit Excel.

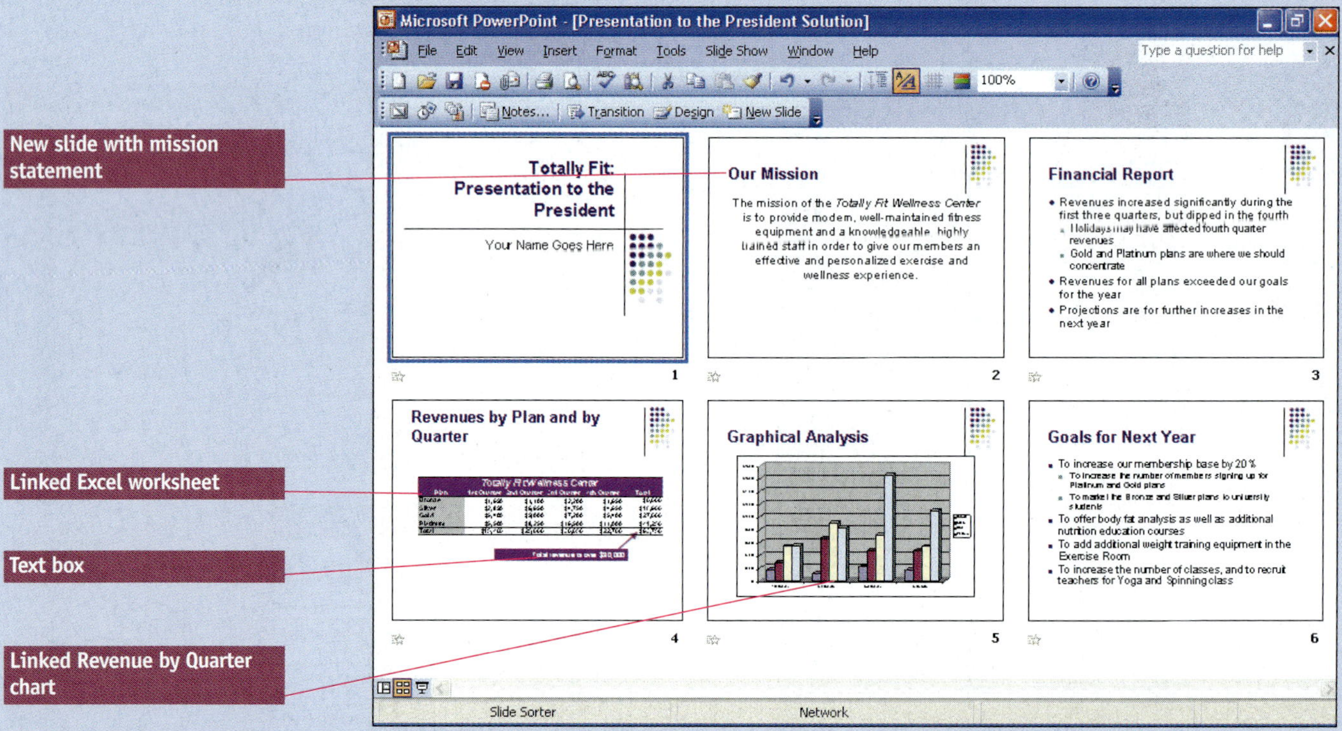

FIGURE 3 Presentation to the President

4. **Last-minute Change (Word, Excel, and PowerPoint):** It was just discovered that the revenue from a few new memberships was not included in the original workbook. Your task is to correct all of the documents that reflect this information. Open the completed *Totally Fit Revenue Solution* workbook from exercise 1.
   a. Click in cell E3 and change the revenue for the Bronze Plan in the fourth quarter to $2,750. Click in cell E4 and change the value of this cell to $5,700. The row and column totals change automatically in the worksheet as do the associated charts. Save the workbook. Exit Excel.
   b. Open the *Report to the President Solution* document from the second exercise. The worksheet and chart should be updated automatically to reflect the corrected revenue data. (The total revenue is now $95,900.) If either the worksheet or the chart is not updated, right click the object to display a context-sensitive menu and click the Update Link command. If the chart is still not updated, right click the object, click the Linked Worksheet (or Chart) Object command, then click the Links command to display the Links dialog box where you can check the source (folder) of the linked objects.
   c. Click at the beginning of the opening paragraph in the memo and enter the new text, which is shown in bold italic in Figure 4. Save and print the completed report. Exit Word.
   d. Start PowerPoint. Open the *Presentation to the President Solution* that you created earlier. PowerPoint detects that a change has been made in the underlying workbook and prompts you to update. Click the button to update the links.
   e. Change to the Slide Sorter view. Press and hold the Shift key as you select the slides containing the Excel worksheet and chart. Pull down the File menu, click the Print command, and print the selection (these two slides) as audience handouts, two slides per page. (Be sure to check the box to frame the slides.)
   f. Save the presentation. Exit PowerPoint.

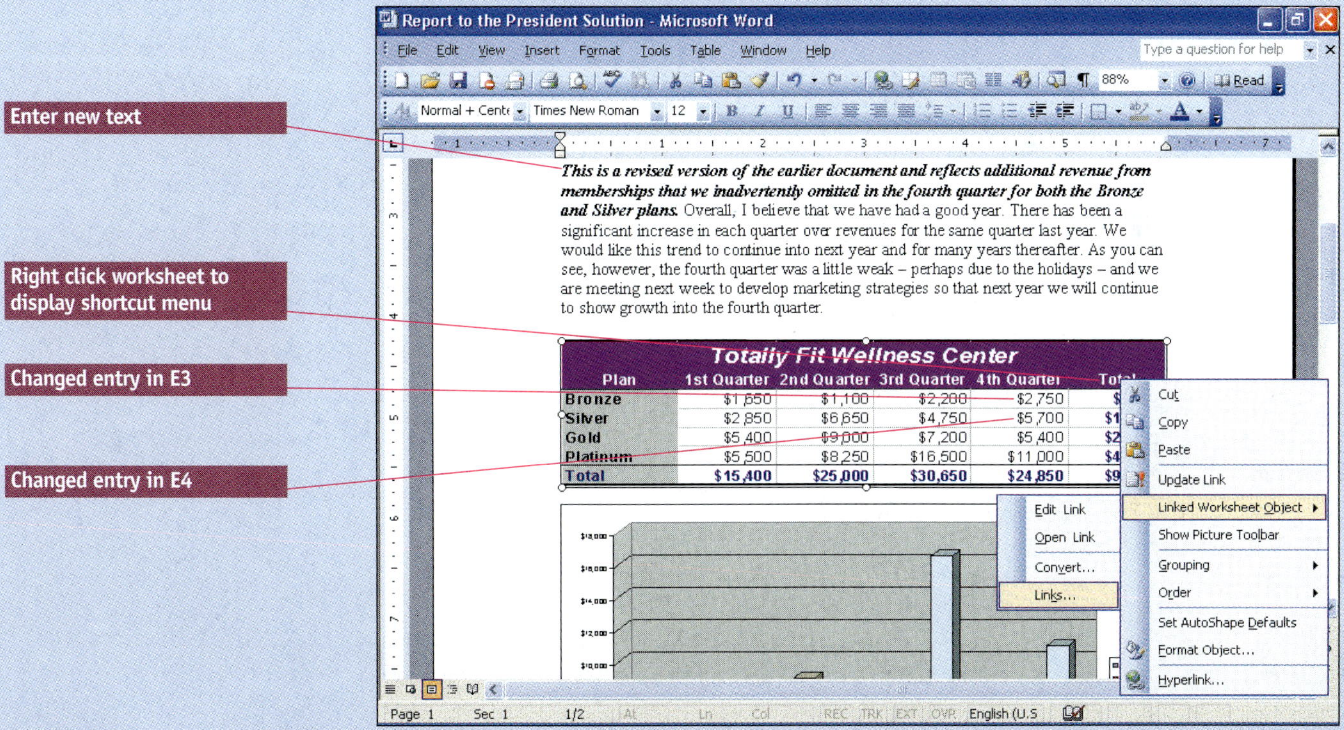

FIGURE 4 Last-minute Change

5. **Importing Data (Access and Excel):** The *Totally Fit* database contains two tables: one for members, and one for the various membership plans that the club offers to its members. The Plan table already exists within the Access database. The member information, however, is in an Excel spreadsheet. Your first task is to import the Excel worksheet into the Access database, where it will be converted to an Access table called Members.
   a. Start Access. Open the *Totally Fit* database in the *Totally Fit Folder*. Click the Tables button if necessary. Pull down the File menu, click (or point to) the Get External Data command, and then click the Import command to display the import dialog box.
   b. Click the down arrow on the Look In list box and change to the *Totally Fit Folder* (the same folder that contains the database). Change the file type to Microsoft Excel. Select the *Members workbook* to start the Import Spreadsheet Wizard.
   c. Click the option button to Show Worksheets. Click Next. Check the box that indicates the first row contains column headings as shown in Figure 5. Click Next. Select the option button to store the data in a new table. Click Next.
   d. You do not need information about the individual fields. Click Next.
   e. Select the option to choose your own primary key. Click the drop-down arrow on the list box and select MemberID. Click Next. Members is entered automatically as the name of the table.
   f. Click the Finish button, then click OK when the wizard indicates that it has imported the table. The Members table appears in the Database window.
   g. Click the Forms button in the Database window and open the Totally Fit Member form. (This form was previously created using the control names in the Members table that was just imported.) Locate the record for Heidi Tamer (record 3) and change her name to your instructor's name. Print the completed form with your instructor's data.

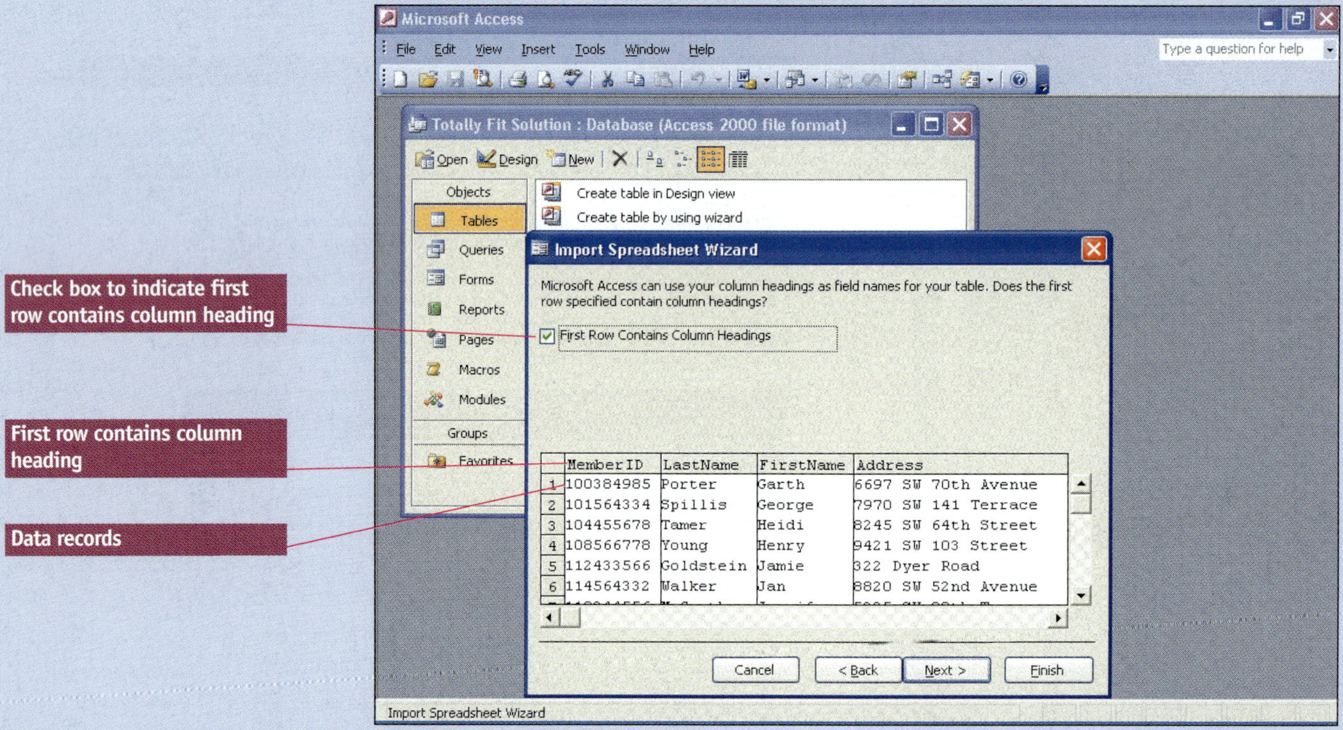

FIGURE 5 Importing Data

6. **A Relational Database (Access):** The *Totally Fit* database contains a one-to-many relationship between the Plan table and the Members table as shown in Figure 6. One plan has many members, but a specific member has chosen only one plan.
   a. Pull down the Tools menu and create the relationships diagram that corresponds to the report in Figure 6. Check the box to enforce referential integrity when you create the relationship.
   b. Pull down the File menu and click the Print Relationships command to create a report containing the relationships diagram. Change to Design view, and then modify the report to match Figure 6. (Use any appropriate clip art.) Print the completed report for your instructor. Close the report and return to the Database window.
   c. Click the Query button in the Database window, and then create a new query in Design view. The query is to contain fields from both tables as shown below:
      i. Select the MemberID, LastName, FirstName, HomePhone, and MembershipDate fields from the Members table.
      ii. Select the PlanID, Cost, and Length fields from the Plan table.
      iii. Display the members in alphabetical order by last name.
      iv. Save the query as Member & Plan Information. You do not have to print the query at this time.
   d. Create a report that groups members by plan, and displays the members alphabetically within each plan. The report should include the member's ID, first and last name, home phone number, and membership date and is to be based on the Member & Plan Information query that you just created. Print this report for your instructor.

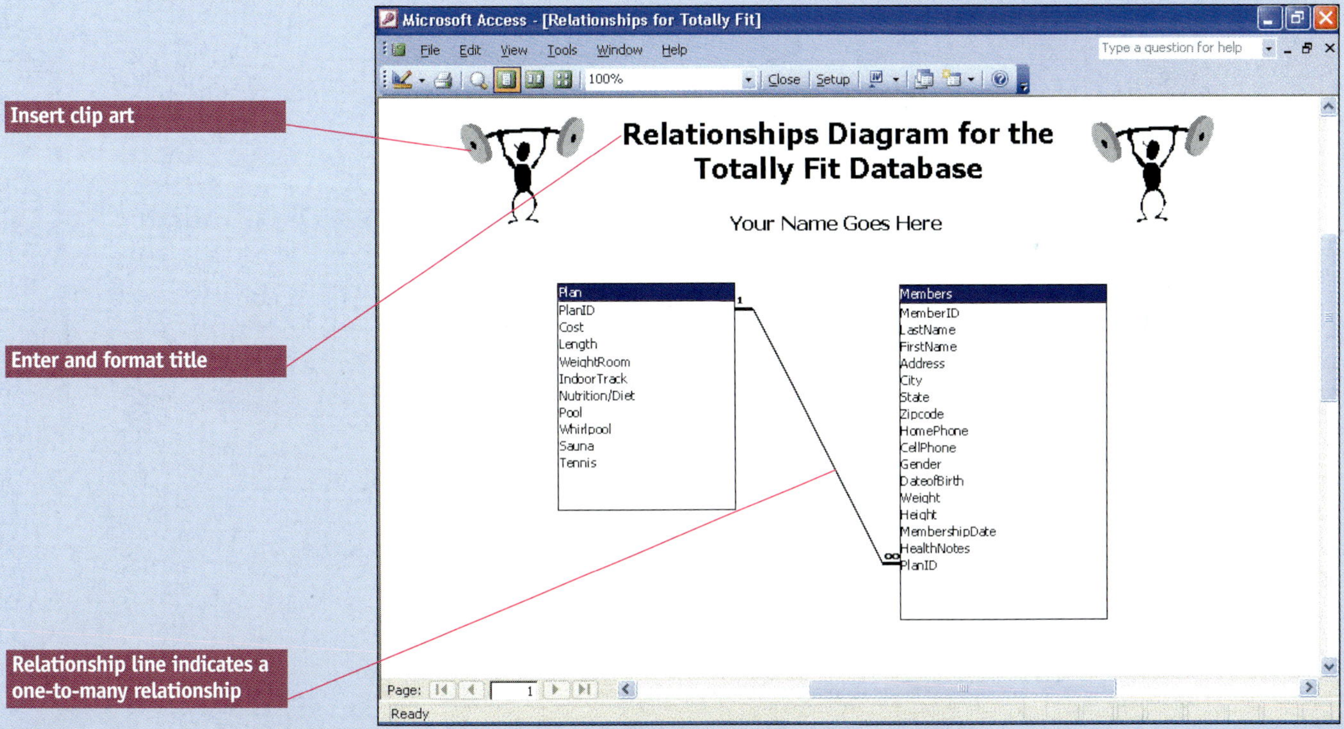

FIGURE 6 A Relational Database

7. **Access Objects: Forms, Queries, and Reports (Access):** Open the *Totally Fit* database in the *Totally Fit Folder* and create the additional objects as described below.
   a. Create the Plan form in Figure 7. You need not follow our design exactly, but you are required to include all of the functionality. (The date of the form is to display the current date.) The middle of the form should contain multiple check boxes to indicate the available facilities within each plan.
   b. Open the Members Form in Design view. Use the Combo Box Wizard to create the control for the plan selected. Check the option to type in the values that you want. Enter the plans: Bronze, Silver, Gold, and Platinum.
   c. Use the completed form to enter data for yourself. Use 111222333 as your MemberID. Complete the rest of the data, selecting the Platinum plan. Print the completed form with your data.
   d. Create a report that shows the member addresses in alphabetical order by member last name. The report should be based on the Members table and should contain the following fields: Last name, First name, PlanID, MemberID, and fields for the mailing address. The address should print on two lines; that is, the street address is on the first line, and the city, state, and zip code are on the second line. The actual report runs 6 pages. You are to print just the page that contains your data.
   e. Create a second report that groups members by gender. The report should include each member's first and last name, date of birth, weight, and height. The members should be listed alphabetically within each gender.
   f. Create a query that will display the members who selected the Platinum plan. The query is to be based on the Members table and should contain the Member ID, Plan ID, first and last name, home phone number, cell phone number, and membership date. Print the dynaset of the query in landscape orientation. Save the query as Platinum Plan.
   g. Create a second query that displays just the female members in alphabetical order by last name. The query should display the Member ID, Plan ID, first and last name, gender, address, date of birth, weight, height, and health notes. Save the query as Female Members.

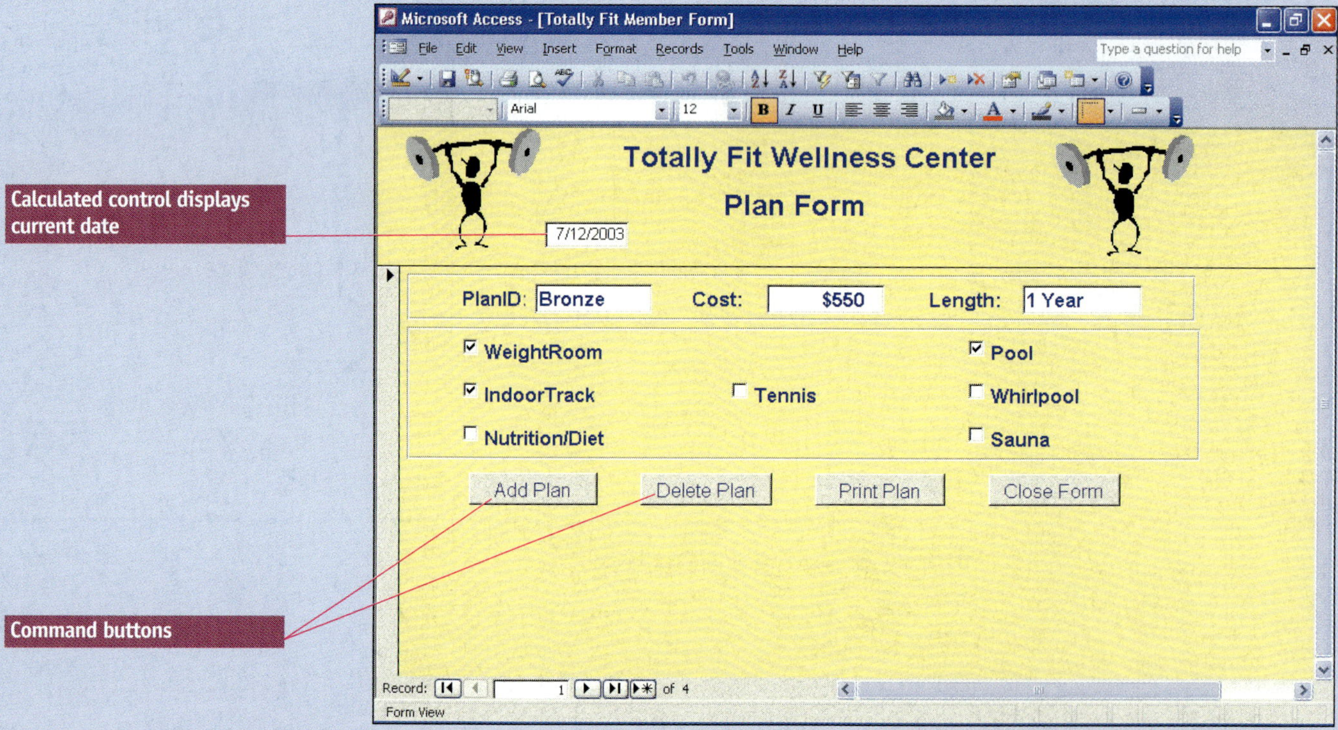

FIGURE 7 Access Objects (Plan Form)

8. **An Access Switchboard (Access):** Create the switchboard in Figure 8 for the *Totally Fit* database. You do not have to match our design exactly, but you are required to have all five buttons. Note, too, that the switchboard contains a Report Menu, which displays a subsidiary switchboard.
   a. The first button on the main switchboard opens the About Totally Fit Wellness Center form as shown in Figure 8. This form has been created for you and can be found in the *Totally Fit* database. You are asked, however, to modify the existing form to include your name in the indicated position.
   b. The second and third buttons display the Members and Plan forms, respectively, in order to maintain data in the associated tables.
   c. The Report Menu button provides access to a subsidiary switchboard that contains the various reports in the database. (These include the relationships diagram and the various reports from exercises 6 and 7.) The report switchboard should also have a button to return to the main switchboard.
   d. The Exit button on the main switchboard closes the database. Add the clip art image at the left of the switchboard. Insert your name under the clip art.
   e. Be sure to test both switchboards completely to be sure that they work correctly. Print the Switchboard Items table, the Main Switchboard form, and the Report Switchboard form for your instructor as proof that you completed the exercise correctly.
   f. Modify the startup property of the database so that the switchboard form opens automatically when you open the database. (You can also create an AutoExec macro to maximize the Database window. Display the Database window, click the Macros button, then click the New button to create a macro. Click the drop-down arrow to display the available actions and scroll until you can select Maximize. Save the macro as AutoExec.)
   g. Close the database, then reopen it. The switchboard should appear automatically and all subsequent objects should appear in a maximized window.
   h. Exit Access and continue with the next exercise.

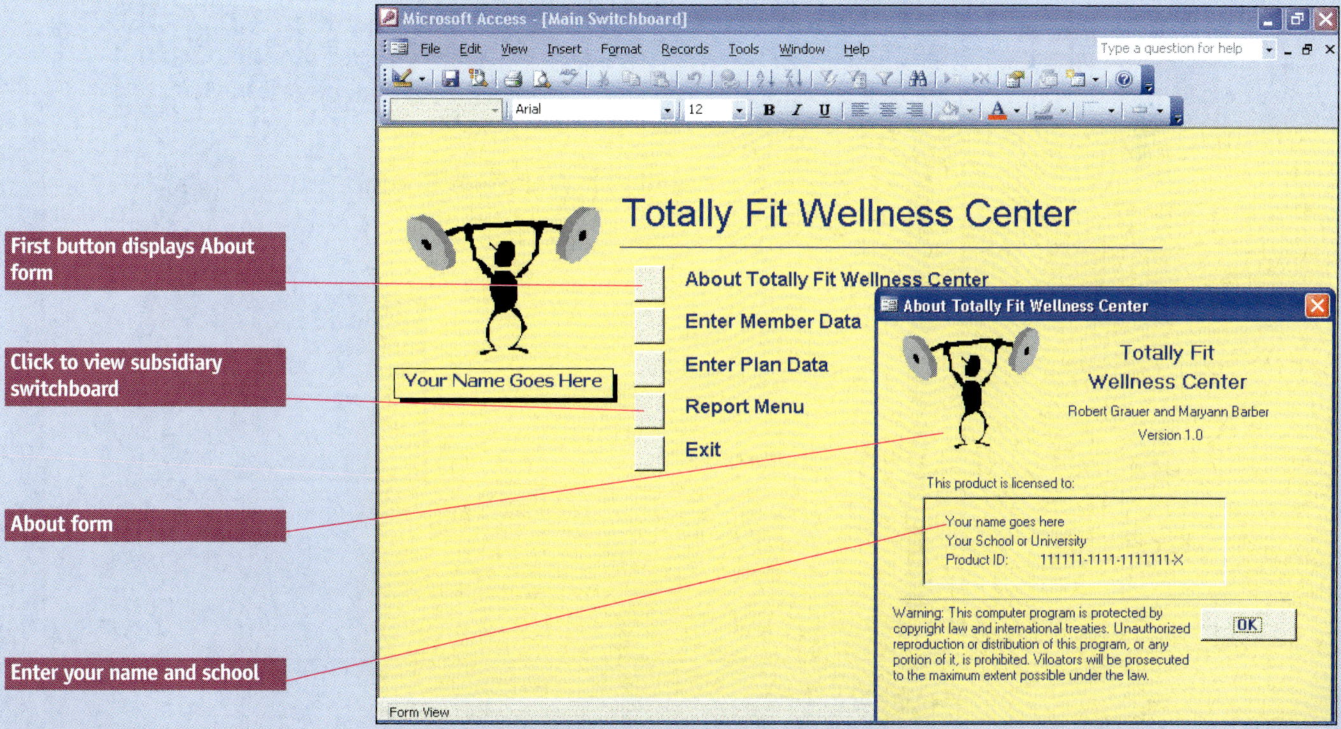

FIGURE 8 An Access Switchboard

9. **Mail Merge (Word and Access):** This exercise uses the Mail Merge utility in Microsoft Word in conjunction with an Access database. You will be asked to create two different form letters. Each letter is sent to a different set of recipients. You can start the merge from either application. Proceed as follows:
   a. Open the partially completed *Letter to Members* document in the *Totally Fit Folder* and save it as *Letter to Members Solution* so that you can return to the original document if necessary.
   b. Pull down the Tools menu, click Letters and Mailings, then click Mail Merge Wizard to open the task pane. Select the Letters option. Click Next. Select the option to use the current document. Click Next.
   c. Select the recipients from an existing list. Choose the *Totally Fit Folder*, select the *Totally Fit* database, and select the Members table to display the Mail Merge Recipients dialog box.
   d. Add the address block and greeting line as shown in Figure 9. Click the Preview Your Letters button to toggle between the field names and the actual data.
   e. Complete the merge and specify the first three records, as shown in Figure 9. (There are more than 60 records in the database.) Print the three letters for your instructor. Save the completed form letter. You do not have to save the merged document. Close Word.
   f. Start Access and open the *Totally Fit* database. Close the switchboard. Click the Queries button in the Database window and open the Female Members query from the earlier exercise. Pull down the Tools menu, click Office Links, then click the Merge It with Microsoft Word command. Select the option to link to an existing document and choose the *Letter to Female Members* document in the *Totally Fit Folder*.
   g. Add the address block and greeting fields to the form letter. Complete the merge and print only the first three letters. Save the completed form letter as *Letter to Female Members Solution*. Exit Word. Exit Access.

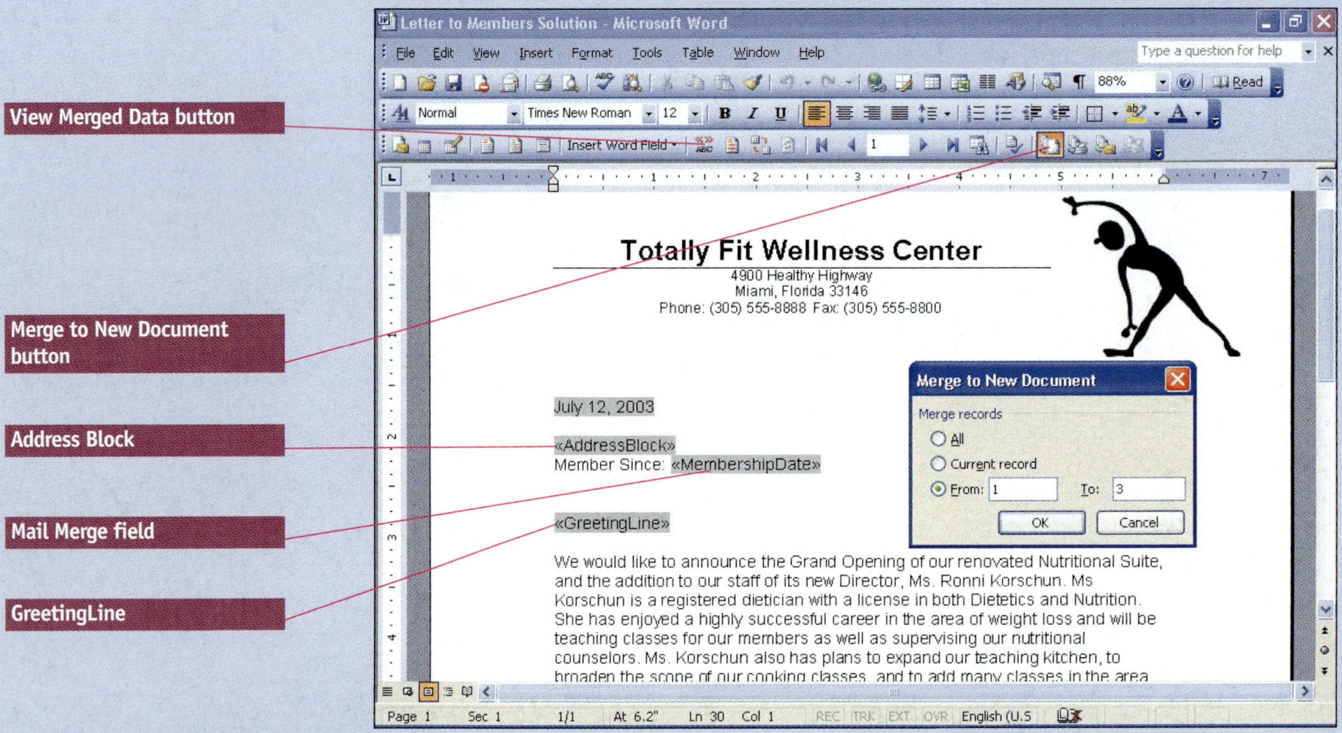

FIGURE 9 Mail Merge

10. **Worksheet References (Excel):** The Board of Directors has asked for a comparison of revenue for this year to last year. An Excel workbook has been created with that information, but it is your task to complete that workbook. Proceed as follows:

   a. Open the *Historical Totally Fit Revenue* workbook in the *Totally Fit Folder* and save it as *Historical Totally Fit Revenue Solution.* (The values in this worksheet reflect the last-minute change that was made in problem 5.)

   b. Click the worksheet tab labeled Year to Year Comparison, then click in cell B3 of this worksheet as shown in Figure 10. Type an equal sign, click the worksheet tab labeled Last Year, click in cell F3 of this worksheet, and press Enter. The formula for this cell appears in the formula bar as ='Last Year'!F3, indicating that the value for this cell is obtained from another worksheet in the same workbook. Enter similar formulas to display the total revenues for all of the plans for both this year and last year.

   c. Complete the entries in column D of the Year to Year Comparison worksheet that show the dollar increase from last year to this year. The cell formulas in this column should reference only the Year to Year Comparison worksheet. Add another set of formulas in column E to compute the percent increase from last year to this year.

   d. Enter your name in the worksheet as shown in Figure 10. Format the completed worksheet, then print the Year to Year Comparison worksheet for your instructor. Print the completed worksheet twice: once to show the displayed values, and once to show the cell formulas.

   e. Create a combination chart that plots both the dollar amount of the increase and the percent of the increase for each plan as shown in Figure 10. Display a data table at the bottom of the chart sheet. Note that the dollar and percent increases for the Platinum Plan alone are $13,750 and 50%, respectively. You do not have to print the combination chart at this time.

   f. Save the completed workbook. Exit Excel.

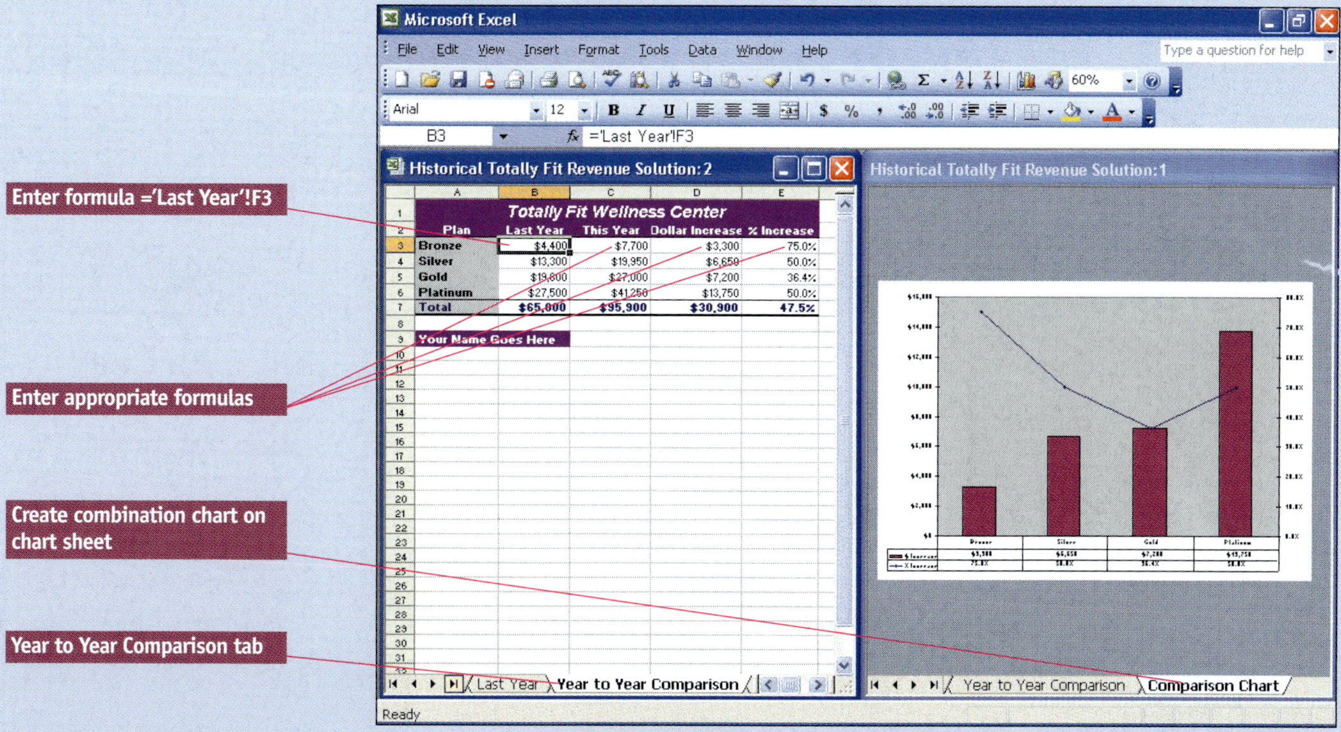

FIGURE 10 Worksheet References

11. **Presentation to the Board (PowerPoint and Excel):** A partially completed version of the presentation in Figure 11 has been saved as *Presentation to the Board* in the *Totally Fit Folder*. Open this presentation and save it as *Presentation to the Board Solution*. Your next task is to link the worksheets and chart from the previous exercise to various slides in this presentation. Linking ensures that you can change the data in the Excel workbook and have the change reflected automatically in the PowerPoint presentation.
   a. Open the *Historical Totally Fit Revenue Solution* workbook from the previous exercise. Select the worksheet that contains revenue data for last year, and link that data to the slide containing the year-to-year comparison (slide 4).
   b. Select the worksheet with the revenue for the current year and link this data to the same slide as in part (a). Move and/or size the worksheets after they have been added to the presentation. Add text boxes to the slide to indicate last year's and this year's performance as appropriate.
   c. Return to Excel. Select the chart sheet containing the combination chart, then link that chart to slide 5 as shown in Figure 11.
   d. Add the mission statement as slide number 2 by importing this slide from the *Presentation to the President*. (Pull down the Insert menu, click the Slides from File command to display the Slide Finder dialog box, and then click the Browse button to locate the earlier presentation.)
   e. Add transition and custom animation effects as you see fit.
   f. Experiment with a different design template, but limit yourself to five minutes. Choose the template you like best. Save the presentation.
   g. Add your name to the title slide in the indicated position. Print the audience handouts of the completed presentation (six per page) for your instructor. (Be sure to check the box to frame the slides.)
   h. Save the completed presentation. Exit PowerPoint. Close the Excel workbook. Exit Excel.

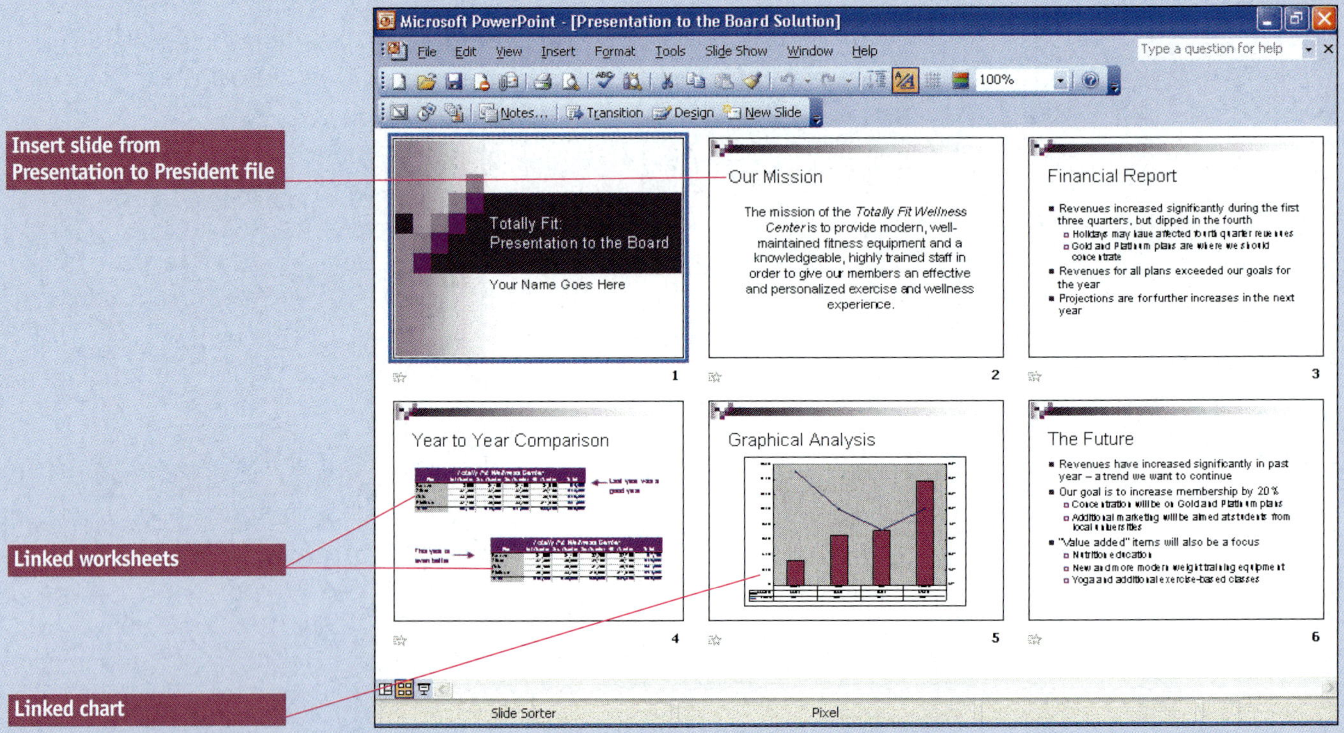

FIGURE 11 Presentation to the Board

12. **Letter to the Board (Word and Excel):** This exercise provides additional practice in linking Excel objects to a Word document. Open the partially completed *Letter to the Board* document in the *Totally Fit Folder*. Save the document as *Letter to the Board Solution* so that you can return to the original document if necessary. Proceed as follows to create the completed document in Figure 12:

   a. Open the *Historical Totally Fit Revenue Solution* workbook from the previous exercise if it is not already open. Select the worksheet containing the revenue for last year and link it to the Word document, immediately after the second paragraph. Place (link) the worksheet containing the revenue for the current year below the first worksheet.

   b. Insert a section break at the end of the first page, and then change the orientation of the second page (section) to landscape as shown in Figure 12.

   c. Return to the Excel workbook. Select the combination chart and link this chart to the Word document. The Excel chart should appear in the document. The chart may be cropped initially. If so, select the entire chart, then click and drag a corner sizing handle to make the chart smaller. Right click the chart and click the command to display the Picture toolbar. Select the Crop tool, then click and drag the side handle at the right of the chart to show the portion of the chart that may have been cropped initially.

   d. Add your name and your instructor's name in the indicated positions. Your instructor is the recipient of the memo and you are the sender. Save the completed document, and then print the completed letter for your instructor.

   e. Exit Word. Exit Excel. You're almost finished. All that remains is the preparation of a cover sheet as described in the next exercise.

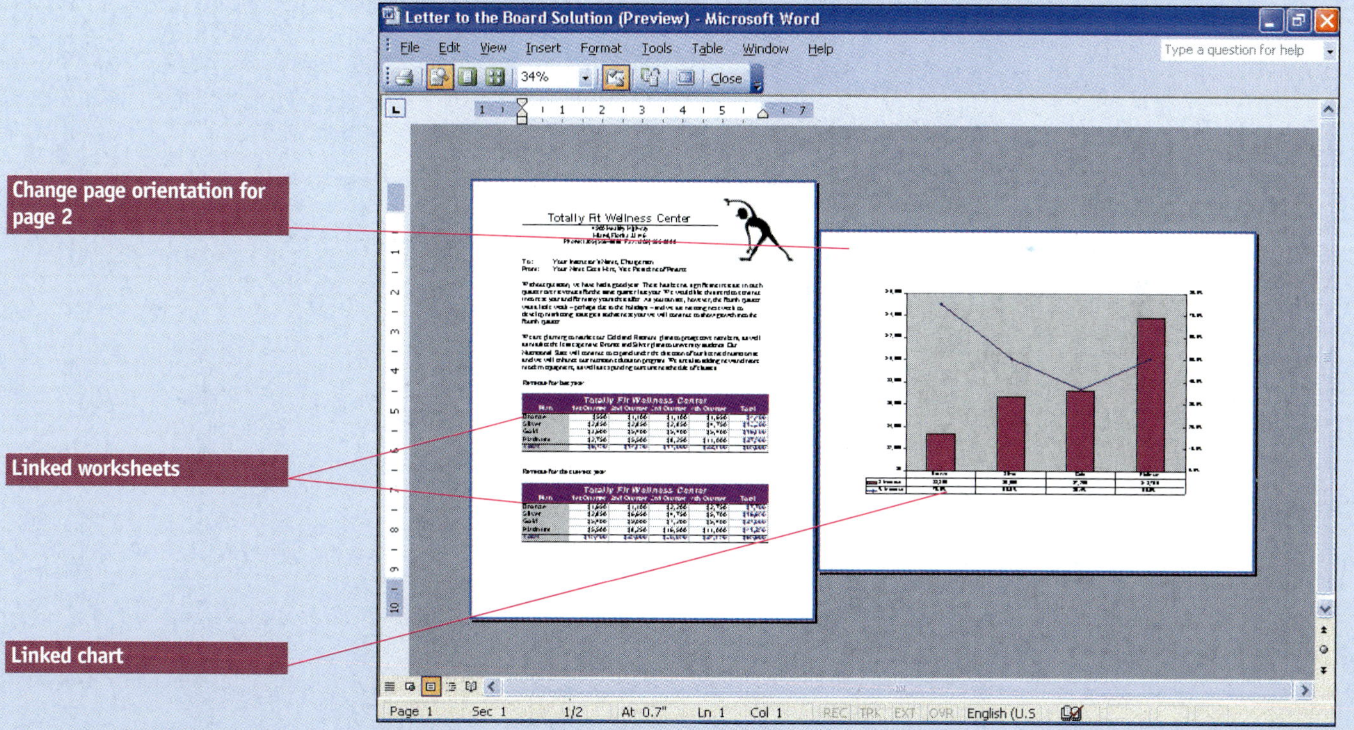

FIGURE 12 Letter to the Board

13. **Create a Home Page (Word):** Open the *Totally Fit Home Page* document in the *Totally Fit Folder*. Pull down the File menu, click the Save as Web Page command, and specify Single File Web Page as the file type to convert the Word document to a Web page. Click Continue when a message appears that indicates pictures with text wrapping will become left or right justified. Review the document and make the basic formatting changes you deem appropriate. Use the Themes command in the Format menu to apply an overall design to the page. Your goal is to create a page similar to Figure 13.

    a. Create a three-by-one table at the top of the document. Place the existing clip art in the left and right cells. Enter the title and other information in the middle cell. Format the text. Size the cells as necessary.

    b. Select the text "e-mail us" that appears in the middle of the document. Pull down the Insert menu and click the Hyperlink command (or click the Insert Hyperlink button on the Standard toolbar), click the E-mail Address button, and then enter your e-mail address.

    c. Create the indicated hyperlinks that appear within the document. Search the Web to find the addresses to our sites, or choose your own. Be sure to enter valid addresses, however, for all selected sites.

    d. Save the document a final time, then exit Word. Start Windows Explorer, then go to the folder containing your Web page, and double click the file you just created. Internet Explorer will start automatically (because your document was saved as a Web page). You should see your document within Internet Explorer as shown in Figure 13. Look carefully at the Address bar and note the local address on drive C, as opposed to a Web address. Print the document for your instructor as proof you completed the assignment.

    e. Creating the home page and viewing it locally is easy. Placing the page on the Web where it can be seen by anyone with an Internet connection is not as straightforward. You will need additional information from your instructor about how to obtain an account on a Web server (if that is available at your school), and further how to upload the Web page from your PC to the server.

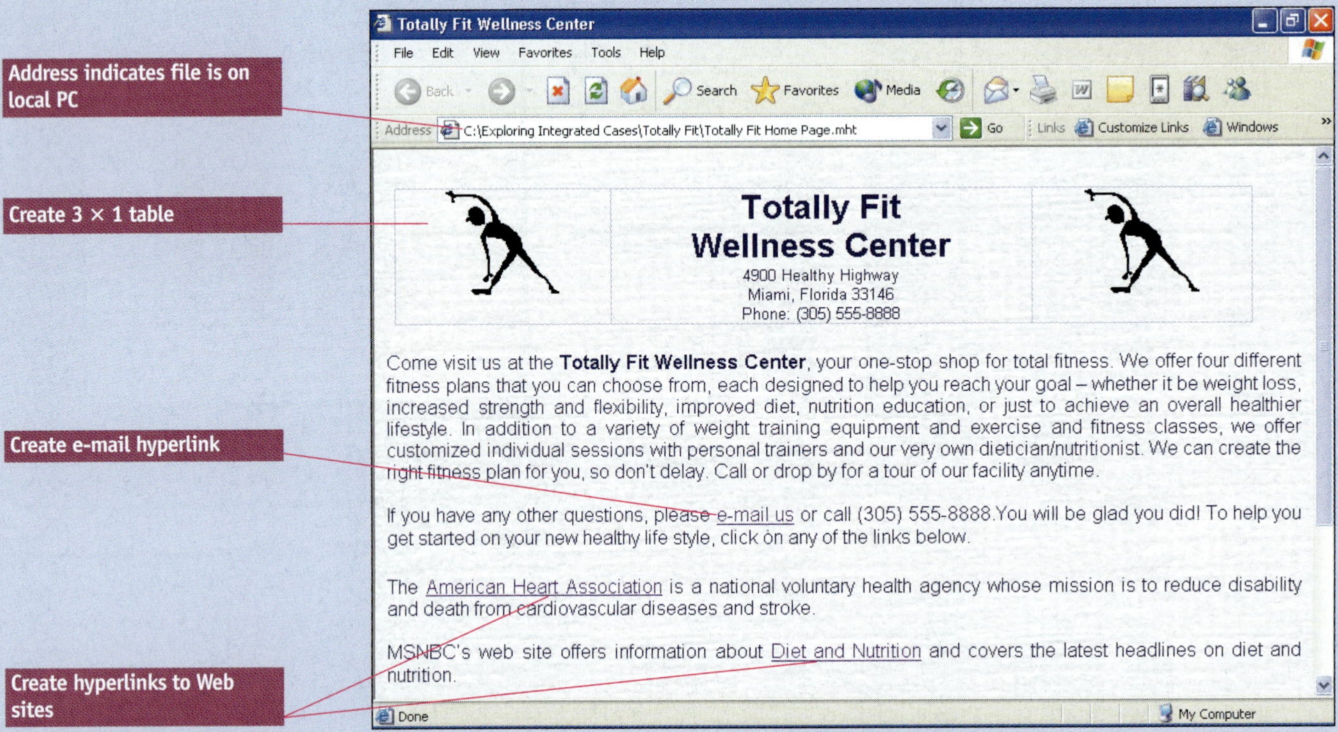

FIGURE 13 Totally Fit Home Page

14. **Submission Checklist (Word):** You have successfully completed multiple exercises within the Totally Fit case study. Each exercise described a specific task(s), required the use of one or more applications in Microsoft Office, and asked you to print one or more documents to show that you completed the exercise. The submissions checklist in Figure 14 will ensure that you have printed all of the required documents.

    a. Open the *Totally Fit Submission Checklist* that is found in the *Totally Fit Folder*. Read the document carefully and check each box after you verify that you have printed the indicated document.

    b. Add your name to the checklist as indicated, then use the checklist as a cover sheet when you submit the material to your instructor.

    c. Think for a minute about all that you have accomplished. You have completed a series of 13 exercises, which required the use of all four major applications within Microsoft Office. You have used the applications individually and in conjunction with one another. You have been able to:

        i. Dynamically link an Excel worksheet and chart to a Word document and PowerPoint presentation, so that changes to the Excel workbook were automatically reflected in the other documents.

        ii. Import an Excel worksheet into an Access database to use a table within the database.

        iii. Use an Access table as the data source for a mail merge in Microsoft Word.

        iv. Use Word to create a home page.

    d. Congratulations on a job well done!

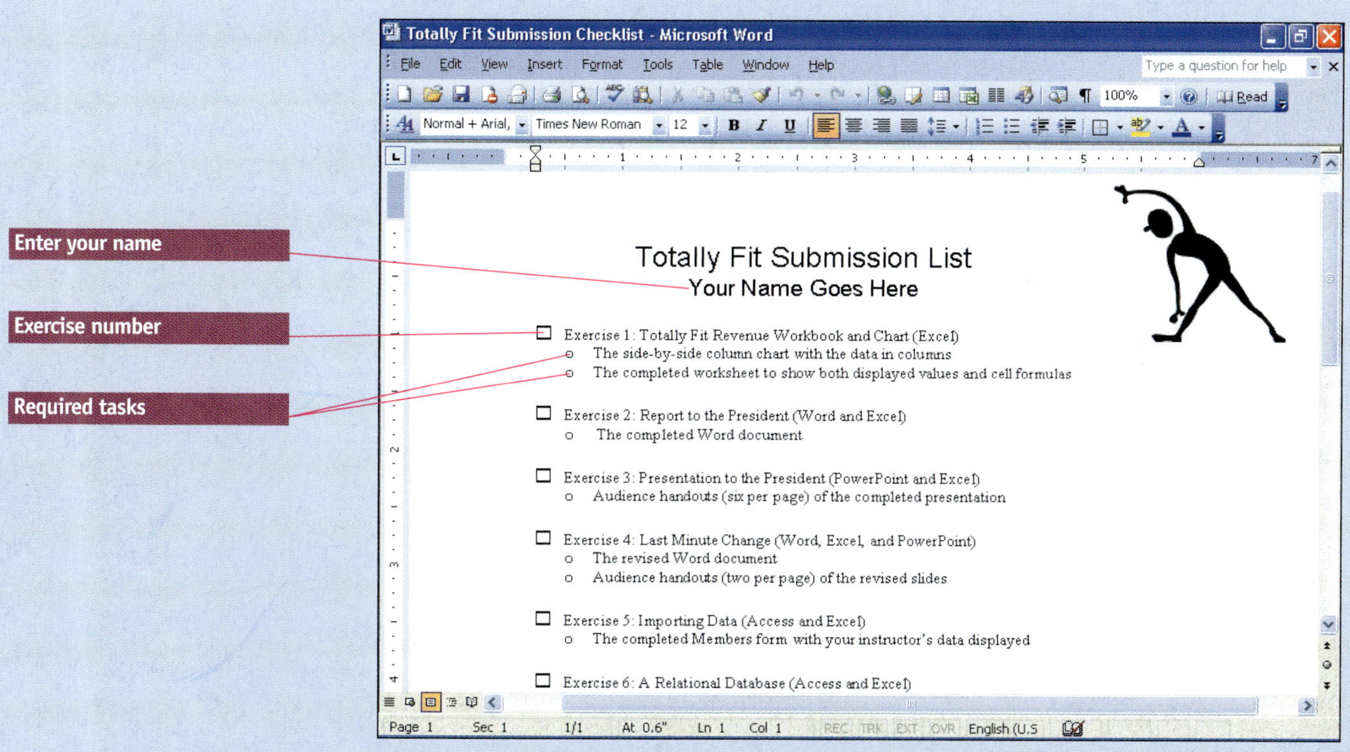

FIGURE 14 Submission Checklist

CASE STUDY 2

Integrated Case Study: Alternate Airways

OBJECTIVES

1. Use the core applications in Office 2003 individually or in conjunction with one another.
2. Link an Excel chart to a Word document and a PowerPoint presentation.
3. Import an Excel worksheet into an Access database.
4. Create Access tables, queries, reports, and forms.
5. Use an Access table as the basis for a mail merge.
6. Use Word to create a Web page for the organization.

integrated exercises

1. Alternate Revenue Workbook and Chart (Excel)
2. Report to the President (Word and Excel)
3. Presentation to the President (PowerPoint and Excel)
4. Last-minute Change (Word, Excel, and PowerPoint)
5. Importing Data (Access and Excel)
6. A Relational Database (Access)
7. Access Objects: Forms, Queries, and Reports (Access)
8. An Access Switchboard (Access)
9. Mail Merge (Word and Access)
10. Worksheet References (Excel)
11. Presentation to the Board (PowerPoint and Excel)
12. Letter to the Board (Word and Excel)
13. Create a Home Page (Word)
14. Submission Checklist (Word)

This document provides a series of 13 exercises in Microsoft Office that relate to Alternate Airways, a small regional carrier. Each exercise describes a specific task for the organization to accomplish and typically requires the use of multiple applications within Microsoft Office for solution. Many of the exercises are cumulative in nature. You may, for example, be asked to create an Excel chart in one exercise, and then incorporate that chart into a Word memo and a PowerPoint presentation in subsequent exercises. Other exercises will ask you to create or modify an Access database, to exchange data between Excel and Access, and to create a Web page for the airline. Collectively, you will gain considerable practice in the core applications of Microsoft Office 2003, and especially in how they work together to accomplish complex tasks.

All of the exercises are based on material from the core application chapters in *Exploring Office 2003 Volume I*. Specific chapter references are deliberately not provided so that the case study is as realistic as possible. Think of this assignment as your first day on the job; you were hired by Alternate Airways because you are proficient in Microsoft Office. This is your chance to show what you know.

Your assignment is to follow the directions of your instructor with respect to which of the exercises you are to complete within the case description. You should begin by downloading the practice files from our Web site at www.prenhall.com/grauer. Go to the site, click the book icon for Office 2003, and then click the Student Downloads tab. Scroll until you can select the link to Integrated Case Studies, and then download the file to your desktop. Double click the file icon and follow the onscreen instructions to install the practice files on your computer. The files you need will be in the Alternate Airways folder within the Exploring Integrated Cases folder.

INTEGRATED EXERCISES

1. **Alternate Revenue Workbook and Chart (Excel):** You will find a partially completed version of the spreadsheet in Figure 1 in the *Alternate Revenue* workbook in the *Alternate Airways Folder.* (You can download the practice files for this case study from our Web site at www.prenhall.com/grauer.) Open the workbook and save it as *Alternate Revenue Solution* so that you can return to the original workbook if necessary. Proceed as follows:
   a. Click in cell F3 and enter the formula to compute the total revenue for the first plane, the Airbus A320. Copy this formula to the remaining cells in column F.
   b. Click in cell B6 and compute the total revenue for the first quarter. Copy this formula to the remaining cells in this row.
   c. Use the AutoFormat command as the basis for formatting your worksheet in an attractive fashion. You can match our formatting, or you can use your own design.
   d. Select the data in cells A2 through E5 to create a side-by-side column chart. Specify that the data series are in columns so that the different planes appear on the X axis. Save this chart in its own sheet. Print this chart for your instructor.
   e. Create a second side-by-side column chart using the same data as in part (d). This time, however, specify that the data is in rows so that the quarters appear on the X axis. Save this chart in its own chart sheet. You do not have to print the chart at this time.
   f. Enter your name in the worksheet as indicated.
   g. Print the completed worksheet twice, once to show displayed values and once to show the cell formulas.
   h. Save the completed workbook for use in subsequent exercises. Exit Excel.

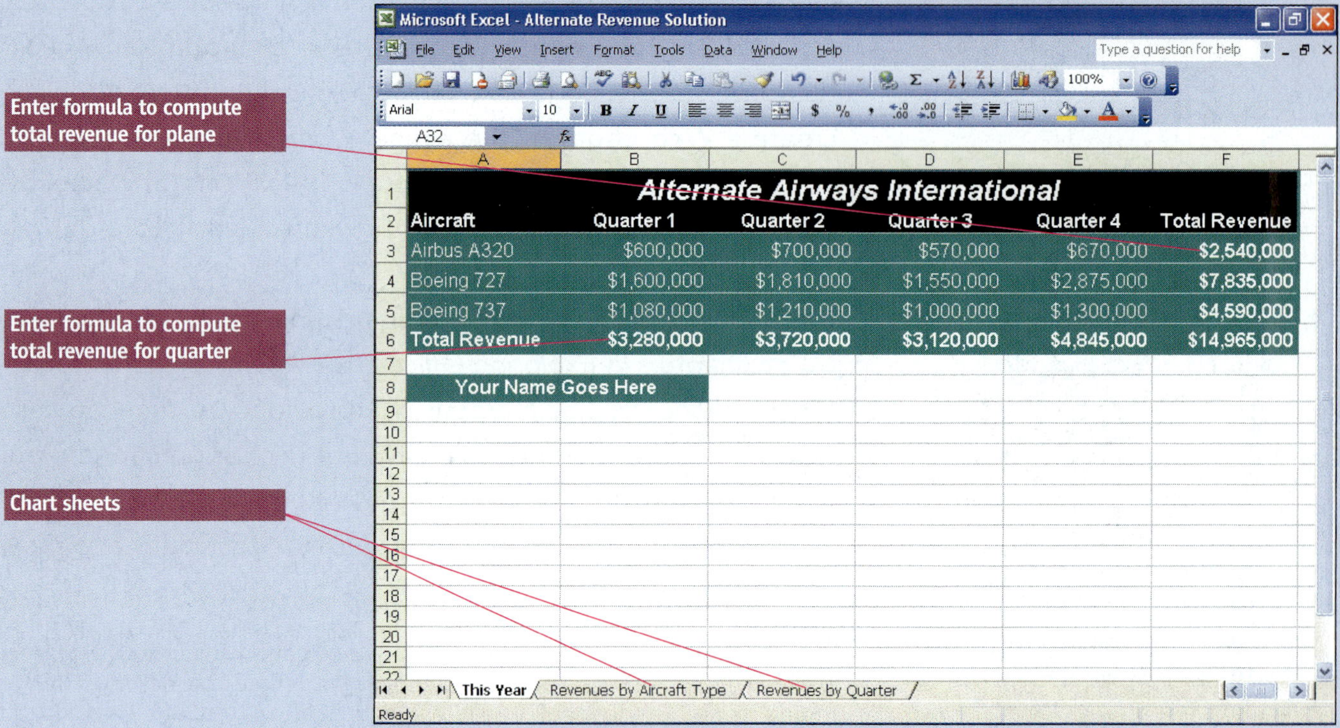

FIGURE 1 Alternate Revenue Workbook and Chart

2. **Report to the President (Word and Excel):** This exercise builds on the previous exercise by creating a Word document that contains the Excel worksheet and a chart. The latter is to be dynamically linked to the Word document, so that any changes in the workbook are automatically reflected in the memo.
   a. You will find a partially completed version of the document in Figure 2 in the *Report to the President* document in the *Alternate Airways Folder.* Open this document and then save it as *Report to the President Solution.* Change the To and From lines in the memo to contain your instructor's name and your name, respectively.
   b. Open the completed workbook from the previous exercise if it is not already open. Click and drag to select the completed worksheet, then click the Copy button on the Standard toolbar.
   c. Click the Microsoft Word button on the Windows taskbar to return to the Word document. Click below the first paragraph. Pull down the Edit menu and click the Paste Special command to display the Paste Special dialog box. Select Microsoft Excel Worksheet Object in the displayed list, click the Paste Link button, and then click OK to insert the worksheet. Do not worry about the size or position at this time.
   d. Use the same technique as in part (b) to link the side-by-side column chart (that displays quarters on the X axis) to the Word document. The Excel chart should appear. The only tricky part (if any) is to display the entire chart (it may be cropped initially). Select the chart, then click and drag a corner sizing handle to make the chart smaller. Right click the chart and click the command to display the Picture toolbar. Select the Crop tool, then click and drag the side handle at the right of the chart to show the portion of the chart that may have been cropped initially.
   e. Move and size the chart within the memo as necessary. You may find it convenient to change the zoom specification to "Whole Page" so that you can position the chart more easily.
   f. Save the completed document. Print the completed document for your instructor. Exit Word.

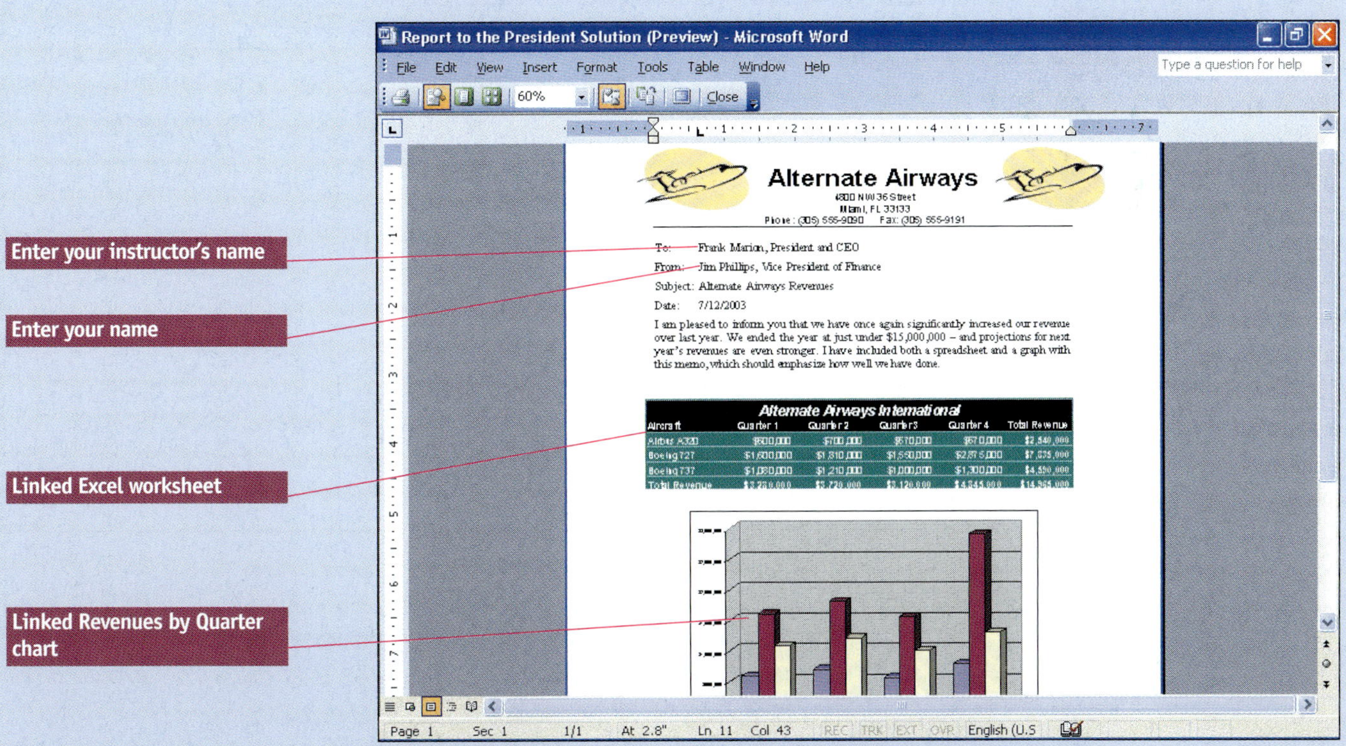

FIGURE 2 Report to the President

3. **Presentation to the President (PowerPoint and Excel):** A partially completed version of the presentation in Figure 3 has been saved as the *Presentation to the President* in the *Alternate Airways Folder.* Open this presentation and save it as *Presentation to the President Solution* so that you can return to the original presentation if necessary.
   a. Insert a new slide that contains a mission statement as the second slide in the presentation. The mission statement should read as follows: *The mission of Alternate Airways is to provide courteous, on-time charter services to our customers in well-maintained aircraft flown by highly trained, professional flight crews.*
   b. Open the completed workbook from exercise 1. Use the same technique as in the previous problem to link the worksheet and the side-by-side column chart (with the data in rows) to the appropriate slides in the presentation, as shown below.
   c. Move and/or size the worksheet and chart after they have been added to the presentation. Save the presentation.
   d. Add to the slide containing the worksheet a text box that points to the total revenue in the worksheet. The text box should indicate that the total revenue is just under $15 million.
   e. Include animation effects as you see fit within a slide and add transition effects from one slide to the next.
   f. Experiment with a different design template, but limit yourself to five minutes. Choose the template you like best. Save the presentation.
   g. Add your name to the title slide. Print the audience handouts of the completed presentation (six per page) for your instructor.
   h. Save the completed presentation. Exit PowerPoint. Close the Excel workbook and exit Excel.

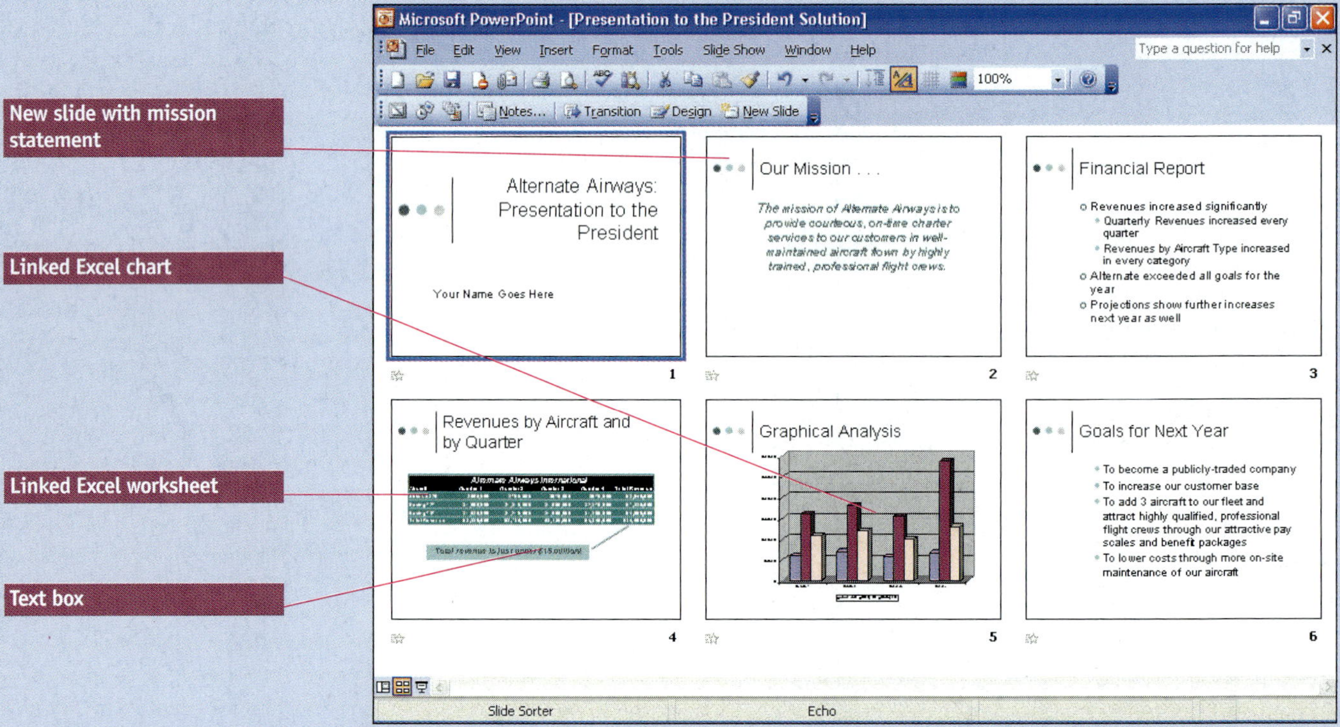

FIGURE 3 Presentation to the President

4. **Last-minute Change (Word, Excel, and PowerPoint):** It was just discovered that the revenue from a few end-of-the year flights was not included in the original workbook. Your task is to correct all of the documents that reflect this information. Open the completed *Alternate Revenue Solution* workbook from exercise 1.
   a. Click in cell E3 and change the revenue for the Airbus A320 in the fourth quarter to $790,000. Click in cell E4 and change the value of this cell to $2,900,000. The row and column totals change automatically in the worksheet as do the associated charts. Save the workbook. Exit Excel.
   b. Open the *Report to the President Solution* document from the second exercise. The worksheet and chart should be updated automatically to reflect the corrected revenue data. (The total revenue is now $15,110,000.) If either the worksheet or the chart is not updated, right click the object to display a context-sensitive menu and click the Update Link command. If the chart is still not updated, right click the object, click the Linked Worksheet (or Chart) Object command, then click the Links command to display the Links dialog box, where you can check the source (folder) of the linked objects.
   c. Click at the beginning of the opening paragraph in the memo and enter the new text, which is shown in bold italic in Figure 4. (Be sure to change the sentence within the paragraph to indicate that revenue is over $15,000,000.) Save and print the completed report. Exit Word.
   d. Start PowerPoint. Open the *Presentation to the President Solution* that you created earlier. PowerPoint detects that a change has been made in the underlying workbook and prompts you to update. Click the button to update the links. (You will have to change the contents of the text box to say that total revenue is just over $15,000,000.)
   e. Change to the Slide Sorter view. Press and hold the Shift key as you select the slides containing the Excel worksheet and chart. Pull down the File menu, click the Print command, and print the selection (these two slides) as audience handouts, two slides per page.
   f. Save the presentation. Exit PowerPoint.

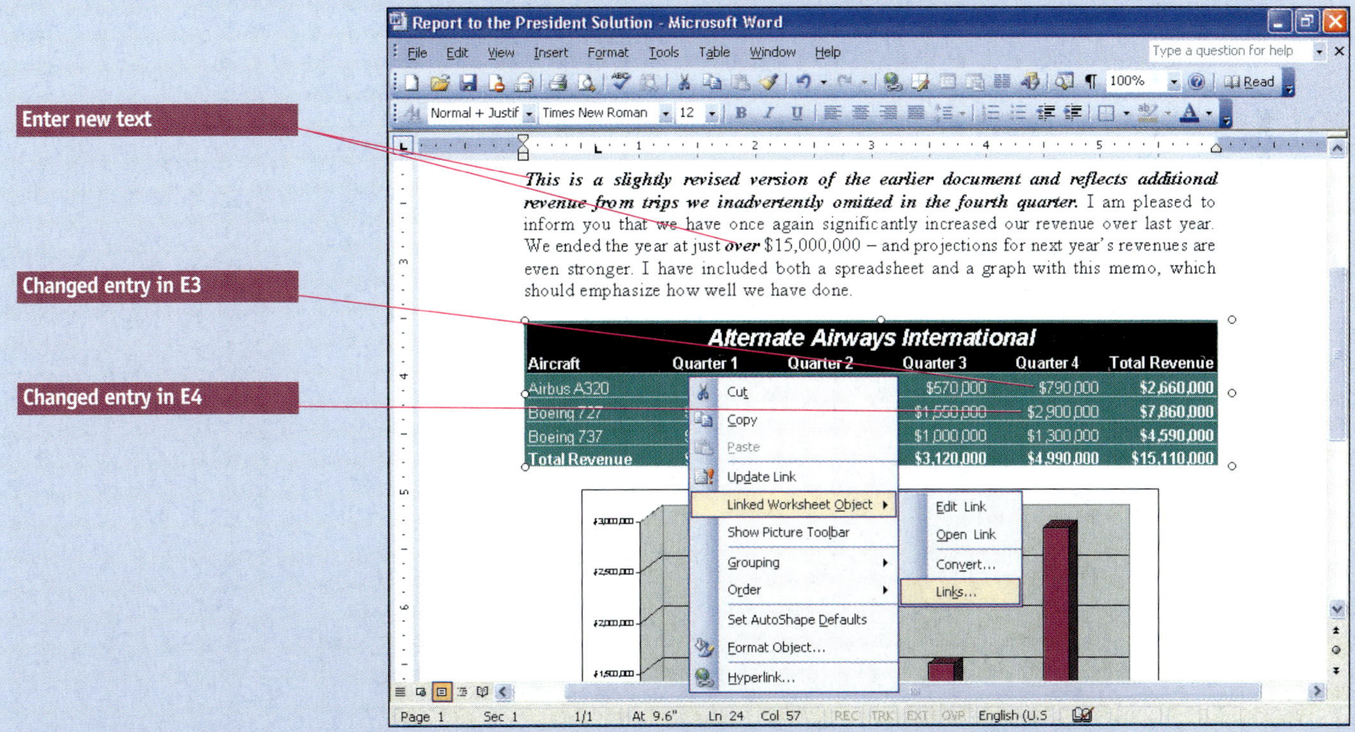

FIGURE 4 Last-minute Change

5. **Importing Data (Access and Excel):** Alternate Airways flies all over the United States. Thus, it maintains bases in different cities to reduce the travel time for its flight crews. The *Alternate Airways database* contains two tables, one for employees (flight crews), and one for the bases of the flight crews. The Employees table already exists within the Access database although data has not been entered for every employee. The base information, however, is in an Excel spreadsheet. Your first task is to import the Excel worksheet into the Access database, where it will be converted to an Access table.
   a. Start Access. Open the *Alternate Airways* database in the *Alternate Airways Folder.* Click the Tables button if necessary. Pull down the File menu, click (or point to) the Get External Data command, and then click the Import command to display the Import dialog box.
   b. Click the down arrow on the Look In list box and change to the *Alternate Airways Folder* (the same folder that contains the database). Change the file type to Microsoft Excel. Select the *Bases* workbook to start the Import Spreadsheet Wizard.
   c. Check the box that indicates the first row contains column headings as shown in Figure 5. Click Next. Select the option button to store the data in a new table. Click Next.
   d. You do not need information about the individual fields. Click Next.
   e. Select the option to choose your own primary key. Click the drop-down arrow on the list box and select BaseID. Click Next. Access indicates that it will import the data into a Bases table.
   f. Click the Finish button, then click OK when the wizard indicates that it has imported the table. The Bases table appears in the Database window.
   g. Click the Forms button in the Database window and open the Bases form. (This form was previously created using the control names in the Bases table that was just imported.) Locate the record for Miami (record 3) and change the supervisor's name to your instructor's name. Print the completed form with your instructor's data.

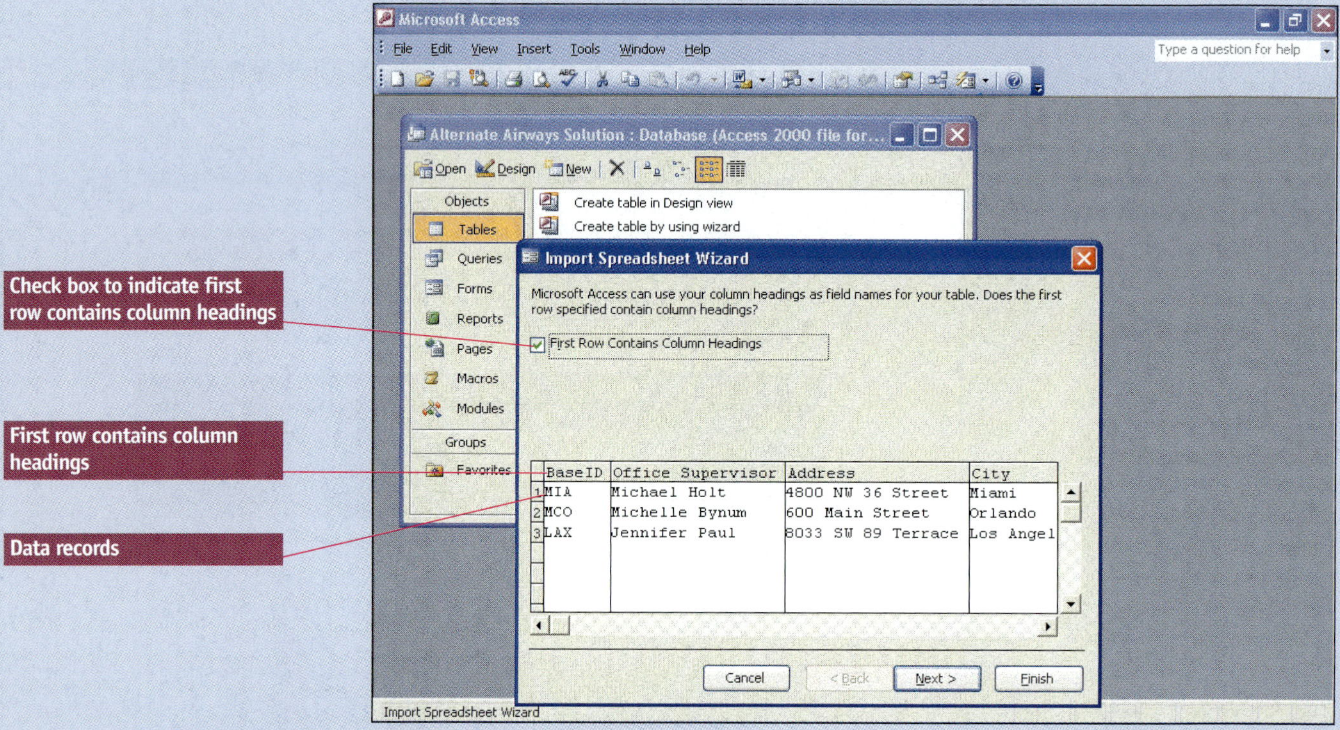

FIGURE 5 Importing Data

6. **A Relational Database (Access):** The *Alternate Airways* database contains a one-to-many relationship between the Bases table and the Employees table as shown in Figure 6. One base has many employees, but a specific employee is assigned to only one base.
   a. Pull down the Tools menu and create the relationships diagram that corresponds to the report in Figure 6. Check the box to enforce referential integrity when you create the relationship.
   b. Pull down the File menu and click the Print Relationships command to create a report containing the relationships diagram. Change to Design view, and then modify the report to match Figure 6. (You can copy the airplane from the Word document in exercise 2.) Print the completed report for your instructor. Close the report and return to the Database window.
   c. Click the Query button in the Database window, and then create a new query in Design view. The query is to contain fields from both tables as shown below:
      i. Select the LastName, FirstName, Position, Address, City, State, ZipCode, and BaseID fields from the Employees table.
      ii. Select the Office Supervisor and Phone fields from the Bases table.
      iii. Display the employees in alphabetical order by last name.
      iv. Save the query as Employee Information. You do not have to print the query at this time.
   d. Create a report that groups employees by position, and displays the employees alphabetically within each position. The report should include the employee's first and last name, base, supervisor, and supervisor's phone number and is to be based on the Employee Information query that you just created. Print this report for your instructor.

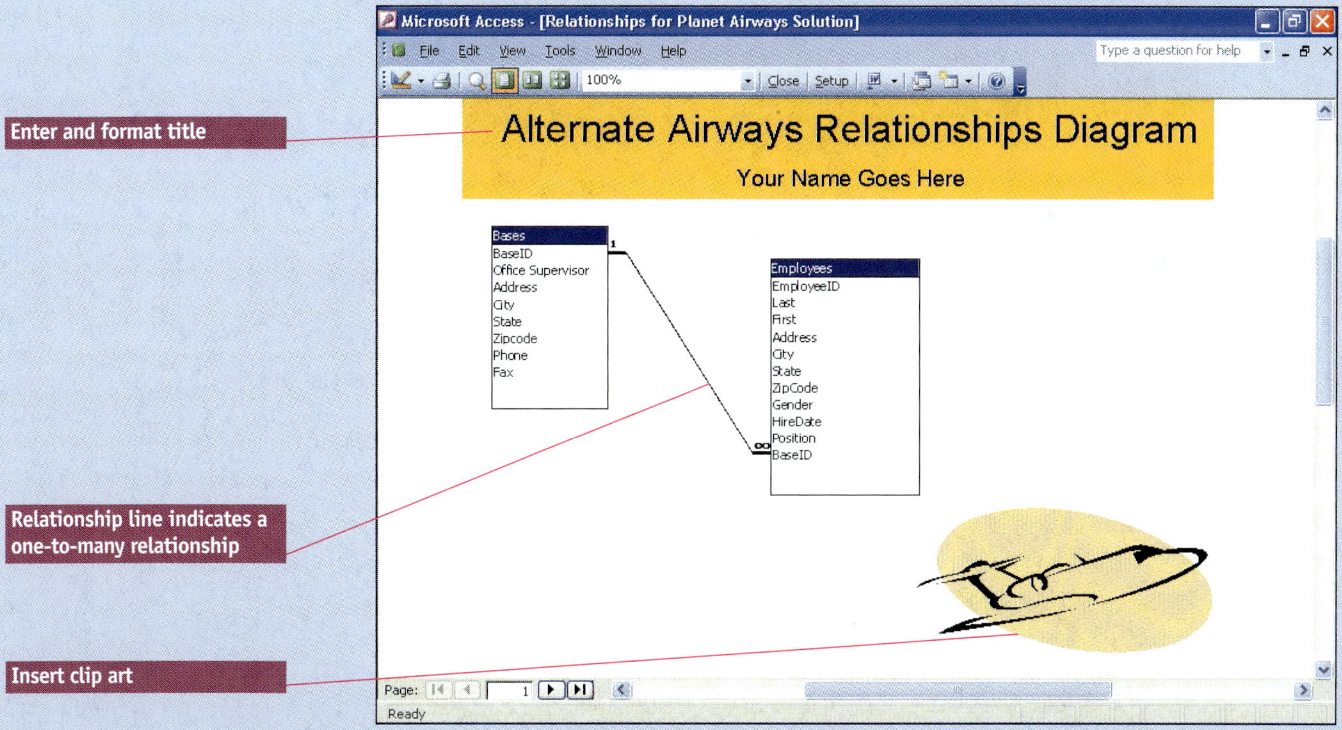

FIGURE 6 A Relational Database

7. **Access Objects: Forms, Queries, and Reports (Access):** Open the *Alternate Airways* database in the *Alternate Airways Folder* and create the additional objects as described below.
   a. Create the Employee form in Figure 7. You need not follow our design exactly, but you are required to include all of the functionality.
   b. Use the Combo Box Wizard to create the control for the employee's position. Check the option to type in the values that you want. Enter the positions: Captain, First Officer, Flight Attendant, Flight Engineer, and Purser.
   c. Use the completed form to enter data for yourself. Use 111222333 as your EmployeeID. You are based in Miami (MIA), and you have been hired as a captain. Print the completed form containing your data. Do not print the forms for the other employees.
   d. Create a report that shows the employee addresses in alphabetical order by employee last name. The report should be based on the Employees table and should contain the following fields: Last name, First name, BaseID, Position, and fields for the mailing address. The address should print on two lines; that is, the street address is on the first line, and the city, state, and zip code are on the second line. The actual report runs 11 pages. You are to print just the page that contains your data.
   e. Create a second report that groups employees by the base to which they are assigned. The report should include each employee's first and last name, position, and date of hire. The employees should be listed alphabetically within each base.
   f. Create a query that will display the employees based in Miami. The query is to be based on the Employees table and should contain each employee's first and last name, complete address, and base assignment. Print the dynaset of the query in landscape orientation.
   g. Create a second query that displays just the flight attendants in alphabetical order by last name. The query should display the first and last name, the fields for the complete mailing address, the BaseID, the position, and the date of hire. You do not have to print the query at this time.

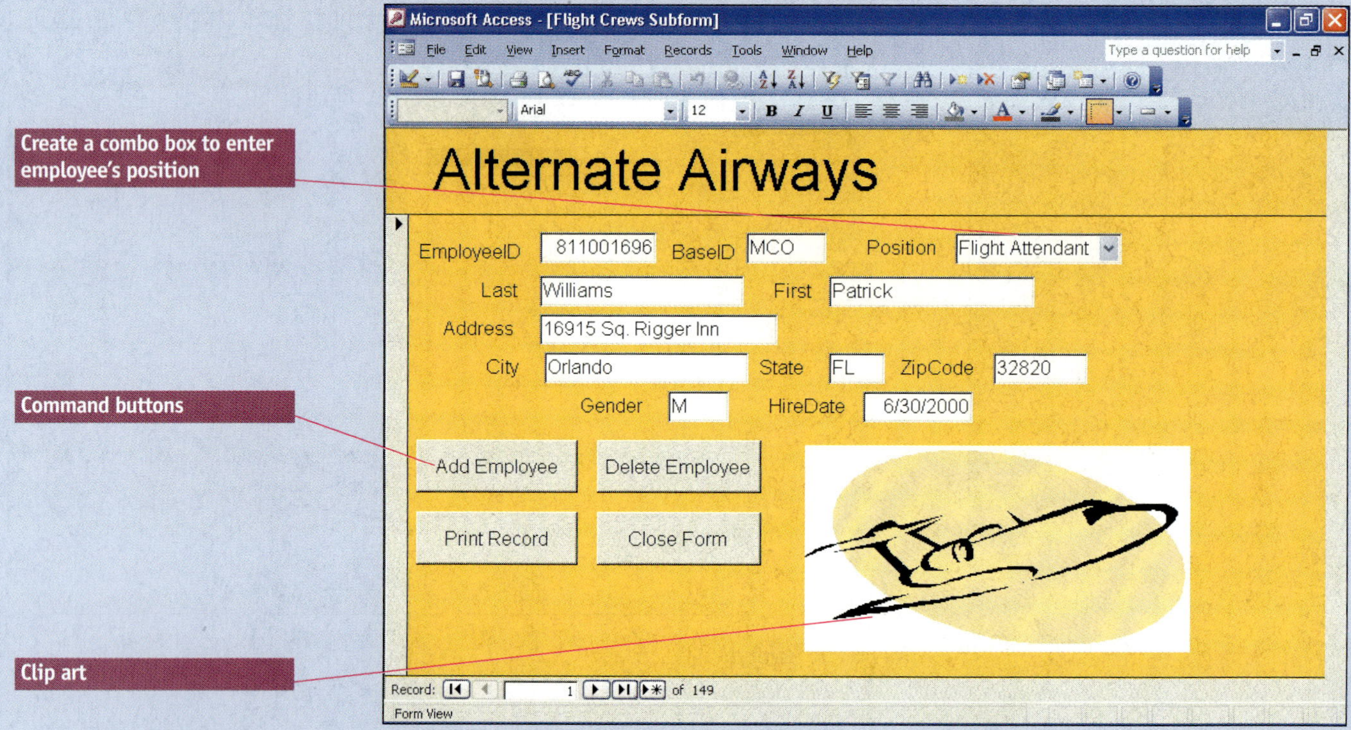

FIGURE 7 Access Objects (Employee Form)

8. **An Access Switchboard (Access):** Create the switchboard in Figure 8 for the *Alternate Airways* database. You do not have to match our design exactly, but you are required to have all five buttons. Note, too, that the switchboard contains a Report Menu, which displays a subsidiary switchboard.
   a. The first button on the main switchboard opens the Alternate Airways form as shown in Figure 8. This form has been created for you and can be found in the *Alternate Airways* database. You are asked, however, to modify the existing form to include your name in the indicated position.
   b. The second and third buttons display the Employee and Base forms, respectively, in order to maintain data in the associated tables.
   c. The Report Menu button provides access to a subsidiary switchboard that contains the various reports in the database. (These include the relationships diagram and the various reports from exercises 6 and 7.) The report switchboard should also have a button to return to the main switchboard.
   d. The Exit button on the main switchboard closes the database. Add the clip art image at the left of the switchboard. Insert your name under the clip art.
   e. Be sure to test both switchboards completely to be sure that they work correctly. Print the Switchboard Items table, the main switchboard, and the report switchboard for your instructor as proof that you completed the exercise correctly.
   f. Modify the startup property of the database so that the switchboard form opens automatically when you open the database. (You can also create an AutoExec macro to maximize the Database window. Display the Database window, click the Macros button, then click the New button to create a macro. Click the drop-down arrow to display the available actions, and scroll until you can select Maximize. Save the macro as AutoExec.)
   g. Close the database, then reopen it. The switchboard should appear automatically, and all subsequent objects should appear in a maximized window.
   h. Exit Access and continue with the next exercise.

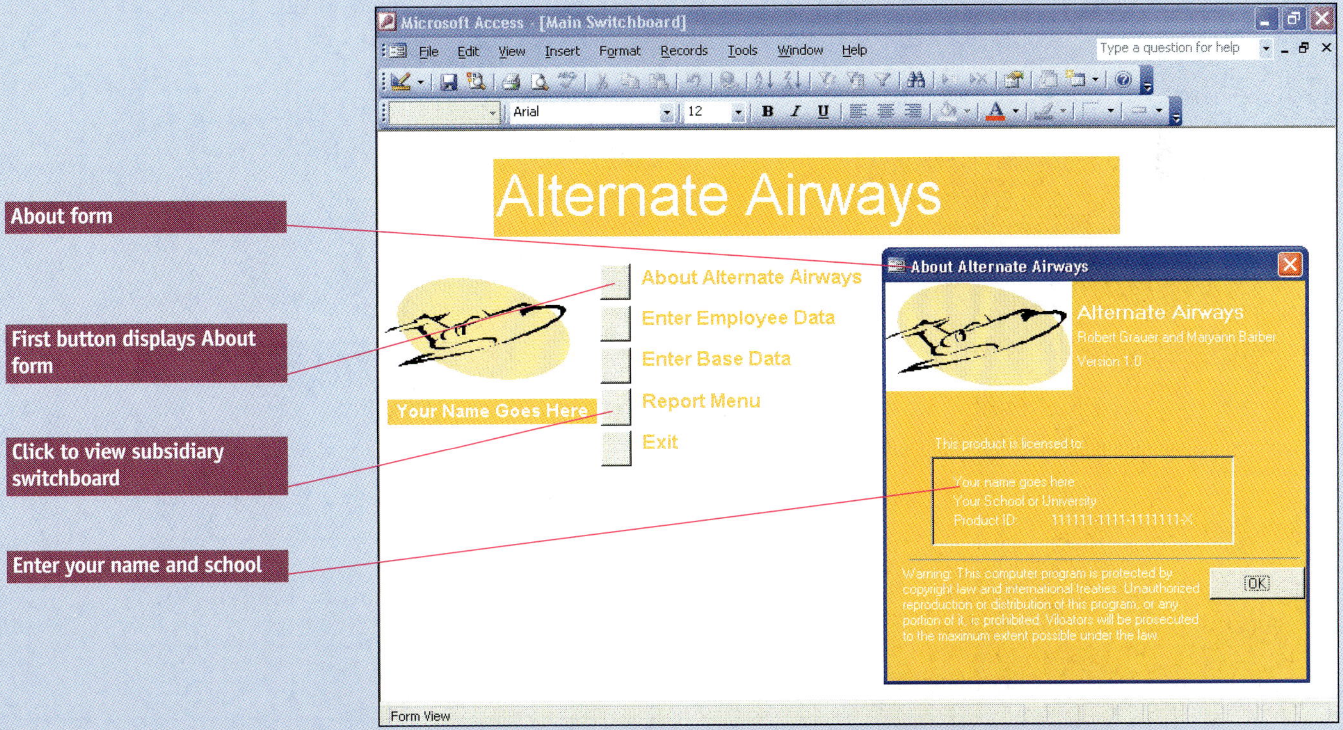

FIGURE 8 An Access Switchboard

9. **Mail Merge (Word and Access):** This exercise uses the Mail Merge facility in Microsoft Word in conjunction with an Access database. You will be asked to create two different form letters. Each letter is sent to a different set of recipients. You can start the merge from either application. Proceed as follows:
   a. Open the partially completed *Letter to Employees* document in the *Alternate Airways Folder* and save it as *Letter to Employees Solution* so that you can return to the original document if necessary.
   b. Pull down the Tools menu, click Letters and Mailings, then click Mail Merge Wizard to open the task pane. Select the Letters option. Click Next. Select the option to use the current document. Click Next.
   c. Select the recipients from an existing list. Choose the *Alternate Airways Folder,* select the *Alternate Airways* database, and select the Employee Information query (which was created in exercise 6) to display the Mail Merge Recipients dialog box.
   d. Add the address block and greeting line as shown in Figure 9. Move to the second paragraph and insert the indicated fields. Click the View Merged Data button to toggle between the field names and the actual data.
   e. Click the Merge to New Document button and specify the first three records, as shown in Figure 9. (There are more than 150 records in the database.) Print the three letters for your instructor. Save the completed form letter. You do not have to save the merged document. Close Word.
   f. Start Access and open the *Alternate Airways* database. Close the switchboard. Click the Queries button in the Database window and open the Flight Attendants query from exercise 7. Pull down the Tools menu, click Office Links, then click the Merge It with Microsoft Word command. Select the option to link to an existing document and choose the *Letter to Flight Attendants* document in the *Alternate Airways Folder.*
   g. Add the address block and greeting fields to the form letter. Complete the merge, and print only the first three letters. Save the completed form letter as *Letter to Flight Attendants Solution.* Exit Word. Exit Access.

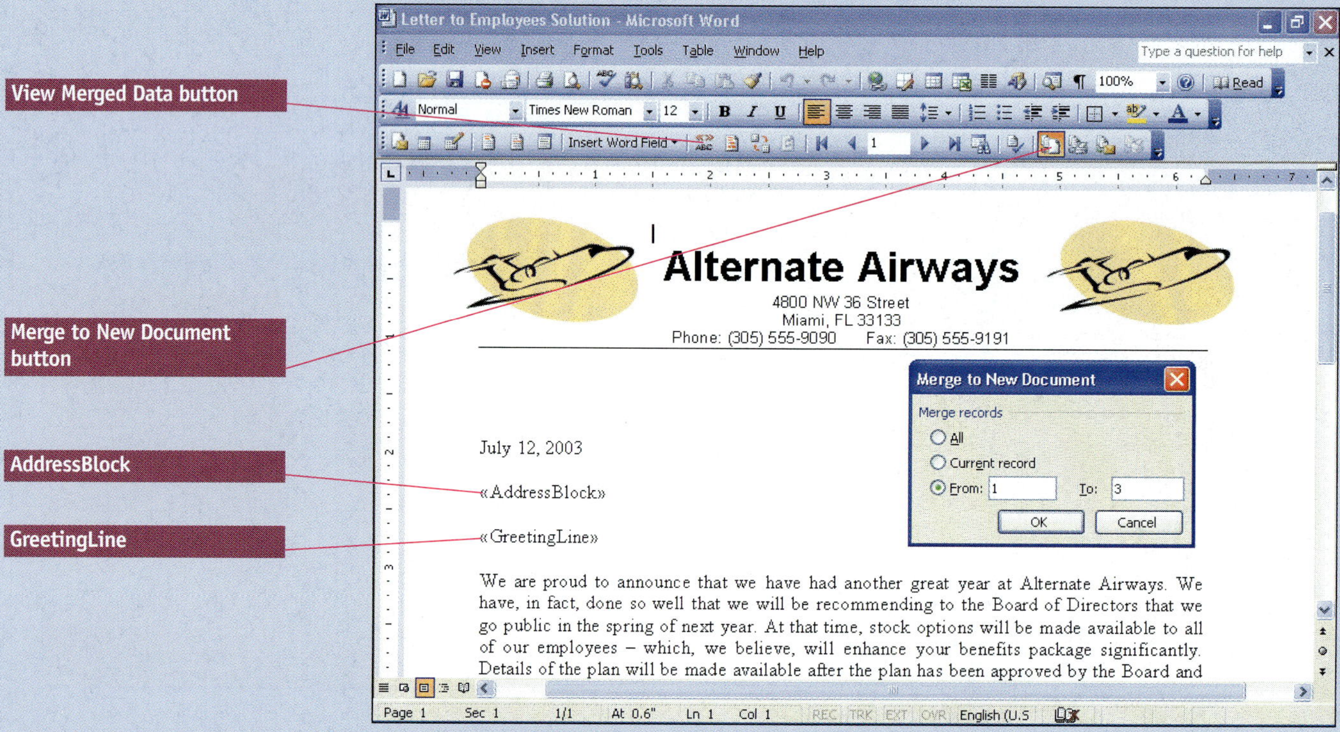

FIGURE 9 Mail Merge

10. **Worksheet References (Excel):** The Board of Directors has asked for a comparison of revenue for this year to last year's revenue. An Excel workbook has been created with that information, but it is your task to complete that workbook. Proceed as follows:

    a. Open the *Historical Alternate Revenue* workbook in the *Alternate Airways Folder* and save it as *Historical Alternate Revenue Solution.* (The values in this worksheet reflect the last-minute change that was made in problem 4 with respect to flight revenue.)

    b. Click the worksheet tab labeled Year to Year Comparison, then click in cell B3 of this worksheet as shown in Figure 10. Type an equal sign, click the worksheet tab labeled Last Year, click in cell F3 of this worksheet, and press Enter. The formula for this cell appears in the formula bar as ='Last Year'!F3, indicating that the value for this cell is obtained from another worksheet in the same workbook. Enter similar formulas to display the total revenues for all of the aircraft for both this year and last year.

    c. Complete the entries in column D of the Year to Year Comparison worksheet that show the dollar increase from last year to this year. The cell formulas in this column should reference only the Year to Year Comparison worksheet. Add another set of formulas in column E (not shown in Figure 10) to compute the percent increase from last year to this year.

    d. Enter your name in the worksheet as shown in Figure 10. Format the completed worksheet, then print the Year to Year Comparison worksheet for your instructor. Print the worksheet two ways, once to show the displayed values, and once to show the cell formulas.

    e. Create a combination chart that plots both the dollar amount of the increase and the percent of the increase for each plane as shown in Figure 10. Display a data table at the bottom of the chart sheet. Note that the dollar and percent increases for total revenue are $4,418,800 and 41.3%, respectively. You do not have to print the combination chart at this time.

    f. Save the completed workbook. Exit Excel.

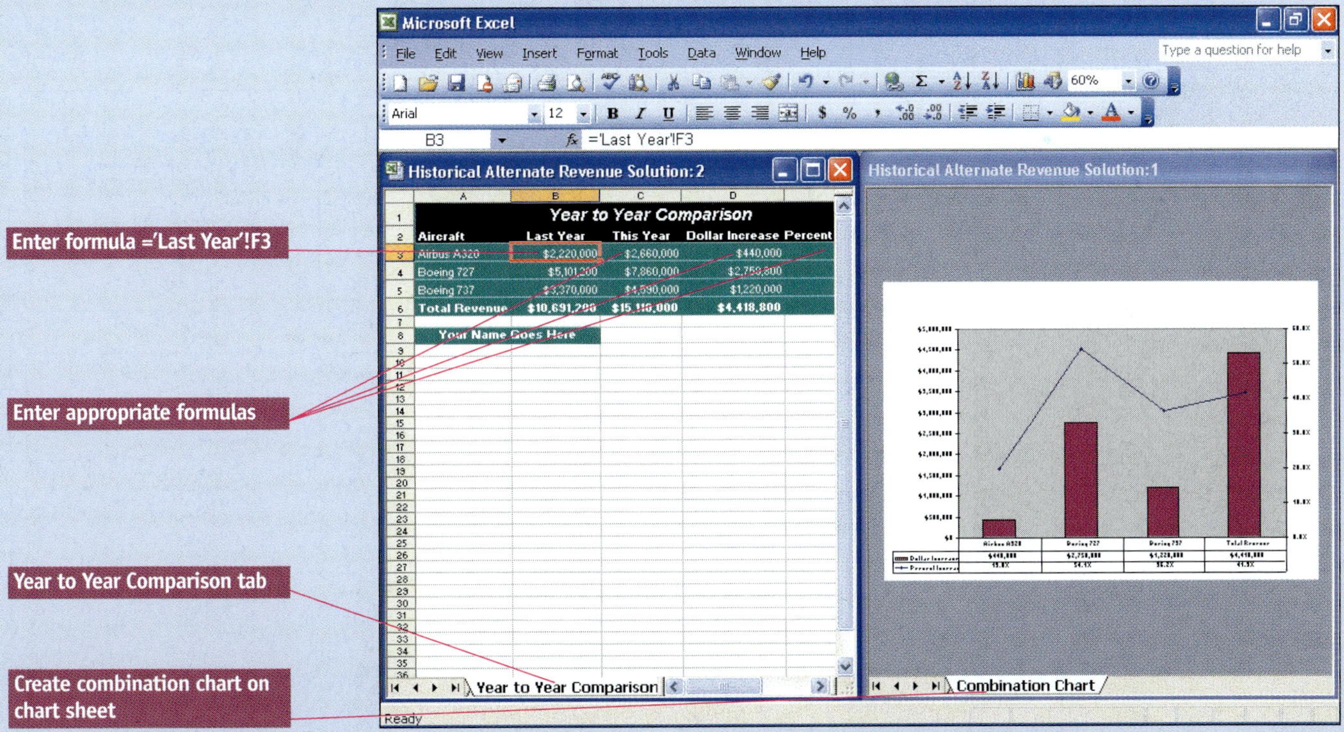

FIGURE 10 Worksheet References

11. **Presentation to the Board (PowerPoint and Excel):** A partially completed version of the presentation in Figure 11 has been saved as *Presentation to the Board* in the *Alternate Airways Folder.* Open this presentation and save it as *Presentation to the Board Solution.* Your next task is to link the worksheets and chart from the previous exercise to various slides in this presentation. Linking ensures that you can change the data in the Excel workbook and have the change reflected automatically in the PowerPoint presentation.

    a. Open the *Historical Alternate Revenue Solution* workbook from the previous exercise. Select the worksheet that contains revenue data for last year, and link that data to the slide containing the Year to Year Comparison (slide 4).

    b. Select the worksheet with the revenue for the current year and link this data to the same slide as in part (a). Move and/or size the worksheets after they have been added to the presentation.

    c. Return to Excel. Select the chart sheet containing the combination chart, then link that chart to slide 5 as shown in Figure 11.

    d. Add the mission statement as slide number 2 by importing this slide from the *Presentation to the President.* (Pull down the Insert menu, click the Slides from File command to display the Slide Finder dialog box, and then click the Browse button to locate the earlier presentation.)

    e. Add transition and custom animation effects as you see fit.

    f. Experiment with a different design template, but limit yourself to five minutes. Choose the template you like best. Save the presentation.

    g. Add your name to the title slide in the indicated position. Print the audience handouts of the completed presentation (six per page) for your instructor.

    h. Save the completed presentation. Exit PowerPoint. Close the Excel workbook. Exit Excel.

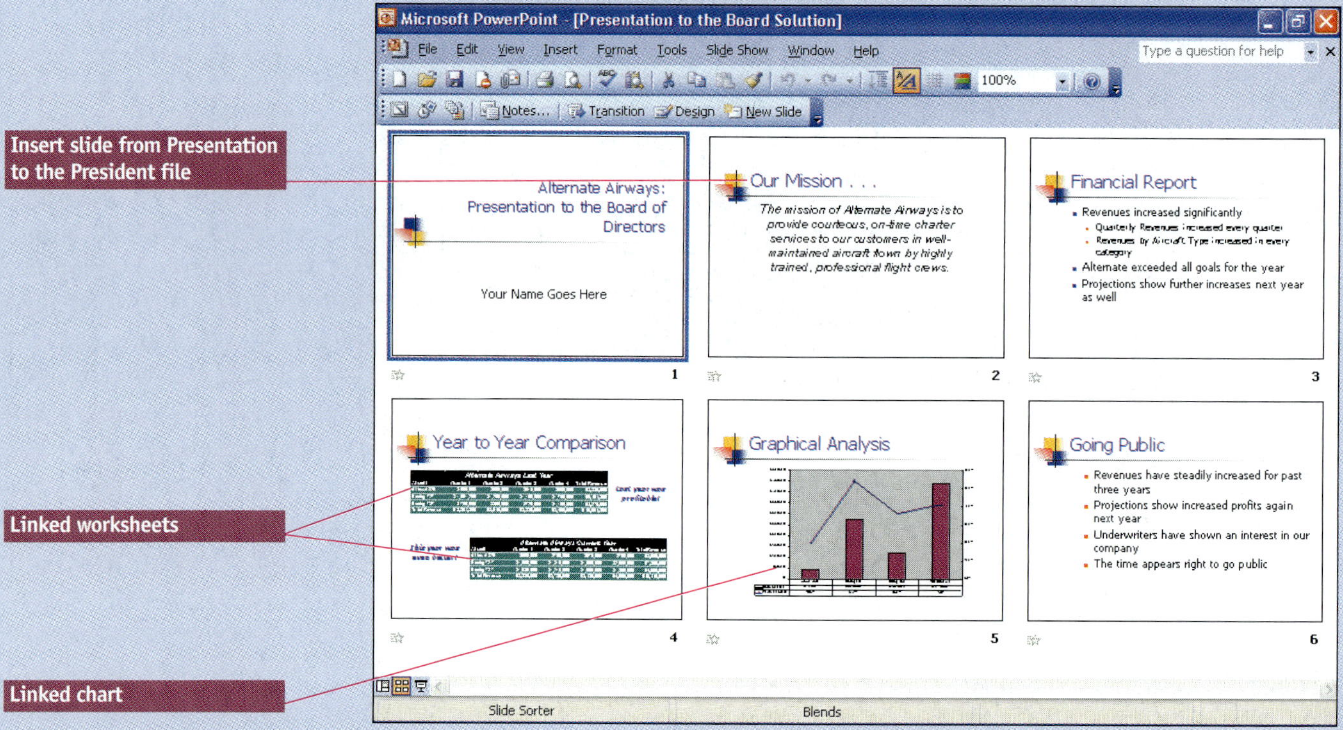

FIGURE 11 Presentation to the Board

12. **Letter to the Board (Word and Excel):** This exercise provides additional practice in linking Excel objects to a Word document. Open the partially completed *Letter to the Board* document in the *Alternate Airways Folder.* Insert your name as the director of Alternate Airways. Save the document as *Letter to the Board Solution* so that you can return to the original document if necessary. Proceed as follows to create the completed document in Figure 12.

    a. Open the *Alternate Airways Historical Sales Solution* workbook from the previous exercise if it is not already open. Select the worksheet containing the revenue for the current year and link it to the Word document, immediately after the first paragraph. Place (link) the worksheet containing the revenue for the previous year below the first worksheet.

    b. Insert a section break at the end of the first page, then change the orientation of the second page (section) to landscape as shown in Figure 12.

    c. Return to the Excel workbook. Select the combination chart and link this chart to the Word document. The Excel chart should appear in the document. The chart may be cropped initially. If so, select the entire chart, then click and drag a corner sizing handle to make the chart smaller. Right click the chart and click the command to display the Picture toolbar. Select the Crop tool, then click and drag the side handle at the right of the chart to show the portion of the chart that may have been cropped initially.

    d. Add your name and your instructor's name in the indicated positions. Your instructor is the recipient of the memo and you are the sender. Save the completed document, and then print the completed letter for your instructor.

    e. Exit Word. Exit Excel. You're almost finished. All that remains is the preparation of a cover sheet as described in the next exercise.

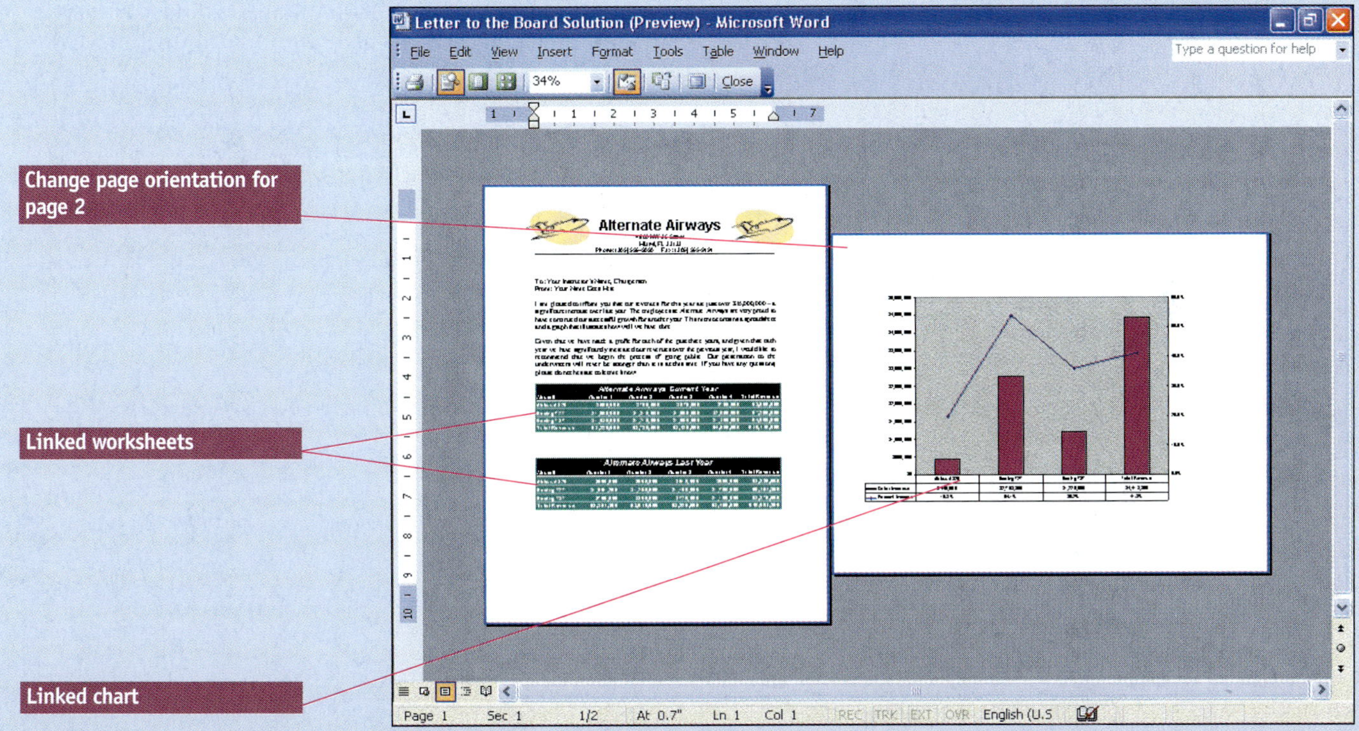

FIGURE 12 Letter to the Board

13. **Create a Home Page (Word):** Open the *Alternate Airways Home Page* document in the *Alternate Airways Folder.* Pull down the File menu, click the Save as Web Page command, and specify Single File Web Page as the file type to convert the Word document to a Web page. Click Continue when a message appears that indicates pictures with text wrapping will become left or right justified.
    a. Review the document and make the basic formatting changes you deem appropriate. Use the Themes command in the Format menu to apply an overall design to the page. Use any theme you like, but the overall document formatting should be similar to the document in Figure 13.
    b. Format the title if you have not already done so. Select the text, "Click here to contact us" that appears toward the top of the document. Pull down the Insert menu and click the Hyperlink command (or click the Insert Hyperlink button on the Standard toolbar), click the E-mail Address button, and then enter your e-mail address.
    c. Go to the last paragraph and insert a hyperlink for the Boeing Company at www.boeing.com. Insert a second link for FlyteComm at www.flytecomm.com, a Web site that lets you track a flight from take-off to landing.
    d. Save the document a final time, then exit Word. Start Windows Explorer, then go to the folder containing your Web page, and double click the file you just created. Internet Explorer will start automatically (because your document was saved as a Web page). You should see your document within Internet Explorer as shown in Figure 13. Look carefully at the Address bar and note the local address on drive C, as opposed to a Web address. Print the document for your instructor as proof you completed the assignment.
    e. Creating the home page and viewing it locally is easy. Placing the page on the Web where it can be seen by anyone with an Internet connection is not as straightforward. You will need additional information from your instructor about how to obtain an account on a Web server (if that is available at your school), and further how to upload the Web page from your PC to the server.

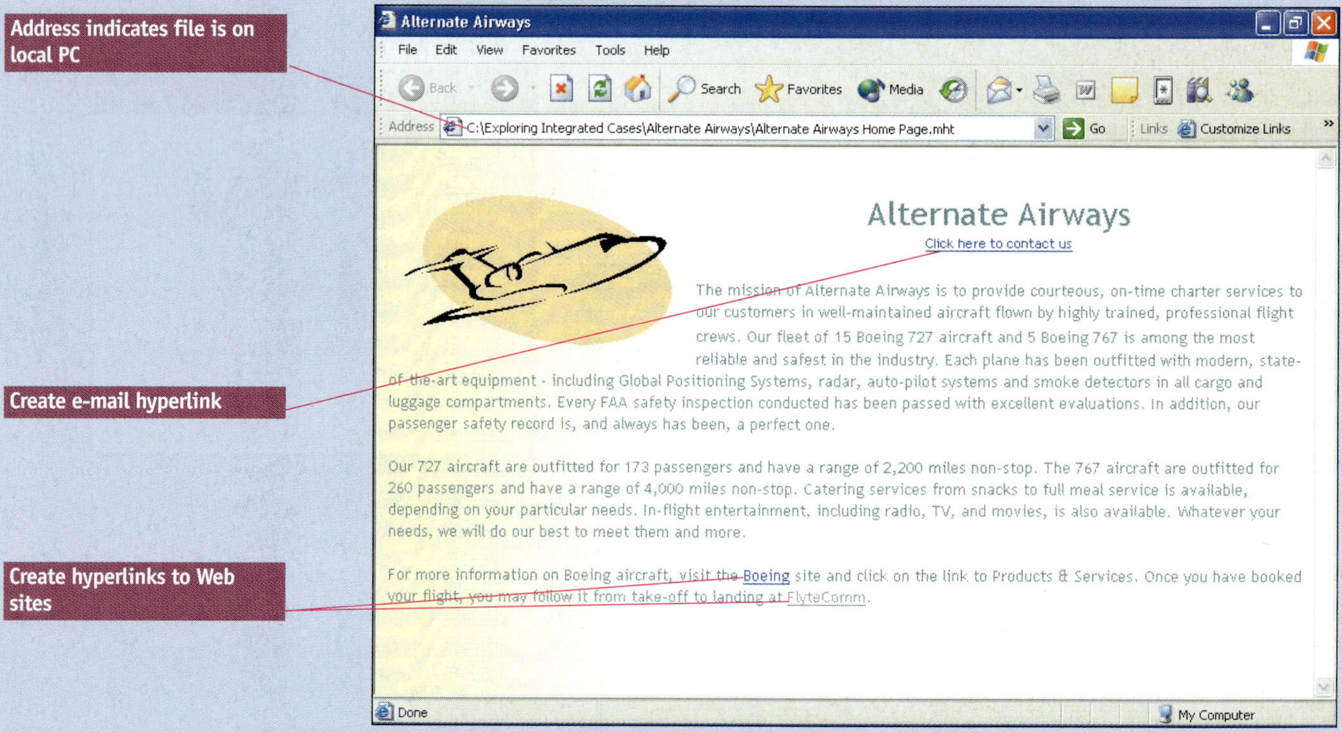

FIGURE 13 Alternate Airways Home Page

14. **Submission Checklist (Word):** You have successfully completed multiple exercises within the Alternate Airways case study. Each exercise described a specific task(s), required the use of one or more applications in Microsoft Office, and asked you to print one or more documents to show that you completed the exercise. The submissions checklist in Figure 14 will ensure that you have printed all of the required documents.
    a. Open the *Alternate Airways Submission Checklist* that is found in the *Alternate Airways Folder.* Read the document carefully and check each box after you verify that you have printed the indicated document.
    b. Add your name to the checklist as indicated, then use the checklist as a cover sheet when you submit the material to your instructor.
    c. Think for a minute about all that you have accomplished. You have completed a series of 13 exercises, which required the use of all four major applications within Microsoft Office. You have used the applications individually and in conjunction with one another. You have been able to:
        i. Dynamically link an Excel worksheet and chart to a Word document and PowerPoint presentation, so that changes to the Excel workbook were automatically reflected in the other documents.
        ii. Import an Excel worksheet into an Access database to use a table within the database.
        iii. Use an Access table as the data source for a mail merge in Microsoft Word.
        iv. Use Word to create a home page.
    d. Congratulations on a job well done!

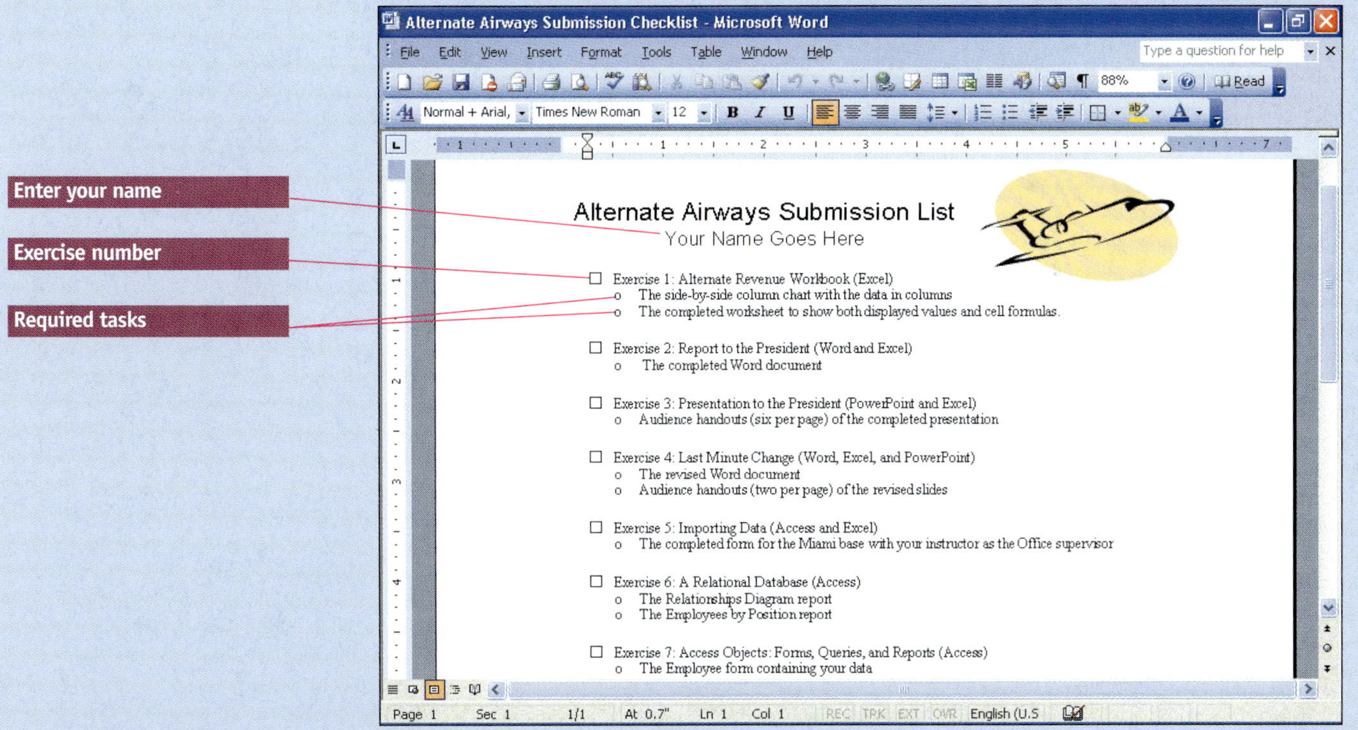

FIGURE 14 Submission Checklist

CASE STUDY

3 Integrated Case Study: University Housing

OBJECTIVES

1. Use the core applications in Office 2003 individually or in conjunction with one another.
2. Link an Excel chart to a Word document and a PowerPoint presentation.
3. Import an Excel worksheet into an Access database.
4. Create Access tables, queries, reports, and forms.
5. Use an Access table as the basis for a mail merge.
6. Use Word to create a Web page for the organization.

integrated exercises

1. University Housing Workbook and Chart (Excel)
2. Report to the Provost (Word and Excel)
3. Presentation to the Provost (PowerPoint and Excel)
4. Last-minute Change (Word, Excel, and PowerPoint)
5. Importing Data (Access and Excel)
6. A Relational Database (Access)
7. Access Objects: Forms, Queries, and Reports (Access)
8. An Access Switchboard (Access)
9. Mail Merge (Word and Access)
10. Worksheet References (Excel)
11. Presentation to the Trustees (PowerPoint and Excel)
12. Letter to the Trustees (Word and Excel)
13. Create a Home Page (Word)
14. Submission Checklist (Word)

This document provides a series of 13 exercises in Microsoft Office that relate to the University Housing Office, as it might exist at your school or university. Each exercise describes a specific task for the organization to accomplish and typically requires the use of multiple applications within Microsoft Office for solution. Many of the exercises are cumulative in nature. You may, for example, be asked to create an Excel chart in one exercise, and then incorporate that chart into a Word memo and a PowerPoint presentation in subsequent exercises. Other exercises will ask you to create or modify an Access database, to exchange data between Excel and Access, and to create a Web page for the Housing Office. Collectively, you will gain considerable practice in the core applications of Microsoft Office 2003, and especially in how they work together to accomplish complex tasks.

All of the exercises are based on material from the core application chapters in *Exploring Office 2003 Volume I*. Specific chapter references are deliberately not provided so that the case study is as realistic as possible. Think of this assignment as your first day on the job; you were hired by University Housing because you are proficient in Microsoft Office. This is your chance to show what you know.

Your assignment is to follow the directions of your instructor with respect to which of the exercises you are to complete within the case description. You should begin by downloading the practice files from our Web site at www.prenhall.com/grauer. Go to the site, click the book icon for Office 2003, and then click the Student Downloads tab. Scroll until you can select the link to Integrated Case Studies, and then download the file to your desktop. Double click the file icon and follow the onscreen instructions to install the practice files on your computer. The files you need will be in the University Housing folder within the Exploring Integrated Cases folder.

INTEGRATED EXERCISES

1. **University Housing Workbook and Chart (Excel):** You will find a partially completed version of the spreadsheet in Figure 1 in the *University Housing* workbook in the *University Housing Folder.* (You can download the practice files for this case study from our Web site at www.prenhall.com/grauer.) Open the workbook and save it as *University Housing Solution* so that you can return to the original workbook if necessary. Proceed as follows:

   a. Click in cell D3 to enter the formula to compute the total room revenue for Ashe Hall. (A double room has two students, both of whom pay cost of the room.) Click in cell E3 and compute the meal revenue for Ashe Hall. Copy the formulas in cells D3 and E3 to remaining cells in these columns.

   b. Click in cell F3 and compute the total revenue for Ashe Hall. Copy this formula to the remaining cells in this column. Enter the formulas to compute the totals in row 8.

   c. Use the AutoFormat command as the basis for formatting your worksheet in an attractive fashion. You can match our formatting, or you can use your own design.

   d. Create a pie chart that shows the percentage of the meal revenue attributable to each dorm. Store this chart in its own chart sheet. Create a column chart that shows the total room revenue for each dorm. Store this chart in its own chart sheet. Print both charts for your instructor.

   e. Create a side-by-side column chart that shows the room revenue and meal revenue for each dorm. Specify that the data series are in columns so that the names of the dorms appear on the X axis. Use the data table option in the Chart Options dialog box to display the numerical data beneath the chart. Save this chart in its own sheet. (You do not have to print the side-by-side chart at this time.)

   f. Enter your name in the worksheet as indicated.

   g. Print the completed Housing Revenue worksheet twice, once to show displayed values and once to show the cell formulas.

   h. Save the completed workbook for use in subsequent exercises. Exit Excel.

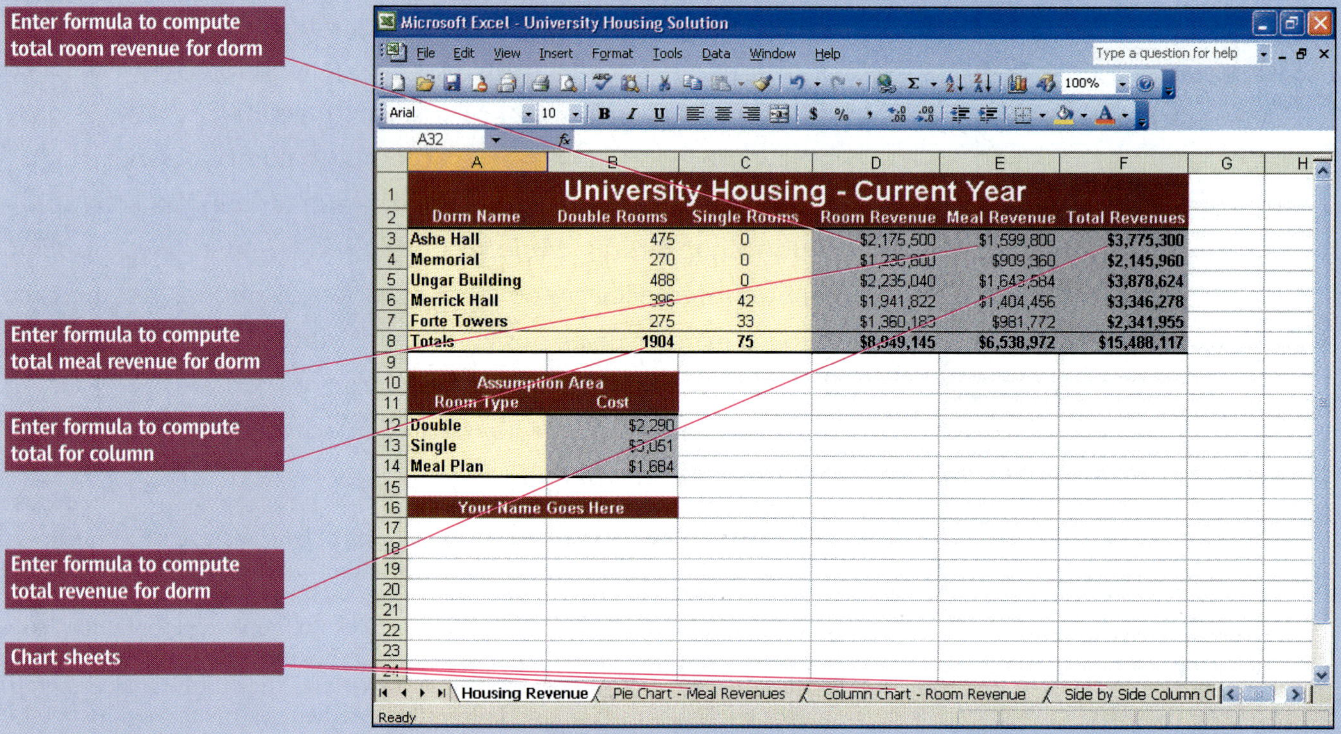

FIGURE 1 University Housing Workbook and Chart

2. **Report to the Provost (Word and Excel):** This exercise builds on the previous exercise by creating a Word document that contains the Excel chart. The latter is to be dynamically linked to the Word document, so that any changes in the Excel workbook are automatically reflected in the memo.
   a. You will find a partially completed version of the document in Figure 2 in the *Report to the Provost* document in the *University Housing Folder.* Open this document and then save it as *Report to the Provost Solution.*
   b. Change the To and From lines in the memo to contain your instructor's name and your name, respectively.
   c. Open the completed workbook from the previous exercise. Click the worksheet tab containing the side-by-side column chart. Click the Zoom button and change the magnification so that you can select the entire chart. Click the Copy button.
   d. Click the appropriate button on the taskbar to return to the Word document. Click below the first paragraph to position the insertion point for the chart. Pull down the Edit menu, click Paste Special, select Microsoft Excel Chart Object, click Paste Link, and click OK.
   e. The Excel chart should appear in the document. The only tricky part (if any) is to display the entire chart (it may be cropped initially). Select the chart, then click and drag a corner sizing handle to make the chart smaller to give yourself room in which to work. Right click the chart and click the command to display the Picture toolbar. Select the Crop tool, then click and drag the side handle at the right of the chart to show the portion of the chart that may have been cropped initially.
   f. Move and size the chart within the memo as necessary. You may find it convenient to change the zoom specification to "Whole Page" so that you can position the chart more easily.
   g. Save the completed document. Print the completed document for your instructor. Exit Word.

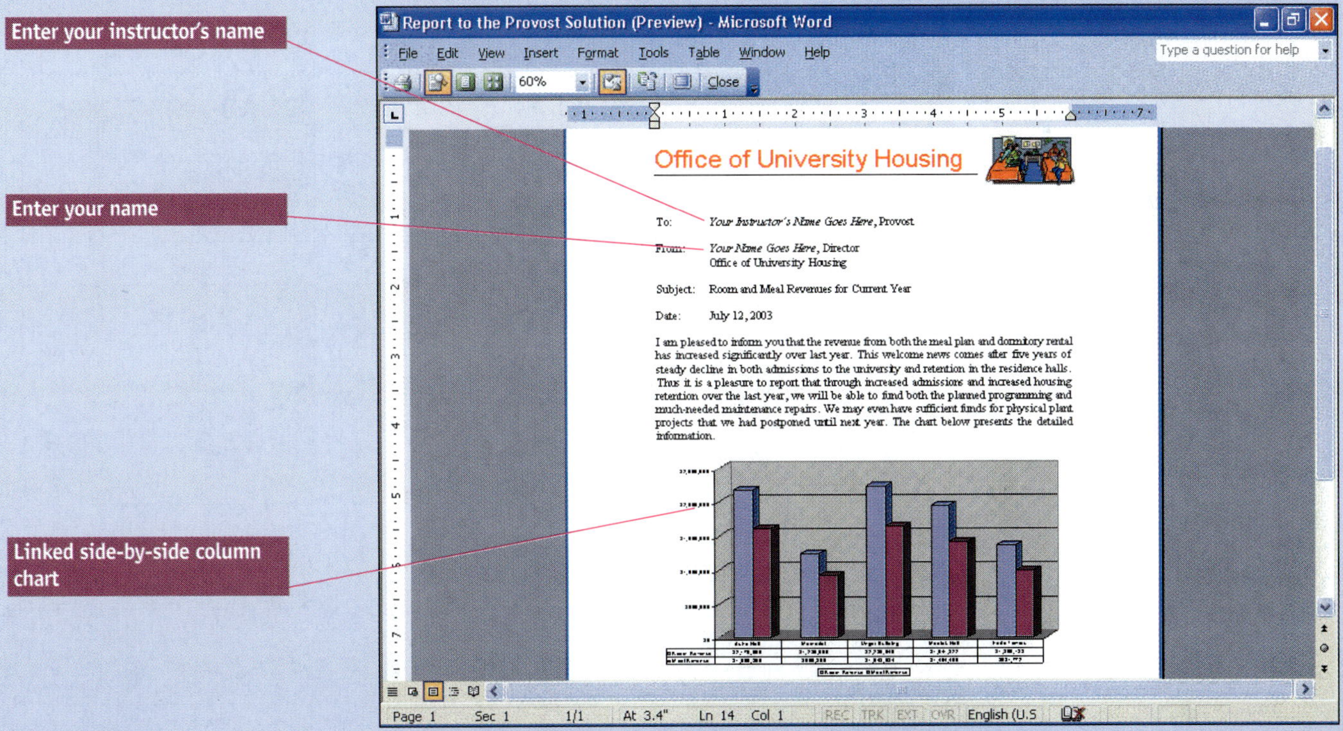

FIGURE 2 Report to the Provost

3. **Presentation to the Provost (PowerPoint and Excel):** A partially completed version of the presentation in Figure 3 has been saved as the *Presentation to the Provost* in the *University Housing Folder.* Open this presentation and save it as *Presentation to the Provost Solution* so that you can return to the original presentation if necessary.
   a. Insert a new slide that contains a mission statement as the fifth slide in the presentation. The mission statement should read as follows: *The mission of the University Housing Office is to provide a total environment that will enrich the educational experience of its residents. It seeks to promote increased interaction between faculty and students through resident masters, special programs, and intramural activities.* Run a spell check after you have added this slide into the presentation.
   b. Open the completed workbook from exercise 1. Use the same technique as in the previous problem to link the worksheet and the chart to the appropriate slides in the presentation, as shown below.
   c. Move and/or size the worksheet and chart after they have been added to the presentation. Save the presentation.
   d. Include animation effects as you see fit within a slide and add transition effects from one slide to the next.
   e. Experiment with a different design template, but limit yourself to five minutes. Choose the template you like best. Save the presentation.
   f. Add your name to the title slide. Print the audience handouts of the completed presentation (six per page) for your instructor.
   g. Save the completed presentation. Exit PowerPoint. Close the Excel workbook and exit Excel.

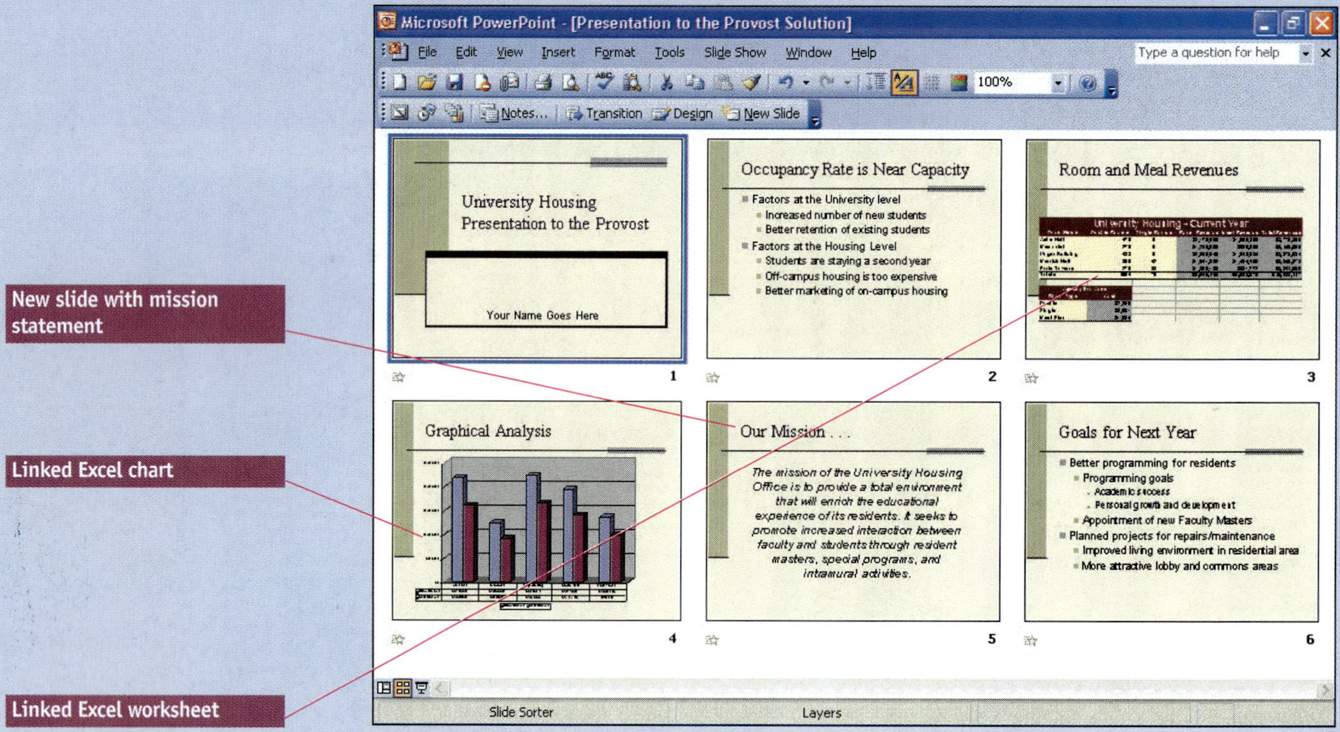

FIGURE 3 Presentation to the Provost

4. **Last-minute Change (Word, Excel, and PowerPoint):** It was just discovered that the single rooms in two of the dorms were not recorded in the year-end worksheet. Your task is to correct all of the documents that reflect this information. Open the completed *University Housing Solution* workbook from exercise 1. Select the Housing Revenue worksheet.

   a. Click in cells C3 and C4. Change the number of single rooms in Ashe Hall and Memorial to 10 and 15, respectively. The revenues change in this worksheet as do all of the associated charts. Save the workbook. Exit Excel.

   b. Open the *Report to the Provost Solution* document from the second exercise. The chart should be updated automatically to reflect the corrected revenue data. (The room revenue for Ashe Hall after the update should be $2,206,010, and this value should appear at the bottom of the chart.) If the chart is not updated, right click the chart to display a context-sensitive menu and click the Update Link command. If the chart is still not updated, right click the chart, click the Linked Chart Object command, then click the Links command to display the Links dialog box, where you can check the source (folder) of the linked objects.

   c. Click at the beginning of the opening paragraph in the memo and enter the new text, which is shown in bold italics in Figure 4. Save and print the completed report. Exit Word.

   d. Start PowerPoint. Open the *Presentation to the Provost Solution* that you created earlier. PowerPoint detects that a change has been made in the underlying workbook and prompts you to update. Click the button to update the links.

   e. Change to the Slide Sorter view. Press and hold the Shift key as you select the slides containing the Excel worksheet and chart. Pull down the File menu, click the Print command, and print the selection (these two slides) as audience handouts, two slides per page.

   f. Save the presentation. Exit PowerPoint.

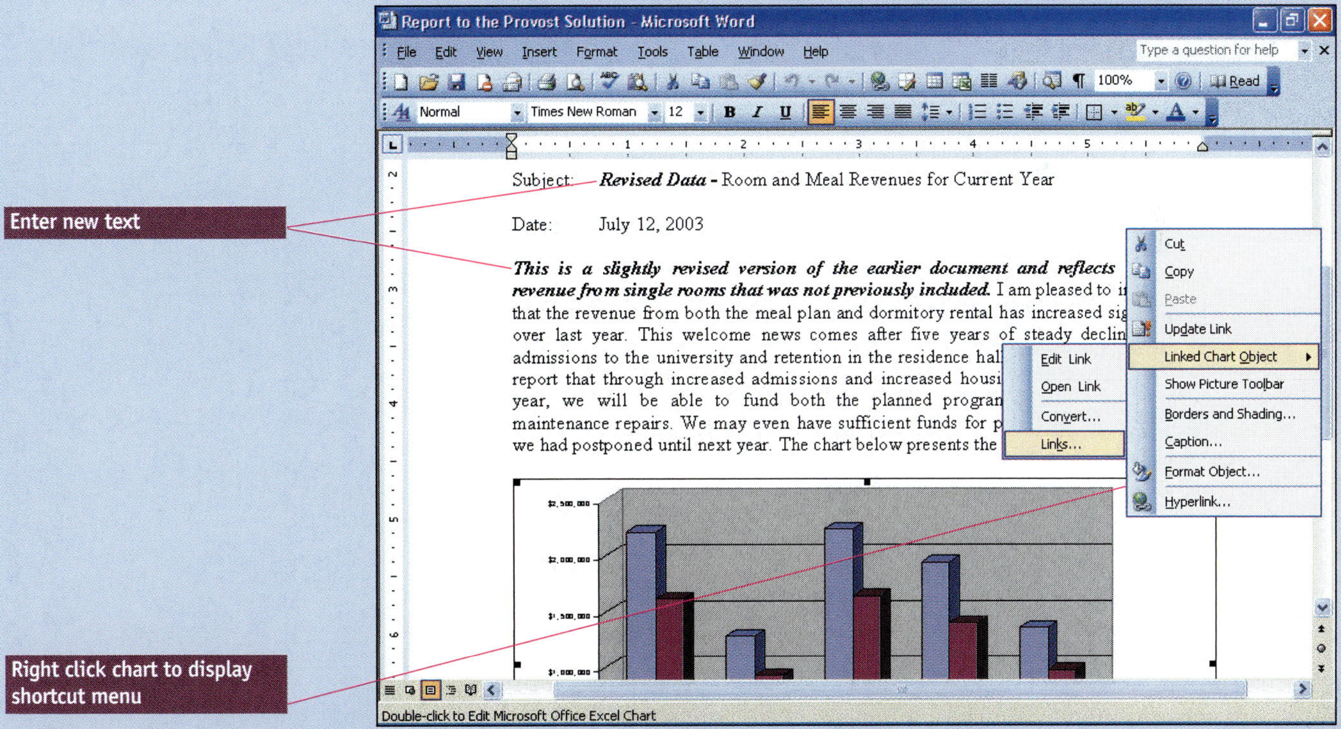

FIGURE 4 Last-minute Change

5. **Importing Data (Access and Excel):** The *University Housing* database contains two tables, one for students, and one for dorms (residence halls). The Students table already exists within the Access database although data has not been entered for every student. The dorm information, however, is in an Excel spreadsheet. Thus, your first task is to import the Excel worksheet into the Access database.
   a. Start Access. Open the *University Housing* database in the *University Housing Folder.* Click the Tables button if necessary. Pull down the File menu, click (or point to) the Get External Data command, and then click the Import command to display the Import dialog box.
   b. Click the down arrow on the Look In list box and change to the *University Housing Folder* (the same folder that contains the database). Change the file type to Microsoft Excel. Select the *Dorms* workbook to start the Import Spreadsheet Wizard.
   c. Check the box that indicates the first row contains column headings as shown in Figure 5. Click Next. Select the option button to store the data in a new table. Click Next.
   d. You do not need information about the individual fields. Click Next.
   e. Select the option to choose your own primary key. Click the drop-down arrow on the list box and select DormID. Click Next. Access indicates that it will import the data into a Dorms table.
   f. Click the Finish button, then click OK when the wizard indicates that it has imported the table. The Dorms table appears in the Database window.
   g. Click the Forms button in the Database window and open the Dorms form. (This form was previously created using the control names in the Dorms table that was just imported.) Locate the record for Merrick Hall (record 3). Change the Master's name to your instructor's name. Modify the e-mail and telephone information as well. Print the completed form with your instructor's data.

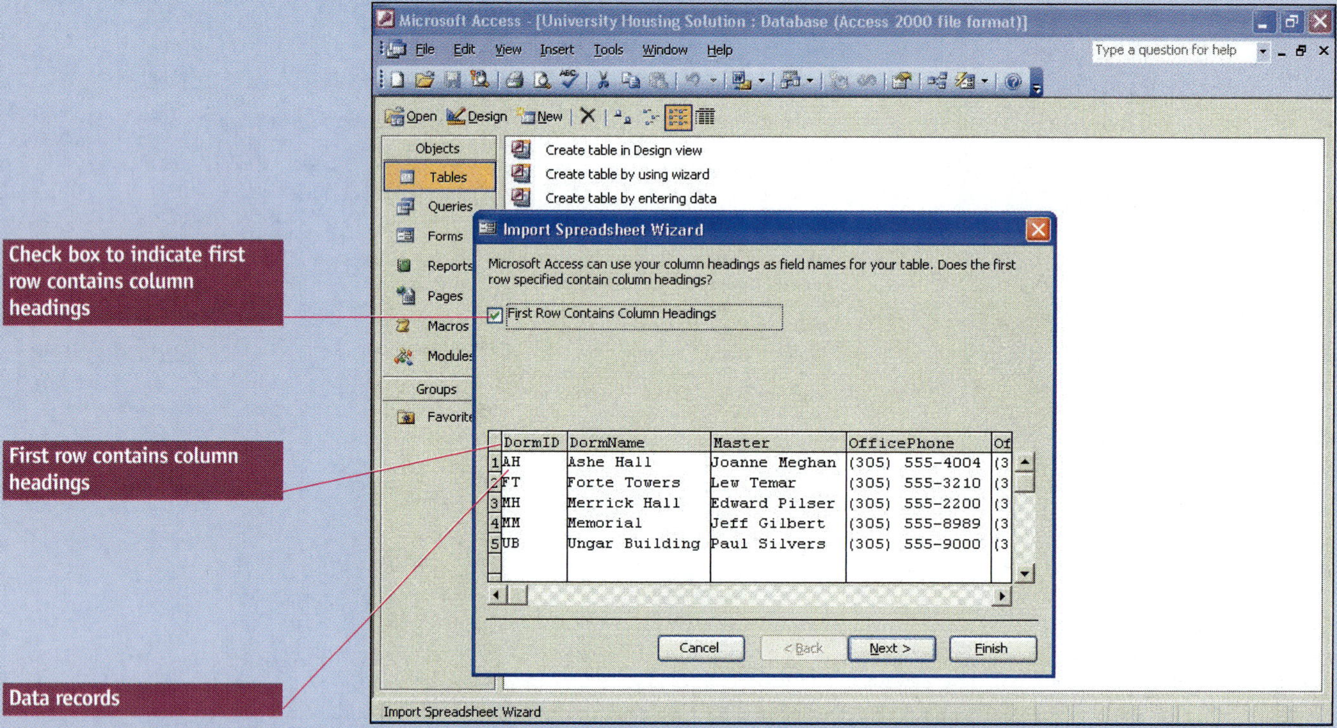

FIGURE 5 Importing Data

6. **A Relational Database (Access):** The *University Housing* database contains a one-to-many relationship between the Dorms table and the Students table as shown in Figure 6. One dorm has many students, but a specific student is assigned to only one dorm.
   a. Pull down the Tools menu and create the relationships diagram that corresponds to the report in Figure 6. Check the box to enforce referential integrity when you create the relationship.
   b. Pull down the File menu and click the Print Relationships command to create a report containing the relationships diagram. Change to Design view, and then modify the report to match Figure 6. (You can enhance the report by importing the clip art from the Word document in exercise 2.) Print the completed report for your instructor. Close the report and return to the Database window.
   c. Click the Query button in the Database window, and then create a new query in Design view. The query is to contain fields from both tables as shown below:
      i. Select the LastName, FirstName, Room, Address, City, State, and ZipCode fields from the Students table.
      ii. Select the DormName, Master, OfficePhone, and EmailAddress from the Dorms table.
      iii. Display the students in alphabetical order by last name.
      iv. Save the query as Student Mailing List. You do not have to print the query at this time.
   d. Create a report that groups students by the dorm to which they are assigned and displays the students alphabetically within each dorm. The report is to be based on the Student Mailing List query that you just created. Print this report for your instructor.

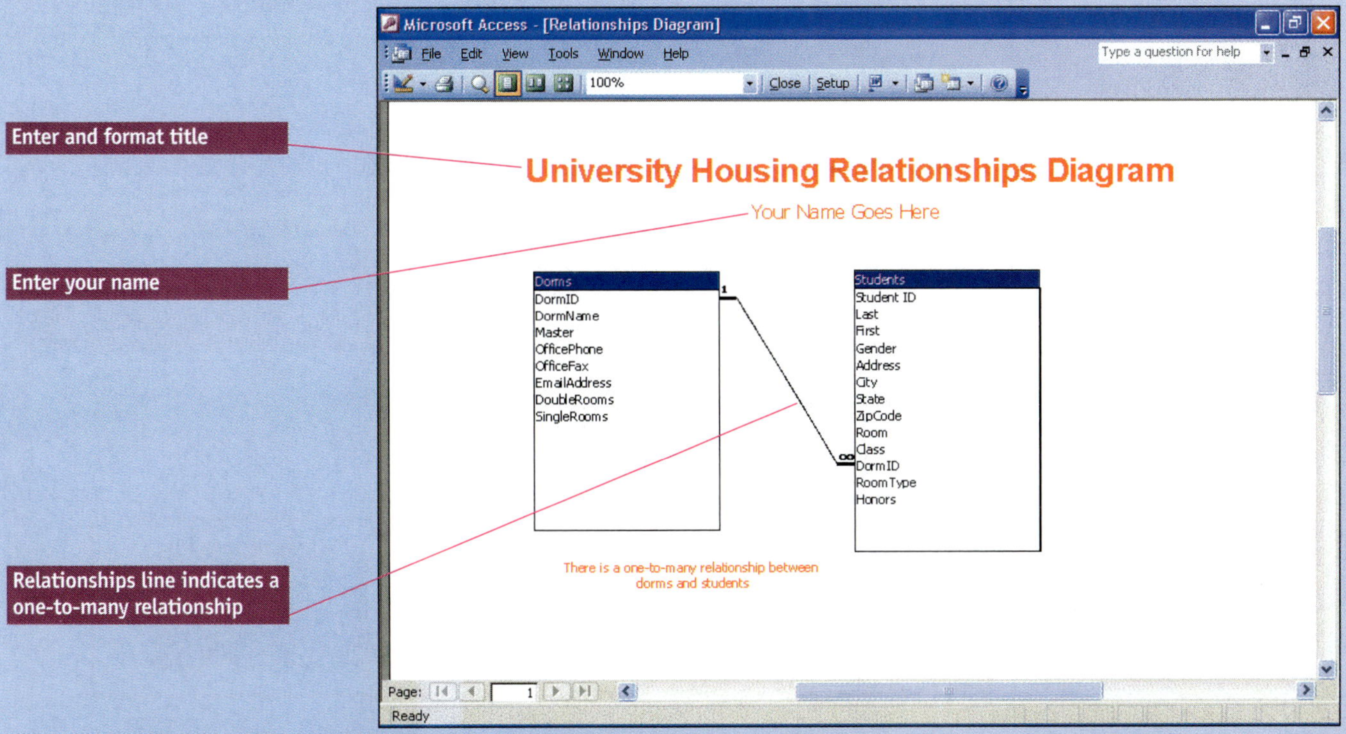

FIGURE 6 A Relational Database

7. **Access Objects: Forms, Queries, and Reports (Access):** Open the *University Housing* database in the *University Housing Folder* and create the additional objects as described below.
   a. Create the Student form in Figure 7. You need not follow our design exactly, but you are required to include all of the functionality. This includes a combo box for the student's class and a second combo box for the student's dorm.
   b. Use the Combo Box Wizard to create the control for the student's class. Check the option to type in the values that you want. Specify that the combo box will contain two columns, one for the numeric class and one for the displayed value. Use 1, 2, 3, and 4 for freshman, sophomore, junior, and senior, respectively. (You will hide the first column so that the user is able to select the text value.)
   c. Use the Combo Box Wizard to create a second control for the student's dorm. Check the option that indicates these values will come from a table or query, and then specify the Dorms table that was imported earlier. Be sure to set the tab order correctly, so that you can tab from one field to the next during data entry.
   d. Use the completed form to enter data for yourself. Use S11223344 as your StudentID. Specify that you will be living in Memorial. Your room is MM8888. Print the completed form containing your data. Do not print the forms for the other students.
   e. Create a report that lists every student in alphabetical order. The report should be based on the Students table and should contain the following fields: StudentID, Last Name, First Name, Address, and Room. The address should print on two lines; that is, the street address is on the first line, and the city, state, and zip code are on the second line. The actual report runs 13 pages. You are to print just the page that contains your data.
   f. Create a query that will display the students living in Memorial. The query is to be based on the Students table and should contain each student's first and last name, complete address, and room assignment. Print the dynaset of the query in landscape orientation.

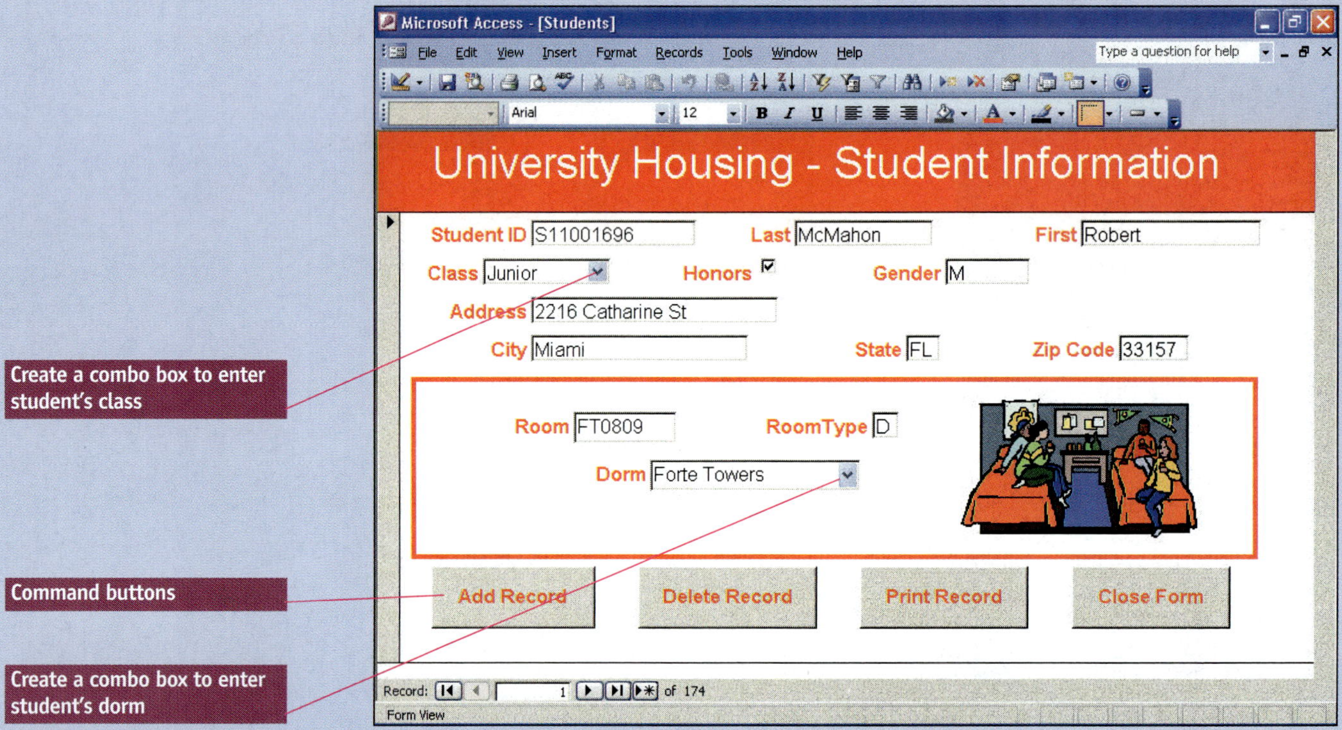

FIGURE 7 Access Objects (Student Form)

8. **An Access Switchboard (Access):** Create the switchboard in Figure 8 for the *University Housing* database. You do not have to match our design exactly, but you are required to have all five buttons. Note, too, that the switchboard contains a Report Menu, which displays a subsidiary switchboard.
   a. The first button on the main switchboard opens the University Housing form as shown in Figure 8. This form has been created for you and can be found in the *University Housing* database. You are asked, however, to modify the existing form to include your name in the indicated position.
   b. The second and third buttons display the Student and Dorm forms in order to maintain data in the associated tables.
   c. The Report Menu button provides access to a subsidiary switchboard that contains the various reports you created in the previous exercise. There should be four buttons on this switchboard, one for each report, and one button to return to the main switchboard.
   d. The Exit button on the main switchboard closes the database.
   e. Add the clip art image to the left of the switchboard. Insert a hyperlink under the clip art that opens the Web page of your school or university.
   f. Be sure to test both switchboards completely to be sure that they work correctly. Print the Switchboard Items table, the main switchboard, and the report switchboard for your instructor as proof that you completed the exercise correctly.
   g. Modify the startup property of the database so that the switchboard form opens automatically when you open the database. (You can also create an AutoExec macro to maximize the Database window. Display the Database window, click the Macros button, then click the New button to create a macro. Click the drop-down arrow to display the available actions and scroll until you can select Maximize. Save the macro as AutoExec.)
   h. Close the database, then reopen it. The switchboard should appear automatically, and all subsequent objects should appear in a maximized window.
   i. Exit Access and continue with the next exercise.

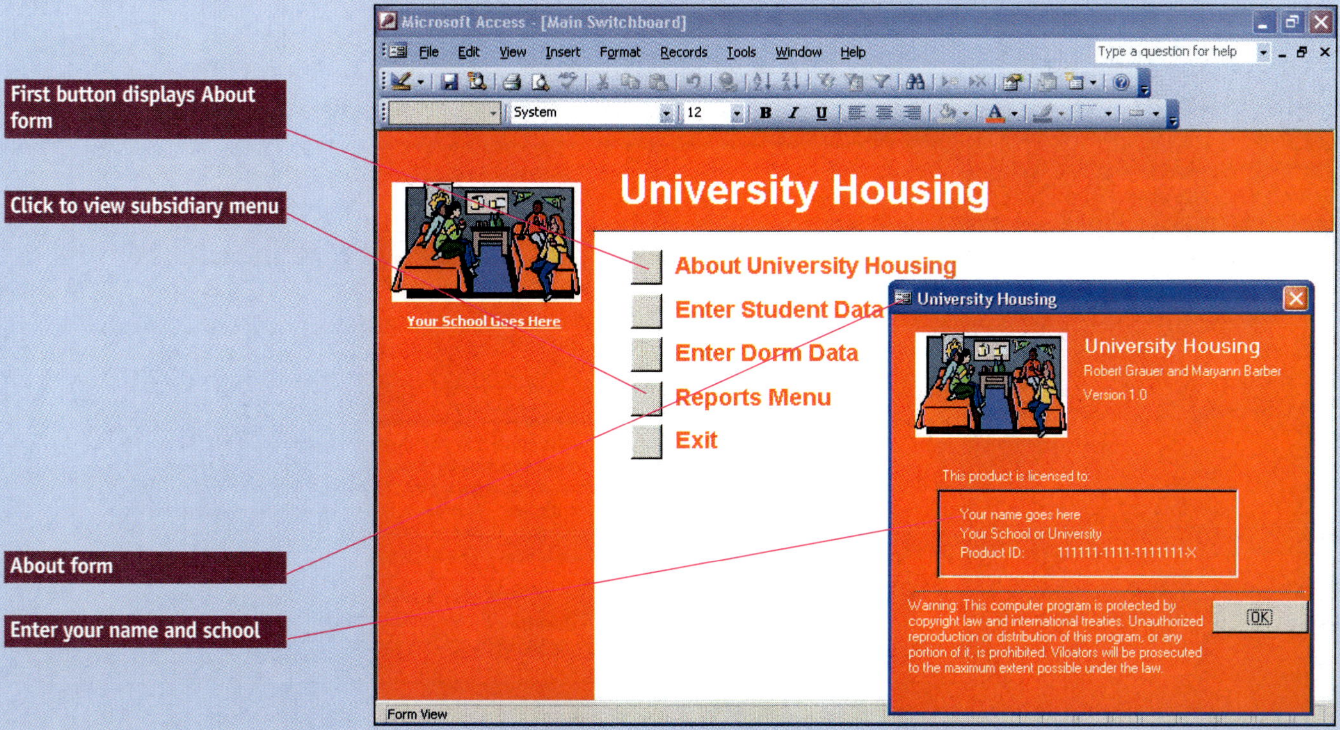

FIGURE 8 An Access Switchboard

9. **Mail Merge (Word and Access):** This exercise uses the Mail Merge facility in Microsoft Word in conjunction with an Access database. You will be asked to create two different form letters. Each letter is sent to a different set of recipients. You can start the merge from either application. Proceed as follows:
   a. Open the partially completed *Introductory Letter* document in the *University Housing Folder* and save it as *Introductory Letter Solution* so that you can return to the original document if necessary.
   b. Pull down the Tools menu, click Letters and Mailings, then click Mail Merge Wizard to open the task pane. Select the Letters option. Click Next. Select the option to use the Current Document. Click Next.
   c. Select the recipients from an existing list. Choose the *University Housing Folder*, select the *University Housing* database, and select the Student Mailing List query (that was created earlier) to display the Mail Merge Recipients dialog box.
   d. Add the address block and greeting line as shown in Figure 9. Move to the second paragraph and insert the indicated fields. Click the View Merged Data button to toggle between the field names and the actual data.
   e. Click the Merge to New Document button and specify the first three records, as shown in Figure 9. (There are more than 150 records in the database.) Print the three letters for your instructor. Save the completed form letter. You do not have to save the merged document. Close Word.
   f. Start Access and open the *University Housing* database. Close the switchboard. Click the Queries button in the Database window and open the Memorial Students query from exercise 7. Pull down the Tools menu, click Office Links, then click the Merge It with Microsoft Word command. Select the option to link to an existing document and choose the *End of Year* document in the *University Housing Folder*.
   g. Add the address block after the phrase, "To the Parents of". Complete the merge and print only the first three letters for your instructor. Save the completed form letter as *End of Year Solution*. Exit Word. Exit Access.

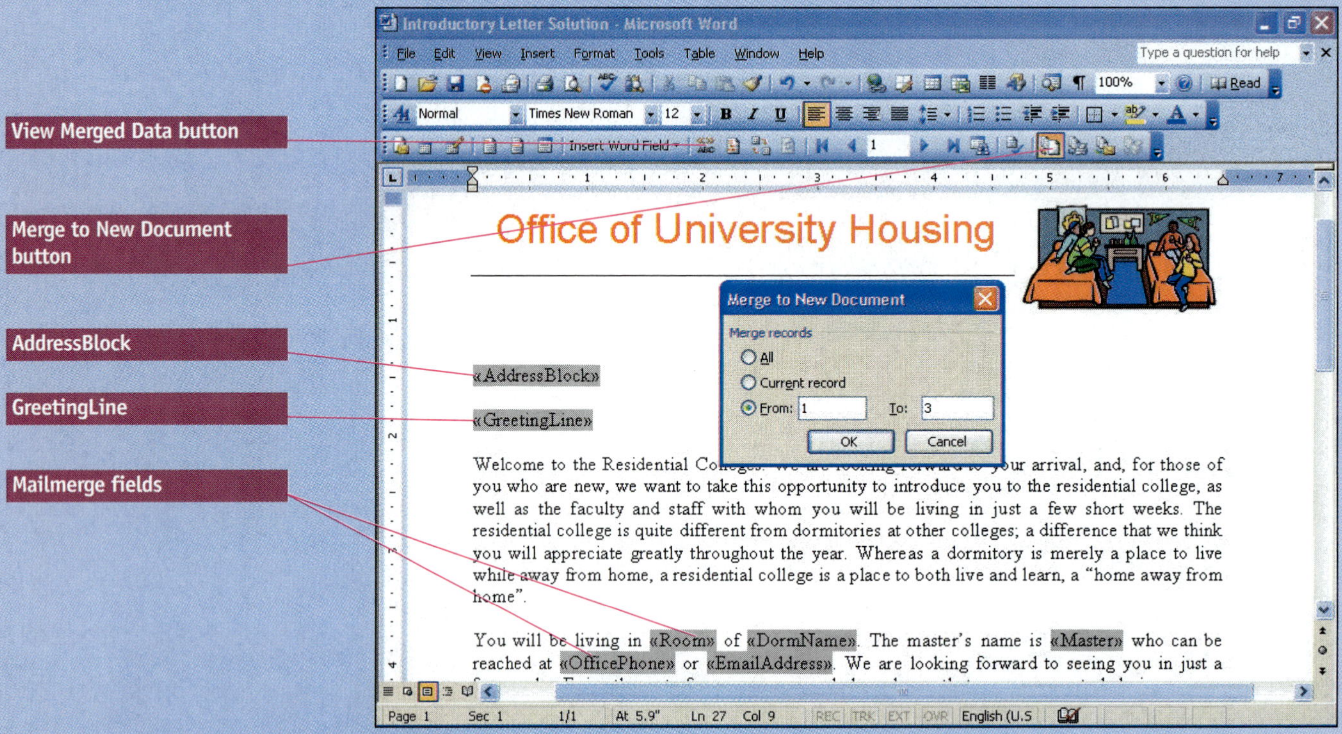

FIGURE 9 Mail Merge

10. **Worksheet References (Excel):** The Trustees have asked for a comparison of the housing revenue for this year to last year's revenue. A second workbook has been created with this information, but it is your task to complete that workbook. Proceed as follows:

    a. Open the *Historical Housing* workbook in the *University Housing Folder* and save it as *Historical Housing Solution.* (The values in this worksheet reflect the last-minute change that was made in problem 4 to the number of single rooms in Ashe Hall and Memorial.)

    b. Click the worksheet tab labeled Year to Year Comparison, then click in cell B3 of this worksheet as shown in Figure 9. Type an equal sign, click the worksheet tab labeled Last Year, click in cell F3 of this worksheet, and press Enter. The formula for this cell appears in the formula bar as ='Last Year'!F3, indicating that the value for this cell is obtained from another worksheet in the same workbook. Enter similar formulas to display the total revenues for all of the dorms for both this year and last year.

    c. Complete the entries in column D of the Year to Year Comparison worksheet that show the dollar increase from last year to this year. The cell formulas in this column should reference only the Year to Year worksheet. Add another set of formulas in column E (not shown in Figure 10) to compute the percent increase from last year to this year.

    d. Format the completed worksheet, then print the Year to Year worksheet for your instructor. Print the worksheet two ways, once to show the displayed values, and once to show the cell formulas.

    e. Create a combination chart that plots both the dollar amount of the increase and the percent of the increase for each dorm as shown in Figure 10. Display a data table at the bottom of the chart sheet. Note that the percent increases for Ashe Hall and Memorial are 6.9% and 39.5%, respectively, and reflect the earlier correction to the number of single rooms in these dorms. You do not have to print the combination chart at this time.

    f. Save the completed workbook. Exit Excel.

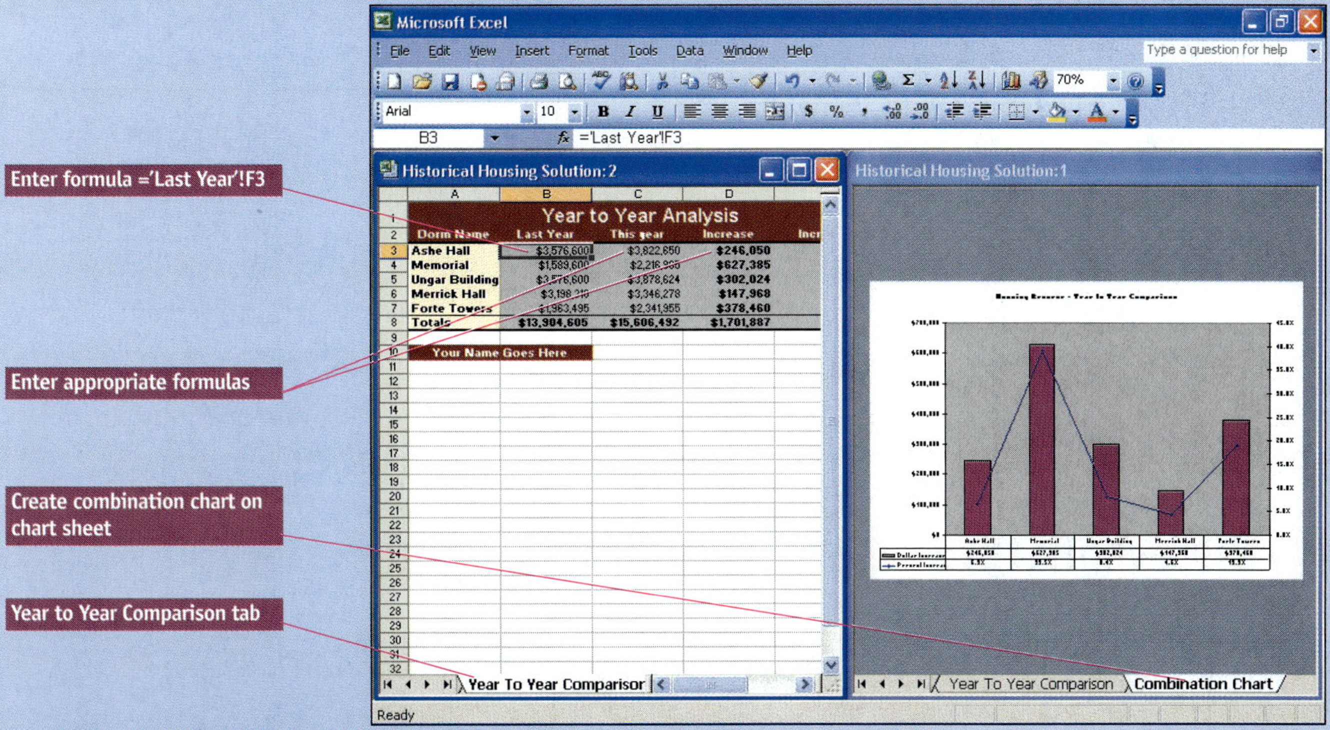

FIGURE 10 Worksheet References

11. **Presentation to the Trustees (PowerPoint and Excel):** A partially completed version of the presentation in Figure 11 has been saved as *Presentation to the Trustees* in the *University Housing Folder.* Open this presentation and save it as *Presentation to the Trustees Solution.* Your next task is to link the worksheets and chart from the previous exercise to various slides in this presentation. Linking ensures that you can change the data in the Excel workbook and have the change reflected automatically in the PowerPoint presentation.
    a. Open the *Historical Housing Solution* workbook from the previous exercise. Select the worksheet that contains revenue data for last year, and link that data to the slide containing the year-to-year comparison (slide 4).
    b. Select the worksheet with the revenue for the current year and link this data to the same slide as in part (a). Move and/or size the worksheets after they have been added to the presentation.
    c. Return to Excel. Select the chart sheet containing the combination chart, then link that chart to slide 5 as shown in Figure 11.
    d. Add the mission statement as slide number 2 by importing this slide from the *Presentation to the Provost.* (Pull down the Insert menu, click the Slides from File command to display the Slide Finder dialog box, and then click the Browse button to locate the earlier presentation.)
    e. Add transition and custom animation effects as you see fit.
    f. Experiment with a different design template, but limit yourself to five minutes. Choose the template you like best. Save the presentation.
    g. Add your name to the title slide in the indicated position. Print the audience handouts of the completed presentation (six per page) for your instructor.
    h. Save the completed presentation. Exit PowerPoint. Close the Excel workbook. Exit Excel.

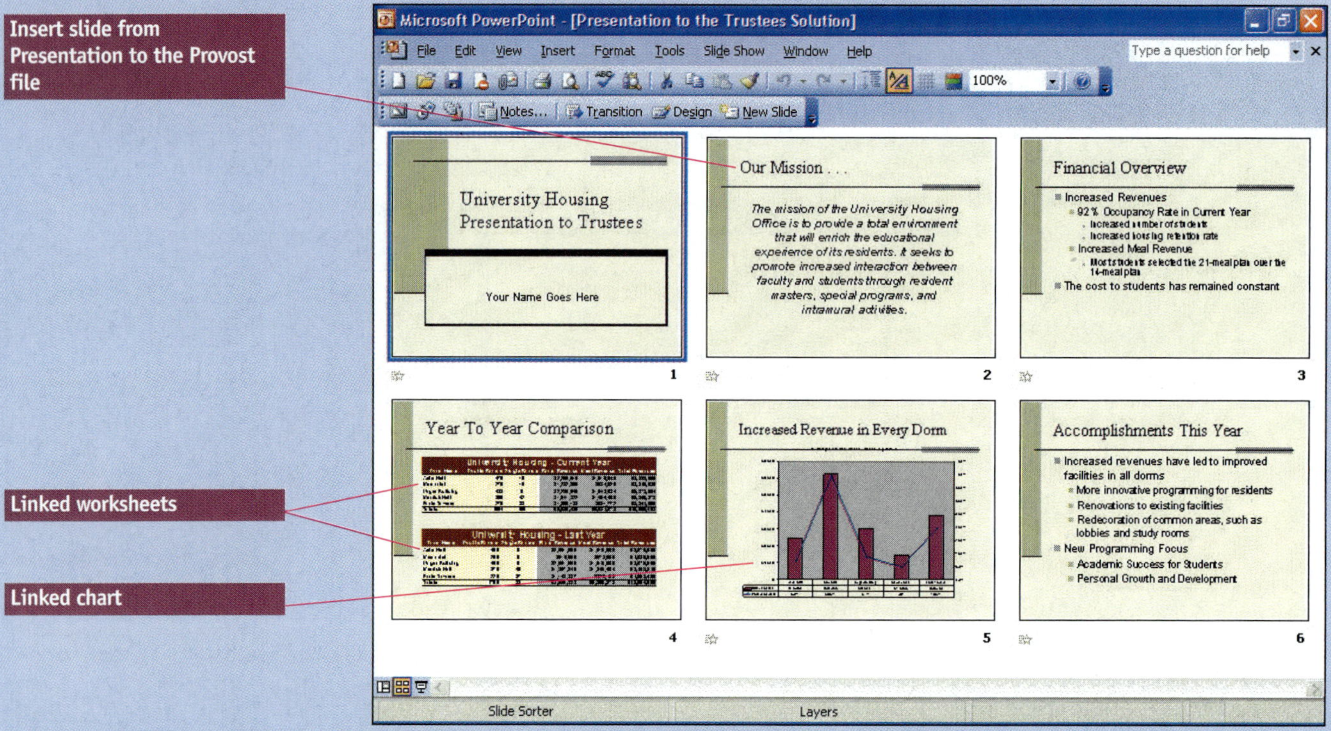

FIGURE 11 Presentation to the Trustees

12. **Letter to the Trustees (Word and Excel):** This exercise provides additional practice in linking Excel objects to a Word document. Open the partially completed *Letter to Trustees* document in the *University Housing Folder.* Insert your name as the director of University Housing. Save the document as *Letter to Trustees Solution* so that you can return to the original document if necessary. Proceed as follows to create the completed document in Figure 12.

    a. Open the *Historical Housing Solution* workbook from exercise 10 if it is not already open. Select the worksheet containing the revenue for the current year and link it to the Word document, immediately after the first paragraph. Place (link) the worksheet containing the revenue for the previous year below the first worksheet.

    b. Insert a section break at the end of the first page, then change the orientation of the second page (section) to landscape as shown in Figure 12.

    c. Return to the Excel workbook. Select the combination chart and link this chart to the Word document. The Excel chart should appear in the document. The chart may be cropped initially. If so, select the entire chart, then click and drag a corner sizing handle to make the chart smaller. Right click the chart and click the command to display the Picture toolbar. Select the Crop tool, then click and drag the side handle at the right of the chart to show the portion of the chart that may have been cropped initially.

    d. Save the completed document, and then print the completed letter for your instructor.

    e. Exit Word. Exit Excel. You're almost finished. All that remains is the preparation of a cover sheet as described in the next exercise.

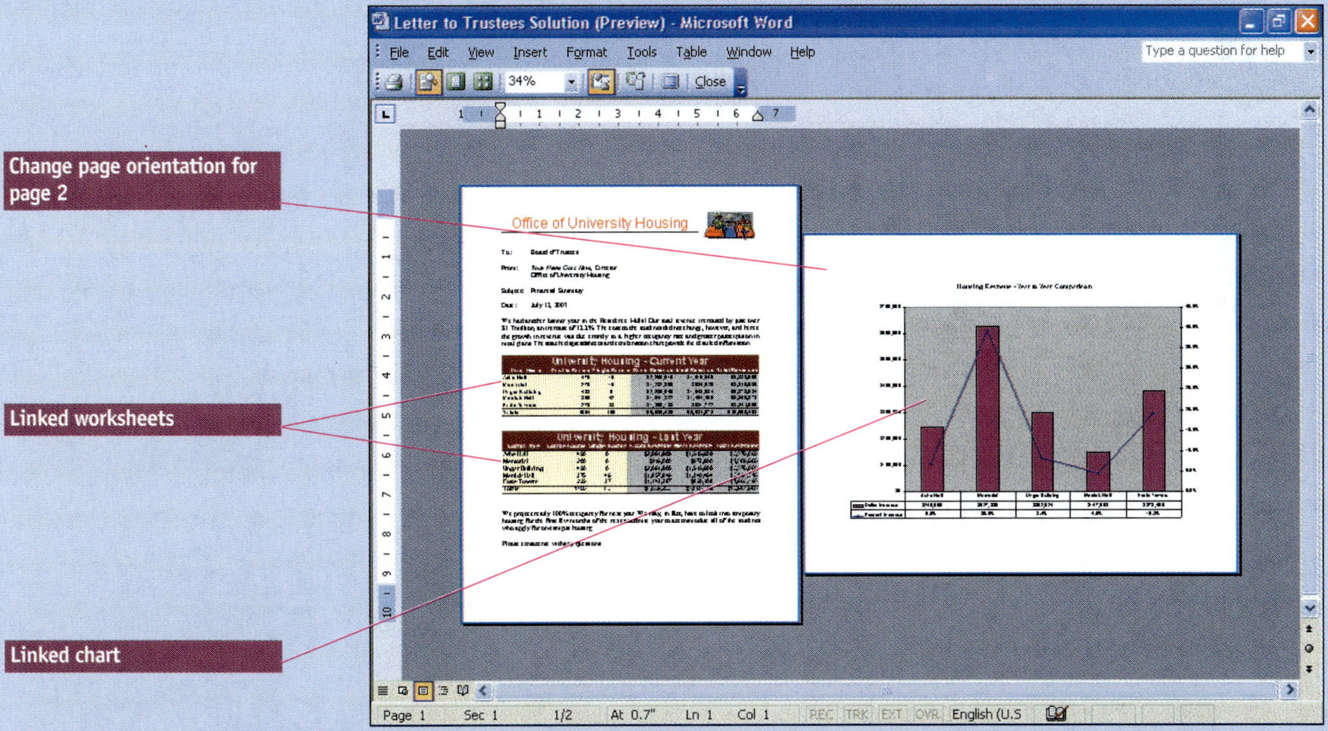

FIGURE 12 Letter to the Trustees

13. **Create a Home Page (Word):** Open the *University Housing Home Page* document in the *University Housing Folder.* Pull down the File menu, click the Save as Web Page command, and specify Single File Web Page as the file type to convert the Word document to a Web page. Click Continue when a message appears that indicates pictures with text wrapping will become left or right justified. Review the document and make the basic formatting changes you deem appropriate. Use the Format Themes command, choose any theme you like, but the overall document formatting should be similar to the document in Figure 13.
    a. Create a one-by-two (one row and two columns) table at the top of the document. Place the existing clip art in the left cell. Enter the title of the Web page in the right cell. Format the title.
    b. Select the text "e-mail us" that appears toward the end of the first paragraph. Pull down the Insert menu and click the Hyperlink command, click the E-mail Address button, and then enter your e-mail address.
    c. Our page does not contain hyperlinks to other Web pages per se; instead it contains links to various places (bookmarks) within the page. Creating a bookmark is a two-step process. First you create the bookmark, and then you create the link to the bookmark. Click immediately to the left of the paragraph on Visitation Rules. Pull down the Insert menu, select Bookmark, then create the VisitationRules bookmark. (Spaces are not permitted in the name.) Now click and drag to select the text, "visitation rules" in the second paragraph and insert a hyperlink to the bookmark you just created.
    d. Insert additional bookmarks for the Rules & Regulations and Payment Options paragraphs, then create hyperlinks to those bookmarks. Go to the end of each paragraph for which you created a bookmark, select the text, "Return to top of page", and insert a hyperlink that returns you to the top of the document.
    e. Save the document a final time, then exit Word. Start Windows Explorer, then go to the folder containing your Web page, and double click the file you just created. Internet Explorer will start automatically (because your document was saved as a Web page). Look carefully at the Address bar and note the local address (e.g., drive C). Print the document for your instructor.

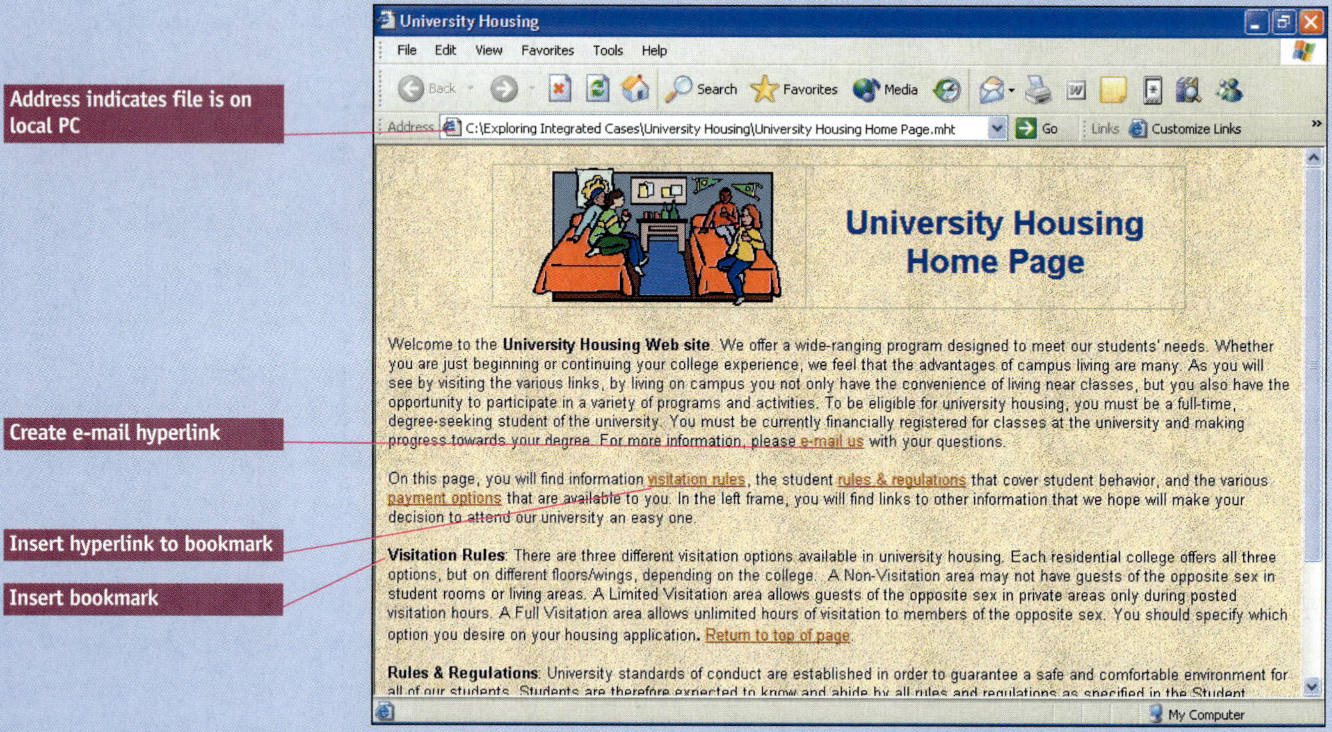

FIGURE 13 University Housing Home Page

14. **Submission Checklist (Word):** You have successfully completed multiple exercises within the University Housing case study. Each exercise described a specific task(s), required the use of one or more applications in Microsoft Office, and asked you to print one or more documents to show that you completed the exercise. The submissions checklist in Figure 14 will ensure that you have printed all of the required documents.
    a. Open the *University Housing Submission Checklist* that is found in the *University Housing Folder.* Read the document carefully and check each box after you verify that you have printed the indicated document.
    b. Add your name to the checklist as indicated, then use the checklist as a cover sheet when you submit the material to your instructor.
    c. Think for a minute about all that you have accomplished. You have completed a series of 13 exercises, which required the use of all four major applications within Microsoft Office. You have used the applications individually and in conjunction with one another. You have been able to:
        i. Dynamically link an Excel worksheet and chart to a Word document and PowerPoint presentation, so that changes to the Excel workbook were automatically reflected in the other documents.
        ii. Import an Excel worksheet into an Access database to use a table within the database.
        iii. Use an Access table as the data source for a mail merge in Microsoft Word.
        iv. Use Word to create a home page.
    d. Congratulations on a job well done!

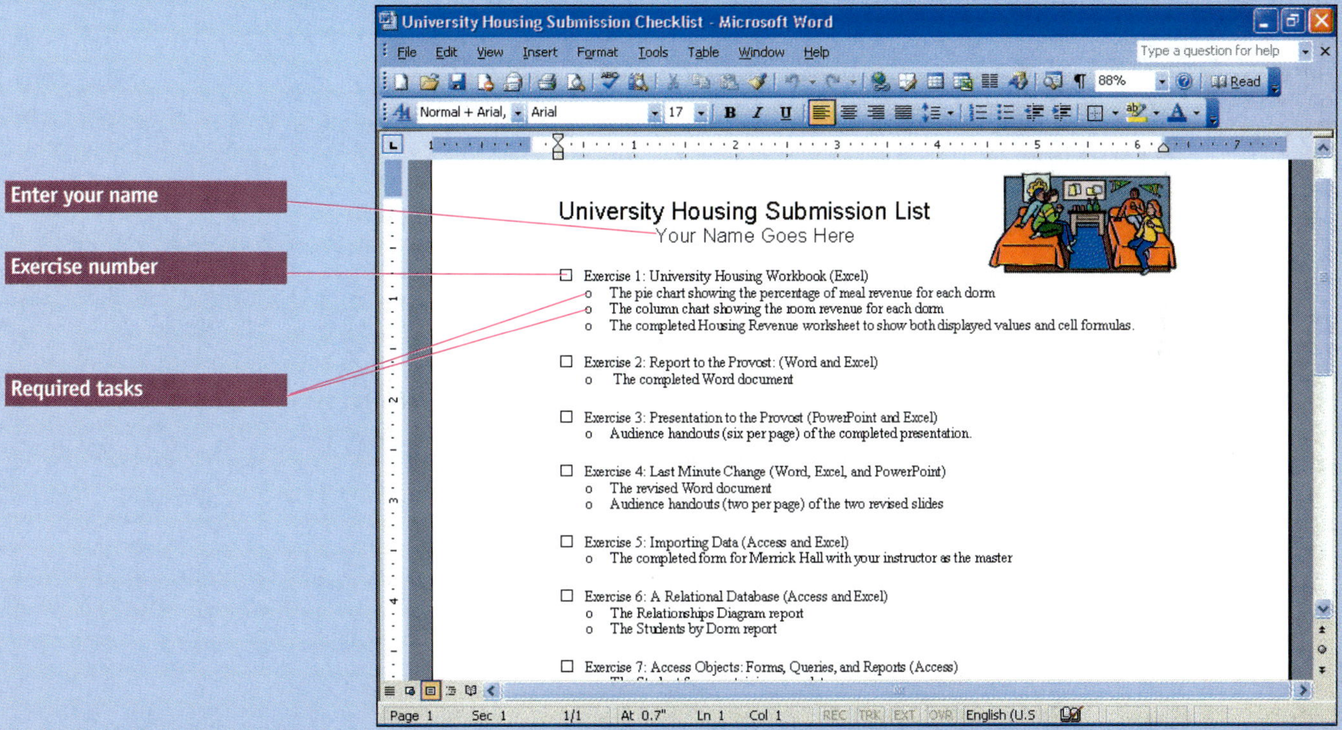

FIGURE 14 Submission Checklist

Enhanced Edition: Additional Exercises and Case Studies

DOWNLOAD THE PRACTICE FILES

1. Go to www.prenhall.com/grauer.
2. Click the book for Office 2003.
3. Click the Student Downloads tab and then click the link to download the Student Data Disk for Office 2003 Volume I Enhanced Edition. Save the file on your desktop.
4. Double click the file after it has been downloaded to your computer. Follow the onscreen instructions to install the practice files on your system.
5. The installation procedure creates four folders, one for each core application; e.g., C:\Exploring Word. (Each folder contains all of the practice files that are referenced throughout the text plus the additional files in this section; that is, you have to download and install only one file.)
6. You can use Windows Explorer to view the various folders and ensure that the installation was correct.
7. A separate installation is required for the integrated case studies that appear toward the end of this section. Follow the instructions in each case to download the appropriate file.

This section contains a set of unstructured chapter-ending case studies, additional end-of-chapter exercises and mini cases, as well as additional integrated case studies that supplement the original exercises in the main body of the text. The material is organized into three distinct sections:

1. A set of chapter-ending case studies that parallel the existing case studies that introduce each chapter: There are 18 cases (one per chapter). The new cases are best used as an end-of-chapter review; that is, they should be attempted after the student completes the chapter.
2. Additional end-of-chapter exercises and mini cases for Word, Excel, Access, and PowerPoint: These exercises are grouped by application (i.e., all of the exercises for Word appear on consecutive pages, followed by the exercises for Excel, Access, and PowerPoint) and indicate which chapter they should be used with. There are three 'common' exercises that appear in each application module. Thus, each module begins with an exercise to review file management (using the practice files for that module) and ends with a Jeopardy-type game in the form of a PowerPoint presentation. Each module also contains a new mini case that provides a series of crossword and word find puzzles written specifically for that application.
3. Two new integrated cases, *The Airport Inn* and *Definitely Needlepoint*, each of which requires the use of multiple applications within Microsoft Office for solution: These cases supplement the existing integrated cases within the original text that ran from pages 993 to 1040. ■

Your assignment is to follow the directions of your instructor with respect to which of the exercises you are to complete within this section. Remember that all of the exercises are provided as supplements to the original exercises in the main body of the text; your instructor will ask you to complete exercises from the main body of the text in addition to these exercises. A table of contents follows on the next page.

Contents

ADDITIONAL EXERCISES AND CASE STUDIES

End-of-chapter Case Studies

End-of-chapter Exercises and Mini Cases

Integrated Case Studies

End-of-chapter Case Studies

Windows Chapter 1: It Should Not Have Happened

Jessica and Brian Street own a property management company in Virginia Beach, specializing in managing vacation and long-term rental homes. It is a small and very successful business, due to the business acumen of the owners. Jessica recently graduated with an MBA, Brian has an MIS degree, and both love living and working out of their home on the beach. Brian is in charge of maintaining their database, which contains information about the rental homes and their owners, existing tenants, and pending rental requests. It is an elaborate, user-friendly system that is backed up daily. The backup files are stored on site for easy access.

The idea for the business stemmed from Jessica's initial experience renting her family's beach home, after her parents had reached a point where they were unable to enjoy the home as often they would like. They were reluctant to sell, however, as they wanted to keep the property in the family, and further, they wanted the additional income it could provide. Jessica and Brian started with one property and built the business from there. That was five years ago and the business has prospered. There were no problems of any kind until the day that Isabel came to town.

Brian backed up his files religiously and assured Jessica that they were protected against computer crashes, viruses, lost files, and so on. He never anticipated a hurricane. Their home was completely destroyed and the backup media were lost in the ensuing flood damage. Brian was stunned. All he could say to Jessica as they sifted through the wreckage was, "It should not have happened."

Your assignment is to read the chapter, paying special attention to file management. Think about how the owners of this business could have avoided the disaster had an appropriate backup strategy been in place; then summarize your thoughts in a brief note to your instructor. Describe the elements of a basic backup strategy. Give several other examples of unforeseen circumstances that can cause data to be lost.

Word Chapter 1: A Question of Ethics

You would never walk into a music store, put a CD under your arm, and walk out without paying for it. What if, however, you could download the same CD from the Web for free? Are you hurting anyone? Or what if you gave a clerk a $5 bill, but received change for a $50? Would you return the extra money? Would you speak up if the person ahead of you on line received change for the $50, when you clearly saw that they gave the clerk $5? Ethical conflicts occur all the time and result when one person or group benefits at the expense of another.

Will Ethridge, your instructor in Business Ethics, has assigned a class project whereby students are divided into teams to consider questions of ethics and society. Each team is to submit a single document that represents the collective efforts of all the team members. The completed project is to include a brief discussion of ethical principles followed by five examples of ethical conflicts. Every member of the team will receive the same grade, regardless of their level of participation; indeed, this might be an ethical dilemma, in and of itself.

Your assignment is to read the chapter and focus on the Track Changes command whereby multiple individuals can enter changes electronically into the same document. You will then open the *Chapter 1 Ending Case Study—A Question of Ethics* document in the Exploring Word folder and display the Reviewing toolbar if it is not already visible. Click the down arrow on the Display for Review list box and select Final Showing Markup to show the changes that have been entered, but not yet reviewed.

This document represents a collaborative effort in which each person's contribution is shown in a different color. Print the document in this format so that the suggested changes appear in the hard copy. Click the Show button on the Reviewing toolbar, and then click Reviewers to match the reviewers with their suggested changes. Accept all of the suggested changes, then print the document in its final form. Read the document carefully in preparation for a class discussion of the ethical decisions involved.

Word Chapter 2: The Neighborhood Association

A neighborhood association promotes interest in a community and encourages neighbors to meet one another. It also gives its members a voice in important issues such as the proposed rezoning of the 63-acre King's Dairy Barn. Mr. King, the patriarch of the family, has recently passed away, and the property is on the market. The Hamilton Investment Company is petitioning the City Council to rezone the land to commercial status in order to build a shopping center. The proposed mall would have two large anchor stores, multiple retail stores, and several restaurants. An alternative proposal by another builder would rezone the property to one-acre residential lots.

You are very concerned about the increased noise and potential crime that another mall would bring to the area. Thus, you have contacted the president of the neighborhood association to ask if there is anything you can do to help fight the proposed mall. Her response was very positive, and she asked you to edit a flyer she created to build support. It is important that you get the attention of as many residents as possible who oppose the idea and encourage them to be present at the upcoming public hearing to voice their opinions. ■

Your assignment is to read the chapter, paying special attention to the various methods of formatting and editing a document. You will then open the original flyer that was provided to you by the president of the association, *Chapter 2 Ending Case Study—The Neighborhood Association*. Your task is to reformat the document to persuade residents to attend the public meeting. You can use color and/or clip art as appropriate. (Use the Help menu to learn how to insert clip art into a document.) Print the completed flyer for your instructor.

Word Chapter 3: The Job Search

As the Director of Human Resources, you are responsible for the overall hiring process for your company. It's a tough economy, and the number of qualified applicants far exceeds the number of available jobs. Although a personal response to each individual is preferable, the volume of résumés for each new position makes this impossible. Hence form letters are routinely used to expedite the process of accepting and rejecting prospective candidates. Your current task is to process the 26 applicants who responded to last week's posting for the Director of Marketing position.

After reviewing the résumés, and conducting a brief phone interview with each candidate, you have narrowed the field to three individuals—Chris Rogers, CJ Johnson, and Helen Nunez, who are to be invited to onsite interviews. The other candidates are to be told that their experience does not meet your current requirements and you regret that you are unable to offer them a position. You want to thank them for applying and wish them every success in finding work. ■

Your assignment is to read the chapter, paying special attention to the topic of a mail merge. You will then write two form letters: the letter inviting the successful candidates to an onsite interview and the rejection letter for the other applicants. Both letters are to use the same corporate letterhead, which you will design. Use your imagination to create a name for your company as well as an attractive logo based on existing clip art.

After you have created the first letter, start the Mail Merge Wizard, then use the *Chapter 3 Ending Case Study—The Job Search* database as your data source, but be sure to select only the three employees that you want to interview. Print the letters to these candidates for your instructor. Open the second form letter and use the same database, but this time select all employees except the three you want to interview. This time, however, print only the form letter. Add a cover sheet to complete the assignment.

Word Chapter 4: The Picky Professor

Every college and university has an instructor or professor with a reputation of being difficult to please because of the high demands that are placed on his/her students. Jerome Grant is that professor in your school. What is interesting, however, is that years later, when you look back at your learning experience, these are the individuals and classes you remember the most because you were forced to work harder than usual. As a result, the lessons you take away from such courses tend to make a lasting impression on you.

This semester you are taking a class from such a professor, who requires a term paper, which is due at the end of the semester. The paper is worth eighty percent of your final grade, and it is absolutely necessary that you submit a polished, appropriately formatted document. The requirements for the paper are included in the syllabus and repeated below. Be sure you do not miss anything!

"The term paper shall include all of the following: an Introduction, Part A, Part B, and Conclusions. Points will be deducted for not using headings, subheadings, and bullets (within appropriate sections). Pages are to be numbered appropriately, and a table of contents should appear after the title page. (The title page should not include page numbers.) Footnotes are required as is a bibliography at the end of the paper. Styles are to be used throughout the document, to promote uniform formatting of similar sections. The paper is to be of an appropriate length, long enough to cover the material, but short enough to keep it interesting. Use a 12-point serif font for the body of the document. The text should be double-spaced, fully justified, with one-inch margins. This is a college-level course, and I will grade accordingly." ■

Your assignment is to read the chapter and focus on working with advanced features such as styles, headers and footers, page numbers, and a table of contents. You will then open up the *Chapter 4 Ending Case Study—The Picky Professor* document and implement the appropriate formatting to meet the requirements of your professor. You are also required to insert four footnotes into the document (your choice of location). Print the completed document as your term paper for submission to your instructor.

Excel Chapter 1: Weddings by Molly

Molly Ketcherside is a wedding consultant who specializes in all aspects of wedding planning for her clients. Although more and more couples are striving to cut costs by handling the majority of the planning on their own, Molly is successfully growing her business based on a proven history of superbly run events resulting in many happy newlyweds. She offers her clients a complete wedding package that includes the cocktail hour, dinner, and beverage (including alcohol). The client chooses the type of dinner (e.g., chicken, salmon, filet mignon, or some type of combination), which determines the cost per guest, specifies the number of guests, and the cost of the reception is obtained by simple multiplication.

Molly provides a detailed budget to all of her clients that divides the cost of a wedding into three major categories—the ceremony, the reception (based on the package selected), and other items such as music and photography. She asks each client for their total budget, and then works closely with the client to allocate that amount over the myriad items that will be necessary. Molly promises to take the stress out of planning, and she advertises a turnkey operation, from invitations to thank-you notes. She assures her clients that their needs will be met without the clients overextending themselves financially. ■

Your assignment is to read the chapter, focusing on spreadsheet formulas and basic spreadsheet commands. You will then open the partially completed *Chapter 1 Ending Case Study—Weddings by Molly* workbook and enter the appropriate formulas to compute the cost of the wedding. (The worksheet already contains the estimated costs.) If you do the assignment correctly, the total cost of the wedding should be $25,000. Molly also wants her clients to see where their money is going, so you are asked to enter formulas to calculate the percentage of the total for each item; for example, the $500 wedding cake represents two percent of the total cost of $25,000. Format the worksheet attractively and add a photograph or clip art showing the happy couple. Copy the completed worksheet, then change the various cost estimates to plan your own affair. Print both worksheets for your instructor. Each worksheet should be printed twice, once to show the displayed values and once to show the cell formulas.

Excel Chapter 2: The Reluctant Entrepreneur

Ken Arnold was living the American dream until globalization and outsourcing disrupted his life. Ken is happily married, he has a beautiful home, and until recently he had a high-paying job at the local manufacturing plant. All of this changed one month ago, when Ken was laid off from the company where he had worked for 15 years. Ken's company offered a relocation package, but he does not want to move because his daughter is in high school and because his wife owns a thriving beauty shop. He has decided to make the best of a bad situation and go into business for himself.

Ken has always enjoyed landscaping and outdoor work. His home is a showplace, and through the years Ken has helped friends and family to design and implement tropical gardens. Now he needs to earn a living from his hobby. You are a close friend and have designed a worksheet for Ken that will compute the required hourly wage, based on the hours worked per week and the number of weeks worked per year, to achieve a desired income level. ■

Your assignment is to read the chapter, paying special attention to the first hands-on exercise, which explains how to use relative and absolute references, and how to create a flexible worksheet by isolating the assumptions on which the worksheet is based. You will then open the partially completed *Chapter 2 Ending Case Study—The Reluctant Entrepreneur* workbook and complete the worksheet.

Your task is to enter the appropriate formulas into the body of the worksheet so that you see the hourly wage necessary to achieve a desired level of income. Start with an initial income of $50,000 and use increments of $5,000 up to an annual income of $250,000. Create the worksheet to accommodate 40-, 50-, and 60-hour work weeks. (If you do the assignment correctly, you will see that Ken can earn $100,000 a year by charging $50, $40, and $33.33 an hour, respectively, for a 40-, 50-, and 60-hour work week.) Add a hyperlink at the top of the worksheet that points to a Web site offering tips for a small business. Format the worksheet in an attractive fashion, then print the completed worksheet for your instructor.

Excel Chapter 3: The Changing Student Population

Congratulations. You have just been hired as a student intern in the Admissions Office. Nicole Beaudry, the Dean of Admissions, has asked you to start tomorrow morning to help her prepare for an upcoming presentation with the Board of Trustees in which she will report on enrollment trends over the past four years. Daytime enrollments have been steady, while enrollments in evening and distance (online) learning are increasing significantly. Nicole has asked for a chart(s) to summarize the data. She would also like your thoughts on what impact (if any) the Internet and the trend to lifelong learning have had on the college population. The dean has asked you to present the information in the form of a memo addressed to the Board of Trustees with the data and graph embedded onto that page.

Dean Beaudry will be presenting her findings on "The Changing Student Population" to the university's Board of Trustees in two weeks. She will speak briefly, and will then open the floor for questions and discussion amongst the group. She has invited you to the meeting to answer specific questions pertaining to these trends from a student's perspective. This is an outstanding opportunity for you to participate with a key group of individuals who support the university. Be prepared to present yourself appropriately! ■

Your assignment is to read the chapter, paying special attention on how to create a Word document that is linked to an Excel worksheet and chart. You will then open up the *Chapter 3 Ending Case Study—The Changing Student Population* workbook and compute the summary totals for each year and each type of enrollment. You are to format the worksheet attractively and create an appropriate chart that shows how each type of enrollment has changed over time. You can then create the Word document, which includes the worksheet and chart, to describe your results. Submit the completed document to your instructor.

Excel Chapter 4: Bill's Autos

Bill Jennings is looking for salespeople to work weekends and a few holidays. You love cars, you need a part-time job, and you can really use the extra money. Bill has a broad inventory of used cars that is popular with college students on a tight budget. Most of his vehicles range in price from ten to fifteen thousand dollars, and Bill has worked out an arrangement with the local credit union to offer special student financing, based on 3-to-5-year time span. For the majority of these auto loans, the interest rates have recently been running between 4% and 9%, depending upon credit history and current income. Interest rates fluctuate constantly, however.

Bill has offered you a job, provided you can create an easy-to-read, one-page car-payment calculator for prospective customers. Bill admits to being a micro-manager, and he has very definite ideas on what he wants it to look like. Therefore he has provided you with a worksheet to help get you started. Knowing the value of making a strong first impression, you realize this is your chance to get started on the right foot, provided the finished product looks great, is flexible, and most importantly, is accurate! ■

Your assignment is to read the chapter, paying special attention to the discussion on financial functions and mixed references. You will then open the *Chapter 4 Ending Case Study—Bill's Autos* worksheet to use as the starting point in creating a flexible car-payment calculator. The user should be able to vary the amount of the loan, interest rate, and/or the term (years) to see the results of varying monthly car payments. It will be important to use the correct financial function and cell references when calculating the payments.

In addition, you need to add appropriate formatting to the worksheet to make it attractive enough for handing out to prospective customers. Be sure to pay attention to how it will look when printed—use various commands within Page Setup to modify the printed document. Upon completion, submit two copies of the worksheet to your instructor, one displaying cell formulas, and one displaying the values.

Access Chapter 1: The South Vancouver Preschool

The South Vancouver Preschool was founded fifty years ago, and it has played a prominent role in the community for much of that time. The school is known for its strong academic and social programs, as well as its ability to provide financial aid to needy students. The school employs a variety of fund-raising techniques, and it has come to depend on an annual auction to raise money to support special programs throughout the year. The school appeals to the parents of its students as well as the local community to donate items for the auction.

The headmaster, Kris King, is your best friend, and Kris has asked you for help in planning the auction. Kris has asked you to maintain the Access database that was created to track the items donated for auction. The hard work has already been done in that the database already exists. Your task is essentially data entry; you will record the donations as they come in, together with the name, address, and telephone number of the donor. You will then print the various reports in the database for Kris to help her plan for the gala event. The reports include a list of all donations, a list of donors and their guests, and a set of mailing labels for all donors. ■

Your assignment is to read the chapter, paying special attention to each of the hands-on exercises. You will then open the *Chapter 1 Ending Case Study—South Vancouver Preschool* database, and examine each of its objects (tables, forms, and reports). You will then use the existing Donors form to enter data about yourself. Enter a gift certificate of your choice (be creative) to be donated, and indicate that two people will be attending, that is, yourself and one guest. Print the completed form containing your data, and then print all of the reports that exist within the database. Submit all of the printed information to your instructor. Add a cover sheet to complete the assignment.

Access Chapter 2: Debbie's Fine Fashions

Debbie Berridge, a talented clothing designer, recently opened a boutique that carries her own line of fine fashions, as well as those of other local designers. Business has been taking off, and she is enjoying both the challenges and joys of owning her own business. One of Debbie's biggest successes is the semi-annual fashion show that features models drawn from her existing clients. Prior to each show, Debbie and her staff make personal calls to each of her customers, inviting them to the show. The calls are very time consuming, but they always produce a good turnout.

The detailed tracking of each customer's individual data has created quite a paper trail, and Debbie has decided to store the data electronically. She will start by collecting simple demographics (name, address, telephone number, and so on). She also wants to store the customer's dress size (P,S,M,L,XL), whether the customer wants to be on her mailing list, whether the customer wants to attend fashion shows, and whether the customer is interested in modeling for these special events. Debbie also plans to add a notes section to keep track of any special preferences for each client. All of this information will help her to reduce the number of calls she has to make prior to each show.

Your assignment is to read the chapter and create a database for Debbie. You can use the Table Wizard to create a Customers table, but you will have to modify the table to include all of the required data as per the case description, and further to set the properties of the individual fields as appropriate. You will also need to create a form in which to enter the data. The Form Wizard is a good place to start, but you will have to modify the result to include command buttons, a suitable piece of clip art in the form header, and appropriate formatting throughout. Use the completed form to enter data about your instructor, indicating whether or not he/she wishes to attend a fashion show.

Access Chapter 3: The Garden Club

The Coral Springs Garden Club is a highly regarded civic organization known for its community projects that are funded in part by the members opening up their homes for an annual garden tour of eight to ten gardens. Stephanie Wall, your favorite aunt, has been an active member for several years, and she was just elected president. It is a prestigious position, but Stephanie needs your help. The membership has grown significantly, yet fundraising is down, and the club has had to cut back on its projects. Your aunt is convinced that the club's enthusiasm is as strong as ever and that all she needs is an efficient way to reach out to its membership.

The club is automated to the extent that it has an Access database with a Members table and associated form. The data entry works well, but little if any information is generated from that data; the database contains only a single membership report. Your aunt would like several additional reports, and she has asked you to take a Saturday afternoon to mine the available data. In particular, she wants to know which members have indicated a willingness to open their homes for the garden tour so that she can begin to plan next year's event. Stephanie also wants a list of members who have donated more than $25 to the club. You love your aunt, and as she stated jokingly, it is one way to get your hands dirty!

Your assignment is to read the chapter and focus on how to create queries and reports that generate specific information. You will then open the *Chapter 3 Ending Case Study—The Garden Club* database and use the existing form to add yourself as a member, indicate that your home is available for garden tours, that your last donation was $100, and that you would like to be included on every mailing. You will then create the reports (and associated queries) that were requested by your aunt. Use the existing report as a guide in the design of the new reports. Print a copy of the two reports you created (your name should appear on both) and submit them to your instructor as proof you completed the case study.

Access Chapter 4: The Disc Jockey

Tim Bozik has loved music as long as he can remember, from rock to rap, from disco to classical. He is very successful professionally, but what he really enjoys are his weekend gigs as a disc jockey. It began innocently enough—he would spin records at fraternity parties and family gatherings. Then a friend submitted his name as a guest DJ on local radio, which led to a regular spot at "The Parthenon." Tim would gladly do it for free, but the fact that he is paid makes it even better.

Tim has an extensive music collection on various media that he wants to catalog within an Access database. He envisions three tables—Artists, Albums, and Songs—with the appropriate one-to-many relationships between Artists and Albums, and between Albums and Songs. The Songs table is the most important, as it is to include an OLE field whereby Tim can store a clip of the actual song. The Albums table should contain the title of the album, the genre, the media type, year of release, the name of the label, and the price that Tim paid for the album. The Artists table should contain the artist's name and notes about the artist. (For the sake of simplicity, Tim has decided on one artist per album.) Be sure to include all necessary fields and set the properties appropriately.

Your assignment is to read the chapter, paying special attention on how to create a one-to-many relationship and enforce referential integrity. You will then create a new database with the required tables for the Disc Jockey database. (You do not have to enter data into all of the tables.)

Your database should also include a basic switchboard, an About form, and a relationships diagram. Use a common clip art image and consistent design elements for each object in the database. Print the switchboard form, the table of switchboard items, the relationships diagram, and the About form for your instructor.

PowerPoint Chapter 1: Go Back in Time

Eileen Clark, your professor in World History, has created a very interesting assignment this semester. Each student is to choose a particular voyage, trip, expedition, or journey of interest and create a ten-minute presentation from the perspective of the individual(s) who traveled. You have been told to create the presentation (text only) in PowerPoint, using information from the Internet, and to keep it to 6–8 slides. However, there is a twist to the presentation—the audience you are presenting to represents the financial sponsors of your travels (i.e., those who are providing you with whatever provisions you will need to successfully complete your trip). It is up to you to convince them that your idea is worthy of their sponsorship.

Your presentation will need to include an explanation of the current situation, detailing potential reasons for the voyage; a brief outline of the plan; a list of provisions; the personal qualifications of the leader(s) of the voyage; and (as that leader) why you think you have what it takes to make the journey. In addition, you need to request what you will want in return for completing a successful expedition!

Professor Clark cited several explorers; among them were Lewis and Clark, Captain Cook, and Christopher Columbus. There are many others for you to choose from—it is up to you to determine who you would want to be and what you might like to have discovered!

Your assignment is to read the chapter, paying special attention to the section on how to use the Internet as a resource when creating PowerPoint presentations. Then you will need to create a PowerPoint presentation from scratch, based on an exploration and explorer of your choice that includes material from the Internet. You will need to conduct your research on the Web and be sure to cite your references. You may want to use an appropriate background or a piece of clip art as well. Submit the completed presentation to your instructor, preferably in handouts of four per page.

PowerPoint Chapter 2: Before and After

It is 3:15 on Friday afternoon, and you are in another meeting, sitting through another dull and unimaginative presentation. You catch the eye of Gitti Lindner, your good friend and colleague, who is as bored as you. Indeed, you can't help thinking what a wasted opportunity this presentation is on the part of the speaker. The subject is important, but the speaker failed to capitalize on the chance to win support for his project; his credibility diminished as he droned on and the audience continued to lose interest. Yes, it is tough to sit through a presentation that doesn't hold your attention, but such presentations are delivered every day in classrooms and companies around the world.

You and Gitti both know that the experienced PowerPoint professional uses a variety of techniques to create interest in a presentation. The right piece of clip art adds a touch of humor, while using a photograph as the background of a slide creates an entirely different look. A chart is almost always better than an endless stream of numbers. Too much color or too many fonts and special effects are just as bad as a monochromatic presentation without any special effect whatsoever. Everyone agrees that creating an interesting presentation is easier said than done, but your instructor has challenged you to enliven an existing and notoriously dull effort.

Your assignment is to read the chapter, paying special attention on how to enhance a presentation by adding appropriate elements as described throughout the chapter. You will then open the *Chapter 2 Ending Case Study—Before and After* presentation, and modify each of the six slides to create a more effective presentation. Change the slides as you see fit; for example, add or delete text to clarify a concept, insert clip art, create a chart, use photographs effectively, add animation, and/or change the template. Retain the original slides in your finished presentation so that you see the effects of your changes and truly have a "before and after" view of the presentation. Use the Rehearse Timing command to practice the presentation, and then save the presentation with the timings in effect. Compare your solution to that of your classmates to see who is the most innovative.

Internet Chapter 1: A Billion Here, a Billion There

"A billion here, a billion there, pretty soon it adds up to real money." This quote is attributed to the late Everett Dirksen, a Republican from the state of Illinois who served in the Senate from 1951 until 1969. Senator Dirksen was referring to the Federal debt, which had reached (the then staggering sum of) more than $300 billion. Thirty-five years later, the deficit is approaching $500 billion and the debt is more then $7 trillion, yet much of the country is blissfully unaware of the potential consequences. Take a quick survey of your classmates to see if they know the current amount of the national debt and/or the difference between the debt and the deficit.

Some debt is acceptable. Most people could not, for example, purchase a home without a mortgage, and many others need to borrow money to buy a car or to finance their education. But how much debt is too much? Excessive credit card balances, for example, threaten your financial security, and virtually everyone should be alarmed by a credit card balance in excess of $1,000. Would it surprise you to learn, therefore, that "your share" of the national debt (the amount of money owed by the United States divided by the population) is approximately $25,000, and that it is currently increasing by $1,500 a year?

Your assignment is to read the chapter and focus on how search engines are used to derive information from the Web. Choose your favorite search engine and obtain the answers to the following questions. What is the difference between the national *debt* and the *deficit*? What is the approximate population of the United States? What is the projected deficit (or surplus) for the current fiscal year? How much is this per person? What is the current amount of the national debt? How much is this per person? What was the national debt in the year you were born? In the year your father was born? What does this information say about the economy and fiscal responsibility of our elected officials over the last 40 years? Submit the answers to your instructor in writing. Be sure to cite the URL (Web page) for each answer.

Concepts Chapter 1: The Case of the Missing Files

Jessica Garcia owns a rapidly growing mortgage brokerage business that specializes in first-time buyers as well as refinancing of existing mortgages. Interest rates have never been lower and business has never been better. There are currently five full-time employees, and Jessica plans additional expansion.

The office runs on a local area network (LAN) with dual servers for reliability. Windows XP Professional is the operating system on the server, and Windows XP Home edition is on each workstation. Stringent backup procedures are in place, consisting of a daily backup of pertinent (data) files, and a weekly backup of all files on the server. The corporate edition of Norton Antivirus is on the server as well as each workstation with automatic updates to maintain current virus protection. Windows Update also runs automatically so that the periodic security patches from Microsoft are continually implemented.

Jessica had, until recently, insisted that all work be done at the office because she was afraid of potential security risks to her system via remote access. The recent crush of new business, however, coupled with two key employees' insistence on telecommuting, has caused her to rethink her strategy, and employees are now permitted to work from home. Just three days after remote access was granted, Jessica received a phone call from a panic-stricken employee who said, "I am in deep trouble! The files I was using yesterday are gone!"

Your assignment is to read the chapter, concentrating on the sections that describe local area networks, backup procedures, and computer viruses. Put yourself in Jessica's place and attempt to troubleshoot the situation by thinking of the different ways that files may "disappear" and the associated recovery procedures. Create a Word document with a list of questions she needs to ask her employee and a list of possible solutions to the problem at hand. Submit the document to your instructor once you have completed the exercise.

Outlook Chapter 1: The Performing Arts Center

The professor in your business policy course has divided the class into teams of four students each. Each team is to select an issue of interest to the local community and conduct a feasibility study of that issue as a semester project. You have been chosen as the team leader, and your group has decided to conduct a feasibility study for a new performing arts center for the city. It will be necessary for you and/or members of your team to meet periodically with community leaders to study the issue and make recommendations.

The most challenging aspect of the project will be to keep everyone up-to-date with the various activities that are taking place throughout the semester. There will be constant e-mail communication as well as face-to-face meetings between members of your group and the local community. Good communication is essential, and you have decided to lean heavily on Outlook to ensure that this takes place. You can assume that everyone is familiar with e-mail, but not everyone is aware of the other functions within Outlook. Thus, it is incumbent on you as the group leader to bring your team up to speed on the other functions within Outlook such as the Contacts list, Calendar, and TaskPad.

Your assignment is to read the chapter and complete the hands-on exercises. Your first task is to add several entries to the Contact list (your professor, three fellow students who will be in your group, and three hypothetical community members), and then assign each contact to an appropriate category. Use the calendar to schedule several appointments for one or more of these contacts. Create a task list with at least five tasks related to your project. Prove to your instructor that you have used Outlook effectively by printing various entries directly from Outlook (e.g., a monthly calendar or selected entries from the Contact list) and/or by capturing various screens as you work with the program.

PRACTICE WITH WORD

1. **Practice with File Management:** You will be using many different Word documents in this class; thus, the ability to move and to copy a file is critical to your success. Download the practice files for *Office 2003 Volume I—Enhanced Edition* as described in Chapter 1 if you have not done so previously. The result will be an Exploring Word folder as shown in Figure 1. (Your screen will differ from ours, depending on where you install the files.) Proceed as follows:
   a. Start Windows Explorer and expand the folders in the tree pane until you can select the newly created Exploring Word folder as shown in Figure 1. Change to the Details view and (if necessary) click the column heading in the Name column to display the files in alphabetical order.
   b. Select the *Chapter 1 Additional Practice 1—Practice with File Management* document in the Exploring Word folder, and write down the date and time the file was last modified. Double click the file to start Microsoft Word and open the document, which contains a series of questions regarding disk and file management using Windows Explorer. Enter your answers into the document, save the completed document, and then print the completed document for your instructor. Close the document, but leave Word open in memory.
   c. Return to Windows Explorer. Pull down the View menu and click the Refresh command. Note that the date and time associated with the *Chapter 1 Additional Practice 1—Practice with File Management* document have changed to reflect the date/time you saved the document.
   d. Click the Date Modified column heading to arrange the files according to the date they were last modified. Click the column heading a second time (if necessary) so that the most recent file (the file you modified in part (b)) appears first. Press the Print Screen key to capture this screen to the Windows clipboard.
   e. Start a new document in Microsoft Word. Press the Enter key several times, then click the Paste button to paste the captured screen into the Word document. Press Ctrl+Home to move to the beginning of the document, and then enter your name and date to complete what will be used as a title page for this assignment. Submit both pages to your instructor.

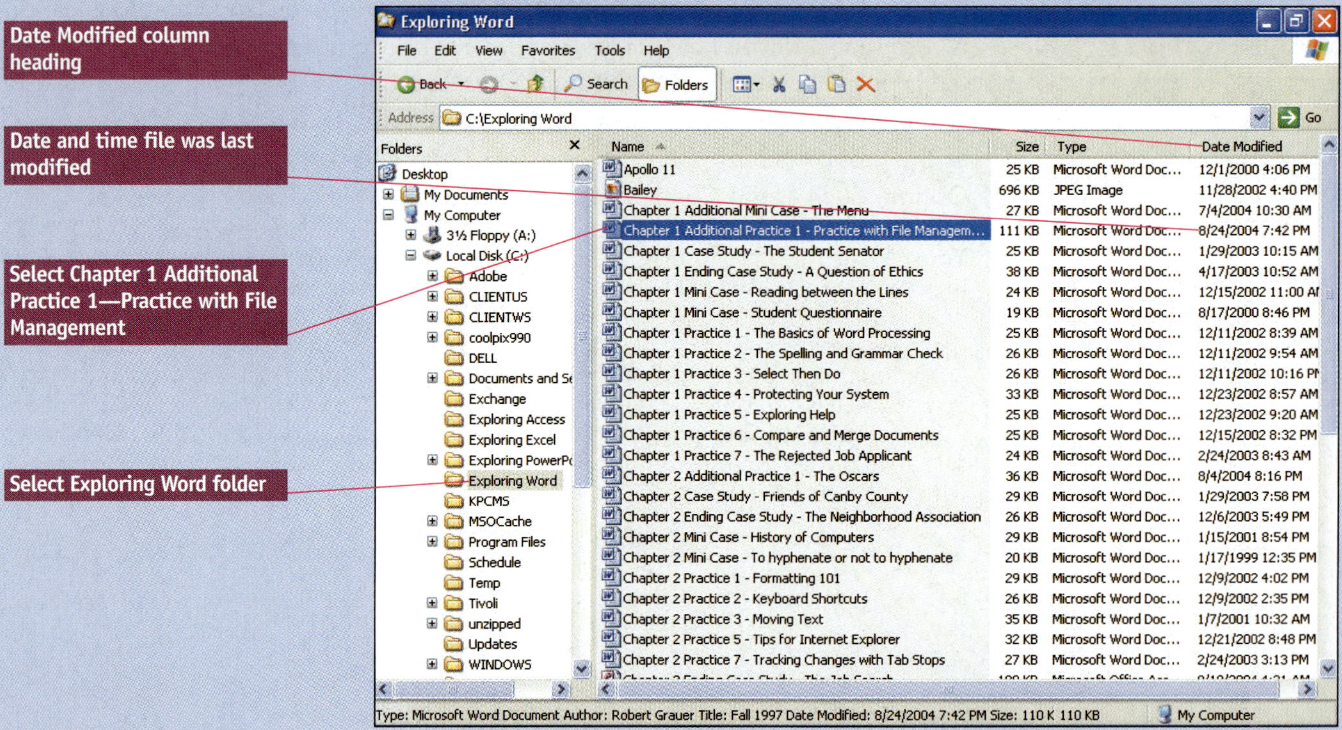

FIGURE 1 Practice with File Management (use with Chapter 1)

2. **Letters Online:** Our text will teach you how to create original documents, but you can also take advantage of existing documents (or templates) to "jump start" the creative process. This example searches for existing templates on the Microsoft Web site that can be used to write a letter. Start Microsoft Word and then proceed as follows:
   a. Pull down the View menu, select the Task Pane command, and choose the New Document task pane. Type "letters" in the Search online for text box, then click the Go button. The system pauses as it searches the Microsoft Web site, then it returns links to various letters that are available. Scroll in the task pane until you can click the link to "Letter with salary requirements". Click the Download button from within the Template Preview dialog box. The document should appear as shown in Figure 2.
   b. The document contains several bracketed fields that require information from you. Click anywhere within Your Name, then type your name, which replaces the original text. Enter your address in similar fashion.
   c. Click and drag to select your name and address, then click the Center button to center the text. Pull down the File menu, click the Page Setup command, and change the top margin to one half an inch.
   d. The date in your document should reflect the current date. Select the Date field. Click the Align Right button on the Formatting toolbar to move the date to the right side of the page.
   e. Click in the first Recipient Name field, and enter your professor's name. Enter the address of your school or university, adding or deleting lines as appropriate.
   f. Move to the body of the letter and replace Recipient Name in the greeting with your professor's name. Click in "Title" and enter "Teaching Assistant". Delete the word "open" that appears to the left of the title that you entered. Click the Justify button on the Formatting toolbar to justify the paragraph.
   g. Click at the end of the first paragraph and insert the sentence, "You also know me from class as a serious and capable student." Complete the remaining fields as appropriate. Justify the remaining paragraphs. Enter your name in the signature line. Print the completed letter for your instructor.

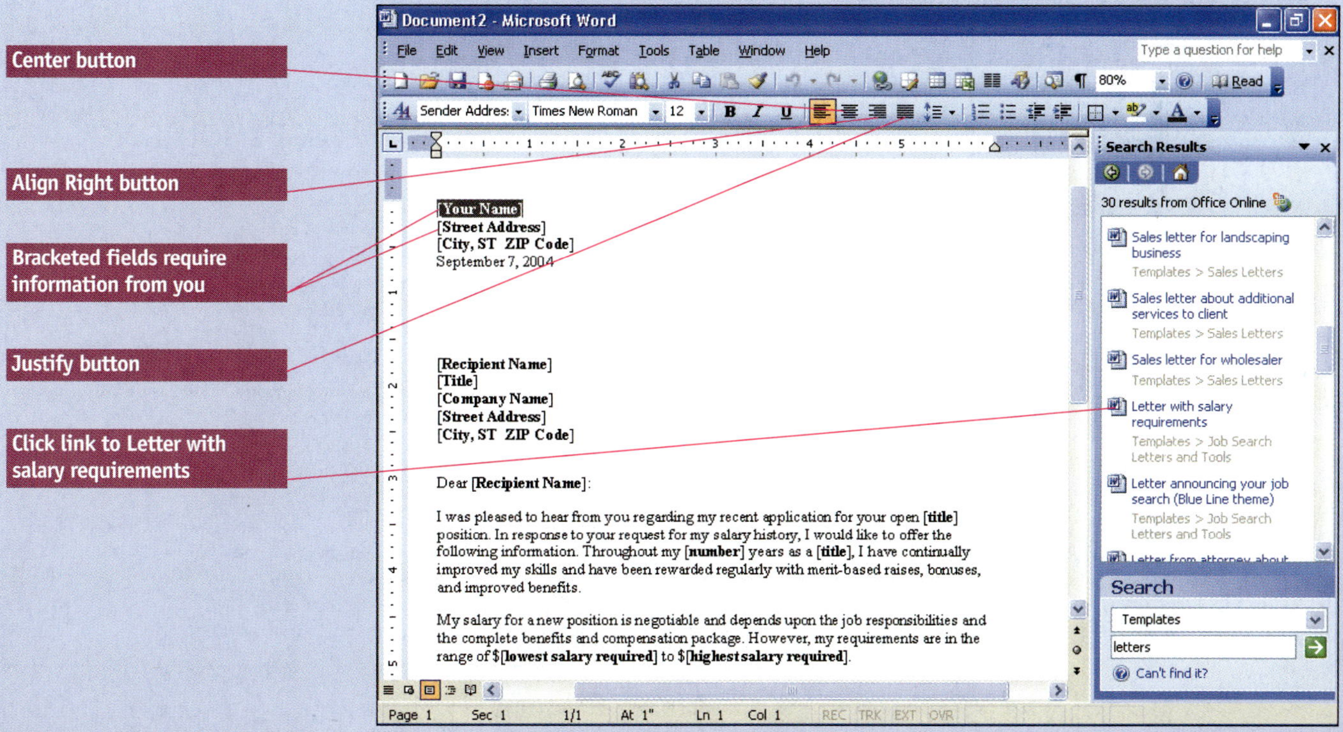

FIGURE 2 Letters Online (use with Chapter 1)

3. **The Oscars:** There are two basic ways to move text within a document. You can use a combination of the Cut and Paste commands, or you can simply click and drag text from one location to another. The latter technique tends to be easier if you are moving text a short distance, whereas cutting and pasting is preferable if the locations are far apart within a document. This exercise will give you a chance to practice both techniques.
   a. Open the partially completed *Chapter 2 Additional Practice 1—The Oscars* document, where you will find a list of Academy Awards for the best picture, starting in 1960. Go to the Oscars Web site at www.oscars.org and add any additional awards that were presented since the publication of our text.
   b. The list is out of order. Thus, your first task is to rearrange the names of the various pictures so that they appear in chronological order.
   c. Center the first two lines of text. Format the title in 25 point Times New Roman. Use a smaller point size for the second line. Use the Insert Hyperlink command (or click the corresponding button on the Standard toolbar) to insert a link to the Oscars Web site.
   d. Display the list of pictures in two columns with a line down the middle as shown in Figure 3. You will have to implement a section break because the first two lines (the title and the hyperlink to the Web site) are in one-column format, whereas the list of movies is in two columns. Click immediately before the first movie, pull down the Insert menu, click the Break command, and then click the option button for a continuous section break. Click OK.
   e. Click anywhere in the second section (check the status bar to confirm that you are in the second section). Pull down the Format menu, click the Columns command, and then change to two columns for this section. Check the box for Line between, and then click OK.
   f. Press Ctrl+End to move to the end of the document and insert a second continuous section break to create two balanced columns.
   g. Add your name to the completed document and submit it to your instructor.

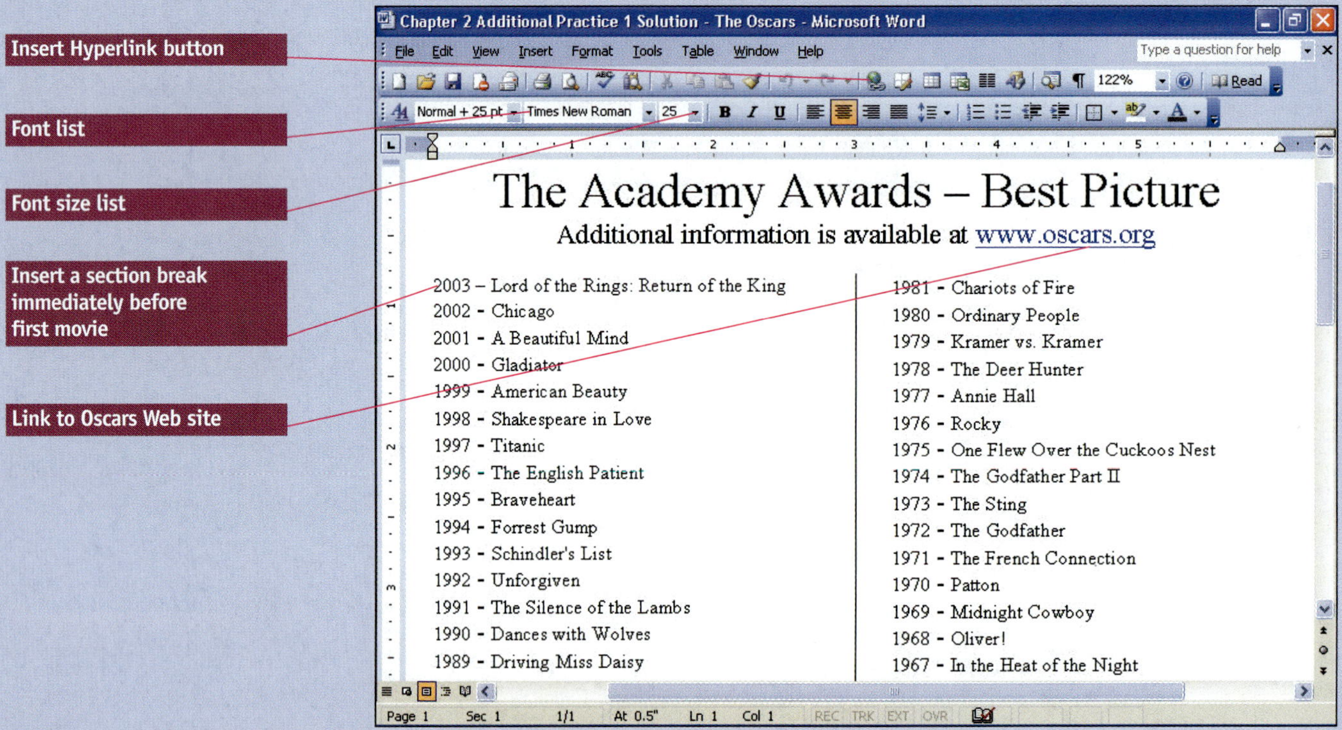

FIGURE 3 The Oscars (use with Chapter 2)

4. **The Flyer:** You can use WordArt, clip art, and photographs to create any type of flyer such as the one describing the study session in Figure 4. You do not have to duplicate our document exactly, but you are to include WordArt and a photograph. Start a new document. Pull down the File menu, click the Page Setup command, and change the left and right margins to .5 inch each, then proceed as follows:
   a. Pull down the Insert menu, click the Picture command, click WordArt, and then choose the third design in the third row. Enter the indicated text in 36 Point Times New Roman, then click OK to create the object. Experiment with the WordArt toolbar to change the shape of the object and/or its color.
   b. Right click the newly created WordArt, click the Format WordArt command to display the associated dialog box, click the Layout tab, and choose the Square layout. Click OK. Move, size, and/or rotate the object as shown in the figure.
   c. Double click below the WordArt to position the insertion point, and then enter the text of our poem. Center the text in 22-point Arial green.
   d. Pull down the Insert menu, click Picture, click the Clip Art command, and enter "computer" in the Search for text box. Click the down arrow in the Results should be list box and limit the file type to photographs. Click Go to search for an appropriate picture (you may get different photographs). Select a photograph and insert it into the document below the text.
   e. Right click the newly inserted photograph and click the Format Picture command to display the associated dialog box. Click the Size tab and change the width to 3.25 inches. Click the Layout tab and change the layout to Square so that you can move the picture more easily. Click OK. Move the picture to the upper left in our group of four photographs.
   f. Select the picture, click the Copy button, then click the Paste button to duplicate the photograph. Click and drag the duplicate picture to the lower right. Select the picture, click the down arrow on the Draw command on the Drawing toolbar, select Rotate or Flip, and then click Flip horizontal to create a mirror image of the picture. Insert a second picture and its mirror image in similar fashion, as shown. Print the completed flyer and submit it to your instructor.

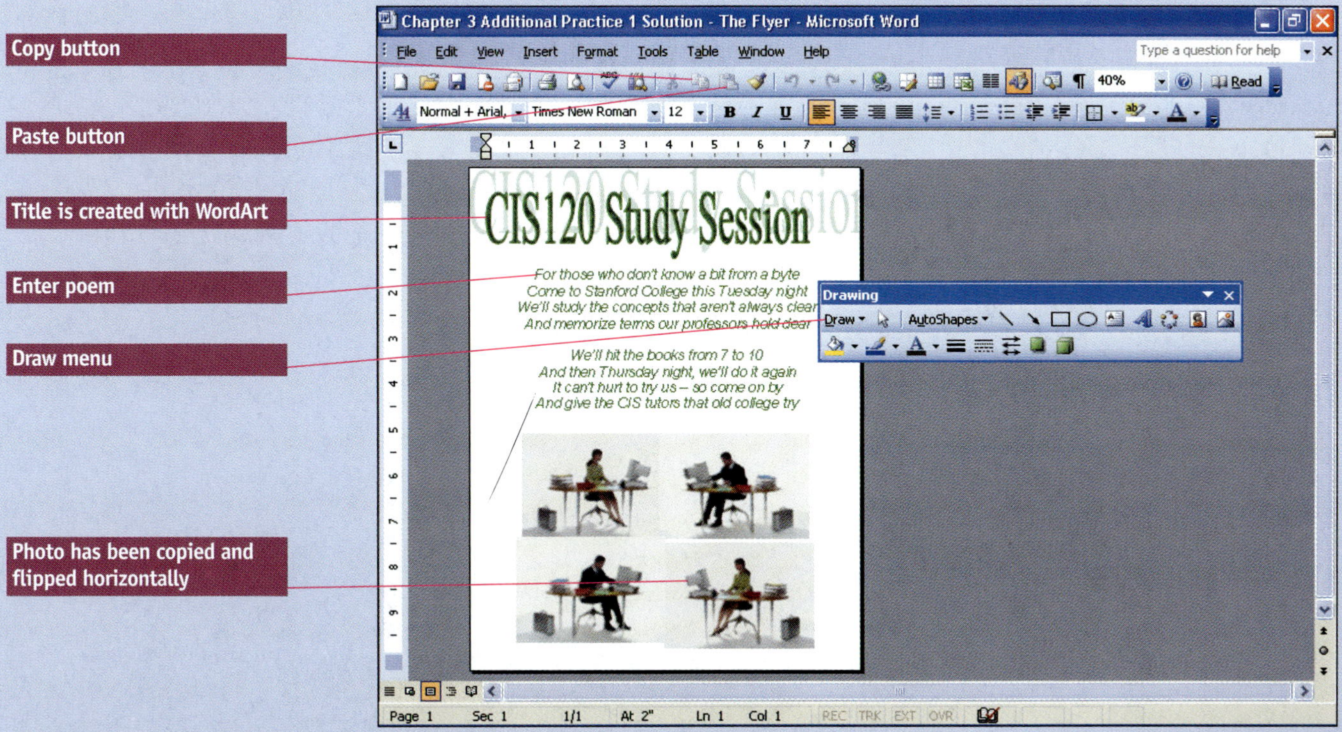

FIGURE 4 The Flyer (use with Chapter 3)

5. **Faculty Evaluations:** Many schools and universities distribute an evaluation form at the end of the semester similar to that of Figure 5. You do not have to duplicate our form exactly, but you are to provide the equivalent functionality, which includes clip art, the use of center tabs, and a symbol. Start a new document and proceed as follows:

   a. Enter the title of the document followed by the three lines of identifying information. Format them accordingly. Insert an appropriate clip art image for your form. Change its wrapping style to Square, then move it and size it as desired. Press Enter two or three times to move to the first question.

   b. Choose the font and point size—for example, 12-point Arial—then enter the first question. Type the number 1 and a period, then press the Tab key. Enter the text of the question. Press Enter to move to the next line. If necessary, press the Backspace key to delete the number 2.

   c. Pull down the Format menu and set center tabs at one-inch increments, from one inch to five inches. Pull down the Insert menu, click the Symbol command, change to the Wingdings font, select the Option button symbol, and click the Insert button. Click the Insert button four additional times so that you have five circles in a row. Close the dialog box. Click in front of the first circle and press the Tab key, click in front of the second circle, press Tab, and so on until you complete the line. Press the End key to move to the end of the line.

   d. Press the Enter key to begin a new line. Change to a smaller point size in the same font (e.g., 8-point Arial). Press Tab, type the first response "Strongly Agree", press Tab, enter the second response, and continue to complete the line. Press Enter. Press Enter a second time to insert a blank line.

   e. Select the four lines (including the blank line) that comprise the first question, click the Copy button, click after the blank line, and then click the Paste button seven times so that you have eight questions in all. Change the text of questions 2 through 4 to match Figure 5. Enter your own text for questions 5 through 8.

   f. Create a "Written Comments" section at the bottom of the document. Print the completed form for your instructor.

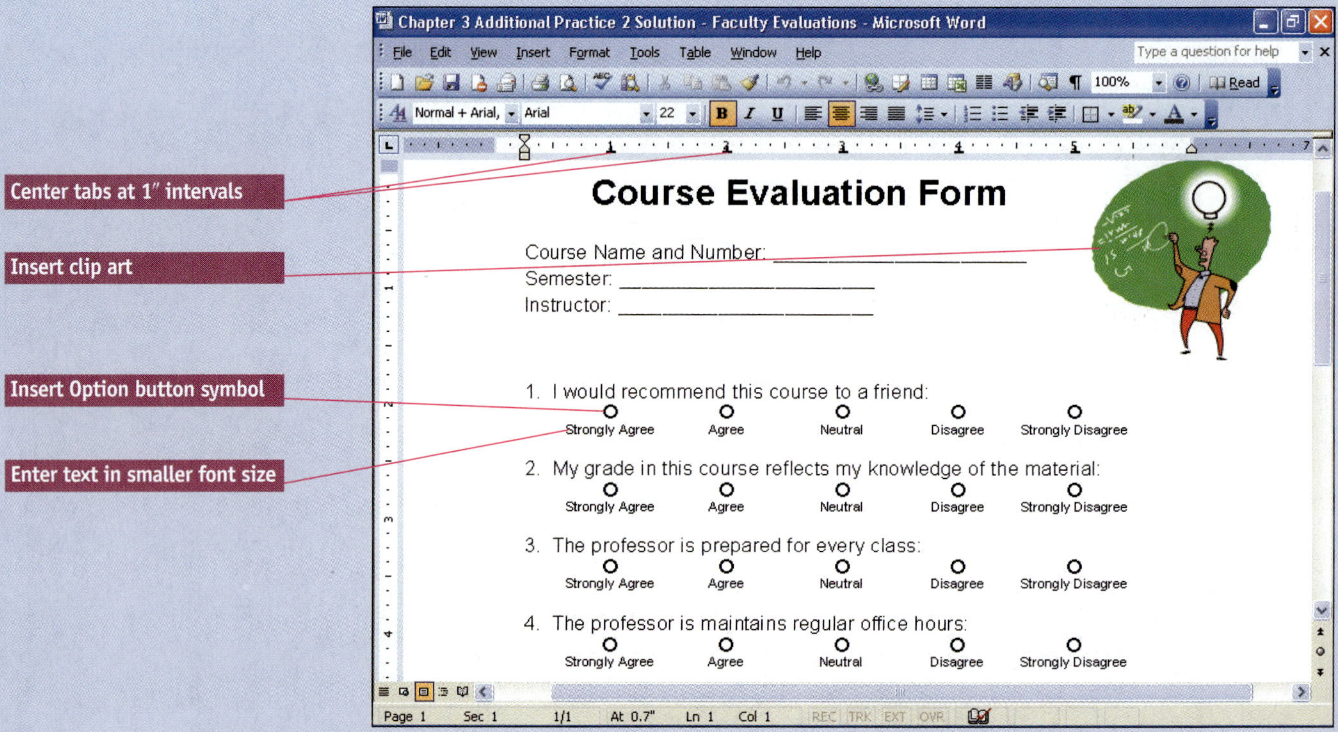

FIGURE 5 Faculty Evaluations (use with Chapter 3)

6. **Create Your Own Clip Art:** There is no way that we could have created the original clip art in the upper-right corner of Figure 6, but it is easy to create the composite document. Start Word, open a new document, and change to landscape orientation. Pull down the Insert menu, click the Picture command, then click Clip Art to open the Clip Art task pane. Enter "Artist" in the Search for text box, and then click the Go button to search for all images pertaining to an artist. Insert the desired clip art image into your document. Proceed as follows:
   a. Right click the newly inserted clip art, click the Format Picture command to display the associated dialog box, click the Layout tab, and then choose Square as the wrapping style. Click OK. This enables you to move and size the object more easily. Select the clip art, click the Copy button, then click the Paste button to duplicate the object. Click and drag the second artist away from the original. Size one of the images so it is approximately 1" square and move it to the upper right corner. Size the copy of the image so that it is approximately 3.25" wide. Move it to the left side of the document.
   b. Duplicate the larger artist, then drag the duplicated object to the right. Select the artist on the left, click the Draw button on the Drawing toolbar, click the Rotate or Flip command, and then click Flip Horizontal to turn the artist around.
   c. Click the Rectangle tool, then click and drag in the document to create a rectangle. Right click the rectangle, click the Format AutoShape command, then use the Colors and Lines tab to change the color and/or fill effect. Use a combination of the Oval and Rectangle tools to create a graphic image.
   d. The only tricky part is changing the color of the artist's smock. Right click the artist, click the Grouping command, click Ungroup, then click "Yes" in response to the message that appears. Click off the group of objects to deselect them all, and then right click the artist's smock, click the Format AutoShape command, and then change the fill color. Right click the border of the artist, click Grouping, then click Regroup to put the artist back together.
   e. Press and hold the Shift key as you click both artists and the graphic image in the middle. Right click all of the selected objects, select the Grouping command, then group the objects. Now copy the composite group as shown.
   f. Add a title to complete the document, and then print it for your instructor.

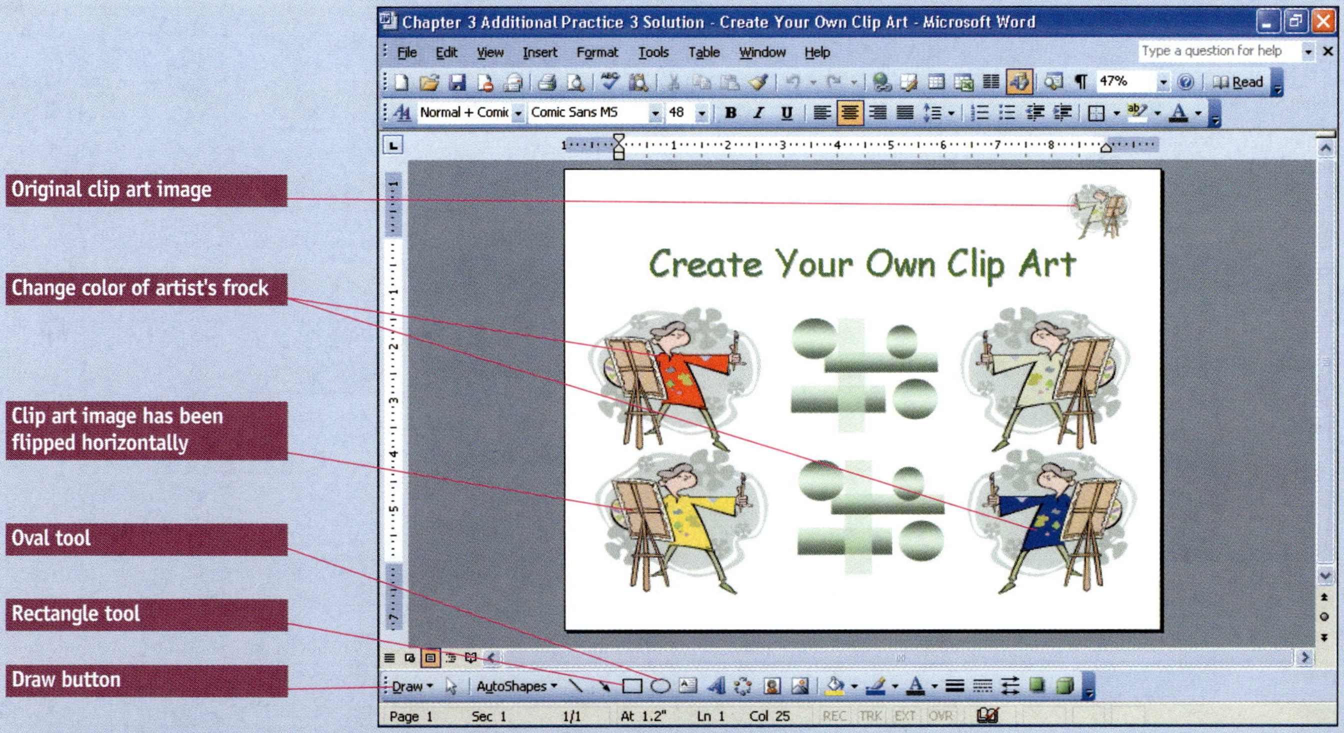

FIGURE 6 Create Your Own Clip Art (use with Chapter 3)

7. **Organization Charts:** All applications in Microsoft Office have access to the Diagram Gallery, which helps you to create and format an organization chart as shown in Figure 7. You have complete flexibility with respect to the content and/or the formatting. You can create any number of levels and/or any number of boxes within a level. You can also change the style or color of the individual boxes and/or the lines connecting the boxes. Proceed as follows:
   a. Start a new document and change to landscape orientation. Type the title of the document, format it, and then center it between the margins. Press Enter two or three times to move down the page. Pull down the Insert menu and click the Diagram command to display the Diagram Gallery dialog box, from where you can select the Organization chart. The default chart consists of four boxes that are displayed on two levels. The lower level has three subordinates reporting to the single box on the top level. Click in the individual boxes to add the names and titles as shown in Figure 7.
   b. Click in the box for the first vice president (which is the leftmost box on the second level). Click the Insert Shape button on the Organization Chart toolbar and choose subordinate. Add the additional boxes and levels in similar fashion until you replicate our organization. Click in the individual boxes to change the titles and individuals associated with each title.
   c. Click anywhere within the drawing area to display a hashed gray line, which is the (invisible) border of the Drawing Canvas, then move and/or size the chart so that it fills the page.
   d. Pull down the Edit menu, click the Select All command (to select the chart as well as the title), and then click the Copy button. Click outside the organization chart to deselect the objects. Press Ctrl+End to move to the end of the document, then press Ctrl+Enter to create a page break. Click the Paste button to create a copy of the chart and the title on the second page.
   e. Click anywhere within the copied chart to display the Organization toolbar, click the AutoFormat button to display the Style Gallery, and then choose a different design for your chart.
   f. Print both charts for your instructor.

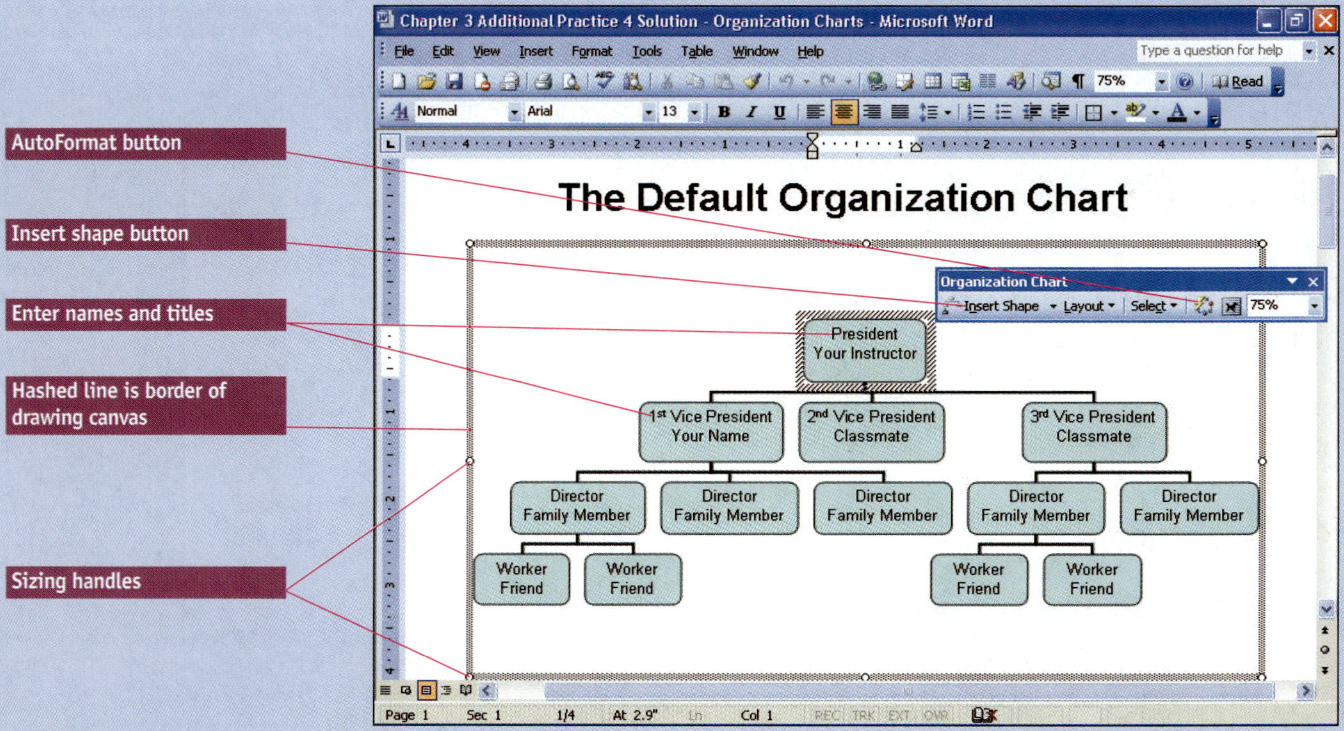

FIGURE 7 Organization Charts (use with Chapter 3)

8. **Multiple Choice Test:** The document in Figure 8 contains a multiple choice test that uses several features that were covered in this chapter. These include headers and footers, bullets and numbering, and a table. Open the partially completed *Chapter 4 Additional Practice 1—Multiple Choice Test* document and proceed as follows:
   a. Select the entire document. Pull down the Format menu, click Bullets and Numbering, and then choose the Outline Numbered tab. Select the appropriate style, then click OK. (The blank line before each question is caused by the Spacing Before option within the Format Paragraph command.)
   b. Press Ctrl+Home to move the insertion point to the beginning of the document. This action also deselects the multiple choice questions. The first question in your document should match the question in our figure. Press Ctrl+End to move the insertion point to the end of the document. The text in question 14 (the last question in the document) corresponds to the second question.
   c. Click and drag to select the five lines that comprise question 14. Click the Cut button, return to the top of the document, click to the right of the number 2, and then click the Paste button. The original question 14 has been moved and now appears as question number 2. All other questions have been renumbered. (If necessary, insert a page break after question 7 so that all parts of question 8 appear together.)
   d. Press Ctrl+End to move to the end of the document, press the Enter key to begin a new question, click the Numbering icon to enter the question number, and then enter the text of an original question. Highlight the question you just created.
   e. Press Ctrl+Home to return to the beginning of the document. Press Enter, move the insertion point to a new line, and then press the Backspace key to turn off the automatic numbering. Enter the title of the document followed by the second line as shown in Figure 8.
   f. Create a three (rows) by five (columns) table that will contain your answer key. Print the document as it currently exists, take the test away from the computer, and then enter the answers into the table within the document.
   g. Pull down the View menu, click the Header and Footer command, and then create the header shown in Figure 8. Print the completed document.

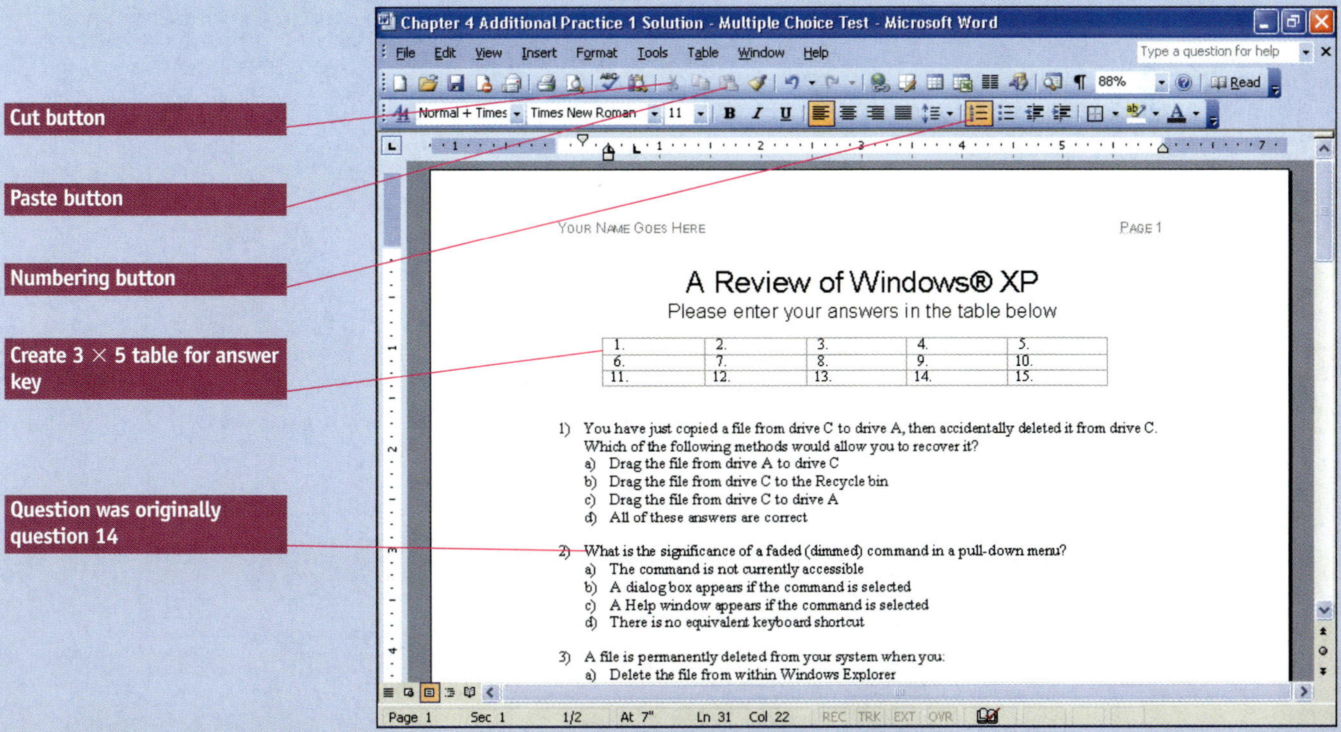

FIGURE 8 Multiple Choice Test (use with Chapter 4)

9. **The Survey:** Everyone complains about the food in the cafeteria. This assignment asks you to put your words into action by creating a survey such as the document in Figure 9. You do not have to duplicate our document exactly; you will make up your own questions and/or you can change our formatting. You are required, however, to use a table as the basis of your document. Proceed as follows:
   a. Display the Tables and Borders toolbar. Create a table with multiple rows and six columns (e.g., 20 rows and six columns). Click outside the table, immediately to the left of the first row, then click the Merge Cells button on the Tables toolbar to combine the cells. Select the new cell, click the Split Cells tool, and specify two columns.
   b. Select the left cell and drag its border to the right to increase its width. Enter and format the 3-line title of the survey in the left cell. Insert an appropriate clip art image in the right cell.
   c. Merge the six cells in the second row into a single cell, then type the instructions to the student as shown in Figure 9.
   d. Enter the potential responses in the third row (Completely Satisfied, Somewhat Satisfied, Neutral, Somewhat Dissatisfied, and Completely Dissatisfied). Do not worry about formatting at this time.
   e. Merge the six cells in the fourth row and then enter "Food Service Facility" as the first category. Type the four questions in this category in the next several rows. The only tricky part (if any) is adjusting the column width. Click and drag to select the cells in the first column, and then drag the right border to the left. The first column becomes wider as the second column becomes narrower. Select all of the cells in the second through fifth columns, then click the Distribute Columns Evenly button on the Tables toolbar.
   f. Merge the cells in row 9, enter "Food Service Staff" into the cell, then create at least three questions for the Food Service Staff category. Create a separate category for Food and enter several additional questions.
   g. Insert an additional row (containing a single cell) at the bottom of the table for written comments. Format the entire table as appropriate.
   h. Print the completed document for your instructor. You may complete the survey (fill in the responses) or not as you see fit.

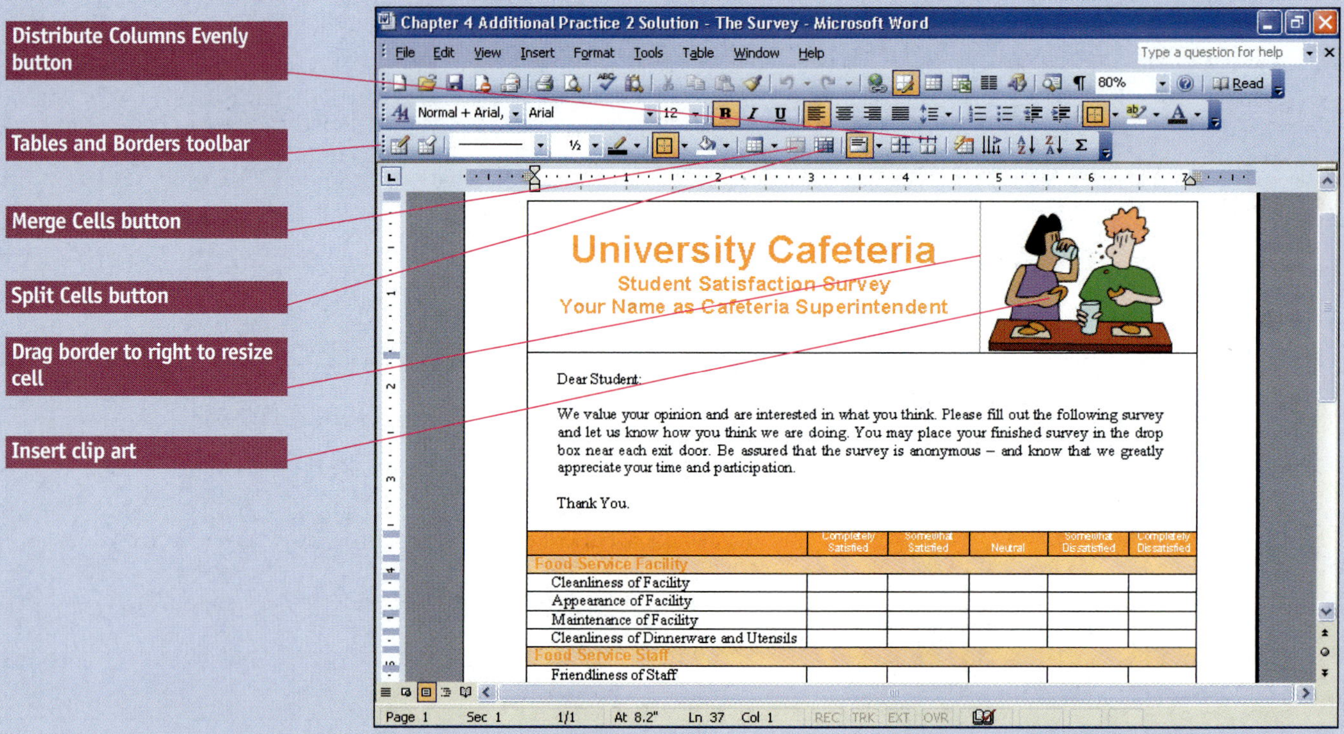

FIGURE 9 The Survey (use with Chapter 4)

10. **Word Jeopardy:** How well do you know Microsoft Word? The presentation in Figure 10 contains a Jeopardy game with 25 answers and questions that review material from Chapters 1 through 4. All you have to do is open the presentation and play the game. Thus, open the *Chapter 4 Additional Practice 3—Word Jeopardy* presentation and proceed as follows:
   a. Pull down the Slide Show menu and click the View Show command (or click the F5 key) to view the slide show, which begins with the title slide. Click the mouse to move to slide 2 (the board). The names of the categories will appear one after another, after which you can select any question in any category. Each dollar amount is a hyperlink to another slide in the presentation.
   b. Select (click) a question, such as the $800 question in the Beyond the Basics category, to display the clue, "Normal, Heading 1, or Body Text, for example". Click the mouse to display the answer "What is a style?" (that appears in the form of a question), then click the answer to return to slide 2 (the board). Before you click, be sure you see the tiny hand indicating that you are clicking the hyperlink, as opposed to clicking the background of the slide.
   c. You should be back on slide 2, the Jeopardy board. Look closely and you will see that the color of the text (i.e., the 800) has changed, indicating that the hyperlink has been followed. Select a different question, view the answer, and return to the game board so that you can be sure of the navigation.
   d. Select a classmate and play the game. There is no buzzer, so you have to determine an equitable way to gain control of the board and keep score. We leave the details to you.
   e. Print the presentation in a variety of ways. Select the first two slides, pull down the File menu, click the Print command, choose the option button for Selection, and select Slides in the Print What list box. Click OK to print. Pull down the Print menu a second time and print the entire presentation in Outline view. Study the outline and be sure that you can answer all of the questions.
   f. You will find additional games for the other Office applications (PowerPoint, Excel, and Access) in the appropriate folders after downloading the practice files from our Web site. The Excel game, for example, is found in the Exploring Excel folder and reviews material from Chapters 1 through 4 in the Excel section.

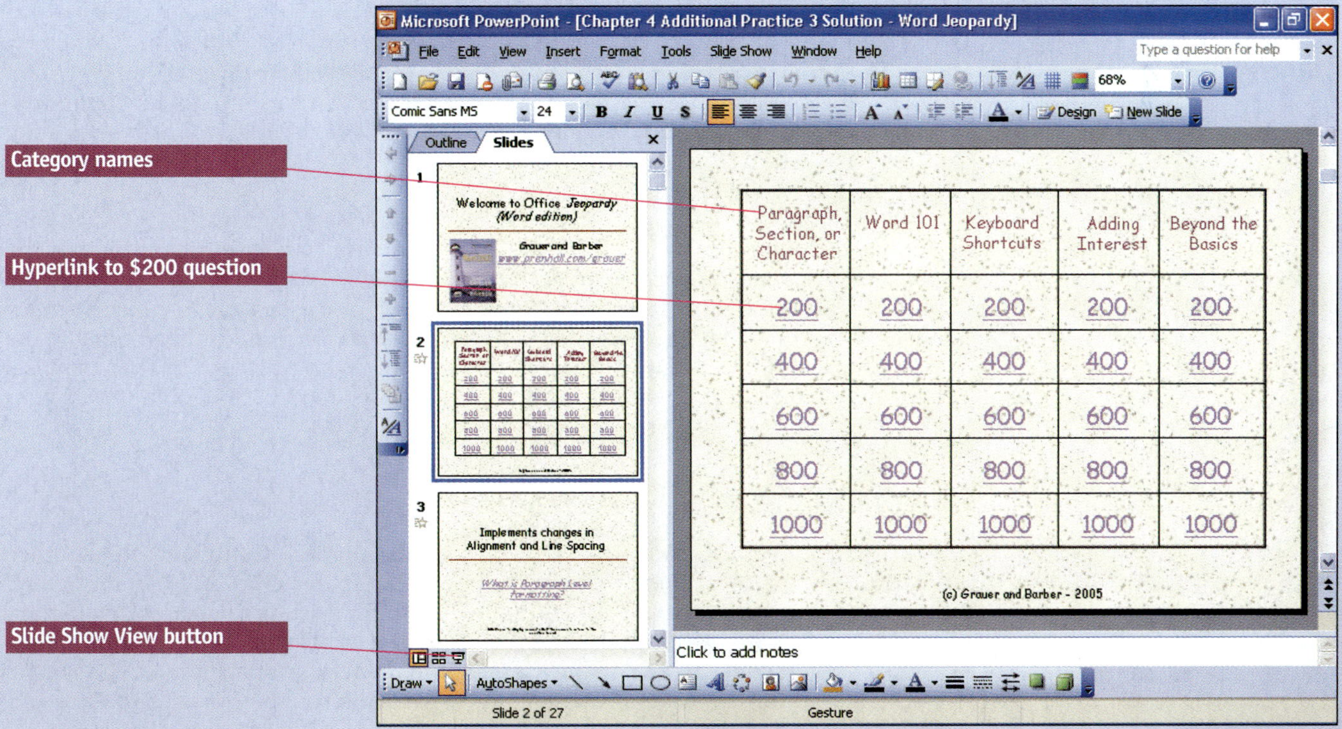

FIGURE 10 Word Jeopardy (use with Chapter 4)

ADDITIONAL MINI CASES

Study Break—Word Find and Crossword Puzzles

Almost everyone enjoys a good puzzle. With this in mind, we have created a series of unique crossword and word find puzzles to accompany the Exploring Office series. Open the *Chapters 1 to 4 Mini Case—Microsoft Word Study Break* document in the Exploring Word folder, and then print the document. You will find two puzzles for each chapter, a word find and a crossword. (You don't have to do every puzzle in every chapter.)

We suggest that you start with the word find and use the list of keywords and concepts at the end of the chapter to determine what each clue represents, and then locate the corresponding word or phrase in the puzzle. You can then try the accompanying crossword, which repeats clues from the word find to reinforce the material, and which adds additional clues to challenge you further. Add your name at the top of the puzzle(s), and then submit the puzzle(s) to your instructor. And if you are up to a challenge, try the composite (Sunday) crossword puzzle that combines the clues from Chapters 1 through 4 in a single puzzle.

Online Study Guide

Every chapter in the Exploring Office series has an online component that helps you to review the conceptual material in the chapter. Go to www.prenhall.com/grauer after you have completed the chapter and click the icon for the Office 2003 book to go to the home page for this series. Click the appropriate title in the left pane, such as Office Volume I or Word, then click the down arrow in the list box at the top of the screen to select the appropriate chapter—Word Chapter 1 for example. Click the link to Online Study Guide in the left pane and take the quiz that consists of objective questions (multiple choice, true/false, and matching).

Click the Submit Answers for Grading button at the bottom of the quiz so that you can see your results. Scroll to the bottom of the answer screen, and then e-mail the results to yourself in HTML format. (If you send the results as text instead of HTML, you will get too many pages of output.) Start your e-mail program, print the e-mail message that contains your results, and bring it to class to submit to your instructor.

The Menu

It's easy to complete a directed formatting exercise when you are given specific instructions as to the font and style to apply. It's more difficult when you have to design the document yourself. Your best friend is getting married, and she has asked for help in creating the menu. It will be a fabulous meal, and all of the menu items have been chosen. All you have to do is format the menu in Microsoft Word.

It's not as simple as it sounds. Good design goes unnoticed, whereas poor design calls attention to itself and detracts from the document. Your assignment is to open the *Chapter 1 Additional Mini Case—The Menu* and complete the document by choosing the appropriate font(s), size(s), and style(s). Your friend has also asked you to create a monogram at the top of the menu, consisting of the first initial of the bride and groom and the first initial of their last name. There is no right or wrong answer to this exercise. Experiment freely, set a time limit, and then print the completed document for your instructor.

Flyers Online

The Office Web site is a valuable resource that contains a variety of templates for all Office applications. Start Word, open the New Document task pane, type "flyer" in the Search online for text box, then click the Go button to search for existing templates that pertain to any type of flyer. You should see more than 20 different documents for various events. Download at least two of these documents and print them for your instructor. The sample flyers should prove very useful because of the attractive formatting, even if you need an entirely different document.

PRACTICE WITH EXCEL

1. **Practice with File Management:** You will be using many different Excel workbooks in this class; thus, the ability to move and to copy a file is critical to your success. Download the practice files for *Office 2003 Volume I—Enhanced Edition* as described in Chapter 1 if you have not done so previously. The result will be an Exploring Excel folder as shown in Figure 11. (Your screen will differ from ours, depending on where you install the files.) Proceed as follows:
    a. Start Windows Explorer and expand the folders in the tree pane until you can select the newly created Exploring Excel folder as shown in Figure 11. Change to the Details view and (if necessary) click the column heading in the Name column to display the files in alphabetical order.
    b. Select the *Chapter 1 Additional Practice 1—Practice with File Management* document in the Exploring Excel folder, and write down the date and time the file was last modified. Double click the file to start Microsoft Word and open the document, which contains a series of questions regarding disk and file management using Windows Explorer. Enter your answers into the document, save the completed document, and then print the completed document for your instructor. Close the document, but leave Word open in memory.
    c. Return to Windows Explorer. Pull down the View menu and click the Refresh command. Note that the date and time associated with the *Chapter 1 Additional Practice 1—Practice with File Management* document have changed to reflect the date/time you saved the document.
    d. Click the Date Modified column heading to arrange the files according to the date they were last modified. Click the column heading a second time (if necessary) so that the most recent file (the file you modified in part (b)) appears first. Press the Print Screen key to capture this screen to the Windows clipboard.
    e. Start a new document in Microsoft Word. Press the Enter key several times, then click the Paste button to paste the captured screen into the Word document. Press Ctrl+Home to move to the beginning of the document, and then enter your name and date to complete what will be used as a title page for this assignment. Submit both pages to your instructor.

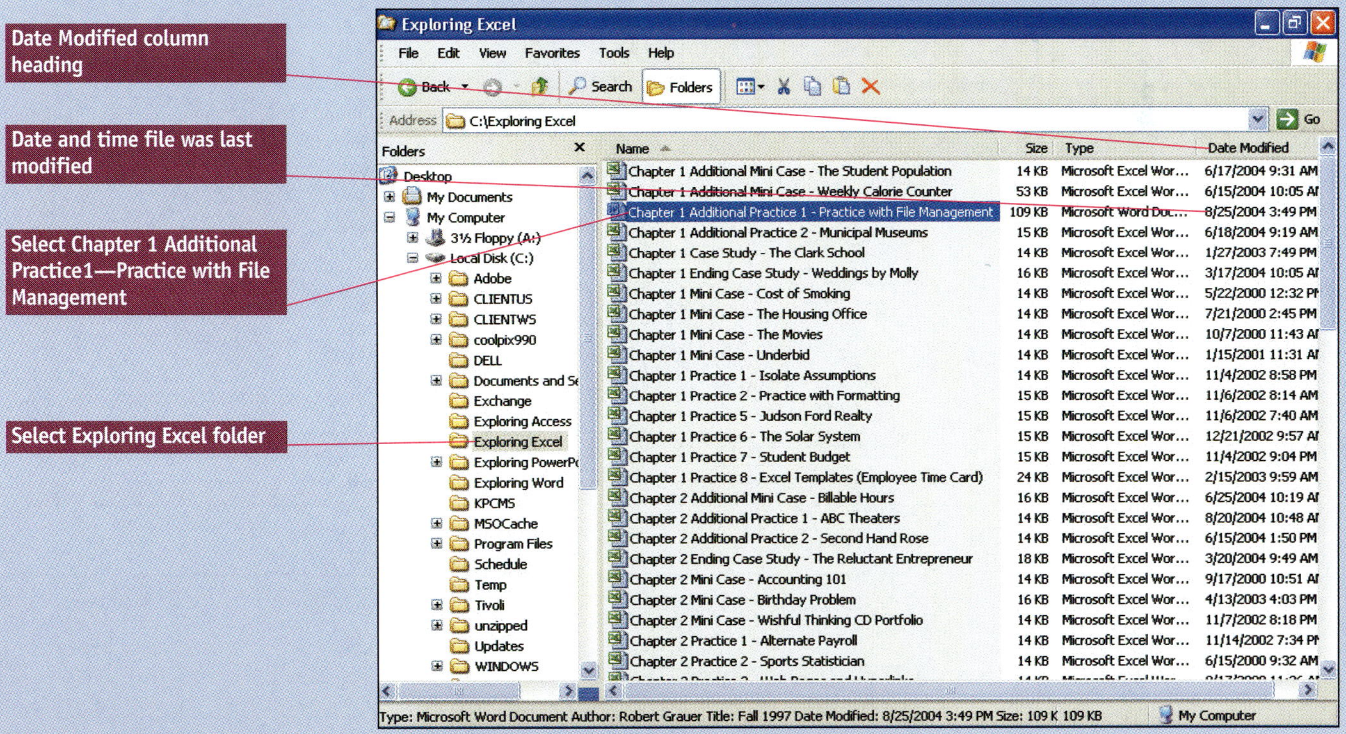

FIGURE 11 Practice with File Management (use with Chapter 1)

2. **Municipal Museums:** Figure 12 displays a spreadsheet that is used to compute the daily revenue for the museums in your city. Open the partially completed workbook in *Chapter 1 Additional Practice 2—Municipal Museums*, and then complete the workbook to match Figure 12. You do not have to match our formatting exactly, but the displayed values should be the same.
   a. Click in cell E5 and enter the formula to compute the ticket revenue for the first museum. Be sure to use the appropriate combination of relative and absolute references so that you can copy this formula to the corresponding cells for the other museums.
   b. Click in cell H5 and enter the formula to compute the gift shop revenue (which is the sum of food and merchandise revenue). Enter the formula for total revenue (ticket revenue plus gift shop revenue) in cell I5. Copy the formulas in cell H5 and I5 to the rows for the other museums.
   c. Click in cell B10 and enter the appropriate Sum function to compute the total number of adult tickets that were sold. Copy the formula in cell B10 to the remaining cells in row 10 to compute the other totals.
   d. Format the worksheet. Click in cell E5 and apply the Currency format (with no decimals). Remain in cell E5, double click the Format Painter tool on the Standard toolbar, then copy this format to the appropriate cells in the worksheet.
   e. Click and drag cells B1 to I1, then click the Merge and Center button on the Formatting toolbar. Change the font size as necessary. Complete the formatting by changing alignments and fonts, using a fill color, and applying borders as you see fit.
   f. Pull down the Insert menu, click the Picture command, click Clip Art, then search for an appropriate museum image. Move and size the clip art as shown.
   g. Use the Page Setup command to create a custom footer that contains the date and time the worksheet is printed, the name of the worksheet, and your name. Be sure to specify landscape printing and appropriate scaling so that the entire worksheet fits on a single page. Print the worksheet twice to show both displayed values and cell formulas.

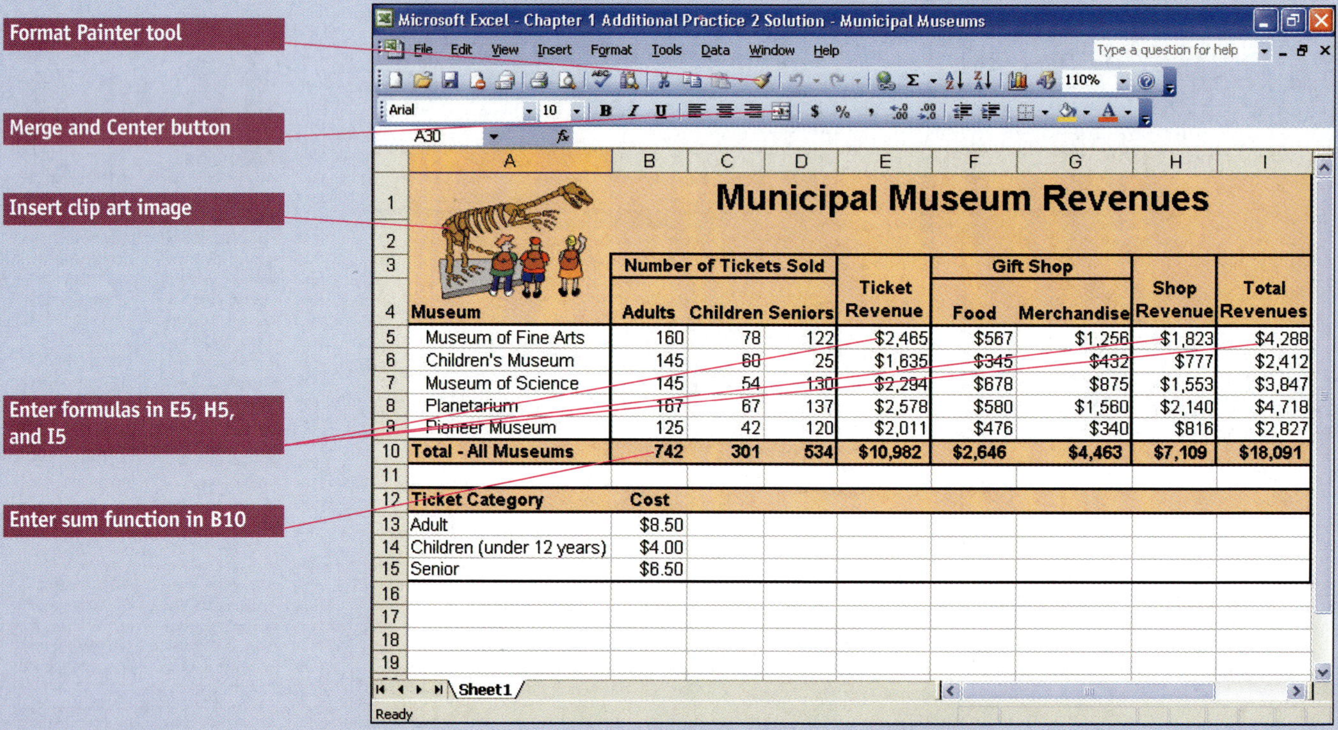

FIGURE 12 Municipal Museums (use with Chapter 1)

3. **ABC Theaters:** Figure 13 displays a spreadsheet that is used to compute the weekly revenue for a chain of movie theatres. Open the partially completed workbook in *Chapter 2 Additional Practice 1—ABC Theaters*, and then complete the workbook to match Figure 13. You do not have to match our formatting exactly, but the displayed values should be the same.
   a. Click in cell D4 and enter a formula, using a combination of relative and absolute references, to compute the ticket revenues for the first theatre.
   b. Enter the appropriate formulas in cells E4 and F4 for the first theatre. Copy the formulas in cells D4, E4, and F4 to the appropriate rows for the other theatres. You can tell that your formulas are correct if you get the same numerical result as in our figure.
   c. Click in cell B9 and enter the function to compute the total number of evening tickets that were sold. Copy this formula to the appropriate cells in row 9 to compute the other totals.
   d. Format the worksheet in attractive fashion. Insert an appropriate clip art image at the upper left, then copy the image as shown in the figure. (Use the Rotate or Flip command in the Draw menu on the Drawing toolbar to flip the figure.) You do not have to match our formatting or clip art.
   e. Use the Page Setup command to create a custom footer that contains the date and time the worksheet is printed, the name of the worksheet, and your name. Be sure to specify landscape printing and appropriate scaling so that the entire worksheet fits on a single page. Print the worksheet twice, to show both displayed values and cell formulas.
   f. Copy the completed worksheet within the current workbook and then rename the new worksheet "Next Year" as shown in the figure. Select the new worksheet, then increase the price of an evening ticket, afternoon ticket, and concession revenue per ticket to $7, $5, and $4, respectively. Change the formatting in the new worksheet to a different background color to distinguish the worksheet. Print the new worksheet to show the displayed values. (The cell formulas are the same as for the previous worksheet.)
   g. Add a cover sheet and submit all three printouts to your instructor.

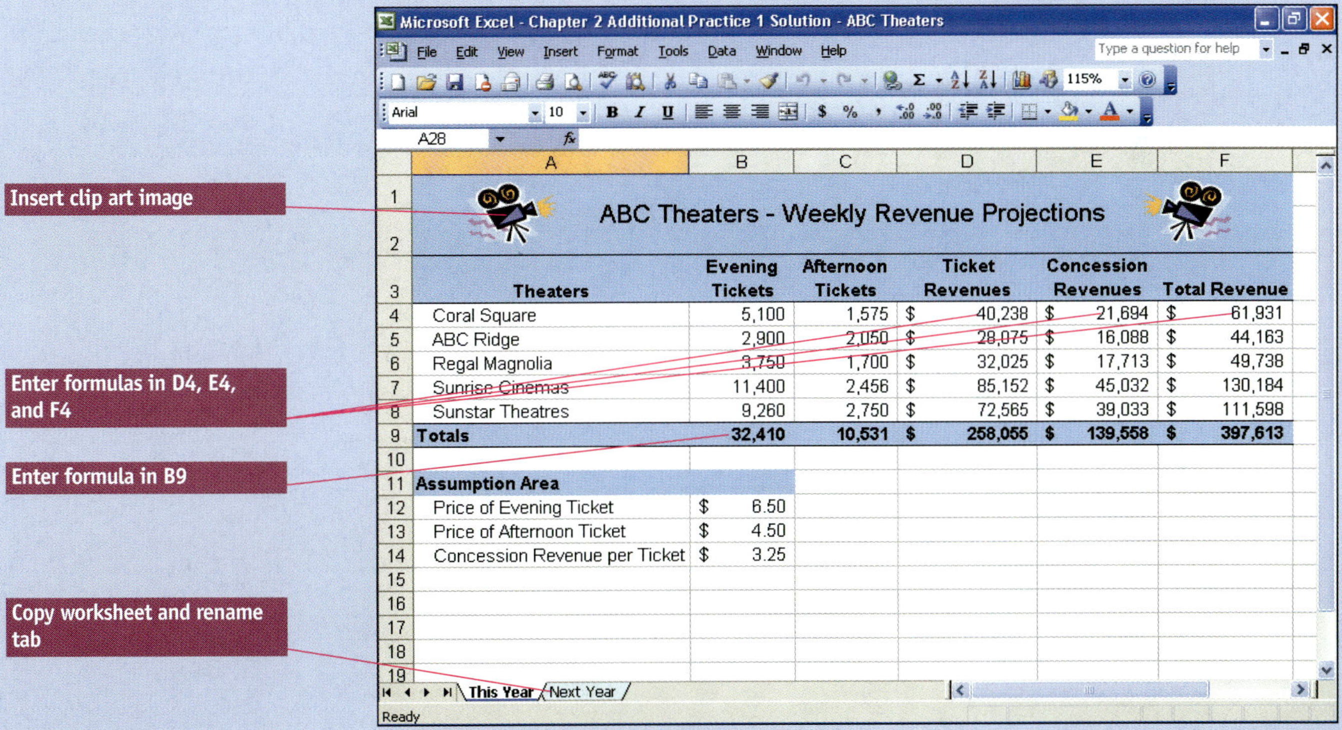

	A	B	C	D	E	F
1	ABC Theaters - Weekly Revenue Projections					
3	Theaters	Evening Tickets	Afternoon Tickets	Ticket Revenues	Concession Revenues	Total Revenue
4	Coral Square	5,100	1,575	$ 40,238	$ 21,694	$ 61,931
5	ABC Ridge	2,900	2,050	$ 28,075	$ 16,088	$ 44,163
6	Regal Magnolia	3,750	1,700	$ 32,025	$ 17,713	$ 49,738
7	Sunrise Cinemas	11,400	2,456	$ 85,152	$ 45,032	$ 130,184
8	Sunstar Theatres	9,260	2,750	$ 72,565	$ 39,033	$ 111,598
9	Totals	32,410	10,531	$ 258,055	$ 139,558	$ 397,613
11	Assumption Area					
12	Price of Evening Ticket	$ 6.50				
13	Price of Afternoon Ticket	$ 4.50				
14	Concession Revenue per Ticket	$ 3.25				

FIGURE 13 ABC Theaters (use with Chapter 2)

4. **Second Hand Rose:** The worksheet in Figure 14 displays the hours worked and associated wages for three employees of the Second Hand Rose consignment shop. Your assignment is to open the partially completed *Chapter 2 Additional Practice 2—Second Hand Rose* workbook and enter the appropriate formulas to determine the hours worked for each employee. Proceed as follows:
   a. Click in cell B4, the "time in" for Maryann on Monday morning, and change the format in this cell so that it displays a time, as opposed to a decimal fraction. Times are stored internally as decimal fractions, from 0 to .9999. Midnight (12:00 AM) is stored as 0. Noon (12:00 PM) is stored as 0.5 as it represents half a day. Use the Format Painter tool to change the time in and time out for all employees.
   b. Click in cell D4 and enter the formula to compute the hours Maryann worked on Monday, then (if necessary) reformat the result as a number. (To calculate the elapsed time between two values, subtract the starting time from the ending time. The result is the fraction of a day that has elapsed, which is then converted to the elapsed time in hours by multiplying by 24.)
   c. Copy the formula in cell D4 to cells D5 through D9 to compute her hours for the remainder of the week. Now copy the formulas in cells D4 through D9 to G4 through G9 and to J4 through J9. The Copy command works because you have used relative references in your formulas.
   d. Compute the total hours worked for Maryann for the week and the associated weekly earnings. Copy the entries in cells C10 and C12 to G10 and G12, and again to J10 and J12.
   e. Format the worksheet in attractive fashion. We used a variety of techniques, including the time format, merging cells, and borders and shading. Change the name of the worksheet tab to reflect the current week—for example, "Week of March 16".
   f. Insert an appropriate piece of clip art in the upper-left portion of the worksheet.
   g. Print the completed workbook twice to show both the displayed values and cell formulas. Use the Page Setup command to display gridlines, row and column headings, and to ensure the entire worksheet fits on one page. Change to landscape printing and center the worksheet horizontally. Add a custom footer that contains your name, the name of the worksheet, the date, and time.

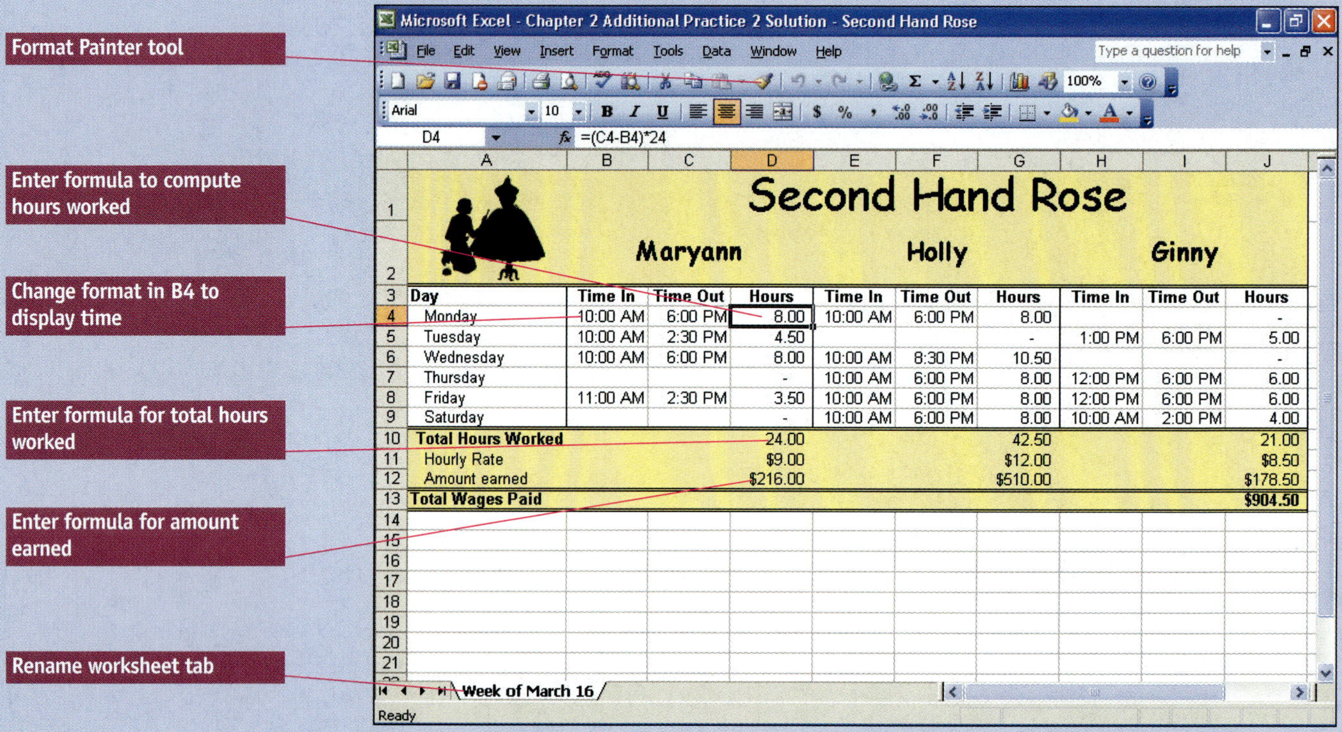

FIGURE 14 Second Hand Rose (use with Chapter 2)

5. **Hotel Bookings:** The workbook in Figure 15 was created by the Director of Marketing for a South Florida hotel chain. The workbook contains a worksheet and several charts that show hotel bookings for different counties according to the source of the booking. Your assignment is to open the partially completed version of the workbook, which is available in the Exploring Excel folder as *Chapter 3 Additional Practice 1—Hotel Bookings,* and proceed as follows:
   a. Use the AutoSum command to enter the formulas to compute the total number of bookings for each county and each source.
   b. Select the entire worksheet (cells A1 through F6), then use the AutoFormat command to format the worksheet. You do not have to accept the entire design nor do you have to use the design we selected. You may also modify the design after it has been applied to the worksheet by changing the font size of selected cells and/or changing boldface and italics.
   c. Create a column chart showing the total dollar amount for each county as shown in Figure 15. Create the graphic to emphasize Monroe's poor bookings.
   d. Create a pie chart that shows the percentage of the total bookings for each source. Create this chart in its own chart sheet. Rename the sheet as appropriate.
   e. Create a stacked column chart that shows the total dollar amount for each booking source and the relative contribution of each county towards the total. Create this chart in its own chart sheet. Rename the sheet as appropriate.
   f. Create a stacked column chart showing the total dollar amount for each county and the relative contribution of each booking source towards the total. Create this chart in its own chart sheet. Rename the sheet as appropriate.
   g. Change the color of each of the worksheet tabs.
   h. Print the entire workbook, consisting of the worksheet in Figure 15 plus the three additional chart sheets that you created. Use portrait orientation for the Sales Data worksheet and landscape orientation for the other sheets. Create a custom footer for each sheet that includes your name, the date and time the sheet is printed, and the name of the sheet. Add a cover sheet, and then submit the completed assignment to your instructor.

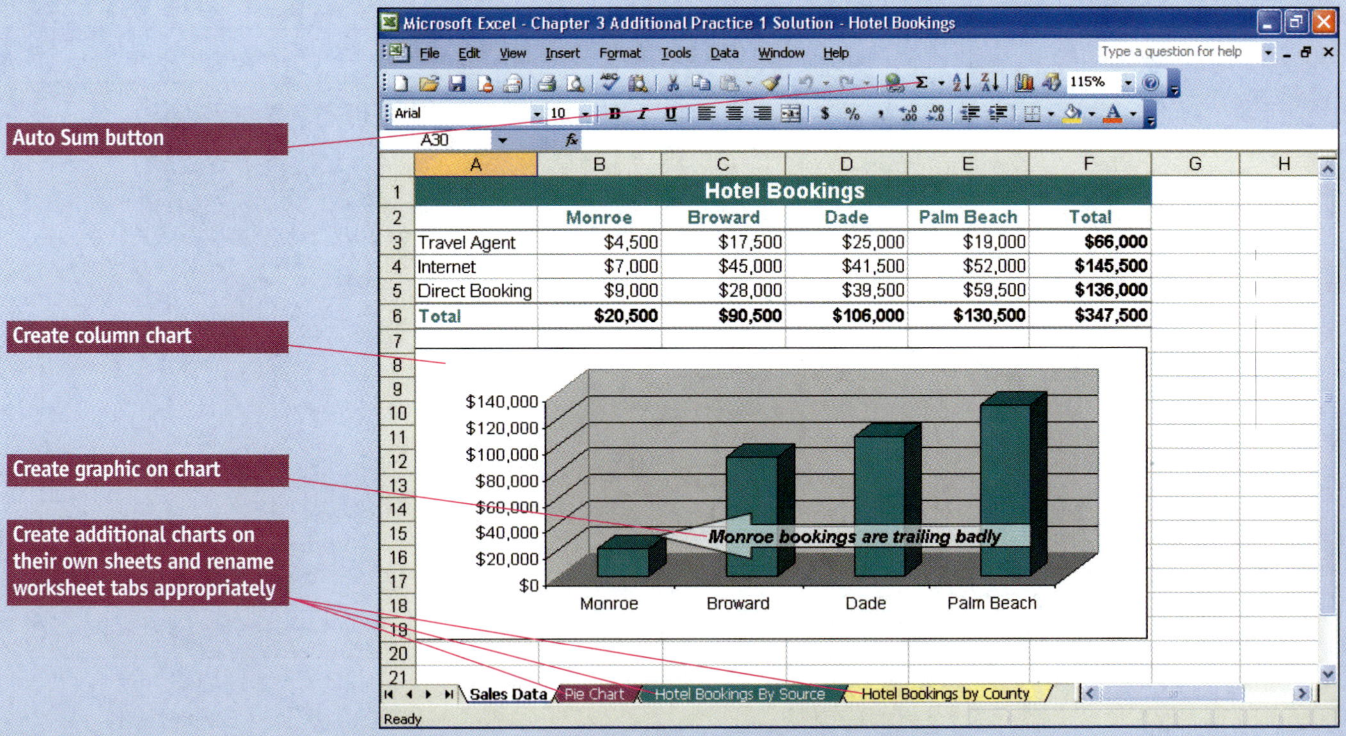

FIGURE 15 Hotel Bookings (use with Chapter 3)

6. **A Combination Chart:** The workbook in Figure 16 is used by a regional airline to compare this year's revenue to that of last year for three classes of aircraft. Your assignment is to open the partially completed *Chapter 3 Additional Practice 2—Combination Chart* workbook, calculate the dollar and percent increases as shown in the Year to Year Comparison worksheet, then create the corresponding combination chart.
   a. Click the worksheet tab labeled Year to Year Comparison, then click in cell B3 of this worksheet as shown in Figure 16. Type an equal sign, click the worksheet tab labeled Last Year, click in cell F3 of this worksheet, and press Enter. The formula for this cell appears in the formula bar as ='Last Year'!F3, indicating that the value for this cell is obtained from another worksheet in the same workbook. Enter a similar formula in cell C3 to display the total revenues for this year.
   b. Click in cell D3 and compute the dollar increase from last year to this year. (This formula does not require reference to the other worksheets.) Click in cell E3 and enter the formula to compute the corresponding percent increase from last year to this year.
   c. Copy the formulas from cells B3:E3 to B4:E5. Add the appropriate formulas in B6:D6 to compute the totals. Copy the formula in cell E5 to cell E6 to determine the percent increase.
   d. Format the completed worksheet so that it approximates Figure 16.
   e. Create a combination chart that plots both the dollar amount of the increase and the percent of the increase for each plane as well as for the company as a whole as shown in Figure 16. Press and hold the Ctrl key as you select cells A2 through A6, D2 through D6, and E2 through E6. Start the Chart Wizard, click the Custom Types tab in step 1 of the Wizard, then choose the Line - Column on 2 axis chart. Specify that the data is in columns and that the legend is to appear at the bottom of the worksheet.
   f. Print the completed workbook to show the displayed values for all three worksheets. Display the cell formulas on the Year to Year Comparison worksheet, then select cells A1 through E6 to show cell values.

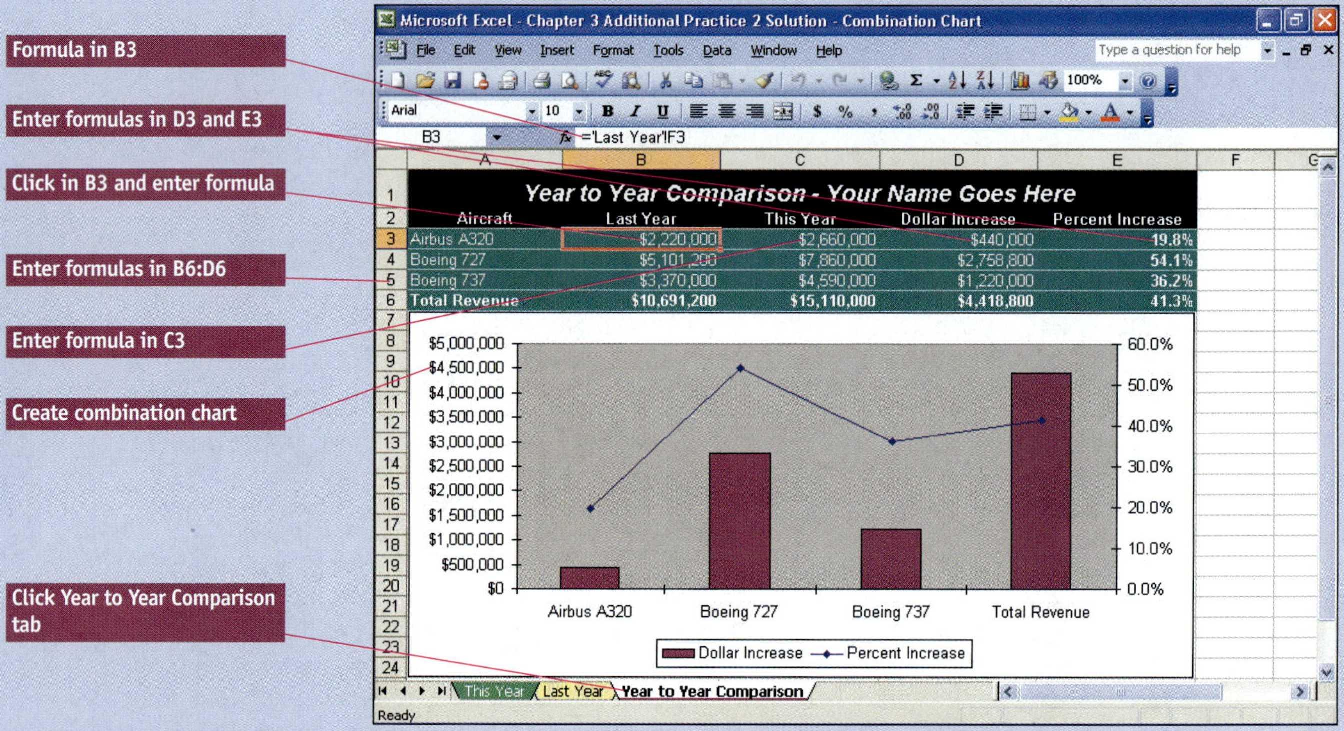

FIGURE 16 A Combination Chart (use with Chapter 3)

7. **Big Bopper Bank:** The workbook in Figure 17 reviews multiple Excel functions that were discussed in the chapter. The selling price and term of each loan are entered in columns B and C. All of the other entries (the interest rate, down payment, amount to be financed, and monthly payment) are determined from these parameters and the table at the bottom of the worksheet. Open the partially completed workbook in *Chapter 4 Additional Practice 1—Big Bopper Bank* and proceed as follows:
   a. Click in cell D4 and enter the appropriate formula to determine the interest rate, which depends on the term of the loan. (You will need to use the VLOOKUP function in your formula to reference the table in cells A15 through C17.) You should see 6.25% since Allen has selected a 30-year loan.
   b. Click in cell C4 and enter 15 years instead of 30 years as the term of the loan. The interest rate should change to 5.75% if your VLOOKUP function is correct. Change the loan back to 30 years.
   c. Click in cell E4 and enter the formula to compute the required down payment, which is found by multiplying the percentage rate for the down payment times the selling price of the home. The percentage rate for the down payment depends on the term of the loan, so you will need to use the VLOOKUP function to determine the correct percentage.
   d. Complete the formulas in row four. The amount to be financed is the selling price minus the down payment. The monthly payment is computed using the PMT function. Copy the formulas to the rows for the other customers.
   e. Enter the appropriate functions to compute the summary statistics at the bottom of the worksheet in cells C19 through C22.
   f. Enter your name in cell A6 in place of Barber, and then highlight the row containing your data. Sort the customers so that they appear in alphabetical order. Be sure you sort the worksheet correctly.
   g. Format the completed worksheet. (You do not have to duplicate our formatting exactly.) Use the Insert Picture command to insert an appropriate graphic.
   h. Print the completed worksheet. Be sure that you print both the displayed values and cell formulas and that the worksheet fits on one page. Include gridlines and row and column headings.

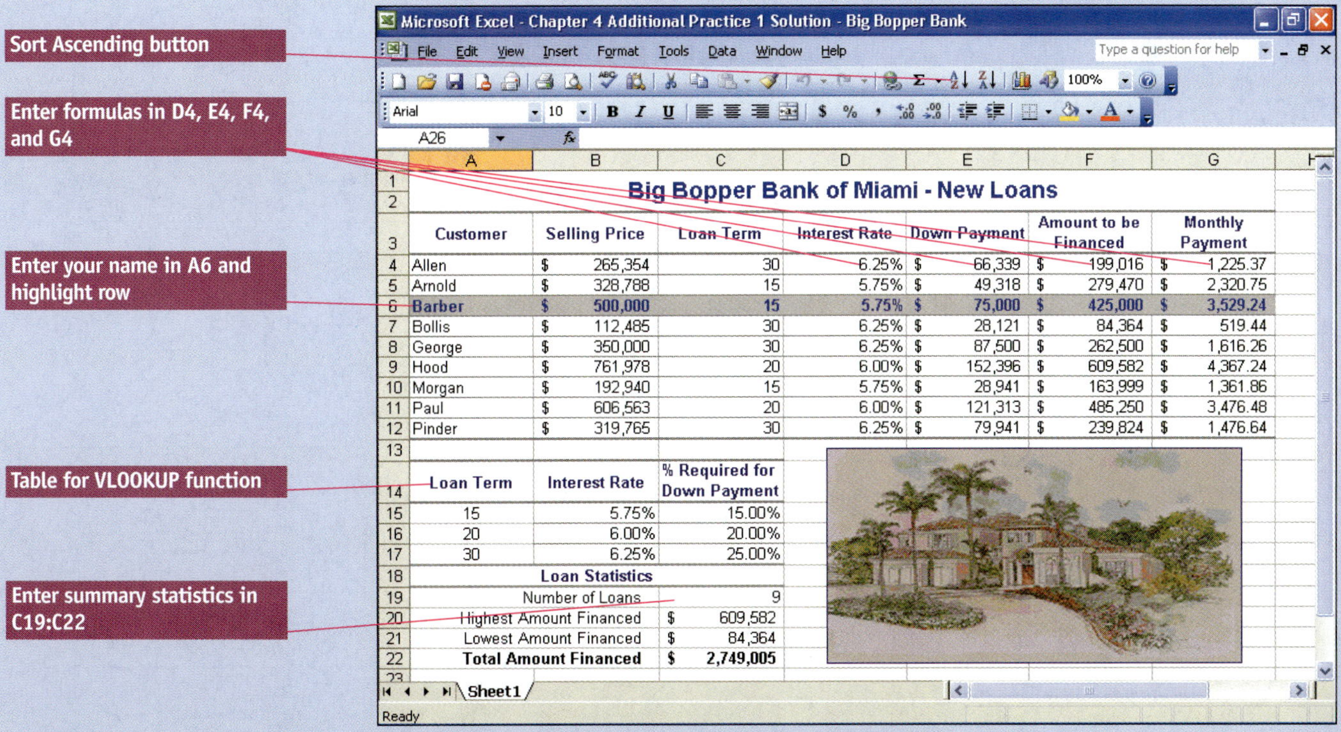

FIGURE 17 Big Bopper Bank (use with Chapter 4)

8. **The Shopping Mall:** The worksheet in Figure 18 displays leasing information for stores in a shopping mall. The data for each store includes the occupancy date, the duration of the lease, and the number of square feet in the store. The assumption area at the bottom of the worksheet contains a table that determines the annual price per square foot (the longer the lease, the cheaper the cost). There are additional adjustments for large stores (a $1.50 reduction in the price per square foot) and small stores (a $1 increase in the price per square foot). Open the partially completed *Chapter 4 Additional Practice 2—The Shopping Mall* workbook and proceed as follows:
   a. Select cells B3 through B13, pull down the Format menu, click the Cells command to display the Format Cells dialog box, click the Number tab, then choose the appropriate Date format as shown in Figure 18.
   b. Click in cell D3 and enter the appropriate formula (as shown in Figure 18) to compute the expiration date. The formula may seem complicated, but it adjusts for leap year and it terminates the lease on the exact date; for example, the expiration date for the five-year lease that began on January 1, 2002 is December 31, 2006.
   c. Click in cell F3 and enter the appropriate VLOOKUP function to determine the annual price per square foot, which is based on the length of the lease.
   d. Enter a nested IF function in cell G3 to compute the adjusted price per square foot, given that those stores larger than 2000 square feet pay a reduced rate, while stores smaller than 1200 square feet pay a premium.
   e. Enter the formulas to compute the annual rent (price per square foot times the square footage) and monthly rent in cells H3 and I3, respectively.
   f. Copy the formulas in row three to the remaining rows of the worksheet. Enter the appropriate SUM or AVERAGE functions in row 14.
   g. Format the completed worksheet. You do not have to match our formatting exactly. Insert a clip art image in the upper left of the worksheet.
   h. Print the completed worksheet to show displayed values and cell formulas. Use the Page Setup command to ensure that the worksheet fits on a single page.

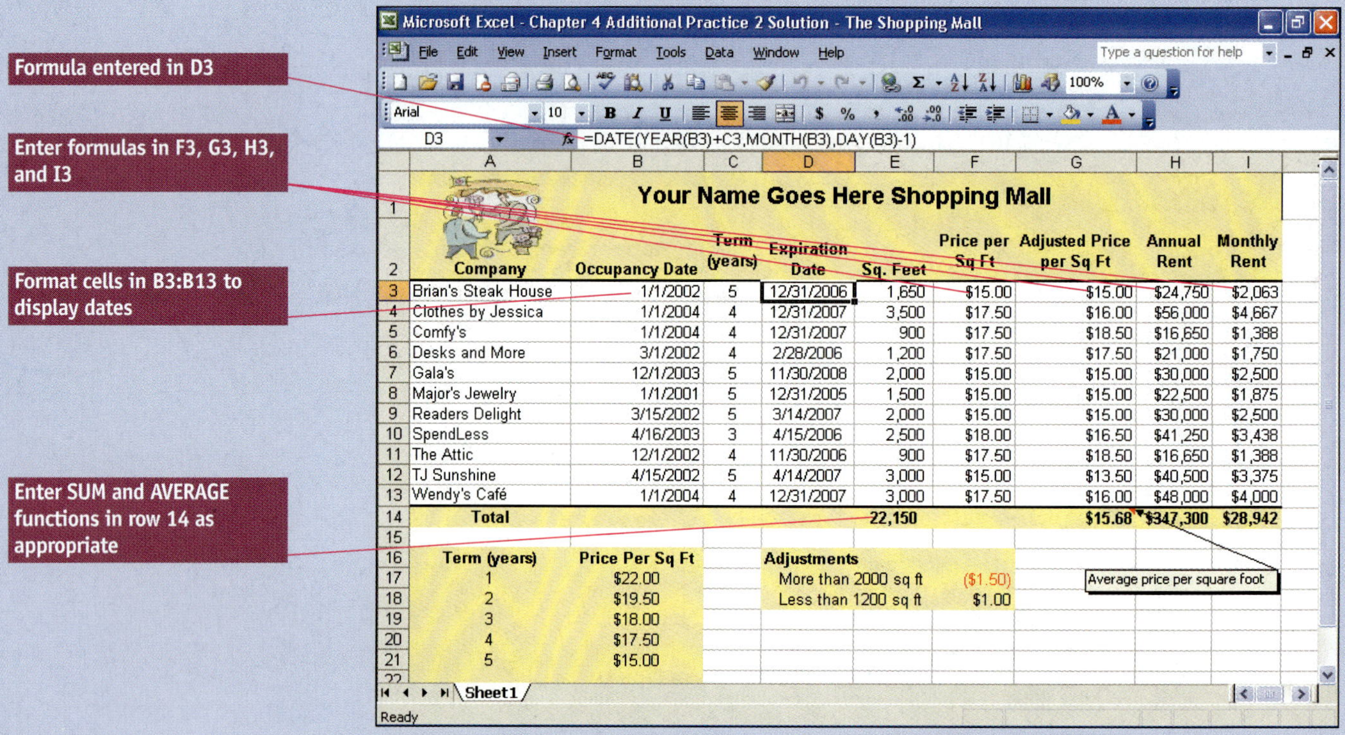

Company	Occupancy Date	Term (years)	Expiration Date	Sq. Feet	Price per Sq Ft	Adjusted Price per Sq Ft	Annual Rent	Monthly Rent
Brian's Steak House	1/1/2002	5	12/31/2006	1,650	$15.00	$15.00	$24,750	$2,063
Clothes by Jessica	1/1/2004	4	12/31/2007	3,500	$17.50	$16.00	$56,000	$4,667
Comfy's	1/1/2004	4	12/31/2007	900	$17.50	$18.50	$16,650	$1,388
Desks and More	3/1/2002	4	2/28/2006	1,200	$17.50	$17.50	$21,000	$1,750
Gala's	12/1/2003	5	11/30/2008	2,000	$15.00	$15.00	$30,000	$2,500
Major's Jewelry	1/1/2001	5	12/31/2005	1,500	$15.00	$15.00	$22,500	$1,875
Readers Delight	3/15/2002	5	3/14/2007	2,000	$15.00	$15.00	$30,000	$2,500
SpendLess	4/16/2003	3	4/15/2006	2,500	$18.00	$16.50	$41,250	$3,438
The Attic	12/1/2002	4	11/30/2006	900	$17.50	$18.50	$16,650	$1,388
TJ Sunshine	4/15/2002	5	4/14/2007	3,000	$15.00	$13.50	$40,500	$3,375
Wendy's Café	1/1/2004	4	12/31/2007	3,000	$17.50	$16.00	$48,000	$4,000
Total				22,150		$15.68	$347,300	$28,942

Term (years)	Price Per Sq Ft
1	$22.00
2	$19.50
3	$18.00
4	$17.50
5	$15.00

Adjustments	
More than 2000 sq ft	($1.50)
Less than 1200 sq ft	$1.00

FIGURE 18 The Shopping Mall (use with Chapter 4)

9. **Barber Academy:** The worksheet in Figure 19 computes the tuition, lunch, insurance, and other fees associated with newly admitted students at an exclusive prep school. The heading information appears at the top of the worksheet, the individual students appear in the middle of the worksheet, and the assumptions and summary calculations appear at the bottom. (This is a large worksheet and hence not all of the students are visible at one time.) Open the partially completed workbook in *Chapter 4 Additional Practice 3—Barber Academy* and proceed as follows:
   a. Click in cell A4 (not shown in Figure 19), pull down the Windows menu, and click the Freeze Panes command so that the first three rows are always visible.
   b. Click in cell C4 and enter the appropriate VLOOKUP function to compute the tuition. Click in cell D4 and enter a second VLOOKUP function to compute the associated cost for lunch. Use a third VLOOKUP function in cell E4 to compute the insurance premium, which is applied to just the tuition. The tuition, lunch fee, and insurance all depend on the level of school in which the student is enrolling, as shown by the table in the assumption area.
   c. Click in cell H4 and enter the formula to determine the cost for bus transportation. The formula requires both an IF function and a VLOOKUP function; that is, you have to determine whether the student requests bus service and then you have to calculate the cost of the service based on the distance from school.
   d. Click in cell I4 and compute the total bill for the first student, which includes the tuition, lunch, insurance, and optional bus transportation. Copy the formulas in row four to the remaining rows of the worksheet. Enter the appropriate SUM functions in row 27 to compute the totals for the academy.
   e. Enter the appropriate functions to compute the summary statistics for the academy as a whole in the lower-right portion of the worksheet.
   f. Format the completed worksheet. (You do not have to match our formatting.) Insert a clip art image as you see fit.
   g. Print the completed worksheet to show both displayed values and cell formulas. Be sure the worksheet fits on a single page.

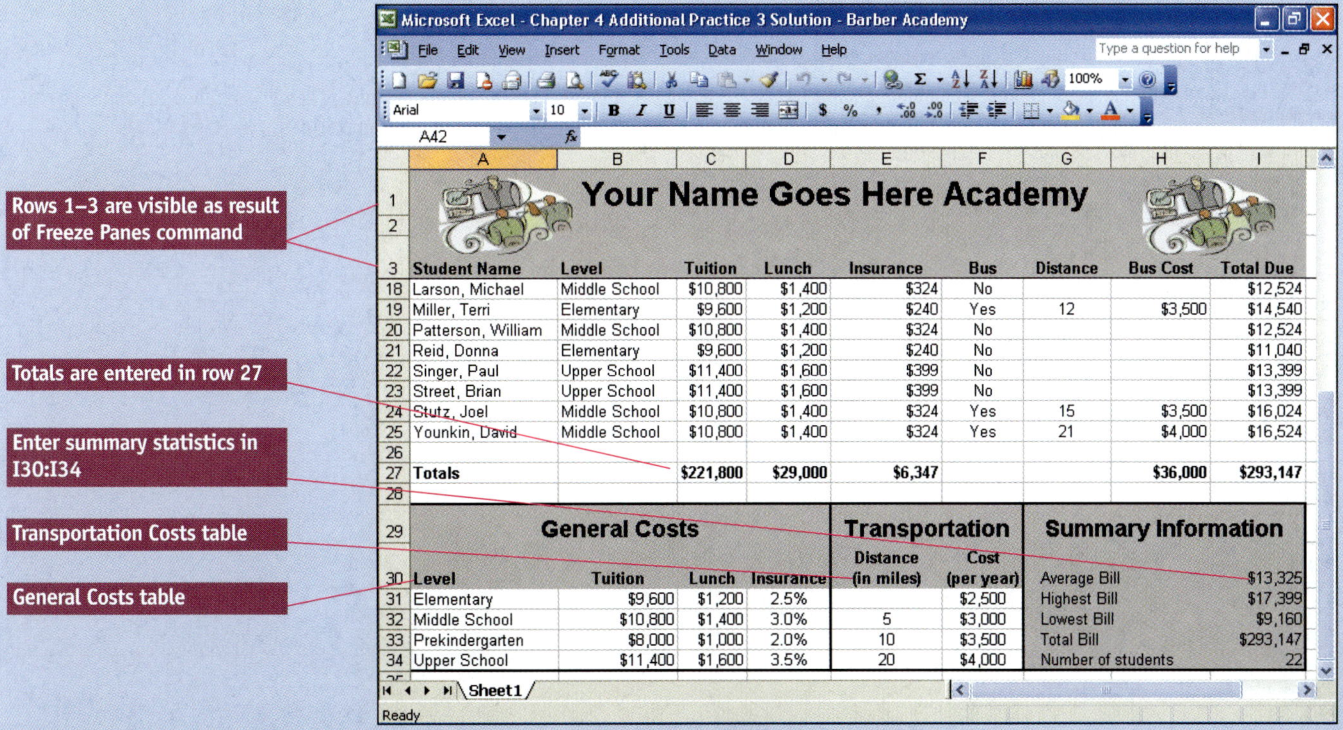

FIGURE 19 Barber Academy (use with Chapter 4)

10. **Mortgage Calculator:** Figure 20 uses mixed references to vary the principal and interest rate in conjunction with the PMT function. The spreadsheet is designed so that the user can change the duration of the mortgage, the initial interest rate and associated increment (5% and .5% in the figure), and/or the initial principle and the associated increment ($150,000 and $5,000). The worksheet then computes the associated payment for the different combinations of interest and principal based on the term of the associated mortgage. Proceed as follows:

    a. Start a new workbook and enter the basic information in rows one through five as shown in the figure. Do not worry about formatting at this time.

    b. Click in cell A8 and enter the formula =B3. Click in cell A9 and enter the formula =A8+$B$4. Copy the formula in cell A9 to the remaining rows in column A.

    c. Click in cell B7 and enter the formula =E3. Click in cell C7 and enter the formula =B7+$E$4. Copy the formula in cell C7 to the remaining columns in row seven.

    d. The trick to this assignment is to develop a formula with the correct mixed references for cell B8 and then copy that formula to the remaining cells in the body of the worksheet. Click in cell B8 and start to enter the PMT function. You know that the interest rate is in cell B7, but you have to determine the appropriate reference. Ask yourself if the interest rate will always come from column B. (No.) Will it always come from row 7? (Yes.) The answer tells you how to enter the mixed reference within the PMT function. You will need to use similar logic to enter the reference to the cell that contains the principal. Once you have the correct formula for cell B8, you can copy it to the remaining cells in the body of the worksheet.

    e. Format the completed worksheet, shading those cells that contain the input parameters. Print the worksheet two ways, once with displayed values and once with the cell formulas. Use the Page Setup command to create a custom footer containing your name, the date, and time, as well as to ensure that the entire worksheet fits on one page.

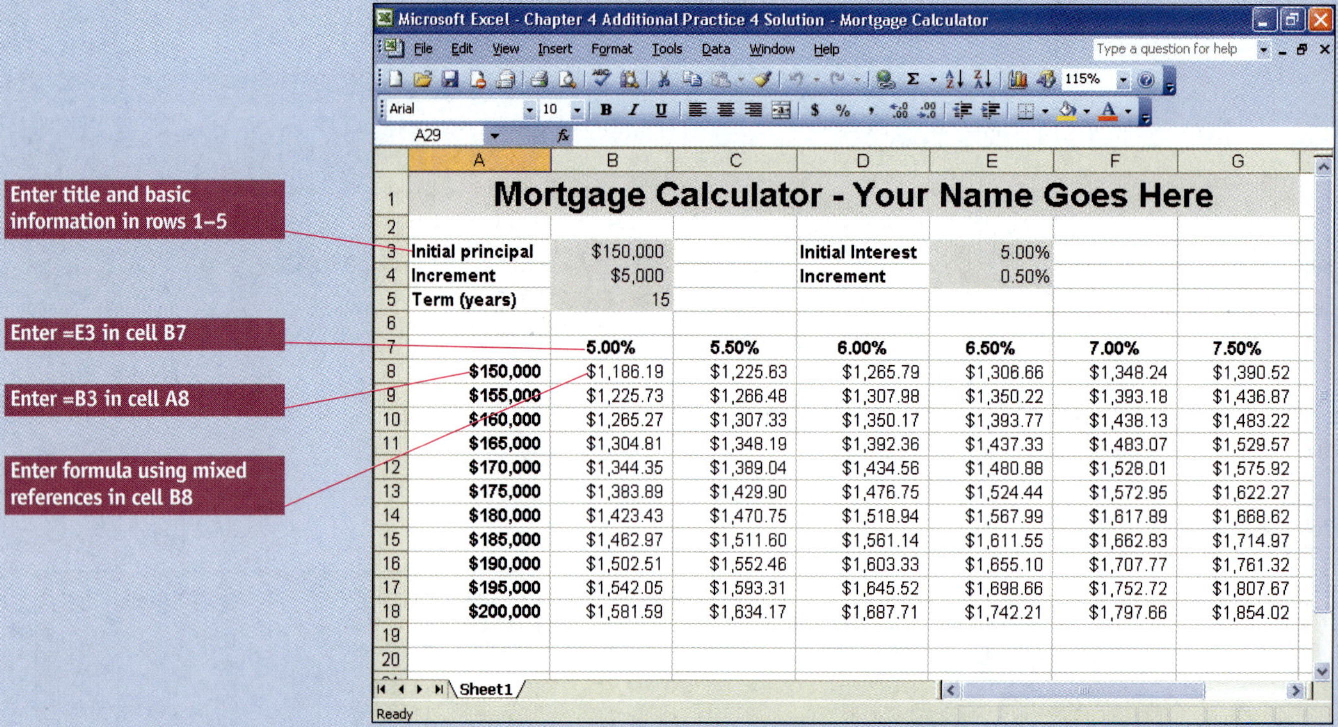

	A	B	C	D	E	F	G
1	Mortgage Calculator - Your Name Goes Here						
2							
3	Initial principal	$150,000		Initial Interest	5.00%		
4	Increment	$5,000		Increment	0.50%		
5	Term (years)	15					
6							
7		5.00%	5.50%	6.00%	6.50%	7.00%	7.50%
8	$150,000	$1,186.19	$1,225.63	$1,265.79	$1,306.66	$1,348.24	$1,390.52
9	$155,000	$1,225.73	$1,266.48	$1,307.98	$1,350.22	$1,393.18	$1,436.87
10	$160,000	$1,265.27	$1,307.33	$1,350.17	$1,393.77	$1,438.13	$1,483.22
11	$165,000	$1,304.81	$1,348.19	$1,392.36	$1,437.33	$1,483.07	$1,529.57
12	$170,000	$1,344.35	$1,389.04	$1,434.56	$1,480.88	$1,528.01	$1,575.92
13	$175,000	$1,383.89	$1,429.90	$1,476.75	$1,524.44	$1,572.95	$1,622.27
14	$180,000	$1,423.43	$1,470.75	$1,518.94	$1,567.99	$1,617.89	$1,668.62
15	$185,000	$1,462.97	$1,511.60	$1,561.14	$1,611.55	$1,662.83	$1,714.97
16	$190,000	$1,502.51	$1,552.46	$1,603.33	$1,655.10	$1,707.77	$1,761.32
17	$195,000	$1,542.05	$1,593.31	$1,645.52	$1,698.66	$1,752.72	$1,807.67
18	$200,000	$1,581.59	$1,634.17	$1,687.71	$1,742.21	$1,797.66	$1,854.02
19							
20							

FIGURE 20 Mortgage Calculator (use with Chapter 4)

11. **Election 2004:** The election has come and gone, but it is interesting to analyze the results of both the popular and electoral votes as shown in Figure 21. (The worksheet was created after 99.9% of the precincts were counted.) You will find a partially completed version of Figure 21 in the file, *Chapter 4 Additional Practice 5—Election 2004*. Open the workbook and proceed as follows:
    a. Enter an appropriate IF function in cells D9 and F9 to determine the number of electoral votes for each candidate. The electoral votes are awarded on an all-or-nothing basis; that is, the candidate with the larger popular vote wins all of that state's electoral votes. The other candidate gets zero votes. (Pull down the Tools menu, click the Options command, click the View tab, and then clear the box to display zero values.)
    b. Copy the entries in cells D9 and F9 to the remaining rows in the respective columns. Format these columns to display red and blue values, for Mr. Bush and Mr. Kerry, respectively.
    c. Enter a formula into cell G9 to determine the difference in the popular vote between the two candidates. The result should always appear as a positive number. You can do this in one of two ways: by using either an absolute value function or an appropriate IF function. Copy this formula to the remaining rows in the column.
    d. Click in cell H9 and determine the percentage differential in the popular vote. This is the difference in the number of votes, divided by the total number of votes.
    e. Enter the appropriate SUM functions in cells B4, B5, C4, and C5 to determine the electoral and popular vote totals for each candidate.
    f. Use the Insert Picture command to add an appropriate clip art image.
    g. Add your name as indicated. Use the Page Setup command to reduce the top and bottom margins to three quarters of an inch and to ensure that the worksheet fits on one page. Adjust the column widths as necessary. Create a custom footer that shows the date the worksheet was printed. Print the displayed values, then print the worksheet a second time to show the cell formulas.
    h. Use the Sort command to display the states in a different sequence, such as the smallest (or largest) vote differential. Print the worksheet in this sequence. Add a title page and submit the completed assignment to your instructor.

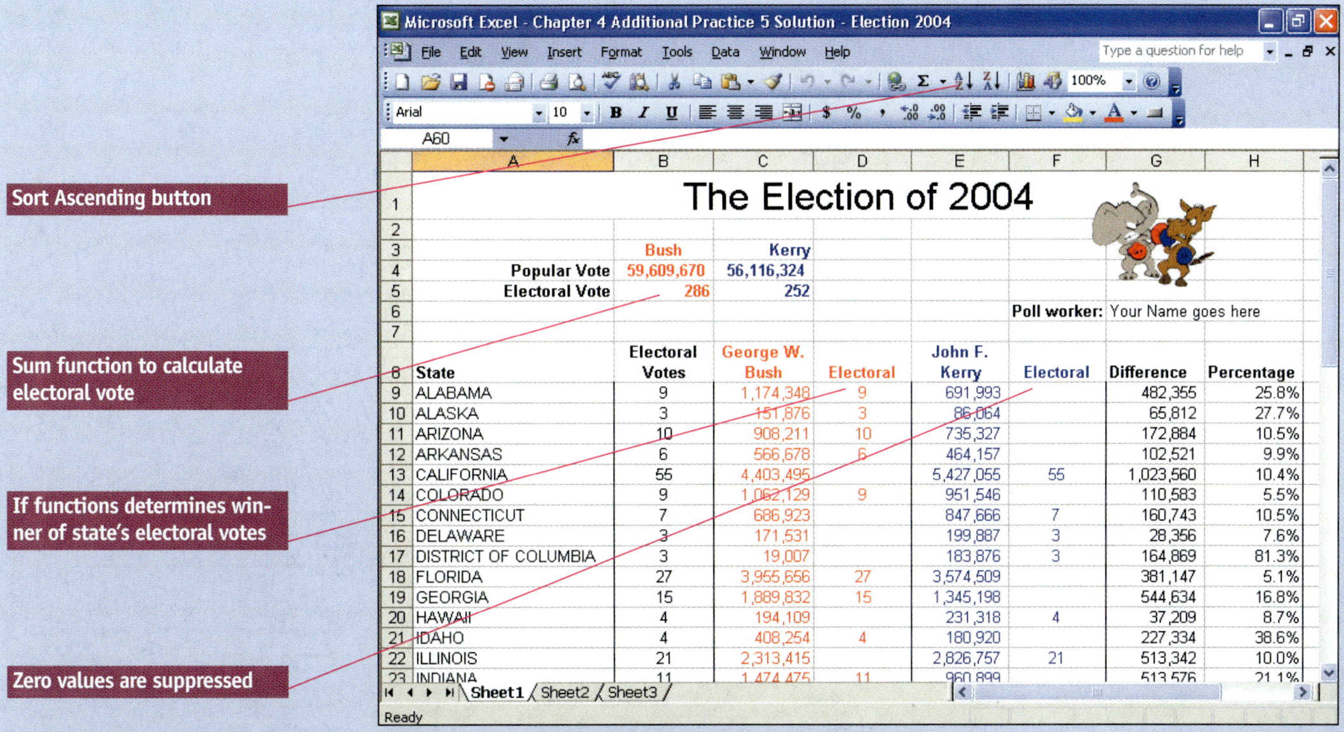

	A	B	C	D	E	F	G	H
1	The Election of 2004							
2								
3		Bush	Kerry					
4	Popular Vote	59,609,670	56,116,324					
5	Electoral Vote	286	252					
6						Poll worker:	Your Name goes here	
7								
8	State	Electoral Votes	George W. Bush	Electoral	John F. Kerry	Electoral	Difference	Percentage
9	ALABAMA	9	1,174,348	9	691,993		482,355	25.8%
10	ALASKA	3	151,876	3	86,064		65,812	27.7%
11	ARIZONA	10	908,211	10	735,327		172,884	10.5%
12	ARKANSAS	6	566,678	6	464,157		102,521	9.9%
13	CALIFORNIA	55	4,403,495		5,427,055	55	1,023,560	10.4%
14	COLORADO	9	1,062,129	9	951,546		110,583	5.5%
15	CONNECTICUT	7	686,923		847,666	7	160,743	10.5%
16	DELAWARE	3	171,531		199,887	3	28,356	7.6%
17	DISTRICT OF COLUMBIA	3	19,007		183,876	3	164,869	81.3%
18	FLORIDA	27	3,955,656	27	3,574,509		381,147	5.1%
19	GEORGIA	15	1,889,832	15	1,345,198		544,634	16.8%
20	HAWAII	4	194,109		231,318	4	37,209	8.7%
21	IDAHO	4	408,254	4	180,920		227,334	38.6%
22	ILLINOIS	21	2,313,415		2,826,757	21	513,342	10.0%
23	INDIANA	11	1,474,475	11	960,899		513,576	21.1%

FIGURE 21 Election 2004 (Use with Chapter 4)

12. **Excel Jeopardy:** How well do you know Microsoft Excel? The presentation in Figure 22 contains a Jeopardy game with 25 answers and questions that review material from Chapters 1 through 4. All you have to do is open the presentation and play the game. Thus, open the *Chapter 4 Additional Practice 6—Excel Jeopardy* presentation and proceed as follows:
    a. Pull down the Slide Show menu and click the View Show command (or click the F5 key) to view the slide show, which begins with the title slide. Click the mouse to move to slide 2 (the board). The names of the categories will appear one after another, after which you can select any question in any category. Each dollar amount is a hyperlink to another slide in the presentation.
    b. Select (click) a question, such as the $400 question in the Excel 101 category, to display the clue, "Used at the beginning of every formula". Click the mouse to display the answer "What is an equal sign?" (that appears in the form of a question), then click the answer to return to slide 2 (the board). Before you click, be sure you see the tiny hand indicating that you are clicking the hyperlink, as opposed to clicking the background of the slide.
    c. You should be back on slide 2, the Jeopardy board. Look closely and you will see that the color of the text (i.e., the 400) has changed, indicating that the hyperlink has been followed. Select a different question, view the answer, and return to the game board so that you can be sure of the navigation.
    d. Select a classmate and play the game. There is no buzzer, so you have to determine an equitable way to gain control of the board and keep score. We leave the details to you.
    e. Print the presentation in a variety of ways. Select the first two slides, pull down the File menu, click the Print command, choose the option button for Selection, and select Slides in the Print What list box. Click OK to print. Pull down the Print menu a second time and print the entire presentation in Outline view. Study the outline and be sure that you can answer all of the questions.
    f. You will find additional games for the other Office applications (Word, PowerPoint, and Access) in the appropriate folders after downloading the practice files from our Web site. The Word game, for example, is found in the Exploring Word folder and reviews material from Chapters 1 through 4 in the Word section.

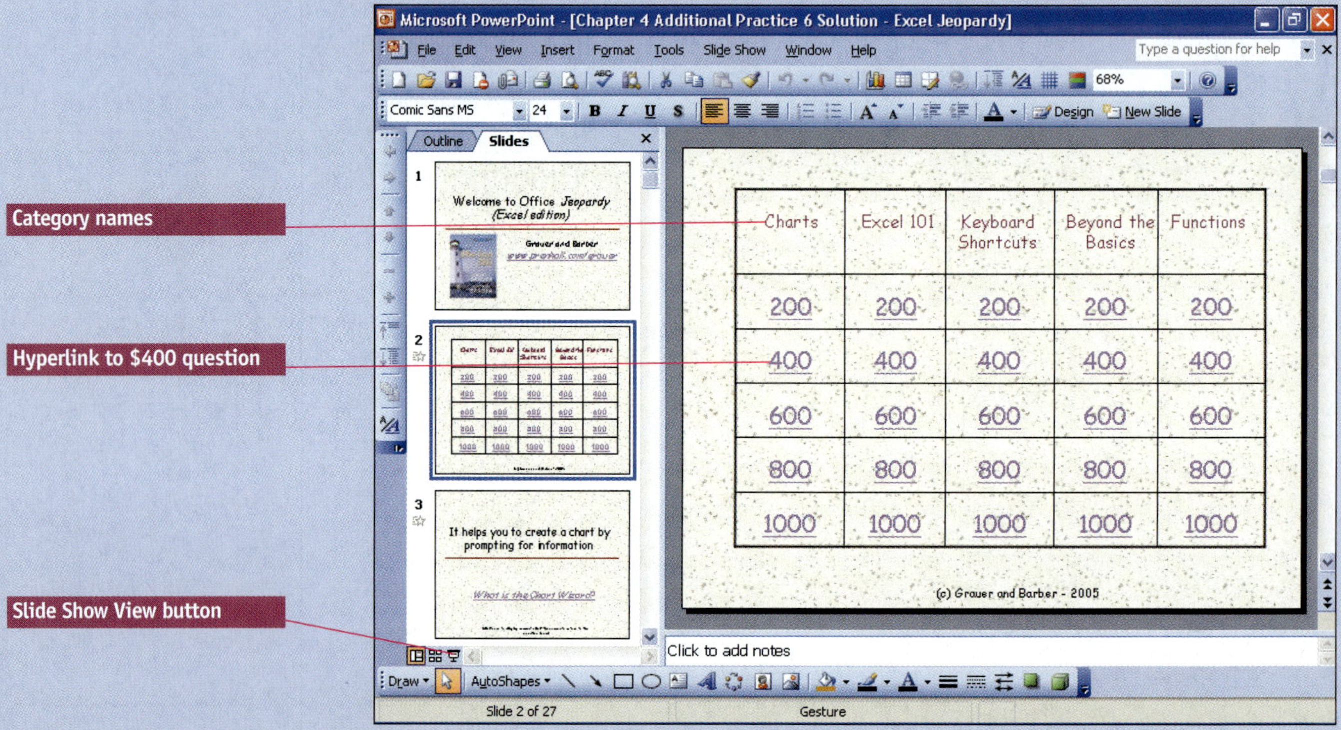

FIGURE 22 Excel Jeopardy (use with Chapter 4)

ADDITIONAL MINI CASES

Study Break—Word Find and Crossword Puzzles

Almost everyone enjoys a good puzzle. With this in mind, we have created a series of unique crossword and word find puzzles to accompany the Exploring Office series. Open the *Chapters 1 to 4 Mini Case—Microsoft Excel Study Break* document in the Exploring Excel folder, and then print the document. You will find two puzzles for each chapter, a word find and a crossword. (You don't have to do every puzzle in every chapter.)

We suggest that you start with the word find and use the list of keywords and concepts at the end of the chapter to determine what each clue represents, and then locate the corresponding word or phrase in the puzzle. You can then try the accompanying crossword, which repeats clues from the word find to reinforce the material, and which adds additional clues to challenge you further. Add your name at the top of the puzzle(s), and then submit the puzzle(s) to your instructor. And if you are up to a challenge, try the composite (Sunday) crossword puzzle that combines the clues from Chapters 1 through 4 in a single puzzle.

Online Study Guide

Every chapter in the Exploring Office series has an online component that helps you to review the conceptual material in the chapter. Go to www.prenhall.com/grauer after you have completed the chapter and click the icon for the Office 2003 book to go to the home page for this series. Click the appropriate title in the left pane, such as, Office Volume I or Excel, then click the down arrow in the list box at the top of the screen to select the appropriate chapter—for example, Excel Chapter 1. Click the link to Online Study Guide in the left pane and take the quiz that consists of objective questions (multiple choice, true/false, and matching).

Click the Submit Answers for Grading button at the bottom of the quiz so that you can see your results. Scroll to the bottom of the answer screen, and then e-mail the results to yourself in HTML format. (If you send the results as text instead of HTML, you will get too many pages of output.) Start your e-mail program, print the e-mail message that contains your results, and bring it to class to submit to your instructor.

Planning for Disaster

This case has nothing to do with spreadsheets per se, but it is perhaps the most important case of all, as it deals with the question of backup. Do you have a backup strategy? Do you even know what a backup strategy is? You had better learn, because eventually you will wish you had one. You will erase a file, be unable to read from a floppy disk, or worse yet, suffer a hardware failure in which you are unable to access the hard drive. The problem always seems to occur the night before an assignment is due. Describe in 250 words or fewer the backup strategy you plan to implement in conjunction with your work in this class.

The Calorie Counter

Everyone has their favorite diet, but eventually it comes down to calories. If you take in more calories than you need, you will gain weight; conversely, if you take in fewer calories than you consume, you will lose weight. One way to count calories is by food group and portion size; for example, each serving of fruit is 60 calories, each serving of protein is 75 calories, and so on. We have done the research for you and created a basic spreadsheet that contains this information.

Your assignment is to open the partially completed, *Chapter 1 Additional Mini Case—Weekly Calorie Counter* workbook and track your meals for one week by entering the number of servings for each food group in the body of the worksheet. You will then enter the appropriate formulas to compute your total calories per meal, total calories per day, and the amount that you are over or under your target goal. You are also asked to compute summary statistics for the week as a whole. *Be sure to check with your physician and/or a licensed dietician before starting your diet.*

E-mail Your Homework

It's easy to send an Excel workbook as an attached file, but we suggest you check with your professor first. He or she may prefer that you print the assignment, rather than mail it, or e-mail may not be available to you. If e-mail is an option, start your e-mail program and create a message to your instructor. Click the Insert (or Attach) button to select the file you want to send, and then click the Send button to mail the message.

The Student Population

Congratulations! You have just been hired as a student assistant in the Registrar's Office due in large part to your excellent work in this course. Your supervisor has collected data on the number of students in each college within the university, and further, has divided that data according to the year in school. Your job is to open the partially completed *Chapter 1 Additional Mini Case—The Student Population* workbook, and compute the total number of students enrolled in each college, as well as the total number of freshmen, sophomores, and so on. In addition, you are to determine the percentage of the student population who are freshmen, sophomores, juniors, and seniors. Add your name as indicated, format the worksheet appropriately, then print it two ways, once with displayed values and once to show the cell formulas. Be sure to include the gridlines and row and column headings. Use the Page Setup command to include a custom footer that shows the date and time the worksheet was completed.

Billable Hours

Attorneys are not shy about billing their clients for all activities associated with a specific legal matter. Open the partially completed *Chapter 2 Additional Mini Case—Billable Hours* workbook and enter the appropriate formula for the first activity to compute the hours worked (or billable hours). Copy this formula to the remaining rows in the worksheet, then total the billable hours for the indicated week. Compute the total amount billed by multiplying the hourly rate by the billable hours. Add your name as indicated, format the worksheet appropriately, then print it two ways, once with displayed values and once to show the cell formulas. Be sure to include the gridlines and row and column headings. Use the Page Setup command to include a custom footer that shows the date and time the worksheet was completed.

Signs of the Zodiac

Many people look forward to reading their daily horoscope, which is based on the sign under which they were born. Your assignment is to open the partially completed *Chapter 4 Additional Mini Case—Signs of the Zodiac* workbook, enter your name and birthday in cells C3 and C4, then enter the appropriate formulas in cells C5 and C6 to compute your age and astrological sign. The latter requires a VLOOKUP function that uses your birth date as an argument to search a table that contains the signs of the Zodiac and the appropriate dates. We have done the hard part for you by creating the table; all you have to do is develop the appropriate VLOOKUP function. Print the completed spreadsheet two ways, once to show displayed values and once to show the cell formulas. Try to explain how the VLOOKUP function works and how the various breakpoints are entered as specific dates, which in turn requires knowledge of the DATE and YEAR functions within Excel. Complete the spreadsheet by adding a hyperlink to a Web site for your horoscope.

PRACTICE WITH ACCESS

1. **Practice with File Management:** You will be working with many different databases in this class; thus, the ability to move and to copy a file is critical to your success. Download the practice files for *Office 2003 Volume I—Enhanced Edition* as described in Chapter 1 if you have not done so previously. The result will be an Exploring Access folder as shown in Figure 23. (Your screen will differ from ours, depending on where you install the files.) Proceed as follows:
   a. Start Windows Explorer and expand the folders in the tree pane until you can select the newly created Exploring Access folder as shown in Figure 23. Change to the Details view and (if necessary) click the column heading in the Name column to display the files in alphabetical order.
   b. Select the *Chapter 1 Additional Practice 1—Practice with File Management* document in the Exploring Access folder, and write down the date and time the file was last modified. Double click the file to start Microsoft Word and open the document, which contains a series of questions regarding disk and file management using Windows Explorer. Enter your answers into the document, save the completed document, and then print the completed document for your instructor. Close the document, but leave Word open in memory.
   c. Return to Windows Explorer. Pull down the View menu and click the Refresh command. Note that the date and time associated with the *Chapter 1 Additional Practice 1—Practice with File Management* document have changed to reflect the date/time you saved the document.
   d. Click the Date Modified column heading to arrange the files according to the date they were last modified. Click the column heading a second time (if necessary) so that the most recent file (the file you modified in part (b)) appears first. Press the Print Screen key to capture this screen to the Windows clipboard.
   e. Start a new document in Microsoft Word. Press the Enter key several times, then click the Paste button to paste the captured screen into the Word document. Press Ctrl+Home to move to the beginning of the document, and then enter your name and date to complete what will be used as a title page for this assignment. Submit both pages to your instructor.

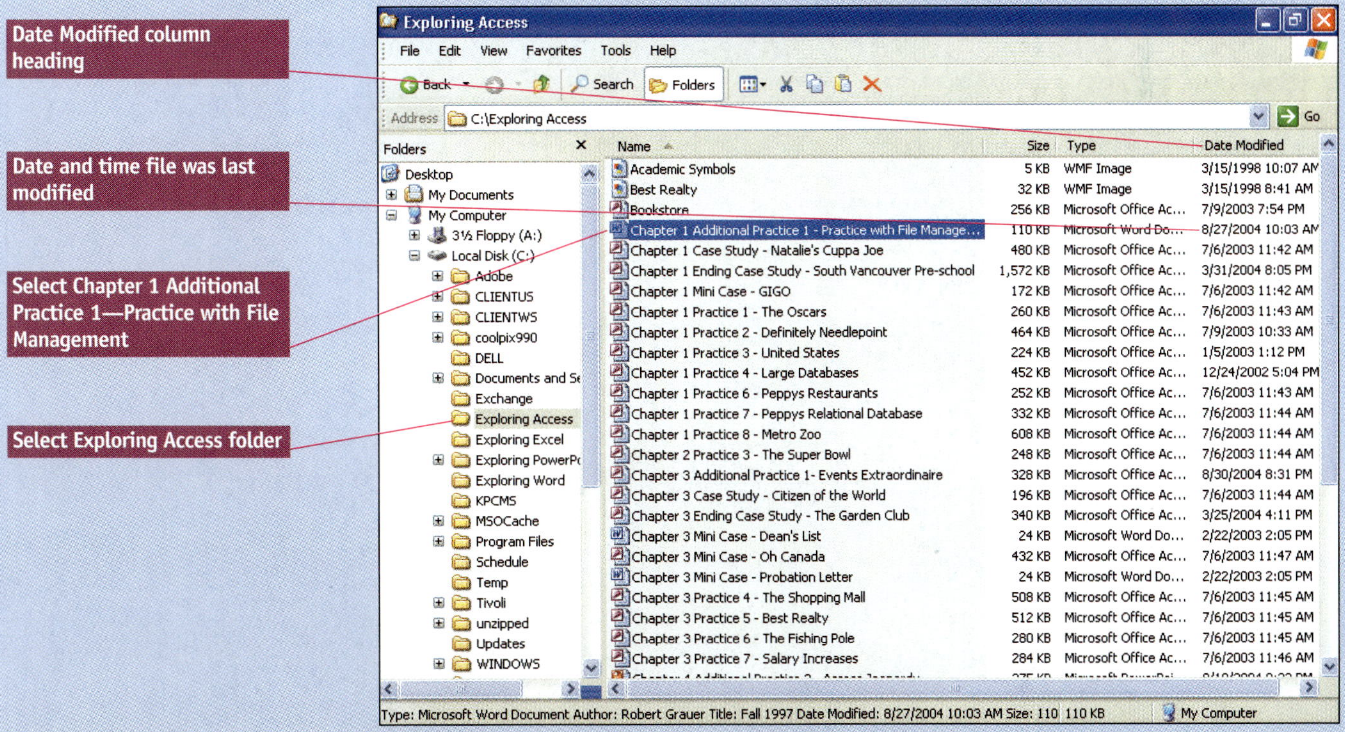

FIGURE 23 Practice with File Management (use with Chapter 1)

2. **Events Extraordinaire:** A close friend, who has started his own event planning business, has asked for your help in creating an Access database. The database is to track the events that your friend's company will coordinate. Your first task is to create the database and associated table as shown in Figure 24. The table is to be developed without benefit of the Table Wizard. Proceed as follows:
   a. Start Access and create a new database. Click the Tables button in the Database window and double click the option to Create table in Design view.
   b. Enter all of the fields and associated field types as shown in Figure 24. (To enter a new field, click in the Field Name column and type the name of the field. Do not use spaces in the field name.) Move to the Data Type column and choose the field type. Note that the EventScope should be created using the Lookup Wizard, and should specify Local, State, National, and International as the event scopes to be listed. Save the table as Events.
   c. Designate the EventID as the primary key (it was established as an AutoNumber field type). Set the Format property to \E000, which will automatically display an EventID that begins with the letter E, followed by a four-digit number. The Event IDs will be generated automatically each time a record is added.
   d. Establish input masks for the sponsor's contact phone number, the starting date, and the ending date. Establish the short date format for both dates.
   e. Set appropriate field sizes for all text fields; for example, change the field size of the Sponsor Contact's Last Name to 15 from the default value of 50.
   f. Select the currency format with zero decimal places for both the cost per person and the planning fee.
   g. Set the Required property to "Yes" for the Event Name, Sponsor, Sponsor Contact First Name, Sponsor Contact Last Name, Start Date, and End Date.
   h. Set the Validation Rule property for the Start Date and End Date to specify a date at least 30 days from today (>Now()+30). Set the Validation Text property to display an appropriate message if the user attempts to enter invalid data.
   i. Enter one record into the completed table using your name as the sponsor contact. Print the table only if you are not doing the next exercise. The table will require two or three pages, even if you change to landscape printing.

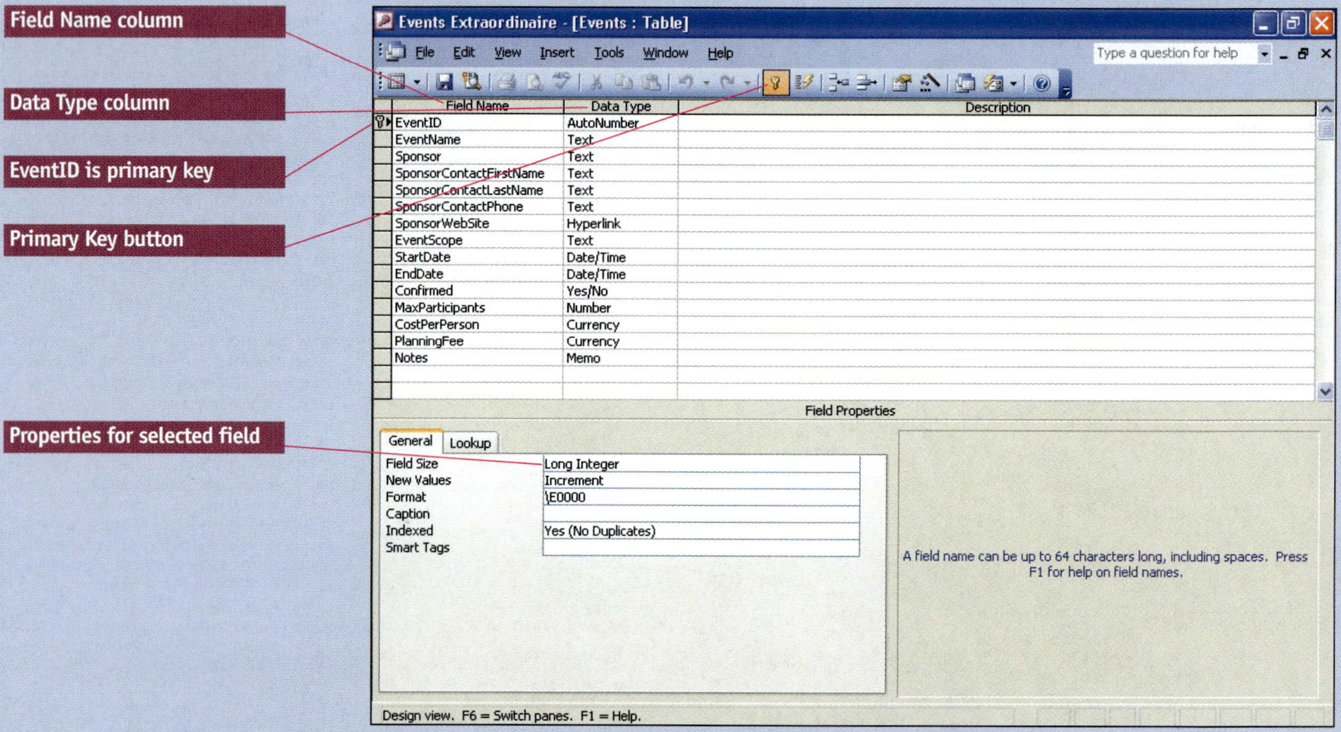

FIGURE 24 Events Extraordinaire (use with Chapter 2)

3. **A Form for Events Extraordinaire:** This assignment asks you to create a form similar to the one in Figure 25, which is based on the Events Extraordinaire database. The design of your form can be different from ours, but you must duplicate the functionality in our figure. Start with the Form Wizard, and then modify the resulting form as necessary so that your finished form accommodates all of the following:
   a. The form should contain a control for every field in the underlying table. In addition, create a calculated control for Potential Revenue (which is equal to the MaxParticipants multiplied by the CostPerPerson). Move, format, align, and size the controls and form background as necessary.
   b. Change the tab order of the controls so that the user tabs through the controls from left to right, top to bottom. Set the Tab Stop property of the EventID to "No" since the user does not input this value (because it is an AutoNumber field). Set the Tab Stop property to "No" for Potential Revenue as well.
   c. Use a different background color for the required fields (such as the Event Name and Sponsor) to emphasize that these fields must be entered. Include a note at the bottom of the form to explain the color change.
   d. Insert a form header with clip art (you do not have to use the same clip art as in our figure) and an appropriate title as shown in Figure 25. Set the Size Mode property of the clip art to Stretch.
   e. Add command buttons as indicated. The command buttons should be a uniform size with equal spacing between them. Test each command button to be sure that it works.
   f. Use the Page Setup command to be sure that the form will fit on a single page when printed. Change the margins and/or orientation of the form as necessary. The completed form should display the data that you entered for yourself when you created the table in the previous problem. Print this form for your instructor.
   g. Click the Add Record button to add a new record to the Events table. Use your instructor's name as the Sponsor Contact person and supply other information as you see fit. Click the Record Selector column to select your instructor's record. Pull down the File menu, click the Print command, then select the option button to print the selected record. Submit both forms to your instructor.

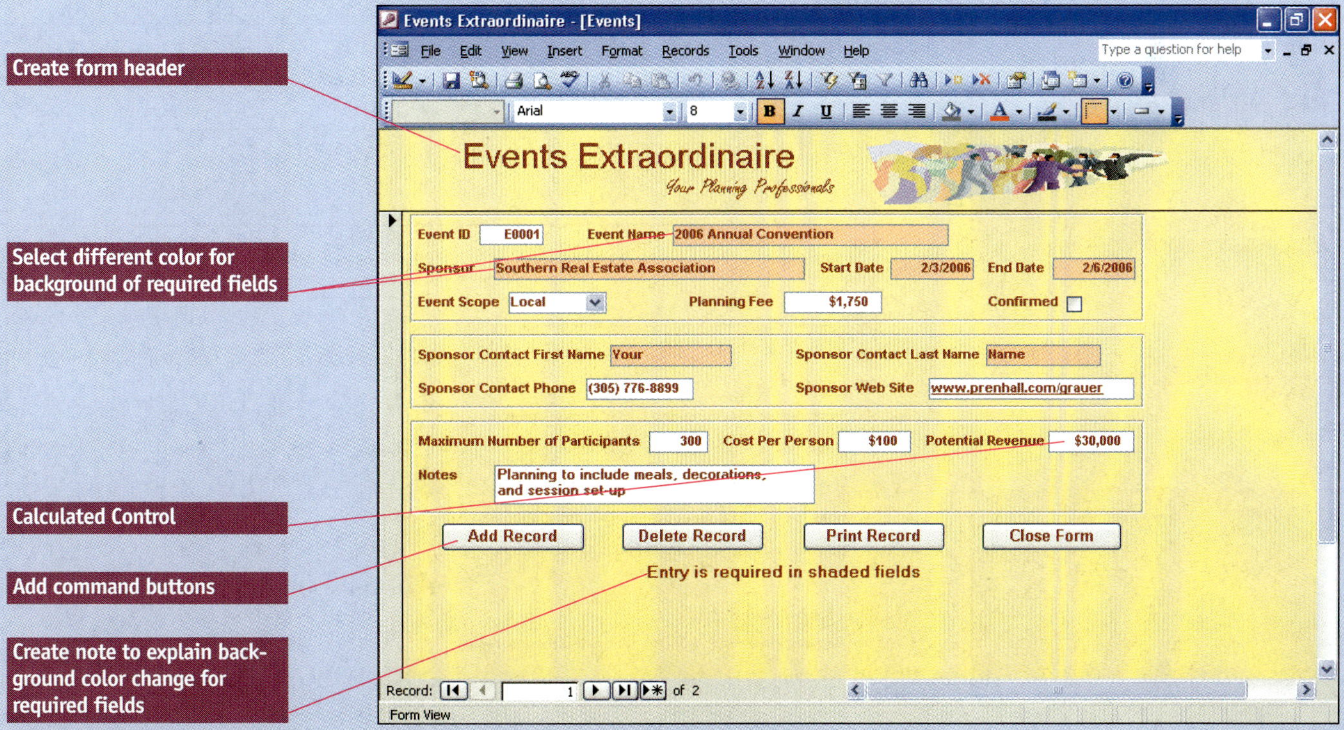

FIGURE 25 A Form for Events Extraordinaire (use with Chapter 2)

4. **Events Extraordinaire:** The partially completed *Chapter 3 Additional Practice 1—Events Extraordinaire* database builds on the previous two exercises. This database contains an Events table with 12 records that is the basis of four reports that are described below. (Only one report is shown in Figure 26.) All four reports are to have the same overall design and logo, but you need not match our design. Each report is required to have a page footer that displays today's date, the page number, and the number of pages in the complete report (e.g., "Page 1 of 2"). You may start with the Report Wizard and then modify the report in Design view, or you may create each report directly in Design view. Proceed as follows:
   a. The first report is to display every event in the database in ascending sequence according to the starting date. This report is to include five fields for each event: Event ID, Sponsor, the event name, the start date, and the planning fee. You are also asked to add a calculated control to the report footer that shows the number of the events (12 in our database).
   b. The second report is to display all local events in alphabetical sequence according to the sponsor's name. The report is to include sponsor, event name, start and end dates, and the maximum number of participants. (This report requires an underlying query.)
   c. The third report is to display the confirmed events in sequence by the starting date. The report is to include the start date, event name, sponsor, contact name (as a concatenated field that includes the first and last name), and the contact phone number. (This report requires an underlying query.)
   d. The fourth report is the group total report that is displayed in Figure 26. The Potential Revenues field is a calculated field that is equal to the maximum number of participants times the cost per person. The report can be based on a query, or you can add a calculated control in Design view. The group footer should show the potential revenue for each group. The report footer should show the total potential revenues for all events.
   e. Print each of the reports and turn them in to your instructor. Change the page orientation and/or margins if necessary to ensure that all of the fields for one record fit on one page.

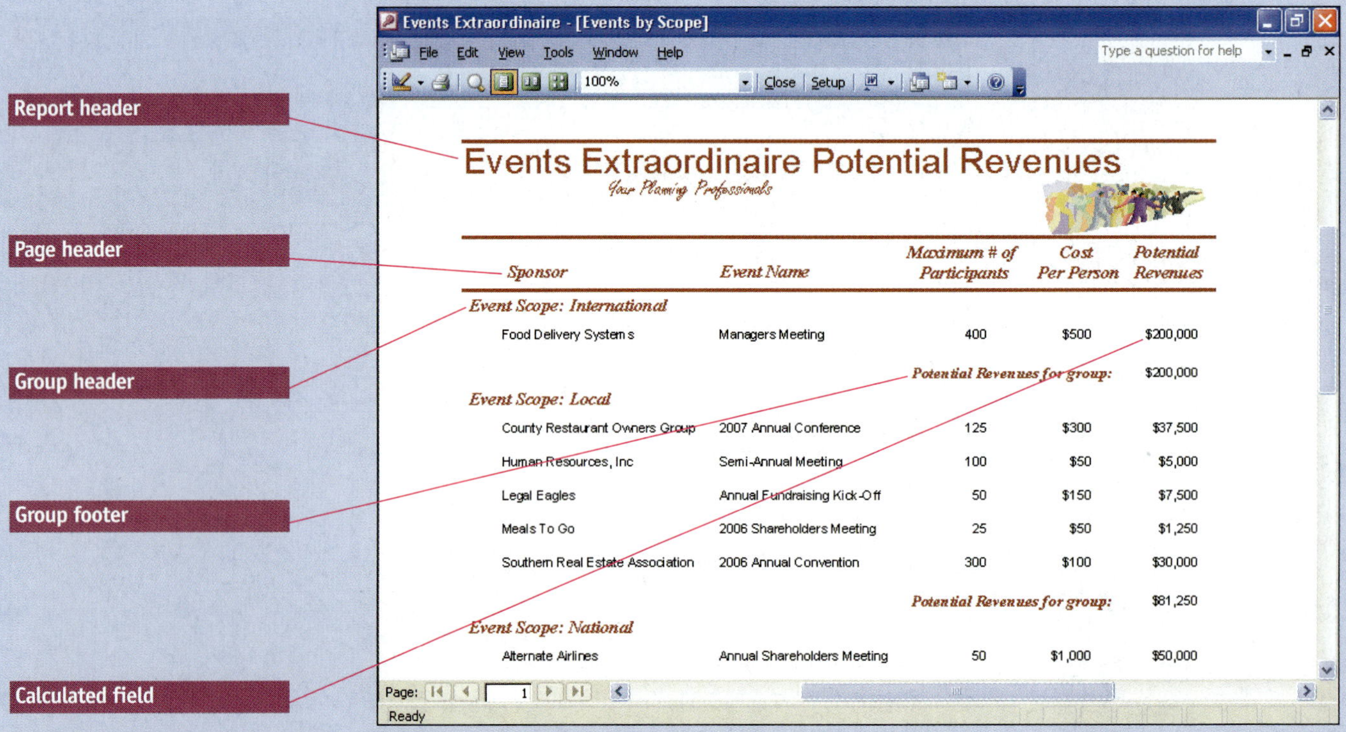

FIGURE 26 Events Extraordinaire (use with Chapter 3)

5. **Events Extraordinaire Report Switchboard:** Figure 27 displays a switchboard for the Events Extraordinaire database that has been developed in the preceding three exercises. Your assignment is to create a comparable switchboard that includes an option to display a report menu. The latter is a second (subsidiary) switchboard that includes commands to print all of the reports in the database, as well as an option to return to the Main Menu. Open the *Chapter 3 Additional Practice 1* database from the previous exercise and proceed as follows:
   a. Start the Switchboard Manager, which will display the Switchboard Manager dialog box. Click New to create a new switchboard (in addition to the main switchboard that is created by default). Enter "Report Menu" as the name of the new switchboard page, then click OK.
   b. You will return to the Switchboard Manager dialog box. Select the Main Switchboard, click Edit, and build the items for the main switchboard (open the About Events Extraordinaire form, which has been provided for you; open the Events form in Edit mode; go to the Report Menu switchboard; and exit the application). After you have built the main switchboard, close the Edit Switchboard Page dialog box to return to the Switchboard Manager dialog box.
   c. Select the Report Menu switchboard and click Edit. Build the items for the Report Menu, which consists of a separate command to open each report in the database, plus a command to return to the main menu. (The latter is a Go To Switchboard command that opens the Main switchboard.) Close the Edit Switchboard Page dialog box. Close the Switchboard Manager.
   d. Open the Switchboard form in Design view to format the switchboard as shown in Figure 27. You do not have to match our design exactly, but your switchboard should be consistent with the design of your forms and reports.
   e. Use the Startup property in the Tools menu to display the switchboard automatically when the database is opened initially. Pull down the Tools menu, click the Database Utilities command, then click the command to Compact and Repair the Database. Access will close the database and then reopen the database and display the switchboard. Test both switchboards completely to be sure that they work correctly.
   f. Print the Switchboard form and Switchboard Items table for your instructor.

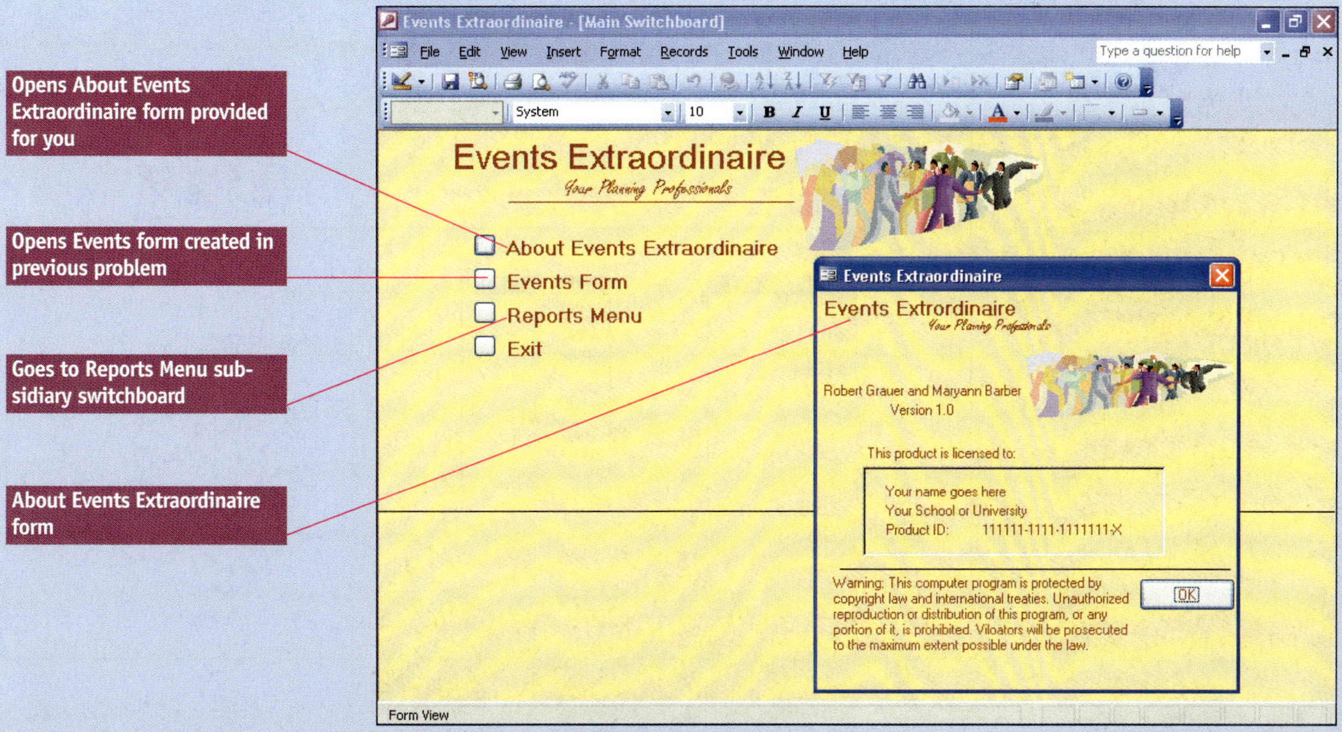

FIGURE 27 Events Extraordinaire Report Switchboard (use with Chapter 4)

6. **Widgets of America Database Design:** Figure 28 displays the relationships diagram in the Widgets of America database that tracks the orders generated by the company's sales staff. There are two one-to-many relationships in the database. One salesperson can have many customers, and one customer can have many orders. Your task is to implement the design in Figure 28 by creating the indicated tables and establishing the relationships. Proceed as follows:
   a. Start Access and create a new database. You do not have to enter data into any of the tables, but you have to create the tables and set all of the field properties in each table. Pay particular attention to the required property as it pertains to the related fields in the various tables. Note that a customer must have an assigned sales representative to place an order. In addition, the company will not accept an order unless the order is associated with a specific customer.
   b. Pull down the Tools menu and click the Relationships command to establish the relationships in Figure 28. Stay in the Relationships window, pull down the File menu, and then click the Print Relationships command to preview the report containing the relationships diagram. Change to the Design view to modify the report header to include a title, today's date, your name, and an appropriate clip art image.
   c. Create a simple About Widgets of America form that is similar to the other About forms that were presented in previous databases. Use the same clip art as in the relationships diagram.
   d. Create a simple switchboard with three menu options—a button to display the About Widgets of America form, a button to print the relationships diagram, and a button to exit the application. The switchboard should contain the same clip art, color scheme, and fonts as the relationships diagram and About form.
   e. Test the switchboard thoroughly to be sure it works correctly. Use the Startup property in the Tools menu to display the switchboard automatically when the database is opened initially. Print the relationships diagram, the Switchboard form, and the Switchboard Items table for your instructor.

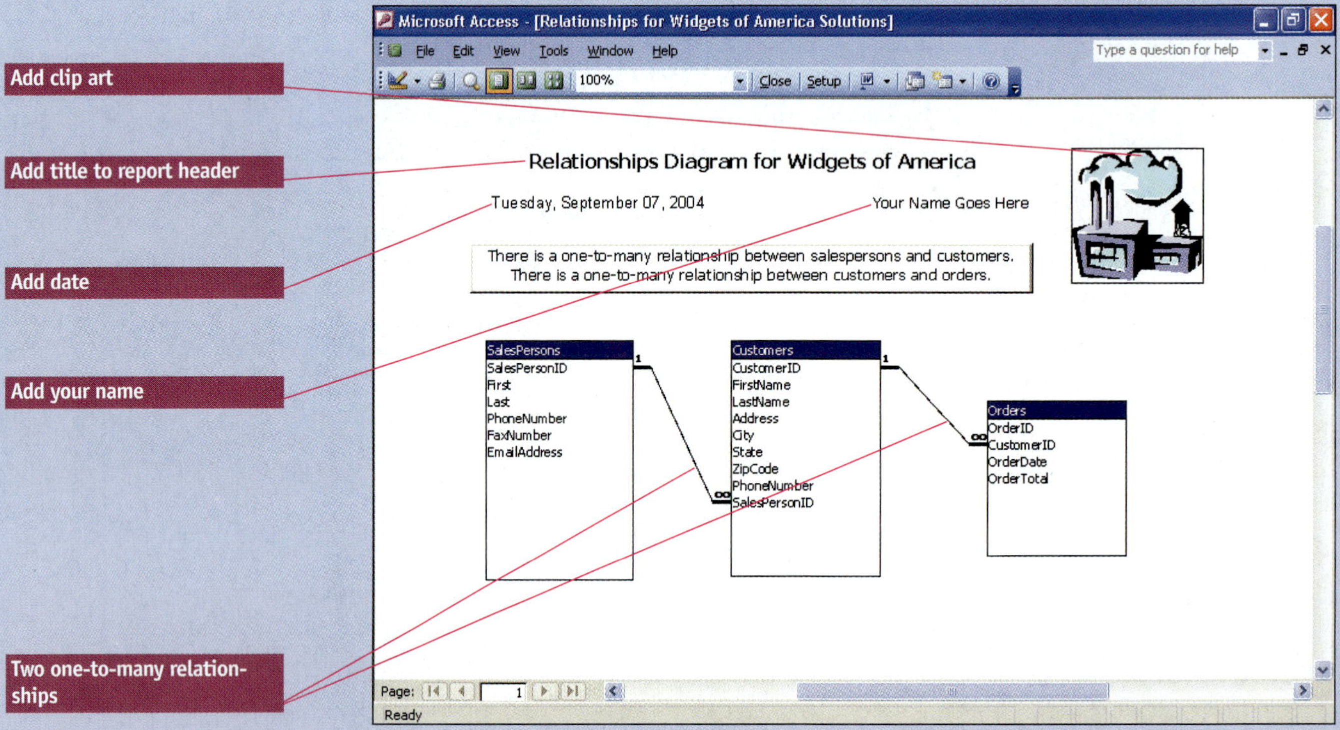

FIGURE 28 Widgets of America Database Design (use with Chapter 4)

7. **Access Jeopardy:** How well do you know Microsoft Access? The presentation in Figure 29 contains a Jeopardy game with 25 answers and questions that review material from Chapters 1 through 4. All you have to do is open the presentation and play the game. Thus, open the *Chapter 4 Additional Practice 3—Access Jeopardy* presentation and proceed as follows:
   a. Pull down the Slide Show menu and click the View Show command (or click the F5 key) to view the slide show, which begins with the title slide. Click the mouse to move to slide 2 (the board). The names of the categories will appear one after another, after which you can select any question in any category. Each dollar amount is a hyperlink to another slide in the presentation.
   b. Select (click) a question, such as the $400 question in the Tables and Forms category, to display the clue, "Recommended field type for phone numbers and zip codes". Click the mouse to display the answer "What is a text field?" (that appears in the form of a question), then click the answer to return to slide 2 (the board). Before you click, be sure you see the tiny hand indicating that you are clicking the hyperlink, as opposed to clicking the background of the slide.
   c. You should be back on slide 2, the Jeopardy board. Look closely and you will see that the color of the text (i.e., the 400) has changed, indicating that the hyperlink has been followed. Select a different question, view the answer, and return to the game board so that you can be sure of the navigation.
   d. Select a classmate and play the game. There is no buzzer, so you have to determine an equitable way to gain control of the board and keep score. We leave the details to you.
   e. Print the presentation in a variety of ways. Select the first two slides, pull down the File menu, click the Print command, choose the option button for Selection, and select Slides in the Print What list box. Click OK to print. Pull down the Print menu a second time and print the entire presentation in Outline view. Study the outline and be sure that you can answer all of the questions.
   f. You will find additional games for the other Office applications (PowerPoint, Excel, and Word) in the appropriate folders after downloading the practice files from our Web site. The Excel game, for example, is found in the Exploring Excel folder and reviews material from Chapters 1 through 4 in the Excel section.

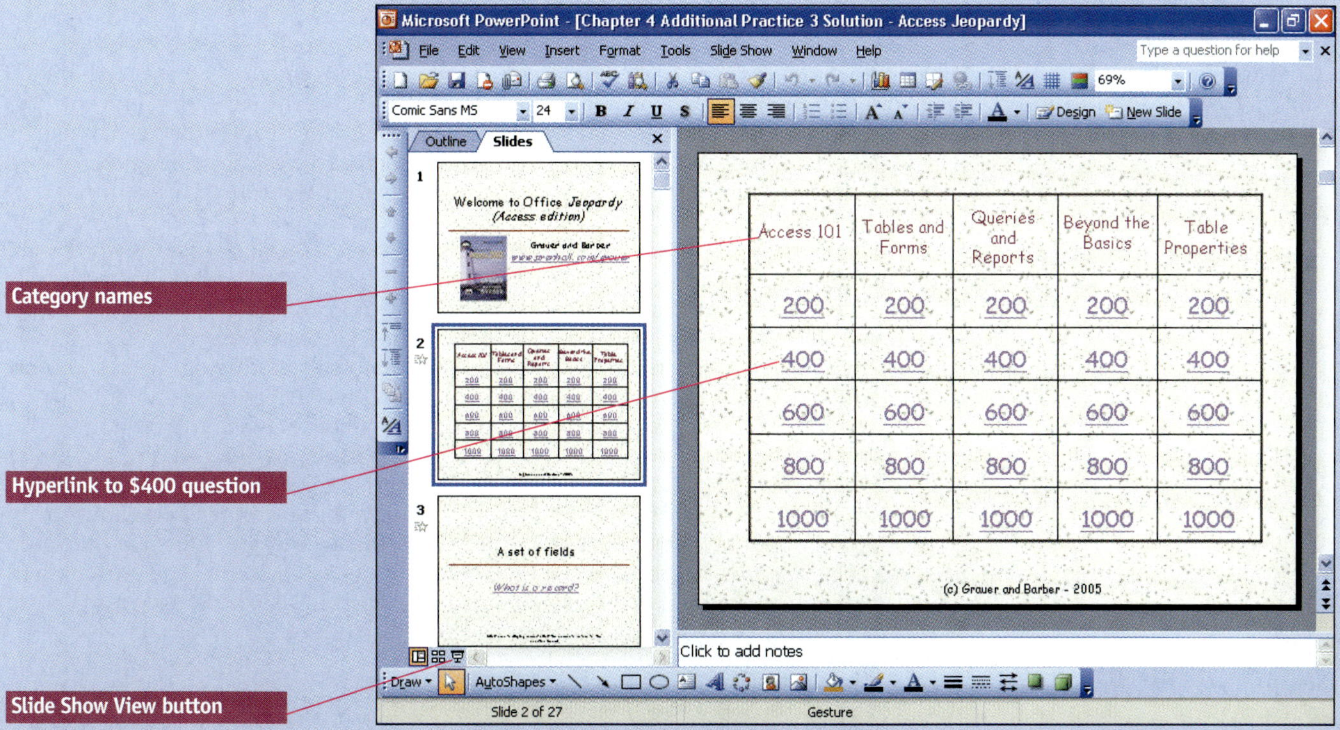

FIGURE 29 Access Jeopardy (use with Chapter 4)

ADDITIONAL MINI CASES

Study Break—Word Find and Crossword Puzzles

Almost everyone enjoys a good puzzle. With this in mind, we have created a series of unique crossword and word find puzzles to accompany the Exploring Office series. Open the *Chapters 1 to 4 Mini Case—Access Study Break* document in the Exploring Access folder, and then print the document. You will find two puzzles for each chapter, a word find and a crossword.

We suggest that you start with the word find and use the list of keywords and concepts at the end of the chapter to determine what each clue represents, and then locate the corresponding word or phrase in the puzzle. You can then try the accompanying crossword, which repeats clues from the word find to reinforce the material, and which adds additional clues to challenge you further. Add your name at the top of the puzzle(s), and then submit the puzzle(s) to your instructor. And if you are up to a challenge, try the composite (Sunday) crossword puzzle that combines the clues from Access Chapters 1 through 4 in a single puzzle.

Online Study Guide

Every chapter in the Exploring Office series has an online component that helps you to review the conceptual material in the chapter. Go to www.prenhall.com/grauer after you have completed the chapter and click the icon for the Office 2003 book to go to the home page for this series. Click the appropriate title in the left pane, such as Office Volume I or Access, then click the down arrow in the list box at the top of the screen to select the appropriate chapter—for example, Access Chapter 1. Click the link to Online Study Guide in the left pane and take the quiz that consists of objective questions (multiple choice, true/false, and matching).

Click the "Submit Answers for Grading" button at the bottom of the quiz so that you can see your results. Scroll to the bottom of the answer screen, and then e-mail the results to yourself in HTML format. (If you send the results as text instead of HTML, you will get too many pages of output.) Start your e-mail program, print the e-mail message that contains your results, and bring it to class to submit to your instructor.

University Apartments

You have just signed your lease for next year at University Apartments, where you have the opportunity to design a database for the complex and thereby save on your rent. The complex has 500 apartments, which are divided into various categories as determined by the number of bedrooms and additional amenities such as a washer/dryer, patio, and so on. There are many apartments in each category, but a given apartment has only one category.

Your database is to track all apartments in the complex and the students who live in those apartments. Each apartment is leased to one or more students, who sign the identical lease with the same rent, and the same starting date and ending date for the lease. The lease information is stored within the Apartment record. Each student pays his or her rent individually each month. Your database should be capable of producing reports to show the total rent received for each apartment and the total rent paid by each student.

Design a database that will satisfy the information requirements. You do not have to enter data into the tables, but you do have to create the tables in order to create the relationships diagram, which you will submit to your instructor. Create an About form similar to the ones presented in previous databases, then develop a simple switchboard with three menu options—a button to display the "About the Apartments" form, a button to print the relationships diagram, and a button to exit the application. The switchboard should contain the same clip art as the relationships diagram. Use the Startup property to display the switchboard when the database is opened.

PRACTICE WITH POWERPOINT

1. **Practice with File Management:** You will be working with many different PowerPoint presentations in this class; thus, the ability to move and to copy a file is critical to your success. Download the practice files for *Office 2003 Volume I—Enhanced Edition* as described in Chapter 1 if you have not done so previously. The result will be an Exploring PowerPoint folder as shown in Figure 30. (Your screen will differ from ours, depending on where you install the files.) Proceed as follows:

    a. Start Windows Explorer and expand the folders in the tree pane until you can select the newly created Exploring PowerPoint folder as shown in Figure 30. Change to the Details view and (if necessary) click the column heading in the Name column to display the files in alphabetical order.

    b. Select the *Chapter 1 Additional Practice 1—Practice with File Management* document in the Exploring PowerPoint folder, and write down the date and time the file was last modified. Double click the file to start Microsoft Word and open the document, which contains a series of questions regarding disk and file management using Windows Explorer. Enter your answers into the document, save the completed document, and then print the completed document for your instructor. Close the document, but leave Word open in memory.

    c. Return to Windows Explorer. Pull down the View menu and click the Refresh command. Note that the date and time associated with the *Chapter 1 Additional Practice 1—Practice with File Management* document have changed to reflect the date/time you saved the document.

    d. Click the Date Modified column heading to arrange the files according to the date they were last modified. Click the column heading a second time (if necessary) so that the most recent file (the file you modified in part (b)) appears first. Press the Print Screen key to capture this screen to the Windows clipboard.

    e. Start a new document in Microsoft Word. Press the Enter key several times, then click the Paste button to paste the captured screen into the Word document. Press Ctrl+Home to move to the beginning of the document, and then enter your name and date to complete what will be used as a title page for this assignment. Submit both pages to your instructor.

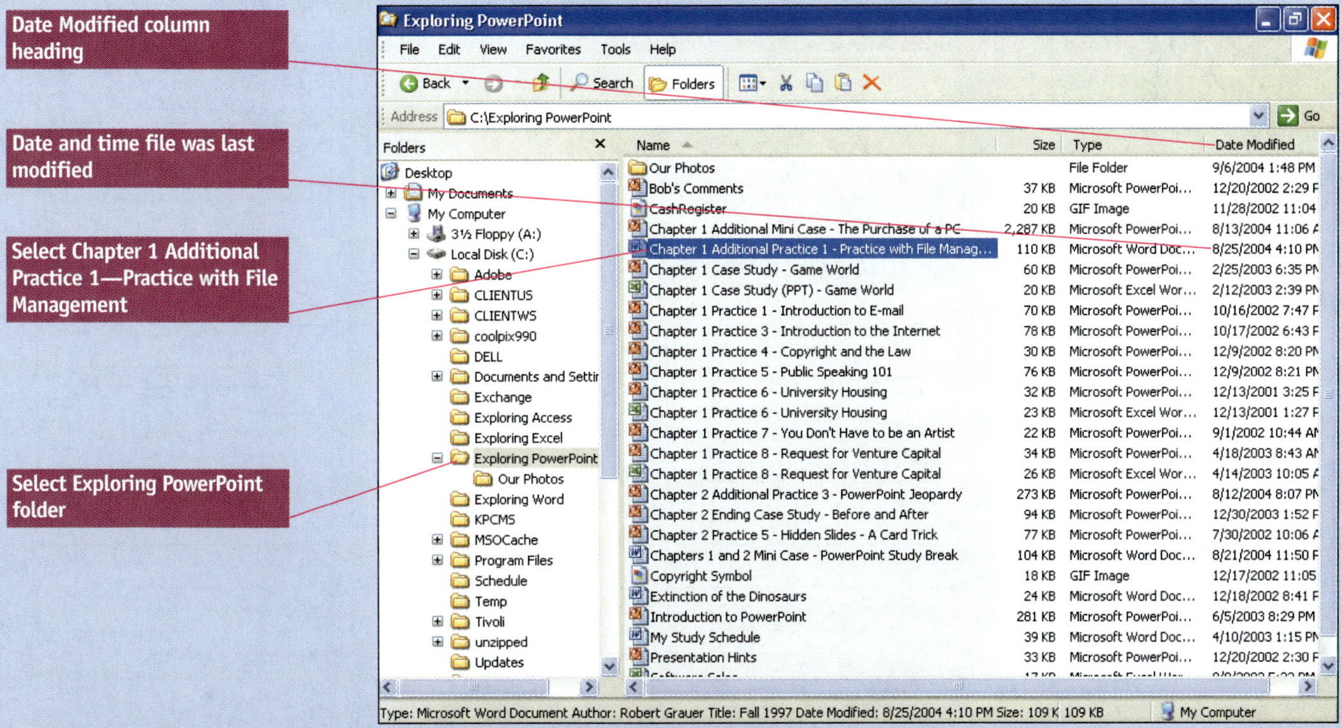

FIGURE 30 Practice with File Management (use with Chapter 1)

2. **PowerPoint Lectures Online:** You can use PowerPoint to create a presentation on virtually anything, so why not create a presentation that describes how to use PowerPoint? This is precisely what the authors have done; we have created a PowerPoint lecture for every chapter in the text. The procedure to download these presentations is identical to downloading the practice files as described in the first hands-on exercise. Proceed as follows:
   a. Go to the Grauer Web site at www.prenhall.com/grauer; click the link to Office 2003, click the Student Resources tab, then scroll until you can click the link to the PowerPoint lectures for the PowerPoint text. Save the file to your desktop, double click the file that you just downloaded, and follow the onscreen instructions to unzip the presentation to the *Exploring Office 2003 PowerPoint Lectures* folder.
   b. Start PowerPoint. Pull down the File menu, click the Open command, and change to the drive and folder where you just unzipped the PowerPoint lectures. Open the presentation for PowerPoint Chapter 1.
   c. Pull down the Slide Show menu and click the View Show command to view the presentation. There are 41 slides in all, and it should take you no more than 10 or 15 minutes to go through the entire presentation. The presentation should be a good review of the material in Chapter 1.
   d. Go to the title slide, click after the authors' names, press the Enter key to start a new line, and enter your name.
   e. Create a new slide immediately after the title slide. Choose the Title and Text layout, title the slide "Things I Learned in This Chapter", and then list at least four facts about PowerPoint that were covered in the chapter.
   f. Print the presentation in multiple ways. Print the title slide as a slide (full page) to serve as a cover page for the assignment. Print audience handouts for the entire presentation (six per page). Be sure to frame the individual slides. Print the outline of the presentation. Submit all of your material to your instructor as proof you completed this assignment.

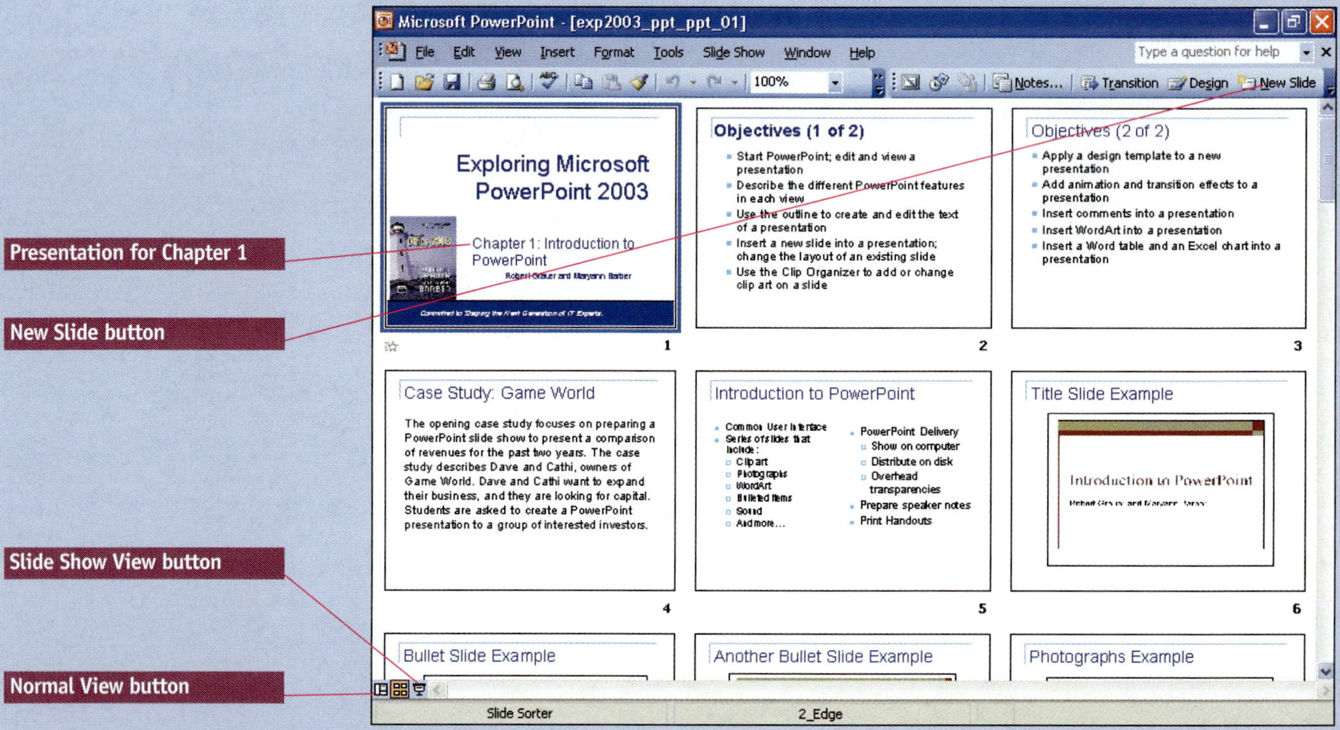

FIGURE 31 PowerPoint Lectures Online (use with Chapter 1)

3. **Working with Photographs:** The presentation in Figure 32 displays a collection of photographs. All of the photographs were obtained by searching the Clip Organizer within Microsoft Office. Click the button to Insert Clip Art to open the task pane, enter "Animals" as the text for your search, and then restrict the results to photographs. (You do not have to use the same photographs as in the figure, and indeed you may work with any subject matter you like.) The exercise is intended for an active Internet connection that extends the search to the Microsoft Web site. Proceed as follows:
   a. Start a new presentation. Create a title slide, and then insert a blank slide. Use the Insert Clip Art command as just described to locate multiple photographs for insertion on the slide. Arrange the pictures in an attractive overlapping fashion.
   b. Select all of the photographs, then use the Format Picture command to apply a black 4-point border around every picture.
   c. Check that all of the photographs are still selected. Click the Compress Photographs tool on the Picture toolbar to compress the pictures and reduce the file sizes.
   d. Click on any picture to deselect all of the pictures. Pull down the Slide Show menu, click Custom Animation, and apply individual entrance effects to each of the photographs. Set each entrance so that it begins automatically after the previous animation.
   e. Insert a second blank slide. Create six separate WordArt objects, each of which is a single letter, (S, A, F, A, R, and I), and each of which uses a different photograph for fill. (You have to save each picture as a separate file in order to use it as fill for a WordArt object.)
   f. Use custom animation so that the objects appear in sequence, one after the other. Include the sound of applause in conjunction with the letter I when "Safari" is spelled out completely.
   g. Print the title slide as a full slide to use as a cover sheet for the assignment. Print the presentation as an audience handout (two slides per page) for your instructor. Add a footer at the bottom of the page that includes your name.

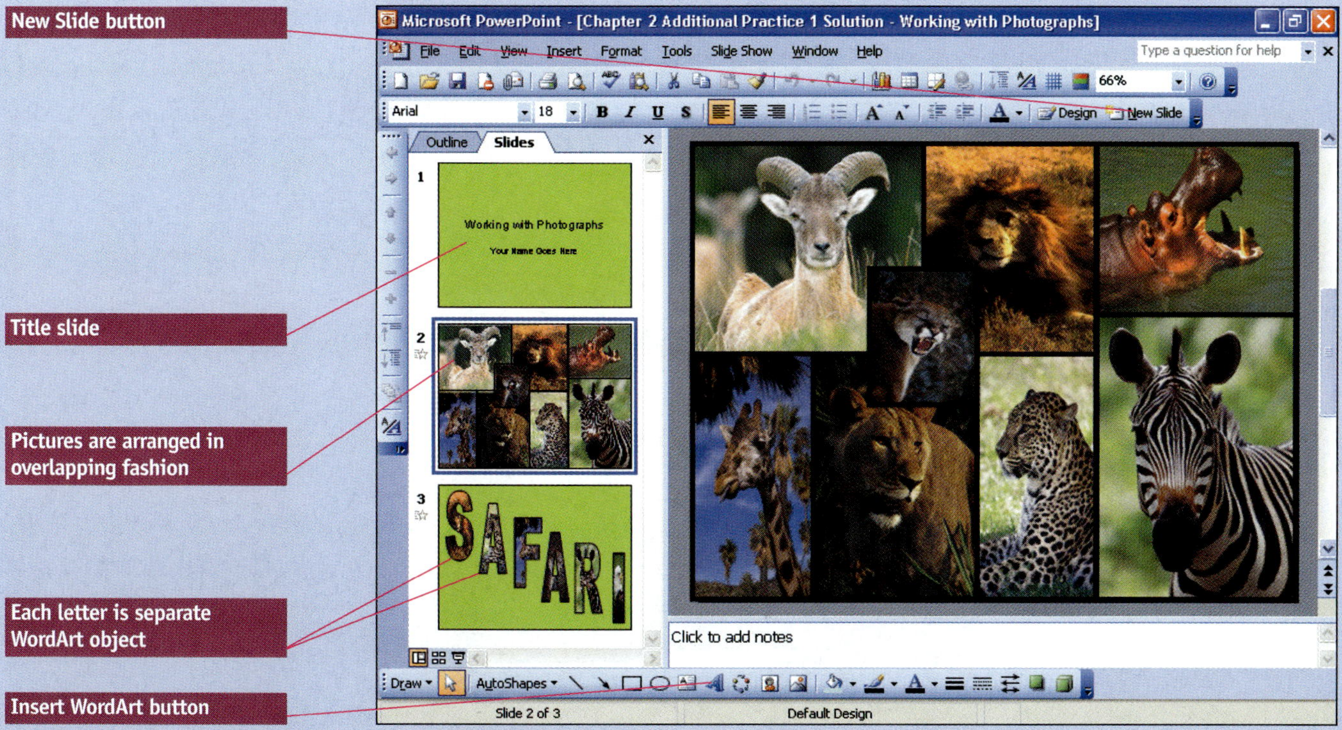

FIGURE 32 Working with Photographs (use with Chapter 2)

4. **Photographs on the Web:** Choose any collection of photographs to create a Web-based presentation similar to the one in Figure 33. You may select your own pictures, download photographs from the Microsoft Design Gallery, and/or use the photographs we supply in the Exploring PowerPoint folder. Each photograph must be saved as a separate file. (The photographs can be stored in different folders.)
   a. Start a new presentation. Create a title slide containing your name. Insert five or six new slides (choose the title only layout) for the photographs.
   b. Select the second slide in your presentation (the slide that will contain the first photograph). Pull down the Format menu, click Background to display the Background dialog box, click the down arrow in the background fill list box, and choose Fill Effects. Click the Picture tab, click the Select Picture button, insert the desired picture, and apply it to this slide. The photograph should fill the entire slide, a technique that adds interest to any presentation.
   c. Enter the title of the picture in the title placeholder, changing the font color and/or the position of the placeholder as necessary to read the title.
   d. Repeat steps (b) and (c) to insert additional photographs and the associated titles on the remaining slides.
   e. Change to the Slide Sorter view after all of the pictures have been inserted into the presentation. Press and hold the Shift key to select multiple slides, pull down the Slide Show menu, and click the Transition command. Add a transition effect for each slide, which includes the camera sound.
   f. Print the audience handouts (six per page) for your instructor. You must specify color (even if you do not have a color printer) within the Color/Grayscale list box within the Print dialog box to see the slide backgrounds.
   g. Save the completed presentation as a Web page, as shown in Figure 33. You do *not* have to upload the presentation to the Web. Print the first slide in the presentation from Internet Explorer to show that you have successfully created a Web document.

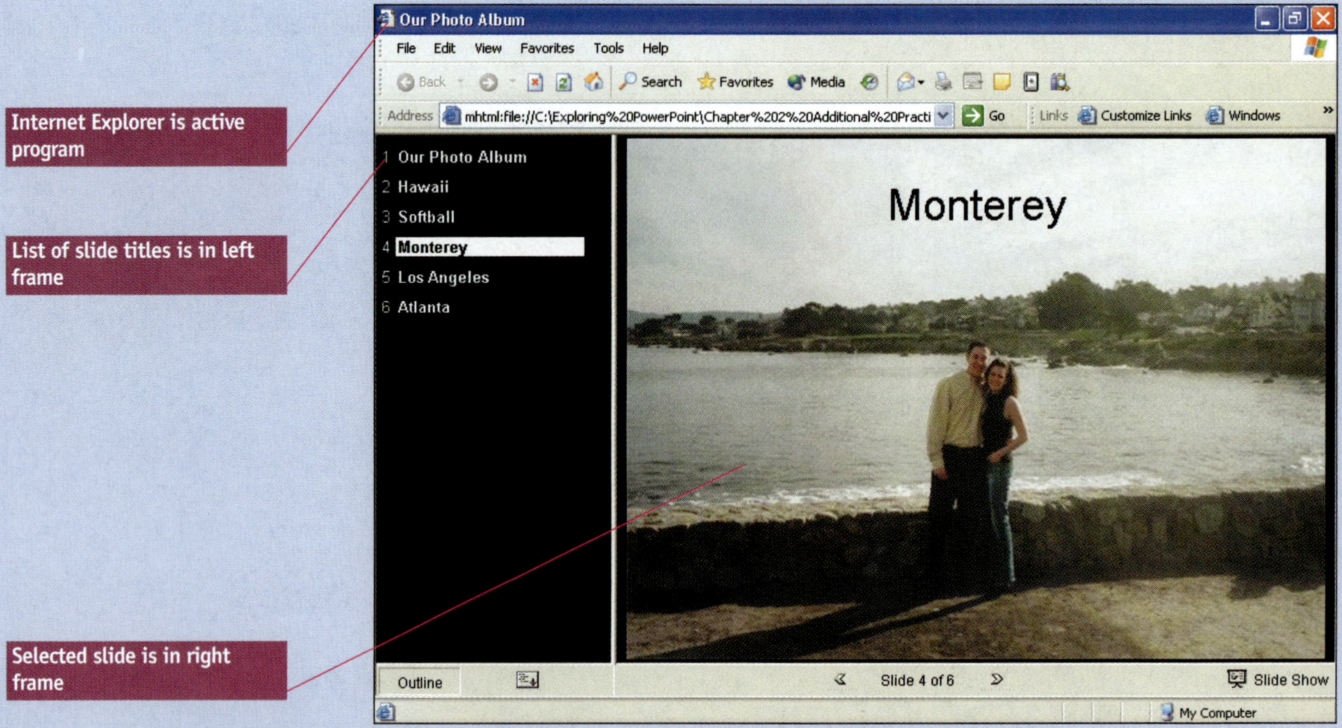

FIGURE 33 Photographs on the Web (use with Chapter 2)

5. **PowerPoint Jeopardy:** How well do you know PowerPoint? The presentation in Figure 34 contains a Jeopardy game with 25 answers and questions that review material from Chapters 1 and 2. All you have to do is open the presentation and play the game. Thus, open the *Chapter 2 Additional Practice 3—PowerPoint Jeopardy* presentation and proceed as follows:
   a. Pull down the Slide Show menu and click the View Show command (or click the F5 key) to view the slide show, which begins with the title slide. Click the mouse to move to slide 2 (the board). The names of the categories will appear one after another, after which you can select any question in any category. Each dollar amount is a hyperlink to another slide in the presentation.
   b. Select (click) a question, such as the $400 question in the Menus and Wizards category, to display the clue, "It contains the Cut, Copy, and Paste commands". Click the mouse to display the answer "What is the Edit menu?" (that appears in the form of a question), then click the answer to return to slide 2 (the board). Before you click, be sure you see the tiny hand indicating that you are clicking the hyperlink, as opposed to clicking the background of the slide.
   c. You should be back on slide 2, the Jeopardy board. Look closely and you will see that the color of the text (i.e., the 400) has changed, indicating that the hyperlink has been followed. Select a different question, view the answer, and return to the game board so that you can be sure of the navigation.
   d. Select a classmate and play the game. There is no buzzer, so you have to determine an equitable way to gain control of the board and keep score. We leave the details to you.
   e. Print the presentation in a variety of ways. Select the first two slides, pull down the File menu, click the Print command, choose the option button for Selection, and select Slides in the Print What list box. Click OK to print. Pull down the Print menu a second time and print the entire presentation in Outline view. Study the outline and be sure that you can answer all of the questions.
   f. You will find additional games for the other Office applications (Word, Excel, and Access) in the appropriate folders after downloading the practice files from our Web site. The Excel game, for example, is found in the Exploring Excel folder and reviews material from Chapters 1 through 4 in the Excel section.

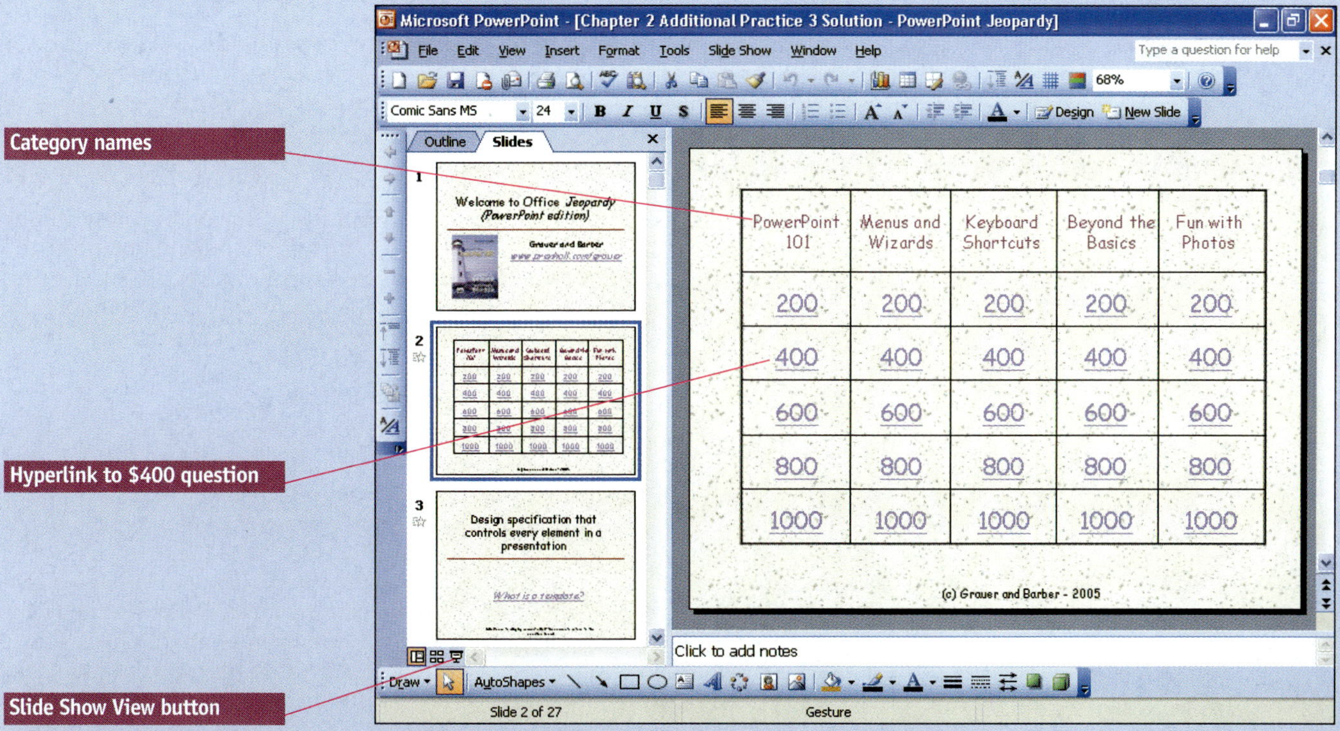

FIGURE 34 PowerPoint Jeopardy (use with Chapter 2)

ADDITIONAL MINI CASES

Study Break—Word Find and Crossword Puzzles

Almost everyone enjoys a good puzzle. With this in mind, we have created a series of unique crossword and word find puzzles to accompany the Exploring Office series. Open the *Chapters 1 and 2 Mini Case—PowerPoint Study Break* document in the Exploring PowerPoint folder, and then print the document. You will find two puzzles for each chapter, a word find and a crossword.

We suggest that you start with the word find and use the list of keywords and concepts at the end of the chapter to determine what each clue represents, and then locate the corresponding word or phrase in the puzzle. You can then try the accompanying crossword, which repeats clues from the word find to reinforce the material, and which adds additional clues to challenge you further. Add your name at the top of the puzzle(s), and then submit the puzzle(s) to your instructor. And if you are up to a challenge, try the composite (Sunday) crossword puzzle that combines the clues from both PowerPoint chapters in a single puzzle.

Online Study Guide

Every chapter in the Exploring Office series has an online component that helps you to review the conceptual material in the chapter. Go to www.prenhall.com/grauer after you have completed the chapter and click the icon for the Office 2003 book to go to the home page for this series. Click the appropriate title in the left pane, such as Office Volume I or PowerPoint, then click the down arrow in the list box at the top of the screen to select the appropriate chapter—for example, PowerPoint Chapter 1. Click the link to Online Study Guide in the left pane and take the quiz that consists of objective questions (multiple choice, true/false, and matching).

Click the Submit Answers for Grading button at the bottom of the quiz so that you can see your results. Scroll to the bottom of the answer screen, and then e-mail the results to yourself in HTML format. (If you send the results as text instead of HTML, you will get too many pages of output.) Start your e-mail program, print the e-mail message that contains your results, and bring it to class to submit to your instructor.

The Purchase of a PC

Are you confused about all the ads for personal computers? The purchase of a PC need not be a trying experience if you approach it just as you would the purchase of any big-ticket item—with research and planning. Be sure you know your hardware requirements before you walk into the store or else you will spend too much money or buy the wrong system. To help you in your research, we have created the *Chapter 1 Additional Mini Case—The Purchase of a PC* presentation in the Exploring PowerPoint folder. (The material in this presentation is taken from the Essential Computing Concepts section in our text, *Exploring Microsoft Office, Volume I.*) All you have to do for this assignment, however, is view the slide show, and then print the presentation in a variety of ways. Print the title slide as a slide (full page) to serve as a cover page, and then print the audience handouts for the entire presentation (six per page). Add a short note to your instructor that summarizes your thoughts on buying a personal computer.

The First Ladies

The *Chapter 2 Practice 3—My Favorite Presidents* presentation (in Chapter 2) asked you to visit the White House Web site to download resources for a presentation on presidents of the United States. We neglected, however, to examine the role of the First Lady. The fact that these women share such an intimate connection with the leaders of the most powerful free nation in the world is reason enough to further examine their role and influence in American life. This assignment asks you to create a parallel presentation on selected first ladies. You need not focus on the spouses of the presidents in the earlier presentation; you should select the first ladies you think were most interesting and/or influential. Print the completed presentation for your instructor.

CASE STUDY

Integrated Case Study
The Airport Inn

OBJECTIVES

1. Use the core applications in Office 2003 individually or in conjunction with one another.
2. Link an Excel chart to a Word document and a PowerPoint presentation.
3. Import an Excel worksheet into an Access database.
4. Create Access tables, queries, reports, and forms.
5. Use an Access table as the basis for a mail merge.
6. Use Word to create a Web page for the organization.

integrated exercises

1. Airport Inn Revenue Workbook and Chart (Excel)
2. Report to the President (Word and Excel)
3. Presentation to the President (PowerPoint and Excel)
4. Last-minute Change (Word, Excel, and PowerPoint)
5. Importing Data (Access and Excel)
6. A Relational Database (Access)
7. Access Objects: Forms, Queries, and Reports (Access)
8. An Access Switchboard (Access)
9. Mail Merge (Word and Access)
10. Worksheet References (Excel)
11. Presentation to the Board (PowerPoint and Excel)
12. Letter to the Board (Word and Excel)
13. Create a Home Page (Word)
14. Submission Checklist (Word)

This document provides a series of 14 exercises in Microsoft Office that relate to the Airport Inn, a hypothetical hotel that is located near an airport. Each exercise describes a specific task for the organization to accomplish and typically requires the use of multiple applications within Microsoft Office for solution. Many of the exercises are cumulative in nature. You may, for example, be asked to create an Excel chart in one exercise, and then incorporate that chart into a Word memo and a PowerPoint presentation in subsequent exercises. Other exercises will ask you to create or modify an Access database, to exchange data between Excel and Access, and to create a Web page for the Airport Inn. Collectively, you will gain considerable practice in the core applications of Microsoft Office 2003, and especially in how they work together to accomplish complex tasks.

All of the exercises are based on material from the core application chapters in *Exploring Office 2003 Volume I.* Specific chapter references are deliberately not provided so that the case study is as realistic as possible. Think of this assignment as your first day on the job; you were hired because you are proficient in Microsoft Office. This is your chance to show what you know. ■

Your assignment is to follow the directions of your instructor with respect to which of the exercises you are to complete within the case description. You should begin by downloading the practice files from our Web site at www.prenhall.com/grauer. Go to the site, click the book icon for Office 2003, and then click the Student Resources tab. Scroll until you can select the link to *Integrated Case Studies (Enhanced Edition)*, and then download the file to your desktop. Double click the file icon and follow the onscreen instructions to install the practice files on your computer. The files you need will be in the Airport Inn folder within the Exploring Integrated Cases folder.

INTEGRATED EXERCISES

1. **Airport Inn Revenue Workbook and Chart (Excel):** You will find a partially completed version of the spreadsheet in Figure 1 in the *Airport Inn Revenue* workbook in the Airport Inn folder. (You can download the practice files for this case study from our Web site at www.prenhall.com/grauer.) Open the workbook and save it as *Airport Inn Revenue Solution* so that you can return to the original workbook if necessary. Proceed as follows:
   a. Click in cell F3 and enter the formula to compute the total revenue for the first revenue source (walk-in reservations). Copy this formula to the remaining cells in column F.
   b. Click in cell B8 and compute the total revenue for the first quarter. Copy this formula to the remaining cells in this row.
   c. Use the AutoFormat command as the basis for formatting your worksheet in an attractive fashion. You can match our formatting, or you can use your own design.
   d. Select the data in cells A2 through E7 to create a side-by-side column chart. Specify that the data series are in columns so that the different sources appear on the X axis. Place the legend at the bottom of the chart. Save this chart in its own sheet called Revenues by Reservation Source. Print the completed chart for your instructor.
   e. Create a second side-by-side column chart using the same data as in part (d). This time, however, specify that the data are in rows so that the quarters appear on the X axis. Save this chart in its own sheet called Revenues by Quarter. You do not have to print this chart at this time.
   f. Enter your name in the worksheet as shown.
   g. Print the completed worksheet twice, once to show displayed values and once to show the cell formulas.
   h. Save the completed workbook for use in subsequent exercises.

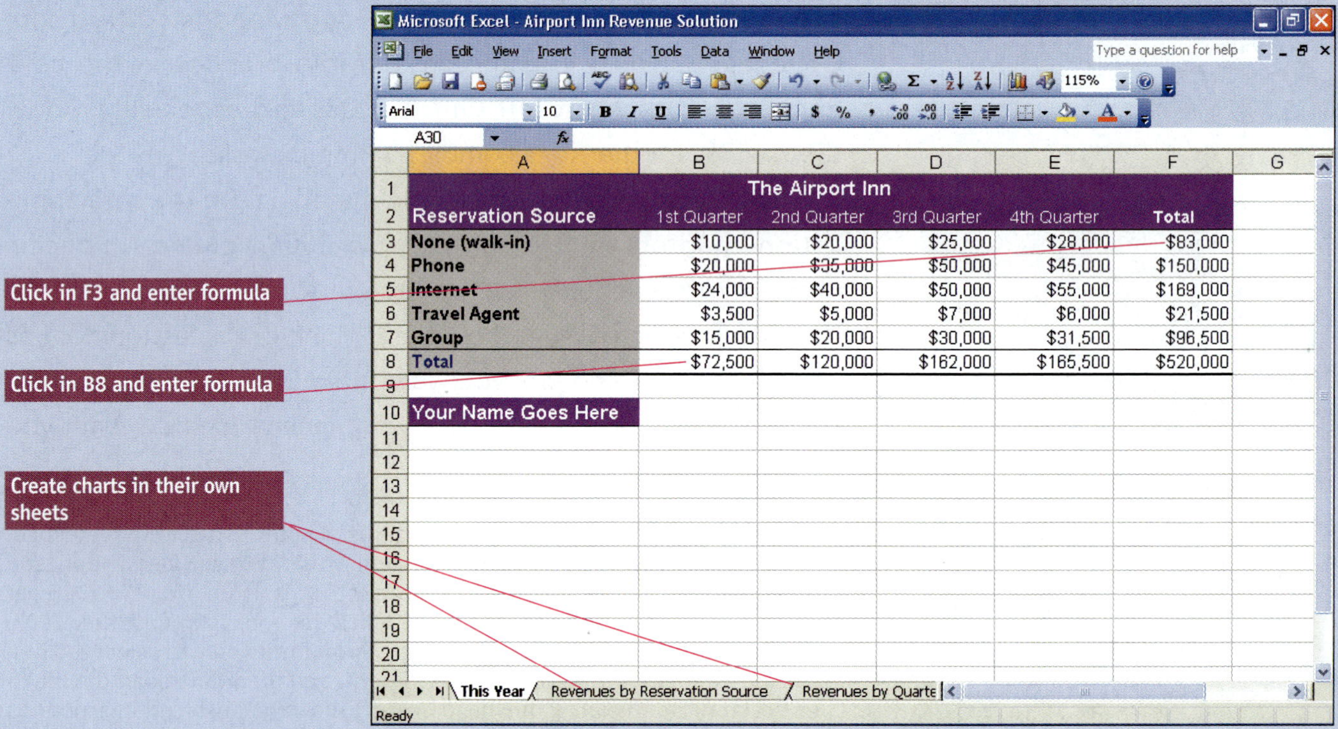

FIGURE 1 Airport Inn Revenue Workbook and Chart

2. **Report to the President: (Word and Excel):** This exercise builds on the previous exercise by creating a Word document that contains the Excel worksheet and a chart. The latter are to be dynamically linked to the Word document so that any changes in the workbook are automatically reflected in the memo.
   a. You will find a partially completed version of the document in Figure 2 in the *Report to the President* document in the Airport Inn folder. Open this document, and then save it as *Report to the President Solution*. Change the To and From lines in the memo to contain your instructor's name and your name, respectively.
   b. Open the completed workbook from the previous exercise if it is not already open. Click and drag to select the completed spreadsheet, then click the Copy button on the Standard toolbar.
   c. Click the Microsoft Word button on the Windows taskbar to return to the Word document. Click below the first paragraph. Pull down the Edit menu and click the Paste Special command to display the Paste Special dialog box. Select Microsoft Excel Worksheet Object in the displayed list, click the Paste Link button, and then click OK to insert the worksheet. Do not worry about the size or position at this time.
   d. Move the cursor so that it is below the worksheet. Press Enter. Use the same technique as in parts (b) and (c) to link the side-by-side column chart (that displays quarters on the X axis) to the Word document. The Excel chart may be too large and/or it may be cropped initially, and hence you will have to move and size the spreadsheet and chart within the memo. Change the wrapping style of each object to square, then change the zoom specification to "Whole Page" so that you can position the objects more easily.
   e. Select the chart, then click and drag a corner sizing handle to make the chart smaller. If the chart is cropped, right click the chart and click the command to display the Picture toolbar. Select the Crop tool, then click and drag the side handle at the right of the chart to show the portion of the chart that may have been cropped initially.
   f. Save the completed document. Print the completed document for your instructor. Exit Word.

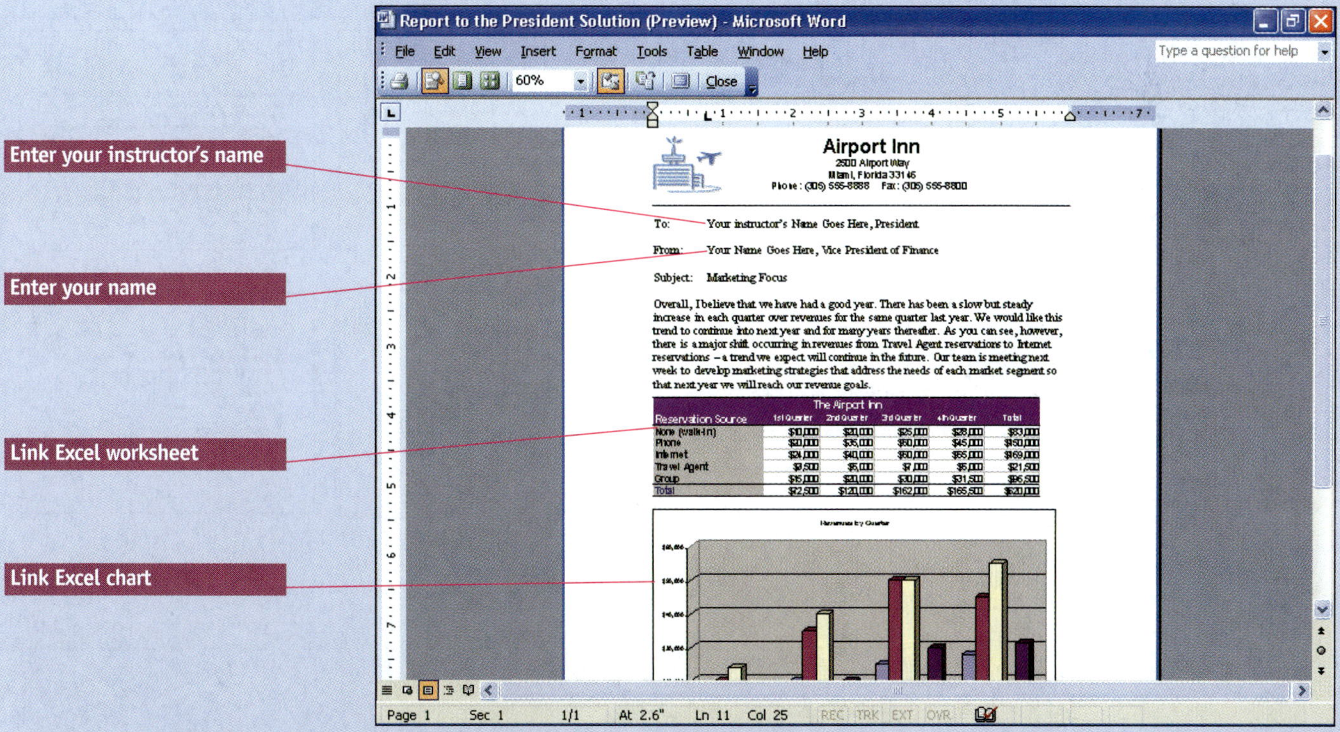

FIGURE 2 Report to the President

3. **Presentation to the President (PowerPoint and Excel):** A partially completed version of the presentation in Figure 3 has been saved as the *Presentation to the President* in the Airport Inn folder. Open this presentation and save it as *Presentation to the President Solution* so that you can return to the original presentation if necessary.

   a. Insert a new slide that contains a mission statement as the second slide in the presentation. The mission statement should read as follows: *The mission of the Airport Inn is to provide modern, well-maintained hotel facilities and a knowledgeable, highly trained staff in order to give our guests a personalized, superior stay.* Increase the font size as appropriate to improve the appearance of the slide.

   b. Open the completed workbook from exercise 1. Use the same technique as described in the previous problem to link the worksheet and the side-by-side column chart (with the data in rows) to the appropriate slides in the presentation, as shown in Figure 3.

   c. Move and/or size the worksheet and chart after they have been added to the presentation. Save the presentation.

   d. Add a textbox to the slide containing the worksheet that points to the total revenue in the worksheet. The text box should indicate that the total revenue is $520,000.

   e. Include animation effects as you see fit within a slide and add transition effects from one slide to the next.

   f. Experiment with a different design template, but limit yourself to five minutes. Chose the template you like best. Save the presentation.

   g. Add your name to the title slide. Print the audience handouts of the completed presentation (six per page) for your instructor. (Be sure to check the box to frame the slides.)

   h. Save the completed presentation. Exit PowerPoint. Close the Excel workbook and exit Excel.

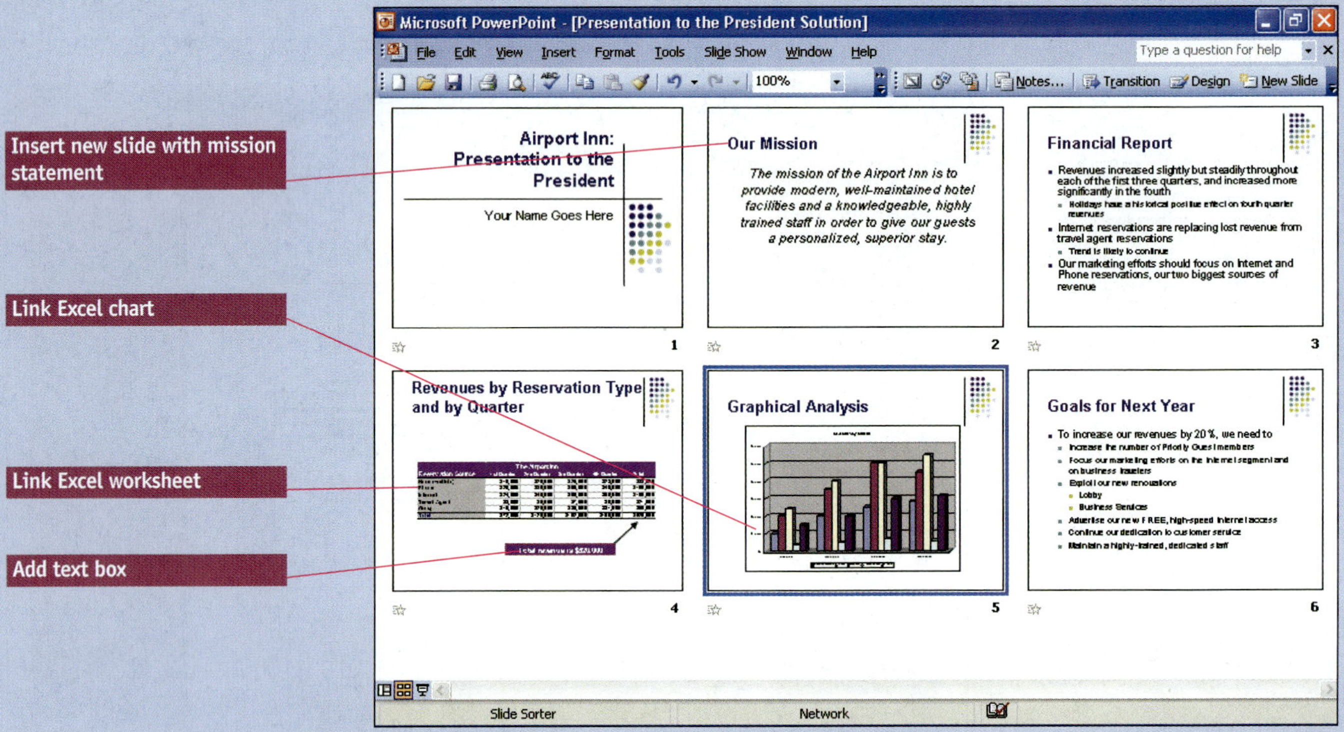

FIGURE 3 Presentation to the President

4. **Last-minute Change (Word, Excel, and PowerPoint):** It was just discovered that the revenue from a few additional Internet and Group reservations were not included in the original workbook. Your task is to correct all of the documents that reflect this information. Open the completed *Airport Inn Revenue Solution* workbook from exercise 1.
   a. Click in cell E3 and change the revenue for the Internet and Group reservations in the fourth quarter. Click in cell E5 and change the value of Internet reservations in the 4th quarter to $60,000. Click in cell E7 and change its value to $35,000. The row and column totals change automatically in the worksheet as do the associated charts. Save the workbook. Exit Excel.
   b. Open the *Report to the President Solution* document from the second exercise. Click the button to update the links to other objects; the worksheet and chart should be updated to reflect the corrected revenue data. (The total revenue is now $528,500.) If either the worksheet or the chart is not updated, right click the object to display a context-sensitive menu and click the Update Link command. If the chart is still not updated, right click the object, click the Linked Worksheet (or Chart) Object command, then click the Links command to display the Links dialog box, where you can check the source (folder) of the linked objects.
   c. Click at the beginning of the opening paragraph in the memo and enter the new text, which is shown in italics in Figure 4. Save and print the completed report. Exit Word.
   d. Start PowerPoint. Open the *Presentation to the President Solution* that you created earlier. PowerPoint detects that a change has been made in the underlying workbook and prompts you to update. Click the button to update the links. Change the text box to indicate the total revenue is $528,500.
   e. Change to the Slide Sorter view. Press and hold the Shift key as you select the slides containing the Excel worksheet and chart. Pull down the File menu, click the Print command, and print the selection (these two slides) as audience handouts, two slides per page. (Check the box to frame the slides.)
   f. Save the presentation. Exit PowerPoint.

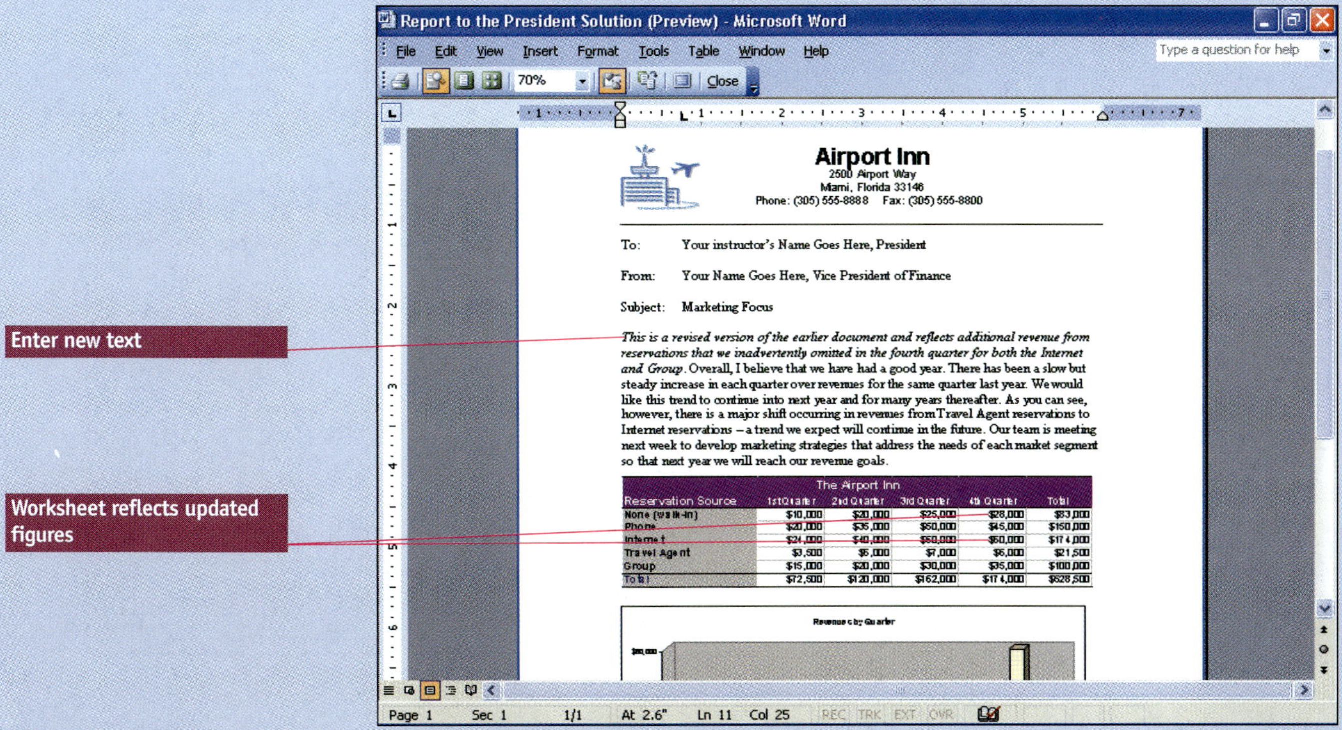

FIGURE 4 Last-minute Change

5. **Importing Data (Access and Excel):** The *Airport Inn* database contains two tables; one for guests, and one for the associated guest status. The Guest Status table already exists within the Access database. The guest information, however, is in an Excel spreadsheet. Your first task is to import the Excel worksheet into the Access database, where it will be converted to an Access table called Guests.

   a. Start Access. Open the *Airport Inn* database in the Airport Inn folder. Click the Tables button if necessary. Pull down the File menu, click (or point to) the Get External Data command, and then click the Import command to display the Import dialog box.

   b. Click the down arrow on the Look in list box and change to the Airport Inn folder (the same folder that contains the database). Change the file type to Microsoft Excel. Select the *Guests* workbook to start the Import Spreadsheet Wizard.

   c. Click the option button to Show Worksheets. Click Next. Check the box that indicates the first row contains column headings as shown in Figure 5. Click Next. Select the option button to store the data in a new table. Click Next.

   d. You do not need information about the individual fields. Click Next.

   e. Select the option that indicates No primary key. (You will add the primary key after the table has been imported.) Click Next. Guests is entered automatically as the name of the table. Click the Finish button, then click OK when the Wizard indicates that it has imported the table. The Guests table appears in the Database window.

   f. Open the Guests table that you just imported in Design view. Insert a new field, GuestID, as the first field in the table; specify AutoNumber as the field type. Designate this field as the primary key. Change the format to \G0000. Modify the properties for the other fields as appropriate; for example, add an input mask for the telephone number.

   g. Change to the Datasheet view and locate the record for Heidi Tamer; change her name to your instructor's name. There is nothing to print at this time. (You will print a report with your instructor's name in exercise 7.)

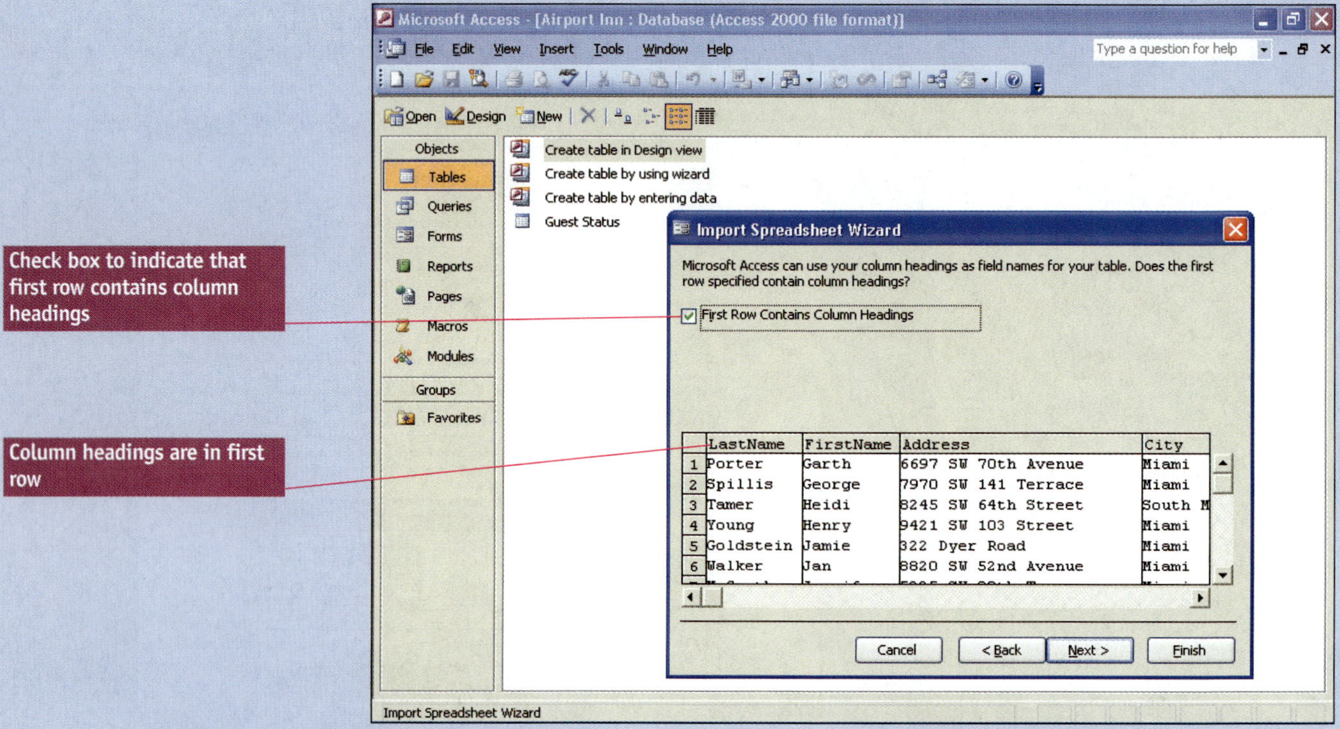

FIGURE 5 Importing Data

6. **A Relational Database (Access):** The *Airport Inn* database contains a one-to-many relationship between the Guest Status table and the Guests table as shown in Figure 6. One Guest Status type (e.g., gold or silver) has many guests, but a specific guest has chosen only one status classification.
   a. Pull down the Tools menu and create the relationships diagram between the two tables as shown in Figure 6. Check the box to enforce referential integrity when you create the relationship.
   b. Pull down the File menu and click the Print Relationships command to create a report containing the relationships diagram. Change to Design view, and then modify the report to match Figure 6. (Use any appropriate clip art.) Print the completed report for your instructor. Close the report and return to the Database window.
   c. Click the Query button in the Database window, and then create a new query in Design view. The query is to contain fields from both tables as described below:
      i. Create a concatenated field in the first column for the guest's name, consisting of the last name, followed by a comma and space, and then the first name.
      ii. Add the GuestStatusID from the Guests table as the second field in the query.
      iii. Select all fields except the GuestStatusID from the Guest Status table.
      iv. Sequence the guests in alphabetical order by last name.
      v. Save the query as Guest Benefits. You do not have to print the query at this time.
   d. Create a report based on the query that you just created. The report will display the guests in alphabetical order by last name, together with their guest status. It will also show each benefit a guest is entitled to, according to his or her guest status.
   e. Add an attractive header to the top of the report. Print the completed report for your instructor.

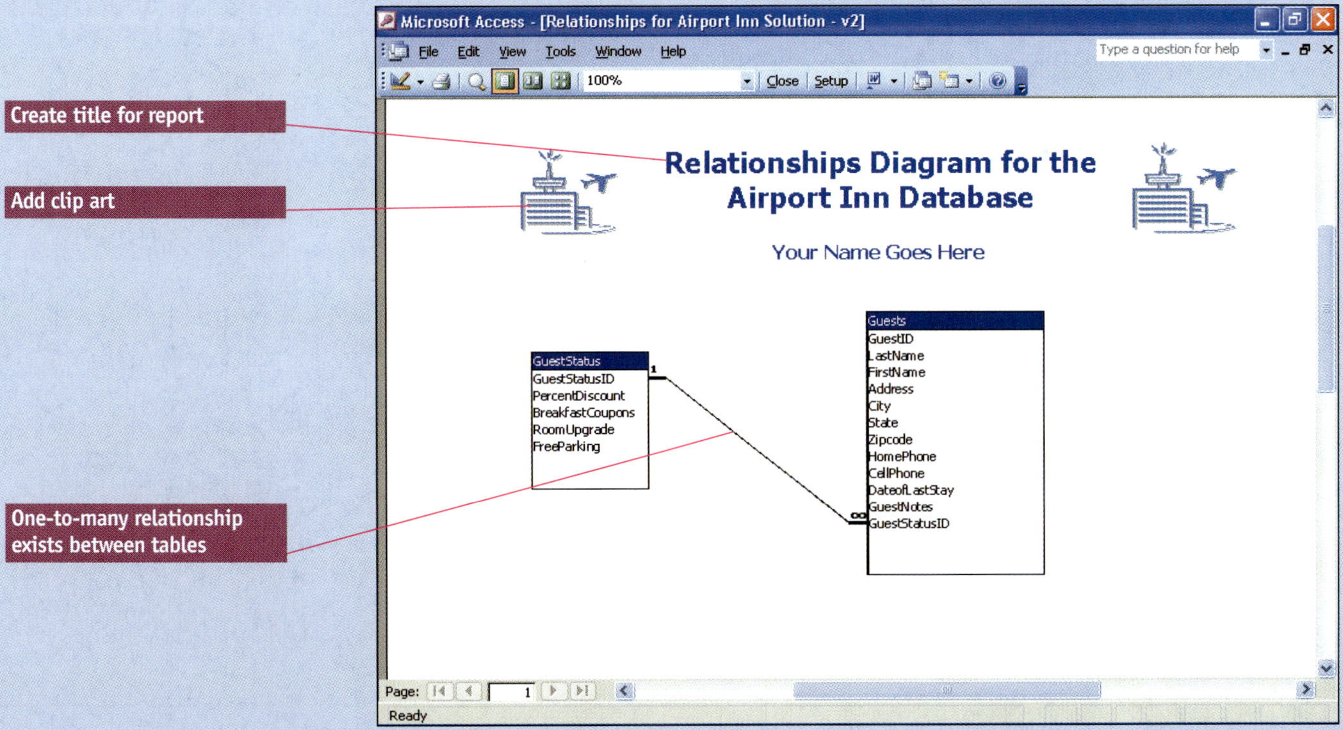

FIGURE 6 A Relational Database

7. **Access Objects: Forms, Queries, and Reports (Access):** Open the *Airport Inn* database in the Airport Inn folder and create the additional objects as described below.
   a. Create the Guests form in Figure 7. You need not follow our design exactly, but you are required to include all of the indicated controls and command buttons. The date in the form header is to display the current date. Use the Combo Box Wizard to create the control for the guest's status.
   b. Use the completed form to enter data for yourself. Your GuestID will be entered automatically since this field is an AutoNumber field. Complete the rest of the data, but give yourself Platinum status. Print the completed form with your data.
   c. Create a report that shows the guest addresses in alphabetical order by guest last name. The report should be based on the Guests table and contain the following fields: Last Name, First Name, GuestID, and fields for the mailing address. The address should print on two lines; that is, the street address is on the first line, and the city, state, and zip code are on the second line.
   d. Create an attractive report header for the report in part (c), then print the completed report for your instructor. The actual report runs several pages. The report should contain your name as well as your instructor's name; part (g) in exercise 5 directed you to modify an existing record to include your instructor's name.
   e. Create a query that displays only the guests with Platinum status. The query should list the guests in alphabetical order by last name, and include the guest's first name, GuestID, address, city, state, zip code, and home phone number.
   f. Create a report based on the query that you just created. The report, however, should include only the name, GuestID, and phone number. (The remaining fields will be used in a mail merge in exercise 9.) Print the report for your instructor.

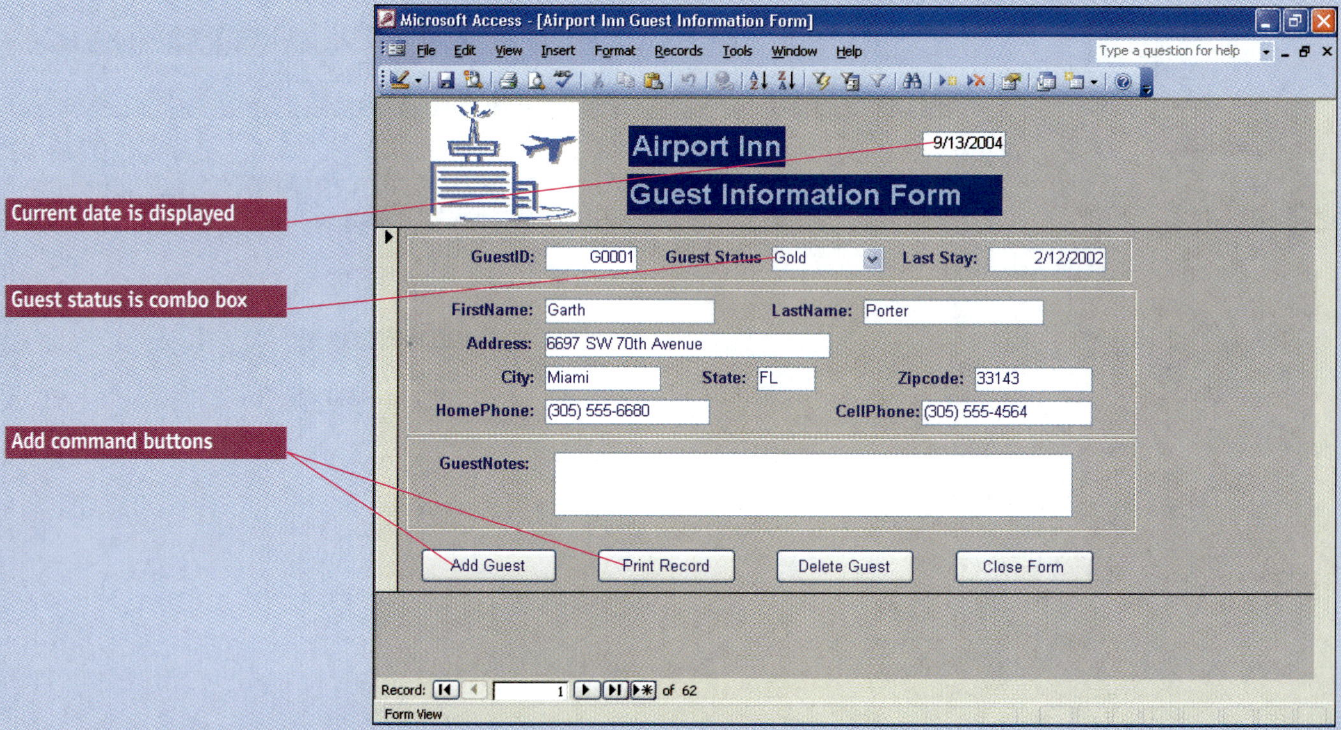

FIGURE 7 Access Objects

8. **An Access Switchboard (Access):** Create the switchboard in Figure 8 for the *Airport Inn* database. You do not have to match our design exactly, but you are required to have all five buttons. Note, too, that the switchboard contains a Report Menu, which displays a subsidiary switchboard.
   a. The first button on the main switchboard opens the About Airport Inn form as shown in Figure 8. This form has been created for you and can be found in the *Airport Inn* database. You are asked, however, to modify the existing form to include your name in the indicated position.
   b. The second and third buttons display the Guests and Guest Status forms, respectively, in order to maintain data in the associated tables.
   c. The Report Menu button provides access to a subsidiary switchboard that contains the various reports in the database. (These include the relationships diagram and the various reports from exercises 6 and 7.) The report switchboard should also have a button to return to the main switchboard.
   d. The Exit button on the main switchboard closes the database. Add the clip art image at the left of the switchboard. Insert your name under the clip art.
   e. Be sure to test both switchboards completely to be sure that they work correctly. Print the Switchboard Items table, the Main Switchboard form, and the Report Switchboard form for your instructor as proof that you completed the exercise correctly.
   f. Modify the startup property of the database so that the switchboard form opens automatically when you open the database. (You can also create an AutoExec macro to maximize the Database window. Display the Database window, click the Macros button, then click the New button to create a macro. Click the drop-down arrow to display the available actions and scroll until you can select Maximize. Save the macro as AutoExec.)
   g. Close the database, then reopen it. The switchboard should appear automatically, and all subsequent objects should appear in a maximized window.
   h. Exit Access.

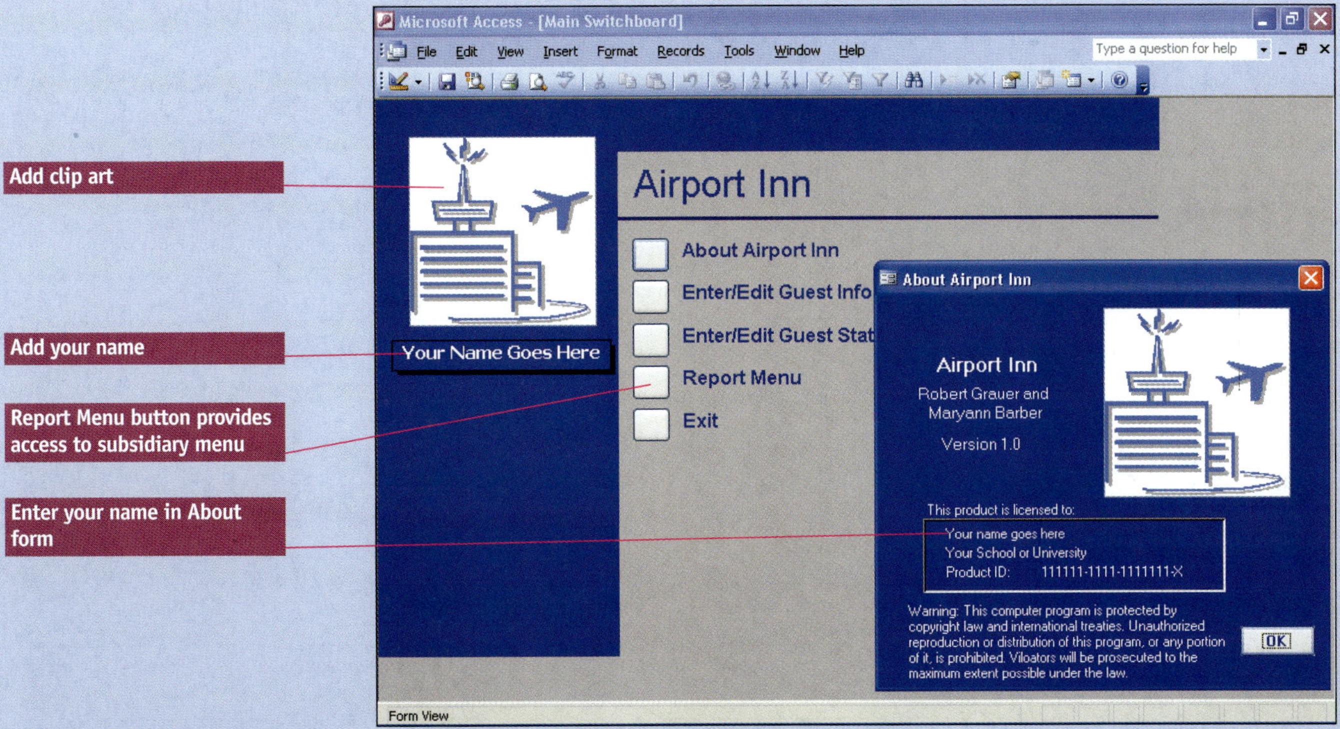

FIGURE 8 An Access Switchboard

9. **Mail Merge (Word and Access):** This exercise uses the Mail Merge utility in Microsoft Word in conjunction with an Access database. You will be asked to create two different form letters. Each letter is sent to a different set of recipients. You can start the merge from either application. Proceed as follows:
   a. Open the partially completed *Letter to Guests* document in the Airport Inn folder and save it as *Letter to Guests Solution* so that you can return to the original document if necessary.
   b. Pull down the Tools menu, click Letters and Mailings, then click Mail Merge to open the task pane. Select the Letters option. Click Next. Select the option to use the current document. Click Next.
   c. Select the recipients from an existing list. Click Browse and choose the Airport Inn folder, select the *Airport Inn* database, and select the Guests table to display the Mail Merge Recipients dialog box. Click OK. Click Next.
   d. Add the address block and greeting line at the beginning of the letter. Click OK. Click Next. Click Preview Your Letters to see the actual data.
   e. Click Next, to complete the merge, click the Print button to display the Merge to Printer dialog box, and then specify the first three records, as shown in Figure 9. (There are more than 60 records in the database.) Print the three letters for your instructor. Save the completed form letter. You do not have to save the merged document. Close Word.
   f. Start Access and open the *Airport Inn* database. Close the switchboard. Click the Queries button in the Database window and open the Platinum Guests query from exercise 7. Pull down the Tools menu, click Office Links, then click the Merge It with Microsoft Office Word command. Select the option to link to an existing document and choose the *Letter to Platinum Guests* document in the Airport Inn folder.
   g. Add the address block and greeting fields to the form letter. Complete the merge and print only the first three letters. Save the completed form letter as *Letter to Platinum Guests Solution*. Exit Word. Exit Access.

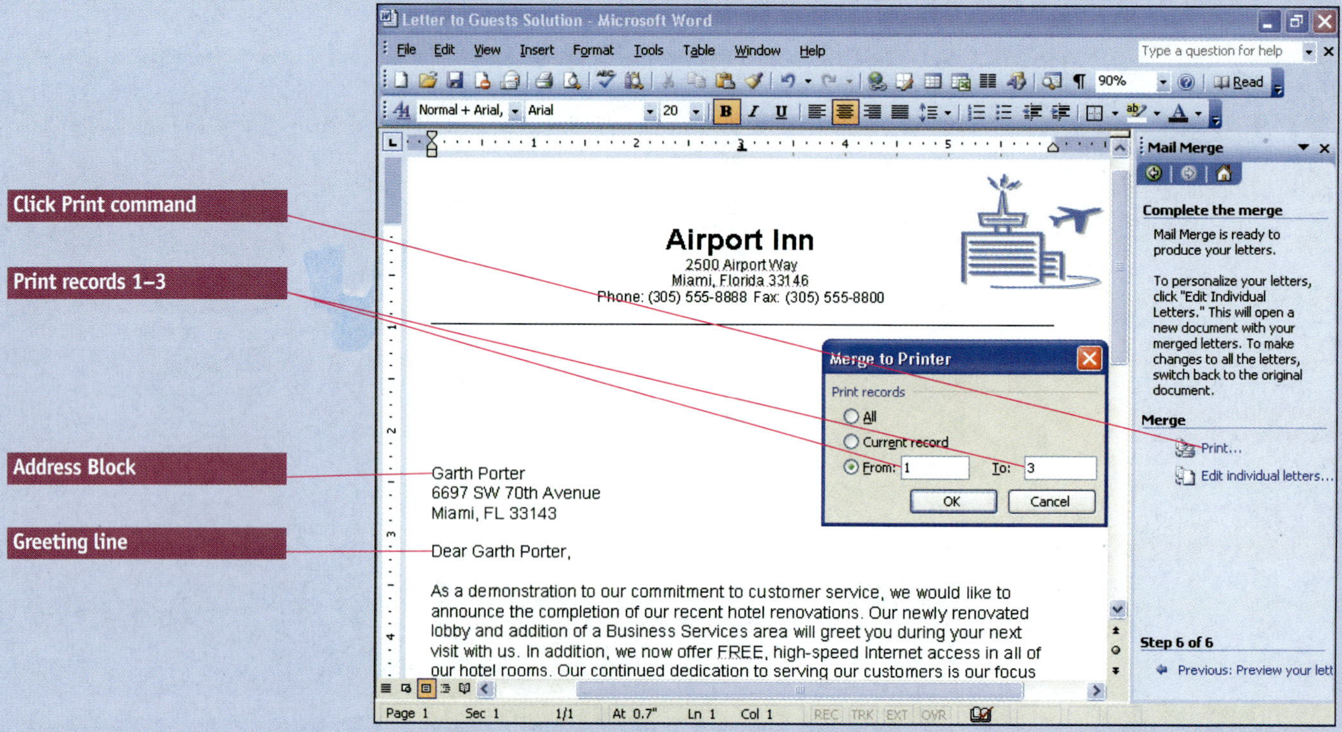

FIGURE 9 Mail Merge

10. **Worksheet References (Excel):** The Board of Directors has asked for a comparison of revenue for this year to last year. An Excel workbook has been created with that information, but it is your task to complete that workbook. Proceed as follows:
    a. Open the *Historical Airport Inn Revenue* workbook in the Airport Inn folder and save it as *Historical Airport Inn Revenue Solution.* (The values in this worksheet reflect the last-minute change that was made in exercise 4.)
    b. Click the worksheet tab labeled Year to Year Comparison, then click in cell B3 of this worksheet. Type an equal sign, click the worksheet tab labeled Last Year, click in cell F3 of this worksheet, and press Enter. The formula for this cell appears in the formula bar as ='Last Year'!F3, indicating that the value for this cell is obtained from another worksheet in the same workbook. Enter similar formulas to display the total revenues for all of the plans for both this year and last year.
    c. Complete the entries in column D of the Year to Year Comparison worksheet that show the dollar increase from last year to this year. The cell formulas in this column should reference only the Year to Year Comparison worksheet. Add another set of formulas in column E to compute the percent increase from last year to this year. Enter totals in row 8.
    d. Enter your name in the worksheet. Format the completed worksheet, then print the Year to Year Comparison worksheet for your instructor. Print the completed worksheet twice, once to show the displayed values and once to show the cell formulas.
    e. Create a combination chart that plots both the dollar amount of the increase as well as the percent of the increase for each reservation source as shown in Figure 10. Display a data table at the bottom of the chart sheet. Note that the dollar and percent increases for the Internet reservations alone are $94,000 and 117.5%, respectively. You do not have to print the combination chart at this time.
    f. Save the completed workbook. Exit Excel.

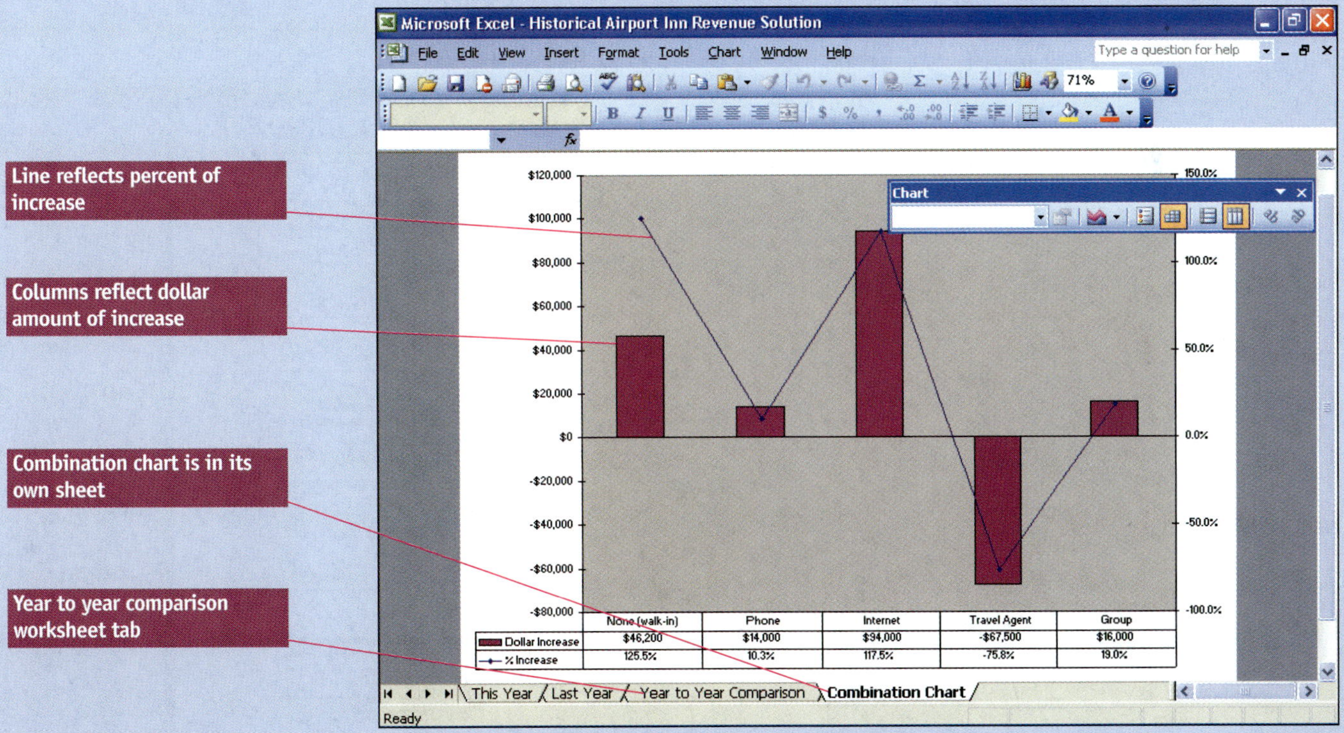

FIGURE 10 Worksheet References

11. **Presentation to the Board (PowerPoint and Excel):** A partially completed version of the presentation in Figure 11 has been saved as *Presentation to the Board* in the Airport Inn folder. Open this presentation and save it as *Presentation to the Board Solution*. Your next task is to link the worksheets and chart from the previous exercise to various slides in this presentation. Linking ensures that you can change the data in the Excel workbook and have the change reflected automatically in the PowerPoint presentation.
    a. Open the *Historical Airport Inn Revenue Solution* workbook from the previous exercise. Select the worksheet that contains revenue data for last year, and link the appropriate cells in that worksheet to the slide containing the Year to Year Comparison (slide 4).
    b. Select the worksheet with the revenue for the current year and link this data to the same slide as in part (a). Move and/or size the worksheets after they have been added to the presentation. Add text boxes to the slide to indicate last year's and this year's performance as appropriate.
    c. Return to Excel. Select the chart sheet containing the combination chart, then link that chart to slide 5 as shown in Figure 11.
    d. Add the mission statement as slide number 2 by importing this slide from the *Presentation to the President*. (Pull down the Insert menu, click the Slides from File command to display the Slide Finder dialog box, and then click the Browse button to locate the earlier presentation.)
    e. Add transition and custom animation effects as you see fit.
    f. Experiment with a different design template, but limit yourself to five minutes. Choose the template you like best. Save the presentation.
    g. Add your name to the title slide in the indicated position. Print the audience handouts of the completed presentation (six per page) for your instructor. (Be sure to check the box to frame the slides.)
    h. Save the completed presentation. Exit PowerPoint. Close the Excel workbook. Exit Excel.

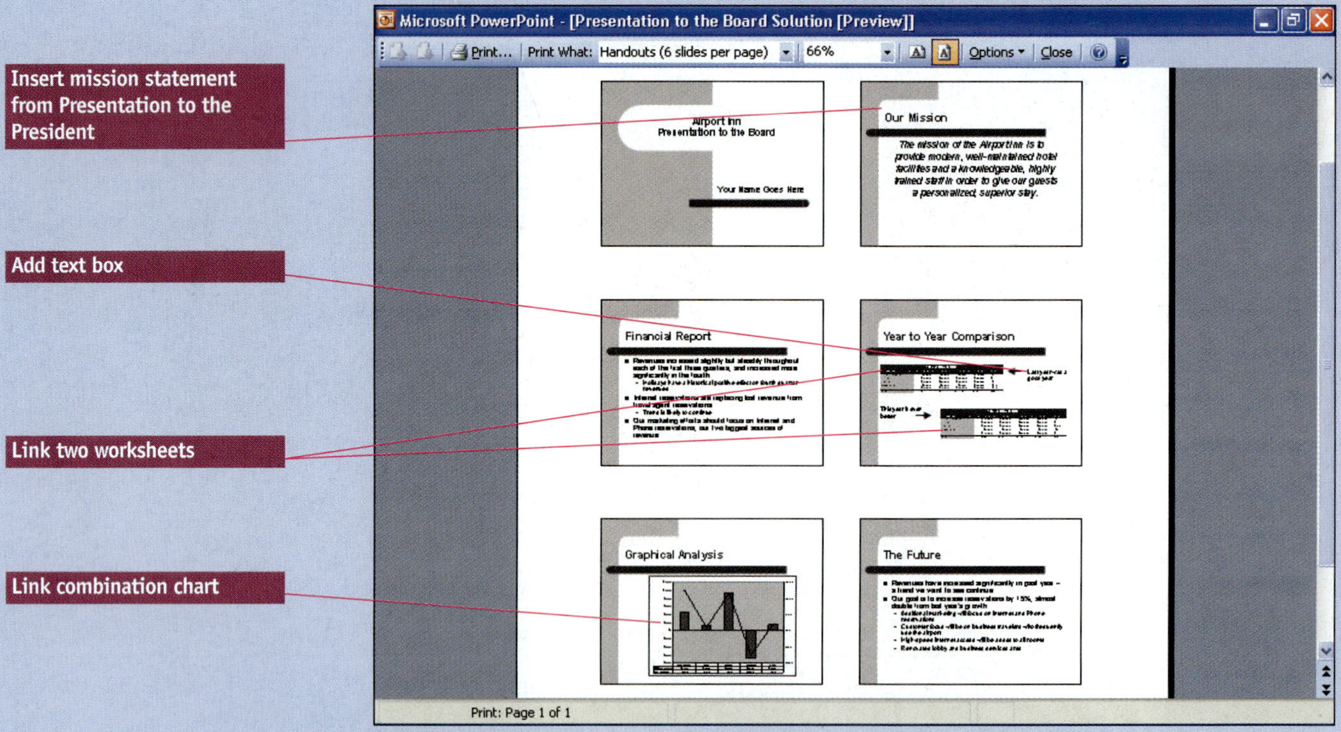

FIGURE 11 Presentation to the Board

12. **Letter to the Board (Word and Excel):** This exercise provides additional practice in linking Excel objects to a Word document. Open the partially completed *Letter to the Board* document in the Airport Inn folder. Save the document as *Letter to the Board Solution* so that you can return to the original document if necessary. Proceed as follows to create the completed document in Figure 12:
    a. Open the *Historical Airport Inn Revenue Solution* workbook from the previous exercise if it is not already open. Select the worksheet containing the revenue for last year and link the appropriate cells in that worksheet to the Word document, immediately after the second paragraph. Place (link) the worksheet containing the revenue for the current year below the first worksheet.
    b. Insert a section break at the end of the first page, and then change the orientation of the second page (section) to landscape as shown in Figure 12.
    c. Return to the Excel workbook. Select the combination chart and link this chart to the Word document. The Excel chart may be too large and/or it may be cropped initially. Change the wrapping style to square, and then change the zoom specification to "Whole Page" so that you can position the object more easily.
    d. Select the chart, then click and drag a corner sizing handle to make the chart smaller. If the chart is cropped, right click the chart and click the command to display the Picture toolbar. Select the Crop tool, then click and drag the side handle at the right of the chart to show the portion of the chart that may have been cropped initially.
    e. Add your name and your instructor's name in the indicated positions. Your instructor is the recipient of the memo and you are the sender. Save the completed document, and then print the completed letter for your instructor.
    f. Exit Word. Exit Excel. You're almost finished. All that remains is the creation of a home page in exercise 13 and the preparation of a cover sheet and checklist in exercise 14.

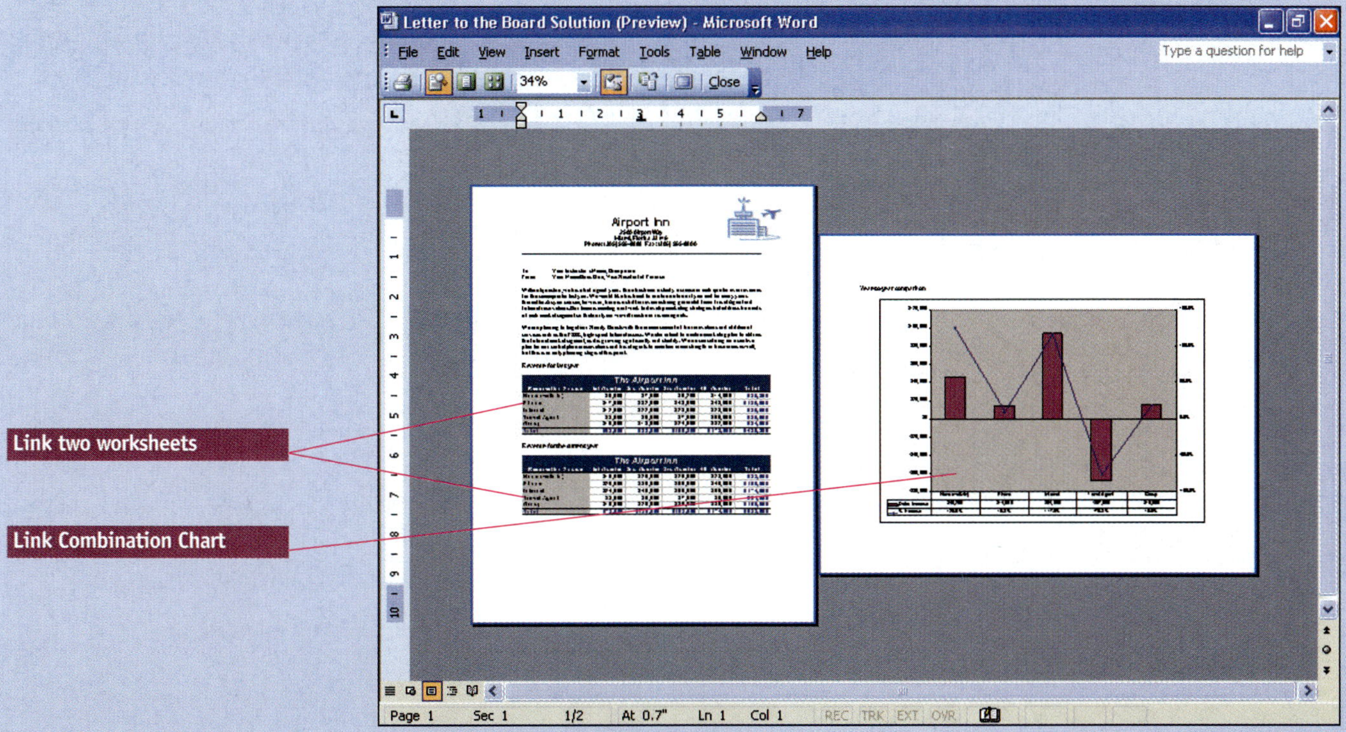

FIGURE 12 Letter to the Board

13. **Create a Home Page (Word):** Open the *Airport Inn Home Page* document in the Airport Inn folder. Pull down the File menu, click the Save as Web Page command, and specify Single File Web Page as the file type to save the Word document to a Web page. (Click Continue if a message appears that indicates pictures with text wrapping will become left or right justified.) Review the document and make the basic formatting changes you deem appropriate. Use the Themes command in the Format menu to apply an overall design to the page. Your goal is to create a page similar to Figure 13.
   a. Create a one-by-three table at the top of the document. Place the existing clip art in the left and right cells. Enter the title and other information in the middle cell. Format the text. Size the cells as necessary. Remove the border around the table.
   b. Select the text "e-mail us" that appears in the middle of the document. Pull down the Insert menu and click the Hyperlink command (or click the Insert Hyperlink button on the Standard toolbar), click the E-mail Address button, and then enter your e-mail address.
   c. Create the indicated hyperlinks that appear within the document. Search the Web to find the addresses to our sites, or choose your own. Be sure to enter valid addresses, however, for all selected sites.
   d. Save the document a final time, then exit Word. Start Windows Explorer, then go to the folder containing your Web page, and double click the file you just created. Internet Explorer will start automatically (because your document was saved as a Web page). You should see your document within Internet Explorer as shown in Figure 13. Look carefully at the Address bar and note the local address on drive C, as opposed to a Web address. Print the document for your instructor as proof you completed the assignment.
   e. Creating the home page and viewing it locally is easy. Placing the page on the Web where it can be seen by anyone with an Internet connection is not as straightforward. You will need additional information from your instructor about how to obtain an account on a Web server (if that is available at your school), and further how to upload the Web page from your PC to the server.

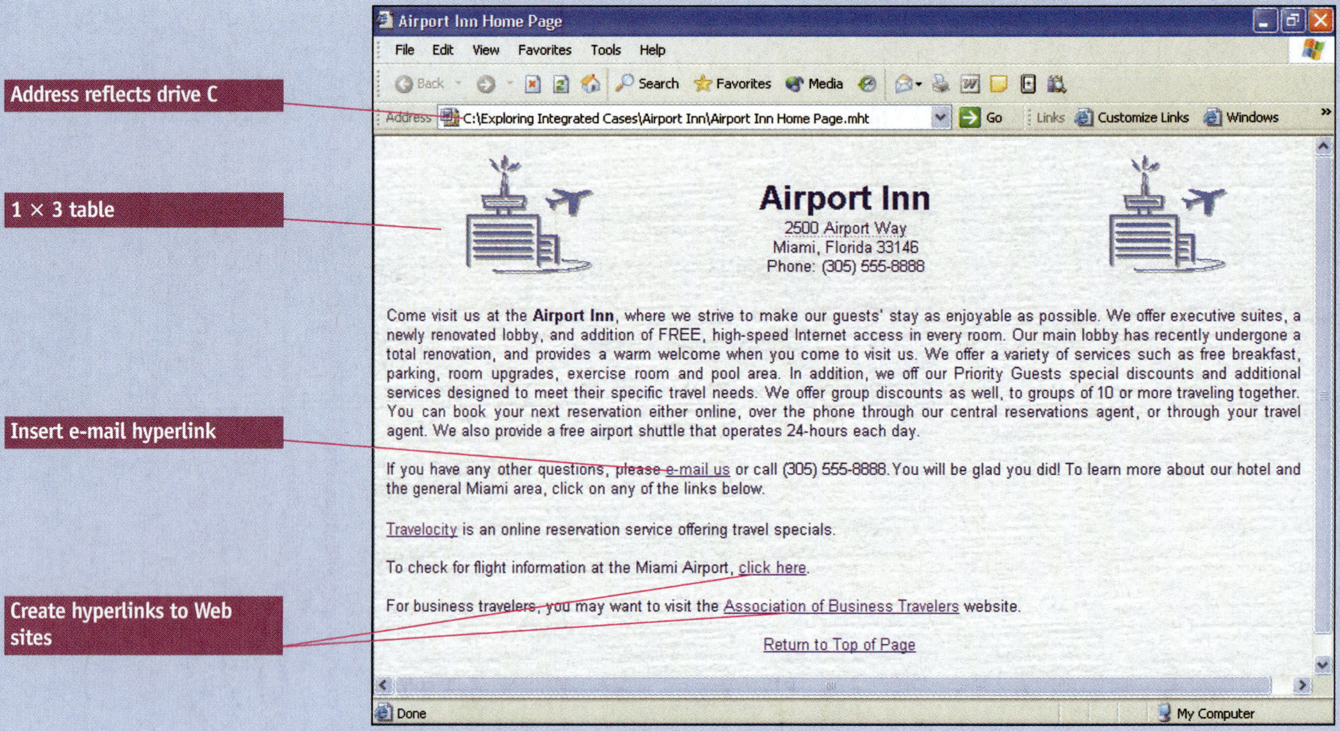

FIGURE 13 Create a Home Page

14. **Submission Checklist (Word):** You have successfully completed multiple exercises within the Airport Inn case study. Each exercise described a specific task(s), required the use of one or more applications in Microsoft Office, and/or asked you to print one or more documents to show that you completed the exercise. The submissions checklist in Figure 14 will ensure that you have printed all of the required documents.
    a. Open the *Airport Inn Submission Checklist* that is found in the Airport Inn folder. Read the document carefully and check each box after you verify that you have printed the indicated document.
    b. Add your name to the checklist as indicated, then use the checklist as a cover sheet when you submit the material to your instructor.
    c. Think for a minute about all that you have accomplished. You have completed a series of 14 exercises, which required the use of all four major applications within Microsoft Office. You have created a home page and may have posted it on the Web.
    d. Congratulations on a job well done!

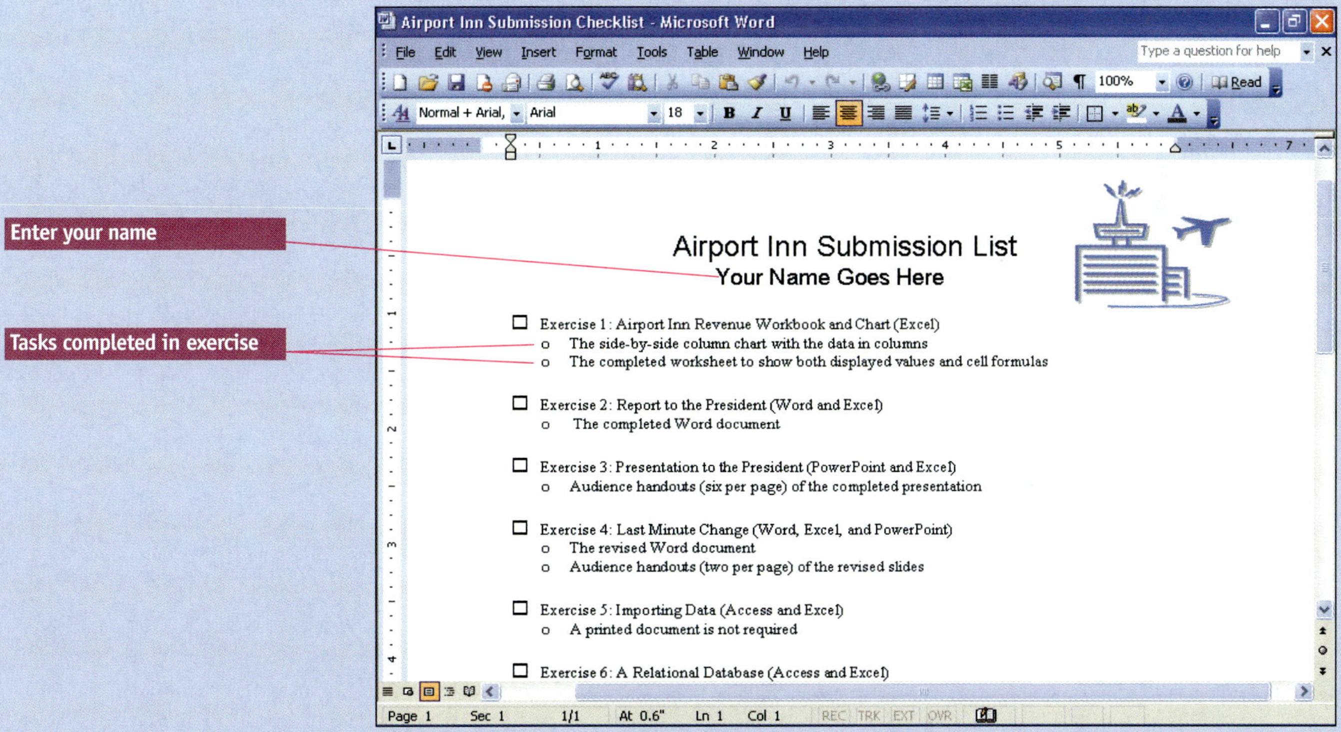

FIGURE 14 Submission Checklist

Integrated Case Study
Definitely Needlepoint

OBJECTIVES

1. Use the core applications in Office 2003 individually or in conjunction with one another.
2. Link an Excel chart to a Word document and a PowerPoint presentation.
3. Import an Excel worksheet into an Access database.
4. Create Access tables, queries, reports, and forms.
5. Use an Access table as the basis for a mail merge.
6. Use Word to create a Web page for the organization.

integrated exercises

1. Sales Summary and Chart (Excel)
2. Report to the Partners (Word and Excel)
3. Presentation to the Partners (PowerPoint and Excel)
4. Last-minute Change (Word, Excel, and PowerPoint)
5. Importing Sales Data (Access and Excel)
6. Access Objects: Forms, Queries, and Reports (Access)
7. An Access Switchboard (Access)
8. Mail Merge (Word and Access)
9. Worksheet References (Excel)
10. Presentation for Venture Capital (PowerPoint and Excel)
11. Letter to Venture Capitalists (Word and Excel)
12. Create a Home Page (Word)
13. Submission Checklist (Word)

This document provides a series of 13 exercises in Microsoft Office that relate to the Definitely Needlepoint boutique, a friendly place to sit and stitch. Each exercise describes a specific task for the organization to accomplish and typically requires the use of multiple applications within Microsoft Office for solution. Many of the exercises are cumulative in nature. You may, for example, be asked to create an Excel chart in one exercise, and then incorporate that chart into a Word memo and a PowerPoint presentation in subsequent exercises. Other exercises will ask you to create or modify an Access database, to exchange data between Excel and Access, and to create a Web page for the boutique. Collectively, you will gain considerable practice in the core applications of Microsoft Office 2003, and especially in how they work together to accomplish complex tasks.

All of the exercises are based on material from the core application chapters in *Exploring Office 2003 Volume I*. Specific chapter references are deliberately not provided so that the case study is as realistic as possible. Think of this assignment as your first day on the job; you were hired because you are proficient in Microsoft Office. This is your chance to show what you know. ■

Your assignment is to follow the directions of your instructor with respect to which of the exercises you are to complete within the case description. You should begin by downloading the practice files from our Web site at www.prenhall.com/grauer. Go to the site, click the book icon for Office 2003, and then click the Student Resources tab. Scroll until you can select the link to *Integrated Case Studies (Enhanced Edition)*, and then download the file to your desktop. Double click the file icon and follow the onscreen instructions to install the practice files on your computer. The files you need will be in the Definitely Needlepoint folder within the Exploring Integrated Cases folder.

INTEGRATED EXERCISES

1. **Sales Summary and Chart (Excel):** You will find a partially completed version of the spreadsheet in Figure 1 in the *Definitely Needlepoint Current Sales* workbook in the Definitely Needlepoint folder. (You can download the practice files for this case study from our Web site at www.prenhall.com/grauer.) Open the workbook and save it as *Definitely Needlepoint Current Sales Solution* so that you can return to the original workbook if necessary. Proceed as follows:
   a. Click in cell F3 and compute the total sales in the canvases category for the entire year. Copy this formula to the remaining cells in column F. Click in cell B8 and compute the total sales for the first quarter, then copy this formula to the remaining cells in this row.
   b. Use the AutoFormat command as the basis for formatting your worksheet in an attractive fashion. You do not have to match our formatting exactly; you can use your own design.
   c. Create a stacked column chart based on the data in cells A2 through E7. Specify that the data series are in rows so that each column represents the total sales (over all categories) for each quarter. The legend will display the different colors used for each category. Display the legend at the bottom of the chart. Save the chart in its own sheet called Graphical Analysis.
   d. Experiment with variations of the chart you just created. Change the chart type from a stacked column chart to a side-by-side column chart and/or change the orientation of the data series from rows to columns. Choose the chart that you think is most appropriate to show the sales by quarter and category.
   e. Change the color of the worksheet tabs. Enter your name in the worksheet as indicated in cell A10.
   f. Use the Page Setup command to display gridlines and row and column headings. Create a custom footer for both worksheets that includes the worksheet tab and current date.
   g. Print the completed Current Year worksheet twice, once to show displayed values and once to show the cell formulas. (You do not have to print the chart at this time.)
   h. Save the completed workbook for use in subsequent exercises. Exit Excel.

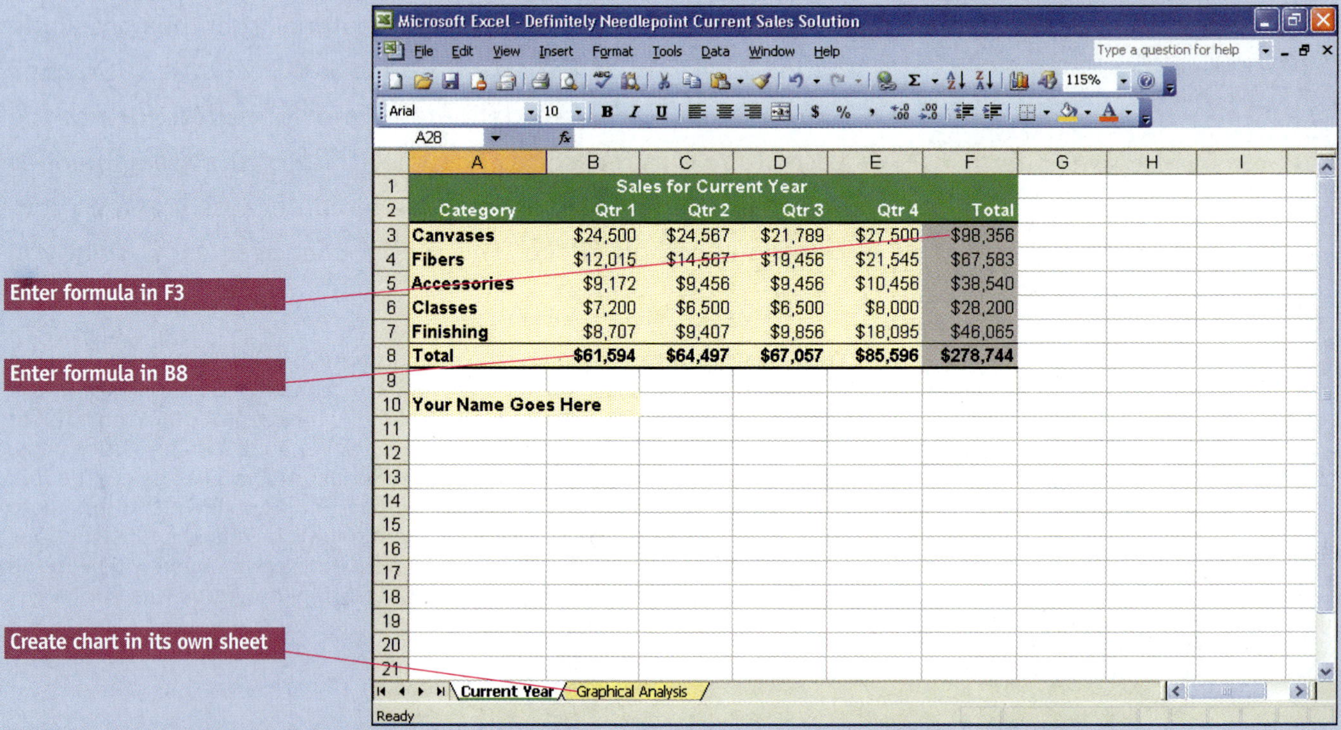

FIGURE 1 Sales Summary and Chart

2. **Report to the Partners: (Word and Excel):** This exercise builds on the previous one by creating a Word document that contains the formatted worksheet and associated chart. The latter is to be dynamically linked to the Word document so that any changes in the Excel workbook will be automatically reflected in the memo.
   a. You will find a partially completed version of the document in Figure 2 in the *Report to Partners* document in the Definitely Needlepoint folder. Open this document, and then save it as *Report to Partners Solution*.
   b. Open the completed workbook from the previous exercise if it is not already open. Click and drag to select the completed worksheet, then click the Copy button on the Standard toolbar.
   c. Click the Microsoft Word button on the Windows taskbar. Pull down the Edit menu and click the Paste Special command to display the Paste Special dialog box. Select Microsoft Excel Worksheet Object in the displayed list, click the Paste Link button, and then click OK to insert the worksheet. Do not worry about the size or position at this time.
   d. Return to the Excel workbook. Click the worksheet tab containing the chart. Click the Zoom button and change the magnification so that you can select the entire chart. Click the Copy button.
   e. Return to the Word document and click below the worksheet to position the insertion point for the chart. Pull down the Edit menu, click Paste Special, select Microsoft Excel Chart Object, click Paste Link, and click OK.
   f. The Excel chart should appear in the document. The only tricky part (if any) is to display the entire chart (it may be cropped initially). Select the chart, then click and drag a corner sizing handle to make the chart smaller. Right click the chart and click the command to display the Picture toolbar. Select the Crop tool, then click and drag the side handle at the right of the chart to show the portion of the chart that may have been cropped initially.
   g. Move and size the worksheet and chart within the memo as necessary. Add your name to the bottom of the memo, and then print the completed report. Save the completed document. Exit Word.

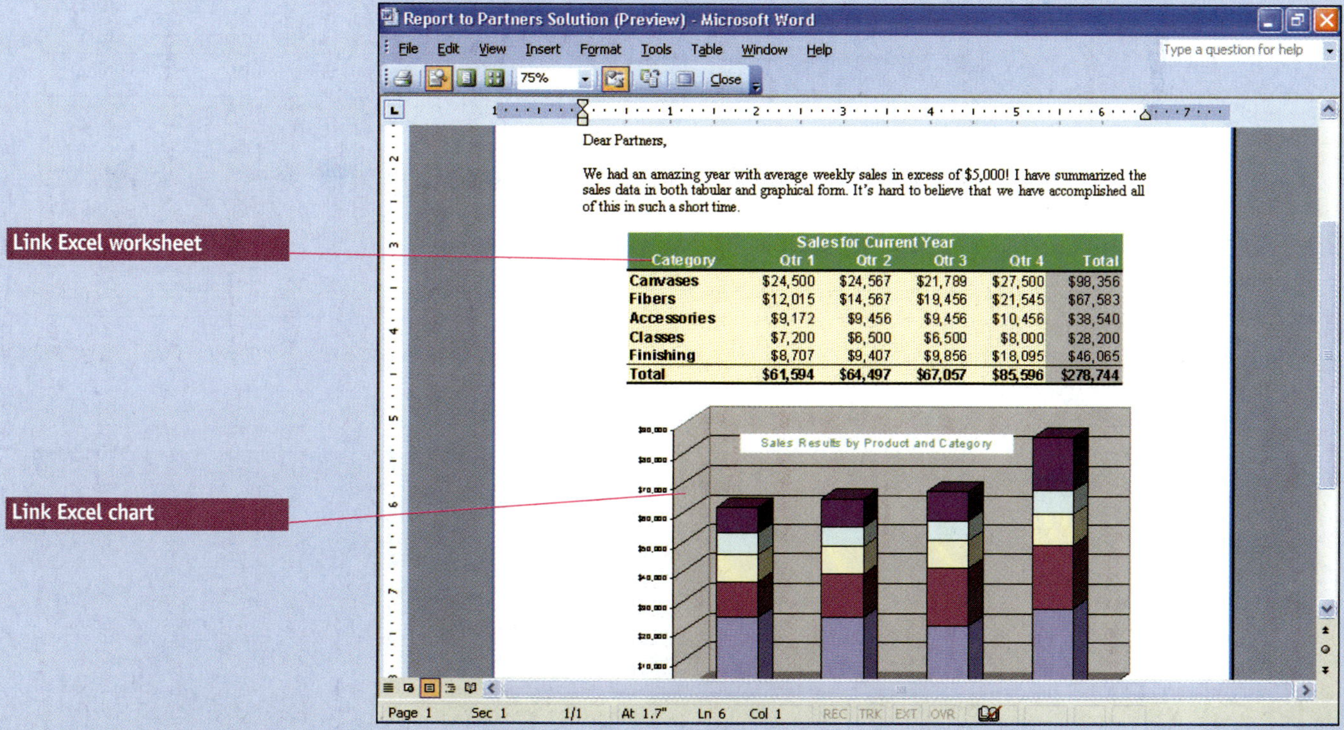

FIGURE 2 Report to the Partners

3. **Presentation to the Partners (PowerPoint and Excel):** You have been asked to present the financial information for last year at a partners' meeting. A partially completed version of the presentation in Figure 3 has been saved as the *Presentation to Partners* in the Definitely Needlepoint folder. Open this presentation and save it as *Presentation to Partners Solution* so that you can return to the original presentation if necessary.
   a. Insert a new slide that contains the mission statement as the third slide in the presentation. The mission statement should read as follows: *Definitely Needlepoint provides an intimate setting in which to stitch. Our customers are our friends and participate in a variety of social and educational activities that encourage and develop the art of needlepoint.*
   b. Open the completed workbook that contains the sales information for the current year. Use the same techniques as in the previous problem to link the worksheet and the chart from the workbook to their respective slides in the presentation, as shown below in Figure 3. Move and/or size these objects after they have been added to the presentation.
   c. Include animation effects as you see fit within a slide and transition effects from one slide to the next.
   d. Add your name to the title slide in the indicated position. Print the audience handouts of the completed presentation (six per page) for your instructor.
   e. Save the completed presentation. Exit PowerPoint. Close the Excel workbook. Exit Excel.

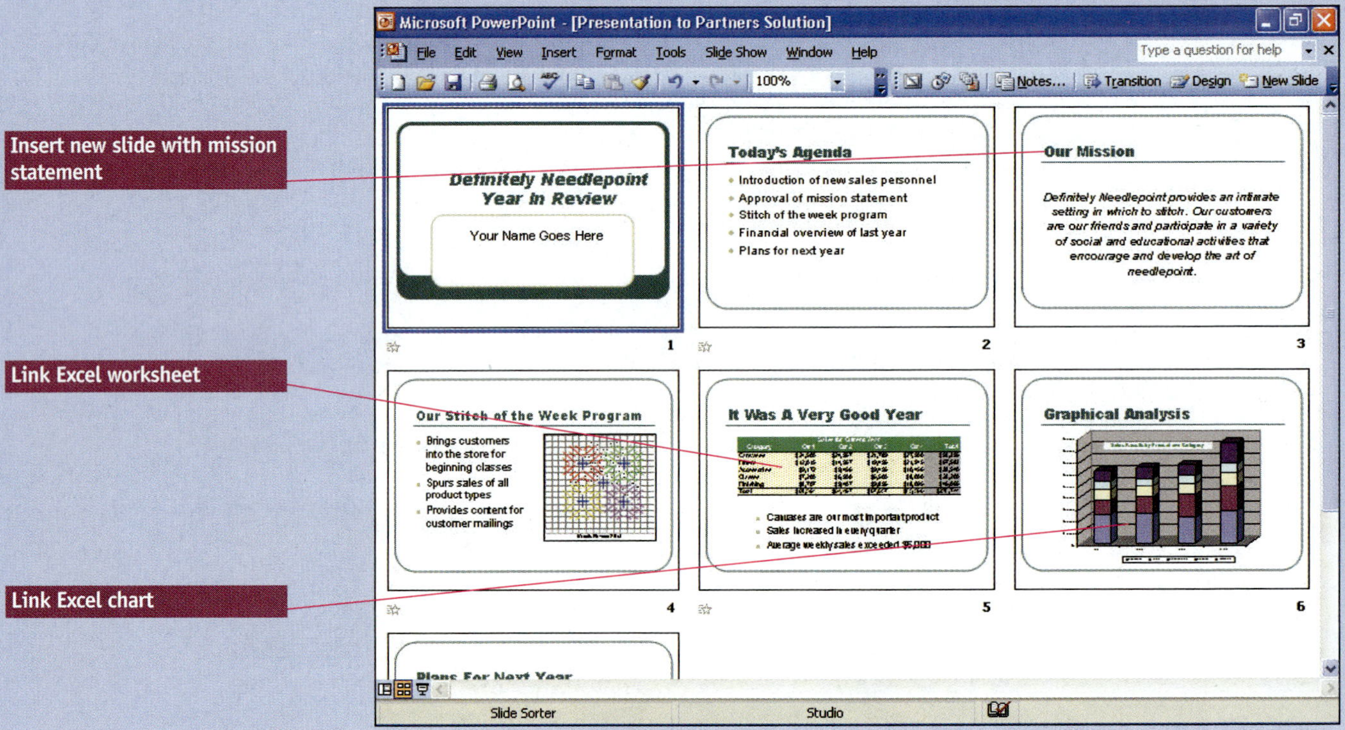

FIGURE 3 Presentation to the Partners

4. **Last-minute Change (Word, Excel, and PowerPoint):** The accountant has just discovered several last-minute sales for canvases and fibers that were not recorded in the year-end worksheet. Your task is to correct all of the documents that reflect this information. Open the completed *Definitely Needlepoint Current Sales Solution* workbook from exercise 1.
   a. Click in cell E3. Change the sale of canvases in the fourth quarter from the current value of $27,500 to the new value of $45,000. Click in cell E4. Change the amount of fibers sold in the fourth quarter from $21,545 to $31,000. Save the workbook. The chart changes automatically to reflect the new values. Exit Excel.
   b. Start Word and open the *Report to Partners Solution* document. The worksheet and chart should be updated automatically to reflect the corrected sales data as shown in Figure 4. (The total sales for last year should be $305,699.) If this is not the case, right click the worksheet to display a context-sensitive menu and click the Update Link command. If the worksheet is still not updated, right click the worksheet to display a context-sensitive menu, click the Linked Worksheet Object command, then click the Links command to display the Links dialog box, where you can check the source (folder) of the linked objects.
   c. Click at the beginning of the opening paragraph in the memo and enter the new text, which is shown in bold italics in Figure 4. Save and print the completed report. Exit Word.
   d. Start PowerPoint. Open the *Presentation to Partners Solution* that you created earlier. PowerPoint detects that a change has been made in the underlying worksheet and chart and prompts you to update. Click the button to update the links.
   e. Change to the Slide Sorter view. Press and hold the Shift key as you select the slides containing the Excel worksheet and chart. Pull down the File menu, click the Print command, and print the selection (these two slides) as audience handouts, two slides per page.
   f. Save the presentation. Exit PowerPoint.

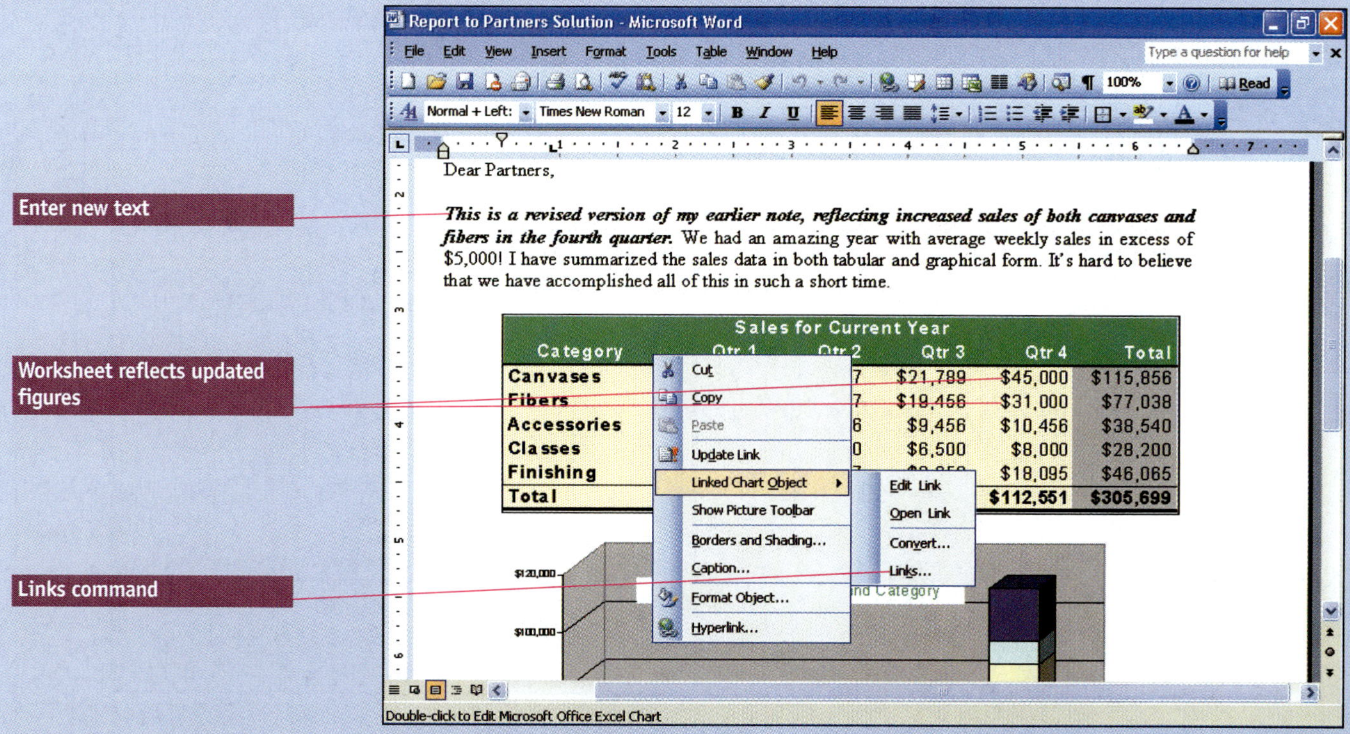

FIGURE 4 Last-minute Change

5. **Importing Sales Data (Access and Excel):** The initial customer mailing list was created in Excel, in part because of the partners' lack of knowledge. The enterprise has grown, however, and it is time to convert the existing customer list into an Access database for more extensive processing. Proceed as follows:
   a. Start Access. Open the *Definitely Needlepoint* database that is found in the Definitely Needlepoint folder. Click the Tables button if necessary.
   b. Pull down the File menu, click (or point to) the Get External Data command, and then click the Import command to display the Import dialog box.
   c. Click the down arrow on the Look in list box and change to the *Definitely Needlepoint* folder (the same folder that contains the *Definitely Needlepoint* database). Change the file type to Microsoft Excel. Select the *Definitely Needlepoint Customer List* workbook to start the Import Spreadsheet Wizard.
   d. The options button to Show worksheets is selected as shown in Figure 5. Click Next. Check the box that indicates the first row contains column headings. Click Next. Select the option button to store the data in a new table. Click Next.
   e. You do not need information about the individual fields. Click Next.
   f. Select the option to choose your own primary key. Click the drop-down arrow on the list box and select CustomerNumber. Click Next.
   g. Access indicates that it will import the data into a Customers table. Click the Finish button, then click OK when the Wizard indicates that it has imported the table. The Customers table appears in the Database window.
   h. Examine the fields in the newly imported Customers table. What data validation (if any) has been established? Which other properties (if any) have been modified from their default settings? What changes would you make to the design of the table? How will your changes affect the existing data?
   i. Continue with the next exercise, in which you will create various objects that are based on the Customers table.

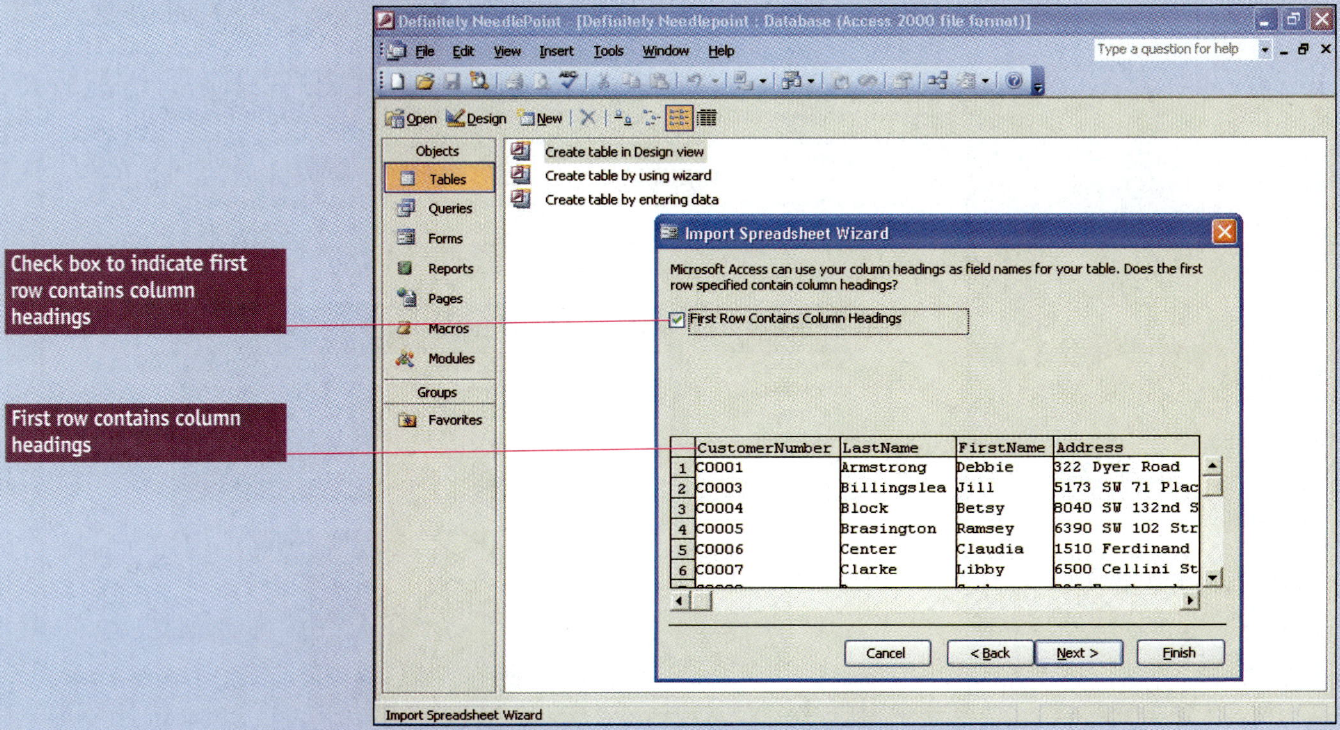

FIGURE 5 Importing Sales Data

6. **Access Objects: Forms, Queries, and Reports (Access):** This assignment asks you to create various objects for the *Definitely Needlepoint* database. All of the objects are based on the Customers table that was imported from the associated Excel workbook in the previous exercise.
   a. Start by creating a Customer form similar to the form in Figure 6. You need not follow our design exactly, but you must have the equivalent functionality. The fields should appear in the same order as on our form. Be sure to set the tab order correctly, so that you can tab from one field to the next during data entry.
   b. The Guild Member control should appear automatically as a check box because the underlying field is defined as a Yes/No field.
   c. The mailing list should be entered as an option group with values of 1, 2, and 3 corresponding to all mailings, semi-annual, and annual mailings, respectively.
   d. Add command buttons to add, print, and delete a record. You also need a command button to close the form.
   e. Use the completed form to enter data for yourself (even if you are not interested in needlepoint). Use customer number C1000 as shown in the figure. Indicate that you are a guild member and that you want to receive all mailings. Print the completed form.
   f. Create a Customer Summary report (not shown) that includes the following five fields from the Customers table: Customer Number, Last Name, First Name, Mailing List Preference (will appear as 1, 2, or 3), and an indication of whether they are a guild member (appears as a check box). The report should display the customers in alphabetical order by last name. Print the page in this report that contains your name.
   g. Create a Customer Address List containing the name and address of every customer. The customers should appear in alphabetical order by last name. Print the page in this report that contains your name.
   h. Create a query that lists guild members in alphabetical order, then create a report based on that query. Include the Customer Number, last name, first name, and a check box showing the customer is a guild member. Print the completed report for your instructor.

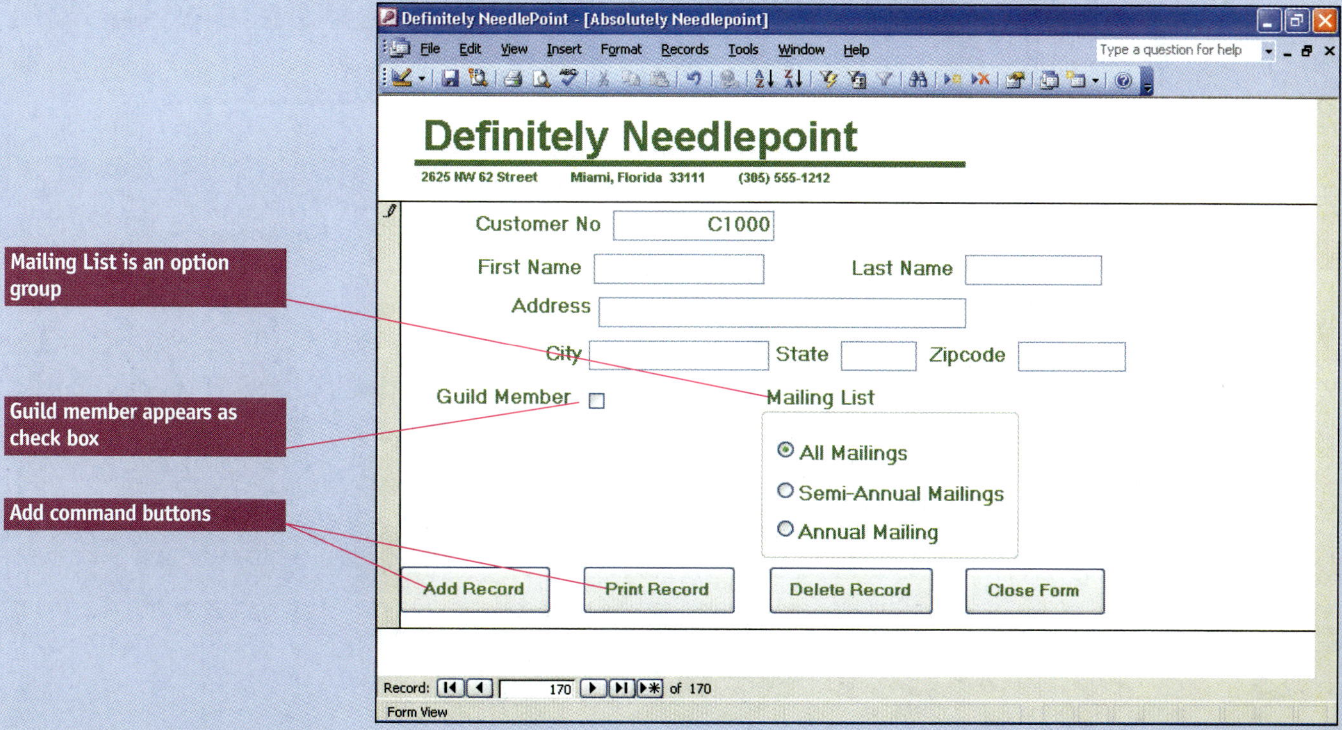

FIGURE 6 Access Objects (A Customer Form)

7. **An Access Switchboard (Access):** Create the switchboard in Figure 7 for use with the *Definitely Needlepoint* database from previous exercises. You do not have to match our design exactly, but you are required to have all four buttons. Note, too, that the switchboard contains a Report menu.
   a. The first button on the main switchboard opens the Definitely Needlepoint form as shown in Figure 7. This form has been created for you and can be found in the *Definitely Needlepoint* database. You are asked, however, to modify the existing form to include your name in the indicated position.
   b. The second button opens the Customer form from the previous exercise.
   c. The Report Menu button provides access to a subsidiary switchboard that contains the various reports you created in the previous exercise. There should be four buttons on this switchboard, one for each report, and one button to return to the main switchboard.
   d. The Exit button on the main switchboard closes the database.
   e. Be sure you test both switchboards completely to be sure that they work correctly. Print the Switchboard Items table, the Main Switchboard form, and the Report Switchboard form for your instructor as proof that you completed the exercise.
   f. Modify the startup property of the database so that the switchboard form opens automatically when you open the database. (You can also create an AutoExec macro to maximize the Database window. Display the Database window, click the Macros button, then click the New button to create a macro. Click the drop-down arrow to display the available actions and scroll until you can select Maximize. Save the macro as AutoExec.)
   g. Close the database, then reopen it. The switchboard should appear automatically, and all subsequent objects should appear in a maximized window.
   h. Exit Access and continue with the next exercise.

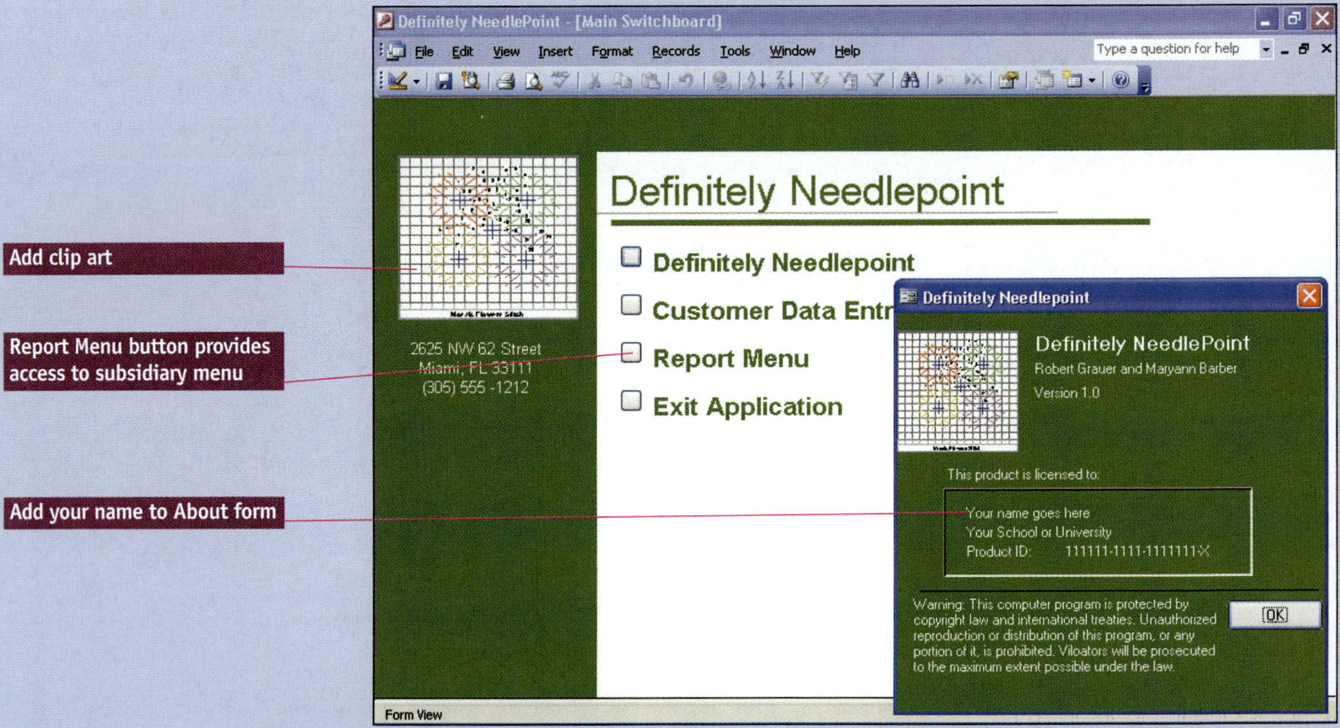

FIGURE 7 An Access Switchboard

8. **Mail Merge (Word and Access):** This exercise asks you to use the Mail Merge Wizard in Microsoft Word in conjunction with an Access database.
   a. Open the partially completed *November Letter* document in the Definitely Needlepoint folder. Save the document as *November Letter Solution* so that you can return to the original document if necessary.
   b. Pull down the Tools menu, click Letters and Mailings, then click Mail Merge Wizard to open the task pane. Select the Letters option. Click Next. Select the option to use the Current Document. Click Next.
   c. Select the recipients from an existing list. Choose the Definitely Needlepoint folder, select the *Definitely Needlepoint* database, and select the Customers table to display the Mail Merge Recipients dialog box. Select all of the recipients.
   d. Complete the form letter by adding an address block and greeting line as shown in Figure 8. Now click the View Merged Data button to toggle between the field names and the actual data. (Figure 8 displays the form letter for Debbie Armstrong.)
   e. Click the Merge to New Document button on the Mail Merge toolbar to display the associated dialog box, and then specify that you want records 1 to 3 as shown in Figure 8. Click OK. There are more than 150 records in the database, so be sure that you print only the first three records.
   f. Word creates a new document consisting of three pages, corresponding to a letter for the first three records in the Customers table in the Access database. Print these letters for your instructor.
   g. Save the completed form letter *(November Letter Solution)*. There is no need to save the document that contains the individual form letters. Exit Word.

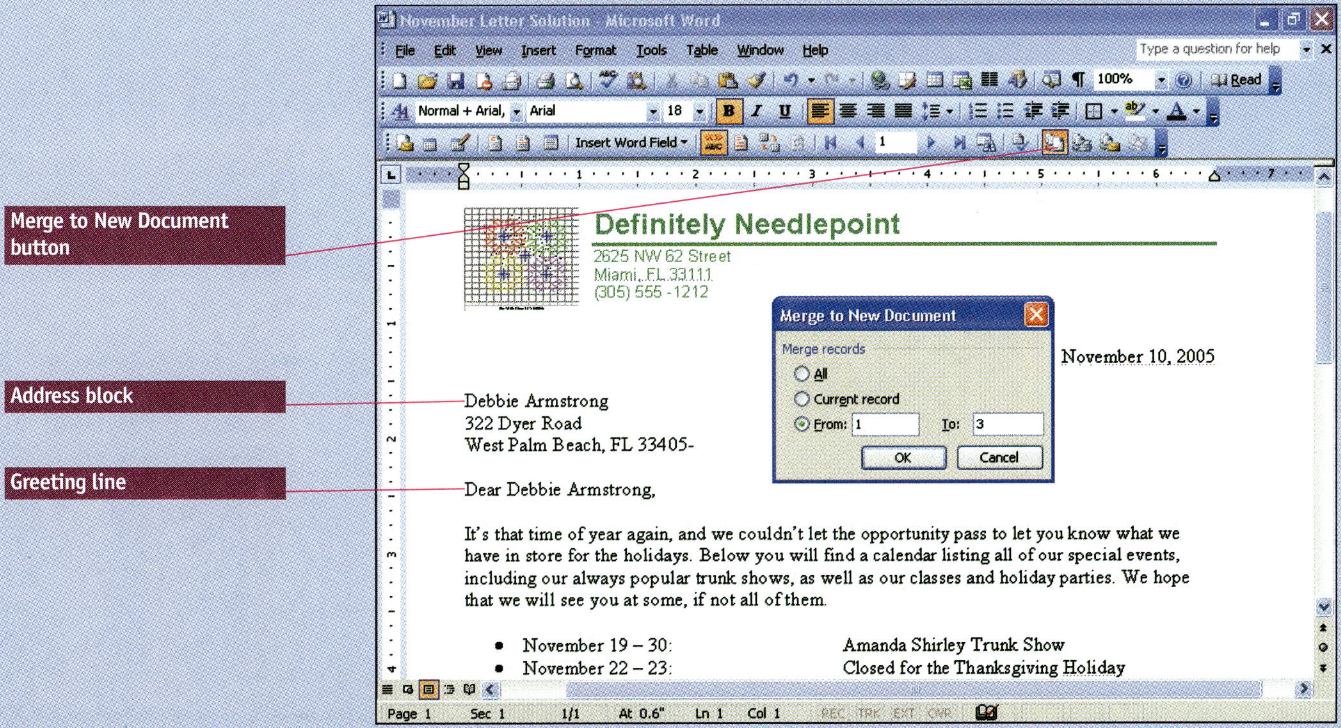

FIGURE 8 Mail Merge

9. **Worksheet References (Excel):** The year that just ended marked the second year of operation for Definitely Needlepoint. The partners are looking for a detailed analysis that will compare the sales for this year to the previous year. Proceed as follows:

   a. Open the *Definitely Needlepoint Historical Sales* workbook in the Definitely Needlepoint folder and save it as *Definitely Needlepoint Historical Sales Solution*. (The values in this worksheet reflect the last-minute correction that was made in problem 4; that is, the total sales for the current year are $305,699.)

   b. Click the worksheet tab labeled Year to Year Comparison, then click in cell B4 of this worksheet as shown in Figure 9. Type an equal sign, click the worksheet tab labeled Previous Year, click in cell F3 of this worksheet, and press Enter. The formula for this cell appears in the formula bar as ='Previous Year'!F3, indicating that the value for this cell is obtained from another worksheet in the same workbook. Complete the formulas for the other cells in this worksheet.

   c. Use the Page Setup command to create a custom footer that contains the worksheet tab, your name, and today's date. Use the Page Setup command to display gridlines, and row and column headings. Print this worksheet for your instructor. Print the worksheet two ways, once to show the displayed values and once to show the cell formulas.

   d. Your next task is to create two charts that reflect the year to year increases. A portion of the chart to show the increases by category can be seen in the right pane of Figure 8. Note that this chart displays the data table below the chart, an option that is found in the Chart menu. Note, too, that we changed the default color of the columns in the chart to green and white. (You do not have to print the chart.)

   e. Create a second chart that shows the increases by quarter. The chart should have the same general appearance as the other chart you created. (You do not have to print the chart.)

   f. Change the tab color of the various worksheets as you see fit. Save the completed workbook. Exit Excel.

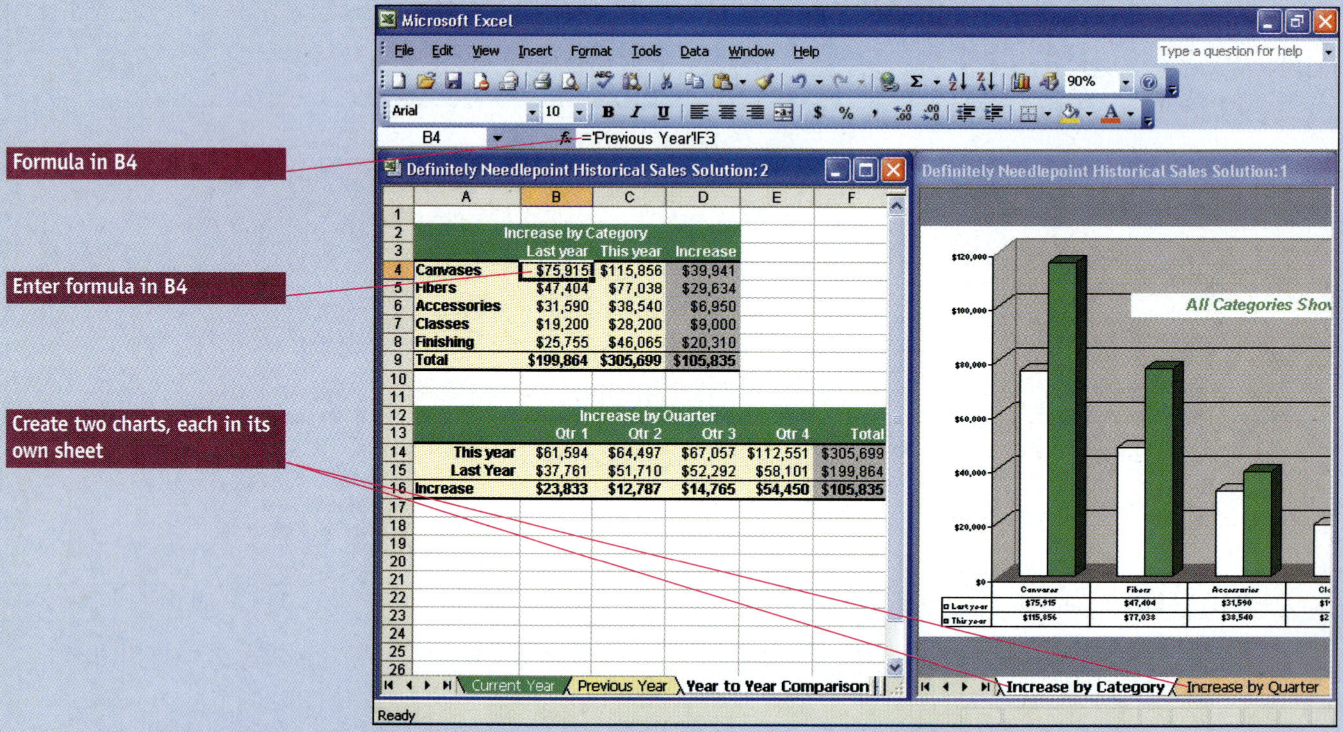

FIGURE 9 Worksheet References

10. **Presentation for Venture Capital (PowerPoint and Excel):** A partially completed version of the presentation in Figure 10 has been saved as the *Request for Venture Capital* presentation in the Definitely Needlepoint folder. Open this presentation and save it as *Request for Venture Capital Solution.* Your next task is to link the worksheets and charts from the previous exercise to various slides in this presentation.

   a. Open the *Definitely Needlepoint Historical Sales Solution* workbook from the previous exercise. Select the worksheet that contains sales data for last year, and link that data to the slide containing the Year to Year Comparison (slide 4). Now select the worksheet with sales data for the current year and link this data to the same slide. Move and/or size the worksheets after they have been added to the presentation.
   b. Locate the worksheet containing the chart that shows the sales increase by category. Link this chart to slide 5.
   c. Locate the chart that shows the sales increase by quarter and link the chart to slide 6.
   d. Add the mission statement as the slide by importing the slide from the *Report to the Partners* presentation. (Pull down the Insert menu, click the Slides from File command to display the Slide Finder dialog box, and then click the Browse button to locate the earlier presentation.)
   e. Add your name to the title slide in the indicated position. Print the audience handouts of the completed presentation (six per page) for your instructor.
   f. Save the completed presentation. Exit PowerPoint. Close the Excel workbook. Exit Excel.

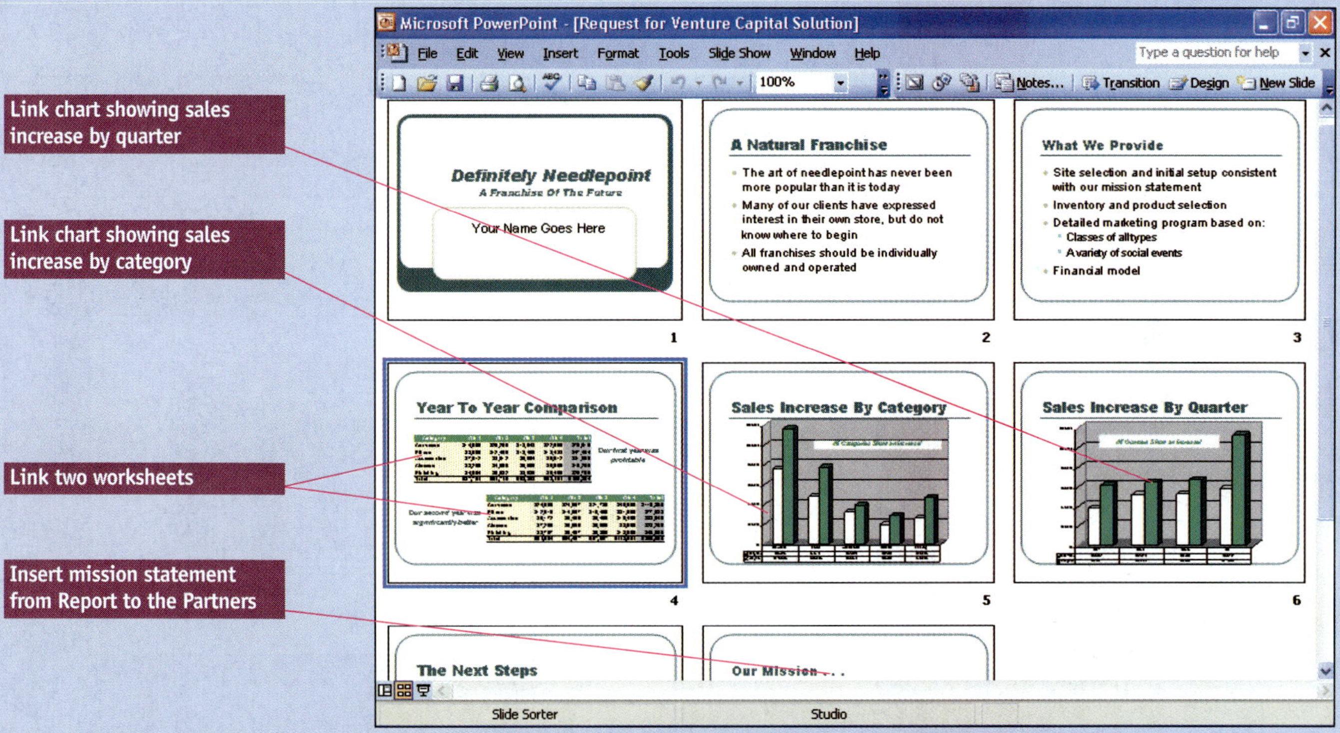

FIGURE 10 Presentation for Venture Capital

11. **Letter to Venture Capitalists (Word and Excel):** This exercise provides additional practice in linking Excel objects to a Word document as well as another chance to practice your skills in a mail merge. Open the partially completed *Letter to Venture Capitalists* document in the Definitely Needlepoint folder, and save it as *Letter to Venture Capitalists Solution*. Insert your name at the bottom of the letter. Now proceed as follows to create the completed document in Figure 11.
    a. Open the *Definitely Needlepoint Historical Sales Solution* workbook from the previous exercise if it is not already open. Use the same techniques as in the previous exercise to link the worksheets containing sales for both the current and previous year to the Word document.
    b. Insert a section break at the end of the first page, then change the orientation of the second page (section) to landscape. Return to the Excel workbook. Select the chart that shows the sales increase by quarter and link this chart to the Word document. The Excel chart should appear in the document. The chart may be cropped initially. If so, select the entire chart, then click and drag a corner sizing handle to make the chart smaller. Right click the chart and click the command to display the Picture toolbar. Select the Crop tool, then click and drag the side handle at the right of the chart to show the portion of the chart that may have been cropped initially.
    c. Use the completed letter as a form letter for a mail merge to venture capitalists. The data for the mailing list is in the Word document, *Venture Capital Mailing List* in the Definitely Needlepoint folder. Pull down the Tools menu, click Letters and Mailings, then click the Mail Merge Wizard command to link to this file. Insert an address block and greeting line, and then print the merged letters for your instructor. You should print three letters. Exit Word.

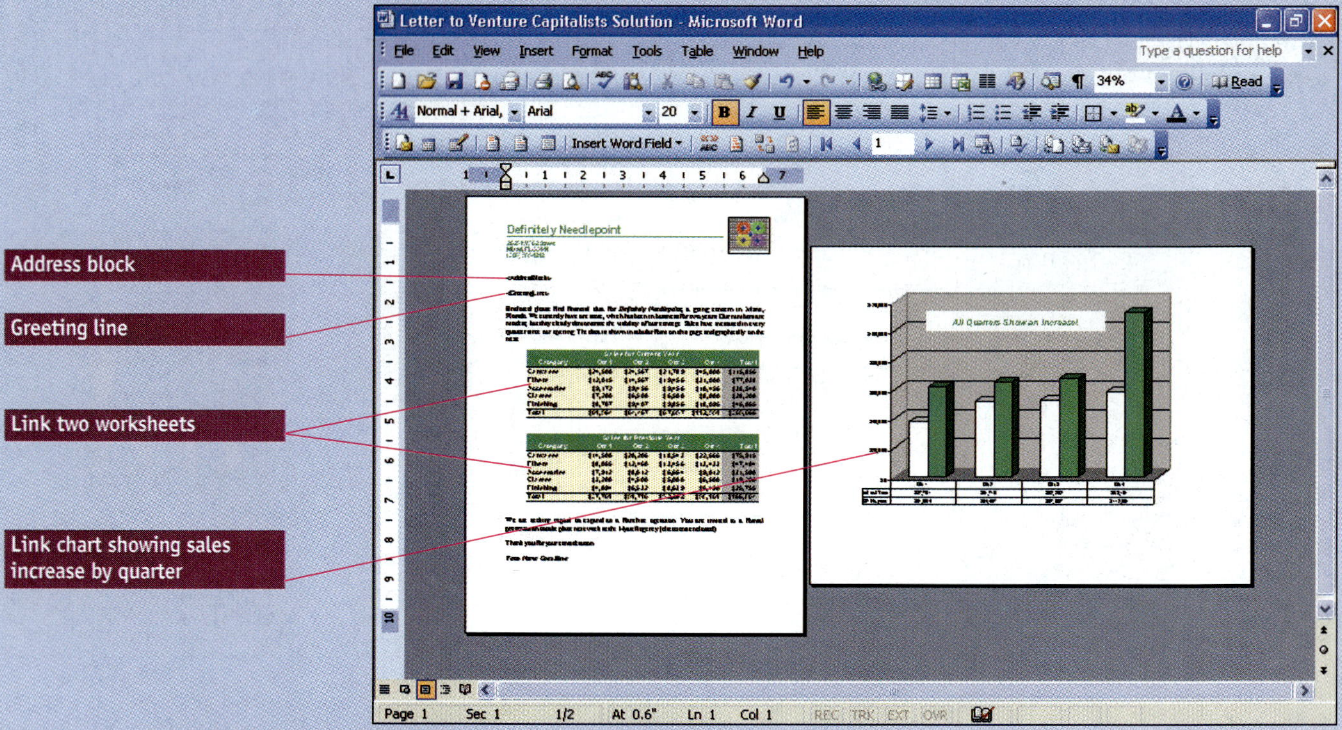

FIGURE 11 Letter to Venture Capitalists

12. **Create a Home Page (Word):** Open the *Definitely Needlepoint Home Page* document in the Definitely Needlepoint folder. Pull down the File menu, click the Save as Web Page command, and specify Single File Web Page as the file type to save the Word document to a Web page. (Click Continue if a message appears that indicates pictures with text wrapping will become left or right justified.) Review the document and make the basic formatting changes you deem appropriate. Use the Themes command in the Format menu to apply an overall design to the page. Your goal is to create a page similar to Figure 12.
   a. Create a one-by-two table at the top of the document. Place the existing clip art in the left cell. Enter the title and other information in the right cell. Format the text. Size the cells as necessary. Remove the border around the table.
   b. Select the text "click here" that appears in the middle of the document. Pull down the Insert menu and click the Hyperlink command (or click the Insert Hyperlink button on the Standard toolbar), click the E-mail Address button, and then enter your e-mail address.
   c. Create the indicated hyperlinks that appear within the document. Search the Web to find the addresses to our sites, or choose your own. Be sure to enter valid addresses, however, for all selected sites.
   d. Save the document a final time, then exit Word. Start Windows Explorer, then go to the folder containing your Web page, and double click the file you just created. Internet Explorer will start automatically (because your document was saved as a Web page). You should see your document within Internet Explorer as shown in Figure 12. Look carefully at the Address bar and note the local address on drive C, as opposed to a Web address. Print the document for your instructor as proof you completed the assignment.
   e. Creating the home page and viewing it locally is easy. Placing the page on the Web where it can be seen by anyone with an Internet connection is not as straightforward. You will need additional information from your instructor about how to obtain an account on a Web server (if that is available at your school), and further how to upload the Web page from your PC to the server.

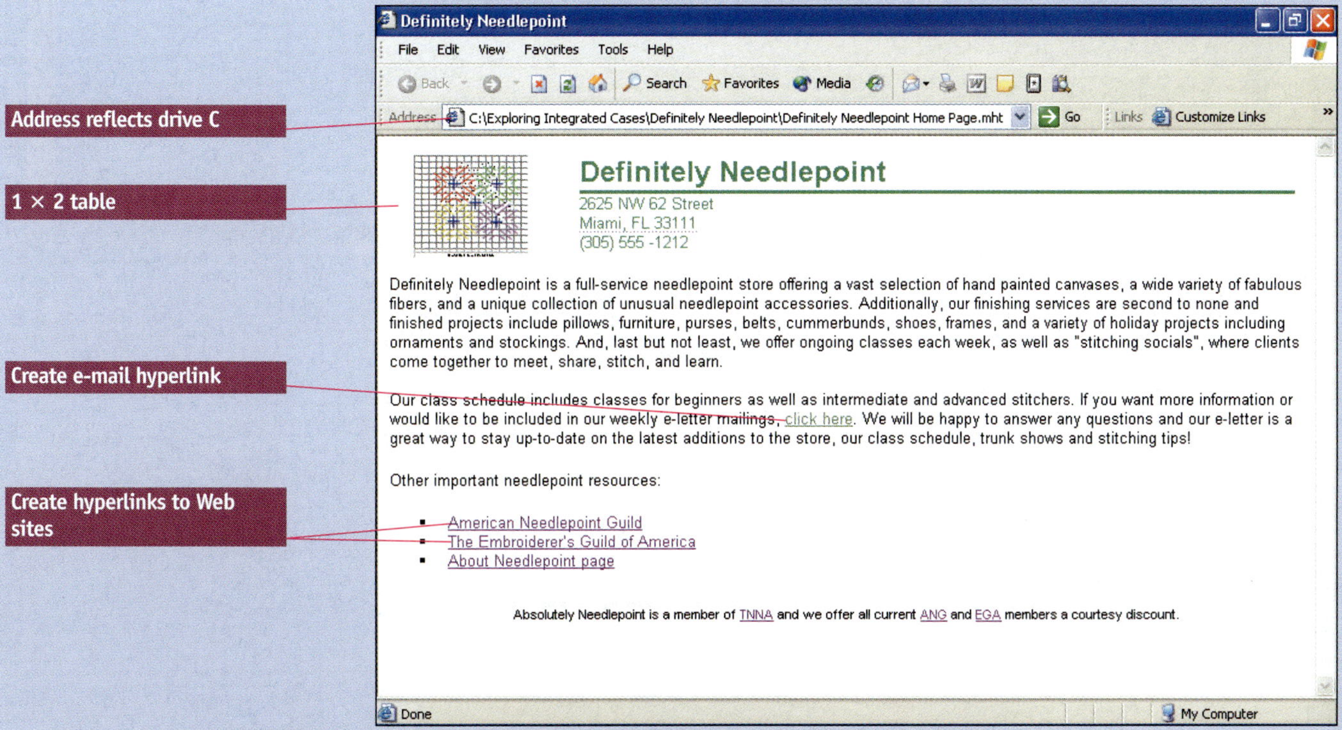

FIGURE 12 Create a Home Page

13. **Submission Checklist (Word):** You have successfully completed multiple exercises with the Definitely Needlepoint case study. Each exercise described a specific task(s), required the use of one or more applications in Microsoft Office, and asked you to print one or more documents to show that you completed the exercise. The submissions checklist in Figure 13 will ensure that you have printed all of the required documents.
    a. Open the *Definitely Needlepoint Submission Checklist* that is found in the Definitely Needlepoint folder. Read the document carefully and check each box after you verify that you have printed the indicated document.
    b. Add your name to the checklist as indicated, then use the checklist as a cover sheet when you submit the material to your instructor.
    c. Think for a minute about all that you have accomplished. You have completed a series of 13 exercises, which required the use of all four major applications within Microsoft Office. Congratulations on a job well done!

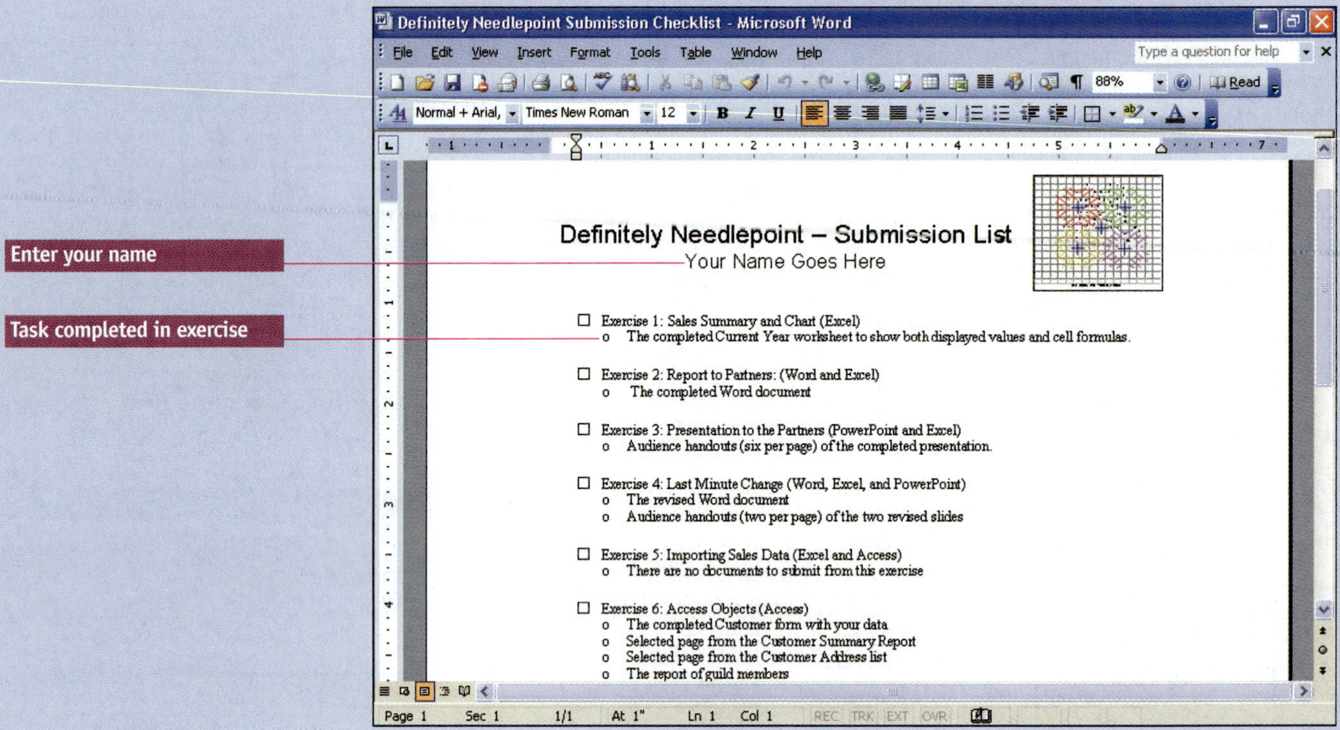

FIGURE 13 Submission Checklist

Glossary

Compiled by Kathleen Voge, University of Alaska

Absolute cell reference In Excel, Absolute cell reference (or address) refers to cell references that will not change when copied to another cell, and is specified with a dollar sign in front of the column and row designation.

Accept and Review Changes command In Word, the Accept and Review Changes command helps users to look over documents and then make desired changes.

Access time All disks have an access time, which on average is the amount of time it takes a disk to retrieve a document.

Accounting format A numeric format that gives users the ability to display a number with the 1000 separator, optional dollar sign, negative values in parentheses, and zero values as hyphens.

Action Items slide In PowerPoint, Action Items slides are slides created during a presentation.

Action query While most queries are generally used to extract information from a database, an Action query allows the user to perform either an update, append, delete, or make-table procedure in the database with a single operation.

Active cell An active cell in Excel is a cell where information or data will be input, indicated by a black border surrounding it.

Address book This function is a section of Outlook that acts like a personal telephone and address book, having the e-mail program retrieve numbers and addresses.

Aggregate (Summary) functions In Access, the Aggregate (Summary) functions are used to determine the total number, average, or maximum values of a group of records.

Alignment In all applications, alignment defines the positioning of text within documents: flush left/flush right, left aligned, right aligned, and centered with the margin.

Allow Zero Length property The Allow Zero Length field property, when set to Yes, will allow text or memo strings of zero length in the field.

AND condition AND condition specifies that records selected must include ALL criteria.

Animation Animations control the appearance of individual elements or objects on a single slide. Animation effects can be used to add interest or excitement to a presentation.

Animation effects In PowerPoint, the program has animation effects, such as stars flying from the top left-hand corner to the bottom right-hand corner.

Append query An Append query is one type of Action query where records from one table are added to the end of the records in another table.

Arguments In Excel, arguments are values as input that perform an indicated calculation, and then return another value as output.

Arial A specific typeface or font. Arial is a sans serif and proportional font.

Arrange command In Excel, once windows are open, the Arrange command under the Windows menu can be used to cascade the open windows.

Ascending sequence In Word, while working on a table, the Ascending Sequence button helps sort information in rows in an ascending manner.

Assumptions In Excel, assumptions are initial conditions or scenarios on which spreadsheets are based.

Asterisks In Access, an asterisk (record selector symbol) is visible next to the end of every table, showing users the status of the record.

AutoContent Wizard In PowerPoint, the AutoContent Wizard helps users to create new presentations.

AutoCorrect The AutoCorrect function instantly changes spelling mistakes as they are typed.

AutoFill capability AutoFill capability allows users to enter data into adjacent cells by dragging the fill handle to desired new cells.

AutoFilter command The AutoFilter command allows users to specify a selected set of data (rows) within a worksheet and display only those rows matching the selected data. The hidden rows are not deleted; they are just not displayed while AutoFilter is activated.

AutoForm An AutoForm is one of several predefined forms that were designed to make form creation easier for the user.

AutoFormat command In Excel, the AutoFormat command presents already formatted designs for users to choose from.

AutoMark The AutoMark command will automatically mark all occurrences of specific text and include the text in an index.

Automatic replacement In Word, automatic replacement is predetermined correction and replacement of words or phrases.

AutoNumber field An AutoNumber field is a data type that makes Access format consecutive numbers every time a new record is added.

AutoOrder The AutoOrder button will allow the Tab key to move to fields in left-to-right, top-to-bottom order as data entry is being completed on a form.

AutoShapes button In PowerPoint, Access, and Word, AutoShapes buttons—located on the Drawing toolbar—can allow users to add lines, rectangles, ovals, callouts, and banners to documents.

AutoSum The AutoSum button on the Standard toolbar causes various cells to add up. By clicking certain rows and columns, their addition is also invoked.

AutoText The AutoText function is similar to AutoCorrect in that it will substitute a predefined item for a specific character string. However, with AutoText, the user must take conscious action for the substitution to occur.

Auxiliary storage Auxiliary storage or secondary storage is a section of the computer whose function is to keep information for an extended period of time and then allow it to be moved to and from the RAM.

AVERAGE function The AVERAGE function in Excel is the statistical function that adds together the values in a specified range and then divides the result by the number of numeric entries in that range.

Avg function The Avg function in Access is the statistical function that adds together the values in a specified field and then divides the result by the number of fields being evaluated.

Background command In PowerPoint, the Background command changes the coloring to all or each slide in a presentation.

Backup The term used to describe an additional copy of a file created to protect the user from loss of or damage to the original file.

Bar chart A bar chart is basically a column chart that has been given a horizontal, not a vertical, orientation.

Between function The Between function selects records that fall within a range of values.

Bit Stands for binary digit, and represents zero and one. Alone, bits do not have significant meaning; however, when combined they equal bytes.

Body Text style The Body Text style is a particular style within Word that can be used to automate the text formatting process and provide a consistent appearance to a document.

Boldface Boldface is the darkening of letters or numbers to emphasize texture in documents.

Bookmark Within a Web browser, bookmarks mark a favorite or frequently used site.

Border tab The Border tab of the Format Cells dialog box allows users to create a border, either with or without special emphasis, around a cell or group of cells.

Borders and Shading command In Word, the Borders and Shading command allows you to apply additional formatting to a paragraph and/or document. Some examples include shadow borders, page borders, and shading.

Bound control Bound controls are fields that are used to change and input data of a table.

Breakpoint A breakpoint is the lowest numeric value for a specific category or series that can be matched in either the VLOOKUP or HLOOKUP functions.

Bug A bug is a mistake in any computer program.

Bulleted list In Word, by clicking on the button with three vertical squares, a list can be made with choices of various bullets.

Bullets and Numbering command In Word, the Bullets and Numbering command under the Format menu gives users a number of choices in styles for bulleting, numbering, and outline numbering.

Byte A byte equals eight bits, and is the smallest addressable unit of memory. Different computers are capable of holding different sizes of bytes or memory; a gigabyte (Gb) is one example.

Calculated control In Access, a calculated control deals with expressions rather than fields for its data source.

Calculated field In Access and Excel, a calculated field is the place where values from formulas that work with a designated field or fields are determined.

Caption property In Access, the Caption property explicitly names labels.

Case statement In Access, the Case statement tests values of a variable as they are input into the program.

Case-insensitive search A search wherein specific text will be matched, but upper- and lowercase differences in that text will not impact the search results.

Case-sensitive search A search wherein text, including upper- and lowercase specifications, will be matched before being included in the search results.

Category labeling In charts, the category labeling is the written language used to describe entries.

CD-ROM An acronym for Compact Disk, Read-Only Memory. It is a disk that stores information in large quantities, but does not allow the user to write on the CD.

Cell In Excel, Access, and Microsoft Office XP, a cell is the intersection of a row and column.

Cell reference In Excel, Access, and Microsoft Office XP, the intersection of a row and column is designated a column and a number equaling the cell reference.

Central processing unit (CPU) The CPU is the main part of a computer responsible for executing computations.

Character style In Access, Word, and PowerPoint, Character Style function harbors the formatting of characters.

Chart A chart in Access and Excel is a graphical representation of data in a worksheet.

Chart sheet A chart sheet is one of the two ways in which you can create a chart in Excel. In a chart sheet, the chart object is the only item on the sheet.

Chart toolbar The Chart toolbar is the toolbar you can work with when creating or modifying charts. You can use the toolbar to change the chart type, the color, shape, or pattern of a data series, along with many other chart manipulation or formatting features.

Chart type There are many different chart types a user can choose from when deciding how to best visually display his/her data. Different chart types include column, bar, line, pie, area, and radar.

Chart Wizard The Chart Wizard is a guide in helping create tables or queries to build desired charts within Access.

Check box In Access, check boxes are used as Yes/No fields for data entry of two choices.

Clip art Clip art in many Microsoft applications is used to create special effects with words, letters, and photographs.

Clip Organizer *See* Microsoft Clip Organizer.

Clipboard The Windows Clipboard area allows you to copy and paste information from one area of a spreadsheet to another. In the normal Windows Clipboard, each subsequent Copy command will replace the current contents of the Windows Clipboard. However, Microsoft Office now provides users with its own clipboard that will allow you to collect multiple text and graphic items (up to 24 items) from different Office documents or other Office programs and then paste them into any other Office document or program.

Clock speed Clock speed is how much time it takes data to be transmitted in a microprocessor.

Close command In any Microsoft program, the Close command allows users to close a document, spreadsheet, or workbook.

Color scheme In PowerPoint, a set of eight colors defines the program's color scheme.

Column chart A column chart in Excel displays data in a column formation and can be converted to a bar chart.

Columnar report A columnar report is the easiest kind of report detailing fields for records in a column.

Columns command In Word, the Columns command calls up the window to insert one to three columns into a document.

Combination chart A combination chart is a chart that uses two or more chart types to display different types of data. It can also be used when different scales are required for multiple data series.

Combo box A type of control that a user can create and add to a form or report.

Command buttons In Access, command buttons help users to modify tables, for example, by clicking on Add Records or New Record.

Comment statements Comment statements are symbols (nonexecutable statements) placed at the beginning of macros to remind users what the macro does.

Comments In PowerPoint, a user can add comments to any presentation to explain his/her thoughts to others who may be reviewing the presentation file.

Common user interface The common user interface is similar design features used within Microsoft Office that provide a sense of familiarity from one Office application to the next. The common user interface contains a common menu structure, consistent methods for executing commands, the Standard and Formatting toolbars, etc.

Compact and Repair Database command The Compact and Repair Database command plays two roles: to eliminate fragmentation and waste on a disk and to repair databases if Access is unable to read them.

Compressed file A compressed file allows users to download large amounts of information from the Web or Internet by reducing the time it takes to transfer the file into the desired program.

Conditional Formatting command The Conditional Formatting command allows users to display values within a spreadsheet in different manners, red values versus blue values.

Constant In any spreadsheet, the entry that does not change is called the constant.

Constraints Constraints in Excel represent restrictions placed in cells or cell ranges.

Controls In Access, a control displays data in numerical or descriptive forms. There are three types of controls: bound, unbound, and calculated controls.

Convert Database command The Convert Database command changes the file format of an Access 2002 database from earlier versions.

Copy command The Copy command is located under the Edit menu, allowing users to copy a desired text, graph, or picture.

Copyright A copyright provides legal protection to an author's written or artistic work. A work that is copyrighted will have limits to its use and/or reproduction.

COUNT function In Excel, the COUNT function returns the number of cells containing numeric entries, or formulas that evaluate to numeric results, within a specified range of cells. In Access, the COUNT function counts the number of records in the group.

COUNTA function The COUNTA function returns the number of cells containing both numeric and text entries within a specified range of cells.

Courier New A specific typeface or font. Courier New is a serif and monospaced font.

Create New Folder command In Word, the Create New Folder command makes new folders for different sets of documents.

Create Subdocument command In Word, the Create Subdocument command allows users to make subdocument files when saving or working on master documents.

Criteria row The Criteria row in the query design grid allows the user to determine the records that will be selected.

Crosstab query A Crosstab query consolidates data from an Access table and presents the information in a row-and-column format, similar to a pivot table in Excel.

Currency field In Access or Excel, the Currency field is used to store monetary figures.

Current record In Access, a current record refers to an active set of fields.

Custom dictionary The dictionary where user-specified words can be added to ensure that they are not flagged as spelling errors in the future.

Custom format A numeric format that gives users the ability to develop specific formatting options.

Cut command The Cut command is located under the Edit menu, letting users cut a desired text, graph, or picture.

Data Data means facts about records or sets of records.

Data points In charts for Excel or Microsoft Graph, data points are numeric values used to describe entries.

Data series In charts for Excel or Microsoft Graph, data series is another way of describing a group of data points on worksheets.

Data type In Access, data types exist in every field of a table, and they determine the types of data limitations and function to be executed within each field.

Data Validation command In Excel and Access, the Data Validation command gives users the ability to prevent errors from happening by restricting the values accepted in cells.

Database In Access, databases are one or more tables.

Database window The Database window shows users the many tables, queries, forms, reports, pages, macros, and modules in Access.

Datasheet In the Microsoft Graph program or Excel, datasheets record data values (data points) to create graphs or data series for presentations.

Datasheet view In Access, the Datasheet View function helps users to add, edit, or delete records.

Date arithmetic Date arithmetic is made possible by Excel storing all dates as integers. Therefore, if a user needs to determine the number of days between two dates, date arithmetic can be used to provide the answer.

Date format A numeric format that gives users the ability to display dates in a variety of different formats.

Date/Time field In Access and Excel, the Date/Time field holds dates or times.

Debugging Debugging is the act of ridding any program of bugs (mistakes).

Default Value property In Access, the Default Value property self-activates a default value each time a record is input into the table.

Delete command The Delete command takes information or lists away from a document or spreadsheet.

Delete query A Delete query is one type of Action query wherein one or more records in a table are deleted according to specified criteria.

Dependent workbook In Excel, the dependent workbook holds the external and is contingent in operation on source workbooks.

Descending sequence In Word, while working on a table, the Descending Sequence button helps sort information in rows in a descending manner.

Design grid The design grid is the lower area of the Query window where specifications for the query are entered.

Design view In Access, the Design view allows users to create and choose tables, and to indicate the fields that will be put into the tables.

Desktop publishing Desktop publishing is bringing text and graphics together to make a polished document without depending on outside sources.

Destination range The cells that you want to copy or move information *to.*

Detail section In an Access report, the Detail section appears in the main body of the report and is printed once for every record in the underlying table or query.

Dialog box Dialog boxes appear immediately after any command has been selected, giving users additional options to complete a command.

Do statement In Excel, the Do statement copies a block of statements until a condition comes to fruition.

Docked toolbar A docked toolbar is any toolbar that has been placed along the edge of the application window. A docked toolbar can be placed on the top, bottom, right, or left edge of the application window.

Documentation worksheets In Excel, documentation worksheets contain descriptive explanations of each worksheet within a workbook.

Drawing canvas The area of work that appears automatically when you select a tool from the Drawing toolbar. The area is identified by a hashed line.

Drawing toolbar In Word, the Drawing toolbar offers users additional choices in drawing lines, shapes, boxes with text, and many other options.

Drop-down list box In Access, drop-down list boxes have choices or indicators to pick from for input into a table.

Dropped-capital letters In Word, a Dropped-capital letter is a larger, dominant bold letter placed at the beginning of a paragraph; used for emphasis.

DVD A DVD is equivalent to a CD-ROM disk, but can store much more data (up to 17 Gb).

Dynaset The results of a query are displayed in a dynaset, which contains the records that satisfy the criteria specified for that query. The dynaset looks and acts like a table, but it is a dynamic subset of the table.

Edit The Edit button changes the contents of a cell or deletes text from a document.

Embedded chart An embedded chart is one of the two ways in which you can create a chart in Excel. An embedded chart is a chart object that is contained within a worksheet along with other worksheet entries.

Embedded object In PowerPoint, embedded objects are placed and stored within a presentation.

Endnote In Word and Access documents, endnotes are like footnotes, but are located at the end of a document.

Event Events are actions, such as clicking a button or closing a file, that are recognized by Access.

Event procedures In Access, event procedures are one of the two kinds found in the Visual Basic code, and are the various actions automatically recognized by Access.

Exit command In any Windows application, the Exit command closes and leaves any application.

Exploded pie chart In Excel, exploded pie charts display relationships among data by dividing data according to slices of a pie.

Export command The Export command allows users to copy an Access database object from an outside source.

Expression In Access, a combination of operators, field names, constants and/or functions are expressions.

External Data toolbar The External Data toolbar is used when working with data that originates from an external data source. It allows the user to refresh external data, specify query ranges, specify query parameters, etc.

Fair use Fair use of any copyrighted material occurs when only a portion of the work is being used for educational or nonprofit use, or for the purpose of critical review. However, you must cite the original work or source in your footnotes and/or bibliography.

Field Fields contain the individual data found in folders.

Field name In Access, field names are located in the first row of a table.

Field row The Field row in the query design grid displays the field name for each field to be included in the query.

Field Size property In Access, the Field Size property restricts and amends the text size of a field.

File While working with spreadsheets, files are in correspondence with manila folders.

File menu The File menu is an integral part of any Windows application, allowing users to open and save documents on a disk.

File name The file name allows users to "name" a document while saving it on a disk.

File Transfer Protocol File Transfer Protocol (FTP) in Word gives users the ability to upload files from PCs to the server.

File type The file type lets users know what application the document was saved under.

Fill handle In Excel, a small black square appearing in the bottom-right corner of a cell allowing data to be entered into cells.

Filter A filter displays a subset of records from the table or query according to user-specified criteria.

Filter by Form In Access, Filter by Form allows users to choose criteria to be input in various relationships within tables or charts, and also can use the and/or function in the criterion selection.

Filter by Selection button In Access, the Filter by Selection button on the Database toolbar allows users to choose only certain desired criteria, and excludes others.

Filter Excluding Selection While the Filter By Selection option selects all records that meet the designated criteria, the Filter Excluding Selection displays all records that do not match the designated criteria.

Filtered list Filtered lists in Excel and Access are the only records that match specific criteria.

Find command The Find command shares a dialog box with the Replace and Go To commands. This command finds various occurrences of the same word or phrase.

First line indent The type of indentation wherein only the first line in a paragraph is indented. It can be implemented by pressing the Tab key at the beginning of the paragraph.

Floating toolbar A floating toolbar is any toolbar that is displayed within the application window and is not in a fixed location on any edge of the window.

Floppy disk A square, plastic apparatus used to store completed documents created on a microprocessor program such as Microsoft Word.

Folder In any Microsoft program, folders organize and store files or documents, and are key components to the Windows storage system.

Font Font (typeface) means the entire group of upper- and lowercase letters, numbers, punctuation marks, and symbols used in documents.

Footer In Word, footers are one or more lines placed at the bottom of a page.

Footnote In Word and Access, footnotes are located at the bottom of document pages detailing additional information.

Foreign key A foreign key is a field in one table that is the primary key in another table.

Form letter A form letter is one that you will create once with only specific pieces of information changing each time you send it. Examples of the information that may change in a form letter include date, name, address, or other pertinent information as deemed necessary. Mail merge is commonly used to easily prepare form letters.

Form view In Access, the Form view allows users to see information on forms without the designs.

Form Wizard In Access, the Form Wizard displays and makes forms for users by asking users a sequence of questions.

Format Cells command Use of the Format Cells command allows users to control the formatting of numbers, alignment, fonts, borders, and patterns.

Format Font command In many applications, the Format Font command allows users to change and alter the typeface, size, and style of text in documents.

Format Painter In Word, the Format Painter tool or feature appears on the Standard toolbar. This feature allows you to reapply both text and graphic formatting options to other specified areas of a document.

Format Paragraph command In Word, this command allows you to specify the alignment, indentation, line spacing, and pagination settings for the selected paragraph(s).

Format Picture command In Word, the Format Picture command gives users the option to alter a picture in documents.

Format property In Access, the Format property alters the method in which a field is shown or printed.

Formatting toolbar In any Microsoft application, it appears under the Standard toolbar, and provides access to common formatting operations such as boldface and italic.

Forms In Access, forms are ways to input, show, and print data in a table.

Forms toolbar In Word, the Forms toolbar allows users to make three kinds of fields: text boxes, check boxes, and drop-down list boxes.

Formula In a spreadsheet, the combination of constants, cell references, arithmetic operations, and/or functions displayed in a calculation is a formula.

Formula bar In Excel or Access, the formula bar shows the contents of the spreadsheet's formula and is located at the top of the worksheet.

Fraction format A numeric format that gives users the ability to display a number as a fraction. Use of this format is appropriate when there is no exact decimal equivalent.

Freeze Panes command When the Freeze Panes command is activated, user-specified rows and/or columns are continuously displayed, or frozen, on the screen regardless of the scrolling currently in effect.

Function In Access or Excel, a function indicates a predefined computational task, such as SUM or AVERAGE.

FV function The FV function returns the future value of an investment, based on constant periodic payments and a constant interest rate.

General format The default format for numeric entries that displays a number according to the way it was originally entered.

General procedure In Access, general procedures are one of the two kinds of procedures. This kind of procedure, however, is not automatically recognized by Access.

Get External Data command In Access or Excel, the Get External Data command brings data from outside sources such as Microsoft Office, a text file, Excel, or Access.

GIGO (garbage in, garbage out) The acronym that describes the observable fact that any information produced by a system is only as good as the information that is entered into the system.

Go To command The Go To command shares a dialog box with the Replace and Find commands. This command finds a word or phrase that the user is looking for.

Goal Seek command In Excel, the Goal Seek command solves mathematical problems and enables the user to set up an end result to determine the input to produce that result.

Grammar check In Word, grammar check allows the user to identify mistakes in punctuation, writing style, sentence structures, and word usage.

Graphics Graphics are designs, pictures, or any other feature used to enhance a document.

Grid A grid in Word is an invisible set of horizontal and vertical lines used to place text in a document.

Group By The Group By specification allows records in a dynaset to be grouped or aggregated according to like values.

Group footer A Group footer reveals the last record and summary information about the group.

Group header A Group header reveals the name of the group of records and is located at a record's beginning.

Hanging indent The type of indentation wherein the first line in a paragraph is usually set at the left margin or leftmost indent, and all remaining lines in the paragraph are indented to some specific amount. Hanging indents are usually used with specific lists.

Hard disk A hard disk or fixed disk is the apparatus located inside of a computer used to store and to access data.

Hard page break In Word, users can put a hard page break in documents on purpose to begin a new page or paragraph

Hard return Hard return takes place when the Enter key is hit at the end of a paragraph.

Header In Word, headers are one or more lines at the top of every printed page.

Header and Footer command In PowerPoint, the Header and Footer command inserts additional information at the bottom or top of slides.

Heading 1 style The Heading 1 style is a particular style within Word that can be used to automate the text formatting process and provide a consistent appearance to a document.

Help command The Help command answers questions that users have about functions of any of the Microsoft programs.

Hidden slide In PowerPoint, experienced speakers who think certain questions may be posed during a presentation use hidden slides to reveal information if needed. Hidden slides can be denoted by a square with a line through it located below the slide in the bottom right-hand corner.

Hide Slide button In PowerPoint, the Hide Slide button allows users to conceal slides during a presentation.

Highlighting The Highlight tool or feature allows you to add color to the background of specific text.

HLOOKUP function The HLOOKUP (or horizontal lookup) function allows a user to search for and match data within a specified table or range and then return a particular value for the matched data. In the HLOOKUP, the data or breakpoint information is organized in a row.

Home page Each time a user logs into a Web browser, the home page of that Web browser or site appears.

Horizontal ruler In Word, the ruler displayed under the toolbars, where the user can change margins, tabs, and/or indents for all or part of the document.

HTML HTML, or HyperText Markup Language, is an address bar recognized by Internet Explorer and Netscape Navigator.

HTML document An HTML document, or basically almost any Web document, is written in HTML (HyperText Markup Language), a universal standard language that is recognized by both Internet Explorer and Netscape Navigator.

Hyperlink A hyperlink can be defined as a reference to another document located on the Internet.

Hyperlink field This is a field that stores Web addresses or URL addresses enabling an Access database to show the Internet link.

Hyphenation Hyphenation is used to eliminate excessive gaps of white space by splitting a word that will not fit on one line. The word is separated by a hyphen (in an appropriate spot), and then completed on the next line.

IF Function The IF function decides on certain numerical augmentations within a worksheet.

IME Mode property The IME Mode property refers to the Input Method Editor for East Asian languages.

Immediate window In Access, during computations in VBA, the VBA editor allows data computations to be shown in the Immediate window.

Import External Data command In Excel, the Import External Data command allows users to bring in information or data from an outside source.

Import Spreadsheet Wizard The Import Spreadsheet Wizard aids users in creating spreadsheets in Excel and imports them into tables for Access.

Imported data Imported data is data that is brought to Access or Excel from an outside source.

Indents In Word, an indent is the spacing between the text and the margins.

Index In Word, after users complete long documents, an index can be created to assist in locating specific information.

Index and Tables command In Word, from the Insert menu, the Index and Tables command helps users to create tables of contents.

Indexed property In Access, the Indexed property ensures speedy and efficient searches for desired fields.

Information Information refers to data that has been rearranged into a form perceived useful by the recipient.

Inheritance Inheritance in databases allows an object or control to inherit or assume the same properties as the object it has been associated with. For example, when a field is added to a form in Access, the properties for that field that were defined during table creation and definition will automatically appear on that field in the form.

In-place editing In the PowerPoint program, modifications to graphs in Microsoft Graph are allowed through in-place editing.

Input devices Any exterior source that takes information, changes it to electronic signals, and transfers it to the CPU. The keyboard, mouse, joystick, scanner, microphone, and auxiliary storage are input devices.

Input Mask property This property places data in a specific pattern wherein numeric data or symbols must be typed in a specific order or way.

InputBox function In Excel, the InputBox function accepts information (input) from users for later use in a procedure. InputBox function information must be placed in parentheses.

Insert Bookmark command The Insert Bookmark command copies sites or Web pages and stores them in folders for future quick access.

Insert Columns command The Insert Columns command puts new columns (fields) onto lists.

Insert command The Insert command within Excel allows users to insert individual cells, rows, or columns into a worksheet.

Insert Comment command This command allows the user to create the equivalent of a ScreenTip containing user-entered information about a cell in a worksheet.

Insert Date command In Word, the Insert Date command puts a date on a document and can be accessed through the Insert menu.

Insert Footnote command In Word, the Insert Footnote command places footnotes at the bottom of desired pages, and gives each note a number.

Insert Function command The Insert Function command in Excel allows users to insert a function into a workbook.

Insert Hyperlink command In many applications, the Insert Hyperlink command lets users bring in a hyperlink from the Web.

Insert menu In Word, the Insert Menu function allows users to make various sections in a document.

Insert mode By pressing the Insert key once, users can amend or add text, missing letters, or symbols

Insert Page Numbers command In Word, located under the Insert menu, the Insert Page Numbers command puts page numbers in five places of alignment and three page positions, according to the user's desired location.

Insert Picture command In PowerPoint, the Insert Picture command downloads pictures into presentations.

Insert Reference command In Word, the Insert Reference command inserts either a footnote or an endnote into a document. The sequential numbering of that note is automatically assigned and maintained by Word.

Insert Rows command The Insert Rows command puts new rows (records) onto lists.

Insert Subdocument command In Word, the Insert Subdocument command creates a subdocument while working on a master document.

Insert Symbol command In Access, Word, and PowerPoint, the Insert Symbol command places symbols and characters in documents.

Insert Table command In PowerPoint, the Insert Table command brings a variety of table choices to users.

Insertion point The Insertion point is a blinking line that allows users to type text where the line appears; present at the beginning of a new document.

Intel Corporation Intel is known for the creation of the microprocessor.

Internet A network of networks that connects computers anywhere in the world.

Internet Explorer When searching for information on the Internet, Internet Explorer is one search tool to be used.

Intranet A network internal to a specific organization that allows employees to access local documents via their Web browser.

IRA (Individual Retirement Account) An IRA account is an account that individuals may open and contribute to in order to save for their retirement years. Individuals will make deposits or contributions to the account, and depositors will accrue or earn interest on the amount they have deposited. IRAs may provide certain tax benefits for individuals.

Key In computer-based systems, keys are the records kept in sequence in particular fields known as Keys.

KeyCode argument In Access, a KeyCode argument finds specific numbers or letters, which may or may not have been used by the user.

Label In Access, Label is an example of an unbound control.

Landscape orientation In many Microsoft applications, landscape orientation allows users to print documents the dimensions of 11 × 8½″.

Leader character A leader character, usually a dot or hyphen, is used to assist the reader in following information across a page. One common use of leader characters is in a Table of Contents.

Left indent The type of indentation wherein the left side of a paragraph can appear to have a different margin. The left indent is normally set to zero in a paragraph. Use of the left indent will offset the paragraph from the established left margin.

Line chart A line chart uses a line between data points and is best used to display time-related information such as trends in sales or profit.

Line spacing The established amount of space between the lines in a paragraph. Line spacing can be set at single, double, line and a half, etc.

Linked data In Access, linked data allows a user to import data from an external source, for example an Excel workbook.

Linked object In PowerPoint, a linked object is an object that is placed and stored in its own file.

Linking In Excel, linking allows multiple data sets to be connected through an external reference in a source workbook.

List In Excel, data is kept in lists, rows of similar data.

List box A list box shows available choices within any dialog box.

Lookup Wizard The Lookup Wizard in Access allows the user to select whether he/she will enter potential values directly into the associated field, or choose to have the values for the lookup come from the data values in another table.

Macro Stored in current workbooks or Personal Macro workbooks, macros are sets of instructions that automatically repeat a task within a program.

Macro Recorder In Excel, the Macro Recorder remembers user instructions and automatically writes the macro.

Mail merge A mail merge can create any type of standardized document, but it is used most often as a way to easily create form letters.

Mail Merge Wizard A wizard in Word specifically designed to guide users through the mail merge process. It ensures that users accomplish each of the tasks needed to successfully create form letters.

Main document In mail merge, two primary files are needed. The main document is the file containing the standardized text of the letter. The main document also includes the placeholders, or merge fields, for the variable data.

Make-table query A Make-table query is one type of Action query wherein a new table is created from the records in an existing table.

Margins tab The Margins tab of the Page Setup command allows you to establish all margin settings (top, bottom, left, right), page orientation, etc., for either a part of or the entire document.

Mark Index entry The Mark Index Entry dialog box in Word allows the user to specify settings associated with a word or phrase to be included in the index.

Master document In Word, master documents have many subdocuments, filed away in separate files.

Masthead In any newsletter, the title identifying a newsletter or paper is called the masthead, and is usually located at the top of the document.

MAX function In Excel, the MAX function is the statistical function that provides the maximum or highest value found in a specified range of cells. In Access, the MAX function determines the maximum value for all records in the group.

Meeting Minder During a PowerPoint presentation, Meeting Minder keeps track of questions or problems arising during a presentation.

Megabyte (Mb) Nowadays the memory of a computer is measured in megabytes (Mb). One Kb and one Mb equal roughly one thousand and one million characters, respectively.

Megahertz (MHz) MHz is defined as *millions of cycles*, and determines how fast a microprocessor works.

Memo field Memo fields in Excel and Access are used to store sentences and paragraphs, and can store up to 640,000 characters in length.

Memory For all computers, memory is another term used to define random access memory or RAM. On a short-term basis, memory stores computer programs and information from other working programs.

Menu bar The menu bar provides users with access to pull-down menus needed to execute tasks within any of the Microsoft programs.

Merge cells Merge cells occur when a user has specified to center an entry across a range of selected cells. The merged cells are then treated as one single cell.

Microcomputer A microcomputer or personal computer (PC) has only one person who can access it at a time, unlike a minicomputer that has many users.

Microprocessor A microprocessor is a single silicon chip containing the PC's or microcomputer's CPU. An example is Intel's Pentium, a well-known microprocessor.

Microsoft Access One of the major applications of the Microsoft Office suite, Microsoft Access is a relational database application that is used to create and manage databases.

Microsoft Clip Gallery In Office, Microsoft Clip Gallery offers users pictures and fancy letters for use in documents and newsletters.

Microsoft Clip Organizer The Clip Organizer is an application that assists users in searching through available media objects. Clip art, sound files, photographs, and movies are examples of what can be stored. The Clip Organizer can be accessed as a stand-alone application or from within Word, Excel, and PowerPoint.

Microsoft Graph A supplementary application found in Microsoft Office XP that allows users to create graphs or charts within an Access report.

Microsoft Organization Chart Microsoft Organization Chart allows users to design an organization chart and import it into PowerPoint.

Microsoft WordArt Microsoft WordArt adds special effects to text and text objects, and can be brought in to PowerPoint by clicking the WordArt tool.

MIN function In Excel, the MIN function is the statistical function that provides the minimum or lowest value found in a specified range of cells. In Access, the MIN function determines the minimum value for all records in the group.

Minicomputer Like mainframes or servers, minicomputers also uphold many users; however, not as many.

Mixed reference A mixed reference occurs when a user is combining the use of an absolute reference with a relative reference. Mixed references are typically used in more sophisticated worksheets by advanced users.

Monospaced typeface A typeface that uses the same amount of space for every character regardless of its width.

Move operation The Move operation transfers the contents of a cell or range of cells from one location to another. When the operation is completed, the cell or cells that contained the moved data are left empty.

Multiple data series When a user is looking at or comparing more than one set of data, multiple data series can be displayed within one chart. For example, if you wanted to compare the sales amounts for January, February, and March for three different locations, multiple data series would be used.

Multitasking Multitasking gives users the choice to work on as many programs as desired at the same time.

Musical Instrument Digital Interface (MIDI) file MIDI files create sounds equivalent to sheet music.

My Documents My Documents is a folder where users can store their working or completed documents.

Name box In Excel, the Name box is another name for the cell reference for the cell being used in the worksheet, and is located at the left of the formula bar.

Navigation controls On the Internet, navigation controls give users additional choices for viewing within Internet Explorer.

Nested IF The Nested IF function, or an IF function within another IF function, is a very common logic structure in programming languages. In Excel, a single IF function contains a condition, a value for IF the condition is true, and a value for IF the condition is false. In a Nested IF function, the true and/or false value within an IF function is simply replaced with another IF function.

New Window command Under the Window menu in Excel, the New Window command creates various windows for users.

Nonbreaking hyphen While hyphenation is used to eliminate excessive gaps of white space in a document, a user may not want a specific word to be broken up between lines in a document. If so, the user can specify a nonbreaking hyphen to ensure that the word will not be hyphenated if it falls at the end of a line.

Normal Style In Word, the Normal Style function contains the typical paragraph settings and is used for every paragraph unless indicated as another style.

Normal view In Word and PowerPoint, the Normal view is the typical way in which a document is seen.

NOT Function During the selection of criteria for records in Access, the NOT function determines that records selected must not be included in the specified value or criteria.

Notes Page view In PowerPoint, the Notes Page view is similar to the Slide view, except it allows users to attach notes below the slide.

Now function The Now function returns the current date and time.

Number field In Access or Excel, a Number field has the values that are in a calculation.

Number format A numeric format that gives the user the ability to display a number with or without the 1000 separator.

Numbered list In Word, by clicking on the button with the numbers one, two, and three, a list using numbers can be incorporated into a document.

Object An object can be data, a chart, a worksheet, a presentation slide, etc.

Object box In Access, the Object box shows the current object being used at the top left of the Module window.

Object Linking and Embedding (OLE) In PowerPoint, OLE gives users the ability to link or embed information designed in other applications.

Office Assistant The animated feature in many Microsoft applications that acts as the gatekeeper or guide to online Help information. It allows the user to enter in a question and then offers different topics the user can select to continue the search for an answer.

Office clipboard *See* Clipboard.

OLE Object field An OLE Object field in Access or Excel contains pictures, sounds, or graphics.

One-to-many relationship When a relationship has been defined between two tables, a one-to-many relationship exists when one occurrence of a data element in the first table can be related to multiple occurrences of the same data element in the other table.

Open command The Open command lets users retrieve documents off of the hard drive or disk.

Operating system An operating system is software that connects the computer's hardware components to each other. This system is located on the hard drive and is loaded into memory when the computer is turned on.

Option group In Access, option groups provide users with choices from lists of three.

OR condition An OR condition during the selection of criteria for records in Access determines that records selected must include only some of the specified criteria.

Orphan An orphan occurs when the first line of a paragraph appears by itself at the bottom of a page while the remainder of that paragraph is continued on the next page. Compare with Widow.

Outline An outline, or outline numbered list, is a list that assists you in organizing information in a document. Normally, an outline allows you to create a numbered list by using several different numbering levels. In Word, an outline can be created and updated automatically.

Outline numbered list In Word, outline numbered lists are lists formed into outlines with numbers that are automatically updated as users add information.

Outline view In Word and PowerPoint, the Outline view gives users the option to view a document's style in an outline form.

Outlining toolbar In Word, the Outlining toolbar helps users to work on master documents, allowing users to collapse and expand subdocuments.

Output devices These devices generally take electronic signals from input devices or the CPU and translate them to the correct output configuration. Typical output devices are monitors, printers, speakers, and the auxiliary storage.

Overtype mode By pressing the Insert key twice, users can amend or add text, missing letters, or symbols.

Pack and Go Wizard In PowerPoint, the Pack and Go Wizard keeps all files from your presentation on a single file, allowing presenters never to be unprepared for a presentation.

Page Break Preview command The Page Break Preview command, located under the View menu option, allows users to see and/or modify the page breaks that will occur when the worksheet is printed.

Page footer The page footer is found at the bottom of each page, showing the page number and descriptive information.

Page header The page header is found at the top of each page, showing the page number, column headings, and other descriptive information.

Page numbers In Access and Word, page numbers can be placed in five alignment locations at the bottom, right, or left side of a document.

Page Setup command The Page Setup command in Access, Excel, and Word allows users to alter the margins, footnotes, and headers of a working document.

Paragraph style In Word, the Paragraph Style function preserves the formatting of paragraphs, such as alignment, indents, and line spacing.

Password protection In Word, password protection is of two different kinds when saving a document: a password to open and a password to amend your document.

Paste command After cutting or copying a text, picture, or graph, the Paste command moves that text, picture, or graph to another location within the document or another document.

Paste Special command The Paste Special command can be used in place of the Paste command to move a text without the associated formatting.

Patterns tab The Patterns tab of the Format Cells dialog box allows users to select a different color or pattern in which to shade a cell or group of cells.

Pen In PowerPoint, during presentations, pens are used to draw or write on the slides.

Pencils In Access, pencils (record selector symbol) show users the record that they are working on and reveal alterations to users.

Percentage format A numeric format that gives the user the ability to display a number as its percentage equivalent. The number entered is multiplied by 100 for display purposes only, a percent sign is added, and any number of decimal places can be specified.

Picture toolbar In Word and PowerPoint, the Picture toolbar has crop options for imported pictures.

Pie charts In Excel, pie charts are one way to display relations that proportions have with each other.

Pivot chart A pivot chart displays the information from a pivot table in graphical form.

Pivot table A pivot table summarizes related data and computes summary statistics for the records in a table (or query) in Access, or a range of data in Excel.

PivotChart view The PivotChart view creates a chart from the associated PivotTable view.

PivotTable view The PivotTable view is similar in concept to an Excel Pivot table and gives the user an easy way to summarize data about groups of data.

Placeholders In PowerPoint, the placeholders are fragmented lines encircling shapes where text, titles, graphs, or photos can be inserted.

Places bar In PowerPoint, the Places bar allows quick access to commonly frequented folders.

PMT function PMT Function in Excel spreadsheets requires three arguments to calculate the periodic payment on a loan.

Pointing In Excel, pointing is using the mouse or arrow keys to select the cell directly in creating a formula in a spreadsheet.

Portrait orientation In many Microsoft applications, portrait orientation can be found under the File menu and then by clicking the PageSetup button. It is the default for printing orientation and documents print as they appear on screen.

Primary key A primary key is a field that can reveal records for tables.

Print command The Print command in any Microsoft program allows users to print documents, spreadsheets, or workbooks.

Print Layout view The Print Layout view is located under the Page Setup of the File button. This view allows users to see how the printed version of the document looks.

Print Preview The Print Preview window allows users to preview the information designated to be printed in various ways.

Program Microsoft Word, Microsoft PowerPoint, and Microsoft Excel are programs whose written guidelines help execute the desired tasks of the users.

Project Explorer In Word, the Project Explorer—like Windows Explorer—shows users open Word documents and/or other Visual Basic projects.

Property A property is what determines an object's role within a program.

Property sheet In Access, property sheets present an object's property, and alterations to the property can be made here.

Proportional typeface A typeface that allocates space according to the width of each individual character.

Public domain When an author gives everyone the right to freely reproduce and distribute his/her material, that material is said to be in the public domain.

Pull-down menus Through the menu bar, pull-down menus allow users to complete commands within any Microsoft program. Pull-down menus are many within each program and can be accessed either by a sequence of commands or by clicking a command button.

Pull-quote In Word, pull-quotes are phrases or sentences set in larger type in order to stand out from other sections of the page.

Query A query allows users to pick records from tables, and put some of those records into other selected tables, and/or perform calculations on that data.

Query window The Query window shows users the field list and design grid in Access.

Range A range is a rectangular group of cells. A range may be a single cell or the entire worksheet. The cell or cells within a range are specified by indicating the diagonally opposite corner cells, typically the upper-left cell and lower-right cell. An example of a range is A1: C13.

Read only memory (ROM) In every computer, this is the memory that is available when a user starts up a computer; it is the set of guidelines that reveal to the computer that it must examine and start up its operating systems into its CPU.

Record When working with spreadsheets, records are the individual files within folders.

Recycle Bin The Recycle Bin stores unwanted documents or files until emptied.

Redo command Located under the Edit button, the Redo command *repeats* the same text by copying it in another location within a working document.

Referential integrity Referential integrity in Access is having the tables in a database harmonious with one another.

Refresh command The Refresh command, represented by the exclamation point button on the External Data toolbar, allows the user to update data in a worksheet that has been originated from an external data source.

Rehearse Timings Rehearse Timings is a feature in PowerPoint that lets users time a presentation while practicing.

Relational database A relational database is a database that has been designed to minimize redundant or repeated data. Common data items that are located in two or more tables can be related; i.e., a relationship can be formed between the two tables based on these common data fields.

Relational operators There are six relational operators that may be used when specifying arguments in functions. They are 1) equal to, 2) not equal to, 3) less than, 4) greater than, 5) less than or equal to, and 6) greater than or equal to.

Relationships window The Relationships window is for users to specify which tables and fields will be related in the database, along with being able to set additional relationship properties such as referential integrity and join types.

Relative reference In Excel, relative reference refers to cell references in the formula that will change when copied to another cell.

Removable mass storage This is another term for Zip drive, an external or internal storage apparatus, which can keep as much as 250Mb of information. It operates like a huge floppy disk.

Remove Filter The Remove Filter feature displays all of the records in the table.

Repeat command Located under the Edit button, the Repeat command lets users paste the same text over again in another location within a working document.

Replace command The Replace command shares a dialog box with the Find and Go To commands. After the Find command finds the text or phrase that the user is looking for, the Replace command allows the user to replace the text or phrase.

Report A report in Access is a printed document for a database.

Report footer A report footer is a section of a report found at the end of a report, containing summary information about the report.

Report header A report header is a section of a report found at the beginning of a report, containing information such as the title and date of the report.

Report Wizard The Report Wizard in Microsoft Access is the simplest way to make and construct a report.

Required property In Access, the Required property discards records not corresponding to the value in field.

Résumé Wizard In Word, the Résumé Wizard aids users in completing professional résumés by asking them a series of questions, and later presenting a template résumé.

Reverse In Word, for text emphasis, reverse is a popular text-and-background technique wherein light text is put on a dark background.

Reviewing toolbar The Reviewing toolbar contains several buttons to aid in the reviewing of and accepting or rejecting changes that have been made to a file.

Revision mark In Word, a vertical line inside of the left margin denotes a revision mark, showing that a change has been made at that place in the document.

Revision toolbar In Word, the Revision toolbar harbors editing tools for users.

Revisions pane The Revisions pane, located at the right of the window, shows how changes will appear for each reviewer of the file.

Right indent The type of indentation wherein the right side of a paragraph can appear to have a different margin. The right indent is normally set to zero in a paragraph. Use of the right indent will offset the paragraph from the established right margin.

Round trip HTML A function that can be found in all applications of Office that enables users to subsequently edit a Web page while in another application and vice versa.

Sans serif typeface Sans serif typeface does not have small lines extending on the bottoms and tops of letters.

Save As command The Save As command lets users change the name of the source where a document is saved or change the place where the document is saved.

Save As Web Page command The Save As Web Page command in Excel allows a worksheet to be changed into a Web page. In other Microsoft programs, this function allows documents on the Web to be transported into programs to be used in working documents.

Save command The Save command allows users to save documents on disks or the hard drive.

Scenario In Excel, scenarios are "what if" situations put into a spreadsheet.

Scenario Manager In Excel, the Scenario Manager enables users to speculate on various situations or outcomes of working spreadsheets.

Scenario summary In Excel, the scenario summary allows users to compare various results of different scenarios in a summary table.

Scientific format A numeric format that gives the user the ability to display a number as a decimal fraction followed by a whole number exponent of 10.

ScreenTip In many applications, ScreenTips pop up and allow users to learn new information about the program.

Scroll bar Vertical and horizontal scroll bars are located within any window and are used to find unseen areas within any working document.

Scrolling In many Microsoft applications, to view different parts of any document, users scroll up and down, or from right to left by pushing the arrow buttons on the keyboard or by using the mouse.

Section In Word, one of the three ways of formatting is by sections which are different parts of a document, and each part can be formatted in various ways.

Section break In a Word document, a section break is a disconnection of space within a document.

Select query The most common type of query, a Select query will search the underlying table and retrieve data that matches the specified criteria.

Selection area The Selection area for a record on a form is the solid colored vertical bar located on the immediate left of the form data in the form window. This vertical bar also has an image of a pencil at the very top.

Selective replacement In Word, by using selective replacement, users can replace words by clicking the Find Next command button, and then the Replace button to change the word.

Select-then-do In Word, the Select-then-do methodology is choosing a text, and then moving it to the desired location and working on it.

Send To command In many Windows applications, the Send To command allows users to send documents or information to e-mail or other applications of their choice.

Serif typeface Serif typeface has small lines extending on the bottoms and tops of letters.

Server On the Internet, information is stored on servers (large computers).

SetFocus method In Access, the SetFocus method brings users back to the point needed to begin work again.

Shared workbook In Excel, when working in workgroups, shared workbooks are placed on networks, making it easier for groups to access and share ideas and amendments.

Show row The Show Row check box in the query design grid controls whether or not the field will be displayed in the dynaset.

Show/Hide ¶ button The toggle button on the Standard toolbar that allows the user to either turn on or off visual display of the nonprinting symbols contained in a document.

Side-by-side column charts Side-by-side column charts are charts with multiple data series wherein similar data will be presented in columns located next to each other. This makes visual comparison of the data much easier.

Simple Query Wizard The Simple Query Wizard is a tool that will assist a user in building a simple query by ensuring that the minimum query specifications are completed.

Sizing handles Sizing handles let users move and size an object such as a picture in documents.

Slide layouts In PowerPoint, there are 24 precreated slide formats that show where different objects, texts, pictures, graphs, and titles belong on the text.

Slide Master In PowerPoint, the Slide Master reveals the formatting for individual slides.

Slide Navigator In PowerPoint, the Slide Navigator gives users the opportunity to find any slide within a presentation.

Slide Show view In PowerPoint, the Slide Show view shows one slide after another as it would appear during the PowerPoint presentation.

Slide Sorter toolbar In PowerPoint, located in the bottom left-hand corner, the Slide Sorter toolbar allows users to change views for their slide show.

Slide Sorter view In PowerPoint, the Slide Sorter view shows users each slide on a smaller scale.

Slide view In PowerPoint, after clicking the Slide View button, users can work on one slide at a time.

Soft page break In Word, the Soft Page Break function pushes text that no longer fits on a page onto the next page.

Soft return A soft return occurs when the word processor moves text from line to line while the user is in a document.

Solver Solver in Excel is an add-in that helps users solve problems with many variables.

Sort In Word, Sort lets users move rows around within tables.

Sort ascending The Sort Ascending feature will sort text data alphabetically from A to Z, and numeric data in increasing order, for example, from 1 to 100.

Sort command The Sort command puts lists in ascending or descending order according to specified keys.

Sort descending The Sort Descending feature will sort text data in reverse alphabetical order from Z to A, and numeric data in decreasing order, for example, from 100 to 1.

Sort row The Sort row in the query design grid allows you to specify the sort order for the data returned in the dynaset.

Sorting and grouping The Sorting and Grouping dialog box allows users to specify group headers and footers as well as sort orders for the grouped data.

Sound Through a sound board and speakers, sound can be used in PowerPoint presentations.

Source range The cells that you want to copy or move information *from*.

Source workbook In Excel, information must be derived from an original source or dependent workbooks.

Special format A numeric format that gives the user the ability to display a number with editing characters, such as hyphens in a Social Security number or parentheses around the area code of a telephone number.

Special indent Two types of indentation, first line and hanging, are considered special indents.

Spellcheck In many Windows applications, Spellcheck is used to make sure users have not made any spelling mistakes; sentence structures can also be checked.

Split cells Split cells is the option that a user can select when a group of previously merged cells needs to be separated.

Spreadsheet In Excel, a spreadsheet is composed of a grid of rows and columns that allow users to organize data and to recompute formulas with any changes made.

SQL view The SQL view allows users to view the query as it appears in SQL (Structured Query Language) statements. Advanced users knowledgeable in SQL can use the SQL view to enter and/or modify query statements.

Stacked column charts Stacked column charts are charts with multiple data series wherein similar data will be presented in one column with each data series being a different color or pattern. This stacked column effect makes it easier to emphasize the total of the data series.

Standard toolbar The Standard toolbar has buttons that give users choices in what to execute next.

Startup property The Startup property is needed to present users with the main switchboard.

Statistical functions A group or category of functions within Excel that allow users to perform common and/or advanced statistical analyses on numeric data in a worksheet.

Status bar In Excel, the status bar can be found at the bottom of the worksheet and allows users to know what is going on as they work.

Style Style is defined as a series of characteristics created for diversity.

Style command In Word, in the Format menu, the Style command adds and changes style types to documents.

Styles and Formatting command The Styles and Formatting command within Word allows the user to create and apply styles in a document.

SUM function In Excel, this function adds up, or sums, the numeric entries within a range of cells. In Access, this function computes the total for a specific field for all records in the group.

Switchboard For nontechnical users to identify pertinent information or data, switchboards let data or objects be moved easily from one place to another within Access or Excel.

Switchboard Items table The Switchboard Items table is the base for the switchboard.

Switchboard Manager The Switchboard Manager is an Access utility used to create switchboards.

Tab key This key when pushed allows the tab to indent for a paragraph or for indentation purposes.

Tab order When moving through the fields on a form, the Tab key is used. The order that you move from field to field is specified by the tab order.

Tab stop A measured position where text will be aligned. It establishes a point where the cursor will move to when the Tab key is pressed.

Table In Access, tables are made up of records and fields organized in rows and columns for the purpose of storing information.

Table feature In Word, the Table feature creates many different kinds of tables for users to choose from.

Table of Contents In Word, a Table of Contents can be created automatically after clicking on the Index and Table command key.

Table row In Access, a table row is a row that is contained in the design grid of the lower half of the Query window to identify the table from which the field was taken.

Table Wizard In Access or Excel, Table Wizard has already created tables for users to choose from.

Tables and Borders toolbar The Tables and Borders toolbar (Table menu) gives users an array of choices when making tables and adding borders to them.

Table menu In Word, after clicking the Table menus, users can choose to draw or to insert tables of varying sizes.

Tabular report A tabular report is a report detailing information in rows rather than columns.

Tape backup unit This is any device to store large amounts of data, like a Zip drive, used for backing up entire systems.

Task Manager The Task Manager helps users to complete tasks, such as shutting down or starting up the computer.

Task pane The pane that allows the user to execute various commands. This pane can serve many functions, and it automatically opens when the user initiates certain actions.

Taskbar The taskbar is the area on the Windows desktop that typically shows all currently open applications. This makes it easier for users to switch between open applications, also known as multitasking. The taskbar can be positioned anywhere on the desktop and can also include quick-launch icons.

Telnet Telnet is a program used with a PC to connect to other programs like the Web or e-mail.

Template Templates are also known as "empty" worksheets or documents in many of the applications.

Terminal session A terminal session is one in which users connect to and maintain a Web page.

Text box In PowerPoint, after clicking onto the empty square in the toolbar, the text box allows text to be inserted into presentations.

Text field A Text field keeps information such as student names, addresses, or numbers, and can store up to 255 characters.

Text format A numeric format that gives the user the ability to left align a numeric entry and is also be used when there are leading zeros in an entry that should be treated as a text entry, such as a ZIP code.

Theme A theme (template) is a set of designs and graphics or colors that could be used in a Microsoft document.

Thesaurus The tool or feature that allows users to search for synonyms—words with similar meanings—to avoid repetition in their writing.

Three-dimensional column chart A three-dimensional column chart is a column chart that has three-dimension effects added to the chart to make it more interesting and visually appealing.

Three-dimensional pie charts In Excel, three-dimensional pie charts are pie charts that are seen in a three-dimensional view.

Thumbnail image A thumbnail image is a miniature view of either a slide or graphical object.

Time format A numeric format that gives users the ability to display times in a variety of different formats.

Times New Roman A specific typeface or font. Times New Roman is a serif and proportional font.

Today () function This function in Excel, when placed in an active cell, always returns to the current date of when the spreadsheet was opened.

Toggle switch A toggle switch is an apparatus that allows the computer to execute two tasks at the same time; for example, the changing of uppercase letters to lowercase letters while pressing the Caps Lock key.

Toolbar The toolbar in any Windows application reveals the buttons available for the execution of various tasks while working within each application.

Top Values property The Top Values property allows users to display a specified percentage or number of the top or bottom records in a list.

Total query In Access, by using one of many summary or aggregate functions, a Total query does calculations on groups of records.

Track Changes command Under the Tools menu in Word, the Track Changes command highlights changes, accepts or rejects changes, or compares documents during the editing process.

Transition effects In PowerPoint, transition effects regulate the way one screen appears on the screen and how the next appears.

Triangle In Access, triangles (record selector symbol) reveal the place where records are being stored (saved).

Type size Type size is a measurement used to determine the size of text in documents. It is measured in points (72 points to the inch).

Type style A type style is the formatting of a typeface, which normally includes regular, bold, or italic settings.

Typeface Typeface is another term for font, meaning the entire group of upper- and lowercase letters, numbers, punctuation marks, and symbols used in documents.

Typography The process of selecting typefaces, type styles, and type sizes to be used within a document.

Unbound control In Access, unbound controls are fields that have no data for entry.

Underlining A formatting option that can be applied to text. It includes single underline, double underline, bold underline, and many other underlining options.

Undo command Located under the Edit button, the Undo command brings back the user's previous work(s) that were erased. This button can be used only when an initial mistake is made.

Unfreeze Panes command When the Unfreeze Panes command is activated, user-specified rows and/or columns that had been continuously displayed are now unfrozen on the screen. Use of the Unfreeze Panes command will return the worksheet to normal scrolling.

Unhiding cells Unhiding cells redisplays any rows or columns that had been previously hidden.

Unicode Compression property The Unicode Compression property, set to "yes" by default, allows Text, Memo, and Hyperlink fields to store data more efficiently.

Update query An Update query is one type of Action query wherein multiple records can be changed or updated in a single query operation.

Validation Rule property In Access, the Validation Rule property discards unknown data records.

Validation Text property In Access, the Validation Text property presents an error message any time the validation rule is broken.

Versions command In Word, instead of using the Save As command, users can click on the Versions command under the File menu, allowing users to save multiple versions of the same document.

Vertical ruler In Word, the ruler displayed on the left of the workspace, where the user can change top and bottom margins in addition to viewing the vertical placement of text on the page.

View menu The View menu supplies various views of a document through different magnifications.

Visual Basic Editor (VBE) In Word, the Visual Basic Editor shows Project Explorer at the left side of the VBE window, and it is used to edit, build, and debug modules.

Visual Basic for Applications (VBA) Easily accessible from any application in Microsoft Office, VBA is an event-driven programming language.

VLOOKUP function The VLOOKUP (or vertical lookup) function allows a user to search for and match data within a specified table or range and then return a particular value for the matched data. In the VLOOKUP, the data or breakpoint information is organized in a column.

WAV file WAV files are digitized recordings of actual sound and are less compact than MIDI files.

Web page A Web page (HTML document) is a document located on the Internet.

Web Page Wizard By asking users many questions, the Web Page Wizard helps users to create their own Web sites.

Web query Web queries can be executed from almost any Web page by pulling the Data menu down, clicking the Import External Data command, clicking New Web Query, and entering the new Web page.

Web site On the Web, Web sites are numerous; these are places where information is distributed about specific topics, companies, or issues.

Whole-word replacement In Word, under the Replace command, whole-word replacement looks for and finds only whole words and replaces them.

Widow A widow occurs when the last line of a paragraph appears by itself at the top of page while the remainder of that paragraph appears on the previous page. Compare with Orphan.

Wild card Wild cards allow users to search for a pattern within a text field.

Windows clipboard Windows clipboard is a transitory place in Windows applications where users can move text or objects by selecting Cut, Copy, and Paste commands located under the Edit menu.

With statement The With statement in Excel allows users to perform many tasks at the same time on objects.

Wizard In many applications, wizards ask users questions and, when finished, create from the questions the desired document.

Word wrap Word wrap occurs as the word processor "wraps" text from line to line.

Workbook A workbook in Excel is made up of one or more worksheets.

Workgroup Workgroups are people who are working on projects. In Excel, the program has the capability to allow changes to the workbook from each member of the workgroup, later to be merged into a single workbook.

Workplace In Excel, a workplace allows users to open multiple workbooks in a single step.

Worksheet Worksheets in Excel refer to spreadsheets (*workbook* and *worksheet* are terms unique to Excel).

Worksheet references In Excel, worksheet references help label cells and remain constant.

World Wide Web The World Wide Web (WWW or the Web) is a smaller part of the Internet.

Write-enabled When open, the square holes located in the upper left- and right-hand corners of any disk allow users to alter files saved on disk.

Write-protected When closed, the square holes located in the upper left- and right-hand corners of any disk allow users to protect files saved on disk.

WYSIWYG WYSIWYG means What You See Is What You Get and is pronounced "wizzywig." This interface means that the way in which a document appears on a microprocessor's screen is how it will look when it prints out.

X axis The X axis on a graph or chart in Excel is the horizontal axis.

Y axis The Y axis on a graph or chart in Excel is the vertical axis.

Yes/No field In Excel and Access, the Yes/No field is used to evaluate these values: Yes/No, True/False, or On/Off.

Zoom command The Zoom command shows a document on the screen at magnifications ranging from 10% to 500%.

Index

Page References for Individual Modules

Windows, 1–72	Access, 497–704	Concepts, 889–944
Word, 73–280	PowerPoint, 705–824	Outlook, 945–992
Excel, 281–496	Internet, 825–888	Integrated Cases, 993–1040

Page References for Individual Modules

Windows, 1–72	Access, 497–704	Concepts, 889–944
Word, 73–280	PowerPoint, 705–824	Outlook, 945–992
Excel, 281–496	Internet, 825–888	Integrated Cases, 993–1040

Page References for Individual Modules

Windows, 1–72	Access, 497–704	Concepts, 889–944
Word, 73–280	PowerPoint, 705–824	Outlook, 945–992
Excel, 281–496	Internet, 825–888	Integrated Cases, 993–1040

O

P

Q

R

Page References for Individual Modules

Windows, 1–72	Access, 497–704	Concepts, 889–944
Word, 73–280	PowerPoint, 705–824	Outlook, 945–992
Excel, 281–496	Internet, 825–888	Integrated Cases, 993–1040

S

T

U

V

W

X

Y

Z